Cassell's German and English Dictionary

Other Cassell's Dictionaries

Cassell's French and English Dictionary

Cassell's Spanish and English Dictionary

Cassell's Latin and English Dictionary

Cassell's

German and English Dictionary

Compiled by

H.-C. SASSE, M.A., M.Litt.

DR. J. HORNE

DR. CHARLOTTE DIXON

Wiley Publishing, Inc.

Published by Wiley Publishing, Inc., New York, NY

For general information on our other products and services or to obtain technical support please contact our Customer Care Department within the U.S. at 800-762-2974, outside the U.S. at 317-572-3993 or fax 317-572-4002.

Wiley also publishes its books in a variety of electronic formats. Some content that appears in print may not be available in electronic books.

Library of Congress Cataloging-in-Publication Data:
Cassell's German and English dictionary.
Reprint. Originally published: Cassell's new compact German-English, English-German dictionary. New York : Funk & Wagnalls, 1966.
1. German language—Dictionaries—English.
2. English language—Dictionaries—German.
I. Sasse, H.-C. II. Horne, J. (Joseph) III. Dixon, Charlotte.
IV. Title. V. Title: Compact German and English dictionary.
PF3640.C28 1986 433'.21 86-8286
ISBN 0-02-024850-4

Manufactured in the United States of America

30 29 28 27 26 25 24 06

Contents

Preface

Among the difficulties that arise in the compilation of a Concise Dictionary that of the selection of words is undoubtedly the most formidable one. The decision as to what to include and, much more difficult, what to exclude, must to a considerable extent depend on the type of student of a foreign language who is most likely to use it. Primarily a dictionary of this kind is intended for the student in the earlier stages of learning German, whether at school or university. As the study of German, even at an early stage, is likely to include the reading of literary texts from the eighteenth century onwards, it was felt that some attention at least must be paid to the inclusion of words no longer in common use today but frequently found in the prescribed texts, whether poetry, drama or prose. That in this respect severe limitations are imposed by the very concept of a 'Concise' Dictionary is of course obvious, but an attempt has been made to include at least some of the most common literary and poetical terms. However, the main emphasis throughout must of course be on straightforward contemporary German. In addition to the needs of the student, those of the traveller and the tourist, of the reader of contemporary literature and of newspapers and magazines, have been kept in mind. It is hoped that the student of science and technology too will find the dictionary useful, though in his case additional reference must of course be made to one of the growing number of specialized works dealing with the technical vocabulary of his particular discipline.

The aim of a Concise Dictionary must be to achieve some kind of viable compromise between conciseness on the one hand and completeness on the other. To make the dictionary as helpful as possible—given only a limited amount of space—certain economies were called for. Omissions were inevitable. What is similarly inevitable is that, except in the most obvious cases, no two experts are likely

to agree as to what may safely be omitted unless (as was attempted here) one makes frequency of usage and general usefulness the main criteria.

It should be remembered, lastly, that this is a concise dictionary which cannot remotely hope to do justice to all the finer meanings and nuances of two highly developed and complex languages. But it is hoped that the student and reader of German, especially in the earlier stages of learning the language, will find here all the help he needs.

For more detailed reference the user will find Cassell's New German Dictionary (ed. Dr. H. T. Betteridge) of considerable help, while the Duden works of reference on German are regarded as the authoritative last word on matters of controversy. In the final analysis there will always be areas of doubt and dispute. That is the prerogative of a living and developing language.

Finally, thanks are due on behalf of the publishers to Prof. W. E. Collinson, late of the University of Liverpool, who acted in a consultative capacity.

H.-C. Sasse

Advice to the User

As a guide to the nature of words which have inevitably been omitted from a dictionary of this size, it may be helpful to state that, when a German *Fremdwort* is identical with the corresponding English term and possesses no grammatical peculiarities, it appears only in the English–German section. For example, it was felt that the word *Atom* (and *a fortiori* derivative compounds such as *Atomphysik*) was unlikely to perplex any English reader and it has therefore been omitted from the German–English, but included in the English–German, section. For the same reason, a somewhat similar plan has been followed with regard to the names of countries. These have mostly been given in German–English only, whereas the corresponding nouns and adjectives of nationality or race are given in English–German only.

Arrangement of Entries

Strict alphabetical order seemed to be most helpful in a dictionary intended primarily for readers in the earlier stages of acquiring a knowledge of German. Within the entries themselves literal meanings and frequency of usage determine the sequence of definitions. Admittedly the second criterion is to a considerable extent a matter of personal linguistic judgment, indeed of *Sprachgefühl*, but it is hoped that in most cases the reader will thereby more readily discover the meaning of any particular word. It can generally be assumed that definitions separated by commas have much the same meaning, whereas differences in meaning or usage are marked by semicolons. Where it was thought desirable and feasible to include idiomatic phrases, relative frequency of usage appeared a more helpful criterion than strict alphabetic sequence.

Words which are spelt alike but are etymologically distinct

Zur Benutzung des Wörterbuches

Ein Hinweis auf die Art der Wörter, auf die in einem Taschenwörterbuch unweigerlich verzichtet werden muss, wird dem Leser die Anwendung dieses Nachschlagwerkes gewiss erleichtern: Ein deutsches Fremdwort, das mit dem entsprechenden englischen Ausdruck identisch ist und keine grammatikalischen Besonderheiten aufweist, erscheint als Stichwort nicht in beiden Sprachen, sondern wird nur im englisch-deutschen Teil aufgeführt. Man darf wohl annehmen, dass ein Wort wie z.B. *Atom* (und *a fortiori* abgeleitete Zusammensetzungen wie *Atomphysik*) einen englischen Leser kaum verwirren wird, weshalb es denn auch im deutsch-englischen Teil weggelassen, indessen im englisch-deutschen Teil berücksichtigt wurde. Aus dem gleichen Grunde wurde bei den Namen von Ländern ein ähnliches Prinzip beachtet. Diese wurden in der Regel nur im deutsch-englischen Teil aufgeführt, während die entsprechenden Substantive und Adjektive der Nationalität oder Rasse nur im englisch-deutschen Teil erscheinen.

Anordnung der Stichwörter

Die strikte alphabetische Reihenfolge schien vorteilhaft für ein Nachschlagwerk, das in erster Linie für Lernende gedacht ist, die die deutsche Sprache noch nicht völlig beherrschen. Bei den gegebenen Übersetzungen eines Stichwortes bestimmen die wörtliche Übertragung sowie die Häufigkeit des Gebrauches die Folge der Definitionen. Gewiss ist das zweite Kriterium weitgehend eine Angelegenheit der persönlichen linguistischen Beurteilung, in der Tat des Sprachgefühls. Doch ist zu hoffen, dass der Leser in den meisten Fällen gerade dadurch der Bedeutung eines Begriffes näher kommt. Allgemein gilt, dass durch ein Komma getrennte Wörter eine annähernd gleiche Bedeutung haben, während Unterschiede in Bedeutung oder Anwendung

have been given separate, numbered entries for the sake of clarity.

A word should be added on the subject of compounds. Most students of German come to realize before long that the notoriously long German nouns, far from complicating the understanding of the language, are merely a matter of syntactical and grammatical convenience, a device for structural conciseness within a given sentence construction. In a 'Concise' Dictionary only such compounds can be given which have a meaning which can be arrived at only with difficulty or not at all. Where a compound is not given, the constituent parts of the word should be looked up. The meaning should then become self-evident.

Grammar

Parts of Speech. These are indicated by abbreviations in italics (*adj.*, *v.a.* etc.), the meaning of which will be found in the List of Abbreviations. It has not been felt necessary to indicate the nature of English proper names.

Genders. In the German-English section nouns are denoted by their gender (*m.*, *f.* or *n.*). In the English-German section gender is shown by the definite article preceding the noun; in a series of nouns the gender is sometimes omitted when it is the same as that of the preceding noun or nouns.

Declension. The Genitive singular and Nominative plural of German nouns are given in parentheses after the gender. The plurals of English nouns are not given, except for certain very irregular forms. The cases governed by prepositions have been included.

Verbs. In both German and English the indication *irr.* refers the user to the tables of Irregular Verbs. Where a compound irregular verb is not given, its forms are identical with those of the simple irregular verb in the table. "To" is omitted from English infinitives throughout. German inseparable verbs are described as such only when there is any possibility of doubt, *e.g.* in the case of prepositional prefixes. Where prefixes are axiomatically always part of an

durch ein Semikolon markiert sind. Wo es als notwendig und durchführbar erachtet wurde, idiomatische Redewendungen zu zitieren, schien die relative Häufigkeit der Anwendung ein nützlicheres Kriterium als die strenge alphabetische Folge. Orthographisch gleiche Wörter, die sich durch ihre etymologische Herkunft unterscheiden, wurden um der Klarheit willen als einzelne Stichwörter aufgeführt und mit Ziffern versehen. Noch ein Wort zum Thema der Wortzusammensetzungen: Die meisten Deutschlernenden werden bald erkennen, dass die berüchtigt langen deutschen Substantive das Verständnis der Sprache keineswegs erschweren. Sie sind lediglich eine Sache syntaktischer und grammatikalischer Vereinfachung, ein Hilfsmittel zu struktureller Kürze und Prägnanz innerhalb einer gegebenen Satzbildung. In einem Taschenwörterbuch können allein solche Wortverbindungen berücksichtigt werden, die nur mit Mühe oder überhaupt nicht abzuleiten sind. Ist eine Wortverbindung nicht angeführt, so sollten die einzelnen Bestandteile nachgesehen werden. Auf diese Weise wird sich der Sinn der Zusammensetzung von selbst ergeben.

Grammatik

Wortarten. Sie sind in abgekürzter Form durch Kursivschrift gekennzeichnet (*adj.*, *v.a.* etc.). Eine Erläuterung der Abkürzungen findet sich im Verzeichnis der Abkürzungen. Es wurde nicht für nötig befunden, die Zugehörigkeit von Eigennamen anzuzeigen.

Geschlecht. Im deutsch–englischen Teil sind die Substantive mit ihrem Geschlecht (*m.*, *f.* oder *n.*) gekennzeichnet. Im englisch–deutschen Teil ist das Geschlecht durch den bestimmten Artikel vor dem Substantiv angegeben. In einer Reihe aufeinanderfolgender Definitionen wurde der Artikel dort weggelassen, wo er mit dem vorhergehenden übereinstimmt.

Deklination. Die Endungen des Genitiv Singular und des Nominativ Plural deutscher Substantive sind in Klammern nach der Bezeichnung des Geschlechtes eingefügt. Der

inseparable verb (*be-*, *ent-*, *zer-* etc.) no such information is given, as it is assumed that the student will be familiar with the function of these prefixes long before he comes to use a dictionary.

Phonetics. Phonetic transcriptions, using the symbols of the International Phonetic Association, are given throughout for all entries in both sections of the dictionary as a help to correct pronunciation. The mark ′ precedes the syllable which carries the stress. The glottal stop is not indicated.

Numbers. Only the most common numerals appear in the body of the dictionary. However, fuller coverage is given in the separate Numerical Tables.

Zur Benutzung des Wörterbuches

Plural englischer Substantive wurde nicht berücksichtigt ausser bei einigen stark unregelmässigen Formen. Fälle, die von Präpositionen regiert werden, wurden aufgenommen.

Verben. Im Deutschen wie im Englischen weist die Anmerkung *irr.* den Leser auf die Tabellen unregelmässiger Verben hin. Ist ein zusammengesetztes Verb nicht angeführt, so sind seine Formen mit denen des einfachen Verbs in der Tabelle identisch. "To" vor englischen Infinitivformen wurde durchgehend weggelassen. Deutsche untrennbare Verben werden nur dort als solche gekennzeichnet, wo Zweifel möglich sind, also bei Verben mit präpositionalen Vorsilben. Wo Vorsilben grundsätzlich Teile eines untrennbaren Verbes (*be-*, *ent-*, *zer-* etc.) bilden, ist kein solcher Hinweis angebracht, da angenommen werden darf, dass der Lernende die Funktion dieser Vorsilben kennt, lange bevor er dazu kommt, ein Wörterbuch zu konsultieren.

Phonetik. Jedes einzelne Stichwort ist auch in seiner phonetischen Transkription wiedergegeben. Dabei wurden die phonetischen Symbole der *International Phonetic Association* benutzt. Der Akzent ' steht jeweils unmittelbar vor der betonten Silbe. Der Knacklaut ist indessen nicht markiert.

Zahlwörter. Nur die gebräuchlichsten Zahlen erscheinen im Hauptteil des Wörterbuches. Eine ausführliche Zusammenstellung findet sich in den besonderen Zahlentabellen.

Key to Pronunciation

Vowels

Phonetic Symbol	German Example
a	lassen ['lasən]
a:	haben ['ha:bən], Haar [ha:r]
ɛ	häßlich ['hɛslɪç], Geld [gɛlt]
ɛ:	Märchen ['mɛ:rçən], Zähne ['tsɛ:nə]
e	Medizin [medi'tsi:n]
e:	leben ['le:bən], See [ze:], lehnen ['le:nən]
ə	rufen ['ru:fən]
ɪ	Fisch [fɪʃ], Mystik ['mɪstɪk]
i	Militär [mili'tɛ:r]
i:	Berlin [bɛr'li:n], Liebe ['li:bə], ihm [i:m]
ɔ	Kopf [kɔpf]
o	mobil [mo'bi:l]
o:	Rose ['ro:zə], Boot [bo:t], ohne ['o:nə]
œ	Mörder ['mœrdər]
ø	möblieren [mø'bli:rən]
ø:	Löwe ['lø:və], Röhre ['rø:ʁə]
u	Hund [hunt]
u:	gut [gu:t], Uhr [u:r]
y	fünf [fynf], Symbol [zym'bo:l]
y:	Lübeck ['ly:bɛk], Mühe ['my:ə]

Phonetic Symbol	English Example
i:	seat [si:t]
i	finish ['finiʃ], physic ['fizik]
e	neck [nek]
æ	man [mæn], malefactor ['mælifæktə]
ɑ:	father ['fɑ:ðə], task [tɑ:sk]
ɔ	block [blɔk], waddle [wɔdl]
ɔ:	shawl [ʃɔ:l], tortoise ['tɔ:təs]
o	domain [do'mein]
u	good [gud], July [dʒu'lai]
u:	moon [mu:n], tooth [tu:θ]
ʌ	cut [kʌt], somewhere ['sʌmwɛə]
ə:	search [sə:tʃ], surgeon ['sə:dʒən]
ə	cathedral [kə'θi:drəl], never ['nevə]

Diphthongs

Phonetic Symbol	German Example
aɪ	Eis [aɪs], Waise ['vaɪzə]
au	Haus [haus]
ɔy	Beute ['bɔytə], Gebäude [gə'bɔydə]

Phonetic Symbol	English Example
ei	great [greit]
ou	show [ʃou]
ai	high [hai]
au	crowd [kraud]
ɔi	boy [bɔi]
iə	steer [stiə]
ɛə	hair [hɛə]
uə	moor [muə]

Key to Pronunciation

Consonants

Phonetic Symbol	German Example
ç	Blech [blɛç], ich [ɪç]
f	Vater ['fa:tər]
j	ja [ja:]
ŋ	bringen ['brɪŋən]
s	beißen ['baɪsən], wißen ['vɪsən], los [lo:s]
ʃ	schon [ʃo:n]
ts	Cäcilie [tsɛ'tsi:ljə], Zimmer ['tsɪmər]
v	weiß [vaɪs]
x	Bach [bax], kochen ['kɔxən], ruchbar ['ru:xba:r]
z	lesen ['le:zən]
b	Biene ['bi:nə]
d	Dach [dax]
g	geben ['ge:bən]
h	hier [hi:r]
k	Koch [kɔx], quartieren [kwar'ti:rən]
l	Lied [li:t]
m	Mirakel [mi'ra:kəl]
n	Nase ['na:zə]
p	Probe ['pro:bə]
r	rot [ro:t]
t	Tisch [tɪʃ]

Phonetic Symbol	English Example
p	paper ['peipə]
b	ball [bɔ:l]
t	tea [ti:], train [trein]
d	deed [di:d]
k	cake [keik], quest [kwest]
g	game [geim]
m	mammoth ['mæməθ]
n	nose [nouz], nanny ['næni]
ŋ	bring [briŋ], finger ['fiŋgə]
f	fair [fɛə], far [fɑ:]
v	vine [vain]
θ	thin [θin], bath [bɑ:θ]
ð	thine [ðain], bathe [beið]
s	since [sins]
z	busy ['bizi]
l	land [lænd], hill [hil]
ʃ	shield [ʃi:ld], sugar ['ʃugə]
ʒ	vision ['viʒən]
r	rat [ræt], train [trein]
h	here [hiə], horse [hɔ:s]
x	coronach ['kɔrənæx], loch [lɔx]

Semi-Consonants

Phonetic Symbol	English Example
j	yellow ['jelou], yes [jes]
w	wall [wɔ:l]

List of Abbreviations

abbr.	abbreviation (of), abbreviated	*m.*	masculine
Acc.	Accusative	*Maths.*	Mathematics
adj.	adjective	*Meas.*	Measurement
adv.	adverb	*Mech.*	Mechanics
Agr.	agriculture	*Med.*	Medicine
Am.	American(ism)	*Met.*	Meteorology
Anat.	Anatomy	*Metall.*	Metallurgy
Archæol.	Archæology	*Mil.*	Military
Archit.	Architecture	*Min.*	Mining
Arith.	Arithmetic	*Motor.*	Motoring
art.	article	*Mount.*	Mountaineering
Astrol.	Astrology	*Mus.*	Music
Astron.	Astronomy	*Myth.*	Mythology
Austr.	Austrian	*n.*	neuter
aux.	auxiliary	*Naut.*	Nautical
Aviat.	Aviation	*Nav.*	Navigation
Bibl.	Biblical	*o.('s)*	one('s)
Bot.	Botany	*o.s.*	oneself
Br.	British	*obs.*	obsolete
Build.	Building	*Orn.*	Ornithology
Carp.	Carpentry	*p.*	person
Chem.	Chemistry	*Parl.*	Parliament
coll.	colloquial	*part.*	particle
collec.	collective	*pej.*	pejorative
Comm.	Commerce	*pers.*	person(al)
comp.	comparative	*Phil.*	Philosophy
conj.	conjunction	*Phonet.*	Phonetics
Cul.	Culinary	*Phot.*	Photography
Dat.	Dative	*Phys.*	Physics
def.	definite	*Physiol.*	Physiology
defect.	defective	*pl.*	plural
dem.	demonstrative	*Poet.*	Poetical
dial.	dialect	*Pol.*	Political
Eccl.	Ecclesiastical	*poss.*	possessive
Econ.	Economics	*p.p.*	past participle
Elec.	Electricity	*prec.*	preceded
emph.	emphatic	*pred.*	predicative
Engin.	Engineering	*prep.*	preposition
Ent.	Entomology	*pron.*	pronoun
excl.	exclamation	*Psych.*	Psychology
f.	feminine	*r.*	reflexive
fig.	figurative	*Rad.*	Radio
Fin.	Finance	*Railw.*	Railways
Footb.	Football	*reg.*	regular
Genit.	Genitive	*Rel.*	Religion
Geog.	Geography	*rel.*	relative
Geol.	Geology	*s.*	substantive
Geom.	Geometry	*Sch.*	School
Gram.	Grammar	*Scot.*	Scottish
Gymn.	Gymnastics	*sing.*	singular
Her.	Heraldry	*sl.*	slang
Hist.	History	*s.th.*	something
Hunt.	Hunting	*Tail.*	Tailoring
imper.	imperative	*Tech.*	Technical
impers.	impersonal	*Teleph.*	Telephone
Ind.	Industry	*temp.*	temporal
indecl.	indeclinable	*Text.*	Textiles
indef.	indefinite	*Theat.*	Theatre
infin.	infinitive	*Theol.*	Theology
insep.	inseparable	*Transp.*	Transport
int.	interjection	*Typ.*	Typography
interr.	interrogative	*Univ.*	University
intim.	intimate	*us.*	usually
iron.	ironical	*v.a.*	active *or* transitive verb
irr.	irregular	*v.n.*	neuter *or* intransitive verb
Ling.	Linguistics	*v.r.*	reflexive verb
Lit.	Literary	*Vet.*	Veterinary Science
Log.	Logic	*vulg.*	vulgar
		Zool.	Zoology

Cassell's German-English Dictionary

A

A, a [a:], *n. das A* (**des —s, die —s**) the letter A; (*Mus.*) the note A; *A Dur*, A major; *A Moll*, A minor.
Aal [a:l], *m.* (**—s**, *pl.* **—e**) eel.
Aas [a:s], *n.* (**—es**, *pl.* **Äser** *or* **—e**) carcass, carrion.
ab [ap], *adv.* off; down; away; (*Theat.*) exit *or* exeunt, — *und zu*, now and again, occasionally; *auf und* —, up and down, to and fro. — *prep.* from; — *Hamburg*, from Hamburg.
abändern ['apɛndərn], *v.a.* alter.
Abart ['apa:rt], *f.* (**—**, *pl.* **—en**) variety, species.
Abbau ['apbau], *m.* (**—s**, *no pl.*) demolition, dismantling; reduction (of staff).
abberufen ['apbəru:fən], *v.a. irr.* recall.
abbestellen ['apbəʃtɛlən], *v.a.* countermand, annul, cancel (an order).
Abbild ['apbɪlt], *n.* (**—es**, *pl.* **—er**) copy, image.
Abbildung ['apbɪlduŋ], *f.* (**—**, *pl.* **—en**) illustration.
Abbitte ['apbɪtə], *f.* (**—**, *pl.* **—n**) apology; — *leisten*, — *tun*, apologise.
abblenden ['apblɛndən], *v.a.* dim (lights).
Abbruch ['apbrux], *m.* (**—s**, *pl.* **⸚e**) breaking off; demolition; *einer Sache — tun*, damage s.th.
abdanken ['apdaŋkən], *v.n.* resign, abdicate, retire (from office).
abdecken ['apdɛkən], *v.a.* uncover, unroof; clear (the table).
Abdruck ['apdruk], *m.* (**—s**, *pl.* **—e**) impression, copy, reprint, cast.
Abend ['a:bənt], *m.* (**—s**, *pl.* **—e**) evening, eve.
Abendbrot ['a:bəntbro:t], *n.* (**—s**, *no pl.*) evening meal, (*Am.*) supper.
Abendland ['a:bəntlant], *n.* (**—es**, *no pl.*) occident, west.
Abendmahl ['a:bəntma:l], *n.* (**—s**, *no pl.*) supper; *das heilige* —, Holy Communion, the Lord's Supper.
abends ['a:bənts], *adv.* in the evening, of an evening.
Abenteuer ['a:bəntɔyər], *n.* (**—s**, *pl.* **—**) adventure.
aber ['a:bər], *conj.* but, however; (*emphatic*) — *ja*! yes, indeed! of course! —*prefix.* again, once more.
Aberglaube ['a:bərglaubə], *m.* (**—ns**, *no pl.*) superstition.
abermals ['a:bərma:ls], *adv.* again, once more.
Abessinien [abɛ'si:njən], *n.* Abyssinia.
abfahren ['apfa:rən], *v.n. irr.* (*aux.* sein) set out, depart, drive off.
Abfall ['apfal], *m.* (**—s**, *pl.* **⸚e**) scrap, remnant; secession; slope; (*pl.*) waste, refuse.
abfallen ['apfalən], *v.n. irr.* (*aux.* sein) fall off; desert; slope.
abfällig ['apfɛlɪç], *adj.* derogatory.
abfangen ['apfaŋən], *v.a. irr.* intercept, catch.
abfärben ['apfɛrbən], *v.n.* (*colours*) run; stain; lose colour.
abfassen ['apfasən], *v.a.* compose, draft.
abfertigen ['apfɛrtɪgən], *v.a.* despatch; deal with, serve (a customer *or* client).
abfeuern ['apfɔyərn], *v.a.* fire (off), launch (rocket, missile).
abfinden ['apfɪndən], *v.a. irr.* indemnify, compound with (o.'s creditors). — *v.r. sich — mit*, put up with, come to terms with.
Abflug ['apflu:k], *m.* (**—s**, *pl.* **⸚e**) take-off, departure (by air).
Abfluß ['apflus], *m.* (**—sses**, *pl.* **⸚sse**) flowing off; drain.
Abfuhr ['apfu:r], *f.* (**—**, *pl.* **—en**) removal, collection (of refuse); (*coll.*) rebuff.
abführen ['apfy:rən], *v.a.* arrest, lead away. —*v.n.* (*Med.*) act as a purgative.
Abführmittel ['apfy:rmɪtəl], *n.* (**—s**, *pl.* **—**) purgative, laxative.
Abgabe ['apga:bə], *f.* (**—**, *pl.* **—n**) delivery, tax, duty, levy.
abgabepflichtig ['apga:bəpflɪçtɪç], *adj.* taxable, subject to duty.
Abgang ['apgaŋ], *m.* (**—(e)s**, *pl.* **⸚e**) wastage, loss; departure; *Schul—*, school-leaving.
abgängig ['apgɛŋɪç], *adj.* lost, missing; (*of goods*) saleable.
abgeben ['apge:bən], *v.a. irr.* deliver, cede; give (an opinion). — *v.r. sich mit etwas*, — concern o.s. with s.th.
abgedroschen ['apgədrɔʃən], *adj.* (*phrases etc.*) trite, hackneyed.
abgefeimt ['apgəfaɪmt], *adj.* cunning, crafty.
abgegriffen ['apgəgrɪfən], *adj.* well thumbed, worn.
abgehen ['apge:ən], *v.n. irr.* (*aux.* sein) leave, retire; branch off; (*Theat.*) make an exit.
abgelebt ['apgəle:pt], *adj.* (*of humans*) decrepit, worn out.
abgelegen ['apgəle:gən], *adj.* remote, distant.
abgemacht ['apgəmaxt], *adj.*, *int.* agreed! done!
abgeneigt ['apgənaɪkt], *adj.* disinclined, averse.
Abgeordnete ['apgəɔrdnətə], *m.*, *f.* (**—n**, *pl.* **—n**) political representative, deputy, Member of Parliament.
Abgesandte ['apgəzantə], *m.*, *f.* (**—n**, *pl.* **—n**) delegate, ambassador.

abgeschieden ['apgəʃi:dən], *adj.* secluded, remote; deceased.
abgeschmackt ['apgəʃmakt], *adj.* insipid.
abgesehen ['apgəze:ən], *adv.* — *von*, apart from, except for.
abgespannt ['apgəʃpant], *adj.* worn out, run down, exhausted.
abgestorben ['apgəʃtɔrbən], *adj.* dead, numb.
abgetan ['apgəta:n], *adj.* finished, over, done with; *damit ist die Sache* —, that finishes the matter.
abgetragen ['apgətra:gən], *adj.* (*clothes*) shabby, threadbare.
abgewöhnen ['apgəvø:nən], *v.a. einem etwas* —, free (rid) s.o. from (of) a habit, wean from.
abgrasen ['apgra:zən], *v.a.* (*animals*) graze.
Abgrund ['apgrunt], *m.* (—**es**, *pl.* ⸚**e**) abyss, precipice.
Abguss ['apgus], *m.* (—**es**, *pl.* ⸚**e**) cast, plaster-cast, mould.
abhalten ['aphaltən], *v.a. irr.* restrain, hold back; hold (meeting etc.).
abhandeln ['aphandəln], *v.a. einem etwas* —, bargain for s.th.
abhanden [ap'handən], *adv.* mislaid; — *kommen*, get lost.
Abhandlung ['aphandluŋ], *f.* (—, *pl.* —**en**) treatise, dissertation; (*pl.*) proceedings.
Abhang ['aphaŋ], *m.* (—**es**, *pl.* ⸚**e**) slope; declivity.
abhängen ['aphɛŋən], *v.a. irr.* take off, unhook; *von etwas* oder *jemandem* —, depend on s.th. *or* s.o.
abhärten ['aphɛrtən], *v.a.* inure against rigours, toughen.
abheben ['aphe:bən], *v.a. irr.* draw (money from bank).
abhold ['aphɔlt], *adj.* averse to (*Dat.*).
abholen ['apho:lən], *v.a. etwas* —, fetch, collect s.th.; *einen* —, meet s.o. (at the station etc.).
Abitur [abi'tu:r], *n.* (—**s**, *no pl.*) matriculation examination.
Abiturient [abitu'rjɛnt], *m.* (—**en**, *pl.* —**en**) matriculation candidate.
Abkehr ['apke:r], *f.* (—, *no pl.*) turning away, renunciation.
abklären ['apklɛ:rən], *v.a.* (*Chem.*) filter, clear.
Abkommen ['apkɔmən], *n.* (—**s**, *pl.* —) treaty, agreement, contract.
Abkömmling ['apkœmlɪŋ], *m.* (—**s**, *pl.* —**e**) descendant.
abkühlen ['apky:lən], *v.a.* cool, chill.
Abkunft ['apkunft], *f.* (—, *no pl.*) descent, origin.
abkürzen ['apkyrtsən], *v.a.* shorten, abridge, curtail.
abladen ['apladən], *v.a. irr.* unload, dump.
Ablaß ['aplas], *m.* (—**sses**, *pl.* ⸚**sse**) (*Eccl.*) indulgence.
ablassen ['aplasən], *v.n. irr. von etwas* —, desist from, refrain from s.th.—*v.a. einem etwas billig* —, reduce the price of s.th. for s.o.
Ablauf ['aplauf], *m.* (—**es**, *no pl.*) (*water*) drainage; (*ticket*) expiration; lapse (of time); (*bill*) maturity.
ablaufen ['aplaufən], *v.n. irr.* (*aux.* sein) (*water*) run off; (*ticket*) expire; *gut* —, turn out well.
Ableben ['aple:bən], *n.* (—**s**, *no pl.*) decease, death.
ablegen ['aple:gən], *v.a.* (*clothes*) take off; (*documents*) file; *Rechenschaft* —, account for; *eine Prüfung* —, take an examination.
Ableger ['aple:gər], *m.* (—**s**, *pl.* —) (*Hort.*) cutting.
Ablegung ['aple:guŋ], *f.* (—, *no pl.*) making (of a vow); taking (of an oath).
ablehnen ['aple:nən], *v.a.* refuse, decline.
ableiten ['aplaɪtən], *v.a.* divert, draw off; (*water*) drain; (*words*) derive from.
ablenken ['aplɛŋkən], *v.a.* (*aux.* haben) *einen von etwas* —, divert s.o.'s attention from s.th., distract.
ablesen ['aple:zən], *v.a. irr.* (*meter*) read off; (*field*) glean.
abliefern ['apli:fərn], *v.a.* deliver.
ablösen ['aplø:zən], *v.a. einen* —, take the place of s.o., (*Mil.*) relieve; detach (a stamp from a letter etc.).
abmachen ['apmaxən], *v.a.* undo, detach; settle, arrange.
abmagern ['apma:gərn], *v.n.* (*aux.* sein) get thinner, waste away.
Abmarsch ['apmarʃ], *m.* (—**es**, *no pl.*) (*Mil.*) marching off.
abmelden ['apmɛldən], *v.r. sich* —, give notice of departure.
abmessen ['apmɛsən], *v.a. irr.* measure (off), gauge.
abmühen ['apmy:ən], *v.r. sich* —, exert o.s., strive.
Abnahme ['apna:mə], *f.* (—, *pl.* —**n**) decline, loss of weight; (*moon*) waning; (*goods*) taking delivery.
abnehmen ['apne:mən], *v.n. irr.* lose weight, (*moon*) wane. — *v.a.* (*hat*) take off; *einem etwas* —, relieve s.o. (of trouble *or* work).
Abneigung ['apnaɪguŋ], *f.* (—, *pl.* —**en**) antipathy, dislike.
abnutzen ['apnutsən], *v.a.* wear out by use.
Abonnement [abɔnə'maŋ], *n.* (—**s**, *pl.* —**s**) (*newspaper*) subscription; (*railway*) season-ticket.
Abonnent [abɔ'nɛnt], *m.* (—**en**, *pl.* —**en**) subscriber.
abonnieren [abɔ'ni:rən], *v.a.* subscribe to (a paper).
Abordnung ['apɔrdnuŋ,] *f.* (—, *pl.* —**en**) delegation, deputation.
Abort [a'bɔrt], *m.* (—**s**, *pl.* —**e**) lavatory, toilet.
Abortus [a'bɔrtus], *m.* (—**us**, *no pl.*) (*Med.*) abortion.
abplagen ['appla:gən], *v.r. sich* —, slave, toil.
abprallen ['appralən], *v.n.* (*aux.* sein) *von etwas* —, bounce off, rebound.

abquälen ['apkvɛ:lən], *v.r. sich* —, toil, make o.s. weary (*mit*, with).
abraten ['apra:tən], *v.n. irr. einem von etwas* —, dissuade s.o. from, advise *or* warn s.o. against.
abräumen ['aprɔymən], *v.a.* remove; *den Tisch* —, clear the table.
abrechnen ['aprɛçnən], *v.a.* reckon up. — *v.n. mit einem* —, settle accounts with s.o., (*coll.*) get even with s.o.
Abrede ['apre:də], *f.* (—, *pl.* —n) agreement, arrangement; *in — stellen*, deny.
abreißen ['apraɪsən], *v.a. irr.* tear off.
abrichten ['aprɪçtən], *v.a.* (*dogs*) train, (*horses*) break in.
abriegeln ['apri:gəln], *v.a.* bolt, bar.
Abriß ['aprɪs], *m.* (—sses, *pl.* —sse) sketch; summary, synopsis.
abrollen ['aprɔlən], *v.a.* uncoil. — *v.n.* (*aux.* sein) roll off.
abrücken ['aprykən], *v.a.* move away. —*v.n.* (*aux.* sein) (*Mil.*) march off.
Abruf ['apru:f], *m.* (—es, *no pl.*) recall (from a post).
abrunden ['aprundən], *v.a.* round off.
abrupfen ['aprupfən], *v.a.* (*feathers*) pluck; (*flowers*) pluck off.
abrüsten ['aprystən], *v.n.* disarm.
Abrüstung ['aprystuŋ], *f.* (—, *no pl.*) disarmament.
abrutschen ['aprutʃən], *v.n.* (*aux.* sein) slide, slither down.
Absage ['apza:gə], *f.* (—, *pl.* —n) cancellation, refusal.
absagen ['apza:gən], *v.n.* refuse, beg to be excused, decline (an invitation).
Absatz ['apzats], *m.* (—es, *pl.* ⸚e) (*shoe*) heel; (*letter*) paragraph; (*Comm.*) *guter* —, ready sale.
abschaffen ['apʃafən], *v.a.* abolish, do away with.
abschälen ['apʃɛ:lən], *v.a.* peel. — *v.r. sich* —, peel off.
abschätzen ['apʃɛtsən], *v.a.* estimate, appraise; (*taxes*) assess.
Abschaum ['apʃaum], *m.* (—es, *no pl.*) scum.
Abscheu ['apʃɔy], *m.* (—s, *no pl.*) abhorrence, detestation, loathing.
abscheulich ['apʃɔylɪç], *adj.* abominable, repulsive.
abschieben ['apʃi:bən], *v.a. irr.* shove off, push off; *schieb ab!* scram!
Abschied ['apʃi:t], *m.* (—s, *pl.* —e) leave, departure, farewell; discharge; resignation.
abschießen ['apʃi:sən], *v.a. irr.* shoot off; discharge; (*gun*) fire; *den Vogel* —, win the prize.
abschinden ['apʃɪndən], *v.r. irr. sich* —, exhaust o.s. with hard work.
abschirren ['apʃɪrən], *v.a.* unharness.
abschlagen ['apʃla:gən], *v.a. irr.* (*attack*) beat off; (*branches*) lop off; *einem etwas* —, deny s.o. s.th.; *eine Bitte* —, refuse a request.
abschlägig ['apʃlɛgɪç], *adj.* negative.
Abschlagszahlung ['apʃlakstsa:luŋ], *f.* (—, *pl.* —en) payment by instalments.
abschleifen ['apʃlaɪfən], *v.a. irr.* grind off.
abschleppen ['apʃlɛpən], *v.a.* (*car*) tow (away). — *v.r. sich* —, wear o.s. out by carrying heavy loads.
abschließen ['apʃli:sən], *v.a. irr.* lock up; (*work*) conclude; (*accounts*) balance; *einen Vertrag* —, conclude an agreement.
Abschluß ['apʃlus], *m.* (—sses, *pl.* ⸚sse) settlement, winding-up.
abschneiden ['apʃnaɪdən], *v.a. irr.* cut off. — *v.n. gut* —, come off well.
Abschnitt ['apʃnɪt], *m.* (—es, *pl.* —e) section; (*book*) paragraph.
abschnüren ['apʃny:rən], *v.a.* lace up, tie up.
abschrecken ['apʃrɛkən], *v.a.* deter, frighten.
abschreiben ['apʃraɪbən], *v.a. irr.* copy, transcribe; crib; *eine Schuld* —, write off a debt.
Abschrift ['apʃrɪft], *f.* (—, *pl.* —en) copy, transcript, duplicate; *beglaubigte* —, certified copy.
Abschuß ['apʃus], *m.* (—sses, *pl.* ⸚sse) act of firing (a gun), shooting down (aircraft).
abschüssig ['apʃysɪç], *adj.* steep.
abschütteln ['apʃytəln], *v.a.* shake off, cast off.
abschwächen ['apʃvɛçən], *v.a.* weaken, diminish.
abschweifen ['apʃvaɪfən], *v.n.* (*aux.* sein) digress (from), deviate.
abschwenken ['apʃvɛŋkən], *v.n.* (*aux.* sein) wheel off (*or* aside).
abschwören ['apʃvø:rən], *v.a. irr.* abjure, renounce by oath.
absehbar ['apze:ba:r], *adj.* imaginable, conceivable, foreseeable.
absehen ['apze:ən], *v.a.*, *v.n. irr. einem etwas* —, copy s.th. from s.o.; *auf etwas* —, aim at s.th.; *von etwas* —, waive s.th.; refrain from s.th.
abseits ['apzaɪts], *adv.*, *prep.* (*Genit.*) aside; — *von*, away from.
Absender ['apzɛndər], *m.* (—s, *pl.*—) sender; (*Comm.*) consigner.
absetzen ['apzɛtsən], *v.a.* set down; dismiss, deprive of office; depose; (*Comm.*) sell, dispose of.
Absicht ['apzɪçt], *f.* (—, *pl.* —en) intention, purpose, aim.
absondern ['apzɔndərn], *v.a.* separate, set apart; (*Med.*) secrete. — *v.r. sich* —, seclude o.s. from.
abspannen ['apʃpanən], *v.a.* unharness.
absparen ['apʃpa:rən], *v.n. sich etwas vom Munde* —, stint o.s. for s.th.
abspenstig ['apʃpɛnstɪç], *adj.* — *machen*, alienate s.o.'s affections, entice s.o. away; — *werden*, desert.
absperren ['apʃpɛrən], *v.a.* (*door*) lock, shut up; (*street*) close, barricade; (*gas, water*) turn off.
absprechen ['apʃprɛçən], *v.a. irr. einem das Recht* —, deprive s.o. of the right to do s.th.

abspülen ['apʃpy:lən], *v.a.* wash up, rinse.
abstammen ['apʃtamən], *v.n.* (*aux.* sein) descend from, originate from.
Abstand ['apʃtant], *m.* (**—es**, pl. **⸚e**) distance; *von etwas — nehmen*, refrain from doing s.th.
abstatten ['apʃtatən], *v.a. einen Besuch —*, pay a visit; *einen Bericht —*, report on; *Dank —*, return thanks.
abstechen ['abʃtɛçən], *v.a. irr. Tiere —*, slaughter animals. — *v.n. von etwas —*, contrast with s.th.
Abstecher ['apʃtɛçər], *m.* (**—s**, *pl.* **—**) short trip, excursion; detour.
abstecken ['apʃtɛkən], *v.a.* mark off, peg out.
absteigen ['apʃtaIgən], *v.n. irr.* (*aux.* sein) descend, alight, dismount.
abstellen ['apʃtɛlən], *v.a.* put s.th. down; (*gas, water*) turn off.
absterben ['apʃtɛrbən], *v.n. irr.* (*aux.* sein) wither; die.
Abstieg ['apʃti:k], *m.* (**—es**, *no pl.*) descent.
Abstimmung ['apʃtImuŋ], *f.* (**—**, *pl.* **—en**) (*Parl.*) division; referendum, voting.
abstoßen ['apʃto:sən], *v.a. irr.* push off, kick off. —*v.n.* (*Naut.*) set sail.
abstoßend ['apʃto:sənt], *adj.* repulsive, repugnant.
abstreifen ['apʃtraIfən], *v.a. irr.* strip off, pull off; cast, shed.
abstufen ['apʃtu:fən], *v.a.* grade.
abstumpfen ['apʃtumpfən], *v.a.* blunt, dull, take the edge off.
abstürzen ['apʃtyrtsən], *v.n.* (*aux.* sein) (*person*) fall; fall down; (*Aviat.*) crash.
Abt [apt], *m.* (**—es**, *pl.* **⸚e**) abbot.
Abtei ['aptaI], *f.* (**—**, *pl.* **—en**) abbey.
Abteil ['aptaIl], *n.* (**—s**, *pl.* **—e**) compartment.
abteilen ['aptaIlən], *v.a.* divide, partition.
Abteilung [ap'taIluŋ], *f.* (**—**, *pl.* **—en**) section, department.
Äbtissin [ɛp'tIsIn], *f.* (**—**, *pl.* **—nen**) abbess.
abtöten ['aptø:tən], *v.a.* mortify, deaden.
abtragen ['aptra:gən], *v.a. irr.* carry away; (*building*) demolish; (*dress, shoes*) wear out; *eine Schuld —*, pay a debt.
abtreiben ['aptraIbən], *v.a. irr.* (*cattle*) drive off; procure an abortion. — *v.n.* (*aux.* sein) (*ship*) drift off.
Abtreibung ['aptraIbuŋ], *f.* (**—**, *pl.* **—en**) abortion.
abtrennen ['aptrɛnən], *v.a.* (*s.th. sewn*) unpick; separate.
Abtretung ['aptre:tuŋ], *f.* (**—**, *pl.* **—en**) cession; conveyance.
Abtritt ['aptrIt], *m.* (**—es**, *pl.* **—e**) W.C.; (*Theat.*) exit *or* exeunt.
abtrocknen ['aptrɔknən], *v.a.* dry.
abtrünnig ['aptrynIç], *adj.* disloyal, faithless.
aburteilen ['apurtaIlən], *v.a.* pass judgment on.
abwägen ['apvɛ:gən], *v.a. gegeneinander —*, weigh against each other.
abwälzen ['apvɛltsən], *v.a. etwas von sich —*, clear o.s. from s.th.
abwandeln ['apvandəln], *v.a.* change; (*verbs*) conjugate; (*nouns*) decline.
abwärts ['apvɛrts], *prep., adv.* downward.
abwaschen ['apvaʃən], *v.a. irr.* wash up.
abwechseln ['apvɛksəln], *v.a.* vary, alternate.
Abweg ['apve:k], *m.* (**—es**, *pl.* **—e**) wrong way; *auf —e geraten*, go astray.
abwehren ['apve:rən], *v.a.* ward off, parry.
abweichen ['apvaIçən], *v.n. irr.* (*aux.* sein) — *von*, deviate from.
abweisen ['apvaIzən], *v.a. irr.* refuse admittance to, rebuff.
abwenden ['apvɛndən], *v.a. irr.* avert, prevent. — *v.r. sich —*, turn away from.
abwesend ['apve:zənt], *adj.* absent.
Abwesenheit ['apve:zənhaIt], *f.* (**—**, *pl.* **—en**) absence.
abwickeln ['apvIkəln], *v.a.* uncoil; (*business*) wind up.
abwischen ['apvIʃən], *v.a.* wipe clean; *sich die Stirn —*, mop o.'s brow.
abzahlen ['aptsa:lən], *v.a.* pay off; pay by instalments.
abzehren ['aptse:rən], *v.n.* (*aux.* sein) waste away.
Abzeichen ['aptsaIçən], *n.* (**—s**, *pl.* **—**) badge, insignia.
abzeichnen ['apsaIçnən], *v.a.* sketch, draw from a model. — *v.r. sich —*, become clear.
abziehen ['aptsi:ən], *v.a. irr.* deduct, subtract; (*knife*) sharpen; strip (a bed). — *v.n.* (*aux.* sein) depart; (*Mil.*) march off.
Abzug ['aptsu:k], *m.* (**—es**, *pl.* **⸚e**) retreat, departure; photographic copy; — *der Kosten*, deduction of charges; (*steam, air*) outlet.
abzweigen ['aptsvaIgən], *v.n.* (*aux.* sein) fork off, branch off.
Achsel ['aksəl], *f.* (**—**, *pl.* **—n**) shoulder; *die —n zucken*, shrug o.'s shoulders.
Acht [axt], *f.* (**—**, *no pl.*) attention, care, caution, heed; *achtgeben*, pay attention; *sich in — acht nehmen*, be careful; ban, excommunication, outlawry; *in — und Bann tun*, outlaw, proscribe.
acht [axt], *num. adj.* eight; *in — Tagen*, in a week; *vor — Tagen*, a week ago.
achtbar ['axtba:r], *adj.* respectable.
achten ['axtən], *v.a.* hold in esteem, value; — *auf*, pay attention to, keep an eye on.
ächten ['ɛxtən], *v.a.* ban, outlaw, proscribe.
achtlos ['axtlo:s], *adj.* inattentive, negligent.
achtsam ['axtza:m], *adj.* attentive, careful.
Achtung ['axtuŋ], *f.* (**—**, *no pl.*) esteem, regard; (*Mil.*) attention!
Ächtung ['ɛxtuŋ], *f.* (**—**, *no pl.*) ban, proscription.
achtzehn ['axtse:n], *num. adj.* eighteen.

achtzig ['axtsɪç], *num. adj.* eighty.
ächzen ['ɛçtsən], *v.n.* groan.
Acker ['akər], *m.* (**—s**, *pl.* ¨) field, arable land; *den — bestellen*, till the soil.
ackern ['akərn], *v.n.* till (the land).
addieren [a'di:rən], *v.a.* add, add up.
Adel ['a:dəl], *m.* (**—s**, *no pl.*) nobility, aristocracy.
ad(e)lig ['a:dlɪç], *adj.* of noble birth, aristocratic.
Ader ['a:dər], *f.* (**—**, *pl.* **—n**) vein; *zu — lassen*, bleed s.o.
Adler ['a:dlər], *m.* (**—s**, *pl.* **—**) eagle.
Adresse [a'drɛsə], *f.* (**—**, *pl.* **—n**) address.
adrett [a'drɛt], *adj.* neat, adroit, smart.
Affe ['afə], *m.* (**—n**, *pl.* **—n**) ape, monkey; (*fig.*) fool.
affektiert [afɛk'ti:rt], *adj.* affected, giving o.s. airs.
äffen ['ɛfən], *v.a.* ape, mimic.
Afghanistan [af'ganistan], *n.* Afghanistan.
Afrika ['a:frika], *n.* Africa.
After ['aftər], *m.* (**—s**, *pl.* **—**) anus.
Agentur [agɛn'tu:r], *f.* (**—**, *pl.* **—en**) agency.
Agraffe [a'grafə], *f.* (**—**, *pl.* **—n**) brooch, clasp.
Agrarier [a'gra:rjər], *m.* (**—s**, *pl.* **—**) landed proprietor.
Ägypten [ɛ'gyptən], *n.* Egypt.
Ahle ['a:lə], *f.* (**—**, *pl.* **—n**) awl, bodkin.
Ahn [a:n], *m.* (**—en**, *pl.* **—en**) ancestor, forefather.
ahnden ['a:ndən], *v.a.* avenge, punish.
Ahne ['a:nə] *see* **Ahn**.
ähneln ['ɛ:nəln], *v.a.* resemble, look like.
ahnen ['a:nən], *v.a.*, *v.n.* have a presentiment, foresee, have a hunch.
ähnlich ['ɛ:nlɪç], *adj.* resembling, like, similar.
Ahnung ['a:nuŋ], *f.* (**—**, *pl.* **—en**) foreboding, presentiment, idea, (*Am.*) hunch.
Ahorn ['a:hɔrn], *m.* (**—s**, *pl.* **—e**) (*Bot.*) maple.
Ähre ['ɛ:rə], *f.* (**—**, *pl.* **—n**) ear of corn.
Akademiker [aka'de:mɪkər], *m.* (**—s**, *pl.* **—**) university graduate.
akademisch [aka'de:mɪʃ], *adj.* academic; *— gebildet*, with a university education.
Akazie [a'ka:tsjə], *f.* (**—**, *pl.* **—n**) (*Bot.*) acacia.
akklimatisieren [aklimati'zi:rən], *v.r. sich —*, become acclimatised.
Akkord [a'kɔrt], *m.* (**—es**, *pl.* **—e**) (*Mus.*) chord; *in — arbeiten*, work on piece-rates.
Akt [akt], *m.* (**—es**, *pl.* **—e**) deed, action; (*Theat.*) act; (*Art*) (depiction of) the nude.
Akte ['aktə], *f.* (**—**, *pl.* **—n**) document, deed; (*pl.*) records, files; *zu den —n legen*, pigeonhole, shelve.
Aktenstück ['aktənʃtyk], *n.* (**—es**, *pl.* **—e**) official document, file.
Aktie ['aktsjə], *f.* (**—**, *pl.* **—n**) (*Comm.*) share, (*Am.*) stock.
Aktiengesellschaft ['aktsjəngəzɛlʃaft], *f.* (**—**, *pl.* **—en**) joint stock company.
Aktionär [aktsjo'nɛ:r], *m.* (**—s**, *pl.* **—e**) shareholder, (*Am.*) stockholder.
Aktiv ['akti:f], *n.* (**—s**, *pl.* **—e**) (*Gram.*) active voice.
Aktiva [ak'ti:va], *n. pl.* (*Comm.*) assets.
aktuell [aktu'ɛl], *adj.* topical.
akzentuieren [aktsɛntu'i:rən], *v.a.* accentuate, stress, emphasize.
Albanien [al'ba:njən], *n.* Albania.
albern ['albərn], *adj.* silly, foolish.
Aliment [ali'mɛnt], *n.* (**—es**, *pl.* **—e**) (*usually pl.* **—e**) alimony, maintenance.
Alkali [al'ka:li], *n.* (**—s**, *pl.* **—en**) alkali.
Alkohol ['alkoho:l], *m.* (**—s**, *no pl.*) alcohol.
Alkoholiker [alko'ho:lɪkər], *m.* (**—s**, *pl.* **—**) drunkard, alcoholic.
All [al], *n.* (**—s**, *no pl.*) the universe, (outer) space.
all [al], *adj.* all, entire, whole; every, each, any.
alle ['alə], *adj.* all, everybody; *— beide*, both of them.
Allee [a'le:], *f.* (**—**, *pl.* **—n**) tree-lined walk, avenue.
allein [a'laɪn], *adj.* alone, sole. — *adv.* solely, only, merely. —*conj.* (*obs.*) only, but, however.
alleinig [a'laɪnɪç], *adj.* sole, only, exclusive.
allenfalls [alən'fals], *adv.* possibly, perhaps, if need be.
allenthalben [alənt'halbən], *adv.* everywhere, in all places.
allerdings [alər'dɪŋs], *adv.* of course, indeed, nevertheless.
allerhand [alər'hant], *adj.* of all sorts *or* kinds, various; *das ist ja —!* I say!
Allerheiligen [alər'haɪlɪgən], *pl.* All Saints' Day.
allerlei [alər'laɪ], *adj.* miscellaneous, various.
allerliebst [alər'li:pst], *adj.* (*Am.*) cute; charming.
allerseits ['alərzaɪts], *adv.* generally, on all sides, universally.
alles ['aləs], *adj.* everything, all.
allgemein [algə'maɪn], *adj.* universal, common, general.
alliieren [ali'i:rən], *v.a.*, *v.n.* ally (o.s.).
allmächtig [al'mɛçtɪç], *adj.* omnipotent.
allmählich [al'mɛ:lɪç], *adj.* by degrees, gradual.
allseitig ['alzaɪtɪç], *adj.* universal, (*Am.*) all-round.
Alltag ['alta:k], *m.* (**—s**, *pl.* **—e**) working day, week-day.
allwissend [al'vɪsənt], *adj.* omniscient.
allzu ['altzu:], *adv.* too, much too.
Alm [alm], *f.* (**—**, *pl.* **—en**) Alpine meadow.
Almosen ['almo:zən], *n.* (**—s**, *pl.* **—**) alms, charity.
Alp [alp], *f.* (**—**, pl. **—en**) (*mostly pl.*) mountain(s), Alps.
Alpdrücken ['alpdrykən], *n.* (**—s**, *no pl.*) nightmare.

als [als], *conj.* than; (*after comparatives*) than; as, like; but; *er hat nichts — Schulden*, he has nothing but debts; (*temp.*) when, as.
alsbald [als'balt], *adv.* forthwith.
also ['alzo:], *adv.* thus, so, in this manner. — *conj.* consequently, therefore.
Alt [alt], *m.* (**—s**, *pl.* **—e**) (*Mus.*) alto.
alt [alt], *adj.* old, ancient; aged; antique.
Altan [al'ta:n], *m.* (**—s**, *pl.* **—e**) balcony, gallery.
Altar [al'ta:r], *m.* (**—s**, *pl.* **¨-e**) altar.
altbacken ['altbakən], *adj.* stale.
Alter ['altər], *n.* (**—s**, *no pl.*) age, old age; epoch.
altern ['altərn], *v.n.* (*aux.* sein) grow old.
Altertum ['altərtu:m], *n.* (**—s**, *pl.* **¨-er**) antiquity.
Altistin [al'tɪstɪn], *f.* (**—**, *pl.* **—nen**) (*Mus.*) contralto.
altklug ['altklu:k], *adj.* precocious.
ältlich ['ɛltlɪç], *adj.* elderly.
Altweibersommer [alt'vaɪbərzɔmər], *m.* (**—s**, *pl.* **—**) Indian summer.
Amboß ['ambɔs], *m.* (**—sses**, *pl.* **—sse**) anvil.
Ameise ['a:maɪzə], *f.* (**—**, *pl.* **—n**) (*Ent.*) ant.
Amerika [a'me:rika], *n.* America.
Amme ['amə], *f.* (**—**, *pl.* **—n**) wet nurse.
Ammoniak [amon'jak], *n.* (**—s**, *no pl.*) ammonia.
Ampel ['ampəl], *f.* (**—**, *pl.* **—n**) (hanging) light, lamp, lantern; traffic light.
Ampfer ['ampfər], *m.* (**—s**, *pl.* **—**) (*Bot.*) sorrel, dock.
Amsel ['amzəl], *f.* (**—**, *pl.* **—n**) (*Orn.*) blackbird.
Amt [amt], *n.* (**—es**, *pl.* **¨-er**) office, post, employment; administration, domain, jurisdiction; place of public business.
amtlich ['amtlɪç], *adj.* official.
Amtmann ['amtman], *m.* (**—s**, *pl.* **¨-er**) bailiff.
Amtsblatt ['amtsblat], *n.* (**—es**, *pl.* **¨-er**) official gazette.
Amtsgericht ['amtsgərɪçt], *n.* (**—s**, *pl.* **—e**) county court; (*Am.*) district court.
amüsieren [amy'zi:rən], *v.a.* amuse.— *v.r. sich* **—**, enjoy o.s.
an [an], *prep.* (*Dat. or Acc.*), at, to, on.
analog [ana'lo:k], *adj.* analogous.
Ananas ['ananas], *f.* (**—**, *pl.* **—**) pineapple.
Anatom [ana'to:m], *m.* (**—en**, *pl.* **—en**) anatomist.
anbahnen ['anba:nən], *v.a.* initiate, open up, pave the way for.
anbändeln ['anbɛndəln], *v.n.* — *mit*, flirt with, make up to.
Anbau ['anbau], *m.* (**—s**, *pl.* **—ten**) (*grain*) cultivation; annex(e), wing (of building).
anbauen ['anbauən], *v.a.* cultivate; add to a building.
anbei [an'baɪ], *adv.* enclosed (in letter).
anbeißen ['anbaɪsən], *v.a. irr.* bite at, take a bite of. — *v.n.* (*fish*) bite; (*coll.*) take the bait.
anbelangen ['anbəlaŋən], *v.a.* concern.
anberaumen ['anbəraumən], *v.a.* fix (a date).
anbeten ['anbe:tən], *v.a.* worship, adore, idolise.
anbiedern ['anbi:dərn], *v.r. sich mit einem* **—**, chum up with s.o.
anbieten ['anbi:tən], *v.a. irr.* offer.
anbinden ['anbɪndən], *v.a. irr.* tie on, bind to; *kurz angebunden sein*, be curt.
Anblick ['anblɪk], *m.* (**—s**, *no pl.*) view, sight, aspect, spectacle.
anbrechen ['anbrɛçən], *v.a. irr.* begin; break; start on. —*v.n.* dawn.
anbrennen ['anbrɛnən], *v.a. irr.* light, set fire to, burn. — *v.n.* (*aux.* sein) catch fire; burn.
anbringen ['anbrɪŋən], *v.a. irr.* fit to, place.
Anbruch ['anbrux], *m.* (**—s**, *no pl.*) beginning; — *der Nacht*, night-fall.
anbrüllen ['anbrylən], *v.a.* roar at.
Andacht ['andaxt], *f.* (**—**, *pl.* **—en**) (*Eccl.*) devotion(s).
andächtig ['andɛxtɪç], *adj.* devout.
andauern ['andauərn], *v.n.* last, continue.
Andenken ['andɛŋkən], *n.* (**—s**, *pl.* **—**) memory; keepsake; souvenir.
anderer ['andərər], *adj.* other, different; *ein* **—**, another.
andermal ['andərma:l], *adv. ein* **—**, another time.
ändern ['ɛndərn], *v.a.* alter, change.
andernfalls ['andərnfals], *adv.* otherwise, or else.
anders ['andərs], *adv.* differently, in another manner, otherwise.
anderthalb ['andərthalp], *adj.* one and a half.
anderweitig ['andərvaɪtɪç], *adj.* elsewhere.
andeuten ['andɔytən], *v.a.* hint at, intimate, indicate.
Andrang ['andraŋ], *m.* (**—es**, *no pl.*) throng, crowd.
aneignen ['anaɪgnən], *v.r. sich etwas* **—**, appropriate s.th.; (*an opinion*) adopt.
anekeln ['ane:kəln], *v.a.* disgust.
Anerbieten ['anɛrbi:tən], *n.* (**—s**, *pl.* **—**) offer.
anerkennen ['anɛrkɛnən], *v.a. irr.* acknowledge, appreciate, recognize, accept.
anfachen ['anfaxən], *v.a.* kindle (a flame).
Anfahrt ['anfa:rt], *f.* (**—**, pl. **—en**) drive; (*down a mine*) descent; (*Am.*) drive-way.
Anfall ['anfal], *m.* (**—s**, *pl.* **¨-e**) attack, assault; (*Med.*) seizure, fit; (*mood*) fit, burst.
anfallen ['anfalən], *v.a. irr. einen* **—**, attack s.o.
Anfang ['anfaŋ], *m.* (**—s**, *pl.* **¨-e**) beginning, start, commencement.

anfangen [ˈanfaŋən], *v.a. irr.* begin, start. — *v.n.* begin, originate.
Anfänger [ˈanfɛŋər], *m.* (**—s**, *pl.* **—**) beginner, novice.
anfänglich [ˈanfɛŋlɪç], *adv.* in the beginning, at first, initially.
anfassen [ˈanfasən], *v.a.* take hold of; touch; seize.
anfechtbar [ˈanfɛçtbaːr], *adj.* disputable, refutable, debatable.
anfechten [ˈanfɛçtən], *v.a.* (*a will, a verdict*) contest; (*jurors*) challenge.
anfeinden [ˈanfaɪndən], *v.a.* show enmity to.
anfertigen [ˈanfɛrtɪgən], *v.a.* make, manufacture, prepare; (*a list*) draw up.
anflehen [ˈanfleːən], *v.a.* implore, beseech.
Anflug [ˈanfluːk], *m.* (**—s**, *pl.* **¨e**) (*Aviat.*) approach; (*beard*) down; touch.
anfordern [ˈanfɔrdərn], *v.a.* demand, claim.
Anfrage [ˈanfraːgə], *f.* (**—**, *pl.* **—n**) enquiry.
anfügen [ˈanfyːgən], *v.a.* join to, annex.
anführen [ˈanfyːrən], *v.a.* lead; adduce, quote (examples), cite; *einen* **—**, dupe s.o., take s.o. in.
Anführungszeichen [ˈanfyːruŋstsaɪçən], *n.* (**—s**, *pl.* **—**) inverted commas, quotation marks.
anfüllen [ˈanfylən], *v.a. wieder* **—**, replenish.
Angabe [ˈangaːbə], *f.* (**—**, *pl.* **—n**) declaration, statement; data; instruction; bragging.
angeben [ˈangeːbən], *v.a. irr.* declare, state; *den Ton* **—**, lead the fashion; *den Wert* **—**, declare the value of.— *v.n. groß* **—**, brag, show off.
Angeber [ˈangeːbər], *m.* (**—s**, *pl.* **—**) informer; braggart.
Angebinde [ˈangəbɪndə], *n.* (**—s**, *pl.* **—**) (*obs.*) present, gift.
angeblich [ˈangeːplɪç], *adj.* ostensible, alleged, so-called.
angeboren [ˈangəboːrən], *adj.* innate, inborn.
Angebot [ˈangəboːt], *n.* (**—es**, *pl.* **—e**) offer, tender, bid; (*Comm.*) **—** *und Nachfrage*, supply and demand.
angebracht [ˈangəbraxt], *adj.* apt, appropriate, opportune.
angedeihen [ˈangədaɪən], *v.n. einem etwas* **—** *lassen*, bestow s.th. on s.o.
angegossen [ˈangəgɔsən], *adj. das sitzt wie* **—**, it fits like a glove.
angehen [ˈangeːən], *v.a. irr. einen um etwas* **—**, apply to s.o. for s.th.; *das geht Dich nichts an*, that is none of your business.
angehören [ˈangəhøːrən], *v.n.* belong to.
Angehörige [ˈangəhøːrɪgə], *m., f.* (**—n**, *pl.* **—n**) near relative; next of kin.
Angeklagte [ˈangəklaːktə], *m., f.* (**—n**, *pl.* **—n**) the accused, defendant, prisoner at the bar.
Angel [ˈaŋəl], *f.* (**—**, *pl.* **—n**) fishing-rod; (*door*) hinge, pivot; *zwischen Tür und* **—**, in passing.
angelegen [ˈangəleːgən], *adj. sich etwas* **—** *sein lassen*, interest o.s. in s.th., concern o.s. in s.th.; *ich werde es mir* **—** *sein lassen*, I shall make it my business.
Angelegenheit [ˈangəleːgənhaɪt], *f.* (**—**, *pl.* **—en**) concern, matter, affair.
angeln [ˈaŋəln], *v.a.* fish, angle.
angemessen [ˈangəmɛsən], *adj.* proper, suitable, appropriate.
angenehm [ˈangəneːm], *adj.* acceptable, agreeable, pleasing, pleasant.
angenommen [ˈangənɔmən], *conj.* **—** *daß*, given that, supposing that, say.
Anger [ˈaŋər], *m.* (**—s**, *pl.* **—**) grass-plot; green, common.
angesehen [ˈangəzeːən], *adj.* respected, esteemed, distinguished.
Angesicht [ˈangəzɪçt], *n.* (**—s**, *pl.* **—er**) face, countenance.
angestammt [ˈangəʃtamt], *adj.* ancestral, hereditary.
Angestellte [ˈangəʃtɛltə], *m., f.* (**—n**, *pl.* **—n**) employee; (*pl.*) staff.
Angler [ˈaŋlər], *m.* (**—s**, *pl.* **—**) angler, fisherman.
angliedern [ˈangliːdərn], *v.a.* annex, attach.
Anglist [aŋˈglɪst], *m.* (**—en**, *pl.* **—en**) (*Univ.*) professor *or* student of English.
angreifen [ˈangraɪfən], *v.a. irr.* handle, touch; (*capital*) break into; attack, assail; *es greift mich an*, it taxes my strength.
angrenzen [ˈangrɛntsən], *v.n.* border upon, adjoin.
Angriff [ˈangrɪf], *m.* (**—s**, *pl.* **—e**) offensive, attack, assault.
Angst [aŋst], *f.* (**—**, *pl.* **¨e**) anxiety; fear; anguish.
ängstigen [ˈɛŋstɪgən], *v.a.* alarm, frighten. — *v.r. sich* **—**, feel uneasy, be afraid.
angucken [ˈangukən], *v.a.* look at.
anhaben [ˈanhaːbən], *v.a. irr.* have on, be dressed in, wear; *einem etwas* **—**, hold s.th. against s.o.
anhaften [ˈanhaftən], *v.n.* stick to, adhere to.
Anhalt [ˈanhalt], *m.* (**—es**, *no pl.*) support, basis.
anhalten [ˈanhaltən], *v.a. irr. einen* **—**, stop s.o. — *v.n.* stop, pull up, halt; *um ein Mädchen* **—**, ask for a girl's hand in marriage. — *v.r. sich an etwas halten*, cling to, hang on to s.th.
Anhaltspunkt [ˈanhaltspuŋkt], *m.* (**—es**, *pl.* **—e**) clue, (*Am.*) lead.
Anhang [ˈanhaŋ], *m.* (**—s**, *pl.* **¨e**) appendix, supplement.
anhängen [ˈanhɛŋən], *v.a. irr.* hang on, fasten to, attach.
Anhänger [ˈanhɛŋər], *m.* (**—s**, *pl.* **—**) follower, adherent; (*Footb.*) supporter; pendant (on a necklace); label; (*Transp.*) trailer.
anhänglich [ˈanhɛŋlɪç], *adj.* attached, affectionate.

Anhängsel [ˈanhɛŋsəl], *n.* (**—s**, *pl.* **—**) appendage.
anhauchen [ˈanhauxən], *v.a.* breathe upon.
anhäufen [ˈanhɔyfən], *v.a.* heap up, pile up, amass. —*v.r. sich* —, accumulate.
anheben [ˈanhe:bən], *v.a. irr.* lift. — *v.n.* (*obs.*) begin.
anheim [anˈhaɪm], *adv.* — *stellen*, leave to s.o.'s discretion.
anheimeln [ˈanhaɪməln], *v.a.* remind one of home.
anheischig [ˈanhaɪʃɪç], *adj. sich — machen*, undertake, pledge o.s.
Anhieb [ˈanhi:p], *m.* (**—s**, *pl.* **—e**) (*fencing*) first stroke; *auf* —, at the first attempt.
Anhöhe [ˈanhø:ə], *f.* (—, *pl.* **—n**) hill, rising ground.
anhören [ˈanhø:rən], *v.a.* listen to; tell by s.o.'s voice *or* accent.
animieren [aniˈmi:rən], *v.a.* instigate, egg on.
ankämpfen [ˈankɛmpfən], *v.n. gegen etwas* —, struggle against s.th.
ankaufen [ˈankaufən], *v.a.* purchase, buy. — *v.r. sich irgendwo* —, buy land somewhere.
Anker [ˈaŋkər], *m.* (**—s**, *pl.* **—**) (*Naut.*) anchor; *den — auswerfen*, cast anchor.
ankern [ˈaŋkərn], *v.a., v.n.* anchor, cast anchor.
Anklage [ˈankla:gə], *f.* (—, *pl.* **—n**) accusation; *gegen einen — erheben*, bring a charge against s.o.
Ankläger [ˈanklɛ:gər], *m.* (**—s**, *pl.* **—**) accuser, prosecutor; plaintiff.
Anklang [ˈanklaŋ], *m.* (**—s**, *pl.* **¨e**) reminiscence; — *finden*, please, meet with approval.
ankleben [ˈankle:bən], *v.a.* stick to, glue to, paste on.
ankleiden [ˈanklaɪdən], *v.a.* dress. — *v.r. sich* —, dress o.s., get dressed.
anklingeln [ˈanklɪŋəln], *v.a.* (*coll.*) *einen* —, ring s.o. up (on the telephone.)
anklopfen [ˈanklɔpfən], *v.n.* knock.
anknüpfen [ˈanknypfən], *v.a.* tie; join on to; *ein Gespräch* —, start a conversation; *wieder* —, resume.
ankommen [ˈankɔmən], *v.n. irr.* (*aux.* sein) arrive; *es kommt darauf an*, it depends upon.
ankreiden [ˈankraɪdən], *v.a.* chalk up.
ankündigen [ˈankyndɪgən], *v.a.* announce, advertise, give notice of, proclaim.
Ankunft [ˈankunft], *f.* (—, *no pl.*) arrival.
ankurbeln [ˈankurbəln], *v.a.* (*Motor.*) crank up.
Anlage [ˈanla:gə], *f.* (—, *pl.* **—n**) (*capital*) investment; enclosure (*with a letter*); (*industrial*) plant; (*building*) lay-out; *öffentliche* —, pleasure grounds; talent.
anlangen [ˈanlaŋən], *v.n.* (*aux.* sein) arrive; concern; *was das anlangt*, as far as this is concerned.
Anlaß [ˈanlas], *m.* (**—sses**, *pl.* **¨sse**) cause, occasion, motive.
anlassen [ˈanlasən], *v.a. irr.* keep on; (*Motor.*) start. — *v.r. sich gut* —, promise well.
Anlasser [ˈanlasər], *m.* (**—s**, *pl.* **—**) (*Motor.*) starter.
anläßlich [ˈanlɛslɪç], *prep.* (*Genit.*) à propos of, on the occasion of.
Anlauf [ˈanlauf], *m.* (**—s**, *pl.* **¨e**) start, run, (*Aviat.*) take-off run.
anlaufen [ˈanlaufən], *v.n. irr.* tarnish; call at (port).
anlegen [ˈanle:gən], *v.a. Geld* —, invest money; *Kleider* —, don clothes; *einen Garten* —, lay out a garden; *Hand* —, give a helping hand; *auf einen* —, take aim at s.o.; (*Naut.*) land, dock.
Anlegestelle '[ˈanle:gəʃtɛlə], *f.* (—, *pl.* **—n**) landing place.
anlehnen [ˈanle:nən], *v.r. sich an etwas* —, lean against s. th.
Anleihe [ˈanlaɪə], *f.* (—, *pl.* **—n**) loan, *öffentliche* —, government loan; *eine — machen*, raise a loan.
anleiten [ˈanlaɪtən], *v.a.* train, instruct.
anlernen [ˈanlɛrnən], *v.a. einen* —, train, apprentice s.o. (in a craft).
Anliegen [ˈanli:gən], *n.* (**—s**, *pl.* **—**) request, petition, concern.
anmachen [ˈanmaxən], *v.a.* fix, fasten; light (a fire).
anmaßen [ˈanma:sən], *v.a. sich etwas* —, arrogate s.th.
anmaßend [ˈanma:sənt], *adj.* arrogant.
anmelden [ˈanmɛldən], *v.a.* announce, (*claim*) give notice of. — *v.r. sich* —, notify o.'s arrival, make an appointment; *sich — lassen*, send in o.'s name.
Anmeldungsformular [anˈmɛlduŋsfɔrmula:r], *n.* (**—s**, *pl.* **—e**) registration form.
Anmerkung [ˈanmɛrkuŋ], *f.* (—, *pl.* **—en**) remark, annotation, footnote.
anmessen [ˈanmɛsən], *v.a. irr.* measure (s.o. for a garment).
Anmut [ˈanmu:t], *f.* (—, *no pl.*) grace, charm.
annähen [ˈannɛ:ən], *v.a.* sew on (to).
annähern [ˈannɛ:ərn], *v.r. sich* —, approach, draw near; (*Maths.*) approximate.
Annäherung [ˈannɛ:əruŋ], *f.* (—, *pl.* **—en**) approach; (*Maths.*) approximation.
Annahme [ˈanna:mə], *f.* (—, *pl.* **—n**) acceptance; assumption, hypothesis.
annehmbar [ˈanne:mba:r], *adj.* acceptable; *ganz* —, passable.
annehmen [ˈanne:mən], *v.a. irr.* take, accept, take delivery of; suppose, assume, presume; *an Kindes Statt* —, adopt.
Annehmlichkeit [ˈanne:mlɪçkaɪt], *f.* (—, *pl.* **—en**) amenity, comfort.
Annonce [anˈnɔ̃:sə], *f.* (—, *pl.* **—n**) (classified) advertisement (in newspaper).
anordnen [ˈanɔrdnən], *v.a.* arrange, regulate; order, direct.

anorganisch ['anɔrga:nɪʃ], *adj.* inorganic.
anpacken ['anpakən], *v.a.* get hold of, seize, grasp.
anpassen ['anpasən], *v.a.* fit, suit. — *v.r. sich* —, adapt o.s.
anpflanzen ['anpflantsən], *v.a.* plant, grow.
Anprall ['anpral], *m.* (—**s**, *no pl.*) impact, bounce, shock.
anpumpen ['anpumpən], *v.a.* (*coll.*) *einen* —, borrow money from s.o.
anrechnen ['anrɛçnən], *v.a. einem etwas* —, charge s.o. with s.th.; *einem etwas hoch* —, think highly of a person for s.th.
Anrecht ['anrɛçt], *n.* (—**es**, *no pl.*) — *auf*, title to, claim to.
Anrede ['anre:də], *f.* (—, *pl.* —**n**) (form of) address, title.
anreden ['anre:dən], *v.a.* address (s.o.).
anregen ['anre:gən], *v.a.* stimulate (s.o.); suggest (s.th.).
Anregung ['anre:guŋ], *f.* (—, *pl.* —**en**) suggestion, hint.
Anreiz ['anraɪts], *m.* (—**es**, *no pl.*) incentive; impulse.
Anrichte ['anrɪçtə], *f.* (—, *pl.* —**n**) dresser, sideboard.
anrichten ['anrɪçtən], *v.a.* (*meal*) prepare, serve (up); *Unheil* —, make mischief.
anrüchig ['anry:çɪç], *adj.* disreputable.
anrücken ['anrykən], *v.a.* bring near to. — *v.n.* (*aux.* sein) approach.
Anruf ['anru:f], *m.* (—**s**, *pl.* —**e**) (*by sentry*) challenge; telephone call.
anrufen ['anru:fən], *v.a. irr.* call to, challenge; implore; ring up; *Gott* —, invoke God.
anrühren ['anry:rən], *v.a.* handle, touch; (*Cul.*) mix.
Ansage ['anza:gə], *f.* (—, *pl.* —**n**) announcement.
ansagen ['anza:gən], *v.a.* announce, notify.
Ansager ['anza:gər], *m.* (—**s**, *pl.* —) announcer; compere.
ansammeln ['anzaməln], *v.a.* accumulate, gather. — *v.r. sich* —, gather, foregather, congregate, collect.
ansässig ['anzɛsɪç], *adj.* domiciled, resident; *sich* — *machen*, settle.
Ansatz ['anzats], *m.* (—**es**, *pl.* ¨**e**) start; (*Maths.*) construction; disposition (to), tendency (to).
anschaffen ['anʃafən], *v.a.* buy, purchase, get.
anschauen ['anʃauən], *v.a.* look at, view.
anschaulich ['anʃaulɪç], *adj.* clear; *einem etwas* — *machen*, give s.o. a clear idea of s.th.
Anschauung ['anʃauuŋ], *f.* (—, *pl.* —**en**) view, perception; *nach meiner* —, in my opinion.
Anschein ['anʃaɪn], *m.* (—**s**, *no pl.*) appearance, semblance.
anscheinend ['anʃaɪnənt], *adj.* apparent, ostensible, seeming.
anschicken ['anʃɪkən], *v.r. sich* — *zu*, prepare for, get ready for.
anschirren ['anʃɪrən], *v.a.* (*horses*) harness.
Anschlag ['anʃla:k], *m.* (—**s**, *pl.* ¨**e**) poster, placard; — *auf das Leben*, attempt at assassination.
Anschlagbrett ['anʃla:kbrɛt], *n.* (—**es**, *pl.* —**er**) notice-board.
anschlagen ['anʃla:gən], *v.a. irr.* (*keys of piano or typewriter*) strike, touch; (*knitting*) cast on; *zu hoch* —, overestimate.
anschließen ['anʃli:sən], *v.a. irr.* fasten with a lock. — *v.r. sich* —, join in; (*club*) join.
Anschluß ['anʃlus], *m.* (—**sses**, *pl.* ¨**sse**) (*Railw.*, *telephone*) connection; (*Pol.*) annexation.
Anschlußpunkt ['anʃluspuŋkt], *m.* (—**es**, *pl.* —**e**) junction; (*Elec.*) inlet point, power point.
anschmiegen ['anʃmi:gən], *v.r. sich* —, nestle closely to.
anschmieren ['anʃmi:rən], *v.a. einen* —, (*coll.*) deceive, cheat s.o.
anschnallen ['anʃnalən], *v.a.* buckle on.
anschnauzen ['anʃnautsən], *v.a.* snarl at, snap at.
anschneiden ['anʃnaɪdən], *v.a. irr.* cut into; *ein Thema* —, broach a subject.
Anschrift ['anʃrɪft], *f.* (—, *pl.* —**en**) address.
anschwellen ['anʃvɛlən], *v.n.* (*aux.* sein) swell.
Ansehen ['anze:ən], *n.* (—**s**, *no pl.*) respect; reputation; authority.
ansehen ['anze:ən], *v.a. irr.* look at *or* upon, consider, regard.
ansehnlich ['anze:nlɪç], *adj.* considerable, appreciable.
anseilen ['anzaɪlən], *v.a.* (*Mount.*) rope together.
ansetzen ['anzɛtsən], *v.a.* join to; (*Maths.*) start, write out (an equation).
Ansicht ['anzɪçt], *f.* (—, *pl.* —**en**) opinion; view; (*Comm.*) approval.
ansichtig ['anzɪçtɪç], *adj.* — *werden*, get a glimpse of.
Ansichts(post)karte ['anzɪçts(pɔst)kartə], *f.* (—, *pl.* —**n**) picture postcard.
ansiedeln ['anzi:dəln], *v.r. sich* —, settle (down), colonize.
Ansinnen ['anzɪnən], *n.* (—**s**, *pl.* —) demand, suggestion.
anspannen ['anʃpanən], *v.a.* tighten yoke, stretch; harness.
anspielen ['anʃpi:lən], *v.n.* (*Game*, *Sport*) lead off; *auf etwas* —, allude to s.th.
Ansporn ['anʃpɔrn], *m.* (—**s**, *no pl.*) spur, incentive.
Ansprache ['anʃpra:xə], *f.* (—, *pl.* —**n**) address, speech, talk.
ansprechen ['anʃprɛçən], *v.a. irr.* address, accost; please.
anspringen ['anʃprɪŋən], *v.a. irr.* leap at. — *v.n.* (*Motor.*) start.

Anspruch ['anʃprux], *m.* (**—s,** *pl.* **¨e**) (*Law*) claim, title.
anspruchsvoll ['anʃpruxsfɔl], *adj.* demanding, hard to please.
anstacheln ['anʃtaxəln], *v.a.* goad, prod.
Anstalt ['anʃtalt], *f.* (**—,** *pl.* **—en**) institution, establishment; *—en treffen*, make arrangements (for).
Anstand ['anʃtant], *m.* (**—es,** *no pl.*) propriety; politeness, good manners, good grace; decency; (*Hunt.*) stand, butts.
anständig ['anʃtɛndɪç], *adj.* decent, proper, respectable.
Anstandsbesuch ['anʃtantsbəzu:x], *m.* (**—es,** *pl.* **—e**) formal visit.
anstandshalber ['anʃtantshalbər], *adv.* for decency's sake.
anstandslos ['anʃtantslo:s], *adv.* unhesitatingly.
anstarren ['anʃtarən], *v.a.* stare at.
anstatt [an'ʃtat], *prep.* (*Genit.*), *conj.* instead of, in lieu of, in the place of.
anstecken ['anʃtɛkən], *v.a.* pin on; set fire to; infect.
Ansteckung ['anʃtɛkuŋ], *f.* (**—,** *pl.* **—en**) infection, contagion.
anstehen ['anʃte:ən], *v.n. irr.* stand in a queue; — *lassen*, put off, delay.
ansteigen ['anʃtaɪgən], *v.n. irr.* (*aux.* sein) rise, increase.
anstellen ['anʃtɛlən], *v.a. einen* —, appoint s.o. to a post; employ; *Betrachtungen* —, speculate. — *v.r. sich* —, form a queue, line up.
anstellig ['anʃtɛlɪç], *adj.* able, skilful, adroit.
Anstellung ['anʃtɛluŋ], *f.* (**—,** *pl.* **—en**) appointment, employment.
anstiften ['anʃtɪftən], *v.a.* instigate.
anstimmen ['anʃtɪmən], *v.a.* intone.
Anstoß ['anʃto:s], *m.* (**—es,** *pl.* **¨e**) (*Footb.*) kick-off; — *erregen*, give offence; *den* — *geben zu*, initiate, give an impetus to; *Stein des —es*, stumbling block; — *nehmen*, take offence.
anstoßen ['anʃto:sən], *v.a. irr.* knock against, push against; give offence; clink (glasses); border on; *mit der Zunge* —, lisp.
anstößig ['anʃtø:sɪç], *adj.* shocking, offensive.
anstreichen ['anʃtraɪçən], *v.a. irr.* paint; *Fehler* —, mark wrong.
Anstreicher ['anʃtraɪçər], *m.* (**—s,** *pl.* **—**) house-painter.
anstrengen ['anʃtrɛŋən], *v.a.* strain exert; *eine Klage gegen einen* —, bring an action against s.o. — *v.r. sich* —, exert o.s.
Anstrengung ['anʃtrɛŋuŋ], *f.* (**—,** *pl.* **—en**) exertion, effort.
Anstrich ['anʃtrɪç], *m.* (**—s,** *pl.* **—e**) coat of paint.
Ansturm ['anʃturm], *m.* (**—s,** *no pl.*) attack, assault, charge.
Ansuchen ['anzu:xən], *n.* (**—s,** *pl.* **—**) application, request, petition.
ansuchen ['anzu:xən], *v.n. bei einem um etwas* —, apply to s.o. for s.th.
Anteil ['antaɪl], *m.* (**—s,** *pl.* **—e**) share, portion; sympathy.
Anteilnahme ['antaɪlna:mə], *f.* (**—,** *no pl.*) sympathy.
Antenne [an'tɛnə], *f.* (**—,** *pl.* **—n**) aerial; antenna.
antik [an'ti:k], *adj.* antique, ancient, classical.
Antike [an'ti:kə], *f.* (**—,** *pl.* **—en**) (classical) antiquity; ancient work of art (statue etc.).
Antiquar [anti'kva:r], *m.* (**—s,** *pl.* **—e**) second-hand dealer; antiquary.
Antiquariat [antikva'rja:t], *n.* (**—s,** *pl.* **—e**) second-hand bookshop.
antiquarisch [anti'kva:rɪʃ], *adj.* antiquarian, second-hand.
Antlitz ['antlɪts], *n.* (**—es,** *pl.* **—e**) countenance, (*Poet.*) face.
Antrag ['antra:k], *m.* (**—s,** *pl.* **¨e**) proposition, proposal, application; *einen* — *stellen*, bring in a motion; make application.
antragen ['antra:gən], *v.a. irr.* propose, make a proposal, offer to.
Antragsformular ['antra:ksfɔrmula:r], *n.* (**—s,** *pl.* **—e**) (*Insurance*) proposal form; application form.
Antragsteller ['antra:kʃtɛlər], *m.* (**—s,** *pl.* **—**) applicant, mover of a resolution.
antreten ['antre:tən], *v.a. irr. ein Amt* —, enter upon an office; *eine Reise* —, set out on a journey. — *v.n.* (*aux.* sein) (*Mil.*) fall in.
Antrieb ['antri:p], *m.* (**—s,** *pl.* **—e**) impulse, motive; incentive; *aus eigenem* —, voluntarily.
Antritt ['antrɪt], *m.* (**—s,** *no pl.*) start, commencement.
Antrittsvorlesung ['antrɪtsforle:zuŋ], *f.* (*Univ.*) inaugural lecture.
antun ['antu:n], *v.a. irr. einem etwas* —, do s.th. to s.o.
Antwort ['antvɔrt], *f.* (**—,** *pl.* **—en**) answer, reply; *abschlägige* —, refusal, rebuff.
antworten ['antvɔrtən], *v.a.* answer, reply to.
anvertrauen ['anfertrauən], *v.a. einem etwas* —, entrust s.o. with s.th.; confide in s.o.
anverwandt ['anfɛrvant] *see* **verwandt.**
Anwalt ['anvalt], *m.* (**—s,** *pl.* **¨e**) lawyer, barrister, solicitor, attorney, advocate.
anwandeln ['anvandəln], *v.a.* befall.
Anwandlung ['anvandluŋ], *f.* (**—,** *pl.* **—en**) fit, turn.
Anwartschaft ['anvartʃaft], *f.* (**—,** *pl.* **—en**) (*Law*) reversion; candidacy.
anweisen ['anvaɪzən], *v.a. irr.* instruct, direct; *angewiesen sein auf*, depend upon.
Anweisung ['anvaɪzuŋ], *f.* (**—,** *pl.* **—en**) instruction, advice, method; (*Comm.*) voucher, credit voucher, cheque.
anwenden ['anvɛndən], *v.a. irr.* use, make use of, apply.

anwerben ['anvɛrbən], *v.a. irr.* (*Mil.*) recruit; *sich — lassen*, enlist.
anwesend ['anve:zənt], *adj.* at hand, present.
Anwesenheit ['anve:zənhaɪt], *f.* (—, *no pl.*) presence, attendance.
anwidern ['anvi:dərn], *v.a.* disgust.
Anzahl ['antsa:l], *f.* (—, *no pl.*) number, quantity.
anzahlen ['antsa:lən], *v.a.* pay a deposit.
Anzahlung ['antsa:luŋ], *f.* (—, *pl.* —**en**) deposit.
Anzeichen ['antsaɪçən], *n.* (—**s**, *pl.* —) indication, omen.
Anzeige ['antsaɪgə], *f.* (—, *pl.* —**n**) notice, (classified) advertisement; denunciation; — *erstatten*, to lay information.
anzeigen ['antsaɪgən], *v.a.* point out, indicate; announce; notify; advertise; denounce.
Anzeiger ['antsaɪgər], *m.* (—**s**, *pl.* —) indicator; (*newspaper*) advertiser.
anzetteln ['antsɛtəln], *v.a.* plot, contrive.
anziehen ['antsi:ən], *v.a. irr.* pull, draw tight, give a tug; attract; stretch; dress; (*screws*) tighten. —, *v.r. sich* —, dress, put on o.'s clothes.
anziehend ['antsi:ənt], *adj.* attractive.
Anziehung ['antsi:uŋ], *f.* (—, *no pl.*) attraction.
Anzug ['antsu:k], *m.* (—**s**, *pl.* ⸚**e**) (man's) suit; approach.
anzüglich ['antsy:klɪç], *adj.* allusive; suggestive; — *werden*, become offensive.
anzünden ['antsyndən], *v.a.* kindle, ignite.
apart [a'part], *adj.* charming, delightful; (*Am.*) cute.
Apfel ['apfəl], *m.* (—**s**, *pl.* ⸚) apple.
Apfelmost ['apfəlmɔst], *m.* (—**s**, *no pl.*) cider.
Apfelsine [apfəl'zi:nə], *f.* (—, *pl.* —**n**) orange.
Apostel [a'pɔstəl], *m.* (—**s**, *pl.* —) apostle.
Apotheke [apɔ'te:kə], *f.* (—, *pl.* —**n**) dispensary, pharmacy, chemist's shop; (*Am.*) drugstore.
Apparat [apa'ra:t], *m.* (—(**e**)**s**, *pl.* —**e**) apparatus; radio *or* television set; telephone.
appellieren [apɛ'li:rən], *v.n.* — *an*, appeal to.
appetitlich [ape'ti:tlɪç], *adj.* appetising, dainty.
Aprikose [aprɪ'ko:zə], *f.* (—, *pl.* —**en**) apricot.
Aquarell [akva'rɛl], *n.* (—**s**, *pl.* —**e**) water-colour (painting).
Ära ['ɛ:ra], *f.* (—, *no pl.*) era.
Arabien [a'ra:bjən], *n.* Arabia.
Arbeit ['arbaɪt], *f.* (—, *pl.* —**en**) work, labour; job; employment; workmanship; *an die — gehen*, set to work.
arbeiten ['arbaɪtən], *v.a., v.n.* work, labour, toil.
Arbeiter ['arbaɪtər], *m.* (—**s**, *pl.* —) worker, workman, labourer, hand.
Arbeiterschaft ['arbaɪtərʃaft], *f.* (—, *no pl.*) working men; workers.
arbeitsam ['arbaɪtza:m], *adj.* industrious, diligent.
Arbeitsamt ['arbaɪtsamt], *n.* (—**s**, *pl.* ⸚**er**) labour exchange.
arbeitsfähig ['arbaɪtsfɛ:ɪç], *adj.* capable of working, able-bodied.
arbeitslos ['arbaɪtslo:s], *adj.* unemployed, out of work.
Arbeitslosigkeit ['arbaɪtslo:zɪçkaɪt], *f.* (—, *no pl.*) unemployment.
Arbeitsnachweis ['arbaɪtsnaxvaɪs], *m.* (—**es**, *no pl.*) labour exchange; (*Am.*) labour registry-office.
Arbeitssperre ['arbaɪtsʃpɛrə], *f.* (—, *pl.* —**n**) (*Ind.*) lock-out.
Archäologe [arçɛo'lo:gə], *m.* (—**n**, *pl.* —**n**) archaeologist.
Arche ['arçə], *f.* (—, *pl.* —**n**) ark.
Archipel [arçi'pe:l], *m.* (—**s**, *pl.* —**e**) archipelago.
architektonisch [arçɪtɛk'to:nɪʃ], *adj.* architectural.
Archivar [arçi'va:r], *m.* (—**s**, *pl.* —**e**) keeper of archives.
arg [ark], *adj.* bad, wicked, mischievous.
Argentinien [argən'ti:njən], *n.* Argentina.
Ärger ['ɛrgər], *m.* (—**s**, *no pl.*) anger, annoyance.
ärgerlich ['ɛrgərlɪç], *adj.* annoying, aggravating, vexing; angry.
ärgern ['ɛrgərn], *v.a.* annoy, vex, make angry. — *v.r. sich* —, get annoyed.
Ärgernis ['ɛrgərnɪs], *n.* (—**ses**, *pl.* —**se**) scandal, nuisance.
arglistig ['arklɪstɪç], *adj.* crafty, sly.
arglos ['arklo:s], *adj.* unsuspecting, guileless, naive.
Argwohn ['arkvo:n], *m.* (—**s**, *no pl.*) mistrust, suspicion.
argwöhnisch ['arkvø:nɪʃ], *adj.* suspicious, distrustful.
Arie ['a:rjə], *f.* (—, *pl.* —**n**) (*Mus.*) aria.
Arm [arm], *m.* (—**s**, *pl.* —**e**) arm.
arm [arm], *adj.* poor, indigent, needy.
Armaturenbrett [arma'tu:rənbrɛt], *n.* (—**s**, *no pl.*) dashboard.
Armband ['armbant], *n.* (—**s**, *pl.* ⸚**er**) bracelet.
Armbanduhr ['armbantu:r], *f.* (—, *pl.* —**en**) wrist-watch.
Armbrust ['armbrust], *f.* (—, *pl.* —**e**) cross-bow.
Ärmel ['ɛrməl], *m.* (—**s**, *pl.* —) sleeve.
Ärmelkanal ['ɛrməlkana:l], *m.* (—**s**, *no pl.*) English Channel.
Armenien [ar'me:njən], *n.* Armenia.
Armenhaus ['armənhaus], *n.* (—**es**, *pl.* ⸚**er**) poor-house, almshouse.
Armenpfleger ['armənpfle:gər], *m.* (—**s**, *pl.* —) almoner.
Armesündermiene [armə'zyndər-mi:nə], *f.* (—, *pl.* —**n**) hangdog look.
ärmlich ['ɛrmlɪç], *adj.* poor, shabby, scanty.
armselig ['armze:lɪç], *adj.* poor, miserable, wretched; paltry.

Armut ['armu:t], *f.* (—, *no pl.*) poverty; *in — geraten*, be reduced to penury.
Arsch [arʃ], *m.* (—es, ¨-e) (*vulg.*) arse.
Arsen(ik) [ar'ze:n(ɪk)], *n.* (—s, *no pl.*) arsenic.
Art [a:rt], *f.* (—, *pl.* —en) kind, species; race; sort; method, way, manner.
artig ['a:rtɪç], *adj.* well-behaved, civil.
Artigkeit ['a:rtɪçkaɪt], *f.* (—, *pl.* —en) politeness, courtesy.
Artikel [ar'ti:kəl], *m.* (—s, *pl.* —) article; commodity.
Artist [ar'tɪst], *m.* (—en, *pl.* —en) artiste (circus, variety).
Arznei [arts'naɪ], *f.* (—, *pl.* —en) medicine.
Arzneimittel [arts'naɪmɪtəl], *n.* (—s, *pl.*—) medicine, drug.
Arzt [artst], *m.* (—es, *pl.* ¨-e) doctor, physician; *praktischer* —, general practitioner.
ärztlich ['ɛrtstlɪç], *adj.* medical.
As (1) [as], *n.* (—ses, *pl.* —se) (*Mus.*) A flat; — *Dur*, A flat major, — *Moll*, A flat minor.
As (2) [as], *n.* (—sses, *pl.* —sse) (*Sport, cards*) ace.
Asbest [as'bɛst], *m.* (—s, *no pl.*) asbestos.
Asche ['aʃə], *f.* (—, *no pl.*) ashes.
Aschenbecher ['aʃənbɛçər], *m.* (—s, *pl.* —) ash-tray.
Aschenbrödel ['aʃənbrø:dəl] *or* **Aschenputtel** ['aʃənputəl], *n.* Cinderella.
Aschkraut ['aʃkraut], *n.* (—s, *pl.* ¨-er) (*Bot.*) cineraria.
Askese [as'ke:zə], *f.* (—, *no pl.*) asceticism.
Asket [as'ke:t], *m.* (—en, *pl.* —en) ascetic.
Assessor [a'sɛsɔr], *m.* (—s, *pl.* —en) assistant; assistant judge.
Ast [ast], *m.* (—es, *pl.* ¨-e) branch, bough.
Aster ['astər], *f.* (—, *pl.* —n) (*Bot.*) aster.
Astronaut [astro'naut], *m.* (—en, *pl.*—en) astronaut.
Astronom [astro'no:m], *m.* (—en, *pl.* —en) astronomer.
Asyl [a'zy:l], *n.* (—s, *pl.* —e) asylum, sanctuary.
Atem ['a:təm], *m.* (—s, *no pl.*) breath, breathing, respiration.
Atemzug ['a:təmtsu:k], *m.* (—s, *pl.* ¨-e) breath.
Äthiopien [ɛti'o:pjən], *n.* Ethiopia.
Atlas (1) ['atlas], *m.* (—sses, *pl.* —sse *and* **Atlanten**) atlas, book of maps.
Atlas (2) ['atlas], *m.* (—sses, *pl.* —asse) satin.
atmen ['a:tmən], *v.n.* breathe.
atomar [ato'ma:r], *adj.* atomic.
Attentat [atɛn'ta:t], *n.* (—s, *pl.* —e) attempt on s.o.'s life.
Attest [a'tɛst], *n.* (—s, *pl.* —e) (*Med.*) certificate.
ätzen ['ɛtsən], *v.a.* corrode; (*Art*) etch; (*Med.*) cauterise.
auch [aux], *conj.*, *adv.* also, too, likewise, as well.
Au(e) ['au(ə)], *f.* (—, *pl.* —en) green meadow, pasture.
auf [auf], *prep.* on, upon; — *der Straße*, in the road; — *deine Gefahr*, at your own risk; — *Befehl*, by order; — *einige Tage*, for a few days; — *dem Lande*, in the country; — *keinen Fall*, on no account.
aufatmen ['aufa:tmən], *v.n.* breathe a sigh of relief.
Aufbau ['aufbau], *m.* (—s, *no pl.*) building; (*Lit.*) composition, structure.
aufbauen ['aufbauən], *v.a.* erect, build, construct.
aufbäumen ['aufbɔymən], *v.r. sich* —, (*horses*) rear.
aufbewahren ['aufbəva:rən], *v.a.* keep, store; (*luggage*) take charge of.
Aufbewahrung ['aufbəva:ruŋ], *f.* (—, *pl.* —en) storage, safe keeping.
aufbieten ['aufbi:tən], *v.a. irr.* call up for service; exert (*energies*).
aufbinden ['aufbɪndən], *v.a. irr.* untie; *einem einen Bären* —, to hoax s.o.
aufblähen ['aufblɛ:ən], *v.a.* puff up, swell, inflate.
aufblühen ['aufbly:ən], *v.n.* (*aux.* sein) flourish, unfold.
aufbrausen ['aufbrauzən], *v.n.* (*aux.* sein) fly into a rage.
aufbringen ['aufbrɪŋən], *v.a. irr.* bring up; afford; annoy (s.o.).
Aufbruch ['aufbrux], *m.* (—s, *no pl.*) departure.
aufbürden ['aufbyrdən], *v.a. einem eine Last* —, burden s.o. with a thing.
aufdecken ['aufdɛkən], *v.a.* uncover, unveil.
aufdonnern ['aufdɔnərn], *v.r. sich* — dress up showily.
aufdrängen ['aufdrɛŋən], *v.a. einem etwas* —, press s.th. upon s.o. — *v.r. sich* —, force o.'s company on.
aufdrehen ['aufdre:ən], *v.a.* (*tap*) turn on.
aufdringlich ['aufdrɪŋlɪç], *adj.* importunate, officious, obtrusive.
Aufdruck ['aufdruk], *m.* (—s, *pl.* —e) imprint.
aufdrücken ['aufdrykən], *v.a.* press open; press on s.th.
Aufenthalt ['aufɛnthalt], *m.* (—s, *pl.* —e) stay, sojourn; delay; stop.
auferlegen ['aufɛrle:gən], *v.a.* impose; enjoin.
auferstehen ['aufɛrʃte:ən], *v.n. irr.* (*aux.* sein) (*Rel.*) rise from the dead.
auffahren ['auffa:rən], *v.n. irr.* (*aux.* sein) start (from o.'s sleep); mount; flare up (in anger).
Auffahrt ['auffa:rt], *f.* (—, *pl.* —en) ascent; approach to a house, drive.
auffallen ['auffalən], *v.n. irr.* (*aux.* sein) strike the ground; *einem* —, strike s.o., astonish.
auffangen ['auffaŋən], *v.a. irr.* (*ball*) catch; (*blow*) parry, ward off; (*letter*) intercept.
auffassen ['auffasən], *v.a.* take in, comprehend.

Auffassung ['auffasuŋ], *f.* (—, *pl.* —**en**) conception, interpretation; view.
aufflackern ['aufflakərn], *v.n.* (*aux.* sein) flare up, flicker.
auffordern ['auffɔrdərn], *v.a.* summon, request, ask, invite.
aufforsten ['auffɔrstən], *v.a.* afforest.
auffressen ['auffrɛsən], *v.a. irr.* devour; (*of animals*) eat up.
auffrischen ['auffrɪʃən], *v.a.* renew, redecorate; (*fig.*) brush up.
aufführen ['auffy:rən], *v.a.* (*Theat.*) perform; *einzeln* —, specify, particularise. — *v.r. sich* —, behave, conduct o.s.
Aufführung ['auffy:ruŋ], *f.* (—, *pl.* —**en**) (*Theat.*) performance.
Aufgabe ['aufga:bə], *f.* (—, *pl.* —**n**) giving up, abandonment; (*letters, telegrams*) posting, despatch; (*work*) task; (*Sch.*) exercise; (*Maths.*) problem.
aufgabeln ['aufga:bəln], *v.a.* (*sl.*) pick up.
Aufgang ['aufgaŋ], *m.* (—**s**, *pl.* ⸚**e**) ascent, stairs.
aufgeben ['aufge:bən], *v.a. irr.* give up, abandon, relinquish; (*Am.*) quit; (*luggage*) check.
aufgeblasen ['aufgəbla:zən], *adj.* conceited, stuck up.
Aufgebot ['aufgəbo:t], *n.* (—**s**, *pl.* —**e**) (*marriage*) banns; (*Mil.*) levy; *mit — aller Kräfte*, with the utmost exertion.
aufgebracht ['aufgəbraxt], *adj.* angry, annoyed.
aufgedunsen ['aufgədunzən], *adj.* bloated, sodden.
aufgehen ['aufge:ən], *v.n. irr.* (*aux.* sein) (*knot*) come undone; (*sun*) rise; (*dough*) swell, rise; (*Maths.*) leave no remainder, cancel out.
aufgehoben ['aufgəho:bən], *adj. gut — sein*, be in good hands.
aufgelegt ['aufgəle:kt], *adj.* disposed, inclined.
aufgeräumt ['aufgərɔymt], *adj.* merry, cheerful, in high spirits.
aufgeweckt ['aufgəvɛkt], *adj.* bright, clever, intelligent.
aufgießen ['aufgi:sən], *v.a. irr. Kaffee* —, make coffee.
aufgreifen ['aufgraɪfən], *v.a. irr.* seize.
Aufguß ['aufgus], *m.* (—**sses**, *pl.* ⸚**sse**) infusion.
aufhalsen ['aufhalzən], *v.a. einem etwas* —, (*coll.*) saddle s.o. with s.th.
aufhalten ['aufhaltən], *v.a. irr.* (*door*) hold open; *einen* —, delay s.o. — *v.r. sich an einem Ort* —, stay at a place; *sich über etwas* —, find fault with s.th.
aufhängen ['aufhɛŋən], *v.a. irr.* hang (up).
aufhäufen ['aufhɔyfən], *v.a.* pile up. — *v.r. sich* —, accumulate.
Aufheben ['aufhe:bən], *n.* (—**s**, *no pl.*) lifting up; ado; *viel —s machen*, make a great fuss.
aufheben ['aufhe:bən], *v.a. irr.* lift (up), pick up; keep, preserve; (*laws*) repeal, abolish; (*agreements*) rescind, annul.
Aufhebung ['aufhe:buŋ], *f.* (—, *pl.* —**en**) abolition, abrogation, annulment, repeal.
aufheitern ['aufhaɪtərn], *v.a.* cheer up; amuse. — *v.r. sich* —, (*weather*) brighten, clear up.
aufhelfen ['aufhɛlfən], *v.n. irr. einem* —, help s.o. up.
aufhellen ['aufhɛlən], *v.r. sich* —, (*weather*) clear up; (*face*) brighten up.
aufhetzen ['aufhɛtsən], *v.a.* rouse (s.o.); *einen — gegen*, incite s.o. against.
aufhorchen ['aufhɔrçən], *v.n.* prick up o.'s ears.
aufhören ['aufhø:rən], *v.n.* cease, stop; (*Am.*) quit; *ohne aufzuhören*, incessantly; *da hört sich doch alles auf!* that is the limit!
aufklären ['aufklɛ:rən], *v.a.* enlighten; clear up; *einen* —, enlighten s.o. —*v.r. sich* —, (*weather*) brighten.
Aufklärung ['aufklɛ:ruŋ], *f.* (—, *no pl.*) (age of) Enlightenment.
aufknacken ['aufknakən], *v.a.* crack (open).
aufknöpfen ['aufknœpfən], *v.a.* unbutton; *aufgeknöpft sein*, be in a talkative mood.
aufkommen ['aufkɔmən], *v.n. irr.* (*aux.* sein) come into use, spring up; *für etwas* —, pay for s.th.; *einen nicht — lassen*, give s.o. no chance.
aufkrempeln ['aufkrɛmpəln], *v.a.* (*coll.*) roll up (o.'s sleeves).
aufkündigen ['aufkyndɪgən], *v.a.* (*money*) recall; *einem die Freundschaft* —, break with s.o.
Auflage ['aufla:gə], *f.* (—, *pl.* —**n**) (*tax*) impost, duty, levy; (*book*) edition, impression; circulation.
auflassen ['auflasən], *v.a. irr.* leave open; (*Law*) cede.
auflauern ['auflauərn], *v.n. einem* —, lie in wait for s.o., waylay s.o.
Auflauf ['auflauf], *m.* (—**s**, *pl.* ⸚**e**) tumult, noisy street gathering; soufflé.
auflaufen ['auflaufən], *v.n. irr.* (*aux.* sein) swell, increase; (*ship*) run aground.
aufleben ['aufle:bən], *v.n.* (*aux.* sein) *wieder* —, revive.
auflegen ['aufle:gən], *v.a. irr.* lay upon, put on; (*book*) publish; (*tax, punishment*) impose, inflict.
auflehnen ['aufle:nən], *v.r. sich gegen einen* (or *etwas*) —, rebel against, mutiny, oppose.
auflesen ['aufle:zən], *v.a. irr.* pick up, gather.
aufleuchten ['auflɔyçtən], *v.n.* light up; (*eyes*) shine.
auflockern ['auflɔkərn], *v.a.* loosen.
auflodern ['auflo:dərn], *v.n.* (*aux.* sein) flare up, blaze up.

auflösen ['aufløːzən], *v.a.* dissolve, loosen; (*puzzle*) solve, guess; (*meeting*) break up; (*business*) wind up; (*partnership*) dissolve; (*army*) disband. — *v.r. sich* —, melt, dissolve, be broken up.

aufmachen ['aufmaxən], *v.a.* (*door, packet*) open; (*knot*) undo; *gut* —, pack nicely. — *v.r. sich* —, get going, set out for.

Aufmachung ['aufmaxuŋ], *f.* (—, *pl.* —**en**) outward appearance, make-up, get-up.

Aufmarsch ['aufmarʃ], *m.* (—**es**, *pl.* ¨**e**) (*Mil.*) parade.

aufmerksam ['aufmɛrkzaːm], *adj.* attentive, observant; civil, kind; *einen — machen auf*, draw s.o.'s attention to.

aufmuntern ['aufmuntərn], *v.a.* encourage, cheer up.

Aufnahme ['aufnaːmə], *f.* (—, *pl.* —**n**) reception; (*Phot.*) snap, photograph; (*Geog.*) mapping out, survey; (*Mus.*) recording.

aufnehmen ['aufneːmən], *v.a. irr.* take up; receive, give shelter to; (*Phot.*) photograph, film; (*Mus.*) record; (*money*) raise, borrow; (*minutes*) draw up; *den Faden wieder* —, take up the thread; *die Arbeit wieder* —, return to work, resume work; *die Fährte* —, (*Hunt.*) recover the scent; *es mit einem* —, be a match for s.o.; (*Comm.*) *Inventar* —, take stock, draw up an inventory.

aufnötigen ['aufnøːtɪgən], *v.a. einem etwas* —, force s.th. upon s.o.

aufpassen ['aufpasən], *v.n.* attend to, pay attention to, take notice of, take care of.

aufpeitschen ['aufpaɪtʃən], *v.a.* whip up.

aufpflanzen ['aufpflantsən], *v.a.* mount, erect. — *v.r. sich vor einem* —, plant o.s. in front of s.o.; *mit aufgepflanztem Bajonett*, with bayonets fixed.

Aufputz ['aufputs], *m.* (—**es**, *no pl.*) finery, trimmings.

aufraffen ['aufrafən], *v.a.* snatch up, rake up. — *v.r. sich wieder* —, pull o.s. together.

aufräumen ['aufrɔymən], *v.a.* put in order, clear away; (*room*) tidy up; *mit etwas* —, make a clean sweep of s.th.; *aufgeräumt sein*, be in a jolly mood.

aufrechnen ['aufrɛçnən], *v.a.* reckon up; set off against.

aufrecht ['aufrɛçt], *adj.* upright, erect; *etwas — erhalten*, maintain s.th.; (*opinion*) stick to, adhere to, uphold.

Aufrechterhaltung ['aufrɛçtərhaltuŋ], *f.* (—, *no pl.*) maintenance, preservation.

aufregen ['aufreːgən], *v.a.* excite, enrage.

aufreiben ['aufraɪbən], *v.a. irr.* rub sore; (*Mil.*) destroy, wipe out. — *v.r. sich* —, exhaust o.s. with worry (*or* work).

aufreizen ['aufraɪtsən], *v.a.* incite, provoke.

aufrichten ['aufrɪçtən], *v.a.* raise, erect, set upright; (*fig.*) comfort, console. — *v.r. sich* —, rise, sit up.

aufrichtig ['aufrɪçtɪç], *adj.* sincere, frank.

aufriegeln ['aufriːgəln], *v.a.* unbolt.

Aufriß ['aufrɪs], *m.* (—**sses**, *pl.* —**sse**) sketch, draft; (*Archit.*) elevation, section.

aufrücken ['aufrykən], *v.n.* (*aux.* sein) rise, be promoted (in rank), advance.

Aufruf ['aufruːf], *m.* (—**s**, *pl.* —**e**) summons, proclamation, appeal; (*Law*) citation.

aufrufen ['aufruːfən], *v.a. irr.* summons; (*Sch.*) call upon.

Aufruhr ['aufruːr], *m.* (—**s**, *pl.* —**e**) uproar, riot, tumult, rebellion, mutiny.

aufrühren ['aufryːrən], *v.a.* stir up, agitate, rouse to rebellion.

Aufrüstung ['aufrystuŋ], *f.* (—, *no pl.*) (*Mil.*) (re-)armament.

aufrütteln ['aufrytəln], *v.a.* rouse, shake s.o. out of his lethargy.

aufsagen ['aufzaːgən], *v.a.* recite.

aufsässig ['aufzɛsɪç], *adj.* refractory, rebellious.

Aufsatz ['aufzats], *m.* (—**es**, *pl.* ¨**e**) top, head-piece, table centre-piece; (*Sch.*) composition, essay; (*newspaper*) article.

aufscheuchen ['aufʃɔyçən], *v.a.* flush (game), startle.

aufschichten ['aufʃɪçtən], *v.a.* stack, pile up in layers.

aufschieben ['aufʃiːbən], *v.a. irr.* push open; delay, postpone, adjourn; (*Parl.*) prorogue.

Aufschlag ['aufʃlaːk], *m.* (—**s**, *pl.* ¨**e**) impact, striking; (*sleeve*) cuff; turn-up; (*uniform*) facings; (*Comm.*) increase in price; (*Tennis*) service.

aufschlagen ['aufʃlaːgən], *v.n. irr.* (*aux.* sein) hit, strike (open); (*Tennis*) serve. — *v.a. die Augen* —, open o.'s eyes; *ein Lager* —, pitch camp; *ein Buch* —, open a book.

aufschlitzen ['aufʃlɪtsən], *v.a.* rip open, slit open.

Aufschluß ['aufʃlus], *m.* (—**sses**, *pl.* ¨**sse**) disclosure, information.

aufschneiden ['aufʃnaɪdən], *v.a. irr.* cut open. — *v.n.* brag, boast.

Aufschneider ['aufʃnaɪdər], *m.* (—**s**, *pl.* —) swaggerer, braggart.

Aufschnitt ['aufʃnɪt], *m.* (—**s**, *no pl.*) slice of cold meat *or* sausage.

aufschnüren ['aufʃnyːrən], *v.a.* unlace, untie.

Aufschrei ['aufʃraɪ], *m.* (—**s**, *pl.* —**e**) outcry, screech, scream, shout, shriek.

Aufschrift ['aufʃrɪft], *f.* (—, *pl.* —**en**) inscription, address; heading.

Aufschub ['aufʃuːp], *m.* (—**s**, *pl.* ¨**e**) delay, adjournment, postponement.

aufschütten ['aufʃytən], *v.a.* (*liquid*) pour upon; (*dam*) raise.

aufschwingen ['aufʃvɪŋən], *v.r. irr. sich* —, soar, rise; *ich kann mich dazu nicht* —, I cannot rise to that.
Aufschwung ['aufʃvuŋ], *m.* (—**s**, *no pl.*) flight, rising; (*Comm.*) improvement, boom.
Aufsehen ['aufze:ən], *n.* (—**s**, *no pl.*) sensation, stir.
Aufseher ['aufze:ər], *m.* (—**s**, *pl.* —) overseer, inspector.
aufsein ['aufzaɪn], *v.n. irr.* (*aux.* sein) be out of bed, be up and about.
aufsetzen ['aufzɛtsən], *v.a.* (*hat*) put on; (*letter, essay*) draft.
Aufsicht ['aufzɪçt], *f.* (—, *no pl.*) inspection, supervision, control.
Aufsichtsrat ['aufzɪçtsra:t], *m.* (—**s**, *pl.* ⸚**e**) (*Comm.*) board of directors.
aufsitzen ['aufzɪtsən], *v.n. irr.* sit up, wait up at night; (*horse*) mount.
aufspannen ['aufʃpanən], *v.a.* (*umbrella*) put up; (*tent*) pitch.
aufspeichern ['aufʃpaɪçərn], *v.a.* store (up), warehouse.
aufsperren ['aufʃpɛrən], *v.a.* open wide, unlock.
aufspielen ['aufʃpi:lən], *v.n. zum Tanz* —, play music for dancing. — *v.r. sich groß* —, give o.s. airs.
aufspießen ['aufʃpi:sən], *v.a.* pierce on a spit; (*joint*) skewer.
aufspringen ['aufʃprɪŋən], *v.n. irr.* (*aux.* sein) leap up, jump up; (*door*) fly open; (*hands in winter*) chap.
aufspüren ['aufʃpy:rən], *v.a.* track, trace.
aufstacheln ['aufʃtaxəln], *v.a.* goad, incite.
Aufstand ['aufʃtant], *m.* (—**s**, *pl.* ⸚**e**) insurrection, revolt, sedition.
aufstapeln ['aufʃta:pəln], *v.a.* pile up, stack, store.
aufstechen ['aufʃtɛçən], *v.a. irr.* (*Med.*) lance.
aufstehen ['aufʃte:ən], *v.n. irr.* (*aux.* sein) (*door*) stand open; stand up; get up (from bed); rise (from a chair).
aufstellen ['aufʃtɛlən], *v.a.* set up, arrange; erect; (*Pol.*) put forward (candidate).
Aufstellung ['aufʃtɛluŋ], *f.* (—, *pl.* —**en**) arrangement; statement; inventory; (*Pol.*) nomination.
aufstemmen ['aufʃtɛmən], *v.a.* prise open.
Aufstieg ['aufʃti:k], *m.* (—**s**, *pl.* —**e**) ascent, rise.
aufstöbern ['aufʃtø:bərn], *v.a.* stir (up); start; (*fig.*) discover, ferret out.
aufstoßen ['aufʃto:sən], *v.a. irr.* push open; bump against. — *v.n.* belch.
aufstreben ['aufʃtre:bən], *v.n.* soar; (*fig.*) aspire.
aufstreichen ['aufʃtraɪçən], *v.a. irr.* (*paint*) lay on; (*butter*) spread.
aufstülpen ['aufʃtylpən], *v.a.* turn up; (*hat*) clap on o.'s head.
auftakeln ['aufta:kəln], *v.a.* (*Naut.*) rig.
Auftakt ['auftakt], *m.* (—**s**, *pl.* —**e**) (*Mus.*) arsis; (*fig.*) opening, prelude.
auftauchen ['auftauxən], *v.n.* (*aux.* sein) appear, emerge, surface.
auftauen ['auftauən], *v.n.* (*aux.* sein) thaw; (*fig.*) lose o.'s reserve.
auftischen ['auftɪʃən], *v.a.* dish up.
Auftrag ['auftra:k], *m.* (—**s**, *pl.* ⸚**e**) assignment, commission, errand; *im — von*, on behalf of.
auftragen ['auftra:gən], *v.a. irr.* (*food*) serve up; (*paint*) apply; *einem etwas* —, charge s.o. with a job; *stark* —, lay it on thick.
auftreiben ['auftraɪbən], *v.a. irr.* raise (*money*); procure, obtain. — *v.n.* (*aux.* sein) (*ship*) run aground.
auftrennen ['auftrɛnən], *v.a.* unstitch; (*hem*) unpick.
Auftreten ['auftre:tən], *n.* (—**s**, *no pl.*) (*Theat.*) appearance; behaviour.
auftreten ['auftre:tən], *v.n. irr.* (*aux.* sein) tread upon, step upon; (*Theat.*) appear, come on; *energisch* —, take strong measures, put o.'s foot down.
Auftritt ['auftrɪt], *m.* (—**s**, *pl.* —**e**) (*Theat.*) scene; altercation, row.
auftun ['auftu:n], *v.a. irr.* open; *den Mund* —, speak. — *v.r. sich* —, (*abyss*) yawn.
auftürmen ['auftyrmən], *v.a.* pile up, heap up. — *v.r. sich* —, tower.
aufwachen ['aufvaxən], *v.n.* (*aux.* sein) awake, wake up.
aufwallen ['aufvalən], *v.n.* (*aux.* sein) boil up, bubble up, rage.
Aufwand ['aufvant], *m.* (—**s**, *no pl.*) expense, expenditure; sumptuousness.
aufwarten ['aufvartən], *v.n.* wait upon, attend on.
aufwärts ['aufvɛrts], *adv.* upward(s), aloft.
Aufwartung ['aufvartuŋ], *f.* (—, *pl.* —**en**) attendance; *seine — machen*, pay a (formal) visit.
aufwaschen ['aufvaʃən], *v.a. irr.* wash the dishes.
aufweisen ['aufvaɪzən], *v.a. irr.* show, produce.
aufwenden ['aufvɛndən], *v.a. irr.* spend upon, expend upon.
aufwickeln ['aufvɪkəln], *v.a.* wind up; unwind.
aufwiegeln ['aufvi:gəln], *v.a.* stir up, incite to rebellion.
aufwiegen ['aufvi:gən], *v.a. irr.* outweigh, counter-balance, make up for.
aufwischen ['aufvɪʃən], *v.a.* wipe away, mop up.
aufwühlen ['aufvy:lən], *v.a.* dig, root up, (*fig.*) stir.
aufzählen ['auftsɛ:lən], *v.a.* count up, enumerate, list.
aufzäumen ['auftsɔymən], *v.a.* bridle (horses).
aufzehren ['auftse:rən], *v.a.* eat up, consume.
aufzeichnen ['auftsaɪçnən], *v.a.* write down, take a note of, record.

aufziehen ['auftsi:ən], *v.a. irr.* draw up, pull up; pull open; (*pennant*) hoist; (*clock*) wind up; (*child*) bring up, rear; *einen* —, tease s.o.; *gelindere Saiten* —, be more lenient.

Aufzucht ['auftsuxt], *f.* (—, *no pl.*) breeding, rearing.

Aufzug ['auftsu:k], *m.* (—s, *pl.* ¨e) lift; (*Am.*) elevator; (*Theat.*) act; dress, array, attire.

aufzwingen ['auftsvɪŋən], *v.a. irr. einem etwas* —, force s.th. on s.o.

Augapfel ['aukapfəl], *m.* (—s, *pl.* ¨) eye-ball; (*fig.*) apple of o.'s eye.

Auge ['augə], *n.* (—s, *pl.* —n) eye; *aus den* —*n, aus dem Sinn*, out of sight, out of mind; *mit einem blauen* — *davonkommen*, escape by the skin of o.'s teeth, get off cheaply; *es wird mir schwarz vor den* —*n*, I feel faint.

Augenblick ['augənblɪk], *m.* (—s, *pl.* —e) moment, instant; *jeden* —, at any moment.

augenblicklich [augən'blɪklɪç], *adj.* momentary, instantaneous.— *adv.* at present, for the moment, immediately.

Augenbraue ['augənbrauə], *f.* (—, *pl.* —n) eye-brow.

augenfällig ['augənfɛlɪç], *adj.* visible, evident, conspicuous.

Augenglas ['augənglas], *n.* (—es, *pl.* ¨er) eye-glass.

Augenhöhle ['augənhø:lə], *f.* (—, *pl.* —n) eye-socket.

Augenlicht ['augənlɪçt], *n.* (—s, *no pl.*) eye-sight.

Augenlid ['augənli:t], *n.* (—s, *pl.* —er) eye-lid.

Augenmaß ['augənma:s], *n.* (—es, *no pl.*) *gutes* —, good measuring ability with the eye, a sure eye.

Augenmerk ['augənmɛrk], *n.* (—s, *no pl.*) attention; *sein* — *auf etwas richten*, focus o.'s attention on s.th.

Augenschein ['augənʃaɪn], *m.* (—s, *no pl.*) appearance; *in* — *nehmen*, view.

augenscheinlich ['augənʃaɪnlɪç], *adj.* apparent, evident.

Augenweide ['augənvaɪdə], *f.* (—, *pl.* —n) delight to the eye, s.th. lovely to look at.

Augenwimper ['augənvɪmpər], *f.* (—, *pl.* —n) eye-lash.

Augenzeuge ['augəntsɔygə], *m.* (—n, *pl.* —n) eye-witness.

August [au'gust], *m.* (—s, *no pl.*) (*month*) August.

Augustiner [augus'ti:nər], *m.* (—s, *pl.* —) (*Eccl.*) Augustinian.

auktionieren [auktsjo'ni:rən], *v.a.* auction(eer), sell by auction.

Aula ['aula], *f.* (—, *pl.* —len) (*Sch, Univ.*) great hall; auditorium maximum.

Aurikel [au'ri:kəl], *f.* (—, *pl.* —n) (*Bot.*) auricula.

aus [aus], *prep.* (*Dat.*) from, out of, of, off. — *adv.* out, over, finished, done with, spent; *es ist alles* —, it is over and done with; *ich weiß weder ein noch* —, I am at my wits' end.

ausarten ['ausartən], *v.n.* (*aux.* sein) degenerate; (*fig.*) deteriorate.

Ausbau ['ausbau], *m.* (—s, *no pl.*) enlargement, extension.

ausbauen ['ausbauən], *v.a.* enlarge (a house); improve on.

ausbedingen ['ausbədɪŋən], *v.a. sich etwas* —, stipulate.

ausbessern ['ausbesərn], *v.a.* (*garment*) mend, repair.

Ausbeute ['ausbɔytə], *f.* (—, *no pl.*) gain, profit, produce.

Ausbeutung ['ausbɔytuŋ], *f.* (—, *no pl.*) exploitation, sweating; (*Min.*) working.

ausbezahlen ['ausbətsa:lən], *v.a.* pay in full.

ausbilden ['ausbɪldən], *v.a.* develop, train; (*Mil.*) drill.

Ausbildung ['ausbɪlduŋ], *f.* (—, *pl.* —en) training, education.

ausbleiben ['ausblaɪbən], *v.n. irr.* (*aux.* sein) fail to appear, be absent.

Ausblick ['ausblɪk], *m.* (—s, *pl.* —e) view (from window); (*fig.*) prospect, outlook.

ausborgen ['ausbɔrgən], *v.a.* (*sich*) *etwas* —, borrow s.th. from.

ausbreiten ['ausbraɪtən], *v.a.* spread (things); stretch out (o.'s arms). — *v.r. sich* —, spread, extend.

Ausbreitung ['ausbraɪtuŋ], *f.* (—, *no pl.*) spreading, extension, distribution, expansion.

ausbringen ['ausbrɪŋən], *v.a. irr. einen Toast auf einen* —, drink s.o.'s health.

Ausbruch ['ausbrux], *m.* (—s, *pl.* ¨e) breaking out, outbreak, eruption, burst (of laughter).

ausbrüten ['ausbry:tən], *v.a.* hatch; (*fig.*) plot.

Ausbund ['ausbunt], *m.* (—s, *pl.* ¨e) paragon, embodiment.

Ausdauer ['ausdauər], *f.* (—, *no pl.*) perseverance, persistence, stamina.

ausdehnen ['ausde:nən], *v.a.* extend, stretch, distend; (*fig.*) prolong, protract. — *v.r. sich* —, expand, extend, stretch.

Ausdehnung ['ausde:nuŋ], *f.* (—, *pl.* —en) extension, expansion; dilation; (*Phys.*) dimension.

ausdenken ['ausdɛŋkən], *v.a. irr.* think out. — *v.r. sich etwas* —, devise s.th., invent s.th.; *das ist gar nicht auszudenken*, that is unimaginable, inconceivable.

Ausdeutung ['ausdɔytuŋ], *f.* (—, *pl.* —en) interpretation, explanation.

ausdörren ['ausdœrən], *v.a.* parch, dry (up).

ausdrehen ['ausdre:ən], *v.a.* (*gas, light, water*) turn off, switch off.

Ausdruck ['ausdruk], *m.* (—s, *pl.* ¨e) expression, phrase.

ausdrücken ['ausdrykən], *v.a.* squeeze out, press out; (*fig.*) express.

ausdrücklich ['ausdryklɪç], *adj.* express, explicit.

Ausdrucksweise ['ausdruksvaɪtsə], *f.* (—, *pl.* —**n**) enunciation, manner of speech, (mode of) expression, style.
ausdünsten ['ausdynstən], *v.a.* exhale, perspire.
auseinander [ausaɪn'andər], *adv.* asunder, apart.
Auseinandersetzung [ausaɪn'andərzɛtsuŋ], *f.* (—, *pl.* —**en**) altercation; discussion, explanation.
auserkoren ['auserko:rən], *adj.* elect, chosen, selected.
auserlesen ['auserle:zən], *adj.* choice, picked, excellent, first class.
auserwählen ['auserve:lən], *v.a.* choose, select.
Ausfahrt ['ausfa:rt], *f.* (—, *pl.* —**en**) drive; gateway; exit.
Ausfall ['ausfal], *m.* (—**s**, *pl.* ⸚**e**) falling out; (*radioactivity*) fall-out; sortie, sally; deficiency, loss, cancellation; result, outcome.
ausfallen ['ausfalən], *v.n. irr.* (*aux.* sein) drop out, fall out; be cancelled, be omitted, fail to take place; turn out (well etc.).
ausfallend ['ausfalənt], *adj.* offensive, abusive; — *werden*, become insulting.
ausfertigen ['ausfertIgən], *v.a.* despatch, draw up, make out, issue.
ausfindig ['ausfIndIç], *adj.* — *machen*, find out, locate, discover.
ausflicken ['ausflIkən], *v.a.* mend, patch.
Ausflucht ['ausfluxt], *f.* (—, *pl.* ⸚**e**) evasion, excuse, subterfuge.
Ausflug ['ausflu:k], *m.* (—**s**, *pl.* ⸚**e**) trip, excursion, outing.
Ausfluß ['ausflus], *m.* (—**sses**, *pl.* ⸚**sse**) (*Engin.*) outflow, outlet; (*Med.*) discharge, suppuration.
ausfragen ['ausfra:gən], *v.a. einen* —, question, quiz s.o.
Ausfuhr ['ausfu:r], *f.* (—, *pl.* —**en**) export.
ausführbar ['ausfy:rba:r], *adj.* practicable, feasible; exportable.
ausführen ['ausfy:rən], *v.a.* take out; lead out; export; carry out, perform, fulfil; point out.
ausführlich [aus'fy:rlIç], *adj.* detailed, full.
Ausführung ['ausfy:ruŋ], *f.* (—, *pl.* —**en**) execution, carrying out; finish; workmanship.
ausfüllen ['ausfylən], *v.a.* (*forms*) fill up, fill in, complete.
ausfüttern ['ausfytərn], *v.a.* line (a dress).
Ausgabe ['ausga:bə], *f.* (—, *pl.* —**en**) issue, distribution; (*goods*) dispatch, issuing counter; delivery; (*book*) edition; (*pl.*) expenses, expenditure.
Ausgang ['ausgaŋ], *m.* (—**s**, *pl.* ⸚**e**) going out; exit; result, upshot; end, conclusion; time off (from duty).
Ausgangspunkt ['ausgaŋspuŋkt], *m.* (—**s**, *pl.* —**e**) starting-point; point of departure.
ausgären ['ausgɛ:rən], *v.n. irr.* (*aux.* sein) ferment; *ausgegoren sein*, have fermented.
ausgeben ['ausge:bən], *v.a. irr.* (*work*) give out, distribute; (*money*) expend, spend; (*tickets*) issue. —*v.r. sich* — *für*, pass o.s. off as.
ausgebreitet ['ausgəbraItət], *adj.* extensive, widespread.
Ausgeburt ['ausgeburt], *f.* (—, *pl.* —**en**) monstrosity; — *des Hirns*, figment of the imagination.
ausgefahren ['ausgəfa:rən], *adj.* (*street*) rutted, well-worn.
ausgehen ['ausge:ən], *v.n. irr.* (*aux.* sein) go out; (*hair*) to fall out; (*colour*) come off, fade; (*breath, patience, money*) become exhausted; result, end in.
ausgelassen ['ausgəlasən], *adj.* boisterous, exuberant, frolicsome, merry, jolly, unbridled.
ausgemacht ['ausgəmaxt], *adj.* arranged, settled, decided; *eine* —*e Sache*, a matter of course, a foregone conclusion; *ein* —*er Schurke*, a downright scoundrel.
ausgeschlossen ['ausgəʃlɔsən], *p.p. das ist* —, that is impossible, out of the question.
ausgewachsen ['ausgəvaksən], *adj.* full-grown, fully grown.
ausgezeichnet ['ausgətsaIçnət], *adj.* excellent, first rate, distinguished.
ausgiebig ['ausgi:bIç], *adj.* abundant, plentiful; (*soil*) fertile, rich.
ausgießen ['ausgi:sən], *v.a. irr.* pour out.
Ausgleich ['ausglaIç], *m.* (—**s**, *no pl.*) settlement, compromise, compensation, equalisation.
ausgleichen ['ausglaIçən], *v.a. irr.* make even, balance, equalise, compensate; (*sport*) equalise, draw.
ausgraben ['ausgra:bən], *v.a. irr.* dig out, dig up, excavate, exhume.
Ausguck ['ausguk], *m.* (—**s**, *pl.* —**e**) look-out; (*Naut.*) crow's nest.
Ausguß ['ausgus], *m.* (—**sses**, *pl.* ⸚**sse**) sink, gutter.
aushalten ['aushaltən], *v.a. irr.* sustain, endure, bear, stand.
aushändigen ['aushɛndIgən], *v.a.* deliver up, hand over.
Aushang ['aushaŋ], *m.* (—**s**, *pl.* ⸚**e**) sign, sign-board, placard.
ausharren ['ausharən], *v.n.* persevere, hold out, wait patiently.
aushecken ['aushɛkən], *v.a.* hatch (a plot).
aushelfen ['aushɛlfən], *v.n. irr.* help out.
Aushilfe ['aushIlfə], *f.* (—, *pl.* —**n**) help, aid, assistance.
aushilfsweise ['aushIlfsvaIzə], *adv.* temporarily, as a stop-gap.
aushöhlen ['aushø:lən], *v.a.* hollow out, excavate.
ausholen ['ausho:lən], *v.a.* pump, sound s.o. — *v.n.* strike out; *weit* —, go far back (in a narration).

auskehren ['auske:rən], *v.a.* sweep out.
auskennen ['auskɛnən], *v.r. irr. sich in etwas* —, know all about s.th.
auskleiden ['ausklaɪdən], *v.a.* undress.
ausklingen ['ausklɪŋən], *v.n. irr.* (*aux.* sein) (*sound*) die away.
ausklügeln ['auskly:gəln], *v.a.* puzzle out, contrive.
auskneifen ['ausknaɪfən], *v.n. irr.* (*aux.* sein) (*coll.*) bolt, run away.
Auskommen ['auskɔmən], *n.* (**—s**, *no pl.*) sufficiency, subsistence, livelihood; *mit dem ist kein* —, there is no getting on with him.
auskommen ['auskɔmən], *v.n. irr.* (*aux.* sein) *mit etwas* —, have enough *or* sufficient of s.th., manage; *mit einem gut* —, be on good terms with s.o., get on well with s.o.
auskömmlich ['auskœmlɪç], *adj.* sufficient.
auskosten ['auskɔstən], *v.a.* taste *or* enjoy to the full.
auskramen ['auskra:mən], *v.a.* rummage out; (*fig.*) reminisce; talk freely.
auskundschaften ['auskuntʃaftən], *v.a.* spy out, reconnoitre, explore.
Auskunft ['auskunft], *f.* (—, *pl.* **⸚e**) information; (*Tel.*) enquiries; (*Mil.*) intelligence, enquiry.
auslachen ['auslaxən], *v.a.* laugh at, deride.
ausladen ['ausla:dən], *v.a. irr.* unload, discharge; cancel (invitation).
Auslage ['ausla:gə], *f.* (—, *pl.* **—n**) outlay, expenses, advance; shop-window display.
Ausland ['auslant], *n.* (**—s**, *no pl.*) foreign country; *ins — fahren*, go abroad.
Ausländer ['auslɛndər], *m.* (**—s**, *pl.* —) foreigner, alien.
auslassen ['auslasən], *v.a. irr.* let off (steam); let out (a dress); melt (butter); leave off, omit. — *v.r. sich über etwas* —, speak o.'s mind about s.th.
Auslassung ['auslasuŋ], *f.* (—, *pl.* **—en**) utterance; omission.
auslaufen ['auslaufən], *v.n. irr.* (*aux.* sein) run out, leak out; (*ship*) put to sea; (*result*) turn out.
Ausläufer ['auslɔyfər], *m.* (**—s**, *pl.* —) errand boy; (*mountain*) spur.
Auslaut ['auslaut], *m.* (**—s**, *pl.* **—e**) (*Phonet.*) final sound.
auslegen ['ausle:gən], *v.a.* lay out, spread out, display; interpret; (*money*) advance.
ausleihen ['auslaɪən], *v.a. irr.* lend, hire out. — *v.r. sich etwas* —, borrow s.th.
auslernen ['auslɛrnən], *v.n.* end o.'s apprenticeship.
ausliefern ['ausli:fərn], *v.a.* hand over, deliver; surrender, give up, extradite.
auslöschen ['auslœʃən], *v.a.* extinguish, put out (fire).
auslosen ['auslo:zən], *v.a.* raffle, draw lots for.
auslösen ['auslø:zən], *v.a.* redeem, ransom, recover; (*fig.*) produce; arouse.
Auslosung ['auslo:zuŋ], *f.* (—, *pl.* **—en**) raffle, draw.
Auslösung ['auslø:zuŋ], *f.* (—, *pl.* **—en**) ransom.
auslüften ['auslyftən], *v.a.* air, ventilate.
ausmachen ['ausmaxən], *v.a.* decide, settle; amount to; *etwas mit einem* —, arrange s.th. with s.o.; *es macht nichts aus*, it does not matter; *wieviel macht das aus?* how much is this? *würde es Ihnen etwas* —? would you mind?
Ausmaß ['ausma:s], *n.* (**—es**, *pl.* **—e**) dimension, amount, extent, scale.
ausmeißeln ['ausmaɪsəln], *v.a.* chisel out, carve out.
ausmerzen ['ausmertsən], *v.a.* expunge, eradicate.
ausmisten ['ausmɪstən], *v.a.* clean, clear up (mess).
ausmustern ['ausmustərn], *v.a.* eliminate, reject; (*Mil.*) discharge.
Ausnahme ['ausna:mə], *f.* (—, *pl.* **—n**) exception.
ausnehmen ['ausne:mən], *v.a. irr.* except, exclude; (*poultry*) draw; (*fish*) clean.
ausnutzen ['ausnutsən], *v.a.* make the most of s.th.; take advantage of s.th.
ausnützen ['ausnytsən], *v.a.* exploit.
auspacken ['auspakən], *v.a.* unpack. — *v.n.* talk freely; (*coll.*) open up.
auspfeifen ['auspfaɪfən], *v.a. irr.* (*Theat.*) hiss at, cat-call.
auspolstern ['auspɔlstərn], *v.a.* stuff.
ausprägen ['ausprɛ:gən], *v.a.* stamp, impress, coin.
ausprobieren ['ausprobi:rən], *v.a.* try out.
Auspuff ['auspuf], *m.* (**—s**, *no pl.*) (*Motor.*) exhaust.
auspusten ['auspu:stən], *v.a.* blow out.
ausputzen ['ausputsən], *v.a.* clean out; adorn.
ausquartieren ['auskvarti:rən], *v.a.* (*Mil.*) billet out.
ausquetschen ['auskvɛtʃən], *v.a.* squeeze out.
ausradieren ['ausradi:rən], *v.a.* erase.
ausrangieren ['ausraŋʒi:rən], *v.a.* cast off, sort out.
ausräuchern ['ausrɔyçərn], *v.a.* fumigate.
ausraufen ['ausraufən], *v.a.* (*obs.*) tear *or* pull out (hair).
ausräumen ['ausrɔymən], *v.a.* clear out, clear away.
ausrechnen ['ausrɛçnən], *v.a.* reckon, compute, calculate; *ausgerechnet du*, (*emph.*) you of all people.
ausrecken ['ausrɛkən], *v.a. sich den Hals* —, crane o.'s neck.
Ausrede ['ausre:də], *f.* (—, *pl.* **—n**) evasion, excuse, subterfuge.
ausreden ['ausre:dən], *v.a. einem etwas* —, dissuade s.o. from s.th. — *v.n.* finish speaking; *einen — lassen*, allow s.o. to finish speaking.

ausreichen ['ausraɪçən], *v.n.* suffice.
ausreißen ['ausraɪsən], *v.a. irr.* pluck, pull out. — *v.n.* (*aux.* sein) run away, bolt.
ausrenken ['ausrɛŋkən], *v.a.* dislocate, sprain.
ausrichten ['ausrɪçtən], *v.a.* adjust, make straight; deliver (a message); accomplish; (*Mil.*) dress.
ausrotten ['ausrɔtən], *v.a.* root up; exterminate, extirpate.
ausrücken ['ausrykən], *v.n.* (*aux.* sein) (*Mil.*) march out; (*coll.*) decamp.
Ausruf ['ausru:f], *m.* (—**s**, *pl.* —**e**) exclamation, interjection, outcry; (*public*) proclamation.
Ausruf(ungs)zeichen ['ausru:f(uŋs)-tsaɪçən], *n.* (—**s**, *pl.* —) exclamation mark.
ausruhen ['ausru:ən], *v.r. sich* —, rest, take a rest.
ausrüsten ['ausrystən], *v.a.* furnish, fit out, equip.
Ausrutschen ['ausrutʃən], *v.n.* (*aux.* sein) slip.
Aussage ['ausza:gə], *f.* (—, *pl.* —**n**) declaration, statement, evidence; (*Law*) deposition, affidavit; (*Gram.*) predicate.
aussagen ['ausza:gən], *v.a.* say, state, utter, declare; (*Law*) depose, give evidence.
Aussatz ['auszats], *m.* (—**es**, *no pl.*) leprosy.
Aussätzige ['auszɛtsɪgə], *m.* (—**n**, *pl.* —**n**) leper.
aussaugen ['auszaugən], *v.a.* suck dry.
ausschalten ['ausʃaltən], *v.a.* switch off.
Ausschank ['ausʃank], *m.* (—**s**, *no pl.*) pub, bar.
Ausschau ['ausʃau], *f.* (—, *no pl.*) watch; — *halten*, look out for.
ausscheiden ['ausʃaɪdən], *v.a. irr.* separate; (*Med.*) secrete. — *v.n.* (*aux.* sein) withdraw from, retire, secede.
Ausscheidung ['ausʃaɪduŋ], *f.* (—, *pl.* —**en**) retirement, withdrawal; (*Med.*) secretion.
Ausschlag ['ausʃla:k], *m.* (—**s**, *pl.* ⸚**e**) turn (of the scales); deflection (of the magnetic needle); (*Med.*) rash, eczema; *den — geben*, clinch the matter; give the casting vote.
ausschlagen ['ausʃla:gən], *v.a. irr.* knock out; refuse, decline (an invitation); *das schlägt dem Faß den Boden aus*, that is the last straw. — *v.n.* (*aux.* sein) (*Hort.*) bud, shoot; *gut* —, turn out well.
auschlaggebend ['ausʃla:kge:bənt], *adj.* decisive; (*vote*) casting.
ausschließen ['ausʃli:sən], *v.a. irr.* lock out; exclude.
ausschließlich ['ausʃli:slɪç], *adj.* exclusive, sole.
ausschlüpfen ['ausʃlypfən], *v.n.* (*aux.* sein) hatch out.
Ausschluß ['ausʃlus], *m.* (—**sses**, *pl.* ⸚**sse**) exclusion; *unter — der Öffentlichkeit*, in camera.
ausschmücken ['ausʃmykən], *v.a.* adorn, decorate, embellish.
Ausschnitt ['ausʃnɪt], *m.* (—**s**, *pl.* —**e**) cutting out; (*newspaper*) cutting; (*dress*) neck (line).
ausschreiben ['ausʃraɪbən], *v.a. irr.* write down in full; make out a bill; advertise (post) as vacant.
ausschreiten ['ausʃraɪtən], *v.n. irr.* (*aux.* sein) step out, stride along.
Ausschreitungen ['ausʃraɪtuŋən], *f. pl.* rioting; excesses.
Ausschuß ['ausʃus], *m.* (—**sses**, *pl.* ⸚**sse**) dross, refuse, rejects, low quality goods; committee, commission, board.
ausschweifend ['ausʃvaɪfənt], *adj.* extravagant; licentious, dissolute.
aussehen ['ausze:ən], *v.n. irr.* look; look like, appear.
außen ['ausən], *adv.* outside, abroad, outward, without.
Außenhandel ['ausənhandəl], *m.* (—**s**, *no pl.*) export trade.
Außenministerium ['ausənmɪnɪste:r-jum], *n.* (—**s**, *pl.* —**terien**) Ministry of Foreign Affairs; (*U.K.*) Foreign Office, (*U.S.*) State Department.
Außenstände ['ausənʃtɛndə], *m. pl.* outstanding claims, liabilities.
außer ['ausər], *prep.* (*Dat.*) in addition to, besides, apart from; out of, at the outside of, beside, without; — *Dienst*, retired. — *conj.* except, save, but.
außerdem ['ausərde:m], *adv.* besides, moreover, furthermore.
Äussere ['ɔysərə], *n.* (—**n**, *no pl.*) exterior.
außerehelich ['ausəre:əlɪç], *adj.* illegitimate.
außergewöhnlich ['ausərgəvø:nlɪç], *adj.* unusual, exceptional.
außerhalb ['ausərhalp], *prep.* outside.
äußerlich ['ɔysərlɪç], *adj.* external.
Äußerlichkeit ['ɔysərlɪçkaɪt], *f.* (—, *pl.* —**en**) formality.
äußern ['ɔysərn], *v.a.* utter, express. — *v.r. sich zu etwas* —, give o.'s opinion on some question; express o.s. on some subject.
außerordentlich [ausər'ɔrdəntlɪç], *adj.* extraordinary, unusual; (*Univ.*) —*er Professor*, senior lecturer *or* reader; (*Am.*) associate professor.
äußerst ['ɔysərst], *adj.* outermost, most remote; extreme, utmost.
außerstande ['ausərʃtandə], *adj.* unable.
Äußerung ['ɔysəruŋ], *f.* (—, *pl.* —**en**) utterance, remark, observation.
aussetzen ['auszɛtsən], *v.a.* set out, put out; offer (a reward); suspend; *etwas an einer Sache* —, find fault with s.th.; *sich einer Gefahr* —, expose o.s. to danger, run a risk. — *v.n.* pause, discontinue; (*Motor.*) stop, misfire.
Aussicht ['auszɪçt], *f.* (—, *pl.* —**en**) view, panorama; prospect, chance; *etwas in — stellen*, hold out the prospect of s.th.; *in — nehmen*, intend.

aussinnen ['auszɪnən], *v. a. irr.* imagine, invent, devise.
aussöhnen ['auszø:nən], *v.r. sich mit einem* —, become reconciled with s.o.
aussondern ['auszɔndərn], *v.a.* single out.
ausspannen ['ausʃpanən], *v.a. (animals)* unharness. — *v.n. (coll.)* relax.
ausspeien ['ausʃpaɪən], *v.a.* spit out, vomit.
aussperren ['ausʃpɛrən], *v.a.* shut out; *(industrial)* lock out.
ausspielen ['ausʃpi:lən], *v.n.* finish playing; *(Sport, Game)* lead (off).
Aussprache ['ausʃpra:xə], *f.* (—, *no pl.*) pronunciation; discussion; confidential talk.
aussprechen ['ausʃprɛçən], *v.a. irr.* have o.'s say; utter; pronounce. — *v.r. sich* —, speak o.'s mind.
Ausspruch ['ausʃprux], *m.* (—**s**, *pl.* ⸚**e**) utterance, dictum.
ausspüren ['ausʃpy:rən], *v.a. (Hunt.)* track down.
ausstaffieren ['ausʃtafi:rən], *v.a.* furnish, equip.
Ausstand ['ausʃtant], *m.* (—**s**, *pl.* ⸚**e**) *(industry)* strike; *(pl.)* outstanding debts, arrears.
ausständig ['ausʃtɛndɪç], *adj.* outstanding; on strike.
ausstatten ['ausʃtatən], *v.a.* endow with, provide with, equip.
Ausstattung ['ausʃtatuŋ], *f.* (—, *pl.* —**en**) outfit; (bridal) trousseau; *(coll.)* get-up.
ausstechen ['ausʃtɛçən], *v.a. irr.* pierce; *einen* —, *(fig.)* excel s.o.
ausstehen ['ausʃte:ən], *v.n. irr.* stand out; *(money)* be overdue. — *v.a.* endure, suffer, bear, undergo; *ich kann ihn nicht* —, I cannot stand him.
aussteigen ['ausʃtaɪgən], *v.n. irr. (aux.* sein) get out, alight; disembark.
ausstellen ['ausʃtɛlən], *v.a.* exhibit; display; make out (bill etc.).
Aussteller ['ausʃtɛlər], *m.* (—**s**, *pl.* —) drawer (of a cheque); exhibitor.
Ausstellung ['ausʃtɛluŋ], *f.* (—, *pl.* —**en**) exhibition; *(Am.)* exposition.
Aussteuer ['ausʃtɔyər], *f.* (—, *pl.* —**n**) trousseau.
ausstopfen ['ausʃtɔpfən], *v.a.* stuff.
ausstoßen ['ausʃtosən], *v.a. irr.* push out, expel; utter.
Ausstrahlung ['ausʃtra:luŋ], *f.* (—, *pl.* —**en**) radiation.
ausstrecken ['ausʃtrɛkən], *v.a.* stretch out, reach out, extend.
ausstreichen ['ausʃtraɪçən], *v.a. irr.* strike out, erase, delete; smoothe.
ausstreuen ['ausʃtrɔyən], *v.a.* scatter, spread, sprinkle; *Gerüchte* —, circulate rumours.
ausstudieren ['ausʃtudi:rən], *v.n.* finish o.'s studies, graduate.
aussuchen ['auszu:xən], *v.a.* select.
Austausch ['austauʃ], *m.* (—**es**, *pl.* —**e**) barter, exchange; *(thoughts, letters)* interchange.
austauschen ['austauʃən], *v.a.* barter, exchange; *(thoughts, letters)* interchange.
austeilen ['austaɪlən], *v.a.* distribute, allocate.
Auster ['austər], *f.* (—, *pl.* —**n**) oyster.
Austerbank ['austərbaŋk], *f.* (—, *pl.* ⸚**e**) oyster-bed.
austilgen ['austɪlgen], *v.a.* exterminate, eradicate, extirpate.
Australien [au'stra:ljən], *n.* Australia.
austreiben ['austraɪbən], *v.a. irr.* drive out, expel; exorcise.
austreten ['austre:tən], *v.a. irr.* tread out; stretch (shoes) by walking; *ausgetretene Stufen*, worn steps. — *v.n. (aux.* sein) retire (from business); withdraw (from a club); *(coll.)* go to the lavatory.
Austritt ['austrɪt], *m.* (—**s**, *pl.* —**e**) withdrawal, retirement.
ausüben ['ausy:bən], *v.a.* exercise, practise; exert, commit.
Ausverkauf ['ausfɛrkauf], *m.* (—**s**, *pl.* ⸚**e**) selling-off, clearance sale.
Auswahl ['ausva:l], *f.* (—, *pl.* —**en**) choice, selection.
Auswanderer ['ausvandərər], *m.* (—**s**, *pl.* —) emigrant.
auswärtig ['ausvɛrtɪç], *adj.* foreign, away.
auswärts ['ausvɛrts], *adv.* outward(s), away from home.
auswechseln ['ausvɛksəln], *v.a.* exchange; fit (spare parts).
Ausweg ['ausve:k], *m.* (—**s**, *pl.* —**e**) expedient; way out; *ich weiß keinen* —, I am at my wits' end.
ausweichen ['ausvaɪçən], *v.n. irr. (aux.* sein) give way; evade, parry.
Ausweis ['ausvaɪs], *m.* (—**es**, *pl.* —**e**) proof of identity, identity card.
ausweisen ['ausvaɪzən], *v.a. irr.* turn out, banish, exile, deport. — *v.r. (aux.* haben) *sich* —, show proof of o.'s identity.
auswendig ['ausvendɪç], *adj.* by heart.
auswirken ['ausvɪrkən], *v.r. sich gut* —, work out well, have a good effect.
Auswuchs ['ausvu:ks], *m.* (—**es**, *pl.* ⸚**e**) sprouting, outgrowth, *(fig.)* excrescence.
Auswurf ['ausvurf], *m.* (—**s**, *pl.* ⸚**e**) excretion; expectoration; — *der Menschheit*, scum of the earth.
auszählen ['austsɛ:lən], *v.n.* count, number. — *v.a.* count out.
Auszahlung ['austsa:luŋ], *f.* (—, *pl.* —**en**) payment.
auszanken ['austsaŋkən], *v.a.* scold, chide.
auszehren ['austse:rən], *v.n. (aux.* sein) waste away, be consumed.
auszeichnen ['austsaɪçnən], *v.a.* mark out, honour, decorate. — *v.r. sich* —, distinguish o.s.
Auszeichnung ['austsaɪçnuŋ], *f.* (—, *pl.* —**en**) distinction, medal.

auszlehen ['austsi:ən], *v.a. irr.* undress, take off (clothes); (*Chem.*) extract; stretch. — *v.n.* (*aux.* sein) move out. — *v.r. sich* —, undress.
auszischen ['austsɪʃən], *v.a.* (*Theat.*) hiss, cat-call.
Auszug ['austsu:k], *m.* (—**s**, *pl.* ¨**e**) removal (from home); marching off; exodus; extract (from a book), abstract (from a deed).
Auto ['auto], *n.* (—**s**, *pl.* —**s**) motor-car, (*Am.*) automobile.
Autogramm [auto'gram], *n.* (—**s**, *pl.* —**e**) autograph.
Automat [auto'ma:t], *m.* (—**en**, *pl.* —**en**) slot machine.
Autor ['autɔr], *m.* (—**s**, *pl.* —**en**) author, writer.
Autorität [autori'tɛ:t], *f.* (—, *pl.* —**en**) authority.
avisieren [avɪ'zi:rən], *v.a.* notify, advise.
Axt [akst], *f.* (—, *pl.* ¨**e**) axe.
Azur [a'tsu:r], *m.* (—**s**, *no pl.*) azure.

B

B [be:], *n.* (—**s**, *pl.* —**s**) the letter B; (*Mus.*) B flat; — *Dur*, B flat major; — *Moll*, B flat minor.
Bach [bax], *m.* (—**es**, *pl.* ¨**e**) brook, rivulet.
Bachstelze ['baxʃtɛltsə], *f.* (—, *pl.* —**n**) wagtail.
Backe ['bakə], *f.* (—, *pl.* —**n**) cheek.
backen ['bakən], *v.a.* bake.
Backenstreich ['bakənʃtraɪç], *m.* (—**s**, *pl.* —**e**) box on the ear.
Bäcker ['bɛkər], *m.* (—**s**, *pl.* —) baker.
Backfisch ['bakfɪʃ], *m.* (—**es**, *pl.* —**e**) (*fig.*) teenage girl.
Backhuhn ['bakhu:n], *n.* (—**s**, *pl.* ¨**er**) fried chicken.
Backobst ['bakopst], *n.* (—**es**, *no pl.*) dried fruit.
Backpfeife ['bakpfaɪfə], *f.* (—, *pl.* —**n**) box on the ear.
Backpflaume ['bakpflaumə], *f.* (—, *pl.* —**n**) prune.
Backstein ['bakʃtaɪn], *m.* (—**s**, *pl.* —**e**) brick.
Backwerk ['bakvɛrk], *n.* (—**s**, *no pl.*) pastry.
Bad [ba:t], *n.* (—**es**, *pl.* ¨**er**) bath; spa, watering-place.
Badeanstalt ['ba:dəanʃtalt], *f.* (—, *pl.* —**en**) public baths.
baden ['ba:dən], *v.n.* bathe, have a bath.
Badewanne ['ba:dəvanə], *f.* (—, *pl.* —**n**) bath-tub.
Bagage [ba'ga:ʒə], *f.* (—, *no pl.*) luggage; (*Am.*) baggage; (*sl.*) mob, rabble.
Bagger ['bagər], *m.* (—**s**, *pl.* —) dredger, dredging-machine.
baggern ['bagərn], *v.a.* dredge.
Bahn [ba:n], *f.* (—, *pl.* —**en**) road, path, course; (*Astr.*) orbit; railway(-line); — *brechen*, open a path.
bahnbrechend ['ba:nbrɛçənt], *adj.* pioneering, epoch-making.
bahnen ['ba:nən], *v.a.* make passable; pave (the way).
Bahngleis ['ba:nglaɪs], *n.* (—**es**, *pl.* —**e**) railway-line, railway-track; (*Am.*) railroad-line, railroad-track.
Bahnhof ['ba:nho:f], *m.* (—**s**, *pl.* ¨**e**) railway-station, (*Am.*) depot.
Bahnsteig ['ba:nʃtaɪk], *m.* (—**s**, *pl.* —**e**) platform.
Bahnwärter ['ba:nvɛrtər], *m.* (—**s**, *pl.* —) signal-man.
Bahre ['ba:rə], *f.* (—, *pl.* —**n**) litter, stretcher; bier.
Bahrtuch ['ba:rtu:x], *n.* (—**s**, *pl.* ¨**er**) pall, shroud.
Bai [baɪ], *f.* (—, *pl.* —**en**) bay, cove.
Baisse ['bɛsə], *f.* (—, *pl.* —**n**) (*Comm.*) fall in share prices.
Bakkalaureat [bakalaure'a:t], *n.* (—**s**, *pl.* —**e**) bachelor's degree.
Bakterie [bak'te:rjə], *f.* (—, *pl.* —**n**) bacterium.
bald [balt], *adv.* soon, shortly, directly, presently.
Baldachin ['baldaxɪn], *m.* (—**s**, *pl.* —**e**) canopy.
baldig ['baldɪç], *adj.* quick, speedy; *auf —es Wiedersehen*, see you again soon.
Baldrian ['baldria:n], *m.* (—**s**, *no pl.*) valerian.
Balearen, die [bale'a:rən, di:], *pl.* Balearic Islands.
Balg (1) [balk], *m.* (—**s**, *pl.* ¨**e**) skin, slough, husk; bellows (of organ *or* forge).
Balg (2) [balk], *n.* (—**s**, *pl.* ¨**er**) brat; naughty child.
balgen ['balgən], *v.r. sich* —, (*children*) fight, romp.
Balgerei ['balgəraɪ], *f.* (—, *pl.* —**en**) scuffle, scrimmage.
Balken ['balkən], *m.* (—**s**, *pl.* —) beam, joist, rafter.
Balkenwerk ['balkənvɛrk], *n.* (—**s**, *no pl.*) building-frame, timbers, woodwork.
Balkon [bal'kɔ̃], *m.* (—**s**, *pl.* —**s**, —**e**) balcony.
Ball [bal], *m.* (—**s**, *pl.* ¨**e**) ball; globe; sphere; dance.
ballen ['balən], *v.a.* form into a ball; clench (o.'s fist).
Ballen ['balən], *m.* (—**s**, *pl.* —) bale, bundle, package; ball (of the hand *or* foot).
ballförmig ['balfœrmɪç], *adj.* spherical.
Ballistik [ba'lɪstɪk], *f.* (—, *no pl.*) ballistics.
Ballon [ba'lɔ̃], *m.* (—**s**, *pl.* —**s**, —**e**) balloon.
Balsam ['balza:m], *m.* (—**s**, *pl.* —**e**) balm, balsam.
Baltikum ['baltɪkum], *n.* (—**s**, *no pl.*) the Baltic countries.

Bambusrohr ['bambusro:r], *n.* (**—s**, *pl.* **—e**) bamboo (cane).

Banane [ba'na:nə], *f.* (—, *pl.* **—n**) banana.

Banause [ba'nauzə], *m.* (**—n**, *pl.* **—n**) narrow-minded person, philistine.

Band (1) [bant], *n.* (**—s**, *pl.* **⸚er**) ribbon, riband, tape; string; (*Bot.*) band; hoop (*for a cask*); (*Anat.*) ligament, tendon.

Band (2) [bant], *n.* (**—s**, *pl.* **—e**) (*fig.*) bond, fetter, chain, (*pl.*) bonds, ties (*of friendship*).

Band (3) [bant], *m.* (**—es**, *pl.* **⸚e**) volume.

Bändchen ['bɛntçən], *n.* (**—s**, *pl.* —) small ribbon, small piece of string; (*book*) small volume.

Bande ['bandə], *f.* (—, *pl.* **—n**) horde, gang, set.

bändigen ['bɛndɪgən], *v.a.* tame, subdue.

Bandmaß ['bantma:s], *n.* (**—es**, *pl.* **—e**) tape-measure.

Bandwurm ['bantvurm], *m.* (**—s**, *pl.* **⸚er**) (*Zool.*) tape-worm.

bange ['baŋə], *adj.* afraid, worried, alarmed.

Bangigkeit ['baŋɪçkaɪt], *f.* (—, *no pl.*) uneasiness, anxiety.

Bank (1) [baŋk], *f.* (—, *pl.* **⸚e**) bench, seat (in a park); *auf die lange — schieben*, delay, shelve; *durch die —*, without exception.

Bank (2) [baŋk], *f.* (—, *pl.* **—en**) bank; *die — sprengen*, break the bank.

Bänkelsänger ['bɛŋkəlzɛŋər], *m.* (**—s**, *pl.* —) ballad singer.

bank(e)rott [baŋk'rɔt], *adj.* bankrupt.

Bankett [baŋ'kɛt], *n.* (**—s**, *pl.* **—e**) banquet.

Bankkonto ['baŋkkɔnto], *n.* (**—s**, *pl.* **—ten**) bank-account.

Bann [ban], *m.* (**—s**, *no pl.*) ban, exile; (*Eccl.*) excommunication; *in den — tun*, outlaw, (*Eccl.*) excommunicate; (*fig.*) charm, spell.

bannen ['banən], *v.a.* banish, exile, cast out.

Banner ['banər], *n.* (**—s**, *pl.* —) banner, standard.

Bannmeile ['banmaɪlə], *f.* (—, *pl.* **—n**) boundary.

bar [ba:r], *adj.* in cash, ready money.

Bar [ba:r], *f.* (—, *pl.* **—s**) bar (for selling drinks etc.).

Bär [bɛ:r], *m.* (**—en**, *pl.* **—en**) (*Zool.*) bear; *einem einen —en aufbinden*, to lead s.o. up the garden-path.

Barauslagen ['barausla:gən], *f. pl.* cash expenses.

Barbar [bar'ba:r], *m.* (**—en**, *pl.* **—en**) barbarian, vandal.

barbarisch [bar'ba:rɪʃ], *adj.* barbarous.

Barbestand ['ba:rbəʃtant], *m.* (**—s**, *pl.* **⸚e**) cash reserve, cash balance.

bärbeißig ['bɛ:rbaɪsɪç], *adj.* surly, morose.

Barchent ['barçənt], *m.* (**—s**, *no pl.*) fustian.

Barde ['bardə], *m.* (**—n**, *pl.* **—n**) bard, minstrel.

Bärenfell ['bɛ:rənfɛl], *n.* (**—s**, *pl.* **—e**) bear-skin.

Bärenmütze ['bɛ:rənmytsə], *f.* (—, *pl.* **—n**) (*Mil.*) busby.

Bärenzwinger ['bɛ:rəntsvɪŋər], *m.* (**—s**, *pl.* —) bear-garden.

Barett [ba'rɛt], *n.* (**—s**, *pl.* **—e**) cap, beret; (*Eccl.*) biretta.

barfuß ['barfus], *adj.* barefoot(ed).

Bargeld ['bargɛlt], *n.* (—(**e**)**s**, *no pl.*) cash.

barhäuptig ['barhɔyptɪç], *adj.* bareheaded.

Barkasse [bar'kasə], *f.* (—, *pl.* **—n**) launch.

Barke ['barkə], *f.* (—, *pl.* **—n**) barge, lighter.

barmherzig [barm'hɛrtsɪç], *adj.* merciful, charitable, compassionate.

Barock [ba'rɔk], *n.* (**—s**, *no pl.*) Baroque.

Baronin [ba'ro:nɪn], *f.* (—, *pl.* **—nen**) baroness.

Barren ['barən], *m.* (**—s**, *pl.* —) parallel bars.

Barsch [barʃ], *m.* (**—es**, *pl.* **—e**) (*Zool.*) perch.

barsch [barʃ], *adj.* rough, harsh, sharp, abrupt, unfriendly.

Barschaft ['ba:rʃaft], *f.* (—, *pl.* **—en**) ready money.

Bart [ba:rt], *m.* (**—s**, *pl.* **⸚e**) beard; (*key*) ward.

Bartflechte ['ba:rtflɛçtə], *f.* (—, *pl.* **—n**) barber's itch.

bärtig ['bɛ:rtɪç], *adj.* bearded.

Basalt [ba'zalt], *m.* (**—s**, *pl.* **—e**) (*Min.*) basalt.

Base ['ba:zə], *f.* (—, *pl.* **—n**) female cousin; (*Chem.*) base.

Basis ['ba:zɪs], *f.* (—, *pl.* **Basen**) base, foundation.

Baskenmütze ['baskənmytsə], *f.* (—, *pl.* **—n**) tam-o'-shanter, beret.

Baß [bas], *m.* (**—sses**, *pl.* **⸚sse**) (*Mus.*) bass.

Baßschlüssel ['basʃlysəl], *m.* (**—s**, *pl.* —) (*Mus.*) bass-clef.

Bassin [ba'sɛ̃], *n.* (**—s**, *pl.* **—s**) basin, reservoir.

Bast [bast], *m.* (**—es**, *pl.* **—e**) inner bark, fibre (*of trees etc.*); bast.

basta ['basta], *int.* and that's that!

Bastei [bas'taɪ], *f.* (—, *pl.* **—en**) bastion.

basteln ['bastəln], *v.a.* work on a hobby, tinker.

Batist [ba'tɪst], *m.* (**—s**, *pl.* **—e**) cambric.

Bau [bau], *m.* (**—es**, *pl.* **—ten**) building, structure, edifice; act of building; *im — begriffen*, in course of construction.

Bauart ['bauart], *f.* (—, *pl.* **—en**) (architectural) style, structure.

Bauch [baux], *m.* (**—es**, *pl.* **⸚e**) belly, stomach.

Bauchfell ['bauxfɛl], *n.* (**—s**, *pl.* **—e**) peritoneum.

bauchig ['bauçɪç], *adj.* bulgy.
Bauchredner ['bauxre:dnər], *m.* (**—s**, *pl.* —) ventriloquist.
bauen ['bauən], *v.a.* build, construct, erect. — *v.n. auf etwas* —, (*fig.*) rely on s.th., count on s.th.
Bauer (1) ['bauər], *m.* (**—n**, *pl.* **—n**) farmer, peasant; (*chess*) pawn.
Bauer (2) ['bauər], *n.* (**—s**, *pl.* —) (*bird*) cage.
Bauernfänger ['bauərnfɛŋər], *m.* (**—s**, *pl.* —) sharper, rook, confidence-trickster.
Bäuerin ['bɔyərɪn], *f.* (—, *pl.* **—nen**) farmer's wife.
Bauernstand ['bauərnʃtant], *m.* (**—s**, *pl.* **¨e**) peasantry.
baufällig ['baufɛlɪç], *adj.* dilapidated, ramshackle.
Baugerüst ['baugəryst], *n.* (**—s**, *pl.* **—e**) scaffolding.
Baugewerbe ['baugəvɛrbə], *n.* (**—s**, *no pl.*) building trade.
Baukunst ['baukunst], *f.* (—, *no pl.*) architecture.
Baum [baum], *m.* (**—(e)s**, *pl.* **¨e**) tree.
Baumeister ['baumaɪstər], *m.* (**—s**, *pl.* —) architect, master-builder.
baumeln ['bauməln], *v.n.* dangle.
Baumkuchen ['baumku:xən], *m.* (**—s**, *pl.* —) pyramid-cake.
Baumschule ['baumʃu:lə], *f.* (—, *pl.* **—n**) plantation of trees, orchard, tree nursery.
Baumstamm ['baumʃtam], *m.* (**—s**, *pl.* **¨e**) stem, trunk.
Baumwolle ['baumvɔlə], *f.* (—, *pl.* **—n**) cotton.
Bauriß ['baurɪs], *m.* (**—sses**, *pl.* **—sse**) plan, architect's drawing.
Bausch [bauʃ], *m.* (**—es**, *pl.* **¨e**) pad, bolster; *in — und Bogen*, in the lump: all at once.
bauschig ['bauʃɪç], *adj.* baggy.
Bauwerk ['bauvɛrk] *see* **Gebäude**.
Bayern ['baɪərn], *n.* Bavaria.
Bazar [ba'za:r], *m.* (**—s**, *pl.* **—e**) bazaar, fair, emporium.
beabsichtigen [bə'apzɪçtɪgən], *v.a.* aim at, intend, have in view.
beachten [bə'axtən], *v.a.* observe, pay attention to.
Beamte [bə'amtə], *m.* (**—n**, *pl.* **—n**) official, officer, civil servant.
Beamtin [bə'amtɪn], *f.* (—, *pl.* **—nen**) female official, female civil servant.
beängstigen [bə'ɛŋstɪgən], *v.a.* alarm, make afraid.
beanspruchen [bə'anʃpruxən], *v.a.* demand, claim, lay claim to.
beanstanden [bə'anʃtandən], *v.a.* object to, raise objections to, query.
beantragen [bə'antra:gən], *v.a.* move, apply, lodge an application.
beantworten [bə'antvɔrtən], *v.a.* answer, reply to.
bearbeiten [bə'arbaɪtən], *v.a.* work (on); (*book, play*) adapt, arrange, revise; (*Agr.*) cultivate; (*fig.*) *einen* —, try to influence s.o., try to convince s.o.
Bearbeitung [bə'arbaɪtuŋ], *f.* (—, *pl.* **—en**) working, manipulation, operation; (*Agr.*) culture, cultivation; (*book, play*) adaptation, revision, arrangement.
beargwöhnen [bə'arkvø:nən], *v.a.* suspect, view with suspicion.
beaufsichtigen [bə'aufzɪçtɪgən], *v.a.* control, supervise, superintend.
beauftragen [bə'auftra:gən], *v.a.* commission, charge, authorize.
bebauen [bə'bauən], *v.a.* build upon; (*Agr.*) cultivate.
beben ['be:bən], *v.n.* shake, quake, tremble; *vor Kälte* —, shiver with cold.
Becher ['bɛçər], *m.* (**—s**, *pl.* —) beaker, cup, goblet, mug; (*dice*) box.
Becken ['bɛkən], *n.* (**—s**, *pl.* —) basin, bowl; (*Anat.*) pelvis; (*Mus.*) cymbal.
Bedacht [bə'daxt], *m.* (**—s**, *no pl.*) consideration; *mit* —, deliberately; *ohne* —, thoughtlessly.
bedächtig [bə'dɛçtɪç], *adj.* circumspect, deliberate, cautious, slow.
bedanken [bə'daŋkən], *v.r. sich für etwas* —, thank s.o. for s.th., decline with thanks (*also iron.*).
Bedarf [bə'darf], *m.* (**—s**, *no pl.*) need, requirement, demand.
bedauerlich [bə'dauərlɪç], *adj.* regrettable, deplorable.
bedauern [bə'dauərn], *v.a.* pity, commiserate, regret; *ich bedaure, daß*, I am sorry that . . .
bedecken [bə'dɛkən], *v.a.* cover (up); *sich mit Ruhm* —, cover o.s. with glory.
bedeckt [bə'dɛkt], *adj.* (*sky*) overcast.
bedenken [bə'dɛŋkən], *v.a. irr.* consider, bear in mind. — *v.r. sich* —, deliberate, hesitate; *sich anders* —, change o.'s mind.
bedenklich [bə'dɛŋklɪç], *adj.* (*persons*) doubtful, dubious; (*things*) risky, delicate, precarious; (*illness*) serious, grave.
Bedenkzeit [bə'dɛŋktsaɪt], *f.* (—, *pl.* **—en**) time to consider, respite.
bedeuten [bə'dɔytən], *v.a.* signify, mean, imply; direct, order.
bedeutend [bə'dɔytənt], *adj.* important, eminent, considerable, outstanding.
bedeutsam [bə'dɔytza:m], *adj.* significant.
Bedeutung [bə'dɔytuŋ], *f.* (—, *pl.* **—en**) significance, meaning; consequence, importance; *nichts von* —, nothing to speak of.
bedienen [bə'di:nən], *v.a.* serve, attend to, wait on; (*machine*) operate; (*Cards*) follow suit. —*v.r. sich* —, help o.s., make use of.
Bediente [bə'di:ntə], *m.* (**—n**, *pl.* **—n**) servant, attendant, footman, lackey.
Bedienung [bə'di:nuŋ], *f.* (—, *pl.* **—en**) service, attendance.
bedingen [bə'dɪŋən], *v.a.* stipulate, postulate, condition, cause.

bedingt [bə'dɪŋkt], *adj.* conditional.
Bedingung [bə'dɪŋuŋ], *f.* (—, *pl.* —**en**) stipulation, condition, term; *unter keiner* —, on no account.
bedingungsweise [bə'dɪŋuŋsvaɪzə], *adv.* on condition, conditionally.
bedrängen [bə'drɛŋən], *v.a.* oppress; press hard, afflict.
Bedrängnis [bə'drɛŋnɪs], *n.* (—**ses**, *pl.* —**se**) oppression, distress.
bedrohen [bə'dro:ən], *v.a.* threaten, menace.
bedrohlich [bə'dro:lɪç], *adj.* threatening, menacing, ominous.
bedrücken [bə'drykən], *v.a.* oppress, harass, depress.
Beduine [bedu'i:nə], *m.* (—**n**, *pl.* —**n**) Bedouin.
bedünken [bə'dyŋkən], *v.a.* appear, seem; *es bedünkt mich*, methinks.
bedürfen [bə'dyrfən], *v.n. irr.* want, need, be in need of.
Bedürfnis [bə'dyrfnɪs], *n.* (—**ses**, *pl.* —**se**) want, need, requirement, necessity; *es ist mir ein* —, I cannot but; *einem dringenden* — *abhelfen*, meet an urgent want *or* need; *ein* — *haben*, (*coll.*) need to relieve o.s.
Bedürfnisanstalt [bə'dyrfnɪsanʃtalt], *f.* (—, *pl.* —**en**) public lavatory, public convenience.
bedürftig [bə'dyrftɪç], *adj.* needy, indigent, poor.
beeidigen [bə'aɪdɪgən], *v.a.* confirm by oath, swear in.
beeifern [bə'aɪfərn], *v.r. sich* —, exert o.s., strive, be zealous.
beeilen [bə'aɪlən], *v.r. sich* —, hurry, hasten, make haste.
beeindrucken [bə'aɪndrukən], *v.a.* impress.
beeinflussen [bə'aɪnflusən], *v.a.* influence.
beeinträchtigen [bə'aɪntrɛçtɪgən], *v.a.* injure, lessen, diminish, detract from, curtail.
beenden [bə'ɛndən], *v.a.* end, finish, terminate, conclude.
beendigen [bə'ɛndɪgən], *v.a.* end, finish, terminate, conclude.
beengen [bə'ɛŋən], *v.a.* cramp, narrow.
beerben [bə'ɛrbən], *v.a. einen* —, inherit from s.o.
beerdigen [bə'e:rdɪgən], *v.a.* bury, inter.
Beere ['be:rə], *f.* (—, *pl.* —**n**) berry.
Beet [be:t], *n.* (—**es**, *pl.* —**e**) (flower) bed.
befähigen [bə'fɛ:ɪgən], *v.a.* fit, enable, qualify.
Befähigung [bə'fɛ:ɪguŋ], *f.* (—, *pl.* —**en**) qualification, capacity, aptitude.
befahren [bə'fa:rən], *v.a. irr.* pass over, travel over; (*Naut.*) navigate.
befallen [bə'falən], *v.a. irr.* befall, fall on; *von Traurigkeit* — *sein*, be overcome by sadness.
befangen [bə'faŋən], *adj.* biased, prejudiced; bashful, embarrassed.
befassen [bə'fasən], *v.a.* touch, handle. — *v.r. sich mit etwas* —, occupy o.s. with s.th.
befehden [bə'fe:dən], *v.a.* make war upon, show enmity towards.
Befehl [bə'fe:l], *m.* (—**s**, *pl.* —**e**) order, command; (*Mil.*) *zu* —, very good, sir; (*Mil.*) *den* — *führen über*, command.
befehlen [bə'fe:lən], *v.a. irr.* order, command.
befehligen [bə'fe:lɪgən], *v.a.* (*Mil.*) command, head.
Befehlshaber [bə'fe:lsha:bər], *m.* (—**s**, *pl.* —) commander, commanding officer, chief.
befehlswidrig [bə'fe:lsvi:drɪç], *adj.* contrary to orders.
befestigen [bə'fɛstɪgən], *v.a.* fasten, fix, attach, affix; (*Mil.*) fortify; strengthen.
befeuchten [bə'fɔyçtən], *v.a.* wet, moisten, dampen.
Befinden [bə'fɪndən], *n.* (—**s**, *no pl.*) state of health.
befinden [bə'fɪndən], *v.a. irr.* think, deem, find. — *v.r. sich an einem Ort* —, be in some place; *sich wohl* —, feel well.
befindlich [bə'fɪntlɪç], *adj.* existing — *sein*, be contained in.
beflecken [bə'flɛkən], *v.a.* stain, spot, blot; defile, pollute.
befleißigen [bə'flaɪsɪgən], *v.r. sich* —, devote o.s. to, take pains to.
beflissen [bə'flɪsən], *adj.* eager to serve, assiduous.
beflügeln [bə'fly:gəln], *v.a.* give wings; (*fig.*) accelerate, animate.
befolgen [bə'fɔlgən], *v.a.* follow, obey; *einen Befehl* —, comply with an order.
befördern [bə'fœrdərn], *v.a.* despatch, forward, send, post, mail, transmit; promote, advance.
Beförderung [bə'fœrdəruŋ], *f.* (—, *pl.* —**en**) forwarding, transmission; (*office*) promotion, advancement.
Beförderungsmittel [bə'fœrdəruŋsmɪtəl], *n.* (—**s**, *pl.* —) conveyance, means of transport.
befragen [bə'fra:gən], *v.a.* question, interrogate, examine.
befreien [bə'fraɪən], *v.a.* free, liberate.
befremden [bə'frɛmdən], *v.a.* appear strange, astonish, surprise.
befreunden [bə'frɔyndən], *v.a.* befriend. — *v.r. sich mit einem* —, make friends with s.o.
befriedigen [bə'fri:dɪgən], *v.a.* content, satisfy; appease, calm.
befruchten [bə'fruxtən], *v.a.* fertilise; impregnate.
Befugnis [bə'fu:knɪs], *f.* (—, *pl.* —**se**) authority, right, warrant.
Befund [bə'funt], *m.* (—**s**, *pl.* —**e**) (*Med.*) diagnosis, findings.
befürchten [bə'fyrçtən], *v.a.* fear, be afraid of.
befürworten [bə'fy:rvɔrtən], *v.a.* support, second.

begabt [bə'ga:pt], *adj.* gifted, talented, able.
Begabung [bə'ga:buŋ], *f.* (—, *pl.* **—en**) ability, talent, gift.
begaffen [bə'gafən], *v.a.* stare at, gape at.
begatten [bə'gatən], *v.r. sich* —, (*Zool.*) copulate.
begeben [bə'ge:bən], *v.r. irr. sich an einen Ort* —, go to a place, betake o.s. to a place; happen, occur.
Begebenheit [bə'ge:bənhaɪt], *f.* (—, *pl.* **—en**) happening, event, occurrence.
begegnen [bə'ge:gnən], *v.n.* (*aux.* sein) meet, meet with, encounter, befall, happen.
begehen [bə'ge:ən], *v.a. irr.* (*road*) walk along, go over; (*festival*) celebrate; (*crime*) commit, perpetrate.
begehren [bə'ge:rən], *v.a.* desire, wish, covet, want.—*v.n. nach etwas* —, long for s.th.
begehrlich [bə'ge:rlɪç], *adj.* covetous, greedy, desirous.
begeifern [bə'gaɪfərn], *v.a.* spit at; (*fig.*) vilify, besmirch.
begeistern [bə'gaɪstərn], *v.a.* inspire, fill with enthusiasm, enrapture.—*v.r. sich für etwas* —, become enthusiastic about s.th.
Begier(de) [bə'gi:r(də)], *f.* (—, *pl.* **—den**) desire, lust, appetite.
begierig [bə'gi:rɪç], *adj.* desirous, lustful; anxious; curious (for news).
begießen [bə'gi:sən], *v.a. irr.* (*plants*) water; (*meat etc.*) baste; *etwas festlich* —, celebrate s.th. by drinking; *sich die Nase* —, (*coll.*) get tight.
Beginn [bə'gɪn], *m.* (**—s**, *no pl.*) beginning, commencement, start.
beginnen [bə'gɪnən], *v.a., v.n. irr.* begin, commence, start.
beglaubigen [bə'glaubɪgən], *v.a.* attest; certify, verify; accredit (an ambassador).
Beglaubigungsschreiben [bə'glaubɪguŋsʃraɪbən], *n.* (**—s**, *pl.* —) credentials.
begleichen [bə'glaɪçən], *v.a. irr.* (*bill*) pay, settle.
begleiten [bə'glaɪtən], *v.a.* accompany, escort, see s.o. off, home etc.
Begleiter [bə'glaɪtər], *m.* (**—s**, *pl.* —) companion, escort; (*Mus.*) accompanist.
Begleiterscheinung [bə'glaɪtərʃaɪnuŋ], *f.* (—, *pl.* **—en**) concomitant; (*Med.*) complication, attendant symptom.
Begleitung [bə'glaɪtuŋ], *f.* (—, *pl.* **—en**) company; (*Mus.*) accompaniment.
beglücken [bə'glykən], *v.a.* make happy.
beglückwünschen [bə'glykvynʃən], *v.a.* congratulate.
begnadet [bə'gna:dət], *adj.* highly talented.
begnadigen [bə'gna:dɪgən], *v.a.* pardon, reprieve.
begnügen [bə'gny:gən], *v.r. sich mit etwas* —, content o.s. with s.th.
Begonie [bə'go:njə], *f.* (—, *pl.* **—n**) (*Bot.*) begonia.
begraben [bə'gra:bən], *v.a. irr.* bury, inter.
Begräbnis [bə'grɛ:pnɪs], *n.* (**—ses**, *pl.* **—se**) burial, funeral, interment.
begreifen [bə'graɪfən], *v.a. irr.* understand, comprehend, conceive.
begreiflich [bə'graɪflɪç], *adj.* comprehensible, conceivable, understandable.
begrenzen [bə'grɛntsən], *v.a.* bound, border, limit.
Begriff [bə'grɪf], *m.* (**—s**, *pl.* **—e**) notion, concept, idea, conception; *im — sein*, be about to . . . .
begriffen [bə'grɪfən], *adj. — sein in*, be engaged in.
begriffsstutzig [bə'grɪfsʃtutsɪç], *adj.* obtuse, dense, slow in the uptake.
begründen [bə'gryndən], *v.a.* base on, justify; found, establish.
begrüßen [bə'gry:sən], *v.a.* greet, salute, welcome.
begünstigen [bə'gynstɪgən], *v.a.* favour, prefer.
Begutachter [bə'gu:taxtər], *m.* (**—s**, *pl.* —) expert; (*Sch.*) assessor, second examiner.
Begutachtung [bə'gu:taxtuŋ], *f.* (—, *pl.* **—en**) expert opinion, assessment, report.
begütert [bə'gy:tərt], *adj.* wealthy, rich, well-to-do.
behaart [bə'ha:rt], *adj.* covered with hair, hairy.
behäbig [bə'hɛ:bɪç], *adj.* comfortable; corpulent, portly.
behaften [bə'haften], *v.a.* charge, burden.
behagen [bə'ha:gən], *v.n.* please, be agreeable; *es behagt mir nicht*, I do not like it.
behaglich [bə'ha:klɪç], *adj.* cosy, comfortable, snug.
behalten [bə'haltən], *v.a. irr.* retain, keep.
Behälter [bə'hɛltər], *m.* (**—s**, *pl.* —) container; box, bin; (*water*) reservoir; tank.
behandeln [bə'handəln], *v.a.* treat, use; (*Med.*) treat; (*subject*) treat; handle.
Behandlung [bə'handluŋ], *f.* (—, *pl.* **—en**) treatment, use; (*Med.*) treatment.
Behang [bə'haŋ], *m.* (**—es**, *pl.* **⸚e**) hanging(s); appendage.
behängen [bə'hɛŋən], *v.a. irr.* festoon with, drape.
beharren [bə'harən], *v.n.* persevere; persist, insist.
beharrlich [bə'harlɪç], *adj.* persevering, persistent, constant, firm.
behauen [bə'hauən], *v.a.* (*stones*) hew, cut.
behaupten [bə'hauptən], *v.a.* claim, assert, affirm, maintain.

Behauptung [bəˈhauptuŋ], *f.* (—, *pl.* —**en**) claim, assertion, affirmation.
Behausung [bəˈhauzuŋ], *f.* (—, *pl.* —**en**) habitation, housing.
behelfen [bəˈhɛlfən], *v.r. irr. sich — mit*, make do with.
behelfsmäßig [bəˈhɛlfsmɛːsɪç], *adj.* makeshift, temporary.
behelligen [bəˈhɛlɪgən], *v.a.* trouble, molest, disturb.
behend(e) [bəˈhɛndə], *adj.* quick, nimble, agile.
beherbergen [bəˈhɛrbɛrgən], *v.a.* give shelter to, put up, harbour.
beherrschen [bəˈhɛrʃən], *v.a.* rule, govern, dominate; *eine Sache* —, master a subject. — *v.r. sich* —, control o.s.
Beherrschung [bəˈhɛrʃuŋ], *f.* (—, *pl.* (*rare*) —**en**) domination, sway; (*subject*) grasp; (*languages*) command.
beherzigen [bəˈhɛrtsɪgən], *v.a.* take to heart, follow, heed.
Beherztheit [bəˈhɛrtsthaɪt], *f.* (—, *no pl.*) courage, spirit.
behexen [bəˈhɛksən], *v.a.* bewitch.
behilflich [bəˈhɪlflɪç], *adj.* helpful, useful.
behindern [bəˈhɪndərn], *v.a.* hinder, hamper.
Behörde [bəˈhœrdə], *f.* (—, *pl.* —**n**) the authorities.
behufs [bəˈhuːfs], *prep.* (*Genit.*) in order to, with a view to.
behüten [bəˈhyːtən], *v.a.* guard, protect; *Gott behüte!* Heaven forbid!
behutsam [bəˈhuːtzaːm], *adj.* careful, cautious.
bei [baɪ], *prep.* (*Dat.*) (*locally*) near by, close by, next to, at.
beibehalten [ˈbaɪbəhaltən], *v.a. irr.* keep, retain.
Beiblatt [ˈbaɪblat], *n.* (—**s**, *pl.* ⸚**er**) supplement (to a newspaper).
beibringen [ˈbaɪbrɪŋən], *v.a. irr.* adduce (proof); produce (witnesses); (*fig.*) teach; impart to.
Beichte [ˈbaɪçtə], *f.* (—, *pl.* —**n**) confession.
Beichtstuhl [ˈbaɪçtʃtuːl], *m.* (—**s**, *pl.* ⸚**e**) confessional.
beide [ˈbaɪdə], *adj.* both, either, the two.
beiderlei [ˈbaɪdərlaɪ], *adj.* of both kinds.
beidrehen [ˈbaɪdreːən], *v.n.* (*Naut.*) heave to.
Beifall [ˈbaɪfal], *m.* (—**s**, *no pl.*) (*verbal*) approbation; (*shouting*) acclamation, acclaim; (*clapping*) applause.
beifällig [ˈbaɪfɛlɪç], *adj.* favourable, approving, assenting.
beifügen [ˈbaɪfyːgən], *v.a.* enclose, attach.
Beifuß [ˈbaɪfuːs], *m.* (—**es**, *no pl.*) (*Bot.*) mugwort.
beigeben [ˈbaɪgeːbən], *v.a. irr.* add, join to. — *v.n. klein* —, give in.
Beigeschmack [ˈbaɪgəʃmak], *m.* (—**s**, *no pl.*) aftertaste, tang.
beigesellen [ˈbaɪgəzɛlən], *v.r. sich* —, associate with.
Beihilfe [ˈbaɪhɪlfə], *f.* (—, *pl.* —**n**) aid, assistance, subsidy.
beikommen [ˈbaɪkɔmən], *v.n. irr.* (*aux.* sein) *einer Sache* —, to grapple with s.th.; *ich kann ihm nicht* —, I cannot catch him out, get at him.
Beil [baɪl], *n.* (—**s**, *pl.* —**e**) hatchet, axe.
Beilage [ˈbaɪlaːgə], *f.* (—, *pl.* —**n**) enclosure (with a letter); supplement (to a newspaper); *Braten mit* —, joint with vegetables.
beiläufig [ˈbaɪlɔyfɪç], *adv.* by the way, incidentally.
beilegen [ˈbaɪleːgən], *v.a.* add, join; enclose (in letter).
beileibe [baɪˈlaɪbə], *int.* — *nicht!* on no account!
Beileid [ˈbaɪlaɪt], *n.* (—**s**, *no pl.*) condolence, sympathy.
beiliegen [ˈbaɪliːgən], *v.n. irr.* be enclosed with.
beimengen [ˈbaɪmɛŋən], *v.a.* (*Cul.*) mix with, add.
beimessen [ˈbaɪmɛsən], *v.a. irr. einem etwas* —, impute s.th. to s.o.; *einem Glauben* —, credit s.o., give credence to.
Bein [baɪn], *n.* (—**s**, *pl.* —**e**) leg; *einem auf die* —*e helfen*, give a helping hand to s.o.
beinahe [baɪˈnaːə], *adv.* almost, nearly.
Beiname [ˈbaɪnaːmə], *m.* (—**ns**, *pl.* —**n**) surname; nickname.
Beinbruch [ˈbaɪnbrux], *m.* (—**s**, *pl.* ⸚**e**) fracture of the leg; (*coll.*) *Hals- und Beinbruch!* good luck!
Beinkleider [ˈbaɪnklaɪdər], *n. pl.* (*obs.*) pants, trousers.
beipflichten [ˈbaɪpflɪçtən], *v.n. einem* —, agree with s.o.
beirren [bəˈɪrən], *v.a. sich nicht — lassen*, not let o.s. be dissuaded *or* put off.
beisammen [baɪˈzamən], *adv.* together.
Beischlaf [ˈbaɪʃlaːf], *m.* (—**s**, *no pl.*) cohabitation, coition.
Beisein [ˈbaɪzaɪn], *n.* (—**s**, *no pl.*) *im — von*, in the presence of.
beiseite [baɪˈzaɪtə], *adv.* apart, aside; (*Theat.*) aside.
beisetzen [ˈbaɪzɛtsən], *v.a.* bury, inter, entomb.
Beispiel [ˈbaɪʃpiːl], *n.* (—**s**, *pl.* —**e**) example, instance; *zum* — (*abbr. z.B.*), for instance, for example.
beißen [ˈbaɪsən], *v.a. irr.* bite; (*pepper, smoke*) burn, sting.
Beißzange [ˈbaɪstsaŋə], *f.* (—, *pl.* —**n**) pair of pincers *or* nippers.
Beistand [ˈbaɪʃtant], *m.* (—**s**, *pl.* ⸚**e**) assistance, help; (*Law*) counsel; — *leisten*, give assistance.
beistehen [ˈbaɪʃteːən], *v.n. irr. einem* —, stand by s.o., help s.o.
beisteuern [ˈbaɪʃtɔyərn], *v.a. zu etwas* —, contribute to s.th.
beistimmen [ˈbaɪʃtɪmən], *v.n.* agree with, assent.

Beistrich ['baɪʃtrɪç], *m.* (—(e)s, *pl.* —e) comma.

beitragen ['baɪtra:gən], *v.a. irr.* contribute; be conducive to.

beitreten ['baɪtre:tən], *v.n. irr.* (*aux.* sein) join (a club); enter into partnership with (a firm).

Beitritt ['baɪtrɪt], *m.* (—s, *no pl.*) accession, joining.

Beiwagen ['baɪva:gən], *m.* (—s, *pl.* —) trailer, sidecar (on motor cycle).

beiwohnen ['baɪvo:nən], *v.n.* be present at, attend.

Beiwort ['baɪvɔrt], *n.* (—s, *pl.* ⸚er) adjective, epithet.

Beize ['baɪtsə], *f.* (—, *pl.* —n) caustic fluid; (*wood*) stain.

beizeiten [baɪ'tsaɪtən], *adv.* betimes, early, in good time.

beizen ['baɪtsən], *v.a.* cauterise; (*wood*) stain.

bejahen [bə'ja:ən], *v.a.* answer in the affirmative.

bejahrt [bə'ja:rt], *adj.* aged, elderly, old.

bejammern [bə'jamərn], *v.a.* bemoan, bewail.

bekannt [bə'kant], *adj.* known, well-known; — *mit*, acquainted with.

Bekannte [bə'kantə], *m.* (—n, *pl.* —n) acquaintance.

bekanntlich [bə'kantlɪç], *adv.* as is well known.

Bekanntmachung [bə'kantmaxuŋ], *f.* (—, *pl.* —en) publication, announcement.

Bekanntschaft [bə'kantʃaft], *f.* (—, *pl.* —en) — *mit einem machen*, strike up an acquaintance with s.o.

bekehren [bə'ke:rən], *v.a.* convert. — *v.r. sich* —, be converted *or* become a convert (to); reform.

bekennen [bə'kɛnən], *v.a. irr.* confess, profess; admit, own up to.

Bekenner [bə'kɛnər], *m.* (—s, *pl.* —) Confessor (as title).

Bekenntnis [bə'kɛntnɪs], *n.* (—ses, *pl.* —se) confession (of faith), avowal, creed.

beklagen [bə'kla:gən], *v.a.* lament, bewail, deplore. — *v.r. sich* — *über*, complain of.

Beklagte [bə'kla:ktə], *m.* (—n, *pl.* —n) (*Law*) defendant.

bekleiden [bə'klaɪdən], *v.a.* clothe, dress, cover; (*office*) hold.

Bekleidung [bə'klaɪduŋ], *f.* (—, *no pl.*) clothing, clothes; (*office*) administration, holding, exercise.

beklemmen [bə'klɛmən], *v.a. irr.* oppress.

Beklemmung [bə'klɛmuŋ], *f.* (—, *pl.* —en) oppression, anguish.

beklommen [bə'klɔmən], *adj.* anxious, uneasy.

bekommen [bə'kɔmən], *v.a. irr.* obtain, get, receive.

bekömmlich [bə'kœmlɪç], *adj.* beneficial; digestible, wholesome.

beköstigen [bə'kœstɪgən], *v.a.* board; feed.

bekräftigen [bə'krɛftɪgən], *v.a.* aver, corroborate, confirm.

bekränzen [bə'krɛntsən], *v.a.* wreathe, crown (with a garland).

bekreuzigen [bə'krɔytsɪgən], *v.r. sich* —, make the sign of the cross, cross o.s.

bekriegen [bə'kri:gən], *v.a.* make war on.

bekritteln [bə'krɪtəln], *v.a.* criticise, carp at, find fault with.

bekritzeln [bə'krɪtsəln], *v.a.* scrawl on, doodle on.

bekümmern [bə'kymərn], *v.a.* grieve, distress, trouble. — *v.r.* trouble o.s. about, grieve over.

bekunden [bə'kundən], *v.a.* manifest, show; declare.

beladen [bə'la:dən], *v.a. irr.* load.

Belag [bə'la:k], *m.* (—s, *pl.* ⸚e) covering, layer; spread (on sandwiches); fur (on the tongue).

belagern [bə'la:gərn], *v.a.* besiege.

Belang [bə'laŋ], *m.* (—s, *pl.* —e) importance; *von* —, of great moment *or* consequence; (*pl.*) concerns, interests.

belangen [bə'laŋən], *v.a.* (*Law*) sue, prosecute.

belanglos [bə'laŋlo:s], *adj.* of small account; irrelevant, unimportant.

belassen [bə'lasən], *v.a. irr. es dabei* —, leave things as they are.

belasten [bə'lastən], *v.a.* load, burden; (*Comm.*) debit, charge; (*Law*) incriminate.

belästigen [bə'lɛstɪgən], *v.a.* bother, pester, molest.

Belastung [bə'lastuŋ], *f.* (—, *pl.* —en) load, burden; (*Comm.*) debiting; (*house*) mortgage; *erbliche* —, hereditary disposition.

Belastungszeuge [bə'lastuŋstsɔygə], *m.* (—n, *pl.* —n) witness for the prosecution.

belaubt [bə'laupt], *adj.* covered with leaves, leafy.

belaufen [bə'laufən], *v.r. irr. sich* — *auf*, amount to, come to.

belauschen [bə'lauʃən], *v.a.* eavesdrop, overhear.

beleben [bə'le:bən], *v.a.* animate, enliven.

Belebtheit [bə'le:pthaɪt], *f.* (—, *no pl.*) animation, liveliness.

Beleg [bə'le:k], *m.* (—s, *pl.* —e) document, proof, receipt, voucher.

belegen [bə'le:gən], *v.a.* cover, overlay; reserve, book (*seat*); support by documents, authenticate, prove.

Belegschaft [bə'le:kʃaft], *f.* (—, *pl.* —en) workers, personnel, staff; (*Min.*) gang, shift.

belegt [bə'le:kt], *adj.* (*tongue*) furred; —*es Brot*, sandwich.

belehnen [bə'le:nən], *v.a.* enfeoff; invest (with a fief).

belehren [bə'le:rən], *v.a.* instruct, advise, inform.

Belehrung [bə'le:ruŋ], *f.* (—, *pl.* —**en**) information, instruction, advice.
beleibt [bə'laipt], *adj.* stout, corpulent, obese.
beleidigen [bə'laɪdɪgən], *v.a.* insult, offend, give offence to.
belesen [bə'le:zən], *adj.* well-read.
beleuchten [bə'lɔyçtən], *v.a.* illumine, illuminate; (*fig.*) throw light on, elucidate.
Beleuchtungskörper [bə'lɔyçtuŋskœrpər], *m.* (—**s**, *pl.* —) lighting fixture, lamp.
Belgien ['bɛlgjən], *n.* Belgium.
belichten [bə'lɪçtən], *v.a.* (*Phot.*) expose.
belieben [bə'li:bən], *v.a.*, *v.n.* please, like, choose.
beliebig [bə'li:bɪç], *adj.* optional; any, whatever.
beliebt [bə'li:pt], *adj.* popular, well-liked.
Beliebtheit [bə'li:pthaɪt], *f.* (—, *no pl.*) popularity.
bellen ['bɛlən], *v.n.* bark.
beloben [bə'lo:bən], *v.a.* praise, approve.
belohnen [bə'lo:nən], *v.a.* reward, recompense.
belügen [bə'ly:gən], *v.a. irr. einen* —, tell lies to s.o., deceive s.o. by lying.
belustigen [bə'lustɪgən], *v.a.* amuse, divert, entertain.
bemächtigen [bə'mɛçtɪgən], *v.r. sich einer Sache* —, take possession of s.th.
bemäkeln [bə'mɛ:kəln], *v.a.* find fault with.
bemalen [bə'ma:lən], *v.a.* paint (over).
bemängeln [bə'mɛŋəln], *v.a.* find fault with.
bemannen [bə'manən], *v.a.* man.
bemänteln [bə'mɛntəln], *v.a.* cloak, hide.
bemeistern [bə'maɪstərn], *v.a.* master.
bemerkbar [bə'mɛrkba:r], *adj.* perceptible, noticeable.
bemerken [bə'mɛrkən], *v.a.* observe, perceive, notice.
Bemerkung [bə'mɛrkuŋ], *f.* (—, *pl.* —**en**) remark, observation, note.
bemessen [bə'mɛsən], *v.a. irr.* measure; curtail.
bemitleiden [bə'mɪtlaɪdən], *v.a.* pity, be sorry for.
bemittelt [bə'mɪtəlt], *adj.* well-off, well-to-do.
bemoost [bə'mo:st], *adj.* mossy.
bemühen [bə'my:ən], *v.a.* trouble, give trouble (to). — *v.r. sich* —, take pains, strive, endeavour.
bemüht [bə'my:t], *adj.* studious; — *sein*, endeavour, try to.
bemuttern [bə'mutərn], *v.a.* mother.
benachbart [bə'naxba:rt], *adj.* neighbouring, adjacent.
benachrichtigen [bə'naxrɪçtɪgən], *v.a.* inform, give notice of, notify.
benachteiligen [bə'naxtaɪlɪgən], *v.a.* prejudice, discriminate against, handicap.
benagen [bə'na:gən], *v.a.* gnaw at.
benebeln [bə'ne:bəln], *v.a.* befog, cloud; (*fig.*) dim, intoxicate.
benedeien [bene'daɪən], *v.a.* bless, glorify.
Benediktiner [benedɪk'ti:nər], *m.* (—**s**, *pl.* —) (monk) Benedictine; Benedictine liqueur.
Benefiz [bene'fi:ts], *n.* (—**es**, *pl.* —**e**) benefit; benefit performance.
Benehmen [bə'ne:mən], *n.* (—**s**, *no pl.*) conduct, behaviour.
benehmen [bə'ne:mən], *v.r. irr. sich* —, behave, conduct o.s.
beneiden [bə'naɪdən], *v.a. einen* — *um*, envy s.o. (s.th.).
benennen [bə'nɛnən], *v.a.* name.
benetzen [bə'nɛtsən], *v.a.* moisten.
Bengel ['bɛŋəl], *m.* (—**s**, *pl.* —) naughty boy, scamp; rascal, lout.
benommen [bə'nɔmən], *adj.* dazed, giddy.
benötigen [bə'nø:tɪgən], *v.a.* be in need of, require.
benutzen [bə'nutsən], *v.a.* make use of, utilise.
Benzin [bɛnt'si:n], *n.* (—**s**, *no pl.*) benzine; (*Motor.*) petrol; (*Am.*) gas, gasoline.
beobachten [bə'o:baxtən], *v.a.* watch, observe.
bequem [bə'kve:m], *adj.* comfortable, easy; convenient; indolent, lazy.
bequemen [bə'kve:mən], *v.r. sich* —, condescend (to), comply (with).
Bequemlichkeit [bə'kve:mlɪçkaɪt], *f.* (—, *pl.* —**en**) convenience, ease, indolence.
beraten [bə'ra:tən], *v.a. irr.* advise, assist with advice, counsel. — *v.r. sich* — *mit*, confer with, consult with.
beratschlagen [bə'ra:tʃla:gən], *v.n.* deliberate with.
Beratung [bə'ra:tuŋ], *f.* (—, *pl.* —**en**) council, deliberation, consultation.
berauben [bə'raubən], *v.a.* rob, deprive (s.o.) of (s.th.).
berauschen [bə'rauʃən], *v.a.* intoxicate.
berechnen [bə'rɛçnən], *v.a.* compute, charge, calculate, estimate.
berechtigen [bə'rɛçtɪgən], *v.a. einen zu etwas* —, entitle s.o. to s.th.; authorise s.o. to have *or* do s.th.
beredsam [bə're:tza:m], *adj.* eloquent.
beredt [bə're:t], *adj.* eloquent.
Bereich [bə'raɪç], *m.* & *n.* (—**s**, *pl.* —**e**) extent, realm, sphere, scope.
bereichern [bə'raɪçərn], *v.a.* enrich, enlarge.
bereisen [bə'raɪzən], *v.a.* travel over *or* through, tour (a country).
bereit [bə'raɪt], *adj.* ready, prepared.
bereiten [bə'raɪtən], *v.a.* prepare, get ready.
bereits [bə'raɪts], *adv.* already.
Bereitschaft [bə'raɪtʃaft], *f.* (—, *no pl.*) readiness, preparedness.
bereitwillig [bə'raɪtvɪlɪç], *adj.* willing, ready, obliging.

bereuen [bəˈrɔyən], *v.a.* repent, be sorry for, regret.
Berg [bɛrk], *m.* (**—es**, *pl.* **—e**) mountain, hill.
bergab [bɛrkˈap], *adj.* downhill.
Bergamt [ˈbɛrkamt], *n.* (**—s**, *pl.* **¨er**) mining-office, mine authority.
bergan [bɛrkˈan], *adj.* uphill.
Bergarbeiter [ˈbɛrkarbaɪtər], *m.* (**—s**, *pl.* **—**) miner, collier.
bergauf [bɛrkˈauf], *adj.* uphill.
Bergbau [ˈbɛrkbau], *m.* (**—s**, *no pl.*) mining, mining industry.
bergen [ˈbɛrgən], *v.a. irr.* shelter, protect, save; (*flotsam*) save, recover, salvage.
bergig [ˈbɛrgɪç], *adj.* mountainous, hilly.
Bergkristall [ˈbɛrkkrɪstal], *m.* (**—s**, *pl.* **—e**) rock-crystal.
Bergleute [ˈbɛrklɔytə], *pl.* miners, colliers.
Bergmann [ˈbɛrkman], *m.* (**—s**, *pl.* **Bergleute**) miner, collier.
Bergpredigt [ˈbɛrkpreːdɪçt], *f.* (**—**, *no pl.*) Sermon on the Mount.
Bergschlucht [ˈbɛrkʃluxt], *f.* (**—**, *pl.* **—en**) ravine, gorge.
Bergsteiger [ˈbɛrkʃtaɪgər], *m.* (**—s**, *pl.* **—**) mountaineer.
Bergstock [ˈbɛrkʃtɔk], *m.* (**—s**, *pl.* **¨e**) alpenstock.
Bergsturz [ˈbɛrkʃturts], *m.* (**—es**, *pl.* **¨e**) landslip, landslide.
Bergung [ˈbɛrguŋ], *f.* (**—**, *pl.* **—en**) sheltering, salvaging; rescue operation.
Bergwerk [ˈbɛrkvɛrk], *n.* (**—s**, *pl.* **—e**) mine, pit.
Bericht [bəˈrɪçt], *m.* (**—s**, *pl.* **—e**) report, account, statement; **—** *erstatten*, report, give an account of.
Berichterstatter [bəˈrɪçtɛrʃtatər], *m.* (**—s**, *pl.* **—**) reporter.
berichtigen [bəˈrɪçtɪgən], *v.a.* set right, correct, rectify, amend.
berieseln [bəˈriːzəln], *v.a.* irrigate.
beritten [bəˈrɪtən], *adj.* mounted on horseback.
Berlin [bɛrˈliːn], *n.* Berlin; **—***er Blau*, Prussian blue.
Bern [bɛrn], *n.* Berne.
Bernhardiner [bɛrnharˈdiːnər], *m.* (**—s**, *pl.* **—**) Cistercian monk; Newfoundland dog, St. Bernard dog.
Bernstein [ˈbɛrnʃtaɪn], *m.* (**—s**, *no pl.*) amber.
bersten [ˈbɛrstən], *v.n. irr.* (*aux.* sein) burst.
berüchtigt [bəˈryçtɪçt], *adj.* notorious, infamous.
berücken [bəˈrykən], *v.a.* enchant, fascinate.
berücksichtigen [bəˈrykzɪçtɪgən], *v.a.* have regard to, take into consideration, allow for.
Beruf [bəˈruːf], *m.* (**—s**, *pl.* **—e**) profession, occupation, calling, trade.
berufen [bəˈruːfən], *v.a. irr.* (*meeting*) call, convene; appoint (to an office). — *v.r. sich* — *auf*, appeal to, refer to. — *adj.* competent, qualified.
berufsmäßig [bəˈruːfsmɛːsɪç], *adj.* professional.
Berufung [bəˈruːfuŋ], *f.* (**—**, *pl.* **—en**) call, vocation, appointment; (*Law*) appeal.
beruhen [bəˈruːən], *v.n. auf etwas* **—**, be based on, be founded on.
beruhigen [bəˈruːɪgən], *v.a.* calm, pacify; comfort, console, set at rest.
Beruhigung [bəˈruːɪguŋ], *f.* (**—**, *pl.* **—en**) reassurance, quieting, calming.
berühmt [bəˈryːmt], *adj.* famous, celebrated, illustrious, renowned.
berühren [bəˈryːrən], *v.a.* touch, handle; (*subject*) mention, touch upon; *peinlich berührt*, unpleasantly affected.
berußt [bəˈruːst], *adj.* sooty.
Beryll [beˈryl], *m.* (**—s**, *pl.* **—e**) beryl.
besagen [bəˈzaːgən], *v.a.* mean, signify.
besagt [bəˈzaːkt], *adj.* aforesaid, abovementioned.
besaiten [bəˈzaɪtən], *v.a.* fit with strings.
Besan [beˈzaːn], *m.* (**—s**, *pl.* **—e**) (*Naut.*) miz(z)en.
besänftigen [bəˈzɛnftɪgən], *v.a.* calm, appease, pacify.
Besatz [bəˈzats], *m.* (**—es**, *pl.* **¨e**) trimming, border.
Besatzung [bəˈzatsuŋ], *f.* (**—**, *pl.* **—en**) crew; (*Mil.*) garrison, occupation.
besaufen [bəˈzaufən], *v.r. irr.* (*vulg.*) *sich* **—**, get drunk.
beschädigen [bəˈʃɛːdɪgən], *v.a.* damage.
beschaffen [bəˈʃafən], *v.a.* procure, get. — *adj.* conditioned, constituted.
Beschaffenheit [bəˈʃafənhaɪt], *f.* (**—**, *no pl.*) nature, kind, quality, condition.
beschäftigen [bəˈʃɛftɪgən], *v.a.* occupy, employ.
beschämen [bəˈʃɛːmən], *v.a.* make ashamed, shame.
beschatten [bəˈʃatən], *v.a.* shade, shadow; follow (s.o.).
Beschau [bəˈʃau], *f.* (**—**, *no pl.*) examination; inspection.
beschauen [bəˈʃauən], *v.a.* view, look at.
beschaulich [bəˈʃaulɪç], *adj.* tranquil, contemplative.
Beschaulichkeit [bəˈʃaulɪçkaɪt], *f.* (**—**, *pl.* **—en**) tranquillity, contemplation.
Bescheid [bəˈʃaɪt], *m.* (**—s**, *pl.* **—e**) answer, information; (*Law*) decision; — *wissen*, know o.'s way about; know what's what.
bescheiden [bəˈʃaɪdən], *v.a. irr.* inform (s.o.); *einen zu sich* **—**, send for s.o. — *adj.* modest, unassuming.
Bescheidenheit [bəˈʃaɪdənhaɪt], *f.* (**—**, *no pl.*) modesty.
bescheinen [bəˈʃaɪnən], *v.a. irr.* shine upon.
bescheinigen [bəˈʃaɪnɪgən], *v.a. einem etwas* **—**, attest, certify.
beschenken [bəˈʃɛŋkən], *v.a.* give a present to.

bescheren [bə'ʃe:rən], *v.a.* give (a present to), bestow (s.th. on s.o.).
Bescherung [bə'ʃe:ruŋ], *f.* (—, *pl.* —**en**) giving (of present); *das ist eine schöne* —, (*fig.*) this is a nice mess!
beschicken [bə'ʃɪkən], *v.a. eine Ausstellung* —, contribute to an exhibition.
beschießen [bə'ʃi:sən], *v.a. irr.* shoot at, fire upon, bombard.
beschiffen [bə'ʃɪfən], *v.a.* navigate, sail.
beschimpfen [bə'ʃɪmpfən], *v.a.* insult, abuse, revile.
beschirmen [bə'ʃɪrmən], *v.a.* protect, shelter, defend.
Beschlag [bə'ʃla:k], *m.* (—**s**, *pl.* ⸚**e**) mounting; metal fitting; (*on stick*) ferrule; *etwas mit — belegen*, or *in — nehmen*, sequestrate, confiscate, seize.
beschlagen [bə'ʃla:gən], *v.a. irr.* shoe (a horse). — *v.n.* (*window*) mist over.
Beschlagnahme [bə'ʃla:kna:mə], *f.* (—, *pl.* —**n**) confiscation, seizure.
beschleunigen [bə'ʃlɔynɪgən], *v.a.* hasten, speed up, accelerate.
beschließen [bə'ʃli:sən], *v.a. irr.* shut, lock up; close, conclude, finish; decide, resolve upon.
Beschluß [bə'ʃlus], *m.* (—**sses**, *pl.* ⸚**sse**) determination, resolution, decree.
beschmieren [bə'ʃmi:rən], *v.a.* soil, smear.
beschmutzen [bə'ʃmutsən], *v.a.* soil, dirty, foul.
beschneiden [bə'ʃnaɪdən], *v.a. irr.* cut, clip; (*Hort.*) lop, prune; (*animals*) crop; circumcise.
Beschneidung [bə'ʃnaɪduŋ], *f.* (—, *pl.* —**en**) lopping, pruning; circumcision.
beschönigen [bə'ʃø:nɪgən], *v.a.* palliate, excuse.
beschränken [bə'ʃrɛnkən], *v.a.* limit, restrict.
beschränkt [bə'ʃrɛŋkt], *adj.* limited; *etwas* —, a little stupid; *Gesellschaft mit —er Haftung*, limited (liability) company.
Beschränkung [bə'ʃrɛŋkuŋ], *f.* (—, *pl.* —**en**) limitation, restriction.
beschreiben [bə'ʃraɪbən], *v.a. irr.* describe; write upon.
beschreiten [bə'ʃraɪtən], *v.a. irr.* tread on.
beschuldigen [bə'ʃuldɪgən], *v.a.* charge (s.o.), accuse.
beschützen [bə'ʃytsən], *v.a.* protect, shelter, guard.
Beschützer [bə'ʃytsər], *m.* (—**s**, *pl.* —) protector, defender.
Beschwerde [bə'ʃve:rdə], *f.* (—, *pl.* —**en**) trouble, hardship, difficulty; complaint, grievance.
beschweren [bə'ʃve:rən], *v.a.* make heavier, weight. — *v.r. sich über etwas* —, complain of s.th.
beschwerlich [bə'ʃve:rlɪç], *adj.* burdensome, hard, troublesome.
beschwichtigen [bə'ʃvɪçtɪgən], *v.a.* soothe, appease, still.
beschwindeln [bə'ʃvɪndəln], *v.a.* cheat, swindle (s.o.).
beschwingt [bə'ʃvɪŋkt], *adj.* winged, light-footed.
beschwipst [bə'ʃvɪpst], *adj.* (*coll.*) tipsy.
beschwören [bə'ʃvø:rən], *v.a. irr.* testify on oath; *einen* —, implore s.o.; conjure (up) (ghosts etc.); exorcize.
beseelen [bə'ze:lən], *v.a.* animate.
besehen [bə'ze:ən], *v.a. irr.* look at, inspect.
beseitigen [bə'zaɪtɪgən], *v.a.* remove.
beseligt [bə'ze:lɪçt], *adj.* enraptured, beatified.
Besen ['be:zən], *m.* (—**s**, *pl.* —) broom, besom.
Besenstiel ['be:zənʃti:l], *m.* (—**s**, *pl.* —**e**) broom-stick.
besessen [bə'zɛsən], *adj.* possessed, obsessed, mad.
besetzen [bə'zɛtsən], *v.a.* (*dress*) trim, lace; (*Mil.*) occupy, garrison; (*office*) fill; (*Theat.*) cast; (*seat*) occupy, take; *besetzt*, engaged.
Besetzung [bə'zɛtsuŋ], *f.* (—, *pl.* —**en**) lacing, trimming; appointment (to post); (*Theat.*) cast.
besichtigen [bə'zɪçtɪgən], *v.a.* view, go over, inspect, examine.
besiedeln [bə'zi:dəln], *v.a.* colonise.
besiegeln [bə'zi:gəln], *v.a.* seal, set o.'s seal to.
besiegen [bə'zi:gən], *v.a.* vanquish, conquer, overcome.
besinnen [bə'zɪnən], *v.r. irr.* reflect; *sich auf etwas* —, recollect, remember, think of.
besinnungslos [bə'zɪnuŋslo:s], *adj.* insensible, unconscious.
Besitz [bə'zɪts], *m.* (—**es**, *no pl.*) possession, property.
besitzanzeigend [bə'zɪtsantsaɪgənt], *adj.* (*Gram.*) possessive.
besitzen [bə'zɪtsən], *v.a. irr.* possess, own, have.
Besitzergreifung [bə'zɪtsɛrgraɪfuŋ], *f.* (—, *no pl.*) occupation, taking possession (of).
besoffen [bə'zɔfən], *adj.* (*vulg.*) drunk.
besohlen [bə'zo:lən], *v.a.* sole (shoes).
besolden [bə'zɔldən], *v.a.* give a salary to, pay.
besonder [bə'zɔndər], *adj.* special, particular.
Besonderheit [bə:zɔndərhaɪt], *f.* (—, *pl.* —**en**) particularity, peculiarity, strangeness.
besonders [bə'zɔndərs], *adv.* especially.
besonnen [bə'zɔnən], *adj.* prudent, cautious, collected, circumspect.
besorgen [bə'zɔrgən], *v.a.* take care of, provide, procure.
Besorgnis [bə'zɔrknɪs], *f.* (—, *pl.* —**se**) care, concern, anxiety, fear.
besorgt [bə'zɔrkt], *adj.* apprehensive, anxious, worried.

Besorgung [bə'zɔrguŋ], *f.* (—, *pl.* —**en**) care, management; purchase, commission; —*en machen*, go shopping.
bespannen [bə'ʃpanən], *v.a.* string (a musical instrument); put horses (to a carriage).
bespötteln [bə'ʃpœtəln], *v.a.* ridicule.
besprechen [bə'ʃprɛçən], *v.a. irr.* discuss, talk over; (book) review. — *v.r. sich* — *mit*, confer with.
bespritzen [bə'ʃprɪtsən], *v.a.* sprinkle, splash.
besser ['bɛsər], *adj.* better; *um so* —, so much the better; *je mehr desto* —, the more the better; — *sein als*, be better than, be preferable to; — *werden*, (*weather*) clear up; (*health*) improve.
bessern ['bɛsərn], *v.a.* better, improve. — *v.r. sich* —, reform, improve, mend o.'s ways.
Besserung ['bɛsəruŋ], *f.* (—*pl.* —**en**) improvement, amendment, reform; (*Med.*) recovery; *gute* —, get well soon.
Besserungsanstalt ['bɛsəruŋsanʃtalt], *f.* (—, *pl.* —**en**) reformatory.
best ['bɛst], *adj.* best.
bestallen [bə'ʃtalən], *v.a.* appoint.
Bestand [bə'ʃtant], *m.* (—**s**, *pl.* ¨—**e**) continuance, duration; stock; balance of cash; — *haben*, endure.
Bestandaufnahme [bə'ʃtantaufna:mə], *f.* (—, *pl.* —**n**) (*Comm.*) stocktaking.
beständig [bə'ʃtɛndɪç], *adj.* continual, perpetual; (*persons*) steady, steadfast, constant.
Bestandteil [bə'ʃtanttaɪl], *m.* (—**s**, *pl.* —**e**) constituent part, component, ingredient, essential part.
bestärken [bə'ʃtɛrkən], *v.a.* confirm, strengthen.
bestätigen [bə'ʃtɛ:tɪgən], *v.a.* confirm, ratify, bear out, sanction; *den Empfang eines Briefes* —, acknowledge receipt of a letter.
bestatten [bə'ʃtatən], *v.a.* bury, inter.
bestäuben [bə'ʃtɔybən], *v.a.* cover with dust, spray; (*Bot.*) pollinate.
bestechen [bə'ʃtɛçən], *v.a. irr.* bribe, corrupt; (*fig.*) captivate.
bestechlich [bə'ʃtɛçlɪç], *adj.* corruptible.
Bestechung [bə'ʃtɛçuŋ], *f.* (—, *pl.* —**en**) corruption, bribery.
Besteck [bə'ʃtɛk], *n.* (—**s**, *pl.* —**e**) set of knife, fork and spoon; set *or* case (of instruments).
Bestehen [bə'ʃte:ən], *n.* (—**s**, *no pl.*) existence.
bestehen [bə'ʃte:ən], *v.a. irr.* undergo, endure, pass (an examination). — *v.n.* exist; *aus etwas* —, consist of s.th.; be composed of s.th.; *auf* (*Dat.*) —, insist upon s.th.
besteigen [bə'ʃtaɪgən], *v.a. irr.* ascend, mount, climb.
bestellen [bə'ʃtɛlən], *v.a.* order, book; appoint; put in order; (*letter, message*) deliver; (*field*) till.
Bestellung [bə'ʃtɛluŋ], *f.* (—, *pl.* —**en**) order, commission, delivery (of letter); tilling (of field); appointment; *auf* —, to order.
bestens ['bɛstəns], *adv.* in the best manner.
besteuern [bə'ʃtɔyərn], *v.a.* tax.
bestialisch [bɛsti'a:lɪʃ], *adj.* beastly, bestial.
Bestie ['bɛstjə], *f.* (—, *pl.* —**n**) beast, brute.
bestimmen [bə'ʃtɪmən], *v.a.* fix, settle; decide (s.th.); determine, define.
bestimmt [bə'ʃtɪmt], *adj.* decided, fixed, appointed; *ganz* —, positively, most decidedly.
Bestimmtheit [bə'ʃtɪmthaɪt], *f.* (—, *no pl.*) certainty.
Bestimmung [bə'ʃtɪmuŋ], *f.* (—, *pl.* —**en**) settlement, decision, determination; provision; destiny.
bestrafen [bə'ʃtra:fən], *v.a.* punish, chastise.
bestrahlen [bə'ʃtra:lən], *v.a.* irradiate; (*Med.*) treat by radiotherapy.
bestreben [bə'ʃtre:bən], *v.r. sich* —, exert o.s., strive (for), endeavour.
Bestrebung [bə'ʃtre:buŋ], *f.* (—, *pl.* —**en**) effort, endeavour, exertion.
bestreichen [bə'ʃtraɪçən], *v.a. irr.* spread.
bestreiten [bə'ʃtraɪtən], *v.a. irr.* contest, deny, dispute; defray (costs).
bestreuen [bə'ʃtrɔyən], *v.a.* sprinkle, strew, powder.
bestricken [bə'ʃtrɪkən], *v.a.* ensnare, entangle.
bestürmen [bə'ʃtyrmən], *v.a.* storm, assail; (*fig.*) importune.
bestürzen [bə'ʃtyrtsən], *v.a.* dismay, confound, perplex.
Besuch [bə'zu:x], *m.* (—**s**, *pl.* —**e**) visit; (*person*) visitor.
besuchen [bə'zu:xən], *v.a.* visit, call on; attend; frequent.
besudeln [bə'zu:dəln], *v.a.* soil, foul.
betagt [bə'ta:kt], *adj.* aged, elderly.
betätigen [bə'tɛ:tɪgən], *v.a.* practise, operate. — *v.r. sich* —, take an active part, work, participate (in).
betäuben [bə'tɔybən], *v.a.* deafen; stun, benumb, anaesthetize.
Betäubung [bə'tɔybuŋ], *f.* (—, *pl.* —**en**) stupor, stupefaction; *örtliche* —, local anaesthetic.
beteiligen [bə'taɪlɪgən], *v.a. einen an etwas* —, give s.o. a share of s.th. — *v.r. sich an etwas* —, participate in s.th.; (*Comm.*) have shares in s.th.
Beteiligte [bə'taɪlɪçtə], *m.* (—**n**, *pl.* —**n**) person concerned.
Beteiligung [bə'taɪlɪguŋ], *f.* (—, *pl.* —**en**) participation, interest.
beten ['be:tən], *v.n.* pray, say o.'s prayers.
beteuern [bə'tɔyərn], *v.a.* aver, affirm solemnly.
betiteln [bə'ti:təln], *v.a.* entitle, name.
Beton [be'tõ], *m.* (—**s**, *no pl.*) concrete.

betonen [bə'to:nən], *v.a.* accentuate, stress, emphasise.
Betonung [bə'to:nuŋ], *f.* (—, *pl.* **—en**) accentuation, emphasis, stress.
betören [bə'tø:rən], *v.a.* delude, infatuate.
Betracht [bə'traxt], *m.* (**—s**, *no pl.*) consideration, respect, regard.
betrachten [bə'traxtən], *v.a.* consider, look at, view; *etwas aufmerksam* **—**, contemplate s.th.
beträchtlich [bə'trɛçtlɪç], *adj.* considerable.
Betrachtung [bə'traxtuŋ], *f.* (—, *pl.* **—en**) contemplation, consideration.
Betrag [bə'tra:k], *m.* (**—s**, *pl.* **¨e**) amount, sum total.
betragen [bə'tra:gən], *v.a. irr.* amount to, come to. — *v.r. sich* **—**, behave, conduct o.s.
Betragen [bə'tra:gən], *n.* (**—s**, *no pl.*) behaviour, conduct, demeanour.
betrauen [bə'trauən], *v.a. einen mit etwas* **—**, entrust s.o. with s.th.
betrauern [bə'trauərn], *v.a.* mourn for, bemoan.
Betreff [bə'trɛf], *m.* (**—s**, *no pl.*) reference; *in* **—**, with regard to.
betreffen [bə'trɛfən], *v.a. irr.* concern, affect, relate to.
Betreiben [bə'traɪbən], *n.* (**—s**, *no pl.*) *auf* **—** *von*, at the instigation of.
betreiben [bə'traɪbən], *v.a. irr.* (*business*) carry on; (*factory*) run; (*trade*) follow, practise.
Betreten [bə'tre:tən], *n.* (**—s**, *no pl.*) entry, entering.
betreten [bə'tre:tən], *v.a. irr.* step upon, set foot on, enter. — *adj.* disconcerted, embarrassed.
betreuen [bə'trɔyən], *v.a.* care for, attend to.
Betrieb [bə'tri:p], *m.* (**—s**, *pl.* **—e**) management, business, factory, plant; *den* **—** *einstellen*, close down; *in* **—** *sein*, be in operation; *in* **—** *setzen*, start working.
betriebsam [bə'tri:pza:m], *adj.* active, busy, industrious, diligent.
Betriebsamkeit [bə'tri:pza:mkaɪt], *f.* (—, *pl.* **—en**) activity, industry, bustle.
betriebsfertig [bə'tri:psfɛrtɪç], *adj.* ready for service; operational.
Betriebsmaterial [bə'tri:psmaterja:l], *n.* (**—s**, *pl.* **—ien**) (*Railw.*) rolling-stock; (*factory*) working-stock.
Betriebspersonal [bə'tri:psperzona:l], *n.* (**—s**, *no pl.*) workmen, employees, staff.
betrinken [bə'trɪŋkən], *v.r. irr. sich* **—**, get drunk.
betroffen [bə'trɔfən], *adj.* perplexed, confounded.
betrüben [bə'try:bən], *v.a.* afflict, grieve.
Betrübnis [bə'trypnɪs], *f.* (**—ses**, *pl.* **—se**) affliction, grief, distress, sorrow.
betrübt [bə'try:pt], *adj.* sad, grieved.
Betrug [bə'tru:k], *m.* (**—s**, *pl.* **¨ereien**) fraud, deceit, deception, imposture; *einen* **—** *begehen*, commit a fraud.
betrügen [bə'try:gən], *v.a. irr.* cheat, deceive.
Betrüger [bə'try:gər], *m.* (**—s**, **—**) swindler, cheat, deceiver, impostor.
betrunken [bə'truŋkən], *adj.* drunk, drunken, tipsy.
Bett [bɛt], *n.* (**—(e)s**, *pl.* **—en**) bed; (*river*) bed, channel.
Bettdecke ['bɛtdɛkə], *f.* (—, *pl.* **—n**) counterpane; (*Am.*) bedspread; *wollene* **—**, blanket; *gesteppte* **—**, quilt.
Bettel ['bɛtəl], *m.* (**—s**, *no pl.*) trash, trifle.
bettelarm ['bɛtəlarm], *adj.* destitute.
Bettelei [bɛtə'laɪ], *f.* (—, *pl.* **—en**) begging, beggary, penury.
betteln ['bɛtəln], *v.a.* beg, ask alms.
betten ['bɛtən], *v.a.* bed, lay to rest. — *v.r.* (*fig.*) *sich* **—**, make o.'s bed.
bettlägerig ['bɛtlɛgərɪç], *adj.* bedridden.
Bettlaken ['bɛtla:kən], *n.* (**—s**, *pl.* **—**) sheet.
Bettler ['bɛtlər], *m.* (**—s**, *pl.* **—**) beggar.
Bettstelle ['bɛtʃtɛlə], *f.* (—, *pl.* **—n**) bedstead.
Bettvorleger ['bɛtfo:rle:gər], *m.* (**—s**, *pl.* **—**) bedside-carpet *or* rug.
Bettwäsche ['bɛtvɛʃə], *f.* (—, *no pl.*) bed linen, bed clothes.
Bettzeug ['bɛttsɔyk], *n.* (**—s**, *no pl.*) bedding.
beugen ['bɔygən], *v.a.* bend, bow. — *v.r. sich* **—**, bend down, stoop.
Beugung ['bɔyguŋ], *f.* (—, *pl.* **—en**) (*Gram.*) inflection.
Beule ['bɔylə], *f.* (—, *pl.* **—n**) bruise, bump, swelling, boil.
beunruhigen [bə'unru:ɪgən], *v.a.* alarm, trouble, disquiet.
beurkunden [bə'u:rkundən], *v.a.* authenticate, verify.
beurlauben [bə'u:rlaubən], *v.a.* grant leave of absence. — *v.r. sich* **—**, take leave.
beurteilen [bə'urtaɪlən], *v.a.* judge, criticise.
Beute ['bɔytə], *f.* (—, *no pl.*) booty, loot; (*animals*) prey; (*Hunt.*) bag.
Beutel ['bɔytəl], *m.* (**—s**, *pl.* **—**) bag; (*money*) purse; (*Zool.*) pouch.
Beuteltier ['bɔytəlti:r], *n.* (**—s**, *pl.* **—e**) marsupial.
bevölkern [bə'fœlkərn], *v.a.* people, populate.
Bevölkerung [bə'fœlkəruŋ], *f.* (—, *pl.* **—en**) population.
bevollmächtigen [bə'fɔlmɛçtɪgən], *v.a.* empower, authorise.
bevor [bə'fo:r], *conj.* before, ere, beforehand.
bevormunden [bə'fo:rmundən], *v.a. insep.* act as guardian to; (*fig.*) browbeat.
bevorrechtigt [bə'fo:rrɛçtɪçt], *adj.* privileged.

bevorstehen [bə'fo:rʃte:ən], *v.n. irr.* impend, lie ahead, be imminent; *einem* —, be in store for s.o.
bevorzugen [bə'fo:rtsu:gən], *v.a. insep.* prefer, favour.
bewachen [bə'vaxən], *v.a.* watch over, guard.
bewachsen [bə'vaksən], *adj.* overgrown.
bewaffnen [bə'vafnən], *v.a.* arm, supply with arms.
Bewahranstalt [bə'va:ranʃtalt], *f.* (— *pl.* **—en**) kindergarten, nursery.
bewahren [bə'va:rən], *v.a.* preserve, keep, take care of.
bewähren [bə'vɛ:rən], *v.r. sich* —, prove o.s.
bewahrheiten [bə'va:rhaltən], *v.r. sich* —, come true.
bewährt [bə'vɛ:rt], *adj.* proved.
Bewährung [bə'vɛ:ruŋ], *f.* (—, *no pl.*) proof, verification.
Bewährungsfrist [bə'vɛ:ruŋsfrɪst], *f.* (—, *no pl.*) probation.
bewaldet [bə'valdət], *adj.* wooded, woody.
bewältigen [bə'vɛltɪgən], *v.a.* overcome; manage, master; cope *or* deal with.
bewandert [bə'vandərt], *adj.* versed, skilled, experienced, conversant.
bewandt [bə'vant], *adj.* such; *damit ist es so* —, it is like this.
Bewandtnis [bə'vantnɪs], *f.* (—, *pl.* **—se**) circumstance, condition, state; *es hat damit folgende* —, the circumstances are as follows.
bewässern [bə'vɛsərn], *v.a.* water, irrigate.
bewegen [bə've:gən], *v.a., v.r.* move, stir; take exercise. — *v.a. irr.* persuade, induce.
Beweggrund [bə've:kgrunt], *m.* (**—es**, *pl.* **¨e**) motive, reason, motivation.
beweglich [bə've:klɪç], *adj.* movable; agile, brisk, sprightly.
Bewegung [bə've:guŋ], *f.* (—, *pl.* **—en**) motion, movement; (*mind*) emotion, agitation.
beweinen [bə'vaɪnən], *v.a.* lament, bemoan, deplore.
Beweis [bə'vaɪs], *m.* (**—es**, *pl.* **—e**) proof, evidence; (*Maths.*) demonstration.
beweisen [bə'vaɪzən], *v.a. irr.* prove, show, demonstrate.
Beweiskraft [bə'vaɪskraft], *f.* (—, *no pl.*) (*Law*) probative force.
Beweismittel [bə'vaɪsmɪtəl], *n.* (**—s**, *pl.* —) evidence, proof.
Bewenden [bə'vendən], *n.* (**—s**, *no pl.*) *es hat damit sein* —, there the matter rests.
bewenden [bə'vendən], *v.n. irr. es dabei — lassen*, leave it at that.
bewerben [bə'vɛrbən], *v.r. irr. sich um etwas* —, apply for s.th.
Bewerber [bə'vɛrbər], *m.* (**—s**, *pl.* —) applicant, candidate; (*marriage*) suitor.
Bewerbung [bə'vɛrbuŋ], *f.* (—, *pl.* **—en**) application, candidature; (*marriage*) courtship.
bewerkstelligen [bə'vɛrkʃtɛlɪgən], *v.a.* perform, bring about.
bewerten [bə'vɛrtən], *v.a.* estimate, value.
bewilligen [bə'vɪlɪgən], *v.a.* grant, allow, permit.
bewillkommnen [bə'vɪlkɔmnən], *v.a.* welcome.
bewirken [bə'vɪrkən], *v.a.* effect, bring about.
bewirten [bə'vɪrtən], *v.a.* entertain, act as host (to).
bewirtschaften [bə'vɪrtʃaftən], *v.a.* manage.
bewohnen [bə'vo:nən], *v.a.* inhabit, occupy.
Bewohner [bə'vo:nər], *m.* (**—s**, *pl.* —) inhabitant, tenant, resident.
bewölken [bə'vœlkən], *v.r. sich* —, become overcast, become cloudy.
bewundern [bə'vundərn], *v.a.* admire.
bewundernswert [bə'vundərnsvɛrt], *adj.* admirable.
bewußt [bə'vust], *adj.* conscious, aware; *es war mir nicht* —, I was not aware of.
bewußtlos [bə'vustlo:s], *adj.* unconscious; — *werden*, faint, lose consciousness.
Bewußtsein [bə'vustzaɪn], *n.* (**—s**, *no pl.*) consciousness; *einem etwas zum — bringen*, bring s.th. home to s.o.
bezahlbar [bə'tsa:lba:r], *adj.* payable.
bezahlen [bə'tsa:lən], *v.a.* pay; (*bill*) settle.
bezähmen [bə'tsɛ:mən], *v.a.* tame, restrain. — *v.r. sich* —, restrain o.s., control o.s.
bezaubern [bə'tsaubərn], *v.a.* bewitch, enchant, fascinate.
bezeichnen [bə'tsaɪçnən], *v.a.* mark, denote, indicate, designate.
bezeichnend [bə'tsaɪçnənt], *adj.* indicative, characteristic, significant.
bezeigen [bə'tsaɪgən], *v.a.* manifest, show.
bezeugen [bə'tsɔygən], *v.a.* attest, bear witness, testify.
bezichtigen [bə'tsɪçtɪgən], *v.a.* accuse (s.o.) of (s.th.).
beziehbar [bə'tsi:ba:r], *adj.* (*goods*) obtainable; (*house*) ready for occupation.
beziehen [bə'tsi:ən], *v.a. irr.* cover; (*house etc.*) move into; (*instrument*) string; make up (a bed); *die Wache* —, mount guard. — *v.r. sich* —, (*sky*) cloud over; *sich auf etwas* —, refer to s.th.
Bezieher [bə'tsi:ər], *m.* (**—s**, *pl.* —) customer; (*newspaper*) subscriber.
Beziehung [bə'tsi:uŋ], *f.* (—, *pl.* **—en**) relation, connection; reference, bearing; *in dieser* —, in this respect; (*Comm.*) *unter — auf*, with reference to.
beziehungsweise [bə'tsi:uŋsvaɪzə], *adv.* respectively, as the case may be, or.

beziffern [bə'tsɪfərn], *v.a.* number.
Bezirk [bə'tsɪrk], *m.* (**—s**, *pl.* **—e**) district; (*Am.*) precinct; (*Parl.*) constituency; (*Law*) circuit.
Bezirksgericht [bə'tsɪrksgərɪçt], *n.* (**—s**, *pl.* **—e**) county court.
Bezug [bə'tsu:k], *m.* (**—s**, *pl.* **¨e**) (*pillow*) case, cover; (*goods*) order, purchase; (*fig.*) relation; **—** *haben auf*, refer to; *mit* **—** *auf*, referring to; (*pl.*) emoluments, income.
bezüglich [bə'tsy:klɪç], *adj.* with regard to, regarding.
Bezugnahme [bə'tsu:kna:mə], *f.* (**—**, *pl.* **—n**) reference; *unter* **—** *auf*, with reference to.
Bezugsbedingung [bə'tsu:ksbədɪŋuŋ], *f.* (**—**, *pl.* **—en**) (*usually pl.*) (*Comm.*) conditions *or* terms of delivery.
Bezugsquelle [bə'tsu:kskvɛlə], *f.* (**—**, *pl.* **—n**) source of supply.
bezwecken [bə'tsvɛkən], *v.a.* aim at, intend.
bezweifeln [bə'tsvaɪfəln], *v.a.* doubt, question.
bezwingen [bə'tsvɪŋən], *v.a. irr.* subdue, conquer. **—** *v.r. sich* **—**, restrain o.s.
Bibel ['bi:bəl], *f.* (**—**, *pl.* **—n**) Bible.
Bibelauslegung ['bi:bəlausle:guŋ], *f.* (**—**, *pl.* **—en**) (Biblical) exegesis.
Biber ['bi:bər], *m.* (**—s**, *pl.* **—**) (*Zool.*) beaver.
Bibliothek [biblio'te:k], *f.* (**—**, *pl.* **—en**) library.
Bibliothekar [bibliote'ka:r], *m.* (**—s**, *pl.* **—e**) librarian.
biblisch ['bi:blɪʃ], *adj.* biblical, scriptural.
Bickbeere ['bɪkbe:rə], *f.* (**—**, *pl.* **—n**) bilberry.
bieder ['bi:dər], *adj.* upright, honest, decent.
Biederkeit ['bi:dərkaɪt], *f.* (**—**, *no pl.*) uprightness, probity.
Biedermann ['bi:dərman], *m.* (**—s**, *pl.* **¨er**) honourable man; (*iron.*) Philistine.
biegen ['bi:gən], *v.a. irr.* bend, bow. **—** *v.n.* (*aux.* sein) *um die Ecke* **—**, turn the corner. **—** *v.r. sich* **—**, curve; **—** *oder brechen*, by hook or by crook.
biegsam ['bi:kza:m], *adj.* flexible, supple, pliant.
Biegung ['bi:guŋ], *f.* (**—**, *pl.* **—en**) curve, bend; (*Gram.*) inflexion.
Biene ['bi:nə], *f.* (**—**, *pl.* **—n**) bee.
Bienenhaus ['bi:nənhaus], *n.* (**—es**, *pl.* **¨er**) apiary.
Bienenkorb ['bi:nənkɔrp], *m.* (**—s**, *pl.* **¨e**) beehive.
Bienenzüchter ['bi:nəntsyçtər], *m.* (**—s**, *pl.* **—**) apiarist, bee-keeper.
Bier ['bi:r], *n.* (**—(e)s**, *pl.* **—e**) beer.
Bierkanne ['bi:rkanə], *f.* (**—**, *pl.* **—n**) tankard.
Biest [bi:st], *n.* (**—es**, *pl.* **—er**) brute, beast.
bieten ['bi:tən], *v.a. irr.* offer; (*auction*) bid.
Bieter ['bi:tər], *m.* (**—s**, *pl.* **—**) (*auction*) bidder.
Bigotterie [bɪgɔtə'ri:], *f.* (**—**, *no pl.*) bigotry.
Bijouterie [bɪʒutə'ri:], *f.* (**—**, *pl.* **—n**) trinkets, dress-jewellery.
Bilanz [bɪ'lants], *f.* (**—**, *pl.* **—en**) (*Comm.*) balance; (financial) statement.
Bild [bɪlt], *n.* (**—es**, *pl.* **—er**) picture, painting, portrait, image; idea; (*coins*) effigy; (*Cards*) court card; (*books*) illustration; (*speech*) figure of speech, metaphor.
bilden ['bɪldən], *v.c.* form, shape; (*mind*) cultivate. **—** *v.r. sich* **—**, improve o.'s mind, educate o.s.
bildend ['bɪldənt], *adj.* instructive, civilising; *die* **—***en Künste*, the fine arts.
bilderreich ['bɪldəraɪç], *adj.* **—***e Sprache*, flowery language, figurative style.
Bilderschrift ['bɪldərʃrɪft], *f.* (**—**, *pl.* **—en**) hieroglyphics.
Bilderstürmer ['bɪldərʃtyrmər], *m.* (**—s**, *pl.* **—**) iconoclast.
Bildhauer ['bɪlthauər], *m.* (**—s**, *pl.* **—**) sculptor.
bildhübsch ['bɪlthypʃ], *adj.* as pretty as a picture.
bildlich ['bɪltlɪç], *adj.* figurative.
Bildnis ['bɪltnɪs], *n.* (**—ses**, *pl.* **—se**) portrait, figure, image, effigy.
bildsam ['bɪltza:m], *adj.* plastic, ductile.
bildschön ['bɪltʃø:n], *adj.* very beautiful.
Bildseite ['bɪltzaɪtə], *f.* (**—**, *pl.* **—n**) (*coin*) face, obverse.
Bildung ['bɪlduŋ], *f.* (**—**, *pl.* (*rare*) **—en**) formation; (*mind*) education, culture; knowledge, learning, accomplishments, attainments.
Billard ['bɪljart], *n.* (**—s**, *pl.* **—s**) billiards.
Billett [bɪl'jɛt], *n.* (**—s**, *pl.* **—s**) ticket.
billig ['bɪlɪç], *adj.* cheap, inexpensive; equitable, just, fair, reasonable.
billigen ['bɪlɪgən], *v.a.* sanction, approve of, consent to.
Billigkeit ['bɪlɪçkaɪt], *f.* (**—**, *no pl.*) cheapness; fairness, equitableness, reasonableness.
Billigung ['bɪlɪguŋ], *f.* (**—**, *no pl.*) approbation, approval, sanction.
Bilsenkraut ['bɪlzənkraut], *n.* (**—s**, *pl.* **¨er**) henbane.
bimmeln ['bɪməln], *v.n.* (*coll.*) tinkle.
Bimsstein ['bɪmsʃtaɪn], *m.* (**—s**, *pl.* **—e**) pumice stone.
Binde ['bɪndə], *f.* (**—**, *pl.* **—n**) band, bandage; tie; ligature; sanitary towel.
Bindeglied ['bɪndegli:t], *n.* (**—s**, *pl.* **—er**) connecting link.
Bindehaut ['bɪndəhaut], *f.* (**—**, *pl.* **¨e**) (*Anat.*) conjunctiva.
Bindehautentzündung ['bɪndəhautɛntsynduŋ], *f.* (**—**, *pl.* **—en**) conjunctivitis.

binden ['bɪndən], *v.a. irr.* bind, tie, fasten.
Bindestrich ['bɪndeʃtrɪç], *m.* (—(e)s, *pl.* —e) hyphen.
Bindewort ['bɪndəvɔrt], *n.* (—s, *pl.* ¨er) conjunction.
Bindfaden ['bɪntfa:dən], *m.* (—s, *pl.* ¨) string, twine.
Bindung ['bɪnduŋ], *f.* (—, *pl.* —en) binding, bond; obligation; (*Mus.*) ligature.
binnen ['bɪnən], *prep.* (*Genit. & Dat.*), *adv.* within.
Binnenhafen ['bɪnənha:fən], *m.* (—s, *pl.* ¨) inland harbour.
Binnenhandel ['bɪnənhandəl], *m.* (—s, *no pl.*) inland trade.
Binse ['bɪnzə], *f.* (—, *pl.* —n) (*Bot.*) rush, reed.
Biographie [biogra'fi:], *f.* (—, *pl.* —n) biography.
Birke ['bɪrkə], *f.* (—, *pl.* —n) (*Bot.*) birch, birch-tree.
Birma ['bɪrma:], *n.* Burma.
Birnbaum ['bɪrnbaum], *m.* (—s, *pl.* ¨e) pear-tree.
Birne ['bɪrnə], *f.* (—, *pl.* —n) pear; (*Elec.*) bulb.
birnförmig ['bɪrnfœrmɪç], *adj.* pear-shaped.
bis [bɪs], *prep.* (*time*) till, until; by; (*place*) to, up to; — *auf*, with the exception of. — *conj.* till, until.
Bisam ['bi:zam], *m.* (—s, *pl.* —e) musk.
Bischof ['bɪʃɔf], *m.* (—s, *pl.* ¨e) bishop.
bischöflich ['bɪʃœflɪç], *adj.* episcopal.
Bischofsstab ['bɪʃɔfsʃta:p], *m.* (—s, *pl.* ¨e) crosier.
bisher ['bɪshe:r], *adv.* hitherto, till now.
bisherig [bɪs'he:rɪç], *adj.* up to this time, hitherto existing.
Biskayischer Meerbusen [bɪs'ka:ɪʃər 'me:rbu:zən]. Bay of Biscay.
Biß [bɪs], *m.* (—sses, *pl.* —sse) bite, sting.
Bißchen ['bɪsçən], *n.* (—s, *pl.* —) morsel; little bit.
Bissen ['bɪsən], *m.* (—s, *pl.* —) bite, morsel.
bissig ['bɪsɪç], *adj.* biting, cutting; sharp, vicious; sarcastic.
Bistum ['bɪstum], *n.* (—s, *pl.* ¨er) bishopric, diocese; see.
bisweilen [bɪs'vaɪlən], *adv.* sometimes, now and then, occasionally.
Bitte ['bɪtə], *f.* (—, *pl.* —n) request, entreaty.
bitte ['bɪtə], *int.* please.
bitten ['bɪtən], *v.a. irr.* ask; request.
bitter ['bɪtər], *adj.* bitter.
Bitterkeit ['bɪtərkaɪt], *f.* (—, *no pl.*) bitterness.
bitterlich ['bɪtərlɪç], *adv.* (*fig.*) bitterly.
Bittersalz ['bɪtərzalts], *n.* (—es, *no pl.*) Epsom salts.
Bittgang ['bɪtgaŋ], *m.* (—(e)s, *pl.* ¨e) (*Eccl.*) procession.
Bittsteller ['bɪtʃtɛlər], *m.* (—s, *pl.* —) petitioner, suppli(c)ant.
Biwak ['bi:vak], *m.* (—s, *pl.* —s) bivouac.
blähen ['blɛ:ən], *v.a.* inflate, puff up, swell.
Blähung ['blɛ:uŋ], *f.* (—, *pl.* —en) (*Med.*) flatulence.
blaken ['bla:kən], *v.n.* smoulder; smoke.
Blamage [bla'ma:ʒə], *f.* (—, *pl.* —n) shame, disgrace.
blamieren [bla'mi:rən], *v.a.*, *v.r.* make (o.s.) ridiculous, make a fool of o.s.
blank [blaŋk], *adj.* shining, bright, smooth, polished.
Bläschen ['blɛ:sçən], *n.* (—s, *pl.* —) little bubble, blister; (*Med.*) vesicle.
Blase ['bla:zə], *f.* (—, *pl.* —n) (*soap*) bubble; (*skin*) blister; (*Anat.*) bladder.
Blasebalg ['bla:zəbalk], *m.* (—s, *pl.* ¨e) pair of bellows.
blasen ['bla:zən], *v.a. irr.* blow; (*Mus.*) sound.
Bläser ['blɛ:zər], *m.* (—s, *pl.* —) (*glass*) blower; (*Mus.*) wind player.
blasiert [bla'zi:rt], *adj.* blasé, haughty.
Blasrohr ['bla:sro:r], *n.* (—s, *pl.* —e) blow-pipe, pea-shooter.
blaß [blas], *adj.* pale, wan, pallid.
Blässe ['blɛsə], *f.* (—, *no pl.*) paleness, pallor.
Blatt [blat], *n.* (—s, *pl.* ¨er) leaf; (*paper*) sheet; blade.
Blatter ['blatər], *f.* (—, *pl.* —n) pustule; (*pl.*) smallpox.
blättern ['blɛtərn], *v.a.* turn the leaves (of a book).
Blätterteig ['blɛtərtaɪk], *m.* (—s, *no pl.*) puff pastry.
Blattgold ['blatgɔlt], *n.* (—es, *no pl.*) gold-leaf.
Blattlaus ['blatlaus], *f.* (—, *pl.* ¨e) (*Ent.*) plant-louse.
Blattpflanze ['blatpflantsə], *f.* (—, *pl.* —n) leaf-plant.
blau [blau], *adj.* blue; *—en Montag machen*, stay away from work; *sein —es Wunder erleben*, be amazed.
blauäugig ['blauɔygɪç], *adj.* blue-eyed.
Blaubeere ['blaube:rə], *f.* (—, *pl.* —n) bilberry, blueberry.
blaublütig ['blaubly:tɪç], *adj.* aristocratic.
bläuen ['blauən], *v.a.* dye blue, rinse in blue.
bläulich ['blɔylɪç], *adj.* pale blue, bluish.
Blausäure ['blauzɔyrə], *f.* (—, *no pl.*) prussic acid.
Blaustrumpf ['blauʃtrumpf], *m.* (—s, *pl.* ¨e) blue-stocking.
Blech [blɛç], *n.* (—s, *pl.* —e) tinplate, sheet metal.
blechen ['blɛçən], *v.n.* (*coll.*) fork out money.
blechern ['blɛçərn], *adj.* made of tin, tinny.
Blechinstrument ['blɛçɪnstrumɛnt], *n.* (—s, *pl.* —e) (*Mus.*) brass instrument.

Blei [blaɪ], *n.* (**—s**, *no pl.*) lead.
bleiben [ˈblaɪbən], *v.n. irr.* (*aux.* sein) remain, stay.
bleich [blaɪç], *adj.* pale, wan, pallid.
Bleiche [ˈblaɪçə], *f.* (—, *pl.* **—n**) pallor; (*laundry*) bleaching-place.
bleichen [ˈblaɪçən], *v.a. irr.* bleach, whiten.
Bleichsucht [ˈblaɪçzuxt], *f.* (—, *no pl.*) chlorosis, anaemia.
bleiern [ˈblaɪərn], *adj.* leaden.
Bleiglanz [ˈblaɪglants], *m.* (**—es**, *no pl.*) (*Min.*) lead sulphide.
Bleisoldat [ˈblaɪzɔlda:t], *m.* (**—en**, *pl.* **—en**) tin soldier.
Bleistift [ˈblaɪʃtɪft], *m.* (**—s**, *pl.* **—e**) pencil.
Blende [ˈblɛndə], *f.* (—, *no pl.*) blind; (*Min.*) blende; (*Phot.*) shutter.
blenden [ˈblɛndən], *v.a.* dazzle, blind.
Blendlaterne [ˈblɛntlatɛrnə], *f.* (—, *pl.* **—n**) dark-lantern.
Blendung [ˈblɛnduŋ], *f.* (—, *pl.* **—en**) blinding, dazzling.
Blendwerk [ˈblɛntvɛrk], *n.* (**—s**, *no pl.*) (optical) illusion, false show.
Blick [blɪk], *m.* (**—s**, *pl.* **—e**) glance, look, glimpse.
blicken [ˈblɪkən], *v.n.* look, glance.
blind [blɪnt], *adj.* blind, sightless; *—er Passagier*, stowaway.
Blinddarm [ˈblɪntdarm], *m.* (**—s**, *pl.* **¨e**) appendix.
Blinddarmentzündung [ˈblɪntdarmɛntsynduŋ], *f.* (—, *pl.* **—en**) appendicitis.
Blindekuh [blɪndəˈku:], *f.* (—, *no pl.*) blind man's buff.
Blindgänger [ˈblɪntgɛŋər], *m.* (**—s**, *pl.* —) misfire, dud, blind.
Blindheit [ˈblɪnthaɪt], *f.* (—, *no pl.*) blindness.
blindlings [ˈblɪntlɪŋs], *adv.* blindly; at random.
Blindschleiche [ˈblɪntʃlaɪçə], *f.* (—, *pl.* **—n**) (*Zool.*) blind-worm.
blinken [ˈblɪŋkən], *v.n.* blink, flash, glitter, gleam.
blinzeln [ˈblɪntsəln], *v.n.* blink.
Blitz [blɪts], *m.* (**—es**, *pl.* **—e**) lightning, flash.
Blitzableiter [ˈblɪtsaplaɪtər], *m.* (**—s**, *pl.* —) lightning-conductor.
blitzblank [ˈblɪtsblaŋk], *adj.* as bright as a new pin; shining.
blitzen [ˈblɪtsən], *v.n.* flash; *es blitzt*, it is lightening; glitter, shine.
Blitzesschnelle [ˈblɪtsəsʃnɛlə], *f.* (—, *no pl.*) lightning-speed.
Blitzlicht [ˈblɪtslɪçt], *n.* (**—s**, *no pl.*) flashlight.
Blitzschlag [ˈblɪtsʃla:k], *m.* (**—s**, *pl.* **¨e**) flash of lightning.
Blitzstrahl [ˈblɪtsʃtra:l], *m.* (**—s**, *pl.* **—en**) flash of lightning.
Block [blɔk], *m.* (**—s**, *pl.* **¨e**) block, log; pad.
Blockhaus [ˈblɔkhaus], *n.* (**—es**, *pl.* **¨er**) log-cabin.
blockieren [blɔˈki:rən], *v.a.* block (up); (*Mil.*) blockade.
blöde [ˈblø:də], *adj.* stupid, dull, thick-headed, dim.
Blödsinn [ˈblø:tsɪn], *m.* (**—s**, *no pl.*) nonsense, idiocy.
blöken [ˈblø:kən], *v.n.* bleat; (*cows*) low.
blond [blɔnt], *adj.* blond, fair, fair-headed.
bloß [blo:s], *adj.* naked, uncovered; bare, mere.
Blöße [ˈblø:sə], *f.* (—, *pl.* **—n**) nakedness, bareness; (*fig.*) weak point.
bloßlegen [ˈblo:sle:gən], *v.a.* uncover, lay bare; (*fig.*) reveal, expose.
bloßstellen [ˈblo:sʃtɛlən], *v.a.* compromise, show up. — *v.r.* *sich* —, compromise o.s.
blühen [ˈbly:ən], *v.n.* bloom, blossom, flower, flourish.
Blümchen [ˈbly:mçən], *n.* (**—s**, *pl.* —) small flower.
Blume [ˈblu:mə], *f.* (—, *pl.* **—n**) flower, bloom; (*wine*) bouquet; (*beer*) froth.
Blumenblatt [ˈblu:mənblat], *n.* (**—s**, *pl.* **¨er**) petal.
Blumenerde [ˈblu:məne:rdə], *f.* (—, *no pl.*) garden mould.
Blumenkelch [ˈblu:mənkɛlç], *m.* (**—es**, *pl.* **—e**) calyx.
Blumenkohl [ˈblu:mənko:l], *m.* (**—s**, *pl.* **—e**) cauliflower.
Blumenstaub [ˈblu:mənʃtaup], *m.* (**—s**, *no pl.*) pollen.
Blumenstrauß [ˈblu:mənʃtraus], *m.* (**—es**, *pl.* **¨e**) bunch of flowers, posy, nosegay.
Blumenzucht [ˈblu:məntsuxt], *f.* (—, *no pl.*) floriculture.
Bluse [ˈblu:zə], *f.* (—, *pl.* **—n**) blouse.
Blut [blu:t], *n.* (**—es**, *no pl.*) blood.
blutarm [ˈblu:tarm], *adj.* anæmic; (*fig.*) very poor.
Blutbad [ˈblu:tba:t], *n.* (**—es**, *pl.* **¨er**) massacre.
blutdürstig [ˈblu:tdyrstɪç], *adj.* bloodthirsty.
Blüte [ˈbly:tə], *f.* (—, *pl.* **—n**) blossom, flower, bloom.
Blutegel [ˈblu:te:gəl], *m.* (**—s**, *pl.* —) leech.
bluten [ˈblu:tən], *v.n.* bleed.
Bluterguß [ˈblu:tɛrgus], *m.* (**—es**, *pl.* **¨e**) effusion of blood.
Blutgefäß [ˈblu:tgəfɛ:s], *n.* (**—es**, *pl.* **—e**) blood-vessel.
blutig [ˈblu:tɪç], *adj.* bloody; cruel.
blutjung [ˈblu:tjuŋ], *adj.* very young.
Blutkörperchen [ˈblu:tkœrpərçən], *n.* (**—s**, *pl.* —) blood-corpuscle.
Blutlassen [ˈblu:tlasən], *n.* (**—s**, *no pl.*) (*Med.*) bloodletting.
Blutrache [ˈblu:traxə], *f.* (—, *no pl.*) vendetta.
Blutsauger [ˈblu:tzaugər], *m.* (**—s**, *pl.* —) vampire.
Blutschande [ˈblu:tʃandə], *f.* (—, *no pl.*) incest.

blutstillend ['blu:ʃtɪlənt], *adj.* styptic, blood-stanching.
Blutsturz ['blu:tʃturts], *m.* (—**es**, *no pl.*) haemorrhage; *einen — haben*, burst a blood-vessel.
Blutsverwandte ['blu:tsfɛrvantə], *m.* or *f.* (—**n**, *pl.* —**n**) blood-relation.
Blutvergießen ['blu:tfɛrgi:sən], *n.* (—**s**, *no pl.*) bloodshed.
Blutvergiftung ['blu:tfɛrgɪftuŋ], *f.* (—, *pl.* —**en**) blood poisoning.
Blutwurst ['blu:tvurst], *f.* (—, *pl.* ⸚**e**) black-pudding.
Blutzeuge ['blu:ttsɔygə], *m.* (—**n**, *pl.* —**n**) martyr.
Bö [bø:], *f.* (—, *pl.* —**en**) (*Naut.*) squall, gust of wind.
Bock [bɔk], *m.* (—**s**, *pl.* ⸚**e**) buck; he-goat; (*Gymn.*) horse; (*horse-drawn carriage*) box seat.
bockbeinig ['bɔkbaɪnɪç], *adj.* bow-legged; pigheaded, obstinate.
Bockbier ['bɔkbi:r], *n.* (—**s**, *no pl.*) bock beer.
bocken ['bɔkən], *v.n.* kick, be refractory; sulk.
Bockfell ['bɔkfɛl], *n.* (—**s**, *pl.* —**e**) buckskin.
bockig ['bɔkɪç], *adj.* pigheaded, obstinate.
Bocksbeutel ['bɔksbɔytəl], *m.* (—**s**, *pl.* —) leather bag; Franconian wine (bottle).
Bockshorn ['bɔkshɔrn], *n.* (—**s**, *pl.* ⸚**er**) buck horn; *einen ins — jagen*, intimidate s.o.
Boden ['bo:dən], *m.* (—**s**, *pl.* ⸚) ground, bottom, soil, floor; garret, loft.
Bodenfenster ['bo:dənfɛnstər], *n.* (—**s**, *pl.* —) attic window.
Bodenkammer ['bo:dənkamər], *f.* (—, *pl.* —**n**) garret, attic.
bodenlos ['bo:dənlo:s], *adj.* bottomless; (*fig.*) unimaginable, enormous.
Bodensatz ['bo:dənzats], *m.* (—**es**, *pl.* ⸚**e**) sediment, dregs, deposit.
Bodensee ['bo:dənze:], *m.* Lake Constance.
Bogen ['bo:gən], *m.* (—**s**, *pl.* —, ⸚) arch, vault, curve; (*Maths.*) arc; (*violin*) bow; (*paper*) sheet; (*Mus.*) ligature.
bogenförmig ['bo:gənfœrmɪç], *adj.* arch-shaped, arched.
Bogenführung ['bo:gənfy:ruŋ], *f.* (—, *no pl.*) (*Mus.*) bowing (technique).
Bogengang ['bo:gəngaŋ], *m.* (—**es**, *pl.* ⸚**e**) arcade.
Bogenlampe ['bo:gənlampə], *f.* (—, *pl.* —**n**) arc-lamp.
Bogenschütze ['bo:gənʃytsə], *m.* (—**n**, *pl.* —**n**) archer.
bogig ['bo:gɪç], *adj.* bent, curved, arched.
Bohle ['bo:lə], *f.* (—, *pl.* —**n**) board, plank.
Böhmen ['bø:mən], *n.* Bohemia.
Bohne ['bo:nə], *f.* (—, *pl.* —**n**) bean; *grüne —n*, French (*Am.* string) beans; *dicke —n*, broad beans; *blaue —n*, (*fig.*) bullets.
Bohnenstange ['bo:nənʃtaŋə], *f.* (—, *pl.* —**n**) bean-pole.
Bohnerbürste ['bo:nərbyrstə], *f.* (—, *pl.* —**n**) polishing-brush.
bohnern ['bo:nərn], *v.a.* polish, wax.
bohren ['bo:rən], *v.a.* bore, pierce, drill.
Bohrer ['bo:rər], *m.* (—**s**, *pl.* —) gimlet; drill.
Bohrturm ['bo:rturm], *m.* (—**s**, *pl.* ⸚**e**) derrick.
Boje ['bo:jə], *f.* (—, *pl.* —**n**) (*Naut.*) buoy.
Bolivien [bɔ'li:vjən], *n.* Bolivia.
Böller ['bœlər], *m.* (—**s**, *pl.* —) (*Mil.*) small mortar.
Bollwerk ['bɔlvɛrk], *n.* (—**s**, *pl.* —**e**) bulwark.
Bolzen ['bɔltsən], *m.* (—**s**, *pl.* —) bolt, arrow, pin; (*smoothing iron*) heater.
Bombe ['bɔmbə], *f.* (—, *pl.* —**n**) bomb, bomb-shell.
Bombenerfolg ['bɔmbənɛrfɔlk], *m.* (—(**e**)**s**, *pl.* —**e**) (*Theat.*) smash hit.
Bonbon [bɔ̃'bɔ̃], *m.* (—**s**, *pl.* —**s**) sweet(s), bonbon; (*Am.*) candy.
Bonbonniere [bɔ̃bɔ'njɛ:rə], *f.* (—, *pl.* —**n**) box of sweets.
Bonze ['bɔntsə], *m.* (—**n**, *pl.* —**n**) (*coll.*) bigwig, (*Am.*) big shot.
Boot [bo:t], *n.* (—**es**, *pl.* —**e**) boat.
Bootsanker ['bo:tsaŋkər], *m.* (—**s**, *pl.* —) grapnel.
Bootsleine ['bo:tslaɪnə], *f.* (—, *pl.* —**n**) tow-rope.
Bor [bɔ:r], *n.* (—**s**, *no pl.*) (*Chem.*) boron.
Bord [bɔrt], *m.* (—**s**, *pl.* —**e**) rim; (*Naut.*) board.
Bordell [bɔr'dɛl], *n.* (—**s**, *pl.* —**e**) brothel.
borgen ['bɔrgən], *v.a.*, *v.n.* borrow; borrow (*von*, from); lend (*Dat.*, to).
Borke ['bɔrkə], *f.* (—, *pl.* —**n**) bark, rind.
Born [bɔrn], *m.* (—**es**, —**e**) (*Poet.*) bourn, spring, well, source.
borniert [bɔr'ni:rt], *adj.* narrow-minded
Borsäure ['bo:rzɔyrə], *f.* (—, *no pl.*) boric acid.
Börse ['børzə], *f.* (—, *pl.* —**n**) purse; (*Comm.*) stock-exchange, bourse.
Börsenbericht ['børzənbərɪçt], *m.* (—**s**, *pl.* —**e**) stock-market report.
Borste ['bɔrstə], *f.* (—, *pl.* —**n**) bristle.
borstig ['bɔrstɪç], *adj.* bristly; (*fig.*) irritable.
Borte ['bɔrtə], *f.* (—, *pl.* —**n**) border, trimming.
bösartig ['bø:sartɪç], *adj.* malevolent, malicious, vicious; (*disease*) malignant.
Böschung ['bøʃuŋ], *f.* (—, *pl.* —**en**) slope, scarp.
böse ['bø:zə], *adj.* bad, wicked; evil; angry, cross (with, *Dat.*); — *auf* (*Acc.*), angry with s.o., (*Am.*) mad at s.o.
Bösewicht ['bø:zəvɪçt], *m.* (—**s**, *pl.* —**er**) villain, ruffian; wretch.

boshaft ['bo:shaft], *adj.* spiteful, malicious.
Bosheit ['bo:shaɪt], *f.* (—, *pl.* **—en**) malice.
böswillig ['bø:svɪlɪç], *adj.* malevolent.
Botanik [bo'ta:nɪk], *f.* (—, *no pl.*) botany.
Botaniker [bo'ta:nɪkər], *m.* (**—s**, *pl.* —) botanist.
Botanisiertrommel [botanɪ'zi:rtrɔməl], *f.* (—, *pl.* **—n**) specimen-box.
Bote ['bo:tə], *m.* (**—n**, *pl.* **—n**) messenger.
Botengang ['bo:təngaŋ], *m.* (**—s**, *pl.* **¨e**) errand.
botmäßig [bo:tmɛ:sɪç], *adj.* subject, subordinate.
Botschaft ['bo:tʃaft], *f.* (—, *pl.* **—en**) message; (*Pol.*) embassy; *gute* —, glad tidings.
Botschafter ['bo:tʃaftər], *m.* (**—s**, *pl.* —) ambassador.
Böttcher ['bœtçər], *m.* (**—s**, *pl.* —) cooper.
Bottich [bɔtɪç], *m.* (**—s**, *pl.* **—e**) vat, tub.
Bouillon [bul'jɔ̃], *f.* (—, *no pl.*) broth, meat soup.
Bowle ['bo:lə], *f.* (—, *no pl.*) bowl; spiced wine.
boxen ['bɔksən], *v.n.* box.
brach [bra:x], *adj.* fallow, unploughed, untilled.
Brand [brant], *m.* (**—es**, *pl.* **¨e**) burning, fire, combustion, conflagration; (*Med.*) gangrene.
Brandblase ['brantbla:zə], *f.* (—, *pl.* **—n**) blister.
branden ['brandən], *v.n.* surge, break (waves).
brandig ['brandɪç], *adj.* blighted; (*Med.*) gangrenous.
Brandmal ['brantma:l], *n.* (**—s**, *pl.* **—e**) burn mark; brand (cattle); (*fig.*) stigma.
brandmarken ['brantmarkən], *v.a.* brand; (*fig.*) stigmatise.
Brandmauer ['brantmauər], *f.* (—, *pl.* **—n**) fire-proof wall.
brandschatzen ['brantʃatsən], *v.a.* levy contributions (from); pillage, plunder.
Brandsohle ['brantzo:lə], *f.* (—, *pl.* **—n**) inner sole, welt (of shoe).
Brandstifter ['brantʃtɪftər], *m.* (**—s**, *pl.* —) incendiary, fire-raiser.
Brandstiftung ['brantʃtɪftuŋ], *f.* (—, *pl.* **—en**) arson.
Brandung ['branduŋ], *f.* (—, *pl.* **—en**) breakers, surf, surge (of sea).
Branntwein ['brantvaɪn], *m.* (**—s**, *pl.* **—e**) brandy.
Brasilien [bra'zi:ljən], *n.* Brazil.
Braten ['bra:tən], *m.* (**—s**, *pl.* —) roast (meat), joint.
braten ['bra:tən], *v.a. reg. & irr.* roast, broil, bake, fry, grill. — *v.n.* (*coll.*) bask (in sun), roast.
Brathering ['bra:the:rɪŋ], *m.* (**—s**, *pl.* **—e**) grilled herring.
Brathuhn ['bra:thu:n], *n.* (**—s**, *pl.* **¨er**) roast chicken.
Bratkartoffeln ['bra:tkartɔfəln], *f. pl.* roast *or* fried potatoes.
Bratpfanne ['bra:tpfanə], *f.* (—, *pl.* **—n**) frying pan.
Bratsche ['bratʃə], *f.* (—, *pl.* **—n**) (*Mus.*) viola.
Bratspieß ['bra:tʃpi:s], *m.* (**—es**, *pl.* **—e**) spit (roasting).
Bratwurst ['bra:tvurst], *f.* (—, *pl.* **¨e**) sausage for frying; fried sausage.
Brau [brau], **Bräu**, [brɔy], *n. & m.* (**—s**, *no pl.*) brew.
Brauch [braux], *m.* (**—es**, *pl.* **¨e**) usage, custom, habit.
brauchbar ['brauxba:r], *adj.* useful, serviceable.
brauchen ['brauxən], *v.a.* make use of, employ; need, require, want; (*time*) take.
Braue ['brauə], *f.* (—, *pl.* **—n**) brow, eye-brow.
brauen ['brauən], *v.a.* brew.
Brauer ['brauər], *m.* (**—s**, *pl.* —) brewer.
Brauerei ['brauəraɪ], *f.* (—, *pl.* **—en**) brewery.
Brauhaus ['brauhaus], *n.* (**—es**, *pl.* **¨er**) brewery.
braun [braun], *adj.* brown.
bräunen ['brɔynən], *v.a.* make brown, tan.
Braunkohl ['braunko:l], *m.* (**—s**, *no pl.*) (*Bot.*) broccoli.
Braunschweig ['braunʃvaɪk], *n.* Brunswick.
Braus [braus], *m.* (**—es**, *no pl.*) bustle, tumult; *in Saus und — leben*, lead a riotous life.
Brause ['brauzə], *f.* (—, *pl.* **—n**) shower (bath); effervescence, (*coll.*) fizzy drink.
Brausekopf ['brauzəkɔpf], *m.* (**—es**, *pl.* **¨e**) hothead.
Brauselimonade ['brauzəlɪmona:də], *f.* (—, *pl.* **—n**) effervescent *or* fizzy lemonade.
brausen ['brauzən], *v.n.* roar, bluster, rush; effervesce.
Brausepulver ['brauzəpulvər], *n.* (**—s**, *pl.* —) effervescent powder.
Braut [braut], *f.* (—, *pl.* **¨e**) bride, betrothed, fiancée.
Brautführer ['brautfy:rər], *m.* (**—s**, *pl.* —) best man.
Bräutigam ['brɔytɪgam], *m.* (**—s**, *pl.* **—e**) bridegroom, betrothed, fiancé.
Brautjungfer ['brautjuŋfər], *f.* (—, *pl.* **—n**) bridesmaid.
bräutlich ['brɔytlɪç], *adj.* bridal.
Brautpaar ['brautpa:r], *n.* (**—es**, *pl.* **—e**) engaged couple.
Brautschau ['brautʃau], *f.* (—, *no pl.*) (*obs.*) search for a wife.
brav [bra:f], *adj.* honest, upright, worthy, honourable; well-behaved, good.
bravo! ['bra:vo], *int.* well done!

Bravourstück [bra'vu:rʃtyk], *n.* (—**s**, *pl.* —**e**) feat of valour.
Brechbohnen ['brɛçbo:nən], *f. pl.* kidney-beans.
Brecheisen ['brɛçaɪzən], *n.* (—**s**, *pl.* —) jemmy.
brechen ['brɛçən], *v.a. irr.* break; (*flowers*) pluck, pick; vomit. — *v.n.* (*aux.* sein) break.
Brechmittel ['brɛçmɪtəl], *n.* (—**s**, *pl.* —) emetic.
Brechruhr ['brɛçru:r], *f.* (—, *no pl.*) cholera.
Brechstange ['brɛçʃtaŋə], *f.* (—, *pl.* —**n**) crow-bar.
Brechung ['brɛçuŋ], *f.* (—, *pl.* —**en**) breaking; (*Phys.*) refraction.
Brei [braɪ], *m.* (—**s**, *pl.* —**e**) pap, pulp, porridge.
breiartig ['braɪa:rtɪç], *adj.* pulpy.
breiig ['braɪɪç], *adj.* pappy.
breit [braɪt], *adj.* broad, wide.
breitbeinig ['braɪtbaɪnɪç], *adj.* straddle-legged.
Breite ['braɪtə], *f.* (—, *pl.* —**n**) breadth, width; (*Geog.*) latitude.
Breitengrad ['braɪtəngra:t], *m.* (—**es**, *pl.* —**e**) (*Geog.*) degree of latitude.
Breitenkreis ['braɪtənkraɪs], *m.* (—**es**, *pl.* —**e**) (*Geog.*) parallel.
breitschultrig ['braɪtʃultrɪç], *adj.* broad-shouldered.
Bremse ['brəmzə], *f.* (—, *pl.* —**n**) (*Ent.*) gad-fly; (*Motor.*) brake; (*horse*) barnacle.
bremsen ['brɛmzən], *v.a.* brake, pull up.
brennbar ['brɛnba:r], *adj.* combustible.
Brenneisen ['brɛnaɪzən], *n.* (—**s**, *pl.* —) branding iron.
brennen ['brɛnən], *v.a. irr.* burn; (*Med.*) cauterise; (*alcohol*) distil; (*hair*) curl; (*coffee*) roast; (*coal*) char; (*bricks*) bake. — *v.n.* burn; (*fig.*) sting; (*eyes*) smart.
Brenner ['brɛnər], *m.* (—**s**, *pl.* —) (*person*) distiller; (*Tech.*) burner.
Brennerei [brɛnə'raɪ], *f.* (—, *pl.* —**en**) distillery.
Brennessel ['brɛnnɛsəl], *f.* (—, *pl.* —**n**) stinging nettle.
Brennholz ['brɛnhɔlts], *n.* (—**es**, *no pl.*) firewood.
Brennmaterial ['brɛnmaterja:l], *n.* (—**s**, *pl.* —**ien**) fuel.
Brennofen ['brɛno:fən], *m.* (—**s**, *pl.* ¨**n**) kiln.
Brennpunkt ['brɛnpuŋkt], *m.* (—**s**, *pl.* —**e**) focus.
Brennschere ['brɛnʃe:rə], *f.* (—, *pl.* —**n**) curling-irons.
Brennstoff ['brɛnʃtɔf], *m.* (—(**e**)**s**, *pl.* —**e**) fuel.
brenzlich ['brɛntslɪç], *adj.* smelling (*or* tasting) of burning; (*fig.*) ticklish.
Bresche ['brɛʃə], *f.* (—, *pl.* —**n**) breach, gap.
Brett [brɛt], *n.* (—**s**, *pl.* —**er**) board, plank, shelf.
Brettspiel ['brɛtʃpi:l], *n.* (—**s**, *pl.* —**e**) table-game.
Brevier [bre'vi:r], *n.* (—**s**, *pl.* (*rare*) —**e**) breviary.
Brezel ['bre:tsəl], *f.* (—, *pl.* —**n**) cracknel, pretzel.
Brief [bri:f], *m.* (—**es**, *pl.* —**e**) letter; epistle.
Briefanschrift ['bri:fanʃrɪft], *f.* (—, *pl.* —**en**) address.
Briefbeschwerer ['bri:fbəʃve:rər], *m.* (—**s**, *pl.* —) letter-weight, paper-weight.
Briefbogen ['bri:fbo:gən], *m.* (—**s**, *pl.* —) sheet of notepaper.
Briefkasten ['bri:fkastən], *m.* (—**s**, *pl.* ¨) (*house*) letter-box; (*street*) pillar-box, (*Am.*) post-box.
brieflich ['bri:flɪç], *adv.* by letter, in writing.
Briefmarke ['bri:fmarkə], *f.* (—, *pl.* —**n**) postage stamp.
Briefpapier ['bri:fpapi:r], *n.* (—**s**, *no pl.*) notepaper.
Briefporto ['bri:fpɔrto], *n.* (—**s**, *pl.* —**ti**) postage.
Brieftasche ['bri:ftaʃə], *f.* (—, *pl.* —**n**) portfolio, wallet; (*Am.*) pocket-book.
Brieftaube ['bri:ftaubə], *f.* (—, *pl.* —**n**) carrier pigeon.
Briefträger ['bri:ftrɛ:gər], *m.* (—**s**, *pl.* —) postman.
Briefumschlag ['bri:fumʃla:k], *m.* (—**s**, *pl.* ¨**e**) envelope.
Briefwechsel ['bri:fvɛksəl], *m.* (—**s**, *no pl.*) correspondence.
Brillant [bril'jant], *m.* (—**en**, *pl.* —**en**) brilliant, diamond. — *adj.* brilliant.
Brille ['brɪle], *f.* (— *pl.* —**n**) spectacles, glasses.
Brillenschlange ['brɪlənʃlaŋə], *f.* (—, *pl.* —**n**) (*Zool.*) hooded cobra.
bringen ['brɪŋən], *v.a. irr.* bring, fetch, carry to, take to, conduct to.
Brise ['bri:zə], *f.* (—, *pl.* —**n**) breeze, light wind.
Britannien [brɪ'tanjən], *n.* Britain.
bröckeln ['brœkəln], *v.a.*, *v.n.* crumble.
Brocken ['brɔkən], *m.* (—**s**, *pl.* —) bit, piece, fragment, scrap; (*bread*) crumb.
bröcklig ['brœklɪç], *adj.* crumbling.
brodeln ['bro:dəln], *v.n.* bubble, simmer.
Brodem ['bro:dəm], *m.* (—**s**, *no pl.*) (*Poet.*) steam, vapour, exhalation.
Brokat [bro'ka:t], *m.* (—**s**, *pl.* —**e**) brocade.
Brom [bro:m], *n.* (—**s**, *no pl.*) (*Chem.*) bromine.
Brombeere ['brɔmbe:rə], *f.* (—, *pl.* —**n**) blackberry, bramble.
Bronze ['brɔ̃:sə], *f.* (—, *pl.* —**n**) bronze.
Brosamen ['bro:za:mən], *pl.* crumbs.
Brosche ['brɔʃə], *f.* (—, *pl.* —**n**) brooch.
Broschüre [brɔ'ʃy:rə], *f.* (—, *pl.* —**n**) pamphlet, brochure, folder.
Brösel ['brø:zəl], *m.* (—**s**, *pl.* —) crumb.
Brot [bro:t], *n.* (—**es**, *pl.* —**e**) bread, loaf; (*fig.*) livelihood.
Brötchen ['brø:tçən], *n.* (—**s**, *pl.* —) roll, bread-roll.

Broterwerb ['bro:tərvɛrp], *m.* (—**s**, *no pl.*) livelihood.
Brotgeber ['bro:tge:bər], *m.* (—**s**, *pl.* —) employer, master.
Brotherr ['bro:thɛr], *m.* (—**n**, *pl.* —**en**) employer, master.
Brotkorb ['bro:tkɔrp], *m.* (—**s**, *pl.* ⁻**e**) bread-basket.
brotlos ['bro:tlo:s], *adj.* unemployed; (*fig.*) unprofitable.
Brotneid ['bro:tnaɪt], *m.* (—**s**, *no pl.*) professional jealousy.
Bruch [brux], *m.* (—**s**, *pl.* ⁻**e**) breakage; rupture; (*Med.*) fracture, rupture, hernia; (*Maths.*) fraction.
Bruchband ['bruxbant], *f.* (—**es**, *pl.* ⁻**er**) abdominal belt, truss.
brüchig ['bryçɪç], *adj.* brittle, full of flaws.
Bruchlandung ['bruxlanduŋ], *f.* (—, —**en**) (*Aviat.*) crash-landing.
Bruchrechnung ['bruxrɛçnuŋ], *f.* (—, *pl.* —**en**) (*Arith.*) fractions.
Bruchstück ['bruxʃtyk], *n.* (—**s**, *pl.* —**e**) fragment, scrap.
Bruchteil ['bruxtaɪl], *m.* (—**s**, *pl.* —**e**) fraction.
Brücke ['brykə], *f.* (—, *pl.* —**n**) bridge.
Brückenpfeiler ['brykənpfaɪlər], *m.* (—**s**, *pl.* —) pier.
Bruder ['bru:dər], *m.* (—**s**, *pl.* ⁻) brother; (*Eccl.*) friar.
brüderlich ['bry:dərlɪç], *adj.* fraternal, brotherly.
Bruderschaft ['bru:dərʃaft], *f.* (—, *pl.* —**en**) fraternity, brotherhood.
Brügge ['brygə], *n.* Bruges.
Brühe ['bry:ə], *f.* (—, *pl.* —**n**) broth, meat-soup.
brühen ['bry:ən], *v.a.* scald.
Brühkartoffeln ['bry:kartɔfəln], *f. pl.* potatoes cooked in broth.
brüllen ['brylən], *v.n.* roar, howl, yell; (*cows*) low, bellow.
Brummbaß ['brumbas], *m.* (—**sses**, *pl.* ⁻**sse**) (*Mus.*) double-bass.
Brummeisen ['brumaɪzən], *n.* (—**s**, *pl.* —) Jew's harp.
brummen ['brumən], *v.n.* growl, grumble, hum.
Brummer ['brumər], *n.* (—**s**, *pl.* —) (*Ent.*) blue-bottle.
Brunnen ['brunən], *m.* (—**s**, *pl.* —) well, fountain, spring.
Brunnenkur ['brunənku:r], *f.* (—, *pl.* —**en**) taking of mineral waters.
Brunst [brunst], *f.* (—, *pl.* ⁻**e**) (*Zool.*) rut, heat.
Brust [brust], *f.* (—, *pl.* ⁻**e**) breast; chest; bosom.
Brustbein ['brustbaɪn], *n.* (—**s**, *pl.* —**e**) breastbone, sternum.
Brustbild ['brustbɪlt], *n.* (—**s**, *pl.* —**er**) half-length portrait.
brüsten ['brystən], *v.r.* *sich* —, boast, brag, plume o.s.
Brustfell ['brustfɛl], *n.* (—**s**, *pl.* —**e**) pleura.
Brustfellentzündung ['brustfɛlɛntsyn-duŋ], *f.* (—, *no pl.*) pleurisy.
Brusthöhle ['brusthø:lə], *f.* (—, *pl.* —**n**) thoracic cavity.
Brustkasten ['brustkastən], *m.* (—**s**, *pl.* ⁻**n**) chest.
Brusttee ['brustte:], *m.* (—**s**, *no pl.*) pectoral (herbal) tea.
Brüstung ['brystuŋ], *f.* (—, *pl.* —**en**) parapet.
Brustwarze ['brustvartsə], *f.* (—, *pl.* —**n**) nipple.
Brustwehr ['brustve:r], *f.* (—, *pl.* —**en**) breastwork, parapet.
Brut [bru:t], *f.* (—, *no pl.*) brood; (*fish*) fry.
brutal [bru'ta:l], *adj.* brutal.
brüten ['bry:tən], *v.a.* brood, hatch.
Brutofen ['bru:to:fən], *m.* (—**s**, *pl.* ⁻) incubator.
brutto ['bruto], *adv.* (*Comm.*) gross.
Bube ['bu:bə], *m.* (—**n**, *pl.* —**n**) boy, lad; (*cards*) knave, (*Am.*) jack; rogue, rascal.
Bubenstreich ['bu:bənʃtraɪç], *m.* (—**s**, *pl.* —**e**) boyish prank; knavish trick.
Bubikopf ['bu:bɪkɔpf], *m.* (—(**e**)**s**, *pl.* ⁻**e**) bobbed hair.
Buch [bu:x], *n.* (—**s**, *pl.* ⁻**er**) book; quire (of paper).
Buchdruckerei ['bu:xdrukəraɪ], *f.* (—, —**en**) printing works, printing office.
Buche ['bu:xə], *f.* (—, *pl.* —**n**) beech (tree).
buchen ['bu:xən], *v.a.* book, enter, reserve; (*fig.*) score.
Bücherei [by:çə'raɪ], *f.* (—, *pl.* —**en**) library.
Buchesche ['bu:xɛʃə], *f.* (—, *pl.* —**n**) hornbeam.
Buchfink ['bu:xfɪŋk], *m.* (—**en**, *pl.* —**en**) (*Orn.*) chaffinch.
Buchhalter ['bu:xhaltər], *m.* (—**s**, *pl.* —) book-keeper.
Buchhändler ['bu:xhɛndlər], *m.* (—**s**, *pl.* —) bookseller.
Buchmarder ['bu:xmardər], *m.* (—**s**, *pl.* —) (*Zool.*) pine-marten.
Buchsbaum ['buksbaum], *m.* (—**s**, *pl.* ⁻**e**) (*Bot.*) box-tree.
Büchse ['byksə], *f.* (—, *pl.* —**n**) box, case; tin, can; rifle, gun.
Büchsenfleisch ['byksənflaɪʃ], *n.* (—**es**, *no pl.*) tinned meat.
Büchsenlauf ['byksənlauf], *m.* (—**s**, *pl.* ⁻**e**) gun-barrel.
Büchsenöffner ['byksənœfnər], *m.* (—**s**, *pl.*—) tin-opener.
Buchstabe ['bu:xʃta:bə], *m.* (—**n**, *pl.* —**n**) letter, character; *großer* —, capital (letter).
Buchstabenrätsel ['bu:xʃta:bənrɛtsəl], *n.* (—**s**, *pl.* —) anagram.
buchstabieren [bu:xʃta'bi:rən], *v.a.* spell (out).
buchstäblich ['bu:xʃtɛplɪç], *adj.* literal.
Bucht [buxt], *f.* (—, *pl.* —**en**) inlet, bay, creek, bight.
Buchung ['bu:xuŋ], *f.* (—, *pl.* —**en**) (*Comm.*) entry (in a book); booking (of tickets).

Buchwissen ['bu:xvɪsən], *n.* (**—s**, *no pl.*) book-learning.
Buckel ['bukəl], *m.* (**—s**, *pl.* **—**) hump, humpback; boss, stud; (*coll.*) back.
bücken ['bykən], *v.r.* *sich* **—**, stoop, bow.
bucklig ['buklɪç], *adj.* humpbacked.
Bückling ['byklɪŋ], *m.* (**—s**, *pl.* **—e**) smoked herring; kipper.
buddeln ['budəln], *v.n.* (*coll.*) dig.
Bude ['bu:də], *f.* (**—**, *pl.* **—n**) shack, stall; (*coll.*) room; (*student's*) digs.
Büfett [by'fɛt], *n.* (**—s**, *pl.* **—s**) sideboard; buffet.
Büffel ['byfəl], *m.* (**—s**, *pl.* **—**) buffalo.
büffeln ['byfəln], *v.n.* (*coll.*) cram (for an examination), swot.
Bug [bu:k], *m.* (**—s**, *pl.* **¨e, —e**) (*Naut.*) bow, (*Aviat.*) nose.
Buganker ['bu:kaŋkər], *m.* (**—s**, *pl.* **—**) bow-anchor.
Bügel ['bygəl], *m.* (**—s**, *pl.* **—**) coat-hanger; (*trigger*) guard; (*horse*) stirrup.
bügeln ['bygəln], *v.a.* iron, smoothe, press.
bugsieren [buk'si:rən], *v.a.* tow.
Bugspriet ['bu:kʃpri:t], *n.* (**—s**, *pl.* **—e**) bowsprit.
Buhle ['bu:lə], *m.* or *f.* (**—n**, *pl.* **—n**) (*Poet.*) paramour, lover.
buhlen ['bu:lən], *v.n.* (*Poet.*) woo, make love (to).
buhlerisch ['bu:lərɪʃ], *adj.* (*Poet.*) amorous, wanton, lewd.
Bühne ['by:nə], *f.* (**—**, *pl.* **—n**) (*Theat.*) stage; scaffold, platform.
Bühnenbild ['by:nənbɪlt], *n.* (**—es**, *pl.* **¨er**) scenery.
Bukett [bu'kɛt], *n.* (**—s**, *pl.* **—s**) bunch of flowers, bouquet; bouquet (*wine*).
Bulgarien [bul'ga:rjən], *n.* Bulgaria.
Bulldogge ['buldɔgə], *f.* (**—**, *pl.* **—n**) bulldog.
Bulle (1) ['bulə], *m.* (**—n**, *pl.* **—n**) bull, bullock.
Bulle (2) ['bulə], *f.* (**—**, *pl.* **—n**) (*Eccl.*) (Papal) Bull.
bumm [bum], *int.* boom! bang!
Bummel ['buməl], *m.* (**—s**, *pl.* **—**) stroll.
Bummelei [bumə'laɪ], *f.* (**—**, *pl.* **—en**) idleness, negligence, casualness, carelessness.
bummeln ['buməln], *v.n.* lounge, waste o.'s time, dawdle; stroll.
Bummelzug ['buməltsu:k], *m.* (**—s**, *pl.* **¨e**) slow train.
bums [bums], *int.* bang! crash!
Bund (1) [bunt], *m.* (**—es**, *pl.* **¨e**) bond, tie, league, alliance, federation, confederacy; (*Eccl.*) covenant.
Bund (2) [bunt], *n.* (**—es**, *pl.* **—e**) bundle, bunch (of keys).
Bündel ['byndəl], *n.* (**—s**, *pl.* **—**) bundle, package.
Bundesgenosse ['bundəsgənɔsə], *m.* (**—n**, *pl.* **—n**) confederate, ally.
Bundesstaat ['bundəsʃta:t], *m.* (**—es**, *pl.* **—en**) federal state; federation.
Bundestag ['bundəsta:k], *m.* (**—es**, *pl.* **—e**) federal parliament.
Bundeswehr ['bundəsve:r], *f.* (**—**, *no pl.*) federal defence; armed forces.
bündig ['byndɪç], *adj.* binding; *kurz und* **—**, concise, terse, to the point.
Bündnis ['byntnɪs], *n.* (**—ses**, *pl.* **—se**) alliance.
Bundschuh ['buntʃu:], *m.* (**—s**, *pl.* **—e**) clog, sandal.
bunt [bunt], *adj.* many-coloured, chequered, variegated, motley; *das ist mir zu* **—**, this is going too far.
buntscheckig ['buntʃɛkɪç], *adj.* dappled, spotted.
Buntspecht ['buntʃpɛçt], *m.* (**—s**, *pl.* **—e**) (*Orn.*) (spotted) woodpecker.
Bürde ['byrdə], *f.* (**—**, *pl.* **—n**) load, burden.
Bure ['bu:rə], *m.* (**—n**, *pl.* **—n**) Boer.
Burg [burk], *f.* (**—**, *pl.* **—en**) castle, fortress, citadel, stronghold.
Bürge ['byrgə], *m.* (**—n**, *pl.* **—n**) surety, bail, guarantee; *einen* **—***n stellen*, offer bail.
bürgen ['byrgən], *v.n.* give security, vouch (for), go bail (for).
Bürger ['byrgər], *m.* (**—s**, *pl.* **—**) citizen, townsman, bourgeois, commoner.
bürgerlich ['byrgərlɪç], *adj.* civic; middle-class, bourgeois; **—***e Küche*, plain cooking.
Bürgermeister ['byrgərmaɪstər], *m.* (**—s**, *pl.* **—**) burgomaster, mayor.
Burggraf ['burkgra:f], *m.* (**—en**, *pl.* **—en**) burgrave.
Bürgschaft ['byrkʃaft], *f.* (**—**, *pl.* **—en**) bail, surety, guarantee; **—** *leisten*, provide security.
Burgund [bur'gunt], *n.* Burgundy.
Burgvogt ['burkfo:kt], *m.* (**—s**, *pl.* **—e**) (*obs.*) castellan, bailiff.
Burgwarte ['burkvartə], *f.* (**—**, *pl.* **—n**) watch-tower.
Büro [by'ro:], *n.* (**—s**, *pl.* **—s**) office, bureau, (professional) chambers.
Bursche ['burʃə], *m.* (**—n**, *pl.* **—n**) lad, boy, fellow; student; (*Mil.*) batman.
Burschenschaft ['burʃənʃaft], *f.* (**—**, *pl.* **—en**) students' association.
Bürste ['byrstə], *f.* (**—**, *pl.* **—n**) brush.
Burundi [bu'rundi], *n.* Burundi.
Busch [buʃ], *m.* (**—es**, *pl.* **¨e**) bush, shrub, copse, thicket.
Büschel ['byʃəl], *n.* (**—s**, *pl.* **—**) bunch; (*hair*) tuft.
buschig ['buʃɪç], *adj.* bushy, tufted.
Buschklepper ['buʃklɛpər], *m.* (**—s**, *pl.* **—**) bushranger.
Busen ['bu:zən], *m.* (**—s**, *pl.* **—**) bosom, breast; (*Geog.*) bay, gulf.
Bussard ['busart], *m.* (**—s**, *pl.* **—e**) (*Orn.*) buzzard.
Buße ['bu:sə], *f.* (**—**, *pl.* **—n**) penance; repentance; penalty.
büßen ['by:sən], *v.a.*, *v.n.* repent, atone, expiate, make amends.
bußfertig ['bu:sfɛrtɪç], *adj.* penitent, repentant.

Büste ['bystə], *f.* (—, *pl.* **—n**) bust.
Büstenhalter ['bystənhaltər], *m.* (**—s**, *pl.* —) brassière.
Bütte ['bytə], *f.* (—, *pl.* **—n**) tub.
Büttel ['bytəl], *m.* (**—s**, *pl.* —) beadle; bailiff.
Büttenpapier ['bytənpapi:r], *n.* (**—s**, *no pl.*) hand-made paper.
Butter ['butər], *f.* (—, *no pl.*) butter.
Butterblume ['butərblu:mə], *f.* (—, *pl.* **—n**) buttercup.
Butterbrot ['butərbro:t], *n.* (**—s**, *pl.* **—e**) bread and butter.
buttern ['butərn], *v.a.*, *v.n.* smear with butter; churn.
Butterteig ['butərtaɪk], *m.* (**—es**, *pl.* **—e**) puff-pastry.
Butzenscheibe ['butsənʃaɪbə], *f.* (—, *pl.* **—n**) bull's-eyed pane.
Byzanz [by'tsants], *n.* Byzantium, Constantinople.

C

C [tse:], *n.* (**—s**, *pl.* **—s**) the letter C; (*Mus.*) *C dur*, C major; *C Moll*, C minor; *C-Schlüssel*, C clef.
Cäsar ['tsɛ:zar], *m.* Cæsar.
Ceylon ['tseilɔn], *n.* Ceylon.
Chaiselongue [ʃɛ:zə'lɔ̃:g], *f.* (—, *pl.* **—s**) couch, settee, sofa.
Champagner [ʃam'panjər], *m.* (**—s**, *pl.* —) champagne.
Champignon [ʃampɪn'jɔ̃], *m.* (**—s**, *pl.* **—s**) mushroom.
chaotisch [ka'o:tɪʃ], *adj.* chaotic.
Charakter [ka'raktər], *m.* (**—s**, *pl.* **—e**) character; mental make-up, disposition.
Charakteristik [karaktər'ɪstɪk], *f.* (—, *pl.* **—en**) characterisation.
charakteristisch [karaktər'ɪstɪʃ], *adj.* characteristic; typical.
Charge ['ʃarʒə], *f.* (—, *pl.* **—n**) office, appointment; (*pl.*) (*Mil.*) non-commissioned officers.
Chaussee [ʃɔ'se:], *f.* (—, *pl.* **—n**) main road, highway.
Chef [ʃɛf], *m.* (**—s**, *pl.* **—s**) chief, head, employer; (*coll.*) boss.
Chefredakteur ['ʃɛfredaktø:r], *m.* (**—s**, *pl.* **—e**) editor-in-chief.
Chemie [çe'mi:], *f.* (—, *no pl.*) chemistry.
Chemikalien [çemɪ'ka:ljən], *f. pl.* chemicals.
Chemiker ['çe:mɪkər], *m.* (**—s**, *pl.* —) (analytical) chemist.
chemisch ['çe:mɪʃ], *adj.* chemical; — *gereinigt*, dry-cleaned.
Chiffre ['ʃɪfər], *f.* (—, *pl.* **—n**) cipher.
chiffrieren [ʃɪ'fri:rən], *v.a.* encipher.
Chile ['tʃi:lə, 'çi:lə], *n.* Chile.
China ['çi:na], *n.* China.
Chinarinde [çi:na'rɪndə], *f.* (—, *no pl.*) Peruvian bark.
Chinin [çi'ni:n], *n.* (**—s**, *no pl.*) quinine.
Chirurg [çi'rurk], *m.* (**—en**, *pl.* **—en**) surgeon.
Chirurgie [çirur'gi:], *f.* (—, *no pl.*) surgery.
Chlor [klo:r], *n.* (**—s**, *no pl.*) chlorine.
Chlorkalk ['klo:rkalk], *m.* (**—s**, *no pl.*) chloride of lime.
Chlornatrium [klo:r'na:trjum], *n.* (**—s**, *no pl.*) sodium chloride.
Choleriker [ko'le:rɪkər], *m.* (**—s**, *pl.* —) irascible person.
Chor [kɔ:r], *m.* (**—s**, *pl.* **¨e**) chorus; choir; (*Archit.*) choir, chancel.
Choral [ko'ra:l], *m.* (**—s**, *pl.* **¨e**) hymn, chorale.
Choramt ['ko:ramt], *n.* (**—s**, *pl.* **¨er**) cathedral service.
Chorgesang ['ko:rgəsaŋ], *m.* (**—s**, *pl.* **¨e**) chorus, choral singing.
Chorhemd ['ko:rhɛmt], *n.* (**—s**, *pl.* **—en**) surplice.
Chorherr ['ko:rhɛr], *m.* (**—n**, *pl.* **—en**) canon, prebendary.
Christ [krɪst], *m.* (**—en**, *pl.* **—en**) Christian.
Christbaum ['krɪstbaum], *m.* (**—s**, *pl.* **¨e**) Christmas tree.
Christentum ['krɪstəntu:m], *n.* (**—s**, *no pl.*) Christendom, Christianity.
Christkind ['krɪstkɪnt], *n.* (**—s**, *no pl.*) Infant Christ, Christ child.
christlich ['krɪstlɪç], *adj.* Christian.
Christmette ['krɪstmɛtə], *f.* (—, *pl.* **—n**) Christmas matins; midnight mass.
Christus ['krɪstus], *m.* (**—i**) Christ; *vor* —, B.C.; *nach* —, A.D.
Chrom [kro:m], *n.* (**—s**, *no pl.*) chrome.
chromatisch [kro'ma:tɪʃ], *adj.* chromatic.
chromsauer ['kro:mzauər], *adj.* — chromate of; *—es Salz*, chromate.
Chronik ['kro:nɪk], *f.* (—, *pl.* **—en**) chronicle.
chronisch ['kro:nɪʃ], *adj.* chronic.
Chronist [kro'nɪst], *m.* (**—en**, *pl.* **—en**) chronicler.
Chrysantheme [kryzan'te:mə], *f.* (—, *pl.* **—n**) chrysanthemum.
Cis [tsɪs]. (*Mus.*) C sharp.
Clique ['klɪkə], *f.* (—, *pl.* **—n**) clique, set.
Coeur [kø:r], *n.* (*Cards*) hearts.
coulant [ku'lant], *adj.* polite, friendly; (*Comm.*) fair, obliging.
Couleur [ku'lø:r], *f.* (—, *pl.* **—en**) colour; students' corporation.
Coupé [ku'pe:], *n.* (**—s**, *pl.* **—s**) (*train*) compartment.
Couplet [ku'ple:], *n.* (**—s**, *pl.* **—s**) comic song.
Coupon [ku'pɔ̃], *m.* (**—s**, *pl.* **—s**) coupon, check, dividend voucher.
Cour [ku:r], *f.* (—, *no pl.*) *einem Mädchen die — machen*, court a girl.

Courtage [kur'ta:ʒə], *f.* (—, *pl.* —**n**) brokerage.
Cousin [ku'zɛ̃], *m.* (—**s**, *pl.* —**s**) cousin.
Cousine [ku'zi:nə], *f.* (—, *pl.* —**n**) (female) cousin.
Cutaway ['katave:], *m.* (—**s**, *pl.* —**s**) morning coat.
Czar [tsa:r], *m.* (—**en**, *pl.* —**en**) Tsar, Czar.

D

D [de:], *n.* (—**s**, *pl.* —**s**) the letter D; (*Mus.*) *D dur*, D major; *D moll*, D minor; *D-Zug*, express train.
da [da:], *adv.* (*local*) there; here; (*temporal*) then, at that moment; (*Mil.*) *wer —?* who goes there? (*Poet. obs.*) where. — *conj.* (*temporal*) when, as; (*causal*) as, because, since.
dabei [da'baɪ], *adv.* nearby; besides, moreover; as well; —*sein*, be present, be about to (*infin.*); — *bleiben*, persist in.
Dach [dax], *n.* (—**es**, *pl.* ⸚**er**) roof.
Dachboden ['daxbo:dən], *m.* (—**s**, *pl.* ⸚) loft.
Dachdecker ['daxdɛkər], *m.* (—**s**, *pl.* —) slater, tiler.
Dachgiebel ['daxgi:bəl], *m.* (—**s**, *pl.* —) gable.
Dachluke ['daxlu:kə], *f.* (—, *pl.* —**n**) dormer window.
Dachpappe ['daxpapə], *f.* (—, *pl.* —**n**) roofing felt.
Dachrinne ['daxrɪnə], *f.* (—, *pl.* —**n**) gutter.
Dachs [daks], *m.* (—**es**, *pl.* —**e**) badger.
Dachstube ['daxʃtu:bə], *f.* (—, *pl.* —**n**) garret, attic (room).
Dachtraufe ['daxtraufə], *f.* (—, *pl.* —**n**) eaves.
dadurch [da'durç], *adv.* (*local*) through it; in that way; (*causal*) thereby.
dafür [da'fy:r], *adv.* for it; instead of it, in return for it; *ich kann nichts* —, it is not my fault, I can't help it.
Dafürhalten [da'fy:rhaltən], *n.* (—**s**, *no pl.*) opinion.
dagegen [da'ge:gən], *adv.* against it, compared to it. — *conj.* on the other hand.
daheim [da'haɪm], *adv.* at home.
daher [da'he:r], *adv.* thence, from that. — *conj.* therefore, for that reason.
dahin [da'hɪn], *adv.* thither, to that place; there; *bis* —, (*local*) thither; (*temporal*) till then; over, past, lost, gone.
dahinbringen [da'hɪnbrɪŋən], *v.a. irr. jemanden* —, induce s.o. to; *es* —, succeed in, manage to.
dahinsiechen [da'hɪnzi:çən], *v.n.* (*aux.* sein) pine away, be failing (in health).
dahinter [da'hɪntər], *adv.* behind that.
Dahlie ['da:ljə], *f.* (—, *pl.* —**n**) (*Bot.*) dahlia.
Dahome ['daome:], *n.* Dahomey.
damalig ['da:malɪç], *adj.* then; of that time; past.
damals ['da:mals], *adv.* then, at that time.
Damast [da'mast], *m.* (—**s**, *no pl.*) damask.
Damaszener [damas'tse:nər], *m.* (—**s**, *pl.* —) Damascene. — *adj.* — *Stahl*, Damascus steel, dagger.
Dame ['da:mə], *f.* (—, *pl.* —**n**) lady; (*cards, chess*) queen; draughts (*game*).
damit [da'mɪt], *adv.* therewith, with that, with it; *und — basta!* and that's all there is to it. — *conj.* in order that, so that; — *nicht*, lest.
dämlich ['dɛ:mlɪç], *adj.* (*coll.*) foolish, silly.
Damm [dam], *m.* (—**es**, *pl.* ⸚**e**) dam, dyke, mole; (*street*) roadway, causeway; (*rail*) embankment.
dämmen ['dɛmən], *v.a.* dam; (*fig.*) stop, restrain.
dämmerig ['dɛmərɪç], *adj.* dusky.
dämmern ['dɛmərn], *v.n.* grow dusky; dawn.
dämonisch [dɛ'mo:nɪʃ], *adj.* demoniac(al), demonlike.
Dampf [dampf], *m.* (—**es**, *pl.* ⸚**e**) vapour, steam, mist, fume; smoke.
dampfen ['dampfən], *v.n.* smoke, fume, steam.
dämpfen ['dɛmpfən], *v.a.* damp, smother, steam; subdue, deaden, muffle, soften down.
Dampfer ['dampfər], *m.* (—**s**, *pl.* —) steamer.
Dämpfer ['dɛmpfər], *m.* (—**s**, *pl.* —) damper; (*Mus.*) mute.
Dampfkessel ['dampfkɛsəl], *m.* (—**s**, *pl.* —) boiler.
Dämpfung ['dɛmpfuŋ], *f.* (—, *pl.* —**en**) damping, smothering, suppression; (*Aviat.*) stabilization.
danach [da'na:x], *adv.* after that, thereafter; accordingly, according to that.
daneben [da'ne:bən], *adv.* near it, by it, close by; *es geht* —, it goes amiss. — *conj.* besides.
Dänemark ['dɛ:nəmark], *n.* Denmark.
Dank [daŋk], *m.* (—**es**, *no pl.*) thanks, gratitude; reward; *Gott sei* —, thank heaven!
dank [daŋk], *prep.* (*Dat.*) owing to, thanks to.
dankbar ['daŋkba:r], *adj.* grateful; thankful.
danken ['daŋkən], *v.n.* (*Dat.*) thank. — *v.a.* owe.
Dankgebet ['daŋkgəbe:t], *n.* (—**s**, *pl.* —**e**) (prayer of) thanksgiving.
dann [dan], *adv.* then, at that time, in that case: — *und wann*, now and then, occasionally.
Danzig ['dantsɪç], *n.* Dantzig

daran, dran [da'ran, dran], *adv.* on it, at it, near that; thereon, thereby; *was liegt —?* what does it matter?
darauf, drauf [da'rauf, drauf], *adv.* (*local*) upon it, on it; (*temporal*) thereupon, thereon, thereafter.
daraufhin [darauf'hɪn], *adv.* thereupon; on the strength of that.
daraus, draus [da'raus, draus], *adv.* therefrom, hence, from that; *ich mache mir nichts —*, I do not care for it.
darben ['darbən], *v.n.* suffer want, go short; famish.
darbieten ['da:rbi:tən], *v.a. irr.* offer, tender, present.
Darbietung ['da:rbi:tuŋ], *f.* (—, *pl.* —**en**) offering, presentation, performance.
darbringen ['da:rbrɪŋən], *v.a. irr.* bring, present, offer.
darein, drein [da'raɪn, draɪn], *adv.* into it, therein.
darin, drin [da'rɪn, drɪn], *adv.* therein, in it, within.
darinnen, drinnen [da'rɪnən, 'drɪnən], *adv.* inside, in there.
darlegen ['da:rle:gən], *v.a.* demonstrate, explain; expound.
Darlehen ['da:rle:ən], *n.* (—**s**, *pl.* —) loan.
Darm [darm], *m.* (—**s**, *pl.* ¨**e**) gut; (*pl.*) intestines, bowels.
Darmsaite ['darmzaɪtə], *f.* (—, *pl.* —**n**) catgut, gut-string.
darob [da'rɔp], *adv.* (*obs.*) on that account, on account of it.
darreichen ['da:raɪçən], *v.a.* offer, tender, present; (*Eccl.*) administer (sacraments).
darstellen ['da:rʃtɛlən], *v.a.* represent, delineate; (*Theat.*) perform.
Darstellung ['da:rʃtɛluŋ], *f.* (—, *pl.* —**en**) representation, exhibition, presentation; (*Theat.*) performance.
dartun ['da:rtu:n], *v.a. irr.* prove, demonstrate.
darüber, drüber [dar'y:bər, 'dry:bər], *adv.* over that, over it; concerning that.
darum, drum [da'rum, drum], *adv.* around it, around that, thereabout; therefore, for that reason.
darunter, drunter [da'runtər, 'druntər], *adv.* under that; thereunder; among; — *und drüber*, topsy-turvy.
das [das], *def. art. n.* the. — *dem. pron.*, *dem. adj.* that, this. —*rel. pron.* which.
Dasein ['da:zaɪn], *n.* (—**s**, *no pl.*) presence, being, existence.
daselbst [da:'zɛlpst], *adv.* there, in that very place.
daß [das], *conj.* that; *es sei denn —*, unless; — *nicht*, lest.
dastehen ['da:ʃte:ən], *v.n. irr.* stand (there).
datieren [da'ti:rən], *v.a.* date, put a date to.
Dativ ['da:ti:f], *m.* (—**s**, *pl.* —**e**) dative.
dato ['da:to], *adv. bis —*, till now, hitherto.
Dattel ['datəl], *f.* (—, *pl.* —**n**) (*Bot.*) date.
Datum ['da:tum], *n.* (—**s**, *pl.* **Daten**) date (*calendar*).
Dauer ['dauər], *f.* (—, *no pl.*) duration, length of time; continuance; permanence.
dauerhaft ['dauərhaft], *adj.* durable, lasting; (*colours*) fast.
Dauerkarte ['dauərkartə], *f.* (—, *pl.* —**n**) season ticket; (*Am.*) commutation ticket.
dauern ['dauərn], *v.n.* continue, last, endure.— *v.a.* move to pity; *er dauert mich*, I am sorry for him.
Dauerpflanze ['dauərpflantsə], *f.* (—, *pl.* —**n**) perennial plant.
Dauerwelle ['dauərvɛlə], *f.* (—, *pl.* —**n**) permanent wave, (*coll.*) perm.
Daumen ['daumən], *m.* (—**s**, *pl.* —) thumb; *einem den — halten*, wish s.o. well, keep o.'s fingers crossed for s.o.
Daune ['daunə], *f.* (—, *pl.* —**n**) down.
davon [da'fɔn], *adv.* thereof, therefrom, from that; off, away.
davonkommen [da'fɔnkɔmən], *v.n. irr.* (*aux.* sein) get off; *mit einem blauen Auge —*, get off lightly.
davor [da'fo:r], *adv.* before that, before it.
dawider [da'vi:dər], *adv.* against it.
dazu [da'tsu:], *adv.* thereto, to that, to it; in addition to that; for that purpose; *noch —*, besides.
dazumal ['da:tsuma:l], *adv.* then, at that time.
dazwischen [da'tsvɪʃən], *adv.* between, among; — *kommen*, intervene, interfere; — *treten*, intervene.
debattieren [deba'ti:rən], *v.a.*, *v.n.* debate.
Debet ['de:bɛt], *n.* (—**s**, *pl.* —**s**) debit.
Debüt [de'by:], *n.* (—**s**, *pl.* —**s**) first appearance, début.
Dechant [de'çant], *m.* (—**en**, *pl.* —**en**) (*Eccl.*) dean.
dechiffrieren [deʃɪf'ri:rən], *v.a.* decode, decipher.
Deck [dɛk], *n.* (—**s**, *pl.* —**e**) (*Naut.*) deck.
Deckbett ['dɛkbɛt], *n.* (—**s**, *pl.* —**en**) coverlet.
Deckblatt ['dɛkblat], *n.* (—**s**, *pl.* ¨**er**) (*Bot.*) bractea; (*cigar*) wrapper.
Decke ['dɛkə], *f.* (—, *pl.* —**n**) cover; blanket, rug; (*bed*) coverlet; (*room*) ceiling.
Deckel ['dɛkəl], *m.* (—**s**, *pl.* —) lid, top; (*book*) cover; (*coll.*) hat.
decken ['dɛkən], *v.a.* cover; (*Comm.*) secure, reimburse. — *v.r. sich —*, *Maths.*) coincide; (*fig.*) square, tally.
Deckfarbe ['dɛkfarbə], *f.* (—, *pl.* —**n**) body colour.
Deckmantel ['dɛkmantəl], *m.* (—**s**, *pl.* ¨) cloak, disguise.
Deckung ['dɛkuŋ], *f.* (—, *pl.* —**en**) covering, protection; (*Comm.*) reimbursement; security; (*Mil.*) cover.
dedizieren [dedɪ'tsi:rən], *v.a.* dedicate.

deduzieren [dedu'tsi:rən], *v.a.* deduce.
defekt [de'fɛkt], *adj.* defective, incomplete, imperfect.
defilieren [defɪ'li:rən], *v.n.* (*Mil.*) pass in review, march past.
definieren [defɪ'ni:rən], *v.a.* define.
Degen ['de:gən], *m.* (**—s**, *pl.* **—**) sword; (*fig.*) brave warrior.
degradieren [degra'di:rən], *v.a.* degrade, demote.
dehnbar ['de:nba:r], *adj.* extensible, ductile.
dehnen ['de:nən], *v.a.* extend, expand, stretch. — *v.r.* *sich* —, stretch o.s.
Deich [daɪç], *m.* (**—es**, *pl.* **—e**) dike, dam, embankment.
Deichsel ['daɪksəl], *f.* (**—**, *pl.* **—n**) thill, shaft, pole.
deichseln ['daɪksəln], *v.a.* (*fig.*) engineer; (*coll.*) manage; wangle.
dein [daɪn], *poss. adj.* your; (*Poet.*) thy. — *poss. pron.* yours; (*Poet.*) thine.
deinesgleichen [daɪnəs'glaɪçən], *adj. pron.* the like of you, such as you.
deinethalben ['daɪnəthalbən], *adv.* on your account, for your sake, on your behalf.
deinetwegen ['daɪnətve:gən], *adv.* because of you, on your account, for your sake, on your behalf.
deinetwillen ['daɪnətvɪlən], *adv.* *um* —, on your account, for your sake, on your behalf.
deinige ['daɪnɪgə], *poss. adj.* your; (*Poet.*) thy. — *poss. pron.* yours; (*Poet.*) thine.
Dekan [de'ka:n], *m.* (**—s**, *pl.* **—e**) (*Eccl., Univ.*) dean.
Dekanat [deka'na:t], *n.* (**—s**, *pl.* **—e**) (*Eccl., Univ.*) deanery, office of dean.
deklamieren [dekla'mi:rən], *v.a., v.n.* recite, declaim.
deklarieren [dekla'ri:rən], *v.a.* declare (for customs duty).
Deklination [deklina'tsjo:n], *f.* (**—**, *pl.* **—en**) (*Gram.*) declension; (*Phys.*) declination.
deklinieren [deklɪ'ni:rən], *v.a.* (*Gram.*) decline.
dekolletiert [dekɔle'ti:rt], *adj.* décolleté, low-necked.
Dekret [de'kre:t], *n.* (**—s**, *pl.* **—e**) decree, edict, official regulation.
dekretieren [dekre'ti:rən], *v.a.* decree, ordain.
delegieren [dele'gi:rən], *v.a.* delegate.
Delegierte [dele'gi:rtə], *m.* (**—n**, *pl.* **—n**) delegate.
delikat [delɪ'ka:t], *adj.* subtle, dainty; tasty; (*coll.*) tricky, difficult.
Delikatesse [delɪka'tɛsə], *f.* (**—**, *pl.* **—n**) delicacy, dainty; (*pl.*) (*Am.*) delicatessen.
Delikt [de'lɪkt], *n.* (**—s**, *pl.* **—e**) (*Law*) crime; misdemeanour.
Delle ['dɛlə], *f.* (**—**, *pl.* **—n**) dent.
Delphin [dɛl'fi:n], *m.* (**—s**, *pl.* **—e**) dolphin.
deltaförmig ['dɛltafœrmɪç], *adj.* deltoid.
dem [de:m], *def. art. Dat.* to the. — *dem. adj.* to this, to that: — *dem. pron.* to this, to that; *wie* — *auch sei*, however that may be. — *rel. pron.* to whom, to which.
demarkieren [demar'ki:rən], *v.a.* mark, demarcate.
Dementi [de'mɛnti], *n.* (**—s**, *pl.* **—s**) (*official*) denial.
dementieren [demɛn'ti:rən], *v.a.* (*Pol.*) deny, contradict.
demgemäß ['de:mgəmɛ:s], *adv.* accordingly.
demnach ['de:mnax], *conj.* therefore, consequently, in accordance with that.
demnächst ['de:mnɛ:çst], *adv.* shortly, soon, in the near future.
demokratisch [demo'kra:tɪʃ], *adj.* democratic.
demolieren [demo'li:rən], *v.a.* demolish.
demonstrieren [demɔn'stri:rən], *v.a., v.n.* demonstrate.
Demut ['de:mu:t], *f.* (**—**, *no pl.*) humility, meekness.
demütig ['de:mytɪç], *adj.* humble, meek, submissive.
demütigen ['de:mytɪgən], *v.a.* humble, humiliate, subdue.
Denkart ['dɛŋka:rt], *f.* (**—**, *pl.* **—en**) way of thinking.
denken ['dɛŋkən], *v.a., v.n. irr.* think, reflect (upon); imagine; (*coll.*) guess.
Denker ['dɛŋkər], *m.* (**—s**, *pl.* **—**) thinker, philosopher.
Denkmal ['dɛŋkma:l], *n.* (**—s**, *pl.* **¨er**) monument.
Denkmünze ['dɛŋkmyntsə], *f.* (**—**, *pl.* **—n**) (commemorative) medal.
Denkschrift ['dɛŋkʃrɪft], *f.* (**—**, *pl.* **—en**) memorandum, memoir.
Denkspruch ['dɛŋkʃprux], *m.* (**—s**, *pl.* **¨e**) aphorism, maxim, motto.
Denkungsart ['dɛŋkuŋsart], *f.* (*pl.* **—en**) *see* **Denkart**.
Denkweise ['dɛŋkvaɪzə], *f.* (**—**, *pl.* **—n**) *see* **Denkart**.
denkwürdig ['dɛŋkvyrdɪç], *adj.* memorable.
Denkzettel ['dɛŋktsɛtəl], *m.* (**—s**, *pl.* **—**) (*fig.*) reminder, punishment, lesson; *einem einen* — *geben*, give s.o. s.th. to think about *or* a sharp reminder.
denn [dɛn], *conj.* for. — *adv.* then; (*after comparatives*) than; *es sei* — *dass*, unless.
dennoch ['dɛnɔx], *conj.* yet, nevertheless, notwithstanding.
Denunziant [denun'tsjant], *m.* (**—en**, *pl.* **—en**) informer.
denunzieren [denun'tsi:rən], *v.a.* inform against, denounce.
Depesche [de'pɛʃə], *f.* (**—**, *pl.* **—n**) dispatch; telegram, wire.
deponieren [depo'ni:rən], *v.a.* deposit; (*Law*) depose.
Depositenbank [depo'zi:tənbaŋk], *f.* (**—**, *pl.* **—en**) deposit-bank.

deprimieren [deprɪ'mi:rən], *v.a.* depress.
Deputierte [depu'ti:rtə], *m.* (—**n**, *pl.* —**n**) deputy.
der [de:r], *def. art. m.* the. — *dem. adj., dem. pron.* this, that. — *rel. pron.* who, which, that.
derart ['de:ra:rt], *adv.* so, in such a manner.
derartig ['de:ra:rtɪç], *adj.* such.
derb [dɛrp], *adj.* firm, solid, coarse, blunt, uncouth; strong, robust.
dereinst [de:r'aɪnst], *adv.* one day (in future).
derenthalben ['de:rənthalbən], *adv.* for her (their) sake, on her (their) account, on whose account.
derentwegen ['de:rəntve:gən], *adv. see* **derenthalben**.
derentwillen ['de:rəntvɪlən], *adv. see* **derenthalben**.
dergestalt ['de:rgəʃtalt], *adv.* in such a manner; so.
dergleichen [de:r'glaɪçən], *adv.* such, such as, suchlike.
derjenige ['de:rje:nɪgə], *dem. adj., dem. pron.* that, this; — *welcher*, he who.
derlei ['de:rlaɪ], *adj.* of that sort.
dermaßen ['de:rma:sən], *adv.* to such an extent, to such a degree.
derselbe [de:r'zɛlbə], *pron.* the same.
derweilen [de:r'vaɪlən], *adv.* meanwhile.
Derwisch ['dɛrvɪʃ], *m.* (—(e)s, *pl.* —e) dervish.
derzeit ['de:rtsaɪt], *adv.* at present.
Des [dɛs], *n.* (—, *pl.* —) (*Mus.*) D flat; — *Dur*, D flat major; — *Moll*, D flat minor.
des [dɛs], *def. art. m. & n. Genit. sing.* of the.
desgleichen [dɛs'glaɪçən], *adj.* such, suchlike. — *adv.* likewise, ditto.
deshalb ['dɛshalp], *adv., conj.* therefore.
desinfizieren [dɛsɪnfit'si:rən], *v.a.* disinfect.
dessen ['dɛsən], *dem. pron. m & n. Genit. sing.* of it, of that. — *rel. pron. m. & n. Genit. sing.* whose, of whom, of which, whereof.
dessenungeachtet [dɛsənunge'axtət], *conj.* notwithstanding that, for all that, despite all that.
Destillateur [dɛstɪla'tø:r], *m.* (—**s**, *pl.* —**e**) distiller.
destillieren [dɛstɪ'li:rən], *v.a.* distil.
desto ['dɛsto], *adv.* the; — *besser*, so much the better; *je* . . . —, the . . . the.
deswegen ['dɛsve:gən], *adv., conj.* therefore.
Detaillist [deta'jɪst], *m.* (—**en**, *pl.* —**en**) retailer.
deucht [dɔyçt] *see* **dünken**; (*obs.*) *mich deucht*, methinks.
deuten ['dɔytən], *v.a.* point to, show; explain, interpret.
deutlich ['dɔytlɪç], *adj.* clear, distinct; evident, plain.
deutsch [dɔytʃ], *adj.* German.
Deutschland ['dɔytʃlant], *n.* Germany.
Deutschmeister ['dɔytʃmaɪstər], *m.* (—**s**, *pl.* —) Grand Master of the Teutonic Order.
Deutschtum ['dɔytʃtu:m], *n.* (—**s**, *no pl.*) German nationality, German customs, German manners.
Deutung ['dɔytuŋ], *f.* (—, *pl.* —**en**) explanation, interpretation.
Devise [de'vi:zə], *f.* (—, *pl.* —**n**) device, motto; (*pl.*) foreign currency.
devot [de'vo:t], *adj.* submissive, respectful, humble.
Dezember [de'tsɛmbər], *m.* December.
dezent [de'tsɛnt], *adj.* modest, decent; unobtrusive.
Dezernent [detsɛr'nɛnt], *m.* (—**en**, *pl.* —**en**) head of section in ministry or city administration.
dezimieren [detsɪ'mi:rən], *v.a.* decimate, reduce.
Diagramm [dia'gram], *n.* (—**s**, *pl.* —**e**) diagram, graph.
Diakon [dia'ko:n], *m.* (—**s**, *pl.* —**e**) (*Eccl.*) deacon.
Diakonisse, Diakonissin [diako'nɪsə, diako'nɪsɪn], *f.* (—, *pl.* —**nen**) deaconess.
Dialektik [dia'lɛktɪk], *f.* (—, *no pl.*) dialectics.
Diamant [dia'mant], *m.* (—**en**, *pl.* —**en**) diamond.
diametral [diame'tra:l], *adj.* diametrical.
Diapositiv [diapozi'ti:f], *n.* (—**s**, *pl.* —**e**) (*lantern, Phot.*) slide.
Diät [di'ɛ:t], *f.* (—, *pl.* —**en**) diet; (*pl.*) daily allowance.
dich [dɪç], *pers. pron.* you. — *refl. pron.* yourself.
dicht [dɪçt], *adj.* tight; impervious (to water); dense, compact, solid, firm; — *bei*, hard by, close to.
Dichte ['dɪçtə], *f.* (—, *no pl.*) density.
dichten ['dɪçtən], *v.a., v.n.* write poetry, compose (*verses etc.*); (*Tech.*) tighten; (*Naut.*) caulk.
Dichter ['dɪçtər], *m.* (—**s**, *pl.* —) poet.
dichterisch ['dɪçtərɪʃ], *adj.* poetic(al).
Dichtigkeit ['dɪçtɪçkaɪt], *f.* (—, *no pl.*) closeness, compactness, thickness, density.
Dichtkunst ['dɪçtkunst], *f.* (—, *no pl.*) (art of) poetry.
Dichtung ['dɪçtuŋ], *f.* (—, *pl.* —**en**) poetry, poem; fiction; (*Tech.*) caulking; washer, gasket.
dick [dɪk], *adj.* thick; fat; (*books*) bulky; voluminous, stout, obese, corpulent.
Dicke ['dɪkə], *f.* (—, *no pl.*) thickness, stoutness.
dickfellig ['dɪkfɛlɪç], *adj.* thick-skinned.
Dickicht ['dɪkɪçt], *n.* (—**s**, *pl.* —**e**) thicket.
die [di:], *def. art. f. & pl.* the. — *dem. adj., dem. pron. f. & pl.* this, these. — *rel. pron. f. & pl.* who, that which.
Dieb [di:p], *m.* (—**s**, *pl.* —**e**) thief.
Diebstahl ['di:pʃta:l], *m.* (—**s**, *pl.* ¨—**e**) theft.

Diele ['di:lə], *f.* (—, *pl.* —**n**) floor; (entrance) hall; plank.
dielen ['di:lən], *v.a.* board, floor.
dienen ['di:nən], *v.n.* *einem* —, serve (s.o.); help (s.o.).
Diener ['di:nər], *m.* (—**s**, *pl.* —) servant, attendant; (*coll.*) bow.
dienlich ['di:nlıç], *adj.* serviceable, useful; *für* — *halten*, think fit.
Dienst [di:nst], *m.* (—**es**, *pl.* —**e**) service, employment, duty; — *haben*, be on duty.
Dienstag ['di:nsta:k], *m.* (—**s**, *pl.* —**e**) Tuesday.
Dienstalter ['di:nstaltər], *n.* (—**s**, *pl.* —) seniority.
dienstbar ['di:nstba:r], *adj.* subject, subservient.
Dienstbarkeit ['di:nstba:rkaıt], *f.* (—, *no pl.*) bondage, servitude.
dienstbeflissen ['di:nstbəflısən], *adj.* assiduous.
Dienstbote ['di:nstbo:te], *m.* (—**n**, *pl.* —**n**) domestic servant.
dienstfertig ['di:nstfɛrtıç], *adj.* obliging, ready to serve.
Dienstleistung ['di:nstlaıstuŋ], *f.* (—, *pl.* —**en**) service.
dienstlich ['di:nstlıç], *adj.* official.
Dienstmädchen ['di:nstmɛ:tçən], *n.* (—**s**, pl. —) maidservant.
Dienstmann ['di:nstman], *m.* (—**s**, *pl.* ¨**er**) commissionaire, porter.
Dienstpflicht ['di:nstpflıçt], *f.* (—, *no pl.*) official duty, liability to serve; (*Mil.*) (compulsory) military service.
Dienststunden ['di:nstʃtundən], *f. pl.* office hours.
diensttauglich ['di:nsttauklıç], *adj.* (*Mil.*) fit for service.
Dienstverhältnis ['di:nstfɛrhɛltnıs], *n.* (—**ses**, *pl.* —**se**) (*pl.*) terms of service.
dies [di:s], *abbr.* **dieses**.
diesbezüglich ['di:sbətsy:klıç], *adj.* concerning this, relating to this matter.
diese ['di:zə], *dem. adj.*, *dem. pron. f. & pl.* this, these.
dieser ['di:zər], *dem. adj.*, *dem. pron. m.* this.
dieses ['di:zəs], *dem. adj.*, *dem. pron. n.* this.
diesjährig ['di:sjɛ:rıç], *adj.* of this year, this year's.
diesmal ['di:sma:l], *adv.* this time, for this once.
Dietrich (1) ['di:trıç], *m.* Derek.
Dietrich (2) ['di:trıç], *m.* (—**s**, *pl.* —**e**) pick lock, master-key, skeleton key.
Differentialrechnung [dıfərɛnts'ja:l-rɛçnuŋ], *f.* (—, *pl.* —**en**) differential calculus.
Differenz [dıfə'rɛnts], *f.* (—, *pl.* —**en**) difference; quarrel.
Diktat [dık'ta:t], *n.* (—**s**, *pl.* —**e**) dictation.
diktatorisch [dıkta'to:rıʃ], *adj.* dictatorial.
Diktatur [dıkta'tu:r], *f.* (—, *pl.* —**en**) dictatorship.
diktieren [dık'ti:rən], *v.a.* dictate.
Ding [dıŋ], *n.* (—**s**, *pl.* —**e**) thing, object, matter.
dingen ['dıŋən], *v.a.* hire, engage (a manual worker).
dingfest ['dıŋfɛst], *adj.* — *machen*, arrest.
dinglich ['dıŋlıç], *adj.* real.
dinieren [di'ni:rən], *v.n.* dine.
Diözese [diø'tse:zə], *f.* (—, *pl.* —**n**) diocese.
Diphtherie [dıftə'ri:], *f.* (—, *no pl.*) diphtheria.
Diplom [di'plo:m], *n.* (—**s**, *pl.* —**e**) diploma.
Diplomatie [dıploma'ti:], *f.* (—, *no pl.*) diplomacy.
dir [dı:r], *pers. pron. Dat.* to you.
direkt [di'rɛkt], *adj.* direct; —*er Wagen*, (*railway*) through carriage; — *danach*, immediately afterwards.
Direktion [dirɛkt'sjo:n], *f.* (—, *pl.* —**en**) direction, management.
Direktor [di'rɛktɔr], *m.* (—**s**, *pl.* —**en**) (managing) director, manager; headmaster, principal.
Direktorium [dirɛk'to:rjum], *n.* (—**s**. *pl.* —**rien**) directorate, board of directors.
Direktrice [dirɛk'tri:sə], *f.* (—, *pl.* —**n**) manageress.
Dirigent [diri'gɛnt], *m.* (—**en**, *pl.* —**en**) (*Mus.*) conductor; (*Austr. Admin.*) head of section in Ministry.
dirigieren [diri'gi:rən], *v.a.* direct, manage; (*Mus.*) conduct.
Dirndl ['dırndl], *n.* (—**s**, *pl.* —) (*dial.*) young girl, country wench; (*fig.*) peasant dress, dirndl.
Dirne ['dırnə], *f.* (—, *pl.* —**n**) (*Poet.*) girl; prostitute.
Dis [dıs], *n.* (—, *no pl.*) (*Mus.*) D sharp.
disharmonisch [dıshar'mo:nıʃ], *adj.* discordant.
Diskant [dıs'kant], *m.* (—**s**, *pl.* —**e**) (*Mus.*) treble, soprano.
Diskont [dıs'kɔnt], *m.* (—(**e**)**s**, *pl.* —**e**) discount, rebate.
diskret [dıs'kre:t], *adj.* discreet.
Diskurs [dıs'kurs], *m.* (—**es**, *pl.* —**e**) discourse.
diskutieren [dısku'ti:rən], *v.a.* discuss, debate.
Dispens [dıs'pɛns], *m.* (—**es**, *pl.* —**e**) dispensation.
dispensieren [dıspɛn'zi:rən], *v.a.* dispense (from), exempt (from).
disponieren [dıspo'ni:rən], *v.n.* — *über*, dispose of; make plans about.
Dissident [dısi'dɛnt], *m.* (—**en**, *pl.* —**en**) dissenter, nonconformist.
distanzieren [dıstan'tsi:rən], *v.r.* *sich* — *von*, keep o.'s distance from; dissociate o.s. from.
Distel ['dıstəl], *f.* (—, *pl.* —**n**) thistle.
Distelfink ['dıstəlfıŋk], *m.* (—**s**, *pl.* —**e**) (*Orn.*) gold-finch.
disziplinarisch [dıstsipli'na:rıʃ], *adj.* diciplinary.
dito ['di:to], *adv.* ditto.

dividieren [dɪvɪ'di:rən], *v.a.* divide.
Diwan ['di:van], *m.* (—**s**, *pl.* —**e**) divan, sofa, couch.
doch [dɔx], *adv.*, *conj.* however, though, although, nevertheless, yet, but; after all, (*emphatic*) yes.
Docht [dɔxt], *m.* (—**es**, *pl.* —**e**) wick.
Dock [dɔk], *n.* (—**s**, *pl.* —**s**, —**e**) dock.
Dogge ['dɔgə], *f.* (—, *pl.* —**n**) bulldog, mastiff; Great Dane.
Dogmatiker [dɔg'ma:tɪkər], *m.* (—**s**, *pl.* —) dogmatist.
dogmatisch [dɔg'ma:tɪʃ], *adj.* dogmatic, doctrinal.
Dohle ['do:lə], *f.* (—, *pl.* —**n**) (*Orn.*) jackdaw.
Doktor ['dɔktɔr], *m.* (—**s**, *pl.* —**en**) doctor; physician, surgeon.
Dolch [dɔlç], *m.* (—**es**, *pl.* —**e**) dagger, dirk.
Dolde ['dɔldə], *f.* (—, *pl.* —**n**) (*Bot.*) umbel.
Dolmetscher ['dɔlmɛtʃər], *m.* (—**s**, *pl.* —) interpreter.
dolmetschen ['dɔlmɛtʃən], *v.a.* interpret.
Dolomiten [dolo'mi:tən], *pl.* Dolomites.
Dom [do:m], *m.* (—**s**, *pl.* —**e**) cathedral; dome, cupola.
Domherr ['do:mhɛr], *m.* (—**n**, *pl.* —**en**) canon, prebendary.
dominieren [domi'ni:rən], *v.a.* dominate, domineer.
Dominikaner [domini'ka:nər], *m.* (—**s**, *pl.* —) Dominican friar.
dominikanische Republik [domini'ka:nɪʃə repu'bli:k], *f.* Dominican Republic.
Domizil [domi'tsi:l], *n.* (—**s**, *pl.* —**e**) domicile, residence, address.
Domkapitel ['do:mkapɪtəl], *n.* (—**s**, *pl.* —) dean and chapter.
Dompfaff ['do:mpfaf], *m.* (—**s**, *pl.* —**en**) (*Orn.*) bullfinch.
Dompropst ['do:mpro:pst], *m.* (—**es**, *pl.* ⸚**e**) provost.
Donau ['do:nau], *f.* (—, *no pl.*) Danube.
Donner ['dɔnər], *m.* (—**s**, *no pl.*) thunder.
donnern ['dɔnərn], *v.n.* thunder; (*fig.*) storm, rage.
Donnerschlag ['dɔnərʃla:k], *m.* (—**s**, *pl.* ⸚**e**) thunderclap.
Donnerstag ['dɔnərsta:k], *m.* (—**s**, *pl.* —**e**) Thursday; *Grün* —, Maundy Thursday.
Donnerwetter ['dɔnərvɛtər], *n.* (—**s**, *pl.* —) thunderstorm; *zum* — (*nochmal*)! hang it all, confound it!
doppeldeutig ['dɔpəldɔytɪç], *adj.* ambiguous.
Doppelgänger ['dɔpəlgɛŋər], *m.* (—**s**, *pl.* —) double.
Doppellaut ['dɔpəllaut], *m.* (—**s**, *pl.* —**e**) diphthong.
doppeln ['dɔpəln] *see* **verdoppeln.**
doppelsinnig ['dɔpəlzɪnɪç] *see* **doppeldeutig.**
doppelt ['dɔpəlt], *adj.* double, twofold.
Doppelzwirn ['dɔpəltsvɪrn], *m.* (—**s**, *no pl.*) double-thread.
Dorf [dɔrf], *n.* (—**es**, *pl.* ⸚**er**) village.
dörflich ['dœrflɪç], *adj.* rural, rustic.
dorisch ['do:rɪʃ], *adj.* Doric.
Dorn [dɔrn], *m.* (—**s**, *pl.* —**en**) thorn, prickle; (*Bot.*) spine; (*buckle*) tongue.
dornig ['dɔrnɪç], *adj.* thorny.
Dornröschen ['dɔrnrø:sçən], *n.* (—**s**, *pl.* —) Sleeping Beauty.
Dorothea [doro'te:a], *f.* Dorothea, Dorothy.
dorren ['dɔrən] *see* **verdorren.**
dörren ['dœrən], *v.a.* dry, make dry, parch.
Dörrobst ['dœrrobst], *n.* (—**es**, *no pl.*) dried fruit.
Dorsch [dɔrʃ], *m.* (—**es**, *pl.* —**e**) cod, codfish.
dort [dɔrt], (*Austr.*) **dorten** ['dɔrtən], *adv.* there, yonder; *von* — *aus*, from that point, from there.
dorther ['dɔrthe:r], *adv.* from there, therefrom, thence.
dorthin ['dɔrthɪn], *adv.* to that place, thereto, thither.
dortig ['dɔrtɪç], *adj.* of that place, local.
Dose ['do:zə], *f.* (—, *pl.* —**n**) box, tin, can.
dösen ['dø:zən], *v.n.* doze, daydream.
Dosis ['do:zɪs], *f.* (—, *pl.* **Dosen**) dose.
Dotter ['dɔtər], *n.* (—**s**, *pl.* —) yolk (of egg).
Dozent [do'tsɛnt], *m.* (—**en**, *pl.* —**en**) university lecturer; (*Am.*) Assistant Professor.
dozieren [do'tsi:rən], *v.n.* lecture.
Drache ['draxə], *m.* (—**n**, *pl.* —**n**) dragon; kite; (*fig.*) termagant, shrew.
Dragoner [dra'go:nər], *m.* (—**s**, *pl.* —) dragoon.
Draht [dra:t], *m.* (—**es**, *pl.* ⸚**e**) wire.
drahten ['dra:tən], *v.a.* wire, telegraph.
Drahtgewebe ['dra:tgəve:bə], *n.* (—**s**, *pl.* —) wire-gauze.
Drahtgitter ['dra:tgɪtər], *m.* (—**s**, *pl.* —) wire grating.
drahtlos ['dra:tlo:s], *adj.* wireless.
Drahtseilbahn ['dra:tzaɪlba:n], *f.* (—, *pl.* —**en**) cable (funicular) railway.
Drahtzange ['dra:ttsaŋə], *f.* (—, *pl.* —**n**) pliers.
drall [dral], *adj.* buxom, plump.
Drama ['dra:ma], *n.* (—**s**, *pl.* —**men**) drama.
Dramatiker [dra'ma:tɪkər], *m.* (—**s**, *pl.* —) dramatist.
dramatisch [dra'ma:tɪʃ], *adj.* dramatic.
dran [dran] *see* **daran.**
Drang [draŋ], *m.* (—**s**, *no pl.*) urge; rush; throng; pressure; impulse.
drängeln ['drɛŋəln], *v.a.* jostle.
drängen ['drɛŋən], *v.a.* press, urge; *die Zeit drängt*, time presses; *es drängt mich*, I feel called upon.
Drangsal ['draŋza:l], *f.* or *n.* (—**s**, *pl.* —**e** *or* —**en**) distress, misery.
drapieren [dra'pi:rən], *v.a.* drape.

drastisch ['drastɪʃ], *adj.* drastic.
drauf [drauf] *see* **darauf.**
Draufgänger ['draufgɛŋər], *m.* (—s, *pl.* —) daredevil.
draußen ['drausən], *adv.* outside, without, out of doors.
drechseln ['drɛksəln], *v.a.* turn (on a lathe); *Phrasen* —, turn phrases.
Drechsler ['drɛkslər], *m.* (—s, *pl.* —) turner.
Dreck [drɛk], *m.* (—s, *no pl.*) dirt, mire, dust, filth, dung.
dreckig ['drɛkɪç], *adj.* dirty, filthy, muddy.
drehbar ['dre:ba:r], *adj.* revolving, swivelling.
Drehbuch ['dre:bu:x], *n.* (—s, *pl.* ¨er) (*film*) script.
drehen ['dre:ən], *v.a.* turn; (*film*) shoot. — *v.n.* turn round, veer.
Drehorgel ['dre:ɔrgəl], *f.* (—, *pl.* —n) barrel-organ.
Drehrad ['dre:ra:t], *n.* (—s, *pl.* ¨er) fly-wheel.
Drehung ['dre:uŋ], *f.* (—, *pl.* —en) rotation, turn, revolution.
drei [draɪ], *num. adj.* three.
dreiblätterig ['draɪblɛtərɪç], *adj.* trifoliate.
Dreieck ['draɪɛk], *n.* (—s, *pl.* —e) triangle.
dreieckig ['draɪɛkɪç], *adj.* triangular, three-cornered.
dreieinig [draɪ'aɪnɪç], *adj.* (*Theol.*) triune.
dreifach ['draɪfax], *adj.* threefold, triple.
Dreifaltigkeit [draɪ'faltɪçkaɪt], *f.* (—, *no pl.*) (*Theol.*) Trinity.
Dreifuß ['draɪfu:s], *m.* (—es, *pl.* ¨e) tripod.
dreijährlich ['draɪjɛrlɪç], *adj.* triennial.
Dreikönigsfest [draɪ'kø:nɪksfɛst], *n.* (—es, *no pl.*) Epiphany.
dreimonatlich ['draɪmo:natlɪç], *adj.* quarterly.
Dreirad ['draɪra:t], *n.* (—s, *pl.* ¨er) tricycle.
dreiseitig ['draɪzaɪtɪç], *adj.* trilateral.
dreißig ['draɪsɪç], *num. adj.* thirty.
dreist [draɪst], *adj.* bold, audacious; impudent.
dreistellig ['draɪʃtɛlɪç], *adj.* —*e Zahl*, number of three figures.
dreistimmig ['draɪʃtɪmɪç], *adj.* for three voices.
Dreistufenrakete ['draɪʃtu:fənra'ke:tə], *f.* (—, *pl.* —n) three-stage rocket.
dreistündig ['draɪʃtyndɪç], *adj.* lasting three hours.
dreitägig ['draɪtɛ:gɪç], *adj.* lasting three days.
dreiteilig ['draɪtaɪlɪç], *adj.* tripartite; three-piece.
dreizehn ['draɪtse:n], *num. adj.* thirteen.
Drell [drɛl], *m.* (—s, *no pl.*) *see* **Drillich.**
Dresche ['drɛʃə], *f.* (—, *no pl.*) thrashing, beating.
dreschen ['drɛʃən], *v.a. irr.* (*corn*) thresh; (*person*) thrash.
Dreschflegel ['drɛʃfle:gəl], *m.* (—s, *pl.* —) flail.
dressieren [drɛ'si:rən], *v.a.* (*animal*) train; break in.
Dressur [drɛ'su:r], *f.* (—, *pl.* —en) training, breaking-in.
Drillbohrer ['drɪlbo:rər], *m.* (—s, *pl.* —) drill.
drillen ['drɪlən], *v.a.* (*a hole*) bore; (*soldiers*) drill.
Drillich ['drɪlɪç], *m.* (—s, *pl.* —e) drill, canvas.
Drilling ['drɪlɪŋ], *m.* (—s, *pl.* —e) three-barrelled gun; (*pl.*) triplets.
drin [drɪn] *see* **darin.**
dringen ['drɪŋən], *v.n. irr.* penetrate, force o.'s way through; *auf etwas* —, insist on s.th.
dringlich ['drɪŋlɪç], *adj.* urgent, pressing.
drinnen ['drɪnən], *adv.* inside, within.
drittens ['drɪtəns], *adv.* thirdly.
droben ['dro:bən], *adv.* up there, above, aloft, overhead.
Droge ['dro:gə], *f.* (—, *pl.* —n) drug.
Drogerie [dro:gə'ri:], *f.* (—, *pl.* —n) druggist's shop, chemist's; (*Am.*) drugstore.
drohen ['dro:ən], *v.a.*, *v.n.* threaten, menace.
Drohne ['dro:nə], *f.* (—, *pl.* —n) drone.
dröhnen ['drø:nən], *v.n.* boom, roar.
Drohung ['dro:uŋ], *f.* (—, *pl.* —en) threat, menace.
drollig ['drɔlɪç], *adj.* droll, odd, quaint.
Dromedar [drɔmə'da:r], *n.* (—s, *pl.* —e) dromedary.
Droschke ['drɔʃkə], *f.* (—, *pl.* —n) cab, hansom, taxi.
Drossel ['drɔsəl], *f.* (—, *pl.* —n) thrush.
Drosselader ['drɔsəla:dər], *f.* (—, *pl.* —n) jugular vein.
Drosselbein ['drɔsəlbaɪn], *n.* (—s, *pl.* —e) collar-bone.
drosseln ['drɔsəln], *v.a.* throttle. *See also* **erdrosseln.**
drüben ['dry:bən], *adv.* over there, on the other side.
drüber ['dry:bər] *see* **darüber.**
Druck [druk], *m.* (—s, *pl.* ¨e, —e) pressure, squeeze; (*Phys.*) compression; (*Typ.*) impression, print; (*fig.*) hardship.
Druckbogen ['drukbo:gən], *m.* (—s, *pl.* —) proof-sheet, proof.
Druckbuchstabe ['drukbu:xʃta:bə], *m.* (—n, *pl.* —n) letter, type.
Drückeberger ['drykəbɛrgər], *m.* (—s, *pl.* —) slacker, shirker.
drucken ['drukən], *v.a.* print.
drücken ['drykən], *v.a.* press, squeeze; trouble, oppress. — *v.r. sich* —, sneak away, shirk.
Drucker ['drukər], *m.* (—s, *pl.* —) printer.
Drücker ['drykər], *m.* (—s, *pl.* —) (*door*) handle, latch; (*gun*) trigger.
Druckerei ['drukəraɪ], *f.* (—, *pl.* —en) printing shop.

Druckerschwärze ['drukərʃvɛrtsə], *f.* (—, *no pl.*) printing-ink.
Druckfehler ['drukfe:lər], *m.* (**—s**, *pl.* —) misprint, printer's error.
druckfertig ['drukfɛrtɪç], *adj.* ready for press.
Drucksache ['drukzaxə], *f.* (—, *pl.* **—n**) (*Postal*) printed matter.
drum [drum] *see* **darum**.
drunten ['druntən], *adv.* down there, below.
drunter ['druntər] *see* **darunter**.
Drüse ['dry:zə], *f.* (—, *pl.* **—n**) gland.
Dschungel ['dʒuŋəl], *m.* or *n.* (**—s**, *pl.* —) jungle.
du [du:], *pers. pron.* thou, you.
ducken ['dukən], *v.a.* bring down, humble. — *v.r. sich* —, duck, stoop, crouch.
dudeln ['du:dəln], *v.n.* play the bagpipes; tootle.
Dudelsack ['du:dəlzak], *m.* (**—s**, *pl.* **¨e**) bagpipe(s).
Duft [duft], *m.* (**—s**, *pl.* **¨e**) scent, odour, fragrance, aroma, perfume.
duften ['duftən], *v.n.* be fragrant.
duftig ['duftɪç], *adj.* fragrant, odoriferous, perfumed.
dulden ['duldən], *v.a.* suffer, endure, bear, tolerate.
duldsam ['dultza:m], *adj.* tolerant, indulgent, patient.
dumm [dum], *adj.* stupid, foolish, dull.
Dummheit ['dumhaɪt], *f.* (—, *pl.* **—en**) stupidity, folly.
dumpf [dumpf], *adj.* musty; (*air*) close; (*sound*) hollow; (*fig.*) gloomy.
dumpfig ['dumpfɪç], *adj.* damp, musty, stuffy.
Düne ['dy:nə], *f.* (—, *pl.* **—n**) dune, sand-hill.
Düngemittel ['dyŋəmɪtəl], *n.* (**—s**, *pl.* —) fertilizer.
düngen ['dyŋən], *v.a.* manure, fertilize.
Dünger ['dyŋər], *m.* (**—s**, *no pl.*) compost, artificial manure.
dunkel ['duŋkəl], *adj.* dark; (*fig.*) obscure, mysterious.
Dünkel ['dyŋkəl], *m.* (**—s**, *no pl.*) conceit, arrogance.
dünkelhaft ['dyŋkəlhaft], *adj.* conceited, arrogant.
Dunkelheit ['duŋkəlhaɪt], *f.* (—, *no pl.*) darkness, obscurity.
dunkeln ['duŋkəln], *v.n.* grow dark.
dünken ['dyŋkən], *v.n.* (*rare*) seem, appear. — *v.r. sich* —, fancy o.s., imagine o.s.
dünn [dyn], *adj.* thin, slim, weak.
Dunst [dunst], *m.* (**—es**, *pl.* **¨e**) vapour, fume; exhalation; haze; *einem blauen — vormachen*, humbug a p.
dünsten ['dynstən], *v.a.* stew.
dunstig ['dunstɪç], *adj.* misty, hazy.
Dunstkreis ['dunstkraɪs], *m.* (**—es**, *pl.* **—e**) atmosphere.
Dunstobst ['dunsto:pst], *n.* (**—es**, *no pl.*) stewed fruit.
duodez [duo'de:ts], *adj.* (*Typ.*) duodecimo (12mo).
Duodezfürst [duo'de:tsfyrst], *m.* (**—en**, *pl.* **—en**) petty prince, princeling.
Dur [du:r], *n.* (*Mus.*) major; sharp.
durch [durç], *prep.* (*Acc.*) (*local*) through, across; (*temporal*) during, throughout; (*manner*) by means of, by. — *adv.* thoroughly, through.
durchaus [durç'aus], *adv.* throughout, quite, by all means, absolutely.
Durchblick ['durçblɪk], *m.* (**—s**, *pl.* **—e**) vista, view.
durchbohren [durç'bo:rən], *v.a. insep.* perforate, pierce.
durchbrennen ['durçbrɛnən], *v.n. irr.* (*aux.* sein) abscond, bolt.
durchbringen ['durçbrɪŋən], *v.a. irr.* bring through, get through; squander (money); pull (a sick person) through. — *v.r. sich redlich* —, make an honest living.
Durchbruch ['durçbrux], *m.* (**—s**, *pl.* **¨e**) breach, break-through.
durchdrängen ['durçdrɛŋən], *v.r. sich* —, force o.'s way through.
durchdringen ['durçdrɪŋən], *v.n. irr. sep.* (*aux.* sein) get through. — [durç'drɪŋən], *v.a. irr. insep.* penetrate, pierce, permeate, pervade.
durchdrücken ['durçdrykən], *v.a.* press through; (*fig.*) carry through.
durcheilen [durç'aɪlən], *v.a. insep.* hurry through.
Durcheinander [durçaɪn'andər], *n.* (**—s**, *no pl.*) confusion, muddle.
durcheinander [durçaɪn'andər], *adv.* in confusion, pell-mell.
Durchfall ['durçfal], *m.* (**—s**, *no pl.*) diarrhoea; (*exams etc.*) failure.
durchfallen ['durçfalən], *v.n. irr.* (*aux.* sein) fall through, come to nought; (*exams etc.*) fail.
durchflechten [durç'flɛçtən], *v.a. irr.* interweave, intertwine.
durchfliegen [durç'fli:gən], *v.a. irr.* fly through; read superficially, skim through.
durchforschen [durç'fɔrʃən], *v.a. insep.* explore, scrutinise, examine thoroughly.
Durchfuhr ['durçfu:r], *f.* (—, *pl.* **—en**) passage, transit.
durchführbar ['durçfy:rba:r], *adj.* practicable, feasible.
durchführen ['durçfy:rən], *v.a.* escort through; (*fig.*) execute, bring about, carry through.
Durchgang ['durçgaŋ], *m.* (**—s**, *pl.* **¨e**) passage, thoroughfare; (*Comm.*) transit.
Durchgänger ['durçgɛŋər], *m.* (**—s**, *pl.* —) runaway horse, bolter; (*fig.*) hothead.
durchgängig ['durçgɛŋɪç], *adj.* general, universal.
durchgehen ['durçge:ən], *v.n. irr.* (*aux.* sein) go through; (*fig.*) abscond; (*horse*) bolt; (*proposal*) be carried. — *v.a. irr.* (*aux.* sein) peruse, review, go over.

durchgreifen ['durçgraɪfən], *v.n. irr.* act decisively, take strong action.
durchhauen ['durçhauən], *v.a.* cut through; *einen* —, flog s.o.
durchkommen ['durçkɔmən], *v.n. irr.* (*aux.* sein) get through; (*exams etc.*) pass.
durchkreuzen [durç'krɔytsən], *v.a. insep.* cross out; (*fig.*) thwart.
durchlassen ['durçlasən], *v.a. irr.* let pass.
Durchlaucht ['durçlauxt], *f.* (— *pl.* —**en**) Highness.
durchleuchten [durç'lɔyçtən], *v.a. insep.* (*Med.*) X-ray.
durchlöchern [durç'lœçərn], *v.a. insep.* perforate, riddle.
durchmachen ['durcmaxən], *v.a.* go through, suffer.
Durchmesser ['durcmɛsər], *m.* (—**s**, *pl.* —) diameter.
durchnässen [durç'nɛsən], *v.a. insep.* wet to the skin, soak.
durchnehmen ['durçne:mən], *v.a. irr.* go over *or* cover (a subject).
durchpausen ['durçpauzən], *v.a.* trace, copy.
durchqueren [durç'kve:rən], *v.a. insep.* cross, traverse.
Durchsage ['durçza:gə], *f.* (—, *pl.* —**n**) (radio) announcement.
durchschauen [durç'ʃauən], *v.a. insep. einen* —, see through s.o.
durchscheinend ['durçʃaɪnənt], *adj.* transparent, translucent.
Durchschlag ['durçʃla:k], *m.* (—**s**, *pl.* ⸚**e**) strainer, sieve, colander, filter; carbon copy.
durchschlagen ['durçʃla:gən], *v.a. irr. insep.* strain, filter. — *v.r. irr. sich* —, fight o.'s way through.
durchschlagend ['durçʃla:gənt], *adj.* thorough, complete, effective.
Durchschnitt ['durçʃnɪt], *m.* (—**s**, *pl.* —**e**) average; (*Med. etc.*) cross section.
durchschnittlich ['durçʃnɪtlɪç], *adj.* average; ordinary.
durchschossen [durç'ʃɔsən], *adj.* interleaved; interwoven.
durchseihen ['durçzaɪən], *v.a. see* **durchsieben**.
durchsetzen [durç'zɛtsən], *v.a. insep.* intersperse; ['durçzɛtsən], *v.a. sep.* have o.'s way (with s.o.). — *v.r. sep. sich* —, make o.'s way successfully, succeed.
Durchsicht ['durçzɪçt], *f.* (—, *no pl.*) revision, inspection, perusal.
durchsichtig ['durçzɪçtɪç], *adj.* transparent.
durchsickern ['durçzɪkərn], *v.n.* (*aux.* sein) trickle through, ooze through.
durchsieben ['durçzi:bən], *v.a.* strain, filter, sift.
durchsprechen ['durçʃprɛxən], *v.a. irr.* talk over, discuss.
durchstöbern [durc'ʃtø:bərn], *v.a. insep.* rummage through.
durchstreichen ['durçʃtraɪçən], *v.a. irr.* cross out, delete.
durchstreifen [durç'ʃtraɪfən], *v.a insep.* roam (through).
durchströmen [durç'ʃtrø:mən], *v.a. insep.* flow through, permeate.
durchsuchen [durç'zu:xən], *v.a. insep.* search thoroughly, examine closely.
durchtrieben [durç'tri:bən], *adj.* artful, sly, cunning, crafty.
durchweben [durç've:bən], *v.a.* interweave.
durchweg(s) ['durçvɛk(s)], *adv.* without exception, every time, throughout.
durchwühlen [durç'vy:lən], *v.a. insep.* search; ransack.
durchziehen [durç'tsi:ən], *v.a. irr. insep.* wander through, traverse; ['durçtsi:ən], *v.a. irr. sep.* interlace (with threads); draw through.
durchzucken [durç'tsukən], *v.a. insep.* flash through, convulse.
Durchzug ['durçtsu:k], *m.* (—**s**, *no pl.*) passage, march through; (*air*) draught.
dürfen ['dyrfən], *v.n. irr.* be permitted; be allowed; dare; be likely.
dürftig ['dyrftɪç], *adj.* paltry, insufficient, poor.
dürr [dyr], *adj.* dry, arid, withered; (*wood*) dead; (*persons*) thin, gaunt.
Dürre ['dyrə], *f.* (—, *pl.* —**n**) aridity, dryness; drought; (*persons*) thinness.
Durst [durst], *m.* (—**es**, *no pl.*) thirst.
dürsten ['dyrstən], *v.n.* thirst.
durstig ['durstɪç], *adj.* thirsty.
Dusche ['du:ʃə], *f.* (—, *pl.* —**n**) shower (bath).
Düse ['dy:zə], *f.* (—, *pl.* —**n**) jet.
duselig ['du:zəlɪç], *adj.* drowsy; silly.
düster ['dy:stər], *adj.* dark, gloomy; sad, mournful; sombre.
Dutzend ['dutsənt], *n.* (—**s**, *pl.* —**e**) dozen.
Duzbruder ['du:tsbru:dər], *m.* (—**s**, *pl.* ⸚) crony, chum; close friend.
duzen ['du:tsen], *v.a.* be on close terms with.
dynamisch [dy'na:mɪʃ], *adj.* dynamic(al).

E

E [e:], *n.* (—**s**, *pl.* —**s**) the letter E; (*Mus.*) *E Dur*, E major; *E Moll*, E minor.
Ebbe ['ɛbə], *f.* (—, *pl.* —**n**) ebb, low tide; — *und Flut*, the tides.
ebben ['ɛbən], *v.n.* ebb.
eben ['e:bən], *adj.* even, level, plane; (*fig.*) plain. — *adv.* precisely, exactly.
Ebenbild ['e:bənbɪlt], *n.* (—**es**, *pl.* —**er**) likeness, image.
ebenbürtig ['e:bənbyrtɪç], *adj.* of equal birth *or* rank; equal.

ebenda ['e:bənda:], *adv.* in the same place.
ebendeswegen ['e:bəndɛsve:gən], *adv.* for that very reason.
Ebene ['e:bənə], *f.* (—, *pl.* —n) plain; level ground; (*Maths.*) plane; *schiefe* —, inclined plane.
ebenfalls ['e:bənfals], *adv.* likewise, also, too, as well.
Ebenholz ['e:bənhɔlts], *n.* (—es, *no pl.*) ebony.
Ebenmaß ['e:bənma:s], *n.* (—es, *pl.* —e) symmetry.
ebenmäßig ['e:bənmɛ:sɪç], *adj.* symmetrical.
ebenso ['e:bənzo:], *adv.* in the same way; — *wie*, just as . . .
Eber ['e:bər], *m.* (—s, *pl.* —) (*Zool.*) boar.
Eberesche ['e:bərɛʃə], *f.* (—, *pl.* —n) (*Bot.*) mountain ash, rowan.
ebnen ['e:bnən], *v.a.* even out, level; smoothe.
echt [ɛçt], *adj.* genuine, real, true, authentic, pure.
Ecke ['ɛkə], *f.* (—, *pl.* —en) corner, nook.
eckig ['ɛkɪç], *adj.* angular.
Eckzahn ['ɛktsa:n], *m.* (—s, *pl.* ¨e) eye tooth; canine tooth.
Eckziegel ['ɛktsi:gəl], *m.* (—s, *pl.* —) (*Build.*) header.
edel ['e:dəl], *adj.* noble; well-born, aristocratic; (*metal*) precious.
Edelmann ['e:dəlman], *m.* (—s, *pl.* **Edelleute**) nobleman, aristocrat.
Edelmut ['e:dəlmu:t], *m.* (—s, *no pl.*) generosity, magnanimity.
Edelstein ['e:dəlʃtaɪn], *m.* (—s, *pl.* —e) precious stone, jewel.
Edeltanne ['e:dəltanə], *f.* (—, *pl.* —n) (*Bot.*) silver fir.
Edelweiß ['edəlvaɪs], *n.* (—sses, *no pl.*) (*Bot.*) edelweiss; lion's foot.
Eduard ['e:duart], *m.* Edward.
Efeu ['e:fɔy], *m.* (—s, *no pl.*) (*Bot.*) ivy.
Effekten [e'fɛktən], *m. pl.* goods and chattels; effects; stocks, securities.
Effektenbörse [e'fɛktənbœrzə], *f.* (—, *pl.* —n) Stock Exchange.
Effekthascherei [e'fɛkthaʃəraɪ], *f.* (—, *pl.* —en) sensationalism, clap-trap.
effektuieren [efɛktu'i:rən], *v.a.* (*Comm.*) execute, effectuate.
egal [e'ga:l], *adj.* equal; all the same.
Egge ['ɛgə], *f.* (—, *pl.* —n) harrow.
Egoismus [ego'ɪsmus], *m.* (—, *no pl.*) selfishness, egoism.
egoistisch [ego'ɪstɪʃ], *adj.* selfish, egoistic(al).
Ehe ['e:ə,] *f.* (—, *pl.* —n) marriage.
ehe ['e:ə], *conj.* before; *adv.* formerly; *je* —*r*, *desto besser*, the sooner, the better.
Ehebrecher ['e:əbrɛçər], *m.* (—s, *pl.* —) adulterer.
Ehebruch ['e:əbrux], *m.* (—s, *pl.* ¨e) adultery.
Ehefrau ['e:əfrau], *f.* (—, *pl.* —en) wife, spouse, consort.
Ehegatte ['e:əgatə], *m.* (—n, *pl.* —n) husband, spouse.
ehelich ['e:əlɪç], *adj.* matrimonial; (*children*) legitimate.
Ehelosigkeit ['e:əlo:zɪçkaɪt], *f.* (—, *no pl.*) celibacy.
ehemalig ['e:əma:lɪç], *adj.* former, late.
ehemals ['e:əma:ls], *adv.* formerly, once, of old.
Ehemann ['e:əman], *m.* (—s, *pl.* ¨er) husband.
ehern ['e:ərn], *adj.* brazen; of brass, of bronze.
Ehestand ['e:əʃtant], *m.* (—s, *no pl.*) matrimony.
ehestens ['e:əstəns], *adv.* as soon as possible.
Ehre ['e:rə], *f.* (—, *pl.* —n) honour, reputation, respect, distinction, glory.
ehren ['e:rən], *v.a.* honour, respect, esteem; *sehr geehrter Herr*, dear Sir.
Ehrenbezeigung ['e:rənbətsaɪguŋ], *f.* (—, *pl.* —en) mark of respect; (*Mil.*) salute.
Ehrenbürger ['e:rənbyrgər], *m.* (—s, *pl.* —) honorary citizen *or* freeman.
Ehrendame ['erənda:mə], *f.* (—, *pl.* —n) maid of honour.
Ehrenerklärung ['e:rənɛrklɛ:ruŋ], *f.* (—, *pl.* —en) reparation, apology.
Ehrengericht ['e:rəngərɪçt], *n.* (—s, *pl.* —e) court of honour.
ehrenhaft ['e:rənhaft], *adj.* honourable, worthy.
Ehrenpreis ['e:rənpraɪs], *m.* (—es, *pl.* —e) prize; (*no pl.*) (*Bot.*) speedwell.
Ehrenrettung ['e:rənrɛtuŋ], *f.* (—, *pl.* —en) vindication.
ehrenrührig ['e:rənry:rɪç], *adj.* defamatory, calumnious.
ehrenvoll ['e:rənfɔl], *adj.* honourable.
ehrenwert ['e:rənvɛrt], *adj.* honourable, respectable.
ehrerbietig ['e:rərbi:tɪç], *adj.* reverential, respectful.
Ehrfurcht ['e:rfurçt], *f.* (—, *no pl.*) reverence, awe.
Ehrgefühl ['e:rgəfy:l], *n.* (—s, *no pl.*) sense of honour.
Ehrgeiz ['e:rgaɪts], *m.* (—es, *no pl.*) ambition.
ehrlich ['e:rlɪç], *adj.* honest; — *währt am längsten*, honesty is the best policy.
ehrlos ['e:rlo:s], *adj.* dishonourable, infamous.
ehrsam ['e:rza:m], *adj.* respectable, honourable.
Ehrwürden ['e:rvyrdən], *m.* & *f.* (*form of address*) *Euer* —, Reverend Sir, Your Reverence.
ehrwürdig ['e:rvyrdɪç], *adj.* venerable, reverend.
Ei [aɪ], *n.* (—s, *pl.* —er) egg, ovum.
ei [aɪ], *int.* ay, indeed.
Eibe ['aɪbə], *f.* (—, *pl.* —n) (*Bot.*) yew.
Eichamt ['aɪçamt], *n.* (—s, *pl.* ¨er) office of weights and measures; (*Am.*) bureau of standards.

Eichapfel [ˈaɪçapfəl], *m.* (—s, *pl.* ¨) oak apple.
Eiche [ˈaɪçə], *f.* (—, *pl.* —n) (*Bot.*) oak.
Eichel [ˈaɪçəl], *f.* (—, *pl.* —n) acorn; (*Anat.*) glans; (*Cards*) clubs.
eichen [ˈaɪçən], *v.a.* gauge, calibrate. — *adj.* made of oak.
Eichhörnchen [ˈaɪçhœrnçən] or **Eichkätzchen** [ˈaɪçkɛtsçən], *n.* (—s, *pl.* —) squirrel.
Eid [aɪt], *m.* (—es, *pl.* —e) oath; *falscher* —, perjury.
Eidam [ˈaɪdam], *m.* (—s, *pl.* —e) (*obs.*) son-in-law.
eidbrüchig [ˈaɪtbryçɪç], *adj.* guilty of perjury.
Eidechse [ˈaɪdɛksə], *f.* (—, *pl.* —n) lizard.
Eidesleistung [ˈaɪdəslaɪstuŋ], *f.* (—, *pl.* —en) affidavit.
Eidgenosse [ˈaɪtgənɔsə], *m.* (—n, *pl.* —n) confederate.
Eidgenossenschaft [ˈaɪtgənɔsənʃaft], *f.* (—, *pl.* —en) confederacy.
eidlich [ˈaɪtlɪç], *adj.* by oath, sworn.
Eidotter [ˈaɪdɔtər], *m.* & *n.* (—s, *pl.* —) yolk of an egg.
Eierbecher [ˈaɪərbɛçər], *m.* (—s, *pl.* —) egg cup.
Eierkuchen [ˈaɪərku:xən], *m.* (—s, *pl.* —) omelet(te), pancake.
Eierschale [ˈaɪərʃa:lə], *f.* (—, *pl.* —n) egg shell.
Eierspeise [ˈaɪərʃpaɪzə], *f.* (—, *pl.* —n) dish prepared with eggs.
Eierstock [ˈaɪərʃtɔk], *m.* (—s, *pl.* ¨e) ovary.
Eifer [ˈaɪfər], *m.* (—s, *no pl.*) zeal, eagerness, ardour, haste, passion, vehemence.
Eiferer [ˈaɪfərər], *m.* (—s, *pl.* —) zealot.
eifern [ˈaɪfərn], *v.n.* be zealous; *gegen einen* —, inveigh against s.o.
eiförmig [ˈaɪfœrmɪç], *adj.* oval, egg-shaped.
eifrig [ˈaɪfrɪç], *adj.* zealous, ardent, eager.
Eigelb [ˈaɪgɛlp], *n.* (—s, *no pl.*) yolk of (an) egg.
eigen [ˈaɪgən], *adj.* own; particular, peculiar.
Eigenart [ˈaɪgəna:rt], *f.* (—, *pl.* —en) peculiarity; idiosyncrasy.
eigenhändig [ˈaɪgənhɛndɪç], *adj.* with o.'s own hand.
Eigenheit [ˈaɪgənhaɪt], *f.* (—, *pl.* —en) peculiarity; idiosyncrasy.
eigenmächtig [ˈaɪgənmɛçtɪç], *adj.* arbitrary, autocratic, high-handed.
Eigenname [ˈaɪgənna:mə], *m.* (—ns, *pl.* —n) proper name.
Eigennutz [ˈaɪgənnuts], *m.* (—es, *no pl.*) self-interest, selfishness.
eigennützig [ˈaɪgənnytsɪç], *adj.* selfish, self-interested, self-seeking.
eigens [ˈaɪgəns], *adv.* particularly, specially.
Eigenschaft [ˈaɪgənʃaft], *f.* (—, *pl.* —en) quality, peculiarity; property.
Eigenschaftswort [ˈaɪgənʃaftsvɔrt], *n.* (—s, *pl.* ¨er) (*Gram.*) adjective.
Eigensinn [ˈaɪgənzɪn], *m.* (—s, *no pl.*) obstinacy.
eigentlich [ˈaɪgəntlɪç], *adj.* true, real; exact, literal.
Eigentum [ˈaɪgəntu:m], *n.* (—s, *pl.* ¨er) property, possession, estate.
Eigentümer [ˈaɪgənty:mər], *m.* (—s, *pl.* —) owner, proprietor.
eigenwillig [ˈaɪgənvɪlɪç], *adj.* self-willed.
eignen [ˈaɪgnən], *v.r.* *sich* — *für* (*zu*), suit, fit, be suitable *or* fit for (to).
Eilbote [ˈaɪlbo:tə], *m.* (—n, *pl.* —n) special messenger.
Eile [ˈaɪlə], *f.* (—, *no pl.*) haste, hurry.
eilen [ˈaɪlən], *v.n.* (*aux.* sein), *v.r.* (*sich* —), hasten, hurry; be urgent.
eilends [ˈaɪlənts], *adv.* hastily.
eilfertig [ˈaɪlfɛrtɪç], *adj.* hasty.
Eilgut [ˈaɪlgu:t], *n.* (—s, *pl.* ¨er) express goods.
eilig [ˈaɪlɪç], *adj.* hasty, speedy; pressing, urgent.
Eilzug [ˈaɪltsu:k], *m.* (—s, *pl.* ¨e) fast train.
Eimer [ˈaɪmər], *m.* (—s, *pl.* —) pail, bucket.
ein(e) [ˈaɪn(ə)], *indef. art*, a, an; *was für* —; what kind of a(n). — *num. adj.* one; — *jeder*, each one.
einander [aɪnˈandər], *adv.* each other, one another.
einarbeiten [ˈaɪnarbaɪtən], *v.a.* train, familiarise s.o. with. —*v.r.* (*aux.* haben) *sich* —, familiarize o.s.
einäschern [ˈaɪnɛʃərn], *v.a.* reduce to ashes, incinerate; cremate.
einatmen [ˈaɪna:tmən], *v.a.* breathe in, inhale.
einätzen [ˈaɪnɛtsən], *v.a.* etch in.
einäugig [ˈaɪnɔygɪç], *adj.* one-eyed.
Einbahnstraße [ˈaɪnba:nʃtra:sə], *f.* (—, *pl.* —n) one-way street.
Einband [ˈaɪnbant], *m.* (—s, *pl.* ¨e) binding, cover of book.
einbändig [ˈaɪnbɛndɪç], *adj.* in one volume.
einbauen [ˈaɪnbauən], *v.a.* build in.
einbegreifen [ˈaɪnbəgraɪfən], *v.a.* *irr.* include, comprise.
einberufen [ˈaɪnbəru:fən], *v.a.* *irr.* convene, convoke; (*Mil.*) call up.
einbeziehen [ˈaɪnbətsi:ən], *v.a.* *irr.* include.
einbiegen [ˈaɪnbi:gən], *v.n.* *irr.* turn into (road).
einbilden [ˈaɪnbɪldən], *v.r.* *sich* —, imagine, fancy.
Einbildung [ˈaɪnbɪlduŋ], *f.* (—, *no pl.*) imagination, fancy, delusion; conceit.
einbinden [ˈaɪnbɪndən], *v.a.* *irr.* (*book*) bind.
Einblick [ˈaɪnblɪk], *m.* (—s, *no pl.*) insight.
Einbrecher [ˈaɪnbrɛçər], *m.* (—s, *pl.* —) burglar; intruder.

Einbrenne ['aɪnbrɛnə], *f.* (—, *pl.* —n) thickening of soup.
einbringen ['aɪnbrɪŋən], *v.a. irr.* bring in, yield, fetch (a price); *wieder* —, retrieve.
einbrocken ['aɪnbrɔkən], *v.a.* crumble; *einem etwas* —, (*fig.*) get s.o. into trouble.
Einbruch ['aɪnbrux], *m.* (—s, *pl.* ⸚e) breaking-in; burglary, house-breaking.
Einbuchtung ['aɪnbuxtuŋ], *f.* (—, *pl.* —en) bight, bay.
einbürgern ['aɪnbyrgərn], *v.a.* naturalise.
Einbuße ['aɪnbu:sə], *f.* (—, *pl.* —n) loss.
einbüßen ['aɪnby:sən], *v.a.* suffer a loss from, lose, forfeit.
eindämmen ['aɪndɛmən], *v.a.* dam in (*or* up).
Eindecker ['aɪndɛkər], *m.* (—s, *pl.* —) (*Aviat.*) monoplane.
eindeutig ['aɪndɔytɪç], *adj.* unequivocal, unambiguous.
eindrängen ['aɪndrɛŋən], *v.r. sich* —, intrude (into), force o.'s way in(to), interfere.
eindrillen ['aɪndrɪlən], *v.a. einem etwas* —, drum s.th. into s.o.
eindringen ['aindrɪŋən], *v.n. irr.* (*aux.* sein) enter, intrude; invade; penetrate.
eindringlich ['aɪndrɪŋlɪç], *adj.* forceful, urgent; impressive.
Eindruck ['aɪndruk], *m.* (—s, *pl.* ⸚e) impression.
eindrücken ['aɪndrykən], *v.a.* press in, squeeze in.
eindrucksfähig ['aɪndruksfɛ:ɪç], *adj.* impressionable.
einengen ['aɪnɛŋən], *v.a.* compress, limit, confine, cramp.
Einer ['aɪnər], *m.* (—s, *pl.* —) (*Maths.*) digit, unit.
einerlei ['aɪnərlaɪ], *adj.* the same, all the same.
einerseits ['aɪnərzaɪts], *adv.* on the one hand.
einfach ['aɪnfax], *adj.* single; simple, plain, uncomplicated; modest, homely.
einfädeln ['aɪnfɛ:dəln], *v.a.* thread.
einfahren ['aɪnfa:rən], *v.n. irr.* (*aux.* sein) drive in, enter. — *v.a.* run in (new car).
Einfahrt ['aɪnfa:rt], *f.* (—, *pl.* —en) entrance, gateway, drive; (*Min.*) descent.
Einfall ['aɪnfal], *m.* (—s, *pl.* ⸚e) falling-in, downfall, fall; (*Mil.*) invasion; (*fig.*) idea, inspiration.
einfallen ['aɪnfalən], *v.n. irr.* (*aux.* sein) fall in, fall into; (*Mil.*) invade; (*fig.*) occur to s.o.
Einfalt ['aɪnfalt], *f.* (—, *no pl.*) simplicity; silliness.
Einfaltspinsel ['aɪnfaltspɪnzəl], *m.* (—s, *pl.* —) simpleton, dunce.
einfangen ['aɪnfaŋən], *v.a. irr.* catch, get hold of.
einfarbig ['aɪnfarbɪç], *adj.* of one colour; monochrome.
einfassen ['aɪnfasən], *v.a.* border, trim; (*diamonds*) set.
Einfassung ['aɪnfasuŋ], *f.* (—, *pl.* —en) bordering, trimming, edging, framing.
einfetten ['aɪnfɛtən], *v.a.* grease, lubricate.
einfinden ['aɪnfɪndən], *v.r. irr. sich* —, appear, be present.
einflechten ['aɪnflɛçtən], *v.a. irr.* plait; (*fig.*) insert.
einfließen ['aɪnfli:sən], *v.n. irr.* (*aux.* sein) flow in; — *lassen*, (*fig.*) mention casually, slip in (a word).
einflößen ['aɪnflø:sən], *v.a.* infuse; (*fig.*) instil, inspire with.
Einfluß ['aɪnflus], *m.* (—sses, *pl.* ⸚sse) influx; (*fig.*) influence.
einflußreich ['aɪnflusraɪç], *adj.* influential.
einflüstern ['aɪnflystərn], *v.n.* suggest, insinuate.
einförmig ['aɪnfœrmɪç], *adj.* uniform; monotonous.
einfriedigen ['aɪnfri:dɪgən], *v.a.* fence in, enclose.
einfügen ['aɪnfy:gən], *v.a.* insert, include, fit in. — *v.r. sich* —, adapt o.s., become a part of.
Einfühlungsvermögen ['aɪnfyluŋsfɛrmø:gən], *n.* (—s, *no pl.*) (*Phil.*) empathy, sympathetic understanding.
Einfuhr ['aɪnfu:r], *f.* (—, *pl.* —en) importation, import.
einführen ['aɪnfy:rən], *v.a.* introduce; (*goods*) import.
Einführung ['aɪnfy:ruŋ], *f.* (—, *pl.* —en) introduction; (*goods*) importation.
einfüllen ['aɪnfylən], *v.a.* fill in, pour into, bottle.
Eingabe ['aɪnga:bə], *f.* (—, *pl.* —n) petitition; application.
Eingang ['aɪngaŋ], *m.* (—s, *pl.* ⸚e) entry, entrance; arrival.
eingangs ['aɪngaŋs], *adv.* in *or* at the beginning.
eingeben ['aɪnge:bən], *v.a. irr.* inspire (with); (*petition*) present, deliver; (*claim*) file; (*complaint*) bring; (*medicine*) administer.
eingeboren ['aɪngəbo:rən], *adj.* native; (*Theol.*) only-begotten.
Eingeborene ['aɪngəbo:rənə], *m.* (—n, *pl.* —n) native.
Eingebrachte ['aɪngəbraxtə], *n.* (—n, *no pl.*) dowry.
Eingebung ['aɪnge:buŋ], *f.* (—, *pl.* —en) inspiration.
eingedenk ['aɪngədɛŋk], *prep.* (*Genit.*) mindful of, remembering.
eingefleischt ['aɪngəflaɪʃt], *adj.* inveterate, confirmed.
eingehen ['aɪnge:ən], *v.n. irr.* (*aux.* sein) (*Comm.*) arrive; *auf etwas* —, enter into s.th., agree to s.th.; *auf etwas näher* —, enter into the details of s.th.; (*animals, plants*) die; (*cloth*) shrink.

eingehend ['aInge:ənt], *adj.* thorough, exhaustive.
Eingemachte ['aIngəmaxtə], *n.* (—**n**, *no pl.*) preserve.
eingenommen ['aIngənɔmən], *adj.* enthusiastic for, infatuated with; — *von sich*, conceited.
Eingeschlossenheit ['aIngəʃlɔsənhaIt], *f.* (—, *no pl.*) isolation, seclusion.
eingeschrieben ['aIngəʃri:bən], *adj.* registered (letter).
eingesessen ['aIngəzεsən], *adj.* old-established; resident.
Eingeständnis ['aIngəʃtεntnIs], *n.* (—**ses**, *pl.* —**se**) confession.
eingestehen ['aIngəʃte:ən], *v.a. irr.* confess to, avow.
Eingeweide ['aIngəvaIdə], *n. pl.* bowels, intestines.
eingewöhnen ['aIngəvø:nən], *v.r. sich* —, accustom o.s. to, get used to.
eingießen ['aIngi:sən], *v.a. irr.* pour in; pour out.
eingleisig ['aInglaIzIç], *adj.* single-track.
eingliedern ['aIngli:dərn], *v.r. sich* —, adapt o.s., fit in.
eingreifen ['aIngraIfən], *v.n. irr.* intervene in; interfere with, encroach on.
Eingriff ['aIngrIf], *m.* (—**s**, *pl.* —**e**) intervention, encroachment, infringement; (*Med.*) operation.
Einguß ['aIngus], *m.* (—**sses**, *pl.* ¨**sse**) infusion; enema.
einhaken ['aInha:kən], *v.a.* hook in. — *v.r. sich* —, (*fig.*) take a p.'s arm.
Einhalt ['aInhalt], *m.* (—**s**, *no pl.*) stop, check, prohibition, cessation; — *gebieten*, check, suppress.
einhalten ['aInhaltən], *v.a. irr.* observe, adhere to.
einhändigen ['aInhεndIgən], *v.a.* hand in, deliver.
einhauen ['aInhauən], *v.a.* hew in, break open.
Einhebung ['aInhe:buŋ], *f.* (—, *pl.* —**en**) (*taxes*) collection.
einheften ['aInhεftən], *v.a.* sew in, stitch in; (*papers*) file.
einhegen ['aInhe:gən], *v.a.* fence in, hedge in.
einheimisch ['aInhaImIʃ], *adj.* native; (*Bot.*) indigenous.
einheimsen ['aInhaImzən], *v.a.* reap.
Einheit ['aInhaIt], *f.* (—, *pl.* —**en**) unit, unity.
einheitlich ['aInhaItlIç], *adj.* uniform, consistent.
einheizen ['aInhaItsən], *v.a.*, *v.n.* heat the stove, light the fire.
einhellig ['aInhεlIç], *adj.* unanimous, harmonious.
einher [aIn'he:r], *adv.* forth, along, on.
einholen ['aInho:lən], *v.a.* obtain; catch up with. — *v.n.* go shopping.
Einhorn ['aInhɔrn], *n.* (—**s**, *pl.* ¨**er**) unicorn.
einhüllen ['aInhylən], *v.a.* wrap up, cover, envelop.

einig ['aInIç], *adj.* at one. — *adv.* in agreement.
einige ['aInIgə], *adj.* some, several.
einigemal ['aInIgəma:l], *adv.* several times.
einigen ['aInIgən], *v.a.* unite. — *v.r. sich* — *mit*, come to an agreement with.
einigermaßen [aInIgər'ma:sən], *adv.* to a certain extent.
Einigkeit ['aInIçkaIt], *f.* (—, *no pl.*) union; unity, unanimity, harmony.
Einigung ['aInIguŋ], *f.* (—, *no pl.*) agreement.
einimpfen ['aInImpfən], *v.a.* inoculate, vaccinate.
einjährig ['aInjε:rIg], *adj.* one-year-old, annual.
einkassieren ['aInkasi:rən], *v.a.* cash (*cheque*), collect (*money*).
Einkauf ['aInkauf], *m.* (—**s**, *pl.* ¨**e**) purchase, buy.
einkaufen ['aInkaufən], *v.a.* purchase, buy. — *v.n.* go shopping.
Einkäufer ['aInkɔyfər], *m.* (—**s**, *pl.* —) (*Comm.*) purchaser, buyer.
Einkehr ['aInke:r], *f.* (—, *no pl.*) stopping (at an inn); (*fig.*) meditation.
einkehren ['aInke:rən], *v.n.* (*aux.* sein) stop *or* put up (at an inn).
einkerkern ['aInkεrkərn], *v.a.* imprison.
einklagen ['aInkla:gən], *v.a.* (*Law*) sue for (money).
einklammern ['aInklamərn], *v.a.* bracket, enclose in brackets.
Einklang ['aInklaŋ], *m.* (—**s**, *no pl.*) accord, unison, harmony.
einkleben ['aInkle:bən], *v.a.* paste in.
einkleiden ['aInklaIdən], *v.a.* clothe; (*fig.*) invest; *sich — lassen*, (*Eccl.*) take the veil.
einklemmen ['aInklεmən], *v.a.* squeeze in, jam in.
einkochen ['aInkɔxen], *v.a.* preserve. — *v.n.* (*aux.* sein) boil down.
Einkommen ['aInkɔmən], *n.* (—**s**, *no pl.*) income, revenue.
einkommen ['aInkɔmən], *v.n. irr.* (*aux.* sein) *bei einem wegen etwas* —, apply to s.o. for s.th.
einkreisen ['aInkraIzən], *v.a.* encircle, isolate.
Einkünfte ['aInkynftə], *pl.* income, revenue; emoluments.
einladen ['aInla:dən], *v.a. irr.* load in; invite.
Einlage ['aInla:gə], *f.* (—, *pl.* —**en**) (*letter*) enclosure; (*Theat.*) addition to programme; (*game*) stake; (*Comm.*) investment.
einlagern ['aInla:gərn], *v.a.* (*goods*) store, warehouse; (*Mil.*) billet, quarter.
Einlaß ['aInlas], *m.* (—**sses**, *no pl.*) admission, admittance; (*water*) inlet.
einlassen ['aInlasən], *v.a. irr.* admit, allow in; let in. — *v.r. sich auf etwas* —, engage in s.th., enter into s.th.
Einlauf ['aInlauf], *m.* (—**s**, *no pl.*) entering; (*Med.*) enema.

einlaufen [ˈaɪnlaufən], *v.n. irr.* (*aux.* sein) (*Naut.*) enter harbour, put into port; (*material*) shrink.
einleben [ˈaɪnle:bən], *v.r.* *sich* —, grow accustomed to, settle down, acclimatise o.s.
einlegen [ˈaɪnle:gən], *v.a.* put in, lay in; enclose; (*money*) deposit; (*food*) pickle, preserve; *Fürbitte* —, intercede; *eingelegte Arbeit*, inlaid work.
einleiten [ˈaɪnlaɪtən], *v.a.* begin, introduce; institute.
Einleitung [ˈaɪnlaɪtuŋ], *f.* (—, *pl.* —**en**) introduction; (*book*) preface; (*Mus.*) prelude; (*Law*) institution.
einlenken [ˈaɪnlɛŋkən], *v.n.* turn in; give in, come round.
einleuchten [ˈaɪnlɔyçtən], *v.n.* become clear.
einlösen [ˈaɪnlø:zən], *v.a.* redeem; (*bill*) honour; (*cheque*) cash.
einmachen [ˈaɪnmaxən], *v.a.* preserve.
einmal [ˈaɪnma:l], *adv.* once; *es war* —, once upon a time; *auf* —, suddenly; *noch* —, once more; *nicht* —, not even.
Einmaleins [ˈaɪnma:laɪns], *n.* (—**es**, *no pl.*) multiplication table.
einmalig [ˈaɪnma:lɪç], *adv.* unique, unrepeatable.
Einmaster [ˈaɪnmastər], *m.* (—**s**, *pl.* —) (*Naut.*) brigantine, cutter.
einmauern [ˈaɪnmauərn], *v.a.* wall in, immure.
einmengen [ˈaɪnmɛŋən], *v.r.* *sich* —, meddle with, interfere.
einmieten [ˈaɪnmi:tən], *v.r.* *sich* —, take lodgings.
einmischen [ˈaɪnmɪʃən], *v.r.* *sich* —, meddle (with), interfere.
einmütig [ˈaɪnmy:tɪç], *adj.* unanimous, in harmony, united.
Einnahme [ˈaɪnna:mə], *f.* (—, *pl.* —**n**) income, revenue; receipts; (*Mil.*) occupation, capture.
einnehmen [ˈaɪnne:mən], *v.a. irr.* take in; (*money*) receive; (*medicine*) take; (*taxes*) collect; (*place*) take up, occupy; (*Mil.*) occupy, conquer; (*fig.*) captivate, fascinate.
einnehmend [ˈaɪnne:mənt], *adj.* fetching, engaging, charming.
einnicken [ˈaɪnnɪkən], *v.n.* (*aux.* sein) nod *or* doze off.
einnisten [ˈaɪnnɪstən], *v.r.* *sich* —, nestle down; (*fig.*) settle in a place.
Einöde [ˈaɪnø:də], *f.* (—, *pl.* —**n**) desert, solitude.
einordnen [ˈaɪnɔrdnən], *v.a.* place in order, file, classify.
einpauken [ˈaɪnpaukən], *v.a.* cram.
einpferchen [ˈaɪnpfɛrçən], *v.a.* pen in, coop up.
einpökeln [ˈaɪnpø:kəln], *v.a.* salt, pickle.
einprägen [ˈaɪnprɛ:gən], *v.a.* imprint; impress.
einquartieren [ˈaɪnkvarti:rən], *v.a.* (*Mil.*) quarter, billet.
einrahmen [ˈaɪnra:mən], *v.a.* frame.
einräumen [ˈaɪnrɔymən], *v.a.* stow (things) away; *einem etwas* —, concede s.th. to s.o.
Einrede [ˈaɪnre:də], *f.* (—, *pl.* —**n**) objection.
einreden [ˈaɪnre:dən], *v.a.* *einem etwas* —, persuade s.o. to. — *v.r.* *sich etwas* —, get s.th. into o.'s head.
einreichen [ˈaɪnraɪçən], *v.a.* hand in, deliver; tender.
einreihen [ˈaɪnraɪən], *v.a.* place in line, arrange.
einreihig [ˈaɪnraɪɪç], *adj.* consisting of a single row; (*Tail.*) single-breasted (suit).
einreißen [ˈaɪnraɪsən], *v.a. irr.* make a tear in; (*houses*) pull down. — *v.n.* (*fig.*) gain ground.
einrenken [ˈaɪnrɛŋkən], *v.a.* (*Med.*) set; (*fig.*) settle.
einrichten [ˈaɪnrɪçtən], *v.a.* put in order, arrange; equip, set up; furnish.
Einrichtung [ˈaɪnrɪctuŋ], *f.* (—, *pl.* —**en**) arrangement, management; furnishing; (*pl.*) facilities; equipment, amenities.
einrücken [ˈaɪnrykən], *v.n.* (*aux.* sein) march in. — *v.a.* insert (in the newspaper).
Eins [aɪns], *f.* (—, *pl.* —**en**, —**er**) one; (*Sch.*) top marks.
eins [aɪns], *num.* one; *es ist mir alles* —, it is all the same to me.
einsalzen [ˈaɪnzaltsən], *v.a.* salt, pickle, cure.
einsam [ˈaɪnza:m], *adj.* lonely, solitary, secluded.
Einsamkeit [ˈaɪnza:mkaɪt], *f.* (—, *no pl.*) loneliness, solitude, seclusion.
Einsatz [ˈaɪnzats], *m.* (—**es**, *pl.* ⸚**e**) (*game*) stake, pool; (*dress*) lace inset; (*Mus.*) entry (of a voice), starting intonation; (*Mil.*) sortie, mission.
einsaugen [ˈaɪnzaugən], *v.a.* suck in; (*fig.*) imbibe.
einsäumen [ˈaɪnzɔymən], *v.a.* hem (in).
einschalten [ˈaɪnʃaltən], *v.a.* insert, interpolate; switch on; put in gear.
einschärfen [ˈaɪnʃɛrfən], *v.a.* impress s.th. on s.o.
einschätzen [ˈaɪnʃɛtsən], *v.a.* assess.
einschenken [ˈaɪnʃɛŋkən], *v.a.* pour in *or* out, fill.
einschieben [ˈaɪnʃi:bən], *v.a.* push in; interpolate, insert.
Einschiebsel [ˈaɪnʃi:psəl], *n.* (—**s**, *pl.* —) interpolation; interpolated part.
einschiffen [ˈaɪnʃɪfən], *v.a.* embark; (*goods*) ship. — *v.r.* *sich* —, go aboard, embark.
einschlafen [ˈaɪnʃla:fən], *v.n. irr.* (*aux.* sein) fall asleep, go to sleep.
einschläfern [ˈaɪnʃlɛ:fərn], *v.a.* lull to sleep.
Einschlag [ˈaɪnʃla:k], *m.* (—**s**, *pl.* ⸚**e**) cover, envelope; (*weaving*) woof, weft; explosion; strike; (*fig.*) streak (of character); touch.

einschlagen ['aɪnʃla:gən], *v.a. irr.* knock in; (*nail*) drive in; (*parcel*) wrap up; (*road*) take. — *v.n.* (*lightning*) strike; be a success.
einschlägig ['aɪnʃlɛ:gɪç], *adj.* bearing on (the subject), pertinent.
einschleppen ['aɪnʃlɛpən], *v.a.* (*disease*) bring in, introduce.
einschließen ['aɪnʃli:sən], *v.a. irr.* lock in *or* up; (*enemy*) surround; (*fig.*) include.
einschlummern ['aɪnʃlumərn], *v.n.* (*aux.* sein) doze off, fall asleep.
Einschluß ['aɪnʃlus], *m.* (**—sses**, *pl.* **¨sse**) inclusion; *mit — von*, inclusive of.
einschmeicheln ['aɪnʃmaɪçəln], *v.r. sich bei einem —*, ingratiate o.s. with s.o.
einschmelzen ['aɪnʃmɛltsən], *v.a. irr.* melt down.
einschmieren ['aɪnʃmi:rən], *v.a.* smear, grease, oil; (*sore*) put ointment on.
einschneidend ['aɪnʃnaɪdənt], *adj.* important, sweeping, incisive, trenchant.
einschneidig ['aɪnʃnaɪdɪç], *adj.* single-edged.
Einschnitt ['aɪnʃnɪt], *m.* (**—s**, *pl.* **—e**) incision, cut, notch; (*verse*) caesura.
einschnüren ['aɪnʃny:rən], *v.a.* lace up; (*parcel*) tie up.
einschränken ['aɪnʃrɛŋkən], *v.a.* confine, limit, restrict. — *v.r. sich —*, curtail o.'s expenses, economize.
einschrauben ['aɪnʃraubən], *v.a.* screw in.
einschreiben ['aɪnʃraɪbən], *v.a. irr.* write in *or* down, inscribe; (*letter*) register. — *v.r. sich —*, enter o.'s name; enrol.
Einschreibesendung ['aɪnʃraɪbəzɛndunŋ], *f.* (**—**, *pl.* **—en**) registered letter, registered parcel.
einschreiten ['aɪnʃraɪtən], *v.n. irr.* (*aux.* sein) step in, intervene.
einschrumpfen ['aɪnʃrumpfən], *v.n.* (*aux.* sein) shrink, shrivel.
einschüchtern ['aɪnʃyçtərn], *v.a.* intimidate, overawe.
Einschuß ['aɪnʃus], *m.* (**—sses**, *pl.* **¨sse**) share, advance of capital; (*weaving*) woof, weft.
einsegnen ['aɪnze:gnən], *v.a.* consecrate, bless; (*Eccl.*) confirm.
Einsehen ['aɪnze:ən], *n.* (**—s**, *no pl.*) realisation; *ein — haben*, be reasonable.
einsehen ['aɪnze:ən], *v.a. irr.* look into, glance over; (*fig.*) comprehend, realise.
einseifen ['aɪnzaɪfən], *v.a.* soap, lather; (*fig.*) take s.o. in.
einseitig ['aɪnzaɪtɪç], *adj.* one-sided; (*fig.*) one-track (mind).
Einsenkung ['aɪnzɛŋkuŋ], *f.* (**—**, *pl.* **—en**) depression (of the ground).
einsetzen ['aɪnzɛtsən], *v.a.* put in, set in; institute, establish; (*money*) stake; (*Hort.*) plant; (*office*) install s.o. — *v.n.* begin.
Einsetzung ['aɪnzɛtsuŋ], *f.* (**—**, *pl.* **—en**) (*office*) investiture, installation; institution.
Einsicht ['aɪnzɪçt], *f.* (**—**, *no pl.*) inspection, examination; insight, understanding.
einsichtig ['aɪnzɪçtɪç], *adj.* intelligent, sensible, judicious.
Einsichtnahme ['aɪnzɪçtna:mə], *f. zur —*, (*Comm.*) on approval, for inspection.
Einsiedler ['aɪnzi:dlər], *m.* (**—s**, *pl.* **—**) hermit, recluse.
einsilbig ['aɪnzɪlbɪç], *adj.* monosyllabic; (*fig.*) taciturn, laconic.
einspannen ['aɪnʃpanən], *v.a.* stretch in a frame; harness; (*coll.*) put to work.
Einspänner ['aɪnʃpɛnər], *m.* (**—s**, *pl.* **—**) one-horse vehicle; one-horse cab, fiacre.
einsperren ['aɪnʃpɛrən], *v.a.* lock in, shut up, imprison.
einspinnen ['aɪnʃpɪnən], *v.r. irr. sich —*, spin a cocoon.
einsprengen ['aɪnʃprɛŋən], *v.a.* sprinkle.
einspringen ['aɪnʃprɪŋən], *v.n. irr.* (*aux.* sein) *auf einen —*, leap at; (*lock*) catch, snap; *für einen —*, deputize for s.o.
Einspruch ['aɪnʃprux], *m.* (**—s**, *pl.* **¨e**) objection, protest; *— erheben*, protest; (*Law*) appeal (against).
einspurig ['aɪnʃpu:rɪç], *adj.* (*Railw.*) single-track line.
einst [aɪnst], *adv.* (*past*) once, once upon a time; (*future*) some day.
Einstand ['aɪnʃtant], *m.* (**—s**, *no pl.*) (*Tennis*) deuce.
einstecken ['aɪnʃtɛkən], *v.a.* put in; pocket; post (a letter).
einstehen ['aɪnʃte:ən], *v.a. irr. zu etwas —*, answer for s.th.; *für einen —*, stand security for s.o.
einsteigen ['aɪnʃtaɪgən], *v.n. irr.* (*aux.* sein) get in, climb on; board.
einstellen ['aɪnʃtɛlən], *v.a.* put in; (*persons*) engage, hire; adjust; (*work*) stop, strike; (*payments*) stop; (*hostilities*) suspend, cease fire. — *v.r. sich —*, turn up, appear.
einstellig ['aɪnʃtɛlɪç], *adj.* (*Maths.*) of one digit.
Einstellung ['aɪnʃtɛluŋ], *f.* (**—**, *pl.* **—en**) putting in; (*persons*) engagement, hiring; adjustment; (*work*) stoppage, strike; (*payments*) suspension; (*hostilities*) suspension, cessation; (*fig.*) opinion, attitude.
einstig ['aɪnstɪç], *adj.* (*past*) former, late, erstwhile; (*future*) future, to be, to come.
einstimmen ['aɪnʃtɪmən], *v.n.* join in, chime in.
einstimmig ['aɪnʃtɪmɪç], *adj.* (*Mus.*) (for) one voice, unison; (*fig.*) unanimous.
einstmals ['aɪnstma:ls], *adv.* once, formerly.

einstöckig ['aɪnʃtœkɪç], *adj.* one-storied.
einstreichen ['aɪnʃtraɪçən], *v.a. irr.* (*money*) take in, pocket.
einstreuen ['aɪnʃtrɔyən], *v.a.* strew; (*fig.*) intersperse.
einstudieren ['aɪnʃtudi:rən], *v.a.* study; (*Theat.*, *Mus.*) rehearse.
einstürmen ['aɪnʃtyrmən], *v.n.* (*aux.* sein) *auf einen* —, rush at, fall upon.
Einsturz ['aɪnʃturts], *m.* (—**es**, *pl.* ⸗**e**) fall, crash; subsidence, collapse.
einstürzen ['aɪnʃtyrtsən], *v.n.* (*aux.* sein) fall in, fall into ruin, fall to pieces, collapse.
einstweilen ['aɪnstvaɪlən], *adv.* in the meantime, meanwhile, for the time being, provisionally.
einstweilig ['aɪnstvaɪlɪç], *adj.* temporary, provisional.
eintägig ['aɪntɛ:gɪç], *adj.* one-day, ephemeral.
Eintagsfliege ['aɪnta:ksfli:gə], *f.* (—, *pl.* —**n**) dayfly.
eintauschen ['aɪntauʃən], *v.a.* — *gegen*, exchange for, barter for.
einteilen ['aɪntaɪlən], *v.a.* divide; distribute; classify.
eintönig ['aɪntø:nɪç], *adj.* monotonous.
Eintracht ['aɪntraxt], *f.* (—, *no pl.*) concord, harmony.
einträchtig ['aɪntrɛçtɪç], *adj.* united, harmonious.
Eintrag ['aɪntra:k], *m.* (—**s**, *pl.* ⸗**e**) entry (in a book); prejudice, damage, detriment.
eintragen ['aɪntra:gən], *v.a. irr.* enter (in a book), register; bring in, yield.
einträglich ['aɪntrɛklɪç], *adj.* profitable, lucrative.
Eintragung ['aɪntra:guŋ], *f.* (—, *pl.* —**en**) entry (in a book); enrolment.
einträufeln ['aɪntrɔyfəln], *v.a.* instil.
eintreffen ['aɪntrɛfən], *v.n. irr.* (*aux.* sein) arrive; happen, come true.
eintreiben ['aɪntraɪbən], *v.a. irr.* drive home (*cattle*); collect (debts etc.).
eintreten ['aɪntre:tən], *v.n. irr.* (*aux.* sein) step in, enter; happen, take place; *in einen Verein* —, join a club; *für einen* —, speak up for s.o.
eintrichtern ['aɪntrɪçtərn], *v.a. einem etwas* —, cram s.th. into s.o.
Eintritt ['aɪntrɪt], *m.* (—**s**, *no pl.*) entry, entrance; beginning; *kein* —, no admission.
eintrocknen ['aɪntrɔknən], *v.n.* (*aux.* sein) shrivel, dry up.
einüben ['aɪny:bən], *v.a.* practise, exercise.
einverleiben ['aɪnfɛrlaɪbən], *v.a.* incorporate in, embody in.
Einvernahme ['aɪnfɛrna:mə], *f.* (—, *pl.* —**n**) (*Austr.*) *see* **Vernehmung**.
Einvernehmen ['aɪnfɛrne:mən], *n.* (—**s**, *no pl.*) understanding; *im besten* —, on the best of terms.
einvernehmen ['aɪnfɛrne:mən], *v.a.* (*aux.* haben) (*Austr.*) *see* **vernehmen**.
einverstanden ['aɪnfɛrʃtandən], (*excl.*) agreed! — *adj.* — *sein*, agree.
Einverständnis ['aɪnfɛrʃtɛntnɪs], *n.* (—**ses**, *no pl.*) consent, agreement, accord.
Einwand ['aɪnvant], *m.* (—**s**, *pl.* ⸗**e**) objection, exception; — *erheben*, raise objections.
einwandern ['aɪnvandərn], *v.n.* (*aux.* sein) immigrate.
einwandfrei ['aɪnvantfraɪ], *adj.* irreproachable, unobjectionable.
einwärts ['aɪnvɛrts], *adv.* inward(s).
einwechseln ['aɪnvɛksəln], *v.a.* change, exchange.
einweichen ['aɪnvaɪçən], *v.a.* steep in water, soak.
einweihen ['aɪnvaɪən], *v.a.* dedicate; (*Eccl.*) consecrate; open (formally), inaugurate; initiate (into).
Einweihung ['aɪnvaɪuŋ], *f.* (—, *pl.* —**en**) (*Eccl.*) consecration; inauguration, formal opening; initiation.
einwenden ['aɪnvɛndən], *v.a. irr.* object to, raise objections, urge against.
einwerfen ['aɪnvɛrfən], *v.a. irr.* throw in; smash in; interject.
einwickeln ['aɪnvɪkəln], *v.a.* wrap up, envelop.
einwilligen ['aɪnvɪlɪgən], *v.n.* consent, assent, agree, accede.
einwirken ['aɪnvɪrkən], *v.n. auf einen* —, influence s.o.
Einwohner ['aɪnvo:nər], *m.* (—**s**, *pl.* —) inhabitant.
Einwohnerschaft ['aɪnvo:nərʃaft], *f.* (—, *no pl.*) population, inhabitants.
Einwurf ['aɪnvurf], *m.* (—**s**, *pl.* ⸗**e**) (*letter box*) opening, slit; slot; objection.
einwurzeln ['aɪnvurtsəln], *v.r. sich* —, take root; *eingewurzelt*, deep-rooted.
Einzahl ['aɪntsa:l], *f.* (—, *no pl.*) singular.
einzahlen ['aɪntsa:lən], *v.a.* pay in, deposit.
einzäunen ['aɪntsɔynən], *v.a.* fence in.
einzeichnen ['aɪntsaɪçnən], *v.a.* draw in, sketch in. — *v.r. sich* —, enter o.'s name, sign.
Einzelhaft ['aɪntsəlhaft], *f.* (—, *no pl.*) solitary confinement.
Einzelheit ['aɪntsəlhaɪt], *f.* (—, *pl.* —**en**) detail, particular.
einzeln ['aɪntsəln], *adj.* single; isolated, detached, apart.
einziehen ['aɪntsi:ən], *v.a. irr.* draw in, retract; (*Law*) confiscate, impound; (*debts*) collect, call in; (*bill of sight*) discount, cash; (*money*) withdraw (from circulation); (*sails*) furl; (*Mil.*) call up.
einzig ['aɪntsɪç], *adj.* sole, single; unique, only.
Einzug ['aɪntsu:k], *m.* (—**s**, *pl.* ⸗**e**) entry, entrance; move (into new house).
einzwängen ['aɪntsvɛŋən], *v.a.* force in, squeeze in.
Eis [aɪs], *n.* (—**es**, *no pl.*) ice; ice-cream.
E-is ['e:ɪs], *n.* (—, *pl.* —) (*Mus.*) E sharp.

Eisbahn ['aɪsba:n], *f.* (—, *pl.* —**en**) ice-rink, skating-rink.
Eisbär ['aɪsbɛ:r], *m.* (—**en**, *pl.* —**en**) polar bear, white bear.
Eisbein ['aɪsbaɪn], *n.* (—**s**, *pl.* —**e**) pig's trotters.
Eisberg ['aɪsbɛrk], *m.* (—**s**, *pl.* —**e**) iceberg.
Eisblumen ['aɪsblu:mən], *f. pl.* frost patterns (*on glass*).
Eisen ['aɪzən], *n.* (—**s**, *pl.* —) iron; *altes* —, scrap iron.
Eisenbahn ['aɪzənba:n], *f.* (—, *pl.* —**en**) railway.
Eisenfleck ['aɪzənflɛk], *m.* (—**s**, *pl.* —**e**) iron mould.
Eisengießerei ['aɪzəngi:səraɪ], *f.* (—, *pl.* —**en**) iron foundry, iron forge.
Eisenguß ['aɪzəngus], *m.* (—**sses**, *pl.* ¨**sse**) cast-iron.
Eisenhändler ['aɪzenhɛndlər], *m.* (—**s**, *pl.* —) ironmonger.
Eisenhütte ['aɪzənhytə], *f.* (—, *pl.* —**n**) *see* **Eisengießerei**.
Eisenschlacke ['aɪzənʃlakə], *f.* (—, *no pl.*) iron dross, iron slag.
eisern ['aɪzərn], *adj.* made of iron; (*coll. & fig.*) strong; strict.
Eisgang ['aɪsgaŋ], *m.* (—**s**, *pl.* ¨**e**) drift of ice.
eisgrau ['aɪsgrau], *adj.* hoary.
eiskalt ['aɪskalt], *adj.* icy cold.
Eislauf ['aɪslauf], *m.* (—**s**, *no pl.*) ice-skating.
Eismeer ['aɪsme:r], *n.* (—**s**, *pl.* —**e**) polar sea; *nördliches* —, Arctic Ocean; *südliches* —, Antarctic Ocean.
Eispickel ['aɪspɪkəl], *m.* (—**s**, *pl.* —) ice axe.
Eisvogel ['aɪsfo:gəl], *m.* (—**s**, *pl.* ¨) (*Orn.*) kingfisher.
Eiszapfen ['aɪstsapfən], *m.* (—**s**, *pl.* —) icicle.
eitel ['aɪtəl], *adj.* vain, frivolous, conceited; (*obs.*) pure.
Eiter ['aɪtər], *m.* (—**s**, *no pl.*) (*Med.*) pus, matter.
Eitergeschwür ['aɪtərgəʃvy:r], *n.* (—**s**, *pl.* —**e**) abscess.
eitern ['aɪtərn], *v.n.* suppurate.
Eiterung ['aɪtəruŋ], *f.* (—, *pl.* —**en**) suppuration.
eitrig ['aɪtrɪç], *adj.* purulent.
Eiweis ['aɪvaɪs], *n.* (—**es**, *no pl.*) white of egg; albumen.
Ekel ['e:kəl], *m.* (—**s**, *no pl.*) nausea, disgust, distaste, aversion.
ekelhaft ['e:kəlhaft], *adj.* loathsome, disgusting, nauseous.
ekeln ['e:kəln], *v.r. sich* — *vor*, be disgusted (by), feel sick, loathe.
Ekuador [ɛkua'dɔr], *n.* Ecuador.
Elan [e'lã], *m.* (—**s**, *no pl.*) verve, vigour.
elastisch [e'lastɪʃ], *adj.* elastic, flexible, buoyant.
Elastizität [elastɪtsɪ'tɛ:t], *f.* (—, *no pl.*) elasticity; (*mind*) buoyancy.
Elch [ɛlç], *m.* (—**s**, *pl.* —**e**) (*Zool.*) elk.
Elegie [ele'gi:], *f.* (—, *pl.* —**n**) elegy.
elektrisieren [elɛktrɪ'zi:rən], *v.a.* electrify.
Elektrizität [elɛktritsɪ'tɛ:t], *f.* (—, *no pl.*) electricity.
Elend ['e:lɛnt], *n.* (—**s**, *no pl.*) misery, distress, wretchedness.
elend ['e:lɛnt], *adj.* miserable, wretched, pitiful; weak; *sich* — *fühlen*, feel poorly.
elendiglich ['e:lɛndɪklɪç], *adv.* miserably, wretchedly.
Elentier ['e:lɛnti:r], *n.* (—**s**, *pl.* —**e**) (*Zool.*) elk.
elf [ɛlf], *num. adj.* eleven.
Elfe ['ɛlfə], *f.* (—, *pl.* —**n**) fairy.
Elfenbein ['ɛlfənbaɪn], *n.* (—**s**, *no pl.*) ivory.
Elisabeth [e'li:zabɛt], *f.* Elizabeth.
Ellbogen ['ɛlbo:gən], *m.* (—**s**, *pl.* —) elbow.
Elle ['ɛlə], *f.* (—, *pl.* —**n**) yard, ell.
Elritze ['ɛlrɪtsə], *f.* (—, *pl.* —**n**) minnow.
Elsaß ['ɛlzas], *n.* Alsace.
Elster ['ɛlstər], *f.* (—, *pl.* —**n**) magpie.
Eltern ['ɛltərn], *pl.* parents.
Emaille [e'ma:j], *n.* (—**s**, *no pl.*) enamel.
emailliert [ema(l)'ji:rt], *adj.* covered with vitreous enamel, enamelled.
Empfang [ɛm'pfaŋ], *m.* (—**s**, *pl.* ¨**e**) receipt; reception.
empfangen [ɛm'pfaŋən], *v.a. irr.* receive, accept, take.
Empfänger [ɛm'pfɛŋər], *m.* (—**s**, *pl.* —) recipient, receiver.
empfänglich [ɛm'pfɛŋlɪç], *adj.* susceptible, impressionable.
Empfängnis [ɛm'pfɛŋnɪs], *f.* (—, *no pl.*) conception.
empfehlen [ɛm'pfe:lən], *v.a. irr.* commend, recommend; give compliments to. — *v.r. sich* —, take leave.
empfinden [ɛm'pfɪndən], *v.a. irr.* feel, perceive.
empfindlich [ɛm'pfɪntlɪç], *adj.* sensitive, susceptible; touchy, thin-skinned.
empfindsam [ɛm'pfɪntsa:m], *adj.* sentimental.
Empfindung [ɛm'pfɪnduŋ], *f.* (—, *pl.* —**en**) sensation, feeling, sentiment.
empor [ɛm'po:r], *adv.* upward(s), up.
Empore [em'po:rə], *f.* (—, *pl.* —**n**) gallery (*in church*).
empören [ɛm'pø:rən], *v.a.* excite, enrage, shock. — *v.r. sich* —, revolt, rebel.
Emporkömmling [ɛm'po:rkœmlɪŋ], *m.* (—**s**, *pl.* —**e**) upstart.
empört [ɛm'pø:rt], *adj.* furious, shocked, disgusted.
Empörung [ɛm'pø:ruŋ], *f.* (—, *pl.* —**en**) rebellion, revolt, mutiny, insurrection; indignation, disgust.
emsig ['ɛmzɪç], *adj.* assiduous, industrious, busy.
Emsigkeit ['ɛmzɪçkaɪt], *f.* (—, *no pl.*) assiduity, diligence.
Ende ['ɛndə], *n.* (—**s**, *pl.* —**n**) end, conclusion.

enden ['ɛndən], *v.n.* end, finish, conclude. — *v.a.* terminate, put an end to.
endgültig ['ɛntgyltɪç], *adj.* definitive, final.
Endivie [ɛn'di:vjə], *f.* (—, *pl.* —**n**) (*Bot.*) endive.
endlich ['ɛntlɪç], *adj.* finite, final, ultimate. — *adv.* at last, at length, finally.
endlos ['ɛntlo:s], *adj.* endless, never-ending, boundless.
Endung ['ɛnduŋ], *f.* (—, *pl.* —**en**) (*Gram.*) ending, termination.
Endziel ['ɛntsi:l], *n.* (—**s**, *pl.* —**e**) final aim.
Energie [enɛr'gi:], *f.* (—, *pl.* —**n**) energy.
energisch [e'nɛrgɪʃ], *adj.* energetic.
eng [ɛŋ], *adj.* narrow, tight; tight-fitting.
engagieren [ãga'ʒi:rən], *v.a.* engage, hire.
Enge ['ɛŋə], *f.* (—, *pl.* —**n**) narrowness, lack of space; *einen in die — treiben* drive s.o. into a corner.
Engel ['ɛŋəl], *m.* (—**s**, *pl.* —) angel.
engelhaft ['ɛŋəlhaft], *adj.* angelic.
Engelschar ['ɛŋəlʃa:r], *f.* (—, *pl.* —**en**) angelic host.
Engelwurzel ['ɛŋəlvurtsəl], *f.* (—, *pl.* —**n**) angelica.
engherzig ['ɛŋkhɛrtsɪc], *adj.* narrow-minded.
England ['ɛŋlant], *n.* England.
englisch (1) ['ɛŋlɪʃ], *adj.* (*obs.*) angelic.
englisch (2) ['ɛŋlɪʃ], *adj.* English; —*e Krankheit*, rickets.
Engpaß ['ɛŋpas], *m.* (—**sses**, *pl.* ⸚**e**) defile, narrow pass; (*fig.*) bottleneck.
engros [ã'gro:], *adj.* wholesale.
engstirnig ['ɛŋʃtɪrnɪç], *adj.* narrow-minded.
Enkel ['ɛŋkəl], *m.* (—**s**, *pl.* —) grandchild, grandson.
enorm [e'nɔrm], *adj.* enormous; (*coll.*) terrific.
entarten [ɛnt'artən], *v.n.* (*aux.* sein) degenerate.
entäußern [ɛnt'ɔysərn], *v.r. sich einer Sache* —, part with s.th.
entbehren [ɛnt'be:rən], *v.a.* lack, be in want of; spare.
entbehrlich [ɛnt'be:rlɪç], *adj.* dispensable, unnecessary, superfluous.
Entbehrung [ɛnt'be:ruŋ], *f.* (—, *pl.* —**en**) privation, want.
entbieten [ɛnt'bi:tən], *v.a. irr. Grüße* —, send o.'s respects.
entbinden [ɛnt'bɪndən], *v.a. irr. einen von etwas* —, release *or* dispense s.o. from s.th.; (*Med.*) deliver (a woman of a child).
Entbindung [ɛnt'bɪnduŋ], *f.* (—, *pl.* —**en**) (*Med.*) delivery, child-birth.
entblättern [ɛnt'blɛtərn], *v.a.* strip of leaves.
entblößen [ɛnt'blø:sən], *v.a.*, *v.r.* (*sich*) —, uncover (o.s.), bare (o.s.).
entdecken [ɛnt'dɛkən], *v.a.* discover, detect.
Ente ['ɛntə], *f.* (—, *pl.* —**n**) duck; *junge* —, duckling; (*fig.*) hoax, fictitious newspaper report.
entehren [ɛnt'e:rən], *v.a.* dishonour, disgrace; deflower, ravish.
enterben [ɛnt'ɛrbən], *v.a.* disinherit.
Enterich ['ɛntərɪç], *m.* (—**s**, *pl.* —**e**) drake.
entfachen [ɛnt'faxən], *v.a.* set ablaze, kindle.
entfahren [ɛnt'fa:rən], *v.n. irr.* (*aux.* sein) slip off, escape.
entfallen [ɛnt'falən], *v.n. irr.* (*aux.* sein) escape o.'s memory; be left off.
entfalten [ɛnt'faltən], *v.a.* unfold; display. — *v.r. sich* —, develop, open up, expand.
entfärben [ɛnt'fɛrbən], *v.r. sich* —, lose colour, grow pale.
entfernen [ɛnt'fɛrnən], *v.a.* remove. — *v.r. sich* —, withdraw.
Entfernung [ɛnt'fɛrnuŋ], *f.* (—, *pl.* —**en**) removal; distance.
entfesseln [ɛnt'fɛsəln], *v.a.* unfetter; let loose.
Entfettungskur [ɛnt'fɛtuŋsku:r], *f.* (—, —**en**) slimming-cure.
entflammen [ɛnt'flamən], *v.a.* inflame.
entfliegen [ɛnt'fli:gən], *v.n. irr.* (*aux.* sein) fly away.
entfliehen [ɛnt'fli:ən], *v.n. irr.* (*aux.* sein) run away, escape, flee.
entfremden [ɛnt'frɛmdən], *v.a.* estrange, alienate.
entführen [ɛnt'fy:rən], *v.a.* abduct, carry off; kidnap; elope with.
entgegen [ɛnt'ge:gən], *prep.* (*Dat.*), *adv.* against, contrary to; towards.
Entgegenkommen [ɛnt'ge:gənkɔmən], *n.* (—**s**, *no pl.*) obliging behaviour, courtesy.
entgegenkommen [ɛnt'ge:gənkɔmən], *v.n. irr.* (*aux.* sein) come towards s.o., come to meet s.o.; do a favour, oblige.
entgegennehmen [ɛnt'ge:gənne:mən], *v.a. irr.* receive, accept.
entgegensehen [ɛnt'ge:gənze:ən], *v.n. irr.* await, look forward to.
entgegnen [ɛnt'gə:gnən], *v.a.* reply, retort.
Entgegnung [ɛnt'ge:gnuŋ], *f.* (—, *pl.* —**en**) reply, retort, rejoinder.
entgehen [ɛnt'ge:ən], *v.n. irr.* (*aux.* sein) (*Dat.*) escape; — *lassen*, let slip.
Entgelt [ɛnt'gɛlt], *n.* (—**s**, *no pl.*) remuneration, recompense.
entgelten [ɛnt'gɛltən], *v.a. irr. einen etwas — lassen*, make s.o. pay for s.th. *or* suffer.
entgleisen [ɛnt'glaɪzən], *v.n.* (*aux.* sein) run off the rails, be derailed.
enthaaren [ɛnt'ha:rən], *v.a.* depilate.
enthalten [ɛnt'haltən], *v.a. irr.* hold, contain. — *v.r. sich* —, abstain from, refrain from.
enthaltsam [ɛnt'haltza:m], *adj.* abstinent, abstemious, temperate.
Enthaltung [ɛnt'haltuŋ], *f.* (—, *no pl.*) abstention.

enthaupten [ɛnt'hauptən], *v.a.* behead, decapitate.
entheben [ɛnt'he:bən], *v.a. irr. einen einer Sache* —, exempt *or* dispense from, suspend from, relieve of.
entheiligen [ɛnt'haılıgən], *v.a.* profane, desecrate.
enthüllen [ɛnt'hylən], *v.a.* unveil; (*fig.*) reveal.
entkleiden [ɛnt'klaıdən], *v.a.* unclothe, undress, strip.
entkommen [ɛnt'kɔmən], *v.n. irr.* (*aux.* sein) escape, get off.
entkräften [ɛnt'krɛftən], *v.a.* enfeeble, debilitate, weaken; (*fig.*) refute (an argument).
entladen [ɛnt'la:dən], *v.a. irr.* unload, discharge. — *v.r. sich* —, burst; (*gun*) go off.
Entladung [ɛnt'la:duŋ], *f.* (—, *pl.* **—en**) unloading, discharge, explosion.
entlang [ɛnt'laŋ], *prep.* along.
entlarven [ɛnt'larfən], *v.a.* unmask; expose.
Entlarvung [ɛnt'larfuŋ], *f.* (—, *pl.* **—en**) unmasking, exposure.
entlassen [ɛnt'lasən], *v.a. irr.* dismiss; (*Am.*) fire; discharge; pension off.
Entlastung [ɛnt'lastuŋ], *f.* (—, *no pl.*) exoneration; credit (to s.o.'s bank account).
entlaufen [ɛnt'laufən], *v.n. irr.* (*aux.* sein) run away.
entlausen [ɛnt'lauzən], *v.a.* delouse.
entledigen [ɛnt'le:dıgən], *v.r. sich einer Sache* —, rid o.s. of *or* get rid of a thing; *sich einer Aufgabe* —, perform a task, discharge a commission.
entleeren [ɛnt'le:rən], *v.a.* empty.
entlegen [ɛnt'le:gən], *adj.* remote, distant, far off.
entlehnen [ɛnt'le:nən], *v.a.* borrow from.
entleihen [ɛnt'laıən], *v.a. irr.* borrow.
entlocken [ɛnt'lɔkən], *v.a.* elicit from.
entmannen [ɛnt'manən], *v.a.* castrate, emasculate.
entmündigen [ɛnt'myndıgən], *v.a.* place under care of a guardian *or* (*Law*) trustees.
Entmündigung [ɛnt'myndıguŋ], *f.* (—, *no pl.*) placing under legal control.
entmutigen [ɛnt'mu:tıgən], *v.a.* discourage, dishearten.
Entnahme [ɛnt'na:mə], *f.* (—, *pl.* **—n**) (*money*) withdrawal.
entnehmen [ɛnt'ne:mən], *v.a. irr.* (*money*) withdraw; understand, gather *or* infer from.
entnerven [ɛnt'nɛrfən], *v.a.* enervate.
entpuppen [ɛnt'pupən], *v.r. sich* —, burst from the cocoon; (*fig.*) turn out to be.
enträtseln [ɛnt'rɛ:tsəln], *v.a.* decipher, make out.
entreißen [ɛnt'raısən], *v.a. irr.* snatch away from; *einer Gefahr* —, save *or* rescue from danger.
entrichten [ɛnt'rıçtən], *v.a.* pay (off).
entrinnen [ɛnt'rınən], *v.n. irr.* (*aux.* sein) escape from.
entrückt [ɛnt'rykt], *adj.* enraptured.
entrüsten [ɛnt'rystən], *v.a.* make angry, exasperate. — *v.r. sich* —, become angry, fly into a passion.
entsagen [ɛnt'za:gən], *v.n.* renounce; waive; abdicate.
Entsatz [ɛnt'zats], *m.* (**—es**, *no pl.*) (*Mil.*) relief.
entschädigen [ɛnt'ʃɛ:dıgən], *v.a.* indemnify, compensate.
entscheiden [ɛnt'ʃaıdən], *v.a. irr.* decide. — *v.r. sich — für*, come to a decision for, decide in favour of.
Entscheidung [ɛnt'ʃaıduŋ], *f.* (—, *pl.* **—en**) decision; verdict.
entschieden [ɛnt'ʃi:dən], *adj.* decided, determined, resolute, peremptory.
Entschiedenheit [ɛnt'ʃi:dənhaıt], *f.* (—, *no pl.*) resolution, firmness, determination.
entschlafen [ɛnt'ʃla:fən], *v.n. irr.* (*aux.* sein) fall asleep; (*fig.*) die, depart this life.
entschleiern [ɛnt'ʃlaıərn], *v.a.* unveil.
entschließen [ɛnt'ʃli:sən], *v.r. irr. sich* —, decide (upon), resolve, make up o.'s mind.
Entschlossenheit [ɛnt'ʃlɔsənhaıt], *f.* (—, *no pl.*) resoluteness, determination.
entschlummern [ɛnt'ʃlumərn], *v.n.* (*aux.* sein) fall asleep.
entschlüpfen [ɛnt'ʃlypfən], *v.n.* (*aux.* sein) slip away; escape.
Entschluß [ɛnt'ʃlus], *m.* (**—sses**, *pl.* **¨—sse**) resolution; *einen — fassen*, resolve (to).
entschuldigen [ɛnt'ʃuldıgən], *v.a.* excuse. — *v.r. sich* —, apologise.
entschwinden [ɛnt'ʃvındən], *v.n. irr.* (*aux.* sein) disappear, vanish.
entseelt [ɛnt'ze:lt], *adj.* inanimate, lifeless.
entsenden [ɛnt'zɛndən], *v.a. irr.* send off, despatch.
Entsetzen [ɛnt'zɛtsən], *n.* (**—s**, *no pl.*) horror, terror.
entsetzen [ɛnt'zɛtsən], *v.a.* (*Mil.*) relieve; frighten, shock, fill with horror. — *v.r. sich — über*, be horrified at.
entsetzlich [ɛnt'zɛtslıç], *adj.* horrible, terrible, dreadful, awful.
entsiegeln [ɛnt'zi:gəln], *v.a.* unseal.
entsinnen [ɛnt'zınən], *v.r. sich einer Sache* —, recollect, remember, call s.th. to mind.
entspannen [ɛnt'ʃpanən], *v.a., v.r.* (*sich*) —, relax.
entspinnen [ɛnt'ʃpınən], *v.r. irr. sich* —, arise, begin.
entsprechen [ɛnt'ʃprɛçən], *v.n. irr.* respond to, correspond to, meet, suit.
entsprechend [ɛnt'ʃprɛçənt], *adj.* corresponding, suitable.
entsprießen [ɛnt'ʃpri:sən], *v.n. irr.* (*aux.* sein) spring up, sprout.
entspringen [ɛnt'ʃprıŋən], *v.n. irr.* (*aux.* sein) escape, originate from; (*river*) have its source at, rise.

entstammen [ɛnt'ʃtamən], *v.n.* (*aux.* sein) spring from, originate from.
entstehen [ɛnt'ʃte:ən], *v.n. irr.* (*aux.* sein) arise, originate, begin, result, spring from.
Entstehung [ɛnt'ʃte:uŋ], *f.* (—, *no pl.*) origin, rise.
entstellen [ɛnt'ʃtɛlən], *v.a.* disfigure, deform, distort; (*fig.*) garble.
entsühnen [ɛnt'zy:nən], *v.a.* free from sin, purify, purge.
enttäuschen [ɛnt'tɔyʃən], *v.a.* disappoint.
entthronen [ɛnt'tro:nən], *v.a.* dethrone.
entvölkern [ɛnt'fœlkərn], *v.a.* depopulate.
entwachsen [ɛnt'vaksən], *v.n. irr.* (*aux.* sein) grow out of, outgrow.
entwaffnen [ɛnt'vafnən], *v.a.* disarm.
entwässern [ɛnt'vɛsərn], *v.a.* drain.
entweder [ɛnt've:dər], *conj.* either; — ......*oder*, either ...... or.
entweichen [ɛnt'vaɪçən], *v.n. irr.* escape, run away.
entweihen [ɛnt'vaɪən], *v.a.* profane, desecrate.
entwenden [ɛnt'vɛndən], *v.a.* take away, steal, embezzle.
entwerfen [ɛnt'vɛrfən], *v.a. irr.* design, sketch, plan, draw up.
entwerten [ɛnt'vɛrtən], *v.a.* reduce in value, depreciate; (*stamps*) cancel.
entwickeln [ɛnt'vɪkəln], *v.a.* unfold, develop; (*ideas*) explain, explicate. — *v.r. sich* —, develop (into), evolve.
Entwicklung [ɛnt'vɪkluŋ], *f.* (—, *pl.* —**en**) unfolding, development, evolution.
entwinden [ɛnt'vɪndən], *v.a. irr.* wrench from, wrest from.
entwirren [ɛnt'vɪrən], *v.a.* unravel, disentangle.
entwischen [ɛnt'vɪʃən], *v.n.* (*aux.* sein) slip away, escape.
entwöhnen [ɛnt'vø:nən], *v.a.* disaccustom; break off a habit; (*baby*) wean.
entwürdigen [ɛnt'vyrdɪgən], *v.a.* disgrace, degrade.
Entwurf [ɛnt'vurf], *m.* (—**s**, *pl.* ⸚**e**) sketch, design, draft, plan, project.
entwurzeln [ɛnt'vurtsəln], *v.a.* uproot.
entziehen [ɛnt'tsi:ən], *v.a. irr.* withdraw, take away, deprive of.
entziffern [ɛnt'tsɪfərn], *v.a.* decipher.
entzücken [ɛnt'tsykən], *v.a.* enchant, delight, charm.
entzündbar [ɛnt'tsyntba:r], *adj.* inflammable.
entzünden [ɛnt'tsyndən], *v.a.* set on fire, light the fire; (*fig.*) inflame. — *v.r. sich* —, catch fire, ignite; (*Med.*) become inflamed.
Entzündung [ɛnt'tsynduŋ], *f.* (—, *pl.* —**en**) kindling, setting on fire; (*Med.*) inflammation.
entzwei [ɛnt'tsvaɪ], *adv.* in two, broken.
entzweien [ɛnt'tsvaɪən], *v.a.* disunite.
Enzian ['ɛntsjan], *m.* (—**s**, *pl.* —**e**) (*Bot.*) gentian.
Enzyklopädie [ɛntsyklopɛ'di:], *f.* (—, *pl.* —**n**) encyclopædia.
Epidemie [epɪde'mi:], *f.* (—, *pl.* —**en**) epidemic.
epidemisch [epɪ'de:mɪʃ], *adj.* epidemic(al).
Epik ['e:pɪk], *f.* (—, *no pl.*) epic poetry.
episch ['e:pɪʃ], *adj.* epic.
Epos ['e:pɔs], *n.* (—, *pl.* **Epen**) epic poem.
Equipage [ekvi'pa:ʒə], *f.* (—, *pl.* —**n**) carriage.
er [e:r], *pers. pron.* he.
Erachten [ɛr'axtən], *n.* (—**s**, *no pl.*) opinion, judgment: *meines* —*s*, in my opinion.
erachten [ɛr'axtən], *v.a.* think, consider.
erarbeiten [ɛr'arbaɪtən], *v.a.* gain *or* achieve by working.
erb ['ɛrb], *adj.* (*in compounds*) hereditary.
erbarmen [ɛr'barmən], *v.r. sich* —, have mercy (on), take pity (on).
erbärmlich [ɛr'bɛrmlɪç], *adj.* miserable, pitiful; contemptible.
erbauen [ɛr'bauən], *v.a.* build, erect; (*fig.*) edify.
erbaulich [ɛr'baulɪç], *adj.* edifying.
Erbauung [ɛr'bauuŋ], *f.* (—, *no pl.*) building, erection; (*fig.*) edification.
Erbbesitz ['ɛrpbəzɪts], *m.* (—**es**, *pl.* —**e**) hereditary possession.
Erbe ['ɛrbə], *m.* (—**n**, *pl.* —**n**) heir. *n.* (—**s**, *no pl.*) inheritance; heritage.
erbeben [ɛr'be:bən], *v.n.* (*aux.* sein) shake, tremble, quake.
erbeigen ['ɛrpaɪgən], *adj.* inherited.
erben ['ɛrbən], *v.a.* inherit.
erbeten [ɛr'be:tən], *v.a. sich etwas* —, ask for s.th. by prayer; request.
erbetteln [ɛr'bɛtəln], *v.a.* obtain by begging.
erbeuten [ɛr'bɔytən], *v.a.* take as booty.
Erbfeind ['ɛrpfaɪnt], *m.* (—**s**, *pl.* —**e**) sworn enemy.
Erbfolge ['ɛrpfɔlgə], *f.* (—, *no pl.*) succession.
erbieten [ɛr'bi:tən], *v.r. irr. sich* —, offer to do s.th.; volunteer; *Ehre* —, do homage.
Erbin ['ɛrbɪn], *f.* (—, *pl.* —**nen**) heiress.
erbitten [ɛr'bɪtən], *v.a. irr.* beg, request, ask for, gain by asking.
erbittern [ɛr'bɪtərn], *v.a.* embitter, anger, exasperate.
erblassen [ɛr'blasən], *v.n.* (*aux.* sein) turn pale.
Erblasser ['ɛrplasər], *m.* (—**s**, *pl.* —) testator.
erbleichen [ɛr'blaɪçən], *v.n. irr.* (*aux.* sein) turn pale, lose colour.
erblich ['ɛrplɪç], *adj.* hereditary, congenital.
erblicken [ɛr'blɪkən], *v.a.* perceive, behold, catch sight of.
erblinden [ɛr'blɪndən], *v.n.* (*aux.* sein) turn blind.
erblos ['ɛrplo:s], *adj.* disinherited; without an heir.

erblühen [ɛrˈbly:ən], *v.n.* (*aux.* sein) blossom (out).
Erbmasse [ˈɛrpmasə], *f.* (—, *no pl.*) estate.
erbosen [ɛrˈbo:zən], *v.a.* make angry. — *v.r. sich* —, become angry.
erbötig [ɛrˈbø:tɪç], *adj.* — *sein*, be willing, be ready.
Erbpacht [ˈɛrppaxt], *f.* (—, *pl.* **—en**) hereditary tenure.
erbrechen [ɛrˈbrɛçən], *v.a. irr.* break open, open by force. — *v.r. sich* —, vomit.
Erbrecht [ˈɛrprɛçt], *n.* (**—s,** *no pl.*) law (*or* right) of succession.
Erbschaft [ˈɛrpʃaft], *f.* (—, *pl.* **—en**) inheritance, heritage, legacy.
Erbse [ˈɛrpsə], *f.* (—, *pl.* **—n**) pea.
Erbstück [ˈɛrpʃtyk], *n.* (**—s,** *pl.* **—e**) heirloom.
Erbsünde [ˈɛrpzyndə], *f.* (—, *no pl.*) original sin.
Erbteil [ˈɛrptaɪl], *n.* (**—s,** *pl.* **—e**) portion of inheritance.
Erdapfel [ˈe:rtapfəl], *m.* (**—s,** *pl.* **¨**) (*Austr.*) potato.
Erdbahn [ˈe:rtba:n], *f.* (—, *no pl.*) orbit of the earth.
Erdball [ˈe:rtbal], *m.* (**—s,** *no pl.*) terrestrial globe.
Erdbeben [ˈe:rtbe:bən], *n.* (**—s,** *pl.* —) earthquake.
Erdbeere [ˈe:rtbe:rə], *f.* (—, *pl.* **—n**) strawberry.
Erde [ˈe:rdə], *f.* (—, *pl.* **—n**) earth, soil ground.
erden [ˈe:rdən], *v.a.* (*Rad.*) earth.
erdenken [ɛrˈdɛŋkən], *v.a. irr.* think out; invent. — *v.r. sich etwas* —, invent s.th., devise s.th.
erdenklich [ɛrˈdɛŋklɪç], *adj.* imaginable, conceivable.
Erdenleben [ˈe:rdənle:bən], *n.* (**—s,** *no pl.*) life on this earth.
Erdfall [ˈe:rtfal], *m.* (**—s,** *pl.* **¨e**) landslip.
Erdfläche [ˈe:rtflɛçə], *f.* (—, *no pl.*) surface of the earth.
Erdgeschoß [ˈe:rtgəʃɔs], *n.* (**—sses,** *pl.* **—sse**) ground floor.
Erdhügel [ˈe:rthy:gəl], *m.* (**—s,** *pl.* —) mound of earth.
erdichten [ɛrˈdɪçtən], *v.a.* think out, invent, feign.
Erdkunde [ˈe:rtkundə], *f.* (—, *no pl.*) geography.
Erdleitung [ˈe:rtlaɪtuŋ], *f.* (—, *pl.* **—en**) earth circuit, earth connexion.
Erdmaus [ˈe:rtmaus], *f.* (—, *pl.* **¨e**) field mouse.
Erdmolch [ˈe:rtmɔlç], *m.* (**—s,** *pl.* **—e**) salamander.
Erdnuß [ˈe:rtnus], *f.* (—, *pl.* **¨sse**) groundnut, peanut.
Erdöl [ˈe:rtø:l], *n.* (**—s,** *no pl.*) petroleum, mineral oil.
erdolchen [ɛrˈdɔlçən], *v.a.* stab (with a dagger).
Erdpech [ˈe:rtpɛç], *n.* (**—s,** *no pl.*) bitumen.
erdreisten [ɛrˈdraɪstən], *v.r. sich* —, dare, have the audacity.
erdrosseln [ɛrˈdrɔsəln], *v.a.* strangle, throttle.
erdrücken [ɛrˈdrykən], *v.a.* crush to death.
Erdrutsch [ˈe:rtrutʃ], *m.* (**—es,** *no pl.*) landslip, landslide.
Erdschicht [ˈe:rtʃɪçt], *f.* (—, *pl.* **—en**) (*Geol.*) layer, stratum.
Erdschnecke [ˈe:rtʃnɛkə], *f.* (—, *pl.* **—n**) slug, snail.
Erdscholle [ˈe:rtʃɔlə], *f.* (—, *pl.* **—n**) clod (of earth).
Erdsturz [ˈe:rtʃturts], *m.* (**—es,** *no pl.*) landslide.
erdulden [ɛrˈduldən], *v.a.* suffer, endure.
Erdumseg(e)lung [ˈe:rtumze:g(ə)luŋ], *f.* (—, *pl.* **—en**) circumnavigation of the earth.
ereifern [ɛrˈaɪfərn], *v.r. sich* —, become heated, get excited.
ereignen [ɛrˈaɪgnən], *v.r. sich* —, happen, come to pass.
Ereignis [ɛrˈaɪknɪs], *n.* (**—ses,** *pl.* **—se**) event, occurrence, happening.
ereilen [ɛrˈaɪlən], *v.a.* overtake, befall.
Eremit [ereˈmi:t], *m.* (**—en,** *pl.* **—en**) hermit, recluse.
erfahren [ɛrˈfa:rən], *v.a. irr.* learn, hear; experience. — *adj.* experienced, practised; conversant with, versed in.
Erfahrenheit [ɛrˈfa:rənhaɪt], *f.* (—, *no pl.*) experience, skill.
Erfahrung [ɛrˈfa:ruŋ], *f.* (—, *pl.* **—en**) experience, knowledge, expertness, skill; *in* — *bringen*, ascertain, come to know.
erfahrungsgemäß [ɛrˈfa:ruŋsgəmɛ:s], *adj.* based on *or* according to experience.
erfahrungsmäßig [ɛrˈfa:ruŋsmɛ:sɪç], *adj.* based on experience; empirical.
erfassen [ɛrˈfasən], *v.a.* get hold of, seize, comprehend, grasp.
erfinden [ɛrˈfɪndən], *v.a. irr.* invent, contrive.
erfinderisch [ɛrˈfɪndərɪʃ], *adj.* inventive, ingenious.
Erfindung [ɛrˈfɪnduŋ], *f.* (—, *pl.* **—en**) invention; contrivance.
Erfolg [ɛrˈfɔlk], *m.* (**—s,** *pl.* **—e**) success; result; effect; — *haben*, succeed, be successful; *keinen* — *haben*, fail.
erfolgen [ɛrˈfɔlgən], *v.n.* (*aux.* sein) ensue, follow, result.
erfolgreich [ɛrˈfɔlkraɪç], *adj.* successful.
erforderlich [ɛrˈfɔrdərlɪç], *adj.* necessary, required.
erfordern [ɛrˈfɔrdərn], *v.a.* demand, require.
Erfordernis [ɛrˈfɔrdərnɪs], *n.* (**—ses,** *pl.* **—se**) necessity, requirement, requisite.
erforschen [ɛrˈfɔrʃən], *v.a.* explore, investigate, conduct research into.
erfragen [ɛrˈfra:gən], *v.a.* find out by asking, ascertain.
erfreuen [ɛrˈfrɔyən], *v.a.* gladden, cheer, delight. — *v.r. sich* — *an*, enjoy, take pleasure in.

erfreulich [ɛr'frɔylɪç], *adj.* pleasing, gratifying.
erfrieren [ɛr'fri:rən], *v.n. irr.* (*aux.* sein) freeze to death, die of exposure; become numb.
erfrischen [ɛr'frɪʃən], *v.a.* refresh.
erfüllen [ɛr'fylən], *v.a.* fulfil, keep (promise); comply with; perform; *seinen Zweck* —, serve its purpose. — *v.r. sich* —, come true, be fulfilled.
Erfüllung [ɛr'fylʊŋ], *f.* (—, *no pl.*) fulfilment; granting; performance; *in — gehen*, come true, be realised.
ergänzen [ɛr'gɛntsən], *v.a.* complete, complement.
Ergänzung [ɛr'gɛntsʊŋ], *f.* (—, *pl.* **—en**) completion; complement, supplement.
ergattern [ɛr'gatərn], *v.a.* pick up.
ergeben [ɛr'ge:bən], *v.a. irr.* give, yield, prove, show. — *v.r. sich* —, surrender (to), acquiesce (in); happen, result, follow. — *adj.* devoted, submissive, humble, obedient.
Ergebenheit [ɛr'ge:bənhaɪt], *f.* (—, *no pl.*) devotion, obedience, humility, fidelity.
ergebenst [ɛr'ge:bənst], *adj. Ihr —er* (*letter ending*), yours very truly, your obedient servant. — *adv.* respectfully.
Ergebnis [ɛr'ge:pnɪs], *n.* (**—ses**, *pl.* **—se**) outcome, result; (*Agr.*) yield.
Ergebung [ɛr'ge:bʊŋ], *f.* (—, *no pl.*) submission, resignation; surrender.
Ergehen [ɛr'ge:ən], *n.* (**—s**, *no pl.*) health, condition, well-being.
ergehen [ɛr'ge:ən], *v.n. irr.* (*aux.* sein) be promulgated *or* issued; — *lassen*, issue, publish; *etwas über sich — lassen*, submit to *or* suffer s.th. patiently. — *v.r. sich* —, (*obs.*) take a stroll.
ergiebig [ɛr'gi:bɪç], *adj.* rich, productive, fertile, profitable.
ergießen [ɛr'gi:sən], *v.r. irr. sich* —, discharge, flow into.
erglänzen [ɛr'glɛntsən], *v.n.* (*aux.* sein) shine forth, sparkle.
erglühen [ɛr'gly:ən], *v.n.* (*aux.* sein) glow; blush.
ergötzen [ɛr'gœtsən], *v.a.* (*obs.*) amuse, delight. — *v.r. sich — an*, delight in.
ergrauen [ɛr'grauən], *v.n.* (*aux.* sein) become grey; grow old.
ergreifen [ɛr'graɪfən], *v.a. irr.* seize, grasp, get hold of; move, touch, affect; *Maßnahmen* —, take measures.
Ergreifung [ɛr'graɪfʊŋ], *f.* (—, *no pl.*) seizure; (*measure*) adoption.
ergriffen [ɛr'grɪfən], *adj.* moved, touched, impressed.
Ergriffenheit [ɛr'grɪfənhaɪt], *f.* (—, *no pl.*) emotion.
ergrimmen [ɛr'grɪmən], *v.n.* (*aux.* sein) grow angry, be enraged.
ergründen [ɛr'gryndən], *v.a.* get to the bottom of, investigate, fathom.
Erguß [ɛr'gus], *m.* (**—sses**, *pl.* **¨sse**) outpouring; (*fig.*) effusion.
erhaben [ɛr'ha:bən], *adj.* sublime, exalted; majestic, elevated.
Erhabenheit [ɛr'ha:bənhaɪt], *f.* (—, *no pl.*) majesty, sublimity.
erhalten [ɛr'haltən], *v.a. irr.* receive, obtain, get, preserve; maintain, keep up. — *v.r. sich — von*, subsist on.
erhältlich [ɛr'hɛltlɪç], *adj.* obtainable.
Erhaltung [ɛr'haltʊŋ], *f.* (—, *no pl.*) preservation, conservation; (*family*) maintenance.
erhärten [ɛr'hɛrtən], *v.a.* make hard; (*fig.*) prove, confirm.
erhaschen [ɛr'haʃən], *v.a.* catch, snatch.
erheben [ɛr'he:bən], *v.a. irr.* lift up, raise; (*fig.*) elevate, exalt; *Klage* —, bring an action; *Geld* —, raise money; *Steuern* —, levy taxes. — *v.r. sich* —, rise, stand up.
erheblich [ɛr'he:plɪç], *adj.* considerable, weighty, appreciable.
Erhebung [ɛr'he:bʊŋ], *f.* (—, *pl.* **—en**) elevation; (*taxes*) levying; revolt, rebellion, rising.
erheischen [ɛr'haɪʃən], *v.a.* (*rare*) require, demand.
erheitern [ɛr'haɪtərn], *v.a.* cheer, exhilarate.
erhellen [ɛr'hɛlən], *v.a.* light up, illuminate; (*fig.*) enlighten. — *v.n.* become evident.
erhitzen [ɛr'hɪtsən], *v.a.* heat; (*fig.*) inflame, excite. — *v.r. sich* —, grow hot; grow angry.
erhöhen [ɛr'hø:ən], *v.a.* heighten, raise, intensify, increase; (*value*) enhance.
erholen [ɛr'ho:lən], *v.r. sich* —, recover, get better; relax (after work); take a rest.
erholungsbedürftig [ɛr'ho:lʊŋsbədyrftɪç], *adj.* in need of a rest.
erhören [ɛr'hø:rən], *v.a.* hear, vouchsafe, grant.
Erich ['e:rɪç], *m.* Eric.
erinnerlich [ɛr'ɪnərlɪç], *adj.* remembered; *soweit mir — ist*, as far as I can remember.
erinnern [ɛr'ɪnərn], *v.a.* remind. — *v.r. sich* —, remember, recollect, recall, call to mind.
Erinnerung [ɛr'ɪnərʊŋ], *f.* (—, *pl.* **—en**) remembrance; recollection; reminiscences.
erjagen [ɛr'ja:gən], *v.a.* hunt (down), chase.
erkalten [ɛr'kaltən], *v.n.* (*aux.* sein) grow cold.
erkälten [ɛr'kɛltən], *v.r. sich* —, catch cold.
Erkältung [ɛr'kɛltʊŋ], *f.* (—, *pl.* **—en**) cold, chill.
erkämpfen [ɛr'kɛmpfən], *v.a.* obtain by fighting; obtain by great exertion.
erkaufen [ɛr'kaufən], *v.a.* purchase; bribe, corrupt.
erkennen [ɛr'kɛnən], *v.a. irr.* recognise; perceive, distinguish, discern; (*Comm.*) credit; *zu — geben*, give to understand; *sich zu — geben*, make o.s. known. — *v.n.* (*Law*) judge; *— auf*, (*Law*) announce verdict, pass sentence.

erkenntlich [ɛr'kɛntlɪç], *adj.* grateful; (*fig.*) *sich — zeigen*, show o.s. grateful.
Erkenntlichkeit [ɛr'kɛntlɪçkaɪt], *f.* (—, *no pl.*) gratitude.
Erkenntnis [ɛr'kɛntnɪs], *f.* (—, *pl.* **—e**) perception, knowledge, comprehension, understanding; realisation, (*Phil.*) cognition.
Erkennung [ɛr'kɛnuŋ], *f.* (—, *no pl.*) recognition.
Erker ['ɛrkər], *m.* (**—s**, *pl.* —) alcove, bay, turret.
Erkerfenster ['ɛrkərfɛnstər], *n.* (**—s**, *pl.* —) bay-window.
erklären [ɛr'klɛ:rən], *v.a.* explain, expound, account for; make a statement on, declare, state.
erklärlich [ɛr'klɛ:rlɪç], *adj.* explicable.
Erklärung [ɛr'klɛ:ruŋ], *f.* (—, *pl.* **—en**) explanation; declaration, statement; (*income tax*) return.
erklecklich [ɛr'klɛklɪç], *adj.* considerable.
erklettern [ɛr'klɛtərn], *v.a.* climb.
erklimmen [ɛr'klɪmən], *v.a. irr.* climb.
erklingen [ɛr'klɪŋən], *v.n. irr.* (*aux.* sein) sound, resound.
erkoren [ɛr'ko:rən], *adj.* select, chosen.
erkranken [ɛr'kraŋkən], *v.n.* (*aux.* sein) fall ill.
erkühnen [ɛr'ky:nən], *v.r. sich —*, dare, make bold, venture.
erkunden [ɛr'kundən], *v.a.* explore, find out; (*Mil.*) reconnoitre.
erkundigen [ɛr'kundɪgən], *v.r. sich —*, enquire (about), make enquiries.
erlaben [ɛr'la:bən], *v.r. sich —*, (*obs.*) refresh o.s.
erlahmen [ɛr'la:mən], *v.n.* (*aux.* sein) become lame; lose o.'s drive; grow tired.
erlangen [ɛr'laŋən], *v.a.* reach, gain, obtain; acquire; attain.
Erlaß [ɛr'las], *m.* (**—sses**, *pl.* **⸚sse**) remission, exemption, release, dispensation; (*Comm.*) deduction; (*Law, Pol.*) proclamation, edict, decree, writ; (*Eccl.*) indulgence; remission.
erlassen [ɛr'lasən], *v.a. irr.* remit, release, let off; (*Law, Pol.*) enact, promulgate.
erläßlich [ɛr'lɛslɪç], *adj.* remissible, dispensable, venial.
erlauben [ɛr'laubən], *v.a.* permit, allow; *sich etwas —*, take the liberty of, make bold to; have the impertinence to.
Erlaubnis [ɛr'laupnɪs], *f.* (—, *no pl.*) permission, leave, permit; *die — haben*, be permitted; *um — bitten*, beg leave; *mit Ihrer —*, by your leave.
erlaucht [ɛr'lauxt], *adj.* illustrious, noble.
erlauschen [ɛr'lauʃən], *v.a.* overhear.
erläutern [ɛr'lɔytərn], *v.a.* explain, illustrate, elucidate.
Erle ['ɛrlə], *f.* (—, *pl.* **—n**) (*Bot.*) alder.
erleben [ɛr'le:bən], *v.a.* live to see; go through, experience.
Erlebnis [ɛr'le:pnɪs], *n.* (**—sses**, *pl.* **—sse**) experience, adventure, occurrence.
erledigen [ɛr'le:dɪgən], *v.a.* settle, finish off, clear up; dispatch; execute (commission etc.).
erledigt [ɛr'le:dɪçt], *adj.* (*coll.*) worn-out; exhausted.
erlegen [ɛr'le:gən], *v.a.* slay; pay down.
erleichtern [ɛr'laɪçtərn], *v.a.* lighten, ease, facilitate.
erleiden [ɛr'laɪdən], *v.a. irr.* suffer, endure, bear, undergo.
erlernen [ɛr'lɛrnən], *v.a.* learn, acquire.
erlesen [ɛr'le:zən], *v.a. irr.* select, choose. — *adj.* select, choice.
erleuchten [ɛr'lɔyçtən], *v.a.* illumine, illuminate, floodlight; (*fig.*) enlighten, inspire.
erliegen [ɛr'li:gən], *v.n. irr.* (*aux.* sein) succumb.
Erlkönig ['ɛrlko:nɪç], *m.* (**—s**, *pl.* **—e**) fairy-king, elf-king.
erlogen [ɛr'lo:gən], *adj.* false, untrue; trumped-up.
Erlös [ɛr'lo:s], *m.* (**—es**, *no pl.*) proceeds.
erlöschen [ɛr'lœʃən], *v.n. irr.* (*aux.* sein) be extinguished, die out; (*fire*) go out; (*contract*) expire.
erlösen [ɛr'lo:zən], *v.a.* redeem; release, save, deliver.
ermächtigen [ɛr'mɛçtɪgən], *v.a.* empower; authorise.
ermahnen [ɛr'ma:nən], *v.a.* admonish, exhort, remind.
ermäßigen [ɛr'mɛ:sɪgən], *v.a.* reduce.
ermatten [ɛr'matən], *v.a.* weaken, weary, tire. — *v.n.* (*aux.* sein) grow weak, become tired.
Ermessen [ɛr'mɛsən], *n.* (**—s**, *no pl.*) judgment, opinion.
ermitteln [ɛr'mɪtəln], *v.a.* ascertain, find out.
ermöglichen [ɛr'mo:klɪçən], *v.a.* make possible.
ermorden [ɛr'mɔrdən], *v.a.* murder.
ermüden [ɛr'my:dən], *v.a.* tire, fatigue. — *v.n.* (*aux.* sein) get tired, grow weary.
ermuntern [ɛr'muntərn], *v.a.* encourage, cheer up.
ermutigen [ɛr'mu:tɪgən], *v.a.* encourage.
ernähren [ɛr'nɛ:rən], *v.a.* nourish, feed.
ernennen [ɛr'nɛnən], *v.a. irr.* nominate, appoint.
erneuern [ɛr'nɔyərn], *v.a.* renew, repair, renovate.
erniedrigen [ɛr'ni:drɪgən], *v.a.* humble, humiliate, degrade. — *v.r. sich —*, humble o.s., abase o.s.
Ernst (1) [ɛrnst], *m.* Ernest.
Ernst (2) [ɛrnst], *m.* (**—es**, *no pl.*) earnestness, seriousness.
ernst [ɛrnst], *adj.* earnest, serious.
Ernte ['ɛrntə], *f.* (—, *pl.* **—n**) harvest, crop.
ernüchtern [ɛr'nyçtərn], *v.a.* sober; (*fig.*) disenchant, disillusion.
erobern [ɛr'o:bərn], *v.a.* (*Mil.*) conquer; take, win.
eröffnen [ɛr'œfnən], *v.a.* open, inaugurate; inform, reveal.
erörtern [ɛr'œrtərn], *v.a.* discuss, debate, argue.

erpicht [ɛr'pɪçt], *adj.* eager for, bent on.
erpressen [ɛr'prɛsən], *v.a.* extort, blackmail.
erquicken [ɛr'kvɪkən], *v.a.* refresh.
erraten [ɛr'ra:tən], *v.a. irr.* guess.
erregen [ɛr're:gən], *v.a.* cause; stir up, excite, agitate; provoke.
erreichen [ɛr'raɪçən], *v.a.* reach, arrive at; (*fig.*) attain, reach.
erretten [ɛr'rɛtən], *v.a.* save, rescue.
errichten [ɛr'rɪçtən], *v.a.* erect, raise, build.
erringen [ɛr'rɪŋən], *v.a. irr.* obtain (by exertion), achieve.
erröten [ɛr'rø:tən], *v.n.* (*aux.* sein) blush, redden.
Errungenschaft [ɛr'ruŋənʃaft], *f.* (—, *pl.* **—en**) achievement, acquisition.
Ersatz [ɛr'zats], *m.* (**—es,** *no pl.*) substitute; compensation, amends: (*Mil. etc.*) replacement.
erschallen [ɛr'ʃalən], *v.n.* (*aux.* sein) resound, sound.
erschaudern [ɛr'ʃaudərn], *v.n.* (*aux.* sein) be seized with horror.
erscheinen [ɛr'ʃaɪnən], *v.n. irr.* (*aux.* sein) appear, make o.'s appearance: seem; be published.
erschießen [ɛr'ʃi:sən], *v.a. irr.* shoot dead.
erschlaffen [ɛr'ʃlafən], *v.n.* (*aux.* sein) flag, slacken.
erschlagen [ɛr'ʃla:gən], *v.a. irr.* slay, kill.
erschließen [ɛr'ʃli:sən], *v.a. irr.* open up.
erschöpfen [ɛr'ʃœpfən], *v.a.* exhaust.
erschrecken [ɛr'ʃrɛkən], *v.a. irr.* startle, shock, terrify. — *v.n.* (*aux.* sein) be startled, be frightened, be terrified.
erschüttern [ɛr'ʃytərn], *v.a.* shake: (*fig.*) move, affect strongly.
erschweren [ɛr'ʃve:rən], *v.a.* (*fig.*) aggravate, make more difficult.
erschwingen [ɛr'ʃvɪŋən], *v.a. irr.* afford, be able to pay.
erschwinglich [ɛr'ʃvɪŋlɪç], *adj.* attainable, within o.'s means.
ersehen [ɛr'ze:ən], *v.a. irr.* — *aus*, gather (from).
ersehnen [ɛr'ze:nən], *v.a.* long for, yearn for.
ersetzen [ɛr'zɛtsən], *v.a.* replace, take the place of; restore, make good; repair; (*money*) refund.
ersichtlich [ɛr'zɪçtlɪç], *adj.* evident.
ersinnen [ɛr'zɪnən], *v.a. irr.* think out; imagine, devise, contrive.
ersparen [ɛr'ʃpa:rən], *v.a.* save.
ersprießlich [ɛr'ʃpri:slɪç], *adj.* useful, profitable, beneficial.
erst [e:rst], *num. adj.* first. — *adv.* first, at first, only, but; — *jetzt*, only now; *nun* — *recht*, now more than ever.
erstatten [ɛr'ʃtatən], *v.a.* reimburse, compensate, repay; *Bericht* —, report.
Erstattung [ɛr'ʃtatuŋ], *f.* (—, *pl.* **—en**) reimbursement, restitution.
Erstaufführung ['e:rstauffy:ruŋ], *f.* (—, *pl.* **—en**) (*Theat.*) first night; première.
Erstaunen [ɛr'ʃtaunən], *n.* (**—s,** *no pl.*) amazement, astonishment, surprise.
erstechen [ɛr'ʃtɛçən], *v.a. irr.* stab.
erstehen [ɛr'ʃte:ən], *v.n. irr.* (*aux.* sein) rise, arise. — *v.a.* buy, purchase.
ersteigen [ɛr'ʃtaɪgən], *v.a. irr.* climb, mount, ascend.
ersticken [ɛr'ʃtɪkən], *v.a. irr.* choke, stifle, suffocate. — *v.n.* (*aux.* sein) choke, suffocate.
erstmalig ['e:rstma:lɪç], *adj.* first. — *adv.* for the first time.
erstreben [ɛr'ʃtre:bən], *v.a.* strive after.
erstrecken [ɛr'ʃtrɛkən], *v.r.* *sich* —, extend, reach to.
ersuchen [ɛr'zu:xən], *v.a.* request, ask.
ertappen [ɛr'tapən], *v.a.* catch, detect.
erteilen [ɛr'taɪlən], *v.a.* bestow, impart; *einen Auftrag* —, issue an order; *Unterricht* —, instruct; *die Erlaubnis* —, give permission.
ertönen [ɛr'tø:nən], *v.n.* (*aux.* sein) sound, resound.
Ertrag [ɛr'tra:k], *m.* (**—s,** *pl.* **¨e**) produce; returns, yield; output; (*sale*) proceeds.
ertragen [ɛr'tra:gən], *v.a. irr.* bear, suffer, endure.
ertränken [ɛr'trɛnkən], *v.a.* drown.
ertrinken [ɛr'trɪŋkən], *v.n. irr.* (*aux.* sein) drown, be drowned.
erübrigen [ɛr'y:brɪgən], *v.a.* save, spare.
erwachen [ɛr'vaxən], *v.n.* (*aux.* sein) awake, wake up.
erwachsen [ɛr'vaksən], *adj.* grown-up, adult. — *v.n. irr.* grow up; ensue, follow, arise.
erwägen [ɛr'vɛ:gən], *v.a. irr.* weigh, ponder, consider.
erwähnen [ɛr'vɛ:nən], *v.a.* mention.
erwärmen [ɛr'vɛrmən], *v.a.* warm (up), make warm.
erwarten [ɛr'vartən], *v.a.* expect, await.
Erwartung [ɛr'vartuŋ], *f.* (—, *pl.* **—en**) expectation.
erwecken [ɛr'vɛkən], *v.a.* wake up, awaken, raise; rouse.
erwehren [ɛr've:rən], *v.r.* *sich* — (*Genit.*), defend o.s.; *ich kann mich des Lachens nicht* —, I cannot help laughing.
erweichen [ɛr'vaɪçən], *v.a.* soften.
erweisen [ɛr'vaɪzən], *v.a. irr.* prove, show; demonstrate.
erweitern [ɛr'vaɪtərn], *v.a.* widen, enlarge, expand.
erwerben [ɛr'vɛrbən], *v.a. irr.* acquire.
erwidern [ɛr'vi:dərn], *v.a.* reply, answer; return.
erwirken [ɛr'vɪrkən], *v.a.* effect, secure.
erwischen [ɛr'vɪʃən], *v.a. see* **ertappen.**
erwünschen [ɛr'vynʃən], *v.a.* desire, wish for.
erwürgen [ɛr'vyrgən], *v.a.* strangle, throttle.
Erz [ɛrts], (**—es,** *pl.* **—e**) ore; brass, bronze.

erzählen [ɛrˈtsɛːlən], *v.a.* narrate, relate, tell.
Erzbischof [ˈɛrtsbɪʃɔf], *m.* (**—s**, *pl.* **¨e**) archbishop.
erzeugen [ɛrˈtsɔygən], *v.a.* engender; beget; produce; (*Elec.*) generate.
Erzherzog [ˈɛrtshɛrtsoːk], *m.* (**—s**, *pl.* **¨e**) archduke.
erziehen [ɛrˈtsiːən], *v.a. irr.* educate, train, bring up, rear.
Erziehungsanstalt [ɛrˈtsiːuŋsanʃtalt], *f.* (**—**, *pl.* **—en**) approved school, reformatory.
erzielen [ɛrˈtsiːlən], *v.a.* obtain; fetch, realize (a price); *Gewinn* **—**, make a profit.
erzittern [ɛrˈtsɪtərn], *v.n.* (*aux.* sein) tremble, shake.
Erzofen [ˈɛrtsoːfən], *m.* (**—s**, *pl.* **¨n**) furnace.
erzürnen [ɛrˈtsyrnən], *v.a.* make angry. — *v.r. sich* **—**, grow angry.
Erzvater [ˈɛrtsfaːtər], *m.* (**—s**, *pl.* **¨**) patriarch.
erzwingen [ɛrˈtsvɪŋən], *v.a. irr.* enforce, force, compel.
es [ɛs], *pron.* it; — *gibt*, there is; — *sind*, there are; — *lebe*, long live!
Es [ɛs], *n.* (**—**, *pl.* **—**) (*Mus.*) E flat.
Esche [ˈɛʃə], *f.* (**—**, *pl.* **—n**) (*Bot.*) ash, ashtree.
Esel [ˈeːzəl], *m.* (**—s**, *pl.* **—**) ass, donkey.
Eselsohr [ˈeːzəlsoːr], *n.* (**—s**, *pl.* **—en**) (*fig.*) dog's ear.
Eskadron [ɛskaˈdroːn], *f.* (**—**, *pl.* **—en**) squadron.
Espe [ˈɛspə], *f.* (**—**, *pl.* **—n**) (*Bot.*) asp, aspen.
eßbar [ˈɛsbaːr], *adj.* edible.
Esse [ˈɛsə], *f.* (**—**, *pl.* **—n**) chimney, forge.
Essen [ˈɛsən], *n.* (**—s**, *no pl.*) meal; eating.
essen [ˈɛsən], *v.a. irr.* eat, have a meal.
Essenz [ɛˈsɛnts], *f.* (**—**, *pl.* **—en**) essence.
Essig [ˈɛsɪç], *m.* (**—s**, *no pl.*) vinegar.
Eßlöffel [ˈɛslœfəl], *m.* (**—s**, *pl.* **—**) table-spoon.
Estland [ˈɛstlant], *n.* Estonia.
Estrade [ɛˈstraːdə], *f.* (**—**, *pl.* **—n**) platform.
Estrich [ˈɛstrɪç], *m.* (**—s**, *no pl.*) floor, flooring, plaster-floor.
etablieren [etaˈbliːrən], *v.a.* establish, set up (business).
Etagenwohnung [eˈtaːʒənvoːnuŋ], *f.* (**—**, *pl.* **—en**) flat; (*Am.*) apartment.
Etappe [eˈtapə], *f.* (**—**, *pl.* **—n**) stage; (*Mil.*) lines of communication.
Etat [eˈtaː], *m.* (**—s**, *pl.* **—s**) (*Parl.*) estimates, budget; (*Comm.*) statement, balance sheet.
ethisch [ˈeːtɪʃ], *adj.* ethical.
Etikett [etiˈkɛt], *n.* (**—s**, *pl.* **—s**) label, ticket, tag.
Etikette [etiˈkɛtə], *f.* (**—**, *no pl.*) etiquette; ceremonial.
etikettieren [etikɛˈtiːrən], *v.a.* label.
etliche [ˈɛtlɪçə], *pl. adj. & pron.* some, several, sundry.
Etui [eˈtviː], *n.* (**—s**, *pl.* **—s**) small case, small box.
etwa [ˈɛtva], *adv.* nearly, about; perhaps, perchance, in some way.
etwaig [ˈɛtvaɪç], *adj.* possible, any, eventual.
etwas [ˈɛtvas], *indef. pron.* some, something. — *adj.* some, any. — *adv.* a little, somewhat.
Etzel [ˈɛtsəl], *m.* Attila.
euch [ɔyç], *pers. pron. pl. Dat. & Acc.* you, yourselves.
euer [ˈɔyər], *poss. adj.* your. — *poss. pron.* yours.
Eule [ˈɔylə], *f.* (**—**, *pl.* **—n**) owl.
eurige [ˈɔyrɪgə], *poss. pron. der, die, das* **—**, yours.
Europa [ɔyˈroːpa], *n.* Europe.
Euter [ˈɔytər], *n.* (**—s**, *pl.* **—**) udder.
evangelisch [evanˈgeːlɪʃ], *adj.* Evangelical, Protestant.
Evangelium [evanˈgeːljum], *n.* (**—s**, *pl.* **—lien**) gospel.
eventuell [evɛntuˈɛl], *adj.* possible.
ewig [ˈeːvɪç], *adj.* eternal; perpetual.
Ewigkeit [ˈeːvɪçkaɪt], *f.* (**—**, *pl.* **—en**) eternity.
explodieren [ɛksploˈdiːrən], *v.n.* explode; detonate.
exponieren [ɛkspoˈniːrən], *v.a.* set forth, explain at length.
Extemporale [ɛkstɛmpoˈraːlə], *n.* (**—s**, *pl.* **—lien**) unprepared exercise.
extrahieren [ɛkstraˈhiːrən], *v.a.* extract.
Extremitäten [ɛkstremɪˈtɛːtən], *f. pl.* extremities.

F

F [ɛf], *n.* (**—s**, *pl.* **—s**) the letter F; (*Mus.*) *F Dur*, F major; *F Moll*, F minor.
Fabel [ˈfaːbəl], *f.* (**—**, *pl.* **—n**) fable; (*fig.*) tale, fiction; (*drama*) plot, story.
fabelhaft [ˈfaːbəlhaft], *adj.* fabulous; phenomenal, gorgeous.
fabeln [ˈfaːbəln], *v.n.* tell fables; talk nonsense.
Fabrik [faˈbriːk], *f.* (**—**, *pl.* **—en**) factory; plant, works.
Fabrikant [fabrɪˈkant], *m.* (**—en**, *pl.* **—en**) manufacturer.
fabrizieren [fabrɪˈtsiːrən], *v.a.* manufacture, make.
fabulieren [fabuˈliːrən], *v.n.* tell fables; (*fig.*) tell tall stories.
Fach [fax], *n.* (**—s**, *pl.* **¨er**) compartment; pigeon-hole, drawer; (*fig.*) subject of study, department, branch.
Fachausdruck [ˈfaxausdruk], *m.* (**—s**, *pl.* **¨e**) technical term.

Fächer [ˈfɛçər], *m.* (**—s**, *pl.* **—**) fan.
Fächertaube [ˈfɛçərtaubə], *f.* (**—**, *pl.* **—n**) fantail.
Fachmann [ˈfaxman], *m.* (**—s**, *pl.* **¨er** *or* **Fachleute**) expert, specialist.
Fachschule [ˈfaxʃu:lə], *f.* (**—**, *pl.* **—n**) technical school.
fachsimpeln [ˈfaxzɪmpəln], *v.n.* talk shop.
Fachwerk [ˈfaxvɛrk], *n.* (**—s**, *no pl.*) timbered framework.
Fackel [ˈfakəl], *f.* (**—**, *pl.* **—n**) torch.
fade [ˈfa:də], *adj.* tasteless; boring, insipid.
Faden [ˈfa:dən], *m.* (**—s**, *pl.* **¨**) thread; (*measure*) fathom.
fadenscheinig [ˈfa:dənʃaɪnɪç], *adj.* threadbare.
Fagott [faˈgɔt], *n.* (**—s**, *pl.* **—e**) (*Mus.*) bassoon.
fähig [ˈfɛ:ɪç], *adj.* able, capable; talented, gifted, competent.
fahl [fa:l], *adj.* pale, sallow.
Fähnchen [ˈfɛ:nçən], *n.* (**—s**, *pl.* **—**) small banner; pennon; (*Mil.*) (*obs.*) small troop.
fahnden [ˈfa:ndən], *v.a.* search for (officially).
Fahne [ˈfa:nə], *f.* (**—**, *pl.* **—n**) flag, banner, standard, colours; (*weather*) vane; (*Typ.*) galley proof.
Fahnenflucht [ˈfa:nənfluxt], *f.* (**—**, *no pl.*) (*Mil.*) desertion.
Fähnrich [ˈfɛ:nrɪç], *m.* (**—s**, *pl.* **—e**) ensign.
Fahrbahn [ˈfa:rba:n], *f.* (**—**, *pl.* **—en**) traffic lane, roadway.
fahrbar [ˈfa:rba:r], *adj.* passable, navigable, negotiable.
Fähre [ˈfɛ:rə], *f.* (**—**, *pl.* **—n**) ferry, ferry-boat.
fahren. [ˈfa:rən], *v.a. irr.* drive. — *v.n.* (*aux.* sein) (*vehicle*) ride (in), be driven; (*vessel*) sail; go, travel.
Fahrer [ˈfa:rər], *m.* (**—s**, *pl.* **—**) driver, chauffeur.
Fahrgast [ˈfa:rgast], *m.* (**—s**, *pl.* **¨e**) passenger.
fahrig [ˈfa:rɪç], *adj.* absent-minded, giddy, thoughtless.
Fahrkarte [ˈfa:rkartə], *f.* (**—**, *pl.* **—n**) ticket.
fahrlässig [ˈfa:rlɛsɪç], *adj.* negligent, careless.
Fährmann [ˈfɛ:rman], *m.* (**—s**, *pl.* **¨er**) ferry-man.
Fahrplan [ˈfa:rplan], *m.* (**—s**, *pl.* **¨e**) timetable, railway-guide.
fahrplanmäßig [ˈfa:rplanmɛ:sɪç], *adj.* according to the timetable, scheduled.
Fahrpreis [ˈfa:rpraɪs], *m.* (**—es**, *pl.* **—e**) cost of ticket, fare.
Fahrrad [ˈfa:rra:t], *n.* (**—s**, *pl.* **¨er**) cycle, bicycle.
Fahrschein [ˈfa:rʃaɪn], *m.* (**—s**, *pl.* **—e**) ticket.
Fahrstraße [ˈfa:rʃtrasə], *f.* (**—**, *pl.* **—n**) roadway.
Fahrstuhl [ˈfa:rʃtu:l], *m.* (**—s**, *pl.* **¨e**) lift; (*Am.*) elevator.
Fahrt [fa:rt], *f.* (**—**, *pl.* **—en**) drive, ride, journey; (*sea*) voyage, cruise.
Fährte [ˈfɛ:rtə], *f.* (**—**, *pl.* **—n**) track, trace, trail.
Fahrzeug [ˈfa:rtsɔyk], *n.* (**—s**, *pl.* **—e**) vehicle, conveyance; vessel, craft.
faktisch [ˈfaktɪʃ], *adj.* real, actual.
Faktor [ˈfaktɔr], *m.* (**—s**, *pl.* **—en**) foreman, overseer, factor; (*Maths.*) factor, component part.
Faktura [fakˈtu:ra], *f.* (**—**, *pl.* **—ren**) (*Comm.*) invoice.
fakturieren [faktuˈri:rən], *v.a.* (*Comm.*) invoice.
Fakultät [fakulˈtɛ:t], *f.* (**—**, *pl.* **—en**) (*Univ.*) faculty.
fakultativ [fakultaˈti:f], *adj.* optional.
Falbel [ˈfalbəl], *f.* (**—**, *pl.* **—n**) flounce, furbelow.
Falke [ˈfalkə], *m.* (**—n**, *pl.* **—n**) (*Orn.*) falcon, hawk.
Fall [fal], *m.* (**—s**, *pl.* **¨e**) fall, falling; case; (*Geog.*) decline, incline, gradient; (*fig.*) fall, decline, downfall, failure.
Fallbaum [ˈfalbaum], *m.* (**—s**, *pl.* **¨e**) tollbar, turnpike.
Fallbeil [ˈfalbaɪl], *n.* (**—s**, *pl.* **—e**) guillotine.
Fallbrücke [ˈfalbrykə], *f.* (**—**, *pl.* **—n**) draw-bridge.
Falle [ˈfalə], *f.* (**—**, *pl.* **—n**) trap, snare.
fallen [ˈfalən], *v.n. irr.* (*aux.* sein) fall, drop; (*Mil.*) be killed.
fällen [ˈfɛlən], *v.a.* fell, cut down, hew down; *ein Urteil* —, (*Law*) pronounce judgment.
Fallensteller [ˈfalənʃtɛlər], *m.* (**—s**, *pl.* **—**) trapper.
fallieren [faˈli:rən], *v.n.* become bankrupt.
fällig [ˈfɛlɪç], *adj.* due, payable.
Fälligkeit [ˈfɛlɪçkaɪt], *f.* (**—**, *pl.* **—en**) (*Comm.*) maturity.
Fallobst [ˈfalo:pst], *n.* (**—es**, *no pl.*) windfall (of fruit).
falls [fals], *conj.* in case, if.
Fallschirm [ˈfalʃɪrm], *m.* (**—s**, *pl.* **—e**) parachute.
Fallstrick [ˈfalʃtrɪk], *m.* (**—s**, *pl.* **—e**) snare, trap.
Fallsucht [ˈfalzuxt], *f.* (**—**, *no pl.*) (*Med.*) epilepsy.
Falltür [ˈfalty:r], *f.* (**—**, *pl.* **—en**) trap-door.
Fällung [ˈfɛluŋ], *f.* (**—**, *pl.* **—en**) cutting down.
falsch [falʃ], *adj.* false, incorrect, wrong; disloyal; counterfeit.
fälschen [ˈfɛlʃən], *v.a.* falsify, forge, tamper with.
Falschheit [ˈfalʃhaɪt], *f.* (**—**, *pl.* **—en**) falsehood, deceit, disloyalty.
fälschlich [ˈfɛlʃlɪç], *adv.* wrongly, falsely.
Fälschung [ˈfɛlʃuŋ], *f.* (**—**, *pl.* **—en**) falsification; forgery.
Falte [ˈfaltə], *f.* (**—**, *pl.* **—n**) fold, pleat; (*face*) wrinkle.
falten [ˈfaltən], *v.a.* fold, plait, pleat; wrinkle.

Falter ['faltər], *m.* (**—s**, *pl.* **—**) (*Ent.*) butterfly.
-fältig ['fɛltɪç], *suffix* (*following numbers*). -fold (*e.g. vierfältig*, fourfold).
Falz [falts], *m.* (**—es**, *pl.* **—e**) groove, notch; joint.
Falzbein ['faltsbaɪn], *n.* (**—s**, *pl.* **—e**) paper-folder, paper-knife.
Falzmaschine ['faltsmaʃi:nə], *f.* (**—**, *pl.* **—n**) folding-machine.
familiär [famil'jɛ:r], *adj.* familiar, intimate.
Familie [fa'mi:ljə], *f.* (**—**, *pl.* **—n**) family.
famos [fa'mo:s], *adj.* (*coll.*) excellent, splendid.
fanatisch [fa'na:tɪʃ], *adj.* fanatic(al), bigoted.
Fanatismus [fana'tɪsmus], *m.* (**—**, *no pl.*) fanaticism.
Fang [faŋ], *m.* (**—es**, *pl.* **⸚e**) catch, capture; (*bird*) talon, claw.
fangen ['faŋən], *v.a. irr.* catch, seize.
Fangzahn ['faŋtsa:n], *m.* (**—s**, *pl.* **⸚e**) fang, tusk.
Fant [fant], *m.* (**—s**, *pl.* **—e**) fop, coxcomb.
Farbe ['farbə], *f.* (**—**, *pl.* **—n**) colour, hue, paint, dye.
färben ['fɛrbən], *v.a.* dye, stain.
Farbenbrett ['farbənbrɛt], *n.* (**—s**, *pl.* **—er**) palette.
Farb(en)druck ['farpdruk, farbəndruk], *m.* (**—s**, *pl.* **—e**) colour-printing.
Farbenspiel ['farbənʃpi:l], *n.* (**—s**, *no pl.*) iridescence.
Färber ['fɛrbər], *m.* (**—s**, *pl.* **—**) dyer.
farbig ['farbɪç], *adj.* coloured.
Farbstift ['farpʃtɪft], *m.* (**—s**, *pl.* **—e**) crayon.
Farbstoff ['farpʃtɔf], *m.* (**—es**, *pl.* **—e**) dye.
Farbton ['farpto:n], *m.* (**—s**, *pl.* **⸚e**) hue, tone, tinge, shade.
Farn [farn], *m.* (**—s**, *pl.* **—e**) (*Bot.*) fern.
Färse ['fɛrzə], *f.* (**—**, *pl.* **—n**) (*Zool.*) heifer.
Fasan [fa'za:n], *m.* (**—s**, *pl.* **—e**) (*Orn.*) pheasant.
Fasching ['faʃɪŋ], *m.* (**—s**, *no pl.*) (Shrovetide) carnival.
Faschismus [fa'ʃɪsmus], *m.* (**—s**, *no pl.*) fascism.
Faselei [fa:zə'laɪ], *f.* (**—**, *pl.* **—en**) silly talk, drivel.
faseln ['fa:zəln], *v.n.* drivel.
Faser ['fa:zər], *f.* (**—**, *pl.* **—n**) thread; string; fibre, filament.
fasern ['fa:zərn], *v.n.* fray.
Faß [fas], *n.* (**—sses**, *pl.* **⸚sser**) barrel, vat, tun, tub, cask, keg; *Bier vom —*, draught beer; *Wein vom —*, wine from the wood.
Fassade [fa'sa:də], *f.* (**—**, *pl.* **—n**) façade.
faßbar ['fasba:r], *adj.* tangible.
Faßbinder ['fasbɪndər], *m.* (**—s**, *pl.* **—**) cooper.
fassen ['fasən], *v.a.* seize, take hold of, grasp; (*jewels*) set; contain, hold. — *v.r.* (*aux.* haben) *sich* —, compose o.s.; *sich kurz* —, be brief.
faßlich ['faslɪç], *adj.* comprehensible, understandable.
Fasson [fa'sɔ̃], *f.* (**—**, *pl.* **—s**) fashion; (*fig.*) cut, style.
Fassung ['fasuŋ], *f.* (**—**, *pl.* **—en**) (*jewels*) setting; (*speech*) wording, version; (*fig.*) composure.
fassungslos ['fasuŋslo:s], *adj.* bewildered, disconcerted; distraught, speechless.
fast [fast], *adv.* almost, nearly.
fasten ['fastən], *v.n.* fast.
Fastenzeit ['fastəntsaɪt], *f.* (**—**, *pl.* **—en**) time of fasting; Lent.
Fastnacht ['fastnaxt], *f*, (**—**, *no pl.*) Shrove Tuesday; Shrovetide.
fauchen ['fauxən], *v.n.* spit, hiss.
faul [faul], *adj.* (*food*) rotten, putrid, decayed; (*persons*) lazy, idle.
Fäule ['fɔylə], *f.* (**—**, *no pl.*) rot.
faulen ['faulən], *v.n.* (*aux.* sein) rot.
faulenzen ['faulɛntsən], *v.n.* laze, idle.
Faulenzer ['faulɛntsər], *m.* (**—s**, *pl.* **—**) idler, sluggard, lazybones.
Faulenzerei ['faulɛntsəraɪ], *f.* (**—**, *pl.* **—en**) idleness, laziness.
Faulheit ['faulhaɪt], *f.* (**—**, *no pl.*) idleness, laziness, sluggishness.
faulig ['faulɪç], *adj.* putrid, rotten.
Fäulnis ['fɔylnɪs], *f.* (**—**, *no pl.*) rottenness, putridity.
Faust [faust], *f.* (**—**, *pl.* **⸚e**) fist.
Fäustchen ['fɔystçən], *n.* (**—s**, *pl.* **—**) small fist; *sich ins — lachen*, laugh in o.'s sleeve.
Faustkampf ['faustkampf], *m.* (**—es**, *pl.* **⸚e**) boxing (match).
Faxen ['faksən], *f. pl.* foolery; — *machen*, play the buffoon.
Fazit ['fatsɪt], *n.* (**—s**, *no pl.*) sum, amount.
Februar ['fe:brua:r], *m.* (**—s**, *no pl.*) February.
fechten ['fɛçtən], *v.n. irr.* fight; fence; (*fig.*) beg.
Feder ['fe:dər], *f.* (**—**, *pl.* **—n**) (*bird*) feather; (*hat*) plume; (*writing*) pen; (*antique*) quill; (*Tech.*) spring.
Federball ['fe:dərbal], *m.* (**—s**, *pl.* **⸚e**) shuttle-cock.
federig ['fe:dərɪç], *adj.* feathery; (*Tech.*) springy, resilient.
Federlesen(s) ['fe:dərle:zən(s)], *n.* (**—s**, *no pl.*) *nicht viel — machen*, make short work of.
Fee [fe:], *f.* (**—**, *pl.* **—n**) fairy.
feenhaft ['fe:ənhaft], *adj.* fairy-like, magical.
Fegefeuer ['fe:gəfɔyər], *n.* (**—s**, *no pl.*) purgatory.
fegen ['fe:gən], *v.a.* clean, sweep. — *v.n.* (*aux.* sein) tear along.
Fehde ['fe:də], *f.* (**—**, *pl.* **—n**) feud, quarrel.
Fehdehandschuh ['fe:dəhantʃu:], *m.* (**—s**, *pl.* **—e**) gauntlet.

fehlbar ['fe:lba:r], *adj.* fallible.
Fehlbetrag ['fe:lbətra:k], *m.* (—**s**, *pl.* ⸚**e**) deficit.
fehlen ['fe:lən], *v.a.* miss. — *v.n.* err, do wrong; be absent; be wanting; *er fehlt mir*, I miss him.
Fehler ['fe:lər], *m.* (—**s**, *pl.* —) fault, defect; mistake, error.
Fehlgeburt ['fe:lgəburt], *f.* (—, *pl.* —**en**) miscarriage.
Fehlschlag ['fe:lʃla:k], *m.* (—**s**, *pl.* ⸚**e**) failure, disappointment.
feien ['faɪən], *v.a. einen — gegen*, charm s.o. against; *gefeit*, proof.
Feier ['faɪər], *f.* (—, *pl.* —**n**) celebration, festival, holiday, festive day.
Feierabend ['faɪəra:bənt], *m.* (—**s**, *pl.* —**e**) time for leaving off work; — *machen*, knock off (work).
feierlich ['faɪərlɪç], *adj.* festive, solemn, stately.
feiern ['faɪərn], *v.a.* celebrate; honour, praise. — *v.n.* rest from work.
Feiertag ['faɪərta:k], *m.* (—**s**, *pl.* —**e**) holiday, festive day.
feig [faɪk], *adj.* cowardly.
Feige ['faɪgə], *f.* (—, *pl.* —**n**) (*Bot.*) fig.
Feigheit ['faɪkhaɪt], *f.* (—, *pl.* —**en**) cowardice, cowardliness.
Feigling ['faɪklɪŋ], *m.* (—**s**, *pl.* —**e**) coward.
Feigwurz ['faɪkvurts], *m.* (—**es**, *no pl.*) (*Bot.*) fennel.
feil [faɪl], *adj.* (*obs.*) for sale; venal.
feilbieten ['faɪlbi:tən], *v.a.* offer for sale.
Feile ['faɪlə], *f.* (—, *pl.* —**n**) file.
feilen ['faɪlən], *v.a.* file.
feilhalten ['faɪlhaltən], *v.a.* have for sale, be ready to sell.
feilschen ['faɪlʃən], *v.n.* bargain, haggle.
Feilspäne ['faɪlʃpɛ:nə], *m. pl.* filings.
fein [faɪn], *adj.* fine; neat, pretty, nice; delicate; (*clothes*) elegant; (*behaviour*) refined, polished.
Feinbäckerei ['faɪnbɛkəraɪ], *f.* (—, *pl.* —**en**) confectioner's shop.
Feind [faɪnt], *m.* (—**es**, *pl.* —**e**) enemy, foe, adversary.
Feindschaft ['faɪntʃaft], *f.* (—, *pl.* —**en**) enmity, hostility.
feindselig ['faɪntze:lɪç], *adj.* hostile, malignant.
feinfühlend ['faɪnfy:lənt], *adj.* delicate, sensitive.
Feinheit ['faɪnhaɪt], *f.* (—, *pl.* —**en**) fineness, elegance, politeness, delicacy.
Feinschmecker ['faɪnʃmɛkər], *m.* (—**s**, *pl.* —), gourmet.
Feinsliebchen [faɪns'li:pçən], *n.* (—**s**, *pl.* —) (*Poet. obs.*) sweetheart.
feist [faɪst], *adj.* fat, obese.
Feld [fɛlt], *n.* (—**es**, *pl.* —**er**) field, plain; (*chess*) square; (*fig.*) sphere, province.
Feldbett ['fɛltbɛt], *n.* (—**s**, *pl.* —**en**) camp-bed.
Feldherr ['fɛlthɛr], *m.* (—**n**, *pl.* —**en**) commander, general.
Feldmesser ['fɛltmɛsər], *m.* (—**s**, *pl.* —) land-surveyor.
Feldscher ['fɛltʃe:r], *m.* (—**s**, *pl.* —**e**) army-surgeon.
Feldstecher ['fɛltʃtɛçər], *m.* (—**s**, *pl.* —) field-glass(es).
Feldwebel ['fɛltve:bəl], *m.* (—**s**, *pl.* —) sergeant-major.
Feldzug ['fɛlttsu:k], *m.* (—**es**, *pl.* ⸚**e**) campaign, expedition.
Felge ['fɛlgə], *f.* (—, *pl.* —**n**) (*wheel*) felloe, felly, rim.
Fell [fɛl], *n.* (—**s**, *pl.* —**e**) hide, skin, pelt.
Felsabhang ['fɛlsaphaŋ], *m.* (—**s**, *pl.* ⸚**e**) rocky slope.
Felsen ['fɛlzən], *m.* (—**s**, *pl.* —) rock, cliff.
Felsengebirge ['fɛlzəngəbɪrgə], *n.* Rocky Mountains.
Felsenriff ['fɛlzənrɪf], *n.* (—**s**, *pl.* —**e**) reef.
felsig ['fɛlzɪç], *adj.* rocky.
Feme ['fe:mə], *f.* (—, *pl.* —**n**) secret tribunal.
Fenchel ['fɛnçəl], *m.* (—**s**, *no pl.*) (*Bot.*) fennel.
Fenster ['fɛnstər], *n.* (—**s**, *pl.* —) window.
Fensterbrett ['fɛnstərbrɛt], *n.* (—**s**, *pl.* —**er**) window-sill.
Fensterflügel ['fɛnstərfly:gəl], *m.* (—**s**, *pl.* —) (window) casement.
Fensterladen ['fɛnstərla:dən], *m.* (—**s**, *pl.* ⸚) shutter.
Fensterscheibe ['fɛnstərʃaɪbə], *f.* (—, *pl.* —**n**) pane.
Ferien ['fe:rjən], *pl.* holidays.
Ferkel ['fɛrkəl], *n.* (—**s**, *pl.* —) young pig, piglet.
Fermate [fɛr'ma:tə], *f.* (—, *pl.* —**n**) (*Mus.*) pause, fermata.
fern [fɛrn], *adj.* far, distant, remote.
Fernbleiben ['fɛrnblaɪbən], *n.* (—**s**, *no pl.*) absence.
Ferne ['fɛrnə], *f.* (—, *pl.* —**n**) distance, remoteness.
ferner ['fɛrnər], *adv.* further, furthermore, moreover.
fernerhin ['fɛrnərhɪn], *adv.* henceforth.
Ferngespräch ['fɛrngəʃprɛx], *n.* (—**s**, *pl.* —**e**) long-distance telephone call, trunk call.
Fernglas ['fɛrngla:s], *n.* (—**es**, *pl.* ⸚**er**) binoculars.
fernhalten ['fɛrnhaltən], *v.a. irr.* keep away.
fernher ['fɛrnhe:r], *adv. von* —, from afar.
fernliegen ['fɛrnli:gən], *v.n. irr.* be far from.
Fernrohr ['fɛrnro:r], *n.* (—**s**, *pl.* —**e**) telescope.
Fernschreiber ['fɛrnʃraɪbər], *m.* (—**s**, *pl.* —) teleprinter.
Fernsehen ['fɛrnze:ən], *n.* (—**s**, *no pl.*) television.
fernsehen ['fɛrnze:ən], *v.n. irr.* watch television.

Fernsehgerät ['fɛrnze:gərɛ:t], *n.* (—**s**, —**e**) television set.
Fernsprechamt ['fɛrnʃprɛçamt], *n.* (—**s**, *pl.* ¨**er**) telephone exchange.
Fernsprecher ['fɛrnʃprɛçər], *m.* (—**s**, *pl.* —) telephone.
Fernstehende ['fɛrnʃte:əndə], *m.* (—**n**, *pl.* —**n**) outsider.
Fernverkehr ['fɛrnfɛrke:r], *m.* (—**s**, *no pl.*) long-distance traffic.
Ferse ['fɛrzə], *f.* (—, *pl.* —**n**) heel.
Fersengeld ['fɛrzəngɛlt], *n.* (—**s**, *no pl.*) — *geben*, take to o.'s heels.
fertig ['fɛrtɪç], *adj.* ready, finished; (*coll.*) worn-out, ruined, done for.
Fertigkeit ['fɛrtɪçkaɪt], *f.* (—, *pl.* —**en**) dexterity, skill.
Fes [fɛs], *n.* (—, *pl.* —) (*Mus.*) F flat.
fesch [fɛʃ], *adj.* smart, stylish; (*dial.*) good-looking.
Fessel ['fɛsəl], *f.* (—, *pl.* —**n**) fetter, shackle.
Fesselballon ['fɛsəlbalɔ̃], *m.* (—**s**, *pl.* —**s**) captive balloon.
Fesselbein ['fɛsəlbaɪn], *n.* (—**s**, *pl.* —**e**) pastern-joint.
fesseln ['fɛsəln], *v.a.* fetter, shackle, chain; (*fig.*) captivate.
Fest [fɛst], *n.* (—**es**, *pl.* —**e**) feast, festival.
fest [fɛst], *adj.* fast, firm; solid, hard; sound; fixed; constant, steadfast.
Feste ['fɛstə], *f.* (—, *pl.* —**n**) fortress, stronghold.
festigen ['fɛstɪgən], *v.a.* make firm; strengthen.
Festland ['fɛstlant], *n.* (—**es**, *pl.* ¨**er**) continent.
festlich ['fɛstlɪç], *adj.* festive, solemn.
festmachen ['fɛstmaxən], *v.a.* fasten.
Festnahme ['fɛstna:mə], *f.* (—, *no pl.*) apprehension, arrest.
festnehmen ['fɛstne:mən], *v.a. irr.* seize, arrest.
Festrede ['fɛstre:də], *f.* (—, *pl.* —**n**) formal address.
festschnallen ['fɛstʃnalən], *v.a.* buckle on, fasten.
Festschrift ['fɛstʃrɪft], *f.* (—, *pl.* —**en**) commemorative volume (in honour of a person or an occasion).
festsetzen ['fɛstzɛtsən], *v.a.* fix, decree.
Festspiel ['fɛstʃpi:l], *n.* (—**s**, *pl.* —**e**) festival (play).
feststehen ['fɛstʃte:ən], *v.n. irr.* stand firm; *es steht fest*, it is certain.
feststellen ['fɛstʃtɛlən], *v.a.* ascertain; state; find; determine; diagnose; establish.
Festtag ['fɛstta:k], *m.* (—**s**, *pl.* —**e**) feast-day, holiday.
Festung ['fɛstuŋ], *f.* (—, *pl.* —**en**) fortress, stronghold, citadel.
festziehen ['fɛsttsi:ən], *v.a. irr.* tighten.
Festzug ['fɛsttsu:k], *m.* (—**s**, *pl.* ¨**e**) procession.
Fett [fɛt], *n.* (—**s**, *pl.* —**e**) fat, grease, lard.
fett [fɛt], *adj.* fat, greasy.
fettartig ['fɛtartɪç], *adj.* fatty.
fetten ['fɛtən], *v.a.* oil, grease.
Fettfleck ['fɛtflɛk], *m.* (—**s**, *pl.* —**e**) spot of grease.
fettgedruckt ['fɛtgədrukt], *adj.* in heavy type.
fetthaltig ['fɛthaltɪç], *adj.* greasy; adipose.
fettig ['fɛtɪç], *adj.* greasy.
fettleibig ['fɛtlaɪbɪç], *adj.* corpulent, obese.
Fetzen ['fɛtsən], *m.* (—**s**, *pl.* —) piece, rag, tatter, shred.
feucht [fɔyçt], *adj.* moist; (*weather*) muggy, wet; (*room*) damp.
Feuchtigkeit ['fɔyçtɪçkaɪt], *f.* (—, *no pl.*) moisture, humidity, dampness, wetness.
feudal [fɔy'da:l], *adj.* feudal; (*coll.*) distinguished, magnificent.
Feuer ['fɔyər], *n.* (—**s**, *pl.* —) fire; (*jewels*) brilliancy; (*fig.*) ardour, passion.
feuerbeständig ['fɔyərbəʃtɛndɪç], *adj.* fire-proof.
Feuerbestattung ['fɔyərbəʃtatuŋ], *f.* (—, *pl.* —**en**) cremation.
Feuereifer ['fɔyəraɪfər], *m.* (—**s**, *no pl.*) ardour.
feuerfest ['fɔyərfɛst], *adj.* fire-proof, incombustible.
feuergefährlich ['fɔyərgəfɛ:rlɪç], *adj.* inflammable.
Feuerlilie ['fɔyərli:ljə], *f.* (—, *pl.* —**n**) tiger lily.
Feuermal ['fɔyərma:l], *n.* (—**s**, *pl.* —**e**) burn, burn-mark.
Feuermauer ['fɔyərmauər], *f.* (—, *pl.* —**n**) fire-proof wall, party-wall.
Feuermelder ['fɔyərmɛldər], *m.* (—**s**, *pl.* —) fire-alarm.
feuern ['fɔyərn], *v.a.* (*Mil.*) fire, discharge; (*coll.*) fire, sack.
Feuerprobe ['fɔyərpro:bə], *f.* (—, *pl.* —**n**) ordeal by fire.
Feuerrad ['fɔyərra:t], *n.* (—**s**, *pl.* ¨**er**) Catherine wheel.
Feuerrohr ['fɔyərro:r], *n.* (—**s**, *pl.* —**e**) gun, matchlock.
Feuersbrunst ['fɔyərsbrunst], *f.* (—, *pl.* ¨**e**) (*rare*) fire, conflagration.
Feuerspritze ['fɔyərʃprɪtsə], *f.* (—, *pl.* —**n**) fire-engine.
Feuerstein ['fɔyərʃtaɪn], *m.* (—**s**, *no pl.*) flint.
Feuertaufe ['fɔyərtaufə], *f.* (—, *pl.* —**n**) baptism of fire.
Feuerwarte ['fɔyərvartə], *f.* (—, *pl.* —**en**) beacon; lighthouse.
Feuerwehr ['fɔyərve:r], *f.* (—, *no pl.*) fire-brigade.
Feuerwerk ['fɔyərvɛrk], *n.* (—, *no pl.* fireworks.
Feuerwerkskunst ['fɔyərvɛrkskunst], *f.* (—, *no pl.*) pyrotechnics.
Feuerzange ['fɔyərtsaŋə], *f.* (—, *pl.* —**n**) fire-tongs.
Feuerzeug ['fɔyərtsɔyk], *n.* (—**s**, *pl.* —**e**) match-box; cigarette-lighter.
feurig ['fɔyrɪç], *adj.* fiery, burning; (*fig.*) ardent, impassioned, fervent; (*wine*) heady.

Fiaker [fi'akər], *m.* (—s, *pl.* —) (*Austr.*) cab, hansom; (*Am.*) coach.
Fiasko [fi'asko:], *n.* (—s, *pl.* —s) failure.
Fibel ['fi:bəl], *f.* (—, *pl.* —n) primer, spelling-book.
Fiber ['fi:bər], *f.* (—, *pl.* —n) fibre.
Fichte ['fɪçtə], *f.* (—, *pl.* —n) (*Bot.*) pine, pine-tree.
fidel [fi'de:l], *adj.* merry, jolly.
Fidibus ['fi:dibus], *m.* (—ses, *pl.* —se) spill, fidibus.
Fidschi ['fɪdʒi:], Fiji.
Fieber ['fi:bər], *n.* (—s, *no pl.*) fever.
fieberhaft ['fi:bərhaft], *adj.* feverish, vehement.
fieberig ['fi:bərɪç], *adj.* feverish, racked by fever.
Fieberkälte ['fi:bərkɛltə], *f.* (—, *no pl.*) chill, shivering (fit).
fiebern ['fi:bərn], *v.n.* have a fever; (*fig.*) rave.
fiebrig ['fi:brɪç], *see* **fieberig**.
Fiedel ['fi:dəl], *f.* (—, *pl.* —n) (*Mus.*) fiddle, violin.
Figur [fi'gu:r], *f.* (—, *pl.* —en) figure, statue, sculpture; chessman.
figürlich [fi'gy:rlɪç], *adj.* figurative.
Filet [fɪ'le:], *n.* (—s, *pl.* —s) netting, net-work; (*meat*) fillet.
Filiale [fɪl'ja:lə], *f.* (—, *pl.* —n) branch, branch-establishment, branch-office.
Filigran [fɪli'gra:n], *n.* (—s, *no pl.*) filigree.
Film [fɪlm], *m.* (—s, *pl.* —e) film; (motion) picture.
Filter ['fɪltər], *m.* (—s, *pl.* —) filter.
filtrieren [fɪl'tri:rən], *v.a.* filter.
Filz [fɪlts], *m.* (—es, *pl.* —e) felt; (*fig.*) niggard, miser, skinflint.
Filzlaus ['fɪltslaus], *f.* (—, *pl.* ¨e) crab-louse.
Finanzamt [fɪ'nantsamt], *n.* (—s, *pl.* ¨er) income-tax office; revenue-office.
Finanzen [fɪ'nantsən], *f. pl.* finances, revenue.
Findelkind ['fɪndəlkɪnt], *n.* (—s, *pl.* —er) foundling.
finden ['fɪndən], *v.a. irr.* find. — *v.r. sich* —, *das wird sich* —, we shall see.
Finder ['fɪndər], *m.* (—s, *pl.* —) finder.
findig ['fɪndɪç], *adj.* resourceful, ingenious.
Findling ['fɪntlɪŋ], *m.* (—s, *pl.* —e) foundling.
Finger ['fɪŋər], *m.* (—s, *pl.* —) finger.
Fingerabdruck ['fɪŋərapdruk], *m.* (—s, *pl.* ¨e) finger-print.
fingerfertig ['fɪŋərfɛrtɪç], *adj.* nimble-fingered.
Fingerhut ['fɪŋərhu:t], *m.* (—s, *pl.* ¨e) thimble; (*Bot.*) foxglove.
fingern ['fɪŋərn], *v.a.* touch with the fingers, finger.
Fingersatz ['fɪŋərzats], *m.* (—es, *pl.* ¨e) (*Mus.*) fingering.
Fingerspitze ['fɪŋərʃpɪtsə], *f.* (—, *pl.* —n) finger-tip.
Fingerzeig ['fɪŋərtsaɪk], *m.* (—s, *pl.* —e) hint.
fingieren [fɪŋ'gi:rən], *v.a.* sham.
fingiert [fɪŋ'gi:rt], *adj.* fictitious.
Fink [fɪŋk], *m.* (—en, *pl.* —en) (*Orn.*) finch.
Finne (1) ['fɪnə], *m.* (—n, *pl.* —n) Finn.
Finne (2) ['fɪnə], *f.* (—, *pl.* —n) pimple; (*fish*) fin.
finnig ['fɪnɪç], *adj.* pimpled; (*fish*) finny.
Finnland ['fɪnlant], *n.* Finland.
finster ['fɪnstər], *adj.* dark, obscure; (*fig.*) gloomy, sinister.
Finsternis ['fɪnstərnɪs], *f.* (—, *no pl.*) darkness, gloom.
Finte ['fɪntə], *f.* (—, *pl.* —n) feint; (*fig.*) pretence, trick.
Firlefanz ['fɪrləfants], *m.* (—es, *no pl.*) foolery.
Firma ['fɪrma], *f.* (—, *pl.* —men) (*business*) firm, company.
Firmung ['fɪrmuŋ], *f.* (—, *pl.* —en) (*Eccl.*) confirmation.
Firnis ['fɪrnɪs], *m.* (—ses, *pl.* —se) varnish.
firnissen ['fɪrnɪsən], *v.a.* varnish.
First [fɪrst], *m.* (—es, *pl.* —e) (*house*) roof-ridge; (*mountain*) top.
Fis [fɪs], *n.* (—, *pl.* —) (*Mus.*) F sharp.
Fisch [fɪʃ], *m.* (—es, *pl.* —e) fish.
Fischadler ['fɪʃa:dlər], *m.* (—s, *pl.* —) osprey, sea-eagle.
Fischbein ['fɪʃbaɪn], *n.* (—s, *no pl.*) whalebone.
fischen ['fɪʃən], *v.a.*, *v.n.* fish, angle.
Fischer ['fɪʃər], *m.* (—s, *pl.* —) fisherman, fisher.
Fischerei [fɪʃə'raɪ], *f.* (—, *no pl.*) fishing; fishery.
Fischergerät ['fɪʃərgərɛ:t], *n.* (—s, *pl.* —e) fishing-tackle.
Fischgräte ['fɪʃgrɛ:tə], *f.* (—, *pl.* —n) fish-bone.
Fischkelle ['fɪʃkɛlə], *f.* (—, *pl.* —n) fish-slice.
Fischlaich ['fɪʃlaɪç], *m.* (—s, *no pl.*) spawn.
Fischmilch ['fɪʃmɪlç], *f.* (—, *no pl.*) soft roe, milt.
Fischotter ['fɪʃɔtər], *m.* (—, *pl.* —n) common otter.
Fischreiher ['fɪʃraɪər], *m.* (—s, *pl.* —) (*Orn.*) heron.
Fischreuse ['fɪʃrɔyzə], *f.* (—, *pl.* —n) bow-net; weir.
Fischrogen ['fɪʃro:gən], *m.* (—s, *no pl.*) roe.
Fischschuppe ['fɪʃʃupə], *f.* (—, *pl.* —n) scale.
Fischtran ['fɪʃtra:n], *m.* (—s, *no pl.*) train-oil.
Fischzucht ['fɪʃtsuxt], *f.* (—, *no pl.*) fish-breeding, pisciculture.
Fiskus ['fɪskus], *m.* (—, *pl.* —ken) Treasury, Exchequer.
Fisole [fɪ'zo:lə], *f.* (—, *pl.* —n) (*Austr.*) French bean.

Fistelstimme [ˈfɪstəlʃtɪmə], *f.* (—, *no pl.*) (*Mus.*) falsetto.
Fittich [ˈfɪtɪç], *m.* (—**es**, *pl.* —**e**) (*Poet.*) wing, pinion.
fix [fɪks], *adj.* quick, sharp; — *und fertig*, quite ready.
Fixum [ˈfɪksum], *n.* (—**s**, *pl.* —**xa**) fixed amount; regular salary.
flach [flax], *adj.* flat, plain, smooth, level; (*water*) shallow.
Fläche [ˈflɛçə], *f.* (—, *pl.* —**n**) plain; (*Maths.*) plane; (*crystal*) face.
Flächeninhalt [ˈflɛçənɪnhalt], *m.* (—**s**, *no pl.*) area.
Flächenmaß [ˈflɛçənma:s], *n.* (—**es**, *pl.* —**e**) square-measure.
Flächenraum [ˈflɛçənraum], *m.* (—**es**, *no pl.*) surface area.
Flachheit [ˈflaxhaɪt], *f.* (—, *no pl.*) flatness; (*fig.*) shallowness.
Flachs [[flaks], *m.* (—**es**, *no pl.*) flax.
flackern [ˈflakərn], *v.n.* flare, flicker.
Fladen [ˈfla:dən], *m.* (—**s**, *pl.* —) flat cake; cow-dung.
Flagge [ˈflagə], *f.* (—, *pl.* —**n**) flag.
Flame [ˈfla:mə], *m.* (—**n**, *pl.* —**n**) Fleming.
flämisch [ˈflɛ:mɪʃ], *adj.* Flemish.
Flamme [ˈflamə], *f.* (—, *pl.* —**n**) flame; blaze.
flammen [ˈflamən], *v.n.* flame, blaze, sparkle.
Flammeri [ˈflaməri:], *m.* (—**s**, *pl.* —**s**) blanc-mange.
Flandern [ˈflandərn], *n.* Flanders.
Flanell [flaˈnɛl], *m.* (—**s**, *pl.* —**e**) flannel.
Flaneur [flaˈnø:r], *m.* (—**s**, *pl.* —**e**) lounger, stroller.
flanieren [flaˈni:rən], *v.n.* lounge, stroll.
Flanke [ˈflaŋkə], *f.* (—, *pl.* —**n**) flank; *in die — fallen*, (*Mil.*) attack in the flank.
Flasche [ˈflaʃə], *f.* (—, *pl.* —**en**) bottle, flask.
Flaschenzug [ˈflaʃəntsu:k], *m.* (—**es**, *pl.* ⸚**e**) pulley.
flatterhaft [ˈflatərhaft], *adj.* fickle, inconstant, flighty.
flattern [ˈflatərn], *v.n.* flutter.
flau [flau], *adj.* insipid, stale; (*fig.*) dull.
Flaum [flaum], *m.* (—**s**, *no pl.*) down.
Flausch [flauʃ], *m.* (—**es**, *no pl.*) pilot-cloth.
Flaute [ˈflautə], *f.* (—, *pl.* —**n**) (*Nav.*) calm; (*fig.*) (*Comm.*) depression.
Flechte [ˈflɛçtə], *f.* (—, *pl.* —**n**) twist, plait, braid; (*Med.*) eruption, ringworm; (*Bot.*) lichen.
flechten [ˈflɛçtən], *v.a.* *irr.* plait; wreathe.
Flechtwerk [ˈflɛçtvɛrk], *n.* (—**s**, *no pl.*) wicker-work, basketry.
Fleck [flɛk], *m.* (—**s**, *pl.* —**e**) spot; place, piece (of ground); (*fig.*) stain, blemish.
Flecken [ˈflɛkən], *m.* (—**s**, *pl.* —) market town, small town.
fleckenlos [ˈflɛkənlo:s], *adj.* spotless.
fleckig [ˈflɛkɪç], *adj.* spotted, speckled.
Fledermaus [ˈfle:dərmaus], *f.* (—, *pl.* ⸚**e**) (*Zool.*) bat.
Flederwisch [ˈfle:dərvɪʃ], *m.* (—**es**, *pl.* —**e**) feather-duster.
Flegel [ˈfle:gəl], *m.* (—**s**, *pl.* —) flail; (*fig.*) boor.
flegelhaft [ˈfle:gəlhaft], *adj.* boorish, churlish, rude.
Flegeljahre [ˈfle:gəlja:rə], *n. pl.* years of indiscretion; teens, adolescence.
flehen [ˈfle:ən], *v.a.*, *v.n.* implore, supplicate, entreat.
Fleisch [flaɪʃ], *n.* (—**es**, *no pl.*) (raw) flesh; (*for cooking*) meat; (*fruit*) pulp.
Fleischbrühe [ˈflaɪʃbry:ə], *f.* (—, *pl.* —**n**) broth, beef-tea.
Fleischer [ˈflaɪʃər], *m.* (—**s**, *pl.* —) butcher.
fleischfressend [ˈflaɪʃfrɛsənt], *adj.* carnivorous.
Fleischhacker [ˈflaɪʃhakər], **Fleischhauer** [ˈflaɪʃhauər], *m.* (—**s**, *pl.* —) butcher.
fleischlich [ˈflaɪʃlɪç], *adj.* fleshly, carnal.
fleischlos [ˈflaɪʃlo:s], *adj.* vegetarian.
Fleischpastete [ˈflaɪʃpaste:tə], *f.* (—, *pl.* —**n**) meat-pie.
Fleiß [flaɪs], *m.* (—**es**, *no pl.*) diligence, assiduity, industry.
fleißig [ˈflaɪsɪç], *adj.* diligent, assiduous, industrious, hard-working.
fletschen [ˈflɛtʃən], *v.a.* *die Zähne* —, show o.'s teeth.
Flicken [ˈflɪkən], *m.* (—**s**, *pl.* —) patch.
flicken [ˈflɪkən], *v.a.* patch, repair, mend; (*shoes*) cobble; (*stockings*) darn.
Flieder [ˈfli:dər], *m.* (—**s**, *pl.* —) (*Bot.*) elder, lilac.
Fliege [ˈfli:gə], *f.* (—, *pl.* —**n**) (*Ent.*) fly; (*beard*) imperial.
fliegen [ˈfli:gən], *v.n.* *irr.* (*aux.* sein) fly; (*coll.*) get the sack, be fired. — *v.a.* fly, pilot (an aircraft).
Flieger [ˈfli:gər], *m.* (—**s**, *pl.* —) airman, aviator; pilot.
fliehen [ˈfli:ən], *v.n.* *irr.* (*aux.* sein) flee, run away; *zu einem* —, take refuge with s.o. — *v.a.* *irr.* avoid, shun (s.o.).
Fliehkraft [ˈfli:kraft], *f.* (—, *no pl.*) centrifugal force.
Fliese [ˈfli:zə], *f.* (—, *pl.* —**n**) floor-tile, flagstone.
Fließband [ˈfli:sbant], *n.* (—(**e**)**s**, *pl.* ⸚**er**) (*Ind.*) assembly line.
fließen [ˈfli:sən], *v.n.* *irr.* (*aux.* sein) flow.
Fließpapier [ˈfli:spapi:r], *n.* (—**s**, *no pl.*) blotting-paper.
Flimmer [ˈflɪmər], *m.* (—**s**, *no pl.*) glittering, sparkling, glimmer.
flimmern [ˈflɪmərn], *v.n.* glisten, glitter.
flink [flɪŋk], *adj.* brisk, agile, quick, sharp, nimble.

Flinte [ˈflɪntə], *f.* (—, *pl.* —**n**) gun, musket, rifle.
Flitter [ˈflɪtər], *m.* (—**s**, *no pl.*) tinsel, spangle, frippery.
Flitterwochen [ˈflɪtərvɔxən], *f. pl.* honeymoon.
flitzen [ˈflɪtsən], *v.n.* (*aux.* sein) *vorbei* —, flit *or* rush past, dash along.
Flocke [ˈflɔkə], *f.* (—, *pl.* —**n**) (*snow*) flake; (*wool*) flock.
Floh [flo:], *m.* (—**s**, *pl.* ⸚**e**) (*Ent.*) flea.
Flor [flo:r], *m.* (—**s**, *pl.* —**e**) bloom; gauze, crape; *in* —, blossoming, blooming.
Florenz [floˈrɛnts], *n.* Florence.
Florett [floˈrɛt], *n.* (—**s**, *pl.* —**e**) (*fencing*) foil.
florieren [floˈri:rən], *v.n.* flourish.
Florstrumpf [ˈflo:rʃtrumpf], *m.* (—**s**, *pl.* ⸚**e**) lisle stocking.
Floskel [ˈflɔskəl], *f.* (—, *pl.* —**n**) rhetorical ornament; oratorical flourish; phrase.
Floß [flo:s], *n.* (—**es**, *pl.* ⸚**e**) raft.
Flosse [ˈflɔsə], *f.* (—, *pl.* —**n**) fin.
flößen [ˈflo:sən], *v.a.* float.
Flößer [ˈflo:sər], *m.* (—**s**, *pl.* —) raftsman.
Flöte [ˈflo:tə], *f.* (—, *pl.* —**n**) (*Mus.*) flute.
Flötenzug [ˈflo:təntsu:k], *m.* (—**es**, *pl.* ⸚**e**) (*organ*) flute-stop.
flott [flɔt], *adj.* (*Naut.*) afloat, floating; (*fig.*) gay, jolly, lively, smart; — *leben*, lead a fast life.
Flotte [ˈflɔtə], *f.* (—, *pl.* —**n**) fleet, navy.
Flottille [flɔˈtɪljə], *f.* (—, *pl.* —**n**) flotilla, squadron.
Flöz [flo:ts], *n.* (—**es**, *pl.* —**e**) layer, stratum; (*coal*) seam.
Fluch [flu:x], *m.* (—**es**, *pl.* ⸚**e**) curse, spell; (*verbal*) curse, oath, swear-word.
fluchen [ˈflu:xən], *v.n.* curse, swear.
Flucht [fluxt], *f.* (—, *pl.* —**en**) flight, fleeing; suite (of rooms).
flüchten [ˈflyçtən], *v.n.* (*aux.* sein), *v.r.* flee, run away, escape.
flüchtig [ˈflyçtɪç], *adj.* fugitive; (*Chem.*) volatile; (*fig.*) superficial; evanescent; hasty; slight.
Flüchtling [ˈflyçtlɪŋ], *m.* (—**s**, *pl.* —**e**) fugitive, refugee.
Flug [flu:k], *m.* (—**s**, *pl.* ⸚**e**) (*Aviat.*) flight.
Flugblatt [ˈflu:kblat], *n.* (—**s**, *pl.* ⸚**er**) broadsheet, leaflet.
Flügel [ˈfly:gəl], *m.* (—**s**, *pl.* —) wing; (*Mus.*) grand piano; (*door*) leaf.
Flügelschlag [ˈfly:gəlʃla:k], *m.* (—**s**, *pl.* ⸚**e**) wing-stroke.
Flügeltür [ˈfly:gəlty:r], *f.* (—, *pl.* —**en**) folding-door.
flügge [ˈflygə], *adj.* fledged.
Flughafen [ˈflu:kha:fən], *m.* (—**s**, *pl.* ⸚) airport; aerodrome.
Flugpost [ˈflu:kpɔst], *f.* (—, *no pl.*) air mail.
flugs [fluks], *adv.* quickly, instantly; (*Lit.*, *obs.*) anon.
Flugsand [ˈflu:kzant], *m.* (—**s**, *no pl.*) quicksand, drifting sand.
Flugzeug [ˈflu:ktsɔyk], *n.* (—**s**, *pl.* —**e**) aeroplane; (*Am.*) airplane.
Flugzeugführer [ˈflu:ktsɔykfy:rər], *m.* (—**s**, *pl.* —) (*Aviat.*) pilot.
Fluidum [ˈflu:idum], *n.* (—**s**, *pl.* —**da**) fluid; (*fig.*) atmosphere.
Flunder [ˈflundər], *f.* (—, *pl.* —**n**) (*fish*) flounder.
Flunkerer [ˈfluŋkərər], *m.* (—**s**, *pl.* —) (*coll.*) fibber, story-teller.
Flur (1) [flu:r], *f.* (—, *pl.* —**en**) field, plain; *auf weiter* —, in the open.
Flur (2) [flu:r], *m.* (—**s**, *pl.* —**e**) (*house*) hall, vestibule; corridor.
Flurschaden [ˈflu:rʃa:dən], *m.* (—**s**, *pl.* ⸚) damage to crops.
Fluß [flus], *m.* (—**sses**, *pl.* ⸚**sse**) river, stream; flow, flowing; flux.
Flußbett [ˈflusbɛt], *n.* (—**s**, *pl.* —**en**) channel, riverbed.
flüssig [ˈflysɪç], *adj.* fluid, liquid; —*e Gelder*, ready cash; liquid assets.
flüstern [ˈflystərn], *v.a.* whisper.
Flut [flu:t], *f.* (—, *pl.* —**en**) flood; high-tide, high water; torrent; deluge.
fluten [ˈflu:tən], *v.n.* flow.
Focksegel [ˈfɔkze:gəl], *n.* (—**s**, *pl.* —) foresail.
Fockmast [ˈfɔkmast], *m.* (—**s**, *pl.* —**en**) foremast.
Föderalismus [fo:dəraˈlɪsmus], *m.* (—, *no pl.*) federalism.
Fohlen [ˈfo:lən], *n.* (—**s**, *pl.* —) foal.
fohlen [ˈfo:lən], *v.n.* foal.
Föhn [fo:n], *m.* (—**s**, *pl.* —**e**) (warm) Alpine wind.
Föhre [ˈfo:rə], *f.* (—, *pl.* —**n**) (*Bot.*) fir, fir-tree.
Folge [ˈfɔlgə], *f.* (—, *pl.* —**n**) succession; series, sequence; continuation; consequence.
folgen [ˈfɔlgən], *v.n.* (*aux.* sein) follow; succeed; result from, be the consequence of; obey.
folgendermaßen [ˈfɔlgəndərma:sən], *adv.* as follows.
folgenschwer [ˈfɔlgənʃve:r], *adj.* momentous, portentous.
folgerichtig [ˈfɔlgərɪçtɪç], *adj.* consistent, logical.
folgern [ˈfɔlgərn], *v.a.* draw a conclusion, infer, conclude, deduce.
Folgerung [ˈfɔlgəruŋ], *f.* (—, *pl.* —**en**) induction, deduction, inference.
folglich [ˈfɔlklɪç], *conj.* consequently, therefore.
folgsam [ˈfɔlkza:m], *adj.* obedient.
Foliant [fo:lˈjant], *m.* (—**en**, *pl.* —**en**) folio-volume, tome.
Folie [ˈfo:ljə], *f.* (—, *pl.* —**n**) foil.
Folter [ˈfɔltər], *f.* (—, *pl.* —**n**) rack, torture.
Folterbank [ˈfɔltərbaŋk], *f.* (—, *pl.* ⸚**e**) rack.
Fond [fɔ̃:], *m.* (—**s**, *pl.* —**s**) back seat.

Fontäne [fɔ̃'tɛ:nə], *f.* (—, *pl.* —**n**) fountain.
foppen ['fɔpən], *v.a.* chaff, banter, tease.
Fopperei [fɔpə'raɪ], *f.* (—, *pl.* —**en**) chaff, banter, teasing.
forcieren [fɔr'si:rən], *v.a.* strain, overdo.
Förderer ['fœrdərər], *m.* (—**s**, *pl.* —) promoter, backer.
Förderkarren ['fœrdərkarən], *m.* (—**s**, *pl.* —) (*Min.*) truck, trolley.
förderlich ['fœrdərlɪç], *adj.* useful, conducive (to).
Fördermaschine ['fœrdərmaʃi:nə], *f.* (—, *pl.* —**n**) hauling-machine.
fordern ['fɔrdərn], *v.a.* demand, claim, ask for; (*duel*) challenge.
fördern ['fœrdərn], *v.a.* further, advance, promote, back; hasten; (*Min.*) haul.
Förderschacht ['fœrdərʃaxt], *m.* (—**s**, *pl.* ¨**e**) (*Min.*) winding shaft.
Forderung ['fɔrdəruŋ], *f.* (—, *pl.* —**en**) demand, claim; (*duel*) challenge.
Förderung ['fœrdəruŋ], *f.* (—, *no pl.*) furtherance, promotion, advancement; (*Min.*) hauling.
Forelle [fo'rɛlə], *f.* (—, *pl.* —**n**) trout.
Forke ['fɔrkə], *f.* (—, *pl.* —**n**) pitchfork, garden-fork.
Form [fɔrm], *f.* (—, *pl.* —**en**) form, shape, figure; manner; condition; (*casting*) mould; (*grammar*) form, voice.
Formalien [fɔr'ma:ljən], *pl.* formalities.
Formalität [fɔrmalɪ'tɛ:t], *f.* (—, *pl.* —**en**) formality, form.
Format [fɔr'ma:t], *n.* (—**s**, *pl.* —**e**) (*book, paper*) size; format; (*fig.*) stature.
Formel ['fɔrməl], *f.* (—, *pl.* —**n**) formula.
formell [fɔr'mɛl], *adj.* formal.
Formfehler ['fɔrmfe:lər], *m.* (—**s**, *pl.* —) faux pas, breach of etiquette.
formieren [fɔr'mi:rən], *v.a.* form. — *v.r.* *sich* —, fall into line.
förmlich ['fœrmlɪç], *adj.* formal; downright.
formlos ['fɔrmlo:s], *adj.* shapeless; (*fig.*) unconventional, informal, unceremonious.
Formular [fɔrmu'la:r], *n.* (—**s**, *pl.* —**e**) (printed) form, schedule.
formulieren [fɔrmu'li:rən], *v.a.* formulate, word.
formvollendet ['fɔrmfɔlɛndət], *adj.* well-rounded, well-finished.
forsch [fɔrʃ], *adj.* dashing.
forschen ['fɔrʃən], *v.n.* search, enquire (after), do research.
Forschung ['fɔrʃuŋ], *f.* (—, *pl.* —**en**) research, investigation; search, exploration.
Forst [fɔrst], *m.* (—**es**, *pl.* —**e**) forest.
Förster ['fœrstər], *m.* (—**s**, *pl.* —) forester, forest-keeper; (*Am.*) ranger.
Forstfrevel ['fɔrstfre:fəl], *m.* (—**s**, *no pl.*) infringement of forest-laws.
Forstrevier ['fɔrstrevi:r], *n.* (—**s**, *pl.* —**e**) section of forest.
Forstwesen ['fɔrstve:zən], *n.* (—**s**, *no pl.*) forestry.
Forstwirtschaft ['fɔrstvɪrtʃaft], *f.* (—, *no pl.*) forestry.
fort [fɔrt], *adv.* away; lost, gone, forth, forward.
Fort [fo:rt], *n.* (—**s**, *pl.* —**s**) fort.
fortan [fɔrt'an], *adv.* henceforth.
fortbilden ['fɔrtbɪldən], *v.r.* *sich* —, improve o.s., receive further education.
fortbleiben ['fɔrtblaɪbən], *v.n. irr.* (*aux.* sein) stay away.
Fortdauer ['fɔrtdauər], *f.* (—, *no pl.*) continuance, duration.
fortfahren ['fɔrtfa:rən], *v.n. irr.* (*aux.* sein) drive off; (*Naut.*) set sail; (*fig.*) continue, go on.
Fortgang ['fɔrtgaŋ], *m.* (—**s**, *no pl.*) going away, departure; (*fig.*) continuation, progress.
Fortkommen ['fɔrtkɔmən], *n.* (—**s**, *no pl.*) advancement, progress; (*fig.*) livelihood.
fortkommen ['fɔrtkɔmən], *v.n. irr.* (*aux.* sein) *gut* —, prosper, succeed.
fortlassen ['fɔrtlasən], *v.a. irr.* allow to go; leave out, omit; *nicht* —, detain.
fortlaufen ['fɔrtlaufən], *v.n. irr.* (*aux.* sein) run away.
fortpflanzen ['fɔrtpflantsən], *v.r.* *sich* —, propagate, multiply; (*sickness*) spread.
forträumen ['fɔrtrɔymən], *v.a.* clear away, remove.
fortschaffen ['fɔrtʃafən], *v.a.* carry away, get rid of.
fortscheren ['fɔrtʃe:rən], *v.r.* *sich* — (*coll.*) beat it, go away.
fortscheuchen ['fɔrtʃɔyçən], *v.a.* scare away.
fortschreiten ['fɔrtʃraɪtən], *v.n. irr.* (*aux.* sein) progress, advance.
Fortschritt ['fɔrtʃrɪt], *m.* (—**s**, *pl.* —**e**) progress, advancement, proficiency.
fortsetzen ['fɔrtzɛtsən], *v.a.* continue, carry on.
fortwährend ['fɔrtvɛ:rənt], *adj.* continual, perpetual, unceasing.
Fracht [fraxt], *f.* (—, *pl.* —**en**) freight, cargo, load.
Frack [frak], *m.* (—**s**, *pl.* —**s**, ¨**e**) dress-suit, evening dress.
Frage ['fra:gə], *f.* (—, *pl.* —**n**) question, query.
Fragebogen ['fra:gəbo:gən], *m.* (—**s**, *pl.* —) questionnaire.
fragen ['fra:gən], *v.a.* ask, enquire, question.
Fragesteller ['fra:gəʃtɛlər], *m.* (—**s**, *pl* —) interrogator, questioner.
fraglich ['fra:klɪç], *adj.* questionable, problematic(al).
fragwürdig ['fra:kvyrdɪç], *adj.* doubtful, questionable.
Fraktion [frak'tsjo:n], *f.* (—, *pl.* —**en**) (*Pol.*) party group.

Frakturschrift [frak'tu:rʃrɪft], *f.* (—, *no pl.*) (*lettering*) Gothic type, Old English type, Black Letter type.
Frank [fraŋk], *m.* (—**en**, *pl.* —**en**) (*money*) franc.
Franke ['fraŋkə], *m.* (—**n**, *pl.* —**n**) Frank, Franconian.
frankieren [fraŋ'ki:rən], *v.a.* (*post*) prepay, frank.
franko ['fraŋko], *adj.* post-paid; *gratis und* —, gratuitously.
Frankreich ['frankraɪx], *n.* France.
Franse ['franzə], *f.* (—, *pl.* —**n**) fringe.
Franzose [fran'tso:zə], *m.* (—**n**, *pl.* —**n**) Frenchman.
französisch [fran'tsø:zɪʃ], *adj.* French.
frappant [fra'pant], *adj.* striking.
frappieren [fra'pi:rən], *v.a.* strike, astonish.
Fraß [fra:s], *m.* (—**es**, *no pl.*) (*animals*) feed, fodder; (*sl.*) grub.
Fratz [frats], *m.* (—**es**, *pl.* —**en**) brat, little monkey.
Fratze ['fratsə], *f.* (—, *pl.* —**en**) grimace, caricature.
Frau [frau], *f.* (—, *pl.* —**en**) woman, wife, lady; (*title*) Mrs.; *gnädige* —, Madam.
Frauenkirche ['frauənkɪrçə], *f.* (—, *no pl.*) Church of Our Lady.
Frauenzimmer ['frauəntsɪmər], *n.* (—**s**, *pl.* —) (*pej.*) woman, female.
Fräulein ['frɔylaɪn], *n.* (—**s**, *pl.* —) young lady; (*title*) Miss.
frech [frɛç], *adj.* insolent, impudent, cheeky, pert, saucy.
Frechheit ['frɛçhaɪt], *f.* (—, *pl.* —**en**) insolence, impudence.
Fregatte [fre'gatə], *f.* (—, *pl.* —**n**) frigate.
frei [fraɪ], *adj.* free, exempt, unhampered, independent, disengaged; vacant; candid, frank.
Freibeuter ['fraɪbɔytər], *m.* (—**s**, *pl.* —) freebooter, pirate.
Freibrief ['fraɪbri:f], *m.* (—**s**, *pl.* —**e**) patent, licence; permit.
freien ['fraɪən], *v.a.* woo, court.
Freier ['fraɪər], *m.* (—**s**, *pl.* —) (*obs.*) suitor.
Freigabe ['fraɪga:bə], *f.* (—, *no pl.*) release.
freigeben ['fraɪge:bən], *v.a. irr.* release.
freigebig ['fraɪge:bɪç], *adj.* liberal, generous.
Freigebigkeit ['fraɪgə:bɪçkaɪt], *f.* (—, *no pl.*) liberality, munificence, generosity.
Freigut ['fraɪgu:t], *n.* (—**s**, *pl.* ⸚**er**) freehold.
Freiheit ['fraɪhaɪt], *f.* (—, *pl.* —**en**) freedom, liberty, immunity, privilege.
Freiherr ['fraɪhɛr], *m.* (—**n**, *pl.* —**en**) baron.
Freikorps ['fraɪko:r], *n.* (—, *no pl.*) volunteer-corps.
Freilauf ['fraɪlauf], *m.* (—**s**, *no pl.*) (*bicycle*) free-wheel.
freilich ['fraɪlɪç], *adv.* to be sure, it is true, indeed, of course.
Freilicht- ['fraɪlɪxt], *adj.* (*in compounds*) open-air.
Freimarke ['fraɪmarkə], *f.* (—, *pl.* —**n**) postage stamp.
freimütig ['fraɪmy:tɪç], *adj.* frank, open, candid.
Freisprechung ['fraɪʃprɛçuŋ], *f.* (—, *no pl.*) acquittal; absolution.
Freistätte ['fraɪʃtɛtə], *f.* (—, *pl.* —**n**) refuge, asylum.
Freistoß ['fraɪʃto:s], *m.* (—**es**, *pl.* ⸚**e**) (*Footb.*) free-kick.
Freitag ['fraɪta:k], *m.* (—**s**, *pl.* —**e**) Friday.
Freitreppe ['fraɪtrɛpə], *f.* (—, *pl.* —**n**) outside staircase.
Freiübung ['fraɪy:buŋ], *f.* (—, *pl.* —**en**) (*mostly pl.*) physical exercises, gymnastics.
freiwillig ['fraɪvɪlɪç], *adj.* voluntary, of o.'s own accord; spontaneous.
Freiwillige ['fraɪvɪlɪgə], *m.* (—**n**, *pl.* —**n**) (*Mil.*) volunteer.
fremd [frɛmt], *adj.* strange, foreign, outlandish; odd.
fremdartig ['frɛmtartɪç], *adj.* strange, odd.
Fremde (1) ['frɛmdə], *f.* (—, *no pl.*) foreign country; *in die* — *gehen*, go abroad.
Fremde (2) ['frɛmdə], *m.* (—**n**, *pl.* —**n**) stranger, foreigner.
Fremdheit ['frɛmthaɪt], *f.* (—, *no pl.*) strangeness.
Freßbeutel ['frɛsbɔytəl], *m.* (—**s**, *pl.* —) nose-bag.
Fresse ['frɛsə], *f.* (—, *pl.* —**n**) (*vulg.*) mouth, snout.
fressen ['frɛsən], *v.a. irr.* (*animals*) eat; (*also fig.*) devour.
Fresserei ['frɛsəraɪ], *f.* (—, *no pl.*) gluttony.
Frettchen ['frɛtçən], *n.* (—**s**, *pl.* —) (*Zool.*) ferret.
Freude ['frɔydə], *f.* (—, *pl.* —**n**) joy, joyfulness, gladness, enjoyment, delight, pleasure.
Freudenfest ['frɔydənfɛst], *n.* (—**s**, *pl.* —**e**) feast, jubilee.
Freudenhaus ['frɔydənhaus], *n.* (—**es**, *pl.* ⸚**er**) brothel.
Freudenmädchen ['frɔydənmɛ:tçən], *n.* (—**s**, *pl.* —) prostitute.
freudig ['frɔydɪç], *adj.* joyful, cheerful, glad.
freudlos ['frɔytlo:s], *adj.* joyless.
freuen ['frɔyən], *v.r. sich* —, rejoice (at), be glad (of); *sich auf etwas* —, look forward to s.th.
Freund [frɔynt], *m.* (—**es**, *pl.* —**e**) friend.
freundlich ['frɔyntlɪç], *adj.* friendly, kind, affable, pleasing, cheerful, pleasant, genial.
Freundschaft ['frɔyntʃaft], *f.* (—, *pl.* —**en**) friendship.
Frevel ['fre:fəl], *m.* (—**s**, *pl.* —) crime, misdeed, offence.

freveln [ˈfreːfəln], *v.n.* do wrong, trespass, commit an outrage.
Friede(n) [ˈfriːdə(n)], *m.* (—**ns**, *no pl.*) peace.
friedfertig [ˈfriːtfertɪç], *adj.* peaceable.
Friedhof [ˈfriːthoːf], *m.* (—**s**, *pl.* ⸚**e**) churchyard, cemetery.
friedlich [ˈfriːtlɪç], *adj.* peaceful.
friedliebend [ˈfriːtliːbənt], *adj.* peaceable, peace-loving.
Friedrich [ˈfriːdrɪç], *m.* Frederic(k).
friedselig [ˈfriːtzeːlɪç], *adj.* peaceable.
frieren [ˈfriːrən], *v.n. irr.* feel cold, freeze.
Fries [friːs], *m.* (—**es**, *pl.* —**e**) frieze.
Friese [ˈfriːzə], *m.* (—**n**, *pl.* —**n**) Frisian.
frisch [frɪʃ], *adj.* fresh; new; (*weather*) crisp; (*fig.*) lively, brisk, gay.
Frische [ˈfrɪʃə], *f.* (—, *no pl.*) freshness, liveliness, gaiety.
Friseur [friˈzøːr], *m.* (—**s**, *pl.* —**e**) hairdresser, barber.
Friseuse [friˈzøːzə], *f.* (—, *pl.* —**n**) female hairdresser.
frisieren [friˈziːrən], *v.a.* dress (s.o.'s) hair.
Frist [frɪst], *f.* (—, *pl.* —**en**) time, term, period; (fixed) term; delay, respite.
fristen [ˈfrɪstən], *v.a. das Leben* —, gain a bare living.
Frisur [friˈzuːr], *f.* (—, *pl.* —**en**) coiffure, hair-style.
frivol [friˈvoːl], *adj.* frivolous.
Frivolität [frivoːliˈtɛːt], *f.* (—, *pl.* —**en**) frivolity.
froh [froː], *adj.* glad, joyful, joyous.
frohgelaunt [ˈfroːgəlaunt], *adj.* good-humoured, cheerful.
fröhlich [ˈfrøːlɪç], *adj.* gay, merry.
frohlocken [froːˈlɔkən], *v.n.* (*rare*) exult.
Frohsinn [ˈfroːzɪn], *m.* (—**s**, *no pl.*) good humour, gaiety.
fromm [frɔm], *adj.* pious, religious, devout.
frommen [ˈfrɔmən], *v.n.* (*obs.*) be of advantage (to s.o.).
Frömmigkeit [ˈfrœmɪçkaɪt], *f.* (—, *no pl.*) piety, devoutness.
Fron [froːn], *f.* (—, *no pl.*) (feudal) service; statute labour.
frönen [ˈfrøːnən], *v.n.* (*fig.*) be a slave to; indulge in (*Dat.*).
Fronleichnam [froːnˈlaɪxnaːm], *m.* (*Eccl.*) (feast of) Corpus Christi.
Front [frɔnt], *f.* (—, *pl.* —**en**) front, forepart; (*building*) elevation; (*Mil.*) front line.
Frosch [frɔʃ], *m.* (—**es**, *pl.* ⸚**e**) (*Zool.*) frog.
Frost [frɔst], *m.* (—**es**, *pl.* ⸚**e**) frost; coldness, chill.
Frostbeule [ˈfrɔstbɔylə], *f.* (—, *pl.* —**n**) chilblain.
frösteln [ˈfrœstəln], *v.n.* feel a chill, shiver.
frostig [ˈfrɔstɪç], *adj.* frosty; cold, chilly.
frottieren [frɔˈtiːrən], *v.a.* rub (down).
Frottiertuch [frɔˈtiːrtuːx], *n.* (—**s**, *pl.* ⸚**er**) Turkish towel, bath towel.
Frucht [fruxt], *f.* (—, *pl.* ⸚**e**) fruit; (*fig.*) result, effect; (*Med.*) fœtus.
fruchtbar [ˈfruxtbaːr], *adj.* fruitful, productive, fertile.
fruchten [ˈfruxtən], *v.n.* produce fruit; (*fig.*) be effectual.
Fruchtknoten [ˈfruxtknoːtən], *m.* (—**s**, *pl.* —) (*Bot.*) seed-vessel.
früh(e) [fryː(ə)], *adj.* early.
Frühe [ˈfryːə], *f.* (—, *no pl.*) early morning, dawn.
früher [ˈfryːər], *adv.* earlier (on), formerly.
frühestens [ˈfryːəstəns], *adv.* at the earliest (possible moment).
Frühjahr [ˈfryːjaːr], *n.*, **Frühling** [ˈfryːlɪŋ], *m.* (—**s**, *pl.* —**e**) spring.
frühreif [ˈfryːraɪf], *adj.* precocious.
Frühschoppen [ˈfryːʃɔpən], *m.* (—**s**, *pl.* —) morning pint (beer *or* wine).
Frühstück [ˈfryːʃtyk], *n.* (—**s**, *pl.* —**e**) breakfast; *zweites* —, lunch.
Fuchs [fuks], *m.* (—**es**, *pl.* ⸚**e**) fox; chestnut (horse); (*fig.*) cunning chap; (*student*) freshman.
Fuchsbau [ˈfuksbau], *m.* (—**s**, *pl.* —**e**) fox-hole.
Fuchseisen [ˈfuksaɪzən], *n.* (—**s**, *pl.* —) fox-trap.
fuchsen [ˈfuksən], *v.r. sich — über*, be annoyed about.
Fuchsie [ˈfuksjə], *f.* (—, *pl.* —**n**) (*Bot.*) fuchsia.
fuchsig [ˈfuksɪç], *adj.* (*coll.*) very angry.
Füchsin [ˈfyksɪn], *f.* (—, *pl.* —**innen**) vixen.
fuchsrot [ˈfuksroːt], *adj.* fox-coloured, sorrel.
Fuchsschwanz [ˈfuksʃvants], *m.* (—**es**, *pl.* ⸚**e**) fox-brush; pad saw.
Fuchtel [ˈfuxtəl], *f.* (—, *pl.* —**n**) sword blade; rod, whip.
Fuder [ˈfuːdər], *n.* (—**s**, *pl.* —) load, cart-load; wine measure (c. 270 gallons).
Fug [ˈfuːk], *m.* (—**s**, *no pl.*) (*rare*) right, justice; *mit — und Recht*, with every right.
Fuge (1) [ˈfuːgə], *f.* (—, *pl.* —**n**) joint, groove.
Fuge (2) [ˈfuːgə], *f.* (—, *pl.* —**n**) (*Mus.*) fugue.
fügen [ˈfyːgən], *v.a.* fit together, join, dovetail. — *v.r. sich* —, submit (to), accommodate o.s. (to).
fügsam [ˈfyːkzaːm], *adj.* pliant, submissive, yielding.
Fügung [ˈfyːguŋ], *f.* (—, *pl.* —**en**) coincidence; dispensation (of Providence); Providence.
fühlbar [ˈfyːlbaːr], *adj.* perceptible; tangible; *sich — machen*, make o.s. felt.
fühlen [ˈfyːlən], *v.a.* feel, touch, sense, be aware of.
Fühler [ˈfyːlər], *m.* (—**s**, *pl.* —) tentacle, feeler.

Fühlhorn [ˈfy:lhɔrn], *n.* (—s, *pl.* ¨er) feeler, antenna, tentacle.
Fühlung [ˈfy:luŋ], *f.* (—, *no pl.*) — *haben mit*, be in touch with.
Fuhre [ˈfu:rə], *f.* (—, *pl.* —n) conveyance, vehicle, cart-load.
führen [ˈfy:rən], *v.a.* lead, guide, conduct, command; (*pen*) wield; (*law-suit*) carry on; (*conversation*) have, keep up; (*name, title*) bear; (*goods*) stock, deal in; *Krieg* —, wage war; *etwas im Schilde* —, have a plan; *das Wort* —, be spokesman; *einen hinters Licht* —, cheat s.o.
Führer [ˈfy:rər], *m.* (—s, *pl.* —) leader, guide; head, manager; conductor; driver, pilot.
Führerschaft [ˈfy:rərʃaft], *f.* (—, *no pl.*) leadership.
Führerschein [ˈfy:rərʃaɪn], *m.* (—s, *pl.* —e) driving-licence.
Führersitz [ˈfy:rərzɪts], *m.* (—es, *pl.* —e) driver's seat; pilot's cockpit.
Fuhrlohn [ˈfu:rlo:n], *m.* (—s, *no pl.*) cartage, carriage.
Fuhrmann [ˈfu:rman], *m.* (—s, *pl.* ¨er) carter, carrier.
Führung [ˈfy:ruŋ], *f.* (—, *no pl.*) guidance; leadership; conducted tour; management, direction; behaviour, conduct.
Führungszeugnis [ˈfy:ruŋstsɔyknɪs], *n.* (—sses, *pl.* —sse) certificate of good conduct.
Fuhrwerk [ˈfu:rvɛrk], *n.* (—s, *pl.* —e) carriage, vehicle, waggon.
Fuhrwesen [ˈfu:rve:zən], *n.* (—s, *no pl.*) transport services, transportation.
Fülle [ˈfylə], *f.* (—, *no pl.*) fullness; abundance, plenty.
Füllen [ˈfylən], *n.* (—s, *pl.* —) foal.
füllen [ˈfylən], *v.a.* fill, fill up; stuff.
Füllfederhalter [ˈfylfe:dərhaltər], *m.* (—s, *pl.* —) fountain-pen.
Füllung [ˈfyluŋ], *f.* (—, *pl.* —en) filling; stuffing; (*door*) panel.
fummeln [ˈfuməln], *v.n.* fumble.
Fund [funt], *m.* (—es, *pl.* —e) find; discovery.
Fundbüro [ˈfuntbyro], *n.* (—s, *pl.* —s) lost property office.
Fundgrube [ˈfuntgru:bə], *f.* (—, *pl.* —n) gold-mine, source, treasure-house.
fundieren [funˈdi:rən], *v.a.* found; establish.
fünf [fynf], *num. adj.* five.
Fünfeck [ˈfynfɛk], *n.* (—s, *pl.* —e) pentagon.
Fünffüßler [ˈfynffy:slər], *m.* (—s, *pl.* —) (*Poet.*) pentameter.
fünfjährig [ˈfynfjɛ:rɪç], *num. adj.* five-year-old.
fünfjährlich [ˈfynfjɛ:rlɪç], *num. adj.* quinquennial, five-yearly.
fünfzehn [ˈfynftse:n], *num. adj.* fifteen.
fünfzig [ˈfynftsɪç], *num. adj.* fifty.
fungieren [funˈgi:rən], *v.n.* — *als*, act as, officiate as.
Funk [fuŋk], *m.* (—s, *no pl.*) radio; wireless; telegraphy.
Funke [ˈfuŋkə], *m.* (—n, *pl.* —n) spark, sparkle.
funkeln [ˈfuŋkəln], *v.n.* sparkle, glitter; (*stars*) twinkle.
funkelnagelneu [ˈfuŋkəlna:gəlnɔy], *adj.* (*coll.*) brand-new.
funken [ˈfuŋkən], *v.a.* flash (messages); telegraph, broadcast.
Funker [ˈfuŋkər], *m.* (—s, *pl.* —) wireless operator.
Funksender [ˈfuŋkzɛndər], *m.* (—s, *pl.* —) radio-transmitter.
Funkspruch [ˈfuŋkʃprux], *m.* (—s, *pl.* ¨e) wireless-message.
Funktelegramm [ˈfuŋktelegram], *n.* (—s, *pl.* —e) radio telegram.
für [fy:r], *prep.* (*Acc.*) for, instead of; *ein* — *allemal*, once and for all; *an und* — *sich*, in itself.
Fürbitte [ˈfy:rbɪtə], *f.* (—, *pl.* —n) intercession.
Furche [ˈfurçə], *f.* (—, *pl.* —n) furrow; (*face*) wrinkle.
furchen [ˈfurçən], *v.a.* furrow; (*face*) wrinkle.
Furcht [furçt], *f.* (—, *no pl.*) fear, worry, anxiety; dread, fright, terror, apprehension.
furchtbar [ˈfurçtba:r], *adj.* dreadful, terrible, frightful.
fürchten [ˈfyrçtən], *v.a.* fear, be afraid of. — *v.r. sich* — *vor*, be afraid of.
fürchterlich [ˈfyrçtərlɪç], *adj.* terrible, horrible, awful.
furchtsam [ˈfurçtza:m], *adj.* timid, fearful, apprehensive.
Furie [ˈfu:rjə], *f.* (—, *pl.* —n) fury, virago.
fürlieb [fyrˈli:p], *adv. mit etwas* — *nehmen*, put up with, be content with s.th.
Furnier [furˈni:r], *n.* (—s, *pl.* —e) veneer, inlay.
Furore [fuˈro:rə], *n.* (—s, *no pl.*) — *machen*, cause a sensation, create an uproar.
Fürsorge [ˈfy:rzɔrgə], *f.* (—, *no pl.*) solicitude; provision; welfare.
fürsorglich [ˈfy:rzɔrglɪç], *adj.* thoughtful, with loving care.
Fürsprache [ˈfy:rʃpra:xə], *f.* (—, *no pl.*) advocacy, intercession.
Fürst [fyrst], *m.* (—en, *pl.* —en) prince, sovereign.
Furt [furt], *f.* (—, *pl.* —en) ford.
Furunkel [fuˈruŋkəl], *m.* (—s, *pl.* —) furuncle, boil.
Fürwort [ˈfy:rvɔrt], *n.* (—s, *pl.* ¨er) pronoun.
Fusel [ˈfu:zəl], *m.* (—s, *no pl.*) bad liquor, (*Am.*) hooch (*sl.*).
Fuß [fu:s], *m.* (—es, *pl.* ¨e) (*human*) foot; (*object*) base.
Fußangel [ˈfu:saŋəl], *f.* (—, *pl.* —n) man-trap.
Fußball [ˈfu:sbal], *m.* (—s, *pl.* ¨e) football.

Fußboden [ˈfu:sbo:dən], *m.* (**—s,** *pl.* **¨**) floor.
fußen [ˈfu:sən], *v.n.* — *auf*, be based upon.
fußfrei [ˈfu:sfraɪ], *adj.* ankle-length.
Fußgänger [ˈfu:sgɛŋər], *m.* (**—s,** *pl.* **—**) pedestrian.
Fußgestell [ˈfu:sgəʃtɛl], *n.* (**—s,** *pl.* **—e**) pedestal.
Fußpflege [ˈfu:spfle:gə], *f.* (**—,** *no pl.*) chiropody.
Fußpunkt [ˈfu:spuŋkt], *m.* (**—s,** *no pl.*) nadir.
Fußtritt [ˈfu:strɪt], *m.* (**—s,** *pl.* **—e**) kick.
futsch [futʃ], *excl.* (*coll.*) gone, lost.
Futter [ˈfutər], *n.* (**—s,** *no pl.*) (*dress*) lining; (*animals*) fodder, feed.
Futteral [futəˈra:l], *n.* (**—s,** *pl.* **—e**) case; sheath.
Futterkräuter [ˈfutərkrɔytər], *n. pl.* herbage.
futtern [ˈfutərn], *v.n.* (*coll.*) feed, stuff o.s.
füttern [ˈfytərn], *v.a.* feed; (*garment*) line.

G

G [ge:], *n.* (**—s,** *pl.* **—s**) the letter G; (*Mus.*) *G Dur*, G major; (*Mus.*) *G Moll*, G minor; (*Mus.*) — *-Saite*, G string.
Gabe [ˈga:bə], *f.* (**—,** *pl.* **—n**) gift, present; donation; *barmherzige* —, alms; (*fig.*) gift, talent.
Gabel [ˈga:bəl], *f.* (**—,** *pl.* **—n**) fork; (*deer*) antler; (*cart*) shafts.
gabelig [ˈga:bəlɪç], *adj.* forked.
Gabelung [ˈga:bəluŋ], *f.* (**—,** *pl.* **—en**) bifurcation, branching (of road).
Gabelzinke [ˈga:bəltsɪŋkə], *f.* (**—,** *pl.* **—n**) prong, tine.
Gabun [gaˈbu:n], *n.* Gaboon.
gackern [ˈgakərn], *v.n.* cackle; (*fig.*) chatter.
gaffen [ˈgafən], *v.n.* gape (at), stare.
Gage [ˈga:ʒə], *f.* (**—,** *pl.* **—n**) salary, pay, fee.
gähnen [ˈgɛ:nən], *v.n.* yawn, gape.
Galan [gaˈla:n], *m.* (**—s,** *pl.* **—e**) lover, gallant.
galant [gaˈlant], *adj.* polite, courteous; *—es Abenteuer*, love affair.
Galanterie [galantəˈri:], *f.* (**—,** *pl.* **—n**) courtesy.
Galanteriewaren [galantəˈri:va:rən], *f. pl.* fancy goods.
Galeere [gaˈle:rə], *f.* (**—,** *pl.* **—n**) galley.
Galerie [galəˈri:], *f.* (**—,** *pl.* **—n**) gallery.
Galgen [ˈgalgən], *m.* (**—s,** *pl.* **—**) gallows, gibbet; scaffold.
Galgenfrist [ˈgalgənfrɪst], *f.* (**—,** *no pl.*) short delay, respite.
Galgenhumor [ˈgalgənhumo:r], *m.* (**—s,** *no pl.*) wry or grim humour.
Galgenvogel [ˈgalgənfo:gəl], *m.* (**—s,** *pl.* **¨**) gallows-bird.
Galizien [gaˈli:tsjən], *n.* Galicia.
Gallapfel [ˈgalapfəl], *m.* (**—s,** *pl.* **¨**) gall-nut.
Galle [ˈgalə], *f.* (**—,** *pl.* **—n**) gall, bile.
Gallenblase [ˈgalənbla:zə], *f.* (**—,** *pl.* **—n**) gall-bladder.
Gallert [ˈgalərt], *n.* (**—s,** *no pl.*) jelly.
Gallien [ˈgaljən], *n.* Gaul.
gallig [ˈgalɪç], *adj.* bilious.
galvanisieren [galvanɪˈzi:rən], *v.a.* galvanize.
Gamaschen [gaˈmaʃən], *f. pl.* spats, gaiters.
Gang [gaŋ], *m.* (**—es,** *pl.* **¨e**) walk, gait; (*horse*) pace; (*house*) passage, corridor; (*meal*) course, dish; (*action*) progress, course; (*sport*) round, bout; (*machine*) motion; stroke; (*Motor.*) gear.
gang [gaŋ], *adj.* — *und gäbe*, customary, usual, common.
Gangart [ˈgaŋa:rt], *f.* (**—,** *pl.* **—en**) gait; (*horse*) pace.
gangbar [ˈgaŋba:r], *adj.* marketable, saleable; (*road*) passable; practicable.
Gans [gans], *f.* (**—,** *pl.* **¨e**) (*Orn.*) goose.
Gänseblümchen [ˈgɛnzəbly:mçən], *n.* (**—s,** *pl.* **—**) daisy.
Gänsefüßchen [ˈgɛnzəfy:sçən], *n. pl.* (*coll.*) inverted commas, quotation marks.
Gänsehaut [ˈgɛnzəhaut], *f.* (**—,** *no pl.*) goose-flesh, goose-pimples.
Gänserich [ˈgɛnzərɪç], *m.* (**—s,** *pl.* **—e**) (*Orn.*) gander.
ganz [ˈgants], *adj.* whole, entire, all; complete, total.
gänzlich [ˈgɛntslɪç], *adj.* whole, total, entire, full, complete.
gar [ga:r], *adj.* sufficiently cooked, done. — *adv.* very, quite.
garantieren [garanˈti:rən], *v.a.* guarantee, warrant.
Garaus [ˈga:raus], *m.* (**—,** *no pl.*) *einem den — machen*, finish s.o., kill s.o.
Garbe [ˈgarbə], *f.* (**—,** *pl.* **—n**) sheaf.
Garde [ˈgardə], *f.* (**—,** *pl.* **—n**) guard, guards.
Garderobe [gardəˈro:bə], *f.* (**—,** *pl.* **—n**) wardrobe; cloak-room; (*Theat.*) dressing-room.
Gardine [garˈdi:nə], *f.* (**—,** *pl.* **—n**) curtain.
Gardist [garˈdɪst], *m.* (**—en,** *pl.* **—en**) guardsman.
gären [ˈgɛ:rən], *v.n.* ferment; effervesce.
Garn [garn], *n.* (**—s,** *pl.* **—e**) yarn, thread.
Garnele [garˈne:lə], *f.* (**—,** *pl.* **—n**) (*Zool.*) shrimp; *große* —, prawn.
garnieren [garˈni:rən], *v.a.* trim, garnish.
Garnison [garniˈzo:n], *f.* (**—,** *pl.* **—en**) garrison.

Garnitur [garni'tu:r], *f.* (—, *pl.* **—en**) trimming; set.
Garnröllchen ['garnrœlçən], *n.* (**—s**, *pl.* —) reel of thread.
garstig ['garstɪç], *adj.* nasty, loathsome, ugly.
Garten ['gartən], *m.* (**—s**, *pl.* **¨**) garden.
Gartenlaube ['gartənlaubə], *f.* (—, *pl.* **—n**) bower, arbour.
Gärtner ['gɛrtnər], *m.* (**—s**, *pl.* —) gardener.
Gärtnerei [gɛrtnə'raɪ], *f.* (—, *pl.* **—en**) horticulture; market-garden; (plant) nursery.
Gärung ['gɛ:ruŋ], *f.* (—, *pl.* **—en**) fermentation, effervescence.
Gas [ga:s], *n.* (**—es, —e**) gas; — *geben*, (*Motor.*) accelerate.
gasartig ['ga:sartɪç], *adj.* gaseous.
Gäßchen ['gɛsçən], *n.* (**—s**, *pl.* —) narrow alley; lane.
Gasse ['gasə], *f.* (—, *pl.* **—n**) alleyway, lane; (*rare*) street.
Gassenbube ['gasənbu:bə] *see* **Gassenjunge**.
Gassenhauer ['gasənhauər], *m.* (**—s**, *pl.* —), street-song, vulgar ballad; pop song.
Gassenjunge ['gasənjuŋə], *m.* (**—n**, *pl.* **—n**) street-urchin.
Gast [gast], *m.* (**—s**, *pl.* **¨e**) guest, visitor.
gastfrei ['gastfraɪ], *adj.* hospitable.
Gastfreund ['gastfrɔynt], *m.* (**—s**, *pl.* **—e**) guest; host.
Gastfreundschaft ['gastfrɔɪntʃaft], *f.* (—, *no pl.*) hospitality.
Gastgeber ['gastge:bər], *m.* (**—s**, *pl.* —) host.
Gasthaus ['gasthaus], *n.* (**—es**, *pl.* **—¨er**), **Gasthof** ['gastho:f], *m.* (**—es**, *pl.* **¨e**) inn, hotel, public house.
gastieren [gas'ti:rən], *v.n.* (*Theat.*) appear as a guest artist; star.
gastlich ['gastlɪç], *adj.* hospitable.
Gastmahl ['gastma:l], *n.* (**—s**, *pl.* **—e**) banquet, feast.
Gastrecht ['gastrɛçt], *n.* (**—s**, *no pl.*) right of hospitality.
Gastspiel ['gastʃpi:l], *n.* (**—s**, *pl.* **—e**) (*Theat.*) performance by visiting company.
Gaststätte ['gaststɛtə], *f.* (—, *pl.* **—n**) restaurant.
Gaststube ['gastʃtu:bə], *f.* (—, *pl.* **—n**) hotel lounge; guest room.
Gastwirt ['gastvɪrt], *m.* (**—s**, *pl.* **—e**) landlord.
Gastwirtin ['gastvɪrtɪn], *f.* (—, *pl.* **—nen**) landlady.
Gastzimmer ['gasttsɪmər], *n.* (**—s**, *pl.* —) *see* **Gaststube**; spare bedroom.
Gatte ['gatə], *m.* (**—n**, *pl.* **—n**) husband, spouse, consort.
Gatter ['gatər], *n.* (**—s**, *pl.* —) grate, lattice, grating.
Gattin ['gatɪn], *f.* (—, *pl.* **—nen**) wife, spouse, consort.
Gattung ['gatuŋ], *f.* (—, *pl.* **—en**) kind, species, sort, class; breed, genus; (*Lit.*) genre.
Gau [gau], *m.* (**—s**, *pl.* **—e**) district, province.
gaukeln ['gaukəln], *v.n.* juggle. — *v.a.* dazzle.
Gaul [gaul], *m.* (**—s**, *pl.* **¨e**) (old) horse, nag; *einem geschenkten — sieht man nicht ins Maul*, never look a gift horse in the mouth.
Gaumen ['gaumən], *m.* (**—s**, *pl.* —) palate.
Gauner ['gaunər], *m.* (**—s**, *pl.* —) rogue, sharper, swindler, cheat.
gaunern ['gaunərn], *v.n.* cheat, trick, swindle.
Gaunersprache ['gaunərʃpra:xə], *f.* (—, *no pl.*) thieves' slang.
Gaze ['ga:zə], *f.* (—, *pl.* **—n**) gauze.
Gazelle [ga'tsɛlə], *f.* (—, *pl.* **—n**) (*Zool.*) gazelle, antelope.
Geächtete [gə'ɛçtətə], *m.* (**—n**, *pl.* **—n**) outlaw.
Geächze [gə'ɛçtsə], *n.* (**—s**, *no pl.*) moaning, groaning.
Geäder [gə'ɛ:dər], *n.* (**—s**, *no pl.*) veins, arteries; veining.
geädert [gə'ɛdərt], *adj.* veined, streaked; grained.
-geartet [gə'a:rtət], *adj.* (*suffix in compounds*) -natured.
Gebäck [gə'bɛk], *n.* (**—s**, *no pl.*) pastry, rolls, cakes.
Gebälk [gə'bɛlk], *n.* (**—s**, *no pl.*) timberwork, timber-frame.
Gebärde [gə'bɛ:rdə], *f.* (—, *pl.* **—n**) gesture.
gebärden [gə'bɛ:rdən], *v.r. sich* —, behave.
Gebaren [gə'ba:rən], *n.* (**—s**, *no pl.*) demeanour.
gebären [gə'bɛ:rən], *v.a. irr.* bear, bring forth, give birth to, be delivered of.
Gebärmutter [gə'bɛ:rmutər], *f.* (—, *no pl.*) womb, uterus.
Gebäude [gə'bɔydə], *n.* (**—s**, *pl.* —) building, edifice.
Gebein [gə'baɪn], *n.* (**—s**, *pl.* **—e**) bones, skeleton; (*fig.*) remains.
Gebell [gə'bɛl], *n.* (**—s**, *no pl.*) barking.
geben ['ge:bən], *v.a. irr.* give, present; confer, bestow; yield; (*cards*) deal. — *v.r. sich* —, show o.s., behave; abate; *das gibt sich*, that won't last long; *es gibt* . . ., there is . . .; *was gibt's?* what's the matter?
Geber ['ge:bər], *m.* (**—s**, *pl.* —) giver, donor.
Gebet [gə'be:t], *n.* (**—s**, *pl.* **—e**) prayer; *sein — verrichten*, say o.'s prayers; *ins — nehmen*, question s.o. thoroughly.
Gebiet [gə'bi:t], *n.* (**—s**, *pl.* **—e**) district, territory; (*Am.*) precinct; jurisdiction; (*fig.*) province, field, sphere, domain.
gebieten [gə'bi:tən], *v.a. irr.* command, order.
Gebieter [gə'bi:tər], *m.* (**—s**, *pl.* —) lord, master, ruler.

Gebilde [gə'bɪldə], *n.* (—**s**, *pl.* —) form, thing; formation, structure; figment.
gebildet [gə'bɪldət], *adj.* educated, cultured, refined.
Gebirge [gə'bɪrgə], *n.* (—**s**, *pl.* —) mountains.
Gebirgskamm [gə'bɪrkskam], *m.* (—**s**, *pl.* ¨**e**) mountain-ridge.
Gebiß [gə'bɪs], *n.* (—**sses**, *pl.* —**sse**) set of (false) teeth, denture; (*horse*) bit.
Gebläse [gə'blɛ:zə], *n.* (—**s**, *pl.* —) bellows; blower.
Gebläsemaschine [gə'blɛ:zəmaʃi:nə], *f.* (—, *pl.* —**n**) blower.
Gebläseofen [gə'blɛ:zəo:fən], *m.* (—**s**, *pl.* ¨) blast-furnace.
geblümt [gə'bly:mt], *adj.* flowered.
Geblüt [gə'bly:t], *n.* (—**s**, *no pl.*) blood; race, line, lineage, stock.
geboren [gə'bo:rən], *adj.* born.
geborgen [gə'bɔrgən], *adj.* saved, hidden, sheltered, rescued.
Gebot [gə'bo:t], *n.* (—**s**, *pl.* —**e**) order, decree, command; (*Bibl.*) Commandment.
geboten [gə'bo:tən], *adj.* necessary, advisable.
Gebräu [gə'brɔy], *n.* (—**s**, *no pl.*) brew, concoction, mixture.
Gebrauch [gə'braux], *m.* (—**s**, *pl.* ¨**e**) use; employment; custom, usage, habit, practice; (*rare*) rite.
gebrauchen [gə'brauxən], *v.a.* use, make use of, employ.
gebräuchlich [gə'brɔyçlɪç], *adj.* usual, customary, common.
Gebrauchsanweisung [gə'brauxsanvaɪzuŋ], *f.* (—, *pl.* —**en**) directions for use.
gebraucht [gə'brauxt], *adj.* used, second-hand.
Gebrechen [gə'brɛçən], *n.* (—**s**, *pl.* —) infirmity.
gebrechen [gə'brɛçən], *v.n. irr. es gebricht mir an*, I am in want of, I lack.
gebrechlich [gə'brɛçlɪç], *adj.* infirm, frail, weak.
gebrochen [gə'brɔxən], *adj.* broken; —*es Deutsch*, broken German.
Gebrüder [gə'bry:dər], *m. pl.* (*Comm.*) brothers.
Gebrüll [gə'bryl], *n.* (—**s**, *no pl.*) roaring; (*cows*) lowing.
Gebühr [gə'by:r], *f.* (—, *pl.* —**en**) charge, due; fee; tax, duty.
gebühren [gə'by:rən], *v.n.* be due to s.o. — *v.r. sich* —, *wie es sich gebührt*, as it ought to be, as is right and proper.
gebunden [gə'bundən], *adj.* (*fig.*) bound, committed; (*Poet.*) metrical.
Geburt [gə'burt], *f.* (—, *pl.* —**en**) birth.
gebürtig [gə'byrtɪç], *adj.* a native of.
Geburtsfehler [gə'burtsfe:lər], *m.* (—**s**, *pl.* —) congenital defect.
Geburtshelfer [gə'burtshɛlfər], *m.* (—**s**, *pl.* —) obstetrician.
Geburtshelferin [gə'burtshɛlfərɪn], *f.* (—, *pl.* —**nen**) midwife.
Geburtsort [gə'burtsɔrt], *m.* (—**s**, *pl.* —**e**) birthplace.
Geburtsschein [gə'burtsʃaɪn], *m.* (—(**e**)**s**, *pl.* —**e**) birth certificate.
Geburtswehen [gə'burtsve:ən], *f. pl.* birthpangs; labour pains.
Gebüsch [gə'byʃ], *n.* (—**es**, *pl.* —**e**) bushes, thicket; underwood.
Geck [gɛk], *m.* (—**en**, *pl.* —**en**) fop, dandy; (*carnival*) fool.
geckenhaft ['gɛkənhaft], *adj.* foppish, dandyish.
Gedächtnis [gə'dɛçtnɪs], *n.* (—**ses**, *no pl.*) memory; remembrance, recollection; *im* — *behalten*, keep in mind.
Gedanke [gə'daŋkə], *m.* (—**ns**, *pl.* —**n**) thought, idea.
Gedankenfolge [gə'daŋkənfɔlgə], *f.* (—, *no pl.*), **Gedankengang** [gə'daŋkəngaŋ], *m.* (—**s**, *pl.* ¨**e**) sequence of thought, train of thought.
Gedankenstrich [gə'daŋkənʃtrɪç], *m.* (—**s**, *pl.* —**e**) dash; hyphen.
Gedärm [gə'dɛrm], *n.* (—**s**, *pl.* —**e**) bowels, intestines, entrails.
Gedeck [gə'dɛk], *n.* (—**s**, *pl.* —**e**) cover; menu; place laid at a table.
gedeihen [gə'daɪən], *v.n. irr.* (*aux.* sein) thrive, prosper; progress.
gedeihlich [gə'daɪlɪç], *adj.* thriving, salutary.
gedenken [gə'dɛŋkən], *v.n. irr.* (*Genit.*) think of, remember; — *etwas zu tun*, intend to do s.th.
Gedenken [gə'dɛŋkən], *n.* (—**s**, *no pl.*) remembrance.
Gedenkfeier [gə'dɛŋkfaɪər], *f.* (—, *pl.* —**n**) commemoration.
Gedicht [gə'dɪçt], *n.* (—**s**, *pl.* —**e**) poem.
gediegen [gə'di:gən], *adj.* solid, sound, genuine, true, honourable, sterling.
Gedränge [gə'drɛŋə], *n.* (—**s**, *no pl.*) crowd, throng; crush.
Gedrängtheit [gə'drɛnkthaɪt], *f.* (—, *no pl.*) conciseness.
gedrungen [gə'druŋən], *adj.* thick-set, stocky; compact; concise (style).
Geduld [gə'dult], *f.* (—, *no pl.*) patience, forbearance.
gedulden [gə'duldən], *v.r. sich* —, be patient.
geduldig [gə'duldɪç], *adj.* patient, forbearing, indulgent.
Geduld(s)spiel [gə'dult(s)ʃpi:l], *n.* (—**s**, *pl.* —**e**) puzzle; (*Cards*) patience.
gedunsen [gə'dunzən], *adj.* bloated.
geeignet [gə'aɪgnet], *adj.* suitable, fit, appropriate, apt.
Gefahr [gə'fa:r], *f.* (—, *pl.* —**en**) danger, peril, hazard, risk; — *laufen*, run the risk.
gefährden [gə'fɛ:rdən], *v.a.* endanger, imperil, jeopardize.
gefährlich [gə'fɛ:rlɪç], *adj.* dangerous, perilous.
Gefährt [gə'fɛ:rt], *n.* (—**s**, *pl.* —**e**) (*obs.*) vehicle, conveyance.
Gefährte [gə'fɛ:rtə], *m.* (—**en**, *pl.* —**en**) comrade, companion, fellow.

Gefälle [gə'fɛlə], *n.* (—**s**, *pl.* —**e**) fall, descent, incline, gradient.
Gefallen [gə'falən], *m.* (—**s**, *no pl.*) pleasure, liking; favour, kindness.
gefallen (1) [gə'falən], *v.n. irr.* please; *es gefällt mir*, I like it; *wie gefällt Ihnen . . .*; how do you like . . ..
gefallen (2) [gə'falən], *adj.* (*Mil.*) fallen, killed in action.
gefällig [gə'fɛlɪç], *adj.* pleasing, accommodating, obliging, anxious to please; *was ist* —? what can I do for you?
Gefälligkeit [gə'fɛlɪçkaɪt], *f.* (—, *pl.* —**en**) courtesy; favour, service, good turn.
gefälligst [gə'fɛlɪçst], *adv.* if you please.
Gefallsucht [gə'falzuxt], *f.* (—, *no pl.*) coquetry.
gefallsüchtig [gə'falzyçtɪç], *adj.* coquettish.
gefangen [gə'faŋən], *adj.* in prison, imprisoned, captive.
Gefangene [gə'faŋənə], *m.* (—**n**, *pl.* —**n**) prisoner, captive.
Gefangennahme [gə'faŋənna:mə], *f.* (—, *no pl.*) arrest, capture.
Gefangenschaft [gə'faŋənʃaft], *f.* (—, *no pl.*) captivity, imprisonment, detention; *in — geraten*, be taken prisoner.
Gefängis [gə'fɛŋnɪs], *n.* (—**sses**, *pl.* —**sse**) prison, gaol.
Gefäß [gə'fɛ:s], *n.* (—**es**, *pl.* —**e**) vessel.
gefaßt [gə'fast], *adj.* collected, composed, ready; calm; *sich auf etwas — machen*, prepare o.s. for s.th.
Gefecht [gə'fɛçt], *n.* (—**s**, *pl.* —**e**) fight, battle, combat; action, engagement.
gefeit [gə'faɪt], *adj.* proof against.
Gefieder [gə'fi:dər], *n.* (—**s**, *no pl.*) plumage, feathers.
Gefilde [gə'fɪldə], *n.* (—**s**, *pl.* —) (*Poet.*) fields, plain.
Geflecht [gə'flɛçt], *n.* (—**s**, *no pl.*) wicker-work, texture.
geflissentlich [gə'flɪsəntlɪç], *adj.* intentional, wilful, with a purpose.
Geflügel [gə'fly:gəl], *n.* (—**s**, *no pl.*) fowls, poultry.
geflügelt [gə'fly:gəlt], *adj.* winged; —*e Worte*, household word, familiar quotation.
Geflüster [gə'flystər], *n.* (—**s**, *no pl.*) whispering, whisper.
Gefolge [gə'fɔlgə], *n.* (—**s**, *no pl.*) retinue, following.
gefräßig [gə'frɛ:sɪç], *adj.* voracious, gluttonous.
Gefreite [gə'fraɪtə], *m.* (—**n**, *pl.* —**n**) (*Mil.*) lance-corporal.
gefrieren [gə'fri:rən], *v.n. irr.* (*aux.* sein) freeze; congeal.
Gefrierpunkt [gə'fri:rpuŋkt], *m.* (—**s**, *no pl.*) freezing point, zero.
Gefrorene [gə'fro:rənə], *n.* (—**n**, *no pl.*) ice-cream.
Gefüge [gə'fy:gə], *n.* (—**s**, *no pl.*) joints, structure, construction; frame.
gefügig [gə'fy:gɪç], *adj.* pliant; docile; *einen — machen*, make s.o. amenable, persuade s.o.
Gefühl [gə'fy:l], *n.* (—**s**, *pl.* —**e**) feeling, sense, sensation.
gegen ['ge:gən], *prep.* (*Acc.*) against; towards; about, near; in comparison with; in the direction of; opposed to; in exchange for; — *Quittung*, against receipt. — *adv.*, *prefix.* counter, opposing, contrary.
Gegend ['ge:gənt], *f.* (—, *pl.* —**en**) region, country, part.
Gegengewicht ['ge:gəngəvɪçt], *n.* (—**s**, *pl.* —**e**) counterweight, counterpoise.
Gegengift ['ge:gəngɪft], *n.* (—**s**, *pl.* —**e**) antidote.
Gegenleistung ['ge:gənlaɪstuŋ], *f.* (—, *pl.* —**en**) return; service in return; *Leistung und* —, give and take.
Gegenrede ['ge:gənre:də], *f.* (—, *pl.* —**n**) contradiction; objection.
Gegensatz ['ge:gənzats], *m.* (—**es**, *pl.* ¨**e**) contrast, opposition, antithesis.
gegensätzlich ['ge:gənzɛtslɪç], *adj.* contrary, adverse.
Gegenseite ['ge:gənzaɪtə], *f.* (—, *pl.* —**n**) opposite side; (*coin*) reverse.
gegenseitig ['ge:gənzaɪtɪç], *adj.* reciprocal, mutual.
Gegenstand ['ge:gənʃtant], *m.* (—**s**, *pl.* ¨**e**) object; subject, matter.
gegenstandslos ['ge:gənʃtantslo:s], *adj.* superfluous, irrelevant.
Gegenstück ['ge:gənʃtyk], *n.* (—**s**, *pl.* —**e**) counterpart.
Gegenteil ['ge:gəntaɪl], *n.* (—**s**, *no pl.*) contrary; *im* —, on the contrary.
gegenüber [ge:gən'y:bər], *prep.* (*Dat.*) opposite to, facing. — *adv.* opposite.
Gegenüberstellung [ge:gən'y:berʃtɛluŋ], *f.* (—, *pl.* —**en**) confrontation.
Gegenwart ['ge:gənvart], *f.* (—, *no pl.*) presence; (*Gram.*) present tense.
Gegenwehr ['ge:gənve:r], *f.* (—, *no pl.*) defence, resistance.
Gegenwirkung ['ge:gənvɪrkuŋ], *f.* (—, *pl.* —**en**) reaction, counter-effect.
gegenzeichnen ['ge:gəntsaɪçnən], *v.a.* countersign.
Gegner ['ge:gnər], *m.* (—**s**, *pl.* —) opponent, adversary, antagonist.
gegnerisch ['ge:gnərɪʃ], *adj.* adverse, antagonistic.
Gegnerschaft ['ge:gnərʃaft], *f.* (—, *no pl.*) antagonism; opposition.
Gehalt (1) [gə'halt], *m.* (—**s**, *no pl.*) contents; (*fig.*) value, standard.
Gehalt (2) [gə'halt], *n.* (—**s**, *pl.* ¨**er**) salary, stipend; pay.
Gehaltszulage [gə'haltstsu:la:gə], *f.* (—, *pl.* —**n**) rise (in salary); increment; (*Am.*) raise.
gehaltvoll [gə'haltfɔl], *adj.* substantial.
Gehänge [gə'hɛŋə], *n.* (—**s**, *pl.* —) slope; festoon, garland.
geharnischt [gə'harnɪʃt], *adj.* armoured, steel-clad; (*fig.*) severe.
gehässig [gə'hɛsɪç], *adj.* malicious, spiteful.

Gehäuse [gəˈhɔyzə], *n.* (—s, *pl.* —) casing, case; (*snail*) shell.
Gehege [gəˈhe:gə], *n.* (—s, *pl.* —) enclosure; *einem ins — kommen*, trespass on s.o.'s preserves.
geheim [gəˈhaɪm], *adj.* secret, clandestine.
Geheimnis [gəˈhaɪmnɪs], *n.* (—ses, *pl.* —se) secret, mystery.
geheimnisvoll [gəˈhaɪmnɪsfɔl], *adj.* mysterious.
Geheimrat [gəˈhaɪmra:t], *m.* (—s, *pl.* ¨e) Privy Councillor.
Geheimschrift [gəˈhaɪmʃrɪft], *f.* (—, *pl.* —en) cryptography.
Geheimsprache [gəˈhaɪmʃpra:xə], *f.* (—, *pl.* —en) cipher.
Geheiß [gəˈhaɪs], *n.* (—es, *no pl.*) command, order, bidding.
gehen [ˈge:ən], *v.n. irr.* (*aux.* sein) go, walk; (*Mach.*) work, function; (*goods*) sell; (*dough*) rise; *er lässt sich —*, he lets himself go; *er lässt es sich gut —*, he enjoys himself; *einem an die Hand —*, lend s.o. a hand, assist s.o.; *in Erfüllung —*, come true; *in sich —*, reflect; *wie geht es dir?* how are you? *es geht mir gut*, I am well.
geheuer [gəˈhɔyər], *adj.* (*only in neg.*) *nicht ganz —*, creepy, eerie, uncanny; (*coll.*) fishy.
Gehilfe [gəˈhɪlfə], *m.* (—n, *pl.* —n) assistant, helper.
Gehirn [gəˈhɪrn], *n.* (—s, *pl.* —e) brain, brains.
Gehirnhautentzündung [gəˈhɪrnhautɛntsyndʊŋ], *f.* (—, *pl.* —en) meningitis, cerebral inflammation.
Gehirnschlag [gəˈhɪrnʃla:k], *m.* (—s, *pl.* ¨e) apoplexy.
Gehöft [gəˈhœft], *n.* (—es, *pl.* —e) farmstead.
Gehör [gəˈhø:r], (—s, *no pl.*) hearing; *gutes —*, musical ear.
gehorchen [gəˈhɔrçən], *v.n.* obey; *nicht —*, disobey.
gehören [gəˈhø:rən], *v.n.* belong. — *v.r. sich —*, be the proper thing to do.
gehörig [gəˈhørɪç], *adj. dazu —*, belonging to, referring to; due, fit, proper, thorough; (*fig.*) sound.
Gehörn [gəˈhœrn], *n.* (—s, *pl.* —e) horns, antlers.
gehörnt [gəˈhœrnt], *adj.* horned; (*fig.*) duped (husband).
Gehorsam [gəˈho:rza:m], *m.* (—s, *no pl.*) obedience; *— leisten*, show obedience; *den — verweigern*, refuse to obey.
gehorsam [gəˈho:rza:m], *adj.* obedient, dutiful, submissive.
Gehrock [ˈge:rɔk], *m.* (—s, *pl.* ¨e) frock-coat.
Geier [ˈgaɪər], *m.* (—s, *pl.* —) (*Orn.*) vulture.
Geifer [ˈgaɪfər], *m.* (—s, *no pl.*) saliva, drivel; (*animals*) foam; (*fig.*) venom, rancour.
geifern [ˈgaɪfərn], *v.n.* slaver, drivel; (*fig.*) foam at the mouth; give vent to o.'s anger.
Geige [ˈgaɪgə], *f.* (—, *pl.* —n) violin, fiddle.
Geigenharz [ˈgaɪgənha:rts], *n.* (—es, *no pl.*) colophony; rosin.
Geigensteg [ˈgaɪgənʃte:k], *m.* (—s, *pl.* —e) bridge of a violin.
Geiger [ˈgaɪgər], *m.* (—s, *pl.* —) violin-player, violinist.
geil [gaɪl], *adj.* rank; lecherous, lascivious.
Geisel [ˈgaɪzəl], *f.* (—, *pl.* —n) hostage.
Geiß [gaɪs], *f.* (—, *pl.* —en) goat, she-goat.
Geißblatt [ˈgaɪsblat], *n.* (—s, *no pl.*) (*Bot.*) honeysuckle.
Geißbock [ˈgaɪsbɔk], *m.* (—s, *pl.* ¨e) billy-goat.
Geißel [ˈgaɪsəl], *f.* (—, *pl.* —n) scourge.
geißeln [ˈgaɪsəln], *v.a.* scourge, whip, flagellate.
Geist [gaɪst], *m.* (—es, *pl.* —er) spirit, mind; brains, intellect; wit; apparition, ghost.
Geisterbeschwörung [ˈgaɪstərbəʃvø:rʊŋ], *f.* (—, *pl.* —en) evocation (of spirits); necromancy; exorcism.
geisterhaft [ˈgaɪstərhaft], *adj.* ghostly, spectral, weird.
Geisterwelt [ˈgaɪstərvɛlt], *f.* (—, *no pl.*) world of spirits.
geistesabwesend [ˈgaɪstəsapve:zənt], *adj.* absent-minded.
Geistesfreiheit [ˈgaɪstəsfraɪhaɪt], *f.* (—, *no pl.*) freedom of thought.
Geistesgegenwart [ˈgaɪstəsge:gənvart], *f.* (—, *no pl.*) presence of mind.
Geisteskraft [ˈgaɪstəskraft], *f.* (—, *pl.* ¨e) faculty of the mind.
Geistesstörung [ˈgaɪstəsʃtø:rʊŋ], *f.* (—, *pl.* —en) mental aberration.
Geistesverfassung [ˈgaɪstəsfɛrfasʊŋ], *f.* (—, *no pl.*) state of mind.
geistesverwandt [ˈgaɪstəsfɛrvant], *adj.* congenial.
Geistesverwirrung [ˈgaɪstəsfɛrvɪrʊŋ], *f.* (—, *no pl.*) bewilderment.
Geisteswissenschaften [ˈgaɪstəsvɪsənʃaftən], *f.pl.* (*Univ.*) Arts, Humanities.
Geisteszerrüttung [ˈgaɪstəstsɛrytʊŋ], *f.* (—, *no pl.*) mental derangement, insanity.
geistig [ˈgaɪstɪç], *adj.* intellectual, mental; spiritual; *—e Getränke*, alcoholic liquors.
geistlich [ˈgaɪstlɪç], *adj.* spiritual; religious; ecclesiastical, clerical; *—er Orden*, religious order; *—er Stand*, holy orders, the Clergy.
Geistliche [ˈgaɪstlɪçə], *m.* (—n, *pl.* —n) priest, clergyman, cleric; minister of religion.
Geistlichkeit [ˈgaɪstlɪçkaɪt], *f.* (—, *no pl.*) clergy.
geistlos [ˈgaɪstlo:s], *adj.* dull, stupid.
geistreich [ˈgaɪstraɪç], *adj.* clever, witty.
Geiz [gaɪts], *m.* (—es, *no pl.*) avarice, covetousness.
geizen [ˈgaɪtsən], *v.n.* be miserly.

Geizhals ['gaɪtshals], *m.* (**—es**, *pl.* **¨e**) miser, niggard.
Geizkragen ['gaɪtskra:gən], *m.* (**—s**, *pl.* **—**) *see* **Geizhals**.
Gekreisch [gə'kraɪʃ], *n.* (**—es**, *no pl.*) screaming, shrieks.
Gekritzel [gə'krɪtsəl], *n.* (**—s**, *no pl.*) scrawling, scribbling.
Gekröse [gə'krø:zə], *n.* (**—s**, *no pl.*) tripe; (*Anat.*) mesentery.
gekünstelt [gə'kynstəlt], *adj.* artificial, affected.
Gelächter [gə'lɛçtər], *n.* (**—s**, *no pl.*) laughter.
Gelage [gə'la:gə], *n.* (**—s**, *pl.* **—**) (*obs.*) feast, banquet.
Gelände [gə'lɛndə], *n.* (**—s**, *pl.* **—**) terrain, region; landscape.
Geländer [gə'lɛndər], *n.* (**—s**, *pl.* **—**) railing, balustrade, banister.
gelangen [gə'laŋən], *v.n.* (*aux.* sein) arrive, come (to).
Gelaß [gə'las], *n.* (**—sses**, *pl.* **—sse**) (*obs.*) room, chamber.
gelassen [gə'lasən], *adj.* calm, composed, collected.
geläufig [gə'lɔyfɪç], *adj.* fluent.
gelaunt [gə'launt], *adj.* disposed.
Geläute [gə'lɔytə], *n.* (**—s**, *no pl.*) ringing, chiming; bells.
geläutert [gə'lɔytərt], *adj.* purified, cleansed.
gelb [gɛlp], *adj.* yellow, amber.
Gelbschnabel ['gɛlpʃna:bəl], *m.* (**—s**, *pl.* **¨**) (*Orn.*) fledg(e)ling; greenhorn.
Gelbsucht ['gɛlpzuxt], *f.* (**—**, *no pl.*) jaundice.
Geld [gɛlt], *n.* (**—es**, *pl.* **—er**) money, currency, coin; *bares* **—**, ready money, hard cash; *kleines* **—**, small change.
Geldanweisung ['gɛltanvaɪzuŋ], *f.* (**—** *pl.* **—en**) money-order.
Geldbuße ['gɛltbu:sə], *f.* (**—**, *pl.* **—n**) fine.
Geldkurs ['gɛltkurs], *m.* (**—es**, *pl.* **—e**) rate of exchange.
Geldmittel ['gɛltmɪtəl], *n. pl.* pecuniary resources, financial resources.
Geldschrank ['gɛltʃraŋk], *m.* (**—s**, *pl.* **¨e**) safe.
Geldstrafe ['gɛltʃtra:fə], *f.* (**—**, *pl.* **—n**) fine.
Geldverlegenheit ['gɛltfɛrle:gənhaɪt], *f.* (**—**, *pl.* **—en**) pecuniary embarrassment, financial difficulty.
Geldwährung ['gɛltvɛ:ruŋ], *f.* (**—**, *pl.* **—en**) currency.
Geldwechsel ['gɛltvɛksəl], *m.* (**—s**, *no pl.*) exchange.
Gelee [ʒə'le:], *n.* (**—s**, *pl.* **—s**) jelly.
gelegen [gə'le:gən], *adj.* situated, situate; *das kommt mir gerade* **—**, that suits me; *mir ist daran* **—**, *dass*, I am anxious that.
Gelegenheit [gə'le:gənhaɪt], *f.* (**—**, *pl.* **—en**) occasion, chance, opportunity; facility; *bei* **—**, one of these days.
Gelegenheitskauf [gə'le:gənhaɪtskauf], *m.* (**—s**, *pl.* **¨e**) bargain.
gelegentlich [gə'le:gəntlɪç], *adj.* occasional.
gelehrig [gə'le:rɪç], *adj.* docile, tractable.
Gelehrsamkeit [gə'le:rza:mkaɪt], *f.* (**—**, *no pl.*) learning, erudition.
gelehrt [gə'le:rt], *adj.* learned, erudite.
Gelehrte [gə'le:rtə], *m.* (**—n**, *pl.* **—n**) scholar, man of learning, savant.
Geleise [gə'laɪzə], *n.* (**—s**, *pl.* **—**) *see* **Gleis**.
Geleit [gə'laɪt], *n.* (**—s**, *no pl.*) escort, accompaniment; (*Naut.*) convoy; *sicheres* **—**, safe conduct.
geleiten [gə'laɪtən], *v.a.* accompany, conduct, escort.
Gelenk [gə'lɛŋk], *n.* (**—s**, *pl.* **—e**) (*human*) joint; (*chain*) link.
Gelenkentzündung [gə'lɛŋkɛnttsyndʊŋ], *f.* (**—**, *pl.* **—en**) (*Med.*) arthritis.
gelenkig [gə'lɛŋkɪç], *adj.* flexible, pliant, nimble, supple.
Gelenkrheumatismus [gə'lɛŋkrɔymatɪsmus], *m.* (**—**, *no pl.*) (*Med.*) rheumatoid arthritis, rheumatic gout.
Gelichter [gə'lɪçtər], *n.* (**—s**, *no pl.*) riff-raff.
Geliebte [gə'li:ptə], *m.* (**—n**, *pl.* **—n**) lover, sweetheart, beloved. — *f.* (**—n**, *pl.* **—n**) mistress; beloved.
gelinde [gə'lɪndə], *adj.* soft, smooth, gentle, mild; **—** *gesagt*, to say the least.
Gelingen [gə'lɪŋən], *n.* (**—s**, *no pl.*) success.
gelingen [gə'lɪŋən], *v.n. irr.* (*aux.* sein) succeed; *es gelingt mir*, I succeed.
gellen ['gɛlən], *v.n.* yell; shrill.
geloben [gə'lo:bən], *v.a.* (*aux.* haben) promise solemnly, vow; *das Gelobte Land*, the Promised Land.
Gelöbnis [gə'lø:pnɪs], *n.* (**—ses**, *pl.* **—se**) vow, promise.
gelt [gɛlt], *inter.* (*coll.*) isn't it? don't you think so?
gelten ['gɛltən], *v.a. irr.* be worth, cost. — *v.n.* count (as), be valid.
Geltung ['gɛltuŋ], *f.* (**—**, *no pl.*) value, importance.
Gelübde [gə'lypdə], *n.* (**—s**, *pl.* **—**) vow, solemn promise *or* undertaking.
gelungen [gə'luŋən], *adj.* (*coll.*) funny, capital.
Gelüst [gə'lyst], *n.* (**—s**, *pl.* **—e**) appetite, desire.
gelüsten [gə'lystən], *v.a.* — *nach*, long for, covet.
Gemach [gə'ma:x], *n.* (**—es**, *pl.* **¨er**) (*Poet.*) chamber, room; apartment.
gemach [gə'ma:x], *adv.* slowly, softly, by degrees.
gemächlich [gə'mɛçlɪç], *adj.* slow, soft, easy, unhurried, leisurely.
Gemahl [gə'ma:l], *m.* (**—s**, *pl.* **—e**) spouse, husband, consort.
Gemahlin [gə'ma:lɪn], *f.* (**—**, *pl.* **—nen**) spouse, wife, consort.
Gemälde [gə'mɛ:ldə], *n.* (**—s**, *pl.* **—**) picture, painting, portrait.
gemäß [gə'mɛ:s], *prep.* (*Dat.*) in accordance with, according to.

gemäßigt [gə'mɛ:sɪçt], *adj.* temperate, moderate; *—es Klima*, temperate climate.
Gemäuer [gə'mɔyər], *n.* (**—s**, *no pl.*) ancient walls, ruins.
gemein [gə'maɪn], *adj.* common, mean, low, vulgar, base.
Gemeinde [gə'maɪndə], *f.* (**—**, *pl.* **—n**) community, parish, municipality; (*Eccl.*) congregation.
Gemeindevorstand [gə'maɪndefor-ʃtant], *m.* (**—es**, *no pl.*) town *or* borough council.
gemeingefährlich [gə'maɪngəfɛ:rlɪç], *adj.* dangerous to the public.
Gemeinheit [gə'maɪnhaɪt], *f.* (**—**, *pl.* **—en**) meanness; baseness; dirty trick.
gemeinhin [gə'maɪnhɪn], *adv.* commonly.
Gemeinplatz [gə'maɪnplats], *m.* (**—es**, *pl.* **⸚e**) commonplace, truism.
gemeinsam [gə'maɪnza:m], *adj.* common, joint; *der — Markt*, (*Pol.*) Common Market; *—e Sache machen*, make common cause. — *adv.* together.
Gemeinschaft [gə'maɪnʃaft], *f.* (**—**, *pl.* **—en**) community; association; *in — mit*, jointly; *in — haben*, hold in common.
gemeinschaftlich [gə'maɪnʃaftlɪç], *adj.* common. — *adv.* in common, together.
Gemeinsinn [gə'maɪnzɪn], *m.* (**—s**, *no pl.*) public spirit.
Gemeinwesen [gə'maɪnve:zən], *n.* (**—s**, *no pl.*) community.
Gemeinwohl [gə'maɪnvo:l], *n.* (**—s**, *no pl.*) common weal; common good.
Gemenge [gə'mɛŋe], *n.* (**—s**, *no pl.*) mixture; (*fig.*) scuffle.
Gemengsel [gə'mɛŋsəl], *n.* (**—s**, *no pl.*) medley, hotchpotch.
gemessen [gə'mɛsən], *adj.* deliberate.
Gemessenheit [gə'mɛsənhaɪt], *f.* (**—**, *no pl.*) precision, deliberation.
Gemetzel [gə'mɛtsəl], *n.* (**—s**, *no pl.*) slaughter, massacre.
Gemisch [gə'mɪʃ], *n.* (**—es**, *pl.* **—e**) mixture, motley.
Gemme ['gɛmə], *f.* (**—**, *pl.* **—n**) gem, cameo.
Gemse ['gɛmzə], *f.* (**—**, *pl.* **—n**) chamois.
Gemüse [gə'my:zə], *n.* (**—s**, *pl.* **—**) vegetables, greens.
Gemüsehändler [gə'my:zəhɛndlər], *m.* (**—s**, *pl.* **—**) greengrocer.
gemustert [gə'mustərt], *adj.* patterned, figured; (*Comm.*) *—e Sendung*, delivery as per sample.
Gemüt [gə'my:t], *n.* (**—s**, *pl.* **—er**) mind, soul, heart; disposition, nature, spirit, temper; feeling.
gemütlich [gə'my:tlɪç], *adj.* cosy, snug, comfortable; genial, friendly, pleasant.
Gemütlichkeit [gə'my:tlɪçkaɪt], *f.* (**—**, *no pl.*) cosiness, snugness; *da hört die — auf*, that is more than I will stand for.
gemütlos [gə'my:tlo:s], *adj.* unfeeling.
Gemütsart [gə'my:tsa:rt], *f.* (**—**, *no pl.*) disposition; character.
Gemütsbewegung [gə'my:tsbəve:guŋ], *f.* (**—**, *pl.* **—en**) emotion.
gemütskrank [gə'my:tskraŋk], *adj.* sick in mind; melancholy.
Gemütsleben [gə'my:tsle:bən], *n.* (**—s**, *no pl.*) emotional life.
Gemütsmensch [gə'my:tsmɛnʃ], *m.* (**—en**, *pl.* **—en**) man of feeling *or* sentiment; (*pej.*) sentimentalist.
gemütvoll [gə'my:tfɔl], *adj.* full of feeling, sympathetic.
gen [gɛn], *prep. contraction* of **gegen**, (*Poet.*) towards, to (*Acc.*).
Genannte [gə'nantə], *m.* (**—n**, *pl.* **—n**) named person, aforesaid.
genäschig [gə'nɛʃɪç], *adj.* fond of sweets, sweet-toothed.
genau [gə'nau], *adj.* precise, exact, accurate; strict, parsimonious.
Genauigkeit [gə'nauɪçkaɪt], *f.* (**—**, *no pl.*) accuracy, exactitude, precision.
Gendarm [ʒã'darm], *m.* (**—en**, *pl.* **—en**) policeman, constable.
genehm [gə'ne:m], *adj.* agreeable, acceptable, convenient.
genehmigen [gə'ne:mɪgən], *v.a.* approve of, agree to, permit; (*contract*) ratify.
geneigt [gə'naɪkt], *adj.* inclined (to), disposed (to), prone (to); *einem — sein*, be well disposed towards s.o.; (*Lit.*) *der —e Leser*, gentle reader.
Geneigtheit [gə'naɪkthaɪt], *f.* (**—**, *no pl.*) inclination, proneness, propensity; favour, kindness.
General [genə'ra:l], *m.* (**—s**, *pl.* **—e**, **⸚e**) general.
Generalfeldmarschall [genə'ra:lfɛlt-marʃal], *m.* (**—s**, *pl.* **⸚e**) field marshal.
Generalkommando [genə'ra:lkɔman-do], *n.* (**—s**, *pl.* **—s**) general's headquarters; (corps) headquarters.
Generalkonsul [genə'ra:lkɔnzul], *m.* (**—s**, *pl.* **—e**) consul-general.
Generalnenner [genə'ra:lnɛnər], *m.* (**—s**, *pl.* **—**) (*Maths.*) common denominator.
Generalprobe [genə'ra:lpro:bə], *f.* (**—**, *pl.* **—n**) dress-rehearsal.
Generalvollmacht [genə'ra:lfɔlmaxt], *f.* (**—**, *pl.* **—en**) (*Law*) general power of attorney.
generell [genə'rɛl], *adj.* general, common.
generös [genə'rø:s], *adj.* generous, magnanimous.
genesen [gə'ne:zən], *v.n. irr.* (*aux.* sein) recover, be restored to health; convalesce.
Genf [gɛnf], *n.* Geneva.
genial [gen'ja:l], *adj.* ingenious; extremely gifted.
Genick [gə'nɪk], *n.* (**—s**, *pl.* **—e**) nape, neck.
Genickstarre [gə'nɪkʃtarə], *f.* (**—**, *no pl.*) (*Med.*) (cerebrospinal) meningitis.
Genie [ʒe'ni:], *n.* (**—s**, *pl.* **—s**) genius.

genieren [ʒe'ni:rən], *v.a.* trouble, embarrass, disturb. — *v.r. sich* —, feel embarrassed; *sich nicht* —, make o.s. at home.
genießbar [gə'ni:sba:r], *adj.* eatable, edible, palatable; drinkable; (*fig.*) pleasant, agreeable.
genießen [gə'ni:sən], *v.a. irr.* enjoy; have the use of; (*food*) eat, partake of; *Ansehen* —, enjoy respect.
Geniestreich [ʒe'ni:ʃtraɪç], *m.* (—**s**, *pl.* —**e**) stroke of genius.
Genitiv ['ge:nɪti:f], *m.* (—**s**, *pl.* —**e**) (*Gram.*) genitive.
Genosse [gə'nɔsə], *m.* (—**n**, *pl.* —**n**) comrade, mate, colleague; (*crime*) accomplice.
Genossenschaft [gə'nɔsənʃaft], *f.* (—, *pl.* —**en**) association, company, confederacy, co-operative, union.
Genre ['ʒãrə], *n.* (—**s**, *pl.* —**s**) genre; style, kind.
Gent [gɛnt], *n.* Ghent.
Genua ['ge:nua], *n.* Genoa.
genug [gə'nu:k], *indecl. adj.* enough, sufficient; —*!* that will do!
Genüge [gə'ny:gə], *f.* (—, *no pl.*) *zur* —, sufficiently; *einem* — *leisten*, give satisfaction to s.o.
genügen [gə'ny:gən], *v.n.* be enough, suffice; *sich etwas* — *lassen*, be content with s.th.
genügsam [gə'ny:kza:m], *adj.* easily satisfied; temperate, sober.
Genügsamkeit [gə'ny:kza:mkaɪt], *f.* (—, *no pl.*) contentedness, moderation; temperateness, sobriety.
Genugtuung [gə'nu:ktuuŋ], *f.* (—, *no pl.*) satisfaction; reparation; atonement.
Genuß [gə'nus], *m.* (—**sses**, *pl.* ⁻**sse**) enjoyment; use; (*food*) consumption.
Genußmittel [gə'nusmɪtəl], *n.* (—**s**, *pl.* —) (*mostly pl.*) luxuries; (*Am.*) delicatessen.
genußreich [gə'nusraɪç], *adj.* enjoyable, delightful.
Genußsucht [gə'nussuxt], *f.* (—, *no pl.*) thirst for pleasure.
Geograph [geo'gra:f], *m.* (—**en**, *pl.* —**en**) geographer.
Geographie [geogra'fi:], *f.* (—, *no pl.*) geography.
Geologe [geo'lo:gə], *m.* (—**n**, *pl.* —**n**) geologist.
Geologie [geolo'gi:], *f.* (—, *no pl.*) geology.
Geometer [geo'me:tər], *m.* (—**s**, *pl.* —) geometrician; land-surveyor.
Geometrie [geome'tri:], *f.* (—, *no pl.*) geometry.
Georg [ge'ɔrk], *m.* George.
Georgine [geɔr'gi:nə], *f.* (—, *pl.* —**n**) (*Bot.*) dahlia.
Gepäck [gə'pɛk], *n.* (—**s**, *no pl.*) luggage; (*Am.*) baggage.
Gepäckaufbewahrung [gə'pɛkaufbəva:ruŋ], *f.* (—, *pl.* —**en**) left luggage office.
Gepäckträger [gə'pɛktrɛ:gər], *m.* (—**s**, *pl.* —) porter.
Gepflogenheit [gə'pflo:gənhaɪt], *f.* (—, *pl.* —**en**) habit, custom, wont.
Geplänkel [gə'plɛnkəl], *n.* (—**s**, *pl.* —) (*rare*) skirmish.
Geplärr [gə'plɛr], *n.* (—**s**, *no pl.*) bawling.
Geplauder [gə'plaudər], *n.* (—**s**, *no pl.*) chatting; small talk.
Gepräge [gə'prɛ:gə], *n.* (—**s**, *no pl.*) impression, stamp.
Gepränge [gə'prɛŋə], *n.* (—**s**, *no pl.*) pomp, ceremony, splendour.
Ger [ge:r], *m.* (—**s**, *pl.* —**e**) (*rare*) spear, javelin.
Gerade [gə'ra:də], *f.* (—**n**, *pl.* —**n**) (*Maths.*) straight line.
gerade [gə'ra:də], *adj.* straight, direct, erect, even; (*fig.*) upright, honest. — *adv.* quite, just; *jetzt* —, now more than ever; *fünf* — *sein lassen*, stretch a point; — *heraus*, in plain terms.
geradeaus [gə'ra:dəaus], *adv.* straight on.
gerädert [gə'rɛ:dərt], *adj.* (*fig.*) fatigued, exhausted, worn out.
geradeswegs [gə'ra:dəsve:ks], *adv.* straightaway, immediately.
geradezu [gə'ra:dətsu:], *adv.* frankly, downright; *das ist* — *scheußlich*, this is downright nasty.
Geradheit [gə'ra:thaɪt], *f.* (—, *no pl.*) straightness; (*fig.*) straightforwardness.
geradlinig [gə'ra:tlɪnɪç], *adj.* rectilinear.
geradsinnig [gə'ra:tzɪnɪç], *adj.* honest, upright.
gerändert [gə'rɛndərt], *adj.* with a milled edge.
Geranie [gə'ra:njə], *f.* (—, *pl.* —**n**) (*Bot.*) geranium.
Gerät [gə'rɛ:t], *n.* (—**s**, *pl.* —**e**) tool, implement, device; appliance; (radio, television) set; apparatus.
geraten [gə'ra:tən], *v.n. irr.* (*aux.* sein) turn out; *gut* —, turn out well; — *auf*, come upon.
Geräteturnen [gə'rɛ:təturnən], *n.* (—**s**, *no pl.*) gymnastics with apparatus.
Geratewohl [gə'ra:təvo:l], *n.* (—**s**, *no pl.*) *aufs* —, at random.
geraum [gə'raum], *adj.* —*e Zeit*, a long time.
geräumig [gə'rɔymɪç], *adj.* spacious, large, wide, roomy.
Geräusch [gə'rɔyʃ], *n.* (—**es**, *pl.* —**e**) noise; sound.
gerben ['gɛrbən], *v.a.* tan, taw; *einem die Haut* —, give s.o. a hiding.
Gerber ['gɛrbər], *m.* (—**s**, *pl.* —) tanner.
Gerbsäure ['gɛrpsɔyrə], *f.* (—, *no pl.*) tannin.
gerecht [gə'rɛçt], *adj.* just, fair; (*Bibl.*) righteous; *einem* — *werden*, do justice to s.o.
Gerechtigkeit [gə'rɛçtɪçkaɪt], *f.* (—, *no pl.*) justice, fairness; (*Bibl.*) righteousness.

Gerede [gə're:də], *n.* (**—s**, *no pl.*) talk, rumour, gossip.
gereichen [gə'raIçən], *v.n.* turn out to be; *einem zur Ehre* —, redound to s.o.'s honour.
gereizt [gə'raItst], *adj.* irritated, annoyed.
gereuen [gə'rɔyən] *see* **reuen.**
Gerhard ['ge:rhart], *m.* Gerard, Gerald.
Gericht [gə'rIçt], *n.* (**—s,** *pl.* **—e**) court of justice, tribunal; (*food*) course, dish; *das Jüngste* —, Last Judgment.
gerichtlich [gə'rIçtlIç], *adj.* judicial, legal; *einen — belangen*, sue s.o.
Gerichtsbarkeit [gə'rIçtsbarkaIt], *f.* (—, *no pl.*) jurisdiction.
Gerichtsdiener [gə'rIçtsdi:nər], *m.* (**—s,** *pl.* —) (*law court*) usher.
Gerichtshof [gə'rIçtsho:f], *m.* (**—es,** *pl.* **¨e**) court of justice.
Gerichtskanzlei [gə'rIçtskantslaI], *f.* (—, *pl.* **—en**) record office.
Gerichtskosten [gə'rIçtskɔstən], *f. pl.* (*Law*) costs.
Gerichtsordnung [gə'rIçtsɔrdnuŋ], *f.* (—, *pl* **—en**) legal procedure.
Gerichtstermin [gə'rIçtstɛrmi:n], *m.* (**—s,** *pl.* **—e**) day fixed for a hearing.
Gerichtsverhandlung [gə'rIçtsfɛrhandluŋ], *f.* (—, *pl.* **—en**) hearing; trial.
Gerichtsvollzieher [gə'rIçtsfɔltsi:ər], *m.* (**—s,** *pl.* —) bailiff.
gerieben [gə'ri:bən], *adj.* ground; crafty, cunning.
gering [gə'rIŋ], *adj.* small, little, mean, petty, unimportant, of little value, trifling; low, base.
geringfügig [gə'rIŋfy:gIç], *adj.* small, petty, insignificant.
geringschätzig [gə'rIŋʃɛtsIç], *adj.* contemptuous, disdainful, supercilious; derogatory.
gerinnen [gə'rInən], *v.n. irr.* (*aux.* sein) coagulate, clot; curdle.
Gerinnsel [gə'rInzəl], *n.* (**—s,** *pl.* —) embolism (of the blood); clot.
Gerippe [gə'rIpə], *n.* (**—s,** *pl.* —) skeleton; frame; (*Aviat.*) air-frame.
gerippt [gə'rIpt], *adj.* ribbed, fluted.
gerissen [gə'rIsən], *adj.* (*coll.*) sharp, cunning.
Germane [gɛr'ma:nə], *m.* (**—n,** *pl.* **—n**) Teuton.
Germanist ['gɛrmanIst], *m.* (**—en,** *pl.* **— en**) (*Univ.*) student of *or* expert in German language and/or literature.
gern [gɛrn], *adv.* gladly, willingly, readily, with pleasure; — *haben*, like.
Geröll [gə'rœl], *n.* (**—s,** *no pl.*) boulders, rubble.
Gerste ['gɛrstə], *f.* (—, *no pl.*) (*Bot.*) barley.
Gerstenschleim ['gɛrstənʃlaIm], *m.* (**—s,** *no pl.*) barley water.
Gerte ['gɛrtə], *f.* (—, *pl.* **—n**) whip, switch, rod.
Geruch [gə'ru:x], *m.* (**—s,** *pl.* **¨e**) smell, odour, scent; *guter* —, fragrance, aroma.
geruchlos [gə'ru:xlo:s], *adj.* scentless, odourless, without smell.
Geruchsinn [gə'ru:xzIn], *m.* (**—es,** *no pl.*) sense of smell.
Gerücht [gə'ryçt], *n.* (**—s,** *pl.* **—e**) rumour, report.
Gerümpel [gə'rympəl], *n.* (**—s,** *no pl.*) lumber, trash.
Gerundium [gə'rundjum], *n.* (**—s,** *pl.* **—dien**) (*Gram.*) gerund.
Gerüst [gə'ryst], *n.* (**—es,** *pl.* **—e**) scaffolding.
Ges [gɛs], *n.* (—, *pl.* —) (*Mus.*) G flat.
gesamt [gə'zamt], *adj.* entire, all, complete.
Gesamtheit [gə'zamthaIt], *f.* (—, *no pl.*) totality.
Gesandte [gə'zantə], *m.* (**—n,** *pl.* **—n**) messenger; ambassador, envoy; *päpstlicher* —, papal nuncio.
Gesandtschaft [gə'zantʃaft], *f.* (—, *pl.* **—en**) embassy, legation.
Gesang [gə'zaŋ], *m.* (**—s,** *pl.* **¨e**) song, air; hymn; (*Lit.*) canto.
Gesangbuch [gə'zaŋbu:x], *n.* (**—s,** *pl.* **¨er**) hymnal, hymn-book.
Gesäß [gə'zɛ:s], *n.* (**—es,** *pl.* **—e**) seat, buttocks.
Geschäft [gə'ʃɛft], *n.* (**—s,** *pl.* **—e**) business; trade, commerce; affairs; occupation; shop; (*Am.*) store.
geschäftig [gə'ʃɛftIç], *adj.* active, bustling, busy.
geschäftlich [gə'ʃɛftlIç], *adj.* concerning business. — *adv.* on business.
Geschäftsführer [gə'ʃɛftsfy:rər], *m.* (**—s,** *pl.* —) manager.
Geschäftshaus [gə'ʃɛftshaus], *n.* (**—es,** *pl.* **¨er**) firm; business premises.
geschäftskundig [gə'ʃɛftskundIç], *adj.* experienced in business.
Geschäftslokal [gə'ʃɛftsloka:l], *n.* (**—s,** *pl.* **—e**) business premises, shop.
Geschäftsordnung [gə'ʃɛftsɔrdnuŋ], *f.* (—, *pl.* **—en**) standing orders; agenda.
Geschäftsträger [gə'ʃɛftstrɛ:gər], *m.* (**—s,** *pl.* —) (*Comm.*) agent; (*Pol.*) chargé d'affaires.
Geschäftsverkehr [gə'ʃɛftsfɛrke:r], *m.* (**—s,** *no pl.*) business dealings.
Geschehen [gə'ʃe:ən], *n.* (**—s,** *no pl.*) happening.
geschehen [gə'ʃe:ən], *v.n. irr.* (*aux.* sein) happen, occur; take place; be done; *das geschieht dir recht*, it serves you right.
gescheit [gə'ʃaIt], *adj.* clever, intelligent.
Geschenk [gə'ʃɛŋk], *n.* (**—s,** *pl.* **—e**) gift, present, donation.
Geschichte [gə'ʃIçtə], *f.* (—, *pl.* **—n**) tale; story; history.
Geschichtenbuch [gə'ʃIçtənbu:x], *n.* (**—es,** *pl.* **¨er**) story-book.
geschichtlich [gə'ʃIçtlIç], *adj.* historical.
Geschichtsschreiber [gə'ʃIçtsʃraIbər], *m.* (**—s,** *pl.* —) historian.
Geschick [gə'ʃIk], *n.* (**—es,** *no pl.*) fate, destiny; dexterity, skill, knack, aptitude.

Geschicklichkeit [gəˈʃɪklɪçkaɪt], *f.* (—, *pl.* —**en**) dexterity, adroitness, skill.
geschickt [gəˈʃɪkt], *adj.* skilled, skilful, clever, able.
Geschirr [gəˈʃɪr], *n.*(—**s**,*no pl.*) crockery, plates and dishes; (*horses*) harness.
Geschlecht [gəˈʃlɛçt], *n.* (—**s**, *pl.* —**er**) sex; kind, race, species, extraction, family; (*Gram.*) gender.
geschlechtlich [gəˈʃlɛçtlɪç], *adj.* sexual; generic.
Geschlechtsart [gəˈʃlɛçtsa:rt], *f.* (—, *pl.* —**en**) generic character.
Geschlechtskrankheit [gəˈʃlɛçtskraŋkhaɪt], *f.* (—, *pl.* —**en**) venereal disease.
Geschlechtskunde [gəˈʃlɛçtskundə], *f.* (—, *no pl.*) genealogy.
Geschlechtsreife [gəˈʃlɛçtsraɪfə], *f.* (—, *no pl.*) puberty.
Geschlechtsteile [gəˈʃlɛçtstaɪlə], *m. pl.* genitals.
Geschlechtstrieb [gəˈʃlɛçtstri:p], *m.* (—**s**, *no pl.*) sexual instinct.
Geschlechtswort [gəˈʃlɛçtsvɔrt], *n.* (—**s**, *pl.* ¨—**er**) (*Gram.*) article.
geschliffen [gəˈʃlɪfən], *adj.* polished; (*glass*) cut.
Geschmack [gəˈʃmak], *m.* (—**s**, *pl.* ¨—**er**) taste, flavour.
geschmacklos [gəˈʃmaklo:s], *adj.* tasteless, insipid; in bad taste.
Geschmacksrichtung [gəˈʃmaksrɪçtuŋ], *f.* (—, *pl.* —**en**) prevailing taste; vogue; tendency.
Geschmeide [gəˈʃmaɪdə], *n.* (—**s**, *pl.* —) jewels, jewellery; trinkets.
geschmeidig [gəˈʃmaɪdɪç], *adj.* flexible, pliant, supple; (*Tech.*) malleable.
Geschmeiß [gəˈʃmaɪs], *n.* (—**es**, *no pl.*) dung; vermin; (*fig.*) rabble.
Geschnatter [gəˈʃnatər], *n.* (—**s**, *no pl.*) cackling.
geschniegelt [gəˈʃni:gəlt], *adj.* spruce, dressed up.
Geschöpf [gəˈʃœpf], *n.* (—**es**, *pl.* —**e**) creature.
Geschoß [gəˈʃɔs], *n.* (—**sses**, *pl.* —**sse**) shot, shell, projectile, missile; (*house*) storey.
geschraubt [gəˈʃraupt], *adj.* (*style*) stilted, affected.
Geschrei [gəˈʃraɪ], *n.* (—**s**, *no pl.*) shrieking, shouting, screaming; (*fig.*) stir, great noise.
Geschreibsel [gəˈʃraɪpsəl], *n.* (—**s**, *no pl.*) scrawl, scribbling.
Geschütz [gəˈʃyts], *n.* (—**es**, *pl.* —**e**) artillery, guns; *schweres — auffahren*, bring o.'s. guns into play.
Geschützweite [gəˈʃytsvaɪtə], *f.* (—, *no pl.*) calibre.
Geschwader [gəˈʃva:dər], *n.* (—**s**, *pl.*—) squadron.
Geschwätz [gəˈʃvɛts], *n.* (—**es**, *no pl.*) chatter, gossip, prattle, tittle-tattle.
geschweige [gəˈʃvaɪgə], *adv.* let alone, to say nothing of.
geschwind [gəˈʃvɪnt], *adj.* quick, nimble, fast, swift, fleet.
Geschwindigkeitsmesser [gəˈʃvɪndɪçkaɪtsmɛsər], *m.* (—**s**, *pl.* —) (*Motor.*) speedometer.
Geschwister [gəˈʃvɪstər], *pl.* brothers and sisters.
geschwollen [gəˈʃvɔlən], *adj.* stilted, turgid, pompous.
Geschworene [gəˈʃvo:rənə], *m.* (—**n**, *pl.* —**n**), juror, juryman; (*pl.*) jury.
Geschwulst [gəˈʃvulst], *f.* (—, *pl.* ¨—**e**) swelling, tumour.
Geschwür [gəˈʃvy:r], *n.* (—**s**, *pl.* —**e**) sore, ulcer, abscess.
Geselle [gəˈzɛlə], *m.* (—**n**, *pl.* —**n**) journeyman; companion, comrade, mate.
gesellen [gəˈzɛlən], *v.a.*, *v.r.* join, associate with, keep company with.
gesellig [gəˈzɛlɪç], *adj.* sociable, companionable; gregarious.
Gesellschaft [gəˈzɛlʃaft], *f.* (—, *pl.* —**en**) society; community; (formal) party; company, club; *geschlossene —*, private party; *einem — leisten*, keep s.o. company; (*Comm.*) *— mit beschränkter Haftung*, (abbr.) *GmbH*, limited company, (*abbr.*) Ltd.
gesellschaftlich [gəˈzɛlʃaftlɪç], *adj.* social.
Gesellschaftsanzug [gəˈzɛlʃaftsantsu:k], *m.* (—**s**, *pl.* ¨—**e**) evening dress.
Gesellschaftsspiel [gəˈzɛlʃaftsʃpi:l], *n.* (—**s**, *pl.* —**e**) round game, party game.
Gesellschaftsvertrag [gəˈzɛlʃaftsfɛrtra:k], *m.* (—**es**, *pl.* ¨—**e**) (*Law*) partnership agreement; deed of partnership.
Gesellschaftszimmer [gəˈzɛlʃaftstsɪmər], *n.* (—**s**, *pl.* —) drawing-room, reception room.
Gesetz [gəˈzɛts], *n.* (—**es**, *pl.* —**e**) law, statute, regulation.
Gesetzbuch [gəˈzɛtsbu:x], *n.* (—**es**, *pl.* ¨—**er**) code of laws; statute book.
Gesetzentwurf [gəˈzɛtsɛntvurf], *m.* (—**es**, *pl.* ¨—**er**) (*Parl.*) draft bill.
gesetzgebend [gəˈzɛtsge:bənt], *adj.* legislative.
gesetzlich [gəˈzɛtslɪç], *adj.* lawful, legal.
Gesetzlichkeit [gəˈzɛtslɪçkaɪt], *f.* (—, *no pl.*) lawfulness, legality.
gesetzlos [gəˈzɛtslo:s], *adj.* lawless, anarchical.
gesetzmäßig [gəˈzɛtsmɛ:sɪç], *adj.* conforming to law, lawful, legitimate.
gesetzt [gəˈzɛtst], *adj.* steady, sedate, staid; *von —em Alter*, of mature age; *— daß*, supposing that.
Gesetztheit [gəˈzɛtsthaɪt], *f.* (—, *no pl.*) sedateness, steadiness.
gesetzwidrig [gəˈzɛtsvi:drɪç], *adj.* illegal, unlawful.
Gesicht (1) [gəˈzɪçt], *n.* (—**s**, *pl.* —**er**) face, physiognomy, look.
Gesicht (2) [gəˈzɪçt], *n.* (—**s**, *pl.* —**e**) sight; vision, apparition.
Gesichtsausdruck [gəˈzɪçtsausdruk], *m.* (—**s**, *no pl.*) face, mien; expression.

Gesichtsfeld [gəˈzɪçtsfɛlt], *n.* (**—es,** *pl.* **—er**) field of vision.
Gesichtskreis [gəˈzɪçtskraɪs], *m.* (**—es,** *pl.* **—e**) horizon.
Gesichtspunkt [gəˈzɪçtspuŋkt], *m.* (**—es,** *pl.* **—e**) point of view.
Gesichtszug [gəˈzɪçtstsu:k], *m.* (**—s,** *pl.* **¨—e**) feature.
Gesims [gəˈzɪms], *n.* (**—es,** *pl.* **—e**) cornice, moulding, ledge.
Gesinde [gəˈzɪndə], *n.* (**—s,** *no pl.*) (domestic) servants.
Gesindel [gəˈzɪndəl], *n.* (**—s,** *no pl.*) mob, rabble.
gesinnt [gəˈzɪnt], *adj.* disposed.
Gesinnung [gəˈzɪnuŋ], *f.* (—, *pl.* **—en**) disposition, sentiment; conviction.
gesinnungslos [gəˈzɪnuŋslo:s], *adj.* unprincipled.
gesinnungstreu [gəˈzɪnuŋstrɔy], *adj.* loyal, staunch.
Gesinnungswechsel [gəˈzɪnuŋsvɛksəl], *m.* (**—s,** *no pl.*) change of opinion, volte-face.
gesittet [gəˈzɪtət], *adj.* civilised, well-mannered.
Gesittung [gəˈzɪtuŋ], *f.* (—, *no pl.*) (*rare*) civilisation, good manners.
gesonnen [gəˈzɔnən] *see* **gesinnt.**
Gespann [gəˈʃpan], *n.* (**—s,** *pl.* **—e**) team, yoke (oxen etc.).
gespannt [gəˈʃpant], *adj.* stretched; intense, thrilled; tense; filled with suspense.
Gespanntheit [gəˈʃpanthaɪt], *f.* (—, *no pl.*) tension, strain, suspense.
Gespenst [gəˈʃpɛnst], *n.* (**—es,** *pl.* **—er**) ghost, spectre, apparition.
gespenstisch [gəˈʃpɛnstɪʃ], *adj.* ghostly, spectral.
Gespiele [gəˈʃpi:lə], *m.* (**—n,** *pl.* **—n**) playmate.
Gespielin [gəˈʃpi:lɪn], *f.* (—, *pl.* **—innen**) (girl) playmate.
Gespinst [gəˈʃpɪnst], *n.* (**—es,** *pl.* **—e**) web.
Gespött [gəˈʃpœt], *n.* (**—s,** *no pl.*) mocking, mockery, jeering, derision; (*fig.*) laughing stock.
Gespräch [gəˈʃprɛ:ç], *n.* (**—s,** *pl.* **—e**) conversation, discourse, talk; (*phone*) call; *ein — anknüpfen*, start a conversation.
gesprächig [gəˈʃprɛ:çɪç], *adj.* talkative, communicative.
gespreizt [gəˈʃpraɪtst], *adj.* wide apart; (*fig.*) affected, pompous.
gesprenkelt [gəˈʃprɛŋkəlt], *adj.* speckled.
gesprungen [gəˈʃpruŋən], *adj.* cracked (glass etc.).
Gestade [gəˈʃta:də], *n.* (**—s,** *pl.* **—**) shore, coast, bank.
Gestalt [gəˈʃtalt], *f.* (—. *pl.* **—en**) form, figure, shape; configuration; stature; fashion; manner, way.
gestalten [gəˈʃtaltən], *v.a.* form, shape, fashion, make. — *v.r. sich* —, turn out.
Gestaltung [gəˈʃtaltuŋ], *f.* (—, *pl.* **—en**) formation; arrangement; planning.
geständig [gəˈʃtɛndɪç], *adj.* confessing; — *sein*, confess.
Geständnis [gəˈʃtɛntnɪs], *n.* (**—ses,** *pl.* **—se**) confession, admission.
Gestank [gəˈʃtaŋk], *m.* (**—s,** *no pl.*) stink, stench.
gestatten [gəˈʃtatən], *v.a.* permit, allow, grant; *wir — uns*, we beg leave to; — *Sie !* pardon me, excuse me.
Geste [ˈgɛstə], *f.* (—, *pl.* **—n**) gesture, gesticulation.
gestehen [gəˈʃte:ən], *v.a. irr.* confess, admit, own; *offen gestanden*, quite frankly.
Gestein [gəˈʃtaɪn], *n.* (**—s,** *pl.* **—e**) (*Poet.*) rock; (*Geol.*) rocks, minerals.
Gestell [gəˈʃtɛl], *n.* (**—s,** *pl.* **—e**) rack, frame; (*table*) trestle; (*books*) stand.
Gestellung [gəˈʃtɛluŋ], *f.* (—, *no pl.*) (*Mil.*) reporting for service.
gestern [ˈgɛstərn], *adv.* yesterday; — *abend*, last night.
gestiefelt [gəˈʃti:fəlt], *adj.* booted; *der —e Kater*, Puss in Boots.
gestielt [gəˈʃti:lt], *adj.* (*axe*) helved; (*Bot.*) stalked, stemmed.
gestikulieren [gɛstikuˈli:rən], *v.n.* gesticulate.
Gestirn [gəˈʃtɪrn], *n.* (**—s,** *pl.* **—e**) star, constellation.
gestirnt [gəˈʃtɪrnt], *adj.* starred, starry.
Gestöber [gəˈʃtø:bər], *n.* (**—s,** *pl.* **—**) (*snow, dust*) drift, storm, blizzard.
Gesträuch [gəˈʃtrɔyç], *n.* (**—es,** *no pl.*) bushes, shrubs; thicket.
gestreift [gəˈʃtraɪft], *adj.* striped.
gestreng [gəˈʃtrɛŋ], *adj.* (*obs.*) strict, severe.
gestrig [ˈgɛstrɪç], *adj.* of yesterday.
Gestrüpp [gəˈʃtryp], *n.* (**—s,** *no pl.*) bushes, underwood, shrubs, shrubbery.
Gestüt [gəˈʃty:t], *n.* (**—s,** *pl.* **—e**) stud (-farm).
Gestüthengst [gəˈʃty:thɛŋst], *m.* (**—es,** *pl.* **—e**) stallion.
Gesuch [gəˈzu:x], *n.* (**—s,** *pl.* **—e**) petition, request, application.
gesucht [gəˈzu:xt], *adj.* in demand; (*style*) far-fetched; affected; studied.
gesund [gəˈzunt], *adj.* healthy, wholesome; *der —e Menschenverstand*, common sense.
Gesundbrunnen [gəˈzuntbrunən], *m.* (**—s,** *pl.* **—**) mineral waters; spa.
gesunden [gəˈzundən], *v.n.* (*aux.* sein) recover o.'s health.
Gesundheit [gəˈzunthaɪt], *f.* (—, *no pl.*) health.
Gesundheitslehre [gəˈzunthaɪtsle:rə], *f.* (—, *no pl.*) hygiene.
Getäfel [gəˈtɛ:fəl], *n.* (**—s,** *no pl.*) wainscot, wainscoting, panelling.
Getändel [gəˈtɛndəl], *n.* (**—s,** *no pl.*) (*rare*) flirting, dallying.
Getier [gəˈti:r], *n.* (**—s,** *no pl.*) (*collective term*) animals.
Getöse [gəˈtø:zə], *n.* (**—s,** *no pl.*) loud noise, din.

Getränk [gə'trɛŋk], *n.* (**—s**, *pl.* **—e**) drink, beverage.
getrauen [gə'trauən], *v.r. sich* —, dare, venture.
Getreide [gə'traɪdə], *n.* (**—s**, *pl.* —) corn, grain.
getreu [gə'trɔy], *adj.* faithful, true, loyal.
getreulich [gə'trɔylɪç], *adv.* faithfully, truly, loyally.
Getriebe [gə'tri:bə], *n.* (**—s**, *pl.* —) machinery; (*Motor.*) gear; drive; *das — der Welt*, the bustle of life.
getrieben [gə'tri:bən], *adj.* (*Tech.*) chased (work.)
Getrödel [gə'trø:dəl], *n.* (**—s**, *no pl.*) dawdling.
getrost [gə'tro:st], *adj.* confident, cheerful; — *sein*, be of good cheer.
Getto ['gɛto], *n.* (**—s**, *pl.* **—s**) ghetto.
Getue [gə'tu:ə], *n.* (**—s**, *no pl.*) pretence, fuss.
Getümmel [gə'tyməl], *n.* (**—s**, *no pl.*) bustle, turmoil.
geübt [gə'y:pt], *adj.* skilled, versed.
Geübtheit [gə'y:pthaɪt], *f.* (—, *no pl.*) skill, experience, dexterity.
Gevatter [gə'fatər], *m.* (**—s**, *pl.* —) (*obs.*) godfather.
gevierteilt [gə'fi:rtaɪlt], *adj.* quartered.
Gewächs [gə'vɛks], *n.* (**—es**, *pl.* **—e**) plant, growth; (*Med.*) excrescence.
gewachsen [gə'vaksən], *adj. einem* (*einer Sache*) *— sein*, be equal to s.o. (s.th.).
Gewächshaus [gə'vɛkshaus], *n.* (**—es**, *pl.* **⸚er**) green-house, hot-house, conservatory.
gewagt [gə'va:kt], *adj.* risky, hazardous; daring.
gewählt [gə'vɛ:lt], *adj.* choice, select.
gewahr [gə'va:r], *adj. einer Sache — werden*, become aware of s.th., perceive s.th.
Gewähr [gə'vɛ:r], *f.* (—, *no pl.*) surety; guarantee; warranty; — *leisten*, guarantee.
gewahren [gə'va:rən], *v.a.* perceive, see, become aware of.
gewähren [gə'vɛ:rən], *v.a.* allow, grant; *einen — lassen*, let s.o. do as he pleases, let be.
Gewährleistung [gə'vɛ:rlaɪstuŋ], *f.* (—, *pl.* **—en**) grant of security (*or* bail); guarantee.
Gewahrsam [gə'va:rza:m], *m.* (**—s**, *no pl.*) safe-keeping, custody.
Gewährsmann [gə'vɛ:rsman], *m.* (**—es**, *pl.* **⸚er**) authority; informant.
Gewährung [gə'vɛ:ruŋ,] *f.* (—, *no pl.*) granting (of request).
Gewalt [gə'valt], *f.* (—, *pl.* **—en**) power, force, might; authority; violence; *höhere* —, (*Law*) act of God, force majeure; *sich in der — haben*, have control over o.s.
Gewalthaber [gə'valtha:bər], *m.* (**—s**, *pl.* —) tyrant; despot, autocrat; person in authority.
gewaltig [gə'valtɪç], *adj.* powerful, mighty, enormous, stupendous.
gewaltsam [gə'valtza:m], *adj.* forcible, violent.
Gewaltstreich [gə'valtʃtraɪç], *m.* (**—s**, *pl.* **—e**) bold stroke; coup d'état.
Gewalttat [gə'valtta:t], *f.* (—, *pl.* **—en**) violent action, violence, outrage.
gewalttätig [gə'valttɛ:tɪç], *adj.* violent, fierce, outrageous.
Gewand [gə'vant], *n.* (**—es**, *pl.* **⸚er**) (*Lit.*) garment, dress; (*Eccl.*) vestment.
gewandt [gə'vant], *adj.* nimble, deft, clever; (*mind*) versatile.
gewärtig [gə'vɛrtɪç], *adj. einer Sache — sein*, expect s.th. to happen.
Gewäsch [gə'vɛʃ], *n.* (**—es**, *no pl.*) stuff and nonsense; rubbish.
Gewässer [gə'vɛsər], *n.* (**—s**, *pl.* —) waters.
Gewebe [gə've:bə], *n.* (**—s**, *pl.* —) (*Physiol.*, *Text.*) tissue; web, weft, texture.
geweckt [gə'vɛkt], *adj.* smart, wide-awake.
Gewehr [gə've:r], *n.* (**—s**, *pl.* **—e**) gun, fire-arm, rifle.
Gewehrlauf [gə've:rlauf], *m.* (**—s**, *pl.* **⸚e**) barrel.
Geweih [gə'vaɪ], *n.* (**—s**, *pl.* **—e**) horns, antlers.
geweiht [gə'vaɪt], *adj.* consecrated; holy.
gewellt [gə'vɛlt], *adj.* corrugated, wavy.
Gewerbe [gə'vɛrbə], *n.* (**—s**, *pl.* —) trade, profession, business; calling; industry.
Gewerbekunde [gə'vɛrbəkundə], *f.* (—, *no pl.*) technology.
Gewerbeschein [gə'vɛrbəʃaɪn], *m.* (**—s**, *pl.* **—e**) trade-licence.
gewerblich [gə'vɛrplɪç], *adj.* industrial.
gewerbsmäßig [gə'vɛrpsmɛ:sɪç], *adj.* professional.
Gewerkschaft [gə'vɛrkʃaft], *f.* (—, *pl.* **—en**) trade union.
Gewicht [gə'vɪçt], *n.* (**—s**, *pl.* **—e**) weight; *schwer ins — fallen*, carry great weight, weigh heavily.
gewichtig [gə'vɪçtɪç], *adj.* weighty, ponderous; (*fig.*) momentous, important, strong.
gewiegt [gə'vi:kt], *adj.* experienced, clever.
gewillt [gə'vɪlt], *adj.* willing.
Gewimmel [gə'vɪməl], *n.* (**—s**, *no pl.*) milling crowd, swarm, throng.
Gewinde [gə'vɪndə], *n.* (**—s**, *pl.* —) (*screw*) thread; (*flowers*) garland.
Gewinn [gə'vɪn], *m.* (**—s**, *pl.* **—e**) gain, profit; (*lottery*) prize; (*gambling*) winnings.
gewinnen [gə'vɪnən], *v.a. irr.* win, gain, obtain, get, earn.
gewinnend [gə'vɪnənt], *adj.* prepossessing; engaging.
Gewinnung [gə'vɪnuŋ], *f.* (—, *no pl.*) (*Ind.*, *Chem.*) extraction; output, production.
Gewinsel [gə'vɪnzəl], *n.* (**—s**, *no pl.*) whimpering.

Gewinst [gə'vɪnst], *m.* (—**es**, *pl.* —**e**) (*obs.*) gain, profit.
Gewirr [gə'vɪr], *n.* (—**s**, *no pl.*) entanglement, confusion.
gewiß [gə'vɪs], *adj.* (*Genit.*) certain, sure. — *adv.* indeed.
Gewissen [gə'vɪsən], *n.* (—**s**, *no pl.*) conscience.
gewissenhaft [gə'vɪsənhaft], *adj.* conscientious, scrupulous.
gewissenlos [gə'vɪsənlo:s], *adj.* unscrupulous.
Gewissensbiß [gə'vɪsənsbɪs], *m.* (—**sses**, *pl.* —**sse**) (*mostly pl.*) pangs of conscience.
gewissermaßen [gə'vɪsərma:sən], *adv.* to a certain extent, so to speak.
Gewißheit [gə'vɪshaɪt], *f.* (—, *no pl.*) certainty.
gewißlich [gə'vɪslɪç], *adv.* surely.
Gewitter [gə'vɪtər], *n.* (—**s**, *pl.* —) thunderstorm.
gewittern [gə'vɪtərn], *v.n.* thunder.
gewitzigt, gewitzt [gə'vɪtsɪçt, gə'vɪtst], *adj.* knowing, clever; shrewd.
gewogen [gə'vo:gən], *adj.* kindly disposed, favourable; *einem — sein*, be favourably inclined towards s.o.
Gewogenheit [gə'vo:gənhaɪt], *f.* (—, *no pl.*) kindness, favour.
gewöhnen [gə'vø:nən], *v.a.* accustom to. — *v.r. sich — an*, get used to, accustom o.s. to.
Gewohnheit [gə'vo:nhaɪt], *f.* (—, *pl.* —**en**) (*general*) custom, usage; (*personal*) habit.
gewohnheitsmäßig [gə'vo:nhaɪtsmɛ:sɪç], *adj.* habitual. — *adv.* by force of habit.
Gewohnheitsrecht [gə'vo:nhaɪtsrɛçt], *n.* (—**s**, *no pl.*) common law.
gewöhnlich [gə'vø:nlɪç], *adj.* customary, usual; (*fig.*) common, mean, vulgar.
gewohnt [gə'vo:nt], *adj.* accustomed to, used to.
Gewöhnung [gə'vø:nuŋ], *f.* (—, *no pl.*) habit, use, habituation.
Gewölbe [gə'vœlbə], *n.* (—**s**, *pl.* —) vault, arch.
Gewölk [gə'vœlk], *n.* (—**s**, *no pl.*) clouds, cloud formation.
Gewühl [gə'vy:l], *n.* (—**s**, *no pl.*) crowd, throng, bustle.
gewunden [gə'vundən], *adj.* tortuous.
Gewürm [gə'vyrm], *n.* (—**s**, *no pl.*) reptiles, worms; vermin.
Gewürz [gə'vyrts], *n.* (—**es**, *pl.* —**e**) spice.
Gewürznelke [gə'vyrtsnɛlkə], *f.* (—, *pl.* —**n**) clove.
Gezänk [gə'tsɛŋk], *n.* (—**s**, *no pl.*) quarrelling, bickering.
Gezeiten [gə'tsaɪtən], *f. pl.* tides.
Gezeter [gə'tse:tər], *n.* (—**s**, *no pl.*) screaming, yelling; (*fig.*) outcry.
geziemen [gə'tsi:mən], *v.r. sich für einen —*, befit *or* become s.o.
geziert [gə'tsi:rt], *adj.* affected.
Gezischel [gə'tsɪʃəl], *n.* (—**s**, *no pl.*) whispering.
Gezücht [gə'tsyçt], *n.* (—**s**, *no pl.*) brood, breed.
Gezweig [gə'tsvaɪk], *n.* (—**s**, *no pl.*) branches, boughs.
Gezwitscher [gə'tsvɪtʃər], *n.* (—**s**, *no pl.*) chirping.
Gezwungenheit [gə'tsvuŋənhaɪt], *f.* (—, *no pl.*) constraint.
Gicht [gɪçt], *f.* (—, *no pl.*) (*Med.*) gout.
gichtbrüchig ['gɪçtbryçɪç], *adj.* (*obs.*) paralytic; gouty.
gichtig ['gɪçtɪç], *adj.* gouty.
Giebel ['gi:bəl], *m.* (—**s**, *pl.* —) gable.
Giebelfenster ['gi:bəlfɛnstər], *n.* (—**s**, *pl.*—) gable-window, dormer-window.
gieb(e)lig ['gi:b(ə)lɪç], *adj.* gabled.
Gier [gi:r], *f.* (—, *no pl.*) greediness, eagerness.
gieren ['gi:rən], *v.n.* (*rare*) — *nach*, thirst for, yearn for.
gierig ['gi:rɪç], *adj.* eager, greedy.
Gießbach ['gi:sbax], *m.* (—**s**, *pl.* ⸚**e**) mountain-torrent.
gießen ['gi:sən], *v.a. irr.* (*liquids*) pour, shed; (*metal*) cast, found.
Gießer ['gi:sər], *m.* (—**s**, *pl.* —) founder.
Gießerei [gi:sə'raɪ], *f.* (—, *pl.* —**en**) foundry.
Gießform ['gi:sfɔrm], *f.* (—, *pl.* —**en**) casting-mould.
Gießkanne ['gi:skanə], *f.* (—, *pl.* —**n**) watering-can.
Gift [gɪft], *n.* (—**es**, *pl.* —**e**) poison, venom; (*fig.*) virulence; (*coll.*) *darauf kannst du — nehmen*, you can bet your life on it.
Giftbaum ['gɪftbaum], *m.* (—**s**, *pl.* ⸚**e**) upas-tree.
Giftdrüse ['gɪftdry:zə], *f.* (—, *pl.* —**n**) poison-gland.
giftig ['gɪftɪç], *adj.* poisonous; (*fig.*) venomous; (*Med.*) toxic.
Giftlehre ['gɪftle:rə], *f.* (—, *no pl.*) toxicology.
Giftpilz ['gɪftpɪlts], *m.* (—**es**, *pl.* —**e**) poisonous toadstool.
Giftschlange ['gɪftʃlaŋə], *f.* (—, *pl.* —**n**) poisonous snake.
Giftstoff ['gɪftʃtɔf], *m.* (—**es**, *pl.* —**e**) poison, virus.
Gigant [gɪ'gant], *m.* (—**en**, *pl.* —**en**) giant.
Gigerl ['gɪ:gərl], *m.* (—**s**, *pl.* —) (*Austr. dial.*) fop, coxcomb.
Gilde ['gɪldə], *f.* (—, *pl.* —**n**) guild, corporation.
Gimpel ['gɪmpəl], *m.* (—**s**, *pl.* —) (*Orn.*) bullfinch, chaffinch; (*fig.*) simpleton.
Ginster ['gɪnstər], *m.* (—**s**, *no pl.*) (*Bot.*) gorse, furze, broom.
Gipfel ['gɪpfəl], *m.* (—**s**, *pl.* —) summit, peak; (*fig.*) acme, culmination, height.
gipfeln ['gɪpfəln], *v.n.* culminate.
Gips [gɪps], *m.* (—**es**, *no pl.*) gypsum, stucco, plaster of Paris.
Gipsabdruck ['gɪpsapdruk], *m.* (—**s**, *pl.* ⸚**e**) plaster-cast.

Gipsbild ['gɪpsbɪlt], *n.* (—**s**, *pl.* —**er**) plaster-figure.
Gipsverband ['gɪpsfɛrbant], *m.* (—**es**, *pl.* ⸚**e**) (*Med.*) plaster of Paris dressing.
girieren [ʒɪ'ri:rən], *v.a.* (*Comm.*) endorse (a bill).
Girlande [gɪr'landə], *f.* (—, *pl.* —**n**) garland.
Girobank ['ʒi:robaŋk], *f.* (—, *pl.* —**en**) transfer *or* clearing bank.
Gis [gɪs], *n.* (—, *pl.* —) (*Mus.*) G sharp; — *Moll*, G sharp minor.
gischen ['gɪʃən], *v.n.* foam, froth.
Gischt [gɪʃt], *f.* (—, *pl.* —**e**) foam, froth; spray.
Gitarre [gi'tarə], *f.* (—, *pl.* —**n**) guitar.
Gitter ['gɪtər], *n.* (—**s**, *pl.* —) trellis, grate, fence; railing; lattice; (*colour-printing*) screen.
Gitterwerk ['gɪtərverk], *n.* (—**s**, *no pl.*) trellis-work.
Glacéhandschuh [gla'se:hantʃu:], *m.* (—**s**, *pl.* —**e**) kid-glove.
Glanz [glants], *m.* (—**es**, *no pl.*) brightness, lustre, gloss; polish, sheen; (*fig.*) splendour.
glänzen ['glɛntsən], *v.n.* shine, glitter, glisten; (*fig.*) sparkle.
glänzend ['glɛntsənt], *adj.* glossy; (*fig.*) splendid, magnificent.
Glanzfirnis ['glantsfɪrnɪs], *m.* (—**ses**, *pl.* —**se**) glazing varnish.
Glanzleder ['glantsle:dər], *n.* (—**s**, *no pl.*) patent leather.
Glanzleinwand ['glantslaɪnvant], *f.* (—, *no pl.*) glazed linen.
glanzlos ['glantslo:s], *adj.* lustreless, dull.
glanzvoll ['glantsfɔl], *adj.* splendid, brilliant.
Glanzzeit ['glantstsaɪt], *f.* (—, *pl.* —**en**) golden age.
Glas [gla:s], *n.* (—**es**, *pl.* ⸚**er**) glass, tumbler.
glasartig ['gla:sa:rtɪç], *adj.* vitreous, glassy.
Glaser ['gla:zər], *m.* (—**s**, *pl.* —) glazier.
Glaserkitt ['gla:zərkɪt], *m.* (—**s**, *no pl.*) putty.
gläsern ['glɛ:zərn], *adj.* vitreous, glassy, made of glass.
Glashütte ['gla:shytə], *f.* (—, *pl.* —**n**) glass-works.
glasieren [gla'zi:rən], *v.a.* glaze; (*cake etc.*) ice.
glasiert [gla'zi:rt], *adj.* glazed; (*Cul.*) frosted, iced; (*Art.*) varnished.
Glasröhre ['gla:srø:rə], *f.* (—, *pl.* —**n**) glass-tube.
Glasscheibe ['gla:sʃaɪbə], *f.* (—, *pl.* —**n**) glass-pane, sheet of glass.
Glassplitter ['gla:sʃplɪtər], *m.* (—**s**, *pl.* —) splinter of glass.
Glasur [gla'zu:r], *f.* (—, *pl.* —**en**) (*potter's*) glaze, glazing; enamel, varnish; (*cake*) icing.
glatt [glat], *adj.* smooth, sleek; even, plain, glossy; glib; downright. — *adv.* entirely; — *rasiert*, close-shaven.
Glätte ['glɛtə], *f.* (—, *no pl.*) smoothness, evenness, slipperiness; polish.
Glatteis ['glataɪs], *n.* (—**es**, *no pl.*) slippery ice; sheet ice; (*Am.*) glaze; *einen aufs — führen*, lead s.o. up the garden path.
glätten ['glɛtən], *v.a.* smooth; (*dial.*) iron.
Glatze ['glatsə], *f.* (—, *pl.* —**n**) bald head.
glatzköpfig ['glatskœpfɪç], *adj.* bald, bald-pated.
Glaube(n) ['glaubə(n)], *m.* (—**ns**, *no pl.*) faith, belief; creed, religion.
glauben ['glaubən], *v.a.* believe; think, suppose. — *v.n. an etwas* (*Acc.*) —, believe in s.th.
Glaubensbekenntnis ['glaubənsbəkɛntnɪs], *n.* (—**ses**, *pl.* —**se**) confession of faith; creed.
Glaubensgericht ['glaubənsgərɪçt], *n.* (—**es**, *no pl.*) inquisition.
Glaubersalz ['glaubərzalts], *n.* (—**es**, *no pl.*) phosphate of soda, Glauber's salts.
glaubhaft ['glauphaft], *adj.* credible, authentic.
gläubig ['glɔybɪç], *adj.* believing, faithful; (*Eccl.*) *die Gläubigen*, the faithful.
Gläubiger ['glɔybɪgər], *m.* (—**s**, *pl.* —) creditor.
glaublich ['glauplɪç], *adj.* credible, believable.
glaubwürdig ['glaupvyrdɪç], *adj.* authentic, worthy of belief; plausible.
gleich [glaɪç], *adj.* same, like, equal, even; *auf —e Weise*, likewise; *es ist mir ganz —*, it is all the same to me. — *adv.* alike, at once; almost; just as; *ich komme —*, I shall be there in a moment; — *und — gesellt sich gern*, birds of a feather flock together.
gleichaltrig ['glaɪçaltrɪç], *adj.* of the same age.
gleichartig ['glaɪça:rtɪç], *adj.* of the same kind, homogeneous.
gleichberechtigt ['glaɪçbərɛçtɪçt], *adj.* entitled to equal rights.
Gleiche ['glaɪçə], *n.* (—**n**, *pl.* —**n**) the like; the same; *etwas ins — bringen*, straighten s.th. out.
gleichen ['glaɪçən], *v.n. irr.* be like, resemble, be equal to.
gleichermaßen ['glaɪçərma:sən], *adv.* in a like manner, likewise.
gleichfalls ['glaɪçfals], *adv.* likewise, equally, as well; *danke —*, thanks, the same to you.
gleichförmig ['glaɪçfœrmɪç], *adj.* uniform; monotonous.
gleichgesinnt ['glaɪçgəzɪnt], *adj.* congenial, of the same mind.
Gleichgewicht ['glaɪçgəvɪçt], *n.* (—**s**, *no pl.*) balance, equilibrium.
gleichgültig ['glaɪçgyltɪç], *adj.* indifferent; *es ist mir —*, it's all the same to me.
Gleichheit ['glaɪçhaɪt], *f.* (—, *pl.* —**en**) equality, likeness.

Gleichklang ['glaɪçklaŋ], *m.* (—**s**, *pl.* ¨**e**) consonance.
gleichmachen ['glaɪçmaxən], *v.a.* level, equate; *dem Erdboden* —, raze to the ground.
Gleichmaß ['glaɪçma:s], *n.* (—**es**, *no pl.*) proportion, symmetry.
gleichmäßig ['glaɪçmɛ:sɪç], *adj.* proportionate, symmetrical.
Gleichmut ['glaɪçmu:t], *m.* (—**s**, *no pl.*) equanimity, calm.
gleichmütig ['glaɪçmy:tɪç], *adj.* even-tempered, calm.
gleichnamig ['glaɪçna:mɪç], *adj.* homonymous.
Gleichnis ['glaɪçnɪs], *n.* (—**ses**, *pl.* —**se**) simile; (*Bibl.*) parable.
gleichsam ['glaɪçza:m], *adv.* as it were, as if.
gleichschenklig ['glaɪçʃɛŋklɪç], *adj.* (*Maths.*) isosceles.
gleichseitig ['glaɪçzaɪtɪç], *adj.* (*Maths.*) equilateral.
Gleichsetzung ['glaɪçzɛtsuŋ], *f.* (—, *no pl.*), **Gleichstellung** ['glaɪçʃtɛluŋ], *f.* (—, *pl.* —**en**) equalisation.
Gleichstrom ['glaɪçʃtro:m], *m.* (—**s**, *no pl.*) (*Elec.*) direct current.
gleichtun ['glaɪçtu:n], *v.a. irr. es einem* —, emulate s.o.
Gleichung ['glaɪçuŋ], *f.* (—, *pl.* —**en**) (*Maths.*) equation.
gleichwohl ['glaɪçvo:l], *adv., conj.* nevertheless, however, yet.
gleichzeitig ['glaɪçtsaɪtɪç], *adj.* simultaneous, contemporary.
Gleis [glaɪs], *n.* (—**es**, *pl.* —**e**) (*Railw.*) track; rails; (*Am.*) track.
gleiten ['glaɪtən], *v.n. irr.* (*aux.* sein) glide, slide, slip.
Gleitflug ['glaɪtflu:k], *m.* (—**es**, *pl.* ¨**e**) (*Aviat.*) gliding.
Gletscher ['glɛtʃər], *m.* (—**s**, *pl.* —) glacier.
Gletscherspalte ['glɛtʃərʃpaltə], *f.* (—, *pl.* —**n**) crevasse.
Glied [gli:t], *n.* (—**es**, *pl.* —**er**) limb, joint; member; link; rank, file.
Gliederlähmung ['gli:dərlɛ:muŋ], *f.* (—, *no pl.*) paralysis.
gliedern ['gli:dərn], *v.a.* articulate, arrange, form.
Gliederreißen ['gli:dərraɪsən], *n.* (—**s**, *no pl.*) pain in the limbs, rheumatism, arthritis etc.
Gliederung ['gli:dəruŋ], *f.* (—, *pl.* —**en**) articulation, disposition, structure, arrangement, organisation.
Gliedmaßen ['gli:tma:sən], *f. pl.* limbs.
glimmen ['glɪmən], *v.n. irr.* glimmer, glow, burn faintly; —*de Asche*, embers.
Glimmer ['glɪmər], *m.* (—**s**, *no pl.*) (*Min.*) mica.
glimpflich ['glɪmpflɪç], *adj.* gentle.
glitschen ['glɪtʃən], *v.n.* (*aux.* sein) (*coll.*) slide.
glitschig ['glɪtʃɪç], *adj.* (*coll.*) slippery.
glitzern ['glɪtsərn], *v.n.* glisten, glitter.
Globus ['glo:bus], *m.* (—**ses**, *pl.* —**se**) globe.
Glöckchen ['glœkçən], *n.* (—**s**, *pl.* —) small bell; hand-bell.
Glocke ['glɔkə], *f.* (—, *pl.* —**n**) bell; *etwas an die große* — *hängen*, make a great fuss about s.th.
Glockenblume ['glɔkənblu:mə], *f.* (—, *pl.* —**n**) (*Bot.*) bluebell.
Glockengießer ['glɔkəngi:sər], *m.* (—**s**, *pl.* —) bell-founder.
glockenklar ['glɔkənkla:r], *adj.* as clear as a bell.
Glockenläuter ['glɔkənlɔytər], *m.* (—**s**, *pl.* —) bell-ringer.
Glockenspiel ['glɔkənʃpi:l], *n.* (—**s**, *pl.* —**e**) chime; (*Mus.*) glockenspiel, carillon.
Glockenstuhl ['glɔkənʃtu:l], *m.* (—**s**, *pl.* ¨**e**) belfry.
Glockenzug ['glɔkəntsu:k], *m.* (—**s**, *pl.* ¨**e**) bell-rope; (*Mus.*) bell-stop.
Glöckner ['glœkner], *m.* (—**s**, *pl.* —) bellringer, sexton.
glorreich ['glo:raɪç], *adj.* glorious.
Glosse ['glɔsə], *f.* (—, *pl.* —**n**) gloss, comment, annotation; —*n machen über*, comment upon; find fault with; scoff at.
glotzen ['glɔtsən], *v.n.* stare wide-eyed; gape.
Glück [glyk], *n.* (—**s**, *no pl.*) luck, good luck, fortune, happiness; — *haben*, be in luck; *auf gut* —, at random; *zum* —, fortunately, luckily; *viel* —, good luck.
Glucke ['glukə], *f.* (—, *pl.* —**n**) (sitting) hen.
glücken ['glykən], *v.n.* succeed; *es ist mir geglückt*, I have succeeded in.
glücklich ['glyklɪç], *adj.* fortunate, lucky, happy.
glückselig [glyk'ze:lɪç], *adj.* blissful, happy.
glucksen ['gluksən], *v.n.* gurgle.
Glücksfall ['glyksfal], *m.* (—**es**, *pl.* ¨**e**) lucky chance, windfall, stroke of good fortune.
Glückspilz ['glykspɪlts], *m.* (—**es**, *pl.* —**e**) (*coll.*) lucky dog.
glückverheißend ['glykfɛrhaɪsənt], *adj.* auspicious, propitious.
Glückwunsch ['glykvunʃ], *m.* (—**es**, *pl.* ¨**e**) congratulation; felicitation.
glühen ['gly:ən], *v.a.* make red-hot; (*wine*) mull. — *v.n.* glow, be red-hot.
glühend ['gly:ənt], *adj.* glowing, burning; red-hot; (*coal*) live; (*fig.*) ardent, fervent.
Glühstrumpf ['gly:ʃtrumpf], *m.* (—**es**, *pl.* ¨**e**) incandescent mantle.
Glühwein ['gly:vaɪn], *m.* (—**s**, *no pl.*) mulled wine.
Glut [glu:t], *f.* (—, *no pl.*) glowing fire; heat; (*fig.*) ardour.
glutrot ['glu:tro:t], *adj.* fiery red.
Glyzerin ['glytsəri:n], *n.* (—**s**, *no pl.*) glycerine.

Gnade ['gna:də], *f.* (—, *pl.* —n) grace; favour; pardon, clemency, mercy; kindness; *Euer —n*, Your Grace.
Gnadenakt ['gna:dənakt], *m.* (—s, *pl.* —e) act of grace.
Gnadenbrot ['gna:dənbro:t], *n.* (—s, *no pl.*) *das — essen*, live on charity.
Gnadenfrist ['gna:dənfrɪst], *f.* (—, *pl.* —en) respite.
Gnadenort ['gna:dənɔrt], *m.* (—(e)s, *pl.* —e) place of pilgrimage.
Gnadenstoß ['gna:dənʃto:s], *m.* (—es, *pl.* ¨e) finishing stroke, coup de grâce, death-blow.
gnadenvoll ['gna:dənfɔl], *adj.* merciful, gracious.
Gnadenweg ['gna:dənve:k], *m.* (—es, *no pl.*) act of grace; *auf dem —*, by reprieve (as an act of grace).
gnädig ['gnɛ:dɪç], *adj.* gracious, merciful, kind; *—e Frau*, Madam; *—er Herr*, Sir.
Gnostiker ['gnɔstɪkər], *m.* (—s, *pl.* —) gnostic.
Gnu [gnu:], *n.* (—s, *pl.* —s) (*Zool.*) gnu.
Gold [gɔlt], *n.* (—(e)s, *no pl.*) gold.
Goldammer ['gɔltamər], *f.* (—, *pl.* —n) (*Orn.*) yellow-hammer.
Goldamsel ['gɔltamzəl], *f.* (—, *pl.* —n) (*Orn.*) yellow-thrush.
Goldarbeiter ['gɔltarbaɪtər], *m.* (—s, *pl.* —) goldsmith.
Goldbarren ['gɔltbarən], *m.* (—s, *pl.* —) ingot of gold.
Goldbergwerk ['gɔltbɛrkvɛrk], *n.* (—s, *pl.* —e) gold-mine.
Goldfisch ['gɔltfɪʃ], *m.* (—es, *pl.* —e) goldfish.
Goldgewicht ['gɔltgəvɪçt], *n.* (—s, *no pl.*) gold-weight, troy-weight.
Goldgrube ['gɔltgru:bə], *f.* (—, *pl.* —n) gold-mine.
goldig ['gɔldɪç], *adj.* golden; (*fig.*) sweet, cute, charming.
Goldklumpen ['gɔltklumpən], *m.* (—s, *pl.* —) nugget (of gold).
Goldlack ['gɔltlak], *m.* (—s, *no pl.*) gold-coloured varnish; (*Bot.*) wallflower.
Goldmacher ['gɔltmaxər], *m.* (—s, *pl.* —) alchemist.
Goldregen ['gɔltre:gən], *m.* (—s, *pl.* —) (*Bot.*) laburnum.
Goldscheider ['gɔltʃaɪdər], *m.* (—s, *pl.* —) gold-refiner.
Goldschmied ['gɔltʃmi:t], *m.* (—s, *pl.* —e) goldsmith.
Goldschnitt ['gɔltʃnɪt], *m.* (—s, *no pl.*) gilt edge.
Golf (1) [gɔlf], *m.* (—s, *pl.* —e) gulf.
Golf (2) [gɔlf], *n.* (—s, *no pl.*) golf.
Gondel ['gɔndəl], *f.* (—, *pl.* —n) gondola.
gondeln ['gɔndəln], *v.n.* (*aux.* sein) ride in a gondola; (*coll.*) travel, get about.
gönnen ['gœnən], *v.a. einem etwas —*, not grudge s.o. s.th.; *wir — es ihm*, we are happy for him.
Gönner ['gœnər], *m.* (—s, *pl.* —) patron, protector.
gönnerhaft ['gœnərhaft], *adj.* patronising.
Gönnerschaft ['gœnərʃaft], *f.* (—, *no pl.*) patronage.
gordisch ['gɔrdɪʃ], *adj.* Gordian; *der —e Knoten*, the Gordian knot.
Göre ['gø:rə], *f.* (—, *pl.* —n) (*coll.*) brat; (*Am.*) kid.
Gosse ['gɔsə], *f.* (—, pl. —n) gutter.
Gote ['go:tə], *m.* (—n, *pl.* —n) Goth.
Gotik ['go:tɪk], *f.* (—, *no pl.*) Gothic style (architecture etc.).
gotisch ['go:tɪʃ], *adj.* Gothic.
Gott [gɔ:t], *m.* (—es, *pl.* ¨er) God, god; *— befohlen*, goodbye; *grüß —!* (*Austr.*) good day; *— sei Dank*, thank God, thank heaven.
gottbegnadet ['gɔtbəgna:dət], *adj.* favoured by God, inspired.
Götterbild ['gœtərbɪlt], *n.* (—es, *pl.* —er) image of a god.
gottergeben ['gɔtɛrge:bən], *adj.* submissive to God's will, devout.
Götterlehre ['gœtərle:rə], *f.* (—, *pl.* —n) mythology.
Götterspeise ['gœtərʃpaɪzə], *f.* (—, *pl.* —n) ambrosia.
Götterspruch ['gœtərʃprux], *m.* (—s, *no pl.*) oracle.
Göttertrank ['gœtərtraŋk], *m.* (—s, *pl.* ¨e) nectar.
Gottesacker ['gɔtəsakər], *m.* (—s, *pl.* —) God's acre, churchyard.
Gottesdienst ['gɔtəsdi:nst], *m.* (—es, *pl.* —e) divine service, public worship.
gottesfürchtig ['gɔtəsfyrçtɪç], *adj.* God-fearing, pious.
Gottesgelehrsamkeit ['gɔtəsgəle:r-za:mkaɪt], *f.* (—, *no pl.*) (*rare*) theology, divinity.
Gottesgericht ['gɔtəsgərɪçt], *n.* (—s, *pl.* —e) ordeal.
Gotteshaus ['gɔtəshaus], *n.* (—es, *pl.* ¨er) house of God; (*rare*) church.
Gotteslästerer ['gɔtəslɛstərər], *m.* (—s, *pl.* —) blasphemer.
Gottesleugner ['gɔtəslɔygnər], *m.* (—s, *pl.* —) atheist.
Gottfried ['gɔtfri:t], *m.* Godfrey, Geoffrey.
gottgefällig ['gɔtgəfɛlɪç], *adj.* pleasing to God.
Gottheit ['gɔthaɪt], *f.* (—, *pl.* —en) deity, divinity.
Göttin ['gœtɪn], *f.* (—, *pl.* —nen) goddess.
göttlich ['gœtlɪç], *adj.* divine, godlike; (*fig.*) heavenly.
gottlob! [gɔt'lo:p], *excl.* thank God!
gottlos ['gɔtlo:s], *adj.* godless, ungodly, impious; (*fig.*) wicked.
gottvergessen ['gɔtfɛrgɛsən], *adj.* reprobate, impious.
gottverlassen ['gɔtfɛrlasən], *adj.* God-forsaken.
Götze ['gœtsə], *m.* (—n, *pl.* —n) idol, false deity.

Götzenbild [ˈgœtsənbɪlt], *n.* (**—es**, *pl.* **—er**) idol.
Götzendienst [ˈgœtsəndiːnst], *m.* (**—es**, *no pl.*) idolatry.
Gouvernante [guvɛrˈnantə], *f.* (**—**, *pl.* **—n**) governess.
Gouverneur [guvɛrˈnøːr], *m.* (**—s**, *pl.* **—e**) governor.
Grab [graːp], *n.* (**—s**, *pl.* **¨er**) grave, tomb; sepulchre.
Graben [ˈgraːbən], *m.* (**—s**, *pl.* **¨**) ditch, trench.
graben [ˈgraːbən], *v.a. irr.* dig.
Grabgeläute [ˈgraːpgəlɔytə], *n.* (**—s**, *no pl.*) death-knell.
Grabhügel [ˈgraːphyːgəl], *m.* (**—s**, *pl.* **—**) tumulus, mound.
Grablegung [ˈgraːpleːguŋ], *f.* (**—**, *no pl.*) (*rare*) burial, interment.
Grabmal [ˈgraːpmaːl], *n.* (**—s**, *pl.* **—e**, **¨er**) tomb, sepulchre, monument.
Grabschrift [ˈgraːpʃrɪft], *f.* (**—**, *pl.* **—n**) epitaph.
Grabstichel [ˈgraːpʃtɪçəl], *m.* (**—s**, *pl.* **—**) graving-tool.
Grad [graːt], *m.* (**—s**, *pl.* **—e**) degree; rank; grade; extent; point; *in gewissem —e*, to a certain degree; *im höchsten —e*, in the highest degree, extremely.
Gradeinteilung [ˈgraːtaɪntaɪluŋ], *f.* (**—**, *pl* **—en**) gradation, graduation.
Gradmesser [ˈgraːtmɛsər], *m.* (**—s**, *pl.* **—**) graduator; (*fig.*) index.
gradweise [ˈgraːtvaɪzə], *adv.* gradually, by degrees.
Graf [graːf], *m.* (**—en**, *pl.* **—en**) count, earl.
Gräfin [ˈgrɛfɪn], *f.* (**—**, *pl.* **—en**) countess.
gräflich [ˈgrɛflɪç], *adj.* belonging to a count *or* earl.
Grafschaft [ˈgraːfʃaft], *f.* (**—**, *pl.* **—en**) county, shire.
Gral [graːl], *m.* (**—s**, *no pl.*) Holy Grail.
Gram [graːm], *m.* (**—s**, *no pl.*) grief, sorrow.
grämen [ˈgrɛːmən], *v.a.* grieve. — *v.r. sich* —, grieve, fret, worry.
gramgebeugt [ˈgraːmgəbɔykt], *adj.* prostrate with grief.
grämlich [ˈgrɛːmlɪç], *adj.* sullen, morose, ill-humoured.
Gramm [gram], *n.* (**—s**, *pl.* **—e**) gramme (15.438 grains); (*Am.*) gram.
Grammatik [graˈmatɪk], *f.* (**—**, *pl.* **—en**) grammar.
grammatikalisch, grammatisch [gramatɪˈkaːlɪʃ, graˈmatɪʃ], *adj.* grammatical.
Gran [graːn], *n.* (**—s**, *pl.* **—e**) (*weight*) grain.
Granat [graˈnaːt], *m.* (**—s**, *pl.* **—e**) garnet.
Granatapfel [graˈnaːtapfəl], *m.* (**—s**, *pl.* **¨e**) (*Bot.*) pomegranate.
Granate [graˈnaːtə], *f.* (**—**, *pl.* **—n**) shell, grenade.
Grande [ˈgrandə], *m.* (**—n**, *pl.* **—n**) grandee.
Grandezza [granˈdɛtsa], *f.* (**—**, *no pl.*) grandeur; sententiousness; pomposity.
grandios [grandɪˈoːs], *adj.* grand.
Granit [graˈniːt], *m.* (**—s**, *pl.* **—e**) granite.
Granne [ˈgranə], *f.* (**—**, *pl.* **—n**) (*corn*) awn, beard.
graphisch [ˈgraːfɪʃ], *adj.* graphic.
Graphit [graˈfiːt], *m.* (**—s**, *no pl.*) blacklead.
Gras [graːs], *n.* (**—es**, *pl.* **¨er**) grass; *ins — beißen*, bite the dust.
grasartig [ˈgraːsaːrtɪç], *adj.* gramineous.
grasen [ˈgraːzən], *v.n.* graze.
Grasfleck [ˈgraːsflɛk], *m.* (**—s**, *pl.* **—e**) grass-stain.
Grashalm [ˈgraːshalm], *m.* (**—s**, *pl.* **—e**) grass-blade.
Grashüpfer [ˈgraːshypfər], *m.* (**—s**, *pl.* **—**) (*Ent.*) grass-hopper.
grasig [ˈgraːzɪç], *adj.* grassy.
Grasmäher [ˈgraːsmɛːər], *m.* (**—s**, *pl.* **—**) lawn-mower.
Grasmücke [ˈgraːsmykə], *f.* (**—**, *pl.* **—n**) (*Orn.*) hedge-sparrow.
grassieren [graˈsiːrən], *v.n.* (*epidemics etc.*) spread, rage.
gräßlich [ˈgrɛslɪç], *adj.* hideous, horrible, ghastly.
Grasweide [ˈgraːsvaɪdə], *f.* (**—**, *pl.* **—n**) pasture.
Grat [graːt], *m.* (**—s**, *pl.* **—e**) edge, ridge.
Gräte [ˈgrɛːtə], *f.* (**—**, *pl.* **—n**) fish-bone.
Grätenstich [ˈgrɛːtənʃtɪç], *m.* (**—s**, *pl.* **—e**) (*embroidery*) herring-bone stitch.
grätig [ˈgrɛːtɪç], *adj.* full of fishbones; (*fig.*) grumpy.
gratis [ˈgraːtɪs], *adj.* gratis; — *und franko*, for nothing.
Gratulation [gratulaˈtsjoːn], *f.* (**—**, *pl.* **—en**) congratulation.
gratulieren [gratuˈliːrən], *v.n. einem zu etwas* —, congratulate s.o. on s.th.
grau [grau], *adj.* grey; (*Am.*) gray; *vor —en Zeiten*, in times of yore.
Grauen [ˈgrauən], *n.* (**—s**, *no pl.*) horror, aversion.
grauen [ˈgrauən], *v.n.* (*morning*) dawn; *es graut mir vor*, I shudder at.
grauenhaft [ˈgrauənhaft], *adj.* horrible, awful, ghastly.
graulen [ˈgraulən], *v.r. sich* —, shudder, be afraid (of ghosts etc.).
graulich [ˈgraulɪç], *adj. mir ist ganz* —, I shudder.
Graupe [ˈgraupə], *f.* (**—**, *pl.* **—n**) groats, peeled barley.
graupeln [ˈgraupəln], *v.n. imp.* (*coll.*) drizzle, sleet.
Graus [graus], *m.* (**—es**, *no pl.*) horror, dread.
grausam [ˈgrauzaːm], *adj.* cruel.
Grauschimmel [ˈgrauʃɪməl], *m.* (**—s**, *pl.* **—**) grey (horse).
grausen [ˈgrauzən], *v.n. es graust mir vor*, I shudder at.
grausig [ˈgrauzɪç], *adj.* dread. gruesome, horrible.

Graveur [gra'vø:r], *m.* (—s, *pl.* —e) engraver.
gravieren [gra'vi:rən], *v.a.* engrave.
Gravität [gravi'tɛ:t], *f.* (—, *no pl.*) gravity.
gravitätisch [gravi'tɛ:tɪʃ], *adj.* grave, solemn.
Grazie ['gra:tsjə], *f.* (—, *pl.* —n) grace, charm; (*goddess*) Grace.
graziös [gra'tsjø:s], *adj.* graceful.
Greif [graɪf], *m.* (—(e)s, *pl.* —e) griffin.
greifbar ['graɪfba:r], *adj.* to hand; (*fig.*) tangible, palpable.
greifen ['graɪfən], *v.a. irr.* grasp, seize, touch, handle; *etwas aus der Luft* —, invent s.th.; *um sick* —, gain ground.
greinen ['graɪnən], *v.n.* (*dial. & coll.*) cry, blubber.
Greis [graɪs], *m.* (—es, *pl.* —e) old man.
greisenhaft ['graɪzənhaft], *adj.* senile.
grell [grɛl], *adj.* (*colour*) glaring; (*light*) dazzling; (*tone*) shrill, sharp.
Grenadier [grena'di:r], *m.* (—s, *pl.* —e) grenadier.
Grenadiermütze [grena'di:rmytsə], *f.* (—, *pl.* —n) busby, bearskin.
Grenze ['grɛntsə], *f.* (—, *pl.* —n) boundary; frontier; borders; (*fig.*) limit.
grenzen ['grɛntsən], *v.n.* — *an*, border on; (*fig.*) verge on.
Grenzlinie ['grɛntsli:njə], *f.* (—, *pl.* —n) boundary-line, line of demarcation.
Greuel ['grɔyəl], *m.* (—s, *pl.* —) horror, abomination; *das ist mir ein* —, I abominate it.
Greueltat ['grɔyəlta:t], *f.* (—, *pl.* —en) atrocity.
greulich ['grɔylɪç], *adj.* horrible, dreadful, shocking, heinous.
Griebe ['gri:bə], *f.* (—, *pl.* —n) (*mostly pl.*) greaves.
Griebs ['gri:ps], *m.* (—es, *pl.* —e) (*dial.*) (*apple*) core.
Grieche ['gri:çə], *m.* (—n, *pl.* —n) Greek.
Griechenland ['gri:çənlant], *n.* Greece.
Griesgram ['gri:sgra:m], *m.* (—s, *pl.* —e) grumbler.
griesgrämig ['gri:sgrɛ:mɪç], *adj.* morose, grumbling.
Grieß ['gri:s], *m.* (—es, *no pl.*) groats, semolina.
Grießbrei ['gri:sbraɪ], *m.* (—s, *pl.* —e) gruel.
Griff [grɪf], *m.* (—s, *pl.* —e) grip, hold, handle.
griffbereit ['grɪfbəraɪt], *adj.* handy.
Grille ['grɪlə], *f.* (—, *pl.* —n) (*Ent.*) cricket; (*fig.*) whim; —*n haben*, be capricious; —*n fangen*, be crotchety, be depressed.
grillenhaft ['grɪlənhaft], *adj.* whimsical; capricious.
Grimasse [gri'masə], *f.* (—, *pl.* —n) grimace.
Grimm [grɪm], *m.* (—s, *no pl.*) fury, rage, wrath.
Grimmen ['grɪmən], *n.* (—s, *no pl.*) gripes; (*Med.*) colic.
grimmig ['grɪmɪç], *adj.* fierce, furious; grim.
Grind [grɪnt], *m.* (—s, *pl.* —e) scab, scurf.
grinsen ['grɪnzən], *v.n.* grin.
Grippe ['grɪpə], *f.* (—, *pl.* —n) influenza, grippe.
Grips [grɪps], *m.* (—es, *no pl.*) (*coll.*) sense, brains; *einen beim — nehmen*, take s.o. by the scruff of his neck.
grob [grɔp], *adj.* coarse; rough; gross; rude, crude, uncouth, impolite; (*jewels*) rough, unpolished.
Grobheit ['grɔphaɪt], *f.* (—, *pl.* —en) rudeness; abusive language.
Grobian ['gro:bja:n], *m.* (—s, *pl.* —e) boor, rude fellow.
Grobschmied ['grɔpʃmi:t], *m.* (—s, *pl.* —e) blacksmith.
Grog [grɔk], *m.* (—s, *pl.* —s) grog, toddy.
grölen ['grø:lən], *v.n.* (*coll.*) scream, squall, bawl.
Groll [grɔl], *m.* (—s, *no pl.*) resentment, anger, rancour; *einen — gegen einen haben*, bear s.o. a grudge.
grollen ['grɔlən], *v.n.* (*thunder*) rumble; *einem* —, bear s.o. ill-will; (*Poet.*) be angry (with).
Grönland ['grø:nlant], *n.* Greenland.
Gros (1) [grɔs], *n.* (—ses, *pl.* —se) gross; twelve dozen.
Gros (2) [gro:], *n.* (—s, *no pl.*) bulk, majority; *en* —, wholesale.
Groschen ['grɔʃən], *m.* (—s, *pl.* —) small coin, penny; one 100th of an Austrian shilling; ten-pfennig piece; *einen schönen — verdienen*, make good money.
groß [gro:s], *adj.* great, big, large; tall; vast; eminent, famous; intense; —*e Augen machen*, stare; *Grosser Ozean*, Pacific (Ocean).
großartig ['gro:sa:rtɪç], *adj.* grand, sublime, magnificent, splendid.
Großbetrieb ['gro:sbətri:p], *m.* (—s, *pl.* —e) large business; large (industrial) concern.
Großbritannien [gro:sbri'tanjən], *n.* Great Britain.
Größe ['grø:sə], *f.* (—, *pl.* —n) size, largeness, greatness; height; quantity; power; celebrity, star; importance.
Großeltern ['gro:sɛltərn], *pl.* grandparents.
Großenkel ['gro:sɛŋkəl], *m.* (—s, *pl.* —) great-grandson.
Größenverhältnis ['grø:sənfɛrhɛltnɪs], *n.* (—ses, *pl.* —se) proportion, ratio.
Größenwahn ['grø:sənva:n], *m.* (—s, *no pl.*) megalomania; delusion of grandeur.
Großfürst ['gro:sfyrst], *m.* (—en, *pl.* —en) grand-duke.

Großfürstin ['gro:sfyrstɪn], *f.* (—, *pl.* —**nen**) grand-duchess.
Großgrundbesitz ['gro:sgruntbəzɪts], *m.* (—**es**, *pl.* —**e**) large landed property, estates.
Großhandel ['gro:shandəl], *m.* (—**s**, *no pl.*) wholesale business.
großherzig ['gro:shɛrtsɪç], *adj.* magnanimous.
Grossist [grɔ'sɪst], *m.* (—**en**, *pl.* —**en**) wholesale merchant.
großjährig ['gro:sjɛ:rɪç], *adj.* of age; — *werden*, come of age.
großmächtig ['gro:smɛçtɪç], *adj.* (*fig.*) high and mighty.
großmäulig ['gro:smɔylɪç], *adj.* bragging, swaggering.
Großmut ['gro:smu:t], *f.* (—, *no pl.*) magnanimity, generosity.
Großmutter ['gro:smutər], *f.* (—, *pl.* ¨) grandmother.
Großsiegelbewahrer [gro:s'zi:gəlbəva:rər], *m.* (—**s**, *pl.* —) Lord Chancellor; Keeper of the Great Seal.
Großstadt ['gro:sʃtat], *f.* (—, *pl.* ¨**e**) large town, city, metropolis.
Großtat ['gro:sta:t], *f.* (—, *pl.* —**en**) achievement, exploit, feat.
Großtuer ['gro:stu:ər], *m.* (—**s**, *pl.* —) boaster, braggart.
großtun ['gro:stu:n], *v.r. irr. sich* — *mit*, brag of; show off, parade.
Großvater ['gro:sfa:tər], *m.* (—**s**, *pl.* ¨) grandfather.
großziehen ['gro:stsi:ən], *v.a. irr.* bring up, rear.
großzügig ['gro:stsy:gɪç], *adj.* boldly conceived; grand, generous.
Grotte ['grɔtə], *f.* (—, *pl.* —**n**) grotto.
Grübchen ['gry:pçən], *n.* (—**s**, *pl.* —) dimple.
Grube ['gru:bə], *f.* (—, *pl.* —**n**) hole, pit; (*Min.*) mine; *in die — fahren*, (*Bibl.*) go down to the grave.
Grübelei ['gry:bəlaɪ], *f.* (—, *pl.* —**en**) brooding, musing.
grübeln ['gry:bəln], *v.n.* brood (over s.th.)
Grubenarbeiter ['gru:bənarbaɪtər], *m.* (—**s**, *pl.* —) miner.
Grubengas ['gru:bənga:s], *n.* (—**es**, *pl.* —**e**) fire-damp.
Grubenlampe ['gru:bənlampə], *f.* (—, *pl.* —**n**) miner's lamp.
Gruft [gruft], *f.* (—, *pl.* ¨**e**) tomb, sepulchre; vault, mausoleum.
grün [gry:n], *adj.* green; *grüne Bohnen*, French beans, runner beans; (*fig.*) unripe, immature, inexperienced; *am —en Tisch*, at the conference table; (*fig.*) in theory; *auf einen —en Zweig kommen*, thrive, get on in the world; *einem nicht — sein*, dislike s.o.
Grund [grunt], *m.* (—**s**, *pl.* ¨**e**) ground, soil; earth; land; bottom; foundation, basis; valley; reason, cause, argument; motive.
Grundbedeutung ['gruntbədɔytuŋ], *f.* (—, *pl.* —**en**) primary meaning, basic meaning.
Grundbesitz ['gruntbəzɪts], *m.* (—**es**, *no pl.*) landed property.
Grundbuch ['gruntbu:x], *n.* (—**s**, *pl.* ¨**er**) land register.
grundehrlich ['grunte:rlɪç], *adj.* thoroughly honest.
Grundeigentum ['gruntaɪgəntu:m], *n.* (—**s**, *pl.* ¨**er**) landed property.
Grundeis ['gruntaɪs], *n.* (—**es**, *no pl.*) ground-ice.
gründen ['gryndən], *v.a.* found, establish, float (a company). — *v.r. sich — auf*, be based on.
grundfalsch ['gruntfalʃ], *adj.* radically false.
Grundfarbe ['gruntfarbə], *f.* (—, *pl.* —**n**) primary colour.
Grundfläche ['gruntflɛçə], *f.* (—, *pl.* —**n**) basis, base.
Grundherr ['grunthɛr], *m.* (—**n**, *pl.* —**en**) lord of the manor, freeholder.
grundieren [grun'di:rən], *v.a.* prime, size, paint the undercoat.
Grundkapital ['gruntkapita:l], *n.* (—**s**, *no pl.*) original stock.
Grundlage ['gruntla:gə], *f.* (—, *pl.* —**n**) foundation, basis.
Grundlegung ['gruntle:guŋ], *f.* (— *no pl.*) laying the foundation.
gründlich ['gryntlɪç], *adj.* thorough, solid.
grundlos ['gruntlo:s], *adj.* bottomless; groundless, unfounded, without foundation.
Grundmauer ['gruntmauər], *f.* (—, *pl.* —**n**) foundation wall.
Gründonnerstag [gry:n'dɔnərsta:k], *m.* (—**s**, *pl.* —**e**) Maundy Thursday.
Grundpfeiler ['gruntpfaɪlər], *m.* (—**s**, *pl.* —) (main) pillar.
Grundriß ['gruntrɪs], *m.* (—**sses**, *pl.* —**sse**) design, groundplan; compendium, elements; blueprint.
Grundsatz ['gruntzats], *m.* (—**es**, *pl.* ¨**e**) principle, maxim; axiom.
grundschlecht ['gruntʃlɛçt], *adj.* thoroughly bad.
Grundschuld ['gruntʃult], *f.* (—, *pl.* —**en**) mortgage (on land).
Grundstein ['gruntʃtaɪn], *m.* (—**s**, *pl.* —**e**) foundation-stone.
Grundsteuer ['gruntʃtɔyər], *f.* (—, *pl.* —**n**) land-tax.
Grundstoff ['gruntʃtɔf], *m.* (—**es**, *pl.* —**e**) raw material.
Grundstück ['gruntʃtyk], *n.* (—**s**, *pl.* —**e**) real estate; plot of land; lot.
Grundtugend ['grunttu:gənt], *f.* (— *pl.* —**en**) cardinal virtue.
Gründung ['gryndʊŋ], *f.* (—, *pl.* —**en**) foundation, establishment.
grundverschieden ['gruntfɛrʃi:dən], *adj.* radically different.
Grundwasser ['gruntvasər], *n.* (—**s**, *no pl.*) underground water.
Grundzahl ['grunttsa:l], *f.* (—, *pl.* —**en**) cardinal number.
Grundzug ['grunttsu:k], *m.* (—**s**, *pl.* ¨**e**) characteristic; distinctive feature.

Grüne ['gry:nə], *n.* (**—n**, *no pl.*) greenness, verdure; *ins — gehen*, take a walk in the open country.
grünen ['gry:nən], *v.n.* become green; (*fig.*) flourish.
Grünfutter ['gry:nfutər], *n.* (**—s**, *no pl.*) green food.
Grünkohl ['gry:nko:l], *m.* (**—s**, *no pl.*) green kale.
Grünkramhändler ['gry:nkra:mhɛndlər], *m.* (**—s**, *pl.* **—**) greengrocer.
Grünschnabel ['gry:nʃna:bəl], *m.* (**—s**, *pl.* **⸚**) greenhorn.
Grünspan ['gry:nʃpa:n], *m.* (**—s**, *no pl.*) verdigris.
Grünspecht ['gry:nʃpɛçt], *m.* (**—s**, *pl.* **—e**) (*Orn.*) green woodpecker.
grunzen ['gruntsən], *v.n.* grunt.
Grünzeug ['gry:ntsɔyk], *n.* (**—s**, *no pl.*) greens, herbs.
Gruppe ['grupə], *f.* (**—**, *pl.* **—n**) group.
gruppieren [gru'pi:rən], *v.a.* group.
gruselig ['gru:zəlɪç], *adj.* creepy, uncanny.
gruseln ['gru:zəln], *v.a. es gruselt mir* I shudder, it gives me the creeps.
Gruß [gru:s], *m.* (**—es**, *pl.* **⸚e**) salutation, greeting; (*pl.*) regards; *mit herzlichem —*, with kind regards; *einen — ausrichten*, convey s.o.'s regards.
grüßen ['gry:sən], *v.a.* greet; *einen — lassen*, send o.'s regards to s.o.; *— Sie ihn von mir*, remember me to him.
Grütze ['grytsə], *f.* (**—**, *pl.* **—n**) peeled grain, groats; (*fig.*) (*coll.*) gumption, brains.
Guatemala [guatə'ma:la], *n.* Guatemala.
gucken ['gukən], *v.n.* look, peep.
Guinea [gɪ'ne:a], *n.* Guinea.
Gulasch ['gulaʃ], *n.* (**—s**, *no pl.*) goulash.
Gulden ['guldən], *m.* (**—s**, *pl.* **—**) florin, guilder.
gülden ['gyldən], *adj.* (*Poet.*) golden.
gültig ['gyltɪç], *adj.* valid; (*money*) current, legal (tender).
Gummi ['gumi:], *m.* (**—s**, *no pl.*) gum, rubber.
Gummiarabikum [gumia'ra:bɪkum], *n.* gum arabic.
gummiartig ['gumia:rtɪç], *adj.* gummy; like rubber.
Gummiball ['gumibal], *m.* (**—s**, *pl.* **⸚e**) rubber-ball.
Gummiband ['gumibant], *n.* (**—s**, *pl.* **⸚er**) rubber-band, elastic.
Gummielastikum [gumie'lastɪkum], *n.* indiarubber.
gummieren [gu'mi:rən], *v.a.* gum.
Gummireifen ['gumiraɪfən], *m.* (**—s**, *pl.* **—**) tyre; (*Am.*) tire.
Gummischuhe ['gumiʃu:ə], *m. pl.* galoshes; (*Am.*) rubbers.
Gunst [gunst], *f.* (**—**, *no pl.*) favour; *zu seinen —en*, in his favour.
Gunstbezeigung ['gunstbətsaɪguŋ], *f.* (**—**, *pl.* **—en**) favour, kindness, goodwill.
günstig ['gynstɪç], *adj.* favourable, propitious.
Günstling ['gynstlɪŋ], *m.* (**—s**, *pl.* **—e**) favourite.
Gurgel ['gurgəl], *f.* (**—**, *pl.* **—n**) gullet, throat.
gurgeln ['gurgəln], *v.n.* gargle; gurgle.
Gurke ['gurkə], *f.* (**—**, *pl.* **—n**) (*Bot.*) cucumber; (*pickled*) gherkin.
Gurt [gurt], *m.* (**—es**, *pl.* **—e**) belt; strap; harness.
Gürtel ['gyrtəl], *m.* (**—s**, *pl.* **—**) girdle, belt; (*Geog.*) zone.
Guß [gus], *m.* (**—sses**, *pl.* **⸚sse**) gush, downpour; founding, cast; (*Cul.*) icing.
Gut [gu:t], *n.* (**—(e)s**, *pl.* **⸚er**) good thing, blessing; property, possession; country seat; estate; (*pl.*) goods.
gut [gu:t], *adj.* good; beneficial; kind; virtuous. — *adv.* well; *es — haben*, be well off; *—er Dinge sein*, be of good cheer; *kurz und —*, in short.
Gutachten ['gu:taxtən], *n.* (**—s**, *pl.* **—**) expert opinion, expert evidence.
gutartig ['gu:ta:rtɪç], *adj.* good-natured; benign.
Güte ['gy:tə], *f.* (**—**, *no pl.*) goodness, kindness, quality.
Güterabfertigung ['gy:tərapfɛrtɪguŋ], *f.* (**—**, *pl.* **—en**) (*Railw.*) goods-depot, goods-office.
Güterabtretung ['gy:təraptre:tuŋ], *f.* (**—**, *pl.* **—en**) cession of goods; (*Law*) surrender of an estate.
gutgelaunt ['gu:tgəlaunt], *adj.* in good spirits, good-humoured.
gutgemeint ['gu:tgəmaɪnt], *adj.* well-meant, well-intentioned.
gutgesinnt ['gu:tgəzɪnt], *adj.* well-intentioned.
Guthaben ['gu:tha:bən], *n.* (**—s**, *pl.* **—**) credit-balance, assets.
gutheißen ['gu:thaɪsən], *v.a. irr.* approve.
gütig ['gy:tɪç], *adj.* kind, benevolent.
gütlich ['gy:tlɪç], *adj.* amicable, friendly; *—er Vergleich*, amicable settlement; *sich — tun*, indulge o.s.
gutmachen ['gu:tmaxən], *v.a. etwas wieder —*, make amends for s.th., compensate.
gutmütig ['gu:tmy:tɪç], *adj.* good-natured, good-tempered.
Gutsbesitzer ['gu:tsbəzɪtsər], *m.* (**—s**, *pl.* **—**) landowner; proprietor of an estate.
gutschreiben ['gu:tʃraɪbən], *v.a. irr. einem etwas —*, enter a sum to s.o.'s credit.
Gutsverwalter ['gu:tsfɛrvaltər], *m.* (**—s**, *pl.* **—**) land-steward, agent, bailiff.
gutwillig ['gu:tvɪlɪç], *adj.* willing, of o.'s own free will.
Gymnasialbildung [gymnaz'ja:lbɪlduŋ], *f.* (**—**, *no pl.*) classical *or* grammar school education.
Gymnasiast [gymnaz'jast], *m.* (**—en**, *pl.* **—en**) grammar-school pupil.

Gymnasium [gym'na:zjum], *n.* (—s, *pl.* —sien) high school.
Gymnastik [gym'nastɪk], *f.* (—, *no pl.*) gymnastics.
gymnastisch [gym'nastɪʃ], *adj.* gymnastic(al); —e *Übungen*, physical exercises.

H

H [ha:], *n.* (—s, *pl.* —s) the letter H; (*Mus.*) *H Dur*, B major; *H Moll*, B minor.
ha! [ha:], *excl.* ha!
Haag, Den [ha:k, de:n], *m.* The Hague.
Haar [ha:r], *n.* (—s, *pl.* —e) hair; wool; nap; *aufs* —, exactly, to a hair; *um ein* —, very nearly, within a hair's breadth.
haaren ['ha:rən], *v.r. sich* —, shed o.'s hair.
haargenau ['ha:rgənau], *adj.* (very) exactly; to a nicety.
haarig ['ha:rɪç], *adj.* hairy.
Haarlocke ['ha:rlɔkə], *f.* (—, *pl.* —n) curl, ringlet.
Haarnadel ['ha:rna:dəl], *f.* (—, *pl.* —n) hairpin.
Haaröl ['ha:rø:l], *n.* (—s, *no pl.*) hair-oil.
Haarpinsel ['ha:rpɪnzəl], *m.* (—s, *pl.* —) camel-hair brush.
Haarröhrchen ['ha:rrø:rçən], *n.* (—s, *pl.* —) capillary tube.
Haarschleife ['ha:rʃlaɪfə], *f.* (—, *pl.* —en) bow in the hair.
Haarschnitt ['ha:rʃnɪt], *m.* (—s, *pl.* —e) hair-cut.
Haarschuppen ['ha:rʃupən], *f. pl.* dandruff.
Haarspalterei ['ha:rʃpaltəraɪ], *f.* (—, *pl.* —en) hair-splitting.
haarsträubend ['ha:rʃtrɔybənt], *adj.* hair-raising, monstrous.
Haarwäsche ['ha:rvɛʃə], *f.* (—, *no pl.*) shampooing.
Haarwickel ['ha:rvɪkəl], *m.* (—s, *pl.* —) curler.
Haarzange ['ha:rtsaŋə], *f.* (—, *pl.* —n) tweezers.
Habe ['ha:be], *f.* (—, *no pl.*) property, belongings, effects; *Hab und Gut*, all o.'s belongings, goods and chattels.
Haben ['ha:bən], *n.* (—s, *no pl.*) credit: *Soll und* —, debit and credit.
haben ['ha:bən], *v.a. irr.* have, possess; *da hast du's*, there you are; *es ist nicht zu* —, it is not available.
Habenichts ['ha:bənɪçts], *m.* (—es, *no pl.*) have-not.
Habgier ['ha:pgi:r], *f.* (—, *no pl.*) greediness, avarice, covetousness.
habhaft ['ha:phaft], *adj. einer Sache* — *werden*, get possession of a thing.
Habicht ['ha:bɪçt], *m.* (—s, *pl.* —e) (*Orn.*) hawk.
Habichtsinseln ['ha:bɪçtsɪnzəln], *f. pl.* the Azores.
Habichtsnase ['ha:bɪçtsna:zə], *f.* (—, *pl.* —n) hooked nose, aquiline nose.
Habilitation [habilita'tsjo:n], *f.* (—, *pl.* —en) admission *or* inauguration as a university lecturer.
habilitieren [habili'ti:rən], *v.r. sich* —, qualify as a university lecturer.
Habseligkeiten ['ha:pzelɪçkaɪtən], *f. pl.* property, effects, chattels.
Habsucht ['ha:pzuxt], *f.* (—, *no pl.*) avarice, greediness.
Hackbeil ['hakbaɪl], *n.* (—s, *pl.* —e) cleaver, chopping-knife.
Hackbrett ['hakbrɛt], *n.* (—s, *pl.* —er) chopping-board.
Hacke ['hakə], *f.* (—, *pl.* —n) hoe, mattock; heel.
Hacken ['hakən], *m.* (—s, *pl.* —) heel; *sich auf die* — *machen*, be off, take to o.'s heels.
hacken ['hakən], *v.a.* hack, chop, hoe; mince; (*birds*) peck.
Hacker ['hakər], *m.* (—s, *pl.* —) chopper.
Häckerling ['hɛkərlɪŋ], *m.* (—s, *no pl.*) chopped straw.
Hackfleisch ['hakflaɪʃ], *n.* (—es, *no pl.*) minced meat
Häcksel ['hɛksəl], *n.* (—s, *no pl.*) chopped straw.
Hader ['ha:dər], *m.* (—s, *no pl.*) quarrel, dispute.
hadern ['ha:dərn], *v.n.* quarrel, have a dispute.
Hafen ['ha:fən], *m.* (—s, *pl.* ¨) harbour, port; refuge, haven.
Hafendamm ['ha:fəndam], *m.* (—s, *pl.* ¨e) jetty, mole, pier.
Hafensperre ['ha:fənʃpɛrə], *f.* (—, *pl.* —n) embargo, blockade.
Hafenzoll ['ha:fəntsɔl], *m.* (—s, *no pl.*) anchorage, harbour due.
Hafer ['ha:fər], *m.* (—s, *no pl.*) oats; *es sticht ihn der* —, he is getting cheeky, insolent.
Haferbrei ['ha:fərbraɪ], *m.* (—s, *no pl.*) porridge.
Hafergrütze ['ha:fərgrytsə], *f.* (—, *no pl.*) ground-oats, oatmeal.
Haferschleim ['ha:fərʃlaɪm], *m.* (—s, *no pl.*) oat-gruel, porridge.
Haff [haf], *n.* (—s, *pl.* —e) bay, lagoon.
Haft [haft], *f.* (—, *no pl.*) custody, imprisonment, arrest.
haftbar ['haftba:r], *adj.* answerable; (*Law*) liable.
Haftbefehl ['haftbəfe:l], *m.* (—s, *pl.* —e) warrant for arrest.
haften ['haftən], *v.n.* stick, cling, adhere; *für einen* —, go bail for s.o.; *für etwas* —, answer for, be liable for s.th.

Häftling ['hɛftlɪŋ], *m.* (**—s**, *pl.* **—e**) prisoner.
Haftpflicht ['haftpflɪçt], *f.* (—, *no pl.*) liability.
Haftung ['haftuŋ], *f.* (—, *no pl.*) liability, security; (*Comm.*) *Gesellschaft mit beschränkter* —, limited liability company, (*abbr.*) Ltd.
Hag [ha:k], *m.* (**—es**, *pl.* **—e**) hedge, enclosure.
Hagebuche ['ha:gəbu:xə], *f.* (—, *pl.* **—n**) hornbeam.
Hagebutte ['ha:gəbutə], *f.* (—, *pl.* **—n**) (*Bot.*) hip, haw.
Hagedorn ['ha:gədɔrn], *m.* (**—s**, *no pl.*) (*Bot.*) hawthorn.
Hagel ['ha:gəl], *m.* (**—s**, *no pl.*) hail.
hageln ['ha:gəln], *v.n.* hail.
Hagelschauer ['ha:gəlʃauər], *m.* (**—s**, *pl.* —) hailstorm.
hager ['ha:gər], *adj.* thin, lean, lank, gaunt.
Häher ['hɛ:ər], *m.* (**—s**, *pl.* —) (*Orn.*) jay.
Hahn [ha:n], *m.* (**—s**, *pl.* **¨e**) (*Orn.*) cockerel, cock; (*water, gas*) cock, tap, faucet; — *im Korbe sein*, rule the roost; *da kräht kein — danach*, nobody cares two hoots about it.
Hahnenbalken ['ha:nənbalkən], *m.* (**—s**, *pl.* —) cock-loft; hen-roost.
Hahnenfuß ['ha:nənfu:s], *m.* (**—es**, *no pl.*) (*Bot.*) crow-foot.
Hahnensporn ['ha:nɛnʃpɔrn], *m.* (**—s**, *no pl.*) cockspur.
Hahnentritt ['ha:nəntrɪt], *m.* (**—s**, *no pl.*) cock's tread.
Hahnrei ['ha:nraɪ], *m.* (**—s**, *pl.* **—e**) cuckold; *einen zum — machen*, cuckold s.o.
Hai [haɪ], *m.* (**—s**, *pl.* **—e**) (*Zool.*) shark.
Haifisch ['haɪfɪʃ], *m.* (**—es**, *pl.* **—e**) (*Zool.*) shark.
Hain [haɪn], *m.* (**—s**, *pl.* **—e**) (*Poet.*) grove, thicket.
Haiti [ha'ɪtɪ], *n.* Haiti.
Häkchen ['hɛ:kçən], *n.* (**—s**, *pl.* —) small hook, crotchet; apostrophe.
häkeln ['hɛ:kəln], *v.a. v.n.* crochet; (*fig.*) tease; (*Am.*) needle (*coll.*).
Haken ['ha:kən], *m.* (**—s**, *pl.* —) hook, clasp; (*fig.*) hitch, snag.
Hakenkreuz ['ha:kənkrɔyts], *n.* (**—es**, *pl.* **—e**) swastika.
halb [halp], *adj.* half; *halb neun*, half past eight.
halbieren [hal'bi:rən], *v.a.* halve, divide into halves; (*Maths.*) bisect.
Halbinsel ['halpɪnzəl], *f.* (—, *pl.* **—n**) peninsula.
Halbmesser ['halpmɛsər], *m.* (**—s**, *pl.* —) radius.
halbpart ['halppart], *adj.* — *mit einem machen*, go halves with s.o.
halbstündig ['halpʃtyndɪç], *adj.* lasting half an hour.
halbstündlich ['halpʃtyntlɪç], *adj.* half-hourly, every half-hour.
halbwegs ['halpve:ks], *adv.* (*coll.*) reasonably, tolerably.
Halbwelt ['halpvɛlt], *f.* (—, *no pl.*) demi-monde.
halbwüchsig ['halpvy:ksɪç], *adj.* teenage.
Halde ['haldə], *f.* (—, *pl.* **—n**) declivity, hill; (*Min.*) waste-heap, slag-heap.
Hälfte ['hɛlftə], *f.* (—, *pl.* **—n**) half; (*obs.*) moiety.
Halfter ['halftər], *f.* (—, *pl.* **—n**) halter.
Hall [hal], *m.* (**—s**, *no pl.*) sound, echo.
Halle ['halə], *f.* (—, *pl.* **—n**) hall, vestibule; portico; porch.
hallen ['halən], *v.n.* sound, resound; clang.
Halm [halm], *m.* **—es**, *pl.* **—e**) stalk; (*grass*) blade.
Hals [hals], *m.* (**—es**, *pl.* **¨e**) neck, throat; — *über Kopf*, head over heels, hastily, hurriedly.
Halsader ['halsa:dər], *f.* (—, *pl.* **—n**) jugular vein.
Halsbinde ['halsbɪndə], *f.* (—, *pl.* **—n**) scarf, tie.
Halsentzündung ['halsɛntsynduŋ], *f.* (—, *pl.* **—en**) inflammation of the throat.
Halskrause ['halskrauzə], *f.* (—, *pl.* **—n**) frill, ruff.
halsstarrig ['halsʃtarɪç], *adj.* stubborn, obstinate.
Halsweh ['halsve:], *n.* (**—s**, *no pl.*) sore throat.
Halt [halt], *m.* (**—es**, *no pl.*) halt; stop; hold; (*also fig.*) support.
haltbar ['haltba:r], *adj.* durable, strong; tenable, valid.
halten ['haltən], *v.a. irr.* hold; keep; detain; deliver (speech, lecture); observe, celebrate. — *v.n.* stop; stand firm; insist; *halt!* stop! stop it! — *v.r. sich* —, hold out, keep, behave.
haltlos ['haltlo:s], *adj.* unprincipled; floundering, unsteady.
Haltung ['haltuŋ], *f.* (—, *pl.* **—en**) carriage, posture, attitude; (*fig.*) behaviour, demeanour; attitude.
Halunke [ha'luŋkə], *m.* (**—n**, *pl.* **—n**) scoundrel, rascal, scamp.
hämisch ['hɛ:mɪʃ], *adj.* malicious, spiteful.
Hammel ['haməl], *m.* (**—s**, *pl.* —) (*meat*) mutton.
Hammelkeule ['haməlkɔylə], *f.* (—, *pl.* **—n**) leg of mutton.
Hammer ['hamər], *m.* (**—s**, *pl.* **¨**) hammer; *unter den — kommen*, be sold by auction.
Hämorrhoiden [hɛmo'ri:dən], *f. pl.* (*Med.*) piles, haemorrhoids.
Hand [hant], *f.* (—, *pl.* **¨e**) hand.
Handarbeit ['hantarbaɪt], *f.* (—, *pl.* **—en**) manual labour; needlework.
Handel ['handəl], *m.* (**—s**, *no pl.*) trade, commerce; — *treiben*, carry on trade, do business.
Händel ['hɛndəl], *m. pl.* quarrel, difference, dispute.

handeln [ˈhandəln], *v.n.* act; — *in,* deal in; *es handelt sich um* . . . it is a question of . . . ; *es handelt von* . . . , it deals with . . . .

handelseinig [ˈhandəlsaınıç], *adj.* — *werden,* come to terms.

Handelsgenossenschaft [ˈhandəlsgənɔsənʃaft], *f.* (—, *pl.* —**en**) trading company.

Handelsgeschäft [ˈhandəlsgəʃɛft], *n.* (—**es,** *pl.* —**e**) commercial transaction.

Handelsgesellschaft [ˈhandəlsgəzelʃaft], *f.* (—, *pl.* —**en**) trading company; joint-stock company.

Handelskammer [ˈhandəlskamər], *f.* (—, *pl.* —**n**) chamber of commerce.

Handelsmarke [ˈhandəlsmarkə], *f.* (—, *pl.* —**n**) trade-mark.

Handelsreisende [ˈhandəlsraızəndə], *m.* (—**n,** *pl.* —**n**) commercial traveller.

händelsüchtig [ˈhɛndəlzyçtıç], *adj.* quarrelsome; litigious.

Handelsvertrag [ˈhandəlsfertra:k], *m.* (—**es,** *pl.* ¨—**e**) commercial treaty; contract.

Handelszweig [ˈhandəlstsvaık], *m.* (—**es,** *pl.* —**e**) branch of trade.

Handfeger [ˈhantfe:gər], *m.* (—**s,** *pl.* —) hand-broom, handbrush.

Handfertigkeit [ˈhantfɛrtıçkaıt], *f.* (—, *no pl.*) dexterity, manual skill; handicrafts.

Handfessel [ˈhantfɛsəl], *f.* (—, *pl.* —**n**) handcuff.

handfest [ˈhantfɛst], *adj.* robust, strong.

Handgeld [ˈhantgɛlt], *n.* (—**es,** *no pl.*) earnest; (*money*) advance.

Handgelenk [ˈhantgəlɛŋk], *n.* (—**s,** *pl.* —**e**) wrist.

handgemein [ˈhanˌgəmaın], *adj.* — *werden,* come to blows.

Handgemenge [ˈhantgəmɛŋə], *n.* (—**s,** *no pl.*) fray, scuffle.

handgreiflich [ˈhantgraıflıç], *adj.* palpable; evident, plain.

Handgriff [ˈhantgrıf], *m.* (—**es,** *pl.* —**e**) handle; (*fig.*) knack.

Handhabe [ˈhantha:bə], *f.* (—, *pl.* —**n**) (*fig.*) hold, handle.

handhaben [ˈhantha:bən], *v.a.* handle, manage; operate.

Handlanger [ˈhantlaŋər], *m.* (—**s,** *pl.* —) helper, carrier.

Händler [ˈhɛndlər], *m.* (—**s,** *pl.* —) dealer, merchant.

handlich [ˈhantlıç], *adj.* handy, manageable.

Handlung [ˈhandluŋ], *f.* (—, *pl.* —**en**) shop; (*Am.*) store; commercial house, mercantile business; action, act, deed; (*Lit.*) plot.

Handrücken [ˈhantrykən], *m.* (—**s,** *pl.* —) back of the hand.

Handschelle [ˈhantʃɛlə], *f.* (—, *pl.* —**n**) manacle, handcuff.

Handschlag [ˈhantʃla:k], *m.* (—**s,** *pl.* ¨—**e**) handshake.

Handschuh [ˈhantʃu:], *m.* (—**s,** *pl.* —**e**) glove; (*of iron*) gauntlet.

Handstreich [ˈhantʃtraıç], *m.* (—**es,** *pl.* —**e**) (*Mil.*) surprise attack, coup de main.

Handtuch [ˈhanttu:x], *n.* (—**es,** *pl.* ¨—**er**) towel.

Handumdrehen [ˈhantumdre:ən], *n.* (—**s,** *no pl.*) *im* —, in no time, in a jiffy.

Handwerk [ˈhantvɛrk], *n.* (—**s,** *pl.* —**e**) handicraft, trade, craft.

Handwörterbuch [ˈhantvœrtərbu:x], *n.* (—**es,** *pl.* ¨—**er**) compact dictionary.

Handwurzel [ˈhantvurtsəl], *f.* (—, *pl.* —**n**) wrist.

Hanf [hanf], *m.* (—**es,** *no pl.*) hemp.

Hänfling [ˈhɛnflıŋ], *m.* (—**s,** *pl.* —**e**) (*Orn.*) linnet.

Hang [haŋ], *m.* (—**es,** *pl.* ¨—**e**) slope, declivity; (*fig.*) (*no pl.*) inclination, propensity.

Hängematte [ˈhɛŋəmatə], *f.* (—, *pl.* —**n**) hammock.

hängen [ˈhɛŋən], *v.a. irr.* hang, suspend. — *v.r. sich* —, hang o.s. — *v.n.* hang, be suspended; be hanged (*execution*).

Hannover [haˈno:fər], *n.* Hanover.

Hänselei [ˈhɛnzəlaı], *f.* (—, *pl.* —**en**) chaffing, leg-pulling, teasing.

hänseln [ˈhɛnzəln], *v.a.* tease, chaff.

Hantel [ˈhantəl], *f.* (—, *pl.* —**n**) dumbbell.

hantieren [hanˈti:rən], *v.n.* busy o.s., work, occupy o.s. (with).

hapern [ˈha:pərn], *v.n.* lack, be deficient; *da hapert es,* that's the snag.

Häppchen [ˈhɛpçən], *n.* (—**s,** *pl.* —) morsel.

Happen [ˈhapən], *m.* (—**s,** *pl.* —) mouthful.

happig [ˈhapıç], *adj.* greedy; excessive.

Härchen [ˈhɛ:rçən], *n.* (—**s,** *pl.* —) short hair.

Harfe [ˈharfə], *f.* (—, *pl.* —**n**) (*Mus.*) harp.

Harke [ˈharkə], *f.* (—, *pl.* —**n**) rake.

Harm [harm], *m.* (—**es,** *no pl.*) grief, sorrow; injury, wrong.

härmen [ˈhɛrmən], *v.r. sich* — *um,* grieve over.

harmlos [ˈharmlo:s], *adj.* harmless, innocuous.

Harmonielehre [harmɔˈni:le:rə], *f.* (—, *pl.* —**n**) (*Mus.*) harmonics; harmony.

harmonieren [harmɔˈni:rən], *v.n. mit einem* —, be in concord with s.o., agree with s.o.

Harmonika [harˈmo:nıka], *f.* (—, *pl.* —**ken**) (*Mus.*) accordion, concertina; mouth-organ.

Harn [harn], *m.* (—**s,** *no pl.*) urine.

Harnisch [ˈharnıʃ], *m.* (—**es,** *pl.* —**e**) harness, armour; *in* — *bringen,* enrage.

Harpune [harˈpu:nə], *f.* (—, *pl.* —**n**) harpoon.

harren [ˈharən], *v.n.* wait for, hope for.

harsch [harʃ], *adj.* harsh; rough; unfriendly.
hart [hart], *adj.* hard, severe, cruel, austere.
Härte ['hɛrtə], *f.* (—, *pl.* —**n**) hardness, severity.
härten ['hɛrtən], *v.a.* harden.
hartleibig ['hartlaɪbɪç], *adj.* constipated.
hartnäckig ['hartnɛkɪç], *adj.* stubborn, obstinate; undaunted.
Harz (1) [harts], *m.* (*Geog.*) (—**es**, *no pl.*) the Hartz mountains.
Harz (2) [harts], *n.* (—**es**, *pl.* —**e**) resin, rosin.
harzig ['hartsɪç], *adj.* resinous.
Hasardspiel [ha'zartʃpi:l], *n.* (—**es**, *pl.* —**e**) game of chance, gamble.
Haschee [ha'ʃe:], *n.* (—**s**, *pl.* —**s**) puree, hash, mash.
haschen ['haʃən], *v.a.* catch, snatch, seize. — *v.n.* — *nach*, strain after, snatch at.
Häschen ['hɛ:sçən], *n.* (—**s**, *pl.* —) (*Zool.*) small hare, leveret.
Häscher ['hɛʃər], *m.* (—**s**, *pl.* —) bailiff.
Hase ['ha:zə], *m.* (—**n**, *pl.* —**n**) (*Zool.*) hare.
Haselrute ['ha:zəlru:tə], *f.* (—, *pl.* —**n**) hazel-switch.
Hasenfuß ['ha:zənfu:s], *m.* (—**es**, *no pl.*) coward.
Hasenklein ['ha:zənklaɪn], *n.* (—**s**, *no pl.*) jugged hare.
Hasenscharte ['ha:zənʃartə], *f.* (—, *pl.* —**n**) hare-lip.
Haspe ['haspə], *f.* (—, *pl.* —**n**) hasp, hinge.
Haspel ['haspəl], *f.* (—, *pl.* —**n**) reel.
haspeln ['haspəln], *v.a.* wind on a reel; (*fig.*) rattle off.
Haß [has], *m.* (—**sses**, *no pl.*) hatred, hate, detestation.
hassen ['hasən], *v.a.* hate, detest.
haßerfüllt ['hasərfylt], *adj.* full of spite, full of hatred.
häßlich ['hɛslɪç], *adj.* ugly, repulsive; (*fig.*) unpleasant, unkind; unseemly.
Hast [hast], *f.* (—, *no pl.*) haste, hurry, hastiness, rashness.
hastig ['hastɪç], *adj.* hasty, hurried.
hätscheln ['hɛtʃəln], *v.a.* pamper, caress, fondle.
Hatz [hats], *f.* (—, *pl.* —**en**) baiting; hunt; revelry.
Haube ['haubə], *f.* (—, *pl.* —**n**) bonnet, cap; (*Motor.*) bonnet, (*Am.*) hood.
Haubenlerche ['haubənlɛrçə], *f.* (—, *pl.* —**n**) (*Orn.*) crested lark.
Haubitze [hau'bɪtsə], *f.* (—, *pl.* —**n**) howitzer.
Hauch [haux], *m.* (—**es**, *no pl.*) breath, whiff; (*fig.*) touch, tinge.
hauchdünn ['haux'dyn], *adj.* extremely thin.
hauchen ['hauxən], *v.n.* breathe.
Hauchlaut ['hauxlaut], *m.* (—**es**, *pl.* —**e**) (*Phonet.*) aspirate.
Haudegen ['haude:gən], *m.* (—**s**, *pl.* —) broad-sword; *ein alter* —, an old bully.
Haue ['hauə], *f.* (—, *no pl.*) (*coll.*) thrashing.
hauen ['hauən], *v.a.* hew; cut; strike; hit; give a hiding to. — *v.n. über die Schnur* —, kick over the traces.
Hauer ['hauər], *m.* (—**s**, *pl.* —) hewer, cutter; (*animal*) fang, tusk.
Häuer ['hɔyər], *m.* (—**s**, *pl.* —) miner.
Haufen ['haufən], *m.* (—**s**, *pl.* —) heap, pile.
häufen ['hɔyfən], *v.a.* heap, pile. — *v.r. sich* —, accumulate, multiply, increase.
häufig ['hɔyfɪç], *adj.* frequent, abundant. — *adv.* frequently, often.
Häufung ['hɔyfuŋ], *f.* (—, *pl.* —**en**) accumulation.
Haupt [haupt], *n.* (—**es**, *pl.* ⸚**er**) head; leader; chief, principal; (*compounds*) main—; *aufs* — *schlagen*, inflict a total defeat on; *ein bemoostes* —, an old student.
Hauptaltar ['hauptalta:r], *m.* (—**s**, *pl.* —**e**) (*Eccl.*) high altar.
Hauptbuch ['hauptbu:x], *n.* (—**es**, *pl.* ⸚**er**) ledger.
Häuptling ['hɔyptlɪŋ], *m.* (—**s**, *pl.* —**e**) chieftain.
Hauptmann ['hauptman], *m.* (—**s**, *pl.* ⸚**er, Hauptleute**) (*Mil.*) captain.
Hauptnenner ['hauptnɛnər], *m.* (—**s**, *pl.* —) (*Maths.*) common denominator.
Hauptquartier ['hauptkvarti:r], *n.* (—**es**, *pl.* —**e**) headquarters.
Hauptsache ['hauptzaxə], *f.* (—, *pl.* —**n**) main thing, substance, main point; *in der* —, in the main.
hauptsächlich ['hauptzɛçlɪç], *adj.* chief, main, principal, essential.
Hauptsatz ['hauptzats], *m.* (—**es**, *pl.* ⸚**e**) (*Gram.*) principal sentence.
Hauptschriftleiter ['hauptʃrɪftlaɪtər], *m.* (—**s**, *pl.* —) editor-in-chief.
Hauptschule ['hauptʃu:lə], *f.* (—, *pl.* —**n**) intermediate school.
Hauptstadt ['hauptʃtat], *f.* (—, *pl.* ⸚**e**) capital, metropolis.
Hauptton ['hauptto:n], *m.* (—**s**, *pl.* ⸚**e**) (*Mus.*) key-note; (*Phonet.*) primary accent.
Haupttreffer ['haupttrɛfər], *m.* (—**s**, *pl.* —) first prize; jackpot.
Hauptverkehrsstunden ['hauptfɛrke:rsʃtundən], *f. pl.* (*traffic etc.*) rush-hour.
Hauptwache ['hauptvaxə], *f.* (—, *pl.* —**n**) central guardroom.
Hauptwort ['hauptvɔrt], *n.* (—**es**, *pl.* ⸚**er**) noun, substantive.
Hauptzahl ['haupttsa:l], *f.* (—, *pl.* —**en**) cardinal number.
Haus [haus], *n.* (—**es**, *pl.* ⸚**er**) house, home; household; firm; *zu* —*e*, at home; *nach* —*e*, home.
Hausarbeit ['hausarbaɪt], *f.* (—, *pl.* —**en**) housework, domestic work: homework.

Hausarrest ['hausarɛst], *m.* (**—es,** *no pl.*) house arrest.
Hausarzt ['hausartst], *m.* (**—es,** *pl.* **¨e**) family doctor.
hausbacken ['hausbakən], *adj.* home-made; homely; humdrum.
Häuschen ['hɔysçən], *n.* (**—s,** *pl.* **—**) small house, cottage; *ganz aus dem — sein*, be beside o.s.
Hausen ['hauzən], *m.* (**—s,** *pl.* **—**) sturgeon.
hausen ['hauzən], *v.n.* reside, be domiciled; *übel —*, play havoc among.
Hausflur ['hausflu:r], *m.* (**—s,** *pl.* **—e**) entrance hall (of a house), vestibule.
Hausfrau ['hausfrau], *f.* (**—,** *pl.* **—en**) housewife, mistress of the house.
Hausfriedensbruch ['hausfri:dənsbrux], *m.* (**—es,** *pl.* **¨e**) (*Law*) intrusion, trespass.
Hausgenosse ['hausgənɔsə], *m.* (**—n,** *pl.* **—n**) fellow-lodger.
Haushalt ['haushalt], *m.* (**—es,** *no pl.*) household.
Haushaltung ['haushaltuŋ], *f.* (**—,** *no pl.*) housekeeping.
Hausherr ['haushɛr], *m.* (**—n,** *pl.* **—en**) master of the house, householder.
Haushofmeister ['haushofmaɪstər], *m.* (**—s,** *pl.* **—**) steward; butler.
hausieren [hau'zi:rən], *v.n.* peddle, hawk.
Hauslehrer ['hausle:rər], *m.* (**—s,** *pl.* **—**) private tutor.
Häusler ['hɔyslər], *m.* (**—s,** *pl.* **—**) cottager.
häuslich ['hɔyslɪç], *adj.* domestic, domesticated.
Hausmädchen ['hausmɛdçən], *n.* (**—s,** *pl.* **—**) housemaid.
Hausmannskost ['hausmanskɔst], *f.* (**—,** *no pl.*) plain fare.
Hausmeister ['hausmaɪstər], *m.* (**—s,** *pl.* **—**) house-porter, caretaker.
Hausmittel ['hausmɪtəl], *n.* (**—s,** *pl.* **—**) household remedy.
Hausrat ['hausra:t], *m.* (**—s,** *no pl.*) household furnishings, household effects.
Hausschlüssel ['hausʃlysəl], *m.* (**—s,** *pl.* **—**) latch-key.
Hausschuh ['hausʃu:], *m.* (**—s,** *pl.* **—e**) slipper.
Hausstand ['hausʃtant], *m.* (**—es,** *pl.* **¨e**) household.
Haustier ['hausti:r], *n.* (**—es,** *pl.* **—e**) domestic animal.
Hausvater ['hausfa:tər], *m.* (**—s,** *pl.* **¨**) paterfamilias.
Hausverwalter ['hausfɛrvaltər], *m.* (**—s,** *pl.* **—**) steward, caretaker; (*Am.*) janitor.
Hauswesen ['hausve:zən], *n.* (**—s,** *no pl.*) household management *or* affairs.
Hauswirt ['hausvɪrt], *m.* (**—es,** *pl.* **—e**) landlord.
Hauswirtin ['hausvɪrtɪn], *f.* (**—,** *pl.* **—nen**) landlady.
Hauswirtschaft ['hausvɪrtʃaft], *f.* (**—,** *no pl.*) housekeeping, domestic economy.
Haut [haut], *f.* (**—,** *pl.* **¨e**) (*human*) skin; (*animal*) hide; (*fruit*) peel; (*on liquid*) skin; membrane; film; *aus der — fahren*, flare up.
Hautausschlag ['hautausʃla:k], *m.* (**—s,** *pl.* **¨e**) rash, eczema.
Häutchen ['hɔytçən], *n.* (**—s,** *pl.* **—**) cuticle, pellicle, membrane.
häuten ['hɔytən], *v.a.* skin, flay, strip off the skin. — *v.r. sich —*, cast off (skin) *or* slough.
Hebamme ['he:pamə], *f.* (**—,** *pl.* **—n**) midwife.
Hebel ['he:bəl], *m.* (**—s,** *pl.* **—**) lever.
heben ['he:bən], *v.a. irr.* raise, lift, hoist, heave; elevate; improve; *aus der Taufe —*, be godfather (godmother) to (s.o.).
Heber ['he:bər], *m.* (**—s,** *pl.* **—**) siphon.
Hebräer [he'brɛ:ər], *m.* (**—s,** *pl.* **—**) Hebrew.
Hechel ['hɛçəl], *f.* (**—,** *pl.* **—n**) hackle, flax-comb.
hecheln ['hɛçəln], *v.a.* dress flax; hackle; (*fig.*) taunt, heckle.
Hecht [hɛçt], *m.* (**—es,** *pl.* **—e**) (*Zool.*) pike; (*swimming*) dive.
Hechtsprung ['hɛçtʃpruŋ], *m.* header.
Heck [hɛk], *n.* (**—s,** *pl.* **—e**) (*Naut.*) stern; (*Motor.*) rear; (*Aviat.*) tail.
Heckbord ['hɛkbɔrt], *m.* (**—s,** *pl.* **—e**) (*Naut.*) taffrail.
Hecke ['hɛkə], *f.* (**—,** *pl.* **—n**) hedge.
hecken ['hɛkən], *v.n.* breed, bring forth.
Heckpfennig ['hɛkpfɛnɪç], *m.* (**—s,** *pl.* **—e**) lucky sixpence.
heda! ['he:da:], *excl.* hey, you!
Heer [he:r], *n.* (**—es,** *pl.* **—e**) army; multitude; *stehendes —*, regular army.
Heeresmacht ['he:rəsmaxt], *f.* (**—,** *pl.* **¨e**) armed forces, troops.
Heerschar ['he:rʃa:r], *f.* (**—,** *pl.* **—en**) host; corps, legion; (*Bibl.*) *der Herr der —en*, the Lord of Hosts.
Heerschau ['he:rʃau], *f.* (**—,** *pl.* **—en**) review, muster, parade.
Heerstraße ['he:rʃtra:sə], *f.* (**—,** *pl.* **—en**) military road; highway; (*Am.*) highroad.
Heerwesen ['he:rve:zən], *n.* (**—s,** *no pl.*) military affairs.
Hefe ['he:fə], *f.* (**—,** *no pl.*) yeast; dregs, sediment.
Hefeteig ['he:fətaɪk], *m.* (**—s,** *pl.* **—e**) leavened dough.
Heft [hɛft], *n.* (**—es,** *pl.* **—e**) exercise-book, copy-book; haft, handle, hilt.
heften ['hɛftən], *v.a.* fasten; baste, stitch, fix, pin.
heftig ['hɛftɪç], *adj.* vehement, violent.
Heftnadel ['hɛftna:dəl], *f.* (**—,** *pl.* **—n**) stitching-needle.
hegen ['he:gən], *v.a.* enclose, protect, preserve; (*fig.*) cherish; entertain; hold; *— und pflegen*, nurse carefully.

Hehl [he:l], *n.* (**—es**, *no pl.*) concealment, secret.
hehlen ['he:lən], *v.n.* receive stolen goods.
Hehler ['hə:lər], *m.* (**—s**, *pl.* **—**) receiver of stolen goods, (*sl.*) fence.
hehr [he:r], *adj.* (*Lit.*) exalted, august, sublime.
Heide (1) ['haɪdə], *m.* (**—n**, *pl.* **—n**) heathen, pagan.
Heide (2) ['haɪdə], *f.* (**—**, *pl.* **—n**) heath.
Heidekraut ['haɪdəkraut], *n.* (**—es**, *no pl.*) heath, heather.
Heidelbeere ['haɪdəlbe:rə], *f.* (**—**, *pl.* **—n**) (*Bot.*) bilberry; (*Am.*) blueberry.
Heidenangst ['haɪdənaŋst], *f.* (**—**, *no pl.*) (*coll.*) mortal fear.
Heidenlärm ['haɪdənlɛrm], *m.* (**—es**, *no pl.*) hullaballoo.
Heidenröschen ['haɪdənrø:sçən], *n.* (**—s**, *pl.* **—**) (*Bot.*) sweet-briar.
Heidentum ['haɪdəntu:m], *n.* (**—s**, *no pl.*) paganism.
heidnisch ['haɪdnɪʃ], *adj.* pagan, heathen.
Heidschnuke ['haɪtʃnu:kə], *f.* (**—**, *pl.* **—n**) moorland sheep.
heikel ['haɪkəl], *adj.* delicate, sensitive, critical.
Heil [haɪl], *n.* (**—(e)s**, *no pl.*) safety, welfare; (*Theol.*) salvation; *sein — versuchen*, have a try, try o.'s luck. — *int.* hail! — *der Königin*, God save the Queen.
heil [haɪl], *adj.* unhurt, intact.
Heiland ['haɪlant], *m.* (**—s**, *no pl.*) Saviour, Redeemer.
Heilanstalt ['haɪlanʃtalt], *f.* (**—**, *pl.* **—en**) sanatorium, convalescent home; (*Am.*) sanitarium.
heilbar ['haɪlba:r], *adj.* curable.
heilbringend ['haɪlbrɪŋənt], *adj.* salutary.
heilen ['haɪlən], *v.a.* cure, heal. — *v.n.* (*aux.* sein) heal.
heilig ['haɪlɪç], *adj.* holy, sacred; *der Heilige Abend*, Christmas Eve; — *sprechen*, canonise; (*before name*) *der, die —e*, Saint.
Heiligenschein ['haɪlɪgənʃaɪn], *m.* (**—s**, *pl.* **—e**) halo; (*clouds*) nimbus.
Heiligkeit ['haɪlɪçkaɪt], *f.* (**—**, *no pl.*) holiness, sanctity, sacredness.
Heiligtum ['haɪlɪçtu:m], *n.* (**—s**, *pl.* **¨er**) sanctuary, shrine; holy relic.
Heiligung ['haɪlɪguŋ], *f.* (**—**, *pl.* **—en**) sanctification, consecration.
heilkräftig ['haɪlkrɛftɪç], *adj.* curative, salubrious.
Heilkunde ['haɪlkundə], *f.* (**—**, *no pl.*) therapeutics.
heillos ['haɪllo:s], *adj.* wicked, mischievous; (*fig.*) awful.
Heilmittel ['haɪlmɪtəl], *n.* (**—s**, *pl.* **—**) remedy.
heilsam ['haɪlza:m], *adj.* salubrious, salutary.
Heilsamkeit ['haɪlza:mkaɪt], *f.* (**—**, *no pl.*) salubrity, salubriousness.
Heilsarmee ['haɪlsarme:], *f.* (**—**, *no pl.*) Salvation Army.
Heilslehre ['haɪlsle:rə], *f.* (**—**, *pl.* **—n**) doctrine of salvation.
Heiltrank ['haɪltraŋk], *m.* (**—es**, *no pl.*) (medicinal) potion.
Heim [haɪm], *n.* (**—es**, *pl.* **—e**) home.
heim [haɪm], *adv. prefix* (*to verbs*) home.
Heimat ['haɪmat], *f.* (**—**, *no pl.*) native place, home, homeland.
Heimatschein ['haɪmatʃaɪn], *m.* (**—es**, *pl.* **—e**) certificate of origin *or* domicile.
Heimchen ['haɪmçən], *n.* (**—s**, *pl.* **—**) (*Ent.*) cricket.
heimführen ['haɪmfy:rən], *v.a.* bring home (a bride); (*fig.*) marry.
Heimgang ['haɪmgaŋ], *m.* (**—es**, *no pl.*) going home; (*fig.*) decease, death.
heimisch ['haɪmɪʃ], *adj.* native, indigenous; *sich — fühlen*, feel at home.
heimkehren ['haɪmke:rən], *v.n.* return (home).
heimleuchten ['haɪmlɔyçtən], *v.n. einem —*, tell s.o. the plain truth, give s.o. a piece of o.'s mind.
heimlich ['haɪmlɪç], *adj.* secret, clandestine, furtive.
heimsuchen ['haɪmzu:xən], *v.a.* visit; afflict, punish.
Heimtücke ['haɪmtykə], *f.* (**—**, *no pl.*) malice.
heimwärts ['haɪmvɛrts], *adv.* homeward.
Heimweh ['haɪmve:], *n.* (**—s**, *no pl.*) homesickness; nostalgia.
heimzahlen ['haɪmtsa:lən], *v.a.* pay back, retaliate.
Hein [haɪn], *m.* (*coll.*) *Freund —*, Death.
Heinzelmännchen ['haɪntsəlmɛnçən], *n.* (**—s**, *pl.* **—**) goblin, brownie, imp.
Heirat ['haɪra:t], *f.* (**—**, *pl.* **—en**) marriage, wedding.
heiraten ['haɪra:tən], *v.a.* marry, wed.
Heiratsgut ['haɪra:tsgu:t], *n.* (**—es**, *pl.* **¨er**) dowry.
heischen ['haɪʃən], *v.a.* (*Poet.*) ask, demand.
heiser ['haɪzər], *adj.* hoarse.
heiß [haɪs], *adj.* hot; (*fig.*) ardent; (*climate*) torrid.
heißen ['haɪsən], *v.a. irr.* bid, command. — *v.n.* be called; be said; signify, mean; *es heißt*, it is said; *das heißt* (*d.h.*), that is to say; *wie — Sie?* what is your name?
heißgeliebt ['haɪsgəli:pt], *adj.* dearly beloved.
heiter ['haɪtər], *adj.* clear; serene; cheerful.
Heiterkeit ['haɪtərkaɪt], *f.* (**—**, *no pl.*) serenity; cheerfulness.
heizen ['haɪtsən], *v.a. v.n.* heat.
Heizkissen ['haɪtskɪsən], *n.* (**—s**, *pl.* **—**) electric pad *or* blanket.
Heizkörper ['haɪtskœrpər], *m.* (**—s**, *pl.* **—**) radiator; heater.
Heizung ['haɪtsuŋ], *f.* (**—**, *pl.* **—en**) heating.
hektisch ['hɛktɪʃ], *adj.* hectic.

hektographieren [hɛktogra'fi:rən], *v.a.* stencil, duplicate.
Hektoliter ['hɛktoli:tər], *m.* (—**s**, *pl.* —) hectolitre (22 gallons).
Held [hɛlt], *m.* (—**en**, *pl.* —**en**) hero.
Heldengedicht ['hɛldəngədɪçt], *n.* (—**es**, *pl.* —**e**) heroic poem, epic.
heldenhaft ['hɛldənhaft], *adj.* heroic. — *adv.* heroically.
Heldenmut ['hɛldənmu:t], *m.* (—**es**, *no pl.*) heroism.
helfen ['hɛlfən], *v.n. irr.* (*Dat.*) help, aid, assist.
Helfershelfer ['hɛlfərshɛlfər], *m.* (—**s**, *pl.* —) accomplice, accessory.
Helgoland ['hɛlgolant], *n.* Heligoland.
hell [hɛl], *adj.* clear, bright, light; (*coll.*) clever, wide awake.
Helldunkel ['hɛlduŋkəl], *n.* (—**s**, *no pl.*) twilight; (*Art*) chiaroscuro.
Helle ['hɛlə], *f.* (—, *no pl.*) clearness; brightness; daylight.
Heller ['hɛlər], *m.* (—**s**, *pl.* —) small coin, farthing.
hellhörig ['hɛlhø:rɪç], *adj.* keen of hearing.
Helligkeit ['hɛlɪçkaɪt], *f.* (—, *no pl.*) clearness; daylight.
Hellseher ['hɛlze:ər], *m.* (—**s**, *pl.* —) clairvoyant.
hellsichtig ['hɛlzɪxtɪç], *adj.* clairvoyant; clear-sighted.
Helm [hɛlm], *m.* (—**es**, *pl.* —**e**) helmet.
Helmbusch ['hɛlmbuʃ], *m.* (—**es**, *pl.* ⸚**e**) crest (of helmet).
Helmgitter ['hɛlmgɪtər], *n.* (—**s**, *pl.* —) eye-slit (in helmet).
Helsingfors ['hɛlzɪŋfɔrs], *n.* Helsinki.
Helsingör [hɛlzɪŋ'ø:r], *n.* Elsinore.
Hemd [hɛmt], *n.* (—**es**, *pl.* —**en**) shirt; vest.
Hemdenstoff ['hɛmdənʃtɔf], *m.* (—**es**, *pl.* —**e**) shirting.
hemmen ['hɛmən], *v.a.* stop, hamper, hinder, restrain; (*fig.*) inhibit.
Hemmschuh ['hɛmʃu:], *m.* (—**s**, *pl.* —**e**) brake; (*fig.*) drag, obstruction.
Hemmung ['hɛmuŋ], *f.* (—, *pl.* —**en**) stoppage, hindrance, restraint; (*watch*) escapement; (*fig.*) inhibition, reluctance.
Hengst [hɛŋkst], *m.* (—**es**, *pl.* —**e**) stallion.
Henkel ['hɛŋkəl], *m.* (—**s**, *pl.* —) handle.
henken ['hɛŋkən], *v.a* hang (s.o.).
Henker ['hɛŋkər], *m.* (—**s**, *pl.* —) hangman, executioner.
Henne ['hɛnə], *f.* (—, *pl.* —**n**) (*Zool.*) hen; *junge* —, pullet.
her [he:r], *adv.* hither, here, to me; (*temp.*) since, ago; *von alters* —, from olden times; *von je* —, from time immemorial; *wo kommst du* —? where do you come from? *wie lange ist es* —? how long ago was it?
herab [hɛ'rap], *adv.* downwards, down to; *die Treppe* —, downstairs.
herablassen [hɛ'raplasən], *v.r. irr. sich* — *etwas zu tun*, condescend to do s.th.
herabsehen [hɛ'rapze:ən], *v.n. irr.* look down; (*fig.*) look down upon s.o.
herabsetzen [hɛ'rapzɛtsən], *v.a.* put down; degrade; (*value*) depreciate; (*price*) reduce, lower; (*fig.*) disparage.
herabwürdigen [hɛ'rapvyrdɪgən], *v.a.* degrade, abase.
herabziehen [hɛ'raptsi:ən], *v.a. irr.* pull down.
Heraldik [he'raldɪk], *f.* (—, *no pl.*) heraldry.
heran [hɛ'ran], *adv.* up to, on, near.
heranbilden [hɛ'ranbɪldən], *v.a.* train. — *v.r. sich* —, train, qualify.
herangehen [hɛ'range:ən], *v.n. irr.* (*aux.* sein) approach, sidle up (to); *an etwas* —, set to work on s.th.
heranmachen [hɛ'ranmaxən], *v.r. sich an etwas* —, set to work on s.th., set about s.th.
herannahen [hɛ'ranna:ən], *v.n.* (*aux.* sein) approach, draw near.
heranrücken [hɛ'ranrykən], *v.a.* move near. — *v.n.* (*aux.* sein) advance, draw near.
heranschleichen [hɛ'ranʃlaɪçən], *v.r. irr. sich* — *an*, sneak up to.
heranwachsen [hɛ'ranvaksən], *v.n. irr.* (*aux.* sein) grow up.
heranwagen [hɛ'ranva:gən], *v.r. sich* —, venture near.
heranziehen [hɛ'rantsi:ən], *v.a. irr.* draw near; *als Beispiel* —, cite as an example; (*fig.*) enlist (s.o.'s aid). — *v.n.* (*aux.* sein) draw near, approach.
herauf [hɛ'rauf], *adv.* up, upwards.
heraufbeschwören [hɛ'raufbeʃvø:rən], *v.a.* conjure up.
heraus [hɛ'raus], *adv.* out, out of.
herausfordern [hɛ'rausfɔrdərn], *v.a.* challenge.
Herausgabe [hɛ'rausga:bə], *f.* (—, *pl.* —**n**) delivery; (*book*) publication; editing.
herausgeben [hɛ'rausge:bən], *v.a. irr.* give out, deliver; (*money*) give change; (*book*) publish, edit.
Herausgeber [hɛ'rausge:bər], *m.* (—**s**, *pl.* —) publisher; editor.
heraushaben [hɛ'rausha:bən], *v.a. irr. etwas* —, have the knack of s.th.
herausputzen [hɛ'rausputsən], *v.r. sich* —, dress up.
herausrücken [hɛ'rausrykən], *v.n. mit Geld* —, fork out money; *mit der Sprache* —, speak out, come out with.
herausschlagen [hɛ'rausʃla:gən], *v.a. irr. die Kosten* —, recover expenses; *viel* —, make the most of; profit by.
herausstellen [hɛ'rausʃtɛlən], *v.a.* put out, expose. — *v.r. sich* — *als*, turn out to be.
herausstreichen [hɛ'rausʃtraɪçən], *v.a. irr.* extol, praise.
heraussuchen [hɛ'rauszu:xən], *v.a.* pick out.

herauswollen [hɛ'rausvɔlən], *v.n. nicht mit der Sprache —*, hesitate to speak out.
herb [hɛrp], *adj.* sour, sharp, tart, acrid; (*fig.*) austere, harsh, bitter; (*wine*) dry.
herbei [hɛr'baɪ], *adv.* hither, near.
herbeischaffen [hɛr'baɪʃafən], *v.a.* procure.
herbeiströmen [hɛr'baɪʃtrø:mən], *v.n.* (*aux.* sein) crowd, flock.
Herberge ['hɛrbɛrgə], *f.* (—, *pl.* **—n**) shelter, lodging, inn.
Herbst [hɛrpst], *m.* (**—es**, *pl.* **—e**) autumn; (*Am.*) fall.
Herbstrose ['hɛrpstro:zə], *f.* (—, *pl.* **—n**) (*Bot.*) hollyhock.
Herbstzeitlose ['hɛrpsttsaɪtlo:zə], *f.* (—, *pl.* **—n**) (*Bot.*) meadow-saffron.
Herd [he:rt], *m.* (**—es**, *pl.* **—e**) hearth, fireplace; cooking-stove; (*fig.*) focus.
Herde ['he:rdə], *f.* (—, *pl.* **—n**) flock, herd; (*fig.*) troop.
herein [hɛ'raɪn], *adv.* in, inside. — *int.* —*!* come in!
hereinbrechen [hɛ'raɪnbrɛçən], *v.n. irr.* (*aux.* sein) *über einen —*, befall s.o., overtake s.o.; (*night*) close in.
hereinfallen [hɛ'raɪnfalən], *v.n. irr.* (*aux.* sein) (*fig.*) be taken in, fall for s.th.
herfallen ['he:rfalən], *v.n. irr.* (*aux.* sein) *über einen —*, go for s.o., set upon s.o.
Hergang ['he:rgaŋ], *m.* (**—es**, *no pl.*) proceedings, course of events; circumstances; story, plot.
hergeben ['he:rge:bən], *v.a. irr.* give up, surrender.
hergebracht ['he:rgəbraxt], *adj.* traditional, time-honoured.
hergehen ['he:rge:ən], *v.n. irr.* (*aux.* sein) proceed; *es geht lustig her*, they are having a gay time.
hergelaufen ['he:rgəlaufən], *adj. ein —er Kerl*, an adventurer, an upstart.
herhalten ['he:rhaltən], *v.n. irr.* suffer, serve (as a butt).
Hering ['he:rɪŋ], *m.* (**—s**, *pl.* **—e**) (*Zool.*) herring; *geräucherter —*, smoked herring, bloater; *gesalzener —*, pickled herring.
herkommen ['he:rkɔmən], *v.n. irr.* (*aux.* sein) come here; be derived from, descend from.
herkömmlich ['he:rkœmlɪç], *adj.* traditional, customary, usual.
Herkunft ['he:rkunft], *f.* (—, *no pl.*) descent, extraction; origin.
herleiern ['he:rlaɪərn], *v.a.* recite monotonously; reel off.
herleiten ['he:rlaɪtən], *v.a.* derive from.
Hermelin [hɛrmə'li:n], *m.* (**—s**, *no pl.*) ermine (*fur*).
hermetisch [hɛr'me:tɪʃ], *adj.* hermetical.
hernach [her'na:x], *adv.* after, afterwards; hereafter.
hernehmen ['he:rne:mən], *v.a. irr.* take, get (from); take (s.o.) to task.
hernieder [hɛr'ni:dər], *adv.* down.
Herr [hɛr], *m.* (**—n**, *pl.* **—en**) master; lord; nobleman; gentleman; (*Theol.*) Lord; principal, governor; *mein —*, Sir; *meine Herren*, gentlemen; *— Schmidt*, Mr. Smith; *einer Sache — werden*, master s.th.
Herrenhaus ['hɛrənhaus], *n.* (**—es**, *pl.* **¨er**) mansion, manor house; (*Parl.*) House of Lords.
Herrenhof ['hɛrənho:f], *m.* (**—es**, *pl.* **¨e**) manor, country-seat.
Herrenstand ['hɛrənʃtant], *m.* (**—es**, *no pl.*) nobility, gentry.
Herrenzimmer ['hɛrəntsɪmər], *n.* (**—s**, *pl.* —) study.
Herrgott ['hɛrgɔt], the Lord God.
herrichten ['he:rrɪçtən], *v.a.* prepare, fix up.
Herrin ['hɛrɪn], *f.* (—, *pl.* **—innen**) mistress, lady.
herrisch ['hɛrɪʃ], *adj.* imperious, lordly.
herrlich ['hɛrlɪç], *adj.* magnificent, splendid, glorious, excellent.
Herrnhuter ['hɛrnhu:tər], *m.* (**—s**, *pl.* —) Moravian; (*pl.*) Moravian brethren.
Herrschaft ['hɛrʃaft], *f.* (—, *pl.* **—en**) mastery, rule, dominion; master, mistress; *meine —en!* ladies and gentlemen!
herrschaftlich ['hɛrʃaftlɪç], *adj.* belonging to a lord; (*fig.*) elegant, fashionable, distinguished.
herrschen ['hɛrʃən], *v.n.* rule, govern, reign.
Herrscher ['hɛrʃər], *m.* (**—s**, *pl.* —) ruler.
herrühren ['he:rry:rən], *v.n.* come from, originate in.
hersagen ['he:rza:gən], *v.a.* recite, reel off.
herschaffen ['he:rʃafən], *v.a.* procure.
herstammen ['he:rʃtamən], *v.n.* come from, stem from, originate from; be derived from.
herstellen ['he:rʃtɛlən], *v.a.* place here; manufacture; *wieder —*, restore; (*sick person*) restore to health.
Herstellung ['he:rʃtɛluŋ], *f.* (—, *no pl.*) manufacture, production.
herstürzen ['he:rʃtyrtsən], *v.n.* (*aux.* sein) *über einen —*, rush at s.o.
herüber [hɛ'ry:bər], *adv.* over, across; *— und hinüber*, there and back.
herum [hɛ'rum], *adv.* round, about; around.
herumbalgen [hɛ'rumbalgən], *v.r. sich —*, scrap; scuffle.
herumbekommen [hɛ'rumbəkɔmən], *v.a. irr.* (*coll.*) talk s.o. over, win s.o. over.
herumbummeln [hɛ'rumbuməln], *v.n.* loaf about.
herumstreichen [hɛ'rumʃtraɪçən], *v.n. irr.* (*aux.* sein) gad about.
herumtreiben [hɛ'rumtraɪbən], *v.r. irr. sich —*, loaf about, gad about.
herumzanken [hɛ'rumtsaŋkən], *v.r. sich —*, squabble, quarrel; live like cat and dog.

herumziehen [hɛ'rumtsi:ən], *v.a. irr.* drag about. — *v.n.* (*aux.* sein) wander about, move from place to place.
herunter [hɛ'runtər], *adj.* down, downward; *ich bin ganz* —, I feel poorly.
heruntergekommen [hɛ'runtərgəkɔmən], *adj.* decayed, broken down; in straitened circumstances; depraved.
herunterhandeln [hɛ'runtərhandəln], *v.a. einem etwas* —, beat s.o. down (in price).
herunterwürgen [hɛ'runtervyrgən], *v.a.* swallow s.th. with dislike.
hervor [hɛr'fo:r], *adv.* forth, forward, out.
hervorheben [hɛr'fo:rhe:bən], *v.a. irr.* emphasize, stress.
hervorragen [hɛr'fo:rra:gən], *v.n.* stand out, project; (*fig.*) be distinguished, excel.
hervorragend [hɛr'fo:rra:gənt], *adj.* prominent; (*fig.*) outstanding, excellent.
hervorrufen [hɛr'fo:rru:fən], *v.a. irr.* call forth; (*fig.*) evoke, bring about, create, cause.
hervorstechen [hɛr'fo:rʃtɛçən], *v.n. irr.* be predominant, stand out.
hervortun [hɛr'fo:rtu:n], *v.r. irr. sich* —, distinguish o.s.
Herz [hɛrts], *n.* (**—ens**, *pl.* **—en**) heart; courage; mind; spirit; feeling; core; (*Cards*) hearts; (*coll.*) darling; *einem etwas ans* — *legen*, impress s.th. upon s.o.; *von —en gern*, with all my heart; *sich etwas zu —en nehmen*, take s.th. to heart.
herzählen ['he:rtsɛ:lən], *v.a.* enumerate.
Herzanfall ['hɛrtsanfal], *m.* (**—s**, *pl.* **¨e**) (*Med.*) heart attack.
Herzbube ['hɛrtsbu:bə], *m.* (**—n**, *pl.* **—n**) (*Cards*) knave *or* jack of hearts.
Herzdame ['hɛrtsda:mə], *f.* (**—**, *pl.* **—n**) (*Cards*) queen of hearts.
Herzeleid ['hɛrtsəlaɪt], *n.* (**—es**, *no pl.*) heartbreak, sorrow, anguish, grief.
herzen ['hɛrtsən], *v.a.* hug.
Herzenseinfalt ['hɛrtsənsaɪnfalt], *f.* (**—**, *no pl.*) simple-mindedness.
Herzensgrund ['hɛrtsənsgrunt], *m.* (**—es**, *no pl.*) *aus* —, with all my heart.
Herzenslust ['hɛrtsənslust], *f.* (**—**, *no pl.*) heart's delight; *nach* —, to o.'s heart's content.
Herzfehler ['hɛrtsfe:lər], *m.* (**—s**, *pl.* **—**) (*Med.*) cardiac defect; organic heart disease.
Herzfell ['hɛrtsfɛl], *n.* (**—s**, *pl.* **—e**) pericardium.
herzförmig ['hɛrtsfœrmɪç], *adj.* heart-shaped.
herzhaft ['hɛrtshaft], *adj.* stout-hearted; courageous, bold; resolute; hearty.
herzig ['hɛrtsɪç], *adj.* lovely, charming, sweet; (*Am.*) cute.
Herzkammer ['hɛrtskamər], *f.* (**—**, *pl.* **—n**) ventricle (of the heart).
Herzklappe ['hɛrtsklapə], *f.* (**—**, *pl.* **—n**) valve of the heart.
Herzklopfen ['hɛrtsklɔpfən], *n.* (**—s**, *no pl.*) palpitations.
herzlich ['hɛrtslɪç], *adj.* hearty, cordial, affectionate; — *gern*, with pleasure; **—e** *Grüße*, kind regards.
Herzog ['hɛrtso:k], *m.* (**—s**, *pl.* **¨e**) duke.
Herzogtum ['hɛrtso:ktu:m], *n.* (**—s**, *pl.* **¨er**) duchy, dukedom.
Herzschlag ['hɛrtsʃla:k], *m.* (**—es**, *pl.* **¨e**) heartbeat; (*Med.*) heart attack, cardiac failure.
Hetäre [he'tɛ:rə], *f.* (**—**, *pl.* **—n**) courtesan.
Hetzblatt ['hɛtsblat], *n.* (**—s**, *pl.* **¨er**) gutter press.
Hetze ['hɛtsə], *f.* (**—**, *pl.* **—n**) chase, hunt, hurry, rush; agitation.
hetzen ['hɛtsən], *v.a.* bait, fluster, chase, hunt, incite. — *v.n. herum* —, rush around.
Hetzer ['hɛtsər], *m.* (**—s**, *pl.* **—**) instigator, rabble-rouser.
Heu [hɔy], *n.* (**—s**, *no pl.*) hay.
Heuboden ['hɔybo:dən], *m.* (**—s**, *pl.* **¨**) hayloft.
Heuchelei [hɔyçə'laɪ], *f.* (**—**, *pl.* **—en**) hypocrisy.
heucheln ['hɔyçəln], *v.n.* play the hypocrite, dissemble. — *v.a.* simulate, affect, feign.
Heuchler ['hɔyçlər], *m.* (**—s**, *pl.* **—**) hypocrite.
Heuer ['hɔyər], *f.* (**—**, *pl.* **—n**) (*Naut.*) engagement; hire, wages.
heuer ['hɔyər], *adv.* (*dial.*) this year, this season.
heuern ['hɔyərn], *v.a.* (*Naut.*) engage, hire.
Heugabel ['hɔyga:bəl], *f.* (**—**, *pl.* **—n**) pitchfork.
heulen ['hɔylən], *v.n.* howl; roar; cry, yell, scream.
Heupferd ['hɔypfɛrt], *n.* (**—es**, *pl.* **—e**) (*Ent.*) grasshopper.
heurig ['hɔyrɪç], *adj.* of this year, this year's (*wine etc.*).
Heuschnupfen ['hɔyʃnupfən], *m.* (**—s**, *no pl.*) hay-fever.
Heuschober ['hɔyʃo:bər], *m.* (**—s**, *pl.* **—**) hayrick.
Heuschrecke ['hɔyʃrɛkə], *f.* (**—**, *pl.* **—n**) (*Ent.*) locust.
heute ['hɔytə], *adv.* today, this day; — *in acht Tagen*, today week, a week today; — *abend*, tonight.
heutig ['hɔytɪç], *adj.* today's, this day's; modern.
heutzutage ['hɔytsuta:gə], *adv.* nowadays.
Hexe ['hɛksə], *f.* (**—**, *pl.* **—n**) witch, sorceress, hag.
hexen ['hɛksən], *v.n.* use witchcraft; practise sorcery.
Hexenschuß ['hɛksənʃus], *m.* (**—sses**, *no pl.*) (*Med.*) lumbago.

Hexerei [hɛksə'raɪ], *f.* (—, *pl.* **—en**) witchcraft, sorcery, juggling.
hie [hi:], *adv.* (*dial.*) here.
Hieb [hi:p], *m.* (**—es**, *pl.* **—e**) cut, stroke; hit, blow; (*pl.*) a thrashing.
hienieden [hi:'ni:dən], *adv.* here below, down here.
hier [hi:r], *adv.* here, in this place.
Hiersein ['hi:rzaɪn], *n.* (**—s**, *no pl.*) presence, attendance.
hiesig ['hi:zɪç], *adj.* of this place, of this country, local.
Hifthorn ['hɪfthɔrn], *n.* (**—s**, *pl.* **¨er**) hunting-horn.
Hilfe ['hɪlfə], *f.* (—, *pl.* **—n**) help, aid, assistance, succour, relief.
hilflos ['hɪlflo:s], *adj.* helpless.
hilfreich ['hɪlfraɪç], *adj.* helpful.
Hilfsmittel ['hɪlfsmɪtəl], *n.* (**—s**, *pl.* —) expedient, remedy.
Hilfsschule ['hɪlfsʃu:lə], *f.* (—, *pl.* **—n**) school for backward children.
Hilfszeitwort ['hɪlfstsaɪtvɔrt], *n.* (**—s**, *pl.* **¨er**) (*Gram.*) auxiliary verb.
Himbeere ['hɪmbe:rə], *f.* (—, *pl.* **—n**) raspberry.
Himmel ['hɪməl], *m.* (**—s**, *pl.* —) heaven, heavens; sky; firmament.
himmelan [hɪməl'an], *adv.* heavenward.
himmelangst ['hɪməlaŋkst], *adv.* *ihm war* —, he was panic-stricken.
Himmelbett ['hɪməlbɛt], *n.* (**—s**, *pl.* **—en**) fourposter.
himmelblau ['hɪməlblau], *adj.* sky-blue.
Himmelfahrt ['hɪməlfa:rt], *f.* (—, *no pl.*) Ascension.
Himmelschlüssel ['hɪməlʃlysəl], *m.* (**—s**, *pl.* —) (*Bot.*) primrose.
himmelschreiend ['hɪməlʃraɪənt], *adj.* atrocious, revolting.
Himmelsgewölbe ['hɪməlsgəvœlbə], *n.* (**—s**, *pl.* —) firmament.
Himmelsstrich ['hɪməlsʃtrɪç], *m.* (**—s**, *pl.* **—e**) climate, zone.
Himmelszeichen ['hɪməlstsaɪçən], *n.* (**—s**, *pl.* —) sign of the zodiac.
himmelweit ['hɪməlvaɪt], *adj.* enormous; — *entfernt*, poles apart.
himmlisch ['hɪmlɪʃ], *adj.* celestial, heavenly.
hin [hɪn], *adv.* there, towards that place; finished, gone; ruined; — *und her*, to and fro.
hinab [hɪn'ap], *adv.* down.
hinan [hɪn'an], *adv.* up.
hinarbeiten ['hɪnarbaɪtən], *v.n.* *auf etwas* —, work towards s.th.
hinauf [hɪn'auf], *adv.* up, up to.
hinaus [hɪn'aus], *adv.* out, out of; *es kommt auf dasselbe* —, it comes to the same thing.
hinauswollen [hɪn'ausvɔlən], *v.n.* wish to go out; (*fig.*) *hoch* —, aim high.
hinausziehen [hɪn'austsi:ən], *v.a. irr.* draw out; drag on; (*fig.*) protract.
Hinblick ['hɪnblɪk], *m.* (**—es**, *no pl.*) *im* — *auf*, in consideration of, with regard to.

hinbringen ['hɪnbrɪŋən], *v.a. irr.* bring to; escort; *Zeit* —, while away time.
hinderlich ['hɪndərlɪç], *adj.* obstructive, cumbersome.
hindern ['hɪndərn], *v.a.* hinder, obstruct, hamper, impede.
hindeuten ['hɪndɔytən], *v.n.* *auf etwas* —, point to s.th., hint at s.th.
Hindin ['hɪndɪn], *f.* (—, *pl.* **—innen**) (*Poet.*) hind.
hindurch [hɪn'durç], *adv.* through; throughout; *die ganze Zeit* —, all the time.
hinein [hɪn'aɪn], *adv.* in, into; *in den Tag* — *leben*, live for the present, lead a life of carefree enjoyment.
hineinfinden [hɪn'aɪnfɪndən], *v.r. irr.* *sich in etwas* —, reconcile *or* adapt o.s. to s.th.
hinfällig ['hɪnfɛlɪç], *adj.* frail, feeble, weak; shaky, void, invalid.
Hingabe ['hɪnga:bə], *f.* (—, *no pl.*) surrender; (*fig.*) devotion.
hingeben ['hɪnge:bən], *v.a. irr.* give up, surrender. — *v.r. sich einer Sache* —, devote o.s. to a task.
hingegen [hɪn'ge:gən], *adv.* on the other hand.
hinhalten ['hɪnhaltən], *v.a. irr.* (*thing*) hold out; (*person*) keep in suspense, put off.
hinken ['hɪŋkən], *v.n.* limp.
hinlänglich ['hɪnlɛŋlɪç], *adj.* sufficient.
hinlegen ['hɪnle:gən], *v.a.* lay down, put away. — *v.r. sich* —, lie down, go to bed.
hinnehmen ['hɪnne:mən], *v.a. irr.* take, submit to, accept.
hinreichen ['hɪnraɪçən], *v.a.* pass to. — *v.n.* suffice, be sufficient.
Hinreise ['hɪnraɪzə], *f.* (—, *pl.* **—n**) outward journey.
hinreißen ['hɪnraɪsən], *v.r. irr.* *sich* — *lassen*, allow o.s. to be carried away.
hinreißend ['hɪnraɪsənt], *adj.* charming, ravishing, enchanting.
hinrichten ['hɪnrɪçtən], *v.a.* execute, put to death.
hinscheiden ['hɪnʃaɪdən], *v.n. irr.* die, pass away.
hinschlängeln ['hɪnʃlɛŋəln], *v.r.* *sich* —, meander, wind along.
Hinsicht ['hɪnzɪçt], *f.* (—, *no pl.*) view, consideration, regard.
hinsichtlich ['hɪnzɪçtlɪç], *prep.* (*Genit.*) with regard to.
hinstellen ['hɪnʃtɛlən], *v.a.* put down; make out to be.
hinten ['hɪntən], *adv.* behind; *von* —, from behind.
hinter ['hɪntər], *prep.* (*Dat.*) behind, after.
Hinterachse ['hɪntəraksə], *f.* (—, *pl.* **—n**) (*Motor.*) rear-axle.
Hinterbein ['hɪntərbaɪn], *n.* (**—s**, *pl.* **—e**) hind-leg; (*fig.*) *sich auf die* **—e** *stellen*, get up on o.'s hind-legs.

Hinterbliebene [hɪntər'bli:bənə], *m.* (—n, *pl.* —n) survivor; mourner; (*pl.*) the bereaved.
hinterbringen [hɪntər'brɪŋən], *v.a. irr.* give information about, (*coll.*) tell on.
Hinterdeck ['hɪntərdɛk], *n.* (—s, *no pl.*) (*Naut.*) quarter deck.
hinterdrein ['hɪntərdraɪn], *adv.* afterwards, after; behind.
hintereinander [hɪntəraɪn'andər], *adv.* in succession, one after another.
Hintergedanke ['hɪntərgədaŋkə], *m.* (—n, *pl.* —n) mental reservation, ulterior motive.
hintergehen [hɪntər'ge:ən], *v.a. irr.* deceive, circumvent.
Hintergrund ['hɪntərgrunt], *m.* (—es, *pl.* ¨e) background; (*Theat.*) backcloth, back-drop.
Hinterhalt ['hɪntərhalt], *m.* (—s, *pl.* —e) ambush; (*fig.*) reserve.
hinterhältig ['hɪntərhɛltɪç], *adj.* furtive, secretive; insidious.
hinterher [hɪntər'he:r], *adv.* behind; in the rear; afterwards.
Hinterindien ['hɪntərɪndjən], *n.* Indo-China.
Hinterkopf ['hɪntərkɔpf], *m.* (—es, *pl.* ¨e) occiput, back of the head.
Hinterlader ['hɪntərla:dər], *m.* (—s, *pl.* —) breech-loader.
hinterlassen [hɪntər'lasən], *v.a. irr.* leave (a legacy), bequeath; leave (word).
Hinterlassenschaft [hɪntər'lasənʃaft], *f.* (—, *pl.* —en) inheritance, bequest.
Hinterlegung [hɪntər'le:guŋ], *f.* (—, *pl.* —en) deposition.
Hinterlist ['hɪntərlɪst], *f.* (—, *no pl.*) fraud, deceit; cunning.
hinterrücks [hɪntər'ryks], *adv.* from behind; (*fig.*) treacherously, behind s.o.'s back.
Hintertreffen ['hɪntərtrɛfən], *n.* (—s, *no pl.*) *ins — geraten*, be left out in the cold, fall behind.
hintertreiben [hɪntər'traɪbən], *v.a. irr.* prevent, frustrate.
Hintertreppe ['hɪntərtrɛpə], *f.* (—, *pl.* —n) back-stairs.
Hintertreppenroman ['hɪntərtrɛpənroma:n], *m.* (—s, *pl.* —e) (*Lit.*) cheap thriller.
hinterziehen ['hɪntərtsi:ən], *v.a. irr. insep.* defraud.
hinträumen ['hɪntrɔymən], *v.n. vor sich —*, daydream.
hinüber [hɪn'y:bər], *adv.* over, across.
hinunter [hɪn'untər], *adv.* down; *den Berg —*, downhill.
hinweg [hɪn'vɛk], *adv.* away, off.
hinwegsetzen [hɪn'vɛkzɛtsən], *v.r. sich über etwas —*, make light of s.th.
Hinweis ['hɪnvaɪs], *m.* (—es, *pl.* —e) hint, indication, reference; *unter — auf*, with reference to.
hinweisen ['hɪnvaɪzən], *v.a. irr. auf etwas —*, refer to, point to s.th.
hinwerfen ['hɪnvɛrfən], *v.a. irr.* throw down; *hingeworfene Bemerkung*, casual remark.
hinziehen ['hɪntsi:ən], *v.a. irr.* draw along; attract. — *v.n.* (*aux.* sein) march along. — *v.r. sich —*, drag on.
hinzielen ['hɪntsi:lən], *v.n. auf etwas —*, aim at s.th., have s.th. in mind.
hinzu [hɪn'tsu:], *adv.* to, near; besides, in addition.
hinzufügen [hɪn'tsu:fy:gən], *v.a.* add.
hinzukommen [hɪn'tsu:kɔmən], *v.n. irr.* (*aux.* sein) be added.
hinzuziehen [hɪn'tsutsi:ən], *v.a. irr.* include, add; call in (expert).
Hiobsbotschaft ['hi:ɔpsbo:tʃaft], *f.* (—, *no pl.*) bad news.
Hirn [hɪrn], *n.* (—es, *pl.* —e) brain, brains. *See also* **Gehirn**.
Hirngespinst ['hɪrngəʃpɪnst], *n.* (—es, *pl.* —e) fancy, chimera, illusion, figment of the imagination.
hirnverbrannt ['hɪrnfɛrbrant], *adj.* crazy, insane, mad; (*coll.*) crack-brained.
Hirsch [hɪrʃ], *m.* (—es, *pl.* —e) (*Zool.*) stag, hart.
Hirschbock ['hɪrʃbɔk], *m.* (—s, *pl.* ¨e) (*Zool.*) stag.
Hirschfänger ['hɪrʃfɛŋər], *m.* (—s, *pl.* —) hunting-knife.
Hirschgeweih ['hɪrʃgəvaɪ], *n.* (—s, *pl.* —e) horns, antlers.
Hirschhorn ['hɪrʃhɔrn], *n.* (—s, *no pl.*) (*Chem.*) hartshorn.
Hirschkäfer ['hɪrʃkɛ:fər], *m.* (—s, *pl.* —) (*Ent.*) stag beetle.
Hirschkeule ['hɪrʃkɔylə], *f.* (—, *pl.* —n) haunch of venison.
Hirschkuh ['hɪrʃku:], *f.* (—, *pl.* ¨e) (*Zool.*) hind, doe.
Hirse ['hɪrzə], *f.* (—, *no pl.*) (*Bot.*) millet.
Hirt [hɪrt], *m.* (—en, *pl.* —en) shepherd, herdsman.
Hirtenbrief ['hɪrtənbri:f], *m.* (—s, *pl.* —e) (*Eccl.*) pastoral letter.
His [hɪs], *n.* (—, *pl.* —) (*Mus.*) B sharp.
hissen ['hɪsən], *v.a.* hoist (the flag).
Historiker [hɪ'sto:rɪkər], *m.* (—s, *pl.* —) historian.
historisch [hɪ'sto:rɪʃ], *adj.* historical.
Hitzblase ['hɪtsbla:zə], *f.* (—, *pl.* —n) blister, heat-rash.
Hitze ['hɪtsə], *f.* (—, *no pl.*) heat, hot weather.
hitzig ['hɪtsɪç], *adj.* hot-headed, hasty, passionate.
Hitzschlag ['hɪtsʃla:k], *m.* (—es, *pl.* ¨e) sunstroke, heat-stroke.
Hobel ['ho:bəl], *m.* (—s, *pl.* —) (*tool*) plane.
Hoch [ho:x], *n.* (—s, *no pl.*) toast (*drink*); (*Met.*) high.
hoch, hoh [ho:x, ho:], *adj.* high; (*fig.*) eminent, sublime.
Hochachtung ['ho:xaxtuŋ], *f.* (—, *no pl.*) esteem, regard, respect.
hochachtungsvoll ['ho:xaxtuŋsfɔl], *adj., adv.* (*letters*) yours faithfully.

Hochamt ['ho:xamt], *n.* (**—es**, *pl.* **¨er**) (*Eccl.*) High Mass.
Hochbau ['ho:xbau], *m.* (**—s**, *pl.* **—ten**) superstructure.
hochbetagt ['ho:xbəta:kt], *adj.* advanced in years.
Hochburg ['ho:xburk], *f.* (**—**, *pl.* **—en**) (*fig.*) stronghold, citadel.
Hochebene ['ho:xe:bənə], *f.* (**—**, *pl.* **—n**) table-land, plateau.
hochfahrend ['ho:xfa:rənt], *adj.* haughty, high-flown; (*coll.*) stuck-up.
Hochgefühl ['ho:xgəfy:l], *n.* (**—s**, *no pl.*) exaltation.
Hochgenuß ['ho:xgənus], *m.* (**—sses**, *pl.* **¨sse**) exquisite enjoyment; treat.
Hochgericht ['ho:xgərɪçt], *n.* (**—s**, *pl.* **—e**) place of execution, scaffold.
hochherzig ['ho:xhɛrtsɪç], *adj.* magnanimous.
Hochmeister ['ho:xmaɪstər], *m.* (**—s**, *pl.* **—**) Grand Master.
Hochmut ['ho:xmu:t], *m.* (**—s**, *no pl.*) haughtiness, pride.
hochnäsig ['ho:xnɛ:zɪç], *adj.* supercilious, stuck-up.
hochnotpeinlich ['ho:xno:tpaɪnlɪç], *adj.* (*obs.*) penal, criminal; *—es Verhör*, criminal investigation.
Hochofen ['ho:xo:fən], *m.* (**—s**, *pl.* **¨**) blast-furnace.
Hochschule ['ho:xʃu:lə], *f.* (**—**, *pl.* **—n**) academy; university.
Hochschüler ['ho:xʃy:lər], *m.* (**—s**, *pl.* **—**) student, undergraduate.
höchst [hœ:çst], *adj.* highest, most. — *adv.* most, extremely.
Hochstapler ['ho:xʃta:plər], *m.* (**—s**, *pl.* **—**) confidence trickster, swindler.
höchstens ['hœ:çstəns], *adv.* at most, at best.
hochtrabend ['ho:xtra:bənt], *adj.* (*horse*) high-stepping; (*fig.*) high-sounding, bombastic.
hochverdient ['ho:xfɛrdi:nt], *adj.* highly meritorious.
Hochverrat ['ho:xfɛra:t], *m.* (**—s**, *no pl.*) high treason.
Hochwild ['ho:xvɪlt], *n.* (**—es**, *no pl.*) deer; big game.
hochwohlgeboren ['ho:xvo:lgəbo:rən], *adj.* (*obs.*) noble; *Euer Hochwohlgeboren*, Right Honourable Sir.
hochwürden ['ho:xvyrdən], *adj.* *Euer Hochwürden*, Reverend Sir.
Hochzeit ['hɔxtsaɪt], *f.* (**—**, *pl.* **—en**) wedding; nuptials.
hochzeitlich ['hɔxtsaɪtlɪç], *adj.* nuptial, bridal.
Hochzeitsreise ['hɔxtsaɪtsraɪzə], *f.* (**—**, *pl.* **—n**) honeymoon.
Hocke ['hɔkə], *f.* (**—**, *pl.* **—n**) squatting posture; shock, stook.
hocken ['hɔkən], *v.n.* crouch, squat; *zu Hause —*, be a stay-at-home.
Hocker ['hɔkər], *m.* (**—s**, *pl.* **—**) stool.
Höcker ['hœkər], *m.* (**—s**, *pl.* **—**) hump.
höckerig ['hœkərɪç], *adj.* hump-backed, hunch-backed.
Hode ['ho:də], *f.* (**—**, *pl.* **—n**) testicle.
Hof [ho:f], *m.* (**—es**, *pl.* **¨e**) yard, courtyard; farm(stead); (*royal*) court; (*moon*) halo; *einem den — machen*, court s.o.
Hofarzt ['ho:fartst], *m.* (**—es**, *pl.* **¨e**) court physician.
hoffähig ['ho:ffɛ:ɪç], *adj.* presentable at court.
Hoffart ['hɔfart], *f.* (**—**, *no pl.*) pride, arrogance.
hoffärtig ['hɔfɛrtɪç], *adj.* proud, arrogant.
hoffen ['hɔfən], *v.n.* hope; *fest auf etwas —*, trust.
hoffentlich ['hɔfəntlɪç], *adv.* as I hope, I trust that.
Hoffnung ['hɔfnuŋ], *f.* (**—**, *pl.* **—en**) hope, expectation, anticipation, expectancy; *guter — sein*, be full of hope; be expecting a baby; *sich — machen auf*, cherish hopes of.
hoffnungslos ['hɔfnuŋslo:s], *adj.* hopeless, past hope.
hofieren [ho'fi:rən], *v.a.* court.
höfisch ['hø:fɪʃ], *adj.* courtlike, courtly.
höflich ['hø:flɪç], *adj.* courteous, civil, polite.
Hoflieferant ['ho:fli:fərant], *m.* (**—en**, *pl.* **—en**) purveyor to His *or* Her Majesty.
Höfling ['hø:flɪŋ], *m.* (**—s**, *pl.* **—e**) courtier.
Hofmarschall ['ho:fmarʃal], *m.* (**—s**, *pl.* **—e**) Lord Chamberlain.
Hofmeister ['ho:fmaɪstər], *m.* (**—s**, *pl.* **—**) (*obs.*) steward; tutor.
Hofnarr ['ho:fnar], *m.* (**—en**, *pl.* **—en**) court jester, court fool.
Hofrat ['ho:fra:t], *m.* (**—s**, *pl.* **¨e**) Privy Councillor.
Hofschranze ['ho:fʃrantsə], *m.* (**—n**, *pl.* **—n**) courtier; flunkey.
Hofsitte ['ho:fzɪtə], *f.* (**—**, *pl.* **—n**) court etiquette.
Höhe ['hø:ə], *f.* (**—**, *pl.* **—n**) height, altitude; *bis zur — von*, up to the level of; *in die —*, upwards; *in die — fahren*, give a start, get excited.
Hoheit ['ho:haɪt], *f.* (**—**, *pl.* **—en**) grandeur; sovereignty; (*title*) Highness.
Hohelied [ho:ə'li:t], *n.* (**—s**, *no pl.*) Song of Solomon.
Höhenmesser ['hø:ənmɛsər], *m.* (**—s**, *pl.* **—**) (*Aviat.*) altimeter.
Höhensonne ['hø:ənzɔnə], *f.* (**—**, *pl.* **—n**) Alpine sun; (*Med.*) ultra-violet lamp.
Höhenzug ['hø:əntsu:k], *m.* (**—s**, *pl.* **¨e**) mountain range.
Höhepunkt ['hø:əpuŋkt], *m.* (**—s**, *pl.* **—e**) climax, culmination, acme; peak.
höher ['hø:ər], *comp. adj.* higher.
hohl [ho:l], *adj.* hollow; (*tooth*) decayed, hollow.
Höhle ['hø:lə], *f.* (**—**, *pl.* **—n**) cave, cavern, den.

hohlgeschliffen ['ho:lgəʃlɪfən], *adj.* concave, hollow-ground.
Hohlheit ['ho:lhaɪt], *f.* (—, *no pl.*) hollowness.
Hohlleiste ['ho:llaɪstə], *f.* (—, *pl.* —**n**) groove, channel.
Hohlmaß ['ho:lma:s], *n.* (—**es**, *pl.* —**e**) dry measure.
Hohlmeißel ['ho:lmaɪsəl], *m.* (—**s**, *pl.* —) gouge.
Hohlsaum ['ho:lzaum], *m.* (—**s**, *pl.* ⸚**e**) hemstitch.
Hohlspiegel ['ho:lʃpi:gəl], *m.* (—**s**, *pl.* —) concave mirror.
Höhlung ['hø:luŋ], *f.* (—, *pl.* —**en**) hollow, cavity.
Hohlziegel ['ho:ltsi:gəl], *m.* (—**s**, *pl.* —) hollow brick.
Hohn [ho:n], *m.* (—**s**, *no pl.*) scorn, derision, mockery; sneer.
höhnen ['hø:nən], *v.a.* deride, sneer at; *see* **verhöhnen.**
Höker ['hø:kər], *m.* (—**s**, *pl.* —) hawker, huckster.
hold [hɔlt], *adj.* kind, friendly; gracious; graceful; sweet.
Holder ['hɔldər] *see* **Holunder.**
holdselig ['hɔltze:lɪç], *adj.* sweet, charming, gracious.
holen ['ho:lən], *v.a.* fetch, collect, get.
Holland ['hɔlant], *n.* Holland.
Hölle ['hœlə], *f.* (—, *no pl.*) hell.
Holm [hɔlm], *m.* (—**es**, *pl.* —**e**) islet, holm; (*Gymn.*) bar.
holperig ['hɔlpərɪç], *adj.* rough, bumpy.
holpern ['hɔlpərn], *v.n.* jolt, stumble; (*fig.*) falter.
Holunder [ho'lundər], *m.* (—**s**, *pl.* —) (*Bot.*) elder; *spanischer* —, lilac.
Holz [hɔlts], *n.* (—**es**, *pl.* ⸚**er**) wood, timber; (*Am.*) lumber; (*no pl.*) forest; bush.
Holzapfel ['hɔltsapfəl], *m.* (—**s**, *pl.* ⸚) (*Bot.*) crab-apple.
holzartig ['hɔltsartɪç], *adj.* woody, ligneous.
holzen ['hɔltsən], *v.a.* cut *or* gather wood.
hölzern ['hœltsərn], *adj.* wooden; (*fig.*) stiff.
Holzhändler ['hɔltshɛndlər], *m.* (—**s**, *pl.* —) timber-merchant; (*Am.*) lumber merchant.
Holzhauer ['hɔltshauər], *m.* (—**s**, *pl.* —) wood-cutter.
holzig ['hɔltsɪç], *adj.* woody, wooded; (*asparagus*) woody, hard; (*beans*) stringy.
Holzkohle ['hɔltsko:lə], *f.* (—, *no pl.*) charcoal.
Holzscheit ['hɔltsʃaɪt], *n.* (—**s**, *pl.* —**e**) log of wood.
Holzschlag ['hɔltsʃla:k], *m.* (—**es**, *pl.* ⸚**e**) clearing; felling area.
Holzschnitt ['hɔltsʃnɪt], *m.* (—**es**, *pl.* —**e**) wood-cut.
Holzschuh ['hɔltsʃu:], *m.* (—**s**, *pl.* —**e**) clog.
Holzweg ['hɔltsve:k], *m.* (—**s**, *pl.* —**e**) timbertrack; (*fig.*) *auf dem — sein*, be on the wrong tack.
Holzwolle ['hɔltsvɔlə], *f.* (—, *no pl.*) wood shavings.
homogen [homo'ge:n], *adj.* homogeneous.
homolog [homo'lo:g], *adj.* homologous.
honett [hɔ'nɛt], *adj.* (*obs.*) respectable, genteel.
Honig ['ho:nɪç], *m.* (—**s**, *no pl.*) honey.
Honigkuchen ['ho:nɪçku:xən], *m.* (—**s**, *pl.* —) ginger-bread.
Honigwabe ['ho:nɪçva:bə], *f.* (—, *pl.* —**n**) honeycomb.
Honorar [hono'ra:r], *n.* (—**s**, *pl.* —**e**) remuneration; (*professional*) fee; honorarium.
Honoratioren [honora'tsjo:rən], *m. pl.* people of rank; dignitaries.
honorieren [hono'ri:rən], *v.a.* pay a fee to, remunerate.
Hopfen ['hɔpfən], *m.* (—**s**, *no pl.*) (*Bot.*) hop, hops; *an dem ist — und Malz verloren*, he is beyond help.
Hopfenstange ['hɔpfənʃtaŋə], *f.* (—, *pl.* —**n**) hop-pole; (*fig.*) tall thin person.
hopsen ['hɔpsən], *v.n.* (*aux.* sein) (*coll.*) hop, jump.
hörbar ['hø:rba:r], *adj.* audible.
horchen ['hɔrçən], *v.n.* listen, eavesdrop.
Horde ['hɔrdə], *f.* (—, *pl.* —**n**) horde.
hören ['hø:rən], *v.a., v.n.* hear.
Hörer ['hø:rər], *m.* (—**s**, *pl.* —) listener; (*Univ.*) student; (*telephone*) receiver.
Hörerin ['hø:rərɪn], *f.* (—, *pl.* —**innen**) female listener; (*Univ.*) woman student.
Hörerschaft ['hø:rərʃaft], *f.* (—, *no pl.*) audience.
Hörgerät ['hø:rgerɛ:t], *n.* (—**es**, *pl.* —**e**) hearing aid.
hörig ['hø:rɪç], *adj.* in bondage, a slave to.
Horizont [hori'tsɔnt], *m.* (—**es**, *pl.* —**e**) horizon.
Horizontale [horitsɔn'ta:lə], *f.* (—, *pl.* —**n**) horizontal line.
Horn [hɔrn], *n.* (—**s**, *pl.* ⸚**er**) horn; (*Mus.*) French horn.
Hörnchen ['hœrnçən], *n.* (—**s**, *pl.* —) French roll, croissant.
hörnern ['hœrnərn], *adj.* horny, made of horn.
Hornhaut ['hɔrnhaut], *f.* (—, *pl.* ⸚**te**) horny skin; (*eye*) cornea.
Hornhautverpflanzung ['hɔrnhautfɛrpflantsuŋ], *f.* (—, *no pl.*) corneal graft.
hornig ['hɔrnɪç], *adj.* hard, horny.
Hornisse [hɔr'nɪsə], *f.* (—, *pl.* —**n**) (*Ent.*) hornet.
horrend [hɔ'rɛnt], *adj.* exorbitant; stupendous.
Hörrohr ['hø:rro:r], *n.* (—**s**, *pl.* —**e**) ear trumpet.
Hörsaal ['hø:rza:l], *m.* (—**s**, *pl.* —**säle**) auditorium, lecture room.

Hörspiel ['hø:rʃpi:l], *n.* (—s, *pl.* —e) radio play.
Horst [hɔrst], *m.* (—es, *pl.* —e) eyrie.
Hort [hɔrt], *m.* (—es, *pl.* —e) (*Poet.*) treasure; stronghold.
Hortensie [hɔr'tɛnzjə], *f.* (—, *pl.* —n) (*Bot.*) hydrangea.
Hose ['ho:zə], *f.* (—, *pl.* —n) trousers, pants, breeches; (*women*) slacks.
Hosenband ['ho:zənbant], *n.* (—es, *pl.* ⸚er) garter.
Hosenträger ['ho:zəntrɛgər], *m. pl.* braces, suspenders.
Hospitant [hɔspɪ'tant], *m.* (—en, *pl.* —en) (*Univ.*) temporary student, non-registered student.
hospitieren [hɔspɪ'ti:rən], *v.n.* attend lectures as a visitor.
Hostie ['hɔstjə], *f.* (—, *pl.* —n) (*Eccl.*) the Host.
hüben ['hy:bən], *adv.* on this side; — *und drüben*, on either side.
hübsch [hypʃ], *adj.* pretty, attractive; handsome; good-looking.
Hubschrauber ['hu:pʃraubər], *m.* (—s, *pl.* —) (*Aviat.*) helicopter.
huckepack ['hukəpak], *adv.* — *tragen*, carry pick-a-back.
Huf [hu:f], *m.* (—es, *pl.* —e) hoof.
Hufe ['hu:fə], *f.* (—, *pl.* —n) hide (of land).
Hufeisen ['hu:faɪzən], *n.* (—s, *pl.* —) horseshoe.
Huflattich ['hu:flatɪç], *m.* (—s, *pl.* —e) (*Bot.*) colt's foot.
Hufschlag ['hu:fʃla:k], *m.* (—s, *pl.* ⸚e) (*of a horse*) hoof-beat.
Hüfte ['hyftə], *f.* (—, *pl.* —n) (*Anat.*) hip; (*animals*) haunch.
Hügel ['hy:gəl], *m.* (—s, *pl.* —) hill, hillock.
hügelig ['hy:gəlɪç], *adj.* hilly.
Huhn [hu:n], *n.* (—s, *pl.* ⸚er) fowl; hen.
Hühnchen ['hy:nçən], *n.* (—s, *pl.* —) pullet, chicken.
Hühnerauge ['hy:nəraugə], *n.* (—s, *pl.* —n) corn (*on the foot*).
Huld [hult], *f.* (—, *no pl.*) grace, favour.
huldigen ['huldɪgən], *v.n.* pay homage.
huldvoll ['hultfɔl], *adj.* gracious.
Hülle ['hylə], *f.* (—, *pl.* —n) cover, covering; veil; *in — und Fülle*, in abundance, in profusion.
hüllen ['hylən], *v.a.* cover, veil, wrap.
Hülse ['hylzə], *f.* (—, *pl.* —n) hull, husk, shell; cartridge-case.
Hülsenfrucht ['hylzənfruxt], *f.* (—, *pl.* ⸚e) (*Bot.*) leguminous plant.
human [hu'ma:n], *adj.* humane.
humanistisch [huma'nɪstɪʃ], *adj.* classical; humanistic.
Hummel ['huməl], *f.* (—, *pl.* —n) (*Ent.*) bumble-bee.
Hummer ['humər], *m.* (—s, *pl.* —) (*Zool.*) lobster.
Humor [hu'mo:r], *m.* (—s, *no pl.*) humour.
humoristisch [humo'rɪstɪʃ], *adj.* humorous, witty.
humpeln ['humpəln], *v.n.* hobble, limp.
Humpen ['humpən], *m.* (—s, *pl.* —) deep drinking-cup, bowl, tankard.
Humus ['hu:mus], *m.* (—, *no pl.*) garden-mould, humus.
Hund [hunt], *m.* (—es, *pl.* —e) dog; (*hunting*) hound; (*fig.*) rascal, scoundrel.
Hundehaus ['hundəhaus], *n.* (—es, *pl.* ⸚er) dog-kennel.
hundert ['hundərt], *num. adj.* a hundred, one hundred.
Hündin ['hyndɪn], *f.* (—, *pl.* —innen) bitch.
Hundstage ['huntsta:gə], *m. pl.* dog days (July to August).
Hundszahn ['huntstsa:n], *m.* (—es, *pl.* ⸚e) (*Bot.*) dandelion.
Hüne ['hy:nə], *m.* (—n, *pl.* —n) giant, colossus; (*fig.*) tall man.
Hünengrab ['hy:nəngra:p], *n.* (—es, *pl.* ⸚er) tumulus, burial mound, barrow, cairn.
Hunger ['huŋər], *m.* (—s, *no pl.*) hunger; starvation.
hungern ['huŋərn], *v.n.* hunger, be hungry.
Hungertuch ['huŋərtu:x], *n.* (—es, *no pl.*) *am — nagen*, go without food; live in poverty.
hungrig ['huŋrɪç], *adj.* hungry; (*fig.*) desirous (of).
Hupe ['hu:pə], *f.* (—, *pl.* —n) motor-horn, hooter (of a car).
hüpfen ['hypfən], *v.n.* (*aux.* sein) hop, skip.
Hürde ['hyrdə], *f.* (—, *pl.* —n) hurdle.
Hure ['hu:rə], *f.* (—, *pl.* —n) whore, prostitute, harlot; (*coll.*) tart.
hurtig ['hurtɪç], *adj.* nimble, agile; quick, speedy, swift.
Husar [hu'za:r], *m.* (—en, *pl.* —en) hussar.
husch! [huʃ], *excl.* quick!
huschen ['huʃən], *v.n.* (*aux.* sein) scurry, slip away.
hüsteln ['hystəln], *v.n.* cough slightly; clear o.'s throat.
husten ['hu:stən], *v.n.* cough.
Hut (1) [hu:t], *m.* (—es, *pl.* ⸚e) hat; *steifer* —, bowler.
Hut (2) [hu:t], *f.* (—, *no pl.*) guard, keeping, care.
hüten ['hy:tən], *v.a.* guard, tend, care for; *Kinder* —, baby-sit; *das Bett* —, be confined to o.'s bed, be ill in bed. — *v.r. sich — vor*, be on o.'s guard against, beware of.
Hüter ['hy:tər], *m.* (—s, *pl.* —) guardian, keeper; (*cattle*) herdsman.
Hutkrempe ['hu:tkrɛmpə], *f.* (—, *pl.* —n) hat-brim.
Hütte ['hytə], *f.* (—, *pl.* —n) hut, cottage; (*Tech.*) furnace, forge, foundry.
Hüttenarbeiter ['hytənarbaɪtər], *m.* (—s, *pl.* —) smelter, foundry worker.
Hyäne [hy'ɛ:nə], *f.* (—, *pl.* —n) (*Zool.*) hyena.

Hyazinthe [hyat'sɪntə], *f.* (—, *pl.* —n) (*Bot.*) hyacinth.
Hyperbel [hy'pɛrbəl], *f.* (—, *pl.* —n) hyperbola.
hypnotisch [hyp'no:tɪʃ], *adj.* hypnotic.
hypnotisieren [hypnoti'zi:rən], *v.a.* hypnotise.
Hypochonder [hypo'xɔndər], *m.* (—s, *pl.* —) hypochondriac.
Hypothek [hypo'te:k], *f.* (—, *pl.* —en) mortgage.
Hysterie [hyste'ri:], *f.* (—, *no pl.*) hysterics, hysteria.
hysterisch [hys'te:rɪʃ], *adj.* hysterical.

I

I [i:], *n.* (—, *no pl.*) the letter I. — *excl.* *i wo!* (*dial.*) certainly not, of course not.
ich [ɪç], *pers. pron.* I, myself.
ideal [ide'a:l], *adj.* ideal.
idealisieren [ideali'zi:rən], *v.a.* idealise.
Idealismus [idea'lɪsmus], *m.* (—, *no pl.*) idealism.
Idee [i'de:], *f.* (—, *pl.* —n) idea, notion, conception.
identifizieren [idɛntifi'tsi:rən], *v.a.* identify.
identisch [i'dɛntɪʃ], *adj.* identical.
Identität [idɛnti'tɛ:t], *f.* (—, *no pl.*) identity.
idiomatisch [idio'ma:tɪʃ], *adj.* idiomatic.
Idyll [i'dyl], *n.* (—s, *pl.* —e) idyll.
Idylle [i'dylə], *f.* (—, *pl.* —n) idyll.
idyllisch [i'dylɪʃ], *adj.* idyllic.
Igel ['i:gəl], *m.* (—s, *pl.* —) (*Zool.*) hedgehog.
ignorieren [ɪgno'ri:rən], *v.a.* ignore, take no notice of.
ihm [i:m], *pers. pron. Dat.* to him, it.
ihn [i:n], *pers. pron. Acc.*, him, it.
Ihnen ['i:nən], *pers. pron. Dat.* you, to you.
ihnen ['i:nən], *pers. pron. pl. Dat.* them, to them.
Ihr [i:r], *poss. adj.* your; of your. —, *poss. pron.* yours.
ihr [i:r], *pers. pron.* to her; (*pl.*) (*intim.*) you. — *poss. adj.* her, their. — *poss. pron.* hers, theirs.
Ihrer ['i:rər], *pers. pron.* of you. — *poss. adj.* of your.
ihrer ['i:rər], *pers. pron.* of her, of it; (*pl.*) of them. — *poss. adj* of her; to her; (*pl.*) of their.
ihresgleichen ['i:rəsglaɪçən], *adv.* of her, its *or* their kind.
ihrethalben ['i:rəthalbən], *adv.* for her sake, for their sake, on her account, on their account.
ihretwegen ['i:rətve:gən] *see* **ihrethalben.**
ihretwillen ['i:rətvɪlən] *see* **ihrethalben.**
Ihrige [i:rɪgə], *poss. pron.* yours.
ihrige ['i:rɪgə], *poss. pron.* hers, its, theirs.
illegitim [ɪlegi'ti:m], *adj.* illegitimate.
illuminieren [ɪlumi'ni:rən], *v.a.* illuminate, floodlight.
illustrieren [ɪlu'stri:rən], *v.a.* illustrate.
Iltis ['ɪltɪs], *m.* (—ses, *pl.* —se) (*Zool.*) polecat, fitchet.
im [ɪm], *contraction of* **in dem**, in the.
Imbiß ['ɪmbɪs], *m.* (—sses, *pl.* —sse) snack, refreshment, light meal.
Imker ['ɪmkər], *m.* (—s, *pl.* —) beekeeper.
immatrikulieren [ɪmmatriku'li:rən], *v.a.* (*Univ.*) matriculate, enrol.
Imme ['ɪmə], *f.* (—, *pl.* —n) (*dial.*, *Poet.*) bee.
immer ['ɪmər], *adv.* always, ever; — *mehr*, more and more; — *noch*, still; — *wieder*, time and again: — *größer*, larger and larger; *auf* —, for ever.
immerdar ['ɪmərda:r], *adv.* for ever.
immerhin ['ɪmərhɪn], *adv.* nevertheless, still, after all.
immerzu ['ɪmərtsu:], *adv.* always, constantly.
Immobilien [ɪmo'bi:ljən], *pl.* real estate.
Immortelle [imɔr'tɛlə], *f.* (—, *pl.* —n) (*Bot.*) everlasting flower.
immun [ɪ'mu:n], *adj.* immune.
impfen ['ɪmpfən], *v.a.* vaccinate, inoculate; (*Hort.*) graft.
imponieren [ɪmpo'ni:rən], *v.n.* impress.
Import [ɪm'pɔrt], *m.* (—s, *pl.* —e) import, importation.
imposant [ɪmpo'zant], *adj.* imposing, impressive.
imstande [ɪm'ʃtandə], *adv.* capable, able; — *sein*, be able.
in [in], *prep.* (*Dat.*, *Acc.*) in, into; at; within.
Inangriffnahme [ɪn'angrɪfna:mə], *f.* (—, *no pl.*) start, beginning, inception.
Inbegriff ['ɪnbəgrɪf], *m.* (—es, *no pl.*) essence, epitome.
inbegriffen ['ɪnbəgrɪfən], *adv.* inclusive.
Inbrunst ['ɪnbrunst], *f.* (—, *no pl.*) ardour, fervour.
indem [ɪn'de:m], *adv.* meanwhile. — *conj.* while, whilst; as, because, in that.
indessen [ɪn'dɛsən], *adv.* meanwhile, in the meantime. — *conj.* however, nevertheless, yet.
Indien ['ɪndjən], *n.* India.
Individualität [ɪndividuali'tɛ:t], *f.* (—, *pl.* —en) individuality, personality.
individuell [ɪndividu'ɛl], *adj.* individual.
Individuum [ɪndi'vi:duum], *n.* (—s, *pl.* —duen) individual.

Indizienbeweis [ɪn'di:tsjənbəvaɪs], *m.* (—**es**, *pl.* —**e**) (*Law*) circumstantial evidence *or* proof.
indossieren [ɪndɔ'si:rən], *v.a.* endorse.
Industrie [ɪndus'tri:], *f.* (—, *pl.* —**n**) industry; manufacture.
industriell [ɪndustri'ɛl], *adj.* industrial.
Industrielle [ɪndustri'ɛlə], *m.* (—**n**, *pl.* —**n**) manufacturer, industrialist.
ineinander [ɪnaɪ'nandər], *adv.* into each other, into one another.
infam [ɪn'fa:m], *adj.* infamous.
Infantin [ɪn'fantɪn], *f.* (—, *pl.* —**en**) Infanta.
infizieren [ɪnfi'tsi:rən], *v.a.* infect.
infolge [ɪn'fɔlgə], *prep.* (*Genit.*) in consequence of, owing to.
informieren [ɪnfɔr'mi:rən], *v.a.* inform, advise.
Ingenieur [ɪnʒen'jø:r], *m.* (—**s**, *pl.* —**e**) engineer.
Ingrimm ['ɪngrɪm], *m.* (—**s**, *no pl.*) anger, rage, wrath.
Ingwer ['ɪŋvər], *m.* (—**s**, *no pl.*) ginger.
Inhaber ['ɪnha:bər], *m.* (—**s**, *pl.* —) possessor, owner; proprietor; occupant.
inhaftieren [ɪnhaf'ti:rən], *v.a.* imprison; arrest.
inhalieren [ɪnha'li:rən], *v.a.* inhale.
Inhalt ['ɪnhalt], *m.* (—(**e**)**s**, *no pl.*) content; contents; tenor.
Inhaltsverzeichnis ['ɪnhaltsfɛrtsaɪçnɪs], *n.* (—**ses**, *pl.* —**se**) (table of) contents; index.
inhibieren [ɪnhi'bi:rən], *v.a.* inhibit, prevent.
Inkasso [ɪn'kaso], *n.* (—**s**, *pl.* —**s**) encashment.
inklinieren [ɪnkli'ni:rən], *v.n.* be inclined to.
inklusive [ɪnklu'zi:və], *adv.* inclusive of, including.
inkonsequent ['ɪnkɔnzəkvɛnt], *adj.* inconsistent.
Inkrafttreten [ɪn'krafttre:tən], *n.* (—**s**, *no pl.*) enactment; coming into force.
Inland ['ɪnlant], *n.* (—**s**, *no pl.*) inland, interior.
Inländer ['ɪnlɛndər], *m.* (—**s**, *pl.* —) native.
Inlett ['ɪnlɛt], *n.* (—**s**, *pl.* —**e**) bed-tick, ticking.
inliegend ['ɪnli:gənt], *adj.* enclosed.
inmitten [ɪn'mɪtən], *prep.* (*Genit.*) in the midst of.
innehaben ['ɪnəha:bən], *v.a.* *irr.* possess; occupy; hold.
innehalten ['ɪnəhaltən], *v.a.* *irr.* (*conditions*) keep to, observe; (*time*) come promptly at. — *v.n.* stop, pause.
innen ['ɪnən], *adv.* within; *nach* —, inwards; *von* —, from within.
Innenminister ['ɪnənmɪnɪstər], *m.* (—**s**, *pl.* —) Minister for Internal Affairs; Home Secretary; (*Am.*) Secretary of the Interior.
inner ['ɪnər], *adj.* inner, interior, internal; intrinsic.
innerhalb ['ɪnərhalp], *prep.* (*Genit.*) within.
innerlich ['ɪnərlɪç], *adj.* internal; inside o.s.; inward.
innerste ['ɪnərstə], *adj.* inmost, innermost.
innewerden ['ɪnəve:rdən], *v.a.* *irr.* (*aux.* sein) perceive, become aware of.
innewohnen ['ɪnəvo:nən], *v.n.* be inherent in.
innig ['ɪnɪç], *adj.* heartfelt, cordial.
Innung ['ɪnuŋ], *f.* (—, *pl.* —**en**) guild, corporation.
Insasse ['ɪnzasə], *m.* (—**n**, *pl.* —**n**) inmate; occupant.
insbesondere [ɪnsbə'zɔndərə], *adv.* especially, particularly, in particular.
Inschrift ['ɪnʃrɪft], *f.* (—, *pl.* —**en**) inscription.
Insel ['ɪnzəl], *f.* (—, *pl.* —**n**) island.
Inserat [ɪnzə'ra:t], *n.* (—**es**, *pl.* —**e**) classified advertisement; (*coll.*) (small) ad.
inserieren [ɪnzə'ri:rən], *v.a.* advertise; insert.
insgeheim [ɪnsgə'haɪm], *adv.* privately, secretly.
insgesamt [ɪnsgə'zamt], *adv.* altogether, in a body.
insofern [ɪnzo'fɛrn], *conj.* — *als*, in so far as, inasmuch as, so far as.
inspirieren [ɪnspi'ri:rən], *v.a.* inspire.
installieren [ɪnsta'li:rən], *v.a.* install, fit.
instandhalten [ɪn'ʃtanthaltən], *v.a.* *irr.* maintain, preserve, keep in repair.
inständig ['ɪnʃtɛndɪç], *adj.* urgent; fervent.
instandsetzen [ɪn'ʃtantzɛtsən], *v.a.* restore, repair; *einen* — *etwas zu tun*, enable s.o. to do s.th.
Instanz [ɪn'stants], *f.* (—, *pl.* —**en**) (*Law*) instance; *letzte* —, highest court of appeal, last resort.
Institut [ɪnsti'tu:t], *n.* (—**es**, *pl.* —**e**) institute, institution, establishment; (*Univ.*) department.
instruieren [ɪnstru'i:rən], *v.a.* instruct.
Insulaner [ɪnzu'la:nər], *m.* (—**s**, *pl.* —) islander.
inszenieren [ɪnstse'ni:rən], *v.a.* put on the stage, produce.
Inszenierung [ɪnstse'ni:ruŋ], *f.* (—, *pl.* —**en**) (*Theat.*) production, staging.
intellektuell [ɪntɛlɛktu'ɛl], *adj.* intellectual.
Intendant [ɪntɛn'dant], *m.* (—**en**, *pl.* —**en**) (*Theat.*) director.
interessant [ɪntərɛ'sant], *adj.* interesting.
Interesse [ɪntə'rɛsə], *n.* (—**s**, *pl.* —**n**) interest.
Interessent [ɪntərɛ'sɛnt], *m.* (—**en**, *pl.* —**en**) interested party.
interessieren [ɪntərɛ'si:rən], *v.a.* interest. — *v.r.* *sich* —, be interested (in).
intern [ɪn'tɛrn], *adj.* internal.
Internat [ɪntɛr'na:t], *n.* (—**es**, *pl.* —**e**) boarding-school.

Interne [ɪn'tɛrnə], *m.* (—n, *pl.* —n) resident (pupil *or* doctor), boarder.
Internist [ɪntɛr'nɪst], *m.* (—en, *pl.* —en) specialist in internal diseases.
interpunktieren [ɪntərpunk'ti:rən], *v.a.* punctuate.
Interpunktion [ɪntərpunkts'jo:n], *f.* (—, *pl.* —en) punctuation.
intim [ɪn'ti:m], *adj.* intimate; *mit einem — sein,* be on close terms with s.o.
intonieren [ɪnto'ni:rən], *v.n.* intone.
Intrigant [ɪntri'gant], *m.* (—en, *pl.* —en) intriguer, schemer.
intrigieren [ɪntri'gi:rən], *v.n.* intrigue, scheme.
Inventar [ɪnvɛn'ta:r], *n.* (—s, *pl.* —e) inventory; *ein — aufnehmen,* draw up an inventory.
Inventur [ɪnvɛn'tu:r], *f.* (—, *pl.* —en) stock-taking.
inwärts ['ɪnvɛrts], *adv.* inwards.
inwendig ['ɪnvɛndɪç], *adj.* inward, internal, inner.
inwiefern [ɪnvi:'fɛrn], *adv.* to what extent.
inwieweit [ɪnvi:'vaɪt], *adv.* how far.
Inzucht ['ɪntsuxt], *f.* (—, *no pl.*) inbreeding.
inzwischen [ɪn'tsvɪʃən], *adv.* meanwhile, in the meantime.
Irak [i'ra:k], *m., n.* Iraq.
Iran [i'ra:n], *n.* Iran.
irden ['ɪrdən], *adj.* earthen.
irdisch ['ɪrdɪʃ], *adj.* earthly, worldly; terrestrial, temporal.
irgend ['ɪrgənt], *adv.* any, some; *wenn es — geht,* if it can possibly be done.
irgendein [ɪrgənt'aɪn], *pron.* any, some.
Irland ['ɪrlant], *n.* Ireland.
ironisch [ɪ'ro:nɪʃ], *adj.* ironic, ironical.
Irre (1) ['ɪrə], *f.* (—, *no pl.*) *in die — gehen,* go astray.
Irre (2) ['ɪrə], *m.* (—n, *pl.* —n) madman, lunatic.
irre ['ɪrə], *adj.* astray; wrong, confused; crazy, demented.
irren ['ɪrən], *v.n.* err, go astray, be wrong. — *v.r. sich —,* be mistaken.
Irrenarzt ['ɪrənartst], *m.* (—es, *pl.* ¨e) psychiatrist.
Irrenhaus ['ɪrənhaus], *n.* (—es, *pl.* ¨er) lunatic asylum, mental hospital.
Irrfahrt ['ɪrfa:rt], *f.* (—, *pl.* —en) wandering.
Irrglaube ['ɪrglaubə], *m.* (—ns, *no pl.*) heresy.
irrig ['ɪrɪç], *adj.* erroneous.
irritieren [ɪri'ti:rən], *v.a.* irritate.
Irrlicht ['ɪrlɪçt], *n.* (—s, *pl.* —er) will-o'-the-wisp.
Irrsinn ['ɪrzɪn], *m.* (—s, *no pl.*) madness, insanity, lunacy.
irrsinnig ['ɪrzɪnɪç], *adj.* insane, deranged.
Irrtum ['ɪrtu:m], *m.* (—s, *pl.* ¨er) error, mistake, fault, oversight.
Irrweg ['ɪrve:k], *m.* (—s, *pl.* —e) wrong track.
Irrwisch ['ɪrvɪʃ], *m.* (—es, *pl.* —e) will-o'-the-wisp.
Ischias ['ɪsçias], *f., m.* (*Med.*) sciatica.
Isegrim ['i:zəgrɪm], *m.* (—s, *pl.* —e) (*fable*) the wolf; a bear (with a sore head) (*also fig.*).
Island ['i:slant], *n.* Iceland.
isolieren [izo'li:rən], *v.a.* (*Electr.*) insulate; (*fig.*) isolate.
Isolierung [izo'li:ruŋ], *f.* (—, *pl.* —en) (*Electr.*) insulation; (*fig.*) isolation.
Italien [i'ta:ljən], *n.* Italy.

J

J [jɔt], *n.* (—, *no pl.*) the letter J.
ja [ja:], *adv., part.* yes; indeed, certainly; even; — *doch,* to be sure; — *freilich,* certainly.
Jacht [jaxt], *f.* (—, *pl.* —en) yacht.
Jacke ['jakə], *f.* (—, *pl.* —n) jacket, tunic.
Jackett [ja'kɛt], *n.* (—s, *pl.* —s) jacket, short coat.
Jagd [ja:kt], *f.* (—, *pl.* —en) hunt, hunting; shooting; chase.
Jagdhund ['ja:kthunt], *m.* (—es, *pl.* —e) retriever, setter; hound.
Jagdrevier ['ja:ktrevi:r], *n.* (—s, *pl.* —e) hunting-ground.
jagen ['ja:gən], *v.a.* hunt; chase; (*fig.*) tear along.
Jäger ['jɛ:gər], *m.* (—s, *pl.* —) hunter, huntsman; game-keeper.
Jägerei [jɛ:gə'raɪ], *f.* (—, *no pl.*) huntsmanship.
jäh [jɛ:], *adj.* abrupt; steep, precipitous; (*fig.*) hasty, rash, sudden.
jählings ['jɛ:lɪŋs], *adv.* abruptly, suddenly, hastily.
Jahr [ja:r], *n.* (—es, *pl.* —e) year.
jähren ['jɛ:rən], *v.r. sich —,* (*anniversary*) come round.
Jahresfeier ['ja:rəsfaɪər], *f.* (—, *pl.* —n) anniversary.
Jahresrente ['ja:rəsrɛntə], *f.* (—, *pl.* —n) annuity.
Jahreszeit ['ja:rəstsaɪt], *f.* (—, *pl.* —en) season.
Jahrgang ['ja:rgaŋ], *m.* (—s, *pl.* ¨e) age group; class; year of publication; vintage.
Jahrhundert [ja:r'hundərt], *n.* (—s, *pl.* —e) century.
jährig ['jɛ:rɪç], *adj.* year-old.
jährlich ['jɛ:rlɪç], *adj.* yearly, annual. — *adv.* every year.
Jahrmarkt ['ja:rmarkt], *m.* (—s, *pl.* ¨e) annual fair.
Jahrtausend [ja:r'tauzənt], *n.* (—s, *pl.* —e) millennium.
Jahrzehnt [ja:r'tse:nt], *n.* (—s, *pl.* —e) decade.
Jähzorn ['jɛ:tsɔrn], *m.* (—s, *no pl.*) irascibility.

Jalousie [ʒalu'zi:], *f.* (—, *pl.* —**n**) Venetian blind.
Jamaika [ja'maika], *n.* Jamaica.
Jambus ['jambus], *m.* (—, *pl.* —**ben**) (*Poet.*) iambic foot.
Jammer ['jamər], *m.* (—**s**, *no pl.*) lamentation; misery; (*fig.*) pity.
jämmerlich ['jɛmərlɪç], *adj.* lamentable, miserable, wretched, piteous.
jammerschade ['jamərʃa:də], *adv.* a thousand pities.
Jänner ['jɛnər] (*Austr.*) *see* **Januar**.
Januar ['janua:r], *m.* (—**s**, *pl.* —**e**) January.
Japan ['ja:pan], *n.* Japan.
Jaspis ['jaspɪs], *m.* (—**ses**, *pl.* —**se**) jasper.
jäten ['jɛ:tən], *v.a.* weed.
Jauche ['jauxə], *f.* (—, *pl.* —**n**) liquid manure.
jauchzen ['jauxtsən], *v.n.* exult, shout with joy.
Jauchzer ['jauxtsər], *m.* (—**s**, *pl.* —) shout of joy.
jawohl [ja'vo:l], *int.* yes, indeed! certainly, of course.
je [je:], *adv.* ever; at any time; at a time; each; *von — her*, always; *— nachdem*, it depends; *— zwei*, in twos; *— eher — besser*, the sooner the better.
jedenfalls ['je:dənfals], *adv.* at all events, in any case, at any rate, anyway.
jeder, –e, –es ['je:dər], *adj.* every, each; *— beliebige*, any. — *pron.* each, each one; everybody.
jederlei ['je:dərlaɪ], *adj.* of every kind.
jedoch [je'dɔx], *adv.*, however, nevertheless, yet, notwithstanding.
jeglicher, –e, –es ['je:klɪçər], *adj.* every, each. — *pron.* every man, each.
jemals ['je:mals], *adv.* ever, at any time.
jemand ['je:mant], *pron.* somebody, someone; anybody, anyone.
Jemen ['je:mən], *n.* Yemen.
jener, –e, –es ['je:nər], *dem. adj.* that, (*Poet.*) yonder. — *dem. pron.* that one, the former.
Jenseits ['jɛnzaɪts], *n.* (—, *no pl.*) the next world, the hereafter, the life to come.
jenseits ['jɛnzaɪts], *prep.* (*Genit.*) on the other side, beyond.
jetzig ['jɛtsɪç], *adj.* present, now existing, current, extant.
jetzt [jɛtst], *adv.* now, at this time, at present.
jeweilig ['je:vaɪlɪç], *adj.* momentary; actual, for the time being.
Joch [jɔx], *n.* (—**es**, *pl.* —**e**) yoke.
Jochbein ['jɔxbaɪn], *n.* (—**s**, *pl.* —**e**) cheek-bone.
Jockei ['jɔkaɪ], *m.* (—**s**, *pl.* —**s**) jockey.
Jod [jo:t], *n.* (—**s**, *no pl.*) iodine.
jodeln ['jo:dəln], *v.n.* yodel.
Jodler ['jo:dlər], *m.* (—**s**, *pl.* —) (*person*) yodeler; (*sound*) yodelling.
Johannisbeere [jo'hanɪsbe:rə], *f.* (—, *pl.* —**n**) (*Bot.*) red currant.
Johannisfest [jo'hanɪsfɛst], *n.* (—**s**, *pl.* —**e**) Midsummer Day, St. John the Baptist's Day (June 24th).
Johanniskäfer [jo'hanɪskɛ:fər], *m.* (—**s**, *pl.* —) (*Ent.*) glow-worm.
Johannisnacht [jo'hanɪsnaxt], *f.* (—, *pl.* ⸗**e**) Midsummer Eve.
johlen ['jo:lən], *v.n.* bawl.
Joppe ['jɔpə], *f.* (—, *pl.* —**n**) shooting jacket
Jota ['jo:ta], *n.* (—**s**, *pl.* —**s**) iota, jot.
Journalismus [ʒurna'lɪsmus], *m.* *see* **Journalistik**.
Journalistik [ʒurna'lɪstɪk], *f.* (—, *no pl.*) journalism.
jubeln ['ju:bəln], *v.n.* rejoice, exult.
Jubilar [ju:bi'la:r], *m.* (—**s**, *pl.* —**e**) person celebrating a jubilee.
Jubiläum [ju:bi'lɛ:um], *n.* (—**s**, *pl.* —**läen**) jubilee.
jubilieren [ju:bi'li:rən], *v.n.* exult, shout with glee.
juchhe [jux'he:], *excl.* hurrah!
Juchten ['juxtən], *m.* (—, *no pl.*) Russian leather.
jucken ['jukən], *v.a.* scratch. — *v.n.* itch.
Jude ['ju:də], *m.* (—**n**, *pl.* —**n**) Jew, Israelite.
Judentum ['ju:dəntu:m], *n.* (—**s**, *no pl.*) Judaism.
Judenviertel ['ju:dənfi:rtəl], *n.* (—**s**, *pl.* —) Jewish quarter, ghetto.
Jüdin ['jy:dɪn], *f.* (—, *pl.* —**innen**) Jewess.
jüdisch ['jy:dɪʃ], *adj.* Jewish.
Jugend ['ju:gənt], *f.* (—, *no pl.*) youth.
jugendlich ['ju:gəntlɪç], *adj.* youthful, juvenile.
Jugoslawien [ju:go'sla:vjən], *n.* Jugoslavia.
Julfest ['ju:lfɛst], *n.* (—**es**, *pl.* —**e**) Yule.
Juli ['ju:li], *m.* (—**s**, *pl.* —**s**) July.
jung [juŋ], *adj.* young.
Junge (1) ['juŋə], *m.* (—**n**, *pl.* —**n**) boy, lad.
Junge (2) ['juŋə], *n.* (—**n**, *pl.* —**n**) young animal.
jungenhaft ['juŋənhaft], *adj.* boyish.
Jünger ['jyŋər], *m.* (—**s**, *pl.* —) disciple, devotee, follower.
Jungfer ['juŋfər], *f.* (—, *pl.* —**n**) (*obs.*) virgin, maid, maiden; lady's maid.
jüngferlich ['jyŋfərlɪç], *adj.* maidenly, coy, prim.
Jungfrau ['juŋfrau], *f.* (—, *pl.* —**en**) virgin.
Junggeselle ['juŋgəzɛlə], *m.* (—**n**, *pl.* —**n**) bachelor; *eingefleischter —*, confirmed bachelor.
Jüngling ['jyŋlɪŋ], *m.* (—**s**, *pl.* —**e**) young man.
jüngst [jyŋst], *adv.* lately, recently.
Juni ['ju:ni], *m.* (—**s**, *pl.* —**s**) June.
Junker ['juŋkər], *m.* (—**s**, *pl.* —) country squire; titled landowner.
Jura ['ju:ra], *n. pl.* jurisprudence, law; (*Univ.*) *— studieren*, read law.
Jurisprudenz [ju:rɪspru'dɛnts], *f.* (—, *no pl.*) jurisprudence.
Jurist [ju:'rɪst], *m.* (—**en**, *pl.* —**en**) lawyer, jurist.

juristisch [ju:'rɪstɪʃ], *adj.* juridical; legal.
just [just], *adv.* just now.
Justiz [jus'ti:ts], *f.* (—, *no pl.*) administration of the law *or* of justice.
Justizrat [jus'ti:tsra:t], *m.* (—s, *pl.* ⸚e) (*Law*) Counsellor; King's (Queen's) Counsel.
Jute ['ju:tə], *f.* (—, *no pl.*) jute.
Juwel [ju've:l], *n.* (—s, *pl.* —en) jewel; (*pl.*) jewellery; (*Am.*) jewelry.
Juwelier [juvə'li:r], *m.* (—s, *pl.* —e) jeweller, goldsmith.

K

K [ka:], *n.* (—, *no pl.*) the letter K.
Kabel ['ka:bəl], *n.* (—s, *pl.* —) cable.
Kabeljau [kabəl'jau], *m.* (—s, *pl.* —e) (*Zool.*) cod, codfish.
kabeln ['ka:bəln], *v.n.* cable, send a cablegram.
Kabine [ka'bi:nə], *f.* (—, *pl.* —n) cabin, cubicle.
Kabinett [kabi'nɛt], *n.* (—s, *pl.* —e) closet; cabinet.
Kabinettsrat [kabi'nɛtsra:t], *m.* (—s, *pl.* ⸚e) cabinet *or* ministerial committee; political adviser.
Kabüse [ka'by:zə], *f.* (—, *pl.* —n) ship's galley.
Kachel ['kaxəl], *f.* (—, *pl.* —n) glazed tile.
Kadaver [ka'da:vər], *m.* (—s, *pl.* —) carrion, carcass; corpse.
Kadenz [ka'dɛnts], *f.* (—, *pl.* —en) (*Mus.*) cadenza.
Kadett [ka'dɛt], *m.* (—en, *pl.* —en) cadet.
Käfer ['kɛ:fər], *m.* (—s, *pl.* —) (*Ent.*) beetle, (*Am.*) bug.
Kaffee ['kafe], *m.* (—s, *no pl.*) coffee.
Käfig ['kɛ:fɪç], *m.* (—s, *pl.* —e) cage.
kahl [ka:l], *adj.* bald; (*trees*) leafless; (*landscape*) barren; — *geschoren*, close-cropped.
Kahn ['ka:n], *m.* (—s, *pl.* ⸚e) boat; punt.
Kai [kaɪ], *m.* (—s, *pl.* —s) quay, wharf, landing-place.
Kaimeister ['kaɪmaɪstər], *m.* (—s, *pl.* —) wharfinger.
Kaiser ['kaɪzər], *m.* (—s, *pl.* —) emperor; *um des —s Bart streiten*, quarrel about nothing.
kaiserlich ['kaɪzərlɪç], *adj.* imperial.
Kaiserschnitt ['kaɪzərʃnɪt], *m.* (—es, *pl.* —e) (*Med.*) Caesarean operation.
Kajüte [ka'jytə], *f.* (—, *pl.* —n) cabin.
Kakadu ['kakadu:], *m.* (—s, *pl.* —s) (*Orn.*) cockatoo.
Kakao [ka'ka:o], *m.* (—s, *no pl.*) cocoa.
Kalauer ['ka:lauər], *m.* (—s, *no pl.*) pun; stale joke.
Kalb [kalp], *n.* (—es, *pl.* ⸚er) calf; (*roe*) fawn; (*fig.*) colt, calf.
Kalbfleisch ['kalpflaɪʃ], *n.* (—es, *no pl.*) veal.
Kälberei [kɛlbə'raɪ], *f.* (—, *pl.* —en) friskiness.
kälbern ['kɛlbərn], *v.n.* frisk, frolic.
Kalbsbraten ['kalpsbra:tən], *m.* (—s, *pl.* —) roast veal.
Kalbshaxe ['kalpshaksə], *f.* (—, *pl.* —n) knuckle of veal.
Kalbskeule ['kalpskɔylə], *f.* (—, *pl.* —n) leg of veal.
Kalbsmilch ['kalpsmɪlç], *f.* (—, *no pl.*) sweetbread.
Kaldaunen [kal'daunən], *f. pl.* (*dial.*) tripe.
Kalesche [ka'lɛʃə], *f.* (—, *pl.* —n) chaise, light carriage.
Kali ['ka:li], *n.* (—s, *no pl.*) potash.
Kaliber [ka'li:bər], *n.* (—s, *pl.* —) calibre; (*fig.*) sort, quality.
kalibrieren [kali'bri:rən], *v.a.* (*Tech.*) calibrate, graduate, gauge.
Kalifornien [kali'fɔrnjən], *n.* California.
Kalium ['ka:ljum], *n.* (—s, *no pl.*) (*Chem.*) potassium.
Kalk [kalk], *m.* (—s, *pl.* —e) lime; *gebrannter* —, quicklime; *mit — bewerfen*, rough-cast.
kalkartig ['kalka:rtɪç], *adj.* calcareous.
Kalkbewurf ['kalkbəvurf], *m.* (—es, *pl.* ⸚e) coat of plaster.
kalken ['kalkən], *v.a.* whitewash; (*Agr.*) lime.
kalkig ['kalkɪç], *adj.* limy, calcareous.
kalkulieren [kalku'li:rən], *v.n.* calculate, reckon.
kalt [kalt], *adj.* cold, frigid; *mir ist* —, I am cold.
kaltblütig ['kaltbly:tɪç], *adj.* cold-blooded, cool.
Kälte ['kɛltə], *f.* (—, *no pl.*) cold, coldness.
Kaltschale ['kaltʃa:lə], *f.* (—, *pl.* —n) cold beer (*or* wine) soup.
Kambodscha [kam'bɔtʃa], *f.* Cambodia.
Kamee [ka'me:], *f.* (—, *pl.* —n) cameo.
Kamel [ka'me:l], *n.* (—s, *pl.* —e) (*Zool.*) camel.
Kamelziege [ka'me:ltsi:gə], *f.* (—, *pl.* —n) (*Zool.*) Angora-goat, llama.
Kamerad [kamə'ra:t], *m.* (—en, *pl.* —en) comrade, companion, mate.
Kameradschaft [kamə'ra:tʃaft], *f.* (—, *pl.* —en) comradeship, fellowship.
Kamerun [kamə'ru:n], *n.* the Cameroons.
Kamille [ka'mɪlə], *f.* (—, *pl.* —n) camomile.
Kamin [ka'mi:n], *m.* (—s, *pl.* —e) chimney; funnel; fireplace, fireside.
Kaminaufsatz [ka'mi:naufzats], *m.* (—es, *pl.* ⸚e) mantel-piece, overmantel.
Kaminfeger [ka'mi:nfe:gər], *m.* (—s, *pl.* —) chimney-sweep.

Kaminsims [ka'mi:nzɪms], *m.* or *n.* (—**es**, *pl.* —**e**) mantel-piece.
Kamm [kam], *m.* (—**es**, *pl.* ⸚**e**) comb; (*cock*) crest; (*mountains*) ridge.
kämmen ['kɛmən], *v.a.* comb; (*wool*) card.
Kammer ['kamər], *f.* (—, *pl.* —**n**) chamber, small room; (*Am.*) closet; (*authority*) board; (*Parl. etc.*) chamber.
Kammerdiener ['kamərdi:nər], *m.* (—**s**, *pl.* —) valet.
Kämmerer ['kɛmərər], *m.* (—**s**, *pl.* —) Chamberlain, Treasurer.
Kammergericht ['kamərgərɪçt], *n.* (—**s**, *pl.* —**e**) Supreme Court of Justice.
Kammergut ['kamərgu:t], *n.* (—**s**, *pl.* ⸚**er**) domain, demesne; crown land.
Kammerherr ['kamərhɛr], *m.* (—**n**, *pl.* —**en**) chamberlain.
Kammersänger ['kamərzɛŋər], *m.* (—**s**, *pl.* —) court singer; title given to prominent singers.
Kammgarn ['kamgarn], *n.* (—**s**, *no pl.*) worsted.
Kammwolle ['kamvɔlə], *f.* (—, *no pl.*) carded wool.
Kampagne [kam'panjə], *f.* (—, *pl.* —**n**) (*Mil.*) campaign.
Kämpe ['kɛmpe], *m.* (—**n**, *pl.* —**n**) (*Poet.*) champion, warrior; *alter* —, old campaigner.
Kampf [kampf], *m.* (—**es**, *pl.* ⸚**e**) combat, fight, struggle; (*fig.*) conflict.
kämpfen ['kɛmpfən], *v.n.* fight, combat, struggle.
Kampfer ['kampfər], *m.* (—**s**, *no pl.*) camphor.
Kämpfer ['kɛmpfər], *m.* (—**s**, *pl.* —) fighter, combatant.
kampfunfähig ['kampfunfɛ:ɪç], *adj.* (*Mil.*) disabled; — *machen*, disable, put out of action.
kampieren [kam'pi:rən], *v.n.* be encamped, camp.
Kanada ['kanada], *n.* Canada.
Kanal [ka'na:l], *m.* (—**s**, *pl.* ⸚**e**) (*natural*) channel; (*artificial*) canal; sewer; *der Ärmelkanal*, the English Channel.
kanalisieren [kanali'zi:rən], *v.a.* canalise; (*streets*) drain by means of sewers.
Kanapee ['kanape:], *n.* (—**s**, *pl.* —**s**) sofa, divan.
Kanarienvogel [ka'na:rjənfo:gəl], *m.* (—**s**, *pl.* ⸚) (*Orn.*) canary.
Kanarische Inseln [ka'na:rɪʃə 'ɪnzəln], *f.pl.* Canary Islands.
Kandare [kan'da:rə], *f.* (—, *pl.* —**n**) bridle, bit.
Kandelaber [kandə'la:bər], *m.* (—**s**, *pl.* —) candelabrum, chandelier.
kandidieren [kandi'di:rən], *v.n.* be a candidate (for), apply (for) (*post*); (*Parl.*) stand (for), (*Am.*) run (for election).
kandieren [kan'di:rən], *v.a.* candy.
Kandiszucker ['kandɪstsukər], *m.* (—, *no pl.*) sugar-candy.
Kanevas ['kanəvas], *m.* (—**ses**, *pl.* —**se**) canvas.
Känguruh ['kɛŋguru:], *n.* (—**s**, *pl.* —**s**) (*Zool.*) kangaroo.
Kaninchen [ka'ni:nçən], *n.* (—**s**, *pl.* —) (*Zool.*) rabbit.
Kaninchenbau [ka'ni:nçənbau], *m.* (—**s**, *pl.* —**e**) rabbit-warren, burrow.
Kanne ['kanə], *f.* (—, *pl.* —**n**) can, tankard, mug; jug; pot; quart.
Kannegießer ['kanəgi:sər], *m.* (—**s**, *pl.* —) pot-house politician.
kannelieren [kanə'li:rən], *v.a.* flute; channel.
Kannibale [kani'ba:lə], *m.* (—**n**, *pl.* —**n**) cannibal.
Kanoe [ka'nu:], *n.* *see* **Kanu.**
Kanone [ka'no:nə], *f.* (—, *pl.* —**n**) cannon, gun; *unter aller* —, beneath contempt; beneath criticism.
Kanonier [kano'ni:r], *m.* (—**s**, *pl.* —**e**) gunner.
Kanonikus [ka'no:nikus], *m.* (—, *pl.* —**ker**) canon, prebendary.
kanonisieren [kanoni'zi:rən], *v.a.* canonise.
Kante ['kantə], *f.* (—, *pl.* —**n**) edge, rim, brim, brink, ledge; (*cloth*) list, selvedge.
Kanten ['kantən], *m.* (—**s**, *pl.* —) (*bread*) crust.
kanten ['kantən], *v.a.* edge, tilt.
Kanthaken ['kantha:kən], *m.* (—**s**, *pl.* —) cant-hook; grapple; grappling hook.
kantig ['kantɪç], *adj.* angular.
Kantine [kan'ti:nə], *f.* (—, *pl.* —**n**), canteen, mess.
Kanton [kan'to:n], *m.* (—**s**, *pl.* —**e**) (Swiss) canton; district, region.
Kantonist [kanto'nɪst], *m.* (—**en**, *pl.* —**en**) *unsicherer* —, shifty fellow.
Kantor ['kantɔr], *m.* (—**s**, *pl.* —**en**) precentor; organist; cantor.
Kanu [ka'nu:], *n.* (—**s**, *pl.* —**s**) canoe.
Kanzel ['kantsəl], *f.* (—, *pl.* —**n**) pulpit; (*Aviat.*) cockpit.
Kanzlei [kants'laɪ], *f.* (—, *pl.* —**en**) office, secretariat; chancellery; chancery office; lawyer's office.
Kanzleipapier [kants'laɪpapi:r], *n.* (—**s**, *no pl.*) foolscap (paper).
Kanzleistil [kants'laɪʃti:l], *m.* (—**s**, *no pl.*) legal jargon.
Kanzler ['kantslər], *m.* (—**s**, *pl.* —) Chancellor.
Kanzlist [kants'lɪst], *m.* (—**en**, *pl.* —**en**) chancery clerk; copying clerk.
Kap [kap], *n.* (—**s**, *pl.* —**s**) (*Geog.*) cape, promontory.
Kapaun [ka'paun], *m.* (—**s**, *pl.* —**e**) capon.
Kapazität [kapatsi'tɛ:t], *f.* (—, *pl.* —**en**) capacity; (*fig.*) (*person*) authority.
Kapelle [ka'pɛlə], *f.* (—, *pl.* —**n**) chapel; (*Mus.*) band.
Kapellmeister [ka'pɛlmaɪstər], *m.* (—**s**, *pl.* —) (*Mus.*) band leader, conductor.
Kaper ['ka:pər], *f.* (—, *pl.* —**n**) (*Bot.*) caper.

kapern ['ka:pərn], *v.a.* capture, catch.
kapieren [ka'pi:rən], *v.a.* (*coll.*) understand, grasp.
Kapital [kapi'ta:l], *n.* (—**s**, *pl.* —**ien**) (*money*) capital, stock.
Kapitäl, Kapitell [kapɪ'tɛ:l, kapɪ'tɛl], *n.* (—**s**, *pl.* —**e**) (*Archit.*) capital.
Kapitalanlage [kapi'talanla:gə], *f.* (—*pl.* —**n**) investment.
kapitalisieren [kapitali'zi:rən], *v.a.* capitalise.
kapitalkräftig [kapi'ta:lkrɛftɪç], *adj.* wealthy, moneyed, affluent; (*business, firm*) sound.
Kapitalverbrechen [kapi'ta:lfɛrbrɛçən], *n.* (—**s**, *pl.* —) capital offence.
Kapitän [kapi'tɛ:n], *m.* (—**s**, *pl.* —**e**) captain (of a ship), master.
Kapitel [ka'pɪtəl], *n.* (—**s**, *pl.* —) chapter.
Kapitulation [kapitulats'jo:n], *f.* (—, *pl.* —**en**) surrender.
kapitulieren [kapitu'li:rən], *v.n.* surrender; capitulate.
Kaplan [kap'la:n], *m.* (—**s**, *pl.* ⸚**e**) chaplain; assistant priest.
Kapotte [ka'pɔtə], *f.* (—, *pl.* —**n**) hood.
Kappe ['kapə], *f.* (—, *pl.* —**n**) cap, bonnet; (*shoe*) toe-cap.
Käppi ['kɛpi], *n.* (—**s**, *pl.* —**s**) military cap.
Kapriole [kapri'o:lə], *f.* (—, *pl.* —**n**) caper.
kaprizieren [kapri'tsi:rən], *v.r.* *sich auf etwas* —, set o.'s heart on s.th., be obstinate about s.th.
kapriziös [kapri'tsjø:s], *adj.* whimsical, capricious.
Kapsel ['kapzəl], *f.* (—, *pl.* —**n**) capsule.
kaputt [ka'put], *adj.* broken, ruined, done for; — *machen*, break, ruin.
Kapuze [ka'pu:tsə], *f.* (—, *pl.* —**n**) hood; monk's cowl.
Kapuziner [kaput'si:nər], *m.* (—**s**, *pl.* —) Capuchin (friar); (*coffee*) cappuccino.
Kapuzinerkresse [kaput'si:nərkrɛsə], *f.* (—, *no pl.*) (*Bot.*) nasturtium.
Karabiner [kara'bi:nər], *m.* (—**s**, *pl.* —) (*rifle*) carbine.
Karaffe [ka'rafə], *f.* (—, *pl.* —**n**) carafe; decanter.
Karambolage [karambo'la:ʒə], *f.* (—, *pl.* —**n**) collision; (*billiards*) cannon.
Karawane [kara'va:nə], *f.* (—, *pl.* —**n**) convoy; caravan.
Karbol [kar'bo:l], *n.* (—**s**, *no pl.*) carbolic acid.
Karbunkel [kar'buŋkəl], *m.* (—**s**, *pl.* —) (*Med.*) carbuncle.
Karfreitag [kar'fraɪta:k], *m.* Good Friday.
Karfunkel [kar'fuŋkəl], *m.* (—**s**, *pl.* —) (*Min.*) carbuncle.
karg [kark], *adj.* scant; meagre; parsimonious.
kargen ['kargən], *v.n.* be stingy, be niggardly.
kärglich ['kɛrklɪç], *adj.* sparing, scanty, poor, paltry.
karieren [ka'ri:rən], *v.a.* checker.
kariert [ka'ri:rt], *adj.* checked, checkered.
Karikatur [karika'tu:r], *f.* (—, *pl.* —**en**) caricature, cartoon.
karikieren [kari'ki:rən], *v.a.* caricature, distort.
Karl [karl], *m.* Charles; — *der Grosse*, Charlemagne.
Karmeliter [karme'li:tər], *m.* (—**s**, *pl.* —) Carmelite (friar).
karminrot [kar'mi:nro:t], *adj.* carmine.
karmoisin [karmoa'zi:n], *adj.* crimson.
Karneol [karne'o:l], *m.* (—**s**, *pl.* —**e**) (*Min.*) cornelian, carnelian.
Karneval ['karnəval], *m.* (—**s**, *pl.* —**s**) carnival; Shrovetide festivities.
Karnickel [kar'nɪkəl], *n.* (—**s**, *pl.* —) rabbit; *er war das* —, he was to blame.
Kärnten ['kɛrntən], *n.* Carinthia.
Karo ['ka:ro], *n.* (—**s**, *pl.* —**s**) check, square; (*cards*) diamonds.
Karosse [ka'rɔsə], *f.* (—, *pl.* —**n**) state-coach.
Karosserie [karɔsə'ri:], *f.* (—, *pl.* —**n**) (*Motor.*) body(-work).
Karotte [ka'rɔtə], *f.* (—, *pl.* —**n**) (*Bot.*) carrot.
Karpfen ['karpfən], *m.* (—**s**, *pl.* —) (*fish*) carp.
Karre ['karə], *f.* (—, *pl.* —**n**) cart, wheelbarrow.
Karren ['karən], *m.* (—**s**, *pl.* —) cart, wheelbarrow, dray.
Karrete [ka're:tə], *f.* (—, *pl.* —**n**) (*Austr.*) rattletrap, rickety coach.
Karriere [ka'rjɛ:rə], *f.* (—, *pl.* —**n**) career; — *machen*, get on well.
Kärrner ['kɛrnər], *m.* (—**s**, *pl.* —) (*obs.*) carter.
Karst [karst], *m.* (—**s**, *pl.* —**e**) mattock.
Karthago [kar'ta:go], *n.* Carthage.
Kartätsche [kar'tɛ:tʃə], *f.* (—, *pl.* —**n**) grape-shot, shrapnel.
Kartäuser [kar'tɔyzər], *m.* (—**s**, *pl.* —) Carthusian (monk).
Karte ['kartə], *f.* (—, *pl.* —**n**) card; ticket; map; chart; (*pl.*) pack ((*Am.*) deck) of cards.
Kartei [kar'taɪ], *f.* (—, *pl.* —**en**) card index.
Kartell [kar'tɛl], *n.* (—**s**, *pl.* —**e**) cartel; ring; syndicate.
Kartoffel [kar'tɔfəl], *f.* (—, *pl.* —**n**) (*Bot.*) potato.
Kartoffelpuffer [kar'tɔfəlpufər], *m.* —**s**, *pl.* —) potato-pancake.
Karton [kar'tɔŋ], *m.* (—**s**, *pl.* —**s**) carton, cardboard-box; (*material*) cardboard, paste-board; cartoon.
Kartusche [kar'tuʃə], *f.* (—, *pl.* —**n**) cartridge.
Karussell [karu'sɛl], *n.* (—**s**, *pl.* —**e**) merry-go-round.
Karwoche ['ka:rvɔxə], *f.* Holy Week.
Karzer ['kartsər], *m.* (—**s**, *pl.* —) lock-up, prison.
Kaschmir ['kaʃmi:r], *m.* (—**s**, *no pl.*) cashmere.

Käse ['kɛ:zə], *m.* (**—s**, *pl.* **—**) cheese.
käseartig ['kɛ:zəa:rtɪç], *adj.* like cheese; caseous.
Kaserne [ka'zɛrnə], *f.* (**—**, *pl.* **—n**) barracks.
kasernieren [kazɛr'ni:rən], *v.a.* put into barracks.
Käsestoff ['kɛ:zəʃtɔf], *m.* (**—s**, *pl.* **—e**) casein.
käseweiß ['kɛ:zəvaɪs], *adj.* deathly pale.
käsig ['kɛ:zɪç], *adj.* cheese-like, cheesy, caseous; (*fig.*) sallow.
Kasperle ['kaspɛrlə], *n.* (**—s**, *pl.* **—**) Punch.
Kasperl(e)theater ['kasparl(ə)tea:tər], *n.* (**—s**, *pl.* **—**) Punch-and-Judy show.
Kaspisches Meer ['kaspɪʃəsme:r], *n.* Caspian Sea.
Kasse ['kasə], *f.* (**—**, *pl.* **—n**) money-box, till; cash-desk; box-office; cash, ready money.
Kassenanweisung ['kasənanvaɪzuŋ], *f.* (**—**, *pl.* **—en**) treasury-bill; cash voucher.
Kassenbuch ['kasənbu:x], *n.* (**—es**, *pl.* **⸚er**) cash-book.
Kassenschrank ['kasənʃraŋk], *m.* (**—s**, *pl.* **⸚e**) strong-box, safe.
Kasserolle [kasə'rɔlə], *f.* (**—**, *pl.* **—n**) stew-pot, casserole.
Kassette [ka'sɛtə], *f.* (**—**, *pl.* **—n**) deed-box; casket; (*Phot.*) plate-holder.
kassieren [ka'si:rən], *v.a.* cash, collect (money); cashier, annul, discharge.
Kastagnette [kastan'jɛtə], *f.* (**—**, *pl.* **—n**) castanet.
Kassierer [ka'si:rər], *m.* (**—s**, *pl.* **—**) cashier; teller.
Kastanie [kas'tanjə], *f.* (**—**, *pl.* **—n**) (*Bot.*) chestnut, (*coll.*) conker; chestnut-tree.
Kästchen ['kɛstçən], *n.* (**—s**, *pl.* **—**) casket, little box.
Kaste ['kastə], *f.* (**—**, *pl.* **—n**) caste.
kasteien [ka'staɪən], *v.r.* *sich* **—**, castigate *or* mortify o.s.
Kastell [ka'stɛl], *n.* (**—s**, *pl.* **—e**) citadel, small fort; castle.
Kastellan [kastɛ'la:n], *m.* (**—s**, *pl.* **—e**) castellan; caretaker.
Kasten ['kastən], *m.* (**—s**, *pl.* **⸚**) box, chest, case, crate.
Kastengeist ['kastəngaɪst], *m.* (**—es**, *no pl.*) exclusiveness; class consciousness.
Kastilien [ka'sti:ljən], *n.* Castile.
Kastrat [ka'stra:t], *m.* (**—en**, *pl.* **—en**) eunuch.
kastrieren [ka'stri:rən], *v.a.* castrate.
Katafalk [kata'falk], *m.* (**—s**, *pl.* **—e**) catafalque.
katalogisieren [katalogi'zi:rən], *v.a.* catalogue.
Katarakt [kata'rakt], *m.* (**—es**, *pl.* **—e**) cataract; waterfall.
Katasteramt [ka'tastəramt], *n.* (**—es**, *pl.* **⸚er**) land-registry office.
katechisieren [kateçi'zi:rən], *v.a.* catechise, instruct.
kategorisch [kate'go:rɪʃ], *adj.* categorical, definite.
Kater ['ka:tər], *m.* (**—s**, *pl.* **—**) tom-cat; (*fig.*) hangover; *der gestiefelte* **—**, Puss-in-Boots.
Katheder [ka'te:dər], *n.* (**—s**, *pl.* **—**) desk; rostrum; lecturing-desk; (*fig.*) professorial chair.
Kathedrale [kate'dra:lə], *f.* (**—**, *pl.* **—n**) cathedral.
Katholik [kato'li:k], *m.* (**—en**, *pl.* **—en**) (Roman) Catholic.
katholisch [ka'to:lɪʃ], *adj.* (Roman) Catholic.
Kattun [ka'tu:n], *m.* (**—s**, *pl.* **—e**) calico, cotton.
Kätzchen ['kɛtsçən], *n.* (**—s**, *pl.* **—**) kitten; (*Bot.*) catkin.
Katze ['katsə], *f.* (**—**, *pl.* **—n**) cat; *die — im Sack kaufen*, buy a pig in a poke; *für die* **—**, no good at all, useless.
katzenartig ['katsəna:rtɪç], *adj.* cat-like, feline.
Katzenauge ['katsənaugə], *n.* (**—s**, *pl.* **—n**) cat's-eye.
Katzenbuckel ['katsənbukəl], *m.* (**—s**, *pl.* **—**) arched back of a cat.
Katzenjammer ['katsənjamər], *m.* (**—s**, *pl.* **—**) hangover.
Katzenmusik ['katsənmuzi:k], *f.* (**—**, *no pl.*) caterwauling; cacophony, discordant music.
Katzensprung ['katsənʃpruŋ], *m.* (**—es**, *no pl.*) (*fig.*) stone's throw
Kauderwelsch ['kaudərvɛlʃ], *n.* (**—es**, *no pl.*) gibberish, double-Dutch.
kauen ['kauən], *v.a.*, *v.n.* chew.
kauern ['kauərn], *v.n.* cower, squat, crouch.
Kauf [kauf], *m.* (**—es**, *pl.* **⸚e**) purchase, buy; bargain.
Kaufbummel ['kaufbuməl], *m.* (**—s**, *no pl.*) shopping-spree.
kaufen ['kaufən], *v.a.* (*things*) buy, purchase; (*persons*) bribe.
Käufer ['kɔyfər], *m.* (**—s**, *pl.* **—**) buyer, purchaser.
Kaufhaus ['kaufhaus], *n.* (**—es**, *pl.* **⸚er**) department store, emporium.
Kaufladen ['kaufla:dən], *m.* (**—s**, *pl.* **⸚**) shop.
käuflich ['kɔyflɪç], *adj.* (*things*) purchasable, marketable; (*persons*) open to bribery, venal.
Kaufmann ['kaufman], *m.* (**—s**, *pl.* **Kaufleute**) merchant; shopkeeper; (*Am.*) store-keeper.
kaufmännisch ['kaufmɛnɪʃ], *adj.* commercial, mercantile.
Kaugummi ['kaugumi], *m.* (**—s**, *no pl.*) chewing gum.
Kaukasus ['kaukazus], *m.* Caucasus (Mountains).
Kaulquappe ['kaulkvapə], *f.* (**—**, *pl.* **—n**) (*Zool.*) tadpole.
kaum [kaum], *adv.* scarcely, hardly; no sooner.
Kaurimuschel ['kaurimuʃəl], *f.* (**—**, *pl.* **—n**) (*Zool.*) cowrie shell.

Kautabak ['kautabak], *m.* (—s, *no pl.*) chewing-tobacco.
Kaution [kau'tsjo:n], *f.* (—, *pl.* —en) security, bail, surety; *eine — stellen*, go, give *or* stand bail.
Kautschuk ['kautʃuk], *m.* (—s, *no pl.*) caoutchouc, India-rubber.
Kauz [kauts], *m.* (—es, *pl.* ¨e) (*Orn.*) screech-owl; (*fig.*) *komischer* —, queer customer.
Käuzchen ['kɔytsçən], *n.* (—s, *pl.* —) little owl; (*fig.*) imp.
Kavalier [kava'li:r], *m.* (—s, *pl.* —e) gentleman; lady's man.
keck [kɛk], *adj.* bold, daring; pert, saucy.
Kegel ['ke:gəl], *m.* (—s, *pl.* —) ninepin, skittle; (*Geom.*) cone; *mit Kind und* —, bag and baggage.
Kegelbahn ['ke:gəlba:n], *f.* (—, *pl.* —en) skittle-alley, bowling-alley.
kegelförmig ['ke:gəlfœrmɪç], *adj.* conical.
kegeln ['ke:gəln], *v.n.* bowl, play at ninepins.
Kehle ['ke:lə], *f.* (—, *pl.* —n) throat, windpipe.
Kehlkopf ['ke:lkɔpf], *m.* (—es, *pl.* ¨e) larynx.
Kehllaut ['ke:llaut], *m.* (—es, *pl.* —e) (*Phonet.*) guttural sound.
Kehlung ['ke:luŋ], *f.* (—, *pl.* —en) channel, flute, groove.
Kehraus ['ke:raus], *m.* (—, *no pl.*) last dance; (*fig.*) break-up, end.
kehren ['ke:rən], *v.a.* sweep; turn; *den Rücken* —, turn o.'s back. — *v.r. sich — an*, pay attention to, regard.
Kehricht ['ke:rɪçt], *m.* (—s, *no pl.*) sweepings; rubbish.
Kehrreim ['ke:rraɪm], *m.* (—s, *pl.* —e) refrain.
Kehrseite ['ke:rzaɪtə], *f.* (—, *pl.* —n) reverse.
kehrtmachen ['ke:rtmaxən], *v.n.* turn around; (*Mil.*) face about; turn back.
keifen ['kaɪfən], *v.n.* scold, nag.
Keil [kaɪl], *m.* (—s, *pl.* —e) wedge.
Keile ['kaɪlə], *f.* (—, *no pl.*) blows; (*coll.*) hiding; — *kriegen*, get a thrashing.
keilen ['kaɪlən], *v.a.* wedge; (*coll.*) thrash.
Keilerei [kaɪlə'raɪ], *f.* (—, *pl.* —en) brawl, fight.
keilförmig ['kaɪlfœrmɪç], *adj.* wedge-shaped.
Keilschrift ['kaɪlʃrɪft], *f.* (—, *pl.* —en) cuneiform writing.
Keim [kaɪm], *m.* (—es, *pl.* —e) germ, seed.
keimen ['kaɪmən], *v.n.* germinate.
keimfrei ['kaɪmfraɪ], *adj.* sterile, germ-free.
keiner, -e, -es [kaɪnər], *adj.* no, not a, not any. — *pron.* no one, none.
keinerlei ['kaɪnərlaɪ], *adj.* no, of no sort, no ... whatever.
keineswegs ['kaɪnəsve:ks], *adv.* by no means, on no account.
Keks [ke:ks], *m.* (—es, *pl.* —e) biscuit.
Kelch [kɛlç], *m.* (—es, *pl.* —e) cup; (*Eccl.*) chalice; (*Bot.*) calyx.
Kelchblatt ['kɛlçblat], *n.* (—es, *pl.* ¨er) sepal.
kelchförmig ['kɛlçfœrmɪç], *adj.* cup-shaped.
Kelle ['kɛlə], *f.* (—, *pl.* —n) ladle; (*mason*) trowel.
Keller ['kɛlər], *m.* (—s, *pl.* —) cellar, basement.
Kellergewölbe ['kɛlərgəvœlbə], *n.* (—s, *pl.* —) vault.
Kellner ['kɛlnər], *m.* (—s, *pl.* —) waiter.
keltern ['kɛltərn], *v.a.* press (*grapes*).
Kenia ['ke:nja], *n.* Kenya.
kennbar ['kɛnba:r], *adj.* recognisable, conspicuous.
kennen ['kɛnən], *v.a. irr.* know, be acquainted with.
Kenner ['kɛnər], *m.* (—s, *pl.* —) connoisseur, expert.
Kennkarte ['kɛnkartə], *f.* (—, *pl.* —n) identity card.
kenntlich ['kɛntlɪç], *adj.* distinguishable.
Kenntnis ['kɛntnɪs], *f.* (—, *pl.* —se) knowledge; (*language*) command.
Kennzeichen ['kɛntsaɪxən], *n.* (—s, *pl.* —) characteristic, distinguishing mark; sign; symptom; criterion.
Kenterhaken ['kɛntərha:kən], *m.* (—s, *pl.* —) grappling-iron.
kentern ['kɛntərn], *v.n.* (*aux.* sein) capsize.
keramisch [ke'ra:mɪʃ], *adj.* ceramic.
Kerbe ['kɛrbə], *f.* (—, *pl.* —n) notch, indentation.
kerben ['kɛrbən], *v.a.* notch.
Kerbholz ['kɛrphɔlts], *n.* (—es, *no pl.*) tally; *auf dem* —, on o.'s conscience, charged against o.
Kerbtier ['kɛrpti:r], *n.* (—es, *pl.* —e) insect.
Kerker ['kɛrkər], *m.* (—s, *pl.* —) prison, jail, gaol; dungeon.
Kerl [kɛrl], *m.* (—s, *pl.* —e) fellow, chap; (*Am.*) guy (*coll.*).
Kern [kɛrn], *m.* (—es, *pl.* —e) (*nut*) kernel; (*fruit*) stone; (*fig.*) heart, crux; pith; (*Phys.*) nucleus.
kerngesund ['kɛrngəzunt], *adj.* hale and hearty, fit as a fiddle.
kernig ['kɛrnɪç], *adj.* solid, pithy.
Kernphysik ['kɛrnfyzi:k], *f.* (—, *no pl.*) nuclear physics.
Kernpunkt ['kɛrnpuŋkt], *m.* (—es, *pl.* —e) gist, essential point.
Kernwaffe ['kɛrnvafə], *f.* (—, *pl.* —n) nuclear weapon.
Kerze ['kɛrtsə], *f.* (—, *pl.* —n) candle.
Kessel ['kɛsəl], *m.* (—s, *pl.* —) kettle, cauldron; (*steam*) boiler.
Kesselschmied ['kɛsəlʃmi:t], *m.* (—s, *pl.* —e) boiler maker.
Kesselstein ['kɛsəlʃtaɪn], *m.* (—s, *no pl.*) fur, deposit, scale (on boiler).
Kette ['kɛtə], *f.* (—, *pl.* —n) chain.
ketten ['kɛtən], *v.a.* chain, fetter.
Kettenstich ['kɛtənʃtɪç], *m.* (—es, *pl.* —e) chain stitch; (*Naut.*) chain knot.

Ketzer ['kɛtsər], *m.* (—**s**, *pl.* —) heretic.
Ketzerei [kɛtsə'raɪ], *f.* (—, *pl.* —**en**) heresy.
ketzerisch ['kɛtsərɪʃ], *adj.* heretical.
keuchen ['kɔyçən], *v.n.* pant, puff, gasp.
Keuchhusten ['kɔyçhu:stən], *m.* (—**s**, *no pl.*) whooping-cough.
Keule ['kɔylə], *f.* (—, *pl.* —**n**) club; (*meat*) leg.
keusch [kɔyʃ], *adj.* chaste, pure.
kichern ['kɪçərn], *v.n.* titter, giggle.
Kiebitz ['ki:bɪts], *m.* (—**es**, *pl.* —**e**) (*Orn.*) lapwing, peewit; (*fig.*) onlooker; (*coll.*) rubber-neck (at chess *or* cards).
Kiefer (1) ['ki:fər], *m.* (—**s**, *pl.* —) jaw, jaw-bone.
Kiefer (2) ['ki:fər], *f.* (—, *pl.* —**n**) (*Bot.*) pine.
Kiel [ki:l], *m.* (—**es**, *pl.* —**e**) keel; (*pen*) quill.
Kielwasser ['ki:lvasər], *n.* (—**s**, *no pl.*) wake.
Kieme ['ki:mə], *f.* (—, *pl.* —**n**) (*fish*) gill.
Kien [ki:n], *m.* (—**s**, *no pl.*) pine-resin, resinous pinewood.
Kienspan ['ki:nʃpa:n], *m.* (—**s**, *pl.* ¨**e**) pine-splinter.
Kiepe ['ki:pə], *f.* (—, *pl.* —**n**) (*dial.*) creel, wicker basket.
Kies [ki:s], *m.* (—**es**, *no pl.*) gravel.
Kiesel ['ki:zəl], *m.* (—**s**, *pl.* —) pebble; flint.
Kieselsäure ['ki:zəlzɔyrə], *f.* (—, *no pl.*) silicic acid.
Kieselstein ['ki:zəlʃtaɪn], *m.* (—**s**, *pl.* —**e**) pebble.
Kilogramm ['ki:logram], *n.* (—**s**, *pl.* —**e**) kilogram (1000 grammes).
Kilometer ['ki:lome:tər], *m.* (—**s**, *pl.* —) kilometre; (*Am.*) kilometer (1000 metres).
Kimme ['kɪmə], *f.* (—, *pl.* —**n**) notch.
Kind [kɪnt], *n.* (—**es**, *pl.* —**er**) child; (*law*) infant; — *und Kegel*, bag and baggage.
Kind(e)l ['kɪnd(ə)l], *n.* (—**s**, *pl.* —) (*dial.*) small child, baby; *Münchner* —, Munich beer.
Kinderei [kɪndə'raɪ], *f.* (—, *pl.* —**en**) childishness; childish prank.
Kinderfräulein ['kɪndərfrɔylaɪn], *n.* (—**s**, *pl.* —) nurse, (*coll.*) nannie.
Kindergarten ['kɪndərgartən], *m.* (—**s**, *pl.* ¨) kindergarten, infant-school.
Kinderhort ['kɪndərhɔrt], *m.* (—**s**, *pl.* —**e**) crèche.
kinderleicht ['kɪndərlaɪçt], *adj.* extremely easy, child's play.
Kindermärchen ['kɪndərmɛ:rçən], *n.* (—**s**, *pl.* —) fairy-tale.
Kinderstube ['kɪndərʃtu:bə], *f.* (—, *pl.* —**n**) nursery; *eine gute* —, a good upbringing.
Kinderwagen ['kɪndərva:gən], *m.* (—**s**, *pl.* —) perambulator, pram.
Kindesbeine ['kɪndəsbaɪnə], *n. pl. von* —*n an*, from infancy.
Kindeskind ['kɪndəskɪnt], *n.* (—**es**, *pl.* —**er**) (*obs.*) grandchild.
Kindheit ['kɪnthaɪt], *f.* (—, *no pl.*) childhood, infancy.
kindisch ['kɪndɪʃ], *adj.* childish.
kindlich ['kɪntlɪç], *adj.* childlike; naïve.
Kinn [kɪn], *n.* (—**s**, *pl.* —**e**) chin.
Kinnbacken ['kɪnbakən], *m.* (—**s**, *pl.* —) (*Anat.*) jaw-bone.
Kinnbackenkrampf ['kɪnbakənkrampf], *m.* (—**s**, *pl.* ¨**e**) (*Med.*) lock-jaw.
Kinnlade ['kɪnla:də], *f.* (—, *pl.* —**n**) (*Anat.*) jaw-bone.
Kino ['ki:no], *n.* (—**s**, *pl.* —**s**) cinema; (*coll.*) pictures; (*Am.*) motion picture theatre; motion pictures, (*coll.*) movies.
Kipfel ['kɪpfəl], *n.* (—**s**, *pl.* —) (*dial.*) roll, croissant.
kippen ['kɪpən], *v.a.* tilt, tip over.
Kirche ['kɪrçə], *f.* (—, *pl.* —**n**) church.
Kirchenbann ['kɪrçənban], *m.* (—**s**, *no. pl.*) excommunication.
Kirchenbuch ['kɪrçənbu:x], *n.* (—**es**, *pl.* ¨**er**) parish-register.
Kirchengut ['kɪrçəngu:t], *n.* (—**es**, *pl.* ¨**er**) church-property.
Kirchenlicht ['kɪrçənlɪçt], *n.* (—**es**, *pl.* —**er**) (*fig.*) shining light, bright spark.
Kirchenrecht ['kɪrçənrɛçt], *n.* (—**es**, *no pl.*) canon law.
Kirchenschiff ['kɪrçənʃɪf], *n.* (—**es**, *pl.* —**e**) nave.
Kirchenstuhl ['kɪrçənʃtu:l], *m.* (—**es**, *pl.* ¨**e**) pew.
Kirchenversammlung ['kɪrçənfɛrzamluŋ], *f.* (—, *pl.* —**en**) synod; convocation.
Kirchenvorsteher ['kɪrçənforʃte:ər], *m.* (—**s**, *pl.* —) churchwarden.
kirchlich ['kɪrçlɪç], *adj.* ecclesiastic(al), religious.
Kirchspiel ['kɪrçʃpi:l], *n.* (—**es**, *pl.* —**e**) parish.
Kirchsprengel ['kɪrçʃprɛŋəl], *m.* (—**s**, *pl.* —) diocese.
Kirchturm ['kɪrçturm], *m.* (—**es**, *pl.* ¨**e**) steeple.
Kirchweih ['kɪrçvaɪ], *f.* (—, *pl.* —**en**) consecration (of a church); church fair.
Kirmes ['kɪrmɛs], *f.* (—, *pl.* —**sen**) *see* **Kirchweih**.
kirre ['kɪrə], *adj.* tame; (*fig.*) amenable.
kirren ['kɪrən], *v.a.* tame, allure. — *v.n.* coo.
Kirsch(branntwein) [kɪrʃ(brantvaɪn)], *m.* (—**s**, *no pl.*) cherry-brandy.
Kirsche ['kɪrʃə], *f.* (—, *pl.* —**n**) (*Bot.*) cherry; *mit ihr ist nicht gut* —*n essen*, she is hard to get on with *or* not pleasant to deal with.
Kirschsaft ['kɪrʃzaft], *m.* (—**es**, *no pl.*) cherry-juice.
Kirschwasser ['kɪrʃvasər], *n.* (—**s**, *no pl.*) cherry-brandy.
Kissen ['kɪsən], *n.* (—**s**, *pl.* —) cushion, pillow.

Kiste ['kɪstə], *f.* (—, *pl.* —n) box, case, chest; crate; coffer.
Kitsch [kɪtʃ], *m.* (—es, *no pl.*) trash; rubbish.
Kitt [kɪt], *m.* (—s, *pl.* —e) cement; (*Glazing*) putty.
Kittel ['kɪtəl], *m.* (—s, *pl.* —) smock; overall, tunic; frock.
kitten ['kɪtən], *v.a.* cement, glue.
Kitzchen ['kɪtsçən], *n.* (—s, *pl.* —) kid; fawn; kitten.
Kitzel ['kɪtsəl], *m.* (—s, *no pl.*) tickling, titillation; itch; (*fig.*) desire, appetite.
kitzeln ['kɪtsəln], *v.a.* tickle, titillate.
kitzlich ['kɪtslɪç], *adj.* ticklish; (*fig.*) delicate.
Kladderadatsch ['kladəradatʃ], *m.* (—es, *no pl.*) bang; mess, muddle.
klaffen ['klafən], *v.n.* gape, yawn.
kläffen ['klɛfən], *v.n.* bark, yelp.
Klafter ['klaftər], *f.* (—, *pl.* —n) fathom; (*wood*) cord.
klagbar ['kla:kba:r], *adj.* (*Law*) actionable.
Klage ['kla:gə], *f.* (—, *pl.* —n) complaint; (*Law*) suit, action.
Klagelied ['kla:gəli:t], *n.* (—es, *pl.* —er) dirge, lamentation.
klagen ['kla:gən], *v.n.* complain, lament; (*Law*) sue.
Kläger ['klɛ:gər], *m.* (—s, *pl.* —) complainant; (*Law*) plaintiff.
Klageschrift ['kla:gəʃrɪft], *f.* (—, *pl.* —en) bill of indictment; written complaint.
kläglich ['klɛ:klɪç], *adj.* woeful, pitiful, deplorable.
klaglos ['kla:klo:s], *adj.* uncomplaining.
Klamm [klam], *f.* (—, *pl.* —en) gorge, ravine.
klamm [klam], *adj.* tight, narrow; numb; clammy.
Klammer ['klamər], *f.* (—, *pl.* —n) clamp, clasp, hook; peg; clip; bracket, parenthesis.
klammern ['klamərn], *v.a.* fasten, peg. — *v.r. sich — an*, cling to.
Klang [klaŋ], *m.* (—es, *pl.* ¨—e) sound, tone; *ohne Sang und —*, unheralded and unsung.
klanglos ['klaŋlo:s], *adj.* soundless.
klangnachahmend ['klaŋnaxa:mənt], *adj.* onomatopoeic.
klangvoll ['klaŋfɔl], *adj.* sonorous.
Klappe ['klapə], *f.* (—, *pl.* —en) flap; (*Tech.*) valve; (*vulg.*) *halt die —!* shut up!
klappen ['klapən], *v.n.* flap; (*fig.*) tally, square; *es hat geklappt*, it worked.
Klapper ['klapər], *f.* (—, *pl.* —n) rattle.
klappern ['klapərn], *v.n.* rattle; (*teeth*) chatter.
Klapperschlange ['klapərʃlaŋə], *f.* (—, *pl.* —n) (*Zool.*) rattle-snake.
Klapphut ['klaphu:t], *m.* (—es, *pl.* ¨—e) opera-hat; chapeau-claque.
Klapps [klaps], *m.* (—es, *pl.* ¨—e) slap, smack; (*fig.*) touch of madness, kink.
Klappstuhl ['klapʃtu:l], *m.* (—s, *pl.* ¨—e) camp-stool, folding-chair.
Klapptisch ['klaptɪʃ], *m.* (—es, *pl.* —e) folding-table.
klar [kla:r], *adj.* clear; bright; (*fig.*) evident; plain, distinct.
Kläranlage ['klɛ:ranla:gə], *f.* (—, *pl.* —n) sewage-farm; filter plant.
klären ['klɛ:rən], *v.a.* clear.
Klarheit ['kla:rhaɪt], *f.* (—, *no pl.*) clearness, plainness.
Klarinette [klari'nɛtə], *f.* (—, *pl.* —n) (*Mus.*) clarinet.
Klärmittel ['klɛ:rmɪtəl], *n.* (—s, *pl.* —) clarifier.
Klärung ['klɛ:ruŋ], *f.* (—, *pl.* —en) clarification; (*fig.*) elucidation.
Klasse ['klasə], *f.* (—, *pl.* —n) class, order; (*Sch.*) form.
klassifizieren [klasifi'tsi:rən], *v.a.* classify.
Klassiker ['klasɪkər], *m.* (—s, *pl.* —) classic.
klassisch ['klasɪʃ], *adj.* classic(al), standard.
Klatsch [klatʃ], *m.* (—es, *no pl.*) gossip, scandal.
klatschen ['klatʃən], *v.n.* clap; gossip; (*rain*) patter; *Beifall* —, applaud.
Klatscherei [klatʃə'raɪ], *f.* (—, *pl.* —en) gossip, scandalmongering.
klauben ['klaubən], *v.a.* pick.
Klaue ['klauə], *f.* (—, *pl.* —n) claw, talon; paw.
klauen ['klauən], *v.a.* steal, (*coll.*) pinch.
Klauenseuche ['klauənzɔyçə], *f.* (—, *pl.* —n) *Maul und* —, foot and mouth disease.
Klause ['klauzə], *f.* (—, *pl.* —n) cell, hermitage; (*coll.*) den.
Klausel ['klauzəl], *f.* (—, *pl.* —n) clause, paragraph.
Klausner ['klausnər], *m.* (—s, *pl.* —) hermit, recluse, anchorite.
Klausur [klau'zu:r], *f.* (—, *pl.* —en) seclusion; written examination.
Klaviatur [klavja'tu:r], *f.* (—, *pl.* —en) keyboard.
Klavier [kla'vi:r], *n.* (—s, *pl.* —e) piano, pianoforte.
Klavierstück [kla'vi:rʃtyk], *n.* (—s, *pl.* —e) piece of piano music.
Klebemittel ['kle:bəmɪtəl], *n.* (—s, *pl.* —) adhesive, glue.
kleben ['kle:bən], *v.a.* paste, stick, glue. — *v.n.* stick, adhere.
klebrig ['kle:brɪç], *adj.* sticky; clammy.
Klebstoff ['kle:pʃtɔf], *m.* (—es, *no pl.*) gum; glue.
Klecks [klɛks], *m.* (—es, *pl.* —e) blot; blotch.
Kleckser ['klɛksər], *m.* (—s, *pl.* —) scrawler; (*painter*) dauber.
Klee [kle:], *m.* (—s, *no pl.*) (*Bot.*) clover, trefoil.
Kleid [klaɪt], *n.* (—es, *pl.* —er) frock, garment, dress, gown; (*Poet.*) garb; (*pl.*) clothes; *—er machen Leute*, clothes make the man.
Kleidchen ['klaɪtçən], *n.* (—s, *pl.* —) child's dress.
kleiden ['klaɪdən], *v.a.* dress, clothe.

Kleiderbügel ['klaidərby:gəl], *m.* (—**s**, *pl.* —) coat-hanger.
Kleiderpuppe ['klaidərpupə], *f.* (—, *pl.* —**n**) tailor's dummy.
Kleiderschrank ['klaidərʃraŋk], *m.* (—**s**, *pl.* ⸚**e**) wardrobe.
kleidsam ['klaitza:m], *adj.* becoming; well-fitting, a good fit.
Kleidung ['klaiduŋ], *f.* (—, *no pl.*) clothing, clothes, dress.
Kleie ['klaiə], *f.* (—, *no pl.*) bran.
klein [klain], *adj.* little, small; minute; petty; *ein — wenig*, a little bit.
Kleinasien [klain'a:zjən], *n.* Asia Minor.
Kleinbahn ['klainba:n], *f.* (—, *pl.* —**en**) narrow-gauge railway.
kleinbürgerlich ['klainbyrgərliç], *adj.* (petit) bourgeois.
Kleingeld ['klaingɛlt], *n.* (—(**e**)**s**, *no pl.*) small change.
kleingläubig ['klainglɔybiç], *adj.* faint-hearted.
Kleinhandel ['klainhandəl], *m.* (—**s**, *no pl.*) retail-trade.
Kleinigkeit ['klainiçkait], *f.* (—, *pl.* —**en**) trifle, small matter.
Kleinkram ['klainkra:m], *m.* (—**s**, *no pl.*) trifles.
kleinlaut ['klainlaut], *adj.* subdued, dejected, low-spirited.
kleinlich ['klainliç], *adj.* petty; mean; narrow-minded; pedantic.
Kleinmut ['klainmu:t], *m.* (—**es**, *no pl.*) faint-heartedness; dejection.
Kleinod ['klaino:t], *n.* (—**s**, *pl.* —**ien**) jewel; trinket.
Kleinstadt ['klainʃtat], *f.* (—, *pl.* ⸚**e**) small town.
Kleister ['klaistər], *m.* (—**s**, *no pl.*) paste.
Klemme ['klɛmə], *f.* (—, *pl.* —**n**) (*Tech.*) vice; clamp; (*fig.*) difficulty, straits; (*coll.*) fix, jam.
klemmen ['klɛmən], *v.a.* pinch, squeeze, jam.
Klemmer ['klɛmər], *m.* (—**s**, *pl.*—) (*eye*) glasses, pince-nez.
Klempner ['klɛmpnər], *m.* (—**s**, *pl.*—) tin-smith; plumber.
Klerus ['kle:rus], *m.* (—, *no pl.*) clergy.
Klette ['klɛtə], *f.* (—, *pl.* —**n**) burdock, bur(r); (*fig.*) hanger-on.
klettern ['klɛtərn], *v.n.* (*aux.* sein) climb, clamber.
Klima ['kli:ma], *n.* (—**s**, *pl.* —**s**) climate.
Klimaanlage ['kli:maanla:gə], *f.* (—, *pl.* —**n**) air conditioning plant.
Klimbim ['klim'bim], *m.* (—**s**, *no pl.*) goings-on; festivity; fuss; *der ganze* —, the whole caboodle.
klimpern ['klimpərn], *v.n.* (*piano*) strum; (*money*) jingle.
Klinge ['kliŋə], *f.* (—, *pl.* —**n**) blade.
Klingel ['kliŋəl], *f.* (—, *pl.* —**n**) (*door, telephone*) bell.
Klingelbeutel ['kliŋəlbɔytəl], *m.* (—**s**, *pl.*—) collecting-bag.
klingeln ['kliŋəln], *v.n.* ring, tinkle.
Klingelzug ['kliŋəltsu:k], *m.* (—**es**, *pl.* ⸚**e**) bell-rope, bell-pull.
klingen ['kliŋən], *v.n. irr.* sound; (*metals*) clang; (*ears*) tingle; —*de Münze*, hard cash, ready money.
Klinke ['kliŋkə], *f.* (—, *pl.* —**en**) (*door*) handle, latch.
klipp [klip], *adv.* — *und klar*, as clear as daylight.
Klippe ['klipə], *f.* (—, *pl.* —**n**) cliff, crag, rock.
klirren ['klirən], *v.n.* clatter, rattle.
Klischee [kli'ʃe:], *n.* (—**s**, *pl.* —**s**) (*Typ.*) plate, printing-block; (*fig.*) cliché, hackneyed expression, tag.
Klistier [kli'sti:r], *n.* (—**s**, *pl.* —**e**) (*Med.*) enema.
Kloake [klo'a:kə], *f.* (—, *pl.* —**n**) sewer, drain.
Kloben ['klo:bən], *m.* (—**s**, *pl.* —) log, block (of wood); pulley.
klopfen ['klɔpfən], *v.a., v.n.* knock, beat.
Klöppel ['klœpəl], *m.* (—**s**, *pl.* —) mallet; (*bell*) tongue, clapper; (*drum*) stick; (*lace*) bobbin.
klöppeln ['klœpəln], *v.a* make (bone) lace.
Klöppelspitze ['klœpəlʃpitsə], *f.* (—, *no pl.*) bone-lace.
Klops [klɔps], *m.* (—**es**, *pl.* —**e**) meat-dumpling.
Klosett [klo'zɛt], *n.* (—**s**, *pl.* —**e**) lavatory, water-closet, toilet.
Kloß [klo:s], *m.* (—**es**, *pl.* ⸚**e**) dumpling.
Kloster ['klo:stər], *n.* (—**s**, *pl.* ⸚) cloister; monastery; convent.
Klostergang ['klo:stərgaŋ], *m.* (—**es**, *pl.* ⸚**e**) cloisters.
Klotz [klɔts], *m.* (—**es**, *pl.* ⸚**e**) block, trunk, stump; (*fig.*) *ein grober* —, a great lout.
klotzig ['klɔtsiç], *adj.* cloddy; lumpish; (*sl.*) enormous.
Klub [klup], *m.* (—**s**, *pl.* —**s**) club.
Kluft [kluft], *f.* (—, *pl.* ⸚**e**) gap; gulf, chasm; (*fig.*) cleavage.
klug [klu:k], *adj.* clever, wise, prudent, judicious, sagacious; *ich kann daraus nicht — werden*, I cannot make head nor tail of it.
klügeln ['kly:gəln], *v.n.* ponder; quibble.
Klugheit ['klu:khait], *f.* (—, *no pl.*) cleverness, wisdom, prudence, judiciousness.
Klumpfuß ['klumpfu:s], *m.* (—**es**, *pl.* ⸚**e**) club-foot.
Klumpen ['klumpən], *m.* (—**s**, *pl.* —) lump, mass, clod; (*blood*) clot; (*metal*) ingot; (*gold*) nugget.
Klüngel ['klyŋəl], *m.* (—**s**, *pl.* —) clique, set.
knabbern ['knabərn], *v.n.* nibble.
Knabe ['kna:bə], *m.* (—**n**, *pl.* —**n**) boy.
Knäblein ['knɛ:blain], *n.* (—**s**, *pl.* —) (*Poet.*) baby boy, small boy.
knack [knak], *int.* crack! snap!
Knäckebrot ['knɛkəbro:t], *n.* (—**es**, *no pl.*) crispbread.
knacken ['knakən], *v.a.* crack.

Knackmandel ['knakmandəl], *f.* (—, *pl.* —**n**) shell-almond.
Knackwurst ['knakvurst], *f.* (—, *pl.* ⸚**e**) saveloy.
Knacks [knaks], *m.* (—**es**, *pl.* —**e**) crack.
knacksen ['knaksən], *v.n.* (*coll.*) crack.
Knall [knal], *m.* (—**es**, *pl.* —**e**) report, bang, detonation; — *und Fall*, quite suddenly, then and there.
Knallbüchse ['knalbyksə], *f.* (—, *pl.* —**n**) pop-gun.
Knalleffekt ['knalɛfɛkt], *m.* (—**s**, *pl.* —**e**) coup de théâtre; sensation.
knallen ['knalən], *v.n.* pop, explode, crack.
Knallgas ['knalga:s], *n.* (—**es**, *no pl.*) oxyhydrogen gas.
knallrot ['knalro:t], *adj.* scarlet; glaring red.
knapp [knap], *adj.* tight; scarce, insufficient; (*style*) concise; (*majority*) narrow, bare.
Knappe ['knapə], *m.* (—**n**, *pl.* —**n**) esquire, shield-bearer; miner.
Knappheit ['knaphaɪt], *f.* (—, *no pl.*) scarcity, shortage.
Knappschaft ['knapʃaft], *f.* (—, *pl.* —**en**) miners' association.
Knarre ['knarə], *f.* (—, *pl.* —**n**) rattle.
knarren ['knarən], *v.n.* rattle, creak.
Knaster ['knastər], *m.* (—**s**, *pl.* —) tobacco.
knattern ['knatərn], *v.n.* crackle.
Knäuel ['knɔyəl], *m.*, *n.* (—**s**, *pl.* —) skein, clew, ball.
Knauf [knauf], *m.* (—**es**, *pl.* ⸚**e**) (*stick*) knob, head; (*Archit.*) capital.
Knauser ['knauzər], *m.* (—**s**, *pl.* —) niggard, skinflint.
knausern ['knauzərn], *v.n.* be stingy, scrimp.
Knebel ['kne:bəl], *m.* (—**s**, *pl.* —) cudgel; gag.
knebeln ['kne:bəln], *v.a.* tie, bind; gag; (*fig.*) muzzle.
Knecht [knɛçt], *m.* (—**es**, *pl.* —**e**) servant, farm hand, menial; vassal, slave.
Knechtschaft ['knɛçtʃaft], *f.* (—, *no pl.*) servitude, slavery.
kneifen ['knaɪfən], *v.a. irr.* pinch. — *v.n.* (*fig. coll.*) back out (of), shirk.
Kneifer ['knaɪfər], *m.* (—**s**, *pl.* —) pince-nez.
Kneifzange ['knaɪftsaŋə], *f.* (—, *pl.* —**n**) pincers.
Kneipe ['knaɪpə], *f.* (—, *pl.* —**n**) pub; saloon.
kneten ['kne:tən], *v.a.* knead; massage.
knick(e)beinig ['knɪk(ə)baɪnɪç], *adj.* knock-kneed.
knicken ['knɪkən], *v.a.* crack, break.
Knicks [knɪks], *m.* (—**es**, *pl.* —**e**) curtsy.
knicksen ['knɪksən], *v.n.* curtsy.
Knie [kni:], *n.* (—**s**, *pl.* —) knee; *etwas übers — brechen*, make short work of.
Kniekehle ['kni:ke:lə], *f.* (—, *pl.* —**n**) hollow of the knee.
knien ['kni:ən], *v.n.* kneel.
Kniescheibe ['kni:ʃaɪbə], *f.* (—, *pl.* —**n**) knee-cap.
Kniff [knɪf], *m.* (—**es**, *pl.* —**e**) fold; (*fig.*) trick, knack, dodge.
knipsen ['knɪpsən], *v.a.* (*tickets*) clip, punch; (*Phot.*) take a snap of.
Knirps [knɪrps], *m.* (—**es**, *pl.* —**e**) pigmy; (*fig.*) urchin.
knirschen ['knɪrʃən], *v.n.* crunch, grate, gnash (teeth).
knistern ['knɪstərn], *v.n.* crackle.
knittern ['knɪtərn], *v.a.* rumple, wrinkle, crinkle, crease.
Knobel ['kno:bəl], *m. pl.* dice.
Knoblauch ['kno:blaux], *m.* (—**s**, *no pl.*) (*Bot.*) garlic.
Knöchel ['knœçəl], *m.* (—**s**, *pl.* —) knuckle, joint; ankle.
Knochen ['knɔxən], *m.* (—**s**, *pl.* —) bone.
Knochengerüst ['knɔxəngəryst], *n.* (—**es**, *pl.* —**e**) skeleton.
knöchern ['knœçərn], *adj.* made of bone.
knochig ['knɔxɪç], *adj.* bony.
Knödel ['knø:dəl], *m.* (—**s**, *pl.* —) dumpling.
Knollen ['knɔlən], *m.* (—**s**, *pl.* —) lump, clod; (*Bot.*) tuber, bulb.
knollig ['knɔlɪç], *adj.* knobby, bulbous.
Knopf [knɔpf], *m.* (—**es**, *pl.* ⸚**e**) button; stud; (*stick*) head, knob.
knöpfen ['knœpfən], *v.a.* button.
Knorpel ['knɔrpəl], *m.* (—**s**, *pl.* —) gristle, cartilage.
knorplig ['knɔrplɪç], *adj.* gristly.
knorrig ['knɔrɪç], *adj.* knotty, gnarled.
Knospe ['knɔspə], *f.* (—, *pl.* —**n**) bud.
Knote ['kno:tə], *m.* (—**n**, *pl.* —**n**) (*fig.*) bounder; lout.
Knoten ['kno:tən], *m.* (—**s**, *pl.* —) knot; (*fig.*) difficulty; (*Theat.*) plot.
Knotenpunkt ['kno:tənpuŋkt], *m.* (—**es**, *pl.* —**e**) (*Railw.*) junction.
Knotenstock ['kno:tənʃtɔk], *m.* (—**es**, *pl.* ⸚**e**) knotty stick.
knotig ['kno:tɪç], *adj.* knotty, nodular.
knüllen ['knylən], *v.a.* crumple.
knüpfen ['knypfən], *v.a.* tie; knot; form (a friendship etc.).
Knüppel ['knypəl], *m.* (—**s**, *pl.* —) cudgel.
knurren ['knurən], *v.n.* grunt, snarl; (*fig.*) growl, grumble.
knurrig ['knurɪç], *adj.* surly, grumpy.
knusprig ['knusprɪç], *adj.* crisp, crunchy.
Knute ['knu:tə], *f.* (—, *pl.* —**n**) knout.
knutschen ['knu:tʃən], *v.r. sich* —, (*coll.*) cuddle; (*Am.*) neck.
Knüttel [knytəl], *m.* (—**s**, *pl.* —) cudgel, bludgeon.
Knüttelvers ['knytəlfɛrs], *m.* (—**es**, *pl.* —**e**) doggerel, rhyme.
Kobalt ['ko:balt], *m.* (—**s**, *no pl.*) cobalt.
Kobaltblau ['ko:baltblau], *n.* (—**s**, *no pl.*) smalt.

Koben [ˈko:bən], *m.* (—s, *pl.* —) pig-sty.
Kober [ˈko:bər], *m.* (—s, *pl.* —) (*dial.*) basket, hamper.
Kobold [ˈko:bɔlt], *m.* (—(e)s, *pl.* —e) goblin, hobgoblin.
Koch [kɔx], *m.* (—es, *pl.* ¨-e) cook, chef.
kochen [ˈkɔxən], *v.a.* cook, boil. — *v.n.* boil; (*fig.*) seethe.
Kocher [ˈkɔxər], *m.* (—s, *pl.* —) boiler.
Köcher [ˈkœçər], *m.* (—s, *pl.* —) quiver.
Köchin [ˈkœçɪn], *f.* (—, *pl.* —innen) (female) cook.
Kochsalz [ˈkɔxzalts], *n.* (—es, *no pl.*) common salt.
Köder [ˈkø:dər], *m.* (—s, *no pl.*) bait, lure; (*fig.*) decoy.
ködern [ˈkø:dərn], *v.a.* bait; (*fig.*) decoy.
Kodex [ˈko:dɛks], *m.* (—es, *pl.* —e) codex; old MS.; (*Law*) code.
kodifizieren [ko:difiˈtsi:rən], *v.a.* codify.
Koffein [kɔfə:ˈi:n], *n.* (—s, *no pl.*) caffeine.
Koffer [ˈkɔfər], *m.* (—s, *pl.* —) box, trunk, suitcase, portmanteau.
Kofferradio [ˈkɔfərra:djo], *n.* (—s, *pl.* —s) portable radio.
Kofferraum [ˈkɔfərraum], *m.* (—s, *no pl.*) (*Motor.*) boot, (*Am.*) trunk.
Kohl [ko:l], *m.* (—s, *no pl.*) (*Bot.*) cabbage; (*fig.*) nonsense, rot.
Kohle [ˈko:lə], *f.* (—, *pl.* —n) coal.
Kohlenflöz [ˈko:lənflø:ts], *n.* (—es, *pl.* —e) coal-seam.
Kohlenoxyd [ˈko:lənɔksy:t], *n.* (—s, *no pl.*) carbon monoxide.
Kohlensäure [ˈko:lənzɔyrə], *f.* (—, *no pl.*) carbonic acid.
Kohlenstift [ˈko:lənʃtɪft], *m.* (—es, *pl.* —e) charcoal-crayon.
Köhler [ˈkø:lər], *m.* (—s, *pl.* —) charcoal-burner.
Koje [ˈko:jə], *f.* (—, *pl.* —n) (*Naut.*) berth, bunk.
Kokarde [kɔˈkardə], *f.* (—, *pl.* —n) cockade.
kokett [koˈkɛt], *adj.* coquettish.
Kokette [koˈkɛtə], *f.* (—, *pl.* —n) coquette, flirt.
kokettieren [kokɛˈti:rən], *v.n.* flirt.
Kokon [koˈkɔ̃], *m.* (—s, *pl.* —s) cocoon.
Kokosnuß [ˈko:kɔsnus], *f.* (—, *pl.* ¨-sse) (*Bot.*) coconut.
Koks [ko:ks], *m.* (—es, *no pl.*) coke.
Kolben [ˈkɔlbən], *m.* (—s, *pl.* —) club; (*rifle*) butt-end; (*engine*) piston; (*Chem.*) retort.
Kolbenstange [ˈkɔlbənʃtaŋə], *f.* (—, *pl.* —n) piston-rod.
Kolibri [ˈko:libri:], *m.* (—s, *pl.* —s) (*Orn.*) humming-bird.
Kolkrabe [ˈkɔlkra:bə], *m.* (—n, *pl.* —n) (*Orn.*) raven.
Kolleg [kɔˈle:k], *n.* (—s, *pl.* —ien) course of lectures; lecture.
Kollege [kɔˈle:gə], *m.* (—n, *pl.* —n) colleague.
Kollekte [kɔˈlɛktə], *f.* (—, *pl.* —n) collection; (*Eccl.*) collect.
Koller [ˈkɔlər], *m.* (—s, *no pl.*) frenzy, rage.
kollidieren [kɔliˈdi:rən], *v.n.* collide.
Köln [kœln], *n.* Cologne.
kölnisch [ˈkœlnɪʃ], *adj.* of Cologne; —*Wasser*, eau de Cologne.
kolonisieren [koloniˈzi:rən], *v.a.* colonise.
Kolonnade [koloˈna:də], *f.* (— *pl.* —n) colonnade.
Koloratur [koloraˈtu:r], *f.* (—, *pl.* —n) coloratura.
kolorieren [koloˈri:rən], *v.a.* colour.
Koloß [koˈlɔs], *m.* (—sses, *pl.* —sse) colossus.
Kolportage [kɔlpɔrˈta:ʒə], *f.* (—, *pl.* —n) colportage, door-to-door sale of books; sensationalism.
Kolportageroman [kɔlpɔrˈta:ʒəroma:n], *m.* (—s, *pl.* —e) penny dreadful, shocker.
kolportieren [kɔlpɔrˈti:rən], *v.a.* hawk; spread, disseminate.
Kombinationsgabe [kɔmbinaˈtsjo:nsga:bə], *f.* (—, *pl.* —en) power of deduction.
kombinieren [kɔmbiˈni:rən], *v.a.* combine; deduce.
Kombüse [kɔmˈby:zə], *f.* (— *pl.* —n) galley, caboose.
Komik [ˈko:mɪk], *f.* (—, *no pl.*) comicality; humour; funny side.
Komiker [ˈko:mɪkər], *m.* (—s, *pl.* —) comedian.
komisch [ˈko:mɪʃ], *adj.* comical, funny; peculiar, strange, odd.
Kommandantur [kɔmandanˈtu:r], *f.* (—, *pl.* —en) commander's office; garrison headquarters.
kommandieren [kɔmanˈdi:rən], *v.a.* command.
Kommanditgesellschaft [kɔmanˈdi:tgəzɛlʃaft], *f.* (—, *pl.* —en) limited partnership.
Kommando [kɔˈmando], *n.* (—s, *pl.* —s) command.
kommen [ˈkɔmən], *v.n. irr.* (*aux.* sein) come, arrive; come about; *um etwas* —, lose s.th.; *zu etwas* —, come by s.th.; *zu sich* —, come to, regain consciousness.
Kommentar [kɔmenˈta:r], *m.* (—s, *pl.* —e) comment, commentary.
Kommers [kɔˈmɛrs], *m.* (—es, *pl.* —e) students' festivity; drinking party.
Kommersbuch [kɔˈmɛrsbu:x], *n.* (—es, *pl.* ¨-er) students' song-book.
kommerziell [kɔmɛrtsˈjɛl], *adj.* commercial.
Kommerzienrat [kɔˈmɛrtsjənra:t], *m.* (—s, *pl.* ¨-e) Councillor to the Chamber of Commerce.
Kommilitone [kɔmiliˈto:nə], *m.* (—n, *pl.* —n) fellow-student.
Kommis [kɔˈmi:], *m.* (—, *pl.* —) clerk.
Kommiß [kɔˈmɪs], *m.* (—sses, *pl.* —) military fatigue-dress; (*fig.*) military service.

Kommißbrot [kɔ'mɪsbro:t], *n.* (**—es,** *no pl.*) (coarse) army bread.
Kommissar [kɔmɪ'sa:r], *m.* (**—s,** *pl.* **—e**) commissioner.
Kommissariat [kɔmɪsar'ja:t], *n.* (**—s,** *pl.* **—e**) commissioner's office.
Kommission [kɔmɪs'jo:n], *f.* (**—,** *pl.* **—en**) commission, mission, committee.
kommod [kɔ'mo:d], *adj.* (*coll.*) snug, comfortable.
Kommode [kɔ'mo:də], *f.* (**—,** *pl.* **—n**) chest of drawers.
Kommune [kɔ'mu:nə], *f.* (**—,** *pl.* **—n**) (*coll.*) Communist Party; Reds.
Kommunismus [kɔmu'nɪsmus], *m.* (**—,** *no pl.*) Communism.
kommunistisch [kɔmu'nɪstɪʃ], *adj.* Communist.
Komödiant [kɔmød'jant], *m.* (**—en,** *pl.* **—en**) comedian, player; humbug.
Komödie [kɔ'mø:djə], *f.* (**—,** *pl.* **—n**) comedy, play; make-believe; **—** *spielen*, (*fig.*) sham, pretend, play-act.
Kompagnon ['kɔmpanjɔ̃], *m.* (**—s,** *pl.* **—s**) partner, associate.
Kompanie [kɔmpa'ni:], *f.* (**—,** *pl.* **—n**) (*Mil.*) company; (*Comm.*) partnership, company.
Kompaß ['kɔmpas], *m.* (**—sses,** *pl.* **—sse**) compass.
Kompaßrose ['kɔmpasro:zə], *f.* (**—,** *pl.* **—n**) compass-card.
kompensieren [kɔmpɛn'zi:rən], *v.a.* compensate.
komplementär [kɔmpləmɛn'tɛ:r], *adj.* complementary.
komplett [kɔm'plɛt], *adj.* complete.
komplimentieren [kɔmplimɛn'ti:rən], *v.a.* compliment, flatter.
Komplize [kɔm'pli:tsə], *m.* (**—n,** *pl.* **—n**) accomplice.
kompliziert [kɔmpli'tsi:rt], *adj.* complicated.
Komplott [kɔm'plɔt], *n.* (**—s,** *pl.* **—e**) plot, conspiracy.
Komponente [kɔmpo'nɛntə], *f.* (**—,** *pl.* —n) component part; constituent.
komponieren [kɔmpo'ni:rən], *v.a.* compose, set to music.
Komponist [kɔmpo'nɪst], *m.* (**—en,** *pl.* **—en**) composer.
Kompositum [kɔm'po:zɪtum], *n.* (**—s,** *pl.* **—ta**) (*Gram.*) compound word.
Kompott [kɔm'pɔt], *n.* (**—s,** *pl.* **—e**) stewed fruit, compote; sweet, dessert.
Kompresse [kɔm'prɛsə], *f.* (**—,** *pl.* **—n**) compress.
komprimieren [kɔmpri'mi:rən], *v.a.* compress.
Kompromiß [kɔmpro'mɪs], *m.* (**—sses,** *pl.* **—sse**) compromise, settlement.
kompromittieren [kɔmpromɪ'ti:rən], *v.a.* compromise. **—** *v.r. sich* **—**, compromise o.s.
kondensieren [kɔndɛn'zi:rən], *v.a.* condense.
Konditor [kɔn'di:tɔr], *m.* (**—s,** *pl.* **—en**) confectioner, pastry-cook.
Konditorei [kɔnditɔ'raɪ], *f.* (**—,** *pl.* **—en**) confectioner's shop, pastry-shop; café.
kondolieren [kɔndo'li:rən], *v.n.* condole with s.o.
Kondukteur [kɔnduk'tø:r], *m.* (**—s,** *pl.* **—e**) (*Swiss & Austr. dial.*) guard (on train), conductor (on tram *or* bus).
Konfekt [kɔn'fɛkt], *n.* (**—s,** *pl.* **—e**) chocolates; (*Am.*) candy.
Konfektion [kɔnfɛk'tsjo:n], *f.* (**—,** *no pl.*) ready-made clothes; outfitting.
Konfektionär [kɔnfɛktsjo'nɛ:r], *m.* (**—s,** *pl.* **—e**) outfitter.
Konferenz [kɔnfe'rɛnts], *f.* (**—,** *pl.* **—en**) conference.
konfessionell [kɔnfɛsjo'nɛl], *adj.* denominational, confessional.
Konfirmand [kɔnfɪr'mant], *m.* (**—en,** *pl.* **—en**) confirmation candidate.
konfirmieren [kɔnfɪr'mi:rən], *v.a.* (*Eccl.*) confirm.
konfiszieren [kɔnfɪs'tsi:rən], *v.a.* confiscate.
Konfitüren [kɔnfɪ'ty:rən], *f. pl.* confectionery, candied fruit, preserves.
konform [kɔn'fɔrm], *adj.* in comformity (with).
konfus [kɔn'fu:s], *adj.* confused, puzzled, disconcerted.
Kongo ['kɔŋgo], *m.* Congo.
Kongruenz [kɔngru'ɛnts], *f.* (**—,** *no pl.*) congruity.
König ['kø:nɪç], *m.* (**—s,** *pl.* **—e**) king.
Königin ['kø:nɪgɪn], *f.* (**—,** *pl.* **—nen**) queen.
königlich ['kø:nɪglɪç], *adj.* royal, regal, kingly, king-like.
Königreich ['kø:nɪçraɪç], *n.* (**—(e)s,** *pl.* **—e**) kingdom.
Königsadler ['kø:nɪçsa:dlər], *m.* (**—s,** *pl.* **—**) golden eagle.
Königsschlange ['kø:nɪçsʃlaŋə], *f.* (**—,** *pl.* **—n**) (*Zool.*) boa constrictor.
Königstiger ['kø:nɪçsti:gər], *m.* (**—s,** *pl.* **—**) (*Zool.*) Bengal tiger.
Königtum ['kø:nɪçtu:m], *n.* (**—s,** *no pl.*) kingship.
Konjunktur [kɔnjuŋk'tu:r], *f.* (**—,** *pl.* **—en**) state of the market, (*coll.*) boom.
Konkordat [kɔnkɔr'da:t], *n.* (**—s,** *pl.* **—e**) concordat.
konkret [kɔn'kre:t], *adj.* concrete.
Konkurrent [kɔnku'rɛnt], *m.* (**—en,** *pl.* **—en**) competitor, (business) rival.
Konkurrenz [kɔnku'rɛnts], *f.* (**—,** *no pl.*) competition.
konkurrieren [kɔnku'ri:rən], *v.n.* compete.
Konkurs [kɔn'kurs], *m.* (**—es,** *pl.* **—e**) bankruptcy.
Konkursmasse [kɔn'kursmasə], *f.* (**—,** *pl.* **—n**) bankrupt's estate, bankrupt's stock.
Können ['kœnən], *n.* (**—s,** *no pl.*) ability; knowledge.
können ['kœnən], *v.a., v.n. irr.* be able to, be capable of; understand; *ich kann,* I can; *er kann Englisch,* he speaks English.

konsequent [kɔnze'kvɛnt], *adj.* consistent.
Konsequenz [kɔnze'kvɛnts], *f.* (—, *pl.* —**en**) (*characteristic*) consistency; (*result*) consequence.
Konservatorium [kɔnzɛrva'to:rjum], *n.* (—**s**, *pl.* —**rien**) (*Mus.*) conservatoire, conservatorium.
Konserve [kɔn'zɛrvə], *f.* (—, *pl.* —**n**) preserve; tinned, *or* (*Am.*) canned food.
konservieren [kɔnzɛr'vi:rən], *v.a.* preserve.
Konsistorium [kɔnzɪs'to:rjum], *n.* (—**s**, *pl.* —**rien**) (*Eccl.*) consistory.
Konsole [kɔn'zo:lə], *f.* (—, *pl.* —**n**) bracket.
konsolidieren [kɔnzoli'di:rən], *v.a.* consolidate.
Konsonant [kɔnzo'nant], *m.* (—**en**, *pl.* —**en**) (*Phonet.*) consonant.
Konsorte [kɔn'zɔrtə], *m.* (—**n**, *pl.* —**n**) associate, accomplice.
Konsortium [kɔn'zɔrtsjum], *n.* (—**s**, *pl.* —**tien**) syndicate.
konstatieren [kɔnsta'ti:rən], *v.a.* state, note, assert.
konsternieren [kɔnstɛr'ni:rən], *v.a.* dismay, disconcert.
konstituieren [kɔnstitu'i:rən], *v.a.* constitute.
konstitutionell [kɔnstitutsjo'nɛl], *adj.* constitutional.
konstruieren [kɔnstru'i:rən], *v.a.* construct; (*Gram.*) construe.
konsularisch [kɔnzu'la:rɪʃ], *adj.* consular.
Konsulat [kɔnzu'la:t], *n.* (—**s**, *pl.* —**e**) consulate.
Konsulent [kɔnzu'lɛnt], *m.* (—**en**, *pl.* —**en**) (*Law*) counsel; consultant.
konsultieren [kɔnzul'ti:rən], *v.a.* consult.
Konsum [kɔn'zu:m], *m.* (—**s**, *no pl.*) (*Econ.*) consumption.
Konsumverein [kɔn'zu:mfɛraɪn], *m.* (—**s**, *pl.* —**e**) cooperative society.
konsumieren [kɔnzu'mi:rən], *v.a.* consume.
Konterbande [kɔntər'bandə], *f.* (—, *no pl.*) contraband.
Konterfei [kɔntər'faɪ], *n.* (—**s**, *pl.* —**e**) (*obs.*) portrait, likeness.
Kontertanz ['kɔntərtants], *m.* (—**es**, *pl.* ¨—**e**) square dance, quadrille.
kontinuierlich [kɔntinu'i:rlɪç], *adj.* continuous.
Kontinuität [kɔntinui'tɛ:t], *f.* (—, *no pl.*) continuity.
Konto ['kɔnto], *n.* (—**s**, *pl.* —**ten**) (*bank*) account; **à** —, on account.
Kontokorrent [kɔntokɔ'rɛnt], *n.* (—**s**, *pl.* —**e**) current account.
Kontor [kɔn'tɔ:r], *n.* (—**s**, *pl.* —**e**) (*obs.*) office.
Kontorist [kɔnto'rɪst], *m.* (—**en**, *pl.* —**en**) clerk.
Kontrabaß ['kɔntrabas], *m.* (—**sses**, *pl.* ¨—**sse**) double-bass.
Kontrapunkt ['kɔntrapuŋkt], *m.* (—**es**, *pl.* —**e**) (*Mus.*) counterpoint.
kontrastieren [kɔntras'ti:rən], *v.a.*, *v.n.* contrast.
kontrollieren [kɔntrɔ'li:rən], *v.a.* check, verify.
Kontroverse [kɔntro'vɛrzə], *f.* (—, *pl.* —**n**) controversy.
Kontur [kɔn'tu:r], *f.* (—, *pl.* —**en**) outline, (*pl.*) contours.
Konvent [kɔn'vɛnt], *m.* (—**s**, *pl.* —**e**) convention, assembly, congress.
konventionell [kɔnvɛntsjo'nɛl], *adj.* conventional, formal.
Konversationslexikon [kɔnvɛrza-'tsjo:nslɛksɪkɔn], *n.* (—**s**, *pl.* —**s**) encyclopaedia.
konvertieren [kɔnvɛr'ti:rən], *v.a.*, *v.n.* convert.
Konvertit [kɔnvɛr'tɪt], *m.* (—**en**, *pl.* —**en**) convert.
Konvolut [kɔnvo'lu:t], *n.* (—**s**, *pl.* —**e**) bundle; scroll.
konvulsivisch [kɔnvul'zi:vɪʃ], *adj.* convulsive.
konzentrieren [kɔntsɛn'tri:rən], *v.a.*, *v.r.* concentrate; *auf etwas* —, centre upon.
konzentrisch [kɔn'tsɛntrɪʃ], *adj.* concentric.
Konzept [kɔn'tsɛpt], *n.* (—**es**, *pl.* —**e**) rough draft, sketch; *aus dem* — *bringen*, unsettle, disconcert.
Konzeptpapier [kɔn'tsɛptpapi:r], *n.* (—**s**, *no pl.*) scribbling paper.
Konzern [kɔn'tsɛrn], *m.* (—**s**, *pl.* —**e**) (*Comm.*) combine.
Konzert [kɔn'tsɛrt], *n.* (—**es**, *pl.* —**e**) concert, (musical) recital.
Konzertflügel [kɔn'tsɛrtfly:gəl], *m.* (—**s**, *pl.* —) grand piano.
konzertieren [kɔntsɛr'ti:rən], *v.n.* give recitals; play in a concert.
Konzertmeister [kɔn'tsɛrtmaɪstər], *m.* (—**s**, *pl.* —) impresario.
Konzession [kɔntsɛ'sjo:n], *f.* (—, *pl.* —**en**) concession, licence.
konzessionieren [kɔntsɛsjo'ni:rən], *v.a.* license.
Konzil [kɔn'tsi:l], *n.* (—**s**, *pl.* —**ien**) (*Eccl.*) council.
konzipieren [kɔntsi'pi:rən], *v.a.* draft, plan.
Koordinierung [ko:ɔrdi'ni:ruŋ], *f.* (—, *pl.* —**en**) co-ordination.
Kopf [kɔpf], *m.* (—**es**, *pl.* ¨—**e**) head; top; heading; (*fig.*) mind, brains, judgment; *aus dem* —, by heart.
köpfen ['kœpfən], *v.a.* behead, decapitate; (*Bot.*) lop.
Kopfhaut ['kɔpfhaut], *f.* (—, *no pl.*) scalp.
Kopfhörer ['kɔpfhø:rər], *m.* (—**s**, *pl.* —) headphone, receiver.
Kopfkissen ['kɔpfkɪsən], *n.* (—**s**, *pl.* —) pillow.
Kopfsalat ['kɔpfzala:t], *m.* (—**s**, *pl.* —**e**) (garden) lettuce.
kopfscheu ['kɔpfʃɔy], *adj.* afraid; alarmed, timid; — *machen*, scare; — *werden*, take fright, jib.

Kopfschmerz ['kɔpfʃmɛrts], *m.* (**—es**, *pl.* **—en**) (*mostly pl.*) headache.
Kopfsprung ['kɔpfʃpruŋ], *m.* (**—s**, *pl.* **⸚e**) (*diving*) header.
kopfüber [kɔpf'y:bər], *adv.* head over heels; headlong.
Kopfweh ['kɔpfve:], *n.* (**—s**, *no pl.*) headache.
Kopfzerbrechen ['kɔpftsɛrbrɛçən], *n.* (**—s**, *no pl.*) racking o.'s brains.
Kopie [ko'pi:] *f.* (**—**, *pl.* **—n**) copy, duplicate.
kopieren [ko'pi:rən], *v.a.* copy, ape, mimic, take off.
Koppe ['kɔpə], *f. see* **Kuppe.**
Koppel ['kɔpəl], *f.* (**—**, *pl.* **—n**) (*dogs*) couple, leash; (*ground*) enclosure, paddock.
koppeln ['kɔpəln], *v.a.* couple, leash.
kopulieren [kopu'li:rən], *v.a.* (*obs.*) marry; pair; (*Hort.*) graft.
Koralle [ko'ralə], *f.* (**—**, *pl.* **—n**) coral.
Korallenriff [ko'ralənrɪf], *n.* (**—es**, *pl.* **—e**) coral-reef.
Korb [kɔrp], *m.* (**—s**, *pl.* **⸚e**) basket, hamper; *einen — geben*, turn s.o. down, refuse an offer of marriage.
Korbweide ['kɔrpvaɪdə], *f.* (**—**, *pl.* **—n**) (*Bot.*) osier.
Kord [kɔrt], *m.* (**—s**, *no pl.*) corduroy.
Kordel ['kɔrdəl], *f.* (**—**, *pl.* **—n**) cord, twine, thread.
Korea [ko're:a], *n.* Korea.
Korinthe [ko'rɪntə], *f.* (**—**, *pl.* **—n**) (*Bot.*) currant.
Korken ['kɔrkən], *m.* (**—s**, *pl.* **—**) cork, stopper.
Korkenzieher ['kɔrkəntsi:ər], *m.* (**—s**, *pl.* **—**) cork-screw.
Korn [kɔrn], *n.* (**—s**, *pl.* **—e**, **⸚er**) (*Bot.*) corn, grain, cereal, rye; (*gun*) sight, *aufs — nehmen*, take aim at.
Kornblume ['kɔrnblu:mə], *f.* (**—**, *pl.* **—n**) (*Bot.*) corn-flower.
Kornbranntwein ['kɔrnbrantvaɪn], *m.* (**—s**, *no pl.*) corn-brandy, whisky.
Kornett [kɔr'nɛt], *m.* (**—s**, *pl.* **—e**) (*Mil.*, *Mus.*) cornet.
körnig ['kœrnɪç], *adj.* granular, granulous; grained.
Kornrade ['kɔrnra:də], *f.* (**—**, *pl.* **—n**) (*Bot.*) corn-cockle.
Kornspeicher ['kɔrnʃpaɪçər], *m.* (**—s**, *pl.* **—**) granary, corn-loft.
Körper ['kœrpər], *m.* (**—s**, *pl.* **—**) body; (*Phys.*) solid.
Körperbau ['kœrpərbau], *m.* (**—s**, *no pl.*) build, frame.
Köpergeruch ['kœrpərgəru:x], *m.* (**—s**, *no pl.*) body odour.
körperlich ['kœrpərlɪç], *adj.* bodily, physical; *—e Züchtigung*, corporal punishment.
Körpermaß ['kœrpərma:s], *n.* (**—es**, *pl.* **—e**) cubic measure.
Körperschaft ['kœrpərʃaft], *f.* (**—**, *pl.* **—en**) corporation.
Korps [ko:r], *n.* (**—**, *pl.* **—**) (*Mil.*) corps; students' corporation.
Korrektheit [kɔ'rɛkthaɪt], *f.* (**—**, *no pl.*) correctness.
Korrektionsanstalt [korɛk'tsjo:nsanʃtalt], *f.* (**—**, *pl.* **—en**) penitentiary, Borstal institution.
Korrektor [kɔ'rɛktɔr], *m.* (**—s**, *pl.* **—en**) proof-reader.
Korrektur [kɔrɛk'tu:r], *f.* (**—**, *pl.* **—en**) correction; proof-correction; revision.
Korrekturbogen [kɔrɛk'tu:rbo:gən], *m.* (**—s**, *pl.* **—**) (*Typ.*) proof-sheet, galley.
Korrespondenzkarte [kɔrɛspɔn'dɛntskartə], *f.* (**—**, *pl.* **—n**) post-card.
korrigieren [kɔri'gi:rən], *v.a.* correct, revise; read (proofs).
Korsett [kɔr'zɛt], *n.* (**—s**, *pl.* **—s**) corset, bodice, stays.
Koryphäe [kɔri'fɛ:ə], *m.* (**—n**, *pl.* **—n**) celebrity, authority, master mind.
Koseform ['ko:zəfɔrm], *f.* (**—**, *pl.* **—en**) term of endearment, pet-name, diminutive.
kosen ['ko:zən], *v.a.*, *v.n.* caress, fondle; make love (to).
Kosinus ['ko:zinus], *m.* (**—**, *pl.* **—**) (*Maths.*) cosine.
Kosmetik [kɔs'me:tɪk], *f.* (**—**, *no pl.*) cosmetics.
kosmetisch [kɔs'me:tɪʃ], *adj.* cosmetic.
kosmisch ['kɔzmɪʃ], *adj.* cosmic.
Kosmopolit [kɔsmopo'li:t], *m.* (**—en**, *pl.* **—en**) cosmopolitan.
kosmopolitisch [kɔsmopo'li:tɪʃ], *adj.* cosmopolitan.
Kost [kɔst], *f.* (**—**, *no pl.*) food, fare; board.
Kostarika [kɔsta'rika], *n.* Costa Rica.
kostbar ['kɔstba:r], *adj.* valuable, precious, costly.
Kostbarkeit ['kɔstba:rkaɪt], *f.* (**—**, *pl.* **—en**) costliness, preciousness; (*pl.*) (*goods*) valuables.
Kosten ['kɔstən], *pl.* cost(s), expenses, charges; (*Law*) costs.
kosten ['kɔstən], *v.a.* taste; (*money*) cost; take, require; *was kostet das?* how much is this?
Kosten(vor)anschlag ['kɔstən(for)anʃla:k], *m.* (**—s**, *pl.* **⸚e**) estimate.
Kostenaufwand ['kɔstənaufvant], *m.* (**—s**, *pl.* **⸚e**) expenditure.
Kostenersatz ['kɔstənɛrzats], *m.* (**—es**, *no pl.*) refund of expenses, compensation.
kostenfrei ['kɔstənfraɪ], *adj.* free (of charge), gratis.
kostenlos ['kɔstənlo:s], *see* **kostenfrei.**
Kostgänger ['kɔstgɛŋər], *m.* (**—s**, *pl.* **—**) boarder.
Kostgeld ['kɔstgɛlt], *n.* (**—es**, *no pl.*) maintenance *or* board allowance.
köstlich ['kœstlɪç], *adj.* excellent, precious; delicious; *ein —er Witz*, a capital joke.
kostspielig ['kɔstʃpi:lɪç], *adj.* expensive, costly.
Kostüm [kɔ'sty:m], *n.* (**—s**, *pl.* **—e**) costume; fancy dress.
Kostümfest [kɔ'sty:mfɛst], *n.* (**—s**, *pl.* **—e**) fancy-dress ball.

kostümieren [kɔsty'mi:rən], *v.a.* dress up.
Kot [ko:t], *m.* (**—es**, *no pl.*) mud, dirt; filth, mire; excrement.
Kotelett [kɔt'lɛt], *n.* (**—s**, *pl.* **—s**) cutlet.
Köter ['kø:tər], *m.* (**—s**, *pl.* **—**) cur, mongrel.
Koterie [ko:tə'ri:], *f.* (**—**, *pl.* **—n**) clique, set, coterie.
Kotflügel ['ko:tfly:gəl], *m.* (**—s**, *pl.* **—**) (*Motor.*) mudguard.
kotig ['ko:tɪç], *adj.* dirty, miry.
kotzen ['kɔtsən], *v.n.* (*vulg.*) vomit.
Koweit ['kɔvaɪt], *n.* Kuwait.
Krabbe ['krabə], *f.* (**—**, *pl.* **—n**) (*Zool.*) crab; shrimp; (*fig.*) brat, imp.
krabbeln ['krabəln], *v.n.* crawl.
Krach [krax], *m.* (**—es**, *pl.* **—e**) crack, crash; din, noise; (*Comm.*) slump; quarrel, row.
krachen ['kraxən], *v.n.* crack, crash.
krächzen ['krɛçtsən], *v.n.* croak.
Kraft [kraft], *f.* (**—**, *pl.* **⁼e**) strength, vigour; force; power, energy; intensity; *in — treten*, come into force.
kraft [kraft], *prep.* (*Genit.*) by virtue of, by authority of, on the strength of.
Kraftausdruck ['kraftausdruk], *m.* (**—s**, *pl.* **⁼e**) forcible expression; expletive.
Kraftbrühe ['kraftbry:ə], *f.* (**—**, *pl.* **—n**) meat-soup, beef-tea.
Kraftfahrer ['kraftfa:rər], *m.* (**—s**, *pl.* **—**) motorist.
kräftig ['krɛftɪç], *adj.* strong, powerful, vigorous, energetic; (*food*) nourishing.
Kraftlehre ['kraftle:rə], *f.* (**—**, *no pl.*) dynamics.
kraftlos ['kraftlo:s], *adj.* weak, feeble.
Kraftwagen ['kraftva:gən], *m.* (**—s**, *pl.* **—**) motor car, automobile, car; lorry, truck.
Kragen ['kra:gən], *m.* (**—s**, *pl.* **—**) collar; *es geht mir an den —*, it will cost me dearly.
Krähe ['krɛ:ə], *f.* (**—**, *pl.* **—n**) (*Orn.*) crow.
krähen ['krɛ:ən], *v.n.* crow.
Krähenfüße ['krɛ:ənfy:sə], *m. pl.* crow's feet (wrinkles).
Krakau ['kra:kau], *n.* Cracow.
krakeelen [kra'ke:lən], *v.n.* (*coll.*) kick up a row.
Kralle ['kralə], *f.* (**—**, *pl.* **—n**) claw, talon.
Kram [kra:m], *m.* (**—s**, *no pl.*) small wares (trade); stuff, rubbish, litter; *es paßt mir nicht in den —*, it does not suit my purpose.
kramen ['kra:mən], *v.n.* rummage.
Krämer ['krɛ:mər], *m.* (**—s**, *pl.* **—**) retailer, general dealer, shopkeeper.
Kramladen ['kra:mla:dən], *m.* (**—s**, *pl.* **⁼**) small retail-shop, general shop *or* store.
Krampe ['krampə], *f.* (**—**, *pl.* **—n**) staple.
Krampf [krampf], *m.* (**—es**, *pl.* **⁼e**) cramp, spasm, convulsion.
Krampfader ['krampfa:dər], *f.* (**—**, *pl.* **—n**) varicose vein.
krampfartig ['krampfa:rtɪc], *adj.* spasmodic.
krampfhaft ['krampfhaft], *adj.* convulsive.
Kran [kra:n], *m.* (**—s**, *pl.* **⁼e**) (*Engin.*) crane.
Kranich ['kra:nɪç], *m.* (**—s**, *pl.* **—e**) (*Orn.*) crane.
krank [kraŋk], *adj.* sick, ill.
kränkeln ['krɛŋkəln], *v.n.* be ailing, be in poor health.
kranken ['kraŋkən], *v.n. an etwas —*, suffer from s.th., be afflicted with s.th.
kränken ['krɛŋkən], *v.a.* vex, grieve; offend, insult.
Krankenbahre ['kraŋkənba:rə], *f.* (**—**, *pl.* **—n**) stretcher.
Krankenhaus ['kraŋkənhaus], *n.* (**—es**, *pl.* **⁼er**) hospital.
Krankenkasse ['kraŋkənkasə], *f.* (**—**, *pl.* **—n**) sick-fund; health insurance.
Krankenkost ['kraŋkənkɔst], *f.* (**—**, *no pl.*) invalid diet.
Krankenschwester ['kraŋkənʃvɛstər], *f.* (**—**, *pl.* **—n**) nurse.
Krankenstuhl ['kraŋkənʃtu:l], *m.* (**—s**, *pl.* **⁼e**) invalid chair.
Krankenversicherung ['kraŋkənfɛrzɪçəruŋ], *f.* (**—**, *pl* **—en**) health insurance.
Krankenwärter ['kraŋkənvɛrtər], *m.* (**—s**, *pl.* **—**) attendant, male nurse.
krankhaft ['kraŋkhaft], *adj.* morbid.
Krankheit ['kraŋkhaɪt], *f.* (**—**, *pl.* **—en**) illness, sickness, disease, malady; complaint; *englische —*, rickets.
Krankheitserscheinung ['kraŋkhaɪtsɛrʃaɪnuŋ], *f.* (**—**, *pl.* **—en**) symptom.
kränklich ['krɛŋklɪç], *adj.* sickly, infirm, in poor health.
Kränkung ['krɛŋkuŋ], *f.* (**—**, *pl.* **—en**) grievance, annoyance; offence, insult.
Kranz [krants], *m.* (**—es**, *pl.* **⁼e**) wreath, garland.
Kränzchen ['krɛntsçən], *n.* (**—s**, *pl.* **—**) little garland; (*fig.*) (ladies') weekly tea party; circle, club.
kränzen ['krɛntsən], *v.a.* garland, wreathe.
Krapfen ['krapfən], *m.* (**—s**, *pl.* **—**) doughnut.
kraß [kras], *adj.* crass, crude.
Krater ['kra:tər], *m.* (**—s**, *pl.* **—**) crater.
Kratzbürste ['kratsbyrstə], *f.* (**—**, *pl.* **—n**) scraper; (*fig.*) cross-patch, irritable person.
Krätze ['krɛtsə], *f.* (**—**, *no pl.*) (*Med.*) scabies, itch, mange.
kratzen ['kratsən], *v.a.*, *v.n.* scratch, scrape, itch.
krauen ['krauən], *v.a.* scratch softly.
kraus [kraus], *adj.* frizzy, curly; crisp, fuzzy; creased; (*fig.*) abstruse; *die Stirn — ziehen*, frown, knit o.'s brow.
Krause ['krauzə], *f.* (**—**, *pl.* **—n**) ruff.
kräuseln ['krɔyzəln], *v.a.*, *v.r.* crisp, curl; ripple.
Krauskohl ['krausko:l], *m.* (**—s**, *no pl.*) Savoy cabbage.

Kraut [kraut], *n.* (—es, *pl.* ⸚er) herb; plant; (*dial.*) cabbage; *wie — und Rüben*, higgledy-piggledy.
krautartig ['krautaːrtɪç], *adj.* herbaceous.
Kräuterkäse ['krɔytərkɛːzə], *m.* (—s, *pl.* —) green cheese.
Kräutertee ['krɔytərteː], *m.* (—s, *no pl.*) herb-tea, infusion of herbs.
Krawall [kra'val], *m.* (—s, *pl.* —e) (*coll.*) row, uproar; shindy.
Krawatte [kra'vatə], *f.* (—, *pl.* —n) cravat, tie.
kraxeln ['kraksəln], *v.n.* (*coll.*) climb, clamber.
Krebs [kreːps], *m.* (—es, *pl.* —e) (*Zool.*) crayfish, crab; (*Med.*) cancer, carcinoma; (*Geog.*) Tropic of Cancer.
krebsartig ['kreːpsaːrtɪç], *adj.* cancerous.
Krebsbutter ['kreːpsbutər], *f.* (—, *no pl.*) crab-cheese.
Krebsgang ['kreːpsgaŋ], *m.* (—es, *no pl.*) crab's walk, sidling; *den — gehen*, retrograde, decline.
Krebsschaden ['kreːpsʃaːdən], *m.* (—s, *pl.* ⸚) cancerous sore *or* affection; (*fig.*) canker, inveterate evil.
Kredenz [kre'dɛnts], *f.* (—, *pl.* —en) buffet, serving table, sideboard.
kredenzen [kre'dɛntsən], *v.a.* taste (*wine*); (*obs.*) present, offer.
kreditieren [kredi'tiːrən], *v.a.* *einem etwas —*, credit s.o. with s.th.
Kreide ['kraɪdə], *f.* (—, *pl.* —n) chalk; (*Art*) crayon.
kreieren [kre'iːrən], *v.a.* create.
Kreis [kraɪs], *m.* (—es, *pl.* —e) circle; (*Astron.*) orbit; district; range; sphere.
Kreisabschnitt ['kraɪsapʃnɪt], *m.* (—s, *pl.* —e) segment.
Kreisausschnitt ['kraɪsausʃnɪt], *m.* (—s, *pl.* —e) sector.
Kreisbogen ['kraɪsboːgən], *m.* (—s, *pl.* ⸚) arc.
kreischen ['kraɪʃən], *v.n.* scream, shriek.
Kreisel ['kraɪzəl], *m.* (—s, *pl.* —) (*toy*) (spinning) top; gyroscope.
kreisen ['kraɪzən], *v.n.* circle, revolve; circulate.
Kreislauf ['kraɪslauf], *m.* (—es, *pl.* ⸚e) circular course; (*Astron.*) orbit; (*blood*) circulation.
kreißen ['kraɪsən], *v.n.* (*Med.*) be in labour.
Kreisstadt ['kraɪsʃtat], *f.* (—, *pl.* ⸚e) county town.
Kreisumfang ['kraɪsumfaŋ], *m.* (—s, *pl.* ⸚e) circumference.
Kreml [krɛml], *m.* (—s, *no pl.*) the Kremlin.
Krempe ['krɛmpə], *f.* (—, *pl.* —n) (*hat*) brim.
Krempel ['krɛmpəl], *m.* (—s, *no pl.*) (*coll.*) refuse, rubbish; stuff.
Kren [kreːn], *m.* (—s, *no pl.*) (*Austr.*) horse-radish.
krepieren [kre'piːrən], *v.n.* (*aux.* sein) (*animals*) die; (*humans*) (*coll.*) perish miserably; explode.
Krepp [krɛp], *m.* (—s, *no pl.*) crape, crêpe.
Kresse ['krɛsə], *f.* (—, *pl.* —n) cress.
Kreta ['kreːta], *n.* Crete.
Kreuz [krɔyts], *n.* (—es, *pl.* —e) cross, crucifix; (*Anat.*) small of the back; (*fig.*) calamity; affliction; *kreuz und quer*, in all directions.
Kreuzband ['krɔytsbant], *n.* (—es, *pl.* ⸚er) wrapper (for printed matter).
kreuzbrav ['krɔytsbraːf], *adj.* as good as gold.
kreuzen ['krɔytsən], *v.a.* cross. — *v.r.* *sich —*, make the sign of the cross.
Kreuzfahrer ['krɔytsfaːrər], *m.* (—s, *pl.* —) crusader.
kreuzfidel ['krɔytsfideːl], *adj.* jolly, merry, as merry as a cricket.
Kreuzgang ['krɔytsgaŋ], *m.* (—es, *pl.* ⸚e) cloisters.
kreuzigen ['krɔytsɪgən], *v.a.* crucify.
Kreuzritter ['krɔɪtsrɪtər], *m.* (—s, *pl.* —) Knight of the Cross; crusader.
Kreuzschmerzen ['krɔytsʃmɛrtsən], *m. pl.* lumbago.
Kreuzstich ['krɔytsʃtɪç], *m.* (—es, *no pl.*) (*Embroidery*) cross-stitch.
Kreuzung ['krɔytsuŋ], *f.* (—, *pl.* —en) (*road*) crossing; (*animals*) cross-breeding.
Kreuzverhör ['krɔytsfɛrhøːr], *n.* (—s, *pl.* —e) cross-examination.
Kreuzweg ['krɔytsveːk], *m.* (—s, *pl.* —e) crossroads; (*Eccl.*) Stations of the Cross.
Kreuzworträtsel ['krɔytsvɔrtrɛːtsəl], *n.* (—s, *pl.* —) crossword-puzzle.
Kreuzzug ['krɔytstsuːk], *m.* (—es, *pl.* ⸚e) crusade.
kriechen ['kriːçən], *v.n. irr.* (*aux.* sein) creep, crawl; (*fig.*) cringe, fawn.
kriecherisch ['kriːçərɪʃ], *adj.* fawning, cringing.
Kriechtier ['kriːçtiːr], *n.* (—s, *pl.* —e) reptile.
Krieg [kriːk], *m.* (—es, *pl.* —e) war.
kriegen ['kriːgən], *v.a.* get, obtain.
Krieger ['kriːgər], *m.* (—s, *pl.* —) warrior.
kriegerisch ['kriːgərɪʃ], *adj.* warlike, martial.
kriegführend ['kriːkfyːrənt], *adj.* belligerent.
Kriegsfuß ['kriːksfuːs], *m.* (—es, *no pl.*) *auf —*, at logger-heads.
Kriegsgewinnler ['kriːksgəvɪnlər], *m.* (—s, *pl.* —) war-profiteer.
Kriegslist ['kriːkslɪst], *f.* (—, *pl.* —en) stratagem.
Kriegsschauplatz ['kriːksʃauplats], *m.* (—es, *pl.* ⸚e) theatre of war.
Kriegsschiff ['kriːksʃɪf], *n.* (—es, *pl.* —e) man-of-war, warship.
Kriegswesen ['kriːksveːzən], *n.* (—s, *no pl.*) military affairs.
Kriegszug ['kriːkstsuːk], *m.* (—es, *pl.* ⸚e) campaign.
Krim [krɪm], *f.* the Crimea.
Kriminalbeamte [krɪmi'naːlbəamtə], *m.* (—n, *pl.* —n) crime investigator.

Kriminalprozeß [krimi'na:lprotsɛs], *m.* (**—sses**, *pl.* **—sse**) criminal procedure *or* trial.
Krimskrams ['krɪmskrams], *m.* (—, *no pl.*) whatnots, knick-knacks, medley.
Krippe ['krɪpə], *f.* (—, *pl.* **—n**) crib, manger; crèche.
Krise ['kri:zə], *f.* (—, *pl.* **—n**) crisis.
Kristall [krɪ'stal], *m.* (**—s**, *pl.* **—e**) crystal; cut glass.
kristallartig [krɪ'stala:rtɪç], *adj.* crystalline.
kristallisieren [krɪstali'zi:rən], *v.a.*, *v.n.* (*aux.* sein), crystallise.
Kristallkunde [krɪ'stalkundə], *f.* (—, *no pl.*) crystallography.
Kriterium [kri'te:rjum], *n.* (**—s**, *pl.* **—rien**) criterion, test.
Kritik [kri'ti:k], *f.* (—, *pl.* **—en**) criticism, review; *unter aller* —, extremely bad.
Kritiker ['kri:tɪkər], *m.* (**—s**, *pl.* —) critic.
kritisch ['kri:tɪʃ], *adj.* critical; precarious, crucial.
kritisieren [kriti'zi:rən], *v.a.* criticise; review; censure.
kritteln ['krɪtəln], *v.n.* cavil (at), find fault.
Krittler ['krɪtlər], *m.* (**—s**, *pl.* —) caviller, fault-finder.
Kritzelei [krɪtsə'laɪ], *f.* (—, *pl.* **—en**) scrawling, scribbling.
kritzeln ['krɪtsəln], *v.a.* scrawl, scribble.
Kroatien [kro'a:tsjən], *n.* Croatia.
Krokodil [kroko'di:l], *n.* (**—s**, *pl.* **—e**) (*Zool.*) crocodile.
Kronbewerber ['kro:nbevɛrbər], *m.* (**—s**, *pl.* —) aspirant to the crown, pretender.
Krone ['kro:nə], *f.* (—, *pl.* **—n**) crown; (*Papal*) tiara; (*fig.*) head, top, flower.
krönen ['krø:nən], *v.a.* crown.
Kronerbe ['kro:nɛrbə], *m.* (**—n**, *pl.* **—n**) heir apparent.
Kronleuchter ['kro:nlɔyçtər], *m.* (**—s**, *pl.* —) chandelier.
Kronsbeere ['kro:nsbe:rə], *f.* (—, *pl.* **—n**) (*Bot.*) cranberry.
Krönung ['krø:nuŋ], *f.* (—, *pl.* **—en**) coronation.
Kropf [krɔpf], *m.* (**—es**, *pl.* **⸚e**) (*human*) goitre, wen; (*birds*) crop, craw.
kropfartig ['krɔpfa:rtɪç], *adj.* goitrous.
kröpfen ['krœpfən], *v.a.* (*birds*) cram.
Kropftaube ['krɔpftaubə], *f.* (—, *pl.* **—n**) (*Orn.*) pouter-pigeon.
Kröte ['krø:tə], *f.* (—, *pl.* **—n**) toad.
Krücke ['krykə], *f.* (—, *pl.* **—n**) crutch; (*fig.*) rake.
Krückstock ['krykʃtɔk], *m.* (**—s**, *pl.* **⸚e**) crutch.
Krug [kru:k], *m.* (**—es**, *pl.* **⸚e**) jug, pitcher, mug; (*fig.*) pub, inn.
Krüger ['kry:gər], *m.* (**—s**, *pl.* —) pub-keeper, tapster.
Krume ['kru:mə], *f.* (—, *pl.* **—n**) crumb.
krüm(e)lig ['kry:m(ə)lɪç], *adj.* crumbly, crumby.
krümeln ['kry:meln], *v.n.* crumble.
krumm [krum], *adj.* crooked, curved; *etwas — nehmen*, take s.th. amiss.
krummbeinig ['krumbaɪnɪç], *adj.* bandy-legged.
krümmen ['krymən], *v.a.* crook, bend, curve. — *v.r. sich* —, (*fig.*) writhe, cringe.
Krummholz ['krumhɔlts], *n.* (**—es**, *no pl.*) (*Bot.*) dwarf-pine.
Krummschnabel ['krumʃna:bəl], *m.* (**—s**, *pl.* ⸚) (*Orn.*) curlew, crook-bill.
Krümmung ['krymuŋ], *f.* (—, *pl.* **—en**) curve; turning, winding.
Krüppel ['krypəl], *m.* (**—s**, *pl.* —) cripple.
krüppelhaft ['krypəlhaft], *adj.* crippled, lame.
krüpp(e)lig ['kryp(ə)lɪç], *adj.* crippled, lame.
Kruste ['krustə], *f.* (—, *pl.* **—n**) crust.
Kübel ['ky:bəl], *m.* (**—s**, *pl.* —) tub, bucket.
Kubikfuß [ku'bi:kfu:s], *m.* (**—es**, *pl.* —) cubic foot.
Kubikinhalt [ku'bi:kɪnhalt], *m.* (**—s**, *no pl.*) cubic content.
Kubismus [ku'bɪsmus], *m.* (—, *no pl.*) cubism.
Küche ['kyçə], *f.* (—, *pl.* **—n**) (*room*) kitchen; (*food*) cooking, cookery, cuisine.
Kuchen ['ku:xən], *m.* (**—s**, *pl.* —) cake.
Küchengeschirr ['kyçəngəʃɪr], *n.* (**—s**, *no pl.*) kitchen utensils.
Küchenherd ['kyçənhe:rt], *m.* (**—es**, *pl.* **—e**) kitchen-range.
Küchenlatein ['kyçənlataɪn], *n.* (**—s**, *no pl.*) dog-Latin.
Küchenmeister ['kyçənmaɪstər], *m.* (**—s**, *pl.* —) chef, head cook.
Küchenschrank ['kyçənʃraŋk], *m.* (**—s**, *pl.* **⸚e**) dresser.
Kuchenteig ['ku:xəntaɪk], *m.* (**—s**, *pl.* **—e**) dough (for cake).
Küchenzettel ['kyçəntsɛtəl], *m.* (**—s**, *pl.* —) bill of fare.
Küchlein ['ky:çlaɪn], *n.* (**—s**, *pl.* —) young chicken, pullet.
Kücken ['kykən], *n.* (**—s**, *pl.* —) young chicken, pullet.
Kuckuck ['kukuk], *m.* (**—s**, *pl.* **—e**) (*Orn.*) cuckoo; *scher Dich zum —!* go to blazes!
Kufe ['ku:fə], *f.* (—, *pl.* **—n**) tub, vat; (*sleigh*) runner; (*cradle*) rocker.
Küfer ['ky:fər], *m.* (**—s**, *pl.* —) cooper.
Kugel ['ku:gəl], *f.* (—, *pl.* **—n**) ball, bullet, sphere; globe.
kugelfest ['ku:gəlfɛst], *adj.* bullet-proof.
kugelförmig ['ku:gəlfœrmɪç], *adj.* spherical, globular.
Kugelgelenk ['ku:gəlgəlɛŋk], *n.* (**—s**, *pl.* **—e**) ball and socket joint.
Kugellager ['ku:gəlla:gər], *n.* (**—s**, *pl.* —) ball-bearing.
Kugelmaß ['ku:gəlma:s], *n.* (**—es**, *pl.* **—e**) ball-calibre.
kugeln ['ku:gəln], *v.a.* roll; bowl.

Kugelregen ['ku:gəlre:gən], *m.* (—**s**, *no pl.*) hail of bullets.
kugelrund ['ku:gəlrunt], *adj.* round as a ball, well-fed.
Kugelschreiber ['ku:gəlʃraɪbər], *m.* (—**s**, *pl.* —) ball-point pen.
Kuh [ku:] *f.* (—, *pl.* ¨**e**) cow; *junge* —, heifer.
Kuhblattern ['ku:blatərn], *f. pl.* cow-pox.
Kuhblume ['ku:blu:mə], *f.* (—, *pl.* —**n**) (*Bot.*) marigold.
Kuhfladen ['ku:fla:dən], *m.* (—**s**, *pl.* —) cow-dung.
Kuhhaut ['ku:haut], *f.* (—, *pl.* ¨**e**) cow-hide; *das geht auf keine* —, that defies description.
kühl [ky:l], *adj.* cool, fresh; (*behaviour*) reserved.
Kühle ['ky:lə], *f.* (—, *no pl.*) coolness, freshness; (*behaviour*) reserve.
kühlen ['ky:lən], *v.a.* cool, freshen.
Kühlraum ['ky:lraum], *m.* (—**es**, *pl.* ¨**e**) refrigerating-chamber.
Kühlschrank ['ky:lʃraŋk], *m.* (—**s**, *pl.* ¨**e**) refrigerator, (*coll.*) fridge.
Kühltruhe ['ky:ltru:ə], *f.* (—, *pl.* —**n**) deep freeze.
Kühlung ['ky:luŋ], *f.* (—, *pl.* —**en**) refrigeration.
Kuhmist ['ku:mɪst], *m.* (—**s**, *no pl.*) cow-dung.
kühn [ky:n], *adj.* bold, daring, audacious.
Kühnheit ['ky:nhaɪt], *f.* (—, *no pl.*) boldness, daring, audacity.
Kujon [ku'jo:n], *m.* (—**s**, *pl.* —**e**) bully, scoundrel.
kujonieren [kujo'ni:rən], *v.a.* bully, exploit.
Kukuruz ['kukuruts], *m.* (—**es**, *no pl.*) (*Austr.*) maize.
kulant [ku'lant], *adj.* obliging; (*terms*) easy.
Kulanz [ku'lants], *f.* (—, *no pl.*) accommodating manner.
Kuli ['ku:li:], *m.* (—**s**, *pl.* —**s**) coolie.
kulinarisch [kuli'na:rɪʃ], *adj.* culinary.
Kulisse [ku'lɪsə], *f.* (—, *pl.* —**n**) (*Theat.*) back-drop, side-scene, wings.
Kulissenfieber [ku'lɪsənfi:bər], *n.* (—**s**, *no pl.*) stage-fright.
kulminieren [kulmi'ni:rən], *v.n.* culminate.
kultivieren [kulti'vi:rən], *v.a.* cultivate.
Kultur [kul'tu:r], *f.* (—, *pl.* —**en**) (*Agr.*) cultivation; (*fig.*) culture, civilization.
Kultus ['kultus], *m.* (—, *pl.* **Kulte**) cult, worship.
Kultusministerium ['kultusmɪnɪste:rjum], *n.* (—**s**, *pl.* —**rien**) Ministry of Education.
Kümmel ['kyməl], *m.* (—**s**, *no pl.*) caraway-seed; (*drink*) kümmel.
Kummer ['kumər], *m.* (—**s**, *no pl.*) grief, sorrow, trouble.
kümmerlich ['kymərlɪç], *adj.* miserable, pitiful.
kummerlos ['kumərlo:s], *adj.* untroubled.
kümmern ['kymərn], *v.r. sich* — *um*, mind, look after, be worried about, care for.
Kümmernis ['kymərnɪs], *f.* (—, *pl.* —**se**) grief, sorrow.
kummervoll ['kumərfɔl], *adj.* sorrowful, painful, grievous.
Kumpan [kum'pa:n], *m.* (—**s**, *pl.* —**e**) companion; mate; *lustiger* —, jolly fellow, good companion.
kund [kunt], *adj.* known, public; *etwas* — *tun*, make s.th. public; — *und zu wissen sei hiermit*, (*obs.*) we hereby give notice.
kundbar ['kuntba:r], *adj.* known; *etwas* — *machen*, announce s.th., make s.th. known.
kündbar ['kyntba:r], *adj.* (*loan, capital etc.*) redeemable; capable of being called in, terminable.
Kunde (1) ['kundə], *m.* (—**n**, *pl.* —**n**) customer; *ein schlauer* —, an artful dodger.
Kunde (2) ['kundə], *f.* (—, *pl.* —**n**) news; information, notification; (*compounds*) science.
Kundgebung ['kuntge:buŋ], *f.* (—, *pl.* —**en**) publication; rally; demonstration.
kundig ['kundɪç], *adj.* versed in, conversant with.
Kundige ['kundɪgə], *m.* (—**n**, *pl.* —**n**) expert, initiate.
kündigen ['kyndɪgən], *v.n.* give notice (*Dat.*).
Kundmachung ['kuntmaxuŋ], *f.* (—, *pl.* —**en**) publication.
Kundschaft ['kuntʃaft], *f.* (—, *no pl.*) clientele, customers; information, reconnaissance.
kundschaften ['kuntʃaftən], *v.n.* reconnoitre, scout.
künftig ['kynftɪç], *adj.* future, prospective, to come.
Kunst [kunst], *f.* (—, *pl.* ¨**e**) art; skill.
Kunstbutter ['kunstbutər], *f.* (—, *no pl.*) margarine.
Künstelei [kynstə'laɪ], *f.* (—, *pl.* —**en**) affectation, mannerism.
kunstfertig ['kunstfɛrtɪç], *adj.* skilled, skilful.
Kunstfreund ['kunstfrɔynt], *m.* (—**es**, *pl.* —**e**) art-lover.
kunstgerecht ['kunstgərɛçt], *adj.* workmanlike.
Kunstgewerbe ['kunstgəvɛrbə], *n.* (—**s**, *no pl.*) arts and crafts.
Kunstgriff ['kunstgrɪf], *m.* (—**es**, *pl.* —**e**) trick, dodge, artifice, knack.
Kunsthändler ['kunsthɛndlər], *m.* (—**s**, *pl.* —) art-dealer.
Kunstkenner ['kunstkɛnər], *m.* (—**s**, *pl.* —) connoisseur.
Künstler ['kynstlər], *m.* (—**s**, *pl.* —) artist, performer.
künstlerisch ['kynstlərɪʃ], *adj.* artistic, elaborate, ingenious.
künstlich ['kynstlɪç], *adj.* artificial.
kunstlos ['kunstlo:s], *adj.* artless, unaffected.

kunstreich ['kunstraɪç], *adj.* ingenious.
Kunstseide ['kunstzaɪdə], *f.* (—, *no pl.*) artificial silk.
Kunststickerei ['kunstʃtɪkəraɪ], *f.* (—, *no pl.*) art needlework.
Kunststoff ['kunstʃtɔf], *m.* (—**es**, *pl.* —**e**) plastics.
Kunststopfen ['kunstʃtɔpfən], *n.* (—**s**, *no pl.*) invisible mending.
Kunststück ['kunstʃtyk], *n.* (—**es**, *pl.* —**e**) trick, feat.
Kunstverständige ['kunstfɛrʃtɛndɪgə], *m.* (—**n**, *pl.* —**n**) art expert.
Küpe ['ky:pə], *f.* (—, *pl.* —**n**) large tub; (*dyeing*) copper.
Kupfer ['kupfər], *n.* (—**s**, *no pl.*) copper.
Kupferblech ['kupfərblɛç], *n.* (—**es**, *no pl.*) copper-sheet.
Kupferdraht ['kupfərdra:t], *m.* (—**es**, *pl.* ⸚**e**) copper-wire.
kupferhaltig ['kupfərhaltɪç], *adj.* containing copper.
Kupferrost ['kupfərrɔst], *m.* (—**es**, *no pl.*) verdigris.
Kupferstecher ['kupfərʃtɛçər], *m.* (—**s**, *pl.* —) (copperplate) engraver.
kupieren [ku'pi:rən], *v.a.* (*rare*) (*ticket*) punch; (*Austr.*) (*horse*) dock.
Kuppe ['kupə], *f.* (—, *pl.* —**n**) (*hill*) top, summit.
Kuppel ['kupəl], *f.* (—, *pl.* —**n**) cupola, dome.
kuppeln ['kupəln], *v.n.* procure, pimp; make a match.
Kuppler ['kuplər], *m.* (—**s**, *pl.* —) procurer, pimp; matchmaker.
Kupplung ['kupluŋ], *f.* (—, *pl.* —**en**) (*Railw.*) coupling, joint; (*Motor.*) clutch.
Kur [ku:r], *f.* (—, *pl.* —**en**) cure; *eine — machen*, undergo medical treatment.
Kuranstalt ['ku:ranʃtalt], *f.* (—, *pl.* —**en**) sanatorium; (*Am.*) sanitarium.
Küraß ['ky:ras], *m.* (—**sses**, *pl.* —**sse**) cuirass.
Kuratel [kura'tɛl], *f.* (—, *pl.* —**en**) guardianship, trusteeship.
Kuratorium [kura'to:rjum], *n.* (—**s**, *pl.* —**rien**) board of guardians *or* trustees; council, governing body.
Kurbel ['kurbəl], *f.* (—, *pl.* —**n**) crank, winch.
Kurbelstange ['kurbəlʃtaŋə], *f.* (—, *pl.* —**n**) connecting rod.
Kurbelwelle ['kurbəlvɛlə], *f.* (—, *pl.* —**n**) crankshaft.
Kürbis ['kyrbɪs], *m.* (—**ses**, *pl.* —**se**) (*Bot.*) pumpkin, gourd.
küren ['ky:rən], *v.a. irr.* (*Poet.*) choose, elect.
Kurfürst ['ku:rfyrst], *m.* (—**en**, *pl.* —**en**) Elector (of the Holy Roman Empire).
Kurhaus ['ku:rhaus], *n.* (—**es**, *pl.* ⸚**er**) spa; hotel; pump room.
Kurie ['ku:rjə], *f.* (—, *pl.* —**n**) (*Eccl.*) Curia; Papal Court.
Kurier [ku'ri:r], *m.* (—**s**, *pl.* —**e**) courier.
kurieren [ku'ri:rən], *v.a.* cure.
kurios [kur'jo:s], *adj.* curious, queer, strange.
Kuriosität [kurjozi'tɛ:t], *f.* (—, *pl.* —**en**) curio, curiosity.
Kurort ['ku:rɔrt], *m.* (—**es**, *pl.* —**e**) spa, watering-place, health-resort.
Kurrentschrift [ku'rɛntʃrɪft], *f.* (—, *no pl.*) running hand, cursive writing.
Kurs [kurs], *m.* (—**es**, *pl.* —**e**) rate of exchange; quotation; circulation; course.
Kursaal ['ku:rza:l], *m.* (—**s**, *pl.* —**säle**) hall, (*spa*) pump-room, casino.
Kursbericht ['kursbərɪçt], *m.* (—**es**, *pl.* —**e**) market report.
Kursbuch ['kursbu:x], *n.* (—**es**, *pl.* ⸚**er**) railway-guide, time-table.
Kürschner ['kyrʃnər], *m.* (—**s**, *pl.* —) furrier, skinner.
kursieren [kur'zi:rən], *v.n.* be current, circulate.
Kursivschrift [kur'zi:fʃrɪft], *f.* (—, *no pl.*) italics.
Kursstand ['kursʃtant], *m.* (—**es**, *no pl.*) rate of exchange.
Kursus ['kurzus], *m.* (—, *pl.* **Kurse**) course (of lectures).
Kurszettel ['kurstsɛtəl], *m.* (—**s**, *pl.* —) quotation-list.
Kurve ['kurvə], *f.* (—, *pl.* —**n**) curve.
kurz [kurts], *adj.* short, brief, concise; curt, abrupt.
kurzangebunden [kurts'angəbundən], *adj.* terse, abrupt, curt.
kurzatmig ['kurtsa:tmɪç], *adj.* short-winded, short of breath.
Kürze ['kyrtsə], *f.* (—, *no pl.*) shortness, brevity.
kürzen ['kyrtsən], *v.a.* shorten, abbreviate, condense; (*Maths.*) reduce.
kürzlich ['kyrtslɪç], *adv.* lately, recently, the other day.
Kurzschluß ['kurtsʃlus], *m.* (—**sses**, *pl.* ⸚**sse**) short circuit.
Kurzschrift ['kurtsʃrɪft], *f.* (—, *no pl.*) shorthand.
kurzsichtig ['kurtszɪçtɪç], *adj.* short-sighted.
kurzum [kurts'um], *adv.* in short.
Kürzung ['kyrtsuŋ], *f.* (—, *pl.* —**en**) abbreviation, abridgement.
Kurzwaren ['kurtsva:rən], *f. pl.* haberdashery.
kurzweg [kurts've:k], *adv.* simply, offhand, briefly.
Kurzweil ['kurtsvaɪl], *f.* (—, *no pl.*) pastime.
kurzweilig ['kurtsvaɪlɪç], *adj.* amusing, diverting, entertaining.
kusch! [kuʃ], *excl.* (*to dogs*) lie down!
kuschen ['kuʃən], *v.n.*, *v.r.* crouch, lie down.
Kuß [kus], *m.* (—**sses**, *pl.* ⸚**sse**) kiss.
küssen ['kysən], *v.a.*, *v.n.*, *v.r.* kiss.
Küste ['kystə], *f.* (—, *pl.* —**n**) coast, shore.

Küstenstadt ['kystənʃtat], *f.* (—, *pl.* ⸚e) seaside town.
Küster ['kystər], *m.* (—s, *pl.* —) sacristan, sexton, verger.
Kustos ['kustɔs], *m.* (—, *pl.* —oden) custodian; director of museum.
Kutschbock ['kutʃbɔk], *m.* (—s, *pl.* ⸚e) box(-seat).
Kutsche ['kutʃə], *f.* (—, *pl.* —n) coach, carriage.
kutschieren [kut'ʃi:rən], *v.n.* drive a coach.
Kutte ['kutə], *f.* (—, *pl.* —n) cowl.
Kutter ['kutər], *m.* (—s, *pl.* —) (*Naut.*) cutter.
Kuvert [ku'vɛ:r], *n.* (—s, *pl.* —s) envelope; (*dinner*) place laid.
kuvertieren [kuvɛr'ti:rən], *v.a.* envelop, wrap.
Kux [kuks], *m.* (—es, *pl.* —e) share in a mining concern.
Kybernetik [ky:bɛr'ne:tɪk], *f.* (—, *no pl.*) cybernetics.

L

L [ɛl], *n.* (—, *pl.* —) the letter L.
Lab [la:p], *n.* (—es, *pl.* —e) rennet.
labbern ['labərn], *v.a.*, *v.n.* dribble, slobber; blab.
Labe ['la:bə], *f.* (—, *no pl.*) (*Poet.*) refreshment; comfort.
laben ['la:bən], *v.a.* refresh, restore, revive.
labil [la'bi:l], *adj.* unstable.
Laborant [labo'rant], *m.* (—en, *pl.* —en) laboratory assistant.
Laboratorium [labora'to:rjum], *n.* (—s, *pl.* —rien) laboratory.
laborieren [labo'ri:rən], *v.n.* experiment; suffer (from).
Labsal ['la:pza:l], *n.* (—s, *pl.* —e) restorative, refreshment.
Labung ['la:buŋ], *f.* (—, *pl.* —en) refreshment, comfort.
Lache ['laxə], *f.* (—, *pl.* —n) pool, puddle.
Lächeln ['lɛçəln], *n.* (—s, *no pl.*) smile; *albernes* —, smirk; *höhnisches* —, sneer.
lächeln ['lɛçəln], *v.n.* smile.
Lachen ['laxən], *n.* (—s, *no pl.*) laugh, laughter.
lachen ['laxən], *v.n.* laugh.
lächerlich ['lɛçərlɪç], *adj.* laughable, ridiculous; preposterous; ludicrous; *sich — machen*, make a fool of o.s.; *etwas — machen*, ridicule s.th.
Lachgas ['laxga:s], *n.* (—es, *no pl.*) nitrous oxide, laughing-gas.
lachhaft ['laxhaft], *adj.* laughable, ridiculous.
Lachkrampf ['laxkrampf], *m.* (—es, *pl.* ⸚e) hysterical laughter, a fit of laughter.
Lachs [laks], *m.* (—es, *pl.* —e) salmon.
Lachsalve ['laxzalvə], *f.* (—, *pl.* —n) peal of laughter.
Lack [lak], *m.* (—s, *pl.* —e) lac, lacquer, varnish.
lackieren [la'ki:rən], *v.a.* lacquer, varnish.
Lackmus ['lakmus], *n.* (—, *no pl.*) litmus.
Lackschuh ['lakʃu:], *m.* (—s, *pl.* —e) patent-leather shoe.
Lackwaren ['lakva:rən], *f. pl.* japanned goods.
Lade ['la:də], *f.* (—, *pl.* —n) box, chest, case, drawer.
Ladebaum ['la:dəbaum], *m.* derrick.
Ladefähigkeit ['la:dəfɛ:ɪçkaɪt], *f.* (—, *pl.* —en), carrying capacity, loading capacity; tonnage.
Ladegeld ['la:dəgɛlt], *n.* (—es, *pl.* —er) loading charges.
Laden ['la:dən], *m.* (—s, *pl.* ⸚) (*window*) shutter; shop, store.
laden ['la:dən], *v.a. irr.* load; (*Elec.*) charge; (*Law*) summon, (*fig.*) incur.
Ladenhüter ['la:dənhy:tər], *m.* (—s, *pl.* —) unsaleable article.
Ladenpreis ['la:dənpraɪs], *m.* (—es, *pl.* —e) retail-price.
Ladentisch ['la:dəntɪʃ], *m.* (—es, *pl.* —e) counter.
Ladeschein ['la:dəʃaɪn], *m.* (—s, *pl.* —e) bill of lading.
Ladestock ['la:dəʃtɔk], *m.* (—es, *pl.* ⸚e) ramrod.
Ladung ['la:duŋ], *f.* (—, *pl.* —en) loading, lading, freight; shipment, cargo; (*gun*) charge; (*Law*) summons.
Laffe ['lafə], *m.* (—n, *pl.* —n) fop.
Lage ['la:gə], *f.* (—, *pl.* —n) site, position, situation; state, condition; stratum, layer.
Lager ['la:gər], *n.* (—s, *pl.* —) couch, bed, divan; (*Geol.*) seam, vein; (*Tech.*) bearing; (*Comm.*) warehouse, store; camp.
Lageraufnahme ['la:gəraufna:mə], *f.* (—, *pl.* —n) stock-taking, inventory.
Lager(bier) ['la:gər(bi:r)], *n.* (—s, *pl.* —e) lager.
Lagergeld ['la:gərgɛlt], *n.* (—es, *pl.* —er) storage charge.
Lagerist [la:gə'rɪst], *m.* (—en, *pl.* —en) warehouse-clerk.
lagern ['la:gərn], *v.a.* store, warehouse.
Lagerstätte ['la:gərʃtɛtə], *f.* (—, *pl.*—n) couch, resting-place; camp site.
Lagerung ['la:gəruŋ], *f.* (—, *pl.* —en) encampment; storage; stratification.
Lagune [la'gu:nə], *f.* (—, *pl.* —n) lagoon.
lahm [la:m], *adj.* lame, paralysed, crippled.
lahmen ['la:mən], *v.n.* be lame, limp.
lähmen ['lɛ:mən], *v.a.* paralyse.
lahmlegen ['la:mle:gən], *v.a.* paralyse.

Lähmung ['lɛ:muŋ], *f.* (—, *pl.* **—en**) paralysis.
Laib [laɪp], *m.* (**—es**, *pl.* **—e**) (*bread*) loaf.
Laich [laɪç], *m.* (**—es**, *pl.* **—e**) spawn.
laichen ['laɪçən], *v.n.* spawn.
Laie ['aɪə], *m.* (**—n**, *pl.* **—n**) layman, (*pl.*) laity.
Lakai [la'kaɪ], *m.* (**—en**, *pl.* **—en**) lackey, flunkey, footman.
Lake ['la:kə], *f.* (—, *pl.* **—n**) brine, pickle.
Laken ['la:kən], *n.* (**—s**, *pl.* —) (*bed*) sheet.
lakonisch [la'ko:nɪʃ], *adj.* laconic.
Lakritze [la'krɪtsə], *f.* (—, *pl.* **—n**) liquorice.
lallen ['lalən], *v.a.*, *v.n.* stammer; babble.
Lama (1) ['la:ma:], *n.* (**—s**, *pl.* **—s**) (*animal*) llama.
Lama (2) ['la:ma:], *m.* (**—s**, *pl.* **—s**) (*priest*) lama.
lamentieren [lamɛn'ti:rən], *v.n.* lament, wail.
Lamm [lam], *n.* (**—es**, *pl.* **¨er**) (*Zool.*) lamb.
Lämmchen ['lɛmçən], *n.* (**—s**, *pl.* —) (*Zool.*) lambkin.
Lämmergeier ['lɛmərgaɪər], *m.* (**—s**, *pl.* —) (*Orn.*) great bearded vulture.
Lampe ['lampə], *f.* (—, *pl.* **—n**) lamp.
Lampenfieber ['lampənfi:bər], *n.* (**—s**, *no pl.*) stage-fright.
Lampenputzer ['lampənputsər], *m.* (**—s**, *pl.* —) lamplighter.
Lampenschirm ['lampənʃɪrm], *m.* (**—s**, *pl.* **—e**) lampshade.
Lampion [lam'pjɔ̃], *m.* & *n.* (**—s**, *pl.* **—s**) Chinese lantern.
lancieren [lã'si:rən], *v.a.* thrust; launch.
Land [lant], *n.* (**—es**, *pl.* **—e** (*Poet.*) and **¨er**) land, country; state; ground, soil; *das Gelobte* —, the Promised Land; *an — gehen*, go ashore; *aufs — gehen*, go into the country.
Landadel ['lanta:dəl], *m.* (**—s**, *no pl.*) landed gentry.
Landarbeiter ['lantarbaɪtər], *m.* (**—s**, *pl.* —) farm-worker.
Landauer ['landauər], *m.* (**—s**, *pl.* —) landau.
Landebahn ['landəba:n], *f.* (—, *pl.* **—en**) (*Aviat.*) runway.
landen ['landən], *v.n.* (*aux. sein*) land, disembark; (*aircraft*) land, touch down.
Landenge ['lantɛŋə], *f.* (—, *pl.* **—n**) isthmus.
Ländereien ['lɛndəraɪən], *f. pl.* landed property, estate.
Landeserzeugnis ['landəsɛrtsɔyknɪs], *n.* (**—sses**, *pl.* **—sse**) home produce.
Landesfürst ['landəsfyrst], *m.* (**—en**, *pl.* **—en**) sovereign.
Landesherr ['landəshɛr], *m.* (**—n**, *pl.* **—en**) (reigning) prince; sovereign.
Landeshoheit ['landəshohaɪt], *f.* (—, *no pl.*) sovereignty.
Landeskirche ['landəskɪrçə], *f.* (—, *pl.* **—n**) established church; national church.
Landesschuld ['landəsʃult], *f.* (—, *no pl.*) national debt.
Landessprache ['landəsʃpra:xə], *f.* (—, *pl.* **—n**) vernacular.
Landestracht ['landəstraxt], *f.* (—, *pl.* **—en**) national costume.
landesüblich ['landəsy:plɪç], *adj.* conventional, usual, customary.
Landesverweisung ['landəsfɛrvaɪzuŋ], *f.* (—, *pl.* **—en**) exile, banishment.
landflüchtig ['lantflyçtɪç], *adj.* fugitive.
Landfrieden ['lantfri:dən], *m.* (**—s**, *no pl.*) King's (*or* Queen's) peace; (*medieval*) public peace.
Landgericht ['lantgərɪçt], *n.* (**—es**, *pl.* **—e**) district court; county court.
Landgraf ['lantgra:f], *m.* (**—en**, *pl.* **—en**) landgrave, count.
Landhaus ['lanthaus], *n.* (**—es**, *pl.* **¨er**) country house.
Landjunker ['lantjuŋkər], *m.* (**—s**, *pl.* —) country squire.
Landkarte ['lantkartə], *f.* (—, *pl.* **—n**) map.
landläufig ['lantlɔyfɪç], *adj.* customary, conventional.
ländlich ['lɛntlɪç], *adj.* rural, rustic.
Landmann ['lantman], *m.* (**—es**, *pl.* **Landleute**) rustic, peasant.
Landmesser ['lantmɛsər], *m.* (**—s**, *pl.* —) surveyor.
Landpartie ['lantparti:], *f.* (—, *pl.* **—n**) country excursion, picnic.
Landplage ['lantpla:gə], *f.* (—, *pl.* **—n**) scourge, calamity; *eine richtige* —, a public nuisance.
Landrat ['lantra:t], *m.* (**—s**, *pl.* **¨e**) district president *or* magistrate.
Landratte ['lantratə], *f.* (—, *pl.* **—n**) landlubber.
Landrecht ['lantrɛçt], *n.* (**—es**, *no pl.*) common law.
Landregen ['lantre:gən], *m.* (**—s**, *no pl.*) steady downpour; persistent rain.
Landschaft ['lantʃaft], *f.* (—, *pl.* **—en**) landscape.
landschaftlich ['lantʃaftlɪç], *adj.* scenic.
Landsknecht ['lantsknɛçt], *m.* (**—es**, *pl.* **—e**) mercenary; hired soldier.
Landsmann ['lantsman], *m.* (**—es**, *pl.* **Landsleute**) fellow-countryman, compatriot.
Landspitze ['lantʃpɪtsə], *f.* (—, *pl.* **—n**) cape, headland, promontory.
Landstraße ['lantʃtra:sə], *f.* (—, *pl.* **—n**) open road, main road, highway.
Landstreicher ['lantʃtraɪçər], *m.* (**—s**, *pl.* —) vagabond, tramp, (*Am.*) hobo.
Landstrich ['lantʃtrɪç], *m.* (**—es**, *pl.* **—e**) tract of land.
Landsturm ['lantʃturm], *m.* (**—s**, *no pl.*) (*Milit.*) militia; Home Guard.
Landtag ['lantta:k], *m.* (**—s**, *pl.* **—e**) (*Parl.*) diet.
Landung ['landuŋ], *f.* (—, *pl.* **—en**) landing.
Landvermesser *see* **Landmesser.**

Landvogt ['lantfo:kt], *m.* (**—es**, *pl.* **⸚e**) (provincial) governor.
Landweg ['lantve:k], *m.* (**—s**, *pl.* **—e**) overland route.
Landwehr ['lantve:r], *f.* (**—**, *pl.* **—en**) militia.
Landwirt ['lantvɪrt], *m.* (**—s**, *pl.* **—e**) farmer, husbandman.
Landwirtschaft ['lantvɪrtʃaft], *f.* (**—**, *no pl.*) agriculture.
Landzunge ['lanttsuŋə], *f.* (**—**, *pl.* **—n**) spit of land.
lang [laŋ], *adj.* long, tall. — *adv.*, *prep.* (*prec. by Acc.*) for, during, long.
langatmig ['laŋa:tmɪç], *adj.* long-winded.
lange ['laŋə], *adv.* a long time; *wie —?* how long? *so — wie*, as long as.
Länge ['lɛŋə], *f.* (**—**, *pl.* **—n**) length; (*Geog.*) longitude.
langen ['laŋən], *v.a.* reach, hand, give s.o. s.th. — *v.n.* suffice, be enough.
Längengrad ['lɛŋəngra:t], *m.* (**—s**, *pl.* **—e**) degree of longitude.
Längenkreis ['lɛŋənkraɪs], *m.* (**—es**, *pl.* **—e**) meridian.
Längenmaß ['lɛŋenma:s], *n.* (**—es**, *pl.* **—e**) linear measure.
Langeweile ['laŋəvaɪlə], *f.* (**—**, *no pl.*) boredom, ennui.
Langfinger ['laŋfɪŋər], *m.* (**—s**, *pl.* **—**) pickpocket.
langjährig ['laŋjɛ:rɪç], *adj.* of long standing.
Langlebigkeit ['laŋle:bɪçkaɪt], *f.* (**—**, *no pl.*) longevity.
länglich ['lɛŋlɪç], *adj.* oblong.
Langmut ['laŋmu:t], *f.* (**—**, *no pl.*) forbearance, patience.
längs [lɛŋs], *prep.* (*Genit.*, *Dat.*) along.
langsam ['laŋza:m], *adj.* slow; deliberate.
längst [lɛŋst], *adv.* long ago, long since.
längstens ['lɛŋstəns], *adv.* at the longest; at the latest.
Languste [laŋ'gustə], *f.* (**—**, *pl.* **—n**) (*Zool.*) spiny lobster.
langweilen ['laŋvaɪlən], *v.a.* (*insep.*) bore, tire. — *v.r. sich —*, feel bored, be bored.
langwierig ['laŋvi:rɪç], *adj.* lengthy, protracted, wearisome.
Lanze ['lantsə], *f.* (**—**, *pl.* **—n**) lance, spear; *eine — brechen*, take up the cudgels, stand up for (s.th. *or* s.o.).
Lanzenstechen ['lantsənʃtɛçən], *n.* (**—s**, *no pl.*) tournament.
Lanzette [lan'tsɛtə], *f.* (**—**, *pl.* **—n**) lancet.
Lanzknecht ['lantsknɛçt], *m.* (**—es**, *pl.* **—e**) *see* **Landsknecht**.
Laos ['la:ɔs], *n.* Laos.
Lappalie [la'paljə], *f.* (**—**, *pl.* **—n**) trifle.
Lappen ['lapən], *m.* (**—s**, *pl.* **—**) rag, duster, patch; (*ear*) lobe.
Läpperschulden ['lɛpərʃuldən], *f. pl.* petty debts.
läppisch ['lɛpɪʃ], *adj.* silly, foolish, trifling.
Lappland ['lapland], *n.* Lapland.
Lärche ['lɛrçə], *f.* (**—**, *pl.* **—n**) (*Bot.*) larch.
Lärm [lɛrm], *m.* (**—s**, *no pl.*) noise, din.
lärmen ['lɛrmən], *v.n.* make a noise, brawl.
Larve ['larfə], *f.* (**—**, *pl.* **—n**) mask; (*Ent.*) grub, larva.
lasch [laʃ], *adj.* limp; insipid.
Lasche ['laʃə], *f.* (**—**, *pl.* **—n**) flap; (*shoe*) gusset, strip.
lassen ['lasən], *v.a.*, *v.n. irr.* let, allow, suffer, permit; leave; make, cause; order, command; desist.
läßlich ['lɛslɪç], *adj.* (*Eccl.*) venial (*sin*).
lässig ['lɛsɪç], *adj.* indolent, sluggish, inactive.
Lässigkeit ['lɛsɪçkaɪt], *f.* (**—**, *no pl.*) lassitude, inaction, indolence; negligence.
Last [last], *f.* (**—**, *pl.* **—en**) load, burden, weight, charge.
lasten ['lastən], *v.n.* be heavy; weigh (on).
lastenfrei ['lastənfraɪ], *adj.* unencumbered.
Laster ['lastər], *n.* (**—s**, *pl.* **—**) vice.
Lästerer ['lɛstərər], *m.* (**—s**, *pl.* **—**) slanderer, calumniator; blasphemer.
lasterhaft ['lastərhaft], *adj.* vicious, wicked; corrupt.
Lasterhöhle ['lastərhø:lə], *f.* (**—**, *pl.* **—n**) den of vice.
lästerlich ['lɛstərlɪç], *adj.* blasphemous.
lästern ['lɛstərn], *v.a.* slander, defame; blaspheme.
lästig ['lɛstɪç], *adj.* tiresome, troublesome.
Lasttier ['lastti:r], *n.* (**—es**, *pl.* **—e**) beast of burden.
Lastwagen ['lastva:gən], *m.* (**—s**, *pl.* **—**) lorry, (*Am.*) truck.
Lasur [la'zu:r], *m.* (**—s**, *pl.* **—e**) lapis-lazuli; ultramarine.
Latein [la'taɪn], *n.* (**—s**, *no pl.*) Latin.
lateinisch [la'taɪnɪʃ], *adj.* Latin.
Laterne [la'tɛrnə], *f.* (**—**, *pl.* **—n**) lantern; (*street*) lamp.
latschen ['la:tʃən], *v.n.* shuffle along.
Latte ['latə], *f.* (**—**, *pl.* **—n**) lath, batten; *eine lange —*, lanky person.
Lattich ['latɪç], *m.* (**—s**, *pl.* **—e**) lettuce.
Latz [lats], *m.* (**—es**, *pl.* **⸚e**) flap, bib; pinafore.
lau [lau], *adj.* tepid, lukewarm, insipid; (*fig.*) half-hearted.
Laub [laup], *n.* (**—es**, *no pl.*) foliage, leaves.
Laube ['laubə], *f.* (**—**, *pl.* **—n**) arbour, summer-house.
Laubengang ['laubəngaŋ], *m.* (**—es**, *pl.* **⸚e**) arcade, covered walk.
Laubfrosch ['laupfrɔʃ], *m.* (**—es**, *pl.* **⸚e**) (*Zool.*) tree-frog.
Laubsäge ['laupzɛ:gə], *f.* (**—**, *pl.* **—n**) fret-saw.
Lauch [laux], *m.* (**—es**, *no pl.*) (*Bot.*) leek.
Lauer ['lauər], *f.* (**—**, *no pl.*) ambush, hiding-place; *auf der — sein*, lie in wait.

lauern ['lauərn], *v.n.* lurk, lie in wait (for), watch (for).
Lauf [lauf], *m.* (**—es**, *pl.* **⸚e**) course, run; running; operation; (*river*) current; (*gun*) barrel; (*fig.*) rein.
Laufbahn ['laufba:n], *f.* (—, *pl.* **—en**) career, *die medizinische — einschlagen*, enter upon a medical career.
Laufband ['laufbant], *n.* (**—s**, *pl.* **⸚er**) (*baby*) rein, leading-string; (*Tech.*) conveyor-belt.
Laufbrücke ['laufbrykə], *f.* (—, *pl.* **—n**) gangway.
Laufbursche ['laufburʃə], *m.* (**—n**, *pl.* **—n**) errand-boy.
laufen ['laufən], *v.n. irr.* (*aux.* sein) run; walk; (*wheel*) turn; flow, trickle down.
laufend ['laufənt], *adj.* current.
Läufer ['lɔyfər], *m.* (**—s**, *pl.* —) runner; (*carpet*) rug; (*Chess*) bishop; (*Footb.*) half-back.
Lauffeuer ['lauffɔyər], *n.* (**—s**, *no pl.*) wildfire.
Laufgraben ['laufgra:bən], *m.* (**—s**, *pl.* **⸚**) trench.
läufig ['lɔyfɪç], *adj.* (*animals*) ruttish.
Laufpaß ['laufpas], *m.* (**—sses**, *no pl.*) *den — geben*, give (s.o.) the sack.
Laufschritt ['laufʃrɪt], *m.* (**—es**, *pl.* **—e**) march; *im —*, at the double.
Laufzeit ['lauftsaɪt], *f.* (—, *pl.* **—en**) running-time; currency; (*animals*) rutting time.
Lauge ['laugə], *f.* (—, *pl.* **—en**) (*Chem.*) lye, alkali.
Lauheit ['lauhaɪt], *f.* (—, *no pl.*) tepidity, lukewarmness; (*fig.*) half-heartedness.
Laune ['launə], *f.* (—, *pl.* **—n**) humour, temper, mood, whim.
launenhaft ['launənhaft], *adj.* moody.
launig ['launɪç], *adj.* humorous.
launisch ['launɪʃ], *adj.* moody, fitful, bad-tempered.
Laus [laus], *f.* (—, *pl.* **⸚e**) (*Zool.*) louse.
Lausbub ['lausbu:p], *m.* (**—en**, *pl.* **—en**) young scamp, rascal.
lauschen ['lauʃən], *v.n.* listen, eavesdrop.
Lausejunge ['lauzəjuŋə], *m.* (**—n**, *pl.* **—n**) rascal, lout.
lausig ['lauzɪç], *adj.* (*vulg.*) sordid, lousy.
laut [laut], *adj.* loud, noisy, audible, clamorous. — *prep.* (*Genit.*) as per, according to, in virtue of.
Laut [laut], *m.* (**—es**, *pl.* **—e**) sound.
lautbar ['lautba:r], *adj.* — *machen*, make known.
Laute ['lautə], *f.* (—, *pl.* **—n**) (*Mus.*) lute.
lauten ['lautən], *v.n.* purport, run, read.
läuten ['lɔytən], *v.a.*, *v.n.* ring; toll; *es läutet*, the bell is ringing.
lauter ['lautər], *adj.* clear, pure; (*fig.*) single-minded; genuine; nothing but. — *adv.* merely.
Lauterkeit ['lautərkaɪt], *f.* (—, *no pl.*) clearness, purity; (*fig.*) single-mindedness, integrity.
läutern ['lɔytərn], *v.a.* clear, purify; refine.
Läuterung ['lɔytəruŋ], *f.* (—, *pl.* **—en**) clearing, purification; refinement.
lautieren [lau'ti:rən], *v.a.* read phonetically.
Lautlehre ['lautle:rə], *f.* (—, *no pl.*) phonetics.
lautlich ['lautlɪç], *adj.* phonetic.
lautlos ['lautlo:s], *adj.* mute, silent; noiseless.
Lautmalerei ['lautma:ləraɪ], *f.* (—, *no pl.*) onomatopoeia.
Lautsprecher ['lautʃprɛçər], *m.* (**—s**, *pl.* —) loudspeaker.
Lautverschiebung ['lautfɛrʃi:buŋ], *f.* (—, *pl.* **—en**) sound shift.
lauwarm ['lauvarm], *adj.* lukewarm, tepid; (*fig.*) half-hearted.
Lava ['la:va], *f.* (—, *no pl.*) lava.
Lavendel [la'vɛndəl], *m.* (**—s**, *no pl.*) (*Bot.*) lavender.
lavieren [la'vi:rən], *v.n.* tack; (*fig.*) wangle.
Lawine [la'vi:nə], *f.* (—, *pl.* **—n**) avalanche.
lax [laks], *adj.* lax, loose.
Laxheit ['lakshaɪt], *f.* (—, *pl.* **—en**) laxity.
Laxiermittel [lak'si:rmɪtəl], *n.* (**—s**, *pl.* —) laxative, aperient.
Lazarett [latsa'rɛt], *n.* (**—s**, *pl.* **—e**) infirmary, military hospital.
Lebemann ['le:bəman], *m.* (**—es**, *pl.* **⸚er**) man about town.
Leben ['le:bən], *n.* (**—s**, *pl.* —) life; (*fig.*) existence; activity; animation, bustle, stir.
leben ['le:bən], *v.n.* live, be alive.
lebend ['le:bənt], *adj.* alive, living; (*language*) modern.
lebendig [le'bɛndɪç], *adj.* living, alive, quick.
Lebensanschauung ['le:bənsanʃauuŋ], *f.* (—, *pl.* **—en**) conception of life, philosophy of life.
Lebensart ['le:bənsa:rt], *f.* (—, *no pl.*) way of living; (*fig.*) behaviour; *gute —*, good manners.
lebensfähig ['le:bənsfɛ:ɪç], *adj.* capable of living, viable.
lebensgefährlich ['le:bənsgəfɛ:rlɪç], *adj.* perilous, extremely dangerous.
Lebensgeister ['le:bənsgaɪstər], *m. pl.* spirits.
lebensgroß ['le:bənsgro:s], *adj.* life-size.
lebenslänglich ['le:bənslɛŋlɪç], *adj.* lifelong, for life; *—e Rente*, life annuity.
Lebenslauf ['le:bənslauf], *m.* (**—es**, *pl.* **⸚e**) curriculum vitae.
Lebensmittel ['le:bənsmɪtəl], *n. pl.* food, provisions, victuals.
lebensmüde ['le:bənsmy:də], *adj.* weary of life.
Lebensunterhalt ['le:bənsuntərhalt], *m.* (**—s**, *no pl.*) livelihood.
Lebenswandel ['le:bənsvandəl], *m.* (**—s**, *no pl.*) conduct, mode of life.

Lebensweise ['le:bənsvaɪzə], *f.* (—, *no pl.*) habits, way of life.
Leber ['le:bər], *f.* (—, *pl.* —**n**) liver; *frisch von der — weg*, frankly, without mincing matters.
Leberblümchen ['le:bərbly:mçən], *n.* (—**s**, *pl.* —) *(Bot.)* liverwort.
Leberfleck ['le:bərflɛk], *m.* (—**s**, *pl.* —**e**) mole.
Lebertran ['le:bərtra:n], *m.* (—**s**, *no pl.*) cod-liver oil.
Leberwurst ['le:bərvurst], *f.* (—, *pl.* ⸚**e**) liver sausage.
Lebewesen ['le:bəve:zən], *n.* (—**s**, *pl.* —) living creature.
Lebewohl ['le:bəvo:l], *n.*, *excl.* farewell, good-bye; — *sagen*, bid farewell.
lebhaft ['le:phaft], *adj.* lively, vivacious, brisk, animated.
Lebkuchen ['le:pku:xən], *m.* (—**s**, *pl.* —) gingerbread.
Lebzeiten ['le:ptsaɪtən], *f. pl. zu — von (Genit.)*, in the lifetime of.
lechzen ['lɛçtsən], *v.n.* be parched with thirst; *nach etwas* —, (*fig.*) long for s.th., pine for s.th.
Leck [lɛk], *n.* (—**s**, *pl.* —**e**) leak; *ein — bekommen*, spring a leak.
leck [lɛk], *adj.* leaky.
lecken ['lɛkən], *v.a.* lick, lap.
lecker ['lɛkər], *adj.* delicate, delicious, dainty.
Leckerbissen ['lɛkərbɪsən], *m.* (—**s**, *pl.* —) delicacy; dainty, tit-bit.
Leckerei [lɛkə'raɪ], *f.* (—, *pl.* —**en**) delicacy.
Leder ['le:dər], *n.* (—**s**, *no pl.*) leather.
ledern ['le:dərn], *adj.* (of) leather, leathery; (*fig.*) dull, boring.
ledig ['le:dɪç], *adj.* unmarried, single; (*fig.*) rid of, free from.
lediglich ['le:dɪklɪç], *adv.* merely, only, solely.
leer [le:r], *adj.* empty, void; blank; (*fig.*) hollow, futile, empty, vain, inane.
Leere ['le:rə], *f.* (—, *no pl.*) emptiness, void, vacuum.
leeren ['le:rən], *v.a.* empty, evacuate.
Leerlauf ['le:rlauf], *m.* (—**s**, *no pl.*) (*Motor.*) idling; (*gear*) neutral.
legalisieren [legali'zi:rən], *v.a.* legalise, authenticate.
Legat (1) [le'ga:t], *m.* (—**en**, *pl.* —**en**) legate.
Legat (2) [le'ga:t], *n.* (—**s**, *pl.* —**e**) legacy, bequest.
Legationsrat [lega'tsjo:nsra:t], *m.* (—**s**, *pl.* ⸚**e**) counsellor in a legation.
legen ['le:gən], *v.a.* lay, put, place. — *v.r. sich* —, lie down; cease, subside.
Legende [le'gɛndə], *f.* (—, *pl.* —**n**) legend.
Legierung [lə'gi:ruŋ], *f.* (—, *pl.* —**en**) alloy.
Legion [le'gjo:n], *f.* (—, *pl.* —**en**) legion.
Legionär [le:gjo'nɛ:r], *m.* (—**s**, *pl.* —**e**) legionary.
legitim [legi'ti:m], *adj.* legitimate.
Legitimation [legitima'tsjo:n], *f.* (—, *pl.* —**en**) proof of identity.
legitimieren [legiti'mi:rən], *v.a.* legitimise. — *v.r. sich* —, prove o.'s identity.
Lehen ['le:ən], *n.* (—**s**, *pl.* —) fief; *zu — geben*, invest with, enfeoff; *zu — tragen*, hold in fee.
Lehensdienst *see* **Lehnsdienst.**
Lehenseid *see* **Lehnseid.**
Lehensmann *see* **Lehnsmann.**
Lehm [le:m], *m.* (—**s**, *no pl.*) loam, clay, mud.
lehmig ['le:mɪç], *adj.* clayey, loamy.
Lehne ['le:nə], *f.* (—, *pl.* —**n**) support, prop; (*chair*) back, arm-rest.
lehnen ['le:nən], *v.a.*, *v.n.* lean. — *v.r. sich — an*, lean against.
Lehnsdienst ['le:nsdi:nst], *m.* (—**es**, *pl.* —**e**) feudal service.
Lehnseid ['le:nsaɪt], *m.* (—**es**, *pl.* —**e**) oath of allegiance.
Lehnsmann ['le:nsman], *m.* (—**es**, *pl.* ⸚**er**) feudal tenant, vassal.
Lehnstuhl ['le:nʃtu:l], *m.* (—**s**, *pl.* ⸚**e**) armchair, easy chair.
Lehramt ['le:ramt], *n.* (—**es**, *pl.* ⸚**er**) professorship; teaching post *or* profession.
Lehrbrief ['le:rbri:f], *m.* (—**es**, *pl.* —**e**) apprentice's indentures; certificate of apprenticeship.
Lehrbuch ['le:rbu:x], *n.* (—**es**, *pl.* ⸚**er**) textbook, manual.
Lehre ['le:rə], *f.* (—, *pl.* —**n**) teaching, advice, rule, doctrine, dogma, moral; (*craft*) apprenticeship.
lehren ['le:rən], *v.a.* teach, inform, instruct; profess.
Lehrer ['le:rər], *m.* (—**s**, *pl.* —) teacher, instructor, schoolmaster.
Lehrgang ['le:rgaŋ], *m.* (—**es**, *pl.* ⸚**e**) course (of instruction).
Lehrgegenstand ['le:rge:gənʃtant], *m.* (—**es**, *pl.* ⸚**e**) subject of instruction; branch of study.
Lehrgeld ['le:rgɛlt], *n.* (—**es**, *pl.* —**er**) premium for apprenticeship; — *zahlen*, (*fig.*) pay for o.'s experience.
Lehrkörper ['le:rkø:rpər], *m.* (—**s**, *no pl.*) teaching staff; (*Univ.*) faculty.
Lehrling ['le:rlɪŋ], *m.* (—**s**, *pl.* —**e**) apprentice.
Lehrmädchen ['le:rmɛ:tçən], *n.* (—**s**, *pl.* —) girl apprentice.
Lehrmeister ['le:rmaɪstər], *m.* (—**s**, *pl.* —) teacher, instructor, master.
Lehrmittel ['le:rmɪtəl], *n.* (—**s**, *pl.* —) teaching appliance *or* aid.
lehrreich ['le:rraɪç], *adj.* instructive.
Lehrsatz ['le:rzats], *m.* (—**es**, *pl.* ⸚**e**) tenet, dogma, rule; (*Maths.*) theorem.
Lehrstuhl ['le:rʃtu:l], *m.* (—**s**, *pl.* ⸚**e**) (*Univ.*) chair; professorship.
Lehrzeit ['le:rtsaɪt], *f.* (—, *pl.* —**en**) apprenticeship.
Leib [laɪp], *m.* (—**es**, *pl.* —**er**) body; abdomen; womb.
Leibarzt ['laɪpa:rtst], *m.* (—**es**, *pl.* ⸚**e**) court surgeon.

Leibbinde ['laipbində], *f.* (—, *pl.* —**n**) abdominal belt.
Leibchen ['laipçən], *n.* (—**s**, *pl.* —) bodice, corset; vest.
leibeigen [laip'aigən], *adj.* in bondage, in thraldom, in serfdom.
Leibeserbe ['laibəserbə], *m.* (—**n**, *pl.* —**n**) heir, descendant, offspring; (*pl.*) issue.
Leibesfrucht ['laibəsfruxt], *f.* (—, *pl.* ⸚**e**) embryo, foetus.
Leibeskraft ['laibəskraft], *f.* (—, *pl.* ⸚**e**) bodily strength; *aus —en*, with might and main.
Leibesübung ['laibəsy:buŋ], *f.* (—, *pl.* —**en**) physical exercise; (*pl.*) gymnastic exercises.
Leibgericht ['laipgəriçt], *n.* (—**s**, *pl.* —**e**) favourite dish.
leibhaftig [laip'haftiç], *adj.* real, incarnate, in person.
leiblich ['laipliç], *adj.* bodily, corporeal.
Leibrente ['laiprεntə], *f.* (—, *pl.* —**n**) life-annuity.
Leibschmerzen ['laipʃmεrtsən], *m.* *pl.* stomach-ache.
Leibspeise ['laipʃpaizə], *f.* (—, *pl.* —**n**) favourite dish.
Leibwache ['laipvaxə], *f.* (—, *no pl.*) body-guard.
Leibwäsche ['laipvεʃə], *f.* (—, *no pl.*) underwear.
Leiche ['laiçə], *f.* (—, *pl.* —**n**) (dead) body, corpse; (*dial.*) funeral.
Leichenbegängnis ['laiçənbəgεŋnis], *n.* (—**ses**, *pl.* —**se**) funeral, burial, interment.
Leichenbeschauer ['laiçənbəʃauər], *m.* (—**s**, *pl.* —) coroner.
Leichenbestatter ['laiçənbəʃtater], *m.* (—**s**, *pl.* —) undertaker; (*Am.*) mortician.
leichenhaft ['laiçenhaft], *adj.* corpse-like, cadaverous.
Leichenschau ['laiçənʃau], *f.* (—, *no pl.*) post mortem (examination), (coroner's) inquest.
Leichentuch ['laiçəntu:x], *n.* (—**es**, *pl.* ⸚**er**) shroud, pall.
Leichenverbrennung ['laiçənfεrbrεnuŋ], *f.* (—, *pl.* —**en**) cremation.
Leichenwagen ['laiçənva:gən], *m.* (—**s**, *pl.* —) hearse.
Leichenzug ['laiçəntsu:k], *m.* (—**es**, *pl.* ⸚**e**) funeral procession.
Leichnam ['laiçna:m], *m.* (—**s**, *pl.* —**e**) (dead) body, corpse.
leicht [laiçt], *adj.* light; slight; weak; easy.
leichtfertig ['laiçtfεrtiç], *adj.* frivolous, irresponsible.
leichtgläubig ['laiçtglɔybiç], *adj.* credulous, gullible.
leichthin ['laiçthin], *adv.* lightly.
Leichtigkeit ['laiçtiçkait], *f.* (—, *no pl.*) ease, facility.
Leichtsinn ['laiçtzin], *m.* (—**s**, *no pl.*) thoughtlessness, carelessness; frivolity.

Leid [lait], *n.* (—**es**, *no pl.*) sorrow, grief; harm, hurt; *einem etwas zu —e tun*, harm s.o.
leid [lait], *adj. es tut mir —*, I am sorry; *du tust mir —*, I am sorry for you.
Leiden ['laidən], *n.* (—**s**, *pl.* —) suffering, misfortune; (*illness*) affliction, complaint; *das — Christi*, the Passion.
leiden ['laidən], *v.a., v.n. irr.* suffer, bear, endure, undergo.
Leidenschaft ['laidənʃaft], *f.* (—, *pl.* —**en**) passion.
leider ['laidər], *adv.* unfortunately.
leidig ['laidiç], *adj.* tiresome, unpleasant.
leidlich ['laitliç], *adj.* tolerable, moderate.
leidtragend ['laittra:gənt], *adj.* in mourning.
Leidtragende ['laittra:gəndə], *m.* or *f.* (—**n**, *pl.* —**n**) mourner.
Leidwesen ['laitve:zən], *n.* (—**s**, *no pl.*) *zu meinem —*, to my regret.
Leier ['laiər], *f.* (—, *pl.* —**n**) lyre.
Leierkasten ['laiərkastən], *m.* (—**s**, *pl.* ⸚) barrel organ.
leiern ['laiərn], *v.n.* drone, drawl on.
leihen ['laiən], *v.a. irr. einem etwas —*, lend s.o. s.th.; *von einem etwas —*, borrow s.th. from s.o.
Leim [laim], *m.* (—**s**, *no pl.*) glue; *einem auf den — gehen*, be taken in by s.o., fall for s.th.
Leimfarbe ['laimfarbə], *f.* (—, *pl.* —**en**) water-colour, distemper.
Lein [lain], *m.* (—**s**, *pl.* —**e**) linseed, flax.
Leine ['lainə], *f.* (—, *pl.* —**n**) line, cord.
Leinen ['lainən], *n.* (—**s**, *no pl.*) linen.
Leinöl ['lainø:l], *n.* (—**s**, *no pl.*) linseed oil.
Leintuch ['laintu:x], *n.* (—**es**, *pl.* ⸚**er**) linen sheet, sheeting.
Leinwand ['lainvant], *f.* (—, *no pl.*) linen, sheeting; (*Art*) canvas; (*film*) screen.
leise ['laizə], *adj.* low, soft, gentle, faint, slight; delicate.
Leiste ['laistə], *f.* (—, *pl.* —**n**) ledge, border; groin.
Leisten ['laistən], *m.* (—**s**, *pl.* —) (*shoe*) last, form.
leisten ['laistən], *v.a.* do, perform; accomplish; *ich kann es mir nicht —*, I cannot afford it.
Leistenbruch ['laistənbrux], *m.* (—**es**, *pl.* ⸚**e**) hernia, rupture.
Leistung ['laistuŋ], *f.* (—, *pl.* —**en**) performance, accomplishment, achievement.
leistungsfähig ['laistuŋksfε:iç], *adj.* efficient.
leiten ['laitən], *v.a.* lead, guide, manage; preside over.
Leiter (1) ['laitər], *m.* (—**s**, *pl.* —) leader, manager; conductor; head.
Leiter (2) ['laitər], *f.* (—, *pl.* —**n**) ladder.
Leiterwagen ['laitərva:gən], *m.* (—**s**, *pl.* —) rack-wagon; (*Austr.*) small hand-cart.

Leitfaden ['laɪtfa:dən], *m.* (—**s**, *pl.* ⸚) (*book*) manual, textbook, guide.
Leitstern ['laɪtʃtɛrn], *m.* (—**s**, *pl.* —**e**) pole-star; (*fig.*) lodestar, guiding star.
Leitung ['laɪtuŋ], *f.* (—, *pl.* —**en**) management, direction; (*Elec.*) lead, connection; line; (water- *or* gas-) main(s); pipeline; *eine lange — haben*, be slow in the uptake.
Leitungsvermögen ['laɪtuŋsfɛrmø:gən], *n.* (—**s**, *no pl.*) conductivity.
Leitwerk ['laɪtvɛrk], *n.* (—**s**, *no pl.*) (*Aviat.*) tail unit.
Lektion [lɛkts'jo:n], *f.* (—, *pl.* —**en**) lesson; *einem eine — geben*, lecture s.o.
Lektor ['lɛktɔr], *m.* (—**s**, *pl.* —**en**) publisher's reader; teacher, lector.
Lektüre [lɛk'ty:rə], *f.* (—, *pl.* —**n**) reading matter, books.
Lende ['lɛndə], *f.* (—, *pl.* —**n**) (*Anat.*) loin.
lendenlahm ['lɛndənla:m], *adj.* weak-kneed, lame.
lenkbar ['lɛŋkba:r], *adj.* dirigible, manageable, tractable, governable.
lenken ['lɛŋkən], *v.a.* drive, steer; (*fig.*) direct, rule, manage.
Lenkstange ['lɛŋkʃtaŋə], *f.* (—, *pl.* —**n**) connecting-rod; (*bicycle*) handle-bar.
Lenz [lɛnts], *m.* (—**es**, *pl.* —**e**) (*Poet.*) spring.
Lepra ['le:pra], *f.* (—, *no pl.*) leprosy.
Lerche ['lɛrçə], *f.* (—, *pl.* —**n**) (*Orn.*) lark, skylark.
lernbegierig ['lɛrnbəgi:rɪç], *adj.* studious, eager to learn.
lernen ['lɛrnən], *v.a.* learn; study; *einen kennen —*, make s.o.'s acquaintance; *auswendig —*, learn by heart.
Lesart ['le:sa:rt], *f.* (—, *pl.* —**en**) reading, version.
lesbar ['le:sba:r], *adj.* legible; readable.
Lese ['le:zə], *f.* (—, *pl.* —**n**) gathering (of fruit); vintage.
lesen ['le:zən], *v.a. irr.* gather; glean; read; *die Messe —*, celebrate *or* say mass; *über etwas —*, (*Univ.*) lecture on s.th.
lesenswert ['le:zənsvɛrt], *adj.* worth reading.
Leser ['le:zər], *m.* (—**s**, *pl.* —) gatherer, gleaner; reader.
leserlich ['le:zərlɪç], *adj.* legible.
Lettland ['lɛtlant], *n.* Latvia.
letzen ['lɛtsən], *v.a.* (*Poet.*) comfort, cheer, refresh.
letzt [lɛtst], *adj.* last, extreme, ultimate, final.
letztens ['lɛtstəns], *adv.* lastly, in the end.
letztere ['lɛtstərə], *adj.* latter.
letzthin ['lɛtsthɪn], *adv.* (*rare*) lately, the other day, recently.
Leu [lɔy], *m.* (—**en**, *pl.* —**en**) (*Poet.*) lion.
Leuchte ['lɔyçtə], *f.* (—, *pl.* —**n**) light, lamp, lantern; (*fig.*) luminary, star.
leuchten ['lɔyçtən], *v.n.* light, shine.
leuchtend ['lɔyçtənt], *adj.* shining, bright; luminous.
Leuchter ['lɔyçtər], *m.* (—**s**, *pl.* —) candlestick, candelabrum.
Leuchtrakete ['lɔyçtrake:tə], *f.* (—, *pl.* —**n**) Roman candle; flare.
Leuchtturm ['lɔyçtturm], *m.* (—**s**, *pl.* ⸚**e**) lighthouse.
leugnen ['lɔygnən], *v.a.* deny, disclaim; *nicht zu —*, undeniable.
Leumund ['lɔymunt], *m.* (—**es**, *no pl.*) renown, reputation.
Leute ['lɔytə], *pl.* persons, people, men; servants, domestic staff.
Leutnant ['lɔytnant], *m.* (—**s**, *pl.* —**s**) lieutenant.
leutselig ['lɔytze:lɪç], *adj.* affable, friendly; condescending.
Levkoje [lɛf'ko:jə], *f.* (—, *pl.* —**n**) (*Bot.*) stock.
Lexikon ['lɛksɪkɔn], *n.* (—**s**, *pl.* —**s**, —**ka**) dictionary, lexicon, encyclopaedia.
Libanon ['li:banɔn], *m.* Lebanon.
Libelle [li'bɛlə], *f.* (—, *pl.* —**n**) (*Ent.*) dragonfly.
Liberia [li'be:rja], *n.* Liberia.
Libyen ['li:bɪən], *n.* Libya.
Licht [lɪçt], *n.* (—**es**, *pl.* —**er**) light, candle; luminary.
licht [lɪçt], *adj.* light, clear, open.
Lichtbild ['lɪçtbɪlt], *n.* (—**es**, *pl.* —**er**) photograph.
Lichtbrechung ['lɪçtbrɛçuŋ], *f.* (—, *pl.* —**en**) refraction of light.
lichten ['lɪçtən], *v.a.* clear, thin; *den Anker —*, weigh anchor.
lichterloh ['lɪçtərlo:], *adj.* blazing, ablaze.
Lichthof ['lɪçtho:f], *m.* (—**s**, *pl.* ⸚**e**) well of a court, quadrangle.
Lichtmeß ['lɪçtmɛs], *f.* (—, *no pl.*) (*Eccl.*) Candlemas.
Lichtschirm ['lɪçtʃɪrm], *m.* (—**s**, *pl.* —**e**) screen, lamp-shade.
Lichtspieltheater ['lɪçtʃpi:ltea:tər], *n.* (—**s**, *pl.* —) cinema.
Lichtung ['lɪçtuŋ], *f.* (—, *pl.* —**en**) glade, clearing.
Lid [li:t], *n.* (—**s**, *pl.* —**er**) eye-lid.
lieb [li:p], *adj.* dear; beloved; good; *das ist mir —*, I am glad of it; *der —e Gott*, God; *unsere —e Frau*, Our Lady; *bei einem — Kind sein*, be a favourite with s.o., curry favour with s.o.
liebäugeln ['li:pɔygəln], *v.n. insep.* ogle.
Liebchen ['li:pçən], *n.* (—**s**, *pl.* —) sweetheart, love, darling.
Liebe ['li:bə], *f.* (—, *no pl.*) love.
Liebelei [li:bə'laɪ], *f.* (—, *pl.* —**en**) flirtation.
lieben ['li:bən], *v.a.* love, like, be fond of.
liebenswürdig ['li:bənsvyrdɪç], *adj.* amiable, kind, charming.
lieber ['li:bər], *adv.* rather, better, sooner; *etwas — tun*, prefer to do s.th.
Liebhaber ['li:pha:bər], *m.* (—**s**, *pl.* —) lover; (*fig.*) amateur, dilettante; (*Theat.*) leading man.
Liebhaberin ['li:phabərɪn], *f.* leading lady.

liebkosen ['li:pko:zən], *v.a. insep.* fondle, caress.
lieblich ['li:plɪç], *adj.* lovely, charming, sweet.
Liebling ['li:plɪŋ], *m.* (—**s**, *pl.* —**e**) darling, favourite.
lieblos ['li:plo:s], *adj.* hard-hearted; unkind.
Liebreiz ['li:praɪts], *m.* (—**es**, *no pl.*) charm, attractiveness.
liebreizend ['li:praɪtsənt], *adj.* charming.
Liebschaft ['li:pʃaft], *f.* (—, *pl.* —**en**) love affair.
Lied [li:t], *n.* (—**es**, *pl.* —**er**) song, air, tune; *geistliches* —, hymn.
liederlich ['li:dərlɪç], *adj.* careless, slovenly; dissolute, debauched; —*es Leben*, profligacy.
Lieferant [li:fə'rant], *m.* (—**en**, *pl.* —**en**) supplier, purveyor, contractor; *Eingang für* —*en*, tradesmen's entrance.
liefern ['li:fərn], *v.a.* deliver, furnish, supply.
Lieferschein ['li:fərʃaɪn], *m.* (—**s**, *pl.* —**e**) delivery note.
liegen ['li:gən], *v.n. irr.* lie; be situated; *es liegt mir daran*, it is of importance to me, I have it at heart; *es liegt mir nichts daran*, it is of no consequence to me.
Liegenschaft ['li:gənʃaft], *f.* (—, *pl.* —**en**) landed property, real estate.
Liga ['li:ga:], *f.* (—, *pl.* —**gen**) league.
Liguster [li'gustər], *m.* (—**s**, *no pl.*) privet.
liieren [li'i:rən], *v.r.* (*aux.* haben) *sich* — *mit*, unite with, combine with.
Likör [li'kø:r], *m.* (—**s**, *pl.* —**e**) liqueur.
lila ['li:la:] *adj.* (*colour*) lilac.
Lilie ['li:ljə], *f.* (—, *pl.* —**n**) (*Bot.*) lily.
Limonade [limo'na:də], *f.* (—, *pl.* —**n**) lemonade.
lind [lɪnt], *adj.* soft, gentle, mild.
Linde ['lɪndə], *f.* (—, *pl.* —**n**) (*Bot.*) lime-tree, linden.
lindern ['lɪndərn], *v.a.* soften, assuage, mitigate, soothe, allay.
Lindwurm ['lɪntvurm], *m.* (—**s**, *pl.* ¨—**er**) (*Poet.*) dragon.
Lineal [line'a:l], *n.* (—**s**, *pl.* —**e**) ruler, rule.
Linie ['li:njə], *f.* (—, *pl.* —**n**) line; lineage, descent; *in erster* —, in the first place.
Linienschiff ['li:njənʃɪf], *n.* (—**es**, *pl.* —**e**) (*Naut.*) liner.
lin(i)ieren [lin'(j)i:rən], *v.a.* rule.
linkisch ['lɪŋkɪʃ], *adj.* awkward, clumsy.
links [lɪŋks], *adv.* to the left, on the left-hand side; —*um!* left about turn!
Linnen ['lɪnən], *n.* (—**s**, *no pl.*) (*Poet.*) linen.
Linse ['lɪnzə], *f.* (—, *pl.* —**n**) (*vegetable*) lentil; (*optical*) lens.
linsenförmig ['lɪnzənfœrmɪç], *adj.* lens-shaped.
Linsengericht ['lɪnzəngərɪçt], *n.* (—**s**, *pl.* —**e**) (*Bibl.*) mess of pottage.
Lippe ['lɪpə], *f.* (—, *pl.* —**n**) lip; (*coll.*) *eine* — *riskieren*, be cheeky.
Lippenlaut ['lɪpənlaut], *m.* (—**s**, *pl.* —**e**) (*Phonet.*) labial.
Lippenstift ['lɪpənʃtɪft], *m.* (—**s**, *pl.* —**e**) lipstick.
liquidieren [lɪkvi'di:rən], *v.a.* liquidate, wind up, settle; charge.
lispeln ['lɪspəln], *v.n.* lisp.
Lissabon [lɪsa'bɔn], *n.* Lisbon.
List [lɪst], *f.* (—, *pl.* —**en**) cunning, craft; trick, stratagem, ruse.
Liste ['lɪstə], *f.* (—, *pl.* —**n**) list, roll, catalogue.
listig ['lɪstɪç], *adj.* cunning, crafty, sly.
Listigkeit ['lɪstɪçkaɪt], *f.* (—, *no pl.*) slyness, craftiness.
Litanei [lita'naɪ], *f.* (—, *pl.* —**en**) litany.
Litauen ['lɪtauən], *n.* Lithuania.
Liter ['li:tər], *m.* & *n.* (—**s**, *pl.* —) litre.
literarisch [litə'ra:rɪʃ], *adj.* literary.
Literatur [litəra'tu:r], *f.* (—, *pl.* —**en**) literature, letters.
Litfaßsäule ['lɪtfaszɔylə], *f.* (—, *pl.* —**n**) advertisement pillar.
Liturgie [litur'gi:], *f.* (—, *pl.* —**n**) liturgy.
Litze ['lɪtsə], *f.* (—, *pl.* —**n**) lace, braid, cord; (*Elec.*) flex.
Livland ['li:flant], *n.* Livonia.
Livree [li'vre:], *f.* (—, *pl.* —**n**) livery.
Lizenz [li'tsɛnts], *f.* (—, *pl.* —**en**) licence.
Lob [lo:p], *n.* (—**es**, *no pl.*) praise, commendation.
loben ['lo:bən], *v.a.* praise, commend.
lobesam ['lo:bəza:m], *adj.* (*Poet.*) worthy, honourable.
Lobgesang ['lo:pgəzaŋ], *m.* (—**s**, *pl.* ¨—**e**) hymn of praise.
Lobhudelei [lo:phu:də'laɪ], *f.* (—, *pl.* —**en**) adulation, flattery, toadying.
löblich ['lø:plɪç], *adj.* laudable, commendable, meritorious.
lobpreisen ['lo:ppraɪzən], *v.a. insep.* eulogise, extol.
Lobrede ['lo:pre:də], *f.* (—, *pl.* —**n**) panegyric, eulogy.
Loch [lɔx], *n.* (—**es**, *pl.* ¨—**er**) hole.
Lochbohrer ['lɔxbo:rər], *m.* (—**s**, *pl.* —) auger.
lochen ['lɔxən], *v.a.* perforate, punch.
Locher ['lɔxər], *m.* (—**s**, *pl.* —) perforator, punch.
löcherig ['lœçərɪç], *adj.* full of holes.
Lochmeißel ['lɔxmaɪsəl], *m.* (—**s**, *pl.* —) mortice-chisel.
Locke ['lɔkə], *f.* (—, *pl.* —**n**) curl, lock, ringlet, tress.
locken ['lɔkən], *v.a.* allure, decoy, entice.
locker ['lɔkər], *adj.* loose; slack; spongy; dissolute; *nicht* — *lassen*, stick to o.'s guns.
lockern ['lɔkərn], *v.a.* loosen.
lockig ['lɔkɪç], *adj.* curled, curly.
Lockmittel ['lɔkmɪtəl], *n.* (—**s**, *pl.* —) inducement, lure, bait.
Lockspeise ['lɔkʃpaɪzə], *f.* (—, *pl.* —**n**) lure, bait.

Lockung [ˈlɔkuŋ], *f.* (—, *pl.* —**en**) allurement, enticement.
Lockvogel [ˈlɔkfo:gəl], *m.* (—**s**, *pl.* ¨) decoy-bird.
Loden [ˈlo:dən], *m.* (—**s**, *pl.* —) coarse cloth, frieze.
lodern [ˈlo:dərn], *v.n.* blaze, flame.
Löffel [ˈlœfəl], *m.* (—**s**, *pl.* —) spoon; (*animal*) ear; *einen über den — barbieren*, take s.o. in.
Logarithmus [logaˈrɪtmus], *m.* (—, *pl.* —**men**) logarithm.
Logbuch [ˈlɔkbu:x], *n.* (—**es**, *pl.* ¨**er**) logbook.
Loge [ˈlo:ʒə], *f.* (—, *pl.* —**n**) (*Theat.*) box; (*Freemasonry*) lodge.
Logenschließer [ˈlo:ʒənʃli:sər], *m.* (—**s**, *pl.* —) (*Theat.*) attendant.
logieren [loˈʒi:rən], *v.n.* board (with).
Logis [loˈʒi:], *n.* (—, *pl.* —) lodgings.
logisch [ˈlo:gɪʃ], *adj.* logical.
Lohe [ˈlo:hə], *f.* (—, *pl.* —**n**) tanning bark; flame.
Lohgerber [ˈlo:gɛrbər], *m.* (—**s**, *pl.* —) tanner.
Lohn [lo:n], *m.* (—**s**, *pl.* ¨**e**) wages, pay; reward; recompense.
lohnen [ˈlo:nən], *v.a.* reward, recompense, remunerate; pay wages to; *es lohnt sich nicht*, it is not worth while.
Lohnstopp [ˈlo:nʃtɔp], *m.* (—**s**, *pl.* —**s**) pay pause, wage freeze.
Löhnung [ˈlø:nuŋ], *f.* (—, *pl.* —**en**) pay, payment.
Lokal [loˈka:l], *n.* (—**s**, *pl* —**e**) locality, premises; inn, pub, café.
lokalisieren [lokaliˈzi:rən], *v.a.* localise.
Lokalität [lokaliˈtɛ:t], *f.* (—, *pl.* —**en**) *see* **Lokal**.
Lokomotive [lokomoˈti:və], *f.* (—, *pl.* —**n**) (*Railw.*) locomotive, engine.
Lokomotivführer [lokomoˈti:ffy:rər], *m.* (—**s**, *pl.* —) (*Railw.*) engine-driver.
Lombard [lɔmˈbart], *m.* (—**s**, *pl.* —**e**) deposit-bank, loan bank.
Lombardei [lɔmbarˈdaɪ], *f.* Lombardy.
Lorbeer [ˈlɔrbe:r], *m.* (—**s**, *pl.* —**en**) laurel.
Lorbeerbaum [ˈlɔrbe:rbaum], *m.* (—**s**, *pl.* ¨**e**) laurel-tree, bay-tree.
Lorbeerspiritus [ˈlɔrbe:rʃpi:ritus], *m.* (—, *no pl.*) bay rum.
Lorgnon [lɔrnˈjɔ̃], *n.* (—**s**, *pl.* —**s**) monocle, eye-glass.
Los [lo:s], *n.* (—**es**, *pl.* —**e**) share, ticket; lot, fate; *das große —*, first prize.
los [lo:s], *adj.* loose, untied; free from, released from, rid of; (*Am.*) quit of; *was ist los?* what is going on? what's the matter? *etwas — werden*, get rid of s.th.; *schieß los!* fire away!
lösbar [ˈlø:sba:r], *adj.* (*question, riddle*) soluble.
losbinden [ˈlo:sbɪndən], *v.a. irr.* untie, unbind, loosen.
losbrechen [ˈlo:sbrɛçən], *v.a. irr.* break off. — *v.n.* (*aux.* sein) break loose.
Löschblatt [ˈlœʃblat], *n.* (—**es**, *pl.* ¨**er**) blotting-paper.
Löscheimer [ˈlœʃaɪmər], *m.* (—**s**, *pl.* —) fire-bucket.
löschen [ˈlœʃən], *v.a.* put out; extinguish; (*debt*) cancel; (*writing*) efface, blot; (*freight*) (*Naut.*) unload; (*thirst*) quench.
Löschpapier [ˈlœʃpapi:r], *n.* (—**s**, *no pl.*) blotting-paper.
Löschung [ˈlœʃuŋ], *f.* (—, *pl.* —**en**) (*freight*) (*Naut.*) discharging, landing, unloading.
losdrücken [ˈlo:sdrykən], *v.n.* discharge, fire.
lose [ˈlo:zə], *adj.* loose, slack; (*fig.*) dissolute; *—s Maul*, malicious tongue.
Lösegeld [ˈlø:zəgɛlt], *n.* (—**es**, *pl.* —**er**) ransom.
losen [ˈlo:zən], *v.n.* draw lots.
lösen [ˈlø:zən], *v.a.* loosen, untie; absolve, free, deliver; dissolve; solve; (*relations*) break off; (*tickets*) take, buy.
losgehen [ˈlo:sge:ən], *v.n. irr.* (*aux.* sein) begin; (*gun*) go off; *auf einen —*, go for s.o.; *jetzt kann's —*, now for it.
loskaufen [ˈlo:skaufən], *v.a.* redeem, ransom.
loskommen [ˈlo:skɔmən], *v.n. irr.* (*aux.* sein) come loose; *von etwas —*, get rid of s.th.
löslich [ˈlø:slɪç], *adj.* (*Chem.*) soluble.
loslösen [ˈlo:slø:zən], *v.a.* detach.
losmachen [ˈlo:smaxən], *v.a.* free from. — *v.r. sich — von*, disengage o.s. from.
losreißen [ˈlo:sraɪsən], *v.a. irr.* pull away, separate. — *v.n.* (*aux.* sein), break loose. — *v.r. sich — von*, tear o.s. away from.
lossagen [ˈlo:sza:gən], *v.r. sich — von*, renounce s.th., dissociate o.s. from s.th.
losschlagen [ˈlo:sʃla:gen], *v.a.* knock loose; let fly; (*fig.*) sell, dispose of.
lossprechen [ˈlo:sʃprɛçən], *v.a. irr.* (*Eccl.*) absolve; (*Law*) acquit.
lossteuern [ˈlo:sʃtɔyərn], *v.n.* — *auf*, make for.
Losung [ˈlo:zuŋ], *f.* (—, *pl.* —**en**) watchword, motto, password, slogan.
Lösung [ˈlø:zuŋ], *f.* (—, *pl.* —**en**) loosening; solution.
losziehen [ˈlo:stsi:ən], *v.n. irr.* (*Mil.*) set out; *gegen einen —*, inveigh against s.o.; (*fig., coll.*) run s.o. down.
Lot [lo:t], *n.* (—**es**, *pl.* —**e**) lead, plummet; (*weight*) half an ounce; (*Maths.*) perpendicular (line).
Löteisen [ˈlø:taɪzən], *n.* (—**s**, *pl.* —) soldering iron.
loten [ˈlo:tən], *v.a., v.n.* (*Naut.*) take soundings, plumb.
löten [ˈlø:tən], *v.a.* solder.
Lothringen [ˈlo:trɪŋən], *n.* Lorraine.
Lötkolben [ˈlø:tkɔlbən], *m.* (—**s**, *pl.* —) soldering iron.
Lotleine [ˈlo:tlaɪnə], *f.* (—, *pl.* —**n**) sounding-line.
Lotrechtstarter [ˈlo:trɛçtʃtartər], *m.* (—**s**, *pl.* —) (*Aviat.*) vertical take-off plane (V.T.O.L.).

Lötrohr ['lø:tro:r], *n.* (—s, *pl.* —e) soldering-pipe.

Lotse ['lo:tsə], *m.* (—n, *pl.* —n) (*Naut.*) pilot.

Lotterbett ['lɔtərbɛt], *n.* (—es, *pl.* —en) bed of idleness; (*obs.*) couch.

Lotterie [lɔtə'ri:], *f.* (—, *pl.* —n) lottery, sweep-stake.

Lotterleben ['lɔtərle:bən], *n.* (—s, *no pl.*) dissolute life.

Löwe ['lø:və], *m.* (—n, *pl.* —n) (*Zool.*) lion.

Löwenbändiger ['lø:vənbɛndɪgər], *m.* (—s, *pl.* —) lion tamer.

Löwengrube ['lø:vəngru:bə], *f.* (—, *pl.* —n) lion's den.

Löwenmaul ['lø:vənmaul], *n.* (—s, *no pl.*) (*Bot.*) snapdragon.

Löwenzahn ['lø:vəntsa:n], *m.* (—s, *no pl.*) (*Bot.*) dandelion.

Löwin ['lø:vɪn], *f.* (—, *pl.* —nen) (*Zool.*) lioness.

Luchs [luks], *m.* (—es, *pl.* —e) lynx.

Lücke ['lykə], *f.* (—, *pl.* —n) gap, breach; (*fig.*) omission, defect, blank.

Lückenbüßer ['lykənby:sər], *m.* (—s, *pl.* —) stop-gap, stand-in.

lückenhaft ['lykənhaft], *adj.* fragmentary, incomplete, imperfect.

Luder ['lu:dər], *n.* (—s, *pl.* —) (*rare*) carrion; (*vulg.*) beast, trollop; *dummes* —, silly ass, fathead.

Luderleben ['lu:dərle:bən], *n.* (—s, *no pl.*) dissolute life.

ludern ['lu:dərn], *v.n.* lead a dissolute life.

Luft [luft], *f.* (—, *pl.* ¨e) air.

Luftbrücke ['luftbrykə], *f.* (—, *no pl.*) air-lift.

Lüftchen ['lyftçən], *n.* (—s, *pl.* —) gentle breeze.

luftdicht ['luftdɪçt], *adj.* airtight.

Luftdruck ['luftdruk], *m.* (—s, *no pl.*) air pressure, atmospheric pressure; blast.

Luftdruckmesser ['luftdrukmesər], *m.* (—s, *pl.* —) barometer, pressure-gauge.

lüften ['lyftən], *v.a.* air, ventilate.

luftförmig ['luftfœrmɪç], *adj.* gaseous.

luftig ['luftɪç], *adj.* airy, windy.

Luftklappe ['luftklapə], *f.* (—, *pl.* —n) air-valve.

Luftkurort ['luftku:rɔrt], *m.* (—s, *pl.* —e) health resort.

Luftlinie ['luftli:njə], *f.* (—, *pl.* —n) bee-line; *in der* —, as the crow flies; (*Aviat.*) airline.

Luftloch ['luftlɔx], *m.* (—s, *pl.* ¨er) air-pocket.

Luftraum ['luftraum], *m.* (—s, *no pl.*) atmosphere; air space.

Luftröhre ['luftrø:rə], *f.* (—, *pl.* —n) windpipe.

Luftschiff ['luftʃɪf], *n.* (—es, *pl.* —e) air-ship.

Luftschiffahrt ['luftʃɪfa:rt], *f.* (—, *no pl.*) aeronautics.

Luftspiegelung ['luftʃpi:gəluŋ], *f.* (—, *pl.* —en) mirage.

Luftsprung ['luftʃpruŋ], *m.* (—s, *pl.* ¨e) caper, gambol; ¨*e machen*, caper, gambol.

Lüftung ['lyftuŋ], *f.* (—, *no pl.*) airing, ventilation.

Lug [lu:k], *m.* (—s, *no pl.*) (*obs.*) lie; — *und Trug*, a pack of lies.

Lüge ['ly:gə], *f.* (—, *pl.* —n) lie, falsehood, fib; *einen* — *strafen*, give s.o. the lie.

lügen ['ly:gən], *v.n. irr.* lie, tell a lie.

lügenhaft ['ly:gənhaft], *adj.* lying, false, untrue.

Lügner ['ly:gnər], *m.* (—s, *pl.* —) liar.

Luke ['lu:kə], *f.* (—, *pl.* —n) dormer-window; (*ship*) hatch.

Lümmel ['lyməl], *m.* (—s, *pl.* —) lout; hooligan.

Lump [lump], *m.* (—s, —en, *pl.* —e, —en) scoundrel, blackguard.

Lumpen ['lumpən], *m.* (—s, *pl.* —) rag, tatter.

Lumpengesindel ['lumpəngəzɪndəl], *n.* (—s, *no pl.*) rabble, riffraff.

Lumpenpack ['lumpənpak], *n.* (—s, *no pl.*) rabble, riffraff.

Lumpensammler ['lumpənzamlər], *m.* (—s, *pl.* —) rag-and-bone-man.

Lumperei [lumpə'raɪ], *f.* (—, *pl.* —en) shabby trick; meanness; trifle.

lumpig ['lumpɪç], *adj.* ragged; (*fig.*) shabby, mean.

Lunge ['luŋə], *f.* (—, *pl.* —n) (*human*) lung; (*animals*) lights.

Lungenentzündung ['luŋənɛntsyndʊŋ], *f.* (—, *pl.* —en) pneumonia.

Lungenkrankheit ['luŋənkraŋkhaɪt], *f.* (—, *pl.* —en) pulmonary disease.

Lungenkraut ['luŋənkraut], *n.* (—s, *pl.* ¨er) lungwort.

Lungenschwindsucht ['luŋənʃvɪntzuxt], *f.* (—, *no pl.*) pulmonary consumption, tuberculosis.

lungern ['luŋərn], *v.n.* idle, loiter.

Lunte ['luntə], *f.* (—, *pl.* —n) fuse, slow-match; — *riechen*, smell a rat.

Lupe ['lu:pə], *f.* (—, *pl.* —n) magnifying glass, lens; *etwas durch die* — *besehen*, examine s.th. closely, scrutinise s.th.; *unter die* — *nehmen*, examine closely.

lüpfen ['lypfən], *v.a.* lift.

Lupine [lu'pi:nə], *f.* (—, *pl.* —n) (*Bot.*) lupin.

Lust [lust], *f.* (—, *pl.* ¨e) enjoyment, pleasure, delight; desire, wish, inclination, liking; — *bekommen zu*, feel inclined to; — *haben auf*, have a mind to, feel like; *nicht übel* — *haben*, have half a mind to.

Lustbarkeit ['lustba:rkaɪt], *f.* (—, *pl.* —en) amusement, diversion, entertainment, pleasure.

Lustdirne ['lustdɪrnə], *f.* (—, *pl.* —n) prostitute.

lüstern ['lystərn], *adj.* lustful, lascivious.

lustig ['lustɪç], *adj.* gay, merry, cheerful, amusing, funny; — *sein*, make merry; *sich über einen* — *machen*, poke fun at s.o.

Lüstling ['lystlɪŋ], *m.* (—**s**, *pl.* —**e**) libertine, lecher.
Lustmord ['lustmɔrt], *m.* (—**es**, *pl.* —**e**) sex murder.
Lustreise ['lustraɪzə], *f.* (—, *pl.* —**n**) pleasure trip.
Lustschloß ['lustʃlɔs], *n.* (—**sses**, *pl.* ¨**sser**) country house, country seat.
Lustspiel ['lustʃpi:l], *n.* (—**s**, *pl.* —**e**) comedy.
lustwandeln ['lustvandəln], *v.n. insep.* (*aux.* sein) stroll, promenade.
Lutherisch ['lutərɪʃ], *adj.* Lutheran.
lutschen ['lutʃən], *v.a.* suck.
Lüttich ['lytɪç], *n.* Liège.
Luxus ['luksus], *m.* (—, *no pl.*) luxury.
Luzern [lu'tsɛrn], *n.* Lucerne.
Luzerne [lut'sɛrnə], *f.* (—, *pl.* —**n**) (*Bot.*) lucerne.
Lymphe ['lymfə], *f.* (—, *pl.* —**n**) lymph.
lynchen ['lynçən], *v.a.* lynch.
Lyrik ['ly:rɪk], *f.* (—, *no pl.*) lyric poetry.
lyrisch ['ly:rɪʃ], *adj.* lyric(al).
Lyzeum [ly'tse:um], *n.* (—**s**, *pl.* **Lyzeen**) lyceum, grammar school *or* high school for girls.

M

M [ɛm], *n.* (—**s**, *pl.* —**s**) the letter *M*.
Maas [ma:s], *f.* River Meuse.
Maat [ma:t], *m.* (—**s**, *pl.* —**s**, —**en**) (*Naut.*) mate.
Mache ['maxə], *f.* (—, *no pl.*) put-up job, humbug, sham, eyewash.
machen ['maxən], *v.a.* make, do, produce, manufacture; cause; amount to; *mach schon*, be quick; *das macht nichts*, it does not matter; *mach's kurz*, cut it short; *etwas — lassen*, have s.th. made; *sich auf den Weg* —, set off; *sich viel (wenig) aus etwas* —, care much (little) for s.th.; *mach, daß du fortkommst!* get out! scram!
Macherlohn ['maxərlo:n], *m.* (—**es**, *pl.* ¨**e**) charge for making s.th.
Macht [maxt], *f.* (—, *pl.* ¨**e**) might, power; force, strength; authority; *mit aller* —, with might and main.
Machtbefugnis ['maxtbəfu:knɪs], *f.* (—, *pl.* —**se**) competence.
Machtgebot ['maxtgəbo:t], *n.* (—**s**, *pl.* —**e**) authoritative order.
Machthaber ['maxtha:bər], *m.* (—**s**, *pl.* —) potentate, ruler.
mächtig ['mɛçtɪç], *adj.* mighty, powerful; *einer Sache — sein*, to have mastered s.th.
machtlos ['maxtlo:s], *adj.* powerless.
Machtspruch ['maxtʃprux], *m.* (—**s**, *pl.* ¨**e**) authoritative dictum; command; decree.
Machtvollkommenheit ['maxtfɔlkɔmənhaɪt], *f.* (—, *pl.* —**en**) absolute power; sovereignty; *aus eigner* —, of o.'s own authority.
Machtwort ['maxtvɔrt], *n.* (—**es**, *pl.* —**e**) word of command, fiat; *ein — sprechen*, bring o.'s authority to bear, speak with authority.
Machwerk ['maxvɛrk], *n.* (—**s**, *pl.* —**e**) shoddy product; bad job; concoction; (*story*) pot-boiler.
Madagaskar [mada'gaskar], *n.* Madagascar.
Mädchen ['mɛ:tçən], *n.* (—**s**, *pl.* —) girl; (*servant*) maid; — *für alles*, maid-of-all-work.
mädchenhaft ['mɛ:tçənhaft], *adj.* girlish, maidenly.
Mädchenhandel ['mɛ:tçənhandəl], *m.* (—**s**, *no pl.*) white slave trade.
Made ['ma:də], *f.* (—, *pl.* —**n**) maggot, mite.
Mädel ['mɛ:dəl], *n.* (—**s**, *pl.* —) (*coll.*) *see* **Mädchen**.
madig ['ma:dɪç], *adj.* maggoty.
Magazin [maga'tsi:n], *n.* (—**s**, *pl.* —**e**) warehouse, storehouse; journal.
Magd [ma:kt], *f.* (—, *pl.* ¨**e**) maid, maidservant; (*Poet.*) maiden.
Magen ['ma:gən], *m.* (—**s**, *pl.* —) (*human*) stomach; (*animals*) maw.
Magengrube ['ma:gəngru:bə], *f.* (—, *pl.* —**n**) pit of the stomach.
Magensaft ['ma:gənzaft], *m.* (—**es**, *pl.* ¨**e**) gastric juice.
mager ['ma:gər], *adj.* lean, thin, slender, slim; (*fig.*) meagre.
Magerkeit ['ma:gərkaɪt], *f.* (—, *no pl.*) leanness, thinness, slenderness.
Magie [ma'gi:], *f.* (—, *no pl.*) magic.
Magier ['ma:gjər], *m.* (—**s**, *pl.* —) magician.
Magister [ma'gɪstər], *m.* (—**s**, *pl.* —) schoolmaster; (*Univ.*) Master; — *der freien Künste*, Master of Arts.
Magistrat [magɪs'tra:t], *m.* (—**s**, *pl.* —**e**) municipal board, local authority.
magnetisch [mag'ne:tɪʃ], *adj.* magnetic.
magnetisieren [magneti'zi:rən], *v.a.* magnetise.
Magnetismus [magne'tɪsmus], *m.* (—, *pl.* —**men**) magnetism; (*person*) mesmerism; *Lehre vom* —, magnetics.
Magnifizenz [magnifi'tsɛnts], *f.* (—, *pl.* —**en**) magnificence; *seine* —, (*Univ.*) title of Vice-Chancellor.
Mahagoni [maha'go:ni], *n.* (—**s**, *no pl.*) mahogany.
Mahd [ma:t], *f.* (—, *pl.* —**en**) mowing.
mähen ['mɛ:ən], *v.a.* mow.
Mäher ['mɛ:ər], *m.* (—**s**, *pl.* —) mower.
Mahl [ma:l], *n.* (—**s**, *pl.* —**e**, ¨**er**) meal, repast.
mahlen ['ma:lən], *v.a.* grind.
Mahlstrom ['ma:lʃtro:m], *m.* (—**s**, *no pl.*) maelstrom, whirlpool, eddy.
Mahlzahn ['ma:ltsa:n], *m.* (—**s**, *pl.* ¨**e**) molar, grinder.

Mahlzeit ['ma:ltsaɪt], *f.* (—, *pl.* **—en**) meal, repast.
Mähmaschine ['mɛ:maʃi:nə], *f.* (—, *pl.* **—n**) reaping-machine; lawn-mower.
Mähne ['mɛ:nə], *f.* (—, *pl.* **—n**) mane.
mahnen ['ma:nən], *v.a.* remind, admonish, warn; (*debtor*) demand payment, dun.
Mähre ['mɛ:rə], *f.* (—, *pl.* **—n**) mare.
Mähren ['mɛ:rən], *n.* Moravia.
Mai [maɪ], *m.* (**—s**, *pl.* **—e**) May.
Maid [maɪt], *f.* (—, *no pl.*) (*Poet.*) maiden.
Maiglöckchen ['maɪglœkçən], *n.* (**—s**, *pl.* —) (*Bot.*) lily of the valley.
Maikäfer ['maɪkɛ:fər], *m.* (**—s**, *pl.* —) (*Ent.*) cockchafer.
Mailand ['maɪlant], *n.* Milan.
Mais [maɪs], *m.* (**—es**, *no pl.*) (*Bot.*) maize, Indian corn.
Majestät [majɛs'tɛ:t], *f.* (—, *pl.* **—en**) majesty.
majestätisch [majes'tɛ:tiʃ], *adj.* majestic.
Major [ma'jo:r], *m.* (**—s**, *pl.* **—e**) (*Mil.*) major.
Majoran [majo'ra:n], *m.* (**—s**, *no pl.*) (*Bot.*) marjoram.
Majorat [majo'ra:t], *n.* (**—s**, *pl.* **—e**) primogeniture; entail.
majorenn [majo'rɛn], *adj.* (*obs.*) of age, over twenty-one.
Majorität [majori'tɛ:t], *f.* (—, *pl.* **—en**) majority.
Makel ['ma:kəl], *m.* (**—s**, *pl.* —) spot, blot; (*fig.*) blemish, flaw, defect.
Mäkelei [mɛ:kə'laɪ], *f.* (—, *pl.* **—en**) fault-finding, carping; fastidiousness.
makellos ['ma:kəllo:s], *adj.* spotless, immaculate.
mäkeln ['mɛ:kəln], *v.n.* find fault (with), cavil (at).
Makkabäer [maka'bɛ:ər], *m.* Maccabee.
Makler ['ma:klər], *m.* (**—s**, *pl.* —) broker.
Mäkler ['mɛ:klər], *m.* (**—s**, *pl.* —) fault-finder, caviller.
Maklergebühr ['ma:klərgəby:r], *f.* (—, *pl.* **—en**) brokerage.
Makrele [ma'kre:lə], *f.* (—, *pl.* **—n**) (*Zool.*) mackerel.
Makrone [ma'kro:nə], *f.* (—, *pl.* **—n**) macaroon.
Makulatur [makula'tu:r], *f.* (—, *no pl.*) waste paper.
Mal [ma:l], *n.* (**—s**, *pl.* **—e**) mark, sign, token; monument; mole, birthmark; stain; time; *dieses* —, this time, this once; *manches* —, sometimes; *mehrere* **—e**, several times; *mit einem* —, all of a sudden.
mal [ma:l], *adv.* & *part.* once; *noch* —, once more; (*coll.*) *hör* —, I say.
Malaya [ma'laɪa], *n.* Malaya.
malen ['ma:lən], *v.a.* paint.
Maler ['ma:lər], *m.* (**—s**, *pl.* —) painter.
Malerei [ma:lə'raɪ], *f.* (—, *pl.* **—en**) painting; picture.
malerisch ['ma:lərɪʃ], *adj.* picturesque.
Malerleinwand ['ma:lərlaɪnvant], *f.* (—, *no pl.*) canvas.
Malheur [ma'lø:r], *n.* (**—s**, *pl.* **—s**) misfortune, mishap.
Mali [ma:li] *n.* Mali.
maliziös [mali'tsjø:s], *adj.* malicious.
Malkasten ['ma:lkastən], *m.* (**—s**, *pl.* ¨) paint-box.
Malstein ['ma:lʃtaɪn], *m.* (**—s**, *pl.* **—e**) monument; boundary stone.
Malstock ['ma:lʃtɔk], *m.* (**—s**, *pl.* ¨**e**) maulstick, mahlstick.
Malteserorden [mal'te:zərɔrdən], *m.* (**—s**, *no pl.*) Order of the Knights of Malta.
malträtieren [maltrɛ'ti:rən], *v.a.* ill-treat.
Malve ['malvə], *f.* (—, *pl.* **—n**) (*Bot.*) mallow.
Malz [malts], *n.* (**—es**, *no pl.*) malt; *an ihm ist Hopfen und — verloren*, he is hopeless.
Malzbonbon ['maltsbɔ̃bɔ̃], *m.* (**—s**, *pl.* **—s**) cough-lozenge, malt drop.
Mälzer ['mɛltsər], *m.* (**—s**, *pl.* —) maltster.
Mama [ma'ma:], *f.* (—, *pl.* **—s**) (*fam.*) mummy, mum, (*Am.*) ma.
Mammon ['mamɔn], *m.* (**—s**, *no pl.*) mammon; *schnöder* —, filthy lucre.
Mammut ['mamut], *n.* (**—s**, *pl.* **—e**) mammoth.
Mamsell [mam'zɛl], *f.* (—, *pl.* **—en**) housekeeper.
man [man], *indef. pron.* one, they, people, men; — *sagt*, they say.
manch [manç], *pron.* (**—er**, **—e**, **—es**) many a, some, several.
mancherlei [mançər'laɪ], *adj.* several; of several kinds.
Manchester [man'çɛstər], *m.* (**—s**, *no pl.*) corduroy.
manchmal ['mançma:l], *adv.* sometimes.
Mandant [man'dant], *m.* (**—en**, *pl.* **—en**) client.
Mandantin [man'dantin], *f.* (—, *pl.* **—innen**) female client.
Mandarine [manda'ri:nə], *f.* (—, *pl.* **—n**) mandarin (orange), tangerine.
Mandat [man'da:t], *n.* (**—s**, *pl.* **—e**) mandate.
Mandel ['mandəl], *f.* (—, *pl.* **—n**) almond; (*Anat.*) tonsil; (*quantity*) fifteen; *eine — Eier*, fifteen eggs.
Mandoline [mando'li:nə], *f.* (—, *pl.* **—n**) mandolin.
Mangan [maŋ'ga:n], *n.* (**—s**, *no pl.*) (*Chem.*) manganese.
Mangel (1) ['maŋəl], *f.* (—, *pl.* **—n**) mangle, wringer.
Mangel (2) ['maŋəl], *m.* (**—s**, *pl.* ¨) deficiency, defect; blemish; lack, shortage, want; *aus — an*, for want of; — *haben an*, be short of, lack(s.th.).
mangelhaft ['maŋəlhaft], *adj.* defective, imperfect.
mangeln (1) ['maŋəln], *v.a.* (*laundry*) mangle.

mangeln (2) ['mangəln], *v.n.* be in want of, be short of; *es —t uns an . . .*, we lack . . . .
mangels ['maŋəls], *prep.* (*Genit.*) for lack of, for want of.
Mangold ['maŋɔlt], *m.* (**—s**, *no pl.*) (*Bot.*) beet, mangel-wurzel.
Manie [ma'ni:], *f.* (**—**, *pl.* **—n**) mania, craze.
Manier [ma'ni:r], *f.* (**—**, *pl.* **—en**) manner, habit; *gute —en haben*, have good manners.
manieriert [mani'ri:rt], *adj.* affected; (*Art*) mannered.
manierlich [ma'ni:rlɪç], *adj.* well behaved, civil, polite.
manipulieren [manipu'li:rən], *v.a.* manipulate.
Manko ['maŋko:], *n.* (**—s**, *pl.* **—s**) deficit, deficiency.
Mann [man], *m.* (**—(e)s**, *pl.* **¨er**, (*Poet.*) **—en**) man; husband; *etwas an den — bringen*, get s.th. off o.'s hands, dispose of s.th.; *seinen — stellen*, hold o.'s own; *bis auf den letzten —*, to a man.
Mannbarkeit ['manba:rkaɪt], *f.* (**—**, *no pl.*) puberty; marriageable age.
Männchen ['mɛnçən], *n.* (**—s**, *pl.* **—**) little man, manikin; (*Zool.*) male; *mein —*, (*coll.*) my hubby; *— machen*, (*dogs*) sit on the hindlegs, beg.
mannhaft ['manhaft], *adj.* manly, stout, valiant.
mannigfaltig ['manɪçfaltɪç], *adj.* manifold, multifarious.
männlich ['mɛnlɪç], *adj.* male; (*fig.*) manly; (*Gram.*) masculine.
Mannsbild ['mansbɪlt], *n.* (**—es**, *pl.* **—er**) (*coll.*) man, male person.
Mannschaft ['manʃaft], *f.* (**—**, *pl.* **—en**) men; crew, team.
mannstoll ['manstɔl], *adj.* man-mad.
Mannszucht ['manstsuxt], *f.* (**—**, *no pl.*) discipline.
Manöver [ma'nø:vər], *n.* (**—s**, *pl.* **—**) manoeuvre.
manövrieren [manø'vri:rən], *v.a.* manoeuvre.
Mansarde [man'zardə], *f.* (**—**, *pl.* **—n**) garret, attic.
manschen ['manʃən], *v.a.*, *v.n.* dabble; splash (about).
Manschette [man'ʃɛtə], *f.* (**—**, *pl.* **—n**) cuff.
Mantel ['mantəl], *m.* (**—s**, *pl.* **¨**) cloak, overcoat, coat, mantle, wrap; *den — nach dem Winde hängen*, be a timeserver.
Manufaktur [manufak'tu:r], *f.* (**—**, *pl.* **—en**) manufacture.
Mappe ['mapə], *f.* (**—**, *pl.* **—n**) portfolio, case, file.
Mär [mɛ:r], *f.* (**—**, *pl.* **—en**) (*Poet.*) tale, tidings, legend.
Märchen ['mɛ:rçən], *n.* (**—s**, *pl.* **—**) fairy-tale, fable; fib.
märchenhaft ['mɛ:rçənhaft], *adj.* fabulous, legendary; (*coll.*) marvellous.
Marder ['mardər], *m.* (**—s**, *pl.* **—**) (*Zool.*) marten.
Maria [ma'ri:a], *f.* Mary; *die Jungfrau —*, the Virgin Mary.
Marienbild [ma'ri:ənbɪlt], *n.* (**—es**, *pl.* **—er**) image of the Virgin Mary.
Marienblume [ma'ri:ənblu:mə], *f.* (**—**, *pl.* **—n**) (*Bot.*) daisy.
Marienglas [ma'ri:ənglas], *n.* (**—es**, *no pl.*) mica.
Marienkäfer [ma'ri:ənkɛ:fər], *m.* (**—s**, *pl.* **—**) (*Ent.*) lady-bird.
Marine [ma'ri:nə], *f.* (**—**, *pl.* **—n**) navy.
marinieren [mari'ni:rən], *v.a.* pickle.
Marionette [mario'nɛtə], *f.* (**—**, *pl.* **—n**) puppet, marionette.
Mark (1) [mark], *n.* (**—s**, *no pl.*) (*bone*) marrow; (*fruit*) pith, pulp.
Mark (2) [mark], *f.* (**—**, *pl.* **—en**) boundary, frontier province.
Mark (3) [mark], *f.* (**—**, *pl.* **—**) (*coin*) mark.
markant [mar'kant], *adj.* striking, prominent; (*remark*) pithy.
Marke ['markə], *f.* (**—**, *pl.* **—n**) (*trade*) mark, brand; (*postage*) stamp; (*game*) counter.
markieren [mar'ki:rən], *v.a.* mark.
markig ['markɪç], *adj.* marrowlike; (*fig.*) pithy, strong.
Markise [mar'ki:zə], *f.* (**—**, *pl.* **—n**) (sun)blind, awning.
Markt [markt], *m.* (**—es**, *pl.* **¨e**) market, market-square, fair.
Marktflecken ['marktflɛkən], *m.* (**—s**, *pl.* **—**) borough; (small) market town.
Marktschreier ['marktʃraɪər], *m.* (**—s**, *pl.* **—**) cheap-jack, quack, charlatan.
Markus ['markus], *m.* Mark.
Marmel ['marməl], *f.* (**—**, *pl.* **—n**) (*obs.*) marble.
Marmelade [marmə'la:də], *f.* (**—**, *pl.* **—n**) marmalade, jam.
Marmor ['marmɔr], *m.* (**—s**, *no pl.*) marble.
Marokko [ma'rɔko], *n.* Morocco.
Marone [ma'ro:nə], *f.* (**—**, *pl.* **—n**) sweet chestnut.
Maroquin [maro'kɛ̃], *n.* (**—s**, *no pl.*) Morocco leather.
Marotte [ma'rɔtə], *f.* (**—**, *pl.* **—n**) whim; fad.
Marquise [mar'ki:zə], *f.* (**—**, *pl.* **—n**) marchioness.
Marsch (1) [marʃ], *m.* (**—es**, *pl.* **¨e**) march; *sich in — setzen*, set out; march off.
Marsch (2) [marʃ], *f.* (**—**, *pl.* **—en**) fen, marsh.
marsch! [marʃ], *int.* march! be off! get out!
Marschboden ['marʃbo:dən], *m.* (**—s**, *no pl.*) marshy soil, marshland.
marschieren [mar'ʃi:rən], *v.n.* (*aux.* sein) march.
Marstall ['marʃtal], *m.* (**—s**, *pl.* **¨e**) royal stud.
Marter ['martər], *f.* (**—**, *pl.* **—n** torture, torment.

martern ['martərn], *v.a.* torture, torment.
Märtyrer ['mɛrtyrər], *m.* (—**s**, *pl.* —) martyr.
Martyrium [mar'ty:rjum], *n.* (—**s**, *pl.* —**rien**) martyrdom.
März [mɛrts], *m.* (—**es**, *pl.* —**e**) (*month*) March.
Masche ['maʃə], *f.* (—, *pl.* —**n**) mesh; (*knitting*) stitch; (*dial.*) bow tie; (*coll.*) racket.
Maschine [ma'ʃi:nə], *f.* (—, *pl.* —**n**) machine; engine; *mit der — geschrieben*, typewritten.
Maschinengarn [ma'ʃi:nəngarn], *n.* (—**s**, *no pl.*) twist.
Maschinerie [maʃinə'ri:], *f.* (—, *pl.* —**en**) machinery.
Maser ['ma:zər], *f.* (—, *pl.* —**n**) (*wood*) vein, streak.
Masern ['ma:zərn], *f. pl.* measles.
Maske ['maskə], *f.* (—, *pl.* —**n**) mask, visor.
Maskerade [maskə'ra:də], *f.* (—, *pl.* —**n**) masquerade.
maskieren [mas'ki:rən], *v.a.* mask. — *v.r. sich* —, put on a mask.
Maß (1) [ma:s], *n.* (—**es**, *pl.* —**e**) measure, size; moderation, propriety; degree, extent; proportion; — *halten*, be moderate; *einem — nehmen*, measure s.o. (for); *in starkem* —, to a high degree; *mit* —, in moderation; *nach* —, to measure; *ohne — und Ziel*, immoderately, with no holds barred; *über alle* —*en*, exceedingly.
Maß (2) [ma:s], *m.* & *f.* (—, *pl.* —**e**) (*drink*) quart.
massakrieren [masa'kri:rən], *v.a.* massacre, slaughter.
Maßarbeit ['ma:sarbaɪt], *f.* (—, *pl.* —**en**) (work) made to measure; bespoke tailoring.
Masse ['masə], *f.* (—, *pl.* —**n**) mass, bulk; multitude; *eine* —, a lot.
Maßeinheit ['ma:saɪnhaɪt], *f.* (—, *pl.* —**n**) measuring-unit.
massenhaft ['masənhaft], *adj.* abundant.
Maßgabe ['ma:sga:bə], *f.* (—, *pl.* —**n**) *nach* —, according to, in proportion to.
maßgebend ['ma:sge:bənt], *adj.* standard; (*fig.*) authoritative.
massieren [ma'si:rən], *v.a.* massage.
mäßig ['mɛ:sɪç], *adj.* moderate, temperate, frugal.
Mäßigkeit ['mɛ:sɪçkaɪt], *f.* (—, *no pl.*) moderation, temperance, frugality.
Mäßigung ['mɛ:sɪguŋ], *f.* (—, *no pl.*) moderation.
Massiv [ma'si:f], *n.* (—**s**, *pl.* —**e**) (*mountains*) massif, range.
Maßliebchen ['ma:sli:pçən], *n.* (—**s**, *pl.* —) (*Bot.*) daisy.
maßlos ['ma:slo:s], *adj.* immoderate; (*fig.*) extravagant.
Maßnahme ['ma:sna:mə], *f.* (—, *pl.* —**n**) measure; —*n ergreifen*, take steps.
Maßregel ['ma:sre:gəl], *f.* (—, *pl.* —**n**) measure.
maßregeln ['ma:sre:gəln], *v.a.* reprove, reprimand.
Maßstab ['ma:sʃta:p], *m.* (—**es**, *pl.* ⸚**e**) standard; (*maps*) scale; *in kleinem* (*großem*) —, on a small (large) scale.
maßvoll ['ma:sfɔl], *adj.* moderate.
Mast (1) [mast], *m.* (—**es**, *pl.* —**e**) mast; pylon.
Mast (2) [mast], *f.* (—, *no pl.*) fattening.
Mastbaum ['mastbaum], *m.* (—**s**, *pl.* ⸚**e**) mast.
Mastdarm ['mastdarm], *m.* (—**s**, *pl.* ⸚**e**) rectum.
mästen ['mɛstən], *v.a.* feed, fatten.
Mastkorb ['mastkɔrp], *m.* (—**s**, *pl.* ⸚**e**) masthead.
Mästung ['mɛstuŋ], *f.* (—, *no pl.*) fattening, cramming.
Materialwaren [mate'rjalva:rən], *f. pl.* groceries; household goods.
materiell [mate'rjɛl], *adj.* material, real; materialistic.
Mathematik [matema'ti:k], *f.* (—, *no pl.*) mathematics.
mathematisch [mate'ma:tɪʃ], *adj.* mathematical.
Matratze [ma'tratsə], *f.* (—, *pl.* —**n**) mattress.
Matrikel [ma'tri:kəl], *f.* (—, *pl.* —**n**) register, roll.
Matrize [ma'tri:tsə], *f.* (—, *pl.* —**n**) matrix, die, stencil.
Matrose [ma'tro:zə], *m.* (—**n**, *pl.* —**n**) sailor, seaman.
Matsch [matʃ], *m.* (—**es**, *no pl.*) slush; mud.
matt [mat], *adj.* tired, exhausted, spent; languid; weak, feeble; (*light*) dim; (*gold*) dull; (*silver*) tarnished; (*Chess*) (check-)mate; — *setzen*, (*Chess*) to (check-)mate.
Matte ['matə], *f.* (—, *pl.* —**n**) mat, matting.
Matthäus [ma'tɛ:us], *m.* Matthew.
Mattheit ['mathaɪt], *f.* (—, *no pl.*) tiredness, exhaustion, languor, feebleness; (*light*) dimness; (*gold*) dullness.
mattherzig ['mathɛrtsɪç], *adj.* poor-spirited, faint-hearted.
Matura [ma'tu:ra], *f.* (—, *pl.* —**en**) (*Austr.*) school-leaving *or* matriculation examination.
Mätzchen ['mɛtsçən], *n.* (—**s**, *pl.* —) nonsense; trick; *mach keine* —, don't be silly.
Mauer ['mauər], *f.* (—, *pl.* —**n**) wall.
Mauerkelle ['mauərkɛlə], *f.* (—, *pl.* —**n**) trowel.
mauern ['mauərn], *v.a.* build. — *v.n.* lay bricks, construct a wall.
Mauerwerk ['mauərvɛrk], *n.* (—**s**, *no pl.*) brick-work.
Maul [maul], *n.* (—**es**, *pl.* ⸚**er**) (*animals*) mouth, muzzle; (*vulg.*) mouth; *das — halten*, shut up, hold o.'s tongue; *ein loses — haben*, have a loose tongue; *nicht aufs — gefallen sein*, have a quick tongue; (*vulg.*) *halt's* —, shut up.

Maulaffe ['maulafə], *m.* (—**n**, *pl.* —**n**) booby; —*n feilhalten*, stand gaping.
Maulbeere ['maulbe:rə], *f.* (—, *pl.* —**n**) (*Bot.*) mulberry.
maulen ['maulən], *v.n.* pout, sulk.
Maulesel ['maule:zəl], *m.* (—**s**, *pl.* —) (*Zool.*) mule.
maulfaul ['maulfaul], *adj.* tongue-tied; taciturn.
Maulheld ['maulhɛlt], *m.* (—**en** *pl.* —**en**) braggart.
Maulkorb ['maulkɔrp], *m.* (—**s**, *pl.* ⸚**e**) muzzle.
Maulschelle ['maulʃɛlə], *f.* (—, *pl.* —**n**) box on the ear.
Maultier ['maulti:r], *n.* (—**s**, *pl.* —**e**) (*Zool.*) mule.
Maulwerk ['maulvɛrk], *n.* (—**s**, *no pl.*) *ein großes — haben*, (*coll.*) have the gift of the gab.
Maulwurf ['maulvurf], *m.* (—**s**, *pl.* ⸚**e**) (*Zool.*) mole.
Maurer ['maurər], *m.* (—**s**, *pl.* —) mason, bricklayer.
Maus [maus], *f.* (—, *pl.* ⸚**e**) mouse.
Mausefalle ['mauzəfalə], *f.* (—, *pl.* —**n**) mouse-trap.
mausen ['mauzən], *v.n.* catch mice. — *v.a.* (*fig.*) pilfer, pinch.
Mauser ['mauzər], *f.* (—, *no pl.*) moulting.
mausern ['mauzərn], *v.r. sich* —, moult.
mausetot ['mauzəto:t], *adj.* dead as a door-nail.
mausig ['mauzɪç], *adj. sich — machen*, put on airs.
Maxime [mak'si:mə], *f.* (—, *pl.* —**n**) maxim, motto, device.
Mazedonien [matsə'do:njən], *n.* Macedonia.
Mäzen [mɛ:'tse:n], *m.* (—**s**, *pl.* —**e**) patron of the arts, Maecenas.
Mechanik [me'ça:nɪk], *f.* (—, *no pl.*) mechanics.
Mechaniker [me'ça:nɪkər], *m.* (—**s**, *pl.* —) mechanic.
mechanisch [me'ça:nɪʃ], *adj.* mechanical.
meckern ['mɛkərn], *v.n.* bleat; (*fig.*) grumble, complain.
Medaille [me'daljə], *f.* (—, *pl.* —**n**) medal.
Medaillon [medal'jɔ̃], *n.* (—**s**, *pl.* —**s**) locket.
meditieren [medi'ti:rən], *v.n.* meditate.
Medizin [medi'tsi:n], *f.* (—, *pl.* —**en**) medicine, physic.
Mediziner [medi'tsi:nər], *m.* (—**s**, *pl.* —) physician, medical practitioner, student of medicine.
medizinisch [medi'tsi:nɪʃ], *adj.* medical, medicinal.
Meer [me:r], *n.* (—**es**, *pl.* —**e**) sea, ocean; *offnes* —, high seas; *am* —, at the seaside; *auf dem* —, at sea; *übers* —, overseas.
Meerbusen ['me:rbu:zən], *m.* (—**s**, *pl.* —) bay, gulf, bight.
Meerenge ['me:rɛŋə], *f.* (—, *pl.* —**n**) straits.
Meeresspiegel ['me:rəsʃpi:gəl], *m.* (—**s**, *no pl.*) sea-level.
Meerkatze ['me:rkatsə], *f.* (—, *pl.* —**n**) long-tailed monkey.
Meerrettich ['me:rrɛtɪç], *m.* (—**s**, *pl.* —**e**) (*Bot.*) horse-radish.
Meerschaum ['me:rʃaum], *m.* (—**s**, *no pl.*) sea-foam; (*pipe*) meerschaum.
Meerschwein ['me:rʃvaɪn], *n.* (—**s**, *pl.* —**e**) (*Zool.*) porpoise.
Meerschweinchen ['me:rʃvaɪnçən], *n.* (—**s**, *pl.* —) (*Zool.*) guinea-pig.
Mehl [me:l], *n.* (—**es**, *no pl.*) flour; meal; dust, powder.
Mehlkleister ['me:lklaɪstər], *m.* (—**s**, *no pl.*) flour paste.
Mehlspeise ['me:lʃpaɪzə], *f.* (—, *pl.* —**n**) (*dial.*) pudding, sweet.
mehr [me:r], *indecl. adj.*, *adv.* more; *umso* —, all the more; *immer* —, more and more; — *als genug*, enough and to spare.
Mehrbetrag ['me:rbətra:k], *m.* (—**s**, *pl.* ⸚**e**) surplus.
mehrdeutig ['me:rdɔytɪç], *adj.* ambiguous.
mehren ['me:rən], *v.r. sich* —, multiply, increase in numbers.
mehrere ['me:rərə], *pl. adj.* several.
mehrfach ['me:rfax], *adj.* repeated.
Mehrheit ['me:rhaɪt], *f.* (—, *pl.* —**en**) majority.
mehrmals ['me:rma:ls], *adv.* several times.
Mehrzahl ['me:rtsa:l], *f.* (—, *no pl.*) (*Gram.*) plural; majority, bulk.
meiden ['maɪdən], *v.a. irr.* shun, avoid.
Meierei [maɪə'raɪ], *f.* (—, *pl.* —**en**) (*dairy*) farm.
Meile ['maɪlə], *f.* (—, *pl.* —**n**) mile; league.
Meiler ['maɪlər], *m.* (—**s**, *pl.* —) charcoal-kiln, charcoal-pile.
mein(e) ['maɪn(ə)], *poss. adj.* my. —*poss. pron.* mine.
Meineid ['maɪnaɪt], *m.* (—**s**, *pl.* —**e**) perjury; *einen — schwören*, perjure o.s.
meineidig ['maɪnaɪdɪç], *adj.* perjured, forsworn.
meinen ['maɪnən], *v.a.* mean, intend, think.
meinerseits ['maɪnərzaɪts], *adv.* I, for my part.
meinethalben ['maɪnəthalbən], *adv.* on my account, speaking for myself, for my sake; I don't care, I don't mind.
meinetwegen ['maɪnətve:gən], *adv.* *see* **meinethalben**.
meinetwillen ['maɪnətvɪlən], *adv.* *um* —, for my sake, on my behalf.
meinige ['maɪnɪgə], *poss. pron.* mine.
Meinung ['maɪnuŋ], *f.* (—, *pl.* —**en**) opinion; meaning; notion; *öffentliche* —, public opinion; *der — sein*, be of the opinion, hold the opinion; *einem die — sagen*, give s.o. a piece of o.'s mind; *meiner — nach*, in my opinion.

Meinungsverschiedenheit ['maɪnuŋsfɛrʃi:dənhaɪt], *f.* (—, *pl.* **—en**) difference of opinion, disagreement.
Meise ['maɪzə], *f.* (—, *pl.* **—n**) (*Orn.*) titmouse.
Meißel ['maɪsəl], *m.* (**—s**, *pl.* —) chisel.
meißeln ['maɪsəln], *v.a.* chisel, sculpt.
meist [maɪst], *adj.* most. — *adv.* usually, generally.
meistens ['maɪstəns], *adv.* mostly.
Meister ['maɪstər], *m.* (**—s**, *pl.* —) (*craft*) master; (*sport*) champion; *seinen — finden*, meet o.'s match.
meisterhaft ['maɪstərhaft], *adj.* masterly.
meisterlich ['maɪstərlɪç], *adj.* masterly.
meistern ['maɪstərn], *v.a.* master.
Meisterschaft ['maɪstərʃaft], *f.* (—, *pl.* **—en**) mastery; (*sport*) championship.
Mekka ['mɛka], *n.* Mecca.
Meldeamt ['mɛldəamt], *n.* (**—s**, *pl.* **¨er**) registration office.
melden ['mɛldən], *v.a.* announce, inform, notify; (*Mil.*) report. — *v.r. sich* —, answer the phone; *sich — lassen*, send in o.'s name, have o.s. announced; *sich zu etwas* —, apply for s.th.
Meldezettel ['mɛldətsɛtəl], *m.* (**—s**, *pl.* —) registration form.
meliert [me'li:rt], *adj.* mixed; (*hair*) iron grey, streaked with grey.
melken ['mɛlkən], *v.a. irr.* milk.
Melodie [melo'di:], *f.* (—, *pl.* **—n**) melody, tune.
Melone [me'lo:nə], *f.* (—, *pl.* **—n**) (*Bot.*) melon; (*coll.*) bowler hat.
Meltau ['me:ltau], *m.* (**—s**, *no pl.*) mildew.
Membrane [mɛm'bra:nə], *f.* (—, *pl.* **—n**) membrane, diaphragm.
Memme ['mɛmə], *f.* (—, *pl.* **—n**) coward, poltroon.
memorieren [memo'ri:rən], *v.a.* memorise, learn by heart.
Menage [me'na:ʒə], *f.* (—, *pl.* **—n**) household.
Menge ['mɛŋə], *f.* (—, *pl.* **—n**) quantity, amount; multitude, crowd; *eine* —, a lot.
mengen ['mɛŋən], *v.a.* mix. — *v.r. sich — in*, interfere in.
Mensch (1) [mɛnʃ], *m.* (**—en**, *pl.* **—en**) human being; man; person; *kein* —, nobody.
Mensch (2) [mɛnʃ], *n.* (**—es**, *pl.* **—er**) (*vulg.*) wench.
Menschenfeind ['mɛnʃənfaɪnt], *m.* (**—es**, *pl.* **—e**) misanthropist.
Menschenfreund ['mɛnʃənfrɔynt], *m.* (**—es**, *pl.* **—e**) philanthropist.
Menschengedenken ['mɛnʃəngədɛŋkən], *n.* (**—s**, *no pl.*) *seit* —, from time immemorial.
Menschenhandel ['mɛnʃənhandəl], *m.* (**—s**, *no pl.*) slave-trade.
Menschenkenner ['mɛnʃənkɛnər], *m.* (**—s**, *pl.* —) judge of character.
Menschenmenge ['mɛnʃənmɛŋə], *f.* (—, *no pl.*) crowd.
Menschenraub ['mɛnʃənraup], *m.* (**—s**, *no pl.*) kidnapping.
Menschenverstand ['mɛnʃənfɛrʃtant], *m.* (**—es**, *no pl.*) human understanding; *gesunder* —, commonsense.
Menschheit ['mɛnʃhaɪt], *f.* (—, *no pl.*) mankind, human race.
menschlich ['mɛnʃlɪç], *adj.* human.
Menschwerdung ['mɛnʃverduŋ], *f.* (—, *no pl.*) incarnation.
Mensur [mɛn'zu:r], *f.* (—, *pl.* **—en**) students' duel.
Mergel ['mɛrgəl], *m.* (**—s**, *no pl.*) marl.
merkbar ['mɛrkba:r], *adj.* perceptible, noticeable.
merken ['mɛrkən], *v.a.* note, perceive, observe, notice; *sich etwas* —, bear in mind; *sich nichts — lassen*, show no sign.
merklich ['mɛrklɪç], *adj.* perceptible, appreciable.
Merkmal ['mɛrkma:l], *n.* (**—s**, *pl.* **—e**) mark, characteristic, feature.
merkwürdig ['mɛrkvyrdɪç], *adj.* remarkable, curious, strange.
Merle ['mɛrlə], *f.* (—, *pl.* **—n**) (*dial.*) blackbird.
Mesner ['mɛsnər], *m.* (**—s**, *pl.* —) sexton, sacristan.
meßbar ['mɛsba:r], *adj.* measurable.
Meßbuch ['mɛsbu:x], *n.* (**—es**, *pl.* **¨er**) missal.
Messe ['mɛsə], *f.* (—, *pl.* **—n**) (*Eccl.*) Mass; *stille* —, Low Mass; (*Comm.*) fair; (*Mil.*) mess.
messen ['mɛsən], *v.a. irr.* measure, gauge. — *v.r. sich mit einem* —, pit oneself against s.o.
Messer (1) ['mɛsər], *m.* (**—s**, *pl.* —) gauge, meter.
Messer (2) ['mɛsər], *n.* (**—s**, *pl.* —) knife.
Messerheld ['mɛsərhɛlt], *m.* (**—en**, *pl.* **—en**) cut-throat, hooligan, rowdy.
Messias [mɛ'si:as], *m.* Messiah.
Meßgewand ['mɛsgəvant], *n.* (**—es**, *pl.* **¨er**) chasuble, vestment.
Meßkunst ['mɛskunst], *f.* (—, *no pl.*) surveying.
Messing ['mɛsɪŋ], *n.* (**—s**, *no pl.*) brass; *aus* —, brazen.
Metall [me'tal], *n.* (**—s**, *pl.* **—e**) metal; *unedle —e*, base metals.
Metallkunde [me'talkundə], *f.* (—, *no pl.*) metallurgy.
meteorologisch [meteoro'lo:gɪʃ], *adj.* meteorological.
Meter ['me:tər], *n. & m.* (**—s**, *pl.* —) (*linear measure*) metre; (*Am.*) meter; (*Poet.*) metre.
methodisch [me'to:dɪʃ], *adj.* methodical.
Metrik ['me:trɪk], *f.* (—, *no pl.*) prosody, versification.
Mette ['mɛtə], *f.* (—, *pl.* **—n**) (*Eccl.*) matins.

Metze ['mɛtsə], *f.* (—, *pl.* **—n**) (*obs.*) prostitute.
Metzelei [mɛtsə'laɪ], *f.* (—, *pl.* **—en**) slaughter, massacre.
metzeln ['mɛtsəln], *v.a.* massacre, butcher.
Metzger ['mɛtsgər], *m.* (**—s**, *pl.* —) butcher.
Meuchelmörder ['mɔyçəlmœrdər], *m.* (**—s**, *pl.* —) assassin.
meucheln ['mɔyçəln], *v.a.* assassinate.
meuchlings ['mɔyçlɪŋs], *adv.* treacherously, insidiously.
Meute ['mɔytə], *f.* (—, *pl.* **—n**) pack of hounds; (*fig.*) gang.
Meuterei [mɔytə'raɪ], *f.* (—, *pl.* **—en**) mutiny, sedition.
meutern ['mɔytərn], *v.n.* mutiny.
Mezzanin ['mɛtsanɪn], *n.* (**—s**, *pl.* **—e**) half-storey, mezzanine.
miauen [mi'auən], *v.n.* mew.
mich [mɪç], *pers. pron.* me, myself.
Michaeli(s) [mɪça'e:li(s)], *n.* Michaelmas.
Michel ['mɪçəl], *m.* Michael; *deutscher* —, plain honest German.
Mieder ['mi:dər], *n.* (**—s**, *pl.* —) bodice.
Miene ['mi:nə], *f.* (—, *pl.* **—n**) mien, air; (facial) expression.
Miete ['mi:tə], *f.* (—, *pl.* **—n**) rent; hire; (*corn*) rick, stack.
mieten ['mi:tən], *v.a.* rent, hire.
Mieter ['mi:tər], *m.* (**—s**, *pl.* —) tenant, lodger.
Mietskaserne ['mi:tskazɛrnə], *f.* (—, *pl.* **—en**) tenement house.
Mietszins ['mi:tstsɪns], *m.* (**—es**, *pl.* **—e**) rent.
Milbe ['mɪlbə], *f.* (—, *pl.* **—n**) mite.
Milch [mɪlç], *f.* (—, *no pl.*) milk; (*fish*) soft roe; *abgerahmte* —, skim(med) milk; *geronnene* —, curdled milk.
Milchbart ['mɪlçba:rt], *m.* (**—s**, *pl.* **⸚e**) milksop.
Milchbruder ['mɪlçbru:dər], *m.* (**—s**, *pl.* ⸚) foster-brother.
milchen ['mɪlçən], *v.n.* yield milk.
Milcher ['mɪlçer], *m.* (**—s**, *pl.* —) (*fish*) milter.
Milchgesicht ['mɪlçgəzɪçt], *n.* (**—s**, *pl.* **—er**) baby face; smooth complexion.
Milchglas ['mɪlçglas], *n.* (**—es**, *no pl.*) opalescent glass, frosted glass.
Milchstraße ['mɪlçʃtra:sə], *f.* (—, *no pl.*) Milky Way.
Milde ['mɪldə], *f.* (—, *no pl.*) mildness, softness; (*fig.*) gentleness, (*rare*) charity, generosity.
mildern ['mɪldərn], *v.a.* soften, alleviate, mitigate, soothe, allay; *—de Umstände*, extenuating circumstances.
Milderung ['mɪldəruŋ], *f.* (—, *pl.* **—en**) mitigation, moderation; soothing.
mildtätig ['mɪlttɛ:tɪç], *adj.* charitable, benevolent, munificent.
Militär [mili'tɛ:r], *n.* (**—s**, *no pl.* military, army; *beim — sein*, serve in the army.
Miliz [mi'li:ts], *f.* (—, *no pl.*) militia.
Milliarde [mɪl'jardə], *f.* (—, *pl.* **—n**) a thousand millions; (*Am.*) billion.
Million [mɪl'jo:n], *f.* (—, *pl.* **—en**) million.
Millionär [mɪljo'nɛ:r], *m.* (**—s**, *pl.* **—e**) millionaire.
Milz [mɪlts], *f.* (—, *pl.* **—en**) spleen.
Mime ['mi:mə], *m.* (**—n**, *pl.* **—n**) mime, actor.
Mimik ['mi:mɪk], *f.* (—, *no pl.*) mime, miming.
Mimiker ['mi:mɪkər], *m.* (**—s**, *pl.* —) mimic.
Mimose [mi'mo:zə], *f.* (—, *pl.* **—n**) (*Bot.*) mimosa.
minder ['mɪndər], *adj.* lesser, smaller, minor, inferior.
Minderheit ['mɪndərhaɪt], *f.* (—, *pl.* **—en**) minority.
minderjährig ['mɪndərjɛ:rɪç], *adj.* (*Law*) under age.
mindern ['mɪndərn], *v.a.* diminish, lessen.
minderwertig ['mɪndərvertɪç], *adj.* inferior, of poor quality.
Minderwertigkeitskomplex ['mɪndərvertɪçkaɪtskɔmplɛks], *m.* (**—es**, *pl.* **—e**) inferiority complex.
mindest ['mɪndəst], *adj.* least, smallest, minimum, lowest; *nicht im —en*, not in the least, not at all.
mindestens ['mɪndəstəns], *adv.* at least.
Mine ['mi:nə], *f.* (—, *pl.* **—n**) mine; (*ball point pen*) refill; (*pencil*) lead.
minimal [mini'ma:l], *adj.* infinitesimal, minimum.
Ministerialrat [minister'ja:lra:t], *m.* (**—s**, *pl.* **⸚e**) senior civil servant.
ministeriell [mɪnɪster'jɛl], *adj.* ministerial.
Ministerium [mini'ste:rjum], *n.* (**—s**, *pl.* **—rien**) ministry.
Ministerpräsident [mi'nɪstərprɛ:zidɛnt], *m.* (**—en**, *pl.* **—en**) prime minister; premier.
Ministerrat [mi'nɪstərra:t], *m.* (**—s**, *pl.* **⸚e**) cabinet, council of ministers.
Ministrant [mini'strant], *m.* (**—en**, *pl.* **—en**) acolyte; sacristan.
Minne ['mɪnə], *f.* (—, *no pl.*) (*obs., Poet.*) love.
Minnesänger [mɪnə'zɛŋər], *m.* (**—s**, *pl.* —) minnesinger; troubadour, minstrel.
Minus ['mi:nus], *n.* (—, *no pl.*) deficit.
Minze ['mɪntsə], *f.* (—, *pl.* **—n**) (*Bot.*) mint.
mir [mi:r], *pers. pron.* to me.
Mirakel [mi'ra:kəl], *n.* (**—s**, *pl.* —) miracle, marvel, wonder.
mischen ['mɪʃən], *v.a.* mix; (*Cards*) shuffle; (*coffee, tea*) blend.
Mischling ['mɪʃlɪŋ], *m.* (**—s**, *pl.* **—e**) mongrel, hybrid.

Mischrasse ['mɪʃrasə], *f.* (—, *pl.* —**n**) cross-breed.
Mischung ['mɪʃuŋ], *f.* (—, *pl.* —**en**) mixture, blend.
Misere [mi'ze:rə], *f.* (—, *no pl.*) unhappiness, misery.
Mispel ['mɪspəl], *f.* (—, *pl.* —**n**) (*Bot.*) medlar (tree).
mißachten [mɪs'axtən], *v.a.* disregard, despise.
mißarten [mɪs'a:rtən], *v.n.* (*aux.* sein) degenerate.
Mißbehagen ['mɪsbəha:gən], *n.* (—**s**, *no pl.*) displeasure, uneasiness.
mißbilligen [mɪs'bɪlɪgən], *v.a.* object (to), disapprove (of).
Mißbrauch ['mɪsbraux], *m.* (—**s**, *pl.* ⸗**e**) abuse, misuse.
missen ['mɪsən], *v.a.* lack, be without, feel the lack of.
Missetat ['mɪsəta:t], *f.* (—, *pl.* —**en**) misdeed, felony.
mißfallen [mɪs'falən], *v.n. irr.* displease.
mißförmig ['mɪsfœrmɪç], *adj.* deformed, misshapen.
Mißgeburt ['mɪsgəburt], *f.* (—, *pl.* —**en**) abortion; monster.
mißgelaunt ['mɪsgəlaunt], *adj.* ill-humoured.
Mißgeschick ['mɪsgeʃɪk], *n.* (—**s**, *no pl.*) mishap, misfortune.
mißgestimmt ['mɪsgəʃtɪmt], *adj.* grumpy, out of sorts.
mißglücken [mɪs'glykən], *v.n.* (*aux.* sein) fail, be unsuccessful.
Mißgriff ['mɪsgrɪf], *m.* (—**s**, *pl.* —**e**) blunder, mistake.
Mißgunst ['mɪsgunst], *f.* (—, *no pl.*) jealousy, envy.
mißhandeln [mɪs'handəln], *v.a.* ill-treat.
Missionar [mɪsjo'na:r], *m.* (—**s**, *pl.* —**e**) missionary.
mißlich ['mɪslɪç], *adj.* awkward; difficult, unpleasant.
mißliebig ['mɪsli:bɪç], *adj.* unpopular, odious.
mißlingen [mɪs'lɪŋən], *v.n. irr.* (*aux.* sein) miscarry, go wrong, misfire, prove a failure, turn out badly.
mißraten [mɪs'ra:tən], *v.n. irr.* (*aux.* sein) miscarry, turn out badly.
Mißstand ['mɪsʃtant], *m.* (—**es**, *pl.* ⸗**e**) grievance, abuse.
Mißton ['mɪsto:n], *m.* (—**s**, *pl.* ⸗**e**) dissonance.
mißtrauen [mɪs'trauən], *v.n.* distrust, mistrust.
Mißverhältnis ['mɪsfɛrhɛltnɪs], *n.* (—**ses**, *no pl.*) disproportion.
Mißverständnis ['mɪsfɛrʃtɛntnɪs], *n.* (—**ses**, *pl.* —**se**) misunderstanding.
Mist [mɪst], *m.* (—**es**, *no pl.*) dung, manure, muck; (*fig.*) rubbish.
Mistel ['mɪstəl], *f.* (—, *pl.* —**n**) (*Bot.*) mistletoe.
Mistfink ['mɪstfɪŋk], *m.* (—**s**, *pl.* —**e**) (*fig.*) dirty child; mudlark.

mit [mɪt], *prep.* (*Dat.*) with. — *adv.* also, along with.
mitarbeiten ['mɪtarbaɪtən], *v.n.* collaborate, cooperate; (*lit. work*) contribute.
mitbringen ['mɪtbrɪŋən], *v.a. irr.* bring along.
Mitbürger ['mɪtbyrgər], *m.* (—**s**, *pl.* —) fellow-citizen.
mitempfinden ['mɪtɛmpfɪndən], *v.a. irr.* sympathise with.
Mitesser ['mɪtɛsər], *m.* (—**s**, *pl.* —) (*Med.*) blackhead.
mitfahren ['mɪtfa:rən], *v.n. irr.* (*aux.* sein) ride with s.o.; *einen — lassen*, give s.o. a lift.
mitfühlen ['mɪtfy:lən], *v.n.* sympathise.
mitgehen ['mɪtge:ən], *v.n. irr.* (*aux.* sein) go along (with), accompany (s.o.); *etwas — heißen* or *lassen*, pilfer, pocket, pinch.
Mitgift ['mɪtgɪft], *f.* (—, *no pl.*) dowry.
Mitglied ['mɪtgli:t], *n.* (—**s**, *pl.* —**er**) member, fellow, associate.
mithin [mɪt'hɪn], *adv., conj.* consequently, therefore.
Mitläufer ['mɪtlɔyfər], *m.* (—**s**, *pl.* —) (*Polit.*) fellow-traveller.
Mitlaut ['mɪtlaut], *m.* (—**s**, *pl.* —**e**) (*Phonet.*) consonant.
Mitleid ['mɪtlaɪt], *n.* (—**s**, *no pl.*) compassion, sympathy, pity; *mit einem — haben*, take pity on s.o.
Mitleidenschaft ['mɪtlaɪdənʃaft], *f.* (—, *no pl.*) *einen in — ziehen*, involve s.o., implicate s.o.
mitmachen ['mɪtmaxən], *v.a., v.n.* join in, participate (in), do as others do; go through, suffer.
Mitmensch ['mɪtmɛnʃ], *m.* (—**en**, *pl.* —**en**) fellow-man; fellow-creature.
mitnehmen ['mɪtne:mən], *v.a. irr.* take along, take with o.; strain, take it out of o., weaken.
mitnichten [mɪt'nɪçtən], *adv.* by no means.
mitreden ['mɪtre:dən], *v.n.* join in a conversation; contribute.
mitsamt [mɪt'zamt], *prep.* (*Dat.*) together with.
Mitschuld ['mɪtʃult], *f.* (—, *no pl.*) complicity.
Mitschüler ['mɪtʃy:lər], *m.* (—**s**, *pl.* —) schoolfellow, fellow-pupil, fellow-student, classmate.
Mittag ['mɪta:k], *m.* (—**s**, *pl.* —**e**) midday, noon, noontide; *zu — essen*, have dinner *or* lunch.
Mittagessen ['mɪta:kɛsən], *n.* (—**s**, *pl.* —) lunch, luncheon.
Mittagsseite ['mɪta:kszaɪtə], *f.* (—, *no pl.*) south side.
Mittäter ['mɪttɛ:tər], *m.* (—**s**, *pl.* —) accomplice.
Mitte ['mɪtə], *f.* (—, *no pl.*) middle, midst.
mitteilen ['mɪttaɪlən], *v.a.* (*Dat.*) communicate, inform, impart.

mitteilsam ['mɪttaɪlza:m], *adj.* communicative.
Mitteilung ['mɪttaɪluŋ], *f.* (—, *pl.* **—en**) communication.
Mittel ['mɪtəl], *n.* (**—s**, *pl.*) means, expedient, way, resource; remedy; (*pl.*) money, funds; *als — zum Zweck*, as a means to an end; *sich ins — legen*, mediate, intercede.
Mittelalter ['mɪtəlaltər], *n.* (**—s**, *no pl.*) Middle Ages.
mittelbar ['mɪtəlba:r], *adj.* indirect.
Mittelding ['mɪtəldɪŋ], *n.* (**—s**, *pl.* **—e**) medium; something in between.
Mittelgebirge ['mɪtəlgəbɪrgə], *n.* (**—s**, *pl.* —) hills; (subalpine) mountains.
mittelländisch ['mɪtəllɛndɪʃ], *adj.* Mediterranean.
mittellos ['mɪtəllo:s], *adj.* penniless, impecunious.
Mittelmaß ['mɪtəlma:s], *n.* (**—es**, *pl.* **—e**) average.
mittelmäßig ['mɪtəlmɛ:sɪç], *adj.* mediocre.
Mittelmeer ['mɪtəlme:r], *n.* (**—s**, *no pl.*) Mediterranean.
Mittelpunkt ['mɪtəlpuŋkt], *m.* (**—s**, *pl.* **—e**) centre; focus.
mittels ['mɪtəls], *prep.* (*Genit.*) by means of.
Mittelschule ['mɪtəlʃu:lə], *f.* (—, *pl.* **—n**) secondary (intermediate) school; (*Austr.*) grammar school; (*Am.*) high school.
Mittelstand ['mɪtəlʃtant], *m.* (**—es**, *no pl.*) middle class.
mittelste ['mɪtəlstə], *adj.* middlemost, central.
Mittelstürmer ['mɪtəlʃtyrmər], *m.* (**—s**, *pl.* —) (*Footb.*) centre-forward.
Mittelwort ['mɪtəlvɔrt], *n.* (**—es**, *pl.* **¨er**) (*Gram.*) participle.
mitten ['mɪtən], *adv.* in the midst; — *am Tage*, in broad daylight.
Mitternacht ['mɪtərnaxt], *f.* (—, *no pl.*) midnight.
Mittler ['mɪtlər], *m.* (**—s**, *pl.* —) mediator.
mittlere ['mɪtlərə], *adj.* middle; average; mean.
Mittwoch ['mɪtvɔx], *m.* (**—s**, *pl.* **—e**) Wednesday.
mitunter [mɪt'untər], *adv.* now and then, occasionally, sometimes.
mitunterzeichnen ['mɪtuntərtsaɪçnən], *v.a.*, *v.n.* countersign; add o.'s signature (to).
Miturheber ['mɪtu:rhe:bər], *m.* (**—s**, *pl.* —) co-author.
Mitwelt ['mɪtvɛlt], *f.* (—, *no pl.*) the present generation, contemporaries, our own times; the world outside.
mitwirken ['mɪtvɪrkən], *v.n.* cooperate.
Mnemotechnik [mne:mo'tɛçnɪk], *f.* (—, *no pl.*) mnemonics.
Möbel ['mø:bəl], *n.* (**—s**, *pl.* —) piece of furniture; (*pl.*) furniture.
mobil [mo'bi:l], *adj.* mobile, active, quick; — *machen*, mobilise, put in motion.
Mobiliar [mobil'ja:r], *n.* (**—s**, *pl.* **Mobilien**) furniture, movables.
mobilisieren [mobili'zi:rən], *v.a.* mobilise.
möblieren [mø'bli:rən], *v.a.* furnish; *neu* —, refurnish.
Mode ['mo:də], *f.* (—, *pl.* **—n**) mode, fashion; custom, use; *in der* —, in fashion, in vogue.
Modell [mo'dɛl], *n.* (**—s**, *pl.* **—e**) model; — *stehen*, model; (*fig.*) be the prototype.
modellieren [modɛ'li:rən], *v.a.* (*dresses*) model; (*Art*) mould.
Moder ['mo:dər], *m.* (**—s**, *no pl.*) mould.
moderig ['mo:drɪç] *see* **modrig**.
modern (1) ['mo:dərn], *v.n.* moulder, rot.
modern (2) [mo'dɛrn], *adj.* modern, fashionable, up-to-date.
modernisieren [modɛrni'zi:rən], *v.a.* modernise.
modifizieren [modifi'tsi:rən], *v.a.* modify.
modisch ['mo:dɪʃ], *adj.* stylish, fashionable.
Modistin [mo'dɪstɪn], *f.* (—, *pl.* **—nen**) milliner.
modrig ['mo:drɪç], *adj.* mouldy.
modulieren [modu'li:rən], *v.a.* modulate.
Modus ['mo:dus], *m.* (—, *pl.* **Modi**) (*Gram.*) mood; mode, manner.
mogeln ['mo:gəln], *v.n.* cheat.
mögen ['mø:gən], *v.n. irr.* like, desire, want, be allowed, have a mind to; (*modal auxiliary*) may, might; *ich möchte gern*, I should like to.
möglich ['mø:klɪç], *adj.* possible, practicable; feasible; *sein —stes tun*, do o.'s utmost; *nicht —!* you don't say (so)!
Möglichkeit ['mø:klɪçkaɪt], *f.* (—, *pl.* **—en**) possibility, feasibility, practicability; (*pl.*) potentialities; contingencies, prospects (of career).
Mohn [mo:n], *m.* (**—es**, *no pl.*) poppy-(seed).
Mohr [mo:r], *m.* (**—en**, *pl.* **—en**) Moor; negro.
Möhre ['mø:rə], *f.* (—, *pl.* **—n**) carrot.
Mohrenkopf ['mo:rənkɔpf], *m.* (**—es**, *pl.* **¨e**) chocolate éclair.
Mohrrübe ['mo:rry:bə], *f.* (—, *pl.* **—n**) carrot.
mokieren [mɔ'ki:rən], *v.r. sich — über*, sneer at, mock at, be amused by.
Mokka ['mɔka], *m.* (**—s**, *no pl.*) Mocha coffee.
Molch [mɔlç], *m.* (**—es**, *pl.* **—e**) (*Zool.*) salamander.
Moldau ['mɔldau], *f.* Moldavia.
Mole ['mo:lə], *f.* (—, *pl.* **—n**) breakwater, jetty, pier.
Molekül [mole'ky:l], *n.* (**—s**, *pl.* **—e**) molecule.
Molke ['mɔlkə], *f.* (—, *pl.* **—n**) whey.
Molkerei [mɔlke'raɪ], *f.* (—, *pl.* **—en** dairy.
moll [mɔl], *adj.* (*Mus.*) minor.

Molluske [mɔ'luskə], *f.* (—, *pl.* —**n**) (*Zool.*) mollusc.
Moment (1) [mo'mɛnt], *m.* (—**s**, *pl.* —**e**) moment, instant.
Moment (2) [mo'mɛnt], *n.* motive, factor; (*Phys.*) momentum.
Momentaufnahme [mo'mɛntaufna:-mə], *f.* (—, *pl.* —**n**) snapshot.
momentan [momɛn'ta:n], *adv.* at the moment, for the present, just now.
Monarch [mo'narç], *m.* (—**en**, *pl.* —**en**) monarch.
Monarchie [monar'çi:], *f.* (—, *pl.* —**n**) monarchy.
Monat ['mo:nat], *m.* (—**s**, *pl.* —**e**) month.
monatlich ['mo:natlɪç], *adj.* monthly.
Monatsfluß ['mo:natsflus], *m.* (—**sses**, *pl.* ¨**sse**) menses.
Monatsschrift ['mo:natsʃrɪft], *f.* (—, *pl.* —**en**) monthly (*journal*).
Mönch [mœnç], *m.* (—**es**, *pl.* —**e**) monk, friar.
Mönchskappe ['mœnçskapə], *f.* (—, *pl.* —**n**) cowl, monk's hood.
Mönchskutte ['mœnçskutə], *f.* (—, *pl.* —**n**) cowl.
Mond [mo:nt], *m.* (—**es**, *pl.* —**e**) moon; *zunehmender* —, waxing moon; *abnehmender* —, waning moon.
Mondfinsternis ['mo:ntfɪnstərnɪs], *f.* (—, *pl.* —**se**) eclipse of the moon.
mondsüchtig ['mo:ntzyçtɪç], *adj.* given to sleep-walking; (*fig.*) moon-struck.
Mondwandlung ['mo:ntvandluŋ], *f.* (—, *pl.* —**en**) phase of the moon.
Moneten [mo'ne:tən], *pl.* (*sl.*) money, cash, funds.
Mongolei [mɔŋgo'laɪ], *f.* Mongolia.
monieren [mo'ni:rən], *v.a.* remind (a debtor); censure.
monogam [mono'ga:m], *adj.* monogamous.
Monopol [mono'po:l], *n.* (—**s**, *pl.* —**e**) monopoly.
monoton [mono'to:n], *adj.* monotonous.
Monstrum ['mɔnstrum], *n.* (—**s**, *pl.* **Monstra**) monster, monstrosity.
Monsun [mɔn'zu:n], *m.* (—**s**, *pl.* —**e**) monsoon.
Montag ['mo:nta:k], *m.* (—**s**, *pl.* —**e**) Monday; *blauer* —, Bank Holiday Monday.
Montage [mɔn'ta:ʒə], *f.* (—, *pl.* —**n**) fitting (up), setting up, installation, assembling.
Montanindustrie [mon'ta:nɪndustri:], *f.* (—, *no pl.*) mining industry.
Montanunion [mɔn'ta:nunjo:n], *f.* (—, *no pl.*) (*Pol.*) European Coal and Steel Community.
Monteur [mɔn'tø:r], *m.* (—**s**, *pl.* —**e**) fitter.
montieren [mɔn'ti:rən], *v.a.* fit (up), set up, mount, install.
Montur [mɔn'tu:r], *f.* (—, *pl.* —**en**) uniform, livery.
Moor [mo:r], *n.* (—**es**, *pl.* —**e**) swamp, fen, bog.
Moos [mo:s], *n.* (—**es**, *pl.* —**e**) moss; (*sl.*) cash.
Moped ['mo:pɛt], *n.* (—**s**, *pl.* —**s**) moped, motorised pedal cycle.
Mops [mɔps], *m.* (—**es**, *pl.* ¨**e**) pug (dog).
mopsen ['mɔpsən], *v.r. sich* —, feel bored.
Moral [mo'ra:l], *f.* (—, *no pl.*) moral, morals.
moralisch [mo'ra:lɪʃ], *adj.* moral.
Morast [mo'rast], *m.* (—**es**, *pl.* ¨**e**) morass, bog, fen, mire.
Moratorium [mora'to:rjum], *n.* (—**s**, *pl.* —**rien**) (*payments etc.*) respite.
Morchel ['mɔrçəl], *f.* (—, *pl.* —**n**) (*Bot.*) morel (edible fungus).
Mord [mɔrt], *m.* (—**es**, *pl.* —**e**) murder.
morden ['mɔrdən], *v.a.*, *v.n.* murder.
Mörder ['mœrdər], *m.* (—**s**, *pl.* —) murderer.
Mordsgeschichte ['mɔrtsgəʃɪçtə], *f.* (—, *pl.* —**n**) (*coll.*) cock-and-bull story.
Mordskerl ['mɔrtskɛrl], *m.* (—**s**, *pl.* —**e**) devil of a fellow; (*Am.*) great guy.
Mordtat ['mɔrtta:t], *f.* (—, *pl.* —**en**) murder.
Morelle [mo'rɛlə], *f.* (—, *pl.* —**n**) (*Bot.*) morello cherry.
Morgen ['mɔrgən], *m.* (—**s**, *pl.* —) morning, daybreak; (*Poet.*) east; measure of land; *eines* —*s*, one morning.
morgen ['mɔrgən], *adv.* tomorrow; — *früh*, tomorrow morning; *heute* —, this morning.
Morgenblatt ['mɔrgənblat], *n.* (—**s**, *pl.* ¨**er**) morning paper.
morgendlich ['mɔrgəntlɪç], *adj.* of *or* in the morning; matutinal.
Morgenland ['mɔrgənlant], *n.* (—**es**, *pl.* —) orient, east.
Morgenrot ['mɔrgənro:t], *n.* (—**s**, *no pl.*) dawn, sunrise.
morgens ['mɔrgəns], *adv.* in the morning.
morgig ['mɔrgɪç], *adj.* tomorrow's.
Morphium ['mɔrfjum], *n.* (—**s**, *no pl.*) morphia, morphine.
morsch [mɔrʃ], *adj.* brittle, rotten, decayed.
Mörser ['mœrzər], *m.* (—**s**, *pl.* —) mortar.
Mörserkeule ['mœrzərkɔylə], *f.* (—, *pl.* —**n**) pestle.
Mörtel ['mœrtəl], *m.* (—**s**, *no pl.*) mortar, plaster.
Mörtelkelle ['mœrtəlkɛlə], *f.* (—, *pl.* —**n**) trowel.
Mosaik [moza'i:k], *n.* (—**s**, *pl.* —**e**) mosaic (work); inlaid work.
mosaisch [mo'za:ɪʃ], *adj.* Mosaic.
Moschee [mo'ʃe:], *f.* (—, *pl.* —**n**) mosque.
Moschus ['mɔʃus], *m.* (—, *no pl.*) musk.
Mosel ['mo:zəl], *f.* Moselle.
Moskau ['mɔskau], *n.* Moscow.

Moskito [mɔs'ki:to], *m.* (**—s**, *pl.* **—s**) (*Ent.*) mosquito.
Most [mɔst], *m.* (**—es**, *no pl.*) new wine, cider.
Mostrich ['mɔstrɪç], *m.* (**—s**, *no pl.*) mustard.
Motiv [mo'ti:f], *n.* (**—es**, *pl.* **—e**) motive; (*Mus.*, *Lit.*) motif, theme.
motivieren [moti'vi:rən], *v.a.* motivate.
Motorrad ['mo:tɔrra:t], *n.* (**—es**, *pl.* **¨er**) motor-cycle.
Motte ['mɔtə], *f.* (**—**, *pl.* **—n**) (*Ent.*) moth.
moussieren [mu'si:rən], *v.n.* effervesce, sparkle.
Möwe ['mø:və], *f.* (**—**, *pl.* **—n**) (*Orn.*) seagull.
Mucke ['mukə], *f.* (**—**, *pl.* **—n**) whim, caprice; obstinacy.
Mücke ['mykə], *f.* (**—**, *pl.* **—n**) (*Ent.*) gnat, fly, mosquito.
Muckerei [mukə'raɪ], *f.* (**—**, *pl.* **—en**) cant.
mucksen ['muksən], *v.n.* stir, move, budge.
müde ['my:də], *adj.* tired, weary; *— machen*, tire.
Muff [muf], *m.* (**—es**, *pl.* **—e**) muff.
muffig ['mufɪç], *adj.* musty, fusty, stuffy.
Mühe ['my:ə], *f.* (**—**, *pl.* **—n**) trouble, pains; effort, labour, toil; *sich — geben*, take pains.
mühelos ['my:əlo:s], *adj.* effortless, easy.
mühen ['my:ən], *v.r. sich —*, exert o.s., take pains.
Mühewaltung ['my:əvaltuŋ], *f.* (**—**, *pl.* **—en**) exertion, effort.
Mühle ['my:lə], *f.* (**—**, *pl.* **—n**) (*flour*) mill; (*coffee*) grinder; game.
Muhme ['mu:mə], *f.* (**—**, *pl.* **—n**) (*obs.*) aunt.
Mühsal ['my:za:l], *f.* (**—**, *pl.* **—e**) hardship, misery, toil.
mühsam ['my:za:m], *adj.* troublesome, laborious.
mühselig ['my:ze:lɪç], *adj.* painful, laborious; miserable.
Mulatte [mu'latə], *m.* (**—n**, *pl.* **—n**) mulatto.
Mulde ['muldə], *f.* (**—**, *pl.* **—n**) trough.
muldenförmig ['muldənfœrmɪç], *adj.* trough-shaped.
Mull [mul], *m.* (**—s**, *no pl.*) Indian muslin.
Müll [myl], *m.* (**—s**, *no pl.*) dust, rubbish; (*Am.*) garbage.
Müller ['mylər], *m.* (**—s**, *pl.* **—**) miller.
mulmig ['mulmɪç], *adj.* dusty, mouldy, decayed.
multiplizieren [multipli'tsi:rən], *v.a.* multiply.
Mumie ['mu:mjə], *f.* (**—**, *pl.* **—n**) (*Archæol.*) mummy.
Mummenschanz ['mumənʃants], *m.* (**—es**, *no pl.*) mummery, masquerade.
München ['mynçən], *n.* Munich.
Mund [munt], *m.* (**—es**, *pl.* **—e**, **¨er**) mouth; *den — halten*, keep quiet; *einen großen — haben*, talk big; *sich den — verbrennen*, put o.'s foot in it.
Mundart ['munta:rt], *f.* (**—**, *pl.* **—en**) (local) dialect.
Mündel ['myndəl], *m.*, *f.* & *n.* (**—s**, *pl.* **—**) ward, minor, child under guardianship.
mündelsicher ['myndəlzɪçər], *adj.* gilt-edged.
munden ['mundən], *v.n. es mundet mir*, I like the taste, I relish it.
münden ['myndən], *v.n.* discharge (into), flow (into).
mundfaul ['muntfaul], *adj.* tongue-tied; taciturn.
mundgerecht ['muntgərɛçt], *adj.* palatable; (*fig.*) suitable.
Mundharmonika ['muntharmo:nɪka], *f.* (**—**, *pl.* **—kas**, **—ken**) mouth organ.
mündig ['myndɪç], *adj.* of age; *— werden*, come of age.
mündlich ['myntlɪç], *adj.* verbal, oral, by word of mouth; (*examination*) viva voce.
Mundschenk ['muntʃɛŋk], *m.* (**—s**, *pl.* **—e**) cupbearer.
mundtot ['muntto:t], *adj.* *— machen*, silence, gag.
Mündung ['mynduŋ], *f.* (**—**, *pl.* **—en**) (*river*) estuary, mouth; (*gun*) muzzle.
Mundvorrat ['muntforra:t], *m.* (**—s**, *pl.* **¨e**) provisions, victuals.
Mundwerk ['muntvɛrk], *n.* (**—s**, *no pl.*) mouth; (*fig.*) gift of the gab.
Munition [muni'tsjo:n], *f.* (**—**, *no pl.*) ammunition.
munkeln ['muŋkəln], *v.n.* whisper; *man munkelt*, it is rumoured.
Münster ['mynstər], *n.* (**—s**, *pl.* **—**) minster, cathedral.
munter ['muntər], *adj.* awake; lively, active, sprightly, vivacious, cheerful, gay.
Münze ['myntsə], *f.* (**—**, *pl.* **—n**) coin.
Münzeinheit ['myntsaɪnhaɪt], *f.* (**—**, *no pl.*) monetary unit.
Münzfälscher ['myntsfɛlʃər], *m.* (**—s**, *pl.* **—**) (counterfeit) coiner.
Münzkunde ['myntskundə], *f.* (**—**, *no pl.*) numismatics.
Münzprobe ['myntspro:bə], *f.* (**—**, *pl.* **—n**) assay of a coin.
mürbe ['myrbə], *adj.* mellow; (*meat*) tender; (*cake*) crisp; brittle; *einen — machen*, soften s.o. up, force s.o. to yield.
Murmel ['murməl], *f.* (**—**, *pl.* **—n**) (*toy*) marble.
murmeln ['murməln], *v.n.* murmur, mutter.
Murmeltier ['murməlti:r], *n.* (**—s**, *pl.* **—e**) (*Zool.*) marmot; *wie ein — schlafen*, sleep like a log.
murren ['murən], *v.n.* grumble, growl.
mürrisch ['myrɪʃ], *adj.* morose, surly, sulky, peevish, sullen.

Mus [mu:s], *n.* (**—es**, *no pl.*) purée, (apple) sauce; pulp.
Muschel [ˈmuʃəl], *f.* (—, *pl.* **—n**) mussel, shell; (*telephone*) ear-piece.
Muse [ˈmu:zə], *f.* (—, *pl.* **—n**) muse.
Muselman [ˈmu:zəlman], *m.* (**—en**, *pl.* **—en**) Muslim, Moslem.
Musik [muˈzi:k], *f.* (—, *no pl.*) music.
musikalisch [muziˈka:lɪʃ], *adj.* musical.
Musikant [muziˈkant], *m.* (**—en**, *pl.* **—en**) musician; performer.
Musiker [ˈmu:zɪkər], *m.* (**—s**, *pl.* —) musician.
musizieren [muziˈtsi:rən], *v.n.* play music.
Muskateller [muskaˈtɛlər], *m.* (**—s**, *no pl.*) muscatel (wine).
Muskatnuß [musˈka:tnus], *f.* (—, *pl.* **⸚sse**) nutmeg.
Muskel [ˈmuskəl], *m.* (**—s**, *pl.* **—n**) muscle.
muskelig [ˈmuskɪlɪç] *see* **musklig**.
Muskete [musˈke:tə], *f.* (—, *pl.* **—n**) musket.
Musketier [muskeˈti:r], *m.* (**—s**, *pl.* **—e**) musketeer.
musklig [ˈmusklɪç], *adj.* muscular.
muskulös [muskuˈlø:s], *adj.* muscular.
Muße [ˈmu:sə], *f.* (—, *no pl.*) leisure; *mit* —, leisurely, at leisure.
Musselin [musəˈli:n], *m.* (**—s**, *pl.* **—e**) muslin.
müssen [ˈmysən], *v.n. irr.* have to, be forced, be compelled, be obliged; *ich muß*, I must, I have to.
müßig [ˈmy:sɪç], *adj.* idle, lazy, unemployed.
Müßiggang [ˈmy:sɪçgaŋ], *m.* (**—s**, *no pl.*) idleness, laziness, sloth.
Muster [ˈmuster], *n.* (**—s**, *pl.* —) sample; pattern; (proto-)type; (*fig.*) example.
Musterbild [ˈmustərbɪlt], *n.* (**—s**, *pl.* **—er**) paragon.
mustergültig [ˈmustərgyltɪç], *adj.* exemplary; standard; excellent.
musterhaft [ˈmustərhaft], *adj.* exemplary.
mustern [ˈmustərn], *v.a.* examine, muster, scan; (*troops*) review, inspect.
Musterung [ˈmustəruŋ], *f.* (—, *pl.* **—en**) review; examination, inspection.
Mut [ˈmu:t], *m.* (**—es**, *no pl.*) courage, spirit; — *fassen*, take heart, muster up courage.
Mutation [mutaˈtsjo:n], *f.* (—, *pl.* **—en**) change.
mutieren [muˈti:rən], *v.n.* change; (*voice*) break.
mutig [ˈmu:tɪç], *adj.* courageous, brave.
mutlos [ˈmu:tlo:s], *adj.* discouraged, dejected, despondent.
mutmaßen [ˈmu:tma:sən], *v.a. insep.* surmise, suppose, conjecture.
Mutter [ˈmutər], *f.* (—, *pl.* ⸚) mother; (*screw*) nut.
Mutterkorn [ˈmutərkɔrn], *n.* (**—s**, *no pl.*) ergot.
Mutterkuchen [ˈmutərku:xən], *m.* (**—s**, *pl.* —) placenta, after-birth.
Mutterleib [ˈmutərlaɪp], *m.* (**—s**, *no pl.*) womb, uterus.
Muttermal [ˈmutərma:l], *n.* (**—s**, *pl.* **—e**) birth-mark.
Mutterschaft [ˈmutərʃaft], *f.* (—, *no pl.*) motherhood, maternity.
mutterseelenallein [ˈmutərze:lənalaɪn], *adj.* quite alone; (*coll.*) all on o.'s own.
Muttersöhnchen [ˈmutərzø:nçən], *n.* (**—s**, *pl.* —) mother's darling, spoilt child.
Mutterwitz [ˈmutərvɪts], *m.* (**—es**, *no pl.*) mother-wit, native wit, common sense.
Mutwille [ˈmu:tvɪlə], *m.* (**—ns**, *no pl.*) mischievousness, wantonness.
Mütze [ˈmytsə], *f.* (—, *pl.* **—n**) cap; bonnet; beret.
Myrrhe [ˈmɪrə], *f.* (—, *pl.* **—n**) myrrh.
Myrte [ˈmɪrtə], *f.* (—, *pl.* **—n**) (*Bot.*) myrtle.
Mysterium [mɪsˈte:rjum], *n.* (**—s**, *pl.* **—rien**) mystery.
Mystik [ˈmɪstɪk], *f.* (—, *no pl.*) mysticism.
Mythologie [mytoloˈgi:], *f.* (—, *pl.* **—n**) mythology.
Mythus [ˈmytus], *m.* (—, *pl.* **Mythen**) myth.

N

N [ɛn], *n.* (**—s**, *pl.* **—s**) the letter N.
na [na], *int.* well, now; *—nu!* well, I never! — *und?* so what?
Nabe [ˈna:bə], *f.* (—, *pl.* **—n**) hub.
Nabel [ˈna:bəl], *m.* (**—s**, *pl.* —) navel.
Nabelschnur [ˈna:bəlʃnu:r], *f.* (—, *pl.* **⸚e**) umbilical cord.
nach [na:x], *prep.* (*Dat.*) after, behind, following; to, towards; according to, in conformity *or* accordance with; in imitation of. — *adv.*, *prefix.* after, behind; afterwards, later; — *und* —, little by little, by degrees, gradually.
nachäffen [ˈna:xɛfən], *v.a.* ape, mimic, imitate; (*coll.*) take off.
nachahmen [ˈna:xa:mən], *v.a.* imitate, copy; counterfeit.
nacharbeiten [ˈna:xarbaɪtən], *v.n.* work after hours *or* overtime. — *v.a.* copy (*Dat.*).
nacharten [ˈna:xa:rtən], *v.n.* (*aux.* sein) resemble, (*coll.*) take after.
Nachbar [ˈnaxba:r], *m.* (**—s**, **—n**, *pl.* **—n**) neighbour.
Nachbarschaft [ˈnaxba:rʃaft], *f.* (—, *no pl.*) neighbourhood, vicinity; (*people*) neighbours.
nachbestellen [ˈna:xbəʃtɛlən], *v.a.* order more, re-order.

nachbilden ['na:xbɪldən], *v.a.* copy, reproduce.
nachdem [na:x'de:m], *adv.* afterwards, after that. — *conj.* after, when; *je* —, according to circumstances, that depends.
nachdenken ['na:xdɛŋkən], *v.n. irr.* think (over), meditate, muse, ponder.
nachdenklich ['na:xdɛŋklɪç], *adj.* reflective, pensive, wistful; — *stimmen,* set thinking.
Nachdruck ['na:xdruk], *m.* (—**s**, *pl.* —**e**) reprint; stress, emphasis.
nachdrucken ['na:xdrukən], *v.a.* reprint.
nachdrücklich ['na:xdryklɪç], *adj.* emphatic; — *betonen,* emphasise.
nacheifern ['na:xaɪfərn], *v.n. einem* —, emulate s.o.
nacheinander ['na:xaɪnandər], *adv.* one after another.
nachempfinden ['na:xɛmpfɪndən], *v.a. irr.* sympathize with, feel for.
Nachen ['naxən], *m.* (—**s**, *pl.* —) (*Poet.*) boat, skiff.
Nachfolge ['na:xfɔlgə], *f.* (—, *pl.* —**n**) succession.
nachfolgend ['na:xfɔlgənt], *adj.* following, subsequent.
Nachfolger ['na:xfɔlgər], *m.* (—**s**, *pl.* —) successor.
nachforschen ['na:xfɔrʃən], *v.a.* search after; enquire into, investigate.
Nachfrage ['na:xfra:gə], *f.* (—, *no pl.*) enquiry; (*Comm.*) demand; *Angebot und* —, supply and demand.
nachfühlen ['na:xfy:lən], *v.a. einem etwas* —, enter into s.o.'s feelings, sympathize with s.o.
nachfüllen ['na:xfylən], *v.a.* replenish, fill up.
nachgeben ['na:xge:bən], *v.n. irr.* relax, slacken, yield; give in, relent, give way.
nachgehen ['na:xge:ən], *v.n. irr.* (*aux.* sein) *einem* —, follow s.o., go after s.o.; (*clock*) be slow; follow up, investigate.
nachgerade ['na:xgəra:də], *adv.* by this time, by now; gradually.
nachgiebig ['na:xgi:bɪç], *adj.* yielding, compliant.
nachgrübeln ['na:xgry:bəln], *v.n.* speculate.
Nachhall ['na:xhal], *m.* (—**s**, *no pl.*) echo, resonance.
nachhaltig ['na:xhaltɪç], *adj.* lasting, enduring.
nachhängen ['na:xhɛŋən], *v.n. irr. seinen Gedanken* —, muse.
nachher ['na:xhe:r], *adv.* afterwards, later on.
nachherig ['na:xhe:rɪç], *adj.* subsequent, later.
Nachhilfestunde ['na:xhɪlfəʃtundə], *f.* (—, *pl.* —**n**) private coaching.
nachholen ['na:xho:lən], *v.a.* make good; make up for.
Nachhut ['na:xhu:t], *f.* (—, *no pl.*) (*Mil.*) rearguard.
nachjagen ['na:xja:gən], *v.n.* (*aux* sein) pursue.
Nachklang ['na:xklaŋ], *m.* (—**s**, *pl.* ⸚**e**) echo; (*fig.*) after-effect, reminiscence.
Nachkomme ['na:xkɔmə], *m.* (—**n**, *pl.* —**n**) descendant, offspring.
nachkommen ['na:xkɔmən], *v.n. irr.* (*aux.* sein) come after, follow; *seiner Pflicht* —, do o.'s duty; comply with; *einem Versprechen* —, keep a promise; *seinen Verpflichtungen nicht* — *können,* be unable to meet o.'s commitments.
Nachkommenschaft ['na:xkɔmənʃaft], *f.* (—, *no pl.*) descendants, offspring, issue, progeny.
Nachlaß ['na:xlas], *m.* (—**sses**, *pl.* ⸚**sse**) inheritance, estate, bequest; remission, discount, allowance.
nachlassen ['na:xlasən], *v.a. irr.* leave behind, bequeath; (*trade*) give a discount of. — *v.n.* abate, subside, slacken.
nachlässig ['na:xlɛsɪç], *adj.* negligent, remiss, careless.
nachlaufen ['na:xlaufən], *v.n. irr.* (*aux.* sein) *einem* —, run after s.o.
Nachlese ['na:xle:zə], *f.* (—, *pl.* —**n**) gleaning.
nachliefern ['na:xli:fərn], *v.a.* supply subsequently, complete delivery of.
nachmachen ['na:xmaxən], *v.a.* copy, imitate; counterfeit, forge.
nachmals ['na:xma:ls], *adv.* afterwards, subsequently.
Nachmittag ['na:xmɪta:k], *m.* (—**s**, *pl.* —**e**) afternoon.
Nachnahme ['na:xna:mə], *f.* (—, *no pl.*) *per* —, cash *or* (*Am.*) collect (payment) on delivery (*abbr.* C.O.D.).
nachplappern ['na:xplapərn], *v.a.* repeat mechanically.
Nachrede ['na:xre:də], *f.* (—, *pl.* —**n**) epilogue; *üble* —, slander.
Nachricht ['na:xrɪçt], *f.* (—, *pl.* —**en**) news, information; (*Mil.*) intelligence; — *geben,* send word.
nachrücken ['na:xrykən], *v.n.* (*aux.* sein) move up.
Nachruf ['na:xru:f], *m.* (—**s**, *pl.* —**e**) obituary.
nachrühmen ['na:xry:mən], *v.a. einem etwas* —, speak well of s.o.
Nachsatz ['na:xzats], *m.* (—**es**, *pl.* ⸚**e**) concluding clause; postscript.
nachschauen ['na:xʃauən], *v.n. jemandem* —, gaze after s.o.
nachschlagen ['na:xʃla:gən], *v.a. irr.* look up, consult (a book).
Nachschlagewerk ['na:xʃla:gəvɛrk], *n.* (—**s**, *pl.* —**e**) work of reference, reference book.
Nachschlüssel ['na:xʃlysəl], *m.* (—**s**, *pl.* —) master-key, skeleton-key.
Nachschrift ['na:xʃrɪft], *f.* (—, *pl.* —**en**) postscript, (*abbr.* P.S.).
Nachschub ['na:xʃu:p], *m.* (—**s**, *pl.* ⸚**e**) (fresh) supply; (*Mil.*) reinforcements.
Nachsehen ['na:xze:ən], *n.* (—**s**, *no pl.*) *das* — *haben,* be left out in the cold.

nachsehen ['na:xze:ən], *v.a., v.n. irr.* look for, look s.th. up, refer to s.th.; *einem etwas* —, be indulgent with s.o.
Nachsicht ['na:xzɪçt], *f.* (—, *no pl.*) forbearance, indulgence.
Nachsilbe ['na:xzɪlbə], *f.* (—, *pl.* —**n**) suffix.
nachsinnen ['na:xzɪnən], *v.n.* muse, reflect.
nachsitzen ['na:xzitsən], *v.n.* be kept in after school.
Nachsommer ['na:xzɔmər], *m.* (—**s**, *pl.* —) Indian summer.
Nachspeise ['na:xʃpaɪzə], *f.* (—, *pl.* —**n**) dessert.
nachspüren ['na:xʃpy:rən], *v.n. einem* —, trace, track.
nächst [nɛ:çst], *prep.* (*Dat.*) next to, nearest to. — *adj.* next.
Nächste ['nɛ:çstə], *m.* (—**n**, *pl.* —**n**) fellow-man, neighbour.
nachstehen ['na:xʃte:ən], *v.n. irr. einem* —, be inferior to s.o.; *keinem* —, be second to none.
nachstehend ['na:xʃte:ənt], *adv.* below, hereinafter. — *adj.* following.
nachstellen ['na:xʃtɛlən], *v.n. einem* —, lie in wait for s.o.
Nachstellung ['na:xʃtɛluŋ], *f.* (—, *pl.* —**en**) persecution, ambush; (*Gram.*) postposition.
nächstens ['nɛ:çstəns], *adv.* soon, shortly.
nachstöbern ['na:xʃtø:bərn], *v.n.* rummage.
nachströmen ['na:xʃtrø:mən], *v.n.* (*aux.* sein) crowd after.
Nacht [naxt], *f.* (—, *pl.* ⸚**e**) night; *die ganze — hindurch*, all night; *bei* —, at night; *gute — wünschen*, bid goodnight; *über* —, overnight; *in der* —, during the night; *bei — und Nebel*, in the dead of night.
Nachteil ['na:xtaɪl], *m.* (—**s**, *pl.* —**e**) disadvantage, damage.
Nachtessen ['naxtɛsən], *n.* (—**s**, *pl.* —) supper; evening meal.
Nachtfalter ['naxtfaltər], *m.* (—**s**, *pl.* —) (*Ent.*) moth.
Nachtgeschirr ['naxtgəʃɪr], *n.* (—**s**, *pl.* —**e**) chamber-pot.
Nachtgleiche ['naxtglaɪçə], *f.* (—, *pl.* —**n**) equinox.
Nachthemd ['naxthɛmt], *n.* (—**es**, *pl.* —**en**) night-dress, night-gown.
Nachtigall ['naxtɪgal], *f.* (—, *pl.* —**en**) (*Orn.*) nightingale.
nächtigen ['nɛçtɪgən], *v.n.* spend the night.
Nachtisch ['naxtɪʃ], *m.* (—**es**, *pl.* —**e**) dessert.
Nachtlager ['naxtla:gər], *n.* (—**s**, *pl.* —) lodgings for the night; (*Mil.*) bivouac.
Nachtmahl ['naxtma:l], *n.* (—**s**, *pl.* —**e**) (*Austr.*) supper.
nachtönen ['na:xtø:nən], *v.n.* resound.
Nachtrag ['na:xtra:k], *m.* (—**s**, *pl.* ⸚**e**) supplement, postscript, addition; (*pl.*) addenda.
nachtragen ['na:xtra:gən], *v.a. irr.* carry after; add; (*fig.*) *einem etwas* —, bear s.o. a grudge.
nachträglich ['na:xtrɛ:klɪç], *adj.* subsequent; supplementary; additional; further; later.
Nachtrupp ['na:xtrup], *m.* (—**s**, *no pl.*) rearguard.
Nachtschwärmer ['naxtʃvɛrmər], *m.* (—**s**, *pl.* —) night-reveller.
Nachttisch ['naxttɪʃ], *m.* (—**es**, *pl.* —**e**) bedside-table.
nachtun ['na:xtu:n], *v.a. irr. einem etwas* —, imitate s.o., emulate s.o.
Nachtwächter ['naxtvɛçtər], *m.* (—**s**, *pl.* —) night-watchman.
Nachtwandler ['naxtvandlər], *m.* (—**s**, *pl.* —) sleep-walker, somnambulist.
Nachwahl ['na:xva:l], *f.* (—, *pl.* —**en**) by(e)-election.
Nachwehen ['na:xve:ən], *f. pl.* aftermath; unpleasant consequences.
Nachweis ['na:xvaɪs], *m.* (—**es**, *pl.* —**e**) proof; (*Lit.*) reference; agency.
nachweisen ['na:xvaɪzən], *v.a. irr.* prove, establish; (*Lit.*) refer.
Nachwelt ['na:xvɛlt], *f.* (—, *no pl.*) posterity.
Nachwort ['na:xvɔrt], *n.* (—**es**, *pl.* —**e**) epilogue.
Nachwuchs ['na:xvu:ks], *m.* (—**es**, *no pl.*) coming generation; recruits.
Nachzahlung ['na:xtsa:luŋ], *f.* (—, *pl.* —**en**) additional payment, supplementary payment.
Nachzählung ['na:xtsɛ:luŋ], *f.* (—, *pl.* —**en**) recount.
nachziehen ['na:xtsi:ən], *v.a. irr.* drag, tow; tighten; trace, pencil. — *v.n.* follow.
Nachzügler ['na:xtsy:glər], *m.* (—**s**, *pl.* —) straggler.
Nacken ['nakən], *m.* (—**s**, *pl.* —) nape, scruff of the neck.
nackend ['nakənt], *adj.* naked.
nackt [nakt], *adj.* nude, naked; (*bird*) callow; (*fig.*) bare; *sich — ausziehen*, strip.
Nadel ['na:dəl], *f.* (—, *pl.* —**n**) needle, pin; *wie auf —n sitzen*, be on tenterhooks.
Nadelöhr ['na:dəlø:r], *n.* (—**s**, *pl.* —**e**) eye of a needle.
Nagel ['na:gəl], *m.* (—**s**, *pl.* ⸚) nail; (*wooden*) peg; (*ornament*) stud; *etwas an den — hängen*, lay s.th. aside, give s.th. up.
nagelneu ['na:gəlnɔy], *adj.* brand new.
nagen ['na:gən], *v.a., v.n.* gnaw; (*fig.*) rankle.
Näharbeit ['nɛ:arbaɪt], *f.* (—, *pl.* —**en**) sewing, needlework.
nahe ['na:ə], *adj., adv.* near, close, nigh; — *bei*, close to; — *daran sein*, be on the point of; *es geht mir* —, it grieves me, it touches me; *einem zu — treten*, hurt s.o.'s feelings; *es liegt* —, it is obvious, it suggests itself.
Nähe ['nɛ:ə], *f.* (—, *no pl.*) nearness, proximity; *in der* —, at hand, close by.

nahen ['na:ən], *v.n.* (*aux.* sein) draw near, approach.
nähen ['nɛ:ən], *v.a.* sew, stitch.
Nähere ['nɛ:ərə], *n.* (—**n**, *no pl.*) details, particulars.
Näherin ['nɛ:ərɪn], *f.* (—, *pl.* — **innen**) seamstress, needlewoman.
nähern ['nɛ:ərn], *v.r.* *sich* —, draw near, approach.
nahestehen ['na:əʃte:ən], *v.n.* be closely connected *or* friendly (with s.o.).
Nährboden ['nɛ:rbo:dən], *m.* (—**s**, *pl.* ¨) rich soil; (*Med.*, *Biol.*) culture-medium.
nähren ['nɛ:rən], *v.a.* nourish, feed. — *v.r. sich* — *von*, feed on; (*fig.*) gain a livelihood.
nahrhaft ['na:rhaft], *adj.* nourishing, nutritive, nutritious.
Nährstand ['nɛ:rʃtant], *m.* (—**es**, *no pl.*) peasants, producers.
Nahrung ['na:ruŋ], *f.* (—, *no pl.*) nourishment.
Nahrungsmittel ['na:ruŋsmɪtəl], *n.* (—**s**, *pl.* —) food, provisions, victuals.
Naht [na:t], *f.* (—, *pl.* ¨**e**) seam.
Nähzeug ['nɛ:tsɔyk], *n.* (—**s**, *no pl.*) sewing kit, work box.
naiv [na'i:f], *adj.* naïve, artless, guileless.
Naivität [naivi'tɛ:t], *f.* (—, *no pl.*) artlessness, guilelessness, naïveté.
Name ['na:mə], *m.* (—**ns**, *pl.* —**n**) name; *guter* —, good name, renown, reputation; *dem* —*n nach*, by name; *etwas beim rechten* —*n nennen*, call a spade a spade.
namens ['na:məns], *adv.* called; by the name of.
Namensvetter ['na:mənsfɛtər], *m.* (—**s**, *pl.* —**n**) namesake.
namentlich ['na:məntlɪç], *adj.* by name; particularly.
Namenverzeichnis ['na:mənfɛrtsaɪçnɪs], *n.* (—**ses**, *pl.* —**se**) list of names; (*scientific*) nomenclature.
namhaft ['na:mhaft], *adj.* distinguished, renowned; considerable; — *machen*, name.
nämlich ['nɛ:mlɪç], *adv.* namely, to wit.
Napf [napf], *m.* (—**es**, *pl.* ¨**e**) bowl, basin.
Napfkuchen ['napfku:xən], *m.* (—**s**, *pl.* —) pound-cake, large cake.
Narbe ['narbə], *f.* (—, *pl.* —**n**) scar; (*leather*) grain.
Narkose [nar'ko:zə], *f.* (—, *pl.* —**n**) anaesthesia; narcosis.
Narr [nar], *m.* (—**en**, *pl.* —**en**) fool; jester, buffoon; *einen zum* —*en haben*, make a fool of s.o.; *an einem einen* —*en gefressen haben*, dote on, be infatuated with s.o.
Narrheit ['narhaɪt], *f.* (—, *pl.* —**en**) foolishness, folly.
närrisch ['nɛrɪʃ], *adj.* foolish, comical; odd; merry; eccentric, mad; — *werden*, go mad.
Narzisse [nar'tsɪsə], *f.* (—, *pl.* —**n**) (*Bot.*) narcissus; *gelbe* —, daffodil.
naschen ['naʃən], *v.a.*, *v.n.* pilfer titbits; nibble at, eat sweets.
Näscherei [nɛʃər'aɪ], *f.* (—, *pl.* —**en**) sweets, dainties, sweetmeats.
naschhaft ['naʃhaft], *adj.* sweet-toothed.
Naschkatze ['naʃkatsə], *f.* (—, *pl.* —**n**) sweet tooth.
Nase ['na:zə], *f.* (—, *pl.* —**n**) nose; (*animal*) snout; scent; *stumpfe* —, snub nose; *gebogene* —, Roman nose; *immer der* — *nach*, follow your nose; *die* — *hoch tragen*, be stuck-up; *eine feine* (*gute*) — *haben*, be good at; not miss much; *die* — *rümpfen*, turn up o.'s nose; *seine* — *in alles stecken*, poke o.'s nose into everything; *einem etwas unter die* — *reiben*, bring s.th. home to s.o.
näseln ['nɛ:zəln], *v.n.* speak with a twang.
Nasenbein ['na:zənbaɪn], *n.* (—**s**, *pl.* —**e**) nasal bone.
Nasenbluten ['na:zənblu:tən], *n.* (—**s**, *no pl.*) nose-bleed.
Nasenflügel ['na:zənfly:gəl], *m.* (—**s**, *pl.* —) side of the nose; nostril.
naseweis ['na:zəvaɪs], *adj.* pert, saucy.
Nashorn ['na:shɔrn], *n.* (—**s**, *pl.* ¨**er**) (*Zool.*) rhinoceros.
Naß [nas], *n.* (—**sses**, *no pl.*) (*Poet.*) fluid.
naß [nas], *adj.* wet, moist, damp.
Nässe ['nɛsə], *f.* (—, *no pl.*) wetness, dampness, moisture, humidity.
nationalisieren [natsjonali'zi:rən], *v.a.* nationalise.
Nationalität [natsjonali'tɛ:t], *f.* (—, *pl.* —**en**) nationality.
Natrium ['na:trjum], *n.* (—**s**, *no pl.*) sodium.
Natron ['natrɔn], *n.* (—**s**, *no pl.*) sodium carbonate; *doppelkohlensaures* —, sodium bicarbonate; bicarbonate of soda.
Natter ['natər,] *f.* (—, *pl.* —**n**) (*Zool.*) adder, viper.
Natur [na'tu:r], *f.* (—, *pl.* —**en**) nature; (*body*) constitution; (*mind*) disposition; *von* —, by nature, constitutionally; *nach der* — *zeichnen*, draw from nature.
naturalisieren [naturali'zi:rən], *v.a.* naturalise.
Naturalleistung [natu'ra:llaɪstuŋ], *f.* (—, *pl.* —**en**) payment in kind.
Naturell [natu'rɛl], *n.* (—**s**, *pl.* —**e**) natural disposition, temper.
Naturforscher [na'tu:rfɔrʃər], *m.* (—**s**, *pl.* —) naturalist.
naturgemäß [na'tu:rgəmɛ:s], *adj.* natural.
Naturgeschichte [na'tu:rgəʃɪçtə], *f.* (—, *no pl.*) natural history.
naturgetreu [na'tu:rgətrɔy], *adj.* true to nature, lifelike.
Naturkunde [na'tu:rkundə], *f.* (—, *no pl.*) natural history.
Naturlehre [na'tu:rle:rə], *f.* (—, *no pl.*) natural philosophy; physics.

natürlich [na'ty:rlıç], *adj.* natural; innate, inherent; unaffected, artless. — *adv.* of course, naturally.
Naturspiel [na'tu:rʃpi:l], *n.* (—**s**, *pl.* —**e**) freak of nature.
Naturtrieb [na'tu:rtri:p], *m.* (—**s**, *no pl.*) natural impulse, instinct.
naturwidrig [na'tu:rvi:drıç], *adj.* contrary to nature, unnatural.
Naturwissenschaft [na'tu:rvısənʃaft], *f.* (—, *pl.* —**en**) (natural) science.
naturwüchsig [na'tu:rvy:ksıç], *adj.* original; unsophisticated.
Nautik ['nautık], *f.* (—, *no pl.*) nautical science.
nautisch ['nautıʃ], *adj.* nautical.
Nazi ['na:tsi], *abbr.* National Socialist.
Neapel [ne'a:pəl], *n.* Naples.
Nebel ['ne:bəl], *m.* (—**s**, *pl.* —) fog; *leichter* —, haze, mist; *dichter* —, (*London*) pea-souper; (*with soot*) smog.
Nebelschicht ['ne:bəlʃıçt], *f.* (—, *pl.* —**n**) fog-bank.
neben ['ne:bən], *prep.* (*Dat.*, *Acc.*) near, by, beside, besides, close to, next to; (*in compounds*) secondary, subsidiary, side-. — *adv.* beside, besides.
nebenan [ne:bən'an], *adv.* next door, nearby.
nebenbei [ne:bən'baı], *adv.* besides, by the way, incidentally.
Nebenbuhler ['ne:bənbu:lər], *m.* (—**s**, *pl.* —) rival.
nebeneinander [ne:bənaın'andər], *adv.* side by side, abreast.
Nebenfluß ['ne:bənflus], *m.* (—**sses**, *pl.* ⸚**sse**) tributary, affluent.
nebenher [ne:bən'he:r], *adv.* by the side of, along with.
Nebenmensch ['ne:bənmenʃ], *m.* (—**en**, *pl.* —**en**) fellow creature.
Nebensatz ['ne:bənzats], *m.* (—**es**, *pl.* ⸚**e**) (*Gram.*) subordinate clause.
Nebenzimmer ['ne:bəntsımər], *n.* (—**s**, *pl.* —) adjoining room.
neblig ['ne:blıç], *adj.* foggy, misty, hazy.
nebst [ne:pst], *prep.* (*Dat.*) together with, including.
necken ['nɛkən], *v.a.* tease, chaff, banter.
neckisch ['nɛkıʃ], *adj.*, droll, playful, arch.
Neffe ['nɛfə], *m.* (—**n**, *pl.* —**n**) nephew.
Neger ['ne:gər], *m.* (—**s**, *pl.* —) Negro.
negerartig ['ne:gəra:rtıç], *adj.* Negroid.
negieren [ne'gi:rən], *v.a.* deny, negate, negative.
nehmen ['ne:mən], *v.a. irr.* take, seize; receive, accept; *einem etwas* —, take s.th. from s.o.; *das lasse ich mir nicht* —, I insist on that, I am not to be done out of that; *ein Ende* —, come to an end; *etwas in die Hand* —, take s.th. in hand; *Schaden* —, suffer damage; *einen beim Wort* —, take s.o. at his word; *sich in acht* —, take care.
Nehrung ['ne:ruŋ], *f.* (—, *pl.* —**en**) narrow tongue of land, spit.
Neid [naıt], *m.* (—**es**, *no pl.*) envy, grudge.
Neidhammel ['naıthaməl], *m.* (—**s**, *pl.* —) dog in the manger.
neidisch ['naıdıʃ], *adj.* envious, grudging, jealous.
Neige ['naıgə], *f.* (—, *pl.* —**n**) remnant, sediment; *zur — gehen*, be on the decline, run short, dwindle.
neigen ['naıgən], *v.a.*, *v.n.* incline, bow, bend; *zu etwas* —, be inclined to, be prone to. — *v.r. sich* —, bow.
Neigung ['naıguŋ], *f.* (—, *pl.* —**en**) inclination, proneness; affection; (*ground*) dip, slope, gradient; (*ship*) list.
Neigungsfläche ['naıguŋsflɛçə], *f.* (—, *pl.* —**n**) inclined plane.
nein [naın], *adv.* no.
Nekrolog [nekro'lo:k], *m.* (—(**e**)**s**, *pl.* —**e**) obituary.
Nelke ['nɛklə], *f.* (—, *pl.* —**n**) (*Bot.*) pink, carnation; (*condiment*) clove.
nennen ['nɛnən], *v.a. irr.* name, call by name, term, style.
Nenner ['nɛnər], *m.* (—**s**, *pl.* —) denominator.
Nennung ['nɛnuŋ], *f.* (—, *pl.* —**en**) naming, mentioning.
Nennwert ['nɛnve:rt], *m.* (—**s**, *pl.* —**e**) nominal value.
Nepal ['ne:pal], *n.* Nepal.
Nerv [nɛrf], *m.* (—**s**, *pl.* —**en**) nerve, sinew; *einem auf die —en gehen*, get on s.o.'s nerves.
Nervenlehre ['nɛrfənle:rə], *f.* (—, *no pl.*) neurology.
nervig ['nɛrvıç], *adj.* strong; (*fig.*) pithy.
nervös [nɛr'vø:s], *adj.* nervous, irritable, fidgety.
Nerz [nɛrts], *m.* (—**es**, *pl.* —**e**) mink.
Nessel ['nɛsəl], *f.* (—, *pl.* —**n**) nettle.
Nesseltuch ['nɛsəltu:x], *n.* (—**es**, *no pl.*) muslin.
Nest [nɛst], *n.* (—**es**, *pl.* —**er**) nest; (*eagle*) eyrie; *kleines* —, small town.
Nesthäkchen ['nɛsthɛ:kçən], *n.* (—**s**, *pl.* —) youngest child.
nett [nɛt], *adj.* nice, kind, friendly; neat, trim.
netto ['nɛto], *adv.* (*Comm.*) net, clear.
Netz [nɛts], *n.* (—**es**, *pl.* —**e**) net; (*Electr.*) grid; *Eisenbahn* —, railway network *or* system.
netzen ['nɛtsən], *v.a.* (*obs.*, *Poet.*) wet, moisten.
Netzhaut ['nɛtshaut], *f.* (—, *pl.* ⸚**e**) retina.
neu [nɔy], *adj.* new, fresh; modern; recent; *aufs —e*, *von —em*, anew, afresh; *—e*, *—ere Sprachen*, modern languages.
Neuenburg ['nɔyənburk], *n.* Neuchâtel.
neuerdings ['nɔyərdıŋs], *adv.* newly, lately.
Neuerer ['nɔyərər], *m.* (—**s**, *pl.* —) innovator.

neuerlich [ˈnɔyərlɪç], *adj.* late, repeated.
Neufundland [nɔyˈfuntlant], *n.* Newfoundland.
Neugier(de) [ˈnɔygiːr(də)], *f.* (—, *no pl.*) inquisitiveness, curiosity.
neugierig [ˈnɔygiːrɪç], *adj.* curious, inquisitive.
Neuheit [ˈnɔyhaɪt], *f.* (—, *pl.* —**en**) novelty.
Neuigkeit [ˈnɔyɪçkaɪt], *f.* (—, *pl.* —**en**) piece of news.
neulich [ˈnɔylɪç], *adv.* lately, recently.
Neuling [ˈnɔylɪŋ], *m.* (—**s**, *pl.* —**e**) novice, beginner, tyro, newcomer; (*Am.*) greenhorn.
neumodisch [ˈnɔymoːdɪʃ], *adj.* newfangled, in vogue.
Neumond [ˈnɔymoːnt], *m.* (—**s**, *pl.* —**e**) new moon.
neun [nɔyn], *num. adj.* nine.
Neunauge [ˈnɔynaugə], *n.* (—**s**, *pl.* —**n**) river lamprey.
neunzehn [ˈnɔyntseːn], *num. adj.* nineteen.
neunzig [ˈnɔyntsɪç], *num. adj.* ninety.
Neuregelung [ˈnɔyreːgəluŋ], *f.* (—, *pl.* —**en**) rearrangement.
Neuseeland [nɔyˈzeːlant], *n.* New Zealand.
neutralisieren [nɔytraliˈziːrən], *v.a.* neutralise.
Neutralität [nɔytraliˈtɛːt], *f.* (—, *no pl.*) neutrality.
Neutrum [ˈnɔytrum], *n.* (—**s**, *pl.* —**ren**) (*Gram.*) neuter.
Neuzeit [ˈnɔytsaɪt], *f.* (—, *no pl.*) modern times.
nicht [nɪçt], *adv.* not; *auch* —, nor; — *doch*, don't; — *einmal*, not even; *durchaus* —, not at all, by no means; — *mehr*, no more, no longer; not any more; *noch* —, not yet; — *wahr?* isn't it? aren't you? (*in compounds*) non–, dis–, a– (*negativing*).
Nichte [ˈnɪçtə], *f.* (—, *pl.* —**n**) niece.
nichten [ˈnɪçtən], *adv.* (*obs.*) *mit*—, by no means, not at all.
nichtig [ˈnɪçtɪç], *adj.* null, void, invalid.
Nichtigkeit [ˈnɪçtɪçkaɪt], *f.* (—, *no pl.*) invalidity, nullity.
nichts [nɪçts], *pron.* nothing, nought; — *als*, nothing but.
nichtsdestoweniger [nɪçtsdɛstoˈveːnɪgər], *adv.* nevertheless.
Nichtsnutz [ˈnɪçtsnuts], *m.* (—**es**, *pl.* —**e**) good for nothing.
Nickel [ˈnɪkəl], *n.* (—**s**, *no pl.*) (*metal*) nickel.
nicken [ˈnɪkən], *v.n.* nod.
nie [niː], *adv.* never, at no time.
nieder [ˈniːdər], *adj.* low, lower, nether; mean, inferior. — *adv.* down.
niedergeschlagen [ˈniːdərgəʃlaːgən], *adj.* dejected, low-spirited, depressed.
niederkommen [ˈniːdərkɔmən], *v.n.* *irr.* (*aux.* sein) (*rare*) be confined.
Niederkunft [ˈniːdərkunft], *f.* (—, *no pl.*) confinement, childbirth.
Niederlage [ˈniːdərlaːgə], *f.* (—, *pl.* —**n**) (*enemy*) defeat, overthrow; (*goods*) depot, warehouse; agency.
Niederlande [ˈniːdərlandə], *n. pl.* the Netherlands.
niederlassen [ˈniːdərlasən], *v.a.* *irr.* let down. — *v.r.* *sich* —, sit down, take a seat; settle; establish o.s. in business.
Niederlassung [ˈniːdərlasuŋ], *f.* (—, *pl.* —**en**) establishment; settlement, colony; branch, branch establishment.
niederlegen [ˈniːdərleːgən], *v.a.* lay down, put down; (*office*) resign, abdicate. — *v.r.* *sich* —, lie down.
Niederschlag [ˈniːdərʃlaːk], *m.* (—**s**, *pl.* ¨**e**) precipitation, sediment, deposit; rain.
niederschlagen [ˈniːdərʃlaːgən], *v.a.* *irr.* strike down; (*fig.*) depress, discourage; (*Law*) quash, cancel; (*eyes*) cast down; (*Chem.*) precipitate; (*Boxing*) knock out.
Niedertracht [ˈniːdərtraxt], *f.* (—, *no pl.*) baseness, meanness, villainy, beastliness.
Niederung [ˈniːdəruŋ], *f.* (—, *pl.* —**en**) low ground, marsh.
niedlich [ˈniːtlɪç], *adj.* pretty, dainty; (*Am.*) cute.
niedrig [ˈniːdrɪç], *adj.* low; (*fig.*) base, vile.
niemals [ˈniːmaːls], *adv.* never, at no time.
niemand [ˈniːmant], *pron.* nobody, no one.
Niere [ˈniːrə], *f.* (—, *pl,* —**n**) kidney.
Nierenbraten [ˈniːrənbraːtən], *m.* (—**s**, *no pl.*) roast loin.
Nierenfett [ˈniːrənfɛt], *n.* (—**s**, *no pl.*) suet.
nieseln [ˈniːzəln], *v.n.* *imp.* drizzle.
niesen [ˈniːzən], *v.n.* sneeze.
Nießbrauch [ˈniːsbraux], *m.* (—**s**, *no pl.*) usufruct, benefit.
Niete [ˈniːtə], *f.* (—, *pl.* —**n**) blank; (*Engin.*) rivet; failure.
Niger [ˈniːgər], *n.* Niger.
Nigeria [niˈgeːrja], *n.* Nigeria.
Nikaragua [nikaˈraːgua], *n.* Nicaragua.
Nikolaus [ˈnɪkolaus], *m.* Nicholas; *Sankt* —, Santa Claus.
Nil [niːl], *m.* (—**s**, *no pl.*) Nile.
Nilpferd [ˈniːlpfeːrt], *n.* (—**s**, *pl.* —**e**) (*Zool.*) hippopotamus.
nimmer (mehr) [ˈnɪmər (meːr)], *adv.* never, never again.
nippen [ˈnɪpən], *v.a., v.n.* sip, (take a) nip (of).
Nippsachen [ˈnɪpzaxən], *f. pl.* knick-knacks.
nirgends [ˈnɪrgənts], *adv.* nowhere.
Nische [ˈniːʃə], *f.* (—, *pl.* —**n**) niche.
Nisse [ˈnɪsə], *f.* (—, *pl.* —**n**) nit.
nisten [ˈnɪstən], *v.n.* nest.
Niveau [niˈvoː], *n.* (—**s**, *pl.* —**s**) level, standard.
nivellieren [nivɛˈliːrən], *v.a.* level.
Nixe [ˈnɪksə], *f.* (—, *pl.* —**n**) water-nymph, mermaid, water-sprite.

Nizza ['nɪtsa], *n.* Nice.
nobel ['no:bəl], *adj.* noble, smart; (*Am.*) swell; munificent, open-handed, magnanimous.
noch [nɔx], *adv.* still, yet; — *einmal*, — *mals*, once more; *weder* . . . — . . ., neither . . . nor . . .; — *nicht*, not yet; — *nie*, never yet, never before.
nochmalig ['nɔxma:lɪç], *adj.* repeated.
Nomade [no'ma:də], *m.* (—**n**, *pl.* —**n**) nomad.
nominell [nomi'nɛl], *adj.* nominal.
nominieren [nomi'ni:rən], *v.a.* nominate.
Nonne ['nɔnə], *f.* (—, *pl.* —**n**) nun.
Noppe ['nɔpə], *f.* (—, *pl.* —**n**) nap.
Norden ['nɔrdən], *m.* (—**s**, *no pl.*) north.
nördlich ['nœrtlɪç], *adj.* northern, northerly.
Nordsee ['nɔrtze:], *f.* North Sea.
nörgeln ['nœrgəln], *v.n.* find fault, cavil, carp, nag.
Norm ['nɔrm], *f.* (—, *pl.* —**en**) standard, rule, norm.
normal [nɔr'ma:l], *adj.* normal, standard.
Norwegen ['nɔrve:gən], *n.* Norway.
Not [no:t], *f.* (—, *pl.* ⸚**e**) need, necessity; misery, want, trouble, distress; (*in compounds*) emergency.
not [no:t], *pred. adj.* — *tun*, be necessary.
Nota ['no:ta], *f.* (—, *pl.* —**s**) bill, statement.
Notar [no'ta:r], *m.* (—**s**, *pl.* —**e**) notary.
Notdurft ['notdurft], *f.* (—, *pl.* ⸚**e**) want, necessaries, necessity; *seine* — *verrichten*, ease o.s.
notdürftig ['no:tdyrftɪç], *adj.* scanty, makeshift.
Note ['no:tə], *f.* (—, *pl.* —**n**) note; (*Mus.*) note; (*School*) mark(s); *nach* —*n*, (*fig.*) with a vengeance.
Notenbank ['no:tənbaŋk], *f.* (—, *pl.* —**en**) bank of issue.
Notenblatt ['no:tənblat], *n.* (—**s**, *pl.* ⸚**er**) sheet of music.
notgedrungen ['no:tgədruŋən], *adj.* compulsory, forced; perforce.
Nothelfer ['no:thɛlfər], *m.* (—**s**, *pl.* —) helper in time of need.
notieren [no'ti:rən], *v.a.* note, book; (*Comm.*) quote.
notifizieren [notifi'tsi:rən], *v.a.* notify.
nötig ['nø:tɪç], *adj.* necessary; — *haben*, want, need.
nötigen ['nø:tɪgən], *v.a.* compel, press, force, urge; necessitate; *sich* — *lassen*, stand upon ceremony.
Notiz [no'ti:ts], *f.* (—, *pl.* —**en**) note, notice; — *nehmen von*, take notice of; (*pl.*) notes, jottings.
notleidend ['no:tlaɪdənt], *adj.* financially distressed, indigent, needy.
notorisch [no'to:rɪʃ], *adj.* notorious.
Notstand ['no:tʃtant], *m.* (—**s**, *no pl.*) state of distress; emergency.
Notverband ['no:tfɛrbant], *m.* (—**es**, *pl.* ⸚**e**) first-aid dressing.
Notwehr ['no:tve:r], *f.* (—, *no pl.*) self-defence.
notwendig ['no:tvɛndɪç], *adj.* necessary, essential, needful.
Notzucht ['no:ttsuxt], *f.* (—, *no pl.*) rape, violation.
Novelle [no'vɛlə], *f.* (—, *pl.* —**n**) (*Lit.*) novella, short story, short novel.
Novize [no'vi:tsə], *m.* (—**n**, *pl.* —**n**) or *f.* (—, *pl.* —**n**) novice.
Nu [nu:], *m.* & *n.* (—, *no pl.*) moment; *im* —, in no time, in an instant.
Nubien ['nu:bjən], *n.* Nubia.
nüchtern ['nyçtərn], *adj.* fasting; sober; jejune; (*fig.*) dry, matter-of-fact, realistic.
Nüchternheit ['nyçtərnhaɪt], *f.* (—, *no pl.*) sobriety; (*fig.*) dryness.
Nudel ['nu:dəl], *f.* (—, *pl.* —**n**) noodles, macaroni, vermicelli; *eine komische* —, a funny person.
Null [nul], *f.* (—, *pl.* —**en**) nought, zero; (*fig.*) nonentity.
null [nul], *adj.* null; nil; — *und nichtig*, null and void; *etwas für* — *und nichtig erklären*, annul.
numerieren [nume'ri:rən], *v.a.* number.
Nummer ['numər], *f.* (—, *pl.* —**n**) number, size, issue.
nun [nu:n], *adv.*, *conj.* now, at present; since; —*!* now! well! *von* — *an*, henceforth; — *und nimmermehr*, nevermore; *was* —*?* what next?
nunmehr ['nu:nme:r], *adv.* now, by this time.
Nunzius ['nuntsjus], *m.* (—, *pl.* —**zien**) (Papal) nuncio.
nur [nu:r], *adv.* only, solely, merely, but; *wenn* —, if only, provided that; — *das nicht*, anything but that; — *zu*, go to it!
Nürnberg ['nyrnbɛrk], *n.* Nuremberg.
Nuß [nus], *f.* (—, *pl.* ⸚**sse**) nut.
Nußhäher ['nushɛ:ər], *m.* (—**s**, *pl.* —) (*Orn.*) jay.
Nüster ['nystər], *f.* (—, *pl.* —**n**) (*horse*) nostril.
Nutzanwendung ['nutsanvɛnduŋ], *f.* (—, *pl.* —**en**) practical application.
nutzbar ['nutsba:r], *adj.* useful, usable, productive.
nütze ['nytsə], *adj.* useful, of use.
Nutzen ['nutsən], *m.* (—**s**, *pl.* —) use, utility; profit, gain, advantage, benefit; — *bringen*, yield profit; — *ziehen aus*, derive profit from.
nützen ['nytsən], *v.a.* make use of, use. — *v.n.* be of use, serve, be effective, work.
nützlich ['nytslɪç], *adj.* useful.
nutzlos ['nutslo:s], *adj.* useless.
Nutznießer ['nutsni:sər], *m.* (—**s**, *pl.* —) beneficiary, usufructuary.
Nymphe ['nymfə], *f.* (—, *pl.* —**en**) nymph.

O

O [o:], *n*, (—s, *pl*. —s) the letter O.
o! [o:], *excl*. oh!
Oase [o'a:zə], *f*. (—, *pl*. —n) oasis.
ob [ɔp], *conj*. whether; if; *als* —, as if; *und* —*!* rather! yes, indeed! — *prep*. (*Genit*., *Dat*.) on account of; upon, on.
Obacht ['o:baxt], *f*. (—, *no pl*.) heed, care; — *geben*, pay attention, look out.
Obdach ['ɔpdax], *n*. (—es, *no pl*.) shelter, lodging.
Obduktion ['ɔpdukts'jo:n], *f*. (—, *pl*. —en) post-mortem examination.
oben [o:bən], *adv*. above, aloft, on top; (*house*) upstairs; (*water*) on the surface; *von* — *bis unten*, from top to bottom; *von* — *herab*, from above; (*fig*.) haughtily, superciliously.
obendrein [o:bən'draIn], *adv*. besides, into the bargain.
obengenannt ['o:bəngənant], *adj*. above-mentioned.
Ober ['o:bər], *m*. (—s, *pl*. —) head waiter; *Herr*—*!*, waiter!; (*in compounds*) upper, chief.
ober ['o:bər], *adj*. upper, higher; chief; superior.
Oberfläche ['o:bərflɛçə], *f*. (—, *pl*. —n) surface.
oberflächlich ['o:bərflɛçlIç], *adj*. superficial, casual.
oberhalb ['o:bərhalp], *adv*., *prep*. (*Genit*.) above.
Oberin ['o:bərIn], *f*. (—, *pl*. —innen) (*Eccl*.) Mother Superior; hospital matron.
Oberschule ['o:bərʃu:lə], *f*. (—, *pl*. —n) high school, secondary school.
Oberst ['o:bərst], *m*. (—en, *pl*. —en) colonel.
Oberstaatsanwalt ['o:bərʃta:tsanvalt], *m*. (—s, *pl*. ⸚e) Attorney-General.
oberste ['o:bərstə], *adj*. uppermost, highest, supreme.
Oberstimme ['o:bərʃtImə], *f*. (—, *pl*. —n) (*Mus*.) treble, soprano.
Oberstübchen ['o:bərʃty:pçən], *n*. (—s, *pl*. —) (*fig*.) *nicht richtig im* — *sein*, have bats in the belfry.
Obervolta ['o:bərvɔlta], *n*. Upper Volta.
obgleich [ɔp'glaIç], *conj*. though, although.
Obhut ['ɔphu:t], *f*. (—, *no pl*.) keeping, care, protection.
obig ['o:bIç], *adj*. foregoing, above-mentioned, aforementioned, aforesaid.
objektiv [ɔpjɛk'ti:f], *adj*. objective, impartial, unprejudiced.
Oblate [o'bla:tə], *f*. (—, *pl*. —n) wafer; (*Eccl*.) Host.
obliegen ['ɔpli:gən], *v.n*. *irr*. be incumbent upon s.o.; be o.'s duty; apply o.s. to.
Obmann ['ɔpman], *m*. (—es, *pl*. ⸚er) chairman; (*jury*) foreman.
Obrigkeit ['o:brIçkaIt], *f*. (—, *pl*. —en) authorities.
obschon [ɔp'ʃo:n] *see under* **obwohl**.
Observatorium ['ɔpzɛrva'to:rjum], *n*. (—s, *pl*. —rien) observatory.
obsiegen ['ɔpzi:gən], *v.n*. (*rare*) be victorious.
Obst [o:pst], *n*. (—es, *no pl*.) fruit.
obszön [ɔps'tsø:n], *adj*. obscene.
obwalten ['ɔpvaltən], *v.n*. (*rare*) exist, prevail, obtain; *unter den* —*den Umständen*, in the circumstances, as matters stand.
obwohl [ɔp'vo:l] (also **obschon** [ɔp'ʃo:n], **obzwar** [ɔp'tsva:r]), *conj*. though, although.
Ochse ['ɔksə], *m*. (—n, *pl*. —n) (*Zool*). ox; bullock; (*fig*.) blockhead.
ochsen ['ɔksən], *v.n*. (*sl*.) swot, cram.
Ochsenauge ['ɔksənaugə], *n*. (—s, *pl*. —n) ox-eye, bull's eye; (*Archit*.) oval dormer window; porthole light.
Ochsenziemer ['ɔksəntsi:mər], *m*. (—s, *pl*. —) (*obs*.) horse-whip.
Ocker ['ɔkər], *m*. (—s, *no pl*.) ochre.
Öde ['ø:də], *f*. (—, *pl*. —n) wilderness.
öde ['ø:də], *adj*. desolate, bleak, dreary.
Odem ['o:dəm], *m*. (—s, *no pl*.) (*Poet*.) breath.
oder ['o:dər], *conj*. or; — *aber*, or else; — *auch*, or rather.
Ofen ['o:fən], *m*. (—s, *pl*. ⸚) stove; oven, furnace.
Ofenpest [o:fən'pɛst], *n*. Budapest.
offen ['ɔfən], *adj*. open; (*fig*.) candid, sincere, frank; — *gestanden*, frankly speaking.
offenbar [ɔfən'ba:r], *adj*. obvious, manifest, evident.
offenbaren [ɔfən'ba:rən], *v.a*. *insep*. make known, reveal, disclose. — *v.r*. *sich einem* —, open o.'s heart to s.o.; unbosom o.s.
Offenheit ['ɔfənhaIt], *f*. (—, *pl*. —en) frankness, candour.
offenkundig ['ɔfənkundIç], *adj*. obvious, manifest.
offensichtlich ['ɔfənzIçtlIç], *adj*. obvious; apparent.
öffentlich ['œfəntlIç], *adj*. public.
offerieren [ɔfe'ri:rən], *v.a*. offer.
Offerte [ɔ'fɛrtə], *f*. (—, *pl*. —n) offer, tender.
offiziell [ɔfi'tsjɛl], *adj*. official.
Offizier [ɔfi'tsi:r], *m*. (—s, *pl*. —e) officer, lieutenant.
Offizierspatent [ɔfi'tsi:rspatɛnt], *n*. (—s, *pl*. —e) (*Mil*.) commission.
offiziös [ɔfi'tsjø:s], *adj*. semi-official.
öffnen ['œfnən], *v.a*. open.
oft [ɔft], **oftmals** ['ɔftma:ls], *adv*. often, frequently.
öfters ['œftərs], *adv*. often, frequently.

Oheim ['o:haɪm], *m.* (**—s**, *pl.* **—e**) (*Poet.*) uncle.
ohne ['o:nə], *prep.* (*Acc.*) without, but for, except.
ohnehin ['o:nəhɪn], *adv.* as it is.
Ohnmacht ['o:nmaxt], *f.* (—, *pl.* **—en**) fainting-fit, swoon; impotence; *in — fallen*, faint.
Ohr [o:r], *n.* (**—es**, *pl.* **—en**) ear; *bis über beide —en*, head over heels; *die —en spitzen*, prick up o.'s ears.
Ohrenbläser ['o:rənblɛ:zər], *m.* (**—s**, *pl.* —) tale-bearer.
Ohrensausen ['o:rənzauzən], *n.* (**—s**, *no pl.*) humming in the ears.
Ohrenschmaus ['o:rənʃmaus], *m.* (**—es**, *no pl.*) musical treat.
Ohrfeige ['o:rfaɪgə], *f.* (—, *pl.* **—n**) box on the ear.
Ohrläppchen ['o:rlɛpçən], *n.* (**—s**, *pl.* —) lobe of the ear.
Ohrmuschel ['o:rmuʃəl], *f.* (—, *pl.* **—n**) auricle.
oktav [ɔk'ta:f], *adj.* octavo.
Oktober [ɔk'to:bər], *m.* (**—s**, *pl.* —) October.
oktroyieren [ɔktroa'ji:rən], *v.a.* dictate, force s.th. upon s.o.
okulieren [oku'li:rən], *v.a.* (*trees*) graft.
Öl [ø:l], *n.* (**—s**, *pl.* **—e**) oil; (*rare*) olive-oil.
Ölanstrich ['ø:lanʃtrɪç], *m.* (**—s**, *pl.* **—e**) coat of oil-paint.
ölen ['ø:lən], *v.a.* oil, lubricate; (*rare*) anoint.
Ölgemälde ['ø:lgəmɛ:ldə], *n.* (**—s**, *pl.* —) oil painting.
Ölung ['ø:luŋ], *f.* (—, *pl.* **—en**) oiling; anointing; (*Eccl.*) *die letzte —*, Extreme Unction.
Olymp [o'lymp], *m.* Mount Olympus.
olympisch [o'lympɪʃ], *adj.* Olympian.
Omelett [ɔmə'lɛt], *n.* (**—s**, *pl.* **—s**) omelette.
Onkel ['ɔŋkəl], *m.* (**—s**, *pl.* —) uncle.
Oper ['o:pər], *f.* (—, *pl.* **—n**) opera.
operieren [opə'ri:rən], *v.a.*, *v.n.* operate (on); *sich — lassen*, be operated on; undergo an operation.
Opfer ['ɔpfər], *n.* (**—s**, *pl.* —) sacrifice; victim.
opfern ['ɔpfərn], *v.a.*, *v.n.* offer (up), sacrifice, immolate.
opponieren [ɔpo'ni:rən], *v.n.* oppose.
Optiker ['ɔptɪkər], *m.* (**—s**, *pl.* —) optician.
oratorisch [ora'to:rɪʃ], *adj.* oratorical.
Orchester [ɔr'kɛstər], *n.* (**—s**, *pl.* —) orchestra, band.
orchestrieren [ɔrkɛs'tri:rən], *v.a.* orchestrate, score for orchestra.
Orchidee [ɔrçi'de:], *f.* (—, *pl.* **—n**) (*Bot.*) orchid
Orden ['ɔrdən], *m.* (**—s**, *pl.* —) medal; (*Eccl.*) (religious) order.
ordentlich ['ɔrdəntlɪç], *adj.* orderly, tidy, methodical, neat; regular; respectable, steady; sound; *—er Professor*, (full) professor.
Order ['ɔrdər], *f.* (—, *pl.* **—s**) (*Comm.*) order.
Ordinarius [ɔrdi'na:rjus], *m.* (—, *pl.* **—ien**) (*Univ.*) professor; (*Eccl.*) ordinary.
ordinär [ɔrdi'nɛ:r], *adj.* common, vulgar.
ordnen ['ɔrdnən], *v.a.* put in order, tidy, arrange, dispose.
Ordnung ['ɔrdnuŋ], *f.* (—, *pl.* **—en**) order, arrangement, disposition, routine; tidiness; class, rank; *in —*, all right, in good trim; *nicht in —*, out of order, wrong.
ordnungsgemäß ['ɔrdnuŋsgəmɛ:s], *adv.* duly.
ordnungsmäßig ['ɔrdnuŋsmɛsɪç], *adj.* regular.
ordnungswidrig ['ɔrdnuŋsvi:drɪç], *adj.* irregular.
Ordnungszahl ['ɔrdnuŋstsa:l], *f.* (—, *pl.* **—en**) ordinal number.
Ordonnanz [ɔrdɔ'nants], *f.* (—, *pl.* **—en**) ordinance; (*Mil.*) orderly.
Organ [ɔr'ga:n], *n.* (**—s**, *pl.* **—e**) organ.
organisieren [ɔrgani'zi:rən], *v.a.* organise.
Orgel ['ɔrgəl], *f.* (—, *pl.* **—n**) (*Mus.*) organ.
Orgelzug ['ɔ:rgəltsu:k], *m.* (**—s**, *pl.* **¨e**) organ-stop.
Orgie ['ɔrgjə], *f.* (—, *pl.* **—n**) orgy.
orientalisch [orjɛn'ta:lɪʃ], *adj.* oriental, eastern.
orientieren [orjɛn'ti:rən], *v.a.* inform, orientate; set s.o. right. — *v.r. sich — über*, orientate o.s., find out about; get o.'s bearings.
Orkan [ɔr'ka:n], *m.* (**—s**, *pl.* **—e**) hurricane, gale, typhoon.
Ornat [ɔr'na:t], *m.* (**—es**, *pl.* **—e**) official robes; vestments.
Ort [ɔrt], *m.* (**—es**, *pl.* **—e**, **¨er**) place, spot; region; (*in compounds*) local.
örtlich ['œrtlɪç], *adj.* local.
Ortschaft ['ɔrtʃaft], *f.* (—, *pl.* **—en**) place, township, village.
Öse ['ø:zə], *f.* (—, *pl.* **—n**) loop; *Haken und —n*, hooks and eyes.
Ostasien ['ɔsta:zjən], *n.* Eastern Asia, the Far East.
Ost(en) ['ɔst(ən)], *m.* (**—s**, *no pl.*) east.
ostentativ [ɔstɛnta'ti:f], *adj.* ostentatious.
Osterei ['o:stəraɪ], *n.* (**—s**, *pl.* **—er**) Easter egg.
Ostern ['o:stərn], *f. pl.* (*used as n. sing.*) Easter.
Österreich ['ø:stərraɪç], *n.* Austria.
Ostindien ['ɔstɪndjən], *n.* the East Indies.
östlich ['œstlɪç], *adj.* eastern, easterly.
Oxyd [ɔk'sy:t], *n.* (**—es**, *pl.* **—e**) oxide.
oxydieren [ɔksy'di:rən], *v.a.*, *v.n.* oxidise.
Ozean ['o:tsea:n], *m.* (**—s**, *pl.* **—e**) ocean, sea; *Grosser —*, Pacific (Ocean).
Ozon [o'tso:n], *n.* (**—s**, *no pl.*) ozone.

P

P [pe:], *n.* (**—s,** *pl.* **—s**) the letter P.
Paar [pa:r], *n.* (**—es,** *pl.* **—e**) pair, couple.
paar [pa:r], *adj. ein* —, a few, some.
Pacht [paxt], *f.* (—, *pl.* **—en**) lease; *in — nehmen*, take on lease.
Pachthof ['paxtho:f], *m.* (**—s,** *pl.* **¨e**) leasehold estate, farm.
Pack (1) [pak], *m.* (**—s,** *pl.* **¨e**) pack, bale, packet; *mit Sack und* —, (with) bag and baggage.
Pack (2) [pak], *n.* (**—s,** *no pl.*) rabble, mob.
Päckchen ['pɛkçən], *n.* (**—s,** *pl.* —) pack, packet; (small) parcel.
packen ['pakən], *v.a.* pack; seize; (*fig.*) **—*d***, thrilling; *pack dich!* be off! scram!
pädagogisch [pɛ:da'go:gɪʃ], *adj.* educational, pedagogic(al).
paddeln ['padəln], *v.n.* paddle.
paff [paf], *excl.* bang! *ich bin ganz* —, I am astounded.
paffen ['pafən], *v.n.* puff; draw (at a pipe).
Page ['pa:ʒə], *m.* (**—n,** *pl.* **—n**) page-boy.
Paket [pa'ke:t], *n.* (**—s,** *pl.* **—e**) packet, package, parcel.
paktieren [pak'ti:rən], *v.n.* come to terms.
Palast [pa'last], *m.* (**—es,** *pl.* **¨e**) palace.
Palästina [palɛ'sti:na], *n.* Palestine.
Paletot ['palәto:], *m.* (**—s,** *pl.* **—s**) overcoat.
Palisanderholz [pali'zandərhɔlts], *n.* (**—es,** *no pl.*) rosewood.
Palme ['palmə], *f.* (—, *pl.* **—n**) (*Bot.*) palm-tree.
Palmkätzchen ['palmkɛtsçən], *n.* (**—s,** *pl.* —) (*Bot.*) catkin.
Palmwoche ['palmvɔxə], *f.* Holy Week.
Pampelmuse ['pampəlmu:zə], *f.* (—, *pl.* **—n**) (*Bot.*) grapefruit.
Panama ['pa:nama], *n.* Panama.
Panier [pa'ni:r], *n.* (**—s,** *pl.* **—e**) standard, banner.
panieren [pa'ni:rən], *v.a.* dress (*meat etc.*), roll in bread-crumbs.
Panne ['panə], *f.* (—, *pl.* **—n**) puncture; (*Motor.*) break-down; mishap.
panschen ['panʃən], *v.n.* splash about in water. — *v.a.* adulterate.
Pantoffel [pan'tɔfəl], *m.* (**—s,** *pl.* **—n**) slipper; *unter dem — stehen*, be henpecked.
Pantoffelheld [pan'tɔfəlhɛlt], *m.* (**—en,** *pl.* **—en**) henpecked husband.
Panzer ['pantsər], *m.* (**—s,** *pl.* —) armour, breast-plate, coat of mail; (*Mil.*) tank.
Papagei [papa'gaɪ], *m.* (**—s,** *pl.* **—en**) (*Orn.*) parrot.
Papier [pa'pi:r], *n.* (**—s,** *pl.* **—e**) paper; (*Comm.*) stocks; (*pl.*) papers, documents; *ein Bogen* —, a sheet of paper.
Papierkrieg [pa'pi:rkri:k], *m.* (**—s,** *no pl.*) (*coll.*) red tape.
Papierwaren [pa'pi:rva:rən], *f. pl.* stationery.
Pappdeckel ['papdɛkəl], *m.* (**—s,** *pl.* —) pasteboard.
Pappe ['papə], *f.* (—, *no pl.*) paste, cardboard, pasteboard.
Pappel ['papəl], *f.* (—, *pl.* **—n**) poplar.
pappen ['papən], *v.a.* stick; glue, paste.
Pappenstiel ['papənʃti:l], *m.* (**—s,** *pl.* **—e**) trifle.
papperlapapp ['papərlapap], *excl.* fiddlesticks! nonsense!
Papst [pa:pst], *m.* (**—es,** *pl.* **¨e**) Pope.
päpstlich ['pɛ:pstlɪç], *adj.* papal; **—*er als der Papst***, fanatically loyal, outheroding Herod; over-zealous.
Parabel [pa'ra:bəl], *f.* (—, *pl.* **—n**) parable; (*Maths.*) parabola.
paradieren [para'di:rən], *v.n.* parade, make a show.
Paradies [para'di:s], *n.* (**—es,** *pl.* **—e**) paradise.
paradox [para'dɔks], *adj.* paradoxical.
Paragraph [para'gra:f], *m.* (**—en,** *pl.* **—en**) paragraph, article, clause, section.
Paraguay ['paragvaɪ, para'gua:ɪ], *n.* Paraguay.
Paralyse [para'ly:zə], *f.* (—, *pl.* **—n**) paralysis.
parat [pa'ra:t], *adj.* prepared, ready.
Pardon [par'dɔ̃], *m.* (**—s,** *no pl.*) pardon, forgiveness.
Parfüm [par'fy:m], *n.* (**—s,** *pl.* **—e**) perfume, scent.
pari ['pa:ri:], *adv.* at par.
parieren [pa'ri:rən], *v.a.* parry, keep off. — *v.n.* obey; *aufs Wort* —, obey implicitly *or* to the letter.
Parität [pari'tɛ:t], *f.* (—, *no pl.*) parity; (religious) equality.
Parkanlagen [park'anla:gən], *f. pl.* parks; public gardens.
parken ['parkən], *v.a.* park.
Parkett [par'kɛt], *n.* (**—s,** *pl.* **—e**) parquet flooring; (*Theat.*) stalls.
Parkuhr [park'u:r], *f.* (—, *pl.* **—en**) parking-meter.
Parlament [parla'mɛnt], *n.* (**—s,** *pl.* **—e**) parliament.
Parlamentär [parlamɛn'tɛ:r], *m.* (**—s,** *pl.* **—e**) officer negotiating a truce.
Parlamentarier [parlamɛn'ta:rjər], *m.* (**—s,** *pl.* —) parliamentarian, member of a parliament.
Parole [pa'ro:lə], *f.* (—, *pl.* **—n**) watchword, cue, motto, slogan, password.

Partei [par'taI], *f.* (—, *pl.* **—en**) party, faction; — *nehmen für*, side with.
Parteigänger [par'taIgɛŋər], *m.* (**—s**, *pl.* —) partisan.
Parteigenosse [par'taIgənɔsə], *m.* (**—n**, *pl.* **—n**) party member (especially National Socialist); comrade.
parteiisch [par'taIIʃ], *adj.* partial, biased, prejudiced.
Parteinahme [par'taIna:mə], *f.* (—, *no pl.*) partisanship.
Parteitag [par'taIta:k], *m.* (**—s**, *pl.* **—e**) party conference; congress.
Parterre [par'tɛrə], *n.* (**—s**, *pl.* **—s**) ground floor; (*Theat.*) pit; stalls.
Partie [par'ti:], *f.* (—, *pl.* **—n**) (*Comm.*) parcel; (*marriage*) match; (*chess etc.*) game; (*bridge*) rubber; outing, excursion, trip.
Partitur [parti'tu:r], *f.* (—, *pl.* **—en**) (*Mus.*) score.
Partizip [parti'tsi:p], *n.* (**—s**, *pl.* **—e, —ien**) (*Gram.*) participle.
Parzelle [par'tsɛlə], *f.* (—, *pl.* **—n**) allotment, lot, parcel.
paschen ['paʃən], *v.a.* smuggle.
Paß [pas], *m.* (**—sses**, *pl.* **¨sse**) (*mountain*) pass; (*travelling*) passport; (*horse*) amble.
Passagier [pasa'ʒi:r], *m.* (**—s**, *pl.* **—e**) passenger; *blinder* —, stowaway.
Passant [pa'sant], *m.* (**—en**, *pl.* **—en**) passer-by.
Passatwind [pa'sa:tvInt], *m.* (**—s**, *pl.* **—e**) trade-wind.
passen ['pasən], *v.n.* fit, suit, be suitable, be convenient; (*Cards*) pass.
passieren [pa'si:rən], *v.a.* sieve; (*road*) pass, cross, negotiate. — *v.n.* (*aux.* sein) pass; happen, take place, come about.
Passif, Passivum [pa'si:f *or* 'pasi:f, pa'si:vum], *n.* (**—s**, *pl.* **—e**; —, *pl.* **—va**) (*Gram.*) passive voice; (*Comm.*) (*pl.*) debts, liabilities.
Passus ['pasus], *m.* (—, *pl.* —) passage (in book).
Pasta, Paste ['pasta, 'pastə], *f.* (—, *pl.* **—ten**) paste.
Pastell [pa'stɛl], *m.* (**—s**, *pl.* **—e**) pastel, crayon; — *malen*, draw in pastel.
Pastete [pa'ste:tə], *f.* (—, *pl.* **—n**) pie, pastry.
Pastille [pa'stIlə], *f.* (—, *pl.* **—n**) lozenge, pastille.
Pastor ['pastɔr], *m.* (**—s**, *pl.* **—en**) minister, pastor; parson; vicar, rector.
Pate ['pa:tə], *m.* (**—n**, *pl.* **—n**) godparent; — *stehen*, be godfather to.
patent [pa'tɛnt], *adj.* fine, grand, (*sl.*) smashing.
Patent [pa'tɛnt], *n.* (**—(e)s**, *pl.* **—e**) patent; charter, licence.
patentieren [patɛn'ti:rən], *v.a.* patent, license.
pathetisch [pa'te:tIʃ], *adj.* elevated, solemn, moving.
Patin ['pa:tIn], *f.* (—, *pl.* **—innen**) godmother.
patriotisch [patri'o:tIʃ], *adj.* patriotic.
Patrone [pa'tro:nə], *f.* (—, *pl.* **—n**) cartridge; stencil, pattern.
Patrouille [pa'truljə], *f.* (—, *pl.* **—n**) (*Mil.*) patrol.
Patsche ['patʃə], *f.* (—, *pl.* **—n**) (*dial.*) hand; (*fig.*) mess, pickle; *in eine — geraten*, get into a jam.
patschen ['patʃən], *v.n.* (*aux.* sein) splash.
Patt [pat], *n.* (**—s**, *pl.* **—s**) (*Chess*) stalemate.
patzig ['patsIç], *adj.* rude; cheeky, saucy.
Pauke ['paukə], *f.* (—, *pl.* **—n**) kettledrum; *mit —n und Trompeten*, with drums beating and colours flying.
pauken ['paukən], *v.n.* beat the kettledrum; (*coll.*) swot, plod, grind; fight a duel.
pausbackig ['pausbakIç], *adj.* chubby-faced, bonny.
Pauschale [pau'ʃa:lə], *f.* (—, *pl.* **—n**) lump sum.
Pause ['pauzə], *f.* (—, *pl.* **—n**) pause, stop; (*Theat.*) interval; (*Sch.*) playtime, break; (*Tech.*) tracing.
pausen ['pauzən], *v.a.* trace.
pausieren [pau'zi:rən], *v.n.* pause.
Pavian ['pa:vja:n], *m.* (**—s**, *pl.* **—e**) (*Zool.*) baboon.
Pech [pɛç], *n.* (**—es**, *no pl.*) pitch; (*shoemaker's*) wax; (*fig.*) bad luck, rotten luck.
pechschwarz ['pɛçʃvarts], *adj.* black as pitch.
Pechvogel ['pɛçfo:gəl], *m.* (**—s**, *pl.* **¨**) unlucky fellow.
Pedell [pe'dɛl], *m.* (**—s**, *pl.* **—e**) beadle; porter, caretaker; (*Univ. sl.*) bulldog.
Pegel ['pe:gəl], *m.* (**—s**, *pl.* —) water-gauge.
peilen ['paIlən], *v.a.*, *v.n.* sound, measure, take bearings (of).
Pein [paIn], *f.* (—, *no pl.*) pain, torment.
peinigen ['paInIgən], *v.a.* torment; harass, distress.
peinlich ['paInlIç], *adj.* painful, disagreeable; embarrassing; delicate; strict, punctilious; (*Law*) capital, penal.
Peitsche ['paItʃə], *f.* (—, *pl.* **—n**) whip.
pekuniär [pekun'jɛ:r], *adj.* financial.
Pelerine [pelə'ri:nə], *f.* (—, *pl.* **—n**) cape.
Pelle ['pɛlə], *f.* (—, *pl.* **—n**) peel, husk.
Pellkartoffeln ['pɛlkartɔfəln], *f. pl.* potatoes in their jackets.
Pelz [pɛlts], *m.* (**—es**, *pl.* **—e**) pelt, fur; fur coat.
pelzig ['pɛltsIç], *adj.* furry.
Pendel ['pɛndəl], *n.* (**—s**, *pl.* —) pendulum.
pendeln ['pɛndəln], *v.n.* swing, oscillate; commute.
pennen ['pɛnən], *v.n.* (*sl.*) sleep.

Pension [pã'sjo:n], *f.* (—, *pl.* —**en**) pension; boarding-house; board and lodging.
Pensionat [pãsjo'na:t], *n.* (—**s**, *pl.* —**e**) boarding-school.
pensionieren [pãsjo'ni:rən], *v.a.* pension off; *sich — lassen*, retire.
Pensum ['pɛnzum], *n.* (—**s**, *pl.* —**sen**) task; curriculum, syllabus.
per [pɛr], *prep.* — *Adresse*, care of.
Perfekt [pɛr'fɛkt], *n.* (—**s**, *pl.* —**e**) (*Gram.*) perfect (tense).
perforieren [pɛrfo'ri:rən], *v.a.* perforate, punch.
Pergament [pɛrga'mɛnt], *n.* (—**s**, *pl.* —**e**) parchment, vellum.
Perle ['pɛrlə], *f.* (—, *pl.* —**n**) pearl; (*glass*) bead; (*fig.*) gem, treasure.
perlen ['pɛrlən], *v.n.* sparkle.
Perlgraupe ['pɛrlgraupə], *f.* (—, *no pl.*) (*Bot.*) pearl-barley.
Perlhuhn ['pɛrlhu:n], *n.* (—**s**, *pl.* ⸚**er**) (*Zool.*) guinea-fowl.
Perlmutter ['pɛrlmutər], *f.* (—, *no pl.*) mother-of-pearl.
Perpendikel [pɛrpən'dɪkəl], *m.* & *n.* (—**s**, *pl.* —) pendulum.
Perser ['pɛrzər], *m.* (—**s**, *pl.* —) Persian; *echter* —, genuine Persian carpet.
Persien ['pɛrzjən], *n.* Persia.
Personal [pɛrzo'na:l], *n.* (—**s**, *no pl.*) personnel, staff.
Personalien [pɛrzo'na:ljən], *n. pl.* particulars (of a person).
Personenverkehr [pɛr'zo:nənfɛrke:r], *m.* (—**s**, *no pl.*) passenger-traffic.
Personenzug [pɛr'zo:nəntsu:k], *m.* (—**s**, *pl.* ⸚**e**) (slow) passenger train.
personifizieren [pɛrzonifi'tsi:rən], *v.a.* personify, embody, impersonate.
Persönlichkeit [pɛr'zø:nlɪçkaɪt], *f.* (—, *pl.* —**en**) personality, person.
perspektivisch [pɛrspɛk'ti:vɪʃ], *adj.* perspective.
Peru [pe'ru:], *n.* Peru.
Perücke [pɛ'rykə], *f.* (—, *pl.* —**n**) wig.
Pest [pɛst], *f.* (—, *no pl.*) plague, pestilence.
pestartig ['pɛsta:rtɪç], *adj.* pestilential.
Petersilie [pe:tər'zi:ljə], *f.* (—, *no pl.*) (*Bot.*) parsley.
petitionieren [petitsjo'ni:rən], *v.a.* petition.
Petschaft ['pɛtʃaft], *n.* (—**s**, *pl.* —**e**) seal, signet.
Petz [pɛts], *m.* (—**es**, *pl.* —**e**) *Meister* —, Bruin (the bear).
petzen ['pɛtsən], *v.n.* tell tales (about), sneak.
Pfad [pfa:t], *m.* (—**es**, *pl.* —**e**) path.
Pfadfinder ['pfa:tfɪndər], *m.* (—**s**, *pl.* —) Boy Scout.
Pfaffe ['pfafə], *m.* (—**n**, *pl.* —**n**) (*pej.*) cleric, priest.
Pfahl [pfa:l], *m.* (—**s**, *pl.* ⸚**e**) post, stake.
Pfahlbauten ['pfa:lbautən], *m. pl.* lake dwellings.
pfählen ['pfɛ:lən], *v.a.* fasten with stakes; impale.
Pfand [pfant], *n.* (—**s**, *pl.* ⸚**er**) pawn, pledge; security; (*game*) forfeit; *ein — einlösen*, redeem a pledge.
pfänden ['pfɛndən], *v.a.* take in pledge; seize.
Pfänderspiel ['pfɛndərʃpi:l], *n.* (—**s**, *pl.* —**e**) game of forfeits.
Pfandgeber ['pfantge:bər], *m.* (—**s**, *pl.* —) pawner.
Pfandleiher ['pfantlaɪər], *m.* (—**s**, *pl.* —) pawnbroker.
Pfandrecht ['pfantrɛçt], *n.* (—**s**, *no pl.*) lien.
Pfändung ['pfɛnduŋ], *f.* (—, *pl.* —**en**) seizure, attachment, distraint.
Pfanne ['pfanə], *f.* (—, *pl.* —**n**) pan, frying-pan.
Pfannkuchen ['pfanku:xən], *m.* (—**s**, *pl.* —) pancake; *Berliner* —, doughnut.
Pfarre ['pfarə], *f.* (—, *pl.* —**n**) living, parish; (*house*) vicarage, parsonage, manse.
Pfarrer ['pfarər], *m.* (—**s**, *pl.* —) parson; vicar, (parish) priest.
Pfau [pfau], *m.* (—**en**, *pl.* —**en**) (*Orn.*) peacock.
Pfauenauge ['pfauənaugə], *n.* (—**s**, *pl.* —**n**) (*Ent.*) peacock butterfly.
Pfeffer ['pfɛfər], *m.* (—**s**, *no pl.*) pepper; *spanischer* —, red pepper, cayenne.
Pfefferkuchen ['pfɛfərku:xən], *m.* (—**s**, *pl.* —) gingerbread, spiced cake.
Pfefferminz ['pfɛfərmɪnts], *n.* (—, *no pl.*) peppermint.
Pfeife ['pfaɪfə], *f.* (—, *pl.* —**n**) whistle, fife; pipe.
pfeifen ['pfaɪfən], *v.a., v.n. irr.* whistle, play the fife; (*Theat.*) boo, hiss; (*bullets*) whiz(z).
Pfeifenrohr ['pfaɪfənro:r], *n.* (—**s**, *pl.* —**e**) pipe-stem.
Pfeil [pfaɪl], *m.* (—**es**, *pl.* —**e**) arrow, dart, bolt.
Pfeiler ['pfaɪlər], *m.* (—**s**, *pl.* —) pillar.
Pfeilwurz ['pfaɪlvurts], *f.* (—, *no pl.*) (*Bot.*) arrow root.
Pfennig ['pfɛnɪç], *m.* (—**s**, *pl.* —**e**) one hundredth of a mark; (*loosely*) penny.
Pferch [pfɛrç], *m.* (—**es**, *pl.* —**e**) fold, pen.
Pferd [pfe:rt], *n.* (—**es**, *pl.* —**e**) horse; *zu* —, on horseback; *vom — steigen*, dismount.
Pferdeknecht ['pfe:rdəknɛçt], *m.* (—**es**, *pl.* —**e**) groom.
Pferdestärke ['pfe:rdəʃtɛrkə], *f.* (—, *no pl.*) horse-power (*abbr.* PS).
Pfiff [pfɪf], *m.* (—**es**, *pl.* —**e**) whistle.
Pfifferling ['pfɪfərlɪŋ], *m.* (—**s**, *pl.* —**e**) (*Bot.*) mushroom; chanterelle; *einen — wert*, worthless.
pfiffig ['pfɪfɪç], *adj.* cunning, sly, crafty.
Pfiffikus ['pfɪfɪkus], *m.* (—, *pl.* —**se**) (*coll.*) sly dog.

Pfingsten ['pfɪŋkstən], *n.* Whitsun (-tide), Pentecost.
Pfingstrose ['pfɪŋkstro:zə], *f.* (—, *pl.* —n) (*Bot.*) peony.
Pfirsich ['pfɪrzɪç], *m.* (—s, *pl.* —e) (*Bot.*) peach.
Pflanze ['pflantsə], *f.* (—, *pl.* —n) plant.
pflanzen ['pflantsən], *v.a.* plant.
Pflanzer ['pflantsər], *m.* (—s, *pl.* —) planter.
pflanzlich ['pflantslɪç], *adj.* vegetable, botanical.
Pflänzling ['pflɛntslɪŋ], *m.* (—s, *pl.* —e) seedling, young plant.
Pflanzung ['pflantsuŋ], *f.* (—, *pl.* —en) plantation.
Pflaster ['pflastər], *n.* (—s, *pl.* —) (*Med.*) plaster; (*street*) pavement; *ein teures* —, an expensive place to live in.
Pflaume ['pflaumə], *f.* (—, *pl.* —n) plum; *getrocknete* —, prune.
Pflege ['pfle:gə], *f.* (—, *no pl.*) care, attention, nursing, fostering.
Pflegeeltern ['pfle:gəɛltərn], *pl.* foster-parents.
pflegen ['pfle:gən], *v.a.* nurse, look after, take care of; *Umgang* — *mit*, associate with. — *v.n.* be used to, be in the habit of.
Pflegling ['pfle:klɪŋ], *m.* (—s, *pl.* —e) foster-child, ward.
Pflicht [pflɪçt], *f.* (—, *pl.* —en) duty, obligation.
Pflichtgefühl ['pflɪçtgəfy:l], *n.* (—s, *no pl.*) sense of duty.
pflichtgemäß ['pflɪçtgəmɛ:s], *adj.* dutiful.
pflichtschuldig ['pflɪçtʃuldɪç], *adj.* in duty bound.
Pflock [pflɔk], *m.* (—s, *pl.* ⸚e) plug, peg.
pflücken ['pflykən], *v.a.* pluck, pick, gather.
Pflug [pflu:k], *m.* (—es, *pl.* ⸚e) plough.
Pflugschar ['pflu:kʃa:r], *f.* (—, *pl.* —en) ploughshare.
Pforte ['pfɔrtə], *f.* (—, *pl.* —n) gate, door, porch.
Pförtner ['pfœrtnər], *m.* (—s, *pl.* —) door-keeper, porter.
Pfosten ['pfɔstən], *m.* (—s, *pl.* —) post, stake; (*door*) jamb.
Pfote ['pfo:tə], *f.* (—, *pl.* —n) paw.
Pfriem [pfri:m], *m.* (—es, *pl.* —e) awl.
Pfropf(en) ['pfrɔpf(ən)], *m.* (—s, *pl.* —en) cork, stopper; (*gun*) wad.
pfropfen ['pfrɔpfən], *v.a.* graft; cork.
Pfründe ['pfryndə], *f.* (—, *pl.* —n) living, benefice.
Pfuhl [pfu:l], *m.* (—es, *pl.* —e) pool, puddle.
Pfühl [pfy:l], *m.* (—es, *pl.* —e) (*Poet.*) bolster, pillow, cushion.
pfui! [pfui], *excl.* shame! ugh! — *Teufel!* shame! a damned shame!
Pfund [pfunt], *n.* (—es, *pl.* —e) pound.
pfuschen ['pfuʃən], *v.n.* botch; *einem ins Handwerk* —, poach on s.o. else's preserve.
Pfütze ['pfytsə], *f.* (—, *pl.* —n) puddle.
Phänomen [fɛ:no'me:n], *n.* (—s, *pl.* —e) phenomenon.
Phantasie [fanta'zi:], *f.* (—, *pl.* —n) fancy, imagination; (*Mus.*) fantasia.
phantasieren [fanta'zi:rən], *v.n.* indulge in fancies; (*sick person*) rave, wander, be delirious; (*Mus.*) improvise.
Phantast [fan'tast], *m.* (—en, *pl.* —en) dreamer, visionary.
Pharisäer [fari'zɛ:ər], *m.* (—s, *pl.* —) Pharisee.
Phase ['fa:zə], *f.* (—, *pl.* —n) phase, stage (of process *or* development).
Philippinen [fili'pi:nən], *f. pl.* Philippines.
Philister [fi'lɪstər], *m.* (—s, *pl.* —) Philistine.
philisterhaft [fi'lɪstərhaft], *adj.* philistine, narrow-minded, conventional.
Philologie [filolo'gi:], *f.* (—, *no pl.*) philology; study of languages.
Philosoph [filo'zo:f], *m.* (—en, *pl.* —en) philosopher.
Philosophie [filozo'fi:], *f.* (—, *pl.* —n) philosophy.
Phiole [fi'o:lə], *f.* (—, *pl.* —n) phial, vial.
Phlegma ['flɛgma], *n.* (—s, *no pl.*) phlegm.
Phonetik [fo'ne:tɪk], *f.* (—, *no pl.*) phonetics.
photogen [foto'ge:n], *adj.* photogenic.
Photograph [foto'gra:f], *m.* (—en, *pl.* —en) photographer.
Photographie [fotogra'fi:], *f.* (—, *pl.* —n) photograph, photo; (*Art*) photography.
photographieren [fotogra'fi:rən], *v.a.* photograph.
Physik [fy'zi:k], *f.* (—, *no pl.*) physics.
physikalisch [fyzi'ka:lɪʃ], *adj.* physical (of physics).
Physiker ['fy:zɪkər], *m.* (—s, *pl.* —) physicist.
Physiologe [fy:zjo'lo:gə], *m.* (—en, *pl.* —en) physiologist.
physiologisch [fy:zjo'lo:gɪʃ], *adj.* physiological.
physisch ['fy:zɪʃ], *adj.* physical.
Picke ['pɪkə], *f.* (—, *pl.* —n) pickaxe, axe.
Pickel ['pɪkəl], *m.* (—s, *pl.* —) pimple.
Piedestal ['pje:dɛsta:l], *n.* (—s, *pl.* —e) pedestal.
piepen ['pi:pən], *v.n.* squeak, chirp.
piepsen ['pi:psən], *v.n.* squeak, chirp.
Pietät [pie'tɛ:t], *f.* (—, *no pl.*) piety, reverence.
Pik [pi:k], *n.* (—s, *pl.* —s) (*cards*) spades.
pikant [pi'kant], *adj.* piquant, spicy; (*fig.*) risqué.
Pikee [pi'ke:], *m.* (—s, *pl.* —s) piqué.
pikiert [pi'ki:rt], *adj.* irritated, annoyed, piqued.
Pikkolo ['pɪkolo], *m.* (—s, *pl.* —s) apprentice waiter, boy (waiter); (*Mus.*) piccolo, flute.

Pilger ['pɪlgər], *m.* (**—s,** *pl.* **—**) pilgrim.
Pille ['pɪlə], *f.* (**—,** *pl.* **—n**) pill.
Pilz [pɪlts], *m.* (**—es,** *pl.* **—e**) fungus, mushroom.
Piment [pi'mɛnt], *n.* (**—s,** *pl.* **—e**) pimento, Jamaican pepper, all-spice.
pimplig ['pɪmplɪç], *adj.* effeminate.
Pinguin [pɪŋgu'i:n], *m.* (**—s,** *pl.* **—e**) (*Orn.*) penguin.
Pinie ['pi:njə], *f.* (**—,** *pl.* **—n**) (*Bot.*) stone-pine.
Pinne ['pɪnə], *f.* (**—,** *pl.* **—n**) drawing-pin; peg.
Pinscher ['pɪnʃər], *m.* (**—s,** *pl.* **—**) terrier.
Pinsel ['pɪnzəl], *m.* (**—s,** *pl.* **—**) (*Painting*) brush, pencil; (*fig.*) simpleton.
Pinzette [pɪn'tsɛtə], *f.* (**—,** *pl.* **—n**) pincers, tweezers.
Pirsch [pɪrʃ], *f.* (**—,** *no pl.*) (deer-) stalking.
Piste ['pɪstə], *f.* (**—,** *pl.* **—n**) track; (*Aviat.*) runway.
pittoresk [pɪto'rɛsk], *adj.* picturesque.
placken ['plakən], *v.r.* *sich* **—**, toil, drudge.
plädieren [plɛ'di:rən], *v.n.* plead.
Plädoyer [plɛ:doa'je:], *n.* (**—s,** *pl.* **—s**) speech for the prosecution *or* the defence (in a court of law), plea, pleading.
Plage ['pla:gə], *f.* (**—,** *pl.* **—n**) torment, trouble; calamity; plague.
plagen ['pla:gən], *v.a.* plague, trouble, torment, vex. — *v.r. sich* —, toil.
Plagiat [plag'ja:t], *n.* (**—es,** *pl.* **—e**) plagiarism.
Plaid [ple:t], *n.* (**—s,** *pl.* **—s**) travelling-rug.
Plakat [pla'ka:t], *n.* (**—(e)s,** *pl.* **—e**) poster, placard, bill.
Plan [pla:n], *n.* (**—es,** *pl.* **¨—e**) plan, scheme, plot; map, ground-plan.
Plane ['pla:nə], *f.* (**—,** *pl.* **—n**) awning, cover.
planieren [pla'ni:rən], *v.a.* level, plane down; bulldoze, flatten.
Planke ['plaŋkə], *f.* (**—,** *pl.* **—n**) plank, board.
Plänkelei [plɛnkə'laɪ], *f.* (**—,** *pl.* **—en**) skirmish.
planmäßig ['pla:nmɛ:sɪç], *adj.* according to plan.
planschen ['planʃən], *v.n.* splash; paddle.
Plantage [plan'ta:ʒə], *f.* (**—,** *pl.* **—n**) plantation.
planvoll ['pla:nfɔl], *adj.* systematic, well-planned.
Planwagen ['pla:nva:gən], *m.* (**—s,** *pl.* **—**) tilt-cart.
plappern ['plapərn], *v.n.* prattle, chatter.
plärren ['plɛrən], *v.n.* blubber, bawl.
Plastik ['plastɪk], *f.* (**—,** *pl.* **—en**) plastic art; plastic (material).
Platane [pla'ta:nə], *f.* (**—,** *pl.* **—n**) plane-tree.
Platin ['pla:ti:n], *n.* (**—s,** *no pl.*) platinum.
platonisch [pla'to:nɪʃ], *adj.* platonic.
plätschern ['plɛtʃərn], *v.n.* splash about.
platt [plat], *adj.* flat, level, even; insipid; downright; **—e** *Redensart*, commonplace, platitude; (*coll.*) *ich bin ganz* —, I am astonished *or* dumbfounded.
Plättbrett ['plɛtbrɛt], *n.* (**—es,** *pl.* **—er**) ironing board.
plattdeutsch ['platdɔytʃ], *adj.* Low German.
Platte ['platə], *f.* (**—,** *pl.* **—n**) plate; dish; board; slab; sheet; ledge; (*fig.*) bald head; (*Mus.*) (gramophone) record.
plätten ['plɛtən], *v.a.* iron (clothes).
Plattfisch ['platfɪʃ], *m.* (**—es,** *pl.* **—e**) (*Zool.*) plaice.
Plattfuß ['platfu:s], *n.* (**—es,** *pl.* **¨—e**) flat foot.
Plattheit ['plathaɪt], *f.* (**—,** *pl.* **—en**) flatness; (*fig.*) platitude.
Platz [plats], *m.* (**—es,** *pl.* **¨—e**) place, town, spot, site; space, room; (*town*) square; seat; — *nehmen*, take a seat, be seated.
Platzanweiserin ['platsanvaɪzərɪn], *f.* (**—,** *pl.* **—nen**) usherette.
Plätzchen ['plɛtsçən], *n.* (**—s,** *pl.* **—**) small place; drop; biscuit.
platzen ['platsən], *v.n.* (*aux.* sein) burst, explode.
Platzregen ['platsre:gən], *m.* (**—s,** *no pl.*) downpour, heavy shower.
Plauderei [plaudə'raɪ], *f.* (**—,** *pl.* **—en**) chat.
Plaudertasche ['plaudərtaʃə], *f.* (**—,** *pl.* **—n**) chatterbox.
Pleite ['plaɪtə], *f.* (**—,** *pl.* **—n**) (*coll.*) bankruptcy; — *machen*, go bankrupt.
Plenum ['ple:num], *n.* (**—s,** *no pl.*) plenary session.
Pleuelstange ['plɔyəlʃtaŋə], *f.* (**—,** *pl.* **—n**) connecting-rod.
Plinsen ['plɪnzən], *f. pl.* (*Austr.*) fritters.
Plissee [plɪ'se:], *n.* (**—s,** *pl.* **—s**) pleating.
Plombe ['plɔmbə], *f.* (**—,** *pl.* **—n**) lead, seal; (*teeth*) filling.
plombieren [plɔm'bi:rən], *v.a.* seal with lead; (*teeth*) fill.
plötzlich ['plœtslɪç], *adj.* sudden.
plump [plump], *adj.* clumsy, ungainly, awkward; crude, coarse.
plumps [plumps], *excl.* bump! oops!
Plunder ['plundər], *m.* (**—s,** *no pl.*) lumber, trash.
plündern ['plyndərn], *v.a.* plunder, pillage.
Plüsch [ply:ʃ], *m.* (**—es,** *no pl.*) plush.
pneumatisch [pnɔy'ma:tɪʃ], *adj.* pneumatic.
Pöbel ['pø:bəl], *m.* (**—s,** *no pl.*) mob, rabble.
pochen ['pɔxən], *v.a., v.n.* knock, beat, throb.

Pocke ['pɔkə], *f.* (—, *pl.* —**n**) pockmark; (*pl.*) smallpox.
pockennarbig ['pɔkənnarbɪç], *adj.* pockmarked.
Podagra ['po:dagra:], *n.* (—**s**, *no pl.*) (*Med.*) gout.
Pointe [po'ɛ̃tə], *f.* (—, *pl.* —**n**) (*of a story*) point.
Pokal [po'ka:l], *m.* (—**s**, *pl.* —**e**) goblet, cup; trophy.
Pökelfleisch ['pø:kəlflaɪʃ], *n.* (—**es**, *no pl.*) salted meat.
Pol [po:l], *m.* (—**s**, *pl.* —**e**) pole.
polemisch [po'le:mɪʃ], *adj.* polemic(al), controversial.
Polen ['po:lən], *n.* Poland.
Police [po'li:sə], *f.* (—, *pl.* —**n**) insurance policy.
polieren [po'li:rən], *v.a.* polish, furbish, burnish.
Poliklinik ['po:likli:nɪk], *f.* (—, *pl.* —**en**) (*Med.*) out-patients' department.
Politik [poli'ti:k], *f.* (—, *no pl.*) politics; policy.
politisieren [politi'zi:rən], *v.n.* talk politics.
Politur [poli'tu:r], *f.* (—, *no pl.*) polish, gloss.
Polizei [poli'tsaɪ], *f.* (—, *no pl.*) police.
polizeilich [poli'tsaɪlɪç], *adj.* of the police.
Polizeistunde [poli'tsaɪʃtundə], *f.* (—, *no pl.*) closing time.
Polizeiwache [poli'tsaɪvaxə], *f.* (—, *pl.* —**n**) police station.
Polizist [poli'tsɪst], *m.* (—**en**, *pl.* —**en**) policeman, constable.
Polizze [po'lɪtsə], *f.* (—, *pl.* —**n**) (*Austr. dial.*) insurance policy.
polnisch ['pɔlnɪʃ], *adj.* Polish.
Polster ['pɔlstər], *n.* (—**s**, *pl.* —) cushion, bolster.
Polterabend ['pɔltəra:bənt], *m.* (—**s**, *pl.* —**e**) wedding-eve party.
Poltergeist ['pɔltərgaɪst], *m.* (—**es**, *pl.* —**er**) poltergeist, hobgoblin.
poltern ['pɔltərn], *v.n.* rumble; make a noise; bluster.
Polyp [po'ly:p], *m.* (—**en**, *pl.* —**en**) (*Zool.*) polyp; (*Med.*) polypus.
Pomeranze [pomə'rantsə], *f.* (—, *pl.* —**n**) (*Bot.*) orange.
Pommern ['pɔmərn], *n.* Pomerania.
Pope ['po:pə], *m.* (—**n**, *pl.* —**n**) Greek Orthodox priest.
Popo [po'po:], *m.* (—**s**, *pl.* —**s**) (*coll.*) backside, bottom.
populär [popu'lɛ:r], *adj.* popular.
porös [po'rø:s], *adj.* porous.
Porree ['pɔre:], *m.* (—**s**, *no pl.*) leek.
Portefeuille [pɔrt'fœj], *n.* (—**s**, *pl.* —**s**) portfolio.
Portier [pɔr'tje:], *m.* (—**s**, *pl.* —**s**) doorkeeper, caretaker; porter.
Porto ['pɔrto:], *n.* (—**s**, *pl.* **Porti**) postage.
Porzellan [pɔrtsɛ'la:n], *n.* (—**s**, *pl.* —**e**) china, porcelain; *Meißner* —, Dresden china.
Posamenten [poza'mɛntən], *n. pl.* trimmings.
Posaune [po'zaunə], *f.* (—, *pl.* —**n**) (*Mus.*) trombone.
Positur [pozi'tu:r], *f.* (—, *pl.* —**en**) posture; *sich in* — *setzen*, strike an attitude.
Posse ['pɔsə], *f.* (—, *pl.* —**n**) (*Theat.*) farce, skit.
Possen ['pɔsən], *m.* (—**s**, *pl.* —) trick; *einem einen* — *spielen*, play a trick on s.o.
possierlich [pɔ'si:rlɪç], *adj.* droll, funny, comic(al).
Post [pɔst], *f.* (—, *pl.* —**en**) post, mail; (*building*) post-office.
Postament [pɔsta'mɛnt], *n.* (—**s**, *pl.* —**e**) plinth, pedestal.
Postanweisung ['pɔstanvaɪzuŋ], *f.* (—, *pl.* —**en**) postal order, money order.
Posten ['pɔstən], *m.* (—**s**, *pl.* —) post, station; place; (*goods*) parcel, lot, job lot; (*Comm.*) item; (*Mil.*) outpost; — *stehen*, stand sentry; *nicht auf dem* — *sein*, be unwell.
Postfach ['pɔstfax], *n.* (—**es**, *pl.* ⸚**er**) post-office box.
postieren [pɔs'ti:rən], *v.a.* post, place, station.
postlagernd ['pɔstla:gərnt], *adj.* poste restante, to be called for.
Postschalter ['pɔstʃaltər], *m.* (—**s**, *pl.* —) post-office counter.
postulieren [pɔstu'li:rən], *v.a.* postulate.
postwendend ['pɔstvɛndənt], *adj.* by return of post.
Postwertzeichen ['pɔstve:rttsaɪçən], *n.* (—**s**, *pl.* —) stamp.
Potenz [po'tɛnts], *f.* (—, *pl.* —**en**) (*Maths.*) power; *zur dritten* —, cubed, to the power of three.
potenzieren [potɛn'tsi:rən], *v.a.* (*Math.*) raise; intensify.
Pottasche ['pɔtaʃə], *f.* (—, *no pl.*) potash.
potzblitz ['pɔtsblɪts], *excl.* good Heavens! good gracious!
potztausend ['pɔtstauzənt], *excl.* great Scott! good Heavens!
Pracht [praxt], *f.* (—, *no pl.*) splendour, magnificence; (*in compounds*) de luxe.
prächtig ['prɛ:çtɪç], *adj.* splendid, magnificent, sumptuous.
prachtvoll ['praxtfɔl], *adj.* gorgeous, magnificent.
Prädikat [prɛ:di'ka:t], *n.* (—**s**, *pl.* —**e**) mark; (*Gram.*) predicate.
Prag [pra:k], *n.* Prague.
prägen ['prɛ:gən], *v.a.* coin, mint, stamp.
prägnant [prɛg'nant], *adj.* meaningful, precise.
prahlen ['pra:lən], *v.n.* boast, brag, talk big, show off.
Praktikant [praktɪ'kant], *m.* (—**en**, *pl.* —**en**) probationer; apprentice.
Praktiken ['praktɪkən], *f. pl.* machinations.

praktisch ['praktɪʃ], *adj.* practical; *—er Arzt*, general practitioner.
praktizieren [prakti'tsi:rən], *v.a.* practise.
Prall [pral], *m.* (—**es**, *pl.* —**e**) impact.
prall [pral], *adj.* tense, tight; (*cheeks*) chubby.
prallen ['pralən], *v.n.* (*aux.* sein) *auf etwas* —, bounce against s.th.
Prämie ['prɛ:mjə], *f.* (—, *pl.* —**n**) prize; (*insurance*) premium; (*dividend*) bonus.
prangen ['praŋən], *v.n.* shine, glitter, make a show.
Pranger ['praŋər], *m.* (—**s**, *pl.* —) pillory; *etwas an den — stellen*, expose s.th., pillory.
präparieren [prɛpa'ri:rən], *v.a.*, *v.r.* prepare.
Präsens ['prɛ:zɛns], *n.* (—, *pl.* —**ntia**) (*Gram.*) present tense.
präsentieren [prɛzɛn'ti:rən], *v.a.* present; *präsentiert das Gewehr!* present arms!
prasseln ['prasəln], *v.n.* (*fire*) crackle; rattle.
prassen ['prasən], *v.n.* revel, gorge (o.s.), guzzle, feast.
Prätendent [prɛtɛn'dɛnt], *m.* (—**en**, *pl.* —**en**) pretender, claimant.
Präteritum [prɛ'te:ritum], *n.* (—**s**, *pl.* —**ta**) (*Gram.*) preterite, past tense.
Praxis ['praksɪs], *f.* (—, *no pl.*) practice.
präzis [prɛ'tsi:s], *adj.* precise, exact.
präzisieren [prɛtsi'zi:rən], *v.a.* define exactly.
predigen ['pre:dɪgən], *v.a.*, *v.n.* preach.
Predigt ['pre:dɪçt], *f.* (—, *pl.* —**en**) sermon; (*fig.*) homily, lecture.
Preis [praɪs], *m.* (—**es**, *pl.* —**e**) price, rate, value; (*reward*) prize; praise; *um jeden* —, at any price, at all costs; *um keinen* —, not for all the world; *feste —e*, fixed prices; no rebate, no discount.
Preisausschreiben ['praɪsausʃraɪbən], *n.* (—**s**, *pl.* —) prize competition.
Preiselbeere ['praɪzəlbe:rə], *f.* (—, *pl.* —**n**) (*Bot.*) bilberry, cranberry.
preisen ['praɪzən], *v.a. irr.* praise, laud; glorify.
preisgeben ['praɪsge:bən], *v.a. irr.* give up, abandon, part with; *dem Spott preisgegeben sein*, become a laughing-stock.
Preisunterbietung ['praɪsuntərbi:tuŋ], *f.* (—, *pl.* —**en**) under-cutting.
Prellbock ['prɛlbɔk], *m.* (—**s**, *pl.* ⸚**e**) buffer (-block).
prellen ['prɛlən], *v.a.* cheat, defraud.
Prellstein ['prɛlʃtaɪn], *m.* (—**s**, *pl.* —**e**) kerbstone.
pressant [prɛ'sant], *adj.* (*Austr*). urgent.
Presse ['prɛsə], *f.* (—, *pl.* —**n**) press; newspapers; (*coll.*) coaching establishment, crammer.
pressieren [prɛ'si:rən], *v.n.* be urgent.
Preßkohle ['prɛsko:lə], *f.* (—, *no pl.*) briquette(s).
Preßkolben ['prɛskɔlbən], *m.* (—**s**, *pl.* —) piston.
Preßluft ['prɛsluft], *f.* (—, *no pl.*) compressed air.
Preußen ['prɔysən], *n.* Prussia.
prickeln ['prɪkəln], *v.n.* prick, prickle, sting, tickle.
Prieme ['pri:mə], *f.* (—, *pl.* —**n**) chew, quid.
Priester ['pri:stər], *m.* (—**s**, *pl.* —) priest; *zum — weihen*, ordain to the priesthood.
Prima ['pri:ma:], *f.* (—, *pl.* **Primen**) highest form at a grammar school (sixth form).
prima ['pri:ma:], *adj.* excellent, splendid, first-rate.
Primaner [pri'ma:nər], *m.* (—**s**, *pl.* —) pupil in the highest form at a grammar school, sixth form boy.
Primel ['pri:məl], *f.* (—, *pl.* —**n**) (*Bot.*) primrose, primula.
Primus ['pri:mus], *m.* (—, *no pl.*) (*School*) head boy, captain of the school.
Prinzip [prɪnt'si:p], *n.* (—**s**, *pl.* —**ien**) principle.
Priorität [priori'tɛ:t], *f.* (—, *no pl.*) priority, precedence.
Prise ['pri:zə], *f.* (—, *pl.* —**n**) pinch of snuff.
Prisma ['prɪsma:], *n.* (—**s**, *pl.* —**men**) prism.
Pritsche ['prɪtʃə], *f.* (—, *pl.* —**n**) plank-bed.
Privatdozent [pri'va:tdotsɛnt], *m.* (—**en**, *pl.* —**en**) (*Univ.*) (unsalaried) lecturer.
privatisieren [privati'zi:rən], *v.n.* have private means.
Probe ['pro:bə], *f.* (—, *pl.* —**n**) experiment, trial, probation, test; (*Theat.*, *Mus.*) rehearsal; sample, pattern; *auf* —, on trial; *auf die — stellen*, put to the test *or* on probation.
Probeabzug ['pro:bəaptsu:k], *m.* (—**s**, *pl.* ⸚**e**) (*Printing*) proof.
proben ['pro:bən], *v.a.* rehearse.
probieren [pro'bi:rən], *v.a.* try, attempt; taste.
Probst [pro:pst], *m.* (—**es**, *pl.* ⸚**e**) provost.
Produzent [produ'tsɛnt], *m.* (—**en**, *pl.* —**en**) producer (of goods), manufacturer.
produzieren [produ'tsi:rən], *v.a.* produce (goods). — *v.r. sich* —, perform, show off.
profanieren [profa'ni:rən], *v.a.* desecrate, profane.
Professur [profɛ'su:r], *f.* (—, *pl.* —**en**) (*Univ.*) professorship, Chair.
profitieren [profi'ti:rən], *v.a.*, *v.n.* profit (by), take advantage (of).
projizieren [proji'tsi:rən], *v.a.* project.
Prokura [pro'ku:ra:], *f.* (—, *no pl.*) (*Law*) power of attorney.
Prokurist [proku'rɪst], *m.* (—**en**, *pl.* —**en**) confidential clerk; company secretary.

prolongieren [prolɔŋ'gi:rən], *v.a.* prolong, extend.
promenieren [promə'ni:rən], *v.n.* take a stroll.
Promotion [promo'tsjo:n], *f.* (—, *pl.* —**en**) graduation, degree ceremony.
promovieren [promo'vi:rən], *v.n.* graduate, take a degree.
promulgieren [promul'gi:rən], *v.a.* promulgate.
Pronomen [pro'no:mən], *n.* (—**s**, *pl.* —**mina**) (*Gram.*) pronoun.
prophezeien [profe'tsaɪən], *v.a.* prophesy, predict, forecast.
prophylaktisch [profy'laktɪʃ], *adj.* preventive, prophylactic.
Propst [pro:pst], *m.* (—**es**, *pl.* ¨—**e**) provost.
Prosa ['pro:za:], *f.* (—, *no pl.*) prose.
prosit ['pro:zɪt], *excl.* cheers! here's to you! your health!
Prospekt [pro'spɛkt], *m.* (—**es**, *pl.* —**e**) prospect; (*booklet*) prospectus.
Prostituierte [prostitu'i:rtə], *f.* (—**n**, *pl.* —**n**) prostitute; (*coll.*) tart.
protegieren [prote'ʒi:rən], *v.a.* favour, patronize.
Protektion [protɛk'tsjo:n], *f.* (—, *no pl.*) patronage, favouritism.
protestieren [protɛs'ti:rən], *v.n.* make a protest, protest (against s.th.).
Protokoll [proto'kɔl], *n.* (—**s**, *pl.* —**e**) minutes, record; protocol; regulations.
Protokollführer [proto'kɔlfy:rər], *m.* (—**s**, *pl.* —) recorder, clerk of the minutes.
Protz [prɔts], *m.* (—**en**, *pl.* —**en**) snob, upstart; show-off.
Proviant [pro'vjant], *m.* (—**s**, *no pl.*) provisions, stores.
provinziell [provɪn'tsjɛl], *adj.* provincial.
Provinzler [pro'vɪntslər], *m.* (—**s**, *pl.* —) provincial.
Provision [provi'zjo:n], *f.* (—, *pl.* —**en**) (*Comm.*) commission, brokerage.
Provisor [pro'vi:zɔr], *m.* (—**s**, *pl.* —**en**) dispenser.
provisorisch [provi'zo:rɪʃ], *adj.* provisional, temporary.
provozieren [provo'tsi:rən], *v.a.* provoke.
Prozedur [protse'du:r], *f.* (—, *pl.* —**en**) proceedings, procedure.
Prozent [pro'tsɛnt], *m.* & *n.* (—**s**, *pl.* —**e**) per cent.
Prozentsatz [pro'tsɛntzats], *m.* (—**es**, *pl.* ¨—**e**) percentage, rate of interest.
Prozeß [pro'tsɛs], *m.* (—**es**, *pl.* —**e**) process; lawsuit, litigation; trial; *mit etwas kurzen — machen*, deal summarily with.
Prozeßwesen [pro'tsɛsve:zən], *n.* (—**s**, *no pl.*) legal procedure.
prüde ['pry:də], *adj.* prudish, prim.
prüfen ['pry:fən], *v.a.* test, examine.
Prüfung ['pry:fuŋ], *f.* (—, *pl.* —**en**) trial, test; examination; (*fig.*) temptation, affliction.
Prügel ['pry:gəl], *m.* (—**s**, *pl.* —) cudgel; (*pl.*) thrashing; *eine Tracht* —, a good hiding.
prügeln ['pry:gəln], *v.a.* beat, give a hiding to.
Prunk [pruŋk], *m.* (—(**e**)**s**, *no pl.*) splendour, ostentation, pomp.
prusten ['pru:stən], *v.n.* snort.
Psalm [psalm], *m.* (—**es**, *pl.* —**e**) psalm.
Psalter ['psaltər], *m.* (—**s**, *pl.* —) (*book*) psalter; (*instrument*) psaltery.
Psychiater [psyçi'a:tər], *m.* (—**s**, *pl.* —) psychiatrist.
Psychologe [psyço'lo:gə], *m.* (—**n**, *pl.* —**n**) psychologist.
Pubertät [pubɛr'tɛ:t], *f.* (—, *no pl.*) puberty.
Publikum ['pu:blɪkum], *n.* (—**s**, *no pl.*) public; (*Theat.*) audience.
publizieren [publi'tsi:rən], *v.a.* publish; promulgate.
Pudel ['pu:dəl], *m.* (—**s**, *pl.* —) poodle; *des —s Kern*, the gist of the matter.
Puder ['pu:dər], *m.* (—**s**, *no pl.*) powder, face-powder.
pudern ['pu:dərn], *v.a.* powder.
Puff [puf], *m.* (—**es**, *pl.* ¨—**e**) cuff, thump.
puffen ['pufən], *v.a.* cuff, thump.
Puffer ['pufər], *m.* (—**s**, *pl.* —) buffer.
Puffspiel ['pufʃpi:l], *n.* (—**s**, *pl.* —**e**) backgammon.
pullen ['pulən], *v.n.* rein in (a horse); (*coll.*) piddle.
Pulsader ['pulsa:dər], *f.* (—, *pl.* —**n**) artery; aorta.
pulsieren [pul'zi:rən], *v.n.* pulsate; pulse, throb.
Pulsschlag ['pulsʃla:k], *m.* (—**s**, *pl.* ¨—**e**) pulse-beat; pulsation.
Pult [pult], *n.* (—**es**, *pl.* —**e**) desk, writing-table; lectern.
Pulver ['pulvər], *n.* (—**s**, *pl.* —) powder.
Pump [pump], *m.* (—**s**, *no pl.*) (*sl.*) credit; *auf* —, on tick.
pumpen ['pumpən], *v.a.*, *v.n.* pump; (*fig.*) (*sl.*) *sich etwas* —, borrow s.th., touch s.o. for s.th.; lend.
Pumpenschwengel ['pumpənʃvɛŋəl], *m.* (—**s**, *pl.* —) pump-handle.
Pumpernickel ['pumpərnɪkəl], *m.* (—**s**, *pl.* —) black bread, Westphalian rye-bread.
Pumphosen ['pumpho:zən], *f. pl.* plus-fours.
Punkt [puŋkt], *m.* (—**es**, *pl.* —**e**) point, dot, spot; (*Gram.*) full stop.
punktieren [puŋk'ti:rən], *v.a.* dot; punctuate.
pünktlich ['pyŋktlɪç], *adj.* punctual.
punktum ['puŋktum], *excl. und damit* —, that's the end of it; that's it.
Puppe ['pupə], *f.* (—, *pl.* —**n**) doll; (*Ent.*) pupa, chrysalis.
pur [pu:r], *adj.* pure, sheer; (*drink*) neat.

Puritaner ['puri'ta:nər], *m.* (—**s**, *pl.* —) puritan.
Purpur ['purpur], *m.* (—**s**, *no pl.*) purple.
Purzelbaum ['purtsəlbaum], *m.* (—**s**, *pl.* ⸚**e**) somersault.
purzeln ['purtsəln], *v.n.* tumble.
Pustel ['pustəl], *f.* (—, *pl.* —**n**) pustule.
pusten ['pu:stən], *v.n.* puff, blow.
Pute ['pu:tə], *f.* (—, *pl.* —**n**) (*Orn.*) turkey-hen; *dumme* —, silly goose.
Puter ['pu:tər], *m.* (—**s**, *pl.* —) turkey-cock.
puterrot ['pu:tərro:t], *adj.* as red as a turkey-cock.
Putsch [putʃ], *m.* (—**es**, *pl.* —**e**) coup de main, insurrection, riot.
Putz [puts], *m.* (—**es**, *no pl.*) finery; cleaning; rough-cast.
putzen ['putsən], *v.a.* polish, shine; clean. — *v.r. sich* —, dress up.
Putzfrau ['putsfrau], *f.* (—, *pl.* —**en**) charwoman.
Putzmacherin ['putsmaxərɪn], *f.* (—, *pl.* —**nen**) milliner.
Pyramide [pyra'mi:də], *f.* (—, *pl.* —**n**) pyramid.
Pyrenäen [pyrə'nɛ:ən], *pl.* Pyrenees; —*halbinsel*, Iberian Peninsula.

Q

Q [ku:], *n.* (—**s**, *pl.* —**s**) the letter Q.
quabbeln ['kvabəln], *v.n.* shake, wobble.
Quacksalber ['kvakzalbər], *m.* (—**s**, *pl.* —) quack, mountebank.
Quacksalberei [kvakzalbə'raɪ], *f.* (—, *pl.* —**en**) quackery.
Quaderstein ['kva:dərʃtaɪn], *m.* (—**s**, *pl.* —**e**) ashlar, hewn stone.
Quadrat [kva'dra:t], *n.* (—**es**, *pl.* —**e**) square; *zum* (or *ins*) — *erheben*, square (a number).
Quadratur [kvadra'tu:r], *f.* (—, *pl.* —**en**) quadrature; *die — des Kreises finden*, square the circle.
quadrieren [kva'dri:rən], *v.a.* square.
quaken ['kva:kən], *v.n.* (*frog*) croak; (*duck*) quack.
quäken ['kvɛ:kən], *v.n.* squeak.
Quäker ['kvɛ:kər], *m.* (—**s**, *pl.* —) Quaker.
Qual [kva:l], *f.* (—, *pl.* —**en**) anguish, agony, torment.
quälen ['kvɛ:lən], *v.a.* torment, torture, vex. — *v.r. sich* —, toil.
qualifizieren [kvalifi'tsi:rən], *v.a.* qualify.
Qualität [kvali'tɛ:t], *f.* (—, *pl.* —**en**) quality.
Qualle ['kvalə], *f.* (—, *pl.* —**n**) (*Zool.*) jelly-fish.
Qualm [kvalm], *m.* (—**es**, *no pl.*) dense smoke.
Quantität [kvanti'tɛ:t], *f.* (—, *pl.* —**en**) quantity.
Quantum ['kvantum], *n.* (—**s**, *pl.* —**ten**) portion, quantity.
Quappe ['kvapə], *f.* (—, *pl.* —**n**) (*Zool.*) tadpole.
Quarantäne [kvaran'tɛ:nə], *f.* (—, *no pl.*) quarantine.
Quark [kvark], *m.* (—**s**, *no pl.*) curds; cream-cheese; (*fig.*) trash, rubbish, nonsense, bilge.
Quarta ['kvarta:], *f.* (—, *no pl.*) fourth form.
Quartal [kvar'ta:l], *n.* (—**s**, *pl.* —**e**) quarter of a year; term.
Quartier [kvar'ti:r], *n.* (—**s**, *pl.* —**e**) quarters, lodging; (*Mil.*) billet.
Quarz [kvarts], *m.* (—**es**, *no pl.*) quartz.
Quaste ['kvastə], *f.* (—, *pl.* —**n**) tassel.
Quatember [kva'tɛmbər], *m.* (—**s**, *pl.* —) quarter day; (*Eccl.*) Ember Day.
Quatsch [kvatʃ], *m.* (—**es**, *no pl.*) nonsense, drivel.
Quecke ['kvɛkə], *f.* (—, *pl.* —**n**) couch-grass, quick-grass.
Quecksilber ['kvɛkzɪlbər], *n.* (—**s**, *no pl.*) quicksilver, mercury.
Quelle ['kvɛlə], *f.* (—, *pl.* —**n**) well, spring, fountain; (*fig.*) source; *aus sicherer* —, on good authority.
Quentchen ['kvɛntçən], *n.* (—**s**, *pl.* —) small amount, dram.
quer [kve:r], *adj.* cross, transverse, oblique, diagonal. — *adv.* across; *kreuz und* —, in all directions.
Querbalken ['kve:rbalken], *m.* (—**s**, *pl.* —) cross-beam.
querdurch ['kve:rdurç], *adv.* across.
querfeldein ['kve:rfɛltaɪn], *adv.* cross-country.
Querkopf ['kve:rkɔpf], *m.* (—**es**, *pl.* ⸚**e**) crank.
Quersattel ['kve:rzatəl], *m.* (—**s**, *pl.* ⸚) side-saddle.
Querschiff ['kve:rʃɪf], *n.* (—**es**, *pl.* —**e**) (*church*) transept.
Querschnitt ['kve:rʃnɪt], *m.* (—**s**, *pl.* —**e**) cross-section; (*fig.*) average.
Querulant [kveru'lant], *m.* (—**en**, *pl.* —**en**) grumbler.
quetschen ['kvɛtʃən], *v.a.* squeeze, crush, mash; bruise.
Queue [kø:], *n.* (—**s**, *pl.* —**s**) (*Billiards*) cue.
quieken ['kvi:kən], *v.n.* squeak.
Quinta ['kvɪnta:], *f.* (—, *no pl.*) fifth form.
Quinte ['kvɪntə], *f.* (—, *pl.* —**n**) (*Mus.*) fifth.
Quirl [kvɪrl], *m.* (—**s**, *pl.* —**e**) whisk; (*Bot.*) whorl.
quitt [kvɪt], *adj.* — *sein*, be quits.
Quitte ['kvɪtə], *f.* (—, *pl.* —**n**) (*Bot.*) quince.

quittegelb ['kvɪtəgɛlp], *adj.* bright yellow.
quittieren [kvɪ'ti:rən], *v.a.* receipt; give a receipt; *den Dienst* —, leave the service.
Quittung ['kvɪtuŋ], *f.* (—, *pl.* —**en**) receipt.
Quodlibet ['kvɔdlɪbɛt], *n.* (—**s**, *pl.* —**s**) medley.
Quote ['kvo:tə], *f.* (—, *pl.* —**n**) quota, share.
quotieren [kvo'ti:rən], *v.a.* (*stock exchange*) quote (prices).

R

R [ɛr], *n.* (—**s**, *pl.* —**s**) the letter R.
Rabatt [ra'bat], *m.* (—**s**, *pl.* —**e**) rebate, discount.
Rabatte [ra'batə], *f.* (—, *pl.* —**n**) flower-border.
Rabbiner [ra'bi:nər], *m.* (—**s**, *pl.* —) rabbi.
Rabe ['ra:bə], *m.* (—**n**, *pl.* —**n**) (*Orn.*) raven; *ein weißer* —, a rare bird.
Rabenaas ['ra:bəna:s], *n.* (—**es**, *pl.* —**e**) carrion.
rabiat [ra'bja:t], *adj.* furious, rabid.
Rache ['raxə], *f.* (—, *no pl.*) revenge, vengeance.
Rachen ['raxən], *m.* (—**s**, *pl.* —) jaws, throat.
rächen ['rɛ:çən], *v.a.* avenge. — *v.r.* *sich* —, avenge o.s., take vengeance.
Rachenbräune ['raxənbrɔynə], *f.* (—, *no pl.*) croup, quinsy.
Rachitis [ra'xi:tɪs], *f.* (—, *no pl.*) (*Med.*) rickets.
rachsüchtig ['raxzyçtɪç], *adj.* vindictive, vengeful.
rackern ['rakərn], *v.r.* *sich* —, (*coll.*) toil, work hard.
Rad [ra:t], *n.* (—**es**, *pl.* ¨—**er**) wheel; bicycle; *ein* — *schlagen*, turn a cart-wheel; (*peacock*) spread the tail.
Radau [ra'dau], *m.* (—**s**, *no pl.*) noise, din, shindy.
Rade ['ra:də], *f.* (—, *pl.* —**n**) corn-cockle.
radebrechen ['ra:dəbrɛçən], *v.a. insep.* murder a language.
radeln ['ra:dəln], *v.n.* (*aux.* sein) (*coll.*) cycle.
Rädelsführer ['rɛ:dəlsfy:rər], *m.* (—**s**, *pl.* —) ringleader.
rädern ['rɛ:dərn], *v.a.* break on the wheel; *gerädert sein*, (*fig.*) ache in all o.'s bones, be exhausted.
Radfahrer ['ra:tfa:rər], *m.* (—**s**, *pl.* —) cyclist.
radieren [ra'di:rən], *v.n.* erase; etch.
Radierung [ra'di:ruŋ], *f.* (—, *pl.* —**en**) etching.
Radieschen [ra'di:sçən], *n.* (—**s**, *pl.* —) (*Bot.*) radish.
Radio ['ra:djo], *n.* (—**s**, *pl.* —**s**) wireless, radio.
raffen ['rafən], *v.a.* snatch up, gather up.
Raffinade [rafi'na:də], *f.* (—, *no pl.*) refined sugar.
Raffinement [rafinə'mã], *n.* (—**s**, *no pl.*) elaborateness.
raffinieren [rafi'ni:rən], *v.a.* refine.
raffiniert [rafi'ni:rt], *adj.* refined; elaborate, crafty, wily, cunning.
ragen ['ra:gən], *v.n.* tower, soar.
Rahm [ra:m], *m.* (—**es**, *no pl.*) cream; *den* — *abschöpfen*, skim; (*fig.*) skim the cream off.
Rahmen ['ra:mən], *m.* (—**s**, *pl.* —) frame; milieu, limit, scope, compass; *im* — *von*, within the framework of.
rahmig ['ra:mɪç], *adj.* creamy.
raisonnieren [rɛzɔ'ni:rən], *v.n.* reason, argue; (*fig.*) grumble, answer back.
Rakete [ra'ke:tə], *f.* (—, *pl.* —**n**) rocket, sky-rocket.
Rakett [ra'kɛt], *n.* (—**s**, *pl.* —**s**) (*tennis*) racket.
rammen ['ramən], *v.a.* ram.
Rampe ['rampə], *f.* (—, *pl.* —**n**) ramp, slope; platform; (*Theat.*) apron.
ramponiert [rampo'ni:rt], *adj.* battered, damaged.
Ramsch [ramʃ], *m.* (—**es**, *pl.* ¨—**e**) odds and ends; (*Comm.*) job lot.
Rand [rant], *m.* (—**es**, *pl.* ¨—**er**) edge, border, verge, rim; (*book*) margin; (*hat*) brim; *am* — *des Grabes*, with one foot in the grave; *außer* — *und Band geraten*, get completely out of hand.
randalieren [randa'li:rən], *v.n.* kick up a row.
Randbemerkung ['rantbəmɛrkuŋ], *f.* (—, *pl.* —**en**) marginal note, gloss.
rändern [rɛndərn], *v.a.* border, edge, mill.
Ränftchen ['rɛnftçən], *n.* (—**s**, *pl.* —) crust (of bread).
Rang [raŋ], *m.* (—**es**, *pl.* ¨—**e**) rank, grade, rate; order, class; standing (in society); (*Theat.*) circle, tier, gallery.
Range ['raŋə], *m.* (—**n**, *pl.* —**n**) scamp, rascal. — *f.* (—, *pl.* —**n**) tomboy, hoyden.
rangieren [rã'ʒi:rən], *v.a.* (*Railw.*) shunt. — *v.n.* rank.
Ranke ['raŋkə], *f.* (—, *pl.* —**n**) tendril, shoot.
Ränke ['rɛŋkə], *m. pl.* intrigues, tricks.
ranken ['raŋkən], *v.r.* (*aux.* haben) *sich* —, (*plant*) climb (with tendrils).
Ränkeschmied ['rɛŋkəʃmi:t], *m.* (—**es**, *pl.* —**e**) plotter, intriguer.
Ranzen ['rantsən], *m.* (—**s**, *pl.* —) satchel, knapsack, rucksack.
ranzig ['rantsɪç], *adj.* rancid, rank.
Rappe ['rapə], *m.* (—**n**, *pl.* —**n**) black horse.

Rappel ['rapəl], *m.* (—**s**, *no pl.*) (*coll.*) slight madness; rage, fit.
Rappen ['rapən], *m.* (—**s**, *pl.* —) small Swiss coin; centime.
rapportieren [rapɔr'ti:rən], *v.a.* report.
Raps [raps], *m.* (—**es**, *no pl.*) rapeseed.
rar [ra:r], *adj.* rare, scarce; exquisite.
rasch [raʃ], *adj.* quick, swift.
rascheln ['raʃəln], *v.n.* rustle.
Rasen ['ra:zən], *m.* (—**s**, *pl.* —) lawn, turf, sod.
rasen ['ra:zən], *v.n.* rave, rage, be delirious; rush, speed; *in —der Eile*, in a tearing hurry.
Raserei [ra:zə'raɪ], *f.* (—, *pl.* —**en**) madness; (*fig.*) fury.
Rasierapparat [ra'zi:rapara:t], *m.* (—**s**, *pl.* —**e**) (safety-)razor; shaver.
rasieren [ra'zi:rən], *v.a.* shave; *sich — lassen*, be shaved, get a shave.
Rasierzeug [ra'zi:rtsɔyk], *n.* (—**s**, *no pl.*) shaving-tackle.
Raspel ['raspəl], *f.* (—, *pl.* —**n**) rasp.
Rasse ['rasə], *f.* (—, *pl.* —**n**) race; breed; *reine —*, thoroughbred; *gekreuzte —*, cross-breed.
Rassel ['rasəl], *f.* (—, *pl.* —**n**) rattle.
rasseln ['rasəln], *v.n.* rattle, clank.
Rassendiskriminierung ['rasəndɪskrimini:ruŋ], *f.* (—, *no pl.*) racial discrimination.
Rast [rast], *f.* (—, *no pl.*) rest, repose.
rasten ['rastən], *v.n.* rest, take a rest; halt.
Raster ['rastər], *m.* (—**s**, *pl.* —) (*Phot.*) screen.
rastlos ['rastlo:s], *adj.* restless.
Rat (1) [ra:t], *m.* (—**es**, *pl.* —**schläge**) advice, counsel; deliberation.
Rat (2) [ra:t], *m.* (—**es**, *pl.* ⸚**e**) council, councillor; *mit — und Tat*, with advice and assistance; *einem einen — geben*, give s.o. advice, counsel s.o.; *einen um — fragen*, consult s.o.; *— schaffen*, find ways and means.
Rate ['ra:tə], *f.* (—, *pl.* —**n**) instalment, rate.
raten ['ra:tən], *v.a.*, *v.n. irr.* advise; guess, conjecture.
Ratgeber ['ra:tge:bər], *m.* (—**s**, *pl.* —) adviser, counsellor.
Rathaus ['ra:thaus], *n.* (—**es**, *pl.* ⸚**er**) town-hall.
Ratifizierung [ratifi'tsi:ruŋ], *f.* (—, *pl.* —**en**) ratification.
Ration [ra'tsjo:n], *f.* (—, *pl.* —**en**) ration, share, portion.
rationell [ratsjo'nɛl], *adj.* rational.
ratlos ['ra:tlo:s], *adj.* helpless, perplexed.
ratsam ['ra:tza:m], *adj.* advisable.
Ratschlag ['ra:tʃla:k], *m.* (—**s**, *pl.* ⸚**e**) advice, counsel.
Ratschluß ['ra:tʃlus], *m.* (—**sses**, *pl.* ⸚**sse**) decision, decree.
Ratsdiener ['ra:tsdi:nər], *m.* (—**s**, *pl.* —) beadle, tipstaff, summoner.
Rätsel ['rɛ:tsəl], *n.* (—**s**, *pl.* —) riddle, puzzle, mystery, enigma, conundrum.
Ratsherr ['ra:tshɛr], *m.* (—**n**, *pl.* —**en**) alderman, (town-)councillor, senator.
Ratte ['ratə], *f.* (—, *pl.* —**n**) (*Zool.*) rat.
Raub [raup], *m.* (—**es**, *no pl.*) robbery; booty, prey.
rauben ['raubən], *v.a.* rob, plunder; *es raubt mir den Atem*, it takes my breath away.
Räuber ['rɔybər], *m.* (—**s**, *pl.* —) robber, thief; highwayman; *— und Gendarm*, cops and robbers.
Raubgier ['raupgi:r], *f.* (—, *no pl.*) rapacity.
Rauch [raux], *m.* (—**s**, *no pl.*) smoke, vapour.
Rauchen ['rauxən], *n.* (—**s**, *no pl.*) smoking; *— verboten*, no smoking.
rauchen ['rauxən], *v.a.*, *v.n.* smoke.
räuchern ['rɔyçərn], *v.a.* (*meat, fish*) smoke-dry, cure; (*disinfect*) fumigate. — *v.n.* (*Eccl.*) burn incense.
Rauchfang ['rauxfaŋ], *m.* (—**s**, *pl.* ⸚**e**) chimney-flue.
Räude ['rɔydə], *f.* (—, *no pl.*) mange.
Raufbold ['raufbɔlt], *m.* (—**s**, *pl.* —**e**) brawler, bully.
raufen ['raufən], *v.a.* (*hair*) tear out, pluck. — *v.n.* fight, brawl. — *v.r. sich — mit*, scuffle with, fight, have a scrap with.
rauh [rau], *adj.* rough; (*fig.*) harsh, rude; hoarse; (*weather*) raw, inclement.
Rauheit ['rauhaɪt], *f.* (—, *no pl.*) roughness; hoarseness; (*fig.*) harshness, rudeness; (*weather*) inclemency; (*landscape*) ruggedness.
rauhen ['rauən], *v.a.* (*cloth*) nap.
Raum [raum], *m.* (—**es**, *pl.* ⸚**e**) space, room; outer space; (*fig.*) scope; *dem Gedanken — geben*, entertain an idea.
räumen ['rɔymən], *v.a.* clear, empty; quit, leave; *das Feld —*, abandon the field, clear out.
Rauminhalt ['raumɪnhalt], *m.* (—**s**, *no pl.*) volume.
räumlich ['rɔymlɪç], *adj.* spatial; (*in compounds*) space-.
Räumlichkeiten ['rɔymlɪçkaɪtən], *f. pl.* premises.
Raumschiff ['raumʃɪf], *n.* (—**es**, *pl.* —**e**) spaceship, spacecraft.
Räumung ['rɔymuŋ], *f.* (—, *pl.* —**en**) evacuation.
raunen ['raunən], *v.a.*, *v.n.* whisper.
Raupe ['raupə], *f.* (—, *pl.* —**n**) (*Ent.*) caterpillar.
Rausch [rauʃ], *m.* (—**es**, *pl.* ⸚**e**) intoxication; delirium, frenzy; *einen — haben*, be drunk, intoxicated; *seinen — ausschlafen*, sleep it off.
rauschen ['rauʃən], *v.n.* rustle, rush, roar.
Rauschgift ['rauʃgɪft], *n.* (—**s**, *pl.* —**e**) drug; narcotic.
Rauschgold ['rauʃgɔlt], *n.* (—**es**, *no pl.*) tinsel.
räuspern ['rɔyspərn], *v.r. sich —*, clear o.'s throat.
Raute ['rautə], *f.* (—, *pl.* —**n**) (*Maths.* rhombus; lozenge; (*Bot.*) rue.

Razzia ['ratsja], *f.* (—, *pl.* **—zzien**) (police-)raid, swoop.
reagieren [rea'gi:rən], *v.n.* react (on).
realisieren [reali'zi:rən], *v.a.* convert into money, realise.
Realschule [re'a:lʃu:lə], *f.* (—, *pl.* **—n**) technical grammar school; secondary modern school.
Rebe ['re:bə], *f.* (—, *pl.* **—n**) vine.
Rebell [re'bɛl], *m.* (**—en**, *pl.* **—en**) rebel, mutineer, insurgent.
Rebensaft ['re:bənzaft], *m.* (**—s**, *pl.* **⸚e**) grape-juice, wine.
Rebhuhn ['re:phu:n], *n.* (**—s**, *pl.* **⸚er**) (*Orn.*) partridge.
Reblaus ['re:plaus], *f.* (—, *pl.* **⸚e**) (*Ent.*) phylloxera.
Rechen ['rɛçən], *m.* (**—s**, *pl.* —) (*garden*) rake; (*clothes*) rack.
Rechenaufgabe ['rɛçənaufga:bə], *f.* (—, *pl.* **—n**) sum; mathematical *or* arithmetical problem.
Rechenmaschine ['rɛçənmaʃi:nə], *f.* (—, *pl.* **—n**) calculating machine, adding-machine.
Rechenschaft ['rɛçənʃaft], *f.* (—, *no pl.*) account; — *ablegen*, account for; *zur — ziehen*, call to account.
Rechenschieber ['rɛçənʃi:bər], *m.* (**—s**, *pl.* —) slide-rule.
Rechentabelle ['rɛçəntabɛlə], *f.* (—, *pl.* **—n**) ready reckoner.
rechnen ['rɛçnən], *v.a.*, *v.n.* reckon, calculate, do sums, compute; *auf etwas* —, count on s.th.; *auf einen* —, rely on s.o.
Rechnung ['rɛçnuŋ], *f.* (—, *pl.* **—en**) reckoning, account, computation; (*document*) invoice, bill, statement, account; *einer Sache — tragen*, make allowances for s.th.; take s.th. into account; *einem einen Strich durch die — machen*, put a spoke in s.o.'s wheel; *eine — begleichen*, settle an account.
Rechnungsabschluß ['rɛçnuŋsapʃlus], *m.* (**—sses**, *pl.* **⸚sse**) balancing of accounts, balance-sheet.
Rechnungsprüfer ['rɛçnuŋspry:fər], *m.* (**—s**, *pl.* —) auditor.
Rechnungsrat ['rɛçnuŋsra:t], *m.* (**—s**, *pl.* **⸚e**) member of the board of accountants, (senior government) auditor.
Recht [rɛçt], *n.* (**—es**, *pl.* **—e**) right, justice; claim on, title to; law, jurisprudence; *von —s wegen*, by right; — *sprechen*, administer justice; *die —e studieren*, study law.
recht [rɛçt], *adj.* right; just; real, true; suitable; proper; *zur —en Zeit*, in time; *es geht nicht mit —en Dingen zu*, there is s.th. queer about it; *was dem einen —, ist dem andern billig*, what is sauce for the goose is sauce for the gander; *einem — geben*, agree with s.o.; — *haben*, be (in the) right.
Rechteck ['rɛçtɛk], *n.* (**—s**, *pl.* **—e**) rectangle.
rechten ['rɛçtən], *v.n.* *mit einem* —, dispute, remonstrate with s.o.
rechtfertigen ['rɛçtfɛrtɪgən], *v.a. insep.* justify. — *v.r. sich* —, exculpate o.s.
rechtgläubig ['rɛçtglɔybɪç], *adj.* orthodox.
rechthaberisch ['rɛçtha:bərɪʃ], *adj.* stubborn, obstinate.
rechtlich ['rɛçtlɪç], *adj.* legal, lawful, legitimate; (*Law*) judicial, juridical.
rechtmäßig ['rɛçtmɛ:sɪç], *adj.* lawful, legitimate, legal.
rechts [rɛçts], *adv.* to the right, on the right.
Rechtsabtretung ['rɛçtsaptre:tuŋ], *f.* (—, *pl.* **—en**) cession, assignment.
Rechtsanwalt ['rɛçtsanvalt], *m.* (**—s**, *pl.* **⸚e**) lawyer, solicitor, attorney.
Rechtsbeistand ['rɛçtsbaɪʃtant], *m.* (**—s**, *pl.* **⸚e**) (legal) counsel.
rechtschaffen ['rɛçtʃafən], *adj.* upright, honest, righteous.
Rechtschreibung ['rɛçtʃraɪbuŋ], *f.* (—, *no pl.*) orthography, spelling.
Rechtshandel ['rɛçtshandəl], *m.* (**—s**, *pl.* **⸚**) action, case, lawsuit.
rechtskräftig ['rɛçtskrɛftɪç], *adj.* legal, valid.
Rechtslehre ['rɛçtsle:rə], *f.* (—, *pl.* **—n**) jurisprudence.
Rechtsspruch ['rɛçtsʃprux], *m.* (**—(e)s**, *pl.* **⸚e**) verdict.
Rechtsverhandlung ['rɛçtsfɛrhandluŋ], *f.* (—, *pl.* **—en**) legal proceedings.
Rechtsweg ['rɛçtsve:k], *m.* (**—(e)s**, *pl.* **—e**) course of law.
rechtswidrig ['rɛçtsvi:drɪç], *adj.* against the law, illegal.
Rechtszuständigkeit ['rɛçtstsu:ʃtɛndɪçkaɪt], *f.* (—, *pl.* **—en**) (legal) competence.
rechtwinklig ['rɛçtvɪŋklɪç], *adj.* rectangular.
rechtzeitig ['rɛçttsaɪtɪç], *adj.* opportune. — *adv.* in time, at the right time.
Reck [rɛk], *n.* (**—s**, *pl.* **—e**) horizontal bar.
Recke ['rɛkə], *m.* (**—n**, *pl.* **—n**) (*Poet.*) hero.
recken ['rɛkən], *v.a.* stretch, extend.
Redakteur [redak'tø:r], *m.* (**—s**, *pl.* **—e**) editor (newspaper, magazine).
Redaktion [redak'tsjo:n], *f.* (—, *pl.* **—en**) editorship, editorial staff; (*room*) editorial office.
Rede ['re:də], *f.* (—, *pl.* **—n**) speech, oration; address; *es geht die* —, people say; *es ist nicht der — wert*, it is not worth mentioning; *eine — halten*, deliver a speech; *zur — stellen*, call to account.
reden ['re:dən], *v.a.* speak, talk, discourse; *einem nach dem Munde* —, humour s.o.; *in den Wind* —, speak in vain, preach to the winds; *mit sich — lassen*, be amenable to reason.

Redensart ['re:dənsa:rt], *f.* (—, *pl.* —en) phrase, idiom; cliché; *einen mit leeren —en abspeisen*, put s.o. off with fine words.
Redewendung ['re:dəvɛnduŋ], *f.* (—, *pl.* —en) turn of phrase.
redigieren [redi'gi:rən], *v.a.* edit.
redlich ['re:tlɪç], *adj.* honest, upright.
Redner ['re:dnər], *m.* (—s, *pl.* —) speaker, orator.
Reede ['re:də], *f.* (—, *pl.* —n) (*Naut.*) roadstead.
Reederei [re:də'raɪ], *f.* (—, *pl.* —en) shipping-business.
reell [re'ɛl], *adj.* honest, fair, sound, bona fide.
Reep [re:p], *n.* (—s, *pl.* —e) (*Naut.*) rope.
Referat [refe'ra:t], *n.* (—s, *pl.* —e) report; paper (to a learned society), lecture.
Referendar [referen'da:r], *m.* (—s, *pl.* —e) junior barrister *or* teacher.
Referent [refe'rɛnt], *m.* (—en, *pl.* —en) reporter, reviewer; lecturer; expert (adviser).
Referenz [refe'rɛnts], *f.* (—, *pl.* —en) reference (to s.o. *or* s.th.).
referieren [refe'ri:rən], *v.a., v.n.* report (on), give a paper (on).
reflektieren [reflɛk'ti:rən], *v.a.* reflect. — *v.n. auf etwas* —, be a prospective buyer of s.th., have o.'s eye on s.th.
Reformator [refɔr'ma:tɔr], *m.* (—s, *pl.* —en) reformer.
reformieren [refɔr'mi:rən], *v.a.* reform.
Regal [re'ga:l], *n.* (—s, *pl.* —e) shelf.
rege ['re:gə], *adj.* brisk, lively, animated.
Regel ['re:gəl], *f.* (—, *pl.* —n) rule, precept, principle; *in der* —, as a rule, generally.
regelmäßig ['re:gəlmɛ:sɪç], *adj.* regular.
regeln ['re:gəln], *v.a.* regulate, arrange, order.
Regelung ['re:gəluŋ], *f.* (—, *pl.* —en) regulation.
regelwidrig ['re:gəlvi:drɪç], *adj.* contrary to rule, irregular, foul.
Regen ['re:gən], *m.* (—s, *no pl.*) rain.
regen ['re:gən], *v.r. sich* —, move, stir.
Regenbogen ['re:gənbo:gən], *m.* (—s, *pl.* —) rainbow.
Regenbogenhaut ['re:gənbo:gənhaut], *f.* (—, *pl.* ¨e) (*eye*) iris.
Regenguß ['re:gəngus], *m.* (—sses, *pl.* ¨sse) downpour, violent shower.
Regenmantel ['re:gənmantəl], *m.* (—s, *pl.* ¨) waterproof, raincoat, mac.
Regenpfeifer ['re:gənpfaɪfər], *m.* (—s, *pl.* —) (*Orn.*) plover.
Regenrinne ['re:gənrɪnə], *f.* (—, *pl.* —n) eaves.
Regenschirm ['re:gənʃɪrm], *m.* (—s, *pl.* —e) umbrella.
Regentschaft [re'gɛntʃaft], *f.* (—, *pl.* —en) regency.
Regie [re'ʒi:], *f.* (—, *pl.* —n) stage management, production, direction.
regieren [re'gi:rən], *v.a.* rule, reign over, govern. — *v.n.* reign; (*fig.*) prevail, predominate.
Regierung [re'gi:ruŋ], *f.* (—, *pl.* —en) government; reign.
Regierungsrat [re'gi:ruŋsra:t], *m.* (—s, *pl.* ¨e) government adviser.
Regiment (1) [regi'mɛnt], *n.* (—s, *pl.* —e) rule, government.
Regiment (2) [regi'mɛnt], *n.* (—s, *pl.* —er) (*Mil.*) regiment.
Regisseur [reʒi'sø:r], *m.* (—s, *pl.* —e) stage-manager, producer, director.
Registrator [regɪs'tra:tɔr], *m.* (—s, *pl.* —en) registrar, recorder; registering machine.
Registratur [regɪstra'tu:r], *f.* (—, *pl.* —en) record office, registry; filing-cabinet.
registrieren [regɪs'tri:rən], *v.a.* register, record, file.
reglos ['re:klo:s], *adj.* motionless.
regnen ['re:gnən], *v.n.* rain; *es regnet in Strömen*, it is raining cats and dogs.
Regreß [re'grɛs], *m.* (—sses, *pl.* —sse) recourse, remedy.
regsam ['re:kza:m], *adj.* quick, alert, lively.
regulieren [regu'li:rən], *v.a.* regulate.
Regung ['re:guŋ], *f.* (—, *pl.* —en) movement; impulse.
Reh [re:], *n.* (—(e)s, *pl.* —e) doe, roe.
rehabilitieren [rehabili'ti:rən], *v.a.* rehabilitate.
Rehbock ['re:bɔk], *m.* (—s, *pl.* ¨e) (*Zool.*) roe-buck.
Rehkeule ['re:kɔylə], *f.* (—, *pl.* —n) haunch of venison.
reiben ['raɪbən], *v.a. irr.* rub, grate, grind; *einem etwas unter die Nase* —, throw s.th. in s.o.'s teeth, bring s.th. home to s.o.
Reibung ['raɪbuŋ], *f.* (—, *pl.* —en) friction.
Reich [raɪç], *n.* (—(e)s, *pl.* —e) kingdom, realm, empire, state.
reich [raɪç], *adj.* rich, wealthy, opulent.
reichen ['raɪçən], *v.a.* reach, pass, hand; *einem die Hand* —, shake hands with s.o. — *v.n.* reach, extend; be sufficient.
reichhaltig ['raɪçhaltɪç], *adj.* abundant, copious.
reichlich ['raɪçlɪç], *adj.* ample, plentiful.
Reichskammergericht [raɪçs'kamərgərɪçt], *n.* (—s, *no pl.*) Imperial High Court of Justice (*Holy Roman Empire*).
Reichskanzlei ['raɪçskantslaɪ], *f.* (—, *pl.* —en) (Imperial) Chancery.
Reichskanzler ['raɪçskantslər], *m.* (—s, *pl.* —) (Imperial) Chancellor.
Reichsstände ['raɪçsʃtɛndə], *m. pl.* Estates (of the Holy Roman Empire).
Reichstag ['raɪçsta:k], *m.* (—s, *pl.* —e) Imperial Parliament, Reichstag, Diet.

Reichtum ['raɪçtu:m], *m.* (—**s**, *pl.* ⸚**er**) riches, wealth, opulence.
Reif (1) [raɪf], *m.* (—**s**, *no pl.*) hoar-frost.
Reif (2) [raɪf], *m.* (—**s**, *pl.* —**e**) ring.
reif [raɪf], *adj.* ripe, mature.
Reifen ['raɪfən], *m.* (—**s**, *pl.* —) hoop; tyre; — *schlagen*, trundle a hoop.
reifen ['raɪfən], *v.n.* (*aux.* sein) ripen, mature, grow ripe.
Reifeprüfung ['raɪfəpry:fuŋ], *f.* (—, *pl.* —**en**) matriculation examination.
reiflich ['raɪflɪç], *adj. sich etwas — überlegen*, give careful consideration to s.th.
Reigen ['raɪgən], *m.* (—**s**, *pl.* —) round-dance, roundelay.
Reihe ['raɪə], *f.* (—, *pl.* —**n**) series; file; row; progression, sequence; (*Theat.*) tier; *in — und Glied*, in closed ranks; *nach der —*, in turns; *ich bin an der —*, it is my turn.
Reihenfolge ['raɪənfɔlgə], *f.* (—, *no pl.*) succession.
Reiher ['raɪər], *m.* (—**s**, *pl.* —) (*Orn.*) heron.
Reim [raɪm], *m.* (—(**e**)**s**, *pl.* —**e**) rhyme.
rein [raɪn], *adj.* clean, pure, clear, neat; —*e Wahrheit*, plain truth; *ins —e bringen*, settle, clear up; *ins —e schreiben*, make a fair copy of; *einem —en Wein einschenken*, have a straight talk with s.o.
Reineke ['raɪnəkə], *m.* (—, *no pl.*) — *Fuchs*, Reynard the Fox.
Reinertrag ['raɪnɛrtra:k], *m.* (—(**e**)**s**, *pl.* ⸚**e**) net proceeds.
Reinfall ['raɪnfal], *m.* (—**s**, *pl.* ⸚**e**) sell, wild-goose chase; disappointment.
reinfallen ['raɪnfalən], *v.n. irr.* (*aux.* sein) be unsuccessful.
Reingewinn ['raɪngəvɪn], *m.* (—**s**, *pl.* —**e**) net proceeds.
Reinheit ['raɪnhaɪt], *f.* (—, *no pl.*) purity.
reinigen ['raɪnɪgən], *v.a.* clean, cleanse; dry-clean; purge.
Reinigung ['raɪnɪguŋ], *f.* (—, *pl.* —**en**) cleaning; (*fig.*) purification, cleansing; *chemische —*, dry-cleaning.
reinlich ['raɪnlɪç], *adj.* clean, neat.
Reis (1) [raɪs], *m.* (—**es**, *no pl.*) rice.
Reis (2) [raɪs], *n.* (—**es**, *pl.* —**er**) twig, sprig; scion; cutting.
Reisbesen ['raɪsbe:zən], *m.* (—**s**, *pl.* —) birch-broom, besom.
Reise ['raɪzə], *f.* (—, *pl.* —**n**) tour, trip, journey, travels; voyage; *gute —!* bon voyage!
reisefertig ['raɪzəfɛrtɪç], *adj.* ready to start.
Reisegeld ['raɪzəgɛlt], *n.* (—**es**, *pl.* —**er**) travel allowance.
reisen ['raɪzən], *v.n.* (*aux.* sein) travel, tour, journey, take a trip.
Reisende ['raɪzəndə], *m.* (—**n**, *pl.* —**n**) traveller; commercial traveller.
Reisig ['raɪzɪç], *n.* (—**s**, *no pl.*) brushwood.
Reisige ['raɪzɪgə], *m.* (—**n**, *pl.* —**n**) (*obs.*) trooper, horseman.
Reißaus [raɪs'aus], *n.* (—, *no pl.*) — *nehmen*, take to o.'s heels.
Reißbrett ['raɪsbrɛt], *n.* (—**es**, *pl.* —**er**) drawing-board.
reißen ['raɪsən], *v.a. irr.* tear; rend; pull; snatch; *etwas an sich —*, seize s.th., usurp.
reißend ['raɪsənt], *adj.* rapid; ravening; carnivorous; (*Comm.*) brisk, rapid (sales).
Reißnagel ['raɪsna:gəl], *m. see* **Reißzwecke**.
Reißschiene ['raɪsʃi:nə], *f.* (—, *pl.* —**n**) T-square.
Reißverschluß ['raɪsfɛrʃlus], *m.* (—**sses**, *pl.* ⸚**sse**) zip-fastener.
Reißzwecke ['raɪstsvɛkə], *f.* (—, *pl.* —**n**) drawing-pin.
reiten ['raɪtən], *v.a. irr.* ride (a horse). — *v.n.* (*aux.* sein) ride, go on horseback.
Reiterei [raɪtə'raɪ], *f.* (—, *pl.* —**en**) cavalry.
Reitknecht ['raɪtknɛçt], *m.* (—**es**, *pl.* —**e**) groom.
Reiz [raɪts], *m.* (—**es**, *pl.* —**e**) charm, attraction, fascination, allure; stimulus; irritation; (*Phys.*) impulse.
reizbar ['raɪtsba:r], *adj.* susceptible; irritable.
reizen ['raɪtsən], *v.a.* irritate; stimulate, charm, entice.
reizend ['raɪtsənt], *adj.* charming.
Reizmittel ['raɪtsmɪtəl], *n.* (—**s**, *pl.* —) stimulant; irritant.
rekeln ['re:kəln], *v.r.* (*dial.*) *sich —*, loll about.
Reklame [re'kla:mə], *f.* (—, *pl.* —**n**) propaganda, advertisement, advertising, publicity.
reklamieren [rekla'mi:rən], *v.a.* claim, reclaim. — *v.n.* complain.
rekognoszieren [rekɔgnɔs'tsi:rən], *v.a.* reconnoitre.
rekommandieren [rekɔman'di:rən], *v.a.* (*Austr.*) register (a letter).
Rekonvaleszent [rekɔnvalɛs'tsɛnt], *m.* (—**en**, *pl.* —**en**) convalescent.
Rekrut [re'kru:t], *m.* (—**en**, *pl.* —**en**) recruit.
rekrutieren [rekru'ti:rən], *v.a.* recruit. — *v.r. sich — aus*, be recruited from.
rektifizieren [rɛktifi'tsi:rən], *v.a.* rectify.
Rektor ['rɛktɔr], *m.* (—**s**, *pl.* —**en**) (school) principal; (*Univ.*) president.
Rektorat [rɛkto'ra:t], *n.* (—**es**, *pl.* —**e**) rectorship, presidency.
relativ [rela'ti:f], *adj.* relative, comparative.
relegieren [rele'gi:rən], *v.a.* expel; (*Univ.*) send down, rusticate.
Relief [rɛl'jɛf], *n.* (—**s**, *pl.* —**s**) (*Art*) relief.
religiös [reli'gjø:s], *adj.* religious.
Reliquie [re'li:kvjə], *f.* (—, *pl.* —**n**) (*Rel.*) relic.

Remise [re'mi:zə], *f.* (—, *pl.* —n) coach-house.
Remittent [remɪ'tent], *m.* (—en, *pl.* —en) remitter.
Renegat [rene'ga:t], *m.* (—en, *pl.* —en) renegade.
Renette [rɛ'nɛtə], *f.* (—, *pl.* —n) rennet(-apple).
renken ['rɛŋkən], *v.a.* wrench, bend, twist.
Rennbahn ['rɛnba:n], *f.* (—, *pl.* —en) race-course; (cinder)-track; (*Motor.*) racing-circuit.
rennen ['rɛnən], *v.n. irr.* (*aux.* sein) run, race, rush.
Renommé [renɔ'me:], *n.* (—s, *no pl.*) renown, repute, reputation.
renommieren [renɔ'mi:rən], *v.n.* brag, boast.
renovieren [reno'vi:rən], *v.a.* renovate, restore, redecorate, renew.
rentabel [rɛn'ta:bəl], *adj.* profitable, lucrative.
Rente ['rɛntə], *f.* (—, *pl.* —n) pension, annuity.
Rentier [rɛn'tje:], *m.* (—s, *pl.* —s) rentier, person of independent means.
rentieren [rɛn'ti:rən], *v.r. sich* —, be profitable, be worthwhile, pay.
Rentner ['rɛntnər], *m.* (—s, *pl.* —) pensioner.
Reparatur [repara'tu:r], *f.* (—, *pl.* —en) repair.
reparieren [repa'ri:rən], *v.a.* repair.
Repräsentant [reprɛzɛn'tant], *m.* (—en, *pl.* —en) representative.
Repräsentantenkammer [reprɛzɛn'tantənkamər], *f.* (—, *pl.* —n) (*Am.*) House of Representatives.
Repressalien [reprɛ'sa:ljən], *f. pl.* reprisals, retaliation.
reproduzieren [reprodu'tsi:rən], *v.a.* reproduce.
Republikaner [republi'ka:nər], *m.* (—s, *pl.* —) republican.
requirieren [rekvi'ri:rən], *v.a.* requisition.
Reseda [re'ze:da], *f.* (—, *pl.* —s) (*Bot.*) mignonette.
Reservat [rezɛr'va:t], *n.* (—es, *pl.* —e) reservation, reserve.
Residenz [rezi'dɛnts], *f.* (—, *pl.* —en) residence, seat of the Court.
residieren [rezi'di:rən], *v.n.* reside.
Residuum [re'zi:duum], *n.* (—s, *pl.* —duen) residue, dregs.
resignieren [rezɪg'ni:rən], *v.n.*, *v.r.* resign; be resigned (to s.th.); give up.
Respekt [re'spɛkt], *m.* (—es, *no pl.*) respect, regard; *mit — zu sagen*, with all due respect.
respektieren [respɛk'ti:rən], *v.a.* respect, honour.
Ressort [rɛ'so:r], *n.* (—s, *pl.* —s) department, domain.
Rest [rɛst], *m.* (—es, *pl.* —e) rest, residue, remainder; remnant; (*money*) balance.
restaurieren [rɛsto'ri:rən], *v.a.* restore, renovate.
Resultat [rezul'ta:t], *n.* (—es, *pl.* —e) result, outcome.
Resümee [rezy'me:], *n.* (—s, *pl.* —s) résumé, précis, digest, summary, synopsis, abstract.
retten ['rɛtən], *v.a.* save, preserve; rescue, deliver; *die Ehre* —, vindicate o.'s honour.
Rettich ['rɛtɪç], *m.* (—s, *pl.* —e) radish.
Rettung ['rɛtuŋ], *f.* (—, *pl.* —en) saving, rescue, deliverance.
retuschieren [retu'ʃi:rən], *v.a.* retouch.
Reue ['rɔyə], *f.* (—, *no pl.*) repentance, remorse, contrition.
reuen ['rɔyən], *v.a.*, *v.n.* repent, regret; *es reut mich*, I am sorry.
Reugeld ['rɔygɛlt], *n.* (—es, *pl.* —er) forfeit-money, penalty.
reüssieren [rey'si:rən], *v.n.* succeed.
Revanche [re'vã:ʃə], *f.* (—, *pl.* —n) revenge; (*fig.*) return.
revanchieren [revã'ʃi:rən], *v.r. sich* —, repay a service, have *or* take o.'s revenge.
Reverenz [reve'rɛnts], *f.* (—, *pl.* —en) bow, curtsy.
revidieren [revi'di:rən], *v.a.* revise, check.
Revier [re'vi:r], *n.* (—s, *pl.* —e) district, precint, quarter; preserve.
Revisor [re'vi:zɔr], *m.* (—s, *pl.* —en) accountant, auditor.
revoltieren [revɔl'ti:rən], *v.n.* rise, revolt.
revolutionieren [revolutsjo'ni:rən], *v.a.* revolutionise.
Revolverblatt [re'vɔlvərblat], *n.* (—s, *pl.* ¨er) gutter press.
Revue [re'vy:], *f.* (—, *pl.* —n) revue; review; — *passieren lassen*, pass in review.
Rezensent [retsɛn'zɛnt], *m.* (—en, *pl.* —en) reviewer, critic.
rezensieren [retsɛn'zi:rən], *v.a.* review.
Rezept [re'tsɛpt], *n.* (—es, *pl.* —e) (*Med.*) prescription; (*Cul.*) recipe.
rezitieren [retsi'ti:rən], *v.a.* recite.
Rhabarber [ra'barbər], *m.* (—s, *no pl.*) (*Bot.*) rhubarb.
Rhein [raɪn], *m.* (—s, *no pl.*) (River) Rhine.
Rhodesien [ro'de:zjən], *n.* Rhodesia.
Rhodus ['ro:dus], *n.* Rhodes.
Rhythmus ['rytmus], *m.* (—, *pl.* —men) rhythm.
Richtbeil ['rɪçtbaɪl], *n.* (—s, *pl.* —e) executioner's axe.
richten ['rɪçtən] *v.a.*, *v.n.* direct, point at; prepare; *die Augen — auf*, fix o.'s eyes upon; *einen zugrunde* —, ruin s.o.; judge, try, pass sentence on, condemn. —*v.r. sich nach* (*Dat.*) —, be guided by.
Richter ['rɪçtər], *m.* (—s, *pl.* —) judge; justice.
richtig ['rɪçtɪç], *adj.* right, correct, exact, true; *nicht ganz — sein*, be not quite right in the head.

Richtlot ['rɪçtlo:t], *n.* (—s, *pl.* —e) plumb-line.
Richtschnur ['rɪçtʃnu:r], *f.* (—, *pl.* —en) plumb-line; (*fig.*) rule, precept.
Richtung ['rɪçtuŋ], *f.* (—, *pl.* —en) direction.
riechen ['ri:çən], *v.a.*, *v.n. irr.* smell, scent, reek; *Lunte* —, smell a rat.
Riege ['ri:gə], *f.* (—, *pl.* —n) row, section.
Riegel ['ri:gəl], *m.* (—s, *pl.* —) bar, bolt; *ein* — *Schokolade*, a bar of chocolate.
Riemen ['ri:mən], *m.* (—s, *pl.* —) strap, thong; oar.
Ries [ri:s], *n.* (—es, *pl.* —e) (*paper*) ream.
Riese ['ri:zə], *m.* (—n, *pl.* —n) giant.
rieseln ['ri:zəln], *v.n.* murmur, babble, ripple, trickle; drizzle.
Riesenschlange ['ri:zənʃlaŋə], *f.* (—, *pl.* —n) anaconda.
Riff [rɪf], *n.* (—es, *pl.* —e) reef.
rigoros [rigo'ro:s], *adj.* strict, rigorous.
Rille ['rɪlə], *f.* (—, *pl.* —n) groove, small furrow; (*Archit.*) flute, chamfer.
Rind [rɪnt], *n.* (—es, *pl.* —er) ox, cow; (*pl.*) cattle, horned cattle, head of cattle.
Rinde ['rɪndə], *f.* (—, *pl.* —n) rind, bark, peel; (*bread*) crust.
Rinderbraten ['rɪndərbra:tən], *m.* (—s, *pl.* —) roast beef.
Rindfleisch ['rɪntflaɪʃ], *n.* (—es, *no pl.*) beef.
Rindvieh ['rɪntfi:], *n.* (—s, *no pl.*) cattle; (*fig.*) blockhead, ass.
Ring [rɪŋ], *m.* (—(e)s, *pl.* —e) ring; (*chain*) link; (*under the eye*) dark circle; (*Comm.*) syndicate, trust.
Ringelblume ['rɪŋəlblu:mə], *f.* (—, *pl.* —n) (*Bot.*) marigold.
ringeln ['rɪŋəln], *v.r. sich* —, curl.
ringen ['rɪŋən], *v.a. irr.* wring. — *v.n.* wrestle.
Ringer ['rɪŋər], *m.* (—s, *pl.* —) wrestler.
Ringmauer ['rɪŋmauər], *f.* (—, *pl.* —n) city *or* town wall.
rings [rɪŋs], *adv.* around.
ringsum(her) [rɪŋ'sum(he:r)], *adv.* round about.
Rinne ['rɪnə], *f.* (—, *pl.* —n) furrow, gutter; groove.
rinnen ['rɪnən], *v.n. irr.* (*aux*, sein) run, leak, drip.
Rinnsal ['rɪnza:l], *n.* (—s, *pl.* —e) channel, water-course.
Rinnstein ['rɪnʃtaɪn], *m.* (—s, *pl.* —e) gutter.
Rippe ['rɪpə], *f.* (—, *pl.* —n) rib.
Rippenfellentzündung ['rɪpənfɛlɛnt-tsynduŋ], *f.* (—, *pl.* —en) pleurisy.
Rippenspeer ['rɪpənʃpe:r], *m.* (—s, *pl.* —e) (*Casseler*) —, spare-rib, ribs of pork.
Rippenstoß ['rɪpənʃto:s], *m.* (—es, *pl.* ⸚e) dig in the ribs, nudge.
Rips [rɪps], *m.* (—es, *no pl.*) rep.
Risiko ['ri:ziko], *n.* (—s, *pl.* —ken) risk.
riskant [rɪs'kant], *adj.* risky.
riskieren [rɪs'ki:rən], *v.a.* risk.
Riß [rɪs], *m.* (—sses, *pl.* —sse) rent, tear; sketch, design, plan.
rissig ['rɪsɪç], *adj.* cracked, torn.
Ritt [rɪt], *m.* (—(e)s, *pl.* —e) ride.
Ritter ['rɪtər], *m.* (—s, *pl.* —) knight; *einen zum* — *schlagen*, dub s.o. a knight.
ritterlich ['rɪtərlɪç], *adj.* knightly; (*fig.*) chivalrous, valiant, gallant.
Ritterschlag ['rɪtərʃla:k], *m.* (—(e)s, *pl.* ⸚e) accolade.
Rittersporn ['rɪtərʃpɔrn], *m.* (—s, *pl.* —e) (*Bot.*) larkspur.
rittlings ['rɪtlɪŋs], *adv.* astride.
Rittmeister ['rɪtmaɪstər], *m.* (—s, *pl.* —) captain (of cavalry).
Ritus ['ri:tus], *m.* (—, *pl.* **Riten**) rite.
Ritz [rɪts], *m.* (—es, *pl.* —e) chink, fissure, cleft, crevice; (*glacier*) crevasse.
ritzen ['rɪtsən], *v.a.* scratch.
Rivale [ri'va:lə], *m.* (—n, *pl.* —n) rival.
Rivalität [rivali'tɛ:t], *f.* (—, *pl.* —en) rivalry.
Rizinusöl ['ri:tsinusø:l], *n.* (—s, *no pl.*) castor oil.
Robbe ['rɔbə], *f.* (—, *pl.* —n) (*Zool.*) seal.
Robe ['ro:bə], *f.* (—, *pl.* —n) dress, robe; gown.
röcheln ['rœçəln], *v.n.* rattle in o.'s throat.
rochieren [rɔ'xi:rən], *v.n.* (*Chess*) castle.
Rock [rɔk], *m.* (—(e)s, *pl.* ⸚e) (*woman*) skirt; (*man*) coat.
rodeln ['ro:dəln], *v.n.* (*aux.* haben *&* sein) toboggan.
roden ['ro:dən], *v.a.* clear, weed, thin out (plants).
Rogen ['ro:gən], *m.* (—s, *no pl.*) (*fish*) roe, spawn.
Roggen ['rɔgən], *m.* (—s, *no pl.*) rye.
roh [ro:], *adj.* raw; rough, rude, coarse, crude; *ein —er Mensch*, a brute; (*in compounds*) rough-; preliminary, unrefined.
Rohbilanz ['ro:bilants], *f.* (—, *pl.* —en) trial balance.
Roheisen ['ro:aɪzən], *n.* (—s, *no pl.*) pig-iron.
Roheit ['ro:haɪt], *f.* (—, *pl.* —en) coarseness, rudeness, crudity.
Rohr [ro:r], *n.* (—es, *pl.* —e, ⸚en) tube, pipe; reed, cane; (*gun*) barrel.
Rohrdommel ['ro:rdɔməl], *f.* (—, *pl.* —n) (*Orn.*) bittern.
Röhre ['rø:rə], *f.* (—, *pl.* —n) tube, pipe; (*Radio*) valve.
Röhricht ['rø:rɪçt], *n.* (—s, *pl.* —e) reeds.
Rohrpfeife ['ro:rpfaɪfə], *f.* (—, *pl.* —n) reed-pipe.
Rohrpost ['ro:rpɔst], *f.* (—, *no pl.*) pneumatic post.
Rohrzucker ['ro:rtsukər], *m.* (—s, *no pl.*) cane-sugar.

Rolladen ['rɔladən], *m.* (—s, *pl.* ⸚) sliding shutter, roller blind.
Rollbahn ['rɔlba:n], *f.* (—, *pl.* —en) (*Aviat.*) runway.
Rolle ['rɔlə], *f.* (—, *pl.* —n) reel, roll; pulley; (*Theat.*) part; rôle; (*laundry*) mangle.
rollen ['rɔlən], *v.a.* roll, reel; (*laundry*) mangle. — *v.n.* (*aux.* sein) roll (along); (*thunder*) roar, roll.
Roller ['rɔlər], *m.* (—s, *pl.* —) scooter.
Rollmops ['rɔlmɔps], *m.* (—es, *pl.* ⸚e) soused herring.
Rollschuh ['rɔlʃu:], *m.* (—s, *pl.* —e) roller-skate.
Rollstuhl ['rɔlʃtu:l], *m.* (—s, *pl.* ⸚e) wheel-chair, bath-chair.
Rolltreppe ['rɔltrɛpə], *f.* (—, *pl.* —n) escalator, moving staircase.
Rom [ro:m], *n.* Rome.
Roman [ro'ma:n], *m.* (—s, *pl.* —e) novel.
romanisch [ro'ma:nɪʃ], *adj.* Romanesque.
Romanliteratur [ro'ma:nlitəratu:r], *f.* (—, *no pl.*) fiction.
Romanschriftsteller [ro'ma:nʃrɪftʃtɛlər], *m.* (—s, *pl.* —) novelist.
Römer ['rø:mər], *m.* (—s, *pl.* —) Roman; (*glass*) rummer.
Rondell [rɔn'dɛl], *n.* (—s, *pl.* —e) circular flower-bed.
Röntgenstrahlen ['rœntgənʃtra:lən], *m. pl.* X-rays.
rosa ['ro:za:], *adj.* pink, rose-coloured.
Rose ['ro:zə], *f.* (—, *pl.* —n) rose.
Rosenkranz ['ro:zənkrants], *m.* (—es, *pl.* ⸚e) garland of roses; (*Eccl.*) rosary.
Rosenkreuzer ['ro:zənkrɔytsər], *m.* (—s, *pl.* —) Rosicrucian.
Rosine [ro'zi:nə], *f.* (—, *pl.* —n) sultana, raisin.
Rosmarin ['rɔsmari:n], *m.* (—s, *no pl.*) (*Bot.*) rosemary.
Roß [rɔs], *n.* (—sses, *pl.* —sse) horse, steed.
Roßbremse ['rɔsbrɛmzə], *f.* (—, *pl.* —n) (*Ent.*) horsefly, gadfly.
Rössel ['rœsəl], *n.* (—s, *pl.* —) (*Chess*) knight.
Roßhaarmatratze ['rɔsha:rmatratsə], *f.* (—, *pl.* —n) hair-mattress.
Roßkastanie ['rɔskasta:njə], *f.* (—, *pl.* —n) (*Bot.*) horse-chestnut.
Rost (1) [rɔst], *m.* (—es, *no pl.*) rust.
Rost (2) [rɔst], *m.* (—s, *pl.* —e) grate; gridiron.
Rostbraten ['rɔstbra:tən], *m.* (—s, *pl.* —) roast meat.
rosten ['rɔstən], *v.n.* go rusty; rust; *alte Liebe rostet nicht*, love that's old rusts not away.
rösten ['rø:stən], *v.a.* toast, roast, grill.
rot [ro:t], *adj.* red; — *werden*, redden, blush.
Rotauge ['ro:taugə], *n.* (—s, *pl.* —n) (*Zool.*) roach.
Röte ['rø:tə], *f.* (—, *no pl.*) redness, red colour.
Röteln ['rø:təln], *m. pl.* (*Med.*) German measles, rubella.
Rotfink ['ro:tfɪŋk], *m.* (—en, *pl.* —en) (*Orn.*) bullfinch.
Rotfuchs ['ro:tfuks], *m.* (—es, *pl.* ⸚e) (*Zool.*) sorrel horse.
rotieren [ro'ti:rən], *v.n.* rotate.
Rotkäppchen ['ro:tkɛpçən], *n.* Little Red Riding Hood.
Rotkehlchen ['ro:tke:lçən], *n.* (—s, *pl.* —) robin.
Rotlauf ['ro:tlauf], *m.* (—s, *no pl.*) (*Med.*) erysipelas.
Rotschimmel ['ro:tʃɪməl], *m.* (—s, *pl.* —) roan-horse.
Rotspon ['ro:tʃpo:n], *m.* (—s, *no pl.*) (*dial.*) claret.
Rotte ['rɔtə], *f.* (—, *pl.* —n) band, gang, rabble; (*Mil.*) file, squad.
Rotwild ['ro:tvɪlt], *n.* (—s, *no pl.*) red deer.
Rotz [rɔts], *m.* (—es, *no pl.*) (*vulg.*) mucus; snot.
Rouleau [ru'lo:], *n.* (—s, *pl.* —s) sun-blind, roller-blind.
routiniert [ruti'ni:rt], *adj.* smart; experienced.
Rübe ['ry:bə], *f.* (—, *pl.* —n) (*Bot.*) turnip; *rote* —, beetroot; *gelbe* —, carrot.
Rubel ['ru:bəl], *m.* (—s, *pl.* —) rouble.
Rübenzucker ['ry:bəntsukər], *m.* (—s, *no pl.*) beet-sugar.
Rubin [ru'bi:n], *m.* (—s, *pl.* —e) ruby.
Rubrik [ru'bri:k], *f.* (—, *pl.* —en) rubric; title, heading, category, column.
Rübsamen ['ry:pza:mən], *m.* (—s, *no pl.*) rape-seed.
ruchbar ['ru:xba:r], *adj.* manifest, known, notorious.
ruchlos ['ru:xlo:s], *adj.* wicked, profligate, vicious.
Ruck [ruk], *m.* (—(e)s, *pl.* —e) pull, jolt, jerk.
Rückblick ['rykblɪk], *m.* (—s, *pl.* —e) retrospect, retrospective view.
Rücken ['rykən], *m.* (—s, *pl.* —) back; (*mountains*) ridge; *einem den — kehren*, turn o.'s back upon s.o.
rücken ['rykən], *v.a.* move, push. — *v.n.* move along.
Rückenmark ['rykənmark], *n.* (—s, *no pl.*) spinal marrow.
Rückenwirbel ['rykənvɪrbəl], *m.* (—s, *pl.* —) dorsal vertebra.
rückerstatten ['rykərʃtatən], *v.a.* refund.
Rückfahrkarte ['rykfa:rkartə], *f.* (—, *pl.* —n) return ticket.
Rückfall ['rykfal], *m.* (—s, *pl.* ⸚e) relapse.
rückgängig ['rykgɛŋɪç], *adj.* — *machen*, cancel, annul, reverse (a decision).
Rückgrat ['rykgra:t], *n.* (—s, *pl.* —e) backbone, spine.
Rückhalt ['rykhalt], *m.* (—s, *no pl.*) reserve; support, backing.

Rückkehr ['rykke:r], *f.* (—, *no pl.*) return.
Rücklicht ['ryklıçt], *n.* (—s, *pl.* —er) (*Motor. etc.*) tail-light.
rücklings ['ryklıŋks], *adv.* from behind.
Rucksack ['rukzak], *m.* (—s, *pl.* ⸚e) rucksack; knapsack.
Rückschritt ['rykʃrıt], *m.* (—es, *pl.* —e) step backward, retrograde step, regression.
Rücksicht ['rykzıçt], *f.* (—, *pl.* —en) consideration, regard.
Rücksprache ['rykʃpra:xə], *f.* (—, *pl.* —n) conference, consultation; — *nehmen mit*, consult, confer with.
rückständig ['rykʃtɛndıç], *adj.* outstanding; old-fashioned; backward.
Rücktritt ['ryktrıt], *m.* (—s, *no pl.*) resignation.
ruckweise ['rukvaızə], *adv.* by fits and starts; jerkily.
Rückwirkung ['rykvırkuŋ], *f.* (—, *pl.* —en) reaction, retroaction.
Rüde ['ry:də], *m.* (—n, *pl.* —n) male (dog, fox etc.).
Rudel ['ru:dəl], *n.* (—s, *pl.* —) flock, herd, pack.
Ruder ['ru:dər], *n.* (—s, *pl.* —) oar, rudder, paddle; *am — sein*, be at the helm; (*Pol.*) be in power.
rudern ['ru:dərn], *v.a., v.n.* row.
Ruf [ru:f], *m.* (—(e)s, *pl.* —e) call; shout; reputation, renown; *einen guten (schlechten) — haben*, have a good (bad) reputation, be well (ill) spoken of.
rufen ['ru:fən], *v.a., v.n. irr.* call, shout; *einen — lassen*, send for s.o.
Rüffel ['ryfəl], *m.* (—s, *pl.* —) (*coll.*) reprimand; (*sl.*) rocket.
Rüge ['ry:gə], *f.* (—, *pl.* —n) censure, blame, reprimand.
Ruhe ['ru:ə], *f.* (—, *no pl.*) rest, repose; quiet, tranquillity; *sich zur — setzen*, retire (from business etc.).
Ruhegehalt ['ru:əgəhalt], *n.* (—es, *pl.* ⸚er) retirement pension, superannuation.
ruhen ['ru:ən], *v.n.* rest, repose, take a rest.
Ruhestand ['ru:əʃtant], *m.* (—es, *no pl.*) retirement.
ruhig ['ru:ıç], *adj.* quiet, tranquil, peaceful, calm; *sich — verhalten*, keep quiet.
Ruhm [ru:m], *m.* (—(e)s, *no pl.*) glory, fame, renown; *einem zum — gereichen*, be *or* redound to s.o.'s credit.
rühmen ['ry:mən], *v.a.* praise, extol, glorify. — *v.r. sich —*, boast.
Ruhr (1) [ru:r], *f.* (River) Ruhr.
Ruhr (2) [ru:r], *f.* (—, *no pl.*) dysentery.
Rührei ['ry:raı], *n.* (—s, *pl.* —er) scrambled egg.
rühren ['ry:rən], *v.a.* stir, move, touch. — *v.r. sich —*, move, stir; get a move on.
rührig ['ry:rıç], *adj.* active, alert.
rührselig ['ry:rze:lıç], *adj.* over-sentimental; lachrymose.
Rührung ['ry:ruŋ], *f.* (—, *no pl.*) emotion.
Ruin [ru'i:n], *m.* (—s, *no pl.*) (*fig.*) ruin; decay; bankruptcy.
Ruine [ru'i:nə], *f.* (—, *pl.* —n) ruin(s).
rülpsen ['rylpsən], *v.n.* belch.
Rum [rum], *m.* (—s, *no pl.*) rum.
Rumänien [ru'mɛ:njən], *n.* Rumania.
Rummel ['ruməl], *m.* (—s, *no pl.*) tumult, row, hubbub.
Rumor [ru'mo:r], *m.* (—s, *no pl.*) noise; rumour.
rumoren [ru'mo:rən], *v.n.* make a noise.
Rumpelkammer ['rumpəlkamər], *f.* (—, *pl.* —n) lumber-room, junk-room.
rumpeln ['rumpəln], *v.n.* rumble.
Rumpf [rumpf], *m.* (—(e)s, *pl.* ⸚e) (*Anat.*) trunk; (*ship*) hull; (*Aviat.*) fuselage.
rümpfen ['rympfən], *v.a. die Nase —*, turn up o.'s nose.
rund [runt], *adj.* round, rotund; — *heraus*, flatly; *etwas — abschlagen*, refuse s.th. flatly; — *herum*, round about.
Runde ['rundə], *f.* (—, *pl.* —n) round; (*Sport*) round, bout; *die — machen*, (*watchman*) patrol.
Rundfunk ['runtfuŋk], *m.* (—s, *no pl.*) broadcasting, wireless; radio.
Rundgang ['runtgaŋ], *m.* (—s, *pl.* ⸚e) round, tour (of inspection).
rundlich ['runtlıç], *adj.* plump.
Rundschau ['runtʃau], *f.* (—, *no pl.*) panorama; review, survey.
Rundschreiben ['runtʃraıbən], *n.* (—s, *pl.* —) circular letter.
rundweg ['runtve:k], *adv.* flatly, plainly.
Rune ['ru:nə], *f.* (—, *pl.* —n) rune; runic writing.
Runkelrübe ['ruŋkəlry:bə], *f.* (—, *pl.* —n) beetroot.
Runzel ['runtsəl], *f.* (—, *pl.* —n) wrinkle, pucker.
Rüpel ['ry:pəl], *m.* (—s, *pl.* —) bounder, lout.
rupfen ['rupfən], *v.a.* pluck; *einen —*, (*fig.*) fleece s.o.
Rupie ['ru:pjə], *f.* (—, *pl.* —n) rupee.
ruppig ['rupıç], *adj.* unfriendly, rude; scruffy.
Ruprecht ['ru:prɛçt], *m. Knecht —*, Santa Claus.
Rüsche ['ry:ʃə], *f.* (—, *pl.* —n) ruche.
Ruß [ru:s], *m.* (—es, *no pl.*) soot.
Rüssel ['rysəl], *m.* (—s, *pl.* —) snout; (*elephant*) trunk.
Rußland ['ruslant], *n.* Russia.
rüsten ['rystən], *v.a.* prepare, fit (out); equip; (*Mil.*) arm, mobilise.
Rüster ['rystər], *f.* (—, *pl.* —n) elm.
rüstig ['rystıç], *adj.* vigorous, robust.
Rüstung ['rystuŋ], *f.* (—, *pl.* —en) armour; preparation; (*Mil.*) armament.

Rüstzeug ['rysttsɔyk], *n.* (—**s**, *no pl.*) equipment.
Rute ['ru:tə], *f.* (—, *pl.* —**n**) rod, twig; (*fox*) brush.
Rutengänger ['ru:təngɛŋər], *m.* (—**s**, *pl.* —) water-diviner.
rutschen ['rutʃən], *v.n.* (*aux.* sein) slip, slide, skid, slither.
rütteln ['rytəln], *v.a.*, *v.n.* shake, jolt.

S

S [ɛs], *n.* (—**s**, *pl.* —**s**) the letter S.
Saal [za:l], *m.* (—(**e**)**s**, *pl.* **Säle**) hall, large room.
Saat [za:t], *f.* (—, *pl.* —**en**) seed; sowing; standing corn.
Sabbat ['zabat], *m.* (—**s**, *pl.* —**e**) sabbath.
sabbern ['zabərn], *v.n.* (*sl.*) slaver, drivel.
Säbel ['zɛ:bəl], *m.* (—**s**, *pl.* —) sabre; *krummer* —, falchion, scimitar.
säbeln ['zɛ:bəln], *v.a.* sabre, hack at.
sachdienlich ['zaxdi:nlɪç], *adj.* relevant, pertinent.
Sache ['zaxə], *f.* (—, *pl.* —**n**) thing, matter, affair; (*Law*) action, case; *die — ist (die) daß*, the fact is that; *das gehört nicht zur* —, that is beside the point; *bei der — sein*, pay attention to the matter in hand; *das ist meine* —, that is my business; *die — der Unterdrückten verteidigen*, take up the cause of the oppressed.
Sachlage ['zaxla:gə], *f.* (—, *no pl.*) state of affairs.
sachlich ['zaxlɪç], *adj.* pertinent; objective.
sächlich ['zɛçlɪç], *adj.* (*Gram.*) neuter.
Sachse ['zaksə], *m.* (—**n**, *pl.* —**n**) Saxon.
Sachsen ['zaksən], *n.* Saxony.
sachte ['zaxtə], *adj.* soft, slow, quiet, careful, gentle.
Sachverhalt ['zaxfɛrhalt], *m.* (—**s**, *no pl.*) facts (of a case), state of things, circumstances.
sachverständig ['zaxfɛrʃtɛndɪç], *adj.* expert, competent, experienced.
Sachwalter ['zaxvaltər], *m.* (—**s**, *pl.* —) manager, counsel, attorney.
Sack [zak], *m.* (—(**e**)**s**, *pl.* ¨**e**) sack, bag; *mit — und Pack*, (with) bag and baggage.
Säckel ['zɛkəl], *m.* (—**s**, *pl.* —) purse.
Sackgasse ['zakgasə], *f.* (—, *pl.* —**n**) cul-de-sac, blind alley; *einen in eine — treiben*, corner s.o.
Sackpfeife ['zakpfaɪfə], *f.* (—, *pl.* —**n**) bagpipe.
Sacktuch ['zaktu:x], *n.* (—**es**, *pl.* ¨**er**) sacking; (*dial.*) pocket-handkerchief.
säen ['zɛ:ən], *v.a.* sow.
Saffian ['zafja:n], *m.* (—**s**, *no pl.*) morocco-leather.
Saft [zaft], *m.* (—(**e**)**s**, *pl.* ¨**e**) juice; (*tree*) sap; (*meat*) gravy; *ohne — und Kraft*, insipid; *im eigenen — schmoren*, stew in o.'s own juice.
Sage ['za:gə], *f.* (—, *pl.* —**n**) legend, fable, myth; *es geht die* —, it is rumoured.
Säge ['zɛ:gə], *f.* (—, *pl.* —**n**) saw.
sagen ['za:gən], *v.a.* say, tell; *einem etwas — lassen*, send word to s.o.; *es hat nichts zu* —, it does not matter; *was Du nicht sagst!* you don't say (so)!
sägen ['zɛ:gən], *v.a.*, *v.n.* saw; (*fig.*) snore.
sagenhaft ['za:gənhaft], *adj.* legendary, mythical; (*fig.*) fabulous.
Sahne ['za:nə], *f.* (—, *no pl.*) cream.
Saite ['zaɪtə], *f.* (—, *pl.* —**n**) string; *strengere —n aufziehen*, (*fig.*) take a stricter line.
Sakko ['zako], *m.* (—**s**, *pl.* —**s**) lounge jacket.
Sakristei [zakrɪ'staɪ], *f.* (—, *pl.* —**en**) vestry.
Salat [za'la:t], *m.* (—(**e**)**s**, *pl.* —**e**) salad; (*plant*) lettuce; (*sl.*) mess.
salbadern ['zalba:dərn], *v.n.* prate, talk nonsense.
Salbe ['zalbə], *f.* (—, *pl.* —**n**) ointment, salve.
Salbei ['zalbaɪ], *m.* (—**s**, *no pl.*) (*Bot.*) sage.
salben ['zalbən], *v.a.* anoint.
salbungsvoll ['zalbuŋsfɔl], *adj.* unctuous.
Saldo ['zaldo], *m.* (—**s**, *pl.* —**s**) balance.
Saline [za'li:nə], *f.* (—, *pl.* —**n**) salt-mine, salt-works.
Salkante ['za:lkantə], *f.* (—, *pl.* —**n**) selvedge, border.
Salm [zalm], *m.* (—**s**, *pl.* —**e**) (*Zool.*) salmon.
Salmiakgeist ['zalmjakgaɪst], *m.* (—**s**, *no pl.*) ammonia.
Salon [za'lɔ̃], *m.* (—**s**, *pl.* —**s**) salon; saloon; drawing-room.
salonfähig [za'lɔ̃fɛ:ɪç], *adj.* presentable, socially acceptable.
salopp [za'lɔp], *adj.* careless, slovenly, shabby, sloppy.
Salpeter [zal'pe:tər], *m.* (—**s**, *no pl.*) nitre, saltpetre.
salutieren [zalu'ti:rən], *v.a.*, *v.n.*, salute.
Salve ['zalvə], *f.* (—, *pl.* —**n**) volley, discharge, salute.
Salz [zalts], *n.* (—**es**, *pl.* —**e**) salt.
Salzfaß ['zaltsfas], *n.* (—**sses**, *pl.* ¨**sser**) salt-cellar.
Salzlake ['zaltsla:kə], *f.* (—, *pl.* —**n**) brine.
Salzsäure ['zaltszɔyrə], *f.* (—, *no pl.*) hydrochloric acid.
Sämann ['zɛ:man], *m.* (—**s**, *pl.* ¨**ner**) sower.
Sambia ['zambia], *n.* Zambia.

Same(n) ['za:mə(n)], *m.* (—**ns**, *pl.* —**n**) seed; sperm; spawn.
Samenstaub ['za:mənʃtaup], *m.* (—**s**, *no pl.*) pollen.
Sämereien [zɛ:mə'raɪən], *f. pl.* seeds, grain.
sämisch ['zɛ:mɪʃ], *adj.* chamois.
Sammelband ['zaməlbant], *m.* (—**es**, *pl.* ⸚**e**) miscellany, anthology.
sammeln ['zaməln], *v.a.* collect, gather. — *v.r. sich* —, meet; collect o.'s thoughts, compose o.s.
Sammler ['zamlər], *m.* (—**s**, *pl.* —) collector; accumulator.
Samstag ['zamsta:k], *m.* (—**s**, *pl.* —**e**) Saturday.
Samt [zamt], *m.* (—(**e**)**s**, *pl.* —**e**) velvet.
samt [zamt], *adv.* together, all together; — *und sonders*, jointly and severally.— *prep.* (*Dat.*) together with.
sämtlich ['zɛmtlɪç], *adj.* each and every.
Sand [zant], *m.* (—**es**, *no pl.*) sand; *feiner* —, grit; *grober* —, gravel.
Sandtorte ['zanttɔrtə], *f.* (—, *pl.* —**n**) sponge-cake, madeira-cake.
Sanduhr ['zantu:r], (—, *pl.* —**en**) hour-glass.
sanft [zanft], *adj.* soft, gentle.
Sänfte ['zɛnftə], *f.* (—, *pl.* —**n**) sedan-chair.
Sang [zaŋ], *m.* (—**es**, *pl.* **Gesänge**) song; *ohne — und Klang*, (*fig.*) unostentatiously, without fuss, without ceremony.
sanieren [za'ni:rən], *v.a.* cure; (*company*) reconstruct, put on a sound financial basis.
sanitär [zani'tɛ:r], *adj.* sanitary.
Sanitäter [zani'tɛ:tər], *m.* (—**s**, *pl.*—) medical orderly; ambulance man.
Sankt [zaŋkt], *indecl. adj.* Saint; (*abbr.*) St.
sanktionieren [zaŋktsjo'ni:rən], *v.a.* sanction.
Sansibar ['zanzɪba:r]. *n.* Zanzibar.
Sardelle [zar'dɛlə], *f.* (—, *pl.* —**n**) (*Zool.*) anchovy.
Sardinien [zar'di:njən], *n.* Sardinia.
Sarg [zark], *m.* (—**es**, *pl.* ⸚**e**) coffin.
sarkastisch [zar'kastɪʃ], *adj.* sarcastic.
Satellit [zatə'li:t], *m.* (—**en**, *pl.* —**en**) satellite.
Satiriker [za'ti:rɪkər], *m.* (—**s**, *pl.* —) satirist.
satt [zat], *adj.* sated, satiated, satisfied; (*colours*) deep, rich; *sich — essen*, eat o.'s fill; *einer Sache — sein*, be sick of s.th., have had enough of s.th.
Sattel ['zatəl], *m.* (—**s**, *pl.* ⸚) saddle; *einen aus dem — heben*, (*fig.*) oust s.o.; *fest im — sitzen*, (*fig.*) be master of a situation; *in allen ⸚n gerecht*, versatile.
satteln ['zatəln], *v.a.* saddle.
Sattheit ['zathaɪt], *f.* (—, *no pl.*) satiety.
sättigen ['zɛtɪgən], *v.a.* satisfy, sate, satiate; (*Chem.*) saturate.
sattsam ['zatza:m], *adv.* enough, sufficiently.
saturieren [zatu'ri:rən], *v.a.* (*Chem.*) saturate.
Satz [zats], *m.* (—**es**, *pl.* ⸚**e**) sentence; proposition; thesis; (*Mus.*) movement; (*Typ.*) composition; (*dregs*) sediment; (*gambling*) stake; *mit einem* —, with one leap (*or* jump *or* bound).
Satzbildung ['zatsbɪlduŋ], *f.* (—, *pl.* —**en**) (*Gram.*) construction; (*Chem.*) sedimentation.
Satzlehre ['zatsle:rə], *f.* (—, *no pl.*) syntax.
Satzung ['zatsuŋ], *f.* (—, *pl.* —**en**) statute.
Satzzeichen ['zatstsaɪçən], *n.* (—**s**, *pl.* —) punctuation-mark.
Sau [zau], *f.* (—, *pl.* ⸚**e**) sow; (*vulg.*) dirty person, slut.
sauber ['zaubər], *adj.* clean, neat, tidy.
säubern ['zɔybərn], *v.a.* clean, cleanse; (*fig.*) purge.
Saubohne ['zaubo:nə], *f.* (—, *pl.* —**n**) broad bean.
Saudiarabien ['zaudiara:bjən], *n.* Saudi Arabia.
sauer ['zauər], *adj.* sour, acid; (*fig.*) troublesome; morose.
Sauerbrunnen ['zauərbrunən], *m.* (—**s**, *pl.* —) mineral water.
Sauerei [zauə'raɪ], *f.* (—, *pl.* —**en**) (*sl.*) filthiness; mess.
Sauerkraut ['zauərkraut], *n.* (—**s**, *no pl.*) pickled cabbage.
säuerlich ['zɔyərlɪç], *adj.* acidulous.
Sauerstoff ['zauərʃtɔf], *m.* (—(**e**)**s**, *no pl.*) oxygen.
Sauerteig ['zauərtaɪk], *m.* (—(**e**)**s**, *pl.* —**e**) leaven.
sauertöpfisch ['zauərtœpfɪʃ], *adj.* morose, peevish.
saufen ['zaufən], *v.a.*, *v.n. irr.* (*animals*) drink; (*humans*) drink to excess.
Säufer ['zɔyfər], *m.* (—**s**, *pl.* —) drunkard, drinker, alcoholic.
saugen ['zaugən], *v.a.*, *v.n.* suck.
säugen ['zɔygən], *v.a.* suckle.
Säugetier ['zɔygəti:r], *n.* (—**s**, *pl.* —**e**) mammal.
Saugheber ['zaukhe:bər], *m.* (—**s**, *pl.* —) suction-pump; siphon.
Säugling ['zɔyklɪŋ], *m.* (—**s**, *pl.* —**e**) suckling, baby.
Saugwarze ['zaukvartsə], *f.* (—, *pl.* —**n**) nipple.
Säule ['zɔylə], *f.* (—, *pl.* —**n**) pillar, column.
Säulenbündel ['zɔylənbyndəl], *n.* (—**s**, *pl.* —) (*Archit.*) clustered column.
Säulenfuß ['zɔylənfu:s], *m.* (—**es**, *pl.* ⸚**e**) (*Archit.*) base, plinth.
Säulengang ['zɔyləngaŋ], *m.* (—**s**, *pl.* ⸚**e**) colonnade.
Saum [zaum], *m.* (—(**e**)**s**, *pl.* ⸚**e**) seam, hem, border, edge; selvedge.
saumäßig ['zaumɛ:sɪç], *adj.* (*sl.*) beastly, filthy, piggish; enormous.
säumen (1) ['zɔymən], *v.a.* hem.
säumen (2) ['zɔymən], *v.n.* delay, tarry.
säumig ['zɔymɪç], *adj.* tardy, slow, dilatory.

Saumpferd ['zaumpfe:rt], *n.* (**—s**, *pl.* **—e**) pack-horse.

saumselig ['zaumze:lɪç], *adj.* tardy, dilatory.

Säure ['zɔyrə], *f.* (—, *pl.* **—n**) acid; (*Med.*) acidity.

Saurier ['zaurjər], *m.* (**—s**, *pl.* **—**) saurian.

Saus [zaus], *m.* (**—es**, *no pl.*) rush; revel, riot; *in — und Braus leben*, live a wild life, live riotously.

säuseln ['zɔyzəln], *v.n.* rustle, murmur.

sausen ['zauzən], *v.n.* bluster, blow, howl, whistle; (*coll.*) rush, dash.

Saustall ['zauʃtal], *m.* (**—s**, *pl.* **¨e**) pigsty.

Schabe ['ʃa:bə], *f.* (—, *pl.* **—n**) (*Ent.*) cockroach.

schaben ['ʃa:bən], *v.a.* scrape, shave, rub.

Schabernack ['ʃa:bərnak], *m.* (**—s**, *pl.* **—e**) practical joke, trick.

schäbig ['ʃɛ:bɪç], *adj.* shabby.

Schablone [ʃa'blo:nə], *f.* (—, *pl.* **—n**) model, mould, pattern, stencil; (*fig.*) routine.

Schach [ʃax], *n.* (**—(e)s**, *no pl.*) chess; *— bieten*, check; *— spielen*, play chess; *in — halten*, keep in check.

Schacher ['ʃaxər], *m.* (**—s**, *no pl.*) haggling, bargaining, barter.

Schächer ['ʃɛçər], *m.* (**—s**, *pl.* **—**) wretch, felon, robber.

Schacht [ʃaxt], *m.* (**—(e)s**, *pl.* **¨e**) shaft.

Schachtel ['ʃaxtəl], *f.* (—, *pl.* **—n**) box, (cardboard) box, (small) case.

Schachtelhalm ['ʃaxtəlhalm], *m.* (**—s**, *pl.* **—e**) (*grass*) horse-tail.

Schächter ['ʃɛçtər], *m.* (**—s**, *pl.* **—**) (kosher) butcher.

schade ['ʃa:də], *int.* a pity, a shame, unfortunate; *wie —*, what a pity; *sehr —*, a great pity.

Schädel ['ʃɛ:dəl], *m.* (**—s**, *pl.* **—**) skull.

Schaden ['ʃa:dən], *m.* (**—s**, *pl.* **¨**) damage, injury, detriment; *zu — kommen*, come to grief.

schaden ['ʃa:dən], *v.n.* do harm, do damage, do injury; *es schadet nichts*, it does not matter.

Schadenersatz ['ʃa:dənɛrzats], *m.* (**—es**, *no pl.*) indemnity, compensation, indemnification; (*money*) damages.

Schadenfreude ['ʃa:dənfrɔydə], *f.* (—, *no pl.*) malicious pleasure.

Schadensforderung ['ʃa:dənsfɔrdəruŋ], *f.* (—, *pl.* **—en**) claim (for damages).

schadhaft ['ʃa:thaft], *adj.* defective, faulty.

schädlich ['ʃɛ:tlɪç], *adj.* injurious, noxious, pernicious, noisome.

schadlos ['ʃa:tlo:s], *adj.* indemnified; *einen — halten*, indemnify s.o., compensate s.o.; *sich an einem — halten*, recoup o.s. from s.o.

Schadlosigkeit ['ʃa:tlo:zɪçkaɪt], *f.* (—, *no pl.*) harmlessness.

Schaf [ʃa:f], *n.* (**—(e)s**, *pl.* **—e**) sheep.

Schafblattern ['ʃa:fblatərn], *f. pl.* (*Med.*) chicken-pox.

Schafdarm ['ʃa:fdarm], *m.* (**—s**, *pl.* **¨e**) sheep-gut.

Schäfer ['ʃɛ:fər], *m.* (**—s**, *pl.* **—**) shepherd.

Schäferstündchen ['ʃɛ:fərʃtyntçən], *n.* (**—s**, *pl.* **—**) tryst; rendezvous.

schaffen ['ʃafən], *v.a.*, *v.n. irr.* make, produce, create. — *v.a. reg.* provide; manage; *aus dem Wege —*, remove. — *v.n. reg.* work; *einem zu — machen*, give s.o. trouble.

Schaffner ['ʃafnər], *m.* (**—s**, *pl.* **—**) (*Railw. etc.*) guard, conductor.

Schafgarbe ['ʃa:fgarbə], *f.* (—, *pl.* **—n**) (*Bot.*) common yarrow.

Schafhürde ['ʃa:fhyrdə], *f.* (—, *pl.* **—n**) sheep-fold.

Schafott [ʃa'fɔt], *n.* (**—(e)s**, *pl.* **—e**) scaffold.

Schafschur ['ʃa:fʃu:r], *f.* (—, *pl.* **—en**) sheep-shearing.

Schaft [ʃaft], *m.* (**—(e)s**, *pl.* **¨e**) shaft; (*gun*) stock.

Schafwolle ['ʃa:fvɔlə], *f.* (—, *no pl.*) sheep's wool, fleece.

Schakal [ʃa'ka:l], *m.* (**—s**, *pl.* **—e**) (*Zool.*) jackal.

Schäkerei [ʃɛ:kə'raɪ], *f.* (—, *pl.* **—en**) playfulness, teasing, dalliance, flirtation.

Schal [ʃa:l], *m.* (**—s**, *pl.* **—e**) scarf, shawl.

schal [ʃa:l], *adj.* stale, flat, insipid.

Schale ['ʃa:lə], *f.* (—, *pl.* **—n**) (*nut, egg*) shell; (*fruit*) peel, rind; dish, bowl; (*Austr.*) cup; (*fig.*) outside.

schälen ['ʃɛ:lən], *v.a.* shell; peel.

Schalk [ʃalk], *m.* (**—(e)s**, *pl.* **—e**) knave; rogue; wag, joker.

Schall [ʃal], *m.* (**—(e)s**, *no pl.*) sound.

Schallbecken ['ʃalbɛkən], *n.* (**—s**, *pl.* **—**) cymbal.

Schallehre ['ʃalle:rə], *f.* (—, *no pl.*) acoustics.

schallen ['ʃalən], *v.n.* sound, reverberate.

Schalmei [ʃal'maɪ], *f.* (—, *pl.* **—en**) (*Poet.*, *Mus.*) shawm.

Schallplatte ['ʃalplatə], *f.* (—, *pl.* **—n**) (gramophone) record.

schalten ['ʃaltən], *v.n.* rule; switch; (*Motor.*) change gear; *— und walten*, manage.

Schalter ['ʃaltər], *m.* (**—s**, *pl.* **—**) (*Elec.*) switch; booking-office; counter.

Schalthebel ['ʃalthe:bəl], *m.* (**—s**, *pl.* **—**) (*Motor.*) gear lever.

Schaltier ['ʃa:lti:r], *n.* (**—s**, *pl.* **—e**) (*Zool.*) crustacean.

Schaltjahr ['ʃaltja:r], *n.* (**—s**, *pl.* **—e**) leap year.

Schalttafel ['ʃaltta:fəl], *f.* (—, *pl.* **—n**) switch-board.

Scham [ʃa:m], *f.* (—, *no pl.*) shame, modesty; private parts.

schämen ['ʃɛ:mən], *v.r. sich —*, be ashamed (of).

schamlos ['ʃa:mlo:s], *adj.* shameless.

schamrot ['ʃa:mro:t], *adj.* blushing; *— werden*, blush.

schandbar [ˈʃantbaːr], *adj.* ignominious, infamous.
Schande [ˈʃandə], *f.* (—, *no pl.*) shame, disgrace; dishonour, ignominy.
schänden [ˈʃɛndən], *v.a.* dishonour, disgrace; violate, ravish.
Schandfleck [ˈʃantflɛk], *m.* (**—s**, *pl.* **—e**) stain, blemish.
schändlich [ˈʃɛntlɪç], *adj.* shameful, disgraceful, infamous.
Schändung [ˈʃɛnduŋ], *f.* (—, *pl.* **—en**) violation.
Schank [ˈʃaŋk], *m.* (**—s**, *no pl.*) sale of liquor.
Schanzarbeiter [ˈʃantsarbaɪtər], *m.* (**—s**, *pl.* —) sapper.
Schanze [ˈʃantsə], *f.* (—, *pl.* **—n**) redoubt, bulwark; *in die — schlagen,* risk, venture.
Schar [ʃaːr], *f.* (—, *pl.* **—en**) troop, band; host.
Scharade [ʃaˈraːdə], *f.* (—, *pl.* **—n**) charade.
scharen [ˈʃaːrən], *v.r. sich — um,* assemble, congregate, gather round.
Schären [ˈʃɛːrən], *f. pl.* reefs, skerries.
scharf [ʃarf], *adj.* sharp, keen, acute, acrid, pungent; piercing; (*fig.*) severe, rigorous.
Schärfe [ˈʃɛrfə], *f.* (—, *no pl.*) sharpness, keenness, acuteness; pungency, acridness; severity, rigour.
schärfen [ˈʃɛrfən], *v.a.* sharpen, whet; (*fig.*) strengthen, intensify.
Scharfrichter [ˈʃarfrɪçtər], *m.* (**—s**, *pl.* —) executioner.
scharfsichtig [ˈʃarfzɪçtɪç], *adj.* sharp-eyed, (*fig.*) penetrating, astute.
scharfsinnig [ˈʃarfzɪnɪç], *adj.* clear-sighted, sagacious, ingenious.
Scharlach [ˈʃarlax], *m.* (**—s**, *no pl.*) scarlet; (*Med.*) scarlet-fever.
Scharlatan [ˈʃarlataːn], *m.* (**—s**, *pl.* **—e**) charlatan, humbug.
scharmant [ʃarˈmant], *adj.* charming.
Scharmützel [ʃarˈmytsəl], *n.* (**—s**, *pl.* —) skirmish.
Scharnier [ʃarˈniːr], *n.* (**—s**, *pl.* **—e**) hinge, joint.
Schärpe [ˈʃɛrpə], *f.* (—, *pl.* **—n**) sash.
Scharpie [ʃarˈpiː], *f.* (—, *no pl.*) lint.
scharren [ˈʃarən], *v.a., v.n.* scrape, rake.
Scharte [ˈʃartə], *f.* (—, *pl.* **—n**) notch, crack; *eine — auswetzen,* repair a mistake, make up for s.th.
Scharteke [ʃarˈteːkə], *f.* (—, *pl.* **—n**) worthless book, trash; *eine alte —,* an old fuddy-duddy, frump.
scharwenzeln [ʃarˈvɛntsəln], *v.n.* dance attendance, be obsequious.
Schatten [ˈʃatən], *m.* (**—s**, *pl.* —) shade, shadow.
Schattenbild [ˈʃatənbɪlt], *n.* (**—s**, *pl.* **—er**) silhouette.
Schattenriß [ˈʃatənrɪs], *m.* (**—sses**, *pl.* **—sse**) silhouette.
schattieren [ʃaˈtiːrən], *v.a.* shade (drawing).
schattig [ˈʃatɪç], *adj.* shady.
Schatulle [ʃaˈtulə], *f.* (—, *pl.* **—n**) cash-box; privy purse.
Schatz [ʃats], *m.* (**—es**, *pl* **¨e**) treasure; (*fig.*) sweetheart, darling.
Schatzamt [ˈʃatsamt], *n.* (**—s**, *pl.* **¨er**) Treasury, Exchequer.
schätzbar [ˈʃɛtsbaːr], *adj.* estimable.
Schätzchen [ˈʃɛtsçən], *n.* (**—s**, *pl.* —) (*coll.*) sweetheart.
schätzen [ˈʃɛtsən], *v.a.* value, estimate; esteem; reckon at.
Schatzkammer [ˈʃatskamər], *f.* (—, *pl.* **—n**) treasury.
Schatzmeister [ˈʃatsmaɪstər], *m.* (**—s**, *pl.* —) treasurer.
Schätzung [ˈʃɛtsuŋ], *f.* (—, *pl.* **—en**) valuation, estimate; (*fig.*) esteem.
Schau [ʃau], *f.* (—, *pl.* **—en**) show, view, spectacle; *zur — stellen,* display; parade.
Schauder [ˈʃaudər], *m.* (**—s**, *pl.* —) shudder, shiver; horror.
schaudern [ˈʃaudərn], *v.n.* shudder, shiver.
schauen [ˈʃauən], *v.a.* see, view. — *v.n.* look, gaze (*auf,* at), *schau mal,* look here.
Schauer [ˈʃauər], *m.* (**—s**, *pl.* —) shiver, paroxysm; (*fig.*) thrill, awe; (*rain*) shower.
schauern [ˈʃauərn], *v.n.* shudder, shiver; (*rain*) shower.
Schauerroman [ˈʃauərromaːn], *m.* (**—s**, *pl.* **—e**) (*novel*) penny dreadful, thriller.
Schaufel [ˈʃaufəl], *f.* (—, *pl.* **—n**) shovel.
Schaufenster [ˈʃaufɛnstər], *n.* (**—s**, *pl.* —) shop-window.
Schaukel [ˈʃaukəl], *f.* (—, *pl.* **—n**) swing.
schaulustig [ˈʃaulustɪç], *adj.* curious.
Schaum [ʃaum], *m.* (**—es**, *pl.* **¨e**) foam, froth; bubbles; scum; *— schlagen,* whip cream.
schäumen [ˈʃɔymən], *v.n.* foam, froth, sparkle.
Schauplatz [ˈʃauplats], *m.* (**—es**, *pl.* **¨e**) scene, stage.
schaurig [ˈʃaurɪç], *adj.* grisly, horrid, horrible.
Schauspiel [ˈʃauʃpiːl], *n.* (**—s**, *pl.* **—e**) spectacle; drama, play.
Schauspieler [ˈʃauʃpiːlər], *m.* (**—s**, *pl.* —) actor, player.
Schaustellung [ˈʃauʃtɛluŋ], *f.* (—, *pl.* **—en**) exhibition.
Scheck [ʃɛk], *m.* (**—s**, *pl.* **—s**) cheque.
scheckig [ˈʃɛkɪç], *adj.* piebald, spotted, dappled.
scheel [ʃeːl], *adj.* squint-eyed; envious; *einen — ansehen,* look askance at s.o.
Scheffel [ˈʃɛfəl], *m.* (**—s**, *pl.* —) bushel.
scheffeln [ˈʃɛfəln], *v.a.* rake in; accumulate.
Scheibe [ˈʃaɪbə], *f.* (—, *pl.* **—n**) disc; (*window*) pane; (*shooting*) target; (*bread*) slice.
Scheibenhonig [ˈʃaɪbənhoːnɪç], *m.* (**—s**, *no pl.*) honey in the comb.

Scheibenschießen ['ʃaɪbənʃiːsən], *n.* (—s, *no pl.*) target-practice.
Scheich [ʃaɪç], *m.* (—s, *pl.* —e) sheikh.
Scheide ['ʃaɪdə], *f.* (—, *pl.* —n) sheath, scabbard; (*Anat.*) vagina.
Scheidemünze ['ʃaɪdəmyntsə], *f.* (—, *pl.* —n) small coin, change.
scheiden ['ʃaɪdən], *v.a. irr.* divide; separate, divorce; *sich — lassen*, obtain a divorce. — *v.n.* (*aux.* sein) part, depart; *aus dem Amte —*, resign office.
Scheidewand ['ʃaɪdəvant], *f.* (—, *pl.* ¨e) partition-wall.
Scheideweg ['ʃaɪdəveːk], *m.* (—s, *pl.* —e) cross-roads; *am — stehen*, be at the parting of the ways.
Scheidung ['ʃaɪduŋ], *f.* (—, *pl.* —en) divorce.
Schein [ʃaɪn], *m.* (—(e)s, *no pl.*) shine, sheen, lustre, splendour; semblance, pretence; *den — wahren*, keep up appearances; *der — trügt*, appearances are deceptive; (*in compounds*) mock, would-be, apparent; (*pl.* —e) (piece of) paper, chit, note; (*fig.*) attestation, certificate.
scheinbar ['ʃaɪnbaːr], *adj.* apparent; ostensible, specious. — *adv.* seemingly.
scheinen ['ʃaɪnən], *v.n. irr.* shine, sparkle; seem, appear.
scheinheilig ['ʃaɪnhaɪlɪç], *adj.* hypocritical.
Scheinheiligkeit ['ʃaɪnhaɪlɪçkaɪt], *f.* (—, *no pl.*) hypocrisy.
scheintot ['ʃaɪntoːt], *adj.* in a cataleptic trance; seemingly dead.
Scheinwerfer ['ʃaɪnvɛrfər], *m.* (—s, *pl.* —) headlight; searchlight; floodlight.
Scheit [ʃaɪt], *n.* (—(e)s, *pl.* —e) piece of wood, billet.
Scheitel ['ʃaɪtəl], *m.* (—s, *pl.* —) (*hair*) parting; top, vertex.
Scheiterhaufen ['ʃaɪtərhaufən], *m.* (—s, *pl.* —) stake; funeral pyre.
scheitern ['ʃaɪtərn], *v.n.* (*aux.* sein) (*ship*) founder, be wrecked; (*fig.*) miscarry, fail.
Schelle ['ʃɛlə], *f.* (—, *pl.* —n) bell.
Schellen ['ʃɛlən], *f. pl.* (*Cards*) diamonds.
schellen ['ʃɛlən], *v.n.* ring the bell.
Schellfisch ['ʃɛlfɪʃ], *m.* (—es, *pl.* —e) (*Zool.*) haddock.
Schelm [ʃɛlm], *m.* (—(e)s, *pl.* —e) rogue, knave, villain.
schelten ['ʃɛltən], *v.a. irr.* scold, chide, rebuke, reprimand.
Schema ['ʃeːma], *n.* (—s, *pl.* —s) schedule, model, plan, scheme.
Schemel ['ʃeːməl], *m.* (—s, *pl.* —) foot-stool.
Schenk ['ʃɛŋk], *m.* (—en, *pl.* —en) cupbearer; publican.
Schenke ['ʃɛŋkə], *f.* (—, *pl.* —n) alehouse, tavern, pub.
Schenkel ['ʃɛnkəl], *m.* (—s, *pl.* —) thigh; (*Geom.*) side of triangle.
schenken ['ʃɛnkən], *v.a.* present s.o. with, donate, give.
Schenkstube ['ʃɛŋkʃtuːbə], *f.* (—, *pl.* —n) tap-room.
Scherbe ['ʃɛrbə], *f.* (—, *pl.* —n) potsherd; fragment of glass etc.
Schere ['ʃeːrə], *f.* (—, *pl.* —n) scissors; (*garden*) shears; (*crab*) claw.
scheren ['ʃeːrən], *v.a.* shave; clip, shear; bother, concern. — *v.r. sich —*, clear off; *scher dich zum Teufel!* go to blazes!
Scherereien [ʃerə'raɪən], *f. pl.* vexation, bother, trouble.
Scherflein ['ʃɛrflaɪn], *n.* (—s, *pl.* —) mite; *sein — beitragen*, contribute o.'s share.
Scherge ['ʃɛrgə], *m.* (—n, *pl.* —n) (*obs.*) beadle.
Scherz [ʃɛrts], *m.* (—es, *pl.* —e) jest, joke; *— beiseite*, joking apart.
scheu [ʃɔy], *adj.* shy, bashful, timid; skittish.
scheuchen ['ʃɔyçən], *v.a.* scare away.
scheuen ['ʃɔyən], *v.a.* shun, avoid, fight shy of, fear. — *v.n.* take fright.
Scheuer ['ʃɔyər], *f.* (—, *pl.* —n) barn.
scheuern ['ʃɔyərn], *v.a.* scour, scrub.
Scheuklappe ['ʃɔyklapə], *f.* (—, *pl.* —n) blinker.
Scheune ['ʃɔynə], *f.* (—, *pl.* —n) barn.
Scheusal ['ʃɔyzaːl], *n.* (—s, *pl.* —e) monster.
scheußlich ['ʃɔyslɪç], *adj.* frightful, dreadful, abominable, hideous.
Schicht [ʃɪçt], *f.* (—, *pl.* —en) layer, stratum, seam; (*society*) class; (*work*) shift.
schick [ʃɪk], *adj.* stylish, chic.
schicken ['ʃɪkən], *v.a.* send, despatch, convey. — *v.r. sich —*, be proper; *sich in etwas —*, put up with s.th., resign o.s. to s.th.
schicklich ['ʃɪklɪç], *adj.* proper, becoming, suitable, seemly.
Schicksal ['ʃɪkzaːl], *n.* (—s, *pl.* —e) fate, destiny, lot.
Schickung ['ʃɪkuŋ], *f.* (—, *pl.* —en) Divine Will, Providence.
schieben ['ʃiːbən], *v.a. irr.* shove, push; *die Schuld auf einen —*, put the blame on s.o.
Schieber ['ʃiːbər], *m.* (—s, *pl.* —) bolt, slide; (*fig.*) profiteer, spiv.
Schiedsgericht ['ʃiːtsgərɪçt], *n.* (—es, *pl.* —e) arbitration tribunal.
Schiedsrichter ['ʃiːtsrɪçtər], *m.* (—s, *pl.* —) referee, umpire, arbiter.
schief [ʃiːf], *adj.* slanting, oblique, bent, crooked; wry; *—e Ebene*, inclined plane; *— gehen*, go wrong.
Schiefe ['ʃiːfə], *f.* (—, *no pl.*) obliquity.
Schiefer ['ʃiːfər], *m.* (—s, *no pl.*) slate.
schiefrig ['ʃiːfrɪç], *adj.* slaty.
schielen ['ʃiːlən], *v.n.* squint, be cross-eyed.
Schienbein ['ʃiːnbaɪn], *n.* (—s, *pl.* —e) shin-bone, shin.

Schiene [ˈʃi:nə], *f.* (—, *pl.* —n) rail; (*Med.*) splint.
schier [ʃi:r], *adj.* (*rare*) sheer, pure. — *adv.* almost, very nearly.
Schierling [ˈʃi:rlɪŋ], *m.* (—s, *pl.* —e) (*Bot.*) hemlock.
schießen [ˈʃi:sən], *v.a., v.n. irr.* shoot, fire, discharge; (*fig.*) rush; *etwas — lassen*, let go of s.th.; *die Zügel — lassen*, loosen o.'s hold on the reins; *ein Kabel — lassen*, pay out a cable; *das ist zum —*, that's very funny.
Schiff [ʃɪf], *n.* (—(e)s, *pl.* —e) ship, vessel, boat; (*church*) nave.
schiffbar [ˈʃɪfba:r], *adj.* navigable.
Schiffbruch [ˈʃɪfbrux], *m.* (—s, *pl* ¨e) shipwreck.
Schiffbrücke [ˈʃɪfbrykə], *f.* (—, *pl.* —n) pontoon-bridge.
schiffen [ˈʃɪfən], *v.n.* sail; navigate.
Schiffsboden [ˈʃɪfsbo:dən], *m.* (—s, *pl.* ¨) (ship's) hold.
Schiffsmaat [ˈʃɪfsma:t], *m.* (—s, *pl.* —e) shipmate.
Schiffsrumpf [ˈʃɪfsrumpf], *m.* (—es, *pl.* ¨e) hull.
Schiffsschnabel [ˈʃɪfsʃna:bəl], *m.* (—s, *pl.* ¨) prow, bows.
Schiffsvorderteil [ˈʃɪfsfɔrdərtaɪl], *n.* (—s, *pl.* —e) forecastle, prow.
Schiffszwieback [ˈʃɪfstsvi:bak], *m.* (—s, *no pl.*) ship's biscuit.
Schikane [ʃiˈka:nə], *f.* (—, *pl.* —n) chicanery.
Schild (1) [ʃɪlt], *m.* (—(e)s, *pl.* —e) shield, buckler, escutcheon; *etwas im — führen*, have designs on s.th., plan s.th.
Schild (2) [ʃɪlt], *n.* (—s, *pl.* —er) signboard, plate.
Schilderhaus [ˈʃɪldərhaus], *n.* (—es, *pl.* ¨er) sentry-box.
Schildermaler [ˈʃɪldərma:lər], *m.* (—s, *pl.* —) sign-painter.
schildern [ˈʃɪldərn], *v.a.* describe, depict.
Schildknappe [ˈʃɪltknapə], *m.* (—n, *pl.* —n) shield-bearer, squire.
Schildkrot [ˈʃɪltkro:t], *n.* (—s, *no pl.*) tortoise-shell.
Schildkröte [ˈʃɪltkrø:tə], *f.* (—, *pl.* —n) (*Zool.*) turtle, tortoise.
Schildpatt [ˈʃɪltpat], *n.* (—s, *no pl.*) tortoise-shell.
Schildwache [ˈʃɪltvaxə], *f.* (—, *pl.* —n) sentinel, sentry; *— stehen*, be on sentry duty, stand guard.
Schilf(rohr) [ˈʃɪlf(ro:r)], *n.* (—(e)s, *no pl.*) (*Bot.*) reed, rush, sedge.
schillern [ˈʃɪlərn], *v.n.* opalesce, glitter, change colour, be iridescent.
Schilling [ˈʃɪlɪŋ], *m.* (—s, *pl.* —e) Austrian coin; shilling.
Schimmel (1) [ˈʃɪməl], *m.* (—s, *pl.* —) white horse.
Schimmel (2) [ˈʃɪməl], *m.* (—s, *no pl.*) mould, mustiness.
schimmeln [ˈʃɪməln], *v.n.* (*aux.* sein) go mouldy, moulder.
Schimmer [ˈʃɪmər], *m.* (—s, *pl.* —) glitter, gleam; *ich habe keinen —*, I haven't a clue.
schimmlig [ˈʃɪmlɪç], *adj.* mouldy, musty, mildewed.
Schimpanse [ʃɪmˈpanzə], *m.* (—n, *pl.* —n) (*Zool.*) chimpanzee.
Schimpf [ʃɪmpf], *m.* (—es, *no pl.*) abuse, affront, insult; *mit — und Schande*, in disgrace.
schimpfen [ˈʃɪmpfən], *v.n.* curse, swear; — *auf*, (*fig.*) run (s.o.) down. — *v.a.* insult (s.o.), call (s.o.) names; scold.
Schindel [ˈʃɪndəl], *f.* (—, *pl.* —n) shingle.
schinden [ˈʃɪndən], *v.a. irr.* flay; (*fig.*) grind, oppress, sweat. — *v.r. sich —*, slave, drudge.
Schindluder [ˈʃɪntlu:dər], *n.* (—s, *pl.* —) worn-out animal; *mit einem — treiben*, exploit s.o.
Schinken [ˈʃɪŋkən], *m.* (—s, *pl.* —) ham.
Schinkenspeck [ˈʃɪŋkənʃpɛk], *m.* (—s, *no pl.*) bacon.
Schippe [ˈʃɪpə], *f.* (—, *pl.* —n) shovel, spade.
Schirm [ʃɪrm], *m.* (—(e)s, *pl.* —e) screen; umbrella; parasol, sunshade; lampshade; (*fig.*) shield, shelter, cover.
schirmen [ˈʃɪrmən], *v.a.* protect (from), shelter.
Schirmherr [ˈʃɪrmhɛr], *m.* (—n, *pl.* —en) protector, patron.
Schlacht [ʃlaxt], *f.* (—, *pl.* —en) battle; fight; *eine — liefern*, give battle; *die — gewinnen*, carry the day, win the battle.
Schlachtbank [ˈʃlaxtbaŋk], *f.* (—, *pl.* ¨e) shambles; *zur — führen*, lead to the slaughter.
schlachten [ˈʃlaxtən], *v.a.* kill, butcher, slaughter.
Schlachtenbummler [ˈʃlaxtənbumlər], *m.* (—s, *pl.* —) camp follower.
Schlachtfeld [ˈʃlaxtfɛlt], *n.* (—s, *pl.* —er) battlefield.
Schlachtruf [ˈʃlaxtru:f], *m.* (—s, *pl.* —e) battle-cry.
Schlacke [ˈʃlakə], *f.* (—, *pl.* —n) slag, clinker, dross.
Schlackwurst [ˈʃlakvurst], *f.* (—, *pl.* ¨e) (*North German*) sausage.
Schlaf [ʃla:f], *m.* (—(e)s, *no pl.*) sleep; slumber, rest; *in tiefem —*, fast asleep; *in den — wiegen*, rock to sleep.
Schläfchen [ˈʃlɛ:fçən], *n.* (—s, *pl.* —) nap; *ein — machen*, have forty winks.
Schläfe [ˈʃlɛ:fə], *f.* (—, *pl.* —n) temple.
schlafen [ˈʃla:fən], *v.n. irr.* sleep; *schlaf wohl*, sleep well; — *gehen*, go to bed.
schlaff [ʃlaf], *adj.* slack, loose, lax, flabby; weak; remiss.
schlaflos [ˈʃla:flo:s], *adj.* sleepless.
Schlafmittel [ˈʃla:fmɪtəl], *n.* (—s, *pl.* —) soporific, sleeping tablet, sleeping draught.
schläfrig [ˈʃlɛ:frɪç], *adj.* drowsy, sleepy.

Schlafrock [ˈʃla:frɔk], *s.* (—**s**, *pl.* ⸚**e**) dressing-gown; *Äpfel im* —, apple fritters.

schlafwandeln [ˈʃla:fvandəln], *v.n.* (*aux.* sein) walk in o.'s sleep, sleep-walk.

Schlag [ʃla:k], *m.* (—(**e**)**s**, *pl.* ⸚**e**) blow, stroke; beat; (*Elec.*) shock; *ein Mann von gutem* —, a good type of man; *vom — gerührt*, struck by apoplexy; — *fünf*, at five o'clock sharp.

Schlagader [ˈʃla:ka:dər], *f.* (—, *pl.* —**n**) artery.

Schlaganfall [ˈʃla:kanfal], *m.* (—**s**, *pl.* ⸚**e**) stroke, apoplexy.

Schlagballspiel [ˈʃla:kbalʃpi:l], *n.* (—**s**, *pl.* —**e**) rounders.

Schlagbaum [ˈʃla:kbaum], *m.* (—**s**, *pl.* ⸚**e**) turnpike.

schlagen [ˈʃla:gən], *v.a. irr.* beat, strike, hit; (*tree*) fell; (*money*) coin; *Alarm* —, sound the alarm; *ans Kreuz* —, crucify; *ein Kreuz* —, make the sign of the cross. — *v.n.* (*clock*) strike; (*birds*) warble; *aus der Art* —, degenerate. — *v.r. sich* —, fight; *sich auf Säbel* —, fight with sabres; *sich an die Brust* —, beat o.'s breast.

Schlager [ˈʃla:gər], *m.* (—**s**, *pl.* —) hit, pop song; (*fig.*) success.

Schläger [ˈʃlɛ:gər], *m.* (—**s**, *pl.* —) rapier; bat; (tennis-)racket; (golf-) club.

Schlägerei [ʃlɛ:gəˈraɪ], *f.* (—, *pl.* —**en**) fray, scuffle.

schlagfertig [ˈʃla:kfɛrtɪç], *adj.* quick-witted.

Schlagkraft [ˈʃla:kkraft], *f.* (—, *no pl.*) striking power.

Schlaglicht [ˈʃla:klɪçt], *n.* (—**s**, *pl.* —**er**) strong direct light.

Schlagsahne [ˈʃla:kza:nə], *f.* (—, *no pl.*) double cream, raw cream; whipped cream.

Schlagschatten [ˈʃla:kʃatən], *m.* (—**s**, *pl.* —) deep shadow.

Schlagseite [ˈʃla:kzaɪtə], *f.* (—, *no pl.*) — *bekommen*, (*Naut.*) list.

Schlagwort [ˈʃla:kvɔrt], *n.* (—**s**, *pl.* ⸚**er**) catchword, slogan; trite saying.

Schlagzeile [ˈʃla:ktsaɪlə], *f.* (—, *pl.* —**n**) headline.

Schlamm [ʃlam], *m.* (—(**e**)**s**, *no pl.*) mud, mire.

Schlampe [ˈʃlampə], *f.* (—, *pl.* —**n**) slut.

Schlange [ˈʃlaŋə], *f.* (—, *pl.* —**n**) snake, serpent; (*fig.*) queue.

schlängeln [ˈʃlɛŋəln], *v.r. sich* —, wind, meander.

schlangenartig [ˈʃlaŋəna:rtɪç], *adj.* snaky, serpentine.

schlank [ʃlaŋk], *adj.* slim, slender.

schlapp [ʃlap], *adj.* limp, tired, weak, slack; — *machen*, break down, collapse.

Schlappe [ˈʃlapə], *f.* (—, *pl.* —**n**) reverse, defeat; *eine — erleiden*, suffer a set-back.

Schlappschwanz [ˈʃlapʃvants], *m.* (—**es**, *pl.* ⸚**e**) weakling; milksop.

Schlaraffenland [ʃlaˈrafənlant], *n.* (—(**e**)**s**, *pl.* ⸚**er**) land of milk and honey.

schlau [ʃlau], *adj.* cunning, crafty, sly, shrewd.

Schlauch [ʃlaux], *m.* (—(**e**)**s**, *pl.* ⸚**e**) hose; tube.

Schlaukopf [ˈʃlaukɔpf], *m.* (—(**e**)**s**, *pl.* ⸚**e**) slyboots; (*Am.*) wiseacre.

schlecht [ʃlɛçt], *adj.* bad, evil, wicked; poor; *mir ist* —, I feel ill; —*e Zeiten*, hard times; —*es Geld*, base money.

schlechterdings [ˈʃlɛçtərdɪŋs], *adv.* simply, positively, absolutely.

schlechthin [ˈʃlɛçthɪn], *adv.* simply, plainly.

Schlechtigkeit [ˈʃlɛçtɪçkaɪt], *f.* (—, *pl.* —**en**) wickedness, baseness.

Schlegel [ˈʃle:gəl], *m.* (—**s**, *pl.* —) mallet; drumstick; (*bell*) clapper.

Schlehdorn [ˈʃle:dɔrn], *m.* (—**s**, *pl.* —**e**) blackthorn, sloe-tree.

schleichen [ˈʃlaɪçən], *v.n. irr.* (*aux.* sein) sneak, prowl, slink; —*de Krankheit*, lingering illness.

Schleichhandel [ˈʃlaɪçhandəl], *m.* (—**s**, *pl.* ⸚) smuggling, black marketeering.

Schleie [ˈʃlaɪə], *f.* (—, *pl.* —**n**) tench.

Schleier [ˈʃlaɪər], *m.* (—**s**, *pl.* —) veil.

Schleife [ˈʃlaɪfə], *f.* (—, *pl.* —**n**) bow, loop, noose.

schleifen [ˈʃlaɪfən], *v.a. irr.* drag along, trail; grind, polish, sharpen, whet, hone; cut.

Schleim [ʃlaɪm], *m.* (—(**e**)**s**, *no pl.*) slime, mucus, phlegm.

Schleimhaut [ˈʃlaɪmhaut], *f.* (—, *pl.* ⸚**e**) mucous membrane.

Schleimsuppe [ˈʃlaɪmzupə], *f.* (—, *pl.* —**n**) gruel.

schleißen [ˈʃlaɪsən], *v.a. irr.* split, slit; (*feathers*) strip.

schlemmen [ˈʃlɛmən], *v.n.* carouse, gormandise.

schlendern [ˈʃlɛndərn], *v.n.* (*aux.* sein) saunter along, stroll.

Schlendrian [ˈʃlɛndria:n], *m.* (—**s**, *no pl.*) old jog-trot, routine.

schlenkern [ˈʃlɛŋkərn], *v.a.* dangle, swing.

Schleppdampfer [ˈʃlɛpdampfər], *m.* (—**s**, *pl.* —) steam-tug, tug-boat, tow-boat.

Schleppe [ˈʃlɛpə], *f.* (—, *pl.* —**n**) train (of a dress).

schleppen [ˈʃlɛpən], *v.a.* carry (s.th. heavy), drag, tow.

Schleppenträger [ˈʃlɛpəntrɛ:gər], (—**s**, *pl.* —) train-bearer.

Schleppnetz [ˈʃlɛpnɛts], *n.* (—**es**, *pl.* —**e**) dragnet.

Schlesien [ˈʃle:zjən], *n.* Silesia.

Schleuder [ˈʃlɔydər], *f.* (—, *pl.* —**n**) sling; catapult.

schleudern [ˈʃlɔydərn], *v.a.* sling, throw, fling away. — *v.n.* (*Motor.*) skid; (*Comm.*) sell cheaply, undersell.

schleunigst ['ʃlɔynɪçst], *adv.* very quickly, with the utmost expedition, promptly.
Schleuse ['ʃlɔyzə], *f.* (—, *pl.* —n) sluice, flood-gate, lock.
Schlich [ʃlɪç], *m.* (—es, *pl.* —e) trick, dodge; *einem hinter seine —e kommen*, be up to s.o.'s tricks.
schlicht [ʃlɪçt], *adj.* plain, simple, homely; *—er Abschied*, curt dismissal.
schlichten ['ʃlɪçtən], *v.a.* level; (*argument*) settle; adjust, compose.
Schlichtheit ['ʃlɪçthaɪt], *f.* (—, *no pl.*) plainness, simplicity, homeliness.
schließen ['ʃli:sən], *v.a. irr.* shut, close; contract; *etwas — aus*, conclude s.th. from; (*meeting*) close; *Frieden —*, make peace; *einen in die Arme —*, embrace s.o.; *etwas in sich —*, imply, entail.
Schließer ['ʃli:sər], *m.* (—s, *pl.* —) doorkeeper; (*prison*) jailer, turnkey.
schließlich ['ʃli:slɪç], *adv.* lastly, finally, in conclusion.
Schliff [ʃlɪf], *m.* (—(e)s, *no pl.*) polish, refinement.
schlimm [ʃlɪm], *adj.* bad, evil, ill; sad; serious, sore; disagreeable; naughty; *um so —er*, so much the worse, worse luck.
Schlinge ['ʃlɪŋə], *f.* (—, *pl.* —n) loop, knot; noose, snare.
Schlingel ['ʃlɪŋəl], *m.* (—s, *pl.* —) little rascal.
schlingen ['ʃlɪŋən], *v.a. irr.* sling, wind; swallow, devour.
Schlips [ʃlɪps], *m.* (—es, *pl.* —e) (neck-)tie, cravat.
Schlitten ['ʃlɪtən], *m.* (—s, *pl.* —) sledge, sled, sleigh.
Schlittschuh ['ʃlɪtʃu:], *m.* (—s, *pl.* —e) skate; *— laufen*, skate.
Schlitz [ʃlɪts], *m.* (—es, *pl.* —e) slit.
schlohweiß ['ʃlo:vaɪs], *adj.* white as sloe-blossom, snow-white.
Schloß [ʃlɔs], *n.* (—sses, *pl.* ⸚sser) (*door*) lock, padlock; (*gun*) lock; palace, castle; *unter — und Riegel*, under lock and key.
Schloße ['ʃlo:sə], *f.* (—, *pl.* —n) hailstone.
Schlosser ['ʃlɔsər], *m.* (—s, *pl.* —) locksmith.
Schlot [ʃlo:t], *m.* (—(e)s, *pl.* —e) chimney, funnel.
schlottern ['ʃlɔtərn], *v.n.* wobble, dodder; tremble.
Schlucht [ʃluxt], *f.* (—, *pl.* —en) deep valley, defile, cleft, glen, ravine, gorge.
schluchzen ['ʃluxtsən], *v.n.* sob.
schlucken ['ʃlukən], *v.a.* gulp down, swallow. — *v.n.* hiccup.
Schlucker ['ʃlukər], *m.* (—s, *pl.* —) *armer —*, poor wretch.
Schlummer ['ʃlumər], *m.* (—s, *no pl.*) slumber.
Schlumpe ['ʃlumpə], *f.* (—, *pl.* —n) slut, slattern.
Schlund [ʃlunt], *m.* (—(e)s, *pl.* ⸚e) throat, gorge, gullet; gulf, abyss.
schlüpfen ['ʃlypfən], *v.n.* (*aux.* sein) slip, slide, glide.
Schlüpfer ['ʃlypfər], *m. pl.* knickers.
schlüpfrig ['ʃlypfrɪç], *adj.* slippery; (*fig.*) obscene, indecent.
schlürfen ['ʃlyrfən], *v.a.* drink noisily, lap up. — *v.n.* (*aux.* sein) (*dial.*) shuffle along.
Schluß [ʃlus], *m.* (—sses, *pl.* ⸚sse) end, termination; conclusion.
Schlüssel ['ʃlysəl], *m.* (—s, *pl.* —) key; (*Mus.*) clef.
Schlüsselbein ['ʃlysəlbaɪn], *n.* (—s, *pl.* —e) collar-bone.
Schlüsselblume ['ʃlysəlblu:mə], *f.* (—, *pl.* —n) (*Bot.*) cowslip, primrose.
Schlußfolgerung ['ʃlusfɔlgəruŋ], *f.* (—, *pl.* —en) conclusion, inference, deduction.
schlüssig ['ʃlysɪç], *adj.* resolved, determined; sure; (*Law*) well-grounded; *sich — werden über*, resolve on.
Schmach [ʃma:x], *f.* (—, *no pl.*) disgrace, ignominy.
schmachten ['ʃmaxtən], *v.n.* languish, pine.
schmächtig ['ʃmɛçtɪç], *adj.* slender, slim, spare.
schmackhaft ['ʃmakhaft], *adj.* tasty, savoury.
schmähen ['ʃmɛ:ən], *v.a.* revile, abuse, calumniate.
Schmähschrift ['ʃmɛ:ʃrɪft], *f.* (—, *pl.* —en) lampoon.
schmal [ʃma:l], *adj.* narrow.
schmälen ['ʃmɛ:lən], *v.a.* chide, scold.
schmälern ['ʃmɛ:lərn], *v.a.* lessen, diminish, curtail; detract from, belittle.
Schmalz [ʃmalts], *n.* (—es, *no pl.*) grease, lard, fat.
schmarotzen [ʃma'rɔtsən], *v.n.* sponge on others.
Schmarren ['ʃmarən], *m.* (—s, *pl.* —) trash; (*dial.*) omelette.
Schmatz [ʃmats], *m.* (—es, *pl.* ⸚e) (*dial.*) smacking kiss.
schmauchen ['ʃmauxən], *v.a., v.n.* smoke.
Schmaus [ʃmaus], *m.* (—es, *pl.* —e) feast, banquet.
schmecken ['ʃmɛkən], *v.a.* taste. — *v.n.* taste; *es schmeckt mir*, I like it.
Schmeichelei [ʃmaɪçə'laɪ], *f.* (—, *pl.* —en) flattery, adulation.
schmeicheln ['ʃmaɪçəln], *v.n.* flatter; fondle, pet.
schmeißen ['ʃmaɪsən], *v a. irr.* throw, hurl, fling; (*sl.*) *ich werde die Sache schon —*, I shall pull it off.
Schmeißfliege ['ʃmaɪsfli:gə], *f.* (—, *pl.* —n) (*Ent.*) bluebottle.
Schmelz [ʃmɛlts], *m.* (—es, *no pl.*) enamel; melting; (*voice*) mellowness.
schmelzbar ['ʃmɛltsba:r], *adj.* fusible.
schmelzen ['ʃmɛltsən], *v.a. irr.* smelt, melt. — *v.n.* (*aux.* sein) (*ice*) melt; (*fig.*) decrease, diminish.

Schmelztiegel ['ʃmɛltsti:gəl], *m.* (—**s**, *pl.* —) crucible; melting pot.
Schmelztopf ['ʃmɛltstɔpf], *m. see* **Schmelztiegel.**
Schmerbauch ['ʃme:rbaux], *m.* (—(**e**)**s**, *pl.* ⸚**e**) (*coll.*) paunch, belly.
Schmerz [ʃmɛrts], *m.* (—**es**, *pl.* —**en**) ache, pain; grief, sorrow; *einem* —*en verursachen*, give *or* cause s.o. pain.
schmerzlich ['ʃmɛrtslɪç], *adj.* painful, distressing.
Schmetterling ['ʃmɛtərlɪŋ], *m.* (—**s**, *pl.* —**e**) (*Ent.*) butterfly, moth.
schmettern ['ʃmɛtərn], *v.n.* resound; (*trumpets*) blare; (*bird*) warble.
Schmied [ʃmi:t], *m.* (—**s**, *pl.* —**e**) (black)smith.
Schmiede ['ʃmi:də], *f.* (—, *pl.* —**n**) forge, smithy.
schmiegen ['ʃmi:gən], *v.r. sich* —, bend, yield; *sich an einen* —, cling to s.o., nestle against s.o.
Schmiere ['ʃmi:rə], *f.* (—, *pl.* —**n**) grease, salve; (*Theat.*) troop of strolling players.
schmieren ['ʃmi:rən], *v.a.* smear, grease, spread; (*fig.*) bribe; (*bread*) butter. — *v.n.* scrawl, scribble.
Schmierfink ['ʃmi:rfɪŋk], *m.* (—**en**, *pl.* —**en**) dirty person; muckraker.
Schmiermittel ['ʃmi:rmɪtəl], *n.* (—**s**, *pl.* —) lubricant.
Schmierseife ['ʃmi:rzaɪfə], *f.* (—, *no pl.*) soft soap.
Schminke ['ʃmɪŋkə], *f.* (—, *pl.* —**n**) greasepaint; rouge; make-up, cosmetics.
Schmirgel ['ʃmɪrgəl], *m.* (—**s**, *no pl.*) emery.
Schmiß [ʃmɪs], *m.* (—**sses**, *pl.* —**sse**) cut in the face, (duelling) scar; (*fig.*) smartness, verve.
Schmöker ['ʃmø:kər], *m.* (—**s**, *pl.* —) trashy book.
schmollen ['ʃmɔlən], *v.n.* sulk, pout.
Schmorbraten ['ʃmo:rbra:tən], *m.* (—**s**, *pl.* —) stewed meat.
Schmuck [ʃmuk], *m.* (—(**e**)**s**, *pl.* —**stücke**) ornament, jewels, jewellery; (*Am.*) jewelry.
schmuck [ʃmuk], *adj.* neat, spruce, dapper, smart.
schmücken ['ʃmykən], *v.a.* adorn, embellish.
Schmucksachen ['ʃmukzaxən], *f. pl.* jewels, finery, jewellery, articles of adornment; (*Am.*) jewelry.
schmuggeln ['ʃmugəln], *v.a.* smuggle.
schmunzeln ['ʃmuntsəln], *v.n.* smirk, grin.
Schmutz [ʃmuts], *m.* (—**es**, *no pl.*) dirt, filth.
schmutzen ['ʃmutsən], *v.n.* get soiled, get dirty.
Schmutzkonkurrenz ['ʃmutskɔnkurɛnts], *f.* (—, *no pl.*) unfair competition.
Schnabel ['ʃna:bəl], *m.* (—**s**, *pl.* ⸚) bill, beak; (*ship*) prow; *halt den* —, keep your mouth shut; *er spricht, wie ihm der* — *gewachsen ist*, he calls a spade a spade.
Schnabeltier ['ʃna:bəlti:r], *n.* (—**s**, *pl.* —**e**) duck-bill, duck-billed platypus.
Schnaderhüpfel ['ʃna:dərhypfəl], *n.* (—**s**, *pl.* —) (*dial.*) Alpine folk-song.
Schnalle ['ʃnalə], *f.* (—, *pl.* —**n**) buckle.
schnalzen ['ʃnaltsən], *v.n.* click; snap.
schnappen ['ʃnapən], *v.n.* snap; snatch at s.th.; *nach Luft* —, gasp for breath.
Schnaps [ʃnaps], *m.* (—**es**, *pl.* ⸚**e**) spirits, brandy, gin.
schnarchen ['ʃnarçən], *v.n.* snore.
Schnarre ['ʃnarə], *f.* (—, *pl.* —**n**) rattle.
schnattern ['ʃnatərn], *v.n.* cackle; gabble; chatter.
schnauben ['ʃnaubən], *v.n.* puff and blow; snort; *vor Zorn* —, fret and fume.
schnaufen ['ʃnaufən], *v.n.* breathe heavily, pant.
Schnauze ['ʃnautsə], *f.* (—, *pl.* —**n**) (*animals*) snout; (*vulg.*) mouth, trap; nozzle.
schnauzen ['ʃnautsən], *v.n.* snarl, shout (at).
Schnecke ['ʃnɛkə], *f.* (—, *pl.* —**n**), (*Zool.*) snail, slug.
Schnee [ʃne:], *m.* (—**s**, *no pl.*) snow.
Schneegestöber ['ʃne:gəʃtø:bər], *n.* (—**s**, *pl.* —) snow-storm.
Schneeglöckchen ['ʃne:glœkçən], *n.* (—**s**, *pl.* —) (*Bot.*) snowdrop.
Schneeschläger ['ʃne:ʃlɛ:gər], *m.* (—**s**, *pl.* —) whisk.
Schneetreiben ['ʃne:traɪbən], *n.* (—**s**, *no pl.*) snow-storm, blizzard.
Schneewittchen [ʃne:'vɪtçən], *n.* (—**s**, *no pl.*) Snow White.
Schneid [ʃnaɪt], *m.* (—**s**, *no pl.*) go, push, dash, courage.
Schneide ['ʃnaɪdə], *f.* (—, *pl.* —**n**) edge.
Schneidebohne ['ʃnaɪdəbo:nə], *f.* (—, *pl.* —**n**) French bean, string-bean.
Schneidemühle ['ʃnaɪdəmy:lə], *f.* (—, *pl.* —**n**) saw mill.
schneiden ['ʃnaɪdən], *v.a. irr.* cut, trim, carve; (*fig.*) ignore, cut; *Gesichter* —, make faces. — *v.r. sich* —, cut o.s.; (*Maths.*) intersect; *sich die Haare* — *lassen*, have o.'s hair cut.
Schneider ['ʃnaɪdər], *m.* (—**s**, *pl.* —) tailor.
Schneiderei [ʃnaɪdə'raɪ], *f.* (—, *no pl.*) tailoring; dressmaking.
Schneidezahn ['ʃnaɪdətsa:n], *m.* (—**s**, *pl.* ⸚**e**) incisor.
schneidig ['ʃnaɪdɪç], *adj.* dashing.
schneien ['ʃnaɪən], *v.n.* snow.
Schneise ['ʃnaɪzə], *f.* (—, *pl.* —**n**) (*forest*) glade, cutting.
schnell [ʃnɛl], *adj.* quick, swift, speedy, fast, rapid; *mach* —, hurry up.
Schnelle ['ʃnɛlə], *f.* (—, *pl.* —**n**) (*river*) rapids.
schnellen ['ʃnɛlən], *v.n.* spring, jump.

Schnelligkeit ['ʃnɛlıçkaıt], *f.* (—, *no pl.*) quickness, speed, swiftness, rapidity; (*Tech.*) velocity.
Schnepfe ['ʃnɛpfə], *f.* (—, *pl.* —**n**) (*Orn.*) snipe, woodcock.
schneuzen ['ʃnɔytsən], *v.r. sich* (*die Nase*) —, blow o.'s nose.
schniegeln ['ʃni:gəln], *v.r. sich* —, (*coll.*) dress up, deck out; *geschniegelt und gebügelt*, spick and span.
Schnippchen ['ʃnıpçən], *n.* (—**s**, *pl.* —) *einem ein — schlagen*, play a trick on s.o.
schnippisch ['ʃnıpıʃ], *adj.* pert, perky.
Schnitt [ʃnıt], *m.* (—(**e**)**s**, *pl.* —**e**) cut, incision; section; (*beer*) small glass; (*dress*) cut-out pattern; (*book*) edge.
Schnittbohne ['ʃnıtbo:nə], *f.* (—, *pl.* —**n**) (*Bot.*) French bean.
Schnitte ['ʃnıtə], *f.* (—, *pl.* —**n**) slice (of bread).
Schnitter ['ʃnıtər], *m.* (—**s**, *pl.* —) reaper.
Schnittlauch ['ʃnıtlaux], *m.* (—**s**, *no pl.*) (*Bot.*) chives.
Schnittmuster ['ʃnıtmustər], *n.* (—**s**, *pl.* —) cut-out pattern.
Schnittwaren ['ʃnıtva:rən], *f. pl.* dry goods, drapery.
Schnitzel ['ʃnıtsəl], *n.* (—**s**, *pl.* —) (*Cul.*) cutlet; *Wiener* —, veal cutlet; snip; (*pl.*) shavings.
schnitzen ['ʃnıtsən], *v.a.* carve (in wood).
schnodd(e)rig ['ʃnɔd(ə)rıç], *adj.* (*coll.*) cheeky, insolent.
schnöde ['ʃnø:də], *adj.* base, heinous, mean, vile; —*r Mammon*, filthy lucre; —*r Undank*, rank ingratitude.
Schnörkel ['ʃnœrkəl], *m.* (—**s**, *pl.* —) (*writing*) flourish.
schnorren ['ʃnɔrən], *v.n.* (*rare*) cadge, beg.
schnüffeln ['ʃnyfəln], *v.n.* sniff; (*fig.*) pry, snoop.
Schnuller ['ʃnulər], *m.* (—**s**, *pl.* —) baby's dummy; (*Am.*) pacifier.
Schnupfen ['ʃnupfən], *m.* (—**s**, *pl.* —) cold (in the head); *den — haben*, have a (running) cold; *den — bekommen*, catch cold.
schnupfen ['ʃnupfən], *v.a., v.n.* take snuff.
Schnupftuch ['ʃnupftu:x], *n.* (—(**e**)**s**, *pl.* ⸚**er**) (*dial.*) (pocket-) handkerchief.
schnuppe ['ʃnupə], *adj.* (*sl.*) *mir ist alles* —, it is all the same to me, I don't care.
schnuppern ['ʃnupərn], *v.n.* smell, snuffle.
Schnur [ʃnu:r], *f.* (—, *pl.* —**en**, ⸚**e**) twine, cord, string; (*Elec.*) lead, extension cord.
Schnurrbart ['ʃnurba:rt], *m.* (—**s**, *pl.* ⸚**e**) moustache; *sich einen — wachsen lassen*, grow a moustache.
Schnürchen ['ʃny:rçən], *n.* (—**s**, *pl.* —) *wie am* —, like clockwork.
schnüren ['ʃny:rən], *v.a.* lace, tie up; *sein Ränzel* —, pack o.'s bag.
Schnurre ['ʃnurə], *f.* (—, *pl.* —**n**) funny story, yarn.
schnurren ['ʃnurən], *v.n.* purr.
Schnürsenkel ['ʃny:rzɛŋkəl], *m.* (—**s**, *pl.* —) (*shoe*) lace.
schnurstracks ['ʃnu:rʃtraks], *adv.* directly, immediately, on the spot.
Schober ['ʃo:bər], *m.* (—**s**, *pl.* —) stack, rick.
Schock (1) [ʃɔk], *n.* (—(**e**)**s**, *pl.* —**e**) sixty, three score.
Schock (2) [ʃɔk], *m.* (—(**e**)**s**, *pl.* —**s**) shock; blow; stroke.
Schöffe ['ʃœfə], *m.* (—**n**, *pl.* —**n**) (*Law*) juror; member of jury.
Schokolade [ʃoko'la:də], *f.* (—, *pl.* —**n**) chocolate; *eine Tafel* —, a bar of chocolate.
Scholle ['ʃɔlə], *f.* (—, *pl.* —**n**) plaice; (*ice*) floe; clod; soil.
schon [ʃo:n], *adv.* already; indeed; yet; *na wenn* —, so what; — *gut*, that'll do; — *gestern*, as early as yesterday.
schön [ʃø:n], *adj.* beautiful, fair, handsome, lovely; —*e Literatur*, belles-lettres, good books.
schonen ['ʃo:nən], *v.a.* spare, save; treat considerately.
Schoner ['ʃo:nər], *m.* (—**s**, *pl.* —) antimacassar; (*Naut.*) schooner.
Schönheit ['ʃø:nhaıt], *f.* (—, *no pl.*) beauty.
Schonung ['ʃo:nuŋ], *f.* (—, *pl.* —**en**) forbearance, considerate treatment; (*forest*) plantation of young trees.
Schonzeit ['ʃo:ntsaıt], *f.* (—, *pl.* —**en**) close season.
Schopf [ʃɔpf], *m.* (—**es**, *pl.* ⸚**e**) tuft, head of hair; (*bird*) crest; *das Glück beim —e fassen*, take time by the forelock, make hay while the sun shines.
Schöpfbrunnen ['ʃœpfbrunən], *m.* (—**s**, *pl.* —) (draw-)well.
schöpfen ['ʃœpfən], *v.a.* (*water*) draw; derive; *Verdacht* —, become suspicious; *frische Luft* —, get a breath of fresh air; *Mut* —, take heart.
Schöpfer ['ʃœpfər], *m.* (—**s**, *pl.* —) creator.
Schöpfkelle ['ʃœpfkɛlə], *f.* (—, *pl.* —**n**) scoop.
Schopflerche ['ʃɔpflɛrçə], *f.* (—, *pl.* —**n**) (*Orn.*) crested lark.
Schöpfung ['ʃœpfuŋ], *f.* (—, *pl.* —**en**) creation.
Schoppen ['ʃɔpən], *m.* (—**s**, *pl.* —) (*approx.*) half a pint.
Schöps [ʃœps], *m.* (—**es**, *pl.* —**e**) (*Zool.*) wether; (*fig.*) simpleton.
Schorf [ʃɔrf], *m.* (—(**e**)**s**, *pl.* —**e**) scab, scurf.
Schornstein ['ʃɔrnʃtaın], *m.* (—**s**, *pl.* —**e**) chimney; (*ship*) funnel.
Schoß [ʃo:s], *m.* (—**es**, *pl.* ⸚**e**) lap; (*Poet.*) womb; skirt, tail; *die Hände in den — legen*, be idle, fold o.'s arms, twiddle o.'s thumbs.

Schößling ['ʃœslɪŋ], *m.* (—s, *pl.* —e) shoot, sprig.
Schote ['ʃo:tə], *f.* (—, *pl.* —n) pod, husk, shell; (*pl.*) green peas.
Schotter ['ʃɔtər], *m.* (—s, *no pl.*) road-metal, broken stones, gravel.
Schottland ['ʃɔtlant], *n.* Scotland.
schraffieren [ʃra'fi:rən], *v.a.* (*Art*) hatch.
schräg ['ʃrɛ:k], *adj.* oblique, sloping, slanting, diagonal.
Schramme ['ʃramə], *f.* (—, *pl.* —n) scratch, scar.
Schrank [ʃraŋk], *m.* (—(e)s, *pl.* ⸚e) cupboard, wardrobe.
Schranken ['ʃraŋkən], *f. pl.* barriers, (level crossing) gates, limits, bounds; *in — halten*, limit, keep within bounds.
schränken ['ʃrɛŋkən], *v.a.* cross; fold.
Schranze ['ʃrantsə], *m.* (—n, *pl.* —n) sycophant, toady.
Schraube ['ʃraubə], *f.* (—, *pl.* —n) screw; bolt; propeller.
Schraubengewinde ['ʃraubəngəvɪndə], *n.* (—s, *pl.* —) thread of a screw.
Schraubenmutter ['ʃraubənmutər], *f.* (—, *pl.* —n) female screw, nut.
Schraubenzieher ['ʃraubəntsi:ər], *m.* (—s, *pl.* —) screw-driver.
Schraubstock ['ʃraupʃtɔk], *m.* (—s, *pl.* ⸚e) (*tool*) vise.
Schreck(en) ['ʃrɛk(ən)], *m.* (—s, *pl.* —) fright, terror, alarm, horror; shock.
Schrecknis ['ʃrɛknɪs], *n.* (—ses, *pl.* —se) terror, horror.
Schrei [ʃraɪ], *m.* (—s, *pl.* —e) cry; scream.
Schreiben ['ʃraɪbən], *n.* (—s, *pl.* —) letter, missive.
schreiben ['ʃraɪbən], *v.a. irr.* write; *ins Reine —*, make a fair copy.
Schreibfehler ['ʃraɪpfe:lər], *m.* (—s, *pl.* —) slip of the pen.
Schreibkrampf ['ʃraɪpkrampf], *m.* (—(e)s, *pl.* ⸚e) writer's cramp.
Schreibmaschine ['ʃraɪpmaʃi:nə], *f.* (—, *pl.* —n) typewriter.
Schreibwaren ['ʃraɪpva:rən], *f. pl.* stationery.
Schreibweise ['ʃraɪpvaɪzə], *f.* (— *pl.* —n) style; spelling.
schreien ['ʃraɪən], *v.a., v.n. irr.* cry, shout, scream, yell.
Schreihals ['ʃraɪhals], *m.* (—es, *pl.* ⸚e) cry-baby, noisy child.
Schrein [ʃraɪn], *m.* (—(e)s, *pl.* —e) box, chest; shrine.
schreiten ['ʃraɪtən], *v.n. irr.* (*aux.* sein) stride, step, pace.
Schrift [ʃrɪft], *f.* (—, *pl.* —en) writing; handwriting, calligraphy; publication; type; *Heilige —*, Holy Writ, Holy Scripture.
Schriftführer ['ʃrɪftfy:rər], *m.* (—s, *pl.* —) secretary.
Schriftgießerei ['ʃrɪftgi:səraɪ], *f.* (—, *pl.* —en) type-foundry.
Schriftleiter ['ʃrɪftlaɪtər], *m.* (—s, *pl.* —) editor.
schriftlich ['ʃrɪftlɪç], *adj.* written. — *adv.* in writing, by letter.
Schriftsetzer ['ʃrɪftzɛtsər], *m.* (—s, *pl.* —) compositor.
Schriftsteller ['ʃrɪftʃtɛlər], *m.* (—s, *pl.* —) writer, author.
Schriftstück ['ʃrɪftʃtyk], *n.* (—s, *pl.* —e) document, deed.
Schriftwechsel ['ʃrɪftvɛksəl], *m.* (—s, *no pl.*) exchange of notes, correspondence.
Schriftzeichen ['ʃrɪftsaɪçən], *n.* (—s, *pl.* —) character, letter (of alphabet).
schrill [ʃrɪl], *adj.* shrill.
Schritt [ʃrɪt], *m.* (—(e)s, *pl.* —e) step, pace, move; *lange —e machen*, stride; *— halten*, keep pace; *— fahren*, drive slowly, drive at walking pace; *aus dem —*, out of step; *in einer Sache —e tun*, make a move *or* take steps about s.th.
schrittweise ['ʃrɪtvaɪzə], *adv.* step by step, gradually.
schroff ['ʃrɔf], *adj.* steep, precipitous; (*fig.*) gruff, blunt, rough, harsh.
schröpfen ['ʃrœpfən], *v.a.* (*Med.*) cup; (*fig.*) fleece.
Schrot [ʃro:t], *m.* & *n.* (—(e)s, *pl.* —e) grape-shot, small shot; *ein Mann vom alten —*, a man of the utmost probity.
Schrotbrot ['ʃro:tbro:t], *n.* (—es, *no pl.*) wholemeal bread.
Schrott [ʃrɔt], *m.* (—(e)s, *pl.* —e), old iron, scrap metal.
Schrulle ['ʃrulə], *f.* (—, *pl.* —n) fad, whim.
schrumpfen ['ʃrumpfən], *v.n.* (*aux.* sein) shrink, shrivel.
Schub [ʃup], *m.* (—s, *pl.* ⸚e) shove, push; batch.
Schubkarren ['ʃupkarən], *m.* (—s, *pl.* —) wheelbarrow.
Schublade ['ʃupla:də], *f.* (—, *pl.* —n) drawer.
schüchtern ['ʃyçtərn], *adj.* shy, bashful, timid.
Schuft [ʃuft], *m.* (—(e)s, *pl.* —e) blackguard, scoundrel.
schuften ['ʃuftən], *v.n.* work hard, toil.
Schufterei [ʃuftə'raɪ], *f.* (—, *no pl.*) drudgery.
schuftig ['ʃuftɪç], *adj.* rascally, mean.
Schuh [ʃu:], *m.* (—s, *pl.* —e) shoe; *einem etwas in die —e schieben*, lay the blame at s.o.'s door.
Schuhwerk ['ʃu:vɛrk], *n.* (—s, *no pl.*) footwear.
Schuhwichse ['ʃu:vɪksə], *f.* (—, *no pl.*) shoe-polish.
Schuld [ʃult], *f.* (—, *pl.* —en) guilt, offence, sin; fault; blame; cause; (*money*) debt; *in —en geraten*, run into debt.
schuld [ʃult], *adj. ich bin —*, it is my fault, I am to blame.
schulden ['ʃuldən], *v.a.* owe, be indebted to.
schuldig ['ʃuldɪç], *adj.* guilty, culpable; *sich — bekennen*, plead guilty; *einen — sprechen*, pronounce s.o. guilty;

ihm ist Anerkennung —, appreciation is due to him.
Schuldigkeit [ˈʃuldɪçkaɪt], *f.* (—, *no pl.*) obligation, duty.
schuldlos [ˈʃultlo:s], *adj.* innocent, guiltless.
Schuldner [ˈʃuldnər], *m.* (—**s**, *pl.* —) debtor.
Schule [ˈʃu:lə], *f.* (—, *pl.* —**n**) school; *in die — gehen*, go to school, attend school; *die — schwänzen*, play truant; *hohe* —, (*Riding*) advanced horsemanship.
schulen [ˈʃu:lən], *v.a.* train, instruct.
Schüler [ˈʃy:lər], *m.* (—**s**, *pl.* —) schoolboy, pupil, student, scholar.
Schulklasse [ˈʃu:lklasə], *f.* (—, *pl.* —**n**) class, form.
Schulleiter [ˈʃu:llaɪtər], *m.* (—**s**, *pl.* —) headmaster.
Schulrat [ˈʃu:lra:t], *m.* (—**s**, *pl.* ⸚**e**) school-inspector.
Schulter [ˈʃultər], *f.* (—, *pl.* —**n**) shoulder.
Schulterblatt [ˈʃultərblat], *n.* (—**s**, *pl.* ⸚**er**) shoulder-blade.
Schultheiß [ˈʃulthaɪs], *m.* (—**en**, *pl.* —**en**) village magistrate, mayor.
Schulunterricht [ˈʃu:luntərrɪçt], *m.* (—**s**, *no pl.*) school teaching, lessons.
schummeln [ˈʃuməln], *v.n.* (*coll.*) cheat.
Schund [ʃunt], *m.* (—(**e**)**s**, *no pl.*) trash.
Schuppe [ˈʃupə], *f.* (—, *pl.* —**n**) scale; (*pl.*) dandruff.
Schuppen [ˈʃupən], *m.* (—**s**, *pl.* —) shed.
Schuppentier [ˈʃupənti:r], *n.* (—**s**, *pl.* —**e**) (*Zool.*) armadillo.
Schur [ʃu:r], *f.* (—, *pl.* —**en**) shearing.
schüren [ˈʃy:rən], *v.a.* (*fire*) poke, rake; (*fig.*) stir up, fan, incite.
schürfen [ˈʃyrfən], *v.a.* scratch. — *v.n.* (*Min.*) prospect.
schurigeln [ˈʃu:rɪgəln], *v.a.* bully, pester.
Schurke [ˈʃurkə], *m.* (—**n**, *pl.* —**n**) scoundrel, villain, blackguard.
Schurz [ʃurts], *m.* (—**es**, *pl.* —**e**) apron, overall.
Schürze [ˈʃyrtsə], *f.* (—, *pl.* —**n**) apron, pinafore.
schürzen [ˈʃyrtsən], *v.a.* tuck up, pin up.
Schürzenjäger [ˈʃyrtsənjɛ:gər], *m.* (—**s**, *pl.* —) ladies' man.
Schurzfell [ˈʃurtsfɛl], *n.* (—**s**, *pl.* —**e**) leather apron.
Schuß [ʃus], *m.* (—**sses**, *pl.* ⸚**sse**) shot, report; dash; *weit vom* —, out of harm's way; wide of the mark.
Schüssel [ˈʃysəl], *f.* (—, *pl.* —**n**) dish.
Schußwaffe [ˈʃusvafə], *f.* (—, *pl.* —**n**) fire-arm.
Schuster [ˈʃu:stər], *m.* (—**s**, *pl.* —) shoemaker, cobbler; *auf —s Rappen*, on Shanks's pony.
schustern [ˈʃu:stərn], *v.n.* cobble, make *or* mend shoes.
Schutt [ʃut], *m.* (—(**e**)**s**, *no pl.*) rubbish, refuse; rubble; — *abladen*, dump refuse.
Schütte [ˈʃytə], *f.* (—, *pl.* —**n**) (*dial.*) bundle, truss.
schütteln [ˈʃytəln], *v.a.* shake, jolt.
schütten [ˈʃytən], *v.a.* shoot, pour; pour out.
schütter [ˈʃytər], *adj.* (*dial.*) (*hair*) thin; scarce.
Schutz [ʃuts], *m.* (—**es**, *no pl.*) protection, shelter, cover; *einen in — nehmen gegen*, defend s.o. against.
Schutzbefohlene [ˈʃutsbəfo:lənə], *m.* (—**n**, *pl.* —**n**) charge, person in o.'s care, ward.
Schutzbündnis [ˈʃutsbyntnɪs], *n.* (—**ses**, *pl.* —**se**) defensive alliance.
Schütze [ˈʃytsə], *m.* (—**n**, *pl.* —**n**) rifleman, sharpshooter, marksman; (*Astrol.*) Sagittarius.
schützen [ˈʃytsən], *v.a.* protect, shelter, defend. — *v.r. sich — vor*, guard o.s. against.
Schützengraben [ˈʃytsəngra:bən], *m.* (—**s**, *pl.* ⸚) trench.
Schutzgebiet [ˈʃutsgəbi:t], *n.* (—**s**, *pl.* —**e**) protectorate.
Schutzgitter [ˈʃutsgɪtər], *n.* (—**s**, *pl.* —) grid, guard.
Schutzheilige [ˈʃutshaɪlɪgə], *m.* (—**n**, *pl.* —**n**) patron saint.
Schützling [ˈʃytslɪŋ], *m.* (—**s**, *pl.* —**e**) protégé, charge.
Schutzmann [ˈʃutsman], *m.* (—**s**, *pl.* ⸚**er**, **Schutzleute**) policeman, constable.
Schutzmarke [ˈʃutsmarkə], *f.* (—, *pl.* —**n**) trade-mark.
Schutzzoll [ˈʃutstsɔl], *m.* (—**s**, *pl.* ⸚**e**) protective duty, tariff.
Schwaben [ˈʃva:bən], *n.* Swabia.
Schwabenstreich [ˈʃva:bənʃtraɪç], *m.* (—**s**, *pl.* —**e**) tomfoolery.
schwach [ʃvax], *adj.* weak, frail, feeble; (*noise*) faint; (*pulse*) low; —*e Seite*, foible; —*e Stunde*, unguarded moment.
Schwäche [ˈʃvɛçə], *f.* (—, *pl.* —**n**) weakness, faintness; infirmity.
schwächen [ˈʃvɛçən], *v.a.* weaken, debilitate.
Schwächling [ˈʃvɛçlɪŋ], *m.* (—**s**, *pl.* —**e**) weakling.
Schwachsinn [ˈʃvaxzɪn], *m.* (—**s**, *no pl.*) feeble-mindedness.
Schwächung [ˈʃvɛçuŋ], *f.* (—, *pl.* —**en**) weakening, lessening.
Schwadron [ʃvaˈdro:n], *f.* (—, *pl.* —**en**) squadron.
Schwadroneur [ʃvadroˈnø:r], *m.* (—**s**, *pl.* —**e**) swaggerer.
schwadronieren [ʃvadroˈni:rən], *v.n.* talk big, swagger.
schwafeln [ˈʃva:fəln], *v.n.* (*sl.*) talk nonsense, waffle.
Schwager [ˈʃva:gər], *m.* (—**s**, *pl.* ⸚) brother-in-law.
Schwägerin [ˈʃvɛ:gərɪn], *f.* (—, *pl.* —**nen**) sister-in-law.
Schwalbe [ˈʃvalbə], *f.* (—, *pl.* —**n**) (*Orn.*) swallow.

Schwalbenschwanz [ˈʃvalbənʃvants], *m.* (—es, *pl.* ⸚e) (*butterfly*) swallow's tail; (*joinery*) dovetail.
Schwall [ʃval], *m.* (—(e)s, *no pl.*) flood; (*fig.*) deluge, torrent.
Schwamm [ʃvam], *m.* (—(e)s, *pl.* ⸚e) sponge; fungus, mushroom; dry rot.
schwammig [ˈʃvamɪç], *adj.* spongy, fungous.
Schwan [ʃvaːn], *m.* (—(e)s, *pl.* ⸚e) swan; *junger* —, cygnet.
schwanen [ˈʃvaːnən], *v.n. imp. es schwant mir*, I have a foreboding.
Schwang [ʃvaŋ], *m. im —e sein*, be in fashion, be the rage.
schwanger [ˈʃvaŋər], *adj.* pregnant.
schwängern [ˈʃvɛŋərn], *v.a.* make pregnant, get with child; (*fig.*) impregnate.
Schwangerschaft [ˈʃvaŋərʃaft], *f.* (—, *pl.* —en) pregnancy.
Schwank [ʃvaŋk], *m.* (—(e)s, *pl.* ⸚e) funny story, joke; (*Theat.*) farce.
schwank [ʃvaŋk], *adj.* flexible, supple; *ein —es Rohr*, a reed shaken by the wind.
schwanken [ˈʃvaŋkən], *v.n.* totter, stagger; (*fig.*) waver, vacillate; (*prices*) fluctuate.
Schwanz [ʃvants], *m.* (—es, *pl.* ⸚e) tail.
schwänzeln [ˈʃvɛntsəln], *v.n.* (*animal*) wag the tail; (*fig.*) fawn, cringe.
schwänzen [ˈʃvɛntsən], *v.a. die Schule* —, play truant.
Schwären [ˈʃvɛːrən], *m.* (—s, *pl.* —) ulcer, abscess.
schwären [ˈʃvɛːrən], *v.n.* fester, suppurate.
Schwarm [ʃvarm], *m.* (—(e)s, *pl.* ⸚e) (*insects*) swarm; (*humans*) crowd; (*birds*) flight.
Schwärmerei [ʃvɛrməˈraɪ], *f.* (—, *pl.* —en) enthusiasm, passion, craze.
Schwarte [ˈʃvartə], *f.* (—, *pl.* —n) rind; crust; *alte* —, (*fig.*) old volume; tome.
schwarz [ʃvarts], *adj.* black.
Schwarzamsel [ˈʃvartsamzəl], *f.* (—, *pl.* —n) (*Orn.*) blackbird.
Schwarzdorn [ˈʃvartsdɔrn], *m.* (—s, *no pl.*) (*Bot.*) blackthorn, sloe.
Schwärze [ˈʃvɛrtsə], *f.* (—, *no pl.*) blackness; printer's ink.
schwärzen [ˈʃvɛrtsən], *v.a.* blacken.
Schwarzkünstler [ˈʃvartskynstlər], *m.* (—s, *pl.* —) magician, necromancer.
Schwarzwald [ˈʃvartsvalt], *m.* Black Forest.
Schwarzwild [ˈʃvartsvɪlt], *n.* (—(e)s, *no pl.*) wild boar.
schwatzen [ˈʃvatsən], *v.n.* chat, chatter, prattle.
Schwätzer [ˈʃvɛtsər], *m.* (—s, *pl.* —) chatterbox.
Schwatzhaftigkeit [ˈʃvatshaftɪçkaɪt], *f.* (—, *no pl.*) loquacity, talkativeness.
Schwebe [ˈʃveːbə], *f.* (—, *pl.* —n) suspense; suspension.
Schwebebaum [ˈʃveːbəbaum], *m.* (—s, *pl.* ⸚e) horizontal bar.
schweben [ˈʃveːbən], *v.n.* be suspended, hover; (*fig.*) be pending; *in Gefahr* —, be in danger; *es schwebt mir auf der Zunge*, it is on the tip of my tongue.
Schwede [ˈʃveːdə], *m.* (—n, *pl.* —n) Swede; *alter* —, (*fig.*) old boy.
Schweden [ˈʃveːdən], *n.* Sweden.
Schwedenhölzer [ˈʃveːdənhœltsər], *n. pl.* (*rare*) matches.
Schwefel [ˈʃveːfəl], *m.* (—s, *no pl.*) sulphur, brimstone.
Schwefelhölzchen [ˈʃveːfəlhœltsçən], *n.* (—s, *pl.* —) (*obs.*) match.
schwefeln [ˈʃveːfəln], *v.a.* impregnate with sulphur, fumigate.
Schwefelsäure [ˈʃveːfəlzɔyrə], *f.* (—, *no pl.*) sulphuric acid.
Schweif [ʃvaɪf], *m.* (—(e)s, *pl.* —e) tail.
schweifen [ˈʃvaɪfən], *v.n.* (*aux.* sein) ramble, stray, wander.
schweifwedeln [ˈʃvaɪfveːdəln], *v.n.* fawn.
Schweigegeld [ˈʃvaɪgəgɛlt], *n.* (—(e)s, *pl.* —er) (*coll.*) hush-money.
Schweigen [ˈʃvaɪgən], *n.* (—s, *no pl.*) silence.
schweigen [ˈʃvaɪgen], *v.n. irr.* be silent; be quiet; *ganz zu — von*, to say nothing of.
schweigsam [ˈʃvaɪkzaːm], *adj.* taciturn.
Schwein [ʃvaɪn], *n.* (—(e)s, *pl.* —e) pig, hog; swine; *wildes* —, boar; (*fig.*) luck, fluke; — *haben*, be lucky.
Schweinekoben [ˈʃvaɪnəkoːbən], *m.* (—s, *pl.* —) pigsty.
Schweinerei [ʃvaɪnəˈraɪ], *f.* (—, *pl.* —en) filth; (*fig.*) smut, filthiness, obscenity; mess.
Schweineschmalz [ˈʃvaɪnəʃmalts], *n.* (—es, *no pl.*) lard.
Schweinigel [ˈʃvaɪnigəl], *m.* (—s, *pl.* —) (*Zool.*) hedgehog, porcupine; (*fig.*) dirty pig, filthy wretch.
Schweinskeule [ˈʃvaɪnskɔylə], *f.* (—, *pl.* —n) leg of pork.
Schweiß [ʃvaɪs], *m.* (—es, *no pl.*) sweat, perspiration.
schweißen [ˈʃvaɪsən], *v.a.* weld, solder.
Schweiz [ʃvaɪts], *f.* Switzerland.
Schweizer [ˈʃvaɪtsər], *m.* (—s, *pl.* —) Swiss; (*fig.*) dairyman.
Schweizerei [ʃvaɪtsəˈraɪ], *f.* (—, *pl.* —en) dairy.
schwelen [ˈʃveːlən], *v.n.* burn slowly, smoulder.
schwelgen [ˈʃvɛlgən], *v.n.* carouse, revel.
Schwelgerei [ʃvɛlgəˈraɪ], *f.* (—, *pl.* —en) revelry.
schwelgerisch [ˈʃvɛlgərɪʃ], *adj.* luxurious, voluptuous.
Schwelle [ˈʃvɛlə], *f.* (—, *pl.* —n) threshold; (*Railw.*) sleeper, tie.
schwellen [ˈʃvɛlən], *v.n. irr.* (*aux.* sein) swell; (*water*) rise.
Schwellung [ˈʃvɛluŋ], *f.* (—, *pl.* —en) swelling.

schwemmen ['ʃvɛmən], *v.a.* wash, soak, carry off.
Schwengel ['ʃvɛŋəl], *m.* (—**s**, *pl.* —) (*bell*) clapper; (*pump*) handle.
schwenken ['ʃvɛŋkən], *v.a.* swing; shake, brandish; (*glasses*) rinse.
Schwenkung ['ʃvɛŋkuŋ], *f.* (—, *pl.* —**en**) change; (*Mil.*) wheeling.
schwer [ʃve:r], *adj.* heavy; difficult, hard; ponderous; severe; — *von Begriff*, obtuse, slow in the uptake; —*e Speise*, indigestible food; *einem das Herz — machen*, grieve s.o.
schwerblütig ['ʃve:rbly:tɪç], *adj.* phlegmatic.
Schwere ['ʃve:rə], *f.* (—, *no pl.*) weight, heaviness; gravity.
Schwerenöter ['ʃve:rənø:tər], *m.* (—**s**, *pl.* —) gay dog, ladies' man.
schwerfällig ['ʃve:rfɛlɪç], *adj.* ungainly, cumbrous, unwieldy; (*fig.*) thickheaded, dense.
Schwergewicht ['ʃve:rgəvɪçt], *n.* (—**s**, *no pl.*) (*Sport*) heavyweight; (*fig.*) emphasis.
schwerhörig ['ʃve:rhø:rɪç], *adj.* hard of hearing, deaf.
Schwerkraft ['ʃve:rkraft], *f.* (—, *no pl.*) gravity.
schwerlich ['ʃve:rlɪç], *adv.* hardly, scarcely.
schwermütig ['ʃve:rmy:tɪç], *adj.* melancholy.
Schwerpunkt ['ʃve:rpuŋkt], *m.* (—**s**, *pl.* —**e**) centre of gravity.
Schwert [ʃve:rt], *n.* (—(**e**)**s**, *pl.* —**er**) sword.
Schwertgriff ['ʃve:rtgrɪf], *m.* (—**s**, *pl.* —**e**) hilt.
Schwertlilie ['ʃve:rtli:ljə], *f.* (—, *pl.* —**n**) (*Bot.*) iris; fleur-de-lys.
Schwertstreich ['ʃve:rtʃtraɪç], *m.* (—(**e**)**s**, *pl.* —**e**) sword-blow, sword-stroke.
schwerwiegend ['ʃve:rvi:gənt], *adj.* weighty.
Schwester ['ʃvɛstər], *f.* (—, *pl.* —**n**) sister; *barmherzige* —, sister of mercy.
Schwesternschaft ['ʃvɛstərnʃaft], *f.* (—, *pl.* —**en**) sisterhood; (*Am.*) sorority.
Schwibbogen ['ʃvɪpbo:gən], *m.* (—**s**, *pl.* —) (*Archit.*) flying buttress.
Schwiegersohn ['ʃvi:gərzo:n], *m.* (—**s**, *pl.* ⸚**e**) son-in-law.
Schwiegertochter ['ʃvi:gərtɔxtər], *f.* (—, *pl.* ⸚) daughter-in-law.
Schwiele ['ʃvi:lə], *f.* (—, *pl.* —**n**) hard skin, callus, weal.
schwielig ['ʃvi:lɪç], *adj.* callous, horny.
schwierig ['ʃvi:rɪç], *adj.* difficult, hard.
Schwierigkeit ['ʃvi:rɪçkaɪt], *f.* (—, *pl.* —**en**) difficulty; *auf —en stoßen*, meet with difficulties.
schwimmen ['ʃvɪmən], *v.n. irr.* (*aux.* sein) swim, float.
Schwimmer ['ʃvɪmər], *m.* (—**s**, *pl.* —) swimmer.
Schwimmgürtel ['ʃvɪmgyrtəl], *m.* (—**s**, *pl.* —) life-belt.
Schwindel ['ʃvɪndəl], *m.* (—**s**, *pl.* —) giddiness, dizziness, vertigo; swindle, fraud.
Schwindelanfall ['ʃvɪndəlanfal], *m.* (—**s**, *pl.* ⸚**e**) attack of giddiness, vertigo.
Schwindelei [ʃvɪndə'laɪ], *f.* (—, *pl.* —**en**) swindle, fraud, deceit.
schwindelhaft ['ʃvɪndəlhaft], *adj.* fraudulent.
schwinden ['ʃvɪndən], *v.n. irr.* (*aux.* sein) dwindle; disappear, vanish.
Schwindler ['ʃvɪndlər], *m.* (—**s**, *pl.* —) swindler, humbug, cheat.
schwindlig ['ʃvɪndlɪç], *adj.* dizzy, giddy.
Schwindsucht ['ʃvɪntzuxt], *f.* (—, *no pl.*) (*Med.*) tuberculosis, consumption.
schwindsüchtig ['ʃvɪntzyçtɪc], *adj.* (*Med.*) tubercular.
Schwinge ['ʃvɪŋə], *f.* (—, *pl.* —**n**) wing.
schwingen ['ʃvɪŋən], *v.a. irr.* brandish. — *v.n.* swing, vibrate. — *v.r. sich* —, vault; *sich auf den Thron* —, usurp *or* take possession of the throne.
Schwingung ['ʃvɪŋuŋ], *f.* (—, *pl.* —**en**) vibration, oscillation.
Schwips [ʃvɪps], *m.* (—**es**, *pl.* —**e**) (*coll.*) tipsiness; *einen — haben*, be tipsy.
schwirren ['ʃvɪrən], *v.n.* whir, buzz.
Schwitzbad ['ʃvɪtsba:t], *n.* (—**es**, *pl.* ⸚**er**) Turkish bath, steam-bath.
schwitzen ['ʃvɪtsən], *v.n.* sweat, perspire.
schwören ['ʃvø:rən], *v.a.*, *v.n. irr.* swear, take an oath; *darauf kannst du* —, you can be quite sure of that, you bet; *falsch* —, forswear o.s., perjure o.s.
schwül [ʃvy:l], *adj.* sultry, close.
Schwüle ['ʃvy:lə], *f.* (—, *no pl.*) sultriness.
Schwulst [ʃvulst], *m.* (—**es**, *no pl.*) bombast.
schwülstig ['ʃvylstɪç], *adj.* bombastic, turgid.
Schwülstigkeit ['ʃvylstɪçkaɪt], *f.* (—, *pl.* —**en**) bombastic style, turgidity.
Schwund [ʃvunt], *m.* (—(**e**)**s**, *no pl.*) dwindling, decline; shrinkage.
Schwung [ʃvuŋ], *m.* (—(**e**)**s**, *pl.* ⸚**e**) swing, leap, bound; (*fig.*) verve, élan; (*Poet.*) flight, soaring.
schwunghaft ['ʃvuŋhaft], *adj.* flourishing, soaring.
Schwungkraft ['ʃvuŋkraft], *f.* (—, *no pl.*) centrifugal force; (*mental*) resilience.
Schwungrad ['ʃvuŋra:t], *n.* (—**s**, *pl.* ⸚**er**) fly-wheel.
schwungvoll ['ʃvuŋfɔl], *adj.* spirited.
Schwur [ʃvu:r], *m.* (—(**e**)**s**, *pl.* ⸚**e**) oath.
Schwurgericht ['ʃvu:rgərɪçt], *n.* (—**s**, *pl.* —**e**) (*Law*) assizes.
sechs [zɛks], *num. adj.* six.
Sechseck ['zɛksɛk], *n.* (—**s**, *pl.* —**e**) hexagon.
sechseckig ['zɛksɛkɪç], *adj.* hexagonal.

Sechser ['zɛksər], *m.* (—**s**, *pl.* —) coin of small value.
sechsspännig ['zɛksʃpɛnɪç], *adj.* drawn by six horses.
sechzehn ['zɛçtse:n], *num. adj.* sixteen.
sechzig ['zɛçtsɪç], *num. adj.* sixty.
Sediment [zedi'mɛnt], *n.* (—**s**, *pl.* —**e**) sediment.
See (1) [ze:], *m.* (—**s**, *pl.* —**n**) lake, pool.
See (2) [ze:], *f.* (—, *no pl.*) sea, ocean; *hohe* —, high seas; *zur* — *gehen*, go to sea, become a sailor.
Seeadler ['ze:adlər], *m.* (—**s**, *pl.* —) (*Orn.*) osprey.
Seebad ['ze:ba:t], *n.* (—**s**, *pl.* ¨**er**) seaside resort; bathe in the sea.
Seebär ['ze:bɛ:r], *m.* (—**en**, *pl.* —**en**) (*fig.*) old salt.
Seefahrer ['ze:fa:rər], *m.* (—**s**, *pl.* —) mariner, navigator.
Seefahrt ['ze:fa:rt], *f.* (—, *pl.* —**en**) seafaring; voyage, cruise.
seefest ['ze:fɛst], *adj.* (*ship*) seaworthy; (*person*) a good sailor.
Seefischerei ['ze:fɪʃəraɪ], *f.* (—, *no pl.*) deep-sea fishing.
Seeflotte ['ze:flɔtə], *f.* (—, *pl.* —**n**) navy, fleet.
Seegang ['ze:gaŋ], *m.* (—**s**, *no pl.*) swell.
Seegras ['ze:gra:s], *n.* (—**es**, *no pl.*) seaweed.
Seehandel ['ze:handəl], *m.* (—**s**, *no pl.*) maritime trade.
Seehund ['ze:hunt], *m.* (—**s**, *pl.* —**e**) (*Zool.*) seal.
Seeigel ['ze:i:gəl], *m.* (—**s**, *pl.* —) (*Zool.*) sea-urchin.
Seejungfrau ['ze:juŋfrau], *f.* (—, *pl.* —**en**) mermaid.
Seekadett ['ze:kadɛt], *m.* (—**en**, *pl.* —**en**) midshipman; (naval) cadet.
Seekarte ['ze:kartə], *f.* (—, *pl.* —**n**) chart.
seekrank ['ze:kraŋk], *adj.* seasick.
Seekrieg ['ze:kri:k], *m.* (—**s**, *pl.* —**e**) naval war.
Seeküste ['ze:kystə], *f.* (—, *pl.* —**n**) sea-coast, shore, beach.
Seele ['ze:lə], *f.* (—, *pl.* —**n**) soul; *mit ganzer* —, with all my heart.
Seelenamt ['ze:lənamt], *n.* (—**s**, *pl.* ¨**er**) (*Eccl.*) office for the dead, requiem.
Seelenangst ['ze:lənaŋkst], *f.* (—, *pl.* ¨**e**) anguish, agony.
Seelenheil ['ze:lənhaɪl], *n.* (—**s**, *no pl.*) (*Theol.*) salvation.
Seelenhirt ['ze:lənhɪrt], *m.* (—**en**, *pl.* —**en**) pastor.
seelenlos ['ze:lənlo:s], *adj.* inanimate.
Seelenmesse ['ze:lənmɛsə], *f.* (—, *pl.* —**n**) requiem; Mass for the dead.
Seelenruhe ['ze:lənru:ə], *f.* (—, *no pl.*) tranquillity of mind.
seelenruhig ['ze:lənru:ɪç], *adj.* cool, calm, collected, unperturbed.
Seelenstärke ['ze:lənʃtɛrkə], *f.* (—, *no pl.*) fortitude; composure.
seelenvergnügt ['ze:lənfɛrgny:kt], *adj.* blissfully happy.
Seelenverwandtschaft ['ze:lənfɛrvantʃaft], *f.* (—, *pl.* —**en**) mental affinity, (mutual) understanding.
seelenvoll ['ze:lənfɔl], *adj.* wistful, soulful.
Seelenwanderung ['ze:lənvandəruŋ], *f.* (—, *no pl.*) transmigration of souls, metempsychosis.
Seeleute ['ze:lɔytə] *see under* **Seemann**.
seelisch ['ze:lɪʃ], *adj.* mental, psychological, psychic(al).
Seelsorge ['ze:lsɔrgə], *f.* (—, *no pl.*) (*Eccl.*) cure of souls; pastoral duties *or* work.
Seemann ['ze:man], *m.* (—**s**, *pl.* ¨**er**, **Seeleute**) seaman, sailor, mariner.
Seemeile ['ze:maɪlə], *f.* (—, *pl.* —**n**) knot, nautical mile.
Seemöwe ['ze:mø:və], *f.* (—, *pl.* —**n**) (*Orn.*) seagull.
Seemuschel ['ze:muʃəl], *f.* (—, *pl.* —**n**) sea-shell.
Seepflanze ['ze:pflantsə], *f.* (—, *pl.* —**n**) marine plant.
Seerabe ['ze:ra:bə], *m.* (—**n**, *pl.* —**n**) (*Orn.*) cormorant.
Seeräuber ['ze:rɔybər], *m.* (—**s**, *pl.* —) pirate.
Seerose ['ze:ro:zə], *f.* (—, *pl.* —**n**) (*Bot.*) water-lily.
Seesalz ['ze:zalts], *n.* (—**es**, *no pl.*) bay salt, sea salt.
Seeschlacht ['ze:ʃlaxt], *f.* (—, *pl.* —**en**) naval engagement, naval battle.
Seestern ['ze:ʃtɛrn], *m.* (—**s**, *pl.* —**e**) (*Zool.*) starfish.
Seestille ['ze:ʃtɪlə], *f.* (—, *no pl.*) calm (at sea).
Seetang ['ze:taŋ], *m.* (—**s**, *no pl.*) (*Bot.*) seaweed.
seetüchtig ['ze:tyçtɪç], *adj.* seaworthy.
Seeuhr ['ze:u:r], *f.* (—, *pl.* —**en**) marine chronometer.
Seeuntüchtigkeit ['ze:untyçtɪçkaɪt], *f.* (—, *no pl.*) unseaworthiness.
Seewasser ['ze:vasər], *n.* (—**s**, *no pl.*) sea-water, brine.
Seewesen ['ze:vezən], *n.* (—**s**, *no pl.*) naval affairs.
Seezunge ['ze:tsuŋə], *f.* (—, *pl.* —**n**) sole (*fish*).
Segel ['ze:gəl], *n.* (—**s**, *pl.* —) sail; *großes* —, mainsail; *unter* — *gehen*, set sail, put to sea; *die* — *streichen*, strike sail.
segelfertig ['ze:gəlfɛrtɪç], *adj.* ready to sail; *sich* — *machen*, get under sail.
Segelflugzeug ['ze:gəlflu:ktsɔyk], *n.* (—**s**, *pl.* —**e**) glider(-plane).
Segelschiff ['ze:gəlʃɪf], *n.* (—**s**, *pl.* —**e**) sailing-vessel.
Segelstange ['ze:gəlʃtaŋə], *f.* (—, *pl.* —**n**) sail-yard.
Segen ['ze:gən], *m.* (—**s**, *no pl.*) blessing, benediction; (*fig.*) abundance; — *sprechen*, give the blessing, say grace.

segensreich ['ze:gənsraıç], *adj.* blessed, full of blessings; prosperous.
Segenswunsch ['ze:gənsvunʃ], *m.* (—**es**, *pl.* ⸚**e**) good wish.
segnen ['ze:gnən], *v.a.* bless.
sehen ['ze:ən], *v.a. irr.* see, behold, perceive; *etwas gern* —, like s.th., approve of s.th. — *v.n.* look, see; *sich — lassen*, parade, show o.s., *wir werden* —, that remains to be seen, we shall see.
sehenswert ['ze:ənsve:rt], *adj.* worth seeing.
Sehenswürdigkeit ['ze:ənsvyrdıçkaıt], *f.* (—, *pl.* —**en**) curiosity, object of interest, tourist attraction; (*pl.*) sights.
Seher ['ze:ər], *m.* (—**s**, *pl.* —) seer, prophet.
Sehne ['ze:nə], *f.* (—, *pl.* —**n**) sinew, tendon; string.
sehnig ['ze:nıç], *adj.* sinewy, muscular; (*meat*) tough.
sehnlich ['ze:nlıç], *adj.* earnest, passionate, eager.
Sehnsucht ['ze:nzuxt], *f.* (—, *no pl.*) longing, yearning, desire.
sehr [ze:r], *adv.* very, much, greatly, very much; *zu* —, too much; — *gut*, very good; — *wohl*, very well.
Sehweite ['ze:vaıtə], *f.* (—, *no pl.*) range of vision.
seicht [zaıçt], *adj.* shallow, superficial.
Seide ['zaıdə], *f.* (—, *pl.* —**n**) silk.
Seidel ['zaıdəl], *n.* (—**s**, *pl.* —) (*dial.*) mug, tankard; pint.
seiden ['zaıdən], *adj.* silk, silken, silky.
Seidenpapier ['zaıdənpapi:r], *n.* (—**s**, *no pl.*) tissue-paper.
Seidenraupe ['zaıdənraupə], *f.* (—, *pl.* —**n**) (*Ent.*) silkworm.
Seidenstoff ['zaıdənʃtɔf], *m.* (—**es**, *pl.* —**e**) spun silk.
Seife ['zaıfə], *f.* (—, *pl.* —**n**) soap; *ein Stück* —, a cake of soap.
seifen ['zaıfən], *v.a.* soap.
Seifenschaum ['zaıfənʃaum], *m.* (—**s**, *no pl.*) lather.
Seifenwasser ['zaıfənvasər], *n.* (—**s**, *no pl.*) soap-suds.
seifig ['zaıfıç], *adj.* soapy, saponaceous.
seihen ['zaıən], *v.a.* strain, filter.
Seil [zaıl], *n.* (—(**e**)**s**, *pl.* —**e**) rope; *straffes* —, taut rope, tight rope; *schlaffes* —, slack rope.
Seilbahn ['zaılba:n], *f.* (—, *pl.* —**en**) funicular railway; cable car.
Seilbrücke ['zaılbrykə], *f.* (—, *pl.* —**n**) rope bridge.
Seiltänzer ['zaıltɛntsər], *m.* (—**s**, *pl.* —) tight-rope walker.
Seilziehen ['zaıltsi:ən], *n.* (—**s**, *no pl.*) tug of war.
Seim [zaım], *m.* (—(**e**)**s**, *pl.* —**e**) strained honey.
Sein [zaın], *n.* (—**s**, *no pl.*) being, existence.
sein (1) [zaın], *v.n. irr.* (*aux.* **sein**) be, exist.
sein (2) [zaın], *poss. adj.* his, her, its; one's. — *pers. pron.* his.
seinerseits ['zaınərzaıts], *adv.* for his part.
seinerzeit ['zaınərtsaıt], *adv.* at that time, at the time, formerly.
seinesgleichen ['zaınəsglaıçən], *indecl. adj. & pron.* of his sort, such as he.
seinethalben ['zaınəthalbən], *adv.* on his account, for his sake, on his behalf.
seinetwegen ['zaınətve:gən], *adv.* on his account, for his sake, on his behalf.
Seinige ['zaınıgə], *n.* (—**n**, *pl.* —**n**) his, his property; (*pl.*) his family, his people; *das* — *tun*, do o.'s share.
seit [zaıt], *prep.* (*Dat.*) since, for; — *gestern*, since yesterday, from yesterday onwards; — *einiger Zeit*, for some time past. — *conj. see* **seitdem**.
seitdem [zaıt'de:m], *adv.* since then, since that time. — *conj.* since.
Seite ['zaıtə], *f.* (—, *pl.* —**n**) side, flank; (*book*) page; *etwas auf die — bringen*, put s.th. aside; *ich bin auf seiner* —, I side with him, I am on his side; *er hat seine guten* —**n**, he has his good points.
Seitenansicht ['zaıtənanzıçt], *f.* (—, *pl.* —**en**) profile.
Seitengleis ['zaıtənglaıs], *n.* (—**es**, *pl.* —**e**) (railway) siding.
Seitenhieb ['zaıtənhi:p], *m.* (—**s**, *pl.* —**e**) innuendo, sly hit, dig.
seitens ['zaıtəns], *prep.* (*Genit.*) on the part of.
Seitensprung ['zaıtənʃpruŋ], *m.* (—**s**, *pl.* ⸚**e**) side-leap, caper; (*fig.*) (amorous) escapade.
Seitenstraße ['zaıtənʃtra:sə], *f.* (—, *pl.* —**n**) side-street.
Seitenstück ['zaıtənʃtyk], *n.* (—**s**, *pl.* —**e**) companion-piece.
Seitenzahl ['zaıtəntsa:l], *f.* (—, *pl.* —**en**) page-number; number of pages.
seither ['zaıthe:r], *adv.* since that time, since then.
seitlich ['zaıtlıç], *adj.* lateral.
Sekretär [zekre'tɛ:r], *m.* (—**s**, *pl.* —**e**) secretary.
Sekretariat [zekreta'rja:t], *n.* (—**s**, *pl.* —**e**) secretariat, secretary's office.
Sekt [zɛkt], *m.* (—**s**, *pl.* —**e**) champagne.
Sekte ['zɛkte], *f.* (—, *pl.* —**n**) sect.
Sektierer [zɛk'ti:rər], *m.* (—**s**, *pl.* —) sectarian.
Sektion [zɛk'tsjo:n) *f.* (—, *pl.* —**en**) section; (*Med.*) dissection.
Sekundaner [zekun'da:nər], *m.* (—**s**, *pl.* —) pupil in the second (highest) form.
Sekundant [zekun'dant], *m.* (—**en**, *pl.* —**en**) (*Duelling*) second.
sekundär [zekun'dɛ:r], *adj.* secondary.
Sekunde [ze'kundə], *f.* (—, *pl.* —**n**) (*time*) second.
Sekundenzeiger [ze'kundəntsaıgər], *m.* (—**s**, *pl.* —) (*clock*) second-hand.
sekundieren [zekun'di:rən], *v.n.* *einem* —, second s.o.
selber ['zɛlbər], *indecl. adj. & pron.* self.
selb(ig) ['zɛlb(ıg)], *adj.* the same.

selbst [zɛlpst], *indecl. adj. & pron.* self; — *ist der Mann*, depend on yourself; *von* —, of its own accord, spontaneously. — *adv.* even; — *wenn*, even if, even though; — *dann nicht*, not even then.
selbständig ['zɛlpʃtɛndɪç], *adj.* independent.
Selbstbestimmung ['zɛlpstbəʃtɪmuŋ], *f.* (—, *no pl.*) self-determination, autonomy.
selbstbewußt ['zɛlpstbəvust], *adj.* self-assertive, self-confident, conceited.
selbstherrlich ['zɛlpsthɛrlɪç], *adj.* autocratic, tyrannical.
Selbstlaut ['zɛlpstlaut], *m.* (—s, *pl.* —e) vowel.
selbstlos ['zɛlpstlo:s], *adj.* unselfish, selfless, altruistic.
Selbstlosigkeit [zɛlpst'lo:zɪçkaɪt], *f.* (—, *no pl.*) unselfishness, altruism.
Selbstmord ['zɛlpstmɔrt], *m.* (—s, *pl.* —e) suicide.
selbstredend ['zɛlpstre:dənt], *adj.* self-evident, obvious.
Selbstsucht ['zɛlpstzuxt], *f.* (—, *no pl.*) selfishness, ego(t)ism.
selbstsüchtig ['zɛlpstzyçtɪç], *adj.* selfish, ego(t)istic(al).
selbstverständlich ['zɛlpstfɛrʃtɛntlɪç], *adj.* self-evident. — *adv.* of course, obviously.
Selbstzweck ['zɛlpsttsvɛk], *m.* (—s, *no pl.*) end in itself.
selig ['ze:lɪç], *adj.* blessed, blissful; (*fig.*) delighted; deceased, late; — *sprechen*, beatify.
Seligkeit ['ze:lɪçkaɪt], *f.* (—, *pl.* —en) bliss, blissfulness; (*Eccl.*) salvation, beatitude.
Seligsprechung ['ze:lɪçʃprɛçuŋ], *f.* (—, *pl.* —en) beatification.
Sellerie ['zɛləri:], *m.* (—s, *pl.* —s) (*Bot.*) celery.
selten ['zɛltən], *adj.* rare, scarce; (*fig.*) remarkable. — *adv.* seldom, rarely, infrequently.
Seltenheit ['zɛltənhaɪt], *f.* (—, *pl.* —en) rarity, curiosity, scarcity; (*fig.*) remarkableness.
Selterwasser ['zɛltərvasər], *n.* (—s, *no pl.*) soda-water.
seltsam ['zɛltza:m], *adj.* strange, unusual, odd, curious.
Semester [ze'mɛstər], *n.* (—s, *pl.* —) university term, semester.
Semit [zɛ'mi:t], *m.* (—en, *pl.* —en) Semite, Jew.
semmelblond ['zɛməlblɔnt], *adj.* flaxen-haired.
Semmelkloß ['zɛməlklo:s], *m.* (—es, *pl.* ⸚e) bread dumpling.
Senator [zɛ'na:tɔr], *m.* (—s, *pl.* —en) senator.
senden ['zɛndən], *v.a. irr.* send, despatch; (*money*) remit. — *v.a. reg.* (*Rad.*) broadcast.
Sender ['zɛndər], *m.* (—s, *pl.* —) sender; (*Rad.*) (broadcasting) station, transmitter.
Sendling ['zɛntlɪŋ], *m.* (—s, *pl.* —e) (*Poet.*) emissary.
Sendschreiben ['zɛntʃraɪbən], *n.* (—s, *pl.* —) epistle, missive.
Sendung ['zɛnduŋ], *f.* (—, *pl.* —en) (*Comm.*) shipment, consignment; (*fig.*) mission; (*Rad.*) broadcast, transmission.
Senegal ['ze:nəgal], *n.* Senegal.
Senf [zɛnf], *m.* (—s, *no pl.*) mustard.
sengen ['zɛŋən], *v.a.* singe, scorch; — *und brennen*, lay waste.
Senkblei ['zɛŋkblaɪ], *n.* (—s, *pl.* —e) plummet.
Senkel ['zɛŋkəl], *m.* (—s, *pl.* —) shoe-lace.
senken ['zɛŋkən], *v.a.* lower, sink. — *v.r. sich* —, sink, go down; dip, slope, subside.
senkrecht ['zɛŋkrɛçt], *adj.* perpendicular.
Senkung ['zɛŋkuŋ], *f.* (—, *pl.* —en) depression, dip, subsidence.
Senn(e) ['zɛn(ə)], *m.* (—n, *pl.* —(e)n) Alpine herdsman.
Sennerin ['zɛnərɪn], *f.* (—, *pl.* —nen) Alpine dairy-woman.
Senneschoten ['zɛnəʃo:tən], *f. pl.* senna pods.
Sennhütte ['zɛnhytə], *f.* (—, *pl.* —n) Alpine dairy; chalet.
sensationell [zɛnzatsjo'nɛl], *adj.* sensational.
Sense ['zɛnzə], *f.* (—, *pl.* —n) scythe.
sensibel [zɛn'zi:bəl], *adj.* sensitive.
Sentenz [zɛn'tɛnts], *f.* (—, *pl.* —en) aphorism.
sentimental [zɛntimɛn'ta:l], *adj.* sentimental.
separat [zepa'ra:t], *adj.* separate, special.
September [zɛp'tɛmbər], *m.* (—s, *pl.* —) September.
Serbien ['zɛrbjən], *n.* Serbia.
Serie ['ze:rjə], *f.* (—, *pl.* —n) series.
Service [zɛr'vi:s], *n.* (—s, *pl.* —) dinner-set, dinner-service.
servieren [zɛr'vi:rən], *v.a., v.n.* serve, wait at table.
Serviertisch [zɛr'vi:rtɪʃ], *m.* (—es, *pl.* —e) sideboard.
Sessel ['zɛsəl], *m.* (—s, *pl.* —) armchair, easy-chair; (*Austr. dial.*) chair.
seßhaft ['zɛshaft], *adj.* settled, domiciled.
setzen ['zɛtsən], *v.a.* set, put, place; (*monument*) erect; (*bet*) stake; (*Typ.*) compose. — *v.r. sich* —, sit down; (*coffee*) settle; *sich bei einem in Gunst* —, ingratiate o.s. with s.o.
Setzer ['zɛtsər], *m.* (—s, *pl.* —) compositor.
Setzling ['zɛtslɪŋ], *m.* (—s, *pl.* —e) young tree, young plant.
Seuche ['zɔyçə], *f.* (—, *pl.* —n) pestilence; epidemic.
seufzen ['zɔyftsən], *v.n.* sigh.
Seufzer ['zɔyftsər], *m.* (—s, *pl.* —) sigh.
Sexta ['zɛksta:], *f.* (—, *pl.* —s) (*Sch.*) sixth form, lowest form.

Sextant [zɛks'tant], *m.* (—**en**, *pl.* —**en**) sextant.
sexuell [zɛksu'ɛl], *adj.* sexual.
sezieren [ze'tsi:rən], *v.a.* dissect.
Seziersaal [ze'tsi:rza:l], *m.* (—**s**, *pl.* —**säle**) dissecting-room.
Sibirien [zi'bi:rjən], *n.* Siberia.
sich [zɪç], *pron.* oneself, himself, herself, itself, themselves; each other.
Sichel ['zɪçəl], *f.* (—, *pl.* —**n**) sickle.
sicher ['zɪçər], *adj.* certain, sure, secure, safe; confident, positive; *seiner Sache — sein*, be sure of o.'s ground; *— stellen*, secure.
Sicherheit ['zɪçərhaɪt], *f.* (—, *pl.* —**en**) certainty; security, safety; confidence, positiveness; *in — bringen*, secure.
sichern ['zɪçərn], *v.a.* secure, make secure; assure, ensure.
Sicherung ['zɪçəruŋ], *f.* (—, *pl.* —**en**) securing; (*Elec.*) fuse; (*gun*) safety-catch.
Sicht [zɪçt], *f.* (—, *no pl.*) sight.
sichtbar ['zɪçtba:r], *adj.* visible; conspicuous.
sichten ['zɪçtən], *v.a.* sift, sort out; sight.
sichtlich ['zɪçtlɪç], *adv.* visibly.
Sichtwechsel ['zɪçtvɛksəl], *m.* (—**s**, *pl.* —) (*Banking*) sight-bill, bill payable on sight.
Sichtweite ['zɪçtvaɪtə], *f.* (—, *no pl.*) range of vision.
sickern ['zɪkərn], *v.n.* (*aux.* sein) leak, ooze, seep.
Sie [zi:], *pron.* (*formal*) you.
sie [zi:], *pers. pron.* she, her; they, them.
Sieb [zi:p], *n.* (—(**e**)**s**, *pl.* —**e**) sieve; riddle; colander.
sieben (1) ['zi:bən], *v.a.* (*Cul.*) sift, strain.
sieben (2) ['zi:bən], *num. adj.* seven; *meine — Sachen*, my belongings.
Siebeneck ['zi:bənɛk], *n.* (—**s**, *pl.* —**e**) heptagon.
Siebengestirn ['zi:bəngəʃtɪrn], *n.* (—**s**, *no pl.*) Pleiades.
siebenmal ['zi:bənma:l], *adv.* seven times.
Siebenmeilenstiefel [zi:bən'maɪlənʃti:fəl], *m. pl.* seven-league boots.
Siebenschläfer ['zi:bənʃlɛ:fər], *m.* (—**s**, *pl.* —) lazy-bones.
siebzehn ['zi:ptse:n], *num. adj.* seventeen.
siebzig ['zi:ptsɪç], *num. adj.* seventy.
siech [zi:ç], *adj.* (*rare*) sick, infirm.
siechen ['zi:çən], *v.n.* be in bad health.
sieden ['zi:dən], *v.a.*, *v.n.* boil, seethe.
siedeln ['zi:dəln], *v.n.* settle.
Siedlung ['zi:dluŋ], *f.* (—, *pl.* —**en**) settlement; housing estate.
Sieg [zi:k], *m.* (—(**e**)**s**, *pl.* —**e**) victory; *den — davontragen*, win the day.
Siegel ['zi:gəl], *n.* (—**s**, *pl.* —) seal; *Brief und —*, sign and seal.
Siegelbewahrer ['zi:gəlbəva:rər], *m.* (—**s**, *pl.* —) Lord Privy Seal; keeper of the seal.
Siegellack ['zi:gəllak], *n.* (—**s**, *no pl.*) sealing wax.
siegeln ['zi:gəln], *v.a.* seal.
siegen ['zi:gən], *v.n.* conquer, win, be victorious, triumph (over).
Sieger ['zi:gər], *m.* (—**s**, *pl.* —) victor, conqueror.
Siegesbogen ['zi:gəsbo:gən], *m.* (—**s**, *pl.* ¨) triumphal arch.
Siegeszeichen ['zi:gəstsaɪçən], *n.* (—**s**, *pl.* —) sign of victory, trophy.
sieghaft ['zi:khaft], *adj.* victorious, triumphant.
siegreich ['zi:kraɪç], *adj.* victorious, triumphant.
siehe! ['zi:ə], *excl.* see! look! lo and behold!
Sierra Leone ['siɛra le'o:nə], *f.* Sierra Leone.
Signal [zɪg'na:l], *n.* (—**s**, *pl.* —**e**) signal.
Signalement [zɪgnalə'mã], *n.* (—**s**, *pl.* —**s**) personal description.
Signalglocke [zɪg'na:lglɔkə], *f.* (—, *pl.* —**n**) warning-bell.
signalisieren [zɪgnali'zi:rən], *v.a.* signal.
Signatarmacht [zɪgna'ta:rmaxt], *f.* (—, *pl.* ¨**e**) signatory power.
signieren [zɪg'ni:rən], *v.a.* sign.
Silbe ['zɪlbə], *f.* (—, *pl.* —**n**) syllable.
Silbenmaß ['zɪlbənma:s], *n.* (—**es**, *pl.* —**e**) (*Poet.*) metre.
Silbenrätsel ['zɪlbənrɛ:tsəl], *n.* (—**s**, *pl.* —) charade.
Silber ['zɪlbər], *n.* (—**s**, *no pl.*) silver; plate.
Silberbuche ['zɪlbərbu:xə], *f.* (—, *pl.* —**n**) white beech(-tree).
Silberfuchs ['zɪlbərfuks], *m.* (—**es**, *pl.* ¨**e**) (*Zool.*) silver fox.
silbern ['zɪlbərn], *adj.* made of silver, silvery.
Silberpappel ['zɪlbərpapəl], *f.* (—, *pl.* —**n**) (*Bot.*) white poplar(-tree).
Silberschimmel ['zɪlbərʃɪməl], *m.* (—**s**, *pl.* —) grey-white horse.
Silberzeug ['zɪlbərtsɔyk], *n.* (—**s**, *no pl.*) (silver) plate.
Silvester [zɪl'vɛstər], *m.* (—**s**, *pl.* —) New Year's Eve.
Similistein ['zi:miliʃtaɪn], *m.* (—**s**, *pl.* —**e**) imitation *or* paste jewellery.
Sims [zɪms], *m.* (—**es**, *pl.* —**e**) cornice, moulding, shelf, ledge.
Simulant [zimu'lant], *m.* (—**en**, *pl.* —**en**) malingerer.
simulieren [zimu'li:rən], *v.a.* simulate.
simultan [zimul'ta:n], *adj.* simultaneous.
Singapur [zɪŋga'pu:r], *n.* Singapore.
Singdrossel ['zɪŋdrɔsəl], *f.* (—, *pl.* —**n**) (*Orn.*) common thrush.
singen ['zɪŋən], *v.a.*, *v.n. irr.* sing.
Singspiel ['zɪŋʃpi:l], *n.* (—**s**, *pl.* —**e**) musical comedy, light opera, opera buffa.
Singular ['zɪŋgula:r], *m.* (—**s**, *pl.* —**e**) singular.

sinken ['zɪŋkən], *v.n. irr.* (*aux.* sein) sink; (*price*) decline, drop, fall; *den Mut — lassen*, lose heart.
Sinn [zɪn], *m.* (—(e)s, *pl.* —e) sense; intellect, mind; consciousness, memory; taste, meaning, purport; wish; *etwas im — haben*, have s.th. in mind, intend s.th.; *leichter —*, lightheartedness; *andern —es werden*, change o's mind; *das hat keinen —*, there is no sense in that; *von —en sein*, be out of o.'s senses; *seine fünf —e beisammen haben*, be in o.'s right mind; *sich etwas aus dem — schlagen*, dismiss s.th. from o.'s mind; *es kommt mir in den —*, it occurs to me.
Sinnbild ['zɪnbɪlt], *n.* (—s, *pl.* —er) symbol, emblem.
sinnen ['zɪnən], *v.n. irr.* meditate, reflect.
Sinnesänderung ['zɪnəsɛndəruŋ], *f.* (—, *pl.* —en) change of mind.
Sinnesart ['zɪnəsa:rt], *f.* (—, *no pl.*) disposition, character.
Sinnesorgan ['zɪnəsɔrga:n], *n.* (—s, *pl.* —e) sense-organ.
Sinnestäuschung ['zɪnəstɔyʃuŋ], *f.* (—, *pl.* —en) illusion, hallucination.
sinnfällig ['zɪnfɛlɪç], *adj.* obvious, striking.
Sinngedicht ['zɪngədɪçt], *n.* (—es, *pl.* —e) epigram.
sinnig ['zɪnɪç], *adj.* thoughtful, meaningful; judicious, fitting.
sinnlich ['zɪnlɪç], *adj.* sensual, sensuous.
Sinnlichkeit ['zɪnlɪçkaɪt], *f.* (—, *no pl.*) sensuality, sensuousness.
sinnlos ['zɪnlo:s], *adj.* senseless, meaningless, pointless.
sinnreich ['zɪnraɪç], *adj.* ingenious.
Sinnspruch ['zɪnʃprux], *m.* (—es, *pl.* ¨e) sentence, maxim, device, motto.
sinnverwandt ['zɪnfɛrvant], *adj.* synonymous.
sinnvoll ['zɪnfɔl], *adj.* meaningful, significant.
sinnwidrig ['zɪnvi:drɪç], *adj.* nonsensical, absurd.
Sintflut ['zɪntflu:t], *f.* (—, *no pl.*) (*Bibl.*) the Flood.
Sinus ['zi:nus], *m.* (—, *pl.* —se) (*Maths.*) sine.
Sippe ['zɪpə], *f.* (—, *pl.* —n) kin, tribe, family, clan.
Sippschaft ['zɪpʃaft], *f.* (—, *pl.* —en) kindred; *die ganze —*, the whole caboodle.
Sirene [zi're:nə], *f.* (—, *pl.* —n) siren.
Sirup ['zi:rup], *m.* (—s, *no pl.*) syrup, treacle.
Sitte ['zɪtə], *f.* (—, *pl.* —n) custom, mode, fashion; (*pl.*) manners, morals; *—n und Gebräuche*, manners and customs.
Sittengesetz ['zɪtəngəzɛts], *n.* (—es, *pl.* —e) moral law.
Sittenlehre ['zɪtənle:rə], *f.* (—, *no pl.*) moral philosophy, ethics.
sittenlos ['zɪtənlo:s], *adj.* immoral, profligate, licentious.
Sittenprediger ['zɪtənpre:dɪgər], *m.* (—s, *pl.* —) moraliser.
Sittich ['zɪtɪç], *m.* (—s, *pl.* —e) (*Orn.*) budgerigar; parakeet.
sittig ['zɪtɪç], *adj.* well-behaved.
sittlich ['zɪtlɪç], *adj.* moral.
Sittlichkeit ['zɪtlɪçkaɪt], *f.* (—, *no pl.*) morality, morals.
sittsam ['zɪtza:m], *adj.* modest, demure.
situiert [zitu'i:rt], *adj. gut (schlecht) —*, well (badly) off.
Sitz [zɪts], *m.* (—es, *pl.* —e) seat, chair; residence, location, place; (*Eccl.*) see.
Sitzarbeit ['zɪtsarbaɪt], *f.* (—, *pl.* —en) sedentary work.
Sitzbad ['zɪtsba:t], *n.* (—(e)s, *pl.* ¨er) hip bath.
sitzen ['zɪtsən], *v.n. irr.* sit, be seated; (*fig.*) be in prison; (*dress*) fit; *— lassen*, throw over, jilt; *— bleiben*, remain seated; (*school*) stay in the same class, not be moved up; be a wallflower; remain unmarried.
Sitzfleisch ['zɪtsflaɪʃ], *n.* (—es, *no pl.*) (*coll.*) *kein — haben*, be restless, lack application.
Sitzplatz ['zɪtsplats], *m.* (—es, *pl.* ¨e) seat.
Sitzung ['zɪtsuŋ], *f.* (—, *pl.* —en) meeting, sitting, session.
Sitzungsprotokoll ['zɪtsuŋsprotokɔl], *n.* (—s, *pl.*—e) minutes (of a meeting).
Sitzungssaal ['zɪtsuŋsza:l], *m.* (—s, *pl.* —säle) board-room, conference room.
Sizilien [zi'tsi:ljən], *n.* Sicily.
Skala ['ska:la], *f.* (—, *pl.* —len) scale; (*Mus.*) gamut.
Skandal [skan'da:l], *m.* (—s, *pl.* —e) scandal; row, riot; *— machen*, kick up a row.
skandalös [skanda'lø:s], *adj.* scandalous.
skandieren [skan'di:rən], *v.a.* (*Poet.*) scan.
Skandinavien [skandɪ'na:vjən], *n.* Scandinavia.
Skelett [ske'lɛt], *n.* (—s, *pl.* —e) skeleton.
Skepsis ['skɛpzɪs], *f.* (—, *no pl.*) scepticism, doubt.
skeptisch ['skɛptɪʃ], *adj.* sceptical, doubtful.
Skizze ['skɪtsə], *f.* (—, *pl.* —n) sketch.
skizzieren [skɪ'tsi:rən], *v.a.* sketch.
Sklave ['skla:və], *m.* (—n, *pl.*—n) slave; *zum —n machen*, enslave.
Sklavendienst ['skla:vəndi:nst], *m.* (—es, *no pl.*) slavery.
Sklaverei [skla:və'raɪ], *f.* (—, *no pl.*) slavery, thraldom.
Skonto ['skɔnto], *m.* & *n.* (—s, *pl.* —s) discount.
Skrupel ['skru:pəl], *m.* (—s, *pl.* —) scruple; *sich — machen*, have scruples.
skrupulös [skrupu'lø:s], *adj.* scrupulous, meticulous.

Skulptur [skulp'tu:r], *f.* (—, *pl.* —**en**) sculpture.
skurril [sku'ri:l], *adj.* ludicrous.
Slawe ['sla:və], *m.* (—**n**, *pl.* —**n**) Slav.
slawisch ['sla:vɪʃ], *adj.* Slav, Slavonic.
Slowake [slo'va:kə], *m.* (—**n**, *pl.* —**n**) Slovakian.
Slowene [slo've:nə], *m.* (—**n**, *pl.* —**n**) Slovenian.
Smaragd [sma'rakt], *m.* (—(**e**)**s**, *pl.* —**e**) emerald.
smaragden [sma'raktən], *adj.* emerald.
Smoking ['smo:kɪŋ], *m.* (—**s**, *pl.* —**s**) dinner-jacket.
so [zo:], *adv.* so, thus, in this way, like this; —*?* really? — *ist es*, that is how it is; — *daß*, so that; — . . . *wie*, as . . . as; *na* — *was!* well, I never! — *conj.* then, therefore.
sobald [zo'balt], *conj.* as soon as, directly.
Socke ['zɔkə], *f.* (—, *pl.* —**n**) sock.
Sockel ['zɔkəl], *m.* (—**s**, *pl.* —) pedestal, plinth, stand, base.
Soda ['zo:da], *n.* (—**s**, *no pl.*) (carbonate of) soda.
sodann [zo'dan], *adv. conj.* then.
Sodbrennen ['zo:tbrɛnən], *n.* (—**s**, *no pl.*) heartburn.
soeben [zo'e:bən], *adv.* just now.
sofern [zo'fɛrn], *conj.* if, in case, so far as.
sofort [zo'fɔrt], *adv.* at once, immediately.
Sog [zo:k], *m.* (—(**e**)**s**, *pl.* —**e**) undertow, suction.
sogar [zo'ga:r], *adv.* even.
sogenannt [zogə'nant], *adj.* so-called, would-be.
sogleich [zo'glaɪç], *adv.* at once, immediately.
Sohle ['zo:lə], *f.* (—, *pl.* —**n**) sole; (*mine*) floor.
Sohn [zo:n], *m.* (—(**e**)**s**, *pl.* ¨**e**) son; *der verlorene* —, the prodigal son.
solange [zo'laŋə], *conj.* as long as.
Solbad ['zo:lba:t], *n.* (—**s**, *pl.* ¨**er**) saline bath.
solch [zɔlç], *adj.*, *dem. pron.* such.
solcherlei ['zɔlçərlaɪ], *adj.* of such a kind, suchlike.
Sold [zɔlt], *m.* (—(**e**)**s**, *no pl.*) army pay.
Soldat [zɔl'da:t], *m.* (—**en**, *pl.* —**en**) soldier.
Soldateska [zɔlda'tɛska], *f.* (—, *pl.* —**s**) soldiery.
Söldner ['zœldnər], *m.* (—**s**, *pl.* —) mercenary, hireling.
Sole ['zo:lə], *f.* (—, *pl.* —**n**) salt-water, brine.
Solei ['zo:laɪ], *n.* (—**s**, *pl.* —**er**) pickled egg.
solidarisch [zoli'dar:ɪʃ], *adj.* joint, jointly responsible; unanimous.
Solidarität [zolidari'tɛ:t], *f.* (—, *no pl.*) solidarity.
Solist [zo'lɪst], *m.* (—**en**, *pl.* —**en**) soloist.
Soll [zɔl], *n.* (—**s**, *no pl.*) debit; — *und Haben*, debit and credit.
sollen ['zɔlən], *v.n. irr.* be obliged, be compelled; have to; be supposed to; (*aux.*) shall, should etc.; *ich soll*, I must, I am to; *er soll krank sein*, he is said to be ill; *ich sollte eigentlich*, I really ought to.
Söller ['zœlər], *m.* (—**s**, *pl.* —) loft, garret, balcony.
Somali [zɔ'ma:li], *n.* Somalia.
somit [zo'mɪt], *adv.* consequently, therefore, accordingly.
Sommer ['zɔmər], *m.* (—**s**, *pl.* —) summer.
Sommerfäden ['zɔmərfɛ:dən], *m. pl.* gossamer.
Sommerfrische ['zɔmərfrɪʃə], *f.* (—, *pl.* —**n**) holiday resort.
Sommergetreide ['zɔmərgətraɪdə], *n.* (—**s**, *no pl.*) spring corn.
Sommersonnenwende ['zɔmərzɔnənvɛndə], *f.* (—, *pl.* —**n**) summer solstice.
Sommersprosse ['zɔmərʃprɔsə], *f.* (—, *pl.* —**n**) freckle.
sonach [zo'na:x], *adv.* therefore, consequently.
Sonate [zo'na:tə], *f.* (—, *pl.* —**n**) sonata.
Sonde ['zɔndə], *f.* (—, *pl.* —**n**) sounding-lead, plummet; probe.
sonder ['zɔndər], (*obs.*) *prep.* (*Acc.*) without.
Sonderausgabe ['zɔndərausga:bə], *f.* (—, *pl.* —**n**) separate edition; special edition.
Sonderausschuß ['zɔndərausʃus], *m.* (—**sses**, *pl.* ¨**sse**) select committee.
sonderbar ['zɔndərba:r], *adj.* strange, odd, queer, singular, peculiar.
sonderlich ['zɔndərlɪç], *adj.* special, especial, particular. — *adv. nicht* —, not much.
Sonderling ['zɔndərlɪŋ], *m.* (—**s**, *pl.* —**e**) freak, odd character, crank.
sondern ['zɔndərn], *v.a.* separate, distinguish, differentiate. — *conj.* but; *nicht nur*, . . . — *auch*, not only . . . but also.
Sonderrecht ['zɔndərrɛçt], *n.* (—**s**, *pl.* —**e**) special privilege.
sonders ['zɔndərs], *adv. samt und* —, all and each, all and sundry.
Sonderstellung ['zɔndərʃtɛluŋ], *f.* (—, *no pl.*) exceptional position.
Sonderung ['zɔndəruŋ], *f.* (—, *pl.* —**en**) separation.
Sonderzug ['zɔndərtsu:k], *m.* (—**s**, *pl.* ¨**e**) special train.
sondieren [zɔn'di:rən], *v.a.* (*wound*) probe; (*ocean*) plumb; (*fig.*) sound.
Sonett [zo'nɛt], *n.* (—(**e**)**s**, *pl.* —**e**) sonnet.
Sonnabend ['zɔna:bənt], *m.* (—**s**, *pl.* —**e**) Saturday.
Sonne ['zɔnə], *f.* (—, *pl.* —**n**) sun.
sonnen ['zɔnən], *v.r. sich* —, sun o.s., bask in the sun, sunbathe.
Sonnenaufgang ['zɔnənaufgaŋ], *m.* (—**s**, *pl.* ¨**e**) sunrise.
Sonnenbrand ['zɔnənbrant], *m.* (—**s**, *pl.* ¨**e**) sunburn.

Sonnendeck ['zɔnəndɛk], *n.* (**—s**, *pl.* **—e**) awning.
Sonnenfinsternis ['zɔnənfɪnstərnɪs], *f.* (**—**, *pl.* **—se**) eclipse of the sun.
sonnenklar ['zɔnənkla:r], *adj.* very clear, as clear as daylight.
Sonnenschirm ['zɔnənʃɪrm], *m.* (**—s**, *pl.* **—e**) parasol, sunshade.
Sonnenstich ['zɔnənʃtɪç], *n.* (**—(e)s**, *no pl.*) sunstroke.
Sonnenuhr ['zɔnənu:r], *f.* (**—**, *pl.* **—en**) sundial.
Sonnenuntergang ['zɔnənuntərgaŋ], *m.* (**—s**, *pl.* **¨e**) sunset.
Sonnenwende ['zɔnənvɛndə], *f.* (**—**, *no pl.*) solstice.
Sonntag ['zɔnta:k], *m.* (**—s**, *pl.* **—e**) Sunday.
sonntags ['zɔnta:ks], *adv.* on Sundays, of a Sunday.
Sonntagsjäger ['zɔnta:ksjɛ:gər], *m.* (**—s**, *pl.* **—**) amateur sportsman.
sonor [zo'no:r], *adj.* sonorous.
sonst [zɔnst], *adv.* else, otherwise, besides, at other times; *— noch etwas?* anything else?
sonstig ['zɔnstɪç], *adj.* other, existing besides.
sonstwo ['zɔnstvo], *adv.* elsewhere, somewhere else.
Sopran [zo'pra:n], *m.* (**—s**, *pl.* **—e**) soprano.
Sorbett ['zɔrbɛt], *n.* (**—s**, *pl.* **—s**) sherbet.
Sorge ['zɔrgə], *f.* (**—**, *pl.* **—n**) care; grief, worry; sorrow; anxiety; concern; (*pl.*) troubles, worries; *— tragen dass . . .* , see to it that . . . ; *— tragen zu*, take care of; *— um*, concern for.
sorgen ['zɔrgən], *v.n.* *— für*, care for, provide for, look after. — *v.r. sich — um*, worry about.
sorgenvoll ['zɔrgənfɔl], *adj.* uneasy, troubled, anxious.
Sorgfalt ['zɔrkfalt], *f.* (**—**, *no pl.*) care, attention.
sorgfältig ['zɔrkfɛltɪç], *adj.* careful, painstaking; elaborate.
sorglos ['zɔrklo:s], *adj.* careless, irresponsible, unconcerned, indifferent; carefree.
sorgsam ['zɔrkza:m], *adj.* careful, heedful.
Sorte ['zɔrtə], *f.* (**—**, *pl.* **—n**) sort, kind, species, brand.
sortieren [zɔr'ti:rən], *v.a.* sort (out).
Sortiment [zɔrti'mɛnt], *n.* (**—s**, *pl.* **—e**) assortment; bookshop.
Sortimentsbuchhändler [zɔrti'mɛnts-bu:xhɛndlər], *m.* (**—s**, *pl.* **—**) retail bookseller.
Soße ['zo:sə], *f.* (**—**, *pl.* **—n**) sauce, gravy.
Souffleur [suf'lø:r], *m.* (**—s**, *pl.* **—e**) prompter.
Soutane [su'ta:nə], *f.* (**—**, *pl.* **—n**) cassock, soutane.
Souterrain [sutɛ'rɛ̃], *n.* (**—s**, *pl.* **—s**) basement.
souverän [su:və'rɛ:n], *adj.* sovereign; (*fig.*) supremely good.
Souveränität [su:vərɛ:ni'tɛ:t], *f.* (**—**, *no pl.*) sovereignty.
soviel [zo'fi:l], *adv.* so much; *— wie*, as much as. — *conj.* so far as; *— ich weiß*, as far as I know.
sowie [zo'vi:], *conj.* as, as well as, as soon as.
Sowjet [sɔv'jɛt], *m.* (**—s**, *pl.* **—s**) Soviet.
sowohl [zo'vo:l], *conj.* *— wie*, as well as.
sozial [zo'tsja:l], *adj.* social.
sozialisieren [zotsjali'zi:rən], *v.a.* nationalise.
Sozialwissenschaft [zo'tsja:lvɪsənʃaft], *f.* (**—**, *pl.* **—en**) sociology; social science.
Sozietät [zotsje'tɛ:t], *f.* (**—**, *pl.* **—en**) partnership.
Sozius ['zotsjus], *m.* (**—**, *pl.* **—se, Socii**) partner; pillion-rider; *—sitz*, (*motor cycle*) pillion (seat).
sozusagen ['zo:tsuza:gən], *adv.* as it were, so to speak.
Spagat [ʃpa'ga:t], *m.* (**—(e)s**, *no pl.*) (*dial.*) string, twine; (*Dancing*) the splits.
spähen ['ʃpɛ:ən], *v.n.* look out, watch; (*Mil.*) scout; spy.
Späher ['ʃpɛ:ər], *m.* (**—s**, *pl.* **—**) scout; spy.
Spalier [ʃpa'li:r], *n.* (**—s**, *pl.* **—e**) trellis; *— bilden*, form a lane (*of people*).
Spalierobst [ʃpa'li:ro:pst], *n.* (**—(e)s**, *no pl.*) wall-fruit.
Spalt [ʃpalt], *m.* (**—(e)s**, *pl.* **—e**) crack, rift, cleft, rent; (*glacier*) crevasse.
Spalte ['ʃpaltə], *f.* (**—**, *pl.* **—n**) (*newspaper*) column.
spalten ['ʃpaltən], *v.a.* split, cleave, slit. — *v.r. sich —*, divide, break up, split up; (*in two*) bifurcate.
Spaltholz ['ʃpalthɔlts], *n.* (**—es**, *no pl.*) fire-wood.
Spaltpilz ['ʃpaltpɪlts], *m.* (**—es**, *pl.* **—e**) fission-fungus.
Spaltung ['ʃpaltuŋ], *f.* (**—**, *pl.* **—en**) cleavage; (*atomic*) fission; (*fig.*) dissension, rupture; (*Eccl.*) schism.
Span [ʃpa:n], *m.* (**—(e)s**, *pl.* **¨e**) chip, chippings, shavings.
Spange ['ʃpaŋə], *f.* (**—**, *pl.* **—n**) clasp, buckle.
Spanien ['ʃpa:njən], *n.* Spain.
spanisch ['ʃpa:nɪʃ], *adj.* Spanish; *—e Wand*, folding screen; *es kommt mir — vor*, it is Greek to me.
Spann [ʃpan], *m.* (**—(e)s**, *pl.* **—e**) instep.
Spanne ['ʃpanə], *f.* (**—**, *pl.* **—n**) span; *eine — Zeit*, a short space of time.
spannen ['ʃpanən], *v.a.* stretch, strain, span.
spannend ['ʃpanənt], *adj.* thrilling, tense.
Spannkraft ['ʃpankraft], *f.* (**—**, *no pl.*) elasticity.
Spannung ['ʃpanuŋ], *f.* (**—**, *pl.* **—en**) tension, suspense, strain; (*fig.*) eager expectation, curiosity, suspense, close attention; (*Elec.*) voltage.

Sparbüchse ['ʃpa:rbyksə], *f.* (—, *pl.* —n) money-box.
sparen ['ʃpa:rən], *v.a.*, *v.n.* save, economise, put by, lay by.
Spargel ['ʃpargəl], *m.* (—s, *pl.* —) asparagus.
Spargelder ['ʃpa:rgɛldər], *n. pl.* savings.
Sparkasse ['ʃpa:rkasə], *f.* (—, *pl.* —n) savings bank.
spärlich ['ʃpɛ:rlɪç], *adj.* scant, scanty, sparse.
Sparpfennig ['ʃpa:rpfɛnɪç], *m.* (—s, *pl.* —e) nest-egg.
Sparren ['ʃparən], *m.* (—s, *pl.* —) spar, rafter; *er hat einen* —, he has a screw loose.
sparsam ['ʃpa:rza:m], *adj.* economical, thrifty, frugal.
Spaß [ʃpa:s], *m.* (—es, *pl.* ⸚e) jest, fun, joke; *aus* —, *im* —, *zum* —, in fun; — *verstehen*, take a joke; *es macht mir* —, it amuses me, it is fun for me.
spaßen ['ʃpa:sən], *v.n.* jest, joke.
spaßhaft ['ʃpa:shaft], *adj.* funny, facetious, jocular.
Spaßverderber ['ʃpa:sfɛrdɛrbər], *m.* (—s, *pl.* —) spoil-sport.
Spaßvogel ['ʃpa:sfo:gəl], *m.* (—s, *pl.* ⸚) wag.
Spat [ʃpa:t], *m.* (—(e)s, *pl.* —e) (*Min.*) spar.
spät [ʃpɛ:t], *adj.* late; *wie* — *ist es?* what is the time? *zu* — *kommen*, be late.
Spätabend ['ʃpɛ:ta:bənt], *m.* (—s, *pl.* —e) latter part of the evening, late evening.
Spatel ['ʃpa:təl], *m.* (—s, *pl.* —) spatula.
Spaten ['ʃpa:tən], *m.* (—s, *pl.* —) spade.
Spatenstich ['ʃpa:tənʃtɪç], *m.* (—(e)s, *pl.* —e) *den ersten* — *tun*, turn the first sod.
später ['ʃpɛ:tər], *adv.* later (on), afterwards.
spätestens ['ʃpɛ:təstəns], *adv.* at the latest.
Spätling ['ʃpɛ:tlɪŋ], *m.* (—s, *pl.* —e) late arrival; late fruit.
Spätsommer ['ʃpɛ:tzɔmər], *m.* (—s, *pl.* —) Indian summer.
Spatz [ʃpats], *m.* (—en *pl.* —en) (*Orn.*) sparrow.
spazieren [ʃpa'tsi:rən], *v.n.* (*aux.* sein) walk leisurely, stroll; — *gehen*, go for a walk, take a stroll; — *führen*, take for a walk.
Spazierfahrt [ʃpa'tsi:rfa:rt], *f.* (—, *pl.* —en) (pleasure-)drive.
Spazierstock [ʃpa'tsi:rʃtɔk], *m.* (—s, *pl.* ⸚e) walking-stick.
Spazierweg [ʃpa'tsi:rve:k], *m.* (—s, *pl.* —e) walk, promenade.
Specht [ʃpɛçt], *m.* (—(e)s, *pl.* —e) (*Orn.*) woodpecker.
Speck [ʃpɛk], *m.* (—(e)s, *no pl.*) bacon; *eine Scheibe* —, a rasher of bacon.
speckig ['ʃpɛkɪç], *adj.* fat.
Speckschwarte ['ʃpɛkʃvartə], *f.* (—, *pl.* —n) bacon-rind.
Speckseite ['ʃpɛkzaɪtə], *f.* (—, *pl.* —n) flitch of bacon.
spedieren [ʃpe'di:rən], *v.a.* forward; despatch.
Spediteur [ʃpedi'tø:r], *m.* (—s, *pl.* —e) forwarding agent, furniture-remover, carrier.
Spedition [ʃpedi'tsjo:n], *f.* (—, *pl.* —en) conveyance; forwarding agency.
Speer [ʃpe:r], *m.* (—(e)s, *pl.* —e) spear, lance.
Speiche ['ʃpaɪçə], *f.* (—, *pl.* —n) spoke.
Speichel ['ʃpaɪçəl], *m.* (—s, *no pl.*) spittle, saliva.
Speicher ['ʃpaɪçər], *m.* (—s, *pl.* —) granary; warehouse, storehouse; loft.
speien ['ʃpaɪən], *v.a.*, *v.n. irr.* spit; vomit, be sick.
Speise ['ʃpaɪzə], *f.* (—, *pl.* —n) food, nourishment, dish.
Speisekammer ['ʃpaɪzəkamər], *f.* (—, *pl.* —n) larder, pantry.
Speisekarte ['ʃpaɪzəkartə], *f.* (—, *pl.* —n) bill of fare, menu.
speisen ['ʃpaɪzən], *v.a.* feed, give to eat. — *v.n.* eat, dine, sup, lunch.
Speiseröhre ['ʃpaɪzərø:rə], *f.* (—, *pl.* —n) gullet.
Speisewagen ['ʃpaɪzəva:gən], *m.* (—s, *pl.* —) (*Railw.*) dining-car.
Spektakel [ʃpɛk'ta:kəl], *m.* (—s, *no pl.*) uproar, hubbub; shindy, rumpus; noise, row.
Spektrum ['ʃpɛktrum], *n.* (—s, *pl.* Spektren) spectrum.
Spekulant [ʃpeku'lant], *m.* (—en, *pl.* —en) speculator.
spekulieren [ʃpeku'li:rən], *v.n.* speculate; theorise.
Spende ['ʃpɛndə], *f.* (—, *pl.* —n) gift, donation; bounty.
spenden ['ʃpɛndən], *v.a.* bestow, donate, contribute.
Spender ['ʃpɛndər], *m.* (—s, *pl.* —) donor, giver, benefactor.
spendieren [ʃpɛn'di:rən], *v.a.* (give a) treat, pay for, stand.
Sperber ['ʃpɛrbər], *m.* (—s, *pl.* —) (*Orn.*) sparrow-hawk.
Sperling ['ʃpɛrlɪŋ], *m.* (—s, *pl.* —e) (*Orn.*) sparrow.
sperrangelweit ['ʃpɛraŋəlvaɪt], *adv.* wide open.
Sperre ['ʃpɛrə], *f.* (—, *pl.* —n) shutting, closing, blockade, blocking; closure; ban; (*Railw.*) barrier.
sperren ['ʃpɛrən], *v.a.* spread out; (*Typ.*) space; shut, close, block; cut off; *ins Gefängnis* —, put in prison. — *v.r. sich* — *gegen*, offer resistance to.
Sperrhaken ['ʃpɛrha:kən], *m.* (—s, *pl.* —) catch, ratchet.
Sperrsitz ['ʃpɛrzɪts], *m.* (—es, *pl.* —e) (*Theat.*) stall.
Sperrung ['ʃpɛruŋ], *f.* (—, *pl.* —en) barring, obstruction, block, blockade; (*Comm.*) embargo.
Sperrzeit ['ʃpɛrtsaɪt], *f.* (—, *pl.* —en) closing-time.
Spesen ['ʃpe:zən], *f. pl.* charges, expenses.

spesenfrei [ˈʃpe:zənfraɪ], *adj.* free of charge; expenses paid.
Spezereien [ʃpe:tsəˈraɪən], *f. pl.* spices.
spezial [ʃpeˈtsja:l], *adj.* special, particular.
spezialisieren [ʃpetsjaliˈzi:rən], *v.a.* specify. — *v.r. sich* —, specialise.
Spezialist [ʃpetsjaˈlɪst], *m.* (—**en**, *pl.* —**en**) specialist, expert.
Spezialität [ʃpetsjaliˈtɛ:t], *f.* (—, *pl.* —**en**) speciality, (*Am.*) specialty.
Spezies [ˈʃpe:tsjɛs], *f.* (—, *pl.* —) species; (*Maths.*) rule.
Spezifikation [ʃpetsifikaˈtsjo:n], *f.* (—, *pl.* —**en**) specification.
spezifisch [ʃpeˈtsi:fɪʃ], *adj.* specific.
spezifizieren [ʃpetsifiˈtsi:rən], *v.a.* specify.
Spezifizierung [ʃpetsifiˈtsi:ruŋ], *f.* (— *pl.* —**en**) specification.
Spezimen [ˈʃpe:tsimən], *n.* (—**s**, *pl.* —**mina**) specimen.
Sphäre [ˈsfɛ:rə], *f.* (—, *pl.* —**n**) sphere.
sphärisch [ˈsfɛ:rɪʃ], *adj.* spherical.
Spickaal [ˈʃpɪka:l], *m.* (—**s**, *pl.* —**e**) smoked eel.
spicken [ˈʃpɪkən], *v.a.* lard; *den Beutel* —, fill o.'s purse.
Spiegel [ˈʃpi:gəl], *m.* (—**s**, *pl.* —) mirror, looking-glass.
spiegelblank [ˈʃpi:gəlblaŋk], *adj.* sparkling, shiny, polished.
Spiegelei [ˈʃpi:gəlaɪ], *n.* (—**s**, *pl.* —**er**) fried egg.
Spiegelfechterei [ˈʃpi:gəlfɛçtəraɪ], *f.* (—, *pl.* —**en**) shadow-boxing, make-believe.
Spiegelfenster [ˈʃpi:gəlfɛnstər], *n.* (—**s**, *pl.* —) plate-glass window.
spiegeln [ˈʃpi:gəln], *v.n.* glitter, shine. — *v.a.* reflect. — *v.r. sich* —, be reflected.
Spiegelscheibe [ˈʃpi:gəlʃaɪbə], *f.* (—, *pl.* —**n**) plate-glass pane.
Spiegelung [ˈʃpi:gəluŋ], *f.* (—, *pl.* —**en**) reflection; mirage.
Spiel [ʃpi:l], *n.* (—(**e**)**s**, *pl.* —**e**) play; game; sport; (*Theat.*) acting, performance; (*Mus.*) playing; *ehrliches* (*unehrliches*) —, fair (foul) play; *leichtes* —, walk-over; *auf dem* — *stehen*, be at stake; *aufs* — *setzen*, stake, risk; *die Hand im* — *haben*, have a finger in the pie; *gewonnenes* — *haben*, gain o.'s point; *ein gewagtes* — *treiben*, play a bold game; *sein* — *mit einem treiben*, trifle with s.o.
Spielart [ˈʃpi:la:rt], *f.* (—, *pl.* —**en**) manner of playing; variety.
Spielbank [ˈʃpi:lbaŋk], *f.* (—, *pl.* —**en**) casino; gambling-table.
Spieldose [ˈʃpi:ldo:zə], *f.* (—, *pl.* —**n**) musical box.
spielen [ˈʃpi:lən], *v.a.*, *v.n.* play; gamble; (*Mus.*) play; (*Theat.*) act; *eine Rolle* —, play a part; *mit dem Gedanken* —, toy with the idea.
spielend [ˈʃpi:lənt], *adv.* easily.
Spieler [ˈʃpi:lər], *m.* (—**s**, *pl.* —) player; gambler; gamester.
Spielerei [ʃpi:ləˈraɪ], *f.* (—, *pl.* —**en**) child's play; trivialities.
Spielhölle [ˈʃpi:lhœlə], *f.* (—, *pl.* —**n**) gambling-den.
Spielmann [ˈʃpi:lman], *m.* (—**s**, *pl.* **Spielleute**) musician, fiddler; (*Middle Ages*) minstrel.
Spielmarke [ˈʃpi:lmarkə], *f.* (—, *pl.* —**n**) counter, chip.
Spielplan [ˈʃpi:lplan], *m.* (—**s**, *pl.* ¨—**e**) (*Theat.*) repertory.
Spielplatz [ˈʃpi:lplats], *m.* (—**es**, *pl.* ¨—**e**) playground.
Spielraum [ˈʃpi:lraum], *m.* (—**s**, *no pl.*) elbow-room; (*fig.*) scope; margin; clearance.
Spielsache [ˈʃpi:lzaxə], *f.* (—, *pl.* —**n**) toy, plaything.
Spielschule [ˈʃpi:lʃu:lə], *f.* (—, *pl.* —**n**) infant-school, kindergarten.
Spieltisch [ˈʃpi:ltɪʃ], *m.* (—**es**, *pl.* —**e**) card-table.
Spieluhr [ˈʃpi:lu:r], *f.* (—, *pl.* —**en**) musical clock.
Spielverderber [ˈʃpi:lfɛrdɛrbər], *m.* (—**s**, *pl.* —) spoilsport.
Spielwaren [ˈʃpi:lva:rən], *f. pl.* toys.
Spielzeit [ˈʃpi:ltsaɪt], *f.* (—, *pl.* —**en**) playtime; (*Theat.*) season.
Spielzeug [ˈʃpi:ltsɔyk], *n.* (—**s**, *pl.* —**e**) plaything, toy.
Spieß [ʃpi:s], *m.* (—**es**, *pl.* —**e**) spear, pike; (*Cul.*) spit.
Spießbürger [ˈʃpi:sbyrgər], *m.* (—**s**, *pl.* —) Philistine.
spießen [ˈʃpi:sən], *v.a.* spear, pierce.
Spießer [ˈʃpi:sər], *m.* (—**s**, *pl.* —) Philistine.
Spießgeselle [ˈʃpi:sgəzɛlə], *m.* (—**n**, *pl.* —**n**) accomplice, companion *or* partner in crime.
spießig [ˈʃpi:sɪç], *adj.* (*coll.*) Philistine, uncultured, narrow-minded.
Spießruten [ˈʃpi:sru:tən], *f. pl.* — *laufen*, run the gauntlet.
Spinat [ʃpiˈna:t], *m.* (—**s**, *no pl.*) spinach.
Spind [ʃpɪnt], *n.* (—(**e**)**s**, *pl.* —**e**) cupboard.
Spindel [ˈʃpɪndəl], *f.* (—, *pl.* —**n**) spindle; distaff; (*staircase*) newel.
spindeldürr [ˈʃpɪndəldyr], *adj.* as thin as a lath.
Spindelholz [ˈʃpɪndəlhɔlts], *n.* (—**es**, *no pl.*) spindle-tree wood.
Spinett [ʃpiˈnɛt], *n.* (—**s**, *pl.* —**e**) spinet.
Spinne [ˈʃpɪnə], *f.* (—, *pl.* —**n**) spider.
spinnefeind [ˈʃpɪnəfaɪnt], *adj. einander* — *sein*, hate each other like poison.
spinnen [ˈʃpɪnən], *v.a. irr.* spin. — *v.n.* (*coll.*) be off o.'s head, be crazy.
Spinnerei [ʃpɪnəˈraɪ], *f.* (—, *pl.* —**en**) spinning-mill.
Spinngewebe [ˈʃpɪngəve:bə], *n.* (—**s**, *pl.* —) cobweb.
Spinnrocken [ˈʃpɪnrɔkən], *m.* (—**s**, *pl.* —) distaff.
spintisieren [ʃpɪntiˈzi:rən], *v.n.* muse, meditate.

Spion [ʃpi'o:n], *m.* (—s, *pl.* —e) spy.
spionieren [ʃpio'ni:rən], *v.n.* spy, pry.
Spirale [ʃpi'ra:lə], *f.* (—, *pl.* —n) spiral.
Spirituosen [ʃpiritu'o:zən], *pl.* spirits, liquors.
Spiritus ['ʃpi:ritus], *m.* (—, *pl.* —se) alcohol, spirits of wine; *denaturierter* —, methylated spirits.
Spiritusbrennerei ['ʃpi:ritusbrɛnərai], *f.* (—, *pl.* —en) distillery.
Spiritusgehalt ['ʃpi:ritusgəhalt], *m.* (—s, *pl.* —e) (*alcoholic*) strength, proof.
Spital [ʃpi'ta:l], *n.* (—s, *pl.* ¨er) infirmary; hospital.
Spitz [ʃpɪts], *m.* (—es, *pl.* —e) Pomeranian dog; *einen — haben*, (*coll.*) be slightly tipsy.
spitz [ʃpɪts], *adj.* pointed; (*fig.*) snappy, biting.
Spitzbart ['ʃpɪtsba:rt], *m.* (—s, *pl.* ¨e) imperial (beard), pointed beard.
Spitzbogen ['ʃpɪtsbo:gən], *m.* (—s, *pl.* —) pointed arch, Gothic arch.
Spitzbogenfenster ['ʃpɪtsbo:gənfɛnstər], *n.* (—s, *pl.* —) lancet window.
Spitzbube ['ʃpɪtsbu:bə], *m.* (—n, *pl.* —n) rogue; rascal; scamp.
Spitzbubenstreich ['ʃpitsbu:bənʃtraɪç], *m.* (—(e)s, *pl.* —e) act of roguery, knavery.
spitzbübisch ['ʃpɪtsby:bɪʃ], *adj.* roguish.
Spitze ['ʃpɪtsə], *f.* (—, *pl.* —n) point; tip; top, peak; extremity; (*pipe*) mouthpiece; (*cigarette*) holder; (*pen*) nib; lace; *etwas auf die — treiben*, carry s.th. to extremes; *an der — stehen*, be at the head of.
Spitzel ['ʃpɪtsəl], *m.* (—s, *pl.* —) police-agent; informer.
spitzen ['ʃpɪtsən], *v.a.* sharpen; *die Ohren* —, prick up o.'s ears; *sich auf etwas* —, await s.th. eagerly, be all agog for s.th.
Spitzenbelastung ['ʃpɪtsənbəlastuŋ], *f.* (—, *pl.* —en) peak load.
Spitzenleistung ['ʃpɪtsənlaɪstuŋ], *f.* (—, *pl.* —en) maximum output; peak performance.
Spitzentuch ['ʃpɪtsəntu:x], *n.* (—(e)s, *pl.* ¨er) lace scarf.
spitzfindig ['ʃpɪtsfɪndɪç], *adj.* subtle, crafty; hair-splitting.
Spitzhacke ['ʃpɪtshakə], *f.* (—, *pl.* —n) pickaxe.
spitzig ['ʃpɪtsɪç], *adj.* pointed, sharp; (*fig.*) biting, poignant.
Spitzmaus ['ʃpɪtsmaus], *f.* (—, *pl.* ¨e) (*Zool.*) shrew.
Spitzname ['ʃpɪtsna:mə], *m.* (—ns, *pl.* —n) nickname.
spitzwinklig ['ʃpɪtsvɪŋklɪç], *adj.* acute-angled.
spleißen ['ʃplaɪsən], *v.a. irr.* split, cleave.
Splitter ['ʃplɪtər], *m.* (—s, *pl.* —) splinter, chip.
splitternackt ['ʃplɪtərnakt], *adj.* stark naked.
splittern ['ʃplɪtərn], *v.n.* (*aux.* sein) splinter.
spontan [ʃpɔn'ta:n], *adj.* spontaneous.
sporadisch [ʃpo'ra:dɪʃ], *adj.* sporadic.
Spore ['ʃpo:rə], *f.* (—, *pl.* —n) spore.
Sporn [ʃpɔrn], *m.* (—s, *pl.* Sporen) spur.
spornstreichs ['ʃpɔrnʃtraɪçs], *adv.* post-haste, at once.
Sportler ['ʃpɔrtlər], *m.* (—s, *pl.* —) athlete, sportsman.
sportlich ['ʃpɔrtlɪç], *adj.* athletic; sporting.
sportsmäßig ['ʃpɔrtsmɛ:sɪç], *adj.* sportsmanlike.
Spott [ʃpɔt], *m.* (—(e)s, *no pl.*) mockery; scorn; *Gegenstand des —s*, laughing-stock; — *treiben mit*, mock, deride; *zum Schaden den — hinzufügen*, add insult to injury.
spottbillig ['ʃpɔtbɪlɪç], *adj.* ridiculously cheap, dirt-cheap.
Spöttelei [ʃpœtə'laɪ], *f.* (—, *pl.* —en) sarcasm.
spötteln ['ʃpœtəln], *v.n.* mock, jeer.
spotten ['ʃpɔtən], *v.a.*, *v.n.* deride, scoff (at); *es spottet jeder Beschreibung*, it defies description.
Spötter ['ʃpœtər], *m.* (—s, *pl.* —) mocker, scoffer.
Spötterei [ʃpœtə'raɪ], *f.* (—, *pl.* —en) mockery, derision.
Spottgedicht ['ʃpɔtgədɪçt], *n.* (—(e)s, *pl.* —e) satirical poem.
spöttisch ['ʃpœtɪʃ], *adj.* mocking, satirical, ironical, scoffing.
spottlustig ['ʃpɔtlustɪç], *adj.* flippant, satirical.
Spottschrift ['ʃpɔtʃrɪft], *f.* (—, *pl.* —en) satire, lampoon.
Sprache ['ʃpra:xə], *f.* (—, *pl.* —n) speech, language, tongue; expression, diction; discussion; *etwas zur — bringen*, bring a subject up; *zur — kommen*, come up for discussion; *heraus mit der —!* speak out!
Sprachfehler ['ʃpra:xfe:lər], *m.* (—s, *pl.* —) impediment in o.'s speech.
sprachfertig ['ʃpra:xfɛrtɪç], *adj.* having a ready tongue; a good linguist, fluent.
Sprachgebrauch ['ʃpra:xgəbraux], *m.* (—(e)s, *no pl.*) (linguistic) usage.
Sprachkenner ['ʃpra:xkɛnər], *m.* (—s, *pl.* —) linguist.
sprachkundig ['ʃpra:xkundɪç], *adj.* proficient in languages.
Sprachlehre ['ʃpra:xle:rə], *f.* (—, *no pl.*) grammar.
sprachlich ['ʃpra:xlɪç], *adj.* linguistic.
sprachlos ['ʃpra:xlo:s], *adj.* speechless, tongue-tied; — *dastehen*, be dumbfounded.
Sprachrohr ['ʃpra:xro:r], *n.* (—s, *pl.* —e) megaphone, speaking-tube; (*fig.*) mouthpiece.
Sprachschatz ['ʃpra:xʃats], *m.* (—es, *no pl.*) vocabulary.
Sprachvergleichung ['ʃpra:xferglaɪçuŋ], *f.* (—, *no pl.*) comparative philology.

Sprachwerkzeug ['ʃpra:xvərktsɔyk], *n.* (—**s**, *pl.* —**e**) organ of speech.
Sprachwissenschaft ['ʃpra:xvisənʃaft], *f.* (—, *pl.* —**en**) linguistics, philology.
sprechen ['ʃprɛçən], *v.a.,v.n. irr.* speak, declare, say; talk; *für einen* —, put in a good word for s.o., speak up for s.o.; *er ist nicht zu* —, he is not available; *auf einen gut zu* — *sein*, feel well disposed towards s.o.; *schuldig* —, pronounce guilty; *das Urteil* —, pass sentence.
sprechend ['ʃprɛçənt], *adj.* expressive; — *ähnlich*, strikingly alike.
Sprecher ['ʃprɛçər], *m.* (—**s**, *pl.* —) speaker, orator, spokesman; (*Rad.*) announcer.
Sprechstunde ['ʃprɛçʃtundə], *f.* (—, *pl.* —**n**) consulting hours, surgery hours; office hours.
Sprechzimmer ['ʃprɛçtsɪmər], *n.* (—**s**, *pl.*—) consulting-room.
spreizen ['ʃpraɪtsən], *v.a.* spread open; *die Beine* —, plant o.'s legs wide apart, straddle. — *v.r. sich* —, give o.s. airs.
Sprengbombe ['ʃprɛŋbɔmbə], *f.* (—, *pl.* —**n**) (high explosive) bomb.
Sprengel ['ʃprɛŋəl], *m.* (—**s**, *pl.* —) diocese.
sprengen ['ʃprɛŋən], *v.a.* sprinkle; water; burst, explode; burst open, blow up; *eine Versammlung* —, break up a meeting. — *v.n.* (*aux.* sein) ride at full speed, gallop.
Sprengpulver ['ʃprɛŋpulvər], *n.* (—**s**, *no pl.*) blasting-powder.
Sprengstoff ['ʃprɛŋʃtɔf], *m.* (—**es**, *pl.* —**e**) explosive.
Sprengwagen ['ʃprɛŋva:gən], *m.* (—**s**, *pl.* —) sprinkler; water-cart.
sprenkeln ['ʃprɛŋkəln], *v.a.* speckle.
Spreu [ʃprɔy], *f.* (—, *no pl.*) chaff.
Sprichwort ['ʃprɪçvɔrt], *n.* (—**s**, *pl.* ⸚**er**) proverb, adage, saying.
sprießen ['ʃpri:sən], *v.n. irr.* sprout, shoot, germinate.
Springbrunnen ['ʃprɪŋbrunən], *m.* (—**s**, *pl.* —) fountain.
springen ['ʃprɪŋən], *v.n. irr.* (*aux.* sein) spring, leap, jump; (*glass*) burst; *etwas* — *lassen*, (*coll.*) treat s.o. to s.th.
Springer ['ʃprɪŋər], *m.* (—**s**, *pl.* —) jumper, acrobat; (*Chess*) knight.
Springflut ['ʃprɪŋflu:t], *f.* (—, *pl.* —**en**) spring-tide.
Springtau ['ʃprɪŋtau], *n.* (—**s**, *pl.* —**e**) skipping-rope; (*Naut.*) slip-rope.
Sprit [ʃprɪt], *m.* (—**s**, *pl.* —**e**) spirit alcohol; (*sl.*) fuel, petrol.
Spritze ['ʃprɪtsə], *f.* (—, *pl.* —**n**) squirt, syringe; fire-engine; (*coll.*) injection.
spritzen ['ʃprɪtsən], *v.a.* squirt, spout, spray, sprinkle; (*coll.*) inject. — *v.n.* gush forth.
Spritzkuchen ['ʃprɪtsku:xən], *m.* (—**s**, *pl.* —) fritter.
Spritztour ['ʃprɪtstu:r], *f.* (—, *pl.* —**en**) (*coll.*) pleasure trip, outing; (*coll.*) spin.
spröde ['ʃprø:də], *adj.* (*material*) brittle; (*person*) stubborn; coy, prim, prudish.
Sprödigkeit ['ʃprø:dɪçkaɪt], *f.* (—, *no pl.*) (*material*) brittleness; (*person*) stubbornness; coyness, primness, prudery.
Sproß [ʃprɔs], *m.* (—**sses**, *pl.* —**sse**) sprout, shoot, germ; (*fig.*) scion, offspring.
Sprosse ['ʃprɔsə], *f.* (—, *pl.* —**n**) (*ladder*) step, rung.
Sprößling ['ʃprœslɪŋ], *m.* (—**s**, *pl.* —**e**) scion, offspring.
Sprotte ['ʃprɔtə], *f.* (—, *pl.* —**n**) sprat.
Spruch [ʃprux], *m.* (—(**e**)**s**, *pl.* ⸚**e**) saying, aphorism; proverb; (*obs.*) saw; (*judge*) sentence, verdict.
spruchreif ['ʃpruxraɪf], *adj.* ripe for judgment; ready for a decision.
Sprudel ['ʃpru:dəl], *m.* (—**s**, *pl.* —) bubbling spring; (*coll.*) soda water.
sprudeln ['ʃpru:dəln], *v.n.* bubble, gush.
sprühen ['ʃpry:ən], *v.a.* sprinkle, scatter, spray. — *v.n.* sparkle, emit sparks; (*rain*) drizzle.
sprühend ['ʃpry:ənt], *adj.* (*fig.*) sparkling, scintillating, brilliant.
Sprühregen ['ʃpry:re:gən], *m.* (—**s**, *no pl.*) drizzling rain, drizzle.
Sprung [ʃpruŋ], *m.* (—(**e**)**s**, *pl.* ⸚**e**) leap, bound, jump; chink, crack; *nur auf einen* — *zu Besuch kommen*, pay a flying visit; *auf dem* — *sein zu*, be on the point of; *sich auf den* — *machen*, cut and run, (*coll.*) fly; *große* ⸚*e machen*, (*coll.*) live it up, cut a dash.
Sprungfeder ['ʃpruŋfe:dər], *f.* (—, *pl.* —**n**) spring.
Sprungkraft ['ʃpruŋkraft], *f.* (—, *no pl.*) springiness, elasticity, buoyancy.
Spucke ['ʃpukə], *f.* (—, *no pl.*) spittle, saliva.
spucken ['ʃpukən], *v.a., v.n.* spit.
Spuk [ʃpu:k], *m.* (—**s**, *pl.* —**e**) haunting; ghost, spectre, apparition; (*coll.*) spook.
spuken ['ʃpu:kən], *v.n.* haunt; be haunted.
spukhaft ['ʃpu:khaft], *adj.* uncanny, phantom-like, ghost-like, spooky.
Spule ['ʃpu:lə], *f.* (—, *pl.* —**n**) spool; (*Elec.*) coil.
Spüleimer ['ʃpy:laɪmər], *m.* (—**s**, *pl.* —) slop-pail.
spülen ['ʃpy:lən], *v.a.* rinse, wash.
Spülicht ['ʃpy:lɪçt], *n.* (—**s**, *no pl.*) dish-water.
Spund [ʃpunt], *m.* (—(**e**)**s**, *pl.* ⸚**e**) bung.
Spundloch ['ʃpuntlɔx], *n.* (—**s**, *pl.* ⸚**er**) bung-hole.
Spur [ʃpu:r], *f.* (—, *pl.* —**en**) footprint, track, trail; spoor; (*fig.*) trace, vestige; *frische* —, hot scent; *einer Sache auf die* — *kommen*, be on the track of s.th.; *keine* — *von*, not a trace of, not an inkling of.
spüren ['ʃpy:rən], *v.a.* trace, track (down); feel, sense, notice.
Spürhund ['ʃpy:rhunt], *m.* (—**s**, *pl.* —**e**) tracker dog, setter, beagle; (*fig.*) spy, sleuth.

spurlos [ˈʃpu:rlo:s], *adj.* trackless, without a trace; *es ging — an ihm vorüber,* it left no mark on him; *— verschwinden,* vanish into thin air.

Spürsinn [ˈʃpy:rzɪn], *m.* (—s, *no pl.*) scent; flair; sagacity, shrewdness.

Spurweite [ˈʃpu:rvaɪtə], *f.* (—, *pl.* —n) gauge, width of track.

sputen [ˈʃpu:tən], *v.r. sich —,* make haste, hurry.

Staat [ʃta:t], *m.* (—(e)s, *pl.* —en) state; government; pomp, show, parade; *— machen,* make a show of.

Staatenbund [ˈʃta:tənbunt], *m.* (—(e)s, *pl.* ¨e) confederacy, federation.

staatlich [ˈʃta:tlɪç], *adj.* belonging to the state, public, national.

Staatsangehörige [ˈʃta:tsangəhø:rɪgə], *m.* (—n, *pl.* —n) citizen (of a country), subject, national.

Staatsangehörigkeit [ˈʃta:tsangəhø:rɪçkaɪt], *f.* (—, *pl.* —en) nationality.

Staatsanwalt [ˈʃta:tsanvalt], *m.* (—s, *pl.* ¨e) public prosecutor, Attorney-General.

Staatsbeamte [ˈʃta:tsbəamtə], *m.* (—n, *pl.* —n) civil servant, employee of the state.

Staatsbürger [ˈʃta:tsbyrgər], *m.* (—s, *pl.* —) citizen, national.

Staatsdienst [ˈʃta:tsdi:nst], *m.* (—(e)s, *pl.* —e) civil service, government service.

Staatseinkünfte [ˈʃta:tsaɪnkynftə], *f. pl.* public revenue.

Staatsgesetz [ˈʃta:tsgəzɛts], *n.* (—es, *pl.* —e) statute law.

Staatsgewalt [ˈʃta:tsgəvalt], *f.* (—, *no pl.*) executive power.

Staatshaushalt [ˈʃta:tshaushalt], *m.* (—s, *no pl.*) state finances, budget.

Staatshaushaltsanschlag [ˈʃta:tshaushaltsanʃla:k], *m.* (—s, *pl.* ¨e) budget estimates.

Staatskanzler [ˈʃta:tskantslər], *m.* (—s, *pl.* —) Chancellor.

Staatskasse [ˈʃta:tskasə], *f.* (—, *no pl.*) public exchequer, treasury.

Staatskörper [ˈʃta:tskœrpər], *m.* (—s, *pl.* —) body politic.

Staatskosten [ˈʃta:tskɔstən], *f. pl. auf —,* at (the) public expense.

Staatskunst [ˈʃta:tskunst], *f.* (—, *no pl.*) statesmanship; statecraft.

Staatsminister [ˈʃta:tsmɪnɪstər], *m.* (—s, *pl.* —) cabinet minister; minister of state.

Staatsrat [ˈʃta:tsra:t], *m.* (—s, *no pl.*) council of state; (*pl.* ¨e) councillor of state.

Staatsrecht [ˈʃta:tsrɛçt], *n.* (—(e)s, *no pl.*) constitutional law.

Staatssiegel [ˈʃta:tszi:gəl], *n.* (—s, *pl.* —) Great Seal, official seal.

Staatsstreich [ˈʃta:tsʃtraɪç], *m.* (—(e)s, *pl.* —e) coup d'état.

Staatswirtschaft [ˈʃta:tsvɪrtʃaft], *f.* (—, *no pl.*) political economy.

Staatszimmer [ˈʃta:tstsɪmər], *n.* (—s, *pl.* —) state apartment.

Stab [ʃta:p], *m.* (—(e)s, *pl.* ¨e) staff; stick, rod, pole; crosier; mace; (*Mil.*) field-officers, staff; *den — über einen brechen,* condemn s.o. (to death).

stabil [ʃtaˈbi:l], *adj.* steady, stable, firm.

stabilisieren [ʃtabiliˈzi:rən], *v.a.* stabilise.

Stabreim [ˈʃta:praɪm], *m.* (—s, *no pl.*) alliteration.

Stabsarzt [ˈʃta:psartst], *m.* (—es, *pl.* ¨e) (*Mil.*) medical officer.

Stabsquartier [ˈʃta:pskvarti:r], *n.* (—s, *pl.* —e) (*Mil.*) headquarters.

Stachel [ˈʃtaxəl], *m.* (—s, *pl.* —n) (*animal*) sting; (*plant*) prickle, thorn; (*fig.*) keen edge, sting; stimulus; *wider den — löcken,* kick against the pricks.

Stachelbeere [ˈʃtaxəlbe:rə], *f.* (—, *pl.* —n) (*Bot.*) gooseberry.

Stachelschwein [ˈʃtaxelʃvaɪn], *n.* (—s, *pl.* —e) (*Zool.*) hedgehog, porcupine.

stachlig [ˈʃtaxlɪç], *adj.* prickly, thorny; (*fig.*) disagreeable.

Stadion [ˈʃta:djɔn], *n.* (—s, *pl.* —dien) sports-arena, stadium.

Stadium [ˈʃta:djum], *n.* (—s, *pl.* —dien) stage (of development), phase.

Stadt [ʃtat], *f.* (—, *pl.* ¨e) town; city.

Stadtbahn [ˈʃtatba:n], *f.* (—, *pl.* —en) metropolitan railway.

Städtchen [ˈʃtɛtçən], *n.* (—s, *pl.* —) small town, township.

Städter [ˈʃtɛtər], *m.* (—s, *pl.* —) townsman.

Stadtgemeinde [ˈʃtatgəmaɪndə], *f.* (—, *pl.* —n) municipality.

städtisch [ˈʃtɛtɪʃ], *adj.* municipal.

Stadtmauer [ˈʃtatmauər], *f.* (—, *pl.* —n) town wall, city wall.

Stadtrat [ˈʃtatra:t], *m.* (—s, *no pl.*) town council; (*pl.* ¨e) town councillor; alderman.

Stadtteil [ˈʃtattaɪl], *m.* (—s, *pl.* —e) ward, district, part of a town.

Stadttor [ˈʃtatto:r], *n.* (—s, *pl.* —e) city-gate.

Stadtverordnete [ˈʃtatfɛrɔrdnətə], *m.* (—n, *pl.* —n) town councillor.

Stafette [ʃtaˈfɛtə], *f.* (—, *pl.* —n) courier; relay.

Staffel [ˈʃtafəl], *f.* (—, *pl.* —n) step, rundle, rung, round; relay; (*fig.*) degree; (*Aviat.*) squadron.

Staffelei [ʃtafəˈlaɪ], *f.* (—, *pl.* —en) easel.

staffeln [ˈʃtafəln], *v.a.* grade; differentiate; stagger.

Staffelung [ˈʃtafəluŋ], *f.* (—, *pl.* —en) gradation.

stagnieren [ʃtagˈni:rən], *v.n.* stagnate.

Stahl [ʃta:l], *m.* (—(e)s, *pl.* ¨e) steel.

stählen [ˈʃtɛ:lən], *v.a.* steel, harden, temper; brace.

stählern [ˈʃtɛ:lərn], *adj.* made of steel, steely.

Stahlquelle [ˈʃta:lkvɛlə], *f.* (—, *pl.* —n) chalybeate spring; mineral spring.

Stahlstich [ˈʃta:lʃtɪç], *m.* (—(e)s, *pl.* —e) steel-engraving.

Stählung [ˈʃtɛ:luŋ], *f.* (—, *no pl.*) steeling; (*fig.*) bracing.
Stahlwaren [ˈʃta:lva:rən], *f. pl.* hardware, cutlery.
Stall [ʃtal], *m.* (—(e)s, *pl.* ¨e) stable; (*pig*) sty; (*dog*) kennel.
Stallbursche [ˈʃtalburʃə], *m.* (—n, *pl.* —n) stable-boy, groom.
Stallungen [ˈʃtaluŋən], *f. pl.* stabling, stables.
Stambul [ˈstambul], *n.* Istanbul.
Stamm [ʃtam], *m.* (—(e)s, *pl.* ¨e) (*tree*) trunk; (*people*) tribe, family, race; (*words*) stem; root.
Stammaktie [ˈʃtamaktsjə], *f.* (—, *pl.* —n) (*Comm.*) original share.
Stammbaum [ˈʃtambaum], *m.* (—s, *pl.* ¨e) pedigree; family tree.
Stammbuch [ˈʃtambu:x], *n.* (—(e)s, *pl.* ¨er) album.
stammeln [ˈʃtaməln], *v.a., v.n.* stammer, stutter; falter.
stammen [ˈʃtamən], *v.n.* (*aux.* sein) be descended from, spring from, originate from, stem from; be derived from.
Stammesgenosse [ˈʃtaməsgənɔsə], *m.* (—n, *pl.* —n) kinsman, clansman.
Stammgast [ˈʃtamgast], *m.* (—es, *pl.* ¨e) regular customer.
Stammgut [ˈʃtamgu:t], *n.* (—s, *pl.* ¨er) family estate.
Stammhalter [ˈʃtamhaltər], *m.* (—s, *pl.* —) son and heir; eldest son.
Stammhaus [ˈʃtamhaus], *n.* (—es, *pl.* ¨er) ancestral mansion; (*royalty*) dynasty; (*Comm.*) business headquarters, head office.
stämmig [ˈʃtɛmɪç], *adj.* sturdy, strong.
Stammler [ˈʃtamlər], *m.* (—s, *pl.* —) stammerer, stutterer.
Stammsilbe [ˈʃtamzɪlbə], *f.* (—, *pl.* —n) (*Ling.*) radical syllable.
Stammtafel [ˈʃtamta:fəl], *f.* (—, *pl.* —n) genealogical table.
Stammvater [ˈʃtamfa:tər], *m.* (—s, *pl.* ¨) ancestor, progenitor.
stammverwandt [ˈʃtamfɛrvant], *adj.* cognate, kindred.
stampfen [ˈʃtampfən], *v.a.* stamp, pound, ram down. — *v.n.* stamp, trample.
Stand [ʃtant], *m.* (—(e)s, *pl.* ¨e) stand; (*market*) stall; situation, state (of affairs), condition; reading, position; rank, station (in life); (*pl.*) the classes, the estates.
Standarte [ʃtanˈdartə], *f.* (—, *pl.* —n) standard, banner.
Standbild [ˈʃtantbɪlt], *n.* (—(e)s, *pl.* —er) statue.
Ständchen [ˈʃtɛntçən], *n.* (—s, *pl.* —) serenade; *einem ein — bringen*, serenade s.o.
Ständehaus [ˈʃtɛndəhaus], *n.* (—es, *pl.* ¨er) state assembly-hall.
Ständer [ˈʃtɛndər], *m.* (—s, *pl.* —) stand, pedestal; post; (upright) desk.
Standesamt [ˈʃtandəsamt], *n.* (—s, *pl.* ¨er) registry office.
Standesbeamte [ˈʃtandəsbəamtə], *m.* (—n, *pl.* —n) registrar (of births, marriages and deaths).
Standesbewußtsein [ˈʃtandəsbəvustzaɪn], *n.* (—s, *no pl.*) class-feeling, class-consciousness.
Standesperson [ˈʃtandəspɛrzo:n], *f.* (—, *pl.* —en) person of rank.
Standgericht [ˈʃtantgərɪçt], *n.* (—es, *pl.* —e) court-martial; summary court of justice.
standhaft [ˈʃtanthaft], *adj.* constant, firm, steadfast.
standhalten [ˈʃtanthaltən], *v.n. irr.* bear up, stand o.'s ground, withstand, resist.
ständig [ˈʃtɛndɪç], *adj.* permanent.
ständisch [ˈʃtɛndɪʃ], *adj.* relating to the estates (of the realm).
Standort [ˈʃtantɔrt], *m.* (—s, *pl.* —e) location; station.
Standpauke [ˈʃtantpaukə], *f.* (—, *pl.* —n) (*coll.*) harangue; severe reprimand.
Standpunkt [ˈʃtantpuŋkt], *m.* (—(e)s, *pl.* —e) standpoint; point of view; *den — vertreten*, take the line; *einem den — klar machen*, give s.o. a piece of o.'s mind.
Standrecht [ˈʃtantrɛçt], *n.* (—(e)s, *no pl.*) martial law.
Standuhr [ˈʃtantu:r], *f.* (—, *pl.* —en) grandfather-clock.
Stange [ˈʃtaŋə], *f.* (—, *pl.* —n) stick, pole; *bei der — bleiben*, stick to the point, persevere.
Stank [ʃtaŋk], *m.* (—s, *no pl.*) (*dial.*) stench; discord, trouble.
Stänker [ˈʃtɛŋkər], *m.* (—s, *pl.* —) (*coll.*) mischief-maker, quarrelsome person.
stänkern [ˈʃtɛŋkərn], *v.n.* pick quarrels; ferret about, make trouble.
Stanniol [ʃtaˈnjo:l], *n.* (—s, *no pl.*) tinfoil.
stanzen [ˈʃtantsən], *v.a.* punch, stamp.
Stapel [ˈʃta:pəl], *m.* (—s, *pl.* —) pile, heap; (*Naut.*) slipway; *ein Schiff vom — lassen*, launch a ship.
Stapellauf [ˈʃta:pəllauf], *m.* (—s, *pl.* ¨e) (*Naut.*) launch, launching.
stapeln [ˈʃta:pəln], *v.a.* pile up.
Stapelnahrung [ˈʃta:pəlna:ruŋ], *f.* (—, *no pl.*) staple diet.
Stapelplatz [ˈʃta:pəlplats], *m.* (—es, *pl.* ¨e) mart, emporium.
Stapelware [ˈʃta:pəlva:rə], *f.* (—, *pl.* —n) staple goods.
Stapfen [ˈʃtapfən], *m.* or *f. pl.* footsteps.
Star (1) [ʃta:r], *m.* (—(e)s, *pl.* —e) (*Med.*) cataract; *einem den — stechen*, operate for cataract; (*fig.*) open s.o's eyes.
Star (2) [ʃta:r], *m.* (—(e)s, *pl.* —en) (*Orn.*) starling.
stark [ʃtark], *adj.* strong, stout; robust; vigorous; heavy; considerable; *—er Esser*, hearty eater. — *adv.* very much.

Stärke ['ʃtɛrkə], *f.* (—, *no pl.*) strength, vigour, robustness; strong point; starch.
Stärkekleister ['ʃtɛrkəklaɪstər], *m.* (—**s**, *no pl.*) starch-paste.
Stärkemehl ['ʃtɛrkəme:l], *n.* (—**s**, *no pl.*) starch-flour.
stärken ['ʃtɛrkən], *v.a.* strengthen; corroborate; starch. — *v.r. sich* —, take some refreshment.
stärkend ['ʃtɛrkənt], *adj.* strengthening, restorative; —*es Mittel*, tonic.
starkleibig ['ʃtarklaɪbɪç], *adj.* corpulent, stout, obese.
Stärkung ['ʃtɛrkuŋ], *f.* (—, *pl.* —**en**) strengthening, invigoration; refreshment.
starr [ʃtar], *adj.* stiff, rigid; fixed; inflexible; stubborn; *einen — ansehen*, stare at s.o.
starren ['ʃtarən], *v.n.* stare.
Starrheit ['ʃtarhaɪt], *f.* (—, *no pl.*) stiffness, rigidity; fixedness; inflexibility; stubbornness.
starrköpfig ['ʃtarkœpfɪç], *adj.* headstrong, stubborn, obstinate, pigheaded.
Starrkrampf ['ʃtarkrampf], *m.* (—(**e**)**s**, *no pl.*) (*Med.*) tetanus.
Starrsinn ['ʃtarzɪn], *m.* (—**s**, *no pl.*) stubbornness, obstinacy.
Station [ʃta'tsjo:n], *f.* (—, *pl.* —**en**) (*Railw.*) station; (*main*) terminus; stop, stopping-place; (*hospital*) ward; *freie* —, board and lodging found.
stationär [ʃtatsjo'nɛ:r], *adj.* stationary.
stationieren [ʃtatsjo'ni:rən], *v.a.* station.
Stationsvorsteher [ʃtat'sjo:nsfɔrʃte:ər], *m.* (—**s**, *pl.* —) station-master.
statisch ['ʃta:tɪʃ], *adj.* static.
Statist [ʃta'tɪst], *m.* (—**en**, *pl.* —**en**) (*Theat.*) extra, walking-on part; (*pl.*) supers.
Statistik [ʃta'tɪstɪk], *f.* (—, *pl.* —**en**) statistics.
Statistiker [ʃta'tɪstɪkər], *m.* (—**s**, *pl.* —) statistician.
Stativ [ʃta'ti:f], *n.* (—**s**, *pl.* —**e**) stand, tripod.
Statt [ʃtat], *f.* (—, *no pl.*) place, stead; *an seiner* —, in his place.
statt [ʃtat], *prep.* (*Genit.*) instead of, in lieu of.
Stätte ['ʃtɛtə], *f.* (—, *pl.* —**n**) place, abode.
stattfinden ['ʃtatfɪndən], *v.n. irr.* take place.
stattgeben ['ʃtatge:bən], *v.n. irr. einer Bitte* —, grant a request.
statthaft ['ʃtathaft], *adj.* admissible, allowable, lawful.
Statthalter ['ʃtathaltər], *m.* (—**s**, *pl.* —) governor.
stattlich ['ʃtatlɪç], *adj.* stately, handsome, distinguished, comely; portly; considerable; *eine* —*e Summe*, a tidy sum.
statuieren [ʃtatu'i:rən], *v.a.* decree; *ein Exempel* —, make an example of.
Statut [ʃta'tu:t], *n.* (—**s**, *pl.* —**en**) statute, regulation.
Staub [ʃtaup], *m.* (—(**e**)**s**, *no pl.*) dust, powder; *sich aus dem — machen*, take French leave; abscond.
Stäubchen ['ʃtɔypçən], *n.* (—**s**, *pl.* —) mote, particle of dust.
stauben ['ʃtaubən], *v.n. es staubt*, it is dusty.
Staubgefäß ['ʃtaupgəfɛ:s], *n.* (—**es**, *pl.* —**e**) stamen.
staubig ['ʃtaubɪç], *adj.* dusty.
Staubkamm ['ʃtaupkam], *m.* (—**s**, *pl.* ¨—**e**) fine-tooth comb.
Staublappen ['ʃtauplapən], *m.* (—**s**, *pl.* —) duster.
Staubmantel ['ʃtaupmantəl], *m.* (—**s**, *pl.* ¨—) overall, smock; dust(er)coat, (*Am.*) duster.
Staubsauger ['ʃtaupzaugər], *m.* (—**s**, *pl.* —) vacuum cleaner.
Staubtuch ['ʃtauptu:x], *n.* (—**es**, *pl.* ¨—**er**) duster.
Staubwedel ['ʃtaupve:dəl], *m.* (—**s**, *pl.* —) feather duster.
Staubwolke ['ʃtaupvɔlkə], *f.* (—, *pl.* —**n**) cloud of dust.
Staubzucker ['ʃtauptsukər], *m.* (—**s**, *no pl.*) castor-sugar, icing-sugar.
Staudamm ['ʃtaudam], *m.* (—**s**, *pl.* ¨—**e**) dam, dyke.
Staude ['ʃtaudə], *f.* (—, *pl.* —**n**) shrub, bush.
stauen ['ʃtauən], *v.a.* stow; (*water*) dam. — *v.r. sich* —, be congested.
staunen ['ʃtaunən], *v.n.* be astonished, be surprised, wonder (at).
Staupe ['ʃtaupə], *f.* (—, *pl.* —**n**) (*animals*) distemper.
stäupen ['ʃtɔypən], *v.a.* (*obs.*) scourge, flog.
Stauung ['ʃtauuŋ], *f.* (—, *pl.* —**en**) stowage; (*water*) damming-up, swell, rising; (*blood*) congestion; (*traffic*) jam, build-up.
stechen ['ʃtɛçən], *v.a. irr.* prick, sting; stab; (*cards*) trump.
stechend ['ʃtɛçənt], *adj.* pungent, biting.
Stechmücke ['ʃtɛçmykə], *f.* (—, *pl.* —**n**) (*Ent.*) gnat, mosquito.
Stechpalme ['ʃtɛçpalmə], *f.* (—, *pl.* —**n**) (*Bot.*) holly.
Steckbrief ['ʃtɛkbri:f], *m.* (—**s**, *pl.* —**e**) warrant (for arrest).
stecken ['ʃtɛkən], *v.a.* stick into, put, place, fix; (*plants*) set, plant; *in Brand* —, set on fire, set fire to. — *v.n. irgendwo* —, be about somewhere; — *bleiben*, get stuck, break down; *er steckt dahinter*, he is at the bottom of it. — *v.r. sich hinter einen* —, shelter behind s.o.
Stecken ['ʃtɛkən], *m.* (—**s**, *pl.* —) stick, staff.
Stecker ['ʃtɛkər], *m.* (—**s**, *pl.* —) (*Elec.*) plug.
Steckkontakt ['ʃtɛkkɔntakt], *m.* (—(**e**)**s**, *pl.* —**e**) (*Elec.*) plug, point.
Stecknadel ['ʃtɛkna:dəl], *f.* (—, *pl.* —**n**) pin.
Steg [ʃte:k], *m.* (—(**e**)**s**, *pl.* —**e**) plank, foot-bridge; jetty; (*violin*) bridge.

Stegreif [ˈʃteːkraɪf], *m.* (—**s**, *pl.* —**e**) (*obs.*) stirrup; *aus dem — sprechen*, extemporise, improvise.
stehen [ˈʃteːən], *v.n. irr.* stand; be; stand still; *einem gut* —, fit *or* suit s.o. well; *mit einem gut* —, be on good terms with s.o.; *gut* —, be in a fair way, look promising; *was steht zu Diensten?* what can I do for you? — *bleiben*, stand still, stop, pull up.
stehlen [ˈʃteːlən], *v.a. irr.* steal.
Steiermark [ˈʃtaɪərmark], *f.* Styria.
steif [ʃtaɪf], *adj.* stiff; (*grog*) strong; awkward; ceremonious, punctilious, formal. — *adv. etwas — und fest behaupten*, swear by all that's holy.
steifen [ˈʃtaɪfən], *v.a.* stiffen, starch.
Steifheit [ˈʃtaɪfhaɪt], *f.* (—, *no pl.*) stiffness; (*fig.*) formality.
Steifleinen [ˈʃtaɪflaɪnən], *n.* (—**s**, *no pl.*) buckram.
Steig [ʃtaɪk], *m.* (—(**e**)**s**, *pl.* —**e**) path, (mountain) track.
Steigbügel [ˈʃtaɪkbyːgəl], *m.* (—**s**, *pl.* —) stirrup.
Steigen [ˈʃtaɪgən], *n.* (—**s**, *no pl.*) rising, increase; (*price*) advance, rise; *im* —, on the increase.
steigen [ˈʃtaɪgən], *v.n. irr.* (*aux.* sein) climb, mount, ascend; (*barometer*) rise; (*population*) increase; (*horse*) rear; (*price*) advance, rise.
Steiger [ˈʃtaɪgər], *m.* (—**s**, *pl.* —) climber, mountaineer; mining-surveyor, overseer.
steigern [ˈʃtaɪgərn], *v.a.* (*price*) raise; (*fig.*) enhance, increase. — *v.r. sich* —, increase.
Steigerung [ˈʃtaɪgəruŋ], *f.* (—, *pl.* —**en**) raising; (*fig.*) enhancement; increase; (*Gram.*) comparison.
Steigung [ˈʃtaɪguŋ], *f.* (—, *pl.* —**en**) gradient.
steil [ʃtaɪl], *adj.* steep.
Stein [ʃtaɪn], *m.* (—(**e**)**s**, *pl.* —**e**) stone, rock; flint; jewel, gem; monument; (*Chess*) piece, chessman; (*Draughts*) man; (*fruit*) stone, kernel; — *des Anstoßes*, stumbling block; *mir fällt ein — vom Herzen*, it is a load off my mind; *bei einem einen — im Brett haben*, be in s.o.'s good books; *einem —e in den Weg legen*, put obstacles in s.o.'s way; *der — des Weisen*, the philosopher's stone.
Steinadler [ˈʃtaɪnaːdlər], *m.* (—**s**, *pl.* —) (*Orn.*) golden eagle.
steinalt [ˈʃtaɪnalt], *adj.* very old.
Steinbock [ˈʃtaɪnbɔk], *m.* (—**s**, *pl.* ⸚**e**) ibex; (*Astrol.*) Capricorn.
Steinbruch [ˈʃtaɪnbrux], *m.* (—**s**, *pl.* ⸚**e**) stone-pit, quarry.
Steinbutt [ˈʃtaɪnbut], *m.* (—**s**, *pl.* —**e**) (*Zool.*) turbot.
Steindruck [ˈʃtaɪndruk], *m.* (—**s**, *no pl.*) lithography.
steinern [ˈʃtaɪnərn], *adj.* stony; built of stone.
Steingut [ˈʃtaɪnguːt], *n.* (—**s**, *no pl.*) earthenware, stoneware, pottery.
Steinhagel [ˈʃtaɪnhaːgəl], *m.* (—**s**, *no pl.*) shower of stones.
Steinhaue [ˈʃtaɪnhauə], *f.* (—, *pl.* —**n**) pickaxe.
Steinhügel [ˈʃtaɪnhyːgəl], *m.* (—**s**, *pl.* —) cairn.
steinig [ˈʃtaɪnɪç], *adj.* stony, rocky.
steinigen [ˈʃtaɪnɪgən], *v.a.* stone.
Steinkalk [ˈʃtaɪnkalk], *m.* (—**s**, *no pl.*) quicklime.
Steinkohle [ˈʃtaɪnkoːlə], *f.* (—, *no pl.*) pit-coal.
Steinkrug [ˈʃtaɪnkruːk], *m.* (—**s**, *pl.* ⸚**e**) stone jar.
Steinmarder [ˈʃtaɪnmardər], *m.* (—**s**, *pl.* —) (*Zool.*) stone-marten.
Steinmetz [ˈʃtaɪnmɛts], *m.* (—**es**, *pl.* —**e**) stone-cutter, stone-mason.
Steinobst [ˈʃtaɪnoːpst], *n.* (—**es**, *no pl.*) stone-fruit.
Steinplatte [ˈʃtaɪnplatə], *f.* (—, *pl.* —**n**) slab, flagstone.
steinreich [ˈʃtaɪnraɪç], *adj.* as rich as Croesus.
Steinsalz [ˈʃtaɪnzalts], *n.* (—**es**, *no pl.*) rock-salt, mineral-salt.
Steinwurf [ˈʃtaɪnvurf], *m.* (—**s**, *pl.* ⸚**e**) *einen — entfernt*, within a stone's throw.
Steiß [ʃtaɪs], *m.* (—**es**, *pl.* —**e**) rump; (*coll.*) buttocks, posterior.
Stellage [ʃtɛˈlaːʒə], *f.* (—, *pl.* —**n**) stand, frame.
Stelldichein [ˈʃtɛldɪçaɪn], *n.* (—**s**, *no pl.*) assignation, rendezvous, tryst; (*coll.*) date.
Stelle [ˈʃtɛlə], *f.* (—, *pl.* —**n**) place, spot; job, position; situation; (*book*) passage; figure, digit; department; *offene* —, vacancy; *auf der* —, at once, immediately; *an deiner* —, if I were you; *nicht von der — kommen*, remain stationary; *zur — sein*, be at hand.
stellen [ˈʃtɛlən], *v.a.* put, place, set; *richtig* —, regulate, correct, amend; (*clock*) set right; *seinen Mann* —, play o.'s part, pull o.'s weight. — *v.r. sich* —, come forward; pretend; *sich krank* —, feign illness, malinger, pretend to be ill.
Stellenbewerber [ˈʃtɛlənbəvɛrbər], *m.* (—**s**, *pl.* —) applicant (for a job).
Stellengesuch [ˈʃtɛləngəzuːx], *n.* (—**s**, *pl.* —**e**) application (for a job).
Stellenvermittlung [ˈʃtɛlənfɛrmɪtluŋ], *f.* (—, *pl.* —**en**) employment office, employment exchange.
stellenweise [ˈʃtɛlənvaɪzə], *adv.* in parts, here and there.
Stellmacher [ˈʃtɛlmaxər], *m.* (—**s**, *pl.* —) wheelwright.
Stellung [ˈʃtɛluŋ], *f.* (—, *pl.* —**en**) position, posture; attitude; situation; job; (*Mil.*) trenches; — *nehmen zu*, express o.'s views on.
Stellvertreter [ˈʃtɛlfɛrtreːtər], *m.* (—**s**, *pl.* —) representative, deputy; substitute, supply, proxy, relief; (*doctor*) locum.
Stelzbein [ˈʃtɛltsbaɪn], *n.* (—**s**, *pl.* —**e**) wooden leg.

Stemmeisen ['ʃtɛmaɪzən], *n.* (—**s**, *pl.* —) crowbar.
stemmen ['ʃtɛmən], *v.a.* (*water*) stem, dam; (*weight*) lift. — *v.r. sich — gegen*, resist fiercely.
Stempel ['ʃtɛmpəl], *m.* (—**s**, *pl.* —) stamp, rubber-stamp, die; pounder; (*Bot.*) pistil.
Stempelgebühr ['ʃtɛmpəlgəby:r], *f.* (—, *pl.* —**en**) stamp-duty.
stempeln ['ʃtɛmpəln], *v.a.* stamp, hallmark; brand; cancel (*postage stamp*). — *v.n.* (*coll.*) — *gehen*, be on the dole.
Stengel ['ʃtɛŋəl], *m.* (—**s**, *pl.* —) stalk.
Stenografie [ʃtenogra'fi:], *f.* (—, *no pl.*) stenography, shorthand.
stenografisch [ʃteno'gra:fɪʃ], *adj.* in shorthand.
Stenogramm [ʃteno'gram], *n.* (—**s**, *pl.* —**e**) shorthand-note.
Stenotypistin [ʃtɛnoty'pɪstɪn], *f.* (—, *pl.* —**nen**) shorthand-typist.
Stephan ['ʃtɛfan], *m.* Stephen.
Steppdecke ['ʃtɛpdɛkə], *f.* (—, *pl.* —**n**) quilt.
Steppe ['ʃtɛpə], *f.* (—, *pl.* —**n**) steppe.
steppen ['ʃtɛpən], *v.a.* stitch, quilt.
Sterbeglocke ['ʃtɛrbəglɔkə], *f.* (—, *pl.* —**n**) passing bell, death bell.
Sterbehemd ['ʃtɛrbəhɛmt], *n.* (—(**e**)**s**, *pl.* —**en**) shroud, winding-sheet.
sterben ['ʃtɛrbən], *v.n. irr.* (*aux.* **sein**) die.
Sterbenswörtchen ['ʃtɛrbənsvœrtçən], *n.* (—**s**, *pl.* —) *nicht ein* —, not a syllable.
Sterbesakramente['ʃtɛrbəzakramɛntə], *n. pl.* (*Eccl.*) last sacraments, last rites.
sterblich ['ʃtɛrplɪç], *adj.* mortal; — *verliebt*, desperately in love.
Sterblichkeit ['ʃtɛrplɪçkaɪt], *f.* (—, *no pl.*) mortality.
stereotyp [stereo'ty:p], *adj.* stereotyped.
sterilisieren [sterili'zi:rən], *v.a.* sterilise.
Sterilität [sterili'tɛ:t], *f.* (—, *no pl.*) sterility.
Stern [ʃtɛrn], *m.* (—(**e**)**s**, *pl.* —**e**) star; (*Typ.*) asterisk.
Sternbild ['ʃtɛrnbɪlt], *n.* (—**s**, *pl.* —**er**) constellation.
Sterndeuter ['ʃtɛrndɔytər], *m.* (—**s**, *pl.* —) astrologer.
Sterndeutung ['ʃtɛrndɔytuŋ], *f.* (—, *no pl.*) astrology.
Sternenschimmer ['ʃtɛrnənʃɪmər], *m.* (—**s**, *no pl.*) starlight.
sternförmig ['ʃtɛrnfœrmɪç], *adj.* star-like, star-shaped.
Sterngucker ['ʃtɛrngukər], *m.* (—**s**, *pl.* —) stargazer.
sternhagelvoll ['ʃtɛrnha:gəlfɔl], *adj.* (*coll.*) as drunk as a lord.
Sternkunde ['ʃtɛrnkundə], *f.* (—, *no pl.*) astronomy.
Sternkundige ['ʃtɛrnkundɪgə], *m.* (—**n**, *pl.* —**n**) astronomer.
Sternschnuppe ['ʃtɛrnʃnupə], *f.* (—, *pl.* —**n**) falling star, shooting star, meteorite.
Sternwarte ['ʃtɛrnvartə], *f.* (—, *pl.* —**n**) observatory.
stetig ['ʃte:tɪç], *adj.* continual, continuous, constant.
stets [ʃte:ts], *adv.* always, ever, continually.
Steuer (1) ['ʃtɔyər], *n.* (—**s**, *pl.* —) rudder, helm, steering wheel.
Steuer (2) ['ʃtɔyər], *f.* (—, *pl.* —**n**) tax; (*local*) rate; (*import*) customs duty.
Steueramt ['ʃtɔyəramt], *n.* (—**s**, *pl.* ¨—**er**) inland revenue office, tax office.
Steuerbeamte ['ʃtɔyərbəamtə], *m.* (—**n**, *pl.* —**n**) revenue officer, tax collector.
Steuerbord ['ʃtɔyərbɔrt], *n.* (—**s**, *no pl.*) starboard.
Steuereinnehmer ['ʃtɔyəraɪnne:mər], *m.* (—**s**, *pl.* —) tax collector.
steuerfrei ['ʃtɔyərfraɪ], *adj.* duty-free, exempt from taxes.
Steuerhinterziehung ['ʃtɔyərhɪntərtsi:uŋ], *f.* (—, *pl.* —**en**) tax evasion.
steuerlos ['ʃtɔyərlo:s], *adj.* rudderless, adrift.
Steuermann ['ʃtɔyərman], *m.* (—**s**, *pl.* ¨—**er**) mate; helmsman.
steuern ['ʃtɔyərn], *v.a.* steer; *einem Unheil* —, avoid *or* steer clear of an evil.
steuerpflichtig ['ʃtɔyərpflɪçtɪç], *adj.* taxable, liable to tax, dutiable.
Steuerrad ['ʃtɔyərra:t], *n.* (—**s**, *pl.* ¨—**er**) steering-wheel.
Steuerung ['ʃtɔyəruŋ], *f.* (—, *no pl.*) steering, controls.
Steuerveranlagung ['ʃtɔyərfɛranla:guŋ], *f.* (—, *pl.* —**en**) tax-assessment.
stibitzen [ʃti'bɪtsən], *v.a.* (*coll.*) pilfer, filch.
Stich [ʃtɪç], *m.* (—(**e**)**s**, *pl.* —**e**) sting; prick; stitch; stab; (*Cards*) trick; (*Art*) engraving; *einen im — lassen*, leave s.o. in the lurch.
Stichel ['ʃtɪçəl], *m.* (—**s**, *pl.* —) (*Art*) graver.
Stichelei [ʃtɪçə'laɪ], *f.* (—, *pl.* —**en**) taunt, sneer, gibe.
sticheln ['ʃtɪçəln], *v.a.* taunt, nag.
stichhaltig ['ʃtɪçhaltɪç], *adj.* valid, sound.
Stichhaltigkeit ['ʃtɪçhaltɪçkaɪt], *f.* (—, *no pl.*) validity, cogency.
Stichprobe ['ʃtɪçpro:bə], *f.* (—, *pl.* —**n**) sample taken at random, sampling.
Stichwahl ['ʃtɪçva:l], *f.* (—, *pl.* —**en**) second ballot.
Stichwort ['ʃtɪçvɔrt], *n.* (—**s**, *pl.* —**e**) key-word; (*Theat.*) cue.
sticken ['ʃtɪkən], *v.a.*, *v.n.* embroider.
Stickerei [ʃtɪkə'raɪ], *f.* (—, *pl.* —**en**) embroidery.
Stickgarn ['ʃtɪkgarn], *n.* (—**s**, *pl.* —**e**) embroidery cotton *or* silk.
Stickhusten ['ʃtɪkhu:stən], *m.* (—**s**, *no pl.*) choking cough.

stickig [ˈʃtɪkɪç], *adj.* stuffy.
Stickmuster [ˈʃtɪkmustər], *n.* (—s, *pl.* —) embroidery-pattern.
Stickstoff [ˈʃtɪkʃtɔf], *m.* (—(e)s, *no pl.*) nitrogen.
stieben [ˈʃtiːbən], *v.n.* (*aux.* sein) scatter, spray; *auseinander* —, disperse.
Stiefbruder [ˈʃtiːfbruːdər], *m.* (—s, *pl.* ¨) step-brother.
Stiefel [ˈʃtiːfəl], *m.* (—s, *pl.* —) boot.
Stiefelknecht [ˈʃtiːfəlknɛçt], *m.* (—(e)s, *pl.* —e) boot-jack.
Stiefelputzer [ˈʃtiːfəlputsər], *m.* (—s, *pl.* —) shoe-black; (*Am.*) shoe-shine; (*hotel*) boots.
Stiefeltern [ˈʃtiːfɛltern], *pl.* step-parents.
Stiefmütterchen [ˈʃtiːfmytərçən], *n.* (—s, *pl.* —) (*Bot.*) pansy.
stiefmütterlich [ˈʃtiːfmytərlɪç], *adj.* like a stepmother; niggardly.
Stiefsohn [ˈʃtiːfzoːn], *m.* (—s, *pl.* ¨e) stepson.
Stiege [ˈʃtiːgə], *f.* (—, *pl.* —n) staircase.
Stieglitz [ˈʃtiːglɪts], *m.* (—es, *pl.* —e) goldfinch.
Stiel [ʃtiːl], *m.* (—(e)s, *pl.* —e) handle; (*plant*) stalk.
Stier [ʃtiːr], *m.* (—(e)s, *pl.* —e) bull; *junger* —, bullock; (*Astrol.*) Taurus.
stieren [ˈʃtiːrən], *v.n.* stare (at), goggle.
Stift (1) [ʃtɪft], *m.* (—(e)s, *pl.* —e) tack, pin, peg; pencil; (*coll.*) apprentice; young chap.
Stift (2) [ʃtɪft], *n.* (—(e)s, *pl.* —e) charitable *or* religious foundation.
stiften [ˈʃtɪftən], *v.a.* establish, give, donate; found, set on foot, originate; *Frieden* —, bring about peace.
Stifter [ˈʃtɪftər], *m.* (—s, *pl.* —) founder, originator, donor.
Stiftung [ˈʃtɪftuŋ], *f.* (—, *pl.* —en) establishment, foundation; institution; charitable foundation; endowment, donation.
Stil [ʃtiːl], *m.* (—(e)s, *pl.* —e) style; (*fig.*) manner.
stilisieren [ʃtiːliˈziːrən], *v.a.* word, draft.
Stilistik [ʃtiːˈlɪstɪk], *f.* (—, *no pl.*) art of composition.
stilistisch [ʃtiːˈlɪstɪʃ], *adj.* stylistic.
still [ʃtɪl], *adj.* quiet, still, silent; calm; —*er Teilhaber*, sleeping partner; *im —en*, secretly, on the sly.
Stille [ˈʃtɪlə], *f.* (—, *no pl.*) silence, quietness, tranquillity; calm, calmness; *in der* —, silently; *in der — der Nacht*, at dead of night.
stillen [ˈʃtɪlən], *v.a.* allay; (*blood*) staunch; (*baby*) suckle, feed, nurse; (*thirst*) quench; (*hunger*) appease.
stillos [ˈʃtiːlloːs], *adj.* incongruous; in bad taste.
Stillung [ˈʃtɪluŋ], *f.* (—, *no pl.*) allaying; (*blood*) staunching; (*baby*) suckling, feeding, nursing; (*thirst*) quenching; (*hunger*) appeasing.
stilvoll [ˈʃtiːlfɔl], *adj.* harmonious; stylish; in good taste.
Stimmband [ˈʃtɪmbant], *n.* (—s, *pl.* ¨er) vocal chord.
stimmberechtigt [ˈʃtɪmbərɛçtɪçt], *adj.* entitled to vote, enfranchised.
Stimmbruch [ˈʃtɪmbrux], *m.* (—s, *no pl.*) breaking of the voice.
Stimme [ˈʃtɪmə], *f.* (—, *pl.* —n) voice; (*election*) vote, suffrage; *die — abgeben*, vote.
stimmen [ˈʃtɪmən], *v.a.* (*piano*) tune; *einen günstig* —, dispose s.o. favourably towards s.th. — *v.n.* agree, tally (with), square (with), accord (with); vote.
Stimmeneinheit [ˈʃtɪmənaɪnhaɪt], *f.* (—, *no pl.*) unanimity.
Stimmengleichheit [ˈʃtɪmənglaɪçhaɪt], *f.* (—, *no pl.*) equality of votes, tie.
Stimmer [ˈʃtɪmər], *m.* (—s, *pl.* —) (*piano*) tuner.
Stimmführer [ˈʃtɪmfyːrər], *m.* (—s, *pl.* —) leader, spokesman.
Stimmgabel [ˈʃtɪmgaːbəl], *f.* (—, *pl.* —n) tuning fork.
stimmhaft [ˈʃtɪmhaft], *adj.* (*Phonet.*) voiced.
Stimmlage [ˈʃtɪmlaːgə], *f.* (—, *pl.* —n) (*Mus.*) register.
stimmlos [ˈʃtɪmloːs], *adj.* voiceless; (*Phonet.*) unvoiced.
Stimmrecht [ˈʃtɪmrɛçt], *n.* (—s, *no pl.*) suffrage, right to vote; *allgemeines* —, universal suffrage.
Stimmung [ˈʃtɪmuŋ], *f.* (—, *no pl.*) tuning; (*fig.*) disposition, humour, mood; atmosphere; *in guter* —, in high spirits, *in gedrückter* —, in low spirits.
stimmungsvoll [ˈʃtɪmuŋsfɔl], *adj.* impressive, full of atmosphere.
Stimmwechsel [ˈʃtɪmvɛksəl], *m.* (—s, *no pl.*) breaking of the voice.
Stimmzettel [ˈʃtɪmtsɛtəl], *m.* (—s, *pl.* —) ballot-paper.
stinken [ˈʃtɪŋkən], *v.n. irr.* stink, reek, smell.
Stinktier [ˈʃtɪŋktiːr], *n.* (—s, *pl.* —e) (*Zool.*) skunk.
Stipendium [ʃtiˈpɛndjum], *n.* (—s, *pl.* —dien) scholarship.
Stirn [ʃtɪrn], *f.* (—, *pl.* —en) forehead, brow; *die — runzeln*, frown, knit o.'s brow; *die — haben zu*, have the cheek to; *einem die — bieten*, face s.o., defy s.o.
Stirnhöhle [ˈʃtɪrnhøːlə], *f.* (—, *pl.* —en) frontal cavity.
Stirnseite [ˈʃtɪrnzaɪtə], *f.* (—, *pl.* —n) front.
stöbern [ˈʃtøːbərn], *v.n.* rummage about; (*snow*) drift.
stochern [ˈʃtɔxərn], *v.a.*, *v.n.* (*food*) pick (at); (*teeth*) pick.
Stock (1) [ʃtɔk], *m.* (—(e)s, *pl.* ¨e) stick, cane, walking-stick; *über — und Stein*, over hedges and ditches.
Stock (2) [ʃtɔk], *m.* (—es, *pl.* —werke) storey, floor.

stocken [ˈʃtɔkən], *v.n.* stop; (*blood*) run cold; (*linen*) go mildewed; hesitate, falter; (*conversation*) flag.

stockfinster [ˈʃtɔkfɪnstər], *adj.* pitch dark.

Stockfisch [ˈʃtɔkfɪʃ], *m.* (—**es**, *pl.* —**e**) dried cod; dried fish.

stöckisch [ˈʃtœkɪʃ], *adj.* obstinate, stubborn.

Stockrose [ˈʃtɔkro:zə], *f.* (—, *pl.* —**n**) (*Bot.*) hollyhock.

Stockschnupfen [ˈʃtɔkʃnupfən], *m.* (—**s**, *no pl.*) heavy *or* chronic cold.

stocksteif [ˈʃtɔkʃtaɪf], *adj.* stiff as a poker.

stockstill [ˈʃtɔkʃtɪl], *adj.* quite still, stock-still.

stocktaub [ˈʃtɔktaup], *adj.* deaf as a post.

Stockung [ˈʃtɔkuŋ], *f.* (—, *pl.* —**en**) stagnation; hesitation; block, blockage; stopping, standstill.

Stockwerk [ˈʃtɔkvɛrk], *n.* (—**s**, *pl.* —**e**) storey, floor.

Stoff [ʃtɔf], *m.* (—(**e**)**s**, *pl.* —**e**) fabric, material; substance; subject matter.

Stoffwechsel [ˈʃtɔfvɛksəl], *m.* (—**s**, *no pl.*) metabolism.

stöhnen [ˈʃtø:nən], *v.n.* groan, moan.

Stoiker [ˈsto:ɪkər], *m.* (—**s**, *pl.* —) stoic.

Stola [ˈsto:la:], *f.* (—, *pl.* —**len**) (*Eccl.*) stole.

Stollen [ˈʃtɔlən], *m.* (—**s**, *pl.* —) fruitcake; (*Min.*) gallery, adit.

stolpern [ˈʃtɔlpərn], *v.n.* (*aux.* sein) stumble, trip.

Stolz [ʃtɔlts], *m.* (—**es**, *no pl.*) haughtiness, pride.

stolz [ʃtɔlts], *adj.* haughty, proud; stuck-up, conceited; (*fig.*) majestic.

stolzieren [ʃtɔlˈtsi:rən], *v.n.* (*aux.* sein) strut; prance.

stopfen [ˈʃtɔpfən], *v.a.* stuff; fill; darn, mend; *einem den Mund* —, cut s.o. short.

Stopfgarn [ˈʃtɔpfgarn], *n.* (—**s**, *pl.* —**e**) darning-thread.

Stoppel [ˈʃtɔpəl], *f.* (—, *pl.* —**n**) stubble.

stoppeln [ˈʃtɔpəln], *v.a.* glean; *etwas zusammen* —, compile s.th. badly.

Stöpsel [ˈʃtœpsəl], *m.* (—**s**, *pl.* —) stopper, cork; *kleiner* —, little mite.

stöpseln [ˈʃtœpsəln], *v.a.* cork.

Stör [ʃtø:r], *m.* (—(**e**)**s**, *pl.* —**e**) (*Zool.*) sturgeon.

Storch [ʃtɔrç], *m.* (—(**e**)**s**, *pl.* ⸚**e**) (*Orn.*) stork.

Storchschnabel [ˈʃtɔrçʃna:bəl], *m.* (—**s**, *pl.* ⸚) stork's bill; (*Tech.*) pantograph.

stören [ˈʃtø:rən], *v.a.* disturb, trouble; (*Rad.*) jam. — *v.n.* intrude, be in the way.

Störenfried [ˈʃtø:rənfri:d], *m.* (—**s**, *pl.* —**e**) intruder, mischief-maker, nuisance.

Störer [ˈʃtø:rər], *m.* (—**s**, *pl.* —) disturber.

stornieren [stɔrˈni:rən], *v.a.* cancel, annul.

störrisch [ˈʃtœrɪʃ], *adj.* stubborn obstinate.

Störung [ˈʃtø:ruŋ], *f.* (—, *pl.* —**en**) disturbance, intrusion; (*Rad.*) jamming.

Stoß [ʃto:s], *m.* (—**es**, *pl.* ⸚**e**) push, thrust; impact; blow, stroke, jolt; (*papers*) heap, pile; (*documents*) bundle.

Stoßdegen [ˈʃto:sde:gən], *m.* (—**s**, *pl.* —) rapier.

Stößel [ˈʃtø:səl], *m.* (—**s**, *pl.* —) pestle; (*Motor.*) tappet.

stoßen [ˈʃto:sən], *v.a. irr.* thrust, push; pound; *vor den Kopf* —, offend. — *v.n.* bump, jolt; — *an*, border upon; *auf etwas* —, come across s.th., stumble on s.th.; *ins Horn* —, blow a horn. — *v.r. sich* —, hurt o.s.; *sich an etwas* —, take offence at s.th., take exception to s.th.

Stoßseufzer [ˈʃto:szɔyftsər], *m.* (—**s**, *pl.* —) deep sigh.

Stoßwaffe [ˈʃto:svafə], *f.* (—, *pl.* —**n**) thrusting *or* stabbing weapon.

stoßweise [ˈʃto:svaɪzə], *adv.* by fits and starts.

Stotterer [ˈʃtɔtərər], *m.* (—**s**, *pl.* —) stutterer, stammerer.

stottern [ˈʃtɔtərn], *v.n.* stutter, stammer.

stracks [ʃtraks], *adv.* straight away, directly.

Strafanstalt [ˈʃtra:fanʃtalt], *f.* (—, *pl.* —**en**) penitentiary, prison.

Strafarbeit [ˈʃtra:farbaɪt], *f.* (—, *pl.* —**en**) (*Sch.*) imposition.

strafbar [ˈʃtra:fba:r], *adj.* punishable, criminal, culpable.

Strafbarkeit [ˈʃtra:fba:rkaɪt], *f.* (—, *no pl.*) culpability.

Strafe [ˈʃtra:fə], *f.* (—, *pl.* —**n**) punishment; (*money*) fine, penalty; *bei* — *von*, on pain of.

strafen [ˈʃtra:fən], *v.a.* punish, rebuke; (*money*) fine.

Straferlaß [ˈʃtra:fərlas], *m.* (—**sses**, *pl.* —**sse**) remission of penalty, amnesty.

straff [ʃtraf], *adj.* tight, tense, taut.

Strafgericht [ˈʃtra:fgərɪçt], *n.* (—**es**, *no pl.*) punishment; judgment; (*Law*) Criminal Court.

Strafgesetzbuch [ˈʃtra:fgəzɛtsbu:x], *n.* (—(**e**)**s**, *pl.* ⸚**er**) penal code.

sträflich [ˈʃtrɛ:flɪç], *adj.* punishable; culpable; reprehensible, blameworthy.

Sträfling [ˈʃtrɛ:flɪŋ], *m.* (—**s**, *pl.* —**e**) convict.

Strafporto [ˈʃtra:fpɔrto], *n.* (—**s**, *pl.* —**ti**) excess postage.

Strafpredigt [ˈʃtra:fpredɪçt], *f.* (—, *pl.* —**en**) severe admonition, stern reprimand.

Strafprozess [ˈʃtra:fprotsɛs], *m.* (—**es**, *pl.* —**e**) criminal proceedings.

Strafrecht [ˈʃtra:frɛçt], *n.* (—(**e**)**s**, *no pl.*) criminal law.

Strafverfahren [ˈʃtra:ffɛrfa:rən], *n.* (—**s**, *pl.* —) criminal procedure.

Strahl [ʃtra:l], *m.* (—(e)s, *pl.* —en) beam, ray; (*water etc.*) jet, spout; (*lightning*) flash; —*en werfen*, emit rays.
Strahlantrieb ['ʃtra:lantri:p], *m.* (—s, *no pl.*) (*Aviat.*) jet propulsion.
strahlen ['ʃtra:lən], *v.n.* radiate, shine, beam, emit rays; (*fig.*) beam (with joy).
strählen ['ʃtrɛ:lən], *v.a.* (*rare*) comb.
Strahlenbrechung ['ʃtra:lənbrɛçuŋ], *f.* (—, *pl.* —en) refraction.
strahlenförmig ['ʃtra:lənfœrmɪç], *adj.* radiate.
Strahlenkrone ['ʃtra:lənkro:nə], *f.* (—, *pl.* —n) aureole, halo.
Strahlung ['ʃtra:luŋ], *f.* (—, *pl.* —en) radiation; (*fig.*) radiance.
Strähne ['ʃtrɛ:nə], *f.* (—, *pl.* —n) skein, hank; *eine — Pech*, a spell of bad luck.
Stramin [ʃtra'mi:n], *m.* (—s, *pl.* —e) embroidery canvas.
stramm [ʃtram], *adj.* tight; rigid; sturdy, strapping.
strampeln ['ʃtrampəln], *v.n.* struggle; (*baby*) kick.
Strand [ʃtrant], *m.* (—(e)s, *pl.* —e) shore, beach, strand.
stranden ['ʃtrandən], *v.n.* be stranded, founder.
Strandkorb ['ʃtrantkɔrp], *m.* (—s, *pl.* ⸚e) beach-chair.
Strandwache ['ʃtrantvaxə], *f.* (—, *no pl.*) coast-guard.
Strang [ʃtraŋ], *m.* (—(e)s, *pl.* ⸚e) rope, cord; *über die ⸚e schlagen*, kick over the traces; *zum — verurteilen*, condemn to be hanged.
strangulieren [ʃtraŋgu'li:rən], *v.a.* strangle.
Strapaze [ʃtra'patsə], *f.* (—, *pl.* —n) over-exertion, fatigue, hardship.
strapazieren [ʃtrapa'tsi:rən], *v.a.* over-exert, fatigue.
strapaziös [ʃtrapa'tsjø:s], *adj.* fatiguing, exacting.
Straße ['ʃtra:sə], *f.* (—, *pl.* —n) (*city*) street; (*country*) road, highway; (*sea*) strait; *auf der* —, in the street; *über die — gehen*, cross the street.
Straßenbahn ['ʃtra:sənba:n], *f.* (—, *pl.* —en) tram; tramcar, (*Am.*) street-car.
Straßendamm ['ʃtra:səndam], *m.* (—s, *pl.* ⸚e) roadway.
Straßendirne ['ʃtra:səndɪrnə], *f.* (—, *pl.* —n) prostitute, street-walker.
Straßenfeger ['ʃtra:sənfe:gər], *m.* (—s, *pl.* —) roadman, road-sweeper, scavenger, crossing-sweeper.
Straßenpflaster ['ʃtra:sənpflastər], *n.* (—s, *no pl.*) pavement.
Straßenraub ['ʃtra:sənraup], *m.* (—s, *no pl.*) highway-robbery.
Stratege [ʃtra'te:gə], *m.* (—n, *pl.* —n) strategist.
sträuben ['ʃtrɔybən], *v.r. sich* —, bristle; (*fig.*) struggle (against), oppose.
Strauch [ʃtraux], *m.* (—(e)s, *pl.* ⸚er) bush, shrub.
straucheln ['ʃtrauxəln], *v.n.* (*aux.* sein) stumble.
Strauchritter ['ʃtrauxrɪtər], *m.* (—s, *pl.* —) footpad, vagabond, highwayman.
Strauß (1) [ʃtraus], *m.* (—es, *pl.* ⸚e) (*Poet.*) fight, tussle; (*flowers*) bunch, bouquet, nosegay.
Strauß (2) [ʃtraus], *m.* (—es, *pl.* —e) (*Orn.*) ostrich.
Sträußchen ['ʃtrɔysçən], *n.* (—s, *pl.* —) small bunch of flowers, nosegay.
Straußfeder ['ʃtrausfe:dər], *f.* (—, *pl.* —n) ostrich-feather.
Strazze ['ʃtratsə], *f.* (—, *pl.* —n) scrapbook.
Strebe ['ʃtre:bə], *f.* (—, *pl.* —n) buttress, prop, stay.
Strebebogen ['ʃtre:bəbo:gən], *m.* (—s, *pl.* —) (*Archit.*) arch, buttress; flying buttress.
Streben ['ʃtre:bən], *n.* (—s, *no pl.*) ambition, aspiration; effort, endeavour, striving.
streben ['ʃtre:bən], *v.n.* strive, aspire, endeavour.
Streber ['ʃtre:bər], *m.* (—s, *pl.* —) pushing person, (social) climber. (*Am. coll.*) go-getter.
strebsam ['ʃtre:pza:m], *adj.* ambitious, assiduous, industrious.
streckbar ['ʃtrɛkba:r], *adj.* ductile, extensible.
Streckbett ['ʃtrɛkbɛt], *n.* (—s, *pl.* —en) orthopaedic bed.
Strecke ['ʃtrɛkə], *f.* (—, *pl.* —n) stretch, reach, extent; distance; tract; line; *zur — bringen*, (*Hunt.*) bag, run to earth.
strecken ['ʃtrɛkən], *v.a.* stretch, extend; (*metal*) hammer out, roll; make (s.th.) last; *die Waffen* —, lay down arms.
Streich [ʃtraɪç], *m.* (—(e)s, *pl.* —e) stroke, blow; (*fig.*) prank; trick; *dummer* —, piece of folly, lark.
streicheln ['ʃtraɪçəln], *v.a.* stroke, caress.
streichen ['ʃtraɪçən], *v.a. irr.* stroke, touch; paint, spread; cancel; strike; (*sail*) lower. — *v.n.* move past, fly past; wander.
Streichholz ['ʃtraɪçhɔlts], *n.* (—es, *pl.* ⸚er) match.
Streichinstrument ['ʃtraɪçɪnstrumɛnt], *n.* (—s, *pl.* —e) stringed instrument.
Streif [ʃtraɪf], *m.* (—(e)s, *pl.* —e) stripe, strip, streak.
Streifband ['ʃtraɪfbant], *n.* (—s, *pl.* ⸚er) wrapper.
Streifblick ['ʃtraɪfblɪk], *m.* (—s, *pl.* —e) glance.
Streife ['ʃtraɪfə], *f.* (—, *pl.* —n) raid; patrol (*police etc*).
Streifen ['ʃtraɪfən], *m.* (—s, *pl.* —) stripe, streak; (*Mil.*) bar.

streifen ['ʃtraɪfən], *v.a.* graze, touch in passing; take off (*remove*). — *v.n.* (*aux.* sein) ramble, roam, rove.
streifig ['ʃtraɪfɪç], *adj.* striped, streaky.
Streik [ʃtraɪk], *m.* (—(e)s, *pl.* —s) strike; *in den — treten*, go on strike.
Streikbrecher ['ʃtraɪkbrɛçər], *m.* (—s, *pl.* —) blackleg.
streiken ['ʃtraɪkən], *v.n.* (*workers*) strike, be on strike.
Streit [ʃtraɪt], *m.* (—(e)s, *pl.* —e) dispute, quarrel, conflict; (*words*) argument; *einen — anfangen*, pick a quarrel.
Streitaxt ['ʃtraɪtakst], *f.* (—, *pl.* ¨e) battle-axe.
streitbar ['ʃtraɪtba:r], *adj.* warlike, martial.
streiten ['ʃtraɪtən], *v.n. irr.* quarrel, fight; *—de Kirche*, Church Militant.
Streitfrage ['ʃtraɪtfra:gə], *f.* (—, *pl.* —n) moot point, point at issue; controversy.
Streithammel ['ʃtraɪthaməl], *m.* (—s, *pl.* —) squabbler.
Streithandel ['ʃtraɪthandəl], *m.* (—s, *pl.* ¨) law-suit.
streitig ['ʃtraɪtɪç], *adj.* disputable, doubtful, at issue; *einem etwas — machen*, contest s.o.'s right to s.th.
Streitkräfte ['ʃtraɪtkrɛftə], *f. pl.* (*Mil.*) forces.
streitlustig ['ʃtraɪtlustɪç], *adj.* argumentative.
Streitschrift ['ʃtraɪtʃrɪft], *f.* (—, *pl.* —en) pamphlet, polemical treatise.
Streitsucht ['ʃtraɪtzuxt], *f.* (—, *no pl.*) quarrelsomeness; (*Law*) litigiousness.
streitsüchtig ['ʃtraɪtzyçtɪç], *adj.* quarrelsome, litigious.
streng [ʃtrɛŋ], *adj.* severe, strict, rigorous; *—e Kälte*, biting cold; *im —sten Winter*, in the depth of winter. — *adv. —genommen*, strictly speaking.
Strenge ['ʃtrɛŋə], *f.* (—, *no pl.*) severity, rigour.
strenggläubig ['ʃtrɛŋglɔybɪç], *adj.* strictly orthodox.
Streu [ʃtrɔy], *f.* (—, *pl.* —en) litter, bed of straw.
Streubüchse ['ʃtrɔybyksə], *f.* (—, *pl.* —n) castor.
streuen ['ʃtrɔyən], *v.a.* strew, scatter, sprinkle.
streunen ['ʃtrɔynən], *v.n.* roam (about).
Streuung ['ʃtrɔyuŋ], *f.* (—, *pl.* —en) strewing; (*shot*) dispersion.
Streuzucker ['ʃtrɔytsukər], *m.* (—s, *no pl.*) castor-sugar.
Strich [ʃtrɪç], *m.* (—(e)s, *pl.* —e) stroke, line, dash; (*land*) tract; (*Art*) touch; region; *gegen den —*, against the grain; *einem einen — durch die Rechnung machen*, put a spoke in s.o.'s wheel, frustrate s.o.
Strichpunkt ['ʃtrɪçpuŋkt], *m.* (—s, *pl.* —e) semicolon.
Strichregen ['ʃtrɪçre:gən], *m.* (—s. *pl.* —) passing shower.
Strick [ʃtrɪk], *m.* (—(e)s, *pl.* —e) cord, line, rope; *du —*, (*fig.*) you scamp! *einem einen — drehen*, give s.o. enough rope to hang himself, lay a trap for s.o.
stricken ['ʃtrɪkən], *v.a.*, *v.n.* knit.
Strickerei [ʃtrɪkə'raɪ], *f.* (—, *pl.* —en) knitting; knitting business, workshop.
Strickleiter ['ʃtrɪklaɪtər], *f.* (—, *pl.* —n) rope-ladder.
Strickzeug ['ʃtrɪktsɔyk], *n.* (—s, *pl.* —e) knitting.
Striegel ['ʃtri:gəl], *m.* (—s, *pl.* —) curry-comb.
striegeln ['ʃtri:gəln], *v.a.* curry.
Strieme ['ʃtri:mə], *f.* (—, *pl.* —n) weal, stripe.
Strippe ['ʃtrɪpə], *f.* (—, *pl.* —n) strap, band, string; cord.
strittig ['ʃtrɪtɪç], *adj.* contentious, debatable.
Stroh [ʃtro:], *n.* (—s, *no pl.*) straw; (*roof*) thatch; *mit — decken*, thatch; *leeres — dreschen*, beat the air.
Strohfeuer ['ʃtro:fɔyər], *n.* (—s, *no pl.*) (*fig.*) flash in the pan; short-lived enthusiasm.
Strohhalm ['ʃtro:halm], *m.* (—s, *pl.* —e) straw.
Strohhut ['ʃtro:hu:t], *m.* (—s, *pl.* ¨e) straw-hat.
Strohkopf ['ʃtro:kɔpf], *m.* (—(e)s, *pl.* ¨e) (*coll.*) stupid person.
Strohmann ['ʃtro:man], *m.* (—s, *pl.* ¨er) (*coll.*) man of straw; (*Cards*) dummy.
Strohmatte ['ʃtro:matə], *f.* (—, *pl.* —n) straw-mat.
Strohwitwe ['ʃtro:vɪtvə], *f.* (—, *pl.* —n) grass-widow.
Strolch [ʃtrɔlç], *m.* (—(e)s, *pl.* —e) vagabond; (*fig.*) scamp.
Strom [ʃtro:m], *m.* (—(e)s, *pl.* ¨e) river, torrent; (*also fig.*) flood; stream; (*also Elec.*) current; (*coll.*) electricity; *gegen den — schwimmen*, swim against the current, be an individualist.
stromab ['ʃtro:map], *adv.* downstream.
stromauf ['ʃtro:mauf], *adv.* upstream.
strömen ['ʃtrø:mən], *v.n.* (*aux.* sein) flow, stream; (*rain*) pour; (*people*) flock.
Stromer ['ʃtro:mər], *m.* (—s, *pl.* —) vagabond, tramp, vagrant.
Stromkreis ['ʃtro:mkraɪs], *m.* (—es, *pl.* —e) (*Elec.*) circuit.
Stromschnelle ['ʃtro:mʃnɛlə], *f.* (—, *pl.* —n) rapids.
Strömung ['ʃtrø:muŋ], *f.* (—, *pl.* —en) current; (*fig.*) tendency.
Strophe ['ʃtro:fə], *f.* (—, *pl.* —n) verse, stanza.
strotzen ['ʃtrɔtsən], *v.n.* be puffed up; overflow, burst, teem.
strotzend ['ʃtrɔtsənt], *adj. vor Gesundheit —*, bursting with health.
Strudel ['ʃtru:dəl], *m.* (—s, *pl.* —) whirl, whirlpool, vortex, eddy; pastry.
Struktur [ʃtruk'tu:r], *f.* (—, *pl.* —en) structure.

Strumpf [ʃtrumpf], *m.* (—(e)s, *pl.* ⸚e) stocking; (*short*) sock.
Strumpfband ['ʃtrumpfbant], *n.* (—(e)s, *pl.* ⸚er) garter.
Strumpfwaren ['ʃtrumpfva:rən], *f. pl.* hosiery.
Strumpfwirker ['ʃtrumpfvɪrkər], *m.* (—s, *pl.* —) stocking-weaver.
Strunk [ʃtruŋk], *m.* (—(e)s, *pl.* ⸚e) (*tree*) stump, trunk; (*plant*) stalk.
struppig ['ʃtrupɪç], *adj.* rough, unkempt, frowsy.
Stube ['ʃtu:bə], *f.* (—, *pl.* —n) room, chamber; *gute* —, sitting-room.
Stubenarrest ['ʃtu:bənarɛst], *m.* (—s, *pl.* —e) confinement to quarters.
Stubenhocker ['ʃtu:bənhɔkər], *m.* (—s, *pl.* —) stay-at-home.
Stubenmädchen ['ʃtu:bənmɛ:tçən], *n.* (—s, *pl.* —) housemaid.
Stuck [ʃtuk], *m.* (—(e)s, *no pl.*) stucco, plaster.
Stück [ʃtyk], *n.* (—(e)s, *pl.* —e) piece; part; lump; (*Theat.*) play; *aus freien —en*, of o.'s own accord; *große —e auf einen halten*, think highly of s.o.
Stückarbeit ['ʃtykarbaɪt], *f.* (—, *pl.* —en) piece-work.
Stückchen ['ʃtykçən], *n.* (—s, *pl.* —) small piece, morsel, bit.
stückeln ['ʃtykəln], *v.a.* cut in(to) pieces; patch, mend.
stückweise ['ʃtykvaɪzə], *adv.* piecemeal.
Stückwerk ['ʃtykvɛrk], *n.* (—s, *no pl.*) (*fig.*) patchy *or* imperfect work, a bungled job.
Stückzucker ['ʃtyktsukər], *m.* (—s, *no pl.*) lump sugar.
Student [ʃtu'dɛnt], *m.* (—en, *pl.* —en) (*Univ.*) student, undergraduate.
studentenhaft [ʃtu'dɛntənhaft], *adj.* student-like.
Studentenverbindung [ʃtu'dɛntənfɛrbɪnduŋ], *f.* (—, *pl.* —en) students' association *or* union.
Studie ['ʃtu:dje], *f.* (—, *pl.* —n) study, (*Art*) sketch; (*Lit.*) essay; (*pl.*) studies.
Studienplan ['ʃtu:djənpla:n], *m.* (—s, *pl.* ⸚e) curriculum.
Studienrat ['ʃtu:djənra:t], *m.* (—s, *pl.* ⸚e) grammar school teacher, assistant master.
studieren [ʃtu'di:rən], *v.a., v.n.* study, read (a subject); be at (the) university.
studiert [ʃtu'di:rt], *adj.* educated; (*fig.*) affected, deliberate, studied.
Studierte [ʃtu'di:rtə], *m.* (*coll.*) egghead.
Studium ['ʃtu:djum], *n.* (—s,) *pl.* —dien study, pursuit; university education.
Stufe ['ʃtu:fə], *f.* (—, *pl.* —n) step; (*fig.*) degree; *auf gleicher — mit*, on a level with.
stufenweise ['ʃtu:fənvaɪzə], *adv.* gradually, by degrees.
Stuhl [ʃtu:l], *m.* (—s, *pl.* ⸚e) chair, seat; *der Heilige* —, the Holy See.
Stuhlgang ['ʃtu:lgaŋ], *m.* (—s, *no pl.*) (*Med.*) stool, evacuation (of the bowels), movement, motion.
Stukkatur [ʃtuka'tu:r], *f.* (—, *no pl.*) stucco-work.
Stulle ['ʃtulə], *f.* (—, *pl.* —n) (*dial.*) slice of bread and butter.
Stulpe ['ʃtulpə], *f.* (—, *pl.* —n) cuff.
stülpen ['ʃtylpən], *v.a.* turn up, invert.
Stulpnase ['ʃtulpna:zə], *f.* (—, *pl.* —n) turned-up nose, pug-nose.
Stulpstiefel ['ʃtulpʃti:fəl], *m.* (—s, *pl.* —) top-boot.
stumm [ʃtum], *adj.* mute, dumb, silent.
Stumme ['ʃtumə], *m.* & *f.* (—n, *pl.* —n) dumb person, mute.
Stummel ['ʃtuməl], *m.* (—s, *pl.* —) stump; (*cigarette*) end, butt.
Stummheit ['ʃtumhaɪt], *f.* (—, *no pl.*) dumbness.
Stümper ['ʃtympər], *m.* (—s, *pl.* —) bungler, botcher.
stümperhaft ['ʃtympərhaft], *adj.* bungling, botchy.
stümpern ['ʃtympərn], *v.a., v.n.* bungle, botch.
Stumpf [ʃtumpf], *m.* (—(e)s, *pl.* ⸚e) stump, trunk; *mit — und Stiel ausrotten*, destroy root and branch.
stumpf [ʃtumpf], *adj.* blunt; (*angle*) obtuse; (*fig.*) dull; — *machen*, blunt, dull.
Stumpfsinn ['ʃtumpfzɪn], *m.* (—s, *no pl.*) stupidity, dullness.
stumpfwinklig ['ʃtumpfvɪŋklɪç], *adj.* obtuse-angled.
Stunde ['ʃtundə], *f.* (—, *pl.* —n) hour; lesson.
stunden ['ʃtundən], *v.a.* give a respite, allow time (to pay up).
Stundenglas ['ʃtundənglas], *n.* (—es, *pl.* ⸚er) hour-glass.
Stundenplan ['ʃtundənpla:n], *m.* (—s, *pl.* ⸚e) (*Sch.*) schedule.
Stundenzeiger ['ʃtundəntsaɪgər], *m.* (—s, *pl.* —) hour-hand.
Stündlein ['ʃtyntlaɪn], *n.* (—s, *pl.* —) *sein — hat geschlagen*, his last hour has come.
Stundung ['ʃtunduŋ], *f.* (—, *pl.* —en) respite, grace.
stupend [ʃtu'pɛnt], *adj.* stupendous.
stur [ʃtu:r], *adj.* obdurate, unwavering, stolid, dour, stubborn.
Sturm [ʃturm], *m.* (—(e)s, *pl.* ⸚e) storm, gale, tempest, hurricane; (*Mil.*) attack, assault; — *und Drang*, (*Lit.*) Storm and Stress; — *im Wasserglas*, storm in a teacup; — *laufen gegen*, storm against.
Sturmband ['ʃturmbant], *n.* (—s, *pl.* ⸚er) chinstrap.
Sturmbock ['ʃturmbɔk], *m.* (—s, *pl.* ⸚e) battering-ram.
stürmen ['ʃtyrmən], *v.a.* storm, take by assault. — *v.n.* be violent, be stormy; (*Mil.*) advance.
Stürmer ['ʃtyrmər], *m.* (—s, *pl.* —) assailant; (*football*) centre-forward.
Sturmglocke ['ʃturmglɔkə], *f.* (—, *pl.* —n) tocsin, alarm-bell.

Sturmhaube ['ʃturmhaubə], *f.* (—, *pl.* —**en**) (*Mil.*) morion, helmet.
stürmisch ['ʃtyrmɪʃ], *adj.* stormy, tempestuous; (*fig.*) boisterous, turbulent, tumultuous, impetuous; —*er Beifall*, frantic applause; —*e Überfahrt*, rough crossing.
Sturmschritt ['ʃturmʃrɪt], *m.* (—**s**, *no pl.*) double march.
Sturmvogel ['ʃturmfo:gəl], *m.* (—**s**, *pl.* ⸚) (*Orn.*) stormy petrel.
Sturz [ʃturts], *m.* (—**es**, *pl.* ⸚**e**) fall, tumble; crash; collapse; (*Comm.*) failure, smash; (*government*) overthrow.
Sturzacker ['ʃturtsakər], *m.* (—**s**, *pl.* ⸚) freshly ploughed field.
Sturzbach ['ʃturtsbax], *m.* (—(**e**)**s**, *pl.* ⸚**e**) torrent.
Stürze ['ʃtyrtsə], *f.* (—, *pl.* —**n**) pot-lid, cover.
stürzen ['ʃtyrtsən], *v.a.* hurl, overthrow; ruin. — *v.n.* (*aux.* sein) (*person*) have a fall; (*object*) tumble down; (*business*) fail; crash; plunge; (*water*) rush. — *v.r.* throw oneself; *sich — auf*, rush at, plunge into.
Sturzhelm ['ʃturtshɛlm], *m.* (—**s**, *pl.* —**e**) crash-helmet.
Sturzsee ['ʃturtsze:], *f.* (—, *no pl.*) heavy sea.
Sturzwelle ['ʃturtsvɛlə], *f.* (—, *pl.* —**n**) breaker, roller.
Stute ['ʃtu:tə], *f.* (—, *pl.* —**n**) mare.
Stutzbart ['ʃtutsba:rt], *m.* (—**s**, *pl.* ⸚**e**) short beard.
Stütze ['ʃtytsə], *f.* (—, *pl.* —**n**) prop, support, stay.
Stutzen ['ʃtutsən], *m.* (—**s**, *pl.* —) short rifle, carbine.
stutzen ['ʃtutsən], *v.a.* (*hair*) clip, trim; (*horse*) dock, crop; (*tree*) prune, lop. — *v.n.* be taken aback, hesitate.
stützen ['ʃtytsən], *v.a.* prop, support; base *or* found (on). — *v.r. sich — auf*, lean upon; (*fig.*) rely upon.
Stutzer ['ʃtutsər], *m.* (—**s**, *pl.* —) dandy, fop, beau.
stutzerhaft ['ʃtutsərhaft], *adj.* dandified.
stutzig ['ʃtutsɪç], *adj.* startled, puzzled; — *werden*, be non-plussed, be taken aback *or* puzzled.
Stützmauer ['ʃtytsmauər], *f.* (—, *pl.* —**n**) buttress, retaining wall.
Stützpunkt ['ʃtytspuŋkt], *m.* (—**s**, *pl.* —**e**) point of support; foothold; (*Mil.*) base; (*Tech.*) fulcrum.
Subjekt [zup'jɛkt], *n.* (—**s**, *pl.* —**e**) subject; (*fig.*) creature.
subjektiv [zupjɛk'ti:f], *adj.* subjective, personal, prejudiced.
sublimieren [zubli'mi:rən], *v.a.* sublimate.
Substantiv [zupstan'ti:f], *n.* (—(**e**)**s**, *pl.* —**e**) (*Gram.*) substantive, noun.
subtil [zup'ti:l], *adj.* subtle.
subtrahieren [zuptra'hi:rən], *v.a.* subtract.
Subvention [zupvɛn'tsjo:n], *f.* (—, *pl.* —**en**) subsidy, grant-in-aid.
Suche ['zu:xə], *f.* (—, *no pl.*) search, quest; *auf der — nach*, in quest of.
suchen ['zu:xən], *v.a., v.n.* seek, look for; attempt, endeavour.
Sucht [zuxt], *f.* (—, *pl.* ⸚**e**) mania, addiction, passion.
süchtig ['zyxtɪç], *adj.* addicted (to).
Sud [zu:d], *m.* (—(**e**)**s**, *pl.* —**e**) boiling, brewing; suds.
Sudan ['zu:dan], *m.* the Sudan.
sudeln ['zu:dəln], *v.a., v.n.* smear, daub, make a mess (of).
Süden ['zy:dən], *m.* (—**s**, *no pl.*) south.
Südfrüchte ['zy:tfryçtə], *f. pl.* Mediterranean *or* tropical fruit.
südlich ['zy:tlɪç], *adj.* southern, southerly; *in —er Richtung*, southward.
Südosten [zy:t'ɔstən], *m.* (—**s**, *no pl.*) south-east.
Suff [zuf], *m.* (—(**e**)**s**, *no pl.*) (*sl.*) boozing, tippling.
suggerieren [zugɛ'ri:rən], *v.a.* suggest.
Sühne ['zy:nə], *f.* (—, *no pl.*) expiation, atonement.
sühnen ['zy:nən], *v.a.* expiate, atone for.
Sühneopfer ['zy:nəɔpfər], *n.* (—**s**, *pl.* —) expiatory sacrifice; atonement.
Suite ['svi:tə], *f.* (—, *pl.* —**n**) retinue, train.
sukzessiv [zuktsɛ'si:f], *adj.* gradual, successive.
Sülze ['zyltsə], *f.* (—, *pl.* —**n**) brawn, aspic, jelly.
Summa [zu'ma:], *f.* (—, *pl.* **Summen**) — *summarum*, sum total.
summarisch [zu'ma:rɪʃ], *adj.* summary.
Summe ['zumə], *f.* (—, *pl.* —**n**) sum, amount.
summen ['zumən], *v.a.* hum. — *v.n.* buzz, hum.
summieren [zu'mi:rən], *v.a.* sum up, add up. — *v.r. sich —*, mount up.
Sumpf [zumpf], *m.* (—(**e**)**s**, *pl.* ⸚**e**) bog, morass, marsh, moor, swamp.
sumpfig ['zumpfɪç], *adj.* boggy, marshy.
Sund [zunt], *m.* (—(**e**)**s**, *pl.* —**e**) straits, sound.
Sünde ['zyndə], *f.* (—, *pl.* —**n**) sin.
Sündenbock ['zyndənbɔk], *m.* (—**s**, *pl.* ⸚**e**) scapegoat.
Sündenfall ['zyndənfal], *m.* (—**s**, *no pl.*) (*Theol.*) the Fall (*of man*).
Sündengeld ['zyndəngɛlt], *n.* (—(**e**)**s**, *no pl.*) ill-gotten gains; (*coll.*) vast sum of money.
sündenlos ['zyndənlo:s], *adj.* sinless, impeccable.
Sündenpfuhl ['zyndənpfu:l], *m.* (—**s**, *pl.* —**e**) sink of iniquity.
Sünder ['zyndər], *m.* (—**s**, *pl.* —) sinner; *armer* —, poor devil; *du alter* —, you old scoundrel.
sündhaft ['zynthaft], *adj.* sinful, iniquitous.
sündig ['zyndɪç], *adj.* sinful.
sündigen ['zyndɪgən], *v.n.* sin, err.
Sündigkeit ['zyndɪçkait], *f.* (—, *no pl.*) sinfulness.
Superlativ ['zu:pərlati:f], *m.* (—**s**, *pl.* —**e**) superlative (degree).

Suppe ['zupə], *f.* (—, *pl.* —**n**) soup; *eingebrannte* —, thick soup; *einem edi — versalzen*, spoil s.o.'s little game.
Suppenfleisch ['zupənflaɪʃ], *n.* (—**es**, *no pl.*) stock-meat.
Suppenkelle ['zupənkɛlə], *f.* (—, *pl.* —**n**) soup ladle.
Suppenterrine ['zupəntɛri:nə], *f.* (—, *pl.* —**n**) tureen.
Surrogat [zuro'ga:t], *n.* (—**s**, *pl.* —**e**) substitute.
süß [zy:s], *adj.* sweet.
Süße ['zy:sə], *f.* (—, *no pl.*) sweetness.
süßen ['zy:sən], *v.a.* sweeten.
Süßholz ['zy:shɔlts], *n.* (—**es**, *no pl.*) liquorice; — *raspeln*, talk sweet nothings, pay compliments.
Süßigkeit ['zy:sɪçkaɪt], *f.* (—, *pl.* —**en**) sweetness; (*pl.*) sweets.
süßlich ['zy:slɪç], *adj.* sweetish; (*fig.*) fulsome, mawkish, cloying.
Süßspeise ['zy:sʃpaɪzə], *f.* (—, *pl.* —**n**) dessert.
Süßwasser ['zy:svasər], *n.* (—**s**, *no pl.*) fresh water.
Symbolik [zym'bo:lɪk], *f.* (—, *no pl.*) symbolism.
symbolisch [zym'bo:lɪʃ], *adj.* symbolic(al).
symbolisieren [zymbɔlɪ'zi:rən], *v.a.* symbolize.
symmetrisch [zy'me:trɪʃ], *adj.* symmetrical.
Sympathie [zympa'ti:], *f.* (—, *no pl.*) sympathy.
sympathisch [zym'pa:tɪʃ], *adj.* congenial, likeable.
Synagoge [zyna'go:gə], *f.* (—, *pl.* —**n**) synagogue.
synchronisieren [zynkroni'zi:rən], *v.a.* synchronise.
Syndikus ['zyndikus], *m.* (—, *pl.* **Syndizi**) syndic.
Synode [zy'no:də], *f.* (—, *pl.* —**n**) synod.
synthetisch [zyn'te:tɪʃ], *adj.* synthetic.
Syrien [zy:rjən], *n.* Syria.
systematisch [zyste'ma:tɪʃ], *adj.* systematic(al).
Szenarium [stse'na:rjum], *n.* (—**s**, *pl.* —**rien**) scenario, stage, scene.
Szene ['stse:nə], *f.* (—, *pl.* —**n**) scene; *in — setzen*, stage, produce; (*coll.*) get up; *sich in — setzen*, show off.
Szenerie [stsenə'ri:], *f.* (—, *pl.* —**n**) scenery.
szenisch ['stse:nɪʃ], *adj.* scenic.
Szepter ['stsɛptər], *n.* (—**s**, *pl.* —) sceptre, mace.

T

T [te:], *n.* (—, *pl.* —) the letter T.
Tabak ['ta:bak], *m.* (—**s**, *pl.* —**e**) tobacco.
Tabaksbeutel ['ta:baksbɔytəl], *m.* (—**s**, *pl.* —) tobacco-pouch.
Tabatiere [ta:ba'tjɛ:rə], *f.* (—, *pl.* —**n**) snuff-box.
tabellarisch [tabɛ'la:rɪʃ], *adj.* in tables, tabular.
Tabelle [ta'bɛlə], *f.* (—, *pl.* —**n**) table, index, schedule.
Tablett [ta'blɛt], *n.* (—**s**, *pl.* —**s**) tray.
Tablette [ta'blɛtə], *f.* (—, *pl.* —**n**) tablet, pill.
Tabulatur [tabula'tu:r], *f.* (—, *pl.* —**en**) tablature, tabling, index.
Tadel ['ta:dəl], *m.* (—**s**, *pl.* —) blame, censure, reproach; (*Sch.*) bad mark; *ohne* —, blameless.
tadellos ['ta:dəllo:s], *adj.* blameless, faultless, impeccable.
tadeln ['ta:dəln], *v.a.* blame, censure, find fault with; reprimand.
tadelnswert ['ta:dəlnsve:rt], *adj.* blameworthy, culpable.
Tafel ['ta:fəl], *f.* (—, *pl.* —**n**) board; (*Sch.*) blackboard; slate; (*fig.*) (*obs.*) dinner, banquet; festive fare; (*chocolate*) slab, bar.
Täfelchen ['tɛ:fəlçən], *n.* (—**s**, *pl.* —) tablet.
tafelförmig ['ta:fəlfœrmɪç], *adj.* tabular.
tafeln ['ta:fəln], *v.n.* dine, feast.
täfeln ['tɛ:fəln], *v.a.* wainscot, panel.
Täfelung ['tɛ:fəluŋ], *f.* (—, *pl.* —**en**) wainscoting, panelling.
Taft, Taffet [taft, 'tafət], *m.* (—(**e**)**s**, *pl.* —**e**) taffeta.
Tag [ta:k], *m.* (—(**e**)**s**, *pl.* —**e**) day; (*fig.*) light; *der jüngste* —, Doomsday; *bei —e*, in the daytime, by daylight; *sich etwas bei —e besehen*, examine s.th. in the light of day; — *für* —, day by day; *von — zu* —, from day to day; *dieser —e*, one of these days, shortly; *etwas an den — bringen*, bring s.th. to light; *in den — hinein leben*, live improvidently; — *und Nachtgleiche*, equinox.
Tagbau ['ta:kbau], *m.* (—**s**, *no pl.*) opencast mining.
Tageblatt ['ta:gəblat], *n.* (—**s**, *pl.* ⸚**er**) daily paper.
Tagebuch ['ta:gəbu:x], *n.* (—(**e**)**s**, *pl.* ⸚**er**) diary, journal.
Tagedieb ['ta:gədi:p], *m.* (—(**e**)**s**, *pl.* —**e**) idler, wastrel.
Tagelöhner ['ta:gəlø:nər], *m.* (—**s**, *pl.* —) day-labourer.
tagen ['ta:gən], *v.n.* dawn; (*gathering*) meet; (*Law*) sit.
Tagesanbruch ['ta:gəsanbrux], *m.* (—**s**, *pl.* ⸚**e**) daybreak, dawn.
Tagesbericht ['ta:gəsbərɪçt], *m.* (—(**e**)**s**, *pl.* —**e**) daily report.
Tagesgespräch ['ta:gəsgəʃprɛ:ç], *n.* (—(**e**)**s**, *pl.* —**e**) topic of the day.
Tagesordnung ['ta:gəsɔrdnuŋ], *f.* (—, *pl.* —**en**) agenda.
Tagewerk ['ta:gəvɛrk], *n.* (—**s**, *no pl.*) day's work, daily round.
täglich ['tɛ:klɪç], *adj.* daily.

tagsüber ['ta:ksy:bər], *adv.* in the daytime, during the day.
Taille ['taljə], *f.* (—, *pl.* —n) waist.
takeln ['ta:kəln], *v.a.* tackle, rig.
Takelwerk ['ta:kəlverk], *n.* (—s, *no pl.*) rigging.
Takt (1) [takt], *m.* (—es, *pl.* —e) (*Mus.*) time, measure, bar; — *schlagen*, beat time.
Takt (2) [takt], *m.* (—es, *no pl.*) tact, discretion.
taktfest ['taktfɛst], *adj.* (*Mus.*) good at keeping time; (*fig.*) firm.
taktieren [tak'ti:rən], *v.n.* (*Mus.*) beat time.
Taktik ['taktɪk], *f.* (—, *pl.* —en) tactics.
Taktiker ['taktɪkər], *m.* (—s, *pl.* —) tactician.
taktisch ['taktɪʃ], *adj.* tactical.
taktlos ['taktlo:s], *adj.* tactless.
Taktmesser ['taktmɛsər], *m.* (—s, *pl.* —) metronome.
Taktstock ['taktʃtɔk], *m.* (—s, *pl.* ⸚e) baton.
Tal [ta:l], *n.* (—(e)s, *pl.* ⸚er) valley, dale, glen.
talab [ta:l'ap], *adv.* downhill.
Talar [ta'la:r], *m.* (—s, *pl.* —e) gown.
Talent [ta'lɛnt], *n.* (—(e)s, *pl.* —e) talent, accomplishment, gift.
talentiert [talən'ti:rt], *adj.* talented, gifted, accomplished.
talentvoll [ta'lɛntfɔl], *adj.* talented, gifted, accomplished.
Taler ['ta:lər], *m.* (—s, *pl.* —) old German coin; thaler.
Talfahrt ['ta:lfa:rt], *f.* (—, *pl.* —en) descent.
Talg [talk], *m.* (—(e)s, *no pl.*) tallow.
Talk [talk], *m.* (—(e)s, *no pl.*) talc.
Talkerde ['talke:rdə], *f.* (—, *no pl.*) magnesia.
Talkessel ['ta:lkɛsəl], *m.* (—s, *pl.* —) (*Geog.*) hollow, narrow valley.
Talmulde ['ta:lmuldə], *f.* (—, *pl.* —n) narrow valley, trough.
Talschlucht ['ta:lʃluxt], *f.* (—, *pl.* —en) glen.
Talsohle ['ta:lzo:lə], *f.* (—, *pl.* —n) floor of a valley.
Talsperre ['ta:lʃperə], *f.* (—, *pl.* —n) dam (across valley); barrage.
Tambour ['tambu:r], *m.* (—s, *pl.* —e) drummer.
Tamtam ['tamtam], *n.* (—s, *no pl.*) tom-tom; (*fig.*) palaver.
Tand [tant], *m.* (—(e)s, *no pl.*) knick-knack, trifle; rubbish.
Tändelei [tɛndə'laɪ], *f.* (—, *pl.* —en) trifling, toying; (*fig.*) flirting.
Tändelmarkt ['tɛndəlmarkt], *m.* (—s, *pl.* ⸚e) rag-fair.
tändeln ['tɛndəln], *v.n.* trifle, dally, toy; (*fig.*) flirt.
Tang [taŋ], *m.* (—s, *pl.* —e) (*Bot.*) seaweed.
Tanganjika [taŋga'nji:ka], *n.* Tanganyika.
Tangente [taŋ'gɛntə], *f.* (—, *pl.* —n) tangent.
Tanger ['taŋər], *n.* Tangier.
Tank [taŋk], *m.* (—(e)s, *pl.* —e) tank.
tanken ['taŋkən], *v.n.* refuel; fill up (with petrol).
Tankstelle ['tankʃtɛlə], *f.* (—, *pl.* —n) filling-station.
Tanne ['tanə], *f.* (—, *pl.* —n) (*Bot.*) fir.
Tannenbaum ['tanənbaum], *m.* (—s, *pl.* ⸚e) (*Bot.*) fir-tree.
Tannenholz ['tanənhɔlts], *n.* (—es, *no pl.*) (*timber*) deal.
Tannenzapfen ['tanəntsapfən], *m.* (—s, *pl.* —) (*Bot.*) fir-cone.
Tansania [tanza'ni:a], *n.* Tanzania.
Tante ['tantə], *f.* (—, *pl.* —n) aunt.
Tantieme [tã'tjɛ:mə], *f.* (—, *pl.* —n) royalty, share (in profits), percentage.
Tanz [tants], *m.* (—es, *pl.* ⸚e) dance.
Tanzboden ['tantsbo:dən], *m.* (—s, *pl.* ⸚) ballroom, dance-hall.
tänzeln ['tɛntsəln], *v.n.* skip about, frisk; (*horses*) amble.
tanzen ['tantsən], *v.a., v.n.* dance.
tanzlustig ['tantslustɪç], *adj.* fond of dancing.
Tapet [ta'pe:t], *n.* (—s, *no pl.*) *aufs — bringen*, broach, bring up for discussion.
Tapete [ta'pe:tə], *f.* (—, *pl.* —n) wall-paper.
tapezieren [tapə'tsi:rən], *v.a.* paper.
Tapezierer [tapə'tsi:rər], *m.* (—s, *pl.* —) paperhanger; upholsterer.
tapfer ['tapfər], *adj.* brave, valiant, gallant, courageous.
Tapferkeit ['tapfərkaɪt], *f.* (—, *no pl.*) valour, bravery, gallantry.
Tapisserie [tapsɪə'ri:], *f.* (—, *no pl.*) needlework; tapestry.
tappen ['tapən], *v.n.* grope about.
täppisch ['tɛpɪʃ], *adj.* clumsy, awkward, unwieldy.
tarnen ['tarnən], *v.a.* camouflage.
Tasche ['taʃə], *f.* (—, *pl.* —n) pocket; bag, pouch; *in die — stecken*, pocket; *in die — greifen*, pay, fork out, put o.'s hand in o.'s pocket.
Taschendieb ['taʃəndi:p], *m.* (—(e)s, *pl.* —e) pickpocket; *vor —en wird gewarnt*, beware of pickpockets.
Taschenformat ['taʃənfɔrma:t], *n.* (—s, *no pl.*) pocket-size.
Taschenspieler ['taʃənʃpi:lər], *m.* (—s, *pl.* —) juggler, conjurer.
Taschentuch ['taʃəntu:x], *n.* (—s, *pl.* ⸚er) (pocket-)handkerchief.
Taschenuhr ['taʃənu:r], *f.* (—, *pl.* —en) pocket-watch.
Tasse ['tasə], *f.* (—, *pl.* —n) cup.
Tastatur [tasta'tu:r], *f.* (—, *pl.* —en) keyboard.
Taste ['tastə], *f.* (—, *pl.* —n) (*Mus.*) key.
tasten ['tastən], *v.n.* grope about, feel o.'s way.
Tastsinn ['tastzɪn], *m.* (—s, *no pl.*) sense of touch.

Tat [ta:t], *f.* (—, *pl.* **—en**) deed, act, action; feat, exploit; *in der* —, in fact, indeed; *auf frischer* —, in the very act; *einem mit Rat und* — *beistehen*, give s.o. advice and guidance, help by word and deed.
Tatbestand ['ta:tbəʃtant], *m.* (**—es**, *pl.* **⸚e**) (*Law*) facts of the case.
Tatendrang ['ta:təndraŋ], *m.* (**—(e)s**, *no pl.*) urge for action; impetuosity.
tatenlos ['ta:tənlo:s], *adj.* inactive.
Täter ['tɛ:tər], *m.* (**—s**, *pl.* —) perpetrator, doer; culprit.
tätig ['tɛ:tɪç], *adj.* active, busy.
Tätigkeit ['tɛ:tɪçkaɪt], *f.* (—, *pl.* **—en**) activity.
Tätigkeitswort ['tɛ:tɪçkaɪtsvɔrt], *n.* (**—(e)s**, *pl.* **⸚er**) (*Gram.*) verb.
Tatkraft ['ta:tkraft], *f.* (—, *no pl.*) energy.
tätlich ['tɛ:tlɪç], *adj.* — *werden*, become violent.
tätowieren [tɛ:to'vi:rən], *v.a.* tattoo.
Tatsache ['ta:tzaxə], *f.* (—, *pl.* **—en**) fact, matter of fact.
tatsächlich ['ta:tzɛçlɪç], *adj.* actual. — *excl.* really!
tätscheln ['tɛ:tʃəln], *v.a.* fondle.
Tatterich ['tatərɪç], *m.* (**—s**, *no pl.*) (*coll.*) trembling, shakiness.
Tatze ['tatsə], *f.* (—, *pl.* **—n**) paw.
Tau (1) [tau], *m.* (**—s**, *no pl.*) thaw; dew.
Tau (2) [tau], *n.* (**—s**, *pl.* **—e**) rope, cable.
taub [taup], *adj.* deaf; (*nut*) hollow, empty; — *machen*, deafen; — *sein gegen*, turn a deaf ear to.
Täubchen ['tɔypçən], *n.* (**—s**, *pl.* —) little dove; (*fig.*) sweetheart.
Taube ['taubə], *f.* (—, *pl.* **—n**) (*Orn.*) pigeon, dove.
Taubenschlag ['taubənʃla:k], *m.* (**—s**, *pl.* **⸚e**) dovecote.
Taubenschwanz ['taubənʃvants], *m.* (**—es**, *pl.* **⸚e**) (*Ent.*) hawkmoth.
Tauber ['taubər], *m.* (**—s**, *pl.* —) (*Orn.*) cock-pigeon.
Taubheit ['tauphaɪt], *f.* (—, *no pl.*) deafness.
Taubnessel ['taupnɛsəl], *f.* (—, *pl.* **—n**) (*Bot.*) deadnettle.
taubstumm ['taupʃtum], *adj.* deaf and dumb, deaf-mute.
tauchen ['tauçən], *v.n.* (*aux.* haben *&* sein) dive, plunge. — *v.a.* immerse, dip.
Tauchsieder ['tauçzi:dər], *m.* (**—s**, *pl.* —) (*Elec.*) immersion heater.
tauen ['tauən], *v.a.*, *v.n.* thaw, melt.
Taufbecken ['taufbɛkən], *n.* (**—s**, *pl.* —) (baptismal) font.
Taufe ['taufə], *f.* (—, *pl.* **—n**) baptism, christening; *aus der — heben*, stand godparent.
taufen ['taufən], *v.a.* baptise, christen.
Taufkleid ['taufklaɪt], *n.* (**—s**, *pl.* **—er**) christening robe.
Täufling ['tɔyflɪŋ], *m.* (**—s**, *pl.* **—e**) infant presented for baptism; neophyte.
Taufname ['taufna:mə], *m.* (**—ns**, *pl.* **—n**) Christian name.
Taufpate ['taufpa:tə], *m.* (**—n**, *pl.* **—n**) godfather, godmother.
Taufstein ['taufʃtaɪn], *n.* (**—s**, *pl.* **—e**) (baptismal) font.
taugen ['taugən], *v.n.* be good for, be fit for; *nichts* —, be good for nothing.
Taugenichts ['taugənɪçts], *m.* (—, *pl.* **—e**) ne'er-do-well, scapegrace, good-for-nothing.
tauglich ['tauklɪç], *adj.* able; useful, fit, suitable.
Taumel ['taumәl], *m.* (**—s**, *no pl.*) giddiness, dizziness, staggering; (*fig.*) whirl; ecstasy, frenzy, delirium, intoxication.
taumeln ['tauməln], *v.n.* (*aux.* sein) reel, stagger.
Tausch [tauʃ], *m.* (**—es**, *no pl.*) exchange, barter.
tauschen ['tauʃən], *v.a.* exchange for, barter against, swop; *die Rollen* —, change places.
täuschen ['tɔyʃən], *v.a.* deceive, delude. — *v.r. sich* —, be mistaken.
Tauschhandel ['tauʃhandəl], *m.* (**—s**, *no pl.*) barter.
Tauschmittel ['tauʃmɪtəl], *n.* (**—s**, *pl.* —) medium of exchange.
Täuschung ['tɔyʃuŋ], *f.* (—, *pl.* **—en**) deceit, deception; illusion.
Täuschungsversuch ['tɔyʃuŋsfɛrzu:ç], *m.* (**—es**, *pl.* **—e**) attempt at deception; (*Mil.*) diversion.
tausend ['tauzənt], *num. adj.* a thousand.
tausendjährig ['tauzəntjɛ:rɪç], *adj.* millennial, of a thousand years; *das —e Reich*, the millennium.
Tausendsasa ['tauzəntzasa], *m.* (**—s**, *pl.* —) devil of a fellow.
Tautropfen ['tautrɔpfən], *m.* (**—s**, *pl.* —) dew-drop.
Tauwetter ['tauvɛtər], *n.* (**—s**, *no pl.*) thaw.
Taxameter [taksa'me:tər], *m.* (**—s**, *pl.* —) taximeter.
Taxe ['taksə], *f.* (—, *pl.* **—n**) set rate, tariff; (taxi)cab; *nach der — verkauft werden*, be sold *ad valorem*.
taxieren [tak'si:rən], *v.a.* appraise, value.
Taxus ['taksus,] *m.* (—, *pl.* —) (*Bot.*) yew(-tree).
Technik ['tɛçnɪk], *f.* (—, *pl.* **—en**) technology, engineering; technique; skill, execution.
Techniker ['tɛçnɪkər], *m.* (**—s**, *pl.* —) technician, technical engineer.
Technikum ['tɛçnɪkum], *n.* (**—s**, *pl.* **—s**) technical school, college.
technisch ['tɛçnɪʃ], *adj.* technical; *—er Ausdruck*, technical term; *—e Störung*, technical hitch *or* breakdown.
technologisch [tɛçno'lo:gɪʃ], *adj.* technological.

Techtelmechtel ['tɛçtəlmɛçtəl], *n.* (—s, *pl.* —) (*coll.*) love affair, flirtation.
Tee [te:], *m.* (—s, *no pl.*) tea.
Teedose ['te:do:zə], *f.* (—, *pl.* —n) tea-caddy.
Teekanne ['te:kanə], *f.* (—, *pl.* —n) tea-pot.
Teelöffel ['te:lœfəl], *m.* (—s, *pl.* —) tea-spoon.
Teemaschine ['te:maʃi:nə], *f.* (—, *pl.* —n) tea-urn.
Teer [te:r], *m.* (—(e)s, *no pl.*) tar.
Teerleinwand ['te:rlaɪnvant], *f.* (—, *no pl.*) tarpaulin.
Teerose ['te:ro:zə], *f.* (—, *pl.* —n) (*Bot.*) tea rose.
Teerpappe ['te:rpapə], *f.* (—, *no pl.*) roofing-felt.
teeren ['te:rən], *v.a.* tar.
Teesieb ['te:zi:p], *n.* (—(e)s, *pl.* —e) tea-strainer.
Teich [taɪç], *m.* (—es, *pl.* —e) pond.
Teig [taɪk], *m.* (—(e)s, *pl.* —e) dough, paste.
teigig ['taɪgɪç], *adj.* doughy.
Teigrolle ['taɪkrɔlə], *f.* (—, *pl.* —n) rolling-pin.
Teil [taɪl], *m.* & *n.* (—(e)s, *pl.* —e) part; portion; piece, component; share; *edler* —, vital part; *zum* —, partly; *zu gleichen* —*en*, share and share alike.
teilbar ['taɪlba:r], *adj.* divisible.
Teilchen ['taɪlçən], *n.* (—s, *pl.* —) particle.
teilen ['taɪlən], *v.a.* divide; share; partition off. — *v.r. sich* —, share in; (*road*) fork.
Teiler ['taɪlər], *m.* (—s, *pl.* —) divider; (*Maths.*) divisor.
teilhaben ['taɪlha:bən], *v.n. irr.* (have a) share in, participate in.
Teilhaber ['taɪlha:bər], *m.* (—s, *pl.* —) partner.
teilhaftig ['taɪlhaftɪç], *adj.* sharing, participating; *einer Sache* — *werden*, partake of s.th., come in for s.th.
Teilnahme ['taɪlna:mə], *f.* (—, *no pl.*) participation; (*fig.*) sympathy, interest.
teilnahmslos ['taɪlna:mslo:s], *adj.* unconcerned, indifferent.
Teilnahmslosigkeit ['taɪlna:mslo:zɪçkaɪt], *f.* (—, *no pl.*) unconcern; listlessness, indifference.
teilnahmsvoll ['taɪlna:msfɔl], *adj.* solicitous.
teilnehmen ['taɪlne:mən], *v.n. irr.* take part (in), participate, partake; (*fig.*) sympathise.
Teilnehmer ['taɪlne:mər], *m.* (—s, *pl.* —) member, participant; (*telephone*) subscriber.
teils [taɪls], *adv.* partly.
Teilstrecke ['taɪlʃtrɛkə], *f.* (—, *pl.* —n) section (of a railway).
Teilung ['taɪluŋ], *f.* (—, *pl.* —en) division, partition; distribution.
Teilungszahl ['taɪluŋstsa:l], *f.* (—, *pl.* —en) (*Maths.*) dividend; quotient.
teilweise ['taɪlvaɪzə], *adv.* partly, in part.
Teilzahlung ['taɪltsa:luŋ], *f.* (—, *pl.* —en) part-payment, instalment.
Teint [tɛ̃], *m.* (—s, *no pl.*) complexion.
telephonieren [telefo'ni:rən], *v.a.*, *v.n.* telephone.
Telegraphie [telegra'fi:], *f.* (—, *no pl.*) telegraphy.
telegraphisch [tele'gra:fɪʃ], *adj.* telegraphic, by telegram.
Telegramm [tele'gram], *n.* (—s, *pl.* —e) telegram, wire, cable.
Telegrammadresse [tele'gramadrɛsə], *f.* (—, *pl.* —n) telegraphic address.
Telegrammformular [tele'gramfɔrmula:r], *n.* (—s, *pl.* —e) telegram-form.
Teleskop [telɛs'ko:p], *n.* (—s, *pl.* —e) telescope.
Teller ['tɛlər], *m.* (—s, *pl.* —) plate.
Tempel ['tɛmpəl], *m.* (—s, *pl.* —) temple.
Temperament [tɛmpəra'mɛnt], *n.* (—s, *pl.* —e) temperament, disposition; (*fig.*) spirits.
temperamentvoll [tɛmpəra'mɛntfɔl], *adj.* full of spirits, vivacious; lively.
Temperatur [tɛmpəra'tu:r], *f.* (—, *pl.* —en) temperature.
Temperenzler [tɛmpə'rɛntslər], *m.* (—s, *pl.* —) total abstainer, teetotaller.
temperieren [tɛmpə'ri:rən], *v.a.* temper.
Tempo ['tɛmpo:], *n.* (—s, *pl.* —s, Tempi) time, measure, speed.
temporisieren [tɛmpori'zi:rən], *v.n.* temporise.
Tendenz [tɛn'dɛnts], *f.* (—, *pl.* —en) tendency.
tendenziös [tɛndɛn'tsjø:s], *adj.* biased, coloured, tendentious.
Tender ['tɛndər], *m.* (—s, *pl.* —) (*Railw.*) tender.
Tenne ['tɛnə], *f.* (—, *pl.* —n) threshing floor.
Tenor [te'no:r], *m.* (—s, *pl.* ¨-e) (*Mus.*) tenor.
Teppich ['tɛpɪç], *m.* (—s, *pl.* —e) carpet.
Termin [tɛr'mi:n], *m.* (—s, *pl.* —e) time, date, appointed day; *einen* — *ansetzen*, fix a day (for a hearing, examination etc.).
Termingeschäft [tɛr'mi:ngəʃɛft], *n.* (—s, *pl.* —e) (business in) futures.
Terminologie [tɛrminolo'gi:], *f.* (—, *pl.* —n) terminology.
Terpentin [tɛrpɛn'ti:n], *n.* (—s, *no pl.*) turpentine.
Terrain [tɛ'rɛ̃], *n.* (—s, *pl.* —s) ground, terrain.
Terrasse [tɛ'rasə], *f.* (—, *pl.* —n) terrace.
Terrine [tɛ'ri:nə], *f.* (—, *pl.* —n) tureen.
territorial [tɛrɪto'rja:l], *adj.* territorial.
Territorium [tɛrɪ'to:rjum], *n.* (—s, *pl.* —torien) territory.

tertiär [tɛr'tsjɛ:r], *adj.* tertiary.
Terzett [tɛr'tsɛt], *n.* (**—s**, *pl.* **—e**) trio.
Testament [tɛsta'mɛnt], *n.* (**—s**, *pl.* **—e**) testament, will; (*Bibl.*) Testament; *ohne* —, intestate.
testamentarisch [tɛstamɛn'ta:rɪʃ], *adj.* testamentary.
Testamentseröffnung [tɛsta'mɛntsɛrœfnuŋ], *f.* (—, *pl.* **—en**) reading of the will.
Testamentsvollstrecker [tɛsta'mɛntsfɔlʃtrɛkər], *m.* (**—s**, *pl.* —) executor.
teuer ['tɔyər], *adj.* dear; costly, expensive; *einem — zu stehen kommen*, cost s.o. dear.
Teuerung ['tɔyəruŋ], *f.* (—, *pl.* **—en**) scarcity, dearth.
Teufel ['tɔyfəl], *m.* (**—s**, *pl.* —) devil, fiend; *armer* —, poor devil; *scher dich zum* —, go to blazes; *den — an die Wand malen*, talk of the devil.
Teufelei [tɔyfə'laɪ], *f.* (—, *pl.* **—en**) devilry, devilish trick.
teuflisch ['tɔyflɪʃ], *adj.* devilish, diabolical.
Thailand ['taɪlant], *n.* Thailand.
Theater [te'a:tər], *n.* (**—s**, *pl.* —) theatre, stage.
Theaterkarte [te'a:tərkartə], *f.* (—, *pl.* **—n**) theatre-ticket.
Theaterkasse [te'a:tərkasə], *f.* (—, *pl.* **—n**) box-office.
Theaterstück [te'a:tərʃtyk], *n.* (**—(e)s**, *pl.* **—e**) play, drama.
Theatervorstellung [te'a:tərfo:rʃtɛluŋ], *f.* (—, *pl.* **—en**) theatre performance.
Theaterzettel [te'a:tərtsɛtəl], *m.* (**—s**, *pl.* —) play-bill.
theatralisch [tea'tra:lɪʃ], *adj.* theatrical; dramatic; histrionic.
Thema ['te:ma:], *n.* (**—s**, *pl.* **—men, Themata**) theme, subject, topic.
Themse ['tɛmzə], *f.* Thames.
Theologe [teo'lo:gə], *m.* (**—n**, *pl.* **—n**) theologian.
Theologie [teolo'gi:], *f.* (—, *no pl.*) theology, divinity.
theoretisch [teo're:tɪʃ], *adj.* theoretical.
theoretisieren [teoreti'zi:rən], *v.n.* theorise.
Theorie [teo'ri:], *f.* (—, *pl.* **—n**) theory.
Therapie [tera'pi:], *f.* (—, *no pl.*) therapy.
Therme ['tɛrmə], *f.* (—, *pl.* **—n**) hot spring.
Thermometer [tɛrmo'me:tər], *n.* (**—s**, *pl.* —) thermometer.
Thermosflasche ['tɛrmɔsflaʃə], *f.* (—, *pl.* **—n**) thermos-flask.
These ['te:zə], *f.* (—, *pl.* **—n**) thesis.
Thron [tro:n], *m.* (**—(e)s**, *pl.* **—e**) throne; *auf den — setzen*, place on the throne, enthrone; *vom — stoßen*, dethrone, depose.
Thronbesteigung ['tro:nbəʃtaɪguŋ], *f.* (—, *pl.* **—en**) accession (to the throne).
Thronbewerber ['tro:nbəvɛrbər], *m.* (**—s**, *pl.* —) claimant to the throne, pretender.
thronen ['tro:nən], *v.n.* sit enthroned.
Thronerbe ['tro:nɛrbə], *m.* (**—n**, *pl.* **—n**) heir apparent, crown prince.
Thronfolge ['tro:nfɔlgə], *f.* (—, *no pl.*) line or order of succession.
Thronfolger ['tro:nfɔlgər], *m.* (**—s**, *pl.* —) heir to the throne, heir apparent.
Thronhimmel ['tro:nhɪməl], *m.* (**—s**, *pl.* —) canopy.
Thronrede ['tro:nre:də], *f.* (—, *pl.* **—n**) speech from the throne.
Thunfisch ['tu:nfɪʃ], *m.* (**—es**, *pl.* **—e**) (*Zool.*) tunny, (*Am.*) tuna.
Thüringen ['ty:rɪŋən], *n.* Thuringia.
Thymian ['ty:mja:n], *m.* (**—s**, *no pl.*) (*Bot.*) thyme.
ticken ['tɪkən], *v.n.* tick.
tief [ti:f], *adj.* deep, profound, low; far; extreme; (*voice*) bass; (*fig.*) profound; *in —ster Nacht*, in the dead of night; *aus —stem Herzen*, from the bottom of o.'s heart. — *adv.* — *atmen*, take a deep breath; — *in Schulden*, head over ears in debt; — *verletzt*, cut to the quick.
Tiefbau ['ti:fbau], *m.* (**—s**, *no pl.*) underground workings.
tiefbedrückt ['ti:fbədrykt], *adj.* deeply distressed; very depressed.
tiefbewegt ['ti:fbəve:kt], *adj.* deeply moved.
Tiefe ['ti:fə], *f.* (—, *pl.* **—en**) depth; (*fig.*) profundity.
tiefgebeugt ['ti:fgəbɔykt], *adj.* bowed down.
tiefgreifend ['ti:fgraɪfənt], *adj.* radical, sweeping.
tiefschürfend ['ti:fʃyrfənt], *adj.* profound; thoroughgoing.
Tiefsee ['ti:fze:], *f.* (—, *no pl.*) deep sea.
Tiefsinn ['ti:fzɪn], *m.* (**—s**, *no pl.*) pensiveness, melancholy.
tiefsinnig ['ti:fzɪnɪç], *adj.* pensive, melancholy, melancholic(al).
Tiegel ['ti:gəl], *m.* (**—s**, *pl.* —) crucible; saucepan.
Tier [ti:r], *n.* (**—(e)s**, *pl.* **—e**) animal, beast; *ein großes* —, (*coll.*) a V.I.P., a bigwig; (*Am.*) a swell, a big shot.
Tierart ['ti:ra:rt], *f.* (—, *pl.* **—en**) (*Zool.*) species.
Tierarzt ['ti:ra:rtst], *m.* (**—es**, *pl.* **¨e**) veterinary surgeon.
Tierbändiger ['ti:rbɛndɪgər], *m.* (**—s**, *pl.* —) animal-tamer.
Tiergarten ['ti:rgartən], *m.* (**—s**, *pl.* **¨**) zoological gardens, zoo.
tierisch ['ti:rɪʃ], *adj.* animal, brute, brutal, bestial.
Tierkreis ['ti:rkraɪs], *m.* (**—es**, *no pl.*) zodiac.
Tierkunde ['ti:rkundə], *f.* (—, *no pl.*) zoology.
Tierquälerei ['ti:rkvɛ:lərаɪ], *f.* (—, *pl.* **—en**) cruelty to animals.
Tierreich ['ti:rraɪç], *n.* (**—(e)s**, *no pl.*) animal kingdom.
Tierschutzverein ['ti:rʃutsfəraɪn], *m.* (**—s**, *pl.* **—e**) society for the prevention of cruelty to animals.

Tierwärter ['ti:rvɛrtər], *m.* (**—s**, *pl.* **—**) keeper (at a zoo).
Tiger ['ti:gər], *m.* (**—s**, *pl.* **—**) (*Zool.*) tiger.
Tigerin ['ti:gərɪn], *f.* (**—**, *pl.* **—nen**) (*Zool.*) tigress.
tilgbar ['tɪlkba:r], *adj.* extinguishable; (*debt*) redeemable.
tilgen ['tɪlgən], *v.a.* strike out, efface, annul; (*debt*) discharge; (*sin*) expiate, atone for.
Tilgung ['tɪlguŋ], *f.* (**—**, *pl.* **—en**) striking out, obliteration; annulment, payment; redemption.
Tilgungsfonds ['tɪlguŋsfɔ̃], *m.* (**—**, *pl.* **—**) sinking fund.
Tingeltangel ['tɪŋəltaŋəl], *m.* & *n.* (**—s**, *pl.* **—**) (*coll.*) music-hall.
Tinktur [tɪŋk'tu:r], *f.* (**—**, *pl.* **—en**) tincture.
Tinte ['tɪntə], *f.* (**—**, *pl.* **—n**) ink; *in der — sein*, be in a jam, be in the soup.
Tintenfaß ['tɪntənfas], *n.* (**—sses**, *pl.* **¨sser**) ink-pot, ink-stand.
Tintenfisch ['tɪntənfɪʃ], *m.* (**—es**, *pl.* **—e**) (*Zool.*) cuttle-fish.
Tintenfleck ['tɪntənflɛk], *m.* (**—s**, *pl.* **—e**) blot, ink-spot.
Tintenklecks ['tɪntənklɛks], *m.* (**—es**, *pl.* **—e**) blot.
Tintenstift ['tɪntənʃtɪft], *m.* (**—s**, *pl.* **—e**) indelible pencil.
Tintenwischer ['tɪntənvɪʃər], *m.* (**—s**, *pl.* **—**) pen-wiper.
tippen ['tɪpən], *v.a.* tap; (*coll.*) type.
Tirol [ti'ro:l], *n.* Tyrol.
Tisch [tɪʃ], *m.* (**—es**, *pl.* **—e**) table, board; *den — decken*, lay the table; *zu — gehen*, sit down to dinner.
Tischdecke ['tɪʃdɛkə], *f.* (**—**, *pl.* **—n**) tablecloth.
Tischgebet ['tɪʃgəbe:t], *n.* (**—s**, *pl.* **—e**) grace.
Tischler ['tɪʃlər], *m.* (**—s**, *pl.* **—**) joiner, cabinet-maker, carpenter.
Tischlerei [tɪʃlə'raɪ], *f.* (**—**, *no pl.*) joinery, cabinet-making, carpentry.
Tischrede ['tɪʃre:də], *f.* (**—**, *pl.* **—n**) after-dinner speech.
Tischrücken ['tɪʃrykən], *n.* (**—s**, *no pl.*) table-turning.
Tischtennis ['tɪʃtɛnɪs], *n.* (**—**, *no pl.*) table-tennis, ping-pong.
Tischtuch ['tɪʃtu:x], *n.* (**—(e)s**, *pl.* **¨er**) tablecloth.
Tischzeit ['tɪʃtsaɪt], *f.* (**—**, *pl.* **—en**) mealtime.
Titane [ti'ta:nə], *m.* (**—n**, *pl.* **—n**) Titan.
titanenhaft [ti'ta:nənhaft], *adj.* titanic.
Titel ['ti:təl], *m.* (**—s**, *pl.* **—**) title; claim; heading, headline.
Titelbild ['ti:təlbɪlt], *n.* (**—(e)s**, *pl.* **—er**) frontispiece.
Titelblatt ['ti:təlblat], *n.* (**—(e)s**, *pl.* **¨er**) title page.
Titelrolle ['ti:təlrɔlə], *f.* (**—**, *pl.* **—n**) title role.
titulieren [titu'li:rən], *v.a.* style, address.
toben ['to:bən], *v.n.* rave; rage, roar; be furious; be wild.
tobsüchtig ['to:pzyçtɪç], *adj.* raving, mad.
Tochter ['tɔxtər], *f.* (**—**, *pl.* **¨**) daughter.
töchterlich ['tœçtərlɪç], *adj.* filial, daughterly.
Tod [to:t], *m.* (**—es**, *pl.* **—esfälle** *or* (*rare*) **—e**) death, decease, demise; *dem — geweiht*, doomed; *Kampf auf — und Leben*, fight to the death; *zum — verurteilen*, condemn to death.
Todesangst ['to:dəsaŋst], *f.* (**—**, *pl.* **¨e**) agony, mortal terror.
Todesanzeige ['to:dəsantsaɪgə], *f.* (**—**, *pl.* **—n**) announcement of death; obituary notice.
Todesfall ['to:dəsfal], *m.* (**—(e)s**, *pl.* **¨e**) death, decease; fatality.
Todesgefahr ['to:dəsgəfa:r], *f.* (**—**, *pl.* **—en**) mortal danger.
Todeskampf ['to:dəskampf], *m.* (**—(e)s**, *pl.* **¨e**) death agony.
todesmutig ['to:dəsmu:tɪç], *adj.* death-defying.
Todesstoß ['to:dəsʃto:s], *m.* (**—es**, *pl.* **¨e**) death-blow.
Todesstrafe ['to:dəsʃtra:fə], *f.* (**—**, *no pl.*) capital punishment.
Todfeind ['to:tfaɪnt], *m.* (**—es**, *pl.* **—e**) mortal enemy.
todkrank ['to:tkraŋk], *adj.* sick unto death, dangerously *or* mortally ill.
tödlich ['tœ:tlɪç], *adj.* mortal, deadly, fatal.
todmüde ['to:tmy:də], *adj.* tired to death.
Todsünde ['to:tzyndə], *f.* (**—**, *pl.* **—n**) mortal sin.
Togo ['to:go], *n.* Togo.
Toilette [toa'lɛtə], *f.* (**—**, *pl.* **—n**) lavatory, toilet; (*fig.*) dress.
tolerant [tɔle'rant], *adj.* tolerant.
Toleranz [tɔle'rants], *f.* (**—**, *no pl.*) toleration; tolerance.
tolerieren [tɔle'ri:rən], *v.a.* tolerate.
toll [tɔl], *adj.* mad, frantic; wild; *—er Streich*, mad prank; *zum — werden*, enough to drive o. mad.
Tolle ['tɔlə], *f.* (**—**, *pl.* **—n**) (*dial.*) fore-lock, tuft of hair, top-knot.
Tollhaus ['tɔlhaus], *n.* (**—es**, *pl.* **¨er**) madhouse, lunatic asylum.
Tollheit ['tɔlhaɪt], *f.* (**—**, *pl.* **—en**) foolhardiness, mad prank.
Tollkirsche ['tɔlkɪrʃə], *f.* (**—**, *pl.* **—n**) belladonna, deadly nightshade.
Tollwut ['tɔlvu:t], *f.* (**—**, *no pl.*) frenzy; rabies.
Tolpatsch ['tɔlpatʃ], *m.* (**—es**, *pl.* **—e**) clumsy person.
Tölpel ['tœlpəl], *m.* (**—s**, *pl.* **—**) blockhead, lout, hobbledehoy.
Tölpelei [tœlpə'laɪ], *f.* (**—**, *pl.* **—en**) clumsiness, awkwardness.
tölpelhaft ['tœlpəlhaft], *adj.* clumsy, doltish, loutish.
Tomate [to'ma:tə], *f.* (**—**, *pl.* **—n**) tomato.

Ton (1) [to:n], *m.* (—(e)s, *pl.* ¨e) sound, tone, accent, note; shade; manners; *guter* (*schlechter*) —, good (bad) form, etiquette; *den — angeben*, set the fashion.
Ton (2) [to:n], *m.* (—s, *no pl.*) clay, potter's earth.
Tonabnehmer ['to:nabne:mər], *m.* (—s, *pl.* —) (*gramophone*) pick-up.
tonangebend ['to:nange:bənt], *adj.* leading in fashion, setting the pace; leading, fashionable.
Tonart ['to:na:rt], *f.* (—, *pl.* —en) (*Mus.*) key.
Tonbandgerät ['to:nbantgerɛ:t], *n.* (—s, *pl.* —e) tape-recorder.
tönen ['tø:nən], *v.n.* sound.
Tonerde ['to:ne:rdə], *f.* (—, *no pl.*) clay.
tönern ['tø:nərn], *adj.* earthen.
Tonfall ['to:nfal], *m.* (—s, *no pl.*) cadence, intonation (of voice).
Tonfolge ['to:nfɔlgə], *f.* (—, *pl.* —n) (*Mus.*) succession of notes.
Tonführung ['to:nfy:ruŋ], *f.* (—, *no pl.*) modulation.
Tonkunst ['to:nkunst], *f.* (—, *no pl.*) music.
Tonkünstler ['to:nkynstlər], *m.* (—s, *pl.* —) musician.
Tonleiter ['to:nlaɪtər], *f.* (—, *pl.* —n) scale, gamut.
Tonne ['tɔnə], *f.* (—, *pl.* —n) tun, cask, barrel; ton.
Tonnengewölbe ['tɔnəngəvœlbə], *n.* (—s, *pl.* —) cylindrical vault.
Tonpfeife ['to:npfaɪfə], *f.* (—, *pl.* —n) clay-pipe.
Tonsatz ['to:nzats], *m.* (—es, *pl.* ¨e) (*Mus.*) composition.
Tonsur [tɔn'zu:r], *f.* (—, *pl.* —en) tonsure.
Tonwelle ['to:nvɛlə], *f.* (—, *pl.* —n) sound-wave.
Topas [to'pa:s], *m.* (—es, *pl.* —e) topaz.
Topf [tɔpf], *m.* (—(e)s, *pl.* ¨e) pot; *alles in einen — werfen*, lump everything together.
Topfblume ['tɔpfblu:mə], *f.* (—, *pl.* —n) pot-plant.
Topfdeckel ['tɔpfdɛkəl], *m.* (—s, *pl.* —) lid of a pot.
Töpfer ['tœpfər], *m.* (—s, *pl.* —) potter.
Töpferarbeit ['tœpfərarbaɪt], *f.* (—, *pl.* —en) pottery.
Töpferscheibe ['tœpfərʃaɪbə], *f.* (—, *pl.* —n) potter's wheel.
Töpferware ['tœpfərva:rə], *f.* (—, *pl.* —n) pottery, earthenware.
Topfgucker ['tɔpfgukər], *m.* (—s, *pl.* —) busybody; inquisitive person.
Topographie [topogra'fi:], *f.* (—, *no pl.*) topography.
Tor (1) [to:r], *m.* (—en, *pl.* —en) (*obs.*) fool, simpleton.
Tor (2) [to:r], *n.* (—(e)s, *pl.* —e) gate; (*Footb.*) goal.
Torangel ['to:raŋəl], *f.* (—, *pl.* —n) hinge.
Tor(es)schluß ['to:r(əs)ʃlus], *m.* (—es, *no pl.*) shutting of the gate; *noch gerade vor* —, at the eleventh hour.
Torf [tɔrf], *m.* (—(e)s, *no pl.*) peat, turf.
Torfgrube ['tɔrfgru:bə], *f.* (—, *pl.* —n) turf-pit.
Torfmoor ['tɔrfmo:r], *n.* (—s, *pl.* —e) peat-bog.
Torfstecher ['tɔrfʃtɛçər], *m.* (—s, *pl.* —) peat-cutter.
Torheit ['to:rhaɪt], *f.* (—, *pl.* —en) foolishness, folly.
Torhüter ['to:rhy:tər], *m.* (—s, *pl.* —) gate-keeper.
töricht ['tø:rɪçt], *adj.* foolish, silly.
Törin ['tø:rɪn], *f.* (—, *pl.* —nen) (*rare*) foolish woman.
torkeln ['tɔrkəln], *v.n.* (*aux.* sein) (*coll.*) stagger, reel.
Tornister [tɔr'nɪstər], *m.* (—s, *pl.* —) knapsack, satchel.
Torpedo [tɔr'pe:do], *m.* (—s, *pl.* —s) torpedo.
Torso ['tɔrzo], *m.* (—s, *pl.* —s) trunk, torso.
Tort [tɔrt], *m.* (—s, *no pl.*) injury, wrong; *einem einen — antun*, wrong s.o.; play a trick on s.o.
Torte ['tɔrtə], *f.* (—, *pl.* —n) cake, pastry, tart.
Tortur [tɔr'tu:r], *f.* (—, *pl.* —en) torture.
Torwächter ['to:rvɛçtər], *m.* (—s, *pl.* —) gate-keeper; porter.
tosen ['to:zən], *v.n.* roar.
tot [to:t], *adj.* dead, deceased.
total [to'ta:l], *adj.* total, complete.
Totalisator [totali'za:tɔr], *m.* (—s, *pl.* —en) totalisator; (*coll.*) tote.
Totalleistung [to'ta:llaɪstuŋ], *f.* (—, *pl.* —en) full effect; total output.
Tote ['to:tə], *m.*, *f.* (—n, *pl.* —n) dead person, the deceased.
töten ['tø:tən], *v.a.* kill, put to death.
Totenacker ['to:tənakər], *m.* (—s, *pl.* ¨) churchyard, cemetery.
Totenamt ['to:tənamt], *n.* (—s, *no pl.*) office for the dead, requiem, Mass for the dead.
Totenbahre ['to:tənba:rə], *f.* (—, *pl.* —n) bier.
Totengräber ['to:təngrɛ:bər], *m.* (—s, *pl.* —) grave-digger.
Totenhemd ['to:tənhɛmt], *n.* (—(e)s, *pl.* —en) shroud, winding-sheet.
Totenklage ['to:tənkla:gə], *f.* (—, *no pl.*) lament.
Totenschein ['to:tənʃaɪn], *m.* (—(e)s, *pl.* —e) death-certificate.
Totenstille ['to:tənʃtɪlə], *f.* (—, *no pl.*) dead calm.
Totenwache ['to:tənvaxə], *f.* (—, *no pl.*) wake.
totgeboren ['to:tgəbo:rən], *adj.* still-born, born dead.
Totschlag ['to:tʃla:k], *m.* (—s, *no pl.*) manslaughter.
totschlagen ['to:tʃla:gən], *v.a.* *irr.* kill, strike dead.

Totschläger ['to:tʃlɛ:gər], *m.* (—**s**, *pl.* —) loaded cane, cudgel.
totschweigen ['to:tʃvaɪgən], *v.a. irr.* hush up.
Tötung ['tø:tuŋ], *f.* (—, *pl.* —**en**) killing.
Tour [tu:r], *f.* (—, *pl.* —**en**) tour, excursion; *in einer* —, ceaselessly; *auf —en bringen,*(*coll.*) (*Motor.*) rev up.
Tournee [tur'ne:], *f.* (—, *pl.* —**n**) (*Theat.*) tour.
Trab [tra:p], *m.* (—(**e**)**s**, *no pl.*) trot.
Trabant [tra'bant], *m.* (—**en**, *pl.* —**en**) satellite.
traben ['tra:bən], *v.n.* (*aux.* sein) trot.
Trabrennen ['tra:prɛnən], *n.* (—**s**, *pl.* —) trotting-race.
Tracht [traxt], *f.* (—, *pl.* —**en**) dress, costume; national costume; native dress; *eine — Prügel*, a good hiding.
trachten ['traxtən], *v.n.* strive, aspire, endeavour; *einem nach dem Leben* —, seek to kill s.o.
trächtig ['trɛçtɪç], *adj.* (*animal*) pregnant, with young.
Trafik [tra'fɪk], *m.* (—**s**, *pl.* —**s**) (*Austr.*) tobacco-kiosk.
Tragbahre ['tra:kba:rə], *f.* (—, *pl.* —**n**) stretcher.
Tragbalken ['tra:kbalkən], *m.* (—**s** *pl.*, —) girder.
tragbar ['tra:kba:r], *adj.* portable; tolerable.
träge ['trɛ:gə], *adj.* lazy, indolent, inert, sluggish.
tragen ['tra:gən], *v.a. irr.* bear, carry; (*dress*) wear; (*fig.*) bear, endure; *Bedenken* —, hesitate, have doubts; *Zinsen* —, yield interest; *einen auf Händen* —, care lovingly for s.o.
Träger ['trɛ:gər], *m.* (—**s**, *pl.* —) porter, carrier; girder.
Trägheit ['trɛ:khaɪt], *f.* (—, *no pl.*) indolence, laziness, inertia.
tragisch ['tra:gɪʃ], *adj.* tragic(al).
Tragkraft ['tra:kkraft], *f.* (—, *no pl.*) carrying *or* load capacity; lifting power.
Tragödie [tra'gø:djə], *f.* (—, *pl.* —**n**) tragedy.
Tragsessel ['tra:kzɛsəl], *m.* (—**s**, *pl.* —) sedan-chair.
Tragweite ['tra:kvaɪtə], *f.* (—, *no pl.*) significance, importance, range.
trainieren [trɛ'ni:rən], *v.a.* train.
Traktat [trak'ta:t], *n.* (—**s**, *pl.* —**e**) treatise, tract.
Traktätchen [trak'tɛ:tçən], *n.* (—**s**, *pl.* —) (short) tract.
traktieren [trak'ti:rən], *v.a.* treat; treat badly.
trällern ['trɛlərn], *v.n.* trill, hum.
Trambahn ['tramba:n], *f.* (—, *pl.* —**en**) tram; (*Am.*) streetcar.
Trampel ['trampəl], *n.* (—**s**, *pl.* —) clumsy person, bumpkin; (*Am.*) hick.
trampeln ['trampəln], *v.n.* trample.
Trampeltier ['trampəlti:r], *n.* (—**s**, *pl.* —**e**) camel; (*fig.*) clumsy person.
Tran [tra:n], *m.* (—(**e**)**s**, *no pl.*) whale-oil.
tranchieren [trã'ʃi:rən], *v.a.* carve.
Tranchiermesser [trã'ʃi:rmɛsər], *n.* (—**s**, *pl.* —) carving-knife.
Träne ['trɛ:nə], *f.* (—, *pl.* —**n**) tear, teardrop; *zu —n gerührt*, moved to tears.
tränen ['trɛ:nən], *v.n.* (*eyes*) water.
Tränendrüse ['trɛ:nəndry:zə], *f.* (—, *pl.* —**n**) lachrymal gland.
tränenleer ['trɛ:nənle:r], *adj.* tearless.
Tränenstrom ['trɛ:nənʃtro:m], *m.* (—**s**, *pl.* ¨**e**) flood of tears.
tränenvoll ['trɛ:nənfɔl], *adj.* tearful.
tranig ['tra:nɪç], *adj.* dull, slow.
Trank [traŋk], *m.* (—(**e**)**s**, *pl.* ¨**e**) drink, beverage, potion.
Tränke ['trɛŋkə], *f.* (—, *pl.* —**n**) (*horse*) watering-place.
tränken ['trɛŋkən], *v.a.* give to drink, water; impregnate, saturate.
transitiv ['tranziti:f], *adj.* transitive.
Transitlager ['tranzɪtla:gər], *n.* (—**s**, *pl.* —) bonded warehouse; transit camp.
transitorisch [tranzi'to:rɪʃ], *adj.* transitory.
transpirieren [transpi'ri:rən], *v.n.* perspire.
transponieren [transpo'ni:rən], *v.a.* transpose.
Transportkosten [trans'pɔrtkɔstən], *f. pl.* shipping charges.
Transportmittel [trans'pɔrtmɪtəl], *n.* (—**s**, *pl.* —) means of carriage, conveyance, transport.
Trapez [tra'pe:ts], *n.* (—**es**, *pl.* —**e**) trapeze; (*Maths.*) trapezoid.
Tratsch [tra:tʃ], *m.* (—**es**, *no pl.*) (*coll.*) gossip, tittle-tattle.
tratschen ['tra:tʃən], *v.n.* (*coll.*) gossip.
Tratte ['tratə], *f.* (—, *pl.* —**n**) (*Comm.*) draft, bill of exchange.
Traube ['traubə], *f.* (—, *pl.* —**n**) (*Bot.*) grape, bunch of grapes.
Traubensaft ['traubənzaft], *m.* (—**s**, *pl.* ¨**e**) grape-juice; (*Poet.*) wine.
traubig ['traubɪç], *adj.* clustered, grape-like.
trauen ['trauən], *v.a.* marry; join in marriage; *sich — lassen*, get married. — *v.n. einem* —, trust s.o., confide in s.o. — *v.r. sich* —, dare, venture.
Trauer ['trauər], *f.* (—, *no pl.*) mourning; sorrow, grief.
Trauermarsch ['trauərmarʃ], *m.* (—**es**, *pl.* ¨**e**) funeral march.
trauern ['trauərn], *v.n.* mourn, be in mourning.
Trauerspiel ['trauərʃpi:l], *n.* (—**s**, *pl.* —**e**) tragedy.
Trauerweide ['trauərvaɪdə], *f.* (—, *pl.* —**n**) (*Bot.*) weeping willow.
Traufe ['traufə], *f.* (—, *pl.* —**n**) eaves; *vom Regen in die* —, out of the frying pan into the fire.
träufeln ['trɔyfəln], *v.a.* drip, drop.
Traufröhre ['traufrø:rə], *f.* (—, *pl.* —**n**) gutter-pipe.

traulich ['traulɪç], *adj.* familiar, homely, cosy.
Traum [traum], *m.* (—(e)s, *pl.* ⸚e) dream; *das fällt mir nicht im —e ein*, I should not dream of it.
Traumbild ['traumbɪlt], *n.* (—s, *pl.* —er) vision.
Traumdeutung ['traumdɔytuŋ], *f.* (—, *no pl.*) interpretation of dreams.
träumen ['trɔymən], *v.n.* dream; *sich etwas nicht — lassen*, have no inkling of, not dream of s.th.; not believe s.th.
Träumer ['trɔymər], *m.* (—s, *pl.* —) dreamer; (*fig.*) visionary.
Träumerei [trɔymə'raɪ], *f.* (—, *pl.* —en) dreaming, reverie.
traumhaft ['traumhaft], *adj.* dreamlike.
traurig ['traurɪç], *adj.* sad, mournful, sorrowful.
Traurigkeit ['traurɪçkaɪt], *f.* (—, *no pl.*) sadness, melancholy.
Trauring ['traurɪŋ], *m.* (—s, *pl.* —e) wedding-ring.
Trauschein ['trauʃaɪn], *m.* (—s, *pl.* —e) marriage certificate.
traut [traut], *adj.* dear, beloved; cosy; *—es Heim Glück allein*, east, west, home's best; there's no place like home.
Trauung ['trauuŋ], *f.* (—, *pl.* —en) marriage ceremony.
Trauzeuge ['trautsɔygə], *m.* (—n, *pl.* —n) witness to a marriage.
trecken ['trɛkən], *v.a.* (*dial.*) draw, drag, tug.
Trecker ['trɛkər], *m.* (—s, *pl.* —) tractor.
Treff [trɛf], *n.* (—s, *no pl.*) (*Cards*) clubs.
Treffen ['trɛfən], *n.* (—s, *pl.* —) action, battle, fight; meeting, gathering; *etwas ins — führen*, put s.th. forward, urge s.th.
treffen ['trɛfən], *v.a. irr.* hit, meet; *nicht —*, miss; *wie vom Donner getroffen*, thunderstruck; *ins Schwarze —*, hit the mark, score a bull's eye. — *v.r. sich —*, happen.
treffend ['trɛfənt], *adj.* appropriate, pertinent.
Treffer ['trɛfər], *m.* (—s, *pl.* —) (*lottery*) win, prize; (*Mil.*) hit.
trefflich ['trɛflɪç], *adj.* excellent.
Treffpunkt ['trɛfpuŋkt], *m.* (—s, *pl.* —e) meeting-place.
Treffsicherheit ['trɛfzɪçərhaɪt], *f.* (—, *no pl.*) accurate aim.
Treibeis ['traɪpaɪs], *n.* (—es, *no pl.*) floating-ice, ice floe.
treiben ['traɪbən], *v.a. irr.* drive, urge; incite; (*trade*) carry on, ply; *Studien —*, study; *was treibst du?* what are you doing? *etwas zu weit —*, carry s.th. too far; *einen in die Enge —*, drive s.o. into a corner. — *v.n.* be adrift, drift.
Treiben ['traɪbən], *n.* (—s, *no pl.*) driving; doings; bustle.
Treiber ['traɪbər], *m.* (—s, *pl.* —) (*Hunt.*) driver; beater.
Treibhaus ['traɪphaus], *n.* (—es, *pl.* ⸚er) hothouse, greenhouse.
Treibkraft ['traɪpkraft], *f.* (—, *no pl.*) impulse, driving power.
Treibriemen ['traɪpri:mən], *m.* (—s, *pl.* —) driving-belt.
Treibsand ['traɪpzant], *m.* (—s, *no pl.*) quicksand, shifting sand.
Treibstange ['traɪpʃtaŋə], *f.* (—, *pl.* —en) main rod, connecting-rod.
Treibstoff ['traɪpʃtɔf], *m.* (—(e)s, *pl.* —e) fuel.
treideln ['traɪdəln], *v.a.* (*Naut.*) tow.
Treidelsteig ['traɪdəlʃtaɪk], *m.* (—s, *pl.* —e) towpath.
trennbar ['trɛnba:r], *adj.* separable.
trennen ['trɛnən], *v.a.* separate, sever. — *v.r. sich —*, part.
Trennung ['trɛnuŋ], *f.* (—, *pl.* —en) separation, segregation; parting; division.
Trennungsstrich ['trɛnuŋsʃtrɪç], *m.* (—es, *pl.* —e) hyphen, dash.
treppab [trɛp'ap], *adv.* downstairs.
treppauf [trɛp'auf], *adv.* upstairs.
Treppe ['trɛpə], *f.* (—, *pl.* —n) stairs, staircase, flight of stairs.
Treppenabsatz ['trɛpənapzats], *m.* (—es, *pl.* ⸚e) (*staircase*) landing.
Treppengeländer ['trɛpəngəlɛndər], *n.* (—s, *pl.* —) balustrade, banisters.
Treppenhaus ['trɛpənhaus], *n.* (—es, *pl.* ⸚er) stair-well, staircase.
Treppenläufer ['trɛpənlɔyfər], *m.* (—s, *pl.* —) stair-carpet.
Treppenstufe ['trɛpənʃtu:fə], *f.* (—, *pl.* —n) step, stair.
Treppenwitz ['trɛpənvɪts], *m.* (—es, *no pl.*) afterthought, esprit de l'escalier.
Tresor [tre'zo:r], *m.* (—s, *pl.* —e) safe, strongroom.
Tresse ['trɛsə], *f.* (—, *pl.* —n) braid, lace, galloon.
treten ['tre:tən], *v.a., v.n. irr.* tread, step, trample upon; go; — *Sie näher*, step this way; *in Verbindung — mit*, make contact with; *in den Ehestand —*, get married; *einem zu nahe —*, offend s.o., tread on s.o.'s toes.
treu [trɔy], *adj.* faithful, loyal, true; conscientious.
Treubruch ['trɔybrux], *m.* (—(e)s, *pl.* ⸚e) breach of faith, disloyalty.
Treue ['trɔyə], *f.* (—, *no pl.*) faithfulness, loyalty, fidelity; *meiner Treu!* upon my soul! *auf Treu und Glauben*, on trust.
Treueid ['trɔyaɪt], *m.* (—s, *pl.* —e) oath of allegiance.
Treuhänder ['trɔyhɛndər], *m.* (—s, *pl.* —) trustee.
treuherzig ['trɔyhɛrtsɪç], *adj.* guileless, trusting.
treulich ['trɔylɪç], *adv.* faithfully.
treulos ['trɔylo:s], *adj.* faithless, perfidious; unfaithful.

Treulosigkeit ['trɔylo:zɪçkaɪt], *f.* (—, *no pl.*) faithlessness, perfidy, disloyalty.
Tribüne [tri'by:nə], *f.* (—, *pl.* **—n**) tribune, platform; (*racing*) grandstand.
Tribut [tri'bu:t], *m.* (**—s**, *pl.* **—e**) tribute.
tributpflichtig [tri'bu:tpflɪçtɪç], *adj.* tributary.
Trichter ['trɪçtər], *m.* (**—s**, *pl.* **—**) funnel.
trichterförmig ['trɪçtərfœrmɪç], *adj.* funnel-shaped.
Trieb [tri:p], *m.* (**—(e)s**, *pl.* **—e**) (*plant*) shoot, growth; instinct, bent, propensity, inclination; (*Psych.*) drive.
Triebfeder ['tri:pfe:dər], *f.* (—, *pl.* **—n**) mainspring; (*fig.*) motive, guiding principle.
Triebkraft ['tri:pkraft], *f.* (—, *pl.* **⸚e**) motive power.
Triebwagen ['tri:pva:gən], *m.* (**—s**, *pl.* **—**) rail-car.
Triebwerk ['tri:pverk], *n.* (**—s**, *pl.* **—e**) power unit, drive.
triefen ['tri:fən], *v.n. irr.* & *reg.* trickle, drip; be wet through, be soaking wet.
Trient [tri'ɛnt], *n.* Trent.
Trier [tri:r], *n.* Treves.
Triest [tri'ɛst], *n.* Trieste.
Trift [trɪft], *f.* (—, *pl.* **—en**) pasture, pasturage, common, meadow.
triftig ['trɪftɪç], *adj.* weighty, valid, conclusive, cogent.
Trikot [tri'ko:], *m.* & *n.* (**—s**, *pl.* **—s**) stockinet; (*circus, ballet*) tights.
Triller ['trɪlər], *m.* (**—s**, *pl.* **—**) (*Mus.*) trill, shake.
trillern ['trɪlərn], *v.n.* trill, quaver, shake; warble.
Trinität ['trini'tɛ:t], *f.* (—, *no pl.*) Trinity.
trinkbar ['trɪŋkba:r], *adj.* drinkable.
Trinkbecher ['trɪŋkbɛçər], *m.* (**—s**, *pl.* **—**) drinking-cup.
trinken ['trɪŋkən], *v.a.*, *v.n. irr.* drink.
Trinker ['trɪŋkər], *m.* (**—s**, *pl.* **—**) drinker, drunkard.
Trinkgelage ['trɪŋkgəla:gə], *n.* (**—s**, *pl.* **—**) drinking-bout.
Trinkgeld ['trɪŋkgɛlt], *n.* (**—s**, *pl.* **—er**) tip, gratuity.
Trinkhalle ['trɪŋkhalə], *f.* (—, *pl.* **—n**) (*spa*) pump-room.
Trinkspruch ['trɪŋkʃprux], *m.* (**—(e)s**, *pl.* **⸚e**) toast.
Trinkstube ['trɪŋkʃtu:bə], *f.* (—, *pl.* **—n**) tap-room.
Tripolis ['tri:polɪs], *n.* Tripoli.
trippeln ['trɪpəln], *v.n.* trip (daintily), patter.
Tripper ['trɪpər], *m.* (**—s**, *no pl.*) (*Med.*) gonorrhoea.
Tritt [trɪt], *m.* (**—(e)s**, *pl.* **—e**) step, pace; kick.
Trittbrett ['trɪtbrɛt], *n.* (**—s**, *pl.* **—er**) foot-board; carriage-step; (*organ*) pedal.
Triumph [tri'umf], *m.* (**—(e)s**, *pl.* **—e**) triumph.
Triumphzug [tri'umftsu:k], *m.* (**—(e)s**, *pl.* **⸚e**) triumphal procession.
Trivialität [trivjali'tɛ:t], *f.* (—, *pl.* **—en**) triviality, platitude.
trocken ['trɔkən], *adj.* dry, arid; (*fig.*) dull, dry as dust; (*wine*) dry.
Trockenfäule ['trɔkənfɔylə], *f.*, **Trockenfäulnis** ['trɔkənfɔylnɪs], *f.* (—, *no pl.*) dry rot.
Trockenboden ['trɔkənbo:dən], *m.* (**—s**, *pl.* **⸚**) loft.
Trockenfutter ['trɔkənfutər], *n.* (**—s**, *no pl.*) fodder.
Trockenfütterung ['trɔkənfytəruŋ], *f.* (—, *pl.* **—en**) dry feeding.
Trockenhaube ['trɔkənhaubə], *f.* (—, *pl.* **—n**) hair drier.
Trockenheit ['trɔkənhaɪt], *f.* (—, *no pl.*) dryness; drought.
Trockenschleuder ['trɔkənʃlɔydər], *f.* (—, *pl.* **—n**) spin-drier.
trocknen ['trɔknən], *v.a.*, *v.n.* dry, air.
Troddel ['trɔdəl], *f.* (—, *pl.* **—n**) tassel.
Trödel ['trø:dəl], *m.* (**—s**, *no pl.*) junk, lumber, rubbish.
Trödelladen ['trø:dəlla:dən], *m.* (**—s**, *pl.* **⸚**) junk-shop.
Trödelmarkt ['trø:dəlmarkt], *m.* (**—s**, *no pl.*) kettle market, jumble sale.
trödeln ['trø:dəln], *v.n.* dawdle, loiter.
Trödler ['trø:dlər], *m.* (**—s**, *pl.* **—**) second-hand dealer; (*coll.*) dawdler, loiterer.
Trog [tro:k], *m.* (**—(e)s**, *pl.* **⸚e**) trough.
Troja ['tro:ja], *n.* Troy.
trollen ['trɔlən], *v.r. sich* **—**, decamp, toddle off, make o.s. scarce.
Trommel ['trɔməl], *f.* (—, *pl.* **—n**) drum; cylinder, barrel; tin box; *die — rühren*, beat the big drum.
Trommelfell ['trɔməlfɛl], *n.* (**—s**, *pl.* **—e**) drum-skin; ear-drum.
trommeln ['trɔməln], *v.n.* drum, beat the drum.
Trommelschlegel ['trɔməlʃle:gəl], *m.* (**—s**, *pl.* **—**) drumstick.
Trommelwirbel ['trɔməlvɪrbəl], *m.* (**—s**, *pl.* **—**) roll of drums.
Trommler ['trɔmlər], *m.* (**—s**, *pl.* **—**) drummer.
Trompete [trɔm'pe:tə], *f.* (—, *pl.* **—n**) trumpet; *die — blasen*, blow the trumpet.
trompeten [trɔm'pe:tən], *v.n.* trumpet, sound the trumpet.
Trompetengeschmetter [trɔm'pe:təngəʃmɛtər], *n.* (**—s**, *no pl.*) flourish of trumpets.
Tropen ['tro:pən], *f. pl.* the tropics.
Tropenfieber ['tro:pənfi:bər], *n.* (**—s**, *no pl.*) tropical fever.
tröpfeln ['trœpfəln], *v.a.*, *v.n.* trickle, sprinkle.
Tropfen ['trɔpfən], *m.* (**—s**, *pl.* **—**) drop; *steter — höhlt den Stein*, constant dripping wears away a stone.
tropfen ['trɔpfən], *v.n.* drop, drip.

Trophäe [tro'fɛə], *f.* (—, *pl.* —**n**) trophy.
tropisch ['tro:pɪʃ], *adj.* tropical, tropic.
Troß [trɔs], *m.* (—**sses**, *pl.* -**sse**) (*Mil.*) baggage-train; (*fig.*) hangers-on, camp-followers.
Troßpferd ['trɔspfe:rt], *n.* (—**s**, *pl.* —**e**) pack-horse.
Trost [tro:st], *m.* (—**es**, *no pl.*) consolation, comfort; *geringer* —, cold comfort; *du bist wohl nicht bei* —? have you taken leave of your senses?
trösten ['trø:stən], *v.a.* comfort, console; *tröste dich*, cheer up.
Tröster ['trø:stər], *m.* (—**s**, *pl.* —) comforter, consoler; (*Theol.*) Holy Ghost, Comforter.
tröstlich ['trø:stlɪç], *adj.* consoling, comforting.
trostlos ['tro:stlo:s], *adj.* disconsolate, inconsolable; desolate, bleak.
Trostlosigkeit ['tro:stlo:zɪçkaɪt], *f.* (—, *no pl.*) disconsolateness; (*fig.*) wretchedness; dreariness.
Trott [trɔt], *m.* (—**s**, *no pl.*) trot.
Trottel ['trɔtəl], *m.* (—**s**, *pl.* —) (*coll.*) idiot.
Trottoir [trɔto'a:r], *n.* (—**s**, *pl.* —**e**) pavement, footpath; (*Am.*) sidewalk.
trotz [trɔts], *prep.* (*Genit.*, *Dat.*) in spite of, despite; — *alledem*, all the same.
Trotz [trɔts], *m.* (—**es**, *no pl.*) defiance, obstinacy, refractoriness; *einem* — *bieten*, defy s.o.; *einem etwas zum* — *machen*, do s.th. in defiance of s.o.
trotzdem [trɔts'de:m], *conj.* notwithstanding that, albeit, although. — *adv.* nevertheless.
trotzen ['trɔtsən], *v.n.* defy; sulk, be obstinate; *Gefahren* —, brave dangers.
trotzig ['trɔtsɪç], *adj.* defiant; sulky, refractory; headstrong, stubborn, obstinate.
Trotzkopf ['trɔtskɔpf], *m.* (—(**e**)**s**, *pl.* ⁻**e**) obstinate child; pig-headed person.
trübe ['try:bə], *adj.* dim, gloomy; (*weather*) dull, cloudy, overcast; (*water*) troubled; (*glass*) misted; —*s Lächeln*, wan smile.
Trubel ['tru:bəl], *m.* (—**s**, *no pl.*) tumult, turmoil, disturbance.
trüben ['try:bən], *v.a.* darken, sadden, trouble; (*glass*) mist; (*metal*) tarnish; (*fig.*) obscure.
Trübsal ['try:pza:l], *f.* (—, *pl.* —**e**), *n.* (—**s**, *pl.* —**e**) misery, trouble, distress; — *blasen*, mope.
trübselig ['try:pze:lɪç], *adj.* woeful, lamentable; woebegone, forlorn.
Trübsinn ['try:pzɪn], *m.* (—**s**, *no pl.*) sadness, dejection.
trübsinnig ['try:pzɪnɪç], *adj.* sad, dejected.
Trüffel ['tryfəl], *f.* (—, *pl.* —**n**) truffle.
Trug [tru:k], *m.* (—(**e**)**s**, *no pl.*) deceit, fraud; *Lug und* —, a pack of lies.
Trugbild ['tru:kbɪlt], *n.* (—**es**, *pl.* —**er**) phantom.
trügen ['try:gən], *v.a. irr.* deceive.
trügerisch ['try:gərɪʃ], *adj.* deceptive, illusory, fallacious.
Truggewebe ['tru:kgəve:bə], *n.* (—**s**, *pl.* —) tissue of lies.
Trugschluß ['tru:kʃlus], *m.* (—**sses**, *pl.* ⁻**sse**) fallacy, false deduction.
Truhe ['tru:ə], *f.* (—, *pl.* —**n**) chest, trunk, coffer.
Trumm [trum], *m.* (—**s**, *pl.* ⁻**er**) lump, broken piece.
Trümmer ['trymər], *m. pl.* fragments, debris, ruins; *in* — *gehen*, go to wrack and ruin; *in* — *schlagen*, wreck.
Trümmerhaufen ['trymərhaufən], *m.* (—**s**, *pl.* —) heap of ruins, heap of rubble.
Trumpf [trumpf], *m.* (—(**e**)**s**, *pl.* ⁻**e**) trump, trump-card.
trumpfen ['trumpfən], *v.a.* trump.
Trumpffarbe ['trumpffarbə], *f.* (—, *pl.* —**n**) trump-suit.
Trunk [truŋk], *m.* (—(**e**)**s**, *pl.* ⁻**e**) draught, potion, drinking; *sich dem* — *ergeben*, take to drink.
trunken ['truŋkən], *adj.* drunk, intoxicated; (*fig.*) elated.
Trunkenbold ['truŋkənbɔlt], *m.* (—**s**, *pl.* —**e**) drunkard.
Trunkenheit ['truŋkənhaɪt], *f.* (—, *no pl.*) drunkenness, intoxication.
Trunksucht ['truŋkzuxt], *f.* (—, *no pl.*) dipsomania, alcoholism.
trunksüchtig ['truŋkzyçtɪç], *adj.* dipsomaniac, addicted to drinking.
Trupp [trup], *m.* (—**s**, *pl.* —**s**) troop, band.
Truppe ['trupə], *f.* (—, *pl.* —**n**) (*Mil.*) company, troops, forces; (*actors*) troupe.
Truppengattung ['trupəngatuŋ], *f.* (—, *pl.* —**en**) branch of the armed forces.
Truthahn ['tru:tha:n], *m.* (—**s**, *pl.* ⁻**e**) (*Orn.*) turkey cock.
Truthenne ['tru:thenə], *f.* (—, *pl.* —**n**) (*Orn.*) turkey hen.
Trtuhühner ['tru:thy:nər], *n. pl.* (*Orn.*) turkey-fowl.
Trutz [truts], *m.* (—**es**, *no pl.*) (*Poet.*) defiance; *zum Schutz und* —, offensively and defensively.
Tschad [tʃat], *n.* Chad.
Tschechoslowakei [tʃɛçoslova'kaɪ], *f.* Czechoslovakia.
Tuch (1) [tu:x], *n.* (—(**e**)**s**, *pl.* ⁻**er**) shawl, wrap.
Tuch (2) [tu:x], *n.* (—**s**, *pl.* —**e**) cloth, fabric.
Tuchhändler ['tu:xhɛndlər], *m.* (—**s**, *pl.* —) draper, clothier.
tüchtig ['tyçtɪç], *adj.* able, competent, efficient. — *adv.* largely, much, heartily.
Tüchtigkeit ['tyçtɪçkaɪt], *f.* (—, *no pl.*) ability, competence, efficiency.
Tücke ['tykə], *f.* (—, *pl.* —**n**) malice, spite.

tückisch ['tykɪʃ], *adj.* malicious, insidious.
Tugend ['tu:gənt], *f.* (—, *pl.* —**en**) virtue.
Tugendbold ['tu:gəntbɔlt], *m.* (—**s**, *pl.* —**e**) paragon.
tugendhaft ['tu:gənthaft], *adj.* virtuous.
Tugendlehre ['tu:gəntle:rə], *f.* (—, *no pl.*) ethics, morals.
Tüll [tyl], *m.* (—**s**, *pl.* —**e**) tulle.
Tulpe ['tulpə], *f.* (—, *pl.* —**n**) (*Bot.*) tulip.
Tulpenzwiebel ['tulpəntsvi:bəl], *f.* (—, *pl.* —**n**) tulip-bulb.
tummeln ['tuməln], *v.r. sich* —, romp about; make haste.
Tummelplatz ['tuməlplats], *m.* (—**es**, *pl.* ⸚**e**) playground, fairground.
Tümpel ['tympəl], *m.* (—**s**, *pl.* —) pond, pool, puddle.
Tun [tu:n], *n.* (—**s**, *no pl.*) doing; *sein — und Lassen*, his conduct.
tun [tu:n], *v.a. irr.* do, make; put; *tut nichts*, it does not matter; *viel zu — haben*, have a lot to do, be busy; *Not* —, be necessary; *Buße* —, repent.
Tünche ['tynçə], *f.* (—, *pl.* —**n**) whitewash.
tünchen ['tynçən], *v.a.* whitewash.
Tunichtgut ['tu:nɪçtgu:t], *m.* (—**s**, *no pl.*) ne'er-do-well, scamp.
Tunke ['tuŋkə], *f.* (—, *pl.* —**n**) sauce, gravy.
tunken ['tuŋkən], *v.a.* dip, steep; (*Am.*) dunk.
tunlich ['tu:nlɪç], *adj.* feasible, practicable, expedient.
tunlichst ['tu:nlɪçst], *adv.* if possible, possibly.
Tunnel ['tunəl], *m.* (—**s**, *pl.* —) tunnel.
Tunnelbau ['tunəlbau], *m.* (—**s**, *no pl.*) tunnelling.
tüpfeln ['typfəln], *v.a.* dot, spot.
Tupfen ['tupfən], *m.* (—**s**, *pl.* —) dot, polka-dot.
Tür [ty:r], *f.* (—, *pl.* —**en**) door; *einem die — weisen*, show s.o. the door; *vor der — stehen*, be imminent; *kehr vor deiner eigenen* —, mind your own business; put your own house in order; *offene —en einrennen*, flog a willing horse; *zwischen — und Angel stecken*, be undecided.
Türangel ['ty:raŋəl], *f.* (—, *pl.* —**n**) door-hinge.
Türhüter ['ty:rhy:tər], *m.* (—**s**, *pl.* —) doorkeeper.
Türkei [tyr'kaɪ], *f.* Turkey.
Türkensäbel ['tyrkənzɛ:bəl], *m.* (—**s**, *pl.* —) scimitar.
Türkis [tyr'ki:s], *m.* (—**es**, *pl.* —**e**) turquoise.
Türklinke ['ty:rklɪŋkə], *f.* (—, *pl.* —**n**) door-handle.
Turm [turm], *m.* (—(**e**)**s**, *pl.* ⸚**e**) tower; spire, steeple; belfry; (*Chess*) castle.
Turmalin [turma'li:n], *m.* (—**s**, *pl.* —**e**) tourmaline.
Türmchen ['tyrmçən], *n.* (—**s**, *pl.* —) turret.
türmen ['tyrmən], *v.a.* pile up. — *v.n.* (*coll.*) bolt, run away. — *v.r. sich* —, rise high, be piled high.
Turmspitze ['turmʃpɪtsə], *f.* (—, *pl.* —**n**) spire.
turnen ['turnən], *v.n.* do exercises *or* gymnastics.
Turnen ['turnən], *n.* (—**s**, *no pl.*) gymnastics, physical training.
Turner ['turnər], *m.* (—**s**, *pl* —) gymnast.
Turngerät ['turngərɛ:t], *n.* (—**es**, *pl.* —**e**) gymnastic apparatus.
Turnhalle ['turnhalə], *f.* (—, *pl.* —**n**) gymnasium.
Turnier [tur'ni:r], *n.* (—**s**, *pl.* —**e**) tournament.
Turnübung ['turny:buŋ], *f.* (—, *pl.* —**en**) gymnastic exercise.
Turnverein ['turnfəraɪn], *m.* (—**s**, *pl.* —**e**) athletics club, gymnastics club.
Türpfosten ['ty:rpfɔstən], *m.* (—**s**, *pl.* —) door-post.
Türriegel ['ty:rri:gəl], *m.* (—**s**, *pl.* —) bolt.
Türschild ['ty:rʃɪlt], *n.* (—(**e**)**s**, *pl.* —**e**) (door)plate.
Türschloß ['ty:rʃlɔs], *n.* (—**sses**, *pl.* ⸚**sser**) lock.
Türschlüssel ['ty:rʃlysəl], *m.* (—**s**, *pl.* —) door-key, latch-key.
Türschwelle ['ty:rʃvɛlə], *f.* (—, *pl.* —**n**) threshold.
Tusch [tuʃ], *m.* (—**es**, *pl.* —**e**) (*Mus.*) flourish.
Tusche ['tuʃə], *f.* (—, *pl.* —**n**) water-colour; Indian ink.
tuscheln ['tuʃəln], *v.n.* whisper.
tuschen ['tuʃən], *v.a.* draw in Indian ink.
Tuschkasten ['tuʃkastən], *m.* (—**s**, *pl.* ⸚) paint-box.
Tüte ['ty:tə], *f.* (—, *pl.* —**n**) paper bag.
Tutel [tu'te:l], *f.* (—, *no pl.*) guardianship.
tuten ['tu:tən], *v.n.* hoot, honk, blow a horn.
Tütendreher ['ty:təndre:ər], *m.* (—**s**, *pl.* —) (*sl.*) small shopkeeper.
Typ [ty:p], *m.* (—**s**, *pl.* —**en**) type.
Type ['ty:pə], *f.* (—, *pl.* —**n**) (*Typ.*) type; (*fig.*) queer fish.
Typhus ['ty:fus], *m.* (—, *no pl.*) (*Med.*) typhoid (fever).
typisch ['ty:pɪʃ], *adj.* typical.
Typus ['ty:pus], *m.* (—, *pl.* **Typen**) type.
Tyrann [ty'ran], *m.* (—**en**, *pl.* —**en**) tyrant.
Tyrannei [tyra'naɪ], *f.* (—, *pl.* —**en**) tyranny, despotism.
tyrannisch [ty'ranɪʃ], *adj.* tyrannical, despotic.
tyrannisieren [tyrani'zi:rən], *v.a.* tyrannize over, oppress, bully.

U

U [u:], *n.* (—**s**, *pl.* —**s**) the letter U.
U-Bahn ['u:ba:n], *f.* (—, *no pl.*) underground (railway); (*Am.*) subway.
Übel ['y:bəl], *n.* (—**s**, *pl.* —) evil, trouble; misfortune; disease.
übel ['y:bəl], *adj.* evil, ill, bad; *mir ist* —, I feel sick; *nicht* —, not too bad; — *daran sein*, be in a bad way, be in a mess.
übelgesinnt ['y:bəlgəzɪnt], *adj.* evil-minded; ill-disposed; *einem* — *sein*, bear s.o. a grudge.
Übelkeit ['y:bəlkaɪt], *f.* (—, *pl.* —**en**) nausea, sickness.
übellaunig ['y:bəllaunɪç], *adj.* ill-humoured, bad-tempered.
übelnehmen ['y:bəlne:mən], *v.a. irr.* take amiss, resent, be offended at.
übelnehmerisch ['y:bəlne:mərɪʃ], *adj.* touchy, easily offended.
Übelstand ['y:bəlʃtant], *m.* (—(**e**)**s**, *pl.* ¨**e**) inconvenience, drawback; (*pl.*) abuses.
Übeltat ['y:bəlta:t], *f.* (—, *pl.* —**en**) misdeed.
Übeltäter ['y:bəltɛ:tər], *m.* (—**s**, *pl.* —) evildoer, malefactor.
übelwollend ['y:bəlvɔlənt], *adj.* malevolent.
üben ['y:bən], *v.a.* practise, exercise; *Rache* —, wreak vengeance.
über ['y:bər], *prep.* (*Dat.*, *Acc.*) over, above; across; about; more than, exceeding; via, by way of; concerning, on. — *adv.* over, above; — *und* —, all over; — *kurz oder lang*, sooner or later; *heute* —*s Jahr*, a year from today.
überall ['y:bəral], *adv.* everywhere, anywhere.
überanstrengen [y:bər'anʃtrɛŋən], *v.a. insep.* overtax s.o.'s strength, strain. — *v.r. sich* —, overtax o.'s strength, overexert o.s.
Überanstrengung [y:bər'anʃtrɛŋuŋ], *f.* (—, *pl.* —**en**) over-exertion, strain.
überantworten [y:bər'antvɔrtən], *v.a. insep.* deliver up, surrender.
überarbeiten [y:bər'arbaɪtən], *v.a. insep.* revise, do again. — *v.r. sich* —, overwork o.s.
überarbeitet [y:bər'arbaɪtət], *adj.* overwrought, overworked.
überaus ['y:bəraus], *adv.* exceedingly, extremely.
überbauen [y:bər'bauən], *v.a. insep.* build over.
überbieten [y:bər'bi:tən], *v.a. irr. insep.* outbid (s.o.); (*fig.*) surpass.
Überbleibsel ['y:bərblaɪpsəl], *n.* (—**s**, *pl.* —) remainder, remnant, residue, rest.
Überblick ['y:bərblɪk], *m.* (—(**e**)**s**, *pl.* —**e**) survey, general view.
überblicken [y:bər'blɪkən], *v.a. insep.* survey, look over.
überbringen [y:bər'brɪŋən], *v.a. irr. insep.* bear, deliver, hand in.
Überbringung [y:bər'brɪŋuŋ], *f.* (—, *no pl.*) delivery.
überbrücken [y:bər'brykən], *v.a. insep.* bridge, span.
überdachen [y:bər'daxən], *v.a. insep.* roof (over).
überdauern [y:bər'dauərn], *v.a. insep.* outlast; tide over.
überdenken [y:bər'dɛŋkən], *v.a. irr. insep.* think over, consider.
überdies [y:bər'di:s], *adv.* besides, moreover.
überdrucken [y:bər'drukən], *v.a. insep.* overprint.
Überdruß ['y:bərdrus], *m.* (—**sses**, *no pl.*) weariness; disgust; *zum* —, ad nauseam.
überdrüssig ['y:bərdrysɪç], *adj.* weary of.
Übereifer ['y:bəraɪfər], *m.* (—**s**, *no pl.*) excessive zeal.
übereifrig ['y:bəraɪfrɪç], *adj.* excessively zealous, officious.
übereilen [y:bər'aɪlən], *v.r. insep. sich* —, hurry too much, overshoot the mark.
übereilt [y:bər'aɪlt], *adj.* overhasty, rash.
übereinkommen [y:bər'aɪnkɔmən], *v.n. irr.* (*aux.* sein) agree.
Übereinkunft [y:bər'aɪnkunft], *f.* (—, *pl.* ¨**e**) agreement, convention.
übereinstimmen [y:bər'aɪnʃtɪmən], *v.n.* agree, concur, harmonize, be of one mind, be of the same opinion; (*things*) tally, square.
Übereinstimmung [y:bər'aɪnʃtɪmuŋ], *f.* (—, *no pl.*) accord, agreement, conformity, harmony.
überfahren (1) [y:bər'fa:rən], *v.a. irr. insep.* traverse, pass over; run over (s.o.).
überfahren (2) ['y:bərfa:rən], *v.a. irr.* ferry across. — *v.n.* (*aux.* sein) cross.
überfahren (3) ['y:bərfa:rən], *v.n.* (*aux.* sein) cross.
Überfahrt ['y:bərfa:rt], *f.* (—, *pl.* —**en**) passage, crossing.
Überfall ['y:bərfal], *m.* (—**s**, *pl.* ¨**e**) sudden attack, raid.
überfallen (1) ['y:bərfalən], *v.n. irr.* (*aux.* sein) (*p.p.* übergefallen) fall over.
überfallen (2) [y:bər'falən], *v.a. irr., insep.* (*p.p.* überfallen) attack suddenly, raid.
überfliegen [y:bər'fli:gən], *v.a. irr. insep.* fly over; (*fig.*) glance over, skim.
überfließen ['y:bərfli:sən], *v.n. irr.* (*aux.* sein) overflow.

überflügeln [y:bər'fly:gəln], *v.a. insep.* surpass, outstrip.
Überfluß ['y:bərflus], *m.* (—**sses**, *no pl.*) abundance, plenty, profusion; surplus; — *haben an*, abound in, have too much of.
überflüssig ['y:bərflysɪç], *adj.* superfluous, unnecessary.
überfluten [y:bər'flu:tən], *v.a. insep.* overflow, flood.
überführen (1) ['y:bərfy:rən], *v.a.* convey, conduct (across).
überführen (2) [y:bər'fy:rən], *v.a. insep.* convict; transport a coffin.
Überführung [y:bər'fy:ruŋ], *f.* (—, *pl.* —**en**) conviction (for a crime); transport (of a coffin).
Überfüllung [y:bər'fyluŋ], *f.* (—, *no pl.*) overcrowding.
Übergabe ['y:bərga:bə], *f.* (—, *no pl.*) surrender, yielding up; delivery, handing over.
Übergang ['y:bərgaŋ], *m.* (—**s**, *pl.* ⸚**e**) passage; (*Railw.*) crossing; (*fig.*) change-over, transition.
übergeben [y:bər'ge:bən], *v.a. irr. insep.* deliver up, hand over. — *v.r. sich* —, vomit.
übergehen (1) ['y:bərge:ən], *v.n. irr.* (*aux.* sein) (*p.p.* übergegangen) go over, change over, turn (into); *zum Feinde* —, go over to the enemy; *in andre Hände* —, change hands.
übergehen (2) [y:bər'ge:ən], *v.a. irr. insep.* (*p.p.* übergangen) pass over, pass by.
Übergehung [y:bər'ge:uŋ], *f.* (—, *no pl.*) omission; passing over.
übergeordnet ['y:bərgəɔrdnət], *adj.* superior.
Übergewicht ['y:bərgəvɪçt], *n.* (—(**e**)**s**, *no pl.*) overweight; (*fig.*) preponderance, superiority.
übergießen [y:bər'gi:sən], *v.a. irr. insep.* pour over, douse with.
überglücklich ['y:bərglyklɪç], *adj.* overjoyed.
übergreifen ['y:bərgraɪfən], *v.n. irr.* overlap; encroach (upon); spread.
Übergriff ['y:bərgrɪf], *m.* (—(**e**)**s**, *pl.* —**e**) encroachment.
übergroß ['y:bərgro:s], *adj.* excessively large, overlarge.
überhaben ['y:bərha:bən], *v.a. irr.* have enough of, be sick of.
überhandnehmen [y:bər'hantne:mən], *v.n. irr.* gain the upper hand; run riot.
überhangen ['y:bərhaŋən], *v.n. irr.* hang over.
überhängen ['y:bərhɛŋən], *v.a. irr.* cover, hang upon.
überhäufen [y:bər'hɔyfən], *v.a. insep.* overwhelm.
überhaupt [y:bər'haupt], *adv.* in general, altogether, at all.
überheben [y:bər'he:bən], *v.r. irr. insep. sich* —, strain o.s. by lifting; (*fig.*) be overbearing.
überheblich [y:bər'he:plɪç], *adj.* overbearing, arrogant.
überheizen [y:bər'haɪtsən], *v.a. insp.* overheat.
überhitzt [y:bər'hɪtst], *adj.* overheated; impassioned.
überholen [y:bər'ho:lən], *v.a. insep.* overtake, out-distance; (*fig.*) overhaul.
überhören [y:bər'hø:rən], *v.a. insep.* hear s.o.'s lessons; ignore, miss (s.th.).
überirdisch ['y:bərɪrdɪʃ], *adj.* celestial, superterrestrial.
Überkleid ['y:bərklaɪt], *n.* (—(**e**)**s**, *pl.* —**er**) outer garment; overall.
überklug ['y:bərklu:k], *adj.* too clever by half, conceited.
überkochen ['y:bərkɔxən], *v.n.* (*aux.* sein) boil over.
überkommen [y:bər'kɔmən], *adj.* — *sein von*, be seized with.
überladen [y:bər'la:dən], *v.a. irr. insep.* overload. — *adj.* overdone, too elaborate; bombastic.
überlassen [y:bər'lasən], *v.a irr. insep.* leave, relinquish, give up, yield.
überlasten [y:bər'lastən], *v.a. insep.* overburden.
überlaufen (1) ['y:bərlaufən], *v.a. irr.* run over; (*to the enemy*) desert.
überlaufen (2) [y:bər'laufən], *v.a. insep.* (*p.p.* überlaufen) overrun.
Überläufer ['y:bərlɔyfər], *m.* (—**s**, *pl.* —) deserter, runaway.
überleben [y:bər'le:bən], *v.a. insep.* survive, outlive; (*fig.*) live (s.th.) down; *sich überlebt haben*, be out of date, be dated.
Überlebende [y:bər'le:bəndə], *m.* (—**n**, *pl.* —**n**) survivor.
überlegen (1) ['y:bərle:gən], *v.a.* lay over, cover.
überlegen (2) [y:bər'le:gən], *v.a. insep.* (*p.p.* überlegt) think over, consider, turn over in o.'s mind. — *adj.* superior; — *sein*, outdo, be superior to.
Überlegenheit [y:bər'le:gənhaɪt], *f.* (—, *no pl.*) superiority.
Überlegung [y:bər'le:guŋ], *f.* (—, *pl.* —**en**) consideration, deliberation; *bei näherer* —, on second thoughts, on thinking it over.
überliefern [y:bər'li:fərn], *v.a. insep.* hand down (to posterity), hand on, pass on.
Überlieferung [y:bər'li:fəruŋ], *f.* (—, *pl.* —**en**) tradition.
überlisten [y:bər'lɪstən], *v.a. insep.* outwit.
Übermacht ['y:bərmaxt], *f.* (—, *no pl.*) superiority, superior force.
übermalen [y:bər'ma:lən], *v.a. insep.* paint over.
übermangansauer [y:bərmaŋ'ga:nzauər], *adj.* permanganate of; —*saueres Kali*, permanganate of potash.
übermannen [y:bər'manən], *v.a. insep.* overpower.
Übermaß ['y:bərma:s], *n.* (—**es**, *no pl.*) excess; *im* —, to excess.

übermäßig ['y:bərmɛ:sɪç], *adj.* excessive, immoderate.
Übermensch ['y:bərmɛnʃ], *m.* (**—en,** *pl.* **—en**) superman.
übermenschlich ['y:bərmɛnʃlɪç], *adj.* superhuman.
übermitteln [y:bər'mɪtəln], *v.a. insep.* convey.
übermorgen ['y:bərmɔrgən], *adv.* the day after tomorrow.
Übermut ['y:bərmu:t], *m.* (**—s,** *no pl.*) wantonness; high spirits.
übermütig ['y:bərmy:tɪç], *adj.* wanton; full of high spirits.
übernachten [y:bər'naxtən], *v.n. insep.* pass *or* spend the night.
übernächtig [y:bər'nɛçtɪç], *adj.* haggard, tired by a sleepless night.
Übernahme ['y:bərna:mə], *f.* (**—,** *no pl.*) taking possession, taking charge.
übernatürlich ['y:bərnaty:rlɪç], *adj.* supernatural.
übernehmen [y:bər'ne:mən], *v.a. irr. insep.* take possession of, take upon o.s., take over. — *v.r. sich* —, overtax o.'s strength.
überordnen ['y:bərɔrdnən], *v.a.* place above.
überprüfen [y:bər'pry:fən], *v.a. insep.* examine, overhaul.
überquellen ['y:bərkvɛlən], *v.n. irr. insep.* (*aux.* sein) bubble over.
überqueren [y:bər'kve:rən], *v.a. insep.* cross.
überragen [y:bər'ra:gən], *v.a. insep.* tower above, overtop; (*fig.*) surpass, outstrip.
überraschen [y:bər'raʃən], *v.a. insep.* surprise, take by surprise.
Überraschung [y:bər'raʃuŋ], *f.* (**—,** *pl.* **—en**) surprise.
überreden [y:bər're:dən], *v.a. insep.* persuade, talk s.o. into (s.th.).
Überredung [y:bər're:duŋ], *f.* (**—,** *no pl.*) persuasion.
überreichen [y:bər'raɪçən], *v.a. insep.* hand over, present formally.
überreichlich ['y:bərraɪçlɪç], *adj.* superabundant.
Überreichung [y:bər'raɪçuŋ], *f.* (**—,** *no pl.*) formal presentation.
überreizen [y:bər'raɪtsən], *v.a. insep.* over-excite, over-stimulate.
überrennen [y:bər'rɛnən], *v.a. irr. insep.* take by storm, overrun.
Überrest ['y:bərrɛst], *m.* (**—es,** *pl.* **—e**) remainder, remnant, residue.
überrumpeln [y:bər'rumpəln], *v.a. insep.* catch unawares, surprise.
übersättigen [y:bər'zɛtɪgən], *v.a. insep.* saturate; surfeit, cloy.
Übersättigung [y:bər'zɛtɪguŋ], *f.* (**—,** *no pl.*) saturation; surfeit.
Überschallgeschwindigkeit ['y:bərʃalgəʃvɪndɪçkaɪt], *f.* (**—,** *no pl.*) supersonic speed.
überschatten [y:bər'ʃatən], *v.a. insep.* overshadow.
überschätzen [y:bər'ʃɛtsən], *v.a. insep.* overrate, over-estimate.
überschauen [y:bər'ʃauən], *v.a. insep.* survey.
überschäumen ['y:bərʃɔymən], *v.n.* (*aux.* sein) bubble over.
überschäumend ['y:bərʃɔymənt], *adj.* ebullient, exuberant.
Überschlag ['y:bərʃla:k], *m.* (**—s,** *pl.* **¨e**) somersault; estimate.
überschlagen [y:bər'ʃla:gən], *v.a. irr. insep.* (*pages*) miss, skip; estimate, compute. — *v.r. sich* —, turn a somersault, overturn. — *adj.* tepid, lukewarm.
überschnappen ['y:bərʃnapən], *v.n.* (*aux.* sein) snap; (*fig., coll.*) go out of o.'s mind.
überschreiben [y:bər'ʃraɪbən], *v.a. irr. insep.* superscribe, entitle.
überschreiten [y:bər'ʃraɪtən], *v.a. irr. insep.* cross; go beyond, exceed.
Überschrift ['y:bərʃrɪft], *f.* (**—,** *pl.* **—en**) heading, headline.
Überschuß ['y:bərʃus], *m.* (**—sses,** *pl.* **¨sse**) surplus.
überschüssig ['y:bərʃysɪç], *adj.* surplus, remaining.
überschütten [y:bər'ʃytən], *v.a. insep.* shower with, overwhelm with.
Überschwang ['y:bərʃvaŋ], *m.* (**—s,** *no pl.*) exaltation, rapture.
überschwemmen [y:bər'ʃvɛmən], *v.a. insep.* flood, inundate.
Überschwemmung [y:bər'ʃvɛmuŋ], *f.* (**—,** *pl.* **—en**) inundation, flood, deluge.
überschwenglich [y:bər'ʃvɛŋlɪç], *adj.* exuberant, exalted.
Übersee ['y:bərze:], *f.* (**—,** *no pl.*) overseas.
übersehen [y:bər'ze:ən], *v.a. irr. insep.* survey, look over; overlook, disregard.
übersenden [y:bər'zɛndən], *v.a. irr. insep.* send, forward, transmit; (*money*) remit.
Übersendung [y:bər'zɛnduŋ], *f.* (**—,** *pl.* **—en**) sending, forwarding, transmission; remittance.
übersetzen (1) ['y:bərzɛtsən], *v.a.* (*p.p.* übergesetzt) ferry across, cross (a river).
übersetzen (2) [y:bər'zɛtsən], *v.a. insep.* (*p.p.* übersetzt) translate.
Übersetzer [y:bər'zɛtsər], *m.* (**—s,** *pl.* **—**) translator.
Übersetzung [y:bər'zɛtsuŋ], *f.* (**—,** *pl.* **—en**) translation.
Übersicht ['y:bərzɪçt], *f.* (**—,** *pl.* **—en**) survey, summary; epitome.
übersichtlich ['y:bərzɪçtlɪç], *adj.* clearly arranged, readable at a glance, lucid.
übersiedeln [y:bər'zi:dəln], *v.n.* (*aux.* sein) remove, move, settle in a different place.
Übersiedlung [y:bər'zi:dluŋ], *f.* (**—,** *pl.* **—en**) removal.
überspannen [y:bər'ʃpanən], *v.a. insep.* overstretch.
überspannt [y:bər'ʃpant], *adj.* eccentric, extravagant.

Überspanntheit [y:bər'ʃpanthaɪt], *f.* (—, *pl.* —**en**) eccentricity.
überspringen [y:bər'ʃprɪŋən], *v.a. irr. insep.* jump over; (*fig.*) skip.
übersprudeln ['y:bərʃpru:dəln], *v.n.* (*aux.* sein) bubble over.
überstechen [y:bər'ʃtɛçən], *v.a. irr.* (*cards*) trump higher.
überstehen [y:bər'ʃte:ən], *v.a. irr. insep.* overcome, endure, get over, weather.
übersteigen [y:bər'ʃtaɪgən], *v.a. irr. insep.* exceed, surpass.
überstrahlen [y:bər'ʃtra:lən], *v.a. insep.* outshine, surpass in splendour.
überstreichen [y:bər'ʃtraɪçən], *v.a. irr. insep.* paint over.
überströmen [y:bər'ʃtrø:mən], *v.a. insep.* flood, overflow.
Überstunde ['y:bərʃtundə], *f.* (—, *pl.* —**n**) extra working time, overtime.
überstürzen [y:bər'ʃtyrtsən], *v.r. insep. sich* —, act in haste.
übertäuben [y:bər'tɔybən], *v.a. insep.* deafen.
überteuern [y:bər'tɔyərn], *v.a. insep.* overcharge.
übertölpeln [y:bər'tœlpəln], *v.a. insep.* cheat.
übertönen [y:bər'tø:nən], *v.a. insep.* (*sound*) drown.
übertragen [y:bər'tra:gən], *v.a. irr. insep.* transfer, hand over; convey; broadcast; translate; (*Comm.*) carry over; *einem ein Amt* —, confer an office on s.o.
Übertragung [y:bər'tra:guŋ], *f.* (—, *pl.* —**en**) cession; transference; handing over; (*Comm.*) carrying over; (*Rad.*) transmission; (*Med.*) transfusion.
übertreffen [y:bər'trɛfən], *v.a. irr. insep.* surpass, excel, outdo.
übertreiben [y:bər'traɪbən], *v.a. irr. insep.* exaggerate.
Übertreibung [y:bər'traɪbuŋ], *f.* (—, *pl.* —**en**) exaggeration.
übertreten (1) ['y:bərtre:tən], *v.n. irr.* (*aux.* sein) go over to; (*river*) overflow; (*religion*) change to, join (*church, party*).
übertreten (2) [y:bər'tre:tən], *v.a. irr. insep.* transgress, trespass against, infringe, violate.
Übertretung [y:bər'tre:tuŋ], *f.* (—, *pl.* —**en**) transgression, trespass, violation, infringement.
übertrieben [y:bər'tri:bən], *adj.* excessive, immoderate, exaggerated.
Übertritt ['y:bərtrɪt], *m.* (—**s**, *no pl.*) defection, going over; (*Rel.*) change, conversion.
übertünchen [y:bər'tynçən], *v.a. insep.* whitewash, rough-cast; (*fig.*) gloss over.
Übervölkerung [y:bər'fœlkəruŋ], *f.* (—, *no pl.*) overpopulation.
übervoll ['y:bərfɔl], *adj.* overful, brimful, chock-full.
übervorteilen [y:bər'fo:rtaɪlən], *v.a. insep.* cheat, defraud.
überwachen [y:bər'vaxən], *v.a. insep.* watch over, superintend, supervise.
Überwachung [y:bər'vaxuŋ], *f.* (—, *no pl.*) superintendence, supervision.
überwachsen [y:bər'vaksən], *v.a. irr. insep.* overgrow.
überwältigen [y:bər'vɛltɪgən], *v.a. insep.* overcome, overpower, subdue.
überwältigend [y:bər'vɛltɪgənt], *adj.* overwhelming.
Überwältigung [y:bər'vɛltɪguŋ], *f.* (—, *no pl.*) overpowering.
überweisen [y:bər'vaɪzən], *v.a. irr. insep.* assign; (*money*) remit.
Überweisung [y:bər'vaɪzuŋ], *f.* (—, *pl.* —**en**) assignment; (*money*) remittance.
überwerfen (1) ['y:bərvɛrfən], *v.a. irr.* throw over; (*clothes*) slip on.
überwerfen (2) [y:bər'vɛrfən], *v.r. irr. insep. sich* — *mit*, fall out with s.o.
überwiegen [y:bər'vi:gən], *v.n. irr. insep.* prevail.
überwiegend [y:bər'vi:gənt], *adj.* paramount, overwhelming, predominant.
überwinden [y:bər'vɪndən], *v.a. irr. insep.* overcome, conquer. — *v.r. sich* —, prevail upon o.s., bring o.s. (to).
Überwindung [y:bər'vɪnduŋ], *f.* (—, *no pl.*) conquest; reluctance.
überwintern [y:bər'vɪntərn], *v.n. insep.* winter, hibernate.
Überwinterung [y:bər'vɪntəruŋ], *f.* (—, *no pl.*) hibernation.
überwölkt [y:bər'vœlkt], *adj.* overcast.
Überwurf ['y:bərvurf], *m.* (—**s**, *pl.* ⸚**e**) wrap, shawl, cloak.
Überzahl ['y:bərtsa:l], *f.* (—, *no pl.*) *in der* —, in the majority.
überzählig ['y:bərtsɛ:lɪç], *adj.* supernumerary, surplus.
überzeichnen ['y:bərtsaɪçnən], *v.a. insep.* (*Comm.*) over-subscribe.
überzeugen [y:bər'tsɔygən], *v.a. insep.* convince. — *v.r. sich*—, satisfy o.s.
Überzeugung [y:bər'tsɔyguŋ], *f.* (—, *no pl.*) conviction.
überziehen (1) ['y:bərtsi:ən], *v.a. irr.* put on (a garment).
überziehen (2) [y:bər'tsi:ən], *v.a. irr. insep.* cover; (*bed*) put fresh linen on; (*Bank*) overdraw.
Überzieher ['y:bərtsi:ər], *m.* (—**s**, *pl.* —) overcoat.
Überzug ['y:bərtsu:k], *m.* (—**s**, *pl.* ⸚**e**) case, cover; bed-tick; coating.
üblich ['y:plɪç], *adj.* usual, customary; *nicht mehr* —, out of use, obsolete.
übrig ['y:brɪç], *adj.* remaining, left over; *die* —*en*, the others; — *bleiben*, be left, remain; — *haben*, have left; — *sein*, be left; *im* —*en*, for the rest; *ein* —*es tun*, stretch a point; *für einen etwas* — *haben*, like s.o.
übrigens ['y:brɪgəns], *adv.* besides, moreover; by the way.
Übung ['y:buŋ], *f.* (—, *pl.* —**en**) exercise, practice.

Ufer ['u:fər], *n.* (**—s**, *pl.* **—**) (*river*) bank; (*sea*) shore, beach.
Uganda [u'ganda], *n.* Uganda.
Uhr [u:r], *f.* (**—**, *pl.* **—en**) clock; watch; *elf* —, eleven o'clock; *wieviel — ist es?* what is the time?
Uhrmacher ['u:rmaxər], *m.* (**—s**, *pl.* **—**) watchmaker, clockmaker.
Uhrwerk ['u:rvɛrk], *n.* (**—s**, *pl.* **—e**) clockwork.
Uhrzeiger ['u:rtsaɪgər], *m.* (**—s**, *pl.* **—**) hand (of clock *or* watch).
Uhu ['u:hu:], *m.* (**—s**, *pl.* **—s**) (*Orn.*) eagle-owl.
ulkig ['ulkɪç], *adj.* funny.
Ulme ['ulmə], *f.* (**—**, *pl.* **—en**) (*Bot*). elm, elm-tree.
Ultrakurzwelle ['ultrakurtsvɛlə], *f.* (**—**, *pl.* **—n**) ultra-short wave.
ultrarot ['ultraro:t], *adj.* infra-red.
Ultrastrahlung ['ultraʃtra:luŋ], *f.* (**—**, *pl.* **—en**) cosmic radiation.
ultraviolett ['ultraviolet], *adj.* ultraviolet.
um [um], *prep.* (*Acc.*) about, around; approximately, near; for, because of; by; — *Geld bitten*, ask for money; — 5 *Uhr*, at five o'clock. — *conj.* to, in order to. — *adv.* up, past, upside down; round about; around.
umarbeiten ['umarbaɪtən], *v.a.* do again, remodel, revise; recast.
umarmen [um'armən], *v.a. insep.* embrace.
Umarmung [um'armuŋ], *f.* (**—**, *pl.* **—en**) embrace.
umbauen (1) ['umbauən], *v.a.* rebuild.
umbauen (2) [um'bauən], *v.a. insep.* surround with buildings.
umbiegen ['umbi:gən], *v.a. irr.* bend.
umbilden ['umbɪldən], *v.a.* transform, reform, recast, remould.
umbinden ['umbɪndən], *v.a. irr. sich etwas* —, tie s.th. around o.s.
umblicken ['umblɪkən], *v.r. sich* —, look round.
umbringen ['umbrɪŋən], *v.a. irr.* kill, slay, murder.
umdrehen ['umdre:ən], *v.a.* turn over, turn round, revolve. — *v.r. sich* —, turn round.
Umdrehung [um'dre:uŋ], *f.* (**—**, *pl.* **—en**) revolution, rotation.
umfahren (1) [um'fa:rən], *v.a. irr. insep.* drive round, circumnavigate.
umfahren (2) ['umfa:ren], *v.a. irr.* run down.
umfallen ['umfalən], *v.n. irr.* (*aux.* sein) fall down, fall over.
Umfang ['umfaŋ], *m.* (**—s**, *pl.* **¨e**) circumference; (*fig.*) extent.
umfangen [um'faŋən], *v.a. irr. insep.* encircle, embrace.
umfangreich ['umfaŋraɪç], *adj.* extensive, voluminous.
umfassen [um'fasən], *v.a. insep.* comprise, contain.
umfassend [um'fasənt], *adj.* comprehensive.
umfließen [um'fli:sən], *v.a. irr. insep.* surround by water.
umformen ['umfɔrmən], *v.a.* transform, remodel.
Umformung ['umfɔrmuŋ], *f.* (**—**, *pl.* **—en**) transformation, remodelling.
Umfrage ['umfra:gə], *f.* (**—**, *pl.* **—n**) enquiry, poll, quiz.
Umfriedung [um'fri:duŋ], *f.* (**—**, *pl.* **—en**) enclosure.
Umgang ['umgaŋ], *m.* (**—s**, *pl.* **¨e**) circuit, procession; (*fig.*) acquaintance, association; relations, connection; — *haben mit*, associate with.
umgänglich ['umgɛŋlɪç], *adj.* sociable, companionable.
Umgangsformen ['umgaŋsfɔrmən], *f. pl.* manners.
Umgangssprache ['umgaŋsʃpra:xə], *f.* (**—** *pl.* **—en**) colloquial speech.
umgeben [um'ge:bən], *v.a. irr. insep.* surround.
Umgebung [um'gə:buŋ], *f.* (**—**, *pl.* **—en**) environment, surroundings.
umgehen (1) ['umge:ən], *v.n. irr.* (*aux.* sein) associate with s.o.; handle s.th.; — *in*, haunt.
umgehen (2) [um'ge:ən], *v.a. irr. insep.* go round; (*flank*) turn; (*fig.*) evade, shirk.
umgehend ['umge:ənt], *adv.* immediately; (*letter*) by return mail.
Umgehung [um'ge:uŋ], *f.* (**—**, *pl.* **—en**) shirking, evasion; detour; (*Mil.*) flank movement, turning.
umgekehrt ['umgəke:rt], *adj.* reverse. — *adv.* conversely.
umgestalten ['umgəʃtaltən], *v.a.* transform, recast.
Umgestaltung ['umgəʃtaltuŋ], *f.* (**—**, *pl.* **—en**) transformation; recasting.
umgraben ['umgra:bən], *v.a. irr.* dig up.
umgrenzen [um'grɛntsən], *v.a. insep.* limit, set bounds to.
Umgrenzung [um'grɛntsuŋ], *f.* (**—**, *pl.* **—en**) boundary; limitation.
umgucken ['umgukən], *v.r. sich* —, look about o.
umhalsen [um'halzən], *v.a. insep.* hug, embrace.
Umhang ['umhaŋ], *m.* (**—s**, *pl.* **¨e**) shawl, cloak.
umher [um'he:r], *adv.* around, round, about.
umherblicken [um'he:rblɪkən], *v.n.* look round.
umherflattern [um'he:rflatərn], *v.n.* (*aux.* sein) flutter about.
umherlaufen [um'he:rlaufən], *v.n. irr.* (*aux.* sein) run about; roam about, ramble, wander.
umherziehend [um'he:rtsi:ənt], *adj.* itinerant.
umhüllen [um'hylən], *v.a. insep.* envelop, wrap up.
Umkehr ['umke:r], *f.* (**—**, *no pl.*) return; change; (*fig.*) conversion.

umkehren ['umke:rən], *v.a.* turn (back), upset, overturn. — *v.n.* (*aux.* sein) turn back, return.
Umkehrung ['umke:ruŋ], *f.* (—, *pl.* —**en**) inversion.
umkippen ['umkɪpən], *v.a.* upset, overturn. — *v.n.* (*aux.* sein) capsize, tilt over.
umklammern [um'klamərn], *v.a. insep.* clasp; clutch; (*fig.*) cling to.
umkleiden (1) ['umklaɪdən], *v.r. sich* —, change o.'s clothes.
umkleiden (2) [um'klaɪdən], *v.a. insep.* cover.
umkommen ['umkɔmən], *v.n. irr.* (*aux.* sein) perish.
Umkreis ['umkraɪs], *m.* (—**es**, *pl.* —**e**) circumference, compass.
Umlauf ['umlauf], *m.* (—**s**, *no pl.*) circulation; *in* — *bringen*, put into circulation.
Umlaut ['umlaut], *m.* (—**s**, *pl.* —**e**) (*Phonet.*) modification of vowels.
umlegen ['umle:gən], *v.a.* lay down, move, shift, put about; (*sl.*) kill.
umleiten ['umlaɪtən], *v.a.* (*traffic*) divert.
umlernen ['umlɛrnən], *v.a.*, *v.n.* relearn; retrain (for new job).
umliegend ['umli:gənt], *adj.* surrounding.
ummodeln ['ummo:dəln], *v.a.* remodel, recast, change, fashion differently.
Umnachtung [um'naxtuŋ], *f.* (—, *no pl.*) mental derangement.
umpacken ['umpakən], *v.a.* repack.
umpflanzen ['umpflantsən], *v.a.* transplant.
Umpflanzung ['umpflantsuŋ], *f.* (—, *pl.* —**en**) transplantation.
umrahmen ['umra:mən], *v.a. insep.* frame, surround.
umrändern [um'rɛndərn], *v.a. insep.* border, edge.
umrechnen ['umrɛçnən], *v.a.* (*figures*) reduce, convert.
umreißen (1) ['umraɪsən], *v.a. irr.* pull down, break up.
umreißen (2) [um'raɪsən], *v.a. irr. insep.* sketch, outline.
umrennen ['umrɛnən], *v.a. irr.* run down, knock over.
umringen [um'rɪŋən], *v.a. insep.* encircle, surround.
Umriß ['umrɪs], *m.* (—**sses**, *pl.* —**sse**) outline, contour.
umrühren ['umry:rən], *v.a.* (*Cul.*) stir.
umsatteln ['umzatəln], *v.n.* (*fig.*) change o.'s profession.
Umsatz ['umzats], *m.* (—**es**, *pl.* ⸚**e**) turnover.
umschalten ['umʃaltən], *v.a.* (*Elec.*) switch (over); reverse (current).
Umschau ['umʃau], *f.* (—, *no pl.*) review, survey; — *halten*, look round, muster, review.
umschauen ['umʃauən], *v.r. sich* —, look round.
umschichtig ['umʃɪçtɪç], *adv.* turn and turn about, in turns.
umschiffen (1) ['umʃɪfən], *v.a.* tranship, transfer (cargo, passengers).
umschiffen (2) [um'ʃɪfən], *v.a. insep.* sail round, circumnavigate.
Umschlag ['umʃla:k], *m.* (—(**e**)**s**, *pl.* ⸚**e**) (*weather*) break, sudden change; (*letter*) envelope; (*Med.*) poultice, compress.
umschlagen ['umʃla:gən], *v.n. irr.* (*aux.* sein) (*weather*) change suddenly; capsize; turn sour.
umschließen [um'ʃli:sən], *v.a. irr. insep.* enclose, surround; comprise.
umschlingen [um'ʃlɪŋən], *v.a. irr. insep.* embrace.
umschnallen ['umʃnalən], *v.a.* buckle on.
umschreiben (1) ['umʃraɪbən], *v.a. irr. insep.* rewrite, write differently.
umschreiben (2) [um'ʃraɪbən], *v.a. irr. insep.* circumscribe, paraphrase.
Umschreibung [um'ʃraɪbuŋ], *f.* (—, *pl.* —**en**) paraphrase.
Umschweife ['umʃvaɪfə], *m.pl.* fuss, talk; circumlocution; *ohne* —, point-blank.
Umschwung ['umʃvuŋ], *m.* (—**s**, *no pl.*) sudden change, revolution.
umsegeln [um'ze:gəln], *v.a. insep.* sail round.
umsehen ['umze:ən], *v.r. irr. sich* —, look round; look out (for), cast about (for).
Umsicht ['umzɪçt], *f.* (—, *no pl.*) circumspection.
umsichtig ['umzɪçtɪç], *adj.* cautious, circumspect.
umsinken ['umzɪŋkən], *v.n. irr.* (*aux.* sein) sink down.
umsonst [um'zɔnst], *adv.* without payment, gratis, for nothing; in vain, vainly, to no purpose.
umspannen (1) ['umʃpanən], *v.a.* change horses.
umspannen (2) [um'ʃpanən], *v.a. insep.* encompass, span.
umspringen ['umʃprɪŋən], *v.n. irr.* (*aux.* sein) (*wind*) change suddenly; *mit einem* —, (*fig.*) deal with s.o.
Umstand ['umʃtant], *m.* (—**s**, *pl.* ⸚**e**) circumstance; fact; factor; (*pl.*) fuss; *in anderen* ⸚*en sein*, be expecting a baby; *unter keinen* ⸚*en*, on no account.
umständlich ['umʃtɛntlɪç], *adj.* circumstantial, ceremonious; complicated, fussy.
Umstandswort ['umʃtantsvɔrt], *n.* (—**es**, *pl.* ⸚**er**) (*Gram.*) adverb.
umstehend ['umʃte:ənt], *adv.* on the next page.
Umstehenden ['umʃte:əndən], *pl.* bystanders.
umsteigen ['umʃtaɪgən], *v.n. irr.* (*aux.* sein) change (trains etc.).
umstellen (1) ['umʃtɛlən], *v.a.* place differently, transpose, change over.
umstellen (2) [um'ʃtɛlən], *v.a. insep.* surround, beset.

Umstellung ['umʃtɛluŋ], *f.* (—, *pl.* —**en**) transposition; (*Gram.*) inversion; change of position in team.
umstimmen ['umʃtɪmən], *v.a.* turn s.o. from his opinion, bring s.o. round to (s.th.).
umstoßen ['umʃto:sən], *v.a. irr.* knock down, upset, overthrow; (*judgment*) reverse.
umstricken [um'ʃtrɪkən], *v.a. insep.* ensnare.
umstritten [um'ʃtrɪtən], *adj.* controversial, disputed.
umstülpen ['umʃtylpən], *v.a.* turn up, turn upside down.
Umsturz ['umʃturts], *m.* (—**es**, *no pl.*) downfall; subversion; revolution.
umstürzen ['umʃtyrtsən], *v.a.* upset, overturn; overthrow.
umtaufen ['umtaufən], *v.a.* rename, rechristen.
Umtausch ['umtauʃ], *m.* (—**s**, *no pl.*) exchange.
umtauschen ['umtauʃən], *v.a.* exchange, change.
Umtriebe ['umtri:bə], *m. pl.* plots, goings-on, intrigues.
umtun ['umtu:n], *v.r. irr. sich — nach,* look for, cast about for.
Umwälzung ['umvɛltsuŋ], *f.* (—, *pl.* —**en**) turning-about; (*fig.*) revolution.
umwandeln ['umvandəln], *v.a.* change, transform; (*Gram.*) inflect.
umwechseln ['umvɛksəln], *v.a.* exchange.
Umweg ['umve:k], *m.* (—**s**, *pl.* —**e**) roundabout way, detour.
Umwelt ['umvɛlt], *f.* (—, *no pl.*) environment, milieu.
umwenden ['umvɛndən], *v.a. irr.* turn round; turn over. — *v.r. sich* —, turn round.
umwerben [um'vɛrbən], *v.a. irr. insep.* court.
umwerfen ['umvɛrfən], *v.a. irr.* overturn, knock over, upset.
umwickeln [um'vɪkəln], *v.a. insep.* wrap round, wind round.
umwölken [um'vœlkən], *v.r. insep. sich* —, (*sky*) darken, become overcast.
umzäunen [um'tsɔynən], *v.a. insep.* hedge in, fence in, enclose.
umziehen (1) ['umtsi:ən], *v.a. irr.* change (clothes). — *v.n.* (*aux.* sein) move (abode).— *v.r. sich* —, change o.'s clothes.
umziehen (2) [um'tsi:ən], *v.r. irr. insep. sich* —, get overcast, cloud over.
umzingeln [um'tsɪŋəln], *v.a. insep.* surround.
Umzug ['umtsu:k], *m.* (—**s**, *pl.* ⸗**e**) procession; removal; move.
unabänderlich [unap'ɛndərlɪç], *adj.* unalterable, irrevocable.
Unabänderlichkeit ['unapɛndərlɪçkaɪt], *f.* (—, *no pl.*) unchangeableness, irrevocability.
unabhängig ['unaphɛŋɪç], *adj.* independent, autonomous; unrelated.
Unabhängigkeit ['unaphɛŋɪçkaɪt], *f.* (—, *no pl.*) independence, self-sufficiency.
unabkömmlich ['unapkœmlɪç], *adj.* indispensable.
unablässig ['unaplɛsɪç], *adj.* unceasing, continual, unremitting.
unabsehbar ['unapze:ba:r], *adj.* immeasurable, immense; unfathomable.
unabsichtlich ['unapzɪçtlɪç], *adj.* unintentional, accidental.
unabwendbar [unap'vɛntba:r], *adj.* irremediable; unavoidable.
unachtsam ['unaxtza:m], *adj.* inattentive, inadvertent, negligent, careless.
Unachtsamkeit ['unaxtza:mkaɪt], *f.* (—, *pl.* —**en**) inadvertence, inattention, negligence, carelessness.
unähnlich ['unɛ:nlɪç], *adj.* unlike, dissimilar.
unanfechtbar ['unanfɛçtba:r], *adj.* indisputable, incontestable.
unangebracht ['unangəbraxt], *adj.* out of place, inapposite.
unangefochten ['unangəfɔxtən], *adj.* undisputed, uncontested.
unangemeldet ['unangəmɛldət], *adj.* unannounced, unheralded.
unangemessen ['unangəmɛsən], *adj.* unsuitable, inappropriate, inadequate.
unangenehm ['unangəne:m], *adj.* disagreeable, unpleasant; *einen — berühren,* jar, grate on s.o.
unangetastet ['unangətastət], *adj.* untouched.
unangreifbar ['unangraɪfba:r], *adj.* unassailable, secure.
unannehmbar ['unanne:mba:r], *adj.* unacceptable.
Unannehmlichkeit ['unanne:mlɪçkaɪt], *f.* (—, *pl.* —**en**) unpleasantness, annoyance.
unansehnlich ['unanze:nlɪç], *adj.* insignificant; unattractive.
unanständig ['unanʃtɛndɪç], *adj.* improper, indecent.
Unanständigkeit ['unanʃtɛndɪçkaɪt], *f.* (—, *pl.* —**en**) indecency, immodesty, impropriety.
unantastbar ['unantastba:r], *adj.* unimpeachable.
unappetitlich ['unapeti:tlɪç], *adj.* distasteful, unsavoury, unappetising.
Unart ['una:rt], *f.* (—, *pl.* —**en**) bad habit, naughtiness.
unartig ['una:rtɪç], *adj.* ill-behaved, naughty.
unästhetisch ['unɛste:tɪʃ], *adj.* offensive, coarse; inartistic.
unauffällig ['unauffɛlɪç], *adj.* unobtrusive.
unaufgefordert ['unaufgəfɔrdərt], *adj.* unbidden.
unaufgeklärt ['unaufgəklɛ:rt], *adj.* unexplained, unsolved.
unaufgeschnitten ['unaufgəʃnɪtən], *adj.* uncut.
unaufhaltsam ['unaufhaltza:m], *adj.* incessant, irresistible.

unaufhörlich [ˈunaufhø:rlɪç], *adj.* incessant, continual.
unauflöslich [ˈunauflø:slɪç], *adj.* indissoluble.
unaufmerksam [ˈunaufmɛrkza:m], *adj.* inattentive.
unaufrichtig [ˈunaufrɪçtɪç], *adj.* insincere.
unaufschiebbar [ˈunaufʃi:pba:r], *adj.* urgent, pressing, brooking no delay.
unausbleiblich [ˈunausblaɪplɪç], *adj.* inevitable, unfailing.
unausführbar [ˈunausfy:rba:r], *adj.* impracticable.
unausgebildet [ˈunausgəbɪldət], *adj.* untrained, unskilled.
unausgefüllt [ˈunausgəfylt], *adj.* not filled up; (*form*) blank.
unausgegoren [ˈunausgəgo:rən], *adj.* crude; (*wine*) unfermented.
unausgesetzt [ˈunausgəzɛtst], *adj.* continual, continuous.
unausgesprochen [ˈunausgəʃprɔxən], *adj.* unsaid; (*fig.*) implied.
unauslöschlich [ˈunauslø:ʃlɪç], *adj.* indelible, inextinguishable.
unaussprechlich [ˈunausʃprɛçlɪç], *adj.* inexpressible, unspeakable.
unausstehlich [ˈunausʃte:lɪç], *adj.* insufferable.
unausweichlich [ˈunausvaɪçlɪç], *adj.* inevitable.
unbändig [ˈunbɛndɪç], *adj.* intractable, unmanageable; (*fig.*) extreme.
unbarmherzig [ˈunbarmhɛrtsɪç], *adj.* merciless.
unbeabsichtigt [ˈunbəapzɪçtɪçt], *adj.* unintentional.
unbeanstandet [ˈunbəanʃtandət], *adj.* unexceptionable; unopposed; with impunity.
unbeantwortlich [ˈunbəantvɔrtlɪç], *adj.* unanswerable.
unbeaufsichtigt [ˈunbəaufzɪçtɪçt], *adj.* unattended to, not looked after; without supervision.
unbebaut [ˈunbəbaut], *adj.* (*Agr.*) uncultivated; undeveloped (by building).
unbedacht [ˈunbədaxt], *adj.* thoughtless.
unbedenklich [ˈunbədɛŋklɪç], *adj.* harmless, innocuous. — *adv.* without hesitation.
unbedeutend [ˈunbədɔytənt], *adj.* insignificant.
unbedingt [ˈunbədɪŋkt], *adj.* unconditional, unlimited, absolute. — *adv.* quite definitely; without fail.
unbeeinflußt [ˈunbəaɪnflust], *adj.* uninfluenced.
unbefahrbar [ˈunbəfa:rba:r], *adj.* impassable, impracticable.
unbefangen [ˈunbəfaŋən], *adj.* unbiased, unprejudiced; easy, unselfconscious, unembarrassed, uninhibited; natural.
Unbefangenheit [ˈunbəfaŋənhaɪt], *f.* (—, *no pl.*) impartiality; ease of manner, unselfconsciousness, openness, naturalness.
unbefestigt [ˈunbəfɛstɪçt], *adj.* unfortified.
unbefleckt [ˈunbəflɛkt], *adj.* immaculate; *—e Empfängnis*, Immaculate Conception.
unbefriedigend [ˈunbəfri:dɪgənt], *adj.* unsatisfactory.
unbefriedigt [ˈunbəfri:dɪçt], *adj.* not satisfied, unsatisfied.
unbefugt [ˈunbəfu:kt], *adj.* unauthorised.
unbegreiflich [ˈunbəgraɪflɪç], *adj.* incomprehensible, inconceivable.
unbegrenzt [ˈunbəgrɛntst], *adj.* unlimited, unbounded.
unbegründet [ˈunbəgryndət], *adj.* unfounded, groundless.
Unbehagen [ˈunbəha:gən], *n.* (**—s**, *no pl.*) uneasiness, discomfort.
unbehaglich [ˈunbəha:klɪç], *adj.* uncomfortable; *sich — fühlen*, feel ill at ease.
unbehelligt [ˈunbəhɛlɪçt], *adj.* unmolested.
unbeholfen [ˈunbəhɔlfən], *adj.* awkward, clumsy.
unbeirrt [ˈunbəɪrt], *adj.* unswerving, uninfluenced, unperturbed.
unbekannt [ˈunbəkant], *adj.* unknown, unacquainted; *ich bin hier —*, I am a stranger here.
unbekümmert [ˈunbəkymərt], *adj.* unconcerned, careless, indifferent.
unbelehrt [ˈunbəle:rt], *adj.* uninstructed.
unbeliebt [ˈunbəli:pt], *adj.* unpopular.
unbemannt [ˈunbəmant], *adj.* without crew, unmanned.
unbemerkbar [ˈunbəmɛrkba:r], *adj.* unnoticeable, imperceptible.
unbemerkt [ˈunbəmɛrkt], *adj.* unnoticed.
unbemittelt [ˈunbəmɪtəlt], *adj.* impecunious, poor.
unbenommen [ˈunbənɔmən], *adj.* *es bleibt dir —*, you are free to.
unbenutzt [ˈunbənutst], *adj.* unused.
unbequem [ˈunbəkve:m], *adj.* uncomfortable, inconvenient, troublesome.
Unbequemlichkeit [ˈunbəkve:mlɪçkaɪt], *f.* (—, *pl.* **—en**) inconvenience.
unberechenbar [ˈunbərɛçənba:r], *adj.* incalculable; (*fig.*) erratic.
unberechtigt [ˈunbərɛçtɪçt], *adj.* unwarranted, unjustified.
unberücksichtigt [ˈunbərykzɪçtɪçt], *adj.* disregarded; *— lassen*, ignore.
unberufen [ˈunbəru:fən], *adj.* unauthorized. — *excl.* touch wood!
unbeschadet [ˈunbəʃa:dət], *prep.* (*Genit.*) without prejudice to.
unbeschädigt [ˈunbəʃɛ:dɪçt], *adj.* undamaged.
unbeschäftigt [ˈunbəʃɛftɪçt], *adj.* unemployed, disengaged.

unbescheiden [ˈunbəʃaɪdən], *adj.* presumptuous, greedy, immodest; unblushing; exorbitant; arrogant.
Unbescheidenheit [ˈunbəʃaɪdənhaɪt], *f.* (—, *no pl.*) presumptuousness, greed.
unbescholten [ˈunbəʃɔltən], *adj.* irreproachable, of unblemished character.
Unbescholtenheit [ˈunbəʃɔltənhaɪt], *f.* (—, *no pl.*) blamelessness, good character, unsullied reputation.
unbeschränkt [ˈunbəʃrɛŋkt], *adj.* unlimited, unbounded; *—e Monarchie*, absolute monarchy.
unbeschreiblich [ˈunbəʃraɪplɪç], *adj.* indescribable.
unbeschrieben [ˈunbəʃriːbən], *adj.* unwritten; *ein —es Papier*, a blank sheet of paper.
unbeschwert [ˈunbəʃveːrt], *adj.* unburdened; easy.
unbeseelt [ˈunbəzeːlt], *adj.* inanimate.
unbesiegbar [unbəˈziːkbaːr], *adj.* invincible.
unbesoldet [ˈunbəzɔldət], *adj.* unpaid, unsalaried.
unbesonnen [ˈunbəzɔnən], *adj.* thoughtless, rash.
Unbesonnenheit [ˈunbəzɔnənhaɪt], *f.* (—, *pl.* **—en**) thoughtlessness.
unbesorgt [ˈunbəzɔrkt], *adj.* unconcerned; *sei —*, never fear.
unbeständig [ˈunbəʃtɛndɪç], *adj.* fickle, inconstant; (*weather*) unsettled.
unbestechlich [ˈunbəʃtɛçlɪç], *adj.* incorruptible.
unbestellbar [ˈunbəʃtɛlbaːr], *adj.* not deliverable; (*letters etc.*) address(ee) unknown.
unbestellt [ˈunbəʃtɛlt], *adj.* not ordered; (*Agr.*) uncultivated, untilled.
unbestimmt [ˈunbəʃtɪmt], *adj.* uncertain, not settled; indefinite; irresolute; vague.
unbestraft [ˈunbəʃtraːft], *adj.* unpunished; without previous conviction.
unbestreitbar [ˈunbəʃtraɪtbaːr], *adj.* indisputable, incontestable.
unbestritten [ˈunbəʃtrɪtən], *adj.* uncontested, undoubted, undisputed.
unbeteiligt [ˈunbətaɪlɪçt], *adj.* unconcerned, indifferent.
unbeträchtlich [ˈunbətrɛçtlɪç], *adj.* inconsiderable, trivial.
unbetreten [ˈunbətreːtən], *adj.* untrodden, untouched.
unbeugsam [ˈunbɔykzaːm], *adj.* inflexible, unyielding.
unbewacht [ˈunbəvaxt], *adj.* unguarded.
unbewaffnet [ˈunbəvafnət], *adj.* unarmed; *mit —em Auge*, with the naked eye.
unbewandert [ˈunbəvandərt], *adj.* unversed in, unfamiliar with.
unbezahlt [ˈunbətsaːlt], *adj.* unpaid.
unbezähmbar [ˈunbətsɛːmbaːr], *adj.* uncontrollable; indomitable.
unbezwinglich [ˈunbətsvɪŋlɪç], *adj.* invincible, unconquerable.
Unbildung [ˈunbɪlduŋ], *f.* (—, *no pl.*) lack of education *or* knowledge *or* culture.
Unbill [ˈunbɪl], *f.* (—, *pl.* **Unbilden**) injustice, wrong, injury; (*weather*) inclemency.
unbillig [ˈunbɪlɪç], *adj.* unreasonable, unfair.
Unbilligkeit [ˈunbɪlɪçkaɪt], *f.* (—, *no pl.*) unreasonableness, injustice, unfairness.
unbotmäßig [ˈunboːtmɛːsɪç], *adj.* unruly, insubordinate.
unbußfertig [ˈunbuːsfɛrtɪç], *adj.* impenitent, unrepentant.
und [unt], *conj.* and; *— nicht*, nor; *— so weiter* (abbr. *u.s.w.*), etc., and so on, and so forth; *— wenn*, even if.
Undank [ˈundaŋk], *m.* (**—s**, *no pl.*) ingratitude.
undankbar [ˈundaŋkbaːr], *adj.* ungrateful; *eine —e Aufgabe*, a thankless task.
Undankbarkeit [ˈundaŋkbaːrkaɪt], *f.* (—, *no pl.*) ingratitude.
undenkbar [ˈundɛŋkbaːr], *adj.* unthinkable, unimaginable, inconceivable.
undenklich [ˈundɛŋklɪç], *adj. seit —en Zeiten*, from time immemorial.
undeutlich [ˈundɔytlɪç], *adj.* indistinct; inarticulate; (*fig.*) unintelligible.
Unding [ˈundɪŋ], *n.* (**—s**, *no pl.*) absurdity.
unduldsam [ˈundultzaːm], *adj.* intolerant.
undurchdringlich [ˈundurçdrɪŋlɪç], *adj.* impenetrable.
undurchführbar [ˈundurçfyːrbaːr], *adj.* impracticable, unworkable.
undurcchsihtig [ˈundurçzɪçtɪç], *adj.* opaque, not transparent.
uneben [ˈuneːbən], *adj.* uneven, rugged; (*coll.*) *nicht —*, not bad.
unecht [ˈunɛçt], *adj.* false, not genuine, spurious, counterfeit.
unedel [ˈunedəl], *adj.* (*metal*) base.
unehelich [ˈuneːəlɪç], *adj.* illegitimate.
Unehre [ˈuneːrə], *f.* (—, *no pl.*) dishonour, disgrace, discredit.
unehrlich [ˈuneːrlɪç], *adj.* dishonest
Unehrlichkeit [ˈuneːrlɪçkaɪt], *f.* (—, *pl.* **—en**) dishonesty.
uneigennützig [ˈunaɪgənnytsɪç], *adj.* unselfish, disinterested, public-spirited.
uneingedenk [ˈunaɪngədɛŋk], *adj.* (*Genit.*) unmindful, forgetful.
uneingeschränkt [ˈunaɪngəʃrɛŋkt], *adj.* unrestrained, unlimited.
uneinig [ˈunaɪnɪç], **uneins** [ˈunaɪns], *adj.* disunited, divided; *— werden*, fall out; *— sein*, disagree.
Uneinigkeit [ˈunaɪnɪçkaɪt], *f.* (—, *pl.* **—en**) disharmony, discord.
uneinnehmbar [ˈunaɪnneːmbaːr], *adj.* unconquerable, impregnable.

uneins *see under* **uneinig.**
unempfänglich ['unɛmpfɛŋlɪç], *adj.* insusceptible; unreceptive.
unempfindlich ['unɛmpfɪntlɪç], *adj.* insensitive, indifferent; unfeeling.
unendlich [un'ɛntlɪç], *adj.* endless, infinite.
unentbehrlich ['unɛntbe:rlɪç], *adj.* indispensable, (absolutely) essential.
unentgeltlich [unɛnt'gɛltlɪç], *adj.* free (of charge).
unentschieden ['unɛntʃi:dən], *adj.* undecided, undetermined; irresolute; (*game*) drawn, tied.
unentschlossen ['unɛntʃlɔsən], *adj.* irresolute.
Unentschlossenheit ['unɛntʃlɔsənhaɪt], *f.* (—, *no pl.*) irresolution, indecision.
unentschuldbar ['unɛntʃultba:r], *adj.* inexcusable.
unentstellt ['unɛntʃtɛlt], *adj.* undistorted.
unentwegt ['unɛntve:kt], *adj.* steadfast, unflinching, unswerving.
unentwickelt ['unɛntvɪkəlt], *adj.* undeveloped; *—e Länder*, underdeveloped countries.
unentwirrbar ['unɛntvɪrba:r], *adj.* inextricable.
unentzifferbar ['unɛnttsɪfərba:r], *adj.* indecipherable.
unentzündbar ['unɛnttsyntba:r], *adj.* non-inflammable.
unerachtet ['unɛraxtət], *prep.* (*Genit.*) (*obs.*) notwithstanding.
unerbeten ['unɛrbe:tən], *adj.* unsolicited.
unerbittlich ['unɛrbɪtlɪç], *adj.* inexorable.
unerfahren ['unɛrfa:rən], *adj.* inexperienced.
unerforschlich ['unɛrfɔrʃlɪç], *adj.* inscrutable.
unerfreulich ['unɛrfrɔylɪç], *adj.* unpleasant, displeasing, disagreeable.
unerfüllbar ['unɛrfylba:r], *adj.* unrealisable.
unerfüllt ['unɛrfylt], *adj.* unfulfilled.
unergründlich ['unɛrgryntlɪç], *adj.* unfathomable, impenetrable.
unerheblich ['unɛrhe:plɪç], *adj.* trifling, unimportant.
unerhört ['unɛrhø:rt], *adj.* unprecedented, unheard of, shocking, outrageous; not granted; turned down.
unerkannt ['unɛrkant], *adj.* unrecognised.
unerkennbar ['unɛrkɛnba:r], *adj.* unrecognisable.
unerklärlich ['unɛrklɛ:rlɪç], *adj.* inexplicable.
unerläßlich ['unɛrlɛslɪç], *adj.* indispensable.
unerlaubt ['unɛrlaupt], *adj.* unlawful, illicit.
unermeßlich ['unɛrmɛslɪç], *adj.* immense, vast.
unermüdlich ['unɛrmy:tlɪç], *adj.* untiring, indefatigable.
unerquicklich ['unɛrkvɪklɪç], *adj.* unedifying, disagreeable.
unerreichbar ['unɛrraɪçba:r], *adj.* unattainable, inaccessible.
unerreicht ['unɛrraɪçt], *adj.* unequalled.
unersättlich ['unɛrzɛtlɪç], *adj.* insatiable, greedy.
unerschöpflich ['unɛrʃœpflɪç], *adj.* inexhaustible.
unerschöpft ['unɛrʃœpft], *adj.* unexhausted.
unerschrocken ['unɛrʃrɔkən], *adj.* intrepid, undaunted.
unerschütterlich ['unɛrʃytərlɪç], *adj.* imperturbable.
unerschüttert ['unɛrʃytərt], *adj.* unshaken, unperturbed.
unerschwinglich ['unɛrʃvɪŋlɪç], *adj.* prohibitive, exorbitant, unattainable.
unersetzlich ['unɛrzɛtslɪç], *adj.* irreplaceable.
unersprießlich ['unɛrʃpri:slɪç], *adj.* unprofitable.
unerträglich ['unɛrtrɛ:klɪç], *adj.* intolerable, insufferable.
unerwartet ['unɛrvartət], *adj.* unexpected.
unerwidert ['unɛrvi:dərt], *adj.* (*love*) unrequited; (*letter*) unanswered.
unerwünscht ['unɛrvynʃt], *adj.* undesirable, unwelcome.
unerzogen ['unɛrtso:gən], *adj.* uneducated; ill-bred, unmannerly.
unfähig ['unfɛ:ɪç], *adj.* incapable, unable, unfit.
Unfähigkeit ['unfɛ:ɪçkaɪt], *f.* (—, *no pl.*) incapability, inability, unfitness.
Unfall ['unfal], *m.* (—s, *pl.* ¨e) accident.
unfaßbar ['unfasba:r], *adj.* incomprehensible, inconceivable.
unfehlbar ['unfɛ:lba:r], *adj.* inevitable; infallible.
Unfehlbarkeit ['unfe:lba:rkaɪt], *f.* (—, *no pl.*) infallibility.
unfein ['unfaɪn], *adj.* indelicate, coarse, impolite.
unfern ['unfɛrn], *prep.* (*Genit.*, *Dat.*) not far from.
unfertig ['unfɛrtɪç], *adj.* unfinished, unready.
unflätig ['unflɛ:tɪç], *adj.* obscene, nasty, filthy.
unfolgsam ['unfɔlkza:m], *adj.* disobedient, recalcitrant.
unförmig ['unfœrmɪç], *adj.* deformed, ill-shaped, misshapen.
unförmlich ['unfœrmlɪç], *adj.* shapeless; free and easy, unceremonious.
unfrankiert ['unfraŋki:rt], *adj.* (*letter*) not prepaid, unstamped, unfranked.
unfrei ['unfraɪ], *adj.* not free; subjugated; constrained.
unfreiwillig ['unfraɪvɪlɪç], *adj.* involuntary.

unfreundlich [ˈunfrɔyntlɪç], *adj.* unfriendly, unkind; (*weather*) inclement.
Unfreundlichkeit [ˈunfrɔyntlɪçkaɪt], *f.* (—, *pl.* —**en**) unfriendliness, unkindness; (*weather*) inclemency.
Unfrieden [ˈunfri:dən], *m.* (—**s**, *no pl.*) discord, dissension.
unfruchtbar [ˈunfruxtba:r], *adj.* barren, sterile; (*fig.*) fruitless.
Unfug [ˈunfu:k], *m.* (—**s**, *no pl.*) disturbance, misconduct; mischief; *grober* —, public nuisance.
unfühlbar [ˈunfy:lba:r], *adj.* imperceptible.
ungangbar [ˈunganŋba:r], *adj.* impassable.
Ungarn [ˈuŋgarn], *n.* Hungary.
ungastlich [ˈungastlɪç], *adj.* inhospitable.
ungeachtet [ˈungəaxtət], *prep.* (*Genit.*) notwithstanding.
ungeahndet [ˈungəa:ndət], *adj.* unpunished, with impunity.
ungeahnt [ˈungəa:nt], *adj.* unexpected, unsuspected, undreamt of.
ungebändigt [ˈungəbɛndɪçt], *adj.* untamed.
ungebärdig [ˈungəbɛ:rdɪç], *adj.* unmannerly, refractory.
ungebeten [ˈungəbe:tən], *adj.* uninvited, unbidden.
ungebleicht [ˈungəblaɪçt], *adj.* unbleached.
ungebraucht [ˈungəbrauxt], *adj.* unused.
Ungebühr [ˈungəby:r], *f.* (—, *no pl.*) unseemliness, impropriety, excess.
ungebührlich [ˈungəby:rlɪç], *adj.* unseemly.
ungebunden [ˈungəbundən], *adj.* unbound, in sheets; unrestrained, loose; unlinked; —*e Rede*, prose.
Ungeduld [ˈungədult], *f.* (—, *no pl.*) impatience.
ungeduldig [ˈungəduldɪç], *adj.* impatient.
ungeeignet [ˈungəaɪgnət], *adj.* unfit, unsuitable.
ungefähr [ˈungəfɛ:r], *adj.* approximate, rough. — *adv.* approximately, roughly, about, round.
ungefährlich [ˈungəfɛ:rlɪç], *adj.* not dangerous, harmless, safe.
ungefällig [ˈungəfɛlɪç], *adj.* ungracious, disobliging.
ungefärbt [ˈungəfɛrpt], *adj.* uncoloured; (*fig.*) unvarnished.
ungefüge [ˈungəfy:gə], *adj.* clumsy.
ungehalten [ˈungəhaltən], *adj.* indignant, angry.
ungeheißen [ˈungəhaɪsən], *adj.* unbidden. — *adv.* of o.'s own accord.
ungehemmt [ˈungəhɛmt], *adj.* unchecked, uninhibited.
ungeheuchelt [ˈungəhɔyçəlt], *adj.* unfeigned.
Ungeheuer [ˈungəhɔyər], *n.* (—**s**, *pl.* —) monster, monstrosity.
ungeheuer [ˈungəhɔyər], *adj.* huge, immense; atrocious, frightful.
ungehobelt [ˈungəho:bəlt], *adj.* unplaned; (*fig.*) boorish, uncultured, unpolished.
ungehörig [ˈungəhø:rɪç], *adj.* unseemly, improper.
Ungehorsam [ˈungəho:rza:m], *m.* (—**s**, *no pl.*) disobedience.
ungehorsam [ˈungəho:rza:m], *adj.* disobedient; — *sein*, disobey.
Ungehorsamkeit [ˈungəho:rza:mkaɪt], *f.* (—, *pl.* —**en**) disobedience, insubordination.
ungekämmt [ˈungəkɛmt], *adj.* unkempt.
ungekünstelt [ˈungəkynstəlt], *adj.* artless, unstudied.
ungeladen [ˈungəla:dən], *adj.* (*gun*) unloaded, not charged; uninvited.
ungeläutert [ˈungəlɔytərt], *adj.* unrefined; unpurified.
ungelegen [ˈungəle:gən], *adj.* inconvenient, inopportune.
Ungelegenheit [ˈungəle:gənhaɪt], *f.* (—, *pl.* —**en**) inconvenience, trouble.
ungelehrig [ˈungəle:rɪç], *adj.* intractable, unintelligent.
ungelenk [ˈungəlɛŋk], *adj.* clumsy, awkward; ungainly.
ungelöscht [ˈungəlœʃt], *adj.* unquenched; (*lime*) unslaked; (*mortgage*) unredeemed.
Ungemach [ˈungəma:x], *n.* (—(**e**)**s**, *no pl.*) adversity, toil, privation.
ungemein [ˈungəmaɪn], *adj.* uncommon, extraordinary. — *adv.* very much, exceedingly.
ungemütlich [ˈungəmy:tlɪç], *adj.* uncomfortable, cheerless, unpleasant.
ungeniert [ˈunʒeni:rt], *adj.* free and easy, unceremonious, unabashed.
ungenießbar [ˈungəˈni:sba:r], *adj.* unpalatable, uneatable, inedible.
ungenügend [ˈungənygənt], *adj.* insufficient, unsatisfactory.
ungenügsam [ˈungəny:kza:m], *adj.* insatiable, greedy.
ungeordnet [ˈungəɔrdnət], *adj.* ill-assorted, confused.
ungepflegt [ˈungəpfle:kt], *adj.* uncared for, neglected.
ungerade [ˈungəra:də], *adj.* uneven; — *Zahl*, odd number.
ungeraten [ˈungəra:tən], *adj.* abortive, unsuccessful, spoiled; undutiful; ill-bred.
ungerecht [ˈungərɛçt], *adj.* unjust, unfair.
ungerechtfertigt [ˈungərɛçtfɛrtɪçt], *adj.* unwarranted, unjustified.
Ungerechtigkeit [ˈungərɛçtɪçkaɪt], *f.* (—, *pl.* —**en**) injustice.
ungeregelt [ˈungəre:gəlt], *adj.* not regulated, irregular.
ungereimt [ˈungəraɪmt], *adj.* rhymeless; —*es Zeug*, nonsense, absurdity.
ungern [ˈungɛrn], *adv.* unwillingly, reluctantly.

ungerufen ['ungəru:fən], *adj.* unbidden.
ungerührt ['ungəry:rt], *adj.* unmoved.
ungesäumt ['ungezɔymt], *adj.* unseamed, unhemmed; (*fig.*) immediate. — *adv.* immediately, without delay.
ungeschehen ['ungəʃe:ən], *adj.* undone; — *machen*, undo.
Ungeschick ['ungəʃɪk], *n.* (—**s**, *no pl.*) awkwardness, clumsiness.
Ungeschicklichkeit ['ungəʃɪklɪçkaɪt], *f.* (—, *pl.* —**en**) awkwardness, clumsiness.
ungeschickt ['ungəʃɪkt], *adj.* awkward, clumsy, unskilful.
ungeschlacht ['ungəʃlaxt], *adj.* uncouth, unwieldy; coarse, rude.
ungeschliffen ['ungəʃlɪfən], *adj.* unpolished; (*fig.*) coarse.
Ungeschliffenheit ['ungəʃlɪfənhaɪt], *f.* (—, *no pl.*) coarseness, uncouthness.
ungeschmälert ['ungəʃmɛ:lərt], *adj.* undiminished, unimpaired.
ungeschminkt ['ungəʃmɪŋkt], *adj.* without cosmetics *or* make-up, not made up; (*truth*) plain, unvarnished.
ungeschoren ['ungəʃo:rən], *adj.* unshorn; *laß mich* —, leave me alone.
ungeschult ['ungəʃu:lt], *adj.* untrained.
ungeschwächt ['ungəʃvɛçt], *adj.* unimpaired.
ungesellig ['ungəzɛlɪç], *adj.* unsociable.
ungesetzlich ['ungəzɛtslɪç], *adj.* illegal, unlawful, illicit.
ungesetzmäßig ['ungəzɛtsmɛ:sɪç], *adj.* illegitimate, lawless; exceptional; not regular.
ungesiegelt ['ungəzi:gəlt], *adj.* unsealed.
Ungestalt ['ungəʃtalt], *f.* (—, *no pl.*) deformity.
ungestalt ['ungəʃtalt], *adj.* misshapen, deformed.
ungestempelt ['ungəʃtɛmpəlt], *adj.* unstamped, uncancelled, not postmarked.
ungestillt ['ungəʃtɪlt], *adj.* unquenched, unslaked; not fed, unsatisfied.
ungestört ['ungəʃtø:rt], *adj.* undisturbed.
ungestraft ['ungəʃtra:ft], *adj.* unpunished. — *adv.* with impunity.
ungestüm ['ungəʃty:m], *adj.* impetuous.
Ungestüm ['ungəʃty:m], *m.* & *n.* (—**s**, *no pl.*) impetuosity.
ungesund ['ungəzunt], *adj.* unwholesome, unhealthy, sickly; (*fig.*) unnatural, morbid.
ungetan ['ungəta:n], *adj.* not done, left undone.
ungetreu ['ungətrɔy], *adj.* disloyal, faithless.
ungetrübt ['ungətry:pt], *adj.* untroubled.
ungewandt ['ungəvant], *adj.* unskilful.
ungewaschen ['ungəvaʃən], *adj.* unwashed; (*sl.*) —*es Mundwerk*, malicious tongue.
ungeweiht ['ungəvaɪt], *adj.* unconsecrated.
ungewiß ['ungəvɪs], *adj.* uncertain, doubtful.
Ungewißheit ['ungəvɪshaɪt], *f.* (—, *no pl.*) uncertainty, suspense.
Ungewitter ['ungəvɪtər], *n.* (—**s**, *pl.* —) storm, thunderstorm.
ungewöhnlich ['ungəvø:nlɪç], *adj.* unusual, uncommon.
Ungewohntheit ['ungəvo:nthaɪt], *f.* (—, *no pl.*) strangeness; want of practice.
ungezähmt ['ungətsɛ:mt], *adj.* untamed; (*fig.*) uncurbed.
Ungeziefer ['ungətsi:fər], *n.* (—**s**, *pl.* —) vermin.
ungeziert ['ungətsi:rt], *adj.* unaffected, natural.
ungezogen ['ungətso:gən], *adj.* ill-mannered, naughty.
ungezügelt ['ungətsy:gəlt], *adj.* unbridled; (*fig.*) unruly.
ungezwungen ['ungətsvuŋən], *adj.* unforced; (*fig.*) unaffected.
Ungezwungenheit ['ungətsvuŋənhaɪt], *f.* (—, *no pl.*) naturalness, ease.
Unglaube ['unglaubə], *m.* (—**ns**, *no pl.*) disbelief.
unglaubhaft ['unglauphaft], *adj.* unauthenticated, incredible.
ungläubig ['unglɔybɪç], *adj.* incredulous, disbelieving.
Ungläubige ['unglɔybɪgə], *m.* (—**n**, *pl.* —**n**) unbeliever.
unglaublich ['unglauplɪç], *adj.* incredible, unbelievable.
unglaubwürdig ['unglaupvyrdɪç], *adj.* unauthenticated, incredible.
ungleichartig ['unglaɪça:rtɪç], *adj.* dissimilar, heterogeneous.
ungleichförmig ['unglaɪçfœrmɪç], *adj.* not uniform; dissimilar.
Ungleichheit ['unglaɪçhaɪt], *f.* (—, *pl.* —**en**) inequality; unlikeness, dissimilarity; unevenness.
ungleichmäßig ['unglaɪçmɛ:sɪç], *adj.* unequal, irregular; changeable, fitful.
Unglimpf ['unglɪmpf], *m.* (—(**e**)**s**, *no pl.*) harshness; insult.
Unglück ['unglyk], *n.* (—**s**, *pl.* —**sfälle**) misfortune, adversity, ill-luck; accident, disaster; distress, sorrow, affliction.
unglückbringend ['unglykbrɪŋənt], *adj.* disastrous, unpropitious.
unglücklich ['unglyklɪç], *adj.* unfortunate, unhappy, unlucky; —*e Liebe*, unrequited love.
unglücklicherweise ['unglyklɪçərvaɪzə], *adv.* unfortunately, unluckily.
Unglücksbotschaft ['unglyksbo:tʃaft], *f.* (—, *pl.* —**en**) bad news.
unglückselig ['unglykze:lɪç], *adj.* luckless, wretched, unfortunate, calamitous.
Unglücksfall ['unglyksfal], *m.* (—(**e**)**s**, *pl.* ¨**e**) accident.

Unglücksgefährte ['unglyksgəfɛ:rtə], *m.* (—n, *pl.* —n) companion in misfortune.
Ungnade ['ungna:də], *f.* (—, *no pl.*) disgrace.
ungültig ['ungyltɪç], *adj.* invalid, void; — *machen*, invalidate, annul.
Ungunst ['ungunst], *f.* (—, *no pl.*) disfavour; unpropitiousness; (*weather*) inclemency.
ungünstig ['ungynstɪç], *adj.* unfavourable, adverse.
ungut ['ungu:t], *adv.* *etwas für — nehmen*, take s.th. amiss.
unhaltbar ['unhaltba:r], *adj.* untenable.
Unheil ['unhaɪl], *n.* (—s, *no pl.*) mischief, harm; disaster.
unheilbar ['unhaɪlba:r], *adj.* incurable.
unheilbringend ['unhaɪlbrɪŋənt], *adj.* ominous, unlucky; disastrous.
Unheilstifter ['unhaɪlʃtɪftər], *m.* (—s, *pl.* —) mischief-maker.
unheilvoll ['unhaɪlfɔl], *adj.* calamitous, disastrous.
unheimlich ['unhaɪmlɪç], *adj.* weird, eerie, uncanny.
unhöflich ['unhø:flɪç], *adj.* impolite, uncivil, discourteous.
Unhold ['unhɔlt], *m.* (—s, *pl.* —e) fiend, monster.
Unhörbarkeit ['unhø:rba:rkaɪt], *f.* (—, *no pl.*) inaudibility.
Uniformität [unifɔrmi'tɛ:t], *f.* (—, *no pl.*) uniformity.
Unikum ['u:nikum], *n.* (—s, *pl.* —s) unique thing *or* person; eccentric.
Universalmittel [univɛr'za:lmɪtəl], *n.* (—s, *pl.* —) panacea, universal remedy.
Universität [univɛrzi'tɛ:t], *f.* (—, *pl.* —en) university.
Universitätsdozent [univɛrzi'tɛ:tsdo-tsɛnt], *m.* (—en, *pl.* —en) university lecturer.
Universum [uni'vɛrzum], *n.* (—s, *no pl.*) universe.
unkaufmännisch ['unkaufmɛnɪʃ], *adj.* unbusinesslike.
Unke ['uŋkə], *f.* (—, *pl.* —n) (*Zool.*) toad; (*fig.*) grumbler, pessimist.
unken ['uŋkən], *v.n.* grumble, grouse.
unkenntlich ['unkɛntlɪç], *adj.* indiscernible, unrecognisable.
Unkenntlichkeit ['unkɛntlɪçkaɪt], *f.* (—, *no pl.*) *bis zur* —, past recognition.
Unkenntnis ['unkɛntnɪs], *f.* (—, *no pl.*) ignorance.
unklug ['unklu:k], *adj.* imprudent.
Unkosten ['unkɔstən], *f. pl.* expenses, costs, charges; overheads.
Unkraut ['unkraut], *n.* (—s, *no pl.*) weed(s).
unkündbar ['unkyntba:r], *adj.* irredeemable; irrevocable, permanent.
unkundig ['unkundɪç], *adj.* ignorant (of), unacquainted (with).
unlängst ['unlɛŋst], *adv.* recently, lately, not long ago.
unlauter ['unlautər], *adj.* sordid, squalid; unfair.
unleidlich ['unlaɪtlɪç], *adj.* intolerable.
unleserlich ['unle:zərlɪç], *adj.* illegible.
unleugbar ['unlɔykba:r], *adj.* undeniable, indisputable.
unlieb ['unli:p], *adj.* disagreeable.
unliebenswürdig ['unli:bənsvyrdɪç], *adj.* sullen, surly.
unlösbar ['unlø:sba:r], *adj.* insoluble.
unlöslich ['unlø:slɪç], *adj.* (*substance*) indissoluble, insoluble.
Unlust ['unlust], *f.* (—, *no pl.*) aversion, disinclination; slackness.
unlustig ['unlustɪç], *adj.* averse, disinclined.
unmanierlich ['unmani:rlɪç], *adj.* ill-mannered.
unmännlich ['unmɛnlɪç], *adj.* unmanly, effeminate.
Unmaß ['unma:s], *n.* (—es, *no pl.*) excess.
Unmasse ['unmasə], *f.* (—, *pl.* —n) vast quantity.
unmaßgeblich ['unma:sge:plɪç], *adj.* unauthoritative, open to correction; (*fig.*) humble.
unmäßig ['unmɛ:sɪç], *adj.* intemperate, excessive.
Unmenge ['unmɛŋə], *f.* (—, *pl.* —n) vast quantity.
Unmensch ['unmɛnʃ], *m.* (—en, *pl.* —en) brute.
unmenschlich ['unmɛnʃlɪç], *adj.* inhuman, brutal; (*coll.*) vast.
unmerklich ['unmɛrklɪç], *adj.* imperceptible.
unmeßbar ['unmɛsba:r], *adj.* immeasurable.
unmittelbar ['unmɪtəlba:r], *adj.* immediate, direct.
unmöglich ['unmø:klɪç], *adj.* impossible.
unmündig ['unmyndɪç], *adj.* under age, minor.
Unmündige ['unmyndɪgə], *m.* (—n, *pl.* —n) (*Law*) minor.
Unmündigkeit ['unmyndɪçkaɪt], *f.* (—, *no pl.*) minority.
Unmut ['unmu:t], *m.* (—s, *no pl.*) ill-humour; displeasure, indignation, petulance.
unmutig ['unmu:tɪç], *adj.* ill-humoured, petulant, indignant.
unnachahmlich ['unnaxa:mlɪç], *adj.* inimitable.
unnachgiebig ['unnaxgi:bɪç], *adj.* relentless, unyielding.
unnachsichtig ['unnaxzɪçtɪç], *adj.* unrelenting, relentless.
unnahbar ['unna:ba:r], *adj.* unapproachable, stand-offish.
unnennbar ['unnɛnba:r], *adj.* unutterable.
unnütz ['unnyts], *adj.* useless.
unordentlich ['unɔrdəntlɪç], *adj.* untidy, slovenly.
Unordnung ['unɔrdnuŋ], *f.* (—, *no pl.*) disorder, untidiness, muddle, confusion.

unparteiisch ['unpartaɪɪʃ], *adj.* impartial, unbiased, objective.
unpassend ['unpasənt], *adj.* unsuitable, inappropriate; improper.
unpassierbar ['unpasi:rba:r], *adj.* impassable.
unpäßlich ['unpɛslɪç], *adj.* indisposed, unwell, out of sorts.
Unpäßlichkeit ['unpɛslɪçkaɪt], *f.* (—, *pl.* —**en**) indisposition.
unproportioniert ['unprɔpɔrtsjoni:rt], *adj.* disproportionate; unshapely.
unqualifizierbar ['unkvalifitsi:rba:r], *adj.* unspeakable, nameless.
Unrat ['unra:t], *m.* (—(**e**)**s**, *no pl.*) dirt, rubbish.
unratsam ['unra:tza:m], *adj.* inadvisable.
Unrecht ['unrɛçt], *n.* (—(**e**)**s**, *no pl.*) wrong, injustice; — *haben*, be in the wrong.
unrecht ['unrɛçt], *adj.* wrong, unjust.
unrechtmäßig ['unrɛçtmɛ:sɪç], *adj.* unlawful, illegal.
unredlich ['unre:tlɪç], *adj.* dishonest.
unregelmäßig ['unre:gəlmɛ:sɪç], *adj.* irregular.
unreif ['unraɪf], *adj.* unripe, immature; (*fig.*) crude, raw.
Unreife ['unraɪfə], *f.* (—, *no pl.*) immaturity.
unrein ['unraɪn], *adj.* unclean; (*fig.*) impure.
Unreinheit ['unraɪnhaɪt], *f.* (—, *pl.* —**en**) impurity.
Unreinlichkeit ['unraɪnlɪçkaɪt], *f.* (—, *no pl.*) uncleanliness.
unrentabel ['unrɛnta:bəl], *adj.* unprofitable.
unrettbar ['unrɛtba:r], *adj.* irretrievable, hopelessly lost.
unrichtig ['unrɪçtɪç], *adj.* incorrect, erroneous, wrong.
Unrichtigkeit ['unrɪçtɪçkaɪt], *f.* (—, *no pl.*) error, falsity, incorrectness.
Unruhe ['unru:ə], *f.* (—, *pl.* —**en**) unrest, restlessness; disquiet, uneasiness; riot, disturbance; (*clock*) balance.
Unruhestifter ['unru:əʃtɪftər], *m.* (—**s**, *pl.* —) disturber (of the peace); troublemaker.
unruhig ['unru:ɪç], *adj.* restless; troublesome, turbulent, uneasy (about), fidgety.
unrühmlich ['unry:mlɪç], *adj.* inglorious.
uns [uns], *pers. pron.* us, ourselves; to us.
unsachlich ['unzaxlɪç], *adj.* subjective; irrelevant.
unsagbar ['unza:kba:r], *adj.* unutterable, unspeakable.
unsanft ['unzanft], *adj.* harsh, violent.
unsauber ['unzaubər], *adj.* unclean, dirty; (*fig.*) squalid.
unschädlich ['unʃɛ:tlɪç], *adj.* harmless, innocuous.
unschätzbar ['unʃɛtsba:r], *adj.* invaluable.
unscheinbar ['unʃaɪnba:r], *adj.* plain, homely, insignificant.
unschicklich ['unʃɪklɪç], *adj.* unbecoming, indecent, improper, unseemly.
unschlüssig ['unʃlysɪç], *adj.* irresolute, undecided.
Unschuld ['unʃult], *f.* (—, *no pl.*) innocence; *verfolgte* —, injured innocence.
unschuldig ['unʃuldɪç], *adj.* innocent, guiltless; chaste; —*es Vergnügen*, harmless pleasure.
unschwer ['unʃve:r], *adv.* easily.
Unsegen ['unze:gən], *m.* (—**s**, *no pl.*) misfortune; curse.
unselbständig ['unzɛlpʃtɛndɪç], *adj.* dependent.
unselig ['unze:lɪç], *adj.* unfortunate, luckless, fatal.
unser ['unzər], *poss. adj.* our. — *pers. pron.* of us.
unsereiner ['unzəraɪnər], *pron.* s.o. in our position; one of us, people in our position.
unserthalben, unsertwegen ['unzərthalbən, unzərtve:gən], *adv.* for our sake, on our account.
unsertwillen ['unzərtvɪlən], *adv. um* —, for our sake, on our account.
unsicher ['unzɪçər], *adj.* unsafe; uncertain, doubtful; (*route*) precarious; (*hand*) unsteady; (*legs*) shaky.
unsichtbar ['unzɪçtba:r], *adj.* invisible.
Unsinn ['unzɪn], *m.* (—**s**, *no pl.*) nonsense.
unsinnig ['unzɪnɪç], *adj.* nonsensical; mad, insane.
Unsitte ['unzɪtə], *f.* (—, *pl.* —**n**) abuse, nuisance; bad habit.
unsittlich ['unzɪtlɪç], *adj.* immoral.
unstät, unstet ['unʃtɛ:t, 'unʃte:t], *adj.* unsteady, inconstant; restless.
unstatthaft ['unʃtathaft], *adj.* illicit.
unsterblich ['unʃtɛrplɪç], *adj.* immortal.
Unsterblichkeit ['unʃtɛrplɪçkaɪt], *f.* (—, *no pl.*) immortality.
unstillbar ['unʃtɪlba:r], *adj.* unappeasable, unquenchable.
unstreitig ['unʃtraɪtɪç], *adj.* indisputable, unquestionable.
Unsumme ['unzumə], *f.* (—, *pl.* —**n**) vast amount (of money).
unsympathisch ['unzympa:tɪʃ], *adj.* uncongenial, disagreeable; *er ist mir* —, I dislike him.
untadelhaft, untadelig ['unta:dəlhaft, 'unta:dəlɪç], *adj.* blameless, irreproachable, unimpeachable.
Untat ['unta:t], *f.* (—, *pl.* —**en**) misdeed, crime.
untätig ['untɛ:tɪç], *adj.* inactive, idle, supine.
untauglich ['untauklɪç], *adj.* unfit, useless; incompetent; (*Mil.*) disabled.
unteilbar [un'taɪlba:r], *adj.* indivisible.

unten ['untən], *adv.* below, beneath; (*house*) downstairs.
unter ['untər], *prep.* (*Dat.*, *Acc.*) under, beneath, below, among, between.
Unterbau ['untərbau], *m.* (**—s**, *pl.* **—ten**) substructure, foundation.
Unterbewußtsein ['untərbəvustzaın], *n.* (**—s**, *no pl.*) subconscious mind, subconsciousness.
unterbieten [untər'bi:tən], *v.a.* *irr.* *insep.* underbid, undersell.
Unterbilanz ['untərbilants], *f.* (**—**, *pl.* **—en**) deficit.
unterbinden [untər'bındən], *v.a.* *irr.* *insep.* tie up, bind up; (*fig.*) prevent, check.
unterbleiben [untər'blaıbən], *v.n.* *irr.* *insep.* (*aux.* sein) remain undone, be left undone, cease.
unterbrechen [untər'brεçən], *v.a.* *irr.* *insep.* interrupt; (*journey*) break; (*speech*) cut short.
Unterbrechung [untər'brεçuŋ], *f.* (**—**, *pl.* **—en**) interruption.
unterbreiten (1) ['untərbraıtən], *v.a.* spread under.
unterbreiten (2) [untər'braıtən], *v.a.* *insep.* submit, lay before.
unterbringen ['untərbrıŋən], *v.a.* *irr.* provide (*a place*) for; (*goods*) dispose of; (*money*) invest; (*people*) accommodate, put up.
Unterbringung ['untərbrıŋuŋ], *f.* (**—**, *no pl.*) provision for; (*goods*) disposal of; (*money*) investment; (*people*) accommodation.
unterdessen [untər'dεsən], *adv.*, *conj.* in the meantime, meanwhile.
unterdrücken [untər'drykən], *v.a.* *insep.* suppress, curb, check; oppress.
Unterdrückung [untər'drykuŋ], *f.* (**—**, *no pl.*) oppression, suppression.
untereinander [untəraın'andər], *adv.* with each other, mutually, among themselves.
unterfangen [untər'faŋən], *v.r.* *irr.* *insep.* *sich* —, dare, venture, presume.
Untergang ['untərgaŋ], *m.* (**—s**, *pl.* **⸚e**) (*sun*) setting; (*ship*) sinking; (*fig.*) decline.
untergeben [untər'ge:bən], *adj.* subject, subordinate.
Untergebene [untər'ge:bənə], *m.* (**—n**, *pl.* **—n**) subordinate.
untergehen ['untərge:ən], *v.n.* *irr.* (*aux.* sein) (*sun*) go down, set; (*ship*) sink; (*fig.*) perish; decline.
Untergeschoß ['untərgəʃɔs], *n.* (**—sses**, *pl.* **—sse**) ground floor; basement.
Untergestell ['untərgəʃtεl], *n.* (**—s**, *pl.* **—e**) undercarriage, chassis.
untergraben [untər'gra:bən], *v.a.* *irr.* *insep.* undermine.
unterhalb ['untərhalp], *prep.* (*Genit.*) below, under.
Unterhalt ['untərhalt], *m.* (**—s**, *no pl.*) maintenance, support, livelihood.
unterhalten (1) ['untərhaltən], *v.a.* *irr.* hold under.
unterhalten (2) [untər'haltən], *v.a.* *irr.* *insep.* maintain, keep, support; entertain. — *v.r.* *sich* —, converse, make conversation; *sich gut* —, enjoy o.s.
unterhaltend [untər'haltənt], *adj.* entertaining, amusing, lively.
Unterhaltskosten ['untərhaltskɔstən], *f. pl.* maintenance; (*house*) cost of repairs.
Unterhaltung [untər'haltuŋ], *f.* (**—**, *pl.* **—en**) maintenance; conversation; amusement, entertainment.
Unterhaltungslektüre [untər'haltuŋslεkty:rə], *f.* (**—**, *no pl.*) light reading, fiction.
unterhandeln [untər'handəln], *v.n.* *insep.* negotiate.
Unterhändler ['untərhεndlər], *m.* (**—s**, *pl.* **—**) negotiator, mediator.
Unterhandlung [untər'handluŋ], *f.* (**—**, *pl.* **—en**) negotiation.
Unterhaus ['untərhaus], *n.* (**—es**, *pl.* **⸚er**) ground floor; (*Parl.*) lower house; House of Commons.
Unterhemd ['untərhεmt], *n.* (**—(e)s**, *pl.* **—en**) vest.
unterhöhlen [untər'hø:lən], *v.a.* *insep.* undermine.
Unterholz ['untərhɔlts], *n.* (**—es**, *no pl.*) undergrowth, underwood.
Unterhosen ['untərho:zən], *f. pl.* (*women*) briefs; (*men*) underpants.
unterirdisch ['untərırdıʃ], *adj.* subterranean, underground.
unterjochen [untər'jɔxən], *v.a.* *insep.* subjugate, subdue.
Unterkiefer ['untərki:fər], *m.* (**—s**, *pl.* **—**) lower jaw.
Unterkleid ['untərklaıt], *n.* (**—s**, *pl.* **—er**) under-garment.
unterkommen ['untərkɔmən], *v.n.* *irr.* (*aux.* sein) find accommodation *or* shelter; (*fig.*) find employment.
Unterkommen ['untərkɔmən], *n.* (**—s**, *no pl.*) shelter, accommodation; (*fig.*) employment, place.
Unterkörper ['untərkœrpər], *m.* (**—s**, *pl.* **—**) lower part of the body.
unterkriegen ['untərkri:gən], *v.a.* get the better of; *lass dich nicht* —, stand firm.
Unterkunft ['untərkunft], *f.* (**—**, *pl.* **⸚e**) shelter, accommodation; employment.
Unterlage ['untərla:gə], *f.* (**—**, *pl.* **—n**) foundation, base; blotting pad; (*pl.*) documents, files.
unterlassen [untər'lasən], *v.a.* *irr.* *insep.* omit (to do), fail (to do), neglect; forbear.
Unterlassung [untər'lasuŋ], *f.* (**—**, *pl.* **—en**) omission, neglect.
Unterlassungssünde [untər'lasuŋszyndə], *f.* (**—**, *pl.* **—n**) sin of omission.
Unterlauf ['untərlauf], *m.* (**—(e)s**, *pl.* **⸚e**) (*river*) lower course.

unterlaufen [untər'laufən], *v.n. irr. insep.* (*aux.* sein) run under; (*mistake*) creep in. — *adj.* suffused, blood-shot.

unterlegen (1) ['untərle:gən], *v.a.* lay under; *einen anderen Sinn* —, put a different construction upon.

unterlegen (2) [untər'le:gən], *adj.* inferior.

Unterleib ['untərlaıp], *m.* (—**s**, *no pl.*) abdomen.

unterliegen [untər'li:gən], *v.n. irr. insep.* (*aux.* sein) succumb, be overcome; be subject (to).

Untermieter ['untərmi:tər], *m.* (—**s**, *pl.* —) subtenant.

unterminieren [untərmi'ni:rən], *v.a. insep.* undermine.

unternehmen [untər'ne:mən], *v.a. irr. insep.* undertake, take upon o.s., attempt.

Unternehmen [untər'ne:mən], *n.* (—**s**, *pl.* —) enterprise, undertaking.

unternehmend [untər'ne:mənt], *adj.* bold, enterprising.

Unternehmer [untər'ne:mər], *m.* (—**s**, *pl.* —) contractor, entrepreneur.

Unteroffizier ['untərɔfitsi:r], *m.* (—**s**, *pl.* —**e**) (*army*) non-commissioned officer; (*navy*) petty officer.

unterordnen ['untərɔrdnən], *v.a.* subordinate. — *v.r. sich* —, submit (to).

Unterordnung ['untərɔrdnuŋ], *f.* (—, *no pl.*) subordination, submission; (*Biol.*) sub-order.

Unterpacht ['untərpaxt], *f.* (—, *no pl.*) sublease.

Unterpfand ['untərpfant], *n.* (—(**e**)**s**, *no pl.*) (*obs.*) pawn, pledge.

Unterredung [untər're:duŋ], *f.* (—, *pl.* —**en**) conference, interview, talk.

Unterricht ['untərrıçt], *m.* (—(**e**)**s**, *no pl.*) instruction, tuition, teaching.

unterrichten [untər'rıçtən], *v.a. insep.* instruct, teach.

Unterrichtsanstalt ['untərrıçtsanʃtalt], *f.* (—, *pl.* —**en**) educational establishment *or* institution.

Unterrichtsgegenstand ['untərrıçtsge:gənʃtant], *m.* (—**s**, *pl.* ¨—**e**) subject of instruction.

Unterrock ['untərrɔk], *m.* (—**s**, *pl.* ¨—**e**) petticoat, slip; underskirt.

untersagen [untər'za:gən], *v.a. insep.* forbid; *Rauchen untersagt*, smoking prohibited.

Untersatz ['untərzats], *m.* (—**es**, *pl.* ¨—**e**) basis, holder, stand, trestle; saucer.

unterschätzen [untər'ʃɛtsən], *v.a. insep.* underrate, underestimate.

unterscheiden [untər'ʃaıdən], *v.a. irr. insep.* distinguish, discriminate, discern, differentiate. — *v.r. sich* —, differ; *ich kann sie nicht* —, I cannot tell them apart.

Unterscheidung [untər'ʃaıduŋ], *f.* (—, *pl.* —**en**) distinction, differentiation.

Unterscheidungsmerkmal [untər'ʃaıduŋsmɛrkma:l], *n.* (—**s**, *pl.* —**e**) distinctive mark, characteristic.

Unterscheidungsvermögen [untər'ʃaıduŋsfɛrmø:gən], *n.* (—**s**, *no pl.*) power of discrimination.

Unterscheidungszeichen [untər'ʃaıduŋstsaıçən], *n.* (—**s**, *pl.* —) criterion.

Unterschenkel ['untərʃɛŋkəl], *m.* (—**s**, *pl.* —) shank, lower part of the thigh.

Unterschicht ['untərʃıçt], *f.* (—, *pl.* —**en**) substratum, subsoil.

unterschieben (1) ['untərʃi:bən], *v.a. irr.* substitute; interpolate; forge; foist upon.

unterschieben (2) [untər'ʃi:bən], *v.a. irr. insep.* (*fig.*) attribute falsely, pass s.o. off as.

Unterschiebung [untər'ʃi:buŋ], *f.* (—, *pl.* —**en**) substitution; forgery.

Unterschied ['untərʃi:t], *m.* (—(**e**)**s**, *pl.* —**e**) difference.

unterschiedlich ['untərʃi:tlıç], *adj.* different, diverse.

unterschiedslos ['untərʃi:tslo:s], *adv.* indiscriminately.

unterschlagen [untər'ʃla:gən], *v.a. irr. insep.* embezzle, intercept.

Unterschlagung [untər'ʃla:guŋ], *f.* (—, *pl.* —**en**) embezzlement.

Unterschlupf ['untərʃlupf], *m.* (—**es**, *pl.* ¨—**e**) shelter, refuge.

unterschlüpfen ['untərʃlypfən], *v.n.* (*aux.* sein) find shelter, slip away; (*fig.*) hide.

unterschreiben [untər'ʃraıbən], *v.a. irr. insep.* sign, subscribe to.

Unterschrift ['untərʃrıft], *f.* (—, *pl.* —**en**) signature.

Unterseeboot ['untərze:bo:t], *n.* (—**s**, *pl.* —**e**) submarine.

untersetzt [untər'zɛtst], *adj.* thickset, dumpy.

untersinken ['untərzıŋkən], *v.n. irr.* (*aux.* sein) go down.

unterst ['untərst], *adj.* lowest, undermost, bottom.

Unterstaatssekretär [untər'ʃta:tszekretɛ:r], *m.* (—**s**, *pl.* —**e**) under-secretary of state.

unterstehen (1) ['untərʃte:ən], *v.n. irr.* (*aux.* sein) find shelter (under).

unterstehen (2) [untər'ʃte:ən], *v.n. irr. insep.* be subordinate. — *v.r. sich* —, dare, venture.

unterstellen (1) ['untərʃtɛlən], *v.a.* place under. — *v.r. sich* —, take shelter (under).

unterstellen (2) [untər'ʃtɛlən], *v.a. insep.* put under the authority of; impute (s.th. to s.o.).

Unterstellung [untər'ʃtɛluŋ], *f.* (—, *pl.* —**en**) imputation, insinuation.

unterstreichen [untər'ʃtraıçən], *v.a. irr. insep.* underline.

Unterstreichung [untər'ʃtraıçuŋ], *f.* (—, *pl.* —**en**) underlining.

Unterströmung ['untərʃtrø:muŋ], *f.* (—, *pl.* —**en**) undercurrent.

unterstützen [untər'ʃtytsən], *v.a. insep.* support, assist, aid; (*fig.*) countenance.

Unterstützung [untər'ʃtytsuŋ], *f.* (—, *pl.* —**en**) support, aid, assistance, relief.
Unterstützungsanstalt [untər'ʃtytsuŋs-anʃtalt], *f.* (—, *pl.* —**en**) charitable institution.
unterstützungsbedürftig [untər'ʃtyt-suŋsbədyrftɪç], *adj.* indigent.
untersuchen [untər'zu:xən], *v.a. insep.* investigate, examine, look over.
Untersuchung [untər'zu:xuŋ], *f.* (—, *pl.* —**en**) investigation, inquiry; (*medical*) examination.
Untersuchungshaft [untər'zu:xuŋs-haft], *f.* (—, *no pl.*) imprisonment pending investigation.
Untersuchungsrichter [untər'zu:-xuŋsrɪçtər], *m.* (—**s**, *pl.* —) examining magistrate.
Untertan ['untərta:n], *m.* (—**s**, *pl.* —**en**) subject, vassal.
untertan ['untərta:n], *adj.* subject.
untertänig ['untərtɛ:nɪç], *adj.* humble, obsequious, submissive, servile.
Untertasse ['untərtasə], *f.* (—, *pl.* —**n**) saucer.
untertauchen ['untərtauxən], *v.a.* dip, duck, submerge. — *v.n.* (*aux.* sein) dive.
unterwegs [untər've:ks], *adv.* on the way.
unterweisen [untər'vaɪzən], *v.a. irr. insep.* teach, instruct.
Unterweisung [untər'vaɪzuŋ], *f.* (—, *pl.* —**en**) instruction, teaching.
Unterwelt ['untərvɛlt], *f.* (—, *no pl.*) Hades, the underworld.
unterwerfen [untər'vɛrfən], *v.a. irr. insep.* subject, subdue. — *v.r. sich* —, submit (to), resign o.s. (to).
Unterwerfung [untər'vɛrfuŋ], *f.* (—, *no pl.*) subjection, submission.
unterwühlen [untər'vy:lən], *v.a. insep.* root up; (*fig.*) undermine.
unterwürfig [untər'vyrfɪç], *adj.* submissive, subject; obsequious.
Unterwürfigkeit [untər'vyrfɪçkaɪt], *f.* (—, *no pl.*) submissiveness; obsequiousness.
unterzeichnen [untər'tsaɪçnən], *v.a. insep.* sign.
Unterzeichner [untər'tsaɪçnər], *m.* (—**s**, *pl.* —) signatory; (*insurance*) underwriter.
Unterzeichnete [untər'tsaɪçnətə], *m.* (—**n**, *pl.* —**n**) undersigned.
Unterzeichnung [untər'tsaɪçnuŋ], *f.* (—, *pl.* —**en**) signature.
unterziehen [untər'tsi:ən], *v.r. irr. insep. sich* —, submit to, undertake; (*operation*) undergo.
Untiefe ['unti:fə], *f.* (—, *pl.* —**n**) shallow water, flat, shoal, sands.
Untier ['unti:r], *n.* (—**s**, *pl.* —**e**) monster.
untilgbar ['untɪlkba:r], *adj.* indelible; (*debt*) irredeemable.
untrennbar ['untrɛnba:r], *adj.* inseparable.
untreu ['untrɔy], *adj.* faithless, unfaithful, disloyal, perfidious.
Untreue ['untrɔyə], *f.* (—, *no pl.*) faithlessness, unfaithfulness, disloyalty, perfidy.
untröstlich ['untrø:stlɪç], *adj.* inconsolable, disconsolate.
untrüglich ['untry:klɪç], *adj.* unmistakable, infallible.
untüchtig ['untyçtɪç], *adj.* inefficient; incompetent.
unüberlegt ['uny:bərle:kt], *adj.* inconsiderate, thoughtless; rash.
unübersehbar ['uny:bərze:ba:r], *adj.* immense, vast.
unübersteiglich ['uny:bərʃtaɪklɪç], *adj.* insurmountable.
unübertrefflich ['uny:bərtrɛflɪç], *adj.* unsurpassable, unequalled, unrivalled.
unübertroffen ['uny:bərtrɔfən], *adj.* unsurpassed.
unüberwindlich ['uny:bərvɪntlɪç], *adj.* invincible, unconquerable.
unumgänglich ['unumgɛŋlɪç], *adj.* indispensable, unavoidable, inevitable.
unumschränkt ['unumʃrɛŋkt], *adj.* unlimited, absolute.
unumstößlich ['unumʃtø:slɪç], *adj.* irrefutable.
unumwunden ['unumvundən], *adj.* frank, plain.
ununterbrochen ['ununtərbrɔxən], *adj.* uninterrupted, unremitting.
unveränderlich ['unfɛrɛndərlɪç], *adj.* unchangeable, unalterable.
unverändert ['unfɛrɛndərt], *adj.* unchanged, unaltered.
unverantwortlich ['unfɛrantvɔrtlɪç], *adj.* irresponsible, inexcusable, unjustifiable.
unveräußerlich ['unfɛrɔysərlɪç], *adj.* not for sale; inalienable.
unverbesserlich ['unfɛrbɛsərlɪç], *adj.* incorrigible.
unverbindlich ['unfɛrbɪntlɪç], *adj.* not binding, without prejudice, without obligation.
unverblümt ['unfɛrblymt], *adj.* blunt, point-blank.
unverbrennlich ['unfɛrbrɛnlɪç], *adj.* incombustible.
unverbrüchlich ['unfɛrbryçlɪç], *adj.* inviolable.
unverbürgt ['unfɛrbyrkt], *adj.* unwarranted, unofficial; unconfirmed.
unverdaulich ['unfɛrdaulɪç], *adj.* indigestible.
unverdaut ['unfɛrdaut], *adj.* undigested.
unverdient ['unfɛrdi:nt], *adj.* unmerited, undeserved.
unverdientermaßen ['unfɛrdi:ntərma:sən], *adv.* undeservedly.
unverdorben ['unfɛrdɔrbən], *adj.* unspoiled, uncorrupted, innocent.
unverdrossen ['unfɛrdrɔsən], *adj.* indefatigable.
unvereidigt ['unfɛraɪdɪçt], *adj.* unsworn.
unvereinbar ['unfɛraɪnba:r], *adj.* incompatible, inconsistent.

Unvereinbarkeit ['unferaInba:rkaIt], *f.* (—, *no pl.*) incompatibility, inconsistency.
unverfälscht ['unferfelʃt], *adj.* unadulterated, genuine, pure.
unverfänglich ['unferfeŋlIç], *adj.* harmless.
unverfroren ['unferfro:rən], *adj.* cheeky, impudent.
unvergeßlich ['unfergeslIç], *adj.* memorable, not to be forgotten, unforgettable.
unvergleichlich ['unferglaIçlIç], *adj.* incomparable.
unverhältnismäßig ['unferheltnIsme:sIç], *adj.* disproportionate.
unverheiratet ['unferhaIra:tət], *adj.* unmarried.
unverhofft ['unferhɔft], *adj.* unexpected.
unverhohlen ['unferho:lən], *adj.* unconcealed, undisguised, candid.
unverkennbar ['unferkenba:r], *adj.* unmistakable.
unverlangt ['unferlaŋkt], *adj.* unsolicited, not ordered.
unverletzlich ['unferletslIç], *adj.* invulnerable; (*fig.*) inviolable.
unverletzt ['unferletst], *adj.* (*persons*) unhurt; (*things*) undamaged, intact.
unvermeidlich ['unfermaItlIç], *adj.* inevitable, unavoidable.
unvermindert ['unfermIndərt], *adj.* undiminished.
unvermittelt ['unfermItəlt], *adj.* sudden, abrupt.
Unvermögen ['unfermø:gən], *n.* (—**s**, *no pl.*) inability, incapacity.
unvermögend ['unfermø:gənt], *adj.* incapable; impecunious.
unvermutet ['unfermu:tət], *adj.* unexpected, unforeseen.
unverrichtet ['unferrIçtət], *adj.* —*er Sache*, empty-handed; unsuccessfully.
unverschämt ['unferʃe:mt], *adj.* impudent, brazen.
unverschuldet ['unferʃuldət], *adj.* not in debt, unencumbered; (*fig.*) undeserved.
unversehens ['unferze:əns], *adv.* unexpectedly, unawares.
unversehrt ['unferze:rt], *adv.* (*persons*) unhurt, safe; (*things*) undamaged.
unversiegbar ['unferzi:kba:r], *adj.* inexhaustible.
unversiegt ['unferzi:kt], *adj.* unexhausted.
unversöhnlich ['unferzø:nlIç], *adj.* implacable, irreconcilable.
unversöhnt ['unferzø:nt], *adj.* unreconciled.
unversorgt ['unferzɔrkt], *adj.* unprovided for.
Unverstand ['unferʃtant], *m.* (—(**e**)**s**, *no pl.*) want of judgment, indiscretion.
unverständig ['unferʃtendIç], *adj.* foolish, unwise, imprudent.
unverständlich ['unferʃtentlIç], *adj.* unintelligible, incomprehensible.
unversteuert ['unferʃtɔyərt], *adj.* with duty *or* tax unpaid.
unversucht ['unferzu:xt], *adj.* untried; *nichts — lassen*, leave no stone unturned.
unverträglich ['unfertre:klIç], *adj.* quarrelsome.
unverwandt ['unfervant], *adj.* unrelated; fixed, constant; immovable.
unverwundbar ['unfervuntba:r], *adj.* invulnerable.
unverwüstlich ['unfervy:stlIç], *adj.* indestructible.
unverzagt ['unfertsa:kt], *adj.* undaunted, intrepid.
unverzeihlich ['unfertsaIlIç], *adj.* unpardonable.
unverzinslich ['unfertsInslIç], *adj.* (*money*) gaining no interest.
unverzollt ['unfertsɔlt], *adj.* duty unpaid.
unverzüglich ['unfertsy:klIç], *adj.* immediate.
unvollendet ['unfɔlendət], *adj.* unfinished.
unvollständig ['unfɔlʃtendIç], *adj.* incomplete.
unvorbereitet ['unfo:rbəraItət], *adj.* unprepared.
unvordenklich ['unfo:rdeŋklIç], *adj.* *seit —en Zeiten*, from time immemorial.
unvorhergesehen ['unfo:rhe:rgəze:ən], *adj.* unforeseen, unlooked for.
unvorsichtig ['unfo:rzIçtIç], *adj.* imprudent, incautious, careless.
unvorteilhaft ['unfɔrtaIlhaft], *adj.* unprofitable, disadvantageous; — *aussehen*, not look o.'s best.
unwägbar ['unve:kba:r], *adj.* imponderable.
unwahr ['unva:r], *adj.* untrue, false.
Unwahrhaftigkeit ['unva:rhaftIçkaIt], *f.* (—, *no pl.*) want of truthfulness, unreliability, dishonesty.
Unwahrheit ['unva:rhaIt], *f.* (—, *pl.* —**en**) lie, untruth, falsehood.
unwegsam ['unve:kza:m], *adj.* impassable, impracticable.
unweigerlich ['unvaIgərlIç], *adj.* unhesitating, unquestioning. — *adv.* without fail.
unweit ['unvaIt], *prep.* (*Genit.*) not far from, near.
Unwesen ['unve:zən], *n.* (—**s**, *no pl.*) nuisance; *sein — treiben*, be up to o.'s tricks.
Unwetter ['unvetər], *n.* (—**s**, *pl.* —) bad weather, thunderstorm.
unwichtig ['unvIçtIç], *adj.* unimportant; insignificant, of no consequence.
unwiderleglich ['unvi:dərle:klIç], *adj.* irrefutable.
unwiderruflich ['unvi:dərru:flIç], *adj.* irrevocable.
unwidersprechlich ['unvi:dərʃpreçlIç], *adj.* incontestable.
unwidersprochen ['unvi:dərʃprɔxən], *adj.* uncontradicted.

unwiderstehlich ['unvi:dərʃte:lıç], *adj.* irresistible.
unwiederbringlich ['unvi:dərbrıŋlıç], *adj.* irrecoverable, irretrievable.
Unwille ['unv:lə], *m.* (**—ns,** *no pl.*) displeasure, indignation.
unwillkürlich ['unvılky:rlıç], *adj.* involuntary; instinctive.
unwirsch ['unvırʃ], *adj.* petulant, testy; curt, uncivil.
unwirtlich ['unvırtlıç], *adj.* inhospitable.
unwirtschaftlich ['unvırtʃaftlıç], *adj.* not economic, uneconomic.
unwissend ['unvısənt], *adj.* illiterate, ignorant.
Unwissenheit ['unvısənhaıt], *f.* (**—,** *no pl.*) ignorance.
unwissenschaftlich ['unvısənʃaftlıç], *adj.* unscholarly; unscientific.
unwissentlich ['unvısəntlıç], *adv.* unknowingly, unconsciously.
unwohl ['unvo:l], *adj.* unwell, indisposed.
Unwohlsein ['unvo:lzaın], *n.* (**—s,** *no pl.*) indisposition.
unwürdig ['unvyrdıç], *adj.* unworthy, undeserving.
Unzahl ['untsa:l], *f.* (**—,** *no pl.*) vast number.
unzählbar [un'tsɛ:lba:r], *adj.* innumerable, numberless.
unzählig [un'tsɛ:lıç], *adj.* innumerable; *—e Male*, over and over again.
unzart ['untsa:rt], *adj.* indelicate, rude, rough; unceremonious.
Unzeit ['untsaıt], *f.* (**—,** *no pl.*) *zur —*, out of season, inopportunely.
unzeitgemäß ['untsaıtgəmɛ:s], *adj.* out of date, behind the times; unfashionable.
unzeitig ['untsaıtıç], *adj.* unseasonable; untimely, inopportune.
unziemlich ['untsi:mlıç], *adj.* unseemly, unbecoming.
Unzier ['untsi:r], *f.* (**—,** *no pl.*) disfigurement; flaw.
Unzucht ['untsuxt], *f.* (**—,** *no pl.*) unchastity; lewdness; fornication.
unzüchtig ['untsyçtıç], *adj.* unchaste, lascivious, lewd.
unzufrieden ['untsufri:dən], *adj.* discontented, dissatisfied.
unzugänglich ['untsugɛŋlıç], *adj.* inaccessible.
unzulänglich ['untsulɛŋlıç], *adj.* inadequate, insufficient.
Unzulänglichkeit ['untsulɛŋlıçkaıt], *f.* (**—,** *no pl.*) inadequacy.
unzulässig ['untsulɛsıç], *adj.* inadmissible.
unzurechnungsfähig ['untsurɛçnuŋsfɛ:ıç], *adj.* not accountable (for o.'s actions), non compos mentis, insane.
Unzurechnungsfähigkeit ['untsurɛçnuŋsfɛ:ıçkaıt], *f.* (**—,** *no pl.*) irresponsibility; feeblemindedness.
unzusammenhängend ['untsuzamənhɛŋənt], *adj.* incoherent.
unzuständig ['untsuʃtɛndıç], *adj.* incompetent, not competent (*Law etc.*).
unzuträglich ['untsutrɛ:klıç], *adj.* unwholesome.
unzutreffend ['untsutrɛfənt], *adj.* inapposite; unfounded; inapplicable.
unzuverlässig ['untsufɛrlɛsıç], *adj.* unreliable.
unzweckmäßig ['untsvɛkmɛ:sıç], *adj.* inexpedient.
unzweideutig ['untsvaıdɔytıç], *adj.* unequivocal, explicit, unambiguous.
üppig ['ypıç], *adj.* abundant; opulent, luxurious, luxuriant, voluptuous.
uralt ['u:ralt], *adj.* very old, old as the hills; ancient.
uranfänglich ['u:ranfɛŋlıç], *adj.* primordial, primeval.
Uraufführung ['urauffy:ruŋ], *f.* (**—,** *pl.* **—en**) (*Theat.*) first night, première.
urbar ['u:rba:r], *adj.* arable, under cultivation; *— machen*, cultivate.
Urbarmachung ['u:rba:rmaxuŋ], *f.* (**—,** *no pl.*) cultivation.
Urbild ['u:rbılt], *n.* (**—(e)s,** *pl.* **—er**) prototype; (*fig.*) ideal.
ureigen ['u:raıgən], *adj.* quite original; idiosyncratic.
Ureltern ['u:rɛltərn], *pl.* ancestors.
Urenkel ['u:rɛŋkəl], *m.* (**—s,** *pl.* **—**) great-grandson, great-grandchild.
Urenkelin ['u:rɛŋkəlın], *f.* (**—,** *pl.* **—nen**) great-granddaughter.
Urfehde ['u:rfe:də], *f.* (**—,** *no pl.*) oath to keep the peace.
Urform ['u:rfɔrm], *f.* (**—,** *pl.* **—en**) primitive form; original form; archetype.
Urgroßmutter ['u:rgro:smutər], *f.* (**—,** *pl.* **⸚**) great-grandmother.
Urgroßvater ['u:rgro:sfa:tər], *m.* (**—s,** *pl.* **⸚**) great-grandfather.
Urheber ['u:rhe:bər], *m.* (**—s,** *pl.* **—**) author, originator.
Urheberrecht ['u:rhe:bərrɛçt], *n.* (**—s,** *pl.* **—e**) copyright.
Urheberschaft ['u:rhe:bərʃaft], *f.* (**—,** *no pl.*) authorship.
Urin [u'ri:n], *m.* (**—s,** *no pl.*) urine.
Urkunde ['u:rkundə], *f.* (**—,** *pl.* **—n**) document, deed, charter; *zur — dessen*, (*obs.*) in witness whereof.
Urkundenbeweis ['u:rkundənbəvaıs], *m.* (**—es,** *pl.* **—e**) documentary evidence.
urkundlich ['u:rkuntlıç], *adj.* documentary.
Urlaub ['u:rlaup], *m.* (**—s,** *pl.* **—e**) leave of absence; vacation; (*Mil.*) furlough.
urplötzlich ['u:rplœtslıç], *adj.* sudden. — *adv.* all at once, suddenly.
Urquell ['u:rkvɛl], *m.* (**—s,** *pl.* **—en**) fountain-head, original source.
Ursache ['u:rzaxə], *f.* (**—,** *pl.* **—n**) cause; *keine —*, don't mention it.
Urschrift ['u:rʃrıft], *f.* (**—,** *pl.* **—en**) original text.
Ursprache ['u:rʃpra:xə], *f.* (**—,** *pl.* **—n**) original language.
Ursprung ['u:rʃpruŋ], *m.* (**—s,** *pl.* **⸚e**) origin; extraction.

ursprünglich ['u:rʃpryŋlɪç], *adj.* original.
Urteil ['urtaɪl], *n.* (—**s**, *pl.* —**e**) opinion; (*Law*) judgment, verdict, sentence; *ein — fällen*, pass judgment on; *nach meinem* —, in my opinion.
urteilen ['urtaɪlən], *v.n.* judge.
Urteilsspruch ['urtaɪlsʃprux], *m.* (—**s**, *pl.* ¨—**e**) judgment, sentence.
Uruguay [uru'gwa:ɪ], *n.* Uruguay.
Urureltern ['u:ru:rɛltərn], *pl.* ancestors.
Urvater ['u:rfa:tər], *m.* (—**s**, *pl.* ¨—) forefather.
Urvolk ['u:rfɔlk], *n.* (—(**e**)**s**, *pl.* ¨—**er**) primitive people, aborigines.
Urwald ['u:rvalt], *m.* (—(**e**)**s**, *pl.* ¨—**er**) primæval forest, virgin forest.
Urwelt ['u:rvɛlt], *f.* (—, *no pl.*) primæval world.
Urzeit ['u:rtsaɪt], *f.* (—, *pl.* —**en**) prehistoric times.

V

V [fau], *n.* (—**s**, *pl.* —**s**) the letter V.
Vagabund [vaga'bunt], *m.* (—**en**, *pl.* —**en**) vagabond, tramp; (*Am.*) hobo.
vag ['va:k], *adj.* vague.
Vakuumbremse ['va:kuumbrɛmzə], *f.* (—, *pl.* —**n**) air-brake, vacuum-brake.
Vase ['va:zə], *f.* (—, *pl.* —**n**) vase.
Vater ['fa:tər], *m.* (—**s**, *pl.* ¨—) father.
Vaterland ['fa:tərlant], *n.* (—(**e**)**s**, *pl.* ¨—**er**) mother-country, native country; *—sliebe*, patriotism.
vaterländisch ['fa:tərlɛndɪʃ], *adj.* patriotic.
vaterlandslos ['fa:tərlantslo:s], *adj.* having no mother country; unpatriotic.
väterlich ['fɛ:tərlɪç], *adj.* fatherly, paternal. — *adv.* like a father.
vaterlos ['fa:tərlo:s], *adj.* fatherless.
Vatermord ['fa:tərmɔrt], *m.* (—(**e**)**s**, *pl.* —**e**) parricide; patricide.
Vatermörder ['fa:tərmœrdər], *m.* (—**s**, *pl.* —) parricide; (*fig.*) high *or* stand-up collar.
Vaterschaft ['fa:tərʃaft], *f.* (—, *no pl.*) paternity.
Vatersname ['fa:tərsna:mə], *m.* (—**ns**, *pl.* —**n**) surname, family name.
Vaterstadt ['fa:tərʃtat], *f.* (—, *pl.* ¨—**e**) native town.
Vaterstelle ['fa:tərʃtɛlə], *f.* (—, *pl.* —**n**) — *vertreten*, act as a father, be a father (to).
Vaterunser [fa:tər'unzər], *n.* (—**s**, *pl.* —) Lord's Prayer.
Vatikan [vati'ka:n], *m.* (—**s**, *no pl.*) Vatican.
vegetieren [vege'ti:rən], *v.n.* vegetate.
Veilchen ['faɪlçən], *n.* (—**s**, *pl.* —) (*Bot.*) violet.
Vene ['ve:nə], *f.* (—, *pl.* —**n**) vein.
Venezuela [vɛnətsu'e:la], *n.* Venezuela.
Ventil [vɛn'ti:l], *n.* (—**s**, *pl.* —**e**) valve.
ventilieren [vɛnti'li:rən], *v.a.* ventilate, air; (*fig.*) discuss, ventilate.
verabfolgen [fɛr'apfɔlgən], *v.a.* deliver, hand over, remit; serve.
Verabfolgung [fɛr'apfɔlguŋ], *f.* (—, *no pl.*) delivery.
verabreden [fɛr'apre:dən], *v.a.* agree (upon); stipulate; *etwas mit einem* —, agree on s.th. with s.o. — *v.r. sich mit einem* —, make an appointment with s.o.; (*coll.*) have a date.
Verabredung [fɛr'apre:duŋ], *f.* (—, *pl.* —**en**) agreement, arrangement, appointment; (*coll.*) date.
verabreichen [fɛr'apraɪçən], *v.a.* deliver, dispense.
verabsäumen [fɛr'apzɔymən], *v.a.* neglect, omit.
verabscheuen [fɛr'apʃɔyən], *v.a.* detest, loathe, abhor.
Verabscheuung [fɛr'apʃɔyuŋ], *f.* (—, *no pl.*) abhorrence, detestation, loathing.
verabscheuungswürdig [fɛr'apʃɔyuŋsvyrdɪç], *adj.* abominable, detestable.
verabschieden [fɛr'apʃi:dən], *v.a.* dismiss, discharge. — *v.r. sich* —, take leave, say good-bye; (*Pol.*) pass (of an Act).
Verabschiedung [fɛr'apʃi:duŋ], *f.* (—, *no pl.*) dismissal; discharge; (*Pol.*) passing (of an Act).
verachten [fɛr'axtən], *v.a.* despise, scorn.
verächtlich [fɛr'ɛçtlɪç], *adj.* despicable, contemptible; contemptuous, scornful.
Verachtung [fɛr'axtuŋ], *f.* (—, *no pl.*) contempt, disdain, scorn.
verallgemeinern [fɛralgə'maɪnərn], *v.a., v.n.* generalise.
veralten [fɛr'altən], *v.n.* (*aux.* sein) become obsolete, date.
veraltet [fɛr'altət], *adj.* obsolete.
Veranda [ve'randa], *f.* (—, *pl.* —**den**) verandah, porch.
veränderlich [fɛr'ɛndərlɪç], *adj.* changeable, variable; (*fig.*) inconstant, fickle.
verändern [fɛr'ɛndərn], *v.a.* change, alter. — *v.r. sich* —, change, vary; change o.'s job.
verankern [fɛr'aŋkərn], *v.a.* anchor.
veranlagt [fɛr'anla:kt], *adj.* inclined; gifted; having a propensity (to); *gut* —, talented; (*tax*) assessed.
Veranlagung [fɛr'anla:guŋ], *f.* (—, *pl.* —**en**) bent; talent; predisposition; (*tax*) assessment.
veranlassen [fɛr'anlasən], *v.a.* bring about, cause, motivate; *einen* —, induce s.o., cause s.o.; *etwas* —, bring s.th. about, cause s.th.

Veranlassung [fɛr'anlasuŋ], *f.* (—, *no pl.*) cause, motive; occasion; inducement; *auf seine —*, at his suggestion; *ohne irgend eine —*, without the slightest provocation.

veranschaulichen [fɛr'anʃaulıçən], *v.a.* illustrate, make clear.

veranschlagen [fɛr'anʃla:gən], *v.a.* estimate, assess.

Veranschlagung [fɛr'anʃla:guŋ], *f.* (—, *pl.* —**en**) estimate.

veranstalten [fɛr'anʃtaltən], *v.a.* organise, arrange.

Veranstalter [fɛr'anʃtaltər], *m.* (—**s**, *pl.* —) organiser.

Veranstaltung [fɛr'anʃtaltuŋ], *f.* (—, *pl.* —**en**) arrangement; entertainment; show; event; (sporting) fixture.

verantworten [fɛr'antvɔrtən], *v.a.* account for. — *v.r. sich —*, answer (for), justify o.s.

verantwortlich [fɛr'antvɔrtlıç], *adj.* responsible, answerable, accountable.

Verantwortlichkeit [fɛr'antvɔrtlıçkaıt], *f.* (—, *no pl.*) responsibility.

Verantwortung [fɛr'antvɔrtuŋ], *f.* (—, *no pl.*) responsibility, justification, excuse; defence; *auf deine —*, at your own risk; *einen zur — ziehen*, call s.o. tc account.

verantwortungsvoll [fɛr'antvɔrtuŋsfɔl], *adj.* responsible.

verarbeiten [fɛr'arbaıtən], *v.a.* manufacture, process; (*fig.*) digest.

Verarbeitung [fɛr'arbaıtuŋ], *f.* (—, *no pl.*) manufacture; process; finish; (*fig.*) digestion.

verargen [fɛr'argən], *v.a. einem etwas —*, blame *or* reproach s.o. for s.th.

verärgern [fɛr'ɛrgərn], *v.a.* annoy, make angry.

Verarmung [fɛr'armuŋ], *f.* (—, *no pl.*) impoverishment.

verausgaben [fɛr'ausga:bən], *v.r. sich —*, overspend, run short of money; spend o.s., wear o.s. out.

veräußern [fɛr'ɔysərn], *v.a.* dispose of, sell.

Veräußerung [fɛr'ɔysəruŋ], *f.* (—, *no pl.*) sale; alienation.

Verband [fɛr'bant], *m.* (—**s**, *pl.* ⸚**e**) bandage, dressing; association, union; unit.

verbannen [fɛr'banən], *v.a.* banish, exile, outlaw.

Verbannte [fɛr'bantə], *m.* (—**n**, *pl.* —**n**) exile, outlaw.

Verbannung [fɛr'banuŋ], *f.* (—, *pl.* —**en**) banishment, exile.

verbauen [fɛr'bauən], *v.n.* obstruct; build up; use up *or* spend in building.

verbeißen [fɛr'baısən], *v.a. irr. sich etwas —*, suppress s.th.; *sich das Lachen —*, stifle a laugh. — *v.r. sich in etwas —*, stick doggedly to s.th.

verbergen [fɛr'bɛrgən], *v.a. irr.* conceal, hide.

verbessern [fɛr'bɛsərn], *v.a.* improve, correct, mend.

Verbesserung [fɛr'bɛsəruŋ], *f.* (—, *pl.* —**en**) improvement; correction.

verbeugen [fɛr'bɔygən], *v.r. sich —*, bow.

Verbeugung [fɛr'bɔyguŋ], *f.* (—, *pl.* —**en**) bow, obeisance.

verbiegen [fɛr'bi:gən], *v.a. irr.* twist, distort, bend the wrong way.

verbieten [fɛr'bi:tən], *v.a. irr.* forbid, prohibit.

verbilligen [fɛr'bıllıgən], *v.a.* cheapen, reduce the price of.

verbinden [fɛr'bındən], *v.a. irr.* tie up, bind up, connect; (*Med.*) dress, bandage; unite, join; *die Augen —*, blindfold. — *v.r. sich —*, unite, join; (*Chem.*) combine.

verbindlich [fɛr'bıntlıç], *adj.* binding; obligatory; obliging; —*en Dank*, my best thanks.

Verbindlichkeit [fɛr'bıntlıçkaıt], *f.* (—, *pl.* —**en**) liability, obligation; compliment.

Verbindung [fɛr'bınduŋ], *f.* (—, *pl.* —**en**) connexion, connection, junction; association; alliance; (*Railw.*) connection; (*Chem.*) compound.

Verbindungsglied [fɛr'bınduŋsgli:t], *n.* (—(**e**)**s**, *pl.* —**er**) connecting link.

Verbindungslinie [fɛr'bınduŋsli:njə], *f.* (—, *pl.* —**n**) line of communication.

verbissen [fɛr'bısən], *adj.* obstinate, grim; soured. — *adv.* doggedly.

verbitten [fɛr'bıtən], *v.a. irr. sich etwas —*, forbid s.th. determinedly; insist on s.th. not being done, object to.

verbittern [fɛr'bıtərn], *v.a.* embitter.

Verbitterung [fɛr'bıtəruŋ], *f.* (—, *no pl.*) exasperation.

verblassen [fɛr'blasən], *v.n.* (*aux.* sein) turn pale.

Verbleib [fɛr'blaıp], *m.* (—(**e**)**s**, *no pl.*) whereabouts.

verbleiben [fɛr'blaıbən], *v.n. irr.* (*aux.* sein) remain.

verblenden [fɛr'blɛndən], *v.a.* dazzle, delude, blind.

Verblendung [fɛr'blɛnduŋ], *f.* (—, *no pl.*) infatuation; delusion.

verblüffen [fɛr'blyfən], *v.n.* amaze, stagger, dumbfound.

Verblüffung [fɛr'blyfuŋ], *f.* (—, *no pl.*) bewilderment.

verblühen [fɛr'bly:ən], *v.n.* (*aux.* sein) wither, fade.

verblümt [fɛr'bly:mt], *adj.* veiled.

verbluten [fɛr'blu:tən], *v.n.* (*aux.* sein) bleed to death.

verborgen (1) [fɛr'bɔrgən], *v.a.* lend out.

verborgen (2) [fɛr'bɔrgən], *adj.* concealed, hidden; *im —en*, secretly.

Verborgenheit [fɛr'bɔrgənhaıt], *f.* (—, *no pl.*) concealment, seclusion.

Verbot [fɛr'bo:t], *n.* (—(**e**)**s**, *pl.* —**e**) prohibition.

verboten [fɛr'bo:tən], *adj.* forbidden, prohibited.

verbrämen [fɛr'brɛ:mən], *v.a.* (*garment*) edge, border.

verbrauchen [fɛr'brauxən], *v.a.* consume, use up; spend.
Verbraucher [fɛr'brauxər], *m.* (—s, *pl.* —) consumer.
Verbrechen [fɛr'brɛçən], *n.* (—s, *pl.* —) crime.
verbrechen [fɛr'brɛçən], *v.a. irr.* commit, perpetrate.
Verbrecher [fɛr'brɛçər], *m.* (—s, *pl.* —) criminal.
Verbrecheralbum [fɛr'brɛçəralbum], *n.* (—s, *no pl.*) rogues' gallery.
verbreiten [fɛr'braɪtən], *v.a.* spread, diffuse.
verbreitern [fɛr'braɪtərn], *v.a.* widen.
Verbreitung [fɛr'braɪtuŋ], *f.* (—, *no pl.*) spread(ing), propaganda, extension.
verbrennbar [fɛr'brɛnba:r], *adj.* combustible.
verbrennen [fɛr'brɛnən], *v.a. irr.* burn; cremate; *von der Sonne verbrannt*, sunburnt. — *v.n.* (*aux.* sein) get burnt. — *v.r. sich* —, scald o.s., burn o.s.
Verbrennung [fɛr'brɛnuŋ], *f.* (—, *pl.* **—en**) burning, combustion; cremation.
verbrieft [fɛr'bri:ft], *adj.* vested; documented.
verbringen [fɛr'brɪŋən], *v.a. irr.* (*time*) spend, pass.
verbrüdern [fɛr'bry:dərn], *v.r. sich* —, fraternise.
verbrühen [fɛr'bry:ən], *v.a.* scald.
verbummeln [fɛr'buməln], *v.a. die Zeit* —, fritter the time away.
verbunden [fɛr'bundən], *adj. einem — sein*, be obliged to s.o.
verbünden [fɛr'byndən], *v.r. sich — mit*, ally o.s. with.
Verbündete [fɛr'byndətə], *m.* (**—n**, *pl.* **—n**) ally, confederate.
verbürgen [fɛr'byrgən], *v.a.* warrant, guarantee. — *v.r. sich für etwas* —, vouch for s.th.; guarantee s.th.
Verdacht [fɛr'daxt], *m.* (**—(e)s**, *no pl.*) suspicion.
verdächtig [fɛr'dɛçtɪç], *adj.* suspicious, doubtful, questionable.
verdächtigen [fɛr'dɛçtɪgən], *v.a.* throw suspicion on, suspect.
verdammen [fɛr'damən], *v.a.* condemn, damn.
verdammenswert [fɛr'damənsve:rt], *adj.* damnable.
Verdammung [fɛr'damuŋ], *f.* (—, *no pl.*) condemnation.
verdampfen [fɛr'dampfən], *v.n.* (*aux.* sein) evaporate.
verdanken [fɛr'daŋkən], *v.a. einem etwas* —, be indebted to s.o. for s.th.; owe s.th. to s.o.
verdauen [fɛr'dauən], *v.a.* digest.
verdaulich [fɛr'daulɪç], *adj.* digestible.
Verdauung [fɛr'dauuŋ], *f.* (—, *no pl.*) digestion.
Verdauungsstörung [fɛr'dauuŋsʃtø:ruŋ], *f.* (—, *pl.* **—en**) indigestion.
Verdeck [fɛr'dɛk], *n.* (**—s**, *pl.* **—e**) awning; (*Naut.*) deck.
verdecken [fɛr'dɛkən], *v.a.* cover, hide.
verdenken [fɛr'dɛŋkən], *v.a. irr. einem etwas* —, blame s.o. for s.th.
Verderb [fɛr'dɛrp], *m.* (**—s**, *no pl.*) ruin, decay.
verderben [fɛr'dɛrbən], *v.a. irr.* spoil, corrupt, pervert. — *v.n.* (*aux.* sein) decay, go bad.
Verderben [fɛr'dɛrbən], *n.* (**—s**, *no pl.*) corruption, ruin.
Verderber [fɛr'dɛrbər], *m.* (**—s**, *pl.* —) corrupter, perverter.
verderblich [fɛr'dɛrplɪç], *adj.* ruinous, pernicious, destructive; (*goods*) perishable.
Verderbnis [fɛr'dɛrpnɪs], *f.* (—, *no pl.*) corruption, depravity; perversion; perdition.
Verderbtheit [fɛr'dɛrpthaɪt], *f.* (—, *no pl.*) corruption, perversion, depravity.
verdeutlichen [fɛr'dɔytlɪçən], *v.a.* illustrate, clarify.
verdichten [fɛr'dɪçtən], *v.a., v.r.* thicken, condense, liquefy.
Verdichtung [fɛr'dɪçtuŋ], *f.* (—, *no pl.*) condensation; solidification.
verdicken [fɛr'dɪkən], *v.a.* thicken; solidify.
verdienen [fɛr'di:nən], *v.a.* earn; deserve.
Verdienst (1) [fɛr'di:nst], *m.* (**—es**, *pl.* **—e**) profit, gain, earnings.
Verdienst (2) [fɛr'di:nst], *n.* (**—es**, *pl.* **—e**) merit, deserts.
verdienstvoll [fɛr'di:nstfɔl], *adj.* meritorious, deserving; distinguished.
verdient [fɛr'di:nt], *adj. sich — machen um*, deserve well of, serve well (a cause etc.).
verdientermaßen [fɛr'di:ntərmasən], *adv.* deservedly.
verdingen [fɛr'dɪŋən], *v.r. irr. sich* —, enter service (with), take a situation (with).
verdolmetschen [fɛr'dɔlmɛtʃən], *v.a.* interpret, translate.
verdoppeln [fɛr'dɔpəln], *v.a.* double.
verdorben [fɛr'dɔrbən], *adj.* spoilt; corrupted, depraved, debauched.
verdrängen [fɛr'drɛŋən], *v.a.* crowd out; (*Phys.*) displace; (*fig.*) supplant, supersede; (*Psych.*) inhibit, repress.
Verdrängung [fɛr'drɛŋuŋ], *f.* (—, *no pl.*) supplanting; (*Phys.*) displacement; (*Psych.*) inhibition, repression.
verdrehen [fɛr'dre:ən], *v.a.* twist (the wrong way); (*fig.*) misrepresent, distort.
verdreht [fɛr'dre:t], *adj.* cracked, cranky, crazy, queer.
Verdrehtheit [fɛr'dre:thaɪt], *f.* (—, *no pl.*) crankiness.
Verdrehung [fɛr'dre:uŋ], *f.* (—, *pl.* **—en**) distortion; (*fig.*) misrepresentation.
verdrießen [fɛr'dri:sən], *v.a. irr.* vex, annoy.
verdrießlich [fɛr'dri:slɪç], *adj.* (*thing*) vexatious, tiresome; (*person*) morose, peevish.

verdrossen [fɛr'drɔsən], *adj.* annoyed; fretful, sulky.
Verdrossenheit [fɛr'drɔsənhaɪt], *f.* (—, *no pl.*) annoyance; fretfulness, sulkiness.
verdrücken [fɛr'drykən], *v.a.* (*sl.*) eat o.'s fill of. — *v.r.* (*coll.*) *sich* —, slink away; sneak away.
Verdruß [fɛr'drus], *m.* (—**sses**, *no pl.*) vexation, annoyance; — *bereiten*, give trouble, cause annoyance.
verduften [fɛr'duftən], *v.n.* (*aux.* sein) evaporate; (*fig.*) (*coll.*) take French leave, clear out.
verdummen [fɛr'dumən], *v.n.* (*aux.* sein) become stupid.
verdunkeln [fɛr'duŋkəln], *v.a.* black-out, obscure; (*fig.*) eclipse.
Verdunk(e)lung [fɛr'duŋk(ə)luŋ], *f.* (—, *no pl.*) darkening, eclipse; black-out.
Verdunk(e)lungsgefahr [vɛr'duŋk(ə)-luŋsgəfa:r], *f.* (—, *no pl.*) (*Law*) danger of prejudicing the course *or* administration of justice.
verdünnen [fɛr'dynən], *v.a.* thin out, dilute.
Verdünnung [fɛr'dynuŋ], *f.* (—, *no pl.*) attenuation; dilution.
verdunsten [fɛr'dunstən], *v.n.* (*aux.* sein) evaporate.
verdursten [fɛr'durstən], *v.n.* (*aux.* sein) die of thirst, perish with thirst.
verdüstern [fɛr'dy:stərn], *v.a.* darken, make gloomy.
verdutzen [fɛr'dutsən], *v.a.* disconcert, bewilder, nonplus.
Veredlung [fɛr'e:dluŋ], *f.* (—, *no pl.*) improvement, refinement.
verehelichen [fɛr'e:əlɪçən], *v.r.* (*obs.*) *sich* —, get married.
verehren [fɛr'e:rən], *v.a.* respect, revere, esteem; worship, adore.
Verehrer [fɛr'e:rər], *m.* (—**s**, *pl.* —) admirer; lover.
verehrlich [fɛr'e:rlɪç], *adj.* venerable.
verehrt [fɛr'e:rt], *adj.* honoured; *sehr —er Herr*, dear Sir.
Verehrung [fɛr'e:ruŋ], *f.* (—, *no pl.*) reverence, veneration; worship, adoration.
verehrungswürdig [fɛr'e:ruŋsvyrdɪç], *adj.* venerable.
vereidigt [fɛr'aɪdɪçt], *adj.* sworn in, bound by oath, under oath; *—er Bücherrevisor*, chartered accountant.
Vereidigung [fɛr'aɪdɪguŋ], *f.* (—, *no pl.*) swearing in; oathtaking.
Verein [fɛr'aɪn], *m.* (—**s**, *pl.* —**e**) union, association, society; club.
vereinbar [fɛr'aɪnba:r], *adj.* compatible.
vereinbaren [fɛr'aɪnba:rən], *v.a.* agree upon, arrange.
Vereinbarung [fɛr'aɪnba:ruŋ], *f.* (—, *pl.* —**en**) arrangement, agreement.
vereinen [fɛr'aɪnən], *v.a.* unite.
vereinfachen [fɛr'aɪnfaxən], *v.a.* simplify.
vereinigen [fɛr'aɪnɪgən], *v.a.* unite. — *v.r. sich — mit*, associate o.s. with, join with.
Vereinigung [fɛr'aɪnɪguŋ], *f.* (—, *pl.* —**en**) union; association.
vereinnahmen [fɛr'aɪnna:mən], *v.a.* receive, take (*money*).
vereinsamen [fɛr'aɪnza:mən], *v.n.* (*aux. sein*) become isolated, become lonely.
vereint [fɛr'aɪnt], *adj.* united, joined. — *adv.* in concert, (all) together.
vereinzelt [fɛr'aɪntsəlt], *adj.* sporadic, isolated. — *adv.* here and there, now and then.
Vereinzelung [fɛr'aɪntsəluŋ], *f.* (—, *pl.* —**en**) isolation; individualization.
vereisen [fɛr'aɪzən], *v.n.* become frozen, freeze; congeal.
Vereisung [fɛr'aɪzuŋ], *f.* (—, *pl.* —**en**) freezing, icing (up).
vereiteln [fɛr'aɪtəln], *v.a.* frustrate, thwart.
Vereitelung [fɛr'aɪtəluŋ], *f.* (—, *pl.* —**en**) frustration, thwarting.
vereitern [fɛr'aɪtərn], *v.n.* suppurate.
Vereiterung [fɛr'aɪtəruŋ], *f.* (—, *pl.* —**en**) suppuration.
verenden [fɛr'ɛndən], *v.n.* (*aux.* sein) (*animal*) die.
verengen [fɛr'ɛŋən], *v.a.* narrow, straighten, constrict.
Verengung [fɛr'ɛŋuŋ], *f.* (—, *pl.* —**en**) narrowing, straightening, contraction.
vererben [fɛr'ɛrbən], *v.a.* leave (by will), bequeath. — *v.r. sich — auf*, devolve upon, be hereditary.
vererblich [fɛr'ɛrplɪç], *adj.* (in)heritable, hereditary.
Vererbung [fɛr'ɛrbuŋ], *f.* (—, *no pl.*) heredity.
verewigen [fɛr'e:vɪgən], *v.a.* immortalise.
Verewigte [fɛr'e:vɪçtə], *m.* (—**n**, *pl.* —**n**) (*Poet.*) deceased.
Verfahren [fɛr'fa:rən], *n.* (—**s**, *pl.* —) process; (*Law*) procedure; proceedings; *das — einstellen*, quash proceedings.
verfahren [fɛr'fa:rən], *v.n. irr.* (*aux.* sein) proceed, act, operate. — *v.a.* spend (*money etc.*) on travelling. — *v.r. sich* —, (*Motor.*) lose o.'s way.
Verfall [fɛr'fal], *m.* (—**s**, *no pl.*) decay, decline; downfall, ruin; (*Comm.*) expiration, maturity; *in — geraten*, fall into ruin, decay.
verfallen [fɛr'falən], *v.n. irr.* (*aux.* sein) decay; go to ruin; lapse; (*Comm.*) fall due, expire; (*pledge*) become forfeit; *einem* —, become the property of, accrue to, devolve upon s.o.; (*fig.*) become the slave of s.o.; (*health*) decline, fail; *auf etwas* —, hit upon an idea. — *adj.* decayed, ruined.
Verfalltag [fɛr'falta:k], *m.* (—**s**, *pl.* —**e**) day of payment; maturity.
verfälschen [fɛr'fɛlʃən], *v.a.* falsify; adulterate.
Verfälschung [fɛr'fɛlʃuŋ], *f.* (—, *pl.* —**en**) falsification; adulteration.

verfangen [fɛr'faŋən], *v.r. irr. sich* —, get entangled; *sich in ein Lügennetz* —, entangle o.s. in a tissue of lies.
verfänglich [fɛr'fɛŋlɪç], *adj.* risky; insidious.
verfärben [fɛr'fɛrbən], *v.r. sich* —, change colour.
verfassen [fɛr'fasən], *v.a.* compose, write, be the author of.
Verfasser [fɛr'fasər], *m.* (—s, *pl.* —) author, writer.
Verfassung [fɛr'fasuŋ], *f.* (—, *pl.* —en) composition; (*state*) constitution; state, condition, disposition.
verfassungsgemäß [fɛr'fasuŋsgəmɛ:s], *adj.* constitutional.
verfassungswidrig [fɛr'fasuŋsvi:drɪç], *adj.* unconstitutional.
verfaulen [fɛr'faulən], *v.n.* (*aux.* sein) rot, putrefy.
verfechten [fɛr'fɛçtən], *v.a. irr.* defend, advocate; maintain.
verfehlen [fɛr'fe:lən], *v.a.* fail, miss; fail to meet; fail to do; *den Weg* —, lose o.'s way.
verfehlt [fɛr'fe:lt], *adj.* unsuccessful, false, abortive; *eine* —*e Sache*, a failure.
Verfehlung [fɛr'fe:luŋ], *f.* (—, *pl.* —en) lapse.
verfeinern [fɛr'faɪnərn], *v.a.* refine, improve.
Verfeinerung [fɛr'faɪnəruŋ], *f.* (—, *pl.* —en) refinement, polish.
verfertigen [fɛr'fɛrtɪgən], *v.a.* make, manufacture.
verfilmen [fɛr'fɪlmən], *v.a.* make a film of, film.
verfinstern [fɛr'fɪnstərn], *v.r. sich* —, get dark; be eclipsed.
verflechten [fɛr'flɛçtən], *v.a. irr.* interweave, interlace. — *v.r. sich* —, (*fig.*) become entangled, become involved.
verfließen [fɛr'fli:sən], *v.n. irr.* (*aux.* sein) flow away; (*time*) elapse, pass.
verflossen [fɛr'flɔsən], *adj.* past, bygone.
verfluchen [fɛr'flu:xən], *v.a.* curse, execrate.
verflucht [fɛr'flu:xt], *excl.* damn!
verflüchtigen [fɛr'flyçtɪgən], *v.r. sich* —, become volatile; evaporate; (*coll.*) make off, make o.s. scarce.
Verfluchung [fɛr'flu:xuŋ], *f.* (—, *pl.* —en) malediction, curse.
Verfolg [fɛr'fɔlk], *m.* (—(e)s, *no pl.*) progress, course.
verfolgen [fɛr'fɔlgən], *v.a.* pursue; persecute; prosecute.
Verfolger [fɛr'fɔlgər], *m.* (—s, *pl.* —) pursuer; persecutor.
Verfolgung [fɛr'fɔlguŋ], *f.* (—, *pl.* —en) pursuit; persecution; prosecution.
Verfolgungswahn [fɛr'fɔlguŋsva:n], *m.* (—s, *no pl.*) persecution mania.
verfrüht [fɛr'fry:t], *adj.* premature.
verfügbar [fɛr'fy:kba:r], *adj.* available.
verfügen [fɛr'fy:gən], *v.a.* decree, order. — *v.n.* — *über etwas*, have control of s.th, have s.th. at o.'s disposal.
Verfügung [fɛr'fy:guŋ], *f.* (—, *pl.* —en) decree, ordinance; disposition, disposal; *einem zur* — *stehen*, be at s.o.'s service *or* disposal.
verführen [fɛr'fy:rən], *v.a.* seduce.
verführerisch [fɛr'fy:rərɪʃ], *adj.* seductive, alluring; (*coll.*) fetching.
Verführung [fɛr'fy:ruŋ], *f.* (—, *no pl.*) seduction.
vergällen [fɛr'gɛlən], *v.a.* spoil, mar.
vergallopieren [fɛrgalɔ'pi:rən], *v.r.* (*coll.*) *sich* —, blunder, overshoot the mark.
vergangen [fɛr'gaŋən], *adj.* past, gone, last.
Vergangenheit [fɛr'gaŋənhaɪt], *f.* (—, *no pl.*) past, time past; (*Gram.*) past tense.
vergänglich [fɛr'gɛŋlɪç], *adj.* transient, transitory.
Vergaser [fɛr'ga:zər], *m.* (—s, *pl.* —) (*Motor.*) carburettor.
vergeben [fɛr'ge:bən], *v.a. irr.* give away; forgive, pardon; confer, bestow.
vergebens [fɛr'ge:bəns], *adv.* in vain, vainly.
vergeblich [fɛr'ge:plɪç], *adj.* vain, futile, fruitless. — *adv.* in vain.
Vergebung [fɛr'ge:buŋ], *f.* (—, *no pl.*) forgiveness, pardon; (*office*) bestowal.
vergegenwärtigen [fɛrge:gən'vɛrtɪgən], *v.a.* bring to mind, imagine.
Vergehen [fɛr'ge:ən], *n.* (—s, *pl.* —) offence lapse.
vergehen [fɛr'ge:ən], *v.n. irr.* (*aux.* sein) go away, pass (away); elapse; perish; (*time*) pass. — *v.r. sich* —, go wrong; offend; violate (*Law*, person).
vergelten [fɛr'gɛltən], *v.a. irr.* repay, reward, recompense.
Vergeltung [fɛr'gɛltuŋ], *f.* (—, *no pl.*) requital, retribution; reward, recompense.
vergessen [fɛr'gɛsən], *v.a. irr.* forget; *bei einem* —, leave behind.
Vergessenheit [fɛr'gɛsənhaɪt], *f.* (— *no pl.*) oblivion.
vergeßlich [fɛr'gɛslɪç], *adj.* forgetful.
vergeuden [fɛr'gɔydən], *v.a.* waste, squander.
vergewaltigen [fɛrgə'valtɪgən], *v.a.* assault criminally, rape, violate; (*fig.*) coerce, force.
Vergewaltigung [fɛrgə'valtɪguŋ], *f.* (—, *no pl.*) criminal assault, rape; (*fig.*) coercion.
vergewissern [fɛrgə'vɪsərn], *v.r. sich* —, ascertain, make sure.
vergießen [fɛr'gi:sən], *v.a. irr.* spill; shed.
vergiften [fɛr'gɪftən], *v.a.* poison.
Vergiftung [fɛr'gɪftuŋ], *f.* (—, *pl.* —en) poisoning.
vergilbt [fɛr'gɪlpt], *adj.* yellow with age.
Vergißmeinnicht [fɛr'gɪsmaɪnnɪçt], *n.* (—s, *pl.* —e) (*Bot.*) forget-me-not.

Vergleich [fɛr'glaɪç], *m.* (—(e)**s**, *pl.* —**e**) comparison; agreement; (*Law*) compromise.
vergleichbar [fɛr'glaɪçba:r], *adj.* comparable.
vergleichen [fɛr'glaɪçən], *v.a. irr.* compare.
vergleichsweise [fɛr'glaɪçsvaɪzə], *adv.* by way of comparison; comparatively; (*Law*) by way of agreement.
Vergnügen [fɛr'gny:gən], *n.* (—**s**, *no pl.*) pleasure, enjoyment, fun.
vergnügen [fɛr'gny:gən], *v.a.* amuse, delight.
Vergnügung [fɛr'gny:guŋ], *f.* (—, *pl.* —**en**) entertainment, amusement.
vergönnen [fɛr'gœnən], *v.a.* grant, allow; not (be)grudge.
vergöttern [fɛr'gœtərn], *v.a.* idolise, worship.
vergraben [fɛr'gra:bən], *v.a. irr.* hide in the ground, bury.
vergrämt [fɛr'grɛ:mt], *adj.* careworn.
vergreifen [fɛr'graɪfən], *v.r. irr. sich — an*, lay violent hands on, violate.
vergriffen [fɛr'grɪfən], *adj.* out of stock, out of print.
vergrößern [fɛr'grø:sərn], *v.a.* enlarge, expand; increase; magnify; (*fig.*) exaggerate.
Vergrößerung [fɛr'grø:səruŋ], *f.* (—, *pl.* —**en**) magnification, enlargement, increase.
Vergrößerungsglas [fɛr'grø:səruŋsglas], *n.* (—**es**, *pl.* ⸚**er**) magnifying glass.
Vergünstigung [fɛr'gynstɪguŋ], *f.* (—, *pl.* —**en**) privilege, favour, special facility, concession.
vergüten [fɛr'gy:tən], *v.a. einem etwas* —, compensate s.o. for s.th.; reimburse s.o. for s.th.
Vergütung [fɛr'gy:tuŋ], *f.* (—, *pl.* —**en**) indemnification, compensation, reimbursement.
verhaften [fɛr'haftən], *v.a.* arrest.
Verhaftung [fɛr'haftuŋ], *f.* (—, *pl.* —**en**) arrest.
verhallen [fɛr'halən], *v.n.* (*aux.* sein) (*sound*) fade, die away.
verhalten [fɛr'haltən], *v.r. irr. sich* —, act, behave.
Verhalten [fɛr'haltən], *n.* (—**s**, *no pl.*) behaviour, conduct, demeanour.
Verhältnis [fɛr'hɛltnɪs], *n.* (—**ses**, *pl.* —**se**) (*Maths.*) proportion, ratio; relation; footing; love-affair, liaison; (*coll.*) mistress.
verhältnismäßig [fɛr'hɛltnɪsmɛsɪç], *adj.* proportionate, comparative.
Verhältniswort [fɛr'hɛltnɪsvɔrt], *n.* (—**es**, *pl.* ⸚**er**) preposition.
Verhältniszahl [fɛr'hɛltnɪstsa:l], *f.* (—, *pl.* —**en**) proportional number.
Verhaltungsmaßregel [fɛr'haltuŋsma:sre:gəl], *f.* (—, *pl.* —**n**) rule of conduct; instruction.
verhandeln [fɛr'handəln], *v.a.* discuss, transact. — *v.n.* negotiate.
Verhandlung [fɛr'handluŋ], *f.* (—, *pl.* —**en**) discussion, negotiation, transaction; (*Law*) proceedings.
verhängen [fɛr'hɛŋən], *v.a.* cover with; decree; inflict (a penalty) on s.o.
Verhängnis [fɛr'hɛŋnɪs], *n.* (—**ses**, *pl.* —**se**) fate, destiny; misfortune.
Verhängnisglaube [fɛr'hɛŋnɪsglaubə], *m.* (—**ns**, *no pl.*) fatalism.
verhängnisvoll [fɛr'hɛŋnɪsfɔl], *adj.* fateful, portentous; fatal.
verhärmt [fɛr'hɛrmt], *adj.* careworn.
verharren [fɛr'harən], *v.n.* remain; persist.
Verhärtung [fɛr'hɛrtuŋ], *f.* (—, *pl.* —**en**) hardening, hardened state; (*skin*) callosity; (*fig.*) obduracy.
verhaßt [fɛr'hast], *adj.* hated, odious.
verhätscheln [fɛr'hɛtʃəln], *v.a.* pamper, coddle.
verhauen [fɛr'hauən], *v.a.* beat, thrash.
Verheerung [fɛr'he:ruŋ], *f.* (—, *pl.* —**en**) devastation.
verhehlen [fɛr'he:lən], *v.a.* conceal, hide.
verheilen [fɛr'haɪlən], *v.n.* (*aux.* sein) heal.
verheimlichen [fɛr'haɪmlɪçən], *v.a.* keep secret, hush up.
verheiraten [fɛr'haɪra:tən], *v.a.* give in marriage, marry off. — *v.r. sich* —, marry, get married.
verheißen [fɛr'haɪsən], *v.a. irr.* promise.
Verheißung [fɛr'haɪsuŋ], *f.* (—, *pl.* —**en**) promise.
verhelfen [fɛr'hɛlfən], *v.n. irr. einem zu etwas* —, help s.o. to s.th.
Verherrlichung [fɛr'hɛrlɪçuŋ], *f.* (—, *no pl.*) glorification.
Verhetzung [fɛr'hɛtsuŋ], *f.* (—, *pl.* —**en**) incitement, instigation.
verhexen [fɛr'hɛksən], *v.a.* bewitch.
verhindern [fɛr'hɪndərn], *v.a.* hinder, prevent.
Verhinderung [fɛr'hɪndəruŋ], *f.* (—, *pl.* —**en**) prevention, obstacle.
verhöhnen [fɛr'hø:nən], *v.a.* deride, scoff at, jeer at.
Verhöhnung [fɛr'hø:nuŋ], *f.* (—, *pl.* —**en**) derision.
Verhör [fɛr'hø:r], *n.* (—**s**, *pl.* —**e**) hearing; (judicial) examination; *ins — nehmen*, question, interrogate, cross-examine.
verhören [fɛr'hø:rən], *v.a.* examine judicially, interrogate. — *v.r. sich* —, misunderstand.
verhüllen [fɛr'hylən], *v.a.* cover, wrap up, veil.
verhungern [fɛr'huŋərn], *v.n.* (*aux.* sein) starve.
verhungert [fɛr'huŋərt], *adj.* famished.
verhunzen [fɛr'huntsən], *v.a.* spoil, bungle.
verhüten [fɛr'hy:tən], *v.a.* prevent, avert.
Verhütung [fɛr'hy:tuŋ], *f.* (—, *no pl.*) prevention, warding off.
verirren [fɛr'ɪrən], *v.r. sich* —, go astray, lose o.'s way.

verirrt [fɛr'ɪrt], *adj.* stray, straying, lost.
verjagen [fɛr'ja:gən], *v.a.* drive away, chase away.
verjährt [fɛr'jɛ:rt], *adj.* statute-barred; prescriptive; obsolete; old.
verjubeln [fɛr'ju:bəln], *v.a.* play ducks and drakes with; squander.
verjüngen [fɛr'jyŋən], *v.a.* make younger; (*Archit.*) taper. — *v.r.* *sich* —, grow younger.
Verjüngung [fɛr'jyŋuŋ], *f.* (—, *pl.* —**en**) rejuvenation.
verkannt [fɛr'kant], *adj.* misunderstood.
verkappt [fɛr'kapt], *adj.* disguised, secret, in disguise.
Verkauf [fɛr'kauf], *m.* (—(**e**)**s**, *pl.* ¨**e**) sale.
verkaufen [fɛr'kaufən], *v.a.* sell.
Verkäufer [fɛr'kɔyfər], *m.* (—**s**, *pl.* —) seller; shop assistant, salesman.
verkäuflich [fɛr'kɔyflɪç], *adj.* for sale, saleable; mercenary.
Verkaufspreis [fɛr'kaufsprais], *m.* (—**es**, *pl.* —**e**) selling-price.
Verkehr [fɛr'ke:r], *m.* (—**s**, *no pl.*) traffic; commerce; intercourse; communication; — *mit*, association with; service (*trains, buses etc.*), transport.
verkehren [fɛr'ke:rən], *v.a.* turn upside down; transform; pervert. — *v.n.* frequent (a place), visit, associate (with); run, operate.
Verkehrsstraße [fɛr'ke:rsʃtra:sə], *f.* (—, *pl.* —**n**) thoroughfare.
Verkehrsstockung [fɛr'ke:rsʃtɔkuŋ], *f.* (—, *pl.* —**en**) traffic jam.
verkehrt [fɛr'ke:rt], *adj.* upside down; (*fig.*) wrong.
Verkehrtheit [fɛr'ke:rthait], *f.* (—, *pl.* —**en**) absurdity, piece of folly.
Verkehrung [fɛr'ke:ruŋ], *f.* (—, *pl.* —**en**) turning; inversion; perversion; misrepresentation; (*Gram.*) inversion.
verkennen [fɛr'kɛnən], *v.a.* *irr.* mistake, fail to recognize; misjudge (s.o.'s intentions).
verklagen [fɛr'kla:gən], *v.a.* sue; accuse.
verklären [fɛr'klɛ:rən], *v.a.* transfigure, illumine.
verklärt [fɛr'klɛ:rt], *adj.* transfigured; radiant.
verkleben [fɛr'kle:bən], *v.a.* paste over.
verkleiden [fɛr'klaidən], *v.a.*, *v.r.* disguise (o.s.).
Verkleidung [fɛr'klaiduŋ], *f.* (— *pl.* —**en**) disguise.
verkleinern [fɛr'klainərn], *v.a.* make smaller, diminish, reduce; belittle, disparage.
Verkleinerung [fɛr'klainəruŋ], *f.* (—, *pl.* —**en**) diminution, reduction; belittling, detraction.
Verkleinerungswort [fɛr'klainəruŋsvɔrt], *n.* (—**s**, *pl.* ¨**er**) (*Gram.*) diminutive.
verkneifen [fɛr'knaifən], *v.r.* *irr.* (*coll.*) *sich etwas* —, deny o.s. s.th.
verkniffen [fɛr'knɪfən], *adj.* pinched; shrewd; hard-bitten.
verknöchern [fɛr'knœçərn], *v.n.* (*aux.* sein) ossify; (*fig.*) become fossilised *or* inflexible.
Verknöcherung [fɛr'knœçəruŋ], *f.* (—, *pl.* —**en**) ossification; (*fig.*) fossilisation.
verknüpfen [fɛr'knypfən], *v.a.* tie, connect, link.
verkochen [fɛr'kɔxən], *v.n.* (*aux.* sein) boil away.
verkommen [fɛr'kɔmən], *v.n.* *irr.* (*aux.* sein) go from bad to worse, go to seed, decay, become depraved. — *adj.* demoralised, down and out, depraved.
Verkommenheit [fɛr'kɔmənhait], *f.* (—, *no pl.*) demoralisation; depravity.
verkörpern [fɛr'kœrpərn], *v.a.* embody.
verkrachen [fɛr'kraxən], *v.r.* *sich* —, quarrel, (*coll.*) have a row.
verkriechen [fɛr'kri:çən], *v.r.* *irr.* *sich* —, creep *or* crawl away; slink away, lie low.
verkümmern [fɛr'kymərn], *v.n.* (*aux.* sein) wear away, waste away; pine away.
verkünden [fɛr'kyndən], *v.a.* proclaim, announce, publish, prophesy.
Verkündigung [fɛr'kyndiguŋ], *f.* (—, *pl.* —**en**) announcement, proclamation; prediction.
Verkündung [fɛr'kynduŋ], *f.* (—, *pl.* —**en**) publication, proclamation.
Verkürzung [fɛr'kyrtsuŋ], *f.* (—, *pl.* —**en**) shortening, curtailment.
verlachen [fɛr'laxən], *v.a.* laugh at, deride.
verladen [fɛr'la:dən], *v.a.* *irr.* load, ship, freight.
Verladung [fɛr'la:duŋ], *f.* (—, *pl.* —**en**) loading, shipping.
Verlag [fɛr'la:k], *m.* (—(**e**)**s**, *pl.* —**e**) publication; publishing-house, (firm of) publishers.
Verlagsrecht [fɛr'la:ksrɛçt], *n.* (—**s**, *pl.* —**e**) copyright.
Verlangen [fɛr'laŋən], *n.* (—**s**, *no pl.*) demand, request; longing, desire.
verlangen [fɛr'laŋən], *v.a.* ask, demand, request.
verlängern [fɛr'lɛŋərn], *v.a.* lengthen, prolong, extend.
Verlängerung [fɛr'lɛŋəruŋ], *f.* (—, *pl.* —**en**) lengthening; (*period*) prolongation, extension.
verlangsamen [fɛr'laŋza:mən], *v.a.* slow down, slacken, decelerate.
Verlaß [fɛr'las], *m.* (—**sses**, *no pl.*) *es ist kein* — *auf dich*, you cannot be relied on.
verlassen [fɛr'lasən], *v.a.* *irr.* leave, abandon. — *v.r.* *sich* — *auf*, rely on, depend upon. — *adj.* forlorn, forsaken, deserted, desolate, lonely.
Verlassenheit [fɛr'lasənhait], *f.* (—, *no pl.*) desolation, loneliness, solitude.
verläßlich [fɛr'lɛslɪç], *adj.* reliable, trustworthy.

Verlauf [fɛr'lauf], *m.* (—(e)s, *no pl.*) lapse, expiration; course.
verlaufen [fɛr'laufən], *v.n. irr.* (*aux.* sein) (*time*) pass; (*period*) expire, elapse; develop(e), turn out. — *v.r. sich* —, lose o.'s way; (*colour*) run.
verlauten [fɛr'lautən], *v.n.* transpire.
verleben [fɛr'le:bən], *v.a.* pass, spend.
verlebt [fɛr'le:pt], *adj.* worn out; spent; (*Am.*) played out.
verlegen [fɛr'le:gən], *v.a.* (*domicile*) move, remove; (*things*) mislay; (*books*) publish; obstruct; adjourn; change to another date *or* place. — *v.r. sich auf etwas* —, devote o.s. to s.th. — *adj.* embarrassed, ill at ease.
Verlegenheit [fɛr'le:gənhaɪt], *f.* (—, *pl.* —en) embarrassment, perplexity; predicament, difficulty.
Verleger [fɛr'le:gər], *m.* (—s, *pl.* —) publisher.
verleiden [fɛr'laɪdən], *v.a. einem etwas* —, spoil s.th. for s.o.
verleihen [fɛr'laɪən], *v.a. irr.* lend; (*honour, title*) confer; bestow, award.
Verleiher [fɛr'laɪər], *m.* (—s, *pl.* —) lender.
Verleihung [fɛr'laɪuŋ], *f.* (—, *pl.* —en) lending, loan; (*medal, prize*) investiture; grant, conferring.
verleiten [fɛr'laɪtən], *v.a.* mislead, entice, induce; seduce.
Verleitung [fɛr'laɪtuŋ], *f.* (—, *no pl.*) misleading, enticement, inducement; seduction.
verlernen [fɛr'lɛrnən], *v.a.* unlearn; forget.
verlesen [fɛr'le:zən], *v.a. irr.* read aloud, read out, recite. — *v.r. sich* —, misread.
verletzen [fɛr'lɛtsən], *v.a.* injure, hurt, wound, violate.
verletzend [fɛr'lɛtsənt], *adj.* offensive, insulting; cutting.
verletzlich [fɛr'lɛtslɪç], *adj.* vulnerable.
Verletzlichkeit [fɛr'lɛtslɪçkaɪt], *f.* (—, *no pl.*) vulnerability.
Verletzung [fɛr'lɛtsuŋ], *f.* (—, *pl.* —en) hurt, wound; (*Law*) violation.
verleugnen [fɛr'lɔygnən], *v.a.* deny, renounce, disown.
Verleugnung [fɛr'lɔygnuŋ], *f.* (—, *pl.* —en) denial, abnegation.
verleumden [fɛr'lɔymdən], *v.a.* slander, calumniate, traduce.
Verleumdung [fɛr'lɔymduŋ], *f.* (—, *pl.* —en) slander, libel, calumny.
verlieben [fɛr'li:bən], *v.r. sich — in*, fall in love with.
Verliebte [fɛr'li:ptə], *m. or f.* (—n, *pl.* —n) person in love, lover.
Verliebtheit [fɛr'li:pthaɪt], *f.* (—, *no pl.*) infatuation, amorousness.
verlieren [fɛr'li:rən], *v.a. irr.* lose.
Verlierer [fɛr'li:rər], *m.* (—s, *pl.* —) loser.
Verlies [fɛr'li:s], *n.* (—(s)es, *pl.* —(s)e) dungeon.
verloben [fɛr'lo:bən], *v.r. sich — mit*, become engaged to.
Verlöbnis [fɛr'lø:pnɪs], *n.* (—ses, *pl.* —se) (*rare*) engagement.
Verlobte [fɛr'lo:ptə], *m.* (—n, *pl.* —n) and *f.* (—n, *pl.* —n) fiancé(e), betrothed.
Verlobung [fɛr'lo:buŋ], *f.* (—, *pl.* —en) engagement, betrothal.
verlocken [fɛr'lɔkən], *v.a.* tempt, entice.
verlogen [fɛr'lo:gən], *adj.* lying, mendacious.
Verlogenheit [fɛr'lo:gənhaɪt], *f.* (—, *no pl.*) mendacity.
verlohnen [fɛr'lo:nən], *v. impers.* be worth while.
verlöschen [fɛr'lœʃən], *v.a.* extinguish.
verlosen [fɛr'lo:zən], *v.a.* raffle; draw *or* cast lots for.
Verlosung [fɛr'lo:zuŋ], *f.* (—, *pl.* —en) raffle, lottery.
verlöten [fɛr'lø:tən], *v.a.* solder.
verlottern [fɛr'lɔtərn], *v.n.* (*aux.* sein) go to the dogs.
Verlust [fɛr'lust], *m.* (—es, *pl.* —e) loss; (*death*) bereavement; (*Mil.*) casualty.
verlustig [fɛr'lustɪç], *adj.* — *gehen*, lose s.th., forfeit s.th.
vermachen [fɛr'maxən], *v.a. einem etwas* —, bequeath s.th. to s.o.
Vermächtnis [fɛr'mɛçtnɪs], *n.* (—ses, *pl.* —sse) will; legacy, bequest; (*fig.*) *heiliges* —, sacred trust.
vermahlen [fɛr'ma:lən], *v.a.* grind (down).
Vermählung [fɛr'mɛ:luŋ], *f.* (—, *pl.* —en) marriage, wedding.
Vermahnung [fɛr'ma:nuŋ], *f.* (—, *pl.* —en) admonition, exhortation.
vermauern [fɛr'mauərn], *v.a.* wall up.
vermehren [fɛr'me:rən], *v.a.* augment, multiply, increase. — *v.r. sich* —, multiply.
Vermehrung [fɛr'me:ruŋ], *f.* (—, *pl.* —en) increase, multiplication.
vermeiden [fɛr'maɪdən], *v.a. irr.* avoid, shun, shirk.
vermeidlich [fɛr'maɪtlɪç], *adj.* avoidable.
Vermeidung [fɛr'maɪduŋ], *f.* (—, *no pl.*) avoidance.
vermeintlich [fɛr'maɪntlɪç], *adj.* supposed, alleged, pretended; (*heir*) presumptive.
vermelden [fɛr'mɛldən], *v.a.* announce, notify.
vermengen [fɛr'mɛŋən], *v.a.* mingle, mix.
Vermerk [fɛr'mɛrk], *m.* (—s, *pl.* —e) entry, notice, note.
vermerken [fɛr'mɛrkən], *v.a.* observe, jot down.
vermessen [fɛr'mɛsən], *v.a. irr.* measure; (*land*) survey. — *adj.* bold, daring, audacious; arrogant.
Vermessenheit [fɛr'mɛsənhaɪt], *f.* (—, *no pl.*) boldness, audacity; arrogance.
Vermesser [fɛr'mɛsər], *m.* (—s, *pl.* —) (*land*) surveyor.

Vermessung [fɛr'mɛsuŋ], *f.* (—, *pl.* —**en**) (*land*) survey; measuring.
vermieten [fɛr'mi:tən], *v.a.* let, lease, hire out.
Vermieter [fɛr'mi:tər], *m.* (—**s**, *pl.* —) landlord; hirer.
vermindern [fɛr'mɪndərn], *v.a.* diminish, lessen.
Verminderung [fɛr'mɪndəruŋ], *f.* (—, *pl.* —**en**) diminution, reduction, decrease, lessening.
vermischen [fɛr'mɪʃən], *v.a.* mix, mingle, blend.
vermissen [fɛr'mɪsən], *v.a.* miss; *vermißt sein*, be missing; *vermißt werden*, be missed.
vermitteln [fɛr'mɪtəln], *v.n.* mediate. — *v.a.* adjust; negotiate, secure.
Vermittler [fɛr'mɪtlər], *m.* (—**s**, *pl.* —) mediator; agent, middleman.
Vermittlung [fɛr'mɪtluŋ], *f.* (—, *pl.* —**en**) mediation, intervention.
vermöbeln [fɛr'mø:bəln], *v.a.* (*sl.*) *einen* —, thrash s.o.
vermodern [fɛr'mo:dərn], *v.n.* (*aux.* sein) moulder, rot.
vermöge [fɛr'mø:gə], *prep.* (*Genit.*) by virtue of, by dint of, on the strength of.
Vermögen [fɛr'mø:gən], *n.* (—**s**, *pl.* —) faculty, power; means, assets; fortune, wealth, riches; *er hat* —, he is a man of property; *nach bestem* —, to the best of o.'s ability.
vermögen [fɛr'mø:gən], *v.a. irr.* be able to, have the power to, be capable of.
vermögend [fɛr'mø:gənt], *adj.* wealthy.
Vermögensbestand [fɛr'mø:gənsbəʃtant], *m.* (—**s**, *pl.* ¨**e**) assets.
Vermögenssteuer [fɛr'mø:gənsʃtɔyər], *f.* (—, *pl.* —**n**) property tax.
vermorscht [fɛr'mɔrʃt], *adj.* mouldering, rotten.
vermuten [fɛr'mu:tən], *v.a.* suppose, conjecture, surmise, presume; guess.
vermutlich [fɛr'mu:tlɪç], *adj.* likely, probable.
Vermutung [fɛr'mu:tuŋ], *f.* (—, *pl.* —**en**) guess, supposition, conjecture.
vernachlässigen [fɛr'naxlɛsɪgən], *v.a.* neglect.
Vernachlässigung [fɛr'naxlɛsɪguŋ], *f.* (—, *pl.* —**en**) neglect, negligence.
vernarren [fɛr'narən], *v.r. sich* — (*in, Acc.*), become infatuated (with).
vernarrt [fɛr'nart], *adj.* madly in love.
vernaschen [fɛr'naʃən], *v.a.* squander (money) on sweets.
vernehmbar [fɛr'ne:mba:r], *adj.* audible; *sich* — *machen*, make o.s. heard.
Vernehmen [fɛr'ne:mən], *n.* (—**s**, *no pl.*) *dem* — *nach*, from what o. hears.
vernehmen [fɛr'ne:mən], *v.a. irr.* hear, learn; (*Law*) examine, interrogate.
vernehmlich [fɛr'ne:mlɪç], *adj.* audible, distinct, clear.
Vernehmlichkeit [fɛr'ne:mlɪçkaɪt], *f.* (—, *no pl.*) audibility.
Vernehmung [fɛr'ne:muŋ], *f.* (—, *pl.* —**en**) (*Law*) interrogation, examination.
verneigen [fɛr'naɪgən], *v.r. sich* —, curts(e)y, bow.
Verneigung [fɛr'naɪguŋ], *f.* (—, *pl.* —**en**) curts(e)y, bow.
verneinen [fɛr'naɪnən], *v.a.* deny, answer in the negative.
Verneinung [fɛr'naɪnuŋ], *f.* (—, *pl.* —**en**) negation, denial; (*Gram.*) negation, negative.
vernichten [fɛr'nɪçtən], *v.a.* annihilate, destroy utterly, exterminate.
Vernichtung [fɛr'nɪçtuŋ], *f.* (—, *no pl.*) annihilation, extinction, destruction.
vernieten [fɛr'ni:tən], *v.a.* rivet.
Vernunft [fɛr'nunft], *f.* (—, *no pl.*) reason, sense, intelligence, judgment; *gesunde* —, common sense; — *annehmen*, listen to reason; *einen zur* — *bringen*, bring s.o. to his senses.
vernünftig [fɛr'nynftɪç], *adj.* sensible, reasonable, rational.
veröden [fɛr'ø:dən], *v.n.* (*aux.* sein) become desolate, become devastated.
Verödung [fɛr'ø:duŋ], *f.* (—, *no pl.*) devastation, desolation.
veröffentlichen [fɛr'œfəntlɪçən], *v.a.* publish.
Veröffentlichung [fɛr'œfəntlɪçuŋ], *f.* (—, *pl.* —**en**) publication.
verordnen [fɛr'ɔrdnən], *v.a.* order, command, ordain; (*Med.*) prescribe.
Verordnung [fɛr'ɔrdnuŋ], *f.* (—, *pl.* —**en**) order; (*Law*) decree, edict, statute; (*Med.*) prescription.
verpassen [fɛr'pasən], *v.a.* lose by delay, let slip; (*train etc.*) miss.
verpfänden [fɛr'pfɛndən], *v.a.* pawn, pledge.
Verpfänder [fɛr'pfɛndər], *m.* (—**s**, *pl.* —) mortgager.
Verpfändung [fɛr'pfɛnduŋ], *f.* (—, *pl.* —**en**) pawning, pledging.
verpflanzen [fɛr'pflantsən], *v.a.* transplant.
Verpflanzung [fɛr'pflantsuŋ], *f.* (—, *pl.* —**en**) transplantation.
verpflegen [fɛr'pfle:gən], *v.a.* board, provide food for, feed; nurse.
Verpflegung [fɛr'pfle:guŋ], *f.* (—, *no pl.*) board, catering; food.
Verpflegungskosten [fɛr'pfle:guŋskɔstən], *f. pl.* (cost of) board and lodging.
verpflichten [fɛr'pflɪçtən], *v.a.* bind, oblige, engage.
verpflichtend [fɛr'pflɪçtənt], *adj.* obligatory.
Verpflichtung [fɛr'pflɪçtuŋ], *f.* (—, *pl.* —**en**) obligation, duty; liability, engagement.
verplaudern [fɛr'plaudərn], *v.a.* spend (time) chatting.
verplempern [fɛr'plɛmpərn], *v.a.* (*coll.*) spend foolishly, fritter away.
verpönt [fɛr'pø:nt], *adj.* frowned upon; taboo.
verprassen [fɛr'prasən], *v.a.* squander (money) in riotous living.

verpuffen [fɛr'pufən], *v.n.* (*aux.* sein) (*coll.*) fizzle out.
verpulvern [fɛr'pulvərn], *v.a.* fritter away.
Verputz [fɛr'puts], *m.* (—**es**, *no pl.*) plaster.
verquicken [fɛr'kvɪkən], *v.a.* amalgamate; mix up.
Verrat [fɛr'ra:t], *m.* (—(**e**)**s**, *no pl.*) treachery, treason.
verraten [fɛr'ra:tən], *v.a. irr.* betray; disclose; *das verrät die Hand des Künstlers*, this proclaims the hand of the artist.
Verräter [fɛr'rɛ:tər], *m.* (—**s**, *pl.* —) traitor.
verräterisch [fɛr'rɛ:tərɪʃ], *adj.* treacherous, treasonable, perfidious; (*fig.*) tell-tale.
verrauchen [fɛr'rauxən], *v.n.* (*aux.* sein) evaporate; (*fig.*) blow over; cool down.
verräuchern [fɛr'rɔyçərn], *v.a.* smoke, fill with smoke.
verräumen [fɛr'rɔymən], *v.a.* misplace, mislay.
verrauschen [fɛr'rauʃən], *v.n.* (*aux.* sein) (*sound*) die away; pass away.
verrechnen [fɛr'rɛçnən], *v.a.* reckon up. — *v.r. sich* —, miscalculate.
Verrechnung [fɛr'rɛçnuŋ], *f.* (—, *pl.* — **en**) reckoning-up.
Verrechnungsscheck [fɛr'rɛçnuŋsʃɛk], *m.* (—**s**, *pl.* —**e**, —**s**) crossed cheque, non-negotiable cheque.
verregnen [fɛr're:gnən], *v.a.* spoil by rain.
verreiben [fɛr'raɪbən], *v.a. irr.* rub away; rub hard.
verreisen [fɛr'raɪzən], *v.n.* (*aux.* sein) go on a journey.
verrenken [fɛr'rɛŋkən], *v.a.* sprain, dislocate.
Verrenkung [fɛr'rɛŋkuŋ], *f.* (—, *pl.* —**en**) sprain, dislocation.
verrichten [fɛr'rɪçtən], *v.a.* do, perform, acquit o.s. of; execute; (*prayer*) say.
verriegeln [fɛr'ri:gəln], *v.a.* bolt.
verringern [fɛr'rɪŋərn], *v.a.* reduce, diminish.
Verringerung [fɛr'rɪŋəruŋ], *f.* (—, *no pl.*) diminution, reduction.
verrinnen [fɛr'rɪnən], *v.n. irr.* (*aux.* sein) run off; (*fig.*) pass, elapse.
verrosten [fɛr'rɔstən], *v.n.* (*aux.* sein) rust.
verrottet [fɛr'rɔtət], *adj.* rotten.
verrucht [fɛr'ru:xt], *adj.* villainous, atrocious, heinous, infamous.
Verruchtheit [fɛr'ru:xthaɪt], *f.* (—, *no pl.*) villainy.
verrücken [fɛr'rykən], *v.a.* shift, displace.
verrückt [fɛr'rykt], *adj.* crazy, mad.
Verrückte [fɛr'ryktə], *m.* (—**n**, *pl.* —**n**) madman. — *f.* (—**n**, *pl.* —**n**) madwoman.
Verrücktheit [fɛr'rykthaɪt], *f.* (—, *pl.* —**en**) craziness; mad act.
Verruf [fɛr'ru:f], *m.* (—**s**, *no pl.*) discredit, ill repute.
verrufen [fɛr'ru:fən], *adj.* notorious, of ill repute.
Vers [fɛrs], *m.* (—**es**, *pl.* —**e**) verse.
versagen [fɛr'za:gən], *v.a. einem etwas* —, deny s.o. s.th., refuse s.o. s.th. — *v.n.* fail, break down; (*voice*) falter; *sich etwas* —, abstain from s.th., deny o.s. s.th.
Versager [fɛr'za:gər], *m.* (—**s**, *pl.* —) misfire; failure, unsuccessful person, flop.
versammeln [fɛr'zaməln], *v.a.* gather around, convene. — *v.r. sich* —, assemble, meet.
Versammlung [fɛr'zamluŋ], *f.* (—, *pl.* —**en**) assembly, meeting, gathering, convention.
Versand [fɛr'zant], *m.* (—**s**, *no pl.*) dispatch, forwarding, shipping, shipment.
versanden [fɛr'zandən], *v.n.* (*aux.* sein) silt up.
Versandgeschäft [fɛr'zantgəʃɛft], *n.* (—**s**, *pl.* —**e**) export business; mail order business.
Versatzamt [fɛr'zatsamt], *n.* (—**s**, *pl.* ⸗**er**) pawn-shop.
versauen [fɛr'zauən], *v.a.* (*sl.*) make a mess of.
versauern [fɛr'zauərn], *v.n.* (*aux.* sein) turn sour; (*fig.*) become morose.
versaufen [fɛr'zaufən], *v.a. irr.* (*sl.*) squander (money) on drink, drink away.
versäumen [fɛr'zɔymən], *v.a.* miss, omit, lose by delay; leave undone; neglect.
Versäumnis [fɛr'zɔymnɪs], *n.* (—**ses**, *pl.* —**se**) neglect, omission; (*time*) loss.
Versbau ['fɛrsbau], *m.* (—**s**, *no pl.*) versification; verse structure.
verschachern [fɛr'ʃaxərn], *v.a.* barter away.
verschaffen [fɛr'ʃafən], *v.a.* provide, procure, obtain, get.
verschämt [fɛr'ʃɛ:mt], *adj.* shamefaced, bashful.
verschanzen [fɛr'ʃantsən], *v.a.* fortify.
Verschanzung [fɛr'ʃantsuŋ], *f.* (—, *pl.* —**en**) fortification, entrenchment.
verschärfen [fɛr'ʃɛrfən], *v.a.* heighten, intensify, sharpen.
verscharren [fɛr'ʃarən], *v.a.* cover with earth; bury hurriedly.
verscheiden [fɛr'ʃaɪdən], *v.n. irr.* (*aux.* sein) die, pass away.
verschenken [fɛr'ʃɛŋkən], *v.a.* make a present of, give away.
verscherzen [fɛr'ʃɛrtsən], *v.a. sich etwas* —, forfeit s.th.
verscheuchen [fɛr'ʃɔyçən], *v.a.* scare away, frighten away; *Sorgen* —, banish care.
verschicken [fɛr'ʃɪkən], *v.a.* send on, send out, forward, transmit; evacuate.
Verschickung [fɛr'ʃɪkuŋ], *f.* (—, *no pl.*) forwarding, transmission; evacuation; banishment, exile.

verschieben [fɛr'ʃi:bən], *v.a. irr.* shift, move; delay, put off, defer, postpone.
Verschiebung [fɛr'ʃi:buŋ], *f.* (—, *pl.* —**en**) removal; postponement; (*fig.*) black marketeering.
verschieden [fɛr'ʃi:dən], *adj.* different, diverse; deceased, departed; (*pl.*) some, several, sundry.
verschiedenartig [fɛr'ʃi:dəna:rtɪç], *adj.* varied, various, heterogeneous.
verschiedenerlei [fɛr'ʃi:dənərlaɪ], *indecl. adj.* diverse, of various kinds.
Verschiedenheit [fɛr'ʃi:dənhaɪt], *f.* (—, *pl.* —**en**) difference; diversity, variety.
verschiedentlich [fɛr'ʃi:dəntlɪç], *adv.* variously, severally; repeatedly.
verschiffen [fɛr'ʃɪfən], *v.a.* export, ship.
verschimmeln [fɛr'ʃɪməln], *v.n.* (*aux.* sein) go mouldy.
verschlafen [fɛr'ʃla:fən], *v.a. irr.* sleep through, sleep away. — *v.r. sich* —, oversleep. — *adj.* sleepy, drowsy.
Verschlag [fɛr'ʃla:k], *m.* (—**s**, *pl.* ⸚**e**) partition, box, cubicle.
verschlagen [fɛr'ʃla:gən], *v.a. irr. es verschlägt mir den Atem*, it takes my breath away. — *adj.* cunning, crafty, sly.
verschlechtern [fɛr'ʃlɛçtərn], *v.a.* worsen, make worse. — *v.r. sich* —, deteriorate.
Verschlechterung [fɛr'ʃlɛçtəruŋ], *f.* (—, *no pl.*) deterioration.
verschleiern [fɛr'ʃlaɪərn], *v.a.* veil.
Verschleierung [fɛr'ʃlaɪəruŋ], *f.* (—, *pl.* —**en**) veiling, concealment; camouflage.
verschleißen [fɛr'ʃlaɪsən], *v.a. irr.* wear out, waste.
verschlemmen [fɛr'ʃlɛmən], *v.a.* squander on eating and drinking.
verschleppen [fɛr'ʃlɛpən], *v.a.* carry off, deport; kidnap; protract, spread; put off, procrastinate.
verschleudern [fɛr'ʃlɔydərn], *v.a.* waste; sell at cut prices.
verschließen [fɛr'ʃli:sən], *v.a. irr.* lock, lock up.
verschlimmern [fɛr'ʃlɪmərn], *v.a.* make worse. — *v.r. sich* —, get worse, worsen, deteriorate.
Verschlimmerung [fɛr'ʃlɪməruŋ], *f.* (—, *no pl.*) worsening, deterioration.
verschlingen [fɛr'ʃlɪŋən], *v.a. irr.* swallow up, devour.
verschlossen [fɛr'ʃlɔsən], *adj.* reserved, uncommunicative, withdrawn.
Verschlossenheit [fɛr'ʃlɔsənhaɪt], *f.* (—, *no pl.*) reserve.
verschlucken [fɛr'ʃlukən], *v.a.* swallow, gulp down; (*fig.*) suppress. — *v.r. sich* —, swallow the wrong way.
verschlungen [fɛr'ʃluŋən], *adj.* intricate, complicated.
Verschluß [fɛr'ʃlus], *m.* (—**sses**, *pl.* ⸚**sse**) lock; clasp; fastening; *unter* — *haben*, keep under lock and key.
Verschlußlaut [fɛr'ʃluslaut], *m.* (—**s**, *pl.* —**e**) (*Phon.*) explosive, plosive, stop.
verschmachten [fɛr'ʃmaxtən], *v.n.* (*aux.* sein) languish, pine; be parched.
Verschmähung [fɛr'ʃmɛ:uŋ], *f.* (—, *no pl.*) disdain, scorn, rejection.
Verschmelzung [fɛr'ʃmɛltsuŋ], *f.* (—, *no pl.*) coalescence, fusion, blending.
verschmerzen [fɛr'ʃmɛrtsən], *v.a.* get over; bear stoically, make the best of.
verschmitzt [fɛr'ʃmɪtst], *adj.* cunning, crafty, mischievous.
verschmutzen [fɛr'ʃmutsən], *v.n.* (*aux.* sein) get dirty.
verschnappen [fɛr'ʃnapən], *v.r. sich* —, blurt out a secret, give o.s. away, let the cat out of the bag.
verschneiden [fɛr'ʃnaɪdən], *v.a. irr.* (*wings*) clip; (*trees*) prune; (*animals*) castrate; (*wine*) blend.
verschneien [fɛr'ʃnaɪən], *v.n.* (*aux.* sein) be snowed up, be covered with snow, be snowbound.
Verschnitt [fɛr'ʃnɪt], *m.* (—**s**, *no pl.*) blended wine, blend.
Verschnittene [fɛr'ʃnɪtənə], *m.* (—**n**, *pl.* —**n**) eunuch.
verschnörkelt [fɛr'ʃnœrkəlt], *adj.* adorned with flourishes.
verschnupft [fɛr'ʃnupft], *adj.* — *sein*, have a cold in the head; (*fig.*) be vexed.
verschnüren [fɛr'ʃny:rən], *v.a.* (*shoes*) lace up; (*parcel*) tie up.
verschonen [fɛr'ʃo:nən], *v.a.* spare, exempt from.
verschönern [fɛr'ʃø:nərn], *v.a.* embellish, beautify.
Verschönerung [fɛr'ʃø:nəruŋ], *f.* (—, *pl.* —**en**) embellishment, adornment.
Verschonung [fɛr'ʃo:nuŋ], *f.* (—, *no pl.*) exemption; forbearance.
verschossen [fɛr'ʃɔsən], *adj.* faded, discoloured; (*fig.*) madly in love.
verschreiben [fɛr'ʃraɪbən], *v.a. irr.* prescribe. — *v.r. sich* —, make a mistake in writing.
verschrien [fɛr'ʃri:ən], *adj.* notorious.
verschroben [fɛr'ʃro:bən], *adj.* cranky, eccentric.
Verschrobenheit [fɛr'ʃro:bənhaɪt], *f.* (—, *pl.* —**en**) crankiness, eccentricity.
verschrumpfen [fɛr'ʃrumpfən], *v.n.* (*aux.* sein) shrivel up.
verschüchtern [fɛr'ʃyçtərn], *v.a.* intimidate.
verschulden [fɛr'ʃuldən], *v.a.* bring on, be the cause of; be guilty of.
verschuldet [fɛr'ʃuldət], *adj.* in debt.
Verschuldung [fɛr'ʃulduŋ], *f.* (—, *no pl.*) indebtedness.
verschütten [fɛr'ʃytən], *v.a.* spill; bury alive.
verschwägern [fɛr'ʃvɛ:gərn], *v.r. sich* —, become related by marriage.
Verschwägerung [fɛr'ʃvɛ:gəruŋ], (—, *no pl.*) relationship by marriage.
verschwatzen [fɛr'ʃvatsən], *v.a.* gossip (the time) away, spend o.'s time gossiping.
verschweigen [fɛr'ʃvaɪgən], *v.a. irr.* keep secret, keep (news) from, hush up.

verschwenden [fɛr'ʃvɛndən], *v.a.* squander, waste.
verschwenderisch [fɛr'ʃvɛndərɪʃ], *adj.* prodigal, profuse, lavish; wasteful.
Verschwendung [fɛr'ʃvɛnduŋ], *f.* (—, *no pl.*) waste, extravagance.
Verschwendungssucht [fɛr'ʃvɛnduŋszuxt], *f.* (—, *no pl.*) prodigality; extravagance.
verschwiegen [fɛr'ʃvi:gən], *adj.* discreet; close, secretive.
Verschwiegenheit [fɛr'ʃvi:gənhaɪt], *f.* (—, *no pl.*) discretion, secrecy.
verschwimmen [fɛr'ʃvɪmən], *v.n. irr.* (*aux.* sein) become blurred.
verschwinden [fɛr'ʃvɪndən], *v.n. irr.* (*aux.* sein) disappear, vanish.
verschwommen [fɛr'ʃvɔmən], *adj.* vague, blurred.
verschwören [fɛr'ʃvø:rən], *v.r. irr.* *sich* —, plot, conspire.
Verschwörer [fɛr'ʃvø:rer], *m.* (—**s**, *pl.* —) conspirator.
Verschwörung [fɛr'ʃvø:ruŋ], *f.* (—, *pl.* —**en**) conspiracy.
Versehen [fɛr'ze:ən], *n.* (—**s**, *pl.* —) error, mistake, oversight.
versehen [fɛr'ze:ən], *v.a. irr.* provide; perform; fill (an office); *einen — mit*, furnish s.o. with. — *v.r. sich* —, make a mistake.
versehren [fɛr'ze:rən], *v.a.* wound; disable.
versenden [fɛr'zɛndən], *v.a. irr.* forward, consign, send off.
Versender [fɛr'zɛndər], *m.* (—**s**, *pl.*—) consigner, exporter.
Versendung [fɛr'zɛnduŋ], *f.* (—, *no pl.*) transmission, shipping.
Versendungskosten [fɛr'zɛnduŋskɔstən], *f. pl.* forwarding charges.
versengen [fɛr'zɛŋən], *v.a.* singe, scorch.
versenken [fɛr'zɛŋkən], *v.a.* sink; (*ship*) scuttle.
Versenkung [fɛr'zɛŋkuŋ], *f.* (—, *no pl.*) sinking; hollow; (*ship*) scuttling; (*Theat.*) trap-door.
versessen [fɛr'zɛsən], *adj.* — *sein auf*, be bent upon, be mad on.
versetzen [fɛr'zɛtsən], *v.a.* transplant, remove; give; pawn, pledge; transfer; (*pupil*) promote to a higher form. — *v.r. sich in die Lage eines anderen* —, put o.s. in s.o. else's position.
versichern [fɛr'zɪçərn], *v.a.* assert, declare, aver, assure (s.o. of s.th); insure (s.th.).
Versicherung [fɛr'zɪçəruŋ], *f.* (—, *pl.* —**en**) assurance, assertion; insurance.
Versicherungsgesellschaft [fɛr'zɪçəruŋsgəzɛlʃaft], *f.* (—, *pl.* —**en**) insurance company.
Versicherungsprämie [fɛr'zɪçəruŋsprɛ:mjə], *f.* (—, *pl.* —**n**) insurance premium.
versiegbar [fɛr'zi:kba:r], *adj.* exhaustible.
versiegeln [fɛr'zi:gəln], *v.a.* seal (up).
versiegen [fɛr'zi:gən], *v.n.* (*aux.* sein) dry up, be exhausted.
versilbern [fɛr'zɪlbərn], *v.a.* plate with silver; (*fig.*) convert into money.
versinken [fɛr'zɪŋkən], *v.n. irr.* sink; (*ship*) founder; sink; *versunken sein*, be absorbed (in s.th.).
Versmaß ['fɛrsma:s], *n.* (—**es**, *pl.* —**e**) metre.
versoffen [fɛr'zɔfən], *adj.* (*vulg.*) drunken.
versohlen [fɛr'zo:lən], *v.a.* (*coll.*) thrash (s.o.).
versöhnen [fɛr'zø:nən], *v.r. sich mit einem* —, become reconciled with s.o.
versöhnlich [fɛr'zø:nlɪç], *adj.* propitiatory, conciliatory.
Versöhnung [fɛr'zø:nuŋ], *f.* (—, *no pl.*) reconciliation.
versorgen [fɛr'zɔrgən], *v.a.* provide with; take care of; support, maintain.
Versorger [fɛr'zɔrgər], *m.* (—**s**, *pl.* —) provider.
Versorgung [fɛr'zɔrguŋ], *f.* (—, *no pl.*) provision, maintenance.
verspäten [fɛr'ʃpɛ:tən], *v.r. sich* —, be late, be behind time; (*train*) be overdue.
Verspätung [fɛr'ʃpɛ:tuŋ], *f.* (—, *no pl.*) delay; lateness.
verspeisen [fɛr'ʃpaɪzən], *v.a.* eat up.
versperren [fɛr'ʃpɛrən], *v.a.* block up, barricade, close.
verspielen [fɛr'ʃpi:lən], *v.a.* lose (at play); gamble away. — *v.r. sich* —, play wrong.
verspielt [fɛr'ʃpi:lt], *adj.* playful.
verspotten [fɛr'ʃpɔtən], *v.a.* deride, scoff at.
versprechen [fɛr'ʃprɛçən], *v.a. irr.* promise. — *v.r. sich* —, make a slip of the tongue.
Versprechen [fɛr'ʃprɛçən], *n.* (—**s**, *pl.* —) promise.
versprengen [fɛr'ʃprɛŋən], *v.a.* disperse.
verspüren [fɛr'ʃpy:rən], *v.a.* feel, perceive.
verstaatlichen [fɛr'ʃta:tlɪçən], *v.a.* nationalise.
Verstand [fɛr'ʃtant], *m.* (—**(e)s**, *no pl.*) intellect, intelligence, sense; understanding, reason, mind.
verstandesmäßig [fɛr'ʃtandəsmɛ:sɪç], *adj.* rational, reasonable.
Verstandesschärfe [fɛr'ʃtandəsʃɛrfə], *f.* (—, *no pl.*) penetration, acumen.
verständig [fɛr'ʃtɛndɪç], *adj.* judicious, sensible, reasonable.
verständigen [fɛr'ʃtɛndɪgən], *v.a.* inform, notify. — *v.r. sich mit einem* —, come to an agreement with s.o.
Verständigung [fɛr'ʃtɛndɪguŋ], *f.* (—, *pl.* —**en**) understanding, agreement; information; arrangement.
verständlich [fɛr'ʃtɛntlɪç], *adj.* intelligible, clear, understandable.
Verständnis [fɛr'ʃtɛntnɪs], (—**ses**, *no pl.*) comprehension, understanding, perception, insight.

verständnisinnig [fɛr'ʃtɛntnɪsɪnɪç], *adj.* sympathetic; having profound insight.
verstärken [fɛr'ʃtɛrkən], *v.a.* strengthen, reinforce, intensify.
Verstärker [fɛr'ʃtɛrkər], *m.* (**—s**, *pl.* **—**) amplifier; magnifier.
Verstärkung [fɛr'ʃtɛrkuŋ], *f.* (**—**, *pl.* **—en**) strengthening, intensification, amplification; (*Mil.*) reinforcements.
verstauben [fɛr'ʃtaubən], *v.n.* (*aux.* sein) get dusty.
verstauchen [fɛr'ʃtauxən], *v.a.* wrench, sprain, dislocate.
verstauen [fɛr'ʃtauən], *v.a.* stow away.
Versteck [fɛr'ʃtɛk], *n.* (**—s**, *pl.* **—e**) hiding-place; place of concealment; —(*en*) *spielen*, play hide-and-seek.
verstecken [fɛr'ʃtɛkən], *v.a.* hide, conceal.
versteckt [fɛr'ʃtɛkt], *adj.* indirect, veiled.
verstehen [fɛr'ʃte:ən], *v.a. irr.* understand, comprehend.
versteigen [fɛr'ʃtaɪgən], *v.r. irr. sich* —, climb too high; (*fig.*) go too far.
versteigern [fɛr'ʃtaɪgərn], *v.a.* sell by auction.
Versteigerung [fɛr'ʃtaɪgəruŋ], *f.* (**—**, *pl.* **—en**) auction, public sale.
versteinern [fɛr'ʃtaɪnərn], *v.n.* (*aux.* sein) turn into stone, petrify.
verstellbar [fɛr'ʃtɛlba:r], *adj.* adjustable.
verstellen [fɛr'ʃtɛlən], *v.a.* adjust; (*voice*) disguise. — *v.r. sich* —, sham, pretend.
versterben [fɛr'ʃtɛrbən], *v.n. irr.* (*aux.* sein) (*Poet.*) die.
versteuern [fɛr'ʃtɔyərn], *v.a.* pay tax on.
verstiegen [fɛr'ʃti:gən], *adj.* eccentric, extravagant.
verstimmen [fɛr'ʃtɪmən], *v.a.* (*Mus.*) put out of tune; (*fig.*) put out of humour, annoy.
Verstimmtheit [fɛr'ʃtɪmthaɪt], *f.* (**—**, *no pl.*) ill-humour, ill-temper, pique.
Verstimmung [fɛr'ʃtɪmuŋ], *f.* (**—**, *pl.* **—en**) bad temper, ill-feeling.
verstockt [fɛr'ʃtɔkt], *adj.* stubborn, obdurate.
Verstocktheit [fɛr'ʃtɔkthaɪt], *f.* (**—**, *no pl.*) stubbornness, obduracy.
verstohlen [fɛr'ʃto:lən], *adj.* surreptitious, clandestine, furtive.
verstopfen [fɛr'ʃtɔpfən], *v.a.* stop up; block (up); *verstopft sein*, be constipated.
Verstopfung [fɛr'ʃtɔpfuŋ], *f.* (**—**, *pl.* **—en**) obstruction; constipation.
verstorben [fɛr'ʃtɔrbən], *adj.* deceased, late.
verstört [fɛr'ʃtø:rt], *adj.* troubled, worried; distracted.
Verstörtheit [fɛr'ʃtø:rthaɪt], *f.* (**—**, *no pl.*) consternation, agitation; distraction; haggardness.
Verstoß [fɛr'ʃto:s], *m.* (**—es**, *pl.* **⸚e**) blunder, mistake; offence.
verstoßen [fɛr'ʃto:sən], *v.a. irr.* cast off, disown, repudiate. — *v.n.* — *gegen*, offend against, act in a manner contrary to.
verstreichen [fɛr'ʃtraɪçən], *v.n. irr.* (*aux.* sein) (*time*) elapse, pass away.
verstricken [fɛr'ʃtrɪkən], *v.a.* entangle, ensnare.
Verstrickung [fɛr'ʃtrɪkuŋ], *f.* (**—**, *pl.* **—en**) entanglement.
verstümmeln [fɛr'ʃtyməln], *v.a.* mutilate, mangle.
verstummen [fɛr'ʃtumən], *v.n.* (*aux.* sein) grow silent; become speechless.
Verstümmlung [fɛr'ʃtymluŋ], *f.* (**—**, *pl.* **—en**) mutilation.
Versuch [fɛr'zu:x], *m.* (**—s**, *pl.* **—e**) attempt, trial, endeavour; (*science*) experiment; (*Lit.*) essay.
versuchen [fɛr'zu:xən], *v.a.* try, attempt, endeavour; (*food*) taste; *einen* —, tempt s.o.
Versucher [fɛr'zu:xər], *m.* (**—s**, *pl.* **—**) tempter.
Versuchskaninchen [fɛr'zu:xskani:nçən], *n.* (**—s**, *pl.* **—**) (*fig.*) guinea-pig.
Versuchung [fɛr'zu:xuŋ], *f.* (**—**, *pl.* **—en**) temptation.
versündigen [fɛr'zyndɪgən], *v.r. sich* —, sin (against).
Versunkenheit [fɛr'zuŋkənhaɪt], *f.* (**—**, *no pl.*) absorption, preoccupation.
vertagen [fɛr'ta:gən], *v.a.* adjourn, prorogue.
Vertagung [fɛr'ta:guŋ], *f.* (**—**, *pl.* **—en**) adjournment, prorogation.
vertauschen [fɛr'tauʃən], *v.a.* exchange, barter, mistake, confuse.
verteidigen [fɛr'taɪdɪgən], *v.a.* defend, uphold, vindicate; (*fig.*) maintain.
Verteidiger [fɛr'taɪdɪgər], *m.* (**—s**, *pl.* **—**) defender; (*Law*) counsel for the defence.
Verteidigung [fɛr'taɪdɪguŋ], *f.* (**—**, *no pl.*) defence; justification.
Verteidigungskrieg [fɛr'taɪdɪguŋskri:k], *m.* (**—(e)s**, *pl.* **—e**) defensive war.
verteilen [fɛr'taɪlən], *v.a.* distribute, allot, allocate.
Verteilung [fɛr'taɪluŋ], *f.* (**—**, *pl.* **—en**) distribution, apportionment.
verteuern [fɛr'tɔyərn], *v.a.* make dearer, raise the price of.
verteufelt [fɛr'tɔyfəlt], *adj.* devilish. — *adv.* (*coll.*) awfully, infernally.
vertiefen [fɛr'ti:fən], *v.a.* deepen.
vertieft [fɛr'ti:ft], *adj.* absorbed, deep in thought.
Vertiefung [fɛr'ti:fuŋ], *f.* (**—**, *pl.* **—en**) cavity, recess, hollow; (*knowledge*) deepening; (*fig.*) absorption.
vertilgen [fɛr'tɪlgən], *v.a.* wipe out, exterminate; (*food*) (*coll.*) polish off.
Vertilgung [fɛr'tɪlguŋ], *f.* (**—**, *no pl.*) extermination, extirpation.
Vertrag [fɛr'tra:k], *m.* (**—(e)s**, *pl.* **⸚e**) contract, agreement; (*Pol.*) treaty, pact, convention.
vertragen [fɛr'tra:gən], *v.a. irr.* suffer, endure; (*food*) digest. — *v.r. sich* — *mit*, get on well with.

vertraglich [fɛrˈtraːklɪç], *adj.* as per contract, according to agreement.
verträglich [fɛrˈtrɛːklɪç], *adj.* accommodating, peaceable.
vertragsmäßig [fɛrˈtraːksmɛːsɪç], *adj.* according to contract.
vertragswidrig [fɛrˈtraːksviːdrɪç], *adj.* contrary to contract.
vertrauen [fɛrˈtrauən], *v.n.* rely (upon), trust (in).
Vertrauen [fɛrˈtrauən], *n.* (—**s**, *no pl.*) confidence, trust, reliance.
vertrauenerweckend [fɛrˈtrauənɛrvɛkənt], *adj.* inspiring confidence.
Vertrauensbruch [fɛrˈtrauənsbrux], *m.* (—**es**, *pl.* ¨**e**) breach of faith.
Vertrauensmann [fɛrˈtrauənsman], *m.* (—**s**, *pl.* ¨**er**) confidant; delegate; person entrusted with s.th.; (*Ind.*) shop steward.
vertrauensselig [fɛrˈtrauənszeːlɪç], *adj.* confiding, trusting.
Vertrauensvotum [fɛrˈtrauənsvoːtum], *n.* (—**s**, *pl.* —**ten**) vote of confidence.
vertrauenswürdig [fɛrˈtrauənsvyrdɪç], *adj.* trustworthy.
vertraulich [fɛrˈtraulɪç], *adj.* confidential; familiar.
Vertraulichkeit [fɛrˈtraulɪçkaɪt], *f.* (—, *pl.* —**en**) familiarity.
verträumt [fɛrˈtrɔymt], *adj.* dreamy.
vertraut [fɛrˈtraut], *adj.* intimate, familiar; conversant.
Vertraute [fɛrˈtrautə], *m.* (—**n**, *pl.* —**n**) close friend, confidant.
Vertrautheit [fɛrˈtrauthaɪt], *f.* (—, *no pl.*) familiarity.
vertreiben [fɛrˈtraɪbən], *v.a. irr.* drive away, expel; eject; (*person*) banish; (*time*) pass, kill; (*goods*) sell.
Vertreibung [fɛrˈtraɪbuŋ], *f.* (—, *no pl.*) expulsion; banishment.
vertreten [fɛrˈtreːtən], *v.a. irr.* represent (s.o.), deputise for (s.o.).
Vertreter [fɛrˈtreːtər], *m.* (—**s**, *pl.* —) representative, deputy; (*Comm.*) agent.
Vertretung [fɛrˈtreːtuŋ], *f.* (—, *pl.* —**en**) representation, agency.
Vertrieb [fɛrˈtriːp], *m.* (—**s**, *pl.* —**e**) sale; distribution.
vertrinken [fɛrˈtrɪŋkən], *v.a. irr.* spend *or* waste money on drink.
vertrocknen [fɛrˈtrɔknən], *v.n.* (*aux.* sein) dry up, wither.
vertrödeln [fɛrˈtrøːdəln], *v.a.* fritter (o.'s time) away.
vertrösten [fɛrːtrøːstən], *v.a.* console; put off; put (s.o.) off with fine words; fob (s.o.) off with vain hopes.
Vertröstung [fɛrˈtrøːstuŋ], *f.* (—, *pl.* —**en**) comfort; empty promises.
vertun [fɛrˈtuːn], *v.a. irr.* squander, waste.
vertuschen [fɛrˈtuʃən], *v.a.* hush up.
verübeln [fɛrˈyːbəln], *v.a.* take amiss.
verüben [fɛrˈyːbən], *v.a.* commit, perpetrate.
verunehren [fɛrˈuneːrən], *v.a.* dishonour, disgrace.
verunglimpfen [fɛrˈunglɪmpfən], *v.a.* bring into disrepute; defame, calumniate.
Verunglimpfung [fɛrˈunglɪmpfuŋ], *f.* (—, *pl.* —**en**) defamation, detraction, calumny.
verunglücken [fɛrˈunglykən], *v.n.* (*aux.* sein) (*person*) meet with an accident; be killed; (*thing*) misfire, fail.
verunreinigen [fɛrˈunraɪnɪgən], *v.a.* contaminate.
Verunreinigung [fɛrˈunraɪnɪguŋ], *f.* (—, *pl.* —**en**) contamination.
verunstalten [fɛrˈunʃtaltən], *v.a.* disfigure, deface.
Verunstaltung [fɛrˈunʃtaltuŋ], *f.* (—, *pl.* —**en**) disfigurement.
Veruntreuung [fɛrˈuntrɔyuŋ], *f.* (—, *pl.* —**en**) embezzlement, misappropriation.
verunzieren [fɛrˈuntsiːrən], *v.a.* disfigure, spoil.
verursachen [fɛrˈuːrzaxən], *v.a.* cause, occasion.
verurteilen [fɛrˈurtaɪlən], *v.a.* condemn; (*Law*) sentence.
Verurteilung [fɛrˈurtaɪluŋ], *f.* (—, *no pl.*) condemnation; (*Law*) sentence.
vervielfältigen [fɛrˈfiːlfɛltɪgən], *v.a.* multiply; duplicate, make copies of.
Vervielfältigung [fɛrˈfiːlfɛltɪguŋ], *f.* (—, *pl.* —**en**) multiplication; duplication, copying.
vervollkommnen [fɛrˈfɔlkɔmnən], *v.a.* improve, perfect.
Vervollkommnung [fɛrˈfɔlkɔmnuŋ], *f.* (—, *no pl.*) improvement, perfection.
vervollständigen [fɛrˈfɔlʃtɛndɪgən], *v.a.* complete.
Vervollständigung [fɛrˈfɔlʃtɛndɪguŋ], *f.* (—, *no pl.*) completion.
verwachsen [fɛrˈvaksən], *v.n. irr.* (*aux.* sein) grow together; be overgrown. — *adj.* deformed.
verwahren [fɛrˈvaːrən], *v.a.* take care of, preserve, secure. — *v.r. sich* — *gegen*, protest against.
verwahrlosen [fɛrˈvaːrloːzən], *v.a.* neglect. — *v.n.* (*aux.* sein) be in need of care and protection, be neglected.
Verwahrlosung [fɛrˈvaːrloːzuŋ], *f.* (—, *no pl.*) neglect.
Verwahrung [fɛrˈvaːruŋ], *f.* (—, *no pl.*) keeping; charge; *in — geben*, deposit, give into s.o.'s charge; — *einlegen gegen*, enter a protest against.
verwalten [fɛrˈvaltən], *v.a.* manage, administer.
Verwalter [fɛrˈvaltər], *m.* (—**s**, *pl.* —) administrator, manager; steward, bailiff.
Verwaltung [fɛrˈvaltuŋ], *f.* (—, *pl.* —**en**) administration, management; Civil Service.
Verwaltungsbezirk [fɛrˈvaltuŋsbətsɪrk], *m.* (—**s**, *pl.* —**e**) administrative district.
Verwandlung [fɛrˈvandluŋ], *f.* (—, *pl.* —**en**) alteration, transformation.

Verwandlungskünstler [fɛr'vandluŋskynstlər], *m.* (—s, *pl.* —) quick-change artist.
verwandt [fɛr'vant], *adj.* related; cognate; congenial.
Verwandte [fɛr'vantə], *m.* (—n, *pl.* —n) relative, relation; kinsman; *der nächste* —, next of kin.
Verwandtschaft [fɛr'vantʃaft], *f.* (—, *pl.* —en) relationship; relations, family; congeniality, sympathy.
verwarnen [fɛr'varnən], *v.a.* admonish, forewarn.
Verwarnung [fɛr'varnuŋ], *f.* (—, *pl.* —en) admonition.
Verwässerung [fɛr'vɛsəruŋ], *f.* (—, *pl.* —en) dilution.
verwechseln [fɛr'vɛksəln], *v.a.* confuse; mistake for.
Verwechslung [fɛr'vɛksluŋ], *f.* (—, *pl.* —en) confusion, mistake.
verwegen [fɛr've:gən], *adj.* bold, audacious.
Verwegenheit [fɛr've:gənhaɪt], *f.* (—, *pl.* —en) boldness, audacity.
verweichlichen [fɛr'vaɪçlɪçən], *v.a.* coddle. — *v.n.* (*aux.* sein) become effeminate.
verweigern [fɛr'vaɪgərn], *v.a.* refuse, deny; reject.
Verweigerung [fɛr'vaɪgəruŋ], *f.* (—, *pl.* —en) refusal, denial; rejection.
verweilen [fɛr'vaɪlən], *v.n.* remain; tarry; stay (with), dwell (on).
verweint [fɛr'vaɪnt], *adj.* (*eyes*) red with weeping.
Verweis [fɛr'vaɪs], *m.* (—es, *pl.* —e) reproof, reprimand, rebuke.
verweisen [fɛr'vaɪzən], *v.a. irr.* reprimand; banish, exile; — *auf etwas*, refer to s.th., hint at s.th.
Verweisung [fɛr'vaɪzuŋ], *f.* (—, *pl.* —en) banishment, exile; reference.
verweltlichen [fɛr'vɛltlɪçən], *v.a.* secularise, profane.
verwenden [fɛr'vɛndən], *v.a.* use, make use of; apply to, employ in, utilize.
Verwendung [fɛr'vɛnduŋ], *f.* (—, *pl.* —en) application, use, expenditure, employment.
verwerfen [fɛr'vɛrfən], *v.a. irr.* reject, disapprove of.
verwerflich [fɛr'vɛrflɪç], *adj.* objectionable.
Verwertung [fɛr've:rtuŋ], *f.* (—, *no pl.*) utilisation.
verwesen [fɛr've:zən], *v.a.* administer. — *v.n.* (*aux.* sein) rot, decompose, putrefy.
Verweser [fɛr've:zər], *m.* (—s, *pl.* —) administrator.
Verwesung [fɛr've:zuŋ], *f.* (—, *no pl.*) (*office*) administration; putrefaction, rotting.
verwickeln [fɛr'vɪkəln], *v.a.* entangle, involve.
verwickelt [fɛr'vɪkəlt], *adj.* intricate, complicated, involved.
Verwicklung [fɛr'vɪkluŋ], *f.* (—, *pl.* —en) entanglement, involvement, complication.
verwildern [fɛr'vɪldərn], *v.n.* (*aux.* sein) run wild.
verwildert [fɛr'vɪldərt], *adj.* wild, uncultivated, overgrown; (*fig.*) intractable.
Verwilderung [fɛr'vɪlderuŋ], *f.* (—, *no pl.*) running wild, growing wild.
verwirken [fɛr'vɪrkən], *v.a.* forfeit.
verwirklichen [fɛr'vɪrklɪçən], *v.a.* realise. — *v.r. sich* —, materialise, come true.
Verwirklichung [fɛr'vɪrklɪçuŋ], *f.* (—, *no pl.*) realisation, materialisation.
Verwirkung [fɛr'vɪrkuŋ], *f.* (—, *no pl.*) forfeiture.
verwirren [fɛr'vɪrən], *v.a.* disarrange, throw into disorder, entangle; puzzle, bewilder, confuse, disconcert.
Verwirrung [fɛr'vɪruŋ], *f.* (—, *pl.* —en) bewilderment, confusion.
verwischen [fɛr'vɪʃən], *v.a.* blot out, smudge, obliterate.
verwittern [fɛr'vɪtərn], *v.n.* (*aux.* sein) be weather-beaten.
verwöhnen [fɛr'vø:nən], *v.a.* spoil, pamper, coddle.
verworfen [fɛr'vɔrfən], *adj.* profligate; rejected, reprobate.
verworren [fɛr'vɔrən], *adj.* confused, perplexed; intricate; (*speech*) rambling.
verwundbar [fɛr'vuntba:r], *adj.* vulnerable.
verwunden [fɛr'vundən], *v.a.* wound, hurt, injure.
verwundern [fɛr'vundərn], *v.r. sich* —, be surprised, wonder, be amazed.
Verwunderung [fɛr'vundəruŋ], *f.* (—, *no pl.*) surprise, astonishment, amazement.
Verwundung [fɛr'vunduŋ], *f.* (—, *pl.* —en) wounding, wound, injury.
verwunschen [fɛr'vunʃən], *adj.* enchanted, spellbound, bewitched.
verwünschen [fɛr'vynʃən], *v.a.* curse; cast a spell on, bewitch.
verwünscht [fɛr'vynʃt], *excl.* confound it!
Verwünschung [fɛr'vynʃuŋ], *f.* (—, *pl.* —en) curse, malediction.
verwüsten [fɛr'vy:stən], *v.a.* devastate, ravage, lay waste.
Verwüstung [fɛr'vy:stuŋ], *f.* (—, *pl.* —en) devastation.
verzagen [fɛr'tsa:gən], *v.n.* (*aux.* sein) lose heart, lose courage.
verzagt [fɛr'tsa:kt], *adj.* fainthearted, discouraged.
Verzagtheit [fɛr'tsa:kthaɪt], *f.* (—, *no pl.*) faintheartedness.
verzählen [fɛr'tsɛ:lən], *v.r. sich* —, miscount.
verzapfen [fɛr'tsapfən], *v.a.* sell (liquor) on draught; (*fig.*) tell (a story), talk (nonsense).
verzärteln [fɛr'tsɛ:rtəln], *v.a.* pamper, coddle; spoil.
verzaubern [fɛr'tsaubərn], *v.a.* bewitch, charm, put a spell on.

verzehren [fɛr'tse:rən], *v.a.* consume, eat. — *v.r. sich* — *in*, pine away with, be consumed with.
Verzehrung [fɛr'tse:ruŋ], *f.* (—, *no pl.*) (*obs.*) consumption, tuberculosis.
verzeichnen [fɛr'tsaɪçnən], *v.a.* draw badly; note down, register, record.
Verzeichnis [fɛr'tsaɪçnɪs], *n.* (—**ses**, *pl.* —**se**) catalogue, list, register.
verzeihen [fɛr'tsaɪən], *v.a. irr.* forgive, pardon.
verzeihlich [fɛr'tsaɪlɪç], *adj.* pardonable, forgivable, excusable, venial.
Verzeihung [fɛr'tsaɪuŋ], *f.* (—, *no pl.*) pardon, forgiveness; *ich bitte um* —, I beg your pardon.
verzerren [fɛr'tsɛrən], *v.a.* distort.
Verzerrung [fɛr'tsɛruŋ], *f.* (—, *pl.* —**en**) distortion; (*face*) grimace.
verzetteln [fɛr'tsɛtəln], *v.a.* disperse, scatter.
Verzicht [fɛr'tsɪçt], *m.* (—(**e**)**s**, *no pl.*) renunciation, resignation.
verzichten [fɛr'tsɪçtən], *v.n.* forgo, renounce.
verziehen [fɛr'tsi:ən], *v.a. irr.* distort; spoil (*child*). — *v.n.* (*aux.* sein) go away, move away.
Verzierung [fɛr'tsi:ruŋ], *f.* (—, *pl.* —**en**) decoration, ornament.
verzögern [fɛr'tsø:gərn], *v.a.* delay, defer, retard, protract, procrastinate. — *v.r. sich* —, be delayed.
Verzögerung [fɛr'tsø:gəruŋ], *f.* (—, *pl.* —**en**) delay, retardation, procrastination; time-lag.
verzollen [fɛr'tsɔlən], *v.a.* pay duty on.
Verzücktheit [fɛr'tsykthaɪt], *f.* (—, *no pl.*) ecstasy, rapture.
Verzug [fɛr'tsu:k], *m.* (—**s**, *no pl.*) delay.
verzweifeln [fɛr'tsvaɪfəln], *v.n.* despair, be desperate.
Verzweiflung [fɛr'tsvaɪfluŋ], *f.* (—, *no pl.*) despair.
verzwickt [fɛr'tsvɪkt], *adj.* complicated, intricate, tricky.
Vesuv [ve'zu:f], *m.* Mount Vesuvius.
Vetter ['vɛtər], *m.* (—**s**, *pl.* —**n**) cousin.
Vetternwirtschaft ['vɛtərnvɪrtʃaft], *f.* (—, *no pl.*) nepotism.
Vexierbild [vɛ'ksi:rbɪlt], *n.* (—**s**, *pl.* —**er**) picture-puzzle.
Vexierspiegel [vɛ'ksi:rʃpi:gəl], *m.* (—**s**, *pl.*—) distorting mirror.
vibrieren [vi'bri:rən], *v.n.* vibrate.
Vieh [fi:], *n.* (—**s**, *no pl.*) cattle, livestock.
Viehfutter ['fi:futər], *n.* (—**s**, *no pl.*) forage, fodder, feeding-stuff.
viehisch ['fi:ɪʃ], *adj.* beastly, brutal.
Viehwagen ['fi:va:gən], *m.* (—**s**, *pl.* —) cattle-truck.
Viehweide ['fi:vaɪdə], *f.* (—, *pl.* —**n**) pasture, pasturage.
Viehzüchter ['fi:tsyçtər], *m.* (—**s**, *pl.* —) cattle-breeder.
viel [fi:l], *adj.* much, a great deal, a lot; (*pl.*) many.
vielartig ['fi:lartɪç], *adj.* multifarious.
vieldeutig ['fi:ldɔytɪç], *adj.* ambiguous, equivocal.
Vieleck ['fi:lɛk], *n.* (—**s**, *pl.* —**e**) polygon.
vielerlei ['fi:lərlaɪ], *adj.* of many kinds, various.
vielfältig ['fi:lfɛltɪç], *adj.* manifold.
vielfarbig ['fi:lfarbɪç], *adj.* multicoloured, variegated.
Vielfraß ['fi:lfra:s], *m.* (—**es**, *pl.* —**e**) glutton.
vielgeliebt ['fi:lgəli:pt], *adj.* much loved.
vielgereist ['fi:lgəraɪst], *adj.* much travelled.
vielleicht [fi'laɪçt], *adv.* perhaps, maybe.
vielmals ['fi:lma:ls], *adv.* many times, frequently, much.
Vielmännerei [fi:lmɛnə'raɪ], *f.* (—, *no pl.*) polyandry.
vielmehr [fi:l'me:r], *adv.* rather, much more. — *conj.* rather, on the other hand.
vielsagend ['fi:lza:gənt], *adj.* expressive, full of meaning.
vielseitig ['fi:lzaɪtɪç], *adj.* multilateral; (*fig.*) versatile.
Vielseitigkeit ['fi:lzaɪtɪçkaɪt], *f.* (—, *no pl.*) versatility.
vielverheißend ['fi:lfɛrhaɪsənt], *adj.* promising, auspicious.
Vielweiberei [fi:lvaɪbe'raɪ], *f.* (—, *no pl.*) polygamy.
vier [fi:r], *num. adj.* four.
Viereck ['fi:rɛk], *n.* (—**s**, *pl.* —**e**) square, quadrangle.
viereckig ['fi:rɛkɪç], *adj.* square.
vierfüßig ['fi:rfy:sɪç], *adj.* four-footed.
vierhändig ['fi:rhɛndɪç], *adj.* four-handed; — *spielen*, (*piano*) play duets.
vierschrötig ['fi:rʃrø:tɪç], *adj.* robust, thick-set, stocky.
vierseitig ['fi:rzaɪtɪç], *adj.* quadrilateral.
vierstimmig ['fi:rʃtɪmɪç], *adj.* (*Mus.*) four-part; for four voices.
vierteilen ['fi:rtaɪlən], *v.a.* quarter, divide into four parts.
Viertel ['fɪrtəl], *n.* (—**s**, *pl.* —) quarter, fourth part.
Viertelstunde [fɪrtəl'ʃtundə], *f.* (—, *pl.* —**n**) quarter of an hour.
viertens ['fi:rtəns], *num. adv.* fourthly, in the fourth place.
Vierwaldstättersee [fi:r'valtʃtɛtərze:], *m.* Lake Lucerne.
vierzehn ['fɪrtse:n], *num. adj.* fourteen; — *Tage*, a fortnight.
vierzig ['fɪrtsɪç], *num. adj.* forty.
Vietnam [viɛt'na:m], *n.* Vietnam.
Vikar [vi'ka:r], *m.* (—**s**, *pl.* —**e**) curate.
Violinschlüssel [vio'li:nʃlysəl], *m.* (—**s**, *pl.* —) (*Mus.*) treble clef.
Virtuosität [vɪrtuozi'tɛ:t], *f.* (—, *no pl.*) mastery, virtuosity.
Visage [vi'za:ʒə], *f.* (—, *pl.* —**n**) (*coll.*) face.
Visier [vi'zi:r], *n.* (—, *pl.* —**e**) visor; (*gun*) sight.
Vision [vi'zjo:n], *f.* (—, *pl.* —**en**) vision.

Visionär [vizjo'nɛ:r], *m.* (—s, *pl.* —e) visionary.
Visitenkarte [vi'zi:tənkartə], *f.* (—, *pl.* —n) card, visiting card.
Visum ['vi:zum], *n.* (—s, *pl.* Visa) visa.
Vizekönig ['vi:tsəkø:nɪç], *m.* (—s, *pl.* —e) viceroy.
Vlies [fli:s], *n.* (—es, *pl.* —e) fleece.
Vogel ['fo:gəl], *m.* (—s, *pl.* ¨) bird; (*coll.*) fellow; *einen — haben*, be off o.'s head.
Vogelbauer ['fo:gəlbauər], *n.* (—s, *pl.* —) bird-cage.
Vogelfänger ['fo:gəlfɛŋər], *m.* (—s, *pl.* —) fowler, bird-catcher.
vogelfrei ['fo:gəlfraɪ], *adj.* outlawed, proscribed.
Vogelfutter ['fo:gəlfutər], *n.* (—s, *no pl.*) bird-seed.
Vogelhändler ['fo:gəlhɛndlər], *m.* (—s, *pl.* —) bird-dealer.
Vogelhaus ['fo:gəlhaus], *n.* (—es, *pl.* ¨er) aviary.
Vogelkenner ['fo:gəlkɛnər], *m.* (—s, *pl.* —) ornithologist.
Vogelkunde ['fo:gəlkundə], *f.* (—, *no pl.*) ornithology.
Vogelperspektive ['fo:gəlpɛrspɛkti:və], *f.* (—, *no pl.*) bird's-eye view.
Vogelschau ['fo:gəlʃau], *f.* (—, *no pl.*) bird's-eye view.
Vogelsteller ['fo:gəlʃtɛlər], *m.* (—s, *pl.* —) fowler, bird-catcher.
Vogesen [vo'ge:zən], *pl.* Vosges Mountains.
Vogler ['fo:glər], *m.* (—s, *pl.* —) fowler.
Vogt [fo:kt], *m.* (—(e)s, *pl.* ¨e) prefect, bailiff, steward, provost.
Vogtei [fo:k'taɪ], *f.* (—, *pl.* —en) prefecture, bailiwick.
Vokabel [vo'ka:bəl], *f.* (—, *pl.* —n) word, vocable.
Vokabelbuch [vo'ka:bəlbu:x], *n.* (—(e)s, *pl.* ¨er) vocabulary (book).
Vokal [vo'ka:l], *m.* (—s, *pl.* —e) vowel.
Vokativ [voka'ti:f], *m.* (—s, *pl.* —e) (*Gram.*) vocative.
Volk [fɔlk], *n.* (—(e)s, *pl.* ¨er) people, nation; *das gemeine* —, mob, the common people.
Völkerkunde ['fœlkərkundə], *f.* (—, *no pl.*) ethnology.
Völkerrecht ['fœlkərrɛçt], *n.* (—s, *no pl.*) international law.
Völkerschaft ['fœlkərʃaft], *f.* (—, *pl.* —en) tribe, people.
Völkerwanderung ['fœlkərvandəruŋ], *f.* (—, *pl.* —en) mass migration.
Volksabstimmung ['fɔlksapʃtɪmuŋ], *f.* (—, *pl.* —en) referendum.
Volksausgabe ['fɔlksausga:bə], *f.* (—, *pl.* —n) popular edition.
Volksbeschluß ['fɔlksbəʃlus], *m.* (—sses, *pl.* ¨sse) plebiscite.
Volksbibliothek ['fɔlksbibliote:k], *f.* (—, *pl.* —en) public library.
Volkscharakter ['fɔlkskaraktər], *m.* (—s, *no pl.*) national character.
Volksentscheid ['fɔlksɛntʃaɪt], *m.* (—s, *pl.* —e) plebiscite.
Volksführer ['fɔlksfy:rər], *m.* (—s, *pl.* —) demagogue.
Volksheer ['fɔlkshe:r], *n.* (—s, *pl.* —e) national army.
Volksherrschaft ['fɔlkshɛrʃaft], *f.* (—, *no pl.*) democracy.
Volkshochschule ['fɔlkshoxʃu:lə], *f.* (—, *no pl.*) adult education (classes).
Volksjustiz ['fɔlksjusti:ts], *f.* (—, *no pl.*) lynch-law.
Volkskunde ['fɔlkskundə], *f.* (—, *no pl.*) folklore.
Volkslied ['fɔlksli:t], *n.* (—s, *pl.* —er) folk-song.
Volksschicht ['fɔlksʃɪçt], *f.* (—, *pl.* —en) class.
Volksschule ['fɔlksʃu:lə], *f.* (—, *pl.* —n) primary school; elementary school.
Volkssitte ['fɔlkszɪtə], *f.* (—, *pl.* —n) national custom.
Volkssprache ['fɔlksʃpra:xə], *f.* (—, *pl.* —n) vernacular.
Volksstamm ['fɔlksʃtam], *m.* (—s, *pl.* ¨e) tribe.
Volkstracht ['fɔlkstraxt], *f.* (—, *pl.* —en) national costume.
volkstümlich ['fɔlksty:mlɪç], *adj.* national, popular.
Volksvertretung ['fɔlksfɛrtre:tuŋ], *f.* (—, *no pl.*) representation of the people, parliamentary representation.
Volkswirt ['fɔlksvɪrt], *m.* (—s, *pl.* —e) political economist.
Volkswirtschaft ['fɔlksvɪrtʃaft], *f.* (—, *no pl.*) political economy.
Volkszählung ['fɔlkstsɛ:luŋ], *f.* (—, *pl.* —en) census.
voll [fɔl], *adj.* full, filled; whole, complete, entire.
vollauf ['fɔlauf], *adv.* abundantly.
Vollbart ['fɔlba:rt], *m.* (—s, *pl.* ¨e) beard.
vollberechtigt ['fɔlbərɛçtɪçt], *adj.* fully entitled.
Vollbild ['fɔlbɪlt], *n.* (—s, *pl.* —er) full-length portrait, full-page illustration.
Vollblut ['fɔlblu:t], *n.* (—s, *pl.* ¨er) thoroughbred.
vollblütig ['fɔlbly:tɪç], *adj.* full-blooded, thoroughbred.
vollbringen [fɔl'brɪŋən], *v.a. irr.* accomplish, achieve, complete.
Vollbringung [fɔl'brɪŋuŋ], *f.* (—, *no pl.*) achievement.
Volldampf ['fɔldampf], *m.* (—es, *no pl.*) full steam.
vollenden [fɔl'ɛndən], *v.a.* finish, complete.
vollendet [fɔl'ɛndət], *adj.* finished; accomplished.
vollends ['fɔlɛnts], *adv.* quite, altogether, wholly, entirely, moreover.
Vollendung [fɔl'ɛnduŋ], *f.* (—, *no pl.*) completion; perfection.
Völlerei [fœlə'raɪ], *f.* (—, *pl.* —en) gluttony.

vollführen [fɔl'fy:rən], *v.a.* execute, carry out.
Vollgefühl ['fɔlgəfy:l], *n.* (**—s**, *no pl.*) consciousness, full awareness.
Vollgenuß ['fɔlgənus], *m.* (**—sses**, *no pl.*) full enjoyment.
vollgültig ['fɔlgyltɪç], *adj.* fully valid; unexceptionable.
Vollheit ['fɔlhaɪt], *f.* (**—**, *no pl.*) fullness, plenitude.
völlig ['fœlɪç], *adj.* entire, whole, complete.
vollinhaltlich ['fɔlɪnhaltlɪç], *adv.* to its full extent.
volljährig ['fɔljɛ:rɪç], *adj.* of age.
Volljährigkeit ['fɔljɛ:rɪçkaɪt], *f.* (**—**, *no pl.*) adult years, majority.
vollkommen ['fɔlkɔmən], *adj.* perfect. — *adv.* entirely.
Vollkommenheit [fɔl'kɔmənhaɪt], *f.* (**—**, *no pl.*) perfection.
Vollmacht ['fɔlmaxt], *f.* (**—**, *pl.* **—en**) authority; fullness of power; power of attorney.
vollsaftig ['fɔlzaftɪç], *adj.* juicy, succulent.
vollständig ['fɔlʃtɛndɪç], *adj.* complete, full. — *adv.* entirely.
vollstrecken [fɔl'ʃtrɛkən], *v.a.* execute, carry out.
Vollstrecker [fɔl'ʃtrɛkər], *m.* (**—s**, *pl.* **—**) executor.
volltönig ['fɔltø:nɪç], *adj.* sonorous.
vollwertig ['fɔlvɛrtɪç], *adj.* standard, sterling.
vollzählig ['fɔltsɛ:lɪç], *adj.* complete.
vollziehen [fɔl'tsi:ən], *v.a. irr.* execute, carry out, ratify.
vollziehend [fɔl'tsi:ənt], *adj.* executive.
Vollziehungsgewalt [fɔl'tsi:uŋsgəvalt], *f.* (**—**, *no pl.*) executive power.
Vollzug [fɔl'tsu:k], *m.* (**—s**, *no pl.*) execution; fulfilment.
Volontär [volɔ̃'tɛ:r], *m.* (**—s**, *pl.* **—e**) volunteer.
von [fɔn] (*von dem* becomes **vom**), *prep.* (*Dat.*) by, from; of; on; concerning, about; — *Shakespeare*, by Shakespeare; — *Beruf*, by profession; *er kommt — London*, he comes from London; — *fern*, from afar; — *jetzt an*, from now on; — *einem sprechen*, speak of s.o.; *dein Breif vom 15.*, your letter of the 15th.
vonnöten [fɔn'nø:tən], *adv.* — *sein*, be necessary.
vonstatten [fɔn'ʃtatən], *adv.* — *gehen*, progress; go off.
vor [fo:r], *prep.* (*Dat.*, *Acc.*) (*place*) before, ahead of, in front of; (*time*) before, prior to, earlier than; from; of; with; above; in presence of, because of; more than; — *dem Hause*, in front of the house; — *Sonnenaufgang*, before sunrise; — *zwei Tagen*, two days ago; *sich — einem verstecken*, hide from s.o.; *sich hüten —*, beware of; *starr — Kälte*, stiff with cold; — *allem*, above all. — *adv.* before; *nach wie —*, now as before.
Vorabend ['fo:ra:bənt], *m.* (**—s**, *pl.* **—e**) eve.
Vorahnung ['fo:ra:nuŋ], *f.* (**—**, *pl.* **—en**) presentiment, foreboding.
voran [fo'ran], *adv.* before, in front, forward, on.
vorangehen [fo'range:ən], *v.n. irr.* (*aux.* sein) take the lead, go ahead.
Voranzeige ['fo:rantsaɪgə], *f.* (**—**, *pl.* **—n**) advance notice; (*film*) trailer.
Vorarbeiter ['fo:rarbaɪtər], *m.* (**—s**, *pl.* **—**) foreman.
voraus [for'aus], *adv.* before, in front, foremost; in advance; *im* or *zum —*, beforehand; (*thanks*) in anticipation.
vorauseilen [for'ausaɪlən], *v.n.* (*aux.* sein) run ahead.
vorausgehen [for'ausge:ən], *v.n. irr.* (*aux.* sein) walk ahead; *einem —*, go before; precede s.o.
vorausshaben [for'ausha:bən], *v.n. irr.* *etwas vor einem —*, have the advantage over s.o.
Voraussage [for'ausza:gə], *f.* (**—**, *pl.* **—n**) prediction, prophecy; (*weather*) forecast.
voraussagen [for'ausza:gən], *v.a.* predict, foretell; (*weather*) forecast.
voraussehen [for'ausze:ən], *v.a. irr.* foresee.
voraussetzen [for'auszɛtsən], *v.a.* presuppose, take for granted.
Voraussetzung [for'auszɛtsuŋ], *f.* (**—**, *pl.* **—en**) supposition, presupposition; *unter der —*, on the understanding.
Voraussicht [for'auszɪçt], *f.* (**—**, *no pl.*) foresight, forethought; *aller — nach*, in all probability.
voraussichtlich [for'auszɪçtlɪç], *adj.* prospective, presumptive, probable, expected. — *adv.* probably, presumably.
Vorbau ['fo:rbau], *m.* (**—s**, *pl.* **—ten**) frontage.
Vorbedacht ['fo:rbədaxt], *m.* (**—s**, *no pl.*) premeditation; *mit —*, on purpose, deliberately.
vorbedacht ['fo:rbədaxt], *adj.* premeditated.
Vorbedeutung ['fo:rbədɔytuŋ], *f.* (**—**, *pl.* **—en**) omen.
Vorbehalt ['fo:rbəhalt], *m.* (**—s**, *pl.* **—e**) reservation, proviso.
vorbehalten ['fo:rbəhaltən], *v.a. irr.* reserve; make reservation that.
vorbehaltlich ['fo:rbəhaltlɪç], *prep.* (*Genit.*) with the proviso that.
vorbei [fo:r'baɪ], *adv.* by; along; past, over, finished, gone.
vorbeigehen [fo:r'baɪge:ən], *v.n. irr.* (*aux.* sein) pass by; go past; march past.
vorbeilassen [fo:r'baɪlasən], *v.a. irr.* let pass.
Vorbemerkung ['fo:rbəmɛrkuŋ], *f.* (**—**, *pl.* **—en**) preface, prefatory note.
vorbereiten ['fo:rbəraɪtən], *v.a.* prepare.
Vorbereitung ['fo:rbəraɪtuŋ], *f.* (**—**, *pl.* **—en**) preparation.

Vorbesitzer ['fo:rbəzɪtsər], *m.* (—**s**, *pl.* —) previous owner.
Vorbesprechung ['fo:rbəʃprɛçuŋ], *f.* (—, *pl.* —**en**) preliminary discussion.
vorbestimmen ['fo:rbəʃtɪmən], *v.a.* predestine, predetermine.
Vorbestimmung ['fo:rbəʃtɪmuŋ], *f.* (—, *no pl.*) predestination.
vorbestraft ['fo:rbəʃtra:ft], *adj.* previously convicted.
vorbeten ['fo:rbe:tən], *v.n.* lead in prayer.
vorbeugen ['fo:rbɔygən], *v.n.* prevent, preclude, obviate. — *v.r. sich* —, bend forward.
Vorbeugung ['fo:rbɔyguŋ], *f.* (—, *no pl.*) prevention; prophylaxis.
Vorbeugungsmaßnahme ['fo:rbɔyguŋsma:sna:mə], *f.* (—, *pl.* —**n**) preventive measure.
Vorbild ['fo:rbɪlt], *n.* (—**s**, *pl.* —**er**) model, example, pattern, ideal.
vorbildlich ['fo:rbɪltlɪç], *adj.* exemplary; typical; — *sein*, be a model.
Vorbildung ['fo:rbɪlduŋ], *f.* (—, *no pl.*) preparatory training.
Vorbote ['fo:rbo:tə], *m.* (—**n**, *pl.* —**n**) herald, precursor, forerunner.
vorbringen ['fo:rbrɪŋən], *v.a. irr.* produce, proffer; advance, utter, allege, assert, claim.
vordatieren ['fo:rdati:rən], *v.a.* antedate.
vordem [for'de:m], *adv.* (*obs.*) formerly, once.
Vorderachse ['fɔrdəraksə], *f.* (—, *pl.* —**n**) front axle.
Vorderansicht ['fɔrdəranzɪçt], *f.* (—, *pl.* —**en**) front view.
Vorderarm ['fɔrdərarm], *m.* (—**s**, *pl.* —**e**) forearm.
Vordergrund ['fɔrdərgrunt], *m.* (—**s**, *pl.* ⸚**e**) foreground
vorderhand ['fɔrdərhant], *adv.* for the present.
Vorderseite ['fɔrdərzaɪtə], *f.* (—, *pl.* —**n**) front.
vorderst ['fɔrdərst], *adj.* foremost, first.
Vordertür ['fɔrdərty:r], *f.* (—, *pl.* —**en**) front door.
Vordertreffen ['fɔrdərtrɛfən], *n.* (—**s**, *no pl.*) *ins — kommen*, be in the vanguard, come to the fore.
vordrängen ['fo:rdrɛŋən], *v.r. sich* —, press forward, jump the queue.
vordringen ['fo:rdrɪŋən], *v.n. irr.* (*aux.* sein) advance, push forward.
vordringlich ['fo:rdrɪŋlɪç], *adj.* urgent; forward, importunate.
Vordruck ['fo:rdruk], *m.* (—**s**, *pl.* —**e**) (*printed*) form.
voreilen ['fo:raɪlən], *v.n.* (*aux.* sein) rush forward.
voreilig ['fo:raɪlɪç], *adj.* over-hasty, rash.
Voreiligkeit ['fo:raɪlɪçkaɪt], *f.* (—, *no pl.*) hastiness, rashness.
voreingenommen ['fo:raɪngənɔmən], *adj.* biased, prejudiced.
Voreingenommenheit ['fo:raɪngənɔmənhaɪt], *f.* (—, *no pl.*) bias, prejudice.
Voreltern ['fo:rɛltərn], *pl.* forefathers, ancestors.
vorenthalten ['fo:rɛnthaltən], *v.a. irr. sep. & insep.* withhold.
Vorentscheidung ['fo:rentʃaɪduŋ], *f.* (—, *pl.* —**en**) preliminary decision.
vorerst [fo:r'e:rst], *adv.* first of all, firstly; for the time being.
vorerwähnt ['fo:rɛrvɛ:nt], *adj.* aforementioned.
Vorfahr ['fo:rfa:r], *m.* (—**en**, *pl.* —**en**) ancestor.
vorfahren ['fo:rfa:rən], *v.n. irr.* (*aux.* sein) drive up (to a house *etc.*).
Vorfall ['fo:rfal], *m.* (—**s**, *pl.* ⸚**e**) occurrence, incident.
vorfinden ['fo:rfɪndən], *v.a. irr.* find, find present, meet with.
Vorfrage ['fo:rfra:gə], *f.* (—, *pl.* —**n**) preliminary question.
vorführen ['fo:rfy:rən], *v.a.* bring forward, produce.
Vorführung ['fo:rfy:ruŋ], *f.* (—, *pl.* —**en**) production, presentation; performance.
Vorgang ['fo:rgaŋ], *m.* (—**s**, *pl.* ⸚**e**) occurrence, event, happening; proceeding, precedent; procedure.
Vorgänger ['fo:rgɛŋər], *m.* (—**s**, *pl.* —) predecessor.
Vorgarten ['fo:rgartən], *m.* (—**s**, *pl.* ⸚) front garden.
vorgeben ['fo:rge:bən], *v.a. irr.* pretend; allow (in advance).
Vorgebirge ['fo:rgəbɪrgə], *n.* (—**s**, *no pl.*) cape, promontory.
vorgeblich ['fo:rge:plɪç], *adj.* pretended; ostensible.
vorgefaßt ['fo:rgəfast], *adj.* preconceived.
Vorgefühl ['fo:rgəfy:l], *n.* (—**s**, *pl.* —**e**) presentiment.
vorgehen ['fo:rge:ən], *v.n. irr.* (*aux.* sein) advance, walk ahead; proceed; (*clock*) be fast, gain; (*fig.*) take precedence; occur, happen; *was geht hier vor?* what's going on here?
Vorgehen ['fo:rge:ən], *n.* (—**s**, *no pl.*) (course of) action, (manner of) procedure.
vorgenannt ['fo:rgənant], *adj.* aforenamed.
Vorgericht ['fo:rgərɪçt], *n.* (—**s**, *pl.* —**e**) hors d'œuvre, entrée.
Vorgeschichte ['fo:rgəʃɪçtə], *f.* (—, *no pl.*) prehistory; early history; antecedents.
vorgeschichtlich ['fo:rgəʃɪçtlɪç], *adj.* prehistoric.
Vorgeschmack ['fo:rgəʃmak], *m.* (—**s**, *no pl.*) foretaste.
Vorgesetzte ['fo:rgəzɛtstə], *m.* (—**n**, *pl.* —**n**) superior, senior; boss.
vorgestern ['fo:rgɛstərn], *adv.* the day before yesterday.
vorgreifen ['fo:rgraɪfən], *v.n. irr.* anticipate, forestall.

Vorhaben ['fo:rha:bən], *m.* (—**s**, *no pl.*) intention, purpose, design.
vorhaben ['fo:rha:bən], *v.a. irr.* intend; be busy with; *etwas mit einem* —, have designs on s.o.; have plans for s.o.
Vorhalle ['fo:rhalə], *f.* (—, *pl.* —**n**) vestibule, hall, porch.
vorhalten ['fo:rhaltən], *v.a. irr.* hold s.th. before s.o.; (*fig.*) remonstrate (with s.o. about s.th.); reproach. — *v.n.* last.
Vorhaltungen ['fo:rhaltuŋən], *f. pl.* remonstrances, expostulations.
vorhanden [for'handən], *adj.* at hand, present, in stock, on hand.
Vorhandensein [for'handənzaın], *n.* (—**s**, *no pl.*) existence; availability.
Vorhang ['fo:rhaŋ], *m.* (—**s**, *pl.* ⸚**e**) curtain.
Vorhängeschloß ['fo:rhɛŋəʃlɔs], *n.* (—**sses**, *pl.* ⸚**sser**) padlock.
vorher ['fo:rhe:r], *adv.* before, beforehand, in advance.
vorhergehen [fo:r'he:rge:ən], *v.n. irr.* (*aux.* sein) go before, precede.
vorhergehend [fo:r'he:rge:ənt], *adj.* foregoing, aforesaid, preceding.
vorherig [fo:r'he:rıç], *adj.* preceding, previous, former.
vorherrschen ['fo:rhɛrʃən], *v.n.* prevail, predominate.
vorhersagen [fo:r'he:rza:gən], *v.a.* predict, foretell.
vorhersehen [fo:r'he:rze:ən], *v.a. irr.* foresee.
vorheucheln ['fo:rhɔyçəln], *v.a. einem etwas* —, pretend s.th. to s.o.
vorhin [fo:r'hın], *adv.* just before, a short while ago.
Vorhof ['fo:rho:f], *m.* (—**s**, *pl.* ⸚**e**) forecourt.
Vorhölle ['fo:rhœlə], *f.* (—, *no pl.*) limbo.
Vorhut ['fo:rhu:t], *f.* (—, *no pl.*) vanguard.
vorig ['fo:rıç], *adj.* former, preceding.
Vorjahr ['fo:rja:r], *n.* (—**s**, *pl.* —**e**) preceding year.
vorjammern ['fo:rjamərn], *v.n. einem etwas* —, moan to s.o. about s.th.
Vorkämpfer ['fo:rkɛmpfər], *m.* (—**s**, *pl.* —) champion; pioneer.
vorkauen ['fo:rkauən], *v.a.* (*fig.*) predigest; spoon-feed.
Vorkaufsrecht ['fo:rkaufsrɛçt], *n.* (—**s**, *no pl.*) right of first refusal, right of pre-emption.
Vorkehrung ['fo:rke:ruŋ], *f.* (—, *pl.* —**en**) preparation; precaution; (*pl.*) arrangements.
Vorkenntnisse ['fo:rkɛntnısə], *f. pl.* rudiments, elements, grounding; previous knowledge.
vorkommen ['fo:rkɔmən], *v.n. irr.* (*aux.* sein) occur, happen; be found.
Vorkommnis ['fo:rkɔmnıs], *n.* (—**ses**, *pl.* —**se**) occurrence, event, happening.
Vorkriegs- ['fo:rkri:ks], *prefix.* prewar.
Vorladung ['fo:rla:duŋ], *f.* (—, *pl.* —**en**) summons, writ, subpœna.
Vorlage ['fo:rla:gə], *f.* (—, *pl.* —**n**) pattern, master-copy.
vorlagern ['fo:rla:gərn], *v.n.* (*aux.* sein) extend (in front of).
Vorland ['fo:rlant], *n.* (—**s**, *pl.* ⸚**er**) cape, foreland, foreshore.
vorlassen ['fo:rlasən], *v.a. irr.* give precedence to; admit, show in.
Vorläufer ['fo:rlɔyfər], *m.* (—**s**, *pl.* —) forerunner, precursor.
vorläufig ['fo:rlɔyfıç], *adj.* provisional, preliminary, temporary. — *adv.* for the time being.
vorlaut ['fo:rlaut], *adj.* pert, forward.
Vorleben ['fo:rle:bən], *n.* (—**s**, *no pl.*) antecedents, past life.
vorlegen ['fo:rle:gən], *v.a.* put before s.o.; submit, propose; (*food*) serve.
Vorleger ['fo:rleg:ər], *m.* (—**s**, *pl.* —) rug, mat.
Vorlegeschloß ['fo:rlegəʃlɔs], *n.* (—**sses**, *pl.* ⸚**sser**) padlock.
vorlesen ['fo:rle:zən], *v.a. irr.* read aloud, read out.
Vorlesung ['fo:rle:zûŋ], *f.* (—, *pl.* —**en**) lecture.
vorletzte ['fo:rlɛtstə], *adj.* last but one, penultimate.
Vorliebe ['fo:rli:bə], *f.* (—, *no pl.*) predilection, partiality.
vorliebnehmen [for'li:pne:mən], *v.n.* — *mit etwas*, be content with s.th., take pot luck.
vorliegen ['fo:rli:gən], *v.n. irr.* (*aux.* sein) be under consideration.
vorlügen ['fo:rly:gən], *v.a. irr. einem etwas* —, tell lies to s.o.
vormachen ['fo:rmaxən], *v.a. einem etwas* —, show s.o. how a thing is done; (*fig.*) play tricks on s.o., deceive s.o.
vormalig ['fo:rma:lıç], *adj.* former, erstwhile, late.
vormals ['fo:rma:ls], *adv.* formerly.
Vormarsch ['fo:rmarʃ], *m.* (—**es**, *pl.* ⸚**e**) (*Mil.*) advance.
vormerken ['fo:rmɛrkən], *v.a.* make a note of, take down; book.
Vormittag ['fo:rmıta:k], *m.* (—**s**, *pl.* —**e**) morning, forenoon.
vormittags ['fo:rmıta:ks], *adv.* in the morning; before noon.
Vormund ['fo:rmunt], *m.* (—**s**, *pl.* ⸚**er**) guardian.
Vormundschaft ['fo:rmuntʃaft], *f.* (—, *pl.* —**en**) guardianship.
Vormundschaftsgericht ['fo:rmuntʃaftsgərıçt], *n.* (—**s**, *pl.* —**e**) Court of Chancery.
vorn [fɔrn], *adv.* before, in front of; in front; (*Naut.*) fore.
Vorname ['fo:rna:mə], *m.* (—**ns**, *pl.* —**n**) first name, Christian name.
vornehm ['fo:rne:m], *adj.* of noble birth, refined; distinguished, elegant.
vornehmen ['fo:rne:mən], *v.a. irr.* take in hand; *sich etwas* —, undertake s.th.; plan *or* intend to do s.th.

Vornehmheit ['fo:rne:mhaɪt], *f.* (—, *no pl.*) refinement, distinction.
vornehmlich ['fo:rne:mlɪç], *adv.* chiefly, principally, especially.
vornherein ['fɔrnhɛraɪn], *adv.* *von* —, from the first; from the beginning.
Vorort ['fo:rɔrt], *m.* (—**s**, *pl.* —**e**) suburb.
Vorortsbahn ['fo:rɔrtsba:n], *f.* (—, *pl.* —**en**) suburban (railway) line.
Vorplatz ['fo:rplats], *m.* (—**es**, *pl.* ¨**e**) forecourt.
Vorposten ['fo:rpɔstən], *m.* (—**s**, *pl.* —) (*Mil.*) outpost, pickets.
Vorpostengefecht ['fo:rpɔstəngəfɛçt], *n.* (—**s**, *pl.* —**e**) outpost skirmish.
Vorprüfung ['fo:rpry:fuŋ], *f.* (—, *pl.* —**en**) preliminary examination.
Vorrang ['fo:rraŋ], *m.* (—**s**, *no pl.*) precedence, first place, priority.
Vorrat ['fo:rra:t], *m.* (—**s**, *pl.* ¨**e**) store, stock, provision.
Vorratskammer ['fo:rra:tskamər], *f.* (—, *pl.* —**n**) store-room; larder.
Vorrecht ['fo:rrɛçt], *n.* (—**s**, *pl.* —**e**) privilege, prerogative.
Vorrede ['fo:rre:də], *f.* (—, *pl.* —**n**) preface; introduction.
Vorredner ['fo:rre:dnər], *m.* (—**s**, *pl.* —) previous speaker.
vorrichten ['fo:rrɪçtən], *v.a.* prepare, fix up, get ready.
Vorrichtung ['fo:rrɪçtuŋ], *f.* (—, *pl.* —**en**) appliance, device, contrivance.
vorrücken ['fo:rrykən], *v.a.* move forward, advance; (*clock*) put on. — *v.n.* (*aux.* sein) (*Mil.*) advance.
Vorsaal ['fo:rza:l], *m.* (—**s**, *pl.* —**säle**) hall, entrance hall.
Vorsatz ['fo:rzats], *m.* (—**es**, *pl.* ¨**e**) purpose, design, intention.
vorsätzlich ['fo:rzɛtslɪç], *adj.* intentional, deliberate.
Vorschein ['fo:rʃaɪn], *m.* *zum* — *kommen*, turn up; appear.
vorschießen ['fo:rʃi:sən], *v.a.* *irr.* (*money*) advance, lend.
Vorschlag ['fo:rʃla:k], *m.* (—**s**, *pl.* ¨**e**) proposal, offer, proposition.
vorschlagen ['fo:rʃla:gən], *v.a.* *irr.* put forward, propose, suggest; recommend.
vorschnell ['fo:rʃnɛl], *adj.* hasty, rash, precipitate.
vorschreiben ['fo:rʃraɪbən], *v.a.* *irr.* write out (for s.o.); (*fig.*) prescribe, order.
Vorschrift ['fo:rʃrɪft], *f.* (—, *pl.* —**en**) prescription, direction, order, command, regulation.
vorschriftsmäßig ['fo:rʃrɪftsmɛ:sɪç], *adj.* according to regulations.
vorschriftswidrig ['fo:rʃrɪftsvi:drɪç], *adj.* contrary to regulations.
Vorschub ['fo:rʃup], *m.* (—**s**, *no pl.*) aid, assistance; — *leisten*, countenance, encourage, abet.
Vorschule ['fo:rʃu:lə], *f.* (—, *pl.* —**n**) preparatory school.
Vorschuß ['fo:rʃus], *m.* (—**sses**, *pl.* ¨**sse**) advance (of cash).

vorschützen ['fo:rʃytsən], *v.a.* use as a pretext, pretend, plead.
vorschweben ['fo:rʃve:bən], *v.n.* be present in o.'s mind.
vorsehen ['fo:rze:ən], *v.r.* *irr.* *sich* —, take heed, be careful, look out, beware.
Vorsehung ['fo:rze:uŋ], *f.* (—, *no pl.*) Providence.
vorsetzen ['fo:rzɛtsən], *v.a.* set before; serve; (*word*) prefix.
Vorsicht ['fo:rzɪçt], *f.* (—, *no pl.*) care, precaution, caution, circumspection.
vorsichtig ['fo:rzɪçtɪç], *adj.* cautious, careful, circumspect.
vorsichtshalber ['fo:rzɪçtshalbər], *adv.* as a precautionary measure.
Vorsichtsmaßnahme ['fo:rzɪçtsma:sna:mə], *f.* (—, *pl.* —**n**) precautionary measure, precaution.
Vorsilbe ['fo:rzɪlbə], *f.* (—, *pl.* —**n**) prefix.
vorsintflutlich ['fo:rzɪntflu:tlɪç], *adj.* antediluvian; (*fig.*) out-of-date.
Vorsitzende ['fo:rzɪtsəndə], *m.* (—**n**, *pl.* —**n**) chairman, president.
Vorsorge ['fo:rzɔrgə], *f.* (—, *no pl.*) care, precaution.
vorsorglich ['fo:rzɔrklɪç], *adj.* provident, careful.
vorspiegeln ['fo:rʃpi:gəln], *v.a.* *einem etwas* —, deceive s.o.; pretend.
Vorspiegelung ['fo:rʃpi:gəluŋ], *f.* (—, *pl.* —**en**) pretence; — *falscher Tatsachen*, false pretences.
Vorspiel ['fo:rʃpi:l], *n.* (—**s**, *pl.* —**e**) prelude; overture.
vorsprechen ['fo:rʃprɛçən], *v.n.* *irr.* *bei einem* —, call on s.o. — *v.a.* *einem etwas* —, say s.th. for s.o.; repeat.
vorspringen ['fo:rʃprɪŋən], *v.n.* *irr.* (*aux.* sein) leap forward; jut out, project.
Vorsprung ['fo:rʃpruŋ], *m.* (—**s**, *pl.* ¨**e**) projection, prominence; (*fig.*) advantage (over), start, lead.
Vorstadt ['fo:rʃtat], *f.* (—, *pl.* ¨**e**) suburb.
vorstädtisch ['fo:rʃtɛtɪʃ], *adj.* suburban.
Vorstand ['fo:rʃtant], *m.* (—**s**, *pl.* ¨**e**) board of directors; director, principal.
Vorstandssitzung ['fo:rʃtantszɪtsuŋ], *f.* (—, *pl.* —**en**) board meeting.
vorstehen ['fo:rʃte:ən], *v.n.* *irr.* project, protrude; (*office*) administer, govern, direct, manage.
vorstehend ['fo:rʃte:ənt], *adj.* projecting, protruding; above-mentioned, foregoing.
Vorsteher ['fo:rʃte:ər], *m.* (—**s**, *pl.* —) director, manager; supervisor.
Vorsteherdrüse ['fo:rʃte:ərdry:zə], *f.* (—, *pl.* —**n**) prostate gland.
vorstellbar ['fo:rʃtɛlba:r], *adj.* imaginable.
vorstellen ['fo:rʃtɛlən], *v.a.* (*thing*) put forward; (*person*) present, introduce; (*Theat.*) impersonate; represent; (*clock*) put on; *sich etwas* —, visualise s.th., imagine s.th.

vorstellig ['fo:rʃtɛlɪç], *adj.* — *werden*, petition; lodge a complaint.
Vorstellung ['fo:rʃtɛluŋ], *f.* (—, *pl.* —**en**) (*person*) presentation, introduction; (*Theat.*) performance; idea, notion, image; representation.
Vorstellungsvermögen ['fo:rʃtɛluŋsfɛr'mø:gən], *n.* (—**s**, *no pl.*) imagination, imaginative faculty.
Vorstoß ['fo:rʃto:s], *m.* (—**es**, *pl.* ¨**e**) (*Mil.*) sudden advance, thrust.
vorstoßen ['fo:rʃto:sən], *v.a. irr.* push forward. — *v.n.* (*aux.* sein) (*Mil.*) advance suddenly.
Vorstrafe ['fo:rʃtra:fə], *f.* (—, *pl.* —**n**) previous conviction.
vorstrecken ['fo:rʃtrɛkən], *v.a.* stretch forward, protrude; (*money*) advance.
Vorstufe ['fo:rʃtu:fə], *f.* (—, *pl.* —**n**) first step.
Vortänzerin ['fo:rtɛntsərɪn], *f.* (—, *pl.* —**nen**) prima ballerina.
Vorteil ['fɔrtaɪl], *m.* (—**s**, *pl.* —**e**) advantage, profit.
vorteilhaft ['fɔrtaɪlhaft], *adj.* advantageous, profitable, lucrative.
Vortrag ['fo:rtra:k], *m.* (—**s**, *pl.* ¨**e**) recitation, delivery, rendering; statement, report; talk, speech, lecture.
vortragen ['fo:rtra:gən], *v.a. irr.* make a report; (*poem*) recite, declaim; make a request; (*Comm.*) carry forward; lecture on.
Vortragskunst ['fo:rtra:kskunst], *f.* (—, *no pl.*) elocution; (art of) public speaking.
vortrefflich [for'trɛflɪç], *adj.* excellent, splendid.
Vortrefflichkeit [for'trɛflɪçkaɪt], *f.* (—, *no pl.*) excellence.
vortreten ['fo:rtre:tən], *v.n. irr.* (*aux.* sein) step forward.
Vortritt ['fo:rtrɪt], *m.* (—**s**, *no pl.*) precedence.
vorüber [for'y:bər], *adv.* past, gone, over, finished, done with.
vorübergehen [for'y:bərge:ən], *v.n. irr.* (*aux.* sein) pass by, pass, go past.
vorübergehend [for'y:bərge:ənt], *adj.* passing, temporary, transitory.
Vorübung ['fo:ry:buŋ], *f.* (—, *pl.* —**en**) preliminary exercise.
Voruntersuchung ['fo:runtərzu:xuŋ], *f.* (—, *pl.* —**en**) preliminary inquiry; trial in magistrate's court.
Vorurteil ['fo:rurtaɪl], *n.* (—**s**, *pl.* —**e**) bias, prejudice.
vorurteilslos ['fo:rurtaɪlslo:s], *adj.* impartial, unprejudiced, unbiased.
Vorvater ['fo:rfa:tər], *m.* (—**s**, *pl.* ¨) progenitor, ancestor.
Vorverkauf ['fo:rferkauf], *m.* (—**s**, *pl.* ¨**e**) booking in advance, advance booking.
vorwagen ['fo:rva:gən], *v.r. sich* —, dare to go (*or* come) forward.
vorwaltend ['fo:rvaltənt], *adj.* prevailing, predominating.
Vorwand ['fo:rvant], *m.* (—**s**, *pl.* ¨**e**) pretence, pretext; *unter dem* —, under pretence of.
vorwärts ['fɔrvɛrts], *adv.* forward.
vorwärtskommen ['fɔrvɛrtskɔmən], *v.n. irr.* (*aux.* sein) make headway, get on.
vorweg [for'vɛk], *adv.* before.
vorwegnehmen [for'vɛkne:mən], *v.a. irr.* anticipate.
vorweisen ['fo:rvaɪzən], *v.a. irr.* show, produce, exhibit.
Vorwelt ['fo:rvɛlt], *f.* (—, *no pl.*) primitive world; former ages.
vorweltlich ['fo:rvɛltlɪç], *adj.* primæval, prehistoric.
vorwerfen ['fo:rvɛrfən], *v.a. irr. einem etwas* —, blame s.o. for s.th.; charge s.o. with s.th., tax s.o. with s.th.
vorwiegen ['fo:rvi:gən], *v.n. irr.* prevail.
vorwiegend ['fo:rvi:gənt], *adv.* mostly, for the most part.
Vorwissen ['fo:rvɪsən], *n.* (—**s**, *no pl.*) foreknowledge, prescience.
Vorwitz ['fo:rvɪts], *m.* (—**es**, *no pl.*) pertness.
vorwitzig ['fo:rvɪtsɪç], *adj.* forward, pert, meddlesome.
Vorwort (1) ['fo:rvɔrt], *n.* (—**s**, *pl.* —**e**) preface.
Vorwort (2) ['fo:rvɔrt], *n.* (—**s**, *pl.* ¨**er**) (*Gram.*) preposition.
Vorwurf ['fo:rvurf], *m.* (—**s**, *pl.* ¨**e**) reproach; theme, subject.
vorwurfsfrei ['fo:rvurfsfraɪ], *adj.* free from blame, irreproachable.
vorwurfsvoll ['fo:rvurfsfɔl], *adj.* reproachful.
Vorzeichen ['fo:rtsaɪxən], *n.* (—**s**, *pl.* —) omen, token; (*Maths.*) sign.
vorzeigen ['fo:rtsaɪgən], *v.a.* show, produce, exhibit, display.
Vorzeit ['fo:rtsaɪt], *f.* (—, *no pl.*) antiquity, olden times.
vorzeiten [for'tsaɪtən], *adv.* (*Poet.*) in olden times, formerly.
vorzeitig ['fo:rtsaɪtɪç], *adj.* premature.
vorziehen ['fo:rtsi:ən], *v.a. irr.* prefer.
Vorzimmer ['fo:rtsɪmər], *n.* (—**s**, *pl.* —) anteroom, antechamber.
Vorzug ['fo:rtsu:k], *m.* (—**s**, *pl.* ¨**e**) preference, advantage; excellence, superiority.
vorzüglich [for'tsy:klɪç], *adj.* superior, excellent, exquisite.
Vorzüglichkeit [for'tsy:klɪçkaɪt], *f.* (—, *no pl.*) excellence, superiority.
Vorzugsaktie ['fo:rtsu:ksaktsjə], *f.* (—, *pl.* —**n**) preference share.
vorzugsweise ['fo:rtsu:ksvaɪzə], *adv.* for choice, preferably.
vulgär [vul'gɛ:r], *adj.* vulgar.
Vulkan [vul'ka:n], *m.* (—**s**, *pl.* —**e**) volcano.
vulkanisch [vul'ka:nɪʃ], *adj.* volcanic.

W

W [ve:] *n.* (**—s**, *pl.* **—s**) the letter W.
Waage ['va:gə], *f.* (—, *pl.* **—n**) balance, pair of scales.
waag(e)recht ['va:g(ə)rɛçt], *adj.* horizontal.
Waagschale ['va:kʃa:lə], *f.* (—, *pl.* **—n**) pan of a balance.
Wabe ['va:bə], *f.* (—, *pl.* **—n**) honeycomb.
Waberlohe ['va:bərlo:ə], *f.* (—, *no pl.*) (*Poet.*) flickering flames, magic fire.
wach [vax], *adj.* awake; alert; *völlig* —, wide awake.
Wachdienst ['vaxdi:nst], *m.* (**—es**, *no pl.*) guard, sentry duty.
Wache ['vaxə], *f.* (—, *pl.* **—n**) guard, watch; (*person*) sentry, sentinel.
wachen ['vaxən], *v.n.* be awake; guard; — *über*, watch, keep an eye on.
Wacholder [va'xɔldər], *m.* (**—s**, *pl.* —) (*Bot.*) juniper.
wachrufen [vax'ru:fən], *v.a. irr.* (*fig.*) call to mind.
Wachs [vaks], *n.* (**—es**, *no pl.*) wax.
wachsam ['vaxza:m], *adj.* watchful, vigilant.
Wachsamkeit ['vaxza:mkaɪt], *f.* (—, *no pl.*) watchfulness, vigilance.
Wachsbild ['vaksbɪlt], *n.* (**—s**, *pl.* **—er**) waxen image.
wachsen ['vaksən], *v.n. irr.* (*aux.* sein) grow, increase.
wächsern ['vɛksərn], *adj.* waxen, made of wax.
Wachsfigur ['vaksfigu:r], *f.* (—, *pl.* **—en**) wax figure.
Wachsfigurenkabinett ['vaksfigu:rənkabinɛt], *n.* (**—s**, *pl.* **—e**) waxworks.
Wachsleinwand ['vakslaɪnvant], *f.* (—, *no pl.*) oil-cloth.
Wachstuch ['vakstu:x], *n.* (**—(e)s**, *no pl.*) oil-cloth; American cloth.
Wachstum ['vakstu:m], *n.* (**—s**, *no pl.*) growth, increase.
Wacht [vaxt], *f.* (—, *pl.* **—en**) watch, guard.
Wachtdienst ['vaxtdi:nst] *see* **Wachdienst**.
Wachtel ['vaxtəl], *f.* (—, *pl.* **—n**) (*Orn.*) quail.
Wachtelhund ['vaxtəlhunt], *m.* (**—(e)s**, *pl.* **—e**) (*Zool.*) spaniel.
Wächter ['vɛçtər], *m.* (**—s**, *pl.* —) watchman, warder, guard.
wachthabend ['vaxtha:bənt], *adj.* on duty.
Wachtmeister ['vaxtmaɪstər], *m.* (**—s**, *pl.* —) sergeant.
Wachtparade [vaxtpara:də], *f.* (—, *pl.* **—n**) mounting of the guard.
Wachtposten ['vaxtpɔstən], *m.* (**—s**, *pl.* —) guard, picket.
Wachtraum ['vaxtraum], *m.* (**—s**, *pl.* ¨**e**) day-dream, waking dream.
Wachtturm ['vaxtturm], *m.* (**—s**, *pl.* ¨**e**) watch-tower.
wackeln ['vakəln], *v.n.* totter, shake, wobble.
wacker ['vakər], *adj.* gallant, brave, valiant; upright.
wacklig ['vaklɪç], *adj.* tottering, shaky; (*furniture*) rickety; (*tooth*) loose.
Wade ['va:də], *f.* (—, *pl.* **—n**) calf (of the leg).
Wadenbein ['va:dənbaɪn], *n.* (**—s**, *pl.* **—e**) shin-bone.
Waffe ['vafə], *f.* (—, *pl.* **—n**) weapon, arm; *die —n strecken*, surrender.
Waffel ['vafəl], *f.* (—, *pl.* **—n**) wafer; waffle.
Waffeleisen ['vafəlaɪzən], *n.* (**—s**, *pl.* —) waffle-iron.
Waffenbruder ['vafənbru:dər], *m.* (**—s**, *pl.* ¨) brother-in-arms, comrade.
waffenfähig ['vafənfɛ:ɪç], *adj.* able to bear arms.
Waffengewalt ['vafəngəvalt], *f.* (—, *no pl.*) *mit* —, by force of arms.
Waffenglück ['vafənglyk], *n.* (**—s**, *no pl.*) fortunes of war.
Waffenrock ['vafənrɔk], *m.* (**—s**, *pl.* ¨**e**) tunic.
Waffenruf ['vafənru:f], *m.* (**—s**, *no pl.*) call to arms.
Waffenschmied [vafənʃmi:t], *m.* (**—s**, *pl.* **—e**) armourer.
Waffenstillstand ['vafənʃtɪlʃtant], *m.* (**—s**, *no pl.*) armistice, truce.
waffnen ['vafnən], *v.a.* arm.
Wage *see* **Waage**.
Wagebalken ['va:gəbalkən], *m.* (**—s**, *pl.* —) scale-beam.
Wagen ['va:gən], *m.* (**—s**, *pl.* —) vehicle, conveyance, carriage, coach, car, cab, wagon, cart, truck, van, dray.
wagen ['va:gən], *v.a.*, *v.n.* dare, venture, risk.
wägen ['vɛ:gən], *v.a.*, *irr.* weigh, balance; (*words*) consider.
Wagenverkehr ['va:gənfɛrke:r], *m.* (**—s**, *no pl.*) vehicular traffic.
wagerecht *see* **waagerecht**.
Waggon [va'gɔ̃], *m.* (**—s**, *pl.* **—s**) railway car, goods van, freight car.
waghalsig ['va:khalzɪç], *adj.* foolhardy, rash, daring.
Wagnis ['va:knɪs], *n.* (**—ses**, *pl.* **—se**) venture, risky undertaking; risk.
Wagschale *see* **Waagschale**.
Wahl [va:l], *f.* (—, *pl.* **—en**) choice; election; selection; alternative.
Wahlakt ['va:lakt], *m.* (**—s**, *pl.* **—e**) poll, election.
Wahlaufruf ['va:laufru:f], *m.* (**—s**, *pl.* **—e**) manifesto, election address.
wählbar ['vɛ:lba:r], *adj.* eligible.
Wählbarkeit ['vɛ:lba:rkaɪt], *f.* (—, *no pl.*) eligibility.

wahlberechtigt ['va:lbərɛçtɪçt], *adj.* entitled to vote.
wählen ['vɛ:lən], *v.a.* choose; (*Parl.*) elect; (*Telephone*) dial.
Wähler ['vɛ:lər], *m.* (**—s**, *pl.* **—**) elector; constituent.
wählerisch ['vɛ:lərɪʃ], *adj.* fastidious, particular.
Wählerschaft ['vɛ:lərʃaft], *f.* (**—**, *pl.* **—en**) constituency.
wahlfähig ['va:lfɛ:ɪç], *adj.* eligible.
Wahlliste ['va:llɪstə], *f.* (**—**, *pl.* **—n**) electoral list, register (of electors).
wahllos ['va:llo:s], *adj.* indiscriminate.
Wahlrecht ['va:lrɛçt], *n.* (**—s**, *no pl.*) franchise.
Wahlspruch ['va:lʃprux], *m.* (**—s**, *pl.* **¨e**) device, motto.
wahlunfähig ['va:lunfɛ:ɪç], *adj.* ineligible.
Wahlurne ['va:lurnə], *f.* (**—**, *pl.* **—n**) ballot-box.
Wahlverwandtschaft ['va:lfɛrvantʃaft], *f.* (**—**, *no pl.*) elective affinity, congeniality.
Wahlzettel ['va:ltsɛtəl], *m.* (**—s**, *pl.* **—**) ballot-paper.
Wahn [va:n], *m.* (**—(e)s**, *no pl.*) delusion.
Wahnbild ['va:nbɪlt], *n.* (**—s**, *pl.* **—er**) hallucination, delusion; phantasm.
wähnen ['vɛ:nən], *v.a.* fancy, believe.
Wahnsinn ['va:nzɪn], *m.* (**—s**, *no pl.*) madness, lunacy.
wahnsinnig ['va:nzɪnɪç], *adj.* insane, mad, lunatic; (*coll.*) terrific.
Wahnsinnige ['va:nzɪnɪgə], *m.* (**—n**, *pl.* **—n**) madman, lunatic.
Wahnwitz ['va:nvɪts], *m.* (**—es**, *no pl.*) madness.
wahnwitzig ['va:nvɪtsɪç], *adj.* mad.
wahr [va:r], *adj.* true, real, genuine.
wahren ['va:rən], *v.a.* guard, watch over.
währen ['vɛ:rən], *v.n.* last.
während ['vɛ:rənt], *prep.* (*Genit.*) during. — *conj.* while, whilst; whereas.
wahrhaft ['va:rhaft], *adj.* truthful, veracious.
wahrhaftig [va:r'haftɪç], *adv.* truly, really, in truth.
Wahrhaftigkeit [va:r'haftɪçkaɪt], *f.* (**—**, *no pl.*) truthfulness, veracity.
Wahrheit ['va:rhaɪt], *f.* (**—**, *pl.* **—en**) truth; reality; *die — sagen*, tell the truth.
Wahrheitsliebe ['va:rhaɪtsli:bə], *f.* (**—**, *no pl.*) love of truth, truthfulness.
wahrlich ['va:rlɪç], *adv.* truly, in truth.
wahrnehmbar ['va:rne:mba:r], *adj.* perceptible.
wahrnehmen ['va:rne:mən], *v.a. irr.* perceive, observe.
Wahrnehmung ['va:rne:muŋ], *f.* (**—**, *pl.* **—en**) perception, observation.
wahrsagen ['va:rza:gən], *v.n.* prophesy; tell fortunes.
Wahrsager ['va:rza:gər], *m.* (**—s**, *pl.* **—**) fortune-teller, soothsayer.
wahrscheinlich [va:r'ʃaɪnlɪç], *adj.* likely, probable; *es wird — regnen*, it will probably rain.
Wahrscheinlichkeit [va:r'ʃaɪnlɪçkaɪt], *f.* (**—**, *pl.* **—en**) likelihood, probability.
Wahrung ['va:ruŋ], *f.* (**—**, *no pl.*) protection, preservation, maintenance.
Währung ['vɛ:ruŋ], *f.* (**—**, *pl.* **—en**) currency, standard.
Wahrzeichen ['va:rtsaɪçən], *n.* (**—s**, *pl.* **—**) landmark; (*fig.*) sign, token.
Waibling(er) ['vaɪblɪŋ(ər)], *m.* Ghibelline.
Waidmann ['vaɪtman], *m.* (**—s**, *pl.* **¨er**) huntsman, hunter.
waidmännisch ['vaɪtmɛnɪʃ], *adj.* sportsmanlike.
Waise ['vaɪzə], *f.* (**—**, *pl.* **—n**) orphan.
Waisenhaus ['vaɪzənhaus], *n.* (**—es**, *pl.* **¨er**) orphanage.
Waisenmutter ['vaɪzənmutər], *f.* (**—**, *pl.* **¨**) foster-mother.
Waisenvater ['vaɪzənfa:tər], *m.* (**—s**, *pl.* **¨**) foster-father.
Wald [valt], *m.* (**—es**, *pl.* **¨er**) wood, forest; woodland.
Waldbrand ['valtbrant], *m.* (**—s**, *pl.* **¨e**) forest-fire.
Waldlichtung ['valtlɪçtuŋ], *f.* (**—**, *pl.* **—en**) forest glade, clearing.
Waldmeister ['valtmaɪstər], *m.* (**—s**, *no pl.*) (*Bot.*) woodruff.
Waldung ['valduŋ], *f.* (**—**, *pl.* **—en**) woods, woodland.
Waldwiese ['valtvi:zə], *f.* (**—**, *pl.* **—en**) forest-glade.
Walfisch ['va:lfɪʃ], *m.* (**—es**, *pl.* **—e**) whale.
Walfischfang ['va:lfɪʃfaŋ], *m.* (**—s**, *no pl.*) whaling.
Walfischfänger ['va:lfɪʃfɛŋər], *m.* (**—s**, *pl.* **—**) whaler, whale fisher.
Walfischtran ['va:lfɪʃtra:n], *m.* (**—s**, *no pl.*) train-oil.
Walküre [val'ky:rə], *f.* (**—**, *pl.* **—n**) Valkyrie.
Wall [val], *m.* (**—(e)s**, *pl.* **¨e**) rampart, dam, vallum; mound.
Wallach ['valax], *m.* (**—s**, *pl.* **—e**) castrated horse, gelding.
wallen ['valən], *v.n.* bubble, boil up; wave, undulate.
Wallfahrer ['valfa:rər], *m.* (**—s**, *pl.* **—**) pilgrim.
Wallfahrt ['valfa:rt], *f.* (**—**, *pl.* **—en**) pilgrimage.
wallfahrten ['valfa:rtən], *v.n.* (*aux.* sein) go on a pilgrimage.
Walnuß ['valnus], *f.* (**—**, *pl.* **¨sse**) (*Bot.*) walnut.
Walpurgisnacht [val'purgɪsnaxt], *f.* witches' sabbath.
Walroß ['valrɔs], *n.* (**—sses**, *pl.* **—sse**) sea-horse, walrus.
Walstatt ['valʃtat], *f.* (**—**, *pl.* **¨en**) (*Poet.*) battlefield.
walten ['valtən], *v.n.* rule; *seines Amtes —*, do o.'s duty, carry out o.'s duties.
Walze ['valtsə], *f.* (**—**, *pl.* **—n**) roller, cylinder.

walzen ['valtsən], *v.a.* roll. — *v.n.* waltz.
wälzen ['vɛltsən], *v.a.* roll, turn about.
walzenförmig ['valtsənfœrmɪç], *adj.* cylindrical.
Walzer ['valtsər], *m.* (—**s**, *pl.* —) waltz.
Wälzer ['vɛltsər], *m.* (—**s**, *pl.* —) tome; thick volume.
Walzwerk ['valtsvɛrk], *n.* (—**s**, *pl.* —**e**) rolling-mill.
Wams [vams], *n.* (—**es**, *pl.* ¨—**e**) (*obs.*) doublet, jerkin.
Wand [vant], *f.* (—, *pl.* ¨—**e**) wall; side.
Wandbekleidung ['vantbəklaɪduŋ], *f.* (—, *pl.* —**en**) wainscot, panelling.
Wandel ['vandəl], *m.* (—**s**, *no pl.*) mutation, change; behaviour, conduct; *Handel und* —, trade and traffic.
wandelbar ['vandəlba:r], *adj.* changeable, inconstant.
Wandelgang ['vandəlgaŋ], *m.* (—**s**, *pl.* ¨—**e**) lobby; lounge, foyer; (*in the open*) covered way, covered walk.
wandeln ['vandəln], *v.a.* (*aux.* haben) change. — *v.n.* (*aux.* sein) walk, wander. — *v.r. sich* —, change.
Wanderbursche ['vandərburʃə], *m.* (—**n**, *pl.* —**n**) travelling journeyman.
Wanderer ['vandərər], *m.* (—**s**, *pl.* —) wanderer, traveller; hiker.
Wanderleben ['vandərle:bən], *n.* (—**s**, *no pl.*) nomadic life.
Wanderlehrer ['vandərle:rər], *m.* (—**s**, *pl.* —) itinerant teacher.
Wanderlust ['vandərlust], *f.* (—, *no pl.*) urge to travel; call of the open.
wandern ['vandərn], *v.n.* (*aux.* sein) wander, travel; migrate.
Wanderschaft ['vandərʃaft], *f.* (—, *no pl.*) wanderings.
Wandersmann ['vandərsman], *m.* (—**s**, *pl.* ¨—**er**) wayfarer.
Wandertruppe ['vandərtrupə], *f.* (—, *pl.* —**n**) (*Theat.*) strolling players.
Wanderung ['vandəruŋ], *f.* (—, *pl.* —**en**) walking tour; hike.
Wandervolk ['vandərfɔlk], *n.* (— (**e**)**s**, *pl.* ¨—**er**) nomadic tribe.
Wandgemälde ['vantgəmɛ:ldə], *n.* (—**s**, *pl.* —) mural painting, mural.
Wandlung ['vandluŋ], *f.* (—, *pl.* —**en**) transformation; (*Theol.*) transubstantiation.
Wandspiegel ['vantʃpi:gəl], *m.* (—**s**, *pl.* —) pier-glass.
Wandtafel ['vantta:fəl], *f.* (—, *pl.* —**n**) blackboard.
Wange ['vaŋə], *f.* (—, *pl.* —**n**) cheek.
Wankelmut ['vaŋkəlmu:t], *m.* (—**s**, *no pl.*) fickleness, inconstancy.
wankelmütig ['vaŋkəlmy:tɪç], *adj.* inconstant, fickle.
wanken ['vaŋkən], *v.n.* totter, stagger; (*fig.*) waver, be irresolute.
wann [van], *adv.* when; *dann und* —, now and then, sometimes.
Wanne ['vanə], *f.* (—, *pl.* —**n**) tub, bath.
wannen ['vanən], *adv.* (*obs.*) *von* —, whence.

Wannenbad ['vanənba:t], *n.* (—**s**, *pl.* ¨—**er**) bath.
Wanst [vanst], *m.* (—**es**, *pl.* ¨—**e**) belly, paunch.
Wanze ['vantsə], *f.* (—, *pl.* —**n**) (*Ent.*) bug.
Wappen ['vapən], *n.* (—**s**, *pl.* —) crest, coat-of-arms.
Wappenbild ['vapənbɪlt], *n.* (—**s**, *pl.* —**er**) heraldic figure.
Wappenkunde ['vapənkundə], *f.* (—, *no pl.*) heraldry.
Wappenschild ['vapənʃɪlt], *m.* (—**s**, *pl.* —**e**) escutcheon.
Wappenspruch ['vapənʃprux], *m.* (—(**e**)**s**, *pl.* ¨—**e**) motto, device.
wappnen ['vapnən], *v.a.* arm.
Ware ['va:rə], *f.* (—, *pl.* —**n**) article, commodity; (*pl.*) merchandise, goods, wares.
Warenausfuhr ['va:rənausfu:r], *f.* (—, *no pl.*) exportation, export.
Warenbörse ['va:rənbœrzə], *f.* (—, *pl.* —**n**) commodity exchange.
Wareneinfuhr ['va:rənaɪnfu:r], *f.* (—, *no pl.*) importation, import.
Warenhaus ['va:rənhaus], *n.* (—**es**, *pl.* ¨—**er**) department store, emporium; (*Am.*) store.
Warenlager ['va:rənla:gər], *n.* (—**s**, *pl.* —) magazine; stock; warehouse.
Warensendung ['va:rənzɛnduŋ], *f.* (—, *pl.* —**en**) consignment of goods.
Warentausch ['va:rəntauʃ], *m.* (—**es**, *no pl.*) barter.
warm [varm], *adj.* warm, hot.
warmblütig ['varmbly:tɪç], *adj.* warm-blooded.
Wärme ['vɛrmə], *f.* (—, *no pl.*) warmth; heat.
Wärmeeinheit ['vɛrməaɪnhaɪt], *f.* (—, *pl.* —**en**) thermal unit; calorie.
Wärmegrad ['vɛrməgra:t], *m.* (—**s**, *pl.* —**e**) degree of heat; temperature.
Wärmeleiter ['vɛrməlaɪtər], *m.* (—**s**, *pl.* —) conductor of heat.
Wärmemesser ['vɛrməmɛsər], *m.* (—**s**, *pl.* —) thermometer.
wärmen ['vɛrmən], *v.a.* warm, heat.
Wärmflasche ['vɛrmflaʃə], *f.* (— *pl.* —**n**) hot-water bottle.
warnen ['varnən], *v.a.* warn; caution.
Warnung ['varnuŋ], *f.* (—, *pl.* —**en**) warning, caution, admonition; notice.
Warschau ['varʃau], *n.* Warsaw.
Warte ['vartə], *f.* (—, *pl.* —**n**) watch-tower, belfry, look-out.
Wartegeld ['vartəgɛlt], *n.* (—**s**, *pl.* —**er**) half pay; (*ship*) demurrage charges.
warten ['vartən], *v.n.* wait; — *auf* (*Acc.*), wait for, await. — *v.a.* tend, nurse.
Wärter ['vɛrtər], *m.* (—**s**, *pl.* —) keeper, attendant; warder; male nurse.
Wartesaal ['vartəza:l], *m.* (—**s**, *pl.* —**säle**) (*Railw.*) waiting-room.
Wartung ['vartuŋ], *f.* (—, *no pl.*) nursing, attendance; servicing; maintenance.

warum [va'rum], *adv.*, *conj.* why, for what reason.
Warze ['vartsə], *f.* (—, *pl.* —n) wart.
was [vas], *interr. pron.* what? — *rel. pron.* what, that which.
Waschanstalt ['vaʃanʃtalt], *f.* (—, *pl.* —en) laundry.
waschbar ['vaʃba:r], *adj.* washable.
Waschbär ['vaʃbɛ:r], *m.* (—en, *pl.* —en) (*Zool.*) raccoon.
Waschbecken ['vaʃbɛkən], *n.* (—s, *pl.* —) wash-basin.
Wäsche ['vɛʃə], *f.* (—, *no pl.*) washing, wash, laundry; linen.
waschecht ['vaʃɛçt], *adj.* washable; (*fig.*) genuine.
waschen ['vaʃən], *v.a. irr.* wash.
Wäscherin ['vɛʃərɪn], *f.* (—, *pl.* —nen) washerwoman, laundress.
Waschhaus ['vaʃhaus], *n.* (—es, *pl.* ¨er) wash-house, laundry; (*reg. trade name*) launderette.
Waschkorb ['vaʃkɔrp], *m.* (—s, *pl.* ¨e) clothes-basket.
Waschküche ['vaʃkyçə], *f.* (—, *pl.* —en) wash-house.
Waschlappen ['vaʃlapən], *m.* (—s, *pl.* —) face-flannel, face-cloth, face-washer; (*fig.*) milksop.
Waschleder ['vaʃle:dər], *n.* (—s, *no pl.*) chamois leather, wash-leather.
Waschmaschine ['vaʃmaʃi:nə], *f.* (—, *pl.* —n) washing-machine.
Waschtisch ['vaʃtɪʃ], *m.* (—es, *pl.* —e) wash-stand.
Waschwanne ['vaʃvanə], *f.* (—, *pl.* —n) wash-tub.
Wasser ['vasər], *n.* (—s, *pl.* —) water; *stille — sind tief*, still waters run deep.
wasserarm ['vasərarm], *adj.* waterless, dry, arid.
Wasserbehälter ['vasərbəhɛltər], *m.* (—s, *pl.* —) reservoir, cistern, tank.
Wasserblase ['vasərbla:zə], *f.* (—, *pl.* —en) bubble.
Wässerchen ['vɛsərçən], *n.* (—s, *pl.* —) brook, streamlet; *er sieht aus, als ob er kein — trüben könnte*, he looks as if butter would not melt in his mouth.
Wasserdampf ['vasərdampf], *m.* (—(e)s, *no pl.*) steam.
wasserdicht ['vasərdɪçt], *adj.* waterproof.
Wasserdruck ['vasərdruk], *m.* (—s, *no pl.*) hydrostatic pressure, hydraulic pressure.
Wassereimer ['vasəraɪmər], *m.* (—s, *pl.* —) pail, water-bucket.
Wasserfall ['vasərfal], *m.* (—s, *pl.* ¨e) waterfall, cataract, cascade.
Wasserfarbe ['vasərfarbə], *f.* (—, *pl.* —n) water-colour.
Wasserheilanstalt ['vasərhaɪlanʃtalt], *f.* (—, *pl.* —en) spa.
wässerig ['vɛsərɪç], *adj.* watery; (*fig.*) insipid, flat, diluted.
Wasserkanne ['vasərkanə], *f.* (—, *pl.* —n) pitcher, ewer.
Wasserkessel ['vasərkɛsəl], *m.* (—s, *pl.* —) boiler; kettle.
Wasserkopf ['vasərkɔpf], *m.* (—(e)s, *pl.* ¨e) (*Med.*) hydrocephalus.
Wasserkur ['vasərku:r], *f.* (—, *pl.* —en) hydropathic treatment.
Wasserleitung ['vasərlaɪtuŋ], *f.* (—, *pl.* —en) aqueduct; water main.
Wasserlinsen ['vasərlɪnzən], *f. pl.* (*Bot.*) duck-weed.
Wassermann ['vasərman], *m.* (—s, *no pl.*) (*Astron.*) Aquarius.
wässern ['vɛsərn], *v.a.* water; irrigate, soak.
Wassernixe ['vasərnɪksə], *f.* (—, *pl.* —n) water nymph.
Wassernot ['vasərno:t], *f.* (—, *no pl.*) drought, scarcity of water.
Wasserrabe ['vasərra:bə], *m.* (—n, *pl.* —n) (*Orn.*) cormorant.
Wasserrinne ['vasərrɪnə], *f.* (—, *pl.* —n) gutter.
Wasserröhre ['vasərrø:rə], *f.* (—, *pl.* —n) water-pipe.
Wasserscheide ['vasərʃaɪdə], *f.* (—, *pl.* —n) watershed.
Wasserscheu ['vasərʃɔy], *f.* (—, *no pl.*) hydrophobia.
Wasserspiegel ['vasərʃpi:gəl], *m.* (—s, *pl.* —) water-level.
Wasserspritze ['vasərʃprɪtsə], *f.* (—, *pl.* —n) squirt; sprinkler.
Wasserstand ['vasərʃtant], *m.* (—s, *no pl.*) water-level.
Wasserstiefel ['vasərʃti:fəl], *m.* (—s, *pl.* —) wader, gumboot.
Wasserstoff ['vasərʃtɔf], *m.* (—(e)s, *no pl.*) hydrogen.
Wassersucht ['vasərzuxt], *f.* (—, *no pl.*) dropsy.
Wassersuppe ['vasərzupə], *f.* (—, *pl.* —n) water-gruel.
Wässerung ['vɛsəruŋ], *f.* (—, *pl.* —en) watering, irrigation.
Wasserverdrängung ['vasərfɛrdrɛŋuŋ], *f.* (—, *no pl.*) displacement (of water).
Wasserwaage ['vasərva:gə], *f.* (—, *pl.* —n) water-balance, water-level; hydrometer.
Wasserweg ['vasərve:k], *m.* (—s, *pl.* —e) waterway; *auf dem —*, by water, by sea.
Wasserzeichen ['vasərtsaɪçən], *n.* (—s, *pl.* —) watermark.
waten ['va:tən], *v.n.* (*aux.* sein) wade.
watscheln ['va:tʃəln], *v.n.* (*aux.* sein) waddle.
Watt (1) [vat], *n.* (—s, *pl.* —e) sandbank; (*pl.*) shallows.
Watt (2) [vat], *n.* (—s, *pl.* —) (*Elec.*) watt.
Watte ['vatə], *f.* (—, *no pl.*) wadding, cotton-wool.
wattieren [va'ti:rən], *v.a.* pad.
Webe ['ve:bə], *f.* (—, *pl.* —n) web, weft.
weben ['ve:bən], *v.a.* weave.
Weber ['ve:bər], *m.* (—s, *pl.* —) weaver.
Weberei [ve:bə'raɪ], *f.* (—, *pl.* —en) weaving-mill.

Weberschiffchen ['ve:bərʃɪfçən], *n.* (—s, *pl.* —) shuttle.
Wechsel ['vɛksəl], *m.* (—s, *pl.* —) change; turn, variation; vicissitude; (*Comm.*) bill of exchange.
Wechselbalg ['vɛksəlbalk], *m.* (—s, *pl.* ⸚e) changeling.
Wechselbank ['vɛksəlbaŋk], *f.* (—, *pl.* ⸚e) discount-bank.
Wechselbeziehung ['vɛksəlbətsi:uŋ], *f.* (—, *pl.* —en) reciprocal relation, correlation.
Wechselfälle ['vɛksəlfɛlə], *m. pl.* vicissitudes.
Wechselfieber ['vɛksəlfi:bər], *n.* (—s, *pl.* —) intermittent fever.
Wechselfolge ['vɛksəlfɔlgə], *f.* (—, *no pl.*) rotation, alternation.
Wechselgeld ['vɛksəlgɛlt], *n.* (—(e)s, *no pl.*) change.
wechseln ['vɛksəln], *v.a.* change, exchange. — *v.n.* change, alternate, change places.
wechselseitig ['vɛksəlzaɪtɪç], *adj.* reciprocal, mutual.
Wechselstrom ['vɛksəlʃtro:m], *m.* (—s, *no pl.*) alternating current.
Wechselstube ['vɛksəlʃtu:bə], *f.* (—, *pl.* —n) exchange office.
wechselvoll ['vɛksəlfɔl], *adj.* eventful, chequered; changeable.
wechselweise ['vɛksəlvaɪzə], *adv.* reciprocally, mutually; by turns, alternately.
Wechselwinkel ['vɛksəlvɪŋkəl], *m.* (—s, *pl.* —) alternate angle.
Wechselwirkung ['vɛksəlvɪrkuŋ], *f.* (—, *pl.* —en) reciprocal effect.
Wechselwirtschaft ['vɛksəlvɪrtʃaft], *f.* (—, *no pl.*) rotation of crops.
Wecken ['vɛkən], *m.* (—s, *pl.* —) (*dial.*) bread-roll.
wecken ['vɛkən], *v.a.* wake, rouse, awaken.
Wecker ['vɛkər], *m.* (—s, *pl.* —) alarm-clock.
Weckuhr ['vɛku:r], *f.* (—, *pl.* —en) alarm-clock.
Wedel ['ve:dəl], *m.* (—s, *pl.* —) feather-duster, fan; tail.
wedeln ['ve:dəln], *v.n. mit dem Schwanz* —, wag its tail.
weder ['ve:dər], *conj.* neither; — . . . *noch*, neither . . . nor.
Weg [ve:k], *m.* (—(e)s, *pl.* —e) way, path, route, road; walk, errand; *am* —, by the wayside.
weg [vɛk], *adv.* away, gone, off, lost.
wegbegeben ['vɛkbəge:bən], *v.r. irr. sich* —, go away, leave.
wegbekommen ['vɛkbəkɔmən], *v.a. irr. etwas* —, get the hang of s.th.; get s.th. off *or* away.
Wegbereiter ['ve:kbəraɪtər], *m.* (—s, *pl.* —) forerunner, pathfinder, pioneer.
wegblasen ['vɛkbla:zən], *v.a. irr.* blow away; *wie weggeblasen*, without leaving a trace.
wegbleiben ['vɛkblaɪbən], *v.n. irr.* (*aux.* sein) stay away.
wegblicken ['vɛkblɪkən], *v.n.* look the other way.
wegbringen ['vɛkbrɪŋən], *v.a. irr. einen* —, get s.o. away.
wegdrängen ['vɛkdrɛŋən], *v.a.* push away.
Wegebau ['ve:gəbau], *m.* (—s, *no pl.*) road-making.
wegeilen ['vɛkaɪlən], *v.n.* (*aux.* sein) hasten away, hurry off.
wegelagern ['ve:gəla:gərn], *v.a.* waylay.
wegen ['ve:gən], *prep.* (*Genit.*, *Dat.*) because of, on account of, owing to, by reason of.
Wegfall ['vɛkfal], *m.* (—s, *no pl.*) omission.
wegfallen ['vɛkfalən], *v.n. irr.* (*aux.* sein) fall off; be omitted; cease.
Weggang ['vɛkgaŋ], *m.* (—s, *no pl.*) departure, going away.
weggießen ['vɛkgi:sən], *v.a. irr.* pour away.
weghaben ['vɛkha:bən], *v.a. irr. etwas* —, understand how to do s.th, have the knack of doing s.th.
wegkommen ['vɛkkɔmən], *v.n. irr.* (*aux.* sein) get away; be lost.
wegkönnen ['vɛkkœnən], *v.n. irr. nicht* —, not be able to get away.
Weglassung ['vɛklasuŋ], *f.* (—, *pl.* —en) omission.
wegmachen ['vɛkmaxən], *v.r. sich* —, decamp, make off.
wegmüssen ['vɛkmysən], *v.n. irr.* be obliged to go; have to go.
Wegnahme ['vɛkna:mə], *f.* (—, *no pl.*) taking, seizure, capture.
Wegreise ['vɛkraɪzə], *f.* (—, *no pl.*) departure.
Wegscheide ['ve:kʃaɪdə], *f.* (—, *pl.* —n) crossroads, crossways.
wegscheren ['vɛkʃe:rən], *v.a.* clip; shave off. — *v.r. sich* —, be off.
wegschnappen ['vɛkʃnapən], *v.a.* snatch away.
wegsehnen ['vɛkze:nən], *v.r. sich* —, wish o.s. far away; long to get away.
wegsein ['vɛkzaɪn], *v.n. irr.* (*aux.* sein) (*person*) be gone, be away; have gone off; (*things*) be lost; *ganz* —, (*coll.*) be beside o.s. *or* amazed.
wegsetzen ['vɛkzɛtsən], *v.a.* put away.
wegspülen ['vɛkʃpy:lən], *v.a.* wash away.
Wegstunde ['ve:kʃtundə], *f.* (—, *pl.* —n) an hour's walk.
Wegweiser ['ve:kvaɪzər], *m.* (—s, *pl.* —) signpost, road-sign.
wegwenden ['vɛkvɛndən], *v.r. irr. sich* —, turn away.
wegwerfen ['vɛkvɛrfən], *v.a. irr.* throw away.
wegwerfend ['vɛkvɛrfənt], *adj.* disparaging, disdainful.
Wegzehrung ['ve:ktse:ruŋ], *f.* (—, *no pl.*) food for the journey; (*Eccl.*) viaticum.

wegziehen ['vɛktsi:ən], *v.a. irr.* draw away, pull away. — *v.n.* (*aux.* sein) march away; (*fig.*) move, remove.
Wegzug ['vɛktsu:k], *m.* (—**s**, *no pl.*) removal; moving away.
Weh [ve:], *n.* (—**s**, *no pl.*) pain; grief, pang; misfortune.
weh [ve:], *adj.* painful, sore; *mir ist — ums Herz*, I am sick at heart; my heart aches. — *adv.* — *tun*, ache; pain, hurt, offend, distress, grieve. — *int.* — *mir!* woe is me!
Wehen ['ve:ən], *n. pl.* birth-pangs, labour-pains.
wehen ['ve:ən], *v.n.* (*wind*) blow.
Wehgeschrei ['ve:gəʃraɪ], *n.* (—**s**, *no pl.*) wailings.
Wehklage ['ve:kla:gə], *f.* (—, *pl.* —**n**) lamentation.
wehklagen ['ve:kla:gən], *v.n. insep.* lament, wail.
wehleidig ['ve:laɪdɪç], *adj.* tearful; easily hurt; self-pitying.
wehmütig ['ve:my:tɪç], *adj.* sad, melancholy, wistful.
Wehr (1) [ve:r], *n.* (—**s**, *pl.* —**e**) weir.
Wehr (2) [ve:r], *f.* (—, *pl.* —**en**) defence, bulwark.
wehren ['ve:rən], *v.r. sich* —, defend o.s., offer resistance.
wehrhaft ['ve:rhaft], *adj.* capable of bearing arms, able-bodied.
wehrlos ['ve:rlo:s], *adj.* defenceless, unarmed; (*fig.*) weak, unprotected.
Wehrpflicht ['ve:rpflɪçt], *f.* (—, *no pl.*) compulsory military service, conscription.
Wehrstand ['ve:rʃtant], *m.* (—**s**, *no pl.*) the military.
Weib [vaɪp], *n.* (—(**e**)**s**, *pl.* —**er**) woman; (*Poet.*) wife.
Weibchen ['vaɪpçən], *n.* (—**s**, *pl.* —) (*animal*) female.
Weiberfeind ['vaɪbərfaɪnt], *m.* (—**s**, *pl.* —**e**) woman-hater, misogynist.
Weiberherrschaft ['vaɪbərhɛrʃaft], *f.* (—, *no pl.*) petticoat rule.
weibisch ['vaɪbɪʃ], *adj.* womanish, effeminate.
weiblich ['vaɪplɪç], *adj.* female, feminine; womanly.
Weiblichkeit ['vaɪplɪçkaɪt], *f.* (—, *no pl.*) womanliness, femininity.
Weibsbild ['vaɪpsbɪlt], *n.* (—**s**, *pl.* —**er**) (*sl.*) female; wench.
weich [vaɪç], *adj.* weak; soft; tender, gentle; effeminate; sensitive; — *machen*, soften; — *werden*, relent.
Weichbild ['vaɪçbɪlt], *n.* (—**s**, *no pl.*) precincts; city boundaries.
Weiche ['vaɪçə], *f.* (—, *pl.* —**n**) (*Railw.*) switch, points.
weichen (1) ['vaɪçən], *v.a.* steep, soak, soften.
weichen (2) ['vaɪçən], *v.n. irr.* (*aux.* sein) yield, make way, give ground.
Weichensteller ['vaɪçənʃtɛlər], *m.* (—**s**, *pl.* —) (*Railw.*) pointsman, signalman.
Weichheit ['vaɪçhaɪt], *f.* (—, *no pl.*) softness; (*fig.*) weakness, tenderness.
weichherzig ['vaɪçhɛrtsɪç], *adj.* soft-hearted, tender-hearted.
weichlich ['vaɪçlɪç], *adj.* soft; (*fig.*) weak, effeminate.
Weichling ['vaɪçlɪŋ], *m.* (—**s**, *pl.* —**e**) weakling.
Weichsel ['vaɪksəl], *f.* Vistula.
Weichselkirsche ['vaɪksəlkɪrʃə], *f.* (—, *pl.* —**n**) sour cherry; morello.
Weide ['vaɪdə], *f.* (—, *pl.* —**n**) pasture, pasturage; (*Bot.*) willow.
Weideland ['vaɪdəlant], *n.* (—**s**, *pl.* ⸚**er**) pasture-ground.
weiden ['vaɪdən], *v.a., v.n.* pasture, feed.
Weidenbaum ['vaɪdənbaum], *m.* (—**s**, *pl.* ⸚**e**) willow-tree.
Weiderich ['vaɪdərɪç], *m.* (—**s**, *pl.* —**e**) willow-herb, loose-strife, rose bay.
Weidgenosse ['vaɪtgənɔsə], *m.* (—**en**, *pl.* —**en**) fellow huntsman.
weidlich ['vaɪtlɪç], *adv.* (*rare*) greatly, thoroughly.
Weidmann ['vaɪtman], *m.* (—**s**, *pl.* ⸚**er**) sportsman, huntsman.
Weidmannsheil! ['vaɪtmanshaɪl], *excl.* tally-ho!
weigern ['vaɪgərn], *v.r. sich* —, refuse, decline.
Weigerung ['vaɪgəruŋ], *f.* (—, *pl.* —**en**) refusal, denial.
Weih [vaɪ], *m.* (—**en**, *pl.* —**en**) (*Orn.*) kite.
Weihbischof ['vaɪbɪʃɔf], *m.* (—**s**, *pl.* ⸚**e**) suffragan bishop.
Weihe ['vaɪə], *f.* (—, *pl.* —**en**) consecration; (*priest*) ordination; initiation; (*fig.*) solemnity.
weihen ['vaɪən], *v.a.* bless, consecrate; ordain. — *v.r. sich* —, devote o.s. (to).
Weiher ['vaɪər], *m.* (—**s**, *pl.* —) pond, fishpond.
weihevoll ['vaɪəfɔl], *adj.* solemn.
Weihnachten ['vaɪnaxtən], *n. or f.* Christmas.
Weihnachtsabend ['vaɪnaxtsa:bənt], *m.* (—**s**, *pl.* —**e**) Christmas Eve.
Weihnachtsfeiertag ['vaɪnaxtsfaɪərta:k], *m.* (—**s**, *pl.* —**e**) Christmas Day; *zweiter* —, Boxing Day.
Weihnachtsgeschenk ['vaɪnaxtsgəʃɛŋk], *n.* (—**s**, *pl.* —**e**) Christmas box, Christmas present.
Weihnachtslied ['vaɪnaxtsli:t], *n.* (—(**e**)**s**, *pl.* —**er**) Christmas carol.
Weihnachtsmann ['vaɪnaxtsman], *m.* (—(**e**)**s**, *pl.* ⸚**er**) Santa Claus, Father Christmas.
Weihrauch ['vaɪraux], *m.* (—**s**, *no pl.*) incense.
Weihwasser ['vaɪvasər], *n.* (—**s**, *no pl.*) holy water.
weil [vaɪl], *conj.* because, as, since.
weiland ['vaɪlant], *adv.* (*obs.*) formerly, once.
Weile ['vaɪlə], *f.* (—, *no pl.*) while, short time; leisure.
weilen ['vaɪlən], *v.n.* tarry, stay, abide.
Wein [vaɪn], *m.* (—(**e**)**s**, *pl.* —**e**) wine; (*plant*) vine; *einem reinen — einschenken*, tell s.o. the truth.

Weinbau ['vaɪnbau], *m.* (**—s,** *no pl.*) vine growing, viticulture.
Weinbeere ['vaɪnbe:rə], *f.* (**—,** *pl.* **—n**) grape.
Weinberg ['vaɪnbɛrk], *m.* (**—s,** *pl.* **—e**) vineyard.
Weinbrand ['vaɪnbrant], *m.* (**—s,** *no pl.*) brandy.
weinen ['vaɪnən], *v.n.* weep, cry.
Weinernte ['vaɪnɛrntə], *f.* (**—,** *pl.* **—n**) vintage.
Weinessig ['vaɪnɛsɪç], *m.* (**—s,** *no pl.*) (wine) vinegar.
Weinfaß ['vaɪnfas], *n.* (**—sses,** *pl.* **¨sser**) wine-cask.
Weingeist ['vaɪngaɪst], *m.* (**—es,** *no pl.*) spirits of wine, alcohol.
Weinhändler ['vaɪnhɛndlər], *m.* (**—s,** *pl.* **—**) wine merchant.
Weinkarte ['vaɪnkartə], *f.* (**—,** *pl.* **—n**) wine-list.
Weinkeller ['vaɪnkɛlər], *m.* (**—s,** *pl.* **—**) wine-cellar; wine-tavern.
Weinkellerei ['vaɪnkɛlərai], *f.* (**—,** *pl.* **—en**) wine-store.
Weinkelter ['vaɪnkɛltər], *f.* (**—,** *pl.* **—n**) wine-press.
Weinkneipe ['vaɪnknaɪpə], *f.* (**—,** *pl.* **—n**) wine-tavern.
Weinkoster ['vaɪnkɔstər], *m.* (**—s,** *pl.* **—**) wine-taster.
Weinlaub ['vaɪnlaup], *n.* (**—s,** *no pl.*) vine-leaves.
Weinlese ['vaɪnle:zə], *f.* (**—,** *pl.* **—n**) vintage, grape harvest.
Weinranke ['vaɪnraŋkə], *f.* (**—,** *pl.* **—n**) vine-branch, tendril.
Weinschenke ['vaɪnʃɛŋkə], *f.* (**—,** *pl.* **—n**) wine-house, tavern.
weinselig ['vaɪnze:lɪç], *adj.* tipsy.
Weinstein ['vaɪnʃtaɪn], *m.* (**—s,** *no pl.*) tartar.
Weinsteinsäure ['vaɪnʃtaɪnzɔyrə], *f.* (**—,** *no pl.*) tartaric acid.
Weinstock ['vaɪnʃtɔk], *m.* (**—s,** *pl.* **¨e**) vine.
Weintraube ['vaɪntraubə], *f.* (**—,** *pl.* **—n**) grape, bunch of grapes.
weinumrankt ['vaɪnumraŋkt], *adj.* vine-clad.
weise ['vaɪzə], *adj.* wise, prudent.
Weise (1) ['vaɪzə], *m.* (**—n,** *pl.* **—n**) wise man, sage.
Weise (2) ['vaɪzə], *f.* (**—,** *pl.* **—n**) manner, fashion; method, way; tune, melody.
weisen ['vaɪzən], *v.a. irr.* point to, point out, show.
Weiser ['vaɪzər], *m.* (**—s,** *pl.* **—**) signpost; indicator; (*clock*) hand.
Weisheit ['vaɪshaɪt], *f.* (**—,** *pl.* **—en**) wisdom, prudence.
Weisheitszahn ['vaɪshaɪtstsa:n], *m.* (**—s,** *pl.* **¨e**) wisdom tooth.
weislich ['vaɪslɪç], *adv.* wisely, prudently, advisedly.
weismachen ['vaɪsmaxən], *v.a.* ***einem etwas* —,** (*coll.*) spin a yarn to s.o.; ***laß dir nichts* —,** don't be taken in.
weissagen ['vaɪsza:gən], *v.a. insep.* prophesy, foretell.
Weissager ['vaɪsza:gər], *m.* (**—s,** *pl.* **—**) prophet, soothsayer.
Weissagung ['vaɪsza:guŋ], *f.* (**—,** *pl.* **—en**) prophecy.
weiß [vaɪs], *adj.* white, clean, blank.
Weißbuche ['vaɪsbu:xə], *f.* (**—,** *pl.* **—n**) (*Bot.*) hornbeam.
Weiße ['vaɪsə], *f.* (**—,** *no pl.*) whiteness; (*fig.*) (*dial.*) pale ale.
weißglühend ['vaɪsgly:ənt], *adj.* at white heat, incandescent, white hot.
Weißnäherin ['vaɪsnɛ:ərɪn], *f.* (**—,** *pl.* **—nen**) seamstress.
Weißwaren ['vaɪsva:rən], *f. pl.* linen.
Weisung ['vaɪzuŋ], *f.* (**—,** *pl.* **—en**) order, direction, instruction; directive.
weit [vaɪt], *adj.* distant, far, far off; wide, broad, vast, extensive; (*clothing*) loose, too big.
weitab [vaɪt'ap], *adv.* far away.
weitaus [vaɪt'aus], *adv.* by far.
weitblickend ['vaɪtblɪkənt], *adj.* far-sighted.
Weite ['vaɪtə], *f.* (**—,** *pl.* **—n**) width, breadth; distance.
weiten ['vaɪtən], *v.a.* widen, expand.
weiter ['vaɪtər], *adj.* further, farther, wider.
weiterbefördern ['vaɪtərbəfœrdərn], *v.a.* send, forward, send on.
weiterbilden ['vaɪtərbɪldən], *v.a.* improve, develop(e), extend.
Weitere ['vaɪtərə], *n.* (**—n,** *no pl.*) rest, remainder.
weiterführen ['vaɪtərfy:rən], *v.a.* continue, carry on.
weitergeben ['vaɪtərge:bən], *v.a. irr.* pass on.
weitergehen ['vaɪtərge:ən], *v.n. irr.* (*aux.* sein) walk on.
weiterhin ['vaɪtərhɪn], *adv.* furthermore; in time to come; in future.
weiterkommen ['vaɪtərkɔmən], *v.n. irr.* (*aux.* sein) get on, advance.
Weiterung ['vaɪtəruŋ], *f.* (**—,** *pl.* **—en**) widening, enlargement.
weitgehend ['vaɪtge:ənt], *adj.* far-reaching, sweeping.
weitläufig ['vaɪtlɔyfɪç], *adj.* ample, large; detailed, elaborate; distant, widespread; diffuse, long-winded.
weitschweifig ['vaɪtʃvaɪfɪç], *adj.* prolix, diffuse, rambling.
weitsichtig ['vaɪtzɪçtɪç], *adj.* long-sighted.
weittragend ['vaɪttra:gənt], *adj.* portentous, far-reaching.
weitverbreitet ['vaɪtfɛrbraɪtət], *adj.* widespread.
Weizen ['vaɪtsən], *m.* (**—s,** *no pl.*) wheat.
Weizengrieß ['vaɪtsəngri:s], *m.* (**—es,** *no pl.*) semolina; grits.
welch [vɛlç], *pron.* what (a).
welcher, -e, -es ['vɛlçər], *interr. pron.* which? what? — *rel. pron.* who which, that; (*indef.*) (*coll.*) some.

welcherlei ['vɛlçərlaɪ], *indecl. adj.* of what kind.
Welfe ['vɛlfə], *m.*(—**n**, *pl.* —**n**) Guelph.
welk [vɛlk], *adj.* faded, withered; — *werden*, fade, wither.
welken ['vɛlkən], *v.n.* (*aux.* sein) wither, fade, decay.
Wellblech ['vɛlblɛç], *n.* (—**s**, *no pl.*) corrugated iron.
Welle ['vɛlə], *f.* (—, *pl.* —**n**) wave, billow.
wellen ['vɛlən], *v.a.* wave.
Wellenbewegung ['vɛlənbəve:guŋ], *f.* (—, *pl.* —**en**) undulation.
Wellenlinie ['vɛlənli:njə], *f.* (—, *pl.* —**n**) wavy line.
wellig ['vɛlɪç], *adj.* wavy, undulating.
welsch [vɛlʃ], *adj.* foreign; Italian; French.
Welschkohl ['vɛlʃko:l], *m.* (—**s**, *no pl.*) (*Bot.*) savoy cabbage.
Welschkorn ['vɛlʃkɔrn], *n.* (—**s**, *no pl.*) (*Bot.*) Indian corn.
Welt [vɛlt], *f.* (—, *pl.* —**en**) world, earth; universe; society.
Weltall ['vɛltal], *n.* (—**s**, *no pl.*) universe, cosmos; (outer) space.
Weltanschauung ['vɛltanʃauuŋ], *f.* (—, *pl.* —**en**) view of life, philosophy of life, ideology.
Weltbeschreibung ['vɛltbəʃraɪbuŋ], *f.* (—, *no pl.*) cosmography.
Weltbürger ['vɛltbyrgər], *m.* (—**s**, *pl.* —) cosmopolitan.
welterschütternd ['vɛltərʃytərnt], *adj.* world-shaking.
weltfremd ['vɛltfrɛmt], *adj.* unwordly, unsophisticated.
Weltgeschichte ['vɛltgəʃɪçtə], *f.* (—, *no pl.*) world history.
Weltherrschaft ['vɛlthɛrʃaft], *f.* (—, *no pl.*) world dominion.
Weltkenntnis ['vɛltkɛntnɪs], *f.* (—, *no pl.*) worldly wisdom.
weltklug ['vɛltklu:k], *adj.* astute, worldly-wise.
Weltkrieg ['vɛltkri:k], *m.* (—**es**, *pl.* —**e**) world war.
weltlich ['vɛltlɪç], *adj.* worldly; (*Eccl.*) temporal, secular.
Weltmacht ['vɛltmaxt], *f.* (—, *pl.* ⸚**e**) world power, great power.
Weltmeer ['vɛltme:r], *n.* (—**s**, *pl.* —**e**) ocean.
Weltmeisterschaft ['vɛltmaɪstərʃaft], *f.* (—, *pl.* —**en**) world championship.
Weltordnung ['vɛltɔrdnuŋ], *f.* (— *pl.* —**en**) cosmic order.
Weltraum ['vɛltraum], *m.* (—**s**, *no pl.*) space.
Weltraumflug ['vɛltraumflu:k], *m.* (—(**e**)**s**, *pl.* ⸚**e**) space flight.
Weltraumforschung ['vɛltraumfɔrʃuŋ], *f.* (—, *no pl.*) space exploration.
Weltraumgeschoss ['vɛltraumgəʃo:s], *n.* (—**es**, *pl.* —**e**) space rocket.
Weltruf ['vɛltru:f], *m.* (—**s**, *no pl.*) world-wide renown.
Weltschmerz ['vɛltʃmɛrts], *m.* (—**es**, *no pl.*) world-weariness, Wertherism; melancholy.
Weltsprache ['vɛltʃpra:xə], *f.* (—, *pl.* —**en**) universal language; world language.
Weltstadt ['vɛltʃtat], *f.* (—, *pl.* ⸚**e**) metropolis.
Weltumseglung ['vɛltumze:gluŋ], *f.* (—, *pl.* —**en**) circumnavigation (of the globe).
Weltuntergang ['vɛltuntərgaŋ], *m.* —**s**, *no pl.*) end of the world.
Weltwirtschaft ['vɛltvɪrtʃaft], *f.* (—, *no pl.*) world trade.
wem [ve:m], *pers. pron.* (*Dat. of* **wer**) to whom — *interr. pron.* to whom?
wen [ve:n], *pers. pron.* (*Acc. of* **wer**) whom — *interr. pron.* whom?
Wende ['vɛndə], *f.* (—, *pl.* —**n**) turn, turning(point).
Wendekreis ['vɛndəkraɪs], *m.* (—**es**, *pl.* —**e**) tropic.
Wendeltreppe ['vɛndəltrɛpə], *f.* (—, *pl.* —**n**) spiral staircase.
wenden ['vɛndən], *v.a. reg. & irr.* turn.
Wendepunkt ['vɛndəpuŋkt], *m.* (—**es**, *pl.* —**e**) turning point; crisis.
Wendung ['vɛnduŋ], *f.* (—, *pl.* —**en**) turn, turning; crisis; (*speech*) phrase.
wenig ['ve:nɪç], *adj.* little, few; *ein* —, a little.
weniger ['ve:nɪgər], *adj.* less, fewer.
wenigstens ['ve:nɪçstəns], *adv.* at least.
wenn [vɛn], *conj.* if; when; whenever, in case; — *nicht*, unless.
wenngleich [vɛn'glaɪç], *conj.* though, although.
wer [ve:r], *rel. pron.* who, he who; — *auch*, whoever. — *interr. pron.* who? which? — *da?* who goes there?
Werbekraft ['vɛrbəkraft], *f.* (—, *no pl.*) (*Advertising*) attraction; appeal; publicity value.
werben ['vɛrbən], *v.n. irr.* advertise, canvass; court, woo. — *v.a.* (*soldiers*) recruit.
Werbung ['vɛrbuŋ], *f.* (—, *pl.* —**en**) advertising, publicity, propaganda; recruiting; courtship.
Werdegang ['ve:rdəgaŋ], *m.* (—**s**, *no pl.*) evolution, development.
werden ['ve:rdən], *v.n. irr.* (*aux.* sein) become, get; grow; turn; *Arzt* —, become a doctor; *alt* —, grow old; *bleich* —, turn pale.
werdend ['ve:rdənt], *adj.* becoming; nascent, incipient, budding.
werfen ['vɛrfən], *v.a. irr.* throw, cast.
Werft (1) [vɛrft], *m.* (—(**e**)**s**, *pl.* —**e**) warp.
Werft (2) [vɛrft], *f.* (—, *pl.* —**en**) dockyard, shipyard, wharf.
Werk [vɛrk], *n.* (— (**e**)**s**, *pl.* —**e**) work, action, deed; undertaking; (*Ind.*) works, plant, mill, factory.
Werkführer ['vɛrkfy:rər], *m.* (—**s**, *pl.* —) foreman.
Werkleute ['vɛrklɔytə], *pl.* workmen.
Werkmeister ['vɛrkmaɪstər], *m.* (—**s**, *pl.* —) overseer.
werktätig ['vɛrktɛ:tɪç], *adj.* active, practical: hard-working.

Werkzeug [ˈvɛrktsɔyk], *n.* (—**s**, *pl.* —**e**) implement, tool, jig, instrument.
Wermut [ˈveːrmuːt], *m.* (—**s**, *no pl.*) absinthe, vermouth.
Wert [veːrt], *m.* (—(**e**)**s**, *pl.* —**e**) value, worth, price; use; merit; importance.
wert [veːrt], *adj.* valuable; worth; dear, esteemed.
Wertangabe [ˈveːrtangaːbə], *f.* (—, *pl.* —**n**) valuation; declared value.
Wertbestimmung [ˈveːrtbəʃtɪmuŋ], *f.* (—, *no pl.*) appraisal, assessment, valuation.
Wertbrief [ˈveːrtbriːf], *m.* (—**s**, *pl.* —**e**) registered letter.
werten [ˈveːrtən], *v.a.* value.
Wertgegenstand [ˈveːrtgeːgənʃtant], *m.* (—**s**, *pl.* ¨—**e**) article of value.
Wertmesser [ˈveːrtmɛsər], *m.* (—**s**, *pl.* —) standard.
Wertpapiere [ˈveːrtpapiːrə], *n. pl.* securities.
Wertsachen [ˈveːrtzaxən], *f. pl.* valuables.
wertschätzen [ˈveːrtʃɛtsən], *v.a.* esteem (highly).
wertvoll [ˈveːrtfɔl], *adj.* of great value, valuable.
Wertzeichen [ˈveːrttsaɪçən], *n.* (—**s**, *pl.* —) stamp; coupon.
wes [vɛs], *pers. pron.* (*obs.*) whose.
Wesen [ˈveːzən], *n.* (—**s**, *pl.* —) being, creature; reality; essence, nature, substance; character, demeanour; (*in compounds*) organisation, affairs.
wesenlos [ˈveːzənloːs], *adj.* disembodied, unsubstantial, shadowy; trivial.
wesensgleich [ˈveːzənsglaɪç], *adj.* identical, substantially the same.
wesentlich [ˈveːzəntlɪç], *adj.* essential, material.
weshalb [vɛsˈhalp], *conj.*, *adv.* wherefore, why; therefore.
Wespe [ˈvɛspə], *f.* (—, *pl.* —**n**) (*Ent.*) wasp.
Wespennest [ˈvɛspənnɛst], *n.* (—**s**, *pl.* —**er**,) wasp's nest; *in ein — stechen*, stir up a hornet's nest.
wessen [ˈvɛsən], *pers .pron.* (*Genit. of* **wer**) whose. — *interr. pron.* whose?
Weste [ˈvɛstə], *f.* (—, *pl.* —**n**) waistcoat.
Westen [ˈvɛstən], *m.* (—**s**, *no pl.*) west; *nach* —, westward.
Westfalen [vɛstˈfaːlən], *n.* Westphalia.
Westindien [vɛstˈɪndjən], *n.* the West Indies.
weswegen [vɛsˈveːgən] *see* **weshalb.**
Wettbewerb [ˈvɛtbəvɛrp], *m.* (—**s**, *pl.* —**e**) competition, rivalry; *unlauterer* —, unfair competition.
Wettbewerber [ˈvɛtbəvɛrbər], *m.* (—**s**, *pl.* —) rival, competitor.
Wette [ˈvɛtə], *f.* (—, *pl.* —**n**) bet, wager; *um die — laufen*, race one another.
Wetteifer [ˈvɛtaɪfər], *m.* (—**s**, *no pl.*) rivalry.
wetteifern [ˈvɛtaɪfərn], *v.n. insep.* vie (with), compete.
wetten [ˈvɛtən], *v.a.*, *v.n.* bet, lay a wager, wager.
Wetter [ˈvɛtər], *n.* (—**s**, *pl.* —) weather; bad weather, storm; *schlagende* —, (*Min.*) fire-damp.
Wetterbeobachtung [ˈvɛtərbəobaxtuŋ], *f.* (—, *pl.* —**en**) meteorological observation.
Wetterbericht [ˈvɛtərbərɪçt], *m.* (—**s**, *pl.* —**e**) weather report *or* forecast.
Wetterfahne [ˈvɛtərfaːnə], *f.* (—, *pl.* —**en**) weather-cock, vane; (*fig.*) turncoat.
wetterfest [ˈvɛtərfɛst], *adj.* weatherproof.
Wetterglas [ˈvɛtərglaːs], *n.* (—**es**, *pl.* ¨—**er**) barometer.
Wetterhahn [ˈvɛtərhaːn], *m.* (—**s**, *pl.* ¨—**e**) weather-cock.
Wetterkunde [ˈvɛtərkundə], *f.* (—, *no pl.*) meteorology.
Wetterleuchten [ˈvɛtərlɔyçtən], *n.* (—**s**, *no pl.*) summer lightning; sheet lightning.
wettern [ˈvɛtərn], *v.n.* be stormy; (*fig.*) curse, swear, thunder (against), storm.
Wettervorhersage [ˈvɛtərfoːrheːrzaːgə], *f.* (—, *pl.* —**n**) weather forecast.
wetterwendisch [ˈvɛtərvɛndɪʃ], *adj.* changeable; irritable, peevish.
Wettkampf [ˈvɛtkampf], *m.* (—(**e**)**s**, *pl.* ¨—**e**) contest, tournament.
Wettlauf [ˈvɛtlauf], *m.* (—**s**, *pl.* ¨—**e**) race.
wettmachen [ˈvɛtmaxən], *v.a.* make up for.
Wettrennen [ˈvɛtrɛnən], *n.* (—**s**, *pl.* —) racing, race.
Wettstreit [ˈvɛtʃtraɪt], *m.* (—**s**, *pl.* —**e**) contest, contention.
wetzen [ˈvɛtsən], *v.a.* whet, hone, sharpen.
Wichse [ˈvɪksə], *f.* (—, *pl.* —**n**) blacking, shoe-polish; (*fig.*) thrashing.
wichsen [ˈvɪksən], *v.a.* black, shine; (*fig.*) thrash.
Wicht [vɪçt], *m.* (—(**e**)**s**, *pl.* —**e**) creature; (*coll.*) chap.
Wichtelmännchen [ˈvɪçtəlmɛnçən], *n.* (—**s**, *pl.* —) pixie, goblin.
wichtig [ˈvɪçtɪç], *adj.* important; weighty; significant; *sich — machen*, put on airs.
Wichtigkeit [ˈvɪçtɪçkaɪt], *f.* (—, *no pl.*) importance; significance.
Wicke [ˈvɪkə], *f.* (—, *pl.* —**n**) (*Bot.*) vetch.
Wickel [ˈvɪkəl], *m.* (—**s**, *pl.* —) roller; (*hair*) curler; (*Med.*) compress.
Wickelkind [ˈvɪkəlkɪnt], *n.* (—**s**, *pl.* —**er**) babe in arms.
wickeln [ˈvɪkəln], *v.a.* roll, coil; wind; wrap (up); (*babies*) swaddle; (*hair*) curl.
Widder [ˈvɪdər], *m.* (—**s**, *pl.* —) ram; (*Astrol.*) Aries.
wider [ˈviːdər], *prep.* (*Acc.*) against, in opposition to, contrary to.

widerfahren [vi:dər'fa:rən], *v.n. irr. insep.* (*aux.* sein) happen to s.o., befall s.o.; *einem Gerechtigkeit — lassen*, give s.o. his due.
Widerhaken ['vi:dərha:kən], *m.* (—s, *pl.* —) barb.
Widerhall ['vi:dərhal], *m.* (—s, *pl.* —e) echo, resonance; (*fig.*) response.
widerlegen [vi:dər'le:gən], *v.a. insep.* refute, disprove, prove (s.o.) wrong.
Widerlegung [vi:dər'le:guŋ], *f.* (—, *pl.* —en) refutation, rebuttal.
widerlich ['vi:dərlɪç], *adj.* disgusting, nauseating, repulsive.
widernatürlich ['vi:dərnaty:rlɪç], *adj.* unnatural; perverse.
widerraten [vi:dər'ra:tən], *v.a. irr. insep.* advise against; dissuade from.
widerrechtlich ['vi:dərrɛçtlɪç], *adj.* illegal, unlawful.
Widerrede ['vi:dərre:də], *f.* (—, *pl.* —n) contradiction.
Widerruf ['vi:dərru:f], *m.* (—s, *pl.* —e) revocation, recantation.
widerrufen [vi:dər'ru:fən], *v.a. irr. insep.* recant, retract, revoke.
Widersacher ['vi:dərzaxər], *m.* (—s, *pl.* —) adversary, antagonist.
Widerschein ['vi:dərʃaɪn], *m.* (—s, *no pl.*) reflection.
widersetzen [vi:dər'zɛtsən], *v.r. insep. sich* —, resist, (*Dat.*) oppose.
widersetzlich [vi:dər'zɛtslɪç], *adj.* refractory, insubordinate.
Widersinn ['vi:dərzɪn], *m.* (—s, *no pl.*) nonsense, absurdity; paradox.
widersinnig ['vi:dərzɪnɪç], *adj.* nonsensical, absurd; paradoxical.
widerspenstig ['vi:dərʃpɛnstɪç], *adj.* refractory, rebellious, obstinate, stubborn.
widerspiegeln [vi:dər'ʃpi:gəln], *v.a.* reflect, mirror.
widersprechen [vi:dər'ʃprɛçən], *v.n. irr. insep.* (*Dat.*) contradict, gainsay.
Widerspruch ['vi:dərʃprux], *m.* (—(es), *pl.* ⸚e) contradiction.
widerspruchsvoll ['vi:derʃpruxsfɔl], *adj.* contradictory.
Widerstand ['vi:dərʃtant], *m.* (—s, *pl.* ⸚e) resistance, opposition.
widerstandsfähig ['vi:dərʃtantsfɛ:ɪç], *adj.* resistant, hardy.
widerstehen [vi:dər'ʃte:ən], *v.n. irr. insep.* (*Dat.*) resist, withstand; be distasteful (to).
Widerstreben [vi:dər'ʃtre:bən], *n.* (—s, *no pl.*) reluctance.
widerstreben [vi:dər'ʃtre:bən], *v.n. insep.* (*Dat.*) strive against, oppose; be distasteful to a p.
Widerstreit ['vi:dərʃtraɪt], *m.* (—s, *no pl.*) contradiction, opposition; conflict.
widerwärtig ['vi:dərvɛrtɪç], *adj.* unpleasant, disagreeable, repugnant, repulsive; hateful, odious.
Widerwille ['vi:dərvɪlə], *m.* (—ns, *no pl.*) aversion (to).
widmen ['vɪdmən], *v.a.* dedicate.
Widmung ['vɪdmuŋ], *f.* (—, *pl.* —en) dedication.
widrig ['vi:drɪç], *adj.* contrary, adverse, inimical, unfavourable.
widrigenfalls ['vi:drɪgənfals], *adv.* failing this, otherwise, else.
wie [vi:], *adv.* how. — *conj.* as, just as, like; — *geht's?* how are you?
wieder ['vi:dər], *adv.* again, anew, afresh; back, in return.
Wiederabdruck ['vi:dərapdruk], *m.* (—s, *pl.* —e) reprint.
Wiederaufbau [vi:dər'aufbau], *m.* (—s, *no pl.*) rebuilding.
Wiederaufnahme [vi:dər'aufna:mə], *f.* (—, *no pl.*) resumption.
Wiederbelebungsversuch ['vi:dərbəle:buŋsfɛrzu:x], *m.* (—es, *pl.* —e) attempt at resuscitation.
Wiederbezahlung ['vi:dərbətsa:luŋ], *f.* (—, *pl.* —en) reimbursement.
wiederbringen ['vi:dərbrɪŋən], *v.a. irr.* bring back, restore.
Wiedereinrichtung ['vi:dəraɪnrɪçtuŋ], *f.* (—, *no pl.*) reorganisation, re-establishment.
Wiedereinsetzung ['vi:dəraɪnzɛtsuŋ], *f.* (—, *pl.* —en) restoration, reinstatement, rehabilitation.
wiedererkennen ['vi:dərɛrkɛnən], *v.a. irr.* recognise.
Wiedererstattung ['vi:dərɛrʃtatuŋ], *f.* (—, *no pl.*) restitution.
Wiedergabe ['vi:dərga:bə], *f.* (—, *no pl.*) restitution, return; (*fig.*) rendering, reproduction.
wiedergeben ['vi:dərge:bən], *v.a. irr.* return, give back; (*fig.*) render.
Wiedergeburt ['vi:dərgəbu:rt], *f.* (—, *no pl.*) rebirth, regeneration, renascence.
Wiedergutmachung [vi:dər'gu:tmaxuŋ], *f.* (—, *no pl.*) reparation.
Wiederherstellung [vi:dər'he:rʃtɛluŋ], *f.* (—, *no pl.*) restoration; recovery.
Wiederherstellungsmittel [vi:dər'he:rʃtɛluŋsmɪtəl], *n.* (—s, *pl.* —) restorative, tonic.
wiederholen [vi:dər'ho:lən], *v.a. insep.* repeat, reiterate.
Wiederholung [vi:dər'ho:luŋ], *f.* (—, *pl.* —en) repetition.
Wiederkäuer ['vi:dərkɔyər], *m.* (—s, *pl.* —) ruminant.
Wiederkehr ['vi:dərke:r], *f.* (—, *no pl.*) return; recurrence.
wiederkehren ['vi:dərke:rən], *v.n.* (*aux.* sein) return.
wiederklingen ['vi:dərklɪŋən], *v.n. irr.* reverberate.
wiederkommen ['vi:dərkɔmən], *v.n. irr.* (*aux.* sein) return, come back.
Wiedersehen ['vi:dərze:ən], *n.* (—s, *no pl.*) reunion, meeting after separation; *auf* —, good-bye; so long! see you again!
wiedersehen ['vi:dərze:ən], *v.a. irr.* see again, meet again.

wiederum ['vi:dərum], *adv.* again, anew, afresh.
Wiedervereinigung ['vi:dərfɛraɪnɪguŋ], *f.* (—, *pl.* —en) reunion, reunification.
Wiedervergeltung ['vi:dərfɛrgɛltuŋ], *f.* (—, *no pl.*) requital, retaliation, reprisal.
Wiederverkauf ['vi:dərfɛrkauf], *m.* (—s, *no pl.*) resale.
Wiederverkäufer ['vi:dərfɛrkɔyfər], *m.* (—s, *pl.* —) retailer.
Wiederversöhnung ['vi:dərfɛrzø:nuŋ], *f.* (—, *no pl.*) reconciliation.
Wiederwahl ['vi:dərva:l], *f.* (—, *no pl.*) re-election.
Wiege ['vi:gə], *f.* (—, *pl.* —n) cradle.
wiegen ['vi:gən], *v.a.* rock (the cradle). — *v.r. sich — in*, delude o.s. with. — *v.a., v.n. irr.* weigh.
Wiegenfest ['vi:gənfɛst], *n.* (—es, *pl.* —e) (*Poet., Lit.*) birthday.
Wiegenlied ['vi:gənli:t], *n.* (—s, *pl.* —er) cradle-song, lullaby.
wiehern ['vi:ərn], *v.n.* neigh.
Wien [vi:n], *n.* Vienna.
Wiese ['vi:zə], *f.* (—, *pl.* —n) meadow.
Wiesel ['vi:zəl], *n.* (—s, *pl.* —) (*Zool.*) weasel.
wieso [vi'zo:] *adv.* why? how do you mean? in what way?
wieviel [vi'fi:l], *adv.* how much, how many; *den —ten haben wir heute?* what is the date today?
wiewohl [vi'vo:l], *conj.* although, though.
Wild [vɪlt], *n.* (—(e)s, *no pl.*) game; venison.
wild [vɪlt], *adj.* wild, savage, fierce; furious.
Wildbach ['vɪltbax], *m.* (—s, *pl.* ⸚e) (mountain) torrent.
Wilddieb ['vɪltdi:p], *m.* (—(e)s, *pl.* —e) poacher.
Wilde ['vɪldə], *m.* (—n, *pl.* —n) savage.
wildern ['vɪldərn], *v.n.* poach.
Wildfang ['vɪltfaŋ], *m.* (—s, *pl.* ⸚e) scamp, tomboy.
wildfremd ['vɪltfrɛmt], *adj.* completely strange.
Wildhüter ['vɪlthy:tər], *m.* (—s, *pl.* —) gamekeeper.
Wildleder ['vɪltle:dər], *n.* (—s, *no pl.*) suède, doeskin, buckskin.
Wildnis ['vɪltnɪs], *f.* (—, *pl.* —se) wilderness, desert.
Wildpark ['vɪltpark], *m.* (—s, *pl.* —s) game-reserve.
Wildpret ['vɪltprɛt], *n.* (—s, *no pl.*) game; venison.
Wildschwein ['vɪltʃvaɪn], *n.* (—s, *pl.* —e) wild boar.
Wille ['vɪlə], *m.* (—ns, *no pl.*) will, wish, design, purpose.
willenlos ['vɪlənlo:s], *adj.* weak-minded.
willens ['vɪləns], *adv.* — *sein*, be willing, have a mind to.
Willenserklärung ['vɪlənsɛrklɛ:ruŋ], *f.* (—, *pl.* —en) (*Law*) declaratory act.
Willensfreiheit ['vɪlənsfraɪhaɪt], *f.* (—, *no pl.*) free will.
Willenskraft ['vɪlənskraft], *f.* (—, *no pl.*) strength of will, will-power.
willentlich ['vɪləntlɪç], *adv.* purposely, on purpose, intentionally, wilfully.
willfahren [vɪl'fa:rən], *v.n. insep.* (*Dat.*) comply with, gratify.
willfährig ['vɪlfɛ:rɪç], *adj.* compliant, complaisant.
willig ['vɪlɪç], *adj.* willing, ready, docile.
willkommen [vɪl'kɔmən], *adj.* welcome; — *heißen*, welcome.
Willkür ['vɪlky:r], *f.* (—, *no pl.*) free will; discretion; caprice, arbitrariness.
willkürlich ['vɪlky:rlɪç], *adj.* arbitrary.
wimmeln ['vɪməln], *v.n.* swarm, teem (with).
wimmern ['vɪmərn], *v.n.* whimper.
Wimpel ['vɪmpəl], *m.* (—s, *pl.* —) pennon, pennant, streamer.
Wimper ['vɪmpər], *f.* (—, *pl.* —n) eyelash; *ohne mit der — zu zucken*, without turning a hair, without batting an eyelid.
Wind [vɪnt], *m.* (—(e)s, *pl.* —e) wind, breeze; *von etwas — bekommen*, get wind of.
Windbeutel ['vɪntbɔytəl], *m.* (—s, *pl.* —) cream puff; (*fig.*) windbag.
Windbüchse ['vɪntbyksə], *f.* (—, *pl.* —n) air-gun.
Winde ['vɪndə], *f.* (—, *pl.* —n) (*Tech.*) windlass; (*Bot.*) bindweed.
Windel ['vɪndəl], *f.* (—, *pl.* —n) (baby's) napkin; (*Am.*) diaper.
windelweich ['vɪndəlvaɪç], *adj.* very soft, limp; *einen — schlagen*, beat s.o. to a jelly.
winden ['vɪndən], *v.a. irr.* wind, reel; wring; (*flowers*) make a wreath of. — *v.r. sich* —, writhe.
Windeseile ['vɪndəsaɪlə], *f.* (—, *no pl.*) lightning speed.
Windfahne ['vɪntfa:nə], *f.* (—, *pl.* —n) weather-cock, vane.
windfrei ['vɪntfraɪ], *adj.* sheltered.
Windhund ['vɪnthunt], *m.* (—s, *pl.* —e) greyhound; (*fig.*) windbag.
windig ['vɪndɪç], *adj.* windy.
Windklappe ['vɪntklapə], *f.* (—, *pl.* —n) air-valve.
Windlicht ['vɪntlɪçt], *n.* (—s, *pl.* —er) torch; storm lantern.
Windmühle ['vɪntmy:lə], *f.* (—, *pl.* —n) windmill.
Windpocken ['vɪntpɔkən], *f. pl.* (*Med.*) chicken-pox.
Windrichtung ['vɪntrɪçtuŋ], *f.* (—, *pl.* —en) direction of the wind.
Windrose ['vɪntro:zə], *f.* (—, *pl.* —n) compass card; windrose.
Windsbraut ['vɪntsbraut], *f.* (—, *no pl.*) gust of wind, squall; gale.
windschief ['vɪntʃi:f], *adj.* warped, bent.
Windschutzscheibe ['vɪntʃutsʃaɪbə], *f.* (—, *pl.* —n) (*Motor.*) windscreen.
Windseite ['vɪntzaɪtə], *f.* (—, *pl.* —n) windward side.

Windspiel ['vɪntʃpi:l], *n.* (**—s**, *pl.* **—e**) greyhound.
windstill ['vɪntʃtɪl], *adj.* calm.
Windung ['vɪnduŋ], *f.* (**—**, *pl.* **—en**) winding; convolution; twist, loop; coil; meandering.
Wink [vɪŋk], *m.* (**—(e)s**, *pl.* **—e**) sign, nod; (*fig.*) hint, suggestion.
Winkel ['vɪŋkəl], *m.* (**—s**, *pl.* **—**) corner; (*Maths.*) angle.
Winkeladvokat ['vɪŋkəlatvoka:t], *m.* (**—en**, *pl.* **—en**) quack lawyer.
Winkelmaß ['vɪŋkəlma:s], *n.* (**—es**, *pl.* **—e**) set-square.
Winkelmesser ['vɪŋkəlmɛsər], *m.* (**—s**, *pl.* **—**) protractor.
Winkelzug ['vɪŋkəltsu:k], *m.* (**—s**, *pl.* **¨e**) evasion, trick, shift.
winken ['vɪŋkən], *v.n.* signal, nod, beckon, wave.
winklig ['vɪŋklɪç], *adj.* angular.
winseln ['vɪnzəln], *v.n.* whimper, whine, wail.
Winter ['vɪntər], *m.* (**—s**, *pl.* **—**) winter.
Wintergarten ['vɪntərgartən], *m.* (**—s**, *pl.* **¨**) conservatory.
Wintergewächs ['vɪntərgəvɛks], *n.* (**—es**, *pl.* **—e**) perennial plant.
Wintergrün ['vɪntərgry:n], *n.* (**—s**, *no pl.*) evergreen; wintergreen.
wintern ['vɪntərn], *v.n.* become wintry.
Winterschlaf ['vɪntərʃla:f], *m.* (**—s**, *no pl.*) hibernation; *den — halten*, hibernate.
Winzer ['vɪntsər], *m.* (**—s**, *pl.* **—**) vine-grower.
winzig ['vɪntsɪç], *adj.* tiny, diminutive.
Wipfel ['vɪpfəl], *m.* (**—s**, *pl.* **—**) top (of a tree), tree-top.
Wippe ['vɪpə], *f.* (**—**, *pl.* **—n**) seesaw.
wippen ['vɪpən], *v.n.* balance, see-saw.
wir [vi:r], *pers. pron.* we.
Wirbel ['vɪrbəl], *m.* (**—s**, *pl.* **—**) (*water*) whirlpool, eddy; whirlwind; (*drum*) roll; (*head*) crown; (*back*) vertebra.
wirbeln ['vɪrbəln], *v.a., v.n.* whirl.
Wirbelsäule ['vɪrbəlzɔylə], *f.* (**—**, *pl.* **—n**) spine, vertebral column.
Wirbelwind ['vɪrbəlvɪnt], *m.* (**—s**, *pl.* **—e**) whirlwind.
Wirken ['vɪrkən], *n.* (**—s**, *no pl.*) activity.
wirken ['vɪrkən], *v.a.* effect, work; bring to pass; (*materials*) weave; (*dough*) knead. — *v.n.* work.
Wirker ['vɪrkər], *m.* (**—s**, *pl.* **—**) weaver.
wirklich ['vɪrklɪç], *adj.* real, actual; true, genuine.
Wirklichkeit ['vɪrklɪçkaɪt], *f.* (**—**, *no pl.*) reality.
wirksam ['vɪrkza:m], *adj.* effective, efficacious.
Wirksamkeit ['vɪrkza:mkaɪt], *f.* (**—**, *no pl.*) efficacy, efficiency.
Wirkung ['vɪrkuŋ], *f.* (**—**, *pl.* **—en**) working, operation; reaction; efficacy; effect, result, consequence; force, influence; *eine — ausüben auf*, have an effect on; influence s.o. *or* s.th.
Wirkungskreis ['vɪrkuŋskraɪs], *m.* (**—es**, *pl.* **—e**) sphere of activity.
wirkungslos ['vɪrkuŋslo:s], *adj.* ineffectual.
wirkungsvoll ['vɪrkuŋsfɔl], *adj.* effective, efficacious; (*fig.*) impressive.
wirr [vɪr], *adj.* tangled, confused; — *durcheinander*, higgledy-piggledy; *mir ist ganz — im Kopf*, my head is going round.
Wirren ['vɪrən], *f. pl.* troubles, disorders, disturbances.
wirrköpfig ['vɪrkœpfɪç], *adj.* muddle-headed.
Wirrsal ['vɪrza:l], *n.* (**—s**, *pl.* **—e**) confusion, disorder.
Wirrwarr ['vɪrvar], *m.* (**—s**, *no pl.*) jumble, hurly-burly, hubbub.
Wirt [vɪrt], *m.* (**—(e)s**, *pl.* **—e**) host; innkeeper; landlord.
Wirtin ['vɪrtɪn], *f.* (**—**, *pl.* **—innen**) hostess, landlady, innkeeper's wife.
wirtlich ['vɪrtlɪç], *adj.* hospitable.
Wirtschaft ['vɪrtʃaft], *f.* (**—**, *pl.* **—en**) housekeeping; administration; economy; household; housekeeping; inn, ale-house; (*coll.*) mess.
wirtschaften ['vɪrtʃaftən], *v.n.* keep house, housekeep; administer, run; (*coll.*) rummage.
Wirtschafterin ['vɪrtʃaftərɪn], *f.* (**—**, *pl.* **—innen**) housekeeper.
wirtschaftlich ['vɪrtʃaftlɪç], *adj.* economical, thrifty.
Wirtschaftlichkeit ['vɪrtʃaftlɪçkaɪt], *f.* (**—**, *no pl.*) economy; profitability.
Wirtschaftsgeld ['vɪrtʃaftsgɛlt], *n.* (**—s**, *pl.* **—er**) housekeeping-money.
Wirtshaus ['vɪrtshaus], *n.* (**—es**, *pl.* **¨er**) inn.
Wisch [vɪʃ], *m.* (**—es**, *pl.* **—e**) scrap of paper, rag.
wischen ['vɪʃən], *v.a.* wipe.
wispern ['vɪspərn], *v.a., v.n.* whisper.
Wißbegier(de) ['vɪsbəgi:r(də)], *f.* (**—**, *no pl.*) craving for knowledge; curiosity.
Wissen ['vɪsən], *n.* (**—s**, *no pl.*) knowledge, learning, erudition.
wissen ['vɪsən], *v.a. irr.* know, be aware of (a fact); be able to.
Wissenschaft ['vɪsənʃaft], *f.* (**—**, *pl.* **—en**) learning, scholarship; science.
wissenschaftlich ['vɪsənʃaftlɪç], *adj.* learned, scholarly; scientific.
wissenswert ['vɪsənsve:rt], *adj.* worth knowing.
Wissenszweig ['vɪsənstsvaɪk], *m.* (**—s**, *pl.* **—e**) branch of knowledge.
wissentlich ['vɪsəntlɪç], *adj.* deliberate, wilful. — *adv.* knowingly.
wittern ['vɪtərn], *v.a.* scent, smell; (*fig.*) suspect.
Witterung ['vɪtəruŋ], *f.* (**—**, *no pl.*) weather; trail; scent.
Witterungsverhältnisse ['vɪtəruŋsfɛrhɛltnɪsə], *n. pl.* atmospheric conditions.

Witterungswechsel ['vɪtəruŋsvɛksəl], *m.* (—s, *no pl.*) change in the weather.
Witwe ['vɪtvə], *f.* (—, *pl.* —n) widow.
Witwer ['vɪtvər], *m.* (—s, *pl.* —) widower.
Witz [vɪts], *m.* (—es, *pl.* —e) wit, brains; joke, jest, witticism; funny story.
Witzblatt ['vɪtsblat], *n.* (—s, *pl.* ¨er) satirical *or* humorous journal.
Witzbold ['vɪtsbɔlt], *m.* (—es, *pl.* —e) wag; wit.
witzeln ['vɪtsəln], *v.n.* poke fun (at).
witzig ['vɪtsɪç], *adj.* witty; funny, comical; bright.
wo [vo:], *interr. adv.* where? — *conj.* when.
wobei [vo:'baɪ], *adv.* by which, at which, in connection with which; whereby; in doing so.
Woche ['vɔxə], *f.* (—, *pl.* —n) week.
Wochenbericht ['vɔxənbərɪçt], *m.* (—s, *pl.* —e) weekly report.
Wochenbett ['vɔxənbɛt], *n.* (—s, *no pl.*) confinement.
Wochenblatt ['vɔxənblat], *n.* (—s, *pl.* ¨er) weekly (paper).
Wochenlohn ['vɔxənlo:n], *m.* (—s, *pl.* ¨e) weekly wage(s).
Wochenschau ['vɔxənʃau], *f.* (—, *no pl.*) newsreel.
Wochentag ['vɔxənta:k], *m.* (—s, *pl.* —e) week-day.
wöchentlich ['vœçəntlɪç], *adj.* weekly, every week.
wodurch [vo:'durç], *adv.* whereby, by which, through which; (*interr.*) by what?
wofern [vo:'fɛrn], *conj.* if, provided that.
wofür [vo:'fy:r], *adv.* for what, for which, wherefore.
Woge ['vo:gə], *f.* (—, *pl.* —n) wave, billow.
wogegen [vo:'ge:gən], *adv.* against what, against which, in return for which.
wogen ['vo:gən], *v.n.* heave, sway; (*fig.*) fluctuate.
woher [vo:'he:r], *adv.* whence, from what place, how.
wohin [vo:'hɪn], *adv.* whither, where.
wohingegen [vo:hɪn'ge:gən], *conj.* (*obs.*) whereas.
Wohl [vo:l], *n.* (—(e)s, *no pl.*) welfare, health; *auf dein* —, your health! cheers!
wohl [vo:l], *adv.* well, fit; indeed, doubtless, certainly; *ja* —, to be sure.
wohlan! [vo:l'an], *excl.* well! now then!
wohlauf! [vo:l'auf], *excl.* cheer up! — *sein*, be in good health.
wohlbedacht ['vo:lbədaxt], *adj.* well considered.
Wohlbefinden ['vo:lbəfɪndən], *n.* (—s, *no pl.*) good health.
Wohlbehagen ['vo:lbəha:gən], *n.* (—s, *no pl.*) comfort, ease, wellbeing.
wohlbehalten ['vo:lbəhaltən], *adj.* safe.
wohlbekannt ['vo:lbəkant], *adj.* well known.
wohlbeleibt ['vo:lbəlaɪpt], *adj.* corpulent, stout.
wohlbestallt ['vo:lbəʃtalt], *adj.* duly installed.
Wohlergehen ['vo:lɛrge:ən], *n.* (—s, *no pl.*) welfare, wellbeing.
wohlerhalten ['vo:lɛrhaltən], *adj.* well preserved.
wohlerzogen ['vo:lɛrtso:gən], *adj.* well bred, well brought up.
Wohlfahrt ['vo:lfa:rt], *f.* (—, *no pl.*) welfare, prosperity.
wohlfeil ['vo:lfaɪl], *adj.* cheap, inexpensive.
Wohlgefallen ['vo:lgəfalən], *n.* (—s, *no pl.*) pleasure, delight, approval.
wohlgefällig ['vo:lgəfɛlɪç], *adj.* pleasant, agreeable.
Wohlgefühl ['vo:lgəfy:l], *n.* (—s, *no pl.*) comfort, ease.
wohlgelitten ['vo:lgəlɪtən], *adj.* popular.
wohlgemeint ['vo:lgəmaɪnt], *adj.* well meant.
wohlgemerkt ['vo:lgəmɛrkt], *adv.* mind you! mark my words!
wohlgemut ['vo:lgəmu:t], *adj.* cheerful, merry.
wohlgeneigt ['vo:lgənaɪkt], *adj.* well disposed (towards).
wohlgepflegt ['vo:lgəpfle:kt], *adj.* well kept.
wohlgeraten ['vo:lgəra:tən], *adj.* successful; well turned out; good, well behaved.
Wohlgeruch ['vo:lgəru:x], *m.* (—es, *pl.* ¨e) sweet scent, perfume, fragrance.
Wohlgeschmack ['vo:lgəʃmak], *m.* (—s, *no pl.*) pleasant flavour, agreeable taste.
wohlgesinnt ['vo:lgəzɪnt], *adj.* well disposed.
wohlgestaltet ['vo:lgəʃtaltət], *adj.* well shaped.
wohlgezielt ['vo:lgətsi:lt], *adj.* well aimed.
wohlhabend ['vo:lha:bənt], *adj.* well-to-do, wealthy, well off.
wohlig ['vo:lɪç], *adj.* comfortable, cosy.
Wohlklang ['vo:lklaŋ], *m.* (—s, *pl.* ¨e) harmony, euphony.
wohlklingend ['vo:lklɪŋənt], *adj.* harmonious, euphonious, sweet-sounding.
Wohlleben ['vo:lle:bən], *n.* (—s, *no pl.*) luxurious living.
wohllöblich ['vo:llø:plɪç], *adj.* worshipful.
wohlmeinend ['vo:lmaɪnənt], *adj.* well-meaning.
wohlschmeckend ['vo:lʃmɛkənt], *adj.* savoury, tasty, delicious.
Wohlsein ['vo:lzaɪn], *n.* (—s, *no pl.*) good health, wellbeing.
Wohlstand ['vo:lʃtant], *m.* (—s, *no pl.*) prosperity.
Wohltat ['vo:lta:t], *f.* (—, *pl.* —en) benefit; kindness; (*pl.*) benefaction, charity; (*fig.*) treat.

Wohltäter [ˈvo:ltɛ:tər], *m.* (—**s**, *pl.* —) benefactor.
Wohltätigkeit [ˈvo:ltɛ:tɪçkaɪt], *f.* (—, *no pl.*) charity.
wohltuend [ˈvo:ltu:ənt], *adj.* soothing.
wohltun [ˈvo:ltu:n], *v.n. irr.* do good; be comforting.
wohlweislich [ˈvo:lvaɪslɪç], *adj.* wisely.
Wohlwollen [ˈvo:lvɔlən], *n.* (—**s**, *no pl.*) benevolence; favour, patronage.
wohnen [ˈvo:nən], *v.n.* reside, dwell, live.
wohnhaft [ˈvo:nhaft], *adj.* domiciled, resident; — *sein*, reside, be domiciled.
Wohnhaus [ˈvo:nhaus], *n.* (—**es**, *pl.* **¨er**) dwelling-house.
wohnlich [ˈvo:nlɪç], *adj.* comfortable; cosy.
Wohnort [ˈvo:nɔrt], *m.* (—**s**, *pl.* —**e**) place of residence.
Wohnsitz [ˈvo:nzɪts], *m.* (—**es**, *pl.* —**e**) domicile, abode, residence.
Wohnstätte [ˈvo:nʃtɛtə], *f.* (—, *pl.* —**n**) abode, home.
Wohnung [ˈvo:nuŋ], *f.* (—, *pl.* —**en**) residence, dwelling; house, flat, lodging; apartment.
Wohnungsmangel [ˈvo:nuŋsmaŋəl], *m.* (—**s**, *no pl.*) housing shortage.
Wohnwagen [ˈvo:nva:gən], *m.* (—**s**, *pl.* —) caravan.
Wohnzimmer [ˈvo:ntsɪmər], *n.* (—**s**, *pl.* —) sitting-room, living-room.
wölben [ˈvœlbən], *v.r. sich* —, vault, arch.
Wölbung [ˈvœlbuŋ], *f.* (—, *pl.* —**en**) vault, vaulting.
Wolf [vɔlf], *m.* (—(**e**)**s**, *pl.* **¨e**) wolf.
Wolke [ˈvɔlkə], *f.* (—, *pl.* —**n**) cloud.
Wolkenbruch [ˈvɔlkənbrux], *m.* (—**s**, *pl.* **¨e**) cloudburst, violent downpour.
Wolkenkratzer [ˈvɔlkənkratsər], *m.* (—**s**, *pl.* —) sky-scraper.
Wolkenkuckucksheim [vɔlkənˈkukukshaɪm], *n.* (—**s**, *no pl.*) Utopia, cloud cuckoo land.
Wolldecke [ˈvɔldɛkə], *f.* (—, *pl.* —**n**) blanket.
Wolle [ˈvɔlə], *f.* (—, *pl.* —**n**) wool.
wollen (1) [ˈvɔlən], *v.a., v.n. irr.* wish, want to, be willing, intend; *was — Sie*, what do you want?
wollen (2) [ˈvɔlən], *ad*. woollen, made of wool.
Wollgarn [ˈvɔlgarn], *n.* (—**s**, *pl.* —**e**) woollen yarn.
Wollhandel [ˈvɔlhandəl], *m.* (—**s**, *no pl.*) wool-trade.
wollig [ˈvɔlɪç], *adj.* woolly.
Wollsamt [ˈvɔlzamt], *m.* (—**s**, *no pl.*) plush, velveteen.
Wollust [ˈvɔlust], *f.* (—, *pl.* **¨e**) voluptuousness; lust.
wollüstig [ˈvɔlystɪç], *adj.* voluptuous.
Wollwaren [ˈvɔlva:rən], *f. pl.* woollen goods.
Wollzupfen [ˈvɔltsupfən], *n.* (—**s**, *no pl.*) wool-picking.
womit [vo:ˈmɪt], *adv.* wherewith, with which; (*interr.*) with what?
womöglich [vo:ˈmø:klɪç], *adv.* if possible, perhaps.
wonach [vo:ˈna:x], *adv.* whereafter, after which; according to which.
Wonne [ˈvɔnə], *f.* (—, *pl.* —**n**) delight, bliss, rapture.
wonnetrunken [ˈvɔnətruŋkən], *adj.* enraptured.
wonnig [ˈvɔnɪç], *adj.* delightful.
woran [vo:ˈran], *adv.* whereat, whereby; (*interr.*) by what? at what?
worauf [vo:ˈrauf], *adv.* upon which, at which; whereupon; (*interr.*) on what?
woraufhin [vo:raufˈhɪn], *conj.* whereupon.
woraus [vo:ˈraus], *adv.* (*rel. & interr.*) whence, from which; by *or* out of which.
worein [vo:ˈraɪn], *adv.* (*rel. & interr.*) into which; into what.
worin [vo:ˈrɪn], *adv.* (*rel.*) wherein; (*interr.*) in what?
Wort [vɔrt], *n.* (—(**e**)**s**, *pl.* **¨er**, —**e**) word, term; expression, saying.
wortarm [ˈvɔrtarm], *adj.* poor in words, deficient in vocabulary.
Wortarmut [ˈvɔrtarmu:t], *f.* (—, *no pl.*) paucity of words, poverty of language.
Wortbildung [ˈvɔrtbɪlduŋ], *f.* (—, *pl.* —**en**) word-formation.
wortbrüchig [ˈvɔrtbryçɪç], *adj.* faithless, disloyal.
Wörterbuch [ˈvœrtərbu:x], *n.* (—(**e**)**s**, *pl.* **¨er**) dictionary.
Worterklärung [ˈvɔrtɛrklɛ:ruŋ], *f.* (—, *pl.* —**en**) definition.
Wortforschung [ˈvɔrtfɔrʃuŋ], *f.* (—, *no pl.*) etymology.
Wortfügung [ˈvɔrtfy:guŋ], *f.* (—, *no pl.*) syntax.
Wortführer [ˈvɔrtfy:rər], *m.* (—**s**, *pl.* —) spokesman.
Wortgefecht [ˈvɔrtgəfɛçt], *n.* (—**es**, *pl.* —**e**) verbal battle.
wortgetreu [ˈvɔrtgətrɔy], *adj.* literal, verbatim.
wortkarg [ˈvɔrtkark], *adj.* laconic, sparing of words, taciturn.
Wortlaut [ˈvɔrtlaut], *m.* (—**s**, *pl.* —**e**) wording, text.
wörtlich [ˈvœrtlɪç], *adj.* verbal; literal, word for word.
wortlos [ˈvɔrtlo:s], *adj.* speechless. — *adv.* without uttering a word.
wortreich [ˈvɔrtraɪç], *adj.* (*language*) rich in words; (*fig.*) verbose, wordy.
Wortreichtum [ˈvɔrtraɪçtum], *m.* (—**s**, *no pl.*) (*language*) wealth of words; (*fig.*) verbosity, wordiness.
Wortschwall [ˈvɔrtʃval], *m.* (—**s**, *no pl.*) bombast; torrent of words.
Wortspiel [ˈvɔrtʃpi:l], *n.* (—**s**, *pl.* —**e**) pun.
Wortversetzung [ˈvɔrtfɛrzɛtsuŋ], *f.* (—, *pl.* —**en**) inversion (of words).
Wortwechsel [ˈvɔrtvɛksəl], *m.* (—**s**, *pl.* —) dispute, altercation.
worüber [voˈry:bər], *adv.* (*rel.*) about which, whereof; (*interr.*) about what?

worunter [vo'runtər], *adv.* (*rel.*) whereunder; (*interr.*) under what?
woselbst [vo:'zɛlpst], *adv.* where.
wovon [vo:'fɔn], *adv.* (*rel.*) whereof; (*interr.*) of what?
wovor [vo:'fo:r], *adv.* (*rel.*) before which; (*interr.*) before what?
wozu [vo:'tsu:], *adv.* (*rel.*) whereto; (*interr.*) why? for what purpose? to what end?
Wrack [vrak], *n.* (**—s**, *pl.* **—s**) wreck.
wringen ['vrɪŋən], *v.a.* wring.
Wringmaschine ['vrɪŋmaʃi:nə], *f.* (**—**, *pl.* **—n**) wringer, mangle.
Wucher ['vu:xər], *m.* (**—s**, *no pl.*) usury.
wucherisch ['vu:xərɪʃ], *adj.* usurious, extortionate.
wuchern ['vu:xərn], *v.n.* practise usury; (*plants*) luxuriate, grow profusely.
Wucherungen ['vu:xəruŋən], *f. pl.* (*Med.*) excrescence, growth.
Wuchs [vu:ks], *m.* (**—es**, *no pl.*) growth; shape, build.
Wucht [vuxt], *f.* (**—**, *no pl.*) power, force; weight; impetus.
wuchten ['vuxtən], *v.n.* (*Poet.*) press heavily. — *v.a.* prise up.
wuchtig ['vuxtɪç], *adj.* weighty, forceful.
Wühlarbeit ['vy:larbaɪt], *f.* (**—**, *pl.* **—en**) subversive activity.
wühlen ['vy:lən], *v.a.*, *v.n.* dig, burrow; (*fig.*) agitate.
Wühler ['vy:lər], *m.* (**—s**, *pl.* **—**) agitator, demagogue.
Wühlmaus ['vy:lmaus], *f.* (**—**, *pl.* **¨e**) (*Zool.*) vole.
Wulst [vulst], *m.* (**—es**, *pl.* **¨e**) roll, pad; swelling.
wülstig ['vylstɪç], *adj.* padded, stuffed; swollen.
wund [vunt], *adj.* sore, wounded.
Wundarzt ['vuntartst], *m.* (**—es**, *pl.* **¨e**) (*obs.*) surgeon.
Wundbalsam ['vuntbalzam], *m.* (**—s**, *pl.* **—e**) balm.
Wunde ['vundə], *f.* (**—**, *pl.* **—n**) wound, hurt.
Wunder ['vundər], *n.* (**—s**, *pl.* **—**) marvel, wonder, miracle.
wunderbar ['vundərba:r], *adj.* wonderful, marvellous.
Wunderding ['vundərdɪŋ], *n.* (**—s**, *pl.* **—e**) marvel.
Wunderdoktor ['vundərdɔktɔr], *m.* (**—s**, *pl.* **—en**) quack doctor.
Wunderglaube ['vundərglaubə], *m.* (**—ns**, *no pl.*) belief in miracles.
wunderhübsch [vundər'hypʃ], *adj.* exceedingly pretty.
Wunderkind ['vundərkɪnt], *n.* (**—s**, *pl.* **—er**) infant prodigy.
Wunderlampe ['vundərlampə], *f.* (**—**, *pl.* **—n**) magic lantern.
wunderlich ['vundərlɪç], *adj.* strange, odd, queer.
wundern ['vundərn], *v.r.* *sich — über*, be surprised at, be astonished at.
wundersam ['vundərza:m], *adj.* wonderful, strange.
wunderschön ['vundərʃø:n], *adj.* lovely, gorgeous; exquisite.
Wundertat ['vundərta:t], *f.* (**—**, *pl.* **—en**) miraculous deed.
wundertätig ['vundərtɛ:tɪç], *adj.* miraculous.
Wundertier ['vundərti:r], *n.* (**—s**, *pl.* **—e**) monster; (*fig.*) prodigy.
Wunderwerk ['vundərverk], *n.* (**—s**, *pl.* **—e**) miracle.
Wundmal ['vuntma:l], *n.* (**—s**, *pl.* **—e**) scar.
Wunsch [vunʃ], *m.* (**—es**, *pl.* **¨e**) wish, desire, aspiration.
Wünschelrute ['vynʃəlru:tə], *f.* (**—**, *pl.* **—n**) divining-rod.
wünschen ['vynʃən], *v.a.* wish, desire, long for.
wünschenswert ['vynʃənsve:rt], *adj.* desirable.
Wunschform ['vunʃfɔrm], *f.* (**—**, *no pl.*) (*Gram.*) optative form.
wuppdich! ['vupdɪç], *excl.* here goes!
Würde ['vyrdə], *f.* (**—**, *pl.* **—n**) dignity, honour.
Würdenträger ['vyrdəntrɛ:gər], *m.* (**—s**, *pl.* **—**) dignitary.
würdevoll ['vyrdəfɔl], *adj.* dignified.
würdig ['vyrdɪç], *adj.* worthy (of), deserving, meritorious.
würdigen ['vyrdɪgən], *v.a.* honour; *ich weiss es zu —*, I appreciate it.
Würdigung ['vyrdɪguŋ], *f.* (**—**, *pl.* **—en**) appreciation.
Wurf [vurf], *m.* (**—(e)s**, *pl.* **¨e**) cast, throw.
Würfel ['vyrfəl], *m.* (**—s**, *pl.* **—**) die; (*Geom.*) cube; *— spielen*, play at dice.
würfelförmig ['vyrfəlfœrmɪç], *adj.* cubic, cubiform.
würfeln ['vyrfəln], *v.n.* play at dice.
Wurfgeschoß ['vurfgəʃo:s], *n.* (**—sses**, *pl.* **—sse**) missile, projectile.
Wurfmaschine ['vurfmaʃi:nə], *f.* (**—**, *pl.* **—n**) catapult.
Wurfscheibe ['vurfʃaɪbə], *f.* (**—**, *pl.* **—n**) discus, quoit.
Wurfspieß ['vurfʃpi:s], *m.* (**—es**, *pl.* **—e**) javelin.
würgen ['vyrgən], *v.a.* strangle, throttle. — *v.n.* choke.
Würgengel ['vyrgɛŋəl], *m.* (**—s**, *no pl.*) avenging angel.
Würger ['vyrgər], *m.* (**—s**, *pl.* **—**) strangler, murderer; (*Poet.*) slayer; (*Orn.*) shrike, butcher-bird.
Wurm [vurm], *m.* (**—(e)s**, *pl.* **¨er**) worm; (*apple*) maggot.
wurmen ['vurmən], *v.a.* vex.
wurmstichig ['vurmʃtɪçɪç], *adj.* worm-eaten.
Wurst [vurst], *f.* (**—**, *pl.* **¨e**) sausage.
wurstig ['vurstɪç], *adj.* (*sl.*) quite indifferent.
Wurstigkeit ['vurstɪçkaɪt], *f.* (**—**, *no pl.*) callousness, indifference.
Würze ['vyrtsə], *f.* (**—**, *pl.* **—n**) seasoning, spice, condiment.
Wurzel ['vurtsəl], *f.* (**—**, *pl.* **—n**) root.
wurzeln ['vurtsəln], *v.n.* be rooted.
würzen ['vyrtsən], *v.a.* season, spice.
würzig ['vyrtsɪç], *adj.* spicy, fragrant.

Wust [vust], *m.* (**—es**, *no pl.*) chaos, trash.
wüst [vy:st], *adj.* waste, desert; desolate; dissolute.
Wüste ['vy:stə], *f.* (—, *pl.* **—n**) desert, wilderness.
Wüstling ['vy:stlɪŋ], *m.* (**—s**, *pl.* **—e**) profligate, libertine.
Wut [vu:t], *f.* (—, *no pl.*) rage, fury, passion.
wüten ['vy:tən], *v.n.* rage, storm, fume.
wutentbrannt ['vu:təntbrant], *adj.* enraged, infuriated.
Wüterich ['vy:tərɪç], *m.* (**—s**, *pl.* **—e**) tyrant; ruthless fellow.
Wutgeschrei ['vu:tgəʃraɪ], *n.* (**—s**, *no pl.*) yell of rage.
wutschnaubend ['vu:tʃnaubənt], *adj.* foaming with rage.

X

X [ɪks], *n.* (**—s**, *pl.* **—s**) the letter X.
X-Beine ['ɪksbaɪnə], *n. pl.* knock-knees.
x-beliebig ['ɪksbəli:bɪç], *adj.* any, whatever (one likes).
Xenie ['kse:njə], *f.* (—, *pl.* **—n**) epigram.
Xereswein ['kse:rəsvaɪn], *m.* (**—s**, *pl.* **—e**) sherry.
x-mal ['ɪksma:l], *adv.* (*coll.*) so many times, umpteen times.
X-Strahlen ['ɪksʃtra:lən], *m. pl.* X-rays.
Xylographie [ksylogra'fi:], *f.* (—, *no pl.*) wood-engraving.
Xylophon [ksylo'fo:n], *n.* (**—s**, *pl.* **—e**) (*Mus.*) xylophone.

Y

Y ['ypsilɔn], *n.* (**—s**, *pl.* **—s**) the letter Y.
Yak [jak], *m.* (**—s**, *pl.* **—s**) (*Zool.*) yak.
Yamswurzel ['jamsvurtsəl], *f.* (—, *pl* **—n**) yam.
Ysop [y'zo:p], *m.* (**—s**, *no pl.*) hyssop.

Z

Z [tsɛt], *n.* (**—s**, *pl.* **—s**) the letter Z.
Zabel ['tsa:bəl], *m.* (**—s**, *pl.* —) (*obs.*) chess-board.
Zacke ['tsakə], *f.* (—, *pl.* **—n**) tooth, spike; (*fork*) prong.
zackig ['tsakɪç], *adj.* pronged, toothed, indented; (*rock*) jagged; (*sl.*) smart.
zagen ['tsa:gən], *v.n.* quail, blench, be disheartened, be fainthearted.
zaghaft ['tsa:khaft], *adj.* faint-hearted.
Zaghaftigkeit ['tsa:khaftɪçkaɪt], *f.* (—, *no pl.*) faintheartedness, timidity.
zäh [tsɛ:], *adj.* tough.
Zähigkeit ['tsɛ:ɪçkaɪt], *f.* (—, *no pl.*) toughness.
Zahl [tsa:l], *f.* (—, *pl.* **—en**) number, figure.
zahlbar ['tsa:lba:r], *adj.* payable, due.
zählbar ['tsɛ:lba:r], *adj.* calculable.
zahlen ['tsa:lən], *v.a.* pay; *Ober!* **—**, waiter! the bill, please.
zählen ['tsɛ:lən], *v.a.*, *v.n.* count, number.
Zahlenfolge ['tsa:lənfɔlgə], *f.* (—, *no pl.*) numerical order.
Zahlenlehre ['tsa:lənle:rə], *f.* (—, *no pl.*) arithmetic.
Zahlenreihe ['tsa:lənraɪə], *f.* (—, *pl.* **—n**) numerical progression.
Zahlensinn ['tsa:lənzɪn], *m.* (**—s**, *no pl.*) head for figures.
Zahler ['tsa:lər], *m.* (**—s**, *pl.* —) payer.
Zähler ['tsɛ:lər], *m.* (**—s**, *pl.* —) counter, teller; meter; (*Maths.*) numerator.
Zahlkellner ['tsa:lkɛlnər], *m.* (**—s**, *pl.* —) head waiter.
Zahlmeister ['tsa:lmaɪstər], *m.* (**—s**, *pl.* —) paymaster, treasurer, bursar.
zahlreich ['tsa:lraɪç], *adj.* numerous.
Zahltag ['tsa:lta:k], *m.* (**—s**, *pl.* **—e**) pay-day.
Zahlung ['tsa:luŋ], *f.* (—, *pl.* **—en**) payment; — *leisten*, make payment; *die —en einstellen*, stop payment.
Zählung ['tsɛ:luŋ], *f.* (—, *pl.* **—en**) counting, computation; census.
Zahlungseinstellung ['tsa:luŋsaɪnʃtɛluŋ], *f.* (—, *pl.* **—en**) suspension of payment.
zahlungsfähig ['tsa:luŋsfɛ:ɪç], *adj.* solvent.
Zahlungsmittel ['tsa:luŋsmɪtəl], *n.* (**—s**, *pl.* —) means of payment; *gesetzliches* —, legal tender.
Zahlungstermin ['tsa:luŋstɛrmi:n], *m.* (**—s**, *pl.* **—e**) time of payment.
zahlungsunfähig ['tsa:luŋsunfɛ:ɪç], *adj.* insolvent.
Zahlwort ['tsa:lvɔrt], *n.* (**—s**, *pl.* **¨er**) (*Gram.*) numeral.
zahm [tsa:m], *adj.* tame; domestic(ated); — *machen*, tame.
zähmen ['tsɛ:mən], *v.a.* tame, domesticate.
Zähmer ['tsɛ:mər], *m.* (**—s**, *pl.* —) tamer.
Zahmheit ['tsa:mhaɪt], *f.* (—, *no pl.*) tameness.
Zähmung ['tsɛ:muŋ], *f.* (—, *no pl.*) taming, domestication.
Zahn [tsa:n], *m.* (**—(e)s**, *pl.* **¨e**) tooth; (*wheel*) cog.

Zahnarzt ['tsa:nartst], *m.* (—es, *pl.* ⸚e) dentist, dental surgeon.
Zahnbürste ['tsa:nbyrstə], *f.* (—, *pl.* —n) tooth-brush.
Zähneklappern ['tsɛ:nəklapərn], *n.* (—s, *no pl.*) chattering of teeth.
Zähneknirschen ['tsɛ:nəknɪrʃən], *n.* (—s, *no pl.*) gnashing of teeth.
zahnen ['tsa:nən], *v.n.* teethe, cut o.'s teeth.
zähnen ['tsɛ:nən], *v.a.* indent, notch.
Zahnfleisch ['tsa:nflaɪʃ], *n.* (—es, *no pl.*) gums.
Zahnfüllung ['tsa:nfyluŋ], *f.* (—, *pl.* —en) filling, stopping (of tooth).
Zahnheilkunde ['tsa:nhaɪlkundə], *f.* (—, *no pl.*) dentistry, dental surgery.
Zahnlücke ['tsa:nlykə], *f.* (—, *pl.* —n) gap in the teeth.
Zahnpaste ['tsa:npastə], *f.* (—, *no pl.*) tooth-paste.
Zahnpulver ['tsa:npulvər], *n.* (—s, *no pl.*) tooth-powder.
Zahnrad ['tsa:nra:t], *n.* (—s, *pl.* ⸚er) cog-wheel.
Zahnradbahn ['tsa:nra:tba:n], *f.* (—, *pl.* —en) rack-railway.
Zahnschmerzen ['tsa:nʃmɛrtsən], *m. pl.* toothache.
Zahnstocher ['tsa:nʃtɔxər], *m.* (—s, *pl.* —) tooth-pick.
Zähre ['tsɛ:rə], *f.* (—, *pl.* —n) (*Poet.*) tear.
Zander ['tsandər], *m.* (—s, *pl.* —) (*fish*) pike.
Zange ['tsaŋə], *f.* (—, *pl.* —n) tongs; pincers; tweezers, nippers; (*Med.*) forceps.
Zank [tsaŋk], *m.* (—es, *pl.* ⸚ereien) quarrel, altercation, tiff.
Zankapfel ['tsaŋkapfəl], *m.* (—s, *pl.* ⸚) bone of contention.
zanken ['tsaŋkən], *v.r.* *sich* —, quarrel, dispute.
zänkisch ['tsɛnkɪʃ], *adj.* quarrelsome.
Zanksucht ['tsaŋkzuxt], *f.* (—, *no pl.*) quarrelsomeness.
zanksüchtig ['tsaŋkzyçtɪç], *adj.* quarrelsome, cantankerous.
Zapfen ['tsapfən], *m.* (—s, *pl.* —) pin, peg; (*cask*) bung, spigot; (*fir*) cone.
zapfen ['tsapfən], *v.a.* tap, draw.
Zapfenstreich ['tsapfənʃtraɪç], *m.* (—s, *no pl.*) (*Mil.*) tattoo, retreat.
zapp(e)lig ['tsap(ə)lɪç], *adj.* fidgety.
zappeln ['tsapəln], *v.n.* kick, struggle, wriggle.
Zar [tsa:r], *m.* (—en, *pl.* —en) Czar, Tsar.
zart [tsart], *adj.* tender, sensitive, delicate, gentle; — *besaitet*, (*iron.*) sensitive, highly strung.
Zartgefühl ['tsartgəfy:l], *n.* (—s, *no pl.*) delicacy, sensitivity.
Zartheit ['tsarthaɪt], *f.* (—, *no pl.*) tenderness, gentleness.
zärtlich ['tsɛ:rtlɪç], *adj.* loving, amorous, tender.
Zärtlichkeit ['tsɛ:rtlɪçkaɪt], *f.* (—, *pl.* —en) tenderness; caresses.
Zartsinn ['tsartzɪn], *m.* (—s, *no pl.*) delicacy.
Zauber ['tsaubər], *m.* (—s, *no pl.*) charm, spell, enchantment; magic; fascination.
Zauberei [tsaubə'raɪ], *f.* (—, *pl.* —en) magic, witchcraft, sorcery.
Zauberer ['tsaubərər], *m.* (—s, *pl.* —) magician, sorcerer, wizard.
zauberisch ['tsaubərɪʃ], *adj.* magical; (*fig.*) enchanting.
Zauberkraft ['tsaubərkraft], *f.* (—, *no pl.*) magic power, witchcraft.
Zaubermittel ['tsaubərmɪtəl], *n.* (—s, *pl.* —) charm.
zaubern ['tsaubərn], *v.n.* practise magic; conjure.
Zauberspruch ['tsaubərʃprux], *m.* (—s, *pl.* ⸚e) spell, charm.
Zauberstab ['tsaubərʃta:p], *m.* (—s, *pl.* ⸚e) magic wand.
Zauderer ['tsaudərər], *m.* (—s, *pl.* —) loiterer, temporizer, procrastinator.
zaudern ['tsaudərn], *v.n.* delay; hesitate, procrastinate.
Zaum [tsaum], *m.* (—(e)s, *pl.* ⸚e) bridle; *im — halten*, check, restrain.
zäumen ['tsɔymən], *v.a.* bridle.
Zaun [tsaun], *m.* (—(e)s, *pl.* ⸚e) hedge, fence; *einen Streit vom — brechen*, pick a quarrel.
Zaungast ['tsaungast], *m.* (—s, *pl.* ⸚e) onlooker, outsider; intruder.
Zaunkönig ['tsaunkø:nɪç], *m.* (—s, *pl.* —e) (*Orn.*) wren.
Zaunpfahl ['tsaunpfa:l], *m.* (—s, *pl.* ⸚e) pale, hedge-pole; *mit dem — winken*, give s.o. a broad hint.
Zaunrebe ['tsaunre:bə], *f.* (—, *pl.* —n) (*Bot.*) Virginia creeper.
zausen ['tsauzən], *v.a.* tousle; (*hair*) disarrange, ruffle.
Zechbruder ['tsɛçbru:dər], *m.* (—s, *pl.* ⸚) tippler, toper.
Zeche ['tsɛçə], *f.* (—, *pl.* —n) bill (in a restaurant); mine; *die — bezahlen*, foot the bill, pay the piper.
Zeder ['tse.dər], *f.* (—, *pl.* —n) (*Bot.*) cedar.
zedieren [tsɛ'di:rən], *v.a.* cede.
Zehe ['tse:ə], *f.* (—, *pl.* —n) toe.
Zehenspitze ['tse:ənʃpɪtsə], *f.* (—, *pl.* —n) tip of the toe, tiptoe.
zehn [tse:n], *num. adj.* ten.
Zehneck ['tse:nɛk], *n.* (—s, *pl.* —e) decagon.
Zehnte ['tse:ntə], *m.* (—n, *pl.* —n) tithe.
zehren ['tse:rən], *v.n.* *von etwas* —, live on s.th., prey upon s.th.
Zehrfieber ['tse:rfi:bər], *n.* (—s, *no pl.*) hectic fever.
Zehrgeld ['tse:rgɛlt], *n.* (—s, *pl.* —er) subsistence, allowance.
Zehrvorrat ['tse:rfo:rra:t], *m.* (—s, *pl.* ⸚e) provisions.
Zehrung ['tse:ruŋ], *f.* (—, *pl.* —en) consumption; victuals; (*Eccl.*) *letzte* —, viaticum.
Zeichen ['tsaɪçən], *n.* (—s, *pl.* —) sign, token, symptom, omen; indication; badge; signal.

Zeichenbrett [ˈtsaɪçənbrɛt], *n.* (—**s**, *pl.* —**er**) drawing-board.
Zeichendeuter [ˈtsaɪçəndɔytər], *m.* (—**s**, *pl.* —) astrologer.
Zeichendeuterei [tsaɪçəndɔytəˈraɪ], *f.* (—, *no pl.*) astrology.
Zeichenerklärung [ˈtsaɪçənɛrklɛ:ruŋ], *f.* (— *pl.*—**en**) legend, key.
Zeichensprache [ˈtsaɪçənʃpra:xə], *f.* (—, *no pl.*) sign-language.
Zeichentinte [ˈtsaɪçəntɪntə], *f.* (—, *no pl.*) marking ink.
zeichnen [ˈtsaɪçnən], *v.a.* draw; mark; (*money*) subscribe; (*letter*) sign.
Zeichner [ˈtsaɪçnər], *m.* (—**s**, *pl.* —) draughtsman, designer.
Zeichnung [ˈtsaɪçnuŋ], *f.* (—, *pl.* —**en**) drawing.
Zeigefinger [ˈtsaɪgəfɪŋər], *m.* (—**s**, *pl.* —) forefinger, index finger.
zeigen [ˈtsaɪgən], *v.a.* show, point to, prove.
Zeiger [ˈtsaɪgər], *m.* (—**s**, *pl.* —) indicator; hand (of watch, clock).
zeihen [ˈtsaɪən], *v.a. irr. einen einer Sache* —, tax s.o. with s.th.
Zeile [ˈtsaɪlə], *f.* (—, *pl.* —**n**) line; furrow; (*pl.*) letter.
Zeisig [ˈtsaɪzɪç], *m.* (—**s**, *pl.* —**e**) (*Orn.*) siskin.
Zeit [tsaɪt], *f.* (—, *pl.* —**en**) time; *zur* —, at present; *auf* —, on credit.
Zeitabschnitt [ˈtsaɪtapʃnɪt], *m.* (—**s**, *pl.* —**e**) period; epoch.
Zeitalter [ˈtsaɪtaltər], *n.* (—**s**, *pl.* —) age, era.
Zeitdauer [ˈtsaɪtdauər], *f.* (—, *no pl.*) space of time.
Zeitfrage [ˈtsaɪtfra:gə], *f.* (—, *pl.* —**n**) topical question; question of time.
Zeitgeist [ˈtsaɪtgaɪst], *m.* (—**s**, *no pl.*) spirit of the age.
zeitgemäß [ˈtsaɪtgəmɛ:s], *adj.* timely, seasonable, opportune, modern.
Zeitgenosse [ˈtsaɪtgənɔsə], *m.* (—**n**, *pl.* —**n**) contemporary.
zeitig [ˈtsaɪtɪç], *adj.* early, timely.
zeitigen [ˈtsaɪtɪgən], *v.a.* engender, generate. — *v.n.* mature, ripen.
Zeitkarte [ˈtsaɪtkartə], *f.* (—, *pl.* —**n**) season ticket.
Zeitlauf [ˈtsaɪtlauf], *m.* (—**s**, *pl.* ⸚**e**) course of time, conjuncture.
zeitlebens [ˈtsaɪtle:bəns], *adv.* for life, (for) all his (*or* her) life.
zeitlich [ˈtsaɪtlɪç], *adj.* temporal, earthly; secular; temporary, transient.
zeitlos [ˈtsaɪtlo:s], *adj.* lasting, permanent.
Zeitmangel [ˈtsaɪtmaŋəl], *m.* (—**s**, *no pl.*) lack of time.
Zeitmesser [ˈtsaɪtmɛsər], *m.* (—**s**, *pl.* —) chronometer, timepiece; metronome.
Zeitpunkt [ˈtsaɪtpuŋkt], *m.* (—**s**, *pl.* —**e**) moment, date; point of time.
zeitraubend [ˈtsaɪtraubənt], *adj.* time-consuming.
Zeitraum [ˈtsaɪtraum], *m.* (—**s**, *pl.* ⸚**e**) space of time, period.
Zeitschrift [ˈtsaɪtʃrɪft], *f.* (—, *pl.* —**en**) periodical, journal, magazine.
Zeitung [ˈtsaɪtuŋ], *f.* (—, *pl.* —**en**) newspaper.
Zeitungsente [ˈtsaɪtuŋsɛntə], *f.* (—, *pl.* —**n**) canard, newspaper hoax.
Zeitungskiosk [ˈtsaɪtuŋskiɔsk], *m.* (—**s**, *pl.* —**e**) newspaper-stall.
Zeitungsnachricht [ˈtsaɪtuŋsna:xrɪçt], *f.* (—, *pl.* —**en**) newspaper report.
Zeitungswesen [ˈtsaɪtuŋsve:zən], *n.* (—**s**, *no pl.*) journalism.
Zeitverlust [ˈtsaɪtfɛrlust], *m.* (—**s**, *no pl.*) loss of time; *ohne* —, without delay.
Zeitvertreib [ˈtsaɪtfɛrtraɪp], *m.* (—**s**, *no pl.*) pastime, amusement; *zum* —, to pass the time.
zeitweilig [ˈtsaɪtvaɪlɪç], *adj.* temporary.
zeitweise [ˈtsaɪtvaɪzə], *adv.* from time to time.
Zeitwort [ˈtsaɪtvɔrt], *n.* (—**s**, *pl.* ⸚**er**) (*Gram.*) verb.
Zelle [ˈtsɛlə], *f.* (—, *pl.* —**n**) cell; booth.
Zelt [tsɛlt], *n.* (—(**e**)**s**, *pl.* —**e**) tent.
Zeltdecke [ˈtsɛltdɛkə], *f.* (—, *pl.* —**n**) awning, marquee.
Zement [tseˈmɛnt], *m.* (—**s**, *no pl.*) cement.
Zenit [tseˈni:t], *m.* (—**s**, *no pl.*) zenith.
zensieren [tsɛnˈzi:rən], *v.a.* review, censure; (*Sch.*) mark.
Zensor [ˈtsɛnzɔr], *m.* (—**s**, *pl.* —**en**) censor.
Zensur [tsɛnˈzu:r], *f.* (—, *pl.* —**en**) censure; (*Sch.*) report, mark; censorship.
Zentimeter [ˈtsɛntime:tər], *m.* (—**s**, *pl.* —) centimetre.
Zentner [ˈtsɛntnər], *m.* (—**s**, *pl.* —) hundredweight.
zentral [tsɛnˈtra:l], *adj.* central.
Zentrale [tsɛnˈtra:lə], *f.* (—, *pl.* —**n**) control room; head office.
zentralisieren [tsɛntraliˈzi:rən], *v.a.* centralise.
Zentrum [ˈtsɛntrum], *n.* (—**s**, *pl.* —**tren**) centre; (*Am.*) center.
Zephir [ˈtsɛ:fɪ:r], *m.* (—**s**, *pl.* —**e**) zephyr.
Zepter [ˈtsɛptər], *m.* & *n.* (—**s**, *pl.* —) sceptre, mace.
zerbrechen [tsɛrˈbrɛçən], *v.a.*, *v.n. irr.* (*aux.* sein) break to pieces; shatter; *sich den Kopf* —, rack o.'s brains.
zerbrechlich [tsɛrˈbrɛçlɪç], *adj.* brittle, fragile.
zerbröckeln [tsɛrˈbrœkəln], *v.a.*, *v.n.* (*aux.* sein) crumble.
zerdrücken [tsɛrˈdrykən], *v.a.* crush, bruise.
Zeremonie [tseremoˈni:], *f.* (—, *pl.* —**n**) ceremony.
zeremoniell [tseremoˈnjɛl], *adj.* ceremonial, formal.
Zerfahrenheit [tsɛrˈfa:rənhaɪt], *f.* (—, *no pl.*) absent-mindedness.
Zerfall [tsɛrˈfal], *m.* (—**s**, *no pl.*) disintegration; decay.
zerfallen [tsɛrˈfalən], *v.n. irr.* (*aux.* sein) fall to pieces. — *adj.* in ruins.

zerfleischen [tsɛr'flaɪʃən], *v.a.* lacerate, tear to pieces.
zerfließen [tsɛr'fli:sən], *v.n. irr.* (*aux.* sein) dissolve, melt.
zerfressen [tsɛr'frɛsən], *v.a. irr.* gnaw, corrode.
zergehen [tsɛr'ge:ən], *v.n. irr.* (*aux.* sein) dissolve, melt.
zergliedern [tsɛr'gli:dərn], *v.a.* dissect; (*fig.*) analyse.
zerhauen [tsɛr'hauən], *v.a.* hew in pieces, chop up.
zerkauen [tsɛr'kauən], *v.a.* chew.
zerkleinern [tsɛr'klaɪnərn], *v.a.* cut into small pieces; (*firewood*) chop.
zerklüftet [tsɛr'klyftət], *adj.* rugged.
zerknirscht [tsɛr'knɪrʃt], *adj.* contrite.
Zerknirschung [tsɛr'knɪrʃuŋ], *f.* (—, *no pl.*) contrition.
zerknittern [tsɛr'knɪtərn], *v.a.* crumple.
zerknüllen [tsɛr'knylən], *v.a.* rumple.
zerlassen [tsɛr'lasən], *v.a. irr.* melt, liquefy.
zerlegen [tsɛr'le:gən], *v.a.* resolve; take to pieces; cut up, carve; (*fig.*) analyse.
zerlumpt [tsɛr'lumpt], *adj.* ragged, tattered.
zermahlen [tsɛr'ma:lən], *v.a.* grind to powder.
zermalmen [tsɛr'malmən], *v.a.* crush.
zermartern [tsɛr'martərn], *v.a.* torment; *sich das Hirn* —, rack o.'s brains.
zernagen [tsɛr'na:gən], *v.a.* gnaw (away).
zerquetschen [tsɛr'kvɛtʃən], *v.a.* squash, crush.
zerraufen [tsɛr'raufən], *v.a.* dishevel.
Zerrbild ['tsɛrbɪlt], *n.* (**—s**, *pl.* **—er**) caricature.
zerreiben [tsɛr'raɪbən], *v.a. irr.* grind to powder, pulverise.
zerreißen [tsɛr'raɪsən], *v.a. irr.* tear, rend, tear up; break; rupture. — *v.n.* (*aux.* sein) be torn; (*clothes*) wear out.
zerren ['tsɛrən], *v.a.* pull, tug, drag; strain.
zerrinnen [tsɛr'rɪnən], *v.n. irr.* (*aux.* sein) dissolve, melt; (*fig.*) vanish.
zerrütten [tsɛr'rytən], *v.a.* unsettle, disorder, unhinge; ruin, destroy.
zerschellen [tsɛr'ʃɛlən], *v.n.* (*aux.* sein) be dashed to pieces, be wrecked.
zerschlagen [tsɛr'ʃla:gən], *v.a. irr.* break, smash to pieces, batter.
zerschmettern [tsɛr'ʃmɛtərn], *v.a.* dash to pieces, break, crush; shatter, overwhelm.
zersetzen [tsɛr'zɛtsən], *v.a.*, *v.r.* break up; disintegrate.
zerspalten [tsɛr'ʃpaltən], *v.a.* cleave, split, slit.
zersprengen [tsɛr'ʃprɛŋən], *v.a.* explode, burst; (*crowd*) disperse; (*Mil.*) rout.
zerspringen [tsɛr'ʃprɪŋən], *v.n. irr.* (*aux.* sein) crack; fly to pieces, split.
zerstampfen [tsɛr'ʃtampfən], *v.a.* crush, pound.
zerstäuben [tsɛr'ʃtɔybən], *v.a.* spray, atomize.
zerstörbar [tsɛr'ʃtø:rba:r], *adj.* destructible.
zerstören [tsɛr'ʃtø:rən], *v.a.* destroy, devastate.
Zerstörer [tsɛr'ʃtø:rər], *m.* (**—s**, *pl.* **—**) destroyer.
Zerstörung [tsɛr'ʃtø:ruŋ], *f.* (—, *pl.* **—en**) destruction.
Zerstörungswut [tsɛr'ʃtø:ruŋsvu:t], *f.* (—, *no pl.*) vandalism.
zerstoßen [tsɛr'ʃto:sən], *v.a. irr.* bruise, pound.
zerstreuen [tsɛr'ʃtrɔyən], *v.a.* scatter, disperse; divert.
zerstreut [tsɛr'ʃtrɔyt], *adj.* absent-minded.
Zerstreuung [tsɛr'ʃtrɔyuŋ], *f.* (—, *pl.* **—en**) dispersion; amusement, diversion, distraction.
zerstückeln [tsɛr'ʃtykəln], *v.a.* dismember.
Zerstückelung [tsɛr'ʃtykəluŋ], *f.* (—, *no pl.*) dismemberment.
zerteilen [tsɛr'taɪlən], *v.a.* divide, separate; disperse, dissipate. — *v.r. sich* —, dissolve.
Zertifikat [tsɛrtifi'ka:t], *n.* (**—s**, *pl.* **—e**) certificate, attestation.
zertrennen [tsɛr'trɛnən], *v.a.* rip up, unstitch.
zertrümmern [tsɛr'trymərn], *v.a.* destroy, break up, demolish.
Zerwürfnis [tsɛr'vyrfnɪs], *n.* (**—ses**, *pl.* **—se**) discord, dissension.
zerzausen [tsɛr'tsauzən], *v.a.* dishevel, tousle.
zerzupfen [tsɛr'tsupfən], *v.a.* pick to pieces, pluck.
Zession [tsɛs'jo:n], *f.* (—, *pl.* **—en**) cession, assignment, transfer.
Zetergeschrei ['tse:tərgəʃraɪ], *n.* (**—s**, *no pl.*) outcry, hullabaloo.
zetern ['tse:tərn], *v.n.* yell; (*coll.*) kick up a row.
Zettel ['tsɛtəl], *m.* (**—s**, *pl.* **—**) slip of paper; label, chit.
Zettelkasten ['tsɛtəlkastən], *m.* (**—s**, *pl.* **¨**) card-index, filing cabinet.
Zeug [tsɔyk], *n.* (**—(e)s**, *no pl.*) stuff, material; implements, kit, utensils; (*coll.*) things.
Zeuge ['tsɔygə], *m.* (**—n**, *pl.* **—n**) witness; *zum —n aufrufen*, call to witness.
zeugen ['tsɔygən], *v.a.* beget, generate, engender. — *v.n.* give evidence.
Zeugenaussage ['tsɔygənausza:gə], *f.* (—, *pl.* **—n**) evidence, deposition.
Zeugenbeweis ['tsɔygənbəvaɪs], *m.* (**—es**, *pl.* **—e**) evidence, proof.
Zeugeneid ['tsɔygənaɪt], *m.* (**—s**, *pl.* **—e**) oath of a witness.
Zeughaus ['tsɔykhaus], *n.* (**—es**, *pl.* **¨er**) (*obs.*) arsenal.
Zeugin ['tsɔygɪn], *f.* (—, *pl.* **—innen**) female witness.

Zeugnis ['tsɔyknɪs], *n.* (—**ses**, *pl.* —**se**) (*Law.*) deposition; testimonial, certificate, reference; character; school report; — *ablegen*, give evidence, bear witness; *einem ein gutes — ausstellen*, give s.o. a good reference.
Zeugung ['tsɔyguŋ], *f.* (—, *pl.* —**en**) procreation, generation.
Zeugungskraft ['tsɔyguŋskraft], *f.* (—, *no pl.*) generative power.
Zeugungstrieb ['tsɔyguŋstri:p], *m.* (—**s**, *no pl.*) procreative instinct.
Zichorie [tsɪ'ço:rjə], *f.* (—, *pl.* —**n**) chicory.
Zicke ['tsɪkə], *f.* (—, *pl.* —**n**) *dial.* for **Ziege**.
Ziege ['tsi:gə], *f.* (—, *pl.* —**n**) goat.
Ziegel ['tsi:gəl], *m.* (—**s**, *pl.* —) (*roof*) tile; (*wall*) brick.
Ziegelbrenner ['tsi:gəlbrɛnər], *m.* (—**s**, *pl.* —) tile-maker, tiler; brickmaker.
Ziegelbrennerei [tsi:gəlbrɛnə'raɪ], *f.* (—, *pl.* —**en**) tile-kiln; brickyard.
Ziegeldach ['tsi:gəldax], *n.* (—**s**, *pl.* ⸚**er**) tiled roof.
Ziegeldecker ['tsi:gəldɛkər], *m.* (—**s**, *pl.* —) tiler.
Ziegelei [tsi:gə'laɪ], *f.* (—, *pl.* —**en**) brickyard, brickworks.
Ziegelerde ['tsi:gəle:rdə], *f.* (—, *no pl.*) brick-clay.
Ziegenbart ['tsi:gənba:rt], *m.* (—**s**, *pl.* ⸚**e**) goat's beard; (*human*) goatee.
Ziegenleder ['tsi:gənle:dər], *n.* (—**s**, *no pl.*) kid (leather).
Ziegenpeter ['tsi:gənpe:tər], *m.* (—**s**, *no pl.*) (*Med.*) mumps.
ziehen ['tsi:ən], *v.a. irr.* draw, pull, drag; pull out; cultivate; breed; (*game*) move. — *v.n.* draw, be an attraction; (*aux.* sein) go, move. — *v.r. sich* —, extend.
Ziehkind ['tsi:kɪnt], *n.* (—**s**, *pl.* —**er**) foster-child.
Ziehmutter ['tsi:mutər], *f.* (—, *pl.* ⸚) foster-mother.
Ziehung ['tsi:uŋ], *f.* (—, *pl.* —**en**) draw (in a lottery).
Ziehvater ['tsi:fa:tər], *m.* (—**s**, *pl.* ⸚) foster-father.
Ziel [tsi:l], *n.* (—**s**, *pl.* —**e**) goal, aim, purpose, intention, end; butt, target; (*Mil.*) objective; (*sports*) winning-post.
zielbewußt ['tsi:lbəvust], *adj.* purposeful; systematic.
zielen ['tsi:lən], *v.n.* aim (at), take aim (at).
Ziellosigkeit ['tsi:llo:zɪçkaɪt], *f.* (—, *no pl.*) aimlessness.
Zielscheibe ['tsi:lʃaɪbə], *f.* (—, *pl.* —**en**) target, butt.
ziemen ['tsi:mən], *v.r. sich* —, become s.o., behove s.o., be proper for, befit.
Ziemer ['tsi:mər], *n.* & *m.* (—**s**, *pl.* —) whip.
ziemlich ['tsi:mlɪç], *adj.* moderate, tolerable, middling, fairly considerable, fair. — *adv.* rather, fairly.
Zier [tsi:r], *f.* (—, *pl.* —**den**) ornament.
Zieraffe ['tsi:rafə], *m.* (—**n**, *pl.* —**n**) fop, affected person.
Zierat ['tsi:ra:t], *m.* (—**s**, *no pl.*) ornament, finery.
Zierde ['tsi:rdə], *f.* (—, *pl.* —**n**) decoration, embellishment; (*fig.*) credit, pride.
Ziererei [tsi:rə'raɪ], *f.* (—, *pl.* —**en**) affectation.
Ziergarten ['tsi:rgartən], *m.* (—**s**, *pl.* ⸚) flower-garden, ornamental garden.
zierlich ['tsi:rlɪç], *adj.* dainty, graceful, pretty.
Zierpflanze ['tsi:rpflantsə], *f.* (—, *pl.* —**n**) ornamental plant.
Zierpuppe ['tsi:rpupə], *f.* (—, *pl.* —**n**) overdressed woman.
Ziffer ['tsɪfər], *f.* (—, *pl.* —**n**) figure, numeral.
Zifferblatt ['tsɪfərblat], *n.* (—**s**, *pl.* ⸚**er**) dial, face.
ziffernmäßig ['tsɪfərnme:sɪç], *adj.* statistical.
Ziffernschrift ['tsɪfərnʃrɪft], *f.* (—, *pl.* —**en**) code.
Zigarette [tsiga'rɛtə], *f.* (—, *pl.* —**n**) cigarette.
Zigarettenetui [tsiga'rɛtənɛtvi:], *n.* (—**s**, *pl.* —**s**) cigarette-case.
Zigarettenspitze [tsiga'rɛtənʃpɪtsə], *f.* (—, *pl.* —**n**) cigarette-holder.
Zigarettenstummel [tsiga'rɛtənʃtuməl], *m.* (—**s**, *pl.* —) cigarette-end.
Zigarre [tsi'garə], *f.* (—, *pl.* —**n**) cigar.
Zigarrenkiste [tsi'garənkɪstə], *f.* (—, *pl.* —**n**) cigar-box.
Zigarrenstummel [tsi'garənʃtuməl], *m.* (—**s**, *pl.* —) cigar-end.
Zigeuner [tsi'gɔynər], *m.* (—**s**, *pl.* —) gipsy.
Zikade [tsi'ka:də], *f.* (—, *pl.* —**n**) (*Ent.*) grasshopper.
Zimmer ['tsɪmər], *n.* (—**s**, *pl.* —) room.
Zimmermädchen ['tsɪmərmɛ:tçən], *n.* (—**s**, *pl.* —) chambermaid.
Zimmermann ['tsɪmərman], *m.* (—**s**, *pl.* **Zimmerleute**) carpenter, joiner.
zimmern ['tsɪmərn], *v.a.* carpenter, construct, build.
Zimmernachweis ['tsɪmərna:xvaɪs], *m.* (—**es**, *pl.* —**e**) accommodation bureau.
Zimmerreihe ['tsɪmərraɪə], *f.* (—, *pl.* —**n**) suite of rooms.
Zimmervermieter ['tsɪmərfɛrmi:tər], *m.* (—**s**, *pl.* —) landlord.
zimperlich ['tsɪmpərlɪç], *adj.* simpering; prim; finicky, hypersensitive.
Zimt [tsɪmt], *m.* (—(**e**)**s**, *no pl.*) cinnamon.
Zink [tsɪŋk], *n.* (—**s**, *no pl.*) zinc.
Zinke ['tsɪŋkə], *f.* (—, *pl.* —**n**) prong, tine.
Zinn [tsɪn], *n.* (—**s**, *no pl.*) tin; pewter.
Zinnblech ['tsɪnblɛç], *n.* (—**s**, *no pl.*) tin-plate.
Zinne ['tsɪnə], *f.* (—, *pl.* —**n**) battlement, pinnacle.

zinnern ['tsɪnern], *adj.* made of pewter, of tin.
Zinnober [tsɪn'o:bər], *m.* (**—s**, *no pl.*) cinnabar; (*coll.*) fuss.
Zinnsäure ['tsɪnzɔyrə], *f.* (**—**, *no pl.*) stannic acid.
Zins [tsɪns], *m.* (**—es**, *pl.* **—en**) duty, tax; rent; (*pl.*) interest.
zinsbar ['tsinsba:r], *adj.* tributary; — *anlegen*, invest at interest; — *machen*, force to pay a tribute.
Zinsen ['tsɪnzən], *m. pl.* interest.
zinsentragend ['tsɪnzəntra:gənt], *adj.* interest-bearing.
Zinseszins ['tsɪnzəstsɪns], *m.* (**—**, *no pl.*) compound interest.
Zinsfuß ['tsɪnsfu:s], *m.* (**—es**, *pl.* **¨e**) rate of interest.
zinspflichtig ['tsɪnspflɪçtɪç], *adj.* subject to tax.
Zinsrechnung ['tsɪnsrɛçnuŋ], *f.* (**—**, *pl.* **—en**) interest account, calculation of interest.
Zinsschein ['tsɪnsʃaɪn], *m.* (**—s**, *pl.* **—e**) coupon, dividend warrant.
Zipfel ['tsɪpfəl], *m.* (**—s**, *pl.* **—**) tassel, edge, point, tip.
Zipperlein ['tsɪpərlaɪn], *n.* (**—s**, *no pl.*) (*coll.*) gout.
zirka ['tsɪrka], *adv.* circa, about, approximately.
Zirkel ['tsɪrkəl], *m.* (**—s**, *pl.* **—**) circle; (*Maths.*) pair of compasses; gathering.
zirkulieren [tsɪrku'li:rən], *v.n.* circulate; — *lassen*, put in circulation.
Zirkus ['tsɪrkus], *m.* (**—**, *pl.* **—se**) circus.
zirpen ['tsɪrpən], *v.n.* chirp.
zischeln ['tsɪʃəln], *v.n.* whisper.
zischen ['tsɪʃən], *v.n.* hiss; sizzle.
Zischlaut ['tsɪʃlaut], *m.* (**—s**, *pl.* **—e**) (*Phon.*) sibilant.
Zisterne [tsɪs'tɛrnə], *f.* (**—**, *pl.* **—n**) cistern.
Zisterzienser [tsɪstɛr'tsjɛnzər], *m.* (**—s**, *pl.* **—**) Cistercian (monk).
Zitadelle [tsɪta'dɛlə], *f.* (**—**, *pl.* **—n**) citadel.
Zitat [tsi'ta:t], *n.* (**—(e)s**, *pl.* **—e**) quotation, reference; *falsches* —, misquotation.
Zither ['tsɪtər], *f.* (**—**, *pl.* **—n**) zither.
zitieren [tsi'ti:rən], *v.a.* cite, quote; *falsch* —, misquote.
Zitronat [tsitro'na:t], *n.* (**—s**, *no pl.*) candied lemon peel.
Zitrone [tsi'tro:nə], *f.* (**—**, *pl.* **—n**) lemon.
Zitronenlimonade [tsi'tro:nənlimona:də], *f.* (**—**, *pl.* **—n**) lemonade, lemon drink.
Zitronensaft [tsi'tro:nənzaft], *m.* (**—s**, *pl.* **¨e**) lemon-juice.
Zitronensäure [tsi'tro:nənzɔyrə], *f.* (**—**, *no pl.*) citric acid.
Zitronenschale [tsi'tro:nənʃa:lə], *f.* (**—**, *pl.* **—n**) lemon-peel.
zitterig ['tsɪtərɪç], *adj.* shaky, shivery.
zittern ['tsɪtərn], *v.n.* tremble, shiver, quake.
Zitterpappel ['tsɪtərpapəl], *f.* (**—**, *pl.* **—n**) (*Bot.*) aspen-tree.
Zivil [tsi'vi:l], *n.* (**—s**, *no pl.*) civilians, *in* —, in plain clothes; (*coll.*) in civvies *or* mufti.
Zivilbeamte [tsi'vi:lbəamtə], *m.* (**—n**, *pl.* **—n**) civil servant.
Zivildienst [tsi'vi:ldi:nst], *m.* (**—es**, *no pl.*) civil service.
Zivilehe [tsi'vi:le:ə], *f.* (**—**, *pl.* **—n**) civil marriage.
Zivilgesetzbuch [tsi'vi:lgəzɛtsbu:x], *n.* (**—s**, *pl.* **¨er**) code of civil law.
Zivilingenieur [tsi'vi:lɪnʒenjø:r], *m.* (**—s**, *pl.* **—e**) civil engineer.
Zivilisation [tsiviliza'tsjo:n], *f.* (**—**, *pl.* **—en**) civilisation.
zivilisatorisch [tsiviliza'to:rɪʃ], *adj.* civilising.
zivilisieren [tsivili'zi:rən], *v.a.* civilise.
Zivilist [tsivi'lɪst], *m.* (**—en**, *pl.* **—en**) civilian.
Zivilkleidung [tsi'vi:lklaɪduŋ], *f.* (**—**, *no pl.*) civilian dress, plain clothes.
Zobel ['tso:bəl], *m.* (**—s**, *pl.* **—**) sable.
Zobelpelz ['tso:bəlpɛlts], *m.* (**—es**, *pl.* **—e**) sable fur; sable-coat.
Zofe ['tso:fə], *f.* (**—**, *pl.* **—n**) lady's maid.
zögern ['tsø:gərn], *v.n.* hesitate, tarry, delay.
Zögerung ['tsø:gəruŋ], *f.* (**—**, *pl.* **—en**) hesitation, delay.
Zögling ['tsø:klɪŋ], *m.* (**—s**, *pl.* **—e**) pupil, charge.
Zölibat [tsø:li'ba:t], *m.* & *n.* (**—s**, *no pl.*) celibacy.
Zoll (1) [tsɔl], *m.* (**—s**, *no pl.*) inch.
Zoll (2) [tsɔl], *m.* (**—s**, *pl.* **¨e**) customs duty; (*bridge*) toll.
Zollabfertigung ['tsɔlapfɛrtɪguŋ], *f.* (**—**, *no pl.*) customs clearance.
Zollamt ['tsɔlamt], *n.* (**—s**, *pl.* **¨er**) custom house.
Zollaufschlag ['tsɔlaufʃla:k], *m.* (**—s**, *pl.* **¨e**) additional duty.
Zollbeamte ['tsɔlbəamtə], *m.* (**—n**, *pl.* **—n**) customs officer.
zollbreit ['tsɔlbraɪt], *adj.* one inch wide.
zollen ['tsɔlən], *v.a. Ehrfurcht* —, pay o.'s respects; *Beifall* —, applaud; *Dank* —, show gratitude.
zollfrei ['tsɔlfraɪ], *adj.* duty-free, exempt from duty.
Zöllner ['tsœlnər], *m.* (**—s**, *pl.* **—**) tax-gatherer.
zollpflichtig ['tsɔlpflɪçtɪç], *adj.* liable to duty, dutiable.
Zollsatz ['tsɔlzats], *m.* (**—es**, *pl.* **¨e**) customs tariff.
Zollverein ['tsɔlfəraɪn], *m.* (**—s**, *no pl.*) customs union.
Zollverschluß ['tsɔlfɛrʃlus], *m.* (**—sses**, *pl.* **¨sse**) bond.
Zone ['tso:nə], *f.* (**—**, *pl.* **—n**) zone.
Zoologe [tso:o'lo:gə], *m.* (**—n**, *pl.* **—n**) zoologist.
Zoologie [tso:olo'gi:], *f.* (**—**, *no pl.*) zoology.

zoologisch [tso:o'lo:gɪʃ], *adj.* zoological; —*er Garten*, zoological gardens, zoo.
Zopf [tsɔpf], *m.* (—(e)s, *pl.* ⸚e) plait, pigtail; (*coll.*) (old-fashioned) pedantry.
Zorn [tsɔrn], *m.* (—(e)s, *no pl.*) wrath, anger, indignation; *seinen — auslassen*, vent o.'s anger; *in — geraten*, get angry.
zornglühend ['tsɔrngly:ənt], *adj.* boiling with rage.
zornig ['tsɔrnɪç], *adj.* angry, wrathful, irate; — *werden*, get angry.
Zote ['tso:tə], *f.* (—, *pl.* —n) smutty story, ribaldry, bawdiness.
zotig ['tso:tɪç], *adj.* loose, ribald, smutty.
zottig ['tsɔtɪç], *adj.* shaggy.
zu [tsu:], *prep.* (*Dat.*) to, towards; in addition to; at, in, on; for; — *Anfang*, in the beginning; — *Fuß*, on foot; — *Hause*, at home; — *Wasser*, at sea, by sea; — *deinem Nutzen*, for your benefit. — *adv.* & *prefix*, to, towards; closed; too; — *sehr*, too; — *viel*, too much.
Zubehör ['tsu:bəhø:r], *n.* (—s, *no pl.*) accessory, appurtenance.
zubekommen ['tsu:bəkɔmən], *v.a. irr.* get in addition.
Zuber ['tsu:bər], *m.* (—s, *pl.* —) tub.
zubereiten ['tsu:bəraɪtən], *v.a.* prepare.
Zubereitung ['tsu:bəraɪtuŋ], *f.* (—, *no pl.*) preparation.
zubilligen ['tsu:bɪlɪgən], *v.a.* allow, grant.
zubleiben ['tsu:blaɪbən], *v.n. irr.* (*aux.* sein) remain shut.
zubringen ['tsu:brɪŋən], *v.a. irr. die Zeit* —, spend the time.
Zubringerdienst ['tsu:brɪŋərdi:nst], *m.* (—es, *pl.* —) shuttle-service, tender-service.
Zubuße ['tsu:bu:sə], *f.* (—, *pl.* —n) (additional) contribution.
Zucht [tsuxt], *f.* (—, *no pl.*) race, breed; discipline; breeding, rearing; education, discipline; (good) manners; *in — halten*, keep in hand.
züchten ['tsyçtən], *v.a.* cultivate; rear, breed; grow.
Züchter ['tsyçtər], *m.* (—s, *pl.* —) (*plants*) nurseryman; (*animals*) breeder.
Zuchthaus ['tsuxthaus], *n.* (—es, *pl.* ⸚er) penitentiary, convict prison.
Zuchthäusler ['tsuxthɔyslər], *m.* (—s, *pl.* —) convict.
Zuchthengst ['tsuxthɛŋst], *m.* (—es, *pl.* —e) stallion.
züchtig ['tsyçtɪç], *adj.* modest, chaste.
züchtigen ['tsyçtɪgən], *v.a.* chastise, lash.
Züchtigkeit ['tsyçtɪçkaɪt], *f.* (—, *no pl.*) modesty, chastity.
Züchtigung ['tsyçtɪguŋ], *f.* (—, *pl.* —en) chastisement; *körperliche* —, corporal punishment.
Zuchtlosigkeit ['tsuxtlo:zɪçkaɪt], *f.* (—, *no pl.*) want of discipline.
Zuchtmeister ['tsuxtmaɪstər], *m.* (—s, *pl.* —) disciplinarian, taskmaster.
Zuchtochse ['tsuxtɔksə], *m.* (—n, *pl.* —n) bull.
Zuchtstute ['tsuxtʃtu:tə], *f.* (—, *pl.* —n) brood-mare.
Züchtung ['tsyçtuŋ], *f.* (—, *pl.* —en) (*plants*) cultivation; (*animals*) rearing, breeding.
Zuchtvieh ['tsuxtfi:], *n.* (—s, *no pl.*) breeding stock.
Zuchtwahl ['tsuxtva:l], *f.* (—, *no pl.*) (*breeding*) selection.
zucken ['tsukən], *v.n.* quiver, twitch; wince; start, jerk.
Zucken ['tsukən], *n.* (—s, *no pl.*) palpitation, convulsion, twitch, tic.
Zucker ['tsukər], *m.* (—s, *no pl.*) sugar.
Zuckerbäcker ['tsukərbɛkər], *m.* (—s, *pl.* —) confectioner.
Zuckerguß ['tsukərgus], *m.* (—es, *no pl.*) (sugar-)icing.
Zuckerkandis ['tsukərkandɪs], *m.* (—, *no pl.*) sugar-candy.
zuckerkrank ['tsukərkraŋk], *adj.* (*Med.*) diabetic.
Zuckerkrankheit ['tsukərkraŋkhaɪt], *f.* (—, *no pl.*) (*Med.*) diabetes.
zuckern ['tsukərn], *v.a.* sugar.
Zuckerpflanzung ['tsukərpflantsuŋ], *f.* (—, *pl.* —en) sugar-plantation.
Zuckerraffinerie ['tsukərrafinəri:], *f.* (—, *pl.* —n) sugar-refinery.
Zuckerrohr ['tsukərro:r], *n.* (—s, *no pl.*) sugar-cane.
Zuckerrübe ['tsukərry:bə], *f.* (—, *pl.* —n) sugar-beet.
Zuckerwerk ['tsukərvɛrk], *n.* (—s, *no pl.*) confectionery.
Zuckerzange ['tsukərtsaŋə], *f.* (—, *pl.* —n) sugar-tongs.
Zuckung ['tsukuŋ], *f.* (—, *pl.* —en) convulsion, spasm.
zudecken ['tsu:dɛkən], *v.a.* cover up.
zudem [tsu'de:m], *adv.* besides, moreover.
Zudrang ['tsu:draŋ], *m.* (—s, *no pl.*) crowd(ing); rush (on), run (on).
zudrehen ['tsu:dre:ən], *v.a.* turn off.
zudringlich ['tsu:drɪŋlɪç], *adj.* importunate; intruding.
zudrücken ['tsu:drykən], *v.a.* close (by pressing), shut.
zueignen ['tsu:aɪgnən], *v.a.* dedicate.
zuerkennen ['tsu:ɛrkɛnən], *v.a. irr.* award, adjudicate.
zuerst [tsu'e:rst], *adv.* at first, first, in the first instance.
Zufahrt ['tsu:fa:rt], *f.* (—, *no pl.*) approach, drive.
Zufall ['tsu:fal], *m.* (—s, *pl.* ⸚e) chance, coincidence; *durch* —, by chance.
zufallen ['tsu:falən], *v.n. irr.* (*aux.* sein) close, fall shut; *einem* —, devolve upon s.o., fall to s.o.'s lot.
zufällig ['tsu:fɛlɪç], *adj.* accidental, casual, fortuitous. — *adv.* by chance.
Zuflucht ['tsu:fluxt], *f.* (—, *no pl.*) refuge, shelter, haven, recourse.

Zufluchtsort ['tsu:fluxtsɔrt], *m.* (—(e)s, *pl.* —e) asylum, shelter, place of refuge.
Zufluß ['tsu:flus], *m.* (—sses, *pl.* ⸚sse) supply; influx.
zuflüstern ['tsu:flystərn], *v.a. einem etwas* —, whisper s.th. to s.o.
zufolge [tsu'fɔlgə], *prep.* (*Genit.*, *Dat.*) in consequence of, owing to, due to, on account of.
zufrieden [tsu'fri:dən], *adj.* content, contented, satisfied; — *lassen*, leave alone.
zufriedenstellen [tsu'fri:dənʃtεlən], *v.a.* satisfy.
zufügen ['tsu:fy:gən], *v.a.* add (to); inflict.
Zufuhr ['tsu:fu:r], *f.* (—, *pl.* —en) (*goods*) supplies.
Zug [tsu:k], *m.* (—(e)s, *pl.* ⸚e) drawing, pull, tug; draught; march, procession; (*Railw.*) train; (*face*) feature; (*chess*) move; (*character*) trait; (*pen*) stroke; (*birds*) flight; migration; (*mountains*) range.
Zugabe ['tsu:ga:bə], *f.* (—, *pl.* —n) addition, make-weight, extra; (*concert*) encore; *als* —, into the bargain.
Zugang ['tsu:gaŋ], *m.* (—s, *pl.* ⸚e) approach, entry, entrance, admittance, access.
zugänglich ['tsu:gεŋlɪç], *adj.* accessible, available; (*person*) affable.
Zugbrücke ['tsu:kbrykə], *f.* (—, *pl.* —n) drawbridge.
zugeben ['tsu:ge:bən], *v.a. irr.* give in addition; concede, admit.
zugegen [tsu'ge:gən], *adv.* present.
zugehen ['tsu:ge:ən], *v.n. irr.* (*aux.* sein) (*door*) shut (of itself), close; happen; *auf einen* —, walk towards s.o.; *so geht es im Leben zu*, such is life; *das geht nicht mit rechten Dingen zu*, there is something uncanny about it.
zugehörig ['tsu:gəhø:rɪç], *adj.* belonging, appertaining.
zugeknöpft ['tsu:gəknœpft], *adj.* reserved, taciturn.
Zügel ['tsy:gəl], *m.* (—s, *pl.* —) rein, bridle.
zügeln ['tsy:gəln], *v.a.* bridle, curb, check.
zugesellen ['tsu:gəzεlən], *v.r. sich* —, associate with, join.
Zugeständnis ['tsu:gəʃtεntnɪs], *n.* (—sses, *pl.* —sse) admission; concession.
zugestehen ['tsu:gəʃte:ən], *v.a. irr.* admit; concede; *einem etwas* —, allow s.o. s.th.
zugetan ['tsu:gəta:n], *adj.* attached, devoted.
Zugführer ['tsu:kfy:rər], *m.* (—s, *pl.* —) (*Railw.*) guard; (*Mil.*) platoon commander.
zugießen ['tsu:gi:sən], *v.a. irr.* fill up, pour on.
zugig ['tsu:gɪç], *adj.* windy, draughty.
Zugkraft ['tsu:kkraft], *f.* (—, *no pl.*) tractive power, magnetic attraction; (*fig.*) pull, attraction; publicity value.
zugleich [tsu'glaɪç], *adv.* at the same time; — *mit*, together with.
Zugluft ['tsu:kluft], *f.* (—, *no pl.*) draught (of air).
zugreifen ['tsu:graɪfən], *v.n. irr.* grab; lend a hand; (*at table*) help o.s.
Zugrolle ['tsu:krɔlə], *f.* (—, *pl.* —n) pulley.
zugrunde [tsu'grundə], *adv.* — *gehen*, perish, go to ruin, go to the dogs; — *legen*, base upon.
Zugstück ['tsu:kʃtyk], *n.* (—s, *pl.* —e) (*Theat.*) popular show; (*coll.*) success, hit.
zugucken ['tsu:gukən], *v.n.* look on, watch.
zugunsten [tsu'gunstən], *prep.* (*Genit.*) for the benefit of.
zugute [tsu'gu:tə], *adv.* — *halten*, make allowances.
Zugvogel ['tsu:kfo:gəl], *m.* (—s, *pl.* ⸚) bird of passage.
zuhalten ['tsu:haltən], *v.a. irr.* keep closed.
Zuhälter ['tsu:hεltər], *m.* (—s, *pl.* —) souteneur; pimp.
Zuhilfenahme [tsu'hɪlfəna:mə], *f.* (—, *no pl.*) *unter* —, with the help of, by means of.
zuhören ['tsu:hø:rən], *v.n.* listen to, attend to.
Zuhörerschaft ['tsu:hø:rərʃaft], *f.* (—, *pl.* —en) audience.
zujubeln ['tsu:ju:bəln], *v.n. einem* —, acclaim s.o., cheer s.o.
zukehren ['tsu:ke:rən], *v.a. einem den Rücken* —, turn o.'s back on s.o.
zuknöpfen ['tsu:knœpfən], *v.a.* button (up).
zukommen ['tsu:kɔmən], *v.n. irr.* (*aux.* sein) *auf einen* —, advance towards s.o.; *einem* —, be due to s.o.; become s.o.; reach s.o.
Zukost ['tsu:kɔst], *f.* (—, *no pl.*) (*food*) trimmings, extras.
Zukunft ['tsu:kunft], *f.* (—, *no pl.*) future; prospects.
zukünftig ['tsu:kynftɪç], *adj.* future, prospective.
Zukunftsmusik ['tsu:kunftsmuzi:k], *f.* (—, *no pl.*) daydreams, pipe-dreams.
zulächeln ['tsu:lεçəln], *v.a. einem* —, smile at s.o.
Zulage ['tsu:la:gə], *f.* (—, *pl.* —n) addition; increase of salary, rise; (*Am.*) raise.
zulangen ['tsu:laŋən], *v.n.* be sufficient; (*at table*) help o.s.
zulänglich ['tsu:lεŋlɪç], *adj.* sufficient, adequate.
zulassen ['tsu:lasən], *v.a. irr.* leave unopened; allow; admit; permit.
zulässig ['tsu:lεsɪç], *adj.* admissible; *das ist nicht* —, that is not allowed.
Zulassung ['tsu:lasuŋ], *f.* (—, *pl.* —en) admission.
Zulauf ['tsu:lauf], *m.* (—s, *no pl.*) run (of customers); crowd, throng.

zulaufen ['tsu:laufən], *v.n. irr.* (*aux.* sein) *auf einen* —, run towards s.o.; *spitz* —, taper, come to a point.
zulegen ['tsu:le:gən], *v.a.* add; increase; *sich etwas* —, make o.s. a present of s.th.; get s.th.
zuletzt [tsu'lɛtst], *adv.* last, at last, lastly, finally, eventually, in the end.
zuliebe [tsu'li:bə], *adv. einem etwas — tun*, oblige s.o.; do s.th. for s.o.'s sake.
zum = **zu dem.**
zumachen ['tsu:maxən], *v.a.* shut, close.
zumal [tsu'ma:l], *adv.* especially, particularly. — *conj.* especially since.
zumeist [tsu'maɪst], *adv.* mostly, for the most part.
zumute [tsu'mu:tə], *adv. mir ist nicht gut* —, I don't feel well.
zumuten ['tsu:mu:tən], *v.a. einem etwas* —, expect *or* demand s.th. of s.o.
Zumutung ['tsu:mu:tuŋ], *f.* (—, *pl.* —**en**) unreasonable demand.
zunächst [tsu'nɛ:çst], *adv.* first, above all.
Zunahme ['tsu:na:mə], *f.* (—, *pl.* —**n**) increase.
Zuname ['tsu:na:mə], *m.* (—**ns**, *pl.* —**n**) surname, family name.
zünden ['tsyndən], *v.n.* catch fire, ignite.
Zunder ['tsundər], *m.* (—**s**, *no pl.*) tinder.
Zünder ['tsyndər], *m.* (—**s**, *pl.* —) lighter, detonator, fuse.
Zündholz ['tsynthɔlts], *n.* (—**es**, *pl.* ¨**er**) match.
Zündkerze ['tsyntkɛrtsə], *f.* (—, *pl.* —**n**) (*Motor.*) sparking-plug.
Zündstoff ['tsyntʃtɔf], *m.* (—**s**, *pl.* —**e**) fuel.
Zündung ['tsynduŋ], *f.* (—, *pl.* —**en**) ignition; detonation.
zunehmen ['tsu:ne:mən], *v.n. irr.* increase, put on weight; (*moon*) wax.
zuneigen ['tsu:naɪgən], *v.r. sich* —, incline towards.
Zuneigung ['tsu:naɪguŋ], *f.* (—, *pl.* —**en**) affection, inclination.
Zunft [tsunft], *f.* (—, *pl.* ¨**e**) company, guild, corporation; (*fig.*) brotherhood.
Zunftgenosse ['tsunftgənɔsə], *m.* (—**n**, *pl.* —**n**) member of a guild.
zünftig ['tsynftɪç], *adj.* professional; proper.
zunftmäßig ['tsunftmɛ:sɪç], *adj.* professional; competent.
Zunge ['tsuŋə], *f.* (—, *pl.* —**n**) tongue; (*buckle*) catch; (*fig.*) language; (*fish*) sole.
züngeln ['tsyŋəln], *v.n.* (*flame*) shoot out, lick.
Zungenband ['tsuŋənbant], *n.* (—**s**, *pl.* ¨**er**) ligament of the tongue.
zungenfertig ['tsuŋənfɛrtɪç], *adj.* voluble, glib.
Zungenlaut ['tsuŋənlaut], *m.* (—**s**, *pl.* —**e**) (*Phon.*) lingual sound.
Zungenspitze ['tsuŋənʃpɪtsə], *f.* (—, *pl.* —**n**) tip of the tongue.
zunichte [tsu'nɪçtə], *adv.* — *machen*, ruin, undo, destroy; — *werden*, come to nothing.
zupfen ['tsupfən], *v.a.* pick, pluck.
zurechnungsfähig ['tsu:rɛçnuŋsfɛ:ɪç], *adj.* accountable, of sane mind, compos mentis.
zurecht [tsu'rɛçt], *adv.* aright, right(ly), in order.
zurechtfinden [tsu'rɛçtfɪndən], *v.r. irr. sich* —, find o.'s way about.
zurechtkommen [tsu'rɛçtkɔmən], *v.n. irr.* (*aux.* sein) arrive in (good) time; *mit einem gut* —, get on well with s.o.
zurechtlegen [tsu'rɛçtle:gən], *v.a.* put in order, get ready.
zurechtmachen [tsu'rɛçtmaxən], *v.a.* get s.th. ready, prepare s.th. — *v.r. sich* —, prepare o.s.; (*women*) make up; (*coll.*) put on o.'s face.
zurechtweisen [tsu'rɛçtvaɪzən], *v.a. irr.* reprove (s.o.), set (s.o.) right; direct.
Zurechtweisung [tsu'rɛçtvaɪzuŋ], *f.* (—, *pl.* —**en**) reprimand.
Zureden ['tsu:re:dən], *n.* (—**s**, *no pl.*) encouragement; entreaties.
zureden ['tsu:re:dən], *v.n.* encourage (s.o.), persuade (s.o.)
zureichen ['tsu:raɪçən], *v.a.* reach, hand. — *v.n.* be sufficient, be enough, suffice.
zurichten ['tsu:rɪçtən], *v.a. etwas* (*einen*) *übel* —, maltreat s.th. (s.o.).
zürnen ['tsyrnən], *v.n.* be angry (with).
zurück [tsu'ryk], *adv.* back; behind; backwards; — *excl.* stand back!
zurückbegeben [tsu'rykbəge:bən], *v.r. irr. sich* —, go back, return.
zurückbehalten [tsu'rykbəhaltən], *v.a. irr.* retain, keep back.
zurückbekommen [tsu'rykbəkɔmən], *v.a. irr.* get back, recover (s.th.).
zurückberufen [tsu'rykbəru:fən], *v.a. irr.* recall.
zurückfordern [tsu'rykfɔrdərn], *v.a.* demand back, demand the return of.
zurückführen [tsu'rykfy:rən], *v.a.* lead back; *auf etwas* —, attribute to; trace back to.
zurückgeblieben [tsu'rykgəbli:bən], *adj.* retarded, mentally deficient, backward.
zurückgezogen [tsu'rykgətso:gən], *adj.* secluded, retired.
zurückhalten [tsu'rykhaltən], *v.a. irr.* keep back, retain.
zurückhaltend [tsu'rykhaltənt], *adj.* reserved.
zurückkehren [tsu'rykke:rən], *v.n.* (*aux.* sein) return.
zurückkommen [tsu'rykkɔmən], *v.n. irr.* (*aux.* sein) come back.
zurücklassen [tsu'ryklasən], *v.a. irr.* leave behind, abandon.

zurücklegen [tsu'rykle:gən], *v.a.* lay aside, put by; *eine Strecke* —, cover a distance. — *v.r. sich* —, lean back; *zurückgelegter Gewinn*, undistributed profits.
zurückmüssen [tsu'rykmysən], *v.n. irr.* be obliged to return.
zurücknehmen [tsu'rykne:mən], *v.a. irr.* take back.
zurückschrecken [tsu'rykʃrɛkən], *v.a.* frighten away. — *v.n. irr.* (*aux.* sein) recoil (from).
zurücksehnen [tsu'rykze:nən], *v.r. sich* —, long to return, wish o.s. back.
zurücksetzen [tsu'rykzɛtsən], *v.a.* put back; slight; discriminate against; neglect.
Zurücksetzung [tsu'rykzɛtsuŋ], *f.* (—, *pl.* —**en**) slight, rebuff.
zurückstrahlen [tsu'rykʃtra:lən], *v.a.* reflect.
zurücktreten [tsu'ryktre:tən], *v.n. irr.* (*aux.* sein) stand back, withdraw; resign.
zurückverlangen [tsu'rykfɛrlaŋən], *v.a.* demand back, request the return of.
zurückversetzen [tsu'rykfɛrzɛtsən], *v.a.* (*Sch.*) put in a lower form. — *v.r. sich* —, turn o.'s thoughts back (to), hark back.
zurückweichen [tsu'rykvaɪçən], *v.n. irr.* (*aux.* sein) withdraw, retreat.
zurückweisen [tsu'rykvaɪzən], *v.a. irr.* refuse, reject, repulse.
zurückwollen [tsu'rykvɔlən], *v.n.* wish to return.
zurückziehen [tsu'ryktsi:ən], *v.a. irr.* draw back; (*fig.*) withdraw, retract, countermand. — *v.r. sich* —, retire, withdraw.
Zuruf ['tsu:ru:f], *m.* (—**s**, *pl.* —**e**) call, acclaim, acclamation.
Zusage ['tsu:za:gə], *f.* (—, *pl.* —**n**) promise; acceptance.
zusagen ['tsu:za:gən], *v.a.* promise; *es sagt mir zu*, I like it. — *v.n.* accept.
zusagend ['tsu:za:gənt], *adj.* affirmative; agreeable.
zusammen [tsu'zamən], *adv.* together, jointly.
zusammenbeißen [tsu'zamənbaɪsən], *v.a. irr. die Zähne* —, set o.'s teeth.
zusammenbetteln [tsu'zamənbɛtəln], *v.a. sich etwas* —, collect (by begging).
zusammenbrechen [tsu'zamənbrɛçən], *v.n. irr.* (*aux.* sein) break down, collapse.
Zusammenbruch [tsu'zamənbrux], *m.* (—**s**, *pl.* ⸚**e**) breakdown, collapse, débâcle.
zusammendrängen [tsu'zaməndrɛŋən], *v.a.* press together; (*fig.*) abridge, condense.
zusammendrücken [tsu'zaməndrykən], *v.a.* compress.
zusammenfahren [tsu'zamənfa:rən], *v.n. irr.* (*aux.* sein) collide; give a start.
zusammenfallen [tsu'zamənfalən], *v.n. irr.* (*aux.* sein) collapse.
zusammenfassen [tsu'zamənfasən], *v.a.* sum up, summarize.
Zusammenfassung [tsu'zamənfasuŋ], *f.* (—, *no pl.*) summing-up, summary.
zusammenfinden [tsu'zamənfɪndən], *v.r. irr. sich* —, discover a mutual affinity, come together.
Zusammenfluß [tsu'zamənflus], *m.* (—**sses**, *pl.* ⸚**sse**) confluence.
zusammengeben [tsu'zamənge:bən], *v.a. irr.* join in marriage.
Zusammengehörigkeit [tsu'zaməngəhø:rɪçkaɪt], *f.* (—, *no pl.*) solidarity; (*Am.*) togetherness.
zusammengesetzt [tsu'zaməngəzɛtst], *adj.* composed (of), consisting (of); complicated; (*Maths.*) composite.
zusammengewürfelt [tsu'zaməngəvyrfəlt], *adj.* motley, mixed.
Zusammenhalt [tsu'zamənhalt], *m.* (—**s**, *no pl.*) holding together; unity.
Zusammenhang [tsu'zamənhaŋ], *m.* (—**s**, *pl.* ⸚**e**) coherence; connection, context.
zusammenhängen [tsu'zamənhɛŋən], *v.n. irr.* hang together, cohere; (*fig.*) be connected (with).
Zusammenklang [tsu'zamənklaŋ], *m.* (—**s**, *pl.* ⸚**e**) unison, harmony.
Zusammenkunft [tsu'zamənkunft], *f.* (—, *pl.* ⸚**e**) meeting, convention, conference; reunion.
zusammenlaufen [tsu'zamənlaufən], *v.n. irr.* (*aux.* sein) crowd together, converge; flock together; (*milk*) curdle; (*material*) shrink.
zusammenlegen [tsu'zamənle:gən], *v.a.* put together; (*money*) collect; (*letter*) fold up.
zusammennehmen [tsu'zamənne:mən], *v.a. irr.* gather up. — *v.r. sich* —, get a firm grip on o.s., pull o.s. together.
zusammenpassen [tsu'zamənpasən], *v.n.* fit together, match; agree; be compatible.
zusammenpferchen [tsu'zamənpfɛrçən], *v.a.* pen up, crowd together in a small space.
zusammenpressen [tsu'zamənprɛsən], *v.a.* squeeze together.
zusammenraffen [tsu'zamənrafən], *v.a.* gather up hurriedly, collect. — *v.r. sich* —, pluck up courage; pull o.s. together.
zusammenrechnen [tsu'zamənrɛçnən], *v.a.* add up.
zusammenreimen [tsu'zamənraɪmən], *v.a. sich etwas* —, figure s.th. out.
zusammenrücken [tsu'zamənrykən], *v.a.* move together, draw closer. — *v.n.* move closer together, move up.
zusammenschießen [tsu'zamənʃi:sən], *v.a. irr.* shoot to pieces, shoot down; *Geld* —, club together, raise a subscription.
zusammenschlagen [tsu'zamənʃla:gən], *v.a. irr.* beat up; strike together; clap, fold.

zusammenschließen [tsu'zamənʃli:sən], *v.r. irr. sich* —, join, unite, ally o.s. (with).
zusammenschweißen [tsu'zamənʃvaɪsən], *v.a.* weld together.
Zusammensein [tsu'zamənzaɪn], *n.* (—**s**, *no pl.*) meeting, social gathering.
Zusammensetzung [tsu'zamənzɛtsuŋ], *f.* (—, *no pl.*) construction; composition.
Zusammenspiel [tsu'zamənʃpi:l], *n.* (—**s**, *no pl.*) (*Theat.*, *Mus.*) ensemble.
zusammenstellen [tsu'zamənʃtɛlən], *v.a.* compose, concoct; put together, compile.
Zusammenstellung [tsu'zamənʃtɛluŋ], *f.* (—, *pl.* —**en**) combination, compilation; juxtaposition.
zusammenstoppeln [tsu'zamənʃtɔpəln], *v.a.* string together, patch up.
Zusammenstoß [tsu'zamənʃto:s], *m.* (—**es**, *pl.* ⸚**e**) clash, conflict; collision.
zusammenstoßen [tsu'zamənʃto:sən], *v.n. irr.* (*aux.* sein) clash; crash, come into collision, collide.
zusammentragen [tsu'zaməntra:gən], *v.a. irr.* collect, compile.
zusammentreffen [tsu'zaməntrɛfən], *v.n. irr.* meet; coincide.
zusammentreten [tsu'zaməntre:tən], *v.n. irr.* (*aux.* sein) meet.
zusammentun [tsu'zaməntu:n], *v.r. irr. sich — mit*, associate with, join.
zusammenwirken [tsu'zamənvɪrkən], *v.n.* cooperate, collaborate.
zusammenwürfeln [tsu'zamənvyrfəln], *v.a.* jumble up.
zusammenzählen [tsu'zaməntsɛ:lən], *v.a.* add up.
zusammenziehen [tsu'zaməntsi:ən], *v.n. irr.* (*aux.* sein) move in together. — *v.a.* draw together, contract. — *v.r. sich* —, shrink; (*storm*) gather; *Zahlen* —, add up.
Zusammenziehung [tsu'zaməntsi:uŋ], *f.* (—, *no pl.*) contraction.
Zusatz ['tsu:zats], *m.* (—**es**, *pl.* ⸚**e**) addition, supplement, admixture; (*will*) codicil.
zuschanzen ['tsu:ʃantsən], *v.a. einem etwas* —, obtain s.th. for s.o.
zuschauen ['tsu:ʃauən], *v.n.* look on, watch.
Zuschauer ['tsu:ʃauər], *m.* (—**s**, *pl.* —) onlooker, spectator.
Zuschauerraum ['tsu:ʃauərraum], *m.* (—**s**, *pl.* ⸚**e**) (*Theat.*) auditorium.
zuschaufeln ['tsu:ʃaufəln], *v.a.* shovel in, fill up.
zuschieben ['tsu:ʃi:bən], *v.a. irr.* push towards; shut; *einem etwas* —, shove (blame) on to s.o.
zuschießen ['tsu:ʃi:sən], *v.a. irr. Geld* —, put money into (an undertaking).
Zuschlag ['tsu:ʃla:k], *m.* (—**s**, *pl.* ⸚**e**) addition; (*Railw.*) excess fare.
zuschlagen ['tsu:ʃla:gən], *v.a. irr.* add; (*door*) bang; (*auction*) knock down to (s.o.). — *v.n.* strike hard.
zuschlag(s)pflichtig ['tsu:ʃla:k(s)pflɪçtɪç], *adj.* liable to a supplementary charge.
zuschmeißen ['tsu:ʃmaɪsən], *v.a. irr.* (*door*) slam to, bang.
zuschneiden ['tsu:ʃnaɪdən], *v.a. irr.* (*pattern*) cut out; cut up.
Zuschneider ['tsu:ʃnaɪdər], *m.* (—**s**, *pl.*—) (*Tail.*) cutter.
Zuschnitt ['tsu:ʃnɪt], *m.* (—**s**, *no pl.*) (*clothing*) cut.
zuschreiben ['tsu:ʃraɪbən], *v.a. irr. einem etwas* —, impute s.th. to s.o.; attribute *or* ascribe s.th. to s.o.
Zuschrift ['tsu:ʃrɪft], *f.* (—, *pl.* —**en**) communication, letter.
Zuschuß ['tsu:ʃus], *m.* (—**sses**, *pl.* ⸚**sse**) additional money, supplementary allowance, subsidy.
zuschütten ['tsu:ʃytən], *v.a.* fill up.
Zusehen ['tsu:ze:ən], *n.* (—**s**, *no pl.*) *das — haben*, be left out in the cold.
zusehen ['tsu:ze:ən], *v.n. irr.* look on, watch; be a spectator; see to it.
zusehends ['tsu:ze:ənts], *adv.* visibly.
zusetzen ['tsu:zɛtsən], *v.a.* add to, admix; lose. — *v.n. einem* —, pester s.o.; attack s.o.
zusichern ['tsu:zɪçərn], *v.a.* promise, assure.
Zusicherung ['tsu:zɪçəruŋ], *f.* (—, *pl.* —**en**) promise, assurance.
Zuspeise ['tsuʃpaɪzə], *f.* (—, *no pl.*) (*dial.*) (*food*) trimmings; vegetables.
zusperren ['tsu:ʃpɛrən], *v.a.* shut, close, lock up.
zuspitzen ['tsu:ʃpɪtsən], *v.a.* sharpen to a point. — *v.r. sich* —, come to a climax.
zusprechen ['tsu:ʃprɛçən], *v.n. irr. dem Wein* —, drink heavily. — *v.a. Mut* —, comfort.
Zuspruch ['tsu:ʃprux], *m.* (—**s**, *pl.* ⸚**e**) exhortation; consolation.
Zustand ['tsu:ʃtant], *m.* (—**s**, *pl.* ⸚**e**) condition, state of affairs, situation.
zustande [tsu'ʃtandə], *adv. — kommen*, come off, be accomplished; — *bringen*, accomplish.
zuständig ['tsu:ʃtɛndɪç], *adj.* competent; appropriate.
Zuständigkeit ['tsu:ʃtɛndɪçkaɪt], *f.* (—, *no pl.*) competence.
zustecken ['tsu:ʃtɛkən], *v.a.* pin up; *einem etwas* —, slip s.th. into s.o.'s hand.
zustehen ['tsu:ʃte:ən], *v.n. irr.* be due to, belong to; be s.o.'s business to.
zustellen ['tsu:ʃtɛlən], *v.a.* deliver, hand over; (*Law*) serve (a writ).
Zustellung ['tsu:ʃtɛluŋ], *f.* (—, *pl.* —**en**) delivery; (*Law*) service.
zusteuern ['tsu:ʃtɔyərn], *v.a.* contribute. — *v.n.* (*aux.* sein) steer for; (*fig.*) aim at.
zustimmen ['tsu:ʃtɪmən], *v.n.* agree to.
Zustimmung ['tsu:ʃtɪmuŋ], *f.* (—, *pl.* —**en**) assent, consent, agreement.

zustopfen ['tsu:ʃtɔpfən], *v.a.* fill up, stop up, plug; darn, mend.
zustoßen ['tsu:ʃto:sən], *v.a. irr.* push to, shut.
zustürzen ['tsu:ʃtyrtsən], *v.n.* (*aux.* sein) *auf einen* —, rush at *or* towards s.o.
Zutaten ['tsu:ta:tən], *f. pl.* ingredients, garnishings.
zuteil [tsu'taɪl], *adv.* — *werden*, fall to s.o.'s share.
zutragen ['tsu:tra:gən], *v.a. irr.* report, tell. — *v.r. sich* —, happen.
Zuträger ['tsu:trɛ:gər], *m.* (—s, *pl.* —) informer, tale-bearer.
zuträglich ['tsu:trɛ:klɪç], *adj.* advantageous, wholesome.
Zutrauen ['tsu:trauən], *n.* (—s, *no pl.*) confidence.
zutrauen ['tsu:trauən], *v.a. einem etwas* —, credit s.o. with s.th.
zutraulich ['tsu:traulɪç], *adj.* trusting; familiar, intimate; tame.
zutreffen ['tsu:trɛfən], *v.n. irr.* prove correct, take place.
zutreffend ['tsu:trɛfənt], *adj.* apposite, pertinent.
Zutritt ['tsu:trɪt], *m.* (—s, *no pl.*) entry; access, admittance; — *verboten*, no admittance.
zutunlich ['tsu:tu:nlɪç], *adj.* confiding; obliging.
zuverlässig ['tsu:fɛrlɛsɪç], *adj.* reliable; authentic.
Zuversicht ['tsu:fɛrzɪçt], *f.* (—, *no pl.*) trust, confidence.
zuversichtlich ['tsu:fɛrzɪçtlɪç], *adj.* confident.
zuvor [tsu'fo:r], *adv.* before, first, formerly.
zuvorkommend [tsu'fo:rkɔmənt], *adj.* obliging, polite.
Zuwachs ['tsu:vaks], *m.* (—es, *no pl.*) increase, accretion, growth.
zuwachsen ['tsu:vaksən], *v.n. irr.* (*aux.* sein) become overgrown.
zuwandern ['tsu:vandərn], *v.n.* (*aux.* sein) immigrate.
zuwegebringen [tsu've:gəbrɪŋən], *v.a. irr.* bring about, effect.
zuweilen [tsu'vaɪlən], *adv.* sometimes, at times.
zuweisen ['tsu:vaɪzən], *v.a. irr.* assign, apportion.
zuwenden ['tsu:vɛndən], *v.a.* turn towards; give.
zuwerfen ['tsu:vɛrfən], *v.a. irr.* throw towards, cast; (*door*) slam.
zuwider ['tsu:vi:dər], *prep.* (*Dat.*) against, contrary to. — *adv.* repugnant.
Zuwiderhandlung [tsu'vi:dərhandluŋ], *f.* (—, *pl.* —en) contravention.
zuwiderlaufen [tsu'vi:dərlaufən], *v.n. irr.* (*aux.* sein) be contrary to, fly in the face of.
zuzählen ['tsu:tsɛ:lən], *v.a.* add to.
zuziehen ['tsu:tsi:ən], *v.a. irr.* draw together; tighten; consult; (*curtain*) draw. — *v.r. sich eine Krankheit* —, catch a disease.
Zuzug ['tsu:tsu:k], *m.* (—s, *no pl.*) immigration; population increase.
zuzüglich ['tsu:tsy:klɪç], *prep.* (*Genit.*) in addition to, including, plus.
Zwang [tsvaŋ], *m.* (—s, *no pl.*) coercion, force; compulsion; (*fig.*) constraint; *sich* — *auferlegen*, restrain o.s.; *tu deinen Gefühlen keinen* — *an*, let yourself go.
zwanglos ['tsvaŋlo:s], *adj.* informal, free and easy.
Zwangsarbeit ['tsvaŋsarbaɪt], *f.* (—, *pl.* —en) forced labour.
Zwangsjacke ['tsvaŋsjakə], *f.* (—, *pl.* —en) strait-jacket.
Zwangsmaßnahme ['tsvaŋsma:sna:mə], *f.* (—, *pl.* —en) compulsory measure, compulsion.
Zwangsversteigerung ['tsvaŋsfɛrʃtaɪgəruŋ], *f.* (—, *pl.* —en) enforced sale.
Zwangsvollstreckung ['tsvaŋsfɔlʃtrɛkuŋ], *f.* (—, *pl.* —en) distraint.
zwangsweise ['tsvaŋsvaɪzə], *adv.* by force, compulsorily.
Zwangswirtschaft ['tsvaŋsvɪrtʃaft], *f.* (—, *no pl.*) price control, controlled economy.
zwanzig ['tsvantsɪç], *num. adj.* twenty.
zwar [tsva:r], *adv.* to be sure, indeed, it is true, true; (*Am.*) sure.
Zweck [tsvɛk], *m.* (—(e)s, *pl.* —e) end, object, purpose.
zweckdienlich ['tsvɛkdi:nlɪç], *adj.* useful, expedient.
Zwecke ['tsvɛkə], *f.* (—, *pl.* —n) tack, drawing-pin.
zweckentsprechend ['tsvɛkɛntʃprɛçənt], *adj.* suitable, appropriate.
zweckmäßig ['tsvɛkmɛ:sɪç], *adj.* expedient, suitable, proper.
zwecks [tsvɛks], *prep.* (*Genit.*) for the purpose of.
zwei [tsvaɪ], *num. adj.* two.
zweibändig ['tsvaɪbɛndɪç], *adj.* in two volumes.
zweideutig ['tsvaɪdɔytɪç], *adj.* ambiguous, equivocal; (*fig.*) suggestive.
Zweideutigkeit ['tsvaɪdɔytɪçkaɪt], *f.* (—, *pl.* —en) ambiguity.
Zweifel ['tsvaɪfəl], *m.* (—s, *pl.* —) doubt, scruple; *ohne* —, no doubt.
zweifelhaft ['tsvaɪfəlhaft], *adj.* doubtful, dubious.
zweifellos ['tsvaɪfəllo:s], *adv.* doubtless.
zweifeln ['tsvaɪfəln], *v.n.* doubt, question; *ich zweifle nicht daran*, I have no doubt about it.
Zweifelsfall ['tsvaɪfəlsfal], *m.* (—s, *pl.* ⸚e) doubtful matter; *im* —, in case of doubt.
Zweifler ['tsvaɪflər], *m.* (—s, *pl.* —) doubter, sceptic.
Zweig [tsvaɪk], *m.* (—(e)s, *pl.* —e) twig, bough, branch.
zweigen ['tsvaɪgən], *v.r. sich* —, bifurcate, fork, branch.
Zweigniederlassung ['tsvaɪkni:dərlasuŋ], *f.* (—, *pl.* —en) branch establishment.

zweihändig ['tsvaɪhɛndɪç], *adj.* two-handed; (*keyboard music*) solo.
Zweihufer ['tsvaɪhu:fər], *m.* (—**s**, *pl.* —) cloven-footed animal.
zweijährig ['tsvaɪjɛ:rɪç], *adj.* two-year-old; of two years' duration.
zweijährlich ['tsvaɪjɛ:rlɪç], *adj.* biennial. — *adv.* every two years.
Zweikampf ['tsvaɪkampf], *m.* (— (**e**)**s**, *pl.* ⸚**e**) duel.
zweimal ['tsvaɪmal], *adv.* twice; — *soviel*, twice as much.
zweimotorig ['tsvaɪmoto:rɪç], *adj.* twin- (*or* two-) engined.
Zweirad ['tsvaɪra:t], *n.* (—**s**, *pl.* ⸚**er**) bicycle.
zweireihig ['tsvaɪraɪɪç], *adj.* (*suit*) double-breasted.
zweischneidig ['tsvaɪʃnaɪdɪç], *adj.* two-edged.
zweiseitig ['tsvaɪzaɪtɪç], *adj.* two-sided, bilateral.
zweisprachig ['tsvaɪʃpra:xɪç], *adj.* bilingual, in two languages.
zweitälteste ['tsvaɪtɛltəstə], *adj.* second (eldest).
zweitbeste ['tsvaɪtbɛstə], *adj.* second best.
zweite ['tsvaɪtə], *num. adj.* second; *aus —r Hand*, secondhand; *zu zweit*, in twos, two of (us, them).
Zweiteilung ['tsvaɪtaɪluŋ], *f.* (—, *pl.* —**en**) bisection.
zweitens ['tsvaɪtəns], *adv.* secondly, in the second place.
zweitletzte ['tsvaɪtlɛtstə], *adj.* last but one, penultimate.
zweitnächste ['tsvaɪtnɛçstə], *adj.* next but one.
Zwerchfell ['tsvɛrçfɛl], *n.* (—**s**, *pl.* —**e**) diaphragm, midriff.
zwerchfellerschütternd ['tsvɛrçfɛlɛrʃytərnt], *adj.* side-splitting.
Zwerg [tsvɛrk], *m.* (—**s**, *pl.* —**e**) dwarf, pigmy.
zwerghaft ['tsvɛrkhaft], *adj.* dwarfish.
Zwetsche ['tsvɛtʃə], *f.* (—, *pl.* —**n**) (*Bot.*) damson.
Zwickel ['tsvɪkəl], *m.* (—**s**, *pl.* —) gusset; *komischer* —, (*coll.*) queer fish.
zwicken ['tsvɪkən], *v.a.* pinch, nip.
Zwicker ['tsvɪkər], *m.* (—**s**, *pl.* —) pince-nez.
Zwickmühle ['tsvɪkmy:lə], *f.* (—, *pl.* —**n**) *in der — sein*, be on the horns of a dilemma, be in a jam.
Zwickzange ['tsvɪktsaŋə], *f.* (—, *pl.* —**n**) pincers.
Zwieback ['tsvɪ:bak], *m.* (—**s**, *pl.* —**e**) rusk.
Zwiebel ['tsvi:bəl], *f.* (—, *pl.* —**n**) onion; bulb.
zwiebelartig ['tsvi:bəla:rtɪç], *adj.* bulbous.
zwiebeln ['tsvi:bəln], *v.a. einen* —, bully, torment s.o.
Zwielicht ['tsvi:lɪçt], *n.* (—**s**, *no pl.*) twilight.
Zwiespalt ['tsvi:ʃpalt], *m.* (—**s**, *pl.* —**e**) difference, dissension; schism.
Zwiesprache ['tsvi:ʃpra:xə], *f.* (—, *pl.* —**n**) dialogue; discussion.
Zwietracht ['tsvi:traxt], *f.* (—, *no pl.*) discord, disharmony.
zwieträchtig ['tsvi:trɛçtɪç], *adj.* discordant, at variance.
Zwillich ['tsvɪlɪç], *m.* (—**s**, *pl.* —**e**) ticking.
Zwilling ['tsvɪlɪŋ], *m.* (—**s**, *pl.* —**e**) twin; (*pl.*) (*Astron.*) Gemini.
Zwingburg ['tsvɪŋburk], *f.* (—, *pl.* —**en**) stronghold.
Zwinge ['tsvɪŋə], *f.* (—, *pl.* —**n**) ferrule.
zwingen ['tsvɪŋən], *v.a. irr.* force, compel; master, overcome, get the better of. — *v.r. sich* —, force o.s. (to), make a great effort (to).
zwingend ['tsvɪŋənt], *adj.* cogent, imperative, convincing.
Zwinger ['tsvɪŋər], *m.* (—**s**, *pl.* —) keep, donjon, fort; bear-pit.
Zwingherrschaft ['tsvɪŋhɛrʃaft], *f.* (—, *pl.* —**en**) despotism, tyranny.
zwinkern ['tsvɪŋkərn], *v.n.* wink; (*stars*) twinkle.
Zwirn [tsvɪrn], *m.* (—(**e**)**s**, *pl.* —**e**) thread, sewing cotton.
Zwirnrolle ['tsvɪrnrɔlə], *f.* (—, *pl.* —**n**) ball of thread, reel of cotton.
zwischen ['tsvɪʃən], *prep.* (*Dat.*, *Acc.*) between; among, amongst.
Zwischenakt ['tsvɪʃənakt], *m.* (—**s**, *pl.* —**e**) (*Theat.*) interval.
Zwischenbemerkung ['tsvɪʃənbəmɛrkuŋ], *f.* (—, *pl.* —**en**) interruption, digression.
Zwischendeck ['tsvɪʃəndɛk], *n.* (—**s**, *pl.* —**e**) (*ship*) steerage, between decks.
zwischendurch ['tsvɪʃəndurç], *adv.* in between, at intervals.
Zwischenfall ['tsvɪʃənfal], *m.* (—**s**, *pl.* ⸚**e**) incident; episode.
Zwischengericht ['tsvɪʃəngərɪçt], *n.* (—**s**, *pl.* —**e**) (*food*) entrée, entremets.
Zwischenglied ['tsvɪʃəngli:t], *n.* (—**s**, *pl.* —**er**) link.
Zwischenhändler ['tsvɪʃənhɛndlər], *m.* (—**s**, *pl.* —) middleman.
Zwischenpause ['tsvɪʃənpauzə], *f.* (—, *pl.* —**n**) interval; pause.
Zwischenraum ['tsvɪʃənraum], *m.* (—**s**, *pl.* ⸚**e**) intermediate space, gap.
Zwischenrede ['tsvɪʃənre:də], *f.* (—, *pl.* —**n**) interruption.
Zwischenruf ['tsvɪʃənru:f], *m.* (—**s**, *pl.* —**e**) interruption, interjection.
Zwischensatz ['tsvɪʃənzats], *m.* (—**es**, *pl.* ⸚**e**) parenthesis; interpolation.
Zwischenspiel ['tsvɪʃənʃpi:l], *n.* (—**s**, *pl.* —**e**) interlude, intermezzo.
Zwischenzeit ['tsvɪʃəntsaɪt], *f.* (—, *no pl.*) interval, interim, meantime; *in der* —, meanwhile.
Zwist [tsvɪst], *m.* (—**es**, *pl.* —**e**) discord, quarrel, dispute.
Zwistigkeiten ['tsvɪstɪçkaɪtən], *f. pl.* hostilities.
zwitschern ['tsvɪtʃərn], *v.n.* chirp, twitter.

Zwitter ['tsvɪtər], *m.* (—s, *pl.* —) hybrid, cross-breed, mongrel; hermaphrodite.
zwitterhaft ['tsvɪtərhaft], *adj.* hybrid; bisexual.
zwölf [svœlf], *num. adj.* twelve.
Zwölffingerdarm ['tsvœlffɪŋərdarm], *m.* (—s, *pl.* ⸚e) duodenum.
Zyankali [tsy:an'ka:li], *n.* (—s, *no pl.*) potassium cyanide.
Zyklon [tsy'klo:n], *m.* (—s, *pl.* —e) cyclone.
Zyklus ['tsyklus], *m.* (—, *pl.* **Zyklen**) cycle; course, series.
zylinderförmig [tsy'lɪndərfœrmɪç], *adj.* cylindric(al).
Zylinderhut [tsy'lɪndərhu:t], *m.* (—s, *pl.* ⸚e) top-hat, silk-hat.
zylindrisch [tsy'lɪndrɪʃ], *adj.* cylindric(al).
Zyniker ['tsy:nɪkər], *m.* (—s, *pl.* —) cynic.
zynisch ['tsy:nɪʃ], *adj.* cynical.
Zynismus [tsy'nɪsmus], *m.* (—, *no pl.*) cynicism.
Zypern ['tsy:pərn], *n.* Cyprus.
Zypresse [tsy'prɛsə], *f.* (—, *pl.* —n) (*Bot.*) cypress.

Cassell's English-German Dictionary

A

A [ei]. das A (*also Mus.*).
a [ə, ei] (**an** [ən, æn] *before vowel or silent* h), *indef. art.* ein, eine, ein; *two at a time*, zwei auf einmal; *many a*, mancher; *two shillings a pound*, zwei Schilling das Pfund.
abacus ['æbəkəs], *s.* das Rechenbrett.
abandon [ə'bændən], *v.a.* (*give up*) aufgeben; (*forsake*) verlassen; (*surrender*) preisgeben.
abandonment [ə'bændənmənt], *s.* das Verlassen (*active*); das Verlassensein (*passive*); die Wildheit, das Sichgehenlassen.
abasement [ə'beismənt], *s.* die Demütigung, Erniedrigung.
abash [ə'bæʃ], *v.a.* beschämen.
abate [ə'beit], *v.n.* nachlassen.
abbess ['æbes], *s.* die Äbtissin.
abbey ['æbi], *s.* die Abtei.
abbot ['æbət], *s.* der Abt.
abbreviate [ə'bri·vieit], *v.a.* abkürzen.
abbreviation [əbri:vi'eiʃən], *s.* die Abkürzung.
abdicate ['æbdikeit], *v.a.*, *v.n.* entsagen (*Dat.*), abdanken.
abdomen [æb'doumən, 'æbdəmən], *s.* (*Anat.*) der Unterleib, Bauch.
abdominal [æb'dɔminəl], *adj.* (*Anat.*) Bauch-, Unterleibs-.
abduct [æb'dʌkt], *v.a.* entführen.
abed [ə'bed], *adv.* zu Bett, im Bett.
aberration [æbə'reiʃən], *s.* die Abirrung; die Verirrung; (*Phys.*) die Strahlenbrechung.
abet [ə'bet], *v.a.* helfen (*Dat.*), unterstützen.
abeyance [ə'beiəns], *s.* die Unentschiedenheit, (der Zustand der) Ungewißheit; *in* —, unentschieden.
abhor [əb'hɔ:], *v.a.* verabscheuen.
abhorrence [əb'hɔrəns], *s.* die Abscheu (*of*, vor, *Dat.*).
abhorrent [əb'hɔrənt], *adj.* widerlich, ekelhaft.
abide [ə'baid], *v.n. irr.* bleiben, verweilen; (*last*) dauern. — *v.a.* aushalten.
ability [ə'biliti], *s.* die Fähigkeit, Tüchtigkeit; (*pl.*) die Geisteskräfte, *f. pl.*
abject ['æbdʒekt], *adj.* elend; (*submissive*) unterwürfig, verächtlich.
ablaze [ə'bleiz], *adj.*, *adv.* in Flammen.
able [eibl], *adj.* fähig; (*clever*) geschickt; (*efficient*) tüchtig.
ablution [ə'blu:ʃən], *s.* die Abwaschung, Waschung.
abnormal [æb'nɔ:məl], *adj.* abnorm, ungewöhnlich.
abnormality [æbnɔ:'mæliti], *s.* die Ungewöhnlichkeit.
aboard [ə'bɔ:d], *adv.* an Bord.
abode [ə'boud], *s.* der Wohnsitz, Wohnort.
abolish [ə'bɔliʃ], *v.a.* aufheben, abschaffen.
abolition [æbo'liʃən], *s.* die Abschaffung, Aufhebung.
abominable [ə'bɔminəbl], *adj.* abscheulich, scheußlich.
abominate [ə'bɔmineit], *v.a.* verabscheuen.
abomination [əbɔmi'neiʃən], *s.* der Abscheu, Greuel.
aboriginal [æbə'ridʒinəl], *adj.* eingeboren, einheimisch. — *s.* der Eingeborene.
aborigines [æbə'ridʒini:z], *s. pl.* die Eingeborenen, Ureinwohner.
abortion [ə'bɔ:ʃən], *s.* die Fehlgeburt; die Abtreibung.
abortive [ə'bɔ:tiv], *adj.* mißlungen.
abound [ə'baund], *v.n.* wimmeln von (*Dat.*).
about [ə'baut], *prep.* um; (*toward*) gegen; *about* 3 *o'clock*, gegen drei; (*concerning*) über, betreffend. — *adv.* umher, herum; (*round*) rund herum; (*nearly*) etwa, ungefähr; (*everywhere*) überall; *to be* — *to*, im Begriffe sein *or* stehen zu . . .
above [ə'bʌv], *prep.* über; — *all things*, vor allen Dingen; *this is* — *me*, das ist mir zu hoch; — *board*, offen, ehrlich. — *adv.* oben, darüber, *over and* —, obendrein; — *mentioned*, obenerwähnt.
abrade [ə'breid], *v.a.* abschaben, abschürfen.
abrasion [ə'breiʒən], *s.* die Abschürfung; Abnutzung.
abreast [ə'brest], *adj.*, *adv.* nebeneinander, Seite an Seite; *keep* —, (sich) auf dem Laufenden halten; Schritt halten (mit).
abridge [ə'bridʒ], *v.a.* (ab)kürzen.
abridgement [ə'bridʒmənt], *s.* die (Ab)kürzung; (*book etc.*) der Auszug.
abroad [ə'brɔ:d], *adv.* im Ausland, auswärts; *to go* —, ins Ausland reisen.
abrogate ['æbrogeit], *v.a.* abschaffen.
abrogation [æbro'geiʃən], *s.* (*Pol.*) die Abschaffung.
abrupt [ə'brʌpt], *adj.* plötzlich; (*curt*) schroff; kurz; jäh.
abruptness [ə'brʌptnis], *s.* (*speech*) die Schroffheit; (*suddenness*) die Plötzlichkeit; (*drop*) die Steilheit.
abscess ['æbses], *s.* das Geschwür, die Schwellung, der Abszeß.

abscond [əb'skɔnd], *v.n.* sich davonmachen.
absence ['æbsəns], *s.* die Abwesenheit; *leave of* —, der Urlaub.
absent (1) ['æbsənt], *adj.* abwesend; —*minded*, zerstreut.
absent (2) [æb'sent], *v.r.* — *oneself*, fehlen, fernbleiben; (*go away*) sich entfernen.
absentee [æbsən'ti:], *s.* der Abwesende.
absolute ['æbsəlu:t], *adj.* absolut, unumschränkt.
absolve [əb'zɔlv], *v.a.* freisprechen (*from*, von), lossprechen, entbinden.
absorb [əb'sɔ:b], *v.a.* absorbieren, aufsaugen; (*attention*) in Anspruch nehmen.
absorbed [əb'sɔ:bd], *adj.* versunken.
absorbent [əb'sɔ:bənt], *adj.* absorbierend.
absorption [əb'sɔ:pʃən], *s.* (*Chem.*) die Absorption; (*attention*) das Versunkensein.
abstain [əb'stein], *v.n.* sich enthalten; — *from voting*, sich der Stimme enthalten.
abstainer [əb'steinə], *s.* der Abstinenzler, Antialkoholiker.
abstemious [əb'sti:miəs], *adj.* enthaltsam.
abstention[əb'stenʃən],*s.*dieEnthaltung.
abstinence ['æbstinəns], *s.* die Enthaltsamkeit, das Fasten (*food*).
abstract [æb'strækt], *v.a.* abstrahieren, abziehen; (*summarize*) kürzen, ausziehen. —['æbstrækt], *adj.* abstrakt; (*Maths.*) rein. — *s.* der Auszug, Abriß (*of article, book, etc.*).
abstracted [æb'stræktid], *adj.* zerstreut, geistesabwesend.
abstraction [æb'strækʃən], *s.* die Abstraktion; der abstrakte Begriff.
abstruse [æb'stru:s], *adj.* schwerverständlich, tiefsinnig.
absurd [əb'sə:d], *adj.* absurd, töricht; (*unreasonable*) unvernünftig, gegen alle Vernunft; (*laughable*) lächerlich.
absurdity [əb'sə:diti], *s.* die Torheit, Unvernünftigkeit.
abundance [ə'bʌndəns], *s.* die Fülle, der Überfluß.
abundant [ə'bʌndənt], *adj.* reichlich.
abuse [ə'bju:z], *v.a.* mißbrauchen; (*insult*) beschimpfen; (*violate*) schänden. —[ə'bju:s], *s.* der Mißbrauch; (*language*) die Beschimpfung; (*violation*) die Schändung.
abusive [ə'bju:siv], *adj.* (*language*) grob; schimpfend, schmähend.
abut [ə'bʌt], *v.n.* anstoßen, angrenzen.
abysmal [ə'bizməl], *adj.* bodenlos.
abyss [ə'bis], *s.* der Abgrund, Schlund.
Abyssinian [æbi'sinjən], *adj.* abessinisch. — *s.* der Abessinier.
acacia [ə'keiʃə], *s.* (*Bot.*) die Akazie.
academic [ækə'demik], *adj.* akademisch. — *s.* der Akademiker.
academy [ə'kædəmi], *s.* die Akademie.
acajou ['ækəʒu:], *s.* (*Bot.*) der Nierenbaum.
accede [æk'si:d], *v.n.* beistimmen; einwilligen; — *to the throne*, den Thron besteigen.
accelerate [æk'seləreit], *v.a.* beschleunigen. — *v.n.* schneller fahren.
acceleration [ækselə'reiʃən], *s.* die Beschleunigung.
accelerator [æk'seləreitə], *s.* (*Motor.*) der Gashebel, das Gaspedal.
accent (1), **accentuate** [æk'sent, æk'sentjueit], *v.a.* akzentuieren, betonen.
accent (2) ['æksənt], *s.* (*Phon.*) der Ton, Wortton, die Betonung; der Akzent (*dialect*), die Aussprache.
accentuation [æksentju'eiʃən], *s.* die Aussprache, Akzentuierung, Betonung.
accept [æk'sept], *v.a.* annehmen.
acceptable [æk'septəbl], *adj.* angenehm, annehmbar, annehmlich.
acceptance [æk'septəns], *s.* die Annahme; (*Comm.*) das Akzept.
access ['ækses], *s.* der Zugang, Zutritt.
accessible [æk'sesibl], *adj.* erreichbar, zugänglich.
accession [æk'seʃən], *s.* der Zuwachs; — *to the throne*, die Thronbesteigung.
accessory [æk'sesəri], *adj.* zugehörig; hinzukommend; (*Law*) mitschuldig; (*subsidiary*) nebensächlich. — *s.* (*Law*) der Mitschuldige; (*pl.*) das Zubehör.
accidence ['æksidəns], *s.* (*Gram.*) die Flexionslehre.
accident ['æksidənt], *s.* (*chance*) der Zufall; (*mishap*) der Unfall, Unglücksfall.
accidental [æksi'dentəl], *adj.* zufällig; (*inessential*) unwesentlich; durch Unfall.
acclaim [ə'kleim], *v.a.* akklamieren, mit Beifall aufnehmen. — *v.n.* zujubeln. — *s.* der Beifall.
acclamation [æklə'meiʃən], *s.* der Beifall, Zuruf.
acclimatize [ə'klaimətaiz], *v.a.*, *v.r.* akklimatisieren; sich anpassen, eingewöhnen.
accommodate [ə'kɔmədeit], *v.a.* (*adapt*) anpassen; (*lodge*) unterbringen, beherbergen, aufnehmen; einem aushelfen; (*with money*) jemandem Geld leihen. — *v.r.* — *oneself to*, sich an etwas anpassen, sich in etwas fügen.
accommodating [ə'kɔmədeitiŋ], *adj.* gefällig, entgegenkommend.
accommodation [əkɔmə'deiʃən], *s.* (*adaptation*) die Anpassung; (*dispute*) die Beilegung; (*room*) die Unterkunft.
accompaniment [ə'kʌmpənimənt], *s.* die Begleitung.
accompany [ə'kʌmpəni], *v.a.* begleiten.
accomplice [ə'kʌmplis *or* ə'kɔmplis], *s.* der Komplize, Mitschuldige, Mittäter.
accomplish [ə'kʌmpliʃ *or* ə'kɔmpliʃ], *v.a.* vollenden, zustandebringen, vollbringen; (*objective*) erreichen.
accomplished [ə'kʌmpliʃd *or* ə'kɔmpliʃd], *adj.* vollendet.

accomplishment [ə'kʌmpliʃmənt *or* ə'kɔmpliʃmənt], *s.* (*of project*) die Ausführung; (*of task*) die Vollendung; (*of prophecy*) die Erfüllung; (*pl.*) die Talente, *n. pl.*, Gaben, Kenntnisse, *f. pl.*

accord [ə'kɔ:d], *s.* (*agreement*) die Übereinstimmung; (*unison*) die Eintracht. — *v.n.* übereinstimmen (*with*, mit) — *v.a.* bewilligen.

accordance [ə'kɔ:dəns], *s.* die Übereinstimmung.

according [ə'kɔ:diŋ], *prep.* — *to*, gemäß, nach, laut.

accordingly [ə'kɔ:diŋli], *adv.* demgemäß, demnach, folglich.

accordion [ə'kɔ:diən], *s.* (*Mus.*) die Ziehharmonika, das Akkordeon.

accost [ə'kɔst], *v.a.* ansprechen, anreden.

account [ə'kaunt], *s.* die Rechnung; (*report*) der Bericht; (*narrative*) die Erzählung; (*importance*) die Bedeutung; (*Fin.*) das Konto, Guthaben; *cash* —, die Kassenrechnung; *on no* —, auf keinen Fall; *on his* —, seinetwegen, um seinetwillen; *on* — *of*, wegen (*Genit.*); *on that* —, darum; *of no* —, unbedeutend. — *v.n.* — *for*, Rechenschaft ablegen über (*Acc.*); (*explain*) erklären.

accountable [ə'kauntəbl], *adj.* verrechenbar (*item*); verantwortlich (*person*).

accountant [ə'kauntənt], *s.* der Bücherrevisor, Rechnungsführer; *junior* —, der Buchhalter.

accredit [ə'kredit], *v.a.* akkreditieren, beglaubigen; (*authorize*) ermächtigen, bevollmächtigen.

accretion [ə'kri:ʃən], *s.* der Zuwachs.

accrue [ə'kru:], *v.n.* (*Comm.*) zuwachsen, erwachsen, zufallen.

accumulate [ə'kju:mjuleit], *v.a.*, *v.n.* anhäufen; sich anhäufen, zunehmen, sich ansammeln.

accumulation [əkju:mju'leiʃən], *s.* die Ansammlung, Anhäufung.

accuracy ['ækjurəsi], *s.* die Genauigkeit.

accurate ['ækjurit], *adj.* genau, richtig.

accursed [ə'kə:sid], *adj.* verflucht, verwünscht.

accusation [ækju'zeiʃən], *s.* die Anklage.

accusative [ə'kju:zətiv], *s.* (*Gram.*) der Akkusativ.

accuse [ə'kju:z], *v.a.* anklagen, beschuldigen (*of*, *Genit.*).

accustom [ə'kʌstəm], *v.a.* gewöhnen (*to*, an, *Acc.*).

ace [eis], *s.* (*Cards*) das As, die Eins.

acerbity [ə'sə:biti], *s.* die Rauheit, Herbheit; (*manner*) die Grobheit.

acetate ['æsiteit], *s.* das Azetat; essigsaures Salz.

acetic [ə'si:tik, ə'setik], *adj.* essigsauer.

acetylene [ə'setili:n], *s.* das Azetylen.

ache [eik], *s.* der Schmerz. — *v.n.* schmerzen, weh(e)tun.

achieve [ə'tʃi:v], *v.a.* erreichen, erlangen; (*accomplish*) vollenden; (*perform*) ausführen; (*gain*) erlangen, erwerben.

achievement [ə'tʃi:vmənt], *s.* (*accomplishment*) die Leistung, der Erfolg; die Errungenschaft; (*gain*) die Erwerbung.

achromatic [ækro'mætik], *adj.* achromatisch, farblos.

acid ['æsid], *adj.* sauer, scharf. — *s.* (*Chem.*) die Säure.

acidulated [ə'sidjuleitid], *adj.* (*Chem.*) angesäuert.

acknowledge [æk'nɔlidʒ], *v.a.* anerkennen; (*admit*) zugeben; (*confess*) bekennen; (*letter*) den Empfang bestätigen.

acknowledgement [æk'nɔlidʒmənt], *s.* die Anerkennung, (*receipt*) Bestätigung, Quittung; (*pl.*) die Dankesbezeigung; die Erkenntlichkeit.

acme ['ækmi], *s.* der Gipfel, Höhepunkt.

acorn ['eikɔ:n], *s.* (*Bot.*) die Eichel.

acoustics [ə'ku:stiks], *s. pl.* die Akustik; (*subject*, *study*) die Schallehre.

acquaint [ə'kweint], *v.a.* bekanntmachen; (*inform*) mitteilen (*Dat.*), informieren; unterrichten.

acquaintance [ə'kweintəns], *s.* die Bekanntschaft; der Bekannte, die Bekannte (*person*); die Kenntnis (*with*, von).

acquiesce [ækwi'es], *v.n.* einwilligen, sich fügen.

acquiescence [ækwi'esəns], *s.* die Einwilligung (*in*, in, *Acc.*), Zustimmung (*in*, zu, *Dat.*)

acquiescent [ækwi'esənt], *adj.* fügsam.

acquire [ə'kwaiə], *v.a.* erlangen, erwerben; (*language*) erlernen.

acquisition [ækwi'ziʃən], *s.* die Erlangung, Erwerbung.

acquit [ə'kwit], *v.a.* freisprechen.

acre ['eikə], *s.* der Acker (*appr.* 0.4 *Hektar*).

acrid ['ækrid], *adj.* scharf, beißend.

acrimonious [ækri'mouniəs], *adj.* scharf, bitter.

across [ə'krɔs, ə'krɔ:s], *adv.* kreuzweise, (quer) hinüber. — *prep.* quer durch, über; *come* —, (zufällig) treffen, *come — a problem*, auf ein Problem stoßen.

act [ækt], *s.* (*deed*) die Tat; (*Theat.*) der Akt; (*Parl. etc.*) die Akte. — *v.a.* (*Theat.*) spielen. — *v.n.* handeln (*do something*); sich benehmen *or* tun, als ob (*act as if*, *pretend*); (*Theat.*) spielen; (*Chem.*) wirken (*react*).

action ['ækʃən], *s.* die Handlung (*play*, *deed*); Wirkung (*effect*); (*Law*) der Prozeß; der Gang.

active ['æktiv], *adj.* (*person*, *Gram.*) aktiv; tätig; rührig (*industrious*); wirksam (*effective*).

activity [æk'tiviti], *s.* die Tätigkeit; (*Chem.*) Wirksamkeit.

actor ['æktə], *s.* der Schauspieler.

actress ['æktrəs], die Schauspielerin.

actual ['æktjuəl], *adj.* tatsächlich, wirklich.

actuality [æktju'æliti], *s.* die Wirklichkeit.
actuary ['æktjuəri], *s.* der Aktuar, Versicherungsbeamte.
actuate ['æktjueit], *v.a.* betreiben, in Bewegung setzen.
acuity [ə'kju:iti], *s.* der Scharfsinn (*mind*), die Schärfe (*vision etc.*).
acute [ə'kju:t], *adj.* scharf, scharfsinnig (*mind*); spitz (*angle*); fein (*sense*); — *accent*, der Akut.
adage ['ædidʒ], *s.* das Sprichwort.
adamant ['ædəmənt], *adj.* sehr hart, unerbittlich (*inexorable*).
adapt [ə'dæpt], *v.a.* anpassen, angleichen; bearbeiten.
adaptable [ə'dæptəbl], *adj.* anpassungsfähig.
adaptation [ædæp'teiʃən], *s.* die Anpassung, die Bearbeitung (*of book*).
adaptive [ə'dæptiv], *adj.* anpassungsfähig.
add [æd], *v.a.* hinzufügen, (*Maths.*) addieren.
adder ['ædə], *s.* (*Zool.*) die Natter.
addict ['ædikt], *s.* der Süchtige.
addiction [ə'dikʃən], *s.* die Sucht.
addicted [ə'diktid], *adj.* verfallen.
addition [ə'diʃən], *s.* die Hinzufügung, Zugabe, (*Maths.*) Addition.
additional [ə'diʃənəl], *adj.* zusätzlich, nachträglich.
address [ə'dres], *s.* die Anschrift, Adresse (*letter*); die Ansprache (*speech*). — *v.a.* (*letter*) adressieren, richten an (*Acc.*).
addressee [ædre'si:], *s.* der Adressat, der Empfänger.
adduce [ə'dju:s], *v.a.* anführen (*proof*, Beweis).
adenoid ['ædinɔid], *s.* (*usually pl.*) (*Med.*) die Wucherung.
adept ['ædept], *adj.* geschickt, erfahren.
adequacy ['ædikwəsi], *s.* die Angemessenheit, das Gewachsensein, die Zulänglichkeit.
adequate ['ædikwət], *adj.* gewachsen (*Dat.*); angemessen, hinreichend (*sufficient*).
adhere [əd'hiə], *v.n.* haften, anhängen; — *to one's opinion*, bei seiner Meinung bleiben.
adherence [əd'hiərəns], *s.* das Festhalten (an, *Dat.*).
adhesion [əd'hi:ʒən], *s.* (*Phys.*) die Adhäsion; das Anhaften.
adhesive [əd'hi:ziv], *adj.* haftend, klebrig; — *plaster*, das Heftpflaster.
adipose ['ædipous], *adj.* fett, feist.
adjacent [ə'dʒeisənt], *adj.* naheliegend, benachbart, angrenzend.
adjective ['ædʒəktiv], *s.* (*Gram.*) das Adjektiv; Eigenschaftswort.
adjoin [ə'dʒɔin], *v.a.* anstoßen, angrenzen.
adjourn [ə'dʒə:n], *v.a.* vertagen, aufschieben.
adjudicate [ə'dʒu:dikeit], *v.a.* beurteilen, richten.
adjunct ['ædʒʌŋkt], *s.* der Zusatz.
adjust [ə'dʒʌst], *v.a.* ordnen; (*adapt*) anpassen; regulieren, einstellen.
adjustable [ə'dʒʌstəbl], *adj.* verstellbar, einstellbar.
adjustment [ə'dʒʌstmənt], *s.* die Einstellung, Anpassung; (*Law*) Schlichtung; Berichtigung.
administer [əd'ministə], *v.a.* verwalten (*an enterprise*); verabreichen (*medicine*); abnehmen (*an oath*, einen Eid).
administration [əd'minis'treiʃən], *s.* die Verwaltung, Regierung; die Darreichung (*sacraments*).
administrative [əd'ministrətiv], *adj.* Verwaltungs-; verwaltend.
admirable ['ædmirəbl], *adj.* bewundernswert.
admiral ['ædmirəl], *s.* der Admiral.
Admiralty ['ædmirəlti], *s.* die Admiralität.
admiration [ædmi'reiʃən], *s.* die Bewunderung.
admire [əd'maiə], *v.a.* bewundern, verehren.
admirer [əd'maiərə], *s.* der Bewunderer, Verehrer.
admissible [əd'misibl], *adj.* zulässig.
admission [əd'miʃən], *s.* die Zulassung; (*entry*) der Eintritt; Zutritt; (*confession*) das Eingeständnis, Zugeständnis.
admit [əd'mit], *v.a.* zulassen; aufnehmen; zugeben (*deed*); gelten lassen (*argument*).
admittance [əd'mitəns], *s.* der Zugang, Eintritt, Zutritt.
admixture [əd'mikstʃə], *s.* die Beimischung, Beigabe.
admonish [əd'mɔniʃ], *v.a.* ermahnen, mahnen, warnen.
admonition [ædmə'niʃən], *s.* die Ermahnung, Warnung.
ado [ə'du:], *s.* der Lärm, das Tun, das Treiben; *without further* —, ohne weiteres.
adolescence [ædo'lesəns], *s.* die Adoleszenz, Jugend, Jugendzeit.
adolescent [ædo'lesənt], *s.* der Jugendliche. — *adj.* jugendlich.
adopt [ə'dɔpt], *v.a.* (*Law*) annehmen, adoptieren.
adoption [ə'dopʃən], *s.* (*Law*) die Annahme, Adoption.
adoptive [ə'dɔptiv], *adj.* Adoptiv-, angenommen.
adorable [ə'dɔ:rəbl], *adj.* anbetungswürdig; (*coll.*) wunderbar, schön.
adoration [ædo'reiʃən], *s.* die Anbetung.
adore [ə'dɔ:], *v.a.* anbeten; verehren.
adorn [ə'dɔ:n], *v.a.* (aus)schmücken, zieren.
Adriatic (Sea) [eidri:'ætik (si:)]. das adriatische Meer.
adrift [ə'drift], *adv.* treibend; *cut o.s.* —, sich absondern.
adroit [ə'drɔit], *adj.* gewandt, geschickt.
adroitness [ə'drɔitnis], *s.* die Gewandtheit, die Geschicklichkeit.

adulation [ædju'leiʃən], *s.* die Schmeichelei.
adulator ['ædjuleitə], *s.* der Schmeichler.
adulatory ['ædjuleitəri], *adj.* schmeichlerisch.
adult [ə'dʌlt *or* 'ædʌlt], *adj.* erwachsen. — *s.* der Erwachsene.
adulterate [ə'dʌltəreit], *v.a.* verfälschen; verwässern.
adulterer [ə'dʌltərə], *s.* der Ehebrecher.
adultery [ə'dʌltəri], *s.* der Ehebruch.
adumbrate [ə'dʌmbreit *or* 'æd-], *v.a.* skizzieren, entwerfen, andeuten.
advance [əd'vɑ:ns], *v.a.* fördern (*a cause*); vorschießen (*money*); geltend machen (*claim*). — *v.n.* vorrücken, vorstoßen; (*make progress, gain promotion*) aufsteigen. — *s.* der Fortschritt (*progress*); der Vorschuß (*money*); *in* —, im voraus.
advancement [əd'vɑ:nsmənt], *s.* der Fortschritt (*progress*), der Aufstieg, die Beförderung (*promotion*); die Förderung (*of a cause*).
advantage [əd'vɑ:ntidʒ], *s.* der Vorteil, Nutzen; (*superiority*) die Überlegenheit.
Advent ['ædvent]. (*Eccl.*) der Advent.
advent ['ædvənt], *s.* die Ankunft.
adventitious [ædven'tiʃəs], *adj.* zufällig.
adventure [əd'ventʃə], *s.* das Abenteuer. — *v.n.* auf Abenteuer ausgehen, wagen.
adventurer [əd'ventʃərə], *s.* der Abenteurer.
adventurous [əd'ventʃərəs], *adj.* abenteuerlich, unternehmungslustig.
adverb ['ædvə:b], *s.* (*Gram.*) das Adverb(ium), Umstandswort.
adverbial [əd'və:biəl], *adj.* adverbial.
adversary ['ædvəsəri], *s.* der Gegner, Widersacher.
adverse ['ædvə:s], *adj.* widrig, feindlich, ungünstig.
adversity [əd'və:siti], *s.* das Unglück, Mißgeschick; *in* —, im Unglück.
advert [əd'və:t], *v.n.* hinweisen.
advertise ['ædvətaiz], *v.a.* anzeigen; annoncieren (*in press*), Reklame machen.
advertisement [əd'və:tizmənt], *s.* die Anzeige, Annonce; Reklame.
advertiser ['ædvətaizə], *s.* der Anzeiger.
advice [əd'vais], *s.* der Rat, Ratschlag; die Nachricht (*information*).
advise [əd'vaiz], *v.a.* raten (*Dat.*), beraten; benachrichtigen (*inform*); verständigen.
advisable [əd'vaizəbl], *adj.* ratsam.
advisedly [əd'vaizidli], *adv.* absichtlich, mit Bedacht.
adviser [əd'vaizə], *s.* der Berater.
advisory [əd'vaizəri], *adj.* beratend, ratgebend, Rats-.
advocacy ['ædvəkəsi], *s.* (*Law*) die Verteidigung; die Fürsprache (*championing of*, für, *Acc.*); die Vertretung (*of view*).
Aegean (Sea) [i:'dʒi:ən (si:)]. das ägäische Meer.
aerated ['ɛəreitid], *adj.* kohlensauer.
aerial ['ɛəriəl], *s.* (*Rad.*) die Antenne. — *adj.* luftig, Luft-.
aerie ['ɛəri, 'iəri], *s. see* **eyrie.**
aerodrome ['ɛərodroum], *s.* der Flugplatz, Flughafen.
aeronautical [ɛəro'nɔ:tikəl], *adj.* aeronautisch.
aeronautics [ɛəro'nɔ:tiks], *s. pl.* die Aeronautik, Luftfahrt.
aeroplane, (*Am.*) **airplane** ['ɛəroplein, 'ɛərplein], *s.* das Flugzeug.
aesthetic(al) [i:s'θetik(əl)], *adj.* ästhetisch.
aesthetics [i:s'θetiks], *s.* die Ästhetik.
afar [ə'fɑ:], *adv.* fern, weit entfernt; *from* —, von weitem, (von) weit her.
affability [æfə'biliti], *s.* die Leutseligkeit, Freundlichkeit.
affable ['æfəbl], *adj.* freundlich, leutselig.
affair [ə'fɛə], *s.* die Affäre; die Angelegenheit (*matter*); das Anliegen (*concern*).
affect [ə'fekt], *v.a.* beeinflußen; rühren; wirken auf; vortäuschen (*pretend*); zur Schau tragen (*exhibit*).
affectation [æfek'teiʃən], *s.* die Ziererei, das Affektieren, die Affektiertheit.
affected [ə'fektid], *adj.* affektiert, gekünstelt, geziert; befallen, angegriffen (*illness*).
affection [ə'fekʃən], *s.* die Zuneigung, Zärtlichkeit.
affectionate [ə'fekʃənit], *adj.* zärtlich, liebevoll; (*in letters*) *yours* —*ly*, herzlichst.
affinity [ə'finiti], *s.* (*Chem.*) die Affinität; die Verwandtschaft (*relationship*).
affirm [ə'fə:m], *v.a.* behaupten, bestätigen, versichern; bekräftigen (*confirm*).
affirmation [æfə'meiʃən], *s.* die Behauptung, Bekräftigung.
affirmative [ə'fə:mətiv], *adj.* bejahend, positiv; *in the* —, bejahend.
affix [ə'fiks], *v.a.* anheften, aufkleben (*stick*); anbringen (*join to*, an, *Acc.*).
afflict [ə'flikt], *v.a.* quälen, plagen.
affliction [ə'flikʃən], *s.* die Plage, Qual; das Mißgeschick; die Not; das Leiden.
affluence ['æfluəns], *s.* der Überfluß (*abundance*); der Reichtum.
affluent ['æfluənt], *adj.* reich, wohlhabend. — *s.* der Nebenfluß (*tributary*).
afford [ə'fɔ:d], *v.a.* geben, bieten; (sich) leisten (*have money for*); gewähren (*give*); hervorbringen (*yield*).
afforest [ə'fɔrist], *v.a.* aufforsten.
affray [ə'frei], *s.* die Schlägerei.
African ['æfrikən], *adj.* afrikanisch. — *s.* der Afrikaner.
affront [ə'frʌnt], *s.* die Beleidigung. — *v.a.* beleidigen.
Afghan ['æfgæn], *adj.* afghanisch. — *s.* der Afghane.
afield [ə'fi:ld], *adj., adv.* im Felde; weit umher; weit weg.
afire [ə'faiə], *adv., adv.* in Flammen.

aflame [ə'fleim], *adj., adv.* in Flammen.
afloat [ə'flout], *adj., adv.* schwimmend, dahintreibend.
afoot [ə'fut], *adj., adv.* im Gange.
afore [ə'fɔ:], *adv.* vorher.
aforesaid [ə'fɔ:sed], *adj. the* —, das Obengesagte, der Vorhergenannte.
afraid [ə'freid], *adj.* ängstlich, furchtsam; *be* —, fürchten (*of s.th.*, etwas, *Acc.*); sich fürchten.
afresh [ə'freʃ], *adv.* von neuem.
aft [ɑ:ft], *adv.* (*Naut.*) achtern.
after ['ɑ:ftə], *prep.* nach (*time*); nach, hinter (*place*); *the day* — *tomorrow*, übermorgen. — *adj.* hinter, später. — *adv.* hinterher, nachher (*time*); darauf, dahinter (*place*). — *conj.* nachdem.
afternoon [ɑ:ftə'nu:n], *s.* der Nachmittag.
afterwards ['ɑ:ftəwədz], *adv.* nachher, daraufhin, später.
again [ə'gein], *adv.* wieder, abermals, noch einmal; zurück (*back*); dagegen (*however*); *as much* —, noch einmal soviel; — *and* —, immer wieder.
against [ə'geinst], *prep.* gegen, wider; nahe bei (*near, Dat.*); bis an (*up to, Acc.*); — *the grain*, wider *or* gegen den Strich.
agate ['ægeit], *s.* der Achat.
agave [ə'geivi], *s.* (*Bot.*) die Agave.
age [eidʒ], *s.* das Alter (*person*); das Zeitalter (*period*); die Reife; *come of* —, volljährig werden; mündig werden; *old* —, das Greisenalter; *for* —*s*, seit einer Ewigkeit. — *v.n.* altern, alt werden.
aged ['eidʒid], *adj.* bejahrt.
agency ['eidʒənsi], *s.* die Agentur (*firm*); die Mitwirkung (*participation*); die Hilfe (*assistance*); die Vermittlung (*mediation*).
agenda [ə'dʒendə], *s.* das Sitzungsprogramm; die Tagesordnung.
agent ['eidʒənt], *s.* der Agent, Vertreter.
agglomerate [ə'glɔməreit], *v.a.* zusammenhäufen. — *v.n.* sich zusammenhäufen, sich ballen.
aggrandisement [ə'grændizmənt], *s.* die Überhebung, Übertreibung, Erweiterung.
aggravate ['ægrəveit], *v.a.* verschlimmern; ärgern.
aggravation [ægrə'veiʃən], *s.* die Verschlimmerung (*of condition*); der Ärger (*annoyance*).
aggregate ['ægrigit], *adj.* gesamt, vereinigt, vereint. — *s.* das Aggregat.
aggregation [ægri'geiʃən], *s.* (*Geol., Chem.*) die Vereinigung, Anhäufung, Ansammlung.
aggression [ə'greʃən], *s.* der Angriff, Überfall.
aggressive [ə'gresiv], *adj.* aggressiv, angreifend.
aggressor [ə'gresə], *s.* der Angreifer.
aggrieve [ə'gri:v], *v.a.* kränken.
aghast [ə'gɑ:st], *adj.* bestürzt; sprachlos; entsetzt.
agile ['ædʒail], *adj.* behend, flink, beweglich.
agitate ['ædʒiteit], *v.a.* bewegen; beunruhigen; aufrühren; stören.
agitation [ædʒi'teiʃən], *s.* (*Pol.*) die Agitation; die Unruhe (*unrest*); der Aufruhr (*revolt*).
agitator ['ædʒiteitə], *s.* (*Pol.*) der Agitator; der Aufwiegler (*inciter*).
aglow [ə'glou], *adv.* glühend.
agnostic [æg'nɔstik], *s.* der Agnostiker.
ago [ə'gou], *adv.* vor; *long* —, vor langer Zeit; *not long* —, kürzlich; *a month* —, vor einem Monat.
agog [ə'gɔg], *adv.* erregt, gespannt, neugierig (*for*, auf, *Acc.*).
agonize ['ægənaiz], *v.a.* quälen, martern. — *v.n.* Qual erleiden; mit dem Tode ringen *or* kämpfen.
agonising ['ægənaiziŋ], *adj.* schmerzhaft, qualvoll.
agony ['ægəni], *s.* die Pein, Qual; der Todeskampf; — *column*, die Seufzerspalte.
agrarian [ə'grɛəriən], *adj.* landwirtschaftlich; — *party*, die Bauernpartei.
agree [ə'gri:], *v.n.* übereinstimmen (*be in agreement*); übereinkommen (*come to an agreement*), sich einigen.
agreeable [ə'gri:əbl], *adj.* angenehm, gefällig.
agreement [ə'gri:mənt], *s.* die Übereinstimmung, das Übereinkommen; der Vertrag, die Verständigung (*understanding*).
agricultural [ægri'kʌltʃərəl], *adj.* landwirtschaftlich.
agriculture ['ægrikʌltʃə], *s.* die Landwirtschaft.
aground [ə'graund], *adj., adv.* (*Naut.*) gestrandet; *to run* —, stranden.
ague ['eigju:], *s.* (*Med.*) der Schüttelfrost.
ah! [ɑ:], *interj.* ach!; aha! (*surprise*).
aha! [ɑ'hɑ:], *interj.* ach so!
ahead [ə'hed], *adv.* vorwärts, voran (*movement*), voraus (*position*), *go* — (*carry on*), fortfahren; *go* — (*make progress*), vorwärtskommen.
ahoy! [ə'hɔi], *interj.* (*Naut.*) ahoi!
aid [eid], *v.a.* helfen (*Dat.*), unterstützen (*Acc.*), beistehen (*Dat.*). — *s.* die Hilfe, der Beistand.
aide-de-camp ['eiddə'kɑ̃], *s.* der Adjutant (eines Generals).
ail [eil], *v.n.* schmerzen; krank sein.
ailing ['eiliŋ], *adj.* kränklich, leidend.
ailment ['eilmənt], *s.* das Leiden.
aim [eim], *v.a.* (*weapon, blow etc.*) richten (*at*, auf). — *v.n.* zielen (auf, *Acc.*); trachten (nach, *strive for*). — *s*, das, Ziel, der Zweck (*purpose*); die Absicht (*intention*).
aimless ['eimlis], *adj.* ziellos, zwecklos.

air [ɛə], *s.* die Luft; die Melodie (*tune*); die Miene (*mien*); *air force*, die Luftwaffe; *air pocket*, das Luftloch; *air raid*, der Luftangriff; *in the open* —, im Freien; *on the* —, im Rundfunk; *to give oneself* —*s*, vornehm tun. — *v.a.* lüften (*room*); trocknen (*washing*); aussprechen (*views*).
airbase ['ɛəbeis], *s.* der Fliegerstützpunkt.
airconditioning ['ɛəkəndiʃəniŋ], *s.* die Klimaanlage.
aircraft ['ɛəkrɑ:ft], *s.* das Luftfahrzeug, Flugzeug.
airgun ['ɛəgʌn], *s.* die Windbüchse, das Luftgewehr.
airiness ['ɛərinis], *s.* die Luftigkeit, Leichtigkeit.
airletter ['ɛəletə], *s.* der Luftpostbrief.
airliner ['ɛəlainə], *s.* das Verkehrsflugzeug.
airmail ['ɛəmeil], *s.* die Luftpost.
airman ['ɛəmən], *s.* der Flieger.
airplane *see* **aeroplane.**
airport ['ɛəpɔ:t], *s.* der Flughafen.
airtight ['ɛətait], *adj.* luftdicht.
airy ['ɛəri], *adj.* luftig.
aisle [ail], *s.* das Seitenschiff (*church*); der Gang.
Aix-la-Chapelle ['eikslaʃæ'pel], Aachen, *n.*
ajar [ə'dʒɑ:], *adv.* angelehnt, halb offen.
akimbo [ə'kimbou], *adv.* Hände an den Hüften, Arme in die Seiten gestemmt.
akin [ə'kin], *adj.* verwandt (*to*, mit, *Dat.*).
alack [ə'læk], *interj.* ach! oh, weh! *alas and* —, ach und wehe!
alacrity [ə'lækriti], *s.* die Bereitwilligkeit; Munterkeit.
alarm [ə'lɑ:m], *s.* der Alarm; Lärm (*noise*); die Warnung; Angst, Bestürzung; — *clock*, der Wecker. — *v.a.* erschrecken.
alas! [ə'læs], *interj.* ach, wehe!
Albanian [æl'beiniən], *adj.* albanisch. — *s.* der Albanier.
album ['ælbəm], *s.* das Album.
albumen [æl'bju:mən], *s.* das Eiweiß, (*Chem.*) der Eiweißstoff.
albuminous [æl'bju:minəs], *adj.* eiweißhaltig, Eiweiß-.
alchemist ['ælkimist], *s.* der Alchimist.
alchemy ['ælkimi], *s.* die Alchimie.
alcohol ['ælkəhɔl], *s.* der Alkohol.
alcoholic [ælkə'hɔlik], *adj.* alkoholisch. — *s.* der Trinker, Alkoholiker.
alcove ['ælkouv], *s.* der Alkoven.
alder ['ɔ:ldə], *s.* (*Bot.*) die Erle.
alderman ['ɔ:ldəmən], *s.* der Ratsherr, der Stadtrat.
ale [eil], *s.* englisches Bier.
alert [ə'lə:t], *adj.* wachsam, aufmerksam; *on the* —, auf der Hut.
algebra ['ældʒibrə], *s.* die Algebra.
Algerian [æl'dʒiəriən], *adj.* algerisch. — *s.* der Algerier.
Algiers [æl'dʒiəz]. Algier, *n.*
alias ['eiliəs], *adv.* sonst genannt.
alien ['eiliən], *adj.* fremd, ausländisch. — *s.* der Fremde, Ausländer.
alienate ['eiliəneit], *v.a.* entfremden.
alienation [eiliə'neiʃən], *s.* die Entfremdung; — *of mind*, die Geisteserkrankung, Geistesgestörtheit.
alienist ['eiliənist], *s.* der Irrenarzt.
alight (1) [ə'lait], *v.n.* absteigen (*from horse*); aussteigen (*from carriage etc.*).
alight (2) [ə'lait], *adj.* brennend, in Flammen.
alike [ə'laik], *adj.* gleich, ähnlich. — *adv. great and small* —, sowohl große wie kleine.
alimentary [æli'mentəri], *adj.* Nahrungs-, Verdauungs-; — *canal*, (*Anat.*) der Darmkanal.
alimentation [ælimen'teiʃən], *s.* die Beköstigung; (*Law*) der Unterhalt.
alimony ['æliməni], *s.* der Unterhaltsbeitrag; (*pl.*) Alimente. , *n.pl.*
alive [ə'laiv], *adj.* lebendig; — *and kicking*, wohlauf, munter; — *to*, empfänglich für.
alkali ['ælkəlai], *s.* (*Chem.*) das Laugensalz, Alkali.
alkaline ['ælkəlain], *adj.* (*Chem.*) alkalisch, laugensalzig.
all [ɔ:l], *adj.*, *pron.* all, ganz (*whole*); sämtliche, alle; *above* —, vor allem; *once and for* —, ein für allemal; *not at* —, keineswegs; *All Saints*, Allerheiligen; *All Souls*, Allerseelen. — *adv.* ganz, gänzlich, völlig; — *the same*, trotzdem; — *the better*, umso besser.
allay [ə'lei], *v.a.* lindern, beruhigen, unterdrücken.
allegation [æli'geiʃən], *s.* die Behauptung.
allege [ə'ledʒ], *v.a.* behaupten, aussagen.
allegiance [ə'li:dʒəns], *s.* die Treue, Ergebenheit; Untertanenpflicht.
allegorical [æli'gɔrikəl], *adj.* allegorisch, sinnbildlich.
alleviate [ə'li:vieit], *v.a.* erleichtern, mildern.
alleviation [əli:vi'eiʃən], *s.* die Erleichterung, Milderung.
alley ['æli], *s.* die Gasse; Seitenstraße; *bowling* —, die Kegelbahn.
alliance [ə'laiəns], *s.* (*Pol.*) die Allianz, das Bündnis (*treaty*); der Bund (*league*).
allied [ə'laid, 'ælaid], *adj.* verbündet, vereinigt; alliiert; verwandt.
alliteration [əlitə'reiʃən], *s.* die Alliteration, der Stabreim.
allocate ['æləkeit], *v.a.* zuweisen, zuteilen.
allot [ə'lɔt], *v.a.* zuteilen (*assign*); verteilen (*distribute*).
allotment [ə'lɔtmənt], *s.* der Anteil; die Zuteilung; die Landparzelle; die Laubenkolonie, der Schrebergarten (*garden*).
allow [ə'lau], *v.a.* gewähren (*grant*); erlauben (*permit*); zulassen (*admit*). — *v.n.* — *for*, Rücksicht nehmen auf (*Acc.*); in Betracht ziehen.

allowance [ə'lauəns], *s.* die Rente; das Taschengeld (*money*); die Erlaubnis (*permission*); die Genehmigung (*approval*); die Nachsicht (*indulgence*).
alloy [ə'lɔi, 'ælɔi], *s.* die Legierung. — *v.a.* (*Metall.*) legieren.
allude [ə'lu:d], *v.a.* anspielen (*to*, auf).
allure [ə'ljuə], *v.a.* locken, anlocken.
allurement [ə'ljuəmənt], *s.* der Reiz, die Lockung.
allusion [ə'lu:ʒən], *s.* die Anspielung.
alluvial [ə'lu:viəl], *adj.* angeschwemmt.
alluvium [ə'lu:viəm], *s.* das Schwemmgebiet, Schwemmland.
ally ['ælai], *s.* der Verbündete, Bundesgenosse, Alliierte. — [ə'lai], *v.a.*, *v.r.* (sich) vereinigen, (sich) verbünden.
almanac ['ɔ:lmənæk], *s.* der Almanach.
almighty [ɔ:l'maiti], *adj.* allmächtig; *God Almighty!* allmächtiger Gott!
almond ['ɑ:mənd], *s.* (*Bot.*) die Mandel.
almoner ['ælmənə], *s.* der Wohlfahrtsbeamte, die Fürsorgerin.
almost ['ɔ:lmoust], *adv.* fast, beinahe.
alms [a:mz], *s.* das Almosen.
aloe ['ælou], *s.* (*Bot.*) die Aloe.
aloft [ə'lɔft], *adv.* droben, (hoch) oben; empor.
alone [ə'loun], *adj.*, *adv.* allein; *all* —, ganz allein; *leave* —, in Ruhe lassen; *let* —, geschweige (denn).
along [ə'lɔŋ], *adv.* längs, der Länge nach; entlang, weiter; *come —!* komm mit!; *get* — (*with*), auskommen. — *prep.* längs; entlang.
alongside [əlɔŋ'said], *adv.* nebenan. — [ə'lɔŋsaid], *prep.* neben.
aloof [ə'lu:f], *adj.*, *adv.* fern, weitab; *keep* —, sich fernhalten.
aloofness [ə'lu:fnis], *s.* das Sichfernhalten; das Vornehmtun.
aloud [ə'laud], *adj.*, *adv.* laut; hörbar.
alphabet ['ælfəbet], *s.* das Alphabet, Abc.
Alpine ['ælpain], *adj.* alpinisch, Alpen-.
Alps, The [ælps, ði]. die Alpen, *pl.*
already [ɔ:l'redi], *adv.* schon, bereits.
Alsatian [æl'seiʃən], *adj.* elsässisch. — *s.* der Elsässer; (*dog*) der Wolfshund, deutscher Schäferhund.
also ['ɔ:lsou], *adv.* (*likewise*) auch, ebenfalls; (*moreover*) ferner.
altar ['ɔ:ltə], *s.* der Altar.
alter ['ɔ:ltə], *v.a.* ändern, verändern. — *v.n.* sich (ver)ändern.
alterable ['ɔ:ltərəbl], *adj.* veränderlich.
alteration [ɔ:ltə'reiʃən], *s.* die Änderung, Veränderung.
altercation [ɔ:ltə'keiʃən], *s.* der Zank, Streit; Wortwechsel.
alternate ['ɔ:ltəneit], *v.a.*, *v.n.* abwechseln lassen, abwechseln.
alternative [ɔ:l'tə:nətiv], *adj.* abwechselnd, alternativ, zur Wahl gestellt. — *s.* die Alternative, die Wahl.
although [ɔ:l'ðou], *conj.* obgleich, obwohl, obschon.
altimeter ['æltimi:tə], *s.* der Höhenmesser.
altitude ['æltitju:d], *s.* die Höhe.
alto ['æltou], *s.* (*Mus.*) die Altstimme, der Alt.
altogether [ɔ:ltu'geðə], *adv.* zusammen, zusammengenommen, allesamt; (*wholly*) ganz und gar, durchaus.
alum ['æləm], *s.* (*Chem.*) der Alaun.
aluminium [ælju'minjəm], (*Am.*) **aluminum** [ə'lu:minəm], *s.* das Aluminium.
always ['ɔ:lweiz], *adv.* immer, stets.
am [æm] *see* **be.**
amalgamate [ə'mælgəmeit], *v.a.* amalgamieren. — *v.n.* sich vereinigen, vermischen.
amalgamation [əmælgə'meiʃən], *s.* die Verbindung, Vereinigung.
amass [ə'mæs], *v.a.* anhäufen, zusammentragen.
amateur [æmə'tə: *or* 'æmətjuə], *s.* der Amateur, Liebhaber.
amatory ['æmətəri], *adj.* Liebes-, verliebt, sinnlich.
amaze [ə'meiz], *v.a.* erstaunen, in Erstaunen versetzen; verblüffen (*baffle*).
amazement [ə'meizmənt], *s.* das Erstaunen, Staunen, die Verwunderung.
amazing [ə'meiziŋ], *adj.* erstaunlich, wunderbar.
Amazon (1) ['æməzən], *s.* (*Myth.*) die Amazone.
Amazon (2) ['æməzən], *s.* (*river*) der Amazonas.
ambassador [æm'bæsədə], *s.* der Botschafter.
ambassadorial [æmbæsə'dɔ:riəl], *adj.* Botschafts-, gesandtschaftlich.
amber ['æmbə], *s.* der Bernstein.
ambidextrous [æmbi'dekstrəs], *adj.* (mit beiden Händen gleich) geschickt.
ambiguity [æmbi'gju:iti], *s.* die Zweideutigkeit, der Doppelsinn.
ambiguous [æm'bigjuəs], *adj.* zweideutig; dunkel (*sense*).
ambit ['æmbit], *s.* der Umkreis, die Umgebung.
ambition [æm'biʃən], *s.* die Ambition, der Ehrgeiz.
ambitious [æm'biʃəs], *adj.* ehrgeizig.
amble [æmbl], *v.n.* schlendern, (gemächlich) spazieren.
ambulance ['æmbjuləns], *s.* der Krankenwagen.
ambush ['æmbuʃ], *v.a.* überfallen (*Acc.*), auflauern (*Dat.*). — *s.* die Falle, der Hinterhalt.
ameliorate [ə'mi:liəreit], *v.a.* verbessern.
amenable [ə'mi:nəbl], *adj.* zugänglich; unterworfen.
amend [ə'mend], *v.a.* verbessern, berichtigen; ändern.
amendment [ə'mendmənt], *s.* die Verbesserung; der Zusatz, die zusätzliche Änderung (*proposal*).
amends [ə'mendz], *s. pl.* der Schadenersatz; *make* —, Schadenersatz leisten; wiedergutmachen.

amenity [ə'mi:niti *or* ə'meniti], *s.* die Behaglichkeit, Annehmlichkeit; (*pl.*) die Vorzüge, *m pl.*; die Einrichtungen, *f. pl.*
American [ə'merikən], *adj.* amerikanisch; — *cloth*, das Wachstuch. — *s.* der Amerikaner.
amiability [eimjə'biliti], *s.* die Liebenswürdigkeit.
amiable ['eimjəbl], *adj.* liebenswürdig.
amicable ['æmikəbl], *adj.* freundschaftlich.
amidst [ə'midst], *prep.* mitten in, mitten unter (*Dat.*), inmitten (*Gen.*).
amiss [ə'mis], *adj.*, *adv.* übel; verkehrt; *take* —, übelnehmen.
amity ['æmiti], *s.* die Freundschaft.
ammonia [ə'mouniə], *s.* das Ammoniak; *liquid* —, der Salmiakgeist.
ammunition [æmju'niʃən], *s.* die Munition.
amnesty ['æmnisti], *s.* die Amnestie, Begnadigung.
among(st) [ə'mʌŋ(st)], *prep.* (mitten) unter, zwischen, bei.
amorous ['æmərəs], *adj.* verliebt.
amorphous [ə'mɔ:fəs], *adj.* amorph, gestaltlos, formlos.
amortization [əmɔ:ti'zeiʃən], *s.* die Amortisierung (*debt*); (*Comm.*) Tilgung, Abtragung.
amount [ə'maunt], *s.* der Betrag (*sum of money*); die Menge (*quantity*). — *v.n.* betragen; — *to*, sich belaufen auf (*Acc.*).
amphibian [æm'fibiən], *adj.* amphibisch. — *s.* (*Zool.*) die Amphibie.
amphibious [æm'fibiəs], *adj.* amphibienhaft.
ample [æmpl], *adj.* weit, breit (*scope*); voll, reichlich; ausgebreitet; genügend.
amplification [æmplifi'keiʃən], *s.* die Ausbreitung; Verbreiterung, Erklärung, Erweiterung; (*Elec.*) die Verstärkung (*sound*).
amplifier ['æmplifaiə], *s.* der Verstärker; der Lautsprecher.
amplify ['æmplifai], *v.a.* erweitern, ausführen, vergrößern; verstärken (*sound*).
amputate ['æmpjuteit], *v.a.* amputieren.
amputation [æmpju'teiʃən], *s.* die Amputation.
amuck [ə'mʌk], *adv.* amok.
amulet ['æmjulit], *s.* das Amulett.
amuse [ə'mju:z], *v.a.* unterhalten, amüsieren.
amusement [ə'mju:zmənt], *s.* die Unterhaltung, das Vergnügen.
an *see under* **a.**
Anabaptist [ænə'bæptist], *s.* der Wiedertäufer.
anachronism [ə'nækrənizm], *s.* der Anachronismus.
anaemia [ə'ni:miə], *s.* (*Med.*) die Blutarmut.
anaemic [ə'ni:mik], *adj.* (*Med.*) blutarm.
anaesthetic [ænəs'θetik], *adj.* schmerzbetäubend. — *s.* die Narkose.
analogous [ə'næləgəs], *adj.* analog.
analogy [ə'nælədʒi], *s.* die Analogie.
analyse ['ænəlaiz], *v.a.* analysieren.
analysis [ə'nælisis], *s.* die Analyse.
anarchic(al) [ə'na:kik(əl)], *adj.* anarchisch.
anarchy ['ænəki], *s.* die Anarchie.
anathema [ə'næθimə], *s.* (*Eccl.*) der Kirchenbann.
anatomical [ænə'tɔmikəl], *adj.* anatomisch.
anatomist [ə'nætəmist], *s.* der Anatom.
anatomize [ə'nætəmaiz], *v.a.* zergliedern, zerlegen.
anatomy [ə'nætəmi], *s.* die Anatomie.
ancestor ['ænsəstə], *s.* der Vorfahre, Ahnherr.
ancestry ['ænsəstri], *s.* die Ahnenreihe, Herkunft, der Stammbaum (*family tree*).
anchor ['æŋkə], *s.* der Anker. — *v.a.* verankern. — *v.n.* ankern.
anchorage ['æŋkəridʒ], *s.* die Verankerung; der Ankerplatz.
anchovy [æn'tʃouvi *or* 'æntʃəvi], *s.* (*Zool.*) die Sardelle.
ancient ['einʃənt], *adj.* alt, uralt, antik; althergebracht (*traditional*). — *s.* (*pl.*) die Alten (Griechen und Römer).
and [ænd], *conj.* und.
Andes, the ['ændi:z, ði]. die Anden, *pl.*
anecdote ['ænekdout], *s.* die Anekdote.
anemone [ə'neməni], *s.* (*Bot.*) die Anemone, das Windröschen; (*Zool.*) *sea* —, die Seeanemone.
anew [ə'nju:], *adv.* von neuem.
angel ['eindʒəl], *s.* der Engel.
angelic [æn'dʒelik], *adj.* engelhaft, engelgleich.
anger ['æŋgə], *s.* der Zorn, Unwille, Ärger. — *v.a.* erzürnen, verärgern, ärgerlich machen.
angle [æŋgl], *s.* (*Geom.*) der Winkel; die Angel (*fishing*). — *v.n.* angeln (*for*, nach).
Angles [æŋglz], *s. pl.* die Angeln, *m. pl.*
Anglo-Saxon [æŋglou'sæksən], *adj.* angelsächsisch. — *s.* der Angelsachse.
anglicism ['æŋglisizm], *s.* der Anglizismus (*style*).
anguish ['æŋgwiʃ], *s.* die Qual, Pein.
angular ['æŋgjulə], *adj.* winklig, eckig.
anhydrous [æn'haidrəs], *adj.* wasserfrei, (*Chem.*) wasserlos.
aniline ['ænilain], *s.* das Anilin. — *adj.* — *dye*, die Anilinfarbe.
animal ['æniməl], *s.* das Tier, Lebewesen.
animate ['ænimeit], *v.a.* beleben, beseelen; (*fig.*) anregen.
animated ['ænimeitid], *adj.* belebt; munter.
animation [æni'meiʃən], *s.* die Belebung.
animosity [æni'mɔsiti], *s.* die Feindseligkeit, Abneigung, Erbitterung.
anise ['ænis], *s.* (*Bot.*) der Anis.

ankle [æŋkl], *s.* (*Anat.*) der Fußknöchel; — *socks*, kurze Socken.
anklet ['æŋklit], *s.* der Fußring.
annalist ['ænəlist], *s.* der Chronist, Geschichtsschreiber.
annals ['ænəlz], *s. pl.* die Annalen (*f. pl.*); die Chronik (*sing.*).
anneal [ə'ni:l], *v.a.* ausglühen.
annex [ə'neks], *v.a.* annektieren, angliedern, sich aneignen.
annex(e) ['æneks], *s.* der Anhang, der Anbau.
annexation [ænek'seiʃən], *s.* die Angliederung, Aneignung.
annihilate [ə'naiileit], *v.a.* vernichten, zerstören.
annihilation [ənaii'leiʃən], *s.* die Vernichtung, Zerstörung.
anniversary [æni'və:səri], *s.* der Jahrestag, die Jahresfeier.
annotate ['ænoteit], *v.a.* anmerken, mit Anmerkungen versehen.
annotation [æno'teiʃən], *s.* die Anmerkung, Notiz.
announce [ə'nauns], *v.a.* melden, ankündigen; anzeigen; (*Rad.*) ansagen.
announcement [ə'naunsmənt], *s.* die Ankündigung, Bekanntmachung; (*Rad.*) die Ansage.
announcer [ə'naunsə], *s.* (*Rad.*) der Ansager.
annoy [ə'nɔi], *v.a.* ärgern; belästigen.
annoyance [ə'nɔiəns], *s.* das Ärgernis; die Belästigung.
annual ['ænjuəl], *adj.* jährlich, Jahres-. — *s.* der Jahresband (*serial publication*); das Jahrbuch; (*Bot.*) die einjährige Pflanze.
annuity [ə'nju:iti], *s.* die Jahresrente, Lebensrente.
annul [ə'nʌl], *v.a.* annullieren, ungültig machen, für ungültig erklären.
annulment [ə'nʌlmənt], *s.* die Annullierung, Ungültigkeitserklärung.
Annunciation [ənʌnsi'eiʃən], *s.* (*Eccl.*) die Verkündigung.
anode ['ænoud], *s.* die Anode.
anodyne ['ænodain], *adj.* schmerzstillend.
anoint [ə'nɔint], *v.a.* salben.
anomalous [ə'nɔmələs], *adj.* abweichend, unregelmäßig, anomal.
anomaly [ə'nɔməli], *s.* die Anomalie, Abweichung, Unregelmäßigkeit.
anon [ə'nɔn], *adv.* sogleich, sofort.
anonymous [ə'nɔniməs], *adj.* (*abbr.* **anon.**) anonym; namenlos; unbekannt.
anonymity [æno'nimiti], *s.* die Anonymität.
another [ə'nʌðə], *adj. & pron.* ein anderer; ein zweiter; noch einer; *one* —, einander.
answer ['ɑ:nsə], *v.a.* beantworten. — *v.n.* antworten. — *s.* die Antwort, Erwiderung.
answerable ['ɑ:nsərəbl], *adj.* verantwortlich (*responsible*); beantwortbar (*capable of being answered*).
ant [ænt], *s.* (*Ent.*) die Ameise.
antagonise [æn'tægənaiz], *v.a.* sich (*Dat.*) jemanden zum Gegner machen.
antagonism [æn'tægənizm], *s.* der Widerstreit, Konflikt; der Antagonismus.
Antarctic [ænt'ɑ:ktik], *adj.* Südpol-, antarktisch. — *s.* der südliche Polarkreis.
antecedence [ænti'si:dəns], *s.* der Vortritt (*rank*).
antecedent [ænti'si:dənt], *s.* (*pl.*) das Vorhergehende, die Vorgeschichte.
antedate ['æntideit], *v.a.* vordatieren.
antediluvian [æntidi'lu:viən], *adj.* vorsintflutlich; (*fig.*) überholt; altmodisch.
antelope ['æntiloup], *s.* (*Zool.*) die Antilope.
antenna [æn'tenə], *s.* (*Ent.*) der Fühler; (*Rad.*) die Antenne.
anterior [æn'tiəriə], *adj.* vorder (*in space*), älter, vorherig, vorhergehend, (*in time*).
anteroom ['æntiru:m], *s.* das Vorzimmer.
anthem ['ænθəm], *s.* die Hymne, der Hymnus.
anther ['ænθə], *s.* (*Bot.*) der Staubbeutel.
antic ['æntik], *s.* die Posse; (*pl.*) komisches Benehmen.
anticipate [æn'tisipeit], *v.a.* vorwegnehmen; zuvorkommen; ahnen (*guess*); erwarten (*await*); vorgreifen.
anticipation [æntisi'peiʃən], *s.* die Vorwegnahme; die Erwartung.
antidote ['æntidout], *s.* das Gegengift.
antipathy [æn'tipəθi], *s.* die Antipathie, der Widerwille.
antipodal [æn'tipədəl], *adj.* antipodisch; entgegengesetzt.
antiquarian [ænti'kwɛəriən], *adj.* altertümlich; antiquarisch.
antiquary ['æntikwəri], *s.* der Altertumsforscher, Antiquar.
antiquated ['æntikweitid], *adj.* überholt, unmodern, veraltet.
antique [æn'ti:k], *s.* die Antike; das alte Kunstwerk. — *adj.* alt, antik; altmodisch.
antiquity [æn'tikwiti], *s.* die Antike, das Altertum; die Vorzeit (*period of history*).
antiseptic [ænti'septik], *adj.* antiseptisch —*s.* das antiseptische Mittel.
antler ['æntlə], *s.* die Geweihsprosse; (*pl.*) das Geweih.
anvil ['ænvil], *s.* der Amboß.
anxiety [æŋ'zaiəti], *s.* die Angst (*fear*); Besorgnis (*uneasiness*); Unruhe.
anxious ['æŋkʃəs], *adj.* ängstlich (*afraid*); besorgt (*worried*); eifrig bemüht (*keen*, um, *on*, *Acc.*).
any ['eni], *adj. & pron.* jeder; irgendein; etwas; (*pl.*) einige; (*neg.*) *not* —, kein.
anybody, anyone ['enibɔdi, 'eniwʌn], *pron.* irgendeiner, jemand; jeder.
anyhow, anyway ['enihau, 'eniwei], *adv.* irgendwie, auf irgendeine Weise; auf alle Fälle.
anyone *see under* **anybody**.

anything ['eniθiŋ], *s.* irgend etwas; alles.
anyway *see under* **anyhow.**
anywhere ['enihwɛə], *adv.* irgendwo; überall; *not* —, nirgends.
apace [ə'peis], *adv.* geschwind, hurtig, flink.
apart [ə'pɑ:t], *adv.* für sich, abgesondert; einzeln; *poles* —, weit entfernt; *take* —, zerlegen; — *from*, abgesehen von.
apartment [ə'pɑ:tmənt], *s.* das Zimmer; (*Am.*) die Wohnung (*flat*).
apathy ['æpəθi], *s.* die Apathie, Interesselosigkeit, Gleichgültigkeit.
apathetic [æpə'θetik], *adj.* apathisch, uninteressiert; teilnahmslos.
ape [eip], *s.* (*Zool.*) der Affe. — *v.a.* nachäffen, nachahmen.
aperient [ə'piəriənt], *adj.* (*Med.*) abführend. — *s.* (*Med.*) das Abführmittel.
aperture ['æpətʃə], *s.* die Öffnung.
apex ['eipeks], *s.* die Spitze, der Gipfel.
aphorism ['æfərizm], *s.* der Aphorismus.
apiary ['eipiəri], *s.* das Bienenhaus.
apiece [ə'pi:s], *adv.* pro Stück, pro Person.
apologetic [əpɔlə'dʒetik], *adj.* entschuldigend, reumütig; verteidigend.
apologize [ə'pɔlədʒaiz], *v.n.* sich entschuldigen (*for*, wegen; *to*, bei).
apology [ə'pɔlədʒi], *s.* die Entschuldigung; Abbitte; Rechtfertigung.
apoplectic [æpə'plektik], *adj.* (*Med.*) apoplektisch.
apoplexy ['æpəpleksi], *s.* (*Med.*) der Schlagfluß, Schlaganfall (*fit*).
apostle [ə'pɔsl], *s.* der Apostel.
apostolic [æpəs'tɔlik], *adj.* apostolisch.
apostrophe [ə'pɔstrəfi], *s.* der Apostroph (*punctuation*); die Anrede (*speech*).
apostrophize [ə'pɔstrəfaiz], *v.a.* apostrophieren; anreden (*speak to*).
apotheosis [əpɔθi'ousis], *s.* die Apotheose.
appal [ə'pɔ:l], *v.a.* erschrecken.
appalling [ə'pɔ:liŋ], *adj.* schrecklich.
apparatus [æpə'reitəs], *s.* das Gerät, die Apparatur; (*coll.*) der Apparat.
apparel [ə'pærəl], *s.* die Kleidung.
apparent [ə'pærənt], *adj.* scheinbar; offensichtlich; augenscheinlich; *heir* —, der rechtmäßige Erbe.
apparition [æpə'riʃən], *s.* die Erscheinung; der Geist, das Gespenst (*ghost*).
appeal [ə'pi:l], *v.n.* appellieren (*make an appeal*); (*Law*) Berufung einlegen; gefallen (*please*). — *s.* (*public, Mil.*) der Appell; die Bitte (*request*).
appear [ə'piə], *v.n.* erscheinen; scheinen; auftreten.
appearance [ə'piərəns], *s.* die Erscheinung; das Auftreten (*stage, etc.*); der Schein (*semblance*); *keep up* —*s*, den Schein wahren; *to all* —*s*, allem Anschein nach.
appease [ə'pi:z], *v.a.* besänftigen.
appeasement [ə'pi:zmənt], *s.* die Besänftigung, (*Pol.*) die Befriedung.
appellation [æpe'leiʃən], *s.* die Benennung.
append [ə'pend], *v.a.* anhängen, beifügen.
appendicitis [əpendi'saitis], *s.* (*Med.*) die Blinddarmentzündung.
appendix [ə'pendiks], *s.* der Anhang; (*Med.*) der Blinddarm.
appertain [æpə'tein], *v.n.* gehören (*to*, zu).
appetite ['æpitait], *s.* der Appetit.
appetizing ['æpitaiziŋ], *adj.* appetitlich, appetitanregend.
applaud [ə'plɔ:d], *v.a.*, *v.n.* applaudieren, Beifall klatschen (*Dat.*).
applause [ə'plɔ:z], *s.* der Applaus, Beifall.
apple [æpl], *s.* der Apfel.
appliance [ə'plaiəns], *s.* das Gerät, die Vorrichtung.
applicable ['æplikəbl], *adj.* anwendbar, passend (*to*, auf).
applicant ['æplikənt], *s.* der Bewerber (*for*, um).
application [æpli'keiʃən], *s.* die Bewerbung (*for*, um); das Gesuch; die Anwendung (*to*, auf); *letter of* —, der Bewerbungsbrief; — *form*, das Bewerbungsformular.
apply [ə'plai], *v.a.* anwenden (auf, *to*, *Acc.*); gebrauchen. — *v.n.* sich bewerben (um, *for*, *Acc.*); (*Dat.*) *this does not* —, das trifft nicht zu; — *within*, drinnen nachfragen.
appoint [ə'pɔint], *v.a.* bestimmen; ernennen; ausrüsten.
appointment [ə'pɔintmənt], *s.* die Festsetzung; die Ernennung; die Bestellung, die Stellung (*position*); *make an* —, jemanden ernennen (*fill a post*), sich verabreden (*arrange to meet*); *by* —, Hoflieferant (*to*, *Genit.*).
apportion [ə'pɔ:ʃən], *v.a.* zuteilen, zuweisen, zumessen.
apposite ['æpəzit], *adj.* passend, angemessen.
appositeness ['æpəzitnis], *s.* die Angemessenheit.
appraise [ə'preiz], *v.a.* beurteilen.
appraisal [ə'preizəl], *s.* die Beurteilung, Abschätzung.
appreciable [ə'pri:ʃəbl], *adj.* merklich; nennenswert.
appreciate [ə'pri:ʃieit], *v.a.* würdigen, schätzen.
appreciation [əpri:ʃi'eiʃən], *s.* die Schätzung, Würdigung.
apprehend [æpri'hend], *v.a.* verhaften, ergreifen (*arrest*); befürchten (*fear*).
apprehension [æpri'henʃən], *s.* die Verhaftung (*arrest*); die Befürchtung (*fear*).
apprehensive [æpri'hensiv], *adj.* besorgt, in Furcht (*for*, um), furchtsam.
apprentice [ə'prentis], *s.* der Lehrling; Praktikant. — *v.a.* in die Lehre geben (*with*, bei, *Dat.*).

apprenticeship [ə'prentiʃip], *s.* die Lehre, Lehrzeit, Praktikantenzeit; *student* —, die Studentenpraxis.
apprise [ə'praiz], *v.a.* benachrichtigen, informieren.
approach [ə'proutʃ], *v.a., v.n.* sich nähern (*Dat.*). — *s.* die Annäherung, das Herankommen, Näherrücken.
approachable [ə'proutʃəbl], *adj.* zugänglich, freundlich.
approbation [æpro'beiʃən], *s.* die (offizielle) Billigung, Zustimmung.
appropriate [ə'proupriit], *adj.* angemessen, gebührend, geeignet (*suitable*). — [ə'prouprieit], *v.a.* requirieren, sich aneignen.
appropriation [əproupri'eiʃən], *s.* die Requisition, Aneignung, Übernahme, Besitznahme.
approval [ə'pru:vəl], *s.* die Billigung, der Beifall, die Zustimmung.
approve [ə'pru:v], *v.a.* loben, billigen; genehmigen; annehmen (*work*).
approved [ə'pru:vd], *adj.* anerkannt.
approximate [ə'prɔksimit], *adj.* ungefähr, annähernd. —*v.n.* & *a.*[ə'prɔksımeıt], sich nähern.
approximation [əprɔksi'meiʃən], *s.* die Annäherung.
approximative [ə'prɔksimətiv], *adj.* annähernd.
appurtenance [ə'pə:tənəns], *s.* das (*or* der) Zubehör.
appurtenant [ə'pə:tənənt], *adj.* zugehörig.
apricot ['eiprikɔt], *s.* (*Bot.*) die Aprikose.
April ['eipril]. der April.
apron ['eiprən], *s.* die Schürze; der Schurz; — *stage*, die Vorbühne, das Proszenium.
apropos [ɑ:prɔ'pou], *adv.* beiläufig; mit Bezug auf, diesbezüglich.
apse [æps], *s.* (*Archit.*) die Apsis.
apt [æpt], *adj.* geeignet, passend; fähig.
aptitude ['æptitju:d], *s.* die Eignung, Fähigkeit.
aptness ['æptnis], *s.* die Angemessenheit, Eignung.
aquatic [ə'kwɔtik *or* ə'kwætik], *adj.* Wasser-, wasser-; — *display*, Wasserkünste. — *s.* (*pl.*) der Wassersport.
aqueduct ['ækwidʌkt], *s.* die Wasserleitung; der Aquädukt.
aqueous ['eikwiəs], *adj.* (*Chem.*) wässerig.
aquiline ['ækwilain], *adj.* adlerartig, Adler-.
Arab ['ærəb], *s.* der Araber.
Arabian [ə'reibiən], *adj.* arabisch; — *Nights*, Tausend-und-eine-Nacht.
Arabic ['ærəbik], *adj.* arabisch (*language, literature*).
arable ['ærəbl], *adj.* pflügbar, bestellbar.
arbiter ['ɑ:bitə], *s.* der Schiedsrichter.
arbitrary ['ɑ:bitrəri], *adj.* willkürlich.
arbitrate ['ɑ:bitreit], *v.n.* vermitteln.
arbitration [ɑ:bi'treiʃən], *s.* die Vermittlung; Entscheidung; (*Comm.*) Arbitrage.
arboriculture ['ɑ:bɔrikʌltʃə], *s.* die Baumzucht.
arbour ['ɑ:bə], *s.* die Laube, Gartenlaube.
arc [ɑ:k], *s.* (*Geom.*) der Bogen; — *lamp*, die Bogenlampe; — *welding*, das Lichtschweißen.
arcade [ɑ:'keid], *s.* die Arkade.
Arcadian [ɑ:'keidiən], *adj.* arkadisch. — *s.* der Arkadier.
arch [ɑ:tʃ], *s.* der Bogen, die Wölbung; —*way*, der Bogengang. — *v.a., v.n.* wölben, sich wölben. — *adj.* schelmisch, listig. — *prefix* oberst; erst Haupt-; — -*enemy*, der Erzfeind.
archaeological [ɑ:kiə'lɔdʒikəl], *adj.* archäologisch.
archaeologist [ɑ:ki'ɔlədʒist], *s.* der Archäologe.
archaeology [ɑ:ki'ɔlədʒi], *s.* die Archäologie.
archaic [ɑ:'keiik], *adj.* altertümlich.
archaism ['ɑ:keiizm], *s.* der Archaismus (*style*).
archbishop [ɑ:tʃ'biʃəp], *s.* der Erzbischof.
archduke [ɑ:tʃ'dju:k], *s.* der Erzherzog.
archer ['ɑ:tʃə], *s.* der Bogenschütze.
archery ['ɑ:tʃəri], *s.* das Bogenschießen.
architect ['ɑ:kitekt], *s.* der Architekt, Baumeister.
architecture ['ɑ:kitektʃə], *s.* die Architektur, Baukunst.
archives ['ɑ:kaivz], *s. pl.* das Archiv.
Arctic ['ɑ:ktik], *adj.* arktisch. — *s.* die Nordpolarländer, *n. pl.*
ardent ['ɑ:dənt], *adj.* heiß, glühend, brennend.
ardour ['ɑ:də], *s.* die Hitze, die Inbrunst, der Eifer.
arduous ['ɑ:djuəs], *adj.* schwierig; mühsam.
area ['ɛəriə], *s.* das Areal (*measurement*); das Gebiet, die Zone; die Fläche (*region*).
arena [ə'ri:nə], *s.* die Arena, der Kampfplatz.
Argentine ['ɑ:dʒəntain], *adj.* argentinisch. — (*Republic*), Argentinien, *n.*
Argentinian [ɑ:dʒən'tiniən], *adj.* argentinisch. — *s.* der Argentin(i)er.
argue ['ɑ:gju:], *v.n.* disputieren, streiten; folgern, schließen.
argument ['ɑ:gjumənt], *s.* das Argument; (*Log.*) der Beweis; der Streit (*dispute*).
argumentative [ɑ:gju'mentətiv], *adj.* streitsüchtig.
arid ['ærid], *adj.* trocken, dürr.
aright [ə'rait], *adv.* richtig, zurecht.
arise [ə'raiz], *v.n. irr.* aufstehen; sich erheben; entstehen (*originate*); *arising from the minutes*, es ergibt sich aus dem Protokoll.
aristocracy [æris'tɔkrəsi], *s.* die Aristokratie, der Adel.
aristocratic [æris'o'krætik], *adj.* aristokratisch, adlig.
arithmetic [ə'riθmətik], *s.* die Arithmetik.

arithmetical [æriθ'metikəl], *adj.* arithmetisch.

ark [ɑ:k], *s.* die Arche; — *of the Covenant*, die Bundeslade.

arm (1) [ɑ:m], *s.* (*Anat.*) der Arm.

arm (2) [ɑ:m], *s.* die Waffe; *up in —s*, in Aufruhr. — *v.a.*, *v.n.* bewaffnen, sich bewaffnen, rüsten, sich rüsten.

armament ['ɑ:məmənt], *s.* die Rüstung, Bewaffnung.

armature ['ɑ:mətiuə], *s.* die Armatur.

armchair ['ɑ:mtʃɛə], *s.* der Lehnstuhl; der Sessel.

Armenian [ɑ:'mi:niən], *adj.* armenisch. — *s.* der Armenier.

armistice ['ɑ:mistis], *s.* der Waffenstillstand.

armour ['ɑ:mə], *s.* die Rüstung, der Harnisch; —*-plated*, gepanzert; —*ed car*, der Panzerwagen.

armourer ['ɑ:mərə], *s.* der Waffenschmied.

armoury ['ɑ:məri], *s.* die Rüstkammer, Waffenschmiede.

army ['ɑ:mi], *s.* die Armee, das Heer.

aroma [ə'roumə], *s.* das Aroma, der Duft.

aromatic [ærə'mætik], *adj.* aromatisch. —*s.* (*Chem.*) das Aromat.

around [ə'raund], *adv.* herum, rund-, ringsherum, umher, im Kreise; *stand* —, herumstehen; *be* —, sich in der Nähe halten. —*prep.* um; bei, um . . . herum.

arouse [ə'rauz], *v.a.* aufwecken, aufrütteln.

arraignment [ə'reinmənt], *s.* die Anklage.

arrange [ə'reindʒ], *v.a.* anordnen, arrangieren, einrichten, vereinbaren.

arrangement [ə'reindʒmənt], *s.* die Anordnung; die Einrichtung; die Vereinbarung (*agreement*); (*Law*) die Vergleichung, der Vergleich.

arrant ['ærənt], *adj.* durchtrieben.

array [ə'rei], *v.a.* schmücken, aufstellen. — *s.* die Ordnung; Aufstellung.

arrears [ə'riəz], *s. pl.* der Rückstand, die Schulden.

arrest [ə'rest], *v.a.* (*Law*) festnehmen, verhaften; festhalten; aufhalten (*hinder*). — *s.* die Festnahme; die Festhaltung.

arrival [ə'raivəl], *s.* die Ankunft.

arrive [ə'raiv], *v.n.* ankommen.

arrogance ['ærəgəns], *s.* die Anmaßung, Überheblichkeit.

arrogant ['ærəgənt], *adj.* anmaßend, hochfahrend, überheblich.

arrow ['ærou], *s.* der Pfeil.

arrowroot ['ærouru:t], *s.* (*Bot.*) die Pfeilwurz.

arsenal ['ɑ:sinəl], *s.* das Arsenal, Zeughaus.

arsenic ['ɑ:sənik], *s.* das Arsen.

arson ['ɑ:sən], *s.* die Brandstiftung.

art [ɑ:t], *s.* die Kunst; *fine* —, schöne Kunst; (*Univ.*) —*s faculty*, die philosophische Fakultät; —*s* (*subject*), das humanistische Fach, die Geisteswissenschaften.

arterial [ɑ:'tiəriəl], *adj.* Pulsader-, Schlagader-; — *road*, die Hauptverkehrsader, die Hauptstraße.

artery ['ɑ:təri], *s.* die Pulsader, Schlagader; der Hauptverkehrsweg.

artesian [ɑ:'ti:ʒən], *adj.* artesisch.

artful ['ɑ:tful], *adj.* listig, schlau.

article ['ɑ:tikl], *s.* (*Gram.*, *Law*, *Press*) der Artikel; der Posten (*item in list*). — *v.a. be —d to a solicitor*, bei einem Advokaten assistieren.

articulate [ɑ:'tikjuleit], *v.a.* artikulieren (*pronounce clearly*). — [—lit], *adj.* deutlich (*speech*).

articulation [a:tikju'leiʃən], *s.* die Artikulation, deutliche Aussprache.

artifice ['ɑ:tifis], *s.* der Kunstgriff, die List.

artificer [ɑ:'tifisə], *s.* der Handwerker.

artificial [ɑ:ti'fiʃəl], *adj.* künstlich, Kunst-; — *silk*, die Kunstseide.

artillery [ɑ:'tiləri], *s.* die Artillerie.

artisan [ɑ:ti'zæn], *s.* der Handwerker.

artist ['ɑ:tist], *s.* der Künstler, die Künstlerin.

artistic [ɑ:'tistik], *adj.* künstlerisch.

artless ['ɑ:tlis], *adj.* arglos, natürlich, naiv.

Aryan ['ɛəriən], *adj.* arisch. — *s.* der Arier.

as [æz], *adv.*, *conj.* so, als, wie, ebenso; als, während, weil; — *big* —, so groß wie; — *well* —, sowohl als auch; *such* —, wie; — *it were*, gleichsam.

asbestos [æz'bestɔs], *s.* der Asbest.

ascend [ə'send], *v.a.*, *v.n.* ersteigen, besteigen; emporsteigen.

ascendancy, -ency [ə'sendənsi], *s.* der Aufstieg; der Einfluß; das Übergewicht.

ascendant, -ent [ə'sendənt], *s. in the* —, aufsteigend.

ascent [ə'sent], *s.* der Aufstieg, die Besteigung.

ascension [ə'senʃən], *s.* (*Astron.*) das Aufsteigen; *Ascension Day*, Himmelfahrt(stag).

ascertain [æsə'tein], *v.a.* in Erfahrung bringen, erkunden, feststellen.

ascertainable [æsə'teinəbl], *adj.* erkundbar, feststellbar.

ascetic [ə'setik], *adj.* asketisch.

asceticism [ə'setisizm], *s.* die Askese.

ascribe [ə'skraib], *v.a.* zuschreiben.

ascribable [ə'skraibəbl], *adj.* zuzuschreiben, zuschreibbar.

ash (1) [æʃ], *s.* (*Bot.*) die Esche.

ash (2) [æʃ], *s.* die Asche.

ashamed [ə'ʃeimd], *adj.* beschämt; *be* —, sich schämen.

ashcan ['æʃkæn] (*Am.*) *see* **dustbin**.

ashen ['æʃən], *adj.* aschgrau, aschfarben.

ashore [ə'ʃɔ:], *adv.* am Land; am Ufer, ans Ufer *or* Land.

ashtray ['æʃtrei], *s.* der Aschenbecher.

Ash Wednesday [æʃ'wenzdei], *s.* der Aschermittwoch.

Asiatic [eiʃi'ætik], *adj.* asiatisch. — *s.* der Asiat.

aside [ə'said], *adv.* seitwärts, zur Seite; abseits.
ask [ɑ:sk], *v.a.*, *v.n.* fragen (*question*); bitten (*request*); fordern (*demand*); einladen (*invite*).
asleep [ə'sli:p], *pred. adj.*, *adv.* schlafend, im Schlaf; eingeschlafen.
asp [æsp], *s.* (*Zool.*) die Natter.
asparagus [æs'pærəgəs], *s.* (*Bot.*) der Spargel.
aspect ['æspekt], *s.* der Anblick, die Ansicht (*view, angle*); der Gesichtspunkt.
aspen ['æspən], *s.* (*Bot.*) die Espe.
asperity [æs'periti], *s.* die Härte; Rauheit.
aspersion [æs'pə:ʃən], *s.* die Verleumdung; Schmähung.
asphalt ['æsfælt], *s.* der Asphalt.
asphyxia [æs'fiksjə], *s.* (*Med.*) die Erstickung.
aspirant [ə'spaiərənt, 'æsp-], *s.* der Bewerber, Anwärter.
aspirate ['æspireit], *v.a.* (*Phon.*) aspirieren. — [—rit] *adj.* aspiriert. — *s.* der Hauchlaut.
aspiration [æspi'reiʃən], *s.* der Atemzug; das Streben (*striving*) ; (*Phon.*) die Aspiration.
aspire [ə'spaiə], *v.n.* streben, verlangen.
ass [æs], *s.* der Esel.
assail [ə'seil], *v.a.* angreifen, anfallen.
assailable [ə'seiləbl], *adj.* angreifbar.
assassin [ə'sæsin], *s.* der Meuchelmörder.
assassinate [ə'sæsineit], *v.a.* meuchlings ermorden.
assassination [əsæsi'neiʃən], *s.* der Meuchelmord, die Ermordung.
assault [ə'sɔ:lt], *v.a.* angreifen, überfallen. — *s.* der Überfall, Angriff.
assay [ə'sei], *s.* die Metallprobe. — *v.a.* (auf Edelmetall hin) prüfen.
assemble [ə'sembl], *v.a.*, *v.n.* versammeln, sich versammeln.
assembly [ə'sembli], *s.* die Versammlung (*assemblage*); — *line*, das laufende Band, das Fließband.
assent [ə'sent], *v.n.* beistimmen (*Dat.*), billigen (*Acc.*). — *s.* die Zustimmung (zu, *Dat.*), Billigung (*Genit.*).
assert [ə'sə:t], *v.a.* behaupten.
assertion [ə'sə:ʃən], *s.* die Behauptung.
assess [ə'ses], *v.a.* schätzen, beurteilen.
assessment [ə'sesmənt], *s.* die Beurteilung, Schätzung, Wertung.
assessor [ə'sesə], *s.* der Beurteiler, Einschätzer, Bewerter, Assessor; der Beisitzer (*second examiner*).
assets ['æsets], *s. pl.* (*Comm.*) die Aktiva; Vorzüge (*personal*).
assiduity [æsi'dju:iti], *s.* der Fleiß, die Emsigkeit.
assiduous [ə'sidjuəs], *adj.* fleißig, unablässig, emsig.
assign [ə'sain], *v.a.* zuteilen, anweisen, zuweisen (*apportion*), festsetzen (*fix*).
assignable [ə'sainəbl], *adj.* zuteilbar; bestimmbar.
assignation [æsig'neiʃən], *s.* die Zuweisung; (*Law*) die Übertragung; die Verabredung.
assignment [ə'sainmənt], *s.* die Zuweisung, Übertragung; die Aufgabe.
assimilate [ə'simileit], *v.a.*, *v.n.* assimilieren, angleichen; sich assimilieren, sich angleichen, ähnlich werden.
assist [ə'sist], *v.a.*, *v.n.* beistehen (*Dat.*), helfen (*Dat.*), unterstützen (*Acc.*).
assistance [ə'sistəns], *s.* der Beistand, die Hilfe; die Aushilfe; (*financial*) der Zuschuß.
assistant [ə'sistənt], *s.* der Assistent, Helfer.
assize [ə'saiz], *s.* die Gerichtssitzung; (*pl.*) das Schwurgericht.
associate [ə'souʃieit], *v.a.* verbinden (*link*). — *v.n.* verkehren (*company*); sich verbinden; (*Comm.*) sich vereinigen. — [—iit], *s.* (*Comm.*) der Partner.
association [əsousi'eiʃən], *s.* die Vereinigung, der Bund, Verein; die Gesellschaft; der Verkehr.
assonance ['æsənəns], *s.* (*Phon.*) die Assonanz, der Gleichlaut.
assort [ə'sɔ:t], *v.a.* ordnen, aussuchen, sortieren; —*ed sweets*, gemischte Bonbons.
assortment [ə'sɔ:tmənt], *s.* die Sammlung, Mischung, Auswahl.
assuage [ə'sweidʒ], *v.a.* mildern, besänftigen, stillen.
assume [ə'sju:m], *v.a.* annehmen; übernehmen, ergreifen.
assuming [ə'sju:miŋ], *adj.* anmaßend; — *that*, angenommen daß . . ., gesetzt den Fall.
assumption [ə'sʌmpʃən], *s.* die Annahme (*opinion*); Übernahme (*taking up*); Aneignung (*appropriation*); *Assumption of the Blessed Virgin*, Mariä Himmelfahrt.
assurance [ə'ʃuərəns], *s.* die Versicherung; Sicherheit (*manner*).
assure [ə'ʃuə], *v.a.* versichern, sicher stellen, ermutigen.
assuredly [ə'ʃuəridli], *adv.* sicherlich, gewiß.
aster ['æstə], *s.* (*Bot.*) die Aster.
asterisk ['æstərisk], *s.* (*Typ.*) das Sternchen.
astern [ə'stə:n], *adv.* (*Naut.*) achteraus.
asthma ['æsθmə], *s.* das Asthma.
asthmatic [æsθ'mætik], *adj.* asthmatisch.
astir [ə'stə:], *adv.* wach, in Bewegung.
astonish [ə'stɔniʃ], *v.a.* in Erstaunen versetzen, verblüffen.
astonishment [ə'stɔniʃmənt], *s.* das Erstaunen, die Verwunderung; die Bestürzung.
astound [ə'staund], *v.a.* in Erstaunen versetzen, bestürzen.
astounding [ə'staundiŋ], *adj.* erstaunlich, verblüffend.
astral ['æstrəl], *adj.* Stern(en)-, gestirnt.

astray [ə'strei], *pred. adj., adv.* irre; *go* —, sich verirren; (*fig.*) abschweifen.
astride [ə'straid], *pred.adj.,adv.* rittlings.
astringent [ə'strindʒənt], *adj.* zusammenziehend.
astrologer [ə'strɔlədʒə], *s.* der Sterndeuter, Astrolog(e).
astrological [æstrə'lɔdʒikəl], *adj.* astrologisch.
astrology [æ'strɔlədʒi], *s.* die Astrologie, Sterndeuterei.
astronaut ['æstrənɔ:t], *s.* der Astronaut.
astronomer [ə'strɔnəmə], *s.* der Astronom.
astronomical [æstrə'nɔmikəl], *adj.* astronomisch.
astronomy [ə'strɔnəmi], *s.* die Astronomie, Sternkunde.
astute [ə'stju:t], *adj.* listig, schlau.
astuteness [ə'stju:tnis], *s.* die Schlauheit, Listigkeit, der Scharfsinn.
asunder [ə'sʌndə], *adv.* auseinander, entzwei.
asylum [ə'sailəm], *s.* das Asyl, der Zufluchtsort (*refuge*); *lunatic* —, das Irrenhaus.
at [æt], *prep.* an; auf; bei, für; in, nach; mit, gegen; um, über; von, aus, zu; — *my expense*, auf meine Kosten; — *all*, überhaupt; — *first*, zuerst; — *last*, zuletzt, endlich; — *peace*, in Frieden; *what are you driving* —? worauf wollen sie hinaus?
atheism ['eiθiizm], *s.* der Atheismus.
atheist ['eiθiist], *s.* der Atheist.
atheistic [eiθi'istik], *adj.* atheistisch, gottlos.
Athens ['æθənz]. Athen, *n.*
Athenian [ə'θi:njən], *s.* der Athener. — *adj.* athenisch.
athlete ['æθli:t], *s.* der Athlet.
athletic [æθ'letik], *adj.* athletisch.
athletics [æθ'letiks], *s. pl.* die Leichtathletik, Athletik.
Atlantic (Ocean) [ət'læntik ('ouʃən)]. der Atlantik.
atlas ['ætləs], *s.* der Atlas.
atmosphere ['ætməsfiə], *s.* die Atmosphäre.
atmospheric(al) [ætməs'ferik(əl)], *adj.* atmosphärisch. — *s.* (*pl.*) atmosphärische Störungen, *f. pl.*
atoll [ə'tɔl], *s.* die Koralleninsel, das Atoll.
atom ['ætəm], *s.* das Atom.
atomic [ə'tɔmik], *adj.* (*Phys.*) Atom–, atomisch, atomar; (*theory*) atomistisch; — *bomb*, die Atombombe; — *pile*, der Atomreaktor; — *armament*, die atomare Aufrüstung.
atone [ə'toun], *v.n.* sühnen, büßen.
atonement [ə'tounmənt], *s.* die Buße, Sühne, Versöhnung.
atonic [ei'tɔnik], *adj.* tonlos, unbetont.
atrocious [ə'trouʃəs], *adj.* gräßlich, schrecklich, entsetzlich.
atrocity [ə'trɔsiti], *s.* die Gräßlichkeit, Grausamkeit, Greueltat.
atrophy ['ætrəfi], *s.* (*Med.*) die Abmagerung, Atrophie. — ['ætrəfai], *v.n.* absterben, auszehren.

attach [ə'tætʃ], *v.a.* anheften, beilegen, anhängen; (*fig.*) beimessen (*attribute*).
attachment [ə'tætʃmənt], *s.* das Anhaften (*sticking to*, an, *Acc.*); das Anhängsel (*appendage*); die Freundschaft (*to*, für, *Acc.*); die Anhänglichkeit (*loyalty*, an, *Acc.*).
attack [ə'tæk], *v.a.* angreifen. — *s.* die Attacke, der Angriff; (*Med.*) der Anfall.
attain [ə'tein], *v.a.* erreichen, erlangen.
attainable [ə'teinəbl], *adj.* erreichbar.
attainment [ə'teinmənt], *s.* die Erlangung, Erreichung; Errungenschaft; (*pl.*) Kenntnisse, *f. pl.*
attempt [ə'tempt], *s.* der Versuch. — *v.a.* versuchen.
attend [ə'tend], *v.a., v.n.* begleiten, anwesend sein (*be present, at*, bei, *Dat.*); beiwohnen (*be present as guest*); zuhören (*listen to*); bedienen (*customer*); behandeln (*patient*).
attendance [ə'tendəns], *s.* die Begleitung (*accompaniment*); die Anwesenheit (*presence*); die Zuhörerschaft (*audience*); *to be in* —, Dienst tun (*at*, bei); anwesend sein (*be present*).
attendant [ə'tendənt], *s.* der Diener, Wärter.
attention [ə'tenʃən], *s.* die Aufmerksamkeit, Achtung.
attentive [ə'tentiv], *adj.* aufmerksam.
attenuate [ə'tenjueit], *v.a.* verdünnen (*dilute*). — *v.n.* abmagern.
attest [ə'test], *v.a.* attestieren, bezeugen, bescheinigen.
attestation [ætes'teiʃən], *s.* die Bescheinigung; das Zeugnis.
Attic ['ætik], *adj.* attisch, klassisch.
attic ['ætik], *s.* die Dachkammer, die Dachstube.
attire [ə'taiə], *v.a.* ankleiden, kleiden. — *s.* die Kleidung.
attitude ['ætitju:d], *s.* die Haltung, Stellung (*toward*, zu), Einstellung.
attorney [ə'tə:ni], *s.* der Anwalt; *Attorney-General*, der Kronanwalt; (*Am.*) der Staatsanwalt; — *at law*, Rechtsanwalt.
attract [ə'trækt], *v.a.* anziehen.
attraction [ə'trækʃən], *s.* die Anziehung; der Reiz (*appeal*); die Anziehungskraft.
attractive [ə'træktiv], *adj.* anziehend, reizvoll.
attribute [ə'tribju:t], *v.a.* zuschreiben, beimessen. — *s.* ['ætribju:t], (*Gram.*) das Attribut, die Eigenschaft.
attributive [ə'tribjutiv], *adj.* (*Gram.*) attributiv; beilegend.
attrition [ə'triʃən], *s.* die Zermürbung, Aufreibung, Reue.
attune [ə'tju:n], *v.a.* (*Mus.*) stimmen, anpassen (*adapt to*, an, *Acc.*).
auburn ['ɔ:bə:n], *adj.* rotbraun.
auction ['ɔ:kʃən], *s.* die Auktion, die Versteigerung.
auctioneer [ɔ:kʃə'niə], *s.* der Auktionator, Versteigerer.

audacious [ɔ:'deiʃəs], *adj.* waghalsig, kühn, dreist.
audacity [ɔ:'dæsiti], *s.* die Kühnheit (*valour*); Frechheit (*impudence*).
audible ['ɔ:dibl], *adj.* hörbar.
audibility [ɔ:di'biliti], *s.* die Hörbarkeit, Vernehmbarkeit.
audience ['ɔ:djəns], *s.* die Audienz (*of the Pope*, beim Papst); (*Theat.*) das Publikum; (*listeners*) die Zuhörer.
audit ['ɔ:dit], *s.* die Rechnungsprüfung, Revision. — *v.a.* revidieren, prüfen.
auditor ['ɔ:ditə], *s.* der Rechnungsrevisor, Buchprüfer.
auditory ['ɔ:ditəri], *adj.* Gehör–, Hör–.
auditorium [ɔ:di'tɔ:riəm], *s.* der Hörsaal, Vortragssaal.
auger ['ɔ:gə], *s.* der (große) Bohrer.
aught [ɔ:t], *pron.* (*obs.*) irgend etwas (*opp. to naught*).
augment [ɔ:g'ment], *v.a.*, *v.n.* vermehren, vergrößern; zunehmen.
augmentation [ɔ:gmen'teiʃən], *s.* die Vergrößerung, Erhöhung, Zunahme.
augur ['ɔ:gə], *v.a.* weissagen, prophezeien.
August ['ɔ:gəst]. der August.
august [ɔ:'gʌst], *adj.* erhaben.
aunt [ɑ:nt], *s.* die Tante.
aurora [ɔ:'rɔ:rə], *s.* die Morgenröte.
auscultation [ɔ:skəl'teiʃən], *s.* (*Med.*) die Auskultation, Untersuchung.
auspices ['ɔ:spisiz], *s.* die Auspizien.
auspicious [ɔ:'spiʃəs], *adj.* unter glücklichem Vorzeichen, verheißungsvoll, günstig.
austere [ɔ:s'tiə], *adj.* streng, ernst, schmucklos.
austerity [ɔ:s'teriti], *s.* die Strenge.
Australian [ə'streiljən], *adj.* australisch. — *s.* der Australier.
Austrian ['ɔ:striən], *adj.* österreichisch. — *s.* der Österreicher.
authentic [ɔ:'θentik], *adj.* authentisch, echt.
authenticity [ɔ:θen'tisiti], *s.* die Authentizität, Echtheit.
author, authoress ['ɔ:θə, ɔ:θər'es], *s.* der Autor, die Autorin; der Verfasser, die Verfasserin.
authoritative [ɔ:'θɔritətiv], *adj.* autoritativ, maßgebend.
authority [ɔ:'θɔriti], *s.* die Autorität, Vollmacht (*power of attorney*); das Ansehen; *the authorities*, die Behörden.
authorization [ɔ:θərai'zeiʃən], *s.* die Bevollmächtigung, Befugnis.
authorize ['ɔ:θəraiz], *v.a.* autorisieren, bevollmächtigen, berechtigen.
authorship ['ɔ:θəʃip], *s.* die Autorschaft.
autobiographical [ɔ:tobaiə'græfikl], *adj.* autobiographisch.
autobiography [ɔ:tobai'ɔgrəfi], *s.* die Autobiographie.
autocracy [ɔ:'tɔkrəsi], *s.* die Selbstherrschaft.
autocrat ['ɔ:tokræt], *s.* der Autokrat, Selbstherrscher.
autograph ['ɔ:togræf, -grɑ:f], *s.* die eigene Handschrift, Unterschrift; das Autogramm.
automatic [ɔ:to'mætik], *adj.* automatisch.
automatize [ɔ:'tɔmətaiz], *v.a.* automatisieren, auf Automation umstellen.
automation [ɔ:to'meiʃən], *s.* (*Engin.*) die Automation; Automatisierung.
automaton [ɔ:'tɔmətən], *s.* der Automat.
automobile ['ɔ:tomobi:l], *s.* der Kraftwagen, das Auto.
autonomous [ɔ:'tɔnəməs], *adj.* autonom, unabhängig.
autonomy [ɔ:'tɔnəmi], *s.* die Autonomie, Unabhängigkeit.
autopsy ['ɔ:tɔpsi], *s.* die Autopsie; Obduktion, Leichenschau.
autumn ['ɔ:təm], *s.* der Herbst.
autumnal [ɔ:'tʌmnəl], *adj.* herbstlich.
auxiliary [ɔ:g'ziljəri], *adj.* Hilfs-.
avail [ə'veil], *v.n.* nützen, helfen, von Vorteil sein. — *v.r.* — *o.s of a th.*, sich einer Sache bedienen. — *s.* der Nutzen; *of no* —, nutzlos.
available [ə'veiləbl], *adj.* vorrätig, verfügbar, zur Verfügung (stehend).
avalanche ['ævəlɑ:nʃ], *s.* die Lawine.
avarice ['ævəris], *s.* der Geiz, die Habsucht, Gier.
avaricious [ævə'riʃəs], *adj.* geizig, habsüchtig, habgierig.
avenge [ə'vendʒ], *v.a.* rächen.
avenue ['ævənju:], *s.* die Allee; der Zugang.
average ['ævəridʒ], *adj.* durchschnittlich; *not more than* —, mäßig. — *s.* der Durchschnitt; *on an* —, durchschnittlich, im Durchschnitt. — *v.a.* den Durchschnitt nehmen.
averse [ə'və:s], *adj.* abgeneigt (*to*, *Dat.*).
aversion [ə'və:ʃən], *s.* die Abneigung, der Widerwille.
avert [ə'və:t], *v.a.* abwenden.
aviary ['eiviəri], *s.* das Vogelhaus.
aviation [eivi'eiʃən], *s.* das Flugwesen.
aviator ['eivieitə], *s.* der Flieger.
avid ['ævid], *adj.* begierig (*of* or *for*, nach).
avidity [æ'viditi], *s.* die Begierde, Gier (*for*, nach).
avoid [ə'vɔid], *v.a.* vermeiden.
avoidable [ə'vɔidəbl], *adj.* vermeidlich, vermeidbar.
avoidance [ə'vɔidəns], *s.* die Vermeidung, das Meiden.
avow [ə'vau], *v.a.* eingestehen, anerkennen (*acknowledge*).
avowal [ə'vauəl], *s.* das Geständnis; die Erklärung.
await [ə'weit], *v.a.* erwarten, warten auf (*Acc.*).
awake(n) [ə'weik(ən)], *v.a.*, *v.n.* *irr.* aufwecken, wecken; aufwachen (*wake up*). — *adj.* *wide awake*, schlau, auf der Hut.

award [ə'wɔ:d], *s.* die Zuerkennung, Auszeichnung; Belohnung (*money*); (*Law*) das Urteil. — *v.a.* zuerkennen; — *damages*, Schadenersatz zusprechen; verleihen (*grant*).
aware [ə'wɛə], *adj.* gewahr, bewußt (*Genit.*).
away [ə'wei], *adv.* weg; hinweg, fort.
awe [ɔ:], *s.* die Ehrfurcht; Furcht.
awful ['ɔ:ful], *adj.* furchtbar, schrecklich.
awhile [ə'wail], *adv.* eine Weile, eine kurze Zeit.
awkward ['ɔ:kwəd], *adv.* ungeschickt, unbeholfen, ungelenk; unangenehm (*difficult*); — *situation*, peinliche Situation, Lage.
awkwardness ['ɔkwədnis], *s.* die Ungeschicklichkeit, Unbeholfenheit.
awl [ɔ:l], *s.* die Ahle, der Pfriem.
awning ['ɔ:niŋ], *s.* die Plane; das Sonnendach.
awry [ə'rai], *adj.* schief, verkehrt.
axe [æks], *s.* die Axt, das Beil.
axiom ['æksiəm], *s.* das Axiom, der Satz, Lehrsatz, Grundsatz.
axiomatic [æksiə'mætik], *adj.* axiomatisch, grundsätzlich; gewiß.
axis ['æksis], *s.* die Achse.
axle [æksl], *s.* die Achse.
ay(e) (1) [ai], *adv.* ja, gewiß.
ay(e) (2) [ei], *adv.* ständig, ewig.
azalea [ə'zeiliə], *s.* (*Bot.*) die Azalie.
azure ['æʒə, 'eiʒə], *adj.* himmelblau, azurblau.

B

B [bi:]. das B; (*Mus.*) das H.
baa [bɑ:], *v.n.* blöken.
babble [bæbl], *v.n.* schwatzen, schwätzen. — *s.* das Geschwätz; das Murmeln (*water*).
babe, baby [beib, 'beibi], *s.* der Säugling, das Baby, das kleine Kind, das Kindlein.
baboon [bə'bu:n], *s.* (*Zool.*) der Pavian.
bachelor ['bætʃələ], *s.* der Junggeselle; (*Univ.*) Bakkalaureus.
back [bæk], *s.* der Rücken, die Rückseite. — *adj.* Hinter-, Rück-; — *door*, die Hintertür; — *stairs*, die Hintertreppe. — *adv.* rückwärts, zurück. — *v.a.* unterstützen; (*Comm.*) indossieren; gegenzeichnen; wetten auf (*Acc.*) (*bet on*).
backbone ['bækboun], *s.* (*Anat.*) das Rückgrat.
backfire ['bækfaiə], *s.* (*Motor.*) die Frühzündung; (*gun*) die Fehlzündung. — [bæk'faiə], *v.n.* (*Motor.*) frühzünden; (*gun*) fehlzünden.
backgammon [bæk'gæmən], *s.* das Bordspiel, das Puffspiel.
background ['bækgraund], *s.* der Hintergrund.
backhand ['bækhænd], *s.* (*Sport*) die Rückhand; *a —ed compliment*, eine verblümte Grobheit.
backside [bæk'said], *s.* (*vulg.*) der Hintere.
backslide [bæk'slaid], *v.n.* abfallen, abtrünnig werden.
backward ['bækwəd], *adj.* zurückgeblieben. **backward(s)** *adv.* rückwärts, zurück.
backwater ['bækwɔ:tə], *s.* das Stauwasser.
backwoods ['bækwudz], *s. pl.* der Hinterwald.
bacon ['beikən], *s.* der Speck.
bad [bæd], *adj.* schlecht, schlimm; böse (*immoral*); (*coll.*) unwohl (*unwell*); *not too —*, ganz gut; *from — to worse*, immer schlimmer; — *language*, unanständige Worte, das Fluchen; — *luck*, Unglück, Pech; *want —ly*, nötig brauchen.
badge [bædʒ], *s.* das Abzeichen; Kennzeichen (*mark*).
badger (1) ['bædʒə], *s.* (*Zool.*) der Dachs.
badger (2) ['bædʒə], *v.a.* ärgern, stören, belästigen.
badness ['bædnis], *s.* die Schlechtigkeit, Bosheit, das schlechte Wesen, die Bösartigkeit.
baffle [bæfl], *v.a.* täuschen, verblüffen. — *s.* (*obs.*) die Täuschung; (*Build.*) Verkleidung; (*Elec.*) Verteilerplatte.
bag [bæg], *s.* der Sack, Beutel; die Tasche; *shopping —*, Einkaufstasche; *travelling —*, Reisehandtasche. — *v.a.* einstecken, als Beute behalten (*hunt*).
bagatelle [bægə'tel], *s.* die Bagatelle, Lappalie, Kleinigkeit; das Kugelspiel (*pin-table ball-game*).
baggage ['bægidʒ], *s.* das Gepäck.
bagging ['bægiŋ], *s.* die Sackleinwand.
baggy ['bægi], *adj.* ungebügelt; bauschig.
bagpipe ['bægpaip], *s.* der Dudelsack.
bagpiper ['bægpaipə], *s.* der Dudelsackpfeifer.
bail [beil], *s.* der Bürge; die Bürgschaft; *stand —*, für einen bürgen; *allow —*, Bürgschaft zulassen. — *v.a.* Bürgschaft leisten; — *out*, (durch Kaution) in Freiheit setzen.
bailiff ['beilif], *s.* der Amtmann; Gerichtsvollzieher.
bait [beit], *s.* der Köder. — *v.a.* ködern, locken (*attract*).
baiter ['beitə], *s.* der Hetzer, Verfolger.
baiting ['beitiŋ], *s.* die Hetze.
bake [beik], *v.a., v.n.* backen.
baker ['beikə], *s.* der Bäcker; *—'s dozen*, 13 Stück.
bakery ['beikəri], *s.* die Bäckerei.
baking ['beikiŋ], *s.* das Backen.

balance ['bæləns], *s.* die Waage (*scales*); die Bilanz (*audit*); das Gleichgewicht (*equilibrium*); (*Comm.*) der Saldo, der Überschuß (*profit*); die Unruhe (*watch*). — *v.a., v.n.* wägen, abwägen (*scales*); ausgleichen (— *up*), einen Saldo ziehen (— *an account*); ins Gleichgewicht bringen (*bring into equilibrium*).
balcony ['bælkəni], *s.* der Balkon, der Söller (*castle*); Altan (*villa*).
bald [bɔ:ld], *adj.* kahl, haarlos; (*fig.*) armselig, schmucklos.
baldness ['bɔ:ldnis], *s.* die Kahlheit (*hairlessness*); Nacktheit (*bareness*).
bale (1) [beil], *s.* der Ballen.
bale (2) [beil], *v.n.* — *out*, abspringen; aussteigen.
Balearic Islands [bæli'ærik ailəndz], *s. pl.* die Balearen, Balearischen Inseln. — *adj.* balearisch.
baleful ['beilful], *adj.* unheilvoll.
balk [bɔ:k], *v.a.* aufhalten, hemmen. — *v.n.* scheuen, zurückscheuen (*at*, vor).
ball (1) [bɔ:l], *s.* der Ball; die Kugel; — *cock*, der Absperrhahn; —*point pen*, der Kugelschreiber.
ball (2) [bɔ:l], *s.* der Ball (*dance*).
ballad ['bæləd], *s.* die Ballade.
ballast ['bæləst], *s.* der Ballast.
ballet ['bælei], *s.* das Ballett.
balloon [bə'lu:n], *s.* der Ballon.
ballot ['bælət], *s.* die geheime Wahl, Abstimmung; — *-box*, die Wahlurne; — *-paper*, der Stimmzettel. —*v. n.* wählen, abstimmen.
balm [ba:m], *s.* der Balsam.
balsam ['bɔlsəm], *s.* der Balsam.
Baltic ['bɔ:ltik], *adj.* baltisch. — (*Sea*), die Ostsee; —*Provinces*, das Baltikum.
balustrade ['bæləstreid], *s.* die Balustrade, das Geländer.
bamboo [bæm'bu:], *s.* (*Bot.*) der Bambus.
bamboozle [bæm'bu:zl], *v.a.* verblüffen; beschwindeln (*cheat*).
ban [bæn], *v.a.* bannen, verbannen; verbieten. — *s.* der Bann, das Verbot.
banal [bæ'næl, 'beinəl], *adj.* banal.
banality [bæ'næliti], *s.* die Banalität, Trivialität.
banana [bə'nɑ:nə], *s.* die Banane.
band [bænd], *s.* das Band (*ribbon etc.*); (*Mus.*) die Kapelle; die Bande (*robbers*). — *v.n.* — *together*, sich verbinden; sich zusammentun.
bandage ['bændidʒ], *s.* der Verband, die Bandage.
bandit ['bændit], *s.* der Bandit.
bandmaster ['bændmɑ:stə], *s.* der Kapellmeister.
bandstand ['bændstænd], *s.* der Musikpavillon.
bandy ['bændi], *adj.* — *-legged*, krummbeinig. — *v.a.* — *words*, Worte wechseln; streiten.
bane [bein], *s.* das Gift; (*fig.*) Verderben.
baneful ['beinful], *adj.* verderblich.
bang [bæŋ], *s.* der Knall (*explosion*), das Krachen (*clap*). — *v.n.* knallen, krachen lassen. — *v.a.* — *a door*, eine Türe zuwerfen.
banish ['bæniʃ], *v.a.* verbannen, bannen.
banisters ['bænistəz], *s. pl.* das Treppengeländer.
bank [bæŋk], *s.* (*Fin.*) die Bank; das Ufer (*river*); der Damm (*dam*). — *v.a.* einlegen, einzahlen, auf die Bank bringen (*sum of money*); eindämmen (*dam up*). — *v.n.* ein Konto haben (*have an account*, *with*, bei).
banker ['bæŋkə], *s.* der Bankier.
bankrupt ['bæŋkrʌpt], *adj.* bankrott; zahlungsunfähig; (*coll.*) pleite.
bankruptcy ['bæŋkrʌptsi], *s.* der Bankrott.
banns [bænz], *s. pl.* das Heiratsaufgebot.
banquet ['bæŋkwit], *s.* das Banquet, Festessen.
bantam ['bæntəm], *s.* das Bantamhuhn, Zwerghuhn; (*Boxing*) — *-weight*, das Bantamgewicht.
banter ['bæntə], *v.n.* scherzen, necken. — *s.* das Scherzen, der Scherz.
baptism ['bæptizm], *s.* die Taufe.
Baptist ['bæptist], *s.* der Täufer; Baptist.
baptize [bæp'taiz], *v.a.* taufen.
bar [bɑ:], *s.* die Barre, Stange (*pole*); der Riegel; Balken; Schlagbaum (*barrier*); (*fig.*) das Hindernis; der Schanktisch (*in public house*); *prisoner at the* —, Gefangener vor (dem) Gericht; *call to the* —, zur Gerichtsadvokatur (*or* als Anwalt) zulassen; (*Mus.*) der Takt. — *v.a.* verriegeln (*door*); (*fig.*) hindern (*from action*); verbieten (*prohibit*); ausschließen (*exclude*).
barb [bɑ:b], *s.* die Spitze (*of wire*); der Widerhaken (*hook*).
barbed [bɑ:bd], *adj.* spitzig; — *remark*, die spitze Bemerkung; — *wire*, der Stacheldraht.
barbarian [bɑ:'bɛəriən], *s.* der Barbar. — *adj.* barbarisch.
barbarism ['bɑ:bərizm], *s.* die Roheit; der Barbarismus.
barber ['bɑ:bə], *s.* der Barbier, Friseur.
barberry ['bɑ:bəri], *s.* (*Bot.*) die Berberitze.
bard [bɑ:d], *s.* der Barde, Sänger.
bare [bɛə], *adj.* nackt, bloß; — *-headed*, barhäuptig. — *v.a.* entblößen.
barefaced ['bɛəfeisd], *adj.* schamlos.
barely ['bɛəli], *adv.* kaum.
bargain ['bɑ:gin], *s.* der Kauf, Gelegenheitskauf; der Handel (*trading*); das Geschäft; *into the* —, noch dazu, obendrein. — *v.n.* feilschen, handeln (*haggle*) (*for*, um).
barge [bɑ:dʒ], *s.* der Lastkahn, die Barke. — *v.n.* (*coll.*) — *in*, stören.
bargee [bɑ:'dʒi:], *s.* der Flußschiffer, Bootsmann.
baritone ['bæritoun], *s.* (*Mus.*) der Bariton.

bark (1) [bɑ:k], *s.* die Rinde (*of tree*).
bark (2) [bɑ:k], *v.n.* bellen (*dog*); — *up the wrong tree*, auf falscher Fährte sein. — *s.* das Gebell (*dog*).
barley ['bɑ:li], *s.* (*Bot.*) die Gerste.
barmaid ['bɑ:meid], *s.* die Kellnerin.
barman ['bɑ:mən], *s.* der Kellner.
barn [bɑ:n], *s.* die Scheune; — *owl*, die Schleiereule.
barnacle ['bɑ:nəkl], *s.* die Entenmuschel; die Klette.
barnstormer ['bɑ:nstɔ:mə], *s.* der Schmierenkomödiant.
barometer [bə'rɔmitə], *s.* das Barometer.
baron ['bærən], *s.* der Baron, Freiherr.
barony ['bærəni], *s.* die Baronswürde.
baroque [bə'rɔk], *adj.* barock. — *s.* das Barock.
barque [bɑ:k], *s.* die Bark.
barracks ['bærəks], *s. pl.* die Kaserne.
barrage ['bærɑ:ʒ, 'bæridʒ], *s.* das Sperrfeuer (*firing*); das Wehr, der Damm.
barrel ['bærəl], *s.* das Faß (*vat*), die Tonne (*tun*); der Gewehrlauf (*rifle*); die Trommel (*cylinder*); — *organ*, die Drehorgel.
barren ['bærən], *adj.* unfruchtbar, dürr.
barrenness ['bærənnis], *s.* die Unfruchtbarkeit.
barricade [bæri'keid], *s.* die Barrikade. — *v.a.* verrammeln, verschanzen.
barrier ['bæriə], *s.* die Barriere, der Schlagbaum; das Hindernis; (*Railw.*) die Schranke.
barrister ['bæristə], *s.* der Rechtsanwalt, Advokat.
barrow (1) ['bærou], *s.* der Schubkarren, Handkarren; — *-boy*, der Höker, Schnellverkäufer.
barrow (2) ['bærou], *s.* (*Archaeol.*) das Hünengrab, Heldengrab.
barter ['bɑ:tə], *v.a.* tauschen, austauschen. — *s.* der Tauschhandel.
Bartholomew [bɑ:'θɔləmju]. Bartholomäus, *m.*; *Massacre of St. Bartholomew's Eve*, Bartholomäusnacht, Pariser Bluthochzeit.
basalt ['bæsɔ:lt, bæ'sɔ:lt], *s.* der Basalt.
base [beis], *s.* die Basis, Grundlage; der Sockel; (*Chem.*) die Base. — *adj.* niedrig, gemein; (*Metall.*) unedel. — *v.a.* basieren, beruhen, fundieren (*upon*, auf).
baseless ['beislis], *adj.* grundlos.
basement ['beismənt], *s.* das Kellergeschoß.
baseness ['beisnis], *s.* die Gemeinheit, Niedrigkeit.
bashful ['bæʃful], *adj.* verschämt, schamhaft, schüchtern.
basic ['beisik], *adj.* grundlegend.
basin ['beisən], *s.* das Becken.
basis ['beisis], *s.* die Basis, Grundlage.
bask [bɑ:sk], *v.n.* sich sonnen.
basket ['bɑ:skit], *s.* der Korb.
bass (1) [beis], *s.* (*Mus.*) der Baß, die Baßstimme.
bass (2) [bæs], *s.* (*Zool.*) der Barsch.
bassoon [bə'su:n], *s.* (*Mus.*) das Fagott.
bastard ['bæstəd], *s.* der Bastard.
baste [beist], *v.a.* mit Fett begießen (*roast meat*); (*coll.*) prügeln.
bastion ['bæstiən], *s.* die Bastion, Festung, das Bollwerk.
bat (1) [bæt], *s.* die Fledermaus.
bat (2) [bæt], *s.* der Schläger. — *v.n.* (den Ball) schlagen; (*cricket*) am Schlagen sein (*be batting*).
batch [bætʃ], *s.* der Stoß (*pile*); die Menge (*people*); (*Mil.*) der Trupp.
bath [bɑ:θ], *s.* das Bad; (*Am.*) —*robe*, der Schlafrock, Bademantel; — *tub*, die Badewanne.
bathe [beið], *v.n.* baden; *bathing pool*, das Schwimmbad; *bathing suit*, der Badeanzug.
batman ['bætmən], *s.* der Offiziersbursche.
baton ['bætən], *s.* der Stab.
batsman ['bætsmən], *s.* der Schläger (*cricket*).
batten [bætn], *s.* die Holzlatte. — *v.a.* mästen, füttern. — *v.n.* fett werden.
batter ['bætə], *s.* der Schlagteig. — *v.a.* schlagen, zertrümmern; —*ing ram*, (*Mil.*) der Sturmbock.
battery ['bætəri], *s.* die Batterie.
battle [bætl], *s.* die Schlacht; — *cruiser*, der Schlachtkreuzer; —*ship*, das Schlachtschiff. — *v.n.* kämpfen (*for*, um).
Bavarian [bə'vɛəriən], *adj.* bayrisch. — *s.* der Bayer.
bawl [bɔ:l], *v.n.* plärren, schreien.
bay (1) [bei], *adj.* rötlich braun.
bay (2) [bei], *s.* die Bucht, Bai; — *window*, das Erkerfenster.
bay (3) [bei], *s. keep at* —, in Schach halten, *stand at* —, sich zur Wehr setzen.
bay (4) [bei], *s.* (*Bot.*) der Lorbeer.
bay (5) [bei], *v.n.* bellen, heulen; — *for the moon*, das Unmögliche wollen.
bayonet ['beiənet], *s.* das Bajonett.
bazaar [bə'zɑ:], *s.* der Basar.
be [bi:], *v.n. irr.* sein, existieren; sich befinden; vorhanden sein; — *off*, sich fortmachen (*move*); ungenießbar sein (*meat, food*); nicht mehr da sein (— *off the menu*).
beach [bi:tʃ], *s.* der Strand, das Gestade.
beacon ['bi:kən], *s.* das Leuchtfeuer; der Leuchtturm; das Lichtsignal.
bead [bi:d], *s.* das Tröpfchen (*drop*); die Perle (*pearl*); (*pl.*) die Perlschnur; der Rosenkranz.
beadle [bi:dl], *s.* (*Univ.*) der Pedell; (*Eccl.*) Kirchendiener.
beagle [bi:gl], *s.* der Jagdhund, Spürhund.
beak [bi:k], *s.* der Schnabel.
beaker ['bi:kə], *s.* der Becher.
beam [bi:m], *s.* der Balken (*wood*); der Strahl (*ray*), Glanz. — *v.n.* strahlen.

bean [bi:n], *s.* (*Bot.*) die Bohne; *not a* —, keinen Heller *or* Pfennig.
bear (1) [bɛə], *s.* (*Zool.*) der Bär.
bear (2) [bɛə], *v.a. irr.* tragen, ertragen; gebären (*a child*); hegen (*sorrow etc.*). — *v.n.* — *upon*, drücken auf (*pressure*), Einfluß haben (*effect*); — *up*, geduldig sein.
bearable ['bɛərəbl], *adj.* tragbar, erträglich.
beard [biəd], *s.* der Bart. — *v.a.* trotzen (*Dat.*).
bearded ['biədid], *adj.* bärtig.
bearer ['bɛərə], *s.* der Träger, Überbringer.
bearing ['bɛəriŋ], *s.* das Benehmen, die Haltung (*manner*); (*pl.*) (*Geog.*) die Richtung; *lose o.'s* —*s*, sich verlaufen; *ball* —*s*, (*Engin.*) das Kugellager.
bearpit ['bɛəpit], *s.* der Bärenzwinger.
beast [bi:st], *s.* das Tier; die Bestie.
beastliness ['bi:stlinis], *s.* das tierische Benehmen; die Grausamkeit (*cruelty*); die Gemeinheit.
beastly ['bi:stli], *adj.* grausam, (*coll.*) schrecklich.
beat [bi:t], *s.* der Schlag, das Schlagen; (*Mus.*) der Takt; die Runde, das Revier (*patrol district*). — *v.a. irr.* schlagen; — *time*, den Takt schlagen; — *carpets*, Teppich klopfen. — *v.n.* — *it*, sich davonmachen.
beater ['bi:tə], *s.* (*Hunt.*) der Treiber.
beatify [bi:'ætifai], *v.a.* seligsprechen.
beau [bou], *s.* der Stutzer, Geck.
beautiful ['bju:tiful], *adj.* schön.
beautify ['bju:tifai], *v.a.* schön machen, verschönern.
beauty ['bju:ti], *s.* die Schönheit; — *salon*, der Schönheitssalon; *Sleeping Beauty*, das Dornröschen.
beaver ['bi:və], *s.* (*Zool.*) der Biber.
becalm [bi'ka:m], *v.a.* besänftigen.
because [bi'kɔz], *conj.* weil, da; — *of*, wegen, um ... willen.
beck [bek], *s.* der Wink; *be at s.o.'s* — *and call*, jemandem zu Gebote stehen.
beckon ['bekən], *v.a.*, *v.n.* winken, heranwinken, zuwinken (*Dat.*).
become [bi'kʌm], *v.n. irr.* werden. — *v.a.* anstehen, sich schicken, passen (*Dat.*).
becoming [bi'kʌmiŋ], *adj.* passend, kleidsam.
bed [bed], *s.* das Bett; Beet (*flowers*); (*Geol.*) das Lager, die Schicht. — *v.a.* betten, einbetten.
bedaub [bi'dɔ:b], *v.a.* beflecken, beschmieren.
bedding ['bediŋ], *s.* das Bettzeug.
bedevil [bi'devəl], *v.a.* behexen, verhexen.
bedew [bi'dju:], *v.a.* betauen.
bedlam ['bedləm], *s.* (*coll.*) das Irrenhaus; *this is* —, die Hölle ist los.
Bedouin ['beduin], *s.* der Beduine.
bedpost ['bedpoust], *s.* der Bettpfosten.
bedraggle [bi'drægl], *v.a.* beschmutzen.
bedridden ['bedridn], *adj.* bettlägerig, ans Bett gefesselt.
bedroom ['bedru:m], *s.* das Schlafzimmer.
bedtime ['bedtaim], *s.* die Schlafenszeit.
bee [bi:], *s.* (*Ent.*) die Biene; *have a* — *in o.'s bonnet*, einen Vogel haben.
beech [bi:tʃ], *s.* (*Bot.*) die Buche.
beef [bi:f], *s.* das Rindfleisch; — *tea*, die Fleischbrühe.
beehive ['bi:haiv], *s.* der Bienenkorb.
beeline ['bi:lain], *s.* die Luftlinie, gerade Linie; *make a* — *for s.th.*, schnurstracks auf etwas losgehen.
beer [biə], *s.* das Bier; *small* —, Dünnbier, (*fig.*) unbedeutend.
beet [bi:t], *s.* (*Bot.*) die Runkelrübe; *sugar* —, die Zuckerrübe.
beetle [bi:tl], *s.* (*Ent.*) der Käfer; — *brows*, buschige Augenbrauen.
beetroot ['bi:tru:t], *s.* (*Bot.*) die rote Rübe.
befall [bi'fɔ:l], *v.a. irr.* widerfahren (*Dat.*). — *v.n.* zustoßen (*happen, Dat.*).
befit [bi'fit], *v.a.* sich geziemen, sich gebühren.
befog [bi'fɔg], *v.a.* in Nebel hüllen; umnebeln.
before [bi'fɔ:], *adv.* vorn; voraus, voran; (*previously*) vorher, früher; (*already*) bereits, schon. — *prep.* vor. — *conj.* bevor, ehe.
beforehand [bi'fɔ:hænd], *adv.* im voraus, vorher.
befoul [bi'faul], *v.a.* beschmutzen.
befriend [bi'frend], *v.a.* befreunden, unterstützen (*support*).
beg [beg], *v.a.*, *v.n.* betteln (um, *for*); ersuchen, bitten (*request*).
beget [bi'get], *v.a. irr.* zeugen.
beggar ['begə], *s.* der Bettler.
begin [bi'gin], *v.a.*, *v.n. irr.* beginnen, anfangen.
beginner [bi'ginə], *s.* der Anfänger.
beginning [bi'giniŋ], *s.* der Anfang.
begone! [bi'gɔn], *interj.* hinweg! fort! mach dich fort!
begrudge [bi'grʌdʒ], *v.a.* nicht gönnen, mißgönnen.
beguile [bi'gail], *v.a.* bestricken, betrügen; — *the time*, die Zeit vertreiben.
behalf [bi'ha:f], *s. on* — *of*, um ... (*Genit.*) willen; im Interesse von, im Namen von.
behave [bi'heiv], *v.n.* sich benehmen, sich betragen.
behaviour [bi'heivjə], *s.* das Benehmen, Gebaren.
behead [bi'hed], *v.a.* enthaupten.
behind [bi'haind], *adv.* hinten, zurück, hinterher. — *prep.* hinter.
behindhand [bi'haindhænd], *adj.*, *adv.* im Rückstand (*in arrears*); zurück (*backward*).
behold [bi'hould], *v.a. irr.* ansehen; erblicken; *lo and* —*!* siehe da!
beholden [bi'houldən], *adj.* verpflichtet (*to, Dat.*).
beholder [bi'houldə], *s.* der Zuschauer.

behove [bi'houv], *v.a.* sich geziemen, ziemen, gebühren.
being ['bi:iŋ], *pres. part for the time* —, vorläufig, für jetzt. — *s.* das Sein, die Existenz; das Wesen (*creature*).
belated [bi'leitid], *adj.* verspätet.
belch [beltʃ], *v.n.* rülpsen, aufstoßen.
belfry ['belfri], *s.* der Glockenturm.
Belgian ['beldʒən], *adj.* belgisch. — *s.* der Belgier.
belie [bi'lai], *v.a.* täuschen, Lügen strafen.
belief [bi'li:f], *s.* der Glaube, die Meinung.
believable [bi'li:vəbl], *adj.* glaubhaft, glaublich.
believe [bi'li:v], *v.a.*, *v.n.* glauben (*an*, *Acc.*), vertrauen (*Dat.*).
believer [bi'li:və], *s.* der Gläubige.
belittle [bi'litl], *v.a.* schmälern, verkleinern, verächtlich machen.
bell [bel], *s.* die Glocke; Schelle, Klingel; — *-founder*, der Glockengießer; — *-boy*, (*Am.*) — *-hop*, der Hotelpage.
belligerent [bi'lidʒərənt], *adj.* kriegführend. — *s.* der Kriegführende.
bellow ['belou], *v.n.* brüllen. — *s.* das Gebrüll.
bellows ['belouz], *s.* der Blasebalg.
belly ['beli], *s.* der Bauch.
belong [bi'lɔŋ], *v.n.* gehören (*Dat.*), angehören (*Dat.*).
belongings [bi'lɔŋiŋz], *s. pl.* die Habe, das Hab und Gut, der Besitz.
beloved [bi'lʌvd, -vid], *adj.* geliebt, lieb.
below [bi'lou], *adv.* unten. — *prep.* unterhalb (*Genit.*), unter (*Dat.*).
Belshazzar [bel'ʃæzə]. Belsazar, *m.*
belt [belt], *s.* der Gürtel, Gurt; der Riemen; (*Tech.*) Treibriemen; *below the* —, unfair. — *v.a.* umgürten; (*coll.*) prügeln.
bemoan [bi'moun], *v.a.* beklagen.
bench [bentʃ], *s.* die Bank; der Gerichtshof (*court of law*); *Queen's Bench*, der oberste Gerichtshof.
bend [bend], *v.a.*, *v.n. irr.* biegen; beugen; sich krümmen. — *s.* die Biegung, Krümmung, Kurve.
bendable ['bendəbl], *adj.* biegsam.
beneath [bi'ni:θ] *see* **below**.
Benedictine [beni'dikti:n], *s.* der Benediktiner.
benediction [beni'dikʃən], *s.* der Segensspruch, der Segen; die Segnung.
benefaction [beni'fækʃən], *s.* die Wohltat.
benefactor ['benifæktə], *s.* der Wohltäter.
benefactress ['benifæktris], *s.* die Wohltäterin.
beneficent [be'nefisənt], *adj.* wohltätig.
beneficial [beni'fiʃəl], *adj.* vorteilhaft, gut (*for*, für), wohltuend.
benefit ['benifit], *s.* der Vorteil, Nutzen. — *v.n.* Nutzen ziehen. — *v.a.* nützen.
benevolence [be'nevələns], *s.* das Wohlwollen.
benevolent [be'nevələnt], *adj.* wohlwollend; — *society*, der Unterstützungsverein, — *fund*, der Unterstützungsfond.
Bengali [ben'gɔ:li], *adj.* bengalisch. — *s.* der Bengale.
benign [bi'nain], *adj.* gütig, mild.
bent [bent], *adj* gebogen, krumm; — *on something*, versessen auf etwas. — *s.* die Neigung, der Hang; — *for*, Vorliebe für.
benzene ['benzi:n], *s.* das Benzol, Kohlenbenzin.
benzine ['benzi:n], *s.* das Benzin.
bequeath [bi'kwi:θ], *v.a.* vermachen, hinterlassen.
bequest [bi'kwest], *s.* das Vermächtnis.
bereave [bi'ri:v], *v.a. irr.* berauben (durch Tod).
bereavement [bi'ri:vmənt], *s.* der Verlust (durch Tod).
beret ['berei], *s.* die Baskenmütze.
Bernard ['bə:nəd]. Bernhard, *m.*; *St.* — *dog*, der Bernhardiner.
berry ['beri], *s.* die Beere.
berth [bə:θ], *s.* (*Naut.*) der Ankerplatz; die Koje. — *v.a.*, *v.n.* anlegen; vor Anker gehen (*boat*).
beseech [bi'si:tʃ], *v.a. irr.* bitten, anflehen.
beset [bi'set], *v.a. irr.* bedrängen, bedrücken, umringen.
beside [bi'said], *prep.* außer, neben, nahe bei; — *the point*, unwesentlich; *quite* — *the mark*, weit vom Schuß.
besides [bi'saidz], *adv.* überdies, außerdem.
besiege [bi'si:dʒ], *v.a.* belagern.
besmirch [bi'smə:tʃ], *v.a.* besudeln.
besom ['bi:zəm], *s.* der Besen.
bespatter [bi'spætə], *v. a.* bespritzen.
bespeak [bi'spi:k], *v.a. irr.* bestellen; (*Tail.*) *bespoke*, nach Maß gemacht *or* gearbeitet.
best [best], *adj.* (*superl. of* **good**) best; — *adv.* am besten. — *s. want the* — *of both worlds*, alles haben wollen; *to the* — *of my ability*, nach besten Kräften; *to the* — *of my knowledge*, soviel ich weiß.
bestial ['bestjəl], *adj.* bestialisch, tierisch.
bestow [bi'stou], *v.a.* verleihen, erteilen.
bet [bet], *s.* die Wette. — *v.a.*, *v.n. irr.* wetten.
betray [bi'trei], *v.a.* verraten.
betrayal [bi'treiəl], *s.* der Verrat.
betrayer [bi'treiə], *s.* der Verräter.
betroth [bi'trouð], *v.a.* verloben.
betrothal [bi'trouðəl], *s.* die Verlobung.
better ['betə], *adj.* (*comp. of* **good**) besser. — *adv. you had* — *go*, es wäre besser, Sie gingen; *think* — *of it*, sich eines Besseren besinnen, sich's überlegen. — *s. get the* — *of*, überwinden; *so much the* —, desto *or* umso besser. — *v.a.* verbessern; — *oneself*, seine Lage verbessern.

betterment ['betəmənt], *s.* die Verbesserung.
between [bi'twi:n], *adv.* dazwischen. — *prep.* zwischen; unter (*among*).
bevel ['bevəl], *s.* der Winkelpasser; die Schräge. — *v.a.* abkanten.
beverage ['bevəridʒ], *s.* das Getränk.
bevy ['bevi], *s.* die Schar (*of beauties*, von Schönen).
bewail [bi'weil], *v.a.*, *v.n.* betrauern, beweinen; trauern um.
beware [bi'wɛə], *v.n.* sich hüten (*of*, vor).
bewilder [bi'wildə], *v.a.* verwirren.
bewitch [bi'witʃ], *v.a.* bezaubern.
beyond [bi'jɔnd], *adv.* jenseits, drüben. — *prep.* über ... hinaus; jenseits; außer.
biannual [bai'ænjuəl], *adj.* halbjährlich.
bias ['baiəs], *s.* die Neigung; das Vorurteil (*prejudice*). — *v.a.* beeinflussen.
bias(s)ed ['baiəsd], *adj.* voreingenommen.
bib [bib], *s.* der Schürzenlatz; das Lätzchen.
Bible [baibl], *s.* die Bibel.
Biblical ['biblikəl], *adj.* biblisch.
bibliography [bibli'ɔgrəfi], *s.* die Bibliographie.
bibliophile ['bibliɔfail], *s.* der Bücherfreund.
biceps ['baiseps], *s.* der Bizeps, Armmuskel.
bicker ['bikə], *v.n.* zanken, hadern.
bickering ['bikəriŋ], *s.* das Gezänk, Hadern, der Hader.
bicycle ['baisikl], (*coll.*) **bike** [baik], *s.* das Fahrrad.
bicyclist ['baisiklist], *s.* der Radfahrer.
bid [bid], *v.a.*, *v.n. irr.* gebieten, befehlen (*Dat.*) (*order*); bieten (*at auction*); — *farewell*, Lebewohl sagen. — *s.* das Gebot, Angebot (*at auction*).
bidding ['bidiŋ], *s.* der Befehl (*order*); das Bieten (*at auction*); die Einladung (*invitation*).
bide [baid], *v.n. irr.* verbleiben, verharren (*in*, *by*, bei).
biennial [bai'eniəl], *adj.* zweijährig, alle zwei Jahre.
bier [biə], *s.* die Bahre, Totenbahre.
big [big], *adj.* groß, dick (*fat*); *talking* —, großsprecherisch; *talk* —, prahlen.
bigamy ['bigəmi], *s.* die Bigamie, die Doppelehe.
bigness ['bignis], *s.* die Größe, Dicke.
bigoted ['bigətid], *adj.* bigott, fanatisch.
bigotry ['bigətri], *s.* die Bigotterie.
bigwig ['bigwig], *s.* (*coll.*) die vornehme Person, der Würdenträger.
bike *see* **bicycle**.
bilberry ['bilbəri], *s.* (*Bot.*) die Heidelbeere.
bile [bail], *s.* die Galle.
bilge [bildʒ], *s.* die Bilge, der Schiffsboden; (*coll.*) Unsinn (*nonsense*).
bilious ['biljəs], *adj.* gallig.
bill (1) [bil], *s.* der Schnabel (*bird*).
bill (2) [bil], die Rechnung (*account*); — *of exchange*, der Wechsel; — *of entry*, die Zolldeklaration; — *of fare*, die Speisekarte; (*Parl.*) der Gesetzentwurf; das Plakat (*poster*). — *v.a.* anzeigen.
billboard ['bilbɔ:d], *s.* (*Am.*) das Anschlagbrett.
billet ['bilit], *s.* das Billett (*card*); das Quartier, die Unterkunft (*army*).
billfold ['bilfould], *s.* (*Am.*) die Brieftasche.
billhook ['bilhuk], *s.* die Hippe.
billiards ['biljədz], *s.* das Billardspiel.
billow ['bilou], *s.* die Woge. — *v.n.* wogen.
bin [bin], *s.* der Behälter.
bind [baind], *v.a. irr.* binden, verpflichten; (*Law*) — *over*, zu gutem Benehmen verpflichten.
binder ['baində], *s.* der Binder, Buchbinder.
bindery ['baindəri], *s.* die Buchbinderei, Binderwerkstatt.
binding ['baindiŋ], *s.* der Einband.
binnacle ['binəkl], *s.* das Kompaßhäuschen.
binocular [bi'nɔkjulə], *adj.* für beide Augen. — *s.* (*pl.*) das Fernglas, der Feldstecher.
binomial [bai'noumiəl], *adj.* binomisch. — *s.* (*pl.*) (*Maths.*) das Binom, der zweigliedrige Ausdruck.
biochemical [baio'kemikəl], *adj.* biochemisch.
biochemistry [baio'kemistri], *s.* die Biochemie.
biographer [bai'ɔgrəfə], *s.* der Biograph.
biographical [baio'græfikəl], *adj.* biographisch.
biography [bai'ɔgrəfi], *s.* die Biographie, die Lebensbeschreibung.
biological [baio'lɔdʒikəl], *adj.* biologisch.
biology [bai'ɔlədʒi], *s.* die Biologie.
biometric(al) [baio'metrik(əl)], *adj.* biometrisch.
biometry [bai'ɔmitri], *s.* die Biometrie.
biophysical [baio'fizikəl], *adj.* biophysisch.
biophysics [baio'fiziks], *s.* die Biophysik.
biped ['baiped], *s.* der Zweifüßler.
biplane ['baiplein], *s.* (*Aviat.*) der Doppeldecker.
birch [bə:tʃ], *s.* (*Bot.*) die Birke; die Birkenrute, Rute (*cane*). — *v.a.* (mit der Rute) züchtigen.
bird [bə:d], *s.* der Vogel; — *of passage*, der Wandervogel, Zugvogel; —*cage*, der Vogelkäfig, das Vogelbauer; — *fancier*, der Vogelzüchter; —*'s-eye view*, die Vogelperspektive.
birth [bə:θ], *s.* die Geburt; — *certificate*, der Geburtsschein.
birthday ['bə:θdei], *s*, der Geburtstag.
biscuit ['biskit], *s.* der *or* das Keks; der Zwieback.

bisect [bai'sekt], *v.a.* entzweischneiden, halbieren.
bisection [bai'sekʃən], *s.* die Zweiteilung, Halbierung.
bishop ['biʃəp], *s.* der Bischof; (*Chess*) der Läufer.
bishopric ['biʃəprik], *s.* das Bistum.
bismuth ['bizməθ], *s.* der *or* das Wismut.
bison ['baisən], *s.* (*Zool.*) der Bison.
bit [bit], *s.* der Bissen (*bite*), das Bißchen (*little* —); das Gebiß (*bridle*); der Bart (*of key*).
bitch [bitʃ], *s.* die Hündin.
bite [bait], *v.a. irr.* beißen. — *s.* das Beißen (*mastication*); der Biß (*morsel*).
biting ['baitiŋ], *adj.* (*also fig.*) beißend, scharf. — *adv.* — *cold*, bitterkalt.
bitter ['bitə], *adj.* bitter.
bitterness ['bitənis], *s.* die Bitterkeit.
bittern ['bitə:n], *s.* (*Orn.*) die Rohrdommel.
bitumen [bi'tju:mən], *s.* der Bergteer, Asphalt.
bivouac ['bivuæk], *s.* (*Mil.*) das Biwak, Lager.
bizarre [bi'zɑ:], *adj.* bizarr, wunderlich.
blab [blæb], *v.a., v.n.* schwatzen, ausplaudern (*give away*).
blabber ['blæbə], *s.* (*coll.*) der Schwätzer.
black [blæk], *adj.* schwarz; — *sheep*, der Taugenichts; — *pudding*, die Blutwurst; *Black Forest*, der Schwarzwald; *Black Maria*, der Polizeiwagen; (*coll.*) die grüne Minna; *Black Sea*, das schwarze Meer.
blackberry ['blækbəri], *s.* (*Bot.*) die Brombeere.
blackbird ['blækbə:d], *s.* (*Orn.*) die Amsel.
blackguard ['blægɑ:d], *s.* der Spitzbube, Schurke.
blackmail ['blækmeil], *v.a.* erpressen. — *s.* die Erpressung.
bladder ['blædə], *s.* (*Anat.*) die Blase.
blacksmith ['blæksmiθ], *s.* der Grobschmied.
blade [bleid], *s.* die Klinge (*razor*); der Halm (*grass*); *shoulder* —, das Schulterblatt.
blamable ['bleiməbl], *adj.* tadelnswert, tadelhaft.
blame [bleim], *s.* der Tadel, die Schuld. — *v.a.* tadeln, beschuldigen, die Schuld zuschreiben (*Dat.*).
blameless ['bleimlis], *adj.* tadellos, schuldlos.
blanch [blɔ:ntʃ], *v.n.* erbleichen, weiß werden. — *v.a.* weiß machen.
bland [blænd], *adj.* mild, sanft.
blandish ['blændiʃ], *v.a.* schmeicheln (*Dat.*).
blandishment ['blændiʃmənt], *s.* (*mostly in pl.*) die Schmeichelei.
blandness ['blændnis], *s.* die Milde, Sanftheit.
blank [blæŋk], *adj.* blank, leer; reimlos (*verse*); *leave a* —, einen Raum freilassen; — *cartridge*, die Platzpatrone.
blanket ['blæŋkit], *s.* die Decke; (*coll.*) *a wet* —, ein langweiliger Kerl, der Spielverderber.
blare [blɛə], *v.n.* schmettern.
blaspheme [blæs'fi:m], *v.a., v.n.* lästern, fluchen.
blasphemous ['blæsfiməs], *adj.* lästerlich.
blasphemy ['blæsfəmi], *s.* die Gotteslästerung.
blast [blɑ:st], *v.a.* sprengen, zerstören. — *s.* der Windstoß (*gust*); der Stoß (*trumpets*); die Explosion (*bomb*); — *furnace*, der Hochofen. — *excl.* (*sl.*) —*!* zum Teufel!
blasting ['blɑ:stiŋ], *s.* das Sprengen.
blatant ['bleitənt], *adj.* laut, lärmend; dreist.
blaze [bleiz], *s.* die Flamme (*flame*); das Feuer; der Glanz (*colour etc.*). — *v.n.* flammen; leuchten (*shine*). — *v.a.* ausposaunen, bekannt machen (*make known*).
blazer ['bleizə], *s.* die Sportjacke, Klubjacke.
blazon ['bleizən], *v.a.* verkünden.
bleach [bli:tʃ], *v.a.* bleichen. — *s.* das Bleichmittel.
bleak [bli:k], *adj.* öde, rauh; trübe, freudlos.
bleakness ['bli:knis], *s.* die Öde (*scenery*); Traurigkeit, Trübheit.
bleary ['bliəri], *adj.* trübe; — *eyed*, triefäugig.
bleat [bli:t], *v.n.* blöken.
bleed [bli:d], *v.n. irr.* bluten. — *v.a.* bluten lassen; erpressen (*blackmail*).
blemish ['blemiʃ], *s.* der Makel, der Fehler. — *v.a.* schänden, entstellen.
blench [blentʃ], *v.n.* zurückweichen, stutzen.
blend [blend], *v.a., v.n.* mischen, vermengen; sich mischen. — *s.* die Mischung, Vermischung.
bless [bles], *v.a.* segnen; beglücken; loben.
blessed [blest, 'blesid], *adj.* gesegnet, selig.
blessing ['blesiŋ], *s.* der Segen.
blight [blait], *s.* der Meltau. — *v.a.* verderben.
blind [blaind], *adj.* blind; — *man's buff*, Blinde Kuh; — *spot*, der schwache Punkt. — *s.* die Blende, das Rouleau; *Venetian* —, die Jalousie. — *v.a.* blind machen, täuschen.
blindfold ['blaindfould], *adj.* mit verbundenen Augen.
blindness ['blaindnis], *s.* die Blindheit.
blindworm ['blaindwə:m], *s.* (*Zool.*) die Blindschleiche.
blink [bliŋk], *s.* das Blinzeln. — *v.n.* blinzeln, blinken. — *v.a.* nicht sehen wollen.
blinkers ['bliŋkəz], *s. pl.* die Scheuklappen.
bliss [blis], *s.* die Wonne, Seligkeit.
blissful ['blisful], *adj.* wonnig, selig.
blister ['blistə], *s.* die Blase. — *v.n.* Blasen ziehen, Blasen bekommen.

blithe [blaið], *adj.* munter, lustig, fröhlich.
blitheness ['blaiðnis], *s.* die Munterkeit, Fröhlichkeit.
blizzard ['blizəd], *s.* der Schneesturm.
bloated ['bloutid], *adj.* aufgeblasen, aufgedunsen.
bloater ['bloutə], *s.* (*Zool.*) der Bückling.
blob [blɔb], *s.* der Kleks.
block [blɔk], *s.* der Block, Klotz (*wood*); Häuserblock (*houses*); — *letters*, große Druckschrift. — *v.a.* blockieren, hemmen (*hinder*); sperren (*road*).
blockade [blɔ'keid], *s.* die Blockade.
blockhead ['blɔkhed], *s.* der Dummkopf.
blonde [blɔnd], *adj.* blond. — *s.* die Blondine.
blood [blʌd], *s.* das Blut; — *vessel*, das Blutgefäß.
bloodcurdling ['blʌdkə:dliŋ], *adj.* haarsträubend.
bloodless ['blʌdlis], *adj.* blutlos, unblutig.
bloodthirsty ['blʌdθə:sti], *adj.* blutdürstig.
bloody ['blʌdi], *adj.* blutig; (*vulg.*) verflucht.
bloom [blu:m], *s.* die Blüte; die Blume. — *v.n.* blühen.
bloomers ['blu:məz], *s. pl.* altmodische Unterhosen für Damen.
blooming ['blu:miŋ], *adj.* blühend.
blossom ['blɔsəm], *s.* die Blüte. — *v.n.* blühen, Blüten treiben.
blot [blɔt], *s.* der Klecks; Fleck; (*fig.*) der Schandfleck. — *v.a.* beflecken; löschen (*ink*); — *out*, ausmerzen, austilgen; *blotting paper*, das Löschpapier.
blotch [blɔtʃ], *s.* der Hautfleck; die Pustel; der Klecks (*blot*).
blotter ['blɔtə], *s.* der Löscher.
blouse [blauz], *s.* die Bluse.
blow (1) [blou], *s.* der Schlag.
blow (2) [blou], *v.a. irr.* blasen; wehen; — *o.'s own trumpet*, prahlen; anfachen (*fire*); — *o.'s nose*, sich schneuzen. — *v.n.* schnaufen, keuchen; — *up*, in die Luft sprengen.
blower ['blouə], *s.* das Gebläse; der Bläser.
blowpipe ['bloupaip], *s.* das Lötrohr.
blubber ['blʌbə], *s.* der Walfischspeck, der Tran. — *v.n.* schluchzen, heulen, flennen.
bludgeon ['blʌdʒən], *s.* der Knüppel; die Keule (*club*). — *v.a.* niederschlagen.
blue [blu:], *adj.* blau; schwermütig (*sad*); — *blooded*, aus edlem Geblüte.
bluebell ['blu:bel], *s.* (*Bot.*) die Glockenblume.
bluebottle ['blu:bɔtl], *s.* (*Ent.*) die Schmeißfliege.
bluestocking ['blu:stɔkiŋ], *s.* der Blaustrumpf.
bluff [blʌf], *adj.* grob, schroff. — *s.* der Bluff, die Täuschung, der Trick. — *v.a.*, *v.n.* vortäuschen (*pretend*), bluffen; verblüffen (*deceive*).
blunder ['blʌndə], *s.* der Fehler, Schnitzer. — *v.n.* einen Fehler machen.
blunderer ['blʌndərə], *s.* der Tölpel.
blunderbuss ['blʌndəbʌs], *s.* die Donnerbüchse.
blunt [blʌnt], *adj.* stumpf (*edge*); derb, offen (*speech*). — *v.a.* abstumpfen; verderben (*appetite*).
bluntness ['blʌntnis], *s.* die Stumpfheit (*edge*); die Derbheit (*speech*).
blur [blə:], *s.* der Fleck. — *v.a.* verwischen.
blurt [blə:t], *v.a.* — *out*, herausplatzen.
blush [blʌʃ], *v.n.* erröten. — *s.* die Schamröte, das Erröten.
bluster ['blʌstə], *s.* das Toben, Brausen. — *v.n.* toben, brausen.
blustering ['blʌstəriŋ], *adj.* lärmend, tobend.
boa ['bouə], *s.* (*Zool.*) die Boa.
boar [bɔ:], *s.* (*Zool.*) der Eber.
board [bɔ:d], *s.* das Brett (*wood*); die Tafel (*notice* —); die Verpflegung (*food*); — *and lodging*, die Vollpension; die Behörde, der Ausschuß (*officials*). — *v.a.* — *up*, vernageln, zumachen; — *someone*, verpflegen; — *a steamer*, an Bord gehen; —*ing school*, das Internat, das Pensionat.
boarder ['bɔ:də], *s.* der Internatsschüler; der Pensionär.
boast [boust], *v.n.* prahlen, sich rühmen. — *s.* der Stolz (*pride*).
boastful ['boustful], *adj.* prahlerisch.
boat [bout], *s.* das Boot; *rowing-* —, das Ruderboot; der Kahn.
bob [bɔb], *s.* der Knicks; (*coll.*) der Schilling. — *v.n.* baumeln; springen; *bobbed hair*, der Bubikopf.
bobbin ['bɔbin], *s.* die Spule, der Klöppel.
bobsleigh ['bɔbslei], *s.* der Bob(sleigh), Rennschlitten.
bodice ['bɔdis], *s.* das Mieder, Leibchen.
bodied ['bɔdid], *adj. suffix; able-* —, gesund, stark.
body ['bɔdi], *s.* der Körper; die Körperschaft (*organisation*).
bodyguard ['bɔdigɑ:d], *s.* die Leibwache.
Boer ['bouə], *s.* der Bure.
bog [bɔg], *s.* der Sumpf. — *v.a.* (*coll.*) — *down*, einsinken.
Bohemian [bo'hi:mjən], *s.* der Böhme. — *adj.* böhmisch; künstlerhaft.
boil (1) [bɔil], *v.a.*, *v.n.* kochen, sieden. — *s.* das Kochen; —*ing point*, der Siedepunkt.
boil (2) [bɔil], *s.* (*Med.*) die Beule, der Furunkel.
boisterous ['bɔistərəs], *adj.* ungestüm; laut (*noisy*).
boisterousness ['bɔistərəsnis], *s.* die Heftigkeit, Lautheit.

bold [bould], *adj.* kühn, dreist; *make* —, sich erkühnen.
boldness ['bouldnis], *s.* die Kühnheit, Dreistigkeit.
Bolivian [bə'livjən], *adj.* bolivianisch. —*s.* der Bolivianer.
bolster ['boulstə], *s.* das Polster, Kissen.
bolt [boult], *s.* der Bolzen, Riegel (*on door*); der Pfeil (*arrow*). — *v.a.* verriegeln (*bar*); verschlingen (*devour*). — *v.n.* davonlaufen (*run away*), durchgehen (*abscond*).
bomb [bɔm], *s.* die Bombe. — *v.a.* bombardieren.
bombard [bɔm'bɑ:d], *v.a.* bombardieren.
bombardment [bɔm'bɑ:dmənt], *s.* die Beschießung.
bombastic [bɔm'bæstik], *adj.* schwülstig, bombastisch (*style*).
bombproof ['bɔmpru:f], *adj.* bombensicher.
bond [bɔnd], *s.* das Band (*link*); die Schuldverschreibung (*debt*); *in* —, unter Zollverschluß; (*pl.*) die Fesseln (*fetters*). — *v.a.* (*Chem.*) binden; (*Comm.*) zollpflichtig erklären (*declare dutiable*).
bondage ['bɔndidʒ], *s.* die Knechtschaft.
bone [boun], *s.* der Knochen; die Gräte (*fish*); — *china*, feines Geschirr, das Porzellan; — *of contention*, der Zankapfel; — *dry*, staubtrocken; — *idle*, stinkfaul; — *lace*, die Klöppelspitze. — *v.a.* Knochen oder Gräten entfernen.
bonfire ['bɔnfaiə], *s.* das Freudenfeuer.
bonnet ['bɔnit], *s.* die Haube, das Häubchen.
bonny ['bɔni], *adj.* hübsch, nett.
bony ['bouni], *adj.* beinern, knöchern.
book [buk], *s.* das Buch. — *v.a.* belegen (*seat*); eine Karte lösen (*ticket*); engagieren (*engage*).
bookbinder ['bukbaində], *s.* der Buchbinder.
bookcase ['bukkeis], *s.* der Bücherschrank.
bookie *see* **bookmaker**.
booking-office ['bukiŋɔfis], *s.* der Fahrkartenschalter; die Kasse (*Theat. etc.*)
book-keeper ['bukki:pə], *s.* der Buchhalter.
book-keeping ['bukki:piŋ], *s.* die Buchhaltung; *double entry* —, doppelte Buchführung, *single entry* —, einfache Buchführung.
bookmaker ['bukmeikə] (*abbr.* **bookie** ['buki]), *s.* (*Racing*) der Buchmacher.
bookmark(er) ['bukmɑ:k(ə)], *s.* das Lesezeichen.
bookseller ['bukselə], *s.* der Buchhändler.
bookshop ['bukʃɔp], *s.* die Buchhandlung.
bookstall ['bukstɔ:l], *s.* der Bücherstand.
bookworm ['bukwə:m], *s.* der Bücherwurm.
boom (1) [bu:m], *s.* der Aufschwung; Boom; (*Comm.*) die Konjunktur; Hausse.
boom (2) [bu:m], *v.n.* dröhnen, (dumpf) schallen.
boon [bu:n], *s.* die Wohltat.
boor [buə], *s.* der Lümmel.
boorish ['buəriʃ], *adj.* lümmelhaft.
boot [bu:t], *s.* der Stiefel, hohe Schuh. — *v.a.* mit dem Stiefel stoßen, kicken.
booth [bu:ð], *s.* die Bude, Zelle (*Teleph.*).
bootlace ['bu:tleis], *s.* der Schnürsenkel, der Schnürriemen.
booty ['bu:ti], *s.* die Beute.
booze [bu:z], *v.n.* (*coll.*) saufen.
boozy ['bu:zi], *adj.* (*coll.*) angeheitert, leicht betrunken.
border ['bɔ:də], *s.* der Rand; die Grenze. — *v.a.*, *v.n.* angrenzen (*on*); einsäumen (*surround*).
borderer ['bɔ:dərə], *s.* der Grenzbewohner.
bore [bɔ:], *v.a.* bohren; langweilen (*be boring*). — *s.* das Bohrloch (*drill-hole*), die Bohrung (*drilling*); der langweilige Kerl (*person*).
boredom ['bɔ:dəm], *s.* die Langeweile.
borer ['bɔ:rə], *s.* der Bohrer (*drill*).
born [bɔ:n], *adj.* geboren.
borrow ['bɔrou], *v.a.* borgen, entlehnen.
borrowing ['bɔrouiŋ], *s.* das Borgen, Entlehnen.
bosom ['buzəm], *s.* der Busen.
boss [bɔs], *s.* der Beschlag, der Buckel; (*coll.*) der Chef.
botanical [bɔ'tænikəl], *adj.* botanisch.
botanist ['bɔtənist], *s.* der Botaniker.
botany ['bɔtəni], *s.* die Botanik.
botch [bɔtʃ], *s.* das Flickwerk. — *v.a.* verderben, verhunzen.
both [bouθ], *adj.*, *pron.* beide, beides; — *of them*, beide. — *conj.* — . . . *and*, sowohl . . . als auch.
bother ['bɔðə], *v.a.* plagen, stören, belästigen; — *it!* zum Henker damit! — *v.n.* sich bemühen. — *s.* die Belästigung, das Ärgernis.
bottle [bɔtl], *s.* die Flasche. — *v.a.* in Flaschen abfüllen.
bottom ['bɔtəm], *s.* der Boden, Grund (*ground*); die Ursache (*cause*); (*Naut.*) der Schiffsboden.
bottomless ['bɔtəmlis], *adj.* grundlos, bodenlos.
bough [bau], *s.* der Zweig, Ast.
boulder ['bouldə], *s.* der Felsblock.
bounce [bauns], *v.a.* aufprallen lassen (*ball*). — *v.n.* aufprallen. — *s.* der Rückprall, Aufprall.
bound (1) [baund], *s.* der Sprung; *by leaps and* —*s*, sehr schnell, sprunghaft. — *v.n.* springen, prallen.
bound (2) [baund], *v.a.* begrenzen, einschränken. — *adj.* verpflichtet; — *to* (*inf.*), wird sicherlich . . .

bound (3) [baund], *adj.* — *for*, auf dem Wege nach.
boundary ['baundəri], *s.* die Grenzlinie, Grenze.
bounder ['baundə], *s.* der ungezogene Bursche.
boundless ['baundlis], *adj.* grenzenlos, unbegrenzt.
bounteous ['bauntiəs], *adj.* freigebig; reichlich (*plenty*).
bounty ['baunti], *s.* die Freigebigkeit (*generosity*); (*Comm.*) Prämie.
bouquet [bu'kei], *s.* das Bukett, der Blumenstrauß; die Blume (*wine*).
bourgeois ['buəʒwa:], *s.* der Bürger; Philister. — *adj.* kleinbürgerlich, philisterhaft.
bow (1) [bau], *s.* (*Naut.*) der Bug; —*sprit*, das Bugspriet.
bow (2) [bau], *s.* die Verbeugung, Verneigung. — *v.n.* sich verneigen, sich verbeugen. — *v.a.* neigen.
bow (3) [bou], *s.* (*Mus.*) der Bogen; die Schleife (*ribbon*). — *v.a.* streichen (*violin*).
bowel ['bauəl], *s.* der Darm; (*pl.*) die Eingeweide.
bowl (1) [boul], *s.* die Schale, der Napf, die Schüssel.
bowl (2) [boul], *s.* die Holzkugel; (*pl.*) das Rasenkugelspiel, Bowlingspiel. — *v.n.* (*Cricket*) den Ball werfen.
bowler (1) ['boulə], *s.* (*hat*) der steife Hut, die Melone.
bowler (2) ['boulə], *s.* (*Sport*) der Ballmann.
box (1) [bɔks], *s.* (*Bot.*) der Buchsbaum.
box (2) [bɔks], *s.* die Büchse, Dose, Schachtel, der Kasten; (*Theat.*) die Loge; — *office*, die Theaterkasse.
box (3) [bɔks], *s.* der Schlag; — *on the ear*, die Ohrfeige. — *v.n.* boxen.
boxer ['bɔksə], *s.* der Boxer; Boxkämpfer.
Boxing Day ['bɔksiŋ'dei], der zweite Weihnachtstag.
boy [bɔi], *s.* der Junge, Knabe; Diener (*servant*).
boyish ['bɔiiʃ], *adj.* knabenhaft.
boyhood ['bɔihud], *s.* das Knabenalter.
brace [breis], *s.* das Band; die Klammer (*clamp*); — *of partridges*, das Paar Rebhühner; die Spange (*denture*). — *v.a.* spannen, straffen. — *v.r.* — *yourself!* stähle dich!
bracelet ['breislit], *s.* das Armband.
braces ['breisiz], *s. pl.* die Hosenträger.
bracken ['brækən], *s.* (*Bot.*) das Farnkraut.
bracket ['brækit], *s.* die Klammer; *income* —, die Einkommensgruppe. — *v.a.* (ein-)klammern; (*Maths.*) in Klammern setzen.
brackish ['brækiʃ], *adj.* salzig.
brad [bræd], *s.* der kopflose Nagel; — *awl*, der Vorstechbohrer.
brag [bræg], *v.n.* prahlen.
braggart ['brægət], *s.* der Prahlhans.
Brahmin ['bra:min], *s.* der Brahmane.
braid [breid], *s.* die Borte; der Saumbesatz. — *v.a.* (mit Borten) besetzen.
Braille [breil], *s.* die Blindenschrift.
brain [brein], *s.* das Gehirn, Hirn; *scatter-* —*ed*, zerstreut.
brainwave ['breinweiv], *s.* der Geistesblitz.
brake [breik], *s.* die Bremse. — *v.a.* bremsen.
bramble [bræmbl], *s.* der (*Bot.*) Brombeerstrauch.
bran [bræn], *s.* die Kleie.
branch [bra:ntʃ], *s.* der Ast, Zweig; (*Comm.*) die Zweigstelle, Filiale. — *v.n.* — *out*, sich verzweigen; — *out into*, sich ausbreiten, etwas Neues anfangen; — *off*, abzweigen.
brand [brænd], *s.* der (Feuer) Brand; das Brandmal (*on skin*); die Sorte, Marke (*make*); — *new*, funkelnagelneu. — *v.a.* brandmarken, kennzeichnen.
brandish ['brændiʃ], *v.a.* schwingen, herumschwenken.
brandy ['brændi], *s.* der Branntwein, Kognac, Weinbrand.
brass [bra:s], *s.* das Messing; — *band*, die Blechmusik, Militärmusikkapelle; — *founder*, Erzgießer, Gelbgießer; (*sl.*) die Frechheit (*impudence*).
brassiere ['bræsiɛə], *s.* der Büstenhalter.
brat [bræt], *s.* (*coll.*) das Kind, der Balg.
brave [breiv], *adj.* tapfer, kühn. — *v.a.* trotzen, standhalten (*Dat.*). — *s.* der Held, Krieger; der Indianer (*redskin*).
bravery ['breivəri], *s.* die Tapferkeit.
brawl [brɔ:l], *s.* der Krawall, die Rauferei. — *v.n.* zanken, lärmen.
brawn [brɔ:n], *s.* die Sülze; (*fig.*) die Körperkraft, Stärke.
brawny ['brɔ:ni], *adj.* stark, sehnig.
bray [brei], *v.n.* iah sagen, Eselslaute von sich geben (*donkey*). — *s.* das Iah des Esels, das Eselsgeschrei.
brazen [breizn], *adj.* (*Metall.*) aus Erz; unverschämt (*shameless*).
brazenfaced ['breiznfeisd], *adj.* unverschämt.
brazier ['breiziə], *s.* der Kupferschmied; die Kohlenpfanne.
Brazil [brə'zil]. Brasilien, *n.*; — *nut*, die Paranuß.
Brazilian [brə'ziliən], *adj.* brasilianisch. — *s.* der Brasilianer.
breach [bri:tʃ], *s.* die Bresche; der Bruch (*break*); die Verletzung; der Vertragsbruch (*of contract*); der Verstoß (*of*, gegen, *etiquette etc.*).
bread [bred], *s.* das Brot; *brown* —, das Schwarzbrot; — *and butter*, das Butterbrot.
breadth [bretθ], *s.* die Breite, Weite.

break [breik], *s.* der Bruch (*breach*); die Lücke (*gap*); die Chance (*chance*); *a lucky* —, ein glücklicher Zufall, ein Glücksfall; die Pause (*from work*). — *v.a., v.n. irr.* brechen; — *off*, Pause machen; — *in*, unterbrechen (*interrupt*); — *in*, (*horse*) einschulen, zureiten; — *up*, abbrechen (*school, work*); — *away*, sich trennen, absondern; — *down*, zusammenbrechen (*health*); (*Am.*) analysieren; auflösen.

breakage ['breikidʒ], *s.* der Bruch, der Schaden (*damage*).

breakdown ['breikdoun], *s.* der Zusammenbruch (*health*); die Panne (*car*); (*Am.*) die Analyse (*analysis*).

breaker ['breikə], *s.* die Brandungswelle, Brandung.

breakfast ['brekfəst], *s.* das Frühstück. *v.n.* frühstücken.

breast [brest], *s.* die Brust.

breath [breθ], *s.* der Atem; der Hauch (*exhalation*); *with bated* —, mit verhaltenem Atem.

breathe [bri:ð], *v.n.* atmen.

breathing ['bri:ðiŋ], *s.* die Atmung.

breathless ['breθlis], *adj.* atemlos.

breech [bri:tʃ], *s.* der Boden; (*pl.*) die Reithosen, *f. pl.*

breed [bri:d], *v.a. irr.* zeugen, züchten (*cattle, etc.*). — *v.n.* sich vermehren. — *s.* die Zucht, die Art (*type*); die Rasse (*race*).

breeder ['bri:də], *s.* der Züchter.

breeding ['bri:diŋ], *s.* die gute Kinderstube (*manners*); die Erziehung; das Züchten (*of plants, cattle etc.*).

breeze [bri:z], *s.* die Briese.

breezy ['bri:zi], *adj.* windig; lebhaft (*manner*), beschwingt (*tone*).

brethren ['breðrən], *s. pl.* (*obs.*) die Brüder.

Breton [bretn], *adj.* bretonisch. — *s.* der Bretagner, Bretone.

brevet ['brevit], *s.* das Patent.

breviary ['bri:viəri], *s.* das Brevier.

brevity ['breviti], *s.* die Kürze.

brew [bru:], *v.a.* brauen. — *s.* das Gebräu, Bräu (*beer*).

brewer ['bru:ə], *s.* der Brauer, Bierbrauer.

brewery ['bru:əri], *s.* die Brauerei, das Brauhaus.

briar, brier ['braiə], *s.* (*Bot.*) der Dornstrauch, die wilde Rose.

bribe [braib], *v.a.* bestechen. — *s.* das Bestechungsgeld.

bribery ['braibəri], *s.* die Bestechung.

brick [brik], *s.* der Ziegel, Backstein; *drop a* —, eine Taktlosigkeit begehen, einen Schnitzer machen.

bricklayer ['brikleiə], *s.* der Maurer.

bridal [braidl], *adj.* bräutlich.

bride [braid], *s.* die Braut.

bridegroom ['braidgru:m], *s.* der Bräutigam.

bridesmaid ['braidzmeid], *s.* die Brautjungfer.

bridge [bridʒ], *s.* die Brücke. — *v.a.* überbrücken; — *the gap*, die Lücke füllen.

bridle [braidl], *s.* der Zaum, Zügel. — *v.a.* aufzäumen. — *v.n.* sich brüsten.

brief [bri:f], *adj.* kurz, bündig, knapp. — *s.* der Schriftsatz, der Rechtsauftrag, die Instruktionen, *f. pl.* (*instructions*). — *v.a.* instruieren, beauftragen; informieren (*inform*).

brigade [bri'geid], *s.* die Brigade.

brigand ['brigənd], *s.* der Brigant, Straßenräuber.

bright [brait], *adj.* hell, glänzend (*shiny*); klug, intelligent (*clever*).

brighten [braitn], *v.a.* glänzend machen (*polish etc.*); erhellen, aufheitern (*cheer*).

brightness ['braitnis], *s.* der Glanz; die Helligkeit; die Klugheit (*cleverness*).

brill [bril], *s.* (*Zool.*) der Glattbutt.

brilliance, brilliancy ['briljəns, -jənsi], *s.* der Glanz, die Pracht.

brim [brim], *s.* der Rand (*glass*); die Krempe (*hat*). — *v.n.* — (*over*) *with*, überfließen von.

brimful ['brimful], *adj.* übervoll.

brimstone ['brimstoun], *s.* der Schwefel; — *butterfly*, der Zitronenfalter.

brindled ['brindld], *adj.* scheckig, gefleckt.

brine [brain], *s.* die Salzsole, das Salzwasser.

bring [briŋ], *v.a. irr.* bringen; — *about*, zustande bringen; — *forth*, hervorbringen; gebären; — *forward*, fördern; anführen; — *on*, herbeiführen; — *up*, erziehen, aufziehen.

brink [briŋk], *s.* (*fig.*) der Rand, — *of a precipice*, Rand eines Abgrundes.

briny ['braini], *adj.* salzig.

brisk [brisk], *adj.* frisch, munter, feurig (*horse*).

brisket ['briskit], *s.* die Brust (eines Tieres).

briskness ['brisknis], *s.* die Lebhaftigkeit.

bristle [brisl], *s.* die Borste. — *v.n.* sich sträuben.

British ['britiʃ], *adj.* britisch.

Britisher, Briton ['britiʃə, 'britən], *s.* der Brite.

brittle [britl], *adj.* zerbrechlich, spröde.

brittleness ['britlnis], *s.* die Sprödigkeit, Zerbrechlichkeit.

broach [broutʃ], *v.a.* anzapfen, anschneiden; — *a subject*, ein Thema berühren.

broad [brɔ:d], *adj.* breit, weit; ordinär, derb (*joke*); — *-minded*, duldsam, weitherzig.

broadcast ['brɔ:dkɑ:st], *v.a.* senden, übertragen (*radio*). — *s.* die Sendung, das Programm.

broadcaster ['brɔ:dkɑ:stə], *s.* der im Radio Vortragende *or* Künstler (*artist*); Ansager.

broadcasting ['brɔ:dkɑ:stiŋ], *s.* das Senden, der Rundfunk; — *station*, der Sender, die Rundfunkstation.

broadcloth ['brɔ:dclɔθ], *s.* das feine Tuch.
broaden [brɔ:dn], *v.a.* erweitern, verbreitern.
brocade [bro'keid], *s.* der Brokat.
brogue [broug], *s.* der grobe Schuh; der irische Akzent.
broil ['brɔil], *v.a.* braten, rösten.
broke [brouk], *adj.* (*coll.*) pleite.
broken ['broukən], *adj.* gebrochen; zerbrochen; unterbrochen (*interrupted*).
broker ['broukə], *s.* der Makler.
bronchial ['brɔŋkjəl], *adj.* (*Anat.*) bronchial, in *or* von der Luftröhre, Luftröhren-.
bronchitis [brɔŋ'kaitis], *s.* (*Med.*) die Luftröhrenentzündung, Bronchitis.
bronze [brɔnz], *s.* (*Metall.*) die Bronze, Bronzefarbe.
brooch [broutʃ], *s.* die Brosche.
brood [bru:d], *s.* die Brut. — *v.n.* brüten; grübeln (*meditate*).
brook (1) [bruk], *s.* der Bach.
brook (2) [bruk], *v.a.* ertragen, leiden.
brooklet ['bruklit], *s.* das Bächlein.
broom [bru:m], *s.* der Besen; (*Bot.*) der Ginster.
broth [brɔθ], *s.* die Brühe; *meat* —, Fleischbrühe.
brothel ['brɔθəl], *s.* das Bordell.
brother ['brʌðə], *s.* der Bruder; — *-in-law*, der Schwager.
brotherhood ['brʌðəhud], *s.* die Bruderschaft.
brotherly ['brʌðəli], *adj.* brüderlich.
brow [brau], *s.* die Braue, Augenbraue; der Kamm (*hill*); die Stirn(e) (*forehead*).
browbeat ['braubi:t], *v.a.* einschüchtern.
brown [braun], *adj.* braun; *in a — study*, in tiefem Nachsinnen.
browse [brauz], *v.n.* weiden (*cattle*); stöbern, (durch-)blättern (*in books etc.*).
Bruin ['bru:in]. Braun, Meister Petz, der Bär.
bruise [bru:z], *v.a.* quetschen, stoßen; (wund) schlagen. — *s.* die Quetschung.
Brunswick ['brʌnzwik]. Braunschweig, *n.*
brunt [brʌnt], *s.* der Anprall; *bear the* —, der Wucht ausgesetzt sein, den Stoß auffangen.
brush [brʌʃ], *s.* die Bürste (*clothes*); der Pinsel (*paint, painting*); — *stroke*, der Pinselstrich. — *v.a., v.n.* bürsten, abbürsten; — *against s.o.*, mit jemandem zusammenstoßen, streifen (*an, Acc.*); — *up one's English*, das Englisch auffrischen; — *off*, abschütteln.
brushwood ['brʌʃwud], *s.* das Gestrüpp.
brusque [brusk], *adj.* brüsk, barsch.
Brussels ['brʌsəlz]. Brüssel, *n.*; — *sprouts*, (*Bot.*) der Rosenkohl.
brutal [bru:tl], *adj.* brutal, grausam.
brutality [bru:'tæliti], *s.* die Brutalität.
brute [bru:t], *s.* der Unmensch.
bubble [bʌbl], *s.* die Blase; (*fig.*) der Schwindel (*swindle*). — *v.n.* sprudeln, wallen, schäumen.
buccaneer [bʌkə'niə], *s.* der Seeräuber.
buck [bʌk], *s.* (*Zool.*) der Bock; (*Am. sl.*) der Dollar. — *v.a.* — *up*, aufmuntern. — *v.n.* — *up*, sich zusammenraffen.
bucket ['bʌkit], *s.* der Eimer, Kübel.
buckle [bʌkl], *s.* die Schnalle. — *v.a.* zuschnallen; biegen. — *v.n.* sich krümmen.
buckler ['bʌklə], *s.* der Schild.
buckram ['bʌkrəm], *s.* die Steifleinwand.
buckskin ['bʌkskin], *s.* das Wildleder.
buckwheat ['bʌkwi:t], *s.* (*Bot.*) der Buchweizen.
bucolic [bju:'kɔlik], *adj.* bukolisch, ländlich, Schäfer-.
bud [bʌd], *s.* (*Bot.*) die Knospe. — *v.n.* knospen.
buddy ['bʌdi], *s.* (*coll. Am.*) der Freund, Kamerad.
budge [bʌdʒ], *v.n.* sich rühren, sich regen.
budget ['bʌdʒit], *s.* das Budget; der Haushaltsplan; der Etat; *present the* —, den Staatsetat vorlegen. — *v.n.* voranschlagen (*for*), planen.
buff [bʌf], *adj.* ledergelb.
buffalo ['bʌfəlou], *s.* (*Zool.*) der Büffel.
buffer ['bʌfə], *s.* der Puffer.
buffet (1) ['bʌfit], *s.* der Puff, Faustschlag (*blow*). — *v.a.* schlagen, stoßen.
buffet (2) ['bufei], *s.* das Buffet, der Anrichtetisch.
buffoon [bʌ'fu:n], *s.* der Possenreißer.
buffoonery [bʌ'fu:nəri], *s.* die Possen, *f. pl.*; das Possenreißen.
bug [bʌg], *s.* (*Ent.*) die Wanze; (*Am.*) der Käfer; (*coll.*) das Insekt.
buggy ['bʌgi], *s.* der Einspänner.
bugle [bju:gl], *s.* (*Mus.*) das Signalhorn, die Signaltrompete.
bugler ['bju:glə], *s.* (*Mus.*) der Trompeter.
build [bild], *v.a., v.n. irr.* bauen; errichten; — *on*, sich verlassen auf (*rely on*). — *s.* die Statur, Figur (*figure*).
builder ['bildə], *s.* der Bauherr, Baumeister (*employer*); Bauarbeiter (*worker*).
building ['bildiŋ], *s.* das Gebäude, der Bau; — *site*, der Bauplatz.
bulb [bʌlb], *s.* (*Bot.*) der Knollen, die Zwiebel; *Dutch* —, die Tulpe; (*Elec.*) die Birne.
bulbous ['bʌlbəs], *adj.* zwiebelartig; dickbäuchig.
Bulgarian [bʌl'gɛəriən], *adj.* bulgarisch. — *s.* der Bulgare.
bulge [bʌldʒ], *s.* die Ausbauchung; die Ausbuchtung (*in fighting line*). — *v.n.* herausragen, anschwellen.
bulk [bʌlk], *s.* die Masse, Menge; *buy in* —, im Großen einkaufen.

bulky ['bʌlki], *adj.* schwer (*heavy*); massig (*stodgy*); unhandlich.
bull (1) [bul], *s.* (*Zool.*) der Bulle, Stier; —*'s eye*, das Schwarze (*target*).
bull (2) [bul], *s.* (*Papal*) die Bulle, der Erlass.
bulldog ['buldɔg], *s.* der Bullenbeißer.
bullet ['bulit], *s.* die Kugel, das Geschoß.
bulletin ['bulitin], *s.* das Bulletin, der Tagesbericht.
bullfight ['bulfait], *s.* der Stierkampf.
bullfinch ['bulfintʃ], *s.* (*Orn.*) der Dompfaff.
bullfrog ['bulfrɔg], *s.* (*Zool.*) der Ochsenfrosch.
bullion ['buljən], *s.* der Goldbarren, Silberbarren.
bullock ['bulək], *s.* (*Zool.*) der Ochse.
bully ['buli], *s.* der Raufbold, Angeber, Großtuer (*braggart*); der Tyrann. — *v.a.* tyrannisieren, einschüchtern.
bulrush ['bulrʌʃ], *s.* (*Bot.*) die Binse.
bulwark ['bulwək], *s.* das Bollwerk, die Verteidigung.
bump [bʌmp], *s.* der Schlag, der Stoß. — *v.a.* stoßen.
bun [bʌn], *s.* das Rosinenbrötchen; das süße Brötchen; (*hair*) der Knoten.
bunch [bʌntʃ], *s.* der Bund (*keys*); der Strauß (*flowers*); die Traube (*grapes*). — *v a.* zusammenfassen, zusammenbinden, zusammenraffen.
bundle [bʌndl], *s.* das Bündel.
bung [bʌŋ], *s.* der Spund (*in barrel*).
bungle [bʌŋgl], *v.a.* verpfuschen, verderben.
bungler ['bʌŋglə], *s.* der Stümper.
bunion ['bʌnjən], *s.* die Fußschwiele.
bunk (1) [bʌŋk], *s.* die (Schlaf-)Koje.
bunk (2) [bʌŋk], *s.* (*coll.*) der Unsinn.
bunker ['bʌŋkə], *s.* der Kohlenraum, Bunker.
bunting ['bʌntiŋ], *s.* das Flaggentuch.
buoy [bɔi], *s.* die Boje.
buoyant ['bɔiənt], *adj.* schwimmend; lebhaft, heiter.
buoyancy ['bɔiənsi], *s.* die Schwimmkraft; die Schwungkraft.
burden (1) [bə:dn], *s.* die Bürde, Last. — *v.a.* belasten, beladen.
burden (2) [bə:dn], *s.* der Refrain; der Hauptinhalt.
burdensome ['bə:dnsəm], *adj.* beschwerlich.
bureau [bjuə'rou], *s.* der Schreibtisch; das Büro.
bureaucracy [bjuə'rɔkrəsi], *s.* die Bürokratie.
burgess ['bə:dʒis], *s.* der Bürger.
burglar ['bə:glə], *s.* der Einbrecher.
burglary ['bə:gləri], *s.* der Einbruch, der Diebstahl.
burgomaster ['bə:gomɑ:stə], *s.* der Bürgermeister.
Burgundian [bə:'gʌndiən], *adj.* burgundisch. —*s.* der Burgunder.
Burgundy (1) ['bə:gəndi], das Burgund.
Burgundy (2) ['bə:gəndi], *s.* der Burgunder(-wein).
burial ['beriəl], das Begräbnis; — *ground*, der Kirchhof, Friedhof; — *service*, die Totenfeier, Trauerfeier.
burlesque [bə:'lesk], *s.* die Burleske, Posse.
burly ['bə:li], *adj.* dick, stark.
Burmese [bə:'mi:z], *adj.* birmesisch. — *s.* der Birmese.
burn [bə:n], *v.a.*, *v.n.* *irr.* brennen, verbrennen. — *s.* das Brandmal.
burner ['bə:nə], *s.* der Brenner.
burnish ['bə:niʃ], *v.a.* polieren.
burred [bə:d], *adj.* überliegend; (*Metall.*) ausgehämmert; — *over*, (*Metall.*) breitgeschmiedet.
burrow ['bʌrou], *s.* der Bau, (*rabbits etc.*). —*v.n.* sich eingraben; wühlen.
burst [bə:st], *v.a.*, *v.n.* *irr.* bersten, platzen, explodieren (*explode*); — *out laughing*, laut auflachen; — *into tears*, in Tränen ausbrechen; — *into flames*, aufflammen; sprengen (*blow up*). — *s.* der Ausbruch; die Explosion.
bury ['beri], *v.a.* begraben; beerdigen.
bus [bʌs], *s.* der Autobus, Omnibus.
busby ['bʌzbi], *s.* (*Mil.*) die Bärenmütze.
bush [buʃ], *s.* der Busch.
bushel [buʃl], *s.* der Scheffel.
bushy ['buʃi], *adj.* buschig.
business ['biznis], *s.* das Geschäft; die Beschäftigung, die Tätigkeit (*activity*); Aufgabe, Obliegenheit; der Handel (*trade*); *on* —, geschäftlich.
businesslike ['biznislaik], *adj.* geschäftsmäßig, nüchtern, praktisch.
businessman ['biznismæn], *s.* der Geschäftsmann.
bust (1) [bʌst], *s.* die Büste.
bust (2) [bʌst], *v.a.*, *v.n.* (*coll.*) sprengen; *go* —, bankrott machen.
bustard ['bʌstəd], *s.* (*Orn.*) die Trappe.
bustle [bʌsl], *s.* der Lärm, die Aufregung. — *v.n.* aufgeregt umherlaufen; rührig sein (*be active*).
busy ['bizi], *adj.* geschäftig (*active*); beschäftigt (*engaged*, mit, *in*); *be* —, zu tun haben.
but [bʌt], *conj.* aber, jedoch; sondern. — *adv.* nur, bloß; — *yesterday*, erst gestern. — *prep.* außer; *all* — *two*, alle außer zwei.
butcher ['butʃə], *s.* der Metzger, Fleischer; —*'s knife*, das Fleischmesser.
butchery ['butʃəri], *s.* die Schlächterei; das Blutbad, das Gemetzel.
butler ['bʌtlə], *s.* der oberste Diener; Kellermeister.
butt [bʌt], *s.* das dicke Ende; der Kolben (*rifle*); der Stoß (*blow*); die Zielscheibe (*target*). — *v.a.* stoßen, spießen.
butter ['bʌtə], *s.* die Butter. — *v.a.* mit Butter bestreichen; — *up*, schmeicheln (*Dat.*).
butterfly ['bʌtəflai], *s.* (*Ent.*) der Schmetterling.
buttery ['bʌtəri], *s.* die Speisekammer.

buttock(s) ['bʌtək(s)], *s.* der Hintere, das Gesäß (*usually pl.*) (*vulg.*).
button [bʌtn], *s.* der Knopf. — *v.a.* — *up*, knöpfen, zumachen.
buttress ['bʌtris], *s.* der Strebepfeiler.
buxom ['bʌksəm], *adj.* drall, gesund.
buy [bai], *v.a. irr.* kaufen.
buzz [bʌz], *s.* das Summen. — *v.n.* summen.
buzzard ['bʌzəd], *s.* (*Orn.*) der Bussard.
by [bai], *prep.* (*beside*) neben, an; (*near*) nahe; (*before*) gegen, um, bei; (*about*) bei; (*from, with*) durch, von, mit; — *the way*, nebenbei bemerkt; — *way of*, mittels. — *adv.* (*nearby*) nahe; nebenan.
by-election ['baiilekʃən], *s.* die Nachwahl; Ersatzwahl.
bygone ['baigɔn], *adj.* vergangen.
bylaw, byelaw ['bailɔ:], *s.* die Bestimmung.
Byzantine [bai'zæntain], *adj.* byzantinisch.

C

C [si:]. das C (*also Mus.*).
cab [kæb], *s.* (*horse-drawn*) die Droschke, der Wagen; das Taxi; —*stand*, der Droschkenhalteplatz; (*Motor.*) der Taxiplatz, Taxistand.
cabaret ['kæbərei], *s.* das Kabarett, die Kleinbühne.
cabbage ['kæbidʒ], *s.* (*Bot.*) der Kohl.
cabin ['kæbin], *s.* die Kabine (*boat*); die Hütte (*hut*); —*-boy*, der Schiffsjunge.
cabinet ['kæbinet], *s.* das Kabinett (*government*); der Schrank (*cupboard*); das kleine Zimmer *or* Nebenzimmer (*mainly Austr.*); (*Rad.*) das Gehäuse; — *maker*, der Kunsttischler.
cable [keibl], *s.* das Kabel (*of metal*), das Seil (*metal or rope*); das Telegramm. — *v.a.* kabeln, telegraphieren.
cablegram ['keiblgræm], *s.* die (Kabel-) Depesche.
cabman ['kæbmən], *s.* der Taxichauffeur.
caboose [kə'bu:s], *s.* die Schiffsküche.
cabriolet [kæbrio'lei], *s.* das Kabriolett.
cackle [kækl], *v.n.* gackern (*hens*); schnattern (*geese*); (*fig.*) schwatzen.
cacophony [kə'kɔfəni], *s.* der Mißklang.
cad [kæd], *s.* der gemeine Kerl, Schuft.
cadaverous [kə'dævərəs], *adj.* leichenhaft.
caddie ['kædi], *s.* der Golfjunge.
caddy ['kædi], *s. tea* —, die Teebüchse, Teedose.
cadence ['keidəns], *s.* (*Phonet.*) der Tonfall; (*Mus.*) die Kadenz.
cadet [kə'det], *s.* (*Mil.*) der Kadett.
cadge [kædʒ], *v.a.* erbetteln.

Caesar ['si:zə]. Cäsar, *m.*
Caesarean [si'zɛəriən], *adj.* cäsarisch; — *operation* or *section*, (*Med.*) der Kaiserschnitt.
cafeteria [kæfə'tiəriə], *s.* das Selbstbedienungsrestaurant.
cage [keidʒ], *s.* (*Zool.*) der Käfig; (*Orn.*) das Vogelbauer. — *v.a.* einfangen, einsperren.
cagey ['keidʒi], *adj.* (*coll.*) argwöhnisch, zurückhaltend; schlau.
cairn [kɛən], *s.* (*Archaeol.*) der Steinhaufen, der Grabhügel.
caitiff ['keitif], *adj.* niederträchtig. — *s.* der Schuft.
cajole [kə'dʒoul], *v.a.* schmeicheln (*Dat.*).
cake [keik], *s.* der Kuchen; — *of soap*, das Stück Seife; *have o.'s — and eat it*, alles haben. — *v.a.*, *v.n.* zusammenbacken; —*d with dirt*, mit Schmutz beschmiert.
calamity [kə'læmiti], *s.* das Unheil, Unglück; Elend.
calcareous [kæl'kɛəriəs], *adj.* (*Geol.*) kalkartig.
calculate ['kælkjuleit], *v.a.* berechnen.
calculation [kælkju'leiʃən], *s.* die Berechnung.
calendar ['kæləndə], *s.* der Kalender.
calf [kɑ:f], *s.* (*Zool.*) das Kalb; (*Anat.*) die Wade; — *love*, die Jugendliebe.
calibre ['kælibə], *s.* das Kaliber.
calico ['kælikou], *s.* der Kaliko, Kattun.
Caliph ['keilif], *s.* der Kalif.
calk (1) [kɔ:k], *v.a.* beschlagen (*horse*).
calk (2), **caulk** [kɔ:k], *v.a.* (*Naut.*) abdichten.
call [kɔ:l], *v.a.*, *v.n.* rufen, herbeirufen; (*Am.*) antelefonieren, anrufen (*ring up*); (*name*) nennen; — *to account*, zur Rechenschaft ziehen; (*summon*) kommen lassen; — *for*, abholen; *this —s for*, das berechtigt zu. — *s.* der Ruf, Anruf; die (innere) Berufung, der Beruf.
callbox ['kɔ:lbɔks] *see* **phone box.**
calling ['kɔ:liŋ], *s.* der Beruf, das Gewerbe (*occupation*).
callous ['kæləs], *adj.* schwielig (*hands*); (*fig.*) unempfindlich, hart, gemein.
callow ['kælou], *adj.* ungefiedert (*bird*); (*fig.*) unerfahren.
calm [kɑ:m], *adj.* ruhig, still; gelassen. — *s.* die Ruhe; (*Naut.*) Windstille. — *v.a.* beruhigen. — *v.n.* — *down*, sich beruhigen, sich legen (*storm etc.*).
caloric [kæ'lɔrik], *adj.* Wärme–, warm; (*Chem.*) kalorisch.
calorie, calory ['kæləri], *s.* die Kalorie.
calumny ['kæləmni], *s.* die Verleumdung.
calve [kɑ:v], *v.n.* kalben, Kälber kriegen.
cambric ['kæmbrik], *s.* der Batist (*textile*).
camel ['kæməl], *s.* (*Zool.*) das Kamel.
cameo ['kæmiou], *s.* die Kamee.
camera ['kæmərə], *s.* (*Phot.*) die Kamera.
camomile ['kæməmail], *s.* (*Bot.*) die Kamille.

camp [kæmp], *s.* das Lager; Zeltlager. — *v.n.* sich lagern, ein Lager aufschlagen, zelten.
campaign [kæm'pein], *s.* der Feldzug. — *v.n.* einen Feldzug mitmachen; (*fig.*) Propaganda machen.
camphor ['kæmfə], *s.* der Kampfer.
camping ['kæmpiŋ], *s.* die Lagerausrüstung (*equipment*); das Lagern (*activity*), das Zelten.
can (1) [kæn], *s.* die Kanne; die Büchse; *watering* —, die Gießkanne. — *v.a.* (*Am.*) einmachen, einkochen (*fruit*).
can (2) [kæn], *v. aux. irr.* können, imstande sein, vermögen.
Canadian [kə'neidiən], *adj.* kanadisch. — *s.* der Kanadier.
canal [kə'næl], *s.* der Kanal; — *lock*, die Kanalschleuse.
canalize ['kænəlaiz], *v.a.* kanalisieren, leiten.
cancel ['kænsəl], *v.a.* widerrufen, absagen (*show*); aufheben, ungültig machen.
cancellation [kænsə'leiʃən], *s.* die Aufhebung, Absage, Widerrufung.
cancer ['kænsə], *s.* (*Med., Astron.*) der Krebs.
cancerous ['kænsərəs], *adj.* (*Med.*) krebsartig.
candelabra [kændi'lɑ:brə], *s.* der Kandelaber, Leuchter.
candid ['kændid], *adj.* offen, aufrichtig.
candidate ['kændideit], *s.* der Kandidat, Bewerber.
candidature ['kændiditʃə], *s.* die Kandidatur, die Bewerbung.
candied ['kændid], *adj.* gezuckert, kandiert (*fruit*).
candle [kændl], *s.* die Kerze, das Licht.
Candlemas ['kændlməs]. (*Eccl.*) Lichtmeß.
candlestick ['kændlstik], *s.* der Kerzenleuchter.
candlewick ['kændlwik], *s.* der Kerzendocht (*textile*).
candour ['kændə], *s.* die Offenheit, Aufrichtigkeit.
candy ['kændi], *s.* (*Am.*) das Zuckerwerk, (*pl.*) Süßigkeiten. — *v.a.* verzuckern.
cane [kein], *s.* (*Bot.*) das Rohr, der Rohrstock; Spazierstock. — *v.a.* (mit dem Stock) schlagen.
canine ['kænain], *adj.* Hunde-, hündisch; — *tooth*, der Eckzahn.
canister ['kænistə], *s.* die Blechbüchse, der Kanister.
canker ['kæŋkə], *s.* (*Bot.*) der Brand; (*Bot.*) der Pflanzenrost; (*fig.*) eine zerfressende Krankheit.
cannibal ['kænibəl], *s.* der Kannibale, Menschenfresser.
cannon ['kænən], *s.* die Kanone, das Geschütz.
canoe [kə'nu:], *s.* das Kanu.
canon ['kænən], *s.* (*Mus., Eccl.*) der Kanon; die Regel; (*Eccl.*) der Domherr; — *law*, das kanonische Recht.
canonize ['kænənaiz], *v.a.* (*Eccl.*) kanonisieren, heiligsprechen.
canopy ['kænəpi], *s.* der Baldachin.
cant [kænt], *s.* die Heuchelei.
can't, cannot [kɑ:nt,'kænɔt] see **can** (2).
cantankerous [kæn'tæŋkərəs], *adj.* zänkisch, mürrisch.
cantata [kæn'tɑ:tə], *s.* (*Mus.*) die Kantate.
canteen [kæn'ti:n], *s.* die Kantine (*restaurant*); die Besteckgarnitur (*set of cutlery*).
canter ['kæntə], *s.* der Galopp, der Kurzgalopp.
canticle ['kæntikl], *s.* (*Eccl.*) der Lobgesang, das Loblied.
canto ['kæntou], *s.* (*Lit.*) der Gesang.
canton ['kæntɔn], *s.* (*Pol.*) der Kanton, der Bezirk.
canvas ['kænvəs], *s.* das Segeltuch; (*Art*) die Malerleinwand; die Zeltplane (*tent*).
canvass ['kænvəs], *v.a., v.n.* (*Pol.*) um Stimmen werben.
canvasser ['kænvəsə], *s.* (*Pol.*) der Werber, Stimmensammler.
cap [kæp], *s.* die Kappe, Mütze; die Haube; der Deckel. — *v.a.* übertreffen.
capability [keipə'biliti], *s.* die Fähigkeit.
capable ['keipəbl], *adj.* fähig (*Genit.*), imstande (*of*, zu); tüchtig.
capacious [kə'peiʃəs], *adj.* geräumig.
capacity [kə'pæsiti], *s.* der Inhalt, die Geräumigkeit; die Fassungskraft (*intellect*); die Leistungsfähigkeit (*ability*); der Fassungsraum (*space*).
cape (1) [keip], *s.* (*Tail.*) der Kragenmantel.
cape (2) [keip], *s.* (*Geog.*) das Kap, das Vorgebirge.
caper ['keipə], *s.* der Sprung, Luftsprung. — *v.n.* in die Luft springen.
capillary [kə'piləri], *adj.* haarfein; — *tubing*, die Haarröhre, die Kapillarröhre.
capital ['kæpitl], *s.* (*Comm.*) das Kapital; die Hauptstadt (*capital city*); — *punishment*, die Todesstrafe; — *letter*, der Großbuchstabe. — *adj.* (*coll.*) ausgezeichnet, vorzüglich.
capitalize ['kæpitəlaiz], *v.a.* (*Comm.*) kapitalisieren; ausnutzen.
capitation [kæpi'teiʃən], *s.* die Kopfsteuer.
capitulate [kə'pitjuleit], *v.n.* kapitulieren.
capon ['keipən], *s.* (*Zool.*) der Kapaun.
caprice [kə'pri:s], *s.* die Kaprize, Laune.
capricious [kə'priʃəs], *adj.* launenhaft, eigensinnig.
Capricorn ['kæprikɔ:n]. (*Astron.*) der Steinbock; *tropic of* —, der Wendekreis des Steinbocks.
capriole ['kæprioul], *s.* der Luftsprung.
capsize [kæp'saiz], *v.n.* umkippen, kentern (*boat*).
capstan ['kæpstən], *s.* (*Engin.*) die Ankerwinde; (*Mech.*) die Erdwinde; (*Naut.*) das Gangspill.
capsular ['kæpsjulə], *adj.* kapselförmig.
capsule ['kæpsju:l], *s.* die Kapsel.
captain ['kæptin], *s.* (*Naut.*) der Kapitän; (*Mil.*) der Hauptmann.

captious ['kæpʃəs], *adj.* zänkisch, streitsüchtig; verfänglich.
captivate ['kæptiveit], *v.a.* einnehmen, gewinnen.
captive ['kæptiv], *s.* der Gefangene. — *adj.* gefangen.
capture ['kæptʃə], *s.* die Gefangennahme (*men*); Erbeutung (*booty*).
Capuchin ['kæputʃin], *s.* (*Eccl.*) der Kapuziner.
car [ka:], *s.* (*Motor.*) der Wagen; das Auto; (*Am.*) der Eisenbahnwagen.
carafe [kæ'ræf], *s.* die Karaffe, Wasserflasche.
caravan ['kærəvæn], *s.* die Karawane; der Wohnwagen.
caraway['kærəwei],*s.*(*Bot.*)derKümmel.
carbine ['ka:bain], *s.* der Karabiner.
carbolic [ka:'bɔlik], *adj.* — *acid*, (*Chem.*) die Karbolsäure.
carbon ['ka:bən], *s.* (*Chem.*) der Kohlenstoff.
carbonate ['ka:bəneit], *s.* (*Chem.*) das kohlensaure Salz, Karbonat.
carbonize ['ka:bənaiz], *v.a.* verkohlen. — *v.n.* (*Chem., Geol.*) zu Kohle werden.
carbuncle ['ka:bʌnkl], *s.* (*Min.*) der Karfunkel; (*Med.*) der Karbunkel.
carburettor [ka:bju'retə], *s.* (*Motor.*) der Vergaser.
carcase, carcass ['ka:kəs], *s.* der Kadaver.
card (1) [ka:d], *s.* die Karte, Postkarte; *playing* —, die Spielkarte; *put your —s on the table*, rück mit der Wahrheit heraus!
card (2) [ka:d], *v.a.* krempeln (*wool*); kardätschen (*cotton*).
cardboard ['ka:dbɔ:d], *s.* die Pappe, der Pappendeckel.
cardiac ['ka:diæk], *adj.* (*Med.*) Herz–.
cardinal ['ka:dinl], *s.* (*Eccl.*) der Kardinal. — *adj.* Kardinal–, grundlegend.
cardiogram ['ka:diogræm], *s.* (*Med.*) das Kardiogramm.
cardsharper ['ka:dʃa:pə], *s.* der Falschspieler.
care [kɛə], *s.* die Sorge (*anxiety*, um, *for*); *with* —, mit Sorgfalt, genau; *care of* (*abbr. c/o on letters*), bei; *take* —, sich in acht nehmen. — *v.n.* — *for*, sich interessieren, gern haben.
careen [kə'ri:n], *v.a.* (*Naut.*) kielholen, umlegen.
career [kə'riə], *s.* die Karriere, Laufbahn.
careful ['kɛəful], *adj.* sorgfältig, vorsichtig, umsichtig.
carefulness ['kɛəfulnis], *s.* die Vorsicht, Sorgfalt, Umsicht.
careless ['kɛəlis], *adj.* unachtsam, nachlässig.
carelessness ['kɛəlisnis], *s.* die Nachlässigkeit, Unachtsamkeit.
caress [kə'res], *v.a.* liebkosen, herzen. — *s.* die Liebkosung, die Zärtlichkeit.
caretaker ['kɛəteikə], *s.* der Hausmeister.
careworn ['kɛəwɔ:n], *adj.* abgehärmt, von Sorgen gebeugt.
cargo ['ka:gou], *s.* die Fracht, die Ladung.
caricature [kærikə'tjuə *or* 'kærikətʃə], *s.* die Karikatur. — *v.a.* karikieren, verzerren.
Carinthian [kə'rinθjən], *adj.* kärntnerisch.
carmine ['ka:main], *s.* der Karmin.
carnage ['ka:nidʒ], *s.* das Blutbad.
carnal [ka:nl], *adj.* fleischlich, sinnlich.
carnation [ka:'neiʃən], *s.* (*Bot.*) die Nelke.
carnival ['ka:nivl], *s.* der Karneval.
carnivorous [ka:'nivərəs], *adj.* fleischfressend.
carol ['kærəl], *s.* *Christmas* —, das Weihnachstlied.
carotid [kə'rɔtid], *s.* (*Anat.*) die Halspulsader.
carousal [kə'rauzəl], *s.* das Gelage, das Gezeche.
carouse [kə'rauz], *v.n.* zechen, schmausen.
carp (1) [ka:p], *s.* (*Zool.*) der Karpfen.
carp (2) [ka:p], *v.n.* bekritteln, tadeln.
Carpathian Mountains [ka:'peiθjən 'mauntinz]. die Karpathen, *f. pl.*
carpenter ['ka:pəntə], *s.* der Zimmermann; Tischler.
carpentry ['ka:pəntri], *s.* die Tischlerei, das Zimmerhandwerk.
carpet ['ka:pit], *s.* der Teppich; — *bag*, die Reisetasche.
carriage ['kæridʒ], *s.* der Wagen, Waggon; das Verhalten, die Haltung (*bearing*); (*Comm.*) — *paid*, einschließlich Zustellung; — *way*, der Straßendamm.
carrier ['kæriə], *s.* der Fuhrmann, Fuhrunternehmer.
carrion ['kæriən], *s.* das Aas.
carrot ['kærət], *s.* (*Bot.*) die Mohrrübe; die Karotte.
carry ['kæri], *v.a.* tragen; bringen; führen (*on vehicle*), fahren (*convey*); — *interest*, Zinsen tragen; (*Comm.*) — *forward*, übertragen; — *two* (*in adding up*), zwei weiter; — *on*, weitermachen, fortfahren; — *through*, durchführen, durchhalten. — *v.n.* vernehmbar sein (*of sound*); — *on*, weiterarbeiten, weiterexistieren.
cart [ka:t], *s.* der Karren, Frachtwagen.
cartel [ka:'tel], *s.* (*Comm.*) das Kartell.
Carthage ['ka:θidʒ]. Karthago, *n.*
carthorse ['ka:thɔ:s], *s.* das Zugpferd.
cartilage ['ka:tilidʒ], *s.* der Knorpel.
carton ['ka:tən], *s.* (*cardboard box*) der Karton, die Schachtel.
cartoon [ka:'tu:n], *s.* die Karikatur; — *film*, der Trickfilm.
cartridge ['ka:tridʒ], *s.* die Patrone.
cartwright ['ka:trait], *s.* der Stellmacher, Wagenbauer.
carve [ka:v], *v.a.* schneiden (*cut*); schnitzen (*wood*), meißeln (*stone*), tranchieren (*meat*).

carver [ˈkɑ:və], *s.* der Schnitzer (*wood*); das Tranchiermesser (*carving knife*).
cascade [kæsˈkeid], *s.* der Wasserfall.
case (1) [keis], *s.* der Kasten, Behälter; das Futteral, Etui (*spectacles*); das Gehäuse (*watch*); die Kiste (*wooden box*); (*Typ.*) der Schriftkasten.
case (2) [keis], *s.* der Fall (*event*); (*Law*) der Rechtsfall, der Umstand (*circumstance*); *in* —, falls.
casement [ˈkeismənt], *s.* der Fensterflügel, das Fenster (*frame*).
caseous [ˈkeisjəs], *adj.* käsig.
cash [kæʃ], *s.* bares Geld; die Barzahlung; — *box*, die Kasse. — *v.a.* einlösen (*cheque*).
cashier [kæˈʃiə], *s.* der Kassierer. — *v.a.* (*Mil.*) entlassen.
cashmere [ˈkæʃmiə], *s.* die Kaschmirwolle (*wool*).
casing [ˈkeisiŋ], *s.* die Hülle; das Gehäuse (*case*); die Haut (*sausage skin*).
cask [ˈkɑ:sk], *s.* das Faß.
casket [ˈkɑ:skit], *s.* das Kästchen; (*Am.*) der Sarg.
Caspian (Sea) [ˈkæspiən (si:)]. das kaspische Meer.
cassock [ˈkæsək], *s.* die Soutane.
cast [kɑ:st], *v.a. irr.* werfen (*throw*); (*Metall.*) gießen; (*Theat.*) besetzen; (*plaster*) formen; — *off*, abwerfen; — *anchor*, ankern; — *o.'s skin*, sich häuten; — *down*, niederschlagen; — *a vote*, die Stimme abgeben. — *s.* der Wurf; (*Metall.*) der Guß; (*Theat.*) die Besetzung; der Abguß (plaster). — *adj.* — *iron*, das Gusseisen; — *steel*, der Gußstahl.
castanets [kæstəˈnets], *s. pl.* (*Mus.*) die Kastagnetten, *f. pl.*
castaway [ˈkɑ:stəwei], *adj.* weggeworfen; (*Naut.*) schiffbrüchig.
caste [kɑ:st], *s.* die Kaste.
caster [ˈkɑ:stə], *s.* der Streuer, die Streubüchse; — *sugar*, Streuzucker.
casting [ˈkɑ:stiŋ], *s.* (*Metall.*) das Gießen, der Guß.
castle [kɑ:sl], *s.* die Burg, das Schloß; (*Chess*) der Turm.
castor (1) [ˈkɑ:stə], *s.* (*Zool.*) der Biber.
castor (2) [ˈkɑ:stə] *see* **caster**.
castor (3) **oil** [ˈkɑ:stər ˈɔil], *s.* das Rizinusöl.
castrate [kæsˈtreit], *v.a.* kastrieren.
castration [kæsˈtreiʃən], *s.* die Kastration.
casual [ˈkæʒjuəl], *adj.* zufällig; gelassen (*manner*); gelegentlich; flüchtig.
casualty [ˈkæʒjuəlti], *s.* der Unglücksfall; — *ward*, die Unfallstation; (*pl.*) die Verluste, *m. pl.*
cat [kæt], *s.* die Katze; *tom* —, der Kater; — *burglar*, der Fassadenkletterer; —*'s eye*, das Katzenauge, der Rückstrahler; der Reflektor.
cataclysm [ˈkætəklizm], *s.* die Sintflut, die Überschwemmung.
catacomb [ˈkætəku:m], *s.* die Katakombe.
catalogue [ˈkætəlɔg], *s.* der Katalog, das Verzeichnis. — *v.a.* im Katalog verzeichnen, katalogisieren.
catapult [ˈkætəpult], *s.* die Schleuder (*hand*); (*Mil.*) die Wurfmaschine. — *v.a.* schleudern.
cataract [ˈkætərækt], *s.* der Wasserfall (*water*); (*Med.*) der Star.
catarrh [kəˈtɑ:], *s.* (*Med.*) der Katarrh.
catastrophe [kəˈtæstrəfi], *s.* die Katastrophe, das Unglück.
catastrophic [kætəsˈtrɔfik], *adj.* katastrophal, unheilvoll.
catch [kætʃ], *v.a. irr.* fangen, auffangen, fassen; überfallen (— *unawares, ambush*); — *a cold*, sich einen Schnupfen zuziehen, sich erkälten; erreichen (*train, etc.*); — *redhanded*, bei frischer Tat ertappen. — *s.* der Fang (*fish*); die Beute (*prey, booty*); der Haken (*hook, also fig.*).
catchpenny [ˈkætʃpeni], *s.* der Flitterkram, Lockartikel. — *adj.* marktschreierisch.
catchphrase, catchword [ˈkætʃfreiz, ˈkætʃwə:d], *s.* das (billige) Schlagwort.
catechism [ˈkætikizm], *s.* der Katechismus.
categorical [kætiˈgɔrikəl], *adj.* kategorisch, entschieden.
category [ˈkætigəri], *s.* die Kategorie, Klasse, Gruppe, Gattung.
cater [ˈkeitə], *v.n.* Lebensmittel einkaufen; verpflegen; (*fig.*) sorgen (*for*, für).
caterer [ˈkeitərə], *s.* der Lebensmittellieferant.
catering [ˈkeitəriŋ], *s.* die Verpflegung.
caterpillar [ˈkætəpilə], *s.* (*Ent.*) die Raupe; (*Mech.*) der Raupenschlepper.
caterwaul [ˈkætəwɔ:l], *v.n.* miauen.
cathedral [kəˈθi:drəl], *s.* der Dom, die Kathedrale.
Catholic [ˈkæθəlik], *adj.* katholisch. — *s.* der Katholik.
catholic [ˈkæθəlik], *adj.* allumfassend.
Catholicism [kəˈθɔlisizm], *s.* der Katholizismus.
catkin [ˈkætkin], *s.* (*Bot.*) das Kätzchen; *pussy-willow* —, das Palmkätzchen.
cattle [kætl], *s. pl.* das Vieh; — *plague*, die Rinderpest; — *show*, die Viehausstellung.
caucus [ˈkɔ:kəs], *s.* die Wahlversammlung; der Wahlausschuß.
caul [kɔ:l], *s.* das Haarnetz; (*Anat.*) die Eihaut.
cauldron [ˈkɔ:ldrən], *s.* der Kessel.
cauliflower [ˈkɔliflauə], *s.* (*Bot.*) der Blumenkohl.
caulk [kɔ:k], *v.a.* kalfatern (*see under* **calk** (2)).
causal [ˈkɔ:zəl], *adj.* ursächlich.
causality [kɔ:ˈzæliti], *s.* der ursächliche Zusammenhang; (*Log.*) die Kausalität.
cause [kɔ:z], *s.* die Ursache. — *v.a.* verursachen.
causeway [ˈkɔ:zwei], *s.* der Damm.
caustic [ˈkɔ:stik], *adj.* ätzend; beißend.

cauterize ['kɔ:təraiz], *v.a.* (*Med.*) ätzen, ausbrennen.
caution ['kɔ:ʃən], *s.* die Vorsicht (*care*); die Warnung (*warning*). — *v.a.* (*Law*) ermahnen; warnen.
cautionary ['kɔ:ʃənəri], *adj.* warnend.
cautious ['kɔ:ʃəs], *adj.* vorsichtig, behutsam.
cautiousness ['kɔ:ʃəsnis], *s.* die Vorsicht, Behutsamkeit.
cavalcade [kævəl'keid], *s.* die Kavalkade; (*Mil.*) der Reiterzug.
cavalry ['kævəlri], *s.* die Kavallerie, die Reiterei.
cave [keiv], *s.* die Höhle. — *v.a.* aushöhlen. — *v.n.* — *in*, einstürzen, einfallen.
caveat ['keiviæt], *s.* (*Law*) die Warnung; der Vorbehalt.
cavern ['kævən], *s.* die Höhle.
cavernous ['kævənəs], *adj.* (*Geog.*, *Geol.*) voll Höhlen.
caviare [kævi'ɑ:], *s.* der Kaviar.
cavil ['kævil], *v.n.* nörgeln (*at*, über), tadeln (*Acc.*).
cavity ['kæviti], *s.* die Höhlung.
caw [kɔ:], *v.n.* (*Orn.*) krächzen.
cease [si:s], *v.a.* einstellen. — *v.n.* aufhören.
ceaseless ['si:slis], *adj.* unaufhörlich.
cedar ['si:də], *s.* (*Bot.*) die Zeder.
cede [si:d], *v.a.* überlassen. — *v.n.* nachgeben.
ceiling ['si:liŋ], *s.* die Decke (*room*); (*Comm.*) die Preisgrenze.
celebrate ['selibreit], *v.a.* feiern; zelebrieren.
celebrated ['selibreitid], *adj.* berühmt.
celebration [seli'breiʃən], *s.* die Feier.
celebrity [si'lebriti], *s.* die Berühmtheit; der „Star".
celerity [si'leriti], *s.* die Behendigkeit, Schnelligkeit.
celery ['seləri], *s.* (*Bot.*) der Sellerie.
celestial [si'lestjəl], *adj.* himmlisch.
celibacy ['selibəsi], *s.* die Ehelosigkeit; (*Eccl.*) das Zölibat.
celibate ['selibit], *adj.* unverheiratet.
cell [sel], *s.* die Zelle.
cellar ['selə], *s.* der Keller; *salt* —, das Salzfaß.
cellarage ['seləridʒ], *s.* die Kellerei; die Einkellerung (*storage*).
cellarer ['selərə], *s.* der Kellermeister.
cellular ['seljulə], *adj.* zellartig, Zell-.
Celt [kelt, selt], *s.* der Kelte.
Celtic ['keltik, 'seltik], *adj.* keltisch.
cement [si'ment], *s.* der Zement, Mörtel. — *v.a.* auszementieren, verkitten.
cemetery ['semətri], *s.* der Kirchhof, der Friedhof.
cenotaph ['senotæf *or* -tɑ:f], *s.* das Ehrengrabmal, Ehrendenkmal.
censer ['sensə], *s.* (*Eccl.*) das Weihrauchfaß.
censor ['sensə], *s.* der Zensor.
censorious [sen'sɔ:riəs], *adj.* kritisch, tadelsüchtig.
censure ['senʃə], *s.* der Tadel, Verweis. — *v.a.* tadeln.
census ['sensəs], *s.* die Volkszählung.
cent [sent], *s.* (*Am.*) der Cent (*coin*); (*Comm.*) *per* —, das Prozent.
centenarian [senti'nɛəriən], *adj.* hundertjährig. — *s.* der Hundertjährige.
centenary [sen'ti:nəri], *s.* die Hundertjahrfeier.
centennial [sen'tenjəl], *adj.* alle hundert Jahre, hundertjährig.
centipede ['sentipi:d], *s.* (*Zool.*) der Tausendfüßler.
central ['sentrəl], *adj.* zentral.
centralize ['sentrəlaiz], *v.a.* zentralisieren.
centre ['sentə], *s.* das Zentrum, der Mittelpunkt; die Mitte.
centric(al) ['sentrik(əl)], *adj.* (*Engin.*, *Maths.*) zentral.
centrifugal [sen'trifjugəl], *adj.* zentrifugal.
centrifuge [sen'trifju:dʒ], *s.* die Zentrifuge.
centripetal [sen'tripitl], *adj.* zentripetal, zum Mittelpunkt hinstrebend.
century ['sentʃuri], *s.* das Jahrhundert.
cereal ['siəriəl], *adj.* vom Getreide, Getreide—. — *s.* die Kornmehlspeise.
cerebral ['seribrəl], *adj.* Gehirn-.
ceremonial [seri'mounjəl], *adj.* feierlich, förmlich (*formal*). — *s.* das Zeremoniell.
ceremonious [seri'mounjəs], *adj.* feierlich, zeremoniell.
ceremony ['seriməni], *s.* die Zeremonie, die Feier.
certain ['sə:tin], *adj.* sicher, gewiß.
certainty ['sə:tinti], *s.* die Gewißheit.
certificate [sə:'tifikit], *s.* das Zeugnis, die Bescheinigung.
certification [sə:tifi'keiʃən], *s.* die Bescheinigung, Bezeugung.
certify ['sə:tifai], *v.a.* bescheinigen, bezeugen, beglaubigen.
certitude ['sə:titju:d], *s.* die Gewißheit.
cerulean [si'ru:ljən], *adj.* himmelblau.
cesspool ['sespu:l], *s.* die Senkgrube.
cessation [se'seiʃən], *s.* das Aufhören; (*of hostilities*) der Waffenstillstand.
cession ['seʃən], *s.* die Abtretung, der Verzicht (*of*, auf).
chafe [tʃeif], *v.a.* wärmen, warmreiben; erzürnen (*annoy*); wundreiben (*skin*). — *v.n.* toben, wüten.
chafer ['tʃeifə], *s.* (*Ent.*) der Käfer.
chaff [tʃɑ:f], *s.* die Spreu; die Neckerei (*teasing*). — *v.a.* necken.
chaffer ['tʃæfə], *v.n.* handeln, schachern (*haggle*).
chaffinch ['tʃæfintʃ], *s.* (*Orn.*) der Buchfink.
chagrin [ʃæ'gri:n], *s.* der Verdruß, der Ärger.
chain [tʃein], *s.* die Kette. — *v.a.* anketten.
chair [tʃɛə], *s.* der Stuhl; (*Univ.*) Lehrstuhl. — *v.a.* vorsitzen (*Dat.*).
chairman ['tʃɛəmən], *s.* der Vorsitzende.
chalice ['tʃælis], *s.* (*Eccl.*) der Kelch.

chalk [tʃɔ:k], *s.* die Kreide. — *v.a.* — *up*, ankreiden, anschreiben.
chalky ['tʃɔ:ki], *adj.* (*Geol.*) kreidig, kreideartig.
challenge ['tʃælindʒ], *v.a.* herausfordern; in Frage stellen (*question*); anhalten (*of a sentry*). — *s.* die Herausforderung; das Anhalten (*by a sentry*); die Einwendung.
chalybeate [kə'libiət], *adj.* (*Med.*) eisenhaltig.
chamber ['tʃeimbə], *s.* das Zimmer, die Kammer.
chamberlain ['tʃeimbəlin], *s.* der Kammerherr.
chambermaid ['tʃeimbəmeid], *s.* das Zimmermädchen, Kammermädchen.
chameleon [kə'mi:ljən], *s.* (*Zool.*) das Chamäleon.
chamois ['ʃæmwɑ:], *s.* (*Zool.*) die Gemse.
champagne [ʃæm'pein], *s.* der Champagner, der Sekt.
champion ['tʃæmpjən], *s.* der Meister, Verteidiger. — *v.a.* vertreten (*cause*); beschützen (*person*).
chance [tʃɑ:ns], *s.* der Zufall; die Gelegenheit (*opportunity*); die Möglichkeit (*possibility*); *take a* —, es darauf ankommen lassen; *by* —, zufällig. — *v.a.* zufällig tun, geraten; riskieren (*risk*).
chancel ['tʃɑ:nsəl], *s.* (*Eccl.*) der Chor, der Altarplatz.
chancellor ['tʃɑ:nsələ], *s.* der Kanzler.
chancery ['tʃɑ:nsəri], *s.* das Kanzleigericht.
chandelier [ʃændə'liə], *s.* der Armleuchter, Kronleuchter.
chandler ['tʃɑ:ndlə], *s.* der Lichtzieher; Krämer; (*corn merchant*) der Kornhändler.
change [tʃeindʒ], *s.* die Änderung; das Umsteigen (*trains*); *small* —, das Kleingeld; die Veränderung; Abwechslung. — *v.a.* ändern (*alter*); wechseln (*money*); umsteigen (*trains*); eintauschen, umtauschen (*exchange*); sich umziehen (*clothes*). — *v.n.* sich (ver)ändern, anders werden, umschlagen; (*Railw.*) — *for*, umsteigen nach.
changeable ['tʃeindʒəbl], *adj.* veränderlich.
changeling ['tʃeindʒliŋ], *s.* der Wechselbalg.
changeover ['tʃeindʒouvə], *s.* der Wechsel; der Umschalter; die Umstellung.
channel ['tʃænəl], *s.* der Kanal. — *v.a.* leiten, kanalisieren.
chant [tʃɑ:nt], *v.a., v.n.* (*Eccl.*) singen. — *s.* (*Mus.*) der Kantus, der liturgische Gesang.
chaos ['keiɔs], *s.* das Chaos.
chaotic [kei'ɔtik], *adj.* chaotisch.
chap (1) [tʃæp], *s.* der Riss (*skin etc.*). — *v.n.* Risse bekommen.
chap (2) [tʃæp], *s.* (*usually in pl.*) der Kinnbacken.
chap (3) [tʃæp], *s.* (*coll.*) der Kerl, der Bursche.
chapel ['tʃæpəl], *s.* (*Eccl.*) die Kapelle.
chaperon ['ʃæpəroun], *s.* die Anstandsdame. — *v.a.* begleiten, bemuttern.
chaplain ['tʃæplin], *s.* der Kaplan.
chapter ['tʃæptə], *s.* das Kapitel.
char [tʃɑ:], *v.a.* verkohlen. — *v.n.* (*coll.*) putzen, Hausarbeit verrichten (*do housework*). — *s.* (*coll.*) die Haushilfe, die Hausgehilfin, Putzfrau.
character ['kærəktə], *s.* der Charakter (*personality*); das Zeichen (*sign, symbol*); (*Maths.*) die Ziffer; das Zeugnis (*testimonial*).
characteristic [kærəktə'ristik], *adj.* charakteristisch, typisch.
characterize ['kærəktəraiz], *v.a.* charakterisieren, kennzeichnen.
charade [ʃə'rɑ:d], *s.* die Scharade, das Silbenrätsel.
charcoal ['tʃɑ:koul], *s.* die Holzkohle; — *burner*, der Köhler.
charge [tʃɑ:dʒ], *v.a.* laden, aufladen; (*Law*) beschuldigen; (*Mil.*) angreifen; belasten (*with a bill*); — *up to s.o.*, jemandem etwas anrechnen; verlangen (*price*). — *s.* die Ladung, der Auftrag (*order*); die Aufsicht: *to be in* —, die Aufsicht haben; (*Law*) die Beschuldigung, Anklage; das Mündel (*of a guardian*); (*pl.*) die Kosten, Spesen.
chargeable ['tʃɑ:dʒəbl], *adj.* anzurechnend; steuerbar (*of objects*).
charger ['tʃɑ:dʒə], *s.* das Schlachtroß.
chariness ['tʃɛərinis], *s.* die Behutsamkeit.
chariot ['tʃæriət], *s.* der Kriegswagen.
charioteer [tʃæriə'tiə], *s.* der Wagenlenker.
charitable ['tʃæritəbl], *adj.* wohltätig, mild, mildtätig.
charitableness ['tʃæritəblnis], *s.* die Wohltätigkeit, Milde.
charity ['tʃæriti], *s.* die Güte; Nächstenliebe; Mildtätigkeit (*alms*); die Barmherzigkeit (*charitableness*); der wohltätige Zweck (*cause*); *sister of* —, barmherzige Schwester.
charlatan ['ʃɑ:lətən], *s.* der Scharlatan, Pfuscher.
charm [tʃɑ:m], *s.* der Zauber (*magic*); der Reiz. — *v.a.* bezaubern.
chart [tʃɑ:t], *s.* (*Geog.*) die Karte. — *v.a.* auf der Karte einzeichnen.
charter ['tʃɑ:tə], *s.* die Urkunde; (*Naut.*) die Schiffsmiete. — *v.a.* mieten, chartern, heuern (*ship, plane*); ein Privileg geben, bevorrechtigen.
charwoman ['tʃɑ:wumən], *s.* die Putzfrau, Reinemacherin.
chary ['tʃɛəri], *adj.* behutsam; vorsichtig (*cautious*); sparsam (*thrifty*).
chase [tʃeis], *v.a.* jagen, verfolgen. — *s.* die Jagd (*hunt*); das Gehege (*game preserve*).
chaser ['tʃeisə], *s.* der Verfolger (*pursuer*); die Schiffskanone (*gun*).
chasm [kæzm], *s.* die Kluft; der Abgrund.
chassis ['ʃæsi], *s.* (*Motor.*) das Fahrgestell.

chaste [tʃeist], *adj.* keusch, züchtig.
chasten [tʃeisn], *v.a.* züchtigen; reinigen.
chastize [tʃæs'taiz], *v.a.* züchtigen.
chastity ['tʃæstiti], *s.* die Keuschheit, Züchtigkeit.
chasuble ['tʃæzjubl], *s.* (*Eccl.*) das Meßgewand.
chat [tʃæt], *v.n.* plaudern. — *s.* das Geplauder.
chattel [tʃætl], *s.* (*usually in pl.*) die Habe; *goods and —s*, Hab und Gut.
chatter ['tʃætə], *v.n.* schwätzen; schnattern. — *s.* das Geschwätz (*talk*).
chatterbox ['tʃætəbɔks], *s.* die Plaudertasche.
chatty ['tʃæti], *adj.* geschwätzig.
chauffeur ['ʃoufə, ʃou'fə:], *s.* (*Motor.*) der Fahrer.
chauffeuse [ʃou'fə:z], *s.* die Fahrerin.
chauvinism ['ʃouvinizm], *s.* der Chauvinismus.
cheap [tʃi:p], *adj.* billig.
cheapen ['tʃi:pən], *v.a.* herabsetzen, erniedrigen (*value*).
cheapness ['tʃi:pnis], *s.* die Billigkeit (*price*).
cheat [tʃi:t], *v.a.*, *v.n.* betrügen. — *s.* der Betrüger.
cheating ['tʃi:tiŋ], *s.* das Betrügen; der Betrug.
check [tʃek], *s.* der Einhalt, der Halt; die Kontrolle; das Hindernis (*obstacle*); (*Chess*) Schach; (*Am.*) *see* **cheque**. — *v.a.* zurückhalten, aufhalten (*stop*); überprüfen. — *v.n.* Schach bieten (*Dat.*).
checker *see under* **chequer**.
checkmate ['tʃekmeit], *s.* das Schachmatt.
cheek [tʃi:k], *s.* die Wange, die Backe; die Unverschämtheit (*impertinence*). — *v.a.* unverschämt sein *or* handeln (*s.o.*, an jemandem).
cheeky ['tʃi:ki], *adj.* frech, unverschämt.
cheer [tʃiə], *v.a.* anfeuern, anspornen; zujubeln; — *up*, aufmuntern. — *v.n.* — *up*, Mut fassen. — *s.* der Zuruf; der Beifallsruf (*acclaim*); *three —s*, ein dreifaches Hoch (*for*, auf).
cheerful ['tʃiəful], *adj.* fröhlich, froh.
cheerless ['tʃiəlis], *adj.* unfreundlich, freudlos.
cheese [tʃi:z], *s.* der Käse; — *straw*, die Käsestange.
cheesecloth ['tʃi:zklɔθ], *s.* (*Am.*) das Nesseltuch.
cheeseparing ['tʃ:izpɛəriŋ], *adj.* knauserig.
cheesy ['tʃi:zi], *adj.* käsig; (*sl.*) schlecht aussehend.
cheetah ['tʃ:itə], *s.* (*Zool.*) der Jagdleopard.
chemical ['kemikəl], *adj.* chemisch. — *s.* die Chemikalie, das chemische Element; das chemische Produkt.
chemise [ʃi'mi:z], *s.* das Frauenhemd.
chemist ['kemist], *s.* der Chemiker; Drogist; Apotheker (*dispenser*).
chemistry ['kemistri], *s.* die Chemie.
cheque, (*Am.*) **check** [tʃek], *s.* (*Fin.*) der Scheck.
chequer, checker ['tʃekə], *s.* das scheckige Muster, Würfelmuster. — *v.a.* würfelig machen, bunt machen.
cherish ['tʃeriʃ], *v.a.* hegen, wertschätzen, lieben.
cherry ['tʃeri], *s.* (*Bot*). die Kirsche; — *brandy*, das Kirschwasser.
chess [tʃes], *s.* das Schachspiel; —*man*, die Schachfigur; —*board*, das Schachbrett.
chest [tʃest], *s.* die Truhe (*box*); die Kiste; (*Anat.*) Brust; — *of drawers*, die Kommode.
chestnut ['tʃestnʌt], *s.* (*Bot.*) die Kastanie; (*horse*) der Braune. — *adj.* kastanienbraun.
chew [tʃu:], *v.a.* kauen; —*ing gum*, der Kaugummi.
chic [ʃi:k], *adj.* elegant, schick.
chicanery [ʃi'keinəri], *s.* die Schikane, Haarspalterei, Kleinlichkeit.
chicken ['tʃikin], *s.* das Huhn, Kücken; — *soup*, die Hühnersuppe.
chickenpox ['tʃikinpɔks], *s.* (*Med.*) die Windpocken.
chicory ['tʃikəri], *s.* (*Bot.*) die Zichorie.
chide [tʃaid], *v.a.* *irr.* schelten.
chief [tʃi:f], *s.* der Häuptling (*of tribe*); (*Am. coll.*) der Chef (*boss*). — *adj.* hauptsächlich, Haupt-, oberst.
chieftain ['tʃi:ftin], *s.* der Häuptling (*of tribe*); Anführer (*leader*).
chilblain ['tʃilblein], *s.* die Frostbeule.
child [tʃaild], *s.* das Kind.
childbirth ['tʃaildbə:θ], *s.* die Niederkunft.
childhood ['tʃaildhud], *s.* die Kindheit.
childish ['tʃaildiʃ], *adj.* kindisch.
childlike ['tʃaildlaik], *adj.* kindlich, wie ein Kind.
Chilean ['tʃiliən], *adj.* chilenisch. — *s.* der Chilene.
chill [tʃil], *s.* die Kälte, der Frost; die Erkältung. — *v.a.* kalt machen (*freeze*); erstarren lassen (*make rigid*); entmutigen (*discourage*).
chilly ['tʃili], *adj.* frostig, eisig, eiskalt.
chime [tʃaim], *s.* das Glockengeläute. — *v.n.* klingen, läuten.
chimera [ki'miərə], *s.* das Hirngespinst, das Trugbild.
chimney ['tʃimni], *s.* der Kamin, der Schornstein; —*pot*, —*stack*, der Schornstein; —*sweep*, der Kaminfeger, Schornsteinfeger.
chimpanzee [tʃimpæn'zi:], *s.* (*Zool.*) der Schimpanse.
chin [tʃin], *s.* (*Anat.*) das Kinn.
china ['tʃainə], *s.* das Porzellan; —*ware*, das Küchengeschirr.
chine (1) [tʃain], *s.* das Rückgrat.
chine (2) [tʃain], *s.* (*Geog.*) der Kamm.
Chinaman ['tʃainəmən], *s.* (*obs.*) der Chinese.
Chinese [tʃai'ni:z], *adj.* chinesisch. — *s.* der Chinese.
chink [tʃink], *s.* die Ritze, der Spalt.

chip [tʃip], *v.a.* schnitzeln (*wood*); ausbrechen (*stone*); in kleine Stücke schneiden. — *v.n.* — *off*, abbröckeln; — *in*, (*coll.*) sich hineinmischen. —*s.* der Span (*wood*); der Splitter (*glass, stone*); (*pl.*) Pommes frites (*pl.*) (*potatoes*).
chiromancy ['kaiərəmænsi], *s.* das Handlesen.
chiropodist [ki'rɔpədist], *s.* der Fußpfleger.
chirp [tʃə:p], *v.n.* zwitschern (*birds*), zirpen (*crickets*).
chirping ['tʃə:piŋ], *s.* das Gezwitscher (*birds*), das Gezirpe (*crickets*).
chisel [tʃizl], *s.* der Meißel. — *v.a.* meißeln.
chit [tʃit], *s.* das Stück Papier; (*coll.*) junges Ding; —*chat*, das Geplauder.
chivalrous ['ʃivəlrəs], *adj.* ritterlich; tapfer (*brave*).
chivalry ['ʃivəlri], *s.* die Ritterlichkeit (*courtesy*); Tapferkeit (*bravery*).
chive [tʃaiv], *s.* (*Bot.*) der Schnittlauch.
chlorate ['klɔ:reit], *s.* (*Chem.*) das Chlorsalz.
chlorine ['klɔ:ri:n], *s.* (*Chem.*) das Chlor, Chlorgas.
chloroform ['klɔrəfɔ:m], *s.* das Chloroform. — *v.a.* chloroformieren.
chocolate ['tʃɔkəlit], *s.* die Schokolade. — *adj.* schokoladefarben.
choice [tʃɔis], *s.* die Wahl; Auswahl (*selection*). — *adj.* auserlesen.
choir ['kwaiə], *s.* der Chor.
choke [tʃouk], *v.a.*, *v.n.* ersticken; verstopfen (*block*). — *s.* (*Elec.*) die Drosselspule; (*Motor.*) die Starterklappe.
choler ['kɔlə], *s.* die Galle; (*fig.*) der Zorn (*anger*).
cholera ['kɔlərə], *s.* (*Med.*) die Cholera.
choleric ['kɔlərik], *adj.* jähzornig, cholerisch.
choose [tʃu:z], *v.a. irr.* wählen, auswählen (*select*).
choosy ['tʃu:zi], *adj.* wählerisch.
chop [tʃɔp], *v.a.* abhacken (*cut off*), hacken (*meat*). — *s.* das Kotelett (*meat*).
chopper ['tʃɔpə], *s.* das Hackbeil (*axe*); das Hackmesser (*knife*).
choppy ['tʃɔpi], *adj.* bewegt (*sea*), stürmisch.
chopstick ['tʃɔpstik], *s.* das Eßstäbchen.
choral ['kɔ:rəl], *adj.* Chor-; — *society*, der Gesangverein.
chorale [kɔ'rɑ:l], *s.* (*Eccl., Mus.*) der Choral.
chord [kɔ:d], *s.* die Saite; (*Geom.*) die Sehne; (*Mus.*) der Akkord.
chorister ['kɔristə], *s.* der Chorknabe (*boy*), Chorsänger.
chorus ['kɔ:rəs], *s.* der Chor (*opera*); der Refrain (*song*).
Christ [kraist]. Christus, *m.*
christen [krisn], *v.a.* taufen (*baptize*); nennen (*name*).
Christendom ['krisndəm], *s.* die Christenheit.
christening ['krisniŋ], *s.* die Taufe.
Christian ['kristjən], *s.* der Christ (*believer in Christ*). — *adj.* christlich; — *name*, der Vorname.
Christianity [kristi'æniti], *s.* die christliche Religion, das Christentum.
Christmas ['krisməs], *s.* (die) Weihnachten; das Weihnachtsfest; — *Eve*, der heilige Abend.
chromatic [kro'mætik], *adj.* (*Mus.*) chromatisch.
chrome [kroum], *s.* das Chrom.
chronic ['krɔnik], *adj.* chronisch.
chronicle ['krɔnikl], *s.* die Chronik. — *v.a.* (in einer Chronik) verzeichnen.
chronological [krɔnə'lɔdʒikəl], *adj.* chronologisch.
chronology [krɔ'nɔlədʒi], *s.* die Chronologie.
chronometer [krɔ'nɔmitə], *s.* das Chronometer.
chrysalis ['krisəlis], *s.* (*Ent.*) die Puppe.
chrysanthemum [kri'zænθəməm], *s.* (*Bot.*) die Chrysantheme.
chub [tʃʌb], *s.* (*Zool.*) der Döbel.
chubby ['tʃʌbi], *adj.* pausbäckig, plump.
chuck [tʃʌk], *v.a.* (*coll.*) — *out*, hinauswerfen. — *v.n.* glucken (*chicken*).
chuckle [tʃʌkl], *v.n.* kichern. — *s.* das Kichern.
chum [tʃʌm], *s.* (*coll.*) der Freund, Kamerad. — *v.n.* (*coll.*) — *up*, sich befreunden (*with*, mit).
chump [tʃʌmp], *s.* der Klotz (*wood*).
chunk [tʃʌnk], *s.* das große Stück (*meat etc.*).
church [tʃə:tʃ], *s.* die Kirche.
churchwarden [tʃə:tʃ'wɔ:dn], *s.* der Kirchenvorsteher.
churchyard ['tʃə:tʃjɑ:d], *s.* der Friedhof.
churl [tʃə:l], *s.* der Grobian, der grobe Kerl.
churlish ['tʃə:liʃ], *adj.* grob, unfein.
churn [tʃə:n], *s.* das Butterfaß. — *v.a.* mischen, schütteln (*butter etc.*); — *up*, aufwühlen (*stir up*).
chute [ʃu:t], *s.* die Gleitbahn.
cider ['saidə], *s.* der Apfelmost.
cigar [si'gɑ:], *s.* die Zigarre; — *case*, das Zigarrenetui.
cigarette [sigə'ret], *s.* die Zigarette; — *holder*, die Zigarettenspitze; — *lighter*, das Feuerzeug.
cinder ['sində], *s.* (*usually in pl.*) die Asche (*fire*); die Schlacke (*furnace*).
Cinderella [sində'relə]. das Aschenbrödel, Aschenputtel.
cinema ['sinimə], *s.* das Kino.
cinematography [sinimə'tɔgrəfi], *s.* die Filmkunst.
Cingalese *see* **Singhalese**.
cinnamon ['sinəmən], *s.* der Zimt.
cipher ['saifə], *s.* die Ziffer; die Geheimschrift (*code*). — *v.n.* rechnen. — *v.a.* chiffrieren (*code*).
Circassian [sə:'kæsiən], *adj.* tscherkessisch. — *s.* der Tscherkesse.

circle [sə:kl], *s.* der Zirkel, Kreis; (*social*) Gesellschaftskreis; (*Theat.*) der Rang. — *v.a.* umringen. — *v.n.* umkreisen; sich drehen (*revolve*).
circuit ['sə:kit], *s.* der Kreislauf; (*Elec.*) der Stromkreis.
circuitous [sə:'kju:itəs], *adj.* weitschweifig, weitläufig.
circular ['sə:kjulə], *adj.* rund, kreisförmig, Rund-; — *tour*, die Rundreise. — *s.* das Rundschreiben (*letter*); der Werbebrief (*advertising*).
circulate ['sə:kjuleit], *v.a.* in Umlauf setzen. — *v.n.* umlaufen, kreisen, zirkulieren.
circulation [sə:kju'leiʃən], *s.* die Zirkulation, der Kreislauf (*blood*); die Verbreitung, Auflage (*newspaper*); der Umlauf (*banknotes*).
circumcise ['sə:kəmsaiz], *v.a.* beschneiden.
circumference [sə:'kʌmfərəns], *s.* der Umfang.
circumscribe ['sə:kəmskraib], *v.a.* beschränken, einengen (*narrow down*); umschreiben (*paraphrase*).
circumspect ['sə:kəmspekt], *adj.* umsichtig, vorsorglich.
circumspection [sə:kəm'spekʃən], *s.* die Umsicht, Vorsicht.
circumstance ['sə:kəmstæns, -stɑ:ns], *s.* der Umstand; *pomp and* —, großer Aufmarsch.
circumstantial [sə:kəm'stænʃəl], *adj.* umständlich; zu einem Umstand gehörig; eingehend; — *evidence*, der Indizienbeweis.
circumvent [sə:kəm'vent], *v.a.* überlisten, hintergehen.
circus ['sə:kəs], *s.* der Zirkus; der Platz.
cirrhus ['sirəs], *s.* die Federwolke.
Cistercian [sis'tə:ʃən], *s.* der Zisterzienser (*monk*).
cistern ['sistən], *s.* die Zisterne, der Wasserbehälter.
citadel ['sitədəl], *s.* die Zitadelle, die Burg.
citation [sai'teiʃən], *s.* das Zitat; (*Law*) die Zitierung, Vorladung; (*Mil.*) die rühmliche Erwähnung.
cite [sait], *v.a.* zitieren (*quote*); (*Law*) vorladen.
citizen ['sitizən], *s.* der Bürger, Staatsbürger (*national*); *fellow* —, der Mitbürger.
citizenship ['sitizənʃip], *s.* das Bürgerrecht, die Staatsangehörigkeit.
citrate ['sitreit], *s.* (*Chem.*) das Zitrat.
citric ['sitrik], *adj.* (*Chem.*) Zitronen-.
citron ['sitrən], *s.* die Zitrone. — *adj.* zitronenfarben.
city ['siti], *s.* die Stadt; die Großstadt; die City. — *adj.* städtisch.
civic ['sivik], *adj.* Stadt-, städtisch (*ceremonial*); bürgerlich.
civil ['sivil], *adj.* zivil; höflich (*polite*); — *engineer*, der Zivilingenieur; — *service*, der Beamtendienst, die Beamtenlaufbahn, der Staatsdienst; — *war*, der Bürgerkrieg.
civilian [si'viljən], *s.* der Zivilist.
civility [si'viliti], *s.* die Höflichkeit.
civilization [sivilai'zeiʃən], *s.* die Zivilisation.
civilize ['sivilaiz], *v.a.* zivilisieren, verfeinern (*refine*).
clack [klæk], *v.n.* klappern (*wood etc.*); plaudern, plappern.
clad [klæd], *adj.* gekleidet.
claim [kleim], *v.a.* Anspruch erheben (*to*, auf); fordern (*demand*); behaupten (*assert*). — *s.* der Anspruch; die Forderung (*demand*); das Recht.
claimant ['kleimənt], *s.* der Beanspruchende, Anspruchserheber.
clairvoyance [klɛə'vɔiəns], *s.* das Hellsehen.
clairvoyant [klɛə'vɔiənt], *s.* der Hellseher.
clam [klæm], *s.* (*Zool.*) die Venusmuschel; *shut up like a* —, verschwiegen sein.
clamber ['klæmbə], *v.n.* klettern.
clamminess ['klæminis], *s.* die Feuchtigkeit, Klebrigkeit.
clammy ['klæmi], *adj.* feucht, klebrig.
clamorous ['klæmərəs], *adj.* lärmend, laut, ungestüm.
clamour ['klæmə], *s.* das Geschrei, der Lärm. — *v.n.* laut schreien (*for*, nach, *Dat.*).
clamp [klæmp], *s.* die Klammer, die Klampe. — *v.a.* festklammern.
clan [klæn], *s.* die Sippe, die Familie.
clandestine [klæn'destin], *adj.* heimlich, verstohlen.
clang [klæŋ], *s.* der Schall, das Geklirr. — *v.n.* erschallen. — *v.a.* erschallen lassen.
clangour ['klæŋə], *s.* das Getöse, der Lärm.
clank [klæŋk], *s.* das Geklirre, das Gerassel (*metal*).
clannish ['klæniʃ], *adj.* stammesbewußt; engherzig (*narrow*).
clap [klæp], *v.a.* schlagen, zusammenschlagen (*hands*). — *v.n.* Beifall klatschen (*Dat.*).
clapperboard ['klæpəbɔ:d], *s.* (*Film*) das Klappbrett, die Klapptafel; der Klöppel (*beater, in lacemaking*).
claptrap ['klæptræp], *s.* der billige Effekt, das eitle Geschwätz (*gossip*).
claret ['klærit], *s.* der Rotwein.
clarification [klærifi'keiʃən], *s.* die Klarstellung, Aufklärung.
clarify ['klærifai], *v.a.* klarstellen.
clari(o)net [klæri(ə)'net], *s.* (*Mus.*) die Klarinette.
clarion ['klæriən], *s.* (*Mus.*) die Zinke, Trompete; — *call*, der laute Ruf.
clash [klæʃ], *v.a.* zusammenschlagen. — *v.n.* aufeinanderprallen, zusammenfallen (*dates*); widerstreiten (*views*). — *s.* (*fig.*) der Zusammenstoß, der Widerstreit.
clasp [klɑ:sp], *v.a.* ergreifen, festhalten. — *s.* der Haken (*hook*); die Schnalle, die Spange (*buckle, brooch*); — *knife*, das Taschenmesser.

class [klɑ:s], *s.* die Klasse.
classic(al) ['klæsik(əl)], *adj.* klassisch.
classics ['klæsiks], *s. pl.* die Klassiker, *m. pl.*; die klassische Philologie (*subject of study*).
classification [klæsifi'keiʃən], *s.* die Klassifizierung.
classify ['klæsifai], *v.a.* klassifizieren.
clatter ['klætə], *s.* das Getöse, Geklirr. — *v.a., v.n.* klappern, klirren.
Claus [klɔ:z]. Claus, Nicholas, *m.*; *Santa* —, der heilige Nikolaus, Knecht Ruprecht, Weihnachtsmann.
clause [klɔ:z], *s.* (*Gram.*) der Nebensatz; die Klausel (*contract*); (*Law*) der Vertragspunkt.
claw [klɔ:], *s.* die Klaue, die Kralle. — *v.a.* kratzen.
clay [klei], *s.* der Ton, Lehm.
clayey [kleii], *adj.* lehmig, tonig.
clean [kli:n], *adj.* rein, reinlich (*habits*); sauber; — *shaven*, glattrasiert. — *v.a.* reinigen, putzen.
cleaner ['kli:nə], *s.* die Reinemacherin, die Putzfrau.
cleanliness ['klenlinis], *s.* die Reinlichkeit, Sauberkeit.
cleanse [klenz], *v.a.* reinigen.
clear [kliə], *adj.* klar, hell; deutlich (*meaning*); schuldlos (*not guilty*). — *s. in the* —, nicht betroffen, schuldlos. — *v.a.* (*Chem.*) klären; (*Law*) für unschuldig erklären; verzollen (*pass through customs*); springen (über, *Acc.*). — *v.n.* (— *up*), sich aufklären, aufhellen (*weather*).
clearance ['kliərəns], *s.* die Räumung; — *sale*, der Ausverkauf; die Verzollung (*customs*).
clearing ['kliəriŋ], *s.* die Lichtung (*in wood*); (*Comm.*) die Verrechnung.
clearness ['kliənis], *s.* die Deutlichkeit, die Klarheit, Helle.
cleave [kli:v], *v.a. irr.* spalten (*wood*). — *v.n.* sich spalten.
cleaver ['kli:və], *s.* das Hackmesser.
cleek [kli:k], *s.* der Golfschläger.
clef [klef], *s.* (*Mus.*) der Schlüssel.
cleft [kleft], *s.* der Spalt. — *adj.* — *palate*, die Gaumenspalte.
clemency ['klemənsi], *s.* die Milde, Gnade (*mercy*).
clement ['klemənt], *adj.* mild (*climate*); gnädig (*merciful*).
clench [klentʃ], *v.a.* zusammenpressen; ballen (*fist*).
clergy ['klə:dʒi], *s.* (*Eccl.*) die Geistlichkeit.
clergyman ['klə:dʒimən], *s.* (*Eccl.*) der Geistliche.
clerical ['klerikl], *adj.* (*Eccl.*) geistlich; beamtlich, Beamten-, Büro- (*office*); — *work*, die Büroarbeit.
clerk [klɑ:k], *s.* der Schreiber, der Bürogehilfe (*junior*), der Bürobeamte, Büroangestellte (*senior*); *bank* —, der Bankbeamte.
clever ['klevə], *adj.* klug; intelligent; geschickt (*deft*); gewandt, listig (*cunning*).
cleverness ['klevənis], *s.* die Klugheit (*intelligence*); die Schlauheit (*cunning*); die Begabung (*talent*); die Geschicklichkeit (*skill*).
clew [klu:] *see* **clue**.
click [klik], *v.a., v.n.* einschnappen (*lock*); zusammenschlagen (*o.'s heels*, die Hacken); schnalzen (*o.'s tongue*); (*sl.*) zusammenpassen (*of two people*). — *s.* das Einschnappen (*lock*); das Zusammenschlagen (*heels*); das Schnalzen (*tongue*).
client ['klaiənt], *s.* (*Law*) der Klient; (*Comm.*) der Kunde.
clientele [kli:ən'tel], *s.* die Klientel, die Kundschaft.
cliff [klif], *s.* die Klippe.
climate ['klaimit], *s.* das Klima.
climatic [klai'mætik], *adj.* klimatisch.
climax ['klaimæks], *s.* der Höhepunkt.
climb [klaim], *v.a.* erklettern, erklimmen. — *v.n.* klettern, bergsteigen; (*Aviat.*) steigen. — *s.* der Aufstieg, die Ersteigung.
climber ['klaimə], *s.* der Bergsteiger (*mountaineer*); (*Bot.*) die Schlingpflanze.
clinch [klintʃ], *v.a.* vernieten, befestigen; — *a deal*, einen Handel abschließen. — *s.* der feste Griff; die Umklammerung (*boxing*).
cling [kliŋ], *v.n. irr.* sich anklammern, festhalten (*to*, an).
clinic ['klinik], *s.* die Klinik.
clinical ['klinikl], *adj.* klinisch.
clink [kliŋk], *s.* das Geklirre; (*coll.*) das Gefängnis. — *v.a.* — *glasses*, mit den Gläsern anstoßen.
clinker ['kliŋkə], *s.* der Backstein; die Schlacke.
clip (1) [klip], *v.a.* stutzen, beschneiden; lochen (*ticket*).
clip (2) [klip], *v.a.* befestigen. —*s. paper* —, die Büroklammer.
clippings ['klipiŋz], *s. pl.* die Abschnitte; die Schnitzel (*waste*); Zeitungsausschnitte, *m. pl.*
cloak [klouk], *s.* der Mantel, der Deckmantel (cover). — *v.a.* verbergen.
cloakroom ['kloukru:m], *s.* die Garderobe; — *free*, keine Garderobegebühr; (*Railw.*) die Gepäckaufbewahrung.
clock [klɔk], *s.* die (große) Uhr, Wanduhr; — *face*, das Zifferblatt.— *v.n.* — *in*, die Zeitkarte (Kontrollkarte) stempeln lassen, eintreffen (*arrive*).
clockwise ['klɔkwaiz], *adv.* im Uhrzeigersinne.
clod [klɔd], *s.* die Erdscholle, der Erdklumpen; (*sl.*) der Lümmel (*lout*).
clog [klɔg], *v.a.* belasten, hemmen, verstopfen. — *v.n.* sich verstopfen. — *s.* der Holzschuh.
cloisters ['klɔistəz], *s. pl.* (*Eccl., Archit.*) der Kreuzgang.

close [klouz], *v.a.* schließen, verschließen; beenden (*meeting etc.*). — *v.n.* — *in on*, über einen hereinbrechen, umzingeln. — *s.* das Ende, der Schluß; [klous] der Domplatz. — [klous], *adj.* nahe (*near*); knapp (*narrow*); nahestehend, vertraut (*friend*); schwül (*weather*); geizig (*miserly*).
closeness ['klousnis], *s.* die Nähe (*nearness*); die Schwüle (*weather*); die Vertrautheit (*familiarity*).
closet ['klɔzit], *s.* der Wandschrank (*cupboard*); das kleine Zimmer; das Klosett (*W.C.*). — *v.r.* — *o.s. with*, sich mit jemandem zurückziehen, sich vertraulich beraten.
closure ['klouʒə], *s.* der Schluß; der Abschluß (einer Debatte).
clot [klɔt], *s.* das Klümpchen. — *v.n.* sich verdicken, gerinnen; —*ted cream*, dicke Sahne.
cloth [klɔθ], *s.* das Tuch; der Stoff; die Leinwand (*bookbinding*); *American* —, das Wachstuch; — *printing*, der Zeugdruck.
clothe [klouð], *v.a.* kleiden. — *v.r.* sich kleiden.
clothes [klouðz], *s. pl.* die Kleider, *n. pl.*; die Kleidung; die Wäsche (*washing*); — *basket*, der Wäschekorb; — *press*, der Kleiderschrank.
clothier ['klouðiə], *s.* der Tuchmacher (*manufacturer*); der Tuchhändler (*dealer*).
clothing ['klouðiŋ], *s.* die Kleidung.
cloud [klaud], *s.* die Wolke; *under a* —, in Ungnade; —*burst*, der Wolkenbruch. — *v.a.* bewölken, verdunkeln. — *v.n.* — *over*, sich umwölken.
cloudiness ['klaudinis], *s.* die Umwölkung, der Wolkenhimmel.
cloudy ['klaudi], *adj.* wolkig, bewölkt, umwölkt.
clout [klaut], *s.* (*obs.*) der Lappen (*rag*); (*coll.*) der Schlag (*hit*). — *v.a.* schlagen (*hit*).
clove [klouv], *s.* die Gewürznelke (*spice*).
clove(n) [klouv(n)], *adj.* gespalten.
clover ['klouvə], *s.* (*Bot.*) der Klee; *to be in* —, Glück haben, es gut haben.
clown [klaun], *s.* der Hanswurst. — *v.n.* den Hanswurst spielen.
clownish ['klauniʃ], *adj.* tölpelhaft.
clownishness ['klauniʃnis], *s.* die Derbheit, Tölpelhaftigkeit.
cloy [klɔi], *v.n.* übersättigen, anwidern, anekeln.
club (1) [klʌb], *s.* die Keule (*stick*). — *v.a.* (einen) mit einer Keule schlagen.
club (2) [klʌb], *s.* der Klub, der Verein. — *v.n.* — *together*, zusammen beitragen, zusammensteuern (*contribute jointly*).
club (3) [klʌb], *s.* (*cards*) das Treff, die Eichel (*German cards*).
clubfoot ['klʌbfut], *s.* der Klumpfuß.
cluck [klʌk], *v.n.* glucken (*hen*).
clue [klu:], *s.* der Anhaltspunkt, Leitfaden, die Richtlinie, die Angabe (*crossword*); *no* —, keine blasse Ahnung.
clump [klʌmp], *s.* der Klumpen; die Gruppe.
clumsiness ['klʌmzinis], *s.* die Unbeholfenheit, Ungeschicklichkeit.
clumsy ['klʌmzi], *adj.* unbeholfen, schwerfällig, ungeschickt.
Cluniac ['klu:njæk]. (*Eccl.*) der Kluniazenser.
cluster ['klʌstə], *s.* die Traube (*grapes*), der Büschel. — *v.n.* in Büschen wachsen *or* stehen, dicht gruppiert sein.
clutch [klʌtʃ], *v.a.* ergreifen, packen (*grip*). — *s.* der Griff; (*Motor.*) die Kupplung.
coach [koutʃ], *s.* die Kutsche; der Wagen, der Autobus; der Privatlehrer (*teacher*). — *v.a.* unterrichten, vorbereiten (*for examinations etc.*).
coachman ['koutʃmən], *s.* der Kutscher.
coagulate [kou'ægjuleit], *v.a.* gerinnen lassen. — *v.n.* gerinnen.
coagulation [kouægju'leiʃən], *s.* das Gerinnen.
coal [koul], *s.* die Kohle; — *mine*, das Kohlenbergwerk; die Kohlengrube; — *miner*, der Bergmann.
coalesce [kouə'les], *v.n.* zusammenwachsen, sich vereinigen.
coalescence [kouə'lesəns], *s.* die Verschmelzung.
coalition [kouə'liʃən], *s.* (*Pol.*) die Koalition, das Bündnis.
coarse [kɔ:s], *adj.* grob; gemein (*manner*).
coarseness ['kɔ:snis], *s.* die Grobheit, Unfeinheit.
coast [koust], *s.* die Küste. — *v.n.* (an der Küste) entlangfahren; gleiten, rodeln.
coat [kout], *s.* der Mantel, Rock; die Jacke (*jacket*); das Fell (*animal*); — *of arms*, das Wappenschild; — *of mail*, das Panzerhemd; — *of paint*, der Anstrich. — *v.a.* überziehen, bemalen (*paint*).
coathanger ['kouthæŋə], *s.* der Kleiderbügel.
coating ['koutiŋ], *s.* der Überzug.
coax [kouks], *v.a.* beschwatzen; überreden (*persuade*).
cob (1) [kɔb], *s.* der Gaul.
cob (2) [kɔb], *s.* (*Orn.*) der Schwan.
cob (3) [kɔb], *s.* der (Mais)Kolben (*corn on the* —).
cobble [kɔbl], *v.a.* flicken (*shoes*).
cobbled ['kɔbld], *adj.* mit Kopfsteinen gepflastert.
cobbler ['kɔblə], *s.* der Schuhflicker.
cobble(stone) ['kɔbl(stoun)], *s.* das Kopfsteinpflaster.
cobweb ['kɔbweb], *s.* das Spinngewebe.
cock [kɔk], *s.* (*Orn.*) der Hahn; (*Engin.*) der Sperrhahn, Hahn; — *sparrow*, das Sperlingsmännchen; — *-a-doodle-doo!* kikeriki!
cockade [kɔ'keid], *s.* die Kokarde.
cockatoo [kɔkə'tu:], *s.* (*Orn.*) der Kakadu.

cockchafer ['kɔktʃeifə], *s.* (*Ent.*) der Maikäfer.
cockerel ['kɔkərəl], *s.* (*Orn.*) der junge Hahn.
cockswain [kɔksn] *see* **coxswain.**
cockle [kɔkl], *s.* (*Zool.*) die Herzmuschel.
cockney ['kɔkni], *s.* der geborene Londoner.
cockpit ['kɔkpit], *s.* (*Aviat.*) der Pilotensitz, die Kanzel, der Führerraum.
cockroach ['kɔkroutʃ], *s.* (*Ent.*) die Schabe.
cocksure ['kɔkʃuə], *adj.* zuversichtlich, allzu sicher.
cocoa ['koukou], *s.* der Kakao.
coconut ['koukonʌt], *s.* die Kokosnuß.
cocoon [kə'ku:n], *s.* der Kokon, die Puppe (*of silkworm*).
cod [kɔd], *s.* der Kabeljau, Dorsch; — *liver oil*, der Lebertran; *dried* —, der Stockfisch.
coddle [kɔdl], *v.a.* verhätscheln, verweichlichen.
code [koud], *s.* das Gesetzbuch, der Kodex; die Chiffre (*cipher*). — *v.a.* chiffrieren, schlüsseln.
codify ['koudifai], *v.a.* kodifizieren.
coerce [kou'ə:s], *v.a.* zwingen.
coercion [kou'ə:ʃən], *s.* der Zwang.
coercive [kou'ə:siv], *adj.* zwingend.
coeval [kou'i:vəl], *adj.* gleichaltrig, gleichzeitig.
coexist [kouig'zist], *v.n.* zugleich existieren, nebeneinander leben.
coffee ['kɔfi], *s.* der Kaffee; — *grinder*, die Kaffeemühle; — *grounds*, der Kaffeesatz; — *pot*, die Kaffeekanne; — *set*, das Kaffee service.
coffer ['kɔfə], *s.* der Kasten, die Truhe.
coffin ['kɔfin], *s.* der Sarg.
cog [kɔg], *s.* der Zahn (*on wheel*); — *wheel*, das Zahnrad.
cogency ['koudʒənsi], *s.* die zwingende Kraft, Triftigkeit.
cogent ['koudʒənt], *adj.* zwingend, triftig.
cogitate ['kɔdʒiteit], *v.n.* nachdenken.
cogitation [kɔdʒi'teiʃən], *s.* die Überlegung, das Nachdenken.
cognate ['kɔgneit], *adj.* verwandt.
cognisance ['kɔgnizəns], *s.* die Erkenntnis; die Kenntnisnahme; (*Law*) die gerichtliche Kenntnisnahme.
cognisant ['kɔgnizənt], *adj.* wissend, in vollem Wissen (*of, Genit.*).
cognition [kɔg'niʃən], *s.* die Kenntnis, das Erkennen.
cohabit [kou'hæbit], *v.n.* zusammenleben.
cohabitation [kouhæbi'teiʃən], *s.* das Zusammenleben.
coheir [kou'ɛə], *s.* der Miterbe.
cohere [kou'hiə], *v.n.* zusammenhängen.
coherence [kou'hiərəns], *s.* der Zusammenhang.
coherent [kou'hiərənt], *adj.* zusammenhängend.
cohesion [kou'hi:ʒən], *s.* (*Phys.*) die Kohäsion.
coiffure [kwæ'fjuə], *s.* die Frisur, die Haartracht.
coil [kɔil], *s.* (*Elec.*) die Spule; die Windung. — *v.a.* aufwickeln; umwickeln, (auf)spulen. — *v.n.* sich winden.
coin [kɔin], *s.* die Münze, das Geldstück. — *v.a.* münzen, prägen; — *a phrase*, eine Redewendung prägen.
coinage ['kɔinidʒ], *s.* die Prägung.
coincide [kouin'said], *v.n.* zusammenfallen, zusammentreffen.
coincidence [kou'insidəns], *s.* das Zusammenfallen, Zusammentreffen; der Zufall (*chance*).
coincident [kou'insidənt], *adj.* zusammentreffend.
coke [kouk], *s.* der Koks. — *v.a.* (*Chem.*, *Engin.*) verkoken.
cold [kould], *adj.* kalt; gefühllos, kühl. — *s.* die Kälte (*temperature*); die Erkältung (*indisposition*).
coldish ['kouldiʃ], *adj.* kühl.
coldness ['kouldnis], *s.* die Kälte (*temperature*); die Kaltherzigkeit (*heartlessness*).
colic ['kɔlik], *s.* die Kolik.
collaborate [kə'læbəreit], *v.n.* zusammenarbeiten.
collaboration [kəlæbə'reiʃən], *s.* die Zusammenarbeit; die Mitwirkung, Mitarbeit (*assistance*).
collaborator [kə'læbəreitə], *s.* der Mitarbeiter.
collapse [kə'læps], *s.* der Zusammenbruch. — *v.n.* zusammenbrechen (*disintegrate*); zerfallen, einstürzen.
collapsible [kə'læpsibl], *adj.* zerlegbar, zusammenlegbar, zusammenklappbar.
collar ['kɔlə], *s.* der Kragen; —*bone*, das Schlüsselbein (*Anat.*); *dog* —, das Halsband; (*coll.*) der Priesterkragen; —*stud*, der Kragenknopf. — *v.a.* beim Kragen fassen, ergreifen.
collate [kɔ'leit], *v.a.* vergleichen (*texts etc.*).
collateral [kɔ'lætərəl], *adj.* Seiten-, von beiden Seiten. — *s.* (*Am.*) die Garantie, Bürgschaft.
collation [kɔ'leiʃən], *s.* die Vergleichung, der Vergleich (*texts etc.*); der Imbiß.
colleague ['kɔli:g], *s.* der Kollege, die Kollegin.
collect [kə'lekt], *v.a.* sammeln, zusammenbringen. — *v.n.* sich versammeln. — ['kɔlikt], *s.* (*Eccl.*) die Kollekte.
collection [kə'lekʃən], *s.* die Sammlung.
collective [kə'lektiv], *adj.* kollektiv, gemeinsam. — *s.* (*Pol.*) das Kollektiv.
collector [kə'lektə], *s.* der Sammler.
college ['kɔlidʒ], *s.* das Kollegium; das College; die Hochschule, Universität.
collide [kə'laid], *v.n.* zusammenstoßen.
collie ['kɔli], *s.* der Schäferhund.
collier ['kɔliə], *s.* der Kohlenarbeiter; das Kohlenfrachtschiff (*boat*).

collision [kə'liʒən], *s.* der Zusammenstoß, Zusammenprall.
collocate ['kɔləkeit], *v.a.* ordnen.
collodion [kə'loudjən], *s.* (*Chem.*) das Kollodium.
colloquial [kə'loukwiəl], *adj.* umgangssprachlich, Umgangs-.
colloquy ['kɔlekwi], *s.* die Unterredung, das Gespräch (*formal*).
collusion [kə'lu:ʒən], *s.* das heimliche Einverständnis, die unstatthafte Partnerschaft; die Verdunkelung.
collusive [kə'lu:ziv], *adj.* abgekartet.
Cologne [kə'loun]. Köln, *n.*; *eau de* —, Kölnisch Wasser.
Colombian [kɔ'lɔmbjən], *adj.* kolumbisch. — *s.* der Kolumbier.
colon (1) ['koulən], *s.* das Kolon, der Doppelpunkt.
colon (2) ['koulɔn], *s.* (*Med.*) der Dickdarm.
colonel [kə:nl], *s.* (*Mil.*) der Oberst; — *-in-chief*, der Generaloberst, der oberste Befehlshaber; *lieutenant-* —, der Oberstleutnant.
colonial [kə'lounjəl], *adj.* kolonial, aus den Kolonien.
colonist ['kɔlənist], *s.* der Siedler; Ansiedler.
colonization [kɔlənai'zeiʃən], *s.* die Kolonisierung, Besiedelung.
colonize ['kɔlənaiz], *v.a.* besiedeln, kolonisieren.
colonnade [kɔlə'neid], *s.* die Kolonnade, der Säulengang.
colony ['kɔləni], *s.* die Kolonie.
colophony [kɔ'lɔfəni], *s.* das Kolophonium (*resin*).
coloration [kʌlə'reiʃən], *s.* die Färbung, Tönung.
colossal [kə'lɔsəl], *adj.* kolossal, riesig, riesenhaft.
colour ['kʌlə], *s.* die Farbe; (*complexion*) die Gesichtsfarbe; (*paint*) die Farbe, der Anstrich; (*dye*) die Färbung. — *v.a.* färben; anstreichen (*paint house etc.*).
colt [koult], *s.* das Füllen.
columbine ['kɔləmbain], *s.* (*Bot.*) die Akelei.
column ['kɔləm], *s.* die Säule; die Spalte (*press*); (*also Mil.*) die Kolonne.
colza ['kɔlzə], *s.* (*Bot.*) der Raps.
coma ['koumə], *s.* (*Med.*) das Koma, die Schlafsucht.
comb [koum], *s.* der Kamm. — *v.a.* kämmen; (*fig.*) genau untersuchen.
combat ['kʌmbət, 'kɔmbət], *s.* der Kampf, das Gefecht; *in single* —, im Duell, Zweikampf. — *v.a.* kämpfen, bekämpfen.
combatant ['kʌmbətənt, 'kɔmb-], *s.* der Kämpfer.
comber ['koumə], *s.* der Wollkämmer.
combination [kɔmbi'neiʃən], *s.* die Kombination, die Verbindung.
combine [kəm'bain], *v.a.* kombinieren, verbinden. — *v.n.* sich verbinden. — ['kɔmbain], *s.* (*Comm.*) der Trust, Ring.
combustible [kəm'bʌstibl], *adj.* verbrennbar; feuergefährlich.
combustion [kəm'bʌstʃən], *s.* die Verbrennung.
come [kʌm], *v.n. irr.* kommen; — *about*, sich ereignen (*event*); — *across*, stoßen auf (*Acc.*); — *by* (*s.th.*), ergattern, erwerben; — *for*, abholen; — *forth*, *forward*, hervorkommen, hervortreten; — *from*, herkommen von, — *in*, hereinkommen; — *off*, (*of object*) loskommen, (*succeed*) glücken; — *out* (*appear*), herauskommen; — *to o.s.*, zu sich kommen; — *of age*, mündig werden; — *to o.'s senses*, zur Besinnung *or* Vernunft kommen; *that is still to* —, das steht uns noch bevor.
comedian [kə'mi:djən], *s.* der Komödiant, Komiker (*stage*).
comedy ['kɔmədi], *s.* die Komödie, das Lustspiel.
comeliness ['kʌmlinis], *s.* die Anmut, Schönheit.
comely ['kʌmli], *adj.* anmutig, schön.
comestible [kə'mestibl], *s.* (*usually pl.*) die Eßwaren, *f. pl.*
comet ['kɔmit], *s.* der Komet.
comfit ['kʌmfit], *s.* das Konfekt, die Bonbons.
comfort ['kʌmfət], *s.* der Trost (*solace*); der Komfort, die Bequemlichkeit. — *v.a.* trösten.
comforter ['kʌmfətə], *s.* der Tröster; (*Am.*) die Steppdecke.
comfortless ['kʌmfətlis], *adj.* trostlos, unbehaglich.
comic ['kɔmik], *adj.* komisch; — *writer*, humoristischer Schriftsteller. — *s.* die Bilderzeitung (*children's paper*).
comical ['kɔmikl], *adj.* lächerlich, zum Lachen, komisch.
comma ['kɔmə], *s.* das Komma, der Beistrich; *inverted* —*s*, die Anführungszeichen.
command [kə'mɑ:nd], *v.a.*, *v.n.* (*Mil.*) kommandieren; über jemanden verfügen (*have s.o. at o.'s disposal*). — *s.* der Befehl.
commandant [kɔmən'dænt], *s.* der Kommandant, Befehlshaber.
commander [kə'mɑ:ndə], *s.* der Befehlshaber.
commandment [kə'mɑ:ndmənt], *s.* (*Rel.*) das Gebot.
commemorate [kə'meməreit], *v.a.* feiern, gedenken (*Genit.*).
commemoration [kəmemə'reiʃən], *s.* die Feier, die Gedächtnisfeier.
commemorative [kə'memərətiv], *adj.* Gedächtnis-.
commence [kə'mens], *v.a.*, *v.n.* beginnen, anfangen.
commencement [kə'mensmənt], *s.* der Anfang, der Beginn.
commend [kə'mend], *v.a.* empfehlen, loben (*praise*).
commendable [kə'mendəbl], *adj.* empfehlenswert.

commendation [kɔmen'deiʃən], *s.* die Empfehlung.
commensurable, commensurate [kə'menʃərəbl, kə'menʃərit], *adj.* kommensurabel, entsprechend; angemessen.
comment ['kɔment], *v.n.* kommentieren (*on*, zu, *Dat.*). — *s.* der Kommentar; die Bemerkung (*remark*).
commentary ['kɔməntəri], *s.* der Kommentar.
commentator ['kɔmənteitə], *s.* der Kommentator, Berichterstatter.
commerce ['kɔmə:s], *s.* der Handel; *college of* —, die Handelsschule.
commercial [kə'mə:ʃəl], *adj.* kommerziell, kaufmännisch, Handels-; — *traveller*, der Handelsreisende, Vertreter; — *manager*, der geschäftliche Leiter.
commingle [kɔ'miŋgl], *v.a.* vermischengefühl.
commiserate [kə'mizəreit], *v.n.* bemitleiden; — *with s.o.*, mit einem Mitgefühl haben.
commissariat [kɔmi'sɛəriət], *s.* (*Pol.*) das Kommissariat.
commissary ['kɔmisəri], *s.* der Kommissar. — *adj.* kommissarisch.
commission [kə'miʃən], *s.* die Kommission; (*Mil.*) der Offiziersrang; die Begehung (*of crime*); (*Law*) die (offizielle) Kommission; der Auftrag, die Bestellung (*order*).
commissionaire [kəmiʃən'ɛə], *s.* der Portier.
commissioned [kə'miʃənd], *adj.* bevollmächtigt.
commissioner [kə'miʃənə], *s.* (*Pol.*) der Kommissar, der Bevollmächtigte.
commit [kə'mit], *v.a.* begehen (*do*); übergeben (*consign*); anvertrauen (*entrust*). — *v.r.* sich verpflichten.
committal [kə'mitl], *s.* das Übergeben; die Überantwortung.
committee [kə'miti], *s.* das Kommitee, der Ausschuß.
commodious [kə'moudiəs], *adj.* bequem, geräumig.
commodity [kə'mɔditi], *s.* (*Comm.*) die Ware, der Artikel.
commodore ['kɔmədɔ:], *s.* (*Naut.*) der Kommodore, der Kommandant eines Geschwaders.
common ['kɔmən], *adj.* gewöhnlich (*usual*); gemein (*vulgar*); allgemein (*general*); *in* —, gemeinschaftlich; — *sense*, der gesunde Menschenverstand; *the — man*, der kleine Mann. — *n. pl. House of Commons*, das Unterhaus.
commoner ['kɔmənə], *s.* der Bürger; (*Parl.*) Mitglied des Unterhauses.
commonness ['kɔmənnis], *s.* die Gemeinheit (*vulgarity*); das häufige Vorkommen (*frequency*).
commonplace ['kɔmənpleis], *adj.* alltäglich. — *s.* der Gemeinplatz.
commonwealth ['kɔmənwelθ], *s.* die Staatengemeinschaft, der Staatenbund; das Commonwealth.
commotion [kə'mouʃən], *s.* die Erschütterung; der Aufruhr; der Lärm.
communal ['kɔmjunəl], *adj.* gemeinschaftlich, allgemein; (*Pol.*) Kommunal-.
commune ['kɔmju:n], *s.* (*Pol.*) die Kommune. — [kə'mju:n], *v.n.* sich unterhalten.
communicable [kə'mju:nikəbl], *adj.* mitteilbar; übertragbar.
communicate [kə'mju:nikeit], *v.a.* mitteilen; verkünden (*proclaim*); benachrichtigen. — *v.n.* in Verbindung stehen.
communication [kəmju:ni'keiʃən], *s.* die Mitteilung; Verlautbarung; die Verkündigung (*proclamation*); die Information; (*Elec.*) die Verbindung; (*pl.*), die Verbindungslinie; —*s engineering*, Fernmeldetechnik.
communion [kə'mju:njən], *s.* (*Eccl.*) die Kommunion; das heilige Abendmahl; die Gemeinschaft (*fellowship*).
Communism ['kɔmjunizm], *s.* (*Pol.*) der Kommunismus.
Communist ['kɔmjunist], *s.* der Kommunist. — *adj.* kommunistisch.
community [kə'mju:niti], *s.* die Gemeinschaft.
commutable [kə'mju:təbl], *adj.* umtauschbar, auswechselbar.
commutation [kɔmju'teiʃən], *s.* der Austausch; (*Law*) die Herabsetzung (*of sentence*).
commutator ['kɔmjuteitə], *s.* (*Elec.*) der Umschalter.
commute [kə'mju:t], *v.n.* hin und her fahren, pendeln, mit Zeitkarte fahren (*travel*). — *v.a.* herabsetzen (*sentence*).
compact ['kɔmpækt], *adj.* kompakt, fest; gedrängt (*succinct*); kurz, bündig (*short*).
companion [kəm'pænjən], *s.* der Gefährte, die Gefährtin.
companionable [kəm'pænjənəbl], *adj.* gesellig, freundlich.
companionship [kəm'pænjənʃip], *s.* die Geselligkeit; die Gesellschaft.
company ['kʌmpəni], *s.* die Gesellschaft; (*Mil.*) die Kompanie; der Freundeskreis (*circle of friends*); (*Comm.*) die Handelsgesellschaft; *limited* (*liability*) —, Gesellschaft mit beschränkter Haftung; *public* (*private*) —, Gesellschaft des öffentlichen (privaten) Rechtes.
comparative [kəm'pærətiv], *adj.* vergleichend, relativ. — *s.* (*Gram.*) der Komparativ.
compare [kəm'pɛə], *v.a.* vergleichen. — *v.n.* sich vergleichen lassen.
comparison [kəm'pærisən], *s.* der Vergleich; das Gleichnis (*simile*).
compartment [kəm'pɑ:tmənt], *s.* (*Railw.*) das Abteil; die Abteilung.
compass ['kʌmpəs], *s.* der Umkreis, Umfang (*scope*); (*Naut.*) der Kompaß; *point of the* —, der Kompaßstrich; (*Engin.*) der Zirkel.

compassion [kəm'pæʃən], *s.* die Barmherzigkeit, das Mitleid, das Erbarmen.
compassionate [kəm'pæʃənit], *adj.* mitleidig; (*Mil.*) — *leave*, der Sonderurlaub.
compatibility [kəmpæti'biliti], *s.* die Verträglichkeit, Vereinbarkeit.
compatible [kəm'pætibl], *adj.* verträglich, vereinbar.
compatriot [kəm'peitriət], *s.* der Landsmann.
compel [kəm'pel], *v.a.* zwingen, nötigen.
compendium [kəm'pendjəm], *s.* das Kompendium, die kurze Schrift, die kurze Darstellung.
compensate ['kɔmpənseit], *v.a.* kompensieren, einem Ersatz leisten.
compensation [kɔmpən'seiʃən], *s.* der Ersatz, die Wiedergutmachung.
compensatory [kɔmpən'seitəri], *adj.* ausgleichend, Ersatz-.
compete [kəm'pi:t], *v.n.* wetteifern, konkurrieren.
competence, competency ['kɔmpitəns, -nsi], *s.* die Kompetenz; Zuständigkeit; Befähigung (*capability*); Tüchtigkeit (*ability*).
competent ['kɔmpitənt], *adj.* kompetent; zuständig; fähig (*capable*); tüchtig (*able*).
competition [kɔmpi'tiʃən], *s.* die Konkurrenz; die Mitbewerbung (*for job*).
competitive [kəm'petitiv], *adj.* Konkurrenz-, konkurrierend.
competitor [kəm'petitə], *s.* (*Comm.*) der Konkurrent; der Mitbewerber (*fellow applicant*), Teilnehmer (*sport*).
complacent [kəm'pleisənt], *adj.* selbstzufrieden, selbstgefällig.
complain [kəm'plein], *v.n.* sich beklagen (*of*, über, *Acc.*).
complaint [kəm'pleint], *s.* die Klage; Beschwerde (*grievance*); das Leiden (*illness*).
complement ['kɔmplimənt], *s.* die Ergänzung, Gesamtzahl. — [-'ment], *v.a.* ergänzen.
complementary [kɔmpli'mentəri], *adj.* Ergänzungs-, ergänzend.
complete [kəm'pli:t], *adj.* komplett; voll (*full up*); vollkommen (*perfect*). — *v.a.* vollenden (*end*); ergänzen (*make whole*).
completeness [kəm'pli:tnis], *s.* die Vollendung (*condition*); Ganzheit (*wholeness*).
completion [kəm'pli:ʃən], *s.* die Vollendung (*fulfilment*); die Beendigung (*ending*); der Abschluß.
complex ['kɔmpleks], *adj.* (*Maths.*) komplex; kompliziert (*complicated*). — *s.* der Komplex (*Archit.*, *Psych.*).
complexion [kəm'plekʃən], *s.* die Gesichtsfarbe; (*fig.*) das Aussehen.
complexity [kəm'pleksiti], *s.* die Kompliziertheit; die Schwierigkeit.
compliance [kəm'plaiəns], *s.* die Willfährigkeit, Einwilligung.
compliant [kəm'plaiənt], *adj.* willig, willfährig.
complicate ['kɔmplikeit], *v.a.* komplizieren, erschweren.
complication [kɔmpli'keiʃən], *s.* die Komplikation, die Erschwerung.
complicity [kəm'plisiti], *s.* (*Law*) die Mitschuld.
compliment ['kɔmplimənt], *s.* das Kompliment. — [-'ment], *v.n.* Komplimente machen.
complimentary [kɔmpli'mentəri], *adj.* lobend; — *ticket*, die Freikarte.
comply [kəm'plai], *v.n.* einwilligen (*with*, in, *Acc.*); sich halten (*an*, *Acc.*).
compose [kəm'pouz], *v.a.*, *v.n.* (*Mus.*) komponieren; beruhigen (*the mind*); (*Lit.*) verfassen; (*Typ.*) setzen.
composed [kəm'pouzd], *adj.* ruhig, gefaßt.
composer [kəm'pouzə], *s.* (*Mus.*) der Komponist.
composite ['kɔmpəzit], *adj.* zusammengesetzt.
composition [kɔmpə'ziʃən], *s.* (*Mus. etc.*) die Komposition; Beschaffenheit Zusammensetzung.
compositor [kəm'pɔzitə], *s.* (*Typ.*) der Schriftsetzer.
compost ['kɔmpɔst], *s.* (*Agr.*) der Dünger, Kompost.
composure [kəm'pouʒə], *s.* die Gelassenheit, die Gemütsruhe, die Fassung.
compound ['kɔmpaund], *s.* (*Chem.*) die Verbindung; die Zusammensetzung. — *adj.* zusammengesetzt; kompliziert; (*Comm.*) — *interest*, die Zinseszinsen. — [kəm'paund], *v.a.* (*Chem.*) mischen, zusammensetzen.
comprehend [kɔmpri'hend], *v.a.* verstehen (*understand*); einschließen (*include*).
comprehensible [kɔmpri'hensibl], *adj.* verständlich, begreiflich.
comprehension [kɔmpri'henʃən], *s.* das Verstehen, das Erfassen; (*Psych.*) — *tests*, die Verständnisprüfung.
comprehensive [kɔmpri'hensiv], *adj.* umfassend.
compress [kəm'pres], *v.a.* komprimieren; zusammendrücken (*press together*). — ['kɔmpres], *s.* (*Med.*) die Kompresse, der Umschlag (*poultice*).
compression [kəm'preʃən], *s.* der Druck; das Zusammendrücken (*pressing together*); die Kürzung (*abridgment*).
comprise [kəm'praiz], *v.a.* umfassen, einschließen.
compromise ['kɔmprəmaiz], *v.a.* kompromittieren. — *v.n.* einen Kompromiß schließen. — *s.* der *or* das Kompromiß.
compulsion [kəm'pʌlʃən], *s.* der Zwang.
compulsory [kəm'pʌlsəri], *adj.* zwingend; Zwangs-; — *subject*, das obligatorische Fach.
compunction [kəm'pʌnkʃən], *s.* die Gewissensbisse, *m. pl.*
computation [kɔmpju'teiʃən], *s.* die Berechnung.

compute [kəm'pju:t], *v.a., v.n.* berechnen.
computer [kəm'pju:tə], *s.* die automatische Rechenmaschine.
comrade ['kɔmrid], *s.* der Kamerad.
comradeship ['kɔmridʃip], *s.* die Kameradschaft.
con [kɔn], *v.a.* genau betrachten, studieren; (*ship*) steuern.
concave ['kɔnkeiv], *adj.* (*Phys.*) konkav.
conceal [kən'si:l], *v.a.* verbergen, verstecken.
concealment [kən'si:lmənt], *s.* die Verhehlung, die Verheimlichung (*act of concealing*); *place of* —, das Versteck.
concede [kən'si:d], *v.a.* zugestehen, einräumen.
conceit [kən'si:t], *s.* die Einbildung, der Eigendünkel (*presumption*); (*obs.*) die Idee; (*Lit.*) die (gedankliche) Spielerei.
conceited [kən'si:tid], *adj.* eingebildet, eitel.
conceivable [kən'si:vəbl], *adj.* denkbar; begreiflich (*understandable*).
conceive [kən'si:v], *v.a., v.n.* empfangen (*become pregnant*); begreifen (*understand*).
concentrate ['kɔnsəntreit], *v.a.* konzentrieren. — *v.n.* sich konzentrieren (*on*, auf, *Acc.*). — *s.* (*Chem.*) das Konzentrat.
concentrated ['kɔnsəntreitid], *adj.* konzentriert.
concentration [kɔnsən'treiʃən], *s.* die Konzentration.
concentric [kɔn'sentrik], *adj.* (*Geom.*) konzentrisch.
conception [kən'sepʃən], *s.* die Vorstellung, der Begriff (*idea*); die Empfängnis (*of a child*).
concern [kən'sə:n], *v.a.* (*affect*) betreffen, angehen; *be concerned with*, zu tun haben (mit, *Dat.*). — *s.* die Angelegenheit (*affair*); die Sorge (*care, business*); das Geschäft, das Unternehmen; *cause grave* —, tiefe Besorgnis erregen.
concerned [kən'sə:nd], *adj.* (*worried*) besorgt; (*involved*) interessiert (*in*, an, *Dat.*).
concerning [kən'sə:niŋ], *prep.* betreffend (*Acc.*), hinsichtlich (*Genit.*).
concert ['kɔnsət], *s.* (*Mus.*) das Konzert; Einverständnis.
concerted [kən'sə:tid], *adj.* gemeinsam, gemeinschaftlich.
concertina [kɔnsə'ti:nə], *s.* (*Mus.*) die Ziehharmonika.
concerto [kən'tʃə:tou], *s.* (*Mus.*) das Konzert.
concession [kən'seʃən], *s.* die Konzession (*licence*); das Zugeständnis.
conch [kɔŋk], *s.* die (große) Muschel.
conciliate [kən'silieit], *v.a.* versöhnen.
conciliation [kənsili'eiʃən], *s.* die Versöhnung.
conciliatory [kən'siliətəri], *adj.* versöhnlich.
concise [kən'sais], *adj.* kurz, knapp.
conciseness [kən'saisnis], *s.* die Kürze, Knappheit.
conclave ['kɔnkleiv], *s.* (*Eccl.*) das Konklave.
conclude [kən'klu:d], *v.a., v.n.* schließen, beenden (*speech etc.*); (*infer*) folgern (*from*, aus, *Dat.*); abschließen (*treaty*).
conclusion [kən'klu:ʒən], *s.* der Abschluß (*treaty*); die Folgerung (*inference*); der Beschluß (*decision*).
conclusive [kən'klu:siv], *adj.* entscheidend, überzeugend.
concoct [kən'kɔkt], *v.a.* zusammenbrauen, aushecken.
concoction [kən'kɔkʃən], *s.* das Gebräu, die Mischung.
concomitant [kɔn'kɔmitənt], *adj.* begleitend; Begleit-, Neben-. — *s.* der Begleitumstand.
concord ['kɔnkɔ:d], *s.* die Eintracht, die Harmonie.
concordance [kən'kɔ:dəns], *s.* die Übereinstimmung; die Konkordanz (*of Bible etc.*).
concordant [kən'kɔ:dənt], *adj.* in Eintracht (mit), übereinstimmend (mit) (*Dat.*).
concordat [kən'kɔ:dæt], *s.* (*Eccl., Pol.*) das Konkordat.
concourse ['kɔnkɔ:s], *s.* das Gedränge (*crowd*).
concrete ['kɔnkri:t], *s.* (*Build.*) der Beton; (*Log.*) das Konkrete. — *adj.* konkret, wirklich.
concur [kən'kə:], *v.n.* übereinstimmen (*with*, mit, *Dat.*).
concurrence [kən'kʌrəns], *s.* die Übereinstimmung.
concurrent [kən'kʌrənt], *adj.* gleichzeitig (*simultaneous*); mitwirkend (*accompanying*).
concussion [kən'kʌʃən], *s.* (*Med.*) die (Gehirn)Erschütterung.
condemn [kən'dem], *v.a.* verurteilen, verdammen.
condemnable [kən'demnəbl], *adj.* verwerflich, verdammenswert.
condemnation [kɔndem'neiʃən], *s.* die Verurteilung, die Verdammung.
condensate ['kɔndenseit], *s.* (*Chem.*) das Kondensat, das Ergebnis der Kondensation.
condensation [kɔnden'seiʃən], *s.* die Kondensation; Verdichtung.
condensed [kən'densd], *adj.* (*Chem.*) kondensiert; (*Chem., Engin.*) verdichtet; gekürzt (*abridged*).
condenser [kən'densə], *s.* (*Chem., Engin.*) der Kondensator; (*Elec.*) der Verstärker.
condescend [kɔndi'send], *v.n.* sich herablassen.
condescending [kɔndi'sendiŋ], *adj.* herablassend.
condescension [kɔndi'senʃən], *s.* die Herablassung.
condiment ['kɔndimənt], *s.* die Würze.
condition [kən'diʃən], *s.* der Zustand; Umstand; die Bedingung (*proviso*); der Gesundheitszustand (*physical state*).

conditional [kən'diʃənəl], *adj.* bedingt; unter der Bedingung; konditionell.
conditioned [kən'diʃənd], *adj.* vorbereitet (*for action*); geartet.
condole [kən'doul], *v.n.* Beileid ausdrücken (*with*, *Dat.*), kondolieren (*with*, *Dat.*).
condolence [kən'douləns], *s.* das Beileid.
condone [kən'doun], *v.a.* verzeihen.
conducive [kən'dju:siv], *adj.* förderlich, dienlich, nützlich (*to*, *Dat.*).
conduct [kən'dʌkt], *v.a.* leiten, führen; (*Phys.*) ein Leiter sein; (*Mus.*) dirigieren. — *v.r.* sich aufführen, sich benehmen. — ['kɔndʌkt], *s.* das Benehmen (*behaviour*); — *of a war*, die Kriegsführung.
conductive [kən'dʌktiv], *adj.* (*Elec.*) leitend.
conductor [kən'dʌktə], *s.* der Leiter, Führer (*leader*); (*Phys.*, *Elec.*) der Leiter; (*Am.*) der Schaffner (*train*); (*Mus.*) der Dirigent.
conduit ['kʌn-, 'kɔndit], *s.* die Leitung, die Röhre.
cone [koun], *s.* (*Geom.*) der Kegel; (*Bot.*) der Zapfen.
coney ['kouni], *s.* (*Zool.*) das Kaninchen.
confection [kən'fekʃən], *s.* das Konfekt.
confectioner [kən'fekʃənə], *s.* der Zuckerbäcker, Konditor.
confectionery [kən'fekʃənəri], *s.* die Zuckerwaren, *f.pl.* (*sweets*); Konditoreiwaren, *f.pl.* (*cakes*); die Zuckerbäckerei (*sweet shop*); die Konditorei.
confederacy [kən'fedərəsi], *s.* der Bund (*of states*); das Bündnis (*treaty*).
confederate [kən'fedərit], *s.* der Bundesgenosse, der Verbündete. — *adj.* verbündet; — *state*, der Bundesstaat. — [-reit], *v.n.* sich verbünden (*with*, mit, *Dat.*).
confederation [kənfedə'reiʃən], *s.* das Bündnis (*treaty*); der Bund (*state*).
confer [kən'fə:], *v.a.* verleihen (*degree*, *title*). — *v.n.* beraten (*with*, mit, *Dat.*), unterhandeln (*negotiate*).
conference ['kɔnfərəns], *s.* die Konferenz, die Besprechung, die Beratung, Tagung.
confess [kən'fes], *v.a.* bekennen; beichten (*sin*); zugestehen (*acknowledge*).
confession [kən'feʃən], *s.* das Bekenntnis; die Beichte (*sin*); das Glaubensbekenntnis (*creed*).
confessor [kən'fesə], *s.* der Bekenner; *father* —, der Beichtvater.
confidant [kɔnfi'dænt], *s.* der Vertraute.
confide [kən'faid], *v.a.* anvertrauen. — *v.n.* vertrauen (*Dat.*).
confidence ['kɔnfidəns], *s.* das Vertrauen; die Zuversicht; — *trick*, die Bauernfängerei, der Schwindel.
confident ['kɔnfidənt], *adj.* zuversichtlich; dreist (*bold*).
confidential [kɔnfi'denʃəl], *adj.* vertraulich, privat.
confine [kən'fain], *v.a.* einschränken (*hem in*); einsperren; *be —d to bed*, bettlägerig sein.
confinement [kən'fainmənt], *s.* die Einschränkung (*limitation*); das Wochenbett, die Niederkunft (*childbirth*).
confines ['kɔnfainz], *s. pl.* die Grenzen, *f. pl.* (*physical*); die Einschränkungen, *f. pl.* (*limitations*).
confirm [kən'fə:m], *v.a.* bestätigen, bekräftigen (*corroborate*); (*Eccl.*) firmen, konfirmieren.
confirmation [kɔnfə'meiʃən], *s.* die Bestätigung (*corroboration*); (*Eccl.*) die Firmung, Konfirmation.
confirmed [kən'fə:md], *adj.* eingefleischt; unverbesserlich.
confiscate ['kɔnfiskeit], *v.a.* konfiszieren, einziehen, beschlagnahmen.
confiscation [kɔnfis'keiʃən], *s.* die Konfiszierung, die Einziehung, die Beschlagnahme (*customs etc.*).
conflagration [kɔnflə'greiʃən], *s.* der (große) Brand.
conflict ['kɔnflikt], *s.* der Konflikt, der Zusammenstoß. — [kən'flikt], *v.n.* in Konflikt geraten; in Widerspruch stehen.
confluence ['kɔnfluəns], *s.* (*Geog.*) der Zusammenfluß.
confluent ['kɔnfluənt], *adj.* zusammenfließend. — *s.* der Nebenfluß (*tributary*).
conform [kən'fɔ:m], *v.n.* sich anpassen.
conformation [kɔnfɔ:'meiʃən], *s.* die Anpassung.
conformist [kən'fɔ:mist], *adj.* fügsam. — *s.* das Mitglied der Staatskirche.
conformity [kən'fɔ:miti], *s.* die Gleichförmigkeit; *in* — *with*, gerade so; gemäß (*Dat.*); die Gleichheit (*equality*.)
confound [kən'faund], *v.a.* verwirren (*confuse*); vernichten (*overthrow*).
confounded [kən'faundid], *adj.* verdammt, verwünscht.
confront [kən'frʌnt], *v.a.* (*Law*) — *s.o. with*, gegenüberstellen (*put in front of*); gegenüberstehen (*stand in front of*).
confrontation [kɔnfrʌn'teiʃən], *s.* die Gegenüberstellung.
confuse [kən'fju:z], *v.a.* verwirren (*muddle*); bestürzen (*perplex*); verwechseln (*mix up*).
confusion [kən'fju:ʒən], *s.* die Verwirrung, das Durcheinander (*muddle*); die Bestürzung (*astonishment*); die Verlegenheit (*dilemma*).
confutation [kɔnfju:'teiʃən], *s.* die Widerlegung.
confute [kən'fju:t], *v.a.* widerlegen.
congeal [kən'dʒi:l], *v.n.* gefrieren (*freeze*); gerinnen.
congenial [kən'dʒi:niəl], *adj.* geistesverwandt, geistig ebenbürtig, sympathisch.
congeniality [kəndʒi:ni'æliti], *s.* die Geistesverwandtschaft.
conger ['kɔŋgə], *s.* (*Zool.*) der Meeraal.

congest [kən'dʒest], *v.a.* anhäufen, überfüllen.
congestion [kən'dʒestʃən], *s.* die Überfüllung; Stauung; die Übervölkerung (*overpopulation*); (*Med.*) der Blutandrang.
conglomerate [kɔn'glɔməreit], *v.n.* sich zusammenballen. — [–rit], *s.* das Konglomerat, die Ballung.
conglomeration [kɔnglɔmə'reiʃən], *s.* die Zusammenhäufung, Zusammenballung.
Congolese [kɔŋgo'li:z], *adj.* kongolesisch. — *s.* der Kongolese.
congratulate [kən'grætjuleit], *v.n.* gratulieren (*on*, zu, *Dat.*).
congratulation [kəngrætju'leiʃən], *s.* (*usually pl.*) die Glückwünsche.
congratulatory [kən'grætjuleitəri], *adj.* Glückwunsch-.
congregate ['kɔŋgrigeit], *v.a.* versammeln. — *v.n.* sich versammeln, sich scharen (*round*, um, *Acc.*).
congregation [kɔŋgri'geiʃən], *s.* die Versammlung, die Schar; (*Eccl.*) die Gemeinde.
congregational [kɔŋgri'geiʃənəl], *adj.* (*Eccl.*) Gemeinde-; *Congregational Church*, unabhängige Gemeindekirche.
congress ['kɔŋgres], *s.* der Kongreß.
congruence ['kɔŋgruəns], *s.* (*Geom.*) die Kongruenz.
congruent ['kɔŋgruənt], *adj.* (*Geom.*) kongruent.
congruity [kɔŋ'gru:iti], *s.* (*Geom.*) die Übereinstimmung; die Kongruenz.
congruous ['kɔŋgruəs], *adj.* übereinstimmend, angemessen.
conic(al) ['kɔnik(əl)], *adj.* konisch, kegelförmig; (*Geom.*) — *section*, der Kegelschnitt.
conifer ['kɔnifə], *s.* (*Bot.*) der Nadelbaum.
conjecture [kən'dʒəktʃə], *s.* die Mutmaßung, die Annahme. — *v.a.* mutmaßen, annehmen.
conjoin [kɔn'dʒɔin], *v.a.* (*Law*) verbinden.
conjugal ['kɔndʒugəl], *adj.* ehelich.
conjugate ['kɔndʒugeit], *v.a.* (*Gram.*) konjugieren.
conjugation [kɔndʒu'geiʃən], *s.* (*Gram.*) die Konjugation.
conjunction [kən'dʒʌŋkʃən], *s.* (*Gram.*) das Bindewort.
conjunctive [kən'dʒʌnktiv], *adj.* verbindend; (*Gram.*) — *mood*, der Konjunktiv.
conjunctivitis [kən'dʒʌŋktivaitis], *s.* (*Med.*) die Bindehautentzündung.
conjuncture [kən'dʒʌŋktʃə], *s.* der Wendepunkt; die Krise (*of events*).
conjure ['kʌŋdʒə], *v.a.* beschwören; — *up*, heraufbeschwören. — *v.n.* zaubern.
conjurer ['kʌndʒərə], *s.* der Zauberer.
connect [kə'nekt], *v.a.* verbinden, in Zusammenhang bringen.
connection, connexion [kə'nekʃən], *s.* die Verbindung, der Zusammenhang.
connivance [kə'naivəns], *s.* die Nachsicht, das Gewährenlassen.
connive [kə'naiv], *v.n.* nachsichtig sein (*at*, bei, *Dat.*); gewähren lassen.
connoisseur [kɔne'sə:], *s.* der Kenner.
connubial [kə'nju:biəl], *adj.* ehelich.
conquer ['kɔŋkə], *v.a.* besiegen (*foe*); erobern (*place*).
conqueror ['kɔŋkərə], *s.* der Eroberer, der Sieger.
conquest ['kɔŋkwest], *s.* der Sieg, die Eroberung.
consanguinity [kɔnsæŋ'gwiniti], *s.* die Blutsverwandtschaft.
conscience ['kɔnʃəns], *s.* das Gewissen; *in all* — wahrhaftig.
conscientious [kɔnʃi'enʃəs], *adj.* gewissenhaft.
conscientiousness [kɔnʃi'enʃəsnis], *s.* die Gewissenhaftigkeit.
conscious ['kɔnʃəs], *adj.* bewußt (*Genit*).
consciousness ['kɔnʃəsnis], *s.* das Bewußtsein.
conscript [kən'skript], *v.a.* (*Mil.*) einziehen, einberufen. — ['kɔnskript], *s.* (*Mil.*) der Rekrut, der Dienstpflichtige.
conscription [kən'skripʃən], *s.* die allgemeine Wehrpflicht.
consecrate ['kɔnsikreit], *v.a.* weihen, widmen.
consecrated ['kɔnsikreitid], *adj.* geweiht (*Dat.*).
consecration [kɔnsi'kreiʃən], *s.* die Weihe, Einweihung (*of church*); die Weihung.
consecutive [kən'sekjutiv], *adj.* aufeinanderfolgend, fortlaufend.
consecutiveness [kən'sekjutivnis], *s.* die Aufeinanderfolge.
consent [kən'sent], *v.n.* zustimmen, beistimmen (*to*, *Dat.*). — *s.* die Zustimmung, die Einwilligung.
consequence ['kɔnsikwəns], *s.* die Konsequenz; (*Log.*) Folgerung; die Folge; die Wichtigkeit (*importance*).
consequent ['kɔnsikwənt], *adj.* folgend, nachfolgend.
consequential [kɔnsi'kwenʃəl], *adj.* wichtigtuend, anmaßend; (*Log.*) folgerichtig.
consequently ['kɔnsikwəntli], *adv.* folglich, infolgedessen.
conservatism [kən'sə:vətizm], *s.* (*Pol.*) der Konservatismus; die konservative Denkweise.
conservative [kən'sə:vətiv], *adj.* (*Pol.*) konservativ.
conservatoire [kən'sə:vətwɑ:], *s.* (*Mus.*) das Konservatorium, die Musikhochschule.
conservatory [kən'sə:vətəri], *s.* (*Bot.*) das Gewächshaus.
conserve [kən'sə:v], *v.a.* konservieren, erhalten, einmachen. — *s.* (*fruit*) das Eingemachte.
consider [kən'sidə], *v.a.* betrachten, in Betracht ziehen (*think over, look at*); berücksichtigen (*have regard to*); nachdenken über (*Acc.*) (*ponder*).

considerable [kən'sidərəbl], *adj.* beträchtlich, ansehnlich.
considerate [kən'sidərit], *adj.* rücksichtsvoll (*thoughtful*).
consideration [kənsidə'reiʃən], *s.* die Betrachtung (*contemplation*); die Rücksicht (*regard*) (*for*, auf, *Acc.*); die Entschädigung (*compensation*); die Belohnung (*reward*).
considering [kən'sidəriŋ], *prep.* in Anbetracht (*Genit.*).
consign [kən'sain], *v.a.* überliefern (*hand over*); übersenden (*remit*).
consignee [kɔnsai'ni:], *s.* (*Comm.*) der Empfänger, der Adressat (*recipient*).
consigner [kən'sainə], *s.* der Absender (*of goods*).
consignment [kən'sainmənt], *s.* die Sendung (*of goods*).
consist [kən'sist], *v.n.* bestehen (*of*, aus, *Dat.*).
consistency [kən'sistənsi], *s.* die Festigkeit, Dichtigkeit; (*Chem.*) die Konsistenz.
consistent [kən'sistənt], *adj.* konsequent; — *with*, übereinstimmend, gemäß (*Dat.*); (*Chem.*) dicht, fest.
consistory [kən'sistəri], *s.* (*Eccl.*) das Konsistorium.
consolable [kən'souləbl], *adj.* tröstlich, zu trösten.
consolation [kɔnso'leiʃən], *s.* der Trost; *draw* —, Trost schöpfen.
console (1) [kən'soul], *v.a.* trösten.
console (2) ['kɔnsoul], *s.* (*Archit.*) die Konsole.
consolidate [kən'sɔlideit], *v.a.* befestigen, konsolidieren. — *v.n.* fest werden.
consolidation [kənsɔli'deiʃən], *s.* die Befestigung; Festigung, Bestärkung (*confirmation*).
consonance ['kɔnsənəns], *s.* (*Phonet.*) die Konsonanz; der Einklang, die Harmonie.
consonant ['kɔnsənənt], *adj.* in Einklang (*with*, mit, *Dat.*). — *s.* der Konsonant.
consort ['kɔnsɔ:t], *s.* der Gemahl, Gatte; die Gemahlin, die Gattin. — [kən'sɔ:t], *v.n.* verkehren (*with*, mit, *Dat.*).
conspicuous [kən'spikjuəs], *adj.* auffallend, deutlich sichtbar, hervorragend.
conspiracy [kən'spirəsi], *s.* die Verschwörung.
conspirator [kən'spirətə], *s.* der Verschwörer.
conspire [kən'spaiə], *v.n.* sich verschwören.
constable ['kʌnstəbl], *s.* der Polizist, der Schutzmann.
Constance ['kɔnstəns]. Konstanze *f.* (*name*); Konstanz (*town*); *Lake* —, der Bodensee.
constancy ['kɔnstənsi], *s.* die Beständigkeit, Treue.
constant ['kɔnstənt], *adj.* (*Chem.*) konstant; treu, beständig.
constellation [kɔnste'leiʃən], *s.* die Konstellation; das Sternbild.
consternation [kɔnstə'neiʃən], *s.* die Bestürzung.
constipation [kɔnsti'peiʃən], *s.* die Verstopfung.
constituency [kən'stitjuənsi], *s.* der Wahlkreis (*electoral district*); die Wählerschaft (*voters*).
constituent [kən'stitjuənt], *adj.* wesentlich. — *s.* der Bestandteil (*component*); (*Pol.*) der Wähler.
constitute ['kɔnstitju:t], *v.a.* ausmachen (*make up*); bilden (*form*); festsetzen (*establish*); (*Pol.*) errichten (*set up*).
constitution [kɔnsti'tju:ʃən], *s.* die Konstitution (*physique*); die Errichtung (*establishment*); die Beschaffenheit, Natur (*nature*); (*Pol.*) die Verfassung.
constitutional [kɔnsti'tju:ʃənəl], *adj.* körperlich bedingt; (*Pol.*) verfassungsmäßig.
constrain [kən'strein], *v.a.* nötigen, zwingen.
constraint [kən'streint], *s.* der Zwang.
constrict [kən'strikt], *v.a.* zusammenziehen.
constriction [kən'strikʃən], *s.* die Zusammenziehung, Beengtheit.
construct [kən'strʌkt], *v.a.* errichten, bauen, konstruieren.
construction [kən'strʌkʃən], *s.* die Errichtung, der Bau, die Konstruktion.
constructive [kən'strʌktiv], *adj.* (*Engin.*) konstruktiv; behilflich (*positive*).
constructor [kən'strʌktə], *s.* der Konstrukteur, der Erbauer (*builder*).
construe [kən'stru:], *v.a.* konstruieren, deuten (*interpret*).
consul ['kɔnsəl], *s.* der Konsul; — -*general*, der Generalkonsul.
consular ['kɔnsjulə], *adj.* konsularisch.
consulate ['kɔnsjulit], *s.* das Konsulat; — -*general*, das Generalkonsulat.
consult [kən'sʌlt], *v.a.* konsultieren, zu Rate ziehen; nachschlagen (*a book*). — *v.n.* sich beraten (*with*, mit, *Dat.*); (*Comm.*) als Berater hinzuziehen.
consultant [kən'sʌltənt], *s.* (*Med.*) der Facharzt; der Berater.
consultation [kɔnsəl'teiʃən], *s.* die Beratung (*advice*); die Besprechung (*discussion*); (*Med.*, *Engin.*) die Konsultation.
consume [kən'sju:m], *v.a.* verzehren (*eat up*); verbrauchen (*use up*).
consumer [kən'sju:mə], *s.* der Verbraucher; (*Comm.*) der Konsument.
consummate [kən'sʌmit], *adj.* vollendet. — ['kɔnsəmeit], *v.a.* vollenden, vollziehen.
consummation [kɔnsə'meiʃən], *s.* die Vollziehung, Vollendung.
consumption [kən'sʌmpʃən], *s.* (*Comm.*) der Verbrauch; (*Med.*) die Schwindsucht.
consumptive [kən'sʌmptiv], *adj.* (*Med.*) schwindsüchtig.

contact ['kɔntækt], *v.a.* berühren (*touch*); in Verbindung treten (mit) (*get into touch* (*with*)). — *s.* (*Elec.*) der Kontakt; die Berührung (*touch*); die Verbindung (*connexion*).
contagion [kən'teidʒən], *s.* (*Med.*) die Ansteckung.
contagious[kən'teidʒəs],*adj.*ansteckend.
contain [kən'tein], *v.a.* enthalten (*hold*); zurückhalten (*restrain*).
container [kən'teinə], *s.* der Behälter.
contaminate [kən'tæmineit], *v.a.* verunreinigen; vergiften.
contemplate ['kɔntəmpleit], *v.a.* betrachten (*consider*). — *v.n.* nachdenken (*ponder*).
contemplation [kɔntəm'pleiʃən], *s.* die Betrachtung (*consideration*); das Sinnen (*pondering*).
contemplative [kən'templətiv], *adj.* nachdenklich, kontemplativ.
contemporaneous [kəntempə'reiniəs], *adj.* gleichzeitig.
contemporary [kən'tempərəri], *adj.* zeitgenössich. — *s.* der Zeitgenosse.
contempt [kən'tempt], *s.* die Verachtung; — *of court*, die Gerichtsbeleidigung.
contemptible [kən'temptibl], *adj.* verächtlich, verachtungswert.
contemptibleness [kən'temptiblnis], *s.* die Verächtlichkeit.
contemptuous [kən'temptjuəs], *adj.* höhnisch, verachtungsvoll.
contemptuousness [kən'temptjuəsnis], *s.* der Hohn, der verachtungsvolle Ton, der Hochmut.
contend [kən'tend], *v.n.* streiten; bestreiten, behaupten.
content [kən'tent], *adj.* zufrieden. — *v.a.* zufriedenstellen. — ['kɔntent], *s.* (*often pl.*) der Inhalt.
contented [kən'tentid], *adj.* zufrieden.
contentedness, contentment [kən-'tentidnis, kən'tentmənt], *s.* die Zufriedenheit.
contention [kən'tenʃən], *s.* der Streit, die Behauptung.
contentious [kən'tenʃəs], *adj.* streitsüchtig (*person*); strittig (*question*).
contest ['kɔntest], *s.* der Streit, Wettstreit, Wettkampf. — [kən'test], *v.a.* um etwas streiten, bestreiten.
context ['kɔntekst], *s.* der Zusammenhang.
contexture [kən'tekstʃə], *s.* (*Engin.*) der Bau, die Zusammensetzung; das Gewebe (*textile*).
contiguity [kɔnti'gju:iti], *s.* die Berührung; die Nachbarschaft.
contiguous [kən'tigjuəs], *adj.* anstossend, anliegend.
continence ['kɔntinəns], *s.* die Mäßigung (*moderation*); die Enthaltsamkeit (*abstemiousness*).
continent (1) ['kɔntinənt], *adj.* enthaltsam, mässig.
continent (2) ['kɔntinənt], *s.* das Festland, der Kontinent.
contingency [kən'tindʒənsi], *s.* der Zufall; die Möglichkeit (*possibility*).
contingent [kən'tindʒənt], *s.* der Beitrag, das Kontingent (*share*). — *adj.* möglich.
continual [kən'tinjuəl], *adj.* fortwährend, beständig.
continuance [kən'tinjuəns], *s.* die Fortdauer.
continuation [kəntinju'eiʃən], *s.* die Fortsetzung.
continue [kən'tinju:], *v.a.* fortsetzen (*go on with*); verlängern (*prolong*). — *v.n.* weitergehen, weiterführen (*of story*).
continuity [kɔnti'nju:iti], *s.* der Zusammenhang, die ununterbrochene Folge, Kontinuität (*Film*); — *girl*, die Drehbuchsekretärin.
continuous [kən'tinjuəs], *adj.* zusammenhängend, ununterbrochen, andauernd.
contort [kən'tɔ:t], *v.a.* verdrehen.
contortion [kən'tɔ:ʃən], *s.* die Verdrehung, Verkrümmung, Verzerrung.
contortionist [kən'tɔ:ʃənist], *s.* der Schlangenmensch.
contour ['kɔntuə], *s.* die Kontur, der Umriß.
contraband ['kɔntrəbænd], *adj.* Schmuggel-, geschmuggelt. — *s.* die Bannware, Schmuggelware.
contract [kən'trækt], *v.a.* zusammenziehen (*pull together*); verengen (*narrow down*); verkürzen (*shorten*); sich eine Krankheit zuziehen (— *a disease*); Schulden machen (— *debts*). — *v.n.* sich zusammenziehen, kürzer werden; einen Kontrakt abschließen (*come to terms*). — ['kɔntrækt], *s.* der Vertrag (*pact*); (*Comm.*) der Kontrakt.
contraction [kən'trækʃən], *s.* die Zusammenziehung; (*Phonet.*) die Kürzung.
contractor [kən'træktə], *s.* (*Comm.*) der Kontrahent; der Lieferant (*supplier*); *building* —, der Bauunternehmer.
contradict [kɔntrə'dikt], *v.n.* widersprechen (*Dat.*).
contradiction [kɔntrə'dikʃən], *s.* der Widerspruch.
contradictory [kɔntrə'diktəri], *adj.* in Widerspruch stehend, widersprechend.
contrarily ['kɔntrərili], *adv.* im Gegensatz dazu, hingegen, dagegen.
contrary ['kɔntrəri], *adj.* entgegengesetzt, *on the* —, im Gegenteil; [kən'trɛəri], widersprechend.
contrast [kən'trɑ:st], *v.a.* einander entgegenstellen, gegenüberstellen. — *v.n.* einen Gegensatz darstellen *or* bilden. — ['kɔntrɑ:st], *s.* der Kontrast (*colours*); der Gegensatz.
contravene [kɔntrə'vi:n], *v.a.* übertreten, zuwiderhandeln (*Dat.*).
contribute [kən'tribju:t], *v.a.* beitragen; beisteuern (*money, energy*).
contribution [kɔntri'bju:ʃən], *s.* der Beitrag.

contributive, contributory [kən'tribjutiv, kən'tribjutəri], *adj.* beitragend, Beitrags-.
contributor [kən'tribjutə], *s.* der Beitragende, der Spender (*of money*); der Mitarbeiter (*journalist etc.*).
contrite ['kɔntrait], *adj.* zerknirscht, reuevoll.
contrition [kən'triʃən], *s.* die Zerknirschung, die Reue.
contrivance [kən'traivəns], *s.* die Vorrichtung, die Erfindung.
contrive [kən'traiv], *v.a.* ausdenken, erfinden; fertigbringen (*accomplish*).
control [kən'troul], *v.a.* kontrollieren (*check*); die Leitung haben (*have command of*); die Aufsicht führen (*supervise*). — *s.* die Kontrolle; die Aufsicht; die Leitung; (*pl.*) (*Motor.*) die Steuerung; (*Aviat.*) das Leitwerk.
controller [kən'troulə], *s.* der Aufseher (*supervisor*); der Direktor (*of corporation*); der Revisor (*examiner, auditor*).
controversial [kɔntro'və:ʃəl], *adj.* umstritten, strittig.
controversy ['kɔntrovə:si], *s.* die Kontroverse, die Streitfrage.
controvert ['kɔntrovə:t], *v.a.* bestreiten, widersprechen (*Dat.*).
contumacious [kɔntju'meiʃəs], *adj.* widerspenstig, halsstarrig.
contumacy ['kɔntjuməsi], *s.* die Widerspenstigkeit (*obstreperousness*); der Ungehorsam (*disobedience*).
contumelious [kɔntju'mi:liəs], *adj.* frech, unverschämt (*insolent*).
contuse [kən'tju:z], *v.a.* quetschen.
conundrum [kə'nʌndrəm], *s.* das Scherzrätsel.
convalescence [kɔnvə'lesəns], *s.* die Gesundung, die Genesung.
convalescent [kɔnvə'lesənt], *adj.* genesend. — *s.* der Genesende, der Rekonvaleszent.
convene [kən'vi:n], *v.a.* zusammenrufen, versammeln. — *v.n.* zusammentreten, sich versammeln.
convenience [kən'vi:niəns], *s.* die Bequemlichkeit; *at your early* —, umgehend; *public* —, öffentliche Bedürfnisanstalt.
convenient [kən'vi:niənt], *adj.* bequem, gelegen; passend (*time*).
convent ['kɔnvənt], *s.* das (Nonnen)-Kloster.
convention [kən'venʃən], *s.* die Konvention, der Kongress (*meeting*); der Vertrag (*treaty*); die Sitte (*tradition, custom*).
conventional [kən'venʃənəl], *adj.* herkömmlich, traditionell.
conventual [kən'ventjuəl], *adj.* klösterlich.
conversation [kɔnvə'seiʃən], *s.* die Konversation, Unterhaltung; das Gespräch.
conversational [kɔnvə'seiʃənəl], *adj.* gesprächig, umgangssprachlich.
converse (1) [kən'və:s], *v.n.* sich unterhalten (*with*, mit, *Dat.*).
converse (2) ['kɔnvə:s], *adj.* umgekehrt.
conversely ['kɔnvə:sli], *adv.* hingegen, dagegen.
conversion [kən'və:ʃən], *s.* die Umkehrung (*reversal*); (*Rel.*) die Bekehrung; (*Comm.*) die Umwechslung.
convert ['kɔnvə:t], *s.* (*Rel.*) der Bekehrte, die Bekehrte; der Konvertit. — [kən'və:t], *v.a.* (*Rel.*) bekehren; (*Comm.*) umwechseln.
converter [kən'və:tə], *s.* (*Rel.*) der Bekehrer; (*Metall., Elec.*) der Umformer.
convertible [kən'və:tibl], *adj.* umwandelbar. — *s.* (*Motor.*) der *or* das Konvertible.
convex ['kɔnveks], *adj.* (*Phys.*) konvex.
convey [kən'vei], *v.a.* transportieren; führen (*bear, carry*); mitteilen (*impart*).
conveyance [kən'veiəns], *s.* die Beförderung (*transport*); das Fuhrwerk (*vehicle*); die Übertragung; (*Law*) das Übertragungsdokument.
conveyancing [kən'veiənsiŋ], *s.* (*Law*) die legale *or* rechtliche Übertragung.
convict ['kɔnvikt], *s.* der Sträfling. — [kən'vikt], *v.a.* für schuldig erklären.
conviction [kən'vikʃən], *s.* die Überzeugung; (*Law*) die Überführung, die Schuldigsprechung.
convince [kən'vins], *v.a.* überzeugen.
convivial [kən'viviəl], *adj.* gesellig (*sociable*).
conviviality [kənvivi'æliti], *s.* die Geselligkeit.
convocation [kɔnvə'keiʃən], *s.* die Zusammenberufung, Festversammlung; (*Eccl.*) die Synode.
convoke [kən'vouk], *v.a.* zusammenberufen.
convolvulus [kən'vɔlvjuləs], *s.* (*Bot.*) die Winde.
convoy ['kɔnvɔi], *s.* das Geleit, die Bedeckung; (*Mil.*) der Begleitzug. — [kɔn'vɔi], *v.a.* geleiten; (*Mil.*) im Geleitzug mitführen.
convulse [kən'vʌls], *v.a.* erschüttern.
convulsion [kən'vʌlʃən], *s.* der Krampf, die Zuckung.
convulsive [kən'vʌlsiv], *adj.* krampfhaft, zuckend.
coo [ku:], *v.n.* girren (*of birds*); *bill and* —, schnäbeln.
cook [kuk], *v.a., v.n.* kochen; (*coll.*) — *the books*, die Bücher(Bilanz)fälschen *or* frisieren. — *s.* der Koch, die Köchin; *too many cooks* (*spoil the broth*), zu viele Köche (verderben den Brei).
cookery ['kukəri], *s.* die Kochkunst; — *school*, die Kochschule.
cool [ku:l], *adj.* kühl (*climate*); kaltblütig (*coldblooded*); unverschämt (*brazen*). — *s.* die Kühle. — *v.a.* abkühlen; (*fig.*) besänftigen. — *v.n.* sich abkühlen.
cooler ['ku:lə], *s.* (*Chem.*) das Kühlfaß; (*coll.*) das Gefängnis; (*sl.*) das Kittchen.

coop [ku:p], *s.* die Kufe; das Faß; *hen* —, der Hühnerkorb. — *v.a.* — *up*, einsperren.
cooper ['ku:pə], *s.* der Böttcher, der Faßbinder.
cooperate [kou'ɔpəreit], *v.n.* zusammenarbeiten; mitarbeiten, mitwirken.
cooperation [kouɔpə'reiʃən], *s.* die Zusammenarbeit, die Mitarbeit.
cooperative [kou'ɔpərətiv], *adj.* willig; mitwirkend. — *s.* die Konsumgenossenschaft, der Konsum.
coordinate [kou'ɔ:dineit], *v.a.* koordinieren, beiordnen. — [-nit], *adj.* (*Gram.*) koordiniert.
coordination [kouɔ:di'neiʃən], *s.* die Koordinierung.
coot [ku:t], *s.* (*Orn.*) das Wasserhuhn.
copartnership [kou'pɑ:tnəʃip], *s.* die Teilhaberschaft; die Partnerschaft in der Industrie.
cope (1) [koup], *s.* (*Eccl.*) das Pluviale, der Priesterrock; (*Build.*) die Decke.
cope (2) [koup], *v.n.* — *with s.th.*, mit etwas fertig werden, es schaffen.
coping ['koupiŋ], *s.* (*Build.*) die Kappe; — *-stone* or *copestone*, der Firststein, Schlußstein, Kappstein.
copious ['koupiəs], *adj.* reichlich; wortreich (*style*).
copiousness ['koupiəsnis], *s.* die Reichhaltigkeit, Fülle.
copper ['kɔpə], *s.* (*Metall.*) das Kupfer; (*sl.*) der Polizist; (*coll.*) der Penny, das Pennystück. — *adj.* kupfern.
copperplate ['kɔpəpleit], *s.* der Kupferstich (*etching*); (*Typ.*) die Kupferplatte.
coppery ['kɔpəri], *adj.* Kupfer-, kupfern, kupferfarben (*colour*).
coppice, copse ['kɔpis, kɔps], *s.* das Unterholz, das Dickicht.
copulate ['kɔpjuleit], *v.n.* sich paaren, begatten.
copulation [kɔpju'leiʃən], *s.* die Paarung; der Beischlaf (*human*).
copy ['kɔpi], *v.a.* kopieren, abschreiben (*write*); imitieren, nachahmen (*imitate*). — *s.* die Kopie; *carbon* —, die Durchschrift; Abschrift; die Nachahmung (*imitation*); die Fälschung (*forgery*).
copybook ['kɔpibuk], *s.* das Heft.
copyist ['kɔpiist], *s.* der Kopist.
coquet, coquette (1) [kɔ'ket], *v.n.* kokettieren.
coquette (2) [kɔ'ket], *s.* die Kokette.
coquettish [kɔ'ketiʃ], *adj.* kokett.
coral ['kɔrəl], *s.* die Koralle. — *adj.* Korallen-.
cord [kɔ:d], *s.* die Schnur, der Strick (*rope*); (*Am.*) der Bindfaden (*string*); die Klafter (*wood measure*); der Kordstoff (*textile*); *vocal* —, das Stimmband.
cordage ['kɔ:didʒ], *s.* (*Naut.*) das Tauwerk.
cordial (1) ['kɔ:diəl], *adj.* herzlich.
cordial (2) ['kɔ:diəl], *s.* der Fruchtsaft (konzentriert), Magenlikör.
cordiality [kɔ:di'æliti], *s.* die Herzlichkeit.
corduroy ['kɔ:djurɔi], *s.* der Kordsamt.
core [kɔ:], *s.* der Kern; das Innere (*innermost part*).
cork [kɔ:k], *s.* der Kork, der Korken. — *v.a.* verkorken.
corkscrew ['kɔ:kskru:], *s.* der Korkzieher.
cormorant ['kɔ:mərənt], *s.* (*Orn.*) der Kormoran, die Scharbe.
corn (1) [kɔ:n], *s.* das Korn, das Getreide (*wheat etc.*); (*Am.*) *sweet* —, der Mais.
corn (2) [kɔ:n], *s.* das Hühnerauge (*on foot*).
corned [kɔ:nd], *adj.* eingesalzt; — *beef*, das Pökelrindfleisch.
cornea ['kɔ:niə], *s.* (*Anat.*) die Hornhaut.
cornel-tree ['kɔ:nəltri:], *s.* (*Bot.*) der Kornelkirschbaum.
cornelian [kɔ:'ni:liən], *s.* (*Geol.*) der Karneol.
corner ['kɔ:nə], *s.* die Ecke; (*Footb.*) der Eckstoß. — *v.a.* in eine Ecke treiben; in die Enge treiben (*force*).
cornered ['kɔ:nəd], *adj.* eckig (*angular*); in die Enge getrieben, gefangen (*caught*).
cornet ['kɔ:nit], *s.* (*Mus.*) die Zinke, das Flügelhorn; (*Mil.*) der Kornett, der Fähnrich.
cornflower ['kɔ:nflauə], *s.* (*Bot.*) die Kornblume.
cornice ['kɔ:nis], *s.* (*Archit.*) das Gesims.
cornucopia [kɔ:nju'koupjə], *s.* das Füllhorn.
corollary [kə'rɔləri], *s.* (*Log.*) der Folgesatz; die Folgeerscheinung (*consequence*).
corona [kə'rounə], *s.* (*Astron.*) der Hof, Lichtkranz.
coronation [kɔrə'neiʃən], *s.* die Krönung.
coroner ['kɔrənə], *s.* der Leichenbeschauer.
coronet ['kɔrənet], *s.* die Adelskrone.
corporal (1) ['kɔ:pərəl], *s.* (*Mil.*) der Korporal, der Unteroffizier, Obergefreite.
corporal (2) ['kɔ:pərəl], *adj.* körperlich; — *punishment*, die Züchtigung.
corporate ['kɔ:pərit], *adj.* (*Law, Comm.*) als Körperschaft; gemeinschaftlich, einheitlich (*as a group or unit.*)
corporation [kɔ:pə'reiʃən], *s.* (*Law, Comm.*) die Körperschaft; die Korporation; die Gemeinde (*municipal*); (*sl.*) der Schmerbauch (*stoutness*).
corps [kɔ:], *s.* das Korps.
corpse [kɔ:ps], *s.* der Leichnam.
corpulence ['kɔ:pjuləns], *s.* die Korpulenz, die Beleibtheit.
corpulent ['kɔ:pjulənt], *adj.* korpulent, dick.
Corpus Christi ['kɔ:pəs 'kristi]. (der) Fronleichnam, das Fronleichnamsfest.
corpuscle ['kɔ:pʌsl], *s.* (*Anat.*) das Körperchen.

correct [kə'rekt], *v.a.* korrigieren (*remove mistakes*); verbessern; tadeln (*reprove*); berichtigen (*rectify*). — *adj.* korrekt, tadellos, richtig.
correction [kə'rekʃən], *s.* die Korrektur (*of mistakes*); die Verbesserung (*improvement*); die Richtigstellung (*restoration*); der Verweis (*censure*).
corrective [kə'rektiv], *adj.* zur Besserung. — *s.* das Korrektiv.
correctness [kə'rektnis], *s.* die Korrektheit (*of manner, action etc.*).
corrector [kə'rektə], *s.* der Korrektor (*proof reader etc.*).
correlate ['kɔrileit], *v.a.* in Beziehung setzen, aufeinander beziehen. — [-lit], *s.* (*Log.*) das Korrelat.
correlative [kɔ'relətiv], *adj.* in Wechselbeziehung stehend.
correspond [kɔris'pɔnd], *v.n.* korrespondieren (*exchange letters*); entsprechen (*to, Dat.*).
correspondence [kɔris'pɔndəns], *s.* die Korrespondenz; der Briefwechsel (*letters*); die Übereinstimmung (*harmony*).
correspondent [kɔris'pɔndənt], *s.* der Korrespondent (*letter-writer*); der Journalist, Berichterstatter (*newspaper*).
corridor ['kɔridɔ:], *s.* der Korridor; der Gang.
corrigible ['kɔridʒibl], *adj.* verbesserlich.
corroborate [kə'rɔbəreit], *v.a.* bestätigen (*confirm*); bestärken (*strengthen*).
corroboration [kərɔbə'reiʃən], *s.* die Bestätigung, die Bekräftigung.
corroborative [kə'rɔbərətiv], *adj.* bekräftigend.
corrode [kə'roud], *v.a.* zerfressen, zersetzen, ätzen (*acid*).
corrosion [kə'rouʒən], *s.* die Anfressung, Ätzung.
corrosive [kə'rouziv], *adj.* ätzend.
corrugated ['kɔrugeitid], *adj.* gewellt, Well-; — *iron*, das Wellblech; — *paper*, die Wellpappe.
corrupt [kə'rʌpt], *v.a.* verderben (*spoil*); bestechen (*bribe*). — *adj.* korrupt (*morals*); verdorben (*spoilt*).
corruptible [kə'rʌptibl], *adj.* verderblich; bestechlich.
corruption [kə'rʌpʃən], *s.* die Korruption; die Bestechung (*bribery*).
corruptness [kə'rʌptnis], *s.* die Verdorbenheit, der Verfall.
corsair ['kɔ:sɛə], *s.* der Korsar, der Seeräuber.
corset ['kɔ:sit], *s.* das Korsett.
coruscate ['kɔrəskeit], *v.n.* schimmern, leuchten.
corvette [kɔ:'vet], *s.* (*Naut.*) die Korvette.
cosine ['kousain], *s.* (*Maths.*) der Kosinus.
cosiness ['kouzinis], *s.* die Bequemlichkeit, die Behaglichkeit (*comfort*).
cosmetic [kɔz'metik], *adj.* kosmetisch. — *s.* (*pl.*) das *or* die (*pl.*) Schönheitsmittel.
cosmic ['kɔzmik], *adj.* kosmisch.
cosmopolitan [kɔzmo'pɔlitən], *adj.* kosmopolitisch, weltbürgerlich. — *s.* der Kosmopolit, der Weltbürger.
Cossack ['kɔsæk], *s.* der Kosak.
cost [kɔst], *v.a. irr.* kosten. — *v.n. irr.* zu stehen kommen. —*s.* die Kosten, *f. pl.* (*expenses*); *at all* —*s*, um jeden Preis.
costermonger ['kɔstəmʌŋgə], *s.* der Straßenhändler.
costly ['kɔstli], *adj.* kostspielig.
costume ['kɔstju:m], *s.* das Kostüm; — *play*, das Zeitstück.
cosy ['kouzi], *adj.* behaglich, bequem.
cot (1) [kɔt], *s.* das Bettchen, Kinderbett.
cot (2) [kɔt], *s.* (*obs.*) die Hütte (*hut*).
cottage ['kɔtidʒ], *s.* die Hütte, das Häuschen.
cottager ['kɔtidʒə], *s.* der Kleinhäusler.
cotton [kɔtn], *s.* die Baumwolle. — *v.n.* — *on to*, (*coll.*) sich anhängen, sich anschließen (*Dat.*); — *on*, folgen können (*understand*).
couch [kautʃ], *s.* die Chaiselongue; der Diwan. — *v.a.* (*express*) in Worte fassen.
cough [kɔf], *v.n.* husten. — *s.* der Husten; *whooping* —, der Keuchhusten.
council ['kaunsil], *s.* der Rat (*body*); die Ratsversammlung.
councillor ['kaunsilə], *s.* der Rat, das Ratsmitglied; der Stadtrat.
counsel ['kaunsəl], *s.* der Rat (*advice*); der Berater (*adviser*); der Anwalt (*lawyer*). — *v.a.* einen Rat geben, beraten (*Acc.*).
counsellor ['kaunsələ], *s.* der Ratgeber; der Ratsherr; (*Am.*) der Anwalt (*lawyer*).
count (1) [kaunt], *v.a.*, *v.n.* zählen; — *on s.o.*, sich auf jemanden verlassen. — *s.* die Zählung.
count (2) [kaunt], *s.* der Graf.
countenance ['kauntənəns], *s.* das Gesicht, die Miene. — *v.a.* begünstigen, unterstützen, zulassen.
counter (1) ['kauntə], *s.* der Rechner, der Zähler (*chip*); die Spielmarke; der Zahltisch (*desk*); Ladentisch (*in shop*); Schalter (*in office*).
counter (2) ['kauntə], *adv.* entgegen.
counteract [kauntə'rækt], *v.a.* entgegenwirken (*Dat.*).
counteraction [kauntə'rækʃən], *s.* die Gegenwirkung; der Widerstand (*resistance*).
counterbalance ['kauntəbæləns], *s.* das Gegengewicht. — [-'bæləns], *v.a.* ausbalancieren, ausgleichen.
countercharge ['kauntətʃɑ:dʒ], *s.* die Gegenklage.
counterfeit ['kauntəfi:t, -fit], *s.* die Fälschung (*forgery*); die Nachahmung (*imitation*). — *adj.* gefälscht, falsch.

counterfoil ['kauntəfɔil], *s.* das Kontrollblatt; der Kupon.
counter-intelligence ['kauntərintelidʒəns], *s.* die Spionageabwehr.
countermand [kauntə'mɑ:nd], *v.a.* widerrufen.
counterpane ['kauntəpein], *s.* die Steppdecke.
counterpart ['kauntəpɑ:t], *s.* das Gegenbild, das Gegenstück.
counterplot ['kauntəplɔt], *s.* der Gegenplan. — *v.n.* einen Gegenplan machen.
counterpoint ['kauntəpɔint], *s.* (*Mus.*) der Kontrapunkt.
counterpoise ['kauntəpɔiz], *s.* das Gegengewicht. — *v.a.* das Gleichgewicht halten.
countersign ['kauntəsain], *v.a.* gegenzeichnen, mitunterschreiben. — *s.* das Gegenzeichen.
countess ['kauntes], *s.* die Gräfin.
counting-house ['kauntiŋhaus], *s.* das Kontor.
countless ['kauntlis], *adj.* zahllos.
country ['kʌntri], *s.* das Land. — *adj.* Land-, ländlich, Bauern-.
county ['kaunti], *s.* die Grafschaft (*British*); der Landbezirk (*U.S.A.*).
couple [kʌpl], *s.* das Paar. — *v.a.* paaren, verbinden. — *v.n.* sich paaren (*pair*); sich verbinden.
couplet ['kʌplit], *s.* das Verspaar.
coupling ['kʌpliŋ], *s.* (*Mech.*) die Kupplung.
courage ['kʌridʒ], *s.* der Mut.
courageous [kə'reidʒəs], *adj.* mutig, tapfer.
courier ['kuriə], *s.* der Eilbote (*messenger*); der Reisebegleiter (*tour leader*).
course [kɔ:s], *s.* der Kurs; der Lauf (*time*); der Ablauf (*lapse of a period etc.*); die Bahn (*racing track*); *in due —*, zu gegebener Zeit; *of —*, natürlich.
courser ['kɔ:sə], *s.* das schnelle Pferd.
court [kɔ:t], *s.* der Hof (*royal etc.*); (*Law*) der Gerichtshof. — *v.a.* (*a lady*) den Hof machen (*Dat.*); — *disaster*, das Unglück herausfordern.
courteous ['kə:tiəs], *adj.* höflich.
courtesan ['kɔ:tizən *or* kɔ:ti'zæn], *s.* die Kurtisane, die Buhlerin.
courtesy ['kə:təsi], *s.* die Höflichkeit; *by — of*, mit freundlicher Erlaubnis von.
courtier ['kɔ:tiə], *s.* der Höfling.
courtly ['kɔ:tli], *adj.* höfisch, Hof-.
court-martial [kɔ:t'mɑ:ʃəl], *s.* das Kriegsgericht.
courtship ['kɔ:tʃip], *s.* das Werben, die Werbung, das Freien.
courtyard ['kɔ:tjɑ:d], *s.* der Hof, der Hofraum.
cousin [kʌzn], *s.* der Vetter (*male*); die Kusine (*female*).
cove [kouv], *s.* die (kleine) Bucht.
covenant ['kʌvənənt], *s.* (*Bibl.*) der Bund; (*Comm.*) der Vertrag.
cover ['kʌvə], *v.a.* decken, bedecken (*table etc.*); schützen (*protect*); — *up*, bemänteln. — *s.* die Decke (*blanket*); der Deckel (*lid*); der Einband (*book*); das Gedeck (*table*); (*Comm.*) die Deckung; — *point*, (*Cricket*) die Deckstellung; *under —*, (*Mil.*) verdeckt, unter Deckung; — *girl*, das Mädchen auf dem Titelblatt (einer Illustrierten.)
covering ['kʌvəriŋ], *s.* die Bedeckung, die Bekleidung (*clothing*).
coverlet, coverlid ['kʌvəlit, 'kʌvəlid], *s.* die Bettdecke.
covert ['kʌvə:t], *s.* der Schlupfwinkel (*hideout*); das Dickicht (*thicket*). — *adj.* verborgen, bedeckt (*covered*); heimlich (*secret*).
covet ['kʌvit], *v.a., v.n.* begehren (*Acc.*), gelüsten (nach (*Dat.*)).
covetous ['kʌvitəs], *adj.* begierig, habsüchtig.
covetousness ['kʌvitəsnis], *s.* die Begierde, die Habsucht.
covey ['kʌvi], *s.* der Flug *or* die Kette (Rebhühner, *partridges*).
cow (1) [kau], *s.* die Kuh; — *-shed*, der Kuhstall.
cow (2) [kau], *v.a.* einschüchtern.
coward ['kauəd], *s.* der Feigling.
cowardice ['kauədis], *s.* die Feigheit.
cower ['kauə], *v.n.* sich kauern.
cowherd ['kauhə:d], *s.* der Kuhhirt.
cowl [kaul], *s.* die Kappe (*of monk*), die Kapuze (*hood*).
cowslip ['kauslip], *s.* (*Bot.*) die Primel, die Schlüsselblume.
coxswain [kɔksn], *s.* (*Naut.*) der Steuermann.
coy [kɔi], *adj.* scheu, spröde, zurückhaltend.
coyness ['kɔinis], *s.* die Sprödigkeit.
crab [kræb], *s.* (*Zool.*) die Krabbe; — *apple*, (*Bot.*) der Holzapfel.
crabbed [kræbd], *adj.* mürrisch (*temper*); unleserlich (*handwriting*).
crack [kræk], *s.* der Riß (*fissure*); der Krach, Schlag; der Sprung; die komische Bemerkung (*remark*). — *adj.* (*coll.*) erstklassig; — *shot*, der Meisterschütze. — *v.a.* aufbrechen; aufknacken (*nut, safe*); — *a joke*, eine witzige Bemerkung machen. — *v.n.* — *under strain*, unter einer Anstrengung zusammenbrechen; bersten (*break*).
cracked, crackers [krækd, 'krækəz], *adj.* (*coll.*) verrückt.
cracker ['krækə], *s.* der Keks; der Frosch (*firework*).
crackle [krækl], *v.n.* knistern, prasseln (*fire*); knallen, platzen (*rocket*).
cracknel ['kræknəl], *s.* die Brezel.
crackpot ['krækpɔt], *s.* (*coll.*) der verrückte Kerl.
cradle [kreidl], *s.* die Wiege. — *v.a.* einwiegen.
craft [krɑ:ft], *s.* die Fertigkeit (*skill*); das Handwerk (*trade*); die List (*cunning*); *arts and —s*, die Handwerkskünste.

craftsman ['kra:ftsmən], *s.* der (gelernte) Handwerker.
crafty ['kra:fti], *adj.* listig, schlau.
crag [kræg], *s.* die Klippe.
cragged, craggy [krægd, 'krægi], *adj.* felsig, schroff.
cram [kræm], *v.a.* vollstopfen (*stuff full*); (*coll.*) pauken (*coach*). — *v.n.* büffeln.
crammer ['kræmə], *s.* (*coll.*) der Einpauker, Privatlehrer (*tutor*).
cramp [kræmp], *s.* (*Med.*) der Krampf; die Klammer (*tool*). — *v.a.* einengen (*narrow*); verkrampfen.
cramped [kræmpd], *adj.* krampfhaft; eingeengt, beengt (*enclosed*).
cranberry ['krænbəri], *s.* (*Bot.*) die Preiselbeere.
crane [krein], *s.* (*Orn.*) der Kranich; (*Engin.*) der Kran. — *v.a.* — *o.'s neck*, den Hals ausrecken.
crank (1) [kræŋk], *s.* (*Motor.*) die Kurbel; — *-handle*, die Andrehwelle; (*Motor.*, *Engin.*) —*shaft*, die Kurbelwelle, die Kurbel.
crank (2) [kræŋk], *s.* der Sonderling, der sonderbare Kauz (*eccentric*).
cranky ['kræŋki], *adj.* sonderbar.
cranny ['kræni], *s.* der Spalt, der Riß; *nook and* —, Eck und Spalt.
crape [kreip], *s.* der Krepp, Flor.
crash [kræʃ], *s.* der Krach; (*Motor.*) Zusammenstoß; (*Aviat.*) Absturz. — *v.n.* krachen (*noise*); stürzen, abstürzen (*fall*).
crass [kræs], *adj.* derb, grob, kraß.
crate [kreit], *s.* der Packkorb (*basket*); die Kiste (*wood*).
crater ['kreitə], *s.* (*Geol.*) der Krater.
cravat [krə'væt], *s.* die breite Halsbinde, das Halstuch (*scarf*); die Krawatte.
crave [kreiv], *v.a.* (dringend) verlangen (*for*, nach, *Dat.*).
craven [kreivn], *adj.* feig, mutlos. — *s.* der Feigling.
craving ['kreiviŋ], *s.* das starke Verlangen.
craw [krɔ:], *s.* (*Zool.*) der Vogelkropf.
crawl [krɔ:l], *v.n.* kriechen; kraulen (*swim*).
crawling ['krɔ:liŋ], *s.* das Kriechen; das Kraulschwimmen.
crayon ['kreiən], *s.* der Farbstift, der Pastellstift.
craze [kreiz], *s.* die Manie; die verrückte Mode (*fashion*).
craziness ['kreizinis], *s.* die Verrücktheit.
crazy ['kreizi], *adj.* verrückt.
creak [kri:k], *v.n.* knarren.
cream [kri:m], *s.* der Rahm, die Sahne; *whipped* —, die Schlagsahne, (*Austr.*) der Schlagobers. — *v.a.* — *off*, (die Sahne) abschöpfen; (*fig.*) das Beste abziehen.
creamery ['kri:məri], *s.* die Molkerei.
creamy ['kri:mi], *adj.* sahnig.
crease [kri:s], *s.* die Falte (*trousers etc.*); — *-resistant*, knitterfrei. — *v.a.* falten (*fold*). — *v.n.* knittern.
create [kri'eit], *v.a.* erschaffen, schaffen.
creation [kri'eiʃən], *s.* die Schöpfung.
creative [kri'eitiv], *adj.* schöpferisch.
creator [kri'eitə], *s.* der Schöpfer.
creature ['kri:tʃə], *s.* das Geschöpf.
credence ['kri:dəns], *s.* der Glaube.
credentials [kri'denʃəlz], *s. pl.* das Zeugnis, das Beglaubigungsschreiben; die Legitimation (*proof of identity*).
credibility [kredi'biliti], *s.* die Glaubwürdigkeit.
credible ['kredibl], *adj.* glaubwürdig, glaublich.
credit ['kredit], *s.* (*Comm.*) der Kredit; der gute Ruf (*reputation*); das Guthaben (*assets*). — *v.a.* — *s.o. with s.th.*, jemandem etwas gutschreiben; glauben (*believe*).
creditable ['kreditəbl], *adj.* ehrenwert, lobenswert.
creditor ['kreditə], *s.* (*Comm.*) der Gläubiger.
credulity [kre'dju:liti], *s.* die Leichtgläubigkeit.
credulous ['kredjuləs], *adj.* leichtgläubig.
creed [kri:d], *s.* das Glaubensbekenntnis.
creek [kri:k], *s.* die kleine Bucht; das Flüßchen (*small river*).
creel [kri:l], *s.* der Fischkorb.
creep [kri:p], *s.* (*Geol.*) der Rutsch; (*pl.*, *coll.*) *the* —*s*, die Gänsehaut, das Gruseln. — *v.n.irr.* kriechen; (*furtively*) sich einschleichen.
creeper ['kri:pə], *s.* die Schlingpflanze, das Rankengewächs; (*Sch.*) der Kriecher; *Virginia* —, der wilde Wein.
creepy ['kri:pi], *adj.* kriechend; gruselig (*frightening*).
cremate [kri'meit], *v.a.* einäschern.
cremation [kri'meiʃən], *s.* die Verbrennung, Einäscherung.
crematorium, (*Am.*) **crematory** [kremə'tɔ:riəm, 'kremətəri], *s.* das Krematorium.
Creole ['kri:oul], *s.* der Kreole.
crepuscular [kri'pʌskjulə], *adj.* dämmerig.
crescent ['kresənt], *adj.* wachsend, zunehmend. — *s.* der (zunehmende) Mond, die Mondsichel; das Hörnchen.
cress [kres], *s.* (*Bot.*) die Kresse; *mustard and* —, die Gartenkresse.
crest [krest], *s.* der Kamm (*cock*); der Gipfel (*hill*); der Kamm (*wave*); der Busch (*helmet*); das Wappenschild (*Heraldry*).
crestfallen ['krestfɔ:lən], *adj.* entmutigt, mutlos, niedergeschlagen.
Cretan ['kri:tən], *adj.* kretisch. — *s.* der Kreter, die Kreterin.
cretonne ['kretɔn], *s.* die Kretonne.
crevasse [krə'væs], *s.* die Gletscherspalte.
crevice ['krevis], *s.* der Riß.
crew (1) [kru:], *s.* (*Naut.*, *Aviat.*) die Besatzung; (*Naut.*) die Schiffsmannschaft; die Mannschaft (*team*); (*Am.*) — *cut*, die Bürstenfrisur.

crew (2) [kru:] *see* **crow**.
crib [krib], *s.* die Krippe (*Christmas*); die Wiege (*cradle*); (*Sch.*) die Eselsbrücke. — *v.a.* (*Sch.*) abschreiben (*copy*).
crick [krik], *s.* (*in neck*) der steife Hals.
cricket ['krikit], *s.* (*Ent.*) das Heimchen, die Grille; (*Sport*) das Cricket(spiel).
crime [kraim], *s.* das Verbrechen; — *fiction*, die Detektivromane, *m. pl.*
criminal ['kriminəl], *s.* der Verbrecher. — *adj.* — *case*, der Kriminalfall; verbrecherisch (*act*); — *investigation*, die Fahndung.
crimp [krimp], *v.a.* kräuseln (*hair*).
crimson ['krimzən], *adj.* karmesinrot.
cringe [krindʒ], *v.n.* kriechen.
crinkle [kriŋkl], *v.a., v.n.* kräuseln.—*s.* die Falte.
crinoline ['krinəlin], *s.* der Reifrock.
cripple [kripl], *s.* der Krüppel. — *v.a.* verkrüppeln; lahmlegen (*immobilize*).
crisis ['kraisis], *s.* die Krise, der Wendepunkt; die Notlage.
crisp [krisp], *adj.* kraus (*hair*); knusperig (*bread*); frisch.
criss-cross ['kriskrɔs], *adv.* kreuz und quer.
criterion [krai'tiəriən], *s.* das Kennzeichen, das Kriterium.
critic ['kritik], *s.* der Kritiker; Rezensent (*reviewer*).
critical ['kritikəl], *adj.* kritisch.
criticism ['kritisizm], *s.* die Kritik (*of*, an, *Dat.*); Rezension, Besprechung (*review*).
criticize ['kritisaiz], *v.a.* kritisieren.
croak [krouk], *v.n.* krächzen (*raven*); quaken (*frog*).
croaking ['kroukiŋ], *s.* das Krächzen, das Gekrächze (*raven*); das Quaken (*frog*).
Croat ['krouæt]. *s.* der Kroate.
Croatian [krou'eiʃən], *adj.* kroatisch.
crochet ['krouʃei], *s.* die Häkelei; — *hook*, die Häkelnadel. — *v.a., v.n.* häkeln.
crock [krɔk], *s.* der Topf, der irdene Krug; der alte Topf; (*coll.*) *old* —, der Invalide, Krüppel.
crockery ['krɔkəri], *s.* (*Comm.*) die Töpferware; das Geschirr (*household*).
crocodile ['krɔkədail], *s.* das Krokodil.
crocus ['kroukəs], *s.* (*Bot.*) der Krokus, die Safranblume.
croft [krɔft], *s.* das Kleinbauerngut.
crofter ['krɔftə], *s.* der Kleinbauer.
crone [kroun], *s.* das alte Weib; die Hexe (*witch*).
crony ['krouni], *s.* (*coll.*) *old* —, der alte Freund.
crook [kruk], *s.* der Krummstab (*staff*); der Schwindler (*cheat*). — *v.a.* krümmen, biegen.
crooked ['krukid], *adj.* krumm; (*fig.*) schwindlerisch, verbrecherisch.
crookedness ['krukidnis], *s.* die Krummheit; die Durchtriebenheit (*slyness*).
croon [kru:n], *v.n.* leise singen; (*Am.*) im modernen Stil singen.
crooner ['kru:nə], *s.* der Jazzsänger.
crop [krɔp], *s.* der Kropf (*bird*); die Ernte (*harvest*); der (kurze) Haarschnitt; *riding* —, die Reitpeitsche. — *v.a.* stutzen (*cut short*). — *v.n.* — *up*, auftauchen.
crosier ['krouziə], *s.* (*Eccl.*) der Bischofsstab.
cross [krɔs], *s.* das Kreuz. — *v.a.* (*Zool.*, *Bot.*) kreuzen; überqueren (*road, on foot*); — *s.o.'s path*, einem in die Quere kommen. — *v.n.* überfahren (übers Wasser); hinübergehen; — *over*, übersetzen (*on boat or ferry*). — *v.r.* sich bekreuzigen. — *adj.* mürrisch (*grumpy*), verstimmt; *at — purposes*, ohne einander zu verstehen; *make* —, verstimmen. — *adv.* kreuzweise; — *-eyed*, schielend; — *-grained*, wider den Strich, schlecht aufgelegt.
crossbow ['krɔsbou], *s.* die Armbrust.
crossbreed ['krɔsbri:d], *s.* die Mischrasse, der Mischling.
cross-examine [krɔsig'zæmin], *v.a.*, *v.n.* (*Law*) ins (Kreuz-)Verhör nehmen.
crossing ['krɔsiŋ], *s.* die Straßenkreuzung; (*Naut.*) die Überfahrt; der Straßenübergang; Kreuzweg.
crossroads ['krɔsroudz], *s.* der Kreuzweg, die Kreuzung.
crossword ['krɔswə:d], *s.* das Kreuzworträtsel.
crotch [krɔtʃ], *s.* der Haken.
crotchet ['krɔtʃit], *s.* (*Mus.*) die Viertelnote; die Grille (*mood*).
crotchety ['krɔtʃiti], *adj.* grillenhaft, verschroben.
crouch [krautʃ], *v.n.* sich ducken (*squat*); sich demütigen (*cringe*).
croup (1) [kru:p], *s.* (*Med.*) der Krupp.
croup (2) [kru:p], *s.* die Kruppe.
crow [krou], *s.* (*Orn.*) die Krähe; das Krähen (*of cock*). — *v.n. irr.* krähen (*cock*).
crowbar ['kroubɑ:], *s.* das Brecheisen.
crowd [kraud], *s.* die Menge (*multitude*); das Gedränge (*throng*). — *v.n.* — *in*, sich hineindrängen, dazudrängen; — *around*, sich herumscharen um (*Acc.*).
crown [kraun], *s.* die Krone (*diadem or coin*); der Gipfel (*mountain*); (*Anat.*) der Scheitel; — *lands*, Krongüter (*n. pl.*), Landeigentum der Krone, *n.*; — *prince*, der Kronprinz; — *of thorns*, die Dornenkrone. — *v.a.* krönen.
crucial ['kru:ʃəl], *adj.* entscheidend, kritisch.
crucifix ['kru:sifiks], *s.* das Kruzifix.
crucify ['kru:sifai], *v.a.* kreuzigen.
crude [kru:d], *adj.* roh, ungekocht, unreif; grob (*manners*), ungeschliffen.
crudity ['kru:diti], *s.* die Rohheit; Grobheit (*manners*).
cruel ['kru:əl], *adj.* grausam.
cruelty ['kru:əlti], *s.* die Grausamkeit.
cruet ['kru:it], *s.* das Salz- *oder* Pfefferfäßchen; das Fläschchen.

cruise [kru:z], *v.n.* (*Naut.*) kreuzen. — *s.* die Seehfahrt, die Seereise; *pleasure* —, die Vergnügungsreise (zu Wasser).
cruiser ['kru:zə], *s.* (*Naut.*) der Kreuzer; *battle* —, der Panzerkreuzer.
crumb [krʌm], *s.* die Krume. — *v.a.* zerbröckeln, zerkrümeln.
crumble [krʌmbl], *v.n.* zerfallen, zerbröckeln.
crumpet ['krʌmpit], *s.* das Teebrötchen, das Teeküchlein.
crumple [krʌmpl], *v.a.* zerknittern (*material*). — *v.n.* — *up*, zusammenbrechen.
crunch [krʌntʃ], *v.a.* zerstoßen, zermalmen. — *v.n.* knirschen.
crusade [kru:'seid], *s.* der Kreuzzug.
crusader [kru:'seidə], *s.* der Kreuzfahrer.
crush [krʌʃ], *v.a.* zerdrücken; zerstoßen (*pulverize*); drängen (*crowd*); zertreten (*tread down*); (*fig.*) vernichten. — *s.* das Gedränge (*throng*); (*coll.*) *have a* — *on*, verknallt sein, in einen verliebt sein.
crust [krʌst], *s.* die Kruste, die Rinde (*bread*). — *v.a.* mit einer Kruste bedecken. — *v.n.* verkrusten.
crustaceous [krʌs'teiʃəs], *adj.* (*Zool.*) krustenartig, Krustentier-.
crusty ['krʌsti], *adj.* krustig, knusperig (*pastry, bread*); mürrisch (*grumpy*).
crutch [krʌtʃ], *s.* die Krücke.
crux [krʌks], *s.* der entscheidende Punkt, der springende Punkt, die Schwierigkeit.
cry [krai], *v.n.* schreien, rufen; weinen (*weep*). — *v.a.* — *down*, niederschreien. — *s.* der Schrei; der Zuruf (*call*).
crypt [kript], *s.* (*Eccl.*) die Krypta, die Gruft.
crystal ['kristəl], *s.* der Kristall.
crystallize ['kristəlaiz], *v.n.* sich kristallisieren, Kristalle bilden.
cub [kʌb], *s.* (*Zool.*) das Junge.— *v.n.* Junge haben, Junge werfen.
Cuban ['kju:bən], *adj.* kubanisch. — *s.* der Kubaner.
cube [kju:b], *s.* der Würfel; (*Maths.*) — *root*, die Kubikwurzel. — *v.a.* zur Dritten (Potenz) erheben; kubieren.
cubic(al) ['kju:bik(əl)], *adj.* kubisch, zur dritten Potenz.
cubit ['kju:bit], *s.* die Elle.
cuckoo ['kuku:], *s.* (*Orn.*) der Kuckuck.
cucumber ['kju:kʌmbə], *s.* (*Bot.*) die Gurke; *cool as a* —, ruhig und gelassen.
cud [kʌd], *s.* das wiedergekäute Futter; *chew the* —, wiederkauen (*also fig.*).
cuddle [kʌdl], *v.a.* liebkosen, an sich drücken. — *v.n.* sich anschmiegen.
cudgel ['kʌdʒəl], *s.* der Knüttel; *take up the* —*s for*, sich für etwas einsetzen.
cue (1) [kju:], *s.* (*Theat.*) das Stichwort. — *v.a.* einem (*Theat.*) das Stichwort *or* (*Mus.*) den Einsatz geben.
cue (2) [kju:], *s.* der Billardstock. — *v.a.* (*Billiards*) abschießen.
cuff (1) [kʌf], *s.* die Manschette, der Aufschlag (*shirt*); —*links*, die Manschettenknöpfe.
cuff (2) [kʌf], *s.* der Schlag. — *v.a.* schlagen, puffen.
culinary ['kju:linəri], *adj.* kulinarisch; Küchen-, Eß-, Speisen-.
cull [kʌl], *v.a.* auswählen, auslesen (*from books*).
culminate ['kʌlmineit], *v.n.* kulminieren, den Höhepunkt erreichen.
culpable ['kʌlpəbl], *adj.* schuldig; strafbar.
culprit ['kʌlprit], *s.* der Schuldige, Verbrecher.
cult [kʌlt], *s.* der Kult, die Verehrung; der Kultus.
cultivate ['kʌltiveit], *v.a.* kultivieren; (*Agr.*) anbauen; pflegen (*acquaintance*); bilden (*mind*).
cultivation [kʌlti'veiʃən], *s.* (*Agr.*) der Anbau; die Bildung (*mind*).
culture ['kʌltʃə], *s.* die Kultur, die Bildung.
cumbersome ['kʌmbəsəm], *adj.* beschwerlich, lästig.
cunning ['kʌniŋ], *s.* die List, die Schlauheit. — *adj.* listig, schlau.
cup [kʌp], *s.* die Tasse (*tea*—); der Becher (*handleless*); (*Eccl.*) der Kelch; der Pokal (*sports*); — *final*, das Endspiel. — *v.a.* (*Med.*) schröpfen.
cupboard ['kʌbəd], *s.* der Schrank.
cupola ['kju:pələ], *s.* (*Archit., Metall.*) die Kuppel.
cur [kə:], *s.* der Köter; (*fig*). der Schurke.
curable ['kjuərəbl], *adj.* heilbar.
curate ['kjuərit], *s.* der Hilfsgeistliche.
curative ['kjuərətiv], *adj.* heilsam, heilend.
curator [kjuə'reitə], *s.* der Kurator, Verwalter, Direktor.
curb [kə:b], *v.a.* zügeln, bändigen. — *s.* der Zaum (*bridle*).
curd [kə:d], *s.* der Rahmkäse, der Milchkäse; (*pl.*) der Quark.
curdle [kə:dl], *v.a.* gerinnen lassen. — *v.n.* gerinnen; erstarren.
cure [kjuə], *s.* die Kur, die Heilung. — *v.a.* kurieren, wieder gesundmachen; einpökeln (*foodstuffs*).
curfew ['kə:fju:], *s.* die Abendglocke (*bells*); das Ausgehverbot, die Polizeistunde (*police*).
curio ['kjuəriou], *s.* die Kuriosität, das Sammlerstück; die Rarität.
curiosity [kjuəri'ɔsiti], *s.* die Neugier; Merkwürdigkeit.
curious ['kjuəriəs], *adj.* neugierig (*inquisitive*); seltsam, sonderbar (*strange*).
curl [kə:l], *v.a.* kräuseln, (in Locken) wickeln. — *v.n.* sich kräuseln. — *s.* die Haarlocke.
curler ['kə:lə], *s.* der Lockenwickler.
curlew ['kə:lju:], *s.* (*Orn.*) der Brachvogel.
curly ['kə:li], *adj.* lockig.
currant ['kʌrənt], *s.* (*Bot.*) die Korinthe, die Johannisbeere.

currency ['kʌrənsi], *s.* die Währung (*money*); der Umlauf (*circulation*).
current ['kʌrənt], *adj.* im Umlauf; allgemein gültig, eben gültig; jetzig (*modern*). — *s.* (*Elect.*) der Strom; die Strömung (*river*); der Zug (*air*).
curry (1) ['kʌri], *v.a.* gerben (*tan*); — *comb*, der Pferdestriegel; — *favour*, sich einschmeicheln.
curry (2) ['kʌri], *s.* das indische Ragout. — *v.a.* würzen.
curse [kə:s], *v.a.*, *v.n.* verfluchen; verwünschen. — *s.* der Fluch; die Verwünschung.
cursive ['kə:siv], *adj.* kursiv, Kursiv-.
cursory ['kə:səri], *adj.* kursorisch, oberflächlich.
curt [kə:t], *adj.* kurz angebunden (*speech*, *manner*).
curtail [kə:'teil], *v.a.* stutzen, beschränken (*scope*); verkürzen (*time*).
curtain ['kə:tin], *s.* die Gardine; der Vorhang; (*Mil.*) — *fire*, das Sperrfeuer; — *lecture*, die Gardinenpredigt; — *speech*, die Ansprache vor dem Vorhang. — *v.a.* verhüllen (*hide*); mit Vorhängen versehen (*hang curtains*).
curtness ['kə:tnis], *s.* die Kürze; die Barschheit.
curts(e)y ['kə:tsi], *s.* der Knicks. — *v.n.* knicksen, einen Knicks machen.
curve [kə:v], *s.* die Krümmung; (*Geom.*) die Kurve. — *v.a.* krümmen, biegen. — *v.n.* sich biegen.
curved [kə:vd], *adj.* krumm, gebogen.
cushion ['kuʃən], *s.* das Kissen. — *v.a.* polstern.
custody ['kʌstədi], *s.* die Obhut; Bewachung, Haft.
custom ['kʌstəm], *s.* die Sitte, die Tradition; der Gebrauch, Brauch (*usage*); die Kundschaft (*trade*); (*pl.*) der Zoll (*duty*).
customary ['kʌstəməri], *adj.* gewohnt, althergebracht, gebräuchlich.
customer ['kʌstəmə], *s.* der Kunde, die Kundin.
cut [kʌt], *v.a. irr.* schneiden; — (*s.o.*), ignorieren; — *o.'s teeth*, zahnen; *this won't — any ice*, das wird nicht viel nützen; — *both ways*, das ist ein zweischneidiges Schwert; — *a lecture*, eine Vorlesung schwänzen; — *short*, unterbrechen. — *adj.* — *out for*, wie gerufen zu *or* für; — *to the quick*, aufs tiefste verletzt; — *glass*, das geschliffene Glas; — *price*, verbilligt. — *s.* der Schnitt (*section*); der Hieb (*gash*); (*Art*) der Stich; — *in salary*, eine Gehaltskürzung; die Abkürzung, die Kürzung (*abridgement*).
cute [kju:t], *adj.* klug, aufgeweckt; (*Am.*) süß, niedlich.
cutler ['kʌtlə], *s.* der Messerschmied.
cutlery ['kʌtləri], *s.* das Besteck (*tableware*); (*Comm.*) die Messerschmiedwaren, *f. pl.*
cutlet ['kʌtlit], *s.* das Kotelett, das Rippchen.
cut-throat ['kʌtθrout], *s.* der Halsabschneider; — *competition*, Konkurrenz auf Leben und Tod.
cuttle [kʌtl], *s.* (*Zool.*) der Tintenfisch.
cyanide ['saiənaid], *s.* (*Chem.*) zyanidsaures Salz; das Zyanid, die Blausäure.
cyclamen ['sikləmən], *s.* (*Bot.*) das Alpenveilchen.
cycle [saikl], *s.* (*Geom.*) der Kreis; (*Mus.*, *Zool.*) der Zyklus; (*coll.*) das Fahrrad. — *v.n.* (*coll.*) radfahren; zirkulieren (*round*, um, *Acc.*).
cyclone ['saikloun], *s.* der Wirbelwind, der Wirbelsturm.
cyclopaedia [saiklo'pi:djə] *see* **encyclopaedia.**
cylinder ['silində], *s.* der Zylinder; die Walze.
cymbal ['simbəl], *s.* (*Mus.*) die Zimbel, das Becken.
cynic ['sinik], *s.* der Zyniker.
cynical ['sinikəl], *adj.* zynisch.
cypress ['saiprəs], *s.* (*Bot.*) die Zypresse.
Cypriot ['sipriət], *adj.* zyprisch. — *s.* der Zypriote.
czar [zɑ:], *s.* der Zar.
Czech, Czechoslovak(ian) [tʃek, tʃeko'slouvæk, tʃekoslo'vækjən], *adj.* tschechisch. —*s.* der Tscheche.

D

D [di:]. das D (*also Mus.*).
dab [dæb], *v.a.* leicht berühren. — *s.* der leichte Schlag (*blow*).
dabble [dæbl], *v.n.* sich in etwas versuchen, pfuschen (*in*, in, *Dat.*).
dabbler ['dæblə], *s.* der Pfuscher, Stümper.
dace [deis], *s.* (*Zool.*) der Weißfisch.
dad, daddy [dæd, 'dædi], *s.* der Papa; Vati; *daddy longlegs*, die Bachmücke, die langbeinige Mücke.
dado ['deidou], *s.* die Täfelung.
daffodil ['dæfədil], *s.* (*Bot.*) die Narzisse.
dagger ['dægə], *s.* der Dolch; *at —s drawn*, spinnefeind; *look —s*, mit Blicken durchbohren.
dahlia ['deiliə], *s.* (*Bot.*) die Dahlie, die Georgine.
daily ['deili], *adj.* täglich; Tages-. — *s.* (*newspaper*) die Tageszeitung; (*woman*) die Putzfrau.
dainties ['deintiz], *s. pl.* das Backwerk, das kleine Gebäck, das Teegebäck.
daintiness ['deintinis], *s.* die Feinheit; die Kleinheit; die Leckerhaftigkeit.
dainty ['deinti], *adj.* fein, klein, zierlich; lecker (*food*).
dairy ['dɛəri], *s.* die Molkerei, die Meierei.
dairyman ['dɛəriman], *s.* der Milchmann; der Senne (*in Alps*).
dais [deis, 'deiis], *s.* das Podium.

daisy ['deizi], *s.* (*Bot.*) das Gänseblümchen, das Marienblümchen.
dale [deil], *s.* das Tal.
dalliance ['dæliəns], *s.* die Tändelei, Liebelei; Verzögerung.
dally ['dæli], *v.n.* die Zeit vertrödeln.
dam (1) [dæm], *s.* der Damm. — *v.a.* eindämmen, abdämmen.
dam (2) [dæm], *s.* (*Zool.*) die Tiermutter.
damage ['dæmidʒ], *s.* der Schaden; der Verlust (*loss*); (*pl.*) (*Law*) der Schadenersatz. — *v.a.* beschädigen.
damageable ['dæmidʒəbl], *adj.* leicht zu beschädigen.
damask ['dæməsk], *s.* der Damast (*textile*). — *adj.* damasten, aus Damast.
dame [deim], *s.* die Dame (*title*); (*Am.*) (*coll.*) die junge Dame, das Fräulein.
damn [dæm], *v.a.* verdammen.
damnable ['dæmnəbl], *adj.* verdammenswert, verdammt.
damnation [dæm'neiʃən], *s.* die Verdammung, Verdammnis.
damn(ed) [dæm(d)], *adj.* & *adv.* verwünscht, verdammt.
damp [dæmp], *adj.* feucht, dumpfig. — *s.* die Feuchtigkeit; (*Build.*) — *course*, die Schutzschicht. — *v.a.* dämpfen, befeuchten; — *the spirits*, die gute Laune verderben.
damsel ['dæmzəl], *s.* die Jungfer; das Mädchen.
damson ['dæmzən], *s.* (*Bot.*) die Damaszenerpflaume.
dance [dɑ:ns], *v.a.*, *v.n.* tanzen. — *s.* der Tanz; *lead s.o. a* —, einem viel Mühe machen.
dandelion ['dændilaiən], *s.* (*Bot.*) der Löwenzahn.
dandle [dændl], *v.a.* hätscheln; schaukeln.
dandy ['dændi], *s.* der Geck, der Stutzer.
Dane [dein], *s.* der Däne.
dane [dein], *s. great* —, die Dogge.
Danish ['deiniʃ], *adj.* dänisch.
danger ['deindʒə], *s.* die Gefahr.
dangerous ['deindʒərəs], *adj.* gefährlich.
dangle [dæŋgl], *v.a.* baumeln lassen. — *v.n.* baumeln, hängen.
dank [dæŋk], *adj.* feucht, naßkalt.
Danube ['dænju:b]. die Donau.
dapper ['dæpə], *adj.* schmuck; niedlich; elegant.
dappled [dæpld], *adj.* scheckig, bunt.
Dardanelles, The [dɑ:də'nelz]. die Dardanellen, *pl.*
dare [dɛə], *v.n. irr.* wagen; *I — say*, das meine ich wohl, ich gebe zu.
daredevil ['dɛədevl], *s.* der Wagehals, der Draufgänger.
daring ['dɛəriŋ], *s.* die Kühnheit.
dark [dɑ:k], *adj.* dunkel, finster. — *s.* die Dunkelheit; *shot in the* —, ein Schuß aufs Geratewohl, ins Blaue.
darken ['dɑ:kən], *v.a.* verdunkeln, verfinstern. — *v.n.* dunkel werden.
darkish ['dɑ:kiʃ], *adj.* nahezu dunkel.
darkness ['dɑ:knis], *s.* die Dunkelheit, Finsternis.
darkroom ['dɑ:kru:m], *s.* die Dunkelkammer.
darling ['dɑ:liŋ], *s.* der Liebling. — *adj.* lieb, teuer.
darn (1) [dɑ:n], *v.a.* stopfen.
darn (2) [dɑ:n], *v.a.* verdammen.
darn(ed) [dɑ:n(d)], (*excl.*) verdammt.
darning ['dɑ:niŋ], *s.* das Stopfen; — *needle*, die Stopfnadel.
dart [dɑ:t], *s.* der Pfeil; der Spieß (*spear*); (*pl.*) das Pfeilwurfspiel. — *v.n.* losstürmen, sich stürzen.
dash [dæʃ], *v.a.* zerschmettern, zerstören (*hopes*). — *v.n.* stürzen. — *s.* der Schlag (*blow*); die Eleganz; (*Typ.*) der Gedankenstrich; (*Motor.*) — *-board*, das Schaltbrett, Armaturenbrett.
dashing ['dæʃiŋ], *adj.* schneidig.
dastard ['dæstəd], *s.* der Feigling, die Memme.
dastardly ['dæstədli], *adj.*, *adv.* feige.
data ['deitə], *s. pl.* (*Science*) die Angaben, die Daten.
date (1) [deit], *s.* das Datum; (*Am.*) die Verabredung; *out of* —, vertetal (*antiquated*), altmodisch (*out of fashion*). — *v.a.* datieren; (*Am.*) ausführen. — *v.n.* das Datum tragen.
date (2) [deit], *s.* (*Bot.*) die Dattel.
dative ['deitiv], *s.* (*Gram.*) der Dativ.
daub [dɔ:b], *v.a.* beklecksen; (*coll.*) bemalen. — *s.* die Kleckserei; (*coll.*) die Malerei.
daughter ['dɔ:tə], *s.* die Tochter; — *-in-law*, die Schwiegertochter.
daunt [dɔ:nt], *v.a.* einschüchtern.
dauphin ['dɔ:fin], *s.* der Dauphin.
daw [dɔ:], *s.* (*Orn.*) die Dohle.
dawdle [dɔ:dl], *v.n.* trödeln, die Zeit vertrödeln.
dawdler ['dɔ:dlə], *s.* der Trödler, Tagedieb, die Schlafmütze.
dawn [dɔ:n], *s.* das Morgengrauen, die Morgendämmerung. — *v.n.* dämmern, tagen.
day [dei], *s.* der Tag; *the other* —, neulich; *every* —, täglich; *one* —, eines Tages; *by* —, bei *or* am Tage.
daybreak ['deibreik], *s.* der Tagesanbruch.
daytime ['deitaim], *s. in the* —, bei Tage.
daze [deiz], *v.a.* blenden (*dazzle*); betäuben (*stupefy*).
dazzle [dæzl], *v.a.* blenden.
deacon ['di:kən], *s.* (*Eccl.*) der Diakon.
deaconess ['di:kənes], *s.* (*Eccl.*) die Diakonisse.
dead [ded], *adj.* tot; *stop* —, plötzlich anhalten; *as — as mutton*, mausetot; — *from the neck up*, (*coll.*) dumm wie die Nacht. — *adv.* — *beat*, erschöpft; (*Am.*) — *sure*, ganz sicher. — *s. in the — of night*, in tiefster Nacht; (*pl.*) die Toten.

deaden [dedn], *v.a.* abschwächen (*weaken*); abtöten (*anæsthetise*).
deadly ['dedli], *adj.* tödlich.
deadness ['dednis], *s.* die Leblosigkeit; Mattheit (*tiredness*).
deaf [def], *adj.* taub; — *and dumb*, taubstumm.
deafen [defn], *v.a.* betäuben.
deafmute ['defmju:t], *s.* der Taubstumme.
deal (1) [di:l], *s.* das Geschäft; die Anzahl; *a fair* or *square* —, eine anständige Behandlung; *a good* —, beträchtlich; *a great* — *of*, sehr viel; *make a* —, ein Geschäft abschliessen; *it's a* —*!* abgemacht! — *v.a. irr.* austeilen; Karten geben (*cards*); — *a blow*, einen Schlag erteilen. — *v.n. irr.* — *with s.th.*, etwas behandeln.
deal (2) [di:l], *s.* (*Bot.*) das Kiefernholz, die Kiefer; — *board*, das Kiefernholzbrett.
dealer ['di:lə], *s.* der Händler.
dean [di:n], *s.* der Dekan.
dear [diə], *adj.* teuer, lieb (*beloved*); teuer, kostspielig (*expensive*); — *me!* ach, Du lieber Himmel! —, —*!* du liebe Zeit! — *John!* Lieber Hans!
dearness ['diənis], *s.* die Teuerung, das Teuersein.
dearth [də:θ], *s.* der Mangel (*of*, an, *Dat.*).
death [deθ], *s.* der Tod; der Todesfall; — *penalty*, die Todesstrafe; — *warrant*, das Todesurteil.
deathbed ['deθbed], *s.* das Totenbett, Sterbebett.
deathblow ['deθblou], *s.* der Todesstoß.
deathless ['deθlis], *adj.* unsterblich.
debar [di'ba:], *v.a.* ausschließen (*from*, von, *Dat.*).
debase [di'beis], *v.a.* erniedrigen, verschlechtern.
debatable [di'beitəbl], *adj.* strittig.
debate [di'beit], *s.* die Debatte. — *v.a.*, *v.n.* debattieren.
debauch [di'bɔ:tʃ], *v.a.*, *v.n.* verführen; verderben.
debauchee [di'bɔ:tʃi:], *s.* der Schwelger, der Wüstling.
debenture [di'bentʃə], *s.* der Schuldschein.
debilitate [di'biliteit], *v.a.* schwächen.
debit ['debit], *s.* die Schuldseite, das Soll (*in account*). — *v.a.* belasten.
debt [det], *s.* die Schuld; *run into* — or *incur* —*s*, Schulden machen.
debtor ['detə], *s.* der Schuldner.
decade ['dekəd, 'dekeid], *s.* das Jahrzehnt; die Dekade.
decadence ['dekədəns], *s.* die Dekadenz, der Verfall.
decalogue ['dekəlɔg], *s.* (*Bibl.*) die zehn Gebote.
decamp [di:'kæmp], *v.n.* aufbrechen, ausreißen.
decant [di'kænt], *v.a.* abfüllen, abgießen.
decanter [di'kæntə], *s.* die Karaffe.
decapitate [di:'kæpiteit], *v.a.* enthaupten köpfen.
decapitation [di:kæpi'teiʃən], *s.* die Enthauptung.
decay [di'kei], *v.n.* in Verfall geraten. — *s.* der Verfall, die Verwesung.
decease [di'si:s], *s.* das Hinscheiden, der Tod. — *v.n.* sterben, dahinscheiden, verscheiden.
deceit [di'si:t], *s.* der Betrug; die List (*cunning*).
deceive [di'si:v], *v.a.* betrügen.
deceiver [di'si:və], *s.* der Betrüger.
December [di'sembə]. der Dezember.
decency ['di:sənsi], *s.* der Anstand; die Anständigkeit, Ehrlichkeit; die Schicklichkeit.
decent ['di:sənt], *adj.* anständig.
decentralize [di:'sentrəlaiz], *v.a.* dezentralisieren.
deception [di'sepʃən], *s.* der Betrug.
deceptive [di'septiv], *adj.* trügerisch.
decide [di'said], *v.a.*, *v.n.* entscheiden; bestimmen (*determine*).
decimal ['desiməl], *adj.* dezimal.
decimate ['desimeit], *v.a.* dezimieren, herabsetzen (*reduce*).
decipher [di'saifə], *v.a.* entziffern (*read*); dechiffrieren (*decode*).
decision [di'siʒən], *s.* die Entscheidung, der Beschluß (*resolution*); die Entschlossenheit (*decisiveness*).
decisive [di'saisiv], *adj.* entscheidend.
decisiveness [di'saisivnis], *s.* die Entschiedenheit.
deck [dek], *s.* (*Naut.*) das Deck; — *chair*, der Liegestuhl. — *v.a.* — (*out*), ausschmücken.
declaim [di'kleim], *v.a.* deklamieren.
declamation [deklə'meiʃən], *s.* die Deklamation.
declamatory [di'klæmətəri], *adj.* Deklamations-, deklamatorisch, Vortrags-.
declaration [deklə'reiʃən], *s.* die Erklärung; die Deklaration.
declare [di'klɛə], *v.a.* erklären. — *v.n.* sich erklären.
declared [di'klɛəd], *adj.* erklärt, offen.
declension [di'klenʃən], *s.* (*Gram.*) die Deklination, die Abwandlung.
declinable [di'klainəbl], *adj.* (*Gram.*) deklinierbar.
declination [dekli'neiʃən], *s.* (*Phys.*) die Abweichung, Deklination.
decline [di'klain], *v.n.* abweichen (*deflect*); abnehmen (*decrease*); sich weigern (*refuse*); fallen (*price*). — *v.a.* (*Gram.*) deklinieren; ablehnen (*turn down*). — *s.* die Abnahme (*decrease*); der Verfall (*decadence*); der Abhang (*slope*).
declivity [di'kliviti], *s.* der Abhang.
decode [di:'koud], *v.a.* entziffern, dechiffrieren.
decompose [di:kəm'pouz], *v.n.* verwesen; zerfallen, sich zersetzen. — *v.a.* auflösen.

decorate ['dekəreit], *v.a.* dekorieren (*honour*); ausschmücken (*beautify*); ausmalen (*paint*).
decoration [dekə'reiʃən], *s.* die Dekoration, der Orden (*medal*); die Ausschmückung (*ornamentation*); die Ausmalung (*décor*).
decorator ['dekəreitə], *s.* der Zimmermaler.
decorous ['dekərəs *or* di'kɔ:rəs], *adj.* anständig, sittsam.
decorum [di'kɔ:rəm], *s.* das Dekorum, das anständige Benehmen.
decoy [di'kɔi], *s.* der Köder (*bait*). — *v.a.* locken, verlocken.
decrease [di'kri:s], *v.a.* vermindern, verringern. — *v.n.* abnehmen. — ['di:kri:s], *s.* die Abnahme, die Verringerung.
decree [di'kri:], *s.* der Beschluß (*resolution*); (*Law*) das Urteil; — *nisi*, das provisorische Scheidungsurteil. — *v.a.*, *v.n.* eine Verordnung erlassen; beschließen (*decide*).
decrepit [di'krepit], *adj.* abgelebt; gebrechlich (*frail*).
decry [di'krai], *v.a.* verrufen; in Verruf bringen.
dedicate ['dedikeit], *v.a.* widmen, weihen, zueignen (*to*, *Dat.*).
dedication [dedi'keiʃən],. *s.* die Widmung, Weihung; die Zueignung.
dedicatory ['dedikeitəri], *adj.* zueignend.
deduce [di'dju:s], *v.a.* schließen (*conclude*); ableiten (*derive*).
deduct [di'dʌkt], *v.a.* abziehen (*subtract*); abrechnen (*take off*).
deduction [di'dʌkʃən], *s.* der Abzug (*subtraction*); die Folgerung (*inference*); der Rabatt (*in price*).
deductive [di'dʌktiv], *adj.* (*Log.*) deduktiv.
deed [di:d], *s.* die Tat, die Handlung (*action*); (*Law*) die Urkunde, das Dokument.
deem [di:m], *v.a.* erachten, halten für.
deep [di:p], *adj.* tief; — *freeze*, die Tiefkühlung; (*fig.*) dunkel. — *s.* die Tiefe (des Meeres).
deepen [di:pn], *v.a.* vertiefen. — *v.n.* tiefer werden; sich vertiefen.
deer [diə], *s.* (*Zool.*) das Rotwild, der Hirsch; — *stalking*, die Pirsch.
deface [di'feis], *v.a.* entstellen, verunstalten.
defalcate [di'fælkeit], *v.n.* Gelder unterschlagen.
defamation [defə'meiʃən], *s.* die Verleumdung.
defamatory [di'fæmətəri], *adj.* verleumderisch.
defame [di'feim], *v.a.* verleumden.
default [di'fɔ:lt], *v.n.* (vor Gericht) ausbleiben. — *s.* der Fehler (*error*); die Unterlassung (*omission*).
defaulter [di'fɔ:ltə], *s.* der Pflichtvergessene; (*Law*) der Schuldige.
defeat [di'fi:t], *v.a.* schlagen, besiegen. — *s.* die Niederlage.
defect [di'fekt], *s.* der Fehler, Makel. —*v.n.* abfallen (*desert*, *from*, von, *Dat.*).
defection [di'fekʃən], *s.* der Abfall.
defective [di'fektiv], *adj.* fehlerhaft, mangelhaft.
defectiveness [di'fektivnis], *s.* die Mangelhaftigkeit, die Fehlerhaftigkeit.
defence [di'fens], *s.* die Verteidigung.
defenceless [di'fenslis], *adj.* wehrlos.
defencelessness [di'fenslisnis], *s.* die Wehrlosigkeit.
defend [di'fend], *v.a.* verteidigen.
defendant [di'fendənt], *s.* (*Law*) der Angeklagte.
defensive [di'fensiv], *adj.* verteidigend. — *s.* die Defensive; *be on the* —, sich verteidigen.
defer [di'fə:], *v.a.* aufschieben (*postpone*). — *v.n.* sich unterordnen, sich fügen (*to*, *Dat.*).
deference ['defərəns], *s.* der Respekt, die Achtung (*to*, vor, *Dat.*).
deferential [defə'renʃəl], *adj.* ehrerbietig, respektvoll.
defiance [di'faiəns], *s.* der Trotz, die Herausforderung.
defiant [di'faiənt], *adj.* trotzig, herausfordernd.
deficiency [di'fiʃənsi], *s.* die Unzulänglichkeit, der Mangel (*quantity*); die Fehlerhaftigkeit (*quality*).
deficient [di'fiʃənt], *adj.* unzulänglich (*quantity*); fehlerhaft (*quality*).
deficit ['defisit], *s.* das Defizit, der Fehlbetrag.
defile (1) [di'fail], *v.a.* schänden, beflecken.
defile (2) ['di:fail], *v.n.* vorbeimarschieren (*march past*) (an, *Dat.*). — *s.* der Engpaß.
defilement [di'failmənt], *s.* die Schändung.
define [di'fain], *v.a.* definieren, begrenzen; bestimmen (*determine*).
definite ['definit], *adj.* bestimmt (*certain*); klar, deutlich (*clear*); endgültig (*final*).
definition [defi'niʃən], *s.* die Definition, die Klarheit; (*Maths.*) die Bestimmung.
definitive [di'finitiv], *adj.* definitiv, endgültig (*final*); bestimmt (*certain*).
deflect [di'flekt], *v.a.* ablenken (*divert*). — *v.n.* abweichen (von, *Dat.*).
defoliation [di:fouli'eiʃən], *s.* der Blätterfall.
deform [di'fɔ:m], *v.a.* verunstalten, entstellen. — *v.n.* (*Metall.*) sich verformen.
deformity [di'fɔ:miti], *s.* die Entstellung; die Häßlichkeit (*ugliness*).
defraud [di'frɔ:d], *v.a.* betrügen.
defray [di'frei], *v.a.* bestreiten, bezahlen (*costs*).
deft [deft], *adj.* geschickt, gewandt.
deftness ['deftnis], *s.* die Gewandtheit, die Geschicktheit.
defunct [di'fʌŋkt], *adj.* verstorben. — *s.* der Verstorbene.

defy [di'fai], *v.a.* trotzen (*Dat.*).
degenerate [di'dʒenəreit], *v.n.* entarten; herabsinken (*sink low*). —[-rit], *adj.* degeneriert, entartet.
degradation [degri'deiʃən], *s.* die Absetzung, Entsetzung, Degradierung.
degrade [di'greid], *v.a.* (*Mil.*) degradieren; entwürdigen; vermindern.
degraded [di'greidid], *adj.* heruntergekommen.
degrading [di'greidiŋ], *adj.* entehrend.
degree [di'gri:], *s.* (*Meas.*, *Univ.*) der Grad; (*Univ.*) die akademische Würde; die Stufe (*step, stage*); die Ordnung, die Klasse (*order, class*); *by —s*, nach und nach, allmählich.
deify ['di:ifai], *v.a.* vergöttern.
deign [dein], *v.n.* geruhen, belieben.
deity ['di:iti], *s.* die Gottheit.
dejected [di'dʒektid], *adj.* niedergeschlagen.
dejection [di'dʒekʃən], *s.* die Niedergeschlagenheit.
delay [di'lei], *v.a.*, *v.n.* aufschieben (*put off*); verzögern (*retard*). — *s.* der Aufschub; die Verzögerung.
delectable [di'lektəbl], *adj.* erfreulich, köstlich.
delectation [delek'teiʃən], *s.* die Freude, das Ergötzen (*in*, an, *Dat.*).
delegate ['deligit], *s.* der Delegierte, Abgeordnete; der Vertreter. — ['deligeit], *v.a.* delegieren, entsenden.
delegation [deli'geiʃən], *s.* die Delegation, die Abordnung.
delete [di'li:t], *v.a.* tilgen, (aus-)streichen, auslöschen (*writing*).
deletion [di'li:ʃən], *s.* die Tilgung, die Auslöschung.
deleterious [deli'tiəriəs], *adj.* schädlich.
delf [delf], *s.* das Delfter Porzellan.
deliberate [di'libərit], *adj.* absichtlich (*intentional*); vorsichtig (*careful*); bedächtig (*thoughtful*). — [-reit], *v.n.* beratschlagen, Rat halten. — *v.a.* überlegen, bedenken.
deliberateness [di'libəritnis], *s.* die Bedächtigkeit (*thoughtfulness*); die Absichtlichkeit (*intention*).
deliberation [dilibə'reiʃən], *s.* die Überlegung, die Beratung.
delicacy ['delikəsi], *s.* die Feinheit, Zartheit (*manner*); der Leckerbissen (*luxury food*); die Schwächlichkeit (*health*).
delicate ['delikit], *adj.* fein (*manner*); schwächlich (*sickly*); kitzlig, heikel (*difficult*).
delicious [di'liʃəs], *adj.* köstlich (*food*).
deliciousness [di'liʃəsnis], *s.* die Köstlichkeit.
delight [di'lait], *s.* das Entzücken, das Vergnügen; *Turkish* —, türkisches Konfekt; *take — in*, an etwas Gefallen finden, sich freuen (an, über). — *v.a.*, *v.n.* entzücken, erfreuen (*in*, an, *Dat.*).
delightful [di'laitful], *adj.* entzückend, bezaubernd.
delimit [di:'limit], *v.a.* abgrenzen, begrenzen.
delimitation [di:limi'teiʃən], *s.* die Begrenzung, Abgrenzung.
delineate [di'linieit], *v.a.* umreißen, entwerfen, skizzieren (*draft, sketch*); schildern, beschreiben (*describe*).
delineation [dilini'eiʃən], *s.* die Skizze, der Entwurf (*sketch, draft*); die Schilderung (*description*).
delinquency [di'liŋkwənsi], *s.* das Verbrechen.
delinquent [di'liŋkwənt], *adj.* verbrecherisch. — *s.* der Verbrecher, Missetäter (*criminal*).
deliquesce [deli'kwes], *v.n.* (*Chem.*) zergehen, zerschmelzen.
deliquescence [deli'kwesəns], *s.* das Zerschmelzen, die Schmelzbarkeit.
deliquescent [deli'kwesənt], *adj.* leicht schmelzbar (*melting*); leicht zerfliessend (*butter etc.*).
delirious [di'liriəs], *adj.* (*Med.*) phantasierend, wahnsinnig.
delirium [di'liriəm], *s.* (*Med.*) das Delirium; der Wahnsinn (*madness*); das Phantasieren (*raving*); — *tremens*, der Säuferwahnsinn.
deliver [di'livə], *v.a.* abliefern, überreichen (*hand over*); liefern (*goods*); befreien (*free*); erlösen (*redeem*); zustellen (*letters etc.*); entbinden (*woman of child*).
deliverance [di'livərəns], *s.* die Erlösung (*redemption*); die Befreiung (*liberation*); die Übergabe.
delivery [di'livəri], *s.* die Befreiung (*liberation*); (*Med.*) die Niederkunft, Entbindung; der Vortrag (*speech*); die Lieferung, die Zustellung (*goods*); — *man*, der Zustellbote; — *van*, der Lieferwagen.
dell [del], *s.* das enge Tal.
delude [di'lu:d], *v.a.* betrügen, täuschen.
deluge ['delju:dʒ], *s.* die Überschwemmung. — *v.a.* überschwemmen.
delusion [di'lu:ʒən], *s.* die Täuschung, das Blendwerk.
delusive, delusory [di'lu:ziv, di'lu:zəri], *adj.* täuschend, trügerisch.
delve [delv], *v.n.* graben.
demagogic(al) [demə'gɔdʒik(əl)], *adj.* demagogisch.
demagogue ['deməgɔg], *s.* der Demagoge, der Aufrührer.
demand [di'ma:nd], *v.a.* verlangen, fordern. — *s.* die Forderung; das Begehren (*desire*); *on* —, auf Verlangen; *in great* —, viel gefragt; *supply and* —, Angebot und Nachfrage.
demarcate [di:'ma:keit], *v.a.* abgrenzen; abstecken (*field*).
demarcation [di:ma:'keiʃən], *s.* die Abgrenzung; — *line*, die Grenzlinie.
demeanour [di'mi:nə], *s.* das Benehmen.
demented [di'mentid], *adj.* wahnsinnig, von Sinnen, toll.
demerit [di:'merit], *s.* der Fehler.

demesne [di'mi:n *or* -'mein], *s.* das Erbgut; die Domäne.
demi- ['demi], *prefix.* halb-.
demigod ['demigɔd], *s.* der Halbgott.
demijohn ['demidʒɔn], *s.* der Glasballon.
demise [di'maiz], *s.* der Tod, das Hinscheiden. — *v.a.* (*Law*) vermachen.
demisemiquaver ['demisemikweivə], *s.* (*Mus.*) die Zweiunddreißigstelnote.
demobilize [di:'moubilaiz], *v.a.* demobilisieren.
democracy [di'mɔkrəsi], *s.* die Demokratie.
democratic [demo'krætik], *adj.* demokratisch.
demolish [di'mɔliʃ], *v.a.* demolieren, zerstören, niederreißen.
demon ['di:mən], *s.* der Dämon, der Teufel; *a — for work,* ein unersättlicher Arbeiter.
demoniac [di'mouniæk], **demoniacal** [di:mə'naiəkl], *adj.* besessen, teuflisch.
demonstrable [di'mɔnstrəbl], *adj.* beweisbar, nachweislich (*verifiable*).
demonstrate ['demənstreit], *v.a., v.n.* beweisen (*prove*); demonstrieren.
demonstration [demən'streiʃən], *s.* der Beweis (*theoretical*); die Demonstration (*practical*); (*Pol.*) Kundgebung.
demonstrative [di'mɔnstrətiv], *adj.* (*Gram.*) demonstrativ; überschwenglich (*emotional*).
demoralize [di:'mɔrəlaiz], *v.a.* demoralisieren.
demote [di:'mout], *v.a.* (*Mil., official*) degradieren.
demotion [di:'mouʃən], *s.* (*Mil., official*) die Degradierung.
demur [di'mə:], *v.n.* Anstand nehmen; Einwendungen machen (*raise objections*); zögern, zaudern (*hesitate*). — *s.* der Zweifel, der Skrupel.
demure [di'mjuə], *adj.* sittsam, zimperlich; spröde (*prim*).
demureness [di'mjuənis], *s.* die Sittsamkeit; die Sprödigkeit (*primness*).
den [den], *s.* die Höhle, Grube; *lion's —,* die Löwengrube.
denial [di'naiəl], *s.* die Verneinung, das Dementi (*negation*); das Ableugnen (*disclaimer*); die Absage (*refusal*).
denizen ['denizən], *s.* der Bürger, der Alteingesessene.
denominate [di'nɔmineit], *v.a.* nennen, benennen (*name*).
denomination [dinɔmi'neiʃən], *s.* die Bezeichnung; der Nennwert (*currency*); (*Rel.*) das Bekenntnis.
denominational [dinɔmi'neiʃənəl], *adj.* konfessionell.
denominator [di'nɔmineitə], *s.* (*Maths.*) der Nenner.
denote [di'nout], *v.a.* bezeichnen, kennzeichnen.
dénouement [dei'nu:mɔ̃], *s.* die Entwicklung, die Darlegung, die Lösung.
denounce [di'nauns], *v.a.* denunzieren, angeben; (*Law*) anzeigen.
dense [dens], *adj.* dicht; (*coll.*) beschränkt (*stupid*).
density ['densiti], *s.* die Dichte; — *of population,* die Bevölkerungsdichte.
dent (1) [dent], *s.* die Beule.
dent (2) [dent], *s.* die Kerbe (*in wood*); der Einschnitt (*cut*).
dental [dentl], *adj.* Zahn-; — *studies,* zahnärztliche Studien; — *treatment,* die Zahnbehandlung. — *s.* (*Phonet.*) der Zahnlaut.
dentist ['dentist], *s.* der Zahnarzt.
dentistry ['dentistri], *s.* die Zahnheilkunde.
denude [di'nju:d], *v.a.* entblößen; berauben (*of, Genit.*).
denunciation [dinʌnsi'eiʃən], *s.* die Denunzierung, die Anzeige.
deny [di'nai], *v.a.* verneinen (*negate*); abschlagen (*refuse*); verleugnen (*refuse to admit*).
deodorant, deodorizer [di:'oudərənt, di:'oudəraizə], *s.* der Geruchsentzieher (*apparatus*); der Deodorant.
deodorize [di:'oudəraiz], *v.a.* geruchlos machen.
depart [di'pɑ:t], *v.n.* abreisen, abfahren (*for,* nach, *Dat.*); scheiden.
department [di'pɑ:tmənt], *s.* die Abteilung; — *store,* das Kaufhaus.
departmental [di:pɑ:t'mentl], *adj.* Abteilungs-.
departure [di'pɑ:tʃə], *s.* die Abreise, die Abfahrt.
depend [di'pend], *v.n.* abhängen, abhängig sein (*upon,* von, *Dat.*); sich verlassen (*upon,* auf, *Acc.*); *that —s,* das kommt darauf an.
dependable [di'pendəbl], *adj.* verläßlich, zuverlässig.
dependant [di'pendənt], *s.* das abhängige Familienmitglied (*member of family*); der Angehörige, Abhängige.
dependence [di'pendəns], *s.* die Abhängigkeit (*need*); das Vertrauen, der Verlaß (*reliance*).
dependency [di'pendənsi], *s.* (*Pol.*) die abhängige Kolonie.
dependent [di'pendənt], *adj.* abhängig (*upon,* von, *Dat.*).
depict [di'pikt], *v.a.* schildern, beschreiben.
deplete [di'pli:t], *v.a.* entleeren (*make empty*); erschöpfen (*exhaust*).
depletion [di'pli:ʃən], *s.* die Entleerung.
deplorable [di'plɔ:rəbl], *adj.* bedauernswert, bedauerlich.
deplore [di'plɔ:], *v.a.* beklagen.
deploy [di'plɔi], *v.a.* entfalten. — *v.n.* sich entfalten; (*Mil.*) aufmarschieren.
deployment [di'plɔimənt], *s.* (*Mil.*) das Deployieren; die Entfaltung.
deponent [di'pounənt], *s.* (*Law*) der vereidigte Zeuge. — *adj.* (*Gram.*) (*verb*) das Deponens.
depopulate [di:'pɔpjuleit], *v.a.* entvölkern.
deport [di'pɔ:t], *v.a.* deportieren.
deportation [di:pɔ:'teiʃən], *s.* die Deportation.

deportment [di'pɔ:tmənt], *s.* die körperliche Haltung (*physical*); das Benehmen (*social*).
depose [di'pouz], *v.a.* absetzen (*remove from office*); (*Law*) zu Papier bringen (*write down*); schriftlich erklären (*declare in writing*).
deposit [di'pɔzit], *s.* (*Comm.*) die Anzahlung; (*Geol.*, *Chem.*) der Niederschlag; (*Geol.*) die Ablagerung; (*Comm.*) — *account*, das Depositenkonto. — *v.a.* (*Geol.*, *Chem.*) absetzen; (*Comm.*) anzahlen, einzahlen.
deposition [di:pə'ziʃən], *s.* die Niederschrift, die schriftliche Erklärung; die Absetzung (*removal from office*).
depositor [di'pɔzitə], *s.* (*Comm.*) der Einzahler.
depository [di'pɔzitəri], *s.* das Lagerhaus.
depot ['depou], *s.* das Depot, das Lagerhaus (*store*); (*Am.*) der Bahnhof.
deprave [di'preiv], *v.a.* verderben.
depraved [di'preivd], *adj.* (moralisch) verdorben.
depravity [di'præviti], *s.* die Verdorbenheit, die Verworfenheit.
deprecate ['deprikeit], *v.a.* mißbilligen (*disapprove of*; *Acc.*); sich verbitten.
deprecation [depri'keiʃən], *s.* die Abbitte; die Mißbilligung (*disapproval*).
depreciate [di'pri:ʃieit], *v.a.* abwerten, herabwürdigen. — *v.n.* an Wert verlieren, im Wert sinken.
depreciation [dipri:ʃi'eiʃən], *s.* die Abwertung; der Verlust (*loss*); (*Pol.*, *Comm.*) die Entwertung.
depredation [depri'deiʃən], *s.* das Plündern, der Raub.
depress [di'pres], *v.a.* niederdrücken (*press down*); deprimieren (*morale*).
depressed [di'prest], *adj.* niedergeschlagen.
depression [di'preʃən], *s.* das Niederdrücken (*action*); (*Pol.*) die Depression; die Niedergeschlagenheit (*despondency*); das Tief (*weather*).
deprivation [depri'veiʃən], *s.* der Verlust (*lack*); die Beraubung (*robbery*).
deprive [di'praiv], *v.a.* berauben (*of*, *Genit.*); wegnehmen (*of*, *Acc.*).
depth [depθ], *s.* die Tiefe; — *charge*, die Unterwasserbombe; *in the —s of night*, in tiefster Nacht; (*Phys.*) — *of focus*, die Tiefenschärfe; *be out of o.'s.* —, den Grund unter seinen Füßen verloren haben, ratlos sein (*be helpless*); — *sounder*, das Echolot.
deputation [depju'teiʃən], *s.* die Deputation, die Abordnung.
depute [di'pju:t], *v.a.* abordnen, entsenden.
deputize ['depjutaiz], *v.n.* vertreten (*for*, *Acc.*).
deputy ['depjuti], *s.* der Abgeordnete, der Deputierte (*delegate*); der Vertreter (*replacement*).
derail [di:'reil], *v.a.* zum Entgleisen bringen. — *v.n.* entgleisen.
derailment [di:'reilmənt], *s.* die Entgleisung.
derange [di'reindʒ], *v.a.* verwirren, stören.
derangement [di'reindʒmənt], *s.* die Verwirrung; die Geistesstörung (*madness*).
derelict ['derilikt], *adj.* verlassen.
dereliction [deri'likʃən], *s.* das Verlassen; — *of duty*, die Pflichtvergessenheit.
deride [di'raid], *v.a.* verlachen, verhöhnen.
derision [di'riʒən], *s.* die Verhöhnung.
derisive [di'raisiv], *adj.* höhnisch, spöttisch.
derivable [di'raivəbl], *adj.* ableitbar.
derivation [deri'veiʃən], *s.* die Ableitung.
derivative [di'rivətiv], *adj.* abgeleitet. — *s.* das abgeleitete Wort.
derive [di'raiv], *v.a.*, *v.n.* ableiten, herleiten.
derogation [dero'geiʃən], *s.* die Herabsetzung.
derrick ['derik], *s.* der Ladebaum.
dervish ['də:viʃ], *s.* der Derwisch.
descant ['deskænt], *s.* (*Mus.*) der Diskant *or* der Sopran. — [dis'kænt], *v.n.* sich verbreiten (*on*, über, *Acc.*).
descend [di'send], *v.n.* hinab- *or* herabsteigen (*go down*); abstammen (*stem from*).
descendant [di'sendənt], *s.* der Nachkomme.
descent [di'sent], *s.* der Abstieg (*going down*); der Fall (*decline*); die Abstammung (*forebears*); der Abhang (*slope*); (*Aviat.*) die Landung.
describable [dis'kraibəbl], *adj.* zu beschreiben, beschreibbar.
describe [dis'kraib], *v.a.* beschreiben, schildern.
description [dis'kripʃən], *s.* die Beschreibung; *of any* —, jeder Art.
descriptive [dis'kriptiv], *adj.* schildernd, beschreibend.
desecrate ['desikreit], *v.a.* entweihen, entheiligen.
desecration [desi'kreiʃən], *s.* die Entweihung, die Schändung.
desert (1) ['dezət], *s.* die Wüste.
desert (2) [di'zə:t], *v.a.* verlassen, im Stiche lassen. — *v.n.* desertieren.
desert (3) [di'zə:t], *s.* (*usually pl.*) das Verdienst.
desertion [di'zə:ʃən], *s.* (*Mil.*) die Fahnenflucht.
deserve [di'zə:v], *v.a.* verdienen.
deserving [di'zə:viŋ], *adj.* verdienstvoll.
design [di'zain], *v.a.* entwerfen (*plan*); vorhaben (*intend*); bestimmen (*determine*). — *s.* der Entwurf (*sketch*); der Plan (*draft*); die Absicht, das Vorhaben (*intention*); das Muster (*pattern*).

designate ['dezigneit], *v.a.* bezeichnen (*mark*); ernennen (*appoint*). — [-nit], *adj.* ernannt; *chairman* —, der künftige Vorsitzende.
designation [dezig'neiʃən], *s.* die Bestimmung, Ernennung (*appointment*); die Bezeichnung (*mark*).
designer [di'zainə], *s.* der Zeichner, der Graphiker (*artist*); der Ränkeschmied (*schemer*).
designing [di'zainiŋ], *adj.* hinterlistig, schlau.
desirable [di'zaiərəbl], *adj.* erwünscht, wünschenswert.
desire [di'zaiə], *s.* der Wunsch, die Begierde; das Verlangen, die Sehnsucht (*longing*). — *v.a.* verlangen, begehren.
desirous [di'zaiərəs], *adj.* begierig (*of*, *inf.*).
desist [di'zist], *v.n.* ablassen, aufhören.
desk [desk], *s.* der Schreibtisch; das Pult; — *lamp*, die Tischlampe *or* Bürolampe.
desolate ['desəlit], *adj.* verlassen, öde; trostlos (*sad*). — [-leit], *v.a.* verwüsten (*lay waste*).
desolation [desə'leiʃən], *s.* die Verwüstung (*of land*); die Trostlosigkeit (*sadness*).
despair [dis'pɛə], *v.n.* verzweifeln (*of*, an, *Dat.*). — *s.* die Verzweiflung.
despatch, dispatch [dis'pætʃ], *v.a.* absenden, befördern (*post*); abfertigen (*send*); erledigen (*deal with*); töten (*kill*). — *s.* die Abfertigung (*clearance*); die Eile (*speed*); die Depesche (*message*).
desperado [despə'reidou, -'rɑ:dou], *s.* der Wagehals, der Draufgänger.
desperate ['despərit], *adj.* verzweifelt.
desperation [despə'reiʃən], *s.* die Verzweiflung.
despicable ['despikəbl], *adj.* verächtlich.
despise [dis'paiz], *v.a.* verachten.
despite [dis'pait], *prep.* trotz (*Genit.*, *Dat.*).
despoil [dis'pɔil], *v.a.* plündern, ausrauben.
despondency [dis'pɔndənsi], *s.* die Verzweiflung, Verzagtheit.
despondent [dis'pɔndənt], *adj.* verzagend, verzweifelnd, mutlos.
despot ['despɔt], *s.* der Despot, der Tyrann.
despotic [des'pɔtik], *adj.* despotisch.
despotism ['despətizm], *s.* (*Pol.*) der Despotismus.
dessert [di'zə:t], *s.* das Dessert, der Nachtisch.
destination [desti'neiʃən], *s.* die Bestimmung, das Ziel; der Bestimmungsort (*address*); das Reiseziel (*journey*).
destine ['destin], *v.a.* bestimmen.
destiny ['destini], *s.* das Geschick; das Schicksal, das Verhängnis (*fate*).
destitute ['destitju:t], *adj.* verlassen (*deserted*); hilflos, mittellos (*poor*); in bitterer Not (*in great distress*).
destitution [desti'tju:ʃən], *s.* die Notlage, die bittere Not.
destroy [dis'trɔi], *v.a.* zerstören (*buildings*); verwüsten; vernichten (*lives*).
destroyer [dis'trɔiə], *s.* der Zerstörer.
destructible [dis'trʌktibl], *adj.* zerstörbar.
destruction [dis'trʌkʃən], *s.* die Zerstörung (*of buildings*), die Verwüstung; die Vernichtung.
destructive [dis'trʌktiv], *adj.* zerstörend, verderblich.
destructiveness [dis'trʌktivnis], *s.* die Zerstörungswut, der Zerstörungssinn.
desultory ['dezəltəri], *adj.* unmethodisch, sprunghaft; oberflächlich (*superficial*).
detach [di'tætʃ], *v.a.* absondern, trennen.
detachment [di'tætʃmənt], *s.* die Absonderung (*separation*); (*Mil.*) das Kommando.
detail [di'teil], *v.a.* im einzelnen beschreiben (*describe minutely*); (*Mil.*) abkommandieren. — ['di:teil], *s.* die Einzelheit.
detailed ['di:teild], *adj.* ausführlich; detailliert, ins Einzelne gehend (*report etc.*); [di'teild], (*Mil.*) abkommandiert.
detain [di'tein], *v.a.* aufhalten, zurückhalten; festhalten (*in prison*).
detect [di'tekt], *v.a.* entdecken, aufdecken.
detection [di'tekʃən], *s.* die Entdeckung, die Aufdeckung.
detective [di'tektiv], *s.* der Detektiv.
detention [di'tenʃən], *s.* (*Law*) die Haft; die Vorenthaltung (*of articles*).
deter [di'tə:], *v.a.* abschrecken.
detergent [di'tə:dʒənt], *s.* das Reinigungsmittel.
deteriorate [di'tiəriəreit], *v.n.* sich verschlimmern, verschlechtern.
deterioration [ditiəriə'reiʃən], *s.* die Verschlimmerung.
determinable [di'tə:minəbl], *adj.* bestimmbar.
determinate [ditə:minit], *adj.* festgesetzt, bestimmt.
determination [di'tə:mi'neiʃən], *s.* die Entschlossenheit (*resoluteness*); die Bestimmung (*identification*); der Entschluß (*resolve*).
determine [di'tə:min], *v.a.* bestimmen (*ascertain*); beschließen (*resolve*).
deterrent [di'terənt], *s.* das Abschreckungsmittel.
detest [di'test], *v.a.* verabscheuen.
detestable [di'testəbl], *adj.* abscheulich.
detestation [detes'teiʃən], *s.* der Abscheu (*of*, vor, *Dat.*).
dethrone [di:'θroun], *v.a.* entthronen, vom Thron verdrängen.
detonate ['di:- *or* 'detoneit], *v.n.* detonieren, explodieren. — *v.a.* explodieren, detonieren lassen, zum Detonieren bringen.

detonation [deto'neiʃən], *s.* die Detonation, die Explosion.
detonator ['detoneitə], *s.* der Zünder, die Zündpatrone; (*Railw.*) die Knallpatrone.
detour ['deituə *or* di'tuə], *s.* der Umweg; (*Civil Engin.*) die Umleitung. — *v.n.* (*Am.*) einen Umweg machen. — *v.a.* (*Am.*) umleiten (*re-route*).
detract [di'trækt], *v.a.*, *v.n.* abziehen; schmälern.
detraction [di'trækʃən], *s.* die Schmälerung, die Verleumdung (*slander*).
detractive [di'træktiv], *adj.* verleumderisch.
detractor [di'træktə], *s.* der Verleumder.
detriment ['detrimənt], *s.* der Nachteil, der Schaden.
detrimental [detri'mentl], *adj.* nachteilig; abträglich; schädlich (*harmful*).
deuce (1) [dju:s], *s.* die Zwei (*game*); (*Tennis*) der Einstand.
deuce (2) [dju:s], *s.* (*coll.*) der Teufel.
devastate ['devəsteit], *v.a.* verwüsten, verheeren.
devastating ['devəsteitiŋ], *adj.* schrecklich, verheerend.
devastation [devəs'teiʃən], *s.* die Verheerung, die Verwüstung.
develop [di'veləp], *v.a.* entwickeln. — *v.n.* sich entwickeln; sich entfalten (*prove, turn out*).
developer [di'veləpə], *s.* (*Phot.*) das Entwicklungsmittel.
development [di'veləpmənt], *s.* die Entwicklung.
developmental [diveləp'mentl], *adj.* Entwicklungs-.
deviate ['di:vieit], *v.n.* abweichen.
deviation [di:vi'eiʃən], *s.* die Abweichung.
device [di'vais], *s.* die Vorrichtung (*equipment*); der Kungstgriff (*trick*).
devil [devl], *s.* der Teufel; der Lehrling, Laufbursche (*printer's, lawyer's*); *the — take the hindmost!* der Teufel hol was dann kommt! — *v.n.* in der Lehre sein (*for*, bei, *Dat.*).
devilish ['devəliʃ], *adj.* teuflisch.
devilment, devilry ['devəlmənt, 'devəlri], *s.* die Teufelei, die Teufelslaune.
devious ['di:viəs], *adj.* abweichend; abgelegen; abwegig.
deviousness ['di:viəsnis], *s.* die Abschweifung, Verirrung.
devise [di'vaiz], *v.a.* erfinden (*invent*); ersinnen (*think out*).
deviser, devisor [di'vaizə], *s.* der Erfinder (*inventor*); der Erblasser (*testator*).
devoid [di'vɔid], *adj.* frei (*of*, von, *Dat.*); ohne (*Acc.*).
devolve [di'vɔlv], *v.a.* übertragen (*transfer*); abwälzen (*pass on burden*) (*to*, auf, *Acc.*). — *v.n.* zufallen (*Dat.*).
devote [di'vout], *v.a.* widmen; aufopfern (*sacrifice*).
devoted [di'voutid], *adj.* ergeben (*affectionate*); geweiht (*consecrated*).
devotee [devo'ti:], *s.* der Anhänger; der Verehrer (*fan*).
devotion [di'vouʃən], *s.* die Hingabe; die Aufopferung (*sacrifice*); die Andacht (*prayer*).
devotional [di'vouʃənəl], *adj.* Andachts-.
devour [di'vauə], *v.a.* verschlingen.
devout [di'vaut], *adj.* andächtig, fromm.
devoutness [di'vautnis], *s.* die Frömmigkeit.
dew [dju:], *s.* der Tau.
dewy [dju:i], *adj.* betaut, taufeucht.
dexterity [deks'teriti], *s.* die Gewandtheit, die Fertigkeit.
dexterous ['dekstərəs], *adj.* gewandt, geschickt.
diabetes [daiə'bi:ti:z], *s.* (*Med.*) die Zuckerkrankheit.
diabetic [daiə'betik], *s.* (*Med.*) der Zuckerkranke. — *adj.* zuckerkrank.
diabolic(al) [daiə'bɔlik(əl)], *adj.* teuflisch.
diadem ['daiədem], *s.* das Diadem, das Stirnband.
diæresis [dai'iərəsis], *s.* die Diärese.
diagnose [daiəg'nouz], *v.a.* diagnostizieren, als Diagnose finden, befinden.
diagnosis [daiəg'nousis], *s.* die Diagnose, der Befund.
diagonal [dai'ægənəl], *adj.* diagonal, schräg. — *s.* (*Geom.*) die Diagonale.
diagram ['daiəgræm], *s.* das Diagramm.
dial ['daiəl], *s.* das Zifferblatt; (*Teleph.*) die Wählerscheibe. — *v.a.*, *v.n.* (*Teleph.*) wählen.
dialect ['daiəlekt], *s.* der Dialekt, die Mundart.
dialectic [daiə'lektik], *s.* (*Phil.*) die Dialektik.
dialektical [daiə'lektikəl], *adj.* dialektisch, logisch.
dialogue ['daiəlɔg], *s.* der Dialog, das Zwiegespräch.
diameter [dai'æmitə], *s.* der Durchmesser.
diametrical [daiə'metrikəl], *adj.* diametral; gerade entgegengesetzt.
diamond ['daiəmənd], *s.* der Diamant; (*Cards*) das Karo.
diaper ['daiəpə], *s.* (*Am.*) die Windel.
diaphragm ['daiəfræm], *s.* (*Anat.*) das Zwerchfell; (*Phys.*) die Membran.
diarrhœa [daiə'riə], *s.* (*Med.*) der Durchfall.
diary ['daiəri], *s.* das Tagebuch, der Kalender.
diatribe ['daiətraib], *s.* der Tadel, der Angriff (*verbal*), die Schmähschrift (*written*).
dibble [dibl], *s.* der Pflanzstock. — *v.n.* Pflanzen stecken, anpflanzen.
dice [dais], *s. pl.* die Würfel (*sing.* **die**). — *v.a.* würfeln, werfen.

dicker ['dikə], *v.n.* (*Am.*) feilschen, handeln.
dicky ['diki], *s.* das Vorhemd.
dictate [dik'teit], *v.a.*, *v.n.* diktieren, vorschreiben.
dictation [dik'teiʃən], *s.* (*Sch.*) das Diktat.
dictator [dik'teitə], *s.* der Diktator.
dictatorship [dik'teitəʃip], *s.* die Diktatur.
diction ['dikʃən], *s.* die Ausdrucksweise (*speech*).
dictionary ['dikʃənri], *s.* das Wörterbuch.
didactic [di'dæktik], *adj.* lehrhaft, Lehr-.
die (1) [dai], *v.n.* sterben (*of*, an, *Dat.*); — *away*, verebben.
die (2) [dai], *s.* der Würfel (*cube*); die Gießform (*mould*); der Stempel (*punch*); (*Metall.*) das Gesenk (*swage*); — *casting*, der Spritzguß; — *castings*, die Spritzgußteile, Gußteile; — *forging*, das Gesenkschmiedestück.
die (3) [dai] *see under* **dice.**
dielectric [daii'lektrik], *adj.* dielektrisch.
diet (1) ['daiət], *s.* (*Pol.*) der Landtag, Reichstag.
diet (2) ['daiət], *s.* (*Med.*) die Diät. — *v.n.* (*Med.*) eine Diät halten. — *v.a.* (*Med.*) eine Diät vorschreiben.
dietary, dietetic ['daiətəri, daiə'tetik], *adj.* diätetisch.
differ ['difə], *v.n.* sich unterscheiden (*be different from*, von, *Dat.*); anderer Meinung sein (*be of different opinion*).
difference ['difərəns], *s.* (*Maths.*) die Differenz; der Unterschied (*discrepancy*); die Meinungsverschiedenheit (*divergence of opinion*).
different ['difərənt], *adj.* verschieden, verschiedenartig.
differentiate [difə'renʃieit], *v.n.* (*Maths.*) differenzieren; einen Unterschied machen (*between*, zwischen, *Dat.*).
difficult ['difikəlt], *adj.* schwierig, schwer.
difficulty ['difikəlti], *s.* die Schwierigkeit.
diffidence ['difidəns], *s.* die Schüchternheit.
diffident ['difidənt], *adj.* schüchtern.
diffraction [di'frækʃən], *s.* die Ablenkung, (*Phys.*, *Optics*) die Brechung.
diffuse [di'fju:z], *v.a.* ausgießen (*pour*); verbreiten (*spread*). — [di'fju:s], *adj.* verbreitet, weitschweifig (*style*); zerstreut.
diffuseness [di'fju:snis], *s.* die Weitläufigkeit (*style*).
diffusion [di'fju:ʒən], *s.* (*Phys.*) die Diffusion, die Zerstreuung, die Verbreitung.
dig (1) [dig], *v.a. irr.* graben; — *in the ribs*, in die Rippen stoßen. — *v.n.* (*coll.*) wohnen (*live in lodgings*).
dig (2) [dig], *v.a.* (*coll.*) verstehen.

digger ['digə], *s.* der Gräber; (*coll.*) der Australier.
digest [di'dʒest], *v.a.* (*Anat.*) verdauen. — ['daidʒest], *s.* (*Am.*) die Sammlung von Auszügen; (*pl.*) Pandekten.
digestibility [didʒesti'biliti], *s.* die Verdaulichkeit.
digestible [di'dʒestibl], *adj.* verdaulich.
digestion [di'dʒestʃən], *s.* die Verdauung.
digestive [di'dʒestiv], *adj.* Verdauungs-; — *biscuit*, das Kornmehlkeks; — *organs*, die Verdauungsorgane.
digit ['didʒit], *s.* (*Maths.*) die (einstellige) Zahl; der Zahlenwert.
digitalis [didʒi'teilis], *s.* (*Bot.*) der Fingerhut.
dignified ['dignifaid], *adj.* würdig, würdevoll.
dignify ['dignifai], *v.a.* ehren (*honour*); zieren (*decorate*).
dignitary ['dignitəri], *s.* der Würdenträger.
dignity ['digniti], *s.* die Würde.
digress [dai'gres], *v.n.* abweichen, abschweifen.
digression [dai'greʃən], *s.* die Abweichung, die Abschweifung.
digressive [dai'gresiv], *adj.* abschweifend (*style*).
digs [digz], *s. pl.* (*coll.*) das (möblierte) Zimmer, die Wohnung.
dike [daik], *s.* der Graben, der Deich. — *v.a.* eindeichen, eindämmen.
dilapidated [di'læpideitid], *adj.* baufällig.
dilapidation [dilæpi'deiʃən], *s.* die Baufälligkeit, der Verfall.
dilate [d(a)i'leit], *v.a.* erweitern, ausdehnen. — *v.n.* sich ausdehnen; sich auslassen (*speak*) (*on*, über, *Acc.*).
dilation [d(a)i'leiʃən], *s.* die Erweiterung (*expansion*); die Auslassung (*speaking*).
dilatoriness ['dilətərinis], *s.* die Saumseligkeit.
dilatory ['dilətəri], *adj.* zögernd, aufschiebend, saumselig.
dilemma [d(a)i'lemə], *s.* das Dilemma, die Klemme.
diligence ['dilidʒəns], *s.* der Fleiß, die Emsigkeit.
diligent ['dilidʒənt], *adj.* fleißig, arbeitsam.
dilly-dally ['dili'dæli], *v.n.* tändeln, zaudern, Zeit vertrödeln.
dilute [d(a)i'lju:t], *v.a.* (*Chem.*) verdünnen; schwächen (*weaken*).
dilution [d(a)i'lju:ʃən], *s.* die Verdünnung.
diluvial, diluvian [d(a)i'lju:viəl, -iən], *adj.* Diluvial-, des Diluviums; sintflutlich.
dim [dim], *adj.* trübe, unklar; (*Phys.*) abgeblendet. — *v.a.* abdunkeln, abblenden.
dimension [d(a)i'menʃən], *s.* die Dimension, das Maß.
dimensional [d(a)i'menʃənəl], *adj.* dimensional.

diminish [di'miniʃ], *v.a.* vermindern. — *v.n.* sich vermindern.
diminution [dimi'nju:ʃən], *s.* die Verringerung, die Verminderung.
diminutive [di'minjutiv], *adj.* verkleinernd, klein. — *s.* (*Gram.*) das Verkleinerungswort.
dimness ['dimnis], *s.* die Trübheit; die Düsterkeit (*dark*).
dimple [dimpl], *s.* das Grübchen.
dimpled [dimpld], *adj.* mit einem Grübchen.
din [din], *s.* das Getöse, der Lärm.
dine [dain], *v.n.* speisen, essen.
dinginess ['dindʒinis], *s.* die Dunkelheit, die Schäbigkeit.
dingy ['dindʒi], *adj.* dunkel, schäbig.
dinner ['dinə], *s.* das Essen; das Festessen (*formal*); — *jacket*, der Smoking.
dint [dint], *s.* der Nachdruck, der Schlag; *by — of*, mittels (*Genit.*).
diocesan [dai'ɔsisən], *adj.* (*Eccl.*) einer Diözese angehörig, Diözesan–.
diocese ['daiəsis], *s.* (*Eccl.*) die Diözese.
dip [dip], *v.a.* eintauchen, eintunken; abblenden (*lights*). — *v.n.* (unter)-tauchen; sinken; sich flüchtig einlassen (*into*, in). — *s.* die Senke; der Abhang (*slope*).
diphtheria [dif'θiəriə], *s.* (*Med.*) die Diphtherie.
diphthong ['difθɔŋ], *s.* (*Phonet.*) der Diphthong.
diploma [di'ploumə], *s.* das Diplom; *teaching* —, das Lehrerdiplom.
diplomacy [di'plouməsi], *s.* die Diplomatie.
diplomatic [diplo'mætik], *adj.* diplomatisch, taktvoll; urkundlich (*documents*). — *s.* (*pl.*) das Studium der Urkunden.
diplomat(ist) ['diplomæt, di'ploumətist], *s.* (*Pol.*) der Diplomat.
dipper ['dipə], *s.* der Taucher.
dire [daiə], *adj.* fürchterlich, schrecklich; — *necessity*, bittere Not.
direct [d(a)i'rekt], *adj.* direkt, unmittelbar. — *v.a.* leiten (*be in charge of*); hinweisen, hinlenken; den Weg zeigen (*tell the way to*); anordnen (*arrange for*).
direction [d(a)i'rekʃən], *s.* die Leitung (*management*); (*Geog.*) die Richtung, Himmelsrichtung; die Anordnung (*arrangement, order*); *—s for use*, die Gebrauchsanweisung.
director [d(a)i'rektə], *s.* der Direktor; der Leiter.
directory [d(a)i'rektəri], *s.* das Adreßbuch; das Telephonbuch.
dirge [də:dʒ], *s.* der Trauergesang.
dirigible ['diridʒibl], *adj.* lenkbar, leitbar.
dirt [də:t], *s.* der Schmutz, der Kot, Dreck. — *adj.* — *cheap*, spottbillig.
dirty ['də:ti], *adj.* schmutzig; gemein (*joke*).
disability [disə'biliti], *s.* die Unfähigkeit, das Unvermögen (*inability*); die Schädigung (*impairment of health*).
disable [dis'eibl], *v.a.* unfähig *or* untauglich machen.
disablement [dis'eiblmənt], *s.* die Versehrung, die Verkrüppelung.
disabuse [disə'bju:z], *v.a.* aufklären, eines Besseren belehren.
disaccustom [disə'kʌstəm], *v.a.* entwöhnen, abgewöhnen.
disadvantage [disəd'vɑ:ntidʒ], *s.* der Nachteil.
disaffection [disə'fekʃən], *s.* die Abneigung; der Widerwille.
disagree [disə'gri:], *v.n.* nicht übereinstimmen, nicht einer Meinung sein.
disagreeable [disə'griəbl], *adj.* unangenehm, verdrießlich; unfreundlich.
disagreement [disə'gri:mənt], *s.* die Uneinigkeit (*disunity*); die Meinungsverschiedenheit (*difference of opinion*).
disallow [disə'lau], *v.a.* nicht gestatten; in Abrede stellen.
disappear [disə'piə], *v.n.* verschwinden.
disappearance [disə'piərəns], *s.* das Verschwinden.
disappoint [disə'pɔint], *v.a.* enttäuschen.
disappointment [disə'pɔintmənt], *s.* die Enttäuschung.
disapprobation [disæpro'beiʃən], *s.* die Mißbilligung.
disapproval [disə'pru:vəl], *s.* die Mißbilligung.
disapprove [disə'pru:v], *v.a.* mißbilligen (*of*, *Acc.*).
disarm [dis'ɑ:m], *v.a.* entwaffnen. —*v.n.* abrüsten.
disarmament [dis'ɑ:məmənt], *s.* die Abrüstung.
disarray [disə'rei], *v.a.* in Unordnung bringen. — *s.* die Unordnung (*disorder*); die Verwirrung (*confusion*).
disaster [di'zɑ:stə], *s.* das Unglück; das Unheil, die Katastrophe.
disastrous [di'zɑ:strəs], *adj.* unheilvoll, schrecklich.
disavow [disə'vau], *v.a.* ableugnen.
disavowal [disə'vauəl], *s.* das Ableugnen.
disband [dis'bænd], *v.a.* entlassen (*dismiss*); auflösen (*dissolve*).
disbar [dis'bɑ:], *v.a.* (*Law*) von der Rechtspraxis ausschließen.
disbelief [disbi'li:f], *s.* der Unglaube (*incredulity*); der Zweifel (*doubt*).
disbelieve [disbi'li:v], *v.a.* nicht glauben; bezweifeln.
disburse [dis'bə:s], *v.a.* auszahlen, ausgeben.
disbursement [dis'bə:smənt], *s.* die Auszahlung, die Ausgabe.
disc [disk], *s.* (*also Med.*) die Scheibe; die Platte (*record*).
discard [dis'kɑ:d], *v.a.* ablegen, beiseite legen, aufgeben.
discern [di'zə:n *or* di'sə:n], *v.a.* unterscheiden; wahrnehmen, bemerken.
discernment [di'sə:nmənt], *s.* die Urteilskraft (*powers of judgment*); die Einsicht.

discharge [dis'tʃɑ:dʒ], *v.a.* entlassen (*dismiss*); abfeuern (*pistol*); abladen, ausladen (*cargo*); bezahlen (*debt*); tun, erfüllen (*duty*). — *s.* die Entladung (*gun*); die Entlassung (*dismissal*); die Bezahlung (*debt*); die Erfüllung (*duty*).
disciple [di'saipl], *s.* (*Bibl.*) der Jünger; der Schüler.
disciplinarian [disipli'nɛəriən], *s.* der Zuchtmeister.
disciplinary ['disiplinəri], *adj.* disziplinarisch.
discipline ['disiplin], *s.* die Disziplin, die Zucht. — *v.a.* disziplinieren, züchtigen.
disclaim [dis'kleim], *v.a.* verleugnen (*deny*); nicht anerkennen (*refuse to acknowledge*); verzichten (*renounce*).
disclaimer [dis'kleimə], *s.* der Widerruf.
disclose [dis'klouz], *v.a.* eröffnen, enthüllen.
disclosure [dis'klouʒə], *s.* die Eröffnung, die Enthüllung.
discoloration [diskʌlə'reiʃən], *s.* die Entfärbung, Verfärbung.
discomfiture [dis'kʌmfitʃə], *s.* die Verwirrung.
discomfort [dis'kʌmfət], *s.* das Unbehagen; die Beschwerde.
disconcert [diskən'sə:t], *v.a.* außer Fassung bringen (*upset*); vereiteln (*frustrate*).
disconnect [diskə'nekt], *v.a.* trennen (*separate*); abstellen.
disconsolate [dis'kɔnsəlit], *adj.* trostlos, untröstlich.
discontent [diskən'tent], *s.* die Unzufriedenheit, das Mißvergnügen. — *v.a.* mißvergnügt stimmen.
discontinuance [diskən'tinjuəns], *s.* die Beendigung (*finish*); das Aufhören (*suspension*); die Unterbrechung (*interruption*).
discontinue [diskən'tinju:], *v.a.* nicht fortsetzen; unterbrechen (*interrupt*); einstellen.
discord ['diskɔ:d], *s.* die Zwietracht (*disagreement*); (*Mus.*) der Mißklang.
discordance [dis'kɔ:dəns], *s.* die Uneinigkeit.
discordant [dis'kɔ:dənt], *adj.* uneinig, widersprechend.
discount ['diskaunt], *s.* (*Comm.*) der Abzug, der Rabatt; *allow a* —, einen Rabatt gewähren; *be at a* —, unbeliebt sein, nicht geschätzt sein; *sell at a* —, unter dem Preis verkaufen. — [dis'kaunt], *v.a.* (*Comm.*) diskontieren, einen Rabatt gewähren; nur mit Vorsicht aufnehmen (*accept with doubt*).
discountable [dis'kauntəbl], *adj.* diskontierbar, in Abzug zu bringen.
discountenance [dis'kauntinəns], *v.a.* mißbilligen.
discourage [dis'kʌridʒ], *v.a.* entmutigen; abraten (*from*, von, *Dat.*).
discouragement [dis'kʌridʒmənt], *s.* die Entmutigung.
discourse [dis'kɔ:s], *v.n.* einen Vortrag halten (*on*, über, *Acc.*); sprechen. — ['diskɔ:s], *s.* der Vortrag; das Gespräch, die Rede.
discourteous [dis'kə:tiəs], *adj.* unhöflich.
discourtesy [dis'kə:təsi], *s.* die Unhöflichkeit.
discover [dis'kʌvə], *v.a.* entdecken.
discovery [dis'kʌvəri], *s.* die Entdeckung.
discredit [dis'kredit], *s.* der üble Ruf; die Schande. — *v.a.* in schlechten Ruf bringen; diskreditieren.
discreditable [dis'kreditəbl], *adj.* schimpflich.
discreet [dis'kri:t], *adj.* diskret, verschwiegen; vorsichtig (*cautious*).
discrepancy [dis'krepənsi], *s.* die Diskrepanz, der Widerspruch; der Unterschied (*difference*).
discretion [dis'kreʃən], *s.* die Diskretion; die Klugheit; der Takt (*tact*); die Verschwiegenheit (*silence*); *at your* —, nach Ihrem Belieben; *use your* —, handle nach deinem Ermessen; handeln Sie nach Ihrem Ermessen.
discretionary [dis'kreʃənəri], *adj.* willkürlich, uneingeschränkt.
discriminate [dis'krimineit], *v.a.*, *v.n.* unterscheiden (*distinguish*); absondern (*separate*).
discriminating [dis'krimineitiŋ], *adj.* scharfsinnig; einsichtig.
discriminatory [dis'krimineitəri], *adj.* einen Unterschied machend; — *legislation*, das Ausnahmegesetz.
discursive [dis'kə:siv], *adj.* diskursiv, ohne Zusammenhang.
discuss [dis'kʌs], *v.a.* besprechen, erörtern.
discussion [dis'kʌʃən], *s.* die Diskussion, das Gespräch.
disdain [dis'dein], *s.* die Verachtung. — *v.a.* verachten, verschmähen; herabsetzen (*belittle*).
disdainful [dis'deinful], *adj.* geringschätzig, verächtlich.
disease [di'zi:z], *s.* die Krankheit.
diseased [di'zi:zd], *adj.* krank.
disembark [disim'bɑ:k], *v.n.* aussteigen, landen. — *v.a.* aussteigen lassen, ausschiffen.
disembarkation [disembɑ:'keiʃən], *s.* die Ausschiffung; die Landung.
disenchant [disin'tʃɑ:nt], *v.a.* ernüchtern.
disenchantment [disin'tʃɑ:ntmənt], *s.* die Ernüchterung.
disengage [disin'geidʒ], *v.a.* losmachen, befreien (*release*); freigeben. — *v.n.* (*Mil.*) sich absetzen.
disengaged [disin'geidʒd], *adj.* frei (*unoccupied*).
disentangle [disin'tæŋgl], *v.a.* entwirren; befreien (*free*).
disentanglement [disin'tæŋglmənt], *s.* die Entwirrung, die Befreiung.

disfavour [dis'feivə], *s.* die Ungunst, die Ungnade.
disfigure [dis'figə], *v.a.* entstellen, verunstalten.
disfiguration [disfigjuə'reiʃən], *s.* die Entstellung, die Verunstaltung.
disfranchise [dis'fræntʃaiz], *v.a.* das Wahlrecht entziehen (*Dat.*).
disgorge [dis'gɔ:dʒ], *v.a.* ausspeien.
disgrace [dis'greis], *v.a.* entehren, Schande bringen. — *s.* die Ungnade, Schande (*shame*); die Entehrung (*putting to shame*).
disgraceful [dis'greisful], *adj.* schändlich, entehrend.
disgruntled [dis'grʌntld], *adj.* verstimmt, unzufrieden.
disguise [dis'gaiz], *v.a.* verkleiden (*dress*); (*fig.*) verstellen. — *s.* die Verkleidung; die Verstellung.
disgust [dis'gʌst], *s.* der Ekel, der Widerwille. — *v.a.* anekeln; *be —ed*, sehr ärgerlich sein; *be —ed with s. th.*, etwas verabscheuen.
dish [diʃ], *s.* die Schüssel (*bowl*); das Gericht (*food*). — *v.a.* (*coll.*) abtun (*frustrate*); — *up*, auftragen (*food*).
dishcloth ['diʃklɔθ], *s.* das Wischtuch; der Abwaschlappen.
dishearten [dis'hɑ:tn], *v.a.* entmutigen, verzagt machen.
dishevelled [di'ʃevəld], *adj.* aufgelöst (*hair*); zerzaust (*hair, clothes*).
dishonest [dis'ɔnist], *adj.* unehrlich.
dishonesty [dis'ɔnisti], *s.* die Unehrlichkeit.
dishonour [dis'ɔnə], *s.* die Schande. — *v.a.* schänden, Schande bringen (über, *Acc.*).
dishonourable [dis'ɔnərəbl], *adj.* ehrlos, schimpflich.
dishwater ['diʃwɔ:tə], *s.* das Spülwasser.
disillusion [disi'lu:ʒən], *s.* die Enttäuschung, die Ernüchterung. — *v.a.* enttäuschen, ernüchtern.
disinclination [disinkli'neiʃən], *s.* die Abneigung.
disincline [disin'klain], *v.a.* abgeneigt machen (*Dat.*).
disinfect [disin'fekt], *v.a.* desinfizieren.
disinfectant [disin'fektənt], *s.* das Desinfektionsmittel.
disinfection [disin'fekʃən], *s.* die Desinfektion.
disingenuous [disin'dʒenjuəs], *adj.* unaufrichtig, unredlich.
disinherit [disin'herit], *v.a.* enterben.
disinter [disin'tə:], *v.a.* exhumieren, ausgraben.
disinterested [dis'intrəstid], *adj.* uneigennützig.
disinterestedness [dis'intrəstidnis], *s.* die Selbstlosigkeit, die Uneigennützigkeit.
disjoin [dis'dʒɔin], *v.a.* trennen.
disjoint [dis'dʒɔint], *v.a.* zerlegen, zerstückeln.
disjointedness [dis'dʒɔintidnis], *s.* die Zerstücktheit, die Zusammenhangslosigkeit (*style of writing etc.*).
disjunction [dis'dʒʌŋkʃən], *s.* die Trennung, die Abtrennung.
disjunctive [dis'dʒʌŋktiv], *adj.* (*Gram.*) trennend, disjunktiv.
disk [disk] *see* **disc.**
dislike [dis'laik], *v.a.* nicht leiden mögen, nicht gerne haben. — *s.* die Abneigung (*of*, gegen, *Acc.*).
dislocate ['dislokeit], *v.a.* verrenken (*bone*); (*fig.*) in Unordnung bringen.
dislocation [dislo'keiʃən], *s.* (*Med.*) die Verrenkung; die Verwirrung (*traffic etc.*).
dislodge [dis'lɔdʒ], *v.a.* vertreiben (*drive out*); entfernen (*remove*).
disloyal [dis'lɔiəl], *adj.* ungetreu; verräterisch.
disloyalty [dis'lɔiəlti], *s.* die Untreue (*sentiment*); der Verrat (*act*).
dismal ['dizməl], *adj.* trostlos, traurig (*mood*); düster, trüb (*weather*).
dismantle [dis'mæntl], *v.a.* niederreißen, zerlegen; abbauen.
dismay [dis'mei], *v.a.* erschrecken, entmutigen. — *s.* die Furcht, der Schrecken, die Bangigkeit.
dismember [dis'membə], *v.a.* zerstückeln.
dismemberment [dis'membəmənt], *s.* die Zerstückelung, die Aufteilung.
dismiss [dis'mis], *v.a.* entlassen (*person*); aufgeben (*idea*).
dismissal [dis'misəl], *s.* die Entlassung; (*Law*) die Abweisung.
dismount [dis'maunt], *v.n.* vom Pferd absteigen. — *v.a.* (die Truppen) absteigen lassen.
disobedience [diso'bi:djəns], *s.* der Ungehorsam.
disobedient [diso'bi:djənt], *adj.* ungehorsam.
disobey [diso'bei], *v.a., v.n.* nicht gehorchen.
disoblige [diso'blaidʒ], *v.a.* verletzen, unhöflich behandeln.
disorder [dis'ɔ:də], *s.* die Unordnung; der Aufruhr (*riot*). — *v.a.* verwirren, in Unordnung bringen.
disorderliness [dis'ɔ:dəlinis], *s.* die Unordentlichkeit.
disorderly [dis'ɔ:dəli], *adj.* unordentlich (*unsystematic*); aufrührerisch, liederlich.
disorganization [disɔ:gəni'zeiʃən *or* -nai'zeiʃən], *s.* die Zerrüttung, die Auflösung (*dissolution*).
disorganize [dis'ɔ:gənaiz], *v.a.* auflösen.
disown [dis'oun], *v.a.* verleugnen.
disparage [dis'pæridʒ], *v.a.* verunglimpfen (*slight*); herabsetzen (*minimize*).
disparagement [dis'pæridʒmənt], *s.* die Herabsetzung.
disparity [dis'pæriti], *s.* die Ungleichheit.
dispatch [dis'pætʃ] *see* **despatch.**
dispel [dis'pel], *v.a.* vertreiben, verscheuchen.

dispensable [dis'pensəbl], *adj.* erläßlich, entbehrlich.
dispensation [dispen'seiʃən], *s.* die Austeilung; (*Eccl.*) die Dispensation.
dispensary [dis'pensəri], *s.* die Apotheke.
dispense [dis'pens], *v.a.* ausgeben, austeilen (*distribute*); — *with*, entbehren können, verzichten (auf, *Acc.*).
dispenser [dis'pensə], *s.* der Apotheker, der Pharmazeut.
dispersal [dis'pə:səl], *s.* das Zerstreuen, die Verteilung.
disperse [dis'pə:s], *v.a.* zerstreuen. — *v.n.* sich zerstreuen, sich verteilen.
dispirit [dis'pirit], *v.a.* mutlos machen, entmutigen.
displace [dis'pleis], *v.a.* verlegen, versetzen; (*Phys.*) verdrängen; —*d person*, der Heimatlose, der Verschleppte, der Flüchtling.
displacement [dis'pleismənt], *s.* die Versetzung (*from one place to another*); die Entwurzelung (*uprooting*); (*Phys.*) die Verdrängung; (*Naut.*) das Deplacement.
display [dis'plei], *v.a.* entfalten, ausstellen, zur Schau stellen (*show*). — *s.* die Entfaltung (*showing*), die Schaustellung, Ausstellung (*exhibition*).
displease [dis'pli:z], *v.a.* mißfallen (*Dat.*).
displeased [dis'pli:zd], *adj.* ungehalten (*at*, über, *Acc.*).
displeasure [dis'pleʒə], *s.* das Mißvergnügen, das Mißfallen (— *at*, an, *Dat.*).
disposable [dis'pouzəbl], *adj.* (*Comm.*) disponibel; zur Verfügung stehend.
disposal [dis'pouzl], *s.* die Verfügung (*ordering*); die Übergabe (*handing over*); *at o.'s* —, zur Verfügung; *bomb* —, die Unschädlichmachung der Bomben.
dispose [dis'pouz], *v.a.* einrichten (*thing*); geneigt machen (*person*); — *of*, etwas loswerden (*Acc.*). — *v.n.* anordnen (*ordain*).
disposed [dis'pouzd], *adj.* geneigt; *be well — towards s.o.*, jemandem zugeneigt sein *or* wohlwollend gegenüberstehen; *well* —, (in) guter Laune.
disposition [dispə'ziʃən], *s.* (*Psych.*) die Anlage; die Gemütsart (*temperament*); die Anordnung (*sequence*); der Plan, die Anlage (*of book etc.*); die Verfügung (*arrangement*).
dispossess [dispə'zes], *v.a.* enteignen, (des Besitzes) berauben (*Genit.*).
disproof [dis'pru:f], *s.* die Widerlegung.
disproportion [disprə'pɔ:ʃən], *s.* das Mißverhältnis.
disproportionate [disprə'pɔ:sənit], *adj.* unverhältnismäßig.
disprove [dis'pru:v], *v.a.* widerlegen.
disputable [dis'pju:təbl], *adj.* bestreitbar.
disputant ['dispjutənt], *s.* der Opponent, der Disputant.
disputation [dispju'teiʃən], *s.* der gelehrte Streit, die Disputation.
dispute [dis'pju:t], *s.* der Disput, die Meinungsverschiedenheit. — *v.a.*, *v.n.* streiten, verschiedener Ansicht sein; disputieren (*debate*); mit Worten streiten (*argue*).
disqualification [diskwɔlifi'keiʃən], *s.* die Disqualifizierung.
disqualify [dis'kwɔlifai], *v.a.* disqualifizieren, ausschließen.
disquiet [dis'kwaiət], *v.a.* beunruhigen, stören. — *s.* die Unruhe, die Störung.
disquisition [diskwi'ziʃən], *s.* die (lange) Abhandlung *or* Rede.
disregard [disri'gɑ:d], *v.a.* mißachten, nicht beachten. — *s.* die Außerachtlassung, die Mißachtung.
disreputable [dis'repjutəbl], *adj.* verrufen, in üblem Rufe stehend.
disrepute [disri'pju:t], *s.* der schlechte Name, der üble Ruf.
disrespect [disris'pekt], *s.* die Geringschätzung, der Mangel an Respekt. — *v.a.* (*obs.*) mißachten, geringschätzen, respektlos behandeln.
disrespectful [disris'pektful], *adj.* respektlos, unhöflich.
disrobe [dis'roub], *v.a.* entkleiden. — *v.n.* sich entkleiden.
disrupt [dis'rʌpt], *v.a.* abreißen, unterbrechen, stören (*disturb*).
disruption [dis'rʌpʃən], *s.* die Störung, die Unterbrechung (*interruption*); der Bruch.
dissatisfaction [dissætis'fækʃən], *s.* die Unzufriedenheit.
dissatisfied [dis'sætisfaid], *adj.* unzufrieden, unbefriedigt.
dissatisfy [dis'sætisfai], *v.a.* unzufrieden lassen.
dissect [di'sekt], *v.a.* zergliedern, zerlegen; (*Anat.*) sezieren.
dissection [di'sekʃən], *s.* die Zergliederung; (*Anat.*) die Sektion.
dissemble [di'sembl], *v.a.*, *v.n.* heucheln; sich verstellen.
disseminate [di'semineit], *v.a.* verbreiten.
dissemination [disemi'neiʃən], *s.* die Verbreitung.
dissension [di'senʃən], *s.* die Uneinigkeit, der Zwist (*conflict*).
dissent [di'sent], *v.n.* anderer Meinung sein; abweichen (*from*, von, *Dat.*). — *s.* die Abweichung, die abweichende Meinung.
dissenter [di'sentə], *s.* der Dissenter, das Mitglied der Freikirche.
dissertation [disə'teiʃən], *s.* die Dissertation, die Abhandlung.
dissever [di'sevə], *v.a.* trennen (*separate*); zerteilen (*divide*).
dissidence ['disidəns], *s.* die Uneinigkeit.
dissident ['disidənt], *adj.* uneinig, anders denkend.

dissimilar [di'similə], *adj.* unähnlich, ungleichartig.
dissimilarity [disimi'læriti], *s.* die Unähnlichkeit, die Ungleichartigkeit.
dissimulate [di'simjuleit], *v.a.* verhehlen (*conceal*). — *v.n.* sich verstellen, heucheln.
dissimulation [disimju'leiʃən], *s.* die Verstellung, Heuchelei, das Vorgeben (*pretence*).
dissipate ['disipeit], *v.a.* zerstreuen (*spread*); verschwenden (*waste*).
dissipation [disi'peiʃən], *s.* die Zerstreuung, die Verschwendung; die Ausschweifung.
dissociate [di'souʃieit], *v.a.* trennen, lösen. — *v.r.* abrücken (von).
dissociation [disouʃi'eiʃən], *s.* die Trennung; die Dissoziation.
dissolubility [disɔlju'biliti], *s.* die Auflösbarkeit.
dissoluble [di'sɔljubl], *adj.* auflösbar.
dissolute ['disəlju:t], *adj.* ausschweifend, lose, liederlich.
dissolution [disə'lju:ʃən], *s.* die Auflösung; der Tod (*death*).
dissolvable [di'zɔlvəbl], *adj.* auflösbar, löslich.
dissolve [di'zɔlv], *v.a.* auflösen; lösen. — *v.n.* sich auflösen, zergehen (*melt*).
dissonance ['disənəns], *s.* die Dissonanz, der Mißklang.
dissonant ['disənənt], *adj.* (*Mus.*) dissonant; mißhellig (*discordant*).
dissuade [di'sweid], *v.a.* abraten (*from*, von, *Dat.*).
dissuasion [di'sweiʒən], *s.* das Abraten.
dissuasive [di'sweisiv], *adj.* abratend.
distaff ['distɑ:f], *s.* der Spinnrocken (*spinning*); *on the — side*, auf der weiblichen Linie.
distance ['distəns], *s.* die Entfernung; die Ferne (*remoteness*). — *v.a.* hinter sich lassen, sich distanzieren (von, *Dat.*)
distant ['distənt], *adj.* entfernt, fern (*space*); kühl (*manner*).
distaste [dis'teist], *s.* die Abneigung (vor, *Dat.*); der Widerwille (gegen, *Acc.*).
distasteful [dis'teistful], *adj.* widerwärtig, zuwider.
distastefulness [dis'teistfulnis], *s.* die Widerwärtigkeit.
distemper (1) [dis'tempə], *s.* die Krankheit; die Staupe (*dogs*).
distemper (2) [dis'tempə]. *s.* die Wasserfarbe (*paint*). — *v.a.* mit Wasserfarbe streichen.
distend [dis'tend], *v.a.* (*Med.*) ausdehnen, strecken. — *v.n.* sich ausdehnen.
distension, distention [dis'tenʃən], *s.* das Dehnen; (*Med.*) die Ausdehnung, die Streckung.
distich ['distik], *s.* (*Poet.*) das Distichon.
distil [dis'til], *v.a.* destillieren. — *v.n.* (*Chem.*) destillieren, herauströpfeln.
distillation [disti'leiʃən], *s.* die Destillierung, (*Chem.*) der Destilliervorgang.
distiller [dis'tilə], *s.* der Branntweinbrenner.
distillery [dis'tiləri], *s.* die (Branntwein)brennerei.
distinct [dis'tiŋkt], *adj.* deutlich, klar; — *from*, verschieden von (*Dat.*).
distinction [dis'tiŋkʃən], *s.* der Unterschied, die Unterscheidung (*differentiation*); die Auszeichnung (*eminence*).
distinctive [dis'tiŋktiv], *adj.* unterscheidend (*differentiating*); deutlich (*clear*); leicht zu unterscheiden (*easy to distinguish*).
distinctiveness [dis'tiŋktivnis], *s.* die Deutlichkeit (*of voice etc.*); die Eigenart, Eigentümlichkeit (*peculiarity*).
distinguish [dis'tiŋgwiʃ], *v.a.* unterscheiden. — *v.r.* — *o.s.*, sich auszeichnen.
distinguishable [dis'tiŋgwiʃəbl], *adj.* unterscheidbar.
distinguished [dis'tiŋgwiʃd], *adj.* berühmt, vornehm.
distort [dis'tɔ:t], *v.a.* verdrehen; verzerren, verrenken.
distortion [dis'tɔ:ʃən], *s.* die Verdrehung, Verzerrung; (*fig.*) die Entstellung (*of truth etc.*).
distract [dis'trækt], *v.a.* abziehen, ablenken (*divert*); stören (*disturb*).
distracted [dis'træktid], *adj.* zerstreut; verrückt (*mentally deranged*).
distraction [dis'trækʃən], *s.* die Ablenkung; die Störung (*disturbance*); *to* —, bis zur Raserei.
distrain [dis'trein], *v.a.* beschlagnahmen, in Beschlag nehmen.
distraint [dis'treint], *s.* die Beschlagnahme.
distress [dis'tres], *s.* die Not, die Trübsal. — *v.a.* betrüben (*sadden*); quälen (*torture*).
distribute [dis'tribju:t], *v.a.* verteilen, austeilen (*among*, unter, *Acc.*).
distribution [distri'bju:ʃən], *s.* die Verteilung; die Austeilung (*giving out*); (*Comm.*) der Vertrieb.
distributive [dis'tribjutiv], *adj.* (*Gram.*) distributiv; — *trades*, die Vertriebsgewerbe.
district ['distrikt], *s.* (*Geog.*, *Pol.*) der Bezirk; die Gegend (*region*); der Kreis (*administrative*); — *commissioner*, der Kreisbeamte, Kreisvorsteher.
distrust [dis'trʌst], *v.a.* mißtrauen (*Dat.*). — *s.* das Mißtrauen (*of*, gegen, *Acc.*).
distrustful [dis'trʌstful], *adj.* mißtrauisch (*of*, gegen, *Acc.*).
disturb [dis'tə:b], *v.a.* stören (*trouble*); in Unordnung bringen (*disorder*).
disturbance [dis'tə:bəns], *s.* die Störung (*interruption etc.*); der Aufruhr (*riot*).
disunion [dis'ju:njən], *s.* die Entzweiung, die Zwietracht.
disunite [disju'nait], *v.a.* entzweien, Zwietracht säen zwischen. — *v.n.* sich trennen.

disuse [dis'ju:z], *v.a.* außer Gebrauch setzen. — [–'ju:s], *s.* der Nichtgebrauch (*abeyance*); die Entwöhnung (*cessation of practice*).
ditch [ditʃ], *s.* der Graben; *dull as —water*, uninteressant, langweilig. — *v.a.* mit einem Graben umgeben (*dig around*); graben.
ditto ['ditou], *adv.* desgleichen, dito.
ditty ['diti], *s.* das Liedchen.
diurnal [dai'ə:nəl], *adj.* täglich.
divan [di'væn], *s.* der Diwan.
dive [daiv], *v.n.* tauchen, springen (ins Wasser); (*Aviat.*) sturzfliegen, einen Sturzflug machen. — *s.* der Hechtsprung (ins Wasser); der Wassersprung; der Kopfsprung; (*Aviat.*) der Sturzflug.
diver ['daivə], *s.* (*Sport, Orn.*) der Taucher.
diverge [dai'və:dʒ], *v.n.* abweichen, auseinandergehen.
divergence [dai'və:dʒəns], *s.* die Abweichung, die Divergenz, Meinungsverschiedenheit.
divergent [dai'və:dʒənt], *adj.* auseinandergehend, abweichend.
divers ['daivəz], *adj. pl.* etliche, verschiedene.
diverse [dai'və:s], *adj.* verschieden, mannigfaltig.
diversify [dai'və:sifai], *v.a.* verschieden machen.
diversion [dai'və:ʃən], *s.* die Zerstreuung; (*Traffic*) die Umleitung.
diversity [dai'və:siti], *s.* die Verschiedenheit; die Ungleichheit (*disparity*).
divert [dai'və:t], *v.a.* ablenken, zerstreuen.
divest [di'vest *or* dai'-], *v.a.* entkleiden, berauben (*of office*, eines Amtes). — *v.r.* — *o.s. of*, auf etwas verzichten (*give up*).
divide [di'vaid], *v.a.* (*Maths.*) dividieren; teilen (*share*); aufteilen (*proportion*); sondern, trennen (*separate*). — *v.n.* sich teilen; (*Maths.*) sich dividieren lassen.
dividend ['dividənd], *s.* (*Comm.*) die Dividende; (*Maths.*) der Dividend.
dividers [di'vaidəz], *s.pl.* der Stechzirkel.
divination [divi'neiʃən], *s.* die Wahrsagung (*prophecy*); die Ahnung.
divine [di'vain], *v.a.* weissagen (*prophesy*); erraten (*guess*). — *adj.* göttlich; (*coll.*) herrlich. —*s.* (*obs.*) der Geistliche (*clergyman*).
divinity [di'viniti], *s.* die Göttlichkeit; die Gottheit (*deity*); die Theologie.
divisibility [divizi'biliti], *s.* (*Maths.*) die Teilbarkeit
divisible [di'vizibl], *adj.* teilbar.
division [di'viʒən], *s.* (*Maths., Mil.*) die Division; die Teilung (*partition*); die Abteilung (*department*); (*Parl.*) die Abstimmung.
divisor [di'vaizə], *s.* (*Maths.*) der Divisor; der Teiler.
divorce [di'vɔ:s], *s.* (*Law*) die Scheidung; die Trennung (*separation*). — *v.a.* sich von einem scheiden lassen.
divulge [dai'vʌldʒ], *v.a.* ausplaudern; verraten (*betray*); verbreiten (*spread*).
dizziness ['dizinis], *s.* der Schwindel.
dizzy ['dizi], *adj.* schwindlig.
do [du:], *v.a. irr.* tun, machen; — *o.'s duty*, seine Pflicht erfüllen; — *o.'s bit*, das Seinige leisten; — *o.'s homework*, seine Aufgaben machen; — *a favour*, einen Gefallen erweisen; vollbringen (*accomplish*); — *away with*, abschaffen (*Acc.*); einpacken. — *v.n. this will* —, das genügt; *this won't* —, so geht's nicht; — *without*, ohne etwas auskommen; *how — you* — ? sehr angenehm (*on introduction to people*).
docile ['dousail], *adj.* gelehrig, lenksam, fügsam.
docility [do'siliti], *s.* die Gelehrigkeit, die Fügsamkeit.
dock (1) [dɔk], *s.* (*Bot.*) das Ampferkraut; — *leaf*, das Ampferblatt.
dock (2) [dɔk], *s.* (*Naut.*) das Dock; —*yard*, die Schiffswerft; (*Law*) die Anklagebank. — *v.a.* (*Naut.*) ein Schiff ins Dock bringen.
dock (3) [dɔk], *v.a.* stutzen (*clip*); kürzen (*wages*).
docket ['dɔkit], *s.* der Zettel (*chit*); der Lieferschein.
doctor ['dɔktə], *s.* (*Med.*) der Arzt, der Doktor. — *v.a.* operieren, kastrieren (*a cat etc.*).
doctorate ['dɔktərit], *s.* das Doktorat, die Doktorwürde.
doctrinaire [dɔktri'nɛə], *s.* der Doktrinär. — *adj.* doktrinär.
doctrinal [dɔk'trainəl], *adj.* Lehr-.
doctrine ['dɔktrin], *s.* die Lehre, die Doktrin.
document ['dɔkjumənt], *s.* das Dokument, die Urkunde.
documentary [dɔkju'mentəri], *adj.* Dokumentar- (*film*); dokumentarisch (*evidence*).
documentation [dɔkjumen'teiʃən], *s.* die Dokumentation, Heranziehung von Dokumenten.
dodge [dɔdʒ], *v.a.* ausweichen (*Dat.*). — *s.* der Kniff.
dodger ['dɔdʒə], *s.* der Schwindler.
doe [dou], *s.* (*Zool.*) das Reh.
doeskin ['douskin], *s.* das Rehleder.
doff [dɔf], *v.a.* abnehmen, ablegen (*clothes*).
dog [dɔg], *s.* der Hund; —*'s ear*, das Eselsohr (*in book*). — *v.a.* verfolgen, auf Schritt und Tritt folgen (*Dat.*) (*follow closely*).
dogfish ['dɔgfiʃ], *s.* (*Zool.*) der Dornhai.
dogged ['dɔgid], *adj.* unverdrossen, zäh.
doggedness ['dɔgidnis], *s.* die Zähigkeit.
doggerel ['dɔgərəl], *s.* der Knüttelvers.
dogma ['dɔgmə], *s.* das Dogma, der Glaubenssatz.

dogmatic [dɔg'mætik], *adj.* dogmatisch.
dogmatism ['dɔgmətizm], *s.* der Dogmatismus.
dogmatize ['dɔgmətaiz], *v.n.* dogmatisieren.
doldrums ['douldrəmz], *s. pl.* die Schwermut, die Depression; (*Naut.*) die Windstillen, *f.pl.*
dole [doul], *s.* das Almosen; die Arbeitslosenunterstützung (*unemployment benefit*); *be on the* —, stempeln gehen, Arbeitslosenunterstützung beziehen. — *v.a.* — *out*, austeilen, verteilen.
doleful ['doulful], *adj.* traurig, bekümmert.
doll [dɔl], *s.* die Puppe.
dollar ['dɔlə], *s.* der Dollar.
dolman ['dɔlmən], *s.* der Dolman.
dolorous ['dɔlərəs], *adj.* (*Lit.*) schmerzlich, schmerzhaft.
dolphin ['dɔlfin], *s.* (*Zool.*) der Delphin.
dolt [doult], *s.* der Tölpel.
doltish ['doultiʃ], *adj.* tölpelhaft.
doltishness ['doultiʃnis], *s.* die Tölpelhaftigkeit.
domain [do'mein], *s.* das Gebiet, der Bereich.
dome [doum], *s.* (*Archit.*) die Kuppel, die Wölbung; der Dom.
domed [doumd], *adj.* gewölbt.
domestic [do'mestik], *adj.* Haus-, häuslich; — *animal*, das Haustier.
domesticate [do'mestikeit], *v.a.* zähmen (*tame*), zivilisieren.
domesticity [dɔmes'tisiti], *s.* die Häuslichkeit.
domicile ['dɔmisail], *s.* das Domizil; der Wohnort.
domiciled ['dɔmisaild], *adj.* wohnhaft (*at*, in, *Dat.*).
dominant ['dɔminənt], *adj.* vorherrschend. — *s.* (*Mus.*) die Dominante.
dominate ['dɔmineit], *v.a.* beherrschen. — *v.n.* herrschen.
domination [dɔmi'neiʃən], *s.* die Herrschaft.
domineer [dɔmi'niə], *v.n.* tyrannisieren.
domineering [dɔmi'niəriŋ], *adj.* überheblich, gebieterisch.
Dominican [do'minikən], *s.* der Dominikaner (*friar*).
dominion [do'minjən], *s.* die Herrschaft (*rule*); das Dominion (*Br. Commonwealth*).
domino ['dɔminou], *s.* (*pl.* **—noes**) der Domino (*mask*); (*pl.*) das Domino (*game*).
don (1) [dɔn], *s.* der Universitätsgelehrte, Universitätsdozent (*scholar*); Don (*Spanish nobleman*).
don (2) [dɔn], *v.a.* anziehen.
donate [do'neit], *v.a.* schenken, stiften.
donation [do'neiʃən], *s.* die Schenkung, die Stiftung; die Gabe (*gift*).
donkey ['dɔŋki], *s.* (*Zool.*) der Esel; — *engine*, die Hilfsmaschine.
donor ['dounə], *s.* der Spender, der Stifter: *blood* —, der Blutspender.
doom [du:m], *s.* die Verurteilung (*judgment*); der Untergang; das jüngste Gericht.
doomed [du:md], *adj.* verurteilt, verdammt (*to*, zu, *Dat.*).
Doomsday ['du:msdei], der jüngste Tag, der Tag des jüngsten Gerichtes.
door [dɔ:], *s.* die Tür(e); *next* —, nebenan; *out of* —*s*, draußen, im Freien; —*bell*, die Türklingel; — *latch*, die Klinke.
doorman ['dɔ:mæn], *s.* der Türsteher, der Pförtner.
dormant ['dɔ:mənt], *adj.* schlafend; unbenutzt.
dormer window ['dɔ:mə 'windou], *s.* das Dachfenster.
dormitory ['dɔmitri], *s.* der Schlafsaal.
dormouse ['dɔ:maus], *s.* (*Zool.*) die Haselmaus.
dose [dous], *s.* (*Med.*) die Dosis. — *v.a.* dosieren.
dot [dɔt], *s.* der Punkt, das Tüpfel. — *v.a.* punktieren; *sign on the* —*ted line*, unterschreiben; — *the i's and cross the t's*, äußerst genau sein.
dotage ['doutidʒ], *s.* die Altersschwäche, das Greisenalter.
dotard ['doutəd], *s.* der alte Dummkopf.
dote [dout], *v.n.* vernarrt sein (*on*, in, *Acc.*).
double [dʌbl], *adj.* (*Maths.*) doppelt; zweideutig (*meaning*); falsch (*false*); — *entry book-keeping*, doppelte Buchführung. — *s.* der Doppelgänger, die Doppelgängerin; *at the* —, im Sturmschritt. — *v.a.* (*Maths.*) verdoppeln; zusammenlegen (*fold in two*). — *v.n.* — *up with pain*, sich vor Schmerzen winden *or* krümmen.
doublet ['dʌblit], *s.* der Wams; — *and hose*, Wams und Hosen; der Pasch (*dice*); (*Ling.*) die Dublette, Doppelform.
doubt [daut], *s.* der Zweifel. — *v.a.* zweifeln (an, *Dat.*); bezweifeln.
doubtful ['dautful], *adj.* zweifelhaft, fraglich (*uncertain*).
doubtless ['dautlis], *adj.* zweifellos, ohne Zweifel.
douche [du:ʃ], *s.* die Dusche.
dough [dou], *s.* der Teig.
doughnut ['dounʌt], *s.* der Krapfen, Pfannkuchen.
doughy ['doui], *adj.* weich, teigig.
douse [daus], *v.a.* begießen, mit Wasser beschütten.
dove [dʌv], *s.* (*Orn.*) die Taube.
dovecote ['dʌvkɔt], *s.* der Taubenschlag.
dovetail ['dʌvteil], *v.a.*, *v.n.* einpassen; fügen; —*ing*, die Einpassung, die Verzinkung.
dowager ['dauədʒə], *s.* die Witwe (*of noble family*, von Stande).
dowdy ['daudi], *adj.* schlampig, unordentlich, unelegant.
dower ['dauə], *s.* die Mitgift, die Ausstattung.

down (1) [daun], *s.* der Flaum, die Daune.
down (2) [daun], *s.* das Hügelland.
down (3) [daun], *adv.* hinunter, herunter; nieder; unter; hinab. — *prep.* herab; hinunter. — *adj. the — train,* der Zug aus London. — *v.a.* niederzwingen, hinunterstürzen.
downcast ['daunka:st], *adj.* niedergeschlagen.
downfall ['daunfɔ:l], *s.* der Sturz.
downhill [daun'hil], *adv.* bergab. — ['daunhil], *adj.* abschüssig.
downpour ['daunpɔ:], *s.* der Platzregen.
downright ['daunrait], *adj.* völlig. — *adv.* geradezu.
downward ['daunwəd], *adj.* abschüssig. — *adv.* (*also* **downwards**) *see* **down.**
dowry ['dauri] *see* **dower.**
doze [douz], *v.n.* dösen, schlummern.
dozen [dʌzn], *s.* das Dutzend.
drab [dræb], *adj.* eintönig; langweilig (*boring*).
draft [dra:ft], *s.* (*Comm.*) die Tratte; der Entwurf (*sketch*); (*Mil.*) das Detachement. — *v.a.* entwerfen (*sketch*); (*Mil.*) abordnen; (*Am.*) einziehen.
drag [dræg], *v.a.* schleppen. — *s.* (*Engin.*) die Schleppbremse, der Dregghaken; der Hemmschuh (*wedge*); *—net,* das Schleppnetz; *—wheel,* das Schlepprad.
dragoman ['drægomən], *s.* der Dolmetscher.
dragon ['drægən], *s.* der Drache.
dragonfly ['drægənflai], *s.* (*Ent.*) die Libelle.
dragoon [drə'gu:n], *v.a.* unterdrücken. — *s.* (*Mil.*) der Dragoner.
drain [drein], *v.a.* entwässern, austrocknen; trockenlegen. — *v.n.* ablaufen, abfließen, auslaufen. — *s.* der Abguß, Abzug, die Gosse (*in street*); (*Engin.*) die Dränage; *—ing board,* das Ablauf- *or* Abwaschbrett; (*Phot.*) *—ing rack,* der Trockenständer; *a — on o.'s income,* eine Belastung des Einkommens.
drainage ['dreinidʒ], *s.* die Trockenlegung, die Kanalisierung.
drainpipe ['dreinpaip], *s.* das Abflußrohr; *— trousers,* die Röhrenhosen, *f. pl.*
drake [dreik], *s.* (*Orn.*) der Enterich.
dram [dræm], *s.* der Trunk; Schluck (*spirits*).
drama ['dra:mə], *s.* das Drama, das Schauspiel.
dramatic [drə'mætik], *adj.* dramatisch.
dramatist ['dra:m— *or* 'dræmətist], *s.* der Dramatiker.
dramatize ['dræmətaiz], *v.a.* dramatisieren.
drape [dreip], *v.a.* drapieren, bedecken; einhüllen (*wrap*). — *s.* (*Am.*) der Vorhang.
draper ['dreipə], *s.* der Stoffhändler, der Tuchhändler.
drapery ['dreipəri], *s.* — *department,* die Stoff- *or* Tuchabteilung; die Tuchhandlung (*shop*).
drastic ['dra:stik *or* 'dræstik], *adj.* drastisch, radikal.
draught [dra:ft], *s.* der Zug (*air*); der Tiefgang (*— of ship*); der Schluck (*drink*); der Schlaftrunk (*sleeping —*); *— horse,* das Zugpferd; *— beer,* das Faßbier; *—board,* das Damespielbrett; (*pl.*) das Damespiel.
draw [drɔ:], *v.a. irr.* ziehen (*pull*); zeichnen (*sketch*); anlocken (*attract*); ausschreiben (*cheque*); *—well,* der Ziehbrunnen. — *s.* das Los, die Verlosung (*lottery*); (*Sport*) das Unentschieden.
drawback ['drɔ:bæk], *s.* der Nachteil, die Schattenseite.
drawbridge ['drɔ:bridʒ], *s.* die Zugbrücke.
drawer ['drɔ:ə], *s.* die Schublade; *chest of —s,* die Kommode; (*pl.*) die Unterhosen, *f. pl.*
drawing ['drɔ:iŋ], *s.* (*Art*) die Zeichnung; *— board,* das Reißbrett; *— office,* das Zeichenbüro, der Zeichensaal.
drawing room ['drɔ:iŋ rum], *s.* das Wohnzimmer, der Salon.
drawl [drɔ:l], *v.n.* gedehnt sprechen. — *s.* die gedehnte Sprechweise.
drawn [drɔ:n], *adj.* (*Sport*) unentschieden.
dray [drei], *s.* der Rollwagen, der Karren; *—man,* der Kutscher, der Fuhrmann.
dread [dred], *s.* der Schrecken. — *adj.* schrecklich. — *v.a.* fürchten. — *v.n.* sich fürchten (vor, *Dat.*).
dreadful ['dredful], *adj.* schrecklich, furchtbar.
dreadnought ['drednɔ:t], *s.* (*Naut.*) das große Schlachtschiff.
dream [dri:m], *s.* der Traum. — *v.n. irr.* träumen; *I would not — of it,* es würde mir nicht im Traum einfallen, ich denke nicht daran.
dreamt [dremt] *see* **dream.**
dreamy ['dri:mi], *adj.* verträumt, träumerisch.
dreariness ['driərinis], *s.* die Öde.
dreary ['driəri], *adj.* traurig, öde.
dredge [dredʒ], *s.* das Schleppnetz. — *v.a.* (*Engin.*) ausbaggern; (*Naut.*) dreggen.
dredger ['dredʒə], *s.* der Bagger, das Baggerschiff; (*Cul.*) die Streubüchse.
dregs [dregz], *s. pl.* der Bodensatz (*in cup etc.*); die Hefe (*yeast*).
drench [drentʃ], *v.a.* durchnässen, tränken.
Dresden ['drezdən]. (*china*) das Meißner Porzellan.
dress [dres], *s.* das Kleid; die Kleidung; *evening —,* die Abendkleidung; *full —,* die Gala(kleidung); *— circle,* erster Rang; *—maker,* die Schneiderin; *— rehearsal,* die Generalprobe; *— shirt,* das Frackhemd; *— suit,* der Frackanzug. — *v.a., v.n.* (sich) anziehen.

dresser [ˈdresə], *s.* der Ankleider (*valet*); der Anrichtetisch (*table*).
dressing [ˈdresiŋ], *s.* (*Build.*) die Verkleidung; der Verband (*bandage*); der Verputz (*interior decoration*); — *gown*, der Schlafrock, Bademantel; (*Theat.*) — *room*, das Künstlerzimmer; Ankleidezimmer; — *table*, der Toilettentisch.
dressy [ˈdresi], *adj.* elegant; modesüchtig.
dribble [dribl], *v.n.* tröpfeln (*trickle*); geifern (*slaver*); (*Footb.*) dribbeln.
driblet [ˈdriblit], *s.* die Kleinigkeit, die Lappalie.
drift [drift], *s.* die Richtung (*direction*); die Strömung (*stream*); das Treiben; Gestöber (*snow*). — *v.a.* treiben. — *v.n.* dahintreiben.
drill (1) [dril], *v.a.* drillen, bohren (*bore*); (*Mil.*) exerzieren; (*Agr.*) eine Furche ziehen; einstudieren (*coach*). — *s.* (*Mil.*) das Exerzieren; (*Agr.*) die Furche; der Bohrer (*tool*); — *hall*, die Übungs- *or* Exerzierhalle.
drill (2) [dril], *s.* der Drillich (*textile*).
drily [ˈdraili], *adv.* trocken.
drink [driŋk], *v.a.*, *v.n. irr.* trinken. — *s.* das Getränk, der Trank (*potion*); etwas zum Trinken (*a* —); *come, have a* —, trinken wir ein Glas (zusammen); *strong* —, geistiges Getränk.
drinkable [ˈdriŋkəbl], *adj.* trinkbar; zum Trinken.
drinker [ˈdriŋkə], *s.* der Trinker, Säufer; der Zecher; der Trunkenbold (*drunkard*).
drip [drip], *v.n.* tröpfeln. — *s.* das Tröpfeln.
dripping [ˈdripiŋ], *s.* (*Cul.*) das Bratenfett, das Schmalz.
drive [draiv], *v.a. irr.* treiben (*sheep etc.*); fahren (*a car*). — *v.n.* fahren; dahinfahren (— *along*). — *s.* die Ausfahrt, Fahrt (*trip*); die Einfahrt (*approach to house*).
driving [ˈdraiviŋ], *s.* das Fahren; — *licence*, der Führerschein; — *school*, die Fahrschule; — *test*, die Fahrprüfung.
drivel [drivl], *s.* der Geifer; der Unsinn (*nonsense*). — *v.n.* Unsinn reden.
driver [ˈdraivə], *s.* der Fahrer, der Chauffeur; (*Railw.*) Führer; (*Hunt.*) der Treiber.
drizzle [drizl], *v.n.* rieseln; leicht regnen. — *s.* das Rieseln, der feine Regen, der Sprühregen.
droll [droul], *adj.* drollig, possierlich.
drollery [ˈdrouləri], *s.* die Possierlichkeit; die Schnurre.
dromedary [ˈdrʌmədəri *or* ˈdrɔm-], *s.* (*Zool.*) das Dromedar.
drone (1) [droun], *s.* das Gedröhn, das Gesumme (*noise*). — *v.n.* dröhnen, summen (*hum loudly*).
drone (2) [droun], *s.* (*Ent.*) die Drohne; der Faulpelz (*lazybones*).
droop [dru:p], *v.a.* hängen lassen. — *v.n.* herabhängen; verwelken (*flowers*); ermatten (*tire*).
drop [drɔp], *s.* der Tropfen (*liquid*); das Fallen (*fall*). — *v.a.* fallen lassen; — *a brick*, eine taktlose Bemerkung machen; — *a hint*, andeuten, auf etwas hindeuten. — *v.n.* fallen.
droppings [ˈdrɔpiŋz], *s. pl.* der Mist, Dünger (*of animals*).
dropsical [ˈdrɔpsikəl], *adj.* (*Med.*) wassersüchtig.
dropsy [ˈdrɔpsi], *s.* (*Med.*) die Wassersucht.
dross [drɔs], *s.* (*Metall.*) die Schlacke; der Unrat, das wertlose Zeug.
drought [draut], *s.* die Dürre, die Trockenheit.
drove [drouv], *s.* die Herde, die Trift (*cattle*).
drover [ˈdrouvə], *s.* der Viehtreiber.
drown [draun], *v.a.* ertränken; überschwemmen (*flood*); übertönen (*noise*). — *v.n.* ertrinken.
drowse [drauz], *v.n.* schlummern, schläfrig sein.
drowsy [ˈdrauzi], *adj.* schläfrig.
drub [drʌb], *v.a.* prügeln.
drudge [drʌdʒ], *s.* das Packtier; der Sklave, der Knecht.
drudgery [ˈdrʌdʒəri], *s.* die Plackerei, die Plagerei (*hard toil*).
drug [drʌg], *s.* die Droge; die Medizin; das Rauschgift. — *v.a.* betäuben.
drugget [ˈdrʌgit], *s.* der (grobe) Wollstoff.
drum [drʌm], *s.* die Trommel. — *v.n.* trommeln, austrommeln.
drunk [drʌŋk], *adj.* betrunken.
drunkard [ˈdrʌŋkəd], *s.* der Trunkenbold.
drunkenness [ˈdrʌŋkənnis], *s.* die Trunkenheit.
dry [drai], *adj.* trocken, dürr; ausgetrocknet, durstig (*thirsty*). — *v.a.* austrocknen, trocken machen, dörren. — *v.n.* trocken werden, trocknen.
dryad [ˈdraiæd], *s.* die Baumnymphe Dryade.
dryness [ˈdrainis], *s.* die Trockenheit, die Dürre.
dual [ˈdju:əl], *adj.* doppelt; Zwei–.
dub (1) [dʌb], *v.a.* zum Ritter schlagen; nennen (*name*).
dub (2) [dʌb], *v.a.* (*Films*) synchronisieren.
dubious [ˈdju:bjəs], *adj.* zweifelhaft.
ducal [ˈdju:kəl], *adj.* herzoglich.
duchess [ˈdʌtʃis], *s.* die Herzogin.
duchy [ˈdʌtʃi], *s.* das Herzogtum.
duck (1) [dʌk], *s.* (*Orn.*) die Ente.
duck (2) [dʌk], *v.n.* sich ducken, sich bücken; untertauchen (*in water*).— *v.a.* untertauchen, ins Wasser tauchen.
duckling [ˈdʌkliŋ], *s.* (*Orn.*) das Entchen.
duct [dʌkt], *s.* (*Anat.*) der Kanal; die Röhre.
ductile [ˈdʌktail], *adj.* dehnbar; fügsam.

dud [dʌd], *s.* (*Mil.*) der Blindgänger; der Fehlschlag.
dude [dju:d], *s.* (*Am.*) der Geck.
dudgeon ['dʌdʒən], *s.* der Groll, der Unwille; *in high* —, sehr aufgebracht.
due [dju:], *adj.* gebührend, fällig, schuldig (*to,Dat.*); angemessen, recht; *this is — to carelessness*, das ist auf Nachlässigkeit zurückzuführen. — *adv.* direkt, gerade. — *s.* (*pl.*) die Gebühren.
duel ['dju:əl], *s.* das Duell. — *v.n.* sich duellieren (mit, *Dat.*).
duet [dju:'et], *s.* (*Mus.*) das Duett.
duffer ['dʌfə], *s.* der Tölpel; (*obs.*) der Hausierer.
duffle, duffel [dʌfl], *s.* der Düffel, das Düffeltuch.
dug [dʌg], *s.* die Zitze.
dug-out ['dʌg-aut], *s.* der Unterstand, der Bunker.
duke [dju:k], *s.* der Herzog; *Grand Duke*, der Großherzog.
dukedom ['dju:kdəm], *s.* das Herzogtum.
dull [dʌl], *adj.* fade, langweilig (*boring*); träge, schwerfällig (*slow to grasp*); stumpfsinnig (*obtuse*); schal, abgeschmackt (*tasteless*); schwach (*perception*); dumpf (*thud, noise*); matt (*colour*); trüb, überwölkt (*weather*); flau (*trade*). — *v.a.* abstumpfen (*senses*).
dullness ['dʌlnis], *s.* die Stumpfheit (*senses*); die Langweile (*boredom*); die Schwerfälligkeit (*stolidity*); die Schwäche (*vision etc.*); die Stumpfsinnigkeit (*stupidity*).
dumb [dʌm], *adj.* stumm; (*sl.*) dumm; —*founded*, verblüfft; — *show*, die Pantomime; —*bell* (*Gymn.*) die Hantel.
dumbness ['dʌmnis], *s.* die Stummheit.
dummy ['dʌmi], *s.* der Strohmann (*cards*); die Kleiderpuppe (*wax figure*); der Blindgänger (*dud shell*); der Schnuller (*baby's*).
dump [dʌmp], *v.a.* kippen, abladen; —*ing ground*, der Abladeplatz. — *s.* (*Am. coll.*) das Bumslokal.
dumpling ['dʌmpliŋ], *s.* der Kloß, (*Austr.*) der Knödel.
dumps [dʌmps], *s. pl.* der Unmut, der Mißmut, die Depression.
dumpy ['dʌmpi], *adj.* untersetzt, kurz und dick.
dun (1) [dʌn], *adj.* schwarzbraun.
dun (2) [dʌn], *s.* der Gläubiger. — *v.a.* energisch mahnen.
dunce [dʌns], *s.* der Dummkopf.
dune [dju:n], *s.* die Düne.
dung [dʌŋ], *s.* der Dünger. — *v.n.* düngen.
dungeon ['dʌndʒən], *s.* der Kerker.
dupe [dju:p], *s.* der Betrogene. — *v.a.* betrügen.
duplicate ['dju:plikeit], *v.a.* verdoppeln; doppelt schreiben *or* ausfüllen (*write twice*); vervielfältigen (*stencil*). — [-kit], *s.* das Duplikat.
duplicity [dju:'plisiti], *s.* die Falschheit, die Doppelzüngigkeit.
durability [djuərə'biliti], *s.* die Dauerhaftigkeit.
durable ['djuərəbl], *adj.* dauerhaft.
duration [djuə'reiʃən], *s.* die Dauer, die Länge (*time*).
duress [djuə'res], *s.* der Zwang; *under* —, zwangsweise.
during ['djuəriŋ], *prep.* während.
dusk [dʌsk], *s.* die Dämmerung.
dusky ['dʌski], *adj.* dunkel, trüb; düster.
dust [dʌst], *s.* der Staub. — *v.a.* abstauben (*clean*); bestäuben (*pollinate*); bestreuen.
dustbin ['dʌstbin], *s.* der Mülleimer.
dusty ['dʌsti], *adj.* staubig; *not so* —, (*coll.*) nicht so übel.
Dutch [dʌtʃ], *adj.* holländisch; niederländisch; — *treat*, auf getrennte Kosten; *double* —, Kauderwelsch, Unsinn.
Dutchman ['dʌtʃmən], *s.* der Holländer, der Niederländer.
dutiful ['dju:tiful], *adj.* gehorsam, pflichttreu, pflichtbewußt.
duty ['dju:ti], *s.* die Pflicht; die Abgabe (*tax*); *customs* —, der Zoll; *be on* —, Dienst haben; (*being*) *on* —, diensthabend; *off* —, dienstfrei; —*free*, zollfrei; *in — bound*, von Rechts wegen, pflichtgemäß.
dwarf [dwɔ:f], *s.* der Zwerg. — *v.a.* am Wachstum hindern (*stunt*); klein erscheinen lassen (*overshadow*).
dwell [dwel], *v.n. irr.* wohnen (*be domiciled*); verweilen (*remain*).
dwelling ['dweliŋ], *s.* die Wohnung; — *place*, der Wohnort.
dwindle [dwindl], *v.n.* abnehmen, kleiner werden.
dye [dai], *v.a.* färben. — *s.* die Farbe; (*Chem.*) der Farbstoff.
dyeing ['daiiŋ], *s.* das Färben; Färbereigewerbe.
dyer ['daiə], *s.* der Färber.
dying ['daiiŋ], *s.* das Sterben; *the* —, (*pl.*) die Sterbenden, *pl.* — *adj.* sterbend.
dynamic [dai'næmik], *adj.* dynamisch.
dynamics [dai'næmiks], *s. pl.* die Dynamik.
dynamite ['dainəmait], *s.* das Dynamit.
dynamo ['dainəmou], *s.* der Dynamo, die Dynamomaschine.
dynasty ['dinəsti], *s.* die Dynastie.
dysentery ['disəntri], *s.* (*Med.*) die Ruhr.
dyspepsia [dis'pepsiə], *s.* (*Med.*) die Magenverstimmung.
dyspeptic [dis'peptik], *adj.* mit verstimmtem Magen; schlecht aufgelegt (*grumpy*).

E

E [i:], das E (*also Mus.*); *E flat*, Es; *E sharp*, Eis; *E minor*, E-moll.

each [i:tʃ], *adj.*, *pron.* jeder, jede, jedes; — *other*, einander; — *one*, jeder einzelne.
eager [ˈi:gə], *adj.* eifrig, begierig.
eagerness [ˈi:gənis], *s.* der Eifer, die Begierde.
eagle [i:gl], *s.* (*Orn.*) der Adler; (*Am.*) das Zehndollarstück.
ear [iə], *s.* das Ohr; —*lap*, das Ohrläppchen; —*phones*, die Kopfhörer; — -*piece*, die Hörmuschel; —*drum*, das Trommelfell; — *of corn*, die Ähre.
earl [ə:l], *s.* der Graf.
earldom [ˈə:ldəm], *s.* die (englische) Grafschaft.
early [ˈə:li], *adj.* früh, frühzeitig.
earmark [ˈiəmɑ:k], *v.a.* kennzeichnen, bezeichnen.
earn [ə:n], *v.a.* verdienen; erwerben.
earnest [ˈə:nist], *s.* der Ernst; der ernste Beweis, das Handgeld; (*Comm.*) die Anzahlung; (*fig.*) der Vorgeschmack. — *adj.* ernst, ernsthaft.
earnings [ˈə:niŋz], *s.* das Einkommen.
earshot [ˈiəʃɔt], *s.* die Hörweite.
earth [ə:θ], *s.* die Erde; der Erdboden (*soil*); der Fuchsbau (*of fox*); *down to* —, praktisch denkend; *move heaven and* —, alles daransetzen; *where on* —, wo in aller Welt.
earthen [ˈə:θən], *adj.* irden, aus Erde; —*ware*, das Steingut.
earthquake [ˈə:θkweik], *s.* das Erdbeben.
earthly [ˈə:θli], *adj.* irdisch.
earthworm [ˈə:θwə:m], *s.* (*Zool.*) der Regenwurm.
earthy [ˈə:θi], *adj.* erdig; irdisch.
earwig [ˈiəwig], *s.* (*Ent.*) der Ohrwurm.
ease [i:z], *s.* die Leichtigkeit (*facility*); die Bequemlichkeit (*comfort*); *feel at* —, sich wie zu Hause fühlen; (*Mil.*) *stand at* —*!* rührt euch! *ill at* —, unbehaglich. — *v.a.* erleichtern, leichter machen; lindern (*pain*). — *v.n.* — *off*, (*Mil.*) sich auflockern.
easel [i:zl], *s.* das Gestell; die Staffelei.
easiness [ˈi:zinis], *s.* die Leichtigkeit, die Ungezwungenheit.
east [i:st], *adj.*, *adv.* Ost-, ostwärts (*direction*). — *s.* der Osten, der Orient.
Easter [ˈi:stə]. das *or* (*n.* or *f. pl.*) die Ostern.
eastern [ˈi:stən], *adj.* östlich; morgenländisch, orientalisch (*oriental*).
easy [ˈi:zi], *adj.* leicht, frei; — *chair*, der Lehnstuhl, Sessel; *stand* —*!* rührt Euch! *take it* —, nimm's nicht so ernst; es sich (*Dat.*) bequem machen (*make o.s. comfortable*); (*Comm.*) — *terms*, Zahlungserleichterungen; — *-going*, gemütlich.
eat [i:t], *v.a.*, *v.n. irr.* essen, speisen (*dine*); fressen (*of animals*); — *humble pie*, sich demütigen; — *o.'s hat*, einen Besen fressen; — *o.'s words* seine Worte bereuen.
eatable [ˈi:təbl], *adj.* genießbar, eßbar.
eaves [i:vz], *s. pl.* die Dachrinne, die Traufe.
eavesdrop [ˈi:vzdrɔp], *v.n.* belauschen (*on s.o.*, *Acc.*).
eavesdropper [ˈi:vzdrɔpə], *s.* der Lauscher.
ebb [eb], *s.* die Ebbe. — *v.n.* nachlassen, abebben, abfließen.
ebonize [ˈebənaiz], *v.a.* wie Ebenholz *or* schwarz beizen.
ebony [ˈebəni], *s.* das Ebenholz.
ebullient [iˈbʌljənt], *adj.* aufwallend.
eccentric [ikˈsentrik], *adj.* exzentrisch, überspannt, wunderlich.
eccentricity [eksenˈtrisiti], *s.* die Exzentrizität, die Überspanntheit.
ecclesiastic [ikli:ziˈæstik], *s.* der Geistliche. — *adj.* (*also* **-ical**) geistlich, kirchlich.
echo [ˈekou], *s.* das Echo, der Widerhall. — *v.a.*, *v.n.* widerhallen (*resound*); wiederholen (*repeat*).
eclectic [iˈklektik], *adj.* eklektisch. — *s.* der Eklektiker.
eclecticism [iˈklektisizm], *s.* (*Phil.*) der Eklektizismus.
eclipse [iˈklips], *s.* die Verfinsterung, Finsternis (*darkness*); die Verdunklung (*darkening*). — *v.a.* verdunkeln.
ecliptic [iˈkliptik], *s.* die Ekliptik, die Sonnenbahn.
economic [i:kəˈnɔmik], *adj.* ökonomisch, wirtschaftlich.
economical [i:kəˈnɔmikl], *adj.* (*frugal*) sparsam, wirtschaftlich.
economics [i:kəˈnɔmiks], *s.* (*pl.*) die Wirtschaftslehre, die Ökonomie.
economist [iˈkɔnəmist], *s.* der Ökonom der Wirtschaftsfachmann.
economize [iˈkɔnəmaiz], *v.n.* sparen (*on*, mit, *Dat.*); sparsam sein mit (*Dat.*).
economy [iˈkɔnəmi], *s.* die Wirtschaft; *political* —, die Nationalökonomie, Staatswirtschaftslehre.
ecstasy [ˈekstəsi], *s.* die Ekstase, die Entzückung, die Verzückung.
ecstatic [iksˈtætik], *adj.* ekstatisch, verzückt; entzückt (*delighted*).
Ecuadorean [ekwəˈdɔ:riən], *adj.* ekuadorianisch. — *n.* der Ekuadorianer.
ecumenical [i:kjuˈmenikəl], *adj.* ökumenisch.
eddy [ˈedi], *s.* der Wirbel, Strudel. — *v.n.* wirbeln.
edge [edʒ], *s.* die Schärfe, die Schneide (*blade*); die Kante (*ledge*); der Rand (*brink*); der Saum (*border*); die Ecke (*corner*); der Schnitt (*book*); die Schärfe (*wit*, *keenness*); *put an* — *on*, schärfen; *be on* —, nervös sein. — *v.a.* besetzen (*decorate*); umgeben; *double-* —*d*, zweischneidig; *two-* —*d*, zweischneidig, zweikantig; —*d with lace*, mit Spitze eingefaßt. — *v.n.* sich bewegen; — *forward*, langsam vorrücken; — *off*, sich abseits halten, sich drücken; — *away from*, abrücken.
edgy [ˈedʒi], *adj.* kantig, eckig; (*fig.*) nervös, reizbar.
edible [ˈedibl], *adj.* eßbar.

edict ['i:dikt], *s.* die Verordnung.
edification [edifi'keiʃən], *s.* die Erbauung.
edifice ['edifis], *s.* der Bau, das Gebäude.
edify ['edifai], *v.a.* erbauen.
edit ['edit], *v.a.* herausgeben (*book etc.*).
edition [i'diʃən], *s.* die Ausgabe.
editor ['editə], *s.* der Herausgeber, der Schriftleiter; (*newspaper*) der Redakteur.
editorial [edi'tɔ:riəl], *adj.* Redaktions-. — *s.* der Leitartikel.
editorship ['editəʃip], *s.* die Redaktion; die Schriftleitung.
educate ['edjukeit], *v.a.* erziehen, (heran)bilden.
education [edju'keiʃən], *s.* die Erziehung (*upbringing*); die Bildung (*general culture*); das Bildungwesen, das Schulwesen (*educational system*); *primary* —, die Grundschulung, das Volksschulwesen; *secondary* —, das Mittelschulwesen, das höhere Schulwesen; *university* —, das Hochschulwesen (*system*), die Universitätsbildung (*of individual*); *local* — *authority*, das Schulamt, die Schulbehörde; *Professor of Education*, Professor der Pädagogik; *further* —, *adult* —, weitere Ausbildung, Erwachsenenbildung.
educational [edju'keiʃənəl], *adj.* erzieherisch (*educative*); Bildungs-, Unterrichts- (*for education*); — *attainment*, der Bildungsgrad, die Schulstufe (*grade*); — *facilities*, die Lehrmittel, Bildungs- *or* Schulungsmöglichkeiten, *f. pl.*
education(al)ist [edju'keiʃən(əl)ist], *s.* der Erzieher, der Pädagoge; der Erziehungsfachmann (*theorist*).
eel [i:l], *s.* (*Zool.*) der Aal.
eerie ['iəri], *adj.* gespenstisch, unheimlich.
efface [i'feis], *v.a.* auslöschen, austilgen.
effacement [i'feismənt], *s.* die Austilgung; *self*- —, die Selbstaufopferung.
effect [i'fekt], *s.* die Wirkung; die Folge, das Ergebnis (*consequence*); der Eindruck (*impression*); *of no* —, ohne jede Wirkung; *carry into* —, ausführen; *take* — *from*, vom . . . in Kraft treten. — *v.a.* bewirken (*bring about*).
effective [i'fektiv], *adj.* wirksam (*having an effect*); gültig (*in force*); dienstfähig (*usable*); wirklich (*actual*).
effectual [i'fektjuəl], *adj.* wirksam (*effective*); kräftig, energisch (*strong*).
effectuate [i'fektjueit], *v.a.* bewerkstelligen (*get done*); bewirken (*bring about*).
effeminacy [i'feminəsi], *s.* die Verweichlichung.
effeminate [i'feminit], *adj.* weichlich, verweichlicht.
effervescence [efə'vesəns], *s.* das Aufbrausen, Schäumen.
effervescent [efə'vesənt], *adj.* aufbrausend, aufschäumend.
effete [i'fi:t], *adj.* abgenutzt, erschöpft.
efficacious [efi'keiʃəs], *adj.* wirksam. energisch.
efficacy ['efikəsi], *s.* die Wirksamkeit, die Energie.
efficiency [i'fiʃənsi], *s.* die Tüchtigkeit (*of person*); die Wirksamkeit; die Leistung.
efficient [i'fiʃənt], *adj.* tüchtig; leistungsfähig; wirksam (*drug etc.*).
effigy ['efidʒi], *s.* das Bild, das Abbild.
efflorescent [eflɔ:'resənt], *adj.* aufblühend.
effluent ['efluənt], *adj.* ausfließend.
effluvium [i'flu:viəm], *s.* die Ausdünstung.
effort ['efət], *s.* die Anstrengung, die Bemühung; *make an* —, sich bemühen, sich anstrengen; *make every* —, alle Kräfte anspannen.
effrontery [i'frʌntəri], *s.* die Frechheit (*cheek*); die Unverschämtheit (*impertinence*).
effortless ['efətlis], *adj.* mühelos.
effulgence [i'fʌldʒəns], *s.* der Glanz, das Strahlen.
effulgent [i'fʌldʒənt], *adj.* schimmernd, strahlend.
effusion [i'fju:ʒən], *s.* die Ausgießung; der Erguß (*verse etc.*); der Überschwang.
effusive [i'fju:ziv], *adj.* überschwenglich.
egg [eg], *s.* das Ei; *fried* —, das Spiegelei; *scrambled* —, das Rührei; — *flip*, der Eierpunsch; —*shell*, die Eierschale. — *v.a.* — *on*, anspornen, anreizen.
eglantine ['egləntain], *s.* (*Bot.*) die wilde Rose.
egoism ['egouizm], *s.* der Egoismus.
ego(t)ist ['ego(t)ist], *s.* der Egoist.
egregious [i'gri:dʒəs], *adj.* ungeheuer(lich).
egress ['i:gres], *s.* der Ausgang, der Ausfluß (*water etc.*).
Egyptian [i'dʒipʃən], *adj.* ägyptisch. — *s.* der Ägypter.
eiderdown ['aidədaun], *s.* die Daunen decke, Steppdecke.
eiderduck ['aidədʌck], *s.* (*Orn.*) die Eidergans.
eight [eit], *num. adj.* acht.
eighteen [ei'ti:n], *num. adj.* achtzehn.
eighty ['eiti], *num. adj.* achtzig.
either ['aiðə], *adj.*, *pron.* einer von beiden. — *conj.* entweder (*or*, oder).
ejaculate [i'dʒækjuleit], *v.a.*, *v.n.* ausstoßen.
eject [i'dʒekt], *v.a.* hinauswerfen; ausstoßen.
ejection [i'dʒekʃən], *s.* die Ausstoßung.
eke [i:k], *v.a.* — *out*, verlängern, ergänzen; — *out an existence*, ein spärliches Auskommen finden.
elaborate [i'læbəreit], *v.a.* ausarbeiten, im einzelnen ausarbeiten. — [-rit], *adj.* detailliert, ausgearbeitet; kunstvoll (*intricate*); umständlich (*involved*).

elaboration [ilæbə'reiʃən], *s.* die Ausarbeitung (im einzelnen); die Detailarbeit.
elapse [i'læps], *v.n.* verstreichen, verfließen (*time*).
elastic [i'læstik], *adj.* elastisch. — *s.* das Gummiband.
elasticity [elæs'tisiti], *s.* (*Phys.*) die Elastizität.
elate [i'leit], *v.a.* stolz machen; ermutigen.
elated [i'leitid], *adj.* in gehobener Stimmung.
elation [i'leiʃən], *s.* der Stolz; die Begeisterung.
elbow ['elbou], *s.* (*Anat.*) der Ellenbogen; *at o.'s* —, bei der Hand; — *room*, der Spielraum. — *v.a.* — *o.'s way through*, sich durchdrängen.
elder (1) ['eldə], *comp. adj.* älter. — *s.* der Alte, der Älteste; Kirchenälteste.
elder (2) ['eldə], *s.* (*Bot.*) der Holunder.
elderly ['eldəli], *adj.* älter; alt; ältlich.
elect [i'lekt], *v.a.* erwählen (*to*, zu, *Dat.*); auswählen (*choose*). — *adj.* erwählt, auserwählt; *chairman* —, der gewählte Vorsitzende.
election [i'lekʃən], *s.* die Auswahl (*selection*); (*Pol.*) die Wahlen, *f.pl.*; die Wahl (*choice*); *by*(*e*) - —, die Bezirkswahl, die Neuwahl; — *broadcast*, eine Radiowahlrede.
electioneering [ilekʃən'iəriŋ], *s.* das Wahlmanöver, die Wahlpropaganda, der Wahlkampf.
elective [i'lektiv], *adj.* durch Wahl bestimmt; Wahl-.
elector [i'lektə], *s.* (*Pol.*) der Wähler; das Mitglied eines Wahlausschusses (*academic etc.*); der Kurfürst (*prince*).
electorate [i'lektərit], *s.* die Wählerschaft.
electress [i'lektrəs], *s.* die Kurfürstin (*princess*).
electric(al) [i'lektrik(əl)], *adj.* elektrisch; *electrical engineer*, der Elektrotechniker; der Student der Elektrotechnik (*trainee*); *electric switch*, der elektrische Schalter; — *razor*, der elektrische Rasierapparat.
electrician [elek'triʃən], *s.* der Elektriker.
electricity [ilek- *or* elek'trisiti], *s.* die Elektrizität.
electrocution [ilektro'kju:ʃən], *s.* die Hinrichtung *or* der Unfall (*accidental*) durch Elektrizität.
electron [i'lektrɔn], *s.* das Elektron.
electroplate [i'lektropleit], *v.a.* galvanisch versilbern.
electrotype [i'lektrotaip], *s.* der galvanische Abdruck, die Galvanographie.
elegance ['eligəns], *s.* die Eleganz.
elegant ['eligənt], *adj.* elegant, fein.
elegy ['elidʒi], *s.* (*Lit.*) die Elegie.
element ['elimənt], *s.* das Element; der Bestandteil (*component*).
elemental [eli'mentl], *adj.* elementar.
elementary [eli'mentri], *adj.* einfach (*simple*); elementar (*for beginners*).
elephant ['elifənt], *s.* (*Zool.*) der Elefant.
elevate ['eliveit], *v.a.* erheben, erhöhen.
elevation [eli'veiʃən], *s.* die Erhebung (*lifting*); (*Geom.*) die Elevation; die Erhöhung (*rise*); der Aufriß (*Engin. drawing*).
elevator ['eliveitə], *s.* (*Am.*) der Lift, der Aufzug, der Fahrstuhl; (*Agr.*) der Getreideheber.
eleven [i'levn], *num. adj.* elf.
elf [elf], *s.* der Elf, der Kobold.
elfin ['elfin], *adj.* Elfen-, elfenhaft.
elicit [i'lisit], *v.a.* herauslocken, entlocken.
eligibility [elidʒi'biliti], *s.* die Wählbarkeit.
eligible ['elidʒibl], *adj.* wählbar, passend.
eliminate [i'limineit], *v.a.* ausschalten, ausscheiden, eliminieren.
elimination [ilimi'neiʃən], *s.* die Ausschaltung, die Ausscheidung.
elision [i'liʒən], *s.* (*Phonet.*) die Auslassung, die Weglassung.
elixir [i'liksə], *s.* das Elixier.
elk [elk], *s.* (*Zool.*) der Elch.
ell [el], *s.* die Elle.
ellipse [i'lips], *s.* (*Geom.*) die Ellipse.
ellipsis [i'lipsis], *s.* (*Gram.*) die Ellipse.
elliptic(al) [i'liptik(əl)], *adj.* (*Gram., Geom.*) elliptisch.
elm [elm], *s.* (*Bot.*) die Ulme.
elocution [elə'kju:ʃən], *s.* der Vortrag (*delivery*); die Vortragskunst.
elocutionist [elə'kju:ʃənist], *s.* der Vortragskünstler.
elongate ['i:lɔŋgeit], *v.a.* verlängern.
elongation [i:lɔŋ'geiʃən], *s.* die Verlängerung.
elope [i'loup], *v.n.* entlaufen, von zu Hause fliehen.
elopement [i'loupmənt], *s.* das Entlaufen, die Flucht von zu Hause.
eloquence ['eləkwəns], *s.* die Beredsamkeit.
eloquent ['eləkwənt], *adj.* beredt, redegewandt.
else [els], *adv.* sonst, außerdem, anders; *or* —, sonst . . .; *how* —? wie denn sonst? *nobody* —, sonst niemand; *anyone* —? sonst noch jemand? — *conj.* sonst.
elsewhere [els'wεə], *adv.* anderswo; anderswohin.
Elsinore ['elsinɔ:]. Helsingör, *n.*
elucidate [i'lju:sideit], *v.a.* erläutern, erklären (*to s.o., Dat.*).
elucidation [ilju:si'deiʃən], *s.* die Erläuterung, die Erklärung.
elude [i'lju:d], *v.a.* ausweichen, entgehen (*Dat.*).
elusive [i'lju:siv], *adj.* schwer faßbar, täuschend.
Elysian [i'liziən], *adj.* elysisch.
emaciate [i'meiʃieit], *v.a.* abmagern, dünn werden.
emaciation [imeiʃi'eiʃən], *s.* die Abmagerung.

emanate ['emәneit], *v.n.* ausgehen, herrühren (*derive*); ausstrahlen (*radiate*).
emancipate [i'mænsipeit], *v.a.* befreien, emanzipieren.
emancipation [imænsi'peiʃәn], *s.* die Emanzipation.
embalm [im'bɑ:m], *v.a.* einbalsamieren.
embankment [im'bæŋkmәnt], *s.* der Flußdamm, der Eisenbahndamm; die Eindämmung.
embarcation *see* **embarkation.**
embargo [im'bɑ:gou], *s.* die Handelssperre.
embark [im'bɑ:k], *v.a.* einschiffen. — *v.n.* sich einschiffen; — *upon s.th.*, an etwas herangehen, unternehmen.
embarkation [embɑ:'keiʃәn], *s.* die Einschiffung.
embarrass [im'bærәs], *v.a.* verlegen machen, in Verlegenheit bringen.
embarrassment [im'bærәsmәnt], *s.* die Verlegenheit.
embassy ['embәsi], *s.* (*Pol.*) die Botschaft, die Gesandtschaft.
embed [im'bed], *v.a.* einbetten.
embellish [im'beliʃ], *v.a.* verschönern, ausschmücken; ausmalen (*story*).
embers ['embәz], *s. pl.* die glühende Asche; die Kohlen, *f. pl.*; *Ember Days*, (*Eccl.*) die Quatembertage, *m. pl.*
embezzle [im'bezl], *v.a.* veruntreuen, unterschlagen.
embitter [im'bitә], *v.a.* verbittern.
emblazon [im'bleizn], *v.a.* ausmalen, auf ein Schild setzen.
emblem ['emblәm], *s.* das Emblem, das Abzeichen.
emblematic(al) [emblә'mætik(әl)], *adj.* sinnbildlich, symbolisch.
embodiment [im'bɔdimәnt], *s.* die Verkörperung.
embody [im'bɔdi], *v.a.* verkörpern.
embolden [im'bouldn], *v.a.* erkühnen, anfeuern, anspornen; *be emboldened*, sich erkühnen.
emboss [im'bɔs], *v.a.* in getriebener Arbeit verfertigen, prägen.
embossed [im'bɔst], *adj.* getrieben, in erhabener Arbeit; gestanzt.
embrace [im'breis], *v.a.* (*fig.*) umarmen, umfassen. — *s.* die Umarmung.
embrasure [im'breiʒә], *s.* die Schießscharte.
embrocation [embro'keiʃәn], *s.* die Einreibung (*act*); (*Pharm.*) die Einreibsalbe.
embroider [im'brɔidә], *v.a.* sticken; verzieren, ausschmücken (*adorn*).
embroidery [im'brɔidәri], *s.* die Stickerei; die Verzierung, Ausschmückung (*of story etc.*).
embroil [im'brɔil], *v.a.* verwickeln.
embryo ['embriou], *s.* der Keim; Embryo.
embryonic [embri'ɔnik], *adj.* im Embryostadium, im Werden.
emend [i'mend], *v.a.* verbessern (*text*), berichtigen.
emendation [i:men'deiʃәn], *s.* die Textverbesserung.
emendator ['i:mendeitә], *s.* der Berichtiger.
emerald ['emәrәld], *s.* der Smaragd.
emerge [i'mә:dʒ], *v.n.* auftauchen, hervortreten, an den Tag kommen.
emergence [i'mә:dʒәns], *s.* das Auftauchen, das Hervortreten.
emergency [i'mә:dʒәnsi], *s.* der Notfall; die kritische Lage; *in case of* —, im Notfalle; — *exit*, der Notausgang; — *landing*, die Notlandung; — *measures*, Notmaßnahmen; — *brake*, die Notbremse.
emery ['emәri], *s.* — *paper*, das Schmirgelpapier.
emetic [i'metik], *s.* das Brechmittel.
emigrant ['emigrәnt], *s.* der Auswanderer.
emigrate ['emigreit], *v.n.* auswandern.
emigration [emi'greiʃәn], *s.* die Auswanderung.
eminence ['eminәns], *s.* die Anhöhe; die Eminenz, der hohe Ruf (*fame*); die eminente Stellung, die Autorität (*authority*); *Your Eminence*, Eure Eminenz.
eminent ['eminәnt], *adj.* eminent, hervorragend.
emissary ['emisәri], *s.* der Abgesandte, der Sendbote.
emission [i'miʃәn], *s.* die Aussendung (*sending out*); die Ausstrahlung (*radiation*).
emit [i'mit], *v.a.* aussenden; ausstrahlen; ausströmen.
emolument [i'mɔljumәnt], *s.* das (Neben)einkommen, das Zusatzgehalt, das Honorar (*fee*).
emotion [i'mouʃәn], *s.* die Rührung, die Bewegung, das Gefühl, die Gemütsbewegung.
emotional [i'mouʃәnәl], *adj.* gefühlvoll.
emperor ['empәrә], *s.* der Kaiser.
emphasis ['emfәsis], *s.* der Nachdruck.
emphasize ['emfәsaiz], *v.a.* betonen.
empire ['empaiә], *s.* das Reich, das Kaiserreich.
empiric(al) [emp'irik(әl)], *adj.* (*Phil.*) empirisch.
empiricism [em'pirisizm], *s.* (*Phil.*) der Empirizismus.
employ [im'plɔi], *v.a.* benutzen (*thing*); beschäftigen, anstellen (*person*).
employee [im'plɔii:], *s.* der Angestellte.
employer [im'plɔiә], *s.* der Arbeitgeber.
employment [im'plɔimәnt], *s.* die Beschäftigung, die Arbeit.
emporium [em'pɔ:riәm], *s.* der Handelsplatz; (*Naut.*) der Stapelplatz; das Warenhaus (*stores*).
empower [em'pauә], *v.a.* bevollmächtigen.
empress ['empres], *s.* die Kaiserin.
emptiness ['emptinis], *s.* die Leere, die Öde.
empty ['empti], *adj.* leer; — *-headed*, geistlos.

emulate ['emjuleit], *v.a.* nacheifern (*Dat.*).
emulation [emju'leiʃən], *s.* der Wetteifer, das Nacheifern.
emulous ['emjuləs], *adj.* nacheifernd, wetteifernd; eifersüchtig (*jealous*).
emulsion [i'mʌlʃən], *s.* (*Pharm.*) die Emulsion.
enable [i'neibl], *v.a.* befähigen; ermächtigen (*empower*).
enact [i'nækt], *v.a.* (*Pol.*) verordnen; verfügen (*order*); darstellen, aufführen (*on stage*).
enactment [i'næktmənt], *s.* die Verordnung.
enamel [i'næml], *v.a.* emaillieren. — *s.* die Emaille; (*Med.*) der Schmelz.
enamour [i'næmə], *v.a.* verliebt machen.
encamp [in'kæmp], *v.n.* (sich) lagern, das Lager aufschlagen.
encampment [in'kæmpmənt], *s.* das Lager.
encase [in'keis], *v.a.* einschließen, in ein Gehäuse schließen.
encashment [in'kæʃmənt], *s.* (*Comm.*) das Inkasso, die Einkassierung.
enchain [in'tʃein], *v.a.* in Ketten legen, anketten.
enchant [in'tʃɑ:nt], *v.a.* bezaubern.
enchantment [in'tʃɑ:ntmənt], *s.* die Bezauberung; der Zauber (*spell*).
encircle [in'sə:kl], *v.a.* umringen, umkreisen; (*Mil.*) einkreisen.
encirclement [in'sə:klmənt], *s.* die Einkreisung.
enclose [in'klouz], *v.a.* einschließen; einlegen (*in letter*).
enclosure [in'klouʒə], *s.* die Einfriedigung; die Beilage, Einlage (*in letter*).
encompass [in'kʌmpəs], *v.a.* umfassen, umspannen (*comprise*).
encore ['ɔnkɔ:, ɔn'kɔ:], *int.* noch einmal! —*s.* die Wiederholung, Zugabe.
encounter [in'kauntə], *v.a.* treffen; begegnen (*Dat.*). — *s.* das Zusammentreffen.
encourage [in'kʌridʒ], *v.a.* ermutigen; anspornen.
encouragement [in'kʌridʒmənt], *s.* die Ermutigung; die Förderung (*promotion*).
encroach [in'kroutʃ], *v.n.* eingreifen (*interfere*); übergreifen.
encroachment [in'kroutʃmənt], *s.* der Eingriff, der Übergriff.
encrust [in'krʌst], *v.a.* inkrustieren; verkrusten.
encumber [in'kʌmbə], *v.a.* belasten.
encumbrance [in'kʌmbrəns], *s.* die Belastung, das Hindernis.
encyclical [en'siklikl], *s.* das (päpstliche) Rundschreiben, die Enzyklika.
encylopaedia [insaiklo'pi:djə], *s.* das Lexikon, die Enzyklopädie.
encyclopaedic [insaiklo'pi:dik], *adj.* enzyklopädisch.
end [end], *s.* das Ende; der Schluß; das Ziel (*aim*); die Absicht (*intention*); *in the* —, am Ende, letzten Endes; *to that* —, zu dem Zweck; *put an* — *to*, einer Sache ein Ende machen; *make* —*s meet*, sein Auskommen finden; *burn the candle at both* —*s*, seine Kräfte verschwenden. — *v.a.* beenden. — *v.n.* enden, Schluß machen.
ending ['endiŋ], *s.* das Ende (*of play etc.*); (*Gram.*) die Endung.
endanger [in'deindʒə], *v.a.* gefährden, in Gefahr bringen.
endear [in'diə], *v.a.* beliebt machen. — *v.r.* — *o.s. to*, sich lieb Kind machen bei.
endearment [in'diəmənt], *s. term of* —, ein Kosewort.
endeavour [in'devə], *v.n.* sich bemühen, sich bestreben. — *s.* das Streben, die Bestrebung, die Bemühung.
endemic(al) [en'demik(əl)], *adj.* einheimisch; endemisch.
endive ['endiv], *s.* (*Bot.*) die Endivie.
endless ['endlis], *adj.* unendlich, endlos.
endorse [in'dɔ:s], *v.a.* bestätigen (*confirm*); beipflichten; (*Fin.*) indossieren (*cheque*).
endorsement [in'dɔ:smənt], *s.* die Bestätigung (*confirmation*); (*Fin.*) das Indossament (*cheque*).
endow [en'dau], *v.a.* begaben (*talents*); ausstatten (*equip*); stiften.
endowment [en'daumənt], *s.* die Begabung (*talents*); die Stiftung; — *policy*, die abgekürzte Lebensversicherung.
endurable [in'djuərəbl], *adj.* erträglich.
endurance [in'djuərəns], *s.* die Ausdauer (*toughness*); die Dauer, Fortdauer (*time*); das Ertragen (*suffering*); — *test*, die Dauerprüfung; (*fig.*) die Geduldsprobe (*patience*).
endure [in'djuə], *v.a.* aushalten, ertragen; leiden (*suffer*).
endways, endwise ['endweiz, -waiz], *adv.* mit dem Ende nach vorne: aufrecht (*vertical*).
enemy ['enəmi], *s.* der Feind, der Gegner.
energetic [enə'dʒetik], *adj.* energisch, tatkräftig.
energy ['enədʒi], *s.* die Energie, die Tatkraft; der Nachdruck (*vehemence*).
enervate ['enə:veit], *v.a.* entkräften, schwächen.
enervation [enə:'veiʃən], *s.* die Entkräftigung, die Schwächung.
enfeeble [in'fi:bl], *v.a.* entkräften, schwächen.
enfold [in'fould], *v.a.* umschließen, umfassen; einhüllen (*veil*).
enforce [in'fɔ:s], *v.a.* erzwingen, durchsetzen.
enforcement [in'fɔ:smənt], *s.* die Erzwingung, die Durchsetzung.
enfranchise [in'fræntʃaiz], *v.a.* freilassen, befreien (*emancipate*); (*Pol.*) das Stimmrecht geben.
enfranchisement [in'fræntʃizmənt], *s.* die Befreiung, die Gewährung des Stimmrechts.

engage [in'geidʒ], *v.a.* verpflichten, engagieren (*pledge, bind*); anstellen (*employ*); verwickeln (*in conversation*); *become —d*, sich verloben. — *v.n.* — *in*, sich einlassen in (*Acc.*), sich befassen mit (*Dat.*).
engagement [in'geidʒmənt], *s.* die Verpflichtung (*pledge*); die Verlobung (*betrothal*); die Verabredung (*appointment*); das Gefecht (*with enemy*).
engaging [in'geidʒiŋ], *adj.* freundlich, verbindlich (*smile etc.*); einnehmend.
engender [in'dʒendə], *v.a.* erzeugen, hervorrufen (*cause*).
engine ['endʒin], *s.* die Maschine; der Motor; (*Railw.*) die Lokomotive; *fire —*, die Feuerspritze; — *driver*, (*Railw.*) der Lokomotivführer.
engineer [endʒi'niə], *s.* der Ingenieur (*professional*); der Techniker (*technician*); (*Am.*) der Lokomotivführer (*engine driver*).
engineering [endʒi'niəriŋ], *s.* das Ingenieurwesen; der Maschinenbau; *chemical —*, die chemische Technik *or* Technologie; *civil —*, das Zivilingenieurwesen; *electrical —*, die Elektrotechnik *or* die Elektrotechnologie; *mechanical —*, der Maschinenbau, die Strukturtechnik; — *laboratory*, das technische Labor; — *workshop*, die technische Werkstatt.
English ['iŋgliʃ], *adj.* englisch; britisch. — *s.* die englische Sprache, das Englisch; (*pl.*) *the —*, die Engländer, *m.pl.*
Englishman ['iŋgliʃmən], *s.* der Engländer.
Englishwoman ['iŋgliʃwumən], *s.* die Engländerin.
engrain [in'grein], *v.a.* tief einprägen.
engrave [in'greiv], *v.a.* gravieren, eingravieren (*art*); einprägen (*impress*).
engraver [in'greivə], *s.* der Graveur, der Kupferstecher.
engraving [in'greiviŋ], *s.* der Kupferstich.
engross [in'grous], *v.a.* ganz in Anspruch nehmen, gefangen halten (*mind*).
engulf [in'gʌlf], *v.a.* verschlingen.
enhance [in'hɑ:ns], *v.a.* erhöhen (*raise*); steigern (*increase*).
enhancement [in'hɑ:nsmənt], *s.* die Erhöhung (*pleasure*); die Steigerung (*growth*).
enigma [i'nigmə], *s.* das Rätsel.
enigmatic(al) [enig'mætik(əl)], *adj.* rätselhaft (*puzzling*); dunkel (*obscure*).
enjoin[in'dʒɔin], *v.a.* (an)befehlen (*s.o.*, *Dat.*), einschärfen (*s.o.*, *Dat.*).
enjoy [in'dʒɔi], *v.a.* genießen (*Acc.*); sich freuen (über, *Acc.*). — *v.r.* — *o.s.*, sich amüsieren.
enjoyable [in'dʒɔiəbl], *adj.* erfreulich, angenehm, genießbar.
enjoyment [in'dʒɔimənt], *s.* der Genuß, die Freude (*of*, an, *Dat.*).
enlarge [in'lɑ:dʒ], *v.a.* vergrößern (*premises etc.*); erweitern (*expand*). — *v.n.* sich verbreiten (*on* or *upon*, über, *Acc.*).
enlargement [in'lɑ:dʒmənt], *s.* die Vergrößerung (*also Phot.*).
enlighten [in'laitn], *v.a.* erleuchten, aufklären (*explain to*).
enlightenment [in'laitnmənt], *s.* (*Eccl.*) die Erleuchtung; (*Phil.*) die Aufklärung.
enlist [in'list], *v.a.* anwerben (*Mil.*); gewinnen (*cooperation*). — *v.n.* (*Mil.*) sich anwerben lassen.
enliven [in'laivn], *v.a.* beleben, aufmuntern.
enmity ['enmiti], *s.* die Feindschaft.
ennoble [i'noubl], *v.a.* adeln; veredeln.
enormity [i'nɔ:miti], *s.* die Ungeheuerlichkeit.
enormous [i'nɔ:məs], *adj.* ungeheuer; ungeheuerlich.
enough [i'nʌf], *adj.*, *adv.* genug; ausreichend; *sure —*, gewiß!; *well —*, ziemlich gut.
enquire *see under* **inquire**.
enquiry *see under* **inquiry**.
enrage [in'reidʒ], *v.a.* wütend machen.
enraged [in'reidʒd], *adj.* wütend, entrüstet.
enrapture [in'ræptʃə], *v.a.* in Entzückung versetzen, entzücken (*delight*).
enrich [in'ritʃ], *v.a.* bereichern; (*Chem.*) verbessern.
enrol [in'roul], *v.a.* einschreiben (*inscribe*); (*Mil.*) anwerben. — *v.n.* sich einschreiben; beitreten (*Dat.*).
enrolment [in'roulmənt], *s.* die Einschreibung; — *form*, das Einschreibeformular.
ensconce [in'skɔns], *v.r.* — *o.s.*, sich niederlassen.
enshrine [in'ʃrain], *v.a.* umhüllen, einschließen; in einem Schrein aufbewahren.
enshroud [in'ʃraud], *v.a.* einhüllen.
ensign ['ensin *or* 'enzən, 'ensain], *s.* (*Naut.*) die Fahne, die Flagge; (*Mil. rank*) der Fähnrich.
enslave [in'sleiv], *v.a.* unterjochen, versklaven.
ensnare [in'snɛə], *v.a.* umgarnen, verführen (*seduce*).
ensue [in'sju:], *v.n.* folgen.
ensure [in'ʃuə], *v.a.* versichern (*assure*); sicherstellen (*make sure*).
entail [in'teil], *v.a.* zur Folge haben, mit sich bringen.
entangle [in'tæŋgl], *v.a.* verwickeln, verwirren (*confuse*).
entanglement [in'tæŋglmənt], *s.* die Verwicklung; die Verwirrung (*confusion*).
enter ['entə], *v.a.* betreten; eintreten; — *o.'s name*, seinen Namen einschreiben. — *v.n.* eintreten (*in*, in, *Acc.*); — *into agreement*, einen Vertrag eingehen; — *on*, sich einlassen in (*Acc.*); — *upon a career*, eine Laufbahn antreten.
enterprise ['entəpraiz], *s.* das Unternehmen; das Wagnis (*daring*); *private —*, das Privatunternehmen; (*Econ.*)

die freie Wirtschaft; *public* —, das staatliche *or* Staatsunternehmen.

enterprising [ˈentəpraiziŋ], *adj.* unternehmungslustig.

entertain [entəˈtein], *v.a.* unterhalten (*amuse*); zu Tisch haben (*person*); hegen (*opinion*).

entertaining [entəˈteiniŋ], *adj.* amüsant, unterhaltend.

entertainment [entəˈteinmənt], *s.* die Unterhaltung, Vergnügung.

enthral [inˈθrɔːl], *v.a.* fesseln, bannen.

enthrone [inˈθroun], *v.a.* auf den Thron bringen *or* setzen.

enthusiasm [inˈθjuːziæzm], *s.* die Begeisterung; die Schwärmerei.

enthusiast [inˈθjuːziæst], *s.* der Enthusiast, der Schwärmer.

enthusiastic [inθjuːziˈæstik], *adj.* enthusiastisch, begeistert, schwärmerisch.

entice [inˈtais], *v.a.* locken, anlocken, verlocken (*lure*).

enticement [inˈtaismənt], *s.* die Lokkung.

entire [inˈtaiə], *adj.* gesamt, ganz; völlig; vollständig (*complete*).

entirety [inˈtaiəriti], *s.* die Gesamtheit (*totality*); das Ganze (*total*).

entitle [inˈtaitl], *v.a.* berechtigen; betiteln (*title*).

entitlement [inˈtaitlmənt], *s.* die Berechtigung.

entity [ˈentiti], *s.* das Wesen.

entomb [inˈtuːm], *v.a.* begraben.

entomologist [entəˈmɔlədʒist], *s.* der Entomologe.

entomology [entəˈmɔlədʒi], *s.* die Entomologie.

entrails [ˈentreilz], *s. pl.* die Eingeweide, *n.pl.*

entrain [inˈtrein], *v.a.* (*Railw., Mil.*) einsteigen lassen. — *v.n.* (*Railw.*) (in den Zug) einsteigen.

entrance (1) [ˈentrəns], *s.* der Eingang (*door*); — *fee*, der Eintritt; — *hall*, der Hausflur, die Vorhalle; *university* —, Zulassung zur Universität.

entrance (2) [inˈtrɑːns], *v.a.* entzücken, hinreißen.

entrant [ˈentrənt], *s.* (*to school, university etc.*) der (neu) Zugelassene; Teilnehmer.

entrap [inˈtræp], *v.a.* fangen, verstricken.

entreat [inˈtriːt], *v.a.* anflehen, ersuchen.

entreaty [inˈtriːti], *s.* die flehentliche *or* dringende Bitte, (*obs.*) das Ansuchen.

entrench [inˈtrentʃ], *v.a.* verschanzen, festsetzen.

entrenchment [inˈtrentʃmənt], *s.* (*Mil.*) die Verschanzung.

entrust [inˈtrʌst], *v.a.* anvertrauen (*s. th.*); betreuen (*s.o. with*, mit, *Dat.*).

entry [ˈentri], *s.* das Eintreten, der Eintritt; der Eingang (*house*); (*Comm.*) die Eintragung (*book-keeping*); *double* —, doppelte Buchführung; die Einfuhr (*import*); — *permit*, die Einreisebewilligung; *no* —, Eintritt verboten!

entwine [inˈtwain], *v.a.* verflechten, herumwickeln.

enumerate [iˈnjuːməreit], *v.a.* aufzählen.

enumeration [injuːməˈreiʃən], *s.* die Aufzählung.

enunciate [iˈnʌnsieit], *v.a.* aussprechen.

enunciation [inʌnsiˈeiʃən], *s.* (*Phonet.*) die Aussprache; die Kundgebung (*declaration*).

envelop [inˈveləp], *v.a.* einhüllen, umhüllen.

envelope [ˈenviloup, ˈɔnvəloup], *s.* die Hülle; der Umschlag, Briefumschlag (*letter*).

enviable [ˈenviəbl], *adj.* beneidenswert.

envious [ˈenviəs], *adj.* neidisch (*of s.o.*, auf, *Acc.*).

environment [inˈvaiərənmənt], *s.* die Umgebung; (*Geog., Zool.*) die Umwelt.

environs [inˈvairənz], *s. pl.* die Umgebung, die Umgegend.

envisage [inˈvizidʒ], *v.a.* sich vorstellen.

envoy [ˈenvɔi], *s.* (*Pol.*) der Gesandte, der Bote.

envy [ˈenvi], *s.* der Neid. — *v.a.* beneiden.

epaulette [epɔːˈlet], *s.* (*Mil.*) das Achselstück, die Epaulette.

ephemeral [iˈfemərəl], *adj.* Eintags-, Tages-; eintägig, vergänglich (*transient*).

epic [ˈepik], *adj.* episch. — *s.* das Epos.

epicure [ˈepikjuə], *s.* der Epikureer, der Feinschmecker, der Genießer.

epidemic [epiˈdemik], *s.* die Epidemie.

epigram [ˈepigræm], *s.* das Epigramm.

epigrammatic [epigrəˈmætik], *adj.* epigrammatisch, kurz; treffend (*apt*).

epilepsy [ˈepilepsi], *s.* (*Med.*) die Epilepsie, die Fallsucht.

epileptik [epiˈleptik], *s.* (*Med.*) der Epileptiker.

epilogue [ˈepilɔg], *s.* der Epilog.

Epiphany [iˈpifəni]. (*Eccl.*) das Fest der heiligen drei Könige, Epiphanias.

episcopal [iˈpiskəpəl], *adj.* bischöflich.

episcopate [iˈpiskəpit], *s.* die Bischofswürde, das Episkopat (*collective*).

episode [ˈepisoud], *s.* die Episode.

epistle [iˈpisl], *s.* die Epistel, das Sendschreiben.

epistolary [iˈpistələri], *adj.* brieflich, Brief-.

epitaph [ˈepitɑːf], *s.* die Grabschrift.

epithet [ˈepiθet], *s.* das Beiwort, die Benennung.

epitome [iˈpitəmi], *s.* die Epitome, der Auszug; der Abriß (*summary*).

epitomize [iˈpitəmaiz], *v.a.* kürzen; einen Auszug machen von (*Dat.*).

epoch [ˈiːpɔk], *s.* die Epoche; — -*making*, bahnbrechend.

equable [ˈekwəbl], *adj.* gleich, gleichmäßig; gleichmütig (*tranquil*).

equal [ˈiːkwəl], *adj.* gleich, ebenbürtig (*to, Dat.*).

equality [i'kwɔliti], *s.* die Gleichheit, Ebenbürtigkeit.
equalization [i:kwəlai'zeiʃən], *s.* der Ausgleich; — *of burdens*, der Lastenausgleich.
equalize ['i:kwəlaiz], *v.a.* gleichmachen. — *v.n.* (*Footb.*) ausgleichen.
equanimity [i:kwə'nimiti], *s.* der Gleichmut.
equate [i'kweit], *v.a.* (*Maths.*) gleichsetzen.
equation [i'kweiʃən], *s.* die Gleichung.
equator[i'kweitə], *s.* (*Geog.*)der Äquator.
equatorial [ekwə'tɔ:riəl], *adj.* (*Geog.*) äquatorial.
equerry ['ekwəri], *s.* der Stallmeister; diensttuender Kammerherr (*of King*).
equestrian [i'kwestriən], *adj.* beritten; Reit-; — *art*, die Reitkunst.
equidistant [i:kwi'distənt], *adj.* gleich weit entfernt.
equilateral [i:kwi'lætərəl], *adj.* gleichseitig.
equilibrium [i:kwi'libriəm], *s.* das Gleichgewicht.
equine ['i:kwain], *adj.* Pferd-, pferdeartig.
equinoctial [i:kwi'nɔkʃəl], *adj.* äquinoktial.
equinox ['i:kwinɔks], *s.* die Tag- und Nachtgleiche.
equip [i'kwip], *v.a.* (*Mil.*) ausrüsten; ausstatten (*furnish*).
equipment [i'kwipmənt], *s.* die Ausrüstung, die Ausstattung; das Zeug.
equitable ['ekwitəbl], *adj.* unparteiisch, gerecht, billig.
equity ['ekwiti], *s.* die Billigkeit, die Unparteilichkeit.
equivalence [i'kwivələns], *s.* die Gleichwertigkeit, die Gleichheit.
equivalent [i'kwivələnt], *adj.* gleichwertig. — *s.* das Äquivalent, der gleiche Wert, der Gegenwert.
equivocal [i'kwivəkəl], *adj.* zweideutig, doppelsinnig, zweifelhaft.
era ['iərə], *s.* die Ära, die Zeitrechnung.
eradicate [i'rædikeit], *v.a.* ausrotten, austilgen, vertilgen.
eradication [irædi'keiʃən], *s.* die Ausrottung, die Vertilgung.
erase [i'reiz], *v.a.* ausradieren.
eraser [i'reizə], *s.* der Radiergummi (*India rubber*).
erasure [i'reiʒjə], *s.* die Ausradierung; die Auskratzung (*scratching*).
ere [ɛə], *prep.* (*obs.*) vor. — *conj.* (*obs.*) ehe, bevor.
erect [i'rekt], *adj.* aufrecht, gerade. — *v.a.* aufrichten; errichten (*build*).
erection [i'rekʃən], *s.* die Errichtung (*structure*); die Aufrichtung (*putting up*).
ermine ['ə:min], *s.* der *or* das Hermelin.
erode [i'roud], *v.a.* (*Geog.*, *Geol.*) ausfressen.
erosion [i'rouʒən], *s.* die Erosion.
erotic [i'rɔtik], *adj.* erotisch.
err [ə:], *v.n.* irren.
errand ['erənd], *s.* der Auftrag, Gang; der Botengang; — *boy*, der Laufbursche.
errant ['erənt], *adj.* herumstreifend; *knight* —, fahrender Ritter.
errata *see under* **erratum**.
erratic [i'rætik], *adj.* regellos, unberechenbar, ohne Verlaß.
erratum [e'reitəm, e'rɑ:təm], *s.* (*pl.* **errata** [e'reitə, e'rɑ:tə]) der Druckfehler.
erroneous [i'rouniəs], *adj.* irrig, irrtümlich.
error ['erə], *s.* der Irrtum, der Fehler.
erudite ['erudait], *adj.* gelehrt.
erudition [eru'diʃən], *s.* die Gelehrsamkeit.
erupt [i'rʌpt], *v.n.* ausbrechen.
eruption [i'rʌpʃən], *s.* der Ausbruch.
eruptive [i'rʌptiv], *adj.* Ausbruchs-, ausbrechend.
escalator ['eskəleitə], *s.* die Rolltreppe.
escapade [eskə'peid], *s.* der Streich (*prank*).
escape [is'keip], *v.a.*, *v.n.* entkommen, entgehen, entfliehen.
escapism [is'keipizm], *s.* die Philosophie der Weltflucht.
escapist [is'keipist], *s.* der Weltflüchtling.
escarpment [is'kɑ:pmənt], *s.* die Böschung.
eschew [is'tʃu:], *v.a.* vermeiden.
escort [is'kɔ:t], *v.a.* geleiten; decken (*cover*). — ['eskɔ:t], *s.* (*Mil.*) die Garde, die Deckung; Begleitung (*persons*); (*Mil.*) das Geleit (*conduct*).
escutcheon [is'kʌtʃən], *s.* das Wappenschild.
esoteric [eso'terik], *adj.* (*Phil.*) esoterisch, geheim, dunkel.
espalier [es'pæljə], *s.* (*Mil.*) das Spalier.
especial [is'peʃəl], *adj.* besonder, außergewöhnlich.
espionage ['espiənɑ:ʒ *or* -nidʒ], *s.* die Spionage, das Spionieren.
espouse [is'pauz], *v.a.* (ver)-heiraten; (*fig.*) eintreten (für, *Acc.*).
espy [is'pai], *v.a.* ausspähen, erspähen.
essay [e'sei], *v.a.* versuchen, probieren. — ['esei], *s.* der Versuch; der Aufsatz, Essay (*composition*).
essayist ['eseiist], *s.* der Essayist.
essence ['esəns], *s.* (*Phil.*, *Chem.*) die Essenz.
essential [i'senʃəl], *adj.* wesentlich; wichtig (*important*).
establish [is'tæbliʃ], *v.a.* feststellen, (*ascertain*); gründen (*found*); —*ed Church*, die englische Staatskirche.
establishment [is'tæbliʃmənt], *s.* die Feststellung (*ascertainment*); die Gründung (*foundation*); die Unternehmung, das Geschäft (*business*); (*Mil.*) die Aufstellung, der Bestand; (*Eccl.*) die Staatskirche.
estate [is'teit], *s.* (*Pol.*) der Stand; das Vermögen; das Gut; (*property*) — *duty*, die Vermögenssteuer; — *manager*, der Gutsverwalter; — *agent*, der

Grundstückmakler; *real* —, der Grundbesitz; (*pl.*) Immobilien, *pl.*
esteem [is'ti:m], *v.a.* schätzen (*value*); achten (*respect*). — *s.* die Wertschätzung, die Achtung.
estimable ['estiməbl], *adj.* schätzenswert.
estimate ['estimeit], *v.a.* schätzen (*evaluate*); berechnen (*calculate*). — ['estimit], *s.* die Schätzung, der Voranschlag.
estimation [esti'meiʃən], *s.* die Wertschätzung; die Achtung (*respect*).
Estonian [es'tounian], *adj.* estnisch, estländisch. — *s.* der Este, Estländer.
estrange [is'treindʒ], *v.a.* entfremden.
estrangement [is'treindʒmənt], *s.* die Entfremdung.
estuary ['estjuəri], *s.* die Mündung (*river*); der Meeresarm (*bay*).
etch [etʃ], *v.a.* (*Metall.*) ätzen; (*Art*) radieren.
etching ['etʃiŋ], *s.* (*Art*) die Radierung.
eternal [i'tə:nl], *adj.* ewig; immerwährend.
eternity [i'tə:niti], *s.* die Ewigkeit.
ether ['i:θə], *s.* der Äther.
ethereal [i'θiəriəl], *adj.* ätherisch, luftig.
ethical ['eθikl], *adj.* ethisch, sittlich.
ethics ['eθiks], *s. pl.* die Ethik, die Sittenlehre; *professional* —, das Berufsethos.
Ethiopian [i:θi'oupiən], *adj.* äthiopisch. — *s.* der Äthiopier.
ethnography [eθ'nɔgrəfi], *s.* die Ethnographie, die Völkerkunde.
etymology [eti'mɔlədʒi], *s.* die Etymologie, die Wortableitung.
eucharist ['ju:kərist], s. (*Eccl.*) die Eucharistie; das heilige Abendmahl.
eulogize ['ju:lədʒaiz], *v.a.* loben, preisen.
euphonium [ju'founiəm], *s.* (*Mus.*) das Bombardon, Baritonhorn.
euphony ['ju:fəni], *s.* der Wohlklang.
European [juərə'piən], *adj.* europäisch. — *s.* der Europäer.
euphemism ['ju:fimizm], *s.* der Euphemismus.
euphuism ['ju:fjuizm], *s.* (*Lit.*) die gezierte Stilart.
evacuate [i'vækjueit], *v.a.* evakuieren, räumen.
evacuation [ivækju'eiʃən], *s.* die Evakuierung, die Räumung.
evade [i'veid], *v.a.* ausweichen (*Dat.*); entgehen (*escape*, *Dat.*).
evanescent [evæ'nesənt], *adj.* verschwindend.
evangelical [i:væn'dʒelikəl], *adj.* evangelisch.
evangelist [i'vændʒəlist], *s.* der Evangelist.
evangelize [i'vændʒəlaiz], *v.a.*, *v.n.* das Evangelium lehren *or* predigen.
evaporate [i'væpəreit], *v.a.* verdunsten lassen, verdampfen lassen. — *v.n.* (*Chem.*) verdunsten.
evaporation [ivæpə'reiʃən], *s.* die Verdampfung, die Verdunstung.
evasion [i'veiʒən], *s.* die Flucht (*escape*) (*from*, von, *Dat.*); die Ausflucht, das Ausweichen.
evasive [i'veiziv], *adj.* ausweichend.
eve, even (1) [i:v,i:vn], *s.* (*Poet.*) der Vorabend; Abend.
even (2) [i:vn], *adj.* eben, glatt (*smooth*); gerade (*number*); quitt (*quits*); gelassen (*temper*); gleich (*equal*). — *v.a.* — *out*, gleichmachen, ebnen.
even (3) [i:vn], *adv.* gerade, selbst, sogar (*emphatic*); *not* —, nicht einmal; — *though*, obwohl.
evening ['i:vniŋ], *s.* der Abend; — *gown*, das Abendkleid; — *dress*, der Abendanzug; der Smoking (*dinner jacket*); der Frack (*tails*).
evenness ['i:vənnis], *s.* die Ebenheit (*of surface*); die Gelassenheit (*of temper*).
event [i'vent], *s.* die Begebenheit, der Vorfall (*happening*); das (große) Ereignis (*state occasion*); *at all* —*s*, auf alle Fälle; *in the* —, im Falle, daß.
eventful [i'ventful], *adj.* ereignisreich.
eventual [i'ventjuəl], *adj.* schließlich, endlich.
ever ['evə], *adv.* je; immer, stets; nur, überhaupt; *for* —, für immer; — *so*, so sehr, sehr; — *since*, seitdem.
evergreen ['evəgri:n], *adj.* immergrün. —*s.* (*Bot.*) das Immergrün.
everlasting [evə'lɑ:stiŋ], *adj.*ewig; dauernd; fortwährend (*continual*).
every ['evri], *adj.* jeder, jeder einzelne (*pl.* alle); — *one*, jeder einzelne; — *now and then*, dann und wann; — *other day*, jeden zweiten Tag; — *day*, alle Tage.
everybody, everyone ['evribɔdi, 'evriwʌn], *s.* jedermann, ein jeder.
everyday ['evridei], *adj.* alltäglich.
everyone *see under* **everybody.**
everything ['evriθiŋ], *s.* alles.
everywhere ['evrihwɛə], *adv.* überall.
evict [i'vikt], *v.a.* vertreiben (*eject*); (*Law*) (gerichtlich) kündigen (*Dat.*).
eviction [i'vikʃən], *s.* die Kündigung, die Vertreibung.
evidence ['evidəns], *s.* der Beweis (*proof*); (*Law*) das Zeugnis; *documentary* —, (*Law*) das Beweisstück; (*Law*) *give* —, eine Zeugenaussage machen.
evident ['evidənt], *adj.* klar, deutlich (*obvious*); augenscheinlich (*visible*); *self-* —, selbstverständlich.
evil ['i:vil], *s.* das Übel, das Böse. — *adj.* übel, böse; — *speaking*, die üble Nachrede.
evildoer ['i:vildu:ə], *s.* der Übeltäter.
evince [i'vins], *v.a.* zeigen, dartun, an den Tag legen.
evocation [i:vo'keiʃən], *s.* die Beschwörung (*magic*); das Hervorrufen.
evocative [i'vɔkətiv], *adj.* hervorrufend, voll Erinnerungen (*of*, *Genit.*).
evoke [i'vouk], *v.a.* hervorrufen (*call forth*); beschwören (*conjure up*).
evolution [i:və'lju:ʃən, ev–], *s.* die Entwicklung, Evolution.

evolutionary [i:və'lju:ʃənri], *adj.* Evolutions-, Entwicklungs-.
evolve [i'vɔlv], *v.a.* entwickeln. — *v.n.* sich entwickeln.
ewe [ju:], *s.* (*Zool.*) das Mutterschaf.
ewer ['juə], *s.* die Wasserkanne.
exact [ig'zækt], *adj.* genau, gewissenhalf, exakt. — *v.a.* fordern; erpressen; eintreiben (*dept.*).
exacting [ig'zæktiŋ], *adj.* genau, anspruchsvoll.
exactitude [ig'zæktitju:d], *s.* die Genauigkeit.
exactly [ig'zæktli], *adv.* (*coll.*) ganz richtig!
exactness [ig'zæktnis], *s.* die Genauigkeit.
exaggerate [ig'zædʒəreit], *v.a.* übertreiben.
exaggeration [igzædʒə'reiʃən], *s.* die Übertreibung.
exalt [ig'zɔ:lt], *v.a.* erhöhen, erheben.
exaltation [egzɔ:l'teiʃən], *s.* die Erhöhung, die Erhebung.
exalted [ig'zɔ:ltid], *adj.* erhaben, hoch.
examination [igzæmi'neiʃən], *s.* die Prüfung; (*Med.*) die Untersuchung; (*Law*) das Verhör, das Untersuchungsverhör; die Ausfragung (*scrutiny*); — *board*, die Prüfungskommission.
examine [ig'zæmin], *v.a.* prüfen; (*Med.*) untersuchen; (*Law*) verhören; ausfragen.
examiner [ig'zæminə], *s.* der Examinator.
example [ig'zɑ:mpl], *s.* das Beispiel; *for* —, zum Beispiel; *set an* —, ein Beispiel geben.
exasperate [ig'zæspəreit], *v.a.* aufreizen; ärgern, aufbringen.
exasperation [igzæspə'reiʃən], *s.* die Entrüstung, die Erbitterung.
excavate ['ekskəveit], *v.a.* ausgraben.
excavation [ekskə'veiʃən], *s.* die Ausgrabung.
exceed [ik'si:d], *v.a.* überschreiten (*go beyond*); übertreffen (*surpass*). — *v.n.* zu weit gehen.
exceeding [ik'si:diŋ], *adj.* (*obs.*) übermäßig, übertrieben.
exceedingly [ik'si:diŋli], *adv.* außerordentlich; äußerst.
excel [ik'sel], *v.a.* übertreffen. — *v.n.* sich auszeichnen (*in*, in, *Dat.*).
excellence ['eksələns], *s.* die Vortrefflichkeit.
excellent ['eksələnt], *adj.* ausgezeichnet, hervorragend.
except [ik'sept], *v.a.* ausnehmen, ausschließen. — *conj.* außer (es sei denn) daß. — *prep.* ausgenommen, mit Ausnahme von (*Dat.*).
exception [ik'sepʃən], *s.* die Ausnahme (*exemption*); der Einwand, Einwurf (*objection*).
exceptionable [ik'sepʃənəbl], *adj.* anfechtbar (*disputable*); anstößig.
exceptional [ik'sepʃənəl], *adj.* außergewöhnlich.
exceptionally [ik'sepʃənəli], *adv.* ausnahmsweise.
excerpt [ik'sə:pt], *v.a.* ausziehen, exzerpieren. — ['eksə:pt], *s.* der Auszug, das Exzerpt.
excess [ik'ses], *s.* das Übermaß; *carry to* —, übertreiben; — *fare*, der Zuschlag; — *luggage*, das Übergewicht.
excessive [ik'sesiv], *adj.* übermäßig, allzuviel.
exchange [iks'tʃeindʒ], *s.* der Austausch; *stock* —, die Börse; *rate of* —, der Kurs; *bill of* —, der Wechsel; der Tausch (*barter*). — *v.a.* wechseln; tauschen (*barter*) (*against*, für, *Acc.*); austauschen (*messages etc.*).
exchangeable [iks'tʃeindʒəbl], *adj.* (*Comm.*) austauschbar.
exchequer [iks'tʃekə], *s.* die Staatskasse; das Finanzamt (*office*); *Chancellor of the Exchequer*, der Schatzkanzler.
excise (1) ['eksaiz], *s.* die Aksize; *customs and* —, das Zollamt, der Zoll; — *officer*, der Zollbeamte, Steuerbeamte.
excise (2) [ek'saiz], *v.a.* (her)ausschneiden.
excision [ek'siʒən], *s.* das Ausschneiden, die Entfernung.
excitable [ik'saitəbl], *adj.* erregbar, reizbar.
excitation [eksi'teiʃən], *s.* (*Phys.*, *Chem.*) die Erregung.
excitement [ik'saitmənt], *s.* die Erregung, Aufregung (*mood*).
exciting [ik'saitiŋ], *adj.* erregend, aufregend, packend (*thrilling*).
exclaim [iks'kleim], *v.a.* ausrufen.
exclamation [ekslə'meiʃən], *s.* der Ausruf (*interjection*); das Geschrei (*shouting*).
exclude [iks'klu:d], *v.a.* ausschließen.
exclusion [iks'klu:ʒən], *s.* der Ausschluß.
exclusive [iks'klu:siv], *adj.* ausschließlich (*sole*); exklusiv (*select*).
exclusiveness [iks'klu:sivnis], *s.* der exklusive Charakter, die Exklusivität.
excommunicate [ekskə'mju:nikeit], *v.a.* (*Eccl.*) von der Kirchengemeinde ausschließen, bannen, exkommunizieren.
excommunication [ekskəmju:ni'keiʃən], *s.* (*Eccl.*) die Exkommunikation, der Bann.
excoriate [eks'kɔ:rieit], *v.a.* häuten; abschälen (*peel*).
excrement ['ekskrimənt], *s.* das Exkrement, der Kot.
excrescence [iks'kresəns], *s.* der Auswuchs.
excretion [eks'kri:ʃən], *s.* die Ausscheidung, der Auswurf.
excruciate [iks'kru:ʃieit], *v.a.* martern, peinigen; *excruciatingly funny*, furchtbar komisch.
exculpate ['ekskʌlpeit], *v.a.* rechtfertigen, entschuldigen.

exculpation [ekskʌl'peiʃən], *s.* die Entschuldigung, die Rechtfertigung.
excursion [iks'kə:ʃən], *s.* der Ausflug, die Exkursion (*outing*); die Digression (*irrelevance*); der Abstecher (*deviation*).
excusable [iks'kju:zəbl], *adj.* entschuldbar, verzeihlich.
excuse [iks'kju:s], *s.* die Entschuldigung. — [-'kju:z], *v.a.* entschuldigen (*Acc.*), verzeihen (*Dat.*).
execrable ['eksikrəbl], *adj.* abscheulich.
execrate ['eksikreit], *v.a.* verfluchen, verwünschen.
execute ['eksikju:t], *v.a.* ausführen (*carry out*); (*Law*) hinrichten (*kill*).
execution [eksi'kju:ʃən], *s.* die Ausführung (*of an order*); (*Law*) die Hinrichtung; die Pfändung (*official forfeit*).
executioner [eksi'kju:ʃənə], *s.* der Henker, der Scharfrichter.
executive [ik'sekjutiv], *adj.* ausübend, vollziehend (*of power etc.*). — *s.* (*Pol.*) die Exekutive; (*Comm.*) das Direktionsmitglied.
executor [ik'sekjutə], *s.* der Testamentsvollstrecker (*of a will*).
exemplar [ig'zemplə], *s.* das Muster, das Beispiel.
exemplary [ig'zempləri], *adj.* musterhaft, vorbildlich.
exemplify [ig'zemplifai], *v.a.* durch Beispiel(e) erläutern.
exempt [ig'zempt], *v.a.* ausnehmen, befreien, verschonen (*spare*).
exemption [ig'zempʃən], *s.* die Ausnahme.
exequies ['eksikwiz], *s. pl.* das Leichenbegängnis, die Totenfeier.
exercise ['eksəsaiz], *s.* die Übung (*practice*); die körperliche Betätigung (*exertion*). — *v.a.* üben; — *o.'s rights*, von seinen Rechten Gebrauch machen; — *discretion*, Diskretion walten lassen; (*Mil.*) — *troops*, exerzieren.
exert [ig'zə:t], *v.a.* ausüben; — *pressure*, Druck ausüben (*upon*, auf, *Acc.*). — *v.r.* — *o.s.*, sich anstrengen.
exertion [ig'zə:ʃən], *s.* die Anstrengung, die Bemühung.
exhale [eks'heil], *v.a.* ausatmen; aushauchen; ausdünsten.
exhalation [ekshə'leiʃən], *s.* die Ausatmung, die Ausdünstung.
exhaust [ig'zɔ:st], *v.a.* erschöpfen. — *s.* (*Motor.*) der Auspuff.
exhaustible [ig'zɔ:stibl], *adj.* erschöpflich.
exhaustion [ig'zɔ:stʃən], *s.* die Erschöpfung.
exhibit [ig'zibit], *v.a.* ausstellen (*display*); zeigen (*demonstrate*). — ['eksibit], *s.* das Ausstellungsobjekt; (*Law*) das Beweisstück.
exhibition [eksi'biʃən], *s.* die Ausstellung (*display*); (*Films*) die Vorführung (*showing*); das Stipendium (*scholarship*).
exhibitioner [eksi'biʃənə], *s.* der Stipendiat.
exhilarate [ig'ziləreit], *v.a.* aufheitern.
exhilaration [igzilə'reiʃən], *s.* die Aufheiterung.
exhort [ig'zɔ:t], *v.a.* ermahnen.
exhortation [egzɔ:'teiʃən], *s.* die Ermahnung.
exigence, exigency ['eksidʒəns, -si], *s.* das Bedürfnis, Erfordernis (*necessity*); der dringende Notfall (*emergency*).
exigent ['eksidʒənt], *adj.* dringend.
exile ['eksail], *s.* der Verbannte (*person*); das Exil, die Verbannung (*state*). — *v.a.* verbannen; des Landes verweisen.
exist [ig'zist], *v.n.* existieren.
existence [ig'zistəns], *s.* das Dasein, die Existenz.
existent [ig'zistənt], *adj.* seiend, wirklich, existierend.
existentialism [egzis'tenʃəlizm], *s.* der Existentialismus.
exit ['eksit], *s.* der Ausgang; (*Theat.*) der Abgang.
exonerate [ig'zɔnəreit], *v.a.* entlasten.
exorbitant [ig'zɔ:bitənt], *adj.* übertrieben, übermäßig.
exorcise ['eksɔ:saiz], *v.a.* bannen, beschwören.
exorcism ['eksɔ:sizm], *s.* die Geisterbeschwörung.
exotic [ig'zɔtik], *adj.* exotisch.
expand [iks'pænd], *v.a.* erweitern, ausbreiten, ausdehnen. — *v.n.* sich erweitern (*broaden*); sich ausdehnen (*stretch*).
expansion [iks'pænʃən], *s.* die Ausdehnung, die Ausbreitung.
expansive [iks'pænsiv], *adj.* ausgedehnt; Ausdehnungs- (*forces*); (*fig.*) mitteilsam.
expatiate [iks'peiʃieit], *v.n.* sich verbreiten (*on*, über, *Acc.*).
expatriate [eks'peitrieit], *v.a.* verbannen.
expect [iks'pekt], *v.a.* erwarten (*wait for*); glauben (*believe*); hoffen (*hope for*); — *a baby*, ein Kind erwarten.
expectant [iks'pektənt], *adj.* schwanger (*with child*); voll Erwartung.
expectation [ekspek'teiʃən], *s.* die Erwartung, die Hoffnung.
expedience, expediency [iks'pi:diəns, -si], *s.* die Zweckmäßigkeit, die Schicklichkeit.
expedient [iks'pi:diənt], *adj.* zweckmäßig, schicklich, ratsam. — *s.* das Mittel; der Ausweg.
expedite ['ekspidait], *v.a.* beschleunigen.
expedition [ekspi'diʃən], *s.* (*Mil. etc.*) die Expedition; die schnelle Abfertigung.
expeditious [ekspi'diʃəs], *adj.* schleunig, schnell.
expel [iks'pel], *v.a.* vertreiben, austreiben; (*Sch.*) verweisen (*from*, von, aus).
expend [iks'pend], *v.a.* ausgeben.
expenditure [iks'penditʃə], *s.* (*Comm.*) die Ausgabe; der Aufwand (*of energy*).

expense [iks'pens], *s.* die Ausgabe; (*pl.*) die Kosten, Auslagen, Spesen, *f. pl.*
expensive [iks'pensiv], *adj.* teuer, kostspielig.
experience [iks'piəriəns], *s.* die Erfahrung, das Erlebnis. — *v.a.* erfahren.
experienced [iks'piəriənsd], *adj.* erfahren.
experiment [iks'perimənt], *s.* das Experiment, der Versuch. — *v.n.* experimentieren, Versuche machen.
experimental [iksperi'mentl], *adj.* Probe-, probeweise, experimentell.
expert ['ekspə:t], *s.* der Fachmann; der Sachverständige.
expertise [ekspə'ti:z], *s.* die Expertise, die Fachkenntnis.
expertness [iks'pə:tnis], *s.* die Gewandtheit.
expiable ['ekspiəbl], *adj.* sühnbar.
expiation [ekspi'eiʃən], *s.* die Sühnung, die Sühne.
expiration [ekspi'reiʃən], *s.* das Ausatmen; (*fig.*) der Tod; der Ablauf (*time*); die Verfallszeit (*lapse of validity*).
expire [iks'paiə], *v.n.* aushauchen (*breathe*); ablaufen (*run out*); sterben (*die*).
expiry [iks'pairi], *s.* die Ablaufsfrist (*of papers*).
explain [iks'plein], *v.a.* erklären, erläutern.
explanation [eksplə'neiʃən], *s.* die Erklärung, Erläuterung.
expletive [iks'pli:tiv], *s.* das Fluchwort, der Kraftausdruck.
explicable ['eksplikəbl], *adj.* erklärlich, erklärbar.
explication [ekspli'keiʃən], *s.* die Erklärung.
explicit [iks'plisit], *adj.* ausdrücklich, deutlich.
explicitness [iks'plisitnis], *s.* die Deutlichkeit, die Bestimmtheit.
explode [iks'ploud], *v.n.* explodieren; (*Mil.*) platzen (*of a shell*). — *v.a.* explodieren lassen.
exploit [iks'plɔit], *v.a.* ausbeuten; ausnützen (*utilize*). — ['eksplɔit], *s.* die Heldentat, die Großtat.
exploitation [eksplɔi'teiʃən], *s.* die Ausbeutung, die Ausnützung.
exploration [eksplɔ:'reiʃən], *s.* die Erforschung.
explore [iks'plɔ:], *v.a.* erforschen, untersuchen (*investigate*).
explosion [iks'plouʒən], *s.* die Explosion.
explosive [iks'plousiv], *adj.* explosiv. — *s.* der Sprengstoff.
exponent [iks'pounənt], *s.* (*Maths.*) der Exponent; der Vertreter (*of a theory*).
export [eks'pɔ:t], *v.a.* ausführen, exportieren. — ['ekspɔ:t], *s.* der Export, die Ausfuhr.
exporter [eks'pɔ:tə], *s.* der Exporteur, der Ausfuhrhändler, der Exportkaufmann.
expose [iks'pouz], *v.a.* entblößen; aussetzen (*to cold etc.*); bloßstellen (*display*); (*Phot.*) belichten; darlegen (*set forth*); ausstellen (*exhibit*).
exposition [ekspo'ziʃən], *s.* die Aussetzung; die Auslegung (*interpretation*); die Darlegung (*deposition, declaration*); die Ausstellung (*exhibition*).
exposure [iks'pouʒə], *s.* die Aussetzung (*to cold etc.*); die Bloßstellung; (*Phot.*) die Belichtung.
expostulate [iks'pɔstjuleit], *v.n.* zur Rede stellen.
expound [iks'paund], *v.a.* auslegen, darlegen.
express [iks'pres], *v.a.* ausdrücken; zum Ausdruck bringen. — *adj.* ausdrücklich, eilig, Eil-; besonder; — *letter*, der Eilbrief; — *train*, der Schnellzug. — *s.* der Eilzug.
expression [iks'preʃən], *s.* der Ausdruck.
expressive [iks'presiv], *adj.* ausdrucksvoll.
expressly [iks'presli], *adv.* ausdrücklich, besonders.
expropriate [eks'prouprieit], *v.a.* enteignen.
expropriation [eksproupri'eiʃən], *s.* die Enteignung.
expulsion [iks'pʌlʃən], *s.* die Ausstoßung; der Ausschluß; die Vertreibung (*of a large number*).
expunge [iks'pʌndʒ], *v.a.* austilgen, auslöschen.
expurgate ['ekspə:geit], *v.a.* reinigen.
exquisite ['ekskwizit], *adj.* auserlesen, vortrefflich.
extant ['ekstənt, ek'stænt], *adj.* noch vorhanden, existierend.
extempore [eks'tempəri], *adv.* aus dem Stegreif, extemporiert.
extemporize [eks'tempəraiz], *v.a.* extemporieren, improvisieren.
extend [iks'tend], *v.a.* ausdehnen (*boundaries etc.*); ausstrecken (*a helping hand*); verlängern (*time*); bieten (*a welcome*); erweitern (*enlarge*). — *v.n.* sich erstrecken, sich ausdehnen; dauern (*time*).
extensible [iks'tensibl], *adj.* ausdehnbar.
extension [iks'tenʃən], *s.* die Ausdehnung; die Verlängerung (*time*); *university — classes*, Abendkurse, *m.pl.* (der Erwachsenenbildung); (*Telephone*) der Apparat.
extensive [iks'tensiv], *adj.* ausgedehnt, umfassend.
extent [iks'tent], *s.* die Ausdehnung, die Weite; die Größe (*size*); *to a certain —*, bis zu einem gewissen Grade; *to the — of £x*, bis zu einem Betrage von x Pfund.
extenuate [iks'tenjueit], *v.a.* beschönigen; mildern; *extenuating circumstances*, (*Law*) mildernde Umstände, *m. pl.*
extenuation [ikstenju'eiʃən], *s.* die Beschönigung, die Abschwächung.

exterior [eks'tiəriə], *adj.* äußerlich. — *s.* das Äußere.
exterminate [iks'tə:mineit], *v.a.* ausrotten, vertilgen.
extermination [ikstə:mi'neiʃən], *s.* die Ausrottung, die Vertilgung.
external [eks'tə:nl], *adj.* äußerlich; auswärtig.
extinct [iks'tiŋkt], *adj.* ausgestorben.
extinction [iks'tiŋkʃən], *s.* das Erlöschen (*dying*); die Vernichtung (*annihilation*); das Aussterben.
extinguish [iks'tiŋgwiʃ], *v.a.* auslöschen; vernichten (*annihilate*). — *v.n.* auslöschen, ausgehen (*of fire* or *life*).
extirpate ['ekstə:peit], *v.a.* ausrotten.
extol [iks'toul], *v.a.* preisen, erheben.
extort [iks'tɔ:t], *v.a.* erpressen.
extortion [iks'tɔ:ʃən], *s.* die Erpressung.
extortionate [iks'tɔ:ʃənit], *adj.* erpresserisch.
extra ['ekstrə], *adj.* zusätzlich. — *s.* (*pl.*) die Nebenausgaben, *f. pl.*
extract [iks'trækt], *v.a.* (aus)ziehen (*pull out*). — ['ekstrækt], *s.* (*Chem.*) der Extrakt; der Auszug (*book*).
extraction [iks'trækʃən], *s.* das Ausziehen (*pulling out*); das Zahnziehen (*tooth*); das Verfertigen eines Auszuges (*book*); die Herkunft (*origin*).
extradite ['ekstrədait], *v.a.* (*Pol.*) ausliefern.
extradition [ekstrə'diʃən], *s.* (*Pol.*) die Auslieferung.
extraneous [eks'treiniəs], *adj.* nicht zur Sache gehörig, unwesentlich.
extraordinary [iks'trɔ:dnəri], *adj.* außerordentlich.
extravagance [iks'trævəgəns], *s.* die Extravaganz; die Verschwendung (*waste*).
extravagant [iks'trævəgənt], *adj.* extravagant; verschwenderisch.
extravaganza [ikstrævə'gænzə], *s.* fantastisches Werk, die Burleske, Posse.
extreme [iks'tri:m], *adj.* äußerst (*uttermost*); höchst (*highest*); extrem (*stringent*); letzt (*last*); — *unction*, (*Eccl.*) die Letzte Ölung; *in the* —, äußerst.
extremity [iks'tremiti], *s.* die äußerste Grenze (*limit*); die Notlage (*straits, emergency*); (*pl.*) die Extremitäten, *f. pl.*
extricate ['ekstrikeit], *v.a.* herauswinden, herauswickeln (*disentangle*), befreien.
extrude [eks'tru:d], *v.a.* ausstoßen; (*Metall.*) ausziehen.
extrusion [eks'tru:ʒən], *s.* die Ausstoßung; die Ausziehung (*of steel etc.*).
exuberant [ig'zju:bərənt], *adj.* überschwenglich, überschäumend.
exude [ik'sju:d], *v.a.* ausschwitzen; von sich geben (*give out*).
exult [ig'zʌlt], *v.n.* frohlocken.
exultant [ig'zʌltənt], *adj.* triumphierend.
exultation [egzʌl'teiʃən], *s.* das Frohlocken, der Jubel.
eye [ai], *v.a.* ansehen, betrachten. — *s.* das Auge; — *of a needle*, das Nadelöhr; *an* — *for an* —, Aug' um Auge; — *witness*, der Augenzeuge.
eyeball ['aibɔ:l], *s.* der Augapfel.
eyebrow ['aibrau], *s.* die Augenbraue.
eyeglass ['aiglɑ:s], *s.* der Zwicker, Klemmer.
eyelash ['ailæʃ], *s.* die Augenwimper.
eyelid ['ailid], *s.* das Augenlid.
eyesight ['aisait], *s.* die Sehkraft, das Augenlicht.
eyrie ['ɛəri, 'iəri], *s.* der Adlerhorst.

F

F [ef]. das F (*also Mus.*).
fable [feibl], *s.* die Fabel; das Märchen.
fabric ['fæbrik], *s.* das Gewebe, der Stoff.
fabricate ['fæbrikeit], *v.a.* herstellen; (*fig.*) fabrizieren; erfinden.
fabrication [fæbri'keiʃən], *s.* (*fig.*) die Erdichtung, die Erfindung.
fabulous ['fæbjuləs], *adj.* fabelhaft; wunderbar.
façade [fə'sɑ:d], *s.* die Fassade.
face [feis], *v.a.* jemandem ins Gesicht sehen (*s.o.*); gegenüberstehen, gegenüberliegen (*lie opposite, Dat.*); — *west*, nach Westen gehen (*of house, window*). — *v.n.* — *about*, sich umdrehen. — *s.* das Gesicht, (*Poet.*) das Angesicht; — *to* — *with*, gegenüber (*Dat.*); *on the* — *of it*, auf den ersten Blick; *lose* —, sich blamieren; *have the* — *to*, die Frechheit haben etwas zu tun.
facet ['fæsit], *s.* die Facette; der Zug (*feature*).
facetious [fə'si:ʃəs], *adj.* scherzhaft.
facetiousness [fə'si:ʃəsnis], *s.* die Scherzhaftigkeit, die Witzigkeit.
facile [f'æsail], *adj.* leicht.
facilitate [fə'siliteit], *v.a.* erleichtern, leicht machen.
facility [fə'siliti], *s.* die Leichtigkeit (*ease*); die Gewandtheit (*deftness*); die Möglichkeit (*possibility*); (*pl.*) die Einrichtungen, die Möglichkeiten, *f. pl.* (*amenities*).
facing ['feisiŋ], *s.* (*Tail.*) der Besatz, der Aufschlag; (*Build.*) die Verkleidung; (*Mil.*) die Schwenkung, die Wendung.
facsimile [fæk'simili], *s.* das Faksimile.
fact [fækt], *s.* die Tatsache; *as a matter of* —, tatsächlich, in Wirklichkeit; —*s and figures*, der Bericht mit Tatsachen und Zahlen; *in* —, tatsächlich; *in point of* —, in der Tat, in Wirklichkeit.
faction ['fækʃən], *s.* (*Pol.*) die Partei, die Faktion.
factitious [fæk'tiʃəs], *adj.* nachgemacht, künstlich.
factor ['fæktə], *s.* der Faktor; (*Comm.*) der Agent; der Umstand (*fact*).

factory ['fæktəri], *s.* die Fabrik; — *hand*, der Fabrikarbeiter.
factual ['fæktjuəl], *adj.* Tatsachen-, tatsächlich.
faculty ['fækəlti], *s.* (*Univ.*) die Fakultät; die Fähigkeit (*sense*); (*pl.*) die Talente, *n. pl.*, die Begabung; Kräfte *f. pl.*
fad [fæd], *s.* die Grille, die Laune; die Marotte.
faddy ['fædi], *adj.* schrullig.
fade [feid], *v.n.* verschießen (*colour*); verwelken (*flower*); vergehen.
fag [fæg], *v.a.* ermüden. — *v.n.* (*Sch.*) Dienste tun, Diener sein (*for*, für). — *s.* die Plackerei; (*coll.*) die Zigarette; (*Sch.*) der Fuchs, der neue Schüler; — *end*, der Zigarettenstummel; (*Naut.*) das offene Tauende; der letze Rest (*remnant*).
faggot ['fægət], *s.* das Reisigbündel.
fail [feil], *v.a.* im Stiche lassen (*let down*); (*Sch.*) durchfallen (*an examination*, in einer Prüfung. — *v.n.* — *to do*, etwas nicht tun, fehlgehen, scheitern; versagen.
failing ['feiliŋ], *adj.* schwach, versagend. — *s.* der Mangel, Fehler.
failure ['feiljə], *s.* der Fehlschlag; das Versagen (*weakness*); das Nichteinhalten (*non-compliance*); das Durchfallen (*in examinations*); der Versager (*person*).
fain [fein], *adv.* (*obs.*) gern, gerne.
faint [feint], *v.n.* in Ohnmacht fallen, ohnmächtig werden. — *adj.* leise, schwach (*noise etc.*); — *hearted*, kleinmütig.
fair (1) [fɛə], *adj.* hübsch, schön (*beautiful*); unparteiisch, fair (*impartial*); anständig, angemessen (*equitable*); blond.
fair (2) [fɛə], *s.* der Jahrmarkt (*market*); (*Comm.*) die Messe, die Handelsmesse.
fairness ['fɛənis], *s.* die Schönheit (*beauty*); die Unparteilichkeit, Fairneß (*objectivity*); die Sportlichkeit (*sportsmanship*); die Anständigkeit (*equity*).
fairy ['fɛəri], *s.* die Fee.
faith [feiθ], *s.* der Glaube; die Treue (*loyalty*); das Vertrauen (*trust*).
faithful ['feiθful], *adj.* (*Rel.*) gläubig; treu (*loyal*); ergeben (*devoted*).
faithless ['feiθlis], *adj.* (*Rel.*) ungläubig; treulos, untreu (*disloyal*).
fake [feik], *s.* der Schwindel.
falcon ['fɔ:(l)kən], *s.* (*Orn.*) der Falke.
falconer ['fɔ:(l)knə], *s.* der Falkner.
falconry ['fɔ:(l)kənri], *s.* die Falknerei.
fall [fɔ:l], *v.n. irr.* fallen, abfallen (*leaves*); einbrechen (*night*); sich legen (*wind*); heruntergehen, sinken (*price*); geboren werden (*pigs, lambs*); — *through*, mißlingen, zunichte werden. — *s.* der Fall; (*Am.*) der Herbst (*autumn*); der Abhang (*precipice*); der Verfall(*decay*);der Untergang(*decline*).
fallacious [fə'leiʃəs], *adj.* trügerisch, trüglich, falsch (*assumption etc.*).
fallacy ['fæləsi], *s.* die Täuschung, der Irrtum, Trugschluß.
fallible ['fælibl], *adj.* fehlbar.
falling ['fɔ:liŋ], *s.* das Fallen; — *sickness*, die Fallsucht; — *off*, das Abnehmen (*decrease*); — *out*, der Zwist, der Streit (*disunity*). — *adj.* — *star*, die Sternschnuppe.
fallow ['fælou], *adj.* brach, fahl.
false [fɔ:ls], *adj.* falsch, unrichtig (*untrue*); — *alarm*, der blinde Alarm; — *bottom*, der Doppelboden; — *start*, der Fehlstart; — *step*, der Fehltritt; — *verdict*, das Fehlurteil; — *pretences*, die Vorspiegelung falscher Tatsachen.
falsehood ['fɔ:lshud], *s.* die Lüge, die Unwahrheit.
falseness ['fɔ:lsnis], *s.* die Falschheit; die Unaufrichtigkeit (*insincerity*).
falsify ['fɔ:lsifai], *v.a.* fälschen, verfälschen.
falsity ['fɔ:lsiti] *see* **falseness**.
falter ['fɔ:ltə], *v.n.* straucheln (*stumble*); stammeln (*stammer*).
fame [feim], *s.* der Ruhm; der Ruf; *ill* —, der üble Ruf.
familiar [fə'miljə], *adj.* vertraut, wohlbekannt, intim; gewohnt (*habitual*); *be on — terms*, auf vertrautem Fuß stehen.
familiarity [fəmili'æriti], *s.* die Vertrautheit, die Vertraulichkeit (*intimacy*).
familiarize [fə'miljəraiz], *v.a.* vertraut machen, bekannt machen.
family ['fæmili], *s.* die Familie; — *doctor*, der Hausarzt; (*Chem.*) die Gruppe; *be in the — way*, in anderen Umständen sein, guter Hoffnung sein, schwanger sein; — *tree*, der Stammbaum.
famine ['fæmin], *s.* die Hungersnot; — *relief*, Hilfe für die Hungernden.
famish ['fæmiʃ], *v.n.* verhungern, hungern; verschmachten.
famous ['feiməs], *adj.* berühmt, wohlbekannt (*for*, wegen).
fan [fæn], *s.* der Fächer (*lady's*); der Ventilator; (*sl.*) der leidenschaftliche Anhänger, der Fan; (*coll.*) Fanatiker (*admirer*). — *v.a.* fächeln; anfachen (*flames*); entfachen (*hatred*). — *v.n.* (*Mil.*) — *out*, sich ausbreiten, ausschwärmen.
fanatic [fə'nætik], *s.* der Fanatiker.
fanatical [fə'nætikəl], *adj.* fanatisch.
fanaticism [fə'nætisizm], *s.* der Fanatismus, die Schwärmerei.
fancier ['fænsiə], *s. pigeon* —, der Taubenzüchter; *bird* —, der Vogelzüchter.
fanciful ['fænsiful], *adj.* schwärmerisch, wunderlich.
fancy ['fænsi], *s.* die Vorliebe (*preference*); die Phantasie; die Laune (*whim*); *take a — to*, liebgewinnen. — *adj.* — *dress*, der Maskenanzug, das Kostüm; — *goods*, Galanteriewaren; — *cakes*, Torten, *f.pl.*; das Feingebäck. — *v.a.* denken, gern haben; (*coll.*) — *oneself as*, sich einbilden, man sei; *just*—! denk doch mal; denk mal an!

fanfare ['fænfεə], *s.* (*Mus.*) die Fanfare, der Tusch.
fang [fæŋ], *s.* (*Zool.*) der Hauzahn, der Giftzahn (*of snake*); (*Engin.*) der Zapfen. — *v.a.* (*Engin.*) vollpumpen, aufpumpen und in Tätigkeit setzen.
fanlight ['fænlait], *s.* die Lünette, das Lichtfenster.
fantastic(al) [fæn'tæstik(əl)], *adj.* fantastisch.
fantasy ['fæntəsi], *s.* (*Poet.*, *Mus.*) die Phantasie; das Hirngespinst (*chimæra*).
far [fɑ:], *adj.* weit; fern, entfernt (*distant*). — *adv.* — *and wide*, weit und breit; *by* —, bei weitem; *go too* —, zu weit gehen; *he will go* —, er wird seinen Weg machen; — *sighted*, weitsichtig.
farce [fɑ:s], *s.* die Farce, die Posse.
fare [fεə], *s.* das Fahrgeld; der Fahrpreis (*of taxi etc.*); der Fahrgast (*one travelling in taxi*); — *stage*, die Fahr- *or* Teilstrecke; das Essen, die Kost (*food*); *bill of* —, die Speisekarte. — *v.n.* ergehen (*Dat.*), daran sein.
farewell [fεə'wel], *interj.* lebewohl! — *dinner*, das Abschiedsessen; — *party*, die Abschiedsgesellschaft.
farinaceous [færi'neiʃəs], *adj.* mehlig, aus Mehl.
farm [fɑ:m], *s.* der Pachthof, der Bauernhof; die Farm; — *hand*, der Landarbeiter, der Farmarbeiter; — *bailiff*, der Gutsverwalter. — *v.a.* bebauen; — *out*, verpachten. — *v.n.* Landwirt sein.
farmer ['fɑ:mə], *s.* der Bauer, Landwirt; der Pächter (*tenant*).
farmland ['fɑ:mlænd], *s.* das Ackerland.
farmyard ['fɑ:mjɑ:d], *s.* der Bauernhof, Gutshof.
farrier ['færiə], *s.* der Hufschmid.
farrow ['færou], *s.* der Wurf (*pigs*). — *v.n.* ferkeln, Junge haben.
farther ['fɑ:ðə], *comp. adj.*, *adv.* ferner, weiter.
farthest ['fɑ:ðist], *superl. adj.*, *adv.* fernst, weitest.
farthing ['fɑ:ðiŋ], *s.* der Farthing, der Heller.
fascinate ['fæsineit], *v.a.* bezaubern, faszinieren.
fascination [fæsi'neiʃən], *s.* die Bezauberung; der Reiz, der Zauberbann (*spell*).
fascism ['fæʃizm], *s.* (*Pol.*) der Faschismus.
fashion ['fæʃən], *s.* die Mode; *out of* —, außer Mode; die Art und Weise (*manner*). — *v.a.* gestalten, bilden (*shape*); *fully —ed*, vollgeformt *or* geformt, angepaßt.
fashionable ['fæʃnəbl], *adj.* modisch, modern; elegant.
fast (1) [fɑ:st], *adj.* schnell (*runner*); fest (*firm*); *my watch is* —, meine Uhr geht vor; *a — woman*, eine leichtlebige Frau; — *train*, der Schnellzug; — *and furious*, schnell wie der Wind. — *adv.* fest.
fast (2) [fɑ:st], *v.n.* (*Rel.*) fasten; (*Rel.*) — *day*, der Fasttag.
fasten [fɑ:sn], *v.a.* festbinden, festmachen (*fix*). — *v.n.* sich festhalten (*on to*, an, *Dat.*).
fastidious [fəs'tidiəs], *adj.* wählerisch, anspruchsvoll.
fastidiousness [fəs'tidiəsnis], *s.* die anspruchsvolle Art.
fat [fæt], *adj.* fett; dick (*person*). — *s.* das Fett; (*Cul.*) das Speisefett.
fatal ['feitəl], *adj.* tödlich (*lethal*); verhängnisvoll.
fatalism ['feitəlizm], *s.* der Fatalismus.
fatality [fə'tæliti], *s.* das Verhängnis; der Todesfall; der tödliche Unfall.
fate [feit], *s.* das Schicksal, Geschick; das Verhängnis (*doom*, *destiny*).
fated ['feitid], *adj.* dem Verderben (Untergang) geweiht.
fateful ['feitful], *adj.* verhängnisvoll, unselig.
father ['fɑ:ðə], *s.* der Vater; (*Eccl.*) Pater; — *-in-law*, der Schwiegervater. — *v.a.* Vater sein *or* werden von (*Dat.*); zeugen (*procreate*).
fatherland ['fɑ:ðəlænd], *s.* das Vaterland.
fatherly ['fɑ:ðəli], *adj.* väterlich; wie ein Vater.
fathom ['fæðəm], *s.* die Klafter. — *v.a.* ergründen, erforschen.
fatigue [fə'ti:g], *s.* die Ermüdung, die Erschöpfung; (*Mil.*) der Arbeitsdienst. — *v.a.* ermüden, erschöpfen.
fatling ['fætliŋ], *s.* (*Agr.*) das Mastvieh.
fatness ['fætnis], *s.* die Beleibtheit (*person*); die Fettheit (*animals*).
fatten [fætn], *v.a.* — *up*, mästen (*animals*); fett werden lassen. — *v.n.* fett werden, sich mästen (an, *Dat.*).
fatty ['fæti], *adj.* (*Chem.*) fett, fettig. — *s.* (*coll.*) der Dickwanst.
fatuity [fə'tju:iti], *s.* die Albernheit, die Dummheit.
fatuous ['fætjuəs], *adj.* albern, dumm, nichtssagend.
faucet ['fɔ:sit], *s.* der Zapfen, der Hahn.
fault [fɔ:lt], *s.* der Fehler; die Schuld; *find — with*, etwas kritisieren; tadeln; *it is my* —, es ist meine Schuld; *at* —, im Irrtum.
faultless ['fɔ:ltlis], *adj.* fehlerlos, fehlerfrei.
faultlessness ['fɔ:ltlisnis], *s.* die Fehlerlosigkeit, die fehlerlose Ausführung.
faulty ['fɔ:lti], *adj.* fehlerhaft, mangelhaft.
faun [fɔ:n], *s.* (*Myth.*) der Faun.
fauna ['fɔ:nə], *s.* die Fauna, die Tierwelt.
favour ['feivə], *s.* die Gunst, das Wohlwollen; (*Comm.*) *in — of*, zugunsten; *do a* —, einen Gefallen tun *or* erweisen; *be in* —, sehr begehrt sein, in hoher Gunst stehen. — *v.a.* bevorzugen, begünstigen, wohlwollend gegenüberstehen (*Dat.*).
favourable ['feivərəbl], *adj.* günstig, vorteilhaft.

favourite ['feivərit], *s.* der Favorit, der Liebling; der Günstling (*of kings*). — *adj.* Lieblings-, bevorzugt.
fawn (1) [fɔ:n], *s.* (*Zool.*) das junge Reh, das Rehkalb; — *coloured*, rehfarben. — *adj.* rehfarben, hellbraun.
fawn (2) [fɔ:n], *v.n.* schmeicheln, kriecherisch sein ((*up*)*on*, *Dat.*).
fawning ['fɔ:niŋ], *adj.* kriecherisch, kriechend.
fear [fiə], *s.* die Furcht, die Angst; *stand in — of s.o.*, sich vor jemandem fürchten; *for — of*, aus Angst vor (*Dat.*). — *v.a.* fürchten, befürchten.
fearful ['fiəful], *adj.* furchtsam (*full of fear*); furchtbar (*causing fear*).
fearless ['fiəlis], *adj.* furchtlos (*of*, vor, *Dat.*).
fearlessness ['fiəlisnis], *s.* die Furchtlosigkeit.
feasibility [fi:zi'biliti], *s.* die Tunlichkeit, die Möglichkeit.
feasible ['fi:zibl], *adj.* tunlich, möglich.
feast [fi:st], *s.* das Fest, der Festtag; der Schmaus (*good meal*). — *v.n.* schmausen (*upon*, von, *Dat.*). — *v.a.* festlich bewirten.
feat [fi:t], *s.* die Tat, die Heldentat; das Kunststück.
feather ['feðə], *s.* die Feder; *show the white* —, Feigheit an den Tag legen; — *bed*, das Federbett. — *v.a.* federn; — *o.'s nest*, sein Schäfchen ins Trockene bringen.
feature ['fi:tʃə], *s.* der Zug (*characteristic*); der Gesichtszug (*facial*). — *v.a.* charakterisieren; (*Film*) in der Hauptrolle zeigen.
February ['februəri], der Februar.
feckless ['feklis], *adj.* hilflos, unfähig.
feculence ['fekjuləns], *s.* (*Chem.*) der Bodensatz, der Hefesatz.
fecund ['fekənd], *adj.* fruchtbar.
fecundate ['fekəndeit], *v.a.* fruchtbar machen, befruchten.
fecundity [fi'kʌnditi], *s.* die Fruchtbarkeit.
federacy ['fedərəsi], *s.* der Bund, die Föderation.
federal ['fedərəl], *adj.* Bundes-, föderativ.
federalism ['fedərəlizm], *s.* der Föderalismus.
federalize ['fedərəlaiz], *v.a.* verbünden.
federation [fedə'reiʃən], *s.* die Föderation, die Verbündung; (*Pol.*) der Bund.
fee [fi:], *s.* die Gebühr (*official dues*); das Honorar (*of doctor etc.*); (*pl.*) (*Sch.*) das Schulgeld.
feeble [fi:bl], *adj.* schwach, matt; — *minded*, schwachsinnig.
feed [fi:d], *v.a. irr.* füttern; verköstigen (*humans*); unterhalten (*maintain*); zuführen (*into machine*, *Dat.*); *be fed up with*, etwas satt haben; — *pipe*, die Speiseröhre. — *v.n.* sich nähren (*on*, von, *Dat.*); weiden (*graze*).
feeder ['fi:də], *s.* der Kinderlatz (*bib*); (*Tech.*) der Zubringer.
feel [fi:l], *v.n. irr.* sich fühlen (*sense*); meinen (*think*). — *v.a.* berühren, betasten (*touch*); empfinden (*be aware of*).
feeler ['fi:lə], *s.* der Fühler; *put out a* —, einen Fühler ausstrecken.
feeling ['fi:liŋ], *s.* das Gefühl; *with* —, bewegt, gerührt (*moved*); grimmig (*in anger*).
feign [fein], *v.a.* vortäuschen, heucheln.
feint [feint], *s.* die Verstellung (*disguise*); die Finte (*fencing*).
felicitate [fi'lisiteit], *v.a.* Glück wünschen (*upon*, zu, *Dat.*), beglückwünschen (*Acc.*).
felicitation [filisi'teiʃən], *s.* die Beglückwünschung, der Glückwunsch.
felicitous [fi'lisitəs], *adj.* glücklich ausgedrückt, gut gesagt (*in speaking*).
felicity [fi'lisiti], *s.* die Glückseligkeit; die glückliche Ausdruckweise (*style*).
feline ['fi:lain], *adj.* Katzen-, katzenartig.
fell (1) [fel], *adj.* grausam; *at one — swoop*, mit einem wilden Schwung.
fell (2) [fel], *v.a.* fällen (*timber*); töten (*kill*).
fell (3) [fel], *s.* das Gebirge, das Felsengelände.
fell (4) [fel], *s.* das Fell, die Haut (*skin*).
fellow ['felou], *s.* der Gefährte, Genosse (*companion*); das Mitglied eines College *or* einer Universität; (*coll.*) der Kerl; *queer* —, seltsamer Kauz; — *feeling*, das Mitgefühl; — *traveller*, der Weggenosse; (*Pol.*) der Mitläufer.
fellowship ['felouʃip], *s.* die Mitgliedschaft (einer Hochschule etc.) (*membership*); die Freundschaft (*friendship*); *good* —, die Geselligkeit.
felly, felloe ['feli,'felou], *s.* die Radfelge.
felon ['felən], *s.* der Verbrecher.
felonious [fi'louniəs], *adj.* verbrecherisch.
felt [felt], *s.* der Filz.
female ['fi:meil], *adj.* weiblich. — *s.* (*Zool.*) das Weibchen.
feminine ['feminin], *adj.* weiblich. — *s.* (*Gram.*) das weibliche Geschlecht; das Weibliche.
fen [fen], *s.* das Moor, das Marschland.
fence [fens], *s.* der Zaun, das Staket. — *v.a.* umzäunen, einzäunen (*enclose*). — *v.n.* fechten (*fight with rapiers*).
fencing ['fensiŋ], *s.* die Einzäunung (*fence*); das Fechten (*with rapiers*); — *master*, der Fechtmeister.
fend [fend], *v.a.* — *off*, abwehren, parieren. — *v.n.* — *for oneself*, sich allein behelfen.
fennel [fenl], *s.* (*Bot.*) der Fenchel.
ferment [fə:'ment], *v.a.* zur Gärung bringen. — *v.n.* gären, fermentieren. — ['fə:ment], *s.* das Gärmittel (*also fig.*); (*Chem.*) das Gärungsprodukt.
fermentation [fə:men'teiʃən], *s.* die Gärung.
fern [fə:n], *s.* (*Bot.*) das Farnkraut.
ferocious [fə'rouʃəs], *adj.* wild, grimmig.

ferocity [fə'rɔsiti], *s.* die Wildheit.
ferret ['ferit], *s.* (*Zool.*) das Frett, das Frettchen. — *v.a.* — *out*, ausspüren.
ferry ['feri], *s.* die Fähre. — *v.a.* — *across*, hinüberrudern, hinüberfahren, übersetzen.
fertile ['fə:tail], *adj.* fruchtbar.
fertility [fə:'tiliti], *s.* die Fruchtbarkeit.
fertilize ['fə:tilaiz], *v.a.* befruchten.
fertilizer ['fə:tilaizə], *s.* das Düngemittel, der Dünger.
fervent ['fə:vənt], *adj.* inbrünstig (*prayer*); heiß (*wish*).
fervid ['fə:vid], *adj.* glühend, heiß (*with zeal*).
fervour ['fə:və], *s.* die Inbrunst (*prayer*); die Sehnsucht (*wish*).
fester ['festə], *v.n.* schwären, eitern.
festival ['festivəl], *s.* das Fest, die Festspiele, *n. pl.*
festive ['festiv], *adj.* festlich, Fest-.
festivity [fes'tiviti], *s.* die Festlichkeit.
festoon [fes'tu:n], *s.* die Girlande. — *v.a.* behängen, mit Girlanden verzieren, schmücken.
fetch [fetʃ], *v.a.* holen, bringen.
fetching ['fetʃiŋ], *adj.* einnehmend.
fetter ['fetə], *v.a.* fesseln, binden. — *s.* (*pl.*) die Fesseln, *f. pl.*
feud [fju:d], *s.* die Fehde.
feudal [fju:dl], *adj.* feudal, Lehns-.
fever ['fi:və], *s.* das Fieber.
few [fju:], *adj.* einige; wenige; *a* —, ein paar.
fiancé [fi'ɔ:nsei], *s.* der Verlobte, Bräutigam.
fiancée [fi'ɔ:nsei], *s.* die Verlobte, Braut.
fib [fib], *s.* (*coll.*) die Lüge. — *v.n.* (*coll.*) lügen.
fibre ['faibə], *s.* die Fiber, Faser.
fibrous ['faibrəs], *adj.* faserartig.
fickle [fikl], *adj.* unbeständig, wankelmütig.
fiction ['fikʃən], *s.* die Erdichtung (*figment*); (*Lit.*) die Romanliteratur.
fictitious [fik'tiʃəs], *adj.* erdichtet, in der Phantasie.
fiddle [fidl], *s.* (*coll.*) die Geige, Fiedel, Violine. — *v.n.* (*coll.*, *Mus.*) geigen; schwindeln (*cheat*).
fiddlesticks! ['fidlstiks], *int.* Unsinn!
fidelity [fi'deliti], *s.* die Treue (*loyalty*); Genauigkeit; (*Engin.*) *high* —, Präzision, High Fidelity.
fidget ['fidʒit], *v.n.* unruhig sein.
fidgety ['fidʒiti], *adj.* nervös.
fie! [fai], *int.* pfui!
field [fi:ld], *s.* das Feld; (*fig.*) das Gebiet; — *glass*, der Feldstecher; (*Hunt.*) — *sports*, die Feldübungen, der Jagdsport. — *v.a.*, *v.n.* abfangen, abpassen (*cricket*).
fiend [fi:nd], *s.* der Unhold, böse Geist; *fresh air* —, ein Freund der frischen Luft.
fiendish ['fi:ndiʃ], *adj.* teuflisch, boshaft.
fierce [fiəs], *adj.* wild, wütend (*beast*); — *weather*, — *cold*, die grimmige Kälte, der grimmige Winter.
fiery ['faiəri], *adj.* feurig; hitzig.
fife [faif], *s.* (*Mus.*) die Querpfeife.
fifteen [fif'ti:n], *num. adj.* fünfzehn.
fifth [fifθ], *num. adj.* der fünfte.
fifty ['fifti], *num. adj.* fünfzig.
fig [fig], *s.* (*Bot.*) die Feige.
fight [fait], *v.a.*, *v.n. irr.* kämpfen, bekämpfen (*in battle*); raufen (*of boys*). — *s.* der Kampf; die Rauferei.
figment ['figmənt], *s.* die Erdichtung.
figurative ['figjuərətiv], *adj.* bildlich (*style*).
figure ['figə], *s.* die Figur (*body*); die Gestalt, Form (*shape*); (*Maths.*) die Zahl, die Ziffer; *cut a* —, einen Eindruck machen; *a fine — of a man!* ein fabelhafter Kerl! — *v.a.* — *out*, ausdenken, ausrechnen. — *v.n.* eine Rolle spielen, rangieren.
figured ['figəd], *adj.* figuriert.
figurehead ['figəhed], *s.* der scheinbare Leiter, die Representationsfigur.
filament ['filəmənt], *s.* der Faden, der Glühfaden (*bulb*).
filbert ['filbə:t], *s.* (*Bot.*) die Haselnuß.
filch [filtʃ], *v.a.* stehlen, klauen.
file [fail], *s.* (*Engin.*) die Feile; (*Mil.*) die Reihe; (*Comm.*) der Aktenstoß, das Aktenbündel, der Ordner; (*pl.*) die Akten, *f. pl.*; *single* —, im Gänsemarsch; *rank and* —, die große Masse; *on the* —, in den Akten. — *v.a.* feilen (*metal*); zu den Akten legen (*papers*); einreichen (*petition*).
filial ['filiəl], *adj.* kindlich.
filibuster ['filibʌstə], *s.* der Freibeuter; (*Am.*) (*Pol.*) die Obstruktion.
filigree ['filigri:], *s.* die Filigranarbeit.
filing ['failiŋ], *s.* (*pl.*) die Feilspäne; das Einheften (*of papers*); — *cabinet*, die Kartei.
fill [fil], *v.a.* füllen; ausfüllen (*place, job*); plombieren (*tooth*); — *up*, tanken (*with petrol*). — *s.* das volle Maß; *eat o.'s* —, sich satt essen.
fillet ['filit], *s.* das Filet (*meat*); das Band, die Binde (*band*).
filling ['filiŋ], *s.* die Plombe (*in tooth*); — *station*, die Tankstelle.
filly ['fili], *s.* das Füllen.
film [film], *s.* der Film (*cinema, Phot.*); die Haut, das Häutchen (*skin*); der Belag (*coating*). — *v.a.* aufnehmen, verfilmen, filmen (*photograph*).
filter ['filtə], *v.a.* filtrieren, filtern. — *v.n.* durchfiltern. — *s.* das Filter.
filth [filθ], *s.* der Schmutz.
filthy ['filθi], *adj.* schmutzig.
filtration [fil'treiʃən], *s.* das Filtrieren, das Durchsickern.
fin [fin], *s.* (*Zool.*) die Finne, die Flosse.
final [fainl], *adj.* letzt, endlich; endgültig. — *s.* (*Sport*) die Endrunde, das Endspiel.
finale [fi'nɑ:li], *s.* (*Mus.*) das Finale.
finality [fai'næliti], *s.* die Endgültigkeit.
finance [fi'næns *or* 'fai-], *s.* die Finanz, das Finanzwesen. — *v.a.* finanzieren.

financial [fi'nænʃəl], *adj.* finanziell, Geld-, Finanz-.
finch [fintʃ], *s.* (*Orn.*) der Fink.
find [faind], *v.a. irr.* finden; — *fault with*, jemanden kritisieren; *all found*, volle Verpflegung (inbegriffen). — *s.* der Fund.
finding ['faindiŋ], *s.* das Finden, der Befund; (*Law*) der Wahrspruch.
fine (1) [fain], *adj.* fein (*delicate*); dünn (*thin*); schön (*beautiful*); scharf (*distinct*); großartig(*splendid*).
fine (2) [fain], *v.a.* zu einer Geldstrafe verurteilen. — *s.* die Geldstrafe.
finery ['fainəri], *s.* der Putz; (*Engin.*) der Frischofen.
finger ['fiŋgə], *s.* der Finger; *have a — in the pie*, die Hand im Spiel haben. — *v.a.* berühren, antasten.
finish ['finiʃ], *v.a.* beenden, fertig machen, vollenden; *—ing touch*, die lezte Hand. — *v.n.* aufhören, enden. — *s.* das Ende (*end*); der letzte Schliff; die Appretur, die Fertigung.
finite ['fainait], *adj.* endlich.
Finn [fin], *s.* der Finne.
Finnish ['finiʃ], *adj.* finnisch.
fir [fə:], *s.* (*Bot.*) die Föhre, die Tanne; — *cone*, der Tannenzapfen.
fire [faiə], *s.* das Feuer; — *brigade*, die Feuerwehr; — *damp*, (*Min.*) schlagende Wetter, *n.pl.*; — *engine*, die Feuerspritze; — *extinguisher*, der Löschapparat, Feuerlöscher; — *escape*, die Rettungsleiter. — *v.a.* brennen (*clay*); anzünden, in Gang setzen (*furnace*); anspornen (*enthuse*); (*coll.*) entlassen (*dismiss*). — *v.n.* feuern (*at*, auf, *Acc.*).
firebrand ['faiəbrænd], *s.* der Aufwiegler.
fireman ['faiəmən], *s.* der Heizer.
fireplace ['faiəpleis], *s.* der Kamin.
fireproof ['faiəpru:f], *adj.* feuerfest.
fireside ['faiəsaid], *s.* der (häusliche) Herd, der Kamin.
firewood ['faiəwud], *s.* das Brennholz.
firework ['faiəwə:k], *s.* (*usually pl.*) das Feuerwerk.
firm [fə:m], *adj.* fest, hart (*solid*); entschlossen (*decided*). — *s.* die Firma.
firmament ['fə:məmənt], *s.* das Firmament, Himmelsgewölbe; der Sternenhimmel.
firmness ['fə:mnis], *s.* die Festigkeit, Entschlossenheit.
first [fə:st], *num. adj.*, *adv.* erst; zuerst; — *of all*, zuallererst; — *born*, erstgeboren; — *rate*, erstklassig. — *s. from the —*, von Anfang an.
fiscal ['fiskəl], *adj.* fiskalisch, von der Staatskasse, Finanz–.
fish [fiʃ], *s.* der Fisch; *like a — out of water*, nicht in seinem Element; *a queer —*, ein seltsamer Kauz; *—bone*, die Gräte. — *v.n.* fischen; — *for compliments*, nach Lob haschen, nach Komplimenten fischen.
fisherman ['fiʃəmən], *s.* der Fischer.
fishery ['fiʃəri], *s.* der Fischfang.
fishing ['fiʃiŋ], *s.* das Fischen, der Fischfang; — *fly*, die Angelfliege; — *line*, die Angelschnur; — *rod*, die Angelrute; — *tackle*, das Angelgerät.
fishy ['fiʃi], *adj.* (*coll.*) anrüchig, verdächtig.
fissile ['fisail], *adj.* (*Phys.*) spaltbar.
fission ['fiʃ(ə)n], *s.* (*Phys.*) die Spaltung.
fist [fist], *s.* die Faust; *hand over —*, im Überfluß; *tight —ed*, geizig.
fisticuffs ['fistikʌfs], *s.* die Schlägerei, das Raufen.
fistula ['fistjulə], *s.* (*Anat.*) die Fistel.
fit (1) [fit], *v.a.* passen, anpassen (*Dat.*); einfügen (— *into s.th.*); — *in*, hineinpassen; — *on a suit*, einen Anzug anprobieren (*Dat.*); — *for a career*, zu einer Laufbahn vorbereiten; — *out*, ausrüsten. — *v.n.* passen, sich fügen (— *into*); — *in*, passen (*in*, zu, *Dat.*). — *adj.* geeignet, fähig (*suitable*); — *to drop*, todmüde; gesund, stark (*healthy*); schicklich (*proper*); (*Sport*) in guter Form.
fit (2) [fit], *s.* der Anfall; *by —s and starts*, ruckweise.
fitful ['fitful], *adj.* launenhaft; unbeständig.
fitness ['fitnis], *s.* die Tauglichkeit (*health*); die Schicklichkeit (*propriety*); die Fähigkeit (*ability*); (*Sport*) die gute Form.
fitter ['fitə], *s.* der Monteur.
fitting, fitment ['fitiŋ, 'fitmənt], *s.* die Armatur; die Montage. — *adj.* passend (*suitable*); geeignet (*appropriate*).
five [faiv], *num. adj.* fünf.
fiver ['faivə], *s.* (*coll.*) die Fünfpfundnote.
fix [fiks], *v.a.* festmachen, befestigen (*make firm*); festsetzen (*a time*); (*Am.*) herrichten, anrichten (*a meal*); — *with a glare* or *stare*, mit den Augen fixieren, scharf ansehen; — *up* (*coll.*), etwas erledigen (*something*); bedienen (*serve s.o.*). — *s.* (*coll.*) die Klemme, die Schwierigkeit, das Dilemma.
fixture ['fikstʃə], *s.* (*Sport*) die Veranstaltung; das Inventarstück (*furniture*).
fizz [fiz], *v.n.* brausen (*drink*).
fizzle [fizl], *v.n.* zischen (*flame*); — *out*, verebben, ausgehen, zunichte werden; (*Am.*, *coll.*) durchfallen (*fail in school*).
fizzy ['fizi], *adj.* mit Kohlensäure, sprudelnd.
flabbergast ['flæbəgɑ:st], *v.a.* (*coll.*) verblüffen.
flabby ['flæbi], *adj.* schlaff.
flaccid ['flæksid], *adj.* schlapp, schlaff.
flag (1) [flæg], *s.* (*Mil.*) die Flagge; die Fahne; — *officer*, der Flaggoffizier; —*staff*, die Fahnenstange.
flag (2) [flæg], *v.n.* ermatten, erschlaffen.
flag (3) [flæg], *s.* (—*stone*) der Fliesstein, die Fliese. — *v.a.* mit Fliesen auslegen, mit Fliessteinen pflastern.

flagon ['flægən], *s.* die Doppelflasche.
flagrant ['fleigrənt], *adj.* entsetzlich (*shocking*); schamlos (*impudent*).
flail [fleil], *s.* der Dreschflegel.
flair [flɛə], *s.* der Instinkt; (*coll.*) die Nase (*for*, für, *Acc.*).
flake [fleik], *s.* die Flocke. — *v.n.* — *off*, abblättern.
flame [fleim], *s.* die Flamme; (*coll.*) *old* —, die (alte) Liebe, Geliebte(r), die Flamme. — *v.n.* flammen, lodern.
flamingo [flə'miŋgou], *s.* (*Orn.*) der Flamingo.
flange [flændʒ], *s.* (*Engin.*) der Flan(t)sch.
flank [flæŋk], *s.* die Flanke, die Seite; die Weiche (*of animal*). — *v.a.* flankieren.
flannel [flænl], *s.* der Flanell.
flap [flæp], *s.* die Klappe; das Ohrläppchen (*earlobe*); der Flügelschlag (— *of wings*).
flare [flɛə], *v.n.* flammen, flackern; — *up*, aufbrausen (*in temper*). — *s.* das Aufflammen, das Aufflackern; die Leuchtkugel.
flash [flæʃ], *s.* der Blitz (*of lightning*); das Aufflammen; (*Phot.*) —*light*, das Blitzlicht. — *v.a.* aufflammen lassen, aufblitzen lassen. — *v.n.* aufflammen, aufblitzen.
flashy ['flæʃi], *adj.* großtuend, angeberisch (*bragging*); buntfarbig (*gaudy*).
flask [flɑ:sk], *s.* die kleine Flasche, das Fläschchen.
flat [flæt], *adj.* flach, eben; abgestanden, schal (*drink*); — *footed*, plattfüßig; (*Mus.*) zu tief, vermindert; platt; albern (*conversation*); — *tyre*, die Panne. — *adv.* — *out*, ausgepumpt, erschöpft. — *s.* die Mietwohnung, Wohnung (*lodgings*); (*Mus.*) das B; (*pl.*) das Flachland; (*Theat.*) (*pl.*) die Bühnenbilder.
flatness ['flætnis], *s.* die Flachheit, die Plattheit (*of conversation etc.*).
flatten [flætn], *v.a.* flach machen; glätten (*smooth*).
flatter ['flætə], *v.a.* schmeicheln (*Dat.*).
flattery ['flætəri], *s.* die Schmeichelei.
flaunt [flɔ:nt], *v.a.* prahlen, prunken (*s.th.*, mit, *Dat.*).
flavour ['fleivə], *s.* der Geschmack, die Würze; das Aroma; die Blume (*bouquet of wine*). — *v.a.* würzen.
flaw [flɔ:], *s.* der Riß (*chink*); der Fehler (*fault*).
flawless ['flɔ:lis], *adj.* fehlerlos.
flax [flæks], *s.* (*Bot.*) der Flachs.
flay [flei], *v.a.* schinden, die Haut abziehen (*Dat.*).
flea [fli:], *s.* (*Ent.*) der Floh.
fleck [flek], *v.a.* sprenkeln.
fledge [fledʒ], *v.a.* befiedern; *fully —d*, flügge; selbständig.
fledgling ['fledʒliŋ], *s.* der Grünschnabel, der Novize.
flee [fli:], *v.a.*, *v.n. irr.* fliehen, entfliehen (*from*, von, *Dat.*); flüchten (vor, *Dat.*).
fleece [fli:s], *s.* das Vlies. — *v.a.* scheren (*sheep*); ausnützen (*exploit*); berauben.
fleet [fli:t], *s.* die Flotte. — *adj.* (*Poet.*) schnellfüßig.
Fleming ['flemiŋ], *s.* der Flame.
Flemish ['flemiʃ], *adj.* flämisch.
flesh [fleʃ], *s.* das (lebende) Fleisch; die Frucht (*of fruit*).
flex [fleks], *s.* (*Elec.*) die Kontaktschnur.
flexible ['fleksibl], *adj.* biegsam; (*fig.*) anpassungsfähig.
flexion ['flekʃən], *s.* (*Gram.*) die Flexion, die Biegung.
flick [flik], *s.* der leichte Schlag. — *v.a.* leicht schlagen, berühren.
flicker ['flikə], *s.* das Flackern, das Flimmern. — *v.n.* flackern, flimmern.
flight [flait], *s.* (*Aviat.*) der Flug; die Flucht (*escape*); — *of stairs*, die Treppe, Treppenflucht.
flimsy ['flimzi], *adj.* hauchdünn (*material*); schwach (*argument*).
flinch [flintʃ], *v.n.* zurückweichen, zurückzucken (*from*, vor, *Dat.*).
fling [fliŋ], *v.a. irr.* schleudern, werfen. — *s.* der Wurf; *highland* —, schottischer Tanz; *have a last* —, sich zum letzten Mal austoben.
flint [flint], *s.* der Feuerstein.
flippancy ['flipənsi], *s.* die Leichtfertigkeit.
flippant ['flipənt], *adj.* leichtfertig, leichtsinnig, schnippisch.
flirt [flə:t], *v.n.* flirten, liebeln, (*with*, *Dat.*).
flirtation [flə:'teiʃən], *s.* die Liebelei.
flit [flit], *v.n.* hin und her flitzen; huschen.
flitch [flitʃ], *s.* die Speckseite.
flitter ['flitə], *v.n.* flattern.
float [flout], *v.n.* obenauf schwimmen, dahingleiten; —*ing ice*, das Treibeis. — *v.a.* schwimmen lassen; (*Naut.*) flott machen; (*Comm.*) gründen (*a company*); ausgeben (*a loan*). — *s.* das Floß (*raft*); der ausgeschmückte Wagen (*decorated vehicle*).
flock [flɔk], *s.* die Herde (*sheep*). — *v.n.* zusammenlaufen, sich scharen.
floe [flou], *s.* die Eisscholle.
flog [flɔg], *v.a.* peitschen (*whip*); antreiben; — *a dead horse*, sich umsonst bemühen; (*coll.*) verkaufen.
flood [flʌd], *s.* die Flut; das Hochwasser, die Überschwemmung (*flooding*); (*fig.*) die Fülle; — *gate*, die Schleuse. — *v.a.* überfluten, überschütten (*with requests*). — *v.n.* überschwemmen (*of river*).
floodlight ['flʌdlait], *s.* das Flutlicht, Scheinwerferlicht.
floor [flɔ:], *s.* der Boden, der Fußboden; das Stockwerk, der Stock (*storey*); *from the* —, aus dem Plenum; — *walker*, die Aufsicht (*in stores*). — *v.a.* zu Boden strecken, überrumpeln (*surprise*).
flop [flɔp], *v.n.* (*coll.*) hinsinken, hinplumpsen; versagen (*fail*). — *s.* das Hinfallen; der Versager (*play, film etc.*).

Florentine ['flɔrəntain], *adj.* florentinisch. — *s.* der Florentiner.
florid ['flɔrid], *adj.* blühend; überladen.
florin ['flɔrin], *s.* das Zweischillingstück.
florist ['flɔrist], *s.* der Blumenhändler.
flotsam ['flɔtsəm], *s.* das Strandgut, Wrackgut.
flounce (1) [flauns], *v.n.* hastig bewegen.
flounce (2) [flauns], *v.a.* mit Falbeln besetzen (*dress*). — *s.* die Falbel (*on dress*).
flounder (1) ['flaundə], *v.n.* umhertappen, unsicher sein.
flounder (2) ['flaundə], *s.* (*Zool.*) die Flunder.
flour ['flauə], *s.* das Mehl.
flourish ['flʌriʃ], *v.n.* blühen; wirken; gedeihen (*thrive*); schnörkeln, verzieren (*in writing*); Fanfaren blasen, schmettern (*trumpets*). — *s.* der Schnörkel; der Trompetenstoß, Tusch (*of trumpets*).
flout [flaut], *v.a.* verhöhnen, verspotten. — *s.* der Hohn, der Spott.
flow [flou], *v.n. irr.* fließen, strömen. — *s.* der Fluß (*of water, goods etc.*); — *of words*, der Redeschwall.
flower ['flauə], *s.* die Blume; die Blüte (*blossom*). — *v.n.* blühen, in Blüte stehen.
flowery ['flauəri], *adj.* gewählt, umständlich, geziert (*style*).
fluctuate ['flʌktjueit], *v.n.* schwanken.
fluctuation [flʌktju'eiʃən], *s.* das Schwanken.
flue [flu:], *s.* der Rauchfang (*of chimney*).
fluency ['flu:ənsi], *s.* das fließende Sprechen, die Geläufigkeit.
fluent ['flu:ənt], *adj.* geläufig, fließend.
fluid ['flu:id], *adj.* fließend, flüssig (*liquid*). — *s.* die Flüssigkeit.
fluke [flu:k], *s.* der glückliche Zufall (*chance*).
flunkey ['flʌŋki], *s.* der Diener, der Bediente.
flurry ['flʌri], *s.* die Unruhe; die Aufregung (*excitement*).
flush (1) [flʌʃ], *s.* das Erröten (*blushing*); die Aufwallung (*of anger*). — *v.a.* nachspülen (*basin*); erröten machen (*make blush*). — *v.n.* erröten.
flush (2) [flʌʃ], *adj.* in gleicher Ebene, eben.
flush (3) [flʌʃ], *v.a.* (*Hunt.*) aufscheuchen.
fluster ['flʌstə], *v.a.* verwirren (*muddle*); aufregen (*excite*).
flute [flu:t], *s.* (*Mus.*) die Flöte; (*Carp.*) die Hohlkehle.— *v.a.* (*Carp., Archit.*) aushöhlen. — *v.n.* (*Mus.*) flöten, Flöte spielen.
flutter ['flʌtə], *v.n.* flattern, unruhig sein. — *s.* die Unruhe.
flux [flʌks], *s.* das Fließen; *be in* —, in der Schwebe sein.
fly [flai], *v.a. irr.* wehen lassen, hissen (*flag*). — *v.n. irr.* (*Aviat.*) fliegen; fliehen (*escape*); eilen (*hurry*). — *s.* (*Ent.*) die Fliege.
flyleaf ['flaili:f], *s.* das Vorsatzblatt.
flying ['flaiiŋ], *adj.* fliegend, Flug-; — *squad*, das Überfallkommando.
flyover ['flaiouvə], *s.* die Brückenkreuzung, Überführung.
flywheel ['flaiwi:l], *s.* das Schwungrad.
foal [foul], *s.* (*Zool.*) das Füllen. — *v.n.* fohlen.
foam [foum], *s.* der Schaum; — *rubber*, das Schaumgummi. — *v.n.* schäumen.
fob [fɔb], *v.a.* — *off*, abfertigen, abspeisen.
focus ['foukəs], *s.* der Brennpunkt; der Mittelpunkt (*of interest*). — *v.a.* (*Phot.*) einstellen. — *v.n.* — *upon*, sich konzentrieren auf (*Acc.*).
fodder ['fɔdə], *s.* das Futter.
foe [fou], *s.* der Feind.
fog [fɔg], *s.* der Nebel.
fogey ['fougi], *s.* der Kerl, Kauz.
foible [fɔibl], *s.* die Schwäche, die schwache Seite.
foil (1) [fɔil], *v.a.* vereiteln. — *s.* das Florett (*fencing rapier*).
foil (2) [fɔil], *s.* die Folie; der Hintergrund (*background*).
foist [fɔist], *v.a.* aufschwatzen (*upon, Dat.*).
fold (1) [fould], *v.a.* falten (*clothes etc.*); umarmen (*in o.'s arms*). — *v.n.* schließen, sich falten. — *s.* die Falte; (*Geol.*) die Vertiefung.
fold (2) [fould], *s.* die Herde (*sheep*); *return to the* —, zu den Seinen zurückkehren.
folder ['fouldə], *s.* die Mappe (*papers*); das Falzbein.
folding ['fouldiŋ], *adj.* Klapp-; — *chair*, der Klappstuhl; — *door*, die Flügeltür.
foliage ['fouljidʒ], *s.* (*Bot.*) das Laub.
folio ['fouliou], *s.* das Folio, der Foliant.
folk [fouk], *s.* (*also pl.*) die Leute; (*pl.*) (*Am.*)Freunde (*mode of address*).
folklore ['fouklɔ:], *s.* die Volkskunde.
folksong ['fouksɔŋ], *s.* das Volkslied.
follow ['fɔlou], *v.a., v.n.* folgen (*Dat.*); — *suit*, dasselbe tun, Farbe bekennen.
follower ['fɔlouə], *s.* der Anhänger (*supporter*); der Nachfolger (*successor*); *camp* —, der Mitläufer.
folly ['fɔli], *s.* die Narrheit; die törichte Handlung (*action*).
foment [fo'ment], *v.a.* anregen (*stimulate*); pflegen (*cultivate*); warm baden.
fond [fɔnd], *adj.* zärtlich, lieb; *be — of*, gern haben.
fondle [fɔndl], *v.a.* liebkosen.
fondness ['fɔndnis], *s.* die Zärtlichkeit, die (Vor-)liebe.
font [fɔnt], *s.* der Taufstein (*baptismal*).
food [fu:d], *s.* die Nahrung, Speise (*nourishment*); Lebensmittel (*n.pl.*); das Futter (*for animals*); *some* —, etwas zum Essen; — *store*, das Lebensmittelgeschäft.
fool [fu:l], *s.* der Narr, Tor. — *v.a.* zum Narren halten, übertölpeln.

foolish ['fu:liʃ], *adj.* töricht, albern, närrisch (*person*); unsinnig (*act*).
foolscap ['fu:lskæp], *s.* das Kanzleipapier.
foot [fut], *s.* der Fuß; *on* —, zu Fuß; — *board*, das Trittbrett; *put o.'s — in it*, eine taktlose Bemerkung fallen lassen, ins Fettnäpfchen treten. — *v.a.* — *the bill*, bezahlen.
footage ['futidʒ], *s.* die Länge in Fuß.
football ['futbɔ:l], *s.* der Fußball.
footbridge ['futbridʒ], *s.* der Steg.
footing ['futiŋ], *s.* die Grundlage, Basis.
footlight ['futlait], *s.* (*usually pl.*) die Rampenlichter, *n. pl.*
footman ['futmən], *s.* der Bediente.
footprint ['futprint], *s.* die Fußstapfe.
footstool ['futstu:l], *s.* der Schemel.
fop [fɔp], *s.* der Geck.
for [fɔ:], *prep.* für (*Acc.*); anstatt (*Genit.*) (*instead of*); *in exchange* —, für, um; — *example*, zum Beispiel; — *heaven's sake*, um Himmels willen; — *two days*, zwei Tage lang; auf zwei Tage; seit zwei Tagen; *now you are — it!* jetzt has du's! *as — me*, meinetwegen, was mich anbelangt; — *all that*, trotz alledem. — *conj.* denn, weil.
forage ['fɔridʒ], *s.* das Futter. — *v.n.* furagieren.
forasmuch [fɔrəz'mʌtʃ], *conj.* (*obs.*) — *as*, insofern als.
foray ['fɔrei], *s.* der Raubzug.
forbear [fɔ:'bɛə], *v.a. irr.* vermeiden, unterlassen (*avoid*); sich enthalten (*abstain*). — *v.n.* (geduldig) hinnehmen, ertragen.
forbid [fə'bid], *v.a. irr.* verbieten; *God —!* Gott behüte!
forbidding [fə'bidiŋ], *adj.* abschreckend.
force [fɔ:s], *s.* (*Phys.*) die Kraft; die Macht (*might*); die Gewalt (*brute* —); (*pl.*) die Streitkräfte, *f. pl.*; (*Phys.*) die Kräfte. — *v.a.* zwingen, nötigen.
forceful ['fɔ:sful], *adj.* kräftig, energisch, kraftvoll.
forceps ['fɔ:seps], *s.* (*Med.*) die Zange; die Pinzette.
forcible ['fɔ:sibl], *adj.* heftig, stark (*strong*); gewaltsam (*violent*).
ford [fɔ:d], *s.* die Furt.
fore- [fɔ:], *pref.* Vorder-, vorder.
forebear ['fɔ:bɛə], *s.* der Vorfahre.
forebode [fɔ:'boud], *v.a.* voraussagen, vorbedeuten.
forecast [fɔ:'kɑ:st], *v.a.* vorhersagen, voraussagen. — ['fɔ:kɑ:st], *s.* die Vorhersage.
foreclose [fɔ:'klouz], *v.a.* ausschließen.
forefather ['fɔ:fɑ:ðə], *s.* der Ahne, der Vorvater.
forefinger ['fɔ:fiŋgə], *s.* (*Anat.*) der Zeigefinger.
forego [fɔ:'gou], *v.a. irr.* vorhergehen.
foreground ['fɔ:graund], *s.* der Vordergrund.
forehead ['fɔrid], *s.* die Stirne.
foreign ['fɔrin], *adj.* fremd; ausländisch.
foreigner ['fɔrinə], *s.* der Fremde, der Ausländer.
foreland ['fɔ:lənd], *s.* das Vorgebirge.
foreman ['fɔ:mən], *s.* der Werkführer, Vorarbeiter.
foremast ['fɔ:mɑ:st], *s.* (*Naut.*) der Fockmast.
foremost ['fɔ:moust], *adj.* vorderst, vornehmlichst, führend. — *adv.* zuerst; *first and* —, zuallererst.
forenoon ['fɔ:nu:n], *s.* der Vormittag.
forensic [fɔ'rensik], *adj.* forensisch, gerichtsmedizinisch.
forerunner ['fɔ:rʌnə], *s.* der Vorläufer.
foresail ['fɔ:seil, 'fɔ:səl], *s.* (*Naut.*) das Focksegel.
foresee [fɔ:'si:], *v.a. irr.* vorhersehen.
foreshadow [fɔ:'ʃædou], *v.a.* vorher andeuten.
foreshorten [fɔ:'ʃɔ:tn], *v.a.* verkürzen.
foresight ['fɔ:sait], *s.* die Vorsorge, der Vorbedacht.
forest ['fɔrist], *s.* der Wald; der Urwald (*jungle*).
forestall [fɔ:'stɔ:l], *v.a.* vorwegnehmen, zuvorkommen (*Dat.*).
forester ['fɔristə], *s.* der Förster.
forestry ['fɔristri], *s.* die Forstwissenschaft (*science*); das Forstwesen (*management*).
foretaste ['fɔ:teist], *s.* der Vorgeschmack.
foretell [fɔ:'tel], *v.a. irr.* voraussagen.
forethought ['fɔ:θɔ:t], *s.* der Vorbedacht.
forewarn [fɔ:'wɔ:n], *v.a.* warnen.
forfeit ['fɔ:fit], *s.* das Pfand (*pledge*); die Einbuße (*fine*); (*pl.*) das Pfänderspiel. — *v.a.* verlieren, verwirken.
forfeiture ['fɔ:fitʃə], *s.* die Verwirkung, die Einbuße, der Verlust.
forge [fɔ:dʒ], *v.a.* schmieden (*iron*); fälschen (*falsify*). — *v.n.* — *ahead*, sich vorwärtsarbeiten. — *s.* die Schmiede (*iron*); der Eisenhammer (*hammer*).
forget [fə'get], *v.a.*, *v.n. irr.* vergessen; — *-me-not*, das Vergißmeinnicht.
forgetful [fə'getful], *adj.* vergeßlich.
forgive [fə'giv], *v.a.*, *v.n. irr.* vergeben, verzeihen.
forgo [fɔ:'gou], *v.a. irr.* verzichten; aufgeben.
fork [fɔ:k], *s.* die Gabel; die Abzweigung (*road*). — *v.n.* sich gabeln, sich spalten.
forlorn [fɔ:'lɔ:n], *adj.* verlassen, verloren, elend.
form [fɔ:m], *s.* die Form, die Gestalt (*shape*); die Formalität (*formality*); das Formular (*document*); *in good* —, (*Sport*) in guter Form; *bad* —, gegen den guten Ton; *a matter of* —, eine Formsache. — *v.a.* formen, gestalten (*shape*); bilden (*an association etc. of*, über, *Acc.*).
formal ['fɔ:məl], *adj.* formal, äußerlich; formell.
formality [fɔ:'mæliti], *s.* die Formalität.

formation [fɔ:'meiʃən], *s.* (*Mil.*) die Formation; (*Geol.*) die Bildung; die Formung; die Aufstellung (*sports team*).
former ['fɔ:mə], *adj.* früher, vorig.
formidable ['fɔ:midəbl], *adj.* schrecklich, furchtbar.
formula ['fɔ:mjulə], *s.* die Formel.
formulate ['fɔ:mjuleit], *v.a.* formulieren.
forsake [fɔ:'seik], *v.a. irr.* verlassen, im Stich lassen.
forsooth [fɔ:'su:θ], *adv.* (*Poet.*) wahrlich, wirklich!
forswear [fɔ:'swεə], *v.a. irr.* abschwören; — *oneself*, einen Meineid schwören.
fort, fortress [fɔ:t, 'fɔ:tris], *s.* das Fort, die Festung.
forth [fɔ:θ], *adv.* vorwärts; weiter (*further*); *and so* —, und so weiter (u.s.w.); fort (*away*).
forthcoming ['fɔ:θkʌmiŋ], *adj.* bevorstehend.
forthwith [fɔ:θ'wiθ], *adv.* sogleich.
fortieth ['fɔ:tiəθ], *num. adj.* vierzigst. — *s.* der Vierzigste.
fortification [fɔ:tifi'keiʃən], *s.* die Befestigung.
fortify ['fɔ:tifai], *v.a.* befestigen; bestärken.
fortitude ['fɔ:titju:d], *s.* die Tapferkeit.
fortnight ['fɔ:tnait], *s.* vierzehn Tage, *m. pl.*
fortuitous [fɔ:'tju:itəs], *adj.* zufällig.
fortunate ['fɔ:tʃənit], *adj.* glücklich, günstig.
fortune ['fɔ:tju:n], *s.* das Glück, das Schicksal; das Vermögen (*wealth*); — *teller*, die Wahrsagerin.
forty ['fɔ:ti], *num. adj.* vierzig.
forward ['fɔ:wəd], *adj.* vorder (*in front*); voreilig, vorlaut (*rash*); früh (*early*). — *adv.* vorne; — *march!* vorwärts! *carry* —, (*Comm.*) übertragen. — *s.* (*Footb.*) der Stürmer, — *line*, der Angriff. — *v.a.* weiterleiten, expedieren; (*letter*) *please* —, bitte nachsenden.
forwardness ['fɔ:wədnis], *s.* die Frühreife; die Voreiligkeit, Dreistigkeit.
fossil ['fɔsil], *s.* das Fossil.
foster ['fɔstə], *v.a.* nähren (*feed*); aufziehen (*bring up*); — *a thought*, einen Gedanken hegen; — *mother*, die Pflegemutter; — *brother*, der Pflegebruder.
foul [faul], *adj.* schmutzig; faul (*rotten*). — *v.a.* beschmutzen. — *v.n.* (*Footb.*) einen Verstoß begehen. — *s.* (*Footb.*) der Verstoß.
found (1) [faund], *v.a.* gründen, begründen.
found (2) [faund], *v.a.* (*Metall.*) gießen (*cast*).
foundation [faun'deiʃən], *s.* das Fundament; die Unterlage; die Begründung, die Gründung (*initiation*); die Stiftung (*establishment*); — *stone*, der Grundstein.
founder (1) ['faundə], *s.* der Gründer, Stifter.
founder (2) ['faundə], *v.n.* scheitern, Schiffbruch erleiden (*on*, an, *Dat.*).
foundling ['faundliŋ], *s.* das Findelkind, der Findling.
foundry ['faundri], *s.* (*Metall.*) die Gießerei.
fount (1) [faunt], *s.* (*Typ.*) der Schriftguss.
fount (2) [faunt] (*Poet.*) *see* **fountain**.
fountain ['fauntin], *s.* die Quelle, der Brunnen; der Springbrunnen; — *pen*, die Füllfeder; — *head*, der Urquell.
four [fɔ:], *num. adj.* vier; — *-in-hand*, das Viergespann.
fowl [faul], *s.* (*Orn.*) das Huhn, das Geflügel.
fowler ['faulə], *s.* der Vogelsteller, Vogelfänger.
fox [fɔks], *s.* (*Zool.*) der Fuchs; (*fig.*) der listige Kauz, Schlauberger (*cunning fellow*). — *v.a.* (*coll.*) überlisten, täuschen.
fraction ['frækʃən], *s.* (*Maths.*) der Bruch; (*Mech.*) der Bruchteil.
fractional ['frækʃənəl], *adj.* (*Maths.*) Bruch–, gebrochen.
fractionate ['frækʃəneit], *v.a.* (*Chem.*) fraktionieren (*oil*).
fractious ['frækʃəs], *adj.* zänkisch, streitsüchtig.
fracture ['fræktʃə], *s.* (*Med.*) der Bruch. — *v.a.* brechen; — *o.'s leg*, sich das Bein brechen.
fragile ['frædʒail], *adj.* zerbrechlich; gebrechlich (*feeble*).
fragment ['frægmənt], *s.* das Bruchstück, das Fragment.
fragrance ['freigrəns], *s.* der Wohlgeruch, Duft.
fragrant ['freigrənt], *adj.* wohlriechend, duftend.
frail [freil], *adj.* gebrechlich, schwach (*feeble*).
frailty ['freilti], *s.* die Schwäche.
frame [freim], *s.* der Rahmen (*of picture*); das Gerüst (*scaffold*); die Form (*shape*). — *v.a.* einrahmen (*a picture*); (*Am.*) in die Enge treiben, reinlegen (*get s.o. wrongly blamed*); (*Comm.*) entwerfen (*a letter*).
framework ['freimwə:k], *s.* der Rahmen (*outline*); das Fachwerk (*construction*).
franchise ['fræntʃaiz], *s.* das Wahlrecht.
Franciscan [fræn'siskən], *s.* der Franziskaner (*friar*).
frank [fræŋk], *adj.* offen, aufrichtig. — *v.a.* frankieren (*letter*). — *s.* der Frankovermerk.
frankincense ['fræŋkinsens], *s.* der Weihrauch.
frantic ['fræntik], *adj.* wahnsinnig, außer sich.
fraternal [frə'tə:nəl], *adj.* brüderlich.
fraternity [frə'tə:niti], *s.* die Bruderschaft; (*Am.*) der Studentenbund, -klub.

fraternize ['frætənaiz], *v.n.* sich verbrüdern, fraternisieren.
fraud [frɔ:d], *s.* der Betrug.
fraudulent ['frɔ:djulənt], *adj.* betrügerisch.
fraught [frɔ:t], *adj.* voll (*with*, von, *Dat.*).
fray (1) [frei], *v.a.* abnutzen; — *the nerves*, auf die Nerven gehen (*Dat.*).
fray (2) [frei], *s.* der Kampf, die Schlägerei.
freak [fri:k], *s.* das Monstrum, die Mißgeburt.
freakish ['fri:kiʃ], *adj.* seltsam; grotesk.
freckle [frekl], *s.* die Sommersprosse.
freckled [frekld], *adj.* sommersprossig.
free [fri:], *adj.* frei; offen (*frank*); — *trade area*, die Freihandelszone; *of my own — will*, aus freien Stücken. — *v.a.* befreien.
freebooter ['fri:bu:tə], *s.* der Freibeuter.
freedom ['fri:dəm], *s.* die Freiheit; — *of a city*, das Ehrenbürgerrecht.
freehold ['fri:hould], *s.* der freie Grundbesitz, der Freigrundbesitz.
freeholder ['fri:houldə], *s.* der (freie) Grundbesitzer.
freeman ['fri:mən], *s.* der Freibürger, Ehrenbürger.
freemason ['fri:meisn], *s.* der Freimaurer.
freewheel ['fri:'wi:l], *s.* der Freilauf, das Freilaufrad. — *v.n.* mit Freilauf fahren.
freeze [fri:z], *v.a. irr.* gefrieren lassen. — *v.n.* frieren, gefrieren; — *up*, zufrieren.
freight [freit], *s.* die Fracht. — *v.a.* verfrachten.
freighter ['freitə], *s.* (*Naut.*) der Frachtdampfer.
French [frentʃ], *adj.* französisch; — *bean*, die Schnittbohne; — *horn*, (*Mus.*) das Horn.
Frenchman ['frentʃmən], *s.* der Franzose.
Frenchwoman ['frentʃwumən], *s.* die Französin.
frenzied ['frenzid], *adj.* wahnsinnig, außer sich.
frequency ['fri:kwənsi], *s.* (*Phys.*) die Frequenz; die Häufigkeit (*of occurrence*).
frequent ['fri:kwənt], *adj.* häufig. — [fri'kwent], *v.a.* (häufig) besuchen.
fresh [freʃ], *adj.* frisch, neu; ungesalzen (*water*); (*sl.*) frech; — *water*, das Süßwasser.
fresher, freshman ['freʃə, 'freʃmən], *s.* der Neuankömmling; (*Univ.*) der Fuchs, Anfänger.
fret (1) [fret], *s.* (*Carp.*) das Gitterwerk, Laubsägewerk. — *v.a.* (*Carp.*) durchbrochen verzieren.
fret (2) [fret], *s.* der Verdruß, Ärger. — *v.n.* sich Sorgen machen.
fretful ['fretful], *adj.* verdrießlich, ärgerlich, mißmutig.
fretsaw ['fretsɔ:], *s.* (*Carp.*) die Laubsäge.
friar ['fraiə], *s.* (*Eccl.*) der Mönch, Bettelmönch.
friction ['frikʃən], *s.* die Reibung; (*fig.*) die Unstimmigkeit.
Friday ['fraid(e)i]. der Freitag; *Good* —, der Karfreitag.
friend [frend], *s.* der (die) Freund(in).
friendly ['frendli], *adj.* freundlich.
friendship ['frendʃip], *s.* die Freundschaft.
frigate ['frigit], *s.* (*Naut.*) die Fregatte.
fright [frait], *s.* die Furcht, der Schreck, das Entsetzen.
frighten [fraitn], *v.a.* erschrecken (*s.o.*).
frightful ['fraitful], *adj.* schrecklich.
frigid ['fridʒid], *adj.* kalt, frostig; kühl.
frill [fril], *s.* die Krause; die Ausschmückung (*style*).
frilly ['frili], *adj.* gekräuselt, geziert.
fringe [frindʒ], *s.* die Franse (*fringed edge*); der Rand (*edge, brink*). — *v.a.* mit Fransen besetzen, einsäumen. — *v.n.* — *on*, grenzen an (*Acc.*).
Frisian ['fri:ʒən], *adj.* friesisch.
frisk [frisk], *v.a.* (*sl.*) durchsuchen (*search*). — *v.n.* hüpfen (*of animals*). — *s.* der Sprung (*of animals*).
frisky ['friski], *adj.* lebhaft, munter.
fritter ['fritə], *s.* der Pfannkuchen; *apple* —, Äpfel im Schlafrock. — *v.a.* zerstückeln (*cut up*); vertrödeln (*waste*), vergeuden.
frivolity [fri'vɔliti], *s.* der Leichtsinn, die Leichtfertigkeit.
frivolous ['frivələs], *adj.* leichtsinnig, leichtfertig.
fro [frou], *adv. to and* —, auf und ab, hin und her.
frock [frɔk], *s.* der Kittel, das Kleid; (*Eccl.*) die Soutane, Kutte.
frog [frɔg], *s.* (*Zool.*) der Frosch.
frogman ['frɔgmən], *s.* der Tauchschwimmer, Froschmann.
frolic ['frɔlik], *s.* der Scherz; der Spaß. — *v.n.* scherzen, ausgelassen sein.
from [frɔm], *prep.* von; von ... her (*hence*); aus ... heraus (*out of*); von ... an (*starting* —); vor (*in the face of*).
front [frʌnt], *s.* die Stirn; die Vorderseite; (*Mil.*) die Front; *in — of*, vor (*Dat.*); — *door*, die Haustür.
frontage ['frʌntidʒ], *s.* die Front, Vorderfront (*of building*).
frontal ['frʌntl], *adj.* Stirn-, Vorder-; (*Mil.*) — *attack*, der Frontalangriff. — *s.* (*Eccl.*) die Altardecke.
frontier ['frʌntjə], *s.* die Grenze; — *police*, die Grenzpolizei.
frontispiece ['frʌntispi:s], *s.* das Titelbild.
frost [frɔst], *s.* der Frost, der Reif.
frostbite ['frɔstbait], *s.* die Frostbeule.
frosted ['frɔstid], *adj.* bereift.
froth [frɔθ], *s.* der Schaum. — *v.n.* schäumen.

frown [fraun], *v.n.* die Stirn runzeln, finster dreinschauen. — *s.* das Stirnrunzeln.
frugal ['fru:gəl], *adj.* frugal, sparsam, einfach.
fruit [fru:t], *s.* die Frucht (*singular*); das Obst (*plural or collective*). — *v.n.* (*Bot.*) Früchte tragen.
frustrate [frʌs'treit], *v.a.* verhindern; vereiteln (*bring to nought*).
fry (1) [frai], *v.a.* braten; *fried potatoes*, Bratkartoffeln, *f. pl.*
fry (2) [frai], *s.* der Rogen (*of fish*); (*fig.*) die Brut, Menge.
frying pan ['fraiiŋpæn], *s.* die Bratpfanne; *out of the — into the fire*, vom Regen in die Traufe.
fuchsia ['fju:ʃə], *s.* (*Bot.*) die Fuchsie.
fudge [fʌdʒ], *s.* weiches Zuckerwerk; (*coll.*) Unsinn!
fuel ['fjuəl], *s.* der Brennstoff, Treibstoff; das Heizmaterial. — *v.a.*, *v.n.* tanken.
fugitive ['fju:dʒitiv], *adj.* flüchtig, auf der Flucht. — *s.* der Flüchtling.
fugue [fju:g], *s.* (*Mus.*) die Fuge.
fulcrum ['fʌlkrəm], *s.* der Stützpunkt, Hebelpunkt.
fulfil [ful'fil], *v.a.* erfüllen; — *a requirement*, einem Gesetz genüge tun.
full [ful], *adj.* voll; vollständig (*complete*); —*time*, hauptberuflich.
fuller ['fulə], *s.* der Walker.
fullness ['fulnis], *s.* die Fülle.
fulsome ['fulsəm], *adj.* widerlich, ekelhaft; übermäßig.
fumble [fʌmbl], *v.n.* tappen (*for*, nach, *Dat.*).
fume [fju:m], *s.* der Rauch, Dunst; der Zorn (*anger*). — *v.n.* zornig sein, wüten (*be angered*).
fun [fʌn], *s.* der Spaß, Scherz; *have* —, sich gut unterhalten, sich amüsieren; *make — of*, zum besten haben.
function ['fʌŋkʃən], *s.* (*also Maths.*) die Funktion; das Amt (*office*); die Feier(lichkeit) (*formal occasion*). — *v.n.* funktionieren (*be in working order*); fungieren (*officiate*).
fund [fʌnd], *s.* der Fonds (*financial*); (*fig.*) die Fülle (*of*, an); *public —s*, die Staatsgelder.
fundamental [fʌndə'mentl], *adj.* grundsätzlich, wesentlich. — *s.* (*pl.*) die Grundlagen, *f.pl.*
funeral ['fju:nərəl], *s.* die Bestattung, Beerdigung.
funereal [fju:'niəriəl], *adj.* wie bei einem Begräbnis, betrübt, traurig.
fungus ['fʌŋgəs], *s.* (*Bot.*) der Pilz; der Schwamm (*mushroom*).
funk [fʌŋk], *s.* (*sl.*) die Angst, Panik. — *v.a.* fürchten.
funnel [fʌnl], *s.* der Trichter.
funny ['fʌni], *adj.* spaßhaft, komisch.
fur [fə:], *s.* der Pelz, das Fell (*coat of animal*); (*Med.*) der Belag (*on tongue*).
furbelow ['fə:bilou], *s.* die Falbel.
furbish ['fə:biʃ], *v.a.* aufputzen.
furious ['fjuəriəs], *adj.* wild, rasend, wütend.
furl [fə:l], *v.a.* (zusammen-)rollen; (*Naut.*) aufrollen.
furlong ['fə:lɔŋ], *s.* ein Achtel einer englischen Meile.
furlough ['fə:lou], *s.* der Urlaub.
furnace ['fə:nis], *s.* der Ofen, Hochofen (*steel*); (*Metall.*) der Schmelzofen.
furnish ['fə:niʃ], *v.a.* ausstatten, versehen (*equip*); möblieren (*a room etc.*).
furnisher ['fə:niʃə], *s.* der Möbelhändler; der Lieferant.
furniture ['fə:nitʃə], *s.* die Möbel, *n. pl.*; die Einrichtung.
furrier ['fʌriə], *s.* der Kürschner.
furrow ['fʌrou], *s.* die Furche (*field*); die Runzel (*brow*). — *v.a.* runzeln (*brow*); Furchen ziehen (*plough up*).
further ['fə:ðə], *comp. adj.*, *adv. see* **farther**. — *v.a.* fördern (*advance*).
furtherance ['fə:ðərəns], *s.* die Förderung (*advancement*).
furthermore ['fə:ðəmɔ:], *adv.* ferner.
furthest ['fə:ðist], *superl. adj.*, *adv. see* **farthest**.
furtive ['fə:tiv], *adj.* verstohlen, heimlich.
fury ['fjuəri], *s.* die Wut; (*Myth.*) die Furie.
furze [fə:z], *s.* (*Bot.*) der Stechginster.
fuse [fju:z], *v.a.*, *v.n.* schmelzen (*melt*); vereinigen (*unite*). — *s.* (*Elec.*) die Sicherung; *blow a* —, eine Sicherung durchbrennen; — *box*, der Sicherungskasten; — *wire*, der Schmelzdraht.
fuselage ['fju:zila:ʒ *or* -lidʒ], *s.* (*Aviat.*) der (Flugzeug-)rumpf.
fusible ['fju:zibl], *adj.* schmelzbar.
fusilier [fju:zi'liə], *s.* (*Mil.*) der Füsilier.
fusion ['fju:ʒən], *s.* die Verschmelzung; die Vereinigung.
fuss [fʌs], *s.* das Getue, die Umständlichkeit; *make a — about*, viel Aufhebens machen.
fussy ['fʌsi], *adj.* übertrieben genau; umständlich; geschäftig (*busy*); — *about*, genau in (*Dat.*).
fusty ['fʌsti], *adj.* moderig, muffig.
futile ['fju:tail], *adj.* nutzlos, vergeblich.
futility [fju:'tiliti], *s.* die Nutzlosigkeit.
future ['fju:tʃə], *s.* die Zukunft. — *adj.* (zu-)künftig.
fuzzy ['fʌzi], *adj.* kraus.

G

G [dʒi:]. das G (*also Mus.*); — *sharp*, das Gis; — *flat*, das Ges; *key of* —, der G Schlüssel, Violinschlüssel.

gab [gæb], *s.* das Geschwätz; *the gift of the* —, ein gutes Mundwerk.
gabble [gæbl], *v.n.* schwatzen.
gable [geibl], *s.* der Giebel.
gad [gæd], *v.n.* — *about*, umherstreifen.
gadfly ['gædflai], *s.* (*Ent.*) die Bremse.
gag [gæg], *s.* der Knebel; (*sl.*) der Witz. — *v.a.* knebeln.
gaiety ['geiəti], *s.* die Fröhlichkeit.
gain [gein], *v.a.* gewinnen, erwerben (*earn*); — *possession*, Besitz ergreifen. — *s.* der Gewinn, Vorteil.
gainful ['geinful], *adj.* — *employment*, die einträgliche Beschäftigung.
gainsay ['geinsei *or* gein'sei], *v.a.* widersprechen (*pers.*, *Dat.*).
gait [geit], *s.* das Schreiten, der Schritt, Gang.
gaiter ['geitə], *s.* die Gamasche.
galaxy ['gæləksi], *s.* (*Astron.*) die Milchstraße; (*fig.*) die glänzende Versammlung.
gale [geil], *s.* der Sturm.
gall [gɔ:l], *s.* die Galle. — *v.a.* verbittern, ärgern.
gallant ['gælənt], *adj.* tapfer (*of soldier*); gallant, höflich (*polite*).
gallantry ['gæləntri], *s.* die Tapferkeit; die Höflichkeit, Galanterie.
gallery ['gæləri], *s.* die Gallerie.
galley ['gæli], *s.* (*Naut.*) die Galeere; (*Typ.*) — *proof*, der Fahnenabzug.
gallon ['gælən], *s.* die Gallone.
gallop ['gæləp], *v.n.* galoppieren. — *s.* der Galopp.
gallows ['gælouz], *s.* der Galgen.
galosh [gə'lɔʃ], *s.* die Galosche.
galvanic [gæl'vænik], *adj.* galvanisch.
galvanize ['gælvənaiz], *v.a.* galvanisieren.
gamble [gæmbl], *v.n.* um Geld spielen; — *away*, verspielen. — *s.* das Risiko.
gambol [gæmbl], *v.n.* herumspringen.
game [geim], *s.* das Spiel (*play*); das Wild, Wildbret (*pheasants etc.*); *fair* —, Freiwild, *n.*, offene Beute, *f.*
gamecock ['geimkɔk], *s.* (*Orn.*) der Kampfhahn.
gamekeeper ['geimki:pə], *s.* der Wildhüter.
gammon ['gæmən], *s.* der (geräucherte) Schinken (*bacon*).
gamut ['gæmət], *s.* die Tonleiter.
gander ['gændə], *s.* (*Orn.*) der Gänserich.
gang [gæŋ], *s.* die Bande; die Mannschaft (*workmen*). — *v.n.* — *up*, eine Bande bilden; — *up on s.o.*, sich gegen jemanden verbünden.
gangrene ['gæŋgri:n], *s.* (*Med.*) der Brand; die Fäulnis.
gangway ['gæŋwei], *s.* die Planke, der Laufgang (*on boat*); der Durchgang.
gaol, jail [dʒeil], *s.* das Gefängnis. — *v.a.* einsperren.
gaoler, jailer ['dʒeilə], *s.* der Kerkermeister.
gap [gæp], *s.* die Lücke; die Bresche (*breach*).
gape [geip], *v.n.* gähnen, (*fig.*) klaffen.
garage ['gærɑ:ʒ *or* 'gæridʒ], *s.* die Garage, die Tankstelle.
garb [gɑ:b], *s.* die Tracht, Kleidung.
garbage ['gɑ:bidʒ], *s.* der Abfall; (*Am.*) — *can*, der Mülleimer.
garble [gɑ:bl], *v.a.* verstümmeln.
garden [gɑ:dn], *s.* der Garten. — *v.n.* im Garten arbeiten.
gardener ['gɑ:dnə], *s.* der Gärtner.
gargle [gɑ:gl], *v.n.* gurgeln, spülen.
gargoyle ['gɑ:gɔil], *s.* (*Archit.*) der Wasserspeier.
garish ['gɛəriʃ], *adj.* grell, auffallend.
garland ['gɑ:lənd], *s.* der Blumenkranz, die Girlande.
garlic ['gɑ:lik], *s.* (*Bot.*) der Knoblauch.
garment ['gɑ:mənt], *s.* das Gewand.
garner ['gɑ:nə], *v.a.* aufspeichern (*store*).
garnet ['gɑ:nit], *s.* der Granat.
garnish ['gɑ:niʃ], *v.a.* ausschmücken, verzieren.
garret ['gærət], *s.* die Dachkammer.
garrison ['gærisən], *s.* (*Mil.*) die Garnison. — *v.a.* stationieren.
garrulity [gæ'ru:liti], *s.* die Schwatzhaftigkeit.
garter ['gɑ:tə], *s.* das Strumpfband, das Hosenband; *Order of the Garter*, der Hosenbandorden.
gas [gæs], *s.* das Gas; (*Am.*) *see* **gasoline**.
gaseous ['geisiəs], *adj.* gasförmig, gasartig.
Gascon ['gæskən], *s.* der Gaskogner.
gasoline ['gæsoli:n], *s.* (*Am.*) das Benzin.
gash [gæʃ], *s.* die Schnittwunde.
gasp [gɑ:sp], *v.n.* keuchen; nach Luft schnappen. — *s.* das Keuchen, das Luftschnappen.
gastric ['gæstrik], *adj.* (*Anat.*) gastrisch; — *ulcer*, das Magengeschwür.
gate [geit], *s.* das Tor, der Eingang. — *v.a.* einsperren, Hausarrest geben (*Dat.*).
gateway ['geitwei], *s.* die Einfahrt.
gather ['gæðə], *v.a.* sammeln, einsammeln (*collect*); versammeln (*assemble*). — *v.n.* entnehmen, schließen (*infer*); sich versammeln (*come together*); aufziehen (*storm*).
gathering ['gæðəriŋ], *s.* die Versammlung (*meeting*).
gauche [gouʃ], *adj.* linkisch, ungeschickt.
gaudy ['gɔ:di], *adj.* übertrieben, grell, prunkhaft.
gauge [geidʒ], *v.a.* (*Engin.*) ausmessen, kalibrieren; eichen (*officially*). — *s.* der Maßstab (*scale*); (*Railw.*) die Spurweite.
gauger ['geidʒə], *s.* der Eichmeister.
Gaul [gɔ:l], *s.* der Gallier.
gaunt [gɔ:nt], *adj.* mager; hager.
gauntlet ['gɔ:ntlit], *s.* der (Panzer)handschuh.
gauze [gɔ:z], *s.* die Gaze.
gavotte [gə'vɔt], *s.* (*Mus.*) die Gavotte.

gay [gei], *adj.* fröhlich, heiter; bunt (*colour*).
gaze [geiz], *v.n.* starren.
gazelle [gə'zel], *s.* (*Zool.*) die Gazelle.
gazette [gə'zet], *s.* die (amtliche) Zeitung; das Amtsblatt.
gear [giə], *s.* das Gerät; (*Mech.*) das Triebwerk; (*Naut.*) das Geschirr; *switch*—, das Schaltgerät; (*Motor.*) der Gang; — *ratio*, die Übersetzung; *differential* —, der Achsenantrieb; *steering* —, die Lenkung (*of car*); — *box*, das Schaltgetriebe, die Gangschaltung; *out of* —, in Unordnung; *in top* —, mit Höchstgeschwindigkeit; *change to bottom* —, auf erste Geschwindigkeit (*or*, auf langsam) einschalten. — *v.a.* — *down*, herabsetzen; (*Engin.*) — *up*, übersetzen; — *to*, anpassen.
gelatine ['dʒeləti:n], *s.* die Gallerte, die Geleemasse.
gem [dʒem], *s.* die Gemme, der Edelstein.
gender ['dʒendə], *s.* (*Gram.*) das Geschlecht.
gene [dʒi:n], *s.* (*Biol.*) das Gen.
genealogy [dʒi:ni'ælədʒi], *s.* die Genealogie; der Stammbaum (*family tree*).
general ['dʒenərəl], *s.* (*Mil.*) der General; *lieutenant*- —, der Generalleutnant. — *adj.* allgemein, General-; — *-purpose*, für alle Zwecke; Allzweck-.
generalization [dʒenərəlai'zeiʃən], *s.* die Verallgemeinerung.
generalize ['dʒenərəlaiz], *v.a.* verallgemeinern.
generate ['dʒenəreit], *v.a.* erzeugen; (*Elec.*) Strom erzeugen.
generation [dʒenə'reiʃən], *s.* die Generation (*contemporaries*); das Zeugen (*production*); (*Elec.*) die Stromerzeugung.
generosity [dʒenə'rɔsiti], *s.* die Großmut (*magnanimity*); die Freigebigkeit (*liberality*).
generous ['dʒenərəs], *adj.* großmütig; freigebig (*with gifts*).
Genevan [dʒi'ni:vən], *adj.* genferisch. — *s.* der Genfer.
genitive ['dʒenitiv], *s.* (*Gram.*) der Wesfall, Genitiv.
genial ['dʒi:niəl], *adj.* freundlich, mild.
geniality [dʒi:ni'æliti], *s.* die Freundlichkeit, Leutseligkeit.
genital ['dʒenitəl], *adj.* Zeugungs-. — *s.* (*pl.*) die Geschlechtsteile, Genitalien, *pl.*
genius ['dʒi:niəs], *s.* das Genie; der Genius.
Genoese [dʒenou'i:z], *adj.* genuesisch. — *s.* der Genuese.
Gentile ['dʒentail], *s.* heidnisch; nicht jüdisch.
gentility [dʒen'tiliti], *s.* die Herkunft aus vornehmem Haus, Vornehmheit.
gentle [dʒentl], *adj.* sanft, mild; gelind (*breeze*).
gentlefolk ['dʒentlfouk], *s.* bessere *or* vornehme Leute, *pl.*
gentleman ['dʒentlmən], *s.* der Gentleman, Herr; feiner Herr.
gentleness ['dʒentlnis], *s.* die Milde, Sanftheit.
gentry ['dʒentri], *s.* der niedere Adel.
genuine ['dʒenjuin], *adj.* echt.
genus ['dʒenəs], *s.* (*Biol.*) die Gattung.
geographer [dʒi'ɔgrəfə], *s.* der Geograph.
geographical [dʒi:o'græfikəl], *adj.* geographisch.
geography [dʒi'ɔgrəfi], die Geographie, Erdkunde.
geological [dʒi:o'lɔdʒikəl], *adj.* geologisch.
geologist [dʒi'ɔlədʒist], *s.* der Geologe.
geology [dʒi'ɔlədʒi], *s.* die Geologie.
geometric(al) [dʒi:o'metrik(əl)], *adj.* geometrisch.
geometrist [dʒi'ɔmətrist], *s.* der Geometer.
geometry [dʒi'ɔmətri], *s.* die Geometrie.
geranium [dʒə'reiniəm], *s.* (*Bot.*) die Geranie, das Germaniu.
germ [dʒə:m], *s.* der Keim; (*pl.*) die Bakterien, *f. pl.*
German ['dʒə:mən], *adj.* deutsch. — *s.* der, die Deutsche.
germane [dʒə:'mein], *adj.* zur Sache gehörig, zugehörig.
germinate ['dʒə:mineit], *v.n.* keimen.
Germanic [dʒə:'mænik], *adj.* germanisch.
gerund ['dʒerənd], *s.* (*Gram.*) das Gerundium.
gerundive [dʒe'rʌndiv], *s.* (*Gram.*) das Gerundiv(um).
gesticulate [dʒes'tikjuleit], *v.n.* Gebärden machen, gestikulieren.
gesture ['dʒestʃə], *s.* die Geste; der Gebärde.
get [get], *v.a. irr.* bekommen, (*coll.*) kriegen; erhalten (*receive*); erwischen (*catch up with*); einholen (*fetch*); — *over* or *across*, klar machen. — *v.n.* gelangen (*arrive*); werden (*become*); — *along*, weiterkommen; — *on* or (*Am.*) *along with s.o.*, mit jemandem auskommen; — *on in the world*, Karriere machen; — *away*, entkommen; — *down to it*, zur Sache kommen; — *in*, hineinkommen; — *off*, aussteigen; *show s.o. where he —s off*, jemandem seine Meinung sagen; (*Sch.*) — *through*, durchkommen (*in examination*); — *up*, aufstehen.
get-up ['getʌp], *s.* das Kostüm; die Ausstattung (*attire*).
Ghanaian [gɑ:'neiən], *adj.* ghanaisch. — *s.* der Ghanaer.
ghastly ['gɑ:stli], *adj.* furchtbar, schrecklich.
gherkin ['gə:kin], *s.* (*Bot.*) die Essiggurke.
ghost [goust], *s.* der Geist, das Gespenst.
giant ['dʒaiənt], *s.* der Riese.
gibberish ['dʒibəriʃ], *s.* das Kauderwelsch.
gibbet ['dʒibit], *s.* der Galgen.

gibe [dʒaib], *v.n.* spotten, höhnen (*at*, über, *Acc.*). — *s.* der Spott, Hohn; die spöttische Bemerkung (*remark*).
giblets ['dʒiblits], *s. pl.* das Gänseklein.
giddiness ['gidinis], *s.* das Schwindelgefühl.
giddy ['gidi], *adj.* schwindelig.
gift [gift], *s.* die Gabe, das Geschenk.
gifted ['giftid], *adj.* begabt.
gig [gig], *s.* der leichte Wagen; (*Naut.*) der Nachen, das Gig.
gigantic [dʒai'gæntik], *adj.* riesig, riesengroß.
giggle [gigl], *v.n.* kichern. — *s.* das Kichern, Gekicher.
gild [gild], *v.a.* vergolden; verschönern; —*ing the pill*, etwas Unangenehmes (die Pille) versüßen.
gill (1) [gil], *s.* (*Biol.*) die Kieme.
gill (2) [dʒil], *s.* das Viertel einer Pinte (0.14 *l.*).
gilt [gilt], *s.* die Vergoldung; — *edged*, mit Goldschnitt; (*Comm.*) hochwertige *or* mündelsichere Staatspapiere.
gimlet ['gimlit], *s.* (*Carp.*) der Handbohrer.
gin [dʒin], *s.* der Gin, der Wachholderbranntwein; — *and tonic*, Gin und Tonic.
ginger ['dʒindʒə], *s.* der Ingwer; — -*haired*, rothaarig; — *nut*, das Ingwer- *or* Pfeffernüßchen, Ingwerkeks; — *beer*, Ingwerbier. — *v.a.* — *up*, aufstacheln, anreizen.
gingerbread ['dʒindʒəbred], *s.* der Lebkuchen, Pfefferkuchen.
gipsy ['dʒipsi], *s.* der Zigeuner.
giraffe [dʒi'rɑ:f], *s.* (*Zool.*) die Giraffe.
gird [gə:d], *v.a. reg.* & *irr.* (*Poet.*) gürten.
girder ['gə:də], *s.* der Balken, Träger.
girdle [gə:dl], *v.a.* gürten, umgürten; — *the earth*, die Erde umkreisen.
girl [gə:l], *s.* das Mädchen.
girlhood ['gə:lhud], *s.* die Mädchenzeit, die Mädchenjahre, *n. pl.*
girlish ['gə:liʃ], *adj.* mädchenhaft, wie ein Mädchen.
gist [dʒist], *s.* das Wesentliche.
give [giv], *v.a. irr.* geben; — *out*, bekanntgeben, bekanntmachen; — *up*, aufgeben; — *way to*, Platz machen. — *v.n.* sich dehnen, sich strecken (*of wood, metal etc.*); — *in*, nachgeben (*to*, *Dat.*).
glacial ['gleiʃəl], *adj.* eisig, Gletscher-.
glacier ['glæsiə], *s.* der Gletscher.
glad [glæd], *adj.* froh, erfreut (*at*, über, *Acc.*).
gladden [glædn], *v.a.* erheitern, erfreuen.
glade [gleid], *s.* die Lichtung.
glamorous ['glæmərəs], *adj.* bezaubernd, blendend glanzvoll.
glamour ['glæmə], *s.* der Zauber; der Glanz.
glance [glɑ:ns], *s.* der Blick; *at a* —, auf den ersten Blick. — *v.n.* flüchtig blicken.
gland [glænd], *s.* (*Anat.*) die Drüse.
glandular ['glændjulə], *adj.* Drüsen-, drüsig.
glare [glɛə], *s.* der blendende Glanz, das Schimmern; der (scharf) durchbohrende Blick (*stare*).
glaring ['glɛəriŋ], *adj.* schreiend (*of colour*); auffallend (*obvious*).
glass [glɑ:s], *s.* das Glas; der Spiegel (*mirror*); das Wetterglas (*barometer*); (*pl.*) die Brille (*spectacles*).
glassblower ['glɑ:sblouə], *s.* der Glasbläser.
glassworks ['glɑ:swə:ks], *s.* die Glashütte.
glassy ['glɑ:si], *adj.* gläsern.
glaze [gleiz], *s.* die Glasur. — *v.a.* glasieren; verglasen.
glazier ['gleiziə], *s.* der Glaser.
gleam [gli:m], *v.n.* strahlen, glänzen (*with*, vor, *Dat.*). — *s.* der Glanz, das Strahlen.
glean [gli:n], *v.a.* auflesen; erfahren (*learn*).
glebe [gli:b], *s.* das Pfarrgut.
glee (1) [gli:], *s.* die Freude, Heiterkeit.
glee (2) [gli:], *s.* (*Mus.*) der Rundgesang; — *club*, die Liedertafel.
glen [glen], *s.* das enge Tal.
glib [glib], *adj.* glatt, geläufig, zungenfertig.
glide [glaid], *v.n.* gleiten. — *s.* das Gleiten.
glider ['glaidə], *s.* (*Aviat.*) das Segelflugzeug.
glimmer ['glimə], *s.* der Schimmer, Glimmer. — *v.n.* schimmern, glimmen.
glimpse [glimps], *s.* der (flüchtige) Blick; *catch a* —, einen Blick erhaschen. — *v.a.* flüchtig blicken (auf, *Acc.*).
glisten [glisn], *v.n.* glitzern, glänzen.
glitter ['glitə], *v.n.* glänzen, schimmern.
gloaming ['gloumiŋ], *s.* die Dämmerung.
globe [gloub], *s.* der Globus, der Erdball; die Kugel.
globular ['glɔbjulə], *adj.* kugelförmig.
gloom [glu:m], *s.* das Dunkel; der Trübsinn, die Traurigkeit.
gloomy ['glu:mi], *adj.* deprimiert, trübsinnig, düster.
glorify ['glɔ:rifai], *v.a.* verherrlichen.
glorious ['glɔ:riəs], *adj.* herrlich; (*Mil.*) glorreich.
glory ['glɔ:ri], *s.* die Herrlichkeit, der Ruhm. — *v.n.* frohlocken (*in*, über, *Acc.*).
gloss [glɔs], *s.* der Glanz; (*Lit.*) die Glosse, Anmerkung. — *v.a.* — *over*, beschönigen; (*Lit.*) glossieren, mit Anmerkungen versehen.
glossary ['glɔsəri], *s.* das Glossar, die Spezialwörterliste; das Wörterbuch.
glossy ['glɔsi], *adj.* glänzend.
glove [glʌv], *s.* der Handschuh.
glow [glou], *v.n.* glühen. — *s.* die Glut, das Glühen; Wohlbehagen.
glower ['glauə], *v.n.* — *at*, feindselig ansehen, anstarren.

glue [glu:], *s.* der Leim. — *v.a.* leimen, zusammenleimen.
glum [glʌm], *adj.* mürrisch, finster.
glut [glʌt], *s.* die Überfülle. — *v.a.* überladen, überfüllen.
glutinous [ˈglu:tinəs], *adj.* zähe, klebrig.
glutton [glʌtn], *s.* der Vielfraß.
gluttony [ˈglʌtəni], *s.* die Schwelgerei, Gefräßigkeit.
glycerine [ˈglisəri:n], *s.* das Glyzerin.
gnarled [nɑ:ld], *adj.* knorrig.
gnash [næʃ], *v.a.* knirschen (*teeth*).
gnat [næt], *s.* (*Ent.*) die Mücke.
gnaw [nɔ:], *v.a., v.n.* nagen (an, *Dat.*), zernagen, zerfressen (at, *Acc.*).
gnome [noum], *s.* der Erdgeist, der Zwerg, Gnom.
go [gou], *v.n. irr.* gehen, fahren, laufen; arbeiten (*engine*); verlaufen (*event*); sich erstrecken (*distance*); — *down in the general esteem*, in der Achtung sinken; — *on*, fortfahren; — *mad*, verrückt werden; — *bald*, die Haare verlieren; — *without*, leer ausgehen, entbehren; *let* —, loslassen; — *for*, auf jemanden losgehen; — *in for*, sich interessieren für (*Acc.*); — *all out for*, energisch unternehmen; *a —ing concern*, ein gutgehendes Unternehmen; *—ing on for 20*, fast 20 Jahre. — *s.* der Versuch; (*coll.*) *plenty of* —, recht lebhaft, voller Schwung.
goad [goud], *v.a.* anstacheln.
goal [goul], *s.* das Ziel; (*Footb.*) das Tor.
goalkeeper [ˈgoulki:pə], *s.* der Torwart.
goalpost [ˈgoulpoust], *s.* der Torpfosten.
goat [gout], *s.* (*Zool.*) die Geiß, Ziege; *billy* —, der Ziegenbock; *nanny* —, die Geiß.
gobble [gɔbl], *v.a.* verschlingen, gierig essen.
goblet [ˈgɔblit], *s.* der Becher.
goblin [ˈgɔblin], *s.* der Kobold, der Gnom; der Schelm.
go-cart [ˈgoukɑ:t], *s.* der Kinderwagen, Gängelwagen.
God [gɔd]. Gott.
god [gɔd], *s.* der Gott.
godchild [ˈgɔdtʃaild], *s.* das Patenkind.
goddess [ˈgɔdes], *s.* die Göttin.
godfather [ˈgɔdfɑ:ðə], *s.* der Pate.
godhead [ˈgɔdhed], *s.* die Gottheit.
godless [ˈgɔdlis], *adj.* gottlos, ungläubig.
godmother [ˈgɔdmʌðə], *s.* die Patin.
goggle [gɔgl], *v.n.* glotzen, starren (*stare*). — *s.* (*pl.*) die Schutzbrille.
going [ˈgouiŋ], *s.* das Gehen, das Funktionieren (*of machinery*); *while the — is good*, zur rechten Zeit.
gold [gould], *s.* das Gold; (*Fin.*) — *standard*, die Goldwährung.
goldfinch [ˈgouldfintʃ], *s.* (*Orn.*) der Stieglitz.
goldsmith [ˈgouldsmiθ], *s.* der Goldschmied.
gondola [ˈgɔndələ], *s.* die Gondel.
good [gud], *adj.* gut; artig, brav; *for* —, auf immer; *in — time*, rechtzeitig; — *and proper*, (*coll.*) wie es sich gehört, anständig; *as — as*, so gut wie; — *looking*, hübsch; — *natured*, gutmütig. — *s. for your own* —, in Ihrem eigenen Interesse; *that's no* —, das taugt nichts; (*pl.*) die Güter, *n.pl.*, Waren, *f.pl.*; *goods station*, der Frachtbahnhof; *goods train*, der Güterzug; *goods yard*, der Güterstapelplatz.
goodbye [gudˈbai], *interj., s.—!* leb wohl! auf Wiedersehen!
goodness [ˈgudnis], *s.* die Güte.
goodwill [gudˈwil], *s.* das Wohlwollen; (*Comm.*) die Kundschaft.
goose [gu:s], *s.* (*Orn.*) die Gans.
gooseberry [ˈguzbəri], *s.* (*Bot.*) die Stachelbeere.
gore [gɔ:], *s.* das geronnene Blut. — *v.a.* durchbohren (*pierce, stab*).
gorge [gɔ:dʒ], *s.* die Felsenschlucht (*ravine*); (*Anat.*) die Kehle. — *v.a.* gierig verschlingen.
gorgeous [ˈgɔ:dʒəs], *adj.* prachtvoll, prächtig.
gorse [gɔ:s], *s.* (*Bot.*) der Stechginster.
gory [ˈgɔ:ri], *adj.* blutig.
goshawk [ˈgɔshɔ:k], *s.* (*Orn.*) der Hühnerhabicht.
gosling [ˈgɔzliŋ], *s.* (*Orn.*) das Gänschen.
gospel [ˈgɔspəl], *s.* das Evangelium; *the — according to*, das Evangelium des . . .
gossamer [ˈgɔsəmə], *s.* das feine Gewebe; die Sommerfäden.
gossip [ˈgɔsip], *v.n.* klatschen; schwatzen, plaudern. — *s.* der Klatsch; der Schwätzer; die Klatschbase.
Gothic [ˈgɔθik], *adj.* gotisch.
gouge [gaudʒ], *s.* der Hohlmeißel. — *v.a.* aushöhlen, ausstechen.
gourd [ˈguəd], *s.* der Kürbis.
gout [gaut], *s.* (*Med.*) die Gicht.
govern [ˈgʌvən], *v.a., v.n.* (*Pol.*) regieren; beherrschen; (*fig.*) leiten, herrschen.
governable [ˈgʌvənəbl], *adj.* lenkbar, lenksam.
governess [ˈgʌvənis], *s.* die Erzieherin, die Gouvernante.
government [ˈgʌvənmənt], *s.* die Regierung; (*Pol.*) — *benches*, die Regierungssitze; — *loan*, die Staatsanleihe.
governor [ˈgʌvənə], *s.* der Gouverneur, Statthalter.
gown [gaun], *s.* das Kleid (*lady's*); (*Univ.*) der Talar; (*official robe*) die Amtstracht.
grab [græb], *v.a.* packen, ergreifen. — *s.* der Zugriff.
grace [greis], *s.* die Gnade; Gunst (*favour*); die Anmut (*gracefulness*); *Your Grace*, Euer Gnaden; das Tischgebet (*prayer at table*); (*Mus.*) — *note*, die Fermate; *ten minutes'* —, zehn Minuten Aufschub. — *v.a.* schmücken, zieren, ehren.
graceful [ˈgreisful], *adj.* anmutig, reizend; graziös (*movement*).

graceless ['greislis], *adj.* ungraziös.
gracious['greiʃəs],*adj.*gnädig,huldreich.
gradation [grə'deiʃən], *s.* die Abstufung, die Stufenleiter.
grade [greid], *s.* der Grad, Rang (*rank*); (*Am.*) (*Sch.*) die Klasse. — *v.a.* sortieren, ordnen.
gradient ['greidiənt], *s.* (*Geog.*) die Steigung; der Steigungswinkel (*angle*).
gradual ['grædjuəl], *adj.* allmählich.
graduate ['grædjueit], *v.n.* promovieren (*receive degree*); — *as a doctor*, als Doktor promovieren, den Doktor machen. — [-djuit], *s.* der Akademiker, Graduierte.
graft (1) [grɑ:ft], *s.* (*Hort.*, *Med.*) die (Haut)übertragung. — *v.a.* (*Hort.*, *Med.*) übertragen, anheften (*on to*, auf, *Acc.*).
graft (2) [grɑ:ft], *s.* (*Am.*) der unerlaubte Gewinn; das Schmiergeld; der Betrug (*swindle*).
grain [grein], *s.* das Korn, Samenkorn; das Getreide; das Gran (=0·065 *gramme*); die Maserung (*in wood*); *against the* —, gegen den Strich.
grammar ['græmə], *s.* die Grammatik; — *school*, das Gymnasium.
grammatical [grə'mætikəl], *adj.* grammatisch.
gramme [græm], *s.* das Gramm.
gramophone ['græməfoun], *s.* das Grammophon.
granary ['grænəri], *s.* der (Korn)-speicher, die Kornkammer.
grand [grænd], *adj.* groß, großartig; wunderbar; *Grand Duke*, der Großherzog. — *s.* (*Am.*) (*sl.*) 1000 Dollar; (*piano*) der Flügel; *baby* —, der Stutzflügel.
grandchild ['grændtʃaild], *s.* der Enkel, die Enkelin.
grandee [græn'di:], *s.* der spanische Grande.
grandeur ['grændjə], *s.* die Größe, Pracht.
grandfather ['grændfɑ:ðə], *s.* der Großvater.
grandiloquent [græn'dilokwənt], *adj.* großsprecherisch.
grandmother ['grændmʌðə], *s.* die Großmutter.
grange [greindʒ], *s.* der Meierhof, das Landhaus.
granite ['grænit], *s.* der Granit.
grannie, granny ['græni], *s.* (*coll.*) die Oma.
grant [grɑ:nt], *s.* die Gewährung (*of permission etc.*); die Zuwendung (*subsidy*); (*Sch.*) das Stipendium. — *v.a.* geben, gewähren; *take for —ed*, als selbstverständlich hinnehmen.
granular ['grænjulə], *adj.* körnig.
granulated ['grænjuleitid], *adj.* feinkörnig, Kristall- (*sugar*).
grape [greip], *s.* (*Bot.*) die Weinbeere; die Traube; — *sugar*, der Traubenzucker; *bunch of —s*, Weintrauben, *f. pl.*
grapefruit ['greipfru:t], *s.* die Pampelmuse.
graphic ['græfik], *adj.* (*Art*) graphisch; deutlich, bildhaft, anschaulich.
grapnel ['græpnəl], *s.* (*Naut.*) der Dregganker.
grapple [græpl], *v.n.* — *with*, raufen, (miteinander) ringen.
grasp [grɑ:sp], *v.a.* (mit der Hand) ergreifen, erfassen. — *s.* das Fassungsvermögen, die Auffassung; der Griff (*hand*).
grasping ['grɑ:spiŋ], *adj.* habgierig, gewinnsüchtig.
grass [grɑ:s], *s.* (*Bot.*) das Gras; der Rasen (*lawn*); — *widow*, die Strohwitwe.
grasshopper ['grɑ:shɔpə], *s.* (*Ent.*) die Heuschrecke.
grate (1) [greit], *s.* der Feuerrost, der Kamin.
grate (2) [greit], *v.a.* reiben (*cheese*); schaben, kratzen. — *v.n.* knirschen; auf die Nerven gehen.
grateful ['greitful], *adj.* dankbar.
grater ['greitə], *s.* das Reibeisen; die Reibe (*electrical*).
gratification [grætifi'keiʃən], *s.* die Genugtuung, Befriedigung.
gratify ['grætifai], *v.a.* befriedigen, erfreuen.
grating ['greitiŋ], *s.* das Gitter.
gratis ['greitis], *adv.* gratis, umsonst, frei, unentgeltlich.
gratitude ['grætitju:d], *s.* die Dankbarkeit.
gratuitous [grə'tju:itəs], *adj.* frei, freiwillig (*voluntary*); unentgeltlich (*free of charge*); grundlos (*baseless*).
gratuity [grə'tju:iti], *s.* das Trinkgeld (*tip*); die Gratifikation.
grave (1) [greiv], *adj.* schwer, ernst (*serious*); feierlich (*solemn*). —*s.* (*Mus.*) das Grave.
grave (2) [greiv], *s.* das Grab (*tomb*).
gravel [grævl], *s.* der Kies.
graveyard ['greivjɑ:d], *s.* der Friedhof.
gravitate ['græviteit], *v.n.* gravitieren, hinstreben.
gravitation [grævi'teiʃən], *s.* die Schwerkraft.
gravitational [grævi'teiʃənəl], *adj.* (*Phys.*) Schwerkrafts-.
gravity ['græviti], *s.* der Ernst (*seriousness*); (*Phys.*) die Schwere, Schwerkraft.
gravy ['greivi], *s.* die Sauce, Soße; der Saft des Fleisches, des Bratens; — *boat*, die Sauciere.
gray, grey [grei], *adj.* grau.
graze (1) [greiz], *v.n.* weiden.
graze (2) [greiz], *v.a.* streifen (*pass closely*), abschürfen.
grazier ['greiziə], *s.* der Viehzüchter.
grease [gri:s], *s.* das Fett; das Schmieröl (*machine*). — *v.a.* einfetten (*pans*); schmieren, einschmieren (*machinery*).
greasy ['gri:si], *adj.* fett, schmierig, ölig.
great [greit], *adj.* groß, bedeutend, wichtig; (*Am.*) wundervoll, wunderbar.

greatcoat ['greitcout], *s.* der Wintermantel.
great-grandfather [greit'grændfɑ:ðə], *s.* der Urgroßvater.
greatly ['greitli], *adv.* stark, sehr.
greatness ['greitnis], *s.* die Größe, Bedeutung.
greedy ['gri:di], *adj.* gierig; gefräßig (*eater*).
Greek [gri:k], *adj.* griechisch. — *s.* der Grieche.
green [gri:n], *adj.* grün; neu (*new*), frisch (*fresh*).
greengage ['gri:ngeidʒ], *s.* (*Bot.*) die Reineclaude.
greengrocer ['gri:ngrousə], *s.* der Grünwarenhändler, Gemüsehändler.
greenhorn ['gri:nhɔ:n], *s.* der Grünschnabel.
greenhouse ['gri:nhaus], *s.* das Gewächshaus, Treibhaus.
Greenlander ['gri:nləndə], *s.* der Grönländer.
greet [gri:t], *v.a.* grüßen, begrüßen.
greeting ['gri:tiŋ], *s.* die Begrüßung; (*pl.*) Grüße, *m. pl.*
gregarious [gri'gɛəriəs], *adj.* gesellig.
grenade [gri'neid], *s.* die Granate.
grey *see under* **gray.**
greyhound ['greihaund], *s.* (*Zool.*) das Windspiel, der Windhund.
grid [grid], *s.* (*Elec.*) das Stromnetz; (*Phys.*) das Gitter.
gridiron ['gridaiən], *s.* der Bratrost, das Bratrostgitter.
grief [gri:f], *s.* der Kummer, die Trauer.
grievance ['gri:vəns], *s.* die Klage, Beschwerde.
grieve [gri:v], *v.a.* kränken. — *v.n.* sich grämen, sich kränken (*over*, über, *Acc.*, wegen, *Genit.*).
grievous ['gri:vəs], *adj.* schmerzlich.
grill [gril], *s.* der Rostbraten, Bratrost. — *v.a.* grillieren, rösten (*meat*); verhören (*question closely*).
grilling ['griliŋ], *s.* das Verhör.
grim [grim], *adj.* grimmig, finster.
grimace [gri'meis], *s.* die Grimasse, die Fratze.
grime [graim], *s.* der Schmutz, der Ruß.
grimy ['graimi], *adj.* schmutzig, rußig.
grin [grin], *v.n.* grinsen; (*coll.*) — *and bear it*, mach gute Miene zum bösen Spiel. — *s.* das Grinsen.
grind [graind], *v.a. irr.* zerreiben (*rub*); schleifen (*sharpen*); mahlen (*pulverize*); — *o.'s teeth*, mit den Zähnen knirschen. — *s.* (*coll.*) die ungeheuere Anstrengung, die Plackerei.
grinder ['graində], *s. coffee* —, die Kaffeemühle; *knife* —, der Schleifer, Wetzer; der Backzahn (*molar*).
grindstone ['graindstoun], *s.* der Schleifstein; *keep o.'s nose to the* —, fest bei der Arbeit bleiben.
grip [grip], *s.* der Griff; *lose o.'s* —, nicht mehr bewältigen können (wie bisher); (*Tech.*) der Handgriff (*handle*). — *v.a.* ergreifen, festhalten.
gripe [graip], *v.n.* (*sl.*) meckern.
gripes [graips], *s. pl.* (*Med.*) das Bauchgrimmen, die Kolik.
gripping ['gripiŋ], *adj.* fesselnd (*story*).
grisly ['grizli], *adj.* scheußlich, gräßlich.
grist [grist], *s.* das Mahlgut, Gemahlene; — *to o.'s mill*, Wasser auf seine Mühle.
gristle [grisl], *s.* der Knorpel.
grit [grit], *s.* das Schrot, der Kies; der Mut (*courage*).
gritty ['griti], *adj.* körnig, kiesig, sandig.
grizzled [grizld], *adj.* grau, graumeliert.
groan [groun], *v.n.* stöhnen.
groats [grouts], *s. pl.* die Hafergrütze.
grocer ['grousə], *s.* der Kolonialwarenhändler, Feinkosthändler.
groin [grɔin], *s.* (*Anat.*) die Leiste; (*Archit.*) die Gewölbekante, Rippe.
groom [gru:m], *s.* der Stallknecht (*stables*); (*obs.*) der Junge (*inn*). — *v.a.* schniegeln, bürsten; schön machen.
groove [gru:v], *s.* die Rinne; die Rille (*of gramophone record*). — *v.a.* rillen; furchen (*dig a furrow*).
grope [group], *v.n.* tappen, tasten (*around*, umher).
gross [grous], *adj.* dick (*fat*); plump (*heavy-handed*); grob (*ill-mannered*); — *weight*, das Bruttogewicht; ungeheuer (*error*).
grotto ['grɔtou], *s.* die Grotte.
ground [graund], *s.* der Grund, Boden (*also pl.*); die Ursache (*cause*); — *floor*, das Erdgeschoß. — *v.n.* stranden (*of ship*).
groundwork ['graundwə:k], *s.* die Grundlagen, *f. pl.*
group [gru:p], *s.* die Gruppe. — *v.a.* gruppieren, anordnen.
grouse (1) [graus], *v.n.* (*coll.*) meckern, sich beklagen. — *s.* der Grund zur Klage, die Beschwerde.
grouse (2) [graus], *s.* (*Orn.*) das Birkhuhn, Moorhuhn.
grove [grouv], *s.* der Hain, das Wäldchen.
grovel [grɔvl], *v.n.* kriechen, schöntun (*Dat.*).
grow [grou], *v.n. irr.* wachsen, sich mehren (*increase*); werden (*become*). — *v.a.* anbauen, anpflanzen.
growl [graul], *v.n.* brummen, knurren. — *s.* das Gebrumme, Geknurre.
grown-up [groun'ʌp], *s.* der Erwachsene. — *adj.* erwachsen.
growth [grouθ], *s.* das Anwachsen (*increase*); das Wachstum (*growing*).
grub [grʌb], *s.* (*Zool.*) die Larve; (*coll.*) das Essen. — *v.n.* — *about*, wühlen.
grudge [grʌdʒ], *s.* der Groll; Neid (*jealousy*). — *v.a.* mißgönnen (*envy*). — *v.n.* — *doing s.th.*, etwas ungerne tun.
gruel ['gru:əl], *s.* der Haferschleim.
gruesome ['gru:səm], *adj.* schauerlich, schrecklich.
gruff [grʌf], *adj.* mürrisch.
grumble [grʌmbl], *v.n.* murren, klagen.

grumbler ['grʌmblə], *s.* der Unzufriedene, Nörgler.
grunt [grʌnt], *v.n.* grunzen. — *s.* das Grunzen.
guarantee [gærən'ti:], *v.a.* bürgen, garantieren. — *s.* die Bürgschaft; (*Comm.*) die Garantie.
guarantor ['gærəntɔ:], *s.* der Bürge; (*Comm.*) der Garant.
guard [gɑ:d], *s.* die Wache (*watch* or *watchman*); (*Railw.*) der Schaffner; die Schutzvorrichtung (*protective device*); (*fire*) —, das Kamingitter ; (*for sword*) das Stichblatt. — *v.a.* bewachen; behüten (*protect*). — *v.n.* auf der Hut sein; — *against*, sich hüten (vor, *Dat.*); vorbeugen.
guarded ['gɑ:did], *adj.* behutsam, vorsichtig.
guardian ['gɑ:djən], *s.* der Vormund (*of child*); der Wächter.
guardianship ['gɑ:djənʃip], *s.* (*Law*) die Vormundschaft.
Guatemalan [gwæti'mɑ:lən], *adj.* guatemaltekisch. — *s.* der Guatemalteke.
Guelph [gwelf], *s.* der Welfe.
guess [ges], *v.a.* raten (*a riddle*). — *v.n.* (*Am.*) glauben, meinen. — *s.* die Vermutung; *have a* —, rate mal!
guest [gest], *s.* der Gast; *paying* —, der Pensionär.
guffaw [gʌ'fɔ:], *s.* das (laute) Gelächter.
guidance ['gaidəns], *s.* die Führung, Anleitung.
guide [gaid], *s.* der Führer, Wegweiser, Reiseführer; (*Phot.*) die Führung. — *v.a.* führen, anleiten.
guided ['gaidid], *adj.* gelenkt; — *missile*, das Ferngeschoß, die Rakete.
guild [gild], *s.* die Gilde, Zunft, Innung.
guildhall ['gildhɔ:l], *s.* das Rathaus.
guile [gail], *s.* der Betrug, die Arglist.
guileless ['gaillis], *adj.* arglos.
guilt [gilt], *s.* die Schuld.
guilty ['gilti], *adj.* schuldig.
guinea ['gini], *s.* die Guinee (21 *shillings*); — *fowl*, das Perlhuhn; — *pig*, das Meerschweinchen.
guise [gaiz], *s.* die Verkleidung (*costume*); die Erscheinung (*appearance*).
guitar [gi'tɑ:], *s.* (*Mus.*) die Gitarre.
gulf [gʌlf], *s.* der Meerbusen, Golf; der Abgrund (*abyss*).
gull [gʌl], *s.* (*Orn.*) die Möwe.
gullet ['gʌlit], *s.* (*Anat.*) der Schlund, die Gurgel.
gullible ['gʌlibl], *adj.* leichtgläubig.
gully ['gʌli], *s.* die Schlucht (*abyss*).
gulp [gʌlp], *v.a.* schlucken. — *s.* der Schluck, Zug.
gum (1) [gʌm], *s.* (*Bot.*) das Gummi. — *v.a.* gummieren; (*coll.*) — *up*, verderben (*spoil*).
gum (2) [gʌm], *s.* (*Anat.*) das Zahnfleisch.
gun [gʌn], *s.* das Gewehr (*rifle*); die Kanone (*cannon*); — *carriage*, die Lafette.
gunpowder ['gʌnpaudə], *s.* das Schießpulver.
gunsmith ['gʌnsmiθ], *s.* der Büchsenmacher.
gurgle [gə:gl], *v.n.* glucksen.
gush [gʌʃ], *v.n.* sich ergießen; schwärmen.
gusset ['gʌsit], *s.* (*Tail.*) der Zwickel.
gust [gʌst], *s.* der Windstoß.
gut [gʌt], *s.* (*Anat.*) der Darm; (*pl.*) die Eingeweide, *n. pl.*; (*coll.*) der Mut. — *v.a.* ausnehmen; ausleeren.
gutter ['gʌtə], *s.* die Rinne, Gosse.
guttersnipe ['gʌtəsnaip], *s.* der Lausbube.
guttural ['gʌtərəl], *adj.* Kehl-. — *s.* (*Phon.*) der Kehllaut.
guy [gai], *s.* die Vogelscheuche, die verkleidete Puppe; (*Am.*) der Kerl.
guzzle [gʌzl], *v.n.* schlemmen.
gymnasium [dʒim'neiziəm], *s.* die Turnhalle.
gymnastics [dʒim'næstiks], *s. pl.* das Turnen; die Gymnastik.
gypsum ['dʒipsəm], *s.* der Gips; der schwefelsaure Kalk.
gyrate [dʒaiə'reit], *v.n.* sich im Kreise bewegen, sich drehen, kreisen.

H

H [eitʃ]. das H.
haberdasher ['hæbədæʃə], *s.* der Kurzwarenhändler.
haberdashery ['hæbədæʃəri], *s.* die Kurzwarenhandlung.
habit ['hæbit], *s.* die Gewohnheit (*custom*); *force of* —, aus Gewohnheit, die Macht der Gewohnheit; die Kleidung (*costume*); *riding* —, das Reitkostüm.
habitable ['hæbitəbl], *adj.* bewohnbar.
habitation [hæbi'teiʃən], *s.* die Wohnung.
habitual [hə'bitjuəl], *adj.* gewohnheitsmäßig.
habituate [hə'bitjueit], *v.a.* gewöhnen.
hack (1) [hæk], *v.a.* hacken (*wood*); treten.
hack (2) [hæk], *s.* der Lohnschreiber; der (alte) Gaul, das Mietpferd (*horse*).
hackle [hækl], *v.a.* hecheln.
hackney ['hækni], *s.* — *carriage*, die Mietskutsche; das Taxi.
haddock ['hædək], *s.* (*Zool.*) der Schellfisch.
haemorrhage ['hemərid3], *s.* (*Med.*) die Blutung, der Blutsturz.
haemorrhoids ['hemərɔidz], *s. pl.* (*Med.*) die Hämorrhoiden, *f. pl.*
hag [hæg], *s.* das alte Weib; die Hexe (*witch*).

haggard [ˈhægəd], *adj.* hager (*lean*); häßlich, abgehärmt.
haggle [hægl], *v.n.* feilschen.
haggler [ˈhæglə], *s.* der Feilscher.
hail (1) [heil], *s.* der Hagel. — *v.n.* hageln.
hail (2) [heil], *v.a.* (mit einem Ruf) begrüßen; rufen. — *interj.* Heil, willkommen! — *s.* der Zuruf, Gruß.
hair [hεə], *s.* das Haar; *split* —*s*, Haarspalterei treiben.
haircut [ˈhεəkʌt], *s.* der Haarschnitt.
hairdresser [ˈhεədresə], *s.* der Friseur.
hale [heil], *adj.* — *and hearty*, frisch und gesund, rüstig.
half [hɑːf], *adj.* halb. — *adv.* — *baked*, unreif; unterentwickelt (*stupid*); (*coll.*) *not* —, und wie! sehr gern. — *s.* die Hälfte; *too clever by* —, allzu gescheit.
halfcaste [ˈhɑːfkɑːst], *s.* der Mischling.
halfpenny [ˈheipni], *s.* der halbe Penny.
halfwit [ˈhɑːfwit], *s.* der Dummkopf.
halibut [ˈhælibət], *s.* (*Zool.*) der Heilbutt.
hall [hɔːl], *s.* der Saal; die Halle; der Hausflur (*entrance* —); (*Univ.*) — (*of residence*), das Studentenheim; — *porter*, der Portier.
hallmark [ˈhɔːlmɑːk], *s.* das Kennzeichen.
hallow [ˈhælou], *v.a.* weihen, heiligen.
Halloween [hælouˈiːn]. der Allerheiligenabend.
halo [ˈheilou], *s.* der Heiligenschein (*of saint*); der Hof (*round the moon*).
hallucination [həluːsiˈneiʃən], *s.* die Halluzination.
halt [hɔːlt], *v.n.* halten, haltmachen; —*!* Halt! zögern (*tarry*); —*ing speech*, die Sprechhemmung. — *v.a.* anhalten, zum Halten bringen. — *s.* (*Railw.*) die (kleine) Haltestelle.
halve [hɑːv], *v.a.* halbieren.
ham [hæm], *s.* (*Cul.*) der Schinken; (*Anat.*) der Schenkel; — *acting*, das Schmierentheater.
hammer [ˈhæmə], *s.* der Hammer. — *v.a.*, *v.n.* hämmern; — *away at*, an etwas emsig arbeiten; — *out a problem*, ein Problem zur Lösung bringen.
hammock [ˈhæmək], *s.* die Hängematte.
hamper (1) [ˈhæmpə], *s.* der Packkorb.
hamper (2) [ˈhæmpə], *v.a.* behindern.
hand [hænd], *s.* die Hand; *a fair* —, eine gute Handschrift; der Uhrzeiger (*on watch, clock*); die Seite (*right, left* —); die Karten, *f. pl.* (*card game*); *play a strong* —, starke Karten halten *or* spielen; *on* —, vorrätig, auf Lager; *get out of* —, unkontrollierbar werden. — *v.a.* — *in*, einhändigen, einreichen; — *out*, austeilen; — *over*, übergeben, einhändigen.
handbag [ˈhændbæg], *s.* die Handtasche.
handbill [ˈhændbil], *s.* der Zettel, Reklamezettel (*advertising*).
handful [ˈhændful], *s.* die Handvoll; *to be quite a* —, genug zu schaffen geben; das Sorgenkind.
handicap [ˈhændikæp], *s.* das Hindernis. — *v.a.* hindern, behindern.
handicraft [ˈhændikrɑːft], *s.* das Handwerk; Kunsthandwerk.
handkerchief [ˈhæŋkətʃif], *s.* das Taschentuch.
handle [hændl], *s.* der Griff; der Henkel (*pot, vase*). — *v.a.* handhaben (*machine*); behandeln (*person*); anpacken (*problem*).
handlebar [ˈhændlbɑː], *s.* die Lenkstange (*bicycle*).
handmaid(en) [ˈhændmeid(n)], *s.* (*obs.*) die Magd.
handrail [ˈhændreil], *s.* das Geländer.
handshake [ˈhændʃeik], *s.* der Händedruck.
handsome [ˈhænsəm], *adj.* hübsch, schön, stattlich.
handy [ˈhændi], *adj.* geschickt; — *man*, der Gelegenheitsarbeiter, Mann für alles.
hang [hæŋ], *v.a. reg. & irr.* hängen; aufhängen (*suspend*); — *it!* zum Henker; — *paper*, ein Zimmer austapezieren; — *dog expression*, den Kopf hängen lassen, die betrübte Miene. — *v.n.* hängen; (*coll.*) — *on!* warte einen Moment! — *about*, herumstehen; herumlungern (*loiter*).
hanger-on [hæŋərˈɔn], *s.* der Anhänger, Mitläufer.
hangman [ˈhæŋmən], *s.* der Henker.
hanker [ˈhæŋkə], *v.n.* sich sehnen.
Hanoverian [hænoˈviəriən], *adj.* hannöversch. — *s.* der Hannoveraner.
hansom [ˈhænsəm], *s.* die zweirädrige Droschke.
haphazard [hæpˈhæzəd], *s.* der Zufall, das Geratewohl.
hapless [ˈhæplis], *adj.* unglücklich.
happen [hæpn], *v.n.* sich ereignen, passieren; — *to* . . ., zufällig . . .
happiness [ˈhæpinis], *s.* das Glück; die Glückseligkeit.
happy [ˈhæpi], *adj.* glücklich, glückselig.
harangue [həˈræŋ], *s.* die Ansprache. — *v.a.* einsprechen (auf, *Acc.*); anreden.
harass [ˈhærəs], *v.a.* plagen, quälen.
harbinger [ˈhɑːbindʒə], *s.* der Vorbote, Bote.
harbour [ˈhɑːbə], *s.* der Hafen. — *v.a.* beherbergen (*shelter*); hegen (*cherish*).
hard [hɑːd], *adj.* schwer (*difficult*); hart (*tough*); hartherzig (*miserly*); — *up*, in Not, in Geldverlegenheit; — *of hearing*, schwerhörig.
harden [hɑːdn], *v.a.* härten. — *v.n.* hart werden.
hardiness [ˈhɑːdinis], *s.* die Kraft, Stärke; die Rüstigkeit.
hardly [ˈhɑːdli], *adv.* kaum.
hardship [ˈhɑːdʃip], *s.* die Not, Bedrängnis (*need*); die Beschwerde (*complaint*).

hardware ['hɑ:dwɛə], *s.* die Eisenware(n).
hardy ['hɑ:di], *adj.* abgehärtet, stark; (*Bot.*) — *annual*, ein widerstandsfähiges Jahresgewächs.
hare [hɛə], *s.* (*Zool.*) der Hase; — *brained*, unbedacht, gedankenlos; — *lip*, die Hasenscharte.
harebell ['hɛəbel], *s.* (*Bot.*) die Glockenblume.
haricot ['hærikou], *s.* (*Bot.*) — *bean*, die welsche Bohne.
hark [hɑ:k], *v.n.* horchen.
harlequin ['hɑ:likwin], *s.* der Harlekin.
harlot ['hɑ:lət], *s.* die Hure.
harm [hɑ:m], *s.* das Leid, Unrecht; *do* — *to*, Schaden zufügen (*Dat.*). — *v.a.* verletzen (*hurt*); schaden (*damage*, *Dat.*).
harmful ['hɑ:mful], *adj.* schädlich.
harmless ['hɑ:mlis], *adj.* harmlos.
harmonious [hɑ:'mouniəs], *adj.* harmonisch; einmütig (*of one mind*).
harmonize ['hɑ:mənaiz], *v.a.* in Einklang bringen. — *v.n.* harmonieren, in Einklang stehen.
harmony ['hɑ:məni], *s.* (*Mus.*) die Harmonie; (*fig.*) der Einklang, die Einmütigkeit.
harness ['hɑ:nis], *s.* der Harnisch. — *v.a.* anschirren, anspannen (*horse*); (*fig.*) nutzbar machen.
harp [hɑ:p], *s.* (*Mus.*) die Harfe. — *v.n.* (*coll.*) — *upon*, herumreiten auf (*Dat.*).
harpoon [hɑ:'pu:n], *s.* die Harpune. — *v.a.* harpunieren.
harrow ['hærou], *s.* die Egge, Harke. — *v.a.* harken, eggen; quälen.
harry ['hæri], *v.a.* verheeren, quälen.
harsh [hɑ:ʃ], *adj.* herb, rauh (*rough*); streng (*severe*).
hart [hɑ:t], *s.* (*Zool.*) der Hirsch.
harvest ['hɑ:vist], *s.* die Ernte; — *home*, das Erntefest.
hash [hæʃ], *v.a.* zerhacken; vermischen (*mix up*). — *s.* das Hackfleisch; *make a* — *of things*, verpfuschen, alles verderben.
hasp [hæsp *or* hɑ:sp], *s.* der Haken, die Spange.
haste [heist], *s.* die Hast, Eile (*hurry*); die Voreiligkeit (*rashness*).
hasten [heisn], *v.n.* eilen, sich beeilen.
hasty ['heisti], *adj.* voreilig.
hat [hæt], *s.* der Hut; (*coll.*) *talk through o.'s* —, Unsinn reden.
hatch (1) [hætʃ], *s.* die Brut (*chickens*). — *v.a.*, *v.n.* (aus-)brüten; aushecken (*cunning*).
hatch (2) [hætʃ], *s.* das Servierfenster (*for serving food*); (*Naut.*) die Luke.
hatch (3) [hætʃ], *v.a.* (*Art*) schraffieren.
hatchet ['hætʃit], *s.* das Beil, die Axt; *bury the* —, das Kriegsbeil begraben.
hate [heit], *v.a.*, *v.n.* hassen; — *to* . . ., nicht . . . wollen. — *s.* der Haß, Widerwille, die Abneigung.
hateful ['heitful], *adj.* verhaßt (*hated*); gehässig (*hating*).
hatred ['heitrid], *s.* der Haß.
hatter ['hætə], *s.* der Hutmacher.
haughty ['hɔ:ti], *adj.* übermütig (*supercilious*); hochmütig, stolz (*proud*); hochnäsig (*giving o.s. airs*).
haul [hɔ:l], *v.a.* schleppen, ziehen. — *s.* das Schleppen; (*coll.*) die Beute.
haulage ['hɔ:lidʒ], *s.* der Schleppdienst, die Spedition.
haunch [hɔ:ntʃ], *s.* (*Anat.*) die Hüfte; der Schenkel (*horse*); die Keule (*venison*).
haunt [hɔ:nt], *v.a.* heimsuchen, spuken (in, *Dat.*); *it is* —*ed*, hier spuktes.
have [hæv], *v.a. irr.* haben, besitzen (*possess*); erhalten; lassen; — *to*, müssen; — *s.th. made, done*, etwas machen lassen.
haven [heivn], *s.* der Zufluchtsort.
haversack ['hævəsæk], *s.* der Brotbeutel.
havoc ['hævək], *s.* die Verwüstung, Verheerung.
hawk (1) [hɔ:k], *s.* (*Orn.*) der Habicht; der Falke (*falcon*).
hawk (2) [hɔ:k], *v.a.* hausieren.
hawker ['hɔ:kə], *s.* der Hausierer.
hawthorn ['hɔ:θɔ:n], *s.* (*Bot.*) der Hagedorn.
hay [hei], *s.* das Heu; — *fever*, der Heuschnupfen; — *loft*, der Heuboden; — *rick*, der Heuschober.
hazard ['hæzəd], *s.* der Zufall (*chance*); die Gefahr (*danger*); das Risiko (*risk*). — *v.a.* aufs Spiel setzen, riskieren.
hazardous ['hæzədəs], *adj.* gefährlich, gewagt.
haze [heiz], *s.* der Dunst, Nebeldunst.
hazel [heizl], *s.* (*Bot.*) die Haselstaude; — *nut*, die Haselnuß.
hazy ['heizi], *adj.* dunstig, nebelig.
he [hi:] *pers. pron.* er; — *who*, derjenige, welcher, wer.
head [hed], *s.* der Kopf; die Spitze (*of arrow*); der Leiter (*of firm*); (*Sch.*) der Direktor; die Überschrift (*heading*); die Krisis (*climax*); (*Pol.*) der Führer, das (Staats-)Oberhaupt. — *v.a.* anführen, führen; (*Mil.*) befehligen: — *v.n.* (*Naut.*) — *for*, Kurs nehmen auf (*Acc.*).
headache ['hedeik], *s.* (*Med.*) die Kopfschmerzen, *m. pl.*
headlamp ['hedlæmp], *s.* der Scheinwerfer.
headphone ['hedfoun], *s.* (*usually pl.*) der Kopfhörer.
headstrong ['hedstrɔŋ], *adj.* halsstarrig.
heady ['hedi], *adj.* hastig, ungestüm; berauschend (*liquor*).
heal [hi:l], *v.a.* heilen. — *v.n.* (zu)heilen, verheilen.
health [helθ], *s.* die Gesundheit; — *resort*, der Kurort; *your* (*good*) —*!* Gesundheit! auf Ihr Wohl! Prosit! (*drinking toast*).
healthy ['helθi], *adj.* gesund.
heap [hi:p], *s.* der Haufen, die Menge. — *v.a.* häufen, aufhäufen.

hear [hiə], *v.a.*, *v.n. irr.* hören; erfahren (*learn*); (*Law*) verhören (*evidence*).
hearing ['hiəriŋ], *s.* das Gehör (*auditory perception*); *within* —, in Hörweite; (*Law*) das Verhör.
hearsay ['hiəsei], *s.* das Hörensagen.
hearse [hə:s], *s.* der Leichenwagen.
heart [hɑ:t], *s.* das Herz; der Mut (*courage*); das Innerste (*core*); *by* —, auswendig; *take to* —, beherzigen; *take — from*, Mut fassen (aus, *Dat.*).
heartburn ['hɑ:tbə:n], *s.* (*Med.*) das Sodbrennen.
heartfelt ['hɑ:tfelt], *adj.* herzlich.
hearth [hɑ:θ], *s.* der Herd.
hearty ['hɑ:ti], *adj.* herzlich; aufrichtig (*sincere*); herzhaft.
heat [hi:t], *s.* die Hitze, Wärme; die Brunst (*animals*). — *v.a.* heizen (*fuel*); erhitzen (*make hot*).
heath [hi:θ], *s.* die Heide.
heathen [hi:ðən], *s.* der Heide, Ungläubige.
heather ['heðə], *s.* (*Bot.*) das Heidekraut.
heating ['hi:tiŋ], *s.* die Heizung.
heave [hi:v], *v.a. reg. & irr.* heben, hieben. — *v.n.* sich heben und senken.
heaven [hevn], *s.* der Himmel; *good —s!* ach, du lieber Himmel!
heaviness ['hevinis], *s.* die Schwere.
heavy ['hevi], *adj.* schwer; schwerwiegend (*grave*).
Hebrew ['hi:bru:], *adj.* hebräisch. — *s.* der Hebräer, der Jude.
hectic ['hektik], *adj.* hektisch, aufgeregt.
hector ['hektə], *v.a.* tyrannisieren (*bully*). — *v.n.* renommieren, prahlen.
hedge [hedʒ], *s.* die Hecke. — *v.a.* einhegen, einzäunen.
hedgehog ['hedʒhɔg], *s.* (*Zool.*) der Igel.
hedgerow ['hedʒrou], *s.* die Baumhecke.
heed [hi:d], *s.* die Hut, Aufmerksamkeit. — *v.a.* beachten.
heedless ['hi:dlis], *adj.* unachtsam.
heel [hi:l], *s.* die Ferse (*foot*); der Absatz (*shoe*); *take to o.'s —s*, die Flucht ergreifen; (*Am. sl.*) der Lump.
heifer ['hefə], *s.* (*Zool.*) die junge Kuh.
height [hait], *s.* die Höhe, Anhöhe; die Größe (*tallness*); der Hügel (*hill*).
heighten [haitn], *v.a.* erhöhen.
heir [εə], *s.* der Erbe (*to*, *Genit.*).
heiress ['εəres], *s.* die Erbin.
heirloom ['εəlu:m], *s.* das Erbstück.
helicopter ['helikɔptə], *s.* (*Aviat.*) der Hubschrauber.
hell [hel], *s.* die Hölle. — *interj.* zum Teufel!
hellish ['heliʃ], *adj.* höllisch.
helm [helm], *s.* das Steuer, Steuerruder.
helmet ['helmit], *s.* der Helm.
helmsman ['helmzmən], *s.* (*Naut.*) der Steuermann.
help [help], *v.a.*, *v.n.* helfen (*Dat.*); *I cannot — laughing*, ich muß lachen; *I cannot — it*, ich kann nichts dafür. — *v.r.* — *o.s.*, sich bedienen. — *s.* die Hilfe, Unterstützung.
helpful ['helpful], *adj.* behilflich, hilfreich.
helping ['helpiŋ], *s.* die Portion.
helpless ['helplis], *adj.* hilflos.
helpmate, helpmeet ['helpmeit, -mi:t], *s.* der Gehilfe, die Gehilfin.
helter-skelter ['heltə'skeltə], *adv.* Hals über Kopf.
hem [hem], *s.* der Saum. — *v.a.* (*Tail.*) einsäumen, säumen.
hemisphere ['hemisfiə], *s.* die Halbkugel, Hemisphäre.
hemlock ['hemlɔk], *s.* der Schierling.
hemp [hemp], *s.* der Hanf.
hemstitch ['hemstitʃ], *s.* der Hohlsaum.
hen [hen], *s.* die Henne (*poultry*); das Weibchen (*other birds*).
hence [hens], *adv.* von hier; von jetzt an.
henceforth ['hens'fɔ:θ], *adv.* fortan, von nun an.
henpecked ['henpekd], *adj.* unter dem Pantoffel stehend.
her [hə:], *pers. pron.* sie (*Acc.*), ihr (*Dat.*). — *poss. adj.* ihr.
herald ['herəld], *s.* der Herold. — *v.a.* ankündigen.
heraldry ['herəldri], *s.* die Wappenkunde.
herb [hə:b], *s.* (*Bot.*) das Kraut.
herbaceous [hə:'beiʃəs], *adj.* krautartig.
herbage ['hə:bidʒ], *s.* das Gras; (*Law*) das Weiderecht.
herbal ['hə:bəl], *adj.* krautartig, Kräuter-, Kraut-.
herd [hə:d], *s.* die Herde. — *v.n.* sich zusammenfinden.
here [hiə], *adv.* hier.
hereafter [hiər'ɑ:ftə], *adv.* hernach, künftig. — *s.* die Zukunft; das Jenseits.
hereby [hiə'bai], *adv.* hiermit.
hereditary [hi'reditəri], *adj.* erblich.
heredity [hi'rediti], *s.* (*Biol.*) die Erblichkeit, Vererbung.
heresy ['herisi], *s.* die Ketzerei.
heretic ['heritik], *s.* der Ketzer.
heretofore ['hiətufɔ:], *adv.* zuvor, vormals.
heritage ['heritidʒ], *s.* die Erbschaft.
hermetic [hə:'metik], *adj.* luftdicht.
hermit ['hə:mit], *s.* der Eremit, Einsiedler.
hero ['hiərou], *s.* der Held.
heroic [hi'rouik], *adj.* heldenhaft, heldenmütig.
heroine ['heroin], *s.* die Heldin.
heroism ['heroizm], *s.* der Heldenmut.
heron ['herən], *s.* (*Orn.*) der Reiher.
herring ['heriŋ], *s.* (*Zool.*) der Hering; *red* —, die Ablenkungsfinte, das Ablenkungsmanöver; — *bone*, die Gräte; *pickled* —, der eingemachte Hering.
hers [hə:z], *poss. pron.* ihr, der ihre, der ihrige.
herself [hə:'self], *pers. pron.* sich; sie selbst.
hesitate ['heziteit], *v.n.* zögern, zaudern; unschlüssig sein (*be undecided*).

hesitation [hezi'teiʃən], *s.* das Zögern, Zaudern; das Bedenken (*deliberation*).
Hessian ['heʃən], *adj.* hessisch. — *s.* der Hesse.
hessian ['hesiən], *s.* die Sackleinwand (*textile*).
heterodox ['hetərədɔks], *adj.* irrgläubig.
heterogeneous [hetəro'dʒi:niəs], *adj.* heterogen, ungleichartig.
hew [hju:], *v.a. irr.* hauen.
hexagonal [hek'sægənəl], *adj.* sechseckig.
hiatus [hai'eitəs], *s.* die Lücke.
hibernate ['haibəneit], *v.n.* überwintern.
hibernation [haibə'neiʃən], *s.* der Winterschlaf.
hiccup ['hikʌp], *s.* (*usually pl.*) (*Med.*) der Schlucken, Schluckauf.
hickory ['hikəri], *s.* (*Bot.*) das Hickoryholz.
hide (1) [haid], *v.a. irr.* verstecken, verbergen. — *v.n. irr.* sich verbergen; — *and seek*, das Versteckspiel.
hide (2) [haid], *s.* die Haut (*of animal*), das Fell, (*tanned*) das Leder.
hideous ['hidiəs], *adj.* häßlich, scheußlich, furchtbar.
hiding (1) ['haidiŋ], *s.* das Versteck.
hiding (2) ['haidiŋ], *s.* die Tracht Prügel.
hierarchy ['haiərɑ:ki], *s.* die Hierarchie.
higgle [higl] *see* **haggle**.
higgledy-piggledy ['higldi'pigldi], *adv.* wüst durcheinander.
high [hai], *adj.* hoch; erhaben, vornehm; angegangen (*meat*); — *school*, die höhere Schule; — *time*, höchste Zeit; (*Am.*) vergnügliche Zeit; *High Church*, die Hochkirche. — *s.* (*Meteor.*) das Hoch.
Highness ['hainis], *s.* die Hoheit (*title*).
highroad, highway ['hairoud, 'haiwei], *s.* die Haupt- *or* Landstraße.
highwayman ['haiweimən], *s.* der Straßenräuber.
hike [haik], *v.n.* wandern, einen Ausflug machen. — *s.* die Wanderung, der Ausflug.
hilarious [hi'lɛəriəs], *adj.* fröhlich, lustig, ausgelassen.
hill [hil], *s.* der Hügel, Berg.
hilt [hilt], *s.* der Griff.
him [him], *pers. pron.* ihn, ihm.
himself [him'self], *pers. pron.* sich; er selbst.
hind [haind], *s.* (*Zool.*) die Hirschkuh, Hindin.
hinder ['hində], *v.a.* hindern.
hindmost ['haindmoust], *adj.* hinterst; *the devil take the* —, den letzten hol der Teufel! nach mir die Sintflut!
hindrance ['hindrəns], *s.* das Hindernis; (*Law*) *without let or* —, ohne Hinderung.
Hindu [hin'du:], *s.* der Hindu.
hinge [hindʒ], *s.* die Angel, der Angelpunkt. — *v.n.* sich um etwas drehen; von etwas abhängen (on, *Dat.*).
hint [hint], *v.n.* zu verstehen geben, auf etwas hindeuten (*at*, auf, *Acc.*), andeuten. — *s.* die Andeutung, der Fingerzeig.
hip (1) [hip], *s.* (*Anat.*) die Hüfte.
hip (2) [hip], *s.* (*Bot.*) die Hagebutte.
hire ['haiə], *v.a.* (ver-)mieten (*car etc.*); anstellen (*man etc.*). — *s.* die Miete; der Lohn (*wage*); — *purchase*, der Abzahlungskauf, die Ratenzahlung.
hireling ['haiəliŋ], *s.* der Mietling.
hirsute ['hə:sju:t], *adj.* behaart, haarig.
his [hiz], *poss. adj.* sein, seine. — *poss. pron.* sein, der seinige, der seine.
hiss [his], *v.n.* zischen (*at*, auf, *Acc.*). — *s.* das Zischen.
historian [his'tɔ:riən], *s.* der Historiker, der Geschichtsschreiber.
historical [his'tɔrikəl], *adj.* historisch, geschichtlich.
history ['histəri], *s.* die Geschichte, die Geschichtswissenschaft.
histrionic [histri'ɔnik], *adj.* schauspielerisch.
hit [hit], *v.a. irr.* schlagen, stoßen. — *s.* der Schlag, der Treffer (*on the target*); (*Am.*) der Schlager, Erfolg (*success*); — *parade*, die Schlagerparade.
hitch [hitʃ], *v.a.* anhaken (*hook*); anhängen; — *a lift*, — *hike*, per Anhalter fahren. — *s.* der Nachteil, der Haken.
hither ['hiðə], *adv.* hierher.
hitherto [hiðə'tu:], *adv.* bisher.
hive [haiv], *s.* der Bienenkorb; Bienenstock; — *of bees*, der Schwarm.
hoar [hɔ:], *adj.* eisgrau, weißlich; — *frost*, der Reif.
hoard [hɔ:d], *v.a.* hamstern. — *s.* der Vorrat, Schatz.
hoarding ['hɔ:diŋ], *s.* die Umzäunung, die Bretterwand; die Reklamewand.
hoarse [hɔ:s], *adj.* heiser.
hoarseness ['hɔ:snis], *s.* die Heiserkeit.
hoax [houks], *s.* der Betrug, die Irreführung; der Schabernack (*in fun*). — *v.a.* betrügen; foppen (*in fun*).
hobble [hɔbl], *v.n.* humpeln. — *v.a.* an den Füßen fesseln.
hobby ['hɔbi], *s.* das Steckenpferd, Hobby, die Liebhaberei.
hobgoblin [hɔb'gɔblin], *s.* der Kobold.
hobnail ['hɔbneil], *s.* der Hufnagel.
hobnailed ['hɔbneild], *adj.* — *boots*, genagelte Stiefel, *m. pl.*
hobnob [hɔb'nɔb], *v.n.* (*coll.*) vertraulich sein.
hock (1) [hɔk], *s.* (*Anat.*) das Sprunggelenk.
hock (2) [hɔk], *s.* (*wine*) der Rheinwein.
hod [hɔd], *s.* (*Build.*) der Trog; der Eimer (*coal*).
hodge-podge *see under* **hotchpotch**.
hoe [hou], *s.* die Hacke, Harke. — *v.a.*, *v.n.* hacken, harken.
hog [hɔg], *s.* das Schwein. — *v.a.* verschlingen (*food*); an sich reißen (*grasp*).
hogshead ['hɔgzhed], *s.* das Oxhoft.
hoist [hɔist], *v.a.* hissen.

hold [hould], *v.a., v.n. irr.* halten (*keep*); enthalten (*contain*); behaupten (*assert*); meinen (*think*); gelten (*be valid*); — *forth*, deklamieren; — *good*, sich bewähren; — *out*, hinhalten (*hope*); (*endure*) aushalten; — *up*, aufhalten. — *s.* (*Naut.*) der Schiffsraum; die Macht (*power*).
holder [ˈhouldə], *s.* der Inhaber, Besitzer.
holding [ˈhouldiŋ], *s.* das Pachtgut (*farm*); der Besitz (*property*); (*Comm.*) der Trust.
hole [houl], *s.* das Loch; die Höhle (*cavity*). — *v.a.* aushöhlen; (*Golf*) ins Loch spielen.
holiday [ˈhɔlidei], *s.* der Feiertag; der Urlaub (*vacation*); (*pl.*) die Ferien, *pl.*
holiness [ˈhoulinis], *s.* die Heiligkeit.
hollow [ˈhɔlou], *adj.* hohl. — *s.* die Höhlung; die Höhle.
holly [ˈhɔli], *s.* (*Bot.*) die Stechpalme.
hollyhock [ˈhɔlihɔk], *s.* (*Bot.*) die Stockrose.
holocaust [ˈhɔlokɔ:st], *s.* das Brandopfer; die Katastrophe.
holster [ˈhoulstə], *s.* die Pistolentasche, die Halfter.
holy [ˈhouli], *adj.* heilig; *Holy Week*, die Karwoche.
homage [ˈhɔmidʒ], *s.* die Huldigung; *pay — to*, huldigen (*Dat.*).
home [houm], *s.* das Heim, die Wohnung; die Heimat; *at —*, zu Hause; *Home Office*, das Innenministerium; — *Rule*, (*Pol.*) die Selbstverwaltung.
homer [ˈhoumə] (*Am.*) *see* **homing pigeon**.
homesick [ˈhoumsik], *adj.* an Heimweh leidend.
homestead [ˈhoumsted], *s.* der Bauernhof.
homicide [ˈhɔmisaid], *s.* der Mord (*crime*); der Mörder (*killer*).
homily [ˈhɔmili], *s.* die Predigt; Moralpredigt.
homing pigeon [ˈhoumiŋˈpidʒən], *s.* die Brieftaube.
homogeneous [hɔməˈdʒi:niəs], *adj.* homogen; gleichartig.
hone [houn], *s.* der Wetzstein. — *v.a.* (*blade, knife*) abziehen.
honest [ˈɔnist], *adj.* ehrlich, aufrichtig.
honesty [ˈɔnisti], *s.* die Ehrlichkeit.
honey [ˈhʌni], *s.* der Honig; (*Am., coll.*) Liebling!
honeycomb [ˈhʌnikoum], *s.* die Honigwabe.
honeymoon [ˈhʌnimu:n], *s.* die Flitterwochen.
honorarium [ɔnəˈrɛəriəm], *s.* das Honorar.
honorary [ˈɔnərəri], *adj.* Ehren-, ehrenamtlich.
honour [ˈɔnə], *s.* die Ehre; *your —*, Euer Ehrwürden, Euer Gnaden (*title*). — *v.a.* ehren, auszeichnen.
honourable [ˈɔnərəbl], *adj.* ehrenwert, ehrenvoll; Hochwohlgeboren (*title*).
hood [hud], *s.* die Kapuze; das akademische Gradabzeichen über dem Talar; (*Hunt.*) die Haube; *—ed falcon*, der Jagdfalke (mit Haube).
hoodwink [ˈhudwiŋk], *v.a.* täuschen.
hoof [hu:f *or* huf], *s.* der Huf (*horse*); die Klaue.
hook [huk], *s.* der Haken; *by — or by crook*, mit allen Mitteln. — *v.a.* angeln, fangen.
hooked [hukd], *adj.* gekrümmt, hakenförmig.
hooligan [ˈhu:ligən], *s.* der Rowdy.
hoop [hu:p], *s.* der Reifen. — *v.a.* (ein Faß) binden.
hooper [ˈhu:pə], *s.* der Böttcher.
hoopoe [ˈhu:pou], *s.* (*Orn.*) der Wiedehopf.
hoot [hu:t], *v.n.* schreien (*owl*); ertönen (*siren*); hupen (*car*).
hooter [ˈhu:tə], *s.* die Sirene (*siren*); die Hupe (*car*).
hop (1) [hɔp], *v.n.* hüpfen, tanzen; *—ping mad*, ganz verrückt.
hop (2) [hɔp], *s.* (*Bot.*) der Hopfen. — *v.a.* (*beer*) hopfen, Hopfen zusetzen (*Dat.*). — *v.n.* Hopfen ernten.
hope [houp], *s.* die Hoffnung. — *v.n.* hoffen (*for*, auf, *Acc.*).
hopeless [ˈhouplis], *adj.* hoffnungslos.
horizon [həˈraizən], *s.* der Horizont.
horizontal [hɔriˈzɔntl], *adj.* horizontal, waagrecht.
horn [hɔ:n], *s.* das Horn; (*Mus.*) *French —*, das Waldhorn, Horn; (*Motor.*) die Hupe.
hornet [ˈhɔ:nit], *s.* (*Ent.*) die Hornisse.
hornpipe [ˈhɔ:npaip], *s.* (*Mus.*) der Matrosentanz; die Hornpfeife.
horrible [ˈhɔribl], *adj.* schrecklich.
horrid [ˈhɔrid], *adj.* abscheulich.
horrific [hɔˈrifik], *adj.* schrecklich, schreckenerregend.
horror [ˈhɔrə], *s.* der Schrecken, das Entsetzen; (*fig.*) der Greuel.
horse [hɔ:s], *s.* das Pferd, Roß; *on —back*, zu Pferd.
horseman [ˈhɔ:smən], *s.* der Reiter.
horsepower [ˈhɔ:spauə], *s.* die Pferdestärke.
horseradish [ˈhɔ:srædiʃ], *s.* der Meerrettich.
horseshoe [ˈhɔ:sʃu:], *s.* das Hufeisen.
horticulture [ˈhɔ:tikʌltʃə], *s.* der Gartenbau.
hose [houz], *s.* die Strümpfe, *m. pl.* (*stockings*); der Schlauch (*water pipe*).
hosiery [ˈhouʒəri], *s.* die Strumpfwarenindustrie; die Strumpfwaren.
hospitable [hɔsˈpitəbl], *adj.* gastlich, gastfreundlich.
hospital [ˈhɔspitl], *s.* das Krankenhaus.
hospitality [hɔspiˈtæliti], *s.* die Gastlichkeit, Gastfreundschaft.
host (1) [houst], *s.* der Gastwirt (*landlord*); der Gastgeber.
host (2) [houst], *s.* (*Rel.*) *angelic —*, die Engelschar; (*Mil.*) das Heer, die Heerschar.
host (3) [houst], *s.* (*Eccl.*) die Hostie.

hostage ['hɔstidʒ], *s.* die Geisel.
hostess ['houstis *or* –tes], *s.* die Gastgeberin; *air* —, die Stewardeß.
hostile ['hɔstail], *adj.* feindlich; feindselig (*inimical*).
hot [hɔt], *adj.* heiß; hitzig (*temperament*); scharf, gewürzt (*of spices*); (*fig.*) heftig, erbittert.
hotchpotch, hodge-podge ['hɔtʃpɔtʃ, 'hɔdʒpɔdʒ], *s.* das Mischmasch.
hotel [ho(u)'tel], *s.* das Hotel, der Gasthof.
hothouse ['hɔthaus], *s.* das Treibhaus.
hound [haund], *s.* (*Zool.*) der Jagdhund. — *v.a.* hetzen.
hour ['auə], *s.* die Stunde; — *hand*, der Stundenzeiger; *for* —*s*, studenlang; *keep early* (*late*) —*s*, früh (spät) zu Bett gehen.
hourglass ['auəglɑ:s], *s.* die Sanduhr.
hourly ['auəli], *adj., adv.*, stündlich.
house [haus], *s.* das Haus; (*Comm.*) die Firma. — [hauz], *v.a.* beherbergen, unterbringen.
houseboat ['hausbout], *s.* das Wohnboot.
housebreaking ['hausbreikiŋ], *s.* der Einbruch.
household ['haushould], *s.* der Haushalt.
housekeeper ['hauski:pə], *s.* die Haushälterin.
housewife ['hauswaif], *s.* die Hausfrau.
housing ['hauziŋ], *s.* die Unterbringung; — *department*, das Wohnungsamt.
hovel ['hɔvl *or* hʌvl], *s.* die Hütte.
hover ['hɔvə *or* 'hʌvə], *v.n.* schweben, schwanken.
how [hau], *adv.* wie; — *do you do?* (*in introduction*) sehr angenehm; — *are you?* wie geht es Ihnen, Dir?
however [hau'evə], *adv.* wie immer, wie auch immer, wie sehr auch. — *conj.* doch, jedoch, dennoch.
howl [haul], *v.n.* heulen. — *s.* das Geheul.
hoyden [hɔidn], *s.* das wilde Mädchen.
hub [hʌb], *s.* die Nabe (am Rad); — *of the universe*, die Mitte der Welt.
hubbub ['hʌbʌb], *s.* der Tumult, Lärm.
huckaback ['hʌkəbæk], *s.* der Zwillich (*textile*).
huckle [hʌkl], *s.* die Hüfte.
huddle [hʌdl], *v.n.* sich drängen, sich zusammenducken. — *s.* das Gedränge.
hue [hju:], *s.* der Farbton, die Tönung.
huff [hʌf], *s.* die schlechte Laune, die Mißstimmung.
huffy ['hʌfi], *adj.* mißmutig, übel gelaunt.
hug [hʌg], *v.a.* umarmen. — *s.* die Umarmung.
huge [hju:dʒ], *adj.* riesig, groß, ungeheuer.
Huguenot ['hju:gənou *or* –nɔt], *s.* der Hugenotte. — *adj.* hugenottisch, Hugenotten-.
hulk [hʌlk], *s.* (*Naut.*) das Schiffsinnere, der Schiffsrumpf; der schwerfällige Mensch.
hull [hʌl], *s.* die Hülse, Schale; (*Naut.*, *Aviat.*) der Rumpf. — *v.a.* (*Engin.*) hülsen.
hullo! [hə'lou], *interj.* hallo!
hum [hʌm], *v.n.* summen, brummen. — *s.* das Summen, Brummen, Gemurmel (*murmuring*).
human ['hju:mən], *adj.* menschlich. — *s.* der Mensch.
humane [hju:'mein], *adj.* menschenfreundlich.
humanity [hju:'mæniti], *s.* die Menschheit (*mankind*); die Menschlichkeit (*compassion*); (*pl.*) die klassischen Fächer, *n. pl.*, die humanistischen Wissenschaften, *f. pl.*
humanize ['hju:mənaiz], *v.a.* menschlich oder gesittet machen.
humble [hʌmbl], *adj.* demütig; bescheiden (*modest*); unterwürfig (*servile*). — *v.a.* erniedrigen (*humiliate*).
humbug ['hʌmbʌg], *s.* die Schwindelei (*swindle*); der Schwindler (*crook*); der Unsinn (*nonsense*).
humdrum ['hʌmdrʌm], *adj.* langweilig, eintönig.
humid ['hju:mid], *adj.* feucht.
humidity [hju:'miditi], *s.* die Feuchtigkeit.
humiliate [hju:'milieit], *v.a.* erniedrigen.
humility [hju:'militi], *s.* die Demut.
humming-bird ['hʌmiŋbə:d], *s.* (*Orn.*) der Kolibri.
humming-top ['hʌmiŋtɔp], *s.* der Brummkreisel.
humorous ['hju:mərəs], *adj.* humoristisch, spaßhaft, komisch.
humour ['hju:mə], *s.* der Humor, die (gute) Laune. — *v.a.* in guter Laune erhalten, gut stimmen; willfahren (*Dat.*).
hump [hʌmp], *s.* der Buckel, der Höcker.
hunch [hʌntʃ], *s.* der Buckel; *have a* —, das Gefühl haben.
hunchback ['hʌntʃbæk], *s.* der Bucklige.
hundred ['hʌndrəd], *num. adj. a* —, hundert.
hundredweight ['hʌndrədweit], *s.* der (englische) Zentner.
Hungarian [hʌŋ'gɛəriən], *adj.* ungarisch. — *s.* der Ungar.
hunger ['hʌŋgə], *s.* der Hunger.
hungry ['hʌŋgri], *adj.* hungrig.
hunt [hʌnt], *s.* die Jagd. — *v.a.*, *v.n.* jagen.
hunter ['hʌntə], *s.* der Jäger.
hurdle [hə:dl], *s.* die Hürde.
hurdy-gurdy ['hə:digə:di], *s.* der Leierkasten.
hurl [hə:l], *v.a.* schleudern, werfen.
hurly-burly ['hə:libə:li], *s.* der Wirrwarr.
hurricane ['hʌrikin], *s.* der Orkan; — *lamp*, die Sturmlaterne.
hurried ['hʌrid], *adj.* eilig, hastig.

hurry ['hʌri], *v.n.* eilen, sich beeilen; — *to do*, eiligst tun. — *v.a.* beschleunigen. — *s.* die Eile, Hast, Beschleunigung.
hurt [hə:t], *v.a. irr.* verletzen; wehetun (*Dat.*); (*verbally*) kränken. — *s.* die Verletzung, Kränkung.
hurtful ['hə:tful], *adj.* schädlich, kränkend.
husband ['hʌzbənd], *s.* der Mann, Ehemann, Gemahl. — *v.a.* verwalten, sparsam verfahren mit (*Dat.*).
husbandman ['hʌzbəndmən], *s.* der Landwirt.
husbandry ['hʌzbəndri], *s.* die Landwirtschaft.
hush [hʌʃ], *v.a.* zum Schweigen bringen. — *s.* die Stille; — *money*, das Schweigegeld.
husky (1) ['hʌski], *adj.* heiser (*voice*).
husky (2) ['hʌski], *s.* (*Zool.*) der Eskimohund.
hussy ['hʌzi], *s.* (*coll.*) das Frauenzimmer.
hustings ['hʌstiŋz], *s.* die Wahltribüne.
hustle [hʌsl], *v.a.* drängen, stoßen. — *s.* das Gedränge.
hut [hʌt], *s.* die Hütte, Baracke.
hutch [hʌtʃ], *s.* der Trog, Kasten (*chest*).
hybrid ['haibrid], *adj.* Bastard-. — *s.* der Bastard.
hydraulic [hai'drɔ:lik], *adj.* hydraulisch.
hydrogen ['haidrədʒən], *s.* der Wasserstoff.
hydroelectric [haidroui'lektrik], *adj.* hydroelektrisch.
hyena [hai'i:nə], *s.* (*Zool.*) die Hyäne.
hygiene ['haidʒi:n], *s.* die Hygiene, Gesundheitslehre.
hymn [him], *s.* die Hymne, das Kirchenlied.
hymnal ['himnəl], *s.* das Gesangbuch.
hyper- ['haipə], *prefix.* über-.
hyperbole [hai'pə:bəli], *s.* die Übertreibung.
hyphen ['haifən], *s.* der Bindestrich.
hypnosis [hip'nousis], *s.* die Hypnose.
hypochondriac [haipo'kɔndriæk], *adj.* hypochondrisch. — *s.* der Hypochonder.
hypocrisy [hi'pɔkrisi], *s.* die Heuchelei.
hypocrite ['hipəkrit], *s.* der Heuchler.
hypothesis [hai'pɔθisis], *s.* die Hypothese.
hypothetical [haipə'θetikəl], *adj.* hypothetisch, angenommen.
hysteria [his'tiəriə], *s.* die Hysterie.

I

I [ai]. das I.
I [ai], *pers. pron.* ich.

ice [ais], *s.* das Eis; — *bound*, eingefroren; (*Naut.*) — *breaker*, der Eisbrecher; (*Am.*) —*box*, der Kühlschrank; — *cream*, das Eis; das Gefrorene. — *v.a.* (*confectionery*) verzuckern; (*cake*) glasieren.
Icelander ['aisləndə], *s.* der Isländer.
Icelandic [ais'lændik], *adj.* isländisch.
icicle ['aisikl], *s.* der Eiszapfen.
icy ['aisi], *adj.* eisig.
idea [ai'diə], *s.* die Idee.
ideal [ai'diəl], *adj.* ideal. — *s.* das Ideal.
idealize [ai'diəlaiz], *v.a.* idealisieren.
identical [ai'dentikəl], *adj.* identisch, gleich.
identification [aidentifi'keiʃən], *s.* die Gleichsetzung, Identifizierung.
identify [ai'dentifai], *v.a.* identifizieren, gleichsetzen.
identity [ai'dentiti], *s.* die Identität, Gleichheit.
idiocy ['idiəsi], *s.* der Blödsinn.
idiom ['idiəm], *s.* das Idiom, die sprachliche Eigentümlichkeit.
idiomatic [idio'mætik], *adj.* idiomatisch.
idiosyncrasy [idio'siŋkrəsi], *s.* die Empfindlichkeit; die Abneigung (gegen, *Acc.*); die Idiosynkrasie.
idle [aidl], *adj.* unnütz (*useless*); müßig, faul (*lazy*). — *v.n.* träge sein.
idleness ['aidlnis], *s.* der Müßiggang, die Faulheit.
idiot ['idiət], *s.* der Idiot.
idol [aidl], *s.* das Götzenbild; das Idol.
idolatry [ai'dɔlətri], *s.* die Götzenverehrung.
idolize ['aidolaiz], *v.a.* vergöttern, abgöttisch lieben.
idyll ['aidil *or* 'idil], *s.* die Idylle, das Idyll.
idyllic [ai'dilik *or* i'dilik], *adj.* idyllisch.
if [if], *conj.* wenn, falls (*in case*); ob (*whether*).
igneous ['igniəs], *adj.* feurig.
ignite [ig'nait], *v.a.* entzünden. — *v.n.* zur Entzündung kommen, sich entzünden.
ignition [ig'niʃən], *s.* die Zündung.
ignoble [ig'noubl], *adj.* unedel, gemein.
ignominious [igno'miniəs], *adj.* schimpflich, schmählich.
ignominy ['ignomini], *s.* die Schande, Schmach.
ignoramus [ignə'reiməs], *s.* der Unwissende.
ignorance ['ignərəns], *s.* die Unwissenheit, Unkenntnis.
ignorant ['ignərənt], *adj.* unwissend.
ignore [ig'nɔ:], *v.a.* ignorieren, nicht beachten.
ill [il], *adj.* böse, schlimm (*bad*); krank (*sick*); — *feeling*, die Verstimmung. — *adv.* — *at ease*, unbequem, verlegen; *can — afford*, kann sich kaum leisten ...; —*timed*, zu unrechter Zeit.
illbred [il'bred], *adj.* ungezogen.
illegal [i'li:gəl], *adj.* illegal, ungesetzlich.
illegibility [iledʒi'biliti], *s.* die Unleserlichkeit.

illegible [i'ledʒibl], *adj.* unleserlich.
illegitimacy [ili'dʒitiməsi], *s.* die Unehelichkeit, Illegitimität.
illegitimate [ili'dʒitimit], *adj.* illegitim, unehelich.
illicit [[i'lisit], *adj.* unerlaubt.
illiteracy [i'litərəsi], *s.* die Unkenntnis des Schreibens und Lesens, das Analphabetentum.
illiterate [i'litərit], *s.* der Analphabet.
illness ['ilnis], *s.* die Krankheit.
illogical [i'lɔdʒikəl], *adj.* unlogisch.
illuminate [i'lju:mineit], *v.a.* erleuchten; (*fig.*) aufklären.
illuminating [i'lju:mineitiŋ], *adj.* aufschlußreich.
illumination [ilju:mi'neiʃən], *s.* die Erleuchtung; die Erklärung (*explanation*).
illusion [i'lju:ʒən], *s.* die Illusion, Täuschung.
illusive, illusory [i'lju:ziv, i'lju:zəri], *adj.* trügerisch, täuschend.
illustrate ['iləstreit], *v.a.* erläutern; illustrieren (*with pictures*).
illustration [iləs'treiʃən], *s.* die Illustration (*pictorial*); Erläuterung, Erklärung; das Beispiel (*instance*).
illustrious [i'lʌstriəs], *adj.* glänzend, berühmt.
image ['imidʒ], *s.* das Bild; das Ebenbild; die Erscheinung (*appearance*).
imagery ['imidʒəri], *s.* der Gebrauch von Stilbildern (*style*), die Bildersprache.
imaginable [i'mædʒinəbl], *adj.* denkbar.
imaginary [i'mædʒinəri], *adj.* eingebildet, nicht wirklich, vermeintlich.
imagination [imædʒi'neiʃən], *s.* die Einbildung; die Vorstellung; die Phantasie.
imaginative [i'mædʒinətiv], *adj.* erfinderisch, voll Phantasie.
imagine [i'mædʒin], *v.a.* sich vorstellen, sich denken.
imbecile ['imbisail *or* 'imbisi:l], *adj.* schwachsinnig. — *s.* der Idiot.
imbecility [imbi'siliti], *s.* der Schwachsinn.
imbibe [im'baib], *v.a.* trinken; (*fig.*) in sich aufnehmen.
imbroglio [im'brouliou], *s.* die Verwicklung.
imbue [im'bju:], *v.a.* erfüllen, sättigen (*fig.*).
imitate ['imiteit], *v.a.* nachahmen, imitieren.
imitation [imi'teiʃən], *s.* die Nachahmung, Imitation; — *leather*, das Kunstleder.
immaculate [i'mækjulit], *adj.* unbefleckt, makellos.
immaterial [imə'tiəriəl], *adj.* unwesentlich, unwichtig.
immature [imə'tjuə], *adj.* unreif.
immeasurable [i'meʒərəbl], *adj.* unermeßlich, unmeßbar.
immediate [i'mi:djit], *adj.* unmittelbar, direkt, sofortig.
immediately [i'mi:djətli], *adv.* sofort.
immemorial [imi'mɔ:riəl], *adj.* undenklich, ewig.
immense [i'mens], *adj.* unermeßlich, ungeheuer.
immerse [i'mə:s], *v.a.* eintauchen.
immersion [i'mə:ʃən], *s.* das Eintauchen, die Versenkung; — *heater*, der Tauchsieder.
immigrant ['imigrənt], *s.* der Einwanderer.
imminent ['iminənt], *adj.* bevorstehend.
immobile [i'moubail], *adj.* unbeweglich.
immoderate [i'mɔdərit], *adj.* unmäßig.
immodest [i'mɔdist], *adj.* unbescheiden; unsittlich, unanständig (*immoral*).
immodesty [i'mɔdisti], *s.* die Unanständigkeit (*indecency*); Unbescheidenheit (*presumption*).
immolate ['iməleit], *v.a.* opfern.
immoral [i'mɔrəl], *adj.* unsittlich, unmoralisch.
immortal [i'mɔ:tl], *adj.* unsterblich.
immortalize [i'mɔ:təlaiz], *v.a.* verewigen, unsterblich machen.
immovable [i'mu:vəbl], *adj.* unbeweglich (*fig.*).
immunity [i'mju:niti], *s.* die Freiheit, Straffreiheit; Immunität.
immutable [im'ju:təbl], *adj.* unabänderlich; unveränderlich.
imp [imp], *s.* der Knirps, Kobold, kleine Schelm.
impair [im'pɛə], *v.a.* beeinträchtigen; vermindern (*reduce*).
impale [im'peil], *v.a.* aufspießen; durchbohren.
impalpable [im'pælpəbl], *adj.* unfühlbar, unmerklich.
impart [im'pɑ:t], *v.a.* erteilen; verleihen (*confer*); mitteilen (*inform*).
impartial [im'pɑ:ʃəl], *adj.* unparteiisch.
impartiality [impɑ:ʃi'æliti], *s.* die Unparteilichkeit, Objektivität.
impassable [im'pɑ:səbl], *adj.* unwegsam; unpassierbar.
impasse [im'pæs], *s.* der völlige Stillstand.
impassioned [im'pæʃənd], *adj.* leidenschaftlich.
impassive [im'pæsiv], *adj.* unempfindlich.
impatience [im'peiʃəns], *s.* die Ungeduld.
impatient [im'peiʃənt], *adj.* ungeduldig.
impeach [im'pi:tʃ], *v.a.* anklagen.
impeachment [im'pi:tʃmənt], *s.* die Anklage.
impecunious [impi'kju:niəs], *adj.* unbemittelt, mittellos.
impede [im'pi:d], *v.a.* behindern, verhindern.
impediment [im'pedimənt], *s.* das Hindernis.
impel [im'pel], *v.a.* antreiben; zwingen (*force*).

impending [im'pendiŋ], *adj.* bevorstehend, drohend.

impenetrable [im'penitrəbl], *adj.* undurchdringlich, unerforschlich.

impenitent [im'penitənt], *adj.* reuelos, unbußfertig.

imperative [im'perətiv], *adj.* zwingend (*cogent*); dringend notwendig. — *s.* (*Gram.*) der Imperativ, die Befehlsform.

imperceptible [impə'septibl], *adj.* unmerklich.

imperfect [im'pə:fikt], *adj.* unvollständig, unvollkommen; fehlerhaft (*goods etc.*). — *s.* (*Gram.*) das Imperfekt.

imperial [im'piəriəl], *adj.* kaiserlich, Kaiser-, Reichs-.

imperil [im'peril], *v.a.* gefährden; in Gefahr bringen, einer Gefahr aussetzen.

imperious [im'piəriəs], *adj.* gebieterisch.

imperishable [im'periʃəbl], *adj.* unverwüstlich, unvergänglich.

impermeable [im'pə:miəbl], *adj.* undurchdringlich.

impersonal [im'pə:sənəl], *adj.* unpersönlich.

impersonate [im'pə:səneit], *v.a.* verkörpern, darstellen; sich ausgeben als.

impertinence [im'pə:tinəns], *s.* die Anmaßung, Frechheit, Unverschämtheit.

impertinent [im'pə:tinənt], *adj.* anmaßend, frech, unverschämt.

imperturbable [impə'tə:bəbl], *adj.* unerschütterlich, ruhig, gelassen.

impervious [im'pə:viəs], *adj.* unwegsam, undurchdringlich.

impetuous [im'petjuəs], *adj.* ungestüm, heftig.

impetus ['impitəs], *s.* die Triebkraft, der Antrieb.

impinge [im'pindʒ], *v.n.* verstoßen (*on*, gegen); übergreifen (*on*, in).

implacable [im'plækəbl], *adj.* unversöhnlich.

implement ['implimənt], *s.* das Gerät. — [impli'ment], *v.a.* (*Law*) erfüllen, in Wirkung setzen, in Kraft treten lassen.

implementation [implimen'teiʃən], *s.* das Inkrafttreten, die Erfüllung, Ausführung.

implicate ['implikeit], *v.a.* verwickeln.

implicit [im'plisit], *adj.* unbedingt; einbegriffen.

implore [im'plɔ:], *v.a.* anflehen.

imply [im'plai], *v.a.* besagen, meinen; andeuten.

impolite [impə'lait], *adj.* unhöflich, grob.

impolitic [im'pɔlitik], *adj.* unklug, unpolitisch, undiplomatisch.

imponderable [im'pɔndərəbl], *adj.* unwägbar. — *s. pl.* unwägbare, unvorhersehbare Umstände, *m.pl.*

import [im'pɔ:t], *v.a.* einführen, importieren; bedeuten, besagen. — ['impɔ:t], *s.* (*Comm.*) die Einfuhr, der Import; die Bedeutung (*importance, meaning*), Wichtigkeit (*significance*); (*Comm.*) — *licence*, die Einfuhrgenehmigung.

importance [im'pɔ:təns], *s.* die Bedeutung, Wichtigkeit.

important [im'pɔ:tənt], *adj.* bedeutend, wichtig.

importation [impɔ:'teiʃən], *s.* die Einfuhr.

importune [impɔ:'tju:n], *v.a.* belästigen, angehen, dringend bitten.

impose [im'pouz], *v.a.* aufbürden, auferlegen. — *v.n.* — *upon s.o.*, einen belästigen.

imposition [impə'ziʃən], *s.* die Belästigung; (*Sch.*) die Strafarbeit.

impossible [im'pɔsibl], *adj.* unmöglich.

impostor [im'pɔstə], *s.* der Schwindler, Betrüger.

impotent ['impətənt], *adj.* schwach, machtlos; impotent (*sexually*).

impound [im'paund], *v.a.* beschlagnahmen, in Beschlag nehmen.

impoverish [im'pɔvəriʃ], *v.a.* arm machen.

impoverished [im'pɔvəriʃd], *adj.* verarmt, armselig.

impracticability [impræktikə'biliti], *s.* die Unmöglichkeit, Unausführbarkeit.

impracticable [im'præktikəbl], *adj.* unausführbar.

imprecate ['imprikeit], *v.a.* verwünschen.

impregnable [im'pregnəbl], *adj.* uneinnehmbar, unbezwinglich.

impregnate [im'pregneit], *v.a.* imprägnieren; (*Chem.*) sättigen.

impress [im'pres], *v.a.* beeindrucken, imponieren (*fig.*); einprägen, einpressen (*print*). — ['impres], *s.* der Eindruck, (*Typ.*) Abdruck.

impression [im'preʃən], *s.* (*fig.*) der Eindruck; die Auflage (*books*).

impressionable [im'preʃənəbl], *adj.* eindrucksfähig, empfänglich.

impressive [im'presiv], *adj.* ergreifend, eindrucksvoll.

imprint ['imprint], *s.* der Name des Verlags oder Druckers. — [im'print], *v.a.* drucken.

imprison [im'prizn], *v.a.* gefangensetzen, in Haft nehmen.

imprisonment [im'priznmənt], *s.* die Haft; (*Law*) der Arrest.

improbability [imprɔbə'biliti], *s.* die Unwahrscheinlichkeit.

improbable [im'prɔbəbl], *adj.* unwahrscheinlich.

improbity [im'proubiti], *s.* die Unredlichkeit.

impromptu [im'prɔmptju:], *adj.*, *adv.* aus dem Stegreif, unvorbereitet.

improper [im'prɔpə], *adj.* unpassend; unanständig (*indecent*).

impropriety [impro'praiiti], *s.* die Unanständigkeit (*indecency*); die Ungehörigkeit.

improve [im'pru:v], *v.a.* verbessern; (*Hort.*) veredeln. — *v.n.* besser werden, sich bessern; (*Med.*) sich erholen.
improvement [im'pru:vmənt], *s.* die Verbesserung; (*Med.*) die Besserung, der Fortschritt.
improvident [im'prɔvidənt], *adj.* unvorsichtig, nicht auf die Zukunft bedacht.
improvise ['imprəvaiz], *v.a.* improvisieren.
imprudent [im'pru:dənt], *adj.* unklug, unvorsichtig.
impudent ['impjudənt], *adj.* unverschämt.
impugn [im'pju:n], *v.a.* anfechten, angreifen.
impulse ['impʌls], *s.* der Impuls; der Anstoß.
impulsive [im'pʌlsiv], *adj.* impulsiv.
impunity [im'pju:niti], *s.* die Straffreiheit.
impure [im'pjuə], *adj.* (*also Metall., Chem.*) unrein, unedel; unsauber.
impute [im'pju:t], *v.a.* beimessen; zurechnen, die Schuld geben für.
in [in], *prep.* in; an; zu, auf; bei; nach, unter; über; von; mit; — *the morning*, vormittags; — *case*, falls; — *any case*, auf jeden Fall; — *German*, auf deutsch; — *my opinion*, meiner Meinung nach; — *the street*, auf der Straße; — *time*, rechtzeitig. — *adv.* drinnen, innen; herein, hinein; zu Hause.
inability [inə'biliti], *s.* die Unfähigkeit.
inaccessible [inæk'sesibl], *adj.* unzugänglich.
inaccurate [i'nækjurit], *adj.* ungenau.
inaction [i'nækʃən], *s.* die Untätigkeit.
inactive [i'næktiv], *adj.* untätig.
inadequate [i'nædikwit], *adj.* unzulänglich.
inadmissible [inəd'misibl], *adj.* unzulässig.
inadvertent [inəd'və:tənt], *adj.* unbeabsichtigt; unachtsam.
inadvertently [inəd'və:təntli], *adv.* unversehens; versehentlich.
inalienable [in'eiliənəbl], *adj.* unveräußerlich.
inane [i'nein], *adj.* hohl, leer, sinnlos.
inanimate [i'nænimit], *adj.* unbeseelt, leblos.
inanity [i'næniti], *s.* die Leere, Nichtigkeit.
inapplicable [i'næplikəbl], *adj.* unanwendbar; unzutreffend.
inappropriate [inə'proupriit], *adj.* unpassend.
inarticulate [inɑ:'tikjulit], *adj.* unartikuliert.
inasmuch [inəz'mʌtʃ], *adv.* insofern(als).
inattentive [inə'tentiv], *adj.* unaufmerksam.
inaudible [i'nɔ:dibl], *adj.* unhörbar.
inaugural [i'nɔ:gjurəl], *adj.* Inaugural-, Eröffnungs-, Antritts-.
inaugurate [i'nɔ:gjureit], *v.a.* einweihen, eröffnen.
inauspicious [inɔ:'spiʃəs], *adj.* ungünstig.
inborn ['inbɔ:n], *adj.* angeboren.
inbred ['inbred], *adj.* in Inzucht geboren; angeboren, ererbt.
inbreeding ['inbri:diŋ], *s.* die Inzucht.
incalculable [in'kælkjuləbl], *adj.* unberechenbar.
incandescence [inkæn'desəns], *s.* die Weißglut.
incandescent [inkæn'desənt], *adj.* weißglühend.
incantation [inkæn'teiʃən], *s.* die Beschwörung.
incapable [in'keipəbl], *adj.* unfähig (*of doing s.th.*, etwas zu tun).
incapacitate [inkə'pæsiteit], *v.a.* unfähig machen.
incapacity [inkə'pæsiti], *s.* die Unfähigkeit.
incarcerate [in'kɑ:səreit], *v.a.* einkerkern, einsperren.
incarnate [in'kɑ:nit], *adj.* eingefleischt; (*Theol.*) verkörpert.
incarnation [inkɑ:'neiʃən], *s.* die Verkörperung; (*Theol.*) Menschwerdung.
incautious [in'kɔ:ʃəs], *adj.* unvorsichtig.
incendiary [in'sendjəri], *adj.* Brand-, brennend. — *s.* der Brandstifter.
incense [in'sens], *v.a.* aufregen, erzürnen (*make angry*); (*Eccl.*) beweihräuchern. — ['insens], *s.* (*Eccl.*) der Weihrauch.
incentive [in'sentiv], *adj.* Ansporn-, Anreiz-. — *s.* der Ansporn, Anreiz; (*Comm.*) — *scheme*, das Inzentivsystem, Akkordsystem.
incessant [in'sesənt], *adj.* unaufhörlich, ununterbrochen.
incest ['insest], *s.* die Blutschande.
incestuous [in'sestjuəs], *adj.* blutschänderisch.
inch [intʃ], *s.* der Zoll. — *v.n.* — *away*, abrücken.
incident ['insidənt], *s.* der Vorfall, Zwischenfall; das Ereignis.
incidental [insi'dentl], *adj.* zufällig. — *s.* (*pl.*) zufällige Ausgaben, *f. pl.*; das Zusätzliche, Nebenausgaben, *f. pl.*
incipient [in'sipiənt], *adj.* beginnend, anfangend.
incise [in'saiz], *v.a.* einschneiden, (*Med.*) einen Einschnitt machen.
incision [in'siʒən], *s.* der Einschnitt.
incisive [in'saisiv], *adj.* einschneidend; energisch (*person*).
incite [in'sait], *v.a.* aufreizen, anspornen.
incivility [insi'viliti], *s.* die Unhöflichkeit.
inclement [in'klemənt], *adj.* unfreundlich (*weather, climate*).
inclination [inkli'neiʃən], *s.* die Neigung (*also fig.*).
incline [in'klain], *v.n.* neigen, sich neigen. — ['inklain], *s.* der Neigungswinkel; der Abhang.
include [in'klu:d], *v.a.* einschließen (*contain*); umfassen (*enclose*).

including [in'klu:diŋ], *prep.* einschließlich.
inclusive [in'klu:siv], *adj.* einschließlich, mitgerechnet.
incoherent [inko'hiərənt], *adj.* unzusammenhängend.
incombustible [inkəm'bʌstibl], *adj.* unverbrennbar.
income ['inkʌm], *s.* das Einkommen.
incommensurable, incommensurate [inkə'menʃərəbl, inkə'menʃərit], *adj.* unvereinbar, unmeßbar.
incomparable [in'kɔmpərəbl], *adj.* unvergleichlich.
incompatible [inkəm'pætibl], *adj.* unvereinbar.
incompetence, incompetency [in'kɔmpitəns, -tənsi], *s.* die Inkompetenz; Unzulänglichkeit.
incompetent [in'kɔmpitənt], *adj.* unzuständig, inkompetent; unzulänglich.
incomplete [inkəm'pli:t], *adj.* unvollständig.
incomprehensible [inkɔmpri'hensibl], *adj.* unverständlich.
inconceivable [inkən'si:vəbl], *adj.* unbegreiflich.
inconclusive [inkən'klu:siv], *adj.* unvollständig (*incomplete*); unüberzeugend; ergebnislos.
incongruity [inkɔŋ'gru:iti], *s.* (*Maths.*) die Inkongruenz; (*fig.*) die Unangemessenheit.
incongruous [in'kɔŋgruəs], *adj.* inkongruent; unangemessen.
inconsequent [in'kɔnsikwənt], *adj.* folgewidrig.
inconsequential [inkɔnsi'kwenʃəl], *adj.* inkonsequent (*inconsistent*); unzusammenhängend.
inconsiderate [inkən'sidərit], *adj.* rücksichtslos, unbedachtsam.
inconsistent [inkən'sistənt], *adj.* inkonsequent.
inconsolable [inkən'souləbl], *adj.* untröstlich.
inconstancy [in'kɔnstənsi], *s.* die Unbeständigkeit; Untreue (*fickleness*).
incontestable [inkən'testəbl], *adj.* unanfechtbar, unbestreitbar.
incontinent [in'kɔntinənt], *adj.* unenthaltsam.
incontrovertible [inkɔntro'və:tibl], *adj.* unstreitig, unanfechtbar.
inconvenience [inkən'vi:niəns], *s.* die Unbequemlichkeit, Unannehmlichkeit.
inconvenient [inkən'vi:niənt], *adj.* unangenehm, unpassend.
inconvertible [inkən'və:tibl], *adj.* unveränderlich; (*Comm.*) unumsetzbar.
incorporate [in'kɔ:pəreit], *v.a.* einverleiben (*Dat.*), eingliedern (*Acc.*).
incorporated [in'kɔ:pəreitid], *adj.* (*Am.*) eingetragene Körperschaft, eingetragener Verein.
incorrect [inkə'rekt], *adj.* unrichtig, fehlerhaft; unschicklich, unpassend.
incorrigible [in'kɔridʒibl], *adj.* unverbesserlich.
incorruptible [inkə'rʌptibl], *adj.* unbestechlich.
increase [in'kri:s], *v.a.* vermehren, vergrößern (*size, volume*); steigern (*heat, intensity*); erhöhen (*price*). — *v.n.* sich vermehren, sich erhöhen; wachsen (*grow*). — ['inkri:s], *s.* die Zunahme; der Zuwachs (*family*); die Erhöhung.
incredible [in'kredibl], *adj.* unglaublich.
incredulity [inkre'dju:liti], *s.* die Ungläubigkeit, der Unglaube.
incredulous [in'kredjuləs], *adj.* ungläubig, schwer zu überzeugen.
increment ['inkrimənt], *s.* (*Comm.*) die Zulage, Gehaltserhöhung.
incriminate [in'krimineit], *v.a.* beschuldigen, inkriminieren.
incubate ['inkjubeit], *v.a.* brüten, ausbrüten. — *v.n.* brüten.
incubator ['inkjubeitə], *s.* der Brutapparat.
inculcate ['inkʌlkeit], *v.a.* einprägen.
inculpate ['inkʌlpeit], *v.a.* beschuldigen.
incumbent [in'kʌmbənt], *adj.* (*upon, Dat.*) obliegend, nötig. — *s.* der Pfründner, Amtsinhaber.
incur [in'kə:], *v.a.* auf sich laden, sich zuziehen.
incurable [in'kjuərəbl], *adj.* unheilbar.
incursion [in'kə:ʃən], *s.* der Einfall, Streifzug.
indebted [in'detid], *adj.* verpflichtet, dankbar (*grateful*); verschuldet (*in debt*).
indecent [in'di:sənt], *adj.* unschicklich, unanständig.
indecision [indi'siʒən], *s.* die Unentschlossenheit.
indecisive [indi'saisiv], *adj.* unentschlossen.
indeclinable [indi'klainəbl], *adj.* (*Gram.*) undeklinierbar.
indecorous [indi'kɔ:rəs *or* in'dekɔrəs], *adj.* unrühmlich, unanständig.
indeed [in'di:d], *adv.* in der Tat, tatsächlich.
indefatigable [indi'fætigəbl], *adj.* unermüdlich.
indefensible [indi'fensibl], *adj.* unhaltbar; unverzeihlich (*unforgivable*).
indefinable [indi'fainəbl], *adj.* unbestimmbar, undefinierbar.
indefinite [in'definit], *adj.* unbestimmt.
indelible [in'delibl], *adj.* unauslöschlich.
indelicate [in'delikit], *adj.* unfein.
indemnify [in'demnifai], *v.a.* entschädigen.
indemnity [in'demniti], die Entschädigung.
indent [in'dent], *v.a.* auszacken, einschneiden.
indenture [in'dentʃə], *s.* der Lehrbrief (*apprentice*); Vertrag.
independence [indi'pendəns], *s.* die Unabhängigkeit, Freiheit.
independent [indi'pendənt], *adj.* unabhängig, frei.

indescribable [indi'skraibəbl], *adj.* unbeschreiblich.
indestructible [indi'strʌktibl], *adj.* unverwüstlich; unzerstörbar.
indeterminable [indi'tə:minəbl], *adj.* unbestimmbar.
indeterminate [indi'tə:minit], *adj.* unbestimmt.
index ['indeks], *s.* (*pl.* **indexes**) das Inhaltsverzeichnis; (*pl.* **indices**) (*Maths.*) der Exponent; — *finger*, der Zeigefinger; (*pl.*) die Finger, Zeiger, *m. pl.* (*pointers*).
India ['indjə], das Indien; — *paper*, das Dünnpapier.
Indian ['indjən], *adj.* indisch; — *ink*, die Tusche. — *s.* der Ind(i)er.
indiarubber ['indjə'rʌbə], *s.* der Radiergummi.
indicate ['indikeit], *v.a.* anzeigen, angeben.
indication [indi'keiʃən], *s.* das Anzeichen, Merkmal, der Hinweis.
indicative [in'dikətiv], *adj.* bezeichnend (für, *Acc.*). — *s.* (*Gram.*) der Indikativ.
indict [in'dait], *v.a.* anklagen.
indictment [in'daitmənt], *s.* die Anklage.
indifference [in'difrəns], *s.* die Gleichgültigkeit.
indifferent [in'difrənt], *adj.* gleichgültig.
indigence ['indidʒəns], *s.* die Armut.
indigenous [in'didʒinəs], *adj.* eingeboren, einheimisch.
indigent ['indidʒənt], *adj.* arm, dürftig.
indigestible [indi'dʒestibl], *adj.* unverdaulich.
indigestion [indi'dʒestʃən], *s.* die Magenbeschwerden, *f. pl.*; die Magenverstimmung.
indignant [in'dignənt], *adj.* empört, unwillig, entrüstet.
indignation [indig'neiʃən], *s.* die Entrüstung, der Unwille.
indignity [in'digniti], *s.* die Schmach, der Schimpf.
indirect [indi'rekt], *adj.* indirekt, mittelbar.
indiscreet [indis'kri:t], *adj.* indiskret, unvorsichtig; unbescheiden (*immodest*); taktlos.
indiscretion [indis'kreʃən], *s.* die Indiskretion, Taktlosigkeit.
indiscriminate [indis'kriminit], *adj.* ohne Unterschied, wahllos, kritiklos.
indispensable [indis'pensəbl], *adj.* unerläßlich, unentbehrlich.
indisposed [indis'pouzd], *adj.* unwohl (*health*); unwillig (*unwilling*).
indisposition [indispə'ziʃən], *s.* das Unwohlsein (*health*); das Abgeneigtsein (*disinclination*).
indisputable [indis'pju:təbl], *adj.* unbestreitbar.
indissoluble [indi'sɔljubl], *adj.* unauflöslich.
indistinct [indis'tiŋkt], *adj.* undeutlich.
indistinguishable [indis'tiŋgwiʃəbl], *adj.* nicht zu unterscheiden, ununterscheidbar.
individual [indi'vidjuəl], *adj.* individuell, persönlich; einzeln (*single*). — *s.* das Individuum, Einzelwesen.
individuality [individju'æliti], *s.* die Individualität.
indivisible [indi'vizibl], *adj.* unteilbar.
Indo-Chinese [indotʃai'ni:z], *adj.* hinterindisch. — *s.* der Hinterind(i)er.
indolent ['indələnt], *adj.* indolent, träge.
Indonesian [indo'ni:ʒən], *adj.* indonesisch. — *s.* der Indonesier.
indoor ['indɔ:], *adj.* im Haus; drinnen (*inside*).
indoors [in'dɔ:z], *adv.* im Hause, zu Hause.
indubitable [in'dju:bitəbl], *adj.* zweifellos, unzweifelhaft.
induce [in'dju:s], *v.a.* veranlassen, bewegen, verleiten (*incite*).
inducement [in'dju:smənt], *s.* der Beweggrund (*cause*); der Anlaß (*reason*); die Verleitung (*incitement*).
induction [in'dʌkʃən], *s.* die Einführung; (*Elec.*) die Induktion.
inductive [in'dʌktiv], *adj.* (*Log.*, *Elec.*) induktiv.
indulge [in'dʌldʒ], *v.a.* nachgeben (*Dat.*); verwöhnen. — *v.n.* — *in*, frönen (*Dat.*).
indulgence [in'dʌldʒəns], *s.* die Nachsicht; das Wohlleben; (*Eccl.*) der Ablaß.
industrial [in'dʌstriəl], *adj.* industriell, Industrie-.
industrious [in'dʌstriəs], *adj.* fleißig, arbeitsam.
industry ['indəstri], *s.* die Industrie (*production*); der Fleiß (*industriousness*).
inebriate [i'ni:brieit], *v.a.* berauschen. — [-iit], *adj.* berauscht.
ineffable [i'nefəbl], *adj.* unaussprechlich.
ineffective, ineffectual [ini'fektiv, ini'fektjuəl], *adj.* unwirksam, wirkungslos; unfähig.
inefficiency [ini'fiʃənsi], *s.* die Erfolglosigkeit, Untauglichkeit.
inefficient [ini'fiʃənt], *adj.* untauglich, untüchtig.
ineligible [in'elidʒibl], *adj.* nicht wählbar.
inept [i'nept], *adj.* untüchtig, albern, dumm.
ineptitude [i'neptitju:d], *s.* die Unfähigkeit; die Dummheit (*stupidity*).
inequality [ini'kwɔliti], *s.* die Ungleichheit.
inert [i'nɔ:t], *adj.* träg.
inestimable [in'estiməbl], *adj.* unschätzbar.
inevitable [in'evitəbl], *adj.* unumgänglich, unvermeidlich.
inexcusable [iniks'kju:zəbl], *adj.* unverzeihlich, unentschuldbar.
inexhaustible [inig'zɔ:stibl], *adj.* unerschöpflich.

inexpedient [iniks'pi:djənt], *adj.* unzweckmäßig, unpraktisch, unpassend.
inexpensive [iniks'pensiv], *adj.* billig, nicht kostspielig.
inexperience [iniks'piəriəns], *s.* die Unerfahrenheit, Naivität.
inexpert [iniks'pə:t], *adj.* ungeübt, unerfahren.
inexpiable [i'nekspiəbl], *adj.* unsühnbar, nicht wieder gut zu machen.
inexplicable [i'neksplikəbl], *adj.* unerklärlich.
inexpressible [iniks'presibl], *adj.* unaussprechlich.
inexpressive [iniks'presiv], *adj.* ausdruckslos.
inextinguishable [iniks'tiŋgwiʃəbl], *adj.* unauslöschlich.
inextricable [i'nekstrikəbl], *adj.* unentwirrbar.
infallible [in'fælibl], *adj.* unfehlbar.
infamous ['infəməs], *adj.* verrufen, abscheulich, berüchtigt.
infamy ['infəmi], *s.* die Schande; Ehrlosigkeit (*dishonour*).
infancy ['infənsi], *s.* die Kindheit, Unmündigkeit; (*fig.*) der Anfang.
infant ['infənt], *s.* das Kind; (*Law*) der Unmündige, das Mündel.
infantry ['infəntri], *s.* die Infanterie.
infatuate [in'fætjueit], *v.a.* betören.
infect [in'fekt], *v.a.* anstecken, infizieren.
infection [in'fekʃən], *s.* (*Med.*) die Ansteckung, Infektion.
infectious [in'fekʃəs], *adj.* (*Med.*) ansteckend.
infer [in'fə:], *v.a.* schließen, herleiten, folgern.
inference ['infərəns], *s.* die Folgerung.
inferior [in'fiəriə], *comp. adj.* geringer; untergeordnet (*subordinate*); schlechter (*worse*).
inferiority [infiəri'ɔriti], *s.* die Inferiorität, Minderwertigkeit.
infernal [in'fə:nəl], *adj.* höllisch.
infest [in'fest], *v.a.* heimsuchen, plagen.
infidel ['infidəl], *adj.* ungläubig. — *s.* der Heide, Ungläubige.
infiltrate ['infiltreit], *v.n.* durchsickern, durchdringen, infiltrieren.
infinite ['infinit], *adj.* unendlich.
infinitive [in'finitiv], *s.* (*Gram.*) der Infinitiv, die Nennform.
infirm [in'fə:m], *adj.* gebrechlich, schwach; siech (*sick*).
infirmary [in'fə:məri], *s.* das Krankenhaus.
infirmity [in'fə:miti], *s.* die Schwäche, Gebrechlichkeit.
inflame [in'fleim], *v.a.* entzünden.
inflammation [inflə'meiʃən], *s.* die Entzündung.
inflate [in'fleit], *v.a.* aufblasen, aufblähen; (*Comm.*) künstlich erhöhen (*values*).
inflation [in'fleiʃən], *s.* die Aufblähung; (*Comm.*) die Inflation.
inflect [in'flekt], *v.a.* (*Gram.*) biegen, flektieren, deklinieren, konjugieren.
inflection [in'flekʃən], *s.* (*Gram.*) die Biegung; (*Phonet.*) der Tonfall.
inflexible [in'fleksibl], *adj.* unbiegsam.
inflexion *see* **inflection**.
inflict [in'flikt], *v.a.* auferlegen (*impose*); beibringen (*administer*).
infliction [in'flikʃən], *s.* die Verhängung, das Beibringen.
influence ['influəns], *v.a.* beeinflussen. — *s.* der Einfluß.
influential [influ'enʃəl], *adj.* einflußreich.
influenza [influ'enzə], *s.* (*Med.*) die Grippe.
inform [in'fɔ:m], *v.a., v.n.* informieren, benachrichtigen; — *against*, jemanden denunzieren.
informal [in'fɔ:məl], *adj.* nicht formell; ungezwungen, zwanglos.
informant [in'fɔ:mənt], *s.* der Angeber.
information [infə'meiʃən], *s.* die Information, Nachricht, Auskunft.
infrequent [in'fri:kwənt], *adj.* selten.
infringe [in'frindʒ], *v.a.* übertreten.
infuriate [in'fjuərieit], *v.a.* wütend machen.
infuse [in'fju:z], *v.a.* einflößen, aufgießen, begießen.
infusion [in'fju:ʒən], *s.* die Eingießung; der Aufguß (*tea*); (*Chem.*) die Infusion.
ingenious [in'dʒi:niəs], *adj.* geistreich, genial.
ingenuity [indʒi'nju:iti], *s.* der Scharfsinn.
ingenuous [in'dʒenjuəs], *adj.* offen, unbefangen, arglos.
ingot ['iŋgət], *s.* der Barren.
ingrained [in'greind], *adj.* eingefleischt.
ingratiate [in'greiʃieit], *v.r.* — *o.s.*, sich beliebt machen, sich einschmeicheln (*with*, bei).
ingratitude [in'grætitju:d], *s.* die Undankbarkeit.
ingredient [in'gri:diənt], *s.* der Bestandteil; die Zutat.
inhabit [in'hæbit], *v.a.* bewohnen.
inhabitant [in'hæbitənt], *s.* der Bewohner; Einwohner.
inhale [in'heil], *v.a.* einatmen.
inherent [in'hiərənt], *adj.* eigen, angeboren (*innate*); in der Sache selbst (*intrinsic*).
inherit [in'herit], *v.a.* erben.
inheritance [in'heritəns], *s.* die Erbschaft, das Erbgut (*patrimony*); (*fig.*) das Erbe.
inhibit [in'hibit], *v.a.* hindern; —*ing factor*, der Hemmfaktor.
inhibition [ini'biʃən], *s.* (*Psych.*) die Hemmung.
inhospitable [inhɔs'pitəbl], *adj.* ungastlich, ungastfreundlich.
inhuman [in'hju:mən], *adj.* unmenschlich.
inhume [in'hju:m], *v.a.* beerdigen.
inimical [i'nimikəl], *adj.* feindlich (gesinnt), feindselig.

inimitable [i'nimitəbl], *adj.* unnachahmlich.
iniquitous [i'nikwitəs], *adj.* ungerecht, schlecht, boshaft.
iniquity [i'nikwiti], *s.* die Ungerechtigkeit (*injustice*); die Schändlichkeit (*shame*).
initial [i'niʃəl], *adj.* anfänglich. — *s.* (*Typ.*) der Anfangsbuchstabe.
initiate [i'niʃieit], *v.a.* einweihen, anfangen.
initiative [i'niʃiətiv], *s.* die Initiative; der erste Anstoß (*impulse*).
injection [in'dʒekʃən], *s.* (*Med.*) die Einspritzung, Injektion.
injudicious [indʒu'diʃəs], *adj.* unbedacht, unbesonnen; übereilt (*rash*).
injunction [in'dʒʌŋkʃən], *s.* die Vorschrift, (*Law*) die gerichtliche Verfügung.
injure ['indʒə], *v.a.* verletzen.
injurious [in'dʒuəriəs], *adj.* verletzend; schädlich (*harmful*).
injury ['indʒəri], *s.* die Verletzung, Verwundung; der Schaden (*damage*).
injustice [in'dʒʌstis], *s.* die Ungerechtigkeit.
ink [iŋk], *s.* die Tinte.
inkling ['iŋkliŋ], *s.* die Ahnung.
inkstand ['iŋkstænd], *s.* das Schreibzeug.
inlaid [in'leid], *adj.* eingelegt.
inland ['inlənd], *adj.* inländisch, Binnen-; — *revenue office*, das Steueramt, Finanzamt.
inlet ['inlit], *s.* (*Geog.*) die kleine Bucht.
inmate ['inmeit], *s.* der Insasse, Bewohner.
inmost ['inmoust], *adj.* innerst.
inn [in], *s.* der Gasthof, das Wirtshaus; *Inns of Court*, die Londoner Rechtskammern, *f. pl.*
innate [i'neit], *adj.* angeboren.
inner ['inə], *adj.* inner; geheim (*secret*).
innings ['iniŋz], *s.* das Daransein (*in Cricket*); die Reihe.
innocence ['inəsəns], *s.* die Unschuld.
innocuous [i'nɔkjuəs], *adj.* unschädlich.
innovate ['inoveit], *v.a.*, *v.n.* als Neuerung einführen, Neuerungen machen.
innovation [ino'veiʃən], *s.* die Neuerung.
innuendo [inju'endou], *s.* das Innuendo, die Anspielung.
innumerable [i'nju:mərəbl], *adj.* unzählig, unzählbar.
inoculate [i'nɔkjuleit], *v.a.* impfen.
inoffensive [ino'fensiv], *adj.* harmlos, unschädlich.
inopportune [in'ɔpətju:n], *adj.* ungelegen.
inordinate [i'nɔ:dinit], *adj.* unmäßig.
inorganic [inɔ:'gænik], *adj.* anorganisch.
inquest ['inkwest], *s.* die gerichtliche Untersuchung (*Law*); *coroner's* —, die Leichenschau.
inquire, enquire [in'kwaiə], *v.n.* sich erkundigen (*after*, nach, *Dat.*), nachfragen.
inquiry, enquiry [in'kwaiəri], *s.* die Nachfrage; — *office*, die Auskunftsstelle.
inquisition [inkwi'ziʃən], *s.* (*Eccl.*) die Inquisition; die gerichtliche Untersuchung.
inquisitive [in'kwizitiv], *adj.* neugierig.
inquisitiveness [in'kwizitivnis], *s.* die Neugier(de).
inroad ['inroud], *s.* der Eingriff, Überfall.
insane [in'sein], *adj.* wahnsinnig.
insanity [in'sæniti], *s.* der Wahnsinn.
insatiable [in'seiʃəbl], *adj.* unersättlich.
inscribe [in'skraib], *v.a.* einschreiben (*enrol*); widmen (*book*).
inscription [in'skripʃən], *s.* die Inschrift.
inscrutable [in'skru:təbl], *adj.* unergründlich, unerforschlich.
insect ['insekt], *s.* das Insekt, Kerbtier.
insecure [insi'kjuə], *adj.* unsicher.
insensate [in'sensit], *adj.* unsinnig (*senseless*); gefühllos..
insensible [in'sensibl], *adj.* unempfindlich; gefühllos.
insensitive [in'sensitiv], *adj.* ohne feineres Gefühl, unempfindlich.
inseparable [in'sepərəbl], *adj.* unzertrennlich, untrennbar.
insert [in'sə:t], *v.a.* einsetzen, einschalten (*add*); inserieren (*in newspaper*).
insertion [in'sə:ʃən], *s.* die Einschaltung (*addition*); die Annonce, das Inserat (*press*).
inside [in'said], *adj.* inner. — *adv.* im Innern. — *prep.* innerhalb. — *s.* das Innere.
insidious [in'sidiəs], *adj.* heimtückisch.
insight ['insait], *s.* der Einblick.
insignia [in'signiə], *s. pl.* die Insignien.
insignificance [insig'nifikəns], *s.* die Geringfügigkeit, Bedeutungslosigkeit.
insignificant [insig'nifikənt], *adj.* unbedeutend, geringfügig.
insincere [insin'siə], *adj.* unaufrichtig.
insincerity [insin'seriti], *s.* die Unaufrichtigkeit.
insinuate [in'sinjueit], *v.a.* zu verstehen geben, andeuten, anspielen auf (*Acc.*).
insinuation [insinju'eiʃən], *s.* der Wink, die Andeutung, Anspielung.
insipid [in'sipid], *adj.* schal, geschmacklos.
insist [in'sist], *v.n.* bestehen (*upon*, auf, *Dat.*).
insistence [in'sistəns], *s.* das Bestehen, Beharren.
insolence ['insələns], *s.* die Frechheit.
insolent ['insələnt], *adj.* frech, unverschämt.
insoluble [in'sɔljubl], *adj.* unlösbar; (*Chem.*) unlöslich.
insolvent [in'sɔlvənt], *adj.* insolvent, zahlungsunfähig, bankrott.
inspect [in'spekt], *v.a.* inspizieren; besichtigen.

inspection [in'spekʃən], *s.* die Inspektion; Besichtigung.
inspiration [inspi'reiʃən], *s.* die Inspiration, Erleuchtung, Begeisterung.
inspire [in'spaiə], *v.a.* inspirieren, begeistern.
instability [instə'biliti], *s.* die Unbeständigkeit, Labilität.
install [in'stɔ:l], *v.a.* einsetzen (*in office*); einbauen.
installation [instə'leiʃən], *s.* die Einsetzung (*inauguration*); die Installation.
instalment [in'stɔ:lmənt], *s.* die Rate; *by —s*, auf Abzahlung; die Fortsetzung (*serial*).
instance ['instəns], *s.* das Beispiel (*example*); (*Law*) die Instanz; *at my —*, auf meine dringende Bitte; *for —*, zum Beispiel. — *v.a.* als Beispiel anführen.
instant ['instənt], *s.* der Augenblick. — *adj.* gegenwärtig; sofortig; laufend (*current month*).
instantaneous [instən'teiniəs], *adj.* augenblicklich, sofortig.
instead [in'sted], *adv.* dafür, stattdessen; — *of*, (an)statt (*Genit.*).
instep ['instep], *s.* (*Anat.*) der Rist.
instigate ['instigeit], *v.a.* aufhetzen, anreizen, anstiften.
instil [in'stil], *v.a.* einflößen.
instinct ['instiŋkt], *s.* der Instinkt, Naturtrieb.
institute ['institju:t], *s.* das Institut. — *v.a.* einrichten (*install*); stiften (*found*).
institution [insti'tju:ʃən], *s.* die Stiftung (*foundation*); die Anstalt (*establishment*).
instruct [in'strʌkt], *v.a.* unterrichten, unterweisen.
instruction [in'strʌkʃən], *s.* der Unterricht (*in schools etc.*); (*pl.*) die Instruktionen, *f. pl.*; die Direktive.
instructive [in'strʌktiv], *adj.* instruktiv, lehrreich.
instrument ['instrumənt], *s.* das Instrument; Werkzeug (*tool*).
insubordination [insəbɔ:di'neiʃən], *s.* der Ungehorsam.
insufferable [in'sʌfərəbl], *adj.* unerträglich.
insufficient [insə'fiʃənt], *adj.* ungenügend, unzulänglich.
insular ['insjulə], *adj.* Insel-; insular (*narrow-minded*).
insulate ['insjuleit], *v.a.* absondern (*separate*); (*Elec.*) isolieren; *insulating tape*, das Isolierband.
insult [in'sʌlt], *v.a.* beleidigen.
insuperable [in'sju:pərəbl], *adj.* unüberwindlich.
insupportable [insə'pɔ:təbl], *adj.* unhaltbar (*argument*); unerträglich (*insufferable*).
insurance [in'ʃuərəns], *s.* die Versicherung; — *policy*, die Police; — *premium*, die Prämie; — *broker*, der Versicherungsmakler.
insure [in'ʃuə], *v.a.* versichern.
insurgent [in'sə:dʒənt], *s.* der Aufständische, Aufrührer.
insurmountable [insə'mauntəbl], *adj.* unüberwindlich.
insurrection [insə'rekʃən], *s.* der Aufstand, Aufruhr; die Empörung.
intact [in'tækt], *adj.* unversehrt, intakt.
intangible [in'tændʒibl], *adj.* unberührbar (*untouchable*); (*Log.*) abstrakt. — *s. pl.* (*Log.*) die Intangibilien, *pl.*
integer ['intidʒə], *s.* (*Maths.*) das Ganze, die ganze Zahl.
integral ['intigrəl], *adj.* wesentlich; vollständig. — *s.* (*Maths.*) das Integral.
integrate ['intigreit], *v.a.* (*Maths.*) integrieren.
integration [inti'greiʃən], *s.* (*Maths.*) die Integrierung; (*fig.*) die Integration, das völlige Aufgehen.
integrity [in'tegriti], *s.* die Rechtschaffenheit, Redlichkeit (*probity*).
intellect ['intilekt], *s.* der Geist, Intellekt, Verstand.
intellectual [inti'lektjuəl], *adj.* intellektuell. — *s.* der Intellektuelle.
intelligence [in'telidʒəns], *s.* die Intelligenz; die Nachricht (*news*).
intelligent [in'telidʒənt], *adj.* intelligent.
intelligible [in'telidʒibl], *adj.* verständlich.
intemperance [in'tempərəns], *s.* die Unmäßigkeit.
intemperate [in'tempərit], *adj.* unmäßig.
intend [in'tend], *v.a.* beabsichtigen, vorhaben.
intendant [in'tendənt], *s.* der Intendant, Verwalter.
intense [in'tens], *adj.* intensiv, heftig.
intent [in'tent], *adj.* gespannt, begierig, bedacht (*on*, auf, *Acc.*). — *s.* die Absicht.
intention [in'tenʃən], *s.* die Absicht.
intentioned [in'tenʃənd], *adj.* *well- —*, wohlgesinnt.
inter [in'tə:], *v.a.* beerdigen.
intercede [intə'si:d], *v.n.* vermitteln (*between*); sich verwenden (*on behalf of*, für, *Acc.*).
intercept [intə'sept], *v.a.* abfangen, auffangen, hemmen.
intercession [intə'seʃən], *s.* die Vermittlung, Fürsprache, Fürbitte.
interchange ['intətʃeindʒ], *s.* der Austausch. — [-'tʃeindʒ], *v.a.* austauschen.
intercourse ['intəkɔ:s], *s.* der Verkehr, Umgang.
interdict [intə'dikt], *v.a.* untersagen, verbieten.
interest ['intrəst], *s.* das Interesse; die Beteiligung; (*Comm.*) die Zinsen, *m. pl.*; *compound —*, die Zinseszinsen, *m. pl.* — *v.a.* interessieren.
interested ['intrəstid], *adj.* (*in*, an, *Dat.*) interessiert; *be — in*, sich interessieren für.

interesting ['intrəstiŋ], *adj.* interessant.
interfere [intə'fiə], *v.n.* sich einmischen, eingreifen (*in*, in, *Acc.*)
interference [intə'fiərəns], *s.* die Einmischung; (*Rad.*) die Störung.
interim ['intərim], *adj.* vorläufig, Zwischen-.
interior [in'tiəriə], *adj.* innerlich. — *s.* das Innere; das Binnenland; — *decorator*, der Innenraumgestalter, der Innenarchitekt; *Ministry of the Interior*, das Innenministerium.
interjection [intə'dʒekʃən], *s.* die Interjektion; der Ausruf.
interlace [intə'leis], *v.a.* einflechten.
interleave [intə'li:v], *v.a.* durchschießen (*a book*).
interlinear [intə'liniə], *adj.* zwischenzeilig.
interlocutor [intə'lɔkjutə], *s.* der Gesprächspartner.
interloper ['intəloupə], *s.* der Eindringling.
interlude ['intəlju:d], *s.* das Zwischenspiel.
intermarry [intə'mæri], *v.n.* untereinander heiraten.
intermediate [intə'mi:diit], *adj.* Mittel-; (*Sch.*) — *certificate*, das Mittelstufenzeugnis.
interment [in'tə:mənt], *s.* die Beerdigung.
interminable [in'tə:minəbl], *adj.* endlos, langwierig.
intermingle [intə'miŋgl], *v.n.* sich vermischen.
intermission [intə'miʃən], *s.* die Pause, Unterbrechung.
intermit [intə'mit], *v.a.* unterbrechen.
intermittent [intə'mitənt], *adj.* Wechsel-, aussetzend.
internal [in'tə:nl], *adj.* intern, innerlich.
international [intə'næʃənəl], *adj.* international; — *law*, das Völkerrecht.
interpolate [in'tə:poleit], *v.a.* interpolieren, einschalten.
interpose [intə'pouz], *v.a.* dazwischenstellen. — *v.n.* vermitteln (*mediate*).
interpret [in'tə:prit], *v.a.* verdolmetschen; erklären (*explain*); auslegen, interpretieren.
interpretation [intə:pri'teiʃən], *s.* die Auslegung, Interpretation.
interpreter [in'tə:pritə], *s.* der Dolmetscher.
interrogate [in'terogeit], *v.a.* ausfragen, befragen, vernehmen.
interrogation [intero'geiʃən], *s.* die Befragung; (*Law*) das Verhör, die Vernehmung.
interrogative [intə'rɔgətiv], *adj.* (*Gram.*) Frage-, Interrogativ-.
interrupt [intə'rʌpt], *v.a.* unterbrechen; stören (*disturb*).
interruption [intə'rʌpʃən], *s.* die Unterbrechung; Störung (*disturbance*).
intersect [intə'sekt], *v.a.* durchschneiden.
intersperse [intə'spə:s], *v.a.* untermengen, vermischen, einstreuen.
intertwine [intə'twain], *v.a.*, *v.n.* (sich) durchflechten.
interval ['intəvəl], *s.* der Zwischenraum; die Pause; (*Mus.*) das Interval.
intervene [intə'vi:n], *v.n.* eingreifen; als Vermittler dienen (*act as mediator*).
intervention [intə'venʃən], *s.* die Vermittlung, Intervention.
interview ['intəvju:], *v.a.* zur Vorsprache einladen (*a candidate*); interviewen. — *s.* die Vorsprache, das Interview.
intestate [in'testit], *adj.* ohne Testament.
intestines [in'testinz], *s. pl.* (*Anat.*) die Eingeweide, *n. pl.*
intimacy ['intiməsi], *s.* die Vertraulichkeit, Intimität.
intimate ['intimit], *adj.* intim, vertraut, vertraulich. — [-meit], *v.a.* andeuten, zu verstehen geben.
intimation [inti'meiʃən], *s.* der Wink, die Andeutung.
intimidate [in'timideit], *v.a.* einschüchtern.
into ['intu], *prep.* (*Acc.*) in, in ... hinein (*towards*).
intolerable [in'tɔlərəbl], *adj.* unerträglich.
intolerance [in'tɔlərəns], *s.* die Unduldsamkeit, Intoleranz.
intonation [into'neiʃən], *s.* (*Phonet.*) die Intonation; (*Mus.*) das Anstimmen, der Tonansatz (*of instruments*).
intoxicate [in'tɔksikeit], *v.a.* berauschen.
intractable [in'træktəbl], *adj.* unbändig, unlenksam.
intransitive [in'trænsitiv *or* in'trɑ:ns-], *adj.* (*Gram.*) intransitiv.
intrepid [in'trepid], *adj.* unerschrocken, furchtlos.
intricacy ['intrikəsi], *s.* die Verwicklung (*tangle*), Schwierigkeit (*difficulty*).
intricate ['intrikit], *adj.* verwickelt, schwierig.
intrigue [in'tri:g], *s.* die Intrige. — *v.n.* intrigieren.
intrinsic [in'trinsik], *adj.* wesentlich; innerlich (*inner*).
introduce [intrə'dju:s], *v.a.* einführen, einleiten (*book etc.*); vorstellen (*person*).
introduction [intrə'dʌkʃən], *s.* die Einführung, das Bekanntmachen; die Einleitung (*preface*); die Vorstellung (*presentation to s.o., Dat.*).
introductory [intrə'dʌktəri], *adj.* einführend.
introspection [intrə'spekʃən], *s.* die Selbstbetrachtung, Introspektion.
introspective [intrə'spektiv], *adj.* nachdenklich, beschaulich.
intrude [in'tru:d], *v.n.* eindringen, sich eindrängen; stören (*be in the way*).
intrusion [in'tru:ʒən], *s.* das Eindringen.

intuition [intju'iʃən], *s.* die Intuition, Eingebung.
intuitive [in'tju:itiv], *adj.* intuitiv, gefühlsmäßig.
inundate ['inʌndeit], *v.a.* überschwemmen.
inure [i'njuə], *v.a.* gewöhnen; abhärten (*harden*).
invade [in'veid], *v.a.* angreifen, einfallen (in, *Dat.*).
invalid [in'vælid], *adj.* ungültig (*void*); ['invəlid] krank (*sick*). — *s.* der Kranke, Invalide.
invalidate [in'vælideit], *v.a.* ungültig machen, für ungültig erklären.
invalidity [invə'liditi], *s.* die Ungültigkeit.
invaluable [in'væljuəbl], *adj.* von hohem Wert, wertvoll, unschätzbar.
invariable [in'vεəriəbl], *adj.* unveränderlich. — *s.* (*Maths.*) die unveränderliche Größe, die Konstante, Unveränderliche.
invasion [in'veiʒən], *s.* die Invasion, der Einfall; Angriff (*of*, auf, *Acc.*).
invective [in'vektiv], *adj.* schmähend. — *s.* die Schmähung.
inveigh [in'vei], *v.n.* schmähen, losziehen (gegen); schimpfen (auf, *Acc.*).
inveigle [in'veigl], *v.a.* verleiten, verführen.
invent [in'vent], *v.a.* erfinden.
invention [in'venʃən], *s.* die Erfindung.
inventor [in'ventə], *s.* der Erfinder.
inventory ['invəntri], *s.* der Bestand, das Inventar; die Liste (*list*).
inverse [in'və:s,'invə:s], *adj.* umgekehrt.
inversion [in'və:ʃən], *s.* die Umkehrung; (*Gram.*, *Maths.*) die Inversion.
invert [in'və:t], *v.a.* umstellen, umkehren. — ['invə:t], *s.* (*Chem.*) — *sugar*, der Invertzucker.
invest [in'vest], *v.a.* bekleiden; bedecken; (*Comm.*) investieren, anlegen.
investigate [in'vestigeit], *v.a.* untersuchen, erforschen.
investiture [in'vestitʃə], *s.* die Investitur; die Belehnung.
investment [in'vestmənt], *s.* die Investierung, Kapitalanlage.
inveterate [in'vetərit], *adj.* eingewurzelt, eingefleischt.
invidious [in'vidiəs], *adj.* neiderregend, verhaßt.
invigorate [in'vigəreit], *v.a.* stärken, beleben.
invincible [in'vinsibl], *adj.* unbesiegbar, unüberwindlich.
inviolable [in'vaiələbl], *adj.* unverletzlich.
invisible [in'vizibl], *adj.* unsichtbar.
invitation [invi'teiʃən], *s.* die Einladung.
invite [in'vait], *v.a.* einladen.
invocation [invo'keiʃən], *s.* die Anrufung.
invoice ['invɔis], *s.* die Rechnung, Faktura. — *v.a.* fakturieren.
invoke [in'vouk], *v.a.* anrufen.
involuntary [in'vɔləntri], *adj.* unfreiwillig (*unwilling*); unwillkürlich (*reflex*).
involve [in'vɔlv], *v.a.* verwickeln.
involved [in'vɔlvd], *adj.* schwierig, verwickelt, kompliziert.
invulnerable [in'vʌlnərəbl], *adj.* unverwundbar, unverletzlich.
inward ['inwəd], *adj.* inner(lich). — *adv.* (*also* **inwards**) einwärts, nach innen, ins Innere.
iodine ['aiədain *or* 'aiədi:n], *s.* (*Chem.*) das Jod.
Iraki, Iraqi [i'rɑ:ki], *adj.* irakisch. — *s.* der Iraker.
Iranian [i'reinjən], *adj.* iranisch. — *s.* der Iranier.
irascible [i'ræsibl], *adj.* jähzornig, aufbrausend.
irate [ai'reit], *adj.* erzürnt, zornig.
ire [aiə], *s.* (*Poet.*) der Zorn.
iridescent [iri'desənt], *adj.* irisierend, schillernd.
iris ['aiəris], *s.* (*Anat.*) die Regenbogenhaut; (*Bot.*) die Schwertlilie.
Irish ['airiʃ], *adj.* irisch, ersisch. — *s.* (*pl.*) *the* —, die Irländer, Iren, *pl.*
Irishman ['airiʃmən], *s.* der Irländer, Ire.
irk [ə:k], *v.a.* verdrießen, verärgern.
irksome ['ə:ksəm], *adj.* lästig, ärgerlich.
iron ['aiən], *s.* (*Metall.*) das Eisen; (*pl.*) die eisernen Fesseln. — *adj.* eisern, Eisen-. — *v.a.* bügeln, plätten; — *out*, schlichten, beilegen.
ironical [ai'rɔnikəl], *adj.* ironisch.
ironmonger ['aiənmʌŋgə], *s.* der Eisenhändler.
ironmould ['aiənmould], *s.* der Rostfleck.
irony ['aiərəni], *s.* die Ironie.
irradiate [i'reidieit], *v.a.* bestrahlen.
irrational [i'ræʃənəl], *adj.* (*Log.*, *Maths.*) irrational; unvernünftig (*without reason*).
irreconcilable [irekən'sailəbl], *adj.* unversöhnlich; unvereinbar (*incompatible*).
irregular [i'regjulə], *adj.* unregelmäßig, gegen die Regel.
irrelevant [i'reləvənt], *adj.* belanglos.
irremediable [iri'mi:diəbl], *adj.* unheilbar; nicht wieder gut zu machen.
irreparable [i'repərəbl], *adj.* unersetzlich.
irrepressible [iri'presibl], *adj.* nicht zu unterdrücken, unbezähmbar.
irreproachable [iri'proutʃəbl], *adj.* untadelhaft, tadellos.
irresistible [iri'zistibl], *adj.* unwiderstehlich.
irresolute [i'rezolju:t], *adj.* unschlüssig, unentschlossen.
irrespective [iris'pektiv], *adj.* ohne Rücksicht (*of*, auf, *Acc.*).
irresponsible [iris'pɔnsibl], *adj.* unverantwortlich.
irretrievable [iri'tri:vəbl], *adj.* unersetzlich, unwiederbringlich.
irreverent [i'revərənt], *adj.* unehrerbietig.
irrevocable [i'revəkəbl], *adj.* unwiderruflich.

irrigate ['irigeit], *v.a.* bewässern.
irritable ['iritəbl], *adj.* reizbar.
irritant ['iritənt], *s.* das Reizmittel.
irritation [iri'teiʃən], *s.* die Reizung, das Reizen; die Erzürnung.
irruption [i'rʌpʃən], *s.* der Einbruch.
island ['ailənd], *s.* die Insel.
isle [ail], *s.* (*Poet.*) die Insel.
isolate ['aisəleit], *v.a.* (*Med.*) isolieren; absondern; (*Chem.*) darstellen.
isolation [aisə'leiʃən], *s.* die Absonderung, Isolierung.
Israeli [iz'reili], *adj.* den Staat Israel betreffend. — *s.* der Israeli.
Israelite ['izreiəlait], *adj.* israelitisch. — *s.* der Israelit.
issue ['isju: *or* 'iʃu:], *s.* der Ausgang, Erfolg (*result*); *main* —, der Hauptpunkt; die Nachkommenschaft (*children*); die Ausgabe (*edition*); Herausgabe (*publication*). — *v.a.* herausgeben; erlassen (*proclaim*); veröffentlichen (*publish*). — *v.n.* herrühren, stammen (*from*).
isthmus ['isθməs], *s.* die Landenge.
it [it], *pron.* es; *with* —, damit.
Italian [i'tæljən], *adj.* italienisch. — *s.* der Italiener.
italics [i'tæliks], *s. pl.* (*Typ.*) der Kursivdruck, die Kursivschrift.
itch [itʃ], *s.* das Jucken. — *v.n.* jucken; — *to do s.th.*, (*coll.*) darauf brennen, etwas zu tun.
item ['aitəm], *s.* der Posten (*in bill*); der Programmpunkt (*agenda*); die Einzelheit.
itemize ['aitəmaiz], *v.a.* (*Comm.*) aufführen; verzeichnen.
iterate ['itəreit], *v.a.* wiederholen.
itinerant [i'tinərənt], *adj.* wandernd.
its [its], *poss. adj.* sein, ihr; dessen, deren.
itself [it'self], *pron.* selber, sich; *of* —, von selbst.
ivory ['aivəri], *s.* das Elfenbein. — *adj.* aus Elfenbein, elfenbeinern.
ivy ['aivi], *s.* (*Bot.*) der Efeu.

J

J [dʒei]. das J.
jabber ['dʒæbə], *v.n.* schnattern.
Jack [dʒæk]. Hans; *Union* —, die britische Flagge; (*Cards*) der Bube.
jack [dʒæk], *s.* (*Motor.*) der Wagenheber. — *v.a.* — *up*, (*Motor.*) hochwinden.
jackal ['dʒækɔ:l], *s.* (*Zool.*) der Schakal.
jackass ['dʒækæs], *s.* (*Zool.*) der Esel.
jackdaw ['dʒækdɔ:], *s.* (*Orn.*) die Dohle.
jacket ['dʒækit], *s.* das Jackett, die Jacke; *dinner* —, der Smoking; *potatoes in their* —*s*, Kartoffeln in der Schale, *f. pl.*
jade [dʒeid], *s.* der Nierenstein.
jaded ['dʒeidid], *adj.* abgeplagt, abgehärmt, ermüdet.
jag [dʒæg], *s.* die Kerbe. — *v.a.* kerben, zacken.
jagged ['dʒægid], *adj.* zackig.
jail *see under* **gaol.**
jailer *see under* **gaoler.**
jam (1) [dʒæm], *s.* die Marmelade, Konfitüre.
jam (2) [dʒæm], *s. traffic* —, die Verkehrsstauung; (*coll.*) *in a* —, in der Klemme. — *v.a.* zusammenpressen (*press together*); (*Rad.*) stören.
Jamaican [dʒə'meikən], *adj.* jamaikanisch. — *s.* der Jamaikaner.
jamb [dʒæm], *s.* der Türpfosten.
jangle [dʒæŋgl], *v.n.* klirren, rasseln. — *s.* das Geklirr, Gerassel.
janitor ['dʒænitə], *s.* der Portier.
January ['dʒænjuəri]. der Januar.
japan [dʒə'pæn], *s.* lakierte Arbeit. — *v.a.* lackieren.
Japanese [dʒæpə'ni:z], *adj.* japanisch. — *s.* der Japaner.
jar (1) [dʒɑ:], *s.* der Topf, das Glas (*preserves*).
jar (2) [dʒɑ:], *v.n.* offenstehen (*door*); mißtönen, knarren.
jargon ['dʒɑ:gən], *s.* der Jargon.
jasmine ['dʒæzmin], *s.* (*Bot.*) der Jasmin.
jasper ['dʒæspə], *s.* der Jaspis.
jaundice ['dʒɔ:ndis], *s.* (*Med.*) die Gelbsucht; (*fig.*) der Neid (*envy*); —*d outlook*, die Verbitterung, Mißstimmung.
jaunt [dʒɔ:nt], *s.* der Ausflug, Spaziergang. — *v.n.* herumstreifen, spazieren.
jaunty ['dʒɔ:nti], *adj.* leicht, munter, lebhaft.
jaw [dʒɔ:], *s.* (*Anat.*) der Kinnbacken; der Rachen (*animals*).
jay [dʒei], *s.* (*Orn.*) der Häher.
jazz [dʒæz], *s.* die Jazzmusik.
jealous ['dʒeləs], *adj.* eifersüchtig.
jealousy ['dʒeləsi], *s.* die Eifersucht.
jeer ['dʒiə], *v.a.*, *v.n.* spotten, verhöhnen.
jejune [dʒi'dʒu:n], *adj.* nüchtern, trocken.
jelly ['dʒeli], *s.* das Gelee.
jellyfish ['dʒelifiʃ], *s.* (*Zool.*) die Qualle.
jeopardize ['dʒepədaiz], *v.a.* gefährden.
jeopardy ['dʒepədi], *s.* die Gefahr.
jerk [dʒə:k], *v.a.* rucken, stoßen (*push*); plötzlich bewegen (*move suddenly*). — *v.n.* zusammenzucken. — *s.* (*Am. coll.*) der Kerl; der Ruck, Stoß.
jersey ['dʒə:zi], *s.* die Wolljacke.
jessamine ['dʒesəmin], *s.* (*Bot.*) der Jasmin.
jest [dʒest], *s.* der Spaß, Scherz. — *v.n.* scherzen.
jester ['dʒestə], *s.* der Spaßmacher, Hofnarr.

jet (1) [dʒet], *s.* der Strahl, Wasserstrahl; (*Aviat.*) die Düse; — *engine*, der Düsenmotor; — *plane*, das Düsenflugzeug. — *v.n.* hervorspringen.
jet (2) [dʒet], *s.* der Gagat; — *black*, pechschwarz.
jetsam [ˈdʒetsəm], *s.* das Strandgut.
jetty [ˈdʒeti], *s.* der Hafendamm, die Landungsbrücke (*landing stage*).
Jew [dʒu:], *s.* der Jude.
jewel [ˈdʒuəl], *s.* das Juwel, der Edelstein.
jewel(le)ry [ˈdʒuəlri], *s.* der Schmuck; die Juwelen, *n. pl.*
Jewish [ˈdʒu:iʃ], *adj.* jüdisch.
Jewry [ˈdʒuəri], *s.* die Judenschaft, das Judentum.
jiffy [ˈdʒifi], *s.* (*coll.*) der Augenblick.
jig (1) [dʒig], *s.* die Gigue (*dance*).
jig (2) [dʒig], *s.* das Werkzeug (*tool*); —*saw*, die Säge; —*saw puzzle*, das Zusammenlegspiel, -setzspiel.
jilt [dʒilt], *v.a.* sitzen lassen.
jingle [dʒiŋgl], *v.a.* klimpern, klimpern lassen (*coins etc.*). —*s.* das Geklimper.
job [dʒɔb], *s.* die Arbeit, Anstellung; die Stellung; das Geschäft; — *in hand*, die Beschäftigung.
jobber [ˈdʒɔbə], *s.* der Makler, Spekulant (*stock exchange*).
jockey [ˈdʒɔki], *s* .der Jockei, Reiter.
jocular [ˈdʒɔkjulə], *adj.* scherzhaft, lustig.
jocund [ˈdʒɔkənd], *adj.* munter, heiter.
jog [dʒɔg], *v.a.* stoßen, antreiben. — *v.n.* gemächlich traben, trotten. — *s.* der Trott.
join [dʒɔin], *v.a.* verbinden, zusammenfügen; (*club etc.*) beitreten (*Dat.*). — *v.n.* (*rivers*) zusammenfließen (mit, *Dat.*); (*Comm.*) sich vereinigen (mit, *Dat.*).
joiner [ˈdʒɔinə], *s.* der Tischler, Schreiner.
joint [dʒɔint], *s.* (*Anat.*) das Gelenk; das Stück Fleisch, der Braten (*meat*); (*sl.*) das Lokal, die Spelunke. — *adj.* vereint, gemeinsam; (*Comm.*) — *stock company*, die Aktiengesellschaft; — *heir*, der Miterbe.
joist [dʒɔist], *s.* (*Carp.*) der Querbalken.
joke [dʒouk], *s.* der Scherz, Witz.
jollity [ˈdʒɔliti], *s.* die Heiterkeit.
jolly [ˈdʒɔli], *adj.* fröhlich, heiter, lustig.
jolt [dʒoult], *v.a.* schütteln, erschüttern (*shake up*). — *s.* der Stoß.
jostle [dʒɔsl], *v.a.* stoßen, drängen. — *v.n.* drängeln.
jot [dʒɔt], *s.* der Punkt, das Iota. — *v.a.* — (*down*), notieren, niederschreiben.
journal [ˈdʒə:nəl], *s.* die Zeitschrift (*periodical*).
journalism [ˈdʒə:nəlizm], *s.* das Zeitungswesen, der Journalistenberuf.
journalist [ˈdʒə:nəlist], *s.* der Journalist.
journey [ˈdʒə:ni], *s.* die Reise.
joust [dʒu:st], *s.* das Turnier.
jovial [ˈdʒouviəl], *adj.* jovial, freundlich; lustig (*gay*).
joy [dʒɔi], *s.* die Freude.
jubilant [ˈdʒu:bilənt], *adj.* frohlockend.
jubilation [dʒu:biˈleiʃən], *s.* der Jubel.
jubilee [ˈdʒu:bili:], *s.* das Jubiläum.
Judaism [dʒuˈdeiizm], *s.* das Judentum.
judge [dʒʌdʒ], *s.* der Richter. — *v.a.* richten, beurteilen, entscheiden.
judgment [ˈdʒʌdʒmənt], *s.* das Urteil; das Urteilsvermögen (*discretion*), die Urteilskraft.
judicial [dʒu:ˈdiʃəl], *adj.* richterlich, gerichtlich.
judicious [dʒu:ˈdiʃəs], *adj.* klug, scharfsinnig.
jug [dʒʌg], *s.* der Krug.
juggle [dʒʌgl], *v.n.* jonglieren, gaukeln.
juggler [ˈdʒʌglə], *s.* der Jongleur.
Jugoslav *see* **Yugoslav.**
jugular [ˈdʒu:g- *or* ˈdʒʌgjulə], *adj.* Kehl-, Hals-, Gurgel-. — *s.* (*vein*) die Halsader.
juice [dʒu:s], *s.* der Saft.
July [dʒuˈlai]. der Juli.
jumble [dʒʌmbl], *v.a.* zusammenmischen, vermischen. — *s.* das gemischte Zeug; — *sale*, der Verkauf, Ausverkauf gebrauchter Dinge, Ramschverkauf.
jump [dʒʌmp], *v.n.* springen. — *s.* der Sprung.
junction [ˈdʒʌŋkʃən], *s.* (*Railw.*) der Knotenpunkt; die Kreuzung.
juncture [ˈdʒʌŋktʃə], *s.* der (kritische) Zeitpunkt.
June [dʒu:n]. der Juni.
jungle [dʒʌŋgl], *s.* der Dschungel.
junior [ˈdʒu:njə], *adj.* jünger; Unter-.
juniper [ˈdʒu:nipə], *s.* (*Bot.*) der Wacholder.
junk [dʒʌŋk], *s.* (*coll.*) das alte Zeug, alte Möbelstücke, *n. pl.*
junket [ˈdʒʌŋkit], *s.* der Schmaus, das Fest; (*Cul.*) dicke Milch mit Sahne. — *v.n.* schmausen, feiern (*celebrate*).
juridical [dʒuəˈridikəl], *adj.* rechtlich; gerichtlich (*in Court*).
jurisdiction [dʒuərizˈdikʃən], *s.* die Gerichtsbarkeit.
juror [ˈdʒuərə], *s.* der, die Geschworene.
jury [ˈdʒuəri], *s.* die Jury, das Geschworenengericht.
just [dʒʌst], *adj.* gerecht; rechtschaffen (*decent*); gehörig (*proper*). — *adv.* soeben, eben; — *as*, eben als, gerade wie.
justice [ˈdʒʌstis], *s.* die Gerechtigkeit; der Richter (*judge*).
justifiable [ˈdʒʌstifaiəbl], *adj.* zu rechtfertigen, berechtigt.
justify [ˈdʒʌstifai], *v.a.* rechtfertigen.
jut [dʒʌt], *v.n.* — (*out*), hervorragen. — *s.* der Vorsprung.
jute [dʒu:t], *s.* die Jute.
juvenile [ˈdʒu:vənail], *adj.* jugendlich, unreif.
juxtaposition [dʒʌkstəpəˈziʃən], *s.* die Nebeneinanderstellung, Gegenüberstellung.

K

K [kei]. das K.
kale [keil], *s.* (*Bot.*) der Krauskohl.
kaleidoscope [kəˈlaidəskoup], *s.* das Kaleidoskop.
kangaroo [kæŋgəˈru:], *s.* (*Zool.*) das Känguruh.
keel [ki:l], *s.* der Kiel; *on an even* —, bei ruhiger See; (*also fig.*) ruhig. — *v.n.* — *over*, umkippen.
keen [ki:n], *adj.* eifrig (*intent*); scharfsinnig (*perspicacious*); scharf (*blade*).
keenness [ˈki:nnis], *s.* der Eifer; Scharfsinn; die Schärfe (*blade*).
keep [ki:p], *v.a. irr.* halten (*hold*); behalten (*retain*); führen (*a shop*); hüten (*gate, dog etc.*). — *v.n.* — *doing*, in etwas fortfahren, — *going*, weitergehen; — *away*, sich fernhalten; — *in, indoors*, zu Hause bleiben; — *off*, abhalten; sich fernhalten; — *out*, draußen bleiben; — *up*, aufrechterhalten. — *s.* das Burgverlies; der Unterhalt.
keeper [ˈki:pə], *s.* der Hüter, Wärter; Museumsbeamte.
keeping [ˈki:piŋ], *s.* die Verwahrung; *in safe* —, in guten Händen, in guter Obhut.
keepsake [ˈki:pseik], *s.* das Andenken.
keg [keg], *s.* das Fäßchen.
ken [ken], *s.* die Kenntnis; *in my* —, meines Wissens. — *v.a.* (*Scottish*) kennen.
kennel [kenl], *s.* die Hundehütte.
kerb(stone) [ˈkə:b(stoun)], *s.* der Prellstein.
kerchief [ˈkə:tʃif], *s.* das Kopftuch, Halstuch.
kernel [kə:nl], *s.* der Kern.
kettle [ketl], *s.* der Kessel; — *drum*, die Kesselpauke.
key [ki:], *s.* der Schlüssel; (*Mus.*) die Tonart; die Taste (*on piano etc.*); — *man*, eine wichtige Person, Person in einer Schlüsselstellung. — *v.a.* — (*in*), einfügen, befestigen.
keyboard [ˈki:bɔ:d], *s.* die Klaviatur; Tastatur (*typewriter*); — *instrument*, das Tasteninstrument.
keyhole [ˈki:houl], *s.* das Schlüsselloch.
keystone [ˈki:stoun], *s.* der Schlußstein.
kick [kik], *v.a., v.n.* mit dem Fuße stoßen *or* treten; — *against s.th.*, sich wehren. — *s.* der Fußstoß, Tritt; (*Footb.*) — *off*, der Ankick; *free* —, der Freistoß; *penalty* —, der Strafstoß, der Elfmeterstoß.
kid (1) [kid], *s.* (*Zool.*) das Geißlein, Zicklein; *with* — *gloves*, mit Glacéhandschuhen; (*coll.*) das Kind.
kid (2) [kid], *v.a.* (*Am. coll.*) zum Narren haben, aufziehen (*tease*).
kidnap [ˈkidnæp], *v.a.* entführen.
kidney [ˈkidni], *s.* (*Anat.*) die Niere; — *bean*, die französische Bohne.
kill [kil], *v.a.* töten; schlachten (*animal*).
kiln [kiln], *s.* der Darrofen; der Ziegelofen (*tiles, bricks*).
kilt [kilt], *s.* der Schottenrock.
kin [kin], *s.* die Verwandtschaft; *kith and* —, die Verwandten, *m. pl.*
kind [kaind], *s.* die Art, Gattung, Art und Weise. — *adj.* freundlich, gütig, liebenswürdig.
kindle [kindl], *v.a.* anzünden, anfachen.
kindliness, kindness [ˈkaindlinis, ˈkaindnis], *s.* die Güte, Freundlichkeit.
kindred [ˈkindrid], *adj.* verwandt.
king [kiŋ], *s.* der König.
kingdom [ˈkiŋdəm], *s.* das Königreich.
kink [kiŋk], *s.* der Knoten; (*coll.*) der Vogel, die Grille (*obsession etc.*).
kinship [ˈkinʃip], *s.* die Sippe, Verwandtschaft.
kipper [ˈkipə], *s.* der geräucherte Hering.
kiss [kis], *v.a.* küssen. — *s.* der Kuß.
kit [kit], *s.* (*Mil.*) die Ausrüstung.
kitbag [ˈkitbæg], *s.* der Tornister.
kitchen [ˈkitʃən], *s.* die Küche; — *garden*, der Gemüsegarten.
kite [kait], *s.* der Drache, Papierdrache; *fly a* —, einen Drachen steigen lassen; (*Orn.*) der Gabelweih, der (rote) Milan; (*sl.*) der Schwindler.
kith [kiθ], *s.* now only in — *and kin*, die Verwandten, *m. pl.*
kitten [kitn], *s.* das Kätzchen.
knack [næk], *s.* der Kniff, Kunstgriff.
knacker [ˈnækə], *s.* der Abdecker (*horse*).
knapsack [ˈnæpsæk], *s.* der Rucksack, Tornister.
knave [neiv], *s.* der Kerl, Schurke; Bube (*cards*).
knead [ni:d], *v.a.* kneten.
knee [ni:], *s.* (*Anat.*) das Knie.
kneel [ni:l], *v.n. irr.* knieen, niederknieen.
knell [nel], *s.* die Totenglocke.
knick-knack [ˈniknæk], *s.* die Nippsache.
knife [naif], *s.* das Messer. — *v.a.* erstechen.
knight [nait], *s.* der Ritter; der Springer (*chess*).
knit [nit], *v.a., v.n. reg. & irr.* stricken; *knitting needle*, die Stricknadel.
knob [nɔb], *s.* der (Tür)knopf, die Türklinke; der Knorren (*wood*).
knock [nɔk], *v.n.* klopfen, schlagen. — *s.* der Schlag, Stoß.
knoll [noul], *s.* der kleine Hügel.
knot [nɔt], *s.* der Knoten; die Schwierigkeit (*difficulty*).
know [nou], *v.a. irr.* kennen (*be acquainted with*); wissen (*possess knowledge (of)*).
knowing [ˈnouiŋ], *adj.* wissend.
knowledge [ˈnɔlidʒ], *s.* die Kenntnis (*acquaintance with*); das Wissen (*by*

study, information etc.); die Kenntnisse (*of language etc.*).
knuckle [nʌkl], *s.* (*Anat.*) der Knöchel. — *v.n.* — *under*, sich fügen.
Kremlin ['kremlin], *s.* der Kreml.
kudos ['kju:dɔs], *s.* der Ruhm, das Ansehen.

L

L [el]. das L.
label [leibl], *s.* die Etikette, das Schildchen.
labial ['leibiəl], *adj.* (*Phonet.*) labial, Lippen-. — *s.* (*Phonet.*) der Lippenlaut.
laboratory [lə'bɔrətəri, (*Am.*) 'læbərətəri], *s.* das Laboratorium, (*coll.*) das Labor.
laborious [lə'bɔ:riəs], *adj.* mühsam.
labour ['leibə], *s.* die Arbeit, Mühe; *Labour Party*, die Arbeiterpartei; (*Med.*) die Geburtswehen, *f. pl.* — *v.n.* sich abmühen, leiden; sich anstrengen.
labourer ['leibərə], *s.* der Arbeiter, Taglöhner.
lace [leis], *s.* die Spitze, Tresse. — *v.a.* verbrämen (*trim with lace*); zuschnüren (*shoe*); stärken (*coffee with rum etc.*).
lacerate ['læsəreit], *v.a.* zerreißen.
lack [læk], *v.a.* ermangeln (*Genit.*). — *v.n.* fehlen (an, *Dat.*). — *s.* der Mangel, das Fehlen.
lackadaisical [lækə'deizikəl], *adj.* schlaff, (*coll.*) schlapp, unbekümmert.
lackey ['læki], *s.* der Lakai, Diener, Bediente.
laconic [lə'kɔnik], *adj.* lakonisch.
lacquer ['lækə], *s.* der Lack. — *v.a.* lackieren.
lad [læd], *s.* der Bursche, Junge.
ladder ['lædə], *s.* die Leiter.
lading ['leidiŋ], *s.* (*Comm.*) das Laden; die Fracht; *bill of* —, der Frachtbrief.
ladle [leidl], *s.* der Schöpflöffel, Suppenlöffel; die Kelle. — *v.a.* ausschöpfen, austeilen.
lady ['leidi], *s.* die Dame; — *-in-waiting*, die Hofdame.
ladybird ['leidibə:d], *s.* (*Ent.*) der Marienkäfer.
ladyship ['leidiʃip], *s.* (*Title*) gnädige Frau.
lag [læg], *v.n.* zurückbleiben. — *v.a.* verkleiden, isolieren (*tank*).
laggard ['lægəd], *s.* der Zauderer. — *adj.* zögernd, zaudernd.
lagoon [lə'gu:n], *s.* die Lagune.
lair [lɛə], *s.* das Lager (*of animal*).
laird [lɛəd], *s.* der schottische Gutsherr.
laity ['leiiti], *s.* die Laien, *m. pl.*
lake [leik], *s.* der See.
lamb [læm], *s.* (*Zool.*) das Lamm. — *v.n.* lammen.
lambent ['læmbənt], *adj.* brennend, lodernd, strahlend.
lame [leim], *adj.* lahm. — *v.a.* lähmen.
lament [lə'ment], *v.a.*, *v.n.* betrauern, beweinen. — *s.* das Klagelied, die Wehklage.
lamp [læmp], *s.* die Lampe; — *-post*, der Laternenpfahl.
lampoon [læm'pu:n], *v.a.* schmähen, lächerlich machen. — *s.* die Schmähschrift.
lamprey ['læmpri], *s.* (*Zool.*) das Neunauge.
lance [lɑ:ns], *s.* (*Mil.*) die Lanze. — *v.a.* durchbohren; (*Med.*) lancieren.
lancer ['lɑ:nsə], *s.* (*Mil.*) der Ulan.
lancet ['lɑ:nsit], *s.* (*Med.*) die Lanzette.
land [lænd], *s.* das Land; das Grundstück (*plot*); — *tax*, die Grundsteuer. — *v.a.* ans Land bringen, fangen (*fish*). — *v.n.* landen.
landlord ['lændlɔ:d], *s.* der Eigentümer, der Hausherr; Wirt (*pub*).
landmark ['lændmɑ:k], *s.* der Grenzstein, das Wahrzeichen.
landscape ['lændskeip], *s.* die Landschaft.
landslide, landslip ['lændslaid, 'lændslip], *s.* der Erdrutsch.
lane [lein], *s.* der Heckenweg, Pfad; die Gasse; (*Motor.*) die Fahrbahn.
language ['læŋgwidʒ], *s.* die Sprache.
languid ['læŋgwid], *adj.* flau, matt.
languor ['læŋgə], *s.* die Mattigkeit, Flauheit.
lank [læŋk], *adj.* mager, schlank.
lantern ['læntən], *s.* die Laterne.
Laotian ['lauʃən], *adj.* laotisch. — *s.* der Laote.
lap (1) [læp], *s.* der Schoß.
lap (2) [læp], *s.* das Plätschern (*of waves*). — *v.a.* auflecken (*lick up*). — *v.n.* plätschern.
lapel [lə'pel], *s.* der Aufschlag (*of jacket*).
lapidary ['læpidəri], *adj.* lapidarisch; wuchtig.
lapse [læps], *v.n.* gleiten, fallen; verlaufen (*time*). — *s.* der Verlauf (*time*); der Fehler (*mistake*); das Verfallen (*into laziness etc.*).
lapwing ['læpwiŋ], *s.* (*Orn.*) der Kiebitz.
larceny ['lɑ:səni], *s.* der Diebstahl.
larch [lɑ:tʃ], *s.* (*Bot.*) die Lärche.
lard [lɑ:d], *s.* das Schweinefett, Schweineschmalz.
larder ['lɑ:də], *s.* die Speisekammer.
large [lɑ:dʒ], *adj.* groß; weit; dick, stark.
largesse ['lɑ:dʒes], *s.* die Freigebigkeit (*generosity*); die Schenkung (*donation*).
lark (1) [lɑ:k], *s.* (*Orn.*) die Lerche.
lark (2) [lɑ:k], *s.* (*coll.*) der Scherz. — *v.n.* scherzen.
larkspur ['lɑ:kspə:], *s.* (*Bot.*) der Rittersporn.
larva ['lɑ:və], *s.* (*Zool.*) die Larve.

larynx ['lærinks], *s.* (*Anat.*) der Kehlkopf.
lascivious [lə'siviəs], *adj.* wollüstig.
lash [læʃ], *s.* die Wimper (*eye*); die Peitschenschnur (*whip*), der Peitschenhieb (*stroke of whip*). — *v.a.* peitschen.
lass [læs], *s.* (*coll.*) das Mädchen.
lassitude ['læsitju:d], *s.* die Mattigkeit.
lasso [lə'su: *or* 'læsou], *s.* das Lasso. — *v.a.* mit einem Lasso fangen.
last (1) [lɑ:st], *adj.* letzt, vorig, äußerst; *at long* —, endlich.
last (2) [lɑ:st], *s.* der Leisten (*shoemaking*).
last (3) [lɑ:st], *v.n.* dauern, anhalten; hinreichen (*be sufficient*).
lastly ['lɑ:stli], *adv.* zuletzt.
latch [lætʃ], *v.a.* verschließen.
latchkey ['lætʃki:], *s.* der Hausschlüssel.
late [leit], *adj.* spät; verspätet; verstorben, selig (*deceased*); neulich (*recent*); *the train is* —, der Zug hat Verspätung; *of late*, jüngst.
latent ['leitənt], *adj.* (*Med.*) latent; verborgen.
lateral ['lætərəl], *adj.* seitlich, Seiten-.
lath [lɑ:θ], *s.* die Latte.
lathe [leið], *s.* die Drehbank.
lather ['læðə], *s.* der Seifenschaum. — *v.n.*, *v.a.* (sich) einseifen.
Latin ['lætin], *adj.* lateinisch. — *s.* das Latein, die lateinische Sprache.
latitude ['lætitju:d], *s.* die geographische Breite; die Weite (*width*); (*fig.*) der Spielraum (*scope*).
latter ['lætə], *adj.* letzter; später (*later*). — *s.* der Letztere.
latterly ['lætəli], *adv.* neulich, neuerdings.
lattice ['lætis], *s.* das Gitter. — *v.a.* vergittern.
Latvian ['lætviən], *adj.* lettisch. — *s.* der Lette.
laud [lɔ:d], *v.a.* loben, preisen.
laudable ['lɔ:dəbl], *adj.* lobenswert.
laudatory ['lɔ:dətəri], *adj.* belobend.
laugh [lɑ:f], *v.n.* lachen; —*ing stock*, der Gegenstand des Gelächters.
laughter ['lɑ:ftə], *s.* das Lachen, Gelächter.
launch [lɔ:ntʃ], *s.* die Barkasse. — *v.a.* vom Stapel lassen.
launching ['lɔ:ntʃiŋ], *s.* der Stapellauf.
laundress ['lɔ:ndris], *s.* die Wäscherin.
laundry ['lɔ:ndri], *s.* die Wäsche (*clothes*); Wäscherei (*place*).
laureate ['lɔ:riit], *s.* der Hofdichter.
laurel ['lɔrəl], *s.* (*Bot.*) der Lorbeer.
lavatory ['lævətri], *s.* das W.C., der Abort, Waschraum; die Toilette; *public* —, die Bedürfnisanstalt.
lavender ['lævəndə], *s.* (*Bot.*) der Lavendel.
lavish ['læviʃ], *adj.* freigebig, verschwenderisch. — *v.a.* vergeuden.
lavishness ['læviʃnis], *s.* die Freigebigkeit, Verschwendung.
law [lɔ:], *s.* das Gesetz (*statute*); das Recht (*justice*); die Jura, Jurisprudenz (*subject of study*).
lawful ['lɔ:ful], *adj.* gesetzlich, gesetzmäßig.
lawless ['lɔ:lis], *adj.* gesetzlos; unrechtmäßig (*illegal*).
lawn (1) [lɔ:n], *s.* der Rasen.
lawn (2) [lɔ:n], *s.* der Batist.
lawsuit ['lɔ:su:t], *s.* der Prozeß.
lawyer ['lɔ:jə], *s.* der Advokat, Rechtsanwalt, Jurist.
lax [læks], *adj.* locker, lax.
laxative ['læksətiv], *s.* das Abführmittel.
laxity ['læksiti], *s.* die Schlaffheit, Lockerheit (*of rope etc.*).
lay (1) [lei], *v.a. irr.* legen; setzen (*put*); stellen (*place*); bannen (*ghost*); — *up*, sammeln. — *v.n.* legen (*eggs*); wetten (*wager*); — *about one*, um sich schlagen.
lay (2) [lei], *s.* (*Poet.*) das Lied.
lay (3) [lei], *adj.* Laien-.
layer ['leiə], *s.* die Schicht; — *cake*, die Cremetorte.
layman ['leimən], *s.* der Laie.
laziness ['leizinis], *s.* die Faulheit.
lazy ['leizi], *adj.* faul, träge.
lea [li:], *s.* (*Poet.*) die Aue.
lead (1) [li:d], *v.a.*, *v.n. irr.* führen, leiten; ausspielen (*cards*). — *s.* die Führung; (*Elec.*) Leitung.
lead (2) [led], *s.* das Blei; Bleilot (*plumbline*).
leader ['li:də], *s.* der Führer; (*Mus.*) der Konzertmeister; der Leitartikel (*leading article*).
leaf [li:f], *s.* (*Bot.*) das Blatt; (*Build.*) der Türflügel. — *v.a.* (*coll.*) — *through*, durchblättern.
leafy ['li:fi], *adj.* belaubt.
league (1) [li:g], *s.* drei englische Meilen, *f.pl.*
league (2) [li:g], *s.* das Bündnis (*pact*); *be in* —, verbündet sein; *League of Nations*, der Völkerbund.
leak [li:k], *v.n.* lecken, ein Loch haben. — *s.* das Loch; (*Naut.*) das Leck.
leaky ['li:ki], *adj.* leck.
lean (1) [li:n], *v.n. irr.*(sich)lehnen (an, *Acc.*), stützen (auf, *Acc.*).
lean (2) [li:n], *adj.* mager, hager.
leap [li:p], *v.n. irr.* springen. — *s.* der Sprung; — *year*, das Schaltjahr.
learn [lə:n], *v.a. irr.* lernen, erfahren.
learned ['lə:nid], *adj.* gelehrt.
learning ['lə:niŋ], *s.* die Gelehrsamkeit.
lease [li:s], *s.* die Pacht, der Mietvertrag (*of house*). — *v.a.* (ver)pachten.
leasehold ['li:should], *s.* die Pachtung.
leash [li:ʃ], *v.a.* koppeln, anbinden. — *s.* die Koppel.
least [li:st], *adj.* wenigst, geringst, mindest, kleinst. — *s. at* (*the*) —, wenigstens, mindestens.
leather ['leðə], *s.* das Leder. — *adj.* Leder-, ledern.
leave [li:v], *v.a. irr.* verlassen (*quit*); lassen (*let*); hinterlassen (*bequeath*). — *v.n.* Abschied nehmen, abreisen. — *s.* der Urlaub; der Abschied (*farewell*); die Erlaubnis (*permission*).

leaven [levn], *s.* der Sauerteig. — *v.a.* säuern.
Lebanese [lebə'ni:z], *adj.* libanesisch. — *s.* der Libanese.
lecture ['lektʃə], *s.* die Vorlesung; der Vortrag.
lecturer ['lektʃərə], *s.* (*Univ.*) der Dozent; der Vortragende (*speaker*).
ledge [ledʒ], *s.* der Sims (*window*).
ledger ['ledʒə], *s.* (*Comm.*) das Hauptbuch.
lee [li:], *s.* die Leeseite (*shelter*).
leech [li:tʃ], *s.* (*Zool.*) der Blutegel.
leek [li:k], *s.* (*Bot.*) der Lauch.
leer ['liə], *s.* das Starren; der Seitenblick. — *v.n.* schielen (*at*, auf, nach); starren.
lees [li:z], *s. pl.* der Bodensatz, die Hefe.
left [left], *adj.* link. — *adv.* inks. — *s.* die linke Seite.
leg [leg], *s.* (*Anat.*) das Bein; der Schaft.
legacy ['legəsi], *s.* das Vermächtnis, das Erbe, Erbgut.
legal ['li:gəl], *adj.* gesetzlich.
legality [li'gæliti], *s.* die Gesetzlichkeit.
legatee [legə'ti:], *s.* (*Law*) der Erbe, die Erbin.
legation [li'geiʃən], *s.* die Gesandtschaft.
legend ['ledʒənd], *s.* die Legende, Sage; die Inschrift (*inscription*).
legendary ['ledʒəndəri], *adj.* legendär, sagenhaft.
leggings ['legiŋz], *s. pl.* die Gamaschen.
legible ['ledʒibl], *adj.* leserlich.
legislation [ledʒis'leiʃən], *s.* die Gesetzgebung.
legislative ['ledʒislətiv], *adj.* gesetzgebend.
legislator ['ledʒisleitə], *s.* der Gesetzgeber.
legitimacy [li'dʒitiməsi], *s.* die Gesetzmäßigkeit; (*Law*) die eheliche Geburt (*of birth*).
legitimate [li'dʒitimit], *adj.* gesetzmäßig; (*Law*) ehelich (*child*). — [-meit], *v.a.* für gesetzlich erklären.
legitimize [li'dʒitimaiz], *v.a.* legitimieren.
leguminous [li'gju:minəs], *adj.* Hülsen–; hülsentragend.
leisure ['leʒə], *s.* die Freizeit, Muße.
leisurely ['leʒəli], *adj.*, *adv.* gelassen, gemächlich.
lemon ['lemən], *s.* (*Bot.*) die Zitrone.
lemonade [lemən'eid], *s.* die Limonade.
lend [lend], *v.a. irr.* leihen; *—ing library*, die Leihbibiothek.
length [leŋθ], *s.* die Länge (*extent*); die Dauer (*duration*); *at* —, ausführlich.
lengthen ['leŋθən], *v.a.*, *v.n.* (sich) verlängern.
lengthy ['leŋθi], *adj.* langwierig, lang.
lenient ['li:niənt], *adj.* nachsichtig, milde.
lens [lenz], *s.* die Linse (*optics*); das Objektiv.
Lent [lent]. die Fastenzeit.
lentil ['lentil], *s.* (*Bot.*) die Linse.
leprosy ['leprəsi], *s.* der Aussatz, die Leprakrankheit.
leprous ['leprəs], *adj.* aussätzig.
lesion ['li:ʒən], *s.* die Verletzung.
less [les], *comp. adj.*, *adv.* weniger, kleiner.
lessee [le'si:], *s.* der Pächter, Mieter.
lessen [lesn], *v.a.*, *v.n.* (sich) verringern, vermindern.
lesser ['lesə], *comp. adj.* geringer; kleiner.
lesson [lesn], *s.* die Lehrstunde, Lektion; (*pl.*) der Unterricht; (*Rel.*) der Bibeltext.
lessor ['lesə], *s.* der Eigentümer, Vermieter.
lest [lest], *conj.* damit nicht; aus Furcht, daß.
let [let], *v.a. irr.* lassen; zulassen; vermieten; (*room*); — *down*, blamieren, enttäuschen; *off*, abschießen. — *s. without — or hindrance*, ohne Hinderung.
lethal ['li:θəl], *adj.* tödlich.
letter ['letə], *s.* der Brief; der Buchstabe (*character*); — *box*, der Briefkasten; (*pl.*) die Literatur.
letterpress ['letəpres], *s.* die Kopierpresse.
lettuce ['letis], *s.* (*Bot.*) der Salat.
level [levl], *adj.* eben, gleich. — *s.* die Ebene; das Niveau. — *v.a.* ebnen, ausgleichen; (*Build.*) planieren.
lever ['li:və], *s.* der Hebel.
levity ['leviti], *s.* der Leichtsinn.
levy ['levi], *v.a.* erheben (*tax*); auferlegen (*penalty*). — *s.* die Steuer.
lewd [lju:d *or* lu:d], *adj.* liederlich, gemein, unzüchtig.
liability [laiə'biliti], *s.* die Verantwortlichkeit; *limited* —, beschränkte Haftung; die Steuerpflichtigkeit (*to tax*), Zollpflichtigkeit (*to duty*).
liable ['laiəbl], *adj.* haftbar, zahlungspflichtig.
liar ['laiə], *s.* der Lügner.
libel ['laibəl], *s.* die Verleumdung. — *v.a.* verleumden, schmähen.
libellous ['laibələs], *adj.* verleumderisch.
liberal ['libərəl], *adj.* (*Pol.*) liberal; freigebig (*generous*); — *arts*, Geisteswissenschaften, *f. pl.*
liberate ['libəreit], *v.a.* befreien, freisetzen; (*Law*) in Freiheit setzen.
Liberian [lai'bi:riən], *adj.* liberisch. — *s.* der Liberier.
libertine ['libəti:n], *s.* der Wüstling.
liberty ['libəti], *s.* die Freiheit; die Erlaubnis (*permission*).
librarian [lai'brεəriən], *s.* der Bibliothekar, die Bibliothekarin.
library ['laibrəri], *s.* die Bibliothek.
Libyan ['libjən], *adj.* libysch. — *s.* der Libyer.
licence ['laisəns], *s.* die Genehmigung, Erlaubnis (*permit*); *driving* —, der Führerschein; die Zügellosigkeit (*licentiousness*).
license ['laisəns], *v.a.* genehmigen, bewilligen; *licensing laws*, Ausschanksgesetze, *n. pl.* (*for alcohol*).

licentiate [lai'senʃiit], *s.* der Lizenziat (*degree*).
licentious [lai'senʃəs], *adj.* ausschweifend, liederlich, locker (*in morals*).
lichen ['laikən, 'litʃən], *s.* (*Bot.*) die Flechte.
lichgate ['litʃgeit], *s.* das Friedhofstor.
lick [lik], *v.a.* lecken; (*Am.*) prügeln, verhauen.
lid [lid], *s.* das Augenlid; der Deckel.
lie [lai], (1) *v.n.* lügen. — *s.* die Lüge (*untruth*).
lie [lai], (2) *v.n. irr.* liegen; — *down*, sich legen, hinlegen; sich fügen (*fig.*).
lieu [lju:], *s. in* —, an Stelle, anstatt (*Genit.*).
lieutenant [lef'tenənt], *s.* der Leutnant.
life [laif], *s.* das Leben.
lifebelt ['laifbelt], *s.* der Rettungsgürtel.
lifeboat ['laifbout], *s.* das Rettungsboot.
lifetime ['laiftaim], *s.* die Lebenszeit, Zeit seines Lebens.
lift [lift], *s.* der Aufzug, Fahrstuhl; (*coll.*) *give a — to*, mitnehmen (im Auto). — *v.a.* heben; aufheben (*abolish*); (*coll.*) klauen, stehlen.
ligament ['ligəmənt], *s.* das Band; (*Anat.*) die Flechse, die Sehne.
ligature ['ligətʃə], *s.* (*Typ.*) die Ligatur; die Verbindung.
light [lait], *adj.* hell, licht; blond (*hair*); leicht (*weight*). — *s.* das Licht; *give a* —, ein Streichholz geben, Feuer geben. — *v.a. irr.* beleuchten (*room*); anzünden (*fire*). — *v.n. irr.* — (*up*), hell werden, leuchten; (*fig.*) aufleuchten.
lighten [laitn], *v.a.* erhellen (*brighten*); erleichtern (*ease*).
lighter ['laitə], *s.* das Feuerzeug (*smoker's*); (*Naut.*) das Lichterschiff.
lighthouse ['laithaus], *s.* der Leuchtturm.
lightning ['laitniŋ], *s.* der Blitz; — *conductor*, der Blitzableiter; — *speed*, die Blitzesschnelle.
ligneous ['ligniəs], *adj.* holzig.
lignite ['lignait], *s.* die Braunkohle.
like (1) [laik], *v.a.* gern haben; *I — to sing*, ich singe gern. — *v.n.* belieben, wollen; *as you* —, wie Sie wollen. — *s. his —s and dislikes*, seine Wünsche und Abneigungen.
like (2) [laik], *adj.* gleich, ähnlich. — *s. his* —, seinesgleichen. — *prep.* gleich, wie; *just — him*! das sieht ihm ähnlich! *feel* —, möchte gern; *what is it* —? wie sieht es aus?
likelihood ['laiklihud], *s.* die Möglichkeit; Wahrscheinlichkeit (*probability*).
likely ['laikli], *adj.* möglich; wahrscheinlich (*probable*).
liken ['laikən], *v.a.* vergleichen.
likeness ['laiknis], *s.* die Ähnlichkeit.
likewise ['laikwaiz], *adv.* ebenso, gleichfalls, auch.
liking ['laikiŋ], *s.* die Vorliebe (*for*, für, *Acc.*); Neigung (*for*, zu, *Dat.*); *to my* —, nach meinem Geschmack *or* Wunsch.
lilac ['lailək], *s.* (*Bot.*) der Flieder.
lilt [lilt], *v.a., v.n.* trällern, summen. — *s.* die Melodie, Weise.
lily ['lili], (*Bot.*) *s.* die Lilie; — *of the valley*, das Maiglöckchen.
limb [lim], *s.* das Glied.
limber ['limbə], *adj.* geschmeidig.
lime (1) [laim], *s.* der Leim, Kalk (*chalk*).
lime (2) [laim], *s.* (*Bot.*) die Linde (*tree*); die Limone (*fruit*); — *juice*, der Limonensaft.
limestone ['laimstoun], *s.* der Kalkstein.
limit ['limit], *s.* die Grenze, das Ende. — *v.a.* begrenzen, beschränken.
limitation [limi'teiʃən], *s.* die Begrenzung.
limn [lim], *v.a.* (*Art.*) zeichnen, malen.
limp [limp], *v.n.* hinken. — *adj.* müde, schlaff.
limpid ['limpid], *adj.* klar, durchsichtig.
linden ['lindən], *s.* (*Bot.*) die Linde.
line (1) [lain], *s.* die Linie, Eisenbahnlinie (*Railw.*); die Zeile; der Strich; (*Mil.*) die Reihe; — *of business*, die Geschäftsbranche; (*Genealogy*) die Abstammung; *take a strong* —, entschlossen auftreten.
line (2) [lain], *v.a.* füttern (*a garment*).
lineage ['liniidʒ], *s.* die Abstammung.
lineament ['liniəmənt], *s.* der Gesichtszug.
linear ['liniə], *adj.* linear, geradlinig.
linen ['linin], *s.* die Leinwand; *bed* —, die Laken, Bettwäsche. — *adj.* leinen.
liner ['lainə], *s.* (*Naut.*) das Passagierschiff.
linger ['liŋgə], *v.n.* zögern; verweilen.
lingerie ['lɛ̃ʒəri:], *s.* die Damenunterwäsche.
linguist ['liŋgwist], *s.* der Sprachkundige, Philologe, Linguist.
liniment ['linimənt], *s.* (*Med.*) die Salbe.
lining ['lainiŋ], *s.* das Futter (*of garment*).
link [liŋk], *s.* das Glied (*in chain*); die Verbindung (*connexion*). — *v.a.* verbinden, verknüpfen.
linnet ['linit], *s.* (*Orn.*) der Hänfling.
linseed ['linsi:d], *s.* der Leinsamen; — *oil*, das Leinöl.
lint [lint], *s.* die Scharpie, das Verbandzeug.
lion ['laiən], *s.* (*Zool.*) der Löwe.
lioness ['laiənes], *s.* (*Zool.*) die Löwin.
lip [lip], *s.* (*Anat., Bot.*) die Lippe (*mouth*); der Rand (*of jug*).
lipstick ['lipstik], *s.* der Lippenstift.
liquefy ['likwifai], *v.a., v.n.* flüssig machen *or* werden.
liqueur [li'kjuə], *s.* der Likör.
liquid ['likwid], *adj.* flüssig. — *s.* die Flüssigkeit.
liquidate ['likwideit], *v.a.* liquidieren; (*Comm.*) flüssig machen (*assets*); bezahlen (*pay off*).

liquor ['likə], *s.* der Alkohol.
liquorice ['likəris], *s.* die Lakritze.
lisp [lisp], *v.n.* lispeln. — *s.* der Sprachfehler, das Anstoßen, Lispeln.
list [list], *s.* die Liste, das Verzeichnis; (*Naut.*) die Schlagseite.
listen [lisn], *v.n.* horchen, zuhören.
listless ['listlis], *adj.* teilnahmslos.
litany ['litəni], *s.* (*Eccl.*) die Litanei.
literal ['litərəl], *adj.* buchstäblich.
literary ['litərəri], *adj.* literarisch, Literatur-.
literature ['litrətʃə], *s.* die Literatur.
lithe [laið], *adj.* geschmeidig.
Lithuanian [liθju'einiən], *adj.* litauisch. — *s.* der Litauer.
litigate ['litigeit], *v.n.* einen Prozeß anstrengen, litigieren, prozessieren.
litigation [liti'geiʃən], *s.* die Litigation, der Prozeß.
litter ['litə], *s.* (*Zool.*) die Jungen, *n. pl.*; die Brut; die Sänfte (*carriage*); der Abfall, die Abfälle (*waste paper etc.*). — *v.n.* (*Zool.*) Junge haben, werfen. — *v.a.* Abfälle wegwerfen, unsauber machen.
little [litl], *adj.* klein (*size, value*); gering (*value*); — *by* —, nach und nach.
liturgy ['litədʒi], *s.* (*Eccl.*) die Liturgie.
live [liv], *v.n.* leben; wohnen (*dwell*).
livelihood ['laivlihud], *s.* der Lebensunterhalt.
liveliness ['laivlinis], *s.* die Lebhaftigkeit.
lively ['laivli], *adj.* lebhaft.
liven [laivn], *v.a.* — *up*, beleben.
liver ['livə], *s.* (*Anat.*) die Leber.
livery ['livəri], *s.* die Livree (*uniform*); — *company*, die Zunftgenossenschaft.
livid ['livid], *adj.* bleich, blaß.
living ['liviŋ], *s.* das Auskommen, der Unterhalt; die Lebensweise; (*Eccl.*) die Pfründe, Pfarrstelle.
lizard ['lizəd], *s.* (*Zool.*) die Eidechse.
lo! [lou], *excl.* (*obs.*) sieh, da! siehe!
load [loud], *s.* die Last, Belastung. — *v.a.* beladen, belasten. — *v.n.* laden, aufladen.
loadstone *see* **lodestone**.
loaf [louf], *s.* der Laib (*bread*); *sugar* —, der Zuckerhut. — *v.n.* herumlungern, nichts tun.
loafer ['loufə], *s.* der Faulenzer, Drückeberger.
loam [loum], *s.* der Lehm.
loan [loun], *s.* die Anleihe. — *v.a.* leihen.
loath [louθ], *adj.* unwillig, abgeneigt.
loathe [louð], *v.a.* verabscheuen, hassen.
loathing ['louðiŋ], *s.* der Abscheu, Ekel.
loathsome ['louθsəm], *adj.* abscheulich, ekelhaft.
lobby ['lɔbi], *s.* die Vorhalle. — *v.a.* (*Pol.*) einen beeinflußen.
lobe [loub], *s.* das Läppchen.
lobster ['lɔbstə], *s.* (*Zool.*) der Hummer.
local ['loukəl], *adj.* lokal, örtlich. — *s.* (*coll.*) das Stammgasthaus (*pub*).
locality [lo'kæliti], *s.* die Lokalität, die Örtlichkeit, der Ort.
localize ['loukəlaiz], *v.a.* lokalisieren, auf einen Ort beschränken.
locate [lo'keit], *v.a.* finden (*find*); ausfindig machen.
location [lo'keiʃən], *s.* die Plazierung (*position*); die Lage; der Standort; *on* —, auf dem Gelände, auf Außenaufnahme (*film*).
loch [lɔx], *s.* (*Scot.*) der See.
lock [lɔk], *s.* das Schloß (*on door*); die Schleuse (*on waterway*); die Locke (*hair*). — *v.a.* schließen, abschließen (*door*); hemmen (*wheel*). — *v.n.* sich schließen; — *in*, ineinandergreifen (*cogs*).
locker ['lɔkə], *s.* der Schließschrank, das Schließfach.
locket ['lɔkit], *s.* das Medaillon.
locksmith ['lɔksmiθ], *s.* der Schlosser.
lock-up ['lɔkʌp], *s.* der Arrest, die Haftzelle; (*coll.*) die Garage.
locust ['loukəst], *s.* (*Ent.*) die Heuschrecke.
lodestone ['loudstoun], *s.* der Magnetstein, Magnet.
lodge [lɔdʒ], *v.n.* wohnen; logieren (*temporary*). — *v.a.* beherbergen (*accommodate*); einbringen (*a complaint, protest*). — *s.* das Haus, das Häuschen; die Loge (*Freemasons*).
lodger ['lɔdʒə], *s.* der (Unter)mieter.
lodgings ['lɔdʒiŋz], *s. pl.* das möblierte Zimmer, die Wohnung.
loft [lɔft], *s.* der Boden, Dachboden.
lofty ['lɔfti], *adj.* hoch; erhaben; stolz (*proud*).
log [lɔg], *s.* der Holzklotz, das Scheit; —*-cabin*, —*-house*, das Blockhaus; (*Naut.*) das Log, das Schiffstagebuch. — *v.a.* (*Naut.*) eintragen.
loggerheads ['lɔgəhedz], *s. pl. at* —, in Widerspruch, Widerstreit, im Konflikt.
logic ['lɔdʒik], *s.* die Logik.
logical ['lɔdʒikəl], *adj.* logisch.
loin [lɔin], *s.* (*Anat.*) die Lende.
loincloth ['lɔinklɔθ], *s.* der Lendenschurz.
loiter ['lɔitə], *v.n.* herumlungern; bummeln.
loiterer ['lɔitərə], *s.* der Lungerer, Faulenzer.
loitering ['lɔitəriŋ], *s.* das Herumlungern, Herumstehen, Faulenzen.
loll [lɔl], *v.n.* herumlungern.
lollipop ['lɔlipɔp], *s.* das Zuckerwerk, die Süßigkeit; (*fig.*) der Leckerbissen.
loneliness ['lounlinis], *s.* die Einsamkeit.
lonely, (*Am.*) **lonesome** ['lounli, 'lounsəm], *adj.* einsam.
long [lɔŋ], *adj.* lang. — *adv.* — *ago*, vor langer Zeit; *before* —, in kurzer Zeit. — *v.n.* sich sehnen (*for*, nach, *Dat.*).
longitude ['lɔndʒitju:d], *s.* die Länge; (*Geog.*) der Längengrad.

longitudinal [lɔndʒi'tju:dinəl], *adj.* in der geographischen Länge, Längen-.
look [luk], *v.n.* blicken, sehen, schauen (*at*, auf, *Acc.*); — *to it*, dafür sorgen; — *out for*, Ausschau halten nach (*Dat.*); — *out!* paß auf! — *after s.o.*, sich um jemanden kümmern; — *into*, prüfen, untersuchen; — *forward to*, sich freuen (auf, *Acc.*); — *over*, durchsehen. — *s.* der Blick (*glance*); das Aussehen (*appearance*).
looking-glass ['lukiŋglɑ:s], *s.* der Spiegel.
look-out ['lukaut], *s.* der Ausblick; die Ausschau.
loom [lu:m], *s.* der Webstuhl. —*v.n.* in der Ferne auftauchen (*emerge*).
loon [lu:n], *s.* (*Orn.*) der Eisvogel, Eistaucher; (*coll.*) der Narr.
loony ['lu:ni], *adj.* (*coll.*) wahnsinnig, närrisch.
loop [lu:p], *s.* die Schlinge, das Schlingband; (*Railw.*) — *line*, die Schleife.
loophole ['lu:phoul], *s.* der Ausweg, die Hintertür.
loose [lu:s], *adj.* locker, lose; liederlich (*morals*). — *v.a.* lösen.
loosen [lu:sn], *v.a.* auflockern, locker machen.
lop [lɔp], *v.a.* stutzen (*trees*).
lopsided [lɔp'saidid], *adj.* einseitig.
loquacious [lo'kweiʃəs], *adj.* geschwätzig.
loquacity [lo'kwæsiti], *s.* die Schwatzhaftigkeit.
Lord [lɔ:d], *s.* (*Rel.*) the —, Gott der Herr; der Lord (*nobleman's title*); — *Mayor*, der Oberbürgermeister.
lord [lɔ:d], *s.* der Herr.
lordly ['lɔ:dli], *adj.* vornehm, stolz.
lore [lɔ:], *s.* die Kunde.
lose [lu:z], *v.a.*, *v.n. irr.* verlieren; nachgehen (*of timepiece*).
loser ['lu:zə], *s.* der Verlierende.
loss [lɔs], *s.* der Verlust.
lot [lɔt], *s.* das Los; der Anteil (*share*); die Menge (*quantity*); die Partie (*auction*); (*Am.*) das Stück Land.
loth *see* **loath**.
lotion ['louʃən], *s.* das Waschmittel, das Wasser.
loud [laud], *adj.* laut; grell (*colour*).
lounge [laundʒ], *s.* der Gesellschaftsraum; (*Obs.*) die Chaiselongue; — *suit*, der Straßenanzug. — *v.n.* nichts tun, herumlungern, herumsitzen.
louse [laus], *s.* (*Zool.*) die Laus.
lout [laut], *s.* der Tölpel.
lovable ['lʌvəbl], *adj.* liebenswürdig, liebenswert.
love [lʌv], *s.* die Liebe; *for the — of God*, um Gottes Willen; *for —*, um nichts; *not for — nor money*, weder für Geld noch gute Worte, auf keinen Fall. — *v.a.*, *v.n.* lieben; — *to*, gern tun.
lover ['lʌvə], *s.* der Liebhaber, der *or* die Geliebte.
low [lou], *adj.* niedrig; nieder, tief; leise; (*Mus.*) tief; (*spirits*) niedergeschlagen. — *v.n.* muhen (*of cattle*).
lowlands ['louləndz], *s. pl.* die Niederungen, *f.pl.*; die Ebene; das Unterland.
lowliness ['loulinis], *s.* die Demut, Bescheidenheit.
lowness ['lounis], *s.* die Niedrigkeit; Tiefe.
loyal ['lɔiəl], *adj.* treu, ergeben, loyal.
loyalty ['lɔiəlti], *s.* die Treue, Ergebenheit, Loyalität.
lozenge ['lɔzindʒ], *s.* die Pastille; (*Geom.*) die Raute.
lubricant ['lu:brikənt], *s.* das Schmiermittel, Schmieröl.
lubricate ['lu:brikeit], *v.a.* ölen, schmieren.
lucid ['lu:sid], *adj.* klar, deutlich.
lucidity [lu:'siditi], *s.* die Klarheit.
luck [lʌk], *s.* das Glück, der Glücksfall.
luckily ['lʌkili], *adv.* glücklicherweise.
lucky ['lʌki], *adj.* mit Glück gesegnet, glücklich.
lucrative ['lu:krətiv], *adj.* einträglich.
lucre ['lu:kə], *s.* der Gewinn.
ludicrous ['lu:dikrəs], *adj.* lächerlich, komisch.
lug [lʌg], *v.a.* schleifen, zerren; (*burden*) schleppen.
luggage ['lʌgidʒ], *s.* das Gepäck.
lugger ['lʌgə], *s.* (*Naut.*) der Logger, Lugger.
lugubrious [lu:'gju:briəs], *adj.* traurig.
lukewarm ['lu:kwɔ:m], *adj.* lauwarm.
lull [lʌl], *s.* die (Wind)stille. — *v.a.* einlullen, beschwichtigen.
lullaby ['lʌləbai], *s.* das Wiegenlied.
lumbago [lʌm'beigou], *s.* (*Med.*) der Hexenschuß.
lumbar ['lʌmbə], *adj.* (*Anat.*) zu den Lenden gehörig, Lenden-.
lumber ['lʌmbə], *s.* der Kram, das alte Zeug; (*timber*) das Bauholz; — *room*, die Rumpelkammer.
luminous ['lu:minəs], *adj.* leuchtend, Leucht-.
lump [lʌmp], *s.* der Klumpen, Haufen; — *sugar*, der Würfelzucker; — *sum*, die Pauschalsumme. — *v.a.* — (*together*), zusammenwerfen.
lumpy ['lʌmpi], *adj.* klumpig.
lunacy ['lu:nəsi], *s.* der Wahnsinn.
lunatic ['lu:nətik], *adj.* wahnsinnig. — *s.* der Wahnsinnige; — *asylum*, das Irrenhaus, die Irrenanstalt.
lunch [lʌntʃ], *v.n.* zu Mittag essen. — *s.* (*also* **luncheon** ['lʌntʃən]) das Mittagessen.
lung [lʌŋ], *s.* (*Anat.*) die Lunge.
lunge [lʌndʒ], *v.n.* stoßen, stürzen. — *s.* der Stoß.
lurch [lə:tʃ], *s. leave in the —*, im Stiche lassen. — *v.n.* taumeln.
lure [luə], *v.a.* locken, ködern (*bait*). — *s.* der Köder (*bait*), die Lockung.
lurid ['ljuərid], *adj.* unheimlich, grell.
lurk [lə:k], *v.n.* lauern.
luscious ['lʌʃəs], *adj.* saftig, süß.
lush [lʌʃ], *adj.* üppig (*vegetation*); übermäßig.

lust [lʌst], *s.* die Wollust, Sucht. — *v.n.* gelüsten (*for*, nach, *Dat.*).
lustre [ˈlʌstə], *s.* der Glanz.
lusty [ˈlʌsti], *adj.* kräftig, laut.
lute [lu:t], *s.* (*Mus.*) die Laute.
lutanist [ˈlu:tənist], *s.* (*Mus.*) der Lautenspieler.
Lutheran [ˈlu:θərən], *adj.* lutherisch. — *s.* der Lutheraner.
luxuriate [lʌgˈzjuərieit, lʌkˈsjuə-], *v.n.* schwelgen; (*Bot.*) üppig wachsen.
luxurious [lʌgˈzjuəriəs, lʌkˈsjuə-], *adj.* üppig; (*rich*) reich ausgeschmückt, prächtig, luxuriös.
luxury [ˈlʌkʃəri], *s.* der Luxus, Aufwand.
lymph [limf], *s.* die Lymphe.
lynx [links], *s.* (*Zool.*) der Luchs.
lyric [ˈlirik], *s.* die Lyrik.
lyrical [ˈlirikəl], *adj.* lyrisch.

M

M [em]. das M.
macaroon [mækəˈru:n], *s.* die Makrone.
mace [meis], *s.* das Zepter.
macerate [ˈmæsəreit], *v.a.* abzehren.
machination [mækiˈneiʃən], *s.* die Machenschaft, Ränke, *m.pl.*
machine [məˈʃi:n], *s.* die Maschine.
mackerel [ˈmækərəl], *s.* (*Zool.*) die Makrele.
mackintosh [ˈmækintɔʃ], *s.* der Regenmantel.
mad [mæd], *adj.* verrückt, wahnsinnig.
madam [ˈmædəm], *s.* (*addr.*) gnädige Frau.
madden [mædn], *v.a.* verrückt machen.
madman [ˈmædmən], *s.* der Wahnsinnige.
madness [ˈmædnis], *s.* der Wahnsinn.
magazine [mægəˈzi:n], *s.* die (illustrierte) Zeitschrift; (*gun*) der Ladestock; der Lagerraum (*storeroom*).
maggot [ˈmægət], *s.* (*Ent.*) die Made.
magic [ˈmædʒik], *adj.* zauberhaft; — *lantern*, die Laterna Magica. — *s.* der Zauber; die Magie, Zauberei.
magician [məˈdʒiʃən], *s.* der Zauberer.
magistracy [ˈmædʒistrəsi], *s.* die Obrigkeit (*authority*).
magistrate [ˈmædʒistr(e)it], *s.* der Richter.
magnanimity [mægnəˈnimiti], *s.* der Großmut.
magnanimous [mægˈnæniməs], *adj.* großmütig.
magnate [ˈmægneit], *s.* der Magnat, Großunternehmer.
magnet [ˈmægnit], *s.* der Magnet.
magnetic [mægˈnetik], *adj.* magnetisch.
magnetize [ˈmægnitaiz], *v.a.* magnetisieren.
magnificence [mægˈnifisəns], *s.* die Herrlichkeit.
magnificent [mægˈnifisənt], *adj.* herrlich, großartig.
magnify [ˈmægnifai], *v.a.* vergrößern (*make larger*); (*Rel.*) verherrlichen.
magnitude [ˈmægnitju:d], *s.* die Größe; *order of* —, die Größenordnung.
magpie [ˈmægpai], *s.* (*Orn.*) die Elster.
Magyar [ˈmægjɑ:], *adj.* madjarisch. — *s.* der Magyar, Madjar.
mahogany [məˈhɔgəni], *s.* das Mahagoni(holz).
maid [meid], *s.* (*Poet.*) das Mädchen; das Stubenmädchen (*servant*).
maiden [meidn], *s.* (*Poet.*) die Jungfrau, das Mädchen; — *aunt*, die unverheiratete Tante.
mail (1) [meil], *s.* die Post. — *v.a.* aufgeben, mit der Post senden.
mail (2) [meil], *s.* (*Mil.*) der Panzer.
maim [meim], *v.a.* verstümmeln, lähmen.
main (1) [mein], *adj.* hauptsächlich, Haupt-; (*Railw.*) — *line*, die Hauptstrecke. — *s.* der Hauptteil; *in the* —, hauptsächlich; (*Poet.*) das Weltmeer; (*pl.*) das Hauptrohr, die Hauptleitung.
main (2) [mein], *s. with might and* —, mit allen Kräften.
mainstay [ˈmeinstei], *s.* die Hauptgrundlage, Hauptstütze.
maintain [meinˈtein], *v.a.* erhalten, unterhalten (*keep*); behaupten (*assert*).
maintenance [ˈmeintənəns], *s.* der Unterhalt, die Unterhaltskosten, *pl.* die Erhaltung.
maize [meiz], *s.* (*Bot.*) der Mais.
majestic [məˈdʒestik], *adj.* majestätisch, prunkvoll.
majesty [ˈmædʒəsti], *s.* die Majestät.
major [ˈmeidʒə], *adj.* größer, älter (*elder brother*); wichtig (*more important*). — *s.* (*Mil.*) der Major; (*Law*) der Mündige. — *v.n.* (*Am.*) sich spezialisieren.
majority [məˈdʒɔriti], *s.* die Mehrheit (*in numbers*); (*Law*) die Mündigkeit; (*Mil.*) der Majorsrang.
make [meik], *v.a. irr.* machen, schaffen, herstellen (*produce*); (*coll.*) verdienen (*money*); *he has made it!* (*coll.*) er hat's geschafft!; — *out*, ausfüllen (*cheque etc.*); entziffern (*decipher*); — *up*, erfinden (*invent*); schminken (*o.'s face*). — *v.n. what do you — of him?* was halten Sie von ihm? — *s.* die Marke.
make-believe [ˈmeikbəli:v], *s.* der Vorwand. — *adj.* vorgeblich.
maladjustment [mæləˈdʒʌstmənt], *s.* die Unfähigkeit sich anzupassen; die falsche Einstellung; das Missverhältnis.
maladroit [mæləˈdrɔit], *adj.* ungeschickt, ungewandt.
malady [ˈmælədi], *s.* das Leiden, die Krankheit.

Malagasy [mælə'gæsi], *adj.* madagassich. — *s.* der Madagasse.
Malaysian [mə'leiziən], *adj.* malaysisch. — *s.* der Malaysier.
malcontent ['mælkəntent], *adj.* mißvergnügt.
male [meil], *adj.* männlich; — *screw*, die Schraubenspindel. — *s.* der Mann; (*Zool.*) das Männchen.
malefactor ['mælifæktə], *s.* der Übeltäter.
malice ['mælis], *s.* die Bosheit.
malicious [mə'liʃəs], *adj.* boshaft, böswillig.
malign [mə'lain], *v.a.* lästern, verleumden.
malignant [mə'lignənt], *adj.* bösartig.
malignity [mə'ligniti], *s.* die Bösartigkeit.
malinger [mə'liŋgə], *v.n.* sich krank stellen.
malleable ['mæliəbl], *adj.* (*Metall.*) leicht zu hämmern; (*fig.*) geschmeidig.
mallet ['mælit], *s.* der Schlegel, Holzhammer.
mallow ['mælou], *s.* (*Bot.*) die Malve.
malpractice [mæl'præktis], *s.* das gesetzwidrige Handeln, der Mißbrauch; die Amtsvergehung.
malt [mɔ:lt], *s.* das Malz.
Maltese [mɔ:l'ti:z], *adj.* maltesisch. — *s.* der Malteser.
maltreat [mæl'tri:t], *v.a.* mißhandeln.
mammal ['mæməl], *s.* (*Zool.*) das Säugetier.
man [mæn], *s.* der Mann (*adult male*); der Mensch (*human being*); — *of war*, das Kriegschiff. — *v.a.* bemannen.
manacle ['mænəkl], *s.* die Handschelle. — *v.a.* fesseln.
manage ['mænidʒ], *v.a.* leiten, handhaben, verwalten; *how did you — it?* wie haben Sie's fertiggebracht?
management ['mænidʒmənt], *s.* die Leitung, Führung.
manager ['mænədʒə], *s.* der Leiter, Geschäftsführer, Manager.
mandatary *see* **mandatory.**
mandate ['mændeit], *s.* das Mandat.
mandatory ['mændətəri], *adj.* befehlend, bevollmächtigt, beauftragt. — *s.* der Bevollmächtigte, Beauftragte.
mandrake ['mændreik], *s.* der Alraun.
mane [mein], *s.* die Mähne.
manganese ['mæŋgəni:z], *s.* (*Chem.*) das Mangan.
mange [meindʒ], *s.* die Räude.
manger ['meindʒə], *s.* die Krippe.
mangle (1) [mæŋgl], *s.* die Mangel. — *v.a.* rollen; mangeln (*laundry*).
mangle (2) [mæŋgl], *v.a.* verstümmeln (*disfigure*).
mango ['mæŋgou], *s.* (*Bot.*) die Mangofrucht.
manhood ['mænhud], *s.* die Mannbarkeit, das Mannesalter.
mania ['meiniə], *s.* der Wahnsinn, die Manie.
maniac ['meiniæk], *s.* der Wahnsinnige. — *adj.* wahnsinnig.
manifest ['mænifest], *adj.* deutlich, klar, offenbar.
manifestation [mænifes'teiʃən], *s.* die Offenbarung.
manifesto [mæni'festou], *s.* das Manifest.
manifold ['mænifould], *adj.* mannigfach.
manipulate [mə'nipjuleit], *v.a.* manipulieren, handhaben.
mankind [mæn'kaind], *s.* die Menschheit.
manly ['mænli], *adj.* mannhaft, männlich.
manner ['mænə], *s.* die Art, Sitte (*custom*); die Manier (*bearing*); das Benehmen (*behaviour*); (*pl.*) gute Sitten.
mannered ['mænəd], *adj.* gesittet, geartet; manieriert, gekünstelt (*artificial*).
manor ['mænə], *s.* — *house*, das Herrenhaus, Schloß.
manorial [mə'nɔ:riəl], *adj.* des Herrenhauses, herrschaftlich.
manservant ['mænsə:vənt], *s.* der Bediente, Diener.
mansion ['mænʃən], *s.* das (herrschaftliche) Wohnhaus, Herrenhaus.
manslaughter ['mænslɔ:tə], *s.* der Totschlag.
mantelpiece ['mæntlpi:s], *s.* der Kaminsims.
mantle [mæntl], *s.* (*gas*) der Glühstrumpf; (*Tail.*) der Mantel. — *v.a.* verhüllen (*cloak*).
manual ['mænjuəl], *s.* das Handbuch; (*Mus.*) das Handregister. — *adj.* Hand-.
manufacture [mænju'fæktʃə], *s.* die Herstellung, Erzeugung (*production*); (*Comm.*) das Fabrikat (*product*).
manufacturer [mænju'fæktʃərə], *s.* der Fabrikant, Erzeuger.
manure [mə'njuə], *s.* der Dünger; der Mist. — *v.a.* düngen.
manuscript ['mænjuskript], *s.* die Handschrift, das Manuskript.
many ['meni], *adj.* viele; *as — as*, ganze . . . (*emphatically*); — *a*, mancher.
map [mæp], *s.* die Landkarte. — *v.a.* —(*out*), nach der Karte planen.
maple [meipl], *s.* (*Bot.*) der Ahorn.
mar [mɑ:], *v.a.* verderben.
marauder [mə'rɔ:də], *s.* der Plünderer.
marble [mɑ:bl], *s.* der Marmor (*rock*); (*pl.*) die Murmel (*game*). — *adj.* marmorn.
March [mɑ:tʃ]. der März.
march [mɑ:tʃ], *s.* der Marsch. — *v.n.* marschieren; *steal a — on s.o.*, jemandem zuvorkommen.
marchioness [mɑ:ʃə'nes], *s.* die Marquise.
mare [mɛə], *s.* (*Zool.*) die Stute.
margin ['mɑ:dʒin], *s.* der Rand.
marginal ['mɑ:dʒinəl], *adj.* Rand-, am Rande gelegen.
marigold ['mærigould], *s.* (*Bot.*) die Dotterblume.

marine [mə'ri:n], *adj.* Marine-, See-. — *s.* (*Mil.*) der Seesoldat; *tell that to the Marines!* der Großmutter erzählen.
mariner ['mærinə], *s.* der Seemann.
marital ['mæritəl], *adj.* ehelich.
maritime ['mæritaim], *adj.* Meeres-, See-.
mark [ma:k], *s.* das Zeichen (*sign*); (*Sch.*) die Zensur, Note; (*Comm.*) die Marke; *wide of the* —, auf dem Holzwege. — *v.a.* markieren (*make sign on*); — *my words*, merk dir das! paß auf! (*Comm.*) — *down*, den Preis heruntersetzen; ins Auge fassen (*observe closely*); *a —ed man*, ein Gezeichneter.
market ['ma:kit], *s.* der Markt. — *v.a.* auf den Markt bringen.
marksman ['ma:ksmən], *s.* der Schütze.
marl [ma:l], *s.* der Mergel.
marmalade ['ma:məleid], *s.* die Orangenmarmelade.
marmot ['ma:mət], *s.* (*Zool.*) das Murmeltier.
maroon (1) [mə'ru:n], *adj.* kastanienbraun, rotbraun.
maroon (2) [mə'ru:n], *v.a.* aussetzen.
marquee [ma:'ki:], *s.* das große Zelt.
marquess, marquis ['ma:kwis], *s.* der Marquis.
marriage ['mæridʒ], *s.* die Ehe, Heirat; die Hochzeit (*wedding*).
marriageable ['mæridʒəbl], *adj.* heiratsfähig.
married ['mærid], *adj.* verheiratet.
marrow ['mærou], *s.* (*Anat.*) das Mark; (*Bot.*) der Kürbis.
marry ['mæri], *v.a.* heiraten; trauen (*perform marriage ceremony*); — *off*, verheiraten (*o.'s daughter*). — *v.n.* sich verheiraten.
marsh [ma:ʃ], *s.* der Morast, Sumpf.
marshal ['ma:ʃəl], *s.* der Marschall.
marshy ['ma:ʃi], *adj.* morastig, sumpfig.
marten ['ma:tin], *s.* (*Zool.*) der Marder.
martial ['ma:ʃəl], *adj.* Kriegs-, kriegerisch.
martin ['ma:tin], *s.* (*Orn.*) die Mauerschwalbe.
martyr ['ma:tə], *s.* der Märtyrer.
martyrdom ['ma:tədəm], *s.* das Märtyrertum, der Märtyrertod.
marvel [ma:vl], *v.n.* staunen (*at*, über, *Acc.*).
marvellous ['ma:v(ə)ləs], *adj.* wunderbar, erstaunlich.
masculine ['mæskjulin], *adj.* männlich. — *s.* (*Gram.*) das Maskulinum, das männliche Geschlecht.
mash [mæʃ], *v.a.* zerquetschen, zerdrücken. — *s.* der Brei.
mask [ma:sk], *v.a., v.n.* maskieren, sich vermummen. — *s.* die Maske.
mason ['meisən], *s.* der Maurer.
masonic [mə'sɔnik], *adj.* freimaurerisch.
masonry ['meisənri], *s.* das Mauerwerk.
masquerade [mæskə'reid], *s.* der Mummenschanz, die Maskerade.
Mass [mæs, ma:s], *s.* (*Eccl.*) die Messe; *Low Mass*, die stille Messe; *High Mass*, das Hochamt; *Requiem Mass*, die Seelenmesse.
mass [mæs], *s.* die Masse; die Menge. — *v.a., v.n.* (sich) massen, ansammeln.
massacre ['mæsəkə], *s.* das Blutbad.
massive ['mæsiv], *adj.* massiv, schwer.
mast [ma:st], *s.* der Mast. — *v.a.* (*Naut.*) bemaston.
Master ['ma:stə], *s.* (*Univ.*) der Magister; der junge Herr (*before boy's name*).
master ['ma:stə], *s.* der Meister (*of a craft*); der Herr, Arbeitgeber (*employer*); — *key*, der Hauptschlüssel. — *v.a.* meistern, beherrschen.
masticate ['mæstikeit] *v.a.* kauen.
mastiff ['mæstif], *s.* (*Zool.*) der Kettenhund, Mastiff.
mat [mæt], *s.* die Matte.
match (1) [mætʃ], *s.* das Streichholz, Zündholz.
match (2) [mætʃ], *s.* der ebenbürtige Partner (*suitable partner*); *find o.'s* —, seinesgleichen finden; (*Sport*) das Wettspiel, der Wettkampf; Fußballkampf; (*Cricket*) das Cricketspiel. — *v.a., v.n.* passen zu, anpassen; ebenbürtig sein (*be equal*).
matchless ['mætʃlis], *adj.* unvergleichlich, ohnegleichen.
mate (1) [meit], *s.* der Gefährte, Genosse; (*Naut.*) der Maat, Steuermann; (*coll.*) Freund. — *v.n.* sich paaren, sich verheiraten.
mate (2) [meit], *v.a.* (*Chess*) matt setzen.
material [mə'tiəriəl], *s.* das Material, der Stoff. — *adj.* wesentlich (*essential*); materiell (*tangible*).
materialism [mə'tiəriəlizm], *s.* der Materialismus.
maternal [mə'tə:nəl], *adj.* mütterlich.
maternity [mə'tə:niti], *s.* die Mutterschaft; — *ward*, die Geburtsklinik.
mathematical [mæθə'mætikəl], *adj.* mathematisch.
mathematics [mæθə'mætiks], *s.* die Mathematik.
matins ['mætinz], *s.* (*Eccl.*) die Frühmette.
matriculate [mə'trikjuleit], *v.n.* sich immatrikulieren (lassen).
matrimonial [mætri'mouniəl], *adj.* Ehe-, ehelich.
matrimony ['mætriməni], *s.* die Ehe.
matron ['meitrən], *s.* die Oberschwester, Oberin (*in hospital etc.*); die Matrone (*older woman*).
matter ['mætə], *s.* der Stoff (*substance*); die Sache, der Gegenstand (*subject*); die Angelegenheit (*case*); *printed* —, Drucksache; *what is the —?* was ist los?; *the heart of the* —, des Pudels Kern; *as a — of fact*, tatsächlich, ernst gesprochen. — *v.n.* bedeutsam sein, wichtig sein.
mattock ['mætək], *s.* die Haue.
mattress ['mætrəs], *s.* die Matratze.
mature [mə'tjuə], *adj.* reif; (*fig.*) gereift. — *v.a., v.n.* reifen, zur Reife bringen; (*Comm.*) fällig werden.

matured [mə'tjuəd], *adj.* abgelagert.
maturity [mə'tjuəriti], *s.* die Reife; (*Comm.*) die Fälligkeit.
maudlin ['mɔ:dlin], *adj.* rührselig, sentimental.
maul [mɔ:l], *v.a.* mißhandeln.
Maundy Thursday ['mɔ:ndi'θə:zd(e)i]. der Gründonnerstag.
mauve [mouv], *adj.* malvenfarbig; violett.
maw [mɔ:], *s.* (*Zool.*) der Magen.
mawkish ['mɔ:kiʃ], *adj.* abgeschmackt, sentimental, rührselig.
maxim ['mæksim], *s.* der Grundsatz.
May [mei]. der Mai.
may (1) [mei], *v.n. aux. irr.* mögen, können; (*permissive*) dürfen.
may (2) [mei], *s.* (*Bot.*) der Weißdorn.
mayor [mɛə], *s.* der Bürgermeister.
maypole ['meipoul], *s.* der Maibaum.
maze [meiz], *s.* das Labyrinth.
me [mi:], *pers. pron.* (*Acc.*) mich; (*Dat.*) mir.
mead [mi:d], *s.* der Met.
meadow ['medou], *s.* die Wiese.
meagre ['mi:gə], *adj.* mager, karg (*lean, poor*); dürftig.
meal (1) [mi:l], *s.* das Mahl, Essen, die Mahlzeit.
meal (2) [mi:l], *s.* das Mehl (*flour*).
mealy ['mi:li], *adj.* mehlig; — *-mouthed*, frömmelnd; kleinlaut (*shy*).
mean (1) [mi:n], *v.a. irr.* bedeuten (*signify*); meinen (*wish to express*); vorhaben (*intend*).
mean (2) [mi:n], *adj.* mittelmäßig, Mittel– (*average*). — *s.* die Mitte.
mean (3) [mi:n], *adj.* gemein, niedrig (*despicable*); geizig.
meander [mi'ændə], *s.* die Windung, das Wellenmuster. — *v.n.* sich winden, sich schlängeln.
meaning ['mi:niŋ], *s.* die Bedeutung (*significance, connotation*); der Sinn.
meaningless ['mi:niŋlis], *adj.* bedeutungslos.
means [mi:nz], *s.* das Mittel; *by all* —, auf jeden Fall, unbedingt; *by no* —, keinesfalls; *by—of*, mittels (*Genit.*).
meantime, meanwhile ['mi:ntaim, 'mi:nwail], *s.* die Zwischenzeit.—*adv.* in der Zwischenzeit, indessen.
measles [mi:zlz], *s.* (*Med.*) die Masern, *f. pl.*; *German* —, die Röteln, *m. pl.*
measurable ['meʒərəbl], *adj.* meßbar.
measure ['meʒə], *s.* das Maß; der Maßstab (*scale*); (*Mus.*) der Takt; das Zeitmaß.—*v.a.* messen, abmessen.
meat [mi:t], *s.* das Fleisch.
mechanic [mi'kænik], *s.* der Mechaniker.
mechanical [mi'kænikəl], *adj.* mechanisch, automatisch; — *engineering*, der Maschinenbau.
mechanics [mi'kæniks], *s.* die Mechanik.
medal [medl], *s.* die Medaille, der Orden.
meddle [medl], *v.n.* sich einmischen (in, *in*, *Acc.*).
mediaeval, medieval [medi'i:vəl], *adj.* mittelalterlich.
mediate ['mi:dieit], *v.n.* vermitteln, intervenieren. — *adj.* mittelbar.
mediator ['mi:dieitə], *s.* der Vermittler.
medical ['medikəl], *adj.* medizinisch, ärztlich; — *orderly*, der Krankenwärter.
medicate ['medikeit], *v.a.* medizinisch behandeln.
medicine ['medsən], *s.* die Medizin, Arznei.
medieval *see* **mediaeval**.
mediocre ['mi:dioukə], *adj.* mittelmäßig.
mediocrity [mi:di'ɔkriti], *s.* die Mittelmäßigkeit.
meditate ['mediteit], *v.n.* nachdenken, sinnen.
meditation [medi'teiʃən], *s.* das Sinnen, Nachdenken.
Mediterranean [meditə'reiniən], *adj.* mittelländisch. — *s.* das Mittelmeer, mittelländische Meer.
medium ['mi:djəm], *s.* das Medium; das Mittel (*means*). — *adj.* mittelgroß.
medlar ['medlə], *s.* (*Bot.*) die Mispel.
medley ['medli], *s.* (*Mus.*) das Potpourri; das Gemisch (*mixture*).
meek [mi:k], *adj.* sanft, mild.
meet [mi:t], *v.a., v.n. irr.* treffen (*Acc.*), sich treffen (mit, *Dat.*), begegnen (*Dat.*). — *s.* (*Hunt.*) die Jagd.
meeting ['mi:tiŋ], *s.* das Zusammentreffen; die Tagung, Sitzung (*conference*).
melancholy ['melənkɔli], *adj.* melancholisch, schwermütig. — *s.* die Melancholie, die Schwermut.
mellifluous [me'lifluəs], *adj.* lieblich, süß (*of sounds*).
mellow ['melou], *adj.* mild, weich, mürbe (*fruit etc.*); freundlich (*mood*). — *v.a.* mürbe machen, reifen lassen. — *v.n.* weich werden.
melodious [mə'loudiəs], *adj.* klangvoll, wohlklingend, melodisch.
melodrama ['melədrɑ:mə], *s.* das Melodrama.
melody ['melədi], *s.* die Melodie.
melon ['melən], *s.* (*Bot.*) die Melone.
melt [melt], *v.a., v.n. reg. & irr.* schmelzen.
member ['membə], *s.* das Mitglied (*of club*); (*Parl.*) der Abgeordnete, das Glied.
membrane ['membrein], *s.* die Membran; (*Anat.*) das Häutchen.
memento [mi'mentou], *s.* das Andenken.
memoir ['memwɑ:], *s.* die Denkschrift; (*pl.*) die Memoiren, *n. pl.*
memorable ['memərəbl], *adj.* denkwürdig.
memorandum [memə'rændəm], *s.* das Memorandum, die Denkschrift.
memorial [mi'mɔ:riəl], *s.* das Denkmal (*monument*). — *adj.* Gedenk-, zum Gedenken, Gedächtnis–.

memory ['meməri], *s.* die Erinnerung; das Gedächtnis (*faculty*); das Andenken (*remembrance*).
menace ['menis], *s.* die Drohung. — *v.a.* bedrohen.
mend [mend], *v.a.* reparieren; verbessern, ausbessern. — *v.n.* sich bessern.
mendacious [men'deiʃəs], *adj.* lügnerisch, verlogen (*lying*).
mendacity [men'dæsiti], *s.* die Lügenhaftigkeit, Verlogenheit.
mendicant ['mendikənt], *adj.* bettlerisch. — *s.* der Bettler.
mendicity [men'disiti], *s.* die Bettelei.
menial ['mi:niəl], *adj.* gemein, grob (*job*).
mental [mentl], *adj.* geistig; (*coll.*) geisteskrank.
mention ['menʃən], *v.a.* erwähnen; *don't — it*, gern geschehen! — *s.* die Erwähnung.
mentor ['mentə], *s.* der Ratgeber.
menu ['menju:], *s.* die Speisekarte.
mercantile ['mə:kəntail], *adj.* Handels-, kaufmännisch.
mercenary ['mə:sənəri], *adj.* für Geld zu haben, käuflich, feil; materiell eingestellt. — *s.* der Söldner.
mercer ['mə:sə], *s.* der Seidenhändler.
mercerised ['mə:səraizd], *adj.* (*Textile*) merzerisiert.
merchandise ['mə:tʃəndaiz], *s.* die Ware.
merchant ['mə:tʃənt], *s.* der Kaufmann.
merchantman ['mə:tʃəntmən], *s.* (*Naut.*) das Handelsschiff, Frachtschiff.
merciful ['mə:siful], *adj.* barmherzig, gnädig.
Mercury ['mə:kjuəri]. (*Myth.*) Merkur, *m.*
mercury ['mə:kjuəri], *s.* (*Chem.*) das Quecksilber.
mercy ['mə:si], *s.* die Barmherzigkeit, Gnade.
mere (1) [miə], *adj.* bloß, allein.
mere (2) [miə], *s.* der Teich.
meretricious [meri'triʃəs], *adj.* falsch, täuschend.
merge [mə:dʒ], *v.n.* aufgehen lassen, verschmelzen (*combine*).
merger ['mə:dʒə], *s.* (*Comm.*) die Fusion, Vereinigung, Zusammenlegung.
meridian [mə'ridiən], *s.* der Meridian; (*fig.*) der Gipfel.
merit ['merit], *s.* das Verdienst, der Wert. — *v.a.* verdienen.
meritorious [meri'tɔ:riəs], *adj.* verdienstlich.
mermaid ['mə:meid], *s.* die Wasserjungfer, Nixe.
merriment ['merimənt], *s.* die Belustigung, das Fröhlichsein, die Fröhlichkeit.
merry ['meri], *adj.* froh, fröhlich; *—go-round*, das Karussel.
mesh [meʃ], *s.* das Netz; die Masche (*knitting*). — *v.a.* einfangen.
mess (1) [mes], *s.* (*Mil.*) die Offiziersmesse.
mess (2) [mes], *s.* die Unordnung (*disorder*).
message ['mesidʒ], *s.* die Nachricht, Mitteilung, Botschaft.
messenger ['mesindʒə], *s.* der Bote.
Messiah [mi'saiə], *s.* der Messias.
metal [metl], *s.* das Metall.
metallurgy ['metələ:dʒi], *s.* die Metallurgie, Hüttenkunde.
metaphor ['metəfɔ:], *s.* die Metapher.
metaphorical [metə'fɔrikəl], *adj.* bildlich.
meter ['mi:tə], *s.* der Messer, Zähler (*gauge*); (*Am.*) *see* **metre** (1).
methinks [mi'θiŋks], *v. impers.* (*obs.*) mich dünkt, ich meine, mir scheint.
method ['meθəd], *s.* die Methode.
methodical [mi'θɔdikəl], *adj.* methodisch, systematisch.
methylate ['meθileit], *v.a.* (*Chem.*) denaturieren.
metre (1) ['mi:tə], *s.* der *or* das Meter (*unit of measurement*).
metre (2) ['mi:tə], *s.* (*Poet.*) das Versmaß.
metric ['metrik], *adj.* metrisch (*system of measurement*).
metrical ['metrikəl], *adj.* (*Poet.*) im Metrum, metrisch, Vers-.
metropolis [mi'trɔpəlis], *s.* die Metropole.
metropolitan [metrə'pɔlitən], *adj.* hauptstädtisch. — *s.* (*Eccl.*) der Erzbischof.
mettle [metl], *s.* der Mut (*courage*); *put s.o. on his —*, einen anspornen.
mew [mju:], *s.* das Miauen (*of cat*). — *v.n.* miauen.
mews [mju:z], *s. pl.* die Stallung.
Mexican ['meksikən], *adj.* mexikanisch. — *s.* der Mexikaner.
microphone ['maikrəfoun], *s.* das Mikrophon.
mid- [mid], *prefix.* mittel, Mittel-, mittler.
midday [mid'dei], *s.* der Mittag.
middle [midl], *s.* die Mitte, das Zentrum.
middling ['midliŋ], *adj.* (*coll.*) mittelmäßig.
midget ['midʒit], *s.* der Zwerg (*dwarf*).
midnight ['midnait], *s.* die Mitternacht.
midriff ['midrif], *s.* das Zwerchfell.
midshipman ['midʃipmən], *s.* (*Naut.*) der Seekadett.
midwife ['midwaif], *s.* die Hebamme.
mien [mi:n], *s.* die Miene.
might [mait], *s.* die Macht, Gewalt.
mighty ['maiti], *adj.* mächtig, stark.
mignonette [minjə'net], *s.* (*Bot.*) die Reseda.
migrate [mai'greit], *v.n.* wandern, migrieren; (*birds*) ziehen.
migratory ['maigrətəri], *adj.* Zug-, Wander-.

Milanese [milə'n:iz], *adj.* mailändisch. — *s.* der Mailänder.
mild [maild], *adj.* mild, sanft.
mildew ['mildju:], *s.* der Meltau.
mile [mail], *s.* die (englische) Meile.
mileage ['mailidʒ], *s.* die Meilenzahl.
milfoil ['milfɔil], *s.* (*Bot.*) die Schafgarbe (*yarrow*).
military ['militəri], *adj.* militärisch. — *s.* das Militär.
militia [mi'liʃə], *s.* die Miliz.
milk [milk], *v.a.* melken. — *s.* die Milch.
milksop ['milksɔp], *s.* die Memme.
milky ['milki], *adj.* milchig; *Milky Way*, die Milchstraße.
mill [mil], *s.* die Mühle; die Spinnerei (*textile*); *rolling* —, das Walzwerk; *run of the* —, gewöhnlich; *through the* —, wohl erfahren, lebenserfahren. — *v.a.* mahlen (*flour*); rollen, walzen (*steel*); rändern (*coins*); —*ed edge*, die Rändelkante. —*v.n.* — (*around*), sich drängen.
miller ['milə], *s.* der Müller.
millet ['milit], *s.* die Hirse.
milliner ['milinə], *s.* die Modistin, Putzmacherin.
millinery ['milinəri], *s.* die Putzwaren, Modewaren, *f. pl.*
million ['miljən], *s.* die Million.
milt [milt], *s.* die Fischmilch; (*Anat.*) die Milz.
mimic ['mimik], *s.* der Mimiker. — *v.a.* nachahmen.
mimicry ['mimikri], *s.* die Nachahmung; (*Zool.*) die Anpassung (*in colour*).
mince [mins], *v.a.* kleinhacken (*meat*); — *o.'s words*, affektiert sprechen; *not* — *o.'s words*, kein Blatt vor den Mund nehmen. — *s.* gehacktes Fleisch; — *pie*, die Dörrobstpastete.
mincemeat ['minsmi:t], *s.* die (gehackte) Dörrobstmischung.
mincing ['minsiŋ], *adj.* affektiert; — *steps*, trippelnde Schritte.
mind [maind], *s.* der Geist, das Gemüt; die Meinung; der Sinn; der Verstand; *what is on your* —? was bedrückt Sie?; *bear in* —, daran denken; *have a* —, Lust haben; *make up o.'s* —, sich entschließen; *with an open* —, unparteiisch. — *v.a.* beachten, achten (auf, *Acc.*). — *v.n. do you* —? macht es Ihnen etwas aus? *never* —, macht nichts; *I don't* —, mir ist's recht, meinetwegen.
minded ['maindid], *adj.* gesinnt, eingestellt.
mine (1) [main], *poss. pron.* mein, meinig.
mine (2) [main], *s.* das Bergwerk (*general*), die Grube (*coal*). — *v.a.* abbauen, graben (*Acc.*, nach, *Dat.*).
miner ['mainə], *s.* der Bergmann, Bergarbeiter; (*coll.*) der Kumpel.
mineral ['minərəl], *s.* das Mineral; (*pl.*) Mineralwasser.
mingle [miŋgl], *v.a.*, *v.n.* (sich) mischen.
minimize ['minimaiz], *v.a.* (möglichst) klein machen.
mining ['mainiŋ], *s.* die Hüttenkunde (*theory*); der Bergbau.
minion ['minjən], *s.* der Liebling.
minister ['ministə], *s.* (*Pol.*) der Minister; *Prime Minister*, der Ministerpräsident; (*Eccl.*) der Geistliche, Pfarrer. — *v.n.* einen Gottesdienst abhalten; dienen (*to*, *Dat.*).
ministration [minis'treiʃən], *s.* der Dienst, die Dienstleistung.
ministry ['ministri], *s.* das Ministerium (*department of state*); (*Eccl.*) der Beruf *or* das Amt des Geistlichen.
minnow ['minou], *s.* (*Zool.*) die Elritze.
minor ['mainə], *adj.* kleiner, geringer; (*Sch.*) jünger (*after boy's name*). — *s.* (*Law*) der Minderjährige, Unmündige.
minority [mai'nɔriti], *s.* die Minorität (*in numbers*); (*Law*) die Unmündigkeit.
minster ['minstə], *s.* (*Eccl.*) das Münster.
minstrel ['minstrəl], *s.* der Spielmann.
mint (1) [mint], *s.* (*Bot.*) die Minze.
mint (2) [mint], *s.* die Münzstätte. — *v.a.* münzen.
minuet [minju'et], *s.* (*Mus.*) das Menuett.
minute (1) ['minit], *s.* die Minute (*time*); (*pl.*) das Protokoll (*of meeting*). — *v.a.* zu Protokoll nehmen, protokollieren.
minute (2) [mai'nju:t], *adj.* winzig, klein.
minutiae [mi'nju:ʃii], *s.pl.* die Details, *n. pl.*, die Einzelheiten, *f. pl.*
miracle ['mirəkl], *s.* das Wunder.
miraculous [mi'rækjuləs], *adj.* wunderbar; wundertätig.
mirage [mi'rɑ:ʒ], *s.* die Luftspiegelung, die Fata Morgana.
mire [maiə], *s.* der Schlamm, Kot.
mirror ['mirə], *s.* der Spiegel. — *v.a.* reflektieren, spiegeln.
mirth [mə:θ], *s.* der Frohsinn.
misadventure [misəd'ventʃə], *s.* das Mißgeschick.
misalliance [misə'laiəns], *s.* die Mißheirat, Mesalliance.
misapply [misə'plai], *v.a.* falsch anwenden.
misapprehend [misæpri'hend], *v.a.* mißverstehen.
misapprehension [misæpri'henʃən], *s.* das Mißverständnis.
misappropriate [misə'prouprieit], *v.a.* unrechtmäßig erwerben, unterschlagen.
misbehave [misbi'heiv], *v.n.* sich schlecht benehmen.
miscalculate [mis'kælkjuleit], *v.a.*, *v.n.* sich verrechnen.
miscarriage [mis'kæridʒ], *s.* das Mißlingen; (*Med.*) die Fehlgeburt.
miscarry [mis'kæri], *v.n.* mißlingen; (*Med.*) fehlgebären.
miscellaneous [misə'leiniəs], *adj.* vermischt.

miscellany [mi'seləni], *s.* der Sammelband (*of writers*); die Mischung, das Gemisch.
mischief ['mistʃif], *s.* der Unfug; *out to make* —, darauf aus, Unfug zu stiften; — *maker*, der Unheilstifter.
mischievous ['mistʃivəs], *adj.* boshaft.
misconceive [miskən'si:v], *v.a.* mißverstehen.
misconception [miskən'sepʃən], *s.* das Mißverständnis.
misconduct [mis'kɔndʌkt], *s.* das unkorrekte Verhalten; der Fehltritt.
misconstruction [miskən'strʌkʃən], *s.* die Mißdeutung.
misconstrue [miskən'stru:], *v.a.* mißdeuten.
misdeed [mis'di:d], *s.* die Missetat.
misdemeanour [misdi'mi:nə], *s.* (*Law.*) das Vergehen; die Missetat.
miser ['maizə], *s.* der Geizhals.
miserable ['mizərəbl], *adj.* elend, kläglich (*wretched*); nichtswürdig (*base*).
miserly ['maizəli], *adj.* geizig.
misery ['mizəri], *s.* das Elend, die Not.
misfortune [mis'fɔ:tʃən], *s.* das Unglück.
misgiving [mis'giviŋ], *s.* die Befürchtung, der Zweifel (*doubt*).
misguide [mis'gaid], *v.a.* irreführen, verleiten.
mishap [mis'hæp], *s.* der Unfall.
misinform [misin'fɔ:m], *v.a.* falsch informieren, falsch unterrichten.
misinterpret [misin'tə:prit], *v.a.* mißdeuten.
misjudge [mis'dʒʌdʒ], *v.a.* falsch beurteilen.
mislay [mis'lei], *v.a. irr.* verlegen.
mislead [mis'li:d], *v.a. irr.* verführen, irreführen.
misnomer [mis'noumə], *s.* der falsche Name.
misogynist [mi'sɔdʒinist], *s.* der Weiberfeind.
misplace [mis'pleis], *v.a.* übel anbringen (*remark*); verlegen (*thing*).
misprint [mis'print], *v.a.* verdrucken, falsch drucken. — ['misprint], *s.* der Druckfehler.
misquote [mis'kwout], *v.a.* falsch zitieren.
misrepresent [misrepri'zent], *v.a.* falsch darstellen.
misrule [mis'ru:l], *s.* die schlechte Regierung; die Unordnung (*disorder*).
miss (1) [mis], *s.* das Fräulein.
miss (2) [mis], *v.a.* vermissen (*yearn for*); versäumen (*a train, lesson etc.*); verfehlen (*target*); — *the boat*, den Anschluß verpassen; *be missing*, fehlen.
missal [misl], *s.* (*Eccl.*) das Meßbuch.
misshapen [mis'ʃeipən], *adj.* mißgestaltet.
missile ['misail], *s.* das Geschoß; *ballistic* —, das Raketengeschoß; *guided* —, ferngesteuertes Raketengeschoss.
mission ['miʃən], *s.* die Mission; Sendung; der Auftrag (*task*).
missionary ['miʃənəri], *adj.* Missions-. — *s.* der Missionar.
missive ['misiv], *s.* das Sendschreiben.
misspell [mis'spel], *v.a.* falsch buchstabieren, falsch schreiben.
mist [mist], *s.* der Dunst; Nebel (*fog*).
mistake [mis'teik], *s.* der Fehler. — *v.a. irr.* verkennen.
mistaken [mis'teikn], *adj.* im Unrecht; irrig; *be* —, sich irren.
mistimed [mis'taimd], *adj.* zur Unzeit, unzeitig.
mistletoe ['misltou], *s.* (*Bot.*) die Mistel, der Mistelzweig.
mistress ['mistrəs], *s.* die Herrin; Hausfrau; Geliebte (*paramour*); Lehrerin (*Sch.*).
mistrust [mis'trʌst], *v.a.* mißtrauen.
misunderstand [misʌndə'stænd], *v.a. irr.* mißverstehen.
misuse [mis'ju:z], *v.a.* mißbrauchen.
mite (1) [mait], *s.* (*Zool.*) die Milbe.
mite (2) [mait], *s.* das Scherflein (*coin*); (*coll.*) das Kindchen, das Kerlchen.
mitigate ['mitigeit], *v.a.* mildern.
mitre ['maitə], *s.* die Bischofsmütze, Mitra.
mitten [mitn], *s.* der Fäustling, Fausthandschuh.
mix [miks], *v.a.* mischen, vermischen. — *v.n.* verkehren.
mixed [miksd], *adj. a — blessing*, eine fragliche Wohltat.
mizzle [mizl], *v.n.* sprühen, rieseln.
mnemonics [ni'mɔniks], *s.* die Gedächtniskunst.
moan [moun], *v.n.* stöhnen (*wail*); klagen (*complain*). — *s.* (*coll.*) die Klage.
moat [mout], *s.* der Burggraben, Wassergraben.
mob [mɔb], *s.* der Pöbel.
mobility [mo'biliti], *s.* die Beweglichkeit.
mobilize ['moubilaiz], *v.a.* mobilisieren.
mock [mɔk], *v.a.* verspotten (*tease*); täuschen (*mislead*). — *v.n.* spotten. — *s.* der Spott, die Täuschung. — *adj.* Schein-; — *heroic*, komisch-heroisch.
modal [moudl], *adj.* (*Gram.*) modal, der Aussageweise nach; (*Mus.*) dem Modus nach.
mode [moud], *s.* (*Mus.*) der Modus, die Art; die Mode (*fashion*).
model [mɔdl], *s.* das Modell; das Muster (*pattern*). — *v.a., v.n.* modellieren.
moderate ['mɔdərit], *adj.* mäßig; (*climate*) gemäßigt. — [-reit], *v.a.* mäßigen; abändern.
modern ['mɔdən], *adj.* modern.
modernize ['mɔdənaiz], *v.a.* modernisieren.
modest ['mɔdist], *adj.* bescheiden.
modesty ['mɔdisti], *s.* die Bescheidenheit.
modify ['mɔdifai], *v.a.* abändern, modifizieren.

modish ['moudiʃ], *adj.* nach der neuesten Mode, modisch.
modulate ['mɔdjuleit], *v.a.* modulieren.
moil [mɔil], *v.n.* sich plagen.
moist [mɔist], *adj.* feucht.
moisten [mɔisn], *v.a.* befeuchten.
moisture ['mɔistʃə], *s.* die Feuchtigkeit.
molasses [mo'læsiz], *s.* die Melasse.
mole (1) [moul], *s.* (*Zool.*) der Maulwurf.
mole (2) [moul], *s.* das Muttermal (*skin mark*).
mole (3) [moul], *s.* der Seedamm, Hafendamm.
molecular [mo'lekjulə], *adj.* molekular.
molecule ['mɔl-, 'moulikju:l], *s.* das Molekül.
molest [mo'lest], *v.a.* belästigen.
mollify ['mɔlifai], *v.a.* besänftigen.
mollusc ['mɔləsk], *s.* (*Zool.*) die Molluske.
molt *see under* **moult**.
molten ['moultən], *adj.* geschmolzen.
moment ['moumənt], *s.* der Augenblick, Moment (*instant*); die Wichtigkeit (*importance*).
momentary ['mouməntəri], *adj.* momentan, einen Augenblick lang.
momentum [mo'mentəm], *s.* das Moment, die Triebkraft.
monarch ['mɔnək], *s.* der Monarch.
monarchy ['mɔnəki], *s.* die Monarchie.
monastery ['mɔnəstri], *s.* das (Mönchs-) kloster.
monastic [mə'næstik], *adj.* klösterlich.
Monday ['mʌndi]. der Montag.
money ['mʌni], *s.* das Geld; *ready* —, bares Geld; *make* —, Geld verdienen; — *order*, die Postanweisung.
Mongolian [mɔŋ'gouliən], *adj.* mongolisch. — *s.* der Mongole.
mongrel ['mʌŋgrəl], *s.* (*Zool.*) der Mischling.
monitor ['mɔnitə], *s.* der Ermahner; (*Rad.*) der Abhörer.
monitoring ['mɔnitəriŋ], *adj.* — *service*, der Abhördienst.
monk [mʌŋk], *s.* (*Eccl.*) der Mönch.
monkey ['mʌŋki], *s.* (*Zool.*) der Affe.
monomania [mɔno'meiniə], *s.* die Monomanie, fixe Idee.
monopolize [mə'nɔpəlaiz], *v.a.* monopolisieren.
monopoly [mə'nɔpəli], *s.* das Monopol.
monosyllabic [mɔnəsi'læbik], *adj.* einsilbig.
monotonous [mə'nɔtənəs], *adj.* monoton, eintönig.
monsoon [mɔn'su:n], *s.* der Monsun.
monster ['mɔnstə], *s.* das Ungeheuer.
monstrance ['mɔnstrəns], *s.* (*Eccl.*) die Monstranz.
monstrosity [mɔns'trɔsiti], *s.* die Ungeheuerlichkeit.
monstrous ['mɔnstrəs], *adj.* ungeheuerlich.
month [mʌnθ], *s.* der Monat.
monthly ['mʌnθli], *adj.* monatlich, Monats-.
mood [mu:d], *s.* die Stimmung, Laune; (*Gram.*, *Mus.*) der Modus.
moodiness ['mu:dinis], *s.* die Launenhaftigkeit.
moody ['mu:di], *adj.* launenhaft.
moon [mu:n], *s.* der Mond.
moonlight ['mu:nlait], *s.* das Mondlicht, der Mondschein.
moonshine ['mu:nʃain], *s.* der Mondschein; (*fig.*) Unsinn.
moonstruck ['mu:nstrʌk], *adj.* mondsüchtig; verliebt.
Moor [muə], *s.* der Mohr.
moor [muə], *s.* das Moor, Heideland.
moorage ['muəridʒ], *s.* der Ankerplatz.
moorhen ['mɔ:hen], *s.* (*Orn.*) das Moorhuhn, Wildhuhn.
moorish ['muəriʃ], *adj.* maurisch.
moot [mu:t], *v.a.* erörtern, besprechen. — *adj. a — point*, ein strittiger Punkt.
mop [mɔp], *s.* der Wischlappen, Mop. — *v.a.* aufwischen (*floor*), wischen (*brow*).
mope [moup], *v.n.* traurig sein.
moral ['mɔrəl], *adj.* moralisch (*high principled*); sittlich (*decent*). — *s.* die Moral (*precept*); (*pl.*) die Sitten, *f. pl.*; die Sittlichkeit.
moralize ['mɔrəlaiz], *v.n.* moralisieren, Moral predigen (*Dat.*).
morass [mo'ræs], *s.* der Morast.
morbid ['mɔ:bid], *adj.* krankhaft.
more [mɔ:], *comp. adj.*, *adv.* mehr; *once* —, noch einmal; *all the* —, umso mehr; *the — the better*, je mehr desto besser.
moreover [mɔ:'rouvə], *adv.* zudem, überdies, weiterhin.
morning ['mɔ:niŋ], *s.* der Morgen, Vormittag; — *coat*, der Cutaway, Frack.
Moroccan [mə'rɔkən], *adj.* marokkanisch. — *s.* der Marokkaner.
Morocco [mə'rɔkou]. Marokko, *n.*
morocco [mə'rɔkou], *s.* der Saffian, das Maroquinleder.
moron ['mɔ:rɔn], *s.* der Schwachsinnige.
morose [mə'rous], *adj.* mürrisch.
morrow ['mɔrou], *s.* (*Poet.*) der Morgen.
morsel [mɔ:sl], *s.* der Bissen, das Stück.
mortal [mɔ:tl], *adj.* sterblich, tödlich; — *sin*, die Todsünde. — *s.* der Sterbliche, der Mensch.
mortality [mɔ:'tæliti], *s.* die Sterblichkeit.
mortar ['mɔ:tə], *s.* (*Build.*) der Mörtel; (*Mil.*) der Mörser.
mortgage ['mɔ:gidʒ], *s.* die Hypothek. — *v.a.* verpfänden; eine Hypothek aufnehmen (auf, *Acc.*).
mortgagee [mɔ:gi'dʒi:], *s.* der Hypothekengläubiger.
mortician [mɔ:'tiʃən], *s.* (*Am.*) *see* **undertaker**.
mortify ['mɔ:tifai], *v.a.* kasteien (*chasten*); kränken (*humiliate*).
mortise ['mɔ:tis], *s.* (*Build.*) das Zapfenloch.

mortuary ['mɔ:tjuəri], *s.* die Leichenhalle.
mosque [mɔsk], *s.* (*Rel.*) die Moschee.
mosquito [mɔs'ki:tou], *s.* (*Ent.*) der Moskito.
moss [mɔs], *s.* (*Bot.*) das Moos.
most [moust], *superl. adj.* meist; (*pl.*) die meisten. — *adv.* meist, meistens; höchst (*before adjectives*).
mostly ['moustli], *adv.* meistenteils.
mote [mout], *s.* das Stäubchen.
moth [mɔθ], *s.* (*Ent.*) die Motte.
mother ['mʌðə], *s.* die Mutter; — *-in-law*, die Schwiegermutter; —*-of-pearl*, die Perlmutter.
motherly ['mʌðəli], *adj.* mütterlich.
motion ['mouʃən], *s.* die Bewegung, der Gang; (*Parl., Rhet.*) der Antrag. — *v.a.* bewegen. — *v.n.* zuwinken (*Dat.*).
motive ['moutiv], *s.* das Motiv, der Beweggrund.
motley ['mɔtli], *adj.* scheckig, bunt.
motor ['moutə], *s.* der Motor.
motoring ['moutəriŋ], *s.* das Autofahren, der Autosport.
mottled [mɔtld], *adj.* gescheckt, gesprenkelt.
motto ['mɔtou], *s.* das Motto, der Wahlspruch.
mould (1) [mould], *s.* die Form; Gußform (*casting*); die Schablone. — *v.a.* formen; (*Metall.*) gießen, formen.
mould (2) [mould], *s.* der Schimmel (*fungus*); (*Hort.*) die Gartenerde. — *v.n.* schimmeln.
moulder (1) ['mouldə], *s.* der Bildner; (*Metall.*) der Gießer.
moulder (2) ['mouldə], *v.n.* vermodern.
mouldy ['mouldi], *adj.* moderig, schimmelig.
moult, (*Am.*) **molt** [moult], *v.n.* (*Zool.*) sich mausern.
mound [maund], *s.* der Erdhügel.
mount [maunt], *v.a.* besteigen (*horse, hill*); montieren, anbringen (*apparatus*). — *v.n.* sich belaufen (*bill*), betragen. — *s.* (*Poet.*) der Berg.
mountain ['mauntin], *s.* der Berg.
mountaineer [maunti'niə], *s.* der Bergsteiger.
mountainous ['mauntinəs], *adj.* gebirgig.
mourn [mɔ:n], *v.a.*, *v.n.* (be)trauern.
mourner ['mɔ:nə], *s.* der Leidtragende.
mournful ['mɔ:nful], *adj.* traurig.
mourning ['mɔ:niŋ], *s.* die Trauer.
mouse [maus], *s.* (*Zool.*) die Maus.
moustache [mə'stɑ:ʃ], *s.* der Schnurrbart.
mouth [mauθ], *s.* (*Anat.*) der Mund; (*Geog.*) die Mündung.
movable ['mu:vəbl], *adj.* beweglich, verschiebbar.
move [mu:v], *v.a.* bewegen; (*emotionally*) rühren; den Antrag stellen (*a motion*). — *v.n.* umziehen; übersiedeln (*change residence*).
movement ['mu:vmənt], *s.* die Bewegung (*motion*); (*Mus.*) der Satz; das Gehwerk (*mechanism*).
movies ['mu:viz], *s. pl.* (*coll.*) das Kino, der Film.
mow [mou], *v.a. irr.* mähen.
much [mʌtʃ], *adj.* viel. — *adv.* sehr, bei weitem; *as* — *as*, ganze . . .; *as* — *again*, noch einmal so viel.
mud [mʌd], *s.* der Schmutz, Schlamm.
muddle [mʌdl], *v.a.* verwirren. — *s.* die Verwirrung.
muff (1) [mʌf], *s.* der Muff.
muff (2) [mʌf], *v.a.* verderben (*mar*).
muffin ['mʌfin], *s.* der dünne Kuchen, der Butterkuchen.
muffle [mʌfl], *v.a.* umwickeln; dämpfen (*a sound*).
muffler ['mʌflə], *s.* das Halstuch; (*Motor.*) der Schalldämpfer.
mug [mʌg], *s.* der Krug; (*coll.*) der Tölpel.
muggy ['mʌgi], *adj.* schwül; feucht (*humid*).
mulatto [mju'lætou], *s.* der Mulatte.
mulberry ['mʌlbəri], *s.* (*Bot.*) die Maulbeere.
mule [mju:l], *s.* (*Zool.*) das Maultier, der Maulesel.
muleteer [mju:li'tiə], *s.* der Mauleseltreiber.
mulish ['mju:liʃ], *adj.* störrisch.
mull (1) [mʌl], *v.a.* würzen (*add spices to*); *mulled wine*, der Glühwein.
mull (2) [mʌl], *v.a.*, *v.n.* — *over*, überlegen, überdenken.
multifarious [mʌlti'fɛəriəs], *adj.* mannigfaltig.
multiple ['mʌltipl], *s.* das Vielfache. — *adj.* vielfach.
multiply ['mʌltiplai], *v.a.*, *v.n.* multiplizieren, (sich) vervielfachen.
multitude ['mʌltitju:d], *s.* die Menge.
multitudinous [mʌlti'tju:dinəs], *adj.* zahlreich, massenhaft.
mumble [mʌmbl], *v.a.*, *v.n.* murmeln.
mummery ['mʌməri], *s.* der Mummenschanz.
mummy (1) ['mʌmi], *s.* die Mumie.
mummy (2) ['mʌmi], *s.* (*coll.*) die Mutti.
mumps [mʌmps], *s.* (*Med.*) der Ziegenpeter.
munch [mʌntʃ], *v.a.*, *v.n.* kauen.
mundane ['mʌndein], *adj.* weltlich.
municipal [mju'nisipəl], *adj.* städtisch.
municipality [mjunisi'pæliti], *s.* die Stadtgemeinde.
munificence [mju'nifisəns], *s.* die Freigebigkeit.
munificent [mju'nifisənt], *adj.* freigebig.
mural ['mjuərəl], *s.* die Wandmalerei; das Wandgemälde. — *adj.* Wand-.
murder ['mə:də], *s.* der Mord. — *v.a.* ermorden, morden.
murderer ['mə:dərə], *s.* der Mörder.
murderous ['mə:dərəs], *adj.* mörderisch.
murky ['mə:ki], *adj.* trübe, unklar.
murmur ['mə:mə], *s.* das Gemurmel.
muscle [mʌsl], *s.* (*Anat.*) der Muskel.
muscular ['mʌskjulə], *adj.* (*Anat.*) muskulös, Muskel-.

muse (1) [mju:z], *v.n.* nachdenken, sinnen.
muse (2) [mju:z], *s.* (*Myth.*) die Muse.
museum [mju:'ziəm], *s.* das Museum.
mushroom ['mʌʃrum], *s.* (*Bot.*) der (eßbare) Pilz.
music ['mju:zik], *s.* die Musik; — *stand*, das Notenpult.
musician [mju'ziʃən], *s.* der Musiker.
musk [mʌsk], *s.* der Moschus, Bisam.
musket ['mʌskit], *s.* die Muskete, Flinte.
muslin ['mʌzlin], *s.* der Musselin.
mussel [mʌsl], *s.* (*Zool.*) die Muschel.
must [mʌst], *v. aux. irr.* müssen; (*with neg.*) dürfen.
mustard ['mʌstəd], *s.* der Senf.
muster ['mʌstə], *v.a.* mustern. — *v.n.* sich sammeln. — *s.* die Musterung; *pass* —, die Prüfung bestehen.
musty ['mʌsti], *adj.* dumpf, dumpfig, muffig.
mutable ['mju:təbl], *adj.* veränderlich.
mutation [mju'teiʃən], *s.* die Veränderung; (*Maths.*, *Genetics*) die Mutation.
mute [mju:t], *adj.* stumm. — *v.a.* (*Mus.*) dämpfen. — *s.* (*Mus.*) der Dämpfer.
mutilate ['mju:tileit], *v.a.* verstümmeln.
mutinous ['mju:tinəs], *adj.* aufrührerisch.
mutiny ['mju:tini], *s.* die Meuterei.
mutter ['mʌtə], *v.a.*, *v.n.* murmeln.
mutton [mʌtn], *s.* das Hammelfleisch; — *chop*, das Hammelkotelett.
mutual ['mju:tjuəl], *adj.* gegenseitig.
muzzle [mʌzl], *s.* der Maulkorb (*of dog*); die Mündung (*of rifle*).
my [mai], *poss. adj.* mein.
myrrh [mə:], *s.* die Myrrhe.
myrtle [mə:tl], *s.* (*Bot.*) die Myrte.
myself [mai'self], *pron.* ich selbst; (*refl.*) mir, mich.
mysterious [mis'tiəriəs], *adj.* geheimnisvoll.
mystery ['mistəri], *s.* das Geheimnis.
mystic ['mistik], *s.* der Mystiker.
mystic(al) ['mistik(əl)], *adj.* mystisch, geheimnisvoll, dunkel.
mystification [mistifi'keiʃən], *s.* die Täuschung, Irreführung.
mystify ['mistifai], *v.a.* täuschen, verblüffen.
myth [miθ], *s.* der Mythos, die Mythe, Sage.

N

N [en]. das N.
nag (1) [næg], *v.a.* nörgeln.
nag (2) [næg], *s.* der Gaul.
nail [neil], *s.* der Nagel. — *v.a.* annageln.
naïve ['naii:v], *adj.* naiv.
naïveté, naïvety [nai'i:vti], *s.* die Naivität, Einfalt.
naked ['neikid], *adj.* nackt.
name [neim], *s.* der Name. — *v.a.* nennen, heißen.
nameless ['neimlis], *adj.* namenlos.
namely ['neimli], *adv.* nämlich.
namesake ['neimseik], *s.* der Namensvetter.
nap [næp], *s.* das Schläfchen. — *v.n.* schlummern, einnicken.
nape [neip], *s.* (*Anat.*) das Genick.
napkin ['næpkin], *s.* die Serviette; Windel (*baby's*).
narrate [nə'reit], *v.a.* erzählen.
narrative ['nærətiv], *s.* die Erzählung, Geschichte.
narrator [nə'reitə], *s.* der Erzähler; (*Rad.*) der Sprecher.
narrow ['nærou], *adj.* eng, schmal; — *gauge*, die Schmalspur; — *minded*, engstirnig.
nasty ['nɑ:sti], *adj.* widerlich, unangenehm.
natal [neitl], *adj.* Geburts-.
nation ['neiʃən], *s.* die Nation, das Volk.
nationality [næʃə'næliti], *s.* die Staatsangehörigkeit, Nationalität.
native ['neitiv], *adj.* einheimisch, eingeboren. — *s.* der Eingeborene.
natural ['nætʃərəl], *adj.* natürlich.
naturalist ['nætʃərəlist], *s.* der Naturforscher.
naturalization [nætʃərəlai'zeiʃən], *s.* die Naturalisierung, Einbürgerung.
naturalize ['nætʃərəlaiz], *v.a.*, *v.n.* naturalisieren, einbürgern.
nature ['neitʃə], *s.* die Natur, das Wesen.
naught [nɔ:t], *s.* die Null.
naughty ['nɔ:ti], *adj.* unartig.
nausea ['nɔ:siə], *s.* (*Med.*) der Brechreiz, das Erbrechen.
nautical ['nɔ:tikəl], *adj.* nautisch, Schiffs-.
naval ['neivəl], *adj.* Marine-.
nave [neiv], *s.* (*Archit.*) das Schiff.
navigable ['nævigəbl], *adj.* schiffbar.
navigate ['nævigeit], *v.a.*, *v.n.* steuern.
navigation [nævi'geiʃən], *s.* die Schifffahrt (*shipping*); das Steuern, die Navigation.
navy ['neivi], *s.* die Flotte, Marine.
Neopolitan [niə'pɔlitən], *adj.* neapolitanisch. — *s.* der Neapolitaner.
near [niə], *adj.*, *adv.* nahe, in der Nähe. — *prep.* nahe (an *or* bei).
nearly ['niəli], *adv.* beinahe, fast.
nearness ['niənis], *s.* die Nähe.
neat [ni:t], *adj.* nett, sauber (*tidy*); rein, unvermischt, pur (*unmixed*).
neatness ['ni:tnis], *s.* die Sauberkeit.
necessary ['nesəsəri], *adj.* notwendig.
necessity [ni'sesiti], *s.* die Not, Notwendigkeit; (*pl.*) das zum Leben Nötige.
neck [nek], *s.* (*Anat.*) der Hals; *stick o.'s — out*, es riskieren. — *v.n.* (*Am. sl.*) knutschen.

necklace ['neklis], *s.* das Halsband, die Halskette.
necktie ['nektai], *s.* der Schlips, die Krawatte.
need [ni:d], *s.* die Not, der Bedarf. — *v.a.* brauchen, nötig haben.
needful ['ni:dful], *adj.* notwendig.
needle [ni:dl], *s.* die Nadel. — *v.a.* (*coll.*) sticheln, ärgern (*annoy*).
needy ['ni:di], *adj.* in Not befindlich, arm, bedürftig.
nefarious [ni'fεəriəs], *adj.* nichtswürdig, schändlich.
negative ['negətiv], *adj.* negativ, verneinend. — *s.* (*Phot.*) das Negativ; die Verneinung (*denial*); *in the* —, verneinend.
neglect [ni'glekt], *v.a.* vernachlässigen, außer acht lassen. — *s.* die Vernachlässigung.
neglectful [ni'glektful], *adj.* nachlässig.
negligence ['neglidʒəns], *s.* die Nachlässigkeit.
negotiate [ni'gouʃieit], *v.a.*, *v.n.* verhandeln, unterhandeln.
negotiation [nigouʃi'eiʃən], *s.* die Unterhandlung.
Negro ['ni:grou], *s.* der Neger.
neigh [nei], *v.n.* wiehern.
neighbour ['neibə], *s.* der Nachbar.
neighbourhood ['neibəhud], *s.* die Nachbarschaft, Umgebung.
neighbouring ['neibəriŋ], *adj.* Nachbar-, benachbart.
neighbourliness ['neibəlinis], *s.* das gute nachbarliche Verhältnis, die Geselligkeit.
neither ['naiðə *or* 'ni:ðə], *adj.*, *pron.* keiner (von beiden). — *conj.* auch nicht; — . . . *nor*, weder . . . noch.
Nepalese [nepə'li:z], *adj.* nepalesisch. — *s.* der Nepalese.
nephew ['nefju *or* 'nevju], *s.* der Neffe.
nerve [nə:v], *s.* der Nerv; der Mut (*courage*); die Frechheit (*impudence*); (*pl.*) die Angst, Nervosität.
nervous ['nə:vəs], *adj.* nervös; — *of*, furchtsam vor (*Dat.*), ängstlich wegen (*Genit.*).
nest [nest], *s.* das Nest; (*fig.*) — *egg*, die Ersparnisse, *f.pl.* — *v.n.* nisten.
nestle [nesl], *v.n.* sich anschmiegen.
net (1) [net], *s.* das Netz. — *v.a.* (Fische) fangen, ins Netz bekommen.
net (2) [net], *adj.* netto; ohne Verpackung; — *weight*, das Nettogewicht.
nettle [netl], *s.* (*Bot.*) die Nessel. — *v.a.* sticheln, ärgern.
neurosis [njuə'rousis], *s.* (*Med.*) die Neurose.
neutrality [nju:'træliti], *s.* die Neutralität.
never ['nevə], *adv.* nie, niemals; — *mind*, mach Dir (machen Sie sich) nichts draus!
nevertheless [nevəðə'les], *conj.* trotzdem, nichtsdestoweniger.
new [nju:], *adj.* neu; *New Year's Day*, der Neujahrstag; *New Zealander*, der Neuseeländer. — *s.* (*pl.*) die Nachrichten, *f. pl.*
newspaper ['nju:speipə], *s.* die Zeitung.
next [nekst], *adj.* nächst. — *adv.* danach.
nib [nib], *s.* die Spitze (*of pen*).
nibble [nibl], *v.a.*, *v.n.* knabbern, nagen (*at*, an, *Dat.*).
nice [nais], *adj.* fein (*scrupulous*); nett, angenehm (*pleasant*).
nicety ['naisəti], *s.* die Feinheit (*of distinction etc.*).
nickel [nikl], *s.* das Nickel; (*Am.*) das Fünfcentstück.
nickname ['nikneim], *s.* der Spitzname.
niece [ni:s], *s.* die Nichte.
Nigerian [nai'dʒiəriən], *adj.* nigerisch. — *s.* der Nigerier.
niggardly ['nigədli], *adj.* geizig.
nigh [nai], *adj.*, *adv.* (*Poet.*) nahe.
night [nait], *s.* die Nacht; *last* —, gestern abend; *the* — *before last*, vorgestern abend; *at* —, nachts.
nightingale ['naitiŋgeil], *s.* (*Orn.*) die Nachtigall.
nightmare ['naitmεə], *s.* der Alpdruck.
nimble [nimbl], *adj.* flink; geschickt (*deft*).
nine [nain], *num. adj.* neun.
nineteen [nain'ti:n], *num. adj.* neunzehn.
ninety ['nainti], *num. adj.* neunzig.
ninth [nainθ], *num. adj.* neunte.
nip [nip], *v.a.* zwicken.
nipple [nipl], *s.* (*Anat.*) die Brustwarze.
nitrogen ['naitrədʒən], *s.* (*Chem.*) der Stickstoff.
no [nou], *part.* nein. — *adj.* kein. — *adv.* nicht; — *one*, niemand.
nobility [no'biliti], *s.* der Adel.
noble [noubl], *adj.* edel; großmütig (*magnanimous*); adlig (*well born*).
nobody ['noubədi], *pron.* niemand.
nod [nɔd], *v.n.* nicken.
noise [nɔiz], *s.* der Lärm, das Geräusch.
noiseless ['nɔizlis], *adj.* geräuschlos.
noisy ['nɔizi], *adj.* laut, lärmend.
nominal ['nɔminəl], *adj.* nominell.
nominate ['nɔmineit], *v.a.* nennen (*name*); ernennen (*appoint*).
nomination [nɔmi'neiʃən], *s.* die Nennung, Ernennung.
none [nʌn], *pron.* keiner, niemand.
nonsense ['nɔnsəns], *s.* der Unsinn.
nook [nuk], *s.* die Ecke, der Winkel.
noon [nu:n], *s.* der Mittag.
noose [nu:s], *s.* die Schlinge.
nor [nɔ:], *conj.* auch nicht; *neither* . . . —, weder . . . noch.
normal [nɔ:məl], *adj.* normal.
normalize ['nɔ:məlaiz], *v.a.* normalisieren.
Norman ['nɔ:mən], *adj.* normannisch. — *s.* der Normanne.
north [nɔ:θ], *s.* der Norden. — *adj.* nördlich.
northerly, northern ['nɔ:ðəli, 'nɔ:ðən], *adj.* nördlich, von Norden.
Norwegian [nɔ:'wi:dʒən], *adj.* norwegisch. — *s.* der Norweger.
nose [nouz], *s.* (*Anat.*) die Nase; — *dive*, der Sturzflug.

nosey ['nouzi], *adj.* (*coll.*) neugierig.
nostalgia [nɔs'tældʒə], *s.* das Heimweh, die Sehnsucht.
nostril ['nɔstril], *s.* (*Anat.*) das Nasenloch.
not [nɔt], *adv.* nicht; — *at all*, keineswegs.
notable ['noutəbl], *adj.* berühmt, wohlbekannt; bemerkenswert.
notary ['noutəri], *s.* der Notar.
notch [nɔtʃ], *s.* die Kerbe. — *v.a.* kerben, einkerben.
note [nout], *s.* die Notiz, der Zettel; (*Mus.*) die Note; die Bedeutung; *take —s*, Notizen machen; *take — of*, zur Kenntnis nehmen. — *v.a.* notieren, aufzeichnen.
notepaper ['noutpeipə], *s.* das Briefpapier.
noteworthy ['noutwə:ði], *adj.* beachtenswert.
nothing ['nʌθiŋ], *pron. s.* nichts; *for —*, umsonst; *good for —*, der Taugenichts.
notice ['noutis], *s.* die Kenntnis (*attention*); die Anzeige (*in press etc.*); Notiz; Bekanntmachung; *give —*, kündigen. — *v.a.* bemerken.
noticeable ['noutisəbl], *adj.* bemerkbar.
notification [noutifi'keiʃən], *s.* die Benachrichtigung, Bekanntmachung.
notify ['noutifai], *v.a.* benachrichtigen, informieren.
notion ['nouʃən], *s.* der Begriff (*concept*); die Idee (*idea*); die Meinung (*opinion*).
notoriety [noutə'raiiti], *s.* der üble Ruf.
notorious [no'tɔ:riəs], *adj.* berüchtigt.
notwithstanding [nɔtwið'stændiŋ], *prep.* ungeachtet (*Genit.*). — *adv.* trotzdem, dennoch. — *conj.* — *that*, obgleich.
nought [nɔ:t], *s.* die Null (*figure 0*); nichts (*nothing*).
noun [naun], *s.* (*Gram.*) das Hauptwort, Substantiv.
nourish ['nʌriʃ], *v.a.* nähren; ernähren.
nourishment ['nʌriʃmənt], *s.* die Nahrung.
Nova Scotian ['nouvə'skouʃən], *adj.* neuschottisch. [Neuschottland]
novel [nɔvl], *s.* (*Lit.*) der Roman. — *adj.* neu; neuartig (*modern*).
novelty ['nɔvlti], *s.* die Neuheit.
November [no'vembə]. der November.
novice ['nɔvis], *s.* der Neuling (*greenhorn*); (*Eccl.*) der, die Novize.
novitiate [no'viʃiit], *s.* die Lehrzeit; (*Eccl.*) das Noviziat.
now [nau], *adv.* nun, jetzt; — *and then*, dann und wann, hin und wieder. — *conj.* — (*that*), da nun.
nowadays ['nauədeiz], *adv.* heutzutage.
nowhere ['nouhwεə], *adv.* nirgends.
noxious ['nɔkʃəs], *adj.* (*Med., Bot.*) schädlich.
nozzle [nɔzl], *s.* die Düse; (*sl.*) die Schnauze.
nuclear ['nju:kliə], *adj.* (*Phys.*) nuklear, Kern-.
nucleus ['nju:kliəs], *s.* der Kern.
nude [nju:d], *adj.* nackt, bloß.
nudge [nʌdʒ], *v.a.* leicht anstoßen.
nudity ['nju:diti], *s.* die Nacktheit.
nugget ['nʌgit], *s.* der Klumpen.
nuisance ['nju:səns], *s.* die Plage, Lästigkeit; das Ärgernis (*annoyance*).
null [nʌl], *adj.* null und nichtig; ungültig.
nullify ['nʌlifai], *v.a.* annullieren, ungültig machen.
nullity ['nʌliti], *s.* die Ungültigkeit.
numb [nʌm], *adj.* erstarrt, gefühllos. — *v.a.* erstarren lassen.
number ['nʌmbə], *s.* die Zahl, Nummer (*telephone etc.*); die Anzahl (*quantity*); *cardinal —*, die Grundzahl; *ordinal —*, die Ordnungszahl. — *v.a.* nummerieren; zählen (*count*).
numbness ['nʌmnis], *s.* die Erstarrung.
numeral ['nju:mərəl], *s.* (*Gram.*) das Zahlwort.
numerical [nju:'merikəl], *adj.* (*Maths.*) Zahlen-, numerisch.
numerous ['nju:mərəs], *adj.* zahlreich.
numismatics [nju:miz'mætiks], *s.* die Münzkunde.
numskull ['nʌmskʌl], *s.* der Dummkopf.
nun [nʌn], *s.* (*Eccl.*) die Nonne.
nunnery ['nʌnəri], *s.* (*Eccl.*) das Nonnenkloster.
nuptials ['nʌpʃəlz], *s. pl.* (*Lit., Poet.*) die Hochzeit, das Hochzeitsfest.
nurse [nə:s], *s.* die Krankenschwester, Pflegerin; die Amme (*wet nurse*). — *v.a.* pflegen.
nursery ['nə:səri], *s.* das Kinderzimmer; (*Bot.*) die Pflanzschule, Baumschule (*for trees*); — *school*, der Kindergarten.
nurture ['nə:tʃə], *v.a.* nähren, aufziehen.
nut [nʌt], *s.* (*Bot.*) die Nuß; (*Tech.*) die Schraubenmutter; (*Am. coll.*) *nuts*, verrückt.
nutcracker ['nʌtkrækə], *s.* (*usually pl.*) der Nußknacker.
nutmeg ['nʌtmeg], *s.* (*Cul.*) die Muskatnuß.
nutriment ['nju:trimənt], *s.* die Nahrung; (*animals*) das Futter.
nutrition [nju'triʃən], *s.* die Ernährung.
nutritious [nju'triʃəs], *adj.* nahrhaft.
nutshell ['nʌtʃel], *s.* die Nußschale; (*fig.*) *put in a —*, kurz ausdrücken.
nymph [nimf], *s.* (*Myth.*) die Nymphe.

O

O [ou]. das O. — *int.* oh!
oaf [ouf], *s.* der Tölpel.
oak [ouk], *s.* (*Bot.*) die Eiche.
oaken ['oukən], *adj.* eichen, aus Eichenholz.

oar [ɔ:], *s.* das Ruder; *put o.'s — in*, sich einmengen.
oasis [ou'eisis], *s.* die Oase.
oath [ouθ], *s.* der Eid; der Fluch (*curse*); *commissioner for —s*, der öffentliche Notar; *take an —*, einen Eid schwören *or* leisten.
oats [outs], *s. pl.* (*Bot.*) der Hafer; *sow o.'s wild —s*, sich austoben, sich die Hörner ablaufen.
obdurate ['ɔbdjurit], *adj.* halsstarrig.
obedience [o'bi:djəns], *s.* der Gehorsam.
obedient [o'bi:djənt], *adj.* gehorsam.
obeisance [o'beisəns], *s.* die Verbeugung, Ehrfurchtsbezeigung.
obese [o'bi:s], *adj.* fettleibig, beleibt.
obey [o'bei], *v.a., v.n.* gehorchen (*Dat.*).
obituary [o'bitjuəri], *s.* der Nachruf, der Nekrolog.
object ['ɔbdʒikt], *s.* der Gegenstand (*thing*); (*Gram.*) das Objekt; der Zweck (*objective, purpose*). — [əb-'dʒekt], *v.n.* — *to*, einwenden (*gainsay*); vorhalten (*remonstrate*).
objection [əb'dʒekʃən], *s.* der Einwand.
objectionable [əb'dʒekʃənəbl], *adj.* anstößig.
objective [əb'dʒektiv], *adj.* objektiv, unparteiisch. — *s.* das Ziel (*aim*).
obligation [ɔbli'geiʃən], *s.* die Verpflichtung.
obligatory [o'bligətəri, 'ɔblig-], *adj.* verbindlich, obligatorisch.
oblige [o'blaidʒ], *v.a.* verpflichten; *much obliged*, vielen Dank; *can you — me?* können Sie mir aushelfen?
obliging [o'blaidʒiŋ], *adj.* gefällig, zuvorkommend.
oblique [o'bli:k], *adj.* schräg, schief; (*fig.*) indirekt.
obliterate [o'blitəreit], *v.a.* auslöschen (*extinguish*); vertilgen (*destroy*).
oblivion [o'bliviən], *s.* die Vergessenheit.
oblivious [o'bliviəs], *adj.* vergeßlich.
oblong ['ɔblɔŋ], *adj.* länglich. — *s.* das Rechteck.
obloquy ['ɔbləkwi], *s.* die Schmähung, Schande.
obnoxious [ɔb'nɔkʃəs], *adj.* verhaßt, scheußlich.
obscene [ɔb'si:n], *adj.* anstößig, obszön.
obscenity [ɔb'sen-, ɔb'si:niti], *s.* die Obszönität.
obscure [əb'skjuə], *adj.* dunkel (*dark*); unbekannt (*unknown*).
obscurity [əb'skjuəriti], *s.* die Dunkelheit (*darkness*); die Unbekanntheit.
obsequies ['ɔbsikwiz], *s. pl.* das Leichenbegängnis.
obsequious [əb'si:kwiəs], *adj.* unterwürfig.
observance [əb'zə:vəns], *s.* die Befolgung, Beobachtung, das Einhalten (*Law etc.*).
observant [əb'zə:vənt], *adj.* aufmerksam; achtsam.
observation [ɔbzə'veiʃən], *s.* die Beobachtung (*watching*); die Bemerkung (*remark*).
observatory [əb'zə:vətri], *s.* die Sternwarte.
observe [əb'zə:v], *v.a.* beobachten (*watch*); bemerken (*notice, remark on*).
obsession [əb'seʃən], *s.* die Besessenheit, fixe Idee.
obsolete ['ɔbsəli:t], *adj.* veraltet.
obstacle ['ɔbstəkl], *s.* das Hindernis.
obstinacy ['ɔbstinəsi], *s.* die Hartnäckigkeit.
obstinate ['ɔbstinit], *adj.* hartnäckig.
obstruct [əb'strʌkt], *v.a.* hemmen, hindern.
obstruction [əb'strʌkʃən], *s.* das Hindernis, die Hemmung, Verstopfung.
obtain [əb'tein], *v.a.* erhalten, erlangen; bekommen (*get*).
obtrude [ɔb'tru:d], *v.n.* sich aufdrängen. — *v.a.* aufdrängen.
obtrusive [əb'tru:siv], *adj.* aufdringlich.
obtuse [ɔb'tju:s], *adj.* stumpf; dumm (*stupid*).
obviate ['ɔbvieit], *v.a.* vorbeugen (*Dat.*).
obvious ['ɔbviəs], *adj.* klar, offenbar, selbstverständlich.
occasion [o'keiʒən], *s.* die Gelegenheit (*chance*); der Anlaß; die Veranlassung (*cause*). — *v.a.* veranlassen; verursachen (*cause*).
occasional [o'keiʒənəl], *adj.* gelegentlich.
occident ['ɔksidənt], *s.* das Abendland, der Westen.
occult [ɔ'kʌlt], *adj.* geheim, Okkult–.
occupancy ['ɔkjupənsi], *s.* der Besitz, das Innehaben (*holding*).
occupant ['ɔkjupənt], *s.* der Inhaber; der Bewohner (*of house*), Insasse.
occupation [ɔkju'peiʃən], *s.* die Besetzung; (*Mil.*) *army of —*, die Besatzung; der Beruf, die Beschäftigung (*job*); — *with*, das Befassen mit (*Dat.*).
occupy ['ɔkjupai], *v.a.* (*Mil.*) besetzen, in Besitz nehmen; beschäftigen (*engage*); bekleiden (*office*).
occur [ə'kə:], *v.n.* geschehen, sich ereignen; — *to s.o.*, jemandem einfallen.
occurrence [ə'kʌrəns], *s.* das Geschehen, Ereignis, der Vorfall.
ocean ['ouʃən], *s.* der Ozean, die See, das Meer. — *adj.* Meeres–.
octagon ['ɔktəgən], *s.* das Achteck.
octagonal [ɔk'tægənəl], *adj.* achteckig.
October [ɔk'toubə]. der Oktober.
octogenarian [ɔktodʒi'neəriən], *s.* der Achtzigjährige.
ocular ['ɔkjulə], *adj.* Augen–.
oculist ['ɔkjulist], *s.* (*Med.*) der Augenarzt.
odd [ɔd], *adj.* ungerade; seltsam (*queer*); einzeln (*solitary*). — *s.* (*pl.*) die Wahrscheinlichkeit.
oddity ['ɔditi], *s.* die Seltenheit, Sonderbarkeit.
oddment ['ɔdmənt], *s.* (*pl.*) die Reste, *m. pl.*
ode [oud], *s.* (*Poet.*) die Ode.
odious ['oudiəs], *adj.* verhaßt, widerwärtig.

odium ['oudiəm], *s.* der Haß.
odorous ['oudərəs], *adj.* duftend, duftig.
odour ['oudə], *s.* der Geruch, Duft.
of [ɔv], *prep.* von (*Dat.*); aus (*out of*) (*Dat.*); — *course*, natürlich.
off [ɔf, ɔ:f], *adv.* fort, weg; entfernt; *make* —, sich davonmachen; *far* —, weit weg; — *and on*, ab und zu; *well* —, wohlhabend. — *prep.* von (*from*); fort von; entfernt von (*distant from*).
offal [ɔfl], *s.* der Abfall.
offence [o'fens], *s.* (*Law*) das Vergehen; die Beleidigung (*insult*).
offend [o'fend], *v.a.* beleidigen (*insult*). — *v.n.* (*Law*) sich vergehen (gegen, *Acc.*).
offensive [o'fensiv], *adj.* beleidigend (*insulting*); anstößig (*indecent*). — *s.* die Offensive, der Angriff (*against*, auf, *Acc.*).
offer ['ɔfə], *v.a.* bieten (*auction*); anbieten (*hold out*). — *s.*das Anerbieten; (*Comm.*) das Angebot, der Antrag.
offering ['ɔfəriŋ], *s.* das Opfer.
office ['ɔfis], *s.* das Amt; die Stellung (*position*); die Funktion (*duties*); das Büro; (*Eccl.*) der Gottesdienst; *high* —, das hohe Amt; — *bearer*, der Amtswalter.
officer ['ɔfisə], *s.* (*Mil.*) der Offizier; der Beamte (*functionary*); *honorary* —, der ehrenamtliche Beamte, der Beamte im Ehrenamt.
official [o'fiʃəl], *adj.* offiziell, amtlich. — *s.* der Beamte.
officiate [o'fiʃieit], *v.n.* amtieren; fungieren.
officious [o'fiʃəs], *adj.* zudringlich, (übertrieben) dienstfertig.
offing ['ɔfiŋ], *s.* (*Naut.*) die hohe See; *in the* —, bevorstehend.
offset [ɔf'set], *v.a.* (*Comm.*) ausgleichen; (*Typ.*) offset drucken, im Offset drucken; (*fig.*) unschädlich machen, wettmachen. — ['ɔfset], *s.* (*Comm.*) die Gegenrechnung, der Ausgleich; (*Typ.*) der Offsetdruck.
offshoot ['ɔfʃu:t], *s.* der Sprößling.
offspring ['ɔfspriŋ], *s.* die Nachkommenschaft.
often, (*Poet.*) **oft** [ɔfn,ɔft], *adv.*oft, häufig.
ogle [ougl], *v.a., v.n.* äugeln, beäugeln, glotzen, anglotzen.
ogre ['ougə], *s.* der Menschenfresser.
oil [ɔil], *s.* das Öl. — *v.a.* einölen, einschmieren.
oilcloth ['ɔilklɔθ], *s.* das Wachstuch.
ointment ['ɔintmənt], *s.* die Salbe.
old [ould], *adj.* alt; —*-fashioned*, altmodisch.
olive ['ɔliv], *s.* (*Bot.*) die Olive; *the Mount of Olives*, der Ölberg.
Olympic [o'limpik], *adj.* olympisch; *the* — *Games*, die Olympischen Spiele.
omelette ['ɔmǝlit], *s.* (*Cul.*) das Omelett, der Eierkuchen.
omen ['oumən], *s.* das (böse) Vorzeichen, das Omen.
ominous ['ɔminəs], *adj.* von schlimmer Vorbedeutung, ominös.
omission [o'miʃən], *s.* die Unterlassung; (*Typ.*) die Auslassung.
omit [o'mit], *v.a.* unterlassen (*leave undone*); auslassen (*leave out*).
omnibus ['ɔmnibəs], *s.* der Omnibus, der Autobus.
omnipotent [ɔm'nipətənt], *adj.* allmächtig.
omniscient [ɔm'nisiənt], *adj.* allwissend.
on [ɔn], *prep.* an; auf; über; vor; bei; zu; nach; um; *call* — (*s.o.*), vorsprechen (bei, *Dat.*); — *fire*, in Flammen; — *condition*, unter der Bedingung (*Comm.*); — *account*, a Konto; — *high*, hoch oben; — *my honour*, auf mein Ehrenwort; — *purpose*, absichtlich; — *sale*, zum Verkauf. — *adv.* weiter, fort (*forward*); gültig, zutreffend (*correct, valid*); *get* —, vorwärtskommen; *get* — *with s.th.*, weitermachen; *get* — *with s.o.*, auskommen (mit, *Dat.*).
once [wʌns], *adv.* einmal; einst (*long ago*); — *more*, nochmals, noch einmal; — *and for all*, ein für alle Mal; *at* —, sogleich; — *in a while*, ab und zu. — *conj.* sobald.
one [wʌn], *num. adj.* ein, eine, ein; — *way street*, die Einbahnstraße. — *pron.* man (*impersonal*). — *s. little* —, der Kleine; — *by* —, eins nach dem anderen, einzeln.
onerous ['ɔnərəs], *adj.* beschwerlich.
onion ['ʌnjən], *s.* (*Bot.*) die Zwiebel.
onlooker ['ɔnlukə], *s.* der Zuschauer.
only ['ounli], *adj.* einzig, allein. — *adv.* nur, bloß. — *conj.* jedoch.
onset ['ɔnset], *s.* der Angriff (*attack*); der Anfang (*beginning*).
onslaught ['ɔnslɔ:t], *s.* der Angriff, Überfall.
onward ['ɔnwəd], *adj.* fortschreitend. — *adv.* (*also* **onwards**) vorwärts.
ooze [u:z], *s.* der Schlamm. — *v.n.* träufeln, sickern.
opacity [o'pæsiti], *s.* (*Phys.*) die Dunkelheit, Undurchsichtigkeit.
opal [oupl], *s.* der Opal.
opaque [o'peik], *adj.* (*Phys.*) dunkel, undurchsichtig.
open [oupn], *adj.* offen; offenherzig (*frank*); — *to suggestions*, einem Vorschlag zugänglich. — *v.a.* öffnen; eröffnen (*start*); — *an account*, ein Konto eröffnen. — *v.n.* sich öffnen, sich auftun.
opening ['oupniŋ], *s.* das Öffnen; die freie Stelle; die Gelegenheit (*opportunity*). — *adj.* einleitend; — *gambit*, (*Chess*) der Eröffnungszug.
openness ['oupənnis], *s.* die Offenheit, Ehrlichkeit (*frankness*).
opera ['ɔpərə], *s.* (*Mus.*) die Oper; *comic* —, die komische Oper; — *hat*, der Zylinderhut, Klapphut.
operatic [ɔpə'rætik], *adj.* (*Mus.*) Opern-.

operate ['ɔpəreit], *v.a.*, *v.n.* (*Engin.*) bedienen; (*Med.*) operieren (*on*, *Acc.*).
operation [ɔpə'reiʃən], *s.* (*Med.*, *Mil.*) die Operation; die Bedienung (*of engine etc.*).
operative ['ɔpərətiv], *adj.* wirksam (*effective*). — *s.* der Arbeiter.
opiate ['oupiit], *s.* das Schlafmittel. — *adj.* einschläfernd.
opine [o'pain], *v.n.* meinen.
opinion [o'pinjən], *s.* die Meinung; *in my* —, meiner Meinung nach.
opinionated [o'pinjəneitid], *adj.* von sich eingenommen, selbstgefällig.
opium ['oupjəm], *s.* das Opium.
opponent [ə'pounənt], *s.* der Gegner.
opportune ['ɔpətju:n], *adj.* gelegen, günstig.
opportunity [ɔpə'tju:niti], *s.* die Gelegenheit, Chance; die Möglichkeit.
oppose [ə'pouz], *v.a.* bekämpfen; widerstehen, entgegentreten (*Dat.*).
opposite ['ɔpəzit], *adj.* entgegengesetzt; gegenüberliegend; gegensätzlich (*contrary*). — *prep.* gegenüber (*Dat.*). — *s.* das Gegenteil.
opposition [ɔpə'ziʃən], *s.* (*Parl.*) die Opposition; der Widerstand.
oppress [ə'pres], *v.a.* unterdrücken.
oppression [ə'preʃən], *s.* die Unterdrückung.
oppressive [ə'presiv], *adj.* drückend, tyrannisch.
opprobrious [ə'proubriəs], *adj.* schändlich, schimpflich.
opprobrium [ə'proubriəm], *s.* die Schande.
optician [ɔp'tiʃən], *s.* der Optiker.
optics ['ɔptiks], *s.* die Optik.
optimism ['ɔptimizm], *s.* der Optimismus.
option ['ɔpʃən], *s.* die Wahl.
optional ['ɔpʃənəl], *adj.* Wahl-, frei, beliebig.
opulence ['ɔpjuləns], *s.* der Reichtum (an, *Dat.*), die Üppigkeit.
opulent ['ɔpjulənt], *adj.* reich, üppig.
or [ɔ:], *conj.* oder; noch (*after neg.*); *either* . . . —, entweder . . . oder.
oracle ['ɔrəkl], *s.* das Orakel.
oral ['ɔ:rəl], *adj.* mündlich. — *s.* die mündliche Prüfung.
orange ['ɔrindʒ],] *s.* (*Bot.*) die Orange, Apfelsine.
oration [ɔ'reiʃən], *s.* die feierliche Rede, Ansprache.
orator ['ɔrətə], *s.* der Redner.
oratorio [ɔrə'tɔ:riou], *s.* (*Mus.*) das Oratorium.
oratory ['ɔrətəri], *s.* (*Eccl.*) die Kapelle; (*Rhet.*) die Redekunst.
orb [ɔ:b], *s.* die Kugel; der Reichsapfel; (*Poet.*) der Himmelskörper.
orbit ['ɔ:bit], *s.* (*Astron.*) die Bahn (der Gestirne), Planetenbahn.
orchard ['ɔ:tʃəd], *s.* der Obstgarten.
orchestra ['ɔ:kistrə], *s.* (*Mus.*) das Orchester.
ordain [ɔ:'dein], *v.a.* ordinieren, anordnen; (*Eccl.*) zum Priester weihen.
ordeal ['ɔ:diəl], *s.* die Feuerprobe; Heimsuchung.
order ['ɔ:də], *s.* die Ordnung (*system*); die Verordnung (*command etc.*); (*Mil.*) der Befehl; (*Comm.*) die Bestellung; (*Biol.*) die Ordnung; der Orden (*Eccl.*; *also decoration*); *take* (*holy*) —*s*, ordiniert werden, Priester werden; *in* — *to*, um zu; *in* — *that*, so daß; *by* —, auf (den) Befehl. — *v.a.* befehlen, verordnen, anordnen: (*Comm.*) bestellen.
orderly ['ɔ:dəli], *adj.* ordentlich, ruhig. —*s.* (*Mil.*) die Ordonanz; (*Med.*) der Gehilfe, Krankenwärter.
ordinal ['ɔ:dinl], *adj.*, *s.* (*number*) die Ordnungszahl.
ordinance ['ɔ:dinəns], *s.* die Verordnung.
ordinary ['ɔ:dinəri], *adj.* gewöhnlich.
ordnance ['ɔ:dnəns], *s.* das schwere Geschütz; (*Mil.*, *Geog.*) — *survey*, die Landesvermessung.
ore [ɔ:], *s.* das Erz, Metall.
organ ['ɔ:gən], *s.* das Organ; (*Mus.*) die Orgel; — *grinder*, der Leierkastenmann.
organic [ɔ:'gænik], *adj.* organisch.
organisation [ɔ:gənai'zeiʃən], *s.* die Organisation.
organise ['ɔ:gənaiz], *v.a.* organisieren.
organism ['ɔ:gənizm], *s.* (*Biol.*) der Organismus.
organist ['ɔ:gənist], *s.* (*Mus.*) der Organist.
orgy ['ɔ:dʒi], *s.* die Orgie.
oriel ['ɔ:riəl], *s.* der Erker; — *window*, das Erkerfenster.
orient ['ɔ:riənt], *s.* der Orient, Osten.
oriental [ɔ:ri'entl], *adj.* östlich.
orifice ['ɔrifis], *s.* die Öffnung, Mündung.
origin ['ɔridʒin], *s.* der Ursprung, die Herkunft.
original [ə'ridʒinl], *adj.* Ursprungs-, ursprünglich; originell (*creative*). — *s.* das Original.
originality [əridʒi'næliti], *s.* die Originalität.
originate [ə'ridʒineit], *v.n.* entstehen, entspringen. — *v.a.* hervorbringen, entstehen lassen.
ornament ['ɔ:nəmənt], *s.* das Ornament; die Verzierung (*decoration*).
ornate [ɔ:'neit], *adj.* geziert, geschmückt.
orphan ['ɔ:fən], *s.* der, die Waise.
orphanage ['ɔ:fənidʒ], *s.* das Waisenhaus.
orthodoxy ['ɔ:θədɔksi], *s.* die Orthodoxie, die Rechtgläubigkeit.
orthography [ɔ:'θɔgrəfi], *s.* die Rechtschreibung.
orthopaedic [ɔ:θə'pi:dik], *adj.* orthopädisch.
oscillate ['ɔsileit], *v.n.* oszillieren, schwingen.
oscillatory ['ɔsileitəri], *adj.* schwingend, oszillierend.
osier ['ouʒiə], *s.* (*Bot.*) die Korbweide.
osprey ['ɔsprei], *s.* (*Orn.*) der Seeadler.

ossify ['ɔsifai], *v.a.* verknöchern lassen; versteinern lassen (*stone*). — *v.n.* verknöchern; versteinern (*stone*).
ostensible [ɔs'tensibl], *adj.* scheinbar, anscheinend, vorgeblich.
ostentation [ɔsten'teiʃən], *s.* die Großtuerei, der Prunk.
ostentatious [ɔsten'teiʃəs], *adj.* großtuerisch, prahlerisch, protzig.
ostler ['ɔslə], *s.* (*obs.*) der Stallknecht.
ostracize ['ɔstrəsaiz], *v.a.* verbannen, ausschließen.
ostrich ['ɔstritʃ], *s.* (*Orn.*) der Strauß.
other ['ʌðə], *adj.* ander. — *pron.*, *s.* *the* —, der, die, das andere.
otherwise ['ʌðəwaiz], *conj.* sonst. — *adv.* andernfalls.
otter ['ɔtə], *s.* (*Zool.*) die Otter.
ought [ɔ:t], *v. aux. defect.* sollte, müßte.
ounce [auns], *s.* die Unze.
our ['auə], *poss. adj.* unser, uns(e)re, unser.
ours ['auəz], *poss. pron.* unsrig, unser, uns(e)re, unser.
ourselves [auə'selvz], *pers. pron.* wir, wir selbst, uns selbst; (*refl.*) uns.
ousel [u:zl], *s.* (*Orn.*) die Amsel.
out [aut], *adv.* aus; draußen (*outside*); außerhalb (*outside, externally*); heraus; hinaus (*outward, away from the speaker*). — *prep.* — *of*, aus, von (*Dat.*).
outer ['autə], *adj.* äußer.
outfit ['autfit], *s.* die Ausrüstung.
outing ['autiŋ], *s.* der Ausflug.
outhouse ['authaus], *s.* das Nebengebäude, der Anbau.
outlaw ['autlɔ:], *s.* der Verbannte, der Vogelfreie.
outlay ['autlei], *s.* (*Comm.*) die Auslagen, die Spesen, *f. pl.*
outlet ['autlit], *s.* der Ausfluß, Abfluß; (*fig.*) das Ventil.
outline ['autlain], *s.* der Umriß, Entwurf. — [aut'lain], *v.a.* skizzieren, umreißen, kurz beschreiben.
outlive [aut'liv], *v.a.* überleben.
outlook ['autluk], *s.* die Aussicht, der Ausblick; die Weltanschauung (*philosophy*).
outlying ['autlaiiŋ], *adj.* außenliegend, außerhalb liegend, entlegen.
outnumber [aut'nʌmbə], *v.a.* an Zahl übertreffen.
outpatient ['autpeiʃənt], *s.* der ambulante Patient.
outrage ['autreidʒ], *s.* die Beleidigung (*insult*); die Gewalttat. — [aut'reidʒ], *v.a.* verletzen, beleidigen, schänden.
outrageous [aut'reidʒəs], *adj.* schändlich, schimpflich, unerhört; übertrieben (*exaggerated*).
outright ['autrait], *adj.* völlig. — [aut'rait], *adv.* gerade heraus, gänzlich.
outrun [aut'rʌn], *v.a. irr.* überholen, einholen.
outset ['autset], *s.* der Anfang.
outshine [aut'ʃain], *v.a. irr.* übertreffen.
outside [aut'said], *adv.* außen, draußen. — ['autsaid], *prep.* außerhalb (*Genit.*). — *adj.* äußere, außenstehend. — *s.* das Äußere, die Außenseite.
outskirts ['autskə:ts], *s. pl.* die Umgebung, Vorstadt.
outstanding [aut'stændiŋ], *adj.* hervorragend (*excellent*); noch unbeglichen (*unpaid*); unerledigt (*undone*).
outstay [aut'stei], *v.a.* länger bleiben, zu lange bleiben.
outvote [aut'vout], *v.a.* überstimmen.
outward ['autwəd], *adj.* äußere, äußerlich, außerhalb befindlich. — *adv.* (*also* **outwards**) auswärts, nach außen.
outweigh [aut'wei], *v.a.* schwerer wiegen als, überwiegen.
outwit [aut'wit], *v.a.* überlisten.
oval [ouvl], *adj.* oval. — *s.* das Oval.
ovary ['ouvəri], *s.* (*Anat.*) der Eierstock.
ovation [o'veiʃən], *s.* die Huldigung, Ovation.
oven [ʌvn], *s.* der Backofen; (kleine) Schmelzofen.
over ['ouvə], *prep.* über; oberhalb. — *adv.* über; herüber; drüben; — *there*, drüben; hinüber (*across*); vorüber (*past*).
overact [ouvər'ækt], *v.n.* übertreiben.
overawe [ouvər'ɔ:], *v.a.* einschüchtern.
overbalance [ouvə'bæləns], *v.a.* überwiegen. — *v.n.* überkippen.
overbear [ouvə'bɛə], *v.a. irr.* überwältigen.
overbearing [ouvə'bɛəriŋ], *adj.* anmaßend.
overboard ['ouvəbɔ:d], *adv.* über Bord.
overburden [ouvə'bə:dn], *v.a.* überlasten.
overcast [ouvə'kɑ:st], *adj.* bewölkt.
overcharge [ouvə'tʃɑ:dʒ], *v.a.* zu viel berechnen (*pers.*, *Dat.*), übervorteilen; überladen (*overload*). — *s.* die Übervorteilung; (*Tech.*) der Überdruck.
overcoat ['ouvəkout], *s.* der Mantel; *light* —, der Überzieher.
overcome [ouvə'kʌm], *v.a.*, *v.n. irr.* überwinden.
overdo [ouvə'du:], *v.a. irr.* übertreiben.
overdone [ouvə'dʌn], *adj.* übergar, zu lange gekocht.
overdrive [ouvə'draiv], *v.a. irr.* abhetzen, zu weit treiben. — ['ouvədraiv] *s.* (*Motor.*) der Schnellgang.
overdue [ouvə'dju:], *adj.* überfällig, verfallen.
overflow [ouvə'flou], *v.a.*, *v.n.* überfließen; überfluten (*banks*). — ['ouvəflou], *s.* der Überfluß (*flood*); die Überschwemmung.
overgrow [ouvə'grou], *v.a. irr.* überwachsen, überwuchern. — *v.n.* zu groß werden.
overhang [ouvə'hæŋ], *v.a. irr.* überhängen.
overhaul [ouvə'hɔ:l], *v.a.* überholen. — ['ouvəhɔ:l], *s.* die Überholung.
overhead [ouvə'hed], *adv.* droben; oben (*above*). — ['ouvəhed], *s.* (*pl.*) (*Comm.*) laufende Unkosten, *pl.*

overhear [ouvə'hiə], *v.a. irr.* zufällig hören.
overjoyed [ouvə'dʒɔid], *adj.* entzückt.
overlap [ouvə'læp], *v.n.* überschneiden, zusammenfallen (*dates etc.*). — ['ouvəlæp], *s.* die Überschneidung, das Zusammenfallen.
overload [ouvə'loud], *v.a.* überlasten; (*Elec.*) überladen.
overlook [ouvə'luk], *v.a.* übersehen; verzeihen (*disregard*).
overmuch [ouvə'mʌtʃ], *adv.* allzusehr.
overpay [ouvə'pei], *v.a., v.n.* zu viel bezahlen.
overpopulated [ouvə'pɔpjuleitid], *adj.* übervölkert.
overpower [ouvə'pauə], *v.a.* überwältigen.
overrate [ouvə'reit], *v.a.* überschätzen.
overreach [ouvə'ri:tʃ], *v.a.* übervorteilen.
override [ouvə'raid], *v.a. irr.* überreiten; unterdrücken (*suppress*).
overrule [ouvə'ru:l], *v.a.* nicht gelten lassen, verwerfen.
overseer ['ouvəsiə], *s.* der Aufseher.
oversleep [ouvə'sli:p], *v.n. irr.* sich verschlafen.
overstep [ouvə'step], *v.a.* überschreiten.
overstrain [ouvə'strein], *v.a., v.n.* (sich) zu sehr anstrengen, überanstrengen.
overt ['ouvə:t], *adj.* offenkundig; öffentlich (*public*).
overtake [ouvə'teik], *v.a. irr.* einholen; (*Mot.*) überholen.
overtax [ouvə'tæks], *v.a.* zu hoch besteuern; (*fig.*) überanstrengen (*strain*).
overthrow [ouvə'θrou], *v.a. irr.* umstürzen; (*Pol.*) stürzen. — ['ouvəθrou], *s.* der Sturz.
overtime ['ouvətaim], *s.* Überstunden, *f. pl.*
overture ['ouvətjuə], *s.* die Ouvertüre.
overturn [ouvə'tə:n], *v.a.* umstürzen. — *v.n.* überschlagen.
overweening [ouvə'wi:niŋ], *adj.* eingebildet.
overweight [ouvə'weit], *s.* das Übergewicht.
overwhelm [ouvə'welm], *v.a.* überwältigen.
overwork [ouvə'wə:k], *v.n.* sich überarbeiten.
overwrought [ouvə'rɔ:t], *adj.* übermäßig erregt, aufgeregt, überreizt.
owe [ou], *v.a.* schulden. — *v.n.* verdanken (*be in debt*).
owing ['ouiŋ], *pred. adj.* — *to*, dank (*Dat.*), zufolge (*Dat.*).
owl [aul], *s.* (*Orn.*) die Eule.
own (1) [oun], *v.a.* besitzen (*possess*). — *adj.* eigen.
own (2) [oun], *v.a.* anerkennen (*acknowledge*).
owner ['ounə], *s.* der Besitzer, Eigentümer.
ox [ɔks], *s.* (*Zool.*) der Ochse.
oxidate ['ɔksideit] *see* **oxidise.**
oxide ['ɔksaid], *s.* (*Chem.*) das Oxyd.
oxidise ['ɔksidaiz], *v.a., v.n.* (*Chem.*) oxydieren.
oxtail ['ɔksteil], *s.* der Ochsenschwanz.
oxygen ['ɔksidʒən], *s.* (*Chem.*) der Sauerstoff.
oyster ['ɔistə], *s.* (*Zool.*) die Auster.
ozone ['ouzoun], *s.* (*Chem.*) das Ozon.

P

P [pi:]. das P.
pa [pɑ:], *s.* (*coll.*) Papa, der Vater.
pace [peis], *s.* der Gang, Schritt (*step*); das Tempo (*rate*). — *v.n.* — *up and down*, auf- und abschreiten. — *v.a.* einschulen (*horse*).
Pacific, The [pə'sifik, θə]. der Stille Ozean.
pacific [pə'sifik], *adj.* friedlich, still.
pacify ['pæsifai], *v.a.* Frieden stiften, beruhigen.
pack [pæk], *s.* das *or* der Pack; der Ballen (*bale*); das Rudel (*wolves*); das Spiel (*cards*); das Paket, die Packung. — *v.a.* packen (*a case*); parteiisch zusammensetzen; die Karten schlecht mischen (*cheat at cards*); *packed like sardines*, dichtgedrängt, eingepfercht. — *v.n.* packen; seine Sachen einpacken.
package ['pækidʒ], *s.* der Ballen (*bale*); das Gepäckstück, Paket.
packet ['pækit], *s.* das Paket; (*Naut.*) — *boat*, das Paketboot, Postschiff.
pact [pækt], *s.* der Pakt, Vertrag.
pad [pæd], *s.* das Polster, Kissen; der Notizblock (*writing block*). — *v.a.* auspolstern; *padded cell*, die Gummizelle.
padding ['pædiŋ], *s.* (*Tail.*) das Futter; (*fig.*) die (nichtssagende) Ausfüllung, das leere Geschwätz.
paddle [pædl], *v.a., v.n.* rudern, paddeln. — *s.* das Paddel, (Doppel)ruder, das Schaufelruder; — *steamer*, der Raddampfer.
paddock ['pædək], *s.* der Sattelplatz; das Gehege.
padlock ['pædlɔk], *s.* das Vorhängeschloß, Vorlegeschloß.
pagan ['peigən], *adj.* heidnisch. — *s.* der Heide.
paganism ['peigənizm], *s.* das Heidentum.
page (1) [peidʒ], *s.* der Page (*court attendant*); Hoteljunge (*hotel boy*). — *v.a.* durch Pagen suchen lassen.
page (2) [peidʒ], die Seite (*of book*). — *v.a.* paginieren (*book*).
pageant ['pædʒənt], *s.* der Aufzug, der Prunkzug; das Schaustück (*dramatic*).
pail [peil], *s.* der Eimer.

pain [pein], *s.* der Schmerz, die Pein; (*pl.*) die Mühe; *go to a lot of* —*s*, sich große Mühe geben. — *v.a.* schmerzen; bekümmern (*mentally*).
paint [peint], *s.* die Farbe (*dye*); die Schminke (*make-up*). — *v.a.* anstreichen, malen.
painter ['peintə], *s.* der Maler.
painting ['peintiŋ], *s.* das Gemälde.
pair [pɛə], *s.* das Paar; *two* —*s of shoes*, zwei Paar Schuhe; *a* — *of spectacles*, die Brille; *a* — *of scissors*, die Schere. — *v.a.* paaren. — *v.n.* sich paaren.
pajamas [pə'dʒɑ:məz] *see under* **pyjamas**.
Pakistani [pɑ:ki'stɑ:ni], *adj.* pakistanisch. — *s.* der Pakistaner.
palace ['pæləs], *s.* der Palast.
palatable ['pælətəbl], *adj.* schmackhaft.
palatal ['pælətl], *adj.* (*Phonet.*) palatal, Gaumen-, Vordergaumen-. — *s.* (*Phonet.*) der Gaumenlaut.
palate ['pælit], *s.* der Gaumen.
Palatinate, The [pə'lætinit, ðə]. die Pfalz, Pfalzgrafschaft.
palaver [pə'lɑ:və], *s.* die Unterredung; das Palaver.
pale (1) [peil], *adj.* blaß, bleich.
pale (2) [peil], *s.* der Pfahl; *beyond the* —, unkultiviert.
Palestinian [pælis'tiniən], *adj.* palästinisch. — *s.* der Palästiner.
palette ['pælit], *s.* die Palette (*see also* **pallet** (1)).
paling ['peiliŋ], *s.* der Lattenzaun; (*pl.*) der Pfahlbau.
pall (1) [pɔ:l], *s.* das Leichentuch.
pall (2) [pɔ:l], *v.n.* schal werden (*become stale*).
pallet (1) ['pælit], *s.* die Palette (*painter's*); — *knife*, das Streichmesser (*potter's etc.*).
pallet (2) ['pælit], *s.* der Strohsack.
palliative ['pæliətiv], *s.* linderndes Mittel; (*fig.*) die Beschönigung.
pallid ['pælid], *adj.* blaß, bleich.
pallor ['pælə], *s.* die Blässe.
palm (1) [pɑ:m], *s.* die Handfläche. — *v.a.* — (*off*) *on to s.o.*, an jemanden loswerden, jemandem etwas andrehen.
palm (2) [pɑ:m], *s.* (*Bot.*) die Palme; *Palm Sunday*, Palmsonntag.
palmer ['pɑ:mə], *s.* (*obs.*) der Pilger (*pilgrim*).
palmist ['pɑ:mist], *s.* der Handleser, Wahrsager.
palmistry ['pɑ:mistri], *s.* die Handwahrsagerei.
palmy ['pɑ:mi], *adj.* glorreich.
palpable ['pælpəbl], *adj.* handgreiflich, greifbar, klar.
palpitate ['pælpiteit], *v.n.* klopfen (*of heart*).
palsied ['pɔ:lzid], *adj.* (*Med.*) gelähmt.
palsy ['pɔ:lzi], *s.* (*Med.*) die Lähmung.
paltry ['pɔ:ltri], *adj.* erbärmlich, armselig.
pamper ['pæmpə], *v.a.* verwöhnen.
pan (1) [pæn], *s.* die Pfanne. — *v.n.* — *out*, sich ausbreiten, sich weiten.
pan (2) [pæn], *v.a.* (*Phot.*) kreisen, im Bogen führen.
panacea [pænə'siə], *s.* das Universalmittel.
pancake ['pænkeik], *s.* der Pfannkuchen.
pander ['pændə], *v.n.* fröhnen (*Dat.*), nachgeben.
pane [pein], *s.* die Glasscheibe.
panel [pænl], *s.* die Holzfüllung, Täfelung (*in room*); die Liste; die Kommission (*of experts etc.*).
pang [pæŋ], *s.* die Angst, Pein; der Schmerz, Stich (*stab of pain*).
panic ['pænik], *s.* die Panik, der Schrecken.
panoply ['pænəpli], *s.* (*Poet.*) die Rüstung.
pansy ['pænzi], *s.* (*Bot.*) das Stiefmütterchen; (*sl.*) der Weichling, Feigling.
pant [pænt], *v.n.* keuchen, schwer atmen.
pantaloons [pæntə'lu:nz] (*usually abbr.* **pants** [pænts]), *s. pl.* die Unterhosen, Hosen, *f.pl.*
panther ['pænθə], *s.* (*Zool.*) der Panther.
pantomime ['pæntəmaim], *s.* die Pantomime, das Weihnachtsstück.
pantry ['pæntri], *s.* die Speisekammer.
pap [pæp], *s.* der Kinderbrei.
papacy ['peipəsi], *s.* das Papsttum.
papal ['peipəl], *adj.* päpstlich.
paper ['peipə], *s.* das Papier (*material*); die Zeitung (*daily* —); die Abhandlung (*essay*); — *knife*, der Brieföffner. — *v.a.* tapezieren (*a room*).
paperhanger ['peipəhæŋə], *s.* der Tapezierer.
paperweight ['peipəweit], *s.* der Briefbeschwerer.
par [pɑ:], *s.* die Gleichheit, das Pari.
parable ['pærəbl], *s.* die Parabel, das Gleichnis.
parabola [pə'ræbələ], *s.* (*Geom.*) die Parabel.
parabolic [pærə'bɔlik], *adj.* parabolisch, gleichnishaft.
parachute ['pærəʃu:t], *s.* (*Aviat.*) der Fallschirm.
parade [pə'reid], *s.* die Parade, der Aufmarsch. — *v.a.* herausstellen; zur Schau tragen (*show off*). — *v.n.* (*Mil.*) vorbeimarschieren.
paradise ['pærədais], *s.* das Paradies.
paraffin ['pærəfin], *s.* das Paraffin.
paragon ['pærəgən], *s.* das Musterkind, Musterbeispiel, Vorbild.
paragraph ['pærəgrɑ:f], *s.* der Abschnitt, Absatz, Paragraph.
Paraguayan [pærə'gwaiən], *adj.* paraguayisch. — *s.* der Paraguayer.
parallel ['pærəlel], *adj.* parallel. — *s.* die Parallele.
paralyse ['pærəlaiz], *v.a.* lähmen.
paralysis [pə'rælisis], *s.* die Lähmung.
paramount ['pærəmaunt], *adj.* oberst.
paramour ['pærəmuə], *s.* der *or* die Geliebte.

parapet ['pærəpit], *s.* das Geländer, die Brüstung.
paraphrase ['pærəfreiz], *s.* die Umschreibung. — *v.a.* umschreiben.
parasite ['pærəsait], *s.* der Schmarotzer, Parasit.
parasol ['pærəsɔl], *s.* der Sonnenschirm.
parboil ['pɑ:bɔil], *v.a.* aufkochen lassen.
parcel [pɑ:sl], *s.* das Paket; Bündel (*bundle*). — *v.a.* — *up*, einpacken.
parch [pɑ:tʃ], *v.a.* austrocknen.
parchment ['pɑ:tʃmənt], *s.* das Pergament.
pardon [pɑ:dn], *v.a.* vergeben, verzeihen (*Dat.*); begnadigen (*Acc.*) (*give amnesty*). — *s.* der Pardon, die Verzeihung; —*!*, *I beg your —!* bitte um Entschuldigung; *I beg your —?* wie bitte?
pare [pɛə], *v.a.* beschneiden (*nails*); schälen (*fruit*).
parent ['pɛərənt], *s.* der Vater, die Mutter, (*pl.*) die Eltern, *pl.*
parentage ['pɛərəntidʒ], *s.* die Abkunft, Herkunft.
parenthesis [pə'renθisis], *s.* die Parenthese, die Klammer.
parish ['pæriʃ], *s.* das Kirchspiel, die Gemeinde, die Pfarre.
parishioner [pə'riʃənə], *s.* das Gemeindemitglied.
Parisian [pə'riziən], *adj.* parisisch. — *s.* der Pariser.
park [pɑ:k], *s.* der Park; (*Motor.*) der Wagenpark, Parkplatz. — *v.a.*, *v.n.* parken.
parking ['pɑ:kiŋ], *s.* (*Motor.*) das Parken; — *meter*, die Parkuhr, der Parkometer.
parley ['pɑ:li], *s.* die Unterredung, Verhandlung. — *v.n.* verhandeln.
parliament ['pɑ:ləmənt], *s.* das Parlament.
parlour ['pɑ:lə], *s.* das Wohnzimmer, die gute Stube: —*maid*, das Dienstmädchen; — *trick*, das Kunststück.
parochial [pə'roukiəl], *adj.* Pfarr-, Gemeinde-; (*fig.*) engstirnig.
parody ['pærədi], *s.* die Parodie. — *v.a.* parodieren.
parole [pə'roul], *s.* das Ehrenwort; (*Mil.*) das Losungswort.
paroxysm ['pærəksizm], *s.* der heftige Anfall.
parquet ['pɑ:ki], *s.* das Parkett; — *floor*, der Parkettfußboden.
parrot ['pærət], *s.* (*Orn.*) der Papagei.
parry ['pæri], *v.a.* parieren, abwehren.
parse [pɑ:s, pɑ:z], *v.a.* (*Gram.*) analysieren.
parsimony ['pɑ:siməni], *s.* die Sparsamkeit.
parsley ['pɑ:sli], *s.* (*Bot.*) die Petersilie.
parson [pɑ:sn], *s.* der Pastor, Pfarrer.
parsonage ['pɑ:sənidʒ], *s.* das Pfarrhaus.
part [pɑ:t], *s.* der Teil; Anteil (*share*); (*Theat.*) die Rolle; (*Mus.*) die Stimme; (*Geog.*) die Gegend; *for his —*, seinerseits. — *v.n.* — (*with*), sich trennen (von, *Dat.*); — *company*, auseinandergehen.
partake [pɑ:'teik], *v.n.* teilnehmen, teilhaben (*in*, an, *Dat.*).
partial [pɑ:ʃl], *adj.* Teil–; parteiisch (*subjective*); — *to*, eingenommen für.
participate [pɑ:'tisipeit], *v.n.* teilnehmen (*in*, an, *Dat.*).
participation [pɑ:tisi'peiʃən], *s.* die Teilnahme.
participle ['pɑ:tisipl], *s.* (*Gram.*) das Mittelwort, Partizip(ium).
particle ['pɑ:tikl], *s.* die Partikel, das Teilchen.
particular [pə'tikjulə], *adj.* besonder (*special*); einzel (*individual*); sonderbar (*queer*); ungewöhnlich; genau. — *s.* (*pl.*) die Details, *n. pl.*, Einzelheiten, *f. pl.*
parting ['pɑ:tiŋ], *s.* der Abschied (*taking leave*); der Scheitel (*hair*).
partisan [pɑ:ti'zæn], *s.* der Partisane, Parteigänger.
partition [pɑ:'tiʃən], *s.* die Teilung (*division*); die Scheidewand (*dividing wall*). — *v.a.* teilen; aufteilen (*divide up*).
partly ['pɑ:tli], *adv.* zum Teil, teils.
partner ['pɑ:tnə], *s.* der Partner; Teilhaber (*in business etc.*).
partnership ['pɑ:tnəʃip], *s.* die Partnerschaft.
partridge ['pɑ:tridʒ], *s.* (*Orn.*) das Rebhuhn.
party ['pɑ:ti], *s.* (*Pol.*) die Partei; (*Law*) die Partei, Seite; die Gesellschaft, die Party (*social gathering*); *throw* or *give a —*, einen Gesellschaftsabend (*or* eine Party) geben; *guilty —*, der schuldige Teil; (*Build.*) — *wall*, die Brandmauer.
Paschal ['pɑ:skəl], *adj.* Oster-.
pass [pɑ:s], *v.a.* passieren; vorbeigehen (an, *Dat.*); durchlassen (*let through*); (*Law*) — *sentence*, das Urteil fällen. — *v.n.* fortgehen, vergehen, geschehen (*happen*); vorübergehen (*of time*); — *for*, gelten; (*Sch.*) durchkommen (*exam*); *come to —*, sich ereignen. — *s.* der Paß; (*Theat.*) die Freikarte.
passable ['pɑ:səbl], *adj.* gangbar; (*fig.*) leidlich, erträglich.
passage ['pæsidʒ], *s.* der Durchgang (*thoroughfare*); das Vergehen (*of time*); die Seereise; die Stelle (*book*).
passenger ['pæsindʒə], *s.* der Reisende, Passagier; — *train*, der Personenzug.
passer-by ['pɑ:səbai], *s.* der Passant, Vorübergehende.
passing ['pɑ:siŋ], *s.* das Vorbeigehen, das Vorübergehen; (*Parl.*) das Durchgehen; das Hinscheiden (*death*). — *adj.* vorübergehend, zeitweilig.
Passion ['pæʃən], *s.* (*Eccl.*) das Leiden; (*Mus.*) die Passion; — *Week*, die Karwoche; — *flower*, die Passionsblume.
passion ['pæʃən], *s.* die Leidenschaft;

fly into a —, aufbrausen.
passive ['pæsiv], *adj.* passiv. — *s.* (*Gram.*) das Passiv(um).
Passover ['pɑ:souvə], *s.* (*Rel.*) das Passahfest.
passport ['pɑ:spɔ:t], *s.* der Reisepaß.
past [pɑ:st], *adj.* vergangen. — *adv.* vorbei. — *prep.* nach (*time*). — *s.* die Vergangenheit; (*Gram.*) das Imperfekt, Präteritum.
paste [peist], *s.* die Paste, der Brei; der Kleister (*glue*). — *v.a.* kleben, kleistern.
pasteboard ['peistbɔ:d], *s.* die Pappe.
pastime ['pɑ:staim], *s.* der Zeitvertreib.
pastor ['pɑ:stə], *s.* (*Rel.*) der Seelsorger, Pfarrer.
pastoral ['pɑ:stərəl], *adj.* Hirten-, pastoral. — *s.* (*Poet*). das Hirtengedicht.
pastry ['peistri], *s.* (*Cul.*) die Pastete; das Gebäck; — *cook*, der Konditor, Zuckerbäcker.
pasture ['pɑ:stʃə], *s.* die Weide, das Grasland. — *v.n.* weiden, grasen.
pasty ['pɑ:sti, 'pæsti], *s.* (*Cul.*) die Pastete. — ['peisti], *adj.* teigig.
pat [pæt], *s.* der Klaps; der Schlag (*slap*). — *v.a.* leicht schlagen, streicheln (*gently*).
patch [pætʃ], *v.a.* flicken, ausbessern. — *s.* der Fleck (*mending material*); der Flecken (*land*); (*coll.*) *no — on him*, kein Vergleich mit ihm; nicht zu vergleichen mit ihm.
patent ['peitənt *or* 'pætənt], *adj.* offen, klar, patent; — *leather*, das Glanzleder. — *s.* das Patent.
patentee [peitən'ti:], *s.* der Patentinhaber.
paternal [pə'tə:nəl], *adj.* väterlich.
path [pɑ:θ], *s.* der Pfad, Weg, Fußsteig.
pathetic [pə'θetik], *adj.* pathetisch, rührend; armselig.
pathology [pə'θɔlədʒi], *s.* (*Med.*) die Pathologie.
pathway ['pɑ:θwei], *s.* der Fußweg, Fußsteig.
patience ['peiʃəns], *s.* die Geduld; die Patience (*card game*).
patient ['peiʃənt], *adj.* geduldig. — *s.* (*Med.*) der Patient.
patrician [pə'triʃən], *adj.* patrizisch. — *s.* der Patrizier.
patrimony ['pætriməni], *s.* das (väterliche) Erbgut.
patriot ['peitriət, 'pætriət], *s.* der Patriot.
patriotism ['peitriətizm, 'pæt-], *s.* die Vaterlandsliebe, der Patriotismus.
patrol [pə'troul], *s.* die Patrouille, Streife. — *v.n.* auf Patrouille gehen.
patron ['peitrən], *s.* der Schutzherr, der Gönner; (*Comm.*) der Kunde; — *saint*, der Schutzheilige.
patronage ['pætrənidʒ], *s.* die Gönnerschaft, Huld.
patronize ['pætrənaiz], *v.a.* besuchen (*frequent*); begünstigen (*favour*).
patronizing ['pætrənaiziŋ], *adj.* herablassend.
patten [pætn], *s.* (*Archit.*) der Sockel; der Holzschuh (*clog*).
patter (1) ['pætə], *s.* das Geplätscher (*rain etc.*). — *v.n.* plätschern.
patter (2) ['pætə], *s.* das Geplauder (*chatter*). — *v.n.* schwätzen.
pattern ['pætən], *s.* das Muster; die Schablone (*in material*).
paucity ['pɔ:siti], *s.* die geringe Anzahl, der Mangel.
paunch [pɔ:ntʃ], *s.* der Wanst.
pauper ['pɔ:pə], *s.* der Arme.
pauperize ['pɔ:pəraiz], *v.a.* arm machen, verarmen lassen.
pause [pɔ:z], *s.* die Pause. — *v.n.* innehalten.
pave [peiv], *v.a.* pflastern.
pavement ['peivmənt], *s.* das Pflaster; der Bürgersteig, Gehsteig.
pavilion [pə'viljən], *s.* das Gartenhaus; der Pavillon.
paw [pɔ:], *s.* die Pfote; die Tatze. — *v.a.* streicheln, betasten.
pawn (1) [pɔ:n], *s.* das Pfand. — *v.a.* verpfänden.
pawn (2) [pɔ:n], *s.* (*Chess*) der Bauer.
pawnbroker ['pɔ:nbroukə], *s.* der Pfandleiher.
pay [pei], *v.a. irr.* zahlen; bezahlen, begleichen (*bill*); — *attention*, aufpassen, Aufmerksamkeit schenken; — *o.'s respects*, Respekt zollen. — *v.n. irr.* sich bezahlt machen, sich lohnen (*it —s to . . .*). — *s.* (*Mil.*) der Sold; (*Comm.*) der Lohn (*wage*), die Bezahlung (*payment*).
payable ['peiəbl], *adj.* zahlbar, zu bezahlen.
payee [pei'i:], *s.* der Empfänger, Präsentant.
payer ['peiə], *s.* der Zahler; (*Comm.*) der Trassat.
payment ['peimənt], *s.* die Bezahlung, Begleichung (*of sum*).
pea [pi:], *s.* (*Bot.*) die Erbse (*see also* **peas(e)**).
peace [pi:s], *s.* der Friede(n); die Ruhe (*restfulness*).
peaceable ['pi:səbl], *adj.* friedlich; friedliebend.
peaceful ['pi:sful], *adj.* friedlich, ruhig (*restful*).
peach [pi:tʃ], *s.* (*Bot.*) der *or* (*Austr.*) die Pfirsich.
peacock ['pi:kɔk], *s.* (*Orn.*) der Pfau.
peahen ['pi:hen], *s.* (*Orn.*) die Pfauhenne.
peak [pi:k], *s.* der Gipfel, die Spitze; der Schirm (*of cap*); — *hour*, die Stunde des Hochbetriebs, Hauptverkehrsstunde.
peal [pi:l], *v.a.* läuten. — *v.n.* erschallen. — *s.* das Läuten, Geläute.
peanut ['pi:nʌt], *s.* (*Bot.*) die Erdnuß.
pear [pɛə], *s.* (*Bot.*) die Birne.
pearl [pə:l], *s.* die Perle; — *barley*, die Perlgraupen, *f. pl.*; *mother of* —, die Perlmutter.

peasant ['pezənt], *s.* der Bauer.
peasantry ['pezəntri], *s.* das Bauernvolk, die Bauernschaft.
peas(e) [pi:z], *s. pl. pease pudding,* der Erbsenbrei, das Erbsenpüree.
peat [pi:t], *s.* der Torf.
pebble [pebl], *s.* der Kiesel(stein).
peck (1) [pek], *s.* der Viertelscheffel (=9 litres.)
peck (2) [pek], *s.* das Picken (*of hen*); (*coll.*) der Kuß. — *v.a.* hacken, hauen.
pecker ['pekə], *s.* die Picke, Haue; *keep your — up!* Mut bewahren!
peckish ['pekiʃ], *adj.* hungrig.
pectoral ['pektərəl], *adj.* Brust-. — *s.* das Brustmittel.
peculiar [pi'kju:liə], *adj.* eigenartig, eigentümlich (*strange*); — *to,* eigen (*Dat.*); besonder (*special*).
peculiarity [pikju:li'æriti], *s.* die Eigentümlichkeit, Eigenartigkeit.
pecuniary [pi'kju:niəri], *adj.* Geld-, geldlich, finanziell, pekuniär.
pedagogue ['pedəgɔg], *s.* der Pädagog(e), Erzieher.
pedal [pedl] *s.* das Pedal; (*Motor.*) der Fußhebel. — *v.n.* radfahren; (*coll.*) radeln.
pedant ['pedənt], *s.* der Pedant.
pedantic [pi'dæntik], *adj.* pedantisch.
pedantry ['pedəntri], *s.* die Pedanterie.
peddle [pedl], *v.a.* hausieren.
peddling ['pedliŋ], *adj.* kleinlich, unbedeutend.
pedestal ['pedistl], *s.* der Sockel.
pedestrian [pi'destriən], *s.* der Fußgänger. — *adj.* Fuß-, Fußgänger-.
pedigree ['pedigri:], *s.* der Stammbaum.
pediment ['pedimənt], *s.* (*Archit.*) der Ziergiebel.
pedlar ['pedlə], *s.* der Hausierer.
peel [pi:l], *s.* die Schale (*of fruit*). — *v.a.* schälen. — *v.n.* sich schälen.
peep [pi:p], *v.n.* gucken. — *s.* der (schnelle) Blick, das Gucken; — *show,* der Guckkasten.
peer (1) [piə], *s.* (*Parl.*) der Pair, Lord; der Ebenbürtige (*equal*).
peer (2) [piə], *v.n.* gucken, blicken, schauen.
peerage ['piəridʒ], *s.* der (Reichs)adel.
peeress ['piəres], *s.* die Gattin eines Pairs.
peerless ['piəlis], *adj.* unvergleichlich.
peevish ['pi:viʃ], *adj.* mürrisch.
pe(e)wit ['pi:wit], *s.* (*Orn.*) der Kiebitz.
peg ['peg], *s.* der Pflock (*stake*); der Holzstift (*in wall*); *clothes* —, die Wäscheklammer. — *v.a.* anpflocken (*to ground*).
pelican ['pelikən], *s.* (*Orn.*) der Pelikan.
pellet ['pelit], *s.* das Kügelchen.
pell-mell ['pel'mel], *adv.* durcheinander.
pelt (1) [pelt], *v.a.* — *with,* bewerfen mit, — *a person with,* werfen nach einem (*Acc.*). — *v.n.* strömen (*rain etc.*); rennen (*hasten*).
pelt (2) [pelt], *s.* der Pelz (*of animal*).

pen (1) [pen], *s. quill* —, die Feder; *fountain* —, die Füllfeder; *ballpoint* —, der Kugelschreiber. — *v.a.* schreiben; verfassen (*compose*).
pen (2) [pen], *s.* das Gehege. — *v.a.* einschliessen (*sheep*).
penal ['pi:nəl], *adj.* Straf-; — *servitude,* die Zuchthausstrafe.
penalize ['pi:nəlaiz], *v.a.* bestrafen.
penalty ['penəlti], *s.* die Strafe.
penance ['penəns], *s.* die Buße.
pence [pens] *see under* **penny.**
pencil ['pensl], *s.* der Bleistift; der Stift; (*Geom.*) der Strahl. — *v.a.* niederschreiben, notieren.
pendant ['pendənt], *s.* das Ohrgehänge; (*fig.*) das Gegenstück.
pendent ['pendənt], *adj.* hängend, schwebend.
pending ['pendiŋ], *adj.* in der Schwebe; unentschieden (*undecided*). — *prep.* während (*during*); bis (zu) (*until*).
pendulum ['pendjuləm], *s.* das Pendel.
penetrate ['penitreit], *v.a.* durchdringen.
peninsula [pi'ninsjulə], *s.* die Halbinsel.
penitent ['penitənt], *s.* der Büßer. — *adj.* bußfertig.
penitentiary [peni'tenʃəri], *s.* (*Am.*) das Zuchthaus (*prison*).
penknife ['pennaif], *s.* das Taschenmesser.
pennant ['penənt], *s.* der Wimpel, das Fähnchen.
penniless ['penilis], *adj.* mittellos, ohne einen Heller Geld, arm.
pennon ['penən] *see* **pennant.**
penny ['peni], *s.* (*pl.* **pence** [pens], **pennies** ['peniz]) der Penny; (*Am.*) das Centstück; — *farthing,* das Hochrad; — *whistle,* die Blechpfeife; *a pretty* —, hübsches Geld.
pension ['penʃən], *s.* die Pension; das Ruhegehalt. — *v.a.* (*off*) pensionieren, in den Ruhestand versetzen.
pensive ['pensiv], *adj.* nachdenklich.
Pentecost ['pentikɔst]. das *or* (*pl.*) die Pfingsten.
penthouse ['penthaus], *s.* das Wetterdach.
penurious [pi'njuəriəs], *adj.* unbemittelt, arm (*poor*); dürftig, karg (*meagre*).
penury ['penjuəri], *s.* die Not, Armut.
peony ['piəni], *s.* (*Bot.*) die Päonie, Pfingstrose.
people [pi:pl], *s. pl.* das Volk (*nation*); die Leute, Menschen (*pl.*). — *v.a.* bevölkern.
pepper ['pepə], *s.* der Pfeffer. — *v.a.* pfeffern.
per [pə:], *prep.* pro; per; durch; *as — account,* laut Rechnung.
peradventure [pə:rəd'ventʃə], *adv.* (*obs.*) von ungefähr; vielleicht (*perhaps*).
perambulator [pə'ræmbjuleitə] (*abbr. coll.*) **pram** [præm]), *s.* der Kinderwagen.

perceive [pə'si:v], *v.a.* wahrnehmen, merken.
percentage [pə'sentidʒ], *s.* der Prozentsatz (*of interest*); Prozente, *n. pl.*
perceptible [pə'septibl], *adj.* wahrnehmbar, merklich.
perception [pə'sepʃən], *s.* die Wahrnehmung, Empfindung.
perch (1) [pə:tʃ], *v.n.* aufsitzen; sitzen (*of birds*). — *s.* die Stange.
perch (2) [pə:tʃ], *s.* (*Zool.*) der Barsch.
perchance [pə'tʃɑ:ns], *adv.* vielleicht.
percolate ['pə:kəleit], *v.n.* durchsickern, durchtröpfeln.
percolator ['pə:kəleitə], *s.* die Kaffeemaschine.
percussion [pə'kʌʃən], *s.* (*Mus.*) das Schlagzeug.
peremptory ['perəmptəri, pə'remptəri], *adj.* entschieden, bestimmt (*decided*); absprechend.
perennial [pə'reniəl], *adj.* (*Bot.*) perennierend; Dauer-.
perfect ['pə:fikt], *adj.* vollkommen, vollendet, perfekt. — *s.* (*tense*) (*Gram.*) das Perfekt(um). — [pə'fekt], *v.a.* vollenden.
perfection [pə'fekʃən], *s.* die Vollendung, Vollkommenheit; *to* —, vollkommen.
perfidious [pə'fidiəs], *adj.* treulos, untreu; tückisch.
perfidy ['pə:fidi], *s.* die Treulosigkeit.
perforate ['pə:fəreit], *v.a.* durchlöchern, perforieren (*paper*); durchbohren (*pierce*).
perforce [pə'fɔ:s], *adv.* mit Gewalt, notgedrungen.
perform [pə'fɔ:m], *v.a.* ausführen (*carry out*); (*Theat.*) aufführen. — *v.n.* spielen, auftreten (*of actor*).
performance [pə'fɔ:məns], *s.* die Ausführung; Verrichtung (*execution of duty etc.*); (*Theat.*) die Aufführung.
perfume ['pə:fju:m], *s.* das Parfüm; der Duft (*scent*). — *v.a.* parfümieren.
perfunctory [pə'fʌŋktəri], *adj.* nachlässig, oberflächlich, flüchtig.
perhaps [pə'hæps], *adv.* vielleicht.
peril ['peril], *s.* die Gefahr.
period ['piəriəd], *s.* die Periode (*time*); der Zeitraum (*span*); (*Am.*) der Punkt (*full stop*).
periodical [piəri'ɔdikəl], *adj.* periodisch. — *s.* die Zeitschrift.
perish ['periʃ], *v.n.* zugrunde gehen, umkommen.
perishable ['periʃəbl], *adj.* vergänglich; (leicht) verderblich (*of food*).
periwig ['periwig], *s.* die Perücke.
periwinkle (1) ['periwiŋkl], *s.* (*Zool.*) die Uferschnecke.
periwinkle (2) ['periwiŋkl], (*Bot.*) das Immergrün.
perjure ['pə:dʒə], *v.r.* meineidig werden.
perjurer ['pə:dʒərə], *s.* der Meineidige.
perjury ['pə:dʒəri], *s.* der Meineid.
permanence, permanency ['pə:mənəns, pə:mənənsi], *s.* die Dauer, Beständigkeit.
permanent ['pə:mənənt], *adj.* Dauer-, dauerhaft, beständig; — *wave*, die Dauerwelle.
permeability [pə:miə'biliti], *s.* die Durchdringbarkeit, Durchlässigkeit.
permeable ['pə:miəbl], *adj.* durchdringlich.
permeate ['pə:mieit], *v.a.* durchdringen.
permissible [pə'misibl], *adj.* zulässig, statthaft.
permission [pə'miʃən], *s.* die Erlaubnis.
permit [pə'mit], *v.a.* zulassen, erlauben. — ['pə:mit], *s.* die Erlaubnis; (*official*) die Genehmigung.
permutation [pə:mju'teiʃən], *s.* (*Maths.*) die Permutation.
pernicious [pə'niʃəs], *adj.* verderblich, schädlich, bösartig.
perorate ['perəreit], *v.n.* eine (lange) Rede beschließen.
perpendicular [pə:pən'dikjulə], *adj.* senkrecht. — *s.* die Senkrechte.
perpetrate ['pə:pitreit], *v.a.* begehen (*commit*).
perpetration [pə:pi'treiʃən], *s.* die Verübung, Begehung.
perpetrator ['pə:pitreitə], *s.* der Begeher, Täter.
perpetual [pə'petjuəl], *adj.* (an-) dauernd; ewig.
perpetuate [pə'petjueit], *v.a.* verewigen.
perpetuity [pə:pi'tju:iti], *s.* die Ewigkeit.
perplex [pə'pleks], *v.a.* bestürzen, verblüffen.
perplexity [pə'pleksiti], *s.* die Bestürzung, Verwirrung.
persecute ['pə:sikju:t], *v.a.* verfolgen.
persecution [pə:si'kju:ʃən], *s.* die Verfolgung.
perseverance [pə:si'viərəns], *s.* die Ausdauer, Beharrlichkeit.
persevere [pə:si'viə], *v.n.* beharren (*in*, bei, *Dat.*).
Persian ['pə:ʃən], *adj.* persisch. — *s.* der Perser.
persist [pə'sist], *v.n.* beharren (*in*, auf, *Dat.*).
persistence [pə'sistəns], *s.* die Beharrlichkeit.
person ['pə:sən], *s.* die Person; *in* —, persönlich.
personal ['pə:sənəl], *adj.* persönlich.
personality [pə:sə'næliti], *s.* die Persönlichkeit.
personify [pə'sɔnifai], *v.a.* verkörpern.
personnel [pə:sə'nel], *s.* das Personal; (*Comm.*) — *manager*, der Personalchef.
perspective [pə'spektiv], *s.* die Perspektive. — *adj.* perspektivisch.
perspicacious [pə:spi'keiʃəs], *adj.* scharfsichtig, scharfsinnig.
perspicacity [pə:spi'kæsiti], *s.* der Scharfblick, Scharfsinn.
perspicuity [pə:spi'kju:iti], *s.* die Durchsichtigkeit, Klarheit.

perspicuous [pə'spikjuəs], *adj.* deutlich, klar.
perspiration [pə:spi'reiʃən], *s.* der Schweiß.
perspire [pə'spaiə], *v.n.* schwitzen.
persuade [pə'sweid], *v.a.* überreden.
persuasion [pə'sweiʒən], *s.* die Überredung.
persuasive [pə'sweiziv], *adj.* überzeugend, überredend.
pert [pə:t], *adj.* naseweis, keck.
pertain [pə'tein], *v.n.* (an)gehören (*to Dat.*).
pertinacious [pə:ti'neiʃəs], *adj.* beharrlich, halsstarrig.
pertinacity [pə:ti'næsiti], *s.* die Beharrlichkeit, Halsstarrigkeit.
pertinence, pertinency ['pə:tinəns, 'pə:tinənsi], *s.* die Angemessenheit.
pertinent ['pə:tinənt], *adj.* angemessen, passend.
pertness ['pə:tnis], *s.* die Keckheit, der Vorwitz.
perturb [pə'tə:b], *v.a.* verwirren, stören, beunruhigen.
perturbation [pə:tə'beiʃən], *s.* die Verwirrung, Störung, Beunruhigung.
peruke [pə'ru:k], *s.* die Perücke.
peruse [pə'ru:z], *v.a.* durchlesen.
Peruvian [pə'ru:viən], *adj.* peruanisch. — *s.* der Peruaner.
pervade [pə'veid], *v.a.* durchdringen.
perverse [pə'və:s], *adj.* verkehrt.
perversion [pə'və:ʃən], *s.* die Perversion.
perversity [pə'və:siti], *s.* die Verdorbenheit, Widernatürlichkeit.
pervert [pə'və:t], *v.a.* verkehren, verderben. — ['pə:və:t], *s.* der Verdorbene, der perverse Mensch.
perverted [pə'və:tid], *adj.* pervers (*sexually*).
pervious ['pə:viəs], *adj.* zugänglich, passierbar; durchlässig.
pessimist ['pesimist], *s.* der Pessimist.
pest [pest], *s.* (*Med.*) die Pest; (*fig.*) die Plage.
pester ['pestə], *v.a.* quälen, auf die Nerven gehen (*Dat.*).
pestiferous [pes'tifərəs], *adj.* verpestend.
pestilence ['pestiləns], *s.* (*Med.*) die Pest, Seuche.
pestle [pesl], *s.* die Mörserkeule.
pet [pet], *s.* das Haustier; der Liebling; — *name*, der Kosename. — *v.a.* liebkosen, streicheln.
petition [pi'tiʃən], *s.* die Bittschrift. — *v.a.* mit einer Bittschrift herantreten an (*Acc.*).
petrel ['petrəl], *s.* (*Orn.*) der Sturmvogel.
petrification [petrifi'keiʃən], *s.* die Versteinerung.
petrify ['petrifai], *v.a.* versteinern; (*fig.*) starr machen, bestürzen; *petrified with fright*, starr vor Entsetzen. — *v.n.* zu Stein werden.
petrol ['petrəl], *s.* das Benzin; (*crude oil*) das Petroleum; — *station*, die Tankstelle.
petticoat ['petikout], *s.* der Unterrock.
pettifogging ['petifɔgiŋ], *adj.* Winkel-, kleinlich, schikanös (*petty*).
pettiness ['petinis], *s.* die Kleinlichkeit.
pettish ['petiʃ], *adj.* verdrießlich.
petty ['peti], *adj.* klein, gering, kleinlich.
petulance ['petjuləns], *s.* die Launenhaftigkeit, Gereiztheit.
petulant ['petjulənt], *adj.* launenhaft.
pew [pju:], *s.* (*Eccl.*) der Kirchensitz; (*coll.*) der Sitz, Stuhl.
pewit ['pi:wit] *see* **pe(e)wit.**
pewter ['pju:tə], *s.* das Zinn; die Zinnwaren, *f. pl.* (*wares*).
pewterer ['pju:tərə], *s.* der Zinngießer.
phantom ['fæntəm], *s.* das Phantom, Trugbild; das Gespenst (*ghost*).
Pharisee ['færisi:], *s.* der Pharisäer.
pharmaceutical [fɑ:mə'sju:tikəl], *adj.* pharmazeutisch.
pharmacy ['fɑ:məsi], *s.* die Apothekerkunst (*dispensing*); die Apotheke (*dispensary*); die Pharmazeutik (*discipline*).
phase [feiz], *s.* die Phase.
pheasant ['fezənt], *s.* (*Orn.*) der Fasan.
phenomenal [fi'nɔminəl], *adj.* außerordentlich, phänomenal.
phenomenon [fi'nɔminən], *s.* das Phänomen.
phial ['faiəl], *s.* die Phiole, das Fläschchen.
philanthropist [fi'lænθrəpist], *s.* der Philanthrop.
philanthropy [fi'lænθrəpi], *s.* die Philanthropie.
philatelist [fi'lætəlist], *s.* der Philatelist, Markensammler.
philately [fi'lætəli], *s.* das Markensammeln, die Philatelie, Briefmarkenkunde.
Philippine ['filipi:n], *adj.* philippinisch.
Philistine ['filistain], *s.* der Philister; (*fig.*) der Spießbürger.
philologist [fi'lɔlədʒist], *s.* der Philologe.
philology [fi'lɔlədʒi], *s.* die Philologie.
philosopher [fi'lɔsəfə], *s.* der Philosoph.
philosophize [fi'lɔsəfaiz], *v.n.* philosophieren.
philosophy [fi'lɔsəfi], *s.* die Philosophie.
phlegm [flem], *s.* das Phlegma (*mood*); (*Med.*) der Schleim.
phlegmatic [fleg'mætik], *adj.* phlegmatisch, gelassen.
phone [foun] *see under* **telephone.**
phonetics [fə'netiks], *s.* die Phonetik.
phosphorescent [fɔsfə'resənt], *adj.* phosphoreszierend, leuchtend.
phosphorus ['fɔsfərəs], *s.* (*Chem.*) der Phosphor.
photograph ['foutəgræf *or* -grɑ:f], *s.* die Photographie, das Lichtbild (*picture*). — *v.a.* photographieren, aufnehmen, (*coll.*) knipsen.
photographer [fə'tɔgrəfə], *s.* der Photograph.

photography [fə'tɔgrəfi], *s.* die Photographie.
phrase [freiz], *s.* die Phrase. — *v.a.* phrasieren, fassen, ausdrücken.
phrenology [fre'nɔlədʒi], *s.* die Phrenologie, Schädellehre.
phthisis ['θaisis], *s.* (*Med.*) die Schwindsucht.
physic ['fizik], *s.* (*obs.*) die Medizin, Arznei.
physical ['fizikəl], *adj.* körperlich (*bodily*); physikalisch (*of physics*).
physician [fi'ziʃən], *s.* der Arzt.
physics ['fiziks], *s.* die Physik.
physiognomy [fizi'ɔnəmi *or* -'ɔgnəmi], *s.* die Physiognomie, die Gesichtsbildung.
physiologist [fizi'ɔlədʒist], *s.* der Physiolog.
physiology [fizi'ɔlədʒi], *s.* die Physiologie.
piano(forte) ['pjænou('fɔ:ti)], *s.* das Klavier.
pick [pik], *v.a.* pflücken (*flowers*); hacken (*hack*); — *up*, auflesen; auswählen (*select*); gewaltsam öffnen (*a lock*); anfangen (*a quarrel*). — *v.n. why — on me?* warum gerade mich auswählen? — *s.* die Picke, Spitzhacke (*axe*); die Auswahl; — *of the bunch*, (*coll.*) das Beste von allen.
picket ['pikit], *s.* die Wache; der Streikposten (*of strikers*); der Pflock (*wood*). — *v.a.* bewachen. — *v.n.* Wache stehen.
pickle [pikl], *s.* (*Cul.*) der Pökel, das Gepökelte; (*coll.*) die unangenehme Lage (*calamity*). — *v.a.* einpökeln.
pickpocket ['pikpɔkit], *s.* der Taschendieb.
picnic ['piknik], *s.* das Picknick. — *v.n.* picknicken.
pictorial [pik'tɔ:riəl], *adj.* illustriert.
picture ['piktʃə], *s.* das Bild; — *book*, das Bilderbuch; — *postcard*, die Ansichtskarte; *pretty as a* —, bildhübsch; der Film; (*pl.*) das Kino. — *v.a.* sich vorstellen.
picturesque [piktʃə'resk], *adj.* pittoresk, malerisch.
pie [pai], *s.* (*Cul.*) die Pastete (*savoury*); das Törtchen (*sweet*).
piebald ['paibɔ:ld], *adj.* scheckig. — *s.* der Schecke (*horse*).
piece [pi:s], *s.* das Stück. — *v.a.* — *together*, zusammenflicken (*mend*), zusammensetzen (*compose*).
piecemeal ['pi:smi:l], *adv.* stückweise.
pied [paid] *see* **piebald**.
pier [piə], *s.* der Hafendamm; der Pfeiler (*column*).
pierce [piəs], *v.a.* durchstechen, durchbohren.
pierglass ['piəglɑ:s], *s.* der Pfeilerspiegel.
piety ['paiəti], *s.* die Pietät, Frömmigkeit.
pig [pig], *s.* (*Zool.*) das Schwein.
pigeon ['pidʒən], *s.* (*Orn.*) die Taube.
pigeonhole ['pidʒənhoul], *s.* das Fach.
pigheaded [pig'hedid], *adj.* starrköpfig, dickköpfig.
piglet ['piglit], *s.* (*Zool.*) das Ferkel.
pigment ['pigmənt], *s.* das Pigment, der (natürliche) Farbstoff.
pigtail ['pigteil], *s.* der Haarzopf.
pike [paik], *s.* (*Zool.*) der Hecht; die Pike (*weapon*).
pile (1) [pail], *s.* der Haufen, Stoß (*paper*). — *v.a.* aufhäufen.
pile (2) [pail], *s.* (*Archit.*) der Pfahl; Pfeiler (*stone*).
pile (3) [pail], *s.* (*Text.*) der Teppichflausch (*carpet*), die Noppe (*cloth*).
piles [pailz], *s. pl.* (*Med. coll.*) die Haemorrhoiden, *pl.*
pilfer ['pilfə], *v.a.* stehlen, mausen.
pilferer ['pilfərə], *s.* der Dieb.
pilgrim ['pilgrim], *s.* der Pilger.
pill [pil], *s.* (*Med.*) die Pille.
pillage ['pilidʒ], *s.* die Plünderung. — *v.a.* ausplündern.
pillar ['pilə], *s.* der Pfeiler, die Säule; — *box*, der Briefkasten.
pillion ['piljən], *s.* der zweite Sitz, Sozius (*motorcycle*).
pillory ['piləri], *s.* der Pranger. — *v.a.* anprangern.
pillow ['pilou], *s.* das Kopfkissen.
pilot ['pailət], *s.* der Pilot; (*Naut.*) der Lotse. — *v.a.* (*Aviat.*) steuern, (*Naut.*) lotsen.
pimento [pi'mentou], *s.* (*Bot.*) der Jamaikapfeffer.
pimp [pimp], *s.* der Kuppler.
pimple [pimpl], *s.* der Pickel; (*pl.*) der Ausschlag.
pin [pin], *s.* die Stecknadel; (*Engin.*) der Bolzen, Stift; (*skittles*) der Kegel. — *v.a.* — *down*, festlegen.
pinafore ['pinəfɔ:], *s.* die Schürze, Kinderschürze.
pincers ['pinsəz], *s. pl.* die Kneifzange, Zange.
pinch [pintʃ], *v.a.* kneifen, zwicken; (*coll.*) klauen, stehlen. — *v.n.* sparen, darben. — *s.* die Prise (*tobacco*); *at a* —, wenn es sein muß.
pine (1) [pain], *s.* (*Bot.*) die Kiefer, Föhre.
pine (2) [pain], *v.n.* — *for*, schmachten (nach, *Dat.*), sich sehnen.
pineapple ['painæpl], *s.* (*Bot.*) die Ananas.
pinion ['pinjən], *s.* der Flügel (*wing*); (*Poet.*) die Schwinge; (*Mech.*) das Zahnrad; — *shaft*, die Ritzelwelle; — *spindle*, die Zahnradwelle. — *v.a.* binden, fesseln.
pink [piŋk], *adj.* rosa. — *s.* (*Bot.*) die (rosa) Nelke; (*Hunt.*) der (rote) Jagdrock; *in the* — (*of condition*), in bester Gesundheit, in bester Form.
pinnacle ['pinəkl], *s.* die Zinne, Spitze; (*fig.*) der Gipfel.
pint [paint], *s.* die Pinte (0.57 litre); (*beer*) der Schoppen.
pioneer [paiə'niə], *s.* der Pionier. — *v.a.* bahnbrechend sein, bahnen.
pious ['paiəs], *adj.* fromm.

pip [pip], *s.* der Obstkern; (*Mil. coll.*) der Leutnantsstern.
pipe [paip], *s.* die Pfeife; (*Engin.*) das Rohr; die Röhre; (*Mus.*) die Pfeife. — *v.a.* pfeifen; durch Rohre leiten.
piping ['paipiŋ], *adj.* — *hot*, kochend heiß.
pipkin ['pipkin], *s.* das Töpfchen.
piquant ['pi:kənt], *adj.* pikant; scharf (*taste*).
pique [pi:k], *s.* der Groll. — *v.a.* reizen.
piracy ['pairəsi], *s.* die Seeräuberei.
pirate ['pairit], *s.* der Pirat, Seeräuber. — [pai'reit], *v.a.* (*fig.*) plagiieren, ohne Erlaubnis drucken (*books*).
pistil ['pistil], *s.* (*Bot.*) der Stempel.
pistol ['pistəl], *s.* die Pistole.
piston ['pistən], *s.* (*Mech.*) der Kolben.
pit [pit], *s.* die Grube; (*Min.*) der Schacht, das Bergwerk; (*Theat.*, *Mus.*) der Orchesterraum; (*Theat.*) das Parterre.
pitch (1) [pitʃ], *s.* der Grad, Gipfel (*height*); (*Mus.*) der Ton, die Tonhöhe (*level*); (*Sport*) das Spielfeld. — *v.a.* werfen; feststecken; (*Mus.*) stimmen; befestigen; (*tent*) (ein Zelt) aufschlagen; — *in*, sich ins Zeug legen.
pitch (2) [pitʃ], *s.* das Pech (*tar*); — *dark*, pechschwarz.
pitchblende ['pitʃblend], *s.* die Pechblende.
pitcher ['pitʃə], *s.* der Krug.
pitchfork ['pitʃfɔ:k], *s.* die Heugabel.
piteous ['pitiəs], *adj.* erbärmlich.
pitfall ['pitfɔ:l], *s.* die Falle.
pith [piθ], *s.* das Mark; (*fig.*) der Kern, das Wesentliche; die Kraft (*strength*).
pithy ['piθi], *adj.* markig, kräftig; prägnant.
pitiable ['pitiəbl], *adj.* erbärmlich.
pitiful ['pitiful], *adj.* erbärmlich (*pitiable*); mitleidig (*sympathetic*).
pitiless ['pitilis], *adj.* erbarmungslos, grausam.
pittance ['pitəns], *s.* der Hungerlohn, das Bißchen, die Kleinigkeit.
pity ['piti], *s.* das Mitleid. — *v.a.* bemitleiden, bedauern.
pivot ['pivət], *s.* (*Mech.*) der Drehpunkt, Zapfen; (*fig.*) der Mittelpunkt, Angelpunkt. — *v.n.* zum Mittelpunkt haben, sich drehen (um).
placard ['plækɑ:d], *s.* das Plakat.
placate [plə'keit], *v.a.* versöhnen.
place [pleis], *s.* der Platz, Ort, die Stelle; — *name*, der Ortsname; (*rank*) der Rang, die Rangstufe. — *v.a.* plazieren (*in a job*); legen, setzen, stellen; — *an order*, einen Auftrag geben.
placid ['plæsid], *adj.* gelassen, sanft, gutmütig.
plagiarism ['pleidʒiərizm], *s.* das Plagiat, das Plagiieren.
plague [pleig], *s.* (*Med.*) die Pest, Seuche; (*fig.*) die Plage. — *v.a.* belästigen, plagen.
plaice [pleis], *s.* (*Zool.*) die Scholle.
plain [plein], *s.* die Ebene, Fläche. — *adj.* eben, flach (*even*); schlicht, einfach, klar; — *dealing*, ehrliche Handlungsweise; — *speaking*, offenes Sprechen, aufrichtiges Reden; (*Mus.*) — *song*, der einstimmige Chorgesang, die gregorianische Kirchenmusik.
plaintiff ['pleintif], *s.* (*Law*) der Kläger.
plaintive ['pleintiv], *adj.* klagend.
plait [plæt], *s.* der Zopf, die Flechte. — — *v.a.* flechten (*hair*); falten.
plan [plæn], *s.* der Plan, Grundriß. — *v.a.* planen, entwerfen.
plane (1) [plein], *v.a.* hobeln (*wood*). — *s.* die Fläche (*surface*); die Stufe (*level*); (*coll.*) das Flugzeug (*aeroplane*).
plane (2) *see* **plane-tree**.
planet ['plænit], *s.* (*Astron.*) der Planet.
plane-tree ['pleintri:], *s.* (*Bot.*) die Platane.
planish ['plæniʃ], *v.a.* (*woodwork*) polieren, glätten.
plank [plæŋk], *s.* die Planke; (*Pol.*) der Programmpunkt.
plant [plɑ:nt], *s.* (*Bot.*) die Pflanze; (*Ind.*) die Anlage, der Betrieb. — *v.a.* anpflanzen, anlegen; — *suspicion*, Verdacht einflößen (*of*, *against*, gegen, *Acc.*).
plantain ['plæntein], *s.* (*Bot.*) der Wegerich; (*fruit*) der Pisang.
plantation [plæn'teiʃən], *s.* die Pflanzung, Plantage.
plaster ['plɑ:stə], *s.* das Pflaster (*adhesive*); (*Build.*) der Mörtel, der Mauerbewurf; — *cast*, der Gipsabdruck; — *of Paris*, der Stuck, der feine Gipsmörtel. — *v.a.* bepflastern, verputzen; (*fig.*) dick auftragen.
plastic ['plæstik], *adj.* plastisch; (*malleable*) formbar; — *surgery*, plastische Chirurgie. — *s.* der Kunststoff.
Plate, River [pleit, 'rivə]. der La Plata Strom.
plate [pleit], *s.* der Teller (*dish*), die Platte, Scheibe; (*coll.*) — *glass*, das Spiegelglas; das Geschirr (*service of crockery*); *gold* —, das Goldgeschirr. — *v.a.* überziehen, versilbern, verchromen.
platform ['plætfɔ:m], *s.* (*Railw.*) der Bahnsteig; die Bühne, das Podium.
platinum ['plætinəm], *s.* das Platin.
platitude ['plætitju:d], *s.* die Plattheit, der Gemeinplatz.
platitudinous [plæti'tju:dinəs], *adj.* nichtssagend.
platoon [plə'tu:n], *s.* (*Mil.*) der Zug.
plaudit ['plɔ:dit], *s.* der Beifall.
plausible ['plɔ:zibl], *adj.* wahrscheinlich, glaubwürdig, einleuchtend.
play [plei], *s.* das Spiel (*game*); (*Theat.*) das Stück. — *v.a.*, *v.n.* spielen.
player ['pleiə], *s.* der Spieler; (*Theat.*) der Schauspieler.
playful ['pleiful], *adj.* spielerisch, spielend.
playground ['pleigraund], *s.* der Spielplatz.
playhouse ['pleihaus], *s.* das Schauspielhaus.

playmate ['pleimeit], *s.* der Spielgefährte.
playwright ['pleirait], *s.* der Dramatiker, Schauspieldichter.
plea [pli:], *s.* die Bitte; das Gesuch; der Vorwand.
plead [pli:d], *v.a.*, *v.n.* plädieren, sich berufen auf; vorschützen (*claim*).
pleasant ['plezənt], *adj.* angenehm, freundlich.
pleasantry ['plezəntri], *s.* das freundliche Wort, der Scherz (*joke*).
please [pli:z], *v.a.*, *v.n.* gefallen; einen Gefallen tun (*do a favour*); *—!* bitte, haben Sie die Güte!; *if you —*, wenn Sie nichts dagegen haben.
pleasing ['pli:ziŋ], *adj.* einnehmend, angenehm.
pleasure ['pleʒə], *s.* das Vergnügen; *at your —*, nach Belieben; *take — in*, Vergnügen finden an (*Dat.*).
pleat [pli:t], *v.a.* plissieren. — *s.* die Falte, das Plissee.
pledge [pledʒ], *s.* das Pfand, die Bürgschaft (*guarantee*); das Versprechen (*promise*). — *v.a.* sich verbürgen, versprechen; zutrinken (*drink to*).
plenary ['pli:nəri], *adj.* Plenar-, vollständig.
plenipotentiary [plenipo'tenʃəri], *s.* der Bevollmächtigte.
plenitude ['plenitju:d], *s.* die Fülle.
plenteous, plentiful ['plentiəs, 'plentiful], *adj.* reichlich, in Fülle.
plenty ['plenti], *s.* die Fülle.
pleurisy ['pluərəsi], *s.* (*Med.*) die Brustfellentzündung.
pliable, pliant ['plaiəbl, 'plaiənt], *adj.* geschmeidig, biegsam.
pliers ['plaiəz], *s. pl.* die Drahtzange.
plight (1) [plait], *s.* die Notlage.
plight (2) [plait], *v.a.* feierlich versprechen.
plod [plɔd], *v.n.* schwerfällig gehen (*walk*); sich plagen (*work hard*).
plot (1) [plɔt], *s.* das Stück Land, der Bauplatz.
plot (2) [plɔt], *s.* das Komplott, die Verschwörung; die Handlung (*book, play etc.*). — *v.a.* aushecken (*ambush etc.*), planen.
plough, plow [plau], *s.* der Pflug. — *v.a.* pflügen; (*coll.*) *be —ed*, durchfallen (*in*, in, *Dat.*).
ploughshare ['plauʃɛə], *s.* die Pflugschar.
plover ['plʌvə], *s.* (*Orn.*) der Kiebitz, Regenpfeifer.
plow *see under* **plough.**
pluck (1) [plʌk], *v.a.* pflücken (*flowers*); rupfen (*feathers*); *— up courage*, Mut fassen.
pluck (2) [plʌk], *s.* (*coll.*) der Mut.
plucky ['plʌki], *adj.* mutig.
plug [plʌg], *s.* (*Elec.*) der Stecker; der Stöpsel (*stopper*); *sparking —*, (*Motor.*) die Zündkerze. — *v.a.* stöpseln, zustopfen (*block*); (*fig.*) betonen, herausstellen (*repeat for advertisement*).
plum [plʌm], *s.* (*Bot.*) die Pflaume; (*coll.*) das Beste.
plumage ['plu:midʒ], *s.* (*Orn.*) das Gefieder.
plumb [plʌm], *s.* das Senkblei, Lot; *— -rule*, die Senkwaage. — *adv.* senkrecht, gerade, lotrecht.
plume [plu:m], *s.* die (Schmuck) feder.
plump [plʌmp], *adj.* dick, drall.
plunder ['plʌndə], *v.a.*, *v.n.* plündern. — *s.* die Beute, der Raub.
plunge [plʌndʒ], *v.a.*, *v.n.* untertauchen, stoßen, hinabstürzen.
plunger ['plʌndʒə], *s.* der Taucher; (*Engin.*) der Tauchkolben.
pluperfect [plu:'pə:fikt], *s.* (*Gram.*) das Plusquamperfektum.
plural ['pluərəl], *s.* (*Gram.*) der Plural, die Mehrzahl.
plurality [pluə'ræliti], *s.* die Mehrzahl, der Plural.
plus [plʌs], *prep.* plus, zuzüglich.
plush [plʌʃ], *s.* (*Text.*) der Plüsch.
ply [plai], *s.* die Falte (*fold*), Lage (*layer*). — *v.a.* ausüben (*trade*).
plywood ['plaiwud], *s.* das Sperrholz, die Sperrholzplatte.
pneumonia [nju'mouniə], *s.* (*Med.*) die Lungenentzündung.
poach (1) [poutʃ], *v.n.* wildern; *— on*, übergreifen auf.
poach (2) [poutʃ], *v.a.* ohne Schale kochen; *poached eggs*, verlorene Eier, *n. pl.*
poacher ['poutʃə], *s.* der Wilderer, Wilddieb.
pocket ['pɔkit], *s.* die Tasche; *— book*, die Brieftasche; das Taschenbuch; *— money*, das Taschengeld.
pod [pɔd], *s.* (*Bot.*) die Schote.
poem ['pouim], *s.* das Gedicht.
poet ['pouit], *s.* der Dichter.
poetic(al) [pou'etik(l)], *adj.* dichterisch.
poignancy ['pɔinjənsi], *s.* die Schärfe.
poignant ['pɔinjənt], *adj.* scharf, beißend, schmerzlich.
point [pɔint], *s.* der Punkt (*of remark, sentence*); die Sache; der Zweck; die Spitze (*of pencil etc.*); *make a —*, es sich zur Aufgabe machen; *in — of fact*, tatsächlich; *come to the —*, zur Sache kommen. — *v.a.*, *v.n.* spitzen, zuspitzen (*pencil*); *— out*, zeigen, (hin)deuten, *— to*, hinweisen auf; *— the moral*, die Moral erklären.
pointblank ['pɔint'blæŋk], *adj.*, *adv.* schnurgerade, direkt.
pointed ['pɔintid], *adj.* scharf, spitzig, deutlich (*remark*).
pointer ['pɔintə], *s.* der Zeiger; (*fig.*) der Fingerzeig (*hint*).
poise [pɔiz], *s.* das Gleichgewicht; (*fig.*) angemessenes Benehmen, die Grazie. — *v.a.* abwägen; im Gleichgewicht halten. — *v.n.* schweben; *—d for action*, tatbereit.
poison [pɔizn], *s.* das Gift. — *v.a.* vergiften.

poke (1) [pouk], *v.a.* schüren (*fire*); stoßen; — *fun at*, sich lustig machen über. — *s.* der Stoß; — *in the ribs*, ein Rippenstoß.
poke (2) [pouk], *s.* der Sack; *a pig in a* —, die Katze im Sack.
poker (1) ['poukə], *s.* der Schürhaken, das Schüreisen.
poker (2) ['poukə], *s.* (*Cards*) das Pokerspiel.
polar ['poulə], *adj.* (*Geog.*) Polar-; (*Phys.*) polar.
polarity [po'læriti], *s.* die Polarität.
Pole [poul], *s.* der Pole.
pole (1) [poul], *s.* (*Geog.*) der Pol.
pole (2) [poul], *s.* die Stange (*rod*); der Pfahl (*upright*).
poleaxe ['poulæks], *s.* die Streitaxt.
polecat ['poulkæt], *s.* (*Zool.*) der Iltis.
polemic [pə'lemik], *s.* die Polemik, der Streit.
police [pə'li:s], *s.* die Polizei. — *v.a.* polizeilich beaufsichtigen.
policeman [pə'li:smən], *s.* der Polizist.
policy (1) ['pɔlisi], *s.* die Politik.
policy (2) ['pɔlisi], *s.* (*Insurance*) die Police.
Polish ['pouliʃ], *adj.* polnisch.
polish ['pɔliʃ], *v.a.* polieren. — *s.* die Politur, der Glanz.
polished ['pɔliʃd], *adj.* glatt (*smooth*); (*fig.*) wohlerzogen, fein (*manners*).
polite [pə'lait], *adj.* höflich.
politeness [pə'laitnis], *s.* die Höflichkeit.
politic ['pɔlitik], *adj.* politisch; schlau (*cunning*).
political [pə'litikəl], *adj.* politisch; staatskundig.
politician [pɔli'tiʃən], *s.* der Politiker, Staatsmann.
politics ['pɔlitiks], *s.* (*sometimes pl.*) die Politik, politische Gesinnung.
poll [poul], *s.* die Wahl (*election*). — *v.n.* abstimmen, wählen, seine Stimme abgeben.
pollard ['pɔləd], *s.* (*Bot.*) der gekappte Baum; (*Zool.*) das hornlose Tier.
pollen ['pɔlən], *s.* (*Bot.*) der Blütenstaub.
pollinate ['pɔlineit], *v.a.* (*Bot.*) bestäuben.
polling ['pouliŋ], *s.* die Wahl, der Wahlgang (*election*); — *station*, das Wahllokal.
pollute [pə'lju:t], *v.a.* verunreinigen.
pollution [pə'lju:ʃən], *s.* die Verunreinigung.
poltroon [pɔl'tru:n], *s.* die Memme.
poly- ['pɔli], *pref.* viel-.
Polynesian [pɔli'ni:ziən], *adj.* polynesisch. — *s.* der Polynesier.
polytechnic [pɔli'teknik], *s.* das Technikum; polytechnische Fachschule.
pomegranate ['pɔm-, 'pʌmgrænit], *s.* (*Bot.*) der Granatapfel.
Pomeranian [pɔmə'reiniən], *adj.* pommerisch. — *s.* der Pommer; der Spitz (*dog*).
pommel [pʌml], *s.* der Sattelknopf; der Knauf (*sword*). — *v.a.* schlagen.
pomp [pɔmp], *s.* der Pomp, das Gepränge.
pompous ['pɔmpəs], *adj.* hochtrabend, prahlerisch; (*manner*) schwerfällig, wichtigtuerisch.
pond [pɔnd], *s.* der Teich.
ponder ['pɔndə], *v.a.*, *v.n.* bedenken, überlegen.
ponderous ['pɔndərəs], *adj.* schwer, schwerfällig.
pontiff ['pɔntif], *s.* der Hohepriester; der Papst.
pontifical [pɔn'tifikəl], *adj.* bischöflich, päpstlich. — *s. pl.* die bischöfliche Amtstracht.
pontificate [pɔn'tifikit], *s.* das (*or* der) Pontifikat. — [-keit], *v.n.* (*coll.*) predigen.
pontoon (1) [pɔn'tu:n], *s.* die Schiffsbrücke, der Brückenkahn.
pontoon (2) [pɔn'tu:n], *s.* (*cards*) das Einundzwanzig, Vingt-et-un.
pony ['pouni], *s.* (*Zool.*) der *or* das Pony.
poodle [pu:dl], *s.* (*Zool.*) der Pudel.
pooh-pooh [pu:'pu:], *v.a.* verspotten.
pool (1) [pu:l], *s.* die Lache, der Pfuhl.
pool (2) [pu:l], *s.* (*fig.*) der gemeinsame Einsatz (*money, forces etc.*). — *v.a.* zusammenschließen.
poop [pu:p], *s.* (*Naut.*) das Heck, Hinterteil.
poor [puə], *adj.* arm, dürftig; *in — health*, bei schwacher Gesundheit; (*fig.*) armselig, schlecht.
pop [pɔp], *v.n.* knallen, explodieren. — *v.a.* (*coll.*) schnell versetzen, verpfänden.
Pope [poup], *s.* (*Eccl.*) der Papst.
poplar ['pɔplə], *s.* (*Bot.*) die Pappel.
poppy ['pɔpi], *s.* (*Bot.*) der Mohn.
populace ['pɔpjulis], *s.* der Pöbel.
popular ['pɔpjulə], *adj.* volkstümlich, beliebt.
popularity [pɔpju'læriti], *s.* die Beliebtheit.
populate ['pɔpjuleit], *v.a.* bevölkern.
population [pɔpju'leiʃən], *s.* die Bevölkerung.
populous ['pɔpjuləs], *adj.* dicht bevölkert.
porcelain ['pɔ:slin], *s.* das Porzellan, das Geschirr.
porch [pɔ:tʃ], *s.* die Eingangshalle, Vorhalle.
porcupine ['pɔ:kjupain], *s.* (*Zool.*) das Stachelschwein.
pore (1) [pɔ:], *s.* die Pore.
pore (2) [pɔ:], *v.n.* sich vertiefen (*over*, in), brüten (über).
pork [pɔ:k], *s.* das Schweinefleisch.
porosity [pɔ:'rɔsiti], *s.* die Porosität.
porous ['pɔ:rəs], *adj.* porös.
porpoise ['pɔ:pəs], *s.* (*Zool.*) der Tümmler, das Meerschwein.
porridge ['pɔridʒ], *s.* (*Cul.*) der Haferbrei.
porringer ['pɔrindʒə], *s.* (*Cul.*) der Napf.
port (1) [pɔ:t], *s.* der Hafen.
port (2) [pɔ:t], *s.* der Portwein (*wine*).

portable [ˈpɔ:təbl], *adj.* tragbar; Koffer- (*radio etc.*).
portcullis [pɔ:tˈkʌlis], *s.* das Fallgatter.
portend [pɔ:ˈtend], *v.a.* vorbedeuten, ahnen lassen.
portent [ˈpɔ:tent], *s.* die Vorbedeutung.
porter [ˈpɔ:tə], *s.* (*Railw.*) der Gepäckträger; der Pförtner, Portier (*caretaker, janitor*); das Porterbier (*beer*).
porterage [ˈpɔ:təridʒ], *s.* der Trägerlohn, die Zustellkosten, *f.pl.*
portfolio [pɔ:tˈfouliou], *s.* die Mappe; (*Pol.*) das Ressort; das Portefeuille.
portico [ˈpɔ:tikou], *s.* (*Archit.*) die Säulenhalle.
portion [ˈpɔ:ʃən], *s.* die Portion, der Anteil. — *v.a.* aufteilen, austeilen (*share out*).
portliness [ˈpɔ:tlinis], *s.* die Stattlichkeit (*dignity*); Behäbigkeit (*corpulence*).
portly [ˈpɔ:tli], *adj.* stattlich (*dignified*); behäbig (*corpulent*).
portmanteau [pɔ:tˈmæntou], *s.* der Handkoffer.
portrait [ˈpɔ:trit], *s.* (*Art*) das Bildnis, Porträt.
portray [pɔ:ˈtrei], *v.a.* im Bilde darstellen, porträtieren; (*fig.*) schildern, darstellen (*describe*).
Portuguese [pɔ:tjuˈgi:z], *adj.* portugiesisch. — *s.* der Portugiese.
pose [pouz], *s.* die Haltung, Stellung (*of model etc.*). — *v.a.* in Pose stellen; aufwerfen (*question*). — *v.n.* (*as model*) stehen, sitzen; — *as*, posieren, sich ausgeben als (*pretend to be*).
poser [ˈpouzə], *s.* die schwierige Frage.
position [pəˈziʃən], *s.* die Lage (*situation*); die Stellung (*job*); der Stand, Rang (*rank*); (*Astron., Mil.*) die Position.
positive [ˈpɔzitiv], *adj.* positiv; (*fig.*) ausdrücklich, sicher (*sure*).
possess [pəˈzes], *v.a.* besitzen.
possession [pəˈzeʃən], *s.* der Besitz, Besitztum.
possessive [pəˈzesiv], *adj.* (*Gram.*) besitzanzeigend, possessiv; (*fig.*) besitzgierig.
possibility [pɔsiˈbiliti], *s.* die Möglichkeit.
possible [ˈpɔsibl], *adj.* möglich.
post (1) [poust], *s.* der Pfosten (*pillar*).
post (2) [poust], *s.* die Post (*mail*); der Posten (*job*). — *v.a.* zur Post geben; (*coll.*) einstecken (*letter*).
postage [ˈpoustidʒ], *s.* das Porto; — *stamp*, die Briefmarke.
postal [poustl], *adj.* Post-.
poster [ˈpoustə], *s.* das Plakat.
posterity [pɔsˈteriti], *s.* die Nachwelt.
posthumous [ˈpɔstjuməs], *adj.* hinterlassen, nach dem Tode, postum.
postman [ˈpoustmən], *s.* der Briefträger.
postmark [ˈpoustma:k], *s.* der Poststempel.
post-mortem [poustˈmɔ:təm], *s.* — — — (*examination*), die Obduktion, Leichenschau.
post-office [ˈpoustɔfis], *s.* das Postamt.
postpone [poustˈpoun], *v.a.* verschieben, aufschieben.
postscript [ˈpoustskript], *s.* die Nachschrift.
postulate [ˈpɔstjuleit], *v.a.* postulieren, voraussetzen.
posture [ˈpɔstʃə], *s.* die Positur, Haltung (*of body*).
pot [pɔt], *s.* der Topf; die Kanne (*beer*); (*coll.*) *go to* —, zugrunde gehen. — *v.a.* einkochen, einmachen; (*fig.*) kürzen.
potash [ˈpɔtæʃ], *s.* (*Chem*) die Pottasche.
potassium [pəˈtæsiəm], *s.* (*Chem.*) das Kalium.
potato [pəˈteitou], *s.* (*Bot.*) die Kartoffel.
potent [ˈpoutənt], *adj.* kräftig, stark, wirksam.
potential [pəˈtenʃəl], *s.* das Potential. — *adj.* möglich, potentiell (*possible*).
potter [ˈpɔtə], *s.* der Töpfer.
pottery [ˈpɔtəri], *s.* die Töpferei; die Töpferwaren, Tonwaren, *f. pl.* (*goods*).
pouch [pautʃ], *s.* der Beutel.
poulterer [ˈpoultərə], *s.* der Geflügelhändler.
poultice [ˈpoultis], *s.* der Umschlag.
poultry [ˈpoultri], *s.* das Geflügel.
pounce (1) [pauns], *s.* (*obs.*) die Klaue. — *v.n.* — *upon*, herfallen (über, *Acc.*).
pounce (2) [pauns], *s.* das Bimssteinpulver. — *v.a.* (mit Bimsstein) abreiben.
pound (1) [paund], *s.* das Pfund; das Pfund Sterling.
pound (2) [paund], *v.a.* zerstoßen.
poundage [ˈpaundidʒ], *s.* das Pfundgeld, die Gebühr pro Pfund.
pour [pɔ:], *v.a.* gießen, schütten, einschenken. — *v.n.* strömen.
pout [paut], *v.n.* schmollen.
poverty [ˈpɔvəti], *s.* die Armut.
powder [ˈpaudə], *s.* (*Mil.*) das Pulver; der Puder (*face etc.*). — *v.a.* zu Pulver machen, stoßen; (*face*) pudern.
power [pauə], *s.* die Macht, Gewalt; Kraft; Fähigkeit; — *of attorney*, die Vollmacht; (*Maths.*) die Potenz; (*Elec.*) der Strom; — *house*, — *station*, das Elektrizitätswerk; — *cut*, die Stromstörung.
powerful [ˈpauəful], *adj.* kräftig, mächtig, einflußreich.
powerless [ˈpauəlis], *adj.* kraftlos, machtlos.
pox [pɔks], *s.* (*Med.*) die Pocken, *f. pl.*; die Syphilis.
practicable [ˈpræktikəbl], *adj.* ausführbar, tunlich.
practical [ˈpræktikəl], *adj.* praktisch.
practice [ˈpræktis], *s.* die Ausübung (*doing, carrying out*); die Praxis.
practise [ˈpræktis], *v.a.* ausführen, ausüben (*a profession etc.*); üben (*rehearse*). — *v.n.* sich üben.

practised ['præktisd], *adj.* geübt, geschult (in).
practitioner [præk'tiʃənə], *s.* (*Med.*) praktischer Arzt; (*Law*) Advokat.
pragmatic [præg'mætik], *adj.* pragmatisch.
prairie ['prɛəri], *s.* die Prärie.
praise [preiz], *v.a.* preisen, loben. — *s.* das Lob.
pram *see under* **perambulator.**
prance [prɑ:ns], *v.n.* sich bäumen; (*fig.*) sich brüsten (*brag*).
prank [præŋk], *s.* der Streich.
prate [preit], *v.n.* plappern, schwatzen.
prattle [prætl], *v.n.* plaudern, schwatzen. — *s.* das Geschwätz.
prawn [prɔ:n], *s.* (*Zool.*) die Steingarnele.
pray [prei], *v.n.* beten. — *v.a.* bitten, ersuchen (*beseech*).
prayer [prɛə], *s.* das Gebet.
preach [pri:tʃ], *v.a., v.n.* predigen.
preacher ['pri:tʃə], *s.* der Prediger.
preamble [pri:'æmbl], *s.* die Vorrede, der Einleitungsparagraph.
precarious [pri'kɛəriəs], *adj.* unsicher, prekär.
precaution [pri'kɔ:ʃən], *s.* die Vorsichtsmaßregel.
precede [pri'si:d], *v.a., v.n.* vorausgehen, den Vortritt haben.
precedence ['presidəns *or* pri'si:dəns], *s.* der Vortritt, Vorrang.
precedent ['presidənt], *s.* der Präzedenzfall.
precept ['pri:sept], *s.* die Vorschrift, Regel.
preceptor [pri'septə], *s.* der Lehrer, Lehrmeister.
precinct ['pri:siŋkt], *s.* das Gebiet, der Bezirk; (*pl.*) die Grenzen, *f. pl.*
precious ['preʃəs], *adj.* wertvoll, kostbar; — *metal*, das Edelmetall.
precipice ['presipis], *s.* der Abgrund.
precipitous [pri'sipitəs], *adj.* jäh, abschüssig.
precise [pri'sais], *adj.* genau, bestimmt.
precision [pri'siʒən], *s.* die Präzision, Genauigkeit; (*Engin.*) — *tool*, das Präzisionswerkzeug.
preclude [pri'klu:d], *v.a.* ausschließen.
precocious [pri'kouʃəs], *adj.* frühreif.
preconceive [pri:kən'si:v], *v.a.* vorher denken.
preconceived [pri:kən'si:vd], *adj.* vorgefaßt.
preconception [pri:kən'sepʃən], *s.* das Vorurteil.
precursor [pri'kə:sə], *s.* der Vorläufer.
predatory ['predətəri], *adj.* räuberisch, Raub-.
predecessor ['pri:disesə], *s.* der Vorgänger.
predestin(at)e [pri:'destin(eit)], *v.a.* vorher bestimmen; (*Theol.*) prädestinieren.
predicament [pri'dikəmənt], *s.* die Verlegenheit.
predicate ['predikit], *s.* (*Gram.*) das Prädikat. — [-keit], *v.a.* behaupten.
predict [pri'dikt], *v.a.* voraussagen, vorhersagen.
prediction [pri'dikʃən], *s.* die Vorhersage (*weather etc.*); die Weissagung (*prophecy*).
predilection [pri:di'lekʃən], *s.* die Vorliebe.
predispose [pri:dis'pouz], *v.a.* vorbereiten; empfänglich machen.
predominant [pri'dɔminənt], *adj.* vorherrschend.
predominate [pri'dɔmineit], *v.n.* vorherrschen.
pre-eminence [pri:'eminəns], *s.* der Vorrang.
prefabricate [pri:'fæbrikeit], *v.a.* vorfabrizieren, als Fertigteil herstellen, in der Fabrik herstellen.
prefabrication [pri:fæbri'keiʃən], *s.* die Vorfabrizierung.
preface ['prefis], *s.* das Vorwort.
prefatory ['prefətəri], *adj.* einleitend.
prefect ['pri:fekt], *s.* der Präfekt.
prefer [pri'fə:], *v.a.* vorziehen.
preference ['prefərəns], *s.* der Vorzug (*Comm.*) — *share*, die Vorzugsaktie.
preferment [pri'fə:mənt], *s.* die Beförderung.
prefix ['pri:fiks], *s.* die Vorsilbe. — [pri:'fiks], *v.a.* vorsetzen.
pregnancy ['pregnənsi], *s.* die Schwangerschaft.
pregnant ['pregnənt], *adj.* schwanger.
prejudge [pri:'dʒʌdʒ], *v.a.* vorher urteilen, voreilig urteilen.
prejudice ['predʒudis], *s.* das Vorurteil. — *v.a.* beeinträchtigen.
prejudicial [predʒu'diʃəl], *adj.* schädlich.
prelate ['prelit], *s.* (*Eccl.*) der Prälat.
preliminary [pri'liminəri], *adj.* vorläufig, Präliminar-. —*s.* (*pl.*) die Vorbereitungen, *f. pl.*
prelude ['prelju:d], *s.* das Vorspiel.
premature ['premətʃə], *adj.* vorschnell, übereilt, vorzeitig.
premeditate [pri:'mediteit], *v.a.* (*Law*) vorher überlegen.
Premier ['premiə], *s.* der Premierminister.
premise (1) ['premis], *s.* (*Log.*) die Prämisse; (*pl.*) das Haus, Grundstück; die Stätte, der Ort; das Lokal (*inn etc.*).
premise (2) [pri:'maiz], *v.a.* vorausschicken.
premium ['pri:miəm], *s.* die Prämie.
premonition [pri:mə'niʃən], *s.* die Vorahnung.
preoccupation [pri:ɔkju'peiʃən], *s.* die Zerstreutheit.
preoccupied [pri:'ɔkjupaid], *adj.* besorgt; zerstreut (*absent-minded*).
preparation [prepə'reiʃən], *s.* die Vorbereitung; Zubereitung (*of meals*).
preparatory [pri'pærətri], *adj.* vorbereitend; — *school*, die Vorschule.
prepare [pri'pɛə], *v.a., v.n.* vorbereiten (*for*, auf); zubereiten (*meals*).
prepay [pri:'pei], *v.a. irr.* vorausbezahlen; (*post*) frankieren.

preponderant [pri'pɔndərənt], *adj.* überwiegend.
preponderate [pri'pɔndəreit], *v.a., v.n.* überwiegen.
preposition [prepə'ziʃən], *s.* (*Gram.*) die Präposition.
prepossess [pri:pə'zes], *v.a.* einnehmen, beeindrucken.
preposterous [pri'pɔstərəs], *adj.* töricht, lächerlich, unerhört.
prerogative [pri'rɔgətiv], *s.* das Vorrecht.
presage [pri'seidʒ], *v.a.* prophezeien. — ['presidʒ], *s.* die Prophezeiung.
prescient ['preʃiənt, 'pri:–], *adj.* vorahnend, vorherwissend.
prescribe [pri'skraib], *v.a., v.n.* vorschreiben; (*Med.*) verschreiben, verordnen.
prescription [pri'skripʃən], *s.* die Vorschrift (*precept*); (*Med.*) das Rezept.
presence ['prezəns], *s.* die Gegenwart, Anwesenheit (*attendance*); das Äußere (*appearance*); — *of mind*, die Geistesgegenwart.
present (1) ['prezənt], *adj.* anwesend, gegenwärtig; jetzig. — *s.* (*Gram.*) das Präsens, die Gegenwart; (*time*) die Gegenwart, heutige Zeit.
present (2) [pri'zənt], *v.a.* darstellen (*on stage*); vorstellen (*introduce*); präsentieren (*arms*); schenken, geben (*gifts*). — ['prezənt], *s.* das Geschenk (*gift*).
presentation [prezən'teiʃən], *s.* die Darstellung (*stage, art*); die Vorstellung (*introduction*); die Überreichung (*of gift*).
presentiment [pri'zentimənt], *s.* das Vorgefühl, die Vorahnung.
presently ['prezəntli], *adv.* bald, sogleich.
preservation [prezə'veiʃən], *s.* die Erhaltung, Bewahrung.
preservative [pri'zə:vətiv], *s.* das Konservierungsmittel.
preserve [pri'zə:v], *v.a.* bewahren, erhalten; (*fruit*) einmachen. — *s.* (*Hunt.*) das Jagdgehege, Jagdrevier, (*pl.*) die Konserven, *f. pl.*
preside [pri'zaid], *v.n.* (*over*) den Vorsitz führen.
president ['prezidənt], *s.* der Präsident.
press [pres], *v.a., v.n.* drücken (*push*); bügeln, plätten (*iron*); nötigen (*force*); dringend bitten (*entreat*). — *s.* die Presse (*newspapers, printing*); der Schrank (*cupboard*); das Gedränge (*crowd*).
pressing ['presiŋ], *adj.* dringend.
pressure ['preʃə], *s.* der Druck.
prestige [pres'ti:ʒ], *s.* das Prestige, Ansehen.
presumable [pri'zju:məbl], *adj.* mutmaßlich, vermutlich.
presume [pri'zju:m], *v.a., v.n.* vermuten; — *on*, sich anmaßen.
presumption [pri'zʌmpʃən], *s.* die Annahme; die Anmaßung (*arrogance*).
presumptive [pri'zʌmptiv], *adj.* mutmaßlich.
presumptuous [pri'zʌmptjuəs], *adj.* anmaßend, dreist, vermessen.
presuppose [pri:sə'pouz], *v.a.* voraussetzen.
pretence [pri'tens], *s.* der Vorwand.
pretend [pri'tend], *v.a., v.n.* vortäuschen, vorgeben.
pretension [pri'tenʃən], *s.* die Anmaßung, der Anspruch (*to*, auf).
pretentious [pri'tenʃəs], *adj.* anspruchsvoll.
preterite ['pretərit], *s.* (*Gram.*) das Präteritum.
pretext ['pri:tekst], *s.* der Vorwand.
pretty ['priti], *adj.* hübsch, nett. — *adv.* (*coll.*) ziemlich.
prevail [pri'veil], *v.n.* vorherrschen, die Oberhand gewinnen.
prevalence ['prevələns], *s.* das Vorherrschen.
prevaricate [pri'værikeit], *v.n.* Ausflüchte machen.
prevent [pri'vent], *v.a.* verhindern.
prevention [pri'venʃən], *s.* die Verhinderung.
preventive [pri'ventiv], *adj.* vorbeugend.
previous ['pri:viəs], *adj.* vorhergehend.
prey [prei], *s.* die Beute, der Raub. — *v.n.* rauben, nachstellen.
price [prais], *s.* der Preis, Wert.
priceless ['praislis], *adj.* unschätzbar, unbezahlbar.
prick [prik], *s.* der Stachel, Stich (*stab*). — *v.a.* stechen (*stab*); punktieren (*puncture*).
prickle [prikl], *s.* (*Bot.*) der Stachel.
pride [praid], *s.* der Stolz. — *v.r.* — *o.s.*, sich brüsten, stolz sein (*on*, auf, *Acc.*).
priest [pri:st], *s.* (*Eccl.*) der Priester.
prig [prig], *s.* der eingebildete Tropf; Tugendheld.
priggish ['prigiʃ], *adj.* dünkelhaft, selbstgefällig.
prim [prim], *adj.* steif, spröde.
primacy ['praiməsi], *s.* der, das Primat.
primæval [prai'mi:vəl], *adj.* Ur-, anfänglich, ursprünglich.
primary ['praiməri], *adj.* erst, ursprünglich; Haupt- (*main*). — *s.* (*pl.*) (*Am.*) die Vorwahlen, *f. pl.* (*Presidential elections*).
prime [praim], *adj.* erst, wichtigst. — *s.* die Blüte, Vollendung, Vollkraft.
primer ['praimə], *s.* das Elementarbuch, die Fibel.
primitive ['primitiv], *adj.* primitiv; ursprünglich (*original*).
primness ['primnis], *s.* die Geziertheit, Steifheit.
primrose ['primrouz], *s.* (*Bot.*) die Primel.
prince [prins], *s.* der Prinz; Fürst (*rank*).
princess [prin'ses], *s.* die Prinzessin.
principal ['prinsipl], *s.* der Direktor (*business*); Rektor (*school etc.*); (*Comm.*) das Kapital; (*Mus.*) der erste Spieler. — *adj.* erst, Haupt-.
principality [prinsi'pæliti], *s.* das Fürstentum.

principle ['prinsipl], *s.* das Prinzip, der Grundsatz.
print [print], *v.a.* drucken, abdrucken. — *s.* (*Typ.*, *Art*) der Druck; *out of* —, vergriffen.
printer ['printə], *s.* der (Buch-drucker.
prior [praiə], *adj.* früher, eher; — *to*, vor (*Dat.*). — *s.* (*Eccl.*) der Prior.
priority [prai'ɔriti], *s.* die Priorität, der Vorrang.
prise [praiz], *v.a.* — *open*, gewaltsam öffnen, aufbrechen.
prism [prizm], *s.* das Prisma.
prison [prizn], *s.* das Gefängnis.
prisoner ['prizənə], *s.* der Gefangene, Sträfling.
pristine ['pristain], *adj.* ehemalig, vormalig, ursprünglich.
privacy ['praivəsi *or* 'privəsi], *s.* die Zurückgezogenheit, Stille.
private ['praivit], *adj.* privat, persönlich, vertraulich (*confidential*). — *s.* (*Mil.*) der Gemeine, Landser.
privation [prai'veiʃən], *s.* der Mangel, die Entbehrung (*lack*); die Beraubung (*deprivation*).
privilege ['privilidʒ], *s.* das Privileg, Vorrecht. — *v.a.* ausnehmen, privilegieren.
privy ['privi], *s.* der Abtritt, Abort. — *adj.* — *to*, mitwissend; *Privy Council*, der Staatsrat.
prize [praiz], *s.* der Preis, die Belohnung; — *v.a.* hochschätzen.
prizewinner ['praizwinə], *s.* der Preisträger; *Nobel* —, der Nobelpreisträger.
probability [prɔbə'biliti], *s.* die Wahrscheinlichkeit.
probable ['prɔbəbl], *adj.* wahrscheinlich.
probate ['proubeit], *s.* (*Law*) die Testamentsbestätigung.
probation [pro'beiʃən], *s.* die Bewährung, Bewährungsfrist (*period*).
probationary [pro'beiʃənəri], *adj.* Bewährungs-.
probe [proub], *v.a.* sondieren, untersuchen. — *s.* die Sonde, Prüfung.
probity ['proubiti], *s.* die Redlichkeit, Anständigkeit.
problem ['prɔbləm], *s.* das Problem.
problematic [prɔblə'mætik], *adj.* zweifelhaft, problematisch.
proboscis [prə'bɔsis], *s.* (*Ent.*) der Rüssel.
procedure [prə'si:dʒə], *s.* der Vorgang, das Verfahren.
proceed [prə'si:d], *v.n.* vorgehen, verfahren.
proceeds ['prousi:dz], *s. pl.* der Ertrag.
process (1) ['prouses], *s.* der Vorgang, Prozeß. — *v.a.* verarbeiten, fertigen.
process (2) [pro'ses], *v.n.* in einem Zuge gehen.
procession [prə'seʃən], *s.* der (feierliche) Umzug, die Prozession.
proclaim [prə'kleim], *v.a.* (*Pol.*) proklamieren, ausrufen.
proclamation [prɔklə'meiʃən], *s.* (*Pol.*) die Ausrufung, Proklamation.
proclivity [prə'kliviti], *s.* der Hang, die Neigung (*tendency*).
procrastinate [prə'kræstineit], *v.a.* aufschieben. — *v.n.* zögern, zaudern.
procreate ['proukrieit], *v.a.* zeugen, hervorbringen.
procurable [prə'kjuərəbl], *adj.* zu verschaffen, erhältlich.
procure [prə'kjuə], *v.a.* verschaffen, besorgen.
prod [prɔd], *v.a.* stoßen.
prodigal ['prɔdigəl], *adj.* verschwenderisch, vergeudend; — *son*, der verlorene Sohn.
prodigious [prə'didʒəs], *adj.* erstaunlich, ungeheuer.
prodigy ['prɔdidʒi], *s.* das Wunderkind.
produce [prə'dju:s], *v.a.* erzeugen, produzieren. — ['prɔdju:s], *s.* das Produkt, Erzeugnis.
producer [prə'dju:sə], *s.* der Erzeuger; (*Theat.*, *Cinema*) der Regisseur.
product ['prɔdʌkt], *s.* das Produkt, Erzeugnis.
production [prə'dʌkʃən], *s.* die Produktion; die Erzeugung (*industrial*); das Zeigen, Vorweisen (*of documents*); (*Theat.*) die Regie.
productive [prə'dʌktiv], *adj.* produktiv, schöpferisch (*mind*); fruchtbar (*soil*).
profane [prə'fein], *adj.* profan; ruchlos.
profanity [prə'fæniti], *s.* die Profanierung; das Lästern.
profess [prə'fes], *v.a.*, *v.n.* bekennen, erklären, sich bekennen zu.
profession [prə'feʃən], *s.* der (höhere) Beruf; (*Eccl.*) das Bekenntnis; die Beteuerung (*protestation*).
professional [prə'feʃənəl], *adj.* beruflich, berufsmäßig.
professor [prə'fesə], *s.* der (Universitäts) Professor.
professorship [prə'fesəʃip], *s.* die Professur.
proffer ['prɔfə], *v.a.* anbieten (*offer*).
proficiency [prə'fiʃənsi], *s.* die Tüchtigkeit; (*skill*) die Beherrschung.
proficient [prə'fiʃənt], *adj.* bewandert, tüchtig; (*in language*) fließend.
profile ['proufail], *s.* das Profil.
profit ['prɔfit], *s.* der Profit, Gewinn, Nutzen. — *v.n.* Nutzen ziehen. — *v.a.* von Nutzen sein (*Dat.*).
profound [prə'faund], *adj.* tief; gründlich (*thorough*).
profuse [prə'fju:s], *adj.* reichlich, verschwenderisch.
profusion [prə'fju:ʒen], *s.* der Überfluß.
progeny ['prɔdʒəni], *s.* der Nachkomme; die Nachkommenschaft.
prognosticate [prɔg'nɔstikeit], *v.a.* vorhersagen.
prognostication [prɔgnɔsti'keiʃən], *s.* die Voraussage.
programme, (*Am.*) **program** ['prougræm], *s.* das Programm.
progress ['prougres], *s.* der Fortschritt. — [prou'gres], *v.n.* fortschreiten, Fortschritte machen.

progression [pro'greʃən], *s.* (*Maths.*) die Reihe, Progression.
progressive [pro'gresiv], *adj.* fortschrittlich (*modern*); fortschreitend (*continuous*); progressiv.
prohibit [prou'hibit], *v.a.* verbieten.
prohibition [proui'biʃən], *s.* das Verbot.
project [prə'dʒekt], *v.a.* projizieren; entwerfen. — ['prɔdʒekt], *s.* das Projekt, der Plan.
projectile [prə'dʒektail], *s.* das Geschoß.
projection [prə'dʒekʃən], *s.* die Projektion (*film*); der Entwurf (*plan*); der Vorsprung (*jutting out*).
proletarian [prouli'tɛəriən], *adj.* proletarisch. — *s.* der Prolet(arier).
prolific [prə'lifik], *adj.* fruchtbar.
prolix ['prouliks], *adj.* weitschweifig.
prologue ['proulɔg], *s.* der Prolog.
prolong [prə'lɔŋ], *v.a.* verlängern, prolongieren.
prominent ['prɔminənt], *adj.* prominent, hervorragend.
promiscuous [prə'miskjuəs], *adj.* unterschiedslos (*indiscriminate*); vermischt (*mixed*).
promise ['prɔmis], *v.a.* versprechen. — *v.n.* Erwartungen erwecken. — *s.* das Versprechen.
promissory ['prɔmisəri], *adj.* versprechend; (*Comm.*) — *note*, der Schuldschein.
promontory ['prɔməntəri], *s.* das Vorgebirge.
promote [prə'mout], *v.a.* befördern; fördern (*foster*).
promotion [prə'mouʃən], *s.* die Beförderung (*advancement*); Förderung (*fostering*); (*Am.*) die Reklame (*publicity*).
prompt [prɔmpt], *adj.* prompt, pünktlich. — *v.a.* (*Theat.*) soufflieren; treiben (*inspire*).
prompter ['prɔmptə], *s.* (*Theat.*) der Souffleur.
promptitude ['prɔmptitju:d], *s.* die Promptheit, Pünktlichkeit.
promulgate ['prɔməlgeit], *v.a.* bekanntmachen, verbreiten.
prone [proun], *adj.* geneigt, neigend.
prong [prɔŋ], *s.* die Zinke, Gabel.
pronominal [pro'nɔminəl], *adj.* (*Gram.*) pronominal.
pronoun ['prounaun], *s.* das Fürwort, Pronomen.
pronounce [prə'nauns], *v.a.*, *v.n.* aussprechen (*words*); feierlich erklären (*proclaim*).
pronunciation [prənʌnsi'eiʃən], *s.* die Aussprache.
proof [pru:f], *s.* der Beweis, die Probe; (*Typ.*) der Korrekturbogen. — *v.a.* (*Engin.*, *Chem.*) impregnieren.
prop [prɔp], *s.* die Stütze, der Stützpfahl. — *v.a.* stützen.
propaganda [prɔpə'gændə], *s.* die Propaganda, Reklame.
propagate ['prɔpəgeit], *v.a.* propagieren; (*Bot.*) fortpflanzen.
propel [prə'pel], *v.a.* forttreiben, vorwärtstreiben.
propeller [prə'pelə], *s.* der Propeller, die Schraube.
propensity [prə'pensiti], *s.* die Neigung, der Hang.
proper ['prɔpə], *adj.* schicklich (*manners*); eigentümlich, eigen (*peculiar*).
property ['prɔpəti], *s.* das Eigentum (*possession*); die Eigenschaft (*quality*).
prophecy ['prɔfisi], *s.* die Prophezeiung, Weissagung.
prophesy ['prɔfisai], *v.a.* prophezeien.
propitiate [prə'piʃieit], *v.a.* versöhnen.
propitiation [prəpiʃi'eiʃən], *s.* die Versöhnung.
propitious [prə'piʃəs], *adj.* gnädig, günstig, geneigt.
proportion [prə'pɔ:ʃən], *s.* das Verhältnis; die Proportion; der Anteil (*portion*); das Ebenmaß (*in art*).
proportionate [prə'pɔ:ʃənit], *adj.* im Verhältnis, verhältnismäßig, proportioniert.
proposal [prə'pouzəl], *s.* der Vorschlag, Antrag.
propose [prə'pouz], *v.a.* antragen, beantragen, vorschlagen. — *v.n.* — *to a lady*, einen Heiratsantrag machen.
proposition [prɔpə'ziʃən], *s.* der Vorschlag, Antrag; die Idee.
propound [prə'paund], *v.a.* vorlegen, vorbringen (*a theory etc.*).
proprietor [prə'praiətə], *s.* der Eigentümer.
propriety [prə'praiəti], *s.* die Schicklichkeit.
propulsion [prə'pʌlʃən], *s.* der Antrieb.
prorogue [prə'roug], *v.a.* vertagen.
prosaic [prə'zeiik], *adj.* prosaisch, nüchtern.
proscribe [pro'skraib], *v.a.* verbieten, ächten.
proscription [pro'skripʃən], *s.* die Verbannung, das Verbot.
prose [prouz], *s.* die Prosa.
prosecute ['prɔsikju:t], *v.a.* verfolgen; (*Law*) gerichtlich verfolgen, anklagen.
prosecutor ['prɔsikju:tə], *s.* (*public*) der Staatsanwalt; der Kläger.
proselyte ['prɔsəlait], *s.* der Neubekehrte, Proselyt.
prospect ['prɔspekt], *s.* die Aussicht; (*pl.*) die Aussichten, Chancen, *f.pl.* — [prɔs'pekt], *v.n.* suchen (*for*, nach, *Dat.*).
prospectus [prə'spektəs], *s.* der Prospekt.
prosper ['prɔspə], *v.n.* gedeihen, blühen. — *v.a.* segnen.
prosperity [prɔs'periti], *s.* der Wohlstand; der Reichtum; das Gedeihen (*thriving*).
prosperous ['prɔspərəs], *adj.* glücklich, wohlhabend.
prostitute ['prɔstitju:t], *s.* die Prostituierte, Dirne. — *v.a.* erniedrigen.
prostrate ['prɔstreit], *adj.* hingestreckt, niedergeworfen, fußfällig. — [prɔs'treit], *v.a.* niederwerfen.

prosy ['prouzi], *adj.* prosaisch, weitschweifig, langweilig.
protect [prə'tekt], *v.a.* beschützen.
protection [prə'tekʃən], *s.* der Schutz; die Protektion (*favour*).
protective [prə'tektiv], *adj.* Schutz-, schützend.
protector [prə'tektə], *s.* der Beschützer; (*Engin.*) der Schutz.
protest [prə'test], *v.a., v.n.* protestieren, einwenden. — ['proutest], *s.* der Protest, Einspruch.
Protestant ['prɔtistənt], *adj.* protestantisch. — *s.* der Protestant.
protestation [prɔtes'teiʃən], *s.* die Beteuerung, Verwahrung.
protocol ['proutəkɔl], *s.* das Protokoll.
prototype ['proutotaip], *s.* das Urbild, Modell, der Prototyp.
protract [prə'trækt], *v.a.* in die Länge ziehen; hinausziehen.
protractor [prə'træktə], *s.* der Winkelmesser, Transporteur, die Schmiege.
protrude [prə'tru:d], *v.n.* herausragen, hervorstehen, vordringen.
protuberance [prə'tju:bərəns], *s.* der Höcker, der Auswuchs, die Protuberanz.
proud [praud], *adj.* stolz (*of*, auf, *Acc.*).
prove [pru:v], *v.a.* beweisen. — *v.n.* sich erweisen (*turn out*).
provender ['prɔvində], *s.* das Viehfutter.
proverb ['prɔvə:b], *s.* das Sprichwort.
proverbial [prə'və:biəl], *adj.* sprichwörtlich.
provide [prə'vaid], *v.a., v.n.* vorsehen, versorgen, verschaffen.
provided [prə'vaidid], *conj.* vorausgesetzt.
providence ['prɔvidəns], *s.* die Vorsehung.
provident ['prɔvidənt], *adj.* vorsorglich.
providential [prɔvi'denʃəl], *adj.* von der Vorsehung bestimmt.
province ['prɔvins], *s.* die Provinz, das Gebiet (*also fig.*).
provincial [prə'vinʃəl], *adj.* ländlich, Provinz-; provinziell.
provision [prə'viʒən], *s.* die Versorgung (*supply*); der Vorrat (*stock*); (*pl.*) die Lebensmittel (*victuals*).
provisional [prə'viʒənəl], *adj.* vorläufig.
proviso [prə'vaizou], *s.* der Vorbehalt.
provocation [prɔvə'keiʃən], *s.* die Herausforderung.
provoke [prə'vouk], *v.a.* herausfordern, provozieren.
prow [prau], *s.* (*Naut.*) der Bug.
prowess ['praues], *s.* die Stärke (*physical*); die körperliche Tüchtigkeit; Tapferkeit.
prowl [praul], *v.n.* herumstreichen.
proximity [prɔk'simiti], *s.* die Nähe.
proxy ['prɔksi], *s.* der Stellvertreter.
prudence ['pru:dəns], *s.* die Klugheit, Vorsicht.
prudent ['pru:dənt], *adj.* klug, vorsichtig.
prudery ['pru:dəri], *s.* die Sprödigkeit.
prudish ['pru:diʃ], *adj.* prüde, spröde, zimperlich.
prune (1) [pru:n], *s.* (*Cul.*) die Backpflaume.
prune (2) [pru:n], *v.a.* beschneiden, stutzen.
Prussian ['prʌʃən], *adj.* preußisch; — *blue*, das Berlinerblau. — *s.* der Preuße.
prussic ['prʌsik], *adj.* blausauer; — *acid*, die Blausäure.
pry [prai], *v.n.* spähen, ausforschen.
psalm [sɑ:m], *s.* der Psalm.
psychology [sai'kɔlədʒi], *s.* die Psychologie.
pub [pʌb], *s.* das Wirtshaus, die Kneipe.
puberty ['pju:bəti], *s.* die Pubertät, Mannbarkeit.
public ['pʌblik], *adj.* öffentlich. — *s.* das Publikum; die Öffentlichkeit.
publican ['pʌblikən], *s.* der Gastwirt.
publication [pʌbli'keiʃən], *s.* die Veröffentlichung, Herausgabe.
publicity [pʌb'lisiti], *s.* die Werbung, die Reklame; — *manager*, der Reklamechef, Werbeleiter.
publicize ['pʌblisaiz], *v.a.* weithin bekannt machen, publizieren.
publish ['pʌbliʃ], *v.a.* veröffentlichen; verlegen (*books*); —*ing house*, der Verlag.
publisher ['pʌbliʃə], *s.* der Verleger.
pucker ['pʌkə], *v.a.* falten; runzeln (*wrinkle*). — *s.* die Falte.
pudding ['pudiŋ], *s.* der Pudding.
puddle [pʌdl], *s.* die Pfütze. — *v.a.* puddeln (*iron*).
puerile ['pjuərail], *adj.* kindisch, knabenhaft.
puff [pʌf], *v.a., v.n.* puffen, paffen, blasen; —*ed-up*, aufgebläht, stolz. — *s.* der Windstoß; — *pastry*, der Blätterteig.
pug [pʌg], *s.* (*Zool.*) der Mops.
pugnacious [pʌg'neiʃəs], *adj.* kampfsüchtig, kampflustig.
puisne ['pju:ni], *adj.* (*Law*) jünger, Unter-.
puissant ['pwi:sənt], *adj.* mächtig, stark.
puke [pju:k], *v.n.* sich erbrechen.
pull [pul], *v.a., v.n.* ziehen, reißen; zerren. — *s.* der Zug, Ruck.
pullet ['pulit], *s.* (*Orn.*) das Hühnchen.
pulley ['puli], *s.* der Flaschenzug.
pulmonary, pulmonic ['pʌlmənəri, pʌl'mɔnik], *adj.* Lungen-.
pulp [pʌlp], *s.* der Brei; das Fleisch (*of fruit*); das Mark (*marrow*); die Pulpa (*tooth*). — *v.a.* zerstampfen, zu Brei stampfen.
pulpit ['pulpit], *s.* (*Eccl.*) die Kanzel.
pulsate [pʌl'seit], *v.n.* pulsieren, schlagen.
pulse (1) [pʌls], *s.* der Puls.
pulse (2) [pʌls], *s.* (*Bot.*) die Hülsenfrüchte, *f. pl.*
pulverize ['pʌlvəraiz], *v.a.* zu Pulver stoßen, zerstoßen.

pumice ['pʌmis], *s.* der Bimsstein.
pump (1) [pʌmp], *s.* die Pumpe. — *v.a.*, *v.n.* pumpen; ausfragen (*question*).
pump (2) [pʌmp], *s.* der Tanzschuh (*dancing shoe*).
pumpkin ['pʌmpkin], *s.* (*Bot.*) der Kürbis.
pun [pʌn], *s.* das Wortspiel. — *v.n.* Wortspiele machen.
Punch [pʌntʃ]. das Kasperle; — *and Judy*, Hanswurst und seine Frau.
punch (1) [pʌntʃ], *v.a.* schlagen, boxen (*box*). — *s.* der Schlag (*hit*); der Faustschlag (*boxing*).
punch (2) [pʌntʃ], *v.a.* lochen (*card*). — *s.* der Pfriem (*tool*).
punch (3) [pʌntʃ], *s.* der Punsch (*drink*).
punchy ['pʌntʃi], *adj.* kurz, dick, untersetzt.
punctilious [pʌŋk'tiliəs], *adj.* sorgfältig, spitzfindig.
punctual ['pʌŋktjuəl], *adj.* pünktlich.
punctuate ['pʌŋktjueit], *v.a.* (*Gram.*) interpunktieren; (*fig.*) betonen.
punctuation [pʌŋktju'eiʃən], *s.* (*Gram.*) die Interpunktion.
puncture ['pʌŋktʃə], *s.* (*Motor.*) der Reifendefekt, die Panne; (*Med.*) die Punktur, der Einstich. — *v.a.* (*Med.*) punktieren.
pungent ['pʌndʒənt], *adj.* scharf, stechend.
punish ['pʌniʃ], *v.a.* bestrafen (*s.o.*); strafen.
punishable ['pʌniʃəbl], *adj.* strafbar.
punishment ['pʌniʃmənt], *s.* die Strafe, Bestrafung.
punt [pʌnt], *s.* das kleine Boot, Flachboot.
puny ['pju:ni], *adj.* schwach, winzig.
pup [pʌp], *s.* der junge Hund; *be sold a* —, einen schlechten Kauf machen. — *v.n.* Junge werfen.
pupil (1) ['pju:pil], *s.* der Schüler.
pupil (2) ['pju:pil], *s.* die Pupille (*eye*).
pupil(l)age ['pju:pilidʒ], *s.* die Minderjährigkeit (*of minor*).
puppet ['pʌpit], *s.* die Puppe, Marionette; der Strohmann (*human tool*).
puppy ['pʌpi] *see* **pup**.
purblind ['pə:blaind], *adj.* halbblind.
purchase ['pə:tʃis], *s.* der Kauf, Einkauf. — *v.a.* kaufen.
pure ['pjuə], *adj.* pur, rein.
purge [pə:dʒ], *v.a.* reinigen. — *s.* die Reinigung; (*Pol.*) die Säuberung.
purify ['pjuərifai], *v.a.* läutern, reinigen.
purl (1) [pə:l], *s.* die Borte; (*knitting*) die Häkelkante.
purl (2) [pə:l], *v.n.* sich drehen, wirbeln; (*sl.*) umkippen.
purl (3) [pə:l], *s.* das Murmeln, Rieseln (*of brook*). — *v.n.* murmeln, rieseln.
purloin [pə:'lɔin], *v.a.* stehlen.
purple [pə:pl], *adj.* purpurn; — *patch*, die Glanzstelle. — *s.* der Purpur.
purport [pə:'pɔ:t], *v.a.* bedeuten, Sinn haben. — ['pə:pət], *s.* der Sinn, die Bedeutung.
purpose ['pə:pəs], *s.* die Absicht, der Zweck.
purposeful ['pə:pəsful], *adj.* zweckbewußt, energisch, zielbewußt.
purr [pə:], *v.n.* schnurren (*of cat*).
purse [pə:s], *s.* die Börse, Geldtasche; das Portemonnaie.
pursuance [pə'sju:əns], *s.* (*Law*) die Verfolgung, Ausführung.
pursuant [pə'sju:ənt], *adj.* (*Law*) zufolge, gemäß (*to*, *Dat.*).
pursue [pə'sju:], *v.a.* verfolgen.
pursuit [pə'sju:t], *s.* die Verfolgung; (*pl.*) die Geschäfte, *n. pl.*; Beschäftigung.
purvey [pə'vei], *v.a.* versorgen, liefern.
purview ['pə:vju:], *s.* der Spielraum; das Blickfeld.
push [puʃ], *v.a.* stoßen, drücken, schieben, drängen; *be —ed for*, in der Klemme sein. — *s.* der Stoß, Schub, das Drängen; *at a* —, wenn absolut nötig.
pusillanimous [pju:si'læniməs], *adj.* kleinmütig.
puss, pussy [pus, 'pusi], *s.* (*coll.*) die Katze, das Kätzchen, Miezchen.
put [put], *v.a. irr.* setzen (*set*), legen (*lay*), stellen (*stand*); — *off*, aufschieben, aus der Fassung bringen (*deflect*); — *on*, anziehen, auflegen; — *it on thickly*, es dick auftragen. — *v.n.* (*Naut.*) — *in*, anlegen.
putrefy ['pju:trifai], *v.a.*, *v.n.* faul werden (*rot*), verwesen.
putrid ['pju:trid], *adj.* faul (*rotten*).
puttee ['pʌti:], *s.* (*Mil.*) die Wickelgamasche.
putty ['pʌti], *s.* der Kitt.
puzzle [pʌzl], *s.* das Rätsel. — *v.a.* zu denken geben (*Dat.*).
pygmy ['pigmi], *s.* der Pygmäe.
pyjamas, (*Am.*) **pajamas** [pi'dʒɑ:məz, pə-], *s. pl.* der Schlafanzug.
pyramid ['pirəmid], *s.* die Pyramide.
pyre [paiə], *s.* der Scheiterhaufen.
pyrotechnics [paiəro'tekniks], *s. pl.* das Feuerwerk, die Feuerwerkskunst.
python ['paiθən], *s.* (*Zool.*) die Riesenschlange.

Q

Q [kju:]. das Q.
qua [kwei], *conj.* als.
quack [kwæk], *v.n.* quaken; (*coll.*) quacksalbern. — *s.* der Quacksalber.
quadrangle ['kwɔdræŋgl], *s.* (*abbr.* **quad** [kwɔd]), das Viereck; der Hof (*in college etc*).
quadrant ['kwɔdrənt], *s.* der Quadrant, Viertelkreis; (*Engin.*) der Winkelmesser.
quadrille [kwɔ'dril], *s.* die Quadrille, der Kontertanz.

quadruped ['kwɔdruped], *s.* (*Zool.*) das vierfüßige Tier.
quadruple ['kwɔdrupl], *adj.* vierfach.
quaff [kwæf], *v.a.* schlucken. — *v.n.* zechen (*drink heavily*).
quagmire ['kwægmaiə], *s.* der Sumpf.
quail (1) [kweil], *s.* (*Orn.*) die Wachtel.
quail (2) [kweil], *v.n.* verzagen.
quaint [kweint], *adj.* seltsam, wunderlich, eigenartig.
quake [kweik], *v.n.* erzittern, beben.
Quaker ['kweikə], *s.* der Quäker.
qualification [kwɔlifi'keiʃən], *s.* die Befähigung, Qualifikation (*ability*); die Einschränkung (*proviso*).
qualify ['kwɔlifai], *v.a.* befähigen (*make able*); beschränken, mäßigen, qualifizieren (*modify*). — *v.n.* sich qualifizieren, das Studium abschließen.
qualitative ['kwɔlitətiv], *adj.* qualitätsmäßig, Wert-, qualitativ.
quality ['kwɔliti], *s.* die Qualität (*high class*); der Wert (*standard*).
qualm [kwɑ:m], *s.* der Skrupel.
quantitative ['kwɔntitətiv], *adj.* quantitativ.
quantity ['kwɔntiti], *s.* die Quantität, Menge.
quantum ['kwɔntəm], *s.* die Menge; das Quantum; — *theory*, die Quantentheorie.
quarantine ['kwɔrənti:n], *s.* die Quarantäne.
quarrel ['kwɔrəl], *s.* der Streit, Zwist. — *v.n.* streiten, zanken.
quarry (1) ['kwɔri], *s.* der Steinbruch.
quarry (2) ['kwɔri], *s.* die Beute (*prey*).
quart [kwɔ:t], *s.* das Viertelmaß (*1.15 litre*).
quarter ['kwɔ:tə], *s.* das Viertel (jahr); (*Arith.*) das Viertel (*also of town*); (*pl.*) das Quartier.
quartermaster ['kwɔ:təmɑ:stə], *s.* (*Mil.*) der Feldzeugmeister.
quartet(te) [kwɔ:'tet], *s.* das Quartett.
quarto ['kwɔ:tou], *s.* das Quartformat.
quartz [kwɔ:ts], *s.* der Quartz.
quash [kwɔʃ], *v.a.* unterdrücken (*suppress*); (*Law*) annullieren.
quaver ['kweivə], *s.* (*Mus.*) die Achtelnote; der Triller (*trill*). — *v.n.* tremolieren, trillern.
quay [ki:], *s.* der Kai, Hafendamm.
queen [kwi:n], *s.* die Königin.
queer [kwiə], *adj.* seltsam, sonderlich.
quell [kwel], *v.a.* unterdrücken.
quench [kwentʃ], *v.a.* löschen; stillen (*thirst*).
querulous ['kweruləs], *adj.* mürrisch, jämmerlich; zänkisch.
query ['kwiəri], *s.* die Frage. — *v.a.* in Frage stellen.
quest [kwest], *s.* das Suchen, Streben; die Suche.
question ['kwestʃən], *s.* die Frage; — *mark*, das Fragezeichen. — *v.a.* fragen, in Frage stellen; ausfragen (*s.o.*).
questionable ['kwestʃənəbl], *adj.* zweifelhaft, fraglich, bedenklich.
queue [kju:], *s.* die Schlange, das Anstellen. — *v.n.* Schlange stehen.
quibble [kwibl], *s.* das Wortspiel, die Ausflucht. — *v.n.* um Worte streiten.
quick [kwik], *adj.* schnell (*fast*); lebendig (*live*).
quicken ['kwikən], *v.a.* beleben, anfeuern.
quicklime ['kwiklaim], *s.* der ungelöschte Kalk.
quicksand ['kwiksænd], *s.* der Flugsand.
quicksilver ['kwiksilvə], *s.* (*Chem.*) das Quecksilber.
quid (1) [kwid], *s.* (*sl.*) das Pfund Sterling.
quid (2) [kwid], *s.* (*Lat.*) etwas; — *pro quo*, Gleiches mit Gleichem.
quiescence [kwi'esəns], *s.* die Ruhe.
quiet ['kwaiət], *adj.* ruhig.
quietism ['kwaiətizm], *s.* der Quietismus.
quietness ['kwaiətnis], *s.* die Ruhe, Stille.
quill [kwil], *s.* der Federkiel, die Feder. — *v.a.* falten, fälteln.
quilt [kwilt], *s.* die Steppdecke.
quince [kwins], *s.* (*Bot.*) die Quitte.
quinine [kwi'ni:n], *s.* (*Med.*) das Chinin.
quinquennial [kwiŋ'kweniəl], *adj.* fünfjährig, fünfjährlich, alle fünf Jahre.
quinsy ['kwinzi], *s.* (*Med.*) die Bräune.
quint [kwint], *s.* (*Mus.*) die Quinte.
quintessence [kwin'tesəns], *s.* die Quintessenz, der Kern, der Inbegriff.
quintuple ['kwintjupl], *adj.* fünffach.
quip [kwip], *s.* die Stichelei; die witzige Bemerkung.
quire [kwaiə], *s.* das Buch Papier.
quirk [kwə:k], *s.* die (unerwartete) Wendung; Spitzfindigkeit.
quit [kwit], *v.a.*, *v.n.* verlassen; weggehen; (*Am.*) aufhören. — *adj.* (*pl.*) (**quits**) quitt, bezahlt.
quite [kwait], *adv.* ganz, völlig.
quiver (1) ['kwivə], *s.* der Köcher.
quiver (2) ['kwivə], *v.n.* erzittern, schauern.
quiz [kwiz], *s.* das Fragespiel, Quizprogramm (*Radio etc.*).
quoit [kɔit], *s.* die Wurfscheibe.
quorum ['kwɔ:rəm], *s.* die beschlußfähige Anzahl.
quota ['kwoutə], *s.* die Quote.
quotation [kwo'teiʃən], *s.* das Zitat; (*Comm.*) der Kostenanschlag, die Notierung.
quote [kwout], *v.a.* zitieren; (*Comm.*) einen Preis zitieren, notieren.

R

R [ɑ:(r)]. das R.
rabbet ['ræbit], *s.* die Fuge, Nute. — *v.a.* einfugen.

rabbi ['ræbai], *s.* (*Rel.*) der Rabbiner.
rabbit ['ræbit], *s.* (*Zool.*) das Kaninchen.
rabble [ræbl], *s.* der Pöbel.
rabid ['ræbid], *adj.* wütend, rasend.
race (1) [reis], *s.* die Rasse; das Geschlecht (*stock*).
race (2) [reis], *s.* das Rennen (*horses etc.*); der Wettlauf (*run*); — *course*, die Rennbahn. — *v.a.*, *v.n.* um die Wette laufen.
racial ['reiʃəl], *adj.* rassisch.
raciness ['reisinis], *s.* das Rassige, die Urwüchsigkeit.
rack [ræk], *s.* die Folterbank; das Reck (*gymnasium*); (*Railw.*) das Gepäcknetz. — *v.a.* recken, strecken; — *o.'s brains*, sich den Kopf zerbrechen.
racket (1), **racquet** ['rækit], *s.* der Tennisschläger.
racket (2) ['rækit], *s.* der Lärm (*noise, din*).
racket (3) ['rækit], *s.* (*coll.*) der Schwindel.
racketeer [ræki'tiə], *s.* der Schwindler.
racy ['reisi], *adj.* stark; pikant.
radar, ['reidɑ:], *s.* das Radar.
radiance ['reidiəns], *s.* der Glanz, das Strahlen.
radiant ['reidiənt], *adj.* strahlend.
radiate ['reidieit], *v.a.*, *v.n.* strahlen, ausstrahlen.
radiator ['reidieitə], *s.* der Heizapparat, Heizkörper; (*Motor.*) der Kühler.
radical ['rædikəl], *adj.* (*Pol.*) radikal; gründlich (*thorough*). — *s.* (*Pol.*) der Radikale; (*Phonet.*) der Grundlaut, Wurzellaut.
radio ['reidiou], *s.* das Radio, der Rundfunk.
radioactive [reidiou'æktiv], *adj.* radioaktiv.
radish ['rædiʃ], *s.* (*Bot.*) der Rettich.
radius ['reidiəs], *s.* der Radius, Halbmesser; (*Phys.*, *Maths.*) der Strahl (*line*).
raffle [ræfl], *s.* die Auslosung. — *v.a.* auslosen, ausspielen.
raft [rɑ:ft], *s.* das Floß.
rafter ['rɑ:ftə], *s.* der Dachsparren.
rag (1) [ræg], *s.* der Lumpen.
rag (2) [ræg], *v.a.* necken, zum Besten haben (*tease*).
ragamuffin ['rægəmʌfin], *s.* der Lumpenkerl.
rage [reidʒ], *s.* die Wut, Raserei; die Manie, Mode (*fashion*). — *v.n.* wüten, rasen.
ragged ['rægid], *adj.* zerlumpt; zackig, rauh (*rough*).
ragout [ra'gu:], *s.* (*Cul.*) das Ragout.
raid [reid], *s.* der Streifzug, die Razzia; der Angriff. — *v.a.* überfallen.
rail (1) [reil], *s.* (*Railw.*) die Schiene; *by* —, mit der Eisenbahn.
rail (2) [reil], *v.n.* schmähen; spotten (*Genit.*).
railing ['reiliŋ], *s.* das Geländer, Gitter.
raillery ['reiləri], *s.* die Spöttelei, das Schmähen.
railway, (*Am.*) **railroad** ['reilwei, 'reilroud], *s.* die Eisenbahn.
raiment ['reimənt], *s.* (*Poet.*) die Kleidung.
rain [rein], *s.* der Regen. — *v.n.* regnen.
rainbow ['reinbou], *s.* der Regenbogen.
raincoat ['reinkout], *s.* der Regenmantel.
raise [reiz], *v.a.* heben (lift); steigern (*prices*); aufbringen (*army*, *money*); züchten (*breed*); aufziehen (*children*). — *s.* (*Am.*) die Steigerung, Erhöhung (*salary*).
raisin ['reizin], *s.* (*Bot.*) die Rosine.
rake (1) [reik], *s.* der Rechen (*tool*). — *v.a.* zusammenrechen, harken; bestreichen (*fire at*).
rake (2) [reik], *s.* der Schlemmer (*roué*).
rakish ['reikiʃ], *adj.* liederlich.
rally ['ræli], *v.a.* sammeln, versammeln. — *v.n.* sich versammeln, sich scharen. — *s.* die Massenversammlung, Kundgebung; das Treffen.
ram [ræm], *s.* der Widder; (*Mil.*) die Ramme. — *v.a.* rammen.
ramble [ræmbl], *v.n.* (im Grünen) wandern; herumschweifen; einen Ausflug machen. — *s.* der Ausflug.
rambler ['ræmblə], *s.* der Wanderer (*hiker*); (*Bot.*) die Heckenrose.
ramification [ræmifi'keiʃən], *s.* die Verzweigung, Verästelung (*also fig.*); (*pl.*) Zweige, *m. pl.* (*also fig.*).
ramp [ræmp], *v.n.* sich ranken (*of plants*). — *s.* die Rampe.
rampant ['ræmpənt], *adj.* zügellos, grassierend (*wild*); (*Her.*) sich bäumend.
rampart ['ræmpɑ:t], *s.* der Wall.
ramshackle ['ræmʃækl], *adj.* wackelig, baufällig.
rancid ['rænsid], *adj.* ranzig.
rancour ['ræŋkə], *s.* der Groll, die Erbitterung.
random ['rændəm], *s.* *at* —, aufs Geratewohl. — *adj.* zufällig, Zufalls-.
range [reindʒ], *s.* die Reihe (*row, series*); (*Geog.*) die Bergkette; der Küchenherd (*stove*); (*Mil.*) die Schießstätte (*shooting ground*); die Schußweite, Reichweite (*distance*). — *v.n.* sich reihen; sich erstrecken (*stretch*). — *v.a.* rangieren, anordnen, durchstreifen.
rangefinder ['reindʒfaində], *s.* (*Phot.*) der Entfernungsmesser.
ranger ['reindʒə], *s.* der Förster, Forstgehilfe; (*Mil.*) der leichte Reiter.
rank (1) [ræŋk], *s.* die Klasse; der Rang (*order*); — *and file*, die Mannschaft (*of members*); die Mitgliedschaft, Masse. — *v.n.* sich reihen; gelten.
rank (2) [ræŋk], *adj.* übermäßig, üppig, allzu stark; ranzig (*of fat etc.*).
rankle [ræŋkl], *v.n.* nagen.
ransack ['rænsæk], *v.a.* plündern.
ransom ['rænsəm], *s.* das Lösegeld; *hold to* —, (gegen Lösegeld) gefangen halten. — *v.a.* loskaufen.

rant [rænt], *v.n.* wüten; großtun; großsprechen.
rap [ræp], *v.a., v.n.* schlagen, klopfen.
rapacious [rə'peiʃəs], *adj.* raubgierig.
rape (1) [reip], *v.a.* vergewaltigen. — *s.* die Vergewaltigung.
rape (2) [reip], *s.* (*Bot.*) der Raps.
rapid ['ræpid], *adj.* rasch, schnell, reißend (*river*). — *s.* (*pl.*) die Stromschnelle.
rapier ['reipiə], *s.* der Degen; (*fencing*) das Rapier.
rapine ['ræpain], *s.* (*Poet.*) der Raub.
rapt [ræpt], *adj.* entzückt; versunken.
rapture ['ræptʃə], *s.* das Entzücken.
rare (1) [rεə], *adj.* selten.
rare (2) [rεə], *adj.* (*meat*) rar.
rarity ['rεəriti], *s.* die Seltenheit.
rascal ['rɑ:skəl], *s.* der Schurke.
rash (1) [ræʃ], *adj.* unbesonnen.
rash (2) [ræʃ], *s.* der Ausschlag (*skin*).
rasher ['ræʃə], *s.* die Speckschnitte.
rasp [rɑ:sp], *s.* die Raspel, Feile. — *v.a., v.n.* raspeln; heiser sein (*speech*).
raspberry ['rɑ:zbəri], *s.* (*Bot.*) die Himbeere.
rat [ræt], *s.* (*Zool.*) die Ratte; (*fig.*) der Verräter.
ratable ['reitəbl], *adj.* steuerpflichtig.
rate (1) [reit], *s.* das Mass; der Tarif; die Geschwindigkeit (*speed*); Gemeindeabgabe (*tax*); das Verhältnis (*proportion*). — *v.a.* schätzen (*estimate*); (*Am.*) einschätzen, halten für.
rate (2) [reit], *v.a.* schelten (*berate*).
rather ['rɑ:ðə], *adv.* vielmehr, eher, lieber (*in comparisons*); — *good*, ziemlich gut.
ratification [rætifi'keiʃən], *s.* die Bestätigung; (*Pol.*) die Ratifizierung.
ratify ['rætifai], *v.a.* bestätigen; (*Pol.*) ratifizieren.
ratio ['reiʃiou], *s.* das Verhältnis.
ration ['ræʃən], *s.* die Ration.
rational ['ræʃənəl], *adj.* Vernunfts-, rationell, vernunftgemäß.
rattle [rætl], *s.* das Geklapper (*noise*); die Klapper (*toy etc.*); *death* —, das Todesröcheln. — *v.a.* klappern, Lärm machen; (*fig.*) aus der Fassung bringen; — *off*, herunterleiern. — *v.n.* rasseln, klappern.
raucous ['rɔ:kəs], *adj.* heiser, rauh.
ravage ['rævidʒ], *v.a.* verheeren. — *s.* (*pl.*) die Verheerung, Verwüstung.
rave [reiv], *v.n.* vernarrt sein (*about*, in); schwärmen (*für*).
raven [reivn], *s.* (*Orn.*) der Rabe.
ravenous ['rævənəs], *adj.* gefräßig, gierig.
ravine [rə'vi:n], *s.* die Schlucht.
ravish ['ræviʃ], *v.a.* schänden, entehren; (*delight*) entzücken.
raw [rɔ:], *adj.* rauh (*rough*); roh (*meat*); jung, grün (*novice*); *a* — *deal*, die unfaire Behandlung.
ray (1) [rei], *s.* (*Phys.*) der Strahl. — *v.n.* strahlen.
ray (2) [rei], *s.* (*Zool.*) der Rochen.
raze [reiz], *v.a.* radieren (*erase*); zerstören (*destroy*).
razor ['reizə], *s.* der Rasierapparat; — *strop*, der Streichriemen.
re* [ri:], *pref.* wieder —, noch einmal, zurück-.

* In the following pages, only those compounds are listed in which the meaning is different from the root word or where no simple stem exists.

reach [ri:tʃ], *v.a.* reichen, erlangen (*attain*); reichen (*hand*); erreichen. — *s.* der Bereich, (*fig.*) die Weite.
react [ri'ækt], *v.n.* reagieren (*to*, auf, *Acc.*).
read (1) [ri:d], *v.a., v.n. irr.* lesen; anzeigen (*meter etc.*); — *for a degree*, studieren.
read (2) [red], *adj. well*—, belesen.
readable ['ri:dəbl], *adj.* gut zu lesen, lesenswert; leserlich (*legible*).
reader ['ri:də], *s.* der Leser; (*Univ.*) der außerordentliche Professor; (*fig.*) das Lesebuch.
readiness ['redinis], *s.* die Bereitschaft, Bereitwilligkeit.
ready ['redi], *adj.* bereit, fertig; prompt; — *money*, das Bargeld.
real [riəl], *adj.* wirklich, wahr, tatsächlich; echt; — *estate*, der Grundbesitz.
realistic [riə'listik], *adj.* realistisch.
reality [ri'æliti], *s.* die Wirklichkeit.
realize ['riəlaiz], *v.a.* (*understand*) begreifen; (*sell*) veräußern; verwirklichen.
realm [relm], *s.* das Reich.
reap [ri:p], *v.a.* ernten.
rear (1) [riə], *adj.* hinter, nach-. — *s.* der Hintergrund; (*Mil.*) die Nachhut.
rear (2) [riə], *v.a.* aufziehen, erziehen (*bring up*). — *v.n.* sich bäumen.
reason ['ri:zən], *s.* die Ursache, der Grund (*cause*); die Vernunft (*reasonableness*). — *v.n.* argumentieren, debattieren.
reasonable ['ri:zənəbl], *adj.* vernünftig; verständig.
reasonably ['ri:zənəbli], *adv.* ziemlich, verhältnismäßig.
rebate ['ri:beit], *s.* der Rabatt.
rebel [rebl], *s.* der Rebell. — [ri'bel], *v.n.* sich empören.
rebound [ri:'baund], *v.n.* zurückprallen. —['ri:baund], *s.* der Rückprall.
rebuff [ri'bʌf], *s.* die Abweisung. — *v.a.* abweisen, zurückweisen.
rebuke [ri'bju:k], *v.a.* zurechtweisen, tadeln. — *s.* der Tadel, die Kritik (an).
rebut [ri'bʌt], *v.a.* zurückweisen.
rebuttal [ri'bʌtl], *s.* die Widerlegung.
recalcitrant [ri'kælsitrənt], *adj.* widerspenstig, störrisch.
recall [ri'kɔ:l], *v.a.* zurückrufen; (*remember*) sich erinnern.
recant [ri'kænt], *v.a., v.n.* widerrufen.
recapitulate [ri:kə'pitjuleit], *v.a.* rekapitulieren, wiederholen.
recast [ri:'kɑ:st], *v.a.* neu fassen, umarbeiten.
recede [ri'si:d], *v.n.* zurückgehen; heruntergehen (*prices etc.*).

receipt [ri'si:t], *s.* die Empfangsbestätigung, Quittung. — *v.a.* quittieren.
receive [ri'si:v], *v.a.* erhalten, empfangen; (*Law*) Diebesgut annehmen.
receiver [ri'si:və], *s.* der Empfänger; (*Law*) der Hehler; (*Telephone*) der Hörer; (*Rad.*) der Apparat.
recent ['ri:sənt], *adj.* jüngst, neuest.
recently ['ri:səntli], *adv.* vor kurzem.
reception [ri'sepʃən], *s.* der Empfang.
receptive [ri'septiv], *adj.* empfänglich.
recess [ri'ses], *s.* (*Parl.*) die Ferien, *pl.*; die Pause; die Nische (*nook*).
recession [ri'seʃən], *s.* (*Econ.*) die Rezession, die Baisse.
recipe ['resipi], *s.* (*Cul.*) das Rezept.
recipient [ri'sipiənt], *s.* der Empfänger (*of donation etc.*).
reciprocal [ri'siprəkəl], *adj.* gegenseitig, wechselseitig.
reciprocate [ri'siprəkeit], *v.a.*, *v.n.* erwidern, vergelten.
recital [ri'saitl], *s.* der Vortrag; (*Mus.*) das Solokonzert, Kammerkonzert.
recite [ri'sait], *v.a.* vortragen; (*story*) erzählen, aufsagen.
reckless ['reklis], *adj.* leichtsinnig.
reckon ['rekən], *v.n.* rechnen (*on*, mit, *Dat.*); dafür halten, denken (*think*).
reclamation [reklə'meiʃən], *s.* (*Agr.*) die Urbarmachung; (*fig.*) die Beschwerde, Reklamation.
recline [ri'klain], *v.n.* sich zurücklehnen.
recluse [ri'klu:s], *s.* der Einsiedler.
recognition [rekəg'niʃən], *s.* die Anerkennung.
recognize ['rekəgnaiz], *v.a.* anerkennen (als) (*acknowledge*); erkennen (*know again*).
recoil [ri'kɔil], *v.n.* zurückprallen, zurückfahren.
recollect [rekə'lekt], *v.a.* sich erinnern (an, *Acc.*).
recollection [rekə'lekʃən], *s.* die Erinnerung, das Gedächtnis.
recommend [rekə'mend], *v.a.* empfehlen.
recompense ['rekəmpens], *v.a.* vergelten, entschädigen, belohnen.
reconcile ['rekənsail], *v.a.* versöhnen.
reconciliation [rekənsili'eiʃən], *s.* die Versöhnung.
recondite ['rekəndait], *adj.* dunkel, verborgen, wenig bekannt.
reconnoitre [rekə'nɔitə], *v.a.* auskundschaften.
record [ri'kɔ:d], *v.a.* notieren, eintragen (*enter*), festhalten; aufnehmen (*tape etc.*). — ['rekɔ:d], *s.* die Aufzeichnung (*in writing*); die Schallplatte (*gramophone*); (*Sports*) der Rekord.
recorder [ri'kɔ:də], *s.* der Protokollführer; (*Law*) der Richter; Syndikus, Registrator; (*Mus.*) die Blockflöte.
recount [ri'kaunt], *v.a.* erzählen
recourse [ri'kɔ:s], *s.* die Zuflucht.
recover [ri'kʌvə], *v.a.* wiedererlangen. — *v.n.* sich erholen.
recovery [ri'kʌvəri], *s.* die Wiedererlangung (*regaining*); (*Med.*) die Genesung, Erholung.
recreation [rekri'eiʃən], *s.* die Erholung.
recrimination [rekrimi'neiʃən], *s.* die Gegenklage.
recruit [ri'kru:t], *v.a.* rekrutieren, anwerben. — *s.* der Rekrut.
rectangle ['rektæŋgl], *s.* das Rechteck.
rectify ['rektifai], *v.a.* richtigstellen; (*Elec.*) gleichrichten, umformen.
rectilinear [rekti'liniə], *adj.* geradlinig.
rectitude ['rektitju:d], *s.* die Aufrichtigkeit.
rector ['rektə], *s.* (*Eccl.*) der Pfarrer; der Rektor, Vorstand (*institution*).
recuperate [ri'kju:pəreit], *v.n.* sich erholen.
recur [ri'kə:], *v.n.* sich wieder ereignen, sich wiederholen.
recurrence [ri'kʌrəns], *s.* die Wiederholung.
red [red], *adj.* rot; — *hot*, glühend heiß.
redbreast ['redbrest], *s.* (*Orn.*) das Rotkehlchen.
redeem [ri'di:m], *v.a.* erlösen.
redemption [ri'dempʃən], *s.* die Erlösung.
redolent ['redolənt], *adj.* duftend.
redound [ri'daund], *v.n.* gereichen, sich erweisen.
redress [ri'dres], *v.a.* abhelfen (*Dat.*); wieder herstellen. — *s.* die Abhilfe.
reduce [ri'dju:s], *v.a.* vermindern, herabsetzen; (*fig.*) degradieren. — *v.n.* (*weight*) abnehmen.
reduction [ri'dʌkʃən], *s.* die Herabsetzung (*price etc.*); die Verminderung (*decrease*); (*Chem.*) die Reduktion.
redundant [ri'dʌndənt], *adj.* überflüssig.
reduplicate [ri:'dju:plikeit], *v.a.* verdoppeln.
reed [ri:d], *s.* (*Bot.*) das Schilfrohr; (*Mus.*) die Rohrpfeife.
reef [ri:f], *s.* das Riff, Felsenriff; (*Naut.*) das Reff.
reek [ri:k], *v.n.* rauchen, dampfen, riechen. — *s.* der Rauch, Dampf, der Gestank.
reel [ri:l], *s.* die Spule, Rolle, Haspel. — *v.a.* — *off*, abrollen; (*fig.*) mechanisch hersagen. — *v.n.* taumeln.
refectory [ri'fektəri], *s.* der Speisesaal; das Refektorium (*in monastery etc.*).
refer [ri'fə:], *v.n.* — *to s.th.*, weiterleiten; überweisen; — *to*, sich beziehen (auf, *Acc.*).
referee [refə'ri:], *s.* der Referent; (*Sport*) der Schiedsrichter.
reference ['refərəns], *s. with* — *to*, in *or* mit Bezug auf; die Referenz, Empfehlung; Verweisung (*to*, auf); — *library*, die Nachschlagebibliothek; — *index*, das (Nachschlags)verzeichnis.
refine [ri'fain], *v.a.* (*Chem.*) raffinieren; (*manners*) verfeinern; (*products*) läutern, veredeln.

reflect [ri'flekt], *v.a.* widerspiegeln (*mirror*); ein Licht werfen (auf, *Acc.*). — *v.n.* — *on*, überlegen (*think over*).
reflection, reflexion [ri'flekʃən], *s.* die Überlegung, das Nachdenken; die Spiegelung, Reflexion.
reform [ri:'fɔ:m], *s.* die Reform, Verbesserung. — *v.a.* reformieren; ['ri:'fɔ:m] (sich) neu bilden. — *v.n.* sich bessern.
refractory [ri'fræktəri], *adj.* widerspenstig.
refrain (1) [ri'frein], *v.n.* — *from*, sich enthalten (*Genit.*); absehen von (*Dat.*).
refrain (2) [ri'frein], *s.* (*Mus.*, *Poet.*) der Kehrreim.
refresh [ri'freʃ], *v.a.* erfrischen.
refrigerator [ri'fridʒəreitə], *s.* der Kühlschrank.
refuge ['refju:dʒ], *s.* die Zuflucht.
refugee [refju'dʒi:], *s.* der Flüchtling. — *adj.* Flüchtlings-.
refund [ri:'fʌnd], *v.a.* ersetzen, zurückzahlen. — ['ri:fʌnd], *s.* die Rückvergütung.
refusal [ri'fju:zəl], *s.* die Verweigerung.
refuse [ri'fju:z], *v.a.* verweigern, abschlagen. — *v.n.* — *to*, sich weigern. — ['refju:s], *s.* der Müll.
refute [ri'fju:t], *v.a.* widerlegen.
regal ['ri:gəl], *adj.* königlich.
regale [ri'geil], *v.a.* bewirten.
regalia [ri'geiliə], *s. pl.* die Kronjuwelen, *n. pl.*; (*fig.*) die Amtstracht, der Amtsschmuck.
regard [ri'gɑ:d], *v.a.* ansehen (*as*, als); beachten (*heed*); *as* —*s*, was ... betrifft. — *s.* die Hochachtung, Achtung (*esteem*);(*pl.*)die Grüsse,*m.pl.*
regarding [ri'gɑ:diŋ], *prep.* bezüglich, mit Bezug auf.
regardless [ri'gɑ:dlis], *adj.* rücksichtslos, ohne Rüchsicht auf.
regency ['ri:dʒənsi], *s.* die Regentschaft.
regent ['ri:dʒənt], *s.* der Regent.
regiment ['redʒimənt], *s.* (*Mil.*) das Regiment. — [-ment], *v.a.* (*fig.*) regimentieren.
region ['ri:dʒən], *s.* die Gegend.
regional ['ri:dʒənəl], *adj.* örtlich, lokal, Bezirks-.
register ['redʒistə], *s.* das Register, die Liste. — *v.n.* sich eintragen.
registrar ['redʒistrɑ:], *s.* der Registrator; der Standesbeamte (*births etc.*); der Kanzleidirektor (*institution*).
registry ['redʒistri], *s.* die Registratur.
regret [ri'gret], *v.a.* bereuen, bedauern. — *s.* die Reue; das Bedauern (*in formal apology*); *with* —, mit Bedauern.
regular ['regjulə], *adj.* regelmäßig; (*Am.*) anständig. — *s.* (*Mil.*) der Berufssoldat.
regulate ['regjuleit], *v.a.* regulieren, regeln.
regulation [regju'leiʃən], *s.* die Regelung; die Anordung (*order*).
rehabilitate [ri:hə'biliteit], *v.a.* rehabilitieren.
rehearsal [ri'hə:sl], *s.* (*Theat.*, *Mus.*) die Probe.
rehearse [ri'hə:s], *v.a.* proben, wiederholen.
reign [rein], *v.n.* herrschen, regieren. — *s.* die Herrschaft, Regierung.
rein [rein], *s.* der Zügel, der Zaum.
reindeer ['reindiə], *s.* (*Zool.*) das Ren, Rentier.
reinforce [ri:in'fɔ:s], *v.a.* betonen, verstärken.
reinforced [ri:in'fɔ:sd], *adj.* verstärkt; — *concrete*, der Eisenbeton.
reject [ri'dʒekt], *v.a.* ausschlagen, verwerfen.
rejection [ri'dʒekʃən], *s.* die Ablehnung, Verwerfung.
rejoice [ri'dʒɔis], *v.n.* sich freuen.
rejoin ['ri:'dʒɔin], *v.a.* wiedervereinigen. — [ri'dʒɔin], *v.n.* erwidern.
rejoinder [ri'dʒɔində], *s.* die Erwiderung.
relapse [ri'læps], *s.* der Rückfall. — *v.n.* fallen, zurückfallen.
relation [ri'leiʃən], *s.* die Beziehung (*connexion*); der, die Verwandte (*relative*); (*pl.*) die Verwandtschaft (*family*).
relative ['relətiv], *adj.* relativ; verhältnismäßig (*in proportion*). — *s.* der, die Verwandte.
relax [ri'læks], *v.n.* sich ausruhen; nachlassen. — *v.a.* entspannen.
relay [ri'lei], *v.a.* (*Rad.*) übertragen. — ['ri:lei], *s.* — *race*, der Staffellauf.
release [ri'li:s], *v.a.* freilassen, freisetzen (*prisoner*); freigeben (*news*). — *s.* die Freigabe (*news etc.*); die Freisetzung (*liberation*).
relegate ['religeit], *v.a.* verweisen, zurückweisen.
relent [ri'lent], *v.n.* nachgeben.
relentless [ri'lentlis], *adj.* unerbittlich, unnachgiebig.
relevance ['reləvəns], *s.* die Wichtigkeit.
relevant ['reləvənt], *adj.* wichtig, sachdienlich.
reliable [ri'laiəbl], *adj.* verläßlich, zuverlässig.
reliance [ri'laiəns], *s.* das Vertrauen.
relic ['relik], *s.* das Überbleibsel; das Andenken; (*Eccl.*) die Reliquie.
relief (1) [ri'li:f], *s.* die Erleichterung, Linderung, (*easement*); die Ablösung (*guard etc.*); die Aushilfe (*extra staff etc.*).
relief (2) [ri'li:f], *s.* (*Art*) das Relief.
relieve [ri'li:v], *v.a.* erleichtern; lindern (*pain*); ablösen (*from duty*).
religion [ri'lidʒən], *s.* die Religion.
religious [ri'lidʒəs], *adj.* religiös, gläubig, fromm.
relinquish [ri'liŋkwiʃ], *v.a.* verlassen, aufgeben.

relish ['reliʃ], *v.a.* Geschmack finden an. — *v.n.* schmecken. — *s.* der Geschmack, die Würze.
reluctance [ri'lʌktəns], *s.* der Widerwille, das Zögern.
reluctant [ri'lʌktənt], *adj.* widerwillig, widerstrebend.
rely [ri'lai], *v.n.* sich verlassen (*on*, auf); vertrauen (auf).
remain [ri'mein], *v.n.* bleiben, zurückbleiben, übrigbleiben.
remainder [ri'meində], *s.* der Rest.
remand [ri'mɑ:nd], *v.a.* — *in custody*, in die Untersuchungshaft zurückschicken. — *s.* — *home*, die Besserungsanstalt.
remark [ri'mɑ:k], *s.* die Bemerkung. — *v.a.* bemerken.
remarkable [ri'mɑ:kəbl], *adj.* bemerkenswert, außerordentlich.
remedial [rə'mi:diəl], *adj.* Heil-, abhelfend.
remedy ['remədi], *s.* das Heilmittel, Hilfsmittel. — *v.a.* abhelfen (*Dat.*).
remember [ri'membə], *v.a.* sich erinnern an; — *s.o. to s.o. else*, jemanden von jemandem grüßen lassen.
remembrance [ri'membrəns], *s.* die Erinnerung.
remind [ri'maind], *v.a.* erinnern (*of*, an), mahnen.
reminiscence [remi'nisəns], *s.* die Erinnerung.
remiss [ri'mis], *adj.* nachlässig.
remission [ri'miʃən], *s.* der Nachlaß; (*Rel.*) die Vergebung (*of sins*).
remit [ri'mit], *v.a.* (*Comm.*) überweisen, einsenden; erlassen (*forgive*).
remittance [ri'mitəns], *s.* (*Comm.*) die Rimesse, die Überweisung.
remnant ['remnənt], *s.* der Überrest.
remonstrate ['remənstreit], *v.n.* Vorstellungen machen.
remorse [ri'mɔ:s], *s.* die Reue.
remote [ri'mout], *adj.* fern, entlegen.
removal [ri'mu:vəl], *s.* das Wegschaffen (*taking away*); die Übersiedlung, der Umzug.
remove [ri'mu:v], *v.a.* entfernen. — *v.n.* umziehen. — *s.* (*Sch.*) die Versetzungsklasse; der Verwandtschaftsgrad (*relationship*).
removed [ri'mu:vd], *adj.* entfernt; *cousin once* —, der Vetter ersten Grades.
remuneration [rimju:nə'reiʃən], *s.* die Besoldung, Entlöhnung.
rend [rend], *v.a.* reißen, zerreißen.
render ['rendə], *v.a.* leisten (*service*); übersetzen (*translate*); wiedergeben; (*Comm.*) — *account*, Rechnung vorlegen.
rendering ['rendəriŋ], *s.* die Wiedergabe, der Vortrag (*of song etc.*); (*Comm.*) die Vorlage; die Übersetzung (*translation*).
renegade ['renigeid], *s.* der Abtrünnige.
renewal [ri'nju:əl], *s.* die Erneuerung; die Verlängerung (*extension*).
rennet ['renit], *s.* das Lab.
renounce [ri'nauns], *v.a.* entsagen (*Dat.*), verzichten auf (*Acc.*).
renown [ri'naun], *s.* der Ruhm.
rent (1) [rent], *v.a.* mieten, pachten. — *s.* die Miete, Pacht (*of land, farm*).
rent (2) [rent], *s.* der Riß (*tear*).
rental [rentl], *s.* die Miete.
renunciation [rinʌnsi'eiʃən], *s.* die Entsagung, der Verzicht.
repair [ri'pɛə], *v.a.* ausbessern, reparieren. — *s.* die Reparatur; *beyond* —, nicht reparierbar.
reparations [repə'reiʃənz], *s. pl.* (*Pol.*) die Reparationen, Wiedergutmachungskosten, *f. pl.*
repartee [repɑ:'ti:], *s.* die treffende Antwort.
repast [ri'pɑ:st], *s.* die Mahlzeit.
repeal [ri'pi:l], *v.a.* (*Parl.*) aufheben, widerrufen. — *s.* die Aufhebung.
repeat [ri'pi:t], *v.a.* wiederholen.
repent [ri'pent], *v.a.* bereuen.
repercussion [ri:pə'kʌʃən], *s.* der Rückstoß, die Rückwirkung.
repertory ['repətəri], *s.* (*Theat. etc.*) das Repertoire, der Spielplan.
repetition [repi'tiʃən], *s.* die Wiederholung.
replace [ri:'pleis], *v.a.* ersetzen.
replete [ri'pli:t], *adj.* voll, angefüllt.
reply [ri'plai], *v.n.* antworten, erwidern. — *s.* die Antwort.
report [ri'pɔ:t], *v.a.*, *v.n.* berichten. — *s.* der Bericht; (*Sch.*) das Zeugnis; der Knall (*of explosion*).
repose [ri'pouz], *v.n.* ruhen. — *v.a.* setzen (*in*, auf). — *s.* die Ruhe, der Friede.
repository [ri'pɔzitəri], *s.* die Niederlage, Aufbewahrungsstätte, Fundstätte.
reprehensible [repri'hensibl], *adj.* tadelnswert.
represent [repri'zent], *v.a.* repräsentieren, vertreten.
representative [repri'zentətiv], *adj.* repräsentativ, typisch. — *s.* der Stellvertreter; (*Pol.*) der Repräsentant.
repress [ri'pres], *v.a.* unterdrücken.
reprieve [ri'pri:v], *v.a.* begnadigen. — *s.* die Gnadenfrist.
reprimand [repri'mɑ:nd], *v.a.* verweisen, tadeln. — *s.* der Tadel.
reprint [ri:'print], *v.a.* neu drucken. — ['ri:print], *s.* der Neudruck.
reprisal [ri'praizəl], *s.* die Vergeltungsmaßregel; (*pl.*) die Repressalien, *f. pl.*
reproach [ri'proutʃ], *v.a.* vorwerfen (*Dat.*), tadeln. — *s.* der Vorwurf, Tadel.
reprobate ['reprəbeit], *adj.* ruchlos, verworfen.
reproduce [ri:prə'dju:s], *v.a.* reproduzieren, erzeugen.
reproof [ri'pru:f], *s.* der Vorwurf, Tadel.
reprove [ri'pru:v], *v.a.* tadeln, rügen (*a person*), mißbilligen (*a practice*).

republic [ri'pʌblik], *s.* die Republik.
repudiate [ri'pju:dieit], *v.a.* zurückweisen, verwerfen.
repugnant [ri'pʌgnənt], *adj.* widerwärtig, ekelhaft.
repulse [ri'pʌls], *v.a.* (*Mil.*) zurückschlagen; abweisen (*s.o.*). — *s.* (*Mil.*) das Zurückschlagen; (*fig.*) die Zurückweisung.
repulsive [ri'pʌlsiv], *adj.* widerwärtig.
reputation [repju'teiʃən], *s.* der (gute) Ruf.
request [ri'kwest], *v.a.* ersuchen. — *s.* das Ersuchen, Ansuchen, die Bitte.
requiem ['rekwiəm], *s.* (*Eccl.*) das Requiem, die Totenmesse.
require [ri'kwaiə], *v.a.* fordern, verlangen, brauchen.
requirement [ri'kwaiəmənt], *s.* die Anforderung, das Erfordernis.
requisite ['rekwizit], *adj.* erforderlich.
requisition [rekwi'ziʃən], *s.* (*Mil.*) die Requisition; die Forderung.
requite [ri'kwait], *v.a.* vergelten.
rescind [ri'sind], *v.a.* für ungültig erklären, aufheben.
rescue ['reskju:], *v.a.* retten. — *s.* die Rettung.
research [ri'sə:tʃ], *v.n.* forschen, Forschung treiben. — *s.* die Forschung.
resemble [ri'zembl], *v.a.* ähnlich sein (*Dat.*), gleichen (*Dat.*).
resent [ri'zent], *v.a.* übelnehmen.
resentful [ri'zentful], *adj.* nachträgerisch; empfindlich (*over-sensitive*).
resentment [ri'zentmənt], *s.* die Empfindlichkeit; der Groll (*spite*).
reservation [rezə'veiʃən], *s.* die Reservierung (*of seat*); der Vorbehalt (*doubt*).
reserve [ri'zə:v], *v.a.* reservieren, belegen (*seat*); (*fig.*) vorbehalten (*o.'s position*). — *s.* die Reserve, die Verschlossenheit (*shyness*); die Einschränkung (*limitation*); die Reserven, *f. pl.* (*money*).
reside [ri'zaid], *v.n.* wohnen.
resident ['rezidənt], *adj.* wohnhaft. — *s.* der Ansässige.
residual [ri'zidjuəl], *adj.* übrig bleibend.
residue ['rezidju:], *s.* der Rückstand, Rest.
resign [ri'zain], *v.a.* abtreten, aufgeben; (ein Amt) niederlegen. — *v.n.* abdanken. — *v.r.* — *o.s. to*, sich in etwas fügen, zurücktreten.
resignation [rezig'neiʃən], *s.* die Resignation, der Rücktritt (*from office*); die Fügung, Resignation (*attitude*).
resin ['rezin], *s.* das Harz.
resist [ri'zist], *v.a.*, *v.n.* widerstehen, Widerstand leisten (*Dat.*).
resistance [ri'zistəns], *s.* der Widerstand.
resolute ['rezəlju:t], *adj.* entschlossen.
resolution [rezə'lju:ʃən], *s.* die Entschlossenheit (*determination*); die Entscheidung (*decision*); der Vorsatz, Entschluß (*vow*).
resolve [ri'zɔlv], *v.a.* auflösen (*solve*); beschließen (*conclude*). — *v.n.* entscheiden (*decide*). — *s.* der Beschluß, die Entscheidung.
resonance ['rezənəns], *s.* die Resonanz.
resort [ri'zɔ:t], *v.n.* — *to*, seine Zuflucht nehmen (zu). — *s. seaside* —, das Seebad, *health* —, der Kurort (*spa*).
resound [ri'zaund], *v.n.* widerhallen.
resource [ri'sɔ:s], *s.* das Hilfsmittel; (*pl.*) die Mittel, *n. pl.*
respect [ri'spekt], *v.a.* respektieren, achten; berücksichtigen (*have regard to*). — *s.* der Respekt, die Achtung; *with* — *to*, mit Bezug auf; *in* — *of*, bezüglich (*Genit.*).
respectability [rispektə'biliti], *s.* die Anständigkeit; Achtbarkeit.
respective [ris'pektiv], *adj.* respektiv.
respectively [ris'pektivli], *adv.* beziehungsweise.
respiration [respi'reiʃən], *s.* die Atmung.
respiratory [ris'paiərətri *or* 'respireitəri], *adj.* Atmungs-.
respire [ri'spaiə], *v.n.* atmen.
respite ['respit], *s.* die Frist, der Aufschub.
resplendent [ri'splendənt], *adj.* glänzend.
respond [ri'spɔnd], *v.n.* antworten, eingehen (*to*, auf).
respondent [ri'spɔndənt], *s.* (*Law*) der Beklagte.
response [ri'spɔns], *s.* die Antwort, Aufnahme, Reaktion; (*fig.*) der Widerhall.
responsibility [rispɔnsi'biliti], *s.* die Verantwortung, Verantwortlichkeit.
responsible [ri'spɔnsibl], *adj.* verantwortlich.
responsive [ri'spɔnsiv], *adj.* empfänglich, zugänglich.
rest (1) [rest], *v.n.* ruhen, rasten. — *s.* die Ruhe, Rast; (*Mus.*) die Pause.
rest (2) [rest], *v.n.* bleiben (*stay*); — *assured*, sei (seien Sie) versichert. — *s.* der Rest; die übrigen, *pl.*
restaurant ['restərɔ̃], *s.* das Restaurant.
restful ['restful], *adj.* ruhig.
restitution [resti'tju:ʃən], *s.* die Wiedergutmachung.
restive ['restiv], *adj.* unruhig, ruhelos.
restless ['restlis], *adj.* rastlos, unruhig.
restoration [restɔ:'reiʃən], *s.* die Wiederherstellung; (*Hist.*) die Restauration.
restore [ri'stɔ:], *v.a.* wiederherstellen.
restrain [ri'strein], *v.a.* zurückhalten, einschränken.
restraint [ri'streint], *s.* die Zurückhaltung.
restrict [ri'strikt], *v.a.* beschränken.
restriction [ri'strikʃən], *s.* die Einschränkung.
restrictive [ri'striktiv], *adj.* einschränkend.

result [ri'zʌlt], *v.n.* folgen, sich ergeben; (*come about*) erfolgen. — *s.* das Ergebnis, Resultat; (*consequence*) die Folge.
resume [ri'zju:m], *v.a.* wiederaufnehmen; (*narrative*) fortsetzen. — *v.n.* fortfahren.
résumé ['rezjumei], *s.* das Resümee, die Zusammenfassung.
resumption [ri'zʌmpʃən], *s.* die Wiederaufnahme.
resurrection [rezə'rekʃən], *s.* (*Rel.*) die Auferstehung.
resuscitate [ri'sʌsiteit], *v.a.* wiederbeleben.
retail ['ri:teil], *s.* der Kleinhandel, Einzelhandel. — [ri'teil], *v.a.* im Detail handeln, verkaufen.
retain [ri'tein], *v.a.* behalten.
retainer [ri'teinə], *s.* der Diener; Gefolgsmann; der Vorschuß (*fee*).
retake [ri:'teik], *v.a. irr.* (*Mil.*) wieder erobern; (*Phot.*, *Film*) noch einmal aufnehmen. — *s.* (*Am.*) die Neuaufnahme (*Phot.*, *Film*).
retaliate [ri'tælieit], *v.n.* sich rächen, vergelten.
retard [ri'tɑ:d], *v.a.* verzögern, verlangsamen.
retch [retʃ], *v.n.* sich erbrechen.
retentive [ri'tentiv], *adj.* behaltend, gut (*memory*).
reticent ['retisənt], *adj.* schweigsam, einsilbig.
retina ['retinə], *s.* (*Anat.*) die Netzhaut.
retinue ['retinju:], *s.* das Gefolge.
retire [ri'taiə], *v.n.* sich zurückziehen (*withdraw*); in den Ruhestand treten (*from work*). — *v.a.* pensionieren.
retirement [ri'taiəmənt], *s.* die Pension, der Ruhestand; die Zurückgezogenheit (*seclusion*).
retort [ri'tɔ:t], *s.* (*Chem.*) die Retorte; die scharfe Antwort (*debate*). — *v.n.* scharf erwidern.
retouch [ri:'tʌtʃ], *v.a.* (*Phot.*) retouchieren.
retrace [ri:'treis], *v.a.* zurückverfolgen.
retreat [ri'tri:t], *v.n.* sich zurückziehen. — *s.* der Rückzug (*Mil.*); Zufluchtsort.
retrench [ri'trentʃ], *v.a.* einschränken (*restrict*); verkürzen (*shorten*). — *v.n.* sich einschränken.
retribution [retri'bju:ʃən], *s.* die Vergeltung.
retrieve [ri'tri:v], *v.a.* wieder bekommen, wieder gewinnen.
retriever [ri'tri:və], *s.* (*Zool.*) der Apportierhund, Stöberhund.
retrograde ['retrogreid], *adj.* rückgängig, rückwärts.
retrospect ['retrospekt], *s.* der Rückblick.
retrospective [retro'spektiv], *adj.* rückblickend.
return [ri'tə:n], *v.a.* zurückgeben; erwidern (*reciprocate*); abordnen, entsenden (*to Parl.*); (*figures*) einsenden. — *v.n.* zurückkehren, zurückkommen. — *s.* die Rückkehr; (*Fin.*) der Gewinn; (*Parl.*) die Entsendung, Mandatierung; (*pl.*) (*figures*) die Einsendung; *by — of post*, umgehend, postwendend; — *ticket*, die Rückfahrkarte.
reunion [ri:'ju:niən], *s.* die Wiedervereinigung.
reveal [ri'vi:l], *v.a.* enthüllen, offenbaren (*show*); verraten (*betray*).
reveille [ri'væli], *s.* (*Mil.*) das Wecken, Wecksignal.
revel [revl], *v.n.* schwelgen.
revelation [revə'leiʃən], *s.* die Offenbarung.
revelry ['revəlri], *s.* die Schwelgerei.
revenge [ri'vendʒ], *s.* die Rache, Revanche. — *v.r.* (also *be revenged*) sich rächen (*on*, an, *Dat.*).
revenue ['revənju:], *s.* das Einkommen; *Inland* —, die Steuereinnahmen.
reverberate [ri'və:bəreit], *v.n.* widerhallen.
revere [ri'viə], *v.a.* verehren.
reverence ['revərəns], *s.* die Ehrerbietung, der Respekt; *show* —, Ehrerbietung zollen.
Reverend ['revərənd]. (*abbr.* **Rev.**) (*Eccl.*) *The* —, Seine Ehrwürden; *The Very* —, Seine Hochwürden.
reverent, reverential ['revərənt, revə'renʃəl], *adj.* ehrerbietig.
reverie ['revəri], *s.* die Träumerei.
reversal [ri'və:səl], *s.* die Umkehrung, Umstoßung.
reverse [ri'və:s], *v.a.*, *v.n.* umkehren, umdrehen. — *s.* das Gegenteil (*contrary*); die Kehrseite (*of coin*).
revert [ri'və:t], *v.a.*, *v.n.* umkehren, zurückkehren.
review [ri'vju:], *v.a.* durchsehen, prüfen (*examine*); rezensieren (*book etc.*). — *s.* die Revision; (*Mil.*) die Parade, Truppenmusterung; die Rezension, Besprechung (*book etc.*).
revile [ri'vail], *v.a.*, *v.n.* schmähen.
revise [ri'vaiz], *v.a.* korrigieren (*correct*); wiederholen (*recapitulate*); umarbeiten (*modify*).
revision [ri'viʒən], *s.* die Revision; Korrektur; Umarbeitung; Wiederholung (*recapitulation*).
revolt [ri'voult], *v.n.* sich empören, revoltieren. — *v.a.* empören. — *s.* die Empörung.
revolting [ri'voultiŋ], *adj.* ekelhaft, empörend.
revolution [revə'lju:ʃən], *s.* (*Pol.*) die Revolution; (*Motor.*) die Umdrehung.
revolve [ri'vɔlv], *v.n.* rotieren, sich drehen.
revolver [ri'vɔlvə], *s.* der Revolver.
revue [ri'vju:], *s.* (*Theat.*) die Revue.
revulsion [ri'vʌlʃən], *s.* der Ekel; der Umschwung.
reward [ri'wɔ:d], *v.a.* belohnen (*person*); vergelten (*deed*). — *s.* die Belohnung.
rheumatic [ru:'mætik], *adj.* (*Med.*) rheumatisch.

rheumatism ['ru:mətizm], *s.* (*Med.*) der Rheumatismus.
rhetoric ['retərik], *s.* die Redekunst.
Rhodesian [ro'di:ʃən, -'di:ʒən], *adj.* rhodesisch. — *s.* der Rhodesier.
rhododendron [roudo'dendrən], *s.* (*Bot.*) die Alpenrose.
rhubarb ['ru:ba:b], *s.* (*Bot.*) der Rhabarber.
rhyme [raim], *s.* der Reim; *no — nor reason*, sinnlos.
rhythm [riðm], *s.* der Rhythmus.
rib [rib], *s.* (*Anat.*) die Rippe.
ribald ['ribəld], *adj.* liederlich; (*joke*) unanständig.
ribbon ['ribən], *s.* das Band.
rice [rais], *s.* der Reis.
rich [ritʃ], *adj.* reich; fruchtbar (*fertile*).
rick [rik], *s.* der Schober.
rickets ['rikits], *s.* (*Med.*) die englische Krankheit, die Rachitis.
rickety ['rikiti], *adj.* gebrechlich, wackelig, baufällig.
rid [rid], *v.a. irr.* befreien, freimachen (*of*, von); — *o.s.*, sich entledigen (*of*, *Genit.*); *get — of*, loswerden (*Acc.*); *be — of*, los sein (*Acc.*).
riddance ['ridəns], *s.* die Befreiung, das Loswerden.
riddle (1) [ridl], *s.* das Rätsel (*puzzle*).
riddle (2) [ridl], *s.* das grobe Sieb (*sieve*). — *v.a.* sieben (*sieve*); durchlöchern.
ride [raid], *v.a.*, *v.n. irr.* reiten (*on horse*), fahren (*on bicycle etc.*); — *at anchor*, vor Anker liegen. — *s.* der Ritt (*on horse*), die Fahrt (*in vehicle*).
rider ['raidə], *s.* der Reiter (*horseman*); der Fahrer (*cyclist etc.*); der Zusatz (*addition*).
ridge [ridʒ], *s.* der Rücken (*edge*); die Bergkette; die Furche (*furrow*). — *v.a.* furchen.
ridicule ['ridikju:l], *s.* der Spott. — *v.a.* lächerlich machen.
ridiculous [ri'dikjuləs], *adj.* lächerlich.
rife [raif], *adj.* häufig, weitverbreitet.
rifle (1) [raifl], *s.* die Büchse, das Gewehr.
rifle (2) [raifl], *v.a.* ausplündern.
rift [rift], *s.* der Riß, Spalt, die Spalte. — *v.a.* spalten.
rig [rig], *s.* (*Naut.*) die Takelung; (*fig.*) —*-out*, die Ausstattung. — *v.a.* (*Naut.*) (auf)takeln; (*Am.*) fälschen (*fake*); — *out*, ausstatten.
right [rait], *adj.* recht; richtig; wahr; gesund; korrekt; — *hand*, rechtsseitig; *you are* —, Sie haben recht; *that's* —, das stimmt. — *s.* das Recht; *by right(s)*, rechtmäßig; *drive on the* —, rechts fahren.
righteous ['raitʃəs], *adj.* rechtschaffen, aufrecht.
rightful ['raitful], *adj.* rechtmäßig.
rigid ['ridʒid], *adj.* steif; unbeugsam; streng (*severe*).
rigidity [ri'dʒiditi], *s.* die Steifheit, Unnachgiebigkeit; die Strenge.
rigmarole ['rigməroul], *s.* die Salbaderei, das Gewäsch.
rigorous ['rigərəs], *adj.* streng; genau.
rigour ['rigə], *s.* die Strenge; die Härte.
rill [ril], *s.* (*Poet.*) das Bächlein.
rim [rim], *s.* der Rand, die Felge.
rime [raim], *s.* (*Poet.*) der Reif.
rind [raind], *s.* die Rinde.
ring (1) [riŋ], *s.* der Ring.
ring (2) [riŋ], *s.* der Schall, das Läuten (*bell*); der Anruf (*telephone*); das Geläute (*bells*). — *v.a. irr.* läuten, klingeln (*bell*). — *v.n.* läuten; ertönen, tönen (*call, voice*).
ringleader ['riŋli:də], *s.* der Rädelsführer.
rink [riŋk], *s.* die Eisbahn; Rollschuhbahn.
rinse [rins], *v.a.* spülen, waschen. — *s.* das Abspülen.
riot ['raiət], *s.* der Aufruhr. — *v.n.* Aufruhr stiften; meutern.
rip [rip], *v.a.* reißen, aufreißen. — *s.* der Riß.
ripe [raip], *adj.* reif.
ripen ['raipən], *v.n.* reifen. — *v.a.* reifen lassen.
ripple [ripl], *s.* die Welle, Kräuselwelle (*water*). — *v.n.* kräuseln (*water*); (*Bot.*) riffeln.
rise [raiz], *v.n.irr.* aufstehen (*get up*); aufsteigen (*ascend*); anschwellen (*swell*); steigen (*price*). — *s.* die Erhöhung; (*Comm.*) der Anstieg; die Steigerung; Erhöhung (*salary*); der Ursprung (*origin*).
rising ['raiziŋ], *s.* der Aufstand (*rebellion*).
risk [risk], *s.* das Risiko. — *v.a.* wagen, riskieren.
rite [rait], *s.* der Ritus.
ritual ['ritjuəl], *s.* das Ritual.
rival [raivl], *s.* der Rivale, Nebenbuhler. — *adj.* nebenbuhlerisch, konkurrierend. — *v.a.* konkurrieren, wetteifern.
river ['rivə], *s.* der Fluß.
rivet ['rivit], *s.* die Niete. — *v.a.* nieten.
roach [routʃ], *s.* (*Zool.*) die Plötze.
road [roud], *s.* die Straße; der Weg.
roam [roum], *v.n.* herumstreifen.
roan [roun], *s.* der Rotschimmel (*horse*).
roar [rɔ:], *v.n.* brüllen (*animals*); brausen (*storm*). — *s.* das Gebrüll (*animal*); das Getöse, Brausen, Rauschen.
roast [roust], *v.a.*, *v.n.* braten, rösten. — *s.* der Braten.
rob [rɔb], *v.a.* berauben.
robbery ['rɔbəri], *s.* der Raub, die Räuberei.
robe [roub], *s.* die Robe.
robin ['rɔbin], *s.* (*Orn.*) das Rotkehlchen.
rock [rɔk], *s.* der Felsen, die Klippe. — *v.a.* schaukeln, wiegen. — *v.n.* wackeln, taumeln.
rocket ['rɔkit], *s.* die Rakete; (*sl.*) die Rüge. — *v.n.* hochfliegen; hochgehen (*prices*).
rocky ['rɔki], *adj.* felsig.

rod [rɔd], *s.* die Rute; (*fishing*) die Angelrute; die Stange (*pole*).
rodent ['roudənt], *s.* (*Zool.*) das Nagetier.
roe (1) [rou], *s.* der Fischrogen.
roe (2) [rou], *s.* (*Zool.*) das Reh, die Hirschkuh.
rogation [ro'geiʃən], *s.* das Gebet, die Litanei; *Rogation Sunday*, der Sonntag Rogate.
rogue [roug], *s.* der Schelm.
role [roul]. *s.* (*Theat.*, *fig.*) die Rolle.
roll [roul], *s.* die Liste; — *call*, der Aufruf, die Parade; die Rolle; die Semmel, das Brötchen (*bread*). — *v.a.* rollen; wälzen. — *v.n.* rollen; sich wälzen; sich drehen; schlingen (*ship*); schlenkern (*person*).
roller ['roulə], *s.* die Rolle; — *bandage*, das Wickelband; — *skates*, die Rollschuhe.
rollick ['rɔlik], *v.n.* herumtollen, lustig sein.
rolling stock ['rouliŋ stɔk], *s.* (*Railw.*) der Wagenbestand.
romance [rou'mæns], *s.* die Romanze.
romantic [rou'mæntik], *adj.* romantisch.
romp [rɔmp], *s.* der Wildfang, das Tollen. — *v.n.* toben.
roof [ru:f], *s.* das Dach. — *v.a.* decken.
rook (1) [ruk], *s.* (*Orn.*) die Saatkrähe.
rook (2) [ruk], *s.* (*Chess*) der Turm.
room [ru:m, rum], *s.* der Raum, das Zimmer. — *v.n.* (*Am.*) ein Zimmer teilen (*with*, mit).
roomy ['ru:mi], *adj.* geräumig.
roost [ru:st], *s.* der Hühnerstall. — *v.n.* aufsitzen, schlafen.
root [ru:t], *s.* die Wurzel. — *v.n.* wurzeln.
rooted ['ru:tid], *adj.* eingewurzelt.
rope [roup], *s.* das Seil. — *v.a.* anseilen (*in climbing*); (*coll.*) — *in*, verwickeln, hereinziehen.
rosary ['rouzəri], *s.* (*Rel.*) der Rosenkranz.
rose [rouz], *s.* (*Bot.*) die Rose.
Rosemary ['rouzməri]. Rosemarie.
rosemary ['rouzməri], *s.* (*Bot.*) der Rosmarin.
rosin ['rɔzin] *see* **resin.**
rosy ['rouzi], *adj.* rosig.
rot [rɔt], *v.n.* faulen, modern. — *s.* die Fäulnis, Verwesung; (*coll.*) der Unsinn.
rotate [ro'teit], *v.a.*, *v.n.* (sich) drehen, rotieren.
rote [rout], *s. by* —, mechanisch, auswendig.
rotten [rɔtn], *adj.* faul, verdorben, schlecht.
rotund [ro'tʌnd], *adj.* rundlich, rund.
rough [rʌf], *adj.* rauh, grob; flüchtig, ungefähr (*approximate*); ungehobelt (*ill-mannered*).
roughshod ['rʌfʃɔd], *adj.* rücksichtslos.
round [raund], *adj.* rund. — *s.* die Runde. — *prep.* (rund) um; um . . . herum. — *adv.* (rings)herum; (*around*) ungefähr; etwa (*approximately*).
roundabout ['raundəbaut], *s.* das Karussel. — *adj.* umständlich.
Roundhead ['raundhed], *s.* (*Eng. Hist.*) der Puritaner.
rouse [rauz], *v.a.* erwecken.
rout [raut], *s.* (*Mil.*) die wilde Flucht. — *v.a.* in die Flucht jagen.
route [ru:t], *s.* der Weg; die Route.
rover ['rouvə], *s.* der Wanderer, ältere Pfadfinder (*scout*); der Seeräuber (*pirate*).
row (1) [rou], *s.* die Reihe.
row (2) [rau], *s.* der Lärm, Streit. — *v.n.* (*coll.*) lärmend streiten, zanken.
row (3) [rou], *v.n.* rudern.
rowdy ['raudi], *s.* der Raufbold. — *adj.* laut, lärmend.
royal ['rɔiəl], *adj.* königlich.
royalty ['rɔiəlti], *s.* das Mitglied des Königshauses, die königliche Hoheit; (*pl.*) (*Law*) die Tantieme.
rub [rʌb], *v.a.*, *v.n.* (sich) reiben. — *s.* die Reibung; die heikle Stelle, das Problem.
rubber (1) ['rʌbə], *s.* der Gummi; Radiergummi.
rubber (2) ['rʌbə], *s.* (*Whist*) der Robber.
rubbish ['rʌbiʃ], *s.* der Abfall, Mist; (*fig.*) der Schund (*book*), der Unsinn (*nonsense*).
ruby ['ru:bi], *s.* der Rubin.
rudder ['rʌdə], *s.* das Steuerruder.
ruddy ['rʌdi], *adj.* rötlich.
rude [ru:d], *adj.* roh; grob; ungebildet; unhöflich.
rudiment ['ru:dimənt], *s.* die Anfangsgründe, die Grundlage.
rue (1) [ru:], *s.* (*Bot.*) die Raute.
rue (2) [ru:], *v.a.* beklagen, bereuen.
ruff [rʌf], *s.* die Halskrause.
ruffian ['rʌfiən], *s.* der Raufbold.
ruffle [rʌfl], *v.a.* zerzausen (*hair*); verwirren (*muddle*). — *s.* die Krause (*on dress*); die Aufregung.
rug [rʌg], *s.* die Wolldecke, der Vorleger.
rugged ['rʌgid], *adj.* rauh; uneben.
ruin ['ru:in], *s.* die Ruine; (*fig.*) der Zusammenbruch. — *v.a.* ruinieren.
rule [ru:l], *s.* die Regel, Vorschrift; die Herrschaft; *slide* —, der Rechenschieber. — *v.a.* beherrschen; regeln; lin(i)ieren (*draw lines on*). —*v.n.* herrschen (*reign*; *be valid*); lin(i)ieren (*draw lines*); entscheiden (*decide*).
ruling ['ru:liŋ], *s.* die Regelung, Entscheidung.
rum (1) [rʌm], *s.* der Rum.
rum (2) [rʌm], *adj.* (*sl.*) seltsam.
Rumanian [ru:'meiniən], *adj.* rumänisch. — *s.* der Rumäne.
rumble [rʌmbl], *v.n.* poltern, rasseln, rumpeln; (*stomach*) knurren.
ruminate ['ru:mineit], *v.n.* wiederkäuen; nachsinnen.
rummage ['rʌmidʒ], *v.a.*, *v.n.* durchstöbern.
rumour ['ru:mə], *s.* das Gerücht.
rump [rʌmp], *s.* der Rumpf, Steiß; — *steak*, das Rumpsteak.

run [rʌn], *v.n. irr.* laufen, rennen; eilen; verkehren (*bus*); fließen (*flow*); (*Theat.*) gegeben werden; lauten (*text*). — *s.* der Lauf, das Rennen; (*Theat.*) die Spieldauer; *in the long* —, am Ende, auf die Dauer.
runaway ['rʌnəwei], *adj.* entlaufen. — *s.* der Ausreißer.
rung [rʌŋ], *s.* die Sprosse.
runway ['rʌnwei], *s.* (*Aviat.*) die Rollbahn, Startbahn, Landebahn.
rupture ['rʌptʃə], *s.* (*Med.*) der Leistenbruch.
rural ['ruərəl], *adj.* ländlich.
rush (1) [rʌʃ], *s.* (*Bot.*) die Binse.
rush (2) [rʌʃ], *s.* der Ansturm, Andrang; die Hetze; der Hochbetrieb. — *v.n.* stürzen, in Eile sein.
Russian ['rʌʃən], *adj.* russisch. — *s.* der Russe.
rust [rʌst], *s.* der Rost. — *v.n.* verrosten.
rustic ['rʌstik], *adj.* ländlich.
rut (1) [rʌt], *s.* die Spur; das Geleise.
rut (2) [rʌt], *s.* (*animals*) die Brunst.
ruthless ['ru:θlis], *adj.* grausam, rücksichtslos.
rye [rai], *s.* (*Bot.*) der Roggen.

S

S [es]. das S.
sable [seibl], *s.* der Zobel. — *adj.* schwarz.
sabotage ['sæbotɑ:ʒ], *s.* die Sabotage. — *v.a.* sabotieren.
sabre ['seibə], *s.* der Säbel.
sack (1) [sæk], *s.* der Sack; (*coll.*) die Entlassung (*get the* —). — *v.a.* (*coll.*) entlassen.
sack (2) [sæk], *v.a.* plündern (*pillage*).
sack (3) [sæk], *s.* (*obs.*) der Weißwein.
sacrament ['sækrəmənt], *s.* das Sakrament.
sacred ['seikrid], *adj.* heilig.
sacrifice ['sækrifais], *s.* das Opfer. — *v.a.* opfern.
sacrilege ['sækrilidʒ], *s.* das Sakrileg, der Frevel.
sad [sæd], *adj.* traurig.
sadden [sædn], *v.a.* betrüben.
saddle [sædl], *s.* der Sattel. — *v.a.* satteln; (*coll.*) — *s.o. with s.th.*, einem etwas aufhalsen.
safe [seif], *adj.* sicher (*secure*); wohlbehalten (*arrival etc.*). — *s.* der Geldschrank, das Safe.
safeguard ['seifgɑ:d], *v.a.* beschützen, garantieren. — *s.* der Schutz, die Sicherheit.
safety ['seifti], *s.* die Sicherheit.
saffron ['sæfrən], *s.* der Safran. — *adj.* safrangelb.
sagacious [sə'geiʃəs], *adj.* scharfsinnig.
sagacity [sə'gæsiti], *s.* der Scharfsinn.
sage (1) [seidʒ], *s.* (*Bot.*) der, die Salbei.
sage (2) [seidʒ], *s.* der Weise. — *adj.* weise, klug.
sail [seil], *s.* das Segel. — *v.n.* segeln, (*Naut.*) fahren.
sailor ['seilə], *s.* der Matrose, Seemann.
Saint [seint, sənt]. (*abbr.* **S.** *or* **St.**) Sankt (*before name*).
saint [seint], *s.* der *or* die Heilige.
sake [seik], *s. for my son's* —, um meines Sohnes willen; *for the* — *of peace*, um des Friedens willen.
salacious [sə'leiʃəs], *adj.* geil; zotig (*joke*).
salad ['sæləd], *s.* der Salat.
salary ['sæləri], *s.* das Gehalt.
sale [seil], *s.* der Verkauf; *annual* —, (*Comm.*) der Ausverkauf.
salesman ['seilzmən], *s.* der Verkäufer.
salient ['seiliənt], *adj.* hervorspringend, wichtig, Haupt-.
saline ['seilain], *s.* die Salzquelle. — *adj.* salzhaltig.
saliva [sə'laivə], *s.* der Speichel.
sallow ['sælou], *adj.* blaß, bleich.
sally ['sæli], *s.* der Ausfall, (*fig.*) der komische Einfall. — *v.n.* ausfallen; — *forth*, losgehen.
salmon ['sæmən], *s.* (*Zool.*) der Lachs.
saloon [sə'lu:n], *s.* der Salon; (*Am.*) das Wirtshaus, die Kneipe.
salt [sɔ:lt], *s.* das Salz; — *cellar*, das Salzfäßchen; (*coll.*) *old* —, der alte Matrose. — *v.a.* salzen.
saltpetre [sɔ:lt'pi:tə], *s.* der Salpeter.
salubrious [sə'lju:briəs], *adj.* gesund (*climate, neighbourhood*).
salutary ['sæljutəri], *adj.* heilsam (*lesson, experience*).
salute [sə'lju:t], *v.a.* grüßen. — *s.* der Gruß, (*Mil.*) Salut.
salvage ['sælvidʒ], *s.* die Bergung, Rettung; das Bergegut. — *v.a.* retten, bergen.
salvation [sæl'veiʃən], *s.* die Rettung; (*Rel.*) die Erlösung, das Heil.
salve [sælv, sɑ:v], *v.a.* einsalben; heilen. — *s.* die Salbe.
salver ['sælvə], *s.* der Präsentierteller.
salvo ['sælvou], *s.* (*Mil.*) die Salve.
Samaritan [sə'mæritən], *s.* der Samariter; (*fig.*) der Wohltäter.
same [seim], *adj.* der-, die-, dasselbe.
sample [sɑ:mpl], *s.* die Probe, das Muster (*test, pack etc.*). — *v.a.* probieren; kosten (*food*).
sampler ['sɑ:mplə], *s.* das Stickmuster.
sanctify ['sæŋktifai], *v.a.* heiligen.
sanctimonious [sæŋkti'mouniəs], *adj.* scheinheilig.
sanction ['sæŋkʃən], *s.* (*Pol.*) die Sanktion; (*fig.*) Genehmigung. — *v.a.* genehmigen, sanktionieren.
sanctuary ['sæŋktjuəri], *s.* das Heiligtum.
sand [sænd], *s.* der Sand. — *v.a.* sanden, bestreuen; (*floors*) abreiben.
sandal [sændl], *s.* die Sandale.

sandwich ['sænwitʃ], *s.* das belegte (Butter)brot.
sane [sein], *adj.* gesund (*mind*); vernünftig.
sanguine ['sæŋgwin], *adj.* optimistisch.
sanitary ['sænitəri], *adj.* Gesundheits-, Sanitäts-; —*towel*, die (Damen)binde.
sanity ['sæniti], *s.* die Vernunft, der gesunde Menschenverstand; (*Law*) die Zurechnungsfähigkeit.
Santa Claus [sæntə'klɔ:z], der heilige Nikolaus, Knecht Ruprecht.
sap (1) [sæp], *s.* der Saft; (*fig.*) die Lebenskraft.
sap (2) [sæp], *v.a.* untergraben, schwächen.
sapling ['sæpliŋ], *s.* (*Bot.*) das Bäumchen, der junge Baum.
sapper ['sæpə], *s.* (*Mil.*) der Sappeur; der Schanzgräber, Pionier.
sapphire ['sæfaiə], *s.* der Saphir.
sarcasm ['sɑ:kæzm], *s.* der Sarkasmus.
sarcastic [sɑ:'kæstik], *adj.* sarkastisch.
sash (1) [sæʃ], *s.* die Schärpe.
sash (2) [sæʃ], *s.* — *window*, das Schiebefenster; — *cord*, die Fensterschnur.
Satan ['seitən], der Satan.
satchel ['sætʃəl], *s.* die Leder(schul)tasche.
sate [seit] *v.a.* sättigen.
satellite ['sætəlait], *s.* der Satellit, Trabant.
satin ['sætin], *s.* (*Text.*) der Atlas.
satire ['sætaiə], *s.* die Satire.
satisfaction [sætis'fækʃən], *s.* die Befriedigung, Zufriedenheit.
satisfactory [sætis'fæktri], *adj.* befriedigend, genügend; zufriedenstellend.
satisfy ['sætisfai], *v.a.* befriedigen, sättigen; (*fig.*) zufriedenstellen.
saturate ['sætʃureit], *v.a.* (*Chem.*) saturieren, sättigen.
Saturday ['sætədei], der Samstag, Sonnabend.
sauce [sɔ:s], *s.* (*Cul.*) die Sauce, Tunke; (*coll.*) die Unverschämtheit.
saucepan ['sɔ:spæn], *s.* (*Cul.*) der Kochtopf.
saucer ['sɔ:sə], *s.* die Untertasse.
saucy ['sɔ:si], *adj.* (*coll.*) unverschämt, frech.
saunter ['sɔ:ntə], *v.n.* schlendern, spazieren.
sausage ['sɔsidʒ], *s.* die Wurst.
savage ['sævidʒ], *adj.* wild. — *s.* der Wilde.
save [seiv], *v.a.* retten (*life*); (*Theol.*) erlösen; sparen (*money*); sich ersparen (*trouble, labour*); aufheben (*keep*). — *v.n.* sparen, sparsam sein. — *prep.*, *conj.* außer, außer daß, ausgenommen.
saving ['seiviŋ], *s.* das Ersparnis; *savings bank*, die Sparkasse.
saviour ['seivjə], *s.* der Retter; (*Rel.*) der Heiland.
savour ['seivə], *s.* der Geschmack; die Würze. — *v.n.* schmecken (*of*, nach, *Dat.*).
savoury ['seivəri], *adj.* schmackhaft. — *s.* pikantes Vor- *or* Nachgericht.
saw (1) [sɔ:], *v.a.* sägen. — *s.* die Säge.
saw (2) [sɔ:], *s.* (*obs.*) das Sprichwort.
sawyer ['sɔ:jə], *s.* der Sägearbeiter, Säger.
Saxon ['sæksən], *adj.* sächsisch. — *s.* der Sachse.
say [sei], *v.a. irr.* sagen; (*lines, prayer*) hersagen. — *v.n.* (*Am. coll.*) —! sagen Sie mal! — *s.* das entscheidende Wort.
saying ['seiiŋ], *s.* das Sprichwort, der Spruch.
scab [skæb], *s.* der Schorf, die Krätze.
scabbard ['skæbəd], *s.* die Degenscheide.
scaffold ['skæfəld], *s.* (*Build.*) das Gerüst; das Schafott (*place of execution*).
scald [skɔ:ld], *v.a.* verbrühen; —*ing hot*, brühheiß.
scale (1) [skeil], *s.* die Waagschale (*balance*).
scale (2) [skeil], *s.* (*Mus.*) die Skala, Tonleiter.
scale (3) [skeil], *s.* (*Geog. etc.*) die Skala, das Ausmaß, der Maßstab; *on a large* —, im großen (Maßstabe). — *v.a.* erklettern (*climb*); — *down*, im Maßstab verringern.
scale (4) [skeil], *s.* (*fish etc.*) die Schuppe. — *v.a.* schuppen, abschälen (*remove* —*s*).
scallop ['skɔləp], *s.* (*Zool.*) die Kammuschel.
scalp [skælp], *s.* (*Anat.*) die Kopfhaut. — *v.a.* skalpieren, die Kopfhaut abziehen.
scamp [skæmp], *s.* (*coll.*) der Taugenichts.
scan [skæn], *v.a.* (*Poet.*) skandieren; (*Rad.*) absuchen.
scandalize ['skændəlaiz], *v.a.* empören, verärgern.
scant [skænt], *adj.* selten; knapp, sparsam.
Scandinavian [skændi'neivjən], *adj.* skandinavisch. — *s.* der Skandinavier.
scanty ['skænti], *adj.* spärlich, knapp.
scapegoat ['skeipgout], *s.* der Sündenbock.
scar [skɑ:], *s.* die Narbe.
scarce [skɛəs], *adj.* selten, spärlich.
scarcely ['skɛəsli], *adv.* kaum.
scarcity ['skɛəsiti], *s.* die Seltenheit, Knappheit.
scare [skɛə], *v.a.* erschrecken, ängstigen. — *s.* der Schreck.
scarecrow ['skɛəkrou], *s.* die Vogelscheuche.
scarf [skɑ:f], *s.* der Schal, das Halstuch.
scarlet ['skɑ:lit], *adj.* scharlachrot. — *s.* der Scharlach.
scarp [skɑ:p], *s.* die Böschung.
scatter ['skætə], *v.a.*, *v.n.* (sich) zerstreuen, (sich) verbreiten; streuen.
scavenge ['skævindʒ], *v.a.* ausreinigen, auswaschen; säubern.
scavenger ['skævindʒə], *s.* der Straßenkehrer; Aasgeier.

scene [si:n], *s.* die Szene, der Schauplatz; *behind the —s*, hinter den Kulissen; *— shifter*, der Kulissenschieber.
scenery ['si:nəri], *s.* die Landschaft (*nature*); (*Theat.*) das Bühnenbild, die Kulissen, *f. pl.*
scent [sent], *s.* der Geruch, Duft, das Parfüm (*perfume*); die Witterung, Fährte (*trail of hunted animal*).
sceptic ['skeptik], *s.* der Skeptiker.
sceptre ['septə], *s.* das Zepter.
schedule ['ʃedju:l, (*Am.*) 'ske-], *s.* der Plan; die Liste; der (Fahr-, Stunden-) plan; (*Law*) der Zusatz (*in documents*). — *v.a.* (*Am.*) einteilen, zuteilen (*apportion*); aufzeichnen.
scheme [ski:m], *s.* das Schema; der Plan; — *of things*, in der Gesamtplanung. — *v.n.* aushecken; Ränke schmieden.
scholar ['skɔlə], *s.* der Gelehrte, der Wissenschaftler; der Schuljunge, Schüler; (*Univ.*) der Stipendiat.
scholarly ['skɔləli], *adj.* gelehrt.
scholarship ['skɔləʃip], *s.* die Gelehrsamkeit (*learning*); das Stipendium (*award*).
scholastic [sko'læstik], *adj.* scholastisch. — *s.* der Scholastiker.
school [sku:l], *s.* die Schule. — *v.a.* abrichten; schulen; erziehen.
schoolboy ['sku:lbɔi], *s.* der Schüler.
schoolgirl ['sku:lgə:l], *s.* die Schülerin.
schoolmaster ['sku:lmɑ:stə], *s.* der Lehrer.
schoolmistress ['sku:lmistrəs], *s.* die Lehrerin.
schooner ['sku:nə], *s.* (*Naut.*) der Schoner.
science ['saiəns], *s.* die Wissenschaft, Naturwissenschaft (*natural — s*).
scientific [saiən'tifik], *adj.* wissenschaftlich, naturwissenschaftlich.
scientist ['saiəntist], *s.* der Gelehrte; Naturwissenschaftler, Naturforscher.
scintillate ['sintileit], *v.n.* funkeln, glänzen.
scion ['saiən], *s.* der Sprößling.
scissors ['sizəz], *s. pl.* die Schere.
scoff [skɔf], *v.a.* verspotten, verhöhnen. — *v.n.* spotten. —*s.* der Spott, Hohn.
scold [skould], *v.a.* schelten. — *v.n.* zanken.
scoop [sku:p], *v.a.* aushöhlen (*hollow out*); ausschöpfen (*ladle out*). — *s.* die Schippe, Schöpfkelle; (*fig.*) die Sensation, Erstmeldung.
scope [skoup], *s.* der Wirkungskreis, Spielraum.
scooter ['sku:tə], *s.* der (Motor)roller.
scorch [skɔ:tʃ], *v.a.* versengen, verbrennen. — *v.n.* versengt werden; (*coll.*) dahinrasen (*speed*).
score [skɔ:], *s.* die Zwanzig; die Rechnung; (*Mus.*) die Partitur; das Spielergebnis (*in game*).
scorn [skɔ:n], *v.a.* verachten. — *s.* der Spott (*scoffing*); die Geringschätzung, Verachtung.
Scot, Scotsman [skɔt, 'skɔtsmən], *s.* der Schotte.
Scotch [skɔtʃ], *s.* der Whisky.
scotch [skɔtʃ], *v.a.* ritzen; (*fig.*) vernichten.
Scotswoman ['skɔtswumən], *s.* die Schottin.
Scottish ['skɔtiʃ], *adj.* schottisch.
scoundrel ['skaundrəl], *s.* der Schurke.
scour ['skauə], *v.a.* scheuern, reinigen.
scourge [skə:dʒ], *s.* die Geißel. — *v.a.* geißeln.
scout [skaut], *s.* der Kundschafter; (*Boy Scout*) der Pfadfinder.
scowl [skaul], *v.n.* finster dreinsehen. — *s.* das finstere Gesicht.
scraggy ['skrægi], *adj.* hager, dürr.
scramble [skræmbl], *v.n.* klettern. — *v.a.* verrühren; *scrambled eggs*, das Rührei.
scrap [skræp], *s.* das Stückchen, der Brocken, Fetzen; — *merchant*, der Altwarenhändler. — *v.a.* zum alten Eisen werfen, verschrotten.
scrapbook ['skræpbuk], *s.* das Sammelbuch, Bilderbuch.
scrape [skreip], *v.a.*, *v.n.* (sich) schaben, kratzen; (*coll.*) — *up*, auflesen. — *s.* (*coll.*) die Klemme (*difficulty*).
scraper ['skreipə], *s.* der Fußabstreifer.
scratch [skrætʃ], *v.a.*, *v.n.* kratzen; sich kratzen; (*Sport*) zurückziehen. — *s.* der Kratzer; *come up to* —, seinen Mann stellen.
scrawl [skrɔ:l], *v.a.*, *v.n.* kritzeln (*scribble*); (*coll.*) unleserlich schreiben. — *s.* das Gekritzel.
scream [skri:m], *v.n.* schreien; kreischen. — *s.* der Schrei; (*coll.*) zum Schreien, zum Lachen.
screech [skri:tʃ], *v.n.* schreien, kreischen (*hoarsely*). — *s.* das Gekreisch.
screen [skri:n], *s.* der Schirm (*protection*); (*Cinema*) die Leinwand. — *v.a.* abschirmen (*shade*); (*Film*) durchspielen, vorführen; (*question*) untersuchen; ausfragen.
screening ['skri:niŋ], *s.* (*Cinema*) die Vorführung; (*Pol.*) die Befragung, Untersuchung.
screw [skru:], *v.a.* schrauben. — *s.* die Schraube.
screwdriver ['skru:draivə], *s.* der Schraubenzieher.
scribble [skribl], *v.a.*, *v.n.* kritzeln, (unleserlich) schreiben. — *s.* das Gekritzel.
scribe [skraib], *s.* der Schreiber.
script [skript], *s.* das Manuskript; (*Film*) das Drehbuch.
scripture ['skriptʃə], *s.* die Heilige Schrift.
scroll [skroul], *s.* die Schriftrolle; (*Typ.*) der Schnörkel; die Urkunde (*document etc.*).
scrub [skrʌb], *v.a.* schrubben, reiben, scheuern.
scruff [skrʌf], *s.* (*of the neck*) das Genick.
scruple [skru:pl], *s.* der Skrupel.
scrupulous ['skru:pjuləs], *adj.* genau, gewissenhaft; azllu bedenklich.

scrutinize ['skru:tinaiz], *v.a.* genau prüfen, untersuchen.
scrutiny ['skru:tini], *s.* die genaue Prüfung; die Untersuchung.
scuffle [skʌfl], *v.n.* sich raufen. — *s.* die Balgerei, Rauferei.
scull [skʌl], *s.* das kurze Ruder.
scullery ['skʌləri], *s.* die Abwaschküche.
scullion ['skʌliən], *s.* (*obs.*) der Küchenjunge.
sculptor ['skʌlptə], *s.* der Bildhauer.
sculpture ['skʌlptʃə], *s.* die Bildhauerei (*activity*); die Skulptur (*piece*).
scum [skʌm], *s.* der Abschaum.
scurf [skə:f], *s.* der Schorf, Grind.
scurrilous ['skʌriləs], *adj.* gemein.
scurvy ['skə:vi], *s.* (*Med.*) der Skorbut. — *adj.* niederträchtig.
scutcheon ['skʌtʃən] *see* **escutcheon.**
scuttle (1) [skʌtl], *s.* (*Naut.*) die Springluke. — *v.a.* (*Naut.*) ein Schiff zum Sinken bringen, versenken.
scuttle (2) [skʌtl], *s.* der Kohleneimer.
scuttle (3) [skʌtl], *v.n.* eilen (*hurry*).
scythe [saið], *s.* die Sense.
sea [si:], *s.* die See, das Meer.
seal (1) [si:l], *s.* das Siegel, Petschaft. — *v.a.* (be)siegeln.
seal (2) [si:l], *s.* (*Zool.*) der Seehund, die Robbe.
seam [si:m], *s.* der Saum; die Naht; (*Min.*) die Ader, das Flöz; (*Metall.*) die Naht. — *v.a.* einsäumen.
seamstress ['si:mstrəs], *s.* die Näherin.
sear [siə], *v.a.* sengen (*burn*); trocknen; verdorren. — *adj. see* **sere.**
search [sə:tʃ], *v.n.* suchen (*for*, nach, *Dat.*); forschen (*for*, nach, *Dat.*). — *v.a.* untersuchen, durchsuchen (*house, case etc.*). — *s.* die Suche (*for person*); die Untersuchung (*of house etc.*).
searchlight ['sə:tʃlait], *s.* der Scheinwerfer.
seasick ['si:sik], *adj.* seekrank.
seaside ['si:said], *s.* die Küste, der Strand.
season [si:zn], *s.* die Jahreszeit, Saison; — *ticket*, die Dauerkarte. — *v.a.* würzen (*spice*). — *v.n.* reifen (*mature*).
seasoning ['si:zniŋ], *s.* die Würze.
seat [si:t], *s.* der Sitz, Sitzplatz, Stuhl. — *v.a.* setzen; fassen (*of room capacity*); *be —ed*, Platz nehmen.
seaweed ['si:wi:d], *s.* (*Bot.*) der Seetang.
secession [si'seʃən], *s.* die Loslösung, Trennung, Spaltung.
seclude [si'klu:d], *v.a.* abschließen, absondern.
seclusion [si'klu:ʒən], *s.* die Abgeschlossenheit.
second ['sekənd], *num. adj.* zweit; (*repeat*) noch ein. — *s.* die Sekunde (*time*); (*Sport*) der Sekundant. — *v.a.* sekundieren (*Dat.*), beipflichten; [si'kɔnd] abkommandieren (zu).
secondary ['sekəndri], *adj.* zweitrangig, sekundär.
secondhand ['sekəndhænd], *adj.* antiquarisch, gebraucht.
secrecy ['si:krəsi], *s.* die Heimlichkeit; *pledge to* —, die Verschwiegenheit.
secret ['si:krit], *s.* das Geheimnis. — *adj.* geheim.
secretary ['sekrətəri], *s.* der Sekretär, die Sekretärin.
secrete [si'kri:t], *v.a.* ausscheiden, absondern.
secretion [si'kri:ʃən], *s.* die Ausscheidung; (*Med.*) das Sekret.
sect [sekt], *s.* die Sekte.
section ['sekʃən], *s.* die Sektion, Abteilung (*department*); der Teil (*part*); Abschnitt (*in book etc.*).
secular ['sekjulə], *adj.* weltlich, säkulär.
secure [sə'kjuə], *adj.* sicher, gesichert. — *v.a.* sichern (*make safe*); besorgen (*obtain*).
security [sə'kjuəriti], *s.* die Sicherheit; (*Comm.*) die Garantie, Bürgschaft; (*pl.*) die Staatspapiere, Wertpapiere, *n. pl.*, Aktien, *f. pl.*
sedate [si'deit], *adj.* gesetzt, ruhig (*placid*).
sedative ['sedətiv], *adj.* beruhigend. — *s.* das Beruhigungsmittel.
sedentary ['sedəntri], *adj.* sitzend, Sitz-.
sediment ['sedimənt], *s.* der Bodensatz; (*Geol.*) das Sediment.
sedition [si'diʃən], *s.* der Aufstand.
seditious [si'diʃəs], *adj.* aufrührerisch.
seduce [si'dju:s], *v.a.* verführen.
sedulous ['sedjuləs], *adj.* emsig, fleißig.
see (1) [si:], *s.* (*Eccl.*) das (Erz)bistum; *Holy See*, der Heilige Stuhl.
see (2) [si:], *v.a., v.n. irr.* sehen; einsehen, verstehen (*understand*).
seed [si:d], *s.* die Saat; der Same (*grain*). — *v.a.* (*Sport*) aussetzen, setzen.
seediness ['si:dinis], *s.* die Schäbigkeit; Armseligkeit, das Elend.
seedy ['si:di], *adj.* elend; schäbig.
seeing ['si:iŋ], *conj.* — *that*, da doch.
seek [si:k], *v.a. irr.* suchen (*object*). — *v.n.* trachten (*to, infin.*).
seem [si:m], *v.n.* scheinen, erscheinen.
seemly ['si:mli], *adj.* schicklich, anständig.
seer [siə], *s.* der Prophet.
seesaw ['si:sɔ:], *s.* die Schaukel.
seethe [si:ð], *v.n.* kochen, (*fig.*) sieden.
segment ['segmənt], *s.* (*Geom.*) der Abschnitt.
segregate ['segrigeit], *v.a.* absondern.
segregation [segri'geiʃən], *s. racial* —, die Rassentrennung.
seize [si:z], *v.a.* ergreifen, packen (*arrest, grasp*); beschlagnahmen (*impound*).
seizure ['si:ʒə], *s.* die Beschlagnahme (*of goods*); (*Med.*) der Anfall.
seldom ['seldəm], *adv.* selten.
select [si'lekt], *v.a.* auswählen; auslesen. — *adj.* auserlesen.
selection [si'lekʃən], *s.* die Wahl, Auswahl.
self [self], *s.* das Selbst; — *- consciousness*, die Befangenheit; — *- denial*, die Selbstverleugnung, Selbstaufopferung.

selfish ['selfiʃ], *adj.* egoistisch, selbstsüchtig.
sell [sel], *v.a. irr.* verkaufen; (*sl.*) — (*s.o.*) *out*, jemanden verraten.
semblance ['sembləns], *s.* der Anschein, die Ähnlichkeit.
semi- ['semi], *pref.* halb.
semibreve ['semibri:v], *s.* (*Mus.*) die ganze Note.
semicircle ['semisə:kl], *s.* der Halbkreis.
semicolon ['semikoulən], *s.* der Strichpunkt.
semiquaver ['semikweivə], *s.* (*Mus.*) die Sechzehntelnote.
senate ['senit], *s.* der Senat.
send [send], *v.a. irr.* senden, schicken; — *for*, holen lassen; — *-off*, die Abschiedsfeier.
Senegalese [senigə'li:z], *adj.* senegal-. — *s.* der Senegalese.
senile ['si:nail], *adj.* altersschwach.
senior ['si:njə], *adj.* älter; dienstälter (*in position*).
seniority [si:ni'ɔriti], *s.* der Rangvortritt, das Dienstalter.
sensation [sen'seiʃən], *s.* die Empfindung; Sensation.
sensational [sen'seiʃənəl], *adj.* sensationell.
sense [sens], *v.a.* fühlen, empfinden. — *s.* der Sinn; das Empfinden, Gefühl; *common* —, gesunder Menschenverstand.
senseless ['senslis], *adj.* sinnlos.
sensibility [sensi'biliti], *s.* die Empfindlichkeit.
sensible ['sensibl], *adj.* vernünftig.
sensitive ['sensitiv], *adj.* feinfühlend, empfindlich.
sensitize ['sensitaiz], *v.a.* (*Phot. etc.*) empfindlich machen.
sensual ['sensjuəl], *adj.* sinnlich, wollüstig.
sensuous ['sensjuəs], *adj.* sinnlich.
sentence ['sentəns], *s.* (*Gram.*) der Satz; (*Law*) das Urteil. — *v.a.* verurteilen.
sententious [sen'tenʃəs], *adj.* spruchreich; affektiert.
sentiment ['sentimənt], *s.* die Empfindung, das Gefühl; die Meinung (*opinion*).
sentimental [senti'mentl], *adj.* sentimental, gefühlvoll; empfindsam.
sentinel ['sentinəl], *s.* (*Mil.*) die Schildwache, Wache.
separable ['sepərəbl], *adj.* trennbar.
separate ['sepəreit], *v.a.* trennen. — [–rit], *adj.* getrennt.
separation [sepə'reiʃən], *s.* die Trennung.
September [sep'tembə]. der September.
sequel ['si:kwəl], *s.* die Folge, Fortsetzung (*serial*).
sequence ['si:kwəns], *s.* die Ordnung, Reihenfolge, Aufeinanderfolge.
sequester [si'kwestə], *v.a.* absondern, entfernen.
sere [siə], *adj.* trocken, dürr.
serene [si'ri:n], *adj.* heiter; gelassen, ruhig (*quiet*).
serf [sə:f], *s.* der Leibeigene.
sergeant ['sɑ:dʒənt], *s.* (*Mil.*) der Feldwebel.
series ['siəri:z *or* 'siərii:z], *s.* die Reihe.
serious ['siəriəs], *adj.* ernst, seriös.
sermon ['sə:mən], *s.* die Predigt.
serpent ['sə:pənt], *s.* (*Zool.*) die Schlange.
serpentine ['sə:pəntain], *adj.* schlangenartig, sich schlängelnd.
serrated [se'reitid], *adj.* (*Bot.*, *Engin.*) zackig, gezackt.
serried ['serid], *adj.* dichtgedrängt.
servant ['sə:vənt], *s.* der Bediente, Diener; die Magd, das Mädchen, Dienstmädchen.
serve [sə:v], *v.a.*, *v.n.* dienen (*Dat.*); (*Law*) abbüßen, absitzen (*sentence*); servieren (*food*); (*Tennis*) angeben.
service ['sə:vis], *s.* der Dienst, die Bedienung; (*Mil.*) der Militärdienst; das Service, Geschirr, Porzellan (*china*).
serviceable ['sə:visəbl], *adj.* brauchbar, dienlich, benutzbar.
servile ['sə:vail], *adj.* knechtisch.
servility [sə:'viliti], *s.* die Kriecherei.
servitude ['sə:vitju:d], *s.* die Knechtschaft.
session ['seʃən], *s.* die Sitzung; das Studienjahr, Hochschuljahr.
set [set], *v.a. irr.* setzen; stellen (*stand*); legen (*lay*); ordnen (— *out*); — *a saw*, eine Sage schärfen, wetzen; fassen (*stone*); — *fire to*, in Brand setzen; — *aside*, beiseitelegen; — *to music*, vertonen; — *about*, anfangen, sich anschicken; herfallen über (*s.o.*); — *up*, einrichten. — *v.n.* — *forth*, *forward*, aufbrechen; — *out to*, streben, trachten; (*sun*) untergehen; fest werden (*solidify*). — *s.* der Satz (*complete collection*); die Garnitur (*garments*); der Kreis, die Clique (*circle of people*); (*Theat.*) das Bühnenbild.
settee [se'ti:], *s.* das Sofa.
setter ['setə], *s.* (*Zool.*) der Vorstehhund; *red* —, der Hühnerhund.
setting ['setiŋ], *s.* das Setzen; die Szene (*of play etc.*); der Sonnenuntergang (*of the sun*); (*Typ.*) — *up*, die Auslegung, Aufstellung.
settle (1) [setl], *v.a.* ordnen, schlichten; (*Comm.*) begleichen, bezahlen. — *v.n.* sich niederlassen, siedeln; (*weather*) sich aufklären.
settle (2) [setl], *s.* der Ruhesitz.
settlement ['setlmənt], *s.* (*Comm.*) die Begleichung; die Siedlung (*habitation*).
seven [sevn], *num. adj.* sieben.
seventeen ['sevnti:n], *num. adj.* siebzehn.
seventh [sevnθ], *num. adj.* siebente.
seventy ['sevnti], *num. adj.* siebzig.
sever ['sevə], *v.a.* trennen.
several ['sevərəl], *adj. pl.* verschiedene, mehrere.

severance ['sevərəns], *s.* die Trennung.
severe [si'viə], *adj.* streng.
severity [si'veriti], *s.* die Strenge.
sew [sou], *v.a., v.n.* nähen.
sewage ['sju:idʒ], *s.* das Abfuhrwasser, Kloakenwasser, Kanalwasser.
sewer (1) ['sju:ə], *s.* die Kanalanlage, der Abzugskanal.
sewer (2) ['souə], *s.* der Näher, die Näherin.
sewing ['souiŋ], *s.* das Nähen; — *machine*, die Nähmaschine.
sex [seks], *s.* das Geschlecht.
sexagenarian [seksədʒə'nɛəriən], *s.* der Sechzigjährige.
sextant ['sekstənt], *s.* der Sextant.
sexton ['sekstən], *s.* (*Eccl.*) der Küster, Totengräber.
sexual ['sekʃuəl], *adj.* geschlechtlich, sexuell.
shabby ['ʃæbi], *adj.* schäbig; (*fig.*) erbärmlich.
shackle [ʃækl], *v.a.* fesseln. — *s.* (*usually pl.*) die Fesseln, *f. pl.*
shade [ʃeid], *s.* der Schatten; (*pl.*) (*Am.*) die Jalousien, *f. pl.* (*blinds*). — *v.a.* beschatten; (*Art*) schattieren, verdunkeln.
shadow ['ʃædou], *s.* der Schatten. — *v.a.* verfolgen.
shady ['ʃeidi], *adj.* schattig; (*fig.*) verdächtig.
shaft [ʃɑ:ft], *s.* der Schaft (*handle*); (*Min.*) der Schacht; die Deichsel (*cart*); der Pfeil (*arrow*).
shag [ʃæg], *s.* der Tabak.
shaggy ['ʃægi], *adj.* zottig.
shake [ʃeik], *v.a. irr.* schütteln; rütteln; (*fig.*) erschüttern. — *v.n.* zittern (*tremble*); wanken (*waver*). — *s.* das Zittern, Beben; (*Mus.*) der Triller.
shaky ['ʃeiki], *adj.* zitternd, wankend; rissig, wackelig (*wobbly*); (*fig.*) unsicher (*insecure*).
shall [ʃæl], *v. aux.* sollen (*be supposed to*); werden (*future*).
shallow ['ʃælou], *adj.* flach, seicht. — *s.* die Untiefe (*sea*).
sham [ʃæm], *adj.* falsch, unecht. — *v.a.* vortäuschen.
shambles [ʃæmblz], *s.* die Unordnung; (*fig.*) das Schlachtfeld.
shame [ʃeim], *s.* die Scham (*remorse*); die Schande (*dishonour*); *what a —!* wie schade! — *v.a.* beschämen.
shamefaced ['ʃeimfeisd], *adj.* verschämt.
shameful ['ʃeimful], *adj.* schändlich (*despicable*).
shampoo [ʃæm'pu:], *s.* das Haarwaschmittel. — *v.a.* das Haar waschen.
shamrock ['ʃæmrɔk], *s.* (*Bot.*) der irische Klee.
shank [ʃæŋk], *s.* der Unterschenkel; (*coll.*) *on Shanks's pony*, zu Fuß.
shanty (1) ['ʃænti], *s.* die Hütte.
shanty (2) ['ʃænti], *s.* *sea —*, das Matrosenlied.
shape [ʃeip], *s.* die Gestalt, Figur, Form. — *v.a.* gestalten, formen. — *v.n.* Gestalt annehmen.
shapely ['ʃeipli], *adj.* wohlgestaltet, schön gestaltet.
share [ʃɛə], *v.a., v.n.* (sich) teilen. — *s.* der Teil, Anteil; (*Comm.*) die Aktie (*in company*).
shareholder ['ʃɛəhouldə], *s.* der Aktionär.
shark [ʃɑ:k], *s.* (*Zool.*) der Haifisch, Hai; (*fig.*) der Wucherer (*profiteer*), Hochstapler.
sharp [ʃɑ:p], *adj.* scharf; (*fig.*) intelligent. — *s.* (*Mus.*) das Kreuz.
sharpen [ʃɑ:pn], *v.a.* schärfen; spitzen (*pencil*).
sharpener ['ʃɑ:pnə], *s.* *pencil —*, der Bleistiftspitzer.
shatter ['ʃætə], *v.a.* zerschmettern. — *v.n.* zerbrechen.
shave [ʃeiv], *v.a., v.n.* (sich) rasieren; abschaben (*pare*). — *s.* die Rasur, das Rasieren.
shavings ['ʃeiviŋz], *s. pl.* die Hobelspäne, *m. pl.*
shawl [ʃɔ:l], *s.* der Schal, das Umschlagetuch.
she [ʃi:], *pers. pron.* sie.
sheaf [ʃi:f], *s.* die Garbe.
shear [ʃiə], *v.a. irr.* scheren (*sheep etc.*).
shears [ʃiəz], *s. pl.* die Schere.
sheath [ʃi:θ], *s.* die Scheide.
sheathe [ʃi:ð], *v.a.* in die Scheide stecken.
shed (1) [ʃed], *s.* der Schuppen.
shed (2) [ʃed], *v.a. irr.* vergießen (*blood, tears*); ausschütten.
sheen [ʃi:n], *s.* der Glanz.
sheep [ʃi:p], *s.* (*Zool.*) das Schaf.
sheer (1) [ʃiə], *adj.* rein, lauter; senkrecht.
sheer (2) [ʃiə], *v.n.* (*Naut.*) gieren, abgieren.
sheet [ʃi:t], *s.* das Bettuch; das Blatt, der Bogen (*paper*); die Platte (*metal*); — *metal*, — *iron*, das Eisenblech; — *lightning*, das Wetterleuchten.
shelf [ʃelf], *s.* das Brett, Regal; der Sims (*mantel*); (*Geog.*) die Sandbank; (*coll.*) *on the —*, sitzengeblieben.
shell [ʃel], *s.* die Schale (*case*); die Muschel (*mussel*); (*Mil.*) die Bombe, Granate. — *v.a.* schälen (*peas*); bombardieren, beschiessen (*town*).
shelter ['ʃeltə], *s.* das Obdach (*lodging*); der Unterstand, Schuppen; der Schutz (*protection*). — *v.a.* Obdach gewähren (*Dat.*); beschützen (*protect*). — *v.n.* sich schützen, unterstellen.
shelve [ʃelv], *v.a.* auf ein Brett legen; (*fig.*) aufschieben (*postpone*).
shelving ['ʃelviŋ], *s.* das Regal.
shepherd ['ʃepəd], *s.* der Schäfer, Hirt.
sheriff ['ʃerif], *s.* der Sheriff.
shew [ʃou] *see* **show**.
shield [ʃi:ld], *s.* der Schild. — *v.a.* schützen.
shift [ʃift], *v.a.* verschieben. — *v.n.* die Lage ändern. — *s.* die Veränderung, der Wechsel; (*Industry*) die Schicht.
shifty ['ʃifti], *adj.* unstet; durchtrieben.

shin [ʃin], *s.* (*Anat.*) das Schienbein.
shindy [ˈʃindi], *s.* der Lärm.
shine [ʃain], *v.n. irr.* scheinen (*sun*); glänzen. — *s.* der Glanz.
shingle (1) [ʃiŋgl], *s.* (*Build.*) die Schindel; (*Hair*) der Herrenschnitt.
shingle (2) [ʃiŋgl], *s.* (*Geol.*) der Kiesel.
shingles [ʃiŋglz], *s. pl.* (*Med.*) die Gürtelrose.
ship [ʃip], *s.* das Schiff. — *v.a.* verschiffen, (*Comm.*) versenden.
shipping [ˈʃipiŋ], *s.* die Schiffahrt; (*Comm.*) der Versand, die Verfrachtung, Verschiffung.
shire [ʃaiə], *s.* die Grafschaft.
shirk [ʃə:k], *v.a.* vermeiden, sich drücken (vor, *Dat.*).
shirt [ʃə:t], *s.* das Hemd.
shirting [ˈʃə:tiŋ], *s.* der Hemdenstoff.
shiver [ˈʃivə], *v.n.* zittern, beben. — *s.* der Schauer, Schauder.
shoal [ʃoul], *s.* der Schwarm; (*Naut.*) die Untiefe.
shock (1) [ʃɔk], *v.a.* entsetzen; erschrecken; schockieren. — *s.* der Schock, das Entsetzen.
shock (2) [ʃɔk], *s.* — *of hair*, zottiges Haar.
shoddy [ˈʃɔdi], *adj.* schlecht, wertlos.
shoe [ʃu:], *s.* der Schuh. — *v.a.* beschuhen; (*horse*) beschlagen.
shoelace, shoestring [ˈʃu:leis, ˈʃu:striŋ], *s.* der Schuhsenkel, (*Austr.*) das Schuhschnürl; *on a shoestring*, fast ohne Geld.
shoeshine [ˈʃu:ʃain], *s.* (*Am.*) der Schuhputzer.
shoestring *see under* **shoelace**.
shoot [ʃu:t], *v.a. irr.* schießen. — *v.n.* sprossen, hervorschießen; (*film*) aufnehmen. — *s.* (*Bot.*) der Sproß.
shooting [ˈʃu:tiŋ], *s.* das Schießen; — *range*, der Schießstand. — *adj.* — *star*, die Sternschnuppe.
shop [ʃɔp], *s.* der Laden, das Geschäft; (*work*) die Werkstatt; *talk* —, fachsimpeln; — *window*, das Schaufenster. — *v.n.* einkaufen.
shopkeeper [ˈʃɔpki:pə], *s.* der Kaufmann, Krämer.
shoplifter [ˈʃɔpliftə], *s.* der Ladendieb.
shore [ʃɔ:], *s.* das Gestade, die Küste; die Stütze. — *v.a.* — *up*, stützen.
short [ʃɔ:t], *adj.* kurz, klein, knapp; (*curt*) kurz angebunden; — *of money*, in Geldnot; *run* —, knapp werden; —*sighted*, kurzsichtig; *be on* — *time working*, kurz arbeiten. — *s.* (*Elect.*) (*coll.*) der Kurzschluß (*short circuit*); (*pl.*) die Kniehose, kurze Hose.
shortcoming [ˈʃɔ:tkʌmiŋ], *s.* der Fehler, Mangel.
shorten [ʃɔ:tn], *v.a.* verkürzen, abkürzen. — *v.n.* kürzer werden.
shorthand [ˈʃɔ:thænd], *s.* die Stenographie; — *typist*, die Stenotypistin.
shot [ʃɔt], *s.* der Schuß; (*man*) der Schütze.
shoulder [ˈʃouldə], *s.* (*Anat.*) die Schulter. — *v.a.* schultern, auf sich nehmen, auf die Achsel nehmen.
shout [ʃaut], *v.n.* schreien, rufen. — *s.* der Schrei, Ruf.
shove [ʃʌv], *v.a.* schieben, stoßen. — *s.* der Schub, Stoß.
shovel [ʃʌvl], *s.* die Schaufel. — *v.a.* schaufeln.
show [ʃou], *v.a. irr.* zeigen; (*fig.*) dartun. — *v.n.* sich zeigen, zu sehen sein; — *off*, prahlen, protzen. — *v.r.* — *o.s. to be*, sich erweisen als. — *s.* (*Theat.*) die Schau, Aufführung.
shower [ʃauə], *s.* der Schauer (*rain*); (*fig.*) die Fülle, der Überfluß; — (*bath*), die Dusche; *take a* —(*bath*), brausen. — *v.a.*, *v.n.* herabregnen; überschütten.
showing [ˈʃouiŋ], *s.* die Vorführung, der Beweis.
showy [ʃoui], *adj.* protzig, angeberisch.
shred [ʃred], *s.* der Fetzen; (*fig.*) die Spur (*of evidence*). — *v.a.* zerreißen, zerfetzen.
shrew [ʃru:], *s.* die Spitzmaus; (*fig.*) das zänkische Weib.
shrewd [ʃru:d], *adj.* schlau, verschlagen, listig.
shriek [ʃri:k], *v.n.* kreischen. — *s.* der Schrei, das Gekreisch.
shrift [ʃrift], *s. give s.o. short* —, mit einem kurzen Prozeß machen.
shrill [ʃril], *adj.* schrill, gellend, durchdringend.
shrimp [ʃrimp], *s.* (*Zool.*) die Garnele.
shrine [ʃrain], *s.* der (Reliquien)-schrein; der Altar.
shrink [ʃriŋk], *v.n. irr.* eingehen, einschrumpfen. — *v.a.* eingehen lassen.
shrinkage [ˈʃriŋkidʒ], *s.* das Eingehen (*fabric*); (*Geol.*) die Schrumpfung.
shrivel [ʃrivl], *v.n.* einschrumpfen, sich runzeln.
shroud [ʃraud], *s.* das Leichentuch. — *v.a.* einhüllen.
Shrove [ʃrouv] **Tuesday**. die Fastnacht.
shrub [ʃrʌb], *s.* (*Bot.*) der Strauch, die Staude.
shrug [ʃrʌg], *v.a.* (*shoulders*) die Achseln zucken. — *s.* das Achselzucken.
shudder [ˈʃʌdə], *s.* der Schauder. — *v.n.* schaudern.
shuffle [ʃʌfl], *v.a.* (*cards*) mischen. — *v.n.* schlürfen, schleppend gehen.
shun [ʃʌn], *v.a.* meiden.
shunt [ʃʌnt], *v.a.*, *v.n.* rangieren.
shut [ʃʌt], *v.a. irr.* schließen. — *v.n.* sich schließen, zugehen; (*coll.*) — *up!* halt's Maul!
shutter [ˈʃʌtə], *s.* der Fensterladen.
shuttle [ʃʌtl], *s.* (*Mech.*) das Weberschiff.
shuttlecock [ˈʃʌtlkɔk], *s.* der Federball.
shy (1) [ʃai], *adj.* scheu, schüchtern. — *v.n.* scheuen (*of horses*).
shy (2) [ʃai], *s.* der Wurf.
sick [sik], *adj.* krank; unwohl, übel; leidend (*suffering*); (*fig.*) — *of*, überdrüssig (*Genit.*).

sicken [sikn], *v.n.* krank werden *or* sein; sich ekeln (*be nauseated*). — *v.a.* anekeln.
sickle [sikl], *s.* die Sichel.
sickness ['siknis], *s.* die Krankheit.
side [said], *s.* die Seite. — *v.n.* — *with*, Partei ergreifen für.
sideboard ['saidbɔ:d], *s.* das Büffet, die Anrichte.
sidereal [sai'diəriəl], *adj.* (*Maths.*, *Phys.*) Sternen-, Stern-.
sidewalk ['saidwɔ:k] (*Am.*) *see* **pavement.**
siding ['saidiŋ], *s.* (*Railw.*) das Nebengleis.
sidle [saidl], *v.n.* — *up to*, sich heranmachen.
siege [si:dʒ], *s.* die Belagerung.
sieve [siv], *s.* das Sieb. — *v.a.* sieben.
sift [sift], *v.a.* sieben; (*fig.*) prüfen.
sigh [sai], *v.n.* seufzen. — *s.* der Seufzer.
sight [sait], *s.* die Sicht (*view*); die Sehkraft (*sense of*); der Anblick; *at* —, auf den ersten Blick; *out of* —, *out of mind*, aus den Augen, aus dem Sinn; (*pl.*) die Sehenswürdigkeiten, *f. pl.*; *—seeing*, die Besichtigung (der Sehenswürdigkeiten). — *v.a.* sichten.
sign [sain], *s.* das Zeichen; der Wink (*hint*); das Aushängeschild (*of pub, shop etc*). — *v.a.* unterschreiben, unterzeichnen. — *v.n.* winken.
signal ['signəl], *s.* das Signal.
signboard ['sainbɔ:d], *s.* das Aushängeschild.
signet ['signit], *s.* das Siegel; — *ring*, der Siegelring.
significance [sig'nifikəns], *s.* die Bedeutung, der Sinn.
significant [sig'nifikənt], *adj.* bedeutend, wichtig.
signify ['signifai], *v.a.* bedeuten (*mean*); anzeigen (*denote*).
silence ['sailəns], *s.* das Schweigen, die Ruhe.
silent ['sailənt], *adj.* still; schweigsam (*taciturn*).
Silesian [sai'li:ʃən], *adj.* schlesisch. — *s.* der Schlesier.
silk [silk], *s.* (*Text.*) die Seide.
silkworm ['silkwə:m], *s.* (*Ent.*) die Seidenraupe.
sill [sil], *s.* die Schwelle; *window* —, das Fensterbrett.
silly ['sili], *adj.* albern, dumm.
silver ['silvə], *s.* das Silber. — *v.a.* versilbern. — *adj.* silbern.
similar ['similə], *adj.* ähnlich.
simile ['simili], *s.* (*Lit.*) das Gleichnis.
simmer ['simə], *v.n.*, *v.a.* langsam kochen.
simper ['simpə], *v.n.* lächeln, grinsen.
simple [simpl], *adj.* einfach; (*fig.*) einfältig.
simpleton ['simpltən], *s.* der Einfaltspinsel, Tor.
simplicity [sim'plisiti], *s.* die Einfachheit; (*fig.*) die Einfalt.
simplify ['simplifai], *v.a.* vereinfachen.
simulate ['simjuleit], *v.a.* nachahmen, heucheln, vortäuschen.
simultaneous [siməl'teinjəs], *adj.* gleichzeitig.
sin [sin], *s.* die Sünde. — *v.n.* sündigen.
since [sins], *prep.* seit (*Dat.*). — *conj.* seit (*time*); weil, da (*cause*). — *adv.* seither, seitdem.
sincere [sin'siə], *adj.* aufrichtig.
sincerely [sin'siəli], *adv.* *yours* —, Ihr ergebener (*letters*).
sincerity [sin'seriti], *s.* die Aufrichtigkeit.
sine [sain], *s.* (*Maths.*) der Sinus, die Sinuskurve.
sinecure ['sainikjuə], *s.* der Ruheposten, die Sinekure.
sinew ['sinju:], *s.* (*Anat.*) die Sehne, der Nerv.
sinful ['sinful], *adj.* sündig, sündhaft.
sing [siŋ], *v.a.*, *v.n.* *irr.* singen; — *of*, besingen.
singe [sindʒ], *v.a.* sengen.
Singhalese [siŋgə'li:z], *adj.* singhalesisch. — *s.* der Singhalese, die Singhalesin.
single [siŋgl], *adj.* einzeln; ledig (*unmarried*; *single-handed*, allein. — *v.a.* — *out*, auswählen.
singlet ['siŋglit], *s.* die Unterjacke.
singly ['siŋgli], *adv.* einzeln (*one by one*).
singular ['siŋgjulə], *adj.* einzigartig, einzig. — *s.* (*Gram.*) die Einzahl.
sinister ['sinistə], *adj.* böse, unheimlich, finster.
sink [siŋk], *v.a.* *irr.* versenken; (*fig.*) (*differences etc.*) begraben. — *v.n.* versinken; (*Naut.*) sinken, versinken. — *s.* das Abwaschbecken, Ausgußbecken.
sinker ['siŋkə], *s.* der Schachtarbeiter (*man*); (*Naut.*) das Senkblei.
sinuous ['sinjuəs], *adj.* gewunden.
sinus ['sainəs], *s.* (*Anat.*) die Knochenhöhle; die Bucht.
sip [sip], *v.a.* schlürfen, nippen. — *s.* das Schlückchen.
siphon ['saifən], *s.* (*Phys.*) der Heber; die Siphonflasche. — *v.a.* auspumpen.
Sir (1) [sə:] (*title preceding Christian name*) Herr von ... (*baronet or knight*).
sir (2) [sə:], *s.* Herr (*respectful form of address*); *dear* —, sehr geehrter Herr (*in letters*).
sire [saiə], *s.* der Ahnherr, Vater. — *v.a.* zeugen (*horses etc.*).
siren ['saiərən], *s.* die Sirene.
sirloin ['sə:lɔin], *s.* das Lendenstück.
siskin ['siskin], *s.* (*Orn.*) der Zeisig.
sister ['sistə], *s.* die Schwester; (*Eccl.*) Nonne; *—in-law*, die Schwägerin.
sit [sit], *v.n.* *irr.* sitzen. — *v.a.* — *an examination*, eine Prüfung machen.
site [sait], *s.* die Lage, der Platz.
sitting ['sitiŋ], *s.* die Sitzung; — *room*, das Wohnzimmer.
situated ['sitjueitid], *adj.* gelegen.
situation [sitju'eiʃən], *s.* die Lage, Situation; der Posten, die Stellung (*post*).

six [siks], *num. adj.* sechs; *be at —es and sevens*, durcheinander, uneinig sein.
sixteen [siks'ti:n], *num. adj.* sechzehn.
sixth [siksθ], *num. adj.* sechste.
sixty ['siksti], *num. adj.* sechzig.
size [saiz], *s.* die Größe, das Maß; (*fig.*) der Umfang.
skate (1) [skeit], *s.* der Schlittschuh. — *v.n.* Schlittschuh laufen.
skate (2) [skeit], *s.* (*Zool.*) der Glattrochen.
skeleton ['skelitən], *s.* das Skelett, Knochengerüst; — *key*, der Dietrich.
sketch [sketʃ], *s.* die Skizze, der Entwurf. — *v.a.* skizzieren, entwerfen. — *v.n.* Skizzen entwerfen.
sketchy ['sketʃi], *adj.* flüchtig.
skew [skju:], *adj.* schief, schräg.
skewer [skju:ə], *s.* der Fleischspieß.
ski [ski:], *s.* der Schi.
skid [skid], *v.n.* gleiten, schleudern, rutschen. — *v.a.* hemmen, bremsen (*wheel*). — *s.* der Hemmschuh, die Bremse (*of wheel*).
skiff [skif], *s.* (*Naut.*) der Nachen, Kahn.
skilful ['skilful], *adj.* geschickt, gewandt; (*fig.*) erfahren.
skill [skil], *s.* die Geschicklichkeit, Gewandtheit; (*fig.*) die Erfahrung.
skim [skim], *v.a.* abschöpfen, abschäumen.
skimp [skimp], *v.a.* knausern, sparsam sein (mit, *Dat.*).
skimpy ['skimpi], *adj.* knapp.
skin [skin], *s.* die Haut; die Schale (*fruit*); — *deep*, oberflächlich. — *v.a.* häuten, schinden.
skinflint ['skinflint], *s.* der Geizhals.
skinner ['skinə], *s.* der Kürschner.
skip [skip], *v.n.* springen, hüpfen. — *v.a.* (*coll.*) auslassen, überspringen. — *s.* der Sprung.
skipper ['skipə], *s.* (*Naut.*) der Kapitän; (*coll.*) der Chef.
skipping rope ['skipiŋ roup], *s.* das Springseil.
skirmish ['skə:miʃ], *s.* das Scharmützel. — *v.n.* scharmützeln.
skirt [skə:t], *s.* der Rock, Rockschoß (*woman's garment*); der Saum (*edge*). — *v.a.* einsäumen (*seam, edge*); grenzen, am Rande entlang gehen.
skirting (board) ['skə:tiŋ (bɔ:d)], *s.* die Fußleiste.
skit [skit], *s.* die Stichelei, die Parodie, Satire.
skittish ['skitiʃ], *adj.* leichtfertig.
skulk [skʌlk], *v.n.* lauern, herumlungern.
skull [skʌl], *s.* der Schädel; — *and crossbones*, der Totenkopf.
skunk [skʌŋk], *s.* (*Zool.*) das Stinktier; (*coll.*) der Schuft.
sky [skai], *s.* der (sichtbare) Himmel.
skylark ['skailɑ:k], *s.* (*Orn.*) die Feldlerche.
skylarking ['skailɑ:kiŋ], *s.* das Possenreißen, die Streiche.
skyline ['skailain], *s.* der Horizont.
skyscraper ['skaiskreipə], *s.* der Wolkenkratzer.

slab [slæb], *s.* die Platte (*stone*); die Tafel, das Stück.
slack [slæk], *adj.* schlaff (*feeble*); locker (*loose*). — *s.* der Kohlengrus. — *v.n.* nachlassen, locker werden, faulenzen.
slacken [slækn], *v.a.*, *v.n.* locker werden, nachlassen.
slackness ['slæknis], *s.* die Schlaffheit, Faulheit.
slag [slæg], *s.* die Schlacke.
slake [sleik], *v.a.* dämpfen, löschen, stillen.
slam (1) [slæm], *v.a.* zuwerfen, zuschlagen (*door*). — *s.* der Schlag.
slam (2) [slæm], *v.a.* (*Cards*) Schlemm ansagen, Schlemm machen. — *s.* (*Cards*) der Stich.
slander ['slɑ:ndə], *v.a.* verleumden. — *s.* die Verleumdung.
slanderer ['slɑ:ndərə], *s.* der Verleumder.
slang [slæŋ], *s.* der Slang.
slant [slɑ:nt], *s.* die schräge Richtung, der Winkel (*angle*).
slap [slæp], *v.a.* schlagen. — *s.* der Klaps, Schlag.
slapdash ['slæpdæʃ], *adj.* oberflächlich.
slash [slæʃ], *v.a.* schlitzen, aufschlitzen; (*coll.*) (*Comm.*) herunterbringen (*prices*). — *s.* der Hieb, Schlag.
slate [sleit], *s.* der Schiefer. — *v.a.* mit Schiefer decken; (*fig.*) ankreiden, ausschelten (*scold*).
slattern ['slætə:n], *s.* die Schlampe.
slaughter ['slɔ:tə], *v.a.* schlachten; niedermetzeln. — *s.* das Schlachten; das Gemetzel.
slave [sleiv], *s.* der Sklave; — *driver*, der Sklavenaufseher. — *v.n.* — (*away*), sich placken, sich rackern.
slavery ['sleivəri], *s.* die Sklaverei.
slavish ['sleiviʃ], *adj.* sklavisch.
slay [slei], *v.a.* erschlagen, töten.
sled, sledge [sled, sledʒ], *s.* der Schlitten.
sleek [sli:k], *adj.* glatt. — *v.a.* glätten.
sleep [sli:p], *v.n. irr.* schlafen. — *s.* der Schlaf.
sleeper ['sli:pə], *s.* der Schläfer; (*Railw.*) die Bahnschwelle; der Schlafwagen (*sleeping car*).
sleepwalker ['sli:pwɔ:kə], *s.* der Nachtwandler.
sleet [sli:t], *s.* der Graupelregen.
sleeve [sli:v], *s.* der Ärmel; der Umschlag (*of record*); *have up o.'s* —, eine Überraschung bereithalten; *laugh in o.'s* —, sich ins Fäustchen lachen.
sleigh [slei], *s.* der Schlitten; — *ride*, die Schlittenfahrt.
sleight [slait], *s.* — *of hand*, der Taschenspielerstreich; der Trick.
slender ['slendə], *adj.* schlank, dünn, gering.
slice [slais], *s.* die Schnitte, Scheibe. — *v.a.* in Scheiben schneiden.
slick [slik], *adj.* glatt.
slide [slaid], *v.n. irr.* gleiten, rutschen (*glide*). — *v.a.* einschieben. — *s.* die Rutschbahn; (*Phot.*) das Dia, Diapositiv; — *rule*, der Rechenschieber.

slight [slait], *adj.* leicht (*light*), gering (*small*); (*fig.*) schwach, dünn (*weak*). — *s.* die Geringschätzung, Respektlosigkeit. — *v.a.* mißachten, geringschätzig behandeln.
slim [slim], *adj.* schlank.
slime [slaim], *s.* der Schleim (*phlegm*); der Schlamm (*mud*).
sling [sliŋ], *v.a. irr.* schleudern, werfen. — *s.* die Schleuder; (*Med.*) die Binde; der Wurf (*throw*).
slink [sliŋk], *v.n. irr.* schleichen.
slip [slip], *v.n.* ausgleiten; — *away*, entschlüpfen; — *up*, einen Fehltritt begehen (*err*). — *v.a.* gleiten lassen, schieben. — *s.* das Ausgleiten; (*fig.*) der Fehltritt; der Fehler (*mistake*); der Unterrock (*petticoat*); *give s.o. the* —, einem entgehen, entschlüpfen.
slipper ['slipə], *s.* der Pantoffel, Hausschuh.
slippery ['slipəri], *adj.* schlüpfrig, glatt.
slipshod ['slipʃɔd], *adj.* nachlässig.
slit [slit], *v.a.* schlitzen, spalten. — *s.* der Schlitz, Spalt.
slither ['sliðə], *v.n.* gleiten, rutschen.
sloe [slou], *s.* (*Bot.*) die Schlehe.
slogan ['slougən], *s.* das Schlagwort.
sloop [slu:p], *s.* (*Naut.*) die Schaluppe.
slop [slɔp], *s.* das Spülicht, Spülwasser.
slope [sloup], *s.* der Abhang, die Abdachung. — *v.n.* sich neigen. — *v.a.* abschrägen.
sloppy ['slɔpi], *adj.* unordentlich, nachlässig.
slot [slɔt], *s.* der Spalt, Schlitz (*slit*); die Kerbe (*notch*); — *machine*, der Automat.
sloth [slouθ], *s.* die Trägheit; (*Zool.*) das Faultier.
slouch [slautʃ], *v.n.* umherschlendern; sich schlaff halten.
slough [slau], *s.* der Morast, Sumpf.
slovenly ['slʌvnli], *adj.* schlampig, schmutzig.
slow [slou], *adj.* langsam; (*Phot.*) — *motion*, die Zeitlupenaufnahme. — *v.n.* — *down*, langsamer fahren *or* laufen.
slow-worm ['slouwə:m], *s.* (*Zool.*) die Blindschleiche.
sludge [slʌdʒ], *s.* der Schlamm, Schmutz.
slug [slʌg], *s.* (*Zool.*) die Wegschnecke; (*Am.*) die Kugel.
sluggish ['slʌgiʃ], *adj.* träg(e).
sluice [slu:s], *s.* die Schleuse. — *v.a.* ablassen (*drain*); begießen (*water*).
slum [slʌm], *s.* das Elendsviertel; Haus im Elendsviertel.
slumber ['slʌmbə], *s.* der Schlummer. — *v.n.* schlummern.
slump [slʌmp], *s.* (*Comm.*) der Tiefstand der Konjunktur; der Preissturz. — *v.n.* stürzen.
slur [slə:], *v.a.* undeutlich sprechen. — *s.* der Schandfleck, die Beleidigung; das Bindezeichen.
slush [slʌʃ], *s.* der Matsch, Schlamm; (*Lit.*) der Kitsch, die Schundliteratur.
slut [slʌt], *s.* die Schlampe.
sly [slai], *adj.* schlau, listig.
smack [smæk], *v.n.* schmecken (*of*, nach, *Dat.*). — *v.a.* schmatzen, lecken. — *s.* der Klaps. — *adv.* (*coll.*) — *in the middle*, gerade in der Mitte.
small [smɔ:l], *adj.* klein; (*fig.*) kleinlich (*petty*); — *talk*, das Geplauder.
smallpox ['smɔ:lpɔks], *s.* (*Med.*) die Blattern, *f. pl.*
smart [smɑ:t], *adj.* schneidig; elegant, schick (*well-dressed*). — *v.n.* schmerzen. — *s.* der Schmerz.
smash [smæʃ], *v.a.* zertrümmern, in Stücke schlagen. — *v.n.* zerschmettern; (*fig.*) zusammenbrechen. — *s.* der Krach.
smattering ['smætəriŋ], *s.* die oberflächliche Kenntnis.
smear [smiə], *v.a.* beschmieren; (*Am. coll.*) den Charakter angreifen, verleumden. — *s.* die Beschmierung, Befleckung.
smell [smel], *v.a. irr.* riechen. — *v.n.* riechen (nach, *Dat.*). — *s.* der Geruch.
smelt (1) [smelt], *v.a.* (*Metall.*) schmelzen.
smelt (2) [smelt], *s.* (*Zool.*) der Stintfisch.
smile [smail], *v.n.* lächeln. — *s.* das Lächeln.
smirk [smə:k], *v.n.* grinsen. — *s.* das Grinsen, die Grimasse.
smite [smait], *v.a. irr.* treffen, schlagen.
smith [smiθ], *s.* der Schmied.
smitten [smitn], *adj.* verliebt.
smock [smɔk], *s.* der Arbeitskittel.
smoke [smouk], *v.a., v.n.* rauchen; räuchern (*fish etc.*). — *s.* der Rauch.
smoked [smoukd], *adj.* — *ham*, der Räucherschinken.
smooth [smu:ð], *adj.* glatt, sanft (*to touch*); (*fig.*) glatt, geschmeidig, wendig. — *v.a.* glätten, ebnen.
smother ['smʌðə], *v.a.* ersticken.
smoulder ['smouldə], *v.n.* schwelen.
smudge [smʌdʒ], *v.a.* beschmutzen. — *v.n.* schmieren, schmutzen. — *s.* der Schmutzfleck, Schmutz.
smug [smʌg], *adj.* selbstgefällig.
smuggle [smʌgl], *v.a.* schmuggeln.
smuggler ['smʌglə], *s.* der Schmuggler.
smut [smʌt], *v.a., v.n.* beschmutzen. — *s.* (*fig.*) der Schmutz.
snack [snæk], *s.* der Imbiß.
snaffle [snæfl], *s.* die Trense.
snag [snæg], *s.* die Schwierigkeit; der Haken.
snail [sneil], *s.* (*Zool.*) die Schnecke.
snake [sneik], *s.* (*Zool.*) die Schlange.
snap [snæp], *v.n.* schnappen (*at*, nach, *Dat.*); (*fig.*) einen anfahren (*shout at s.o.*). — *v.a.* (er)schnappen; (*Phot.*) knipsen. — *s.* (*abbr. for* **snapshot** ['snæpʃɔt]) (*Phot.*) das Photo.
snare [snɛə], *s.* die Schlinge. — *v.a.* *see* **ensnare**.
snarl [snɑ:l], *v.n.* knurren (*dog*); — *at s.o.*, einen anfahren, anschnauzen.

snatch [snætʃ], *v.a.* erschnappen, erhaschen.
sneak [sni:k], *v.n.* kriechen, schleichen. — *s.* der Kriecher.
sneer [sniə], *v.n.* höhnen, verhöhnen (*at*, *Acc.*). — *s.* der Spott.
sneeze [sni:z], *v.n.* niesen. — *s.* das Niesen.
sniff [snif], *v.a.*, *v.n.* schnüffeln.
snigger ['snigə], *v.n.* kichern. — *s.* das Kichern.
snip [snip], *v.a.* schneiden, schnippeln.
snipe (1) [snaip], *s.* (*Orn.*) die Schnepfe.
snipe (2) [snaip], *v.n.* schießen.
snivel [snivl], *v.n.* schluchzen (*from weeping*); verschnupft sein (*with a cold*).
snob [snɔb], *s.* der Snob.
snobbish ['snɔbiʃ], *adj.* vornehm tuend; protzig, snobistisch.
snooze [snu:z], *s.* das Schläfchen. — *v.n.* einschlafen, ein Schläfchen machen.
snore [snɔ:], *v.n.* schnarchen. — *s.* das Schnarchen.
snort [snɔ:t], *v.n.* schnaufen; schnarchen (*snore*).
snout [snaut], *s.* die Schnauze, der Rüssel.
snow [snou], *s.* der Schnee. — *v.n.* schneien.
snowdrift ['snoudrift], *s.* das Schneegestöber.
snowdrop ['snoudrɔp], *s.* (*Bot.*) das Schneeglöckchen.
snub [snʌb], *v.a.* kurz abfertigen; (*fig.*) schneiden (*ignore*). — *adj.* — *nosed*, stumpfnasig. — *s.* die Geringschätzung, das Ignorieren.
snuff [snʌf], *s.* der Schnupftabak. — *v.a.* ausblasen (*candle*).
snug [snʌg], *adj.* behaglich; geborgen (*protected*).
so [sou], *adv.* so, also; *not — as*, nicht so wie. — *conj.* so.
soak [souk], *v.a.* einweichen, durchtränken. — *v.n.* weichen, durchsickern (*in*(*to*), in, *Acc.*). — *s.* der Regenguß.
soap [soup], *s.* die Seife. — *v.a.* einseifen.
soar [sɔ:], *v.n.* sich aufschwingen, schweben.
sob [sɔb], *v.n.* schluchzen. — *s.* das Schluchzen.
sober ['soubə], *adj.* nüchtern. — *v.a.*, *v.n.* — (*down*), (sich) ernüchtern.
sobriety [so'braiəti], *s.* die Nüchternheit.
soccer ['sɔkə], *s.* (*Sport*) das Fußballspiel.
sociable ['souʃəbl], *adj.* gesellig.
social ['souʃəl], *adj.* sozial, gesellschaftlich. — *s.* die Gesellschaft (*party*).
socialism ['souʃəlizm], *s.* (*Pol.*) der Sozialismus.
socialist ['souʃəlist], *adj.* (*Pol.*) sozialistisch, Sozial-. — *s.* der Sozialist.
society [sə'saiəti], *s.* die Gesellschaft (*human* —); der Verein (*association*); (*Comm.*) die (Handels)gesellschaft.
sock (1) [sɔk], *s.* der Strumpf.
sock (2) [sɔk], *v.a.* (*sl.*) schlagen, boxen.
socket ['sɔkit], *s.* *eye* —, die Augenhöhle; (*Elec.*) die Steckdose.
sod [sɔd], *s.* der Rasen, die Erde.
sodden [sɔdn], *adj.* durchweicht.
sofa ['soufə], *s.* das Sofa.
soft [sɔft], *adj.* weich, sanft; einfältig (*stupid*).
soften [sɔfn], *v.a.* weich machen, erweichen. — *v.n.* weich werden, erweichen.
soil [sɔil], *s.* der Boden, die Erde. — *v.a.* beschmutzen.
sojourn ['sʌdʒən *or* 'sɔdʒən], *s.* der Aufenthalt. — *v.n.* sich aufhalten.
solace ['sɔlis], *s.* der Trost.
solar ['soulə], *adj.* Sonnen-.
solder ['sɔldə *or* 'sɔ:də], *v.a.* löten. — *s.* das Lötmittel.
soldier ['souldʒə], *s.* der Soldat. — *v.n.* dienen, Soldat sein.
sole (1) [soul], *s.* (*Zool.*) die Seezunge.
sole (2) [soul], *s.* die Sohle (*foot*).
sole (3) [soul], *adj.* allein, einzig.
solecism ['sɔlisizm], *s.* der Sprachschnitzer.
solemn ['sɔləm], *adj.* feierlich.
solemnize ['sɔləmnaiz], *v.a.* feiern, feierlich begehen.
solicit [sə'lisit], *v.a.* direkt erbitten, angehen, anhalten (*for*, um).
solicitor [sə'lisitə], *s.* (*Law*) der Anwalt, Rechtsanwalt.
solicitous [sə'lisitəs], *adj.* besorgt.
solid ['sɔlid], *adj.* fest; solide; (*fig.*) gediegen; massiv (*bulky*).
solidify [sə'lidifai], *v.a.* verdichten, fest machen. — *v.n.* sich verfestigen.
soliloquy [sə'liləkwi], *s.* das Selbstgespräch, der Monolog.
solitaire [sɔli'tɛə], *s.* der Solitär; (*Am.*) die Patience.
solitary ['sɔlitəri], *adj.* einzeln (*single*); einsam (*lonely*).
solitude ['sɔlitju:d], *s.* die Einsamkeit.
solstice ['sɔlstis], *s.* die Sonnenwende.
soluble ['sɔljubl], *adj.* (*Chem.*) löslich; lösbar.
solution [sə'lju:ʃən], *s.* die Lösung.
solvable ['sɔlvəbl], *adj.* (auf)lösbar (*problem, puzzle*).
solve [sɔlv], *v.a.* lösen (*problem, puzzle*).
solvent ['sɔlvənt], *adj.* (*Chem.*) auflösend; (*Comm.*) zahlungsfähig. — *s.* das Lösungsmittel.
sombre ['sɔmbə], *adj.* düster; schwermütig, traurig.
some [sʌm], *adj.* irgend ein, etwas; (*pl.*) einige, manche; etliche.
somebody ['sʌmbɔdi], *s.* jemand.
somersault ['sʌməsɔ:lt], *s.* der Purzelbaum.
sometimes ['sʌmtaimz], *adv.* manchmal, zuweilen.
somewhat ['sʌmwɔt], *adv.* etwas, ziemlich.
somewhere ['sʌmwɛə], *adv.* irgendwo(hin).

somnambulist [sɔm'næmbjulist], *s.* der Nachtwandler.
somnolent ['sɔmnələnt], *adj.* schläfrig, schlafsüchtig.
son [sʌn], *s.* der Sohn; —*-in-law*, der Schwiegersohn.
song [sɔŋ], *s.* (*Mus.*) das Lied; der Gesang; *for a* —, spottbillig.
sonnet ['sɔnit], *s.* (*Poet.*) das Sonett.
sonorous ['sɔnərəs], *adj.* wohlklingend.
soon [su:n], *adv.* bald.
sooner ['su:nə], *comp. adv.* lieber (*rather*); früher, eher (*earlier*), *no — said than done*, gesagt, getan.
soot [sut], *s.* der Ruß.
soothe [su:ð], *v.a.* besänftigen.
soothsayer ['su:θseiə], *s.* der Wahrsager.
sop [sɔp], *s.* der eingetunkte Bissen; (*fig.*) die Bestechung (*bribe*).
soporific [sɔpə'rifik], *adj.* einschläfernd.
soprano [sə'prɑ:nou], *s.* (*Mus.*) der Sopran.
sorcerer ['sɔ:sərə], *s.* der Zauberer.
sorceress ['sɔ:səres], *s.* die Hexe.
sorcery ['sɔ:səri], *s.* die Zauberei, Hexerei.
sordid ['sɔ:did], *adj.* schmutzig; gemein.
sore [sɔ:], *adj.* wund, schmerzhaft; empfindlich. — *s.* die wunde Stelle.
sorrel (1) ['sɔrəl], *s.* (*Bot.*) der Sauerampfer.
sorrel (2) ['sɔrəl], *s.* (*Zool.*) der Rotfuchs.
sorrow ['sɔrou], *s.* der Kummer, das Leid, der Gram.
sorry ['sɔri], *adj.* traurig; *I am* —, es tut mir leid.
sort [sɔ:t], *s.* die Art, Gattung, Sorte. — *v.a.* aussortieren.
sortie ['sɔ:ti:], *s.* (*Mil.*) der Ausfall.
sot [sɔt], *s.* der Trunkenbold.
soul [soul], *s.* die Seele; *not a* —, niemand, keine Menschenseele.
sound (1) [saund], *v.n.*, *v.a.* tönen, klingen, erklingen lassen. — *s.* der Klang, Ton, Laut.
sound (2) [saund], *adj.* gesund; (*fig.*) vernünftig (*plan etc.*); solide.
soup [su:p], *s.* die Suppe.
sour [sauə], *adj.* sauer; (*fig.*) mürrisch.
source [sɔ:s], *s.* die Quelle; der Ursprung (*origin*).
souse [saus], *v.a.* einpökeln, einsalzen.
south [sauθ], *s.* der Süden.
South African [sauθ 'æfrikən], *adj.* südafrikanisch. — *s.* der Südafrikaner.
southern ['sʌðən], *adj.* südlich, Süd-.
sou(th)-wester [sau(θ)'westə], *s.* (*Naut.*) der Südwester.
souvenir ['su:vəniə], *s.* das Andenken.
sovereign ['sɔvrin], *s.* der Herrscher (*ruler*); das Goldstück (*£1 coin*). — *adj.* allerhöchst, souverän.
Soviet ['souviit], *adj.* sowjetisch. — *s.* der Sowjet.
sow (1) [sau], *s.* (*Zool.*) die Sau.
sow (2) [sou], *v.a. irr.* säen, ausstreuen (*cast*).
spa [spɑ:], *s.* das Bad; der Kurort.
space [speis], *s.* der Zwischenraum (*interval*); der Raum, das Weltall, der Kosmos (*interplanetary*); der Platz (*room*). — *v.a.* sperren, richtig plazieren.
spacious ['speiʃəs], *adj.* geräumig.
spade [speid], *s.* der Spaten; *call a — a* —, das Kind beim rechten Namen nennen; (*Cards*) das Pik.
span [spæn], *s.* die Spanne (*time*); die Spannweite. — *v.a.* überspannen (*bridge*); ausmessen.
spangle [spæŋgl], *s.* der Flitter. — *v.a.* beflittern, schmücken.
Spaniard ['spænjəd], *s.* der Spanier.
spaniel ['spænjəl], *s.* (*Zool.*) der Wachtelhund.
Spanish ['spæniʃ], *adj.* spanisch.
spanner ['spænə], *s.* der Schraubenschlüssel.
spar (1) [spɑ:], *s.* (*Naut.*) der Sparren.
spar (2) [spɑ:], *s.* (*Geol.*) der Spat.
spar (3) [spɑ:], *v.n.* boxen.
spare [spɛə], *v.a.* schonen (*save*); sparsam sein; übrig haben. — *v.n.* sparen; sparsam sein. — *adj.* übrig (*extra*); mager, hager (*lean*); Reserve- (*tyre etc.*).
sparing ['spɛəriŋ], *adj.* sparsam, karg.
spark [spɑ:k], *s.* der Funken; (*fig.*) der helle Kopf.
sparkle [spɑ:kl], *v.n.* glänzen, funkeln. — *s.* das Funkeln.
sparrow ['spærou], *s.* (*Orn.*) der Sperling.
sparrowhawk ['spærouhɔ:k], *s.* (*Orn.*) der Sperber.
sparse [spɑ:s], *adj.* spärlich, dünn.
spasm [spæzm], *s.* der Krampf.
spasmodic [spæz'mɔdik], *adj.* krampfhaft; (*fig.*) ab und zu auftretend.
spats [spæts], *s. pl.* die Gamaschen, *f.pl.*
spatter ['spætə], *v.a.* bespritzen, besudeln.
spatula ['spætjulə], *s.* der Spachtel.
spawn [spɔ:n], *s.* der Laich, die Brut.
speak [spi:k], *v.a.*, *v.n. irr.* sprechen, reden; — *out*, frei heraussprechen.
speaker ['spi:kə], *s.* der Sprecher.
spear [spiə], *s.* der Spieß, Speer, die Lanze. — *v.a.* aufspießen.
special [speʃl], *adj.* besonder, speziell, Sonder-.
specific [spi'sifik], *adj.* spezifisch, eigentümlich.
specify ['spesifai], *v.a.* spezifizieren.
specimen ['spesimən], *s.* die Probe; (*Comm.*) das Muster.
specious ['spi:ʃəs], *adj.* bestechend, trügerisch.
speck [spek], *s.* der Fleck.
speckle [spekl], *s.* der Tüpfel, Sprenkel. — *v.a.* sprenkeln.
spectacle ['spektəkl], *s.* das Schauspiel, der Anblick; (*pl.*) die Brille.
spectator [spek'teitə], *s.* der Zuschauer.
spectre ['spektə], *s.* das Gespenst.
speculate ['spekjuleit], *v.n.* nachsinnen, grübeln (*ponder*); spekulieren.

speculative ['spekjulətiv], *adj.* spekulativ; sinnend.
speech [spi:tʃ], *s.* die Rede, Ansprache; das Sprechen (*articulation*); *figure of —*, die Redewendung; *make a —*, eine Rede halten.
speechify ['spi:tʃifai], *v.n.* viele Worte machen, unermüdlich reden.
speed [spi:d], *s.* die Eile; die Geschwindigkeit (*velocity*); (*Mus.*) das Tempo. — *v.a.* (eilig) fortschicken. — *v.n.* eilen, schnell fahren; — *up*, sich beeilen.
spell (1) [spel], *s.* der Zauber (*enchantment*). — *v.a.* buchstabieren (*verbally*); richtig schreiben (*in writing*).
spell (2) [spel], *s.* die Zeitlang, Zeit (*period*).
spellbound ['spelbaund], *adj.* bezaubert, gebannt.
spend [spend], *v.a. irr.* ausgeben (*money*); verbringen (*time*); aufwenden (*energy*); erschöpfen (*exhaust*).
spendthrift ['spendθrift], *s.* der Verschwender.
spew [spju:], *v.a.* speien; ausspeien.
sphere [sfiə], *s.* die Sphäre (*also fig.*); (*Geom.*) die Kugel.
spice [spais], *s.* die Würze (*seasoning*); das Gewürz (*herb*). — *v.a.* würzen.
spider ['spaidə], *s.* (*Zool.*) die Spinne.
spigot ['spigət], *s.* (*Mech.*) der Zapfen.
spike [spaik], *s.* die Spitze, der lange Nagel; (*fig.*) der Dorn. — *v.a.* durchbohren, spießen; (*Mil.*) vernageln (*a gun*).
spill (1) [spil], *v.a. irr.* ausschütten, vergießen; (*Am. coll.*) — *the beans*, mit der Sprache herausrücken, alles verraten; *it's no good crying over spilt milk*, was geschehen ist, ist geschehen.
spill (2) [spil], *s.* der Fidibus.
spin [spin], *v.a. irr.* spinnen, drehen, wirbeln. — *v.n.* wirbeln, sich schnell drehen; — *dry*, schleudern. — *s.* die schnelle Drehung; — *drier*, die Wäscheschleuder.
spinach ['spinidʒ], *s.* (*Bot.*) der Spinat.
spinal ['spainəl], *adj.* Rückgrats-.
spine [spain], *s.* (*Anat.*) die Wirbelsäule; der Rücken (*of book*).
spinney ['spini], *s.* das Gestrüpp.
spinster ['spinstə], *s.* die (alte) Jungfer; die unverheiratete Dame.
spiral ['spaiərəl], *adj.* Spiral-, gewunden. — *s.* (*Geom.*) die Spirale.
spirant ['spaiərənt], *s.* (*Phonet.*) der Spirant.
spire [spaiə], *s.* (*Archit.*) die Turmspitze.
spirit ['spirit], *s.* der Geist; das Gespenst (*ghost*); der Mut (*courage*); die Stimmung, Verfassung (*mood*); das geistige Getränk (*drink*), (*pl.*) Spirituosen, *pl.*; *in high —s*, in guter Stimmung, Laune. — *v.a.* — *away*, entführen, verschwinden lassen.
spiritual ['spiritjuəl], *adj.* geistig (*mental*); (*Rel.*) geistlich. — *s.* (*Mus.*) das Negerlied.
spit (1) [spit], *s.* der Spieß, Bratspieß. — *v.a.* aufspießen.
spit (2) [spit], *v.n. irr.* ausspucken. — *s.* die Spucke.
spite [spait], *s.* der Groll; *in — of*, trotz (*Genit.*). — *v.a.* ärgern.
spiteful ['spaitful], *adj.* boshaft.
spittle [spitl], *s.* der Speichel.
spittoon, [spi'tu:n], *s.* der Spucknapf.
splash [splæʃ], *s.* der Spritzer; *make a —*, Aufsehen erregen. — *v.a., v.n.* spritzen; (*fig.*) um sich werfen (*money etc.*).
splay [splei], *v.a.* ausrenken, verrenken.
spleen [spli:n], *s.* (*Anat.*) die Milz; (*fig.*) der Spleen, die Laune, Marotte.
splendour ['splendə], *s.* die Pracht, der Glanz.
splice [splais], *v.a.* splissen; (*Naut.*) — *the mainbrace*, das Hauptfaß öffnen!
splint [splint], *s.* (*Med.*) die Schiene.
splinter ['splintə], *s.* der Span; der Splitter (*fragment*).
split [split], *v.a. irr.* spalten; (*fig.*) verteilen, teilen (*divide*). — *v.n.* sich trennen; (*coll.*) — *on s.o.*, einen verraten. — *adj.* — *second timing*, auf den Bruchteil einer Sekunde. — *s.* die Spaltung.
splutter ['splʌtə], *v.n.* sprudeln. — *s.* das Sprudeln.
spoil [spɔil], *v.a. irr.* verderben; (*child*) verwöhnen; (*Mil.*) plündern, berauben. — *v.n.* verderben. — *s.* (*pl.*) die Beute.
spoilsport ['spɔilspɔ:t], *s.* der Spielverderber.
spoke [spouk], *s.* die Speiche; die Sprosse.
spokesman ['spouksmən], *s.* der Wortführer, Sprecher.
sponge [spʌndʒ], *s.* der Schwamm; — *cake*, die Sandtorte. — *v.a.* mit dem Schwamm wischen. — *v.n.* (*coll.*) schmarotzen (*on*, bei, *Dat.*).
sponger ['spʌndʒə], *s.* (*coll.*) der Schmarotzer (*parasite*).
sponsor ['spɔnsə], *s.* der Bürge (*guarantor*); der Förderer; Pate. — *v.a.* fördern, unterstützen.
spontaneous [spɔn'teiniəs], *adj.* spontan, freiwillig.
spook [spuk], *s.* der Spuk, Geist, das Gespenst.
spool [spu:l], *s.* die Spule. — *v.a.* aufspulen.
spoon [spu:n], *s.* der Löffel. — *v.a.* mit dem Löffel essen, löffeln.
sport [spɔ:t], *s.* der Sport; (*fig.*) der Scherz. — *v.a.* tragen (*wear*). — *v.n.* scherzen.
spot [spɔt], *s.* die Stelle, der Ort, Platz; (*stain*) der Fleck; (*fig.*) der Schandfleck (*on o.'s honour*); *on the —*, sogleich; auf der Stelle; *in a —*, (*Am. coll.*) in Verlegenheit; — *cash*, Barzahlung, *f.* — *v.a.* entdecken, finden.
spotted ['spɔtid], *adj.* fleckig, gefleckt; befleckt; pickelig.
spouse [spauz], *s.* der Gatte; die Gattin.

spout [spaut], *v.a.*, *v.n.* ausspeien, sprudeln, sprudeln lassen; (*sl.*) predigen, schwatzen. — *s.* die Tülle (*teapot etc.*); die Abflußröhre.
sprain [sprein], *v.a.* (*Med.*) verrenken. — *s.* die Verrenkung.
sprat [spræt], *s.* (*Zool.*) die Sprotte.
sprawl [sprɔ:l], *v.n.* sich spreizen, ausbreiten.
spray [sprei], *v.a.*, *v.n.* sprühen spritzen. — *s.* die Sprühe; der Sprühregen.
spread [spred], *v.a.*, *v.n. irr.* ausbreiten; verbreiten (*get abroad*); streichen (*overlay with*). — *s.* die Ausbreitung; Verbreitung.
spree [spri:], *s.* das Vergnügen, der lustige Abend, Bummel.
sprig [sprig], *s.* der Zweig, Sprößling.
sprightly ['spraitli], *adj.* munter, lebhaft.
spring [spriŋ], *s.* die Quelle (*water*); der Ursprung (*origin*); der Frühling (*season*); (*Mech.*) die Feder, Sprungfeder, Spirale. — *v.n. irr.* springen (*jump*); entspringen (*originate*). — *v.a.* — *a surprise*, eine Überraschung bereiten.
springe [sprindʒ], *s.* der Sprenkel.
sprinkle [spriŋkl], *v.a.* (be)sprengen; (*Hort.*) berieseln.
sprint [sprint], *s.* der Kurzstreckenlauf, Wettlauf.
sprite [sprait], *s.* der Geist, Kobold.
sprout [spraut], *s.* (*Bot.*) die Sprosse, der Sprößling; *Brussels —s*, der Rosenkohl.
spruce (1) [spru:s], *adj.* sauber, geputzt; schmuck.
spruce (2) [spru:s], *s.* (*Bot.*) die Fichte, Rottanne.
spume [spju:m], *s.* der Schaum.
spur [spə:], *s.* der Sporn (*goad*); (*fig.*) der Stachel; der Ansporn, Antrieb; (*Geog.*) der Ausläufer (*of range*). — *v.a.* anspornen.
spurious ['spjuəriəs], *adj.* unecht, falsch.
spurn [spə:n], *v.a.* verschmähen, verachten.
spurt [spə:t], *v.a.* spritzen. — *v.n.* sich anstrengen. — *s.* die Anstrengung.
sputter ['spʌtə], *v.a.* heraussprudeln. — *v.n.* sprühen, sprudeln.
spy [spai], *s.* der Spion. — *v.n.* spionieren (*on*, bei, *Dat.*).
squabble [skwɔbl], *v.n.* zanken. — *s.* der Zank, Streit.
squad [skwɔd], *s.* der Trupp.
squadron ['skwɔdrən], *s.* die Schwadron, das Geschwader.
squalid ['skwɔlid], *adj.* schmutzig, elend, eklig.
squall [skwɔ:l], *s.* der Windstoß.
squalor ['skwɔlə], *s.* der Schmutz.
squander ['skwɔndə], *v.a.* verschwenden, vergeuden.
square [skwɛə], *s.* das Quadrat; der Platz; (*coll.*) der Philister, Spießer. — *v.a.* ausrichten; (*coll.*) ins Reine bringen. — *adj.* viereckig; quadratisch; redlich (*honest*); quitt (*quits*).
squash (1) [skwɔʃ], *v.a.* zerquetschen, zerdrücken (*press together*). — *s.* das Gedränge (*crowd*); der Fruchtsaft (*drink*).
squash (2) [skwɔʃ], *s.* (*Sport*) eine Art Racketspiel.
squat [skwɔt], *v.n.* kauern; sich niederlassen. — *adj.* stämmig, untersetzt.
squatter ['skwɔtə], *s.* der Ansiedler.
squaw [skwɔ:], *s.* die Indianerfrau.
squeak [skwi:k], *v.n.* quieken, quietschen. — *s.* das Gequiek.
squeal [skwi:l], *v.n.* quieken; (*Am. coll.*) verraten, preisgeben.
squeamish ['skwi:miʃ], *adj.* empfindlich, zimperlich.
squeeze [skwi:z], *v.a.* drücken, quetschen. — *s.* das Gedränge.
squib [skwib], *s.* der Frosch (*firework*); (*Lit.*) das Spottgedicht.
squint [skwint], *v.n.* schielen. — *s.* das Schielen.
squire [skwaiə], *s.* der Landedelmann, Junker.
squirrel ['skwirəl], *s.* (*Zool.*) das Eichhörnchen.
squirt [skwə:t], *v.a.* spritzen. — *s.* der Spritzer, Wasserstrahl; (*sl.*) der Wicht.
stab [stæb], *v.a.* erstechen, erdolchen. — *s.* der Dolchstich, Dolchstoß.
stability [stə'biliti], *s.* die Beständigkeit, Stabilität.
stable (1) [steibl], *adj.* fest, beständig; (*Phys.*) stabil.
stable (2) [steibl], *s.* der Stall.
stack [stæk], *s.* der Stoß (*pile*); der Schornstein (*chimneys*). — *v.a.* aufschichten.
staff [stɑ:f], *s.* der Stab, Stock; (*Mil.*) der Stab, Generalstab; (*Sch.*) der Lehrkörper; das Personal. — *v.a.* besetzen.
stag [stæg], *s.* (*Zool.*) der Hirsch; — *party*, die Herrengesellschaft.
stage [steidʒ], *s.* (*Theat.*) die Bühne; die Stufe, das Stadium (*phase*); (*fig.*) der Schauplatz; *fare —*, die Teilstrecke. — *v.a.* (*Theat.*) inszenieren, abhalten (*hold*).
stagecoach ['steidʒkoutʃ], *s.* die Postkutsche.
stagger ['stægə], *v.n.* schwanken, wanken, taumeln. — *v.a.* (*coll.*) verblüffen (*astonish*); staffeln (*graduate*).
stagnate [stæg'neit], *v.n.* stocken, stillstehen.
staid [steid], *adj.* gesetzt, gelassen.
stain [stein], *s.* der Fleck, Makel. — *v.a.* beflecken; beizen; färben (*dye*).
stained [steind], *adj.* — *glass window*, buntes Fenster.
stainless ['steinlis], *adj.* rostfrei.
stair [stɛə], *s.* die Stufe, Stiege.
staircase ['stɛəkeis], *s.* das Treppenhaus; die Treppe.
stake [steik], *s.* der Pfahl, Pfosten; Scheiterhaufen; (*Gambling*) der Einsatz; *at —*, auf dem Spiel. — *v.a.* aufs Spiel setzen.
stale [steil], *adj.* abgestanden, schal.

stalemate ['steilmeit], *s.* (*Chess*) das Patt; der Stillstand.
stalk (1) [stɔ:k], *s.* (*Bot.*) der Stengel, Halm.
stalk (2) [stɔ:k], *v.n.* stolzieren, steif gehen. — *v.a.* pirschen (*hunt*).
stall [stɔ:l], *s.* die Bude (*booth*), der Stand (*stand*); (*Eccl.*) der Chorstuhl; (*Theat.*) der Sperrsitz; Parterresitz. — *v.n.* (*Motor.*) stehenbleiben.
stallion ['stæljən], *s.* (*Zool.*) der Hengst.
stalwart ['stɔ:lwət], *adj.* kräftig, stark, verläßlich.
stamina ['stæminə], *s.* die Ausdauer, Widerstandskraft.
stammer ['stæmə], *v.n.* stammeln, stottern.
stamp [stæmp], *s.* der Stempel (*rubber* —); die Marke (*postage*); die Stampfe, Stanze (*die* —). — *v.a.* stempeln; (*Mech.*) stanzen; frankieren (*letters*). — *v.n.* stampfen.
stampede [stæm'pi:d], *s.* die wilde Flucht. — *v.n.* in wilder Flucht davonlaufen.
stand [stænd], *v.n. irr.* stehen. — *v.a.* aushalten, standhalten (*Dat.*). — *s.* der Ständer (*hats etc.*); der Stand (*stall*); (*fig.*) die Stellung.
standard ['stændəd], *s.* der Standard (*level*); (*Mil.*) die Standarte; der Maßstab (*yardstick*). — *adj.* normal.
standing ['stændiŋ], *s.* der Rang, das Ansehen. — *adj.* — *orders*, die Geschäftsordnung; (*Mil.*) die Vorschriften, *f. pl.*, Dauerbefehle, *m. pl.*
standpoint ['stændpɔint], *s.* der Standpunkt (*point of view*).
standstill ['stændstil], *s.* der Stillstand.
stanza ['stænzə], *s.* (*Poet.*) die Stanze, Strophe.
staple [steipl], *s.* das Haupterzeugnis; der Stapelplatz. — *adj.* Haupt-. — *v.a.* stapeln; heften (*paper*).
stapler ['steiplə], *s.* die Heftmaschine.
star [stɑ:], *s.* der Stern; (*Theat. etc.*) der Star. — *v.n.* (*Theat. etc.*) die Hauptrolle spielen.
starboard ['stɑ:bəd], *s.* das Steuerbord.
starch [stɑ:tʃ], *s.* die Stärke (*laundry*). — *v.a.* stärken.
stare [stɛə], *v.n.* starren. — *s.* der starre Blick, das Starren.
stark [stɑ:k], *adj.* völlig, ganz.
starling ['stɑ:liŋ], *s.* (*Orn.*) der Star.
start [stɑ:t], *v.n.* anfangen; aufbrechen; auffahren, aufspringen; stutzen (*jerk*); abfahren (*depart*). — *v.a.* starten (*car etc.*), in Gang setzen. — *s.* der Anfang; (*Sport*) der Start, Anlauf; der Aufbruch (*departure*); *by fits and —s*, ruckweise.
starter ['stɑ:tə], *s.* (*Sport*) der Starter, Teilnehmer (*participant*); das Rennpferd (*horse*); (*Motor.*) der Anlasser.
startle [stɑ:tl], *v.a.* erschrecken.
starve [stɑ:v], *v.n.* verhungern, hungern. — *v.a.* aushungern.
state [steit], *s.* der Zustand, die Lage; (*Pol.*) der Staat; (*personal*) der Stand (*single etc.*). — *v.a.* erklären, darlegen.
stately ['steitli], *adj.* stattlich, prachtvoll.
statement ['steitmənt], *s.* die Feststellung; *bank* —, der Kontoauszug.
statesman ['steitsmən], *s.* der Staatsmann, Politiker.
statics ['stætiks], *s.* die Statik.
station ['steiʃən], *s.* (*Railw.*) die Station; der Bahnhof; die Stellung, der Rang (*position*); (*Mil.*) die Stationierung. — *v.a.* (*Mil.*) aufstellen, stationieren; (*fig.*) hinstellen.
stationary ['steiʃənri], *adj.* stationär, stillstehend.
stationer ['steiʃənə], *s.* der Papierhändler.
stationery ['steiʃənri], *s.* das Briefpapier, Schreibpapier; die Papierwaren, *f. pl.*
statuary ['stætjuəri], *s.* die Bildhauerkunst.
statue ['stætju:], *s.* das Standbild.
status ['steitəs], *s.* die Stellung (*rank, position*).
statute ['stætju:t], *s.* das Statut; — *law*, das Landesrecht, Gesetzesrecht.
staunch [stɔ:ntʃ], *adj.* zuverlässig.
stave [steiv], *s.* die Faßdaube (*of vat*); (*Poet.*) die Strophe; (*Mus.*) die Linie. — *v.a.* — *off*, abwehren.
stay [stei], *v.n.* bleiben, verweilen, wohnen. — *v.a.* hindern, aufhalten. — *s.* der Aufenthalt; (*pl.*) das Korsett.
stead [sted], *s.* die Stelle; *in his* —, an seiner Statt.
steadfast ['stedfɑ:st], *adj.* standhaft, fest.
steadiness ['stedinis], *s.* die Beständigkeit.
steady ['stedi], *adj.* fest, sicher; beständig, treu.
steak [steik], *s.* das Steak.
steal [sti:l], *v.a. irr.* stehlen. — *v.n.* sich stehlen, schleichen.
stealth [stelθ], *s.* die Heimlichkeit.
stealthy ['stelθi], *adj.* heimlich, verstohlen.
steam [sti:m], *s.* der Dampf; *get up* —, in Gang bringen *or* kommen; — *boiler*, der Dampfkessel. — *v.n.* dampfen; davondampfen. — *v.a.* dämpfen, (*Cul.*) dünsten.
steed [sti:d], *s.* das Schlachtroß.
steel [sti:l], *s.* der Stahl. — *adj.* stählern. — *v.n.* — *o.s.*, sich stählen.
steep (1) [sti:p], *adj.* steil; (*fig.*) hoch; (*coll.*) gesalzen (*price*).
steep (2) [sti:p], *v.a.* einweichen, sättigen.
steeple [sti:pl], *s.* (*Archit.*) der Kirchturm.
steeplechase ['sti:pltʃeis], *s.* das Hindernisrennen.
steeplejack ['sti:pldʒæk], *s.* der Turmdecker.
steer (1) [stiə], *s.* (*Zool.*) der junge Stier.
steer (2) [stiə], *v.a.* steuern (*guide*).
steerage ['stiəridʒ], *s.* die Steuerung; (*Naut.*) das Zwischendeck.

stellar ['stelə], *adj.* Stern-, Sternen-.
stem (1) [stem], *s.* der Stamm; (*Phonet.*) der Stamm; der Stiel, die Wurzel. — *v.n.* —*from*, kommen von, abstammen.
stem (2) [stem], *v.a.* sich entgegenstemmen (*Dat.*); (*fig.*) eindämmen.
stench [stentʃ], *s.* der Gestank.
stencil ['stensil], *s.* die Schablone, Matrize; *cut a* —, auf Matrize schreiben.
step [step], *s.* der Schritt, Tritt; (*of ladder*) die Sprosse; (*of stairs*) die Stufe. — *v.n.* treten, schreiten (*stride*). — *v.a.* (*coll.*) — *up*, beschleunigen.
step- [step], *pref.* Stief- (*brother, mother etc.*).
stereo- ['stiəriou], *pref.* Stereo-.
sterile ['sterail], *adj.* steril.
sterling ['stə:liŋ], *adj.* echt, vollwertig; *pound* —, ein Pfund Sterling.
stern (1) [stə:n], *adj.* streng.
stern (2) [stə:n], *s.* (*Naut.*) das Heck.
stevedore ['sti:vədɔ:], *s.* der Hafenarbeiter.
stew [stju:], *s.* (*Cul.*) das Schmorfleisch, das Gulasch.
steward ['stju:əd], *s.* der Verwalter; der Haushofmeister; (*Naut.*) der Steward.
stick [stik], *s.* der Stock, Stecken. — *v.a.* stecken (*insert*); kleben (*glue*). — *v.n.* stecken, haften bleiben; (*fig., coll.*) — *to s.o.*, zu jemandem halten (*be loyal*).
sticky ['stiki], *adj.* klebrig; (*fig.*) prekär, schwierig (*difficult*); *come to a — end*, ein böses Ende nehmen.
stiff [stif], *adj.* steif; schwer, schwierig (*examination*); formell (*manner*).
stiffen [stifn], *v.a.* steifen, versteifen. — *v.n.* steif werden, sich versteifen.
stifle [staifl], *v.a., v.n.* ersticken; (*fig.*) unterdrücken.
stigmatize ['stigmətaiz], *v.a.* stigmatisieren, brandmarken.
stile [stail], *s.* der Zauntritt, Übergang.
still (1) [stil], *adj.* still, ruhig. — *adv.* immer noch. — *conj.* doch, dennoch. — *v.a.* stillen, beruhigen.
still (2) [stil], *s.* die Destillierflasche, der Destillierkolben.
stilt [stilt], *s.* die Stelze.
stilted ['stiltid], *adj.* auf Stelzen; (*fig.*) hochtrabend, geschraubt.
stimulant ['stimjulənt], *s.* das Reizmittel. — *adj.* anreizend, anregend.
stimulate ['stimjuleit], *v.a.* anreizen, stimulieren, anregen.
stimulus ['stimjuləs], *s.* der Reiz, die Anregung.
sting [stiŋ], *v.a. irr.* stechen; (*fig.*) kränken, verwunden. — *v.n. irr.* stechen, brennen, schmerzen. — *s.* der Stachel (*prick*); der Stich (*stab*).
stink [stiŋk], *v.n. irr.* stinken. — *s.* der Gestank.
stint [stint], *s.* die Einschränkung (*limit*); das Maß, Tagespensum. — *v.a.* beschränken, einschränken.
stipend ['staipend], *s.* die Besoldung, das Gehalt.
stipendiary [stai'pendiəri], *adj.* besoldet, bezahlt.
stipulate ['stipjuleit], *v.a.* festsetzen, ausbedingen.
stir [stə:], *v.a.* rühren, bewegen. — *v.n.* sich rühren. — *s.* die Aufregung; *cause a* —, Aufsehen erregen.
stirrup ['stirəp], *s.* der Steigbügel.
stitch [stitʃ], *v.a.* sticken, nähen. — *s.* der Stich; der stechende Schmerz, der Seitenstich (*pain*).
stoat [stout], *s.* (*Zool.*) das Hermelin.
stock [stɔk], *s.* das Lager; *in* —, auf Lager; vorrätig; der Stamm, die Familie; (*Fin.*) das Kapital; — *exchange*, die Börse; (*pl.*) die Börsenpapiere, *n. pl.*, Aktien, *f.pl.* — *v.a.* halten, führen.
stockade [stɔ'keid], *s.* das Staket.
stockbroker ['stɔkbroukə], *s.* (*Fin.*) der Börsenmakler.
stockholder ['stɔkhouldə], *s.* (*Fin., Am.*) der Aktionär.
stocking ['stɔkiŋ], *s.* der Strumpf.
stocktaking ['stɔkteikiŋ], *s.* die Inventuraufnahme.
stoical ['stouikəl], *adj.* stoisch.
stoke [stouk], *v.a.* schüren.
stoker ['stoukə], *s.* der Heizer.
stole [stoul], *s.* (*Eccl.*) die Stola; der Pelzkragen (*fur*).
stolid ['stɔlid], *adj.* schwerfällig, gleichgültig.
stomach ['stʌmək], *s.* der Magen; (*fig.*) der Appetit.
stone [stoun], *s.* der Stein; der Kern (*fruit*). — *v.a.* steinigen (*throw —s at*); entsteinen (*fruit*).
stony ['stouni], *adj.* steinig; (*sl.*) — *broke*, pleite.
stool [stu:l], *s.* der Schemel, Hocker; (*Med.*) der Stuhlgang.
stoop [stu:p], *v.n.* sich bücken; (*fig.*) sich herablassen.
stooping ['stu:piŋ], *adj.* gebückt.
stop [stɔp], *v.a.* halten, stoppen; aufhören; aufhalten (*halt*); — *up*, verstopfen, versperren (*block*); (*tooth*) plombieren. — *v.n.* stehen bleiben (*stand*); sich aufhalten (*stay*). — *s.* der Halt, die Haltestelle (*of bus etc.*); das Aufhalten, Innehalten (*stoppage*); das Register (*organ*); (*Gram.*) der Punkt.
stoppage ['stɔpidʒ], *s.* die Stockung, Hemmung (*hindrance*); die Arbeitseinstellung (*strike*).
stopper ['stɔpə], *s.* der Stöpsel.
storage ['stɔ:ridʒ], *s.* das Lagern.
store [stɔ:], *s.* der Vorrat, das Lagerhaus, Magazin; (*Am.*) das Kaufhaus; (*fig.*) die Menge (*of anecdotes etc.*). — *v.a.* lagern.
storey ['stɔ:ri], *s.* das Stockwerk.
stork [stɔ:k], *s.* (*Orn.*) der Storch.
storm [stɔ:m], *s.* der Sturm, das Gewitter.
story ['stɔ:ri], *s.* die Geschichte, Erzählung (*narrative*).

stout [staut], *adj.* fest; stark, kräftig. — *s.* das starke Bier.
stove [stouv], *s.* der Ofen.
stow [stou], *v.a.* verstauen, packen. — *v.n.* — *away*, als blinder Passagier fahren.
stowaway ['stouəwei], *s.* der blinde Passagier.
straddle [strædl], *v.n.* rittlings sitzen.
straggle [strægl], *v.n.* umherschweifen, streifen; (*Bot.*) wuchern.
straight [streit], *adj.* gerade, offen. — *adv.* — *away*, sofort, sogleich.
straighten [streitn], *v.a.* ausrichten, gerade richten. — *v.n.* sich ausrichten.
strain [strein], *s.* die Anstrengung, Anspannung; (*Mus.*) der Ton, Stil; der Hang. — *v.a.* anstrengen, filtrieren; seihen. — *v.n.* sich anstrengen.
strainer ['streinə], *s.* der Seiher, der Filter, das Sieb.
strait [streit], *adj.* eng. — *s.* (*usually pl.*) die Enge, Meerenge.
strand (1) [strænd], *s.* der Strand.
strand (2) [strænd], *s.* die Litze (*of rope, string*).
strange [streindʒ], *adj.* fremd (*unknown*); seltsam (*queer*).
stranger ['streindʒə], *s.* der Fremdling, Fremde; der Unbekannte.
strangle [strængl], *v.a.* erdrosseln, erwürgen.
strangulation [strængju'leiʃən], *s.* die Erdrosselung, Erwürgung.
strap [stræp], *v.a.* festschnallen, anschnallen. — *s.* der Gurt, Riemen.
strapping ['stræpiŋ], *adj.* stark, stämmig.
strata *see under* **stratum.**
stratagem ['strætədʒəm], *s.* die List; (*Mil.*) der Plan.
strategy ['strætədʒi], *s.* die Strategie.
stratification [strætifi'keiʃən], *s.* die Schichtung; (*Geol.*) die Lagerung.
stratum ['streitəm], *s.* (*pl.* **strata** ['streitə]) die Schicht, Lage.
straw [strɔ:], *s.* das Stroh; *that's the last* —, das ist die Höhe!
strawberry ['strɔ:bəri], *s.* (*Bot.*) die Erdbeere.
stray [strei], *v.n.* irregehen, schweifen; sich verirren. — *adj.* irr, verirrt.
streak [stri:k], *s.* der Strich; der Streifen; (*fig.*) der Anflug.
streaky ['stri:ki], *adj.* gestreift; (*bacon*) durchwachsen.
stream [stri:m], *v.n.* strömen, wehen (*in the wind*). — *s.* die Strömung (*flow*); der Bach (*brook*), der Strom (*river*).
streamer ['stri:mə], *s.* der Wimpel, das Band, die Papierschlange.
street [stri:t], *s.* die Straße; —*s ahead*, weit voraus.
streetcar ['stri:tkɑ:], *s.* (*Am.*) *see* **tram.**
streetlamp ['stri:tlæmp], *s.* die Straßenlaterne.
strength [streŋθ], *s.* die Stärke; die Kraft.
strengthen ['streŋθən], *v.a.* stärken; (*fig.*) bekräftigen (*support*).
strenuous ['strenjuəs], *adj.* anstrengend.
stress [stres], *v.a.* (*Phonet.*) betonen; (*fig.*) hervorheben. — *s.* die Betonung (*emphasis*); der Druck (*pressure*).
stretch [stretʃ], *v.a.* spannen; strecken, ausstrecken; — *a point*, eine Ausnahme machen. — *s.* die Strecke (*distance*); (*coll.*) die Zuchthausstrafe (*penal sentence*).
stretcher ['stretʃə], *s.* die Tragbahre.
strew [stru:], *v.a.* streuen, ausstreuen.
strict [strikt], *adj.* streng (*severe*); genau (*exact*).
stricture ['striktʃə], *s.* der Tadel, die Kritik; (*pl.*) die kritische Rede.
stride [straid], *v.n. irr.* schreiten. — *s.* der Schritt; *take in o.'s* —, leicht bewältigen.
strident ['straidənt], *adj.* laut, lärmend; grell.
strife [straif], *s.* der Streit, Zank.
strike [straik], *v.a.*, *v.n. irr.* schlagen; abmachen (*bargain*); (*Mus.*) — *up*, anstimmen (*song*), aufspielen (*instrument*); beginnen; — *the eye*, auffallen; streiken, in Streik treten. — *s.* der Streik, die Arbeitseinstellung.
striking ['straikiŋ], *adj.* auffallend.
string [striŋ], *s.* die Schnur; (*Mus.*) die Saite; — *quartet*, das Streichquartett; die Reihe (*series*). — *v.a.* anreihen (*beads etc.*); — *together*, verbinden. — *v.n.* — *along*, sich anschließen.
stringency ['strindʒənsi], *s.* die Strenge (*severity*); die Knappheit (*shortage*).
stringent ['strindʒənt], *adj.* streng (*severe*); knapp (*short*).
strip [strip], *s.* der Streifen. — *v.a.*, *v.n.* abstreifen, (sich) entkleiden; (sich) entblößen.
stripe [straip], *s.* der (Farb)streifen; die Strieme (*mark on body*). — *v.a.* streifen, bestreifen.
strive [straiv], *v.n. irr.* sich bemühen (*for*, um, *Acc.*), streben (*for*, nach, *Dat.*).
stroke (1) [strouk], *v.a.* streicheln.
stroke (2) [strouk], *s.* der Strich (*brush*); der Streich (*sword*), der Stoß (*blow*); (*Med.*) der Schlaganfall.
stroll [stroul], *v.n.* schlendern.
strolling ['strouliŋ], *adj.* — *players*, die Wandertruppe.
strong [strɔŋ], *adj.* stark.
strongbox ['strɔŋbɔks], *s.* die Geldkassette.
strongroom ['strɔŋrum], *s.* der Geldtresor.
strop [strɔp], *s.* der Streichriemen.
structure ['strʌktʃə], *s.* der Bau, Aufbau; die Struktur.
struggle [strʌgl], *s.* der Kampf, das Ringen. — *v.n.* kämpfen, ringen.
strut [strʌt], *v.n.* stolzieren.
stub [stʌb], *s.* der Stumpf, Stummel (*cigarette*). — *v.a.* — *out*, ausmachen, auslöschen (*cigarette etc.*).

stubble [stʌbl], *s.* die Stoppel, das Stoppelfeld; die (Bart)stoppeln, *f. pl.* (*beard*).
stubborn ['stʌbən], *adj.* eigensinnig, hartnäckig.
stucco ['stʌkou], *s.* die Stuckarbeit.
stud (1) [stʌd], *s.* der Hemdenknopf, Kragenknopf (*collar* —). — *v.a.* beschlagen (*nail*); besetzen (*bejewel*).
stud (2) [stʌd], *s.* das Gestüt (*horses*).
student ['stju:dənt], *s.* der Student.
studied ['stʌdid], *adj.* geziert, absichtlich (*deliberate*); gelehrt (*learned*).
studio ['stju:diou], *s.* (*Phot.*) das Atelier; (*Film, Rad.*) das Studio.
studious ['stju:diəs], *adj.* beflissen, fleißig; lernbegierig.
study ['stʌdi], *v.a., v.n.* studieren. — *s.* das Studium; das Arbeitszimmer (*room*); (*Mus. etc.*) die Studie; (*Art*) der Entwurf; die Untersuchung (*investigation*).
stuff [stʌf], *s.* der Stoff, das Material; (*coll.*) das Zeug (*rubbish*). — *v.a.* stopfen, ausstopfen (*animals*); (*Cul.*) füllen.
stuffing ['stʌfiŋ], *s.* die Füllung, das Füllsel.
stultify ['stʌltifai], *v.a.* dumm machen.
stumble [stʌmbl], *v.n.* stolpern; — *upon*, zufällig stoßen (auf, *Acc.*).
stumbling ['stʌmbliŋ], *s.* das Stolpern; — *block*, das Hindernis, der Stein des Anstoßes.
stump [stʌmp], *s.* der Stumpf. — *v.a.* verblüffen; abstumpfen. — *v.n.* schwerfällig gehen.
stun [stʌn], *v.a.* betäuben, verdutzen.
stunning ['stʌniŋ], *adj.* betörend, fabelhaft, überwältigend.
stunt (1) [stʌnt], *v.a.* am Wachstum behindern, klein halten.
stunt (2) [stʌnt], *s.* der Trick, das Kunststück; (*Aviat.*) der Kunstflug.
stupefy ['stju:pifai], *v.a.* betäuben.
stupendous [stju:'pendəs], *adj.* erstaunlich.
stupid ['stju:pid], *adj.* dumm.
stupor ['stju:pə], *s.* die Erstarrung, Lähmung (*of mind*).
sturdy ['stə:di], *adj.* derb, stark, stämmig.
sturgeon ['stə:dʒən], *s.* (*Zool.*) der Stör.
stutter ['stʌtə], *v.n.* stottern.
sty [stai], *s.* der Schweinestall.
sty(e) [stai], *s.* (*Med.*) das Gerstenkorn (*on eyelid*).
style [stail], *s.* (*Lit.*) der Stil; der Griffel (*stylus*); die Mode (*fashion*); die Anrede (*address*). — *v.a.* anreden.
stylish ['stailiʃ], *adj.* elegant, modern.
suave [sweiv, swɑ:v], *adj.* höflich, gewinnend.
sub- [sʌb], *pref.* Unter–.
subaltern ['sʌbəltən], *s.* (*Mil.*) der Leutnant, Oberleutnant.
subject ['sʌbdʒikt], *s.* (*Gram.*) das Subjekt; (*Pol.*) der Untertan; der Gegenstand. — *adj.* untertan (*to, Dat.*); — *to*, abhängig von. — [səb'dʒekt], *v.a.* unterwerfen (*to, Dat.*); aussetzen (*Dat.*).
subjunctive [səb'dʒʌŋktiv], *s.* (*Gram.*) der Konjunktiv.
sublet [sʌb'let], *v.a.* in Untermiete vermieten, untervermieten.
sublimate ['sʌblimeit], *v.a.* sublimieren.
submarine ['sʌbməri:n], *s.* das Unterseeboot.
submission [səb'miʃən], *s.* die Unterwerfung (*subjection*); der Vorschlag (*suggestion*).
submit [səb'mit], *v.a.* unterwerfen (*subjugate*); vorlegen. — *v.n.* sich beugen (*to, Dat.*).
suborn [sʌ'bɔ:n], *v.a.* anstiften; bestechen (*corrupt*).
subpoena [sʌb'pi:nə], *s.* (*Law*) die Vorladung.
subscribe [səb'skraib], *v.a.* unterschreiben. — *v.n.* zeichnen (*to*, zu); abonnieren (*paper*).
subscription [səb'skripʃən], *s.* das Abonnement (*to, Genit.*); (*club*) der Beitrag.
subsequent ['sʌbsikwənt], *adj.* folgend.
subservient [sʌb'sə:viənt], *adj.* unterwürfig.
subside [səb'said], *v.n.* sinken; abnehmen (*decrease*).
subsidence [sʌb'saidəns, 'sʌbsidəns], *s.* das Sinken, Sichsetzen.
subsidiary [sʌb'sidjəri], *adj.* Hilfs-, Neben-.
subsidize ['sʌbsidaiz], *v.a.* unterstützen (*with money*), subventionieren.
subsidy ['sʌbsidi], *s.* die Unterstützung, Subvention.
subsist [səb'sist], *v.n.* leben, existieren.
subsistence [səb'sistəns], *s.* das Dasein, Auskommen; der Lebensunterhalt.
substance ['sʌbstəns], *s.* das Wesen, der Stoff, die Substanz.
substantial [səb'stænʃəl], *adj.* wesentlich, beträchtlich.
substantiate [səb'stænʃieit], *v.a.* dartun, nachweisen, bestätigen.
substantive ['sʌbstəntiv], *s.* (*Gram.*) das Substantiv, Hauptwort. — *adj.* (*Mil.*) effektiv, wirklich.
substitute ['sʌbstitju:t], *v.a.* ersetzen, an die Stelle setzen. — *s.* der Ersatzmann, Vertreter.
subterfuge ['sʌbtəfju:dʒ], *s.* die Ausflucht.
subtle [sʌtl], *adj.* fein, schlau, subtil.
subtract [səb'trækt], *v.a.* abziehen; (*Maths.*) subtrahieren.
suburb ['sʌbə:b], *s.* die Vorstadt, der Vorort.
subversion [səb'və:ʃən], *s.* (*Pol.*) der Umsturz.
subversive [səb'və:siv], *adj.* umstürzlerisch, umstürzend.
subway ['sʌbwei], *s.* die Unterführung; (*Am.*) die Untergrundbahn.
succeed [sək'si:d], *v.n.* erfolgreich sein, Erfolg haben. — *v.a.* nachfolgen (*Dat.*) (*follow*).

success [sək'ses], *s.* der Erfolg.
successful [sək'sesful], *adj.* erfolgreich.
succession [sək'seʃən], *s.* die Nachfolge.
successive [sək'sesiv], *adj.* der Reihe nach, aufeinanderfolgend.
succinct [sək'siŋkt], *adj.* bündig, kurz.
succour ['sʌkə], *v.a.* beistehen (*Dat.*), helfen (*Dat.*).
succulent ['sʌkjulənt], *adj.* saftig.
succumb [sə'kʌm], *v.n.* unterliegen (*to*, *Dat.*).
such [sʌtʃ], *adj.* solch, derartig. — *pron.* ein solcher; — *as*, diejenigen, alle die.
suchlike ['sʌtʃlaik], *pron.* (*coll.*) dergleichen.
suck [sʌk], *v.a.*, *v.n.* saugen.
suckle [sʌkl], *v.a.* säugen, stillen.
suction ['sʌkʃən], *s.* das Saugen; (*Engin.*) Saug-.
Sudanese [su:də'ni:z], *adj.* sudanisch, sudanesisch. — *s.* der Sudan(es)er.
sudden [sʌdn], *adj.* plötzlich.
suds [sʌdz], *s. pl.* das Seifenwasser.
sue [sju:], *v.a.* gerichtlich belangen, verklagen.
suède [sweid], *s.* das Wildleder.
suet ['su:it], *s.* das Nierenfett.
suffer ['sʌfə], *v.a.* ertragen, dulden. — *v.n.* leiden (*from*, an).
sufferance ['sʌfərəns], *s.* die Duldung; *on* —, nur widerwillig.
suffice [sə'fais], *v.n.* genügen, langen, (aus)reichen.
sufficient [sə'fiʃənt], *adj.* genügend, hinreichend.
suffocate ['sʌfəkeit], *v.a.*, *v.n.* ersticken.
suffragan ['sʌfrəgən], *s.* (*Eccl.*) der Weihbischof.
suffrage ['sʌfridʒ], *s.* das Wahlrecht, Stimmrecht.
suffuse [sə'fju:z], *v.a.* übergießen, überfließen.
sugar ['ʃugə], *s.* der Zucker; — *basin*, die Zuckerdose.
suggest [sə'dʒest], *v.a.* vorschlagen, anregen.
suggestion [sə'dʒestʃən], *s.* der Vorschlag.
suggestive [sə'dʒestiv], *adj.* zweideutig.
suicide ['sju:isaid], *s.* der Selbstmord, Freitod.
suit [su:t], *s.* das Gesuch, die Bitte (*request*); die Farbe (*cards*); (*Law*) der Prozeß; der Anzug (*clothes*). — *v.n.* passen (*Dat.*) (*be convenient to*); passen zu (*look well with*). — *v.a.* anpassen (*match*).
suitcase ['su:tkeis], *s.* der Handkoffer.
suitable ['su:təbl], *adj.* passend.
suite [swi:t], *s.* das Gefolge (*following*); die Zimmerflucht (*rooms*); die Reihe (*cards*).
suitor ['su:tə], *s.* der Brautwerber, Freier.
sulk [sʌlk], *v.n.* schmollen.
sullen ['sʌlən], *adj.* düster, mürrisch.
sully ['sʌli], *v.a.* beschmutzen.
sulphur ['sʌlfə], *s.* (*Chem.*) der Schwefel.
Sultan ['sʌltən], *s.* der Sultan.
Sultana [sʌl'tɑ:nə], *s.* die Sultanin.
sultana [sʌl'tɑ:nə], *s.* (*Bot.*) die Sultanine.
sultry ['sʌltri], *adj.* schwül.
sum [sʌm], *s.* die Summe; (*fig.*) der Inbegriff. — *v.a.*, *v.n.* — *up*, zusammenfassen.
summary ['sʌməri], *s.* die Zusammenfassung, der Auszug. — *adj.* summarisch.
summer ['sʌmə], *s.* der Sommer; *Indian* —, der Spätsommer, Altweibersommer, Nachsommer.
summit ['sʌmit], *s.* der Gipfel, die Spitze.
summon(s) ['sʌmən(z)], *v.a.* (*Law*) vorladen. — *s.* (**summons**) die Vorladung.
sump [sʌmp], *s.* (*Motor.*) die Ölwanne.
sumptuous ['sʌmptjuəs], *adj.* prächtig, mit Aufwand, kostbar.
sun [sʌn], *s.* die Sonne. — *v.r.* sich sonnen.
sunburn ['sʌnbə:n], *s.* der Sonnenbrand.
Sunday ['sʌnd(e)i]. der Sonntag.
sundial ['sʌndaiəl], *s.* die Sonnenuhr.
sundown ['sʌndaun] *see* **sunset**.
sundry ['sʌndri], *adj.* mehrere, verschiedene. — *s.* (*pl.*) Gemischtwaren, *f. pl.*
sunny ['sʌni], *adj.* sonnig.
sunrise ['sʌnraiz], *s.* der Sonnenaufgang.
sunset ['sʌnset], *s.* der Sonnenuntergang.
sunshade ['sʌnʃeid], *s.* das Sonnendach, der Sonnenschirm (*parasol*).
super ['su:pə], *s.* (*Theat.*) der Statist. — *adj.* (*coll.*) fein, famos.
super- ['su:pə], *pref.* über-, hinzu-.
superannuation [su:pərænju'eiʃən], *s.* die Pensionierung.
superb [su'pə:b], *adj.* hervorragend, herrlich.
supercilious [su:pə'siliəs], *adj.* hochmütig, anmaßend.
superficial [su:pə'fiʃəl], *adj.* oberflächlich.
superfluous [su:'pə:fluəs], *adj.* überflüssig.
superintendent [su:pərin'tendənt], *s.* der Oberaufseher.
superior [su:'piəriə], *adj.* ober, höher. — *s.* der Vorgesetzte.
superiority [su:piəri'ɔriti], *s.* die Überlegenheit.
superlative [su:'pə:lətiv], *s.* (*Gram.*) der Superlativ. — *adj.* ausnehmend gut.
supermarket ['su:pəmɑ:kit], *s.* das Selbstbedienungsgeschäft, SB-Geschäft, der grosse Lebensmittelladen.
supersede [su:pə'si:d], *v.a.* verdrängen.
superstition [su:pə'stiʃən], *s.* der Aberglaube.
superstitious [su:pə'stiʃəs], *adj.* abergläubisch.
supervise ['su:pəvaiz], *v.a.* beaufsichtigen, überwachen.

supine [su'pain], *adj.* auf dem Rücken liegend. — ['su:pain], *s.* (*Gram.*) das Supinum.
supper ['sʌpə], *s.* das Abendessen; *Last Supper*, das Heilige Abendmahl.
supplant [sə'plɑ:nt], *v.a.* verdrängen.
supple [sʌpl], *adj.* geschmeidig, biegsam.
supplement ['sʌplimənt], *s.* die Beilage (*paper*); der Zusatz.
supplementary [sʌpli'mentri], *adj.* zusätzlich.
supplier [sə'plaiə], *s.* der Lieferant.
supply [sə'plai], *v.a.* liefern (*s. th.*); beliefern, versorgen (*s.o.*). — *s.* die Versorgung.
support [sə'pɔ:t], *v.a.* unterstützen. — *s.* die Stütze (*prop*); die Unterstützung (*financial etc.*).
suppose [sə'pouz], *v.a.* annehmen, vermuten.
supposition [sʌpə'ziʃən], *s.* die Annahme, Vermutung, Voraussetzung.
suppress [sə'pres], *v.a.* unterdrücken.
suppurate ['sʌpjureit], *v.n.* eitern.
supremacy [su'preməsi], *s.* die Überlegenheit (*pre-eminence*); Obergewalt (*power*).
supreme [su'pri:m], *adj.* höchst, oberst.
surcharge ['sə:tʃɑ:dʒ], *s.* die Sonderzahlung, der Aufschlag, Zuschlag.
sure [ʃuə], *adj.* sicher; *to be* —, sicherlich; *make* —, sich überzeugen.
surety ['ʃuəti], *s.* (*Law*) die Kaution.
surf [sə:f], *s.* die Brandung.
surface ['sə:fis], *s.* die Oberfläche.
surfeit ['sə:fit], *s.* die Übersättigung, das Übermaß. — *v.a.* übersättigen.
surge [sə:dʒ], *v.n.* wogen, rauschen. — *s.* die Woge, das Aufwallen.
surgeon ['sə:dʒən], *s.* (*Med.*) der Chirurg.
surgery ['sə:dʒəri], *s.* (*Med.*) die Chirurgie (*subject*); — *hours*, die Sprechstunde.
surgical ['sə:dʒikəl], *adj.* chirurgisch.
surly ['sə:li], *adj.* mürrisch.
surmise [sə:'maiz], *v.a.* mutmaßen, vermuten. — *s.* die Mutmaßung, Vermutung.
surmount [sə'maunt], *v.a.* übersteigen; überwinden (*overcome*).
surname ['sə:neim], *s.* der Zuname.
surpass [sə'pɑ:s], *v.a.* übertreffen.
surplice ['sə:plis], *s.* das Chorhemd.
surplus ['sə:pləs], *s.* der Überfluß.
surprise [sə'praiz], *s.* die Überraschung. — *v.a.* überraschen.
surrender [sə'rendə], *v.a.* übergeben, aufgeben. — *v.n.* sich ergeben. — *s.* die Waffenstreckung, Kapitulation.
surreptitious [sʌrəp'tiʃəs], *adj.* heimlich.
surround [sə'raund], *v.a.* umgeben, einschließen.
surroundings [sə'raundiŋz], *s. pl.* die Umgegend, Umgebung.
survey ['sə:vei], *s.* die Übersicht; die Vermessung. — [sə'vei], *v.a.* überblicken; vermessen.
surveyor [sə'veiə], *s.* der Vermesser, Feldmesser.
survival [sə'vaivəl], *s.* das Überleben.
survive [sə'vaiv], *v.a.*, *v.n.* überleben, überstehen.
susceptibility [səsepti'biliti], *s.* die Empfänglichkeit.
susceptible [sə'septibl], *adj.* empfänglich, empfindlich.
suspect [səs'pekt], *v.a.* verdächtigen. — ['sʌspekt], *adj.* verdächtig. — *s.* die Verdachtsperson, der Verdächtigte.
suspend [səs'pend], *v.a.* aufhängen; unterbrechen (*procedure*); einstellen (*work*).
suspense [səs'pens], *s.* die Spannung (*tension*); Ungewißheit (*uncertainty*).
suspension [səs'penʃən], *s.* (*Law*) die Suspension; die Einstellung (*stoppage*); die Aufhängung, Suspension; (*Motor.*) die Federung; — *bridge*, die Kettenbrücke, Hängebrücke.
suspicion [səs'piʃən], *s.* der Verdacht, Argwohn.
suspicious [səs'piʃəs], *adj.* verdächtig; argwöhnisch.
sustain [səs'tein], *v.a.* erleiden (*suffer*); ertragen (*bear*); aufrechterhalten (*maintain*).
sustenance ['sʌstinəns], *s.* der Unterhalt (*maintenance*); die Nahrung (*food*).
suture ['sju:tʃə], *s.* (*Med.*) die Naht.
suzerain ['sju:zərein], *s.* der Oberherr, Oberlehnsherr.
swab [swɔb], *s.* (*Med.*) die Laborprobe, der Abstrich; der Schrubber (*scrubber*). — *v.a.* (*Med.*) eine Probe entnehmen; schrubben (*scrub*).
swaddle [swɔdl], *s.* die Windel.
swaddling ['swɔdliŋ], *adj.* — *clothes*, die Windeln, *f. pl.*
swagger ['swægə], *v.n.* großtun. — *s.* das Großtun, Renommieren.
swallow (1) ['swɔlou], *s.* (*Orn.*) die Schwalbe.
swallow (2) ['swɔlou], *v.a.* schlucken; verschlingen (*devour*).
swamp [swɔmp], *s.* der Sumpf. — *v.a.* versenken; (*fig.*) überschütten.
swan [swɔn], *s.* (*Orn.*) der Schwan.
swank [swæŋk], *v.n.* großtun, angeben, aufschneiden. — *s.* der Großtuer.
swap, swop [swɔp], *v.a.* eintauschen, tauschen. — *v.n.* tauschen. — *s.* der Tausch.
sward [swɔ:d], *s.* (*Poet.*) der Rasen.
swarm [swɔ:m], *v.n.* schwärmen. — *s.* der Schwarm.
swarthy ['swɔ:ði], *adj.* dunkel, dunkelbraun.
swashbuckler ['swɔʃbʌklə], *s.* der Aufschneider, Angeber, Renommist.
swastika ['swɔstikə], *s.* das Hakenkreuz.
swathe [sweið], *v.a.* einhüllen, einwickeln.
sway [swei], *v.a.* schwenken; beeinflußen. — *v.n.* schwanken, sich schwingen. — *s.* der Einfluß, die Macht.

swear [swɛə], *v.a., v.n. irr.* schwören (*an oath*); fluchen (*curse*).
sweat [swet], *v.n.* schwitzen. — *s.* der Schweiß.
Swede [swi:d], *s.* der Schwede.
Swedish ['swi:diʃ], *adj.* schwedisch.
sweep [swi:p], *v.a., v.n. irr.* fegen, kehren; *a new broom —s clean,* neue Besen kehren gut. — *s.* der Schornsteinfeger (*chimney —*).
sweet [swi:t], *adj.* süß. — *s.* der Nachtisch; (*pl.*) Süßigkeiten, *f. pl.*
swell [swel], *v.a. irr.* anschwellen lassen. — *v.n.* anschwellen. — *adj., adv.* (*Am. sl.*) ausgezeichnet. — *s.* (*sl.*) der feine Kerl.
swelter ['sweltə], *v.n.* vor Hitze vergehen.
swerve [swə:v], *v.n.* abschweifen, abbiegen.
swift (1) [swift], *adj.* schnell, behende, rasch.
swift (2) [swift], *s.* (*Orn.*) die Turmschwalbe.
swill [swil], *v.a.* spülen (*rinse*); (*sl.*) saufen (*drink heavily*). — *s.* das Spülicht (*dishwater*); (*coll.*) das Gesöff.
swim [swim], *v.n. irr.* schwimmen. — *s.* das Schwimmen.
swindle [swindl], *v.a.* beschwindeln. — *s.* der Schwindel.
swine [swain], *s. pl.* die Schweine; (*sing.*) der Schweinehund, das Schwein.
swing [swiŋ], *v.a., v.n. irr.* schwingen, schaukeln. — *s.* der Schwung; die Schaukel.
swipe [swaip], *v.a.* schlagen; (*fig.*) stehlen. — *s.* der Schlag.
swirl [swə:l], *v.a., v.n.* wirbeln (*in air*). — *s.* der Wirbel.
Swiss [swis], *s.* der Schweizer. — *adj.* schweizerisch, Schweizer-.
switch [switʃ], *v.a.* (*Elec.*) — *on,* andrehen, einschalten; — *off,* abschalten; (*fig.*) wechseln, vertauschen (*change*). — *v.n.* umstellen, umschalten. — *s.* (*Elec.*) der Schalter.
switchboard ['switʃbɔ:d], *s.* die Telephonzentrale, das Schaltbrett.
switchgear ['switʃgiə], *s.* (*Elec.*) das Schaltgerät, die Schaltung.
swivel [swivl], *v.n.* drehen. — *s.* der Drehring; — *chair,* der Drehstuhl.
swoon [swu:n], *v.n.* in Ohnmacht fallen. — *s.* die Ohnmacht.
swoop [swu:p], *s.* der Stoß. — *v.n.* (herab)stoßen; stürzen; (nieder)-schießen.
swop *see* **swap.**
sword [sɔ:d], *s.* das Schwert.
syllable ['siləbl], *s.* die Silbe.
syllabus ['siləbəs], *s.* das Verzeichnis, der Lehrplan.
symbol ['simbəl], *s.* das Symbol, Sinnbild.
sympathetic [simpə'θetik], *adj.* mitfühlend, teilnehmend; sympathisch.
sympathy ['simpəθi], *s.* die Sympathie, das Mitgefühl.
symphony ['simfəni], *s.* (*Mus.*) die Symphonie.
synchronize ['siŋkrənaiz], *v.a.* synchronisieren.
syndicate ['sindikit], *s.* die Arbeitsgruppe, das Syndikat.
synod ['sinəd], *s.* die Synode, Kirchentagung.
synonymous [si'nɔniməs], *adj.* synonym.
synopsis [si'nɔpsis], *s.* die Zusammenfassung, Übersicht.
Syrian ['siriən], *adj.* syrisch. — *s.* der Syrer.
syringe ['sirindʒ], *s.* die Spritze.
syrup ['sirəp], *s.* der Sirup.
system ['sistəm], *s.* das System.
systematize ['sistəmətaiz], *v.a.* ordnen, in ein System bringen.

T

T [ti:]. das T.
tab [tæb], *s.* das Schildchen, der Streifen.
tabard ['tæbəd], *s.* der Wappenrock, Heroldsrock.
tabby ['tæbi], *s.* (*cat*) die getigerte Katze.
table [teibl], *s.* der Tisch; (*Maths.*) die Tabelle, das Einmaleins. — *v.a.* (*Parl.*) einen Entwurf einbringen; (*Am.*) auf die lange Bank schieben.
tablecloth ['teiblklɔθ], *s.* das Tischtuch.
tablemat ['teiblmæt], *s.* der Untersatz.
tablenapkin ['teiblnæpkin], *s.* die Serviette.
tablespoon ['teiblspu:n], *s.* der Eßlöffel.
tablet ['tæblit], *s.* die Tablette (*pill*); die Schreibtafel, der Block (*writing*).
taboo [tə'bu:], *s.* das Verbot, Tabu.
tabular ['tæbjulə], *adj.* tabellarisch; wie eine Tafel.
tacit ['tæsit], *adj.* stillschweigend.
taciturn ['tæsitə:n], *adj.* schweigsam, einsilbig.
tack [tæk], *s.* der Stift; der Stich (*sewing*). — *v.a.* nageln; heften (*sew*).
tackle [tækl], *v.a.* (*Naut.*) takeln; (*Footb., fig.*) angreifen; anpacken. — *s.* (*Naut.*) das Takel; (*fig.*) das Zeug; (*Footb.*) das Angreifen.
tact [tækt], *s.* der Takt; das Zartgefühl.
tactics ['tæktiks], *s. pl.* die Taktik.
tadpole ['tædpoul], *s.* (*Zool.*) die Kaulquappe.
taffeta ['tæfitə], *s.* (*Text.*) der Taft.
tag [tæg], *s.* der Anhängezettel; das Sprichwort (*saying*). — *v.a.* anhängen. — *v.n.* — *on to,* sich anschließen.

tail [teil], *s.* der Schwanz; (*fig.*) das Ende; (*pl.*) der Frack (*tailcoat*). — *v.a.* (*Am.*) folgen (*Dat.*).
tailor ['teilə], *s.* der Schneider; —*made*, geschneidert, nach Maß gemacht. — *v.a.* schneidern.
taint [teint], *v.a.* beflecken; verderben (*corrupt*). — *s.* der Fleck.
take [teik], *v.a. irr.* nehmen; bringen, ergreifen (*seize*); erfordern (*require*); — *up*, aufnehmen, beginnen; ertragen (*suffer, tolerate*); — *breath*, Atem holen; — *care*, sich in acht nehmen; — *offence at*, Anstoß nehmen an; — *place*, stattfinden; — *for*, halten für. — *v.n.* wirken (*be effective*); — *to*, Gefallen finden (an, *Dat.*); — *to flight* or *o.'s heels*, sich aus dem Staube machen; — *after*, ähnlich sein.
takings ['teikiŋz], *s.* (*pl.*) die Einnahmen, *f. pl.*
tale [teil], *s.* das Märchen, die Geschichte.
talent ['tælənt], *s.* das Talent, die Begabung.
talented ['tæləntid], *adj.* talentiert, begabt.
talk [tɔ:k], *v.a., v.n.* reden, sprechen. — *s.* das Gespräch (*discussion*); der Vortrag (*lecture*); das Reden, Gerede (*speaking*).
talkative ['tɔ:kətiv], *adj.* geschwätzig, redselig, gesprächig.
tall [tɔ:l], *adj.* hoch (*high*); groß (*grown high*); *a — order*, eine schwierige Aufgabe; *a — story*, eine Aufschneiderei, das Seemannsgarn.
tallow ['tælou], *s.* der Talg.
tally ['tæli], *v.n.* passen (*match*); stimmen (*be correct*).
talon ['tælən], *s.* die Klaue, Kralle.
tame [teim], *adj.* zahm. — *v.a.* zähmen.
tamper ['tæmpə], *v.n.* hineinpfuschen (*with*, in, *Acc.*).
tan [tæn], *s.* die Lohe; die braune Farbe; der Sonnenbrand (*sun*). — *v.a.* bräunen; (*leather*) gerben; (*fig.*) verbleuen (*beat*).
tang [tæŋ], *s.* der Seetang; (*fig.*) der Beigeschmack.
tangible ['tændʒibl], *adj.* greifbar.
tangle [tæŋgl], *v.a.* verwickeln (*entangle*). — *s.* die Verwirrung, Verwicklung.
tank [tæŋk], *s.* der Tank; (*Mil.*) der Panzer; der Wasserspeicher (*cistern*). — *v.a., v.n.* tanken.
tankard ['tæŋkəd], *s.* der Maßkrug, Bierkrug.
tanner (1) ['tænə], *s.* der Gerber.
tanner (2) ['tænə], *s.* (*sl.*) das Sechspencestück.
tantalize ['tæntəlaiz], *v.a.* quälen.
tantamount ['tæntəmaunt], *adj.* gleich, gleichwertig.
tap [tæp], *v.a.* anzapfen (*barrel*); klopfen; tippen (*on shoulder etc.*); (*fig.*) anpumpen (*for money*). — *s.* der Hahn; der Zapfen (*barrel*); der leichte Schlag (*on shoulder etc.*).
tape [teip], *s.* das Band; *red* —, die Bürokratie, der Bürokratismus; — *measure*, das Bandmaß; — *recorder*, das Tonbandgerät.
taper ['teipə], *v.n.* spitz zulaufen. — *v.a.* spitzen. — *s.* die (spitze) Kerze.
tapestry ['tæpistri], *s.* die Tapete, der Wandteppich.
tapeworm ['teipwə:m], *s.* der Bandwurm.
taproot ['tæpru:t], *s.* die Pfahlwurzel, Hauptwurzel.
tar [tɑ:], *s.* der Teer; (*Naut. sl.*) der Matrose. — *v.a.* teeren.
tardy ['tɑ:di], *adj.* träge (*sluggish*), langsam.
tare (1) [tɛə], das Taragewicht, die Tara (*weight*). — *v.a.* auswägen, tarieren.
tare (2) [tɛə], *s.* (*Bot.*) die Wicke.
target ['tɑ:git], *s.* das Ziel; die Zielscheibe (*board*).
tariff ['tærif], *s.* der Tarif.
tarnish ['tɑ:niʃ], *v.a.* trüben. — *v.n.* anlaufen.
tarpaulin [tɑ:'pɔ:lin], *s.* die Persenning.
tarry (1) ['tæri], *v.n.* zögern (*hesitate*); warten (*wait*).
tarry (2) ['tɑ:ri], *adj.* teerig.
tart (1) [tɑ:t], *s.* die Torte.
tart (2) [tɑ:t], *adj.* herb, sauer.
tart (3) [tɑ:t], *s.* (*sl.*) die Dirne.
Tartar ['tɑ:tə], *s.* der Tatar; (*fig.*) der Tyrann.
tartar ['tɑ:tə], *s.* (*Chem.*) der Weinstein.
task [tɑ:sk], *s.* die Aufgabe, das Tagewerk; *take to* —, zur Rechenschaft ziehen.
tassel [tæsl], *s.* die Quaste.
taste [teist], *v.a.* schmecken; versuchen, kosten. — *s.* die Probe (*tasting*); der Geschmack (*flavour*).
tasteful ['teistful], *adj.* geschmackvoll.
tasteless ['teistlis], *adj.* geschmacklos.
tasty ['teisti], *adj.* schmackhaft.
tatter ['tætə], *s.* der Lumpen. — *v.a.* in Fetzen reißen, zerfetzen.
tattle [tætl], *v.n.* schwatzen. — *s.* das Geschwätz.
tattoo (1) [tə'tu:], *s.* (*Mil.*) der Zapfenstreich, das militärische Schaustück, die Parade.
tattoo (2) [tə'tu:], *v.a.* tätowieren. — *s.* die Tätowierung.
taunt [tɔ:nt], *v.a.* höhnen, schmähen. — *s.* der Hohn, Spott.
tavern ['tævən], *s.* die Schenke.
tawdry ['tɔ:dri], *adj.* kitschig, flitterhaft.
tawny ['tɔ:ni], *adj.* braungelb, lohfarbig.
tax [tæks], *s.* die Abgabe, Steuer; Besteuerung (*taxation*). — *v.a.* besteuern; (*fig.*) anstrengen, ermüden (*strain*).
taxi ['tæksi], *s.* das Taxi.
tea [ti:], *s.* der Tee.
teach [ti:tʃ], *v.a., v.n. irr.* lehren, unterrichten.
teacher ['ti:tʃə], *s.* der Lehrer, die Lehrerin.

team [ti:m], *s.* (*Sport*) die Mannschaft; das Gespann (*horses*); (*fig.*) der Stab; — *spirit*, der Korpsgeist.
tear (1) [tεə], *s.* der Riß (*rent*). — *v.a. irr.* zerreißen (*rend*).
tear (2) [tiə], *s.* die Träne.
tearing ['tεəriŋ], *adj.* — *hurry*, rasende Eile.
tease [ti:z], *v.a.* necken (*mock*); aufrauhen (*roughen*).
teat [ti:t], *s.* die Brustwarze, Zitze.
technical ['teknikəl], *adj.* technisch.
technique [tek'ni:k], *s.* die Technik, Methode.
techy *see* **tetchy.**
tedious ['ti:diəs], *adj.* langweilig, lästig.
tedium ['ti:diəm], *s.* der Überdruß, die Langeweile.
tee [ti:], *s.* (*Sport*) der Golfballhalter.
teem [ti:m], *v.n.* wimmeln.
teenager ['ti:neidʒə], *s.* der, die Jugendliche; Teenager.
teeth *see under* **tooth.**
teethe [ti:ð], *v.n.* Zähne bekommen, zahnen.
teetotal [ti:'toutl], *adj.* abstinent, antialkoholisch.
teetotaller [ti:'toutlə], *s.* der Antialkoholiker.
telegram ['teligræm], *s.* das Telegramm.
telephone ['telifoun], *s.* (*abbr.* **phone**) das Telephon; – *booth*, die Fernsprechzelle; — *exchange*, das Fernsprechamt.
television [teli'viʒən], *s.* das Fernsehen; — *set*, der Fernsehapparat.
tell [tel], *v.a. irr.* erzählen, berichten (*relate*); verraten (*reveal*).
tell-tale ['telteil], *s.* der Angeber, Zuträger. — *adj.* sprechend; Warnungs-.
teller ['telə], *s.* der Zähler; der Kassier (*cashier*).
temerity [ti'meriti], *s.* die Verwegenheit, Tollkühnheit.
temper ['tempə], *v.a.* vermischen (*mix*); mäßigen (*moderate*); (*Metall.*) härten. — *s.* die üble Stimmung, Wut, Laune; (*Metall.*) die Härte.
temperance ['tempərəns], *s.* die Mäßigkeit, Enthaltsamkeit.
temperate ['tempərit], *adj.* gemäßigt, temperiert.
temperature ['temprətʃə], *s.* die Temperatur.
tempest ['tempist], *s.* der Sturm.
tempestuous [tem'pestjuəs], *adj.* stürmisch.
temple (1) [templ], *s.* der Tempel.
temple (2) [templ], *s.* (*Anat.*) die Schläfe (*side of brow*).
temporal ['tempərəl], *adj.* weltlich, zeitlich.
temporary ['tempərəri], *adj.* zeitweilig, vorläufig, provisorisch.
temporize ['tempəraiz], *v.n.* zögern, Zeit zu gewinnen suchen.
tempt [tempt], *v.a.* versuchen.
temptation [temp'teiʃən], *s.* die Versuchung.
ten [ten], *num. adj.* zehn.
tenth [tenθ], *num. adj.* zehnte. — *s.* der Zehnte.
tenable ['tenəbl], *adj.* haltbar.
tenacious [ti'neiʃəs], *adj.* zähe, festhaltend, hartnäckig.
tenacity [ti'næsiti], *s.* die Zähigkeit, Ausdauer.
tenancy ['tenənsi], *s.* das Mietverhältnis; die Mietdauer.
tenant ['tenənt], *s.* der Mieter, Pächter.
tench [tentʃ], *s.* (*Zool.*) die Schleie.
tend (1) [tend], *v.a.*, *v.n.* warten, pflegen (*nurse*).
tend (2) [tend], *v.n.* neigen, gerichtet sein (*be inclined*).
tendency ['tendənsi], *s.* die Tendenz, Neigung.
tender (1) ['tendə], *s.* das Angebot (*offer*); *legal* —, das Zahlungsmittel. — *v.a.* einreichen.
tender (2) ['tendə], *adj.* sanft (*affectionate*); zart, zärtlich, weich (*delicate*).
tender (3) ['tendə], *s.* (*Railw.*) der Tender.
tendon ['tendən], *s.* (*Anat.*) die Sehne, Flechse.
tendril ['tendril], *s.* (*Bot.*) die Ranke.
tenement ['tenimənt], *s.* die Mietswohnung, die Mietskaserne.
tenet ['tenit], *s.* der Grundsatz (*principle*); die Lehre (*doctrine*).
tenfold ['tenfould], *adj.* zehnfach.
tennis ['tenis], *s.* das Tennis.
tenor ['tenə], *s.* (*Mus.*) der Tenor; der Sinn, Inhalt (*meaning*).
tense (1) [tens], *adj.* gespannt; straff (*taut*).
tense (2) [tens], *s.* (*Gram.*) die Zeitform.
tension ['tenʃən], *s.* die Spannung.
tent [tent], *s.* das Zelt.
tentacle ['tentəkl], *s.* (*Zool.*) das Fühlhorn, der Fühler.
tentative ['tentətiv], *adj.* versuchend, vorsichtig; (*fig.*) vorläufig.
tenterhooks ['tentəhuks], *s. pl.* die Spannhaken, *m. pl.*; *be on* —, in größter Spannung sein.
tenuous ['tenjuəs], *adj.* dünn, fadenscheinig, spärlich.
tenure ['tenjuə], *s.* der Mietbesitz, die Mietvertragslänge, das Mietrecht; — *of office*, die Amtsdauer.
tepid ['tepid], *adj.* lau, lauwarm.
term [tə:m], *s.* der Ausdruck (*expression*); die Bedingung (*condition*); der Termin, die Frist (*period*); (*Sch.*) das Semester, Trimester; *be on good —s with* (*s.o.*), auf gutem Fuß stehen mit. — *v.a.* benennen, bezeichen.
terminate ['tə:mineit], *v.a.* beenden, zu Ende bringen. — *v.n.* zu Ende kommen.
terminus ['tə:minəs], *s.* die Endstation.
terrace ['teris], *s.* die Terrasse.
terrestrial [tə'restriəl], *adj.* irdisch.
terrible ['teribl], *adj.* schrecklich, furchtbar.
terrific [tə'rifik], *adj.* fürchterlich; (*coll.*) ungeheuer.

terrify ['terifai], *v.a.* erschrecken.
territory ['teritəri], *s.* das Gebiet.
terror ['terə], *s.* der Schrecken.
terse [tə:s], *adj.* bündig, kurz.
tertiary ['tə:ʃəri], *adj.* tertiär.
test [test], *s.* die Prüfung; (*Chem.*) die Probe; — *-tube*, das Reagensglas *or* Reagenzglas. — *v.a.* prüfen.
testament ['testəmənt], *s.* das Testament.
testator [tes'teitə], *s.* der Erblasser.
testicle ['testikl], *s.* (*Anat.*) die Hode.
testify ['testifai], *v.a.* bezeugen.
testimonial [testi'mouniəl], *s.* das Zeugnis.
testimony ['testiməni], *s.* das Zeugnis, die Zeugenaussage (*oral*).
testiness ['testinis], *s.* die Verdrießlichkeit.
testy ['testi], *adj.* verdrießlich, reizbar.
tetanus ['tetənəs], *s.* (*Med.*) der Starrkrampf.
tetchy, techy ['tetʃi], *adj.* mürrisch, reizbar.
tether ['teðə], *s.* das Spannseil; (*fig.*) *at the end of o.'s* —, am Ende seiner Geduld. — *v.a.* anbinden.
text ['tekst], *s.* der Text, Wortlaut.
textile ['tekstail], *s.* die Textilware, der Webstoff.
textual ['tekstjuəl], *adj.* textlich, Text-.
texture ['tekstʃə], *s.* das Gewebe, die Struktur.
Thai [tai], *adj.* Thai-, siamesisch. — *s. pl.* die Thaivölker, *pl.*
than [ðæn], *conj.* als (*after comparatives*).
thank [θæŋk], *v.a.* danken (*Dat.*). — *s.* (*pl.*) der Dank.
that [ðæt], *dem. adj.* der, die, das, jener. — *dem. pron.* der, die, das; (*absolute, no pl.*) das. — *rel. pron.* der, die, das, welcher, was. — *conj.* daß; damit (*in order* —).
thatch [θætʃ], *v.a.* decken (mit Stroh). — *s.* das Strohdach.
thaw [θɔ:], *v.n.* tauen; auftauen. — *s.* das Tauwetter.
the [ðə, *before vowel* ði], *def. art.* der, die, das. — *adv.* — *bigger* — *better*, je grösser desto *or* umso besser.
theatre ['θiətə], *s.* das Theater; (*fig.*) der Schauplatz.
theatrical [θi'ætrikəl], *adj.* bühnenhaft (*of the stage*); theatralisch; Bühnen-, Theater-.
theft [θeft], *s.* der Diebstahl.
their [ðɛə], *poss. adj.* ihr.
theirs [ðɛəz], *poss. pron.* der, die, das ihrige, der, die, das ihre.
them [ðem], *pers. pron.* sie, ihnen.
theme [θi:m], *s.* das Thema; (*Mus.*) das Thema, Motiv.
then [ðen], *adv.* dann, damals; *by* —, *till* —, bis dahin. — *conj.* dann, denn. — *adj.* damalig.
thence [ðens], *adv.* von da; daher.
theology [θi'ɔlədʒi], *s.* die Theologie.
theorem ['θiərəm], *s.* (*Maths.*) der Lehrsatz, Grundsatz.
theorize ['θiəraiz], *v.n.* theoretisieren.
therapeutics [θerə'pju:tiks], *s. pl.* die Heilkunde.
therapy ['θerəpi], *s.* die Therapie.
there [ðɛə], *adv.* dort, da; dorthin, dahin (*thereto*); — *is*, — *are*, es gibt; *here and* —, hier und da.
thereabout(s) [ðɛərəbaut(s)], *adv.* ungefähr, da herum.
thereafter [ðɛər'a:ftə], *adv.* hernach, danach.
thereby [ðɛə'bai], *adv.* dadurch.
therefore ['ðɛəfɔ:], *adv.* darum, deshalb.
thermal, thermic ['θə:məl, 'θə:mik], *adj.* thermisch; warm; Wärme-.
thermometer [θə'mɔmitə], *s.* das Thermometer.
these [ði:z], *dem. adj. & pron. pl.* diese.
thesis ['θi:sis], *s.* die These; die Dissertation.
they [ðei], *pers. pron. pl.* sie.
thick [θik], *adj.* dick; dicht; (*fig.*) dick befreundet; — *as thieves*, wie eine Diebsbande.
thicken ['θikən], *v.a.* verdicken. — *v.n* dick werden.
thicket ['θikit], *s.* das Dickicht.
thickness ['θiknis], *s.* die Dicke.
thief [θi:f], *s.* der Dieb.
thieve [θi:v], *v.n.* stehlen.
thigh [θai], *s.* (*Anat.*) der Oberschenkel.
thimble [θimbl], *s.* der Fingerhut.
thin [θin], *adj.* dünn. — *v.a., v.n.* (sich) verdünnen.
thine [ðain], *poss. pron.* (*Poet.*) dein, der, die, das deinige.
thing [θiŋ], *s.* das Ding; die Sache (*matter*).
think [θiŋk], *v.a., v.n. irr.* denken; meinen, glauben.
thinker ['θiŋkə], *s.* der Denker.
third [θə:d], *num. adj.* der, die, das dritte. — *s.* das Drittel.
thirdly ['θə:dli], *adv.* drittens.
thirst [θə:st], *s.* der Durst (*for*, nach). — *v.n.* dürsten.
thirsty ['θə:sti], *adj.* durstig; *be* —, Durst haben.
thirteen [θə:'ti:n], *num. adj.* dreizehn.
thirty ['θə:ti], *num. adj.* dreißig.
this [ðis], *dem. adj.* dieser, diese, dieses. — *dem. pron.* dieser, diese, dieses; dies.
thistle [θisl], *s.* (*Bot.*) die Distel.
thither ['ðiðə], *adv.* dahin, dorthin.
tho' [ðou] *see under* **though.**
thong [θɔŋ], *s.* der Riemen (*strap*); die Peitschenschnur.
thorn [θɔ:n], *s.* (*Bot.*) der Dorn.
thorough ['θʌrə], *adj.* gründlich; völlig (*complete*).
thoroughbred ['θʌrəbred], *s.* das Vollblut, der Vollblüter. — *adj.* Vollblut-.
thoroughfare ['θʌrəfɛə], *s.* der Durchgang (*path*); die Durchfahrt.
those [ðouz], *dem. adj. pl.* die, jene. — *dem. pron. pl.* jene, diejenigen.
thou [ðau], *pers. pron.* (*Poet.*) du.
though [ðou], *conj.* (*abbr.* **tho'**) obgleich, obwohl, wenn auch (*even if*). — *adv.* doch, zwar.

thought [θɔ:t], *s.* der Gedanke; *also past tense and participle of* **think** *q.v.*
thoughtful ['θɔ:tful], *adj.* rücksichtsvoll, nachdenklich.
thoughtless ['θɔ:tlis], *adj.* gedankenlos.
thousand ['θauzənd], *num. adj. a* —, tausend. — *s.* das Tausend.
thrash [θræʃ], *v.a.* dreschen (*corn*); prügeln (*s.o.*).
thread [θred], *s.* der Faden. — *v.a.* einfädeln. — *v.n.* sich schlängeln, sich winden.
threadbare ['θredbεə], *adj.* fadenscheinig.
threat [θret], *s.* die Drohung.
threaten [θretn], *v.a.* drohen, androhen (*Dat.*).
three [θri:], *num. adj.* drei.
threescore ['θri:skɔ:], *num. adj.* sechzig.
thresh [θreʃ], *v.a.* dreschen (*corn*). — *See also* **thrash.**
threshold ['θreʃould], *s.* die Schwelle (*of door*).
thrice [θrais], *num. adv.* dreimal.
thrift [θrift], *s.* die Sparsamkeit; (*Bot.*) die Grasnelke, Meernelke.
thrill [θril], *v.a.* packen (*grip*). — *v.n.* erschauern, zittern (vor, *Dat.*). — *s.* der Schauer; die Spannung.
thriller ['θrilə], *s.* der Thriller, der spannende Roman *or* Film etc.
thrive [θraiv], *v.n.* gedeihen (*also fig.*); (*fig.*) gut weiterkommen, Glück haben.
thriving ['θraiviŋ], *adj.* blühend, (*Comm.*) gut gehend.
throat [θrout], *s.* (*Anat.*) der Schlund, die Kehle.
throb [θrɔb], *v.n.* pochen, klopfen.
throes [θrouz], *s. pl.* die Wehen, *f. pl.*; die Schmerzen, *m. pl.*
throne [θroun], *s.* der Thron.
throng [θrɔŋ], *s.* die Menge, das Gedränge. — *v.a., v.n.* (sich) drängen.
throttle [θrɔtl], *s.* die Kehle, Luftröhre; (*Mech.*) das Drosselventil; (*Motor.*) *open the* —, Gas geben.
through [θru:], *prep.* durch (*Acc.*); mittels (*Genit.*) (*by means of*). — *adv.* (mitten) durch.
throughout [θru:'aut], *prep.* ganz (hin)durch (*space*); während, hindurch (*time*). — *adv.* durchaus, in jeder Beziehung.
throw [θrou], *v.a. irr.* werfen; — *open*, eröffnen. — *s.* der Wurf.
thrush [θrʌʃ], *s.* (*Orn.*) die Drossel.
thrust [θrʌst], *v.a.* stoßen, drängen. — *v.n.* stoßen (*at*, nach); sich drängen. — *s.* der Stoß, Angriff; *cut and* —, Hieb und Gegenhieb.
thud [θʌd], *s.* der Schlag, das Dröhnen, der dumpfe Ton. — *v.n.* dröhnen, aufschlagen.
thumb [θʌm], *s.* (*Anat.*) der Daumen; *rule of* —, die Faustregel; (*Am.*) — *tack* see **drawing pin.** — *v.a.* durchblättern (*book*); — *a lift*, per Anhalter fahren.
thump [θʌmp], *v.a.* schlagen, puffen. — *v.n.* schlagen (*on*, auf; *against*, gegen). — *s.* der Schlag, Stoß.
thunder ['θʌndə], *s.* der Donner. — *v.n.* donnern.
thunderstruck ['θʌndəstrʌk], *adj.* wie vom Donner gerührt.
Thursday ['θə:zdi]. der Donnerstag.
Thuringian [θuə'rindʒiən], *adj.* thüringisch. — *s.* der Thüringer.
thus [ðʌs], *adv.* so, auf diese Weise (*in this way*).
thwart [θwɔ:t], *v.a.* vereiteln, durchkreuzen.
thy [ðai], *poss. adj.* (*Poet.*) dein, deine, dein.
thyme [taim], *s.* (*Bot.*) der Thymian.
tic [tik], *s.* (*Med.*) das Zucken.
tick (1) [tik], *s.* das Ticken (*watch*). — *v.n.* ticken.
tick (2) [tik], *s.* (*coll.*) der Kredit, Borg.
ticket ['tikit], *s.* die Fahrkarte (*travel*); die Eintrittskarte (*entry*); (*Am.*) der Strafzettel (*driving*).
ticking (1) ['tikiŋ], *s.* das Ticken (*of watch*).
ticking (2) ['tikiŋ], *s.* (*Text.*) der Zwillich.
tickle [tikl], *v.a., v.n.* kitzeln. — *s.* das Kitzeln.
ticklish ['tikliʃ], *adj.* kitzlig.
tidal [taidl], *adj.* Gezeiten-, Ebbe-, Flut-.
tide [taid], *s.* die Gezeiten, *f.pl.*, die Ebbe und Flut. — *v.a.* — *over*, hinweghelfen (über, *Acc.*).
tidiness ['taidinis], *s.* die Sauberkeit, Ordnung.
tidings ['taidiŋz], *s. pl.* (*Poet.*) die Nachricht.
tidy ['taidi], *adj.* nett, sauber, ordentlich. — *v.a.* — *up*, sauber machen.
tie [tai], *v.a.* binden, knüpfen. — *v.n.* (*Sport*) unentschieden sein. — *s.* die Binde, Krawatte; (*Sport*) das Unentschieden.
tier [tiə], *s.* der Rang, die Reihe, Sitzreihe.
tiger ['taigə], *s.* (*Zool.*) der Tiger.
tight [tait], *adj.* fest, eng, dicht (*close*); (*coll.*) betrunken (*drunk*); — *fisted*, geizig (*stingy*). — *s. pl.* die Trikothosen, *f.pl.*
tighten [taitn], *v.a.* festziehen.
tile [tail], *s.* der Ziegel (*roof etc.*); die Kachel (*glazed*). — *v.a.* kacheln, ziegeln.
till (1) [til], *prep., conj.* bis.
till (2) [til], *v.a.* aufbauen, beackern (*land*).
till (3) [til], *s.* die Ladenkasse.
tilt [tilt], *v.a.* kippen, neigen, umschlagen (*tip over*). — *v.n.* sich neigen, kippen, kentern. — *s.* die Neigung.
timber ['timbə], *s.* das Holz, Bauholz.
time [taim], *s.* die Zeit; (*Mus.*) das Tempo, Zeitmaß; *in* —, zur rechten Zeit; *every* —, jedesmal; *what is the* —? wievel Uhr ist es? — *v.a.* zeitlich messen, rechtzeitig einrichten.
timely ['taimli], *adj.* rechtzeitig.

timetable ['taimteibl], *s.* (*Railw.*) der Fahrplan; (*Sch.*) der Stundenplan.
timid ['timid], *adj.* furchtsam.
timpani ['timpəni], *s. pl.* (*Mus.*) die Kesselpauken, *f. pl.*
tin [tin], *s.* das Zinn, Weißblech; die Dose, Büchse (*preserved foods*); — *opener*, der Büchsenöffner.
tincture ['tiŋktʃə], *s.* die Tinktur, das Färbungsmittel.
tinder ['tində], *s.* der Zunder.
tinfoil ['tinfɔil], *s.* das Stanniol.
tinge [tindʒ], *v.a.* färben, anfärben. — *s.* die Färbung, leichte Farbe; (*fig.*) die Spur.
tingle [tiŋgl], *v.n.* klingen (*bells*); (*Anat.*) prickeln. — *s.* das Klingen; Prickeln.
tinker ['tiŋkə], *s.* der Kesselflicker. — *v.n.* basteln.
tinkle [tiŋkl], *v.a.* klingeln.
tinsel ['tinsəl], *s.* das Lametta, Flittergold.
tint [tint], *v.a.* färben. — *s.* die Farbe; der Farbton.
tiny ['taini], *adj.* winzig.
tip (1) [tip], *v.a.* kippen; (*coll.*) ein Trinkgeld geben (*Dat.*). — *s.* (*Sport etc.*) (*coll.*) der Tip; das Trinkgeld (*gratuity*).
tip (2) [tip], *s.* die Spitze; das Mundstück (*cigarette*).
tipple [tipl], *v.n.* (viel) trinken, zechen.
tipsy ['tipsi], *adj.* beschwipst.
tiptoe ['tiptou], *s. on* —, auf Zehenspitzen.
tiptop ['tiptɔp], *adj.* (*coll.*) erstklassig.
tirade [ti'reid *or* tai'reid], *s.* der Wortschwall, die Tirade.
tire (1) [taiə], *v.a., v.n.* ermüden.
tire (2) *see under* **tyre**.
tired ['taiəd], *adj.* müde.
tiresome ['taiəsəm], *adj.* langweilig (*boring*); auf die Nerven gehend (*annoying*).
tissue ['tiʃju:], *s.* das Gewebe; — *paper*, das Seidenpapier.
titbit ['titbit], *s.* der Leckerbissen.
tithe [taið], *s.* der Zehnte.
title [taitl], *s.* der Titel, die Überschrift; (*fig.*) der Anspruch (*claim*).
titmouse ['titmaus], *s.* (*Orn.*) die Meise.
titter ['titə], *v.n.* kichern. — *s.* das Kichern.
tittle [titl], *s.* das Tüpfelchen; — *tattle*, das Geschwätz.
titular ['titjulə], *adj.* Titular-.
to [tu], *prep.* zu (*Dat.*), gegen (*Acc.*); bis (*until, as far as*), nach, an, auf; *in order* —, um zu. — [tu:], *adv.* zu; — *and fro*, hin und her.
toad [toud], *s.* (*Zool.*) die Kröte.
toadstool ['toudstu:l], *s.* (*Bot.*) der Giftpilz.
toady ['toudi], *v.n.* kriechen. — *s.* der Kriecher.
toast [toust], *s.* der Toast, das Röstbrot; der Trinkspruch. — *v.a.* toasten, rösten; trinken auf; — *s.o.*, einen Trinkspruch ausbringen auf einen.
tobacco [tə'bækou], *s.* der Tabak.
toboggan [tə'bɔgən], *s.* der Rodel, der Schlitten. — *v.n.* rodeln, Schlitten fahren.
tocsin ['tɔksin], *s.* die Sturmglocke.
today [tə'dei], *adv.* heute.
toddle [tɔdl], *v.n.* watscheln; abschieben (— *off*).
toddler ['tɔdlə], *s.* (*coll.*) das kleine Kind (das gehen lernt).
toe [tou], *s.* (*Anat.*) die Zehe.
toffee ['tɔfi], *s.* der Sahnebonbon.
together [tə'geðə], *adv.* zusammen.
toil [tɔil], *v.n.* hart arbeiten. — *s.* die schwere, harte Arbeit.
toilet ['tɔilit], *s.* das Anziehen, Ankleiden; die Toilette, der Abort, das Klosett (*lavatory*).
token ['toukən], *s.* das Zeichen (*sign*); der Beweis (*proof*); das Andenken (*keepsake*).
tolerable ['tɔlərəbl], *adj.* erträglich, leidlich.
tolerance ['tɔlərəns], *s.* die Toleranz, Duldsamkeit; (*Tech.*) die Toleranz.
tolerant ['tɔlərənt], *adj.* tolerant, duldsam.
tolerate ['tɔləreit], *v.a.* ertragen, dulden.
toll [toul], *v.a., v.n.* läuten. — *s.* der Zoll; — *gate*, — *bar*, der Schlagbaum.
tomato [tə'mɑ:tou], *s.* (*Bot.*) die Tomate.
tomb [tu:m], *s.* das Grab, Grabmal.
tomboy ['tɔmbɔi], *s.* der Wildfang.
tomcat ['tɔmkæt], *s.* (*Zool.*) der Kater.
tome [toum], *s.* der große Band, (*coll.*) der Wälzer.
tomfoolery [tɔm'fu:ləri], *s.* die Narretei.
Tommy ['tɔmi], *s.* (*Mil.*) (*coll.*) der englische Soldat.
tomorrow [tə'mɔrou], *adv.* morgen; — *morning*, morgen früh; *the day after* —, übermorgen.
ton [tʌn], *s.* die Tonne.
tone [toun], *s.* der Ton, Klang; (*fig.*) die Stimmung (*mood*). — *v.a.* — *down*, abtönen, abstimmen.
tongs [tɔŋz], *s. pl.* die Zange.
tongue [tʌŋ], *s.* (*Anat.*) die Zunge.
tonic ['tɔnik], *s.* das Stärkungsmittel. — *adj.* tonisch, stärkend.
tonight [tu'nait], *adv.* heute abend, heute nacht.
tonnage ['tʌnidʒ], *s.* die Tonnage, das Tonnengeld.
tonsil ['tɔnsil], *s.* (*Anat.*) die Mandel.
tonsilitis [tɔnsi'laitis], *s.* (*Med.*) die Mandelentzündung.
tonsure ['tɔnʃə], *s.* die Tonsur.
too [tu:], *adv.* allzu, zu, allzusehr; auch (*also*).
tool [tu:l], *s.* das Werkzeug, das Gerät; *machine* —, die Werkzeugmaschine.
tooth [tu:θ], *s.* (*pl.* **teeth** [ti:θ]) der Zahn.
toothache ['tu:θeik], *s.* das Zahnweh.
toothbrush ['tu:θbrʌʃ], *s.* die Zahnbürste.

toothpaste ['tu:θpeist], *s.* die Zahnpaste.
top (1) [tɔp], *s.* die Spitze; der Gipfel (*mountain*); der Wipfel (*tree*); der Giebel (*house*); die Oberfläche (*surface*); *big* —, das Zirkuszeltdach; — *hat*, der Zylinder. — *v.a.* übertreffen (*surpass*); bedecken (*cover*).
top (2) [tɔp], *s.* der Kreisel (*spinning* —).
topaz ['toupæz], *s.* der Topas.
tope [toup], *v.n.* zechen, saufen.
toper ['toupə], *s.* der Zecher.
topic ['tɔpik], *s.* das Thema, der Gegenstand.
topical ['tɔpikəl], *adj.* aktuell (*up to date*).
topmost ['tɔpmoust], *adj.* höchst, oberst.
topsy-turvy ['tɔpsi 'tə:vi], *adv.* durcheinander, auf den Kopf gestellt.
torch [tɔ:tʃ], *s.* die Fackel; (*Elec.*) die Taschenlampe.
torment ['tɔ:mənt], *s.* die Qual, Marter. — [tɔ:'ment], *v.a.* quälen, martern, peinigen.
tornado [tɔ:'neidou], *s.* der Wirbelsturm.
torpid ['tɔ:pid], *adj.* starr, betäubt; (*fig.*) stumpfsinnig.
torpor ['tɔ:pə], *s.* die Starre; die Stumpfheit, Stumpfsinnigkeit.
torrent ['tɔrənt], *s.* der Gießbach, der (reißende) Strom.
torrid ['tɔrid], *adj.* brennend heiß, verbrannt.
torsion ['tɔ:ʃən], *s.* die Drehung, Windung.
tortoise ['tɔ:təs], *s.* (*Zool.*) die Schildkröte.
tortoiseshell ['tɔ:təʃel], *s.* das Schildpatt.
tortuous ['tɔ:tjuəs], *adj.* gewunden.
torture ['tɔ:tʃə], *s.* die Folter; (*fig.*) die Folterqualen, *f. pl.* — *v.a.* foltern.
Tory ['tɔ:ri], *s.* (*Pol.*) der englische Konservative.
toss [tɔs], *s.* der Wurf (*of coin, etc.*); *argue the* —, sich streiten. — *v.a.* werfen. — *v.n.* — *up*, losen.
total [toutl], *adj.* ganz, gänzlich, total. — *s.* die Gesamtsumme. — *v.a.* sich (im ganzen) belaufen auf.
totality [tou'tæliti], *s.* die Gesamtheit.
totter ['tɔtə], *v.n.* wanken, schwanken, torkeln.
touch [tʌtʃ], *v.a.* berühren; anfassen; (*coll.*) anpumpen (*for money*); — *up*, auffrischen. — *s.* die Berührung (*contact*); (*Mus.*) der Anschlag.
touching ['tʌtʃiŋ], *adj.* rührend, ergreifend.
touchline ['tʌtʃlain], *s.* (*Sport*) der Rand des Spielfeldes, die Seitenlinie.
touchy ['tʌtʃi], *adj.* empfindlich.
tough [tʌf], *adj.* zäh, widerstandsfähig (*resistant*); *get* —, grob werden; — *luck*, Pech! — *s.* (*Am. coll.*) der Grobian.
tour [tuə], *s.* die Tour, Reise; (*Theat.*) die Tournee. — *v.a., v.n.* touren, bereisen.
tourist ['tuərist], *s.* der Tourist.
tournament ['tuə- *or* 'tə:nəmənt], *s.* der Wettkampf, das Turnier.
tout [taut], *v.n.* Kunden suchen, anlocken. — *s.* der Kundenfänger.
tow [tou], *s.* das Schlepptau. — *v.a.* ziehen, schleppen.
toward(s) [tu'wɔ:d(z), tɔ:d(z)], *prep.* gegen; gegenüber; zu . . . hin; auf . . . zu; für.
towel ['tauəl], *s.* das Handtuch.
towelling ['tauəliŋ], *s.* der Handtuchdrell; *Turkish* —, das Frottiertuch.
tower [tauə], *s.* der Turm, Zwinger. — *v.n.* emporragen, hervorragen (über).
towing path ['tou(iŋ) pɑ:θ] *see* **towpath**.
town [taun], *s.* die Stadt; — *crier*, der Ausrufer; — *hall*, das Rathaus (*offices*).
townsman ['taunzmən], *s.* der Städter.
towpath ['toupɑ:θ], *s.* der Treidelpfad.
toy [tɔi], *s.* das Spielzeug; (*pl.*) Spielsachen, Speilwaren, *f. pl.*; — *shop*, der Speilwarenladen. — *v.n.* spielen.
trace [treis], *s.* die Spur. — *v.a.* suchen, aufspüren; pausen (*through paper*).
track [træk], *s.* die Spur, Fährte (*path*); (*Railw.*) das Geleis(e).
tract [trækt], *s.* der Traktat (*pamphlet*); die Strecke (*stretch*).
traction ['trækʃən], *s.* das Ziehen (*pulling*); (*Tech.*) der Zug.
tractor ['træktə], *s.* der Traktor.
trade [treid], *s.* der Handel (*commerce*); das Gewerbe (*craft*); — *wind*, der Passatwind; — *union*, die Gewerkschaft. — *v.a.* — *in*, in Zahlung geben. — *v.n.* handeln, Handel treiben; — *in*, eintauschen.
trademark ['treidmɑ:k], *s.* die (Schutz)-marke, das Warenzeichen.
tradesman ['treidzmən], *s.* der Lieferant.
traduce [trə'dju:s], *v.a.* verleumden.
traffic ['træfik], *s.* der Verkehr; (*Comm.*) der Handel; — *light*, die Verkehrsampel.
trafficator ['træfikeitə], *s.* (*Motor.*) der Winker.
tragedy ['trædʒədi], *s.* die Tragödie, das Trauerspiel.
tragic ['trædʒik], *adj.* tragisch.
tradition [trə'diʃən], *s.* die Tradition.
traditional [trə'diʃənəl], *adj.* traditionell.
trail [treil], *s.* die Spur, Fährte; (*Am.*) der Pfad. — *v.a.* nach sich ziehen, schleppen; (*Am.*) nachfolgen (*Dat.*).
trailer ['treilə], *s.* (*Motor.*) der Anhänger; (*Film*) die Voranzeige.
train [trein], *v.a.* ausbilden; (*Sport*) trainieren, abrichten, dressieren (*animal*). — *v.n.* (*Sport*) sich vorbereiten; sich ausbilden (*for profession*). — *s.* (*Railw.*) der Zug; (*Mil.*) der Zug, Transport; die Schleppe (*bridal gown, etc.*); — *of thought*, die Gedankenfolge.

training ['treiniŋ], *s.* die Erziehung; Ausbildung; — *college*, das Lehrerseminar, die pädagogische Hochschule.
trait [trei, treit], *s.* der Zug, Wesenszug.
traitor ['treitə], *s.* der Verräter.
tram(car) ['træm(kɑ:)], *s.* die Straßenbahn, der Strassenbahnwagen.
trammelled [træmld], *adj.* gebunden, gefesselt.
tramp [træmp], *s.* der Landstreicher, Strolch. — *v.n.* trampeln; (zu Fuß) wandern.
trample [træmpl], *v.a.* niedertrampeln. — *v.n.* trampeln, treten.
tramway ['træmwei], *s.* die Strassenbahn.
trance [trɑ:ns], *s.* die Verzückung.
tranquil ['træŋkwil], *adj.* ruhig, still, friedlich.
tranquillizer ['træŋkwilaizə], *s.* (*Med.*) das Beruhigungsmittel.
transact [træn'zækt], *v.a.* abmachen; verrichten (*conclude*), erledigen.
transaction [træn'zækʃən], *s.* die Verhandlung, Abmachung, Durchführung.
transcend [træn'send], *v.a.* übersteigen.
transcendental [trænsen'dentl], *adj.* transzendental.
transcribe [træn'skraib], *v.a.* übertragen; umschreiben (*cipher etc.*); abschreiben.
transcription [træn'skripʃən], *s.* die Umschrift; die Abschrift (*copy*).
transept ['trænsept], *s.* (*Archit.*) das Querschiff.
transfer [træns'fə:], *v.a.* versetzen, überführen; übertragen; überweisen (*money*). — *v.n.* verlegt werden. —['trænsfə:], *s.* der Wechsel, Transfer; die Versetzung; Überweisung.
transfigure [træns'figə], *v.a.* verklären.
transfix [træns'fiks], *v.a.* durchbohren.
transform [træns'fɔ:m], *v.a.* verändern, umwandeln. — *v.r.* sich verwandeln.
transgress [træns'gres], *v.a.* überschreiten (*trespass on*). — *v.n.* sich vergehen.
transient ['trænsiənt], *adj.* vergänglich.
transit ['trænsit, 'trænzit], *s.* der Durchgang; die Durchfahrt, Durchfuhr (*travel*); (*Comm.*) der Transit. — *v.n.* (*Am.*) durchfahren (*of goods*).
transitive ['trænsitiv], *adj.* (*Gram.*) transitiv.
transitory ['trænsitəri], *adj.* vergänglich, flüchtig.
translate [træns'leit], *v.a.* übersetzen; versetzen (*office*).
translation [træns'leiʃən], *s.* die Übersetzung, die Übertragung.
translucent [trænz'lju:sənt], *adj.* durchscheinend.
transmission [trænz'miʃən], *s.* die Übersendung, Übermittlung; (*Rad.*) die Sendung; (*Motor.*) die Transmission.
transmit [trænz'mit], *v.a.* übersenden, übermitteln; (*Rad., T.V.*) übertragen, senden.
transmutation [trænzmju'teiʃən], *s.* die Verwandlung.
transparent [træns'pɛərənt], *adj.* durchsichtig.
transpire [træns'paiə, trænz-], *v.n.* bekannt werden.
transplant [træns'plɑ:nt, trænz-], *v.a.* verpflanzen; (*Med.*) übertragen.
transport [træns'pɔ:t], *v.a.* transportieren; (*fig.*) entzücken. — ['trænspɔ:t], *s.* der Transport; die Versendung (*sending*); (*fig.*) die Entzückung.
transpose [træns'pouz], *v.a.* (*Mus.*) transponieren.
transverse [trænz'və:s], *adj.* quer; schräg (*oblique*).
trap [træp], *v.a.* in eine Falle führen; ertappen (*detect*). — *s.* die Falle; der Einspänner (*gig*).
trapeze [trə'pi:z], *s.* das Trapez.
trapper ['træpə], *s.* der Fallensteller.
trappings ['træpiŋz], *s. pl.* der Schmuck; (*fig.*) die Äußerlichkeiten, *f. pl.*
trash [træʃ], *s.* (*Lit.*) der Schund; der Kitsch; das wertlose Zeug.
trashy ['træʃi], *adj.* wertlos, kitschig.
travail ['træveil], *s.* die Wehen, Sorgen, die Mühe.
travel [trævl], *v.n.* reisen. — *v.a.* bereisen. — *s.* das Reisen; — *agency*, das Reisebüro.
traveller ['trævələ], *s.* der Reisende; (*Comm.*) der Handelsreisende, Vertreter.
traverse ['trævə:s], *adj.* quer. — *s.* die Traverse, der Querbalken. — [trə'və:s], *v.a.* durchqueren; (*fig.*) durchwandern.
trawl [trɔ:l], *v.n.* (mit Schleppnetz) fischen.
trawler ['trɔ:lə], *s.* das Fischerboot, der Fischdampfer.
tray [trei], *s.* das Tablett.
treacherous ['tretʃərəs], *adj.* verräterisch; (*fig.*) gefährlich.
treachery ['tretʃəri], *s.* der Verrat.
treacle [tri:kl], *s.* der Sirup.
tread [tred], *v.a., v.n. irr.* (be)treten, auftreten. — *s.* der Tritt, Schritt; die Lauffläche (*of a tyre*).
treason [tri:zn], *s.* der Verrat.
treasure ['treʒə], *s.* der Schatz.
treasurer ['treʒərə], *s.* der Schatzmeister.
treasury ['treʒəri], *s.* die Schatzkammer; (*U.K.*) *the Treasury*, das Schatzamt, Finanzministerium.
treat [tri:t], *v.a.* behandeln; bewirten (*as host*). — *v.n.* (*Pol.*) unterhandeln (*negotiate*). — *s.* der Genuß (*pleasure*).
treatise ['tri:tis], *s.* die Abhandlung.
treatment ['tri:tmənt], *s.* die Behandlung.
treaty ['tri:ti], *s.* der Vertrag.
treble [trebl], *s.* (*Mus.*) die Sopranstimme, Knabenstimme, der Diskant; (*Maths.*) das Dreifache. — *v.a.* verdreifachen.

tree [tri:], *s.* (*Bot.*) der Baum.
trefoil ['tri:fɔil], *s.* (*Bot.*) der dreiblätt(e)rige Klee; das Dreiblatt.
trellis ['trelis], *s.* das Gitter.
tremble [trembl], *v.n.* zittern. — *s.* das Zittern.
tremendous [tri'mendəs], *adj.* ungeheuer (groß); schrecklich.
tremor ['tremə], *s.* das Zittern; (*Geol.*) das Beben; (*Med.*) das Zucken.
trench [trentʃ], *s.* der Graben.
trenchant ['trentʃənt], *adj.* einschneidend, scharf.
trend [trend], *s.* die Tendenz; (*Comm.*) der Trend.
trepidation [trepi'deiʃən], *s.* die Angst, das Zittern.
trespass ['trespəs], *v.n.* sich vergehen, übertreten (*law*); — *on*, unbefugt betreten. — *s.* die Übertretung.
tress [tres], *s.* die Flechte, Haarlocke.
trestle [tresl], *s.* das Gestell; — *table*, der Klapptisch.
trial ['traiəl], *s.* die Probe, der Versuch; (*Law*) die Verhandlung, der Prozeß, das Verhör.
triangle ['traiæŋgl], *s.* das Dreieck; (*Mus.*) der Triangel.
tribe [traib], *s.* der Stamm.
tribulation [tribju'leiʃən], *s.* die Trübsal, Drangsal.
tribunal [trai'bju:nəl], *s.* das Tribunal, der Gerichtshof.
tributary ['tribjutəri], *adj.* Neben-. — *s.* der Nebenfluß.
tribute ['tribju:t], *s.* der Tribut.
trice [trais], *s.* *in a* —, im Nu.
trick [trik], *s.* der Kniff, Trick. — *v.a.* betrügen.
trickery ['trikəri], *s.* der Betrug.
trickle [trikl], *v.n.* tröpfeln, sickern. — *s.* das Tröpfein.
tricky ['triki], *adj.* verwickelt; (*fig.*) bedenklich, heikel.
tricycle ['traisikl], *s.* das Dreirad.
tried [traid], *adj.* erprobt, bewährt.
triennial [trai'eniəl], *adj.* dreijährlich.
trifle [traifl], *v.n.* scherzen, spielen. — *s.* die Kleinigkeit; (*Cul.*) der süße Auflauf.
trigger ['trigə], *s.* der Drücker. — *v.a.* — *off*, auslösen.
trilateral [trai'lætərəl], *adj.* dreiseitig.
trill [tril], *s.* (*Mus.*) der Triller. — *v.a.*, *v.n.* trillern.
trim [trim], *adj.* niedlich, schmuck; nett (*dress*). — *v.a.* beschneiden; (*Naut.*) — *sails*, einziehen. — *s.* die Ausrüstung; (*Naut.*) das Gleichgewicht.
trimmer ['trimə], *s.* die Putzmacherin; (*fig.*) der Opportunist.
trimmings ['triminz], *s. pl.* (*fig.*) der Kleinkram; (*Tail.*) der Besatz.
Trinity ['triniti], *s.* (*Theol.*) die Dreifaltigkeit, Dreieinigkeit.
trinket ['triŋkit], *s.* das Geschmeide; (*pl.*) Schmucksachen, *f. pl.*
trip [trip], *s.* der Ausflug, die Reise. — *v.a.* — *up*, ein Bein stellen (*Dat.*). — *v.n.* stolpern.
tripe [traip], *s.* die Kaldaunen, *f. pl.*; (*fig.*) der Unsinn.
triple [tripl], *adj.* dreifach.
triplet ['triplit], *s.* der Drilling; (*Mus.*) die Triole; (*Poet.*) der Dreireim.
tripod ['traipɔd], *s.* der Dreifuß.
tripos ['traipɔs], *s.* das Schlußexamen (*Cambridge Univ.*).
trite [trait], *adj.* abgedroschen.
triumph ['traiʌmf], *s.* der Triumph. — *v.n.* triumphieren.
triumphant [trai'ʌmfənt], *adj.* triumphierend.
trivial ['triviəl], *adj.* trivial, platt, alltäglich.
troll (1) [troul], *v.n.* trällern (*hum*); fischen. — *s.* der Rundgesang (*song*).
troll (2) [troul], *s.* der Kobold (*gnome*).
trolley ['trɔli], *s.* der Teewagen (*furniture*); (*Tech.*) die Dräsine, der Karren.
trollop ['trɔləp], *s.* die Schlampe.
trombone [trɔm'boun], *s.* (*Mus.*) die Posaune.
troop [tru:p], *s.* der Haufe; (*Mil.*) die Truppe, der Trupp. — *v.n.* sich sammeln. — *v.a.* *Trooping the Colour*, die Fahnenparade.
trophy ['troufi], *s.* die Trophäe, das Siegeszeichen.
tropic ['trɔpik], *s.* (*Geog.*) der Wendekreis; (*pl.*) die Tropen, *f. pl.*
tropical ['trɔpikəl], *adj.* tropisch.
trot [trɔt], *v.n.* traben. — *s.* der Trab, Trott.
troth [trouθ], *s.* (*obs.*) die Treue; *pledge o.'s* —, Treue geloben.
trouble [trʌbl], *s.* die Mühe, Sorge (*worry*); der Kummer (*sadness*); die Störung (*disturbance*). — *v.a.* bemühen (*ask favour of*); bekümmern (*worry*); stören (*disturb*).
troublesome ['trʌblsəm], *adj.* ärgerlich, schwierig, unangenehm.
trough [trɔf], *s.* der Trog; (*Met.*) das Tief.
trounce [trauns], *v.a.* verprügeln.
trouncing ['traunsiŋ], *s.* die Tracht Prügel.
trousers ['trauzəz], *s. pl.* die Hosen, *f. pl.*
trout [traut], *s.* (*Zool.*) die Forelle.
trowel ['trauəl], *s.* die Kelle.
troy(weight) ['trɔi(weit)], *s.* das Troygewicht.
truant ['tru:ənt], *s.* (*Sch.*) der Schulschwänzer; *play* —, die Schule schwänzen.
truce [tru:s], *s.* der Waffenstillstand.
truck (1) [trʌk], *s.* (*Rail.*) der Güterwagen; (*Am.*) *see* **lorry**.
truck (2) [trʌk], *s.* *have no* — *with*, nichts zu tun haben mit.
truculent ['trʌkjulənt], *adj.* streitsüchtig.
trudge [trʌdʒ], *v.n.* sich schleppen.
true [tru:], *adj.* wahr; treu (*faithful*); echt (*genuine*); richtig (*correct*).

truffle [trʌfl], *s.* die Trüffel.
truism ['tru:izm], *s.* der Gemeinplatz, die Binsenwahrheit.
truly ['tru:li], *adv. yours* —, Ihr ergebener.
trump [trʌmp], *s.* der Trumpf; — *card*, die Trumpfkarte. — *v.a.* — *up*, erfinden, erdichten.
trumpery ['trʌmpəri], *s.* der Plunder, Schund. — *adj.* wertlos, belanglos.
trumpet ['trʌmpit], *s.* (*Mus.*) die Trompete. — *v.a.* stolz austrompeten, ausposaunen. — *v.n.* trompeten.
truncate [trʌŋ'keit], *v.a.* verstümmeln, stutzen.
truncheon ['trʌnʃən], *s.* der Knüppel. — *v.a.* durchprügeln.
trundle [trʌndl], *v.n.* trudeln; sich wälzen. — *v.a.* — *a hoop*, Reifen schlagen.
trunk [trʌŋk], *s.* der Stamm (*tree*); der Rüssel (*of elephant*); der (große) Koffer (*chest*); — *call*, das Ferngespräch.
truss [trʌs], *s.* das Band, Bruchband. — *v.a.* zäumen, stützen; aufschürzen.
trust [trʌst], *v.a., v.n.* trauen (*Dat.*), vertrauen (*Dat.*); anvertrauen (*Dat., Acc.*). — *s.* das Vertrauen; *in* —, zu treuen Händen, als Treuhänder; (*Comm.*) der Trust.
trustworthy ['trʌstwə:ði], *adj.* zuverläßig.
truth [tru:θ], *s.* die Wahrheit.
truthful ['tru:θful], *adj.* wahrhaftig.
try [trai], *v.a. irr.* versuchen (*s. th.*); (*Law*) verhören; — *on* (*clothes*), anprobieren; — *out*, ausprobieren. — *v.n.* versuchen, sich bemühen. — *s.* der Versuch (*attempt*); (*Rugby*) der Try.
Tsar [zɑ:], *s.* der Zar.
tub [tʌb], *s.* das Faß; die Wanne (*bath*); (*Naut.*) das Übungsboot.
tube [tju:b], *s.* die Tube (*paste etc.*); die Röhre (*pipe, also Elec.*); der Schlauch (*tyre*); das Rohr (*tubing*); (*Transport*) die Londoner Untergrundbahn.
tuberous ['tju:bərəs], *adj.* knollenartig, knollig.
tubular ['tju:bjulə], *adj.* röhrenförmig.
tuck [tʌk], *s.* (*Tail.*) die Falte; (*Sch. sl.*) der Leckerbissen. — *v.a.* — *up*, zudecken; — *in*, einschlagen. — *v.n.* (*sl.*) — *in*, tüchtig zugreifen.
tucker ['tʌkə], *s.* (*sl.*) das Essen.
tuckshop ['tʌkʃɔp], *s.* der Schulladen.
Tuesday ['tju:zdi]. der Dienstag.
tuft [tʌft], *s.* der Büschel.
tug [tʌg], *v.a.* ziehen, zerren. — *s.* (*Naut.*) der Schlepper; — *of war*, das Tauziehen.
tuition [tju:'iʃən], *s.* der Unterricht, Privatunterricht.
tulip ['tju:lip], *s.* (*Bot.*) die Tulpe.
tumble [tʌmbl], *v.n.* purzeln. — *s.* der Sturz, Fall.
tumbril ['tʌmbril], *s.* der Karren.
tumid ['tju:mid], *adj.* geschwollen.
tumour ['tju:mə], *s.* (*Med.*) die Geschwulst, der Tumor.
tumult ['tju:mʌlt], *s.* der Tumult, Auflauf; der Lärm (*noise*).
tun [tʌn], *s.* die Tonne, das Faß.
tune [tju:n], *s.* die Melodie. — *v.a.* stimmen; (*Rad.*) — *in* (*to*), einstellen(auf).
tuneful ['tju:nful], *adj.* melodisch.
tuner ['tju:nə], *s.* der (Klavier)stimmer.
tunic ['tju:nik], *s.* der Kittel.
tuning ['tju:niŋ], *s.* das Stimmen; die Abstimmung (*also Rad.*); — *fork*, die Stimmgabel.
tunnel [tʌnl], *s.* der Tunnel. — *v.n.* graben, einen Tunnel bauen.
turbid ['tə:bid], *adj.* trüb, dick.
turbot ['tə:bət], *s.* (*Zool.*) der Steinbutt.
turbulence ['tə:bjuləns], *s.* der Sturm, das Ungestüm; (*Aviat.*) die Turbulenz.
tureen [tjuə'ri:n], *s.* die Suppenterrine, Suppenschüssel.
turf [tə:f], *s.* der Rasen; (*Sport*) die Rennbahn, der Turf. — *v.a.* mit Rasen belegen; (*sl.*) — *out*, hinausschmeißen.
turgid ['tə:dʒid], *adj.* schwülstig (*style*).
Turk [tə:k], *s.* der Türke.
turkey ['tə:ki], *s.* (*Orn.*) der Truthahn.
Turkish ['tə:kiʃ], *adj.* türkisch.
turmoil ['tə:mɔil], *s.* die Unruhe, der Aufruhr.
turn [tə:n], *v.a.* wenden, drehen, kehren (*to*); — *down*, ablehnen; (*coll.*) — *in*, abgeben (*hand over*); — *on*, andrehen (*tap etc.*); — *off*, ausdrehen; — *out*, produzieren. — *v.n.* sich drehen, sich ändern; werden; — *on s.o.*, jemanden verraten; (*coll.*) — *out*, ausrücken; (*coll.*) — *up*, auftauchen. — *s.* die Drehung, Windung; der Hang; die Reihe; die Nummer (*act*); *it is my* —, ich bin an der Reihe.
turncoat ['tə:nkout], *s.* der Überläufer.
turner ['tə:nə], *s.* der Drechsler.
turnip ['tə:nip], *s.* (*Bot.*) die Rübe.
turnpike ['tə:npaik], *s.* der Schlagbaum.
turnstile ['tə:nstail], *s.* das Drehkreuz.
turntable ['tə:nteibl], *s.* die Drehscheibe.
turpentine ['tə:pəntain], *s.* der *or* das Terpentin.
turquoise ['tə:kwɔiz *or* 'tə:kɔiz], *s.* der Türkis.
turret ['tʌrit], *s.* (*Archit.*) der Turm, das Türmchen.
turtle [tə:tl], *s.* (*Zool.*) die Schildkröte; (*Orn.*) — *-dove*, die Turteltaube.
tusk [tʌsk], *s.* (*Zool.*) der Stoßzahn.
tussle [tʌsl], *s.* der Streit, die Rauferei.
tutelage ['tju:tilidʒ], *s.* die Vormundschaft.
tutor ['tju:tə], *s.* der Privatlehrer; der Tutor, Studienleiter. — *v.a.* unterrichten.
twaddle [twɔdl], *s.* das Geschwätz. — *v.n.* schwätzen.
twang [twæŋ], *s.* der scharfe Ton. — *v.n.* scharf klingen.
tweed [twi:d], *s.* (*Text.*) der Tweed.
twelfth [twelfθ], *num.adj.* zwölft; *Twelfth Night*, das Fest der Heiligen Drei Könige (*6th January*).

twelve [twelv], *num. adj.* zwölf.
twenty ['twenti], *num. adj.* zwanzig.
twice [twais], *num. adv.* zweimal, doppelt.
twig [twig], *s.* (*Bot.*) der Zweig, die Rute.
twilight ['twailait], *s.* das Zwielicht, die Dämmerung.
twill [twil], *s.* (*Text.*) der Köper. — *v.a.* köpern.
twin [twin], *s.* der Zwilling.
twine [twain], *s.* der Bindfaden, die Schnur. — *v.a.* drehen, zwirnen. — *v.n.* sich verflechten; sich winden (*plant*).
twinge [twindʒ], *s.* der Zwick, Stich.
twinkle [twiŋkl], *v.n.* blinzeln, blinken. — *s.* das Zwinkern, der Blick.
twirl [twə:l], *s.* der Wirbel. — *v.a.* schnell drehen, wirbeln.
twist [twist], *v.a.* flechten, drehen; verdrehen. — *s.* die Drehung, Krümmung; das Geflecht; (*fig.*) die Wendung (*sudden change*).
twitch [twitʃ], *v.a.* zupfen, zucken. — — *v.n.* zucken. — *s.* das Zucken, der Krampf.
twitter ['twitə], *v.n.* zwitschern; (*fig.*) zittern. — *s.* das Gezwitscher; (*fig.*) die Angst.
two [tu:], *num. adj.* zwei; — *-faced*, falsch.
twofold ['tu:fould], *adj.* zweifach.
tympanum ['timpənəm], *s.* (*Med.*) das Trommelfell.
type [taip], *s.* (*Typ.*) die Type; (*Psych.*) der Typ, Typus. — *v.a.*, *v.n.* tippen; mit der Maschine schreiben.
typewriter ['taipraitə], *s.* die Schreibmaschine.
typhoid ['taifɔid], *s.* (*Med.*) der (Unterleibs)typhus. — *adj.* typhusartig.
typist ['taipist], *s.* der (die) Maschinenschreiber(in).
typhoon [tai'fu:n], *s.* der Taifun.
typical ['tipikəl], *adj.* typisch, charakteristisch.
typography [tai'pɔgrəfi], *s.* die Typographie, Buchdruckerkunst.
tyrannical [ti'rænikəl], *adj.* tyrannisch.
tyranny ['tirəni], *s.* die Tyrannei.
tyrant ['taiərənt], *s.* der Tyrann.
tyre, (*Am.*) **tire** [taiə], *s.* der Reifen.
tyro ['taiərou], *s.* der Anfänger.
Tyrolese [tiro'li:z], *adj.* tirolisch, Tiroler-. — *s.* der Tiroler.

U

U [ju:]. das U.
ubiquitous [ju'bikwitəs], *adj.* überall da, überall zu finden.
udder ['ʌdə], *s.* (*Zool.*) das Euter.
ugly ['ʌgli], *adj.* häßlich.
Ukrainian [ju:'kreiniən], *adj.* ukrainisch. — *s.* der Ukrainer.
ulcer ['ʌlsə], *s.* (*Med.*) das Geschwür.
ulcerate ['ʌlsəreit], *v.n.* (*Med.*) schwären.
ulcerous ['ʌlsərəs], *adj.* (*Med.*) geschwürig.
ulterior [ʌl'tiəriə], *adj.* weiter, ferner, weiterliegend.
ultimate ['ʌltimit], *adj.* letzt, endlich, äußerst.
ultimatum [ʌlti'meitəm], *s.* das Ultimatum.
umbrage ['ʌmbridʒ], *s.* der Schatten; *take* —, Anstoß nehmen (an, *Dat.*).
umbrella [ʌm'brelə], *s.* der Schirm, Regenschirm.
umpire ['ʌmpaiə], *s.* (*Sport*) der Schiedsrichter.
umpteen ['ʌmpti:n], *adj.* zahlreiche, verschiedene.
un- [ʌn], *negating pref.* un-, nicht-; with *verbs*, auf-, ent-, los-, ver-; *where a word is not given, see the simple form.*
unable [ʌn'eibl], *adj.* unfähig; *be* —, nicht können.
unaccustomed [ʌnə'kʌstəmd], *adj.* ungewohnt.
unaided [ʌn'eidid], *adj.* allein, ohne Hilfe.
unaware [ʌnə'wɛə], *adj.* unbewußt.
uncertain [ʌn'sə:tin], *adj.* unsicher.
uncle [ʌŋkl], *s.* der Onkel.
unconscious [ʌn'kɔnʃəs], *adj.* bewußtlos; unbewusst.
uncouth [ʌn'ku:θ], *adj.* ungehobelt, roh.
unction ['ʌnkʃən], *s.* die Salbung (*anointing*); die Salbe; *Extreme Unction*, (*Eccl.*) die Letzte Ölung.
unctuous ['ʌŋktjuəs], *adj.* salbungsvoll.
under ['ʌndə], *prep.* unter. — *adv.* darunter, unten (*underneath*); *pref.* (*compounds*) unter-.
undercarriage ['ʌndəkæridʒ], *s.* (*Aviat.*) das Fahrwerk.
underfed [ʌndə'fed], *adj.* unterernährt.
undergo [ʌndə'gou], *v.a. irr.* durchmachen, erdulden.
undergraduate [ʌndə'grædjuit], *s.* (*Univ.*) der Student.
underground ['ʌndəgraund], *adj.* unterirdisch; — *railway* die Untergrundbahn. — [ʌndə'graund], *adv.* unterirdisch.
underhand [ʌndə'hænd], *adj.* heimlich, hinterlistig.
underline [ʌndə'lain], *v.a.* unterstreichen.
undermine [ʌndə'main], *v.a.* untergraben.
underneath [ʌndə'ni:θ], *adv.* unten, darunter. — ['ʌndəni:θ], *prep.* unter.
undersigned ['ʌndəsaind], *adj.* unterzeichnet. —*s.* der Unterzeichnete.
understand [ʌndə'stænd], *v.a. irr.* verstehen, begreifen.
understatement ['ʌndəsteitmənt], *s.* die zu bescheidene Festellung, Unterbewertung.

undertaker ['ʌndəteikə], *s.* der Leichenbestatter.
undertaking [ʌndə'teikiŋ], *s.* das Unternehmen (*business*); das Versprechen (*promise*).
undertone ['ʌndətoun], *s.* der Unterton.
underwrite [ʌndə'rait], *v.a. irr.* (*Comm.*) versichern.
underwriter ['ʌndəraitə], *s.* (*Comm.*) der Assekurant, Versicherer, Mitversicherer.
undeserved [ʌndi'zə:vd], *adj.* unverdient.
undeserving [ʌndi'zə:viŋ], *adj.* unwürdig.
undignified [ʌn'dignifaid], *adj.* würdelos.
undiscerning [ʌndi'zə:niŋ], *adj.* geschmacklos.
undiscriminating [ʌndis'krimineitiŋ], *adj.* unterschiedslos, unkritisch.
undisputed [ʌndis'pju:tid], *adj.* unbestritten.
undo [ʌn'du:], *v.a. irr.* zerstören (*destroy*); öffnen (*open*).
undoubted [ʌn'dautid], *adj.* zweifellos.
undress [ʌn'dres], *v.a.*, *v.n.* — (sich)ausziehen. — ['ʌndres], *s.* das Hauskleid.
undue [ʌn'dju:], *adj.* unangemessen.
undulate ['ʌndjuleit], *v.n.* wallen, Wellen schlagen.
unduly [ʌn'dju:li], *adv.* ungebührlich, übermäßig.
unearth [ʌn'ə:θ], *v.a.* ausgraben.
unearthly [ʌn'ə:θli], *adj.* überirdisch.
uneasy [ʌn'i:zi], *adj.* unruhig, unbehaglich.
unemployed [ʌnim'plɔid], *adj.* arbeitslos.
unemployment [ʌnim'plɔimənt], *s.* die Arbeitslosigkeit.
unending [ʌn'endiŋ], *adj.* endlos.
uneven [ʌn'i:vən], *adj.* uneben; ungerade.
unexceptionable [ʌnik'sepʃənəbl], *adj.* tadellos.
unexpired [ʌniks'paiəd], *adj.* noch nicht abgelaufen, noch gültig.
unfair [ʌn'fɛə], *adj.* unfair; unehrlich.
unfeeling [ʌn'fi:liŋ], *adj.* gefühllos.
unfit [ʌn'fit], *adj.* (*Mil.*, *Med.*) untauglich, schwach; (*food etc.*) ungenießbar.
unfold [ʌn'fould], *v.a.* entfalten.
unforeseen [ʌnfɔ:'si:n], *adj.* unerwartet.
unfounded [ʌn'faundid], *adj.* grundlos.
unfurnished [ʌn'fə:niʃd], *adj.* unmöbliert.
ungrudging [ʌn'grʌdʒiŋ], *adj.* bereitwillig.
unhappy [ʌn'hæpi], *adj.* unglücklich.
unhinge [ʌn'hindʒ], *v.a.* aus den Angeln heben.
unicorn ['ju:nikɔ:n], *s.* (*Myth.*) das Einhorn.
uniform ['ju:nifɔ:m], *s.* die Uniform. — *adj.* gleichförmig, einförmig.
union ['ju:niən], *s.* die Vereinigung; *trade* —, die Gewerkschaft; *Union Jack*, die britische Nationalflagge.
unique [ju'ni:k], *adj.* einzigartig.
unison ['ju:nisən], *s.* (*Mus.*) der Einklang, die Harmonie.
unit ['ju:nit], *s.* die Einheit (*measure etc.*).
unite [ju'nait], *v.a.* vereinen. — *v.n.* sich vereinen, verbünden.
unity ['ju:niti], *s.* die Einigkeit.
universal [ju:ni'və:səl], *adj.* allgemein.
universe ['ju:nivə:s], *s.* das Weltall.
university [ju:ni'və:siti], *s.* die Universität, Hochschule; — *degree*, der akademische Grad.
unkempt [ʌn'kempt], *adj.* ungekämmt, ungepflegt.
unleavened [ʌn'levənd], *adj.* ungesäuert.
unless [ʌn'les], *conj.* außer, wenn nicht, es sei denn.
unlettered [ʌn'letəd], *adj.* ungebildet.
unlicensed [ʌn'laisənsd], *adj.* nicht (für Alkoholverkauf) lizenziert.
unlike [ʌn'laik], *adj.* ungleich. — ['ʌnlaik], *prep.* anders als, verschieden von.
unlikely [ʌn'laikli], *adj.*, *adv.* unwahrscheinlich.
unlock [ʌn'lɔk], *v.a.* aufschließen.
unmask [ʌn'mɑ:sk], *v.a.* entlarven.
unpack [ʌn'pæk], *v.a.*, *v.n.* auspacken.
unpleasant [ʌn'pleznt], *adj.* unangenehm.
unreliable [ʌnri'laiəbl], *adj.* unzuverlässig.
unremitting [ʌnri'mitiŋ], *adj.* unablässig.
unrepentant [ʌnri'pentənt], *adj.* reuelos.
unrest [ʌn'rest], *s.* die Unruhe.
unsafe [ʌn'seif], *adj.* unsicher.
unscathed [ʌn'skeiðd], *adj.* unversehrt.
unscrew [ʌn'skru:], *v.a.* abschrauben.
unscrupulous [ʌn'skru:pjuləs], *adj.* skrupellos, gewissenlos.
unseat [ʌn'si:t], *v.a.* aus dem Sattel heben; absetzen.
unselfish [ʌn'selfiʃ], *adj.* selbstlos.
unsettle [ʌn'setl], *v.a.* verwirren; (*fig.*) aus dem Konzept bringen.
unsew [ʌn'sou], *v.a.* auftrennen.
unshrinking [ʌn'ʃriŋkiŋ], *adj.* unverzagt.
unsophisticated [ʌnsə'fistikeitid], *adj.* naiv, natürlich.
unsparing [ʌn'spɛəriŋ], *adj.* schonungslos.
unstable [ʌn'steibl], *adj.* unsicher; labil.
unstitch [ʌn'stitʃ], *v.a.* auftrennen.
unstop [ʌn'stɔp], *v.a.* aufstöpseln, öffnen (*a bottle*).
unstudied [ʌn'stʌdid], *adj.* ungekünstelt.
unsuccessful [ʌnsək'sesful], *adj.* erfolglos.
unsuspecting [ʌnsə'spektiŋ], *adj.* arglos.
untie [ʌn'tai], *v.a.* losbinden.
until [ʌn'til], *prep.*, *conj.* bis.

untimely [ʌn'taimli], *adj.* vorzeitig, unzeitig.
untiring [ʌn'taiəriŋ], *adj.* unermüdlich.
unto ['ʌntu], *prep.* (*Poet.*) zu.
untold [ʌn'tould], *adj.* ungezählt, unermeßlich.
untoward [ʌn'tɔ:d *or* ʌn'touəd], *adj.* unangenehm; widerspenstig (*recalcitrant*).
untrustworthy [ʌn'trʌstwə:ði], *adj.* unzuverlässig.
unveil [ʌn'veil], *v.a.* enthüllen.
unwieldy [ʌn'wi:ldi], *adj.* sperrig, schwerfällig.
unwind [ʌn'waind], *v.a.* abwickeln.
unwitting [ʌn'witiŋ], *adj.* unwissentlich, unbewusst.
unwonted [ʌn'wountid], *adj.* ungewohnt.
unwrap [ʌn'ræp], *v.a.* auspacken, auswickeln.
unyielding [ʌn'ji:ldiŋ], *adj.* unnachgiebig; hartnäckig.
unyoke [ʌn'jouk], *v.a.* ausspannen.
up [ʌp], *adv.* auf, aufwärts (*upward*); aufgestanden (*out of bed*); — (*there*), oben; *what's up?* was ist los? — *to*, bis zu; *be* — *to s.th.*, auf etwas aus sein, etwas im Schilde führen; *it's* — *to you*, es liegt an dir. — *prep.* auf, hinauf. — *s. ups and downs*, das wechselnde Schicksal, Auf und Ab.
upbraid [ʌp'breid], *v.a.* tadeln.
upheaval [ʌp'hi:vl], *s.* das Chaos, Durcheinander, die Umwälzung.
uphill [ʌp'hil], *adv.* bergauf(wärts). — ['ʌphil], *adj.* (an)steigend; (*fig.*) mühsam.
uphold [ʌp'hould], *v.a.* aufrechterhalten.
upholster [ʌp'houlstə], *v.a.* polstern.
upholstery [ʌp'houlstəri], *s.* die Polsterung.
upon [ʌ'pɔn] *see* **on.**
upper ['ʌpə], *adj.* ober, höher; — *hand*, die Oberhand.
uppish ['ʌpiʃ], *adj.* anmaßend.
upright ['ʌprait], *adj.* aufrecht, gerade; (*fig.*) aufrichtig, rechtschaffen.
uproar ['ʌprɔ:], *s.* der Lärm, Aufruhr.
uproot [ʌp'ru:t], *v.a.* entwurzeln.
upset [ʌp'set], *v.a.* umwerfen; (*fig.*) aus der Fassung bringen. — ['ʌpset], *s.* das Umwerfen; (*fig.*) die Bestürzung.
upshot ['ʌpʃɔt], *s.* der Ausgang, das Ergebnis.
upside ['ʌpsaid], *s.* die Oberseite; — *down*, auf den Kopf gestellt.
upstairs [ʌp'stɛəz], *adv.* oben, nach oben.
upstart ['ʌpstɑ:t], *s.* der Parvenü, Emporkömmling.
upward ['ʌpwəd], *adj.* steigend, aufwärtsgehend. — *adv.* (*also* **upwards**) aufwärts; — *of*, mehr als.
urban ['ə:bən], *adj.* städtisch.
urbane [ə:'bein], *adj.* zivilisiert.
urbanity [ə:'bæniti], *s.* die Bildung, der Schliff.
urchin ['ə:tʃin], *s.* der Schelm; (*Zool.*) *sea* —, der Seeigel.
urge [ə:dʒ], *v.a.* drängen. — *s.* der Drang.
urgent ['ə:dʒənt], *adj.* dringend, drängend, dringlich.
urine ['juərin], *s.* der Urin.
urn [ə:n], *s.* die Urne.
Uruguayan [ju:ru'gwaiən], *adj.* uruguayisch. — *s.* der Uruguayer.
us [ʌs], *pers. pron.* uns.
usage ['ju:sidʒ], *s.* der (Sprach)gebrauch; die Sitte.
use [ju:z], *v.a.* gebrauchen, benutzen. — [ju:s], *s.* der Gebrauch, die Benutzung; der Nutzen (*usefulness*).
usher ['ʌʃə], *s.* der Türhüter, Platzanweiser. — *v.a.* — *in*, anmelden, einführen.
usherette [ʌʃə'ret], *s.* die Platzanweiserin, Programmverkäuferin.
usual ['ju:ʒuəl], *adj.* gewöhnlich, üblich.
usurer ['ju:ʒərə *or* 'ju:zjuərə], *s.* der Wucherer.
usurp [ju'zə:p], *v.a.* an sich reißen, usurpieren.
usury ['ju:ʒjuəri], *s.* der Wucher.
utensil [ju:'tensil], *s.* das Gerät, Werkzeug.
utility [ju:'tiliti], *s.* die Nützlichkeit (*usefulness*); der Nutzen; *public* —, (die) öffentliche Einrichtung.
utilize ['ju:tilaiz], *v.a.* nutzbar machen, ausbeuten, ausnützen.
utmost ['ʌtmoust], *adj.* äußerst, weitest, höchst. — *s.* das Höchste, Äußerste.
utter ['ʌtə], *adj.* äußerst, gänzlich. — *v.a.* äußern, aussprechen.
utterly ['ʌtəli], *adv.* äußerst, völlig.
uvula ['ju:vjulə], *s.* (*Anat.*) das Zäpfchen.

V

V [vi:]. das V.
vacancy ['veikənsi], *s.* die freie Stelle, die Vakanz.
vacant ['veikənt], *adj.* frei; leer.
vacate [və'keit], *v.a.* frei machen.
vacation [və'keiʃən], *s.* die Niederlegung (*of a post*); die Ferien, *pl.* (*school*); der Urlaub (*holiday*).
vaccinate ['væksineit], *v.a.* (*Med.*) impfen.
vaccine ['væksi:n], *s.* (*Med.*) der Impfstoff.
vacillate ['væsileit], *v.n.* schwanken.
vacuity [væ'kju:iti], *s.* die Leere.
vacuous ['vækjuəs], *adj.* leer.
vacuum ['vækjuəm], *s.* das Vakuum; — *cleaner*, der Staubsauger.
vagabond ['vægəbɔnd], *s.* der Landstreicher.
vagary [və'gɛəri], *s.* die Laune, Grille.

vagrant ['veigrənt], *adj.* herumstreichend. — *s.* der Landstreicher.
vague [veig], *adj.* vage, unbestimmt, unklar.
vain [vein], *adj.* nichtig, vergeblich, eitel; *in* —, vergebens, umsonst.
vale [veil], *s.* (*Poet.*) das Tal.
valerian [və'liəriən], *s.* (*Bot.*) der Baldrian.
valet ['vælei, 'vælit], *s.* der Diener.
valiant ['væljənt], *adj.* mutig, tapfer.
valid ['vælid], *adj.* gültig, stichhaltig.
valley ['væli], *s.* das Tal.
valuable ['væljuəbl], *adj.* wertvoll, kostbar.
valuation [vælju'eiʃən], *s.* die Schätzung.
value ['vælju:], *s.* der Wert. — *v.a.* wertschätzen, schätzen.
valve [vælv], *s.* (*Mech.*) das Ventil; (*Rad.*) die Röhre.
vamp (I) [væmp], *s.* das Oberleder.
vamp (2) [væmp], *s.* (*Am. coll.*) der Vamp.
vampire ['væmpaiə], *s.* der Vampir.
van [væn], *s.* der Lieferwagen.
vane [vein], *s.* die Wetterfahne.
vanguard ['væŋgɑ:d], *s.* die Vorhut, der Vortrupp.
vanilla [və'nilə], *s.* die Vanille.
vanish ['væniʃ], *v.n.* verschwinden.
vanity ['væniti], *s.* die Nichtigkeit; die Eitelkeit (*conceit*).
vanquish ['væŋkwiʃ], *v.a.* besiegen.
vantage ['vɑ:ntidʒ], *s.* der Vorteil; — *point*, die günstige Position.
vapid ['væpid], *adj.* leer, schal.
vapour ['veipə], *s.* der Dunst; (*Chem.*) der Dampf.
variable ['vɛəriəbl], *adj.* variabel, veränderlich.
variance ['vɛəriəns], *s.* die Uneinigkeit.
variation [vɛəri'eiʃən], *s.* die Variation; die Veränderung, Abweichung.
varicose ['værikəs], *adj.* Krampf-, krampfaderig.
variegated ['vɛərigeitid], *adj.* bunt, vielfarbig.
variety [və'raiəti], *s.* die Mannigfaltigkeit; (*Bot.*) die Varietät, Abart; (*Theat.*) das Varieté, das Varietétheater.
various ['vɛəriəs], *adj.* verschieden; mannigfaltig.
varnish ['vɑ:niʃ], *s.* der Firnis, der Lack. — *v.a.* mit Firnis anstreichen, lackieren.
vary ['vɛəri], *v.a.* abändern. — *v.n.* sich ändern, variieren.
vase [vɑ:z], *s.* die Vase.
vassal [væsl], *s.* der Vasall, Lehnsmann.
vast [vɑ:st], *adj.* ungeheuer, groß.
vat [væt], *s.* die Kufe, das große Faß.
vault [vɔ:lt], *s.* das Gewölbe; die Gruft (*grave*); (*Sport*) der Sprung, *pole* —, der Stabhochsprung. — *v.n.* springen.
vaunt [vɔ:nt], *v.a.* rühmen. — *v.n.* prahlen, sich rühmen. — *s.* die Prahlerei.
veal [vi:l], *s.* das Kalbfleisch.
veer [viə], *v.n.* sich drehen.
vegetable ['vedʒitəbl], *s.* das Gemüse.
vegetarian [vedʒi'tɛəriən], *adj.* vegetarisch. — *s.* der Vegetarier.
vegetate ['vedʒiteit], *v.n.* vegetieren.
vehemence ['vi:əməns], *s.* die Vehemenz, Heftigkeit.
vehicle ['vi:ikl], *s.* das Fahrzeug, Fuhrwerk; (*Motor.*) der Wagen.
veil [veil], *s.* der Schleier. — *v.a.* verschleiern.
vein [vein], *s.* die Ader.
vellum ['veləm], *s.* das feine Pergamentpapier.
velocity [vi'lɔsiti], *s.* die Geschwindigkeit, Schnelligkeit.
velvet ['velvit], *s.* (*Text.*) der Samt.
venal ['vi:nəl], *adj.* käuflich.
vend [vend], *v.a.* verkaufen; —*ing machine*, der Automat.
veneer [və'niə], *s.* das Furnier. — *v.a.* furnieren.
venerable ['venərəbl], *adj.* ehrwürdig.
venerate ['venəreit], *v.a.* verehren.
venereal [və'niəriəl], *adj.* Geschlechts-.
Venezuelan [veni'zweilən], *adj.* venezolanisch. — *s.* der Venezolaner.
vengeance ['vendʒəns], *s.* die Rache.
venison ['venizn *or* venzn], *s.* das Wildpret.
venom ['venəm], *s.* das Gift.
vent [vent], *v.a.* Luft machen (*Dat.*). — *s.* das Luftloch, die Öffnung.
ventilate ['ventileit], *v.a.* ventilieren, lüften.
ventricle ['ventrikl], *s.* (*Anat.*) die Herzkammer.
ventriloquist [ven'triləkwist], *s.* der Bauchredner.
venture ['ventʃə], *s.* das Wagnis, Unternehmen. — *v.a.* wagen, riskieren. — *v.n.* sich erlauben, (sich) wagen.
venue ['venju:], *s.* der Treffpunkt, Versammlungsort.
veracity [və'ræsiti], *s.* die Glaubwürdigkeit, Wahrhaftigkeit.
verbose [və:'bous], *adj.* wortreich, weitschweifig.
verdant ['və:dənt], *adj.* grünend, grün.
verdict ['və:dikt], *s.* das Urteil, die Entscheidung.
verdigris ['və:digri:s], *s.* der Grünspan.
verdure ['və:djə], *s.* das Grün.
verge [və:dʒ], *s.* der Rand, die Einfassung. — *v.n.* grenzen (*on*, an, *Acc.*).
verify ['verifai], *v.a.* bestätigen; (*Law*) beglaubigen.
verily ['verili], *adv.* (*Bibl.*) wahrlich.
veritable ['veritəbl], *adj.* wahr, echt.
vermicelli [və:mi'seli], *s.* die Nudeln, *f. pl.*
vermilion [və'miljən], *s.* das Zinnober (*paint*).
vermin ['və:min], *s. pl.* das Ungeziefer.
vermouth ['və:mu:θ, -mu:t], *s.* der Wermut.
vernacular [və'nækjulə], *s.* die Landessprache. — *adj.* einheimisch.
vernal ['və:nəl], *adj.* frühlingsartig, Frühlings-.

versatile ['və:sətail], *adj.* gewandt; vielseitig.
verse [və:s], *s.* der Vers; (*Poet.*) die Strophe.
versed [və:sd], *adj.* bewandert.
version ['və:ʃən], *s.* die Version, Fassung, Lesart; (*fig.*) die Darstellung.
vertebrate ['və:tibrət], *s.* (*Zool.*) das Wirbeltier. — *adj.* mit Rückenwirbeln versehen.
vertex ['və:teks], *s.* der Zenit.
vertigo ['və:tigou], *s.* (*Med.*) der Schwindel, das Schwindelgefühl.
verve [və:v], *s.* der Schwung.
very ['veri], *adv.* sehr. — *adj.* echt, wirklich,wahrhaftig.
vespers ['vespəz], *s. pl.* (*Eccl.*) der Abendgottesdienst, die Vesper.
vessel [vesl], *s.* das Gefäß (*container*); (*Naut.*) das Fahrzeug, Schiff.
vest [vest], *s.* das Gewand; (*Tail.*) die Weste; das Unterhemd (*undergarment*). — *v.a.* übertragen.
vested ['vestid], *adj.* — *interests*, das Eigeninteresse.
vestige ['vestidʒ], *s.* die Spur.
vestment ['vestmənt], *s.* (*Eccl.*) das Meßgewand.
vestry ['vestri], *s.* (*Eccl.*) die Sakristei.
vetch [vetʃ], *s.* (*Bot.*) die Wicke.
veterinary ['vetərinri], *adj.* tierärztlich; — *surgeon*, der Tierarzt.
veto ['vi:tou], *s.* (*Pol.*) der Einspruch, das Veto.
vex [veks], *v.a.* quälen, plagen.
vexation [vek'seiʃən], *s.* die Plage, der Verdruß.
via [vaiə], *prep.* über.
vibrate [vai'breit], *v.n.* schwingen, vibrieren.
vicar ['vikə], *s.* (*Eccl.*) der Pfarrer, Vikar.
vicarious [vi'kɛəriəs], *adj.* stellvertretend.
vice (1) [vais], *s.* das Laster (*immorality*).
vice (2) [vais], *s.* (*Mech.*) der Schraubstock.
vice- [vais], *pref.* Vize-, zweiter (*chairman etc.*).
vicinity [vi'siniti], *s.* die Nachbarschaft, Nähe.
vicious ['viʃəs], *adj.* böse, bösartig.
vicissitude [vi'sisitju:d], *s.* der Wechsel, Wandel; (*pl.*) Wechselfälle, *m. pl.*
victim ['viktim], *s.* das Opfer.
victuals [vitlz], *s. pl.* die Lebensmittel, *n. pl.*
vie [vai], *v.n.* wetteifern.
Vietnamese [vjetnə'mi:z], *adj.* vietnamesisch. — *s.* der Vietnamese.
view [vju:], *s.* der Anblick, die Aussicht (*panorama*); die Ansicht (*opinion*); die Absicht (*intention*). — *v.a.* betrachten; besichtigen (*inspect*).
vigil ['vidʒil], *s.* die Nachtwache.
vigilance ['vidʒiləns], *s.* die Wachsamkeit.
vigorous ['vigərəs], *adj.* kräftig, rüstig, energisch.
vigour ['vigə], *s.* die Kraft, Energie.
vile [vail], *adj.* schlecht, niedrig.
vilify ['vilifai], *v.a.* beschimpfen, erniedrigen.
villa ['vilə], *s.* das Landhaus, die Villa.
village ['vilidʒ], *s.* das Dorf.
villain ['vilən], *s.* der Schurke.
villainous ['vilənəs], *adj.* niederträchtig.
villainy ['viləni], *s.* die Niedertracht, Schändlichkeit.
vindicate ['vindikeit], *v.a.* behaupten, verteidigen; rechtfertigen (*justify*).
vindictive [vin'diktiv], *adj.* rachsüchtig.
vine [vain], *s.* (*Bot.*) der Weinstock, die Rebe.
vinegar ['vinigə], *s.* der Essig.
vintage ['vintidʒ], *s.* die Weinernte; der Jahrgang (*also fig.*).
vintner ['vintnə], *s.* der Weinbauer, Winzer.
viola [vi'oulə], *s.* (*Mus.*) die Viola, Bratsche.
violate ['vaiəleit], *v.a.* verletzen, schänden.
violence ['vaiələns], *s.* die Gewalt; die Gewalttätigkeit.
violent ['vaiələnt], *adj.* gewalttätig (*brutal*); heftig (*vehement*).
violet ['vaiəlit], *s.* (*Bot.*) das Veilchen. — *adj.* veilchenblau, violett.
violin [vaiə'lin], *s.* (*Mus.*) die Violine, Geige.
viper ['vaipə], *s.* (*Zool.*) die Viper, Natter.
virago [vi'rɑ:gou], *s.* das Mannweib.
virgin ['və:dʒin], *s.* die Jungfrau.
virile ['virail], *adj.* männlich, kräftig.
virtual ['və:tjuəl], *adj.* eigentlich.
virtue ['və:tju:], *s.* die Tugend; *by — of*, kraft (*Genit.*).
virtuoso [və:tju'ousou], *s.* der Virtuose.
virtuous ['və:tjuəs], *adj.* tugendhaft.
virulent ['virulənt], *adj.* bösartig, giftig.
virus ['vaiərəs], *s.* (*Med.*) das Gift, Virus.
viscosity [vis'kɔsiti], *s.* die Zähigkeit, Zähflüssigkeit.
viscount ['vaikaunt], *s.* der Vicomte.
viscous ['viskəs], *adj.* zähflüssig, klebrig.
visibility [vizi'biliti], *s.* die Sichtbarkeit, Sicht.
visible ['vizibl], *adj.* sichtbar.
vision ['viʒən], *s.* die Sehkraft; (*fig.*) die Vision (*dream*); die Erscheinung (*apparition*).
visionary ['viʒənri], *s.* der Träumer, (*Poet.*) der Seher. — *adj.* visionär, phantastisch, seherisch.
visit ['vizit], *s.* der Besuch. — *v.a.* besuchen.
visitation [vizi'teiʃən], *s.* die Heimsuchung.
visor ['vaizə], *s.* das Visier.
vista ['vistə], *s.* (*Art*) die Aussicht, der Ausblick.
visual ['viʒjuəl], *adj.* visuell, Seh-.
vital [vaitl], *adj.* lebenswichtig; (*fig.*) wesentlich.
vitality [vai'tæliti], *s.* die Lebenskraft, Vitalität.

vitiate ['viʃieit], *v.a.* verderben, umstoßen.
vitreous ['vitriəs], *adj.* gläsern, glasartig.
vitrify ['vitrifai], *v.a.* verglasen.
vivacious [vi'veiʃəs], *adj.* lebhaft, munter.
viva (voce) ['vaivə ('vousi)], *s.* die mündliche Prüfung.
vivacity [vi'væsiti], *s.* die Lebhaftigkeit.
vivid ['vivid], *adj.* lebhaft.
vixen ['viksən], *s.* (*Zool.*) die Füchsin; (*fig.*) das zänkische Weib.
vizier [vi'ziə], *s.* der Wesir.
vocabulary [vo'kæbjuləri], *s.* das Vokabular; der Wortschatz.
vocal ['voukəl], *adj.* laut; (*Mus.*) Stimm-, Sing-.
vocation [vo'keiʃən], *s.* die Berufung (*call*); der Beruf (*occupation*).
vociferous [vo'sifərəs], *adj.* schreiend, laut.
vogue [voug], *s.* die Mode.
voice [vɔis], *s.* die Stimme.
void [vɔid], *adj.* leer (*empty*); ungültig, (*invalid*); *null and* —, null und nichtig. — *s.* die Leere.
volatile ['vɔlətail], *adj.* flüchtig.
volcanic [vɔl'kænik], *adj.* vulkanisch.
volcano [vɔl'keinou], *s.* der Vulkan.
volition [və'liʃən], *s.* der Wille.
volley ['vɔli], *s.* (*Mil.*) die Salve; (*Footb.*) der Volleyschuß; (*Tennis*) der Flugball.
volt [voult], *s.* (*Elec.*) das Volt.
voltage ['voultidʒ], *s.* die Spannung.
voluble ['vɔljubl], *adj.* gesprächig, zungenfertig.
volume ['vɔlju:m], *s.* (*Phys.*) das Volumen; der Band (*book*); (*fig.*) der Umfang.
voluminous [və'lju:minəs], *adj.* umfangreich.
voluntary ['vɔləntri], *adj.* freiwillig. — *s.* (*Mus.*) das Orgelsolo.
volunteer [vɔlən'tiə], *s.* der Freiwillige. — *v.n.* sich freiwillig melden.
voluptuous [və'lʌptjuəs], *adj.* wollüstig, lüstern.
vomit ['vɔmit], *v.a.*, *v.n.* (sich) erbrechen, übergeben.
voracious [vɔ'reiʃəs], *adj.* gierig, gefräßig.
vortex ['vɔ:teks], *s.* der Wirbel, Strudel.
vote [vout], *v.n.* (*Pol.*) wählen, abstimmen, die Stimme abgeben. — *s.* (*Pol.*) die Stimme.
voter ['voutə], *s.* der Wähler.
votive ['voutiv], *adj.* (*Eccl.*) geweiht, gelobt; Votiv-.
vouch [vautʃ], *v.a.*, *v.n.* (sich) verbürgen, einstehen(für).
voucher ['vautʃə], *s.* der Beleg; (*Comm.*) der Gutschein.
vouchsafe [vautʃ'seif], *v.a.* bewilligen, gewähren. — *v.n.* geruhen, sich herablassen.
vow [vau], *s.* das Gelübde. — *v.a.* schwören, geloben.
vowel ['vauəl], *s.* der Vokal.
voyage ['vɔiidʒ], *s.* die Seereise. — *v.n.* zur See reisen.
vulcanize ['vʌlkənaiz], *v.a.* vulkanisieren.
vulgar ['vʌlgə], *adj.* gemein, pöbelhaft, ordinär, vulgär.
vulnerable ['vʌlnərəbl], *adj.* verwundbar, verletzbar.
vulture ['vʌltʃə], *s.* (*Orn.*) der Geier.

W

W ['dʌblju:]. das W.
wabble *see* **wobble**.
wad [wɔd], *s.* das Bündel (*notes*); der Bausch (*cotton wool*).
waddle [wɔdl], *v.n.* watscheln.
wade [weid], *v.n.* waten, durchwaten.
wafer ['weifə], *s.* die Oblate, die Waffel; (*Eccl.*) die Hostie.
waffle [wɔfl], *s.* (*Cul.*) die Waffel. — *v.n.* (*coll.*) schwafeln.
waft [wæft], *v.a.* wegwehen.
wag (1) [wæg], *v.a.* wedeln, schütteln.
wag (2) [wæg], *s.* der Spaßvogel.
wage (1) [weidʒ], *v.a.* unternehmen; — *war*, Krieg führen.
wage (2) ['weidʒ], *s.* (*often in pl.*) der Lohn.
wager ['weidʒə], *v.a.* wetten. — *s.* die Wette.
waggish ['wægiʃ], *adj.* spaßhaft, mutwillig, schelmisch.
wag(g)on ['wægən], *s.* der Wagen, Güterwagen.
wagtail ['wægteil], *s.* (*Orn.*) die Bachstelze.
waif [weif], *s.* das verwahrloste Kind; das herrenlose Gut.
wail [weil], *v.n.* wehklagen. — *s.* das Wehklagen, die Klage.
waist [weist], *s.* (*Anat.*) die Taille.
waistcoat ['weiskout, 'weskət], *s.* die Weste, das Wams.
wait [weit], *v.n.* warten; — *for*, warten auf; — *upon*, bedienen. — *v.a.* erwarten.
waiter ['weitə], *s.* der Kellner; *head* —, der Oberkellner, (*coll.*) der Ober.
waiting room ['weitiŋ rum], *s.* das Wartezimmer; (*Railw.*) der Wartesaal.
waive [weiv], *v.a.* aufgeben, verzichten (auf, *Acc.*)
wake (1) [weik], *v.n. irr.* wachen, aufwachen, wach sein. — *v.a.* aufwecken.
wake (2) [weik], *s.* (*Naut.*) das Kielwasser; (*fig.*) die Spur; *in the* — *of*, in den Fußstapfen (*Genit.*).
waken ['weikən], *v.a.* aufwecken. — *v.n.* aufwachen.
walk [wɔ:k], *v.n.* (zu Fuß) gehen. — *s.* der Gang (*gait*); der Spaziergang.

wall [wɔ:l], *s.* die Wand, Mauer.
wallet ['wɔlit], *s.* die Brieftasche.
wallflower ['wɔ:lflauə], *s.* (*Bot.*) der Goldlack; (*fig.*) das Mauerblümchen.
wallow ['wɔlou], *v.n.* schwelgen; sich wälzen.
walnut ['wɔ:lnʌt], *s.* (*Bot.*) die Walnuß.
walrus ['wɔ:lrəs], *s.* (*Zool.*) das Walroß.
waltz [wɔ:lts], *s.* der Walzer.
wan [wɔn], *adj.* blaß, bleich.
wand [wɔnd], *s.* der Stab.
wander ['wɔndə], *v.n.* wandern, durchwandern; (*fig.*) — *from the subject*, vom Thema abkommen.
wane [wein], *v.n.* abnehmen, verfallen.
want [wɔnt], *v.a.* brauchen, wollen, nötig haben, wünschen. — *v.n.* mangeln, fehlen. — *s.* die Not.
wanton ['wɔntən], *adj.* mutwillig, ausgelassen.
war [wɔ:], *s.* der Krieg.
warble [wɔ:bl], *v.a., v.n.* singen; (*Mus.*) trillern.
warbler ['wɔ:blə], *s.* (*Orn.*) der Singvogel.
ward [wɔ:d], *s.* die Verwahrung; das *or* der Mündel (*child in care*); (*Pol.*) der Wahlbezirk; die Station (*hospital*). — *v.a.* — *off*, abwehren.
warden [wɔ:dn], *s.* der Vorstand, Vorsteher; Rektor.
warder ['wɔ:də], *s.* der Wächter; (*in prison*) der Wärter, Gefängniswärter.
wardrobe ['wɔ:droub], *s.* der Kleiderschrank.
ware [wεə], *s.* die Ware.
warehouse ['wεəhaus], *s.* das Warenlager.
warfare ['wɔ:fεə], *s.* der Krieg, die Kriegsführung.
warlike ['wɔ:laik], *adj.* kriegerisch.
warm [wɔ:m], *adj.* warm.
warn [wɔ:n], *v.a.* warnen, ermahnen.
warning ['wɔ:niŋ], *s.* die Warnung.
warp [wɔ:p], *v.a.* krümmen, verziehen (*of wood*); (*fig.*) verderben; verzerren, verdrehen. — *v.n.* sich werfen, krümmen.
warrant ['wɔrənt], *s.* (*Law*) der Haftbefehl; — *officer*, der Unteroffizier; (*Comm.*) die Vollmacht, Bürgschaft. — *v.a.* garantieren (*vouch for*); versichern (*assure*).
warranty ['wɔrənti], *s.* (*Law*) die Gewähr; Garantie.
warren ['wɔrən], *s.* das Gehege.
warrior ['wɔriə], *s.* der Krieger.
wart [wɔ:t], *s.* (*Med.*) die Warze.
wary ['wεəri], *adj.* vorsichtig, achtsam (*careful*).
wash [wɔʃ], *v.a., v.n.* (sich) waschen; — *up*, spülen, abwaschen. — *s.* die Wäsche (*laundry*).
wasp [wɔsp], *s.* (*Ent.*) die Wespe.
waspish ['wɔspiʃ], *adj.* reizbar, zänkisch, bissig.
wassail [wɔsl], *s.* das Trinkgelage. — *v.n.* zechen.
waste [weist], *v.a.* zerstören, verwüsten; verschwenden. — *adj.* wüst, öde. — *s.* die Verschwendung (*process*); der Abfall (*product*); — *paper*, die Makulatur; — *paper basket*, der Papierkorb.
wasteful ['weistful], *adj.* verschwenderisch.
watch [wɔtʃ], *v.a.* bewachen; beobachten (*observe*); hüten (*guard*). — *s.* die Wache (*guard*); die Uhr, Taschenuhr (*time-piece*).
watchful ['wɔtʃful], *adj.* wachsam.
watchman ['wɔtʃmən], *s.* der Nachtwächter.
water ['wɔ:tə], *s.* das Wasser; (*pl.*) die Kur; — *colour*, das Aquarell; — *gauge*, der Pegel. — *v.a.* wässern; begießen (*flowers*).
watercress ['wɔ:təkres], *s.* (*Bot.*) die Brunnenkresse.
waterproof ['wɔ:təpru:f], *adj.* wasserdicht.
watt [wɔt], *s.* (*Elec.*) das Watt.
wattle [wɔtl], *s.* (*Bot.*) die Hürde.
wave [weiv], *s.* die Welle; *permanent* —, die Dauerwelle. — *v.n.* zuwinken (*Dat.*); wehen; winken. — *v.a.* schwenken (*handkerchief*).
waver ['weivə], *v.n.* schwanken, unentschlossen sein.
wax [wæks], *s.* das Wachs, der Siegellack. — *v.a.* wachsen, bohnern.
waxen [wæksn], *adj.* aus Wachs, wächsern.
way [wei], *s.* der Weg (*road etc.*); die Strecke; Richtung; *in no* —, keineswegs; (*pl.*) die Art und Weise; *Milky Way*, die Milchstraße.
wayward ['weiwəd], *adj.* eigensinnig.
we [wi:], *pers. pron.* wir.
weak [wi:k], *adj.* schwach, kraftlos.
weaken ['wi:kən], *v.a.* schwächen. — *v.n.* schwach werden.
weakling ['wi:kliŋ], *s.* der Schwächling.
wealth [welθ], *s.* der Wohlstand, Reichtum.
wealthy ['welθi], *adj.* wohlhabend, reich.
wean [wi:n], *v.a.* entwöhnen.
weapon ['wepən], *s.* die Waffe.
wear [wεə], *v.a. irr.* tragen (*clothes*). — *v.n.* — *off*, sich abtragen, schäbig werden; — *out*, sich erschöpfen. — *s.* die Abnutzung.
weariness ['wiərinis], *s.* die Müdigkeit, der Überdruß.
weary ['wiəri], *adj.* müde, überdrüssig.
weasel [wi:zl], *s.* (*Zool.*) das Wiesel.
weather ['weðə], *s.* das Wetter. — *v.a.* überstehen. — *v.n.* (*Geol.*) verwittern.
weatherbeaten ['weðəbi:tn], *adj.* abgehärtet, wetterhart.
weathercock ['weðəkɔk], *s.* der Wetterhahn; (*fig.*) wetterwendischer Mensch.
weave [wi:v], *v.a. irr.* (*Text.*) weben, — *s.* das Gewebe.
web [web], *s.* das Gewebe.
wed [wed], *v.a.* heiraten; trauen (*a couple*). — *v.n.* (sich ver)heiraten.
wedding ['wediŋ], *s.* die Hochzeit; Trauung (*ceremony*).

wedge [wedʒ], *s.* der Keil. — *v.a.* keilen.
wedlock ['wedlɔk], *s.* die Ehe.
Wednesday ['wenzd(e)i]. der Mittwoch.
wee [wi:], *adj.* (*Scot.*) winzig, klein.
weed [wi:d], *s.* das Unkraut. — *v.a.* ausjäten, jäten.
week [wi:k], *s.* die Woche.
weep [wi:p], *v.n. irr.* weinen; —*ing willow*, die Trauerweide.
weigh [wei], *v.a.* wiegen, wägen; (*fig.*) abwägen, beurteilen; (*Naut.*) — *anchor*, den Anker lichten. — *v.n.* wiegen.
weighing machine ['weiiŋ mə'ʃi:n], *s.* die Waage.
weight [weit], *s.* das Gewicht; *gross* —, das Bruttogewicht; *net* —, das Nettogewicht.
weighty ['weiti], *adj.* (ge)wichtig; (*fig.*) schwer.
weir [wiə], *s.* das Wehr.
weird [wiəd], *adj.* unheimlich.
welcome ['welkəm], *adj.* willkommen. — *s.* der *or* das Willkommen. — *v.a.* willkommen heißen, begrüßen.
weld [weld], *v.a.* schweißen.
welfare ['welfɛə], *s.* die Wohlfahrt, soziale Fürsorge.
well (1) [wel], *s.* der Brunnen. — *v.n.* hervorsprudeln.
well (2) [wel], *adv.* gut, wohl; durchaus; — *bred*, wohlerzogen. — *pred. adj.* gesund, wohl.
Welsh [welʃ], *adj.* walisisch. — *s. pl.* die Waliser, *m.pl.*
Welshman ['welʃmən], *s.* der Waliser.
welt [welt], *s.* der Rand, die Einfassung.
welter ['weltə], *s.* die Masse, das Chaos. — *v.n.* sich wälzen.
wen [wen], *s.* (*Med.*) die Schwellung.
wench [wentʃ], *s.* die Magd, das Mädchen.
west [west], *s.* der Westen. — *adj.* (*also* **westerly, western** ['westəli, 'westən]) westlich.
Westphalian [west'feiliən], *adj.* westfälisch. — *s.* der Westfale.
wet [wet], *adj.* naß, feucht; — *paint*, frisch gestrichen. — *v.a.* anfeuchten, benetzen, naß machen.
whack [hwæk], *v.a.* durchprügeln. — *s.* die Tracht Prügel, der Schlag.
whale [hweil], *s.* (*Zool.*) der Walfisch.
whalebone ['hweilboun], *s.* das Fischbein.
wharf [hwɔ:f], *s.* der Kai.
wharfinger ['hwɔ:findʒə], *s.* der Kaimeister.
what [hwɔt], *rel. & interr. pron.* was; welcher, welche, welches; was für.
what(so)ever [hwɔt(sou)'evə], *rel. pron.* was auch immer. — *adj.* einerlei welche-r, -s, -n.
wheat [hwi:t], *s.* (*Bot.*) der Weizen.
wheedle [hwi:dl], *v.a.* beschwatzen.
wheel [hwi:l], *s.* das Rad; die Umdrehung, Drehung. — *v.a., v.n.* drehen, sich drehen, schieben.
wheelbarrow ['hwi:lbærou], *s.* der Schubkarren.
wheeze [hwi:z], *v.n.* keuchen, schnaufen. — *s.* das Keuchen.
whelp [hwelp], *s.* (*Zool.*) das Junge, der junge Hund. — *v.n.* Junge werfen.
when [hwen], *adv.* (*interr.*) wann? — *conj.* als (*in past*), wenn, während.
whence [hwens], *adv.* woher, von wo.
where [hwɛə], *adv.* wo, wohin; (*interr.*) wo? wohin?
whereabout(s) ['hwɛərəbaut(s)], *adv.* wo, wo etwa. — *s.* (**whereabouts**) der zeitweilige Aufenthalt *or* Wohnort.
whereas [hwɛər'æz], *conj.* wohingegen, während.
whereupon [hwɛərə'pɔn], *conj.* woraufhin.
wherewithal ['hwɛəwiðɔ:l], *s.* die gesamte Habe, das Nötige. — *adv.* (*obs.*) womit.
whet [hwet], *v.a.* wetzen, schleifen.
whether ['hweðə], *conj.* ob.
whey [hwei], *s.* die Molke.
which [hwitʃ], *rel. & interr. pron.* welcher, welche, welches; der, die, das.
whiff [hwif], *s.* der Hauch, Luftzug.
while [hwail], *s.* die Weile, Zeit. — *v.a.* — *away the time*, dahinbringen, vertreiben. — *conj.* (*also* **whilst**) während, so lange als.
whim [hwim], *s.* die Laune, Grille.
whimper ['hwimpə], *v.n.* winseln.
whimsical ['hwimzikəl], *adj.* grillenhaft.
whine [hwain], *v.n.* weinen, wimmern, klagen. — *s.* das Gewimmer, Gejammer.
whinny ['hwini], *v.n.* wiehern.
whip [hwip], *s.* die Peitsche; (*Pol.*) der Einpeitscher. — *v.a.* peitschen.
whir [hwə:], *v.n.* schwirren. — *s.* das Schwirren.
whirl [hwə:l], *s.* der Wirbel, Strudel. — *v.a., v.n.* wirbeln.
whirligig ['hwə:ligig], *s.* der Karussel.
whirlpool ['hwə:lpu:l], *s.* der Strudel.
whirr *see* **whir**.
whisk [hwisk], *v.a.* fegen; schlagen; — *away or off*, schnell wegtun (*a th.*), schnell fortnehmen (*a p.*). — *v.n.* — *away*, dahinhuschen. — *s.* der Schläger.
whiskers ['hwiskəz], *s.* der Backenbart, Bart.
whisky ['hwiski], *s.* der Whisky.
whisper ['hwispə], *s.* das Geflüster. *v.a., v.n.* flüstern.
whistle [hwisl], *s.* die Pfeife (*instrument*); der Pfiff (*sound*). — *v.a., v.n.* pfeifen.
whit [hwit], *s.* die Kleinigkeit; *not a* —, nicht im geringsten.
white [hwait], *adj.* weiß; — *lead*, das Bleiweiß; — *lie*, die Notlüge.
whitebait ['hwaitbeit], *s.* (*Zool.*) der Breitling.
whiten [hwaitn], *v.a.* weißen, bleichen.
whitewash ['hwaitwɔʃ], *s.* die Tünche. — *v.a.* reinwaschen.

whither ['hwiðə], *adv.* wohin; dahin wo.
whiting ['hwaitiŋ], *s.* (*Zool.*) der Weißfisch; die Schlämmkreide (*chalk*).
whitlow ['hwitlou], *s.* (*Med.*) das Nagelgeschwür.
Whitsun(tide) ['hwitsən(taid)], *s.* (das) Pfingsten; *Whit Sunday*, der Pfingstsonntag.
whittle [hwitl], *v.a.* schnitzen, abschaben.
whiz [hwiz], *v.n.* zischen; (*fig.*) vorbeiflitzen.
who [hu:], *interr. pron.* wer?, welcher?, welche? — *rel. pron.* welcher, welche, welches, der, die, das.
whoever [hu:'evə], *rel. pron.* wer auch immer.
whole [houl], *adj.* ganz, völlig. — *s.* das Ganze.
wholesale ['houlseil], *adv.* im Engros. — *adj.* Engros-, Großhandels-.
wholesome ['houlsəm], *adj.* gesund.
whoop [hu:p], *s.* das Geschrei; — *v.n.* laut keuchen; —*ing cough*, der Keuchhusten.
whortleberry ['hwə:tlbəri], *s.* (*Bot.*) die Heidelbeere.
whose [hu:z], *pron.* wessen, dessen, deren.
whosoever [hu:sou'evə] *see* **whoever**.
why [hwai], *rel. & interr. adv.* warum?
wick [wik], *s.* der Docht.
wicked ['wikid], *adj.* böse, schlecht.
wicker ['wikə], *adj.* Rohr-, geflochten.
wicket ['wikit], *s.* das Pförtchen.
wide [waid], *adj.* weit, breit; (*fig.*) umfangreich, groß, reich(*experience*).—*adv. far and* —, weit und breit; — *awake*, völlig wach.
widen [waidn], *v.a.*, erweitern.
widgeon ['widʒən], *s.* die Pfeifente.
widow ['widou], *s.* die Witwe.
widower ['widouə], *s.* der Witwer.
width [widθ], *s.* die Weite, Breite.
wield [wi:ld], *v.a.* schwingen; — *power*, die Macht ausüben.
wife [waif], *s.* die Frau, Gattin.
wig [wig], *s.* die Perücke.
wild [waild], *adj.* wild.
wilderness ['wildənis], *s.* die Wildnis.
wildfire ['waildfaiə], *s.* das Lauffeuer.
wilful ['wilful], *adj.* absichtlich; vorsätzlich.
wiliness ['wailinis], *s.* die Schlauheit, Arglist.
will [wil], *s.* der Wille; (*Law*) der letzte Wille, das Testament. — *v.n.* wollen. — *v.a.* (*Law*) vermachen, hinterlassen.
willing ['wiliŋ], *adj.* bereitwillig.
will-o'-the-wisp [wiləðə'wisp], *s.* das Irrlicht.
willow ['wilou], *s.* (*Bot.*) die Weide.
wily ['waili], *adj.* schlau, verschmitzt.
wimple [wimpl], *s.* der Schleier.
win [win], *v.a.*, *v.n. irr.* gewinnen, siegen, erringen.
wince [wins], *v.n.* zucken, zusammenzucken.
winch [wintʃ], *s.* die Kurbel, Winde.
wind (1) [wind], *s.* der Wind; der Atem (*breath*); *get — of s.th.*, von etwas hören.
wind (2) [waind], *v.a. irr.* winden; wenden, drehen (*turn*); —(*up*), aufziehen (*timepiece*); — *up*, (*business, debate*) beenden. — *v.n.* sich schlängeln, winden.
windfall ['windfɔ:l], *s.* das Fallobst (*fruit*); (*fig.*) der Glücksfall.
windlass ['windləs], *s.* die Winde.
window ['windou], *s.* das Fenster; — *sill*, das Fensterbrett.
windpipe ['windpaip], *s.* (*Anat.*) die Luftröhre.
windscreen ['windskri:n], *s.* (*Motor.*) die Windschutzscheibe.
windshield ['windʃi:ld] (*Am.*) *see* **windscreen**.
windy ['windi], *adj.* windig.
wine [wain], *s.* der Wein; — *merchant*, der Weinhändler.
wing [wiŋ], *s.* der Flügel; (*Poet.*) die Schwinge.
wink [wiŋk], *s.* das Zwinkern; der Augenblick. —*v.n.* blinzeln, zwinkern.
winner ['winə], *s.* der Sieger, Gewinner.
winning ['winiŋ], *adj.* einnehmend.
winsome ['winsəm], *adj.* reizend, einnehmend.
winter ['wintə], *s.* der Winter.
wintry ['wintri], *adj.* winterlich.
wipe [waip], *v.a.* wischen, abwischen.
wire [waiə], *s.* der Draht; (*coll.*) das Telegramm; *barbed* —, der Stacheldraht. — *v.a.* verbinden; (*fig.*) telegraphieren. — *v.n.* telegraphieren.
wireless ['waiəlis], *s.* das Radio. — *adj.* drahtlos.
wirepuller ['waiəpulə], *s.* der Puppenspieler; (*fig.*) der Intrigant.
wiry ['waiəri], *adj.* zäh, stark.
wisdom ['wizdəm], *s.* die Weisheit.
wise [waiz], *adj.* weise, verständig, klug.
wiseacre ['waizeikə], *s.* der Allzuschlaue, Naseweis.
wish [wiʃ], *v.a.*, *v.n.* wünschen. — *s.* der Wunsch.
wistful ['wistful], *adj.* nachdenklich (*pensive*); wehmütig (*sad*).
wit [wit], *s.* der Witz; Geist; Verstand; der witzige Mensch; der Witzbold.
witch [witʃ], *s.* die Hexe, Zauberin.
witchcraft ['witʃkra:ft], *s.* die Zauberkunst, Hexerei.
with [wið], *prep.* mit, mitsamt, bei, durch, von.
withal [wi'ðɔ:l], *adv.* obendrein.
withdraw [wið'drɔ:], *v.a.*, *v.n. irr.* (sich) zurückziehen; widerrufen; abheben (*money from bank*).
withdrawal [wið'drɔ:əl], *s.* der Rückzug; (*Comm. etc.*) die Widerrufung; Abhebung (*bank*).
wither ['wiðə], *v.a.* welk machen. — *v.n.* verwelken; ausdorren, verdorren (*dry up*); (*fig.*) vergehen.
withhold [wið'hould], *v.a. irr.* zurückhalten, vorenthalten.

within [wi'ðin], *prep.* innerhalb; (*time*) binnen (*Genit.*). — *adv.* darin, drinnen.
without [wi'ðaut], *prep.* ohne; (*obs.*) außerhalb (*outside*); *do* —, entbehren. — *adv.* draußen, außen.
withstand [wið'stænd], *v.a. irr.* widerstehen (*Dat.*).
withy ['wiθi], *s.* der Weidenzweig.
witless ['witlis], *adj.* einfältig.
witness ['witnis], *s.* der Zeuge. — *v.a.* bezeugen, Zeuge sein von. — *v.n.* zeugen, Zeuge sein.
witticism ['witisizm], *s.* das Bonmot, die witzige Bemerkung.
witty ['witi], *adj.* witzig, geistreich.
wizard ['wizəd], *s.* der Zauberer.
wizened ['wizənd], *adj.* verwelkt, vertrocknet, runzlig.
wobble [wɔbl], *v.n.* wackeln.
woe [wou], *s.* (*Poet.*) das Weh, Leid.
wolf [wulf], *s.* (*Zool.*) der Wolf.
woman ['wumən], *s.* die Frau, das Weib.
womanly ['wumənli], *adj.* weiblich.
womb [wu:m], *s.* der Mutterleib, Schoß; (*Anat.*) die Gebärmutter.
wonder ['wʌndə], *s.* das Wunder. — *v.n.* sich wundern (*be amazed*); gern wissen mögen (*like to know*); sich fragen.
wonderful ['wʌndəful], *adj.* wunderbar.
wondrous ['wʌndrəs], *adj.* (*Poet.*) wunderbar.
wont [wount], *s.* die Gewohnheit. — *pred. adj.* gewohnt.
won't [wount] = **will not.**
woo [wu:], *v.a.* freien, werben (um).
wood [wud], *s.* das Holz (*timber*); der Wald (*forest*).
woodbine ['wudbain], *s.* das Geißblatt.
woodcock ['wudkɔk], *s.* (*Orn.*) die Waldschnepfe.
woodcut ['wudkʌt], *s.* (*Art*) der Holzschnitt.
wooded ['wudid], *adj.* bewaldet.
wooden [wudn], *adj.* hölzern, Holz–.
woodlark ['wudlɑ:k], *s.* (*Orn.*) die Heidelerche.
woodpecker ['wudpekə], *s.* (*Orn.*) der Specht.
woodruff ['wudrʌf], *s.* (*Bot.*) der Waldmeister.
woof [wu:f], *s.* (*Text.*) der Einschlag, das Gewebe.
wool [wul], *s.* die Wolle; — *gathering*, zerstreut.
woollen ['wulən], *adj.* wollen, aus Wolle.
woolly ['wuli], *adj.* wollig; (*fig.*) unklar, verschwommen.
word [wə:d], *s.* das Wort; *send* —, Botschaft senden. — *v.a.* ausdrücken.
wording ['wə:diŋ], *s.* die Fassung, der Stil.
work [wə:k], *s.* die Arbeit; *out of* —, arbeitslos; das Werk (*opus*); (*pl.*) die Fabrik. — *v.a., v.n.* arbeiten, bearbeiten; (*engine*) funktionieren.
worker ['wə:kə], *s.* der Arbeiter.
workhouse ['wə:khaus], *s.* das Armenhaus.
workshop ['wə:kʃɔp], *s.* die Werkstatt.
world [wə:ld], *s.* die Welt.
worldly ['wə:ldli], *adj.* weltlich, zeitlich.
worm [wə:m], *s.* (*Zool.*) der Wurm. — *v.a.* — *o.'s way*, sich einschleichen. — *v.n.* sich einschleichen.
wormeaten ['wə:mi:tn], *adj.* wurmstichig.
worry ['wʌri], *v.a., v.n.* plagen, quälen, sorgen, ängstigen; sich beunruhigen; *don't* —, bitte machen Sie sich keine Mühe. — *s.* die Plage, Mühe, Qual, Sorge (*about*, um, *Acc.*).
worse [wə:s], *comp. adj., adv.* schlechter, schlimmer.
worship ['wə:ʃip], *s.* die Verehrung; der Gottesdienst (*divine* —).
worst [wə:st], *superl. adj.* schlechtest, schlimmst. — *adv.* am schlimmsten *or* schlechtesten. — *s.* das Schlimmste.
worsted ['wustid], *s.* (*Text.*) das Kammgarn.
worth [wə:θ], *adj.* wert. — *s.* der Wert.
worthy ['wə:ði], *adj.* würdig, wert, verdient.
would [wud] *past tense of* **will,** *q.v.*
wound [wu:nd], *s.* die Wunde. — *v.a.* verwunden.
wraith [reiθ], *s.* das Gespenst.
wrangle [ræŋgl], *v.n.* zanken, streiten. — *s.* der Zank, Streit.
wrap [ræp], *v.a.* einwickeln, einhüllen. — *s.* (*Am.*) der Mantel (*coat*), Pelz (*fur*), Schal (*stole*).
wrapper ['ræpə], *s.* der Umschlag, die Hülle.
wrath [rɔ:θ], *s.* der Zorn, Grimm.
wreak [ri:k], *v.a.* (*Lit.*) auslassen, üben.
wreath [ri:θ], *s.* der Kranz.
wreathe [ri:ð], *v.a.* winden, bekränzen.
wreck [rek], *s.* der Schiffbruch; das Wrack (*debris*). — *v.a.* zerstören, zertrümmern, (*fig.*) verderben.
wren [ren], *s.* (*Orn.*) der Zaunkönig.
wrench [rentʃ], *v.a.* entreißen (*tear from*); verdrehen. — *s.* heftiger Ruck; (*fig.*) der (Trennungs)schmerz.
wrest [rest], *v.a.* zerren.
wrestle [resl], *v.n.* ringen, im Ringkampf kämpfen.
wrestling ['resliŋ], *s.* der Ringkampf.
wretch [retʃ], *s.* der Schuft, Lump (*scoundrel*).
wretched ['retʃid], *adj.* elend.
wriggle [rigl], *v.n.* sich winden, schlängeln.
wring [riŋ], *v.a. irr.* auswinden, ausringen.
wrinkle [riŋkl], *s.* die Hautfalte, Runzel. — *v.a.* runzeln (*brow*); rümpfen (*nose*).
wrist [rist], *s.* (*Anat.*) das Handgelenk.
wristwatch ['ristwɔtʃ], *s.* die Armbanduhr.
writ [rit], *s.* die Schrift; (*Law*) die Vorladung.

write [rait], *v.a.*, *v.n. irr.* schreiben, verfassen.
writer ['raitə], *s.* der Schreiber; (*Lit.*) der Schriftsteller.
writhe [raið], *v.n.* sich winden.
writing ['raitiŋ], *s.* die Schrift; der Stil (*style*).
wrong [rɔŋ], *adj.* falsch, verkehrt; *to be* —, unrecht haben. — *s.* das Unrecht. — *v.a.* Unrecht *or* Schaden tun (*Dat.*).
wrongful ['rɔŋful], *adj.* unrechtmäßig.
wrongheaded [rɔŋ'hedid], *adj.* querköpfig.
wroth [rouθ], *adj.* (*Lit.*) zornig.
wrought [rɔ:t], *adj.* (*work*) gearbeitet; — *iron*, das Schmiedeeisen.
wry [rai], *adj.* verkehrt, krumm, schief, verdreht.

X

X [eks]. das X.
X-ray ['eksrei], *s.* (der) Röntgenstrahl.
xylophone ['zailəfoun], *s.* (*Mus.*) das Xylophon.

Y

Y [wai]. das Y, Ypsilon.
yacht [jɔt], *s.* (*Naut.*) die Jacht.
yachtsman ['jɔtsmən], *s.* (*Naut.*) der Segelsportler.
yap [jæp], *v.n.* kläffen.
yard (1) [jɑ:d], *s.* der Hof.
yard (2) [jɑ:d], *s.* die englische Elle, der Yard.
yarn [jɑ:n], *s.* das Garn; (*coll.*) die Geschichte (*tale*).
yarrow ['jærou], *s.* (*Bot.*) die Schafgarbe.
yawl [jɔ:l], *s.* (*Naut.*) die Yawl.
yawn [jɔ:n], *v.n.* gähnen. — *s.* das Gähnen.
ye [ji:], *pron.* (*obs.*) *see* **you.**
year [jə: *or* jiə], *s.* das Jahr; *every other* —, alle zwei Jahre.
yearly ['jiəli], *adj.*, *adv.* jährlich.
yearn [jə:n], *v.n.* sich sehnen (nach, *Dat.*).
yeast [ji:st], *s.* die Hefe.
yell [jel], *v.n.* gellen, schreien. — *s.* der Schrei.
yellow ['jelou], *adj.* gelb; (*sl.*) feige.
yelp [jelp], *v.n.* kläffen, bellen. — *s.* das Gebelle.
yeoman ['jouman], *s.* der Freisasse; (*Mil.*) der Leibgardist (*Yeoman of the Guard*).
yes [jes], *adv.* ja; jawohl.
yesterday ['jestəd(e)i], *adv.* gestern; *the day before* —, vorgestern.
yet [jet], *conj.* doch, dennoch. — *adv.* noch, außerdem; *as* —, bisher; *not* —, noch nicht.
yew [ju:], *s.* (*Bot.*) die Eibe.
yield [ji:ld], *v.a.* hervorbringen, ergeben; abwerfen (*profit*). — *v.n.* nachgeben (*to*, *Dat.*). — *s.* der Ertrag.
yoke [jouk], *s.* das Joch (Ochsen). — *v.a.* einspannen, anspannen.
yolk [jouk], *s.* das Eidotter.
yon, yonder [jɔn, 'jɔndə], *dem. adj.* (*obs.*) jener, jene, jenes; der *or* die *or* das da drüben.
yore [jɔ:], *adv.* (*obs.*) *of* —, von damals; ehedem.
you [ju:], *pers. pron.* du, dich, ihr, euch; (*formal*) sie (*in letters*, Du, Dich *etc.*).
young [jʌŋ], *adj.* jung. — *s.* (*Zool.*) das Junge.
your [juə], *poss. adj.* dein, deine, dein; euer, eure, euer; (*formal*) ihr, ihre, ihr (*in letters* Dein, Euer *etc.*).
yours [jɔ:z], *poss. pron.* deinig, eurig; der, die *or* das ihrige (*in letters* Deinig, der Ihrige *etc.*).
yourself [juə'self], *pers. pron.* du selbst, Sie selbst; ihr selbst; dich (selbst), euch (selbst) (*in letters* Du selbst; Dich (selbst) *etc.*).
youth [ju:θ], *s.* die Jugend.
youthful ['ju:θful], *adj.* jugendlich.
Yugoslav [ju:go'slɑ:v], *adj.* jugoslawisch. — *s.* der Jugoslawe.
Yule, Yuletide [ju:l, 'ju:ltaid], *s.* das Julfest, die Weihnachtszeit.

Z

Z [zed, (*Am.*) zi:]. das Z.
zany ['zeini], *s.* der Hanswurst.
zeal [zi:l], *s.* der Eifer.
zealous ['zeləs], *adj.* eifrig.
zebra ['zi:brə], *s.* (*Zool.*) das Zebra.
zenith ['zeniθ], *s.* der Zenit, Scheitelpunkt.
zero ['ziərou], *s.* der Nullpunkt, die (Ziffer) Null; — *hour*, die festgesetzte Stunde; festgesetzter Zeitpunkt.
zest [zest], *s.* die Lust; der Genuß; die Würze.
zigzag ['zigzæg], *s.* der Zickzack. — *adj.* Zickzack-.
zinc [ziŋk], *s.* das Zink.
zip(per) ['zip(ə)], *s.* der Reißverschluß (*zip fastener*).
zone [zoun], *s.* die Zone.
zoological gardens [zouə'lɔdʒikəl gɑ:dnz], *s.* (*abbr.* **zoo** [zu:]) zoologischer Garten, der Zoo, Tiergarten.

German Irregular Verbs

Note: *Where a compound irregular verb is not given, its forms are identical with those of the simple irregular verb as listed.*

Infin.	*Pres. Indic. 3rd Pers. Sing.*	*Imperf. Indic.*	*Imperf. Subj.*
backen	**bäckt**	**backte (buk)**	**backte**
befehlen	**befiehlt**	**befahl**	**beföhle**
beginnen	**beginnt**	**begann**	**begönne**
beißen	**beißt**	**biß**	**bisse**
bergen	**birgt**	**barg**	**bürge**
bersten	**birst**	**barst**	**börste**
bewegen	**bewegt**	**bewog**	**bewöge**
biegen	**biegt**	**bog**	**böge**
bieten	**bietet**	**bot**	**böte**
binden	**bindet**	**band**	**bände**
bitten	**bittet**	**bat**	**bäte**
blasen	**bläst**	**blies**	**bliese**
bleiben	**bleibt**	**blieb**	**bliebe**
braten	**brät**	**briet**	**briete**
brechen	**bricht**	**brach**	**bräche**
brennen	**brennt**	**brannte**	**brennte**
bringen	**bringt**	**brachte**	**brächte**
denken	**denkt**	**dachte**	**dächte**
dreschen	**drischt**	**drosch**	**dräsche**
dringen	**dringt**	**drang**	**dränge**
dürfen	**darf**	**durfte**	**dürfte**
empfangen	**empfängt**	**empfing**	**empfinge**
empfehlen	**empfiehlt**	**empfahl**	**empföhle**
empfinden	**empfindet**	**empfand**	**empfände**
erlöschen	**erlischt**	**erlosch**	**erlösche**

German Irregular Verbs

Imper.	*Past Participle*	*English*
backe	gebacken	bake
befiehl	befohlen	order, command
beginn(e)	begonnen	begin
beiß(e)	gebissen	bite
birg	geborgen	save, conceal
birst	geborsten	burst
beweg(e)	bewogen	induce
bieg(e)	gebogen	bend
biet(e)	geboten	offer
bind(e)	gebunden	tie, bind
bitte	gebeten	request
blas(e)	geblasen	blow
bleib(e)	geblieben	remain
brat(e)	gebraten	roast
brich	gebrochen	break
brenne	gebrannt	burn
bring(e)	gebracht	bring
denk(e)	gedacht	think
drisch	gedroschen	thrash
dring(e)	gedrungen	press forward
	gedurft	be permitted
empfang(e)	empfangen	receive
empfiehl	empfohlen	(re)commend
empfind(e)	empfunden	feel, perceive
erlisch	·rloschen	extinguish

German Irregular Verbs

Infin.	*Pres. Indic. 3rd Pers. Sing.*	*Imperf. Indic.*	*Imperf. Subj.*
erschrecken (*v.n.*)	erschrickt	erschrak	erschräke
essen	ißt	aß	äße
fahren	fährt	fuhr	führe
fallen	fällt	fiel	fiele
fangen	fängt	fing	finge
fechten	ficht	focht	föchte
finden	findet	fand	fände
flechten	flicht	flocht	flöchte
fliegen	fliegt	flog	flöge
fliehen	flieht	floh	flöhe
fließen	fließt	floß	flösse
fressen	frißt	fraß	fräße
frieren	friert	fror	fröre
gebären	gebiert	gebar	gebäre
geben	gibt	gab	gäbe
gedeihen	gedeiht	gedieh	gediehe
gehen	geht	ging	ginge
gelingen (*impers.*)	(mir) gelingt	gelang	gelänge
gelten	gilt	galt	gälte
genesen	genest	genas	genäse
genießen	genießt	genoß	genösse
geschehen (*impers.*)	(mir) geschieht	geschah	geschähe
gewinnen	gewinnt	gewann	gewönne
gießen	gießt	goß	gösse
gleichen	gleicht	glich	gliche
gleiten	gleitet	glitt	glitte
graben	gräbt	grub	grübe
greifen	greift	griff	griffe

German Irregular Verbs

Imper.	*Past Participle*	*English*
erschrick	erschrocken	be frightened
iß	gegessen	eat
fahr(e)	gefahren	travel
fall(e)	gefallen	fall
fang(e)	gefangen	catch
ficht	gefochten	fight
find(e)	gefunden	find
flicht	geflochten	twine together
flieg(e)	geflogen	fly
flieh(e)	geflohen	flee
fließ(e)	geflossen	flow
friß	gefressen	eat (of animals)
frier(e)	gefroren	freeze
gebier	geboren	give birth to
gib	gegeben	give
gedeih(e)	gediehen	thrive
geh(e)	gegangen	go
geling(e)	gelungen	succeed
gilt	gegolten	be worth, be valid
genese	genesen	recover
genieß(e)	genossen	enjoy
	geschehen	happen
gewinn(e)	gewonnen	win
gieß(e)	gegossen	pour
gleich(e)	geglichen	equal, resemble
gleit(e)	geglitten	glide
grab(e)	gegraben	dig
greif(e)	gegriffen	grasp

German Irregular Verbs

Infin.	*Pres. Indic. 3rd Pers. Sing.*	*Imperf. Indic.*	*Imperf. Subj.*
haben	hat	hatte	hätte
halten	hält	hielt	hielte
hangen (*v.n.*)	hängt	hing	hinge
heben	hebt	hob	höbe
heißen	heißt	hieß	hieße
helfen	hilft	half	hülfe
kennen	kennt	kannte	kennte
klimmen	klimmt	klomm	klömme
klingen	klingt	klang	klänge
kneifen	kneift	kniff	kniffe
kommen	kommt	kam	käme
können	kann	konnte	könnte
kriechen	kriecht	kroch	kröche
laden	lädt	lud	lüde
lassen	läßt	ließ	ließe
laufen	läuft	lief	liefe
leiden	leidet	litt	litte
leihen	leiht	lieh	liehe
lesen	liest	las	läse
liegen	liegt	lag	läge
lügen	lügt	log	löge
mahlen	mahlt	mahlte	mahlte
meiden	meidet	mied	miede
messen	mißt	maß	mäße
mißlingen (*impers.*)	(mir) mißlingt	mißlang	mißlänge
mögen	mag	mochte	möchte
müssen	muß	mußte	müßte
nehmen	nimmt	nahm	nähme

Imper.	*Past Participle*	*English*
habe	gehabt	have
halt(e)	gehalten	hold
häng(e)	gehangen	hang
hebe	gehoben	lift
heiß(e)	geheißen	be called
hilf	geholfen	help
kenn(e)	gekannt	know
klimm(e)	geklommen	climb
kling(e)	geklungen	ring, sound
kneif(e)	gekniffen	pinch
komm(e)	gekommen	come
	gekonnt	be able
kriech(e)	gekrochen	creep
lad(e)	geladen	load
laß	gelassen	let
lauf(e)	gelaufen	run
leid(e)	gelitten	suffer
leih(e)	geliehen	lend
lies	gelesen	read
lieg(e)	gelegen	lie
lüg(e)	gelogen	lie, be untruthful
mahle	gemahlen	grind
meid(e)	gemieden	avoid
miß	gemessen	measure
	mißlungen	fail
	gemocht	wish, be willing
	gemußt	have to
nimm	genommen	take

German Irregular Verbs

Infin.	*Pres. Indic. 3rd Pers. Sing.*	*Imperf. Indic.*	*Imperf. Subj.*
nennen	nennt	nannte	nennte
pfeifen	pfeift	pfiff	pfiffe
preisen	preist	pries	priese
quellen (*v.n.*)	quillt	quoll	quölle
raten	rät	riet	riete
reiben	reibt	rieb	riebe
reißen	reißt	riß	risse
reiten	reitet	ritt	ritte
rennen	rennt	rannte	rennte
riechen	riecht	roch	röche
ringen	ringt	rang	ränge
rinnen	rinnt	rann	rönne
rufen	ruft	rief	riefe
saufen	säuft	soff	söffe
saugen	saugt	sog	söge
schaffen	schafft	schuf	schüfe
scheiden	scheidet	schied	schiede
scheinen	scheint	schien	schiene
schelten	schilt	schalt	schölte
schieben	schiebt	schob	schöbe
schießen	schießt	schoß	schösse
schinden	schindet	schund	schünde
schlafen	schläft	schlief	schliefe
schlagen	schlägt	schlug	schlüge
schleichen	schleicht	schlich	schliche
schleifen	schleift	schliff	schliffe
schließen	schließt	schloß	schlösse
schlingen	schlingt	schlang	schlänge

German Irregular Verbs

Imper.	*Past Participle*	*English*
nenne	genannt	name
pfeif(e)	gepfiffen	whistle
preis(e)	gepriesen	praise
quill	gequollen	spring
rat(e)	geraten	counsel
reib(e)	gerieben	rub
reiß(e)	gerissen	`ear
reit(e)	geritten	ride
renn(e)	gerannt	run
riech(e)	gerochen	smell
ring(e)	gerungen	struggle
rinn(e)	geronnen	flow
ruf(e)	gerufen	call
sauf(e)	gesoffen	drink (to excess)
saug(e)	gesogen	suck
schaff(e)	geschaffen	create
scheid(e)	geschieden	separate
schein(e)	geschienen	appear
schilt	gescholten	scold
schieb(e)	geschoben	shove
schieß(e)	geschossen	shoot
schind(e)	geschunden	skin
schlaf(e)	geschlafen	sleep
schlag(e)	geschlagen	beat
schleich(e)	geschlichen	slink, creep
schleif(e)	geschliffen	slide, polish
schließ(e)	geschlossen	shut, close
schling(e)	geschlungen	wind, devour

German Irregular Verbs

Infin.	*Pres. Indic. 3rd Pers. Sing.*	*Imperf. Indic.*	*Imperf. Subj.*
schmeißen	schmeißt	schmiß	schmisse
schmelzen (*v.n.*)	schmilzt	schmolz	schmölze
schneiden	schneidet	schnitt	schnitte
schrecken (*v.n.*)	schrickt	schrak	schräke
schreiben	schreibt	schrieb	schriebe
schreien	schreit	schrie	schriee
schreiten	schreitet	schritt	schritte
schweigen	schweigt	schwieg	schwiege
schwellen	schwillt	schwoll	schwölle
schwimmen	schwimmt	schwamm	schwömme
schwinden	schwindet	schwand	schwände
schwingen	schwingt	schwang	schwänge
schwören	schwört	schwur	schwüre
sehen	sieht	sah	sähe
sein	ist	war	wäre
senden	sendet	sandte *or* sendete	sendete
singen	singt	sang	sänge
sinken	sinkt	sank	sänke
sinnen	sinnt	sann	sänne
sitzen	sitzt	saß	säße
sollen	soll	sollte	sollte
speien	speit	spie	spiee
spinnen	spinnt	spann	spönne
sprechen	spricht	sprach	spräche
sprießen	sprießt	sproß	sprösse
springen	springt	sprang	spränge
stechen	sticht	stach	stäche
stehen	steht	stand	stände

Imper.	*Past Participle*	*English*
schmeiß(e)	geschmissen	hurl
schmilz	geschmolzen	melt
schneid(e)	geschnitten	cut
schrick	(erschrocken)	frighten
schreib(e)	geschrieben	write
schrei(e)	geschrien	cry
schreit(e)	geschritten	stride
schweig(e)	geschwiegen	be silent
schwill	geschwollen	swell
schwimm(e)	geschwommen	swim
schwind(e)	geschwunden	vanish
schwing(e)	geschwungen	swing
schwör(e)	geschworen	swear
sieh	gesehen	see
sei	gewesen	be
send(e)	gesandt *or* gesendet	send
sing(e)	gesungen	sing
sink(e)	gesunken	sink
sinn(e)	gesonnen	meditate
sitz(e)	gesessen	sit
	gesollt	be obliged
spei(e)	gespieen	spit
spinn(e)	gesponnen	spin
sprich	gesprochen	speak
sprieß(e)	gesprossen	sprout
spring(e)	gesprungen	leap
stich	gestochen	prick
steh(e)	gestanden	stand

German Irregular Verbs

Infin.	*Pres. Indic. 3rd Pers. Sing.*	*Imperf. Indic.*	*Imperf. Subj.*
stehlen	**stiehlt**	**stahl**	**stöhle**
steigen	**steigt**	**stieg**	**stiege**
sterben	**stirbt**	**starb**	**stürbe**
stinken	**stinkt**	**stank**	**stänke**
stoßen	**stößt**	**stieß**	**stieße**
streichen	**streicht**	**strich**	**striche**
streiten	**streitet**	**stritt**	**stritte**
tragen	**trägt**	**trug**	**trüge**
treffen	**trifft**	**traf**	**träfe**
treiben	**treibt**	**trieb**	**triebe**
treten	**tritt**	**trat**	**träte**
trinken	**trinkt**	**trank**	**tränke**
trügen	**trügt**	**trog**	**tröge**
tun	**tut**	**tat**	**täte**
verderben	**verdirbt**	**verdarb**	**verdürbe**
verdrießen	**verdrießt**	**verdroß**	**verdrösse**
vergessen	**vergißt**	**vergaß**	**vergäße**
verlieren	**verliert**	**verlor**	**verlöre**
wachsen	**wächst**	**wuchs**	**wüchse**
wägen	**wägt**	**wog**	**wöge**
waschen	**wäscht**	**wusch**	**wüsche**
weichen	**weicht**	**wich**	**wiche**
weisen	**weist**	**wies**	**wiese**
werben	**wirbt**	**warb**	**würbe**
werden	**wird**	**wurde**	**würde**
werfen	**wirft**	**warf**	**würfe**
wiegen	**wiegt**	**wog**	**wöge**
winden (*v.a.*)	**windet**	**wand**	**wände**

Imper.	Past Participle	English
stiehl	gestohlen	steal
steig(e)	gestiegen	climb
stirb	gestorben	die
stink(e)	gestunken	stink
stoß(e)	gestoßen	push
streich(e)	gestrichen	stroke, touch
streit(e)	gestritten	quarrel, fight
trag(e)	getragen	carry
triff	getroffen	meet
treib(e)	getrieben	drive
tritt	getreten	step
trink(e)	getrunken	drink
trüg(e)	getrogen	deceive
tu(e)	getan	do
verdirb	verdorben (and verderbt)	spoil
verdrieß(e)	verdrossen	grieve
vergiß	vergessen	forget
verlier(e)	verloren	lose
wachs(e)	gewachsen	grow
wäg(e)	gewogen	weigh
wasch(e)	gewaschen	wash
weich(e)	gewichen	yield
weis(e)	gewiesen	show
wirb	geworben	court
werde	geworden	become
wirf	geworfen	throw
wieg(e)	gewogen	weigh
wind(e)	gewunden	wind

German Irregular Verbs

Infin.	*Pres. Indic. 3rd. Pers. Sing.*	*Imperf. Indic.*	*Imperf. Subj.*
wissen	weiß	wußte	wüßte
wollen	will	wollte	wollte
zeihen	zeiht	zieh	ziehe
ziehen	zieht	zog	zöge
zwingen	zwingt	zwang	zwänge

Imper.	*Past Participle*	*English*
wisse	gewußt	know
wolle	gewollt	wish, want
zeih(e)	geziehen	accuse
zieh(e)	gezogen	draw, pull
zwing(e)	gezwungen	force, compel

English Irregular Verbs

Infin.	*Past Indic.*	*Past Participle*	*German*
abide	abode	abode	bleiben
arise	arose	arisen	aufstehen
awake	awoke	awoke	aufwecken
be	was, were	been	sein
bear	bore	borne	tragen
beat	beat	beaten	schlagen
become	became	become	werden
beget	begot	begotten	zeugen
begin	began	begun	beginnen
bend	bent	bent	biegen
bereave	bereaved,bereft	bereaved, bereft	berauben
beseech	besought	besought	bitten
bid	bade, bid	bidden, bid	gebieten
bide	bided, bode	bided	verbleiben
bind	bound	bound	binden
bite	bit	bitten	beißen
bleed	bled	bled	bluten
blow	blew	blown	blasen
break	broke	broken	brechen
breed	bred	bred	zeugen
bring	brought	brought	bringen
build	built	built	bauen
burn	burnt, burned	burnt, burned	brennen
burst	burst	burst	bersten
buy	bought	bought	kaufen

English Irregular Verbs

Infin.	*Past Indic.*	*Past Participle*	*German*
can (*pres. indic.*)	could	—	können
cast	cast	cast	werfen
catch	caught	caught	fangen
chide	chid	chidden, chid	schelten
choose	chose	chosen	wählen
cleave	cleft, clove	cleft, cloven	spalten
cling	clung	clung	sich anklammern
clothe	clothed, clad	clothed, clad	kleiden
come	came	come	kommen
cost	cost	cost	kosten
creep	crept	crept	kriechen
crow	crowed, crew	crowed	krähen
cut	cut	cut	schneiden
dare	dared, durst	dared	wagen
deal	dealt	dealt	austeilen, handeln
dig	dug	dug	graben
do	did	done	tun
draw	drew	drawn	ziehen
dream	dreamt, dreamed	dreamt, dreamed	träumen
drink	drank	drunk	trinken
drive	drove	driven	treiben
dwell	dwelt	dwelt	wohnen
eat	ate	eaten	essen
fall	fell	fallen	fallen
feed	fed	fed	füttern
feel	felt	felt	fühlen
fight	fought	fought	kämpfen
find	found	found	finden

English Irregular Verbs

Infin.	*Past Indic.*	*Past Participle*	*German*
flee	fled	fled	fliehen
fling	flung	flung	schleudern
fly	flew	flown	fliegen
forbid	forbad(e)	forbidden	verbieten
forget	forgot	forgotten	vergessen
forgive	forgave	forgiven	vergeben
forsake	forsook	forsaken	verlassen
freeze	froze	frozen	frieren
get	got	got	bekommen
gird	girded, girt	girden, girt	gürten
give	gave	given	geben
go	went	gone	gehen
grind	ground	ground	mahlen
grow	grew	grown	wachsen
hang	hung	hung	hängen
have	had	had	haben
hear	heard	heard	hören
heave	heaved, hove	heaved, hove	heben
hew	hewed	hewn, hewed	hauen
hide	hid	hidden, hid	verstecken
hit	hit	hit	schlagen
hold	held	held	halten
hurt	hurt	hurt	verletzen
keep	kept	kept	halten
kneel	knelt	knelt	knien
knit	knitted, knit	knitted, knit	stricken
know	knew	known	kennen, wissen
lay	laid	laid	legen

English Irregular Verbs

Infin.	*Past Indic.*	*Past Participle*	*German*
lead	led	led	führen
lean	leant, leaned	leant, leaned	lehnen
leap	leaped, leapt	leaped, leapt	springen
learn	learned, learnt	learned, learnt	lernen
leave	left	left	lassen
lend	lent	lent	leihen
let	let	let	lassen
lie (=recline)	lay	lain	liegen
light	lit, lighted	lit, lighted	beleuchten
lost	lost	lost	verlieren
make	made	made	machen
may (*pres. indic.*)	might	—	mögen
mean	meant	meant	meinen
meet	met	met	treffen, begegnen
melt	melted	melted, molten	schmelzen
mow	mowed	mown	mähen
must (*pres. indic.*)	—	—	müssen
pay	paid	paid	zahlen
put	put	put	stellen
quit	quit(ted)	quit(ted)	verlassen
—	quoth	—	sagte
read	read	read	lesen
rend	rent	rent	reissen
rid	rid	rid	befreien
ride	rode	ridden	reiten, fahren
ring	rang	rung	klingeln
rise	rose	risen	aufstehen
run	ran	run	laufen

English Irregular Verbs

Infin.	*Past Indic.*	*Past Participle*	*German*
saw	sawed	sawn	sägen
say	said	said	sagen
see	saw	seen	sehen
seek	sought	sought	suchen
sell	sold	sold	verkaufen
send	sent	sent	senden
set	set	set	setzen
shake	shook	shaken	schütteln
shall (*pres. indic.*)	should	—	werden, sollen
shape	shaped	shaped, shapen	formen
shear	sheared	shorn	scheren
shed	shed	shed	vergiessen
shine	shone	shone	scheinen
shoe	shod	shod	beschuhen
shoot	shot	shot	schiessen
show	showed	shown	zeigen
shrink	shrank	shrunk	schrumpfen
shut	shut	shut	schliessen
sing	sang	sung	singen
sink	sank	sunk	sinken
sit	sat	sat	sitzen
slay	slew	slain	erschlagen
sleep	slept	slept	schlafen
slide	slid	slid	gleiten
sling	slung	slung	schleudern
slink	slunk	slunk	schleichen
slit	slit	slit	schlitzen
smell	smelt, smelled	smelt, smelled	riechen

English Irregular Verbs

Infin.	*Past Indic.*	*Past Participle*	*German*
smit	smote	smitten	schlagen
sow	sowed	sown, sowed	säen
speak	spoke	spoken	sprechen
speed	sped, speeded	sped, speeded	eilen
spell	spelt, spelled	spelt, spelled	buchstabieren
spend	spent	spent	ausgeben
spill	spilled, spilt	spilled, spilt	verschütten
spin	spun, span	spun	spinnen
spit	spat	spat	speien
split	split	split	spalten
spread	spread	spread	ausbreiten
spring	sprang	sprung	springen
stand	stood	stood	stehen
steal	stole	stolen	stehlen
stick	stuck	stuck	stecken
sting	stung	stung	stechen
stink	stank, stunk	stunk	stinken
strew	strewed	strewed, strewn	streuen
stride	strode	stridden	schreiten
strike	struck	struck, stricken	schlagen
string	strung	strung	(auf)reihen
strive	strove	striven	streben
swear	swore	sworn	schwören
sweep	swept	swept	kehren
swell	swelled	swollen, swelled	schwellen
swim	swam	swum	schwimmen
swing	swung	swung	schwingen
take	took	taken	nehmen

English Irregular Verbs

Infin.	*Past Indic.*	*Past Participle*	*German*
teach	taught	taught	lehren
tear	tore	torn	zerreißen
tell	told	told	erzählen
think	thought	thought	denken
thrive	thrived, throve	thrived, thriven	gedeihen
throw	threw	thrown	werfen
thrust	thrust	thrust	stoßen
tread	trod	trodden	treten
wake	woke, waked	waked, woken woke	wachen
wear	wore	worn	tragen
weave	wove	woven	weben
weep	wept	wept	weinen
will	would	—	wollen
win	won	won	gewinnen
wind	wound	wound	winden
work	worked, wrought	worked, wrought	arbeiten
wring	wrung	wrung	ringen
write	wrote	written	schreiben

Numerical Tables

Cardinal Numbers

0	nought, zero	null
1	one	eins
2	two	zwei
3	three	drei
4	four	vier
5	five	fünf
6	six	sechs
7	seven	sieben
8	eight	acht
9	nine	neun
10	ten	zehn
11	eleven	elf
12	twelve	zwölf
13	thirteen	dreizehn
14	fourteen	vierzehn
15	fifteen	fünfzehn
16	sixteen	sechzehn
17	seventeen	siebzehn
18	eighteen	achtzehn
19	nineteen	neunzehn
20	twenty	zwanzig
21	twenty-one	einundzwanzig
22	twenty-two	zweiundzwanzig
25	twenty-five	fünfundzwanzig
30	thirty	dreißig
36	thirty-six	sechsunddreißig
40	forty	vierzig
50	fifty	fünfzig
60	sixty	sechzig
70	seventy	siebzig
80	eighty	achtzig
90	ninety	neunzig
100	(one)hundred	hundert
101	(a)hundred and one	hundert(und)eins
102	(a)hundred and two	hundert(und)zwei
200	two hundred	zweihundert
300	three hundred	dreihundert
600	six hundred	sechshundert
625	six hundred and twenty-five	sechshundertfünfundzwanzig
1000	(a)thousand	tausend
1965	nineteen hundred and sixty-five	neunzehnhundertfünfundsechzig
2000	two thousand	zweitausend
1,000,000	a million	eine Million
2,000,000	two million	zwei Millionen

Various suffixes may be added to German numerals, the commonest of which are cited in the following examples:

zehnfach	tenfold
dreisilbig	trisyllabic
vierstimmig	four-part (*i.e.* for four voices)
sechsteilig	in six parts

Ordinal Numbers

1st	first	erste (abbr. 1.)
2nd	second	zweite (abbr. 2.)
3rd	third	dritte (abbr. 3.)
4th	fourth	vierte
5th	fifth	fünfte
6th	sixth	sechste
7th	seventh	siebte
8th	eighth	achte
9th	ninth	neunte
10th	tenth	zehnte
11th	eleventh	elfte
12th	twelfth	zwölfte
13th	thirteenth	dreizehnte
14th	fourteenth	vierzehnte
15th	fifteenth	fünfzehnte
16th	sixteenth	sechzehnte
17th	seventeenth	siebzehnte
18th	eighteenth	achtzehnte
19th	nineteenth	neunzehnte
20th	twentieth	zwanzigste
21st	twenty-first	einundzwanzigste
22nd	twenty-second	zweiundzwanzigste
25th	twenty-fifth	fünfundzwanzigste
30th	thirtieth	dreißigste
40th	fortieth	vierzigste
50th	fiftieth	fünfzigste
60th	sixtieth	sechzigste
70th	seventieth	siebzigste
80th	eightieth	achtzigste
90th	ninetieth	neunzigste
100th	hundredth	hundertste
102nd	hundred and second	hundert(und)zweite
200th	two hundredth	zweihundertste
300th	three hundredth	dreihundertste
625th	six hundred and twenty-fifth	sechshundertfünfundzwanzigste
1000th	thousandth	tausendste
2000th	two thousandth	zweitausendste
1,000,000th	millionth	millionste

Fractions etc.

$\frac{1}{4}$	a quarter	ein Viertel
$\frac{1}{3}$	a third	ein Drittel
$\frac{1}{2}$	a half	(ein)halb
$\frac{2}{3}$	two thirds	zwei Drittel
$\frac{3}{4}$	three quarters	drei Viertel
$1\frac{1}{4}$	one and a quarter	ein ein Viertel
$1\frac{1}{2}$	one and a half	anderthalb
$5\frac{1}{2}$	five and a half	fünfeinhalb
$7\frac{2}{5}$	seven and two-fifths	sieben zwei Fünftel
$\frac{15}{20}$	fifteen-twentieths	fünfzehn Zwanzigstel
.7	point seven	0,7 Null Komma sieben